A MODERN APPROACH TO EVIDENCE

TEXT, PROBLEMS, TRANSCRIPTS AND CASES

Fifth Edition

■ ■ ■

by

Richard O. Lempert
Eric Stein Distinguished University Professor of Law and Sociology, Emeritus
University of Michigan

Samuel R. Gross
Thomas and Mabel Long Professor of Law
University of Michigan

James S. Liebman
Simon H. Rifkind Professor of Law
Columbia Law School

John H. Blume
Professor of Law
Cornell University

Stephan Landsman
Robert A. Clifford Professor of Tort Law and Social Policy
DePaul University College of Law

Fredric I. Lederer
Chancellor Professor of Law
William & Mary School of Law

AMERICAN CASEBOOK SERIES®

WEST ACADEMIC PUBLISHING

Mat #41433424

American Casebook Series is a trademark registered in the U.S. Patent and Trademark Office.

ISBN: 978–0–314–28765–6

For Elliot, Phoebe, Janet, Diane and to the Memory of Lee Lowrey III

PREFACE TO THE FIFTH EDITION

When we finished the Fourth Edition in 2011, we did not expect to be producing a new edition this soon, and we would not have done so but for the redrafting of the Federal Rules of Evidence. Although the redrafting was intended to do no more than improve readability consistent with similar changes in other federal rules of procedure, and although the updated language changes almost nothing beyond clarifying ambiguities that occasionally led to varying judicial interpretations, the rules figure so prominently in our textual discussion that we felt an update to accord with the new language was essential. Except for Chapter 7, parts of which have been substantially rewritten to account for recent cases that appear to have wrought important changes in the protections accorded by the Confrontation Clause, little of substance has changed, although we have dropped Appendix One in Chapter 2 on the history of codification, corrected some misspellings and similar errors and done some minor updating. In particular, except in Chapter 7, all problems and their analyses remain as they were in the Fourth Edition. Teachers will find that material they prepared to use when teaching from the Fourth Edition should still be usable in the same way, and a careful student working with the Fourth Edition and attending closely to a current version of the Federal Rules of Evidence could manage, although we would not recommend it.

In preparing this edition we were helped immensely by the hard work and careful eye of Laura Harlow. We thank her very much.

RICHARD O. LEMPERT
SAMUEL R. GROSS
JAMES S. LIEBMAN
JOHN H. BLUME
STEPHAN LANDSMAN
FREDRIC L. LEDERER

October, 2013

ACKNOWLEDGMENTS

Excerpts from the following books and articles appear with the kind permission of the copyright holders.

Buckley, Bill, Day in the Life Videos: Why Hire a Professional? National Trial Lawyer (March 1991). Copyright © 1991 Bill Buckley. Reprinted by permission of author.

Chernow, Eli, Video in the Courtroom: More Than a Talking Head, 15 Litigation 3 (Fall 1998). Copyright © 1998 by American Bar Association. Reprinted by permission.

Freedman, Monroe H., Professional Responsibility of the Criminal Defense Lawyer: The Three Hardest Questions, 64 Mich. L. Rev. 1469 (1966). Reprinted by permission of the Michigan Law Review.

Gass, J. Ric, Defending Against Day-in-the-Life Videos, 34 For the Defense 8–9, 15 (July 1992). Copyright © 1992 by Defense Research Institute, Inc. Reprinted by permission.

Krane, Dan E., figures 6.2 and 6.3, in Guide to Forensic DNA Evidence, William Thompson. In Bert Black and Patrick Lee, eds., Expert Evidence: A Practitioner's Guide to Law, Science, and the FJC Manual. Reprinted by permission of author.

McCrystal, James L., Videotaped Trials: A Primer, 61 Judicature 250 (1978). Copyright © 1978 by Judicature, the Journal of the American Judicature Society. Reprinted by permission.

Saltzburg, Stephen A., Michael M. Martin, and Daniel J. Capra, Federal Rules of Evidence Manual (7th ed. 1998). Copyright © 1998 by Matthew Bender & Company, a part of LexisNexis. Reprinted by permission.

Stefan, Susan, The Protection Racket: Rape Trauma Syndrome, Psychiatric Labeling and Law, 88 NW. U. L. Rev. 1271, 1333–39 (1994). Copyright © 1994 by the Northwestern University School of Law, *Law Review*. Reprinted by permission.

Stewart, I. Daniel, Jr., Perception, Memory, and Hearsay: A Criticism of Present Law and the Proposed Federal Rules of Evidence, 1970 Utah L. Rev. 1. Reprinted by permission of Utah Law Review.

Thompson, William, Guide to Forensic DNA Evidence, in Bert Black and Patrick Lee, eds., Expert Evidence: A Practitioner's Guide to Law, Science, and the FJC Manual (1997). Copyright © 1997 by West Group. Reprinted by permission.

Tigar, Michael E., Examining Witnesses (1993). Copyright © 1993 by Section of Litigation, American Bar Association. Reprinted by permission.

Weinstein, Jack B., Probative Force of Hearsay, 46 Iowa L. Rev. 331 (1961). Reprinted by permission of the author and the Iowa Law Review.

Werth, Barry, Damages: One Family's Legal Struggles in the World of Medicine. Copyright ©1998 by Barry Werth, Reprinted with the permission of Simon & Schuster, Inc.

USING THIS BOOK

I. AN APPROACH TO EVIDENCE

This is not a casebook. It bears little resemblance to the materials used in most law school courses. This book consists largely of text, problems and transcripts. The cases we include are used primarily to raise policy issues, not to teach substantive points of law. We have found that teaching the substantive law of evidence primarily through case analysis makes little sense. Great amounts of time are devoted to reading and analyzing cases in order to extract principles that can be stated in a paragraph or less. Often little time is left for serious policy analysis. Codifications of evidence law, increasingly important to the modern practitioner, are inevitably slighted. The case approach can also frustrate students who correctly sense that appellate courts are far removed from the setting in which most evidentiary battles are resolved.

Nor is this a treatise or handbook. Although we provide an orderly description of evidentiary law and practice in the US, we go beyond description to critically analyze the way courts and lawyers make evidentiary decisions, and we offer our considered opinions—as a trigger to yours—on how to improve things. We pay particular attention to the realities of how evidence rules come to be adopted and are applied; the validity of the policies usually offered to justify the rules, and the possibility that unstated explanations are actually at work; and the real-world implications of the rules for parties, witnesses, and others who are affected by litigation (e.g., the victims of sexual abuse, insurance companies, government agencies). As befits a book on evidence, this one is attentive to the actual facts of all these matters and routinely cites examples from practice and the available social scientific research.

We believe that evidence is one of the most interesting and exciting courses in the law school curriculum. It is at once eminently practical and highly intellectual. There are rules to be learned and concepts to be pondered. The rules of evidence may be examined from historical, logical and psychological perspectives. They may also be examined as tools that lawyers use to win cases. Ethical issues are close to the surface in this course and are important to an understanding of what it is to be a lawyer. Underlying everything is the often unexplored relationship between rules of evidence and the quality of justice that a legal system delivers. We have found that by using textual material, critical analysis and problems, we can explore each of these aspects of evidence law in greater depth than we could by using either the case method or a handbook format.

Most students who take evidence are concerned primarily with the practicalities of litigation. Nonetheless, we believe that even the most practically oriented will benefit from serious reflection on the policies behind the rules. In evidence, as in much of law, practical and philosophic concerns complement each other. We hope our book vindicates this point of view and that future Thayers, Wigmores, Morgans, McCormicks and Weinsteins will benefit from considering the issues we raise.

A strength of our approach lies in the ability it gives students to learn the rudiments of evidence law from the text itself and to use the problems to test their mastery. To facilitate independent learning, we try to be as straightforward as possible in our explication of the rules. Discussion of the problems in class then provides an excellent vehicle for assuring that students understand the basic application of the rules, for addressing issues that students find most difficult to grasp and for bringing out nuances and ambiguities and confronting questions of policy.

This book is designed to be a self-contained teaching device. It is written so that students will not have to resort to hornbooks, nutshells, texts or other works in order to understand these materials or to answer the problems. Nevertheless we recognize that some students find two treatments of an issue more helpful than one. For them, we recommend McCormick's excellent treatise, although there is significant overlap between that work and this one.

Those who have not taught or learned from problems before may find that using problems takes considerably more time than they anticipate. A problem only a paragraph in length may present all the salient facts of a reported case. In writing this book we faced a choice: either to include only the problems that we like best and believe can all be taught in a three—or four—hour course, or to include many more problems than could ever be covered in a single course, so that instructors can pick the problems that they find most interesting or most relevant to the needs of their students. We opted for a compromise. At various points in the text we insert a problem, or occasionally two problems, which the instructor can assign to review the material that has just been covered. It should be possible to discuss all these problems (and a few more) in a standard length evidence course. Then at the end of chapters and major subsections we provide "Additional Problems" of varying difficulty, which are designed to highlight both basic and finer points of the material discussed. There are far too many of these to be covered in a single course. Hence some instructors may choose to assign only the problems embedded in the text; others may decide to substitute a problem or problems from the additional offerings for the embedded problems, and still others may choose to assign both embedded and additional problems, or make different choices for different chapters. No option is foreclosed. In the interest of time, instructors may also want to eliminate certain textual material. In some chapters, such as those on exhibits and on expert evidence, we offer several detailed examples of the use of these types of evidence, knowing that most instructors will not want (or have time) to explore every example. In other chapters, instructors may not want to discuss every evidence rule or subrule that we choose to analyze or every case excerpt that we present as an illustration. The book was written with the expectation that instructors would feel no compulsion to assign every chapter, or everything that is in a particular chapter, or to discuss everything that is assigned, or to cover the topics in the order in which we present them. Our hope was to include enough material to allow instructors to emphasize those areas of evidence law that they believe are most important, in the order that works best for them.

The book is organized around the Federal Rules of Evidence ("FREs"). This was a sensible choice in 1977, when the first edition was published, two years after the Federal Rules went into effect. By now it is all but inevitable. The Federal Rules serve as the basis for evidence codes in over forty states, the United States Military, the Commonwealth of Puerto Rico—and, of course, they govern directly in federal courts. We reproduce all of the rules that we discuss in the text, but they are scattered throughout the chapters. Several comparatively unimportant rules are not reproduced any place, and—far more important—we do not systematically reprint the Advisory Committee Notes on the rules, or any portions of their legislative history. For these purposes, it is useful to assign a current version of the Federal Rules of Evidence, including the Advisory Committee Notes, together with this book.

II. NOTES ON STYLE

To avoid lengthy citations and make our text read more smoothly, we have adopted the following conventions for the works we cite most frequently. We cite Wigmore's *Treatise on Evidence*, as "Wigmore," Weinstein and Berger's *Weinstein's Federal Evidence* as "Weinstein," and McCormick's treatise, *McCormick on Evidence*, as "McCormick." Unless otherwise noted all such citations are to the most recent version of the work. For Wigmore that is the Fourth Edition, which posthumously revised the author's multi-volume 1940 edition and was published in stages between 1961 and 1988; for Weinstein it is the Second Edition, a looseleaf publication published in 1997 and updated by regular releases; for McCormick it is the Sixth Edition, published in 2006 under the general editorship of Kenneth S. Broun.*

---

* McCormick now appears in two versions, a one-volume Hornbook Series "Student Edition" with very few references, and a two-volume "Practitioner's Treatise Series" edition that is much longer because it has many detailed references. The text and the chapter and section numbers of the two versions are identical, but the pagination is not. To facilitate use of either version, our citations to McCormick include section numbers but not page numbers. A new edition of the Practitioner's Treatise appeared in 2013, but since as we write the most recent edition of the Hornbook in the 2006 edition our citations are to that edition of the Treatise as well.

We save space and make judicial opinions read more easily by eliminating most internal citations. These deletions are not noted. Deletions of textual material in opinions and articles are noted by ellipses. We also delete most footnotes found in opinions and articles without indicating the deletions. Where we choose to keep footnotes appearing in the material we reproduce, we identify these footnotes by lower-case letters. Our own footnotes are noted by Arabic numerals.

We have given names to the characters that appear in most problems in order to make them seem more human. Except in some instances where names are drawn from actual cases, the characters are not intended to bear any relationship to real people. If we have inadvertently used your name for a hypothetical axe murderer, we hope you are not offended by the coincidence.

III. BIBLIOGRAPHY

Many sources are cited in the footnotes. In addition, each chapter but the first ends with a suggested list of additional readings. These sources might be of special interest to those who wish to pursue particular topics in greater depth and to those who believe that we have treated some familiar doctrines inadequately or unfairly.

For general coverage of the law of evidence, the updated version of Wigmore's treatise remains a respected source, and for a quicker overview the latest edition of McCormick's Student Hornbook or the citation rich Practitioner's Treatise are excellent sources. Earlier editions of Wigmore's treatise should be consulted by those interested in delving into the common law of evidence and its historical development, for Wigmore's efforts not only reflect but also helped create both modern evidence law and widely accepted, although not always correct, understandings of its history. The historically minded may also wish to inspect Thayer's Preliminary Treatise on Evidence, a superb work of scholarship, published in 1898 and the dominant synthesis until Wigmore's first edition. Shorter classics of the common law and efforts to improve it and Maguire's *Evidence—Common Sense and Common Law* (1947) and Morgan's *Basic Problems of Evidence* (1962).

The Advisory Committee Notes to the Federal Rules are an exceptionally useful treatment of many important interpretive and historical questions, and students are well-advised to read carefully the Notes accompanying each rule they read. For further discussion of the Federal Rules of Evidence, you might investigate several multivolume works: Weinstein and Berger's *Weinstein's Federal Evidence (2nd ed)*; Wright and Graham's *Federal Practice and Procedure* § 5000 et seq.; and Mueller and Kirkpatrick's *Federal Evidence*. For a useful and concise single-volume handbook, see Paul C. Giannelli, Understanding Evidence (3d ed. 2009).

SUMMARY OF CONTENTS

———

TABLE OF CONTENTS

TABLE OF CASES

The principal cases are in bold type.

TABLE OF RULES

TABLE OF AUTHORITIES

A MODERN APPROACH TO EVIDENCE

TEXT, PROBLEMS, TRANSCRIPTS AND CASES

Fifth Edition

CHAPTER 1

SOME BASICS

• • •

I. INTRODUCTION TO EVIDENCE

A. THE TRIAL GAME

Do you remember when you first decided to become a lawyer? Chances are that in your earliest fantasies you saw yourself before a jury, arguing eloquently to save your innocent client from undeserved punishment, or prosecuting a vicious criminal, or fighting an evil corporate conspiracy. Your role models were probably drawn from fiction—The Practice, or To Kill a Mockingbird, or Law and Order—all stalwart warriors, fighting the good fight, facing skilled and determined opponents.

Fictional depictions of trials are often misleading, but some aspects of the picture they paint are accurate. Trials *are* sometimes dramatic, although more often they are mundane or even dull. More important, a trial really is a contest, a two-sided game of the kind that economists call a zero-sum game: whatever one side wins the other side loses. As in most games, the roles of the players are well-defined, and their goals are clear. There are rules that define permissible moves, and a judge who ensures that the most important rules are followed. The stakes may be enormous: millions of dollars, years in prison, or even life itself. Unlike most, however, this game is played by proxy. The main players—the opposing attorneys—have less at risk than those they represent, the parties who sit beside them. But the stakes for the lawyers are also high. Success and satisfaction in one's career may turn on courtroom performance. To be given the opportunity to stave off injustice and to fail is painful, whatever the odds against success. An attorney must be prepared to do her or his best.

The rules of evidence are among the most important procedural rules that govern trials. They determine the information that will reach the fact-finder—the judge or the jury. You may have the strongest possible case, but unless the fact-finder can hear the evidence you wish to present, these facts cannot influence the decision. Conversely, your opponent's case may appeal to base prejudice or impermissible sentiment, but if the fact-finder hears that appeal it may act in response.

The rules of evidence are not always clear. Like the rules of many games, it is often uncertain how they should apply to particular

1

situations. It is the lawyer's task to convince the judge that her or his interpretation should be adopted. This is not a trial practice book, but we do hope to familiarize you with the rules of evidence so that you may perform as well as you possibly can in your trial work. We hope also to teach you that knowledge of evidence law is useful only if it is integrated into a well thought-out litigation strategy. Finally, we pose some policy questions in an attempt to evaluate the implications of our system of evidence law for the quality of the justice we administer.

Two further points before we leave the metaphor of trial as game. *First*, to the extent that rulings on evidence law determine the outcome of the game, the game is almost always won or lost at trial rather than on appeal. This may seem strange to second-and third-year law students who have been fed a steady diet of appellate opinions. But appellate judges seek generally to ensure that justice was done below; they are less concerned with upholding the letter of the law, especially procedural law. Except occasionally when constitutional values are implicated, an appellate court will rarely reverse a trial court for mistaken rulings on evidentiary issues even if it believes that the errors may have affected the verdict—unless the appellate court doubts the substantive justice of the outcome of the trial.[1] For the most part, when it comes to the law of evidence, the trial court is the court of last resort.

Second, as in all games, the quality of refereeing may be spotty. Judges, like attorneys, vary in the skill and knowledge which they bring to their task. Judges, like referees, almost always have the last word. In this book you will be taught the rules of evidence in a relatively precise form, and you will learn nice distinctions between particular aspects of various rules. In court, the rules may be fuzzy and the distinctions may disappear, or they may disappear in one judge's court and reappear in another's. Phrases like "res gestae" may serve to dispose of several matters that you will learn to treat as a series of distinct exceptions to the hearsay rule. You will, no doubt, learn to adapt your arguments to the judges you appear before. Even so, the distinctions you learn in this course should serve you in good stead. They will help you appreciate the rationale (if any) behind the fuzzy rules that often prevail. When you

---

[1] See Anna-Rose Mathieson & Samuel R. Gross, Review for Error, 2 Law, Probability and Risk 259 (2004). If you are skeptical of this claim (or even if you are not), try a simple test. Go to the Federal Reporter or the appropriate reporter of appellate decisions for your state. Look at a number of criminal appeals in which questions of evidence are raised. Note the propensity of the courts to dispose of evidence issues without discussion in a catch-all paragraph, to rationalize rulings below as correct, or to conclude, without reasons, that possible errors below could not have affected the trial results. Are you as confident as the court that the alleged errors did not influence the verdict? Now look at those few convictions that were reversed on non-constitutional evidentiary grounds. Are the errors cited in the reversals clearly more substantial than errors for which the same court has refused to reverse? On the other hand, are the defendants' cases more generally sympathetic? Does there seem to be a higher probability (totally apart from the evidentiary points at issue) that an injustice was done at trial? See Margaret A. Berger, When, If Ever, Does Evidentiary Error Constitute Reversible Error?, 25 Loy. L.A. L. Rev. 893 (1992).

have an appealable case they will suggest arguments that justify a decision in your favor. And, if you should someday ascend the bench, they might help you become one of the judges to whom this paragraph does not apply.

In most American jurisdictions, evidence law is codified. Most American evidence codes are modeled on the Federal Rules of Evidence, which were adopted by Congress in 1975, and have since also been adopted (with various modifications) by forty-two states, Guam, Puerto Rico, the Virgin Islands, and the United States military. Because of their pervasive presence, we use the Federal Rules of Evidence ("FREs") as an organizing principle throughout this book; when appropriate, we note how these rules differ from other codifications (e.g., the California Evidence Code) and from un-codified common law rules.

As you know, the overwhelming majority of litigated disputes, civil or criminal, never go to trial. Moreover, many attorneys devote all or most of their time to matters other than litigation—contract negotiations, taxes, estate planning, and so forth. As a result, many, perhaps most lawyers complete successful and rewarding careers without once standing before a jury. You may already expect to be in this group. If you do not see yourself as a trial lawyer, what use is a course in evidence to you?

Though you may never appear in court, the possibility of litigation may be present in many of the things you do. When you draft instruments or advise clients you will have to keep an eye to possible court tests; to do this effectively you must know what kinds of information the court would be willing to admit in reaching a decision. As a negotiator you must be aware that the strength of your client's position may turn on the probability that particular kinds of evidence will be admitted or excluded if the matter reaches trial. If you work as an appellate lawyer you obviously must be able to evaluate a trial transcript for evidentiary errors as well as for grander errors of law. In addition, one of the interesting features of evidence law is that many of these apparently neutral procedural rules in fact disproportionately advantage one group of litigants over another. When an issue of evidence law is before your legislature, you or your clients may have a significant stake in the outcome regardless of the nature of your practice. Finally, you will be a lawyer. You will be expected by your non-lawyer associates to possess some of the basic knowledge that, in the popular mind, characterizes your profession. Evidence is one of those fields which you will be expected to know something about.

B. BASIC TERMINOLOGY

Most of this chapter consists of an annotated transcript of a trial. We believe this is a useful way to introduce the rules of evidence in the context in which they are actually used. Before we begin, however, it will help to define some basic terms that will crop up repeatedly in this transcript and throughout the course. For the present we will merely give rough and quick definitions of concepts that we will explore in detail in the remainder of the book,[2] followed by a brief description of how a trial record—such as this transcript—is created.

A **witness** is a person who gives **testimony** in court. The term is also sometimes used to refer to people who have perceived events relevant to legal proceedings whether or not they are called to testify.

Testimony is a sworn oral report by a **witness** of information relating to a legal dispute.

An **exhibit** is a physical object—a contract, a picture, a gun, etc.—that is presented in evidence because it provides information relating to a legal dispute.

An **objection** is a motion by a party (frequently with supporting reasons) asking the judge to exclude evidence offered by an opposing party.

An **offer of proof** is information that a party provides to the judge to show the contents of evidence that it has offered and to which an opposing party has made an **objection**.

A **foundation** is a fact on which evidence must be presented before a litigant is allowed to present evidence on some related matter. For example, a foundation is required before a **witness** is allowed to testify as an expert neurologist: the lawyer who calls her must present evidence that she *is* an expert in neurology.

Direct examination is the examination of a **witness**, almost always by the lawyer who calls her to the stand.

Cross examination is the examination of a **witness**, almost always by a lawyer for a party other than the one that called her to the stand.

A **leading question** is a question that suggests the desired answer. Leading questions are allowed on **cross examination**; with some exceptions, they are prohibited on **direct examination**.

Impeachment is evidence that is used to show that a **witness** has made a mistake, or has lied, or for some other reason has testified inaccurately.

Rehabilitation is evidence that is used to show that a **witness** who has been **impeached** did in fact testify truthfully and accurately.

---

[2] Since this list is intended as an introduction rather than a dictionary, the definitions are ordered by content rather than alphabetically, in a sequence which reflects (imperfectly) the order in which issues are discussed in this book.

Personal knowledge of a fact is knowledge based on a person's own sensory perceptions—seeing, hearing, touching, smelling or tasting—as opposed to knowledge that is based on what the witness heard from another person, read about, figured out, or guessed. In general, **witnesses** can only testify to matters within their personal knowledge.

Opinion evidence is evidence of something the **witness** has not seen, heard, or otherwise perceived directly, but rather has inferred from other information. Opinion evidence by **expert witnesses** is generally admissible; other **witnesses** can only testify to a narrow range of opinions, based on their own sensory perceptions.

Relevant evidence is evidence which has a tendency to make some fact that matters in the case more likely or less likely. Relevance is a requirement for admissibility; irrelevant evidence is inadmissible.

Unfair prejudice is the effect of evidence that confuses or misleads the trier of fact, or causes the trier of fact to decide the case on a legally improper basis, such as hatred toward a party.

Character evidence is evidence that is offered to prove that a person is likely to have behaved in a certain way because she has a propensity to act that way, that is, because she's the sort of person who does things like that. Character evidence is generally inadmissible to prove how a person behaved *out of court*, but some types of character evidence may be used to show that a **witness** *lied in court* (**impeachment**) or to respond to such a charge (**rehabilitation**).

Hearsay is evidence of a statement that was made at some earlier time, which is presented at trial to prove that what the statement says is true. For example, if a **witness testifies**: "Jane ran in and told me that it was raining," that would be hearsay if the **testimony** is offered to show that Jane's statement was true—that it was indeed raining—but not hearsay if it was offered to show that Jane speaks English. Hearsay is generally inadmissible, but there are many exceptions.

An **admission** is any statement that was made by one party in the case, and is then introduced in evidence by an opposing party. Admissions are treated very differently from other statements. Evidence of an admission may be admitted even if it is **hearsay**, and even if it was not based on **personal knowledge** or expresses an otherwise inadmissible **opinion**.

A **privileged communication** is one that occurred within a legally recognized confidential relationship—for example, the relationship between lawyer and client or between husband and wife.

If the appropriate criteria are met, evidence of a privileged communication is inadmissible.

Privileged information is information that a person or an organization has a right to withhold from judicial proceedings. For example, the government can withhold state secrets.

An **expert witness** is a **witness** who has special knowledge or training that may be useful to the trier of fact—for example, a physician or an engineer. Expert witnesses are allowed to testify to a much broader range of **opinions** than other witnesses, and frequently may base their opinions on **hearsay** or other inadmissible evidence.

C. "FOR THE RECORD"

After a trial, there is often an appeal. In our system, an appellate court is generally restricted to reviewing a trial "on the record": it must base its decision solely on information that was presented in the trial court and preserved in the record of the trial. But the importance of trial records is not restricted to their use on appeal. The record is the authoritative source of information about the trial for *all* purposes. Since nobody can remember everything that happens in a case that stretches over weeks or months, not to mention years, the lawyers and the judge will consult the record regularly in order to address questions of substantive or procedural law, or to prepare the examination of a witness or an argument to the jury. Later, during deliberations, the jury is allowed to review documents and to view exhibits that are in the record, and may ask to have excerpts of the recorded testimony read or played back to it. When the trial is over, there may be related hearings in the same case—on sentencing, probation, modification, enforcement, contempt, and so forth—which may take place days, months or years later. If the participants in these hearings need to find out about what happened at trial, or to remind themselves, they too must look to the record.

What is this "record" that is so central to our system of litigation? It consists of three types of things:

- Pleadings, memoranda, and other court documents,
- Transcripts (or sometimes recordings) of oral proceedings, and
- Exhibits.

All of these items are placed in the record by the lawyers and the judge, in one manner or another. Since the record is so important, lawyers must make sure both that the items they rely on are in the record, and that their meaning is clear. We will give a brief sketch of how to do this for each of the three categories of things that make up the record.[3]

1. Pleadings and Other Court Documents

The record in a case includes the pleadings and other legal documents in a case—the complaint, answer, motions, memoranda of law, declarations, etc. These papers are incorporated into the record when they are *filed* with the clerk of the court. Once a case is underway and the parties have appeared in court, an attorney who wishes to file a document must generally show that it has been served on all other parties in the case. (This is usually done by filing a sworn document called a "proof of service" which describes how service was accomplished.) In addition, rules of court may prescribe the format for court documents: the type of paper, the style of the heading, the length, the supporting documents that may be required, etc. Some court rules now permit or require electronic filing of some types of documents, and prescribe their format and length (often in terms of word counts).

There are numerous types of court documents that may be filed, but they share an essential characteristic: they are all *prepared for* the trial or hearing in which they are used. Although court documents are not generally considered *evidence*, they may have important evidentiary implications because they frequently express the parties' factual contentions. Consider, for example, a defendant in a civil case who files an answer to the complaint in which, among other things, he admits that he is a resident of New York. Strictly speaking, that admission is not "evidence" of his residence (although it could be presented in evidence if the need arose), but it is a dispositive statement that obviates the need for evidence on this point. On occasion, however, documents prepared for litigation *are* evidence. In deciding legal issues—including the admissibility of evidence—a judge may use affidavits and declarations as evidence. For example, in order to rule on a hearsay objection it may be necessary to decide whether the person who made the statement that is the subject of the objection was at that time employed by the party who made the objection. If so, the statement is considered an "admission" and is admissible even if it is hearsay. In deciding this issue, the judge may consider as evidence an affidavit from the alleged employee that was prepared just for the hearing on that issue.

2. Transcripts

a. How Transcripts Are Made

When journalists or politicians say that a statement is "on the

---

[3] For more detailed treatments of the issues we discuss in this section, see Jon Waltz & John Kaplan, Making the Record (1982); and Thomas A. Mauet, Trial Techniques (8th ed. 2010).

record" they simply mean that it is made openly and publicly. When trial lawyers say that a statement is "in the record" they mean something more specific: that it was made during formal proceedings in the case, and recorded by the official method in use in that court. In court, the traditional method of choice is stenographic transcription by a certified court reporter using a special high-speed note-taking machine. The reporter who takes these notes can "read back" from them during the trial—to remind the participants of things that were said minutes or hours or days before—and he can use them to prepare an official *transcript* of all or part of the proceedings: a verbatim record of what was said, which the reporter certifies as complete and accurate. Transcripts are usually prepared for appeals. For most trials, if there is no appeal the court reporter's notes are never transcribed, and there is no generally intelligible record of what was said in court. In some high-stakes cases— capital cases (in some states), or civil cases where the possible damages are very high—the court or the parties will pay to have an on-going "daily" transcript made for use in the trial itself, or even a contemporaneous "real time" transcription. But this is an uncommon and often expensive procedure.[4] And sometimes an outsider will pay for a transcript—usually a partial transcript—to use in another court case, or in a news story, or for some other purpose.[5]

Many courts do not rely on short-hand reporters, but instead use electronic recording devices. The simpler sorts of systems produce audio-recording, from which transcripts are made when necessary; this is not always easy, since it is sometimes difficult to identify the speakers. In the past two decades, more elaborate audio-and video-recording systems have become increasingly common. The video records they create do not have the high production values of broadcast video, but they do show the speakers (who are therefore easy to identify for transcription)—their gestures, mannerisms, movements and facial expressions. Unfortunately, much of this information is lost on appeal, because the record that is used at that stage is usually a conventional transcript that a stenographer prepares from the recording. Even so, this method (or something similar) is likely to become increasingly common in the future, partly because of the intrinsic advantages of electronic recording, especially the ability to provide instant records of proceeding, but mostly because even the most sophisticated electronic recording systems are cheaper than employing full-time court reporters.

---

[4] To prepare daily transcripts the court must employ several court reporters who work in relays, alternating between transcribing, generating transcripts, and checking the transcripts they produce. Modern stenographic note-taking machines are electronic and use software that makes it possible to produce a rough version of a transcript virtually contemporaneously and at a much lower cost than was possible with old fashioned machines.

[5] That is how the transcript in People v. Tellez, the case that follows, was produced: it was prepared specifically for this book. There was no appeal in the Tellez case because the defendant was acquitted, and under the double jeopardy clause of the Fifth Amendment, the state may not appeal an acquittal.

b.   *What Gets Transcribed*

Testimony.   The most obvious and essential purpose of a trial transcript is to report the testimony of the witnesses. From the time a witness is sworn in, everything that is said during her examination will appear in the transcript: questions by the lawyers on direct and cross examination, answers by the witness, objections by opposing lawyers, rulings by the judge. This method provides the appellate court with the maximum amount of information, and the maximum amount of paper— hundreds, thousands, sometimes hundreds of thousands of transcript pages. By contrast, some judicial systems rely on summary records. For example, in Germany—where the scope of appellate review is *wider* than in the United States—trial judges (who hear civil cases without juries) dictate summaries of the testimony, and those summaries, with additions and comments from the lawyers, are used on appeal instead of verbatim transcripts.[6]

Sometimes a judge will "strike" testimony from the record because it is inadmissible. This may happen, for example, if the opposing party could not object soon enough to prevent the witness from giving the improper testimony in the first place. Testimony that is "stricken" may not be considered by the jurors (at least they're not *supposed* to consider it) but it still appears in the transcript, together with the motion to strike and the ruling of the court. For example:

Question (by Direct Examiner): How did they open the door?

Answer: I didn't see, but Brad told me they used a crowbar.

Opposing Counsel: I object, Your Honor. Hearsay.

The Court: Sustained.

Opposing Counsel: And I move to strike the answer.

The Court: Yes. The answer will be stricken starting from when Brad told him. Ladies and gentlemen, you should disregard what the witness said about what Brad told him.

Objections, rulings, and offers of proof.   You can't complain on appeal about an error in admitting evidence if you didn't make a timely objection, on the record, at trial.[7] Sometimes evidentiary objections are made in writing, but 99 times out of 100 objections are spoken, recorded and (if necessary) transcribed. The objection must be "specific"—unless it's obvious from the context, you have to state the legal basis for the objection: irrelevant, hearsay, inadmissible character evidence, etc. In

---

[6]   John H. Langbein, The German Advantage in Civil Procedure, 52 U. Chi. L. Rev. 823, 828–29, 857 (1985).

[7]   As usual, there is an exception to this rule. Even in the absence of an objection, an appellate court may consider "a plain error affecting a substantial right." FRE 103(e); see Chapter Two, p. 170.

addition, the objecting party must secure a ruling on the record. For example:

> **Q. (by Direct Examiner)** Did he ever threaten any of his other customers, to your knowledge?
>
> **A.** Well, I remember . . .

> **Opposing Counsel:** Objection, irrelevant and unfairly prejudicial.

> **Direct Examiner:** No, your Honor. It goes to the witness's state of mind.

> **A.** Well, in March I think he told the guy at Lucky's that if he didn't order 200 cases there'd be blood all over the loading dock.

In this example the objecting party would probably not be allowed to complain on appeal that the testimony was improperly admitted. Although the attorney did object, she did not insist upon and did not receive a ruling from the judge. That failure will be said to waive the objection. In effect, she is inviting the inference that she reconsidered her position, most likely because she was satisfied with the examining attorney's explanation.

If an objection is sustained, the party that asked the question may wish to argue on appeal that it was an error to *exclude* the evidence. There is a precondition for that claim as well: the record must show what the excluded evidence *would have been*, so that the appellate court can decide whether it should have been admitted, and, if so, assess the impact of the improper exclusion on the trial. Sometimes the content of the excluded evidence is apparent from the context; otherwise the attorney who asked the question must put it on the record by making an "offer of proof."

There are many ways to make an offer of proof, ranging from a written statement by the attorney to actual testimony by the witness, under oath, outside the hearing of the jury. The most common by far is for the attorney to *just say it*:

> **Q. (by Direct Examiner)** Had you had any prior business dealings with the defendant?

> **Opposing Counsel**: Objection, Judge. Irrelevant.

> **Direct Examiner**: May we approach the bench?

> **The Court**: You may.

> **Direct Examiner** (outside of the hearing of the jury): Your Honor, I offer to prove that the witness, if permitted, will testify that over the past 18 months he leased five trucks from the defendant, and that the terms always included liability insurance coverage to one million dollars.

The Court: Sustained.

This example also illustrates how an offer of proof may be useful at the trial itself: telling the judge what you expect to show is often the best way to argue that the evidence should be admitted. In this case, for example, the direct examiner is arguing that the terms of previous leases are relevant to the transaction at hand. It didn't work—the objection was sustained—but that is common, no matter how well you do your job.

Jury selection, opening statements, closing argument, instructions, etc. Trials include several essential stages in addition to testimony: jury selection and opening statements by the lawyers come before the testimony; instructions on the law and closing arguments come after it. All of these proceedings take place in open court in the presence of the jurors (or the prospective jurors), and normally they are recorded and may be transcribed. In some courts, however, it is customary not to record jury selection, or (less frequently) the attorneys' opening statements or closing arguments. An attorney can always have a record made of these stages, but she may be required to pay the cost of hiring a court reporter to do it.

Sidebar conferences and meetings in chambers. In a jury trial, the jury is the trier of fact, but the judge is the trier of law and general referee. Many of the rules the judge administers are designed to limit or channel the information the jury receives. Therefore, the judge and the lawyers discuss many issues—the qualifications of a juror, admissibility of a letter from the defendant to his mother, the starting time after lunch, the wording of the jury instruction on proximate cause—outside the presence of the jury. Sometimes these discussions are formal arguments to the court, in public session, on the record. Often, however, as in our last example, they take the form of whispered "sidebar" discussions between the judge and the lawyers at the bench, or informal conversations in the judge's chambers. Despite their informality, these meetings may resolve significant issues and produce rulings that are important enough to raise on appeal. But there's a hitch: often such proceedings are not recorded, and in order to appeal a ruling both the trial court's decision and the party's objection must be in the record. There are a couple of ways around this problem. An attorney can ask to have the court reporter present at these conferences, but this may annoy the judge because it slows things down, or because it's physically awkward (e.g., there may be no place for the reporter to sit at a sidebar conference). Alternatively, after the conference, the lawyer can ask to make a statement in open court, or to have the judge make a statement, that summarizes the issues, rulings and objections and "puts them on the record." This procedure can be used for other purposes as well. In some trials judges will not permit the lawyers to make detailed objections or offers of proof in the presence of the jury, but are happy to let them state these matters "for the record" after the jury is excused for the day or during breaks in the testimony, or to file them in writing.

c.   *The Need for Clarity*

Court reporters generally do an excellent job of recording courtroom proceedings, provided three conditions are met: they must hear what is said; it must be stated unambiguously; and it must be in a form that can be reproduced in a transcript. Lawyers have an obligation to help make a clear record by being sensitive to the requirements of the reporters' job. Here's a list of some of the most common issues, all of which are also problematic for electronic recording:

Indistinct speech.   Lawyers must not only speak clearly and distinctly, they must also make sure that their witnesses speak clearly enough so that the court reporter (not to mention the jury and judge) can understand them.

Inaudible responses. The reporter can only record words. If the witness answers a question by nodding her head or shrugging her shoulders the lawyer must ask for an audible response ("Please answer out loud so the court reporter can take down what you say," or "You shrugged in response to my last question. Does that mean you don't know?"), or supply one ("Let the record reflect that the witness nodded her head in agreement with the last question.").

Simultaneous speech. A transcript is a linear medium. It can only reproduce one speaker at a time—even if the reporter can hear and record multiple speakers. Sometimes it may be necessary to interrupt a witness in order to stop him from giving inadmissible testimony; otherwise, court proceedings are supposed to have only one speaker at a time.

Proper names and technical terms. Even common names may have multiple spellings—Cooke and Koch are often pronounced the same as Cook; Bower, Baur, Bauer and Bour may all sound alike—and the spelling of an uncommon name is sometimes a surprise to everybody. Ditto for unusual or technical words—e.g., N,N-diethylmetatoloamide. Have pity. Spell these words out for the court reporter, or better yet, if you know that an examination will include a lot of difficult names or technical terms, give the reporter a printed list of them in advance.

Ambiguity. A lot of things that seem perfectly clear when they are said are ambiguous when you read them months or years later. This often happens with numbers. Did "It cost two-fifty" mean the price was $2.50 or $250? When the witness said "I called a meeting for nine-thirty" did he mean 9:30 a.m., 9:30 p.m., or September 30th? The same problem can also happen with negative answers to negatively phrased questions:

Q. You didn't recognize him, did you?

A. No.

Does the answer mean, "No, I didn't recognize him," or, "No, you're wrong, I did"? It's hard to notice and avoid all these pitfalls in advance, but part of your job is to do just that.

Gestures. When we talk, we gesture. We point—"It was him!"; we illustrate—"like this" (clapping three times quickly); we indicate—"about that wide" (spreading thumb and forefinger). None of these gestures can make it into a transcript, even if the transcript is made from a videotape that does record them. In order to complete the record, the lawyer conducting the examination must reduce them to words. Sometimes this can be done by a follow-up question:

> **Q.** Where did he hit you?
>
> **A.** He hit me right here.
>
> **Q.** He hit you below your left eye, is that correct?
>
> **A.** Yes.

Often the best or only thing to do is make a statement "for the record."

> **Q.** Do you see the man who hit you in court?
>
> **A.** Yes, over there in the green suit.
>
> **Q.** Let the record reflect that the witness has identified the defendant.

In the absence of an objection from the opposing party, or a disagreement from the judge, that statement will be taken as an accurate description of the witness's gesture. Similarly, if the witness says, "he was about as far from me as you are," the lawyer can follow that up with, "for the record, Your Honor, about eight feet."

One final note on clarity. Witnesses are not the only offenders. Lawyers also often speak in "this's" and "that's", "here's" and "there's", or gesture and point, or use proper names without spelling them—and the record that's produced is just as ambiguous.

3. Exhibits

The last category of items that go in the record is *exhibits*: objects or documents that have evidentiary value in themselves, or that help clarify or illustrate the testimony of a witness. Exhibits can range from a knife that was found in the victim's back, to a signed lease agreement for an office, to a map of the sewage system for a subdivision. Unlike court documents which are filed, exhibits are presented as evidence or in conjunction with other evidence, for the benefit of the trier of fact.

"Gimme a 'D'!   Gimme an 'N'!   Gimme an 'A'!!"

The procedure for using exhibits is somewhat elaborate. We will describe it here in cursory form, and again in more detail in Chapter Ten.

First, an exhibit must be *marked* for identification by the clerk of the court. That makes it a part of the record. A marked exhibit (or sometimes, a copy of the exhibit) will be retained in the record even if it is not admitted in evidence so that a reviewing court will be aware of its nature or contents. For that purpose, the exhibit itself serves as a substitute for an offer of proof, which is used to inform the trial judge and the appellate courts of the contents of excluded oral evidence. Once an exhibit is marked participants in the trial should refer to it by its exhibit number, in order to eliminate any ambiguity about the object of a reference. You're supposed to say "When did you first see *Plaintiff's Exhibit Number 12*" rather than "When did you first see *this letter?*"

Second, an exhibit must be *shown* to the opposing party—if that party is not already aware of its contents.

Third, the exhibit must be *admitted* in evidence. In most cases this requires testimony from a witness that the exhibit is indeed what the offering party claims it to be: the knife that was found in the victim's back, the signed lease, etc. This type of foundational testimony is called *authentication.* However, some types of documents—for example, government publications—are considered *self-authenticating* and do not require authenticating testimony as a prerequisite for admission in evidence.

Last, after the exhibit is admitted in evidence it may be *published* to the trier of fact—i.e. its contents may be made known by showing it to the jury, passing it around, reading it out loud, etc.

II.   PEOPLE V. TELLEZ

A. INTRODUCTION

The transcript that follows is from a comparatively short criminal trial, less than 3 days of testimony, plus opening statements, closing arguments, and legal instructions. The trial, *The People of the State of Illinois v. Ronald Tellez*, took place in the Cook County (Chicago), Illinois, Circuit Court in January of 1989. The defendant, Mr. Tellez, was an ex-police officer who had been arrested and was awaiting trial for capital murder. While the murder case was pending, Mr. Tellez allegedly assaulted a sheriff's officer who was guarding him and attempted to escape from custody. The prosecution decided to try the aggravated assault and attempted escape case first and the murder case second. This is the transcript of the first trial. However, because of the pending murder charge, this trial can also be viewed as the opening act of the longer and much more serious capital trial that came later: the prosecution hoped to get a conviction on these lesser charges and use it to help obtain a conviction and a death sentence at the later murder trial. As a result, this assault and attempted escape case was handled with uncommon care on both sides. The prosecution is represented by two experienced Assistant State's Attorneys, the defense by two experienced Assistant Public Defenders.

Even though it is short as trial transcripts go, the transcript of the *Tellez* case is too long to reproduce in its entirety. We have edited it down to about half of the total length. The portion that is printed includes all of the opening statements, closing arguments and final instructions to the jury; virtually all of the testimony of the defendant and the alleged victim; most of the testimony of the prosecution's second most important witness; and a portion of the testimony of one defense witness in addition to the defendant. We have omitted several minor witnesses (much of whose testimony was not controverted), and a great deal of discussion between the judge and the lawyers on legal and housekeeping issues. Short excerpts from some of this omitted material are reproduced in later chapters. We believe that the portion of the transcript printed here—together with the footnotes that help explain and raise questions about it—will give you a complete view of the issues in the *Tellez* trial, and a good introduction to the use of evidence and to the rules of evidence in action.   To help you follow the transcript, we begin with a concise summary of all the evidence that was presented in the *Tellez* trial, whether it is reproduced here or not.

B. SUMMARY OF THE EVIDENCE

The prosecution called five witnesses, beginning with the alleged victim, **Nicholas Alfieri**, a Deputy Sheriff whose job was to escort the Defendant from a fourth floor courtroom back to the basement tunnel leading to the jail.   Alfieri testified that he handcuffed the Defendant and took him down in the elevator, but when the doors opened on the basement, the Defendant suddenly kicked him in the groin.   Alfieri fell forward and out of the elevator, and when he attempted to get up and keep the door from closing, the Defendant kicked him again.   This happened repeatedly until help arrived.   Alfieri further testified that when the other officers arrived, one asked the Defendant to get off the elevator, and one said something about a loose handcuff key.   These details were questioned on cross-examination, when Alfieri admitted that he had failed to mention them in his incident report or in several interviews.

The prosecution then called **Surander Singhal**, the emergency room doctor who examined Alfieri after the incident.   He testified that he found bruises in the groin area, on the left inner thigh, and on both knees, and that he prescribed Tylenol for pain.

Michael Daly, the third witness, was another Deputy Sheriff, the first to arrive at the scene by the elevator.   He testified that when he got there, the Defendant had one handcuff on, with the other dangling open.   Daly testified that he came running when he heard Alfieri yelling, "Escape, escape," but he admitted on cross-exam that he did not write this in his report or mention it in earlier interviews.

The last prosecution witnesses were **Robert Sykes** and **William DeValle**, two Sheriff's Department Corrections Officers who arrived at the elevator scene just after Daly did.   Both testified that they heard someone yelling for help, and, after locking up their area, came running, and found Alfieri lying on his back in the elevator doorway, and Daly standing near him.   Both officers entered the elevator to subdue the Defendant and noted that one handcuff was on, and the other was dangling open.   Sykes further testified that he saw a key in the handcuff lock, and that he struck the Defendant once in the face to subdue him.   On cross, Sykes admitted that he did not mention the handcuff key in his first report, and that no loose handcuff key was ever found in the area.

The defense presented its case through eight live witnesses and one witness to whose testimony the prosecution stipulated. **Juanita Lilly**, a Sheriff's Deputy assigned to the courtroom, testified that she let Alfieri and the Defendant through a locked door to the elevator, and locked the door behind them before returning to the courtroom. **Meggs McKinney**, an Emergency Medical Technician at the jail, testified that he responded to the incident when called, examined the Defendant, and sent him to the emergency room for further evaluation of head trauma. **Ralph Willer**, an Internal Affairs officer who investigated the incident, testified that both Deputy Alfieri and Deputy Daly changed their stories in different interviews.

Russell Gardner, the Security Supervisor of the Courthouse, testified that he arrived after the incident, had the Defendant stripped to his underwear for safety, and called both the Cook County paramedics and the Chicago Fire Department paramedics. Although he saw the Cook County paramedics place the Defendant on a stretcher for transport to the emergency room, he admitted on cross-examination by the prosecution that he did not see any injuries on the Defendant's body. **Jose Cruz**, Chief of Court Services Personnel, testified that he had pictures taken of Alfieri's injuries, but did not have pictures taken of the Defendant because it was not his job to do so. Cruz also testified that Alfieri never told him anything about a loose handcuff key.

Dipankar Banerjee, a doctor who examined the Defendant at the hospital, said that the Defendant complained of blurred vision and pain in his left eye. Banerjee referred him to an ophthalmologist because his vision was worse than it normally was, and to an optometrist because he had lost his glasses in the incident. **Floyd Turner**, an investigator at the Public Defender's office, appeared and authenticated various photographs he had taken to show the layout of the court building.

The last live witness to appear was the defendant, **Ronald Tellez**, testifying on his own behalf. He testified that while the elevator was moving, Alfieri started a fight by pushing him into the elevator wall. Tellez fought back by kicking. He further testified that there was no loose handcuff key, and that he was able to work one hand out of one cuff just before the other officers arrived. He also stated that he was not attempting to escape, he was only trying to defend himself.

Finally, the defense read a stipulation to the jury: if **Dr. Ross Romine** were called he would testify that he examined the Defendant at the hospital and took multiple x-rays, and that both the x-rays and the visual exam were unremarkable.

C. TRANSCRIPT

IN THE CIRCUIT COURT OF COOK COUNTY
COUNTY DEPARTMENT-CRIMINAL DIVISION

THE PEOPLE OF THE	)	
STATE OF ILLINOIS,	)	
Plaintiff,	)	No. 87–12500
	)	
vs.	)	Charge: Aggravated
	)	Battery and
	)	Attempted Escape
RONALD TELLEZ,	)	
Defendant.	)	

REPORT OF PROCEEDINGS of the hearings before the Honorable LORETTA HALL MORGAN, January, 19 through 24, 1989.

APPEARANCES:

HONORABLE RICHARD M. DALEY, State's Attorney of Cook County, by MR. THOMAS GARDINER & MR. JAMES REILLY, Assistant State's Attorneys, for the People of the State of Illinois.

MR. RANDOLPH N. STONE, Public Defender of Cook County, by MS. ANDREA LYON & MS. JENNIFER SOULE, Assistant Public Defenders, for the Defendant.

. . .

THURSDAY, JANUARY 19, 1981

THE COURT: Can we bring the jury out?[8]

MS. LYON: We should probably have a motion to exclude witnesses.

MR. REILLY: We will join in that motion.

THE COURT: Are you joining in that motion?

---

[8]　The trial proper is just about to begin, but a great deal has already taken place. The jury that will try the case has been chosen, and the two sides have conducted the preparation that is necessary to conduct a trial. On the prosecution side, an investigation took place before charges were filed—witnesses were interviewed, statements taken, physical evidence collected, etc. On the defense side, this process could only begin after the defendant had been charged. Both sides have prepared their witnesses to testify, and served them with subpoenas to insure their attendance, if necessary. See Chapter Two, pp. 198–212.

MR. REILLY: We join in it.

MS. LYON: I have no witnesses in court.[9]

THE COURT: We are ready for the jury.

(The following proceedings were had in the presence of the jury.)

THE COURT: Is all the jury present and accounted for? There should be thirteen persons.[10]

THE SHERIFF: Yes.

THE COURT: Be seated. Good afternoon, ladies and gentlemen. Let me welcome you back to Courtroom 302 on behalf of the Court and the parties in this case and the attorneys.

I hope you all had a very pleasant evening and a pleasant morning before you joined us here again today.

You have now been sworn as a jury to try this case. The People of the State of Illinois v. Tellez. By your verdicts you will, in fact, decide the disputed issues in this case.[11]

As I mentioned to you yesterday, the Court will decide questions of law, and you will decide questions of fact.[12]

---

[9] Both parties have joined in exercising their right to have non-party witnesses excluded from the court until after the conclusion of their testimony. In federal cases, FRE 615 requires the court to exclude most witnesses upon request of a party, and also gives the judge discretion to order exclusion on her own. Illinois, where the *Tellez* case was tried, still has no codified rules of evidence, but judges generally stick to that pattern.

FRE 615 follows the general practice and exempts three specific types of witnesses from exclusion: a party; an officer or representative of a non-natural party; and a person whose presence is essential to the presentation of a case. The most controversial aspect of the rule is that which allows a governmental or corporate party to designate a representative who may not be excluded. Most courts that have addressed the question have allowed the government to designate an investigative officer to be present in a criminal case even if the officer is a crucial witness whose presence throughout the trial does not obviously aid the government's attorney. The court does have the power under FRE 611(a) to make such witnesses testify at the start of the government's case. However, the Supreme Court has held that a court may not force a defendant who wishes to testify on his own behalf to choose between testifying at the outset of his case or not at all. Brooks v. Tennessee, 406 U.S. 605 (1972).

FRE 615(d) also exempts witnesses who are "authorized by statute to be present." In federal cases, under 18 USC § 3771(a)(3) a victim of a crime has "[t]he right not to be excluded from . . . public court proceedings [relating to the crime] unless the court . . . [receives] clear and convincing evidence" that the victim's testimony "would be materially altered if the victim heard other testimony at that proceeding."

[10] Felony juries in Illinois have 12 members. Why are there 13 jurors here?

[11] The judge begins the trial by "pre-instructing" the jury—giving them some basic information on their duties, the structure of the trial that will follow, and some of the basic rules that will govern it. Courts vary in the extent to which they do this, although it seems a useful practice.

[12] Judge Morgan has given the conventional description of the division of labor between judge and jury: judge—law; jury—facts. As usual, it's a little more complicated than that. In deciding issues of *law* the judge may have to resolve questions of *fact*, and sometimes the judge and jury have to decide the *same* factual question. See Chapter Two, pp. 181–183. On the whole, however, this is a good description of the distinction, in part because it's tautological: if

Before you retire at the close of the evidence in this case, the Court will instruct you both orally and by written instruction on the law that is applicable to this case, and that is the law that you will be required to follow in reaching your verdict.

I will ask you to give very careful attention to the testimony and to the evidence as it is received and presented for your consideration. I will caution you further not to form or express any opinion until you are all together at the close of the evidence and you have been instructed to begin your deliberations. That will be after arguments by counsel and instruction by the Court.

Even during the course of the trial, which we still anticipate as I told you yesterday might well conclude tomorrow afternoon, you should not discuss the case with anyone, even among yourselves.

I would further caution you when you arrive tomorrow, and should it be that you had to return on Monday, although I doubt that, but for the pendency of this trial and while you are an impaneled jury, when you arrive at the building, come straight to this courtroom, straight into the courtroom, and straight into the jury room. Do not linger in the hallways.

You are not to have contact with other persons outside of the court personnel, the deputy sheriffs who are charged with the responsibility of looking after you and protecting you. By protecting you, I do not mean from any physical harm but protecting you against contamination by outside sources around this case.[13]

From time to time during the trial, I will be called upon to rule on objections that may be made by either side or motions that may be made by either side.

In some instances, my ruling will come immediately. You will hear it, and we will move on. You will hear however I rule.

In other cases, we may have to retire out of your hearing for legal argument and for a ruling on that legal argument. You are not in any way, shape, or form to infer anything as to my opinion as to the merits of this case from any ruling I might make.

If there is an objection while a witness is testifying and I sustain that objection, which means that I agree with the objecting party and that the witness is not going to be allowed to answer that question, it is essentially the same admonition.

Do not consider that as the Court trying to keep something from you

---

the judge decides an issue, that *means* it's a question of law; if the jury decides it, that *means* it's a question of fact.

[13] The judge has told the jury in some detail what *not* to do: *not* to talk about the case with outsiders; *not* to discuss it among themselves until deliberations; *not* to form preliminary opinions; even *not* to linger in the hall. Why all these negative injunctions? What do they say about our view of juries?

or the objecting attorney trying to keep something from you.[14]

The prosecution in this case are the assistant state's attorneys that you met yesterday, and we usually begin the trial of cases with opening statements by the attorneys. Because the State has the burden throughout a criminal trial, they proceed first, and they put on their case first.

One or the other of the state's attorneys to whom you were introduced yesterday will rise very shortly, approach the podium, and make what is called an opening statement to you.[15]

Listen to it carefully, as you should listen to everything carefully that is said in the courtroom during this trial. It is important to understand that the statements of either the defense attorneys or the prosecuting attorneys are not evidence.

It is an opportunity for each counsel, for each side to give you a kind of road map through the case.

Essentially the opening statement tells you what that side expects the evidence to show, and listen to it carefully because it will give you a bird's-eye view and will give you a frame of reference to begin listening to evidence that will come from the witness stand.

When the state's attorney concludes his opening statement, one of the defense attorneys will rise and make an opening statement. Obviously while we are talking about the same case, the two viewpoints will be different. The defense will tell you what it expects the evidence to show.

At the conclusion of the opening statements, the State will proceed to present its case to you by means of witnesses who will be called and sworn, and they will answer questions from that witness stand.

At the conclusion of the State's presentation of its case in chief, the defense, the defense attorneys, may, if they choose to, present evidence.

It is important to understand the defense is not required to do anything. It is not required to present any evidence. The defendant is not required to testify. He is not required to do anything.

---

[14] Another negative injunction: The jury must *not* infer anything from the fact that objections are made or that evidence is excluded. Right!

[15] The prosecution's right to go first may be a considerable advantage. There is a body of social psychological literature which suggests that the party speaking first has the opportunity to prepare a neutral audience so that it will not be fully receptive to the arguments of a second speaker. What is crucial is that the first party expose the audience to some of the arguments of the other party and provide a framework in which these arguments may be rejected. See William J. McGuire, Inducing Resistance to Persuasion: Some Contemporary Approaches, in Advances in Experimental Social Psychology, L. Berkowitz, ed., Vol. 1 (1964). The defendant's opening statement may, as in this case, immediately follow the prosecution's statement, or the defendant may reserve the right to make an opening statement until the presentation of the defendant's case-in-chief.

I have no idea whether the defense will be presenting evidence to you or not, but let me caution you that should the defense not present evidence, that is nothing upon which you should draw any inferences.

It is very important that you understand the defendant is not required to present any evidence. The burden is on the State. In order to move the case forward, the State must present its evidence.

At the close of the State's case in chief, there may or may not be evidence presented by the defense. Should the defense, in fact, present evidence, the State again, really because of the fact that they have the burden to prove the defendant guilty beyond a reasonable doubt, is allowed to present more evidence if they choose. That evidence being evidence in rebuttal. That may or may not occur.

At the close of all the evidence each side will be allowed to make closing arguments to you. If you will notice, I said opening statements. Each side will talk about what they think the evidence will show, but when I am talking about the closing, I am talking about closing argument. That is the opportunity for each side to argue the evidence and the fair inferences that may be drawn from the evidence.

At the conclusion of all the arguments you will be instructed in the law applicable to this case. You will be tendered a set of written instructions that will have been discussed and gone over with by the Court and each counsel, and then you will retire to the jury room to deliberate this case.

The Court has given you a sort of sense of how we will proceed hoping that that may help you not worry about incidentals and procedures so much and will free you completely to listen carefully to the evidence, and as I look at that jury, and as I watched you being selected yesterday, I feel confident that this jury is going to do its job as the trier of fact in an exemplary way.

If there is nothing further, we may begin our opening statements.

OPENING STATEMENT FOR THE PROSECUTION

BY MR. GARDINER:

Ladies and gentlemen of the jury, on August 28, 1987, this defendant, Ronald Tellez, was brought over to the building here at 26th and California. He was dressed in a suit. He was brought up to the courtroom of Judge Robert Collins, Room 400, just one floor above us here. He was brought in because he had a case pending in that courtroom. He was charged with murder in that case.

He was handcuffed to a chair in the jury room, in the back of Judge Collins' courtroom and his case was called and he came out on the case and then was brought back to the jury room where he was handcuffed again.

There was a deputy sheriff that handcuffed him. His name is Michael Daly.

Now Michael Daly was called down to an area below the courthouse here in the basement area where he was to man a desk, and the custody, the looking after, of the defendant was then handled by a person named Nicholas Alfieri who at that time was also a deputy sheriff assigned to the courtroom.

It was around noon that Nicholas Alfieri went back to the jury room. Deputy Sheriff Alfieri was dressed in his uniform. He was not armed. The deputy sheriffs are not armed when they escort prisoners.

Deputy Sheriff Alfieri unhooked the handcuffs, then proceeded to walk the defendant with handcuffs behind his back to a door that entered an area in back of the courtroom and, in fact, in back of all of the courtrooms here at 26th Street, and they went through a door and into an area that led to an elevator, an elevator whose shaft, in fact, is in the back of this courtroom and every other courtroom here.

At the elevator Deputy Sheriff Alfieri got in. The defendant got in. They proceed downstairs to the basement. There the elevator doors opened, but the defendant did not get off. Instead he kicked Deputy Sheriff Alfieri in the groin, and the deputy sheriff was knocked back and out of the elevator.

The deputy sheriff moved in trying to keep the door open with his arm, and again he was kicked and again he was thrown back outside of the elevator and it happened again and again.

Throughout this time, Deputy Sheriff Alfieri was yelling for help. Deputy Sheriff Michael Daly was down the hallway and he came to the area, and two other Cook County correctional officers, further down the tunnel that runs between this building and the Cook County Jail, came running when they heard the yelling.

But when Deputy Sheriff Michael Daly arrived, he stood there as Nicholas Alfieri was being kicked, and he said, "Ronnie, please come off the elevator," but he never laid a hand on this defendant.

The two correctional officers came running, and they moved into the elevator. What they saw before they entered that elevator was a kick to Nicholas Alfieri who had sustained more kicks during that time.

Alfieri was on his back, and he had a foot in the elevator door to try to keep it open. They saw the defendant kick that foot.

The officers, Officer William DeValle and Officer Robert Sykes, moved into the elevator. What they saw was the defendant with one handcuff on his wrist and an open handcuff there, and they saw him swinging. Alfieri was on his back at the time.

It was Officer Sykes that saw him swinging as they came into the elevator, and Officer Sykes struck this defendant, and they were able to place him back into custody, back into their control. They took him to the lockup area.

Nicholas Alfieri went to the lockup area himself and back to his courtroom and ultimately to St. Anthony's Hospital where he was treated for injuries to the upper portion of his leg and to his groin area. He was given a support for the groin area. He was given Tylenol as a pain killer.[16]

Ladies and gentlemen, there are two charges in this case, aggravated battery, in that this defendant struck a person that he knew to be a Cook County deputy sheriff, Nicholas Alfieri, and attempt escape, in that he attempted to escape from the custody of Deputy Sheriff Alfieri.

Throughout the incident that you will hear about, you will hear about the struggle that Nicholas Alfieri had to keep those elevator doors open, to prevent those doors from closing, to prevent the elevator from going up.

You will hear the testimony of the other officers in this case, and at the conclusion of that testimony, we believe that you will find the defendant guilty of attempt escape and aggravated battery.

Thank you.

THE COURT: Thank you, Mr. Gardiner.

OPENING STATEMENT FOR THE DEFENSE

BY MS. LYON:

This is not a case about an attempt escape in custody. As you will see, as the evidence is explored in this case and as we hope to demonstrate introductorily to you in this opening statement, there was no place for Ron [17] to go, no place for him to escape to. That fact was obvious as the evidence will show.

This is not a case about an aggravated battery either. It is a case about a fight. It is a case about a fight between two men, one of whom happened to be a deputy sheriff at the time, and Ron Tellez.

Mr. Alfieri quit shortly after this incident. But since he was at that time a deputy sheriff and because Ron was an inmate, according to the prosecution this makes this an aggravated battery. In other words, Ron's

---

[16] Notice the form of the opening statement up to this point: a simple story, told in chronological order. The evidence, of course, will not be that simple. For one thing, some points will be in dispute. Furthermore, the testimony will not be in the form of a narrative but of questions and answers, and, since different witnesses will describe different parts of these events, it will not all come out in any simple story-like order. Mr. Gardiner could have organized his opening as follows: "Ladies and gentlemen of the jury, you will hear from Mr. Alfieri who will testify that. . . . After that you will hear from Officer Daly who will testify that. . . ." Which format do you think is more effective as a method of explanation and persuasion?

[17] Who's "Ron"? Why does Ms. Lyon refer to him by first name only?

status as an inmate and Mr. Alfieri's status as a deputy sheriff makes it an aggravated battery.

MR. REILLY: Objection. Objection.

THE COURT: There is an objection pending. Yes, counsel.

MR. REILLY: Objection. It is argumentative.[18]

MS. LYON: Isn't that what they said their evidence was going to show?

THE COURT: You may continue.[19]

MS. LYON: Thank you, your Honor.

Let me tell you a little bit about what the evidence is going to show as to what happened on August 28 of last year.

First of all, you will find from the evidence that at the time that Ron was arrested, which was about a month prior to this and he was arrested on a murder charge and we will speak about that in a minute, he was a police officer. He was a police officer for the Blue Island Police Department, and he was, in fact, under arrest and he was in jail.

As you found out yesterday during the examination that the Court gave, he was in jail charged with the crime of murder, and he is still charged with that crime. He has not been tried on that case.

As the judge instructed you, as he sits here now he is presumed innocent of this case. He is equally presumed innocent of that case. He has not been tried as of yet.

When this trial is over, he will be tried on that case, and the prosecution, for whatever reason, has chosen to try this case first.

Now you will find, and you probably already know this, you will find from the evidence that being an inmate is an inherently dangerous thing, being in jail. I do not think this would come as any particular surprise to you, and I think the evidence will show that is true.

The dangers are obvious, but the dangers are more for someone who is a police officer or was a police officer than for another person.

The evidence will show that, in fact, a police officer may need special protection from other inmates. It should come as no particular surprise

---

[18] As the judge has told the jury, in the opening statement (as opposed to the closing argument) an attorney is supposed to restrict herself to *describing* the evidence she expects the jury to hear, and not *argue* for inferences or conclusions that may follow from that evidence. That means that the opposing lawyer can object to an opening statement that is "argumentative." The line is hard to draw. At one extreme, a statement that describes admissible testimony is always okay. At the other, an appeal to commonsense or reason is always an argument, although it can be dressed up to *sound* like a description: "*The evidence will show* that there is only one reasonable explanation for this sequence of events. . . ."

[19] What's the judge's ruling on the objection? Is she correct?

that inmates are not particularly fond of police officers.

In addition, there can be problems with guards who, perhaps, not presuming innocence think that this is a police officer who has somehow gone bad. So there are extra problems associated for a person who is a police officer, who had been in custody a very short time at that point, who is in custody.

What I would like to do now is show you a little bit about what the evidence is going to show about what happened in Room 400, and you will also find from the evidence that there was a court order that had been entered to segregate Ron away from the rest of the inmates for the reasons, for the obvious reasons that he is a police officer and he needed some special protection.

Although there is a lockup area which I am going to describe to you in a moment where most of the inmates are kept, he was kept separate. He was locked, handcuffed in the jury room.

. . .

When it was time for him to be transported, Deputy Alfieri handcuffed him behind his back and he was escorted into the lockup area by Deputy Lilly.

Deputy Lilly is a woman sheriff who was assigned at that time to Judge Collins' courtroom.

She followed him down this hallway and this area here where the dots are, that is all bars, and behind here is where the lockup area itself is, where the other inmates are kept.[20] There is a gate here also with bars which can be locked.

They walked through here, and you come to another gate area, okay? This gate area also has bars and is locked and there is a really large key, metal key. You will see that that goes to this particular area.

Now Mr. Alfieri did not have that key. Deputy Lilly has that key because she is the person who was in control of that courtroom, okay? So she unlocks the door, and Mr. Alfieri with Ron comes in here. The door is locked behind them, and Deputy Lilly who has the key, Alfieri does not, walks back and goes to the courtroom to attend to the other courtroom business.

He is then brought through here. There is like another holding area. This is all bars here. This area here goes into another courtroom. The lockups are all adjacent to each other. There is the south side of the building and the north side of the building and so they are all adjacent to each other so the sheriffs can take care of these transportation problems.

He is brought through this gate, which was not locked that day, was

---

[20] Ms. Lyon is using a chart to help the jury follow her client's movements.

brought back through here and into the elevator. The elevator then descended to the basement.

Now the basement area is connected as the prosecutor told you directly with the jail itself.

This is the elevator area and this is the hallway and here is another set of barred gates, which also can be locked, and this is a hallway that leads to—you will see some photographs, we have some photographs to show you later—which leads to an area about midway down this hall, where there is a desk in front of the holding area, into which the prisoners were put, and they would be divided into the various divisions that they were going to and taken back to the jail at some point later.

It is at this desk that Deputy Daly was seated at the time this occurred. Mr. Sykes and Mr. DeValle were somewhere between 100 and 150 feet further away than Deputy Daly.

What happened is as he came down from the lockup, he is handcuffed behind his back, and that is a normal procedure and a sensible procedure. Nobody is saying that should not happen.

He is handcuffed behind his back. He is brought downstairs. What happens is he is pushed into the wall of the elevator, okay? He is shoved, and Ron Tellez is a police officer. He fought back. That is what happened.

There was a fight, and somehow during the fight managed to—he is struggling and he pulls one hand out of the handcuff. I do not know how, and that is what this case is about.

Mr. Alfieri starts yelling for help because he was kicked—I am not saying he was not kicked. There is evidence that he was kicked.

There is evidence that Ron was hurt. Ron was treated. Ron was seen by doctors as well.

He starts calling for help. Deputy Daly arrives. Deputy Daly does not quite know what to do. He is standing there. Seconds later Sykes and DeValle come up, and they make the assumption that their fellow officer is in some kind of trouble and they help him. Nothing wrong with that, nothing wrong with that, but they were not there at the beginning of the incident. They have no way of knowing other than to rely on what Nicholas Alfieri, the former deputy sheriff, said as to how this began.

Now I believe that the evidence will show that there are rules that the deputy sheriffs have, that the sheriff's department has, and there should be rules.

There are rules that police officers have. There are rules that lawyers and judges have. We are a nation of laws as the judge told you yesterday.

There are rules, the evidence will show, against hitting an inmate or hurting an inmate for no reason.

We believe that the evidence will show that, in fact, Mr. Alfieri was covering himself. That is what it was about.

If he said Ron Tellez was attempting to escape, and maybe he was trying to stay in the elevator and stay away from Nicholas Alfieri, where on earth was he going to go? Where?

He could run out into the hall and into the arms of more sheriffs. He could take the elevator up to one of the other floors and get back into this area which is the same area in every single courtroom. It would be locked. He would be locked in a little cell area.

Where was he going? Attempt escape? That is ridiculous. That is ridiculous.[21]

This is not a case about an attempt escape. It is not a case about an aggravated battery. It is a case about a fight, and it is a case about a cover-up.

Ron Tellez is not guilty. Thank you.

. . .

THE COURT: Mr. Gardiner, if you are ready, call your first witness please.

MR. GARDINER: We call Nicholas Alfieri to the stand.

(Witness sworn)

NICHOLAS ALFIERI,

called as a witness on behalf of the People of the State of Illinois, having been first duly sworn, was examined and testified as follows:

DIRECT EXAMINATION

BY MR. GARDINER:

Q. Sir, can you please state your name and spell your last name? **A.** Nicholas Alfieri, A-L-F-I-E-R-I.

Q. Mr. Alfieri, are you employed? **A.** Yes.

Q. Where are you currently employed? **A.** JB Corporation.

Q. What do you do with that company? **A.** Sales.

Q. What state do you live in now? **A.** Texas.

Q. Were you formerly employed as a deputy sheriff? **A.** Yes.

---

[21] Reread the last couple of paragraphs. Doesn't this portion of Ms. Lyon's opening statement strike you as *more* argumentative than the part the prosecutor objected to at the beginning? Why doesn't he object here?

Q. How long did you work as deputy sheriff? **A.** Approximately two-and-a-half years.

Q. What responsibilities did you have as a deputy sheriff? **A.** Courtroom duties. Bringing out prisoners who were in custody in front of the judge for court business, taking them back to the lockup, picking them up downstairs at the jail bridge, and bringing them up to the lockup area and in back of the courtrooms.

Q. When you say taking them from the jail bridge, what is the jail bridge? **A.** The jail bridge is an area that the prisoners are in in the morning and they are brought up to the courtroom area. It is downstairs. It is in the basement of this facility.

Q. Now you mentioned people in custody. What do you mean by "custody"? **A.** Custody is an individual who is housed at the jail, at a jail facility.

Q. In the course of your duties as a deputy sheriff, were you familiar with the elevators in this building? **A.** Yes.

Q. Where do those elevators lead? What elevators would you deal with as a deputy sheriff? **A.** The elevators are in back of the courtroom areas throughout the building. They are in the back area behind the courtrooms.

Q. Where do those elevators go to? **A.** Well they could go to any floor or to the basement. They can go to any floor or the basement.[22]

Q. On August 28, 1987, were you working as deputy sheriff? **A.** Yes.

Q. Were you in uniform? **A.** Yes.

Q. The uniform that you would wear would be much like those deputy sheriffs in the courtroom today? **A.** No. I believe we had different uniforms at the time.

Q. Were you armed? **A.** No.

Q. On that date what responsibilities did you have? **A.** I had the general responsibilities of a courtroom, to bring prisoners out and bring them back, just the general responsibilities of a courtroom.

Q. What courtroom were you assigned to? **A.** Room 400.

---

[22] We're still in the introductory part of Mr. Alfieri's testimony, but the basic pattern is set. As we all have learned to expect, the testimony is in the form of questions and answers. Although no rule specifically prohibits testimony in the form of unbroken narratives (e.g., "Mr. Alfieri, please give us a complete account of your dealings with Ronald Tellez on August 28, 1987") judges generally prefer, and usually require, questions and answers. See Chapter Two, pp. 156–157. The most important consequence of this practice should already be evident: it gives the examining lawyer great control over the content and the organization of the witness's testimony. In this case, since it is direct examination, most of the questions are non-leading: "Where do those elevators go?" as opposed to "The elevators go to any floor in the building, don't they?"

Q. Who was the judge in that courtroom? **A.** Judge Collins.

Q. That courtroom is in this building? **A.** Yes.

Q. Just one floor above us here? **A.** Yes.

Q. Now in the course of your duties on August 28, 1987, did you see a person that you know to be Ronald Tellez? **A.** Yes.

Q. Do you see that person in court today? **A.** Yes.

MS. LYON: Your Honor, we will stipulate to the identification if they want the stipulation.[23]

MR. GARDINER: We will accept the stipulation, your Honor.

Q. Where did you see the defendant? **A.** He was in the back in the jury room handcuffed to a chair, right in the space where the door is open and you can see him with an open door there.

Q. When did you see the defendant? **A.** In the morning, early morning. The exact time, I do not know, but early in the morning.

Q. Did you have him in your custody at that time? **A.** He was in the courtroom's custody. Specifically I do not know if he was in my custody.

Q. Who were you working with that day? **A.** Deputy Daly, Deputy Lilly, Deputies Daly and Lilly.

Q. Where were they assigned? **A.** Same courtroom.

Q. When you saw the defendant sitting in the jury room, could you describe how he appeared? **A.** He was sitting there. He would have been cuffed to a chair, and he was just sitting there.

Q. How was he dressed? **A.** He had a suit on. I recall that.

Q. Did you have contact with the defendant on that day? **A.** At some point I did. Yes.

Q. What point did you have contact? **A.** At the lunch recess.

Q. What time was that approximately? **A.** Approximately 12:00; right around 12:00 o'clock I believe.

Q. What other deputy sheriffs were working with you at that time? **A.** At that time just Deputy Lilly.

Q. Deputy Sheriff Daly was not working with you? **A.** I think Deputy Daly had been called on the phone to be reassigned to another area. They needed him somewhere else.

---

[23] A stipulation is an agreement between the parties about the accuracy of some undisputed fact. See Chapter Eleven, pp. 1393–1397. In this case, Ms. Lyon has offered a simple stipulation: that the defendant in court is the same person that Mr. Alfieri saw a year-and-a-half before, in Courtroom 400. The prosecutor accepts the stipulation, which means that the fact stipulated to is now officially determined to be true, and no more evidence on that point need be offered.

Q. Around noon you went over to the defendant? **A.** Yes.

Q. What did you do? **A.** I took his handcuff off, handcuffed him in back, and I was taking him down to the bridge area to bring him back to the jail area.

Q. Could you describe for the jurors where you first went with the defendant? **A.** Okay. We walked through a little area to a door. We opened that door. We walked down a corridor. I do not know if it is about fifty feet or so. It is a corridor that leads toward the elevator. It goes right past the holding cell that is in back of the courtroom. There is a gate there. That gate is opened. We turn a little bit to the left, to the elevator. The elevator is right there.

Q. When you arrived with the defendant at the elevator, were you alone? **A.** Deputy Lilly walked us back there.

Q. What did you do when you arrived at the elevator? **A.** Pushed the button for the elevator to come up.

Q. What happened next? **A.** The elevator came up.

Q. What did you do? **A.** He stepped on the elevator, went toward the back. I stepped on the elevator, was off to the side a little bit, pressed the button down to the basement, and the elevator proceeded down.

Q. Who was in the elevator at that time? **A.** He and myself.

Q. Did you arrive at the basement? **A.** Yes.

Q. What happened in the basement? **A.** The door opened all the way, suddenly he kicked me in the testicles.

Q. What happened to you? **A.** I jumped forward and I was—

Q. When you say forward, what direction would that be in relation to the elevator? **A.** Out of the elevator toward the front of the elevator, and out of the elevator.

Q. What did you do after you were kicked in the testicles and moved outside the elevator? **A.** I realized the doors were closing and he was on the elevator and I was off it. So I rushed the elevator, put my arm up like that, pushed the elevator door, you know, so that it would open, and at that time I received another kick either in the testicles or right next to it in the leg and I fell down.

Q. After receiving that second kick, where were you? **A.** Down on the ground somewhere off the elevator.

Q. What did you do then? **A.** Started yelling help, help, help, help. Got back up, rushed the elevator, did the same thing. Pushed the door so that it would open, received another kick, fell back down.

Q. What was happening to the elevator door each time you were kicked and you fell back? **A.** It would jar open. I would push it open.

Q. During those times when you were not pushing it open, what would happen with that elevator? **A.** It would start to close again.

Q. The third time that you were kicked, what happened? **A.** I still would have been yelling help, help, help, getting up, rushing back to the elevator, pushing it open, getting kicked again, falling back down, yelling help, help, help.

Q. Where was the defendant in the elevator? **A.** I didn't see him as I was rushing the elevator. I saw him one time. He was all the way in the back, his hands behind his back just looking motionless, straight ahead, just motionless. I do not know if he was looking straight at me. I saw him one time. When I would rush the elevator and push it, I did not see him, but I felt the kick and I fell back.

Q. After you were kicked the fourth time, what happened? **A.** Same thing. Falling back, screaming, rushing the elevator, and I do not know if it was after that time or shortly after that Deputy Daly came.

Q. When you say that Deputy Daly came, where did he come? **A.** He just came up. He was on the right side of me, and he was there.

Q. Where were you when you saw Deputy Daly? **A.** Probably on the ground. I can't really recall if I was on the ground or if I was getting up to rush the elevator. I just knew he was there.

Q. What did Deputy Daly do? **A.** He was trying to coax him. He was saying, come on. Stop that. Quit it. Come off. Quit it. Stuff like that.

Q. Who was he trying to coax? **A.** The defendant.

Q. How did he address the defendant? **A.** By the first name, Ron or Ronnie, something like that.

Q. Did Deputy Daly touch the defendant at any time? **A.** No.

Q. Now during the time that Deputy Daly was coaxing the defendant, what was happening to you? **A.** I was still proceeding the same way, rushing it, banging the thing open, getting kicked, falling back down, and yelling help.

Q. What happened after you were kicked? **A.** I was kicked maybe a few more times and I looked up to my right and then I saw two correctional guards turn the corner and they were coming.

Q. Do you know the names of those correctional guards? **A.** I believe DeValle and Sykes.

Q. Throughout this time, were you running? **A.** Yes.

Q. What did you see Officers DeValle and Sykes do? **A.** Well they rushed on the elevator, bodies were all over, and I was laying on the ground at that point and I was looking up. It looked like they were pushing him up, like he had slid down or something, and they were pushing him up by the underarms.

Q. Where were they in relation to you? **A.** They were on the elevator. I was laying on the ground. At that point I had my foot up against the elevator. I had it up, my left foot up against the elevator. I was laying completely on the ground looking up like this, and they rushed on. So their bodies were in front of me.

Q. Was that the first time that you had fallen on your back on the ground? **A.** No. I think I fell on my back almost every time.

Q. Now you said that you saw the two officers hold the defendant? **A.** Looked like they took him by his underarms and pushed him up.

Q. What happened after that? **A.** Then it looked like they did something in back with his cuffs which I saw their hands going back.

Q. What happened to the defendant? What did they do with the defendant? **A.** Well they took him off the elevator, but they did something before then. Before then, somebody yelled—one of them said something about there is a key. There is a key. Alfieri pick up the key.

Q. What happened then? **A.** I said, that can't be. That can't be.

Q. After you said that, what happened? **A.** They took him off the elevator.

Q. Where did you go? **A.** I was still laying there.

Q. Did you get up? **A.** Yeah.

Q. What did you do once you got up? **A.** I asked Daly, could you have dropped some keys or something? He said, no.

Q. Where did you go? **A.** Then I walked up toward the elevator and I looked down like this and I said, there's nothing here, there's nothing here because they were still off to the side a ways.

Q. Did you pick anything up? **A.** Yeah. I picked up papers. Paperwork and maybe his glasses.

Q. Where did you go with the papers? **A.** I went back to the bridge area.

Q. What happened then? **A.** I went into the bridge area. I made a phone call to Sergeant Hoff indicating what had happened.

Q. What did you do after making that phone call? **A.** After a while, we went upstairs, a number of individuals, and I spoke or I waited to speak to a state's attorney.

Q. Did you later seek medical treatment? **A.** Yes.

Q. Where did you go? **A.** St. Anthony's Hospital.

Q. What happened at St. Anthony's Hospital? **A.** They took a look at me, I guess the leg and the testicles. My finger on my hand was bothering me, and I was a little bit bruised here. They gave me some medication of some sort, like Tylenol or something, and they gave me some support for the testicles, some kind of strap.

Q. Now the kicks that the defendant gave to you, where were those kicks? Where did he strike you? **A.** All of them were to the testicle area, the groin area, or the leg right next to it.

MR. GARDINER: Your Honor, may I approach the witness?

THE COURT: Yes. You may.[24]

BY MR. GARDINER:

Q. Mr. Alfieri, I will hand to you People's Exhibit Numbers 1 through 5 for identification. I direct your attention, first, to People's Exhibit Number 1. Could you identify that photograph? **A.** A picture of me.[25]

Q. When was that taken? **A.** It would have been taken the Monday after, whatever date that was, a few days after.

Q. What day of the week was August 28, 1987? **A.** A Friday.

Q. So that would be the 31st? **A.** It would be Monday. Monday would be the 31st. That sounds reasonable.

Q. Directing your attention to People's Exhibit Number 1, does that picture truly and accurately depict you as you appeared on August 31, 1987? **A.** Yes.

Q. Now I direct your attention to People's Exhibit Number 2 for identification. Do you recognize that picture? **A.** Yes.

Q. What is that a picture of? **A.** Forearm area, some bruises over it.

Q. Is that the forearm area where you show those bruises? How did you receive those injuries? **A.** It must have been when I hit the door like that, pushing it, because I am looking at where they are and it had to have been that way when I was pushing at the door. I was maybe

---

[24] Some judges require attorneys to examine witnesses from a podium in the center of the court; others permit the lawyers to stand (or even sit) at counsel table, or to move about the court. In most courts, however (contrary to what you often see on TV), the lawyer must address the witness from a respectful distance—perhaps 8 or 10 feet. The purpose of this restriction is to prevent lawyers from physically intimidating witnesses. If a lawyer needs to move close to the witness—typically to hand the witness a document—she asks permission of the judge. Since the purpose of the rule is to prevent intimidation, some judges only require lawyers to ask for permission to approach a witness on cross-examination, or on direct examination of a hostile witness.

[25] Mr. Gardiner is having the witness authenticate several exhibits, photographs of the witness a few days after the events at issue. Note the elements that he covers: The exhibits have been pre-marked for identification (presumably before the testimony began), he refers to them by exhibit numbers, and he elicits testimony that they are what he claims: photographs of Mr. Alfieri's injuries.

catching it with my hand and I was catching it with this part too and I was pushing it that way. So I believe I received it in that manner.

Q. Does People's Exhibit 2 for identification truly and accurately depict the injuries that you received on August 28, 1987? A. Yes.

Q. I ask that you go to People's Exhibit Number 3 for identification please. Do you recognize that picture? A. Yes.

Q. What is that? A. It looks like the same picture, my arm, but a closer view from the camera.

Q. What injury does that show? A. It shows some bruises.

Q. How did you receive that injury? A. With my arm pushing against the door like that.

Q. Does People's Exhibit Number 3 for identification truly and accurately depict the injury that you received from the defendant on August 28, 1987? A. Yes.

Q. I will ask that you move to People's Exhibit Number 4 for identification please. What is that? A. It is a picture of my leg with black-and-blue marks and bruises.

Q. How did you receive the injury depicted in that photograph? A. From kicks.

Q. From whom? A. Kicks from the defendant.

Q. Does that photograph, People's Exhibit Number 4 for identification, truly and accurately depict the injuries you received from the defendant on August 28, 1987? A. Yes.

Q. I ask that you go to People's Exhibit Number 5 for identification please. Do you recognize that item? A. Yes.

Q. What do you recognize that to be? A. It is another view of my leg with the black-and-blue marks and the bruises.

Q. How did you receive those injuries? A. Kicks from the defendant.

Q. Does that exhibit, People's Exhibit Number 5 for identification, truly and accurately show the injuries you received from the defendant on August 28, 1987? A. Yes.[26]

Q. Mr. Alfieri, at any time did you strike the defendant on August 28, 1987? A. No.

---

[26] Mr. Gardiner does not move the admission of the exhibits in evidence. That means he may not "publish"—show—them to the jury at this point. If he had moved for admission the defense attorneys would have had an opportunity to object and to conduct an examination of the witness at that time on the issue of authenticity. See Chapter Ten, pp. 1282–1286. Mr. Gardiner also does not make a record of showing the exhibits to the defense. Most likely they have seen them before trial; if not, they would probably object and ask to see the photographs before they were given to the witness.

Q. At any time did you push or shove him? **A.** No.

Q. Did you know the defendant before August 28, 1987? **A.** No.

MR. GARDINER: If I could have a moment, your Honor.[27]

Q. Mr. Alfieri, how tall are you? **A.** Five-foot-five.

Q. How much did you weigh back in 1987? **A.** Approximately 160.

Q. On that August date or on any date prior to that had you ever had an argument with the defendant? **A.** No.

Q. Had he given you any trouble at any time prior to that day? **A.** No.

Q. Did he give you any trouble on that date prior to going down to the basement on the elevator? **A.** No.

MR. GARDINER: Nothing further, your Honor.

THE COURT: Thank you. Cross examination.

CROSS EXAMINATION

BY MS. LYON:

Q. Mr. Alfieri, you testified that you had been a deputy sheriff for approximately two-and-a-half years? **A.** Yes.

Q. Shortly after this incident, you quit the department, isn't that true? **A.** Yes.

Q. Before you became a deputy sheriff, you had training? **A.** Actually, no.

Q. You had no training to become a deputy sheriff? **A.** No.

Q. You never went to an academy of any kind? **A.** You indicated before I started as a deputy sheriff you had training.[28]

Q. I beg your pardon. Before you actually got hired, right? **A.** Yes.

Q. After you got hired, you got trained? **A.** I never went to an academy. I came the same day to this facility, and I worked here for about three months and then I went to an academy.

Q. Would it be fair to say that before August 28, 1987, you had been to the academy? **A.** Yes.

Q. So you had received some training? **A.** Yes.

---

[27] Why does Mr. Gardiner ask for a moment at this point in his examination of Mr. Alfieri? There's no way to tell for sure from the transcript, but many experienced trial attorneys are careful to pause a couple of questions before the end of an examination in order to confer with co-counsel, to check on whether they missed something that should be asked.

[28] Ms. Lyon has inadvertently incorporated an unnecessary fact into her question—that he went to the academy *before* he was hired, and the witness is answering very literally. Does this make his testimony more effective?

Q. That would be training in various things associated with your job? **A.** Yes.

Q. You were, in fact, an officer with the sheriff's department? **A.** Yes.

Q. You were trained in various things such as self-defense? **A.** Yes.

Q. You were trained about the rules of the department? **A.** Yes.

Q. The regulations of the department? **A.** Yes.

Q. The various procedures of the department? **A.** Yes.

Q. There is a lot of paperwork involved with the department? **A.** Yes.

Q. And what you had to do and who you had to talk to, right? **A.** Yes.

Q. You were trained in what to do in an emergency situation, is that right? **A.** Yes.[29]

Q. For instance, if there was a fire? **A.** I believe so. Yes.

Q. If a prisoner became ill? **A.** Yes.

Q. Who to call, what to do basically, is that right? **A.** Yeah.

Q. You also learned something or were trained in some degree as to the law? **A.** Yes.

Q. What offenses were? **A.** Yes.

Q. For instance, you know that under our law a person has a right to self-defense? **A.** Yes.

Q. That includes you? **A.** Yes.

Q. That includes Ron Tellez? **A.** Yes.

Q. You also know that it is against the law to use violence against a person with no reason? **A.** Yes.

Q. It is your contention here that that is what Ron did to you? **A.** Yes.

Q. A reason for violence, an acceptable reason for violence to be used against an inmate, might be an attempt escape, wouldn't it? **A.**

---

[29] Read back through the last ten questions and answers. How many words has the witness spoken? These, obviously, are *leading* questions. As we have mentioned, supra p. 4, leading questions are allowed on cross-examination. In practice, they are not only permitted but heavily favored. See Chapter Two, pp. 151–153. What information does an attorney need to be able to prepare and conduct this sort of interrogation?

Since this is cross examination, the questions are supposed to be restricted to "the subject matter of the direct examination"—which includes, at least, anything having to do with Mr. Alfieri's dealings with Mr. Tellez on August 28, 1987—"and matters affecting the witness's credibility." FRE 611(b). See Chapter Two, pp. 153–154.

Would you repeat that please?

Q. Sure. If for some reason you needed to justify the use of force against an inmate, one good justification would be an attempt escape, wouldn't it?

MR. REILLY: Objection to the form of the question.[30]

THE COURT: Sustained. Sustained.[31]

BY MS. LYON:

Q. You testified earlier when the prosecutor was asking you questions that you are five-five and weighed about 160 at the time of this incident? **A.** Right.

Q. As part of your training, did you learn how to estimate heights and weights? **A.** I do not know how really good I am at estimating heights and weights. I do not know if we would be trained on that. I think my ability is kind of poor on estimating heights and weights.

MS. LYON: With the judge's permission, may I ask that the witness come off the stand for a moment?[32]

MR. GARDINER: Objection, your Honor. I fail to see the relevance.

MS. LYON: I would like to—

THE COURT: Step up here.

(The following proceedings were had out of the hearing of the jury and the court reporter.)[33]

(The following proceedings were had in the hearing of the jury.)

BY MS. LYON:

Q. Mr. Alfieri, would you step down and stand in the middle of the courtroom please? **A.** Sure.

(Witness stepped down.)

MS. LYON: Ron, would you do me a favor and stand up?

Q. Would you be able to estimate at all? **A.** About five-foot-six or five-foot-seven.

MS. LYON: Thank you very much. You can resume the stand.

---

[30] Presumably the objection is that the question, in the process of asking whether it is permissible to use violence to thwart an attempted escape, implies that the witness might have "*needed to justify* the use of force. . . ."

[31] Does it matter how the court rules? Does it matter that the question is never answered?

[32] As with approaching the witness, a lawyer may have to ask for permission to request the witness move from his usual position on the witness stand, depending on the practice in the particular court.

[33] What was said in this brief "sidebar" conference at the bench? If the judge made a significant ruling in that discussion, could the losing party complain about it on appeal? In this case, the matter was probably inconsequential.

(Witness resumed the stand.)

BY MS. LYON:

Q. Let's talk for a few moments, if we might, about what happened on August 28, 1987. You said you were assigned to Courtroom 400, Judge Collins' courtroom? **A.** Yes.

Q. They are bigger courtrooms than this courtroom, is that right? **A.** Yes. Bigger courtrooms than this courtroom we are in?

Q. Than we are in right now? **A.** Yes.

Q. In fact, those courtrooms are the older courtrooms that have been around longer. These are new? **A.** Yeah. Yeah.

Q. Those courtrooms have a lockup behind them as does every courtroom? **A.** Yeah.

Q. And in the lockup is where prisoners are kept generally? **A.** Yes.

Q. But in certain circumstances, special circumstances, a prisoner might be kept segregated from other prisoners, is that right? **A.** Yes.

Q. Such as where there is a court order to that effect? **A.** Yes.

Q. You were aware, were you not, that there was a court order to keep Ron, who was a police officer at the time of his arrest, segregated from the rest of the prisoners? **A.** Yes.

Q. That is the reason he was in the jury room rather than in the lockup area with the rest of the prisoners? **A.** Yes.

Q. I would like you to take a look at what has been marked as Defense Exhibit Number 1. If you would come off the stand. Can you see from here, jury? Well can you tell what this is looking from the diagram? **A.** Yes.[34]

Q. Would you tell the ladies and gentlemen of the jury what it is? **A.** This would be a door right here to the area that you walk all the way down the hall. There is another gate here. You turn in here. There is a small room, and then there is the elevator.

Q. Is this the lockup area of Courtroom 400? **A.** Yeah. Well the lockup you had it further—The area would be here.

Q. Behind this dotted line, is that right? **A.** Yes.

Q. Where the dotted line is, that is bars, isn't that right? **A.** Okay.

Q. If you walked out of this room and kept going straight, you

---

[34] Ms. Lyon is having the witness authenticate a defense exhibit, which has been pre-marked for identification. Apparently it is a large diagram, and is visible to the jury. In other words, it is being "published" before it is admitted in evidence. The prosecutors do not object, probably because it is an indisputably accurate diagram that will inevitably be admitted. Note that the witness has come off the witness stand, but this time Ms. Lyon does not ask for permission from the judge.

would go through some doors into the courtroom? **A.** Yes. Yes.

Q. The jury room would be just a little further east as you walked out of the door, is that right? **A.** As you walked out here, yeah.

Q. You would turn to your left and it would be—**A.** Yes. Yes.

Q. And it would be right in this area? **A.** Yes.

Q. The door that you spoke about was right about here that it was opened? **A.** Yes.

Q. That you could see Mr. Ron Tellez? **A.** Yes.

Q. Would you with this red pen put a "D" where this door was please?

The area of the jury room, could you put "JR" for jury room? You can resume the stand.

(Witness resumed the stand.)

BY MS. LYON:

Q. You testified briefly about your duties as a courtroom assistant, but basically what you were there to do was to keep order in the courtroom, right? **A.** Yes.

Q. If there was noise, to tell people to be quiet? **A.** Yes.

Q. To bring prisoners in and out of the lockup? **A.** Yes.

Q. To appear in front of the judge? **A.** Yes.

Q. To transport prisoners to and from the courtroom? **A.** Yes.

Q. And to attend to the needs of, perhaps, if there was a jury trial, of the jurors? **A.** Yes.

Q. Various things like that, is that right? **A.** Right.

Q. What happens when a case is called is the sheriffs are informed that the case has been called in front of the judge, right? **A.** Right.

Q. If you are on duty, you would go and you would get the prisoner? **A.** Yes.

Q. You would bring the prisoner out in front of the judge? **A.** Yes.

Q. And you would remain there with the prisoner—**A.** Yes.

Q.—For whatever business was taking place? **A.** Yes.

Q. And then you would return the prisoner back to the lockup or, in Ron's case, back to the jury room where he would be seated and handcuffed? **A.** Yes.

Q. On this particular day you did not bring Ron Tellez out in front of the judge? **A.** No.

Q. That was Deputy Daly who did that? **A.** Yes.

Q. He was brought out twice? **A.** I do not recall.

Q. Did you bring him out either time? **A.** No.

Q. That was Deputy Daly that would have done that? **A.** Yes.

Q. You transported him or you were going to transport him back to the lockup area and onto the bridge? **A.** Yes.

Q. Deputy Lilly, that is a female sheriff, is that right? **A.** Yes.

Q. She had the key to the gate that you pointed at before, isn't that right? **A.** Yes.

Q. This is a large key, is it not? **A.** Yes.

MS. LYON: Mr. Anderson, do you have a key like that?

THE SHERIFF: Yes. She does.[35]

BY MS. LYON:

Q. I am going to show you what I will consider marked as Defense Exhibit Number—

Do we have to mark it?

THE COURT: Well you have to be able to identify it in the report somehow, counsel.

BY MS. LYON:

Q. We will consider it marked as Defense Exhibit 1-A for the record.

Does that look like the kind of key we are discussing? **A.** Yes.

Q. You did not have these keys, is that right? **A.** Deputy Lilly and I both walked with the defendant. I cannot remember who put the key inside, if it was me or her, to open the door. We were both walking together. I believe she had the keys in her hand.

Q. You got on the elevator with Ron? **A.** Yeah.

Q. She left? **A.** Yeah.

Q. And locked it back? **A.** I guess she locked it back. I do not know exactly.

Q. You did not have the keys with you? **A.** No.

Q. By the way, during the day Deputy Daly had gone down to take care of an arraignment, is that right? **A.** I believe he had been transferred to the bridge area. There is a chair in an area down by the bridge.

---

[35] "Mr. Anderson" and "she" are, presumably, deputy sheriffs assigned to the Tellez trial as bailiffs. But the record does not reflect that.

Q. Prior to that, he had taken a prisoner down to the chief judge, and when he came back, you told him he had been transferred down to the bridge? **A.** There was a phone call. There was a phone call for him to be transferred. I cannot remember if I told him to call or if he called to get the information, but there had been a phone call I believe from Sergeant Hoff, somebody from the office reassigning him.

Q. You have already told us when the prosecutor was asking you questions your version of what happened downstairs in the basement, right? **A.** Yes. Except the word version. It is the truth not version.

. . .

Q. Now, Mr. Alfieri, there was an investigation that was done in this case, isn't that true? **A.** Yes.

Q. That was done by the Internal Affairs Division of what was then your office, the Sheriff's Office, is that right? **A.** Yes.

Q. The Internal Affairs Section investigates problems that might have occurred in the Sheriff's Department, is that correct? **A.** Yes.

Q. Complaints? **A.** Yes.

Q. By sheriffs against other sheriffs? **A.** Yes.

Q. By inmates against sheriffs? **A.** Yes.

Q. By sheriffs against inmates? **A.** Yes.

Q. Basically anything that goes wrong involving sheriffs they may investigate, is that fair to say? **A.** Yes.

Q. They investigated this case, isn't that true? **A.** Yes.

Q. You gave a number of statements to them regarding what happened in this case? **A.** Yes.

Q. You were questioned quite extensively? **A.** Yes.

Q. Five or six times, is that about right? **A.** I do not know if it was that many times.

Q. Four? **A.** Maybe less, maybe even three.

Q. In fact, you wrote a memorandum to your sergeant regarding this, isn't that true? **A.** Yes.

Q. And you were interviewed by an investigator by the name of Willer, is that correct? **A.** Yes.

Q. At least twice? **A.** Yes.

Q. When you were describing this incident for the prosecutor a few moments ago, you said that you were kicked, knocked back, kicked, knocked back, kicked, knocked back, and it took you quite a while to describe that, isn't that right? **A.** I do not know what you mean to describe it.

Q. As you answered each question, that took a few moments? **A.** Yes.

Q. It took longer than the entire incident took isn't that true? **A.** Yes.

Q. The entire incident from the time you say that Ron just started kicking you for no reason until Sykes, DeValle, and Daly came on the scene and subdued him, that whole thing took about a minute? **A.** It probably took a little bit longer than that to the best of my recollection. Being kicked back and forth, all I can do is approximate time, but I think it was little bit longer than that.

Q. How long do you think it was? **A.** A minute and a half.

Q. You do recall writing a memorandum as I said before to Sergeant Lewis, isn't that right? **A.** Yes.

Q. And in that memorandum you said that it took about a minute? **A.** If I recall, they were asking me when Daly came. It took about a minute. I thought it took about a minute for Daly to come, and then somebody came afterwards.

Q. When you write reports, you were trained about paperwork as you said earlier, is that right? **A.** Yes. Yes.

Q. Paperwork is important in your job, isn't that right? **A.** Yes.

Q. You are trained to write complete reports? **A.** Yes.

Q. Accurate reports? **A.** Yes.

Q. Include every important detail? **A.** Yes.

Q. It would be fair to say, wouldn't it, Mr. Alfieri, that if a prisoner somehow had hold of a handcuff key, that would be important, wouldn't it? **A.** Yes.

Q. If someone said in the course of an incident like this that there was a handcuff key loose somewhere, that would be important, wouldn't it? **A.** Yes.

Q. If you searched for a handcuff key, that would be important, wouldn't it? **A.** Yes.

Q. I would like to show you what I am going to mark as Defense Exhibit Number 22 for identification and ask you if you recognize this. **A.** Yes.

Q. Would you tell the ladies and gentlemen of the jury what that is? **A.** That was my report directly afterwards.

Q. That is what you wrote to your sergeant? **A.** Yeah.

Q. The sergeant is your boss? **A.** Yes.

Q. Would you read that report over again, and when you get to the part where you say anything about a key, would you raise your hand?

MR. REILLY: Objection. He never said he said that in his report. That assumes a fact not in evidence. It is an improper question.[36]

MS. LYON: It is impeachment by omission, and it is totally proper, Mr. Reilly.

THE COURT: Not in the form that you put the question. Rephrase the question.

BY MS. LYON:

Q. Is there anywhere in that report where you say one word about a key? **A.** No.

Q. Thank you. Now you say you were interviewed a number of times, isn't that true? **A.** Yes.

Q. That was by Mr. Willer, isn't that right? **A.** Yes.

Q. Before you were interviewed, you were given your rights, weren't you? **A.** Yes.

Q. An administrative proceedings rights form, isn't that true? **A.** Yes.

Q. You were told—

MR. REILLY: Objection, Judge.

THE COURT: Basis?

MR. REILLY: It is irrelevant, judge, in this proceeding.

THE COURT: Do you want to come forward?

(The following proceedings were had out of the hearing of the jury.)[37]

MR. REILLY: For the record, I do not see why counsel has to show him an administrative form that shows he was advised of certain rights he has administratively as a sheriff's deputy.

I do not see the relevance in presenting it to a jury at this time in a trial for aggravated battery and attempt escape against Mr. Tellez. I fail

---

[36] Mr. Reilly is correct. Ms. Lyon has implied that the report refers to a key, and asked the witness to indicate *where* that happens. But there's no evidence that the report contains any such reference; in fact it does not, and Ms. Lyon is using this format to try to emphasize that fact.

[37] This time the side-bar conference has been transcribed, no doubt because the judge and the lawyers anticipate that it could include an important ruling that might be the subject of an appeal. Presumably the conference is being conducted in the courtroom in such a manner that the court reporter can hear it, but not the jury. Depending on the architecture of the court and the volume of the speakers' voices, jurors sometimes do hear what is said at side-bar.

to see the relevance.[38]

THE COURT: Counsel?

MS. LYON: The relevance is it goes to his bias and his reason to change his story as time goes on.

THE COURT: I do not see how giving him rights in an administrative proceeding goes to that.

MS. LYON: Because he had something to lose.

THE COURT: That can be inferred from a lot of the evidence.

I do not see whether or not they gave him his rights in an administrative proceeding has to do with anything.

MS. LYON: I disagree with your Honor. I think it goes to his bias and his interest. He has an interest in keeping his job. He has an interest in not getting suspended.

THE COURT: If you are talking about the substance of what he said in a statement to someone, you are absolutely right.

Whether or not he was given any rights which really have no relevance to the issues in here, but they have relevance to what happened over there—It has no relevance in this case. I have no problem with you going into what he said to them.

MS. LYON: It does have relevance in that he had a motive at that time to change his story, to conform to other people.

THE COURT: Whether or not he was given any rights, that would be true.

MS. LYON: Yes, but it makes it very clear what was the intervening factor that made him start changing his story. The story keeps getting better every time he gets talked to and he gets his rights.

THE COURT: You can go into whatever it is he said. I am sort of understanding what you are saying.

You have to do this on a piece-by-piece basis. The problem I have with that is that it starts out sounding like he was under arrest. He was not under arrest. There was no arresting authority.[39]

You have a right to deal with whatever he said. If he changed his story, impeach him. I do not see the relevance in anything except—

---

[38] Consider the definition of relevance, supra p. 5. Isn't the fact that Mr. Alfieri was warned of his rights *relevant* to his credibility?

[39] The judge has supplied the real reason to exclude the evidence: the "unfair prejudice" (supra p. 5) that might flow from the implication that Mr. Alfieri was under arrest. In practice, lawyers often object to evidence as "irrelevant"—as Mr. Reilly has done here—when the real objection is "unfair prejudice." But *why* is it unfairly prejudicial to imply that Mr. Alfieri was under arrest?

MS. LYON: Obviously I disagree with you, but I have made my point on that.

Let me ask you this so I do not get stopped again in the middle.

I intend to ask him what he had to lose. I intend to talk to him about the fact that he had reason to start adding things to his story.

THE COURT: Well I will be frank with you. As soon as this issue comes up, you are going to be concerned about whether or not you are going to keep your job.

It is so obviously patent to the facts even as they have already come out. Certainly I would have no objection.

If you have something to lose, the State may object. I do not have any problem with that. Of course, he was worried about losing his job.

MS. LYON: I wanted to clear it up now as long as we are here.

(The following proceedings were had in the hearing of the jury.)

THE COURT: May I have the last question read back, the one that precipitated read back?

(Record read back by the reporter.)

THE COURT: Counsel, I am assuming we can proceed. I was not sure where we broke in with the objection. I am assuming we can proceed at this point.

Go ahead, Miss Lyon.

BY MS. LYON:

Q. Now you were interviewed by Mr. Willer of the Internal Affairs Division, isn't that right? A. Yes.

Q. One of the interviews occurred on the 31st of August, 1987? A. Yeah.

Q. It was a few days later? A. Yeah.

Q. In that interview he asked you to describe what happened, is that right? A. Yes.

Q. You described what happened? A. Yeah.

Q. Never in that interview did you ever say one word about a key to Mr. Willer, did you?

MR. GARDINER: Objection.

THE COURT: Overruled.

THE WITNESS: I do not believe so, but I do not remember that interview very well. I did not realize at the time that I had some stress problems and was not remembering things that I should have remembered.

BY MS. LYON:

Q. You had stress problems so that is why you did not remember then? **A.** I do not remember the full conversation. They told me I did not tell them that. I had no reason to doubt that, but I do not recall it because I did find out afterwards I was having some stress problems and forgetting things that basically I would not forget normally.

Q. Your stress problems are fine, your memory is fine now, but it was not fine a few days later, is that what you were saying? **A.** I guess so because I never consciously deleted or left anything out consciously. Never.

Q. Returning back to the report that you made on the day of the incident, the report that you typed and you sent to your sergeants, to Sergeant Lewis? **A.** Yes.

Q. Nowhere in that report did you say one word about Mr. Daly saying, come on, Ron, get off the elevator, did you? **A.** No.

Q. Nowhere in that report did you say one word about—When you were interviewed on August 31, you did not say anything about this, come on, Ron, get off the elevator stuff either, did you? **A.** I don't recall. I don't recall that interview real well.

Q. You remember that now though is what you are telling us, that he said that now? That is what you are telling us now?

MR. REILLY: Objection.

THE WITNESS: I did not understand the question.

MR. REILLY: I will withdraw the objection.

THE WITNESS: I did not understand it as you phrased it.

MS. LYON: I will ask the question again.

Q. You are telling us now today that Deputy Daly said, come on, Ron, get off the elevator, right? **A.** Yeah.

Q. But did nothing to help you, right? **A.** Yeah.

Q. You did not see him grab for Ron? **A.** No.

Q. You did not see anything like that? **A.** I am being kicked back and forth. I know what I didn't see. I do not know if anything happened, but that is as I remember it.

Q. You said earlier that you are on the floor and so there are all these people in your way and you are having trouble seeing what is going on in the elevator, right?

MR. REILLY: Objection. As to what point in time, Judge?[40]

THE COURT: Please clarify, Miss Lyon.

BY MS. LYON:

Q. After Mr. Daly, Mr. Sykes, and Mr. DeValle arrive on the scene, you testified you were laying on the floor? **A.** Mr. Daly arrived on the scene before the other two.

Q. I am talking about when all three were there, okay. Are we understanding each other? **A.** Yes.

Q. Fine. All three were there. You said you were on the floor? **A.** Yes.

Q. You were on the floor because you say Ron, for no reason, had kicked you? **A.** Yes.

Q. You also said when the prosecutor was asking you questions that you couldn't see very clearly what was going on in the elevator? **A.** I do not know. Yeah. There was two bodies that rushed in, and I thought I saw them pick him up by the underarms. Like this.

Q. You say you thought they did something about—**A.** They reached—

Q. In the back, right? **A.** Yes.

Q. Let me return just a moment to before Mr. Daly gets there, just at that moment before Mr. Daley gets there. **A.** All right.

Q. You say you are being knocked back, you are being kicked, you are somehow getting up, you are holding the door open, you are being kicked, and all of this stuff? **A.** Yes.

Q. While all this is going on, you did not happen to notice that Ron had managed to struggle out of one of the handcuffs and only had one on there? **A.** No. I did not.

Q. You never put that in your report? **A.** No.

Q. In fact, in your report, you said he was handcuffed behind his back, isn't that right? **A.** Yes.

Q. He was handcuffed behind his back, kicked you once, is that right? **A.** First time, yes.

Q. You fell back, right? **A.** I jumped forward. Are you talking about the first time?

Q. First time off the elevator, right? **A.** Yeah. Yeah.

Q. You started to get back on the elevator, is that right? **A.** No. I just went for the door like this.

---

[40] The basis for the objection is that the question is ambiguous or vague.

Q. You did not go to grab Ron who was handcuffed behind his back, did you? **A.** No. I did not.

Q. You did not try to get in the elevator with him, did you? **A.** No.

Q. You say that you just pushed it and he kicked you and then you fell back? **A.** Yeah.

Q. And then you got up and, oh, you fell back again, right? **A.** Yes.

Q. Any number of times? **A.** Yes.

Q. While this is going on, you are yelling for help? **A.** Yes.

Q. Ron's handcuffed behind his back? **A.** Yes.

Q. That is a normal procedure, isn't that right? **A.** Yes.

Q. When you transport a prisoner? **A.** Yes.

Q. The reason that you have someone handcuffed behind their back is so that they are relative to you in a more helpless position, isn't that true? **A.** Yes.

Q. So you are in a superior position to them, isn't that correct? **A.** Yes.

Q. When you were interviewed by Mr. Willer, the interview you are having trouble remembering today, when you were interviewed by him, do you recall saying you saw Mr. Sykes and Mr. DeValle bump Ron up against the elevator door, knock his glasses off? **A.** No. I recall that—

Q. The question is do you remember saying that to Mr. Willer that you saw Mr. Sykes and/or Mr. DeValle push him or bump him into the elevator and that is how he got his injury?

MR. REILLY: Objection. There were two questions. The other thing had something to do with knocking his glasses off.

MS. LYON: Well I rephrased the question, if that is all right with you, sir.

THE COURT: Just a minute.

Which question is before the witness now?

MS. LYON: It was a compound question. I wanted to make it simpler.

Q. Do you recall when you spoke to Mr. Willer on August 31, 1987, telling him that Mr. Sykes and/or Mr. DeValle pushed Ron up into the wall or up against the wall in the elevator? Do you remember saying that? **A.** In the manner that I described it—in the manner that I described it, pushing up this way, he had sloped down and pushing up this way to get him upright.

Q. Do you recall saying that Tellez pushed sideways and slightly bumped his head on the inside elevator wall? **A.** I think I recall the cheek might have touched the wall. I believe so.

Q. Touched the wall? **A.** Touch I think. Touch, bump.

Q. You said earlier that you are or were trained in knowing the rules and the regulations of the Sheriff's Department? **A.** Yes.

Q. You were familiar with the following rule, are you not: Conduct regarding the performance of duties, general discharge of duties. Employees shall discharge their duties in a firm and efficient manner and shall assist each other in the performance of their duties? **A.** Yes.

Q. You were found to have violated that, were you not?

MR. GARDINER: Objection.

MR. REILLY: Objection.

THE COURT: Come forward.

(The following proceedings were had out of the hearing of the jury.)

THE COURT: Where are you going? Why don't we do this in chambers.

MS. LYON: That will give the jury a break too.

THE COURT: They have been out here for almost two hours.

(The following proceedings were had in the hearing of the jury.)

THE COURT: Ladies and gentlemen, I think this might be a good time for you to get water and otherwise stretch your legs before we come back in. This is something that can be done in chambers. Rather than have you sit there under those hot lights, why don't you adjourn, and we will call you out as soon as we are ready.

[The conference in chambers that follows is long and rambling. Obviously the defense wants the jury to hear that Mr. Alfieri was found to have violated sheriff's department rules by giving an inaccurate report of the incident, and the prosecution wants to keep it out. The only part we reproduce is the judge's ruling.]

. . .

THE COURT: The only question that I would allow is did anything happen to you as a result of this incident, and his answer to that would be, no. . . . The way you establish that is to, if it is there, I have no idea what the evidence will show, that he said A to one thing and B to somebody else and C to somebody else, but the issue of whether or not he lied is something for the jury to determine. They are not bound by somebody else's conclusion of what happened here. That is why we have them all sitting there.

I do not know why the whole thing is so elusive, but Mr. Gardiner's point about that conclusion somehow coming in as a piece of evidence, that is troublesome. That can't be. The evidence did come in in such a way that they can make a conclusion. They can draw the conclusion that he lied or didn't lie.

If you were talking to the person who, in fact, made the recommendation, I think you are pretty limited in what I would allow in terms of what all his mental processes were.

You could ask him something like, at the conclusion of the investigation did you interview other people? Yes. I did. You interviewed Mr. Alfieri? Yes. I did. At the conclusion of your investigation did you take any action? Yes. I did. What was that? There was a recommendation.

I think that is as far as you can go with that for whatever that's worth. Even if that person were here, I would not want you getting into the machination that went on in his head to lead him wherever he went because I do think that is the province of the jury in this case, for whatever all that evidence is worth, because frankly I do not think any of that, I am being very frank, because I do not think any of that goes. I think that is very illusory. That is my honest feeling.

I would certainly allow you to elicit the fact that something did happen administratively. If you put somebody on the stand, you can ask them what action they took based upon their investigation of the incident and in their supervisory capacity, whatever action they took.[41]

MS. LYON: I got you.

(A recess was taken.)

. . .

CROSS-EXAMINATION RESUMED BY MS. LYON:

Q. Mr. Alfieri, I would like to go back again to this statement that you said today about how Mr. Daley was saying, Ron, please get off the elevator and stuff like that? A. Yes.

Q. We talked earlier about this report that you wrote on the date of the incident. Do you recall that? A. Yes.

Q. On that report, you never said anything in that report about Mr.

---

[41] One of the issues debated in the argument on this objection was hearsay: a *finding* that Mr. Alfieri lied could be described as a *statement* by someone other than the witness, offered to show that the statement is true. The judge focuses more on the fact that such a finding is a *conclusion*—an opinion of the person who made the finding—and that opinions of that sort are generally inadmissible. See Chapter Two, pp. 141–145. But note that the judge will allow a witness to testify to any *action he took* on the basis of such an inadmissible conclusion. Does this make sense? If a supervising officer is permitted to testify that on the basis of his investigation he suspended Mr. Alfieri without pay, what will the jury infer about his evaluation of Mr. Alfieri's truthfulness? And, other than as a basis for inferring what the supervisor thought about Mr. Alfieri's conduct or his credibility, would the suspension be relevant to this trial?

Daly saying anything like, Ron, get off the elevator, is that correct? **A.** I believe so.

Q. We also talked about the first interview that you had with Mr. Willer of the Internal Affairs Division, right? **A.** Yes.

Q. He asked you questions? **A.** Yes.

Q. You gave answers? **A.** Yes.

Q. He let you talk as long as you want? He did not cut you off? **A.** The first interview—I remember part of it. I remember taking the pictures. I do not remember it all.

Q. You never told him in that interview anything about this stuff about Ron, Ron, please get off the elevator? **A.** I do not recall. I do not recall every detail. I could forget details. If details did not stick in my mind, I do not know, but I know that happened and I know I have said that any number of times.

Q. Did you say it to Investigator Willer, the Internal Affairs Division of the Sheriff's Department, on the 31st of August of 1987? **A.** I do not recall.

Q. You also were interviewed by him on the 1st of September, isn't that true? **A.** Yes.

Q. That was the second time that you were interviewed by him, is that correct? **A.** Yes.

Q. At that time you said something about hearing something about a key. Finally, that third time that you spoke or wrote to the department you said something about a key then?

MR. REILLY: Objection.

THE WITNESS: Yes.

THE COURT: Basis?

THE WITNESS: Which date? At some point somebody reminded me. I said, yes, yeah. I remembered and told them everything I know.

MR. GARDINER: I will withdraw it.

BY MS. LYON:

Q. When you were reminded, then you said something about the key? **A.** Yes. Yes.

Q. In that interview on September 1 of 1987 with Investigator Willer of the Sheriff's Department Internal Affairs Division, you never said anything about this stuff about Ron, Ron, please get off the elevator, did you? **A.** I don't know. I can't recall.

When people would remind me, if I forgot something, I will tell them.

I cannot remember every single word I said to them at that date. I do not remember which interview was which.

Q. Is your answer, I don't remember? Yes or no? **A.** I don't remember.

Q. Fine. You were aware when you were being interviewed by the Internal Affairs Division that there could be some consequences as to what they found, right? **A.** Yeah.

Q. You could lose your job possibly? **A.** Possibly.

Q. It possibly could be referred to some other authority for criminal prosecution possibly? **A.** Possibly.

Q. You could be suspended? **A.** Yes.

Q. You could lose pay? **A.** Yes.

Q. It could reflect badly on your ability to be promoted? **A.** Yeah.

Q. You said earlier I believe when we took the break that you were familiar with some of the regulations or with the regulations of your department, is that correct? **A.** Familiar. Yes.

Q. We went through one regulation with which you are familiar. Are you also familiar with the following regulation:

Conduct regarding the performance of duty, general discharge of duties.

Number 2: Employees of the department who shall in the performance of their official duties display reluctance to perform their assigned duties properly or who act in a manner continuing to bring discredit upon themselves or the department or who fail to assume responsibility or exercise diligence and interest in the pursuit of their duties or whose actions or performance in a position, rank, or assignment are below acceptable standards may be deemed incompetent and may be subject to dismissal from the department.

Are you familiar with that regulation? **A.** It is common sense what you are saying. I understand it, but as far as actually being familiar, that I have ever read it, I have probably never read it.

Q. What about this regulation?

Conduct regarding the performance of duty, regarding reports. Employees shall not—

MR. REILLY: Objection, Judge. May we have a side-bar?

THE COURT: Yes.

(The following proceedings were had out of the hearing of the jury.)

MR. REILLY: Judge, I object to defense counsel reading Sheriff's

Department regulations. In just reading them, I think it creates the inference, and it misleads the jury in leading them to believe, that somehow he has violated these rules and regulations. Simply reading them and asking him if he is familiar with them, these lengthy regulations, I think is misleading to the jury.

I do not know where counsel is going with this line of questioning.

MS. LYON: My understanding was, your Honor, from the ruling that you made previously, which, Mr. Reilly, you were not there for all of it, was that although I was not allowed to ask him what conclusion other people came to regarding these regulations, that he was the improper witness for that, that it would be all right for me to inquire whether he was familiar with certain regulations so I could tie this up later.

THE COURT: I think you have got one difficulty. That is it has not been established that those are, in fact, regulations of the Cook County Department of Corrections. It has not been established.

Who knows what you are reading?

MS. LYON: I am relying on the Cook County Department of Corrections' own report which they say this is what he, in fact, violated. It is not like I am doing something in bad faith here.[42]

THE COURT: In terms of the evidence that is in the record at this time, this Court, and I am sure that jury, would have no idea what you are reading from. It could be the regulations of the Chicago Fire Department. Who knows what those regulations are or even if they are regulations, much less who they are the regulations of.[43]

MS. LYON: I intend to prove that they are the regulations. I have someone under subpoena to bring the book of regulations and prove it. It puts me in a position of having to ask Mr. Alfieri to come back if he is familiar with them. That seems a little ridiculous.

THE COURT: I think there is something you can do with that, but I am not going to try the case. I think you have a problem at this point because I do not know where all this is going to. They do not know what this is for.

MS. LYON: I have to tie it up later. That is what you told me. I am trying to lay the foundation to do that, that he was found in violation.

---

[42] It's "bad faith" to ask questions that convey a misleading impression to the jury, usually by implying facts that the examiner does not have a good reason to believe are true.

[43] What is the judge concerned about? It's hard to believe that there is any real dispute about the content of the regulations of the Cook County Department of Corrections. Certainly the prosecutor didn't suggest that problem in his objection. This type of problem occurs in trials: the judge gets bothered by something that neither side cares about, and, because the judge's concern is so unanticipated, it is hard to address on the spot. Ms. Lyon has asked the deputy whether he is *familiar* with a regulation; strictly speaking he can answer that question just as easily whether she's reading from the printed regulations, or from her notes, or reciting from memory. But the judge wants to know what she is reading from.

THE COURT: I do not see any problem with you dealing with the regulations. I am just suggesting that there is again a problem that we probably ought to be concerned with before we ever get to that.

Do you understand what I am saying?

MS. LYON: I am afraid I don't.

THE COURT: I am saying you are simply reading something that nobody knows what it is and asking him if he is familiar with it.

Why should he be familiar with it?

MS. LYON: Because he said he was trained on the rules and regulations of the department.

THE COURT: I am saying you have not established that you are, in fact, questioning him about those rules. You are questioning him about some rules.

MS. LYON: I do not have the book of regulations with me today. They are under subpoena for tomorrow. They are. I am quoting right out of their report. I did not make this up.

THE COURT: I do not know that their report is something to base your questions on. Do you understand what I am saying?

For all we know, the report may have been miswritten, misquoted. It is kind of like the best evidence rule.

I thought, perhaps, there was going to be an objection on that basis. The objection came from something different obviously.

MS. LYON: What is your ruling, your Honor? Would you tell me what your ruling is?

THE COURT: The original objection as I understood it was the fact that she is dealing with the specific regulations that he is purported to have violated.

MR. REILLY: I do not even know if that is true.

MS. LYON: You have the reports.

MR. REILLY: Besides the foundation question, even if she were to bring in the keeper of the records, what does that prove? This is regulation.

THE COURT: That is for the jury to decide, not us. I do not think there is anything wrong with him bringing in the regulations of his job. We are talking about the performance of his duties. I disagree with you, counsel. I do not think that is an area she cannot go into, but I think the way it is coming in is the problem.

MR. REILLY: My objection is to foundation then also.

THE COURT: That objection will be well-taken.[44]

MS. LYON: Give me a minute to try to figure out what I did wrong. I can't figure it out.

(The following proceedings were had in the hearing of the jury.)

BY MS. LYON:

Q. Mr. Alfieri, you stated earlier that you are familiar with the rules and regulations of the Sheriff's Department? **A.** Familiar. That does not mean I know them all or know them well. I am familiar.

MS. LYON: I am going to ask leave to mark this as Defense Exhibit Number 23 or am I on 24?

MS. SOULE: Twenty-three.

THE COURT: Twenty-three.

BY MS. LYON:

Q. This is Defense Exhibit Number 23 for identification, and I am going to show it to you.

I am going to ask you to take a look at this paragraph right here, indicating for the record I am pointing to I believe the third paragraph on the page. **A.** From what point? This?

Q. This, right here. **A.** Okay.

Q. Are you familiar with that regulation, what I just showed you? **A.** Yes. Yes.

Q. That regulation is that employees shall not knowingly falsify or cause to be entered, either orally or in writing, any inaccurate, false, or improper information on any report, document, or record of this department or any other department.

Any alteration or destruction of such reports, documents, or records is also prohibited unless properly authorized.

Right? **A.** That is what it said. Yes.[45]

Q. I am going to also ask leave to mark as Defense Exhibit Number 24 the next page. I ask you to take a look at the top paragraph on this

---

[44] The judge holds, in effect that the departmental regulations are admissible, overruling the objection that they are misleading or unfairly prejudicial. But she offers another objection that the prosecutors snap up: that the questions as framed are improper in the absence of a better foundational showing that these are in fact the regulations in question. So far, Ms. Lyon hasn't been able to get a hold of a copy of the official book of regulations, and therefore cannot satisfy that requirement.

[45] Apparently Ms. Lyon has marked the Cook County Department of Corrections report on this incident as an exhibit, shown to the witness, and gotten him to acknowledge familiarity with the regulation *before* describing it; and apparently the judge considers that an adequate foundation— or else the prosecutor didn't figure out how to renew the objection the judge raised earlier; see note 44 supra.

page and ask you if you are familiar with that regulation. **A.** Right here.

Q. There. **A.** Yes.

Q. That regulation says all employees shall cooperate fully with competent authority conducting any department investigations and shall answer all questions truthfully and submit documents and statements as required, is that correct? **A.** I am familiar with that, yes.

Q. There was an administrative action recommended against you in this case, correct? **A.** I don't know.

Q. Mr. Alfieri, you stated that you are familiar with most of the rules and regulations of the department? **A.** Yes.

Q. And you know something about the law? **A.** Yes.

Q. You certainly know that it would be against the law for you to strike Mr. Tellez with no provocation? **A.** Certainly. Yes.

Q. You certainly know that if you did that that he would have a right to defend himself? **A.** If I did that, but I never did that.

Q. Mr. Alfieri, you said you were a sheriff for two-and-a-half years? **A.** Yes.

Q. You have been in other situations where there have been problems with inmates and sheriffs that either you were aware of or heard about? **A.** I did not understand the way you phrased that.

Q. In your whole two-and-a-half years—**A.** Yes.

Q.—Did you ever hear about any other sheriff having a problem with an inmate?

MR. REILLY: Objection, Judge, relevance.

THE COURT: Sustained.

BY MS. LYON:

Q. In your experience as a sheriff, you are certainly aware of instances where a sheriff might, might have lied to cover his own behavior, aren't you?

MR. GARDINER: Objection.

MR. REILLY: Objection. I ask that the jury disregard that question.

THE COURT: The objection is sustained, Miss Lyon.[46]

MS. LYON: I have no other questions.

THE COURT: Redirect.

MR. GARDINER: If we may have a moment.

---

[46] The question was clearly objectionable, on several different grounds, as Ms. Lyon no doubt knew. Is it ethical to ask a question that you know is objectionable?

THE COURT: The jury is instructed to disregard the last question asked by counsel.

REDIRECT EXAMINATION
BY MR. GARDINER:[47]

Q. Mr. Alfieri, in August of 1987 when this defendant was in your custody, you knew he was a former police officer, is that right? **A.** Yes.

Q. You knew what he was charged with, is that right? **A.** Yes.

Q. What was he charged with? **A.** Murder.

. . .

Q. Defense counsel showed you your report. I think it was Defense Exhibit Number 22. Now what is this report? **A.** Could I see it? Are you talking about the report directly afterwards?

THE COURT: I believe it is Defendant's Exhibit Number 22.

BY MR. GARDINER:

Q. This report here, that is the report that the defense showed you, is that right? **A.** Yes.

Q. Is that report meant to contain every detail that would appear? **A.** No.

Q. What would you call this report? **A.** It is a report to give some basic information.

Q. A summary? **A.** Yes. Yes.

Q. Now when situations occur in which deputy sheriffs or guards are injured, are there usually investigations that take place? **A.** Yes.

Q. Ordinarily there are interviews that take place, is that right? **A.** Yes. Yes.

Q. At the time you wrote this report, did you expect there would be other interviews coming up? **A.** Yeah. I believe so. I never really been through anything that I was thinking consciously, but common sense would say that there would be other interviews.

Q. The defense has made much of one interview to Investigator Willer. In fact, you did tell Investigator Willer on September 1, 1987, that you heard one of the officers behind you say something to the effect, one cuff is off and there is a key. Is that right? **A.** I remember something

---

[47] Re-direct examination is generally allowed to permit the direct examiner to address new issues that were brought up for the first time on cross-examination. In theory, this is a much tighter restriction than the limitation of the scope of cross-examination: it only permits questioning about matters that were brought up *for the first time* on cross. By the same token, recross, if permitted, should be restricted to matters that came up for the first time on re-direct; and so on. In practice, some judges permit more wide-ranging re-examinations. See Chapter Two, p. 154.

about a key. I remember the key. I do not remember about the cuff.

Q. Now you never were accused of striking the defendant, were you? **A.** No.

Q. You did not lose your job? **A.** No.

Q. You never received any suspension of any duration, is that correct? **A.** Correct.

MS. LYON: Objection, your Honor. Duration? Ten days' duration.

THE COURT: Duration is any period of time.

BY MR. GARDINER:

Q. You never received any suspension, is that right? **A.** No.

Q. Now you did state that you resigned, is that correct? **A.** Yes.

Q. Why did you resign?

MS. LYON: Objection, your Honor.

THE COURT: Basis? You established that he resigned, counsel.[48]

THE WITNESS: I resigned because the job is just too stressful for me, and I never want to work at it again.

BY MR. GARDINER:

Q. After this incident, after August 28, 1987, did you continue to work as a deputy sheriff? **A.** Yes.

Q. Did you do anything else? **A.** After I worked? I continued to work for a period of two weeks.

Q. What did you do at that point? **A.** At that point—afterwards I went into the hospital.

MS. LYON: Your Honor, objection.

THE WITNESS: I don't—

THE COURT: Basis?

Hold on, Mr. Witness.

THE WITNESS: I am sorry.

THE COURT: Hold on, Mr. Witness.

MS. LYON: Do you want me to argue an objection in front of the jury?

THE COURT: Would you like a side-bar?

---

48 Ms. Lyon is probably objecting on the ground that Mr. Alfieri's reason for resigning is irrelevant. The judge responds that she "opened the door" to this inquiry: since she established that he did resign, the prosecutor is entitled to show *why* he did so; by bringing up the subject, she waived any objection to other questions in the same area. The limits of this doctrine are extremely fuzzy.

MS. LYON: Probably a good idea.

(The following proceedings were had out of the hearing of the jury.)

MS. LYON: Your Honor, I assume that he is about to talk about how this incident was so stressful to him that he had to check into a hospital and get psychiatric treatment and a bunch of other stuff like that, and I do not see how that is relevant at all to this.

THE COURT: You opened the door on your cross-examination.

MS. LYON: They can bring in all his psychological problems as a result?

THE COURT: The fact that there is some manifestations of stress.[49]

You elicited on cross-examination the fact that in two of his responses—

I do not know where they are going. I will not allow them to get into any detailed delineation of what problems he had. If they indicate that he was still feeling badly and he went to the hospital, I will let them do that. I am not going to allow a lot of exploration.

MS. LYON: May I make a request? Could you ask that Mr. Gardiner lead him and ask the one question and stop.

Mr. Alfieri likes to talk a lot. Who knows what else he might tell us?[50]

THE COURT: Assuming Mr. Gardiner can lead his own witness.

MR. GARDINER: I can lead him to an extent.

THE COURT: He is your witness. It will be fine for you to say, Mr. Alfieri, just answer what I ask you and wait until I ask another question. Indicate that. I do not want him to ramble on.

(The following proceedings were had in the hearing of the jury.)

BY MR. GARDINER:

Q. Mr. Alfieri, I am going to ask you some questions and I ask that you just respond to the questions themselves as I put them to you.

When you resigned from the Cook County Deputy Sheriff's Office, you resigned because of the stress from this incident, is that right? **A.** Yes.

---

[49] Once again, Ms. Lyon is precluded from objecting to an issue she herself raised on cross-examination.

[50] A major function of leading questions is to limit what the witness can say in response. That is allowed on cross-examination to enable the lawyer to get information from a potentially hostile witness. Here Ms. Lyon is asking the judge to *require* leading questions on *direct examination* for a different purpose: to prevent the witness from volunteering inadmissible evidence by restricting his answers to Yes or No. That is a legitimate but uncommon function of leading questions. What is Ms. Lyon afraid of hearing from the witness?

Q. In fact, because of this incident, you sought medical attention, is that correct? **A.** Yes.

Q. You went to Skokie Valley Community Hospital? **A.** I believe that is the name of the hospital.

Q. It was a hospital in Skokie for stress-related problems? **A.** Yes.

Q. A psychiatric-type hospital? **A.** Yes. Yes.

Q. You spent six weeks in the hospital, is that correct? **A.** Yes.

Q. That is because you couldn't face your job after this defendant attacked you, is that correct? **A.** Yes.

Q. It is because of the stress that was caused by this incident that you spent the time at that hospital, is that correct? **A.** Yes.

Q. In fact, after leaving that hospital, you moved to a different employment, is that correct? **A.** Yes.

Q. In fact, you resigned because of this incident, is that correct? **A.** Yes.

Q. And because of the stress that came from this incident, is that right? **A.** Yes.

Q. You never hit this defendant, is that right? **A.** No.

Q. You never touched this defendant, isn't that right? **A.** Never touched him.

MR. GARDINER: One moment, judge.

. . .

Q. Mr. Alfieri, you testified that the elevator bank behind this courtroom opens at every floor, is that correct? **A.** Yes. Yes.

Q. It opens into the back of the courtroom? **A.** Yes.

Q. And leads to any of these floors? **A.** Yes.

Q. There are certain times of day that the lockup area around those elevators is open, is that right? **A.** Yeah. It is supposed to be closed, but sometimes they are open.

Q. In fact, sometimes they are open for cleaning, is that right? **A.** Yes.

Q. Sometimes they could be open through inadvertence? **A.** For what?

Q. Through a mistake by someone, is that right? **A.** Yeah. Yeah.

Q. Carelessness, is that right? **A.** Yes.

Q. In fact, the custodians have keys to the lockup areas in the back and the elevators to open up and clean out those areas? **A.** Yes.

Q. Those areas can then be open and a person getting off that elevator could walk through a courtroom and out the door, is that right? **A.** Yes.

Q. That would be true in any courtroom, is that right? **A.** Yes.

Q. At certain times of day, is that right? **A.** Sure. Anything is possible.

Q. From your experience working here at 26th and California, Fridays are days that are shorter days generally, is that right? **A.** Generally, yes.

Q. A greater number of courtrooms tend to close earlier, is that right? **A.** Yes.

Q. A greater number of courtrooms will close for the day around noon or a little after, is that right? **A.** Yes.

MS. LYON: I want to object. This is about the tenth or eleventh leading question of his own witness.[51]

THE COURT: Try not to lead, counsel.

BY MR. GARDINER:

Q. In fact, Mr. Alfieri, if you were to walk in the back of this courtroom today, what would the condition of the area near the elevator be?

MS. LYON: Its condition today is irrelevant. That is what you ruled.

THE COURT: Sustained.

BY MR. GARDINER:

Q. Back in August of 1987, could access to the elevator area be open?

MS. LYON: Objection, your Honor. Vague. Speculative.

THE COURT: Rephrase the question, Mr. Gardiner.

BY MR. GARDINER:

Q. In August of 1987, under what circumstances could the lockup area near the elevators be open on any floor? **A.** If someone made a mistake, if someone was careless and didn't lock it. If a custodian came and was cleaning up and walked down a ways a little bit, they might leave it open. It is conceivable that somebody could leave it open.

Q. Mr. Alfieri, you testified regarding what occurred in the

---

[51] Actually it's the fifteenth leading question in a row. In fact, despite the fact that leading questions are prohibited on redirect as well as on direct, this examination reads much more like Ms. Lyon's cross than Mr. Gardiner's initial direct. Why? Also, how does it sound to the jury when an attorney conducts the examination of one of his own critical witnesses in this fashion? See Chapter Two, pp. 148–151.

basement of this building with the defendant.

Why were you trying to keep those doors open? **A.** To contain him, just to contain him so he could not get up.

Q. To contain him so he could not get up to go, where? **A.** Any floor up.

Q. What could happen there? **A.** Possibly if he found a door or a gate open he could have just walked right through.

MR. GARDINER: Nothing further, your Honor.

THE COURT: Any recross?

MS. LYON: Yes, your Honor.

RECROSS EXAMINATION
BY MS. LYON:

Q. Mr. Alfieri, you said that you did mention this key stuff to Mr. Willer the second time he interviewed you on September 1, right? **A.** Yes.

Q. That was after you were reminded of it, right? **A.** Yeah.

Q. Also the prosecutor asked you about the report that you wrote the day of the incident? **A.** Yes.

Q. You said it was a summary, right? **A.** Yes.

Q. Didn't have every word in it? **A.** Yeah.

Q. You also said that you were trained to write down the important details in your report, is that right? **A.** Yeah. It does not mean I am perfect or I never make mistakes or I am not sloppy. You are trained to do some things. It does not mean that you do not make mistakes.

Q. Mr. Alfieri? **A.** Yes.

Q. You would agree with me, would you not, that if there was something about a key to a pair of handcuffs in an incident like this, you would agree that that was an important fact, would you not? **A.** Yes. Yes.

Q. That important fact was not in your report, isn't that true? **A.** That is true.

MR. GARDINER: Objection, your Honor. It is asked and answered, and I think it is a misstatement.

THE COURT: Sustained. Sustained.[52]

---

[52] Strictly speaking, "asked and answered" may not be the appropriate objection (see Chapter Two, p. 149), and there does not appear to be any misstatement in Ms. Lyon's question. But the objection is good, and is properly sustained. First, the question is cumulative; Ms. Lyon has been over this ground before. Second, it's not appropriate re-cross examination since this issue was not newly brought up in the redirect. See supra note 47. Both of these grounds are

BY MS. LYON:

Q. You testified about how sometimes those gates are open, right?
A. Yeah.

Q. When the prosecutor was asking you questions? **A.** Yes.

Q. You also said that they are supposed to be locked at all times?
A. Yes.

Q. That is a regulation too, isn't it? **A.** Yes.

Q. If a courtroom is empty, that is if all business is done, there are
no more prisoners, the courtroom is empty, closed for the day, one of two
things is true. Either a sheriff is in the courtroom, or the courtroom door
is locked, isn't that true? **A.** Normally. I couldn't state that absolutely
every single time.

Q. That is the regulation, isn't it? **A.** I guess so. I am not sure. The
regulation? That the doors are supposed to be locked is a regulation.
Yeah.

Q. Isn't that true? **A.** Yeah.

Q. You were talking about how sometimes the gates are not open
and that you were aware of this, right? That the gates are open when
they are supposed to be locked? **A.** I have seen it sometimes.

Q. Even though that is against the rules? **A.** Yeah.

Q. And regulations are clear. They are supposed to be locked at all
times? **A.** Yes.

Q. For the very reason so that there will not be access to the
courtroom from the elevator, right? **A.** Sure.

Q. You had been with the department approximately two-and-a-half
years, is that right? **A.** Yes.

Q. On some occasions you had seen that rule broken. That is what
you are saying? **A.** Yes.

Q. Ron Tellez was not a Cook County sheriff, was he? **A.** No.

Q. You had not taken him on an inspection tour of all of the
courtrooms in the building, had you? **A.** No.

Q. You had not discussed with him that sometimes those gates are
open, had you? **A.** No.

Q. When you took him down there, he saw the deputy who did not

---

within the court's plenary control over the manner of questioning. See FRE 611, Chapter Two,
pp. 156–157.

Note that the witness answered the question before the objection. If it mattered (it doesn't),
what would Mr. Gardiner have to do to preserve a possible claim of error based on the argument
that this evidence was inadmissible? See Chapter Two, pp. 165–167.

go with you use one of those big keys like I showed you before to open a gate to let you in, didn't he?

MR. REILLY: Objection to what he saw, Judge.[53]

THE COURT: As to what who saw?

MR. REILLY: What Mr. Tellez saw.

THE COURT: Sustained.

BY MS. LYON:

Q. He was with you when you saw—**A.** He was there. What he saw, I don't know.

Q. The custodians in this building generally come to clean at the end of the day, isn't that right? **A.** Yes.

Q. They work from 4:00 until midnight, isn't that correct? **A.** I think so.

Q. This happened at 12:00 noon, isn't that correct? **A.** Yes.

MS. LYON: Your Honor, that is all.

MR. GARDINER: Nothing further, Judge.

THE COURT: Thank you, Mr. Alfieri. You are excused.

. . .

FRIDAY, JANUARY 20, 1989

THE CLERK: Ronald Tellez

(The following proceedings were had in the presence and hearing of the jury)

THE COURT: Good morning. Be seated.

I hope you had a nice evening. We are ready to begin. State, would you call your next witness?

MR. REILLY: Deputy Michael Daly.

(Witness sworn)

MICHAEL DALY,

called as a witness on behalf of the People of the State of Illinois, having been first duly sworn, was examined and testified as follows:

DIRECT EXAMINATION

BY MR. REILLY:

MR. REILLY: Judge, if I may proceed?

---

[53] What is the basis for this objection? See supra, p. 4. Notice that the judge does not explain her ruling to the jury, so they have to guess why they can't hear the answer to this question. That's common. Should judges explain evidentiary ruling more often?

THE COURT: Yes, you may.

BY MR. REILLY:

Q. Sir, you have been sworn. Would you please tell us your name and spell your last name for the benefit of the court reporter? **A.** Michael Daly.

Q. How old are you, Mr. Daly? **A.** 30.

Q. What is your business or occupation, sir? **A.** I work for the Cook County Sheriff's Department.

Q. And in what capacity? **A.** I work as a deputy sheriff in the courtroom assigned to the Daley Center.

Q. How long have you been a Cook County Sheriff? **A.** Approximately 7 and a half years.

Q. Where are you currently assigned? **A.** At the Daley Center right now.

Q. Okay. And I would like to direct your attention back to August of 1987. Where were you assigned? **A.** I was assigned at 2650 South California.

Q. That is located in Chicago, Cook County, Illinois? **A.** That's correct.

Q. You worked in this criminal court building, is that correct? **A.** Yes, sir.

Q. What courtroom were you assigned to August 28, 1987? **A.** Courtroom 400.

Q. And that was the courtroom of Judge Robert Collins, is that correct? **A.** Yes, sir.

Q. And being assigned to that courtroom you were assigned as a courtroom deputy, is that correct? **A.** Yes, sir.

Q. Your duties included basically those as any other courtroom sheriff, is that correct? **A.** Yes.

Q. I would like to direct your attention to a particular day, August the 28th of 1987, Friday. Do you recall working in Judge Collins' courtroom that morning? **A.** Yes, I do.

Q. Sometime early this morning at around 9:30 shortly before your court call, did you receive custody of a prisoner by the name of Ronald Tellez? **A.** Yes, I did.

Q. Do you see Mr. Tellez in court today? **A.** Yes, I do.

MS. LYON: Stipulate to the identification.[54]

---

[54] Why does Ms. Lyon offer this stipulation? If she hadn't, what would happen next?

MR. REILLY: I will accept the stipulation that the defense would stipulate that Deputy Daly would make an in-court identification of the defendant Ronald Tellez. We would accept that.

THE COURT: So stipulated, counsel?

MS. LYON: Yes, your Honor.

BY MR. REILLY:

Q. And Mr. Tellez had a case pending in Judge Collins' courtroom that morning, is that correct? A. That's correct.

Q. And physically what was done with Mr. Tellez when he was put into your custody? A. He was brought up from the bridge area and he—I put him personally into the jury room, alongside the courtroom.

Q. Okay. And when you put him into the jury room was he handcuffed in any way? A. He was taken out of the handcuffs when he was put into the jury room then rehandcuffed and handcuffed to a chair in the jury room.

Q. You handcuffed him? A. Yes, sir.

Q. You used your handcuffs? A. Yes, sir.

Q. To handcuff him. And you were aware that he was a police officer or had been a police officer, is that correct? A. Yes, sir.

Q. Sometime later that same morning, that Friday morning, were you called away from courtroom 400? A. Yes, I was.

Q. And where were you reassigned? A. To the bridge area downstairs in the basement of the facility.

Q. For the benefit of jury would you tell us where, specifically, the bridge area is where you were assigned, Mr. Daly? A. It is downstairs in the basement and it divides the courthouse between the courthouse and the Department of Corrections.

. . .

Q. Okay. And are you alone when you are at that position at that station? A. Yes.

Q. I would like to then direct your attention to approximately noon on that Friday. Were you at your station at that time? A. Yes.

Q. And would you tell the Ladies and Gentlemen of the jury what you heard or you saw at noon time? A. Well, approximately noon time I was at that particular point and I heard some yelling from the north elevator and the yelling was just—what was said was escape, escape. So I ran up to that particular point and I—

Q. How far is it from your station to this elevator where you heard escape, escape? A. Approximately one hundred feet.

Q. Okay. And did you run there? **A.** Yes, sir.

Q. And when you got to that elevator would you tell us what you saw? **A.** Well, I saw Deputy Alfieri on his knees and he was being kicked by someone in the elevator.

Q. And did you look in to see who the person was that was kicking Deputy Alfieri? **A.** Yes, I did.

Q. Who was that? **A.** Mr. Tellez.

Q. Was Mr. Cbesides kicking Deputy Alfieri, who was on his knees, was Mr. Tellez saying anything at that time? **A.** Not at this particular point.

Q. Did he say anything at that—while you were at that elevator? **A.** Yes, he did.

Q. What, if anything, did he say? **A.** He told—either talking to me or both of us and he said get out of here.

Q. When you arrived at that bank of the elevators in the basement there and you saw this, what did you do? **A.** I made sure that the door was opened because the door was closing and I just held the door open at that particular point.

Q. And was Deputy Alfieri still on the ground? **A.** Yes, sir.

Q. And Mr. Tellez still kicking him? **A.** Yes, sir.

Q. Okay. And did you ever—strike that. Did you enter the elevator at that time? **A.** No.

Q. Did you say anything to Mr. Tellez? **A.** I might have said something to the effect of what are you doing or something like that.

Q. Did you call him by name? **A.** Yes. I called him by his first name.

Q. Ron or Ronnie? **A.** Ronnie.

Q. Now, when you first arrived there at the elevator door, and saw Mr. Tellez kicking Deputy Alfieri, did you observe or did you notice any type of injury to Mr. Tellez? **A.** No, sir.

Q. Were his glasses still on? **A.** Yes, sir.

Q. You didn't observe my bruises or marks or cuts on his face? **A.** No, I did not.

Q. While in the elevator will you describe the—strike that. Did you see the defendant's hands at that time? **A.** Yes, I did.

Q. Where were his hands at when you arrived at the elevator? **A.** His hands were by his chest, you know, out, outward from his chest trying to close the elevator.

Q. Were there any handcuffs on his hands? **A.** Yes, there were.

Q. Okay. Describe the condition of those handcuffs as you saw them when you arrived at the elevator? **A.** I'm not really sure which particular handcuff was cuffed. Either the right hand or left hand and the other particular handcuff was lost and it was opened.

Q. So what you are telling us, on one hand a handcuff was closed and locked, is that correct? **A.** That is correct.

Q. And the other portion of the other—part of that handcuff was not connected to his hand, is that correct? **A.** That's correct.

Q. And, in fact, it was opened? **A.** Yes, sir.

Q. It wasn't locked and off the hand, it was off the hand and opened? **A.** Yes.

Q. So somehow that cuff had been opened, correct? **A.** Yes, sir.

Q. Did you observe a handcuff key at that time? **A.** No, sir.

Q. At any time did you observe a handcuff key? **A.** No, sir.

Q. That elevator, the elevator that goes behind room 400 and goes to the basement, that is the same bank of elevators behind this court-room, is that correct? **A.** Yes, sir.

Q. Okay. And that elevator gives you access to the back of all of these courtrooms on this side of the building, is that correct? **A.** That is correct.

Q. And how long did you work in this building, Deputy Daly? **A.** Approximately five years.

Q. Okay. Have you worked in most of the courtrooms in this building? **A.** Yes, sir.

Q. And back in August of 1987, was it uncommon for the gates or the bars behind these courtrooms next to the elevators to be opened at different times, parts of the days? **A.** No, it wasn't uncommon.

Q. That was against procedure though, correct? **A.** Yes, sir.

Q. They should be locked at all times? **A.** That's correct.

Q. Did you, at any time, while at the elevator door, see Deputy Alfieri get up off the ground and try to strike Mr. Tellez? **A.** No, sir.

Q. How was Mr. Tellez dressed that day? **A.** Similar to what he is dressed today.

Q. Did he have a suit on? **A.** Yes.

Q. Did he have a tie on? **A.** Yes.

Q. Was he clean shaven? **A.** Yes.[55]

Q. Did you, at any time, try and go into the elevator and restrain Mr. Tellez? **A.** No, I did not.

Q. Other than try and keep those elevator doors opened, did you do anything else to assist Deputy Alfieri? **A.** No.

Q. Sometime after you arrived two correctional officers arrived, is that correct? **A.** Yes, sir.

Q. About how much time went by from the time you first got there to the time these two correctional officers came on the scene? **A.** Between ten and fifteen seconds.

Q. And now, when the correctional officers arrived where were you at? **A.** I am right in front of the elevator.

Q. And where is Deputy Alfieri? **A.** He is still on the ground, on his knees.

Q. When these two correctional officers arrived what did they do? **A.** They went by me when I was in the elevator with the door and they went into the elevator.

Q. Okay. And you later learned them to be Officer Sykes and DeValle, is that correct? **A.** Yes.

Q. And did they take custody of Mr. Tellez? **A.** Yes, they did.

Q. Incidentally, when Officer Sykes and Officer DeValle went in the elevator did either Sykes or DeValle hit Mr. Tellez? **A.** Sykes did.

Q. How many times did he hit him? **A.** Once.

Q. Did you see any other blows struck at Mr. Tellez? **A.** No, I did not.

Q. Did Mr. Tellez struggle or fight after the one blow was struck by Officer Sykes? **A.** No, he did not.

Q. Before he was taken out of that elevator was he handcuffed? **A.** Yes, he was.

Q. Did you handcuff him or one of the two correctional officers? **A.** I believe it was one of the correctional officers that handcuffed him.

Q. Do you remember, did your handcuffs remain dangling on the prisoner at that time? **A.** I don't recall.

Q. Did you ever eventually get your handcuffs back? **A.** Yes, I did.

Q. Did you see any injury on Mr. Tellez after he was struck by correctional Officer Sykes? **A.** He had an abrasion on the cheek. I believe it was the left cheek.

---

[55] Why does the prosecutor ask these questions about the defendant's appearance?

Q. And that wasn't there when you arrived though, was it? **A.** No, sir.

Q. How long did you know Deputy Nicholas Alfieri? **A.** I have known him at that particular point for about three years.

Q. And at that time you were working in the same courtroom together, is that correct? **A.** Yes, sir.

Q. Work on day to day basis with prisoners? **A.** Yes.

Q. Would you watch Deputy Alfieri handle other prisoners? **A.** Yes.

Q. Did you ever see him strike any other prisoner? **A.** No.

MS. LYON: Objection. Is this an attempt to do character evidence?

THE COURT: I'll overrule it.[56]

BY MR. REILLY:

Q. Well, beside working with him, have you talked to other people about Deputy Alfieri's reputation for peacefulness? **A.** Yes, I have.

Q. And what is, or what was Deputy Alfieri's reputation for peacefulness back in August of 1987? **A.** He was a very good officer and he was very good with the inmates. He was very peaceful with them. He wasn't argumentative or anything to that extent.[57]

Q. You never saw him demonstrate any violence? **A.** No, sir.

Q. After the prisoner, inmate Tellez was removed in the elevator, where was he taken? **A.** He was taken to the holding cell in the Department of Corrections.

Q. Sometime later that afternoon, approximately 5:30, did you have an opportunity to see Mr. Tellez again? **A.** Yes, I did.

Q. Where was that at? **A.** It was downstairs in the Department of Corrections in another holding cell where he was staying at.

Q. And did Mr. Tellez say anything to you at that time? **A.** He motioned me over when I got down there with another prisoner.

Q. And did you go over? **A.** Yes, sir.

---

[56] The judge's ruling is wrong. Mr. Reilly is using character evidence to try to prove how Mr. Alfieri behaved in his dealings with Mr. Tellez. Character evidence is sometimes allowed in criminal cases to show how the alleged victim is likely to have behaved, but only: (1) if the defendant initiates the use of character evidence (which hasn't happened); and (2) if the evidence is in the form of the witness's opinion of the victim's character, or testimony about the victim's reputation, rather than testimony about particular incidents of conduct by the victim (which it isn't). See Chapter Five, pp. 405–410; People v. Whiters, 146 Ill.2d 437, 440, 167 Ill.Dec. 1042, 588 N.E.2d 1172, 1173 (1992).

[57] This is character evidence in the form of reputation testimony, or at least the question called for reputation evidence—the answer sounds more like an expression of the witness's opinion. Assuming it is reputation evidence, it might be admissible—*if* the defendant had initiated the use of evidence of the alleged victim's character; but he did not. See supra, note 56.

Q. What did he say to you at that time? **A.** He just said that he was sorry about what had happened to the deputy that was working in 400 with me at the time and he just said he didn't want to go back to jail.

Q. Did he tell you that he had been assaulted by Nicholas Alfieri? **A.** No, he did not.

Q. Did he tell you that he had been pushed or shoved by Nicholas Alfieri? **A.** No, he did not.

Q. Did he tell you he had been punched or struck in any way by Nicholas Alfieri? **A.** No. Nicholas Alfieri? No, he did not.

Q. Incidentally Deputy, you know Ronald Tellez, correct? **A.** Yes, I do.

Q. You knew him before he was a prisoner here, correct? **A.** Yes, sir.

Q. You knew that he was a Blue Island policeman, is that correct? **A.** Yes, I did.

Q. Where did you know him from? **A.** I used to live in Blue Island a few years back and I knew him just through saying hi to him and say hi to me and through a bar that we used to frequent.

Q. Oh, the two of you would—used to drink in the same bar, is that right? **A.** That's correct.

Q. Had you had any dispute or argument with Mr. Tellez that day? **A.** Not at all.

Q. Were you present for any argument or dispute between Nicholas Alfieri and Mr. Tellez prior to the assault on Mr. Alfieri? **A.** No, sir.

MR. REILLY: If I may have a moment, Judge?

Judge, I have nothing further at this time.

MS. LYON: May I inquire, your Honor?

CROSS EXAMINATION

BY MS. LYON:

Q. Now, Mr. Daly, you didn't see what happened before you got to the elevator obviously? **A.** That's correct.

Q. You don't know what precipitated this, do you? **A.** No, I don't.

Q. Now, you say today that you heard someone shouting escape, escape, is that what you said today? **A.** Yes, that is what I said.

Q. You've written a number of reports and answered a lot of questions in the investigation of this matter, haven't you? **A.** Yes, I have.

Q. In fact, you wrote a report on the 31st of August, 1987, didn't you? **A.** If that is what the report says.

Q. And that was to Assistant Chief Jose Cruz, isn't that right? **A.** If that is what it says.

Q. What exhibit are we on? 25?

MS. SOULE: Yes.

MR. REILLY: Judge, I object to counsel showing the deputy this. He said he wrote a report. He has acknowledged that. I don't see the purpose in showing him the report.

THE COURT: I think she is entitled to do that. Have you shown it to them?

MS. LYON: Yes, I just did.

THE COURT: Is it marked?

MS. LYON: Defense Exhibit Number 25, your Honor.

I ask you to take look at that. Is that your report?

A. Yes, it is.

Q. Is there anywhere in this report that you say that you heard the words escape, escape? **A.** No, there is not.[58]

Q. Now, you also talked to Investigator Willer in this case, isn't that right? **A.** Yes, ma'am.

Q. And that would have been on—excuse me. Before we get to that, you also wrote another report on the 2nd of September, 1987. Marking that Defense Exhibit Number 26 for identification. Would you take a look at that, please? Do you recognize that? **A.** Yes.

Q. And that is your report from September 2nd, 1987? **A.** Yes.

Q. And nowhere in that report do you say anything about the words escape, escape, is that correct? To these new words, escape, escape?

MR. REILLY: Objection to "new words."

THE COURT: Sustained. Strike.

BY MS. LYON:

Q. These words escape, escape. You don't see it in that report, do you? **A.** To—it is not in that report.

Q. You also gave a statement on the 2nd of September, 1987 in room 702 at Internal Affairs, isn't that true? **A.** I don't recall the date but I did give a report.

Q. Well, can I have that marked as Defense Exhibit Number 27 for identification? I will let you take a look at that report. Actually,

---

[58] Ms. Lyon is impeaching Officer Daly by showing that his initial report on this incident is, at least arguably, inconsistent with his testimony in that it includes no mention of an apparently critical fact. See Chapter Five, pp. 450–459.

verbatim statement. **A.** I read that.

Q. Is that your statement? **A.** Yes, ma'am.

Q. And in that statement you never said one word about what you heard was yelled escape, escape, did you? **A.** No, ma'am.

Q. In fact, no place in any report that you ever made before today, anything written, any of these official documents did you ever come up with escape, escape before?

MR. REILLY: Objection to the phrasing of that question.[59]

THE COURT: Sustained.

BY MS. LYON:

Q. Did you ever say it before, Mr. Daly, in any of these reports? **A.** No.

Q. Now, you went to the academy for the Sheriff's Department, didn't you? **A.** Yes, ma'am.

Q. You were trained, were you not? **A.** Yes.

Q. You were trained in procedures of the department? **A.** Yes.

Q. You were trained about the rules and regulations of the Sheriff's Department? **A.** Yes.

Q. You were trained in what you are supposed to do as a courtroom sheriff? **A.** Yes.

Q. How to handle emergencies? **A.** Yes.

Q. You were taught something about the law? **A.** Yes.

Q. You were taught something about self-defense? **A.** Yes.

Q. And a little bit about the law of self-defense, right? **A.** Yes.

Q. And you were also taught something about how to write reports, isn't that true? **A.** Yes.

Q. Report writing is a function of your job, isn't that true? **A.** Sometimes, yes.

Q. And you were taught, were you not, to make full, accurate and complete reports, isn't that true? **A.** A summary, not verbatim.

Q. Well, would you like to go back to the statement that was Defense Exhibit Number 27? What kind of a statement is that, Mr. Daly? **A.** It is a summary of what happened.

Q. It is a question and answer statement, is it not? **A.** Yes.

Q. You were asked questions? **A.** Yes.

---

[59] What phrase is Mr. Reilly objecting to?

Q. You were given the opportunity to answer? **A.** Yes.

Q. And every word you said was written down, isn't that true? **A.** Yes.

Q. And this report is one, two, three and a half pages long, isn't that right? **A.** Yes.

Q. Nobody said, Mr. Daly, we heard enough from you, you can't talk any more, did they? **A.** No, they didn't say that.

Q. Nobody said, we don't want you to answer more fully, did they? **A.** No.

Q. In fact, you were encouraged to answer questions fully and completely, isn't that true? **A.** I was encouraged to tell the truth.

Q. And to be full and complete, isn't that true? **A.** To the best of my ability, yes.

Q. Now, one of the things that you are trained in, Mr. Daly, is—if you are handling prisoners is to try and avoid escapes? **A.** Yes, ma'am.

Q. In fact, if this was an attempted escape and somebody was hollering escape, escape from the elevator that would be an important fact, would it not? **A.** Possible.

Q. Possible. Okay.

Now, you testified earlier for the portion that you were—I think a fair assessment, acquainted with Ron Tellez? **A.** Yes.

Q. Not a personal friend? **A.** No.

Q. But someone you knew socially? **A.** Yes.

Q. You knew he was a police officer? **A.** Yes.

Q. You knew he was in custody on a serious charge? **A.** Yes.

Q. You knew he was charged with murder? **A.** Yes.

Q. And you knew because you have been trained something about the law, that there is a presumption of innocence, didn't you? **A.** That's correct.

Q. You knew that he was charged with murder, right? **A.** Yes.

Q. You know he hasn't yet been tried on that case?

MR. REILLY: Objection to this line of questioning, Judge.

THE COURT: Where are you going, counsel?

MS. LYON: I'll be glad to tell in a side-bar.

THE COURT: No. I would say get off it.[60]

MS. LYON: I will.

Q. The prosecution asked you about the fact that Ron was wearing a suit on the day in question, on August 28th, right? **A.** Yes.

Q. And you are also aware that prisoners are allowed to wear civilian clothes to court? **A.** Yes, they are.

Q. In this jurisdiction any way, right? **A.** Yes.

Q. In some jurisdictions they must come in prison garb but this jurisdiction they can have something civilian to wear to court, isn't that true? **A.** Yes, ma'am.

Q. And many prisoners do? **A.** Yes.

. . .

(Witness excused)

. . .

MR. GARDINER: Judge, if we can be heard at side-bar?

(The following proceedings were had out of the presence and hearing of the jury)

MR. REILLY: People move exhibits 1 through 5 in evidence and ask the identifying marks be stricken.

THE COURT: There being no objection there that evidence will be admitted.

MS. LYON: Okay.

MR. GARDINER: Move those into evidence before the jury now.

(The following proceedings were had in the presence and hearing of the jury)

MR. GARDINER: Your Honor, the People would move People's Exhibits 1, which is a picture of Nicholas Alfieri; 2, which is a picture of Nicholas Alfieri's arm; 3, which is another picture of Nicholas Alfieri's arm; 4, which is a picture of the leg area of Nicholas Alfieri; and People's Exhibit Number 5, which is another picture of the lower portion of the body of Nicholas Alfieri into evidence.

MS. LYON: No objection.

THE COURT: Their being no objection, People's Exhibits 1, 2, 3, 4, and 5, the identifying marks may be struck, and they will be admitted into evidence.

---

[60] The judge's position seems simple: The jury has been told that Mr. Tellez has been charged with murder, and that he hasn't yet been tried; they should not hear anything else about the murder case.

MR. GARDINER: We would seek to publish these exhibits to the jury.

MS. LYON: No objection to that either.

THE COURT: Proceed.

(Photographs were published to the jury)[61]

MR. GARDINER: Your Honor, for the record we have published People's Exhibits 1 through 5 to the jury. With the addition of those exhibits the People would rest.

THE COURT: Thank you, Mr. Gardiner.

Ladies and Gentlemen of the jury, the State has now completed the presentation of its case in chief, and you have only been back in the box for a few minutes but I am going to have the deputy take you out for a few minutes while we deal with legal issues before we move forward with further evidence from the defense.

(The following proceedings were had out of the presence and hearing of the jury)

THE COURT: Are there any motions?

MS. LYON: We make a motion without argument for a directed verdict at this time.[62]

THE COURT: Any response?

MR. GARDINER: We would ask that it be denied.

THE COURT: Motion for directed verdict will be denied.

MS. LYON: We appreciate if we can have a few minutes. The witnesses should be coming in.

. . .

(Witness sworn)

RALPH WILLER,

called as a witness on behalf of the Defendant, having been first duly sworn, was examined and testified as follows:

----

[61] The prosecution waited until the end of its case to have the pictures of Mr. Alfieri's injuries admitted in evidence, and to show them to the jury. In addition to the tactical considerations mentioned in note 26, supra, are there other advantages to proceeding in this order?

[62] This is a pro forma motion: If Ms. Lyon thought she had a hope of winning, she would argue the motion. The reason is clear. The prosecution has presented witnesses who have produced more than sufficient evidence for a jury to conclude that the defendant committed the crimes charged—if those witnesses are believed. That's all that's required to get by a motion for a directed verdict. By failing to argue the motion Ms. Lyon is saying to the judge, in effect: "I have to make this motion, but it's a dead loser, so I won't waste your time." Given that unmistakable signal, why bother?

DIRECT EXAMINATION
BY MS. LYON:

Q. Mr. Willer, state your full name and spell your last name for the court reporter? **A.** Ralph Willer, W-I-L-L-E-R.

Q. Mr. Willer, how are you employed? **A.** A Sheriff's police officer.

Q. And how long you have you been a Sheriff's police officer? **A.** Twenty years.

Q. Where are you currently assigned? **A.** Fugitive division which is the basement of the next door building.

Q. What does the fugitive division do? **A.** We locate and arrest people that are wanted on felony warrants.

Q. If we can go back a little bit in your twenty years, what have been some of your other assignments? **A.** I spent four years in uniform, ten years assigned to the State's Attorney's office and one year I was assigned to detach duty assigned to court services, Internal Affairs.[63]

Q. Now, would you tell the Ladies and Gentlemen of the jury what court services, Internal Affairs is? **A.** Internal Affairs for court services investigates anything that involves a deputy sheriff's allegations against him or injuries to that deputy sheriff, anything that involves a deputy sheriff as opposed to a correctional officer or a Sheriff's police officer.

. . .

Q. Okay. And when you were assigned to the Internal Affairs Division what were your duties there? **A.** Well, we would investigate any allegations made against a deputy sheriff or if a deputy sheriff got injured, how that happened, and with an eye towards trying to prevent it from happening again. Anything investigating a deputy sheriff.

Q. Okay. And you said you were assigned there or detailed there for a year? **A.** Yes, that is correct.

Q. Okay. Now, I would like to call your attention to an investigation regarding what—well, what started out as an investigation of some injuries that were received by Deputy Sheriff Nicholas Alfieri which occurred on August the 28th, 1987? **A.** Yes.

Q. Are you familiar with that investigation? **A.** Yes.

Q. And could you tell the Ladies and Gentlemen of the jury how it is

---

[63] The testimony by officer Willer so far is "background evidence"—testimony that tells the jury a bit about who the witness is, rather than informing them about the facts of the case. We have not seen much background testimony in this trial, perhaps because the major witnesses are all police officers, and that status alone may constitute enough of a basic introduction. Strictly speaking, background testimony is not *relevant* to the issues at hand, but it is widely accepted. See Chapter Three, p. 217. Courts vary greatly in the amount of detail they will permit as background evidence.

you are familiar with that investigation? **A.** Well, Deputy Alfieri sustained some injuries and we were notified. Well, I was assigned to it a couple days after it happened and the way it was told to me was that he sustained these injuries in an attempted escape.

Q. And so you began an investigation, is that right? **A.** That's correct.

Q. You spoke to Mr. Alfieri, is that true? **A.** Yes, ma'am.

Q. And that was on two different occasions? **A.** Two or three. I'm not sure. It is a while back. Two or three times. At least twice.

. . .

Q. Now, when you interview somebody, in fact, you interview more than just Mr. Alfieri regarding this case, is that right? **A.** Yes.

Q. You interviewed Mr. Daly? **A.** Yes.

Q. And officer—Cook County Department of Corrections Officer Sykes? **A.** Right.

Q. Also a Cook County Department of Corrections Officer DeValle? **A.** Yes.

Q. And when you interviewed Mr. Alfieri you say you did so two or three times? **A.** Yes.

Q. Why?

MR. GARDINER: Objection.

THE COURT: The form of the question, yes.

MS. LYON: **Q.** Was there a reason why you interviewed him more than once? **A.** Yes.

Q. Could you tell us what that is, please?

THE COURT: It is the same question.

MR. GARDINER: Objection.

THE WITNESS: I should answer, your Honor?

THE COURT: It is the same question, was there a reason why and why is the same question.

MS. LYON: Perhaps I'm not understanding your Honor's ruling. Can you explain to me in a side-bar?

THE COURT: Well, counsel, why is generally taken to call for the witness to probe his own mental processes and draw conclusions. That generally is not permissible. I would ask you to rephrase the question.

MS. LYON: I'll try.[64]

Had there been no differences between or discrepancies—

MR. GARDINER: Objection.

THE COURT: Sustained.

BY MS. LYON:

Q. Did Mr. Alfieri tell you different things at different times?

MR. GARDINER: Objection.

THE COURT: Overruled.

A. Yes, he did.[65]

Q. And did Mr. Daly tell you different things at different times? A. Yes, he did.

Q. Before we go into some of the specifics, Mr. Willer, what is—do I call you Deputy Willer? A. Officer will be fine.

. . .

MS. LYON: Q. As part of your investigation in this case, did you have occasion to, on the 4th of September, 1987, to check under the elevator, on the north side of the court building? A. I can't say for sure that was the date but I did check under the elevator you mentioned.

Q. Would you like to see the reports to refresh your memory as to the date? A. Sure would.

Q. Okay. This would be Defense Exhibit Number 30. A. Okay. 4th of September, '87.[66]

Q. When you checked under the elevator what exactly did you do? A. I had to go get the elevator repairman for the building and have him come out there and raise the elevator so we could get under it and jump

---

[64] What is Ms. Lyon getting at by asking officer Willer *why* he re-interviewed Mr. Alfieri? Why is it so difficult? Remember that this is *direct* examination, so she can't use leading questions freely, and yet the witness—a police officer—is not likely to be sympathetic to her client, an accused murderer on trial for allegedly assaulting another officer and attempting to escape.

[65] Finally, after four objections, and at least as many questions, we have it: Alfieri changed his story. What effect are the objections by the prosecutor likely to have had on the jury? See Chapter Two, pp. 186–191.

[66] The witness has "refreshed his memory" by looking at his report. In theory, after doing so he now *remembers* the date and can testify to it; therefore the report itself doesn't need to be marked or introduced in evidence—it's merely a prop, a device that helped trigger the memory that enables him to answer this question. In practice, many witnesses—especially police officers— are allowed to informally "refresh" their memories from reports and memoranda while they are testifying; along the way they no doubt testify to facts that they do not independently remember but merely believe to be true because they are written down—which, in theory, is impermissible under the rubric of "refreshing memory." See Chapter Six, pp. 664–665. If a witness does use a report or memorandum to refresh his memory, the opposing party has the right to see the memorandum, to cross examine the witness about it, and to introduce any relevant portions in evidence. See FRE 612.

down in the pit.

Q. And why did you do that? **A.** I was looking for a key, a handcuff key.

Q. Did you find one? **A.** No, I did not.

Q. Did you find some other keys? **A.** I sure did.

Q. What kind of keys did you find? **A.** They were keys to the lockup doors and tunnel doors in the bridge, which is how they move prisoners from the jail to the courts here and back and forth.

Q. Okay. No handcuff key? **A.** No.

Q. Now, you said that you interviewed Mr. Alfieri at least twice and the first time that you interviewed him here in this building could you describe his demeanor, please? **A.** Well, he was fine. There was nothing wrong with him otherwise I wouldn't have talked to him. He seemed fine except for the injuries that I saw later on him but mentally, emotionally, he was calm and answered the questions right up front.

Q. Did he have any problem understanding you? **A.** Not to my knowledge.

Q. Did he seem to have any problems with his memory? **A.** No.

Q. Did you give him a full opportunity to discuss with you everything that happened? **A.** Yes.

. . .

CROSS EXAMINATION
BY MR. GARDINER:

MR. GARDINER: Officer Willer, you testified regarding certain rules, is that right?

A. Yes.

Q. And there is a rule against a deputy sheriff allowing a prisoner to escape from handcuff, isn't that right? **A.** Certainly.

Q. During the course of your investigation, was there any—ever any evidence that Nicholas Alfieri struck the defendant? **A.** None whatsoever.

Q. No further questions.

MONDAY, JANUARY 23, 1989

THE COURT: Bring out the jury.

(The following proceedings were within the presence and hearing of the jury:)

MS. LYON: Your Honor, the defense, Mr. Tellez would like to testify in his own behalf.[67]

THE COURT: Mr. Tellez, would you take the stand and be sworn?

(Witness sworn)

RONALD TELLEZ,

the defendant, called as a witness in his own behalf, having been first duly sworn, was examined and testified as follows:

THE COURT: You may proceed.

MS. LYON: Thank you, your Honor.

DIRECT EXAMINATION

BY MS. LYON:

Q. Would you tell the ladies and gentlemen of the jury your name, please? A. Ronald Tellez, T-e-l-l-e-z.

Q. Mr. Tellez, before your arrest, you were employed? A. Yes, I was.

Q. What did you do? A. I was a police officer.

Q. How long had you been a police officer? A. Eight and a half years.

---

[67] The Fifth Amendment to the Constitution gives the defendant in a criminal case the right not to take the stand. Furthermore, neither the prosecutor nor the judge may comment on the defendant's failure to testify. See Chapter Eight, pp. 1070–1072. Nevertheless, the jury cannot help but notice the defendant's silence and may be influenced by this in the jury room. Thus, it is dangerous for defense counsel to keep a client off the stand. However, it may also be dangerous to allow one's client to testify. Once the defendant takes the stand he is treated more or less like any other witness. This means that he is subject to cross-examination, and that aspects of his past which arguably bear on his veracity may be brought out to impeach him. In particular, if he has previously been convicted of a felony (or of some misdemeanors) the jury will probably hear about it if he testifies, but very likely will not if he doesn't testify. See Chapter Five, pp. 424–438. Mr. Tellez doesn't face this problem. He is *charged* with another very serious felony—murder—but the jury knows about that anyway because it's related to the charges for which he is on trial. Mr. Tellez also has another advantage over some criminal defendants. As an ex-police officer, he is an experienced witness, and likely to make a decent impression from the stand. Some criminal defendants are both uncomfortable and hostile in court. This may be understandable, but it does not impress juries well.

Under the Fifth, Sixth, and Fourteenth Amendments, a criminal defendant also has the right *to testify* in his own behalf if he chooses to do so. Rock v. Arkansas, 483 U.S. 44, 50–53 (1987). This was not always the case. At one time defendants in criminal cases, parties on both sides in civil cases, and other people who had direct pecuniary or proprietary interests in the outcome of litigation, were precluded from testifying. These and other common law "incompetencies" have long since been abolished. See Chapter Two, pp. 146–147.

In most criminal cases, the defendant, if he does take the stand, will testify last. There are two reasons for this choice. First, it gives the defendant (who cannot be excluded from the court) the opportunity to hear the other witnesses for the defense before he speaks, and to phrase his testimony to avoid, or minimize, or explain conflicts with those witnesses. See supra, note 9. Second, going last may give the defendant's testimony greater emphasis than coming somewhere in the middle. (For similar reasons, prosecutors frequently have the victim testify first, if that's feasible, as Mr. Alfieri did here.) Of course, putting the defendant last can backfire. The last major part of the defendant's testimony is the cross-examination; if the cross-examination goes badly for the defendant, that may be what the jurors remember best.

Q. And that was where? **A.** In the City of Blue Island.

Q. Now, you were arrested for the crime of murder? **A.** Yes, I was.

Q. And you were in jail? **A.** Yes, I was.

Q. I want to call your attention now to the date of August 28th of 1987, okay? **A.** Yes.

Q. And you were brought to court that day to Room 400, is that right? **A.** Yes.

Q. Calling your attention to around noon, all right, physically where were you at that time? **A.** I was in the jury room.

Q. Now, when you say the jury room, where physically within the jury room where were you? **A.** At the large table sitting in a chair.

Q. When you say the large table, there's a table in the jury room? **A.** Yes.

Q. And relative to the door, where were you sitting? **A.** I can see directly out to the courtroom.

Q. To the door to the courtroom? **A.** Yes.

Q. And you say you were sitting in a chair? **A.** Yes.

Q. Were you handcuffed? **A.** Yes, I was.

Q. And how were you handcuffed? Could you show the ladies and gentlemen of the jury where your hand was? **A.** Left hand to the armrest of the chair.

Q. Now, about noon did you see Deputy Alfieri, the man who testified against you a few days ago? **A.** Yes, I did.

Q. What happened when you first saw him? **A.** He came inside and told me I was going downstairs.

Q. When you say came inside the jury room? **A.** Yes, came inside the jury room.

Q. So when he came inside the jury room, did he do something? **A.** Yes, he removed the left handcuff from me and then told me to stand up.

Q. Now, when you say removed the handcuff from you, did he remove it from the arm first or the chair first? **A.** From my arm first.

Q. And told you to stand up? **A.** Yes, he did.

Q. Did you do that? **A.** Yes, I did.

Q. Then what did he do? **A.** He took the other section of the handcuff off the armrest.

Q. What did he do next? **A.** He told me to turn around and put my hands behind my back.

Q. And did you do that? **A.** Yes, I did.

Q. Now, for the sake of the jury, you had your hands behind your back like this, is that right? **A.** That is correct.

Q. And he handcuffed you from behind? **A.** Yes, he did.

Q. Did you say anything to him, was there any conversation about the handcuffing process? **A.** Yes, the right handcuff wasn't on properly.

Q. When you say it wasn't on properly, what do you mean? **A.** It was on long ways instead of, it's hard to explain. Instead of the curve of the handcuff, it was long ways against the curve of my wrist. It's hard to explain without showing you.

Q. Do any of you have a set of handcuffs? Do you have a pair. Thank you, Mr. Anderson.

Can we consider this as marked as Defense Exhibit Number 34, I think, your Honor? I'm going to show you what is being considered marked as Defense Exhibit Number 34 for identification.

Could you tell the jury what you mean when you say long ways? Just show them what you mean.

A. Instead of being this way, it's long way, this way.

Q. How was your wrist placed within it? **A.** Instead of being, wrist going this way, it was this way.

THE COURT: Counsel, can you see?

MR. REILLY: Yes, Judge.

MS. LYON: **Q.** Did you tell him; that is, did you tell Mr. Alfieri that he had the cuff on wrong? **A.** Yes, I did.

Q. Why did you tell him, did it hurt? **A.** If you do it the wrong way, it hits the inner nerve of your wrist, you know that it's done wrong that way.

Q. I mean obviously it was behind your back. Could you see him do it that way? **A.** No, you can feel the way the groove is.

Q. What did you tell him? **A.** I told him, "You got it on wrong." He said, "Don't worry about it, you're not going to have it on that long."

Q. Did you say anything else about it? **A.** No, he then double locked it and that was it.

Q. Now, after he locked the handcuffs, did he take you somewhere?

A. Yes, he took me down to the bullpen to the next gate that leads to the elevator.

Q. Now, when you went towards the bullpen that leads to the elevator, I'm going to show you Defense Exhibit Number 1 for identification. This is the bullpen, is that right? **A.** The bullpen is in this section right here.

Q. When you were walking down that hall, were you with someone or was it just you and Alfieri? **A.** The woman security officer.

Q. The same lady who testified here Friday, rather?[68] **A.** Yes.

Q. So you walked down the hallway, is that right? **A.** Yes, I did.

Q. And who unlocked the gate? **A.** I think he did, and then we went through it and then she, he gave her the keys and she locked the gate.

Q. And when the gate was locked, where did you go? **A.** We went standing by the elevator.

Q. You stood by the elevator waiting for the elevator? **A.** Waiting for the elevator.

Q. When you got in the elevator, who was in the elevator with you? **A.** Nobody else, just me and him.

Q. Where physically within the elevator did you stand? **A.** I stand in the middle of the elevator facing the wall.

Q. When you say facing the wall—just a moment, your Honor, I have to find a picture.

I'm going to show you what's been previously identified as Defense Exhibit Number 13. Can you see where you were standing there? **A.** Yes, right in the center of the elevator facing the wall.

Q. Your Honor, indicating for the record, that the witness has pointed to the center panel of three panels in the photograph.

Now, which way were you facing in the elevator? **A.** You have to face the wall, they tell you to face the wall.

Q. So you were facing the wall with your hands behind your back, is that right? **A.** Yes.

Q. And Mr. Alfieri was in there with you? **A.** Yes.

Q. Where did you go when you got in the elevator? **A.** We went up.

Q. Why did you go up? **A.** Somebody else wanted the elevator upstairs.

Q. So you went up first? **A.** We went up first.

Q. Did you pick up anyone there? **A.** I think we picked up another officer.

Q. Did you see who it was? **A.** No.

Q. And then what happened after you picked up this other person?

---

68 Sheriff's Officer Juanita Lilly.

A. We went down and we stopped on another floor.

Q. Do you know what floor it was? **A.** No, I don't.

Q. When you stopped at this other floor, what happened, did anyone else get on or off? **A.** Before the officer, when the officer entered the elevator, I forget—

Q. Mr. Alfieri? **A.** Alfieri told me to move to the left, to the corner of the elevator.

Q. So you moved to your left? **A.** Yes.

Q. And then what happened? **A.** And then the officer got in and we went down to another floor, I don't know what floor, and the officer got off.

Q. When you say the officer, are you assuming it's an officer or did you see him? **A.** I didn't see him, but it had to be an officer.

Q. Then did you continue down in the elevator? **A.** Yes, but when the officer left, I went back to my original spot.

Q. You moved back to the center? **A.** To the center.

Q. The elevator began to go down? **A.** Yes.

Q. What happened as the elevator began to go down? **A.** When I moved from the corner to the center, I forget the officer—

Q. Alfieri? **A.** Alfieri grabbed me and he pulled me to the left side of the elevator.

Q. When you say he grabbed you physically, where did he grab you? **A.** He grabbed my left arm.

Q. You were handcuffed behind your back? **A.** Yes, I was.

Q. So you moved over to the left? **A.** Well, when I went to the left, I hit the left side of the elevator.

Q. When you say you hit the left side of the elevator, what part of your body hit the left side of the elevator? **A.** My face.

Q. What did you say when that happened? **A.** Well, when I hit the elevator, the left lens of my glasses broke and cut my left cheek underneath my glasses.

Q. What happened then? **A.** I swore, I told him, "Look what you did, that wasn't necessary." During all that when it happened, he just, I took a step back and he pushed me back forward again.

Q. Now, when you say took a step back, you stepped backwards? **A.** I stepped back, I wanted to find, I didn't want to step on my lens.

Q. And you stepped backwards and he pushed you again? **A.** He pushed me again forward to the elevator.

Q. When you say forward to the elevator, to what part? **A.** To the same corner that I was where I hit, the area I hit.

Q. When he pushed you again, what did you do? **A.** I hit the corner, hit the section, I went back again and then he pulled me down.

Q. When you say he pulled you down, where did he pull you down to? **A.** He grabbed me from the back of my collar, I don't know if he grabbed my left arm or right arm, but I went down to the floor.

Q. When you say you went down to the floor, onto your knees? **A.** On my right side.

Q. You fell all the way onto the floor? **A.** I went to the right side of my body, yes.

Q. Ron, the elevator was still going down at this time? **A.** No, as soon as I hit the ground it stopped.

Q. You were on the basement at that point? **A.** We were in the basement.

Q. What did you do when he did this to you? **A.** Nothing, the door was opening and he grabbed my tie and told me to come out.

Q. What did you do? **A.** He started pulling on my tie, I was trying to get in a sitting position. When he was pulling me out of the elevator, he stopped because the door started closing again, so he pushed the door open and then he went around, let go of the tie. He went around to the button and he was pressing buttons, so I don't know what buttons he was pressing.

Q. What did you do to Mr. Alfieri? **A.** I got around, I turned around and when I started kicking him.

Q. Why did you start kicking him? **A.** Because I thought he was going to grab me again the same way he did before.

Q. What did you think he was going to do to you? **A.** I don't know, you know. I don't know if he was going to hit me again, I don't know what he was going to do next, it's hard to say.

Q. Ron, you knew he was a correctional officer? **A.** I know.

Q. You knew you shouldn't have kicked him? **A.** I know that, but when he grabbed me around my tie and started pulling me out of the elevator, I had no choice. If he would have grabbed me again or, you know, when I spun around I didn't want him to come near me, keep away from me. Then he started hollering, "Help, help."

Q. Now, you heard his testimony that you just started kicking him for no reason, right? **A.** Yes, I heard that.

Q. Did you do that? **A.** I didn't kick him for no reason, I had a reason.

Q. And when you were kicking him, did he fall backwards or forwards? **A.** No.

Q. Did he fall at all? **A.** No, he turned around the corner, when I kicked him the first time he went around the corner and started yelling, "Help, help," he came back.

He went to kick me, he missed. It wasn't a good kick, he nicked me. Second time I went around, I tried to turn my body to the right side to get back up. He kicked, he got me in the back of the neck.

I turned around again, I was on my face now. He left the elevator and kept screaming, "Help, help," and he came back. The door was closing, he put his arm up. The door went back, went open again, and he stayed there.

I got back on my feet. At that time Mike Daly came around.

Q. That's Mr. Daly who testified here also, is that right? **A.** Yes.

Q. And you said Mike Daly, is that right? **A.** Mike Daly.

Q. You knew who he was from before, is that right? **A.** Yes.

Q. When you were a police officer? **A.** Yes.

Q. Is he like a best friend of yours? **A.** No, he's not a best friend.

Q. Just an acquaintance? **A.** Just an acquaintance.

Q. And you heard him say that Mr. Alfieri was on the floor at some point, didn't you? **A.** Yes.

Q. And he was on the floor at some point? **A.** I never saw him hit the ground, I never saw him hit the ground.

Q. What did Mr. Daly do when he got there? **A.** Daly was right behind him and Alfieri was standing by the elevator door with his arm against the elevator, and every time I got near him, he would start kicking, so I went back and I told Daly, I said, "Grab him," and Daly grabbed his right shoulder and Alfieri pulled away from him and Daly just stood there doing nothing, just stood there.

Q. Ron, you have heard the testimony of Mr. Sykes and Mr. DeValle, right? **A.** Yes.

Q. They testified when they got there, that Mr. Alfieri was on the floor, do you remember, do you remember them testifying to that? **A.** Yes, I do.

Q. Could he have been on the floor? **A.** He could, but I never saw him on the floor. His leg was always extended by the elevator, he could have looked like he was on the floor, maybe a knee, but not on the floor.

Q. Ron, you also heard testimony that you had only one handcuff on? **A.** Yes.

Q. Did you manage to get one of your hands out of the handcuff? **A.** Yes, I did.

Q. Which hand was that? **A.** The right hand.

Q. The one that you were demonstrating earlier with, is that right? **A.** Yes.

Q. How did you do that? **A.** Just turn your wrist completely around.

Q. And pulled out of it? **A.** And pulled out of it, it will take awhile to pull out of it.

Q. Why did you pull out of it? **A.** Because he was coming back in the elevator.

Q. Were you scared? **A.** Yeah, I mean, all you have is your feet, you don't have, you don't have your hands. They have the advantage, I don't.

Q. Do you have any idea why he pushed you or grabbed you by the tie or any of that, do you have any idea why Mr. Alfieri did that? **A.** I think he panicked, I think he saw what—

MR. REILLY: Objection.

THE COURT: Sustained.[69]

MS. LYON: **Q.** Ron, when you went down in that elevator, did you just start kicking Mr. Alfieri in the groin? **A.** No.

Q. Did you go down in that elevator, attack Mr. Alfieri, and attempt to escape? **A.** No.

Q. Were you trying to escape? **A.** No.

Q. Why did you kick him? **A.** Because he grabbed me around the tie. He was pulling me out of the elevator by my tie. I had to turn around, I had to stop him from letting go of my tie.

MS. LYON: No further questions.

---

[69] What's the basis for this objection? See supra, note 53.

*"If it slows down, just ask my father about the murder
he always swears he did not commit."*

CROSS EXAMINATION

BY MR. REILLY:

Q. If I may inquire, Judge. Mr. Tellez, you have testified in court before, is that right? **A.** Yes, I have.

Q. Lots of times? **A.** Yes.

Q. Over the last eight or nine years, you have appeared in front of judges and juries, is that right? **A.** Juries twice, yes.[70]

Q. And you were incarcerated for about six weeks at the time this incident happened, is that right? **A.** Yes, sir.

Q. You had been in Division 1 at Cook County Jail? **A.** Yes, sir.

Q. Charged with murder, is that right? **A.** Yes, sir.

Q. Now, the day this happened, August 28th, you were up in Room 400 above here, is that right? **A.** Yes, sir.

---

[70] Why does Mr. Reilly start his cross-examination with these first three questions?

Q. That's right above this courtroom, is that correct? **A.** I don't know if it's above this courtroom.

Q. Is that the first time you had met Nicholas Alfieri? **A.** I think so.

Q. And up until the time that he moved you at noon, you hadn't had any problems with him, had you? **A.** I had no problems with any officer.

Q. You hadn't given him any problems, is that right? **A.** No, sir.

Q. You were very nice, very polite, just as you are today, correct? **A.** Yes, sir, try to be.

Q. Followed any of the requests the sheriffs made of you, is that right? **A.** Yes, sir.

Q. And when he first handcuffed you to take you downstairs, you say he put the handcuff on you wrong? **A.** Yes, sir.

Q. And it was a little bit too tight on you? **A.** No, sir, it wasn't. It was tight, but it was done improperly.

Q. And you were able to slip out of that, is that your testimony? **A.** Yes, sir.

Q. Slip out of that locked handcuff? **A.** Yes, sir.

Q. So when you slipped out of it later in the elevator, it wasn't open, you had just slipped out of it, that's your testimony? **A.** Yes, sir.

Q. And when you got on the elevator, after making these couple of stops, you say that you were about to move back to the center of the elevator, is that right? **A.** Yes, sir.

Q. And it's at that point in time that you're telling us that Nicholas Alfieri grabbed you and threw you up against the wall, is that right? **A.** He grabbed me, sir.

Q. Did he throw you up against the wall? **A.** As a result of the grab, it resulted in me hitting the wall.

Q. That's not my question. Did he take you and did he throw you up against the wall? **A.** Yes, sir.

Q. And when he did that, you're telling these people that your glasses broke? **A.** My left lens broke.

Q. Broke? **A.** Yes.

Q. Shattered and cut you? **A.** No, sir, it didn't shatter.

Q. It broke? **A.** It broke.

Q. And cut you? **A.** And cut me right here.

Q. So the glass was sharp that cut your left side of your check? **A.** Yes, sir.

Q. You were bleeding? **A.** Yes, sir.

Q. So you were bleeding there in the elevator. Are your glasses still on or off? **A.** The right side is still on, the right side lens is still on, yes.

Q. The right side lens is on, but the left side lens has broken and it's on the floor? **A.** It's on the floor.

Q. How many different pieces? **A.** None.

Q. One piece? **A.** Just one piece.

Q. And you have a cut underneath your left eye? **A.** Yes, sir.

Q. And you're still standing, right? **A.** Yes, sir.

Q. Nicholas Alfieri is still standing, right? **A.** Yes, sir, he's behind me.

Q. And you begin to bleed from the face? **A.** Yes, sir.

Q. And what do you say then? **A.** I swore at him and I told him look what he did, and I took a step back to look for the lens.

Q. And that's when he grabbed you by the tie? **A.** No, sir.

Q. What did he do next? **A.** He pushed me forward again.

Q. When you say forward, into the elevator doors? **A.** Not the elevator doors, again to the same section I was on before.

Q. Alfieri is doing this, right? **A.** Yes, sir.

Q. And is he swearing back at you now? **A.** No, sir.

Q. You were swearing at him, though, right? **A.** I swore at him, sir.

Q. Because he had hurt you when he threw you up against the wall, right? **A.** Yes, sir.

Q. Glasses had broken, right? **A.** The lens fell off, yes, sir.

Q. You were bleeding now, right? **A.** Yes, sir.

Q. But he wasn't swearing back, he wasn't saying anything? **A.** No, sir.

Q. Then he pushed you up again, is that right? **A.** Yes, sir.

Q. You got madder, right? **A.** Yes, sir.

Q. And then you kicked him? **A.** Pardon me, sir?

Q. Then you kicked him? **A.** No, sir.

Q. What did you do next? **A.** He grabbed me from the back of my coat and I think my left arm and he pushed me down to the ground.

Q. You had a suit and tie on, is that right? **A.** Yes, sir.

Q. So he had to come over to you and he threw you on the ground, is that right? **A.** He pulled me down to the ground.

Q. He pulled you down to the ground? **A.** Yes, sir.

Q. You had been a police officer eight and a half years, right? **A.** Yes, sir.

Q. Did you resist him when he pulled you to the ground? **A.** No, sir.

Q. You showed no resistance at all? **A.** I wasn't expecting it.

Q. So he surprised you when he threw you down on the floor of the elevator?

MS. LYON: Objection, he said three times pulled, not thrown.

MR. REILLY: **Q.** I'll rephrase it. You were surprised when you were pulled down to the floor? **A.** Yes, sir.

Q. So now you're down on the ground? **A.** Yes, sir.

Q. Face down? **A.** On my right side.

Q. Glasses still on or off? **A.** At that time, I think they were off.

Q. Still bleeding? **A.** Yes, sir, I think so.

Q. You're down on the right side, on your right side laying in the elevator, right? **A.** Yes, sir.

Q. Were you screaming? **A.** I was swearing.

Q. You were screaming? **A.** I was swearing, sir.

Q. Swearing at Alfieri? **A.** Yes.

Q. Asking him to cut it out, right? **A.** I just told him, "Look what you did."

Q. Telling him to stop? **A.** I told him to stop, it wasn't necessary.

Q. It wasn't necessary? **A.** No, sir.

Q. But he kept coming at you, didn't he? **A.** No, sir, he just grabbed my tie.

Q. Now, you're on the ground? **A.** Yes, sir.

Q. And he grabbed your tie? **A.** Yes, sir.

Q. So he didn't keep coming after you, after you go to the ground he didn't back up again, right? **A.** No, sir, he reached for my tie.

Q. Came towards you, right? **A.** Yes, sir.

Q. He's only five foot five, right? **A.** Yes, sir.

Q. So now you're down on the ground and he grabs you by the tie? **A.** Yes, sir.

Q. You're still handcuffed, right? **A.** Yes, sir.

Q. You don't have a handcuff free now, do you? **A.** No, sir.

Q. And you're laying on your right side? **A.** Yes, sir.

Q. Pulls you by your tie? **A.** Yes, sir.

Q. You kick him? **A.** Not yet, sir.

Q. What do you do after he kicks you, strike that, after he pulls your tie? **A.** He started pulling me towards the elevator door.

Q. So he's dragging you now on the floor of the elevator, is that what you're telling us? **A.** He's pulling me by the tie, sir.

Q. If he's pulling you by the tie, you're moving? **A.** Yes, sir, but not as quickly.

Q. Nobody else is in there, just Nicholas Alfieri, right? **A.** Yes, sir.

Q. And how far, does he pull you in the elevator? **A.** Toward the elevator.

Q. You're still moving? **A.** Still moving towards the elevator door.

Q. The elevator is still moving? **A.** No, sir.

Q. Elevator stopped? **A.** Elevator was stopped.

Q. Are you in the basement now? **A.** We are in the basement.

Q. And the doors are open? **A.** Doors open.

Q. And he's trying to drag you out, pull you out of the elevator? **A.** Yes, sir.

Q. You're screaming? **A.** No, sir.

Q. You're not saying anything? **A.** No, sir.

Q. And you're not resisting this little guy pulling you out of the elevator? **A.** There's no way you can resist.

Q. At some point in time, you're telling us while on the ground there you were able to kick him, right? **A.** No, sir, not then.

Q. How far does he drag you out of the elevator? **A.** To the door entrance.

Q. To the entrance of the door? Then what happens? **A.** He stops.

Q. Backs up? **A.** The door started closing again.

Q. You're in the doorway, though, right? **A.** Yes, sir.

Q. So the elevator couldn't have closed, right? **A.** Door started closing, sir.

Q. But for it to close all the way, it would have had to hit you, right? **A.** Yes, sir.

Q. And you're still laying on your right side? **A.** No, sir, I'm on my back.

Q. You're on your back now? **A.** Yes, sir.

Q. So before he had pulled you out of that elevator or towards the door, you had gone from your right side onto your back, is that right? **A.** Yes, sir.

Q. So your arms are behind you handcuffed, is that right? **A.** Yes, sir.

Q. With handcuffs on, is that right? **A.** Yes, sir.

Q. And you're laying on your back, right? **A.** Yes, sir.

Q. And your hands would be between the floor and your back, correct? **A.** Yes, sir.

Q. And this fellow is pulling you, dragging you towards the elevator door, is that your testimony? **A.** Yes, sir.

Q. When you get to the elevator door, he stops? **A.** Yes, sir.

Q. You get up? **A.** Yes, sir—no, sir, I didn't get up.

Q. Tell us what you did. **A.** He stopped.

Q. What did you do? **A.** I started turning around.

Q. You had to roll over, I take it? **A.** Yes, sir.

Q. Roll over on your stomach now? **A.** Yes, sir, I tried.

Q. Then what do you do? Tell us what you did.

MS. LYON: Objection, your Honor. I mean, if the next thing that happens is something he did.

THE COURT: Counsel, the question was what did you do. The witness should be responsive in answering that question.

THE WITNESS: I tried to get up on my knees.

MR. REILLY: **Q.** Did you get up? **A.** No, sir.

Q. What did do next after you tried to get on your knees? **A.** I turned my body around, my feet facing the door.

Q. Are you on your back or stomach? **A.** I'm on my back.

Q. Still on your back? **A.** Yes, sir.

Q. Handcuffs behind you on your back? **A.** Yes, sir.

Q. Now, this is all happening in the basement there, the elevator doors are there and it's still just you and Nicholas Alfieri? **A.** Yes, sir.

Q. After you turned yourself around, now, do you get up then? **A.** No, sir.

Q. Stay laying on the ground? **A.** Yes, sir.

Q. Hands behind your back? **A.** Yes, sir.

Q. Weight of your body on your hands, on your handcuffed hands? **A.** Yes, sir.

Q. Alfieri comes after you again? **A.** He left the elevator, sir.

Q. He left the elevator? **A.** Yes, sir.

Q. He had already gone out of the elevator to drag you out of there, isn't that right? **A.** Yes, sir, but he stopped.

Q. He stopped? **A.** Yes, sir.

Q. He had dragged you all the way to the door of the elevator, right? **A.** Yes, sir.

Q. And he dragged you by your tie? **A.** Yes, sir.

Q. That's what you're telling us, right? **A.** Yes, sir.

Q. So he was outside of the elevator at that point in time? **A.** It's hard to determine what part of his body was out of the elevator.

Q. You're in the doorway laying there on your back, he's outside the elevator, is that correct? **A.** No, sir, he let go of the tie and he went to press some buttons inside the elevator.

Q. So you're in the basement, right? **A.** Yes, sir.

Q. He told you that you were through with court, going back to Division 1, right? He had told you that? **A.** Yes, sir.

Q. You knew that you were down in the basement and you expected to go down that tunnel, right? **A.** Yes, sir.

Q. That's what you expected? **A.** Yes, sir.

Q. But now you see Alfieri in there pressing buttons, right? **A.** Yes, sir.

Q. So he's back inside the elevator now? **A.** Sir, when he was pulling the tie, the doors started to close. He put his arm up to push the door open, he went inside the elevator again to press some buttons.

Q. You didn't see what buttons he pressed? **A.** No, sir.

Q. You're still on the ground? **A.** Yes, sir.

Q. Still bleeding? **A.** Yes, sir.

Q. You don't know where your glass lens is? **A.** No, sir.

Q. Does he hit you again while you're on the ground? **A.** Yes, sir.

Q. Where does he hit you? **A.** He missed the first time.

Q. Tried to kick you while you were down there on the ground? **A.** Yes, sir.

Q. This is Alfieri, right? **A.** Yes, sir.

Q. What is he saying when he's trying to kick you? **A.** I don't remember what he said to me.

Q. Was he saying anything? **A.** He was saying something, but he was yelling most of the time.

Q. Yelling at you? **A.** Back and forth, I don't know if he was yelling at me.

Q. But he was yelling most of the time? **A.** He was yelling, "Help, help, somebody."

Q. He's yelling, "Help, help, somebody"? **A.** Yes, sir.

Q. You were the guy that was laying on the ground, right? **A.** Yes, sir.

Q. You were the guy with his hands handcuffed behind him laying on the ground, right? **A.** Yes, sir.

Q. You were the guy that was bleeding, right? **A.** Yes, sir.

Q. And he's yelling, "Help, help"? **A.** Yes, sir.

Q. He's not yelling at you? **A.** No, sir.

Q. No remarks, no swearing towards you? **A.** No, sir.

Q. Tries to keep kick you once and he misses? **A.** Yes, sir.

Q. Just you and him in that elevator? **A.** Yes, sir.

Q. And he kicks you once and he misses you? **A.** Yes, sir.

Q. You're laying on the ground? **A.** Yes, sir.

Q. You're handcuffed? **A.** Yes, sir.

Q. And he kicks you and misses you? **A.** He missed me the first time.

Q. Then you kick him? **A.** No, sir.

Q. Then he kicks you again? **A.** Yes, sir.

Q. Hits you this time? **A.** Yes, sir.

Q. Where does he kick you this time? **A.** Back of the neck.

Q. Back of the neck? **A.** Yes.

Q. You're laying on your back, right? **A.** Yes, sir.

Q. Feet are towards the door? **A.** Yes, sir.

Q. That's what you told, isn't it? **A.** Yes.

Q. He had to come inside the elevator somehow and kick you on the back of the neck? **A.** No, sir.

Q. Was he outside the elevator when he kicked you on the back of the neck? **A.** When he was pressing the buttons.

Q. And what side of the neck did he kick you? **A.** The back side of the neck.

Q. Right in the middle of the back side of your head? Yes, sir.

Q. You're laying on your back still? **A.** Yes.

Q. Is that correct? **A.** Yes, sir.

Q. Now, you start swearing even more at him, right? **A.** Yes, sir.

Q. Sir? **A.** Yes, sir.

Q. As he still yelling, "Help, help"? **A.** Yes, sir.

Q. Now, these people haven't been in the downstairs there but that tunnel, in that tunnel it echoes, doesn't it? **A.** Yes, sir.

Q. It's very loud in that tunnel, right? **A.** Yes, sir.

Q. So somebody yelling or screaming in that tunnel, you'd hear it for a long way? **A.** Yes, sir.

Q. And he's yelling, "Help, help," and you're swearing at him, is that right? **A.** Yes, sir.

Q. Now, after you catch—now, is he wearing, was he wearing similar type of shoes as these gentlemen in this courtroom? **A.** Black shoes, sir.

Q. Police issue? **A.** I don't know if they are police issue.

Q. You have never seen shoes like that before? **A.** Yes, sir, but I don't know if they are police issues, every officer wears different shoes.

Q. But he caught you in the back of the neck finally with this kick, is that right? **A.** Yes, sir.

Q. That hurt you quite a bit? **A.** It hurt.

Q. Knock your glasses off? **A.** No, sir.

Q. Glasses still on the head, right? **A.** No, sir.

Q. Glasses were off the head? **A.** Glasses were off the head.

Q. Glasses were off the head? Where are the glasses? **A.** On the floor, I assume.

Q. You don't know where they were? **A.** No, sir.

Q. Now you kick him, is that right? **A.** Yes, sir.

Q. Now you hit him, is that right? **A.** I kicked him.

Q. Where did you kick him at? You're laying on the ground. **A.** I don't know, sir.

Q. What part of his body do you strike with your foot? **A.** I kicked several times, sir. I didn't anticipate where I was going to kick.

Q. While you're laying on the ground? **A.** Yes, sir.

Q. You're laying on your back still, right? **A.** Yes, sir.

Q. In the doorway of the elevator? **A.** Yes, sir, pretty close to it.

Q. And very shortly after being kicked in the neck by Nicholas Alfieri, you kick back? **A.** Yes, sir.

Q. And you don't know where you struck him? **A.** No, sir, I kicked.

Q. You just kicked? **A.** Kicked several times.

Q. You didn't see where you were kicking? **A.** No, sir.

Q. You're not blind without your glasses, are you? **A.** I'm pretty close to it.

Q. You need your glasses at all times? **A.** Yes, sir.

Q. Pardon me? **A.** Yes, sir.

Q. And you kicked how many times? **A.** I don't know, seven, eight times maybe, a lot, like bicycle kicks.

Q. Mr. Tellez, you were laying on the ground handcuffed, right? **A.** Yes, sir.

Q. There was nothing stopping Nicholas Alfieri from moving around, right? **A.** No, sir.

Q. Is that correct? **A.** Yes, sir.

Q. Now, your first kick, you kicked up, is that right, or was it sideways? **A.** I just kicked, I don't know where.

Q. Did you kick up or did you kick sideways? **A.** Kicked straight out.

Q. This way? **A.** Yes, sir.

Q. Well, if you were to kick straight out in the position you were in, am I correct to assume you would hit him about his ankles? **A.** Yes, sir.

Q. So you just kicked straight out? **A.** Yes.

Q. Where is he at when you kick him the first time? **A.** Standing by the doorway area.

Q. Now, he moves out of the way, then, after you kick him the first time, right? **A.** No, sir.

Q. Stays there? **A.** Yes, sir.

Q. You kick him again? **A.** Yes, sir.

Q. Where do you kick him this time? **A.** Caught my left foot.

Q. Where do you kick him, what part of his body? **A.** I don't know.

Q. You kick him this time with your left foot, right? **A.** Yes, sir.

Q. Correct? **A.** Yes, sir.

Q. Straight out again? **A.** Straight out again.

Q. These are straight out kicks, and you're still laying on the ground still, is that right? **A.** Yes, sir.

Q. You catch him a second time with this kick now? **A.** He caught my left foot.

Q. I'm sorry? **A.** He caught my foot.

Q. Well, when you kicked him the second time, did you strike his body? **A.** It's hard to say, he caught it and it hit his side, I mean it's hard.

Q. It hit his side? **A.** Hit his side of his leg, wasn't an accurate kick.

Q. Is the blood running in your eye now at this point in time? **A.** No, sir.

Q. Now, after the second kick, he moves out of the way? **A.** No, he caught my leg.

Q. He caught your leg? **A.** Yes, sir.

Q. He's holding onto your leg now? **A.** Yes, sir.

Q. And you're handcuffed? **A.** Yes, sir.

Q. And you told us you were afraid he was going to grab your tie again too? **A.** Yes, sir.

Q. What is he saying, what is Alfieri saying when he's got your leg in the elevator? **A.** I don't know, sir.

Q. Was he saying something to you? **A.** Yes, sir, but I don't recall what he was saying.

Q. Still yelling, "Help, help"? **A.** Oh, yes, sir.

Q. Yelling for help. Are you able to kick him again after he's holding onto your left leg there? **A.** Yes, sir, I used my right leg.

Q. Now you kick with your right leg? **A.** Yes, sir.

Q. Still laying on your back, right? **A.** Yes, sir.

Q. Still have your hands handcuffed behind you? **A.** Yes, sir.

Q. With your weight laying on your handcuffs? **A.** Yes, sir.

Q. Kick him now with your right leg? **A.** Yes, sir.

Q. Where do you hit him? **A.** I don't know, sir.

Q. You don't know? Did you hit him, though, did you make contact? **A.** Yes, sir.

Q. Straight out kick again? **A.** It was a little higher.

Q. Higher up this time, maybe about the knees maybe? **A.** I don't know, sir, those are wild kicks, those are not something—

Q. They were wild kicks? **A.** Wild kicks.

Q. You weren't trying to concentrate them all in one area, were you? **A.** No.

Q. Wild kicks? **A.** They were wild kicks.

Q. But you strike him this time with the right leg, correct? **A.** I think so.

Q. Now his hands are free, correct? **A.** Yes, sir.

Q. Except for the fact I assume one of his arms has your leg, is that correct? **A.** Yes, sir.

Q. Is he punching you at all? **A.** No, sir.

Q. Knocking you around at all with the other hand? **A.** No, sir, I was on the floor.

Q. Pardon me? **A.** I was on the floor.

Q. Did he kick you anymore while you were down there? **A.** No, sir, not then.

Q. He's holding onto your leg, what do you do next, strike that. He's holding onto your leg, you kick him with the right leg a little higher up this time. What do you do next? **A.** It was just, you kick, you just kick wildly, you don't kick, you don't count how many times you throw your legs out, you just kick.

Q. You kick several more times? **A.** Yes, sir.

Q. With which leg? **A.** The right leg.

Q. Where is Mr. Alfieri at now? You can't see him? **A.** Still right in front of me, he's holding onto my leg.

Q. Holding onto your ankle, leg, or thigh? **A.** Ankle.

Q. Holding onto your ankle, trying to? **A.** Yes, sir.

Q. Were you resisting him? **A.** No, sir.

Q. So you just had your left leg out there and he was holding onto it? **A.** He was holding onto it.

Q. Was he dragging you on the elevator? **A.** No, sir.

Q. Just holding onto the left leg? **A.** Yes, sir.

Q. Is that correct? **A.** Yes, sir.

Q. Just standing there, right? **A.** Yes, sir.

Q. And you're kicking him away with your right leg, is that right? **A.** Yes, sir.

Q. He just stood there for that, is that right? **A.** Yes, sir.

Q. Wasn't kicking you back? **A.** No, sir.

Q. Wasn't hitting you with a free hand? **A.** No, sir.

Q. And you kicked him a whole bunch more times, is that right? **A.** Yes, sir.

Q. You don't know how many more times? **A.** No, sir.

Q. You never jumped back when you kicked him, when you hit him? **A.** He eventually let go of my leg.

Q. Did he ever scream out when you kicked him? **A.** No, sir.

Q. Never screamed out in pain when you kicked him? **A.** No, sir.

Q. How many more blows did you strike him with the right leg, how many more times did you hit him? **A.** I don't know, sir.

Q. He just wouldn't let go, would he? **A.** He eventually let go.

Q. He did let go? **A.** Yes, sir.

Q. Then Mike Daly shows up, right? **A.** Yes, sir.

Q. You're still on the ground there, right? **A.** I was getting up, sir.

Q. You were getting up now? **A.** Yes, sir.

Q. Alfieri had backed off, is that right? **A.** Yes, sir.

Q. Off the elevator? **A.** No, sir, he was standing by the doorway area still.

Q. You're laying in the doorway, right? **A.** No, sir, not now.

Q. Where are you at now? **A.** I moved up.

Q. Up into the elevator? **A.** Up in the elevator, sir.

Q. Were you able to do so on your back, is that right? **A.** Yes, sir.

Q. Able to slide along the floor? **A.** Yes, sir.

Q. With your hands in handcuffs behind you? **A.** Yes, sir.

Q. And Daly walks up, you're in the process of getting up, is that right? **A.** Yes, sir.

Q. Alfieri is just standing there at the doorway? **A.** Yes, sir.

Q. And you know Mike Daly, right? **A.** Yes, sir.

Q. You had known him for several years, right? **A.** I have seen him, I don't know him personally for several years.

Q. The two of you had talked before, right? **A.** We have talked in court, sir.

Q. You talked in Maplewood Tavern, right? **A.** Yes, sir.

Q. Used to see him in there with some frequency, correct? **A.** No, sir, not often.

Q. Well, you used to see him there, right? **A.** Once in awhile.

Q. You knew he lived in Blue Island, right? **A.** Yes, sir.

Q. He knew you were a Blue Island policeman? **A.** Yes, sir.

Q. You knew he was a sheriff's officer, right? **A.** Yes.

Q. You knew all this? **A.** Yes.

Q. And you had talked to Mike Daly earlier that day, right? **A.** I don't know if I did, sir.

Q. Mike Daly was the sheriff working in the courtroom that morning when you were brought over to Room 400, do you remember that? **A.** Yes, sir.

Q. Did you have a conversation with Mike at that time? **A.** I don't know if I had a conversation with him.

Q. Well, they were Mike's handcuffs on you? **A.** Yes, sir.

Q. Mike Daly is the one that handcuffed you to the chair, right? **A.** Yes, sir.

Q. And then Mike Daly had to suddenly, sometime that morning, had to leave, right? **A.** Yes, sir.

Q. Was working down in the bridge area, right? **A.** I don't know that, sir.

Q. Well, he was the first one to show up when you were swearing and screaming and Nick Alfieri was yelling for help, right? **A.** Yes, sir.

Q. And he had a station, you did learn he had a station right there in the bridge area, right? **A.** Yes, sir.

Q. And it's your testimony that when Mike Daly walks up, you're just getting up off the floor, right? **A.** Yes, sir.

Q. Your glasses are off? **A.** Yes, sir.

Q. One glass, the lens is off somewhere on the floor? **A.** Yes, sir.

Q. You're bleeding? **A.** Yes, sir.

Q. Tie had been pulled from your person, is that right? **A.** No, sir, it wasn't pulled off my person.

Q. It was all disheveled, though, right? **A.** I wasn't paying attention to my tie, sir.

Q. You had been kicked in the neck? **A.** Kicked in the back of the neck, yes, sir.

Q. And you're asking Mike Daly for some help now, right? **A.** When I was getting up, sir.

Q. Right? **A.** Not right then and there.

Q. Well, you had just been dragged around this elevator, got kicked while you were down, thrown around that elevator, your glasses knocked off. This is all true, isn't it? **A.** Yes, sir.

Q. This fellow kept coming after you, right, Alfieri? **A.** He kept coming.

Q. He kept coming, didn't he? **A.** Yes, sir.

Q. You saw Mike Daly, that was a friendly face, right? **A.** Yes, sir.

Q. You asked him for help? **A.** No, sir, not right then and there.

Q. Did you trust Michael Daly? **A.** I don't know him well enough to trust him.

Q. I'll withdraw the question. Did you think maybe Michael Daly was going to jump on you then? **A.** I don't know.

Q. Well, when Michael Daly showed up, were you in fear of Michael Daly? **A.** You cannot anticipate what another officer is going to do, I can't. I don't know what he's going to do.

Q. You have seen Michael Daly lots of times before? **A.** No, sir, not lots of times.

Q. You have talked to him before? **A.** I have had conversations with him.

Q. Conversations have always been friendly with him? **A.** Hi, how you doing, what's going on, nothing more than just regular personal information.

Q. Never had any arguments with him, right, Daly? **A.** Never had any arguments with any officers.

Q. He didn't threaten you or anything that morning, did he, when he handcuffed you? **A.** No, sir.

Q. You were comfortable when he handcuffed you to the chair, right? **A.** Yes, sir.

Q. So my question is when Michael Daly shows up, did he make any threatening moves towards you? **A.** No, sir.

Q. You were still afraid that Nicholas Alfieri was going to keep coming after you, though, right? **A.** He, how can you, I don't know what he's thinking. I don't know what he's going—

Q. What about you, what were you thinking, were you thinking this Nick Alfieri, this guy is just beating me up in this elevator, dragged me around this elevator, knocked my glasses off, made me bleed, kicked me in the back of the head while I'm down, you were afraid he was going to keep coming, is that fair? **A.** He had the advantage.

Q. That's not my question. Were you afraid he was still going to keep coming after you? **A.** I don't know if he was going to keep coming, I just wanted him to stop.

Q. So then you decide you're going to take the handcuffs off? **A.** No, sir.

Q. Well, then you got your handcuffs off, right? **A.** Yes, sir.

Q. While Daly's there? **A.** Yes, sir.

Q. And you said it takes, your testimony was it takes some time, but if you turn the wrist around it takes awhile and you can take your hand out, is that your testimony? **A.** You have to turn your wrist in order—

Q. The other way? **A.** Yes, and it's painful to do that.

Q. But you had just been subjected to so much pain that you were willing to subject yourself to even some more pain and try and get that wrist free, isn't that right? **A.** If I want to get my butt kicked, I'm going to have my hands free.

Q. So you were ready to fight then, right? **A.** Yes, sir.

Q. And you went through the time and the pain to get your one wrist free, right? **A.** Yes, sir.

Q. And Daly's there and Alfieri's there, right? **A.** Yes, sir.

Q. And now you've got your hands free, is that right? **A.** Yes, sir.

Q. It's your testimony now that that one handcuff is still cuffed, it's still locked, but you have slipped out of it? **A.** Yes, sir.

Q. That's your testimony, is that correct? **A.** Yes, sir.

Q. The handcuff isn't open? **A.** No, sir.

Q. You heard all the other witnesses testify here, is that correct? **A.** Yes, sir.

Q. But you're telling us you just were able to slide out of that handcuff, right? **A.** It took some doing, yes, sir.

Q. And you had some time to do it on the elevator, right? **A.** I was struggling with it, yes, sir.

Q. Now, while you're struggling with that handcuff, I take it it takes some movement, is that right? **A.** Yes, sir.

Q. Tell us what Daly and Alfieri are doing? **A.** Daly, when he arrived, he called out my name. I told him right there, you know, grab him, keep him away from me.

Q. You're telling Daly to hold Nick Alfieri away from you, keep him back? **A.** Yes, sir.

Q. Alfieri looked like he was going to charge and come after you again? **A.** No, sir, he was kicking.

Q. He was still kicking? **A.** He was kicking, he came in to the elevator door and he was kicking.

Q. Still even after Daly was there? **A.** Yes, sir.

Q. Alfieri's kicking at you? **A.** Yes, sir.

Q. So he's still coming at you, charging towards you. Is that right? **A.** It was, he's by the elevator door, he's kicking, I'm kicking when I got up.

Q. He's five foot five, sir? **A.** Yes, sir.

Q. For his legs to hit you, he'd have to get right up on you to kick him? **A.** I understand.

Q. So he came back in the elevator then, right? **A.** Yes, sir.

Q. And started kicking at you again? **A.** Not into the elevator, by the doorway area of the elevator.

Q. Stayed off the elevator? **A.** By the doorway area, he's in the center of the doorway area.

Q. In the elevator or out of the elevator? **A.** In the middle, it's the only way I can describe it.

Q. Right where the doors close, is that fair? **A.** Yes, sir.

Q. You're in the back of the elevator now? **A.** I'm in the center of the elevator.

Q. Center of the elevator, begging Daly to keep him away? **A.** No, I didn't beg him, sir.

Q. What did you say? **A.** I said, "Grab him, keep him away."

Q. Grab him, keep him away? And does Daly grab him then? **A.** He reached for his right arm.

Q. The question is did he grab him, did he grab his right arm? **A.** I think he did.

Q. He did? So now you've got Daly holding Alfieri's right arm?

MS. LYON: Objection, he said he thought he did. I know it's cross examination, but he should accept the witness's answer.

THE COURT: Overruled.

MR. REILLY: **Q.** You think Daly's got him by the right arm, is that right? **A.** It's hard to be looking at the person's body when you're looking at his feet.

Q. And he's still kicking away, though, right, Alfieri? **A.** We are both kicking each other.

Q. You're still kicking too? **A.** Yes, sir, when I got up.

Q. And also taking your cuffs off at the same time? **A.** I'm doing that.

Q. And again, you're still in the basement area, right, the elevator hasn't moved? **A.** No, sir, elevator hasn't moved.

Q. There's still screaming going on, you're telling Daley to keep him off, hold him back? **A.** Yes, sir.

Q. In that same tunnel area, right? **A.** Yes, sir.

Q. Echoing throughout the tunnel, is that right? **A.** I don't know if it's echoing where I'm at.

Q. Now, you get your handcuffs free, right? **A.** Yes, sir.

Q. Got both your hands free, right? **A.** Yes, sir.

Q. You're ready to fight now, right? **A.** No, sir.

Q. Daly and Alfieri are still in the doorway, is that correct? **A.** Yes, sir.

Q. What do you do when you get your handcuffs free? **A.** As soon as I got them free, the other officers arrived.

Q. So right as Sykes and DeValle show up, right at that moment the cuffs come off? **A.** Just maybe a second or two before.

Q. And again, defense counsel went over this, as far as you know, Alfieri is still standing? **A.** Yes, sir, moving around in the elevator facing down the floor, moving around, don't get to see the person all the time, you're struggling to get up, you don't keep your eye on the person all the time.

Q. Was he screaming at any point in time, Alfieri, screaming out in pain? **A.** Not in, he seemed more pissed than in pain.

Q. And these two jail guards coming into the elevator and they come right over to you, right? **A.** Yes, sir.

Q. And you don't want to fight then, right? **A.** No, sir.

Q. You just have your hands straight down, is that correct? **A.** Yes, sir.

Q. And the first thing the one jail guard does is go in there and cold cocked you, is that right? **A.** Hit me in the, right above my ear, yes, sir.

Q. Hit you with a hand, is that right, fist? **A.** I don't know if it was an open hand or closed fist, sir.

Q. Above your right ear? **A.** Side of the head, sir, yes.

Q. Which side of the head? **A.** This side.

Q. That's your left side? **A.** Yes, sir.

Q. That's the same side, your left side, that's bleeding, right, left side of your—**A.** Yes, sir.

Q. Your cheek? **A.** Yes, sir.

Q. And he hits you, do you go down then? **A.** No, sir.

Q. You stay standing? **A.** Yes, sir.

Q. They have to handcuff you, right? **A.** Yes, sir.

Q. Officer Sykes, he's the first gentleman that testified, he puts handcuffs on you again, right? **A.** Both officers grabbed me, sir.

Q. Both of them handcuffed you? **A.** Yes, sir.

Q. Never heard anybody yell, "There's a key," never heard that? **A.** No, sir.

Q. And it's still your testimony that that one cuff was locked, it wasn't open? **A.** It was double locked, sir.

Q. Double locked? Couldn't have been opened, is that your testimony? **A.** Yes, sir.

Q. Without a key? **A.** Yes, sir.

Q. The correctional officers take you down to the bridge area, is that right, then? **A.** I don't know, sir.

Q. Well, they took you down the tunnel, didn't they? **A.** I don't know, sir.

Q. Were you passed out at this point in time? **A.** When the officers, correctional officer grabbed me, they had to re-handcuff me with their set of handcuffs because they couldn't open the other handcuff.[71]

Q. Sir, my question is were you passed out at this point in time? **A.** Yes, I was out cold.

Q. You were unconscious? **A.** Yes, sir.

Q. You don't remember anything that happened after that? **A.** Until I woke.

---

[71] This answer does not respond to the question; therefore Mr. Reilly could have asked to have it stricken. Instead, he simply re-asks the question. Which procedure is likely to be more effective from his point of view?

Q. You told us after you got hit you were still standing? **A.** Yes, sir.

Q. And is it then that we don't remember anything? **A.** No, sir, I still remember a few things afterwards.

Q. Do you remember being down in the bridge area into another holding cell? **A.** No, sir.

Q. You don't remember that at all? **A.** No, sir.

Q. It's all a fog? **A.** I don't remember, sir.

Q. Well, where were you at when you woke up or came to? **A.** In courtroom 400.

Q. And you had blood all over you at that time? **A.** No, sir.

Q. Well, your cheek had been bleeding, you had been knocked around, pulled around this elevator. Did you have blood all over your clothes? **A.** Some was on my shirt, sir.

Q. Some was on your shirt? **A.** Yes.

Q. What about your suit, you had your suit on too? **A.** I didn't have any clothes on upstairs, I couldn't determine.

Q. And that's when, so you remember being up in Room 400, right? **A.** Yes, sir.

Q. And that's when you heard the fellow testify last week, Lieutenant Russell Gardner, taller white haired older guy, you remember him testifying? **A.** Yes.

Q. They had the Chicago Fire Department paramedics look at you then, right? You don't remember that? **A.** I never saw them, sir.

Q. Never saw them? **A.** No, sir.

Q. Well, you heard Lieutenant Gardner testify that they came and looked at you said you were all right and left? **A.** I never saw them, sir.

Q. You don't remember that? **A.** I never saw them, I never was treated or anything.

Q. Well, were you conscious when you were in Room 400 there? **A.** When I was woken up by the paramedics, yes, sir.

Q. Well, I'm talking about the Chicago Fire Department, sir, **A.** I never seen them, sir.

Q. You never saw them? **A.** No, sir.

Q. Did you hear Lieutenant Gardner testify Friday here? **A.** Yes, sir.

Q. Do you remember seeing Lieutenant Gardner? **A.** Yes, sir.

Q. You do remember seeing him? **A.** Yes, sir.

Q. But you don't remember the Chicago Fire Department paramedics looking at you? **A.** No, sir.

Q. You were having some trouble with your glasses anyway as of August, is that right? **A.** Trouble with my glasses?

Q. Trouble with them being broken? **A.** No, sir.

Q. Do you remember being examined when you were admitted to the jail here in July? **A.** Yes, sir.

Q. Did you tell them you were having a problem with your glasses? **A.** I don't remember anything about that.

Q. Did you tell them that you wore glasses? **A.** Yes, I had glasses.

Q. Now, at the time you had been, at the time of this incident in August, August 28th, you had been to see the doctor for a chest problem and respiratory problem, right? **A.** Yes, sir.

Q. Taking medication at the time? **A.** I don't know if they gave me any medication, sir.

Q. Now, later that afternoon around 5:30, you ran into Michael Daly again, right? **A.** Yes, sir.

Q. Had a conversation with Michael Daly, right? **A.** Yes, sir.

Q. And you told Michael Daly to tell Officer Alfieri I'm sorry and apologize for you? **A.** No, sir.

Q. Never said that? **A.** No, sir.

Q. Never told Michael Daly that you just didn't feel like going back to Division 1, never said that? **A.** In some words, yes, sir.

Q. Well, never told him to apologize to Nicholas Alfieri? **A.** I apologized to him.

Q. Sir? **A.** I apologized to Mike.

Q. Did you tell Mike Daly to apologize to Nicholas Alfieri for you? **A.** No, sir.

Q. You were still mad at Alfieri, right? **A.** Yes, sir.

Q. He was the one that came after you, right? **A.** Yes, sir.

Q. You did nothing to provoke this, right? **A.** No, sir.

Q. You had done everything you could to cooperate with Nicholas Alfieri, right? **A.** Up to that point, yes, sir.

Q. You do remember talking to Daly later in the afternoon, though, right? **A.** Yes, sir.

Q. The two of you, again, knew each other, right? **A.** Yes, sir.

Q. And no one gave you a handcuff key that day, did they? **A.** No, sir.

Q. No one helped you get out of that handcuff on the elevator, right? **A.** No, sir.

Q. Nobody opened that handcuff for you, right, other than to take you downstairs? **A.** No, sir.

Q. You just slipped out of it on your own, is that right? **A.** Yes, sir.

Q. If I may have a moment, Judge.

Mike Daly walked up, did you tell him that Alfieri had just attacked you there in the elevator? **A.** Not when he walked up, sir.

Q. Sometime that day did you tell him? **A.** Yes, sir.

Q. Tell him that they had thrown you, pulled you up against the wall? **A.** Yes, sir.

Q. Told you that he had broken your glasses? **A.** I told him he cut my left eye, sir.

Q. It was obvious that you had a cut underneath your eye, is that right? **A.** Yes, sir.

Q. You had been bleeding, right? **A.** Yes, sir.

Q. They brought you up to Room 400 in front of Judge Collins, right? **A.** No, sir.

Q. Not in front of the judge? **A.** No, sir.

Q. Back up into the lockup, though, right? **A.** Yes, sir.

Q. Were you telling anybody there that you had been beat up by Nicholas Alfieri had attacked you? **A.** They wouldn't let me, sir.

Q. Nobody would let you? **A.** No, sir.

Q. How about that Lieutenant Russ Gardner, the older white-haired guy, did you tell him that Nicholas Alfieri had attacked you? **A.** In the position I was in, sir, I couldn't talk.

Q. That's not my question. Did you tell him? **A.** No, sir.

Q. Was Nick Alfieri hovering over you when you were up in Room 400, then? **A.** I saw him, sir.

Q. He was around, right? **A.** Yes, sir.

Q. You were still afraid of him then, right? **A.** No, sir.

MR. REILLY: Nothing further, Judge.[72]

---

[72] Obviously Mr. Reilly wants to persuade the jury to disbelieve Mr. Tellez's story. How successful is he in this endeavor? If you compare this cross examination to Ms. Lyon's cross examination of Mr. Alfieri, you'll see two main differences. First, Ms. Lyon spends a great deal of time focusing on inconsistencies between Mr. Alfieri's testimony and the statements he made

THE COURT: Any redirect?

MS. LYON: No.

THE COURT: You may be excused, Mr. Tellez.

(Witness excused.)

. . .

(Defense rests)

TUESDAY, JANUARY 24, 1989

THE CLERK:

(The following proceedings were had in the presence and hearing of the jury)

THE COURT: Good morning, Ladies and Gentlemen. Have a seat. I do apologize for the delay. This morning was one of the emergencies that you have come to understand what it means that the Cook County Circuit Court is the busiest circuit system in the world.

As I indicated to you last night, you are going to hear the closing arguments of counsel this morning. The State having the burden to prove the defendant guilty beyond a reasonable doubt will address you first, then Miss Lyon on behalf of the defendant Mr. Tellez will address you in closing argument and then the State will have an opportunity to address you in rebuttal.

At the conclusion of those arguments, you will be instructed by the Court on the law applicable to this case. You will then retire to deliberate on your verdict.

Are we ready, State?

MR. GARDINER: Yes, your Honor.

THE COURT: You may proceed.

INITIAL CLOSING ARGUMENT FOR THE PROSECUTION

BY MR. GARDINER:

Ladies and Gentlemen of the jury, on August 28th, 1987, the defendant was brought to room 400 where he appeared before Judge Collins, was placed in the jury room and then removed from the jury room by Nicholas Alfieri around noon. Alfieri took him handcuffed through the door into the elevator. And they went down in the elevator to the basement area leading to the tunnel.

---

to the officers investigating the incident; Mr. Reilly apparently does not have any inconsistent pretrial statements from Mr. Tellez, so he is limited to working on internal inconsistencies and implausibilities in the witness's testimony. Second, Mr. Reilly spends most of his time going over the same ground that was covered in the direct examination of Mr. Tellez, while Ms. Lyon devotes much more attention to issues that were not touched in the direct examination of Mr. Alfieri.

It was there that you heard testimony that the defendant began kicking Nicholas Alfieri. He kicked him in the groin, in the leg area and the first time it knocked him out of the elevator and he came back in to open the door and he was kicked a second time and again and again as he moved out of the elevator and attempted to get into the elevator to keep the doors opened. And ultimately, Officer Sykes and DeValle arrived and they were able to get a hold of the defendant and once again take custody of this defendant.

The account of Nicholas Alfieri in this case does not stand alone. It is corroborated. It is supported by the other witnesses that you have heard in this case, and those accounts refute the account the defendant gave to you on this witness stand.

You heard Michael Daly testify that when he arrived at the scene the defendant was kicking Nicholas Alfieri, that Alfieri's handcuff was opened, contrary to what the defendant said from the stand. And that the defendant said get away. Daly didn't testify that he attempted to stop Nicholas Alfieri. Instead, what he was doing on the scene was—he described what occurred and he described the actions of this defendant in much the same way as they were described by Nicholas Alfieri. And that account of Nicholas Alfieri is supported by the officers who responded to the scene, by Officer Sykes and DeValle.

They arrived at the scene after hearing the words help, help, help repeatedly. In fact, those words were so loud that Russ Gardner, on the first floor, could hear those. The words coming from a person that the defense contends was himself, the aggressor in the case. Instead what do they find?

They didn't find Mike Tyson. They didn't find somebody dragging the defendant by a tie. They found Nicholas Alfieri laying on the floor with his foot propped in the elevator trying to keep it opened crying for help in a position consistent with what Alfieri said. The man that had been struck repeatedly by this defendant. And they also saw the handcuff open and they saw the defendant showing his intent in this case, the intent to get out of that area, to escape, that intent shown by him trying to close the doors and to get away, in kicking Nicholas Alfieri as he lay on the floor. And that intent was also shown by his actions when the officers came into that elevator.

The defendant was swinging his arms and one of the blows was blocked by Officer Sykes. That conduct is consistent with how the defendant was operating before that time with Nicholas Alfieri. Sykes blocked the blow and then gave a blow himself, a blow that you will be instructed he was entitled to give, to prevent this type of action, and then they were able to place the defendant in custody.

That was the testimony of Officer DeValle as well, that the defendant was the aggressor, that the defendant was taking advantage of the man on the ground, Nicholas Alfieri.

A few words about the defense case. You have heard testimony from a paramedic, Mr. McKinney. You heard testimony from a doctor. You heard a stipulation regarding Dr. Romine (phonetic spelling) who had observed the defendant. There was no diagnosis by any person that saw this defendant have any harm other than the harm to the eye. In fact, Russ Gardner told you when the Chicago paramedics arrived they took a look at the defendant and left. Russ Gardner saw the defendant stripped at the time. He didn't see any injury.

Think of the defendant's account of the way that he was manhandled as he would have you believe in that elevator. Wouldn't there have been other injuries? Other injuries as he claims he was being kicked, as he claims that he is on his back with the handcuffs under him? Wouldn't those cuffs be hurting his wrist? As he was shoved against the door he says? But no, the only injury that exists, the only injury is to his eye. The injury inflicted by Officer Sykes, as he told you, as he had to do to prevent the harm that the defendant was causing.

And one of the other accounts by the defense of how things occurred. He claimed he was kicked in the middle of the back of his head. Even as he was laying on the floor. Nicholas Alfieri picked up his head and kicked him and put him back down?

On cross examination the truth comes out. Your common sense can be applied to the facts that you heard during the defense testimony, the defendant's testimony. And, of course, he weaves his tale around the facts as best he can. When do those handcuffs come off? Right before the officers arrive. When does he stand up? Right before those officers arrive. He has to tell you that tale, Ladies and Gentlemen. He has to weave a story as best he can. And he is a man that has been in court before. He has testified before juries. He testifies in that soft voice because he knows that maybe he can portray himself as the person he wasn't on that date, August 28th, 1987.

And what more does he tell you? He has no idea why Nicholas Alfieri would have pushed him against the wall. No idea. No prior contact with this person, no words are spoken by Nicholas Alfieri to him. Alfieri just in a sudden whim decides to push him against the wall and go through all the other gyrations that the defendant invented for you to hear. He says that he was kicking wildly.

Might I suggest, Ladies and Gentlemen, you had a chance to look at the pictures. Those pictures show injuries that are pointed to an area to disable Nicholas Alfieri. All of those injuries occurred to the groin and the leg area. They are not the result of wild kicks. They are not the result of kicks that this defendant told you he had no idea where they were going. They are the result of the same kicks that Nicholas Alfieri described and described consistently to you and that was supported by the other testimony that you heard in our case.

Ladies and Gentlemen, you will be instructed at the conclusion of this case that to prove the offense of aggravated battery we need to prove that the defendant was in the custody of a person he knew to be a peace officer, Nicholas Alfieri, and that bodily harm was caused to him and that he did not act in a justified way.

I submit the evidence has proven all of those factors and to prove attempt escape we need to prove that the defendant was charged with a crime, murder, and that he attempted to escape, that his intent was to escape on that day.

Now, you heard testimony from even the chief of the criminal courts that the courtrooms in this building in back of the courtrooms near the elevators, the gates can be unlocked. It happens every day. Even the person in charge of those gates admitted to that. But you will also be instructed that is not a defense in this case. Even if on that particular day the defendant had been able to close those doors before Sykes and DeValle arrived, even if he had been able to do that and arrived at a floor where the gates had been locked, that is not a defense. It is not a defense that he has a misapprehension under the circumstances.

And I submit, that given the testimony that you heard from people that work here every day, that very well could have occurred. This defendant in his suit, with his knowledge of the courts in this county could have walked right out the door. But his intent on that date was the key. What did he intend to do?

You saw his actions. You heard the testimony. You can tell with your common sense exactly what this defendant intended to do. The man charged with murder at the time, he has no idea why Nicholas Alfieri did the things that he says Alfieri did but think of the defendant's position at the time and think of his words to Michael Daly as well. I am sorry. I just didn't want to go back to Division 1 of the Cook County Jail. That shows his intent, Ladies and Gentlemen.

Ladies and Gentleman, you heard the testimony, you viewed the exhibits and after doing so I would ask that when you return to the jury room you consider that evidence and find the defendant guilty on both counts.

THE COURT: Thank you, Mr. Gardiner.

Are you ready, Miss Lyon?

MS. LYON: I am, your Honor. Thank you.

CLOSING ARGUMENT FOR THE DEFENSE

BY MS. LYON:

This has not been a case about an aggravated battery, nor has it been a case about an attempt escape. It has been a case about a fight and a cover-up. If you have any doubt, if you have any doubt about the cover-up part just take a look at all the lies that were told by Alfieri and Daly. Just take a look at it and ask yourself why.

I am going to discuss them in some detail and I hope you will be patient with me as I do that. You see, what happens is they add more facts as time goes on. The story gets better as time goes on. They keep changing things as time goes on. Each time they're interviewed they add something. To try and make it better, to try and make it an attempt escape, to try and justify their behavior in this case, and because—and I think the Judge is going to instruct you—I know the Judge will instruct you to use your common sense.

I think you know that people who work together, particularly people who work together in a law enforcement type of situation often times they stick together. They stick together. They try to support each other. And in this context, please remember one important thing. Not one of the sheriffs that the prosecution called in their case, not even Mr. Sykes or Mr. DeValle, who basically told what happened, what they saw, not one of them ever said at the beginning in their first interview, in their first report, anywhere one word about an opened handcuff. Nobody. None of them said it at first. Oh, they said it later, some in their second interview, some in their third interview, but they never said it at first and you know why? Because it wasn't opened. It wasn't opened.

I'm going to discuss the handcuffs with you a little bit later on in more detail and the other reason why it became important for a handcuff to be opened I will also discuss with you, which is that an attempt escape charge covers all their ground for them. I will explain that in a moment.

Let me talk to you a little bit about Investigator Willer. Now, he told you that the different stories were told to him by Alfieri each time he talked to him and by Daly each time he talked to him. And maybe, I don't know, maybe you are wondering why is that important? Why did we spend all the time talking about this report and running up and down with all the different exhibits of reports and interviews and all the rest of that? Well, it is important because one of the instructions the Judge will give you, which has to do with impeachment of a witness; that is, if a witness has said A on day one and says B on day two you should take that into consideration. You take that into consideration in deciding whether to believe the witness or not. That is basically what the instruction says, although it says it better than I just did. But also because—also because these witnesses have a point of view, a bias, a perspective of their own.

They have something to protect. That is the reason that Investigator Willer's testimony, that the facts of an investigation into their behavior was important. This was not intended to embarrass anybody or to make them uncomfortable, but we are trying to bring you all of the facts. That is why we brought in all of the witnesses that we did, the witnesses that the prosecution chose not to call.

Now, what is this bias? Well, again your common sense. Mr. Alfieri had something to lose. His job. Mr. Daly had something to lose. His job. If they had done something illegal perhaps they had even more to fear. That is the reason that Investigator Willer's testimony is so important.

And, in fact, you will be instructed regarding the correct, rather the believability of witnesses and you will be told to take into account their bias, and I'm sure right now that the prosecutor who bets to see when I'm finished is furiously writing down how he has a bias. He has a murder charge so he has a reason to lie.

Well, that is a very awkward position because every time someone is charged with a crime, if they testify they have a bias. If they don't testify you have something to hide. You are stuck. We tried and I think we did, to bring to you everything about this case.

Back to Investigator Willer. One of the things you will be instructed to do is to take into account the demeanor of the witnesses. I know the prosecution is very upset with Mr. Tellez's demeanor. They didn't like it. They wished he was the kind of person that would blow up. That would make them feel better but he is who he is.

You saw on cross examination how Mr. Alfieri, how he could remember things when the prosecutor was asking him questions but his memory would fade when I was asking him questions. How he would evade answers. How Mr. Daly would evade answers and get, if I may, I think I can appropriately characterize his testimony as kind of smart aleck with me? You didn't see any of that with Mr. Tellez and that upset the prosecution so they're going to try and characterize his good demeanor as a bad point. Well, I guess that that is what they have to do.

But Mr. Willer's demeanor. One of the members of their own department, who is part of, just for one year, part of internal investigations, how clear it was from his demeanor what he thought of the different stories that were told to him by Alfieri and Daly. So let's talk about what they lied about and let's try to examine why if we can.

And by the way, the sorry excuses that were made on redirect examination for all the things that were missing from reports. Well, you are not very well trained in reports. You don't write reports very often. Well, do they have to be trained to tell the truth?

I mean, if an attempt escape occurred wouldn't it be a pretty big fact that there was an opened handcuff, or that someone said something about a key? Of course, it would be. That would be the first thing you would say. This is an attempt escape and that is how you know.

But it wasn't the first thing anyone said because they hadn't figured out what to say yet. That is why. And just because they all said it eventually, doesn't mean—don't know if they all sat and talked to each other. I have no way of knowing that. But what we do know is one thing, and if you remember, when Mr. Alfieri was being cross examined he said well, yes, on the third interview or the fourth interview, whatever it was, that he did mention the key when he was quote, reminded of it. Remember that? He had to be reminded.

MR. REILLY: Not the testimony.

MS. LYON: That is the testimony. You are perfectly free to argue, Mr. Prosecutor.

THE COURT: I'm sorry, Miss Lyon. I didn't hear the point. Would you read it back?

(The reporter read back the statement)

THE COURT: Overruled.[73]

MS. LYON: All of them were interviewed by Mr. Willer who was the investigator in the case and they all were asked questions about what each other had said. I mean, how else do you check out what happened?

So, it is not particularly surprising that as time went on they all began to adopt the story of each other because they had something to protect, their job, and possibly, possibly, criminal liability. And they lied about how it started. Alfieri, because he started it and Daly because when he got there he was torn. He was torn. He knew Ron Tellez from before. Not a friend but an acquaintance. He knew he was a police officer.

Imagine, if you will, for a moment, yourselves in a situation like that, where you got divided loyalties to deal with. You come up on a situation, you got a feeling that the person you work with is doing wrong, you grab at him and don't know what to do so you are, in fact, immobilized. That is exactly what he was. He did nothing because he didn't know what to do. Being torn between two loyalties, between what he thought was right and what he was supposed to do to protect his co-worker.

---

[73] Attorneys are allowed a great deal of leeway in closing argument. They may try to persuade the jury by appealing to commonsense, they may construct plausible explanations, they may criticize and praise, they may characterize evidence as true or false and witnesses as honest or deceptive. But there are limits. An attorney may not state her own belief about the facts of the case or the truthfulness of the witness, or appeal to racism or sexism or other improper biases, or refer to evidence that is not in the record. The mildest form of this last sin is probably the most common type of improper argument: misrepresenting the record. That, apparently, is the basis for Mr. Reilly's objection. But he is wrong, and the judge correctly overrules the objection—as most judges will during closing argument, unless the violation is clear.

Let's talk for a moment about how we know that this is not an aggravated battery. First, it is true that we don't know, I don't know, Mr. Tellez doesn't know, no one knows why Mr. Alfieri started what he started.

The Judge will instruct you that the defense doesn't have the burden of proof, the prosecution does. They are the ones that have to prove things beyond a reasonable doubt and all that. And we don't have to prove why. But maybe, just maybe, Ron was right.

Remember the testimony about how they're down in the elevator and just about the time that they hit the bottom he had moved back to the center of the elevator? Remember that? He moved back to the center and Alfieri shoved him into the corner. Well perhaps—again, I don't know and remember Ron's back is to Alfieri. He can't see his face at that point. Perhaps Alfieri didn't intend to shove him. Perhaps the combination of a little bit too much force, the elevator dropping down, the angle in which he was pushing him pushed him into the corner and, in fact, just like Ron tried to tell you he panicked. He panicked because he saw a cut. He panicked because he had caused an injury. And then just lost it. Perhaps that is the reason.

Another possible reason is because Ron is a police officer and there are people who feel, you know, if they are in law enforcement somehow it is embarrassing to have one of your own do something wrong. I know perhaps he felt like, you know, he had let him down. I know he is supposed to presume him innocent until he has been tried and he hasn't been tried on the murder but that is hard to do. That is hard to do.

Well, how do we know that Alfieri started it? First of all, one of the things we know for sure is Mr. Sykes hit him one time and we know there are other injuries. Okay. We don't have pictures. We didn't have a picture of bruises and I wish we did. But you see, we didn't have control over what pictures were taken. We didn't have control over what pictures were taken. Mr. Cruz did that. And that is one of the reasons—that is a reason we called Chief Cruz.

You know we subpoenaed him to court to tell you that he was the one that had control over what photographs were taken. We had no way—we weren't even his lawyers then—of taking these pictures. So the pictures you will see or you have seen of Mr. Alfieri of the bruises three or four days later—and I think you can use your common sense and know bruises look darker as time goes on and show more as time goes on and look worse as time goes on, until they start to heal—that we were not in a position to take photographs. That there were no photographs taken because that was the choice of the prosecuting authority at that time.

Another indication that Alfieri started it. Mr. Alfieri said that Mr. Sykes pushed him into the wall. Now, on cross examination he said well, his cheek touched the wall. I think it was his language, if I remember properly. And if I don't you are right. I am wrong. You are the ones who count.

Where did he come up with this pushing him into the wall? Mr. Sykes didn't say he pushed him into the wall. Mr. DeValle didn't say he pushed him into the wall. Where did he come up with pushed him into the wall? He came up with it to explain what he, in fact, had done. It is a psychological clue to what he was feeling guilty about. To what he was feeling guilty about, and I would like to say a few words about Mr. Alfieri's personal revelation to you that he found it so stressful that he quit after two weeks, conveniently, just at the time the investigation was wrapping up and that he checked himself into a psychiatric hospital for treatment, et cetera, et cetera.

First of all, if someone needs help, whether it is psychiatric help or medical help they should get it. Please don't misunderstand me or the defense when I say that if they need psychiatric help they should get it. But he said it was the stress from this incident. It could equally be the stress from guilty knowledge, from a guilty conscience and from the consequences of what happened. Just as likely. I do not mean in any way to deny him. If he needs psychiatric help he needs it. But I wish you would consider that.

The glasses. Another reason that we know. The fact of more than one injury. Another reason that we know. Because Sykes is only responsible for one. And Alfieri's story. It is improbable that he was kicked in the groin from behind and that he fell forward and then he fell backwards and then all of this kind of stuff. It is an improbability. That is another way that we know.

The reasonable inference from his behavior is that he was lying, that he was protecting his job, and all of this nonsense about how he can't remember that first interview. He was under so much stress.

Well, you heard Investigator Willer testify. Investigator Willer who has—he is no friend of Ron Tellez's. He has no ax to grind. He is not a defense friend. He works with the other side. You heard him testify that, in fact, he had no problem remembering things, talking, that he was never cut-off, you know, we heard enough now. That he could talk as long as he wanted. Chief Cruz was there. His boss was there. And at that point, at that point it was just a routine investigation. They hadn't begun to investigate any wrongdoings. It was just a natural thing. The first interview later became something else.

Just a few words about Ron's testimony. I know I have already covered it but it makes sense—was to respond to proceed to a real threat. Let's talk for a minute about the handcuffs. Okay.

We have a prosecution theory that the handcuffs were opened, dangling open and Ron telling you that he had pulled out of it because it was closed the wrong way. It was closed lengthwise and able to twist his hand and pull out. Okay.

Now, Sykes and DeValle subdue him. Right. Nobody is saying, by the way, that Mr. Sykes shouldn't have hit him when he was with the fist opened. Remember? Mr. Sykes couldn't remember. Nobody is saying that. One is on one side of him and one is on the other side of him. They push him against the wall. This is their testimony. They push him up, you know, and they are handcuffing him from behind. And Sykes says that they got—I don't remember if it was Mr. Sykes' handcuffs or Mr. DeValle's handcuffs but one of their handcuffs. Remember that? Got their handcuffs and put them on the ground.

Now, you are in an emergency situation. You got this man subdued. He has half of a set of handcuffs on him. All you have to do to put the other handcuff on is close it if it is open. That is all you have to do. If you want to you can then put on a second set of handcuffs or something if that is what you need but why is it that they didn't do that? Because it wasn't open. It was locked. That is why. That is why there was a second pair of handcuffs.

Just think about it. It makes sense. It makes all the sense in the world. That is all they had to do was close that other pair on him. If they were worried that the pair was defective or something they could have put a second pair on in addition. But they didn't because they couldn't. That is why.

During the prosecutor's cross examination of Ron, he tried to make it seem as though what Ron would—what happened in that elevator took a long time. It didn't. It took seconds. A minute. Who knows? It happened fast. You know, you are not able—it is not like a film where you can stop and slow things down and count how many times you get kicked, and examining where people are and when you are laying on the floor tell if someone else is laying on the floor necessarily. It is not like that. You don't have a moment for calm reflection.

Self-defense doesn't require you to sit down and say now, is there a better way I can handle this? Because the law recognizes, the law recognizes that human beings are human beings. That we are—what did I say, ten percent logic and ninety percent emotion. That is what we are. We react to things as they appear. That we feel things. So if you are afraid, you react and you do whatever you can to protect yourself.

Ron told you. He knew he was wrong. He wasn't supposed to hit a guard. He shouldn't have done it. He knows that now. But at the time what are you thinking about? You aren't. You aren't calmly reflecting what would be the best thing to do. You are you just reacting because you are scared.

We know all of this happened fast. We know it was confusing. We know it was frightening, and undoubtedly frightening for Mr. Alfieri as well. Undoubtedly was.

Now, also, the prosecutor tried to make it seem as though that being dragged by the tie through the elevator was totally impossible. You know because as he cross examined he took a tie and he walks all the way, you know. It was very good. But the elevator is six feet eleven inches by five feet seven inches. Five feet seven inches in depth and six feet eleven inches in length. You will get these diagrams and photographs back in the jury room so you can look at them at your leisure, and so this is done to scale and anybody who can, you know, who can measure it can see the elevator is small.

So, if someone is around here, which is where Ron says he was, and being dragged forward, we are talking about dragging him forward what, a foot, two feet? Does that outwit the realm of possibility? Does that not make sense? Of course it makes sense. Of course it makes sense. We need to keep the things in perspective when you are examining the evidence in this case.

Now, in fact, cross examination basically was a sarcastic reiteration of what Ron told us on direct examination. That was basically it. And you know, there is one thing that Ron said. Maybe he felt a little embarrassed when he said it, but when he was explaining how he pulled out of the handcuffs remember what he said about why. He just had the uttering of truth to it. He said if I was going to get my butt kicked I was going to fight. I was going to have my hands free. I mean, the man was a police officer for eight and a half years. He stands accused of a very serious crime that will happen in another trial. Not that this isn't serious, this is plenty serious. The natural instinct of maybe to defend himself, I would think that that gets doubled or tripled or who knows by a police officer who has for years put his life on the line defending the public.

I spoke to you earlier with the photographs and about why we had to call Cruz and to get in the fact that that is how the photographs were ordered by him and only ordered of Mr. Alfieri. And we felt it important, even though it seemed fairly clear, that Mr. Cruz was definitely taking sides, and it wasn't ours. But we felt that it was fair and right to try and tell you as much as possible about the case and so we subpoenaed people, even people that were likely to not want to testify for Ron.

And you noticed that each of the deputies would testify for the prosecutor on cross examination, the ones that we called and the ones that they called on direct examination about how Mr. Alfieri was such a peaceful person. You know, that he would never do anything like this.

Of course, none of them know him at home, none of them have ever seen him lose his temper or ever seen him in a fight situation but in working with him every day he seemed okay with them. They never seen him panicked. They never seen whatever it was that caused him to either feel so guilty or so stressed or both to feel he needed to check into a psychiatric hospital but they gave their opinion as to peacefulness. Yet the prosecution did not want you to hear the opinion of Mr. Willer as to Alfieri and Daly's truthfulness. They didn't want you to hear that.

We do know that at least one of the injuries that he received was serious. The one to the eye. We know that it required aftercare, glasses, ophthalmologists, all the rest of that. Fortunately, it wasn't—didn't put his eye out. He wasn't left with a scar but it was a serious injury. One that should be taken serious. And isn't it more likely, isn't it more likely that a cut under the eye would occur from the lens of a glass being pushed in, you know, the edge of the lens of a glass than the opened hand as Sykes may he have hit him with? Or even a fist? Isn't that more likely? Doesn't that make more sense? He did have X-rays for the back of his neck, head and chest. Those were X-rays ordered by the doctor.

You also heard him say that he, Ron, tell you that he kind of faded in and out of consciousness. Next thing there were a few moments in the elevator after he was—Sergeant DeValle had him cuffed, that he was awakened and the next thing he really clearly knew was when he was in courtroom 400, and you also heard Sykes and DeValle say I had to help him down the corridor. You know that something happened to him and he was injured.

And please, don't misunderstand me. He injured Mr. Alfieri. We are not saying that he didn't. We are not saying that it is good. Just that he was acting in self-defense and fear. Let's talk now about how we know that this is not an attempt escape. Isn't it interesting how, even Chief Cruz, the chief of security, tried to help out the prosecution theory by saying well, you know, we have these rules but we don't always obey them? Wasn't it interesting that act of desperation of re-examination when Mr. Alfieri was testifying when they started to go into well, sometimes the doors are opened, and all this other kind of stuff? But do you remember recross examination when I asked him questions after they had asked him the second time? Do you remember that?

Isn't it true, Mr. Alfieri, that you have a rule that the gate should be locked? Yes. Isn't it true, Mr. Alfieri that the gates are usually locked because that is the rule? Yes. And isn't it true, Mr. Alfieri, that one of two things is always true, either there is a sheriff in the courtroom or it is double bolt locked shut? Isn't that true? Answer, yes. Where was he going? Where was he going?

I'm talking about the cleaning people have keys but they don't come until four o'clock and this happened at noon. And the little, you know, I suppose I shouldn't say this. I don't mean to sound demeaning but cute remark about Friday saying it was get-a-way day. Wasn't that nice? We were here Friday and what time did we leave? Five o'clock. There are lots of courts that work a full day. I suppose there are some that don't. I suppose there are some that don't.

Why do you suppose everyone in the prosecution case was so anxious to say how possible all of this was? Because they need to make this into an attempt escape. If they can somehow make this into an attempt escape, any injuries to Ron are explained, not that even shooting him in the back would be excusable.

You are going to be instructed that a guard or other peace officer is justified in the use of force including force likely to cause death or great bodily harm which he reasonably believes to be necessary to prevent the escape from a penal institution of a person whom the officer reasonably believes to be lawfully detained in the institution awaiting trial for an offense. You are going to be instructed on that. That you will get it in writing and the Judge will read it to you as well.

In other words, anything they did, if this was an attempt escape would be justified. That is a very good reason to try and make it into an attempt escape. No matter what happens. They have no way of knowing if there are facial bones broken or injury to the cervical spine. They have no way of knowing that.

There is a kind of division between the weights. In fact, you may remember Chief Cruz saying, Mr. Sykes was—they don't work for me. Mr. Daly, Mr. Alfieri they did. There are two basically—sort of two organizations that work more or less together but they have their separate domains. The court personnel sheriffs and the Cook County Department of Corrections sheriffs and they are different and they have different responsibilities and they have different biases and interests. They do.

And you remember that Mr. Sykes and Mr. DeValle told you that they don't know how this began. That they just, without any question, went to Alfieri's aid. Well, why didn't Daly?

Well, the prosecution may want to say they were kind of trying to imply it. I thought in their examination but perhaps in and out that Mr. Daly was acquainted with Ron and maybe in some kind of way he was trying to sort of help Ron escape. It was kind of the implication in some of their questioning. Which is utter nonsense. That is utter nonsense.

You heard the testimony that Mr. Daly was the person who, in fact, locked him in the jury room. If there was some kind of plot or plan between Mr. Daly and Ron Tellez and you are going to try and help someone to escape in some kind of way, wouldn't it make a little bit more sense to just fail to lock the handcuffs to the chair or to do something where there is some, at least some chance of him getting out? It makes no sense logically, and if I misinterpret the reason for the prosecution's questions I will apologize.

But you see, he did nothing because when he first got there he knew Alfieri was in the wrong, or he suspected he was in the wrong and he didn't know what to do. He was immobilized and that is everybody's testimony. That he was, in fact, immobilized, that he did nothing.

He told Mr. Daly that he was sorry. Ron told him. And I think the reasonable inference and clear inference for that was he was sorry for putting him in the middle. Ron was police officer. He understands the brotherhood. Now brotherhood and sisterhood. Now women get to be police officers too. He understands that. How you need to stick with your own. How he might understand how Mr. Daly could be immobilized by being torn by conflicting loyalties, by conflicting views of what was right and what was wrong.

And he did say and, you know, as again the statements kept changing and getting better and better for Mr. Daly to explain his behavior or in his case his lack of behavior that he didn't want to go back to Division 1. Well, I really don't want to go back to Division 1, Mr. Daly, because I'm afraid of my safety there.

And I think there is no question—I don't think anyone on this jury has any question that a police officer, who is in custody, charged with a crime is in much more danger than another kind of inmate. I don't think that I even have to spend any time persuading you of that. Even though lots of witnesses admitted that on cross examination that that is, in fact, the truth. And it is obvious why.

He might have arrested a particular inmate who is in there or it gets around he is a police officer. Inmates are not necessarily fond of police officers and some guards feel like, you know, you let us down and I'm going to make it even harder on you. So being in Division 1 of the jail— and there are six divisions of the jail by the way, not the only one—may have been difficult for him and he may have been discussing that with Mr. Daly. That is hardly evidence of an intent to escape. You may remember that there was discussion about this court order that kept him apart from other prisoners. There was a court order keeping him apart from other prisoners for exactly this reason.

I know I discussed with you already about the handcuffs. I just want to point out to you another instruction that the Judge is going to read to you. And this is an instruction regarding circumstantial evidence.

It says, circumstantial evidence is the proof of facts or circumstances which give rise to a reasonable inference of other facts which intend to show the guilt or innocence of the defendant. Circumstantial evidence should be considered by you together with all of the other evidence in the case at arriving at your verdict.

What I mean by that, in regards to the cuffs is, the circumstantial evidence of them putting on a second set of cuffs argues that Ron was telling the truth, that he pulled one hand out because it was closed wrong, he was able to twist his hand and pull out in his depression and his fear and that it was still locked. And that that is why they put on the second set of cuffs.

And the key. The elusive key. The key that appears in second, third and fourth reports of people. The key that appears. Sykes saw it but DeValle, who he says was paying attention to the cuff, didn't see it and it wasn't on the floor and they searched the elevator and searched below the elevator and found others keys. What key? There was no key. There never was a key. It is a bunch of nonsense. It is a bunch of attempting to make this into an attempt escape to justify all the injuries that may have been on Ron. He wasn't seriously hurt except for the eye, which is good. I'm glad Mr. Alfieri wasn't seriously hurt. He was bruised and uncomfortable but I'm glad he wasn't seriously hurt either.

But you see if it is an attempt escape everything is justified. Everything is justified. And how do we know for sure that is not an attempt escape? I know I'm talking a long time. I hope you forgive me. We know because of the changeable physical evidence. All these photographs that you saw showing not only what is the fact of what is behind courtroom 400 and you know what is in the jail, but the facts that Ron Tellez knew.

Mr. Alfieri told you he didn't take him on a tour of all of the courtrooms so he can take a look and see if some of them were opened or not opened. I mean, if we are going to—for goodness sakes he was taken from the lockup to the courtroom. He was supposed to be in and back.

THE COURT: Five minutes, Miss Lyon

MS. LYON: Five minutes.

THE COURT: I am giving you five minutes.

MS. LYON: Okay. Can I have ten, please?

THE COURT: Five.

MS. LYON: Well, I'll try.

If I talk too fast you have to really forgive me.

The photos definitely show you that not only—you see the prosecution has to prove to you intent. They have to prove to you that he intended to escape. That means that they have to, to some degree, prove what was in his mind. What did he say going down there? Locked doors. Keys going to other sheriffs. He is locked in. Bars. Walls. Bricks. Everywhere he can go. He is going to try and escape from one part of the jail to another part of the jail, from one arm of one set of sheriffs to the arms of another? It makes no sense.

I am sure that the prosecution plans in rebuttal to talk about the following two instructions, one of which is a definition of attempt and the other one is that—the one that the other prosecution referred to as—it is not a defense to the charge of attempt that because of a misapprehension of the circumstances it would have been impossible to commit the offense attempt. That is true. That is the law. But if he only saw what he saw that you will see in these photos.

Where on earth would he form the intent to run? Run where? Go where? Escape where? Maybe to get away from Alfieri. Maybe to try and fight his way from Alfieri, yes. But not escape, no intent. They haven't proven it. They haven't come close.

I need to talk to you briefly because I have—about the murder charge, the fact he is charged with murder and the prosecution says it is important because it goes to state of mind because he has a serious charge. And that is the reason that it is admissible even though he is not being tried on the murder now.

The prosecution has chosen to try this case first; that is their right. That is what they have done. He has not been tried. He is innocent. You will receive an instruction about presumption of innocence and I am—I have to ask you to try to pay attention to it as regarding the murder charge and I think you know from voir dire how difficult it is. If my memory serves me right, 20 or 22 people said they couldn't presume his innocence if he knew that he was charged with murder in another case. It is very, very hard to do. It is hard to do. But you said that you could do it and we all trust that that is true.

In a few moments I will stop talking and the prosecutor has the opportunity to rebut those questions that I have raised. The prosecution doesn't choose the facts that they are given. They don't choose the witnesses they are given, and I mean no disrespect to either of these two fine prosecutors when I speak about their case perhaps in disparaging terms.

You will hear about the evils of crimes and necessity of protecting sheriffs and that is why they are have the more serious law, aggravated battery instead of battery when the sheriff is the victim. That is all true. We all agree with that. But that is not the point. We don't need to protect liars who are trying to cover themselves.

I am just about finished and I want to thank you for your attention and obviously, I have gone overtime. I want to thank Judge Morgan and the prosecutors and everybody in here for a fair trial and there have been sometimes when Judge Morgan and I have disagreed but I suppose that is just natural.

Also at times, perhaps I have gone too far and I raised my voice or yelled a little bit too much and I hopefully have not offended you. I don't intend to. It is just that this is serious. This is serious. This is serious to Ron Tellez. He has a very serious case pending here. It has serious implications for his other case.

And also, by my demeanor, if in any way I have given you the impression that the defense, or I or anyone in the defense team dislikes or doesn't respect Cook County sheriffs I wish to disabuse you of that. That is not the case. In fact, the opposite is the case.

Finally, I would like to leave you with one thought. Each of you, each of you can sit here right now, raise your hand to God, swear to God and promise yourselves, me and anyone else that it is important to you that you will never commit a crime. You can promise us that. But you cannot promise, but what you cannot promise is that you will never be accused of one. That you can't promise.

Ron Tellez sits here accused of a crime. A crime that he is not guilty of. I ask you to find him not guilty of aggravated battery, of attempt escape.

Thank you.

THE COURT: Thank you, Miss Lyon.

Mr. Reilly.

MR. REILLY: Thank you. If I may.

FINAL CLOSING ARGUMENT FOR THE PROSECUTION [74]

BY MR. REILLY:

Ladies and Gentlemen, that is a very important thought to leave you with. It is Ron Tellez that is accused here. Who is on trial here, Nicholas Alfieri, the Cook County Sheriff's Department, Michael Daly? Of course not. It is Ronald Tellez. He is the person who stands charged and accused of aggravated battery and attempt escape. Nicholas Alfieri, five foot five, one hundred sixty pounds, the raging bull of 26th and California if you believe Mr. Tellez.

Well, all twelve of you were chosen for your common sense, for your own experiences in life. Both sides and the Court felt that you can be fair.

---

[74] In most jurisdictions the prosecution has the right to speak both first and last at the close of the trial. However, a few jurisdictions restrict the prosecutor to one closing argument and do not allow the prosecutor to speak after defense counsel argues. The psychological literature on persuasion suggests that the ability to speak both first and last on an issue should be a substantial advantage, but there is no good empirical evidence which indicates the degree to which this is in fact the case in trials. The justification for giving the prosecution this advantage is that the prosecution has the burden of proving the state's case beyond a reasonable doubt. Yet, the plaintiff in a civil case usually has a similar advantage though the plaintiff may prevail upon a mere preponderance of the evidence. As defense counsel what might you do to minimize the advantage of the prosecutor?

No way does all of the evidence in this case justify Nicholas Alfieri savagely attacking and beating and brutalizing poor Ron Tellez. That is not what all of the evidence shows.

The suggestion—not the suggestion, the statement by the defense that this is a giant cover-up, it is a giant conspiracy, that all of the sheriffs, deputies and correctional officers and lieutenants and chiefs got together and got their stories straight and they're going to get Ron Tellez.

Well, there is no love lost between Michael Daly and Nicholas Alfieri and that should be clear to everybody here because Michael Daly did nothing to help Nicholas Alfieri while he is laying on the ground being kicked by this man. And if it isn't clear to everyone here today, and it should have been clear to you the first day that Nicholas Alfieri testified, he was an easy mark. Nicholas Alfieri was an easy mark. He was an easy set-up for a guy that knows the ropes.

It was noon time. It was Friday. Michael Daly just happens to get— to disappear and reassigned. It just happened to be Michael Daly's handcuffs that are on Nicholas Alfieri's—strike that, on Ronald Tellez. It happens to be a noon recess. It is time for Ron Tellez to go back. The only one helping out Nicholas Alfieri then is Deputy Lilly. You heard her testify. And now he is alone with Mr. Tellez.

And if you look in the basement here, when you come down in the elevator there is a hallway that leads to the jail. The only person between that elevator and the jail, at noon time that Friday, was Michael Daly, who just happened to be stationed there, midway between the jail and that elevator shaft. That elevator shaft that gives you access to seven different floors in this building, and you can look at all of those defense pictures about how secure it is up in room 400, and no doubt that it is. And it may have been that day, but there is access to seven different floors from that elevator shaft and that is the evidence.

Mr. Tellez is a trained policeman. He has his handcuffs off. He has his business suit and tie on. All of that, that is evidence. All of that is evidence that you should consider carefully.

And Michael Daly offers no help to Nicholas Alfieri. And that is clear. That is very clear. So to suggest that Alfieri and Daly are now involved in this conspiracy to get Ron Tellez does not jive.

MS. LYON: Objection, your Honor, that is not what I said.

THE COURT: It is just argument.

MR. REILLY: Thank you, Judge.[75]

The suggestion that Deputies Sykes and DeValle are also involved in

---

[75] This time Ms. Lyon's objection to the closing argument is properly overruled. Although she never said there was a "conspiracy," the prosecutor is entitled to argue that she implied it, and that the implication is ridiculous.

this conspiracy and this cover-up, again don't jive with what they saw, what they heard, and defense counsel's own argument, when they came on the scene they told you what they saw. And what they heard and what they did.

The testimony from a variety of witnesses that Nicholas Alfieri was a peaceful person, he wasn't the type of guy to be grabbing policemen, throwing them up against the wall, breaking their glasses, slamming them to the ground, kicking them, dragging them by their tie, that is not the type of person that Nicholas Alfieri was.

And you heard testimony from a variety of people; Deputy Lilly, Chief Cruz, they all came in here, they took the stand, they were under oath, they were questioned by both sides and that is the testimony. That is the evidence you have in front of you.

All of the questions you heard about the Internal Affairs Division investigation conducted by the Sheriff's deputy. Why was it conducted? You have an attempt escape and you have a Sheriff's deputy who is injured. And not for one minute do we suggest, would anyone suggest that there weren't some major procedural and rule violations by Alfieri, by Daly.

Nicholas Alfieri has a murder suspect, high security prisoner, gets his handcuffs off and get them on the ground and disarms them and disables them. That is a big problem for Nicholas Alfieri.

Michael Daly comes on the scene and does nothing. Does nothing. He broke some rules. Absolutely. But if you recall what the Judge said, the Internal Affairs Investigations is not what is on trial here. What is on trial here is Ronald Tellez for battering a Sheriff's deputy and attempting to escape from this building.

So all of the questions about, did he write his report right, what should Daly have done, did Alfieri not handcuff him right, those are all very interesting questions but they are not what you should be concerned about today. Judge Morgan will instruct you on the law, and instruct you as to what you should concern yourself with.

The defense put forth to you, by Mr. Tellez, through his attorneys, he said he was acting in self-defense. Well, Ladies and Gentlemen, that is pretty much the only defense that could be put forth to you. It is pretty obvious that he couldn't say I didn't do it. I wasn't there. It wasn't me. That is pretty obvious. He had four people testify that he is kicking Nicholas Alfieri.

MS. LYON: Your Honor, I object to all the defenses that we—that is not a proper argument.

THE COURT: Counsel, this is argument. He can respond to your closing argument.

MR. REILLY: And it is pretty obvious that he couldn't say I didn't do anything because Alfieri is gravely injured at the time and believe me, he felt those kicks in the place of where they were kicked. So his defense is he started it. I was defending myself. That is his only option. And now he tries to put it on a one on one. Alfieri is lying. He started it. He is the one that knocked me around and abused me and brutalized me in that elevator.

So when you as jurors are confronted with that situation then you have to look at all the rest of the evidence.

You heard Alfieri testify and you heard Tellez's testimony. Now, you look at what everybody else says. And everybody else has got Alfieri down on the ground. Everybody but Ronald Tellez. Everybody else has him down on the ground. Everybody else has Tellez kicking him while he is on the ground. So that supports what Nicholas Alfieri tells you. Nicholas Alfieri's reputation for peacefulness. You can and should consider that. That is evidence.

And please remember what the lawyers say and what the lawyers argue is not evidence. The evidence that you should base your decision on came from that witness stand, from the people that came into this courtroom, took an oath and testified. That is what you use to make your decision in this case.

Clearly the defendant had a motive and a reason to get out of 26th and California having been charged with murder, and I think Miss Lyon has covered that topic. He had a good reason to get out of here. And he had an excellent opportunity and he had an easy mark and Nicholas Alfieri at noon on August 28th, 1987.

The photos that you have had an opportunity to look at of the injuries to Nicholas Alfieri clearly show, as Mr. Gardiner told you that, those were well placed, well designed kicks. Those were not the kicks of someone who is laying on the ground with his hands handcuffed behind him and the weight of his body on his hands kicking wildly. Those are well placed, well designed and well intended kicks because Ronald Tellez knew exactly what he was doing when he kicked Nicholas Alfieri in the groin.

And poor Nicholas Alfieri knowing that he had broken the rules, knowing that he goofed up, knowing that he made mistakes is desperately trying to keep that elevator door opened because if those doors close and Mr. Tellez goes up he goes anywhere on seven floors in this building and he conceivably escapes from the custody and that would be a major, major problem. And that is why poor Nicholas Alfieri left himself opened to so many painful kicks because this poor guy is laying on the floor in the basement there trying to keep that door opened and rather than trying to defend himself and protect himself against these kicks, and I think common sense will tell you you get kicked in the groin like that you will cover up and you will try and protect yourself. But he had a greater interest, a greater concern to keep those doors opened because if Tellez got in that elevator and those doors closed and he went up to the second floor or the third floor behind this courtroom, anything was possible so that is why Nicholas Alfieri has such concentrated localized injuries because the poor guy was laying on the ground trying to keep the he elevator door opened.

And why are there no pictures of Mr. Tellez? Well, remember very carefully the testimony of all of the witnesses. There were no visible injuries on the defendant that day. Several days later a Dr. Banerjee testified that there was a bruise around the left eye, but the testimony from the defense witnesses and from the State witnesses was there were no visible injuries.

The Chicago Fire Department paramedics left. There is nothing wrong with him. Lieutenant Russ Gardner called by the defense, no visible injuries. I saw him with his clothes off. What did they want him to take a picture of? No allegations that he had been attacked by Nicholas Alfieri. There was no reason to take pictures of the defendant at that time.

The suggestion that this was a fight is ludicrous and again, when you look at Nicholas Alfieri versus Ronald Tellez look at everybody else's testimony. And again, the testimony of correctional Officer Sykes and DeValle is very telling. They don't work with these two individuals while they are all sheriffs. They work in the Department of Corrections at 26th Street and Alfieri and Daly work here in the building. And it was asked, do you have any personal relationship with Alfieri or Daly? No. Then who are they?

They came in here and told you that when they arrived on the scene Alfieri is on the ground, he is being kicked by Tellez, the cuffs are off, the cuffs, the one cuff is opened, and this guy took a swing at Robert Sykes. And Sykes did what he could to deflect that blow and he cracked him with a right punch, therefore, striking him on the left side of the eye. All of that jives, all of that makes sense.

Then he says the only one that said he saw a key in this case was Robert Sykes. That is the testimony. Nobody will dispute that. The only one that said he saw a key was Robert Sykes. Alfieri is still on the ground. He didn't think the guy ever got his handcuffs off. Sykes is the only one who testified that he saw a key, and he has no motive to lie or to make that up.

At one point in time defense counsel says well, Sykes and DeValle they told you what they saw. They were just doing their job. You can't have it both ways. They can't be part of the conspiracy also. He got those cuffs opened with a key because the handcuff was opened and when

Sykes. got into that elevator with DeValle they weren't looking to use somebody else's handcuff and get somebody else's key to put those handcuffs on. He is a trained correctional officer. He is going to go in there and he is going to use his cuffs and that is what he did.

Again, the medical testimony that you heard in this case simply boils down to the fact that there were no visible injuries to the defendant. He complained of injuries absolutely. He complained of injuries, complained of some trauma to the head and he was X-rayed for those things, checked out by a doctor. X-rays were negative. Unremarkable. No substantial injuries. Certainly doesn't jive with the beating that he says he got by Nicholas Alfieri.

Dr. Banerjee and all of the Chicago Fire Department paramedics, Meggs McKinney—I think that was the fellow's name—they didn't see a man that had just been beaten up in that small little elevator, beaten up and kicked. They saw a fellow that complained of some injuries to his head. Sent him over for an evaluation but didn't see this cut over—under the cheek, didn't see this badly beaten up man. That is the testimony. That is the evidence.

The testimony of the defendant, the reason we went into such detail about the position he was in—is if you consider an individual who is handcuffed, double locked as he said in those handcuffs, laying on the ground, all the weight of his body on his hands, which are handcuffed, you are not going to have much movement at all. You can try it. Common sense will tell you that. You get down on the ground, put your hands behind you and handcuff them and immobilize them you are not going to have much movement. You will have not much of an opportunity to inflict the types of injuries that were inflicted on Nicholas Alfieri.

Ladies and Gentlemen, Judge Morgan will instruct you as to the law you are to follow in this case. And regarding the escape, the attempt escape, she is going to instruct you that the offense attempted need not be committed. Only that there was a substantial step taken towards the commission of that offense. And if you can get a little five foot five jail guard alone in the basement of this building with an elevator that has access to seven floors, if you can get him down on the ground and sufficiently immobilized and if you can get your handcuffs off, if you can have a suit and tie on, if you can act cool, if you can act calm, if you know what you are doing, you have taken a substantial step to getting out of this place.

I am not saying he is going to succeed. I don't know what floor he may or may not have intended to get off on, but that is a substantial step towards the commission of the offense of escape.

The other charge is aggravated battery to a peace officer. Clearly the evidence shows that Nicholas Alfieri was battered. Clearly it shows that he was a peace officer, and from all of the evidence you should be able to determine that Mr. Tellez was not justified in inflicting that type of a beating on Mr. Alfieri.

If you use your common sense, if you use the law as Judge Morgan instructs you, the only fair verdict, the only just verdict in this case is a verdict of guilty on both counts.

Thank you.[76]

THE COURT: Thank you, Mr. Reilly.

Ladies and Gentlemen, that concludes the argument of counsel. We have now reached that point in the trial where the Court will instruct you as to the law that you are to apply in this case. I'm going to read them to you orally and at the point in which you retire you will be able to take them in written form into the jury room with you.[77]

Members of the jury, the evidence and arguments in this case have been completed and I will now instruct you as to the law.

The law that applies to the case is stated in these instructions and it is your duty to follow all of them. You must not single out certain instructions and disregard others. It is your duty to determine the facts and to determine them only from the evidence in this case. You are to apply the law to the facts and in this way decide the case. Neither sympathy nor prejudice should influence you. You should not be

---

[76] Consider the amount of time devoted to the closing arguments. What the attorneys say may not be "evidence," but it can greatly influence the jury's thinking.

[77] Needless to say, the instructions the judge gives are not cut from whole cloth. Illinois, like most American jurisdictions, has an official set of pattern instructions for use in criminal cases. The current version for criminal trials is Illinois Pattern Jury Instructions—Criminal (4th ed. 2000) (with annual supplements). The instructions in this publication are derived from, or have been approved in, state case law. That means that judges are unlikely to be reversed for misstating the law if they use these pattern instructions. Equally important, pattern instructions are a convenient aid to busy judges and trial lawyers. Whatever their source, the function of judicial instructions is to educate and guide jurors. How useful are they for that purpose? There is good deal of psychological research on this point, and it's pretty depressing. In general, the studies show that while jurors make good use of the evidence, they do not understand or remember the instructions well at all. See, e.g., Peter Tiersma, The Rocky Road to Legal Reform: Improving the Language of Jury Instructions, 66 Brooklyn L. Rev. 1081 (2001); Alan Reifman, Spencer M. Gusick & Phoebe C. Ellsworth, Real Jurors' Understanding of the Law in Real Cases, 16 Law & Hum. Behav. 539 (1992); Phoebe C. Ellsworth, Are Twelve Heads Better Than One?, 52 Law & Contemp. Probs., No. 4, 205 (1989); R.P. Charrow & V.R. Charrow, Making Legal Language Understandable, 79 Colum. L. Rev. 1306 (1979). Judge Morgan at least gives the jurors a written copy of the instructions, to help them in their deliberations. Surprisingly few judges follow this simple sensible practice.

The decision on which instructions to give (and, in some cases, on the wording of instructions that are not taken directly from the form book) is usually made at a conference between the judge and the lawyers. Judge Morgan held two such conferences, which we have not reproduced, one before Mr. Tellez testified, and one after the defense rested. As a result, the lawyers knew in advance how the judge would instruct the jury and could organize their arguments in terms of those instructions. In some jurisdictions the attorneys make their closing arguments *after* the jury has been instructed on the law. The advantage to this procedure is that the jury is familiar with the law as well as the facts before hearing finally from the lawyers. It has the disadvantage of further separating the arguments from the evidence.

influenced by any person's race, color, religion or national ancestry.

From time to time it has been the duty of the court to rule on the admissibility of evidence. You should not concern yourselves with the reasons for these rulings. You should disregard questions and exhibits which were withdrawn or to which objections were sustained.

Any evidence that was received for a limited purpose should not be considered by you for any other purpose. You should disregard testimony and exhibits which the Court has refused or stricken. The evidence which you should consider consists only of the testimony of the witnesses and the exhibits which the Court has received. You should consider all the evidence in the light of your own observations and experience in life. Neither by these instructions nor by any ruling or remark which I have made do I mean to indicate any opinion as to the facts or as to what your verdict should be. Faithful performance by you of your duties as jurors is vital to the administration of justice.

You are the sole judges of the believability of the witnesses and of the weight to be given to the testimony of each of them. In considering the testimony of any witness, you may take into account his ability and opportunity to observe, his memory, his manner while testifying, any interest, bias or prejudice that he may have, and the reasonableness of his testimony considered in the light of all of the evidence in the case. You should judge the testimony of the defendant in the same manner as you judge the testimony of any other witness.

Opening statements are made by the attorneys to acquaint you with the facts they expect to prove. Closing arguments are made by the attorneys to discuss the facts and circumstances in the case and should be confined to the evidence and to reasonable inferences to be drawn from the evidence. Neither opening statements nor closing arguments are evidence, and any statement or argument made by the attorneys which is not based on the evidence should be disregarded.

The defendant is charged with the offense of aggravated battery and attempt escape. The defendant has pleaded not guilty.

The indictment in this case is the formal method of accusing the defendant of an offense and placing him on trial. It is not any evidence against the defendant and does not create any inference of guilt.

The defendant is presumed to be innocent of the charges against him.

This presumption remains with him throughout every stage of the trial and during your deliberations on the verdict and is not overcome unless from all of the evidence in the case you are convinced beyond a reasonable doubt that the defendant is guilty.

The State has the burden of proving the guilt of the defendant beyond a reasonable doubt, and this burden remains on the State throughout the case. The defendant is not required to prove his innocence.

Circumstantial evidence is the proof of facts or circumstances which give rise to a reasonable inference of other facts, which tend to show the guilt or innocence of the defendant. Circumstantial evidence should be considered by you together with all the other evidence in the case in arriving at your verdict.

You have before you evidence that the defendant made a statement relating to the offense charged in the indictment. It is for you to determine whether the defendant made the statement, and if so, what weight should be given to the statement. In determining the weight to be given to a statement you should consider all of the circumstances under which it was made.

The believability of a witness may be challenged by evidence that on some former occasion he made a statement that was not consistent with his testimony in this case. When evidence is received for that purpose only, you may use it only to decide the weight to be given the testimony you heard from the witness in this courtroom.

The term "peace officer" means any person who, by virtue of his office of public employment, is vested by law with a duty to maintain public order or to make arrests for offenses, whether that duty extends to all offenses or is limited to specific offenses.

The term "penal institution" means a penitentiary, state farm, reformatory, prison, jail, house of corrections, or other institution for the incarceration or custody of persons under sentence for offenses, or awaiting trial or sentence for offenses.

A person commits the offense of attempt when he, with the intent to commit the offense of escape, does any act which constitutes a substantial step toward the commission of the offense of escape. The offense attempted need not have been committed. It is not a defense to the charge of attempt that, because of a misapprehension of the circumstances, it would have been impossible to commit the offense attempted.

A person charged with the commission of a murder, a felony, commits the offense of escape when he intentionally escapes from the custody of an employee of a penal institution.

To sustain the charge of attempt, the State must prove the following propositions:

First: That the defendant performed an act which constituted a substantial step toward the commission of the offense of escape; and

Second: That the defendant did so with intent to commit the offense of escape.

If you find from your consideration of all the evidence that each one of these propositions has been proved beyond a reasonable doubt you should find the defendant guilty.

If you find from your consideration of all the evidence that any one of these propositions has not been proved beyond a reasonable doubt you should find the defendant not guilty.

A person commits the offense of battery when he intentionally and by any means causes bodily harm to another person.

A person commits the offense of aggravated battery when he, in committing a battery, knows the individual harmed is a peace officer engaged in the execution of any of his official duties.

To sustain the charge of aggravated battery, the State must prove the following propositions:

First: That the defendant knowingly or intentionally without legal justification caused bodily harm to Nicholas Alfieri; and

Second: That the defendant knew Nicholas Alfieri to be a correctional officer engaged in the execution of his official duties, and

Third: That the defendant was not justified in using the force which he used.

If you find from your consideration of all the evidence that each one of these propositions has been proved beyond a reasonable doubt, you should find the defendant guilty.

If you find from your consideration of all the evidence that any one of these propositions has not been proved beyond a reasonable doubt, you should find the defendant not guilty.

A person is justified in the use of force when and to the extent that he reasonably believes that such conduct is necessary to defend himself against the imminent use of unlawful force.

A guard or other peace officer is justified in the use of force, including force likely to cause death or great bodily harm, which he reasonably believes to be necessary to prevent the escape from a penal institution of a person whom the officer reasonably believes to be lawfully detained in the institution awaiting trial for an offense.

When you retire to the jury room you will first elect one of your members as your foreperson. He or she will preside during the your deliberations upon your verdict.

Your agreement upon a verdict must be unanimous. Your verdicts must be in writing and signed by all of you, including your foreperson.

The defendant is charged with the offenses of aggravated battery and attempt escape. You will receive four forms of verdict. As to each charge you will be provided both a "not guilty" and a "guilty" form of verdict.

THE COURT: Miss Clerk, will you swear the bailiff?[78]

(Bailiffs sworn)

. . .

(Proceedings passed)

(The following proceedings were had out of the presence and hearing of the jury)

THE COURT: The question. "Will the next jury have this verdict brought out as testimony?"

They could if it were a guilty in a provable.

MR. REILLY: That is not their concern.

THE COURT: It is not their concern. Unless someone convinces me otherwise. It is not a concern of theirs at all.

MS. LYON: Why don't you write that. Something along those lines. That is not a relevant issue to this case or something along those lines.

THE COURT: I guess I can write it as oppose to bringing them out. Is everyone agreeable?

MR. REILLY: No objection.

MS. LYON: Go ahead.

THE COURT: I will put, "This factor has no relevance to your deliberations."

MR. REILLY: Fine.[79]

. . .

THE CLERK: Ronald Tellez.

---

[78] At this point the jury is committed to the custody of the bailiff for the duration of its deliberations. The bailiff is "sworn" to properly oversee the deliberations by making sure that the jurors are able to deliberate without communication or interference from the outside.

[79] The jurors—no fools—have honed in on the real key issue in the case: How will a verdict in Mr. Tellez's attempted escape and aggravated assault trial affect his murder trial? As the judge acknowledges to the lawyers, if Mr. Tellez is convicted the jury in the murder case may well hear about it. It may be admissible as evidence of "consciousness of guilt," on the theory that a person would be unlikely to try to escape from pre-trial custody unless he knew he was guilty and expected to be convicted. In addition, if Mr. Tellez is convicted of murder and the jury in that case has to decide whether or not he should be sentenced to death, the assault and attempted escape conviction would be admissible on the question of penalty. Clearly it is because of these possible uses of a conviction that the prosecution is trying this case first. Otherwise, why would they go to all this trouble to get Mr. Tellez sentenced to a term of years in prison, *before* trying him on much more serious charges, for which the punishment is life imprisonment or death? But the jurors are not supposed to consider any of this, so the judge—with the concurrence of the attorneys on both sides—tells them "this factor has no relevance to your deliberations." If you were one of the jurors who asked this question, how would that answer make your feel?

(The following proceedings were had out of the presence and hearing of the jury)

THE COURT: The jury has two more questions in addition to screaming and yelling at each other. . . . The second question is, "Can the jury find the defendant guilty of a lesser charge than aggravated battery?" This issue obviously came up as we were doing the instructions. The Court took its position, which is why we did not give instructions on the lesser included, and I have not changed that position in terms of the Court. Certainly everyone is free to make their record.

MS. LYON: Your Honor, I would be renewing my motion that you submit the lesser included offense of battery. They do have the definition of it already. That you submit the issues instruction and the verdict forms and allow them to see that.

MR. REILLY: It is our position it is a legal definition and legal issue, and the Court ruled properly and they should be instructed that they have the applicable law and they have the applicable verdicts.[80]

THE COURT: I will briefly restate my position, my ruling on this issue when it came up in the instruction conference. Namely, there is no controversy around the fact that Mr. Alfieri was a correctional officer, a peace officer within the legal definition of a peace officer. The law is clear that if one commits a battery on a person of that status it is by operation of law an aggravated battery. The Court's feeling was then, as it is now, if they find a battery at all, by operation of law it has to be an aggravated battery.

. . .

(The following proceedings were had in the presence and hearing of the jury)

THE COURT: Be seated. Would the foreman identify himself.

JUROR BOBER: Walter Bober. Should I read?

THE COURT: Mr. Foreman, have you reached a verdict in this matter?

JUROR BOBER: Yes, we have.

THE COURT: And have you signed your verdict forms?

JUROR BOBER: Yes, we have.

THE COURT: Would you tender those to the sheriff, please?

Miss Sheriff, if you would deliver those to the clerk.

Miss Tally, would you read the verdicts?

---

[80] The defense attorney wants the jury to have the option of a lesser included conviction; the prosecutor opposes it. Why do you suppose they take these opposing positions?

THE CLERK: We, the jury, find the defendant Ronald Tellez not guilty of the offense of aggravated battery.

We, the jury, find the defendant, Ronald Tellez not guilty of the offense of attempt escape.[81]

THE COURT: Are there any requests by either counsel?

MR. REILLY: Ask that the jury be polled.

. . .

THE COURT: Ladies and Gentlemen of the jury, I want to thank you on behalf of the Circuit Court of Cook County and all the people of the County of Cook for the service you have rendered here. You have certainly carried out your obligations of citizenship in an exemplary way. And you should understand that the system could not operate without the participation of people such as yourself.

It really is one of the highest services you can pay to your country and to your community short of serving in the military and giving your life for your country.

The jury trial system is an old system in this country. It is one of our cherished aspects of government and while we know that a lot of people find it bothersome and you may have over the course of this trial, other things that you would rather be doing, you choose to discharge those obligations to citizenship and come and sit in the trial of this matter.

I know that some of you may have served before and I commend you for coming back and serving the people of your community again.

I wish you all the best in your future. I hope that if you are ever called upon again that you might consider, and try to work it out so that you can serve again.

. . .

Postscript

From November 6 to November 18, 1989, Mr. Tellez was tried in Cook County Circuit Court for capital murder, with Mr. Gardiner and Mr. Reilly prosecuting, and Ms. Lyon defending with Mr. Michael Morrissey, another Cook County Assistant Public Defender. Tellez was convicted as charged, but at the penalty phase the jury sentenced him to life imprisonment rather than death by lethal injection.

---

[81] From your reading of the record, what factors do you think are most likely to have led the jury to acquit Mr. Tellez?

CHAPTER 2

TAKING EVIDENCE

■ ■ ■

The traditional form of evidence in American trials is oral testimony, from sworn witnesses, in the presence of the trier of fact. In this chapter we discuss the process of taking testimony: the requirements for testifying; the process of questioning witnesses; the general nature of the objections to testimony; and the procedures for making, opposing and ruling on objections. While the focus of the chapter is testimony, most of what we say—especially in the third section, on objections—applies as well to the other category of evidence that is used at trial: documents and other tangible items that are presented to the trier of fact as exhibits. Exhibits are discussed in more detail in Chapter Ten.[1]

I.   PRECONDITIONS TO TESTIMONY

A. PERSONAL KNOWLEDGE AND
THE LAY OPINION RULE

I was gratified to be able to answer promptly, and I did.

I said I didn't know.

—Mark Twain, *Life on the Mississippi*

It is often said that the most basic rule of evidence is relevance. From the point of view of the *case*, this is true: regardless of source, only evidence that is relevant to the issues on trial may be introduced. From the point of view of the *witness*, however, the fundamental limitation is *personal knowledge*: regardless of the case, or the issue, a person may only testify to things she has perceived. Federal Rule of Evidence 602 states a common version of this restriction:

---

[1]   To be admitted in evidence most exhibits must be "authenticated" by testimony from a witness. See FRE 901. Some exhibits, however, are "self-authenticating"—they may be admitted in evidence without any foundational testimony whatever. See FRE 902. Self-authenticating exhibits are the only complete exception to the rule that evidence requires testimony from witnesses. In addition, there are several *substitutes* for evidence that are discussed in Chapter Eleven: *stipulations* by the parties, who agree that certain factual premises may be accepted without dispute; *presumptions* that tell the trier of fact how to regard particular issues in the absence of sufficiently powerful evidence to overcome the presumptions; and *judicial notice*, a finding by the judge that a proposition is indisputably true and must be accepted as a fact.

A witness may testify to a matter only if evidence is introduced sufficient to support a finding that the witness has personal knowledge of the matter. . . .

The personal knowledge requirement means that a witness can testify only to what she saw, heard, or otherwise perceived. Note, however, that the testimony "Virginia told me that her car broke down" is not objectionable on this basis if the witness heard Virginia make that statement. If that testimony is offered to prove that Virginia's car did break down, it may be objectionable on a different ground: hearsay. On the other hand, if the witness who heard that statement from Virginia (but knew nothing more on the subject) testifies: "Virginia's car broke down" the testimony would be objectionable for lack of personal knowledge. In this second version the witness is asserting something she did not perceive.

Personal knowledge does not necessarily mean precise knowledge. A witness is only required to do her best, to relate what she can about the subject of her testimony. Testimony that "there were three or four, or maybe five people in the room," or that "I don't remember his words, but I know he agreed to the deal," or that "it took somewhere between an hour and two hours" is not objectionable for lack of personal knowledge. If the testimony is based on the witness's perceptions and represents her best memory it is admissible, even if the perception and memory are foggy or incomplete.

There are two major exceptions to the personal knowledge requirement:

(1) The first exception concerns "admissions." As we will see in Chapter Six, statements by a party to a trial that are offered in evidence by the opposing party—"admissions"—are a major exception to the hearsay rule. In addition, an "admission" by the opposing party may be used in evidence even if it is based on second-hand information or guess-work rather than perception. (On the other hand, as we will also see, other hearsay exceptions do require personal knowledge on the part of the person who made the statement.)

(2) The second exception is codified in the last sentence of FRE 602 itself:

This rule does not apply to a witness's expert testimony under Rule 703.

In other words, as we will see in Chapter Nine, opinion testimony by expert witnesses is largely exempt from the personal knowledge rule.

Lay witnesses are also allowed to express opinions, but within a narrow range. In the nineteenth century, some American courts developed a doctrine that lay witnesses must testify to "facts" only, not to "inferences" or "opinions." But description and inference are inextricably intertwined. When we say that "it was going at least 60 miles per hour," or that "he was standing 10, 15 feet away," or that "he was angry," we are reporting our *opinions* (or conclusions, or inferences) based on what we saw, rather than the actual sensory data on which those opinions are based. There is no way to avoid doing this. As a result, the ostensible prohibition of lay opinion testimony never really worked; it was applied inconsistently, and developed a succession of exceptions.[2] The modern rule, as exemplified by FRE 701, is more liberal:

> If a witness is not testifying as an expert, testimony in the form of an opinion is limited to one that is:
>
> **(a)** rationally based on the witness's perception;
>
> **(b)** helpful to clearly understanding the witness's testimony or to determining a fact in issue; and
>
> **(c)** not based on scientific, technical, or other specialized knowledge within the scope of Rule 702.

FRE 701(a) requires personal knowledge as a basis for lay opinion evidence: only opinions based directly on the witness's own perception are admissible. You can testify that your neighbor was speeding (an opinion) if you saw his car whiz by—but not if you believe it because somebody told you that "Carl just whizzed by," or because you know that he usually does that. FRE 701(b) is a rule of preference: if more precise sensory data are available and easy to convey, use them; if not, you may fill in with inferences. Testimony that a car was "pricey" might be "helpful" if the witness doesn't remember or didn't recognize the model, but not if he can testify that it was a 2012 Porsche. Testimony that a vote was "lopsided" would not be "helpful" if the witness could give an actual count, 8 to 10. On the other hand, opinions about more complex or ambiguous conditions are typically allowed even if the witness made more specific observations, on the theory that the opinion conveys more information than most people can describe in specific concrete terms. Thus the opinion that a person was "angry" is admissible even though the witness can testify that he was shouting, had a flushed face, and gestured quickly with trembling hands. (But testimony that a person seen shouting at 100 feet was "angry" probably would be excluded, not for lack

---

[2] See McCormick § 11 for an excellent treatment of this issue. As the New Hampshire Supreme Court explained a hundred and forty years ago:

A constant observer of the trial of cases, examining the testimony for the purpose of ascertaining how many opinions are received and how many rejected, will find ten of the former as often as he finds one of the latter; and, if he is very critical, he will find the ratio much greater than that. Opinions are constantly given. A case can hardly be tried without them. Their number is so vast, and their use so habitual, that they are not noticed as opinions distinguished from other evidence. State v. Pike, 49 N.H. 399, 423 (1870).

of helpfulness but because it is not "rationally based on the witness's perception.")

(FRE 701(c) was added in 2000. Its purpose, as the Advisory Committee on Evidence Rules explained in its Note, is simply to avoid any overlap between expert and lay opinion evidence, and prevent some expert opinion testimony being presented as lay opinion testimony. See Chapter Nine.)

Older common-law evidence cases often purported to prohibit witnesses from testifying to opinions on "ultimate issues," basic questions that had to be resolved by the trier of fact. Like the opinion rule itself, this prohibition proved unworkable and was never consistently applied. In some cases, adherence to the rule required nothing more than an artificial caution in expressing an opinion that would otherwise be objectionable: an expert would not be allowed to testify that a defendant physician's conduct "caused" the plaintiff's injuries, but would be allowed to say that it "might have" done so. For other issues that are "ultimate" in the sense that they are the critical factual question in dispute— intoxication, speed, identity of a person—this "rule" was simply disregarded. Not surprisingly, commentators were scornful of the "ultimate issue rule";[3] Wigmore described its usual justification—to prevent the witness from "usurping the function of the jury"—as "empty rhetoric."[4] The fact is that many witnesses, whether they utter "opinions" or not, testify to propositions which, if accepted by the jury, are dispositive of central issues in dispute.

Modern codified rules of evidence have dispensed with the ultimate issue rule. FRE 704(a) states:

> **In General—Not Automatically Objectionable.** An opinion is not objectionable just because it embraces an ultimate issue.

Subdivision (b) of FRE 704, which was added by amendment in 1984, provides an exception to general rule in FRE 704(a) by restoring a version of the "ultimate issue" rule for expert testimony on the mental state of a criminal defendant. In that context, no witness may state an opinion about the defendant's mental state in terms of the legal standards that define "an element of the crime charged or of a defense." Thus a psychiatrist may testify that the defendant was mentally ill at the time of the crime with which she is charged, but may not testify that the defendant was unable to distinguish right from wrong (assuming that is the test for lack of criminal responsibility in the jurisdiction).

The formal abolition of the ultimate opinion rule does not mean that any opinion on any relevant issue is admissible. As the Advisory Committee for the Federal Rules points out in its Note to Rule 704, Rules

---

[3]   McCormick § 12; 7 Wigmore § 1920–21 at 18–26.

[4]   Id. § 1920 at 18.

701 and 702 require that opinions be *helpful*, and Rule 403 permits the exclusion of opinions that are unfairly prejudicial or waste the court's time. "These provisions afford ample assurances against the admission of opinions which would merely tell the jury what result to reach. . . ." Thus testimony by a witness who says: "In my opinion, you should find the defendant guilty," would be excluded as unhelpful. Similarly, opinions couched in terms of legal criteria are often excluded. Thus "the defendant was driving negligently" is objectionable as "a legal conclusion," but a similar opinion expressed in more "factual" terms—"the defendant was driving at an excessive speed for the road conditions"— may be allowed. The problem with the first statement is not that it addresses an "ultimate issue" but rather that few witnesses are considered experts on the law, and even when legal experts are available jurors are expected to decide legal issues based solely on the judge's instructions and their own lay judgment. Finally, judges almost never allow a witness to express an opinion about the credibility of the testimony of another witness.[5] Courts regard the assessment of the credibility of testimony as a special and exclusive preserve of the trier of fact.[6]

B. OATH

Oath, n. In law, a solemn appeal to the Deity, made binding upon the conscience by a penalty for perjury.

—Ambrose Bierce, THE DEVIL'S DICTIONARY

Traditionally, a witness raises his hand and "swears" to tell "the truth, the whole truth and nothing but the truth, so help me God." This form is conventional rather than mandatory. "Swearing" is not required; referring to God is optional. FRE 603 states:

Before testifying, a witness must give an oath or affirmation to testify truthfully. It must be in a form designed to impress that duty on the witness's conscience.

The Advisory Committee notes underline the open nature of the rule: "no special verbal formula is required."[7]

What is required is a solemn promise to tell the truth. This promise, made in a judicial proceeding, subjects the witness to prosecution for perjury if he is later proven to have willfully lied. Perjury must be

---

[5] By contrast, as we will see in Chapter Five, a witness may sometimes testify that, in her opinion, another witness is *generally* a truthful or an untruthful person.

[6] We saw an example of this special concern to exclude testimony that may embody an opinion or a conclusion about a witness's credibility in Judge Morgan's rulings on the admissibility of evidence about a pre-trial internal Sheriff's Office investigation of the incident at issue in People v. Tellez, Chapter One, pp. 50–51.

[7] Some states do prescribe specific words for the testimonial oath, but nonetheless provide for variations to accommodate witnesses who object to swearing or who do not believe in a deity. See e.g., California Code of Civil Procedure § 2094.

reasonably common. There are lots of trials in which witnesses testify to diametrically opposing versions of the facts, and often the only plausible explanation is that some or all of them are lying. But perjury prosecutions are rare. Perjury requires a specific intent to deceive, which makes it a notoriously difficult crime to prove, and suspected perjury often has a low claim on prosecutorial resources. This is no accident; it reflects a diffuse legal judgment that it is better to let some liars get away with it than to discourage honest testimony by making the threat of prosecution for perjury too menacing.[8] Nonetheless, taking an oath is likely to increase the probability of honest testimony. Some witnesses view oaths very seriously for religious or for civic reasons unrelated to the prospect of prosecution. Others may be motivated by the remote threat of prosecution for perjury, perhaps because they have exaggerated fears of this danger. But probably the most common effect is that taking an oath changes the context of a statement and raises the stakes. To not merely deceive but also to break an oath and commit a felony in the process may offend the values and clash with the self-image of many casual liars. Equally important, the oath may encourage care. A witness who might otherwise guess or unconsciously make up facts to improve her story may stick more closely to what she knows for sure.

C. COMPETENCE

At common law several categories of people were not allowed to testify at all, including: atheists, convicted felons, the parties, and the parties' spouses. These disqualifications have all been swept away, although some of these formerly disqualifying facts (e.g., a felony record) are commonly used to impeach witnesses who do testify. The general rule now is that "Every person is competent to be a witness. . . . " FRE 601.

There are exceptions to this general rule of competence, but they are very narrow. A judge may not testify at a trial in which she presides (FRE 605), and a juror may not testify in a case in which he is sitting (FRE 606(a)). In addition, many states retain "Dead Man Statutes"— rules that prohibit the opposing parties in lawsuits by or against dead people from testifying about dealings with their deceased opponents. The justification for this rule is that since death has sealed the lips of one side to the dispute, the law should prevent the other side from taking unfair advantage by giving an account that cannot be contradicted. There is no such disqualification in the Federal Rules of Evidence, but the second sentence of FRE 601 tells federal courts to apply state-law competence rules in cases which, under the *Erie* doctrine,[9] are subject to state substantive law:

---

[8]   See generally, Comment, Perjury: The Forgotten Offense, 65 J. Crim. L. & Criminology 361 (1974).

[9]   See Erie Railroad v. Tompkins, 304 U.S. 64 (1938).

But in a civil case, state law governs the witness's competency regarding a claim or defense for which state law supplies the rule of decision.

The most common state-law disqualifications that might be subject to this rule are "dead man statutes," and this language was inserted with these laws in mind.

At common law, children and insane people were also incompetent to testify. Some modern codifications include provisions that specifically address these issues. For example, Texas Rule of Evidence 601 disqualifies children, insane persons, and other witnesses who "after being examined by the court, appear not to possess sufficient intellect to relate transactions with respect to which they are interrogated." The Federal Rules contain no such provision. Still, federal judges do conduct preliminary inquiries—commonly for young witnesses but sometimes for those with mental disabilities—to see if they understand the nature of the proceedings and their duties as witnesses. The best formal justification for this procedure is the oath requirement of FRE 603: since a witness must promise to testify truthfully, the judge is impliedly authorized to determine whether the witness understands the meaning of that promise to testify truthfully and has the capacity to keep it.[10]

Problem II-1. Able is charged with arson in New York City. The fire started at about 3 p.m. on Labor Day, 2008. At trial, Able calls his eight-year old son, Jimmy, who, if permitted, will testify: "I called my father around 4 o'clock on Labor Day—after I got back from the picnic—at the number he'd given me. It was a long distance call to Chicago. Uncle Sid answered, and said that Daddy was there but he was outside, walking the dog." The prosecutor objects: "This witness has no personal knowledge as a basis for his testimony." **Assuming Jimmy knows Uncle Sid well and recognized his voice, is the objection valid? Is there another objection the prosecutor could make?**

Problem II-2. Defendant is charged with bank robbery. At trial the teller who paid over the money is called and testifies that he gave the money to a man wearing a bandanna over his face. Asked if he can identify the bandit, the teller says, "I'm not sure, but I think so." Asked if he sees anyone resembling the bandit in the courtroom, he replies, "That man, sitting at the table there, I think he is the robber." (Indicating the defendant.) Asked by the prosecutor whether he is certain, the teller replies, "No, I can't be certain, but I think he looks like the robber." Defendant moves to strike. **Should the motion be granted?**

---

[10] A judge could also exclude testimony from an "incompetent" witness under FRE 403, which gives courts the authority to exclude evidence if its probative value is substantially outweighed by the danger of unfair prejudice, confusion, or waste of time.

II.   INTERROGATION

A. DIRECT EXAMINATION

The distinctive feature of our system of adversarial fact-finding is that the parties present the evidence. In particular, lawyers for the parties call and question witnesses. By contrast, under the civil law systems of adjudication that are used in most continental European countries, the judge calls the witnesses and conducts the primary examinations, with limited supplementary interrogation by the lawyers.

Testifying in a common-law trial is a tricky job. The witness is required to be passive—to answer friendly and hostile questions alike while asking none—to avoid the numerous objections you are now studying, and yet somehow to make sense to a panel of inexperienced jurors. This process only works if the attorneys "prepare" the witnesses: talk to them in advance, learn what they have to say, explain the procedure, rehearse their testimony. Partisan preparation of witnesses has obvious costs: it allows the parties to shape the evidence, and it gives them opportunities to play on the biases of the witnesses. In some countries—for example, Holland—pre-trial contacts between lawyers and witnesses are prohibited. In our system, partisan preparation is not only permitted, it is essential.[11] The lawyer who calls a witness has not just the right but the duty to prepare the witness to testify if the witness is willing, and the opposing lawyer has a corresponding duty to learn as much as possible about the witness's testimony in advance, through interviewing or formal discovery. If everything works as it should, a trial is not a procedure for *obtaining* evidence (since both sides know what's coming) but a forum for *presenting* evidence.[12]

This system gives a great deal of power over the testimony to lawyers in general, and to the direct examiner in particular—the lawyer who chooses the witness and questions her first. To restrict that power, we limit the ability of lawyers to control testimony *during* direct examinations. The major way we do so is by limiting the use of leading questions on direct examination. FRE 611(c) states:

---

[11] The task of preparing a friendly witness to testify is discussed in more detail in the Appendix to this Chapter, infra, pp. 204–209.

[12] This description, of course, is an ideal case. Even with the best possible preparation, some surprises are inevitable in any trial. Moreover, in some cases the parties are unable to prepare thoroughly enough to anticipate all of the evidence. This is most likely in criminal trials in those jurisdictions that still have limited discovery in criminal cases. See Wayne R. LaFave, Jerold H. Israel, Nancy J. King & Orin S. Kerr, Criminal Procedure, § 20.1 (5th ed. 2009). In civil trials, where discovery procedures are usually extensive (see Fed.R.Civ.P. 26), well-prepared lawyers are often able to approximate this ideal.

Leading Questions. Leading questions should not be used on direct examination except as necessary to develop the witness's testimony. . . .

A leading question is a question that suggests the answer. Clear cases are easy to spot: "You're eighteen, aren't you?" "And that took place *before* you ever heard of the Ramco offer, right?" And so forth. Leading questions are disfavored because they allow the direct examiner to tell the witness what to say, and because the direct examiner is presumed to be on good terms with the witness—to represent the side the witness might favor. Leading questions give the direct examiner too much control, and they prevent the jury from hearing the witness relate the details of her observations in her own words. Out-of-court preparation may be necessary, but once they get into court witnesses are expected to testify on direct in their own words and without explicit cues from the lawyers who call them.

A closely related prohibition is captured by the objection that a question has been "asked and answered." This objection (which ordinarily is available only against direct examiners) is designed to deal with a different method of cuing a witness: If the first answer isn't what you had in mind, repeat the question:

Q. How many shots did you hear?

A. Five.

Q. I'm sorry. How many shots were there?

A. Oh, that's right. Six.

If caught in time, the second question may be objectionable as "asked and answered," although judges often allow lawyers more than one chance at posing questions.[13]

As with most rules, the problem with the objection to leading questions is dealing with close calls. Most questions suggest at least some aspects of the expected answer: "You heard six shots in quick succession, didn't you?" is obviously suggestive. But "What did you hear?" already suggests that the witness heard something, and so does "Did you hear anything?" Whether a particular level of suggestiveness matters depends on the context. For example, if a policeman has already testified about making an arrest with his partner, the question "Where was your partner standing when you put the cuffs on Mr. Sullivan?" is not very

---

[13] On cross-examination, the examiner is *entitled* to try to get the witness to change her testimony; indeed, that is one of the purposes of cross-examination. Therefore, the mere fact that a question has been already answered is not an objection. But there is a related objection that may be made if the examiner keeps asking the same question and repeatedly refuses to accept the answer. The problem in that situation is that since the witness clearly will not change her testimony the examination is a waste of the court's time, or abusive to the witness, or perhaps argumentative. Nonetheless, such objections on cross-examination are sometimes mischaracterized as "asked and answered."

suggestive. But what if he hadn't yet mentioned his partner, and the questioning went like this:

Q. Was anybody standing near you when you cuffed Mr. Sullivan?

A. Not that I recall.

Q. Where was your partner standing?

A. Oh, yeah. He was right near me.

In that context, "Where was your partner standing?" is much more suggestive and may be impermissibly leading on direct examination. Trial courts have virtually unlimited discretion in ruling on objections to leading questions.

FRE 611(c), following the common law, permits leading questions on direct examination "as necessary to develop the witness's testimony." This provision allows leading questions on direct to *help* witnesses— for example, to remind a witness of something she has forgotten:

Q. What day was that, when you signed the lease?

A. I don't remember.

Q. Was it Monday, July 10?

A. Yes, that's right.

Leading on direct is also permitted to help witnesses who may have some general difficulty testifying—young children, witnesses with limited mental capacity, and witnesses with imperfect command of English. Finally, leading is permitted on direct examinations concerning "preliminary matters," which in this context means issues that are not disputed. This makes it possible to move quickly through uncontested terrain, and focus on what needs to be decided. For example:

Q. Officer Clam, you are a patrolman for the New York City Police Department, in the 44th Precinct in the Bronx, isn't that so?

A. Yes sir.

Q. And you were on duty on the night of Tuesday, May 25, 2010, in a police cruiser, right?

A. Yes sir.

Q. And at about 11:30 p.m. that night you were in your police car on the Grand Concourse in the vicinity of East 173rd Street, isn't that so?

A· Yes, I was.

So far, the testimony by the officer is merely the frame for the picture that follows. None of what he said is likely to be in dispute, so an objection to the questions as leading ought to be overruled.

From the point of view of the direct examiner, the main vice of leading a witness is not that it is objectionable, but that it diminishes the power of the testimony. A lawyer is not the most credible source of information in a courtroom; everybody knows that you are obliged to say and do whatever serves your client's interests. If a witness sounds like she is following your suggestions and saying what you want her to say, her credibility is reduced. It is far better (if possible) to have a friendly witness give useful testimony in her own words, in response to minimal open-ended inquiries. On the other hand, if your opponent is leading his own witness like a dog on a leash, you may want to let him go ahead and do so rather than object and force him to let the witness speak.

B. CROSS-EXAMINATION

On cross-examination, the rules on leading questions—practical as well as formal—are reversed. The rules permit them—"Ordinarily, the court should allow leading questions . . . on cross-examination . . ." (FRE 611(c))—and in practice, cross-examination of a hostile witness may consist of little but leading questions. The lawyer is best able to prepare such an examination if she has a previous statement from the witness that gives a reasonably complete account of what the witness knows about the matter: a deposition, a signed statement, a recorded interview, testimony at an earlier hearing. With a prior statement in hand the lawyer knows what propositions the witness must agree to, and she can organize those propositions into a set of leading questions that give the witness little opportunity to wander, or indeed to talk:

Q. Within five minutes after my client left, you too left your office, didn't you?

A. Yes.

Q. And you went to Mr. Sterling's office?

A. Yes.

Q. Mr. Sterling was in his office, right?

A. Yes, he was.

Q. When you arrived at his office, Mr. Sterling was alone, wasn't he?

A. Yes.

Q. Incidentally, Mr. Sterling is the District Sales Manager for Impco, right?

A. Right.

Q. He's your immediate supervisor, your boss?

A. Yes.

Q. You told Mr. Sterling that my client had complained about the performance of his rotary mower, didn't you?

A. Yes, I did.

Q. And Mr. Sterling said, "Who cares," or words to that effect?

A. Right.

We have seen several excellent examples of this mode of questioning in the *Tellez* transcript. It enables you to maintain control over a witness who may be out to undermine your case, and who ordinarily will not be available for friendly pre-trial preparation. If the witness strays from the paved path and says more than necessary to respond, you can object to the "non-responsive answer," since a witness is supposed to answer each question on its own terms and not to volunteer additional information.[14] Since this is a hostile cross-examination, you have no interest in enhancing the witness's credibility by giving him a chance to speak in his own voice. On the contrary, this mode of questioning may help to undermine his credibility by creating the impression that he's grudgingly conceding things he'd rather not mention. The type of witness control that is possible with careful preparation and disciplined execution makes cross-examination a powerful tool, for good or ill. Wigmore, a great fan of cross-examination, famously wrote that: "[I]t is beyond any doubt the greatest legal engine ever invented for the discovery of truth."[15] But Wigmore added (less famously), in the same paragraph, that: "A lawyer can do anything with cross examination—if he is skillful enough not to impale his own cause upon it. He may, it is true, do more than he ought to do; he may . . . make the truth appear like falsehood."[16]

The key to a friendly direct examination is to prepare the witness to testify effectively in response to limited cues (non-leading questions) from the examining attorney. The key to a hostile cross-examination is to prepare a set of leading questions that enable the examiner to control the witness, and by doing so to present a useful piece of the picture the examiner intends to paint. Volumes have been written advising attorneys how to do this.[17] We will mention only a few of the key points:

---

[14] In theory, the objection that an answer is non-responsive may only be made by the examining attorney. If the examiner is happy with the answer, and there is no other objection to it, why force the examiner to ask another question to which this answer would be responsive? In practice, some judges let either side object to non-responsive answers. This makes sense as a mechanism to control a witness who keeps volunteering inadmissible evidence that the non-examining attorney cannot anticipate or stop before it has been said and heard.

[15] 5 Wigmore § 1367, p. 32.

[16] Id.

[17] See, e.g., Francis Lewis Wellman, The Art of Cross Examination (1904); Robert E. Keeton, Trial Tactics and Methods, Ch. 3 (1954); Irving Younger, The Advocate's Deskbook: The

• Know what answers the witness must give to every question.

• Only cross-examine with a purpose, and keep to that purpose as economically as possible.

• Ask only leading questions.[18]

• Absolutely never ask the witness to explain.[19]

If you do all that successfully, you can control the examination so tightly that, in the limiting case, the witness can hardly get a word in edgewise.[20]

Direct examination may cover any relevant matter. Cross examination is more restricted. In federal court and in most states you are limited (in some respects) to the same ground that was covered in the direct examination. FRE 611(b):

Essentials of Trying a Case, Ch. 15 (1988); Thomas A. Mauet, Trial Techniques, Ch. VII (7th ed. 2007).

[18] By asking a question, on direct or on cross-examination, you waive any objection to any responsive answer. Let's say you're defending a suspect in a robbery case who was seen at the building where the robbery took place near the time of the crime. You know from a prior statement that a prosecution witness will say he saw your client—William Blake—leave the building at about 11:00 p.m. That helps you because other witnesses will say that the robbery took place after 11:30. If you lead consistently you can make this point without a problem.

Q. A little while later you saw Mr. Blake leave the building? A. Right.

Q. And then you saw him walk south on Darby Street? A. Yes.

Q. And that was right about 11:00 p.m., wasn't it? A. Yes

But if you ask even one innocent sounding open-ended question, everything can change:

Q.   After he left the building, *what did Mr. Blake do*? A. He took out a pint—I think it was gin—drained it, and smashed the bottle on the sidewalk.

The answer is harmful, and might have been objectionable if the prosecutor had elicited it, but you asked for it.

[19] There are hundreds of telling and amusing stories of lawyers shooting themselves in the foot by asking for explanations. Perhaps the most famous is this old and probably apocryphal examination in a criminal trial in which the defendant was charged with felonious assault and battery for biting off the victim's ear:

Q. This fight took place on a dusty field, didn't it? A. Yes.

Q. My client and Mr. Smith were on the ground? A. Yes.

Q. Rolling in the dirt? A. Yes.

Q. And you were about, what, 15 feet away weren't you? A. More or less.

Q. You never saw my client put his mouth on Mr. Smith's ear, did you? A. No.

Q. You never saw him bite Mr. Smith at all did you? A. No.

Q. So *how can you say* that my client bit off Mr. Smith's ear? A. Because I saw him spit it out.

[20] In practice, of course this extreme scenario may be an unrealizable ideal, or even a false goal. Some judges allow witnesses to give more elaborate answers than the questions call for because they feel the limited answers the cross-examiner wants will be misleading. And some witnesses ask for the opportunity to explain their answers, or simply give non-responsive run-on answers. When this happens, a cross-examiner who cuts the witness off runs the risk of looking like a bully, or creating the impression that she has something to hide. The details of dealing with the complexities of the art of cross-examination are beyond the scope of this chapter. Our basic message, however, is simple. The most common problems on cross-examination are not knowing what the witness will say, losing control of the witness and allowing the witness to talk too much.

Scope of Cross-Examination. Cross-examination should not go beyond the subject matter of the direct examination and matters affecting the witness's credibility. The court may allow inquiry into additional matters as if on direct examination.

At common law, a minority of American jurisdictions rejected this limitation and permitted cross examination on any relevant issue. FRE 611(b) codifies the majority rule that the direct examiner controls the scope of testimony—more or less. Many rules of evidence are ambiguous in application, and this one is a good example. For example, if a witness in a spouse abuse case testifies on direct that she saw the defendant beat his wife with a stick on Saturday around 9 p.m., what is the "subject matter" of her direct testimony: what the defendant did around 9 p.m. or what happened between the defendant and his wife that night or the defendant's history of wife beating?

After the cross-examination, the judge will usually permit re-direct examination by the attorney who originally called the witness. Although no Federal Rule specifically speaks to the scope of re-examinations, the usual rule is that re-direct is limited to issues that were brought up for the first time on cross. This makes sense: if re-direct examination were permitted on anything within the "subject matter" of the cross, then, in many cases, it could repeat the entire direct examination, and more. After re-direct, the judge may permit re-cross-examination on any new matters addressed for the first time on re-direct. In practice, judges sometimes allow re-examinations that range beyond these theoretical restrictions.

If the judge decides that a question is outside the scope of the direct, it may still be asked on cross-examination if it bears on the witness's *credibility*, i.e., if it tends to show that he was mistaken or lying. This means that any of the forms of impeachment that are discussed in Chapter Five are proper subjects of cross-examination, regardless of the content of the direct. And even if the judge decides that some questions by the cross-examiner—e.g., about the defendant's behavior two weeks earlier—are both beyond the scope of the direct and not pertinent to credibility, that doesn't mean they can't be asked. The judge "may allow inquiry" into these matters "as if on direct examination"—i.e., without the cross-examiner's unrestricted freedom to use leading questions. Of course the judge can also refuse to "allow inquiry," in which case the cross-examiner will be forced to recall the witness and ask these questions in a real direct examination later in the case, but that is likely to inconvenience the witness and eat up time.

C. IMPEACHING AND LEADING ON DIRECT

Traditionally, at common law, a party was said to "vouch" for the credibility of any witness he called to the stand. One consequence of this rule was that a party could not ordinarily impeach his own witness—call a witness and then present evidence or argument that the witness should not be believed. This archaic rule has been abandoned by the Federal Rules and other codifications of evidence law, which permit any party to impeach any witness. FRE 607 states:

> Any party, including the party that called the witness, may attack the witness's credibility.

The modern rule recognizes that litigants typically cannot choose their witnesses but must call those who happen to know something about the case. A party is not responsible for what a witness says, and shouldn't be bound by it, especially since a witness whom you call to provide crucial evidence on one issue (the light was green) may go ahead and provide damaging testimony that you intend to dispute on another issue (your client was speeding).

The right to impeach, however, is not the same as the right to cross-examine. You are free to impeach on direct, but ordinarily you must do so without leading questions. However, you may use leading questions on direct (whether or not you are impeaching) if you call "a hostile witness, an adverse party, or a witness identified with an adverse party." FRE 611(c)(2). This version of an old common-law rule is based on the realization that sometimes the assumptions that justify the usual rules for direct and cross-examination do not apply. Rule 611(c)(2) recognizes three types of situations in which leading questions should be permitted on direct because the witness is not likely to cooperate with the direct examiner: (1) when one party in a civil case calls the opposing party as a hostile witness,[21] (2) when a party calls an employee, relative, or other person "identified" with the opposing party, (3) when the witness demonstrates hostility to the direct examiner by being evasive, or changing her story, or acting truculent, or unexpectedly giving evidence that damages the direct examiner's case. If the witness is the adverse party, the reversal should be complete: the direct examiner may use leading questions freely, and the party's own attorney, questioning her client on what is formally cross-examination, is restricted to non-leading questions. If the witness is "identified with the adverse party" that will usually be the case. However, if the witness is hostile but unaffiliated, both sides may get to interrogate with leading questions—which makes perfect sense: an ornery outsider can be equally difficult for all parties.

---

[21] In a criminal case, the Fifth Amendment prohibition against compulsory self-incrimination prevents the prosecution from calling the defendant as a witness, and the plaintiff is not a person but a collective entity—the state or "the people"—which cannot take the stand and testify.

"Be advised, Counsellor, the court will not
tolerate a circuslike atmosphere."

D. THE JUDGE'S PLENARY CONTROL

The rules that govern the interrogation of witnesses are subject to an overarching super-rule: The judge controls. FRE 611(a):

Control by the Court; Purposes. The court should exercise reasonable control over the mode and order of examining witnesses and presenting evidence so as to:

    (1) make those procedures effective for determining the truth;

    (2) avoid wasting time; and

    (3) protect witnesses from harassment or undue embarrassment.

In practice, "reasonable control" means that the judge has virtually unreviewable authority to decide how and when questions are put to witnesses. The nature of this authority is reflected in the use of permissive verbs throughout FRE 611: "Cross-examination *should* be limited to the subject matter of the direct examination," "Leading questions *should not* be used on the direct examination of a witness," and so forth. Except in the rarest and most extreme circumstances, rulings on the issues we've discussed in this section are not the stuff of successful appeals.

Most of the practices we've described evolved within this sphere of judicial discretion, and some continue to exist there without specific codified authority. There are no specific federal rules that permit leading questions on direct examination when the witness is a child, or to help a witness who can't remember what she once knew, or on preliminary matters; and there are no codified objections that a question has been asked and answered, or that an answer is non-responsive. Nonetheless, federal judges generally apply these traditional rules in one way or another. Similarly, while no rule refers to the practice, judges sometimes entertain objections that a question "calls for a narrative answer," presumably on the ground that shorter questions and answers give the court and the opposing party better advance notice of potentially objectionable testimony. On the other hand, in other courts or in other cases some witnesses are permitted to narrate at length.

Problem II-3. Laura Adderley was a passenger in a car driven by Walter Cane; she was severely injured in a crash between Walter's car and a car driven by Derek Black. Adderley sues Black for negligence, claiming that he was speeding at the time of the accident, and that his negligent driving caused her injuries. She calls Cane as a witness, and Cane testifies on direct examination about his driving up to the moment of the accident, which, he claims, he did not see coming at all. On cross-examination, the attorney for Black wishes to elicit testimony to the effect that after the collision—while Adderley was lying unconscious in a drug store to which she had been carried—Cane left the scene of the accident without notifying anyone of his identity. **Should the judge permit this line of inquiry? What objection can Laura make?**

III.   OBJECTIONS

A. WHY HAVE EXCLUSIONARY RULES OF EVIDENCE?

The main subject of the law of evidence is the body of exclusionary rules of evidence that lawyers evoke by making objections: irrelevant, unfair prejudice, hearsay, etc. Most of this book is devoted to describing and explaining these rules and their exceptions. In this initial section we discuss the procedures that govern evidentiary objections in general: how to make them and when, who rules on them and how, the effect of errors, and so forth. But first, let's pause to consider a more basic question: Why not let the parties present whatever they will, in whatever form they will, and trust in the self-interest of the adversaries to produce the best available evidence on each side? Couldn't we get along just as well—or better—without all those objections? And if you think this is a ridiculous fantasy, remember that in France, Germany, Spain, Holland, and other civil-law countries, trials are conducted every day without most of these exclusionary rules. Why not do the same here?

There are many answers to these questions, but most of them boil down to two words: lawyers and juries. In civil-law adjudication, the selection and interrogation of witnesses are handled primarily by judges who are specifically trained for that task, and who (presumably) can be trusted to be fair and efficient. In our system lawyers perform these tasks, and they may need rules to push them to serve rather than obstruct the ends of justice. In civil-law trials the evidence is also evaluated primarily by judges—who (presumably) have the experience and discipline to use it appropriately. In common-law trials, the trier of fact is often a jury of lay people, inexperienced in judging cases, whom we do not fully trust; therefore, we exclude evidence that they might misuse.[22]

Jury trials are at the base of the rules of evidence in another respect as well. The use of a bifurcated tribunal, with a jury that decides issues of fact and a judge who decides questions of law, makes it possible to exclude evidence and actually keep the triers of fact from hearing it.[23] The judge, on the other hand, will usually hear evidence even if she does exclude it. Attorneys sometimes seek bench trials when they fear the opposition will attempt to introduce evidence on one point which is likely to have an impermissible but devastating impact in another area. They apparently believe that judges, unlike juries, can separate permissible inferences from the impermissible ones—presumably because they are forced to hear inadmissible evidence all the time. This may be so; but it is unlikely that even judges can make this separation complete. Indeed, Professors Kalven and Zeisel in their pathbreaking study, *The American Jury,* found a number of judges willing to admit that they would have decided cases differently from the jury because they would not have

---

[22] We do not wish this brief contrast between the continental and Anglo-American systems to be read as suggesting that the civil system of judicial fact-finding is superior to the Anglo-American system of jury trial. There is considerable evidence that juries are excellent fact-finders (though they often have trouble understanding the law as it is provided to them); in celebrated cases, juries have been bulwarks of individual liberty and collective freedom; in ordinary cases, they infuse community values into a largely bureaucratic legal system; and as groups, juries have advantages in fact-finding and decision making that even trained individuals cannot match. On the other side, the continental system's obvious advantages are inextricably linked to their methods of training and selecting judges and lawyers, and, in criminal cases, to their procedures for investigating crime. Replacing American jury trials with bench trials would not automatically bring with it many of the strengths of the continental system. Instead, it might create new problems by undermining one of the unique strengths of the system of adjudication that we have developed.

[23] See Mirjan R. Damaska, Evidence Law Adrift 47 (1997).

ignored facts they knew which had not been entered into evidence.[24] Occasionally judges have devised systems in which the litigants in bench trials can have a judge other than the one before whom the case is to be tried rule on some evidentiary objections. This structure would solve the problem, but it is awkward at best, and impossible for unanticipated objections that arise during testimony. In any event, it has rarely been tried.

Most of the exclusionary rules of evidence are designed to prod lawyers or shield jurors, in order to accomplish one or more of the following three goals, in the context of the trial itself:[25]

(i) To Save Time. Evidence that wastes the court's time is not likely to be persuasive, and for the most part experienced lawyers will avoid using it. But lawyers might present wasteful evidence because they don't know any better, or, worse, because they want to delay a decision, or extend some part of a trial to the end of the day or the end of the week, or run up the costs for the other side. If they could do it, lawyers in some cases would filibuster to prevent any decision at all. The rules that exclude evidence that is irrelevant, repetitious, or unduly time consuming are designed to prevent those abuses.

(ii) To Encourage the Presentation of Reliable Information. Some evidence is excluded in order to encourage the parties to present more probative and reliable evidence. Left to their own devices, parties would frequently use the best available evidence simply because it is the most persuasive, but not always. The witness's testimony in person may sound more shaky and less certain than an investigator's sanitized rendition of his story; if it weren't for the hearsay rule, a litigant might prefer to use the second-hand version. Similarly, some of the rules of evidence force parties and their lawyers to obtain and preserve evidence that might otherwise be lost or destroyed—for example the "chain of custody" requirement for many exhibits in criminal cases (see Chapter Ten), and the "best evidence" or original document rule for documentary exhibits (see Chapter Ten).

(iii) To Prevent Misuse. Jurors can misuse evidence in various ways. They can overvalue information; they can undervalue it; they can decide the case on the basis of extraneous facts that make

---

[24]   Harry Kalven, Jr. & Hans Zeisel, The American Jury 115 (1966).

[25]   Most trials are heard by judges alone, without juries, either because the parties waive their rights to trial by jury, or because they have no legal right to a jury trial in the first instance. See infra, note 88 and accompamying text. Nonetheless, we will assume throughout this book that the trier of fact is a jury, for two related reasons: (1) Jury trials present the trickiest problems in the use of evidence, and (2), as a consequence, the rules of evidence have been designed with jury trials in mind. In Section III(H) of this chapter we discuss how these rules are applied in bench trials.

them love or hate a party or a witness; or they can simply fail to understand the evidence and become confused. We try to prevent these problems by giving the jury legal instructions that tell them how to reach a verdict, but—since we don't believe that strategy always works—we also use the more extreme remedy of excluding altogether evidence that may be particularly likely to confuse lead the jury or lead it astray. Many exclusionary rules—including those on relevance, unfair prejudice, hearsay, and character evidence—are designed to serve this purpose.

The three justifications that we have discussed so far are addressed to a single purpose: effective fact-finding in the case at hand. In addition, some exclusionary rules are justified entirely or in part because they serve other purposes altogether:

(iv) To Serve Goals Other Than Accurate Fact-Finding. Several common-law rules exclude evidence of particular types of conduct that are connected to the case: fixing a dangerous condition after an accident, having liability insurance for damage claims caused by the type of accident that occurred, attempting to negotiate a settlement or a plea bargain, offering to help a victim. Some of these items may not be very probative (e.g., insurance), but some are very telling (e.g., an offer to settle for a large sum). All are excluded at least in part in order to encourage people to do those things without fear that their conduct will be used against them in court. In addition, a great deal of highly probative evidence is excluded in order to protect values such as privacy, confidentiality and personal autonomy. These values are the bases for the evidentiary privileges that shield confidential communications between spouses or between attorneys and clients, and that prohibit the state from compelling a person to testify against herself.[26] Privileges such as these are not designed to preserve or improve the accuracy of the fact-finding process, and the justifications for them are unrelated to the form of the trial. They make as much sense in judge-run civil-law trials as in our familiar adversarial common-law trials. And indeed, the major common-law privileges are also available in France, Germany and other civil law countries, frequently in broader forms than those that apply in this country.[27]

Having outlined the main arguments for the exclusionary rules of evidence, we add a caveat. We do not mean to say that all these rules are

---

[26] In criminal cases, prosecution evidence is sometimes excluded because it is the fruit of an illegal search and seizure in violation of the Fourth Amendment, or an illegal interrogation in violation of the Fifth Amendment, or was obtained in violation of the defendant's Sixth Amendment right to counsel. The logic of these exclusions is similar to the logic of evidentiary privileges, although they are traditionally considered rules of criminal procedure rather than rules of evidence.

[27] See Kurt Riechenberg, The Recognition of Foreign Privileges in United States Discovery Proceedings, 9 Nw. J. Int'l L. & Bus. 80 (1988).

necessary or even effective means for achieving those ends. These are the reasons that are commonly given; as you will see in the chapters that follow, sometimes we think they are persuasive, sometimes not.

B. A CLASSIFICATION OF OBJECTIONS

You may object to evidence for many reasons. But the way you do it is usually the same: stand and say "Objection, Your Honor, [blank]," filling in the blank with "irrelevant," or "calls for hearsay," or "leading," or whatever. The phrases you insert may sound similar in context, but they mean very different things. What follows is a simple classification of objections. Some of the objections we list are already familiar; others may be new to you. Don't worry if you aren't sure what a particular objection means. At this point, our aim is just to provide an overview of the different types of issues to which objections may be addressed.

(i) Objections to the Content of Evidence. Objections in this category basically make the argument, *"This evidence is not admissible at all"*—that is, it's not admissible at the trial in which it is offered. Most of the major rules of evidence are implemented by objections of this sort: irrelevant, hearsay, undue prejudice, privileged, improper opinion, inadmissible settlement negotiation, etc.

(ii) Objections to the Foundation for Evidence. These objections, if fully spelled out, say in effect, *"This item of evidence is inadmissible unless the proponent can show something else first."* The main objections in this category are stated in terms of the lack of evidence (or insufficient evidence) on some *foundational issue*: lack of authentication of an exhibit, lack of qualifications for an expert, lack of evidence on some fact that is necessary to make the evidence relevant.[28]

(iii) Objections to the Form of a Question. These objections basically say, *"The testimony may be admissible, but you've asked the wrong sort of question."* The most important objection to the form of a question is that it is leading (on direct); other objections in this

---

[28] A related objection is that a question "assumes a fact not in evidence"—i.e., that it implies something that is not in evidence, and cannot be denied by a responsive answer. Thus, "Have you stopped beating your wife," is objectionable if the witness has not already admitted to beating his wife, but okay if he has. In other words, the question is objectionable until the record contains a statement from the witness that he did beat his wife. (On the other hand, "You beat your wife, didn't you" is not objectionable on this ground. It does imply that the witness beats his wife, but that implication can be unambiguously denied by saying, "No." Even so, the question should not be asked unless the questioner expects, in good faith, that the answer will be "Yes," since even if beating is denied the jury may think that something improper was going on. See Chapter Five, pp. 401–403.)

group are that the question calls for a narrative answer, or is compound or confusing.[29]

(iv) Objections to Timing and Sequence. Sometimes the only thing wrong with evidence is that it is coming *at the wrong time.* A non-responsive or volunteered answer is objectionable because it didn't follow an appropriate question; cross examination beyond the scope of the direct is objectionable because it's not the cross-examiner's turn to open up new issues; cumulative or repetitive evidence is objectionable because it comes after other similar evidence on the same issue; and a question that's been asked and answered is objectionable on direct because the same question was asked before.

These categories of objections were not created equal. Objections to content are the most important, they are subject to the most explicit regulation by rules and statutes, and they are the most likely to be addressed on appeal. Foundational questions are sometimes quite important, and occasionally at issue on appeal, but the range of judicial discretion is greater than with questions of content. Objections to the form of questions, or to timing or sequence, are considerably less important, and almost entirely within the trial judge's unreviewable discretion.

C. WAIVING, PRESERVING, AND REVIEWING ERROR

1. General Principles

As we have mentioned,[30] to invoke an exclusionary rule of evidence you must make a timely and specific objection. Otherwise, the trial judge can ignore your problem and you won't be allowed to raise it on appeal. On the other side, if you want to be able to complain on appeal about an improper exclusion you must make an offer of proof to inform the judge of the content of the excluded evidence, unless it was apparent from the context. But what does all this really mean? What do you have to do and what are the consequences of failing to do so? Perhaps the best way to

---

[29] The objection that a question is "argumentative" is often described as an objection "to the form of the question." In terms of this classification, it is better categorized as an objection to the content of the evidence. An "argumentative" question to a friendly witness is often an attempt to get impermissible lay opinion testimony; e.g., "so all in all, the best explanation for the accident is that your accelerator stuck after you lifted your foot off the clutch?" And an argumentative question to the hostile witness is typically designed to insinuate the *questioner's* opinion into the evidence: "Do you expect us to believe that after ten years in San Francisco you didn't know that it's foggy in the summer?" It is called "argumentative" not because the attorney is necessarily arguing with the witness, but because the attorney is making the kind of point that should be reserved for closing argument to the jury.

[30] See Chapter One, pp. 9–10

answer this question is by reference to four general policies that apply across the range of evidentiary rules:

a. *Evidence Is Presumed Admissible*

The general rule of admissibility is codified by FRE 402:

Relevant evidence is admissible unless any of the following provides otherwise:

- the United States Constitution;
- a federal statute;
- these rules; or
- other rules prescribed by the Supreme Court.

Irrelevant evidence is not admissible.

In other words, if there's no specific rule excluding relevant evidence, it comes in.[31] In addition, although it's not stated explicitly in the rules, the drafters intended that close calls go to the proponent of the evidence.[32] Thus, for example, the Advisory Committee Notes on FRE 801(a) (concerning the definition of hearsay) state: "ambiguous and doubtful cases will be resolved . . . in favor of admissibility."

b. *The Parties Control the Case*

Trial in our system is viewed as a method of sorting out differences between the parties. The parties frame the issues, and present the evidence. If neither side makes a claim, it is not heard; if neither side calls a witness, she does not testify.[33] Similarly, the parties are responsible for invoking the rules of evidence, for two reasons: (1) The parties are entitled to decide which objections to raise, and when. (2) In many cases the judge needs to hear from the parties in order to know how to rule. Without the information the attorneys supply in their objections, arguments, and offers of proof, the judge would not understand the

---

[31] FRE 402 also has the apparent effect of abolishing common law objections. In theory, the only objections that can be raised in federal court are those that are spelled out in a rule or statute. In fact, federal courts and state courts applying similar rules often entertain traditional objections that are not mentioned in the text of any rule or statute. Presumably, their authority to do so stems from FRE 403, which allows courts to exclude relevant evidence if it is likely to be unduly prejudicial, confusing, or time consuming; from FRE 611, which give judges "reasonable control" over the interrogation of witnesses; and perhaps from FRE 102 which provides that "[T]hese rules should be construed so as to administer every proceeding fairly, eliminate unjustifiable expense and delay, and promote the development of evidence law, to the end of ascertaining the truth and securing a just determination."

[32] See Thomas M. Mengler, The Theory of Discretion in the Federal Rules of Evidence, 74 Iowa L. Rev. 413, n.4 (1989) describing Congressional testimony by members of the Advisory Committee emphasizing that the proposed rules favor admissibility.

[33] Judges do have the authority, codified in FRE 614, to call and question witnesses. In practice, they rarely call witnesses. They are more likely to ask questions of witnesses called by the parties, but if they do, they generally ask only a few. Most American judges believe in party control—which is hardly surprising, since they are mostly recruited from the ranks of experienced trial lawyers, for whom party control is almost universally an article of faith.

purpose of evidence that seems irrelevant, or the danger of evidence that seems innocuous.

c. Objections Can be Waived

This follows from the first two principles: the parties are not required to assert available objections, and, if they don't do so, we fall back on the general principle that evidence is presumed to be admissible. Indeed, in the absence of an objection evidence is almost always admissible, and evidence that is admitted without objection may be fully relied upon by the jury, even if it would have been reversible error to admit that evidence over a proper objection.

d. The Trial Judge Is Rarely Reversed

We made this point at the beginning of the book, but it's worth repeating: Appellate courts rarely reverse judgments because of errors in evidentiary rulings, and on many issues the trial-court judge has such a wide discretion that it's hard for her to err in the first place.[34] In *General Electric v. Joiner* [35] the Supreme Court wrote that "abuse of discretion is the proper standard of review of a district court's evidentiary rulings."[36] As a categorical statement of law, this is simply wrong. As we will see, there are many rules of evidence for which the judge's task is to apply the law to the facts, not to exercise discretion. For example, a federal court has no discretion to admit evidence of a confidential statement made by a client to her attorney (see Chapter Eight), and no discretion to exclude evidence, offered for the purpose of impeachment, that a witness was convicted of a crime involving dishonesty or false statement (see Chapter Five, discussing FRE 609(a)(2)). But the practical implication of the Supreme Court's statement is more important. The Court is so accustomed to deferring to trial court judges on evidentiary issues that it has come to assume that trial judges have discretion to admit or exclude evidence in all situations.

---

[34] A 1982 study of 544 criminal appeals in the California Court of Appeal found that improper admission of prejudicial evidence was the most common claim on appeal. The issue was presented in 216 cases, 40% of the total, but defendants obtained reversal or modification in only 6 of those cases—a success rate of 2.8%. Claims of improper exclusion of defense evidence were raised in 85 cases—16% of the total—but not one was successful. Thomas Y. Davis, Affirmed: A Study of Criminal Appeals and Decision-Making Norms in a California Court of Appeal, 1982 Am. B. Found. Res. J. 543, 564, 616. Another study found that in 1990 only 30 federal judgments were reversed because of evidentiary error—in a system that conducts approximately 20,000 trials each year! Margaret A. Berger, When, If Ever, Does Evidentiary Error Constitute Reversible Error?, 25 Loy. L.A. L. Rev. 893 (1992). Moreover, "Examination of [those thirty] cases indicates (1) that some of the alleged errors are not really evidentiary errors, and (2) that in a number of cases an element other than evidentiary error may have accounted for the appellate court's response. . . . " Id. at 895.

[35] 522 U.S. 136 (1997).

[36] Id. at 517. See also Kumho Tire v. Carmichael, 526 U.S. 137 (1999).

2. Avoiding Waiver

How do these principles play out in practice? FRE 103 sets out what amounts to an obstacle course for a party that wants to raise evidence issues on appeal—or rather two parallel obstacle courses, the objection, and the offer of proof:

(a) Preserving a Claim of Error. A party may claim error in a ruling to admit or exclude evidence only if the error affects a substantial right of the party and:

> **(1)** if the ruling admits evidence, a party, on the record:
>
>> **(A)** timely objects or moves to strike; and
>>
>> **(B)** states the specific ground, unless it was apparent from the context; or
>
> **(2)** if the ruling excludes evidence, a party informs the court of its substance by an offer of proof, unless the substance was apparent from the context.

(b) Not Needing to Renew an Objection or Offer of Proof. Once the court rules definitively on the record—either before or at trial—a party need not renew an objection or offer of proof to preserve a claim of error for appeal.

a. *Objections to Admission of Evidence*

Waiving an objection is easier than falling off a log—all you have to do is keep your mouth shut. You don't even have to keep it shut for long, since you're supposed to object to evidence at the earliest available opportunity. If a question calls for inadmissible testimony, you're supposed to object immediately, if possible before the answer is given. If an unanticipated answer is inadmissible, you're supposed to object and move to strike the testimony right away. If you wait you'll probably find that you're late, that the objection has been waived. The purpose of this timeliness requirement is to minimize the harm—to keep out the inadmissible evidence in the first place, or to let the judge know about the problem in time to give cautionary instructions or otherwise limit the damage. In addition, a timely objection gives the opposing party a chance to try to cure the problem and get the evidence admitted, if that can be done.

A particular trap is keeping quiet because you have already made an adequate objection to a similar question. Unless the judge allows you to make a "continuing objection" to a category of questions,[37] you must object every time a witness is asked an objectionable question or gives an objectionable answer. For example, suppose a witness mentioned a hearsay statement ("Mary told me that Dr. Ellis was out"), and an

---

[37] See infra pp. 168–170.

appropriate objection was made and overruled. That objection must be repeated (though perhaps with less specificity) each time the witness repeats that hearsay statement. A failure to repeat the objection might even be taken as a waiver of the original objection that *was* made.

Keeping quiet is not the only way to waive an objection. You not only need to speak, you have to say the right thing: you must make a *specific* and *correct* objection. Consider the following situation:

OPPOSING ATTORNEY: Q. What did Mr. Barnes do after he hung up the phone?

WITNESS: A. He told me that Jane Nichols just told him she had already sold the house.

YOU: I object, Your Honor, and move to strike. The answer is. . .

Let's assume that the objection "hearsay" is correct and should be sustained, and the objection "irrelevant" is incorrect and should be overruled. (Incidentally, either way the objection is timely, even though it comes after the answer, because the objectionable nature of the testimony was not apparent from the question.)

If you say "hearsay" everything is fine. If the objection is overruled, you can appeal the error. On the other hand, if you say "irrelevant" then there is no error to appeal—the objection on that ground was *properly* overruled.[38] You had a good objection on hearsay grounds, but you waived it by not making it. But what if you make a "general objection"— you add no grounds at all, or a meaningless catchall formula like "irrelevant, incompetent and immaterial"? Again, you can't appeal. You didn't help the judge enough by telling her what was wrong with the evidence you wanted her to exclude.[39] In short, you waive an objection unless you say the right thing, and say it quickly. (And even so, you may waive it by other means—by agreeing to a waiver in advance,[40] or by "opening the door" to the inadmissible evidence by presenting the same

---

[38] See, e.g., United States v. Wilson, 966 F.2d 243, 246 (7th Cir. 1992) (objection based on relevance (FREs 401 and 402) did not alert court to claim that evidence was unduly prejudicial (FRE 403)). The requirement that an objection be specific may apply to the legal authority for the objection as well as the underlying issue. In some courts, if you don't say that you are objecting under the federal constitution—or more specifically under the, say, the Fifth or the Sixth Amendment—you may not claim federal constitutional error on appeal even if you raised a similar claim under state law.

[39] See, e.g., Een v. Consolidated Freightways, 220 F.2d 82, 87–88 (8th Cir. 1955) (Objection that the question was "incompetent, irrelevant, immaterial, calling for speculation, guess and conjecture, obviously invading the province of the jury, calling for a conclusion" is not sufficiently specific where the counsel's objection was that either the witness was not qualified to answer the question or that the question was not a proper question for expert testimony.)

[40] See e.g., United States v. Mezzanatto, 513 U.S. 196 (1995), holding that an agreement to waive FRE 410, which excludes evidence of statements made during plea negotiations, is enforceable, at least when the evidence is used to impeach testimony by the defendant who made the statement.

evidence or related evidence,[41] or other evidence on the same inadmissible issue.[42])

What if the judge sustains the general objection? Would that ruling be reversed on appeal because it was insufficiently specific? No; in most cases the appellate court (if it says anything at all on the issue) will affirm a ruling sustaining a general objection if there was any plausible basis for properly excluding the evidence. In effect, the higher courts will assume that the trial judge had the correct ruling in mind. But what if the trial judge excludes the evidence on the *erroneous* basis that it was irrelevant? Again, some appellate courts will affirm the ruling, despite the error, because there was another unstated ground on which the evidence could properly have been excluded. The theory is that it makes little sense to send the case back for retrial just so the judge can make the same ruling on a different basis.[43]

Stepping back for a second, it's easy to see that these rules of review are direct applications of the principles that we started with. We expect evidence to be admissible, so you have to make a clear and specific argument to keep it out. You don't have to object if you don't want to—we're happy to admit objectionable evidence if no one complains—but if you do object you have to do it in a manner that is most helpful to the judge. And finally, whether she says the evidence is In or Out, the judge always wins if you don't dot your i's and cross your t's—and if you do, the judge usually wins anyway.

b. *Claims of Erroneous Exclusion of Evidence*

Strictly speaking, you don't need to object to the exclusion of your own evidence. Your main move is to *offer* it; it's the opposition that *objects*. However, you do have to respond to any objection that's raised and alert the court to the "substance of the evidence" by making an "offer of proof." How you do so may vary, as we have noted,[44] from a simple statement by the attorney to a dress rehearsal of sworn testimony outside the presence of the jury. But regardless of its form, if the offer of proof to the trial judge doesn't include the information that is necessary to make

---

[41] See e.g., United States v. Silvers, 374 F.2d 828, 832 (7th Cir. 1967), holding that the defendant's use of his prison experience to present an insanity defense waived any objection to erroneously admitted testimony on his prior convictions.

[42] See Warren Live Stock Co. v. Farr, 142 F. 116, 117 (C.C.A.Colo.1905), holding that the introduction of an inadmissible issue allows one's adversary to introduce counter evidence on the same issue. See also All American Life and Casualty Co. v. Oceanic Trade Alliance Council International, Inc., 756 F.2d 474, 479 (6th Cir. 1985). The issue of "door opening" came up in the *Tellez* case, Chapter One, p. 60. Notice in those passages how the claim that the objecting party himself introduced related evidence makes it unnecessary for the judge to decide whether the evidence at stake *is* in fact inadmissible.

[43] See, e.g., Tooley v. Bacon, 70 N.Y. 34, 37 (1877); Palm v. Kulesza, 333 Mass. 461, 131 N.E.2d 472, 473 (Mass. 1956); G.E.B. v. S.R.W., 422 Mass. 158, 661 N.E.2d 646, 654 (Mass. 1996); Utley v. Healy, 663 N.E.2d 229, 232 (Ind.Ct.App.1996); Bowman v. McDonald's Corp., 916 S.W.2d 270, 279 (Mo.Ct.App.1995).

[44] See Chapter One, pp. 10–11.

your argument on appeal, you may be out of luck. For example, in *Saltzman v. Fullerton Metals Co.*[45] the issue was whether a management training program run by the defendant was "bona fide" for the purposes of the Equal Pay Act. After three witnesses had testified on the subject, the plaintiff attempted to ask similar questions of a fourth witness and was cut short by the judge. In challenging that exclusion, the plaintiff's attorney made the following offer of proof:

> I think that the evidence would show that the training program was not a formal training program and it did not reach the level that would sustain the burden of proof of defendant's affirmative defense in regard to a bona fide training program.[46]

In other words, the plaintiff's attorney explained (in general terms) what the evidence would show and why it was *relevant* to the case—which sounds like the "substance" of the evidence that is mentioned in FRE 103(a)(2). Unfortunately for him, the issue on appeal was whether the evidence was properly excluded as *cumulative*—i.e., redundant—given that three previous witnesses had testified on the same issue. The plaintiff had an answer in the Circuit Court. This witness "would have provided more specific information about the training program than [the previous witnesses] because he appeared to possess more authority over the program"[47]—but apparently he never made that point in the trial court, so the appellate court would not consider it:

> If plaintiff's counsel had alerted the district court to the . . . particular reasons for Riskind's continued testimony now asserted on appeal, the district court may have reversed its earlier position. Such is the salutary purpose behind an offer of proof.[48]

Of course, at the trial itself it might not have been nearly so clear that the testimony was being excluded because it appeared to be cumulative. In other words, to avoid being shut out on appeal, you may have to let the judge know why your evidence ought to be admitted over any plausible objection, stated or unstated.

3. Escape Clauses

FRE 103(a)(1)(B), like the common law from which it was derived, recognizes that the specific ground for an objection need not be stated if it is "apparent from the context." Appellate courts occasionally rest on this ground. If, over your objection that it's irrelevant, three witnesses have been allowed to testify to the sequence of floats in the Macy's

---

[45] 661 F.2d 647 (7th Cir. 1981).

[46] Id. at 652.

[47] Id.

[48] Id. at 653.

Thanksgiving Day Parade, a general objection to a fourth witness on the same topic will suffice. Sometimes the basis for the objection may be inferred simply from the evidence that you seek to exclude. If the question is: "How did Ms. Blye describe the accident?" the objection "hearsay" is so obvious that you may not need to state it specifically (provided you *do* object).[49] But don't count on this sort of treatment, especially if the specific basis hasn't been stated in an earlier objection.

If an objection applies to a whole category of questions, you may ask the judge to dispense with the requirement of a specific objection to each question and to allow you to make a "continuing objection:"

> Your Honor, may we have a continuing objection to any testimony by this witness about the Macy's Thanksgiving Day Parade, on the ground that it is irrelevant under Rules 401 and 402?

If the request is granted, similar testimony by other witnesses may also be brought within its terms. ("I'd like to renew our continuing objection to any testimony pertaining to the Macy's parade.")

For offers of proof the escape clause is more powerful: If the substance of the evidence "was apparent from the context" (FRE 103(a)(2)) you don't have to make any offer of proof at all. The common case is when you ask a leading question. If the judge sustains an objection to: "You never saw Mr. Shapiro again, did you?" you're not going to be faulted for failing to put on the record that you believe the witness, if permitted, would testify that he never saw Mr. Shapiro again.

In some jurisdictions attorneys are specifically exempt from the duty of making offers of proof in order to preserve a claim of error if the evidence at issue was excluded during cross-examination.[50] To the extent that leading questions are used on cross-examination, offers of proof may be needed less often, but that doesn't justify an exemption in cases where the substance of the excluded evidence is *not* apparent. The exception is sometimes explained on the ground that in cross-examination, unlike direct examination, a lawyer is not held to *know* what a witness will say, but the argument doesn't wash. In fact, lawyers should (and often do) know what answers they will get to questions on cross-examination,[51] and when they don't they can still say what they *hope* to prove. Perhaps the strongest argument for this special dispensation is that "such an offer would reveal to the witness and opposing counsel the direction of the

---

[49] See, e.g., Floy v. Hibbard, 227 Iowa 149, 287 N.W. 829 (1939).

[50] See, e.g., Ohio Evid. R 103(A)(2); California Evidence Code § 354(c).

[51] See supra, pp. 151–153.

questioning,"[52] and give them a chance to undermine effective cross-examination.

FRE 103(a)(2) makes no distinction between direct and cross-examination. Some argue that even without any special provision, the requirement of offers of proof should be relaxed on cross-examination,[53] and many trial court judges do just that. On the other hand, even courts that operate under blanket exemptions from offers of proof on cross sometimes require cross-examiners to explain what they're up to. For example, in *People v. Coleman* [54] the California Court of Appeal held that despite California's Evidence Code § 354(c) (which exempts cross-examiners from the offer of proof requirement), "it should have been clear that the judge was unaware of the materiality of the question if, indeed it had a material purpose." Therefore, since "the defense counsel made no offer of proof or other attempt to explain a relevant purpose of the question" the defendant can raise no claim on appeal because "[t]here was not abuse of discretion upon which error can be predicated."[55] In short, on this issue (and on many others) the formal rules of evidence make less difference than you might expect. With or without a codified exemption, appellate judges may be less demanding on offers of proof on cross than on direct examination, and, with or without an explicit exemption, they may find that the failure to make an offer of proof is a waiver.

Finally, there is the mother of all escape clauses—the plain error rule—which is codified in FRE 103(e):

> **Taking Notice of Plain Error.** A court may take notice of a plain error affecting a substantial right, even if the claim of error was not properly preserved.

In other words, an appellate court can decide to excuse non-compliance with these rules and to consider a claim that has been waived, if it thinks an injustice has been done. As the Advisory Committee points out, "In the nature of things, the application of the plain error rule will be more likely with respect to the admission of evidence than to exclusion, since failure to comply with normal requirements of offers of proof is likely to produce a record which simply does not disclose the error."

Do not rely on the plain error doctrine. It is a discretionary power of appellate courts. It is available for serious errors of any sort, but it is

---

[52] In re Anthony P., 167 Cal.App.3d 502, 511, 213 Cal.Rptr. 424, 429 (1985). With respect to the witness, this problem can be avoided by making the offer outside the witness's hearing, but that takes time and may be awkward.

[53] McCormick § 51; cf. Saltzman v. Fullerton Metals Co., supra note 45, at 653 n.8.

[54] 8 Cal.App.3d 722, 87 Cal.Rptr. 554 (1970).

[55] Id. at 8 Cal.App.3d at 730–31, 87 Cal.Rptr. at 559. For a pre-evidence code case to the same effect, see People v. Diaz, 206 Cal.App.2d 651, 666, 24 Cal.Rptr. 367, 375–376 (1962). In some cases, courts operating under Cal. Evid. Codes § 354(c) or similar rules simply ignore the exception for cross-examination and uphold exclusionary rulings because no offer of proof was made, e.g., People v. Alfaro, 61 Cal.App.3d 414, 422, 132 Cal.Rptr. 356, 360 (1976).

rarely exercised—and especially not for errors in admitting or excluding evidence.[56] Moreover, even in the context of the plain error rule—which specifically allows courts to consider objections that have been waived— courts may find a way to use the silence of the trial lawyer against his client. For example, in *Helminski v. Ayerst Labs.*[57] the Sixth Circuit noted that the inadmissible statements at issue were made several times without objection. From this the court reasoned that there was no plain error, since the party's own attorney apparently did not "perceive the issue as one which affected the substantial rights of his client."[58]

D. HARMLESS ERROR

The harmless error doctrine pervades American appellate review. It requires courts to consider an error in the context of the trial as a whole and decide "what effect the error had or reasonably may be taken to have had upon the jury's decision."[59] The question is whether, considering everything else that happened "the error itself had substantial influence."[60] If so, the judgment must be reversed; if not, the error is harmless. If the error is constitutional, the court must be convinced that it was harmless beyond a reasonable doubt.[61] For evidentiary rulings in federal court, the harmless error doctrine is codified in FRE 103(a): "A party may claim error in a ruling to admit or exclude evidence only if the error affects a substantial right of the party . . ." Other jurisdictions use stronger language. California Evidence Code Sections 353 and 354, for example, state that relief on appeal will be denied unless the error "resulted in a *miscarriage of justice.*"

Harmless error is an imprecise, case-specific concept. It's hard to say what it means, and it is applied differently in different areas of the law. For evidentiary rulings, it is a powerful force limiting the scope of review. Appellate courts often find error in evidentiary rulings but say it was harmless, or, less visibly but probably more frequently, ignore evidentiary issues entirely if they think any error would have been harmless in the context of the case as a whole. This has two related consequences for trials, as explained by Professor Thomas Mengler.[62] *First*, it focuses attention on the overall fairness of the trial rather than on the correctness of individual rulings:

---

[56] "[T]he plain error exception to the contemporaneous objection rule is to be 'used sparingly, solely in those circumstances in which a miscarriage of justice would otherwise result.' " United States v. Young, 470 U.S. 1, 15 (1985) (quoting United States v. Frady, 456 U.S. 152, 163 n. 14 (1982)).

[57] 766 F.2d 208 (6th Cir. 1985).

[58] Id. at 211.

[59] Kotteakos v. United States, 328 U.S. 750, 764 (1946).

[60] Id. at 765.

[61] Chapman v. California, 386 U.S. 18, 24 (1967).

[62] Mengler, supra note 32.

By making evidentiary errors grounds for reversal only if they affect a substantial right of the party, the harmless error rule tells losing litigants they have no cause to complain if they were able to present the core of their case fairly to the fact-finder, without too much prejudice poisoning their presentation.[63]

Second, it undermines the value of appellate decisions as precedents that interpret and give content to the rules of evidence:

Because the harmless error rule tells the appellate courts to base their decisions on a gestalt view of the overall fairness of each trial, appellate evidence decisions usually do not tell third parties what counts as reversible error [since to understand that one needs to be familiar with the entire record]. By its operation, the harmless error rule consequently takes some of the ruleness out of the Federal Rules.[64]

On the other hand, the harmless error rule may also serve to protect the rules of evidence. The possibility of finding harmless error reduces the number of "hard cases" that might make "bad law"—cases in which an appellate court is convinced the outcome is just despite procedural flaws, and which therefore tempt that court to distort procedural rules in order to uphold the trial court's judgment. From this perspective, the harmless error rule may be underused. Throughout this book you will see instances in which evidentiary rules have been altered or ignored when a more principled decision might have acknowledged error and affirmed nonetheless.

––––––––––

Problem II-4. Jocelyn Normand is injured when she falls from a ski lift in a 50 mile-per-hour gust of wind. She sues Sky Lift, Inc., the manufacturer of the lift, and the Snow Bird Ski Resort, alleging that Sky Lift designed and manufactured a defective lift that was dangerous in windy conditions, and that Snow Bird negligently operated the lift in dangerous conditions. The claims are tried jointly. At trial Normand calls Martin Sales, the Snow Bird Ski Resort lift supervisor who was on duty at the time of the accident. The following is a portion of Mr. Sales' direct examination:

Q. (by counsel for plaintiff Jocelyn Normand) Didn't Bob Turlow—the state safety engineer who investigated this accident—say that lifts like that should never be operated with winds over 35 miles-per-hour?

COUNSEL FOR DEFENDANT SNOW BIRD SKI RESORT: Objection, Your Honor, irrelevant.

––––––––––––––––––––

[63] Id. at 454.

[64] Id. at 456–57.

COUNSEL FOR DEFENDANT SKY LIFT, INC.: And also hearsay, Your Honor.

THE COURT: Overruled. You may answer.

A. Yes.

The jury finds for defendant Sky Lift, Inc., on the products' liability claim, but for the Plaintiff Normand and against Defendant Snow Bird Ski Resort on the negligence claim. Snow Bird appeals. Assume that the evidence described above was in fact relevant but inadmissible hearsay. **How should the appellate court treat Snow Bird's claim on appeal that this evidence was improperly admitted?**

Problem II-5. Plaintiffs Darci and Linda White sue the Black & Tan Oil Company for nuisance, negligence and trespass, claiming that leaks, fumes and other pollution from drilling operations on Black & Tan's land killed vegetation and caused bare areas on the Whites' adjacent property. At trial the Whites' called Jim Plank, district operations manager of Black & Tan Oil. Here is a portion of his direct examination.

Q. (by counsel for the plaintiff): You had pollution complaints from other land owners in the area, didn't you? **A.** Yes, a few.

Q. In fact, Black & Tan bought two tracts of land in this area to resolve other pollution complaints, didn't it?

DEFENSE COUNSEL: Objection, Your Honor.

THE COURT: Counsel, please approach the bench.

THE FOLLOWING PROCEEDINGS WERE HAD IN OPEN COURT OUT OF THE HEARING OF THE JURY.

PLAINTIFF'S COUNSEL: It's relevant because it shows that there was pollution nearby.

DEFENSE COUNSEL: Your Honor, it's irrelevant. There were no bare patches on those plots.

THE COURT: Do you say there were bare patches on the parcels they bought?

PLAINTIFF'S COUNSEL: No, Your Honor.

THE COURT: The objection is sustained.

The jury finds for the defendant, the Black & Tan Oil Company, and the Whites appeal. They claim, among other issues, that the testimony described above was excluded in error since it would have shown, if they had been permitted to proceed, that the parcels that Black & Tan bought were polluted with the same chemicals that they claim polluted their own land. **How should the appellate court treat this assignment of error?**

E. THE ROLES OF JUDGE AND JURY

1. Issues of Law

When evidence is offered and objected to, the decision on admissibility may turn on an interpretation of law or on a finding of fact. When the decision turns on an interpretation of law, courts have no difficulty allocating responsibility: only the judge is responsible. Suppose that Peter turns to Rita for confidential legal advice; Rita is a recent law school graduate but has not taken a bar examination. These facts are not in dispute. Later, at a trial, Rita is placed on the witness stand and asked to reveal Peter's confidences. Peter claims the attorney-client privilege. The party seeking Rita's testimony responds that the privilege does not apply because Rita was not a member of the bar at the time Peter confided in her. Whether a person must be a member of the bar for communications with that person to qualify for the protection of the attorney-client privilege is purely a question of law which the judge will decide without in any way involving the jury.

2. Most Preliminary Issues of Fact

Matters are only slightly more difficult when the admissibility of evidence turns on findings of fact. FRE 104(a) states the general rule:

> **In General.** The court must decide any preliminary question about whether a witness is qualified, a privilege exists, or evidence is admissible. In so deciding, the court is not bound by evidence rules, except those on privilege.

In general, the judge determines all questions of admissibility. (The exceptions to this general rule are governed by FRE 104(b), and related provisions. They are discussed in the next subsection.) If the admissibility of evidence turns in whole or in part on some matter of fact, the judge is usually responsible for determining whether that fact exists. Ordinarily, allocating this fact-finding responsibility to the judge serves six goals:[65] minimizing the complexity of the jury's task; enhancing the predictability of results; preserving with precision issues for appeal; keeping the prejudicial material from the jury; vindicating the policies of the privileges and other exclusionary rules; and saving time at the trial.

---

[65] These six policies were first identified in John M. Maguire & Charles S.S. Epstein, Preliminary Questions of Fact in Determining the Admissibility of Evidence, 40 Harv. L. Rev. 392, 393–95, 412 (1927). We do not necessarily agree with all the arguments made in favor of the division of responsibility. See, e.g., Stephen A. Saltzburg, Standards of Proof and Preliminary Questions of Fact, 27 Stan. L. Rev. 271, 272 n.2 (1975). See also Edmund M. Morgan, Functions of Judge and Jury in the Determination of Preliminary Questions of Fact, 43 Harv. L. Rev. 165, 169 (1929). But these arguments have been accepted in many jurisdictions.

Let us vary our earlier example so that Peter's right to claim the attorney-client privilege turns on an issue of fact. Assume that Peter claims that he reasonably believed that Rita was an attorney, and that under the laws of the forum state a reasonable belief that a confidant is an attorney will justify a claim of privilege. In that situation the judge must determine whether Peter believed Rita was an attorney, and if so, whether this belief was reasonable. This determination may be made out of the presence of the jury. The hearing is likely to be relatively brief. The judge is likely to have had experience in deciding cases of this kind; he may know how other courts have dealt with similar cases, and he may, through his own questioning, be able to pinpoint those aspects of the matter which he thinks are crucial to a resolution of the issue. If the judge relies on evidence which is inadmissible under the ordinary rules of evidence, as he is generally allowed to do, the jury will not learn of it. The jury will also not learn of information that is relevant to the preliminary question, but irrelevant and perhaps prejudicial on the main issue on trial. If, as sometimes happens, the possible privilege must be breached slightly to determine whether any privilege exists, this may occur in chambers so that the dissemination of privileged information is kept to a minimum. Finally, if the judge decides that the privilege applies and the testimony should be excluded, care may be taken that the jurors do not learn of the kind of information that has been kept from them.

But what if the decision on the availability of the privilege were given to the jury? This might be done in one of two ways. First, the trial might be interrupted and the jury asked for an interlocutory judgment on the issue of whether Peter reasonably believed Rita to be a lawyer. This would be time-consuming, if for no other reason than the jury's need to deliberate. The jury's concentration on the main issues in the case would be disrupted. Problems of inadmissible or prejudicial evidence might also exist. Finally, the jury would learn of the kind of evidence one party was seeking to keep from them, and its decision on the preliminary factual issue might be influenced by a desire to receive the evidence in question.

The other approach would be to present the privileged testimony to the jury together with the evidence pertaining to the availability of the privilege. At the conclusion of the trial, the jurors would be instructed that they are not to consider Rita's testimony if they find that Peter's statements to Rita were privileged. This has many of the disadvantages of the interlocutory verdict and some additional ones. One obvious disadvantage is that, regardless of whether the privilege is found applicable, the privileged material will be revealed, thus destroying a principal value of the privilege. A second disadvantage is the possibility that the jurors will not be able to dismiss Rita's testimony from their minds even if they find that it should not be admitted. Finally, the usual practice of general verdicts would make appellate review impossible.

Unless the jury returns a special verdict on this (and every other) objection, the appellate court would never know whether the objection was sustained or overruled.

When the judge acts as a fact-finder to determine the admissibility of evidence, he must allow the parties to be heard on the issue. The "hearing" may be anything from a two-minute argument over evidence that is already in the record, to a two-week trial at which half-a-dozen witnesses are called by each side. FRE 104(c) governs the circumstances under which this hearing must be conducted outside the hearing of the jury:

Conducting a Hearing So That the Jury Cannot Hear It. The court must conduct any hearing on a preliminary question so that the jury cannot hear it if:

(1) the hearing involves the admissibility of a confession;

(2) a defendant in a criminal case is a witness and so requests; or

(3) justice so requires.

Except when the admissibility of a confession is in issue, or when a criminal defendant who intends to testify on the preliminary issue so requests, the judge has discretion to hear facts relating to admissibility either in front of or away from the jury. If a hearing on the admissibility of evidence is brief and the evidence offered innocuous, there is little reason to send the jury out. In some situations, such as the qualification of an expert witness, it may be desirable for the jury to hear the evidence to avoid the need to repeat the same testimony for their use if the evidence is admitted. But if allegedly objectionable evidence will have to be presented during the hearing, or if evidence on admissibility is irrelevant to the main issues of the case and possibly prejudicial, the better procedure is to determine admissibility outside the hearing of the jury.

A criminal defendant may testify on issues relating to the admissibility of evidence without waiving his Fifth Amendment right to remain silent at the trial. If the jurors saw the defendant testify on certain issues, they might be particularly suspicious of the defendant's failure to testify on the substantive issues in the case. So as not to burden the defendant's right to testify on preliminary issues, FRE 104(c)(2) gives the defendant the right to testify on preliminary issues outside the presence of the jury.[66]

---

[66] On its face, FRE 104(c) gives an accused only the right to have his testimony taken outside the *hearing* of the jury. In certain circumstances the court may be able to listen to testimony and arguments concerning the admissibility of evidence in the presence of the jury but out of their hearing. If the issue is simple and the evidence slight, a conference at the bench may be all that is needed to resolve the matter. However, the defendant's right under FRE 104(c)

Under FRE 104(d), "[b]y testifying on a preliminary question, a defendant in a criminal case does not become subject to cross-examination on other issues in the case." However, if the defendant's testimony on direct examination extends beyond the preliminary matter in dispute, the defendant may find that he has opened the door to cross-examination on the new issues he has raised. Although the jury may not be present at the hearing on admissibility, the prosecution might later be allowed to introduce the defendant's testimony on issues not relating to the preliminary matter. Thus defense counsel must be very careful in questioning a client on a preliminary matter, even if the jury is absent.[67]

FRE 104(a) exempts hearings on preliminary factual issues that affect admissibility from the operation of the rules of evidence themselves, except those that govern privileges. Some states give the judge similar freedom, while others purport to apply the ordinary rules of evidence to determinations of preliminary facts. However, even in the latter states, the rules of evidence are likely to be quite relaxed in practice. Most rules of evidence are designed in large part to avoid prejudicing the jury. As a result, these rules are ordinarily somewhat relaxed when trial is to a judge, and there is even less reason to adhere to them when only a preliminary fact is in issue. The rules on privileges, however, are intended to serve a different goal: protecting confidential relationships. Since confidentiality can be destroyed by disclosure to a judge as well as to a jury, the rules on privileges do apply in FRE 104(a) hearings.

When otherwise inadmissible evidence is introduced on a preliminary issue, it typically falls into one of two categories: (1) *Affidavits*, or other forms of written evidence. Such documents may not, ordinarily, be introduced at trial because (as we will see in Chapter Six) that would violate the rule against hearsay.[68] (2) *The evidence that is itself the subject of the objection.* For example, FRE 104(a) permits a judge to consider the contents of a statement for the purpose of deciding whether it is within the hearsay exception for a statement that is "against the interests" of the person who made it. Without the rule, one could argue that the statement is inadmissible in a hearing on its own admissibility.[69] On the other hand, FRE 104(a) does not permit a party to question a witness about an allegedly privileged communication in order to try to

---

should be interpreted as a right not to be *seen* giving testimony. This requires that the defendant's testimony be taken out of the *presence* of the jury when the defendant so demands.

[67] If the defendant's testimony is confined to the preliminary matter, it cannot subsequently be introduced as evidence of guilt, but it might be admissible for impeachment purposes if the defendant later testifies. See Walder v. United States, 347 U.S. 62 (1954); Simmons v. United States, 390 U.S. 377, 389–94 (1968); United States v. Havens, 446 U.S. 620 (1980); cf. Harris v. New York, 401 U.S. 222 (1971).

[68] See Advisory Committee Note to FRE 104(a).

[69] See id.; Bourjaily v. United States, 483 U.S. 171 (1987).

show from the contents of the communication that the privilege does not apply.

FRE 104(a) does not say what burden of proof the judge should apply in deciding factual questions that determine the admissibility of evidence. The issue was resolved authoritatively in 1987, when the Supreme Court decided in *Bourjaily v. United States*[70] that for preliminary facts the required burden under the Federal Rules is proof by a preponderance of the evidence.[71] This burden falls on whichever party seeks to rely on the fact at issue. A party that seeks to admit evidence under an exception to the hearsay rule must prove any facts that are essential to that exception by a preponderance of the evidence, and a party that seeks to exclude evidence as privileged must prove the existence of the privilege by the same standard.

When the judge admits evidence over objection, the objecting party is permitted nonetheless to attack the admitted evidence by any permissible means, and then argue that the evidence in question is not worthy of belief. FRE 104(e) emphasizes this right:

> **Evidence Relevant to Weight and Credibility.** This rule does not limit a party's right to introduce before the jury evidence that is relevant to the weight or credibility of other evidence.

Some facts that bear on the admissibility of the evidence also go to weight and credibility, and some do not. For example, if a party was overruled on a claim of attorney-client privilege, he could not plausibly attack the credibility of the statement he made to his alleged attorney by showing that they were made in confidence for the purpose of securing legal advice. On the other hand, if the judge determines over objection that a witness' credentials, while minimal, are sufficient to qualify her as an expert, the opponent is not precluded from attacking those credentials in front of the jury and arguing that the witness's expert opinions should not be trusted. Similarly, if the judge finds that a statement was sufficiently against interest when made to qualify for that hearsay exception, the opponent will be permitted to show the jury that in some ways the statement was also self-serving because that issue affects the statement's probative value.

FRE 104 does not require the judge to make explicit findings on factual issues that determine the admissibility of evidence. Appellate courts occasionally say that it is good practice to do so, but they almost never reverse a judgment on that ground. In most cases, the appellate

---

[70]   483 U.S. 171 (1987).

[71]   In Lego v. Twomey, 404 U.S. 477 (1972), the Supreme Court decided that due process was not offended when the trial judge determined whether a confession was voluntary by a preponderance of the evidence. Since the case for deciding preliminary questions by some stricter standard than the preponderance of the evidence is probably strongest when the voluntariness of a confession is at issue, *Lego* almost certainly means that as a matter of constitutional law no higher standard will ever be required.

court will simply assume from the trial court's ruling on admissibility that the appropriate factual findings were made.

3. Preliminary Factual Issues That Go to Relevance and Personal Knowledge (and Authentication)

The general rule that the judge decides questions of fact that go to admissibility is subject to some exceptions. The central one is codified in FRE 104(b):

> **Relevance That Depends on a Fact.** When the relevance of evidence depends on whether a fact exists, proof must be introduced sufficient to support a finding that the fact does exist. The court may admit the proposed evidence on the condition that the proof be introduced later.

This rule reflects a judgment that when the only objection to proffered evidence is that it is not logically relevant unless certain other facts exist, the advantages of giving the judge responsibility for finding those preliminary facts are outweighed by the possibility that the judge's findings will deprive the jury of the opportunity to pass on central issues in the case.[72]

Take a murder prosecution in which the prosecution wants to introduce evidence that the defendant stood to inherit $500,000 from the deceased, to show that she had a motive to kill him. The defendant argues, and will testify, that the $500,000 bequest is irrelevant because she did not know about it, and therefore could not possibly have been motivated by it. Who should determine what the defendant knew? This is the kind of question that the jury is clearly able to decide. No interlocutory procedures are necessary or desirable; rather the question is a natural step in reaching a general verdict. If the judge were responsible for finding the preliminary fact, it is possible that his best judgment would be that the weight of the evidence suggests that the defendant did not know of the bequest. If on the basis of this decision the judge excluded the evidence his action might seriously damage the prosecution's case in a situation where reasonable people might well disagree with the judge's assessment of who was telling the truth. Presumably the parties chose a jury trial rather than a bench trial to get the judgment of twelve lay people on these issues. If the rule made the judge responsible for finding all the facts on which proffered evidence was conditionally relevant, jury trials would often be aborted at the bench.

The judge does not avoid all responsibility when the jury is assigned the task of finding facts on which the relevance of other evidence is

---

[72] This situation is known as "conditional relevance;" it is discussed in greater detail in Chapter Three, pp. 223–228. At this point we address the procedure for admitting or excluding evidence that is "conditionally relevant." In Chapter Three we discuss the considerations that determine whether or not an item of evidence is subject to this rule.

conditioned. The judge must determine whether the evidence bearing on the preliminary fact is such that reasonable people could find that it exists. If not, evidence conditioned on a finding of that fact must be excluded. What the judge avoids is the need to decide, by some standard, whether he believes the preliminary fact exists.

FRE 104(b) says that conditionally relevant evidence may be admitted either after or before the introduction of sufficient evidence of the preliminary fact. Under the latter procedure, which is known as "connecting up," the judge might require the proponent to describe the connecting evidence that will be presented. More often conditionally relevant evidence is admitted on the attorney's assurance that the connection will be made. If connecting evidence is not presented, the opposing party should ask the judge to strike the conditionally relevant evidence from the record. If she does not move to strike by the end of the proponent's case, any objection on this ground may be waived.

Conditional relevance is not the only context in which the jury decides factual questions that bear on admissibility. Under FRE 602, the personal knowledge requirement is subject to the same procedure: A witness may only testify if there is evidence "sufficient to support a finding that the witness has personal knowledge of the matter." The Advisory Committee's Note to FRE 602 says that "The rule is in fact a specialized application of the provisions of Rule 104(b) on conditional relevance." This is wrong. When the issue is conditional relevance, if the condition is not met the evidence has no value whatever in deciding the case. Thus, in the previous example, if the defendant did not know of the money she stood to inherit, the inheritance—however well established— has no implications for her guilt, one way or the other. But what if a witness in a automobile accident case testifies that "The blue sedan drove straight through the red light," and it is later determined that he never saw the event but was relying on a description from his sister who did see it? That witness's testimony is not based on personal knowledge; as a result, it may be less persuasive than first-hand evidence, and it will certainly be inadmissible. But it is not irrelevant. Even a second-hand story has some tendency to make the facts that it recounts more likely. In this case, for example, there is a good chance that the testimony is an accurate reflection of accurate first-hand observations by the witness's sister.[73]

---

[73] FRE 901(a), which governs authentication of exhibits and identification of voices, also assigns fact-finding authority to the jury:

> **In General.** To satisfy the requirement of authenticating or identifying an item of evidence, the proponent must produce evidence sufficient to support a finding that the item is what the proponent claims it is.

As with the personal knowledge requirement, the Advisory Committee's Note to FRE 901 says that "[t]his requirement of showing authenticity or identity falls in the category of relevancy dependent upon the fulfillment of a condition of fact. . . . " As we will see in Chapter Ten, in some

When evidence is admitted subject to a factual finding by the jury, the opposing party may ask the judge to instruct the jurors that if they do not find that the preliminary fact existed, they must ignore the evidence. When the issue truly is only *conditionally* relevant, no instruction is necessary. A judge hardly needs to point out to jurors of average intelligence that if the defendant never heard of a bequest, its existence could have no bearing on her motivation and her conduct. But if the issue is personal knowledge rather than conditional relevance, or if the evidence may have a tendency to prejudice or confuse the jury, it may be important to tell the jury to disregard the evidence if the factual conditions for its admission are not met.

———————

Problem II-6. Northern Resources (NR), a North Dakota mining company sued Great Plains Construction (GPC) for the cost of asbestos removal from NR's headquarters in Bismarck, North Dakota, which was built by GPC starting in September 1968. NR claims that at the time of construction GPC (but not NR) knew that a fireproofing product called "Monokote"— which GPC sprayed over structural steel and decking for the building—contained 20% asbestos, and posed a health hazard. At trial, to show that GPC was aware of the health hazard of asbestos before construction began, NR sought to introduce in evidence an undated memorandum to GPC from its insurance company summarizing a 1966 article on the dangers of construction materials that contained asbestos. The memo was found in a GPC folder that contained more than twenty documents, most but not all of which were dated before September 1968. The judge excluded the memo because he found that NR had not proved that GPC received the document before work began on NR's building. The jury found for the defendant, GPC, and NR appeals claiming that the exclusion of the memo was error. **How should the appellate court rule on this claim?**

———————

4. Preliminary Factual Questions That Go to "Ultimate Issues"

Consider a criminal prosecution for bigamy in which the prosecutor wishes to call the defendant's ostensible wife to testify that he told her that he was already married to another woman when he married her. The defendant, who denies the previous marriage, objects on the ground that his wife is precluded from testifying against him by a spousal

———————

situations that are governed by FRE 901, this statement is correct—the unauthenticated evidence is truly irrelevant—and in some situations it's false.

privilege;[74] the prosecution counters that since the defendant was already married, his marriage to the proposed witness was invalid and therefore the privilege does not apply. Obviously, in this situation the question of admissibility and the ultimate question of guilt are the same. If the defendant married twice, his second marriage was invalid, therefore the privilege does not apply—and he's guilty of bigamy. If he married only once, the second marriage is valid, his wife may not testify—and he's innocent. Who should decide the issue for the purpose of ruling on the evidentiary objection?

Under the Federal Rules, it appears that when an issue that goes to admissibility coincides with an ultimate issue, the judge decides admissibility unless there is a specific rule that provides otherwise.[75] State court decisions vary; in some cases, issues that the Federal Rules assign to the judge will go to the jury instead.[76] Where the overlap of preliminary and ultimate issue is complete, courts should be wary of keeping from the jury evidence that might reasonably be found admissible when that evidence may be the best that's available on a matter the jury is expected to resolve. Furthermore, when the coincidence of issues is complete the danger of confusing or prejudicing the jurors may be minimal. In this case, for example, the jurors hardly need to be told to disregard the wife's testimony if they find that the defendant's second marriage is valid. They need only be instructed that in that situation, the defendant is entitled to a judgment of acquittal.[77]

When a judge does decide as a preliminary matter a factual issue that is also submitted to the jury, the jury is not told of the judge's factual finding. Thus, in our example, if the judge found that the witness could testify because her marriage to the defendant was bigamous and therefore invalid, the jurors would not know of that decision; they would

---

[74] The privilege at issue is the privilege of confidential marital communications. See Chapter Eight, pp. 1040–1045; Uniform Rule of Evidence 504(a). (As we will see in Chapter Eight, there are no codified Federal Rules of Evidence that govern evidentiary privileges. See FRE 501.) In addition, if the wife was unwilling to testify against her husband she could object under the "adverse testimony" privilege, which allows one spouse to refuse to testify against the other in a criminal prosecution. See Uniform Rule of Evidence 504(b), Chapter Eight, pp. 1037–1039.

[75] As we will see in Chapter Ten, pp. 1305–1307, FRE 1008, which deals with the "original document rule," assigns one such fact-finding task to the jury: When the genuineness of a document must be determined both to decide its admissibility and to decide the ultimate merits of the case, that issue is resolved by the jury alone, as is the case with other issues of fact.

[76] See cases cited in McCormick § 53, Practitioners' Treatise edition.

[77] Of course, if the evidence is admitted the confidentiality of the relationship is breached, even if the jury later determines that the marriage is valid. Some evidentiary privileges are subject to exceptions that are specifically designed to avoid such conundrums. For example, if an attorney sues a client for her fee, the client might claim both that no attorney-client relationship existed, and that the attorney cannot reveal the client's statements to prove the relationship because if the attorney's claim is correct, the client's statements are privileged. The judge need not resolve this dilemma because the attorney-client privilege does not prevent the disclosure of information pertaining to disputes over fees. See, e.g., Uniform Rule of Evidence 502(d)(3). Similarly, in the situation covered in the example in the text, some jurisdictions specify that spousal privileges do not apply in bigamy prosecutions. See Calif. Evidence Code § 972 (e)(3).

only know that the witness did testify. If the jurors were told of the judge's decision, there is a great danger that they would be unduly influenced by it, and would not reach an independent judgment. To avoid that danger, any hearing on a preliminary matter that is also an issue for the jury ought to be held outside the presence of the jury.

It is perfectly possible for the judge, deciding an issue as a preliminary matter, and for the jury, deciding it as an ultimate issue, to reach apparently inconsistent decisions. In our example, if the judge concludes that the defendant's second marriage was bigamous and permits the witness to testify, the jury may nonetheless acquit the defendant of bigamy. One obvious reason is that different burdens of proof may apply. In this case, the judge's decision, under FRE 104(a), should be based on a preponderance of the evidence, but the jury can only convict on proof beyond a reasonable doubt. Even when the burdens of proof are the same, however, the judge and the jury are required to reach independent judgments on the issue, and if the evidence is susceptible to two interpretations, those judgments may conflict. And in some situations, the judge and the jury may also differ because their decisions are based on different information. In particular, under FRE 104(a) the judge may consider inadmissible evidence in deciding preliminary issues, but the jury, of course, is only supposed to consider admissible evidence.

"The jury will disregard the witness's last remarks."

F. CAUTIONARY INSTRUCTIONS AND LIMITED ADMISSIBILITY

Juries hear inadmissible evidence in almost every trial. Sometimes the evidence is given before the opponent has a chance to object; sometimes the basis for the objection isn't apparent until later. When this happens, the opposing party is required to move to strike the evidence from the record, as we have already seen.[78] If the judge grants the motion to strike, she may, on her own motion or at the request of a party, give the jury a "cautionary instruction" to disregard the evidence that they have already heard.

FRE 105 describes a similar procedure that may be used when evidence has limited admissibility.

> If the court admits evidence that is admissible against a party or for a purpose—but not against another party or for another purpose—the court, on timely request, must restrict the evidence to its proper scope and instruct the jury accordingly.

For example, under FRE 407 evidence that the defendant in a slip-and-fall personal injury trial fixed the sidewalk on which the plaintiff was injured is admissible to prove that the defendant owned or controlled the sidewalk, but inadmissible to prove that he was negligent in maintaining the sidewalk—as we will see in Chapter Four. If the repair evidence comes in, the defendant's lawyer may ask the judge to tell the jurors that they can use it for the first purpose but not the second.

Do cautionary and limiting instructions work? Courts talk about this issue in three different modes. The question usually comes up when evidence that was inadmissible for all purposes or for some purposes was heard by the jury, a cautionary instruction was given, and the objecting party lost at trial and then argues on appeal that permitting the jury to hear the evidence was prejudicial error. The appellate courts (as always) generally affirm; in this context, they usually do it by official presumption: "This limiting instruction is clear. It must be presumed that the jury conscientiously observed it."[79] Sometimes courts are more explicit in explaining the basis for this presumption. As the Supreme Court put it in the context of a criminal prosecution:

> The rule that juries are presumed to follow their instructions is a pragmatic one, rooted less in the absolute certitude that the presumption is true than in the belief that it represents a reasonable practical accommodation of the interests of the state and the defendant in the criminal justice process.[80]

---

[78] Supra, p. 165; see FRE 103(a)(1).

[79] Shotwell Mfg. Co. v. United States, 371 U.S. 341, 367 (1963).

[80] Richardson v. Marsh, 481 U.S. 200, 211 (1987).

And occasionally (typically still in the course of affirming a judgment) courts express cynicism about the entire process. Judge Learned Hand, for example, wrote that such instructions may ask the jury to perform "a mental gymnastic which is beyond, not only their powers, but anybody else,"[81] and called the procedure a legal "placebo."[82]

Social scientific studies using simulated juries generally support the cynical view.[83] The evidence does suggest that cautionary instructions can limit jury discussion of impermissible inferences. Nonetheless, most studies show that experimental juries that hear inadmissible evidence are more likely to reach verdicts that are consistent with that evidence than juries that never hear such evidence, and that instructions don't change that effect. Indeed, some studies show that cautionary instructions can have a boomerang effect—they can magnify the impact of inadmissible evidence. On the other hand, there are also indications that jurors sometimes are able to disregard inadmissible evidence, if they understand that it has been excluded because it is unreliable and not because it is considered privileged, or unfairly prejudicial, or constitutionally improper.

Courts recognize that in some situations cautionary instructions are not protective enough. The most important example is when two criminal defendants are prosecuted jointly, and the prosecution wishes to introduce in evidence a confession by one of the defendants who elects not to testify. In that situation under the hearsay rule, the confession is admissible as an "admission" against the defendant who made it, but it is inadmissible against her co-defendant—as we will see in Chapter Seven. Frequently, if evidence is admissible against only one of two defendants, the jury will hear it, the judge will tell the jurors not to use it in deciding the guilt of the other defendant, and the appellate courts will be satisfied. But if the evidence is a confession that implicates a co-defendant against

---

[81] Nash v. United States, 54 F.2d 1006, 1007 (2d Cir. 1932).

[82] United States v. Delli Paoli, 229 F.2d 319, 321 (2d Cir. 1956). See Note, Social Science Findings and the Jury's Ability To Disregard Evidence Under the Federal Rules of Evidence, 52 Law & Contemp. Probs. No. 4, 341 (1989).

[83] See Saul M. Kassin & Christina A. Studebaker, "Instructions to Disregard and The Jury: Curative and Paradoxical Effects," in J. M. Golding & C. M. MacLeod (eds.), Intentional Forgetting: Interdisciplinary Approaches (Hillsdale, N.J.: Erlbaum, 1997); Carretta & Moreland, The Direct and Indirect Effects of Inadmissible Evidence, 13 J. App. Soc. Psych. 291–309 (1983); Valerie P. Hans & Anthony N. Doob, Section 12 of the Canada Evidence Act and the Deliberations of Simulated Juries, 18 Crim. L. Q. 235–253 (1976); Sarah Tanford & Michele Cox, Decision Processes in Civil Cases: The Impact of Impeachment Evidence on Liability and Credibility Judgments, 2 Soc. Behav. 165–182 (1987); Roselle L. Wissler & Michael J. Saks, On the Inefficacy of Limiting Instructions: When Jurors Use Credibility Evidence to Decide on Guilt, 9 Law & Hum. Behav. 37–48 (1985); Sharon Wolf & David A. Montgomery, Effects of Inadmissible Evidence and Level of Judicial Admonishment to Disregard on the Judgments of Mock Jurors, 7 J. App. Soc. Psych. 205–219 (1977); but see Evelyn O. Schaefer & Kristine L. Hansen, Similar Fact Evidence and Limited Use Instructions: An Empirical Investigation, 14 Crim. L. J. 157–179 (1990); Steven Fein, et al., Can the Jury Disregard That Information? The Use of Suspicion to Reduce the Prejudicial Effect of Pretrial Publicity and Inadmissible Testimony, 23 Personality & Soc. Psychology Bult. 1215 (1997).

whom it is inadmissible, the Supreme Court has held that a limiting instruction is not enough to protect the co-defendant's constitutional rights:

> [T]here are some contexts in which the risk that the jury will not, or cannot, follow instructions is so great, and the consequences of failure so vital to the defendant, that the practical and human limitations of the jury system cannot be ignored. Such a context is presented here, where the powerfully incriminating extrajudicial statements of a codefendant, who stands accused side-by-side with the defendant, are deliberately spread before the jury in a joint trial.[84]

FRE 105 says that the court shall give a limiting instruction "on timely request." The qualification is important; it means that when evidence is admissible for a limited purpose, the party that might suffer unfair prejudice from the evidence gets to decide whether it wants a cautionary instruction. Frequently, an experienced trial attorney will conclude that a cautionary instruction would do more harm than good by emphasizing damaging evidence that might have gone unnoticed, or by making a connection that the jurors might otherwise have missed. Imagine the unspoken reaction of a juror who's told by the judge that he should *not* consider evidence of insurance on the issue of damages: "Oh yeah, I see your point—if he's insured he won't actually have to pay. But of course, I shouldn't pay any attention to that."

G. SOME TACTICAL CONSIDERATIONS

Why make an objection? At first blush, the answer seems obvious: because the evidence is inadmissible. But that is never a sufficient reason to object, and sometimes not even a necessary condition. In an actual trial, where everything you do is designed to impress the jury with the justice of your client's case, there are many possible reasons to make objections, and just as many competing reasons not to object even if the evidence is inadmissible. The decision to object or not to object is complex and difficult, not least because it often must be made in a split second. True skill at the task can only be acquired with practice; we certainly cannot teach you how to do it in these few pages. Our goal instead is to outline the main considerations that determine the general shape of practice in most trials.

1. How to Object

The basic rule is that an objection should be stated clearly and simply: "Objection your Honor, hearsay," or "I object, your Honor; the question calls for speculation." You need to get the judge's attention, and

---

[84] Bruton v. United States, 391 U.S. 123, 135–36 (1968). See Chapter Seven, pp. 817–823.

if you are objecting to a question it is also important to get the attention of the witness in order to stop her from answering. That requires you to speak clearly and audibly; beyond that, it rarely helps to raise your voice or to express anger. Some judges require you to stand to make an objection. Even if it's not required, standing is often a good idea. It draws attention in a civil, respectful manner, and it allows you to signal that you intend to object before you begin to speak, which can be useful if the judge does not want you to state your objection until the interrogating attorney has completed the question. You are required to state the grounds for the objection,[85] but that just means identifying the category of objection— irrelevant, unduly prejudicial, hearsay, and so forth. You are not required to *argue* for your position, although it may be a good idea to do so, if you are permitted. Practice varies. Some judges permit arguments in front of the jury unless a party objects; some will only hear arguments in chambers or at the bench, out of the hearing of the jury; and some judges will not hear argument on evidentiary objections at all— except that which is necessarily contained in objections and in offers of proof—unless they themselves request it.

2. Reasons to Object

There are three possible reasons to make an objection for the benefit of the record on appeal:

- To preserve a specific error as an issue for appeal.

- To make a record that may demonstrate that the trial was unfair in general.

- To exclude evidence in order to be able to argue that there is insufficient evidence in the record to support a claim by the opposition.

In addition, there are several possible reasons to make an objection for the purpose of improving one's chances at the trial itself:

- To keep the evidence out—presumably because it would be harmful.

- To disrupt a hostile witness who's on a roll, and possibly to distract the jury.

- To disrupt the opposing attorney, who might forget a question or make a mistake.

- To protect, or help, or provide information to a friendly witness under cross-examination.

---

[85] See supra pp. 165–167.

• To emphasize testimony to which you object, assuming it is helpful to your side and will be admitted despite the objection.

• To argue the objection within the hearing of the jury (if you are permitted to do so).

• To eat up the clock.

Some of these purposes are ethically problematic, but in practice they are all tolerated unless they are pushed too far.

3.   Reasons Not to Object

The only reason to pass on an available objection for the benefit of a later appeal is the obvious one: you want the evidence in question to be in the record. There are, however, several important reasons not to object for the purposes of the trial:

• Because the evidence does not hurt your side.

• Because the evidence helps your side.

• Because the evidence, if it's admitted, will allow you to respond with otherwise inadmissible evidence that will help your case.

• To avoid emphasizing harmful evidence.

• To avoid creating the impression that you think the evidence *is* harmful to your case.

• To avoid annoying the jury or the judge.

• Because by objecting to an improper or ineffective examination you may force your opponent to do a better job.

• To set a pattern: if you don't object during their examinations, the opposing attorneys may be more reluctant to make objections during your examinations, or they may look more disruptive, deceptive, or obnoxious by contrast if they do.

How do these reasons pro and con stack up? For the purposes of an appeal, the more objections the better. The more you object, the more issues you can raise. The trial judge and jury may get angry and frustrated with a lawyer who disrupts the testimony with frequent objections, but not an appellate court that sees the case as parts of a transcript highlighting those few objections that appear substantial, and briefs arguing the merits of assignments of error. But appeals on evidentiary issues are rarely successful anyway. The main event is always the trial, and at trial the reasons not to object in front of the jury are often much stronger than the reasons to object. The last thing you want to do is make the jury think that you have something to hide, or that you can't be trusted. As a result, in many trials the jurors hear very few objections, and in some trials they hear none at all.

4. Motions in Limine

Sometimes you can get the major benefits of making an objection without paying any significant cost. The way to do that is by making the objection in advance, outside the presence of the jury. This procedure is known as a motion "in limine," which is Latin for "at the threshold." Preparation is key. In order to make a motion in limine, you must anticipate the issue. If you see the problem coming, and if the judge is willing to hear it, a motion in limine permits you to exclude evidence without giving the jury the impression that you have something to hide; to keep any reference to the objectionable evidence out of the trial, so that the jury never knows that something is missing and never speculates about what it may be; and to object to evidence that is ultimately admitted without giving it added emphasis. In addition, it's easier to prepare your case if you know in advance how the judge will rule on a major objection that may result in the exclusion of an important part of your evidence, or of your opponent's evidence.

A motion in limine is usually an objection to anticipated evidence from the other side. It is also possible, however, to ask the court *in limine* to overrule an anticipated objection and decide in advance that evidence that you wish to present is in fact admissible. One way or the other, a ruling on a motion in limine is not a final judgment, but merely an interlocutory decision by the trial judge. The judge has the authority to reconsider and reverse it at anytime—as, indeed, she may reconsider and reverse any other ruling on an evidentiary objection. In practice, this rarely happens. If the judge makes an unqualified ruling on an objection *in limine*, that ruling (as long as it stands) ought to satisfy the FRE 103 requirement that the party that wishes to complain about the admission of evidence must have made a timely and specific objection. Conversely, an offer of proof made at a hearing on a motion in limine should satisfy the requirement that a party that wishes to claim error in the exclusion of evidence must have informed the court of the content of the excluded evidence, unless the judge says otherwise. This procedure gives the judge the option to require a party to reraise the issue at trial if it wants to preserve a claim of error.

FRE 103(b), which was added by amendment in 2000, addresses this issue:

> **Not Needing to Renew an Objection or Offer of Proof.** Once the court rules definitively on the record—either before or at trial—a party need not renew an objection or offer of proof to preserve a claim of error for appeal.

The trick, of course, is telling when a ruling is "definitive." The Advisory Committee's Note to this amendment states that "the amendment imposes an obligation on counsel to clarify whether an *in limine* or other evidentiary ruling is definitive when there is doubt on that point." In other words, if you want to rely on a ruling in limine, you'd best get the judge to agree that it is "definitive."

There are limitations on the usefulness of motions in limine. The obvious one is that it is often not possible to anticipate objections, even important ones. Moreover, when you have correctly anticipated an important evidentiary issue, it is sometimes best not to advertise that fact. Your opponent may be less well informed, less conscientious, less skillful, or less lucky than you; he may have misunderstood the issue, or missed it altogether. As a result, it is sometimes worth giving up the advantages of an advance ruling to preserve the advantage of surprise. But the most important limitation on the value of motions in limine is that they are discretionary. Judges do not have to rule on evidentiary objections in advance. Their practice in this regard is extremely variable. Some judges favor motions in limine; on some issues they may even require that objections be made in advance, when possible. Other judges are almost never willing to consider an objection to an item of evidence before it is actually offered at trial.

5.   A General Approach to Objections

The circumstances in which evidentiary objections might be made are far too varied for any single formula on how and when to object. In some situations, any one of the considerations we have listed above, and others, may be a sufficient reason to make or to forgo an objection. Cases vary, judges vary, juries vary, and the styles of different attorneys—even the best and the most experienced—vary as much as any of these. Nonetheless, with trepidation, we hazard a general approach as a useful starting point for thinking about a strategy for dealing with evidentiary objections at an upcoming trial.

• Identify in advance significant items of the opposing parties' evidence that you want and may be able to exclude, and attempt to do so before trial by motions in limine.

• Attempt to anticipate objections that cannot be handled in limine, so you can lay your plans in advance.

• For every item of evidence, ask yourself two questions: (1) Does it hurt my case? (2) Is it important? If the answer to both questions is *"Yes,"* you *might* want to object. If the answer to either question is *"No,"* do not object unless there are compelling tactical reasons to do so.

• If the evidence is important and does hurt your case, ask yourself, "Is there some way I might be able to keep it out?" If the answer is *"Yes,"* ask yourself, "Is the possibility of excluding the evidence worth the costs of objecting before the jury?" If the answer is *"Yes"* again, object; otherwise do not.

This is a lot to do in the ten, or five, or two seconds that you may have to decide whether to object or to let a possible objection pass. What makes the task doable is preparation. Preparation enables you to identify issues that can be handled invisibly in advance by motions in limine; preparation helps you spot problems as soon as they occur, or even to anticipate them; preparation helps you phrase your objections in ways that are most likely to prevail and least likely to damage your case. But most of all, with careful preparation you can gauge what matters and what doesn't matter, what's important and what's unimportant—which will solve half of your problems, because if it doesn't matter, it doesn't matter, and if it's unimportant you don't need to object.

———————

Problem II-7. You are defending Landco, a real estate management firm that manages an apartment building in Seattle, in a lawsuit brought by Linda Lopez, a resident of the building who was robbed and beaten on the sidewalk immediately outside the front entrance. Lopez claims that Landco was negligent in not providing adequate security in that area. Landco contends that its security arrangements were reasonable, and that in any event it was not responsible for security on the sidewalk outside the building. Before trial you make a motion in limine to exclude evidence that Landco paid $250,000 to settle a prior lawsuit in which a resident sued for damages for slipping on ice outside the rear entrance of the same building. You argue that this evidence is irrelevant, inadmissible under the rules of evidence (see FRE 408), and that its unfairly prejudicial impact substantially outweighs any probative value. The judge rules that the evidence is inadmissible to show negligence, but admissible on the issue of Landco's control over and responsibility for the sidewalk areas surrounding the building. You believe the judge's ruling is error.

At trial, the attorney for Ms. Lopez calls the plaintiff in the slip-and-fall case, apparently for the purpose of presenting evidence on that lawsuit and settlement. **What should you do?**

———————

H. OBJECTIONS TO EVIDENCE IN NON-JURY TRIALS

In theory, the same rules of evidence apply in a jury trial and in a trial before a judge sitting alone. This was true at common law, and remains true under the Federal Rules. FRE 101, which defines the scope of the Rules, simply says: "These rules apply to proceedings in United States courts. . . ." No exception is made for bench trials.[86] In practice,

_____
[86] The wording of some rules does refer specifically to the jury. Some are procedural rules that can only apply when the jury is the trier of fact and the judge the trier of law: FREs 103

however, the rules that apply in non-jury proceedings are likely to be quite different.

Most judges and commentators agree that by and large the exclusionary rules of evidence that govern our trials were developed in response to a deep-seated mistrust of juries. It follows that when a case is tried without a jury, these rules need not be applied, at least not in their usual form—with the exception of the rules that govern privileges, which exist to protect confidential relationships from intrusions by any type of tribunal.[87]   In practice, the rules of evidence are frequently relaxed in the absence of a jury. Given this wide spread practice, it would make sense to acknowledge the difference and write separate, simpler rules of evidence for bench trials—especially since the great majority of American trials are conducted without juries.[88]   But suggestions to that effect have been ignored: "The courts appear persistent in refusing either to apply formal evidence doctrine or to change it."[89]

There is one necessary difference in the application of the rules of evidence between bench trials and jury trials. The judge will ordinarily know the content of evidence that is excluded. Often the evidence must be disclosed to determine its admissibility, and even when that isn't necessary, the proponent must make the content known by way of an offer of proof in order to present any claim of error. The jury, on the other hand, will usually not hear excluded evidence, and in many situations may not even know that any evidence was excluded. This inevitable difference in procedure has led to another common difference in practice: In bench trials, decisions on objections are often postponed. Since the judge will hear the evidence anyway, she can receive it "subject to objection," and then rule on the objection at the end of the trial, if it is renewed.

In reviewing evidentiary rulings in a bench trial, appellate courts are even more deferential than usual to trial court judgments, and even less likely to find that error was harmful. If important contested evidence

---

and 104 discuss, among other issues, the conditions under which hearings on evidentiary issues may or must be conducted outside the hearing of the jury; FRE 105 is about instructions to the jury on limited admissibility; and FRE 201 addresses jury instructions on judicial notice. Others rules reflect a background concern that juries might be more readily biased than judges. FRE 403 refers to "misleading the jury"—apparently misleading the judge as trier of fact is less worrisome. FRE 703 (another balancing rule) prohibits disclosing "to the jury," but not to the judge as trier of fact, inadmissible evidence that an expert witness relied on in reaching an admissible expert opinion, unless the probative value of the disclosure "substantially outweighs [its] prejudicial effect."

[87] See, e.g., McCormick § 60; Note, Exclusionary Rules of Evidence in Non-Jury Proceedings, 46 Ill. L. Rev. 915 (1952). There are dissents from this point of view. See Dale A. Nance, The Best Evidence Principle, 73 Iowa L. Rev. 227, 229–30 (1988).

[88] Kevin M. Clermont & Theodore Eisenberg, Trial by Jury or Judge: Transcending Empiricism, 77 Cornell L. Rev. 1124, 1127 n.7 (1992); Kenneth C. Davis, An Approach to Rules of Evidence for Nonjury Cases, 50 A.B.A.J. 723 (1964).

[89] Leo Levin & Harold K. Cohen, The Exclusionary Rules in Nonjury Criminal Cases, 119 U. Pa. L. Rev. 905, 908 (1971).

was excluded, they may occasionally find error. But if the evidence was admitted, they indulge in a peculiar presumption: If a trial judge admitted evidence in error, the appellate court will often presume that she disregarded the inadmissible evidence and based her findings solely on admissible evidence, if there is sufficient admissible evidence to support the findings.[90] This means that except in dealing with privileges, it is all but impossible for a judge in a bench trial to commit reversible error by admitting evidence over objection, unless she makes the tactical mistake of announcing in her opinion that she relied on the objectionable evidence.

Taken together, the practice of postponing rulings and the presumption that inadmissible evidence is disregarded mean that in bench trials the rules of evidence can largely be ignored, in the name of efficiency. McCormick has drawn a road map for all to see:

> In practice . . . most trial judges . . . apply the rules of evidence in a nonjury trial to exclude evidence that "is *clearly* inadmissible, privileged, or too time consuming in order to guard against reversal." However, where the admissibility of evidence is debatable . . . experienced trial judges in nonjury case[s] [avoid reversal by] . . . provisionally admit[ting] all arguably admissible evidence, even if objected to with the announcement that all admissibility questions are reserved until the evidence is all in. In considering any objections renewed by motion to strike at the end of the case, the judge leans toward admission rather than exclusion but seeks to find clearly admissible testimony on which to base his findings of fact. This practice lessens the time spent in arguing objections and helps ensure that appellate courts have in the record the evidence that was rejected as well as that which was received.[91]

A judge who uses McCormick's method can effectively discourage attorneys in bench trials from even bothering to raise most available objections. This is common. Of course, a judge *may* apply the rules of evidence in a bench trial just as strictly as in a jury trial. The rules of evidence do apply to bench trials, in theory, and sometimes they are actually applied in court.

---

[90]   See, e.g., Plummer v. Western Int. Hotels Co., 656 F.2d 502, 505 (9th Cir. 1981); Clark v. United States, 61 F.2d 695, 708 (8th Cir. 1932). There are cases that go the other way—e.g., People v. DeGroot, 108 Ill.App.2d 1, 11, 247 N.E.2d 177, 181–82 (1969)—but they are rare.

[91]   McCormick § 60.

ADDITIONAL PROBLEMS

Problem II-8. Peter Strand was injured in a highway accident when a truck driven by Dale Bumpers crossed the median strip and overturned in the opposing lanes. Strand sues Bumpers. Bumpers calls Amy Short, who was driving a car directly behind his truck. Ms. Short testifies without objection that Bumper's truck was sideswiped by a van shortly before it crossed the median strip. Her testimony then continues as follows:

> **Q. (by defense counsel)** How would you describe the driving of the truck driver before the truck was hit by the van?

> **MS. SHORT:** He was in complete control of his vehicle until he was sideswiped by that van.

> **PLAINTIFF'S COUNSEL:** Objection, Your Honor. Improper opinion.

> **THE COURT:** Ms. Short, do you mean to say that he was driving in a safe and prudent manner and at a safe rate of speed in the proper lane of travel?

> **MS. SHORT:** Yes, Your Honor.

> **THE COURT:** I'll allow it.

> **PLAINTIFF'S COUNSEL:** Thank you, Your Honor.

The jury finds for the defendant, and on appeal the plaintiff argues that this testimony was improper. **How will this objection be treated on appeal?**

Problem II-9. Hamilton Jones placed title to all of his real property in the name of his son Tom. Jones placed the title in Tom's name for the purpose of holding title for Tom's brothers and sisters. After the death of Hamilton Jones, Tom conveyed the title to the property to himself in fee simple. Tom died leaving all his property to Joyce and naming her sole executor of his estate. Joyce refused to convey the property to Tom's brothers and sisters, whereupon they sued her as executor asking the court to impose a constructive trust on the property held by the estate. At trial, plaintiffs wished to testify to conversations between Tom and themselves in which Tom allegedly acknowledged that he held title as their trustee. Joyce objected to the admission of this testimony, contending that none of the plaintiffs was competent to testify. **What is the basis of Joyce's argument? Should she prevail?**

Problem II-10. Defendant was driving his car when it crashed into and broke the show window of Plaintiff's jewelry store. The accident imperiled Plaintiff's life, as he was pinned beneath Defendant's car. Plaintiff sues Defendant in tort. Plaintiff contends that the accident was caused by Defendant's driving at an excessive rate of speed. At the trial

Plaintiff calls witness A, a merchant who owns a bakery three doors down from Plaintiff's store. The merchant testifies, "I first saw Defendant's car whiz by the bakery window. It was then going 75 miles per hour." Defendant objects to his testimony. **What is the basis of the objection? What is the proper ruling?** Defendant calls witness B who was standing on the street corner, and B testifies that Defendant's car was going 35 miles per hour. Plaintiff objects. **On what grounds? What is the proper ruling?**

Problem II-11. Sandra Chamallas brought an action to recover damages for personal injuries allegedly caused by the negligence of Acme's employee, Shane. Chamallas claims that Shane, while driving one of Acme's trucks, plowed into her car as she was stopped for a red light. In order to establish *respondeat superior* liability, Chamallas calls Shane as her first witness. She asks him only whether at the time of the collision he was in the employ of Acme and engaged in Acme's business, and to identify an accident report he had filled out. On cross-examination, Acme seeks to elicit Shane's description of the collision and of the events preceding and following it. **On what ground might an objection be made? What should the ruling be? If the cross-examination is allowed, should the defense counsel be allowed to use leading questions?**

Problem II-12. Plaintiff was driving his car when he was struck by a truck owned by Defendant and operated by a third party. In his suit against the Defendant, Plaintiff's attorney moves to call both the third party and the Defendant as hostile witnesses. **Is this permissible? If a direct action could be brought against the insurance company that insures both the Defendant and the third-party, should both of them be treated as hostile witnesses?**

Problem II-13. Defendant was responsible for a metal filler lid in the sidewalk in front of his store on which pedestrians were expected to walk. Plaintiff Jones sued Defendant for injuries he sustained in a fall which he said was caused by the fact that the lid in question was old and rusted and that it slipped as he put his weight on it. Defendant contended that Jones fell because he was so intoxicated that he could not maintain his balance. At trial, Defendant offers a witness named Smith to testify that he was following Jones about twenty feet to the rear prior to the accident; that in his opinion, from what he observed, Jones was grossly intoxicated; that he saw Jones fall; and that it was his impression that Jones fell because he was so intoxicated that he could not maintain his equilibrium. Jones objects to his entire testimony. **Should the court allow any of it to be admitted?** Assume that Smith had not seen Jones fall but had heard a noise and rushed up while Jones was on the ground. **If Smith smelled alcohol on Jones' breath, could he so testify? Could Smith testify that Jones was intoxicated? Why or why not?**

Problem II-14. A guest in an automobile brings an action against the owner and driver. The guest calls as a witness a third party who had been sitting on her front porch about 75 yards from where the defendant's automobile left the road. Although she could not see the car, the witness heard tires squealing and heard the automobile strike some trees on the side of the road immediately before it plunged into a ravine. Plaintiff asks the witness to give her estimate of the speed of the automobile based upon the sound which she heard. **An objection is made. What result?**

Problem II-15. The Defendant is on trial for murder. The star witness for the prosecution, Sam Peabody, testifies that he heard two shots coming from around a corner, at which point he ran to the corner to see what had happened. The prosecutor's next question is, "What did you see next?" Peabody responds, "I saw the Defendant about twenty yards from the house running as fast as he could away from that house because he had just shot the murder victim." **Is Peabody's answer objectionable? All of it? Some of it?**

Problem II-16. Plaintiff brought an action to recover rent claimed to be due from the Defendant under certain leases. The leases in question covered an entire business block. Plaintiff leased the premises to one Littlefield who assigned the leases to Defendant on June 30, 2003. Littlefield then fled the jurisdiction. On the day of Littlefield's departure, Defendant paid to Plaintiff the rent then in arrears and occupied the premises. Thereafter Defendant sublet parts of the building, paid for repairs, and, from rents collected from the subtenants, paid the Plaintiff the rents due under the leases—except for $300,000, which was owed when the lease expired. The issue was whether Defendant was Littlefield's agent or whether he was the beneficiary of an outright assignment and liable for the outstanding balance. Defendant took the stand and testified as follows: "Littlefield made me his agent. There was no absolute assignment at all. It is true that Littlefield owed me money and that the assignment was collateral security for his debt, but both of us intended an agency arrangement only." Plaintiff introduces no direct evidence rebutting Defendant's testimony, nor does Plaintiff cross-examine or object to the evidence. (If the assignment was only as security for a debt, and not absolute, then the Defendant was operating the leased premises in his capacity as agent and not assignee and would not be liable for the balance. In this jurisdiction, whether an assignment is absolute where given as collateral for a debt depends on the value of the assignment, the amount of the debt, and the powers the assignee is given with respect to the assigned leasehold.) **Is there any possible ground for objection? Assuming an objection might have prevailed but was not raised, what weight should the trial judge accord the evidence?**

Problem II-17. Defendant is charged with forcible rape and assault. The defense at trial is consent; the case turns on whether the jury believes the victim or the defendant. Defendant produces a witness who testifies that he saw the victim at the home of the defendant at the time of the alleged crime. After stating that he heard no threats, or crying or shouting, the witness is about to relate the conversations he had overheard when the prosecution objects. Defense counsel states: "Your Honor, the conversations shed light on who is telling the truth and who is lying in this case. Either there was a rape committed or there was consent. Let's find out." The judge sustains the objection and the defendant is convicted, and appeals. **Assuming arguendo it was error to exclude the evidence, is the offer of proof adequate to justify an appellate court's reversing the conviction?**

Problem II-18. Mary Denhable is indicted for assault with a deadly weapon and for the attempted murder of the supervisor at the law firm where she worked. The supervisor testifies that he fired Mary two days before the alleged assault. He then describes the assault. A portion of his direct examination follows:

> **Q.** Okay, now, after she stabbed you, backed off with the knife, and started coming at you again, were you scared at that point? **A.** Sure, yes.
>
> **Q.** What were you afraid she was going to do to you? **A.** She was going to kill me. Thought she was going to stab me again.
>
> **Q.** So you—at that time you were in fear for your life? **A.** Yes, sir.
>
> **Q.** And this particular knife, did you feel that it was a deadly weapon? **A.** Yes, sir.
>
> **Q.** Did you feel that it could kill you? **A.** Yes, sir.
>
> **Q.** How long was the blade again, about how long? **A.** (Indicating)
>
> **Q.** About like that, about what—seven, eight inches? **A.** About seven or eight inches.
>
> **Q.** It's a butcher knife, is that right? **A.** Butcher, yes, sir.

Mary's attorney vigorously protests this line of questioning and asks that the answers be stricken. **What is the most likely basis for the lawyer's objections and motion to strike? Should the motion be granted in federal court? In a common law jurisdiction?**

Problem II-19. Francis Speedy is charged with operating an automobile at 60 miles per hour in a 45 mile per hour zone. The speed was determined by radar. In laying the foundation for testimony based upon radar readings, State Trooper X testifies that he is familiar with the use of radar equipment to measure vehicular speed; that, while working with State Trooper Y, he set up at the location in question a radar machine used by the state police; that the state police follow a regular procedure to test the accuracy of radar machines both before and after they are put in operation at a particular location; and that the procedure is to set up the equipment and allow a short time for it to "warm-up," after which one officer drives his automobile through the zone of operation at speeds of 70, 60 and 50 miles per hour while the second officer reads the radar meter. Trooper Y is in the hospital on the day of the trial, but Trooper X offers to testify that the standard procedure was followed immediately prior to Speedy's arrest, and that after the radar machine was set up and allowed to "warm-up," he drove his automobile through the zone of operations at speeds of 70, 60, and 50 miles per hour while Trooper Y read the radar meter. Speedy objects to this evidence. **Is it admissible? Does it matter if Trooper Y is in the hospital with a bullet wound? On vacation? Too busy to show up in court?**

IV.   APPENDIX
THE PRODUCTION OF EVIDENCE

A. THE NEED TO PREPARE

A spectator watching an advocate perform, or a student reading the record in a trial like the *Tellez* case, might well underestimate the difficulty of the lawyer's job. Direct examination may appear simple and natural to one watching the parties' chosen witnesses parade their knowledge in their own words before the trier of fact. One may wonder what accounts for the high hourly fees of lawyers who appear to do little more than ask, "Where were you?" or "What did he do?", or "What did you do next?" Cross-examination, while more obviously dependent on the examining counsel, often seems to be little more than an effort to rephrase what the witness has said in a way which emphasizes its least favorable side—though one also sees attempts to tease, chastise, and cajole witnesses into adding to, subtracting from, or modifying what they said, as well as attacks on credibility ranging from the reluctant suggestion that even good and honest people may err to the gleeful demolition of a witness's story and sometimes the witness's character as well.

No one who has tried even a single case will minimize the skill and effort which lie behind the careful examination of witnesses. As in great tennis or a Robert Frost poem, apparent simplicity is the result of training and hard work; it is not inherent in the nature of things. Preparing a case is difficult, time-consuming, and often expensive, but it is more important to success at trial than fine oratorical skills or the best tactical sense. The noted trial lawyer, Louis Nizer, made the point this way:

> [I]n a certain sense there is no right or wrong way to try a case, any more than there is right or wrong way to paint a painting or to write a poem. That is, the right way to try a case which expresses your personality and your talents to the full. . . .
>
>   . . .
>
> There is only one thing that I shall be didactic about . . . I shall brook no disagreement on this subject. . . . [T]he most important qualification for an able trial lawyer is *thorough preparation, hard work and industry.*[92]

Investigation, preparation and cogitation are not only prerequisites for effective trial advocacy; they are also essential in settling civil suits and negotiating guilty pleas.

The testimony, documents, expert opinions, and exhibits which comprise the evidence that forms a lawyer's case are not always available when the decision to represent a client is made. They must be discovered, compiled and interpreted. An ethical attorney does not make up evidence in the sense of creating appearances with no basis in reality, but in a very real sense he or she must generate the evidence that is later presented in negotiations or in court. This appendix discusses some of the ways in which lawyers generate this evidence.

One of the most important aspects of preparation for trial is discovery. In civil cases, discovery is usually regulated by rule or statute,[93] and the scope of available discovery is very broad. Criminal discovery is typically much more limited, and its scope is determined in part by appellate court interpretations of the requirements of the due process clauses of the Fifth and Fourteenth Amendments.[94] We will not discuss either type of discovery, since they are covered in detail in courses on civil and criminal procedure. Instead, we will focus on the process of investigation and preparation that takes place without any specific legal procedure to compel cooperation from witnesses, or from others who may control the relevant information.

Investigation and preparation begin before a case is filed, and continue until the last witness is called. Early investigation helps a lawyer decide whether to take a case; it may turn up facts which will convince the opposition to drop the case at the inception; and it can uncover or preserve evidence which would otherwise be lost forever.

---

[92] Louis Nizer, The Art of Jury Trial, 32 Cornell L. Q. 59, 59–60 (1946) (emphasis in original).

[93] E.g., Fed. R. Civ. P. 26.

[94] See Wayne R. LaFave, Jerold H. Israel, Nancy J. King & Orin S. Kerr, Criminal Procedure, § 20.4 (5th ed. 2009).

Later investigation is necessary for counsel to maximize the benefits of available discovery. And witness preparation is a constant process, the backdrop against which trials are conducted.

Before going further we should alert you to the fact that although interviewing, investigation, and witness preparation are among the most basic ways in which lawyers generate evidence, we can barely scratch the surface of these topics in a book devoted to the rules that govern the admissibility of evidence at trial. Books on trial practice and preparation go into the matter more deeply,[95] and clinical or other practical experience is necessary in order to learn to practice these arts.

B. INTERVIEWS, INVESTIGATION, AND WITNESS PREPARATION

1. Interviewing the Client

Imagine that a client comes to your office to inquire about the possibility of bringing a lawsuit against a police officer. The client complains that the officer in question filed a false charge against him for selling narcotics, that as result the client was arrested and his house searched, but that ultimately all charges were dismissed. The client's main specific complaints are that: (1) the entire prosecution for sale of narcotics was maliciously brought, and based upon false and perjurious evidence; (2) the search of the client's house was baseless and made unnecessarily offensive by the large number of officers participating; and (3) the officer's false statements on the witness stand at the preliminary hearing, which he repeated for the local press after testifying, injured the client's reputation among his friends and in the community. On the assumption that this angry and somewhat rambling story is true, you see five possible causes of action: malicious prosecution, trespass, slander, false arrest, and a federal action for invasion of constitutionally protected rights.

Does the fact that the client's story suggests several different causes of action warrant filing suit? Plainly the answer is no. Before you become involved you want to know more about the case. The easiest and most important way to learn more is to question your prospective client.

The client interview is more than just a fact-gathering mission. It is an interpersonal process which provides an early opportunity for you to

---

[95] See, e.g., Robert M. Bastress & Joseph D. Harbaugh, Interviewing, Counseling, and Negotiating: Skills for Effective Representation (1990); David A. Binder & Paul Bergman, Fact Investigation: From Hypothesis to Proof (1984); and Michael E. Tigar, Examining Witnesses (2nd ed. 2003).

evaluate your potential client and his or her story, and for the client to evaluate you.[96]

Needless to say, a major goal of the client interview is to obtain information. But you should have other goals as well, such as establishing rapport with the client. Try to obtain the facts without unnecessarily interrupting the client's story. You should ask questions to clarify confusing points and to adjust the pace of the interview, but remember that useful questions are well-timed and usually open-ended, inviting the client to elaborate. *Listen* to the client. This may seem like unnecessary advice, but it is sometimes difficult to follow. Remember that you and the client may have very different goals, as well as prejudices and conflicting frames of reference which can impede communication. Try to be aware of these factors, and make an effort to listen to what the client does *not* say, as well. Build rapport by empathizing with the client, and avoiding the temptation to make judgments. Finally, you should seek to determine what the client needs, and whether it is something you can provide. Do not assume that because the client has sought a lawyer, the client really needs legal services.

2. Interviewing Witnesses

"The lawyer who would have a success in advocacy must see and talk to his witnesses."[97] Or he must be sure that someone he trusts interviews witnesses for him. There are advantages in the lawyer conducting his own interviews.[98] He gets to know the witnesses, their strengths, weaknesses, and temperaments, and he gets an idea of their credibility. But there are also costs. The time of a senior lawyer may be prohibitively expensive, and he may not be as good an interviewer as someone associated with him or those he can hire. Professional investigators may be particularly valuable since they often have law enforcement experience and law enforcement friends.

Discussing the advantages of an investigator, John Flinn, who worked as a private investigator in the State of Virginia, and who had prior experience in an FBI lab, as a Virginia State Trooper and as a United States Treasury agent, made the following observations:

> Just to say that any police officer is going to cooperate with any investigator, or any police officer is not going to cooperate with any attorney would be wrong. But some attorneys can do

---

[96] For a more detailed discussion of client interviewing, see Harrop A. Freeman & Henry Weihofen, Clinical Law Training: Interviewing and Counseling, 25–27 (1972); see also Robert Bastress & Joseph Harbaugh, Interviewing Counseling and Negotiating 59–196 (1990).

[97] F. Busch, Law and Tactics in Jury Trials § 204, at 294 (1949).

[98] We are talking here about an early interview to gather information. The litigator will always want to talk to those who will testify for his client in order to prepare their testimony. See infra, Section II(c).

wonders with *some* policemen and some investigators can do wonders with *most* policemen. We've got a sort of relationship there—being a policeman is something like I guess being a fraternity brother—once you've been there you've got a lot of things to share with the guys who are out there now and they'll open up to you, so to speak, or rap with you. But attorneys have about two strikes against them every time they contact a police officer. . . .

. . .

Police officers make mistakes, and I think any really good police officer knows his own limitations and the limitations of the people he works with. And whereas the one case you're working on may be the most important thing in your life, for the moment anyway, and for the people you represent it may be the most important thing, for this police officer it's just one of several cases. He knows when he comes to court there are some areas he is weak in and he also knows that if we have been working on the case, or any good investigator has, that investigator has been working just on that one case probably and may be in a position to trip him up on some things that he may have overlooked. But as far as impeaching a dishonest police officer I don't think any good investigator would have any hesitancy about doing that. Nor would any good police officer regret to see it done.

. . .

What may happen to prospective plaintiffs and their counsel is that they will wait several months before deciding that an investigation in addition to the government's investigation would be conducted. By that time everything is going to be working against us, I'm afraid, because things will have quieted down and people will have been advised what to say and what not to say and they will have gotten all their stories straight. If I was an attorney, . . . and I had a client whose child was involved in an automobile accident or whose family was in any way involved in some type of an episode that might end up in court, I would have an independent investigation conducted just as soon as possible after the thing happened. I think that would be Number 1, because to rely upon a government agency to investigate anything and think that's going to benefit everybody involved is wrong. I know that from experience, because most government agencies from the . . . Sheriff's Office on up to the FBI conduct sort of an assembly line process, and it's not a real in depth study of any specific occurrence. There are always areas that the investigator wishes he had time to dig into, but doesn't. A private investigator is able to concentrate on one case at a time if he has the resources coming in and he can cover everything right down the line. And we've found a lot of police officers are real happy to see us come around because they wish, as I did when I was on the force, that they could have spent more time on a particular case. Thus, they will steer us to things that they would have checked into if they had more time. And they know that we understand why they don't have more time.

. . .

I don't know if things have changed or what. When I was a police officer I always thought everything was stacked on the side of the defense. Now that I am on the other side, I begin to think that everything is stacked on the side of the police. Overall, I think everything works out well many times. But both sides must be prepared. The investigation for both sides must be thorough, the lawyers must be prepared, and the adversaries must be evenly matched.[99]

Contrary to what one may gather from television, investigation is not easy. Witnesses are not all cooperative; they are certainly not all accurate; and, sadly they are not all honest.

Considerable ingenuity may be required to locate persons who observed the criminal act charged or who have information concerning it. After they are located, their cooperation must be secured. It may be necessary to approach a witness several times to raise new questions stemming from facts learned from others.[100]

The following paragraphs summarize one approach to identifying and overcoming various difficulties which are inherent in interviewing witnesses.[101]

Before a lawyer can begin the interviewing process, there are several issues that should be considered, including the importance of talking to any particular witness. It is also important to determine whether the lawyer needs to become more familiar with the scene of the events, and with tangible and documentary evidence, and whether the lawyer should first speak to any other witness or witnesses. After these issues have been addressed, a lawyer who wants to obtain information from a witness must motivate the witness to share that information.

---

[99] Talk given at the University of Virginia Law School, Sept. 7, 1973.

[100] ABA Standards for Criminal Justice, Prosecution Function and Defense Function, Defense Function 182 (3rd ed. 1993).

[101] This excerpt is based on David A. Binder & Paul Bergman, Fact Investigation: From Hypothesis to Proof 221–243 (1984).

There are many factors which cause people to withhold information. A witness might fear the loss of self-esteem, such as occurs if she provides information when it seems morally wrong to do so, or if that information might help an unpopular litigant, or harm a popular one. A witness might also believe that providing information is improper, in light of her relationship to the parties; for instance, a person who is to testify for one party may be reluctant to talk to the lawyer for the opposing party. Social etiquette can also be a barrier. A person might feel that speaking to a lawyer—or to anyone of another gender, or race, or station in life—is improper, even when the topic would be freely discussed among that person's peers. Many witnesses are reluctant to recall and speak about traumatic events, and other witnesses are reluctant to talk when they believe that the upshot will be testimony in court, and that their testimony will cost them money or, more frequently, time. Witnesses may withhold information because they do not see its relevance, believing perhaps that the interviewer has an improper reason for seeking that information. Finally, some witnesses are unable to provide full attention and accurate information because they are deeply involved in some task or event that is not, in itself, important.

Fortunately, there are also a number of methods that may be used to motivate witnesses to provide information. One important approach is continual empathy: the interviewer should listen actively, paying attention to the witness's statement, and then reflecting it back to him or her; the interviewer should also acknowledge and respond to both expressed and unexpressed feelings. Other important techniques include: showing personal interest in the witness; explicitly recognizing the importance of the witness, and appealing to the witness's sense of justice and fair play. It is often helpful to ask questions which imply an expectation that the witness will reply, because we have all been socialized to respond to that expectation. Finally, where it is possible to do so, it may also be helpful to the interviewer to provide some information to the witness, especially if that information will explain the relevance of the information that is sought from the witness.

3. Preparing the Friendly Witness to Testify

A lawyer prepares for cross-examination on her own. As we saw in Section II, pp. 151–153, a hostile cross-examination is a process that does not depend on the cooperation of one witness; quite the contrary, the usual operating assumption is that the witness must be forced to toe the line. But the direct examination of a friendly witness is another matter. It requires cooperation between the examining attorney and the witness. One of your main tasks is to educate, prepare, and build rapport with your own witnesses. Remember that most witnesses know little or nothing about courtroom procedure and the role of the witness, or, worse, they have picked up a lot of misinformation from movies or TV. If you and the witness are to perform successfully from a common script, you must teach her what to do, and demonstrate that she can rely on your judgment and experience. As an experienced trial lawyer explains:[102]

> You and the witness are in your office. It is days or weeks before the witness will testify. Here are some things you might say. Edit the narrative as needed, because procedures vary. In real life, it will not be one-sided. The witness will want to interrupt with questions. Make sure someone else from your office, or connected with the case in a way not to disrupt the lawyer-client privilege is sitting in. Think about whether notes you take are discoverable.

> "Hello. Have a seat. Can I get you some coffee, or a soft drink or water?"

> Do not order somebody else to do this.

> "I wanted to get a chance to talk about the trial and answer your questions. This should take a couple of hours, but I think you set aside time so we can do a really good job.

> "Have you ever been a witness in court before? Tell me about that. . . . Well, just for myself, I'd like to go through it all with you, but I'll cut it short if I am talking about something you already know. Every case is different. Every judge, jury, and courtroom are different.

> "Here is a diagram of the courtroom we are going to be in. It might not be just like this one, because there can always be changes. But this is basically it. You will be out here in the witness room until we call you. They have this rule that you can't sit in and listen to the testimony of any other witness. Now, when you are done testifying, we can ask the judge to let you stay for the rest of the trial, and usually she'll grant that.

> "When you are called, the bailiff will walk with you into the courtroom. I'll make sure that Mr. Wilson from my office is there, too. I know you'll be a little nervous, but just walk right in. You'll walk up to this desk here, where a woman is sitting, just in front of the judge's bench. She should stand up, if she's paying attention. She'll say, 'Raise your right hand.' Do that, and she'll ask you to swear that you'll tell the truth. Do you have a religious objection to swearing the oath—I mean, would you rather affirm that you will tell the truth?"

---

[102] Michael E. Tigar, Examining Witnesses 51–57 (2nd ed. 2003). Reprinted by permission of ABA Publishing. Copyright 2003 by American Bar Association.

Always ask this, and if the answer is "yes," work it out beforehand with the clerk.

"Then, you take your seat right here in the witness chair. Put your hands in your lap, sit up straight, and look at me. I'll be standing right here.

"Now comes the hard part. You know more about what you saw than anybody else in the world. More than I do, more than [the client], certainly more than the other side. The lawyer on the other side knows you know what you're talking about, and he might try to make some objections or interrupt us to keep you from telling what you know in the most effective way possible.

"I need a big favor from you. I need you to trust me on this. I am the lawyer for [the client]. It's my job to make sure that if the lawyer on the other side makes some objection or interruption, that gets handled.

"Another thing. There are all these rules in court. They don't let you just come in and tell your story like you know it. Maybe some of what you know is based on what you heard from other people. Or the jury can understand it better if we show them some pictures of the scene. For a lot of reasons, the way we do this is that I ask questions and you answer to the jury.

"In a few minutes, we will go over all the things you know. I have some pictures here, and I will be making sure they show the intersection the way it was. Everything you have to do in court can be summed up like this: Listen to every question, no matter if I ask it, the other side's lawyer asks it, or the judge asks it. Listen to it. Then take a second or two to make sure you've got the question in mind. Then answer that question straight and true. If the question is not clear, just say, 'I'm sorry, I don't understand what you're asking.'" At this point, you might have a chart with the rules on it.

1. Listen to the question.

2. Take a second or two.

3. If the question isn't clear, say so.

4. If the question is clear, answer that question.

"If you remember these principles, you'll do fine. Now, maybe you're thinking, 'Who is this bozo telling me I'll do fine? What if I get confused and flustered in there and he asks me a question and I forget what I'm supposed to say?' Or maybe you watched some lawyer program on television and you're thinking, 'What do I do when the other side's lawyer puts his face about a foot from mine and hollers cross examination at me?'

"For what it's worth, I think those are great questions. The answer to both of them is the same. Do just what's on the chart. Let's go through it.

"I ask a question. I don't know as much about the case as you do, so the question doesn't seem to make sense. You pause and say, 'I don't understand.' Or suppose I ask you, 'Did the red Ford stop here at the stop sign?' And you know it did, but then it started right up again and went on through, even though Stacy Wilson was in the crosswalk.

"All I'm asking is, please, you've got to trust me to know the case, trust me to know that you know all the important facts, and I want the jury to hear all you know. So just answer the question I asked, and then I will ask the next question that brings out more of the story. Also, there are all these rules about the form of questions I can ask, and the way things have to be done. If you let me ask the questions, then I can try to make sure we let the jury know the truth, and do that in the way the rules require.

"There's whole other reason for listening, pausing, and just answering the question. That's the way we're going to control the lawyer on the other side. Because you are going to treat him the same way you treat me. Listen to his question. Then pause. In that pause, I get a chance to do my job. If the question is improper, or if he is being abusive and in your face, I can stand up and object. If the judge sustains the objection, good. If she overrules it and says 'Answer the question,' you have had a few more seconds to focus on rules 3 and 4, so you do the next right thing."

. . . "Now suppose my question is clear, but you just plain forgot the answer for a moment. That happens to everybody, especially sitting up there in the witness chair. Maybe it'll happen today on something and we can practice. If you forget, smile and say something like 'I know that, but it just escapes me at the moment.' Then I get to ask, 'Is your memory exhausted on this right now?' And you say, 'Yes.' Then I can remind you of that fact, and we go ahead.

"You probably wonder who you should look at when you are answering. Half of that is easy. When I, or the other lawyer, or the judge is asking you a question, look at whoever is asking."

We have to step out of the narrative here because courtrooms and judges are so different. Do you examine from a seated position at the counsel table, from behind a lectern, standing at your table, or from wherever you like? How is the courtroom laid out? How far are you from the witness—that is, does the witness have to pan the courtroom with her eyes to look from the jury to you and back again?

Will you be in one of those small, almost intimate, courtrooms of the modern type where counsel, parties, jurors, witnesses, and spectators are seated in a kind of circle, so that it really looks like anybody can talk to everybody?

Whatever the rule and whatever the interior design, you want your witnesses to be comfortable. You do not want them jerking their heads back and forth and looking agitated. I operate on several key assumptions born of experience. Jurors may not forgive the normal signs of nervousness, which may seem to betoken insincerity. You must be in charge, and every witness on your side needs to be reminded. You assert your control by preparation and by adopting techniques of examination that preserve your options.

You and the witness may benefit from videotaping a part of the proposed examination. Beware of any requirement that you turn the tape over to your opponent, and make sure your witness is able to answer cross-examination questions about the process. I prefer to videotape only a few questions and answers so that the witness can truthfully say, "They just wanted me to see how I looked to other people, so they videotaped about a dozen questions and answers."

Your relationship with a friendly witness, particularly one who will testify at length or on an important subject, will say a great deal to the jury. The respect you and the witness show one another and to the other trial participants is vital. You are the only person who can help the novice witness know how to "relate" to the jury. Once, Lady Bird Johnson was a character witness for a defendant I represented. She came in over the weekend to be prepared to testify, accompanied by a Secret Service agent and our mutual friend Bob Strauss.

The questions one asks a character witness, and the answers she is permitted to give, are well confined. I was surprised that Mrs. Johnson worried about the basic matters of how to look, act, and present herself to the jurors. I made the mistake of thinking that with all those years in public life, this cameo role as a witness would not concern her. She was concerned, not only because the experience was novel. She is so gracious and accomplished that she wanted her testimony to be effective. She cared in the same way that most friendly witnesses care.

I described the courtroom. Then I said something like, "Mrs. Johnson, when I first came to Washington, D.C., in 1966, we lived on Capitol Hill. Your husband was president. And I still remember how you would dedicate those 'vest-pocket parks' and other green spaces. The children in the neighborhood and their parents would come to hear you. Those jurors are the mothers and fathers you were so effective at talking with. They are concerned about the same issues, and they have the same common sense they always did."

That explanation, Mrs. Johnson said, and Bob Strauss told me later, worked because it tied the experience of being a witness to other events in Mrs. Johnson's life. Every witness you will ever meet has—sometime, somewhere—explained something to somebody. That may be a good place to start.

How did this episode come out? Mrs. Johnson was asked, and answered, the standard character witness questions. The last one was, "Do you have an opinion about his integrity and honesty?" She said, "Yes. He has integrity, and he is honest." And then she turned to the jurors, looked them in the eyes, and said in tones redolent of those speeches in the parks, "You know, there's many people who don't like John, but nobody ever said he wasn't honest."

Almost every witness has special qualities that can make their testimony real. The nurse can say, "I checked the blood pressure," or, "I checked the blood pressure, just as I was trained to do." The second answer dignifies the witness in the jurors' eyes and lets the witness exhibit a quality of which she is proud. An experienced employee, well-briefed on antitrust risks, is better able to know if anything improper happened at a meeting than someone with less experience. A bank teller may have been trained to observe the characteristics of those at his workstation. A court official will have been trained to notice whether certain procedures were or were not followed. Learn your witness's special qualities, and integrate them into the direct examination. To this extent at least, the witness's story helps the client's story.

4. Examining Places, Instruments and Documents

No matter how lucid a client's or witness' description of a place or an item of tangible evidence, it would be folly to rely upon the description and fail to look for yourself. In some circumstances your own impressions will suffice, but often you will need the help of others to preserve or appreciate what is there. You may wish to photograph a scene or photocopy documents for use in interviewing witnesses and at trial. You may also need expert help to analyze blood, verify questioned documents, conduct ballistics test or engage in the countless other scientific analyses which can make or break a case. The details of such analyses are quite technical, and we can not go into them here, but it may be essential that you have access to those who have mastered them.[103]

5. Miscellaneous Sources of Information

Since many government agencies, both state and federal, investigate a host of subjects and often compile reports on their investigation, a diligent lawyer will always try to find reports of governmental inquiries

---

[103] See Chapter Nine.

that may bear on her case. In an automobile accident case, for example, a police officer may appear promptly at the scene and attempt to reconstruct what happened. The officer's report may contain the names of potential witnesses, statements made by witnesses and parties, and some indication of the physical characteristics of the scene such as the type of damage done to the vehicles or the length of skid marks, if any. If an airplane crashes, there is likely to be a study by the regulatory authorities which, if available, may be of tremendous help in litigation. The resources and expertise which a federal agency can put into such an investigation far exceed those available to private attorneys. The apparent disinterest of the government will also enhance the credibility of the report if there is some way of using it at trial.[104] Another way of generating information that may be helpful in developing a case is the obvious, but underrated method of perusing the technical or scientific literature in areas relevant to your case. Many diligent lawyers spend considerable time researching the history, the purpose and the competing interpretations of the law upon which they rely or against which they must labor; yet if they are unable to convey clearly the factual basis of their case or to cross-examine their opponent's experts intelligently, they are likely to lose the benefits of their legal learning.[105] Skilled lawyers

---

[104] It may be difficult to actually use such a report at trial, since the written report itself might be inadmissible hearsay. But see FRE 803(8), discussed in Chapter Six. Where cooperation with government investigators is mandated by law, information given to satisfy the statute will often be protected by a privilege. Indeed, some government reports are classified as confidential, either by custom or by statute, so the attorney may find that she is unable to get access to such reports even for the purpose of a pretrial investigation.

The Freedom of Information Act (FOIA), 5 U.S.C. § 552, and similar state laws, may serve as discovery substitutes. The federal statute provides that governmental agencies must make agency records promptly available to any person, regardless of her identity or need for disclosure, unless the records are exempted from the compulsory disclosure requirements of the Act. The federal exemptions cover the following matters: 1) national security information, 2) records relating solely to internal personnel rules and practices, 3) information protected against disclosure by other federal statutes, 4) trade secrets and commercial or financial information, 5) pre-decisional internal communications, 6) information which would constitute a clearly unwarranted invasion of personal privacy, 7) investigatory records compiled for "law enforcement purposes", 8) reports prepared by an agency responsible for the regulation or supervision of financial institutions and 9) geological and geophysical information and data.

The Supreme Court has said that "the FOIA was not intended to supplement or displace rules of discovery." John Doe Agency v. John Doe Corporation, 493 U.S. 146, 153 (1989). Circuit courts have emphasized that the purpose of the FOIA is public disclosure, not private litigation. See, e.g., Metex Corporation v. ACS Industries, Inc., 748 F.2d 150 (3d Cir. 1984). Thus, it may be difficult to use the FOIA for discovery, especially in light of Exemption Three, but the Act has nevertheless been used for this purpose. Procedurally, it has certain advantages. Under the Act, an agency has twenty days in which to reply to an initial request for information, and 20 days to make a determination with respect to an appeal (§ 552(a)(6)(A)). Thus, obtaining covered information can greatly expedite a proceeding. An adverse FOIA decision is immediately appealable as a final decision (5 U.S.C. § 552(a)(6)(C)). A discovery motion under the Federal Rules of Civil Procedure is review able only by obtaining a writ of mandamus or upon appeal after an adverse decision on the merits. A court in a FOIA action may also assess costs and reasonable attorney fees against the government when the complainant substantially prevails (§ 552(a)(4)(E)).

[105] Expert witnesses may also be used for the same purpose. One of the most valuable services the expert performs is educating the attorney about the technical background of the case and helping her prepare for direct and cross-examination.

will tell you that the facts and not the law most often decide the outcomes of their cases.[106]

6.   Access to Witnesses

Any lawyer representing any party in any type of case may have difficulty interviewing a crucial witness. Cases that address this issue, however, almost always concern problems faced by criminal defense attorneys. The main reason for this pattern, no doubt, is that in most American jurisdictions a criminal defense attorney has no power to compel a witness to talk to her before trial. In a civil case, under most modern rules of discovery, a lawyer can subpoena a reluctant witness to a deposition. Similarly, a criminal prosecutor can usually subpoena an unwilling witness to testify before a grand jury (and even that is rarely necessary, since few witnesses refuse to talk to police officers or other investigators for the prosecution). But a criminal defense attorney is vulnerable to actions that obstruct her access to witnesses.

Courts that have faced this issue have uniformly recognized two separate rights: (1) A criminal defendant (and by extension, probably, any party) has the right, through his counsel, to approach a witness and attempt to interview her, unobstructed by the court or the government. (2) The witness has the right to decline to be interviewed. As one comment explains:[107]

> The courts of the United States have generally looked with favor on defense interviewing witnesses. It is not only a right of the defendant but a duty of his counsel. It is often found to be a constitutional right, sometimes based on due process, sometimes on the right to summon witnesses. Some courts have found a manifest unfairness in allowing the prosecution access to a witness while estranging the defense.

> However, the right of the defendant has been a right against the court or against the district attorney and not against the witness. A court may order an interview with someone under its jurisdiction or it may restrain the prosecution from interfering with an interview, but a court will not ordinarily order an unwilling witness to submit to an interview.

In other words, while it is perfectly legitimate for the witness to refuse to talk to a defense lawyer or a defense investigator, the prosecutor and the police may not order, or persuade, or suggest to the witness that she do

---

[106] See, e.g., Lloyd Striker, The Art of Advocacy (1954).

[107] Raymond J. Hagen, Interviewing Witnesses in Criminal Cases, 28 Brooklyn L. Rev. 207, 225 (1962).

so;[108] and they may not place the witness beyond the reach of the defense—for example, by deporting her.[109] If the witness is in public custody, the government has an affirmative obligation to produce her and give the defense a fair opportunity to attempt to interview the witness, but having done so, the final choice is up to the witness.[110]

V. BIBLIOGRAPHY

McCormick, Chs. 1, 2, 3, 4, 6, 7.

Weinstein, Chs. 103–105, 601–606, 611, 614–615, 701 (1999).

Bastress, Robert M. and Joseph D. Harbaugh, Interviewing, Counseling, and Negotiating: Skills for Effective Representation (1990).

Binder, David B. and Paul Bergman, Fact Investigation: From Hypothesis to Proof (1993).

Damaska, Mirjan R., Evidence Law Adrift (1997).

Kalven, Harry Jr. and Hans Zeisel, The American Jury (1966).

Kassin, Saul M. and Christina A. Studebaker, "Instructions to Disregard and The Jury: Curative and Paradoxical Effects," in J.M. Golding & C.M. MacLeod (eds.), Intentional Forgetting: Interdisciplinary Approaches (Hillsdale, N.J.: Erlbaum, in press).

Wayne R. LaFave, Jerold H. Israel, Nancy J. King & Orin S. Kerr, Criminal Procedure, §§ 20.1, 20.4 (5th ed. 2009).

Mauet, Thomas A., Trial Techniques (8th ed. 2010).

Tigar, Michael E., Examining Witnesses (2nd ed. 2003).

Wellman, Francis Lewis, The Art of Cross Examination (1904).

Berger, Margaret A., When, If Ever, Does Evidentiary Error Constitute Reversible Error?, 25 Loy. L.A. L. Rev. 893 (1992).

Carretta, T.R. and R.C. Moreland, The Direct and Indirect Effects of Inadmissible Evidence, 13 J. App. Soc. Psych. 291 (1983).

---

[108] E.g., People v. Mitchell, 16 Ill.App.2d 189, 147 N.E.2d 883 (1958); Walker v. Superior Court, 155 Cal.App.2d 134, 317 P.2d 130 (1957); Cern, Interference by Prosecutor with Defense Counsel's Pretrial Interrogation of Witnesses, 90 A.L.R.3d 1231 (1979).

[109] E.g., United States v. Mendez-Rodriguez, 450 F.2d 1 (9th Cir. 1971); Eunice A. Eichelberger, Effect on Federal Criminal Proceeding of Unavailability to Defendant of Alien Witness Through Deportation or other Government Action, 56 A.L.R. Fed. 698 (1994).

[110] E.g., W. E. Shipley, Accused Right to Interview Witness Held in Public Custody, 14 A.L.R.3d 652 (1952).

Clermont, Kevin M. and Theodore Eisenberg, Trial by Jury or Judge: Transcending Empiricism, 77 Cornell L. Rev. 1124 (1992).

Comment, Perjury: The Forgotten Offense, 65 J. Crim. L. and Criminology 361 (1974).

Davis, Kenneth C., An Approach to Rules of Evidence for Nonjury Cases, 50 A.B. A. J. 723 (1964).

Davis, Thomas Y., Affirmed: A Study of Criminal Appeals and Decision-Making Norms in a California Court of Appeal, 1982 Am. B. Found. Res. J. 543.

Fein, Steven, et al., Can the Jury Disregard That Information? The Use of Suspicion to Reduce the Prejudicial Effect of Pretrial Publicity and Inadmissible Testimony, 23 Personality and Soc. Psychology Bull. 1215 (1997).

Hans, Valerie P. and Anthony N. Doob, Section 12 of the Canada Evidence Act and the Deliberations of Simulated Juries, 18 Crim. L. Q. 235 (1976).

Levin, Leo and Harold K. Cohen, The Exclusionary Rules in Nonjury Criminal Cases, 119 U. Pa. L. Rev. 905 (1971).

Maguire, John MacArthur and Charles S.S. Epstein, Preliminary Questions of Fact in Determining the Admissibility of Evidence, 40 Harv. L. Rev. 392 (1927).

Mengler, Thomas M., The Theory of Discretion in the Federal Rules of Evidence, 74 Iowa L. Rev. 413 (1989).

Morgan, Edmund M., Functions of Judge and Jury in the Determination of Preliminary Questions of Fact, 43 Harv. L. Rev. 165 (1929).

Nance, Dale A., The Best Evidence Principle, 73 Iowa L. Rev. 227 (1988).

Nizer, Louis, The Art of Jury Trial, 32 Cornell L.Q. 59 (1946).

Note, Exclusionary Rules of Evidence in Non-Jury Proceedings, 46 Ill. L. Rev. 915 (1952).

Note, Social Science Findings and the Jury's Ability To Disregard Evidence Under the Federal Rules of Evidence, 52 Law and Contemp. Probs. No. 4, 341 (1989).

Riechenberg, Kurt, The Recognition of Foreign Privileges in United States Discovery Proceedings, 9 Nw. J. Int'l L. and Bus. 80 (1988).

Saltzburg, Stephen A., Standards of Proof and Preliminary Questions of Fact, 27 Stan. L. Rev. 271 (1975).

Schaefer, Evelyn O. and Kristine L. Hansen, Similar Fact Evidence and Limited Use Instructions: An Empirical Investigation, 14 Crim. L. J. 157 (1990).

Tanford, Sarah and Michele Cox, Decision Processes in Civil Cases: The Impact of Impeachment Evidence on Liability and Credibility Judgments, 2 Soc. Behav. 165 (1987).

Wissler, Roselle L. and Michael J. Saks, On the Inefficacy of Limiting Instructions: When Jurors Use Credibility Evidence to Decide on Guilt, 9 Law and Hum. Behav. 37 (1985).

Wolf, Sharon and David A. Montgomery, Effects of Inadmissible Evidence and Level of Judicial Admonishment to Disregard on the Judgments of Mock Jurors, 7 J. App. Soc. Psych. 205 (1977).

CHAPTER 3

RELEVANCE

■ ■ ■

I. ASPECTS OF RELEVANCE

A. THE BASIC POLICY

Trials may be thought of in many ways. They may be seen as battles between two "champions," something akin to medieval Europe's trial by combat. From this perspective, there is an aesthetic satisfaction in watching skillful lawyers joust, and the excitement when a battle pits "our side" against "theirs" may rise to a fever pitch. Some modern procedural rules (for example, the rules governing discovery in civil cases) are designed in part to reduce the gamesmanship of trials. But so long as lawyers remain dependent on clients for their livelihood, and so long as clients prefer winning to abstract justice, the modern trial is unlikely to shed entirely its contentious atmosphere. From another perspective, the trial may be seen as an elaborate ritual designed to convince litigants that they have been heard. The attorney's role here is not so much to win as to convince the client that she has had the opportunity to voice her proof and views. From this perspective it is the *appearance* of fairness that is essential.[1] From a third point of view, a trial is simply a form of dispute resolution. This perspective holds that ultimately it is more important that a dispute be resolved than that it be resolved perfectly. This view justifies limited rights of collateral and direct appeal, rules of res judicata and statutes of limitations. Finally, a trial may be seen as a way of finding the truth so that disputes are resolved correctly. Procedures for discovery and penalties for perjury respond to this concern.

These perspectives are not mutually exclusive, and the litigation process reflects elements of each. But in modern evidence law the "truth-finding" model predominates. This model presumes that rules of evidence should be judged by whether or not they increase the chance that the jury will reach the correct verdict.[2] The law is too practical to concern itself

---

[1] See generally Tom Tyler, Procedural Justice (vol. 1) (2005).

[2] As we have already seen in Chapter Two, evidence law responds to other values as well. But where these values conflict with truth-finding, there is sure to be tension, and some people argue that the value of truth-finding should prevail. The controversies surrounding the Fourth Amendment exclusionary rule, especially as applied to the states in *Mapp v. Ohio*, 367 U.S. 643 (1961), and the exclusion of confessions obtained in violation of *Miranda v. Arizona*, 384 U.S. 436 (1966), are examples of both these points. The discussion of privileges in Chapter Eight provides other examples of policies which override truth-finding.

with the nice epistemological question of whether the truth can ever be known. It assumes that it can, and it assumes that the way to find truth is to present the fact-finder with all the evidence that bears on the issue to be decided, except when there is *good reason* to do otherwise. This policy permeates the law of evidence. As we saw when we discussed competence in Chapter Two, and as we shall see in our discussion of other rules, the tendency over the past century has been to increase the range of evidence available to the decision maker.[3] This basic policy is expressed in FRE 402:

> Relevant evidence is admissible unless any of the following provides otherwise:
>
> - the United States Constitution;
>
> - a federal statute;
>
> - these rules; or
>
> - other rules prescribed by the Supreme Court.
>
> Irrelevant evidence is not admissible.

And in FRE 403:

> The court may exclude relevant evidence if its probative value is substantially outweighed by the danger of one or more of the following: unfair prejudice, confusing the issues, misleading the jury, undue delay, wasting time, or needlessly presenting cumulative evidence.[4]

But what evidence is relevant? FRE 401 defines the term:

> Evidence is relevant if:
>
> **(a)** it has any tendency to make a fact more or less probable than it would be without the evidence; and
>
> **(b)** the fact is of consequence in determining the action.

---

[3] The history of privileges contains counter examples, which makes sense, since privileges are the major category of evidentiary rules that are *not* justified by their tendency to promote accurate fact-finding. Yet, generally speaking, the tendency holds with privileges as well. The matter is discussed more fully in Chapter Eight

[4] These rules are in an intellectual tradition traceable to James Bradley Thayer, who wrote:

> There is a principle—not so much a rule of evidence as a presupposition involved in the very conception of a rational system of evidence, as contrasted with the old formal and mechanical systems—which forbids receiving anything irrelevant, not logically probative. James B. Thayer, Preliminary Treatise on Evidence, 264 (1898).

> The two leading principles should be brought into conspicuous relief, (1) that nothing is to be received which is not logically probative of some matter requiring to be proved; and (2) that everything which is thus probative should come in, unless a clear ground of policy or law excludes it. Id. at 530.

Thayer's view of this matter is generally accepted by courts and scholars.

B. "OF CONSEQUENCE IN DETERMINING THE ACTION"—MATERIALITY

Let us examine each part of this definition, starting with FRE 401(b). Evidence may bear on a fact that is of no consequence to a legal action because it does not relate to a matter in issue. Such evidence is called *immaterial* regardless of how probative it is of facts on which it does bear. Immateriality is one reason why evidence may lack relevance. If the victim of a traffic accident sues the owner of a truck under the doctrine of *respondeat superior*, evidence that the owner is a careful driver is immaterial because it is the actual driver's carefulness that is at issue, and not the care of the owner. Where a sailor sues a ship owner for maintenance and cure, evidence of contributory negligence is immaterial. The owner's duty of maintenance and cure exists whether or not the injury was caused by the sailor's negligence.

The term "materiality" is usually reserved for the relationship between offered evidence and a legal issue raised by the pleadings in the case, but evidence may be material in the sense that it is properly of consequence to the litigation in question even where it does not bear directly on a legal issue. Evidence affecting the credibility of a witness, for example, is always material. Also, by convention materiality includes "background evidence": basic information about the identity of witnesses, their ages, occupations, places of residence and so forth. Information that aids in the understanding of other material evidence is also considered material. Thus, maps, diagrams and graphs are not excludable as irrelevant even if there is no dispute about what they portray.

At one time, when pleadings were strictly construed and only limited amendment allowed, a lawyer might find that evidence which seemed highly probative of the general matter in question was excluded as immaterial due to improvidently drafted pleadings. Under liberalized modern rules of procedure, this difficulty has almost disappeared. As the art of pleading has diminished in importance, so has the importance of nice distinctions between materiality and relevance.[5] Today the concept of materiality is generally treated as we treat it here—a subcategory of relevance. The term itself is not mentioned in the federal rules and may eventually linger only as part of the ritualistic objection "incompetent, immaterial, and irrelevant," used by some lawyers in an attempt to touch the maximum number of bases with the least amount of thought.

C. CIRCUMSTANTIAL AND DIRECT EVIDENCE

As FRE 401(a) provides, evidence which is offered for its bearing on a fact in issue is irrelevant if, after receipt of the evidence, the existence of

---

[5] There is some question, however, whether Ashcroft v. Iqbal, 129 S.Ct. 1937 (2009) and its progeny will resurrect these issues.

that fact appears no more or less probable than it did before the evidence was offered. Thus evidence that a driver involved in a Texas accident was a Democrat would, in most cases, be irrelevant on the issue of whether that driver was speeding because there is no reason to believe that Democrats, as a class, drive faster than Republicans or independents.

Evidence may be irrelevant in this logical sense only if it is *circumstantial* rather than *direct* proof of a fact in issue. Direct evidence is testimonial evidence which, if believed, resolves a matter in issue. Circumstantial evidence offers no such direct resolution, but serves as a basis from which the trier of fact may make reasonable inferences about a matter in issue. It too is often testimonial in nature. For example, testimony by a witness, Walters, that she saw the defendant, Clark, pull a gun out and shoot the victim, Hill, is direct evidence on the issue of who shot Hill. If believed, we know that Clark was the shooter. Testimony by Walters that she saw Clark standing over Hill's body with a smoking gun, by contrast, is only circumstantial evidence that Clark shot Hill. Even if believed, it only justifies an inference that Clark did the shooting. Other inferences are possible: Clark, for example, might have heard the shot, rushed to the scene, and picked up the gun just as Walters approached.

When we say that evidence is irrelevant in this logical sense, we are saying that knowing an item of circumstantial evidence does not allow the trier of fact to *reasonably* infer anything about the likely existence of a fact in issue. To return to our earlier example, if Texas jurors knew the defendant in tort was a Democrat, they could not from this information alone reasonably infer anything about the likelihood the defendant was speeding. We would say that evidence of the defendant's political affiliation was logically irrelevant.

Conversely, when we say that evidence of some fact, which we shall call the *evidentiary fact,* is logically relevant, we mean only that it has some tendency, however slight, to make a consequential fact in issue more or less likely than it would be if that fact did not exist. Ordinarily what is contemplated is an objective empirical relationship between the evidentiary fact and a fact in issue such that when the former exists the latter is, as an objective matter, more or less likely to exist. This is the situation when the evidentiary fact, either directly or as part of an inferential chain, has a greater-than-chance association with the existence or non-existence of a fact in issue in a case.

There are no degrees of relevance; evidence is either relevant or it is not. Strictly speaking, it is a mistake to say that one item of admissible evidence is "*more relevant*" than another. What differentiates items of different evidentiary weight is *probative value,* i.e. their power to persuade a reasonable person about a fact in issue. Admissible evidence varies widely in probative value.

The difference between direct and circumstantial evidence does not mean that direct evidence is always, or even presumptively, of greater probative value. The difference is that direct evidence, *if believed*, requires no further inference for its bearing on a fact in issue. However, direct evidence need not be believed and may not be very persuasive, as where an eyewitness to a crime admits he is almost blind. Circumstantial evidence, like a fingerprint on a gun, may be far more probative than direct evidence from an unreliable witness. Direct and circumstantial evidence pose different inferential problems, but the differences do not mean that one type is necessarily more probative than the other.

D. REALITY HYPOTHESES

Usually it is so easy to decide that evidence is relevant that we don't stop to wonder why we think so. But underlying every judgment of relevance is a theory of reality: that is, a theory about why people act in various ways and how things are linked in the real world. These theories are ordinarily widely shared and taken for granted. Thus, no one would ask why evidence of Clark's standing over Hill's dead body with a smoking gun in his hand is relevant on the issue of who shot Hill. We believe that the world works in such a way that guns smoke when they have been recently fired, and that someone who possesses a recently fired gun near a dead person is more likely than someone without these characteristics to have killed that person. Occasionally, however, a link is not obvious, and the proponent of evidence must advance what we call a *reality hypothesis*: that is, some plausible view of how the world works that explains why the facts offered in evidence are linked with facts the party must prove. Thus, the prosecutor in the Texas speeding case, if asked why she thought the defendant's political affiliation was a relevant fact, might reply: "You have to be crazy to be a Democrat; crazy people are more likely than sane people to speed; therefore, showing that the defendant is a Democrat, shows that he is especially likely to speed." The defendant may dispute this view of reality by persuading the court of the invalidity of any of the empirical propositions on which it rests. In this case, the prosecutor's world view seems wrong. The claim that crazy people drive faster than sane people has, at best, a weak basis in common experience, and the proposition that a person has to be crazy to be a Democrat is untenable. Therefore, the prosecutor's evidence should be excluded because she has not produced a plausible argument that the defendant's political association is relevant (although a Texas jury in some parts of Texas might decide otherwise the week before an election).

As another example, consider a defendant charged with robbing a postal carrier in the lobby of a building. The prosecution wants to show that the defendant lives in the building. The argument for relevance is obvious: because he lived there, the defendant had ready access to the lobby and an easy opportunity to commit the crime. If forced to expand this argument, the prosecutor would, no doubt, incorporate the fact at issue—the defendant's residence—into a robbery story. He could argue that the defendant lay in wait in his apartment, rushed out to rob his victim and then returned to his apartment; or his theory might be that on his way home the defendant happened upon the mail carrier in the deserted lobby, took advantage of the opportunity to rob him, and then let himself into his apartment as if nothing had happened. Either way, in order to meet the test of relevance the prosecutor does not have to present evidence on any of the other elements of this story; the most he has to do is articulate a story that is at least minimally plausible and consistent with the evidence he offers. The defense attorney will get nowhere by objecting that there is no evidence that robbers are more likely to commit crimes near their own homes than elsewhere. Indeed, the defense attorney will lose a relevance objection even if she has statistics that show that robbers seldom rob in their own back yards. Even if these statistics are conceded to be accurate, the prosecutor is entitled to argue that this defendant robbed this victim in that manner. Unless the argument is laughable (failing the so-called "straight face test")—and this one is not—it is sufficient to meet the weak test that the evidence—here proof of the defendant's address—has *any* tendency to make the defendant's guilt more probable.

But the defense attorney's argument is also plausible. It may well be that robbers are careful to rob away from home. This argument too can be expanded: The last thing a robber would want to do is rob his own postal carrier. That would disrupt his mail service, anger his neighbors, and—worst of all—vastly increase his chance of being recognized. Since this argument too is not laughable, the defendant's address could also be introduced by the defense, over objection, as relevant evidence of innocence. This situation is common. Relevance simply means that an item of evidence can be fit into an argument that advances the proponent's case and that the argument cannot be dismissed as ridiculous or scientifically impossible. Frequently, a single item of evidence will fit comfortably into diametrically opposing arguments (and many other stories as well). In fact, some facts are so central that they have to be a part of any story about the case, on either side. For example, in a murder case, if you hear that the victim was the defendant's father, you know that will be a central relevant fact for both the prosecutor and the defense, even if you know nothing else about the case and have no idea what the specific arguments on each side will be.

On some issues, neither judges nor jurors know enough about how the world operates to evaluate relevance claims without assistance. When that's true, experts may be called to establish the reality hypotheses on which the relevance of the evidence rests.[6] For example, when DNA

---

[6] In these situations the expert typically first testifies before the judge to convince her, in accord with FRE 104(a), that the evidence qualifies for admission as relevant. Later the expert

identifications were in their infancy, experts had to be called to establish not just that a defendant's DNA matched DNA associated with the crime, but also the validity of the techniques used to preserve, extract and match that DNA, the fact that no two people, except identical twins, have DNA that matches throughout the genome, and the validity of the statistical techniques used to establish the likely probative value of DNA matches. Today, judges often will decide these issues by taking judicial notice of most aspects of DNA technology,[7] although proponents of DNA evidence sometimes prefer testimony on these points to judicial notice because explaining the premises of DNA analysis to a jury may make for a more persuasive identification story.

The fact that evidence is scientific does not mean there are no plausible conflicting reality hypotheses. Indeed, differences of opinion about some of the assumptions underlying DNA identification testimony grew so heated that those involved in the controversies spoke of the *DNA Wars*.[8] Clashes of this sort between experts pose special problems for courts because often neither judges nor jurors possess the knowledge needed to intelligently choose between contending experts. Usually when conflicting views of how the world works are plausible, the court will admit the evidence and allow the jury to decide which position appears more likely. When the dispute focuses on scientific evidence, however, the courts sometimes demand more than the minimal requirement of relevance as a precondition of admissibility. In the seminal case of *Daubert v. Merrell Dow Pharmaceuticals*,[9] the Supreme Court, interpreting FRE 702, invited judges to take a more active role in determining the likely validity of scientific evidence before admitting it, and judges today frequently accept the Court's invitation.

Problem III-1. Phoebe Francis, on vacation in Nome, Alaska, was injured by a glass shard when a bottle of Kookie Kola, which a friend had bought from a vending machine and tossed gently to her, exploded in mid-air. Phoebe brought suit against the Nome Bottling Company, relying solely on the argument that the defendant was liable for her injuries under the theory of *res ipsa loquitur* (i.e., accidents of this sort "speak for themselves" and do not happen unless the defendant has been negligent). At trial, Phoebe might offer the following items of evidence:

---

may testify before the jury to explain why the evidence should affect its decision, which is to say why the evidence is relevant.

    [7]   See Chapter Eleven, pp. 1399–1407 on judicial notice.

    [8]   See, e.g., Richard O. Lempert, After the DNA Wars: Skirmishing with NRC II, 37 Jurimetrics J. 439–468 (1997).

    [9]   509 U.S. 579 (1993). See Chapter Nine, pp. 1159–1163 for a discussion of this important case.

(1) Her own testimony that the bottle exploded in mid-air, and that a piece of glass from the bottle opened a two-inch cut on her leg.

(2) Her friend's testimony to the same effect.

(3) Her friend's testimony that he had put $2.00 into a soda machine and pressed the button labeled Kookie Kola.

(4) Her friend's testimony that what he took from the machine was a bottle of Kookie Kola.

(5) Testimony by Phoebe's mother that her family's vacation had been ruined by her daughter's injury.

(6) Testimony by Phoebe's mother that her daughter could catch anything thrown to her.

(7) Jill Janitor's testimony that she was called to the scene of the accident and cleaned up a mess, consisting of broken glass and a substance she recognized as the residue of a cola beverage, which was spread throughout the room.

(8) Janitor's testimony that while cleaning up she found a large fragment of a bottle with most of the label attached. The portion she found said "ie Kol," and in the lower right hand corner it read "Nome Bottling Company."

(9) A sketch Janitor had made of the pattern of cola stains and embedded glass on the room's floor, walls and ceiling.

(10) The fragment of a bottle that Janitor described.

(11) A copy of a contract between the Nome Bottling Company and the Kookie Kola Company, giving Nome Bottling the exclusive right to bottle Kookie Kola in the Nome area.

(12) Testimony by a former employee of Nome's that employees did not regularly check the pressure at which it was bottling soda.

(13) Expert testimony that Nome's bottling equipment was old and prone to over pressurize or under pressurize soda it bottled.

(14) Testimony by an emergency room physician that she used three stitches to close a wound on Phoebe's leg that "was consistent with being caused by a piece of flying glass."

Are any of these items of evidence immaterial? Is any of the evidence Phoebe might offer otherwise irrelevant? Are any of these items direct evidence that Phoebe was injured by glass from an exploding soda bottle? Are any of them circumstantial evidence that Phoebe was injured by glass from an exploding soda bottle? Is there any direct evidence that the glass that allegedly injured Phoebe came from a bottle of Kookie Kola? That it came from soda bottled by the Nome Bottling Company?

What reality hypotheses support the admissibility of the testimony that Jill Janitor is prepared to give?

E. CONDITIONAL RELEVANCE

In a trial, evidence can only unfold gradually; it cannot all be presented at once. This may cause difficulties because the relevance of one item of circumstantial evidence may be apparent only when other items are known. Consider the Texas Democrat again. If it could be shown that at the time of the accident the polls were about to close in a hotly contested Democratic electoral primary, his political affiliation becomes a relevant fact because it is reasonable to hypothesize that a politically active individual might risk speeding to insure that he could cast his ballot.

Where the relevance of one item of evidence depends on the receipt of another item to place it in context, the first item may be received in evidence over objection with the understanding that later evidence will "connect it up" to matters at issue in the case. Under the Federal Rules, the issue is described as "conditional relevance" and is governed by FRE 104(b), which provides:

> **(b) Relevance That Depends on a Fact.** When the relevance of evidence depends on whether a fact exists, proof must be introduced sufficient to support a finding that the fact does exist. The court may admit the proposed evidence on the condition that the proof be introduced later.

The notion is that one fact standing alone may not appear relevant, but two facts taken together may establish a relevant proposition. Typically the judge will accept an attorney's word that evidence will be connected up, but where a matter is likely to be prejudicial or excessively time-consuming, she may ask the attorney to briefly describe the way in which the matter relates to the case.[10] Whether the connection is actually proven is a question for the jury. The judge's only function is to decide whether the party offering the evidence at issue has presented sufficient other evidence to support a jury finding that the connecting condition exists.

On close examination, the concept of conditional relevance is more complex and problematic than it may seem at first. Professor Vaughn

---

[10] It is a breach of ethics to offer evidence subject to "connecting up" when one knows the connecting evidence is unavailable. Occasionally, however, evidence will not be connected up because crucial testimony proves inadmissible on non-relevance grounds, because witnesses change their stories or don't show up, or through sheer inadvertence. When, for any reason, there is a failure to connect up evidence, the earlier evidence will, upon request of the opposing party, be stricken from the record, and the jury will be instructed to disregard it. If the stricken evidence is particularly prejudicial, a mistrial might be appropriate. Failure to request that unconnected evidence be stricken is likely to waive all objections to the receipt of that evidence. See Chapter Two, supra pp. 165–167

Ball has called the idea of conditional relevance a "myth."[11] His basic argument is that (1) "conditionally relevant" evidence is necessarily logically relevant (i.e., it adds some quantum of useful information, however modest, to the facts in the case), and (2) the logical relevance of most if not all circumstantial evidence depends on other facts in evidence. To illustrate, consider the case of a criminal defendant, whom we shall call Tracy, who is charged with dynamiting the Federal Building in Omaha, Nebraska. Evidence of one fact, **A**—that two weeks before the bombing, a large quantity of dynamite was delivered to a house in Omaha—would be considered irrelevant and inadmissible unless the prosecution also presented evidence of another fact, **B**—that Tracy, either directly or through others, had access to that house. But, as Professor Ball points out, evidence of **A** is by itself logically relevant because it makes the conjunction of **A** and **B** more likely than it would be without that evidence. In the terms of our example, evidence tending to show that explosives were delivered to the Omaha house makes what the prosecutor needs to show—namely, that Tracy had access to explosives at that house—more likely than it would be without the delivery evidence, for the prosecutor must show both that there were explosives in the house and that Tracy was able to enter the house.

Now consider the other side of the problem. What if in addition to (**A**)—evidence of the delivery, the prosecution presents a credible eyewitness who would testify to fact **B**—that Tracy lived in the house where the dynamite was delivered? Does that prove Tracy's guilt without regard to other facts? No. It's only relevant if fact **C** is also true—that Tracy knew the material delivered was an explosive.[12] But, unlike Tracy's access to the dynamite (**B**), Tracy's knowledge that it was dynamite that had been delivered (**C**) will not be considered a necessary factual condition on which the relevance of fact **A** depends. Why? One reason is that facts **A** and **B** are sufficient to tie Tracy to the dynamite regardless of his knowledge though neither would alone. Beyond this no evidence need be produced that Tracy knows what dynamite looks like for, absent evidence to the contrary, that would be presumed.

---

[11] Vaughn C. Ball, The Myth of Conditional Relevance, 14 Ga. L. Rev. 435 (1980). (Professor Ball has specifically disavowed an article by the same title to which his name is attached, which appeared in the Arizona State Law Journal.)

[12] The creative mind can easily think of factual conditions for relevance in addition to **B** and **C**—for example, that the dynamite was stored in an accessible location rather than placed in a locked basement that Tracy could not enter. One can similarly think of prosecutorial theories of what happened under which **A**'s relevance would not depend on **B** and **C**. For example, Tracy's buddy may have arranged for the delivery of dynamite to his own house, and then taken the package of explosives that was delivered and placed it unopened in Tracy's car. The fact that explosives had been delivered to a house in Omaha would still be relevant, but Tracy's knowledge that a box delivered to his buddy's house contained dynamite and his ability to gain access to the house and to the dynamite in it would not bear on the likelihood of his guilt under the prosecutor's theory. Of course, that theory entails its own factual conditions for the relevance of fact **A**. For example, Tracy would need to know the nature of, and have access to, the dynamite in his car.

Or consider another example: Victor Victim is overheard saying that the next time he sees Doris Defendant, he will shoot her on sight. Doris, charged with murder for shooting Victor as he reached into his pocket for a fountain pen, seeks to introduce evidence of Victor's threat to support her claim of self-defense. Logically, Victor's threat against Doris is relevant to her self-defense claim only if she knew of the threat (step 1), and she honestly feared that Victor would carry it out (step 2). Evidence of Victor's threat does not tend to show Doris shot in self-defense unless both conditions are met.[13] But courts would treat these conditions differently. Most judges would say that only step 1 (knowledge of Victor's threat) is a *condition* for the relevance of the threat evidence; that is, knowledge is the only fact Doris must try to prove as a condition for admitting Victor's threat. Step 2 (fear) is equally necessary to the argument that the threat supports a self-defense claim, but it will not be treated as a factual predicate for the admissibility of the threat evidence. Instead, the jury will be allowed to infer fear from the circumstances.

The conditional relevance principle recognized in the FRE grew out of the belief that the jury, rather than the judge, should determine whether the requisite condition (Doris's knowledge of the threat in our example) has been satisfied. Otherwise, the judge would be allowed excessive control over factfinding at trial.[14] That said, concern remained that allowing the litigants free reign with respect to the introduction of certain sorts of evidence, like that concerning a party's alleged notice or knowledge of critical information, would throw the court open to an excessive volume of potentially prejudicial material. To prevent this, the judge is authorized under FRE 104(b) to inquire whether there is evidence "sufficient to support a finding" that the conditioning or preliminary fact (that Doris knew of the threat) exists to allow a reasonable jury to so find. This division of responsibility preserves the jury's role as factfinder while allowing the judge to function as gatekeeper. Some have argued that this still gives the judge too much power over factfinding.[15] True or not, the FRE 104(b) process imposes a

---

[13] One might argue that the fact that the deceased uttered one threat, even if it was not known to the defendant, makes it more likely that he uttered other threats, some of which the defendant may have learned of, or that it makes it more likely that he had in the past tried to assault the defendant. This is a valid observation, but to simplify our analysis we will assume that the defendant in our hypothetical stipulates that the threat her witness reports was the only threat or action that might have placed her in fear of the defendant.

[14] In Gila Valley, Globe & Northern Railway Company v. Hall, 232 U.S. 94, 102–103 (1914), the Supreme Court held that the trial judge was to determine the preliminary fact whether the plaintiff railroad employee had overheard a statement uttered in a normal tone of voice some twenty yards away, remarking on the dangerous condition of a gasoline-powered three-wheel railcar that he was about to operate. Professor Edmund Morgan sharply criticized this ruling as granting trial judges too much power over fact-finding and proposed a precursor to FRE 104(b). See Edmund M. Morgan, Functions of Judge and Jury in the Determination of Preliminary Questions of Fact, 43 Harv. L. Rev. 165 (1929).

[15] See, e.g., Dale A. Nance, Conditional Relevance Reinterpreted, 70 B.U.L. Rev. 447, 455 (1990); Richard D. Friedman, Conditional Probative Value: Neoclassicism Without Myth, 93 Mich. L. Rev. 439, 445–48 (1994).

somewhat higher standard for the admission of evidence deemed to be covered by the rule than the simple relevance standard used elsewhere.[16]

How does a court choose between requiring evidence on one factual link in a chain of reasoning as a condition for considering another link and letting the jury infer the link without additional evidence? In other words, how does a court decide whether the relevance of an item of evidence is *conditional*? FRE 104(b) offers no guidance, but in practice, courts seem to be guided by two concerns:

(1) *Does evidence of the conditioning fact greatly increase the probative value of the item of evidence that is offered?*[17] Consider our first example above: Although technically relevant, the probative value of evidence that explosives were delivered to a house in Omaha, without any evidence connecting Tracy to the house, seems tiny. By contrast, the probative value of evidence that dynamite was delivered to Tracy's house seems reasonably high even without specific evidence that Tracy knew that what had been delivered was dynamite, since most people who have dynamite delivered to them receive it knowingly and deliberately. Similarly a court would not require more specific evidence that Tracy could get at the dynamite while it was in his home. Since most people have access to things in their own homes, evidence that the dynamite was delivered to Tracy's home is strong circumstantial evidence of access.

(2) *Is good evidence of the factual condition likely to be available?*[18] In our example involving Doris, evidence that she had been threatened by the defendant may be reasonably probative standing alone, since threats are often delivered face to face or the target otherwise learns of them. But Doris ought to be able to put on evidence that speaks directly to this step. She can testify to a direct threat or report how she learned she had been threatened. Even if she declines to testify (as she is entitled to do under the Fifth Amendment) she will often be able to produce witnesses who were present when she was threatened or when she learned she had been. But her belief in the threat, the second logical step, cannot be directly observed by any independent witness (apart from actions Doris may have taken that circumstantially suggested her fear). Of course, the defendant can herself testify to that effect (if she chooses to do so), but her testimony

---

[16] See Craig R. Callen, Rationality and Relevancy: Conditional Relevance and Constrained Resources, 2003 Mich. St. L. Rev. 1243 (2003).

[17] See, e.g., Dale A. Nance, Conditional Relevance Reinterpreted, 70 B. U. L. Rev. 447 (1990) (arguing that many applications of the doctrine of "conditional relevance," especially in the early part of this century, are best understood as attempts by courts to require something more than mere logical relevance for admissibility—a variant of the debate over "legal relevance" versus "logical relevance" that is discussed below in subsection G); Richard D. Friedman, Conditional Probative Value: Neoclassicism Without Myth, 93 Mich. L. Rev. 439 (1994) (arguing that "conditional relevance" is a misnomer, and that the concept should be renamed "conditional probative value").

[18] See Nance, supra note 17 (arguing that a major purpose of the "conditional relevance" rule is to implement a general policy of forcing litigants to produce the most probative evidence that is available on an issue).

would do little to aid the jury since it is in her interest to say that she believed the threat regardless of how she actually felt.

In deciding when testimony to one fact is conditioned on proof of another, courts are also influenced by precedent and by the centrality of evidence. Thus, in some jurisdictions, an additional reason why courts condition evidence of a threat on a person's having heard that threat is, because precedential cases have imposed this requirement. Conversely, where a matter is relatively peripheral in a case, courts may be less attentive to the niceties of conditional relevance than they would be if the fact conditioned on some other fact were central.

We do not mean to say that courts are always predictable in applying FRE 104(b) and similar provisions. As with most evidence rules, there is a great deal of variability in trial court rulings on conditional relevance, and most of those rulings—whichever way they go—are upheld on appeal. Judging from reported decisions, however, rulings under FRE 104(b) are rarely appealed, which suggests that in practice, the rule on conditional relevance operates reasonably smoothly.[19]

The converse of conditional relevance, the situation in which apparently relevant evidence appears irrelevant when placed in context, has received little attention from courts or commentators. Consider, for example, a suspect who attempts to escape from custody while being transported to jail. In a later trial, evidence of the attempt will be considered relevant, for flight from pre-trial custody may be reasonably interpreted as an attempt to avoid conviction, and it is reasonable to suppose that suspects conscious of their guilt are more likely to fear

---

[19] Unfortunately, courts and legislatures have confused the issue of conditional relevance by using the term in contexts in which it does not properly belong. What seems to happen is that: *First*, for reasons of policy or tradition, a court or a drafting committee decides that some foundational issue should be determined by the jury rather than by the judge and that the judge's role should be restricted to deciding if there is sufficient evidence to support a jury finding that the foundational fact exists. *Second*, since this standard for admissibility is the same as that which applies to conditional relevance, the court or committee decides that the issue is one of conditional relevance. In Chapter Two, supra pp. 180–181, we saw an example of this in the personal knowledge requirement. FRE 602 requires "evidence sufficient to support a finding that the witness has personal knowledge of the matter," and the Advisory Committee's Note on FRE 602 explains that "the rule is in fact a specialized application of the provisions of Rule 104(b) on conditional relevance." But the Advisory Committee's analysis is mistaken. A witness's testimony can be *relevant* even if it is based on guess-work or second-hand information; it is just less probative in most cases than testimony based on personal knowledge. In Chapter Ten we will see the same error again, this time with respect to the requirement of authentication of an exhibit or identification of a voice under FRE 901. Similarly, California Evidence Code § 403 gives the jury the power to decide, among other things, the identity of a person who made a statement when the admissibility of the statement turns on that issue. The California Law Revision Commission's comment on that section explains that this allocation of responsibility is appropriate because the issue "involves the relevancy of the evidence." But as Justice Otto Kaus of the California Supreme Court pointed out, "This is nonsense. On D's trial for the murder of V, the statement 'D murdered V' is relevant whoever made it." Otto M. Kaus, All Power to the Jury—California's Democratic Evidence Code, 4 Loy. L.A. L. Rev. 233, 238 (1971). Under the hearsay rule and its exceptions, the *admissibility* of the statement may depend on the identity of the speaker, but its relevance does not depend on this unless it is clear from the speaker's identity that she had no rational basis for making her claim.

conviction than those who believe themselves innocent. But if the suspect could show that he had read a recent newspaper story which pictured the local jail as overcrowded, unsanitary and a hotbed of sexual assaults, or that the local jailor had threatened to kill him if he were ever in his custody, the escape attempt might be seen as equally likely whether the suspect were guilty or innocent. Nonetheless, a court would probably admit evidence of the escape attempt on the issue of the suspect's consciousness of guilt, and deny a motion to strike it from the record even after an explanation consistent with innocence was presented. There is a good reason for this. The jury, which is responsible for judging the credibility of witnesses, might not believe testimony that the defendant had read of the jail conditions or been threatened by the jailor. And even if the jury believed that the defendant *might* have been motivated by fear of the jail conditions or the jailor, it could still rationally conclude that a more important motivation was fear that because he had committed the crime a strong case could be mustered against him. Still, if you are confident that an opponent's evidence will appear utterly irrelevant when seen in context, you might object on this ground. But first be sure there are no significant tactical advantages to be gained from presenting the jury with the facts from which it can make its own relevance determination.

Problem III-2. Alan is charged with killing his wife. One item of evidence offered by the prosecution is the fact that Alan is the beneficiary of a $25,000 insurance policy issued on the life of his wife. Alan objects on the ground that there is absolutely no evidence indicating that he needed money, and that, on the contrary, he has $100,000 in the bank and is free of all debts. **Is the evidence of the insurance policy admissible?** Would you answer differently if the policy were in the amount of $250,000?

F.   RELEVANT AND IRRELEVANT

Evidence is often relevant for one purpose and irrelevant for others. In the example of the escape attempt, evidence of the story on jail conditions would be relevant on the issue of whether the attempt evinced consciousness of guilt, but the story would probably be found logically irrelevant on the issue of whether the suspect committed the crime charged and immaterial if offered as an indictment of the local penal system. As we noted in Chapter Two, where evidence is admissible for only one of several possible purposes, the evidence will almost always be admitted for that purpose. The opponent has the right to have the jury instructed that the evidence should be used only for the permitted purpose, but it is not clear that the jury can or will follow such instructions. In fact, attorneys frequently waive their right to *limiting instructions* for fear that such instructions will only call the jury's attention to the impermissible inferences.[20]

Difficult situations arise when evidence that might prejudice a jury is offered to prove a peripheral point—or a point on which other evidence is readily available. Although a case may be made for excluding the evidence, even in these situations, courts are reluctant to interfere with counsel's preferred method of proving her case. Thus, in a murder trial, the condition of a stabbing victim may ordinarily be shown by a series of bloody pictures rather than through the colorless testimony of an autopsy surgeon, and plaintiffs in tort actions are given great leeway in choosing how to prove the extent of their injuries. The issue in these cases is not logical relevance—the evidence is clearly relevant—but rather how FRE 403 (which requires a weighing of the probative value and the various risks associated with the evidence) should be administered and whether, in administering FRE 403, courts may consider the availability of alternative ways of proving a point.

We shall consider FRE 403 shortly and look closely at a case that in one special circumstance constrains the proof a prosecutor can offer. But ordinarily the principle at work here is one that is general to the nonconstitutional areas of evidence law. *Evidence which is admissible for one purpose will not be excluded simply because it is inadmissible for other purposes.* Instead, the jury will be instructed, if opposing counsel so requests or if the judge chooses to act *sua sponte*, to consider the evidence only for the proper purpose. Think of the jury as sitting in a house with many doors. To reach the jury you need only go through one door. It does not matter if the rest are barred. The key to finding the open door is knowing evidence law and knowing the substantive law on which theories of admission can be based. The latter is as important as the former. *No matter how well you know the rules of evidence, you cannot use them well unless you also master the substantive law that bears on your case.*

———

Problem III-3. Darlene is a self-employed pipe fitter. She is the defendant in a criminal case in which she is charged with breaking into and emptying the vault of the New Phoenix National Bank using an acetylene torch or similar tool. The prosecution seeks to introduce in evidence an oxy-acetylene torch found in Darlene's garage. **Is the evidence relevant? How probative is it? Can you answer this without knowing anything about pipe fitting? Could you conduct a proper defense without knowing anything about that occupation?**

———

[20] See Chapter Two, supra pp. 184–186.

G. LOGICAL OR LEGAL RELEVANCE?

Thayer, in his *A Preliminary Treatise on Evidence at the Common Law*, asserted, "The law furnishes no test of relevance. For this, it tacitly refers to logic and general experience. . . . "[21] The Federal Rules reflect Thayer's position. For evidence to be relevant and hence presumptively admissible, it need only tend logically to prove or disprove some fact in issue. There is, however, another view that was once popular with some courts and given weight by some commentators;[22] this is the view that a mere logical relationship between proffered evidence and a fact in issue is not enough to justify admissibility. There must be something more, some "plus value." Evidence lacking such plus value might be *logically* relevant, but it is not *legally* so. This concept of plus value is, however, confusing; it is not clear what it is or how it can be determined. Ultimately the concept "legal relevance" is probably just a less precise way of acknowledging, as modern courts do, that even relevant evidence may be excluded if it seems likely to be unduly prejudicial, misleading or time-consuming. Of course, the less probative the evidence and the less need for it in a party's case, the more likely it is to be excluded on one of these grounds despite some probative value. The judge's task is to balance the probative value of and need for the evidence against the harm that may result from its admission.

Return to the example of evidence of jail conditions offered to show that the defendant did not commit a crime. We suggested above that on this issue the evidence would probably be regarded as irrelevant. But counsel might argue: "My client knew of these conditions and consequently was terrified at the prospect of going to jail. Surely this knowledge makes it unlikely that he would commit the crime that might lead him to be arrested and thrown in jail." The argument is not devoid of reason. Some courts might dispose of it without analysis by saying that the jail condition evidence lacks plus value and so is not legally relevant. A more thoughtful court would say that in view of the large number of crimes committed despite widespread knowledge of prison conditions, evidence of prison conditions, even if it is relevant, has minimal probative value. Any contributions the evidence might make to deciding whether the defendant committed the crime is greatly outweighed by its tendency to interject confusing collateral issues, by the time the prosecution might require to dispute the defendant's contentions, and by the possibility that the jury would improperly acquit

---

[21] James Bradley Thayer, A Preliminary Treatise on Evidence at the Common Law 265 (1898).

[22] Most notably Wigmore, without whose support this approach might have died out long ago. Wigmore writes, "[L]egal relevancy denotes . . . *something more than a minimum of probative value.*" 1 Wigmore § 28, at 409–10. Wigmore suggests that "plus value" is necessary "to prevent the jury from being satisfied by matters of slight value, capable of being exaggerated by prejudice and hasty reasoning." Id. at 409.

a guilty defendant because the jurors didn't want him to be sent to such a jail.

The prime danger of the "legal relevance" approach is that it invites courts to confuse the question of whether evidence is *relevant* with the question of whether it is *sufficient* to support a verdict. *Evidence is relevant if alone or in context it has any tendency to prove or disprove a fact in issue; evidence is sufficient if a reasonable jury could conclude from the evidence introduced that the party with the burden of proof has met that burden.*[23]

Legal relevance may be used in a sense other than a requirement that minimally relevant evidence have some "plus value." There are certain *recurring* situations in which various courts have declared evidence to be irrelevant despite some logical relationship between the evidence and facts in issue. By using the language of relevance, these courts obscure the fact that their decisions to exclude the evidence are based on considerations of legal policy rather than on pure logic. We treat this evidence in Chapters Four and Five for what it is: logically relevant evidence declared inadmissible on policy grounds. However, most treatments and codifications of evidence law discuss these principles under the rubric of relevance. You should remember that these principles exclude evidence for a variety of different policy reasons, each of which must be evaluated on its own merits. These rules often exclude evidence of low probative value on certain issues, but they exist precisely because the evidence they exclude is not ordinarily irrelevant. If it were, these exclusionary rules would not be needed.

There are a number of principles of evidence law which at their root reflect a concern for relevance. A desire to ensure that evidence is not only relevant but also has something more than minimal probative value permeates many of the exclusionary rules we shall discuss, most notably the rule against hearsay. Concerns for relevance most obviously drive the rules of authentication discussed in Chapter Ten, the requirement of a chain of custody for certain real evidence (also Chapter Ten), and some requirements pertaining to the competence of witnesses and the admission of opinion testimony which we encountered in Chapter Two. For example, if an IOU offered by the plaintiff in a debt action is signed by a Jane Doe other than defendant Jane Doe, its existence does not tend to prove that the Ms. Doe in court owes the plaintiff money.[24] Hence we

---

[23] For example, evidence that defendant attempted to escape is relevant on the issue of whether the defendant is guilty of a crime with which he is charged, but if this were the only evidence connecting the defendant to the crime, it would not be sufficient to support a conviction.

[24] Arguably, the evidence tends to prove the opposite, for it suggests that the money that the plaintiff claims is actually owed by some other Jane Doe. However, although FRE 401 speaks of evidence that makes a consequential fact *"more* or *less probable"* a party is not ordinarily allowed to introduce evidence over an opposing party's objection when its relevance lies entirely in its tendency to prove the opponent's case. The likelihood that the evidence is offered to take advantage of impermissible inferences is too great. The major exception is

require *authentication*: as a precondition to introducing the IOU, the plaintiff must present evidence sufficient for a reasonable jury to find that the note was in fact written by the defendant. Those rules that most directly reflect a concern for relevance are more than applications of FRE 401, for they go beyond the requirement of minimal logical relevance that Rule 401 embodies. To use authentication as the example again, consider a situation in which the only evidence of authenticity is the name on the note. As we will see in Chapter Ten, that showing is insufficient for authentication, and the note will be kept from the jury—despite the fact that it has some logical tendency to show that the defendant owes the stated sum to the plaintiff. In considering principles that, like authentication, are based substantially on a concern for relevance, ask yourself whether it makes sense for rules to require more than minimal logical relevance.

"Your Honor, the relevance of this line of questioning will become apparent in a moment."

---

evidence that undercuts the credibility of a party's own witnesses. This exception is justified because parties should be candid about factors that limit the value of the evidence they offer, and if a party is willing to reveal such evidence, an opponent should not be able to make it look as if he was trying to hide it. This process is sometimes referred to as "defanging the tiger" or "taking the sting out" of the discrediting information.

H. WITNESS CREDIBILITY AND OTHER EVIDENTIARY DEFICIENCIES

Consider a law suit in which the plaintiff, Paula Pedestrian, sues the defendant, Doreen Driver, alleging that Driver ran a red light and hit her, causing serious injuries. Neither the likelihood of Driver's negligence nor the extent of Pedestrian's injuries is related to Dick Doctor's fees, Sam Souse's drinking habits or Wilma Worker's latest job. Yet evidence pertaining to each of these matters might be admitted in the case of Pedestrian v. Driver. If Doctor testified that Pedestrian suffered a permanent nerve injury, Driver could show he had been paid $10,000 to examine Pedestrian and testify on her behalf. If Souse testified that Driver ran a red light at 10:45 a.m., Driver could introduce evidence tending to prove that Souse had consumed a fifth of whiskey between 9:00 a.m. and 10:45 a.m. And if Worker backed up Souse's story, Driver could call Pedestrian's husband to testify that three days after the accident he had given Worker a job.

The principle at work here is obvious and sensible. The probative value of evidence depends not just on the abstract relationship of an evidentiary fact to a fact in issue but also on the likelihood that the evidentiary fact actually exists. An evidentiary fact that is highly probative of a consequential fact may have little persuasive value if it is unlikely to exist. Thus, if Driver ran a red light that fact is almost conclusive of her negligence. But if the only reason to believe Driver ran a red light is that someone who was drunk at the time says so, there may be little reason to believe Driver was negligent. Thus, evidence that affects the credibility of reports of relevant facts is itself relevant. For this reason, as we will see in Chapter Five, witnesses can be impeached by showings of bias, perceptual problems, an exceptional willingness to lie and the like. For similar reasons, as we shall see in Chapter Ten, the genuineness and accuracy of documents may be questioned even if the conditions for their admission are met. Ordinarily the judge's task is only to assess the relationship of reported facts to facts in issue. Judging credibility is left to juries.

———————

Problem III-4. Sam Park is on trial for assaulting and robbing Kim Lee, a young Korean woman who had come to this country some four months before the attack. The case against Park turns on the accuracy of Lee's eyewitness identification. Both before and at trial Lee describes her assailant as a clean-shaven man. Park, on the other hand, produces several witnesses who testify that on the date of the crime he wore a mustache. Park also wants to call Rev. Kun who was born in Korea and lived there for 40 years before emigrating to the United States some 10 years ago. Rev. Kun is familiar with Korean culture and would testify that facial hair is culturally significant as a mark of dignity, age and respect in Korea; that it is a "folkway" in Korea; and that Ms. Lee, as a Korean, would have paid particular attention to a mustache had one been worn by her assailant. **Is Rev. Kun's testimony relevant? If so, on what issues?** Ms. Lee also testifies that her assailant was sloppily dressed at the time she was attacked. The defendant wants to put on several witnesses to testify that he was normally neat and clean in his dress. **Is that evidence admissible? If so, for what purpose?**

I.   FRE 403 BALANCING

Ultimately, the jury decides the evidentiary value of all evidence submitted to it; indeed, this weighing of evidence is its principal function. In any given case it is possible that the jury ultimately decides that much of the evidence introduced doesn't bear on the questions it must resolve. However, when evidence is objected to as irrelevant, the judge must decide whether the jury should receive the information in the first place. Where the only issue is logical relevance, the judge's sole task is to determine the logical relationship of the evidence to matters in issue. If the evidence might influence a reasonable trier of fact, it should be admitted regardless of the value that the judge personally places on it. Where the relevance of evidence is disputable, the judge is likely to admit the evidence "for what it's worth" since the jury is trusted to discount the evidence if it is not relevant or has only slight probative value.

The judge's task is not, however, always easy. Problems arise when evidence that bears some logical relationship to a matter in issue threatens to confuse the jury, or to be unduly repetitious or time-consuming or, worse yet, to unfairly bias the jury in its evaluation of the case. In these circumstances, the judge cannot escape the chore assigned to her by FRE 403. She must weigh the probative value of the evidence and balance it against the possible detrimental effects of its admission.

FRE 403 provides:

> The court may exclude relevant evidence if its probative value is substantially outweighed by a danger of one or more of the following: unfair prejudice, confusing the issues, misleading the jury, undue delay, wasting time, or needlessly presenting cumulative evidence.

The availability of other evidence on the same point may affect the judge's decision under FRE 403 as will opposing counsel's willingness to stipulate to whatever facts the evidence she objects to might legitimately be used to prove. If the evidence is unique and important, and if no stipulation is forthcoming, the need for information almost always outweighs associated detrimental effects. Where evidence is not unique or the opposing party is willing to stipulate to everything the evidence tends legitimately to prove, the judge's decision can go either way—

although the Supreme Court (by a one vote margin) carved out a narrow area in which it has removed some of the discretion from the trial judge.

The case in which the Court did this, *Old Chief v. United States*,[25] arose when the petitioner, Johnny Lynn Old Chief, was charged not only with assault with a dangerous weapon and using a firearm in the commission of a crime of violence, but also with violating a law that precludes a person with a prior felony conviction from possessing firearms. To prove the latter charge, the government wanted to introduce a record of Old Chief's prior conviction, which disclosed that Old Chief had received a sentence of five years imprisonment for an unlawful assault that had resulted in serious bodily injury.

If not for the "felon in possession" charge, information about the prior assault would have been inadmissible. Old Chief was afraid that the evidence that he had committed a past violent assault would prejudice the jury against him or lead some jurors to make the impermissible inference that because he had assaulted someone in the past, he was likely to have committed the crimes he was now charged with.[26] Thus, Old Chief offered to stipulate that he had been previously convicted of a serious enough crime that if he were found to have possessed a gun, he would have been in violation of the "felon in possession" law.[27] His defense was that he had not had a gun.

The prosecutor refused to agree to the stipulation, and insisted that he had a right to prove his case as he wished. The trial judge agreed with the prosecutor, and the Ninth Circuit affirmed, noting that under Ninth Circuit law a stipulation is not proof and has no place in the FRE 403 balancing process.

The Supreme Court majority began its discussion of the case by rejecting Old Chief's argument that the name of his prior offense, as contained in the prior conviction record, is irrelevant. Since this evidence shows Old Chief to be a convicted felon, which is an element of the offense charged, it properly bears on a fact in issue and so is relevant under FRE

---

[25]   519 U.S. 172 (1997).

[26]   FRE 404, as we will see in Chapter Five, generally prohibits evidence of other crimes to show that a defendant has a propensity to commit the crime charged.

[27]   See Chapter Eleven, pp. 1393–1397 for a general discussion of stipulations. In fact, Old Chief's stipulation was inartfully drawn and did not mandate the conclusion we state in the text. The Supreme Court majority, while recognizing this, assumed that the stipulation's defects did not motivate the trial judge's rejection of the stipulation, but rather that the judge's view that the government had a right to prove its case as it wished led to the rejection. In proceeding on this assumption, the Court was reaching out to make a statement, for the conventional result in a situation of this sort is to deny the appeal because in offering an inadequate stipulation the petitioner failed to generate or preserve error. We suspect that when the Court decided to hear this case the Justices did not realize that there was a problem with the stipulation. Although the Court could (some would say "should") have dismissed the case when the Justices learned that the stipulation was inadequate, *Old Chief* provided a good vehicle for resolving a conflict between the Circuits, and the Justices may have seen no gains from waiting for another case to do this.

401 and presumptively admissible under FRE 402. Citing the Advisory Committee note to Rule 401, the Court went on to say that the existence of other evidence that proves the same thing, such as the proposed stipulation, does not render the conviction record irrelevant.

This required the Court to confront the FRE 403 issue directly and decide whether the probative value of the government's evidence was so substantially outweighed by its tendency toward unfair prejudice that the trial judge had no discretion to admit the evidence once the defendant offered a stipulation conceding everything the conviction record could legitimately have been offered to prove. In addressing this question, the Court distinguished relevance, which it regards as inhering in an item of evidence, from probative value, which it regards as an evidentiary feature that can vary with the availability of alternative ways of proving a point. Speaking for the five person majority, Justice Souter wrote:

> Thus the [Advisory Committee's] notes leave no question that when Rule 403 confers discretion by providing that evidence "may" be excluded, the discretionary judgment may be informed not only by assessing an evidentiary item's twin tendencies, but by placing the result of that assessment alongside similar assessments of evidentiary alternatives.[28]

Earlier in the opinion, Souter described the judgment process in more detail:

> On objection, the court would decide whether a particular item of evidence raised a danger of unfair prejudice. If it did, the judge would go on to evaluate the degrees of probative value and unfair prejudice not only for the item in question but for any actually available substitutes as well. If an alternative were found to have substantially the same or greater probative value but a lower danger of unfair prejudice, sound judicial discretion would discount the value of the item first offered and exclude it if its discounted probative value were substantially outweighed by unfairly prejudicial risk. . . . [Thus] a judge applying Rule 403 could reasonably apply some discount to the probative value of an item of evidence when faced with less risky alternative proof going to the same point.[29]

The majority, applying this standard, went on to find that the conviction record raised a substantial danger of unfair prejudice because it might lure a jury into reasoning impermissibly that Old Chief had a bad character which made him likely to commit crimes like the violent crimes charged. Old Chief's admission of the prior felony conviction, whether

---

[28] 519 U.S. at 184–85.

[29] Id. at 182–83.

accepted as a stipulation or not,[30] was seen as less prejudicial but "seemingly conclusive evidence" of everything the conviction record could legitimately have been offered to prove. In these circumstances, the Court held it was an abuse of discretion to admit the conviction record when Old Chief's admission could be used to prove the same point.

If this were all there were to *Old Chief*, one could easily imagine a cottage industry of consultants arising to advise lawyers about when they should prefer conceding points through judicial admissions to having their opponents attempt to prove them with potentially prejudicial evidence. However, in reaching their conclusion, the Court's majority sought to foreclose most such tactical uses of admissions. Justice Souter wrote:

> The "fair and legitimate weight" of conventional evidence showing individual thoughts and acts amounting to a crime reflects the fact that making a case with testimony and tangible things not only satisfies the formal definition of an offense, but tells a colorful story with descriptive richness.... Evidence ... has force beyond any linear scheme of reasoning, and as its pieces come together a narrative gains momentum, with power not only to support conclusions but to sustain the willingness of jurors to draw the inferences, whatever they may be, necessary to reach an honest verdict. This persuasive power of the concrete and particular is often essential to the capacity of jurors to satisfy the obligations that the law places on them.... [T]he evidentiary account of what a defendant has thought and done can accomplish what no set of abstract statements ever could, not just to prove a fact but to establish its human significance, and so to implicate the law's moral underpinnings and a juror's obligation to sit in judgment. Thus, the prosecution may fairly seek to place its evidence before the jurors, as much to tell a story of guiltiness as to support an inference of guilt, to convince the jurors that a guilty verdict would be morally reasonable as much as to point to the discrete elements of a defendant's legal fault.

> But there is something even more to the prosecution's interest in resisting efforts to replace the evidence of its choice with admissions and stipulations, for ... there lies the need for evidence in all its particularity to satisfy the jurors' expectations about what proper proof should be. Some such demands they bring with them to the courthouse, assuming, for example, that a charge of using a firearm to commit an offense will be proven by

---

[30] A stipulation must be agreed to by both parties to be entered into evidence. However, a party may unilaterally make a *judicial admission*, which is a formal statement, usually in writing, that binds the party to everything conceded. Since the government refused to join in Old Chief's stipulation, the Court treated the offer to stipulate as a proffered judicial admission. See Chapter Eleven.

introducing a gun in evidence. A prosecutor who fails to produce one, or some good reason for his failure, has something to be concerned about. . . . Expectations may also arise in jurors' minds simply from the experience of a trial itself. The use of witnesses to describe a train of events naturally related can raise the prospect of learning about every ingredient of that natural sequence the same way. If suddenly the prosecution presents some occurrence in the series differently, as by announcing a stipulation or admission, the effect may be like saying, "never mind what's behind the door," and jurors may well wonder what they are being kept from knowing. A party seemingly responsible for cloaking something has reason for apprehension, and the prosecution with its burden of proof may prudently demur at a defense request to interrupt the flow of evidence telling the story in the usual way.

In sum, the accepted rule that the prosecution is entitled to prove its case free from any defendant's option to stipulate the evidence away rests on good sense. A syllogism is not a story, and a naked proposition in a courtroom may be no match for the robust evidence that would be used to prove it. . . . A convincing tale can be told with economy, but when economy becomes a break in the natural sequence of narrative evidence, an assurance that the missing link is really there is never more than second best.[31]

In writing as he does, Justice Souter seems to recognize a new kind of relevance, one that does not fit nicely into the definition of FRE 401. We might call this *narrative relevance*.[32] The concept recognizes that most trials are in some measure, if not entirely, contests between stories. Convincing jurors is not just a matter of laying facts out before them; how the facts are laid out may be as important as what they are. For example, social psychologists Nancy Pennington and Reid Hastie experimented with giving mock jurors the same facts in either "witness order" or "story order."[33] When evidence was presented in witness order, witnesses appeared once and the jurors received all the information each witness knew, without regard to how the facts fit into the case. When evidence was presented in story order, the mock jurors received the information in

---

[31] Id. at 187–89.

[32] Lempert, Richard, "Narrative Relevance, Imagined Juries, and a Supreme Court Inspired Agenda for Jury Research." 1 Int'l Comment on Evidence 1 (1999). The Supreme Court seemed to have narrative relevance in mind in House v. Bell, 547 U.S. 518 (2006), when it reversed the denial of federal habeas corpus relief because the only direct evidence of sexual assault dropped out of the case in light of subsequently obtained DNA evidence. The Court said the effect of this evidence was to undermine the "central theme in the State's narrative linking House to the crime." Id. at 541.

[33] Nancy Pennington and Reid Hastie, Explaining the Evidence: Tests of the Story Model for Juror Decision Making, 62 J. Per. & Soc. Psychol. 189–206 (1992).

the order events happened, the kind of temporal order most stories follow. This meant that a witness might appear several times to present evidence. Although the logical content of the facts reported did not vary, jurors hearing the facts in story order were more persuaded.

Justice Souter seems to be telling us that in reaching decisions under FRE 403, a court should give considerable, and often dispositive weight to a party's need to tell an effective, coherent story. If, for example, a man's wife and a dispassionate stranger together stumbled upon the dead body of the woman's husband, *Old Chief* would not require the prosecutor to call only the stranger to testify to where the body was found. She could call the widow, even if the widow would be dressed in black and might break into tears describing what she saw. Not only is the widow's reaction part of the reality of the crime—however irrelevant to any issue the jury needs to decide—but if the jurors knew (or suspected) that the stranger who found the body was accompanied by the dead man's wife, they might be curious or concerned if they never heard from the wife. Some might speculate that she was a suspect in the killing or that she was absent because the victim treated her cruelly.

From a narrative perspective the issue in *Old Chief*, as Souter took pains to emphasize, was special. While Old Chief's status as a convicted felon was legally crucial, it had nothing to do with the story of what had transpired. Either Old Chief had brandished a gun or he had not. This is the issue that required the jury to decide between conflicting stories. Old Chief's status as a convicted felon determined whether he had violated the "felon in possession" law, so the jury also had to decide whether Old Chief was a convicted felon or not. But here there was no conflict of stories. Indeed, Old Chief's admission is conclusive on this point. Equally important, the Justices in the majority saw no *permissible* way that information about Old Chief's past conviction could have affected the jury's decision on the issue of whether Old Chief had possessed a gun, but they saw considerable danger that this information might have influenced the jury in impermissible ways. In particular, the fact that Old Chief had been previously convicted of a serious assault might lead the jury to the impermissible inference that since he had once committed a serious assault, he was probably guilty of the assault he was now charged with.[34]

Courts usually confine *Old Chief* to its facts and apply it only to situations where evidence bears entirely on a formal legal issue that has no relationship to the story conflict that constitutes the heart of the parties' dispute.[35] But while there is much about *Old Chief* that cautions

---

[34]   519 U.S. at 180.

[35]   See, e.g., United States v. Phillippi, 442 F.3d 1061, 1064 (7th Cir. 2006); United States v. Dorsey, 523 F.3d 878, 880 (8th Cir. 2008). See also David P. Leonard, The Legacy of Old Chief and the Definition of Relevant Evidence: Implications for Uncharged Misconduct Evidence, 36 Sw. U.L. Rev. 819, 839 (2008).

against an expansive reading, nothing suggests it must be read this narrowly.

Since probative value, dangers of prejudice, the adequacy of alternative evidence, jurors' expectations about what evidence they will hear and the importance of evidence to a persuasive narrative all vary by degree, there is considerable room for case-by-case judicial discretion in applying *Old Chief*. Indeed, *Old Chief* can be read to cut against exclusions for prejudice. Some judges, who have been using their discretion to exclude bloody photos as proof of death when only the fact and not the manner of death is in issue, may be persuaded to the contrary by Justice Souter's paean to the importance of narrative. We believe that would be a mistake. Nothing about *Old Chief* tells judges that they should be less concerned about prejudice in striking FRE 403 balances than they were before the decision. The dicta on narrative are there to confirm that judges ordinarily retain their discretion under FRE 403 to admit potentially prejudicial relevant evidence, although a party could prove the same point using apparently less prejudicial means. But it is also unclear how far the dictum extends. Some judges may read *Old Chief* as mandating the substitution of less emotion-rousing proof in a wide variety of circumstances.

The majority in *Old Chief* saw a danger of substantial prejudice in the evidence the state sought to present, and, given the admission Old Chief was prepared to make, believed the incremental probative value of the state's evidence was zero or close to it. Usually tradeoffs will not be so stark. Where the tradeoff between probative value and prejudicial danger is a close one, FRE 403 mandates admissibility since it allows relevant evidence to be excluded only if its probative value is *"substantially outweighed"* by threats to fair and efficient fact-finding. However, the difference between merely "outweighing" and "substantially outweighing" has never been clarified. What is clear is that appellate courts regard decisions under FRE 403 as committed largely to the discretion of the trial judge. Decisions at trial are unlikely to be overturned on appeal. Trial judges should, however, explain why they reach the decisions they do. Some appellate courts have disapproved of trial judges who strike an FRE 403 balance but refuse counsel's request to state the reasons for their ruling.

FRE 403's importance and the discretion it accords trial judges cannot be overstated. Although it codifies what was the law in most jurisdictions before 1975, its explicit recognition of the broad balancing power accorded trial judges has made FRE 403 and its state equivalents the most frequent ground of objection in most federal and some state courts. You need only take a quick glance at reported decisions to appreciate the number and variety of occasions in which FRE 403 balancing is invoked.

J. THE MEANING OF PREJUDICE

In casual conversation the word "prejudice" is often used as if it were synonymous with "harm." We often say we were prejudiced by something when we mean that we were harmed by it. When the law speaks of prejudice, it is not speaking so casually. Prejudice refers to a specific kind of harm: harm which results when evidence is inappropriately influential because it appeals to the biases or emotions of the fact-finder. To be sure that there was no mistaking their meaning, the drafters of the Federal Rules modified the term "prejudice" with the word "unfair." But the modifier should not have been necessary. Prejudice, properly understood, is unfair.[36]

Evidence may destroy a party's case without being prejudicial within the meaning of FRE 403. For example, consider a driver arrested for exceeding a 20 mile per hour school zone speed limit. If the arresting officer testifies that the driver was clocked by radar at 35 miles per hour within a block of the school, the driver's case may be destroyed, for unless the officer's testimony is discredited, conviction is almost certain. Yet the testimony is not prejudicial in the sense of being unfairly influential, nor is the driver prejudiced by it. If the driver's protestations of innocence are overwhelmed by the officer's testimony, it is because of the probative force of that evidence; that is, its tendency to convince a *rational* fact-finder, devoid of biases and emotions, of the existence of a fact in issue.

Conversely, although prejudice may not exist without harm, even slight harm may be prejudicial. Thus, in the case of the Texas speeder, evidence that the defendant is a registered Democrat would probably not cause great harm even before a jury composed entirely of Republicans, since political differences are unlikely to affect verdicts in matters as mundane as speeding. Yet so long as any harm might be attributable to the partisan identification, evidence of the driver's political affiliation is potentially prejudicial. It is prejudicial because so far as we know, political affiliation has no plausible relationship to the probability a driver would speed, but it might conceivably affect a speeding verdict by appealing to the fact-finder's biases or emotions. It is this appeal that the law regards as impermissible.[37]

---

[36] In *Old Chief* Justice Souter wrote:

The term "unfair prejudice," as to a criminal defendant, speaks to the capacity of some concededly relevant evidence to lure the fact-finder into declaring guilt on a ground different from proof specific to the offense charged. So, the [Advisory] Committee Notes to Rule 403 explain, "'Unfair prejudice' within its context means an undue tendency to suggest decision on an improper basis, commonly, though not necessarily, an emotional one."

519 U.S. at 180.

[37] Evidence of the driver's political affiliation would be inadmissible *even if* the prosecutor had excellent statistical evidence that 90% of speeders in that jurisdiction are Democrats. The inference that such evidence invites—that the defendant is the sort of person who speeds; therefore he probably was speeding on this occasion—is a forbidden character inference. See Chapter Five. Even worse, it is an inference based on evidence of the behavior of a *group* to

If, however, testimony about the driver's political affiliation were admitted, a subsequent conviction would probably not be overturned on appeal.   As we have seen, the prejudicial potential of evidence may appear so slight, or other evidence in a case may be so overwhelming, that the admission of the evidence is harmless error.[38] This seems true of our speeding example.   But harmless error is error even if it does not justify overturning a decision, and trial courts should be vigilant in excluding evidence that can be prejudicial yet bears no rational relation to the existence of a fact in issue.

Often, however, evidence has both probative value and the potential to prejudice a fact-finder.   In our speeding case, evidence that the arresting officer had been threatened with dismissal if he did not ticket a certain number of drivers each day would be relevant because it might rationally lead a jury to question the officer's testimony.   At the same time, it might prejudice the state's case because a jury might be so incensed by the existence of ticket quotas that it would acquit a guilty driver to express its disapproval of the state's policing system.   Where probative value and prejudicial potential are mixed in this way, the judge applying FRE 403 must decide whether the harm to accurate fact-finding that is likely to result from the evidence's impermissible appeal is considerably greater than the evidence's likely incremental contribution to accurate fact-finding.   Only if the likely harm is much greater should the evidence be barred.   Where the prejudicial potential is obvious but the evidence has important probative value, the judge in admitting the evidence may also issue a limiting instruction directing the jury to consider the evidence only for its proper purposes.   But, as we have previously pointed out, it is not clear that such instructions help.[39]

Problem III-5. David Rollin is indicted for arson.   Specifically, he is alleged to have set fire to the home of Vilma and Juan Rodriguez.   At the trial, the prosecution offers in evidence a large authenticated photograph showing a portion of the smoldering remains of the house in the background, with the anguished faces of Mr. and Mrs. Rodriguez prominently featured in the foreground. **Is the photo relevant? How might the defendant protect against its admission?**

---

which the defendant belongs rather than on his own individual behavior or character, a type of evidence that American courts almost never consider. In other words, even if the inference from party membership to speeding were factually plausible, it would be legally forbidden.

[38] Chapter Two, supra, pp. 171–172. In the wake of the *Old Chief* decision, most reviewing panels faced with the question have held that a district court's refusal to require the prosecution to stipulate rather than present proof of the existence and nature of a prior offense is "harmless error." See Jana L. Torok, (Note) The Undoing of Old Chief: Harmless Error and Felon-in-Possession-of-Firearms Cases, 48 U. Kan. L. Rev. 431 (1999–2000).

[39] See Chapter Two, supra, pp. 184–186.

Problem III-6. Bertie Wooster is charged with burglary of a home. He pleads not guilty. The prosecution seeks to introduce evidence that on the night of the burglary Wooster was arrested three houses away from the scene of the burglary for selling narcotics. **Is the evidence relevant? Is it admissible? Assume the judge thinks it is both relevant and admissible, what steps might counsel for Wooster take to minimize the prejudicial effect of the evidence?**

II.   A MATHEMATICAL RESTATEMENT

We hope that what is written above is clear, but we now intend to restate some of what is written and to extend our remarks in another, more precise language—the language of mathematics. While some of you may have chosen a career in law in part because of your preference for verbal as opposed to mathematical analysis, we have found that mathematical models can clarify thinking about questions of relevance.

The excerpt that follows is taken from an article written by one of the authors.[40] Changes from the original are not noted in this excerpt.

Mathematics as a language can help clarify those legal rules that involve weighing evidence in an essentially probabilistic fashion. Two simple models, Bayes' Theorem and regret matrices, are helpful in thinking about the meaning of relevance and in analyzing certain of the rules generally associated with this topic. The following discussion assumes that the fact-finder is a jury and, unless otherwise noted, that the issue to be resolved is the defendant's guilt. However, the analysis may readily be generalized to the situation where the fact-finder is a judge and/or a question other than guilt is at issue. The two models are here applied to a simplified situation where the fact-finder must evaluate only one item of indisputably accurate testimony.[41]

A. BAYES' THEOREM

First we must attend to Bayes' Theorem. This theorem follows directly from two elementary formulas of probability theory: If A and B are any two propositions, then:

$$P(A \ \& \ B) = P(A \mid B) \cdot P(B) \text{[42] (1)}$$

$$P(A) = P(A \ \& \ B) \ v \ P(A \ \& \ \text{not-}B) \text{[43] (2)}$$

---

[40] Richard O. Lempert, Modeling Relevance, 75 Mich. L. Rev. 1021 (1977).

[41] See id. at pp. 1048–1062, for an exploration of complexities that can arise when a case involves two or more items of possibly unreliable evidence.

[42] These symbols mean that the probability that events A and B will both occur is equal to the probability that A will occur if B has occurred times the probability that B will occur (the ampersand is "and," the vertical line means "given," and the dot is "times"). For example, if A = a warm day and B = a sunny day, the probability that it will be both warm and sunny equals the probability that it will be warm if it is in fact sunny times the probability that it will be sunny.

From these rather basic equations the following formula may be derived (expressed in terms of "odds" rather than "probability"):

$$O(G \mid E) \ = \ \frac{P(E \mid G)}{P(E \mid \text{not-}G)} \cdot O(G) \quad (3)$$

This formula describes the way knowledge of a new item of evidence (E) would influence a Bayesian rational decision maker's evaluation of the odds that a defendant is guilty (G). Since the law assumes that a fact-finder *should* be rational in this Bayesian logical sense, this is a normative model (i.e. one seeking to express the proper or desired approach to be utilized by the ideal juror). What this equation says is that the odds (O) that a defendant is guilty, given the introduction of a new item of evidence, is equal to (1) the probability that the evidence would be presented to the jury if the defendant is in fact guilty, (2) divided by the probability that that same evidence would be presented to the jury if the defendant is in fact not guilty, (3) times the prior odds of the defendant's guilt. The prior odds are the odds that would have been given of the defendant's guilt before receipt of the item of evidence in question.[44]

For example, suppose at some point in a criminal trial the fact-finder believes that the odds are fifty-fifty, or 1:1, that the defendant is guilty. A more familiar way of stating this is that the fact-finder believes that the probability of the defendant's guilt is .50.[45] The evidence next received proves the following: that the perpetrator's blood, shed at the scene of the crime, was type A; that the defendant has type A blood; and that fifty per

---

[43] These symbols mean that the probability that an event A will occur equals the probability that event A will occur with event B, plus the probability that event A will occur with any event that is not B. If A = a warm day and B = a sunny day, the probability that it will be a warm day equals the probability that it will be warm and sunny plus the probability that it will be warm and not sunny.

[44] The figure for these odds is not important to the following analysis, though it might be important in analyzing other problems such as harmless error. It seems unlikely that jurors consciously think in terms of the odds of guilt after each item of evidence is received. It is possible, however, that without stopping to quantify, jurors, after hearing an item of evidence, make incremental changes in their perception of the party's position in much the way Bayes' Theorem suggests, and that if asked, they might be able to express these odds in mathematical terms. Research suggests that jurors can do the latter, but that at best they are inconsistent and often inaccurate Bayesians. See, B.C. Smith, S.D. Penrod, A.L. Otto & R.C. Park, Jurors' Use of Probabilistic Evidence, 20 Law & Hum. Behav. 49–82 (1996).

[45] One-to-one [1:1] odds (or "odds of 1") means that the existence of a state or an event is thought to be as likely as its non-existence, so the associated probability of its existence is .50 or 50%. Two-to-one [2:1] odds (or "odds of 2") means that the existence of a state or event is regarded as twice as likely as its non-existence so the associated probability of its existence is .67 or 67% since, allowing for rounding, .67 is twice .33. In general, the relationship between odds and probability is defined as follows, where O stands for odds and P stands for probability.

$$O \ = \ \frac{P}{(1\text{-}P)}$$

cent of the suspect population [46] has type A blood. Thus, if the defendant were the perpetrator, the probability that the blood found at the scene would be type A is 1.0.[47] The probability that the blood would be type A if someone else committed the crime is .50, or ½, since half of the other possible suspects have type A blood. Plugging these figures into the formula indicates that after receiving the blood evidence a rational decision maker would evaluate the odds of guilt as:

$$O(G \mid E) \ = \ \frac{1}{.5} \ \cdot \ \frac{1}{1} \ = \ \frac{1}{.5} \ = \ 2$$

The new evidence has raised the odds in favor of the defendant's guilt to 2, or 2:1. Another way of stating this result is that the fact-finder's best estimate of the probability that the defendant is guilty is now .67. Evidence that changes an estimated probability of guilt in this fashion is clearly relevant in a criminal trial.

Consider another case. Assume that the range of possible suspects has been limited to voters in a community so conservative that only one out of ten voters supports the liberal candidate. While a group of conservative jurors drawn from this community might be angered by evidence that the defendant supports the liberal candidate, such a showing would not influence the judgment of an ideal juror. Absent some reason to believe that liberals are more prone to commit the crime in question, the probability that the defendant could have been shown to be a liberal were he guilty is .1, the same as the probability that he could have been shown to be a liberal were he not guilty. Solving the Bayesian equation we find:

$$O(G \mid E) \ = \ \frac{.1}{.1} \ \cdot \ O(G) \ = \ (O(G))$$

The odds of the defendant's guilt remains O(G); the same as they were before the jury learned of the defendant's political affiliation. In these circumstances evidence of the defendant's political affiliation is not relevant.

---

[46] The suspect population could be people in the United States, people in a particular locality, males in a locality, black people, white people, etc. It turns on what is already known about the characteristics of the perpetrator. See, Richard O. Lempert, The Suspect Population and DNA Identification, 34 Jurimetrics 1–7 (1993). The textual example assumes that the suspect population is relatively large.

[47] At this point some might object that it can never be completely clear that the blood found was the perpetrator's. The point is well taken, but the fact that absolute certainty may never exist with respect to an item of evidence does not affect the basic argument.

1. Logical Relevance

In both examples the effect of the evidence on the decision maker's final judgment as to guilt turns entirely on the ratio,

$$\frac{P(E \mid G)}{P(E \mid \text{not-}G)}$$

conventionally called the *likelihood ratio*. In the first example $P(E \mid G)$ was twice $P(E \mid \text{not-}G)$, and the fact-finder doubled its prior odds of the defendant's guilt. In the second example $P(E \mid G)$ and $P(E \mid \text{not-}G)$ were the same, so the likelihood ratio was one, and the fact-finder's prior estimate of the defendant's guilt remained unchanged. In terms of the Bayesian model, it will always be the case that the impact of new evidence on the prior odds of guilt, or on any other disputed hypothesis, will be solely a function of the likelihood ratio for that evidence. Where the likelihood ratio for an item of evidence differs from one, that evidence is *logically relevant*. This is the mathematical equivalent of the statement in FRE 401 that "relevant evidence" is "evidence having *any* tendency to make the existence of any fact that is of consequence to the determination of the action more probable or less probable than it would be without the evidence." (Emphasis added.) Hence, an item of evidence is logically relevant only when the probability of finding that item of evidence given the truth of some hypothesis at issue in the case differs from the probability of finding the same item of evidence given the falsity of the hypothesis in issue. In a criminal trial, if a particular item of evidence is as likely to be found if the defendant is guilty as it is if he is innocent, the evidence is logically irrelevant on the issue of the defendant's guilt.

As a practical matter courts may be justified in treating evidence as logically irrelevant when the likelihood ratio for that evidence is only *slightly* different from one, since such evidence will have little effect on the odds that the disputed hypothesis is true. A slight difference in this context must be very small indeed, since a likelihood ratio of 1.5 would lead a fact-finder to increase by fifty percent his prior estimate of the odds in question and a likelihood ratio of 2.0 would result in a doubling of the prior odds.

It is clear from the model that the likelihood ratio depends entirely on the relative magnitudes of $P(E \mid G)$ and $P(E \mid \text{not-}G)$ and not on the absolute size of either. Thus, evidence that is unlikely to be associated with a guilty defendant will nevertheless be probative of guilt so long as the evidence is more (or less) likely to be associated with someone who is not guilty. Suppose, for example, that in an assault case the state can show both that the defendant is a heroin addict and that one in 500 criminal assailants are heroin addicts. Thus, it is quite unlikely that any given criminal assailant is a heroin addict, but this does not necessarily make the additional evidence exonerative or irrelevant. If the state can also show that only one in 1000 people who never engage in criminal assaults are heroin addicts, knowing the defendant is an addict should lead a fact-finder to double her prior odds that the defendant was the assailant. Conversely, if there was one heroin addict for every 250 non-assailants, evidence of the defendant's addiction should lead the fact-finder to halve her prior odds on the defendant's guilt. In either of these supposed cases there may be good reason to keep evidence of the defendant's addiction from the jury, but the reason is not that the information is logically irrelevant.

2. Estimation Problems

Courts declare evidence irrelevant for several reasons. Sometimes they are concerned that the likelihood ratio may be one or very close to it. This problem, examined above, is properly called the problem of "logical relevance." On other occasions courts are concerned with the possibility that the fact-finder will misestimate the probabilities that make up the likelihood ratio; i.e., $P(E|G)$ and/or $P(E|not\text{-}G)$. Overestimating the numerator or underestimating the denominator makes the conclusion favored by the person offering the evidence appear more probable than it actually is; underestimating the numerator or overestimating the denominator has the opposite result. In the above assault hypothetical, if the fact-finder thought that one in 10,000 rather than one in 1,000 non-assailants were heroin addicts, her misestimation would lead to a twenty-fold increase in the odds that the defendant was the assailant rather than the twofold increase that was in fact justified. We call such problems "estimation problems."

Estimation problems take several forms. The most obvious is that evidence may be given more weight than it deserves. The jurors may exaggerate the probative value of evidence because they believe that the association between an item of evidence and the hypothesis it bears on is more powerful than it in fact is, or because they are not estimating probative worth in the proper context given the facts of the case. The heroin example of the preceding paragraph is a situation in which the jurors misestimate the strength of a crucial association, throwing the denominator of the likelihood ratio off by a factor of ten. When courts reject evidence fearing this type of misestimation, they often categorize the problem as one of prejudice, a term better reserved for another situation,[48] or they may speak of the danger of confusing or misleading the jury.

An estimation problem also exists when there is so little information about the relationship of certain evidence to the hypothesis in question that the evidence's implications are unclear. In these circumstances

---

[48] See Section I, Subsection J, supra, of this Chapter and Section II, Subsection B, infra.

courts may exclude evidence as irrelevant rather than let the jurors speculate on its import. Since such evidence might well relate to the probability of guilt or innocence if its true implications were known, a more precise justification for exclusion is "relevance unknown." If the textual example that posited a relationship between heroin addiction and assault did not ring true, it is probably because we lack the base rate information needed to evaluate the relationship between heroin addiction and the likelihood of engaging in an assault. Although the image of the "dope fiend" is that of a violent personality, effects associated with ingesting heroin suggest that addicts are less likely than non-addicts to engage in physical violence for its own sake.[49] With no good evidence of appropriate base rates and conflicting images of the violent propensities of heroin addicts, it makes sense to keep evidence of heroin addiction from a jury in assault cases because its relevance is unknown.

Under FRE 403 and at common law, courts have discretion to exclude logically relevant evidence likely to pose estimation problems if the probative value of the evidence is substantially outweighed by the danger that it will mislead the jury. The Bayesian model suggests that in exercising this discretion, the more the court's estimation of the proper likelihood ratio for an item of evidence deviates from 1:1, the less willing the court should be to exclude that evidence despite a danger of substantial misestimation. If the likelihood ratio for an item of evidence is 2:1 and the fact-finder perceives it as 20:1 the misevaluation might well be of critical importance. However, if the likelihood ratio for the evidence is 100:1 and the fact-finder misperceives it as 1000:1, the error is unlikely to be critical because the evidence whether properly weighed or overweighted will usually lead to the same conclusion: that the favored hypothesis is established by the appropriate standard of proof. Furthermore, excluding evidence where the likelihood ratio deviates substantially from 1:1 deprives the fact-finder of information that might aid considerably in the rational resolution of disputed factual claims and may prevent a party from making what is, on a *fair* reading of all the evidence, a powerful case. Thus courts are right in rarely, if ever, excluding evidence of substantial probative value simply because the jury appears likely to give it even more weight than it deserves, or because the precise weight it deserves is unclear.[50] The preferred solution is to provide the jury with the information needed to assess accurately the probative value of the offered evidence.

---

[49] Since there is good reason to believe that addicts often find it necessary to resort to crime in order to support their habits, if the assault were with an intent to rob the probative value of the evidence of addiction would, no doubt, be higher and the likely direction of the relationship would be clearer.

[50] There are other concerns that may justify the exclusion of highly probative evidence, e.g., the rules of privilege and the rules regarding illegally seized evidence.

A similar analysis applies when a court is called on to weigh the probative value of evidence against such factors as confusion of the issues, delay, and waste of time. Where the likelihood ratio for the evidence is far from 1:1, exclusion on these grounds is almost never justified except in the special case where, after considering all other admissible evidence, the court is convinced that the prior odds in favor of the disputed hypothesis are so high or so low that even highly probative evidence is unlikely to change the jury's judgment. This means that courts should be more reluctant in close cases than in clear ones to exclude probative evidence on such grounds as threatened delay, confusion, or waste of time. Appellate courts are certainly influenced by the closeness of cases in reviewing claims that excluding evidence for these reasons was erroneous.

The Bayesian model presented thus far aids in understanding the following aspects of the law relating to relevance: (1) the meaning of logical relevance, (2) the principle that only logically relevant evidence is admissible, (3) the discretion that courts have to exclude relevant evidence when the jury is likely to give it undue weight, and (4) the reluctance of courts to exclude highly probative evidence even though the jury is likely to give it undue weight.

The Bayesian model does not, however, indicate why in some cases it might be desirable to exclude probative evidence not likely to raise estimation problems nor why it should be reversible error for a court to admit logically irrelevant evidence. However, another model drawn from decision theory helps clarify these aspects of the law of relevance. This model, called a *regret matrix*, aids in thinking about prejudice.

B. PREJUDICE AND THE REGRET MATRIX

A regret matrix[51] is not a normative model since the law does not necessarily expect its ideal decision maker to act in a manner consistent with it. It may, however, be a good descriptive model of the way decision makers, be they jurors or judges, actually behave, and values may be inserted into the model that are, arguably, normative. The model assumes that individuals wish to minimize the expected regret felt in the long run as a result of their decisions. In law, for example, a decision maker might wish to find for plaintiffs only when defendants were negligent. In terms of this model, the decision maker would have no regret in finding for plaintiffs when defendants were negligent and no regret in finding for defendants when they were not negligent.[52] Since in the uncertain world of litigation the decision maker can never be

---

[51] What we refer to as a "regret" matrix is a form of what is generally called a "utility" matrix in the decision theory literature.

[52] The example assumes that defenses such as contributory negligence are unavailable in this case, so liability turns solely on the issue of the defendant's negligence.

absolutely sure that a particular defendant was or was not negligent, the decision maker can never be absolutely sure of avoiding outcomes that would be regretted if the truth were known.

Although absolute certainty is impossible, the decision maker might be able to estimate a probability that the defendant was negligent, e.g., .6 or .7. If this can be done and if the decision maker can articulate the *relative* regret associated with different possible outcomes, a regret matrix can be constructed that indicates which decision—given the probabilities—leads to the least total regret in the long run. Consider the situation portrayed in Figure 1.

Figure 1

Decision Maker's
Regret Matrix

		True State of Affairs	
		D **Negligent**	**D Not** **Negligent**
Verdict	For P	0	1
	For D	1	0

If the Decision Maker's Estimated Probabilities are:

Prob. D was negligent = .6; Prob. D was not negligent = .4

Then the Decision Maker's Expected Regret is:

If Verdict for P, 0 x .6 + 1 x .4 = .4

If Verdict for D, 1 x .6 + 0 x .4 = .6

In this matrix no regret is associated with a decision for P (the plaintiff) when D (the defendant) was negligent or with a decision for D when D was not negligent. One unit of regret is associated with each mistake, that of finding for P when D was not negligent and that of finding for D when D was negligent. How should a decision maker with these values decide? That depends on his estimate of the probability that D was negligent. In the above example this probability is estimated at .6, making the estimated probability that D was not negligent (1 - .6) or .4. Knowing these probabilities, the expected regret for each verdict can be calculated by multiplying the regret associated with the verdict, given the defendant's actual negligence or non-negligence, times the probability that the defendant actually was negligent or not negligent. The sum of these products for a given verdict equals the total regret to be expected (in the long run) if that verdict were reached in all cases having the same regret matrix and probability of negligence. In our example, there is a .6 probability that D was negligent. Hence there is a .6 probability that the decision maker who decides for P will feel no regret [.6 x 0 = 0]. Conversely, there is a .4 probability that D was not negligent and that a decision for P will result in one unit of regret [.4 x 1 = .4]. Thus, the regret expected from deciding for P, given the perceived probability of D's negligence, will, in the long run, average .4 of whatever unit regret is measured in [0 + .4 = .4]. The situation is reversed when the decision is for D. This decision brings with it a .6 probability that the decision maker will feel one unit of regret and a .4 probability that the decision maker will feel no regret. Consequently, the average expected regret from deciding for D is .6 units in the long run. An individual concerned with minimizing expected regret will decide for P in this circumstance.

The regret matrix used in this example is normative (i.e. predictive of the socially desirable or appropriate outcome) for most civil cases. A judge or juror *should* feel the same regret in mistakenly finding for P as she does in mistakenly finding for D.[53] If this is the case (i.e., if this particular regret matrix actually models the decision maker's values), one can show algebraically that regret is minimized by deciding for P whenever the probability of negligence is greater than .5 and deciding for D whenever the probability of negligence is less than .5.[54]

There are many civil cases in which a fact-finder might not in fact feel equal regret at the two kinds of mistakes, even if this is how things should be. In these circumstances the fact-finder may strain to reach decisions that run counter to the weight of the evidence. For example, if an insurance company executive were seated on a jury, she might regret mistakenly deciding for P when D was not negligent twice as much as mistakenly exonerating the defendant. (This may be portrayed by changing the value in the upper right-hand cell of the matrix in Figure One to 2 while leaving the value in the lower left-hand cell at 1.) With this relative regret and the same probability that D is negligent as in the earlier example, .6 units of regret would be associated with a decision for

---

[53] This standard, even without the law's tie breaker giving decisions to defendants where the evidence is in equipoise, does not necessarily mean that a fact-finder will make mistakes that favor P with the same frequency as she makes mistakes that favor D. The ratio of erroneous plaintiff decisions to erroneous defense decisions in trials turns not just on the burden of proof, but also on the proportion of justified law suits in the mix of cases fact-finders hear and on the fact-finder's ability to determine accurately the questions those cases pose. To choose an extreme example, if the defendants are in fact liable in all (or virtually all) civil cases that go to trial, then all (or virtually all) errors that juries make will occur in cases in which the defendants were in fact at fault. Similarly, the "beyond a reasonable doubt" standard in criminal cases, even if expressed in terms of a quantitative tradeoff, does not necessarily imply that some given number of guilty criminals will be acquitted for each innocent person who is convicted. The mathematically inclined who are interested in this matter should read Michael L. Dekay's excellent article, The Difference Between Blackstone-Like Error Ratios and Probabilistic Standards of Proof, 21 Law & Soc. Inq. 95 (1996).

[54] This is what a burden of proof by the preponderance of the evidence means. Regret is equal when the probability of negligence is exactly .5. Here the law has decided that the defendant should prevail.

D (the same as before) and .8 units of regret [0 x .6 + 2 x .4] with a decision for P. Hence a decision for D could be expected, although the executive's estimated probability of D's negligence is sixty percent.[55]

At law the burden of proof needed to win a judgment or sustain a conviction, is in theory, the same for all defendants: good or evil, young or old, attractive or unattractive, dangerous or non-threatening. Yet most jurors are likely to regret wrong decisions that harm seemingly good people more than similar mistakes that harm seemingly evil people. Where a person is mistakenly helped, as in a wrongful acquittal, regret will be less the more favorable the juror's attitude toward the person. If a juror cannot avoid being influenced by her attitude preferences in reaching a verdict, the burden of proof she imposes is effectively changed by any information that affects these preferences.

The law's ideal juror estimates only the probabilities pertaining to the matter in issue; she does not estimate or respond to the regret associated with possible mistakes. Relative regret is a normative not a personal matter (i.e., focusing on a general standard of correctness), and the court's instructions on the burden of proof are intended to convey the law's norms. The requirement that guilt be proved beyond a reasonable doubt may mean that an accused should not be convicted unless the probability of guilt is judged to be at least .91, which can be seen as a quantification of the idea that the law regards a wrongful conviction as being ten times more regrettable than a wrongful acquittal, or it may mean that conviction should not follow unless some other minimum probability of guilt is obtained; but whatever the degree of certainty associated with proof beyond a reasonable doubt, the law does not contemplate that the standard for proof of guilt will vary with the defendant's personal characteristics or with the sordid details of the crime someone committed.

In practice, the ideal of an unvarying standard is not achieved. Instructions on burden of proof, particularly in criminal cases, are so ambiguous that jurors necessarily exercise discretion in determining the degree of certainty needed to support possible verdicts. There is also considerable evidence that the personal characteristics of victims and defendants influence jury verdicts as do aspects of criminal activity that do not logically relate to the issue of guilt or innocence. Where this occurs one may properly speak of prejudice, for prejudicial evidence is best thought of as: *any evidence that influences jury verdicts without relating logically to the legal questions a jury must answer.*[56]   Evidence that

---

[55] This assumes that the executive would choose to minimize regret rather than follow the court's instruction that P should prevail if he has established his case by a preponderance of the evidence.

[56] To be sure that prejudicial evidence is not interpreted as any evidence that harms a party's case, FRE 403 speaks of "unfair prejudice." We believe that if the law's concept of prejudice is properly understood, the word "unfair" is redundant. See supra, pp. 241–243. The

relates logically to a disputed issue may in addition have a prejudicial effect, since the probative value of evidence may not fully determine its impact in the case. In terms of the regret model, one can conceptualize the prejudicial *potential* of evidence as the degree to which it can affect the regret matrix of a juror viewing the case. The prejudicial *impact* of evidence is its prejudicial potential discounted by the juror's ability to ignore sentiment and similar personal preferences in interpreting the evidence and applying the court's instructions. Often the law fictively assumes that this ability is complete so long as the juror is instructed not to use evidence inappropriately, but practicing lawyers know that limiting instructions are no curealls.

Much of the law relating to relevance is concerned with the possible effects of potentially prejudicial information on jury decision making. The danger of prejudice justifies the exclusion of some logically relevant evidence that does not pose estimation problems, and the same danger explains why the admission of logically irrelevant evidence may be reversible error. As we shall see in Chapters Four and Five, a number of relevance rules are justified in part because the evidence they exclude is fraught with prejudicial potential. We shall conclude this discussion by looking briefly at two rules by way of example.

FRE 411 provides that evidence of liability insurance may not be introduced to show negligence. The Rule seems justified, since possessing liability insurance appears to have little bearing on carefulness.[57] Thinking solely in terms of Bayes' Theorem, evidence of the defendant's insurance coverage might be objectionable on the ground that its introduction wastes the court's time, but there is no reason to believe that such evidence will hurt either party. If it doesn't, reversing a case for a FRE 411 violation seems silly since that only wastes more time. However, the regret matrix suggests a more substantial reason for excluding evidence of insurance and a justification for reversing cases for FRE 411 violations. A fact-finder who knows that a defendant was insured may feel less regret at mistakenly holding that defendant liable than she would if she thought the defendant himself would have to pay for the harm. Interestingly, some have argued that jurors should be informed of the existence of insurance because jurors assume insurance exists and construct their regret matrices accordingly. Insurance companies are not worse off when their interest in the case is revealed, so the argument goes, but uninsured defendants are harmed if jurors do not know they lack insurance.[58]

---

idea of "narrative relevance," sanctioned by the Supreme Court in *Old Chief*, suggests that the Supreme Court might, for example, regard the influence of a testifying victim's tears on a jury verdict as "fair prejudice." The definitions the *Old Chief* majority provide for "prejudice" do not, however, suggest that the majority had an idea of "fair prejudice" in mind.

[57] See Chapter Four, Section II, Subsection E, especially note 47.

[58] Id. and note 48.

Consider also a rule to be discussed in Chapter Five; namely, that evidence of other crimes is ordinarily inadmissible to show a defendant's propensity to commit crimes. At least three reasons may be given for this rule. First, regardless of the association between a past criminal record and recent criminal activity, there is social value in officially refusing to treat a person as more likely to engage in a current crime because of a past conviction. Even though the connection might exist in a probabilistic sense, recognizing it in the law would increase the harm the label "deviant" brings to people who in fact lead blameless lives after having been convicted of crimes. Second, the fact-finder in criminal cases might substantially overestimate the relationship between past convictions and subsequent behavior and thus overestimate the probability that the defendant is guilty of the crime in question. Third, and probably most important, knowledge of an individual's past crimes may increase the regret the fact-finder associates with mistakenly acquitting while diminishing the regret an erroneous conviction might bring. Thus a juror might think it a terrible tragedy to erroneously convict if that means sending someone who has led a blameless life to prison, but she might be relatively untroubled by the thought of erroneously incarcerating someone who has spent a lifetime shuffling in and out of prison. The juror might reason, even if the defendant did not commit the charged crime, he probably committed other crimes without being caught.

These regret matrix models speak not only to the reasons behind the relevance rules, but they also indicate why lawyers work so hard to circumvent those rules that prohibit the mention of past crimes and similarly loaded evidence. They also pose starkly the question of whether it is ethical to introduce evidence solely for the purpose of changing a fact-finder's regret matrix.

. . .

If you find these models a helpful way to think about relevance problems, experiment a bit with different hypothetical values in the Bayesian equation or the regret matrix. If you are interested in pursuing the matter further, two good articles which deal with Bayesian statistics (for somewhat different purposes) are: Finkelstein and Fairley, "A Bayesian Approach to Identification Evidence," 83 Harv. L. Rev. 489 (1970) and Tribe, "Trial by Mathematics: Precision and Ritual in the Legal Process," 84 Harv. L. Rev. 1329 (1971). Either of these will present you with a derivation of Bayes' Theorem from the two basic propositions of probability theory presented above. An article you might want to consult on decision theory and regret matrices is: Kaplan, "Decision Theory and the Fact-finding Process," 20 Stan. L. Rev. 1065 (1968). For a discussion of more subtle issues see the article by Dekay cited in note 53. If you are interested in challenges to the Bayesian model of rational thought, the places to begin are Jonathan L. Cohen's book, *The Probable and the Provable* and the special issue of The Boston University Law Review, which occupies pages 377–452 of Volume 66 (1986). Also numerous articles by David A. Schum, some with coauthors, speak intelligently to issues raised by different models of logical thought. See, for example, his discussion of why hearsay is problematic, "Hearsay From a Layperson," and the comments by Professors Friedman and Swift that follow.[59] Finally David Kaye has written extensively and clearly on uses of Bayes' Theorem.[60]

―――――――

Problem III-7. Sharon Cohn's home is severely damaged when a large chunk of ice from the landing gear of a jet airliner crashes through the roof. Cohn sues National Airlines. Cohn lives two miles from the Metro City Airport, and sixty percent of the flights over her home are National's. **If Cohn was out of town on the date of the accident, and doesn't know what time it happened, may she introduce statistics to show the total number of flights over her house and the number of National flights, and argue on that basis that the probability is six out of ten that a National plane caused the damage?** Assume that Cohn claims that the damage occurred between about 10:30 and 11:00 p.m. on Tuesday, July 21, 2008. The flight records from Metro City Airport are presented in evidence, and show the following arrival times for flights that went over Cohn's house on that date: 10:20 p.m. National, 10:35 p.m. National, 10:48 p.m. National, 10:56 p.m. National, 11:02 p.m. Spirit. **May Cohn argue on this basis that the probability of National being responsible for the damage is 80%? On that record is there sufficient evidence to support a verdict for the plaintiff?**

III.   EXPLANATORY OR SUBJECTIVE RELEVANCE

A.   EXPERT OPINION

The principles expressed by Federal Rules 401, 402 and 403 are at the core of the law of evidence. Most evidence rules sound variations on the theme that all relevant evidence should be admitted unless its probative value is outweighed by a tendency to prejudice, mislead or otherwise confuse the jury. The hearsay rule, for example, seeks to specify situations where the probative value of evidence is likely to be so

――――――――――

[59] Schum, Hearsay From a Layperson, 14 Cardozo L. Rev. 1–77 (1992); Richard D. Friedman, Infinite Strands, Infinitesimally Thin: Storytelling, Bayesianism, Hearsay and Other Evidence, 14 Cardozo L. Rev. 79–101 (1992); Swift, A Response to the "Probative Value" Theory of Hearsay Suggested by "Hearsay From a Layperson," 14 Cardozo L. Rev. 103–119 (1992).

[60] E.g., David H. Kaye, Clarifying the Burden of Persuasion: What Bayesian Decision Rules Do and Do Not Do, 3 Int. J. of Evid. & Proof 1–29 (1999).

low or so indeterminate that it makes sense to keep information from the jury. The rules regarding authentication require special guarantees of relevance where it seems feasible to demand such guarantees and where the evidence involved is of a type that is likely to be of particular importance. Indeed, of those rules commonly used to exclude evidence, only privileges are justified by values that have little to do with the themes of this chapter.

Perhaps no rule comes closer to restating the basic relevance theme than FRE 702, which defines the occasions when expert opinion testimony will be received. Under FRE 702 the key to admissibility is helpfulness: the expert witness's opinion must "help the trier of fact to understand the evidence or to determine a fact in issue."

At first blush, it seems that evidence that merely helps the jury to understand other evidence is not relevant, because the explanation does not in itself make any fact that matters more likely or less likely. But opinions offered to aid a jury's understanding of other evidence are admissible. This is because for good reasons there is a subjective side to FRE 401.[61] An item of observational evidence (an x-ray of a fracture of the victim's skull, for example), may have a strong objective tendency to make the existence of a consequential fact (that the victim was killed by a blow to the head) more probable or less probable than it otherwise would be, but it cannot help a jury unless the jurors understand that this tendency exists. For this reason, if the implications of facts in evidence cannot be understood without scientific, technical or other specialized knowledge, experts are allowed to tell the jury how the facts might or should be interpreted.[62] If relevance were only an objective phenomenon, the expert's testimony would be excludable as irrelevant (except where the expert reports an investigation of factual matters), for an expert's belief about what evidence implies for the existence of consequential facts does not make the existence of these facts more or less probable than they

---

[61] In a certain sense all evidence is only subjectively relevant because what it affects is the *appearance* to the fact-finder of the plausibility of some fact in issue. But underlying the relevance of most ordinary factual evidence is the sense that there is an objective relationship between the evidence offered and the fact in issue such that if the evidence offered is true, the fact in issue is more or less likely to have existed. The judge usually assumes that if there is an objective relationship, the jurors' subjective judgments will be appropriately influenced. The judge also ordinarily does not try to decide whether the offered evidence is subjectively credible, but leaves that determination to the jury.

[62] Expert testimony is not limited to interpretations and opinions. An expert may present facts to the jury that are every bit as concrete as the facts lay people testify to. Thus a DNA expert reporting that DNA taken from a suspect matches DNA found at a crime scene is reporting facts in much the same sense as an eyewitness who testifies that the defendant sitting in court looks like the person who robbed him. To some degree what each witness says is, of course, a matter of opinion, but the DNA expert's opinion is, if anything, more objective than that of the eyewitness in the sense that another DNA expert who did the same analysis of a DNA sample as the testifying expert would be more likely to make the same DNA identification than another eyewitness who saw the bank robbery would be to identify the same person as the robber.

otherwise would be, given the evidence.[63] The expert's testimony as to her beliefs does, however, make consequential facts *appear to the jury* to be more or less probable, because the jury learns from the expert's opinion what these esoteric facts imply to one who knows how to interpret them.   Thus, if expert testimony is well presented, the jury should understand the reason why the factual evidence in the case justifies particular conclusions.   Evidence that instructs jurors how better to understand evidence that would otherwise not make sense to them is properly treated as relevant, for fact-finding is a subjective process, and better understanding of admitted evidence should lead to more rational judgments.

To give an example, consider an auto accident in which one of the jury's tasks is to determine whether the defendant was speeding when her car collided with the plaintiff's car. During the plaintiff's case a police officer testifies to the damage done to the cars involved, the length of the skid marks laid down by the defendant's car, the condition of the road, and the like. If an accident reconstruction expert then testifies for the plaintiff and offers an expert opinion that the defendant was speeding, what she says will not make it objectively more probable that the defendant was in fact speeding, for that objective probability is established by the information that has already been presented regarding the accident. The expert's testimony will, however, give the jury a better idea of what that probability is, for without expert help the ordinary juror will have no idea what to make of the police officer's testimony. Thus, the expert's testimony makes the probability the defendant was speeding *appear* greater than it otherwise might seem, for the expert instructs the jurors on how to make sense of the evidence and tells them what it implies. Experts are routinely allowed to instruct jurors in this fashion. With the law's approval, experts give jurors their views about how to think about facts in the case, and their opinions of what those facts imply, with the aim of encouraging the jurors to adopt these views and opinions as their own. Lay opinion on the other hand is not admitted to interpret core facts that jurors are thought unable to evaluate on their own; rather, it is allowed (within a much narrower scope) because it captures or summarizes facts that are not amenable to more concrete presentation. Lay opinion is allowed because it is otherwise difficult to present relevant factual information.

---

[63] There is a special sense in which this is not true. The very fact that the expert is testifying for a party may bear some objective relationship to the likelihood the party's claim is true since some experts are good at discerning the truth and would not testify in support of an invalid claim.

As Professor Schum has emphasized in various articles, a similar situation exists where a jury believes a witness knows more than she testifies to, and thinks the witness's willingness to testify for a party or what she says is influenced by information she does not report. (See e.g., Schum, supra note 59). Interestingly, one of the earliest forms of English trials, which we tend to regard today as irrational, was built on the value of the fact of witnessing. If an accused party was able to get a certain number of people of a particular status to swear for him, he prevailed.

Courts welcome expert opinion so long as the expert interprets facts of a kind that lay people are not ordinarily called upon to evaluate. They are much less hospitable to experts who seek to apply a body of specialized knowledge to problems that lay people are accustomed to dealing with, or who seek to sharpen the jury's common sense by telling the jurors how an expert would approach their problem or what aspects of the evidence an expert would deem important. Thus, despite years of campaigning by Wigmore, few courts ever allowed psychiatrists to testify to the credibility of rape victims [64]; and in a celebrated case that forms the basis for one of the problems that follow, a guilty verdict was reversed because the trial judge allowed a statistician to describe how a mathematical decision theorist might assess the implications of certain circumstantial evidence.[65]

"I urge this jury not to let the evidence prejudice you against my client."

In excluding expert testimony of this kind, courts sometimes speak of the offered evidence as "invading the province of the jury." Behind this rhetoric is the idea that the expert's testimony will not aid the jurors because the testimony seeks to instruct them on matters that an unassisted group of lay people can intelligently evaluate. There is also the notion that the jurors, as the law's chosen fact-finders, should not be told how to view evidence unless their unaided judgment is likely to be

---

[64] Wigmore's campaign should give us pause about proposals similar to his, for the "science" of his day would probably have fostered conclusions that today's science would reject.

[65] People v. Collins, 68 Cal.2d 319, 66 Cal.Rptr. 497, 438 P.2d 33 (1968).

deficient in some respect. If their unaided judgment is not deficient, the expert testimony will not assist the jury because the jury needs no help; therefore, it will not qualify for admission under FRE 702, and will be properly excluded under FRE 403 for its tendency to waste time and the possibility it might mislead or confuse the jury. A long history of trusting juries to make certain kinds of evaluations does not, however, mean that expert instruction will be useless to the jury, for scientifically based expertise has been acquired about matters that were once confined to the realm of intuitive judgment. Nevertheless, courts are much more skeptical about the ability of experts to aid jurors in thinking about ordinary testimony than they are when evidence is more esoteric.

B. EYEWITNESS EXPERTS, DNA EXPERTS, AND PERMITTED OPINIONS

It is instructive to contrast eyewitness identifications in criminal cases with DNA identifications. Ordinary people judge the credibility of eyewitnesses all the time. Much of our daily conversation is with eyewitnesses to events, and frequently we must decide whether to believe them ("The fish was *how* big?" "You saw Sheila with David? I don't believe it!"). So, one would think that jurors need no help in evaluating the probative force of eyewitness testimony. DNA evidence, on the other hand, is completely foreign to most jurors' experience. Even those who know something about DNA are unlikely to have had prior occasions to judge the probative force of a DNA match.

Another difference is that an expert in the psychology of eyewitness identification adds nothing to the objective probability of the existence of any fact in issue. Whether or not the eyewitness expert testifies, the jury has all the evidence that tends to establish that a defendant has committed a charged crime, including the fact that an eyewitness says the defendant did it. The only problem (according to the defendant who proffers the eyewitness expert) is that the jurors do not appreciate how fallible eyewitness testimony can be. The DNA expert, by contrast, gives the jury new evidence that tends to establish the defendant's presence at a crime scene: evidence that the defendant's DNA matches DNA extracted from blood, semen or other biological material apparently left by the perpetrator.

What the eyewitness expert provides the jury is information that bears on the likelihood that an eyewitness testified accurately. In some respects, the expert's testimony is similar to an ordinary lay witness's testimony that some other witness is biased against the defendant. But testimony on bias gives the jury a reason why the *particular* person testifying against this defendant may not be as credible as she seems. The eyewitness expert ordinarily only gives the jury information that may help it evaluate the testimony of eyewitnesses *in general.* If she is appearing for the defense, that will usually be testimony reporting research which suggests that eyewitnesses who report on observations similar in certain respects to those of the eyewitnesses in the case at hand are not as credible as they may seem, for example, when those witnesses are white and are attempting to make cross-race identifications.[66]

The eyewitness expert's testimony is also similar in some respects to the testimony a DNA expert provides. In addition to reporting the DNA match, the DNA expert tells the jury the probability that a randomly selected person would have DNA matching the crime scene DNA. Only with this information can the jury know how incriminating a DNA match is. If, for example, one in five people has DNA like that left at the crime scene, we haven't learned a great deal beyond the fact that the defendant is not excluded as a suspect. If, on the other hand, only one in 100 billion people has DNA like that at the crime scene, the reported match seems like overwhelming evidence of the defendant's involvement in the crime.[67] The proponent of eyewitness expert testimony would similarly argue that the jury needs expert testimony to evaluate the probative value of the eyewitness's report that the defendant's appearance matches the appearance of the person she saw at the crime scene. There is a difference, however. The typical judge recognizes that the jurors would not know what to make of the DNA evidence if an expert didn't explain it to them, but the judge is likely to believe that jurors are able to assess eyewitness testimony without expert help. The jurors, no doubt, would share the judge's views.[68]

We have already suggested that an eyewitness expert's testimony is analogous to that of a bias witness, except that the latter provides a reason to discount testimony that is specific to a particular witness, while the former provides reasons to discount the testimony of all witnesses in situations similar to that of the eyewitness in question. Neither the bias witness nor the eyewitness expert can know that the causes for concern she raises have in fact colored an opposing witness's testimony, but the bias witness can ordinarily purport to be certain that the concern she

---

[66] For this, and other eyewitness research see Phoebe C. Ellsworth and Robert Mauro, "Psychology and Law" in Daniel Gilbert et al. eds. The Handbook of Social Psychology, 702–707 (1998).

[67] In fact, astronomical numbers like this, which are common in expert DNA testimony, overstate the weight of the evidence, for the probability of a laboratory or police processing error far exceeds the probability of a random match. If there is, for example, a one in a thousand chance that a laboratory error contaminated the crime scene DNA with the defendant's, a much smaller probability that the two would match by chance, like the one in 100 million figure mentioned in the text, tells the jury little about the likelihood that a match would be reported if the defendant did not leave the DNA at the scene of the crime. See, Lempert, Some Caveats Concerning DNA as Criminal Identification Evidence: With Thanks to the Reverend Bayes, 13 Cardozo L. Rev. 303 (1991); Lempert, After the DNA Wars: Skirmishing With NRC II, 37 Jurimetrics J. 439 (1997).

[68] The process of obtaining DNA identification evidence is in fact complicated and extremely remote from most people's experience, and the interpretation of that evidence raises an additional set of complex technical issues. See Chapter Nine, pp. 1247–1260.

raises specifically *applies* to an opposition witness while the eyewitness expert typically cannot make this claim.[69] Some courts have found that these differences are sufficient to justify excluding eyewitness expert testimony. However, it is usually not the basic relevance hurdle that precludes eyewitness expert testimony. Nor should it be. Eyewitness expert testimony, like much expert testimony that is routinely admitted, and like testimony about witness bias, can enhance the jury's ability to accurately assess the value of other evidence in the case.

When eyewitness expert testimony is excluded it is usually by judicial discretion on FRE 403 grounds, or on the basis of a similar analysis of the "helpfulness" requirement of FRE 702. One argument is that the jurors do not need an expert's help since, in their day-to-day lives, they regularly assess the stories of people who claim to have witnessed events, and often are able to refine their judgment skills by checking these stories and hence their assessments. This is a questionable ground for exclusion. In our robbery example, for instance, it might appear that no juror needs an expert to point out that an identification may be untrustworthy because the robber's face was poorly lit and the witness viewed the robber from a distance. Yet even in regard to such obvious considerations, an expert's testimony might be helpful. Without it, jurors might not focus on these aspects of the identification, or they might underestimate the degree to which bad lighting and distance can undermine the accuracy of identifications. On other matters, such as the functional size of lineups[70] or the tenuous nature of the relationship between a witness's confidence and his accuracy[71], the information the eyewitness expert relates is likely to be news to most jurors.

A more justifiable reason to bar eyewitness expert testimony is that it might mislead or confuse the jury. On some issues, such as the "weapon focus" phenomenon or the suggestibility of school age children, the scientific evidence is conflicting. If expert testimony is allowed, there might be a battle of experts on issues that bear on the credibility of factual witnesses. This might distract jurors from the core issues in the case, and waste time. Moreover, even if an eyewitness expert accurately

---

[69] Some matters that the eyewitness expert might testify to, like the effects of monochromatic lighting on color perception, will necessarily affect what an eyewitness can credibly report.

[70] Because line-ups and photo arrays may be constructed so that one person stands out, the fact that a witness identified the suspect may not be as surprising as it might seem given the number of people the witness chose from. The decrement from actual to functional size may be estimated by showing the line-up to people who never saw the crime and asking them to point to the suspect. If a six-person line-up is shown to a group of people with no connection to the crime and one-third point to the suspect this indicates that something about the line-up construction has caused the suspect to stand out as the likely culprit apart from the possibility that he committed the crime. Although the line-up had a nominal size of six its functional size would be three.

[71] People often think that a witness's confidence in making an identification is a good indicator of the witness's accuracy. In fact, confidence is a weak signal of accuracy if it is a signal at all.

identifics a series of case-related phenomena that hamper eyewitness accuracy in general, these features may not have affected the accuracy of the eyewitness in the case. This possibility does not make the expert's testimony irrelevant any more than the possibility that a friend of the plaintiff is testifying accurately makes testimony about the friend's biases irrelevant, but it seems to be the factor which most influences judicial discretion in the reported cases. Where an eyewitness's identification is corroborated by other evidence and so appears likely to be true, trial judges frequently exclude eyewitness expert testimony on FRE 403 grounds, and their decisions are invariably upheld on appeal.[72] Conversely where eyewitness testimony is all or almost all that implicates a defendant, trial courts often admit eyewitness expert testimony, and it is in such cases that one finds the few appellate court decisions reversing convictions because an eyewitness expert was barred from testifying.

Making a decision to admit evidence by looking to see how strongly other evidence inculpates a defendant conflicts with the idea that evidence law is an autonomous set of procedural norms which itself determines the admissibility of the evidence parties offer. But in the eyewitness expert area, this appears to be a sensible, practical solution and one consistent with FRE 403 which invites balancing between probative value and opposing concerns. Eyewitness expert testimony is commonly allowed in situations where giving too much weight to an eyewitness's testimony could well lead to a wrongful conviction, and it is commonly barred where other evidence suggests the eyewitness is likely to be accurate despite conditions that are known to diminish the accuracy of eyewitness testimony generally. In other areas of evidence law one seldom finds such a neat example of how a judge's view of the merits affects her exercise of discretion. But whenever judges have discretion to admit or exclude evidence—and on appeal as well—one is likely to find that judges' assessments of who should prevail on the merits have a subtle, and occasionally not so subtle, tug on their decisions about what evidence should be considered.

FRE 401 has an objective ring to it when it provides that relevant evidence is evidence that "has any tendency to make a fact more or less probable than it would be without the evidence." No evidence can

---

[72] Because this is an issue that is usually committed to the discretion of the trial judge, the pattern of trial court rulings cannot be determined from appellate opinions. The problem is not simply that the trial court is generally upheld on appeal. Because the ruling is so discretionary, it may not even be cited as error by the losing side, or if it is it may not be mentioned in the appellate opinion. Moreover, eyewitness experts are usually presented by defendants in criminal cases. Since the prosecution usually has no opportunity to appeal, that means that rulings *permitting* eyewitness experts to testify are rarely subject to review, even under the lax standard that governs FRE 403. Psychologists who are frequently called to testify as eyewitness experts report that in recent years they have usually been permitted to testify. But even that impressionistic assessment may be misleading, since lawyers may be less likely to call the expert in the first place if they are facing a judge who they anticipate will not admit the evidence.

literally meet the test of affecting the existence of a consequential fact since these facts are all in the past and at the time of trial either exist or do not exist. But evidence can relate to these facts in the objective sense of being a reasonable basis for concluding that crucial facts did or did not exist. It is this requirement of a reasonable nexus between offered evidence and some material fact the evidence purports to prove that the drafters of FRE 401 were trying to capture.

We have seen that the idea of an objective connection between evidence and material fact doesn't explain the admissibility of much expert opinion evidence, for jurors hearing an expert's opinion will often have before them all the evidence which makes a consequential fact more or less likely. What they lack is knowledge about how that evidence relates to the factual questions that they must answer. Expert opinion tells jurors how to think about evidence they would otherwise poorly understand; often, indeed, it does that thinking for them. An accident reconstruction expert, for example, may explain to the jurors how physical facts—the skid marks, the type of damage to the vehicles, the road conditions—can be used to help determine the likely cause of an accident; in addition, she may also give the jury her opinion of what that cause is; or, under the Federal Rules, she may simply give the jury her opinion and leave it to the cross-examiner to bring out the facts on which she relied. In each case, the expert is telling the jury how, in her view, to best make use of evidence that renders a particular hypothesis about the cause of the accident more (or less) likely.

Even if the jury never learns the facts behind the expert's causal assessment, it is those facts and not the expert's opinion that make the expert's conclusion about the factual cause of the accident more (or less) likely. For this reason, we have associated expert opinion with what we have called "subjective relevance." Without making the existence of a particular consequential fact (like the fact that the defendant was speeding in our accident reconstruction example) more or less likely, the expert's opinion gives the jury *reason to believe* in that fact's existence (or non-existence). The underlying factual evidence does both these things, but only for those who understand its implications. The expert provides that understanding. She instructs the jurors so they understand the facts they have heard, and/or she supplies an understanding the jurors can substitute for their own. Given this well-established use of expert testimony, a more adequate definition of relevance would have been evidence that "has any tendency to make a material fact *reasonably appear* more or less probable than it would be without the evidence." This definition would have covered both ordinary factual testimony and the information supplied by reliable expert opinions.

Problem III-8. Ryan and Claire McDonald brought their 6-month old child Tara to the hospital emergency room one night. Tara had multiple recent bruises on her chest and had stopped breathing. Despite the ER staff's best efforts to revive her, Tara died. Ryan is charged with second degree murder. A neighbor testifies that she saw Ryan on one occasion carry Tara by one of her arms and roughly pinch her cheek. An ER nurse testifies he heard Claire ask Ryan several times "What happened?" and that Ryan finally said he thought the baby fell off the couch, the same thing he told the police when they questioned him. Now the state wants to introduce the testimony of Doctor Kerbs who will testify that her autopsy revealed that Tara had 17 contusions on her chest, a partially healed rib fracture at least 7 weeks old, evidence of rectal tearing which was at least 6 weeks old, a split liver, a split pancreas and a number of other trauma-associated injuries. It is the doctor's opinion, based on the autopsy, that Tara suffered from battered child syndrome, a syndrome, he will tell the jury, "which exists when a child has sustained repeated and/or serious injuries by non-accidental means." Ryan claims Dr. Kerbs's testimony is inadmissible because there is no evidence linking Ryan to these injuries. **Should the court sustain Ryan's objection? Would it make a difference if Claire, testifying under a grant of transactional immunity, surprises the prosecutor by testifying that she had beaten Tara the day of her death before Ryan had arrived home?**

IV. NARRATIVE RELEVANCE AND DEMONSTRATIVE EVIDENCE

Demonstrative or illustrative evidence poses conceptual problems for a theory of relevance beyond those posed by expert opinions. It is non-testimonial evidence, most often visual in nature, though it may appeal to any of the senses. Charts, models, computer simulations, graphs, reenactments, maps and diagrams are common kinds of demonstrative evidence. We cover the use of demonstrative evidence in Chapter Ten. Here we discuss it to expand on the idea of relevance.

At the outset it is important to recognize that even though demonstrative evidence is non-testimonial, it can be part and parcel of testimony or even a substitute for it. Thus, a police officer may trace on a map the escape route a robber took and not mention every street, or a doctor may use a model or a computerized simulation to show aspects of his impression of a person's injury that are difficult to put into words. Demonstrative evidence can be the best, and sometimes the only, way to communicate some aspect of what a witness saw or inferred. Our analysis concerns only what one might think of as pure demonstrative evidence, by which we mean evidence offered only for its value in illustrating information already presented to the court. Robert Brain and

Daniel Broderick are referring to demonstrative evidence of this pure sort when they write:

> [T]o be admissible under the Federal Rules of Evidence, a piece of evidence must be relevant, and to be relevant, a piece of evidence must make the existence of a fact of consequence in the action more or less probable than it would be without that evidence. No piece of demonstrative evidence can meet this test. The only purpose of demonstrative evidence is to illustrate or clarify previously admitted *other* evidence.[73]

Brain and Broderick are right. Demonstrative evidence does nothing to affect the probability that a consequential fact was true, for if it is purely demonstrative, it adds nothing in the way of new information bearing on the existence of that fact. Nor does it provide new information of the kind expert opinion provides, for it is not admitted to instruct jurors on how they should think about other evidence, nor does it tell jurors how an expert would interpret evidence too esoteric or technical for most people to understand. Indeed, it might be argued that pure demonstrative evidence is not evidence at all. It is more like lawyer argument, which juries are instructed is not evidence, in that it is used to enhance the persuasiveness of other evidence that has already been admitted in the case. It is no wonder that it is difficult to fit demonstrative evidence into the definition FRE 401 provides. Thus it is hard to justify its admissibility given FRE 402's injunction that "I*rrelevant evidence is not admissible.*"

But we saw in *Old Chief* that the Supreme Court recognizes another kind of relevance, what we have called, following Justice Souter's analysis, *narrative relevance.* Demonstrative evidence is part of the *way* lawyers tell their case stories to juries, and it has become an increasingly important part as trials have grown longer, evidence has become more complex and new technologies for presenting hypotheses and illustrating facts have been developed. There is nothing illegitimate about employing demonstrative evidence; properly used it helps jurors understand the facts of cases. Thus jurors who might have trouble understanding a verbal description of where one apartment in a building was located relative to another, are likely to have little trouble if, after verbally describing the relative locations of apartments, the witness points to the location of the apartments on a building plan. Similarly, a juror who is puzzled by the unfamiliar vocabulary of a doctor who describes how the lower jaw is linked to the skull may understand fully if a model of a skull is used to illustrate the doctor's testimony. And jurors who are unsure of what the evidence from various witnesses implies for the cause of a traffic accident may appreciate how the evidence fits together after viewing a

---

[73] Brain & Broderick, The Derivative Relevance of Demonstrative Evidence: Charting Its Proper Evidentiary Status, 25 U.C. Davis L. Rev. 957 (1992) (emphasis added).

computer animation incorporating the facts the witnesses have testified to.

The probative value of purely demonstrative evidence is entirely subjective, for its admission is justified only by its likely effect on a fact-finder's mind. This is so because demonstrative evidence legitimately tends to prove a party's case only to the extent it *accurately* clarifies for the fact-finder the import of evidence that has already been received. This probative value may be outweighed by the various counterweights FRE 403 lists, and in particular, the tendency of the evidence to prejudice or mislead the jury or waste the court's time.

Demonstrative evidence can cause problems because, although, in theory, pure demonstrative evidence provides the jurors only with a better way of appreciating what they have already learned, in practice it is almost impossible to present demonstrative evidence that does not convey new information. Even a simple chart, which lists the most important points several witnesses have testified to, tells the jury that the points listed are regarded as especially important. In this respect demonstrative evidence can convey claims that would otherwise have to be reserved for closing argument.

Demonstrative evidence can mislead by selectively including facts in evidence or by incorporating facts not in evidence in ways that are not obvious. Demonstrative evidence that puts together evidence from several sources may be persuasive because a compelling overall portrait draws jurors' attention away from the inadequately proven underpinnings of what they see. A filmed reenactment of a crime, for example, may leave jurors with the feeling that what they have seen is the most plausible version of what happened, but also leave them unaware that no one has testified to some of the actions they saw portrayed on the screen, or that to the extent they are inferring intention from appearance and body language, there is no evidence that the defendant looked or moved like the actor on the screen. It can similarly induce jurors to overlook a powerful piece of defense evidence that has been omitted from the reenactment they are viewing. Thus in deciding whether to admit demonstrative evidence, a court should ask whether it fairly illustrates what it is supposed to illustrate, and it may refuse admission if the material suggests consequential facts not in evidence.

Justice Souter used the idea we call narrative relevance to explain why, despite the decision in *Old Chief*, lawyers should not be expected to prove points with only the most colorless or dispassionate proof available. It seems clear from Souter's opinion that, in striking an FRE 403 balance, judges need not regard as illegitimate the tendency of some evidence to engage a juror's interest and emotions, which is a relief, since many trials are dull enough as it is. But under the *Old Chief* opinion, narrative relevance alone does not justify admissibility. Thus, the prosecution may be allowed to prove who died through a grieving widow's testimony even though the defense is willing to stipulate to the dead person's identity, or it may be allowed to show the jury the bloody hatchet used in a killing when the defense is willing to stipulate that the murder weapon was an axe. But the widow's testimony would not be admissible if the identity of the deceased did not matter, and the bloody hatchet would be inadmissible if the deceased had been shot rather than hacked to death. In other words before a judge allows narrative relevance to weigh in the 403 balance, *she should be satisfied that the narratively relevant evidence also has, or relates to evidence that has, logical relevance as defined by FRE 401.*

It might seem that demonstrative evidence is an exception to the FRE 402's mandate that only relevant evidence is admissible. But in a fundamental sense it is not. Just as the narratively relevant spouse's tears must come attached to otherwise relevant testimony of the deceased's identity, so must demonstrative evidence be linked to the otherwise relevant facts it illustrates. Nevertheless, given a Supreme Court that sometimes interprets the Federal Rules of Evidence literally, there could be a problem here. For this reason Brain and Broderick have proposed amending FRE 401 to read:

> "Relevant evidence" means: (a) evidence having any tendency to make the *apparent* existence of any fact that is of consequence to the determination of the action more probable or less probable than it would be without the evidence [. . .]; *or (b) evidence that fairly and accurately explains, illustrates, or clarifies other admissible evidence.*[74]

An amendment, however, is not necessary, for Brain and Broderick's proposed language seems to capture what courts now do.

Problem III-9. Gary Grant, a police officer, is accused of shooting a 16 year old youth, Paul Power, when Power had his hands raised in surrender. Grant alleges he shot in self-defense when Power was reaching for a pocket in which a gun was later found. The prosecution seeks to introduce an animated video in which a light representing the bullet from Grant's gun is shown hitting a computer graphic model designed to represent Power's height and weight. The model is wearing a coat like the one Power wore the night he was killed. The model's arms are in various positions. After each "shot" the model's coat is projected on the screen and a red circle indicates the exit point of the bullet. The circle's location matches the location of the bullet hole in Power's coat when the model's hands are in the air. It does not match the bullet's exit

---

[74] Id. at 1023 (emphasis in original to indicate suggested new wording).

hole when the hands are reaching down toward the pocket. **Should the jury be allowed to see the computer animation? What foundation is needed? Why not just have an expert testify?**

V. SUMMARY

In this Chapter we have identified relevance as the core concept on which the admissibility of evidence turns. Questions of logical relevance are by definition problematic only when the admissibility of circumstantial evidence is in issue. Under FRE 401, which defines logical relevance, the concept is most naturally understood as the objective tendency of a fact offered in evidence to make the existence of a fact that is legally consequential (i.e. material) more or less probable than it would be without the evidence. Although the determination of logical relevance may usually be made without regard to the other evidence a party can offer, a fact suggested by one item of evidence may bear on a fact in issue only if some other fact exists. In certain circumstances where the other fact's existence appears problematic and/or where it should be easy for a party to prove that fact if it is true, the relevance of the first fact will be said to be *conditional* on the existence of the second. In these circumstances, a judge will, upon appropriate objection, not allow the jury to consider the first fact unless the proponent of the evidence is able to provide the jury with sufficient evidence to find the second.

Although FRE 401 may be read narrowly to encompass only evidence which objectively relates to the probable existence of a fact in issue, we know from the kinds of evidence courts admit that it must encompass more. First, it includes evidence that bears on the credibility of witnesses and the value of documents and physical evidence. Second, it includes evidence that is subjectively relevant in the sense that it aids the jury in understanding how or why particular evidence relates to a fact in issue. Third, it includes evidence that is narratively relevant either in the sense that it illustrates or clarifies other admissible evidence or in its tendency to engage jurors in a story that the evidence reasonably tells.

Finally, relevant evidence is presumptively admissible, and irrelevant evidence is not admissible. The judge, however, has discretion under FRE 403 to exclude relevant evidence if its probative value is substantially outweighed by its tendency to prejudice a party's case, mislead a jury, waste the court's time and the like. The most important of these countervailing considerations is prejudice, which refers not to all the harm evidence does to an opponent's case, but only to harm which is not attributable to its legitimate probative value. Most often prejudicial harm is associated with evidence that arouses a fact-finder's emotions and gives that person a reason, apart from the weight of the evidence, to reach a particular verdict. In deciding whether the likely prejudicial impact of evidence substantially outweighs its probative value, the judge may consider other evidence in the case, including a party's evidentiary concessions.   At least in some situations—like the one the Court confronted in *Old Chief*—the FRE 403 balance must take an opponent's evidentiary concessions into account.

ADDITIONAL PROBLEMS

Problem III-10.   In 2010, the Anderson Company sued the Brice Company for the costs of removing asbestos that the Brice Company had used in September 1968 to fireproof a five-story office building it owned. Anderson claimed that Brice was negligent in using a dangerous asbestos-containing product, Abcote, to fireproof its building.   Brice claimed that in 1968, at the time it fireproofed Anderson's building, Abcote was state of the art, and it had no idea of the dangers of asbestos. During discovery Anderson asked for all material discussing the presence of asbestos in Abcote in the Brice Company files.   In response to the subpoena Brice turned over to Anderson five sheets of paper from the insurance carrier that are stapled together.   The first four sheets, which have nothing to do with asbestos, are stamped with dates ranging from July 1967 through April 1968.   The last sheet is a summary of a technical article from a chemistry journal published in 1966 on the dangers of asbestos and suggests that Brice might want to consider whether the information should affect its use of Abcote.   This page is undated. Anderson offers the fifth sheet to show that Brice knew Abcote might pose a serious hazard if it began to deteriorate.   Brice argued that since it could not be shown that it was aware of the contents of the summary before September 1968, the page is irrelevant and hence inadmissible. **What should the court do? If the court admits the evidence, how should the jury use the evidence?**

Problem III-11.   Jeremy Foster is on trial for armed robbery and attempted murder growing out of a convenience store holdup in which a clerk was stabbed.   The government wishes to introduce a witness who will testify that although a black shoe print found in the store was too smeared for a positive identification it is very likely to have been left by a beat up Air Jordan first edition and that Air Jordan first editions are worth more than $1000 because so few of them are around.   The government also will introduce a detective who will testify that when she arrested the defendant four days after the robbery, he was wearing a beat up pair of Air Jordan first editions.   Foster argues that both the expert's testimony and the detective's are irrelevant because no eye witness said anything about the shoes the robber was wearing and any one of a number of people who rushed to the clerk's aid might have left the bloody shoe print.   **What should the court do? If the court admits the evidence how should the jury use the evidence?**

Problem III-12. Carrie Miles is charged with mail fraud in connection with the advertisement and sale of her "Magnetic Oil Detector." The crux of the charge is that she circulated advertisements through the mails in which she claimed that the machine is effective at detecting oil up to seven thousand feet below the earth's surface, when in fact it is useless. At trial Miles persists in her claim that the device is effective. As proof she offers to testify that before marketing the device she tested it on 60 different occasions, and in each test the device correctly indicated the presence or absence of oil. The prosecutor convinces the judge that the tests were not sufficiently accurate to warrant relying on them as proof that the device works. **Should the judge nevertheless admit the testimony on Miles' theory? Is there any other theory on which the testimony might be allowed? If you were the prosecutor and had convincing evidence that Miles' tests were scientifically unsound would you have wanted her testimony to be excluded?** Suppose Miles wants to introduce testimony from two of the ten thousand people who bought the device. Each will testify that they drilled wells where the device indicated and found oil. **Should their testimony be allowed? Does it matter if these two people are Miles' cousins?**

Problem III-13.   Karen Himber was partially paralyzed when she misjudged the depth of a pool she dove into. Karen sued the Prefab Pool Company under a theory of strict liability claiming that their pools were defective because the bottoms were dyed light blue which made them look deeper in the ground than they in fact were.   She also sued Joan Friedman, doing business as Pool Installers, alleging that her workers were negligent in installing the pool because they failed to paint depth markers on the pool's apron. Karen asked for $8 million in damages, but before trial she settled with Pool Installers and its insurance company for its policy limit of $500,000. At trial Joan Friedman, the proprietor of Pool Installers, testifies that in her experience pools that are painted light blue on the bottom look deeper than pools with white bottoms or dark blue bottoms.   Prefab Pool argues that Friedman's testimony is irrelevant because the jury could be taken to view pools with different colored bottoms and could judge for itself how the color of a pool bottom affects its apparent depth.

Should the judge allow the testimony? How should Karen's attorney respond to Prefab's argument?   On cross-examination, Prefab Pool's attorney asks Joan, "Isn't it true that you settled the negligence suit brought against you by Karen for your policy limit of $500,000?" Karen objects, arguing that testimony on the settlement is irrelevant because even if Pool Installers was negligent in installing the pool, its negligence would not relieve Prefab Pools of any liability it has under a strict products liability theory. **How should Prefab Pool's attorney respond to the argument? How should the court rule?**

Problem III-14. Max Nugent is charged as the "Sidewalk Slasher," a serial killer who stabbed to death homeless people sleeping on sidewalks. He is charged in connection with these deaths on the basis of eyewitness testimony linking him to two of the deaths, his possession of a wallet belonging to a third victim (which Nugent claims to have found), and evidence that a kitchen knife could have caused all of the victims' wounds. The prosecutor wants to project before the jury slides of all three victims, showing their throats cut, their clothes smeared with blood and, in the case of one victim, his limbs hacked off. Nugent offers to stipulate that each of the victims was stabbed to death. **Can the prosecutor introduce the pictures over Nugent's objection? Can the prosecutor introduce the pictures if Nugent offers to stipulate that all of the dead were victims of premeditated murder and to promise that his only defense will be one of mistaken identity?**

Problem III-15. Wanda Wiley is charged with bank robbery. Two witnesses to the robbery, a passerby and a bank teller, have identified Wanda as the robber, but both admit they are somewhat uncertain. Another teller who witnessed the robbery said that Wanda may have been the robber, but she is unable to make a positive identification. Perhaps the most important items of evidence in the case are photographs that were taken during the robbery by the bank's hidden cameras. The photographs show the robber to be a young woman with long blond hair and a ponytail. At trial Wanda has short brown hair. At the time of the robbery Wanda was on parole following a conviction for grand larceny. The prosecutor wants to introduce Wanda's parole officer, who has known Wanda for two years, to testify that about the time of the robbery she had long blond hair which she wore in a ponytail. He would also testify that he recognizes her to be the person pictured in the surveillance photographs. The defendant points out that many people saw Wanda at least as regularly as the parole officer during the preceding two years—Wanda's friends and relatives, patrons of the diner where she worked, her fellow employees, and several shopkeepers in the neighborhood where she lived. **In these circumstances should the parole officer be allowed to testify? If you were representing Wanda, would you be satisfied if the prosecutor agreed that he would not ask the parole officer how it was that she knew Wanda but instead would allude to the basis of their acquaintance as a "business relationship"? If Wanda's appearance had not changed between the time of the robbery and the time of the trial, could a witness who knew Wanda identify her as the woman depicted in the bank surveillance photographs? Should the trial judge grant the defendant's request to instruct the jury that "It is natural for people to want to change their hair styles, so the fact that Wanda cut and dyed her hair sometime after the robbery may not be taken as evidence that she participated in the robbery"?**

Problem III-16. You are the trier of fact in a civil case. The plaintiff is suing on an insurance policy to recover compensation for the destruction of her building by fire. The insurance company raises a defense of arson. After most of the evidence relating to the defense is presented, you remain skeptical. You think there is only a one in three chance the plaintiff was the "torch." In fact you believe it is twice as likely that there was no arson. The insurance company presents testimony that nine months before the fire the plaintiff insured her building for a figure more than 25% above its fair market value. The insurance company then introduces an industry-wide survey reporting that in two of every five fires shown to be arson, the burned buildings were insured within the year preceding the fire for a figure that was 25% or more above their fair market value. The survey also reports that in only one of a thousand fires not shown to be arson were burned buildings insured for a figure 25% or more above their fair market value. Would you be willing to multiply your prior odds on arson of 1:2 by 400 (2/5 divided by 1/1000 = 2 x 1000/5 = 400) to arrive at odds of 200 to 1 that arson has been committed by the plaintiff? **If not, why don't you use the probabilities in the manner suggested? Is the evidence the insurance company wishes to offer irrelevant? Should we treat the Bayesian model as only a heuristic device and not as a technique to be used by trial courts to resolve factual disputes?** (If you are intrigued by this question, you might be interested in reading Joseph Kadane and David Schum, *A Probabilistic Analysis of the Sacco and Vanzetti Evidence*, John Wiley and Sons, New York, 1996).

Problem III-17. (a) Susan Sharp calls 911 and asks the police to come quickly because her husband Barry is hitting her, and she is afraid she will be killed. When the police arrive they hear Barry screaming at Susan and note that Susan is bruised on her upper arms and has a bruise under one eye. They ask Susan how long this has been going on and she replies, "I have had seven years of Hell, almost since I married the man." Susan later does not want to press charges, but pursuant to local policy, Barry is tried anyway for misdemeanor spouse abuse. Barry calls Susan who testifies on his behalf that she started the fight by throwing a saucer at Barry; that she may have been bruised on her arms as Barry tried to keep her from throwing other things; that she received the bruise under her eye the day before from walking into a door knob in the dark and that Barry had not hit her on the day in question. In rebuttal, the state wishes to call Dr. Wang, a psychologist who will testify (1) that in her opinion Ms. Sharp suffers from Battered Women's Syndrome (BWS), (2) that BWS is characterized by, among other things, self blame for violence, learned helplessness, fear of harm from leaving a husband, great dependence on the husband, a belief that when husbands apologize after violence that things will improve, and anxiety and depression, and (3) that in her experience it is common for battered women to call the police when they are being assaulted, yet later refuse to press charges. **Is Dr. Wang's testimony admissible against Barry? Would the testimony be admissible as part of the prosecutor's rebuttal case had Susan not testified? Would it be admissible as part of the prosecutor's case-in-chief if Susan had said she would not testify for the prosecution, but it was not known whether she would testify for the defense? Does it matter whether Dr. Wang's testimony is based on (1) the facts the prosecutor presented, (2) watching Susan testify, or (3) an hour-long interview with Susan in which she denied that her husband was an abuser but according to Wang seemed quite agitated when she did so and admitted there were frequent quarrels in her marriage to Barry, but that they were mostly her fault?**

(b) Assume that Susan Sharp, whose situation is described above, one afternoon took out a gun her husband owned and killed him as he slept in front of the TV set. The state charged her with first degree murder. At her trial she testifies to a long history of abuse by her husband Barry and says that she felt he would kill her if she didn't leave him. The prosecutor on cross-examination tries to punch holes in her story by establishing that Barry had a $500,000 life insurance policy with Susan as beneficiary; that although Barry never did anything to hold her captive, she had never moved out or gone to a divorce attorney; that she had retracted charges of spouse abuse three times after she had called the police and had testified on Barry's behalf in the one case that had gone to trial; and that she regularly made love to her husband, including the evenings of the three days she had called the police. The defense wants to call Dr. Wang to rehabilitate Susan. **May the defense do this?**

(c) Suppose Susan, on trial for murder, argues both temporary insanity and self-defense. She establishes through her own testimony and the testimony of relatives and neighbors that Barry often hit her and that twice in seven years the beatings were so serious she had to go to the a hospital emergency room. She also testifies that before he sat down to watch television her husband had said that unless the house was spic and span by the time the football game he was watching ended, he would beat her within an inch of her life. Finally, she says that it never occurred to her that she might escape from Barry by calling the police, going to a battered women's shelter or returning to her parents' home and getting a divorce. Susan next wants to call Dr. Wang to testify that as someone suffering from BWS Susan might reasonably have felt that it was as impossible for her to escape from Barry as it would have been had her back literally been against a wall, and that it was also natural for her to think that Barry would kill her if she didn't kill him first. **Is Dr. Wang's testimony admissible?**

Problem III-18. On June 18, 1964, Mrs. Juanita Brooks was the victim of a purse snatching while walking down an alley in the San Pedro area of Los Angeles. She neither heard nor saw her assailant as she was pushed from behind, but as she got to her feet she observed a young blonde woman with a ponytail running from the scene. Another witness, who heard her scream, saw a blond woman with a ponytail run out of the alley in which Mrs. Brooks had been attacked, and dash into a yellow automobile. The car started immediately. It was, according to the witness, driven by a black man who had a beard and a mustache. Neither Ms. Brooks nor the witness saw enough to be able to identify the participants in the crime. The police arrested Janet and Malcolm Collins for the crime. Janet had dark blonde hair which she wore in a ponytail. Malcolm was a black man who at the time of his arrest on June 22 had a mustache but no beard. The couple owned a yellow Lincoln automobile with an off-white top. In addition to the testimony of the witnesses described above, the prosecution introduced the following evidence:

a. Testimony that when the police came to arrest the Collinses, Malcolm was seen streaking from the back door of the house.

b. Testimony that Malcolm had a beard when he paid fines on two traffic tickets on June 19. There is other testimony in the case that Malcolm shaved his beard on June 2 when he married Janet.

c. Testimony that Malcolm paid $35.00 for fines on two traffic tickets on June 19, together with testimony that between $35.00 and $40.00 was in Mrs. Brooks' purse when it was stolen, that the couple had only $12.00 when they were married on June 2, that Malcolm had not worked since that time and that Janet's earnings were not much more than $12.00 a week.

d. Testimony from a mathematician describing the "product rule"; i.e. a mathematical rule which holds that the probability that a number of independent events will occur together is equal to the product of the probabilities that the individual events will occur. (e.g. the probability that one die will come up six is 1/6. The probability that two dice will each come up six is 1/36 or 1/6 x 1/6.) The prosecutor asked the witness to assume that the following probabilities were associated with the characteristics that had been established by the testimony of the other witnesses in the case:

Characteristic	Individual Probability
A. Partly yellow automobile	1/10
B. Man with mustache	1/4
C. Girl with ponytail	1/10
D. Girl with blond hair	1/3
E. Negro man with beard	1/10
F. Interracial couple in car	1/1000

The prosecutor then asked the mathematician to illustrate how the product rule would work if the probabilities of the different events were as assumed. The mathematician responded that applying the product rule to the assumed factors yielded a probability that there was about one chance in twelve million that any couple possessed the distinctive characteristics of the defendants. **Should any of the evidence described above have been admitted in this case? How is it relevant? Should its admission constitute reversible error? Do you see any special problems with the mathematician's testimony? Would your judgment about the admissibility of the mathematician's testimony be different if after presenting the testimony the prosecutor in questioning the witness made it clear that the frequencies the witness had used were arbitrary and the jurors should use their own probabilities?** (This problem is based on the case of *People v. Collins*, 68 Cal.2d 319, 66 Cal.Rptr. 497, 438 P.2d 33 (1968) (cited in note 65 supra.) To learn more about this case, how it arose, and why it stimulated thinking about the use of probability theory for legal factfinding see the essay by George Fisher which appears as the first chapter in *Evidence Stories* (R. Lempert, ed.) (Foundation Press, 2006.)

Problem III–19. In the quaint old days when music was on vinyl, Mission Incorporated was a company owned by a small group of priests who wrote, produced, and published musical compositions and recordings. Music Corporation was a corporation that distributed and promoted music. In 1989 Mission signed an agreement with Music regarding a rock opera entitled VIRGIN which the priests had composed. Music agreed to promote the record as well as at least four singles taken from the album in exchange for exclusive rights to distribute the album in the United States. One single taken from the record, "Fear No Evil," reached #80 on the "Hot Soul Singles" chart of Billboard Magazine when Music breached its agreement, ceased promoting the single, and started withdrawing it from record stores. Even so the record's momentum carried it to an additional 10,000 sales, which placed it at #61 on the Billboard chart. Mission sued Music for the damages it suffered from the breach of contract, one item of which was lost royalties. In support of this they offered a statistical analysis of every one of the 324 songs that had reached #61 on the chart during 1989. This analysis showed that 76% ultimately reached the top 40, 65% the top 30, 51% the top 20, 34% the top 10, 21% the top 5, and 10% #1. Mission had an expert available who would have converted this information concerning other singles into projected sales figures for "Fear No Evil" and the sales figures into lost royalties. They also had an expert available who would have testified about the possibility that a hit single taken from the album would have led to concert tours, substantially more sales of the two-record VIRGIN album, and to a decision to produce VIRGIN on Broadway. The trial judge did not admit any of this evidence. **Was the trial judge's decision correct with regard to any or all of this evidence?**

Problem III-20. Plaintiff was injured in an industrial accident, losing a leg and a hand. In the resulting lawsuit Plaintiff seeks to introduce a film which shows him engaged in a series of activities around his house. The film was taken by a professional photographer over a period of three hours. Plaintiff's activities were not rehearsed, no special camera effects were used, and the film was not edited. However, only 25 minutes of activity were filmed during the time the photographer was in the house. The film shows the Plaintiff doing normal household activities or attempting to do them. These include such things as raking leaves in his yard, setting the dinner table, moving furniture, getting out of bed and strapping on his prosthetic devices, driving a car, loading a gun, and operating a fishing reel (although he was not actually fishing). In addition, it shows him hugging his daughter and placing a cigarette in the mouth of his quadriplegic brother. The Plaintiff is clearly handicapped in all these activities, although the degree of handicap varies. He manages to do all of them in some way. Plaintiff would like to introduce this film as part of his effort to prove damages at the trial. Defendant objects, saying the film is redundant and irrelevant as well as prejudicial. **How should the trial court rule? Should it rule differently with respect to some of the behaviors depicted than with respect to others? If so, why?**

Problem III-21. Jim Maldin is charged with the premeditated murder of his brother Sam. Jim claims to have blacked out the night of the crime and to remember nothing about it except (he claims) that his brother was in a foul mood. The prosecution introduces evidence that a book was found on the floor in Sam's bedroom; Jim's fingerprints were found on the murder weapon; that Sam was shot in the leg, side and heart; that three bullet holes were found in the living room, two were found in both the dining room and Sam's bedroom and one was found in the hall, and that some blood was found in the dining room and more blood in the living room where Sam was found dead. The prosecution seeks to follow the testimony establishing these facts with a videotaped reenactment of the crime. The reenactment begins with a shot of the actor playing Sam sitting on his bed reading. The actor playing Jim enters Sam's bedroom with a gun; he shoots twice at Sam but misses. Sam drops the book on the floor and dashes into the hall as Jim fires a shot that misses him. Sam races through the kitchen with Jim following him and into the dining room. Jim fires twice and Sam's leg drags as he moves to the living room. Jim fires once and Sam twists as if hit in the side. Jim fires twice and Sam falls down clutching his heart. **Is the videotape admissible? Does it matter if Sam's prints along with Jim's were found on the gun?** Suppose that instead of a reenactment this were a computer animation with Jim represented by a dot of light that pulsed when a shot was fired at Sam by a humanoid figure. **Would the animation be admissible? Would it make any difference if Sam were represented by a grey dot?**

Problem III–22. Summer Goodwin is charged with attempted blackmail. She allegedly called noted comedian Harry Barnes and told him that unless he paid her $10 million she would sell a story to *The National Peeper* naming him as her father and telling the press how poorly he had treated her, his illegitimate daughter, over the years. Barnes, instead of paying the money, called the police. At trial, Goodwin wants to introduce evidence that she agreed to a DNA test to show Barnes was her father and that Barnes refused. May she? Goodwin also offers evidence that some years before she and Barnes had had DNA tests which proved he was her father. **Should the trial judge allow this evidence?** Suppose Goodwin had never threatened Barnes but had sold a story to *The National Peeper* naming Barnes as her father. **Should the trial judge admit the evidence of the DNA test offer or of its results in a civil suit for libel brought by Barnes against Goodwin? Should the same evidence be admitted if Barnes instead brings his suit against *The National Peeper*?**

Problem III–23. After losing both legs in an automobile accident, Ralph Lawrence brings a negligence suit against the driver of the car that hit him. **At the trial may Ralph: (1) Unstrap his artificial limbs and have them passed around the jury box so that the jurors can judge their weight for themselves? (2) Present films of his early rehabilitation, which show him in obvious pain from wearing the artificial limbs and often falling down? (3) Show films taken of him before the accident in which he is starring in pick-up basketball games and winning a slam dunk contest? (Does it matter if the films were taken 8 years before the accident? Suppose Ralph testifies that he played basketball up until he was injured, but these were the only films he had?) (4) Play a police videotape made after the accident which shows the driver who injured him having trouble walking a straight line and balancing on one foot? Does it matter whether the driver had later been charged with drunk driving? (5) Show a film of the driver, the day after the accident, dancing at a disco? (6) Show a film taken a year after the accident, showing the driver playing in a pick-up basketball game?**

May the driver—the defendant in this case—introduce: (7) Evidence that Ralph, who was living as a "beach bum" and working part-time as a waiter in a restaurant before the accident, went back to school after the accident, had graduated with honors, and is now a first year MBA student at Big Bucks Business School? (8) Evidence that the average Big Bucks

business student takes a job paying $90,000 a year after graduation and after 15 years is earning $410,000? (9) Show a film of Ralph playing wheelchair basketball and accepting an MVP award at a state tournament? (10) Pass around for the jury to examine a pair of artificial legs considerably lighter than those Ralph used? **Does the admissibility of any of this evidence depend on what Ralph was allowed to introduce?**

After Ralph testifies to the pain and disruption the accident caused him, could the driver bring out on cross-examination that: (11) Ralph had later married the surgeon who operated on him? (12) That they were still as much in love as the day they married and that they had one child and another was on the way? (13) That Ralph was the father of these children, and they were conceived by "natural" means? (14) That, when he married his wife she was earning $310,000 a year which was about 15 times more than Ralph had ever earned? (15) That relative to other players, Ralph was far better at wheel chair basketball than he had been as an ordinary basketball player?

Problem III-24. Plaintiff sued to recover from the defendant the purchase price of a drum of paint. Plaintiff had purchased another drum of paint from the defendant at an earlier time—6 months earlier—and after the purchase of the second drum, plaintiff found that the first was defective. As a result of using the defective paint, plaintiff's barn roof rotted. Thus, plaintiff returned the second drum unopened and unexamined to the defendant and asked for the return of the purchase price. Defendant refused. At trial, plaintiff sought to introduce evidence tending to show the defective nature of the first batch of paint. **Should the evidence be admitted on the issue of whether the paint in the second drum was defective? On some other issue? Is it important that the case on which this problem is based arose in the 1920s and not today?**

Problem III-25. Peggy Pender sues Daphne Defoe, alleging that she was injured when Defoe's car in which she, Peggy, was a passenger went off the road because Defoe was driving far over the speed limit. At trial, Pender offers evidence that two years before Defoe had been arrested three times in the space of eight months for drunk driving. Defoe objects to this evidence because there is no allegation that she was drunk at the time of the accident. The judge overrules the objection and admits the evidence, "for what it's worth." **Is this decision correct? May Defoe in her case-in-chief introduce evidence proving any of the following:**

> (a) That for sixteen months she has been attending Alcoholics Anonymous meetings on a regular basis and that during that time she hasn't touched a drop of alcohol?

(b) That for a year she has been working as a truck driver and that she has been recently cited as her company's "safe driver of the year," the first time a "rookie" has won that honor?

(c) That she was giving Pender a ride because Pender had recently lost her license after being convicted for the fourth time for drunk driving?

Would your ruling on any of these items of evidence be different if Pender did not succeed in introducing evidence of Defoe's history of drunk driving?

Problem III-26. Samantha Seller sues to recover $5,000 from Bob Buyer, allegedly owing from the sale of an automobile by Seller to Buyer. Seller contends that the parties orally agreed that the car would be transferred from Seller to Buyer in exchange for Buyer's paying $20,000. The money was to be paid in three installments: first, there would be $5,000 down; next, there would be a payment of $10,000 one month after the down-payment; and finally, there would be a payment of $5,000 one month after the second installment. Alleging that only $15,000 was paid, Seller claims that she is entitled to recover the remaining $5,000. Buyer alleges that the contract called for a total sales price of only $15,000. Seller offers to introduce the testimony of Oliver Offeree, who will testify that two days before the sale was consummated between Seller and Buyer, Seller offered him the car for $20,000. Buyer objects to this testimony. **Should it be admitted? Would it make any difference if Seller offered the testimony not just of Oliver Offeree, but also of Owen Offeree, Ophelia Offeree, and Oscar Offeree, who will each testify that a short time before the sale was made between Buyer and Seller, Seller offered each of them the car for $20,000. Is this additional testimony likely to make the probability greater that Oliver's testimony will be admitted? Is it likely that all four witnesses will be permitted to testify, or will their testimony be deemed cumulative? Would your conclusion be the same if the other sales offers had been made in early August and the sale occurred in late October?**

Problem III-27. At about 6:00 p.m. on a cold winter's night in Boston, two experienced policemen stopped a car that resembled a get-away car that had been used in the armed robbery of a supermarket at about 2:30 that afternoon. What happened next is unclear, but what is clear is that Sam Brown, the driver, ended up dead. He was shot by the police officers, who fired through the windows from both sides of the car. Plaintiff, Brown's widow, sued the officers for wrongful death. The defendant officers claim that when they ordered Brown to get out of his car, he responded by driving into one of them, knocking him down, backing up, trying to run him over, and then shooting at him. However, no gun was found on Brown or in the car after Brown's death. Defendants sought to introduce testimony from two grocery store employees that Brown was one of two people who had robbed them at 2:30 the afternoon of the killing. The trial judge excluded the employees' testimony, noting that the witnesses' credibility was questionable and that the probative force of their testimony was outweighed by its tendency to prejudice the jury. **On what theory is the defendant's evidence relevant? Should the trial judge's ruling be overturned on appeal?** Ms. Brown, knowing the police would say they stopped her husband's car because it resembled one used in a robbery, presented in her case-in-chief a witness who testified that Sam was seen at the hospital where he worked at about 2:30 on the afternoon of the robbery. **Does this change the way the appellate court should deal with the decision below?** Suppose that in her closing argument to the jury Brown's lawyer said "Sam Brown never did anything wrong in his life. Defendants never brought anybody to the stand to say that Sam Brown robbed them." Suppose the defendants did not object to this closing argument but had given a sufficient offer of proof when the employees' testimony was excluded. **Should the plaintiff's closing argument affect the decision on appeal?**

Problem III-28. Plaintiff's wife, Doreen, was killed at age 39 when her car failed to negotiate a mountain turn and skidded off the road over a cliff. The accident occurred in mid-afternoon; the wife had not been drinking or taking drugs; the road surface was dry, and the car was apparently in good condition. Plaintiff seeks to recover on a life insurance policy which provides that the beneficiary will receive double indemnity should the insured die by accidental means. The insurance company claims that only the face amount is owing because Doreen committed suicide. As part of its defense the company seeks to introduce evidence that, five years before, Doreen had taken an overdose of sleeping pills and almost died. It also wants to introduce evidence that Doreen had changed jobs three times in the past year; that three months before she died she had signed a "living will" providing that "heroic" measures should not be used to sustain her life in case of terminal illness or irreversible brain damage; that twice within the preceding eighteen months Doreen had sued her husband for divorce, alleging marital infidelity, but had each time withdrawn the action, and that off and on she had been under a psychiatrist's care for depression for almost 10 years. **Should the judge admit any of this evidence over the plaintiff's objection? May the insurance company present a psychologist who will testify that the wife had been suffering from "self destruction syndrome"; that about 70% of "self destruction syndrome" sufferers who die before age 40 have killed themselves, and that "self destruction syndrome" sufferers are about six times more likely than others to be involved in fatal single car accidents where alcohol is not a cause?**

Should a court be more or less reluctant to admit the psychologist's testimony if the witness is the person who invented the term "self destruction syndrome," has devoted her entire career to studying the syndrome, has written the definitive book on the subject, and is one of a handful of people who claim expertise in this area? Would there be a better or weaker case for admitting this syndrome evidence if the expert testimony came from one of the psychiatrist's who had treated Doreen for depression?

Problem III-29. Sally Zanger, is an attorney representing a white man accused of robbing a black woman. She knows that the prosecution's case consists largely of an eyewitness identification by the woman who was robbed. In a pretrial motion, Zanger asks the court to rule that at the trial the prosecution may not ask the victim to point out the person who robbed her. Zanger argues that because the defendant will be the only person sitting with her at the counsel's table, any courtroom identification of the defendant will have little probative value but, because of its dramatic aspect, will have substantial prejudicial effect. She is willing to stipulate that two weeks after the robbery the victim identified the defendant, from a photograph, as the person who robbed her. Zanger says she will not object to testimony describing that identification. (There was a lineup identification two days after the photo identification, but it did not meet the requisite constitutional standards for admissibility.) **Has Zanger acted wisely in making her motion coupled with the stipulation? Should the court grant Zanger's motion?**

Zanger is thinking about asking the judge to place her client in a lineup in court, along with nine other men, and requesting that any identification by the witness be made from this lineup. Coincidentally, the prosecutor is thinking about making a similar request. (He would like the lineup to include only three other men.) **Is the request a wise one for either party to make? If one party makes such a request and the other does not object, should the judge allow the courtroom lineup? Should the judge allow a courtroom lineup on the defendant's motion if the prosecution objects? On the prosecution's motion if the defendant objects?**

Zanger makes her motion to bar a courtroom identification or, in the alternative, to have any courtroom identification made in a lineup. The judge denies the motion in both respects. Zanger then decides to seat the defendant, who is out on bail, in the spectator section of the courtroom and have the defendant's brother sit at the counsel's table. **Is it proper for an attorney to take such action without the permission of the court?** The victim points to the defendant's brother sitting at counsel table as the one who robbed her. At the close of the prosecution's case, Zanger reveals her subterfuge and, as there is insufficient evidence to convict the defendant without the eyewitness identification, moves for a directed acquittal. The prosecutor protests and is allowed to reopen his case. He asks the defendant to sit at counsel's table where he belongs. Then he puts the robbery victim back on the stand and asks her to point to the person who robbed her. This time the woman points to the defendant. Zanger renews her motion for a directed verdict of acquittal. **Should the court grant it?** Assume that the woman, when asked if she recognizes the one who robbed her, points not to the defendant but to one of the male jurors. After some minutes of confusion and further questioning by the prosecutor, she changes her mind and points to the defendant. **Would the defendant be entitled to a directed verdict of acquittal or a mistrial?**

Problem III-30. Julien Prince, a sixteen year old, is on trial for a murder he allegedly committed when he was fifteen. The strongest evidence against him is a confession he made after eight hours of police questioning.

The prosecutor, knowing from his suppression motion that Prince will claim the confession was coerced, takes care to have the officer who questioned Prince not only deny the use of force or other coercive tactics but also to point to five different places in the confession where it refers to facts only the killer could have known. When Prince testifies he claims he signed the confession because he was tired and scared and the police had told him that only if he signed the confession would he be allowed to go home. He says he doesn't know how the confession came to contain facts only the killer would have known but he supposes the police told him these facts. Prince wants to introduce the testimony of Sam Gross, a law professor who is one of the country's leading experts on convicting the innocent. Gross will testify that among the several hundred people whose convictions were disproved by DNA or similarly convincing evidence, there were a number of cases where the conviction had been based on a confession which contained information only the perpetrator could have known. **Should Gross be allowed to testify? Should the court decide differently if in addition to the confession the prosecutor had introduced evidence that a partial print found on the murder weapon was consistent with Prince's thumb print as well as the testimony of a witness who reported having heard two shots and then seen someone, whom he identified as Prince, flee the crime scene and toss a gun down a sewer as he ran.** (Note, this problem was not written by Sam Gross who is a co-author of this book. RL)

VI.   BIBLIOGRAPHY

Weinstein Chs. 401.01–403.07 (1999).

Wigmore, John.H., Evidence in Trials at Common Law (4th ed.) Boston: Little, Brown (1961–1988) 1, §§ 27–36.

Wright, Charles Alan and Kenneth W. Graham, Federal Practice and Procedure: Evidence, St. Paul, Minn.: West Pub. Co., Vol. 22 §§ 5161–5224 (1978).

Allen, Ronald J., The Myth of Conditional Relevancy, 25 Loy. L.A. L. Rev. 871 (1992).

Ball, Vaughn C., The Moment of Truth: Probability Theory and the Standards of Proof, 14 Vand. L. Rev. 807 (1961).

Ball, Vaughn C., The Myth of Conditional Relevancy, 14 Ga. L. Rev. 435 (1980).

Brain, Robert D. and Daniel J. Broderick, The Derivative Relevance of Demonstrative Evidence: Charting Its Proper Evidentiary Status, 25 U.C. Davis L. Rev. 957 (1992).

Callen, Craig R., Rationality and Relevancy: Conditional Relevance and Constrained Resources, 2003 L. Rev. M.S.U.-D.C.L. 1243 (2003).

Carretta, T.R. and R.L. Moreland, The Direct and Indirect Effects of Inadmissible Evidence, 13 J. App. Soc. Psych. 291 (1983).

Dolan, Andrew K., Rule 403: The Prejudice Rule in Evidence, 49 S. Cal. L. Rev. 220 (1976).

Ellsworth, Phoebe C., and Robert Mauro, Psychology and Law in Daniel Gilbert et al., eds., The Handbook of Social Psychology 702–07 (1998).

Fairley, William B. and Frederick Mosteller, A Conversation About Collins, 41 U. Chi. L. Rev. 242 (1974).

Finkelstein, Michael O. and William B. Fairley, A Comment on "Trial by Mathematics," 84 Harv. L. Rev. 1801 (1971).

Friedman, Richard D., Infinite Strands Infinitesimally Thin: Storytelling Bayesianism, Hearsay and Other Evidence, 14 Cardozo L. Rev. 79 (1992).

Friedman, Richard D., Conditional Probative Value: Neoclassicism Without Myth, 93 Mich. L. Rev. 439 (1994).

Hennes, David B., Manufacturing Evidence For Trial: The Prejudicial Implications of Videotaped Crime Scene Reenactments, 142 U. Pa. L. Rev. 2125 (1994).

James, George F., Relevancy, Probability and the Law, 29 Cal. L. Rev. 689 (1941).

Kaye, David H., Clarifying the Burden of Persuasion: What Bayesian Decision Rules Do and Do Not Do, 3 Ind. J. of Evid. and Proof 1 (1999).

Lempert, Richard, "Narrative Relevance, Imagined Juries, and a Supreme Court Inspired Agenda for Jury Research." 1 Int'l Comment on Evidence 1 (1999).

Leonard, David P., The Legacy of *Old Chief* and the Definition of Relevant Evidence: Implications for Uncharged Misconduct Evidence, 36 S.W. L. Rev. 819 (2007–8).

Morgan, Edmund M., Functions of Judge and Jury in the Determination of Preliminary Questions of Fact, 43 Harv. L. Rev. 165 (1929).

Morgan, Edmund and John. M. Maguire, Looking Backward and Forward at Evidence 1886–1936, 50 Harv. L. Rev. 909 (1937).

Mosteller, Robert P., Syndromes and Politics in Criminal Trials and Evidence Law, 46 Duke L. J. 461 (1996).

Nance, Dale A., Conditional Relevance Reinterpretation, 70 B.U. L. Rev. 447 (1990).

Nance, Dale A., Conditional Probative Value and the Reconstruction of the Federal Rules of Evidence, 95 Mich. L. Rev. 419 (1995).

Saltzburg, Stephen A., Special Aspects of Relevance: Countering Negative Inferences Associated With the Absence of Evidence, 66 Cal. L. Rev. 1011 (1978).

Schaefer, Evelyn G. and Kristine L. Hansen, Similar Fact Evidence and Limited Use Instructions: An Empirical Investigation, 14 Crim. L.J. 157 (1990).

Torok, Jana L., (Comment) The Undoing of *Old Chief*: Harmless Error and Felon-in-Possession-of-Firearms Cases, 48 Kan. L. Rev. 431 (1999–2000).

Travers, Arthur H., Jr., An Essay on the Determination of Relevancy Under the Federal Rules of Evidence, 1977 Ariz. St. L.J. 327.

Tribe, Laurence H., Trial by Mathematics: Precision and Ritual in the Legal Process, 84 Harv. L. Rev. 1329 (1971).

Tyler, Tom, Procedural Justice (vol. 1) 2005.

Weyrauch, Walter O., Law as Mask—Legal Ritual and Relevance, 66 Cal. L. Rev. 699 (1978).

Wissler, Roselle L. and Michael J. Saks, On the Inefficacy of Limiting Instructions: When Jurors Use Credibility Evidence to Decide on Guilt, 9 Law & Hum. Behav. 37 (1985).

CHAPTER 4

RELEVANT BUT INADMISSIBLE: CATEGORICAL BALANCING AND THE "RELEVANCE RULES"

▪ ▪ ▪

I. AN OVERVIEW

A. INTRODUCTION TO THE RULES

American evidence law includes a group of exclusionary rules that often are discussed under the general rubric of "relevance." But as thoughtful commentators and judges have long noted, the evidence these rules exclude is not, strictly speaking, irrelevant. Rather, the evidence is excluded because its probative value frequently is low and its potential for prejudice often is high.

Evidence governed by these exclusionary rules is common enough that courts have repeatedly had to balance its probative value against its prejudicial potential. The many appellate decisions discussing the evidence have enabled judges, codifiers and commentators to extract a set of more or less coherent rules that strike that balance categorically, instead of requiring judges and trial attorneys to strike it case by case. In some instances, however, the balance struck has had as much to do with the political or economic influences of those advantaged as any other factor.

Simplifying greatly, the general rules are as follows: (1) *Character.* Subject to some important exceptions, evidence of a person's trait of character (for example, a robbery defendant's propensity to violence or a tort defendant's reputation for carelessness) may not be introduced to establish that the person behaved in conformity with that character trait on a particular occasion. Among the exceptions to this rule are certain types of "character evidence" that are admissible to show that a witness was truthful or untruthful while testifying in court.[1] (2) *Other crimes.* As a corollary to the first rule, evidence of a criminal defendant's other

---

[1] Most of the rules discussed in this and the next chapter are collected in Article IV of the FRE ("Relevancy and Its Limits"). The remaining rules are in Article VI of the FRE ("Witnesses"). Three of the rules covered in the next chapter (FRE 607–609, cross-referenced in FRE 404(a)(3)) identify exceptional situations in which evidence of a witness's character may be introduced to support or refute a claim that she lied in court. A fourth rule, FRE 610, broadens the ban on character evidence to include a type of ideological evidence—a witness's religious beliefs, which cannot be used to prove that the witness is or is not credible.

crimes is usually inadmissible to show that the defendant committed the crime charged. A witness's criminal convictions, however, may sometimes be introduced to suggest that the witness lacks credibility. (3) *Habit.* Evidence that a person or enterprise had a certain habit generally *is* admissible to show that the subject acted in accord with that habit on a specific occasion. (4) *Subsequent remedial measures.* Evidence that a party took remedial measures after an accident may not be introduced to show that the party is legally liable for creating or maintaining the pre-accident state of affairs. (5) *Payment of medical expenses.* Evidence that one person paid or offered to pay the medical expenses of another person may not be introduced to prove that the paying person negligently caused the injuries of the person paid. (6) *Offers to compromise or plead guilty.* Evidence that a party offered to compromise a claim or to plead guilty to a crime, and certain statements made by a party during the course of settlement or plea negotiations, may not be introduced to show the party's liability or guilt. (7) *Liability insurance.* Evidence that a party did or did not have liability insurance may not be introduced to show that the party was or was not negligent. (8) *Similar events.* Evidence of an event offered to show that another event occurred in a particular way is scrutinized carefully to assure that the two events are sufficiently similar to support the intended inference. In general, *these rules exclude evidence when used for the purpose specified in the rule but not when used for other purposes.*[2]

This chapter discusses the last five of these rules. The next chapter discusses the first three. The rules discussed here provide a helpful introduction to problems encountered throughout the book: recognizing the multiple uses of evidence; figuring out how to bar some uses while allowing other uses of the same evidence; disentangling truth-focused reasons for excluding relevant evidence from other reasons for doing so; assessing the behavioral assumptions that underlie many of these reasons; evaluating rules that are mainly promoted by self-interested repeat-player litigators; and choosing between a large set of narrow rules that closely constrain judicial behavior in particular situations, and a small number of general rules that confer broad judicial discretion in a variety of contexts.

---

[2]   There are two exceptions to this pattern. Pursuant to FRE 408(a) not only are compromises and offers to compromise excluded "to prove or disprove the validity or amount of a disputed claim," they are also barred if offered "to impeach by a prior inconsistent statement or a contradiction." Under FRE 410, evidence of withdrawn guilty pleas, pleas of nolo contendere, offers to plead guilty and statements in plea negotiations, if they are covered by the rule, are inadmissible for all purposes against the defendant who made them. In practice this means primarily that such evidence is unavailable for impeachment as well as to prove the defendant's guilt.

B. TWO TYPES OF EVIDENCE

Evidence may be divided into two broad categories—substantive evidence, which answers the question "What happened?" and credibility evidence, which answers the question "Is it believable?". The first category includes evidence that tends to show that an element of a cause of action or a defense is more or less likely to have occurred. For example, testimony that the defendant drank several beers before a car accident makes it more likely that the defendant was negligent. The second category consists of evidence that reflects on the value of other evidence. For example, evidence that the witness who testified to the defendant's drinking despised the defendant undermines the believability of that witness's testimony. Of course, such impeaching evidence, like evidence attacking the validity of nontestimonial evidence, helps a party prove his own substantive case or disprove his opponent's case. But it accomplishes its goal indirectly, by discrediting the other side's substantive evidence. "Credibility" evidence thus is relevant because it tends to make the jury disbelieve the opposing side's substantive evidence about what happened.[3]

As we explain in the next chapter, the rules governing "character," "other crimes" and "habit" evidence tend to *exclude* evidence offered for substantive purposes while *regulating the form* of evidence offered for credibility purposes. The rules covered in this chapter exclude substantive evidence but—with two exceptions[4]—have *no effect* on evidence offered on credibility.

Although the "relevance rules" typically distinguish between evidence offered for substantive and impeachment purposes, jurors apparently have trouble making the distinction. Even when instructed otherwise, jurors are likely to be influenced by evidence that is admissible only for impeachment in deciding aspects of the case that do *not* relate to witness credibility or the weight of other evidence. The inability of jurors to limit the use of credibility evidence to its permissible purpose is a subspecies of a broader problem that many evidence rules pose.[5] These rules frequently make evidence admissible for one purpose (*e.g.*, to prove damages) but inadmissible for another purpose (*e.g.*, to prove liability). Lawyers sometimes offer evidence that is properly admissible for one purpose in the hope that jurors will use it for another purpose. Although this practice is so common that some count it among the litigator's arts, it also can be unethical, as when the only motive for offering evidence is to get jurors to misuse it.

---

[3] Although we often assume that the trier of fact is a jury, much of what we say about juries also applies to judges who try facts. Indeed, psychological inquiry has suggested substantial similarity between laypersons and judges as factfinders. See Chris Guthrie, Jeffrey J. Rachlinski and Andrew J. Wistrich, Inside the Judicial Mind, 86 Cornell L. Rev. 777 (2001).

[4] See supra, note 2.

[5] See especially Chapter Two, Section III.F., pp. 184–186.

C. REASONS FOR THE RULES

The "relevance" rules share a number of features. First, the evidence they exclude generally is not very probative of the issues on which introduction is forbidden. Furthermore, the more probable the inference such evidence is introduced to support, the more likely it is that the proponent of the evidence is able to introduce other, stronger evidence. Consider an example involving subsequent repairs. Suppose the defendant has added a railing to the stairway in which the plaintiff fell. If the defendant were indeed negligent in maintaining the stairway without a railing, a simple description of the unguarded stairway might show that the defendant's failure to provide a railing was negligent, and the plaintiff also should be able to produce expert testimony that explains why it was unsafe. If, on the other hand, the plaintiff can offer no reason besides the subsequent repair to believe the defendant was negligent, the inference of negligence is weak.[6] Of course, low probative value or lack of strategic significance does not by itself justify a decision to exclude evidence. In combination, items with low probative value may make a strong case that cannot otherwise be made. But the confluence of low probative value and low importance may justify a receptive attitude towards categorical exclusion.

The "relevance rules" also respond to estimation problems. Consider an offer to plead guilty to a lesser offense. Such offers have probative value; an innocent person is probably less likely to offer to admit culpability than a guilty one. But there are many factors that might lead an innocent individual to offer a plea to a lesser charge: she might be

---

[6] Stated in the Bayesian terms introduced in Chapter Three, Section II.A., pp. 243–245, the probability that a subsequent repair would be the only evidence of negligence the plaintiff could produce would be lower if the defendant were negligent than if the defendant were not negligent. Because the denominator thus exceeds the numerator, the likelihood ratio is less than one, and any prior estimate of the odds of the defendant's negligence would be revised *downward* by this pattern of evidence. This does not mean either that the subsequent repair evidence is irrelevant or that it provides no support for the plaintiff's case: Even if it is the only evidence, the fact of the later repair still provides some indication of negligence because the downward revision of the prior odds is less than would be the case if there were *no* evidence of negligence at all.

On the other hand, the probability that the unguarded stairway would appear dangerous to the lay person, that an expert would testify that it was dangerous, *and* that a subsequent repair occurred, is greater if the defendant had not exercised reasonable care than if the defendant had done so. This confluence of evidence might increase the estimate of the likelihood that the defendant was negligent one hundred fold. In this case, excluding the evidence of the subsequent repair will weaken the plaintiff's case somewhat but will nevertheless leave a strong case: The remaining evidence of negligence still may increase the estimate of the likelihood that the defendant was negligent by, say, fifty fold.

This analysis is an argument that, although logically relevant, the evidence of the subsequent repair may not be very important on the issue of negligence. If the argument is correct, then, as a practical matter, few cases will arise in which the evidence of negligence is so close that the subsequent repair will make a difference. As noted in the text, however, this analysis does not necessarily mean that a rule excluding all evidence of subsequent remedial measures is preferable to the general rule that relevant evidence is admissible unless its probative value is substantially outweighed by its negative effect on the fact-finding process.

unable to make bail while waiting for trial, and the likely sentence on the lesser charge might be less than the expected period of pretrial detention; the likely penalty if convicted on the greater charge might be so severe that she does not wish to take the risk; or she might have been advised that the trial will come down to her word against a police officer's and that in such circumstances juries usually convict.

Most jurors are unaware of the factors that might lead innocent people to plead guilty. This ignorance will cause them to underestimate substantially the probability that an innocent defendant would offer to plead guilty, and to overestimate the degree to which the evidence suggests the defendant's guilt. In addition, the cost of providing jurors with the facts needed to make a proper estimate—the usual cure for estimation problems—may be high. Informing jurors about the plea process through which most criminal cases are resolved, and about the pressures that lead innocent individuals to plead guilty, would consume considerable time, might prejudice the defendant or the state, and would probably undermine the jurors' confidence in the criminal process in which they are asked to play a part. Moreover, the attempt to avoid misestimation might not work. Even if the jury does hear about the pressures that might lead an innocent defendant to plead guilty, most jurors have not been and do not anticipate being in such a situation. So, regardless of what they hear, many jurors might still overestimate the likelihood that they (and by extension, other innocent individuals) would refuse to admit guilt when falsely accused.

The categorical exclusion rules also seek to avoid extended litigation on collateral issues. Consider a tort plaintiff's offer to show that the defendant is careless by presenting evidence that she caused another accident. Such evidence can magnify the dispute. The defendant might want to argue that the prior accident never occurred, or that her carelessness did not cause it. A jury hearing this argument might be distracted from evidence that bears directly on the accident at issue in the case. In addition, the defendant might not expect the evidence because it is not an integral part of the plaintiff's case. In that event, the defendant either will be unable to present what might have been a convincing response, or she will have to secure a costly continuance.

The "relevance rules" also respond to problems of prejudice that inhere in some of the categories of excluded evidence. "Other crimes" evidence provides an example. Although such evidence is easy to prove, hard to dispute and apparently probative, it might lead jurors to convict an accused not because they believe he committed the crime charged, but rather because he is a bad person. In "regret matrix" terms (see Chapter Three, Section II.B.), evidence of other crimes might improperly decrease juror regret at convicting a defendant who is innocent of the crime charged and increase regret at acquitting a defendant who is guilty.

Other policy reasons used to justify the "relevance rules" have nothing to do with probative value or its usual counterweights (misestimation, confusion of the issues, surprise, prejudice, and waste of time). For instance, an offer of a large settlement early in a law suit for breach of contract may be quite probative of liability, but is excluded to foster openness in settlement negotiations. Similarly, the rule concerning subsequent remedial measures often is explained on the ground that society should not discourage post-accident repairs by making them admissible to prove liability.

At least two of these justifications (limited persuasive power and some asserted policy advantage) support each of the "relevance rules." Generally speaking, therefore, if one considers all the factors, the rules are defensible—that is, they make at least as much sense as most other accepted rules governing whether or not to admit particular categories of evidence.[7]

D. LIMITED SCOPE

Even our simplified summary of the relevance rules reveals that each of them classifies types of evidence as inadmissible *only for certain purposes*.[8] When evidence of an excluded type is offered for some other, nonprohibited purpose, the evidence is not automatically excluded. Evidence with little probative value and considerable prejudicial potential when offered to prove one fact may have considerable probative value and less prejudicial potential when offered to prove another fact. Courts accordingly have refused to extend the relevance rules beyond their well-defined, narrow range. Much can be learned about the policies underlying each rule by closely attending to the uses for which the evidence is and is not forbidden.

Consider again the example of subsequent remedial measures. We have already suggested that such evidence is unlikely to be crucial on the issue of negligence. But suppose the issue instead is control. An accident occurs in a hallway of a condominium apartment building. The defendant condominium association claims the hallway was under the control of a condominium unit owner; the owner claims the hallway was under the control of the association; the condominium agreement is unclear on the point. The fact that the association repaired the hallway carpeting after the accident may be the most convincing evidence the plaintiff can offer on the question of control. Because the probative value of subsequent repair evidence when offered to prove control is likely to be greater than its value when offered to prove negligence, the line drawn by the rule—

---

[7]   Using defensibility in this weak sense does not answer the more complicated question whether categorical rules of exclusion are preferable to resting discretion with trial judges.

[8]   With the exception noted above, supra, note 2.

which permits the use of subsequent remedial measures to show control—seems sensible.

As we already have noted, when evidence is admitted for a limited purpose, the jurors still might use it for a forbidden purpose—even if they are instructed otherwise. In this way, the many permissible uses of evidence subject to the "relevance rules" may frustrate the policies behind the rules. Application of the usual case-by-case balancing codified in FRE 403 lets judges resist this tendency by excluding such evidence if its probative value for a permissible purpose is overwhelmed by any of the recognized counterweights, including the possibility that the jury will use the evidence for a prohibited purpose. Too often, however, trial and appellate courts treat a commonly permitted use of evidence otherwise subject to a "relevance rule" as a categorical "exception" to the exclusionary rule, and conclude that evidence within the "exception" is admissible for the permitted purpose regardless of its probative value or the fact that it is fraught with danger of prejudice. This conclusion is a *non sequitur*. When a rule prohibits the use of evidence only for one purpose, evidence offered for another purpose does not fall within an *exception* to the rule but rather is a matter that lies *outside* the rule and instead is governed by *other* rules of evidence—including FRE 402's presumption of admissibility of relevant evidence and FRE 403's discretion to exclude the evidence if prejudice substantially outweighs probative value. The mistaken application of "exceptions" of this sort is particularly serious with respect to character evidence, which we discuss in the next chapter.

Although a court can exclude evidence subject to one of the "relevance rules" even though the conditions for an "exception" are met,[9] the converse is not true. Ad hoc balancing is not appropriate when a "relevance rule" applies and the evidence has no permissible purpose that avoids the rule. In that event, Congress has decided for the courts, and the evidence must be excluded.

E. AVOIDING MISUSE

An attorney who is worried that the jury will misuse evidence admissible for a permitted purpose has two ways of trying to keep it out, both of which are discussed in more depth in Chapter Eleven, Section II.A. *First*, the lawyer may stipulate to *everything* the evidence might properly be used to prove—assuming, of course, that the client has more to gain than to lose from the stipulation. Courts often let the opposing side reject a stipulation, however, on the theory that a party is entitled to

---

[9]   Only FRE 609(a)(2), discussed in Chapter Five, Section IV.B.3, pp. 433–437, forbids any version of the traditional balancing. Under Rule 609(a)(2), if a witness has been convicted of a crime involving dishonesty or false statement during the last ten years, or if any part of a sentence for such a conviction was served during that same period, the court "shall" admit the conviction to impeach the witness.

prove the elements of the case by any competent evidence the party chooses.[10] *Second*, the attorney may make a "judicial admission"—a binding concession that removes an entire issue (e.g., an element of a crime) from the class of disputed fact questions. If evidence addresses an issue that is no longer in dispute, the evidence is irrelevant under FRE 401 and inadmissible under FRE 402. This technique can be costly if a party concedes a fact that her opponent otherwise might not be able to prove.

If a party cannot persuade a judge to use FRE 403 to exclude evidence that is likely to be misused, and if the party is unwilling or unable to make an acceptable stipulation or judicial admission, she still may request a limiting instruction under FRE 105 telling the jury to consider evidence only for its bearing on a particular issue. As we discuss in Chapter Two,[11] however, attorneys often feel that limiting instructions only make matters worse, by alerting jurors to forbidden inferences, and so they forgo requesting instruction and hope for the best.

II.   THE RULES IN DETAIL

A. SUBSEQUENT REMEDIAL MEASURES

1.   The Rule

FRE 407 provides:

When measures are taken that would have made an earlier injury or harm less likely to occur, evidence of the subsequent measures is not admissible to prove:

- negligence;
- culpable conduct;
- a defect in a product or its design; or
- a need for a warning or instruction.

But the court may admit this evidence for another purpose, such as impeachment or—if disputed—proving ownership, control, or feasibility of precautionary measures.

---

[10] Cf. Chapter Three, Section I.I., pp. 234–240, discussing the Supreme Court's holding in Old Chief v. United States, 519 U.S. 172 (1997), that, under the limited circumstances of the case, the prosecution was obliged to accept the defendant's offer to stipulate that he previously had been convicted of a crime that made him subject to the prohibition against ex-felons' possessing firearms. The trial court had permitted the prosecutor to reject the stipulation and prove the highly prejudicial facts of the prior conviction.

[11] See Chapter Two Section III.F., pp. 184–186.

The common law has a rule that precludes the introduction of evidence of subsequent repairs to show negligence.[12] Although FRE 407's reference to "subsequent remedial measures" sounds broader than the common law's "subsequent repairs" formulation, the federal rule essentially codifies the common law rule, which has been applied, for example, to lowered speed limits, new chemical formulas, the posting of warnings, revised rules and practices, installation of safety devices, and the discharge of employees.

FRE 407 also follows the common law in excluding evidence of subsequent remedial measures only when the evidence is offered to prove negligence, culpable conduct or, more recently, a modern alternative to negligence, such as a defect in a product design.[13] The *permitted* purposes listed in the final sentence of FRE 407 are ones for which evidence of subsequent remedial measures has commonly been admitted. They are mentioned only as examples, however, and do not exhaust the permitted purposes. Adept lawyers frequently find permitted evidentiary uses of subsequent remedial actions. For example, lawyers often cross-examine opposing witnesses about the safety of pre-accident conditions and then are allowed to use subsequent modifications to impeach the witness's answer that the original condition was as safe as possible.

The loophole the rule provides for alternative uses of subsequent repair evidence is narrowed somewhat by the rule's requirement that the issue on which the evidence is admitted be disputed. This limitation is particularly important with respect to the feasibility of precautionary measures. Proof of the defendant's ability to behave more safely usually is necessary to show negligence. Accordingly, evidence of the feasibility of safer conduct almost always is relevant in negligence cases, and evidence of subsequent remedial measures almost always would be admissible to show "feasibility" if relevance were the only criterion. However, because the ability to conduct an activity more safely does not by itself establish negligence, defendants often concede that issue so it is not "disputed" and the "feasibility" exception does not apply.[14]

---

[12] The common law rule was authoritatively articulated by Baron Bramwell in Hart v. Lancashire & Yorkshire Ry. Co., 21 L.T. 261 (1869).

[13] As we discuss infra, Subsection 3, pp. 300–302, the states are divided on whether to admit evidence of subsequent remedial measures to prove product and design defects and other alternatives to negligence. Until 1997, when FRE 407 was amended to cover that use of evidence of subsequent remedial measures in products liability cases, the federal courts also were divided on the question and, despite the rule change, federal courts in diversity cases still honor state evidence rules allowing the use of subsequent remedial measures in strict liability actions when they conclude that the rule is part of the state's substantive law of accidents. See Call, Fire & Cas. Co. v. State Indus., 221 F.3d 1351 (10th Cir. 2000).

[14] As we point out above, most permitted evidentiary uses of subsequent measures are not, strictly speaking, exceptions to FRE 407 but simply matters lying *outside* the rule's prohibition against using the evidence to prove negligence or culpable conduct. But feasibility of safer action *is* used to prove negligence, so admission of the evidence to show "feasibility" (when disputed) is a true exception. Cf. infra, note 22 and accompanying text on the broader impact of the "feasibility" exception on design defect cases.

2.   The Rationale in Negligence Cases

Two reasons are commonly given for excluding evidence of subsequent remedial measures on the issue of negligence: (1) The evidence has little probative value.   (2) Admitting the evidence might deter people from taking socially beneficial post-accident precautions.   In this subsection, we consider the validity of these explanations for the subsequent repair rule in negligence cases and suggest an additional rationale.   In the next subsection, we ask whether it makes sense for the rule to apply in strict liability cases.

If the making of a remedial modification after an accident has probative weight on the issue of negligence, it is because the precaution tends to show the actor's belief that due care requires the remedial measure.   The actor's post-accident belief that due care requires the measure suggests that, even *before* the accident, he believed or should have believed that the measure was necessary.   This suggests, in turn, that due care did require the measure before the accident, and that the actor was negligent for not having taken it.

Even if these inferences are appropriate, the probative value of evidence of subsequent repairs is likely to be low, for two reasons.   First, conscientious individuals, newly alerted to a dangerous condition, may be expected to do everything feasible to remedy that condition regardless of the reasonableness of their earlier care.   Accidents thus are likely to prompt protective measures because they provide *new* information about hitherto *unnoticed* dangers.   Consequently, the taking of subsequent remedial measures may not be much more likely if there was pre-accident negligence than if there was not.   The actor's belief that due care now requires a measure only weakly tends to prove that due care previously required the measure.

Second, subsequent repair evidence relates to negligence in a strange way—via inferences to and from a party's *opinion* or *opinions* about what constitutes due care.   Yet, evidence rules generally bar witnesses—even experts—from expressing opinions that synthesize the facts of a case into a conclusion of law. Although the opinion of a *party* is not barred—the "party admissions" rule (see Chapter Six, Section III.B.) holds parties especially accountable for their words, actions and opinions—the fact remains that the conclusions of a non-lawyer about the legal

---

Although opinions differ and the rule's syntax is unclear, most courts apply FRE 407's "if disputed" language to all alternative uses of subsequent repair evidence and not just to its use to show the feasibility of precautionary measures.

FRE 407's loophole for alternative uses of subsequent remedial measures evidence is also narrowed somewhat by the phrasing of the rule's last sentence.   Saying that "the court *may* admit this evidence" emphasizes the trial judge's obligation to exercise the discretion afforded by FRE 403 when subsequent remedial measures evidence is offered for purposes other than proving culpability or defect.   If prejudice substantially outweighs probative value, the judge should exclude the evidence.

consequences of her actions often will be mistaken. When relevance depends upon treating an action as merely *implying* an opinion on negligence, the chain of inference is even more tenuous. This does not mean that nothing would be gained by requiring parties to explain why post-accident remedial measures do not acknowledge pre-accident carelessness. The fact that convincing explanations often exist does not detract from the value of the exercise when they do not. But a risk would remain. Jurors might give too much credence to the suggestion of negligence and too little credence to the party's seemingly self-serving explanation of why the subsequent measure was taken. If so, they would underestimate the likelihood that the measure would have been taken even if the party had not been negligent.[15] (Estimation problems of this sort often affect evidence of actions offered to show a consciousness of liability or guilt.)

When the issue of due care at the time of an accident depends on the feasibility of precautionary steps, the probative value of post-accident remedial measures increases in both ways we have discussed. Suppose that "feasibility" is the main issue in a suit because the defendant admits knowing before the accident that a condition was unsafe but claims the danger was unavoidable. Now, the subsequent cure has considerable probative value. Absent recent technological innovation, the fact of a post-accident cure is strong evidence of the feasibility of a pre-accident cure. Also, the inference here proceeds from the actual existence of the cure at the time the remedial step is taken, and not from anybody's *opinion* about a remedy's existence, much less an opinion about "due care." This difference in probative value helps explain why subsequent repairs are admissible to show the feasibility of precautionary measures but not to show other aspects of negligence.

While these considerations generally tend to suggest the limited probative value of subsequent remedial measures evidence in negligence cases, they do not, alone, justify categorical exclusion. It is easy to imagine cases where such evidence will be sufficiently probative to surmount a challenge on FRE 401 or FRE 403 grounds. Consider the case of a fatal car/train collision at a railroad crossing. If the defendant railroad makes repairs after the accident that it had delayed for several years because of bureaucratic bungling, the tardy repair work provides valuable evidence of the railroad's prior unreasonable conduct. One

---

[15] Misestimation error may be inevitable in negligence trials. Just hearing that an accident occurred may lead jurors to overestimate the accident's foreseeability (and thus the likelihood of negligence) through a process of 20–20 hindsight. See Baruch Fischoff, Hindsight-Foresight: The Effect of Outcome Knowledge on Judgment Under Uncertainty, 1 J. of Exper. Psych. Hum. Percep. & Perf. 288 (1975); Baruch Fischoff & R. Beyth, "I Knew it Would Happen": Remembered Probabilities of Once-Future Things, 13 Org. Beh. & Hum. Perf. 1 (1975); Jeffrey J. Rachlinski, A Positive Psychological Theory of Judging in Hindsight, 65 U. Chi. L. Rev. 571 (1998). If that is true, then the key issue here is the extent of any *added* risk of overestimation of negligence from admitting evidence of subsequent remedial measures.

needs to look further to defend blanket exclusion. One rationale has been that parties would not make repairs after an accident if evidence of the repairs could be used against them.

If unquestioning repetition by courts and commentators could make a statement true, then this proposition would certainly be true and would justify excluding the evidence. But, as a matter of behavioral psychology, the proposition is dubious at best. Actors sufficiently schooled in the law to realize that evidence of subsequent remedial measures will not be admissible on the issue of fault are also likely to realize that such evidence *may* be admissible for other purposes, and also that a failure to repair after being warned by an accident may constitute gross negligence and justify punitive damages should another accident occur. Thus, any likely increase in repairs seems too small to justify the rule's blanket exclusion of evidence that often may be at least modestly probative. Moreover, there is no empirical evidence to support the traditional claim that actors in the real world refrain from making repairs because of a fear of liability.

There are, however, two additional rationales that help explain the rule, though courts rarely articulate them. First, the rule preserves the integrity of a certain conception of a negligence regime (albeit one that relies on a debatable understanding of how duty is or should be determined in negligence law). Under this conception, actors may do as they please until they become aware that their actions harm others, at which point they acquire a duty to avoid harms that cost the victim more than they profit the actor. An example might be a dog owner who need not muzzle the beast until it reveals its proclivity to bite. The subsequent repair rule preserves this "one bite for free" conception of negligence by assuring that the actor's response to the event that arguably marks the onset of the duty—the accident that reveals the hazard and prompts remedial action—is not used to extend the duty backwards in time to a point prior to any awareness of the hazard.

In a similar vein, the rule prevents courts from punishing actors for taking remedial steps that the law and good citizenship require. It may be precisely because legal and moral duties often compel post-accident precautionary measures, no matter what the evidence rules say, that those rules seek to ensure that jurors do not hold the actors' remedial actions against them. This fairness rationale also may explain why some courts exclude subsequent repairs that are required by statute, even though legally mandated repairs are especially unlikely to be deterred by allowing their admission into evidence. It may also help explain why defendants who take subsequent remedial steps without having received notice of the plaintiff's injuries are also covered by the rule.

Even this Samaritan rationale is not entirely convincing, however. One might argue that accepted notions of negligence (and good citizenship) require *more* than just a response to accidents after they occur: they also require anticipation and avoidance. People are responsible for hazards they *should* have known about as well as ones they actually recognize. By affording some protection to actors who failed to take the step that tort policy most favors (anticipatory measures) as long as they took a less favored step (subsequent measures) and did not take the least favored step (no measures at all), the subsequent repair rule might actually clash with accepted tort policies. One state has so concluded and adopted a rule specifically permitting introduction of subsequent remedial measures in both negligence and strict liability cases.[16]

At least as long as the action is for negligence, the subsequent repair rule has been applied to large corporations in much the same way as to individuals. This need not be the case, however. A rule that envisions an individual tortfeasor alerted to danger by an accident and contemplating a repair does not apply with the same force to a corporation's broad remedial changes—for example, in product design or safety rules. Unlike repairs undertaken by individuals, large-scale remedial measures by corporations typically do not respond to a specific plaintiff's accident but rather are impersonal bureaucratic responses to a number of reported accidents or to the kinds of precautionary safety evaluations that modern tort law and government regulations encourage. Note, though, that when corporations are sued for personal injuries based on negligence, they are often simultaneously sued for the same injuries based on strict liability. As we shall shortly see, a significant number of state courts (unlike the federal courts) have refused to apply the subsequent repair rule to strict liability suits, thus indirectly limiting the rule's application when corporations take remedial steps.

The reasons courts give to justify their decisions exert real influence on the law. For example, the idea that evidence of subsequent repairs is excluded to avoid discouraging such repairs has led courts to allow parties to prove negligence with evidence of repairs by *non-parties*, because a non-party is unlikely to forego making a repair out of fear that it might be used to prove *someone else's* negligence. (The one bite and fairness rationales described above also may be used to justify the admissibility of third party repairs.) If the courts instead explained the rule mainly on the basis of low probative value, then non-party repair evidence would be inadmissible, because the probative value of non-party repairs to show a party's negligence is even lower than the probative value of the party's own repairs.

---

[16] Rhode Island's version of Rule 407 states: "When, after an event, measures are taken which, if taken previously, would have made the event less likely to occur, evidence of the subsequent measures is admissible." See Brian Fielding, Note: Rhode Island's 407 Subsequent Remedial Measure Exception: Why It Informs What Goes Around Comes Around in Restatements (Second) & (Third) of Torts, and a Modest Proposal, 14 Roger Williams U. L. Rev. 298 (2009).

Discrepancies between the reasons courts give to explain legal rules and the courts' actual application of the rules also can be enlightening. For example, as we mention above, some courts that explain FRE 407 as designed to keep courts from discouraging voluntary repairs nonetheless also exclude evidence of repairs required by statute, which almost certainly would not be deterred by their admissibility in evidence.[17] Such discrepancies suggest that unstated policies are also at work—for example, the one bite and fairness rationales—although courts tend to explain such decisions as encouraging prompt obedience to statutory mandates when legal resistance might, otherwise, be mounted.[18]

3. The Rationale in Strict Liability Cases

Until 1997, FRE 407 excluded evidence of subsequent remedial measures only when offered to prove "negligence or culpable conduct." On its face, this language limited the rule to cases in which the required level of blame was at least a "lack of due care" and, arguably, made the rule inapplicable to product liability lawsuits brought under a theory of strict liability. Nonetheless, the dominant (though not uniform) view in the federal courts was that FRE 407 applied in strict liability as well as in negligence actions. In 1997, FRE 407 was amended to conform to the majority rule in the federal courts and to bar subsequent remedial measures evidence when used to prove "a defect in a product or its design" or "a need for a warning or instruction." The view in a significant number of state courts is the opposite—that evidence of subsequent remedial measures is *admissible* in strict liability cases as long as prejudicial potential does not substantially outweigh probative value.[19] In the authors' view, these state courts have the better of this debate. However, the persuasive power of federal codification has led a number of states to embrace the amended FRE 407 formula.

The most common explanation for applying the subsequent repair rule in strict liability actions is the desire not to deter remedial measures. This explanation seems at least as unconvincing here as in the negligence

---

[17] See, e.g., Werner v. Upjohn Co., 628 F.2d 848 (4th Cir. 1980). Other courts admit evidence of remedial measures required by governmental regulations on the ground that doing so will not deter such measures. See, e.g., O'Dell v. Hercules, Inc., 904 F.2d 1194 (8th Cir. 1990). See generally E. Lee Reichert, Note, The "Superior Authority Exception" to Federal Rule of Evidence 407: The "Remedial Measure" Required to Clarify a Confused State of Evidence, 1991 U. Ill. L. Forum 843.

[18] See, e.g., Vockie v. General Motors Corp., Chevrolet Division, 66 F.R.D. 57 (E.D. Pa. 1975), aff'd 523 F.2d 1052 (3d Cir. 1975).

[19] The contrary trend in the state courts began with Ault v. International Harvester Co., 13 Cal.3d 113, 117 Cal.Rptr. 812, 528 P.2d 1148 (1974), which interpreted California's subsequent repair rule, Cal. Evid. Code § 1151, to allow admission of subsequent remedial measures to prove products defective. For discussions of the competing positions, see, e.g., Randolph L. Burns, Note, Subsequent Remedial Measures and Strict Products Liability: A New—Relevant—Answer to an Old Problem, 81 Va. L. Rev. 1144 (1995); Lev Dassin, Note, Design Defects in the Rules Enabling Act: The Misapplication of Federal Rule of Evidence 407 to Strict Liability, 65 N.Y.U. L. Rev. 736 (1990).

context. Most strict liability defendants are big corporations as to which the rationale of promoting repairs has little force. True, if remedial measures are deterred, considerable harm could ensue because the dangers that corporations create may affect many victims. Nonetheless, corporations' common statutory duties to repair, and their heightened concern about the risk of punitive damages if they ignore known dangers, are likely to overwhelm any incentive a different set of rules of evidence might have given them to forgo making repairs.[20]

There are especially strong reasons to abandon the subsequent remedial measures rule in design defect cases. Unless the defect is obvious (as when a car's rear mounted auto gas tank explodes on impact), the plaintiff usually must show that an alternative design was both feasible and safer. Because a business is not likely to change a product unless doing so is feasible and improves the product's safety, a subsequent improvement is highly probative on both crucial issues.[21] (Of course, this means that feasibility will often be controverted and, if so, that FRE 407 will not apply. But the rule's availability will lead to more disputes over what is and is not controverted.) Also, strict liability for design defects is a legal regime that does not give the party responsible for the dangerous condition "one bite for free," but instead encourages manufacturers to anticipate and avoid dangers. In design defect cases, therefore, the rule's preservation of a one-bite regime, and its protection of actors who "conscientiously" react after accidents occur, seems neither necessary nor appropriate.

---

[20] This is true even though accidents are low probability events, and the use of subsequent repair evidence once a suit is filed (if permitted) is a high probability event. Applied to a large number of mass-produced products, even a very low probability of accidents may mean a lot of accidents. Because each accident caused by the failure to modify after the first accident may be subject to punitive as well as actual damages, the cost of not modifying is likely to overwhelm the cost of reasonable modification, plus added actual-damages liability (if any). But see Flaminio v. Honda Motor Co., 733 F.2d 463 (7th Cir. 1984) (Posner, J.). Evidence of prior accidents may be admissible on the question of liability as well as on damages, see infra, Section II.F., pp. 320–323. This fact adds to the cost of not modifying because each new accident increases the pool of potential evidence that may be offered against the manufacturer when new accidents occur. Of course, if the subsequent repair rule has no *adverse* effects, then its application makes sense though it only rarely prompts additional safety measures. But we suspect that enforcing the rule in lieu of the usual FRE 403 balance *does* have adverse effects—that excluding subsequent repair evidence that is probative and not very prejudicial lets more manufacturers escape liability for defective products than it shields from liability for products that are safe. If we are right, the rule actually *deters* safety measures by enabling manufacturers on average to bear less than the full costs of the harms their defective products cause. This point is of particular importance where design defects are in issue. These are particularly difficult to prove and, since the adoption of the Restatement (Third) of Torts, have become particularly challenging for plaintiffs since they are required to show a practical alternative design to win. Some courts have admitted such proof via the feasibility exception, others have not.

[21] Although it is true that designs are changed for many reasons, including "to decrease costs, increase efficiency or increase the marketability of a product," James M. Wood, Liability and Evidentiary Issues Involving Prescription Production Recall, 74 Def. Couns. J. 64, 66 (2007), if the change improves the product's safety, changes made for these reasons strongly support the claim that safer alternatives were available and feasible from a cost and business perspective.

With the shift toward the Restatement (Third) of Tort's requirement of a demonstration of a practical alternative design, applying the subsequent repair rule to product liability cases could have the perverse effect of making liability more difficult to prove in design defect cases than in otherwise similar negligence cases.[22] This may, indeed, have been the objective of the sustained lobbying and law reform effort mounted by the representatives of manufacturing interests.[23]

Problem IV-1. The plaintiff's wife and children were killed when a railroad train collided with their car. The collision occurred at a crossing protected only by a flashing red light. The plaintiff brought an action to recover damages for the railway company's negligence. At trial, the plaintiff seeks to introduce:

(a) A photograph of the intersection taken two weeks after the accident. The photograph shows the way the crossing looked at the time of the accident, except that by the time the picture was taken the railroad had augmented the flashing red light with a wooden barrier to block automobile traffic when a train was coming.

(b) Testimony that a week after the accident the railroad added the wooden barrier.

(c) The same evidence as in (b) after the railroad alleged in its pleadings that the county highway commission and not the railroad was responsible for maintaining the safety of railroad crossings.

(d) The same evidence as in (b) after an expert testifying on behalf of the railroad told the jury that a flashing light was the only kind of automatic device for which maintenance could be effectively provided at the rural crossing in question.

(e) Testimony from an employee of the defendant describing how the railroad determines speed limits for different portions of its track and stating that the speed limit for the portion of the track on which the

---

[22] Under our analysis, the difference between negligence and design defect liability subsides sufficiently to justify FRE 407's application in the design defect context only if the definition of "defect" includes the negligence-based requirement that the hazard created by the product was reasonably foreseeable. This is what most federal courts of appeal have concluded based on the definition of design defect included in Restatement (Second) of Torts §402(a). Otherwise, application of the subsequent repair rule is difficult to justify, even in jurisdictions that define "defect" in a manner that incorporates *other* aspects of negligence—e.g., the failure to utilize a safer design that was *reasonably* available or was at least as safe as the "state of the art" design. Note, however, that even under the revised FRE 407, the closer the feasibility of a safer design is to being sufficient to establish design defect liability, the more likely it is that defendants will "dispute[ ]" the "feasibility of precautionary measures" and, thus, that subsequent repair evidence will be admissible under the "feasibility" exception. Although this mitigates the harm of the revised rule, the rule also, as we point out in the text, invites needless disputes at trial and on appeal.

[23] See Frances E. Zollers, et al., Looking Backward, Looking Forward: Reflections on Twenty Years of Product Liability Reform, 50 Syracuse L. Rev. 1019 (2000).

accident occurred had been reduced from 90 m.p.h. to 70 m.p.h. nine months after the accident.

Should any of this evidence be admitted over objections based on FRE 407?

Problem IV-2. Pastie Palate is injured by his Cuisinecraft while making cream of avocado soup. Palate sues Cuisinecraft Co. on a strict products liability theory. Two months later, the company redesigns the product to keep injuries such as Palate's from occurring. At trial, Palate wants to introduce evidence of the redesign. Cuisinecraft objects under the longstanding common law rule forbidding evidence of subsequent repairs in tort cases. The jurisdiction, which has no codified rules of evidence and follows the common law, has not yet decided whether its subsequent repair rule bars evidence of subsequent remedial measures in strict liability cases. **What are the best arguments for admitting the evidence? What are the best arguments for excluding the evidence? How would you rule?**

"The proof was in the pudding, but the pudding was ruled inadmissible as evidence."

B. COMPROMISES OFFERS AND NEGOTIATIONS

FRE 408 provides:

(a) Prohibited uses.—Evidence of the following is not admissible—on behalf of any party—either to prove or disprove the validity or amount of a disputed claim or to impeach by a prior inconsistent statement or contradiction:

(1) furnishing, promising, or offering—or accepting, promising to accept, or offering to accept—a valuable consideration in compromising or attempting to compromise the claim; and

(2) conduct or a statement made during compromise negotiations about the claim—except when offered in a criminal case and when the negotiations related to a claim by a public office in the exercise of its regulatory, investigative, or enforcement authority.

(b) Exceptions.—The court may admit this evidence for another purpose, such as proving a witness's bias or prejudice, negating a contention of undue delay, or proving an effort to obstruct a criminal investigation or prosecution.

In providing that offers of compromise are not admissible to prove the validity or invalidity of a claim or its amount, FRE 408 follows the common law. Two justifications often are given. The first is the familiar claim of low probative value: a compromise offer may reflect a desire to buy peace rather than the offeror's belief about her liability. This rationale is sound when applied to an offer to pay a small fraction of a contested claim—say, $5000 on a $100,000 claim. It wanes, however, when applied to an offer to pay most of a claim—say, $85,000 on a $100,000 claim—which strongly suggests a belief that one's position is weak. Even given the problems with "inferred opinion" evidence discussed in connection with the subsequent remedial measures rule, the relevance rationale does not justify denying courts discretion to distinguish offers that were probably extended to buy peace from offers that strongly imply a consciousness of liability.[24] A related and more broadly applicable policy is a fear of misestimation. By focusing on the high likelihood that individuals *at fault* will want to settle, jurors may lose sight of the high if somewhat lesser likelihood that individuals *not at fault* also will want to settle. If jurors do so, they will overestimate the probative weight of the evidence.[25]

---

[24] See McCormick § 266, at 466.

[25] Stated in the Bayesian terms introduced in Chapter Three, Section II.A., pp. 243–245 jurors may mistake a high numerator value (reflecting the likelihood that a party at fault will want to settle) for high probativeness, thus ignoring the fact that the denominator value (reflecting the likelihood that a party not at fault will want to settle) also may be high, if not *as* high.

The second justification for the rule is that it promotes compromise, which has become the law's favored method of settling disputes.[26] Individuals might resist initiating compromise negotiations if they knew their offers could be used against them in court. Unlike the comparable assumption with respect to remedial measures, this assumption seems reasonable. The purpose of a settlement offer is to achieve a relatively favorable outcome to a lawsuit. The negative evidentiary impact of an offer, if disclosed at trial, is likely to be recognized by any party considering settlement, since the offeror is likely to be represented by counsel. By contrast, in the remedial repair situation, incentives unrelated to specific legal cases predominate, so the evidentiary effect of making a safety improvement is unlikely to be decisive for the actor, assuming she is even aware of the evidentiary consideration.

There is a related noninstrumental rationale for FRE 408. Following the logic of our remedial repairs discussion, this rationale might be stated as follows: "In fairness, the judicial system should not use a person's socially desirable offer to compromise against her." Or, more philosophically: "An adversarial judicial system that values individual over state control of dispute resolution should not penalize steps asserting individual control of dispute resolution—namely, a party's offer to settle a claim without court control or involvement." These rationales explain FRE 408's availability to non-lawyer settlement negotiators, who are likely to be unaware of the evidentiary consequences of their actions.[27]

In excluding evidence of conduct or statements made in compromise negotiations, FRE 408 gives more protection than the common law—and in the process erases any claim that low probative value explains the rule. Consider a libel action in which the defendant tells the plaintiff, "You're right, the story is false, and I offer you $10,000 to soothe your feelings." Following the probative value rationale, the common law rule protects only the compromise offer, but not the accompanying statement touching on the merits. By contrast, FRE 408 protects the entire utterance as long as it was made in compromise negotiations.[28]

---

[26] See Samuel R. Gross & Kent D. Syverud, Don't Try: Civil Jury Verdicts in a System Geared to Settlement, 44 U.C.L.A. L. Rev. 1 (1996).

[27] Some authorities think the rationale of promoting settlement is so strong as to "privilege" settlement offers against disclosure; and so, would empower the offeror to block any public disclosure, whether in discovery or litigation, of the privileged material. In fact, FRE 408 creates no privilege; it does not shield offers from disclosure—neither in pretrial discovery nor in court—but only forbids certain uses of the evidence at trial. See Phoenix Solutions, Inc. v. Wells Fargo Bank, N.A., 254 F.R.D. 568 (N.D. Cal. 2008).

[28] FRE 408 has been held by some courts to sweeps even further. It has been held to protect internal memoranda and discussions undertaken *in preparation* for settlement negotiations. See Affiliated Mfrs., Inc. v. Aluminum Co. of America, 56 F.3d 521 (3d Cir. 1995); Xcoal Energy & Resources, LP v. Smith, 635 F. Supp. 2d 453 (W.D. Va. 2009). This should be contrasted with the likely outcome under FRE 407 where post-accident reports, root-cause analyses and similar investigative materials are not rendered inadmissible by the rule. See Benitez-Allende v. Alcan Aluminio do Brasil, S.A., 857 F.2d 26 (1st Cir. 1988).

The common law rule's narrow reach also explains the ritual that one finds in settlement negotiations in common law jurisdictions and which still lingers in some Federal Rules jurisdictions. In order to render inadmissible (as irrelevant) statements independent of the compromise offer, common law negotiators typically commence each statement, or at least the negotiation as a whole, with the incantation that all factual statements are "hypothetical" or (in the English phrase) "without prejudice."

Freedom from stifling formalisms in settlement negotiations easily justifies FRE 408's broadened exclusion.[29] So does the protection FRE 408 affords parties who try to settle their differences without lawyers and judges, blissfully unaware of the technicalities of common law compromise doctrine—such as the need to speak hypothetically. However, by using rigid definitions of both a claim disputed as to "validity or amount" and "compromise negotiations," some federal courts have risked reimposing the formalisms and traps for the unwary that the revised rule sought to avoid. The prospect of losing evidence that sometimes is so probative as to be dispositive, in service of an informal compromise negotiation that failed, strikes some courts as too high a price to pay. Those courts treat what from one perspective are embryonic negotiations to settle expected lawsuits as, instead, the closing stages of the failed business relationship that precipitated the suit. For example, courts have admitted evidence of an employer's offer to award severance pay to a dismissed employee if the employee agreed not to initiate an age discrimination suit,[30] and a trademark user's offer to remunerate a competing user of the same trademark after the competing user threatened to sue.[31] Understandable as such outcomes are, they may lead parties to engage lawyers, file suits and conduct negotiations via boilerplate in just the costly ways the liberalized rule was designed to prevent.

Disapproval of extortionate or nuisance litigation explains FRE 408's requirement that the proposed settlement relate to a claim that is *"disputed"* as to "validity or amount." If during settlement negotiations the plaintiff admits she has no case but asks the defendant to pay something anyway to avoid the expense of trial or the danger that the jury will be fooled, FRE 408 does not protect the statements. If, however, *either* "validity" *or* "amount" is disputed, the rule's full protection is available, even if the excluded evidence relates to an aspect of the claim that is *not* disputed. For example, FRE 408 would preclude a plaintiff

---

[29] FRE 408's broadened exclusion, as well as the basic common law rule, also serve to avoid the ethically awkward situations in which one or both parties' attorneys are required to testify at trial about their settlement negotiations, and to discourage attorneys from wastefully embellishing settlement offers and negotiations with statements designed to "make a record" for trial.

[30] Cassino v. Reichhold Chemicals Inc., 817 F.2d 1338 (9th Cir. 1987).

[31] Big O Tire Dealers, Inc. v. Goodyear Tire & Rubber Co., 561 F.2d 1365 (10th Cir. 1977).

from proving negligence by offering the defendant's statement during settlement negotiations that, "I carelessly ran you over, but your damages are a lot less than you claim." By protecting such statements, FRE 408 decreases the potential costs, and increases the likelihood of success, of all settlement efforts that have a capacity to resolve *some* kind of genuine dispute that the courts otherwise would have to resolve.

FRE 408 is also more liberal than prior common law practice in covering completed compromises as well as offers. It clearly excludes evidence of a settlement that was reached but then abandoned for some reason, if the evidence is offered to prove the existence or amount of liability. The rule's impact on evidence of settlements of *separate* disputes involving some or all of the same parties is less clear, because the rule only applies to settlements of "the" particular claim in dispute. Nonetheless, the Advisory Committee Note says that the rule applies "when a party to the present litigation has compromised with a third person." This statement, and the rule's policy of promoting settlements, has led most courts to apply the rule to exclude evidence of compromises of separate disputes between the same parties, or between a party and a third person, at least when the transaction at issue in the prior settlement is the same as, or related to, the transaction at issue in the current suit. The rule's restriction to evidence used "to prove or disprove the validity or amount of a disputed claim" may be intended to limit its application to lawsuits in which liability for the underlying conduct is in dispute regardless of who the parties to the compromise were. Thus if a party brings suit to enforce the settlement agreement, or to rescind the agreement (e.g., for fraud), FRE 408 permits introduction of the completed compromise as well as statements made during the negotiations that produced it. In this situation, the issue is no longer liability for the original claim but liability on a contract, and the negotiations are evidence of the contract and its contents.

As with evidence affected by the other categorical balancing rules, evidence of an offer to compromise is not excluded for all purposes. FRE 408 lists some of the purposes for which courts may admit evidence of an offer to compromise or statements made during compromise negotiations. One common purpose is to show "a witness's bias or prejudice." Consider the common three-way accident situation in which Arthur, the driver of one car, pays Bea, his passenger, a compromise settlement, and Bea then testifies for Arthur against Carmen, the driver of the second car. If Carmen seeks to introduce evidence of the compromise settlement, the courts sometimes exclude it on the theory that Carmen wants to use it to show Arthur's negligence in the accident. A careful attorney for Carmen will make clear, however, that evidence of the compromise is offered to show that Arthur and Bea have had prior dealings that are likely to dispose Bea to favor Arthur, for instance, Arthur's payment to Bea of a generous settlement. The evidence thus is not barred by FRE 408, although it may be barred, in the judge's discretion, under FRE 403. The more generous Arthur's settlement, the more the evidence tends to show bias on Bea's part. But if the settlement is well within the bounds of reason, exclusion might be warranted because its impeachment value diminishes while the jury's inclination to use it improperly to suggest Arthur's liability may not.[32]

The purpose for which evidence of civil compromise negotiations *is* excluded is broader than that for which evidence of subsequent remedial measures is excluded: to prove or disprove the validity or amount of a disputed claim, rather than to prove "negligence", "culpable conduct" or "a defect in a product or its design." This means, for example, that while subsequent remedial measures may be used to show ownership or control of a vehicle or of premises involved in an accident, a compromise offer may not. The logic of this distinction is simple. Any aspect of a claim of liability—ownership and control as well as negligence—may be in dispute, and may be settled by compromise. The purposes of the rule are just as important when the issue in contention is "Who's car was it?" rather than "How fast was it going?"

Rule 408 was amended in 2006 to resolve a conflict among the federal circuits regarding whether the rule's exclusion applies when compromise materials are offered in a subsequent criminal prosecution.[33] The Department of Justice was the chief advocate for an amendment that would permit unfettered use of such materials in criminal trials. Public reaction to the government's proposal was intensely hostile. Critics argued that under such a rule settlement discussions would be chilled in a wide range of cases, unsophisticated parties might be unfairly trapped and there might be a return to the "bad" old days of "hypothetical"

---

[32] In contrast to FRE 407, which refers to "impeachment" generally, FRE 408 refers only to "bias or prejudice." Although in theory this should make no difference because the list of permitted purposes is exemplary, not exclusive, there may be good reason for using the narrower formulation in the FRE 408 context, and for giving weight to the language difference when courts interpret the rule. Consider this situation: Paolo claims Danya breached a contract causing $100,000 in damages. In ensuing negotiations, Danya offers to settle for $50,000, saying, "you're right, I breached." Paolo refuses and sues. At trial, Danya testifies that she did not breach the contract. Can the court admit Danya's offer and statement on the ground that its inconsistency with Danya's testimony "impeaches" her? The problem with admitting the evidence (especially when it is Paolo who elicited Danya's testimony) is that it lets Paolo and the jury surrepititiously use Danya's offer and statement mainly for its bearing on Danya's liability, thus neutralizing the purpose of the rule. Impelled by a distaste for liars, however, and also by the probative weight of the evidence (albeit, on a forbidden issue), some courts admit the evidence on the ground that it comes in to impeach, not to prove liability or amount. See, e.g., Brocklesby v. United States, 767 F.2d 1288 (9th Cir. 1985); County of Hennepin v. AFG Indus., Inc., 726 F.2d 149 (8th Cir. 1984). In 2006, FRE 408(a) was amended to resolve this dispute, by making settlement efforts and statements inadmissible "to impeach by a prior inconsistent statement or contradiction." In making this change, the drafters again opted strongly in favor of the policy of promoting the settlement of lawsuits and (by allowing probable liars to get away with it) further eroded the rationale that the evidence the rule excludes is weak and makes little contribution to getting at the truth in the matter before the court.

[33] Compare United States v. Prewitt, 34 F.3d 436 (7th Cir. 1994) (materials admissible) with United States v. Bailey, 327 F.3d 1131 (10th Cir. 2003) (materials inadmissible).

incantations. A deal was struck in which Rule 408's exclusion remained largely intact except when the government, as a "regulatory, investigative or enforcement authority" was involved in civil negotiations and later sought use of compromise materials generated in the civil proceedings.[34]

Problem IV-3. Driver, driving Owner's car without permission, collides with Plaintiff at an intersection fracturing Plaintiff's tibia. Plaintiff sues Owner, claiming that the defective condition of the brakes on Owner's car caused the accident. Plaintiff calls Driver to testify that the brakes were not working and the accident was not Driver's fault. Owner wants to introduce evidence showing that Driver settled out of court with Plaintiff by paying Plaintiff $500. **Is Owner permitted to do so? Would the situation be different if Plaintiff had been paralyzed? If Plaintiff were only bruised but claimed that he suffered recurrent nightmares since the accident?**

Problem IV-4. In the same case as in the preceding problem, Plaintiff and Owner engage in pretrial settlement negotiations during which Plaintiff says, "Look, you and I both know that the accident was Driver's fault, but he and I have settled, and I know you're going to lose if a jury gets this case, especially because Driver will testify for me—so let's settle. I'll take $1,000." **Can Owner introduce this offer and accompanying statement into evidence?** Suppose Owner begins negotiations by saying, "Look, I can't waste my time. You'll take $100 to get off my back or you'll find there are a lot worse accidents than the one you were just in." **Admissible?**

Problem IV-5. On the same facts as the preceding two problems, suppose that immediately after hearing of the accident, Owner called Plaintiff and said, "I'm truly sorry about the accident. I've been meaning to fix those lousy brakes. Will you take a couple hundred bucks and call it even?" **Admissible? On what issues?**

C. NOLO CONTENDERE PLEAS, WITHDRAWN GUILTY PLEAS AND STATEMENTS DURING PLEA DISCUSSIONS

FRE 410 provides:

(a) **Prohibited Uses**. In a civil or criminal case, evidence of the following is not admissible against the defendant who made the plea or participated in the plea discussions:

---

[34] See Robet A. Weninger, Amended Federal Rule of Evidence 408: Trapping the Unwary, 26 Rev. Litig. 401 (2007); Mikah K. Story Thompson, To Speak or Not to Speak? Navigating the Treacherous Waters of Parallel Investigations Following the Amendment of Federal Rule of Evidence 408, 76 U. Cin. L. Rev. 939 (2008).

(1) a guilty plea that was later withdrawn;

(2) a nolo contendere plea;

(3) a statement made during a proceeding on either of those pleas under Federal Rule of Criminal Procedure 11 or a comparable state procedure; or

(4) a statement made during plea discussions with an attorney for the prosecuting authority if the discussions did not result in a guilty plea or they resulted in a later-withdrawn guilty plea.

(b) **Exceptions.** The court may admit a statement described in Rule 410(a)(3) or (4):

(1) in any proceeding in which another statement made during the same plea or plea discussions has been introduced, if in fairness the statements ought to be considered together; or

(2) in a criminal proceeding for perjury or false statement, if the defendant made the statement under oath, on the record, and with counsel present.

FRE 410 follows prior common law practice in excluding evidence of pleas of nolo contendere and of withdrawn guilty pleas. Unlike the other "relevance rules" *this exclusion makes the evidence inadmissible "against the defendant" for all purposes rather than inadmissible to prove some particular claim.*

The two main arguments for this rule are similar to those for the exclusion of offers to compromise civil claims: to avoid misestimation by the jury, and to encourage—or at least not discourage—guilty pleas. The misestimation rationale may be stronger in the criminal than in the civil setting, however. Even jurors who can appreciate why an "innocent" tort defendant might offer a nuisance value settlement, might find it difficult to understand why an innocent criminal defendant would accept jail time and the stigma of conviction.[35] This is particularly true because jurors typically are not told about, and might well underestimate, (1) the time the defendant would have to serve if convicted of the offense originally charged, rather than the lesser offense to which she pled guilty, or (2) the sentencing advantages of pleading guilty or nolo to the crime charged. We have already mentioned these and other reasons why an innocent defendant might plead guilty.[36] In addition, it is often difficult to infer

---

[35] Research on individuals wrongfully convicted of murder or rape indicate that false confessions occur with some frequency in these cases. See Samuel R. Gross et al., Exonerations in the United States: 1989 Through 2003, 95 J. Crim. L. & Criminology 523 (2005); Brandon L. Garrett, The Substance of False Confessions, 62 Stan. L. Rev. 1051 (2010). If people will confess falsely to serious crimes, it is not surprising that the incentives available for pleading guilty yield false pleas.

[36] See supra, Section I.C., pp. 290–292.

the degree of a defendant's consciousness of guilt from either the charge to which she pleads guilty (which may be determined by the prosecutor's charging or plea negotiating policies or by either party's view of the appropriate sentence) or the sentence imposed which can reflect judicial discretion within the limits set by the crime charged (which some jurisdictions insulate from the bargaining process by leaving it entirely to the judge).

Plea bargaining has never been popular and is sometimes subject to intense criticism. It has however, become accepted as a necessary method of moving criminal cases through the courts, many of which dispose of 80 or 90 percent of their criminal dockets in this manner.[37] Recognizing that the defendants who "cop a plea" are serving the needs of the system while serving their own interests, FRE 410 promotes plea bargains by generally protecting defendants from having their actions and statements used against them in court. Here, the rationales for FRE 408 and FRE 410 are not identical. In moving from the civil to the criminal setting, the greater significance of social and institutional considerations (e.g., law enforcement policies, administrative efficiency and the need for public faith in the outcome) makes it less appropriate to facilitate a free market in settlements and more important to preserve governmental and judicial control over the outcome of the suit.

Federal law and the law of most states grant courts the discretion to accept pleas of nolo contendere, or "no contest," at least in misdemeanor cases. A plea of nolo contendere avoids one major consequence of a plea of guilty. A valid guilty plea may be introduced in a subsequent civil or criminal case as the pleading party's admission of any fact necessary to a finding of guilt of the offense to which the party pled guilty. By contrast, under FRE 410 and similar rules, a plea of nolo contendere can *never* be used as an admission of facts essential to a finding of guilt, because the rule prevents the opposing party from presenting evidence of a nolo contendere plea.[38] FRE 410 thus creates a mild stimulus for "nolo" pleas. "Nolo" pleas also provide a face-saving mechanism for defendants seeking

---

[37] See *Blackledge v. Allison*, 431 U.S. 63, 71 (1977) ("whatever might be the situation in an ideal world, the fact is that the guilty plea and the often concomitant plea bargain are important components of this country's criminal justice system. Properly administered they can benefit all concerned.") This acceptance has been formalized in the federal sentencing guidelines which typically provide sentence reductions for those who plead guilty.

[38] When used as evidence of guilt of the offense charged, a guilty plea is hearsay—i.e., the pleading party's prior statement that she committed the offense, which is offered to prove that she did. Nonetheless, as we discuss in Chapter Six, Section III.B.3., pp. 595–597, the plea is admissible under the "party admissions" exception to the hearsay rule. A judgment of conviction, whether based on a guilty plea or a jury verdict, is also hearsay if offered as evidence of the facts necessary to a finding of guilt—it is the convicting court's statement that the facts necessary to a finding of guilt were proved beyond a reasonable doubt. FRE 803(22) creates a hearsay exception for felony convictions used to show the facts that were necessary to support the convictions, if the convictions were "entered after a trial or guilty plea." Like FRE 410, however, FRE 803(22) protects defendants who plead nolo contendere by withholding the hearsay exception from judgments of conviction based on nolo contendere pleas.

the benefits of pleading—e.g., less stringent sentences under the Federal Sentencing Guidelines—but who are unwilling to admit guilt.

The plea of nolo contendere is particularly important in situations in which criminal liability and civil liability attach to the same conduct. This is especially so when multiple plaintiffs are likely to claim civil damages stemming from the criminal conduct, and most especially so, when the defendant is a corporation that cannot be imprisoned but only fined. Under the Clayton Act, for example, final criminal judgments in actions brought by the United States under the antitrust laws provide prima facie evidence in subsequent private civil actions that the guilty party has committed antitrust violations subject to treble damages. The Act, however, exempts "consent judgments . . . entered before any testimony has been taken,"[39] which the courts have construed to include pleas of nolo contendere but not pleas of guilty. A corporation charged with a criminal antitrust violation thus has a strong incentive to plead nolo contendere, even if the probability of conviction seems low, because the criminal penalty (a fine) is likely to be substantially smaller than the damages that might be awarded in a series of private treble damage actions in which a conviction would be admissible and potentially devastating evidence of liability. FRE 410 provides similar protection to corporate defendants who plead nolo contendere to criminal charges in antitrust, securities, oil spill, airplane crash and similar cases.

Withdrawn guilty pleas pose special problems. The federal rule and most state rules make withdrawn pleas inadmissible in both criminal and civil trials. When guilty pleas may be withdrawn only with the court's permission, a withdrawal lowers a plea's probative value because the findings necessary to permit the withdrawal—that the plea was not entirely voluntary or fully informed, or was otherwise defective— undermine its value as an admission of guilt. The argument based on low probative value is weaker in jurisdictions that permit withdrawal of guilty pleas as a matter of right. Accordingly, some such jurisdictions admit evidence of the withdrawn plea while allowing defendants to explain their actions. Others forbid the evidence on one or more of several grounds: that jurors will persistently overestimate the probative weight of the withdrawn plea, however valid the defendant's explanation; that courts should not penalize defendants who elect to go to trial by obliging them to waive their Fifth Amendment privilege against testifying in order to explain the withdrawal; and that the workload of the courts might increase if withdrawn pleas were admissible and if, as a result, fewer defendants pleaded guilty in the first place.

Defense attorneys (who typically negotiate plea bargains with prosecutors) rarely make—or allow their clients to make—unqualified (i.e., nonhypothetical) admissions of guilt during plea negotiations.

---

[39]   15 U.S.C. § 16(a).

Judges, who have a strong interest in facilitating free-ranging discussions that may lead to plea agreements, resist admitting such improvident statements when they are made. FRE 410 formalizes this resistance by excluding such statements at trial, for all purposes, with two narrow exceptions.[40] The settlement value of free-ranging discussions notwithstanding, rule makers and judges have, since 1980, progressively narrowed the protection offered defendants by FRE 410. They have reshaped the rule in ways that allow an expanding range of statements made by defendants when dealing with government representatives to be used at trial after plea negotiations have broken down.[41] One of the most powerful tools in limiting the reach of FRE 410 is the prosecution's refusal to engage in plea negotiations unless defendants agree beforehand to waive their FRE 410 objections if the prosecutor offers statements made during negotiations to impeach the defendant's contradictory testimony at trial (assuming the case gets that far). The Supreme Court has enforced a "knowing and voluntary" advance waiver of FRE 410 objection under these circumstances.[42]

FRE 410 is apparently asymmetrical because it only excludes evidence offered "against the *defendant*." The rule does not bar the defense from rebutting the state's case or bolstering its own case using otherwise admissible statements made by prosecutors during plea negotiations. If a defendant introduces such a statement, however, the exception in subsection (b)(1) lets the government introduce other statements made in the negotiations—including ones damaging to the defendant—if they place in context or otherwise elucidate the statement introduced by the defendant. In practice, moreover, courts rarely allow defendants to introduce evidence that a prosecutor offered to accept a plea or said that the state's case was weak.[43] This practice is a sensible application of FRE 403. A prosecutor's belief about the defendant's factual guilt, although not irrelevant, is merely an opinion—one that is particularly susceptible to misestimation by jurors and is explainable only through testimony by a lawyer in the case. The drafters of FRE 410 make

---

[40] FRE 410(b)(1) allows the prosecutor to use evidence of such a statement if the defendant introduced another statement from the same negotiation and fairness requires that the jury hear both statements; and FRE 410(b)(2) permits evidence of a statement made under oath in plea negotiations that is itself the subject of a perjury prosecution, if it was made on the record in the presence of counsel.

[41] See Michael H. Graham, Plea Bargaining Pursuant to Fed. R. Evid. 410: "Criminal Defendant Beware!!!," 44 No. 6 Crim. Law Bull. Art. 8 (2008).

[42] United States v. Mezzanatto, 513 U.S. 196 (1995). In a separate opinion, three of the seven Justices in the majority expressed uncertainty whether FRE 410 objections can be waived in advance as to statements the government offers in its case-in-chief and not just for impeachment purposes. A number of lower court cases decided since *Mezzanatto* have, however, approved such use. See, e.g., United States v. Young 223 F.3d 905 (8th Cir. 2000).

[43] See, e.g., United States v. Verdoorn, 528 F.2d 103 (8th Cir. 1976).

clear in their commentary that the "against the defendant" limitation implies no disapproval of this practice.[44]

The exception in subsection (b)(2) applies almost exclusively to statements made in the course of proceedings under Rule 11 of the Federal Rules of Criminal Procedure or other formal judicial proceedings in which guilty pleas are offered, because only such proceedings are likely to be under oath, on the record, and in the presence of counsel. Before accepting a plea, a court must be convinced—typically by the defendant's statements on the record—that he is competent to plead and that the plea is voluntary and has a basis in fact. The defendant's statements in this context are protected by FRE 410, unless they were made under oath (as is required in some but not all courts), in which event subsection (b)(2) makes the statements admissible against the defendant in a prosecution for perjury allegedly committed in the plea proceeding. Perjury charges might be brought, for example, against a defendant who is alleged to have made false exculpatory statements during plea proceedings in hopes of convincing the judge to impose a lighter sentence.

FRE 410 has been amended twice. The most important difference between the current version and the one it replaced is that the existing rule only protects statements made in the course of "plea discussions with an attorney for the prosecuting authority," while the former rule also protected unilateral offers to plead guilty made by defendants to officials other than prosecuting attorneys. By requiring formalities that are largely in the control of government attorneys—actual negotiations and a government attorney's participation—the current rule avoids factually difficult questions that previously arose when defendants sought the rule's protection for what looked suspiciously like run-of-the-mill admissions to police officers, IRS agents, postal inspectors and the like. The revised rule serves the *government's* and the *courts'* interests, but it risks prejudicing the legally unsophisticated defendant who offers a police investigator inculpatory information in the belief, encouraged by the investigator, that a plea is being negotiated. Some judges have begun to resist abuses by extending FRE 410 to statements made during plea negotiations between defendants and nonlawyer government agents acting or purporting to act at the behest of government lawyers. The *Miranda* rule, due process constraints on police officers' ability to make and then break promises to criminal suspects, and the courts' supervisory powers over police conduct may provide additional safeguards against the introduction of admissions made under a reasonable expectation that they were part of confidential plea negotiations.

---

[44] Multiple defendant cases can present problems if a defendant, or a prosecutor in response to a defendant, seeks to introduce plea negotiation statements prejudicial to a co-defendant. In that event, the judge must at least instruct the jury not to use the statements against the codefendant, and she probably should grant the codefendant a separate trial upon request.

Courts still confront the difficult task of distinguishing conversations between defendants and prosecutors directed towards possible pleas from those directed towards obtaining confessions. The courts generally apply a two-tiered test: Did the defendant have and exhibit a subjective understanding that he was negotiating a plea at the time he made the statements in question? And if so, was that understanding reasonable under the circumstances? As interpreted, the rule mainly protects actions by, or in the presence of, defense attorneys.

Problem IV-6. Betty Breakin is charged with burglary, a felony. The prosecutor, Ajay Ada, offers to reduce the charge to a misdemeanor, loitering near a building at night, if Breakin pleads guilty. Breakin refuses, and Ada proceeds to trial on the felony charge. **Can Breakin introduce evidence of Ada's offer to accept a misdemeanor plea?** Assume defense counsel asks Ada, "Why the big reduction?" and Ada responds, "Frankly, I don't believe the principal eyewitness." **Can Breakin introduce this statement?** Suppose Ada instead replies, "Your client's prints don't match the prints on the burglar's tool found at the scene," and Ada introduces no burglar's tools or fingerprint evidence at trial. **Is Ada's statement admissible?**

Problem IV-7. Assume that in the plea negotiations referred to in the preceding problem Breakin, in defense counsel's presence, told Ada, "No way I'm gonna plead. I was at the movies when that burglary went down, and I got two friends who was with me." **Can Ada introduce this statement if the defense rests without presenting any evidence? If Breakin testifies that she was home in bed at the time of the alleged burglary? If Breakin presents her two roommates, each of whom testifies that she was home in bed when the burglary occurred? As defense counsel, what factors would you consider before resting without presenting any evidence? Before presenting Breakin's or the roommates' testimony that she was home in bed? If Ada had refused to negotiate a plea unless Breakin agreed to waive any FRE 410 objections at trial, what effect should and would the trial judge give to Breakin's pretrial waiver agreement in the situations addressed in each of the preceding questions?**

Herman ® is reprinted with permission from Laughing Stock Licensing Inc., Ottawa, Canada. All Rights Reserved.

D. PAYMENT OF MEDICAL EXPENSES

FRE 409 restates the common law with respect to evidence of the payment of medical and similar expenses after accidents:

> Evidence of furnishing, promising to pay, or offering to pay medical, hospital, or similar expenses resulting from an injury is not admissible to prove liability for the injury.

There are two familiar justifications for the rule. (1) Because many people act from humanitarian motives in providing post-accident medical care the probative weight of any implied admission of liability is low, but prejudice from juror overvaluation of the evidence may be high. One manifestation of this rationale is that in some states the exclusionary rule applies only if a humanitarian motivation is shown. The fact that many insurance policies now authorize limited payments for medical expenses of injured third parties, regardless of the policyholder's negligence, adds weight to the relevance-based justification. Some have suggested that the humanitarian rationale may, in fact, mask hard-headed business motivations which have led many insurance companies to adopt "advance payment programs" because studies indicate that these tend to decrease the number of lawsuits and reduce total outlays.[45]

---

[45] Charles Alan Wright and Kenneth Graham, Jr., 23 Fed. Prac. & Proced. Evid. § 5322.

(2) Paying or offering to pay for post-accident medical care is socially desirable conduct and should not be discouraged. Partially undermining this policy, courts traditionally have treated admissions made in connection with an offer or the furnishing of medical care as admissible to prove liability, judging them to have high probative value. FRE 409 follows this pattern by excluding evidence of payments or offers to pay while not mentioning associated "statements." A middle position favored by some authorities is to exclude accompanying statements only if they are inextricably linked to the offer or provision of medical payments.

FRE 409 has no "exceptions" clause, but still excludes the evidence *only* when it is offered to prove the payer's liability. The evidence is not excluded when offered for other purposes, such as showing the defendant's responsibility for the condition that caused the accident. FRE 409's formulation shows that the "exceptions" clauses in the other categorical balancing rules are, strictly speaking, superfluous. With or without listed exceptions, a rule that excludes evidence for one purpose (here, "to prove liability") does not prevent its admission for other purposes.

There have been some recent efforts to extend the protections offered by FRE 409 to statements of regret or apology, most particularly in the medical malpractice context. If protection is warranted for such statements, it would seem far better to craft purpose-made legislation, a step that has been taken in a significant number of states.[46]

Problem IV-8. Rollo Rico, relishing a chaufferless spin in his Rolls Royce, ran over Sluggo Snyder while Sluggo was crossing the street. Rollo, rushed out of his Rolls, revived Sluggo and said, "I'm so remorseful. I feel just rotten. I've never run this contraption before. I don't know what happened, but I'm sure the responsibility is all mine. I want you to receive the best medical care. Please, repair to the Ritz Hospital immediately, and I'll reimburse your expenses there." Sluggo went to the Ritz, a luxurious private hospital, rather than to the public hospital to which he ordinarily would have gone, and ran up $80,000 in health care expenses during a twelve day recuperation. When Sluggo was released, Rollo refused to pay, saying, "Because you recklessly ran in front of my car, I have no obligation to remit the monies you request." **If Sluggo sues Rollo in tort, which of Rollo's post-accident statements can come in on the issue of negligence? Can they come in on any other issue? Can Sluggo sue Rollo on some other theory under which the statements are admissible?**

---

[46] See Jennifer Robbennolt, Apologies and Legal Settlement: An Empirical Examination, 102 Mich. L. Rev. 460, 470–73 (2003).

E. LIABILITY INSURANCE

FRE 411 codifies the common law on evidence of liability insurance:

Evidence that a person was or was not insured against liability is not admissible to prove whether the person acted negligently or otherwise wrongfully. But the court may admit this evidence for another purpose, such as proving a witness's bias or prejudice or proving agency, ownership, or control.

Evidence of liability insurance is inadmissible if offered by a plaintiff as a basis for inferring that an insured defendant, having no fear of paying accident costs, was careless at a particular time. Such evidence also is inadmissible if offered by a defendant who wishes to argue that low policy limits or a lack of insurance gave her an incentive to be careful. The low probative value of insurance evidence is revealed by the fact that, but for the rule, the same parties just as plausibly might argue for the same inferences based on the *opposite* evidence—plaintiffs might claim that defendants who do not purchase liability insurance are reckless generally; defendants might claim that their care in purchasing liability protection reflects their care generally.[47]

As noted in Chapter Three, Section III.B., insurance evidence also may pose a risk of prejudice because it may lower a jury's regret at inaccurately finding the insured party liable. Social scientific studies, however, question this expectation. People typically assume (correctly) that most civil defendants have insurance, and subjects in jury experiments are not much affected by evidence of its presence or

---

[47] Even if FRE 411 did not exclude evidence of liability insurance offered for these purposes, FRE 404 would do so. See Chapter Five, Section II.A., pp. 347–356. Another way to illustrate the near irrelevance and possible prejudice of evidence about liability insurance offered to prove or disprove liability is by considering why jurors *care* about insurance in tort cases. They care not because the information helps them decide liability, but because they are curious to know whether the defendant or an insurance company will pay any damages they award. Evidence offered to satisfy this curiosity is, of course, irrelevant; it makes no material fact relating to liability or damages more or less likely than before the evidence was offered. That jurors are more likely to use insurance evidence for this irrelevant purpose than for its minimal contribution to an assessment of liability provides an independent reason for FRE 411, *if* the forbidden use is prejudicial in some way—the question to which we next turn in the text. It should be noted, however, that one recent study suggests that state initiatives mandating automobile insurance coverage appear to *reduce precaution* among the formerly uninsured and lead to an appreciable increase in accidents and fatalities, displaying a so-called "moral hazard" effect. Alma Cohen, et al., The Effect of Automobile Insurance and Accident Liability Laws on Traffic Fatalities, 47 J. of Law and Econ. 357 (2004).

Whatever its effect on behavior the presence or absence of insurance is of immense importance in determining the context in which civil trials take place. It determines who sues (plaintiffs injured by insured or adequately self-insured defendants); who is sued; who defends and pays for suits; who pays damages; and what damages are likely to be collected—which, in turn, drives settlements. It is the mechanism through which the various incentives that constitute our system of tort compensation usually operate. Is it worrisome, or merely ironic, that a fact so central to the legal system is inadmissible when cases actually go to trial? See Samuel R. Gross, Make-Believe: The Rules Excluding Evidence of Character and Liability Insurance, 49 Hast. L. Rev. 843 (1998); Shari S. Diamond, et al., Blindfolding the Jury, 52 Law and Contemp. Probs. 247 (1989).

absence.[48]   Still, plaintiffs' lawyers believe in the power of insurance evidence and typically do what they can to let the jurors know that the defendant is insured.   Lawyers often achieve this goal by (1) asking prospective jurors on voir dire about their connections to the insurance business, (2) using evidence of liability insurance to show the defendant's responsibility for the individual or instrumentality that caused the accident, or (3) impeaching investigators or expert witnesses by showing that an insurance company hired them to testify for the defendant.

Ultimately, FRE 411 is so easy to circumvent that it accomplishes little or nothing that is not already achieved by FRE 402 and FRE 403. It does, however, impose additional litigation costs (rulings under FRE 411 may be easier to challenge on appeal than rulings under FRE 403), and it may prejudice *uninsured* defendants by preventing them from disabusing jurors of the assumption that all defendants are insured.   For these reasons, many commentators argue that the rule should be abandoned. The rule's survival despite its weaknesses may reveal the power of "repeat player" insurance company lawyers, who value the rule not only for its limited impact at trial but also because it generates issues on appeal in the many cases in which insurance evidence is admitted.[49]

Problem IV-9. In the same situation as in problem 8 above, Rollo has no insurance. **May he introduce evidence that he lacks insurance to support his argument that he was driving with extreme caution on the day in question? May Rollo introduce evidence that his Rolls Royce was custom built for him and that he has always lavished the greatest love and care on it, in order to prove that he was driving cautiously at the time?**

Problem IV-10. Silver-Screen (S-S), a movie production company, buys its film stock from PhotoFair (PF), a film manufacturer. Each canister of

---

[48]   See, e.g., Valerie P. Hans & William Lofquist, Jurors' Judgments of Business Liability in Torts Cases: Implications for the Litigation Explosion Debate, 26 Law & Soc. Rev. 85 (1992) (jurors are skeptical of claims against business defendants and try to moderate damage awards); Elizabeth Loftus, Insurance Advertising and Jury Awards, 65 A.B.A.J. 68 (1979) (mock jurors exposed to evidence that the defendant is insured award *lower* damages than jurors from whom such evidence is withheld).   Shari S. Diamond & Neil Vidmar, Jury Room Ruminations on Forbidden Topics, 87 Va. L. Rev. 1857, 1875–1896 (2001) (analysis of the deliberations of forty real Arizona juries found unauthorized juror discussions of insurance in 85% of the cases, with an average of four mentions per case. Most often speculation focused on whether the plaintiff had already received funds from his or her own insurance company. Many jurors were inclined to reject the collateral source rule, which requires jurors in tort cases to disregard whether an injured party has received first-party insurance payments.)

[49]   Having legitimate arguments on appeal is particularly valuable for defendants. In a few cases, such arguments prevail. In many more cases, the risk that the argument they will prevail—and the delays in enforcing judgments while appeals occur—put pressure on winning plaintiffs to settle pending appeals for less than the juries' verdicts. Even if the value of such arguments is small in any single case, their aggregate value may be large for insurance companies, which defend many cases.

film contains a notice stating that in the event that the film provided by PF should prove defective, PF's liability is limited to the replacement cost of the film.   No S-S executive ever opens new canisters of film, and the cinematographers who do open them discard the notices unread. Upon developing fifty canisters of film shot for its new epic *Cast of Thousands*, S-S found that scratches caused more than half the exposed film to be worthless. S-S sued PF for the cost of reshooting the ruined film and for lost profits caused by the delay. PF responded that the scratches were due not to defective film but to S-S's negligence in developing the film and, in the alternative, that PF's liability, if any, was limited to the cost of replacing the damaged film. S-S denied the allegation of negligence and claimed it was not bound by the disclaimers in the canisters because none of its executives had seen them. PF responded that it was industry custom to limit liability to replacement costs and that, as experienced film producers, S-S executives would know of the custom whether or not they read the notices. PF wants to show that S-S had an insurance policy that indemnified S-S against defective film and other hazards. S-S argues that the evidence is inadmissible under FRE 411 and also under FRE 402 and FRE 403 because S-S is only suing for losses that were not covered by insurance. **On what ground, if any, is evidence of the insurance policy admissible?**

F. SIMILAR HAPPENINGS

The fact that trial judges repeatedly balance the probative weight and the prejudice associated with a particular type of evidence need not lead to well defined or codified rules governing the admissibility of the evidence. Absent policy considerations extrinsic to the ascertainment of truth in the particular case, and especially absent "repeat players" such as insurance companies that consistently seek a particular ruling on certain types of evidence, even recurrent problems of misestimation and prejudice may not cause a departure from the usual practice of balancing competing considerations on a case-by-case basis under FRE 403 or its common law analogues. Evidence of similar happenings is a case in point.

A plaintiff in a negligence action may offer evidence that other individuals tripped and fell on a certain stair tread in order to show that the tread was defective, or that the defect posed an unreasonable risk, or that the proprietor knew of the risk, or that the condition could cause an accident and injuries like those suffered by the plaintiff. Or a party to a condemnation proceeding may offer evidence of the price at which similar parcels of land are selling to show that the opponent's suggested price is unreasonable. Even though "similar event" evidence of this sort often is offered, and judges often are suspicious of it, most jurisdictions—and the Federal Rules—have no hard and fast rules governing its use. Instead, objections to evidence of similar happenings trigger case-by-case analyses of probative value and the risk of prejudice under FRE 403 and its common law analogues.

In many cases, the relevance of other experiences similar to the one at issue is obvious. Nonetheless, the courts approach evidence of other happenings skeptically because of its capacity to mislead the jury. Pressed to visualize what happened on a particular occasion based on incomplete information, jurors may naturally rely on a more complete and vivid image of what happened on *another* occasion, if that image is available. In that situation, jurors may overvalue evidence of the other event, while ignoring ways in which the two events differ. Aware of this problem, courts demand proof that two events are substantially similar before allowing information about one event to influence judgment about what happened in the course of the other. This solution, however, does not eliminate all the problems with similar events evidence. In deciding whether to admit such evidence, courts also consider whether the evidence will require delays to allow the opposing party to respond, whether it will cause excessive attention to collateral issues such as the accuracy with which the other event is reported, whether it will confuse jurors about which event is in issue, and whether it will prejudice jurors by informing them that the event giving rise to the trial is not the only such incident in which the party has been involved.

What counts as "substantial" similarity varies from court to court, case to case and issue to issue, although courts almost always pay close attention to similarity in place and time. In the stair tread example, proof of other accidents on different stairs may say little about the safety of the stair on which the plaintiff tripped. Likewise, an accident in the winter on a stair that was icy may have little bearing on what happened in the summer when the stair was dry. And an accident on the same stair two years before the accident in question probably would be excluded given the likelihood that conditions changed between the two accidents.

Skepticism about similar events evidence declines as the uniformity of conditions across space and time increases. (This may account for the fact that judicial receptivity to similar events evidence seems to have increased as mass production and mass culture have taken hold.) In the stair tread example, if the tread were of the same age and material throughout, a court might allow a plaintiff to show that frayed treads on other stairs caused people to trip in much the same way as the plaintiff claims to have tripped on the stair in question, or to show that tripping on frayed treads can cause injuries like those suffered by the plaintiff. Evidence of prior accidents on other stairs is especially likely to be admitted to show that the defendant had reason to inspect all the treads, assuming the plaintiff can show that the defendant knew of the earlier accidents.

The counterpart of the plaintiff's use of similar accidents to help prove liability is the defendant's use of the absence of other accidents to show a safe condition, or to show that the defendant was reasonable in not anticipating a dangerous condition. The fact that hundreds of people climbed the same staircase on the same day as the plaintiff without tripping suggests that a clumsy plaintiff and not a defective tread caused the fall. The probative value of such evidence is limited, however, because of the tenuous link between the number of complaints and the number of mishaps that actually may have occurred. Stair climbers other than the plaintiff may have tripped but not fallen, or fallen without being hurt, or been hurt without complaining, or complained to someone other than the witness who testifies to the lack of complaints. Moreover, the plaintiff may have been the first to pass after a deteriorating condition became sufficiently dangerous to cause a serious accident. These difficulties have led some courts that admit evidence of similar accidents to show danger to forbid evidence of good safety records. Most courts, however, admit both kinds of evidence when warranted by the requisite balancing—which usually means that evidence of the absence of accidents encounters more resistance. The absence of complaints is uniformly admissible when relevant to show lack of notice.

Similar events evidence poses problems in contracts as well as negligence contexts. When the other contract involves *only* nonparties, nearly all courts exclude it. Some courts also follow a blanket practice of refusing to admit evidence of the terms of a contract between a party and a third party to show the terms of a contract between the plaintiff and the defendant. In this situation, the epigram *res inter alios acta* (a thing done between others) often is invoked as a substitute for close analysis. There is some sense to the epigram when bargaining power and skill are not evenly distributed and their distribution matters. The fact that Honest Joe, the used car dealer, offered Tough Tessa a 2010 Prius for $13,000 does not mean that he did not sell the same car to Soft Simon for $15,000. Even in this situation, however, the earlier offer is clearly *relevant* to the price agreed to by Joe and Simon, and some courts would admit it on this issue. Probative weight increases and prejudice decreases when business practices are more uniform than on used car lots.

Standardization or fungibility also explains the courts' willingness to admit evidence of similar sales (including sales between nonparties), as well as price lists and market reports, to establish the fair market value of nonunique items. Even as to unique items, such as jewels and thoroughbred horses, evidence of other sales may be offered as the basis for an expert appraiser's opinion. In the case of land, sales of other parcels may be admitted into evidence directly, assuming a showing of substantial similarity.

In the next chapter, we discuss limitations on evidence of a person's prior acts to show his propensity to act in a particular way. As we point out there, evidence of a person's prior acts often is relevant (and sometimes is admissible) to show things other than propensity. For example, other acts may reveal a party's guilty knowledge, tortious or criminal intent, or plan or design. Evidence of similar acts also may be useful to impeach a party or a witness by undermining the validity of claims or the credibility of testimony, as when an unusual claim about how an accident occurred is shown to be identical to a claim on which the plaintiff recovered years before.[50] When similar acts evidence is offered for some reason other than to show propensity, the considerations discussed in this section—primarily, the courts' insistence upon proof of substantial similarity—come into play.

Another issue at the intersection of similar happenings and propensity evidence is the admissibility of evidence of an individual's alleged "accident proneness." When used to show negligent causation of an accident, the courts resist such evidence.[51] Sometimes, however, courts admit evidence of a particular individual's reputation for accident proneness or involvement in a series of accidents in a suit alleging an employer's negligence for hiring or continuing to employ that individual.

Problem IV-11. While descending a stairway in a theater, Plaintiff fell and broke her ankle after catching her foot in a space between the end of a row of seats and the edge of a step. She sues, claiming negligence. **Can Defendant introduce the theater manager's testimony that in fifteen years no one had suffered a similar accident when leaving that row? When leaving other rows? Can Plaintiff present the testimony of a witness who five years earlier sprained his ankle in a similar space in a row twenty feet closer to the screen than the row where Plaintiff's accident occurred? Can Plaintiff offer**

---

[50] Courts resist admitting evidence of a party's claims or testimony in other cases to undermine the credibility of the party's claims and testimony in the current case, unless the prior and current claims or testimony either are virtually identical or are quite similar and the prior claims or testimony are shown to have been fraudulent. Only then is a dishonest intent clear.

[51] The courts' resistance to such evidence makes sense. An individual who is clumsy or is employed in a risky activity may have an exceptionally high number of accidents without ever engaging in behavior that rises to the level of negligence or contributory negligence. Also, involvement in a series of accidents may simply involve a run of bad luck. Assume, for example, that 100 accidents occur in a village of 100 people each year and that the accidents are assigned to people at random by drawing names out of a hat and replacing the names after each drawing. Many people in the village would draw their fair share of accidents: one. Others would be lucky and draw no accidents, while some unlucky souls would draw two, three or even four accidents. Although the odds that any one individual would draw four accidents are very low, the odds that one out of all 100 individuals would be so unlucky may be fairly high. To describe the unlucky individual who does draw four accidents as "accident prone" would be factually inaccurate, even though he may *appear* accident prone to jurors who overlook the fact that *someone* is likely to end up in the unfortunate predicament by chance alone.

evidence of three similar injuries that occurred in a different theater that was designed by the architect who designed Defendant's building?

Problem IV-12. Plaintiff is suing for injuries alleged to have occurred when alighting from a bus. Defendant wishes to show that during the previous year the plaintiff brought negligence actions against two other individuals. Defendant wants the court to instruct the jury that it may consider how unusual it is for an individual not engaged in hazardous activities to suffer repeated injuries due to the negligence of different people during a short period of time. **Would you admit the evidence? Would you give the requested instruction?**

Problem IV-13. Another Plaintiff sues a bus company, claiming that a bus driver negligently started too suddenly while Plaintiff was alighting. Defendant wishes to show that, during a four-months period, Plaintiff and his relatives (sisters, cousins and aunts) brought 17 claims against the same bus company for injuries allegedly sustained while alighting from buses. The plaintiff made one of these claims. **Is the evidence admissible?**

III. CONCLUSION

In discussing the various "relevance rules" in this chapter, we have suggested that a single theme unites most of them. As we will see in Chapter Five, the same theme applies to the character evidence rules (FRE 404–406 and 413–415) and to the rape victim's shield rule (FRE 412). In general, the low probative value associated with the excluded evidence has freed the courts and codifiers to give special attention to other values that are served by categorical exclusion. The following factors most commonly lead to this conclusion (particularly when "repeat player" opponents of the evidence persistently argue for exclusion): the risk that jurors will overestimate the probative weight of the evidence; the possibilities of confusion, surprise, and waste of time inherent in disputes over collateral facts; the danger of prejudice to parties who may be judged on the basis of actions unrelated to those in issue in the case; and extrinsic policy reasons peculiar to specific rules.

Even if the types of evidence we have been discussing generally have low probative value, they are not worthless. These forbidden kinds of evidence almost always have some probative value, and on occasion they may be quite persuasive. If there were no other substantial reasons to exclude the evidence, the appropriate decision would be to admit.

This discussion of the "relevance rules," with its emphasis on reasons for exclusion, previews not only the next chapter but the rest of the book. Much of evidence law deals with categorical justifications for excluding evidence that has some probative value. Hearsay statements are excluded, despite their relevance, because we fear that they are comparatively unreliable and that the jury will be unable to give them their proper weight. Privileged communications are excluded in order to protect valued relationships or to promote certain behavior. We reject much opinion evidence because there are certain issues on which we want the jury's decision to be entirely its own. In these areas and others, there is a tension between the factors that justify exclusion and the value of the evidence, if properly used. As we already have seen—and will see again—this tension often leads to more exceptions than there are rules.

We close this chapter with a fundamental question—not only about the rules we have just analyzed, but about many yet to be discussed: *Are the rules necessary? Would it make more sense to abolish the specific rules and exceptions and instead allow courts to decide these matters guided by common sense and the principles specified in FRE 402 and 403?*

ADDITIONAL PROBLEMS

Problem IV-14. Pat was injured while walking down the west side of Broadway near a site where the Daft Construction Co. was putting up a building. The sidewalk near the site was closed to pedestrians, so Pat walked in the adjacent street near the curb. As Pat walked past, the operator of a small crane on the site swiveled the crane around, knocking Pat down and seriously injuring her neck. At the time, no human look-out was posted on the sidewalk or in the street, but signs in various languages directed pedestrians to walk on the sidewalk on the other side of the street. Pat sues Daft alleging negligence. The jurisdiction applies a comparative fault rule. A reasonable estimate of Pat's damages is $1,000,000. Daft offers to settle for $100,000.

a) In addition to the above facts, Pat's evidence shows that the forewoman at the construction site posted a notice several days before Pat passed by forbidding construction workers to operate heavy equipment anywhere near the sidewalk unless a human look-out was posted to keep pedestrians off the sidewalk and out of the adjacent street. **What advice would you give Pat about the likelihood that she will win at trial and receive damages exceeding the settlement offer?**

(b) **Would your advice change if the forewoman posted the notice described in (a) above the day after the accident occurred; if the notice was posted the day after the accident but the forewoman had ordered it posted the day before the accident; if no notice was involved in the case, but the site forewoman fired the crane operator an hour after the accident; if the notice was posted the day after the accident by the Municipal Construction Safety Board, a government agency not a party to the litigation?**

(c) Rule 407 of the Rhode Island Rules of Evidence makes subsequent remedial measures admissible as evidence of fault in personal injury cases. **Would your advice to Pat change if the forewoman had posted the notice the day after the accident, which occurred in downtown Providence, Rhode Island, and the action was filed as a diversity case in the United States District Court for the District of Rhode Island? If the action were filed in state court?**

Problem IV-15. Sandra Harvey, an employee of Mid-Central Packers, lost the tips of two fingers when the bacon slicing machine she was cleaning started suddenly after she had stopped it by raising a safety shield. The shield was supposed to stop the blade from rotating by disengaging a clutch connecting the motor and the blade. Three weeks after the accident, the manufacturer of the machine, Chimera Corp., rewired the machine so that the motor itself shut off when the safety shield was raised. Explaining the modification, Chimera's president wrote a letter to Mid-Central stating that the rewiring would "prevent accidental actuation of the blade and possible injury." Hardy sued Chimera, claiming that her injuries were the result of the machine's negligently designed wiring system, which shorted out in the presence of grease and moisture, disenabling the safety device on the shield. Chimera's expert witness made the following statements on direct or cross-examination:

(a) "The safety features of the slicing machine were reasonable."

(b) "The machine was the best and safest machine of its kind on the market at the time of the accident."

(c) "Improper wiring did not cause the accident. The grease on the wires due to Mid-Central's improper maintenance caused the accident."

(d) "The circuit breaker could've been rewired to cut off the motor instead of the clutch. But that would've reduced the life of the motor and wouldn't have helped much, because a short-circuit could still cause the motor to run when the shield is up."

(e) "I base my opinion in part on the fact that I visited the plant several days after the accident, and the machine was working fine."

In response to the expert's five statements, Harvey proffers rebuttal evidence of the rewiring and the letter. Chimera objects, citing FRE 407. **Do any or all of the five statements justify admitting the evidence that Chimera rewired the machine? Should the letter be treated differently from the rewiring? What other objection might Chimera have made, with what result? Can Harvey ask the Chimera engineer who rewired the machine to describe the condition of the wires when she took apart the machine? Would the discarded wires be admissible if found by Harvey's investigator? During pretrial discovery, could the court have forced Chimera, over objection, to produce a copy of the letter?**

Problem IV-16. Eduardo García was injured in 2010 when his car, an Aardvark he bought new in 2008, went off the road while he was trying to negotiate a sharp curve. García testifies that, just as he entered the curve, the steering wheel on the vehicle locked, causing the mishap. He claims that a defective pin in the steering wheel column caused the locking and sues the Aardvark Auto Company (AAC), the maker of the vehicle, on both negligence and strict liability theories. In support of his claim, García introduces the testimony of an expert who examined his car after the crash. He also proffers a recall letter distributed by AAC pursuant to the National Traffic and Motor Vehicle Safety Act of 1966 that says in part: "In certain of our 2008 Aardvarks one of the steering column pins was damaged in the assembly process. Although the damage is unlikely to cause problems, in rare instances it may cause steering malfunctions. Therefore, if you own a 2008 Aardvark please take it to any AAC dealership for an inspection of the pin. If the pin is defective, the dealer will replace it at no cost to you." AAC distributed the letter three months after García's accident. **Is the recall letter admissible in support of the negligence claim? In support of the strict liability claim? How would your answer differ if the company had distributed the letter three months before García's accident? As counsel for each side, what arguments would you offer as bases for admitting or excluding the evidence on the strict liability claim in a state court that has not yet ruled on the applicability of the state's subsequent remedial measures rule to strict liability cases? Would your arguments change if the state had the following subsequent remedial measures rule, which is the same as FRE 407 before its 1997 revision, and is the rule in effect in a number of states today?**

> *When, after an event, measures are taken which, if taken previously, would have made the event less likely to occur, evidence of the subsequent measures is not admissible to prove negligence or culpable conduct in connection with the event. This rule does not require the exclusion of evidence of subsequent measures when offered for another purpose, such as proving ownership, control or feasibility of precautionary measures, if controverted, or impeachment.*

Problem IV-17. Ace was injured when a motorcycle she was driving on a two-lane highway crashed into an oncoming car as she tried to pass a car in her own lane. Ace sues the D'Press Accelerator Co. (DAC), claiming it made the accelerator of the motorcycle she was driving, and that the accelerator was negligently and defectively designed so that it suddenly cut off the flow of fuel to the engine when the machine traveled in excess of 75 mph on a bumpy surface. DAC calls Dr. X, who testifies that in his expert opinion (1) the badly mangled accelerator found in the wreckage of the motorcycle was not manufactured by DAC but was a different kind of accelerator manufactured by one of DAC's competitors, and (2) DAC's accelerator was not negligently designed or defective because there was no other safe and efficient way to design it. On cross-examination, Ace's lawyer asks Dr. X the following questions:

(a) Q. It's your opinion that DAC didn't make the accelerator in Ace's cycle, right?

    A. Right.

    Q. But you know that a week after the accident, DAC's safety director wrote owners of cycles with its accelerator telling them to stay off bumpy roads?

(b) Q. And it's your opinion that DAC's accelerator had the best available design as of the date of the accident?

    A. Yes, it is.

    Q. Did DAC tell you that a month after Ace's accident, it reengineered its accelerator to be less sensitive to bumps?

As DAC's lawyer, what objections would you make? As Ace's lawyer, what responses would you make? What actions should DAC ask the court to take, apart from barring the question?

Problem IV-18. (a) Same facts as in Problem IV-17. During settlement negotiations DAC's CEO denies there is anything wrong with the accelerator, saying he would gladly pay all Ace's damages if he thought the accelerator were defective. The CEO says he will reconsider his offer to settle the case for 10 percent of Ace's claimed damages if a panel of independent experts tests the accelerator and finds that it causes stalling at 80 mph on bumpy roads. The expert panel so finds. DAC offers to pay two-thirds of the damages Ace claims. Ace declines the offer and at trial calls one of the independent experts to testify that the accelerator causes stalling at high speeds on bumpy roads. Defendant objects to the expert's testimony. **What ruling?**

(b) Same situation, except that after negotiations break off, Ace makes a discovery request for the experts' written report, which DAC controls. DAC objects, citing FRE 408. Ace files a motion to compel discovery. **What ruling?**

(c) Same situation, except that the president hired the experts to examine and report on the accelerator before negotiations began. During negotiations, DAC cites the experts' findings as its reason for offering to pay half of Ace's damages. Negotiations break off, Ace obtains the experts' report from one of them, and Ace offers it at trial. Citing only FRE 408, DAC objects. **What ruling?**

(d) Same situation, except that liability and damages issues are tried separately, and the jury finds for Ace on liability. At the damages phase of trial, Ace calls a witness to describe DAC's offer during the last set of negotiations to pay two-thirds of Ace's damages. DAC objects. **What ruling?**

(e) Same situation, except that during her case in chief at a nonbifurcated trial, Ace offers to show that DAC recently paid $2,000,000 to another motorcycle crash victim to settle a law suit claiming that DAC's defective accelerator caused the cycle to stall and crash. Defendant objects. **What ruling? Is that same settlement admissible in a trial against DAC for criminally negligent homicide stemming from its knowing marketing of a defective accelerator, causing the death of a different victim?**

(f) **What ruling if DAC offered evidence of a settlement growing out of the same accident and covering half of Ace's alleged damages between Ace and the manufacturer of the motorcycle's brakes? What ruling if, instead, DAC wants to ask about Ace's settlement with the brake company on cross-examination of the brake company's chief engineer whom Ace called to testify that the brakes did not cause the accident?**

Problem IV-19. Dale's car collides with Pauline's, badly damaging Pauline's front left fender. The drivers jump out of their cars and begin arguing. Pauline demands $2000 to cover the damage to her car. Dale says, "Well, maybe I did run the light. Let's not quibble over peanuts. Take $1000 and call it even." Dale gives Pauline a check for $1000. The check bounces. Pauline sues. At trial, Pauline's lawyer calls her to testify to Dale's statements after the accident. Dale's lawyer objects.

(a) **How should Pauline's lawyer respond? How should the judge rule?**

(b) **What if Dale instead had said: "We can work it out. Sure, I ran the light. And no doubt your fender is worth at least $2000. But think of all the time and trouble you'll waste if it comes to a lawsuit. Life is very short. You'll accept $1000, *won't* you?"**

(c) **What if Dale had said: "Let's work this out. It's true I ran the red light, but your ratty old fender isn't worth $2000. Take $1000 and call it even."**

(d) **What if Dale instead had given Pauline a (rubber) check for $3000, saying: "Maybe I did run the light. Let's not quibble over peanuts. Take $3000 and call it even?"**

(e) **In the original scenario, suppose Pauline received and successfully cashed Dale's check but then sues for an additional $2000. Can Dale testify to his conversation with Pauline?**

(f) **In the original scenario, suppose the injury under discussion was to Pauline's right leg not her left front fender. On what ground(s) should Dale's lawyer object to the introduction of his statement? How should Pauline's lawyer respond? How should the judge rule?**

Problem IV-20. From 1999 to 2007, Haile Ellis and Samantha Dupuy were the two shareholders in a closely held company that sold and installed fiberglass insulation products. In 2007, following an acrimonious dispute, Ellis and Dupuy, dissolved the corporation and ended their business association. Thereafter, each sued the other in a series of cases involving the division of the former corporation's assets and also a "noncompete" agreement into which the two allegedly had entered when they formed their closely held company. By 2010, all the suits had been settled. In 2011, Ellis' new company, Fiber Snug, Inc. (FSI), sued Dupuy and several other individuals and companies under the Sherman Act alleging that the defendants successfully eliminated FSI from the local market by engaging in predatory pricing. After jury selection, all of the defendants save Dupuy settled with FSI for $50,000 each. A former FSI attorney, Melanie Memory claims that, during a negotiation to settle one of the prior lawsuits between Dupuy and Ellis, Dupuy told her he had "every intention of competing against Ellis and cutting prices to the bone—and further—if that's what it takes to drive Ellis out of business." At trial, FSI's lawyers (1) ask the judge to tell the jury that the defendants who were present at jury selection but now are absent settled with FSI, each paying FSI $50,000; and (2) call Memory to testify to Dupuy's statement. **As Dupuy's attorney, what objections would you make? As the judge, what rulings would you make if Dupuy objects to all of FSI's requests?**

Problem IV-21. In 2010, Corpoindustria de Venezuela employed Gonzalez to arrange a short-term loan of $4,000,000 from American Bank. Gonzalez arranged the loan, and Corpoindustria promptly paid back the principal and interest. In 2011, Gonzalez arranged another short-term loan of $4,000,000 from American to Corpoindustria, which American paid into a bank account designated by Gonzalez. Corpoindustria claims that it terminated its relationship with Gonzalez in 2010, that its officers did not sign the 2010 loan papers submitted by Gonzalez, and that no money reached it on the 2010 transaction. American sues Gonzalez for return of the $4,000,000 plus interest. American's attorney is prepared to testify that, during settlement negotiations, Gonzalez admitted forging the signatures of Corpoindustria executives in order to secure the loan. American also produces a Settlement Agreement signed by Gonzalez and American's lawyers, saying "The undersigned parties agree that, due to certain irregularities in connection with the aforesaid loan, Gonzalez will pay American $4,000,100, and that American accepts that sum in settlement of its claim against Gonzalez." Gonzalez contends that Corpoindustria orally authorized the 2010 loan arrangement, that its officers signed the papers submitted to American, that he lost the money in commodity trading setbacks, and that he never admitted forgery during negotiations with American. **At Gonzalez' trial on wire and mail fraud charges in connection with his solicitation of loans**

from American, may the government introduce the testimony of American's lawyer about Gonzalez' statements during settlement negotiations? If Gonzalez fails to pay American the $4,000,100, and American sues Corpoindustria, may Corpoindustria introduce American's Settlement Agreement with Gonzalez to refute American's claim that Gonzalez was Corpoindustria's agent?

Problem IV-22. The City of Troy wishes to purchase some farmland owned by Helen Homer in order to extend a horse path. Homer knows from a neighbor that the City can condemn property for this purpose, as it did previously when extending the horse path through the neighbor's property. The City Attorney made the following statements when negotiating with Homer and her attorney over the price of the land: (1) "We'll give you $45,000 for your land." (2) "The market value of your land is $50,000; we'll give you $45,000." (3) "We'll give you 10% less than the market value of your land which, by our calculation, comes to $45,000." Helen refuses. The City proceeds to condemn the property. **If the City argues in court that the market value of the land is only $40,000, which, if any of the above statements would be admitted at common law as tending to prove that the market value of the land is more than $40,000? Which would be admitted under the Federal Rules? Would it make a difference if Homer had a For Sale sign on the property when the discussions with the City began?**

Problem IV-23. Harry Converse was involved in an automobile accident with Paula Potts in which Potts suffered severe injuries. Potts sued Converse for $2,000,000. Converse was present during the negotiations at which his $600,000 offer was rejected. **May Potts introduce evidence that during the negotiations Converse appeared very tense, wrung his hands throughout and even started crying and got up and left when Potts described her injuries? Would your answer be different if Converse's attorney had opened the negotiations with the statement, "Now, of course, all this is without prejudice"?**

Problem IV-24. The Internal Revenue Service notifies Dr. Dorothy Blair, a physician, that it believes she has substantially understated her income in recent years, and it wishes to audit her books. After the audit, she is "invited" to see the IRS agent in charge of the case. The agent gives Blair *Miranda* warnings; states that Blair is in big trouble because the audit shows that she understated her income for the two preceding years by $100,000; and tells Blair she faces up to ten years in prison. Blair asks whether she can do anything to keep out of trouble. The agent replies that if Blair immediately pays the entire amount owing plus interest and applicable penalties and if she agrees to plead guilty to a misdemeanor tax offense if the IRS decides to prosecute her criminally, the agent is confident based on prior experience that felony charges will not be brought. Blair responds that her own audit shows that she understated her income by no more than $60,000, but because she should have been more careful and wants to keep her license, she will pay the IRS what it wants and plead guilty to a misdemeanor if charges are brought. **If Blair changes her mind and decides not to pay the $100,000 and the IRS, after a re-audit, sues her civilly for $55,000, are Blair's statements to the IRS agent admissible against her? If the government charges Blair with felony (i.e., intentional) tax fraud, can it introduce her statements to the agent to show that she knew she understated her income?** Would it make a **difference if the local U.S. Attorney had authorized IRS agents to negotiate pleas in tax cases?** Suppose Blair paid the IRS the $100,000 plus interest and penalties to avoid prosecution, then sued the government for a refund of $80,000. **Could the government introduce Blair's statements to the IRS agent to show that it owed Blair no more than $40,000?**

Problem IV-25. An individual in a ski mask robbed a bank, then got into the passenger side of a car waiting outside and sped away. Teen Young and her boyfriend, Ralph Rand, are charged with the robbery. During the lunch break in a pretrial hearing, Young and her attorney run into Assistant United States Attorney (ASA) Henri Prolix while all three are waiting in line at the courthouse cafeteria. Young says to Prolix, "Can we talk?" The ASA says, "Shoot." Young says, "Ralph didn't have anything to do with the robbery. He thought I went in to use the cash machine. Can we work something out for Ralph?" To which Prolix responds, before walking away, "What are we talking about here? The robber in the surveillance photos doesn't look a thing like you." **As the ASA at a separate trial against Young at which the surveillance photos are in evidence, could you—and would you—introduce Young's statements? As defense counsel, could you—and would you—introduce Prolix's statement? Assuming Prolix and Rand agreed that charges against Rand would be dropped if Rand testified against Young, could Young introduce evidence of the bargain between the government and Rand?**

Problem IV-26. Same facts as problem 25, but assume that the ASA speaks to Young alone immediately after she is arrested and given *Miranda* warnings. Young confesses to being the getaway driver after the ASA says, "Tell me who the guy was behind the mask and I'll skip the gun count and tell the judge you cooperated." **At Young's trial for aiding and abetting bank robbery, is her confession admissible?**

Problem IV-27. Poe, an employee of D-Way Mom and Pop Laundry Shop, was injured while operating a pressing machine at D-Way. Poe sues

D-Way for negligent maintenance of the pressing machine. **What ruling on D-Way's objection to Poe's evidence that D-Way has liability insurance covering employee injuries? What ruling on Poe's objection to Mom's testimony on behalf of D-Way that she takes all reasonable precautions, as exemplified by her purchase of liability insurance against all foreseeable kinds of mishaps? Suppose Poe and D-Way agree before trial that neither will object to the other's evidence of D-Way's liability insurance. May they bind the judge to admit the evidence? Consider FRE 103(a)(1) and (d). In the original scenario, what ruling on D-Way's objection to each of the following cross-examination questions put to its expert witness after she testifies that D-Way's pressing machine was in "tip top shape" when the accident occurred?**

Q. Dr. Expert, you were paid to testify in this case by the Mutual of New Mexico Insurance Co., correct?

Q. And Mutual of New Mexico insures D-Way, right?

Q. Indeed, Mutual of New Mexico insures D-Way for up to $3,000,000 in liability, correct?

Problem IV-28. The Acme Encyclopedia Company sells its books on a door-to-door basis. It will hire anyone who has access to a car as a sales representative. Acme pays its sales representatives on a straight commission basis. Sales representatives are expected to pay all their expenses, except that any salesperson who has been with the company for more than three months receives 15 cents a mile for automobile expenses incurred on company business and is covered by a $200,000 liability insurance policy for any accidents that occur while on company business. On rare occasions, the company dismisses individuals after three months if they have very poor sales records. Leslie Keslie has been a sales representative for Acme for seven months. One evening, while going to visit a prospective purchaser, Leslie hits Peter Pedestrian causing severe injuries. Pedestrian sues Acme for his $500,000 in medical expenses. Acme's attorneys are thinking of defending at least in part on the ground that they are not responsible for Leslie's actions because Leslie is an independent contractor who sets her own hours, chooses her own route and contacts her own prospects. **What factors should the attorneys consider before deciding whether to raise the defense?**

Problem IV-29. An expert in reconstructing accidents testifies that after a careful examination of the skid marks, the point of impact and the location of the cars when they came to rest, she has concluded that Defendant's car was not speeding when it struck Plaintiff's car. **Can Plaintiff ask the expert if she works for Costate, Defendant's liability insurer? If so, can she then be asked to confirm that she has testified for Costate on 20 prior occasions, in each case**

concluding that the Costate driver was not speeding at the time of an accident?

Problem IV-30. DSC employees James and Keeler quit DSC and formed their own company, Next Level. DSC sued James, Keeler and Next Level claiming they stole trade secrets from DSC. After the suit was filed, General Instrument Corp. (GI) purchased Next Level from James and Keeler for $91,000,000 and stock options. GI also agreed to indemnify James and Keeler (but not Next Level) against all expenses, judgments, penalties, fines and amounts paid in the settlement of DSC's law suit. At a trial at which the indemnity agreement was admitted against James, Keeler and Next Level, the jury found for DSC and awarded $126,500,000 in compensatory damages and $10,200,000 in punitive damages ($10,000,000 against Next Level and $100,000 each against James and Keeler). In deciding whether particular arrangements qualify as liability insurance subject to FRE 411, the courts have identified six attributes of liability insurance: (1) the insurer is paid to take a risk; (2) the insurer is well able to pay if the risk eventuates in injury; (3) the insurer agrees to indemnify the insured from liability to third persons, not for harm to the insured; (4) the insurer spreads any losses among its policy holders; (5) the insured is disinclined to incur risks because doing so may cause its premiums to rise; and (6) the insurer insures against future risk. **Are all of the listed factors relevant to a decision whether a particular arrangement qualifies as liability insurance for purposes of FRE 411? Do they exhaust the relevant factors? Which factors are the most, and which are the least, important? Which factors suggest that the indemnity agreement in question is, and which suggest that it is not, a liability insurance arrangement? Considering the relevant factors and their relative importance, should the indemnity agreement be treated as liability insurance, or not?** In addition to deciding whether the indemnity agreement qualified as liability insurance, the district court that decided this case (*DSC Communications Corp. v. Next Level Communications*, 929 F.Supp. 239 (E.D. Tex. 1996)) reached five conclusions:

(a) FRE 411 did not bar the admission of the indemnity agreement (assuming it qualified as liability insurance) because it was offered to establish damages, not liability. Because Next Level's only assets were the stolen trade secrets and their fruits, and because the technology at issue had yet to produce a marketable product, the best measure of the value of the stolen trade secrets was GI's purchase price for Next Level. Because the purchase price included the value of the indemnity agreement, it was admissible on the question of damages. (Does it matter that the court was unable to attach even an approximate value to the indemnity agreement based on the evidence at trial?)

(b) FRE 411 bars the use of liability insurance to show that "the [insured] person acted negligently or otherwise wrongfully" but not to prove "ownership[ ] or control." "[T]he fact that James and Keeler felt it necessary to 'insure' against the contingency that they might be found to have stolen DSC's trade secrets is evidence that they believed that they may not have owned the trade secrets. As such, this evidence is relevant to [and admissible on] the issue of whether James or Keeler owned the alleged trade secrets."

(c) FRE 411 is waived by an insured that "engages in 'poor-mouthing,' " i.e., pleading poverty to discourage the jury from awarding damages that would "break" the defendant. James and Keeler's attorney told the jury in opening argument that "this case was 'a question of life and death' to Mr. James and Mr. Keeler." Doing so "opened the door" to—or established the "curative admissibility" of—proof that the two were insured against liability.

(d) The probative value of the indemnity agreement was not substantially outweighed by its prejudicial effect.

(e) Any error under FRE 411 in admitting the indemnity agreement was harmless.

On appeal, how would you rule on challenges to each of the district court's five conclusions?

Problem IV-31. Plaintiff, Reginald Ray, an employee of Wanda's Hamburger Joint, suffered third-degree burns while using a Universal Eclectic (UE) french fryer. In order to filter hot grease in the manner specified by UE, Ray had to lift a six-pound pan containing fifteen pounds of grease at a temperature of 350 degrees and pour the grease through a paper cone filter into a second pan on the floor. As Ray was pouring grease from one pan to the other, a pressurized asthma inhaler fell from his shirt pocket into the grease in the top pan and exploded, severely burning Ray. Ray sued UE for negligent design. UE answered that the fryer was not dangerous and that Ray's dropping the inhaler and its explosion were negligent and unforeseeable occurrences for which UE bore no responsibility. After introducing evidence that UE could have avoided the pouring procedure by installing a manual siphon for $100 on an $800 machine, Ray offers testimony describing burns suffered by eight other employees of fast food restaurants while filtering grease in the operation of a UE fryer. Seven accidents occurred before Ray's and involved first-degree through third-degree burns (third degree burns being the most serious) following spillage of grease during the pouring process. The eighth accident, involving first-degree burns, occurred after Ray's: An employee's hat fell into the bottom pan, causing grease to splatter onto the employee's legs and feet. UE objects. **As Ray's attorney, on what theories would you argue that the other-incidents evidence is admissible? As judge, would you admit any or all of the other-incidents evidence? If so, on what theory or theories?** Assume that Ray instead sues Wanda's Hamburger Joint for negligently failing to adopt and enforce a rule forbidding employees to operate the UE french fryer without first emptying their shirt pockets. **Should Ray be permitted to show that at the time of the accident five other Wanda's franchises in the same city had adopted such a rule? Should he be permitted to show that two accidents occurred at other Wanda's franchises in the City when pocket pens fell into the pan, spattering grease? Would your answer be different if the two accidents had occurred at the Wanda's where Ray works? Would your answers be the same if the other spatter accidents only damaged the clothes of the employees involved?**

Problem IV-32. Polychrome Paint Co. supplies paint to Eddie Miss, a home builder. Miss asks to return the most recently acquired drum of paint, stating that paint he previously purchased from Polychrome but used only after the second drum was acquired was defective. Polychrome refuses to accept the return and sues Miss for the purchase price. Miss seeks to introduce evidence that five months earlier the same Polychrome sales agent sold him paint of the same brand as the paint he tried to return, and that the paint ruined roof shingles he had coated with it, causing leakage. **Is the evidence admissible? Would your answer differ if there were no way to test the quality of the paint before applying it?** Assume instead that Miss sues Polychrome for damages to a roof painted with the most recently acquired drum of paint. **Can Miss introduce evidence that application of the same type of paint five months earlier damaged another roof? Would it make a difference if the other roof was a neighbor's barn roof? Would your answers to any of these questions change if the labels on the two paint drums have batch numbers and the batch numbers are the same? What if the batch numbers are different? Could Polychrome introduce evidence that in the past five years it has received no complaints about the particular brand of paint?**

Problem IV-33. Darren Daigaku was severely injured while driving his 2008 Cross Pickup Truck to college when another driver ran a stop sign and hit the driver's side of the truck bed, rupturing the gas tank and causing an explosion. Daigaku sues Cross Motor Co. alleging that Cross defectively and negligently designed its Pickup Truck so that the gas tank was located outside the outer frame of the truck bed, creating a high risk of explosions on impact. Daigaku claims that the car that hit him was traveling 20 m.p.h. in a 30 m.p.h. zone. Cross claims the car was traveling 75 m.p.h. Daigaku offers a video tape produced for and aired on a Front Page television program on the dangers of trucks designed with the gas tank outside the truck frame. The tape (prepared several months after Daigaku's accident) shows a fiery explosion after a car traveling 30 m.p.h. crashes into the driver's side of a stationary 2006 Cross Pick-up Truck, rupturing the gas tank. The experts who staged the crash for Front Page would testify that, in order to avoid having to stage multiple crashes until one generated sparks capable of igniting gasoline, they installed an electric "sparking" device on the front bumper of the crash car. Cross objects to the Front Page evidence. **Is the evidence admissible? Can Daigaku introduce 25 letters Front Page received after the show reporting similar crashes? Could Daigaku introduce the letters if they had been sent to Cross rather than Front Page? Would it matter if all the letter writers were clients of the same lawyer?**

Problem IV-34. City of Angles wishes to condemn land owned by Jack Quartersin. In order to prove the market value of land, City wishes to introduce testimony as to the purchase price paid on two recent sales of property in the same neighborhood. **Under what conditions, if any, should the testimony be admitted? Would it matter if the two earlier sales were to City after it threatened to condemn the land? What is City's best strategy if it feels that the evidence of other purchase prices is essential to its case? Assuming the above evidence is unavailable, may City introduce evidence that offers to purchase at certain prices had been made?**

Problem IV-35. Sondra Skid sues for damages allegedly incurred when she slipped on the floor of the lobby of Darius Damp's office building between 11:15 and 11:30 a.m. on February 13 and broke her hip. Skid claims that the wet and slippery condition of the lobby's linoleum floor caused the accident. The day was cold, and snow had gently been falling all morning. A few minutes after paramedics took Skid to the hospital, and shortly before noon, a messenger entered the same lobby. Skid calls the messenger to testify. After preliminary questions about when and where the messenger entered defendant's building, the following exchange occurs:

P.   Counsel: Tell us what, if anything, happened as you passed through the door and entered the lobby.

D.   Counsel Objection. What happened when this witness went in the front door has no relation to this case.

Court: Objection sustained.

P.   Counsel: [At the bench.] We offer to prove by this witness that at 15 minutes before noon on February 13, when Sondra Skid was at the hospital after she had been injured, this messenger walked into the lobby of Darius Damp's building and that, within four or five feet of the door, his feet slipped out from under him and he nearly fell. This witness will further testify that, although he caught himself without falling, the reason he slipped and nearly fell was that the floor was slick because it was wet.

What is the best basis for Damp's objection? What is Skid's best response? What is the proper ruling? Would the result change if

the messenger had slipped in the same place on the same type of winter's day but on February 11? On February 15? Would the result change if, in cross-examining Skid, defense counsel had tried to suggest that Skid was clumsy and had asked whether she was accident prone?

Problem IV-36. Impyous Press is indicted under an obscenity statute for publishing and selling in New York City *Lord Chastity's Mistress*, an illustrated novel about an adulterer. The Supreme Court's test for obscenity is whether to the average individual, applying contemporary community standards, the dominant theme of the materials taken as a whole appeals to the prurient interest and is without social importance. Through a qualified expert, Impyous wants to introduce an illustrated edition of D.H. Lawrence's *Lady Chatterly's Lover*. Using the expert, Impyous wants to prove that the two books are comparable in theme, treatment and illustration, and that Lawrence's novel has been a best seller throughout New York City and State for three years. Impyous also wants to call a private investigator to testify that he found copies of other similarly illustrated novels about adulterers on sale at a number of bookstores and newsstands in each of the five largest cities in New York State. The prosecutor objects to all this evidence. **As judge, would you admit the evidence? What additional information would you want before ruling? Would you admit testimony that Impyous's book is a best seller in Boston?**

Problem IV-37. Townco Refining Co., contracted with Soloho Crude Oil Co. to supply Townco with oil. Paragraph 7 of the contract says that "the term of this agreement shall be for a period of 11 months commencing on October 1, 2013 and ending on August 31, 2014 and continuing thereafter unless terminated by either party providing not less than six (6) months notice of termination in writing." On January 23, 2014, Soloho informed Townco that it intended to, and it thereafter did, terminate delivery of oil under the contract on July 23, 2014. Townco sued, claiming that, under Paragraph 7, the six-months termination period could not commence until after August 31, 2014, thus giving Townco the right to oil at the contract price until at least the end of February 2015. Soloho contends that Paragraph 7 permitted termination of the agreement at any time following six-months notice. Over objection, Townco offers five contracts entered into between Soloho and various oil refining companies during the fall of 2013. Each contract contains a provision similar to Paragraph 7, except that each provision states that "notice may be given at any time" or that "notice of termination may be given at any time during the agreement." **Is the evidence admissible? Whose case does it tend to support?**

Problem IV-38. As an advertising device, employees of Foxy-Loxy Super-hardware have glued 600 tubes of Vaux Epoxy together to form a large "V" with a single tube at the bottom glued to a shelf. A banner is strung between the two sides of the "V" reading "The Strength of Epoxy." This promotion has tripled Foxy-Loxy's sales of Vaux Epoxy. One day when Marjorie Chang was shopping in Foxy-Loxy, the bottom tube came loose causing the "V" to fall on Chang with such force that it broke her arm. Chang offers evidence that the "V" broke loose from its moorings at least twice before, once breaking a shopper's collarbone and the other time fracturing a child's skull. Foxy-Loxy's attorney objects, pointing out that the store's manager is prepared to testify in response that both previous accidents were caused by someone reaching in from the aisle behind the epoxy display and accidentally hitting the "V." After the second accident the store added a barrier preventing customers in the adjacent aisle from reaching through the shelves and hitting the "V." **Given the manager's available response, is there any theory on which Chang might succeed in introducing the evidence? What is Foxy-Loxy's strongest argument as to why it should not be put in the position of having to present the manager's testimony? If Chang learns that the manager glued the bottom tube of epoxy to the shelf not with epoxy but with a weaker glue to avoid damaging the shelf, is there any way Chang can get that information before the jury in hopes that evidence of Foxy-Loxy's false advertising will improve Chang's chances of securing relief on her negligence claim? What instructions can Foxy-Loxy request if the other-glue evidence is admitted? As Foxy-Loxy's attorney, what instructions would you request?**

Problem IV-39. Olivia Kalamity Corral rents Liberty Valance 200 acres of pasture land for $6000 a year. Valance intends to graze cattle on the land during the growing season. Valance visits the land and finds Corral's cattle grazing along with his own animals. Valance sues. Corral defends on the ground that the oral rental agreement included her reservation of a right to pasture up to 50 of her own cattle on the land. **Can Valance introduce the testimony of Shane Gray that eight days before Valance rented the land from Corral, Corral had offered the grazing rights to Gray for $5800 a year and had not mentioned any reservation of rights with respect to Corral's own cattle? Would your answer be the same if the earlier asking price was $6200? $7500?**

Problem IV-40. Carla Cluney enters Thomas Green's Rare Book Emporium & Tobacco Shop one rainy day, slips, hits a ladder that jars a shelf that dislodges a musty history book that falls on Cluney's head. Cluney claims she slipped on water that Green negligently let accumulate. Green claims that no water was on the floor and that Cluney tripped over her own feet. **Can Green introduce the testimony of Cluney's former dance teacher that he "gave up on Cluney because she was constantly tripping over her own feet?" Can**

Green introduce the testimony of several witnesses that they have seen Cluney fall for no apparent reason? Can Green follow these witnesses with a psychologist who will testify that, on the basis of what she has heard in court, Cluney is accident prone? Can Green introduce evidence that Cluney has a mild form of epilepsy, a symptom of which is falling down for no apparent reason?

IV.   BIBLIOGRAPHY

McCormick, Chs. 18, 19, 25 (§§ 266, 267).

Weinstein Chs. 407–411.

Wright, Charles Alan and Kenneth Graham, Jr., 23 Fed. Prac. & Proced. Evid § 5322.

Bell, George M., Admissions Arising Out of Compromise: Are They Irrelevant?, 31 Tex. L. Rev. 239 (1953).

Brazil, Wayne D., Protecting the Confidentiality of Settlement Negotiations, 39 Hastings L.J. 955 (1988).

Cohen, Alma, et al., The Effect of Automobile Insurance and Accident Liability Laws on Traffic Fatalities, 47 J. of Law and Econ. 357 (2004).

Calnan, Alan, The Insurance Exclusionary Rule Revisited: Are Reports of its Demise Exaggerated? 52 Ohio St. L.J. 1177 (1991).

Diamond, Shari S., et al., Blindfolding the Jury, 52 Law and Contemp. Probs. 247 (1989).

Diamond, Shari S. and Neil Vidmar, Jury Room Ruminations on Forbidden Topics, 87 Va. L. Rev. 1857 (2001).

DiLisio, Karen A., The Admissibility of Subsequent Remedial Measures in a Products Liability Case, 3 Prob. Liab. L.J. 222 (1992).

Eichhorn, Lisa, Note, Social Science Findings and the Jury's Ability to Disregard Evidence Under the Federal Rules of Evidence, 52 Law and Contemp. Prob. 341 (1989).

Falkner, Judson F., Extrinsic Policies Affecting Admissibility, 10 Rutgers L. Rev. 574 (1956).

Fannin, Paul Robert, Disclosure of Insurance in Negligence Trials—The Arizona Rule, 5 Ariz. L. Rev. 83 (1963).

Fielding, Brian, Note: Rhode Island's 407 Subsequent Remedial Measure Exception: Why It Informs What Goes Around Comes Around in

Restatement (Second) & (Third) of Torts, and a Modest Proposal, 14 Roger Williams U. L. Rev. 298 (2009).

Flink, Andrea Lynne, Note, Admissibility of Subsequent Remedial Measures Evidence in Diversity Actions Based on Strict Products Liability, 53 Ford. L. Rev. 1485 (1985).

Garrett, Brandon L., The Substance of False Confessions, 62 Stan. L. Rev. 1051 (2010).

Graham, Michael, Plea Bargaining Pursuant to Fed. R. Evid. 410: "Criminal Defendant Beware!!!," 44 No. 6 Crim. Law Bull. Art. 8 (2008).

Green, Eric, A Heretical View of the Mediation Privilege, 2 Ohio St. J. Disp. Res. 1 (1986).

Green, Thomas F., Jr., Relevancy and its Limits, Law and Social Order 553 (1969).

Gross, Samuel R., Make-Believe: The Rules Excluding Evidence of Character and Liability Insurance, 49 Hast. L. J. 843 (1998).

Gross, Samuel R., et al., Exonerations in the United States: 1989 Through 2003, 95 J. Crim. L. & Criminology 523 (2005).

Guthrie, Chris, Jeffrey J. Rachlinski, & Andrew J. Wistrich, Inside the Judicial Mind, 86 Cornell L. Rev. 777 (2001).

Harris, Robert K., The Impeachment Exception to Rule 407: Limitations on the Introduction of Evidence of Subsequent Measures, 42 U. Miami L. Rev. 901 (1988).

Henderson, Roger C., Product Liability and Admissibility of Subsequent Remedial Measures: Resolving the Conflict by Recognizing the Difference Between Negligence and Strict Tort Liability, 64 Neb. L. Rev. 1 (1985).

Hjelmeset, Fred S., Impeachment of Party by Prior Inconsistent Statement in Compromise Negotiations: Admissibility Under Federal Rules of Evidence 408, 43 Clev. St. L. Rev. 75 (1995).

Imwinkelried, Edward J., The Meaning of Probative Value and Prejudice in Federal Rule of Evidence 403: Can Rule 403 Be Used to Resurrect the Common Law of Evidence, 41 Vand. L. Rev. 879 (1988).

Kalven, Harry, Jr., The Jury, the Law, and the Personal Injury Damage Award, 19 Ohio St. L.J. 158 (1958).

Ladd, Mason, Determination of Relevancy, 31 Tulane L. Rev. 81 (1956).

Leonard, David P., Codifying a Privilege for Self-Critical Analysis, 25 Harv. J. Legisl. 113 (1988).

Likert, George H., Precautionary Measures and Compromises, 1945 Wis. L. Rev. 399.

Mangrum, R. Collin, Nebraska's Evidentiary Rules of Relevance, 29 Creighton L. Rev. 119 (1995).

Michaels, Jane, Rule 408: A Litigation Mine Field, 19 Litigation, Fall 1992, at 36.

Perino, Michael A., Drafting Mediation Privileges: Lessons from the Civil Justice Reform Act, 26 Seton Hall L. Rev. 1 (1995).

Rachlinski, Jeffrey J., A Positive Psychological Theory of Judging in Hindsight, 65 U. Chi. L. Rev. 571 (1998).

Richardson, Thais L., Comment, The Proposed Amendment to Federal Rule of Evidence 407: A Subsequent Remedial Measure that Does Not Fix the Problem, 45 Am. U. L. Rev. 1453 (1996).

Robbennolt, Jennifer, Apologies and Legal Settlement: An Empirical Examination, 102 Mich. L. Rev. 460 (2003).

Schmertz, John R., Jr., Relevance and its Policy Counterweights: A Brief Excursion Through Article IV of the Proposed Rules of Evidence, 33 Fed. B.J. 1 (1974).

Schwartz, Victor E., The Exclusionary Rule on Subsequent Repairs—A Rule in Need of Repair, 7 The Forum 1 (1971).

Slough, M. C., Relevancy Unraveled, 5 Kan. L. Rev. 404, 675 and 6 Kan. L. Rev. 38 (1957).

Stone, Julius, The Rule of Exclusion of Similar Fact Evidence: America, 51 Harv. L. Rev. 988 (1938).

Story Thompson, Mikah K., To Speak or Not to Speak? Navigating the Treacherous Waters of Parallel Investigations Following the Amendment of Federal Rule of Evidence 408, 76 U. Cin. L. Rev. 939 (2008).

Tracy, John E., Admissibility of Statements of Fact Made During Negotiations for Compromise, 34 Mich. L. Rev. 524 (1936).

Waltz, Jon R. and J. Patrick Huston, The Rules of Evidence in Settlement, 5 Litigation 11 (1981).

Wellborn, Olin Guy, III, The Federal Rules of Evidence and the Application of State Law in the Federal Courts, 55 Tex. L. Rev. 371 (1977).

Weninger, Robert A., Amending Federal Rule of Evidence 408: Trapping the Unwary, 26 Rev. Litig. 401 (2007).

Williams, C. R., The Problem of Similar Fact Evidence, 5 Dalhousie L. J. 281 (1979).

Wood, James M., Liability and Evidentiary Issues Involving Prescription Production Recalls, 74 Def. Couns. J. 64 (2007).

Zollers, Frances E., et al., Looking Backward, Looking Forward: Reflections on Twenty Years of Product Liability Reform, 50 Syracuse L. Rev. 1019 (2000).

CHAPTER 5

CHARACTER AND CREDIBILITY

■ ■ ■

I. CHARACTER AND CREDIBILITY IN GENERAL

The rules discussed in this chapter address two interrelated issues: the use of evidence of a person's "character" to show that he or she acted in conformity or in accordance with that character outside of court; and the use of any sort of relevant evidence—character evidence or several other types—to show that a witness testified truthfully or untruthfully on the witness stand. Our discussion begins with FRE 404—which contains the so-called "propensity rule," forbidding the use of character evidence to prove conforming conduct, as well as several exceptions to and exclusions from that rule. FRE 404 provides:

(a) Character Evidence.

(1) Prohibited Uses. Evidence of a person's character or character trait is not admissible to prove that on a particular occasion the person acted in accordance with the character or trait.

(2) Exceptions for a Defendant or Victim in a Criminal Case. The following exceptions apply in a criminal case:

(A) a defendant may offer evidence of the defendant's pertinent trait, and if the evidence is admitted, the prosecutor may offer evidence to rebut it;

(B) subject to the limitations in Rule 412, a defendant may offer evidence of an alleged victim's pertinent trait, and if the evidence is admitted, the prosecutor may:

(i) offer evidence to rebut it; and

(ii) offer evidence of the defendant's same trait; and

(C) in a homicide case, the prosecutor may offer evidence of the alleged victim's trait of peacefulness to rebut evidence that the victim was the first aggressor.

(3) Exceptions for a Witness. Evidence of a witness's character may be admitted under Rules 607, 608, and 609.

(b) Crimes, Wrongs, or Other Acts.

(1) Prohibited Uses. Evidence of a crime, wrong, or other act is not admissible to prove a person's character in order to show that on a particular occasion the person acted in accordance with the character.

(2) Permitted Uses; Notice in a Criminal Case. This evidence may be admissible for another purpose, such as proving motive, opportunity, intent, preparation, plan, knowledge, identity, absence of mistake, or lack of accident. On request by a defendant in a criminal case, the prosecutor must:

(A) provide reasonable notice of the general nature of any such evidence that the prosecutor intends to offer at trial; and

(B) do so before trial — or during trial if the court, for good cause, excuses lack of pretrial notice.

In the next section of this chapter, Section II, we introduce the propensity rule, and describe several common *nonpropensity* uses of evidence which that rule does not bar—including but not limited to those listed in FRE 404(b)(2). As we will see, courts interpret some of these "nonpropensity" uses so broadly that the distinction between them and proof of propensity threatens to break down. Section II concludes with an overview of how character evidence, broadly conceived, is used in trials.

In Section III we discuss two of the *true* exceptions to the propensity rule: FRE 404(a)(2)(A), which permits a criminal defendant to use evidence of his own character to prove his conforming conduct, and FRE 404(a)(2)(B), which allows the criminal defendant to use evidence of the alleged victim's character to prove the victim's conforming conduct. Both rules, in addition, allow the prosecution to respond with evidence of the criminal defendant's bad character, and FRE 404(2)(B) allows the prosecutor to respond with evidence of the alleged victim's good character, to prove conforming conduct.

In Section IV we address FRE 404(a)(3), a third true exception to FRE 404(a)(1), which provides that some types of character evidence may be used as "[e]vidence of a *witness's* character" (emphasis added)—i.e., to *impeach* or *rehabilitate* a *witness's credibility*—as provided in FREs 607, 608 and 609.

In Section V we move from the use of character evidence to other methods of impeaching the credibility of witnesses: evidence of bias, factual contradictions, prior inconsistent statements, defects of perception, memory or narration, and religious beliefs. For the most part, these noncharacter methods of impeachment—despite their importance at trial—are not governed by specific Federal Rules. In Section VI we briefly discuss the rehabilitation of impeached witnesses, and in Section VII we address the ethics of impeachment.

Finally, in Section VIII, we discuss four more recently adopted rules that govern the use of character and related evidence in sexual assault and child molestation trials. FRE 412—the federal "rape shield rule"— greatly *limits* the use of evidence of sexual predisposition or prior sexual behavior of the alleged victim of a sexual assault, for all purposes— propensity, nonpropensity and impeachment. FREs 413–415 *permit* the introduction against defendants in criminal or civil trials for sexual assault or child molestation of evidence of the defendant's other similar acts—also for all purposes, including to show the defendant's action in accordance with the propensities revealed by the other similar acts.

Covering such a large number of issues makes for a long chapter. We treat them together because several common underlying themes make them easier to understand as a group. First, there are common procedural and formal threads. For example, when evidence of propensity is admitted, there is a general (but not universal) preference for evidence in the form of a person's reputation for a particular character trait ("He's generally thought to be a liar.") or in the form of the witness's opinion ("I believe he is untrustworthy.") over testimony about telling acts ("I twice caught him cheating at cards."). Similarly, courts generally prefer that impeachment—whether based on a witness's propensity to lie or by other means—be conducted by asking the witness questions on cross-examination rather than by calling additional witnesses. This preference ranges from mild in some contexts to an outright prohibition of "extrinsic evidence" in others.

Second, there is a unifying analytic theme. Courts tend to be more wary of evidence to the extent that its probative value depends on inferences about the general personality or character of a person, and more open to evidence to the extent that its probative value depends on inferences that are specifically linked to the facts (the particular stimuli and responses) at issue in the case. The degree to which particular rules reflect that preference, however, depends on a host of additional factors, including historical accident, judicial habit and political pressures.

II. THE PROPENSITY RULE: WHAT IT DOES AND DOES NOT EXCLUDE, AND WHY

A. REASONS FOR THE RULE

The propensity rule bars the circumstantial use of character evidence to show action in accordance with character. For example, all of the evidence in the following examples would be excluded by the rule:

• **Patricia sues Donna for negligently running into Patricia's car while both were driving on the interstate.** Donna's defense is contributory negligence. In her case in chief, Donna offers a psychiatrist who has examined Patricia and has concluded that she fits the psychological profile of an accident-prone individual. Donna also calls an insurance agent to testify that Patricia's insurance was recently canceled because she was involved in three car accidents during the past two years.

• **Wally, a waiter, is prosecuted for submitting false bills, and embezzling a portion of what diners paid him at the restaurant where he works.** The prosecutor, in his case in chief, calls an IRS auditor to testify that she audited Wally's income tax returns for three of the past five years, and found that in all three years Wally understated his tips by at least 50 percent. In Wally's defense, his attorney calls Harry, the owner of another restaurant where Wally once worked, to testify about three occasions when Wally scrupulously returned excess payments to customers who accidentally overpaid for meals.

By excluding such evidence, the propensity rule contradicts everyday experience. If asked whether we believe an accusation against someone we know, we might very well say: "I don't doubt for a minute that Frank did it. He did something like it to me two months ago. Ask everyone who knows Frank; they'll all say the same thing." Employers routinely ask people furnishing references to discuss the applicant's character and prior behavior in situations similar to those she is likely to encounter on the job. After a motorman was accused of recklessly operating a subway train on the Lexington Avenue line in New York City, causing a derailment that killed five passengers and injured 200 others, the *New York Times* thought its readers would want to know the following about the motorman: "Colleagues said they knew Robert R. to take a drink or two before squeezing into the motorman's cab but expressed disbelief that he might have been so impaired that he lost control." "Despite two reprimands from the Transit Authority, they said they never knew him to be unable to drive safely." "[Several months earlier,] Mr. R ran a red signal while operating a train at 167th Street. After the incident he was suspended without pay for three days. He was also reprimanded in March for a minor rules violation."[1] If the *Times* served its readers well by reporting this information about how the tragic accident occurred, why should a judge keep the same evidence—all of which is probably excludable under the propensity rule—from a civil or criminal jury trying to answer the same question? More broadly, if trials are supposed to help jurors construct a story of what happened, why should judges exclude

---

[1]   N. R. Kleinfeld, *Motorman's Colleagues Say He Drank at Work*, N.Y. Times, Aug. 30, 1991, at B5.

evidence of a classic ingredient of stories—the virtues and frailties of the main characters that impel them, tragically or comically, to act in particular ways?[2]

The propensity rule is also contrary to everyday experience *inside* the courtroom. As we discuss more fully in Section II.C. below, jurors almost never deliberate on a case without substantial evidence on the character of the parties and the witnesses. Often, evidence reflecting on character is admitted for a purpose other than propensity, or is apparent to the jury even though it is never technically "admitted." Think of the defense attorney who makes a show during trial of respectfully consulting a client charged with a brutal murder, or the prosecutor in the same case who strategically seats members of the victim's family in the front row of the courtroom so the jury can see their behavior and their reactions throughout the trial. Or consider the tendency of lawyers calling witnesses to refer to them by honorifics, such as "doctor," "professor," or "most reverend," and of opposing lawyers to refer to them, instead, as merely "mister," "miz," or just "you." The rules that govern trials permit the adversaries to present all these images and messages to the jury. Parties have a right to be present in the courtroom; criminal defendants are entitled to appear in court without visible shackles and dressed in a manner calculated to make a good impression; and witnesses regularly testify to their names, addresses and occupations, and frequently to other "background facts" that suggest character traits.

If inferences from character to actions are so common in our daily lives, in story-telling and, indeed, in trials themselves—why then does the propensity rule exclude evidence offered to support such inferences? Irrelevance is not the explanation. As Judge Cardozo said, "there may be cogency in the argument that a quarrelsome defendant is more likely [than the average person] to start a quarrel. . . ."[3] Or, as Justice Jackson said, it "might logically be persuasive that [the defendant] is by propensity a probable perpetrator of the crime."[4] Certainly recidivism rates suggest that, at least for some offenses, a person's past criminality has some bearing on the likelihood that he committed a similar crime more recently.[5]

Evidently, "the principle back of the exclusion is one not of logic, but of policy."[6] Several policies are at work. The most obvious is a desire to avoid evidence that invites sympathy or antipathy towards a party irrespective of his behavior on the occasion in question. Jurors with a

---

[2] See Nancy Pennington & Reid Hastie, The Story Model for Juror Decision Making, in Inside the Juror: The Psychology of Juror Decision Making (R. Hastie ed. 1993).

[3] People v. Zackowitz, 254 N.Y. 192, 172 N.E. 466, 468 (N.Y. 1930).

[4] Michelson v. United States, 335 U.S. 469, 475 (1948).

[5] Recidivism rates are discussed infra, p. 504, note 251.

[6] People v. Zackowitz, supra, 172 N.E. at 468 (citing 1 Wigmore §§ 57, 197; People v. Richardson, 222 N.Y. 103, 118 N.E. 514 (N.Y. 1917)).

reasonable doubt about the defendant's guilt may convict nonetheless if they think that he committed other crimes or has a propensity to act in a dangerously violent manner. In the "regret matrix" terms introduced in Chapter Three, Section II.B., other crimes evidence may improperly diminish the regret the jurors would feel if they reached a false guilty verdict or increase their regret at a false *not* guilty verdict. This is true whether or not the defendant's prior misbehavior has resulted in conviction and punishment. If the jurors think that the defendant has committed crimes but escaped punishment they may vote to convict not because they are convinced that the defendant is guilty of the charged crime, but in order to punish the defendant for his other crimes.[7] If a defendant's other crimes *have* resulted in convictions, jurors may demand less evidence of guilt because they believe that an erroneous conviction would cause less damage of a personal, economic and dignitary nature than it would if he had no record. Also, common misconceptions about sentencing and parole policies may lead some jurors to believe that felons serve less time in prison for their crimes than they deserve and that additional punishment for *past* crimes is appropriate regardless of the punishment required for the crime at issue in the current trial.[8]

Another reason for the propensity rule is that jurors faced with evidence of bad character or other crimes may overestimate its probative value. The impulse to treat character traits and prior behavior as predictive of current behavior is very strong. Although we should not lightly doubt instincts and habits of mind that guide our daily lives, there are good reasons to mistrust the weight jurors might instinctively give to propensity evidence. Social psychological evidence suggests that people give too much weight to evidence of personality traits—such as accident proneness and criminal predisposition—and too little weight to evidence about the context of the specific case. The explanation for this phenomenon proceeds in two steps. First, people usually overestimate the extent to which two facts occurring in association with each other are causally related, and especially overestimate the causal role that *human beings* play in events occurring around them.[9] In trying to understand events involving other people, it's easier to generate theories based on

---

[7] See State v. Derbyshire, 349 Mont. 114, 201 P.3d 811, 817 (2009) (basing the propensity rule on the principle that "[a] defendant must not be convicted merely because he is an unsavory person").

[8] See, e.g., Simmons v. South Carolina, 512 U.S. 154, 159, 170 n. 9 (1994) (plurality opinion); id. at 173 (Souter, J. concurring) (discussing studies showing that, unless instructed otherwise, jurors responsible for determining whether to sentence convicted defendants to life imprisonment or to death routinely underestimate the amount of time persons sentenced to life imprisonment are required to serve before becoming eligible for parole).

[9] Richard Nisbett & Lee Ross, Human Inference: Strategies and Shortcomings of Social Judgment (1980). Nisbett and Ross call this tendency to impute more causal responsibility than is merited to other persons and less than is merited to the persons' environment or the context in which they act "the fundamental attribution error." Although this error leads people to overestimate the responsibility of *others* for events, it does not generally lead them to overestimate their *own* responsibility!

human agency than to appreciate how the context may have shaped what happened. Thus, jurors hearing an automobile accident case may be overly prone to attribute the accident to the driver rather than, for example, to unexpected road conditions. Second, people are especially likely to overestimate the role of human agency when a familiar explanatory theory is handy. Jurors in an automobile accident case who learn that the driver was involved in other accidents may find it extremely easy to explain the accident on the theory that she was careless, or is "accident prone," even though information of this sort is only a weak predictor of traffic accidents and more diligent inquiry would likely reveal a better explanation.

The problem may be especially acute when the issue is identity, as opposed to fault or causation, for then another cognitive bias comes into play. People tend to base their estimates of the likelihood that someone committed a particular act on the degree to which the act resembles a form of behavior that is thought to be typical of people like him.[10] So, in deciding whether a person with certain incriminating character traits is responsible for an untoward event, people tend to focus on the traits and ignore the context. In particular, they pay little attention to the total number of possible suspects, and to the proportion of those suspects with the trait in question. To illustrate, assume that a person with a long record of prior assaults is ten times more likely to start a brawl than a person whose record is clean, and that a brawl broke out in a bar when Gordon, a person with a long prior record of assaults, was among 100 people present. Despite Gordon's background, the chances are 10 to 1 that someone without a record, that is someone other than Gordon, started the fight. Yet the police, if they have no good leads, might well focus their initial investigation on Gordon, and selectively obtain and record evidence implicating him, without considering evidence against other patrons. For example, Gordon might be the only person placed in a lineup. The same bias could lead *jurors* to give great weight to Gordon's record of brawling and to pay little attention to the possibility that other patrons might be implicated by more specific evidence. The propensity rule can help counteract this bias by preventing Gordon's resemblance to the jurors' stereotype of an aggressor from overwhelming the base-rate evidence—namely, the large number of other potential suspects who, as a group, are (in the absence of other evidence) more likely than Gordon to have committed the crime.[11]

---

[10] Amos Tversky & Daniel Kahneman, Judgments of and by Representativeness, in Judgment Under Uncertainty: Heuristics and Biases 84 (Daniel Kahneman, Paul Slovic & Amos Tversky eds. 1982). Tversky and Kahneman call this tendency the "representativeness heuristic."

[11] To give another example, suppose that 10 of 10,110 people who attend a rock concert are multiple-offending brawlers (i.e., have started fights on multiple occasions in the past); 100 are one-time offending brawlers; and 10,000 have never started a fight. Suppose also that, on average, prior multiple-offending brawlers start a fight on 1 out of 10 occasions when they are in

In addition, there is a good deal of psychological evidence that character traits are not always static aspects of personality or good predictors of behavior. Character traits and conduct reflecting them vary over time and across situations, and they change as people change and mature, as contexts change, and when competing aspects of personality are called into play.[12] Evidence that a building inspector regularly takes bribes may have considerably less bearing on whether he acted honestly as church treasurer than jurors might believe if they are among the many who view character as largely immutable and think that personality overwhelms context in determining behavior.

---

a crowd; prior one-time brawlers do so on 1 out of 50 occasions; and persons with clean records do so on 1 out of 1000 occasions. We thus would expect 13 fights to break out at the concert in question—1 (i.e., 10 x 1/10) started by a prior multiple brawler; 2 (i.e., 100 x 1/50) started by prior one-time brawlers; and 10 (i.e., 10,000 x 1/1000) started by persons with previously clean records. If we chose a fight at random among those occurring at the concert, there is only 1 chance in 13 that a prior multiple brawler started the fight and 10 chances in 13 that someone with a previously clean record did so. If, however, one of the fights leads to a police investigation, the police are likely to suspect first and try to build a case against one of the multiple offenders. This police tactic is not silly; although there is a less than 8% chance that the person who started the fight was a prior multiple brawler (and a less than 1% chance that any *particular* one of the 10 prior multiple brawlers did so), there is a much greater chance that each of the 10 prior multiple brawlers started the fight than that any single one of the prior one-time or no-time offenders did so.

Difficulties arise, however, if the police investigation ends where it began, with the 10 prior multiple brawlers. Say, the police show pictures of those 10 people to a number of concert-goers, three of whom identify one of the prior multiple brawlers as most like the brawler in question. Suppose that person is charged with starting the fight, and that the state's evidence consists of one eyewitness who said he saw the person in a bathroom near where the fight began between 10 and 15 minutes before the fight broke out, and two eyewitnesses who say he looks like the person who threw the beer bottle that started the fight, but they can't be certain. The accused's defense is a ticket stub for a seat located some distance from where the fight started, and his girlfriend's testimony that he was with her all the time except when he went to the bathroom for five minutes at least 20 minutes before the fight started. What do you think the chances are that a jury will convict the defendant on that evidence? If the state also shows that he was involved in 10 previous barroom brawls or fights at sporting events, what do you think the chances of a conviction are now? How would that probability change if the jury were told what they will, in fact, never learn—namely, that the crowd at the event contained 9 other people with records like the defendant's and 100 others who had been involved in one previous brawl?

[12] Most researchers agree that static character "traits" and dynamic "situations" interact to influence behavior. See Susan M. Davies, Evidence of Character to Prove Conduct: A Reassessment of Relevancy, 27 Crim. L. Bull. 504 (1991) (discussing "trait" theory, "situationism" and "inter-actionism"). Traits are almost certainly most predictive when defined in terms of an individual's behavior in well-specified and highly similar situations. See Edward J. Imwinkelried, Reshaping the "Grotesque" Doctrine of Character Evidence: The Reform Implications of the Most Recent Psychological Research, 36 Southwestern U.L. Rev. 741, 754, 758 (2007) (recent studies have consistently yielded the finding that predictions of behavior based on interactions between fixed traits and situational features are more accurate than predictions based solely on either trait or situation; a consensus is emerging around "the proposition that each person possesses relatively stable 'if . . . , then . . . ' behavioral signatures," and that "the condition in the signature—the 'if . . . '—is the occurrence of a situation that falls within a particular class of events that have certain psychological salience for the person"). But cf. Chris William Sanchirico, Character Evidence and the Object of Trial, 101 Colum. L. Rev. 1227, 1233, 1241 (2001) (although there is general agreement among personality psychologists that individual behavior is determined by a combination of cross-situational attributes and situation-specific factors, recent research suggests that some "cross-situation attributes, as evidenced by past acts, may be quite probative of conduct" in criminal and torts cases, given "the stability of certain personality features such as 'low empathy' or lack of 'self control' ").

Trials, particularly criminal trials, create their own set of cognitive biases. Jurors, for example, might accurately conclude that a high proportion of guilty robbery defendants have committed past robberies.[13] But as we saw in Chapter Three, assessing the probative value of that assumption (the numerator in the "likelihood ratio" estimate discussed in Chapter Three) requires jurors to estimate an additional probability, namely, the likelihood that *innocent* robbery defendants have committed past robberies (the denominator in the "likelihood ratio" estimate). Jurors might try to answer this question by estimating the proportion of, say, all adult citizens with robbery convictions. Because that proportion is very low, and the proportion of guilty robbery defendants with prior records is quite high, the jurors will conclude that a prior record is highly probative of guilt. In fact, the evidence is *not* very probative because police and prosecutors do not pluck robbery defendants randomly from the adult population, but concentrate instead on the pool of known robbers. Like Claude Rains in the famous closing scene of *Casablanca*, the police may, for good and obvious reasons, focus their attention on "the usual suspects"—people who have prior records or known "bad character." One important aspect of this process is that the photographs shown to crime victims and other eyewitnesses for the purpose of identifying the criminal usually come from files on people with records for similar crimes. When mistakes are made and innocent defendants are prosecuted, they will very often be innocent defendants *with* prior similar records.[14] Moreover, despite the propensity rule, a prior record is a serious handicap at trial. Sometimes evidence of prior convictions gets in during the prosecution's case-in-chief. More often it is either admissible for impeachment if the defendant testifies, or it keeps the defendant from testifying at all; either way, the defendant is more likely to be convicted. This means that a prosecutor is more likely to try a weak case if the defendant has a criminal record. The net effect is that at trial the proportion of *innocent* robbery defendants who have prior records—like

---

[13] Data on recidivism among robbers are reported infra, p. 504, note 251.

[14] See Samuel R. Gross, Loss of Innocence: Eyewitness Identification and Proof of Guilt, 16 J. of Legal Studies 395, 417 (1987). Overestimation will be especially great if jurors treat the defendant's prior record as "independently" corroborating the eyewitness identification when the two items of evidence are, in fact, interdependent and may even be cumulative. The two items are interdependent because the defendant's prior record led the police to show the victim the defendant's photograph. They will be cumulative if the witness's confidence in the identification was enhanced by the witness's knowledge at the time of the identification (prompted by the use of a "mug shot" or, sometimes, by improper police comments) that the individual in the photograph had committed similar crimes in the past.

If not discouraged by the propensity rule, the police practices discussed in text might also impede law enforcement efforts over the long haul by increasing recidivism. Consider the suggestion that letting law enforcement officials rely liberally on prior crimes as a basis for arresting and convicting defendants would lessen the incentive of prior offenders to reform. "If I'm going to be branded as a robber forever, and repeatedly arrested and convicted for it," the rational prior offender might reason, "I might as well get the benefits of being a robber in the meantime." See Joel Schrag & Suzanne Scotchmer, Crime and Prejudice: The Use of Character Evidence in Criminal Trials, 10 J.L. & Econ. Org. 319, 323 (1994). See also Usual Suspects (Poly-Gram Pictures 1995).

the proportion of guilty defendants with prior records—is likely to be pretty high.

Plea bargaining practices may further erode the probative value of prior crimes evidence in criminal cases. Consider the following assumptions: (1) Guilty defendants with prior records are particularly likely to accept plea bargains if any leniency at all is offered, given the severe disadvantages they face at trial (even with the propensity rule), and the likely strength of the evidence against them. (2) Innocent defendants without records also are comparatively unlikely to go to trial because the probable weakness of the evidence against them and the absence of a prior record will encourage prosecutors to dismiss their cases or offer "sweetheart" pleas (minor misdemeanors or time served awaiting trial), if they are charged at all. If these assumptions are correct, then the pool of defendants who go to trial is disproportionately composed of two types of defendants: (1) guilty defendants without records (who do not face the disadvantages that cause many guilty defendants with prior records to plead); and (2) innocent defendants with prior records (who may be driven to trial by their sense of injustice and by the fact that they have an honest "innocence" defense, combined with their inability to secure dismissals or favorable bargains from prosecutors who see them as predictable recidivists, and who can play the "prior record" card at trial). As a result, at trial guilty defendants would be *less* likely than innocent defendants to have prior records. This would make prior crimes evidence positively misleading, because it would tend to predict innocence, although jurors would treat it as evidence of guilt. Of course, these assumptions may be wrong, at least some of the time.[15] Even so, they

---

[15] The assumptions underlying this suggestion are speculative and controversial. They have three premises—that criminal defense counsel, who have a lot of say over whether their clients plead guilty, have good information about when their clients are and are not guilty, and share their clients' incentives when both conditions are present; that judges impose higher sentences on defendants who go to trial than on ones who plead guilty, giving defendants incentives to plead guilty when they are guilty; and that defendants with prior records are not routinely given sentences that are so much higher than those given defendants without such records that guilty defendants with prior records have "nothing to lose" by going to trial. Modern mandatory sentencing practices typified by the Federal Sentencing Guidelines support the second assumption by imposing stiff sentencing penalties on defendants who insist on trials. Although modern sentencing guidelines and the imposition in some jurisdictions of mandatory sentences of life or life without parole for "three-time-losers" undermine somewhat the validity of the third assumption, the effect is tempered by prosecutors' ability to limit the charges to which defendants plead guilty to ones that do not trigger mandatory enhancements based on prior records.

A fourth assumption explains how even close observers might fail to perceive that prior records are probative of the innocence of defendants who go to trial. Assume that most trial defendants are guilty. If this "base rate" assumption is true, then most trial defendants with prior records are guilty even if, for defendants who go to trial, prior records are associated with innocence. Thus, if 90% of all criminal trial defendants are guilty and only 10% are innocent, and if 70% of the former have prior records while 80% of the latter do (so that prior records are more often associated with innocence than guilt), the proportion of trial defendants with prior records who are guilty would still be about 89%. (Prior odds x likelihood ratio = subsequent odds; 9/1 x .7/.8 = 6.3/.8 = 7.9; subsequent odds expressed as a probability = 7.9/(7.9 v 1) = .89, or 89%; given these assumptions, the proportion of defendants without records who are guilty is 93%.) If this is true, the accurate perception that a very high proportion of trial defendants with criminal

illustrate how the probative value of a prior criminal record may be greatly exaggerated by jurors who know little about the plea bargaining process that shapes the cases they see at trial.

This analysis suggests that the propensity rule shares an important justification with the privilege against self-incrimination and the ban on coerced confessions. By excluding evidence that is easy to obtain but less reliable than it is persuasive, all three rules encourage the police to conduct more thorough investigations. Whatever the probative value of propensity evidence may be, it is not generally *as* probative as ballistics, DNA or fingerprint evidence; the testimony of witnesses to the offense; evidence about the defendant's motivations and intentions with regard to the victim; or other evidence specifically linking the defendant to the crime.[16] Although the stakes are different, the same policy applies to criminal defendants and to both parties in civil cases. They too have to work harder to find more probative case-specific evidence because they cannot freely rely on propensity evidence.

Propensity evidence is also subject to the problems of proof and presentation that we discussed in Chapter Four. We have been using prior convictions as an illustration, but character evidence often deals with conduct that has never been the subject of any official proceedings. If there is a dispute about the underlying facts, the jurors may be confused and distracted. They will have to set aside consideration of the facts of the case on trial to decide if some other event actually took place—and only then (if they get it right), can they even attempt, against all odds, to give the prior conduct its appropriate probative weight. The quality of the evidence on this side issue may be low, and jurors may be misled by the thin evidence. Even if they doubt the precise past behavior occurred, they might believe that there must be some fire under all the smoke—especially if the opposition's rebuttal is weak because the propensity evidence took it by surprise or didn't seem like it would be the "main event" at the trial. If the opposition is surprised, and if the issue is important, fairness might require a continuance, which is a heavy cost in a jury trial. And the issue may be important, because character evidence often has a big impact on jurors. Finally, even if the issue is painstakingly aired, it is likely to be a distracting and inconclusive side show, because most people do things, at one time or another, that suggest diametrically opposite character traits.

A final justification for the propensity rule is that it reflects two related notions about human reformability and responsibility that have nothing to do with a search for the truth, but are fundamental to our

---

records are guilty would probably prevent even close observers from realizing that the presence of a prior record makes guilt less, not more, likely.

[16] The same logic applies to drug-smuggler and terrorist profiles, which sometimes justify investigative actions but are excluded at trials, as character evidence. See United States v. Baldwin, 418 F.3d 575 (6th Cir. 2005).

social aspirations, even if we do not always adhere to them. The first is that individuals should not be defined by past acts or by immutable traits of "character." We believe, instead, that even criminals can reform, and that once they have "paid their debt to society," they should be taken back and treated like everyone else. Accordingly, the presumption of innocence should (and in theory at least, does) attach in the same way regardless of past record. The second notion is that people should be judged by what they do and not by who they are—by their behavior and not by the generalized characteristics of a class or category to which they belong.

The courts that apply the propensity rule do not necessarily endorse all of these explanations for it. But these arguments do help explain the origin of the rule, and its persistence. Together, they have led courts to take seriously the claim that the rule is constitutionally required in criminal cases.[17] But persistence is not immutability. In 1994, Congress adopted a broad exception to the propensity rule for sexual assault and child molestation cases (which we discuss in Section VIII below), and some states apply similar, if often narrower, exceptions by statute, rule or case law. Although these changes have been explained on grounds peculiar to sexual assault and child molestation cases, they pose a more basic question: Will the justifications for the propensity rule continue to sustain it against the criticisms that it offends commonsense, is unnecessary (nearly all other nations get along without it, and even England has largely abandoned it[18]), and impedes law enforcement (at least in the short run) by making conviction of the guilty (as well as the innocent) more difficult?[19]

––––––––––

Problem V-1. The prosecution charges Zachary with the first-degree (i.e., premeditated) murder of Victor using a pistol. In her opening statement, Zachary's lawyer claims that the offense is at most voluntary manslaughter because Zachary shot Victor under the influence of an extreme emotional disturbance after Victor insulted Zachary's wife. To prove that Zachary is disposed to look for opportunities to kill, that he did

---

[17] See Estelle v. McGuire, 502 U.S. 62 (1991). See also State v. Ellison, 239 S.W.3d 603, 608 (Mo. 2007) ("Evidence of a defendant's prior criminal acts, when admitted purely to demonstrate the defendant's criminal propensity, violates [a Missouri state] constitutional protection[ ] vital to the integrity of our criminal justice system."). Cf. United States v. Castillo, 140 F.3d 874 (10th Cir. 1998) (upholding the constitutionality of FRE 413's suspension of the propensity rule in cases in which the criminal defendant is charged with sexual assault, see infra, Section VIII, as long as the continued application of FRE 403 protects against the worst abuses that the character rule had previously avoided).

[18] See Boardman v. Department of Public Prosecutor, [1974] 3 All E.R. 887. Of course, nearly all nations get along without a jury system, especially in civil cases, which may explain the idiosyncratic nature of American evidence rules.

[19] See, e.g., H. Richard Uviller, Evidence of Character to Prove Conduct: Illusion, Illogic, and Injustice in the Courtroom, 130 U. Pa. L. Rev. 845, 848–49, 882–85 (1982). See also David P. Bryden & Roger C. Park, "Other Crimes" Evidence in Sex Offense Cases, 78 Minn. L. Rev. 529 (1994).

so in this instance, and that he coolly premeditated the killing, the prosecution offers evidence in its case-in-chief that Zachary keeps an arsenal of guns in his home. The prosecution also offers evidence in its case-in-chief that Zachary has been convicted in the past of assault with a deadly weapon, robbery and second-degree (i.e., intentional) murder. The prosecution also offers the testimony of the bartender at a tavern Zachary frequents that Zachary has a reputation as a violent person. **Should these various items of evidence be admitted or excluded? Would it make any difference to your treatment of the arsenal evidence that Zachary dropped his wife off at home before returning to the site of his encounter with Victor and shooting him?**

B. EVIDENCE THAT IS NOT EXCLUDED BY THE PROPENSITY RULE

1. Other Purposes Generally

Read the text of FRE 404 at the beginning of Section I, pp. 345–346 above. In its first sentence, FRE 404(a)(1), emphasizes that the propensity rule excludes character evidence only if offered as a basis for inferring action in accordance with a trait of character. This is the *"inclusionary"* form of the rule. Evidence of character traits is admissible for all purposes except as a basis of inferences from propensity. In some jurisdictions the rule is stated in an *"exclusionary"* form, which excludes evidence of traits of character except when offered for specifically permitted purposes, which usually include those listed as examples of permitted purposes in FRE 404(b)(2). The inclusionary version seems more permissive, but the difference is more theoretical than real because courts applying exclusionary versions of the rule often exercise great ingenuity in fitting other acts evidence into one of the permitted categories.

The very presence of FRE 404(b) further emphasizes that character evidence may be offered for permitted purposes—because the provision is almost entirely superfluous. FRE 404(b)'s initial subsection, FRE 404(b)(1), simply applies to evidence of "other act[s]" the ban on propensity uses that FRE 404(a)(1) applies to *all* forms of character evidence. And (apart from a "notice" proviso) FRE 404(b)'s second subsection, FRE 404(b)(2) merely makes the "inclusionary" consequences of this rule explicit—nonforbidden uses of evidence are not forbidden— and adds a nonexclusive (and therefore logically unnecessary) list of "[ ]other purpose[s]" for which evidence of character traits *"may be admissible"* (emphasis added): to show "motive, opportunity, intent, preparation, plan, knowledge, identity, absence of mistake, or lack of accident." FRE 404(b)'s unnecessary presence is no accident. The Rule's drafters wanted to be clear that character evidence is admissible for many purposes, and Congress redrafted the rule to give even greater emphasis to those purposes. These efforts succeeded. Although superfluous, FRE 404(b) is cited by courts in written opinions more often than any other rule of evidence, except FRE 403. Moreover, it usually is cited to justify the *admission* of "other crimes" evidence.[20]

Unless we naively assume that jurors always follow instructions to consider evidence indicative of bad character only for the limited purpose for which it is admitted, the dangers the propensity rule is designed to guard against will be present whenever such evidence is admitted, for any purpose.[21] Admitting such evidence on issues besides propensity without incurring excessive prejudice requires that the line between propensity and other uses be drawn with care. Yet courts all too frequently admit dangerously prejudicial evidence on the theory that it is not excluded by the propensity rule, even though it probably should be excluded for lack of *any* permissible purpose, or because it does not bear on a matter that is genuinely in dispute. Moreover, as we shall see, courts sometimes admit evidence of traits of character, especially "other acts" evidence, in situations in which it is likely to have severe prejudicial effects yet aid little in the resolution of the issue on which it is admissible for a nonpropensity purpose. As a number of courts have held, however, a good deal of unnecessary prejudice can be eliminated if the proponent of "other acts" evidence, and the trial judge before admitting it, (1) articulate clearly the chain of inferences for which the evidence is being admitted, making sure that no link in the chain depends on an inference of action in accordance with bad character, and (2) sensitively balance the probative value and prejudicial potential of the evidence under FRE 403, with due regard for the probability that the jury will misuse the evidence for the forbidden inference.[22] Courts also may reduce prejudice by limiting character evidence to issues that actually are "in dispute," given the defense the accused actually presents. Because "other crimes" evidence is most frequently and badly misused when offered to prove "intent",[23] we

---

[20] See Abraham P. Ordover, Balancing the Presumptions of Guilt and Innocence: Rules 404(b), 608(b) and 609(a), 38 Emory L.J. 135, 142–43 & nn.31-34 (1989).

[21] Considerable empirical research suggests that, even when instructed otherwise, jurors presented with evidence of bad character, particularly "other acts" evidence, use it to infer both that the defendant acted in conformity with the character trait on the occasion in question and that he is a bad person who deserves to be punished regardless of guilt on the particular occasion. See Edward J. Imwinkelried, The Need to Amend Federal Rule of Evidence 404(b): The Threat to the Future of the Federal Rules of Evidence, 30 Vill. L. Rev. 1465, 1470, 1487–88 (1985).

[22] See, e.g., United States v. Daraio, 445 F.3d 253 (3d Cir. 2006), cert. denied, 549 U.S. 1111 (2007); United States v. Murphy, 241 F.3d 447 (6th Cir. 2001), cert. denied 532 U.S. 1044 (2001); United States v. Youts, 229 F.3d 1312 (10th Cir. 2000); United States v. Hernandez-Guevara, 162 F.3d 863 (5th Cir. 1998); United States v. Beasley, 809 F.2d 1273 (7th Cir. 1987).

[23] See Edward J. Imwinkelried, The Use of an Accused Uncharged Misconduct to Prove Mens Rea: The Doctrine Which Threatens to Engulf the Character Evidence Prohibition, 51 Ohio St. L.J. 575 (1990); David P. Leonard, The Use of Uncharged Misconduct Evidence to Prove Knowledge, 81 Neb. L. Rev. 115, 148 (2002) (the misuse of "other acts" evidence to show

return to this problem and possible solutions after discussing intent below.

The remainder of this section discusses some of the most important *permitted* uses of character evidence, beginning with some of the least controversial.

2. Character in Issue

Sometimes evidence of a character trait is offered not so the jury may *infer* some other material fact but because that trait of character is *itself* of consequence in the suit. Examples include evidence that an individual is an unfit parent, when parental "fitness" is at issue in a custody battle; evidence that the plaintiff is "corrupt" when offered by the defendant in a defamation action to show the truth of an accusation of corruption; evidence that the operator of a passenger train was a reckless driver when offered to show that the railroad company negligently entrusted its trains to a careless person; evidence that the alleged victim of the offense of seduction was "chaste" where chastity is an element of the offense; evidence that the defendant is a convicted robber, when offered to prove that she violated a penal statute forbidding convicted felons to possess firearms; evidence of uncharged offenses to show the existence of a criminal enterprise in a prosecution for racketeering; and evidence in a drug possession case that a defendant often used illicit drugs when offered to rebut the claim that government agents entrapped a defendant who was not otherwise "predisposed" to commit the crime.[24] This *non*inferential use of character evidence is a necessary and obvious "other purpose" for such evidence that is permitted (because not excluded) by FRE 404.

There may be less danger of prejudice when character itself is at issue than when it is used to prove other conduct. Because the legally significant fact is the very fact that the character evidence most directly proves—for example, that the person in possession of a firearm *was* an ex-felon—the jury is unlikely to be influenced by the evidence unless it is convinced on that legally relevant issue.[25] But there is some danger of

---

knowledge is "perhaps most common" in prosecutions for drug offenses, particularly possession with intent to distribute).

[24] See Sorrells v. United States, 287 U.S. 435, 451 (1932) (once an entrapment defense is raised, the prosecutor may present evidence of the defendant's propensity to commit the alleged crime). Although not barred by the propensity rule, character evidence offered to prove character in issue might still be excluded if prejudicial effect substantially outweighs probative value, as might occur if the other acts are old ones.

[25] Consider, by way of contrast, evidence offered to show that the defendant is the person who committed a bank robbery because he committed several prior bank robberies using the same *modus operandi*. In that situation, the evidence can prejudice the defendant in multiple ways (e.g., by encouraging the jury to convict the defendant because he is a bad man or because he is by disposition a bank robber, hence is likely to be the bank robber in question) even if the jury does not draw the inference for which the evidence is offered—that the prior and the current robberies were carried out in so similar a fashion that the perpetrator of all of them must be the same person.

prejudice nonetheless. The jury may, for example, use evidence that the defendant committed a prior felony not only for the permitted noninferential purpose of deciding that she is an ex-felon, but also for the forbidden inferential purpose of deciding that she very likely was in possession of a gun, and may also alter its view of the importance of proof beyond a reasonable doubt, given that the defendant has a felony record. This type of prejudice is built into statutes that make such character issues elements of criminal offenses.[26] The magnitude of the problem depends on the content of the criminal statute. For example, in *People v. Gardeley,*[27] the defendants were charged with attempted murder, felonious assault and robbery, with an enhancement if the jury found that their conduct was "for the benefit of, at the direction of, or in association with any criminal street gangs." At trial the prosecutor was allowed to present opinion evidence that the defendants were gang members, and evidence of particular prior gang crimes that they were alleged to have committed. The California Supreme Court affirmed the convictions, despite the fact that this sort of evidence could easily have prejudiced the jury in its decision on the underlying crimes. Although we find the Gardeley opinion disturbing on several counts, the court's decision does not offend the propensity rule.[28] The essential problem is the underlying statute, which requires the jury simultaneously to determine guilt and make vague and potentially highly prejudicial findings about the defendants' character, associations and past behavior.

FRE 405(b) recognizes the special nature of cases in which "a person's character or character trait is an essential element of a charge, claim, or defense" by providing that in that situation a person's character may be proven by "specific instances of the person's conduct" as well as by reputation or opinion testimony. Only the latter two types of proof are available under FRE 405(a) when the exceptions to the propensity rule found in FRE 404(a)(2)(A) and (B) and FRE 608 allow character to be used as evidence of conduct. FRE 405(b) reflects a recognition that when character itself is at issue, character evidence, and especially evidence of specific instances of conduct, is likely to be more important and less dangerous than when such evidence is used to prove behavior circumstantially. The types of evidence that may be used to prove a person's character are discussed in greater detail below.

---

[26] Cf. Chapter Three, Section I.I., pp. 234–240 (discussing Old Chief v. United States, 519 U.S. 172 (1997), a "felon in possession" case in which the Court ruled under the circumstances that, in order to exclude highly prejudicial evidence detailing a prior offense, the trial judge should have required the prosecutor to accept the defendant's stipulation that he was an ex-felon).

[27] 14 Cal.4th 605, 59 Cal.Rptr.2d 356, 927 P.2d 713 (Cal.1996).

[28] The opinion evidence that the defendants were gang members came from a police officer testifying as an expert on gang activities, and was based in part on hearsay reports that the defendants had committed various gang-related crimes. We believe this was a serious abuse of the rules governing expert testimony, discussed in Chapter Nine.

Problem V-2. The plaintiff sues the defendant for the wrongful death of her son. She alleges that the defendant was negligent in retaining one Peter Elrod as a blasting crew foreman and that Elrod's negligence in failing to warn of an imminent detonation was the proximate cause of her son's death. The plaintiff seeks to introduce general reputation evidence concerning the foreman's character for carelessness, testimony from two people who had worked with Elrod that in their opinion he was the most careless foreman they had worked under, and testimony describing three instances when the foreman had failed to give sufficient warning that a blast was imminent. **Is any of this evidence admissible? On what issues?**

Problem V-3. Darlene Duvall is charged with conspiracy to sell cocaine. She claims that the Government, through an undercover agent, entrapped her into taking part in the conspiracy. The Government offers evidence that a month before the alleged entrapment began, Duvall approached the undercover agent offering to sell him cocaine. The Defendant objects. **What ruling and why?**

3. Other Crimes, Wrongs or Acts

a. Introduction

FRE 404(a)(1) does not bar evidence of a person's character if the inference it is offered to support is something other than that the person acted in conformity with the character trait. As we note above, FRE 404(b)(2) emphasizes this point, by providing that evidence of "Crimes, Wrongs, or Other Acts" may be admissible for nonpropensity purposes "such as proving motive, opportunity, intent, preparation, plan, knowledge, identity, absence of mistake or lack of accident." Consider a bank robbery in which the masked robber escapes by commandeering a car outside the bank, taking the driver hostage, running a red light and crashing into a sanitation truck. At trial, the prosecutor might offer evidence of the car theft, kidnapping and reckless driving—not to support an inference that the defendant has a propensity to commit criminal acts, but rather to show that the defendant (the person pulled from the car that hit the garbage truck) was the bank robber. It's hard to imagine a trial judge who would not admit the evidence for this purpose.

FRE 404(b)(2) permits evidence of what the title to FRE 404(b) calls Crimes, Wrongs, or Acts" that are not at issue in the trial for any nonpropensity purpose. Given the permission for evidence of "Acts", the more limited categories that precede "Acts"—"Crimes, Wrongs"—are logically superfluous. The function of these terms—like the function of FRE 404(b)(2) in its entirety—is to highlight common but controversial situations in which nonpropensity uses of other-act evidence is permitted. Thus, under FRE 404(b)(2), evidence that the defendant flew jets for the Air Force will be admissible to show that he was able to fly the plane he is charged with stealing; and evidence that the plaintiff drove on a particular road five days a week for ten years will be admissible to show that she was familiar with its twists and turns. But these uses of prior "acts," and countless others, are too innocuous to raise an eyebrow. Problems occur only when there is a serious potential for prejudice, and that usually happens when the other "acts" are "crimes" or "wrongs." Accordingly, most disputes arising under FRE 404(b)(2)—and our discussion of that rule—focus on the latter two types of acts.

In this subsection we discuss some of the most common nonpropensity uses of evidence of other crimes or wrongs, and some of the problems peculiar to each such use. We also cover the "issue in dispute" prerequisite for such uses, and procedural questions. The names that are used to describe particular nonpropensity uses are often arbitrary; as you will see, some uses can be described equally well under two or three separate headings. Most of our examples—and most actual trials in which "other crimes" evidence is used—are criminal cases. But "other acts" evidence also may be offered in civil cases. For example, in a civil suit growing out of a hit-and-run car accident the plaintiff might use evidence of the defendant's commission of bank robbery and car theft near the time and place of the accident to show that the defendant was at the scene of the accident, and that he had a motive to drive recklessly and to leave the accident scene without stopping.

Problem V-4. Dan Dooley is charged with the illegal sale of narcotics. At his trial the prosecution seeks to introduce evidence that Dooley attempted to hire someone to kill the main prosecution witness. Dooley objects. **Does the testimony come in?**

b. *"Res Gestae"*

Courts frequently hold that wrongs committed or detected simultaneously with the conduct at issue in the case are admissible to give the jury a fuller understanding of the events surrounding the crime charged.[29] This exception is sensible, for often the story of one crime

---

[29] This category is sometimes said to be comprised of two types of situations: (1) where the alleged crime or tort occurred contemporaneously with a separate one, and both must be described to give the jury a convincing account of what happened; and (2) where the alleged crime or tort is an aggregate of multiple offenses or wrongs over a period of time, only some of which are charged in the case. For a discussion of the difference between the two and an example of the latter in a civil case, see Elliot v. Turner Constr. Co., 381 F.3d 995 (10th Cir.

cannot be intelligibly told without some discussion of other crimes. If the defendant is on trial for a murder that occurred during a robbery, it is difficult to describe the murder—and it may be impossible to suggest a motive for it—without mentioning the robbery.

Courts, however, sometimes use this theory to admit evidence of other crimes that are *not* needed to understand the offense charged. In a Texas trial for drunken driving, for example, a prosecutor was allowed to introduce evidence of a gun found concealed in the defendant's car at the time of his arrest.[30] And in a New York prosecution for possession with intent to distribute based on heroin found in a car search incident to arrest, the trial judge permitted the prosecutor to introduce evidence of the uncharged crime that triggered the arrest, even though the jurors' lack of knowledge of the reason for the arrest would have left no ambiguity about the facts of the case.[31]

Problem V-5. Orly Overstreet is charged with possession of a controlled substance known as Angel Dust. Eunice Mercury is prepared to testify that she was working at The Chasm Clothing Store when Overstreet tried to purchase two pairs of blue jeans with a credit card. Mercury discovered that the credit card was stolen and confronted Overstreet, who grabbed the pants and ran out of the store. Mercury gave chase, screaming for onlookers to call the police. Moments before Mercury caught up with Overstreet and tackled her, Mercury saw Overstreet pull a brown paper bag from her purse and throw it down a storm sewer. When the police arrived they recovered a brown bag from the sewer; the bag contained a controlled substance, Angel Dust. Overstreet objects to the part of Mercury's proposed testimony about the credit card and pants. **How should the judge rule?**

c. *Identity*

Courts frequently admit other-crimes evidence to show identity. Unfortunately, they do not consistently define the situations in which the concept applies. Without a limiting definition, this use could swallow the

---

2004) (to establish defendant's negligent planning of a bridge construction project, plaintiff could introduce evidence of multiple negligent acts reflecting the poorly conceived plan). See also United States v. McGauley, 279 F.3d 62 (1st Cir. 2002) (evidence of uncharged instances of the fraudulent scheme at issue in the case was admissible to explain the fraud.)

[30] Dowdy v. State, 385 S.W.2d 678 (Tex.Crim.Ct.App. 1964).

[31] See People v. Resek, 3 N.Y.3d 385, 787 N.Y.S.2d 683, 821 N.E.2d 108, 110 (2004) (reversing the conviction because evidence of the uncharged crime was not necessary to help the jury "sort out ambiguous but material facts," and any ambiguity could have been avoided by "instruct[ing] the jurors that the arrest was lawful and that they were not to speculate as to its reasons"). See also United States v. Bowie, 232 F.3d 923, 928 (D.C. Cir. 2000) (criticizing overbroad use of res gestae to admit other-crimes evidence because it "threatens to override" the propensity rule).

propensity rule whole, because one of the classic propensity inferences is from past crimes to present identity—from the fact that the defendant committed other offenses to the conclusion the he is the person who committed the offense in question. This misuse of the identity concept illustrates an important fact about the FRE 404(b)(2) list of permitted uses of prior-crimes evidence. That list not only is under-inclusive because it is illustrative rather than exhaustive;[32] it is also over-inclusive because evidence offered for a listed purpose is still inadmissible (or, at least, *should* be inadmissible) if it relies on the forbidden propensity inference to serve that purpose.

Evidence that an item the defendant acquired in a previous crime was used by the otherwise unidentified perpetrator in committing the charged crime may properly be used to prove identity, as when a gun the defendant is known to have stolen from a sporting goods store is later used to commit a homicide. Likewise, in our bank robbery example, the defendant's commission of a series of crimes that suggest a hasty escape from a location near the bank—reckless driving, running a red light, leaving the scene of an accident, etc.—is admissible to support the inference that the defendant is the one who robbed the bank moments before. In both examples, the link between the two crimes is relatively strong; there is no need to puzzle over degrees of similarity. But a caution is in order. The inference that the defendant committed the offense charged can be no stronger than the evidence that the defendant committed the other crimes. The weaker the evidence that the defendant committed the other crimes, the greater the likelihood that the prior-crimes evidence will waste the court's time and unfairly prejudice the defendant. Below, we discuss the question of how much evidence that the defendant committed the other act is needed to justify admitting evidence of the act.

FRE 404(b)(2) also lists "opportunity" as a permissible purpose for evidence of other crimes. But "opportunity," "ability," "skill" and various related issues are really just bases for inferring "identity"—that the defendant is the person who did it. For example, evidence that the defendant stole a car half an hour after a homicide, in the same remote hamlet, demonstrates that he was at the crime scene at the right time and could have done the killing ("opportunity"). Similarly, evidence that in a previous robbery the defendant shot the lock off a door at 40 feet demonstrates that she has the skill to commit a similar feat in the course of the charged crime ("skill"). In both cases, the other crimes support the argument that the defendant *could* have been the person who committed this crime as well. As we discuss below, certain uses of FRE 404(b)(2)'s common "plan" category also goes to identity.

---

[32] For example, evidence that the defendant bribed a potential witness in the defendant's narcotics trial is admissible to prove the defendant's consciousness of guilt, even though that use is not listed in FRE 404(b). See United States v. Mendez-Ortiz, 810 F.2d 76 (6th Cir. 1986).

Problem V-6. Sandy Suttry is charged with theft from a safe in the Knoxville Supermarket on April 3. The theft occurred while the supermarket was open for business. There was no evidence of forced entry into the safe. The prosecution offers evidence showing: (1) that when Suttry was arrested the next day, on April 4, he was holding a leather bag containing metal files, a small crowbar, a stethoscope and skeleton keys; (2) that eight weeks earlier on February 11, Suttry made a bank deposit that included a marked bill stolen three days earlier during business hours from the same safe; and (3) that ten weeks before that, on November 23, Suttry was the getaway driver for a bank robbery committed by Colleen McCarty, whose brother, Gene, was a Knoxville Supermarket employee during the entire period in question. **What objections should Suttry make to this evidence? How should the judge rule?**

d. Motive

In our earlier bank robbery example, the robbery created the motive for the car theft, kidnapping and the traffic offenses and linked the perpetrator of those crimes to the crime on trial. Frequently, the argument runs the other way: The defendant's commission of a prior offense is used as evidence that he had a motive to commit the offense charged, as when a prominent citizen's involvement in various criminal enterprises is used to establish a motive for hiring someone to kill a prosecutor.[33] Other crimes evidence is particularly important in circumstances such as these because the jury might regard the absence of evidence of a motive as evidence of innocence. The case for other-crimes evidence is less compelling when the jury is more likely to assume that a sufficient motive exists. The desire for money, for example, is so common that there is no need to demonstrate it in order to secure a conviction for theft or robbery. Nevertheless, some courts admit evidence tending to show that a defendant is a drug addict with an expensive "habit" or outstanding drug debts in order to establish a motive for theft. Such evidence is not logically irrelevant, but it may be so fraught with the danger of prejudice that its probative value (at least when offered in the

---

[33] See United States v. Vance, 871 F.2d 572 (6th Cir. 1989); United States v. Siegel, 536 F.3d 306 (4th Cir.), cert. denied, 129 S.Ct. 770 (2008) (defendant's extensive history of frauds and crimes was admissible to establish her motive to kill the victim who was in a position to report the crimes to authorities). Although usually used to establish identity or conduct, a motive created by prior crimes also may establish intent. See United States v. Palmer, 809 F.2d 1504 (11th Cir. 1987) (acquisition of wealth through unlawful drug dealing permits inference of motive, and thus of intent, to evade taxes).

prosecution's case-in-chief before the defendant has made an issue of motive) is substantially outweighed by its prejudicial effect.[34]

"Other crimes" evidence has also been used to suggest that a motive for the prior offenses carried over to the offense charged. Where the defendant assaulted a murder victim several times in the past, evidence of the prior assaults might be offered to show that the defendant "hated" the victim. Although no less an authority than Wigmore has approved this use of other crimes evidence to show motive,[35] there is little to distinguish it from the forbidden inference that defendant had a propensity to attack the victim. From this, hate is inferred, and hate is then posited as a motive to assault and kill the victim. But the same inference from previous assaults to the assault charged could be made without reference to the intervening emotion of hate (or jealousy or sadistic pleasure). The intuition persists, however, that this situation presents a stronger case for using prior-crimes evidence than most uses that trigger a propensity inference. Perhaps the defendant's record of committing crimes against a particular victim is so probative of whether he committed a similar crime against the same victim that its value outweighs the associated dangers. Indeed, as we suggest in Subsection 5 below, the propensity rule may be defined so that it does not exclude evidence offered for this explicit purpose. If this is the basis for admissibility, however, courts should face the policy issues directly, rather than applying the potentially over-inclusive label of "motive."

———————

Problem V-7. Tom Harford is charged with murdering a store clerk in an attempted robbery. The prosecution offers evidence that Harford (1) was homeless on the day of the robbery; (2) had a $200-a-day morphine addiction at the time; (3) physically threatened a friend, a week before the robbery, when the friend said she couldn't pay up on a loan Harford had made to her; and (4) was turned over to the police six months earlier for shoplifting, by the same store clerk. **Is any of this evidence admissible in the prosecution's case-in-chief? Would it make a difference if the attempted robbery were of a pharmacy?**

———————————————

[34] Compare United States v. LaFlam, 369 F.3d 153 (2d Cir.), cert. denied, 543 U.S. 951 (2004) (defendant's drug use and debts around the time of the alleged bank robberies were admissible to establish his motive to commit, and thus an inference the he did commit, the alleged robberies) with United States v. Madden, 38 F.3d 747 (4th Cir. 1994) (evidence of drug use and addiction is not admissible to establish the defendant's motive to commit bank robbery absent specific evidence, in addition, that he didn't have the financial resources to support his addiction).

[35] 2 Wigmore § 306, at 206. See, e.g., Government of Virgin Islands v. Harris, 938 F.2d 401 (3d Cir. 1991) (admitting evidence of defendant's prior acts of violence against his wife to establish his negative feelings towards her and an inference that he was the one who killed her).

e. Common Plan or Scheme

Perhaps the most elastic and bewildering category of nonpropensity uses of other-acts evidence is that referred to as "common plan or scheme." This label is applied in several distinct situations. Sometimes, one crime is in fact predicated on the commission of another. An example is setting a building on fire to cover up a theft. Because the crime charged (arson) cannot be understood without knowing of the associated crime (theft), the case for admission is strong. This use of the other-crimes evidence can also be understood as a variant of the res gestae category that we discuss above.

The "common plan or scheme" label is also sometimes used when the defendant is charged with an offense based on his connection to an event with innocent as well as criminal explanations. Here, evidence of a connection to several similar events is offered to rule out the innocent explanations. Suppose, for example, that an infant under the care of a baby sitter dies suddenly in her crib when her breathing stops. Although suspicion might focus on the baby sitter, the possibility of Sudden Infant Death Syndrome or "crib death" would justify a failure to prosecute. Suppose, however, that the prosecutor shows that the same baby sitter previously was present when five other children died under similar circumstances. This evidence is highly probative of the claim that the baby sitter suffocated the sixth victim (and some or all of the others). Although the probability that any one of the unusual incidents occurred by accident may be relatively high, the probability that all six occurred innocently while the same baby sitter was on duty is extremely low.[36] This other-acts evidence also is less prejudicial than usual because the *forbidden* propensity inference does not arise unless the *desired* inference is drawn. The trier of fact is unlikely to conclude, based on the five other deaths, that the defendant has a propensity to kill children without first concluding, based on the low probability of six innocent deaths occurring in the same way, that foul play caused the charged homicide. This version of "common plan or scheme" evidence is also sometimes treated as evidence of "absence of mistake, or lack of accident." FRE 404(b)(2).

The "common plan or scheme" justification is most frequently used when two or more crimes appear to have been plotted by the same individual because they exhibit a similar unusual pattern. The similarity between the other-crimes and the crime charged supports an inference that the same individual committed all of them. As such, anything that serves to link the defendant to the similar crimes also links her to the crime charged. Because courts usually require other crimes admitted under this theory to bear some peculiar similarity to the crime charged,[37]

---

[36] See United States v. Woods, 484 F.2d 127 (4th Cir. 1973).

[37] The charged and other crimes should be similar in important respects that clearly distinguish them from crimes of the same generic sort. Compare United States v. Robinson, 161 F.3d 463 (7th Cir. 1998), cert. denied, 526 U.S. 1078 (1999) (defendant's subsequent bank

they sometimes classify this use of other-crimes evidence as "novel means," "distinctive modus operandi," "behavioral fingerprint"—or simply "identity"—rather than "common scheme or plan."

Here again, the strength of the inference from the other-crimes evidence depends on how strongly the defendant is linked to the other crimes. If the crime charged is one in a series of bizarrely similar crimes, a rational trier of fact may be satisfied that the same person committed them all. Yet, if there is no evidence linking the defendant to the other crimes, evidence about them can only be prejudicial. Though it may be less intuitively obvious, the other-crimes evidence may be equally weak and prejudicial if the defendant is only linked to the other crimes by evidence that already links him to the crime charged. Consider, for example, a series of armed robberies in which ballistics tests indicate that all shots fired were from the same gun.[38] Suppose the defendant is arrested for speeding, and the gun that fired the shots is found in the car. She is charged with the one robbery in which there is an eyewitness identification. She answers the charge by attempting to discredit the eyewitness and claiming that she bought the gun from a stranger two days before being arrested. The jurors will not be aided in evaluating the competing theories by knowing that the same gun was used in three, five, or fifty robberies rather than just in the one charged. They may, however, be prejudicially swayed by their knowledge of other crimes. The more robberies it appears the defendant might have committed, the more the jurors may regret the mistake of acquitting her though she is guilty, and the less evidence it may take to persuade them to convict.[39] Only if there is evidence besides the gun that the defendant committed one or more of the other robberies in which shots were fired by the assailant will the state's case be legitimately strengthened by the fact that the defendant possessed the gun used in all the robberies.

---

robbery was admissible to link him to the prior, charged bank robbery, given a common modus operandi: the robber in both cases wore an orange ski mask with a distinctive slit; carried a large Louis Vuitton duffel bag; vaulted the teller counter, bag and pistol in hand; demanded money at gunpoint; laid the gun down while emptying the teller drawers himself; and fled in a blue Chevrolet Cavalier) with United States v. Luna, 21 F.3d 874 (9th Cir. 1994) ("take over" feature of two other bank robberies and the one charged is too "generic" to justify admission of the other crimes). In addition, there should be no important attributes that distinguish the other offenses from the charged crime. McCormick, § 190, aptly describes the appropriate standard: "The pattern and characteristics of the crime must be so unusual and distinctive as to be like a signature." Regrettably, some courts see a scrawled John Hancock when faced with little more than a printed John Doe.

[38] Cf. Williams v. State, 143 So.2d 484 (Fla.1962).

[39] See Chapter III, Section II.B., pp. 249–255. Jurors surely would anticipate feeling more regret upon finding out that they acquitted a guilty defendant whom they had reason to think was a career criminal than a defendant who appeared to be a first-time offender. But the presumption of innocence and other societal values discussed above suggest that criminal jurors' regret matrices should take into account only the regret associated with inaccurately punishing or not punishing the perpetrator of the charged offense and not that associated with the possibility that the defendant will be punished or escape punishment for other offenses. This helps explain why jurors (as opposed to the sentencing judge) are not routinely presented with evidence of the defendant's prior record (unless the defendant testifies, see infra, Section IV.B.3).

Even when the evidence linking the defendant to the other offenses is strong and those offenses are distinctively similar to the one charged, one still might ask whether the permitted "distinctive modus operandi" inference differs from the forbidden propensity inference. The jury arguably is still being invited to convict the defendant of the offense charged because he has a propensity to commit offenses just like it. Evidently a different outcome is warranted—despite the fact that the prejudice caused by hearing about other criminal conduct by the defendant is similar—because the probative value of "modus operandi" evidence is far greater than most other propensity evidence, and the danger of overestimation is far smaller. Even so, courts should explain why and where they draw the line between the two types of evidence.[40] We attempt to do just that in Subsection 5 below.

Problem V-8. Maude Margarette is charged with robbing a grocery store after pulling a snub-nosed revolver on the proprietor. The prosecution has two other grocery store owners who will identify Maude as the person who robbed their stores at the point of a snub-nosed revolver. **Should the testimony from these witnesses be allowed? Would the prosecution's chance of getting this testimony admitted be greater, lesser, or the same if the person allegedly involved in the three robberies were a man rather than a woman?**

f.   Knowledge

Occasionally, the prosecutor or plaintiff in a civil case has to prove, as part of its case-in-chief or to meet a defense, that the defendant knew certain facts. In some situations, evidence of other crimes tends to demonstrate that knowledge. Suppose, for example, that the defendant is charged with passing a counterfeit twenty dollar bill. The defendant denies knowing the bill was counterfeit. If the state can show that the defendant had in the past engaged in counterfeiting, this would tend to show that he had the expertise to recognize a counterfeit twenty when he saw one.[41] The same inference might be drawn from the defendant's possession of equipment used to counterfeit money. Knowledge also

---

[40] One alternative explanation is that modus operandi evidence does not link defendants to crimes via a propensity inference but instead via "trace" or "resemblance" inferences like those raised by such circumstantial evidence of identity as matching DNA or carpet fibers. It arguably is no more appropriate to say that "John was convicted of being the bank robber in the Bozo mask because he was shown to have a propensity to rob banks while wearing clown masks" than it is to say that "Jane was convicted of being the bank robber who left behind a type AB blood stain because she has a propensity to shed type AB blood." Still, the former may more appropriately be called a propensity inference than the latter, given the higher degree of choice and opprobrium associated with the apparently matching trait and the higher likelihood of some unnoticed dissimilarity between the trait reflected in the case at hand and the trait revealed by the prior cases.

[41] See United States v. Crachy, 800 F.2d 83 (6th Cir. 1986).

sometimes is used to prove identity on theories that we describe in subsection c. above as "opportunity" or "ability."

Problem V-9 (review problem). In the past year, Officer Ronald Howard has seen Alice Kidboy smoking a marijuana cigarette (once) and carrying paraphernalia used in smoking marijuana (twice). **At which of the following seven trials is Howard's testimony admissible against Kidboy?** (1) Kidboy's trial for possessing marijuana, which she claims a police officer planted in her purse after her arrest on other charges; (2) the same trial, after Kidboy instead testifies that an undercover police officer entrapped her into taking the drugs from him; (3) the same trial, at which Kidboy instead claims a friend put an ounce of marijuana in her purse a week before her arrest without telling her; (4) the same trial, at which the crucial issue instead is whether an expertly rolled marijuana cigarette—found on a bar in a restaurant—belonged to Kidboy (who admits seeing the "joint" on the bar but says she never touched it), or to the man sitting next to her at the bar; (5) Kidboy's trial on charges of being a felon in possession of a controlled substance, namely, cocaine; (6) a libel trial in which Kidboy is suing *The Manhattaner* magazine for publishing an article calling her "a doper"; (7) the same libel trial, except that the alleged libel is that Kidboy is "a petty thief"? **In which of these trials is "knowledge" the best theory of admissibility? What turns on correctly labeling that theory? In which of these trials is Kidboy's character "at issue"? What turns on correctly answering that question?**

g. *Intent*

When a party's commission of the alleged act is conceded or easily established, courts often admit other-acts evidence to prove that the act was not done innocently but with the intent required to establish criminal or civil liability. Suppose the defendant is charged with bribing college basketball players to "shave" points in violation of a statute making it an offense to pay players money with "the intent to influence their play."[42] Evidence that the defendant had paid players to shave points in other states bears on the defendant's intent through inferences that do not depend on character. The past payment of bribes suggests that, when the same person gave money to the players involved in the instant case, he was not providing a token of affection or an under the table scholarship or making a mistake, but was acting with the hope and knowledge, based on past experience, that the recipients would alter their play.

The admission of prior-act evidence to prove intent is easier to justify when the intent at issue is actually in dispute, especially when the

---

[42] Cf. State v. Goldberg, 261 N.C. 181, 134 S.E.2d 334, cert. denied, 377 U.S. 978 (1964).

commission of the prior act is conceded. Consider how a jury would evaluate a defendant's testimony that he administered poison to his wife believing the substance was harmless after the prosecution shows that the victim was the third spouse poisoned by the defendant's "mistakes." Not only is the evidence highly probative on the issue of intent, but it may also be the only evidence available to counter the defendant's claim of honest error. Notice, however, even in these relatively noncontroversial circumstances, how thin the line is between the argument that the prior crimes indicate that the defendant did not make an honest mistake and the argument that the prior crimes show that the defendant has a propensity to do evil acts.[43] We attempt to make that line more distinct in Subsection 5 below.

When the commission of the prior act is *not* admitted, or when its circumstances are not clearly established by other evidence, prior-acts evidence offered to prove intent presents more serious problems. Suppose Mark is charged with killing his daughter, whom he rushed to the hospital with a head injury. He claims that the girl fell off a couch and hit her head on a coffee table. The state claims he struck the child. A court might admit evidence of prior wounds likely to have been caused by beatings (so-called "battered child syndrome" evidence) on the theory that, although not linked by any direct evidence to Mark, "proof of [the daughter's] battered child status . . . demonstrated that [her] death was the result of an *intentional act* by *someone*, and not an accident."[44] Even if instructed not to consider this evidence on the question whether *Mark* inflicted the head wound, the jury is almost sure to use the evidence in that very prejudicial way, as well as on the issue of intent.

Although the use of prior acts to prove intent is usually discussed in the context of criminal cases, it is also a common feature in some sorts of civil trials. Such evidence may be used, of course, in trials of civil claims for fraud or conversion, or other types of misconduct that are also criminal, but the most frequent use may be in discrimination cases that have no criminal overtones. In a typical case, there is no dispute about *what* the defendant did—that he hired five male job applicants, but not the female plaintiff, for example—and the entire case turns on *why* he did so: Was it because the plaintiff is a woman, or for some other reason? In such cases, the defendant's general hiring practices (and sometimes other

---

[43] Consider, for example, an attorney who is charged with making fraudulent statements to a bankruptcy court to obscure his possible conflicts of interest. He admits making inaccurate statements but denies any intent to deceive. Does evidence that he had misrepresented his bar memberships in prior filings in other courts tend to prove that he knows a false statement when he makes one to a court, or does it show that he has a propensity to lie to courts? To us, the evidence falls on the propensity side of the line. But in the case from which the facts are taken, the trial and appellate courts admitted the evidence as permissible, nonpropensity proof of intent. United States v. Gellene, 182 F.3d 578 (7th Cir. 1999).

[44] Estelle v. McGuire, 502 U.S. 62, 69 (1991) (emphasis added) (admission of evidence under similar circumstances does not violate the federal Constitution, whether or not it violated state evidence law).

conduct as well) are routinely admitted as circumstantial evidence of his intent. Because intent is the central (often, the sole) issue in such cases, and because the defendant's actual conduct is rarely in dispute, the use of prior-acts evidence in civil discrimination trials is less controversial.

In criminal cases, where the practice often *is* controversial, there are three major safeguards against the inappropriate use of prior-acts evidence to prove intent—though courts are often quite lax in applying them. The first two are discussed above: The judge's power (1) to require the party offering the evidence to articulate clearly the chain of inferences for which the evidence is offered and to review the explanation to be sure it involves no inference of action in conformity with bad character, and (2) to undertake an explicit balance of probative value against unfair prejudice, with prejudice including the likelihood that the jury will use the evidence for impermissible purposes. The third safeguard—exclusion of the evidence when intent is not actually in dispute—is discussed in the next subsection.

Problem V-10. Dave meets Vivian at Dorian's Red Hand Bar. The two go home together to Vivian's apartment. Towards morning, according to Vivian, Dave ties her up, beats and rapes her, then appears to fall asleep. Vivian frees herself, leaves and calls the police, who return with Vivian to her apartment. Vivian and the police find Dave in the shower merrily singing away, calm and collected as can be. Upon questioning by the police, Dave expresses shock at Vivian's story and claims that, as far as he knew, everything occurring the night before was with Vivian's consent. At trial, the prosecutor offers testimony by Anita and Brenda that they, too, met Dave at Dorian's, took Dave home with them, were tied up, beaten and raped, escaped, returned to their apartments with the police, and found Dave merrily showering and singing. **Is Anita's and Brenda's testimony admissible? If so, on what theory? Suppose instead that Dave is accused of being the masked rapist who lured Vivian into the hallway outside her apartment with a call on her unlisted cell phone number. Is evidence that Dave purloined Vivian's purse two months earlier at Dorian's Bar admissible? If so, on what theory?**

h. Issue in Dispute

Before permitting a party to use other-crimes evidence to show something besides propensity, the court should determine that the issue on which the evidence is offered is actually in dispute. Some courts see this as a simple mechanical process: An issue is in dispute when it is an element of a charged offense, a civil cause of action, or a defense to either, and the opposing party has not expressly admitted to that element. This formalistic approach is misguided because parties often do not truly dispute issues that technically must be proved in order to establish or avoid liability. For example, prior-crimes evidence may be introduced to show a criminal defendant's state of mind in situations in which the only real issue is identity. Recall the example of the defendant charged with bribing college basketball players. The "prior-bribes" evidence would be highly probative if, for example, the defendant claimed she gave the players the money as a "prize" for stellar past performance but with no intent to influence their behavior in the future. But if the defendant instead denied that she gave the players any money, intent, though technically part of the prosecution's case, is not really in issue. The mistaken identity defense implicitly concedes that whoever paid the players did it so that they would shave points. In these circumstances, jurors are likely to use the "prior bribes" evidence not to draw a nonpropensity inference on the uncontested issue of intent but rather to draw a propensity inference on the disputed issue of identity: Knowing that the defendant bribed basketball players in the past may lead the jury to conclude that she's the person who bribed these players on this occasion.

Other courts recognize this danger and refuse to admit evidence to prove intent if the charged crime clearly was committed by *someone* with the required mental state, and if the defendant does not claim otherwise and instead defends on the ground that she was not the culprit.[45] Better courts go further and disallow bad-acts evidence offered to prove *any* element that the prosecution can sufficiently establish with other evidence and that the defendant does not contest. Many courts, however, treat the defendant's not guilty plea as placing all elements of the offense in issue. A defendant in such courts may try to counter the prosecution's offer of other-crimes evidence by formally stipulating to the element the evidence is theoretically offered to prove (e.g., intent), but courts often let the prosecutors refuse such a stipulation.[46]

In courts that limit other-crimes evidence to issues actually in dispute, the defendant's attorney must be careful not to open the door to such evidence by casting doubt on facts that otherwise are undisputed. If, for example, the defendant testifies that he gave his wife a poisonous

---

[45] See, e.g., United States v. Bell, 516 F.3d 432 (6th Cir. 2008); United States v. Sumner, 119 F.3d 658 (8th Cir. 1997); State v. Lipka, 174 Vt. 377, 817 A.2d 27, 38 (2002).

[46] See, e.g., United States v. Tan, 254 F.3d 1204 (10th Cir. 2001). Cf. Old Chief v. United States, 519 U.S. 172 (1997), discussed supra, in note 26, and also discussed in Chapter Three, Section I.I., pp. 234–240. As *Old Chief* makes clear, parties are permitted to refuse stipulations in order to get the benefit of more salient evidence they prefer to present. If, however, that additional salience is substantially outweighed by the prejudicial effect of the preferred evidence, the trial court should exclude the evidence under FRE 403, which usually has the effect of forcing the party to accept the stipulation. See United States v. Crowder, 141 F.3d 1202 (D.C. Cir. 1998). Such stipulations may not be without cost to the party making them; they may confuse jurors into thinking that more is being conceded than the issue the stipulation is designed to take out of the case. Stipulations are discussed more generally in Chapter Eleven, Section II.A., pp. 1393–1399.

substance by accident after mistaking it for medicine, the prosecutor would probably be allowed to respond by showing that the defendant had poisoned someone else, or had attacked his wife in any manner, or had attempted to hire someone to kill her.

———————

Problem V-11. Patricia Poitras claims that Quinn Quimby and Rex Robbins kidnapped her in St. Louis and drove her to Des Moines. Quimby is indicted for that single offense. In an opening statement— before any evidence is presented—Quimby's lawyer claims the evidence will show that Poitras willingly joined the two men on the trip. The prosecutor, in her case in chief, seeks to elicit testimony from Poitras that Quimby and Robbins raped her during the trip from St. Louis to Des Moines. Quimby objects. **Is this testimony admissible? Would it be admissible if Quimby's announced defense instead were mistaken identity? Under either scenario, may the prosecutor call Stella Stetler to testify that she saw Quimby shoot Robbins dead in Des Moines two days after Poitras testifies that she arrived there? What if Stetler will testify that, just before shooting Robbins, Quimby said, "Dead men don't talk"?** Assume the alleged rape occurred in the same jurisdiction where the kidnapping case was being tried. **What might a prosecutor in that jurisdiction do to avoid any possible objection to evidence of the rape? What kind of motion might defense counsel make in response to that tactic? How would you expect the judge to rule on defense counsel's motion?**

i.   Notice; Proof of Involvement in Other Crimes

As we emphasize above, other-crimes evidence offered for nonpropensity purposes is no stronger than the proof that the other crimes occurred or than the link connecting them to the defendant. If either issue is disputable, the parties must be prepared to litigate the question. To assure that criminal defendants are not surprised by the need to try issues collateral to the ones charged, FRE 404(b)(2) requires prosecutors, "[o]n request by a defendant in a criminal case," to provide reasonable notice before trial (or, for good cause, during trial) of the general nature of any other-crimes evidence the state intends to introduce at trial.[47]

The link between the defendant and the proffered bad acts will sometimes be weak because other acts evidence is admissible under FRE 404(b)(2) without proof of a criminal conviction. Indeed, the other acts might not have violated any criminal law. Even if they did, the conduct

———————

[47]   FRE 404(b)(2) limits the notice requirement to criminal cases, where the effects of surprise are more serious and other means of discovery are more limited than in civil cases.

might not have led to charges or, if charges were brought, the defendant might have been acquitted. The last situation is particularly troublesome. Although a verdict of not guilty does not necessarily mean that the defendant was more likely than not innocent, acquittals are given that meaning for many purposes, and juries that acquit may do so because some or even all jurors think the defendant is in fact innocent. Few jurisdictions, however, regard acquittals as conclusive proof of the defendant's noninvolvement in prior bad acts, and the Supreme Court has held that there is no constitutional double jeopardy or collateral estoppel bar to admitting evidence of such acts following acquittals.[48] Admission of such evidence occasionally makes sense, as in our example of the baby sitter who claimed he lost six charges to "crib death," or the classic example of the man who claimed he accidentally poisoned three wives. In such cases, unless evidence of the earlier crimes is admitted despite the acquittals, the defendants might go on murdering with impunity, as long as prosecutors bring separate charges after each death. Situations as clear as these are rare, however, and would be adequately covered by a rule forbidding admission of evidence of another crime following acquittal unless later developments (as opposed to evidence that was available at the time of trial) suggest the acquittal was factually mistaken.

A prosecutor may not ethically offer evidence of a defendant's bad act unless she believes in good faith that the defendant committed it. When the prosecutor believes this and the defendant denies it, the court must decide whether the evidence linking the defendant to the bad act is strong enough to justify admitting evidence of that act. Different courts have applied different tests in assessing whether the link is strong enough, ranging from proof beyond a reasonable doubt, to "clear and convincing" evidence, to a preponderance of the evidence, to proof sufficient to support a reasonable juror's finding by a preponderance of the evidence (even if the judge herself is not convinced by a preponderance). We believe that a

---

[48] Dowling v. United States, 493 U.S. 342 (1990). In *Dowling*, the Court upheld the introduction of evidence of a subsequent attempted robbery on a modus operandi theory, even though the defendant had been acquitted of the subsequent offense. The Court ruled that the collateral estoppel aspect of the Fifth Amendment guarantee against double jeopardy applies only if the prior verdict unequivocally rests on a factual determination contrary to the one sought in the case at hand. In the case before the Court, the prior acquittal reflected only a determination that the defendant had not been proven guilty of the other offense *beyond a reasonable doubt*. The jury could use the other-crime evidence without contradicting the prior jury's determination, simply by considering that evidence along with everything else the government introduced. For even if the jury concluded only that the defendant *probably* (though not undoubtedly) committed the other offense, and thus that he probably committed the charged offense using the same modus operandi, it still could have convicted him beyond a reasonable doubt based, in addition, on an eyewitness identification of the defendant as the perpetrator of the charged offense and testimony linking him to a taxicab that the robber hijacked outside the bank. See also United States v. Felix, 503 U.S. 378 (1992) (prosecution's use of evidence of an uncharged crime to convict the defendant on a charged offense does not create a double jeopardy bar to the defendant's subsequent conviction for the uncharged crime). Unlike the federal courts, which rarely inform jurors of the acquittal, most state courts allow, or even require, the trial judge to instruct the jury, on request, that the accused was previously acquitted of the alleged other offense. See Kinney v. People, 187 P.3d 548 (Colo. 2008) (discussing cases).

relatively strict test—such as the "clear and convincing" standard—is warranted, for several reasons.   Prior-crimes evidence always creates a risk of misuse for propensity purposes, and it invites other kinds of prejudice as well.   Even if the evidence is properly probative, the balance of probative value and prejudice is likely to be close.   When there are serious doubts about the defendant's guilt of the other offense, probative weight declines and the likelihood of prejudice increases—which ordinarily should tip the balance in favor of exclusion.   Furthermore, if there is a genuine dispute about the defendant's involvement in the other crime, the defendant often will want to contest the matter before the jury. Because such collateral disputes draw the jury's attention away from the central issue in the case, it becomes difficult to provide the jury with enough information to permit a reliable resolution of the collateral issue without creating a substantial danger that the jury will be misled or confused as to the decisive issue in the case.   If, instead, a preliminary hearing is held before the judge alone, a full airing of the evidence of the other crime can occur relatively quickly.   Then, a strict standard of admissibility can minimize the danger that the jury will mistakenly attribute the crime to the defendant or be confused about the decisive issue, while still admitting other-crimes evidence when its probative value warrants.

In *Huddleston v. United States*,[49] the Supreme Court rejected these considerations.   Instead, taking a literal approach to the Federal Rules, the Court applied the broad rule of admissibility in FRE 104(b).[50]   That "conditional relevance" rule[51] requires the judge to admit other-crimes evidence as long as a reasonable juror, considering all the evidence, could find by a preponderance that the defendant committed the other crime— and as long as the judge concludes that the likely prejudice from the evidence (including the possibility of misuse for propensity purposes) does not substantially outweigh probative value.   Upon request, the judge must instruct the jurors that they cannot rely on the other-crimes evidence until they find by a preponderance that the defendant committed the other crimes.

The Court in *Huddleston* thought the weak FRE 104(b) test justified because it lets the government build its case out of "individual pieces of evidence" that are "insufficient in themselves to prove a point [but that]

---

[49]   485 U.S. 681 (1988).

[50]   Without considering probativeness or prejudice or other policy concerns, the Court simply noted that FRE 104(b) provides the general standard of admissibility when the relevance of one item of evidence is conditioned on proof of a fact, that FRE 404(b) has no contrary standard. and that the latter rule was drafted to emphasize the admissibility of prior crimes for nonpropensity purposes. Id. at 687–88.   Before *Huddleston*, most courts had applied at least a "clear and convincing evidence" test.

[51]   See Chapter Two, Section III.E.3. pp. 179–181, and Chapter Three, Section I.E., pp. 223– 228.

may in cumulation prove it."[52] The Court pointed out that the flexible standard of FRE 403 also applies, giving trial judges a satisfactory response to the prejudice inherent in other-crimes evidence when probative value is low because of doubts about the defendant's connection to the other crimes. Relying on this last point, courts may use the weakness of the evidence linking the defendant to other offenses as a basis for excluding them under FRE 403.[53]

Problem V-12. Milo Massey is charged with burglarizing the home of Fannie Finley, aged 79, on September 15. Finley testifies that she awoke one night to find a prowler in her room. It was dark, but she could see that the prowler had a piece of white cloth over his hand. When Finley stirred, the prowler fled. After calling the police, Finley discovered that someone had cut a six-inch square out of a white sheet in her spare bedroom. She never found the cloth square, but nothing else was missing. The prosecutor next offers the testimony of Cordelia Cox, aged 82, who lives twelve blocks from the Finley residence. Cox is prepared to testify that, three weeks later, on the night of October 6, she awoke to find a man in her bedroom with one of her white dish towels over his hand. When the man left, Cox got out of bed, found $11 missing and called the police. The police arrested Massey on the street near Cox's home and took him there, where Cox identified him as the burglar. Prior to the trial on the Finley burglary, Massey was tried for the Cox burglary and acquitted. Massey objects to Cox's testimony. **How should the judge rule? Would you rule differently if the case arose as a matter of first impression in a jurisdiction that has adopted the FREs but does not necessarily follow U.S. Supreme Court interpretations of particular FREs?**

j.   Summary of Other Crimes and Acts

We have devoted a good deal of space to questions involving evidence of other crimes and bad acts. It is a complicated and fascinating topic. It poses the problem of probative value versus prejudice in its starkest form. It vividly demonstrates that rules of evidence are not always neutral rules of procedure, but rather often carry systematic implications for the fate of particular categories of litigating parties. Any change that increases the probability that other-crimes evidence will be admitted at trial should increase the proportion of criminal defendants who are convicted, both at trial and by guilty plea. Some of those additional defendants who are convicted will be guilty, others will be innocent.

---

[52]   485 U.S. at 691 (quoting Bourjaily v. United States, 483 U.S. 171, 179–80 (1987)).

[53]   See, e.g., United States v. Fortenberry, 860 F.2d 628 (5th Cir. 1988).

Regrettably, we lack the knowledge to make even a good guess as to the proportion of defendants in each category.

The discussion also shows how courts can manipulate labels to reach decisions that are not justified by rigorous analysis. One reason judges do this is that lawyers fail in their tasks. Too often, lawyers only argue that precedent is more consistent with their preferred categorization than with that of their opponents. This argument is often fruitless, for appellate judges are adept at distinguishing or ignoring precedent they wish to avoid. A good advocate is able to explain *why* the case advanced as the controlling precedent or, more generally, the outcome the lawyer advocates makes sense, forcing the court to face the disturbing legal or logical implications of an adverse decision. Inability to do this is a legacy of learning rules without learning the reasons for them. Policy matters.

The following protocol may help when the admissibility of other-acts evidence is at issue. *First*, identify all the ways in which the other-acts evidence tends to establish a material and contested fact. *Second*, decide whether any of those uses proceeds without relying on the forbidden inference that the person acted in accordance with a character trait that the other acts suggest. If the only value of the evidence is by way of the propensity inference, it should be excluded unless it is covered by one of the exceptions to the propensity rule, which we discuss below. *Third*, if the evidence supports a disputed material fact both through the propensity inference and through an inference other than propensity, determine whether the prejudicial effect of the evidence substantially outweighs its probative value when offered for the permissible purpose. In reaching this last conclusion, probative value should be discounted by any doubts about the defendant's connection to the other acts, and prejudice should include the probability that the evidence will be used for the forbidden propensity inference despite a limiting instruction to the contrary. It is also appropriate to consider other ways the party offering the evidence can prove the same point, bearing in mind that parties generally have great discretion to prove their cases by any admissible evidence.

As this protocol suggests, much depends upon a clear distinction between evidence used for the forbidden propensity inference and evidence used for some other purpose. Considering some of the uses that are permitted to show "motive," "common scheme or plan" and "intent," you can see the difficulty of making this distinction. We will return to the question in a moment, but first we must consider one final purpose for which evidence of a pattern of conduct is admissible without resort to an exception to the propensity rule—namely, to show action in accordance with a habit or routine practice.

Problem V-13. In November and December 2012, Officer Rich of the Iowa City Police Department issued three speeding tickets to Nancy Jean. Shortly thereafter Rich, her husband, and the police department began to receive numerous telephone calls in which the caller remained silent or hung up. These calls continued for almost a year. During that period Rich and her husband received two threatening letters, both in March of 2013, which referred to Rich as a "pig" and threatened a gruesome death for her and her family. Jean was later arrested and charged on two counts of mailing threatening letters. At the trial the government introduced evidence that Rich had given Jean the three speeding tickets, evidence that one of the anonymous telephone calls had been traced to her telephone, testimony of a friend of Jean's that Jean had admitted making the calls, and testimony from the arresting officer that when he went to arrest Jean he found in her home three handguns, two rifles, a jar of cyanide poison and a homemade gasoline bomb. Jean objected to the admission of the evidence pertaining to her speeding, and her possession of firearms, poison and a bomb. **Should this evidence be admitted? On what theories?**

Problem V-14. Two men wearing ski masks and waving pistols rob a bank. Justin Jones and Thurston Thule are charged with the offense and tried separately. At Jones's trial, the prosecution wants to introduce: (1) Surveillance photographs of the robbery taken at a point when the mask of one of the robbers came off; (2) photographs of Jones's alleged accomplice, Thule, revealing that he strongly resembles the man whose mask came off during the bank robbery; (3) the testimony of Cheri Cheng that two men wearing ski masks robbed her at knife point in her home, two weeks after the bank robbery, taking some jewelry—men whom she would identify, based on their voices, as Jones (who lives on the first floor of her townhouse) and Thule (who lives next door). Jones objects to this evidence, citing FRE 402, 403, and 404(a)(1). **How should the judge rule? What if Jones had previously been acquitted of the Cheng robbery?**

4. Habit and Routine Practice

FRE 406 says:

> Evidence of a person's habit or an organization's routine practice may be admitted to prove that on a particular occasion the person or organization acted in accordance with the habit or routine practice. The court may admit this evidence regardless of whether it is corroborated or whether there was an eyewitness.

Under FRE 406, evidence of a person's habit or an organization's routine practice "may be admitted" to prove conduct in accordance with that habit or practice, unless—as is indicated by the word "may"—some other rule of exclusion (including FRE 403) applies. As we will see, however, this would be so without the rule, making FRE 406 superfluous in the same way as FRE 404(b)(2) is superfluous (see Section II.B.1, pp. 357–359, and II.B.3.a, pp. 361–362, above).

FRE 406 is not without purpose, however, because it explicitly rejects the so-called *eyewitness rule* that some common law jurisdictions followed. The eyewitness rule excluded evidence of a habit to prove conduct unless there were no eyewitnesses who could testify to what occurred. This inflexible preference for reconstructing events from eyewitness testimony alone, rather than from such testimony coupled with circumstantial inferences based on habit, was misguided. Because witnesses' perception and memory are subject to many kinds of distortion,[54] an eyewitness's testimony may be no more reliable as an indicator of behavior than an established habit—indeed, it may be less so. Moreover, witnesses to events may be few in number or biased, while witnesses to longstanding habits may be numerous and less interested in the outcome. When, for example, the only witness to a fatal accident is the driver of the defendant transit company's bus, the bus driver's testimony that the decedent ran a stop sign may be less persuasive than testimony by the decedent's neighbors that he always stopped and looked both ways before crossing the intersection where the accident occurred. Yet, in an "eyewitness rule" jurisdiction, the bus driver's availability might preclude the habit evidence.

FRE 406's more important objective is to confirm—albeit without quite saying—that FRE 404(a)(1)'s ban on character evidence does not apply to habit evidence; although FRE 406's word "may" suggests that the rule does not trump other evidence rules that would exclude habit evidence, the rule would be senseless if FRE 404(a)(1)'s ban on character evidence entirely neutralized it. There must, then, be a distinction between evidence proving action in accordance with a *character trait* and evidence proving action in accordance with a *habit* or a *routine practice*. Understanding that distinction may help us understand the general distinction between evidence offered for propensity and evidence offered for another reason.

There are good reasons to be wary of habit evidence, at least if "habit" is broadly defined. Were courts to admit evidence of a so-called "habit for care," or a "habit of robbing gas stations" or a "habit of lying," the propensity rule would be nullified. But "habit" need not be defined so loosely or so similarly to "character."[55] McCormick distinguishes the two concepts as follows:

---

[54] See, e.g., infra, p. 411, note 105.

[55] Nor *is* the term "habit" as used in FRE 406 interpreted this loosely. See, e.g., United States v. Angwin, 271 F.3d 786 (9th Cir. 2001) (evidence that the defendant was trained to act, and that in a number of instances he did act, in a nonconfrontational manner in dangerous situations is not admissible to establish a habit of nonconfrontational behavior); Jones v. Southern Pacific R.R., 962 F.2d 447 (5th Cir. 1992) (records showing that train operator was

> Character is a generalized description of a person's disposition, or of the disposition in respect to a general trait, such as honesty, temperance, or peacefulness. Habit . . . is more specific. It denotes one's regular responses to a repeated [specific] situation. If we speak of a character for care, we think of the person's tendency to act prudently in all the varying situations of life—in business, at home, in handling automobiles and in walking across the street. A habit, on the other hand, is the person's regular practice of responding to a particular kind of situation with a specific type of conduct. Thus, a person may be in the habit of bounding down a certain stairway two or three steps at a time. . . . The doing of the habitual acts may become semiautomatic, as with a driver who invariably signals before changing lanes.[56]

McCormick's definition is consistent with the ordinary meaning of the term "habit," and suggests why the law allows habit evidence to prove action in conformity therewith while excluding character evidence offered for the same purpose. First, habit evidence is more probative of behavior. When a specific, well-defined stimulus (e.g., a stop sign, or a desire to get down a particular stairway) always or nearly always prompts a specific and well-defined response (e.g., putting on the brakes until the car stops or bounding down two steps at a time), we have a lot more to go on in predicting behavior than when the evidence reveals a less defined propensity (e.g., a violent personality). The former suggests that the person regularly stops or routinely takes the stairs two steps at a time, while the latter suggests only a higher than normal probability of some undefined aggressive act.

Second, prejudice is less of a threat. Most habits are unlikely to move a jury to sympathy, anger or other emotions likely to distort judgment. Moreover, the clear specification of the circumstances that

---

reprimanded seven times in seven years for variety of infractions while driving trains were inadmissible to show habit of careless operation of trains; court says in dicta that even if all the reprimands had been for the same offense and had occurred in a shorter period, they still probably would not establish a habit); Priest v. Rotary, 98 F.R.D. 755 (N.D.Cal.1983) (repeated instances of forming intimate relationships with other persons for economic benefit do not reveal "habit"). In addition to considering the generic or specific nature of the stimulus and response characterizing the alleged habit, courts consider the frequency with which the conduct is known to have manifested itself, both in general and relative to the number of opportunities for it to have done so. See, e.g., Leonard v. Nationwide Mut. Ins. Co., 499 F.3d 419 (5th Cir. 2007) (evidence of advice about flood insurance that an employee with hundreds of clients gave to only five of them over a decade is not admissible to establish that the employee habitually gave the advice); U.S. Football League v. National Football League, 842 F.2d 1335 (2d Cir. 1988) (four instances over 20-year period does not show "routine practice" of ignoring antitrust advice). Evidence of heavy drinking is usually inadmissible to prove drunkenness on a particular occasion. See Advisory Committee Note to FRE 406. Cf. Loughan v. Firestone Tire & Rubber Co., 749 F.2d 1519 (11th Cir. 1985) (evidence, including plaintiffs' own testimony, that he routinely drank to excess at the specific time of day and place involved in the lawsuit was properly admitted under FRE 406).

[56] McCormick § 195.

stimulate the habitual action and the ease of identifying inconsistencies between those circumstances and the situation at issue help the jury evaluate the evidence. If the facts in the case are unlike those that ordinarily prompt the habitual conduct, the inference of action in accordance with habit is destroyed. For example, if the plaintiff in a lawsuit was in the habit of taking stairs two steps at a time when late for meetings, but was not late for anything when he fell down the stairs, the inference that he may have caused the fall by skipping steps is weakened. Inferences from bad character are much more difficult to evaluate. Someone who embezzles money from a bank, for example, probably takes advantage of only a small fraction of the opportunities to do so, and may be honest in his personal dealings. If he is charged with taking money that disappeared from the church treasury during his term as treasurer, the inference to be drawn from his "character," or his bank embezzlement, is far from clear.

Habit evidence does not, however, entirely avoid the problems that make us wary of character evidence. Even well-established habits do not always govern behavior. A person in the habit of signaling before changing lanes may not do so when in a hurry. Indeed, accidents may be particularly likely to occur on the rare occasions when safe habits are neglected. Moreover, an individual may consciously deviate from a well-known habit in order to create an alibi, as when a person who regularly takes the six o'clock bus home from work kills a coworker at six-fifteen. Thus, a case may be made for excluding habit evidence when an accident almost certainly would not have occurred if the victim had acted habitually (a pedestrian run over by a train probably did not follow her habit of looking both ways before crossing the tracks), or when the charged behavior suggests a motive for deliberate nonhabitual behavior. The alternative of leaving the matter to the jury is also reasonable, however. Jurors know that the existence of a habit does not guarantee conforming behavior and can determine when events are inconsistent with habitual behaviors or when there are motives to deviate from habits. Jurors also can be relied upon to detect fabricated or exaggerated claims of habit, as when a surviving relative with an interest in the outcome of a lawsuit describes the decedent's pattern of stopping at most stop signs as a habit of *always* doing so.

Even less troublesome is evidence of the customs or routine practices of businesses and other organizations. The need for regularity in institutional settings, and the institutional sanctions that often apply when rules or customs are violated, provide extra guarantees that an activity followed usual practice. With respect to business custom, therefore, FRE 406's liberal standard generally prevails, even in jurisdictions that bar evidence of an individual's habit unless there are no eyewitnesses to what happened. A mail clerk's testimony that he routinely mailed letters placed in out boxes, and that he followed this routine on the day in question, would be accepted everywhere as evidence that a letter was mailed, even if the clerk had no recollection of mailing the letter at issue in the lawsuit. Many jurisdictions permit anyone who knows of or relies on a routine practice to testify about it. Some states, however, require the individual whose customary behavior is at issue to testify that, even though he does not remember the activity, he is sure that he followed his customary practice on the occasion in question.

The differences between character and habit evidence are important, but, especially with habits that inspire sympathy or animosity, those differences may be more of degree than of kind. We thus can understand the impulse to exclude habit evidence in order to avoid the judgment calls needed to distinguish it from character evidence, and to help guarantee that character will remain inadmissible. But the impulse should be resisted. Evidence as probative as habit evidence should not be presumptively excluded.

———————

Problem V-15. Molly Farelayn was injured when Chet Chiklit's car collided with hers on the highway. Only the driver was in each car. Farelayn sues Chiklit, claiming he was not paying full attention when he changed lanes in front of her because he was taking a piece of gum from a wrapper and putting it in his mouth. Although several gum wrappers were found along with other debris on the floor of the driver's side of Chiklit's car immediately after the accident, Chiklit denies having any gum with him on the trip in question. He claims he hit Farelayn's car when she unexpectedly sped up as he was changing lanes in front of her. In her case-in-chief, Farelayn calls Terry Traetor, who occasionally carpools to work with Chiklit. Traetor is prepared to testify that each of the six times she and Chiklit drove to and from work together, he was obsessively chewing gum. Chiklit objects to the proposed testimony. **What ruling? What else would you want to know from Traetor before ruling? Would the outcome of this lawsuit be more reliable in a jurisdiction that does, or does not, follow the eyewitness rule? Why?**

5. Forbidden and Permitted Inferences

Suppose that Pam sues Dennis, alleging that Dennis hit her car after failing to make a complete stop at a red light before turning right. Dennis claims he made a complete stop, and that he hit Pam's car because she recklessly changed from the left to the right lane in the middle of the intersection without signaling. Wilbur owns a gas station at the corner where the accident occurred. Wilbur saw Dennis rush past the station in his distinctive lime green Fiat on three occasions on the afternoon in question, each time turning right on a red light without fully stopping.

Wilbur did not, however, see the turn that led to the accident. Should a court let Wilbur testify for plaintiff? On the one hand, Dennis's other acts permit an inference that he was in a rush that afternoon (or that he had a "motive" to rush) and that his haste caused the accident. The evidence arguably is highly probative of a lack of caution at the time in question, and not very prejudicial. On the other hand, the series of acts on a single afternoon do not reveal a "habit" and do not easily fit within a recognized category of admissible other-acts evidence. ("Motive" as used in FRE 404(b)(2) typically means circumstantial evidence that tends to point to someone as the person who did some action.) Pam's argument, presumably, is that Dan was in a rush and driving carelessly that whole afternoon. This claim is certainly relevant to the issues at hand, but isn't it just a version of the forbidden inference—that Dennis had a propensity to rush that day?

The case is a close one, but a court might properly admit the evidence, particularly because the jury is unlikely to loathe Dennis for not quite stopping before turning right. True, the evidence arguably demonstrates a "propensity." The same thing might be said, however, when courts properly admit evidence of a defendant's motive to hurt the homicide victim as revealed by prior beatings; evidence of a common scheme or plan to kill children under one's care and claim "crib death"; evidence that the defendant robbed four other banks using the same distinctive modus operandi; evidence of prior "point-shaving" bribes to show that the money handed over on the occasion in question was intended to influence behavior and not as a prize or gift; and evidence of an individual's habitual mode of descending a staircase two steps at a time. What connects these types of evidence, and what distinguishes them from run-of-the-mill character evidence, is that in each case the stimulus and response associated with the evidence is clearly specified and is very similar to the stimulus and alleged response associated with the events in the lawsuit. The behavior in question doesn't *always* happen—it may even be quite rare—but the claim is that a particular stimulus produces a specific type of behavior far more frequently than we normally expect.[57] As a result, probative value is fairly high and the probability of misestimation (if not of other kinds of prejudice) is fairly low. Generalizing the point, we can say that the propensity rule does not seem to bar evidence when: (1) the evidence reveals a behavioral trait that is highly specific in time and place (or sufficiently habitual that it semi-automatically appears *across* time and space) and manifests itself in only a limited range of actions; and (2) the action alleged in the lawsuit occurred at or in that particular time, place and manner.[58]

---

[57] See supra, p. 352, note 12, discussing the consensus among psychologists that personality traits are far more predictive of behavior in specified situations than in general.

[58] The propensity rule thus bars inferences of conformity with the kinds of general traits that are not very predictive of conduct but does not bar inferences of conformity with the

Under this analysis, there is no clear qualitative distinction between evidence of, say, business practice, habit, modus operandi, intent or motive, and propensity. Rather, the bases for inferring action in accordance with a behavioral trait may be aligned along a *strength-of-inference* continuum in approximately this stated order.[59] Our earlier explanation of why habit evidence lies at the opposite end of that continuum from evidence of a general character trait, such as dishonesty, helps locate the dividing line between permissible and forbidden inferences that link personal traits to action in accordance with them. Habit may be defined by a specific and almost reflexively repeated *response* (say, Alice puts on the brakes) to a particular *stimulus* (say, Alice sees a stop sign). Compared to character evidence (say, Bob's dishonesty inferred from a prior act of embezzlement), habit evidence is stronger both because of the clarity and specificity of the stimulus and response, and because of the greater confidence that a particular stimulus leads to a particular response. We are likely to have reliable evidence that seeing a stop sign always (or almost always) causes Alice to press on the brakes, and we may have equally clear evidence that she probably saw the stop sign that was at the intersection. By contrast Bob's "dishonest character" must be inferred from comparatively weak evidence (it can't be observed like the repetitive conduct that makes a habit); it will only occasionally lead to dishonest acts; and it will have widely varying effects in different contexts—all of which establishes a classic case for exclusion. Similarly, evidence that the defendant in a homicide case had repeatedly assaulted the victim is a more specific predictor of his behavior in the incident at issue than evidence that he frequently assaulted other people. Predictably, prior assaults against the victim of the crime on trial are very likely to be admitted, even if the legal theory for admission ("motive") is strained.

So, in our example of Dennis who is alleged to have made a right turn on a red light without coming to a complete stop, Pam might offer evidence that Dennis often speeds, that he received a ticket for passing in a no-passing zone, and that he recently backed into a car in a parking lot. The trait this evidence reveals—careless driving—can manifest itself in a variety of behaviors ranging from due care (when the person tries hard or just happens to pay attention), to minor and momentary lapses, to extremely dangerous driving. How that trait of "being careless" might manifest itself on a particular occasion when the person approaches a red light at a busy intersection is anybody's guess. The evidence thus falls far towards the propensity end of the continuum and presents an obvious case for exclusion. By contrast, Wilbur's testimony that Dennis thrice

---

situation-specific traits that behavioral scientists believe *do* best predict conduct. See supra, p. 352, note 12.

[59] "Character in issue" falls at the very end of the continuum, where the behavioral trait does not manifest itself in conduct "similar" to that alleged in the suit but is the very trait alleged in the suit.

failed to make a complete stop before turning right at the same red light on the very afternoon of the accident reveals a trait that is more closely tied to the situation in the suit (a tendency not to stop at that light before turning, at least on the day in question)—although we still can't tell whether it's a reliable and lasting habit, a short-term pattern, or a coincidence. This evidence falls towards the middle of the continuum; it presents a close case, in which the evidence might or might not be admitted. The line drawn by FRE 404(a)(1) cannot be defined precisely because many factors might properly influence judges in close cases, including the linkage between situation, trait and behavior and the prejudice likely to be associated with the trait evidence.[60] As an advocate and as a student, the best you can hope to do in advance is to identify the factors that are likely to affect the decision and the lines of argument that have the best chance of persuading a judge.

Problem V-16. Paula sues Drake for injuries incurred in an automobile accident. Paula claims Drake ran a stop sign and struck Paula. Drake claims he made a proper stop at the stop sign and that Paula ran in front of his car. Paula offers the testimony of Fred that, the day before the accident involving Paula, he saw Drake driving the wrong way down a one-way street, honking his horn in a hospital zone and steering with his feet. Drake objects to Fred's testimony. **What ruling and why?**

Problem V-17. Same facts as in Problem V-16, except that Paula offers the testimony of Frieda, rather than Fred. Frieda is prepared to testify that she runs a gas station at the intersection at which the accident involving Paula occurred; that she knows Drake who lives in the neighborhood and buys gasoline from Frieda; that Drake passes by the gas station every morning on his way to work; that on most but not all mornings, Frieda sees Drake make a so-called "California stop" at the intersection (Drake slows down as he approaches the intersection, looks both ways for cars, then, if the intersection is clear, proceeds through the intersection without quite coming to a complete stop); and that Drake makes full stops at the intersection on some mornings, for example, when a car is coming the other way, when it is raining or when there is a police officer in the vicinity. Drake objects to Frieda's testimony. **What ruling and why?**

Problem V-18. Faith Farnsworth sues the Dallas Rapid Transit System for injuries received when she was alighting from a DRTS bus. She claims the bus driver sped away from the stop as she was taking the last step off

---

[60] See generally United States v. Beasley, 809 F.2d 1273 (7th Cir. 1987) ("There are no bright line rules; it is easy to identify polar cases but impossible to draw a line of demarcation. . . . Rules 403 and 404(b) establish standards rather than rules. [The objective] is to ensure that standards not be applied as if they were rules, as if they established mechanical indicia. . . .").

the bus, causing her to fall and break her hip. At trial Farnsworth offers the testimony of other passengers of buses operated by the same driver that, on different occasions, he ran red lights, changed lanes without signaling, nearly struck pedestrians, barely missed colliding with cars and sped away from stops before passengers had safely exited the bus, and that the driver has a reputation for recklessness among the town's bus riders. The defense objects to all this testimony. **How should the judge rule, and why?**

Problem V-19. Same facts as in Problem V-18, except that Farnsworth is herself prepared to testify that during her ride on the bus on the day of the accident, the driver appeared to be speeding between stops and that, at three of the five stops before her own, he barely waited for passengers to step out of the bus before rushing away. The defense objects to this testimony. **How should the judge rule, and why?**

"Never mind what I did, Your Honor. I want to be judged for who I am, as an individual."

C.   FURTHER OBSERVATIONS ON THE NATURE OF "CHARACTER EVIDENCE"

The theory of the propensity rule is that (subject to the exceptions we discuss below) a jury is supposed to base its judgment on evidence of what the relevant actors in a case *did*, not on what sort of people they *are*. As we have noted, people do not ordinarily make this distinction. When the question is "*Did* Emma steal?" we inevitably think "*Would* she?" If she's done it before, then yes; if she never has, probably not. Because this type of reasoning is so common, so much a part of human nature, lawyers learn to exploit it by developing character images to suit their purposes. Indeed, it is probably only a slight exaggeration to say that almost everything trial lawyers do in court is designed, at least in part, to serve this end. What we label "character evidence," however, plays only a modest role in this pervasive practice of character development; in many cases, none whatever.

Lawyers don't usually *say* "My client is an honest, thoughtful, soft-spoken, well-dressed, middle class man, just like you." They are not generally allowed to do that, and in any case—like all good dramatists—they would rather show it. Parties and witnesses are told to dress and behave in ways that are appropriate to the images the lawyers want to convey. They are taught to testify in character—to be polite, low key, thoughtful, whatever. Cross-examiners try to get witnesses—especially opposing parties—to lose control and break from their assigned characters, usually by showing anger. Family members and friends are recruited to show up and play supporting roles. When the jury is watching, lawyers treat their clients in the manner that is appropriate to the characters they want the jury to see—friendly, intelligent, trusting, respectful. Lawyers dress and act to convey the impression that they themselves are the sort of people the jurors can trust. And so forth.[61]

---

[61] Sometimes, an implicit courtroom characterization is made explicit by the opposition, to discredit it. Consider, for example, an excerpt from the closing argument for the defendant in a drug sale case where the defense was entrapment:

> What about Don Howe? On the day this sale took place, he was not the same clean-cut, well-dressed man that you saw and heard in this courtroom. In fact, on that day he wasn't even Don Howe. He was using the name Gene Hall. He was not wearing his coat and tie then. He had long hair to his shoulders; he had a full growth of beard on his face; he was drinking wine; and according to the testimony of Mel Gabe, he had been smoking marijuana. In short, he was doing everything in his power to win the confidence of these young people so he could trap them into allowing him to persuade them to commit an unlawful act so that he could come into court and prosecute them.

Jacob A. Stein, Closing Arguments § 3:355 (2010–2011 electronic ed.). Occasionally we might hear a lawyer with a particularly hard hand to play forthrightly argue that his client does have a human character:

> When you were chosen for this jury, you agreed to decide this case fairly and impartially. Now, I represent a corporation and Mr. Gursky represents an individual. You might think of a corporation as impersonal, but Memorex consists of *people*, decent, hard-working people like Joe and Richard. And *those people* are counting on you to give them the same consideration as plaintiff, as I am sure you will.

We have seen that many permitted uses of character evidence border on the propensity inference, or are all but indistinguishable from it. Others—"knowledge" or "opportunity," for instance—are more analytically distinct, but how much difference does that make? Character arguments, whether or not they speak in terms of propensity, can bias the fact-finder by creating sympathy or antipathy; frequently that's the main point of making them. Nonetheless, courts often allow lawyers not only to introduce character evidence for a variety of purposes, but also to *describe* the character of parties and others in highly emotive terms—as long as the characterizations can be said to be based on evidence about the conduct that is at issue in the trial. In *Williams v. State*,[62] the defendant was sentenced to life imprisonment for raping an eight-year-old girl. In the course of his closing argument, the prosecutor said, among other things, that the defendant "was under the record the vilest type of character known to humanity," that he had "a warped brain, a degenerate mind," and that he "should be killed just as a person would kill a rattlesnake."[63] The appellate court had no difficulty with this:

> We agree with the prosecutor that an adult who would commit the acts done by the defendant shows that he is "lowdown, degenerate, and filthy." He richly deserves the punishment which he received.[64]

Williams is an extreme case, but there is no shortage of less extreme cases in which courts permitted prosecutors to describe criminal defendants as, for example, a "professional assassin,"[65] a "hired gunfighter,"[66] a "dope pusher,"[67] an "executioner,"[68] an "animal,"[69] a "punk,"[70] a "type of worm,"[71] or a "mad dog."[72] To be sure, there are cases on the other side in which judgments were reversed for very similar arguments: "cheap, scaly, slimy crook,"[73] "leech off society,"[74] or "junkie,

---

Id. at § 3:5 (emphasis in original).

[62] 93 Okla.Crim. 260, 226 P.2d 989 (Okla.Crim.App.1951).

[63] Id. at 997.

[64] Id.

[65] State v. Hunt, 323 N.C. 407, 373 S.E.2d 400 (N.C. 1988).

[66] Johnston v. United States, 154 F. 445, 449 (9th Cir. 1907).

[67] State v. Prince, 713 S.W.2d 914 (Tenn.Crim.App.1986).

[68] People v. Franklin, 135 Ill.2d 78, 142 Ill.Dec. 152, 552 N.E.2d 743 (1990); People v. Cunningham, 177 Ill.App.3d 544, 126 Ill.Dec. 826, 532 N.E.2d 511 (1988).

[69] Williams v. Alabama, 377 So.2d 634 (Ala.Crim.App.1979); see State v. Craig, 308 N.C. 446, 302 S.E.2d 740 (N.C. 1983) ("a pack of wolves").

[70] State v. Canisales, 126 Ariz. 331, 615 P.2d 9 (Ariz.App.1980).

[71] United States v. Walker, 190 F.2d 481, 484 (2d Cir. 1951).

[72] Commonwealth v. Capps, 382 Pa. 72, 114 A.2d 338, 342 (1955); Miller v. Georgia, 226 Ga. 730, 731, 177 S.E.2d 253, 254 (1970).

[73] Volkmor v. United States, 13 F.2d 594, 595 (6th Cir. 1926).

[74] State v. Owen, 73 Idaho 394, 408, 253 P.2d 203, 211 (1953).

rat and 'sculptor' with a knife."[75]   But they were not reversed because these arguments violate the character evidence rule. Rather, the courts have drawn a weaving, inconsistent, frequently invisible line between arguments that are permissibly "harsh," and those that are prejudicially "inflammatory."

There is a fine logical distinction at issue. If the claim that the defendant is "the vilest type of character known to humanity" is based solely on evidence that he committed the crime with which he is charged, then to argue that he has this character trait is not to claim that he acted in accord with that trait on a particular occasion. The causal inference runs in the opposite direction: Evidence that the defendant committed the crime is the basis for the argument that he is vile. Ergo, it is not a propensity argument. Q.E.D.

So what? Whether they are "inflammatory" or merely "passionate," these arguments are designed to arouse the jury. It may be hard to see why a court would permit a lawyer to make an emotional appeal of this sort—when it is allowed, there's rarely any explanation for it—but it's easy to understand why a lawyer would want to do it. It's done in the hope that the anger and horror that are evoked will drive the jurors' judgment before them—which is, precisely, one of the principal dangers that propensity rule is supposed to guard against. Furthermore, such arguments can trigger an inferential feedback loop that amounts to a judgment from propensity: "You have convinced me that the evidence that he committed this vicious crime shows that he is a vicious beast; and because he is a vicious beast, I am reassured in my conviction that he committed this vicious crime." This is circular, of course, but that doesn't mean it has no impact. Indeed, were the judgment that the defendant is a "beast" only a byproduct—and not a *cause*—of guilty verdicts, prosecutors would spend much less energy promoting those judgments, and their relevance would be hard to defend. Moreover such arguments do speak to *character*, if that term has any consistent meaning. That they are not within the ambit of the character evidence rule says a lot about the rule's modesty.

Odder yet, *explicit* propensity *arguments* are regularly tolerated in contexts in which propensity *evidence* would be—or ought to be—excluded. The simplest example is when otherwise admissible evidence is used by a lawyer for a favorable propensity argument about the party she represents. For example, in the *Tellez* case,[76] the defendant was a former

---

[75] People v. Hickman, 34 App.Div.2d 831, 312 N.Y.S.2d 644 (1970). Frequently, courts disapprove such arguments on ethical or other grounds but nonetheless affirm the conviction, concluding that the argument violated no constitutional or other legal proscription or was harmless error. See, e.g., Darden v. Wainwright, 477 U.S. 168 (1986), and the lower court decisions in the case.

[76] Chapter One, Section II.C., pp. 18, 122.

police officer. His lawyer used that fact in her closing argument, without objection:

> The natural instinct of [anybody] to defend himself, I would think that that gets doubled or who knows by a police officer who has for years put his life on the line defending the public.

No one, we trust, would argue that evidence that a defendant was a police officer is *admissible* to prove that the force he used was more likely in self-defense, than, as was alleged in *Tellez*, in an attempt to escape from jail. But once that evidence is before the jury anyway, nobody thinks to object when a lawyer draws that "character" inference.

Character arguments are routinely made in other situations as well. For example, in the O.J. Simpson murder trial, his chief defense attorney made the following argument about a witness who happened to sit next to Mr. Simpson on a plane ride from Chicago to Los Angeles:

> And I thought very interesting about this man, Partridge. Remember, he's the man who was a patent lawyer, who had gone to Harvard, and he observed O.J. Simpson on this flight back. He saw him make these phone calls. He saw his emotional state. . . . He wrote notes about what took place—not to publish them. He's a patent lawyer, so he understood. . . . [77]

During the presentation of the defense case, Simpson's lawyer could not properly have argued that evidence that Mr. Partridge was a patent lawyer, or that he went to Harvard, was admissible to show that Partridge should be believed. (As we will see, some types of character evidence are admissible on credibility, but not this.) But once the evidence came in (probably as "background"), nobody thought to object when a lawyer made that precise point in argument.

One last example, this one from a treatise on closing argument:[78]

> Ladies and gentlemen, I submit to you that the evidence has shown beyond a reasonable doubt that this young man, Thaddeus Cydzik, was more than an innocent bystander in this matter not just in the commission of the armed robbery but in the commission of the killing. He knew what was going to happen, ladies and gentlemen. He certainly had a good idea what could happen and I submit he had a good idea what was in fact going to happen. *This is an intelligent young man. He was almost a straight A student in high school, an honor student. He is a young man who has had everything placed at his disposal, a good family, a strict family, and a family that saw to it that he did not have to work when he went to college.* He certainly didn't need

---

[77] People v. Simpson, No. BA-097211, Superior Court, Los Angeles County (California), Dept. 103, September 1995, 1995 WL 686429, at 55.

[78] Stein, supra, note 61, at § 577 (emphasis added).

money from an armed robbery to further his education, ladies and gentlemen.

But my point is that this young man was and is a leader, and not a follower. If you want to believe that this young man followed Donald Paulson in everything he did, then so be it. If you want to believe that the defendant was directed by someone who had not had the benefit of a higher education, then so be it. This young man knew what he was going to do when he went in there. He knew what could happen during the course of an armed robbery. He knew that someone could get killed but he just didn't think it would happen this time. Well, it did.

Here, favorable evidence about the defendant is used against him. The argument is seamless and plausible; it does not sound even mildly objectionable. And yet, as the italicized portions highlight, it is in part a propensity argument. Mr. Cydzik is intelligent and able; he is a leader; therefore, he is unlikely to have been an ignorant follower in this crime.

We would not allow other exclusionary rules to be undermined in this way. Consider a case in which evidence of a subsequent repair to a stairway banister was admitted to show the defendant landlord's control over the place in which the plaintiff was injured. What if the plaintiff's attorney argued to the jury:

> You've heard that after this terrible accident it was Mr. Markman, the landlord, who replaced the old, cracked wooden railings on the stairs with steel rods. Why would he do that, unless the wooden railings were dangerous?

Surely that lawyer would be stopped, perhaps even by the court *sua sponte* if there was no immediate objection. The argument is a flagrant violation of FRE 407. But equally flagrant propensity arguments are not stopped; the fact that they undercut FRE 404(a)(1) seems to go totally unnoticed. The difference is that evidence and arguments on subsequent repairs occupy a small corner of the trial process, they are relatively easy to isolate and exclude. By contrast, "character" and "propensity" are ubiquitous, and characterological attributions of cause seem built into human reasoning.

Most people who study trials have come to believe that successful courtroom advocacy is usually structured as storytelling rather than as logical proof.[79] To be effective, a story must correspond to the jurors' image of what a story should be,[80] and that image is drawn from the most numerous and vivid stories they read, hear and see—from fiction.[81] Our

---

[79] See, e.g., Nancy Pennington & Reid Hastie, A Cognitive Theory of Juror Decision-Making: The Story Model, 13 Cardozo L. Rev. 519 (1991).

[80] Id. at 525–27.

[81] Some common stories we consume are not strictly speaking fiction, but biography or "news." Even there, however, the writers tend to construct the stories along the lines of common

relationship to fictional characters is fundamentally different from our relationship to people in the world. We *know* why fictional characters act as they do because we are told. Their actions are plausible and their stories are compelling when their motivation is based on their "nature"—their character—which we also know because we are told, as we rarely are in life. As we have seen, there is a great deal of evidence that "character" and "personality" traits are an unreliable basis for predicting human behavior—in life.[82] But in *stories*, character is a strong predictor of conduct, by authorial fiat. The ambition of trial lawyers is to achieve in court the control a writer enjoys on paper—to author the winning courtroom story. To succeed, they work with familiar, proven forms. Their art imitates art.

In short, character is central to the trial lawyer's task. As in fiction, it is more important, more central, in court than in life. If we really did manage to exclude character evidence and character argument, we'd drain half the fun from the game. So we don't force the issue. Much of the *evidence* that goes into character construction is not touched by the rules pertaining to character evidence, and we don't even bother thinking about character *arguments* unless a lawyer crosses a heavily contested line—typically, by insinuating inadmissible evidence of prior crimes that are not in the record,[83] or by transparently arguing propensity from evidence of prior misconduct that was admitted solely for impeachment.[84]

Does the prominent role that character evidence and argument play in trial advocacy prove that the propensity rule is a sham and should be abandoned? We think not. The powerful impulse of jurors to rely on unreliable propensity reasoning—and the ability of lawyers to exploit that impulse—make a rule that imposes some restraint all the more important. Absent the rule, reasoning from character might entirely overwhelm trials. None of us can refrain entirely from focusing our suspicions on "the usual suspects" while overlooking "the usually upright," but we can resist having a judicial system that does little else.

Problem V-20. Lauren Winokur is charged with robbing a gas station using a .38 caliber pistol with a wooden handle. Evidence at trial places Winokur near the gas station a half hour before it was robbed, and she generally matches the description of the masked robber. When Winokur

---

fictional narratives, with well-defined "characters" whose behavior runs true to form. An example is the *New York Times*' portrayal of the subway driver in the Lexington line crash discussed supra, p. 348.

[82] See supra, Section II. A., p. 352 & note 12.

[83] See, e.g., People v. Mejias, 72 A.D.2d 570, 420 N.Y.S.2d 737 (1979); People v. Wright, 41 N.Y.2d 172, 391 N.Y.S.2d 101, 359 N.E.2d 696 (N.Y. 1976).

[84] See, e.g., People v. Fields, 258 Ill.App.3d 912, 197 Ill.Dec. 300, 631 N.E.2d 303 (1994); State v. Sanders, 634 S.W.2d 525 (Mo.Ct.App.1982); State v. Moran, 141 Vt. 10, 444 A.2d 879 (Vt. 1982).

was arrested a half mile from the station forty minutes after the robbery, she had $372 in her handbag in small bills. The station's cash register receipts suggest that $357 were taken. The handbag also contained a .38 caliber revolver with a fake wood handle (actually it was plastic) registered to her boyfriend. The owners of two different gas stations in the same town identify Winokur as the person who robbed them with a wood-handled pistol three and five months before the robbery at issue. The trial judge lets the prosecutor make the following closing argument, over objection: "You see Lauren Winokur sitting there all dressed up, trying to pretend she's a respectable citizen. And you see those kids in the first row she turns and talks to every chance she gets, trying to pretend she's just a mother. Well she's not a respectable citizen. She's not just a mother. You've heard the testimony: Three good hardworking people and a cop on the beat, showing beyond doubt that Lauren Winokur is a common criminal who makes a living by robbing people at gunpoint. A criminal usually dressed in a black leather jacket and a mask. That's why she robbed Sam's Gasomat. That's why she's here. She's just a common criminal, a common armed robber, who does nothing well but rob." **Is any of this argument improper? On what grounds? As an appellate judge, would you reverse Winokur's conviction based on the argument? Would it matter if the prosecutor, in a bench conference after the defendant objected, said, "Judge, those aren't even her kids; they're her sister's kids?" What if the prosecutor knows Winokur has children, just not those in the courtroom? Should the court have insisted on evidence of the children's relationship to Winokur? How might such a record have been made? How should the judge rule on a motion by the prosecutor early in the trial to forbid Winokur to speak to the children in court?** Suppose Winokur testified and introduced records showing that she got a job as a bank teller a week before the alleged robbery and, on the day of the robbery, cashed her first pay check of $387. Suppose her lawyer later makes the following closing argument to the jury: "You heard Ms. Winokur testify. You saw the paycheck she cashed the day of the robbery. Why would a smart woman like Ms. Winokur, a talented woman with a plum job and a fat paycheck, want to rob a gas station? Where's the logic? Where's the motive? It doesn't add up." **Is any of this argument improper? Is your answer affected by the judge's ruling on the prosecutor's argument?**

III. EXCEPTIONS TO THE PROPENSITY RULE: SUBSTANTIVE EVIDENCE

The propensity rule has several exceptions. In this section we discuss the two oldest and best established exceptions permitting propensity evidence on "substantive" issues: evidence of the good character of a criminal defendant, and evidence of the bad character of the alleged crime victim. In Section IV we discuss the use of character evidence to impeach or support "credibility"—to help the trier of fact decide whether to believe a particular witness, rather than as direct evidence of the events to which the witness testifies. And in Section VIII below we discuss the broadest and newest exceptions to the propensity rule—FRE 413–415, which permit all uses of evidence of similar offenses to prove that the defendant committed sexual assault or child molestation—together with FRE 412, the federal "rape shield rule," which forbids nearly all uses of character evidence in sexual assault trials to prove that the victim consented to sexual relations.

A. THE CRIMINAL DEFENDANT'S GOOD CHARACTER

FRE 404(a)(2)(A) contains an exception to the propensity rule that applies only to "a criminal case." Under the exception, "a defendant may offer evidence of the defendant's pertinent trait [of character], and if the evidence is admitted the prosecutor may offer evidence to rebut it." This exception follows the common law rule permitting an accused to attempt to prove that she possesses traits of character that make it unlikely that she committed the crime for which she is on trial.[85] Because the criminal defendant decides whether to open up the issue, prejudicing the jury against the defendant is not considered a problem, and the probative value of the evidence is thought to outweigh the disadvantages of admitting it. Also, allowing criminal defendants to introduce evidence of good character can help protect a mistakenly accused defendant's good *reputation*. If a case is publicized, the press will report on respected members of the community who came to the accused's defense;[86] in run-of-the-mill cases, at least those in the courtroom will learn that respectable people think well of the accused. In addition, a "good character" trait—unlike a trait of "bad character"—is strongly predictive of behavior, *if* we truly know that the trait exists. A defendant who really is "a life-long forger" may nonetheless be innocent of the forgery for which he is on trial; but a defendant who really is a "completely honest man" will never be guilty of that crime.

---

[85] A defendant who attempts to exonerate himself through character evidence is sometimes said to have "put his character in issue." This terminology is unfortunate, for it invites confusion with the situation in which the quality of an individual's character is in fact *an issue* in the case. See supra, Section II.B.2, pp. 359–361. When character evidence is used circumstantially to support the propensity inference, as under FRE 404(a)(2)(A), character is not "in issue" except in the sense that the validity of any item of admissible evidence is open to dispute. We prefer to say that the defendant has "opened the door" to evidence of his character—and in the process assumed the risk that he will be prejudiced by whatever rebuttal the prosecutor presents.

[86] The rule works, if John Connally's case is any measure. Connally was Secretary of the Treasury under President Richard Nixon and the only prominent official charged in the Watergate scandal who escaped conviction. His defense relied heavily on the character testimony of a former First Lady, the Bishop of Dallas, and other luminaries. A few years later, Connally made a credible run for the Republican nomination for President.

Despite its justifications, this exception to the propensity rule has its costs. Evidence of an accused's good character may be misleading. Even the vicious have friends, and most people can find witnesses to testify to their good character even though their lives have been far from exemplary. As we note below, however, this problem is largely avoided by letting the prosecutor respond to evidence of a defendant's good character with questions about the defendant's "pertinent" bad acts. Other problems are not as easily avoided. Evidence of good character may prejudice the jurors in the defendant's favor, because their regret at mistakenly convicting an innocent defendant of good character is likely to be high, while their regret at mistakenly acquitting a guilty defendant is likely to be less than it otherwise would be. Moreover, good character is harder to show than bad character. We *know* that someone is "a murderer" if he has been caught murdering just once; we can only *infer* that someone is "honest to a fault" from the fact that he never seems to lie. But we may be deceived. Our apparently honest friend may have fooled us—most people do their best to hide their worst deeds, and his well-known predilection for truth-telling may lead him to think he can get away with particularly important lies now and then—or he may be less honest in some contexts than others, or he may never have previously faced a situation that provoked his dishonest impulses, or if he had we may not have been present. In short, evidence of bad character often reliably shows the trait in question—as when the defendant in a robbery prosecution has been twice convicted of robbery—but that trait usually has low probative value as evidence of the conduct at issue. By contrast, many good character traits would be extremely probative of the relevant conduct, but those traits cannot be observed directly, and inferential evidence about them is unreliable.

The weak justifications for the good-character rule are reflected in the many practical and procedural limits on its application. Only defendants with genuinely good reputations and nearly spotless histories are wise to offer evidence of their good character. Under FRE 404(a)(2)(A), as we discuss in more detail below, once the accused offers evidence of good character, the prosecution may present evidence of bad character. More important, as we will see, a defendant's character witnesses may be cross-examined about particular bad acts she may have committed. Even a person of generally good character is likely to be seriously hurt if she has behaved shamefully on one or two occasions, because evidence of bad acts is more likely to stick in the jurors' minds than general evidence of good character and jurors may get the impression that the few incidents they learn about are just the tip of the iceberg. As a French proverb says: If you mix a cup of wine with a barrel of sewage, you have a barrel of sewage; if you mix a cup of sewage with a barrel of wine, you have a barrel of sewage.

At common law and under the Federal Rules, the 404(a)(2)(A)-type exception applies only to *pertinent* traits of character. An accused embezzler might offer evidence that he is trustworthy or honest but not evidence that he is peaceable or nonviolent. A person charged with assault is in the opposite situation.[87] More general traits—such as a disposition to abide by the law—arguably are relevant to rebut almost any accusation, and courts often allow such evidence or give defendants leeway in presenting evidence of more specific traits that are not directly pertinent but permit an inference of law-abidance. The pertinence requirement is probably more successful in keeping defendants from offering evidence of good character at times remote from the events in issue, and in preventing prosecutors on rebuttal from offering evidence about a defendant's reputation after it had been tarnished by the instant charges.

The exception for evidence of the defendant's character traditionally has been limited to criminal cases. Its usefulness in protecting reputation, however, has led a growing number of states to extend the exception to civil cases in which the plaintiff's complaint charges behavior that would be actionable under the criminal law. A few jurisdictions admit character evidence in civil cases whenever there are no eyewitnesses to the event to which the evidence is circumstantially relevant. Even jurisdictions that generally do not admit character evidence in civil cases sometimes make an exception when an action for civil assault is countered by a claim of self-defense. In these jurisdictions, if there is some dispute about who committed the first act of aggression, each party is allowed to show his own reputation for peaceableness and his opponent's reputation for turbulence and violence. The drafters of the precursor to FRE 404(a)(2)(A) clearly intended it to apply only in criminal cases, but a few federal courts followed the emerging state practice and extended the exception to civil cases involving potentially criminal conduct. This triggered a 2006 amendment making even clearer than before that the exception is limited to "a criminal case"; in federal courts, defendants enjoy no exception to the propensity rule in civil actions.

Still other limiting rules apply when evidence of an accused's character is offered as circumstantial proof of likely conduct. At common law, evidence of good character had to take the form of testimony about the defendant's reputation in some relevant community. Specific acts consistent with the subject's alleged reputation could not be shown—thus reversing the preferred mode of proof in most other situations, including when character evidence has been used for nonpropensity purposes. Dean Ladd gave this explanation for preferring reputation to specific acts testimony:

---

[87] See, e.g., United States v. Harris, 491 F.3d 440 (D.C.Cir. 2007), cert. denied, 552 U.S. 1157 (2008) (testimony that the defendant is a devoted family man is inadmissible evidence of good character in a prosecution for possession of cocaine with intent to distribute).

The object of the law in making reputation the test of character is to get the aggregate judgment of a community rather than the personal opinion of the witness which might be considered to be warped by his own feeling or prejudice. Even reputation must, to be admitted, be general in a community rather than based upon a limited class. While it is not necessary that a character witness know what the majority of a neighborhood thinks of a person, he must know of the general regard with which the party is commonly held.

It is the general concurrence of a great number of people reflecting the sentiment toward the party whose character is subject to inquiry that is necessary to establish a reputation and to warrant its use as evidence. In this, the theory of the law is that trustworthiness is gained from the expressions of many people in their estimation of a person which would not be obtained by the individual opinion of a single witness however well acquainted he might be with the party's character. . . . The reputed character of a person is created from the slow spreading influence of community opinion growing out of his behavior in the society in which he moves and is known and upon this basis is accepted as proof of what his character actually is.[88]

Ladd's explanation may have made some sense when most communities were small and everyone knew and talked about everyone. Because many people in small towns might know a person's reputation and agree on it, reputation had an attractive concreteness. Today, however, many people are far more anonymous, or have fleeting connections to a variety of communities. As a result, courts have held that reputation testimony need not be based on actual public comment about an individual. Testimony that nothing bad has been heard is sufficient to support the inference of good reputation. The courts also have altered the historical limitation that defined "relevant community" as the neighborhood in which one lived. Now the workplace is commonly accepted as a relevant community, and reputation in other places where individuals have spent considerable amounts of time may also be acceptable. Even in earlier periods, Dean Ladd's assumptions about the reliability of reputation evidence were countered by doubts about reliance on "the secondhand product of multiplied guesses and gossip."[89]

A better explanation for the preference for reputation testimony is the law's basic ambivalence about the circumstantial use of character as evidence of conduct. Testimony about reputation takes much less time than testimony about a series of specific events and—unlike much

---

[88] Mason Ladd, Techniques and Theory of Character Testimony, 24 Iowa L. Rev. 498, 513 (1939).

[89] 7 Wigmore § 296, at 244.

specific-events testimony—is typically bloodless, ritualistic and a bit dull. Because reputation "compacts into the brief phrase of a verdict the teaching of many incidents and the conduct of years,"[90] it minimizes the time devoted to a type of evidence the law generally resists and moderates its impact without wholly excluding it.   The traditional restriction to reputation evidence is particularly sensible if we are right that the exception for proof of the defendant's character is designed as much to protect reputation itself as to prove conduct and to generate accurate trial outcomes.

Dean Ladd has suggested that questions of the following sort are ideal in a case in which Y, charged with homicide, has called W to testify to Y's character:[91]

(1) General questions identifying W and suggesting that the jury can rely on W's evaluation of public comments about Y.

(2) General questions to show that W personally knew Y, so that the jury may be sure that W is associating what he has heard with the right individual.

(3) **Q.** Mr. W have you heard remarks or comments about Y made by people generally in and around the community of Z town? **A.** Yes, I have.

(4) **Q.** Have these remarks and comments been many or few in number? **A.** I have heard many people talk about Y on numerous occasions.

(5) **Q.** Were these persons members of any particular group? **A.** No. The remarks I have heard came from individuals in various parts of the community.

(6) **Q.** Over how long a period of time have you heard comments about Y by people generally in and around Z town? **A.** For the last several years and quite recently.

(7) **Q.** Have these comments and remarks related to Y's character as a quiet, peaceable, law-abiding citizen? **A.** Yes, there have been many remarks about Y concerning his disposition as a peaceful, quiet and law-abiding citizen in the community.

(8) **Q.** Does Y have a *general* reputation for being a quiet, peaceable, law-abiding citizen in and around the community of Z town? [Italicized word emphasizes that Y's reputation is not confined to a specific group.] **A.** Yes, he does.

(9) **Q.** Do you know the *general* reputation of Y for being a quiet, peaceable, law-abiding citizen in and around the community of Z town prior to and on [the date of the commission of the offense]? **A.** Yes, I do.

---

[90]   Michelson v. United States, 335 U.S. 469, 477 (1948).

[91]   Ladd, supra, note 88, at 398.

(10) **Q.** Will you please tell the jury whether that reputation was good
or bad? **A.** It was good.

Presenting character evidence this way reduces the emotional appeal
of propensity evidence. And though it might put some jurors to sleep, it is
unlikely to draw their attention from the central issues in the case or to
prompt disputes concerning the existence of collateral facts, as might
occur if character could be proved by specific acts. As silly as the
reputation ritual at first appears, therefore, it may make a good deal of
sense as a compromise—assuming it makes some sense to let criminal
defendants defend themselves and their reputations through character in
the first place.

Defense lawyers try to increase the impact of character evidence by
impressing the jury with the distinction of the witnesses who are willing
to testify to the defendant's good character or at least with how many
there are. As with all potentially redundant evidence, judges have
discretion to limit the number of character witnesses who testify.
Because the emphasis is less on what is said and more on the status or
numbers of the people saying it, character evidence invites an inference of
innocence not so much from the defendant's good character as from the
fact that notable or numerous people think highly of him. Whatever its
content, therefore, reputation testimony gives the impression that the
witness is presenting a personal opinion about the defendant's character
even if the witness speaks only to reputation. Indeed, it is likely, as
Wigmore argued, that jurors learn more from "witnesses whose personal
intimacy gives to their belief a first and highest value [than from] those
who merely repeat a form of words in which the term 'reputation'
occurs."[92] Wigmore's view that the limitation on the form of character
evidence should be relaxed to allow opinion as well as reputation
testimony prevailed with the drafters of the Federal Rules. FRE 405(a)
provides:

> **By Reputation or Opinion.** When evidence of a person's
> character or character trait is admissible, it may be proved by
> testimony about the person's reputation *or by testimony in the
> form of an opinion.* On cross-examination of the character
> witness, the court may allow an inquiry into relevant specific
> instances of the persons' conduct. (Emphasis added.)

This change makes sense as long as the rule allows opinions only
from witnesses whose close relationship to the defendant suggests special
knowledge of his character. In order to maintain the compromise that
has developed around reputation evidence, opinion testimony should also
be kept short and uncomplicated. Ideally it consists of a brief statement
of the witness's opportunity to observe the defendant's behavior and form

---

[92]   7 Wigmore § 1986, at 166.

an opinion, followed by that opinion. On its face, FRE 405(a) contains neither of these limitations. Nothing in its language prevents a police officer who knows the defendant only as an arrestee from responding to the defendant's character evidence with an opinion that the defendant is violent; nothing keeps a psychologist from giving her expert opinion that the defendant would find it difficult to hurt anyone; and nothing prevents a lengthy explication of a character witness's opinion. In interpreting FRE 405(a), however, the courts have usually applied sensible and fairly tight restrictions. Typically, a foundation is required, expert testimony is disallowed,[93] and testimony is limited to a litany very like the one we borrow from Dean Ladd above except that the word "opinion" is substituted for the word "reputation," and references to what the witness "knows" or "believes" are substituted for references to what the witness has "heard."

The character exception gives criminal defendants the unusual advantage of being able to choose witnesses freely from among their friends and associates.[94] As we have noted, however, only a small number of defendants can take advantage of this opportunity because of two offsetting benefits the prosecutor gains once the defendant presents character testimony. First, after defense witnesses testify that the defendant's reputation is good, prosecution witnesses may testify that it is bad.[95] More important, as the last sentence in FRE 405(a) provides, the ban on specific-instance testimony that applies when the defendant calls a character witness does not bind the prosecutor when she cross-examines that witness. Unless a defendant has led a previously blameless life, the prosecutor's ability to question character witnesses about the defendant's relevant past transgressions may be devastating. The effect is only modestly alleviated by the defendant's ability (to the extent the trial judge permits) to respond to cross-examination about specific instances of bad character with redirect examination eliciting specific instances of good character.

A defendant's *reputation* witnesses may be asked whether they have *heard* of a defendant's bad acts, while *opinion* witnesses may be asked if they *know* of them. The theory in both cases is that inquiry into specific

---

[93] For a rare and questionable exception, see United States v. Roberts, 887 F.2d 534 (5th Cir. 1989) (the defendant in a prosecution for importing cocaine should have been allowed to present expert psychological testimony that his personality was consistent with his defense— that he came to possess the drugs while acting as a self-appointed vigilante seeking to expose drug dealers).

[94] Parties also may choose expert witnesses. See Chapter Nine. Parties are more or less stuck with most other witnesses, who either were involved in the underlying events or were fortuitously present when one of those events occurred.

[95] As we discuss in the next section, prosecution witnesses may also give reputation or opinion testimony about aspects of the defendant's bad character in response to defense witnesses who offer reputation or opinion testimony attacking the same aspects of the *victim's* character. This may occur, for example, in an assault or homicide case in which the defendant claims he acted in self-defense after being threatened by the victim.

bad acts tests the credibility of the character witness. A character witness who has not heard (or does not know) of the defendant's bad acts may not be very familiar with the defendant's reputation (or have an inadequate basis for her opinion).[96] A witness who admits that she has heard (or knows) of bad acts but still thinks the defendant's reputation or character is good (or has a high opinion of the defendant's character) may be a poor judge of character.

Under this theory, jurors should consider the bad acts inquired into only for their bearing on the character witness's credibility, and they are instructed not to treat the acts mentioned as evidence of the defendant's character. Almost no one believes that jurors abide by this instruction. Under the same theory, inquiry into bad acts is useful to test a character witness's credibility even if the defendant did not commit the acts in question, for a rumor need not be true to affect a person's reputation or opinions about his character. Here, too, the theory breaks down in practice. Courts forbid inquiry about bad acts unless the prosecutor believes in good faith, not simply that the allegations are sufficiently credible and well known to affect a person's reputation and opinions about her,[97] but also that the defendant actually *committed* the alleged bad acts. The only basis for the latter requirement is a fear that the jurors will assume the defendant committed any act that is asked about and will hold it against the defendant even when instructed that the inquiry is limited to testing the credibility of the character witness. Thus, the system concerns itself with the prejudicial misuse of evidence when the misuse would paint an inaccurate picture of the defendant's character but treats this likely misuse as a price defendants must pay when they attempt to introduce character evidence that probably makes them appear more upstanding than they are. These compromises are not without wisdom.[98]

---

[96] Once the witness admits that she has not heard or does not know of a particular bad act, the prosecutor generally will not be permitted to emphasize the acts further by asking what the community, or what the opinion witness, "would think" if informed that the defendant had committed the act. See United States v. Shwayder, 312 F.3d 1109 (9th Cir. 2002) (surveying cases).

[97] Cf. United States v. Monteleone, 77 F.3d 1086 (8th Cir. 1996) (the prosecutor's good faith belief that the defendant lied to the grand jury in the case did not provide a basis for asking the defendant reputation witness whether he had heard about the lie because grand jury proceedings are secret and don't affect community beliefs).

[98] Throughout this discussion we encounter a basic problem that permeates the law of evidence and makes its study so interesting. Certain procedures make perfect analytic sense when evidence law is treated as a self-contained system of rules and assumptions, but make almost no sense when their actual operation in jury trials is considered. Court decisions reflect this tension between evidence law as an abstract scheme of analysis and as a practical scheme for regulating the flow of information to juries. At times, rulings are justified on the basis of logical but artificial abstract analysis. At other times, analytically perfect answers are rejected because the system cannot make the fine discriminations in practice that are possible in abstract analysis. Analytically, the prosecutor should be allowed to ask a reputation witness if she has heard of an actual but unfounded charge against the defendant. Such charges affect reputation, and the witness's knowledge of the charge bears on the degree to which the witness is acquainted with defendant's reputation. Yet most jurisdictions forbid such questions because of the danger

Because reputation and opinions about character may be affected by arrests or bad acts that have not resulted in convictions, it is appropriate to ask reputation witnesses whether they have heard about the defendant's involvement in such events (and to ask opinion witnesses if they know of them). If a witness admits to knowledge, the defendant may ask the witness on redirect examination why the event did not affect the defendant's reputation (or the witness's opinion). The witness may reply by saying that most people believe that the event did not occur, that charges were dropped or the defendant was found innocent after trial, or with some other remark that pulls the sting of the cross-examination. Alternatively, the defense on redirect may ask questions of the following type: "Have you also heard that charges were dropped for lack of evidence?"—assuming the defense attorney believes that the information about which she inquires is true.

Cross-examination is limited to "relevant" bad acts—i.e., ones that relate to the character trait about which the witness has testified. Thus, it is technically improper to ask a witness who has testified that the defendant has a good reputation for peacefulness whether she has heard that the defendant was once convicted for embezzlement. Courts, however, vary greatly in their enforcement of the "relevant trait" limitation.

Courts also must consider how far back in time a cross-examiner may go in search of bad acts. Technically, the issue is whether the act is so old that a knowledgeable reputation or opinion witness would not be expected to have heard or know of it. Because the jury is likely to treat any apparent claim of bad acts as reflecting directly on the defendant's character, the court also should be concerned with the point at which past

---

that they will unfairly prejudice the defendant. This more pragmatic approach, however, might lead to the conclusion that *well-founded* charges are "fairly" allowed to prejudice the defendant (and, thus, in truth, are more than simply a basis for testing the credibility of character witnesses), given that the law permits such questions to be asked. If this is true, then perhaps a whole series of pragmatic compromises might be operating. To keep the defendant's favorable propensity evidence from unduly skewing the jury's deliberations, the defendant is limited to reputation and opinion testimony while the prosecutor is permitted to ask specific-instance questions on cross-examination. Recognizing, however, that allowing such questions might unfairly skew deliberations in the other direction, the law modestly readjusts the balance of advantages in the defendant's favor by requiring jurors to be instructed to consider questions about specific bad acts only as they bear on the credibility of the character witness and not as they bear on the defendant's character. The adjustment is intended to be only modest, however, given the recognition that jurors will make some, at least subliminal, judgments about the defendant's character based on the prosecutor's well-founded innuendoes and the answers to the prosecutor's questions. A similarly illogical but possibly expedient effort to moderate the advantage afforded by the defendant's exception is the common but not universal practice of refusing to instruct juries that character evidence by itself can create a reasonable doubt even though in theory it can do so. Compare Edgington v. United States, 164 U.S. 361, 366 (1896) ("The circumstances may be such that an established reputation for good character, if it is relevant to the issue, would alone create a reasonable doubt, although without it, the other evidence would be convincing.") with United States v. Pujana-Mena, 949 F.2d 24 (2d Cir. 1991) (following majority rule in refusing to give an instruction that evidence of good character can by itself establish reasonable doubt). See also infra, pp. 405–406.

acts are no longer probative of current character. The leading case on the issue and more generally on testing reputation witnesses for knowledge of specific acts is *Michelson v. United States.*[99]

Michelson was tried in 1947 for bribing a revenue agent. He pleaded entrapment, and the question was whom to believe, Michelson or the tax man. Michelson called five character witnesses, three of whom testified that he had a very good reputation for honesty, truthfulness and being a law-abiding citizen, and two of whom said they had never heard anything against Michelson. Two of the witnesses said they had known the defendant for about thirty years, and the others said they had known him for at least fifteen years. On cross-examination four of the witnesses were asked, "Did you ever hear that on October 11, 1920, the defendant, Solomon Michelson, was arrested for receiving stolen goods?" The question apparently was asked in good faith; a paper record of the arrest, which the defense did not challenge, was exhibited.[100] In an opinion by Justice Jackson that is often celebrated as the most intelligent judicial essay on the proof of character by reputation evidence, the Supreme Court rejected the defendant's claim that the question constituted reversible error tainting his conviction.

Jackson identified three issues that had to be dealt with before the decision below could be affirmed. First was whether inquiry about the arrest was proper. He answered this question in the standard manner, pointing out that even a false arrest may cloud one's reputation and stating that an inquiry into arrests tests the witness's qualifications to report community opinion. Second was whether, in a trial for bribery, an inquiry into the crime of receiving stolen goods was proper. The Court of Appeals forced this question on the Supreme Court by suggesting, in the process of affirming Michelson's conviction on the basis of circuit precedent, that the Court should reverse the decision and adopt the Illinois rule, which allows inquiries only about arrests on similar or identical charges. Jackson noted that the Illinois rule was inconsistent with the great weight of authority and concluded that Michelson's own trial showed the proposed rule to be unwise. Michelson, he pointed out, had offered evidence of good character broader than the crime charged, including the traits of honesty, truthfulness and law-abidance,

---

[99] 335 U.S. 469 (1948).

[100] The judge charged the jury as follows:

I instruct the jury that what is happening now is this: the defendant has called character witnesses, and the basis for the evidence given by those character witnesses is the reputation of the defendant in the community, and since the defendant tenders the issue of his reputation the prosecution may ask the witness if she has heard of various incidents in his career. I say to you that regardless of her answer you are not to assume that the incidents asked about actually took place. All that is happening is that this witness' standard of opinion of the reputation of the defendant is being tested. Is that clear?

Id. at 472 n.3.

characteristics that seem as incompatible with knowingly receiving stolen goods as with offering a bribe to a revenue agent.

The third issue was the lapse of time between the 1920 arrest and the events that gave rise to the trial. Here Jackson equivocated. After suggesting that the judge would have had discretion to exclude the inquiry, he pointed out that two of the witnesses traced their acquaintance with Michelson to a time before the 1920 arrest, that Michelson himself had pointed out a 1927 conviction for violating New York City trademark law with regard to watches and that there had been no objection at trial because of lapse of time.

What makes the Jackson opinion memorable is not the specific decisions reached on the issues in the case. Jackson disposed of the first two in a narrowly analytic manner and never fully faced up to the third. Jackson's opinion stands out because it frankly recognizes the anomalies of the reputation rule and acknowledges the likelihood that the jury will not comprehend limiting instructions designed to avoid the problems. Then, the opinion attempts to convert inconsistency and illogic into pragmatic virtues:

> We concur in the general opinion of courts, text-writers and the profession that much of this law is archaic, paradoxical and full of compromises and compensations by which an irrational advantage to one side is offset by a poorly reasoned counter privilege to the other. But somehow it has proved a workable even if clumsy system when moderated by discretionary controls in the hands of a wise and strong trial court. To pull one misshapen stone out of the grotesque structure is more likely simply to upset its present balance between adverse interests than to establish a rational edifice.[101]

This statement makes the important point that analytically illogical evidence rules may be sensible from a practical standpoint. We saw this already in noting the possibly wise compromise among competing interests that occurs when patently feeble reputation testimony (or only slightly more substantial opinion testimony) is required in lieu of testimony about specific instances of conduct. For this reason, Justice Jackson's analysis of the complicated set of compromises qualifying the defendant's exception to the propensity rule is justly celebrated even by commentators who are quick to criticize other aspects of evidence law as illogical.

But Justice Jackson's opinion is also widely accepted as a justification for placing almost no limits on the specific acts on which a defendant's character witnesses may be cross-examined.[102] And on this

---

[101] Id. at 486.

[102] See, e.g., United States v. Holt, 170 F.3d 698 (7th Cir. 1999) (permissible to ask witnesses to defendant's reputation for honesty and law-abiding behavior whether they had

point Jackson's position is not so much a thoughtful argument for the status quo as a call for thoughtless surrender. Even if Justice Jackson is correct that the character rule is an irrational set of compromises, the conclusion that changing any aspect of the scheme can only be detrimental does not follow. All the argument fairly suggests is that one should be careful and expect the unexpected in deciding whether to change a rule of evidence. As Justice Jackson points out, the law seems to have arrived at its current state through a series of adjustments that offset unfair advantages created by prior adjustments. Artificially declaring an end to this process of "compromises and compensations" may be just as damaging to fair trials as failing to see that it occurred in the first place.

Justice Jackson thus gives no good reason to allow cross-examination about twenty-five-year-old arrests and convictions. In FRE 609 (discussed infra, Section IV.B.3), the drafters of the federal rules included a strong presumption against using old convictions for impeachment. Justice Jackson's analysis may have kept the drafters of FRE 405(a) from imposing a similar limitation on the use of ancient arrests and convictions in cross-examining character witnesses for the accused. Even so, FRE 403 gives courts the discretion to preclude cross-examination on bad acts that are so dated that their prejudicial impact greatly exceeds their probative force.

We have expressed strong views in discussing the legal system's treatment of character evidence. Here and elsewhere you should consider our critical comments critically. You may, for example, find less to celebrate than we do in Justice Jackson's general defense of the "grotesque structure" of pragmatically developed evidence rules, or more to celebrate than we do in his specific defense of broad cross-examination of reputation witnesses. Our task is to encourage you to think about these matters; it is not to tell you what to think.

Problem V-21. Sigmund Sign-Felled is charged with armed robbery for allegedly mugging an elderly man on Broadway and 112th Street. Sign-Felled opens his defense at trial by calling Tom Spoon, who testifies that he has known Sign-Felled well for the last five years and that the two are "like brothers." Without further ado, defense counsel asks the following questions: (1) "Describe Sign-Felled's reputation for honesty?" (2) "What is your opinion of Sign-Felled's character for violence or nonviolence?" (3)

---

heard allegations that he was behind on his child-support payments and had engaged in sexual harassment at work); United States v. Alvarez, 860 F.2d 801, modified, 868 F.2d 201 (7th Cir. 1989) (permissible to ask character witnesses in narcotics and racketeering case whether they knew or had heard the defendant violated the immigration laws, though the violations occurred years before and in cities other than where the witnesses lived); United States v. Glass, 709 F.2d 669 (11th Cir. 1983) (permissible to ask character witnesses for sheriff charged with dealing drugs about his acceptance of money in return for fixing traffic tickets).

(Assuming objections to question (2) are overruled) "What is the basis of your opinion?" (4) "Would you give us an example of the defendant's nonviolent behavior?" **How should the judge rule on the prosecutor's objections to these questions? May Spoon instead testify that he gave Sign-Felled the Core Battery Personality Test and Sign-Felled scored in the 98th percentile for nonviolence— assuming Spoon is an expert in giving the test and interpreting its results, and that the test validly measures nonviolent disposition? Why or why not?**

Problem V-22. Same facts as Problem V-21. Suppose the judge permits Spoon to testify that, "In my opinion, Sign-Felled is as nonviolent as the day is long." On cross-examination, the prosecutor asks the following questions: (1) "Have you heard that four years ago, Sign-Felled used false pretenses to swindle the Widower Constancia out of his entire pension?" (2) "Did you know that seven years ago, Sign-Felled was convicted of the felony of forcibly stealing candy from babies in Bryant Park at Broadway and 42nd Street?" (3) "Did you know that Sign-Felled was arrested only last year for smoking marijuana on the street at Broadway and 113th Street?" **How should the judge rule on defense counsel's objections to these questions? Assuming the court permits the questions, and Spoon denies hearing or knowing about any of the incidents, may the prosecutor present the testimony of Constancia, or either of the two arresting officers, that the events occurred? If the judge overrules an objection and allows question (1), and Spoon answers "No," may Sign-Felled call Constancia to testify that the alleged swindle never took place, and that all Sign-Felled's many dealings with Constancia have been honorable? What other use might Sign-Felled make of Constancia? If instead of testifying about Sign-Felled's nonviolence, Spoon testifies that Sign-Felled and he were volunteering at a soup kitchen when the mugging occurred, may the prosecutor then ask Spoon question (1), (2) or (3)?**

B. THE ALLEGED VICTIM'S BAD CHARACTER

FRE 404(a)(2)(B) (which is quoted in full on p. 345) restates the common law exception to the propensity rule which provides that a defendant in a criminal case "may offer evidence of an alleged victim's pertinent trait" of character (FRE 404(a)(2)(B)), and "if the evidence is admitted, the prosecutor may . . . offer evidence to rebut it" (FRE 404(a)(2)(B)(i)).[103] Evidence of this sort is most commonly offered to support claims of self-defense in criminal trials for assault or homicide.

---

[103] The common law exception applied only to criminal cases. Prior to 2006, a few federal courts had extended the precursor to FRE 404(a)(2)(B) to civil cases involving claims of self-defense in response to allegations of assault or wrongful death. An amendment in 2006 made clear that the exception applies only to criminal cases.

Although the rule includes no foundational requirement, some courts interpret FRE 404(a)(2)(B) to require defendants to introduce other evidence of self-defense before attacking the alleged victim's character. Under FRE 405(a), a defendant is restricted to attacking the alleged victim's character with reputation or opinion testimony; he may not present evidence showing, for example, that the victim is known to have started several other fights. Questions about specific instances of the alleged victim's conduct are permitted on cross-examination by the prosecutor but only (in theory) to test the credibility of the character witness and not as substantive evidence of the alleged victim's character. The justification for allowing evidence on the victim's character, the way the inquiry is handled, and the issues raised are all similar to those we discussed in the preceding section on criminal defendants' use of evidence of their own good character; we will not repeat that discussion here.

When self-defense is claimed, FRE 404(a)(2)(B) allows the accused to introduce propensity evidence to suggest that the alleged victim was the first aggressor. The defendant may also show that she knew the alleged victim was or was reported to be a violent person to support a claim that her use of force was reasonable. This latter use of character evidence does not violate (and thus is not an exception to) the propensity rule because it is offered not as circumstantial evidence that the alleged victim acted in accordance with his character but, instead, to show the defendant's good faith belief that she needed to defend herself. Because this is a *non*propensity use of character evidence, it is not governed by FRE 405(a), so the defendant may offer evidence of specific instances of the alleged victim's conduct that she knew or had heard about.[104] She also may introduce evidence of the victim's reputation for violence if she knew of that reputation at the time of her alleged crime, or evidence of another's opinion that the victim was violent if that opinion had been shared with her before the alleged crime. Because these uses of evidence of the alleged victim's character are not designed to show that the victim in fact acted in accordance with a violent character, but only that the defendant had reason to *believe* the victim was dangerous, the evidence does not trigger the prosecutor's various rights, discussed below, to rebut evidence of the victim's propensity for violence by showing the victim's good character or the defendant's bad character.

In addition to cross-examining witnesses to the alleged victim's bad character, the prosecutor may respond with rebuttal witnesses who offer reputation or opinion testimony attesting to the victim's good character. FRE 404(a)(2)(C) also permits the prosecution "in a homicide case" to present "evidence of the alleged victim's trait of peacefulness to rebut

---

[104] In FRE 405(a) (quoted in full supra, p. 400), as elsewhere in the rules, the "evidence of character" that triggers the rule's application is a shorthand for evidence of a trait of character offered for the single purpose of proving action in accordance with the trait. When character evidence is offered for some *other*, nonpropensity purpose, FRE 405(a) does not apply.

[*any*, even noncharacter] evidence that the victim was the first aggressor." This latter provision reflects what had been the minority position at common law. Before states began revising their evidence codes on the model of the Federal Rules, defendants in most jurisdictions could plead self-defense and introduce *non*character evidence suggesting that the deceased was the first aggressor without opening the door to character evidence suggesting that the deceased was a peaceable person. This procedure works well in assault cases in which the defendant argues self-defense, because the prosecutor can call the victim to testify to what happened. In homicide cases, however, the victim cannot testify, so FRE 405(a) lets the prosecutor answer the defense with character evidence about the victim in the form of reputation or opinion testimony. The relatively weak form of such evidence may deter jurors from giving it too much weight; it may not deter them, however, from being incensed that such a fine person was killed, or from being unduly moved by the grief of those called as character witnesses. When these reactions are likely, they may provide a basis for exclusion under FRE 403. This narrow exception for self-defense claims in homicide cases is the only time the prosecution may present evidence of a criminal defendant's bad character or an alleged victim's good character if the defendant did not first open the door by presenting character evidence of her own.

Under FRE 404(a)(2)(B) and (C), therefore, the prosecutor may use evidence of the alleged victim's law-abiding propensities to defend the character of the victim in one of two situations: in response to a direct attack on the victim's character, or—in the case of a homicide—in response to a claim of self-defense.

A 2000 amendment to FRE 404 further expanded the prosecutor's ability to use propensity evidence to respond to a defendant's attack on the alleged victim's character. In an effort to equalize the treatment of alleged victims and criminal defendants, the 2000 amendment lets the prosecutor use reputation or opinion testimony to demonstrate the *defendant's* aggressive or violent character whenever the defendant first attacks the *victim's* character for that same trait. See FRE 404(a)(2)(B)(ii). Prior to 2000, the only time a prosecutor could introduce evidence of a defendant's propensity to commit crimes of the sort charged was in response to the defendant's introduction of evidence under the precursor to FRE 404(a)(2)(A) that such a crime was out of character for him. Now, defendants open themselves up to character attack either by defending their own character under FRE 404(a)(2)(A) or by attacking the victim's character under FRE 404(a)(2)(B). It remains the case, however, that a defendant's claim of self-defense supported only by *nonpropensity* evidence does not trigger the prosecutor's ability to attack the defendant's character, even in homicide cases. It also remains the case that if the defendant chooses to vaunt his own good character without attacking the alleged victim's character, the prosecutor may not show that the victim was just as nice a guy.

The impulse to protect victims' rights relative to those of criminal defendants triggered another recent amendment to FRE 404(a)(2)(B). Until relatively recently, a common use of the exception permitting defendants to present evidence of the alleged victim's character was to support a claim of consent in a rape case. FRE 412 and similar state "rape victim's shield statutes" now bar character evidence when offered to show that the alleged victim has a propensity to engage in sexual conduct. This narrowing of the reach of the FRE 404(a)(2)(B) exception was implied by FRE 412's adoption in 1978 and was made explicit in a 2006 amendment confirming that the exception is "subject to the limitations imposed by Rule 412." We discuss FRE 412 infra, Section VIII.B.

Problem V-23. Daniel Duker is alleged to have hit Paul Paster over the head with a whiskey bottle one evening when both were drinking at Out for the Count Inn. Both are long-time habitués of that establishment. Duker says he acted in self-defense after Paster threatened him with a pool cue. At trial, Duker wants (1) to testify to his opinion, based on his long association with Paster at Out for the Count Inn, that Paster is a violent man. Duker also wants (2) to give ten examples of occasions when he observed Paster's pugnacious and pugilistic behavior, (3) to introduce evidence of Paster's reputation for unprovoked violence among patrons of the Tenth Round Tavern, a place Paster frequently patronizes but Duker has never visited, and (4) to present testimony about two fights Paster had previously started at Tenth Round Tavern. **Is any of this evidence admissible in Paster's suit against Duker for assault and battery? In a criminal trial at which Duker is charged with assault?** Assume Duker is charged with homicide growing out of the whiskey bottle fray, and presents only item (1) above as part of his defense. **Should the plaintiff or prosecutor be permitted to introduce the testimony of George Frazier, the long-time bartender at Out for the Count Inn, that in his opinion Paster is as gentle as a lamb? That in his opinion Duker has a violent temper? That on three separate occasions he has seen Duker attack patrons for little or no reason? Would your answers to any of these questions be different if item (2) were the only evidence of Paster's aggressive nature that Duker presented?**

IV. EXCEPTIONS TO THE PROPENSITY RULE: IMPEACHMENT EVIDENCE

A. IMPEACHMENT GENERALLY

Subparagraph (3) of FRE 404(a) establishes another exception to the propensity rule: "Evidence of a witness's character may be admitted under Rules 607, 608, and 609." FREs 607–609 govern the use of character evidence to impeach a witness, the subject of this section. FREs 607, 610 and 613 and some additional rules govern the use of other kinds of evidence for impeachment purposes and are discussed in Section V. Before proceeding to those topics, however, it is useful to consider briefly the general question of impeachment.

As is noted in Chapter Two, the most common method of discrediting adverse testimony is by cross-examining the witness who offered it. By pointing out gaps or inconsistencies in a witness's testimony, or by exposing failures of perception, memory or communication, the adroit cross-examiner may weaken or even neutralize what appeared on direct examination to be a convincing presentation. Cross-examination is not, however, the only means of attacking the truthfulness or reliability of a witness's testimony. A party seeking to discredit testimony may offer independent evidence designed to show that the testimony cannot be believed. A party may impeach an adverse witness's testimony by showing flaws in the testimony, the witness or both. Witnesses on cross-examination often will cooperate in revealing the limits of their perception or memory of an event or in their ability to describe what they saw, and may be candid in revealing motives they have to favor the party that called them.[105] Witnesses are less likely to cooperate in showing that their perception, memory, narrative ability and, especially, their character for truthfulness are generally bad.

At common law a party could not impeach a witness she had called except in special circumstances. This rule was the consequence of the broader common law principle that a party "vouched" for the credibility of the witnesses she called. The usual rationale for both propositions was that they deterred parties from calling witnesses known to be untrustworthy. The problem with this rationale was that a party often "has little or no choice of witnesses. The party must call those who happen to have observed the particular facts in controversy."[106] A rule that prevents a party from questioning the accuracy of the witnesses she calls may keep her from calling important witnesses or from giving the

---

[105] Consider the witness who had only a partial view of the events, is related to a party, is being paid as an expert or is called to testify by a prosecutor who has brought charges against the same witness in another case. Because the witness knows that these bases for doubting his testimony can easily be shown, he is likely to acknowledge them on cross-examination; indeed, the direct examiner may bring up these problems in advance to "pull the sting."

[106] McCormick § 38.

jury an accurate picture of the credibility of those she does call. It also ignores the possibility that a lawyer may credit one part of a witness's account but not another.[107]

The rule forbidding impeachment on direct examination did avoid one problem. Juries may give *substantive* effect to evidence that is admitted solely for *impeachment* purposes. For example, one way of impeaching a witness is to show that she said something out of court that contradicts what she said on the stand. Often, however, such evidence may not be used to support an argument that the out-of-court statement is true (it usually is inadmissible hearsay if offered for its truth) and may only be used to suggest that a person who tells contradictory stories cannot be believed no matter what she says. Yet even when told not to, a jury may take a witness's prior inconsistent statements as true, and a lawyer may call a witness solely in order to impeach her with otherwise inadmissible prior statements that he hopes the jury will believe. Still, the temptation to call witnesses solely to impeach them and thus get inadmissible evidence before the jury can be countered by evidence and ethics rules forbidding that particular practice.[108] Not all impeachment of a party's own witnesses need be precluded.

Because there are often good reasons for a party to impeach witnesses on direct examination, the common law rule precluding such impeachment had many exceptions. Parties ordinarily could impeach a witness they called if they were surprised by unfavorable testimony, if the witness was an opposing party or for some other reason was declared to be "hostile," or if the party was required by law to call the witness, as in the case of an attesting witness to a will. Common law courts also sometimes avoided the impact of the rule by having the judge call the witness, thus permitting both sides to impeach.[109]

The arguments against limiting impeachment on direct examination prevailed with the drafters of the Federal Rules. FRE 607 provides that

---

[107] No more convincing is the argument that attorneys armed with the ability to impeach their own witnesses can coerce favorable but inaccurate testimony. An attorney unethical enough to threaten to reveal embarrassing information to secure falsely favorable testimony and a witness weak-willed enough to bow to the pressure would hardly be deterred by a rule that forces the attorney to threaten embarrassing disclosure outside of court. The common law rule thus accomplishes little besides keeping ethical lawyers from revealing accurate information about the foibles of witnesses they believe are only partially trustworthy.

[108] See infra, pp. 457–458, discussing some of those rules. The problem here also could be avoided by adopting the minority rule among state jurisdictions, not followed by the Federal Rules, which admits all prior inconsistent statements of a witness for the truth of the matter asserted. See Chapter Six, Section IV.D., pp. 757–770. See also infra, p. 451, note 156 and p. 454, note 159.

[109] Courts in jurisdictions that retain the common law rule also often let parties try to "refresh" the recollection of uncooperative witnesses on direct examination by reminding them of statements they previously made. If this last practice is allowed, most of the justification for the common law rule, as applied to impeachment by inconsistent statements, evaporates. See infra, Section V.C., pp. 450–459. The jury is as likely to ignore instructions not to make substantive or impeachment use of evidence offered solely to refresh recollection as it is to ignore instructions not to make substantive use of identical evidence offered solely to impeach.

"[a]ny party, including the party that called the witness, may attack the witness's credibility." The constitutional rights of the accused to impeach adverse witnesses and to present evidence in defense, discussed in Chapter Seven, dictate the same result in criminal cases whenever there are strong reasons to let the accused impeach a witness she called, or weak reasons to forbid her to do so.[110]

Under common law practice, the exceptional circumstances that let a party impeach her own witness (e.g., the witness's hostility) are the same circumstances that permit leading questions on direct examination. Under FRE 607, however, a party presenting a witness may "impeach" any unfavorable aspect of the witness's testimony, even if the bulk of the testimony is friendly. May a party use leading questions to facilitate the impeachment of a nonhostile witness on direct examination? Generally, FRE 611(c) follows the common law in limiting leading questions to cross-examination and the direct examination of hostile or adverse witnesses. FRE 611(c) also, however, permits leading questions on direct examination "as necessary to develop the witness's testimony." It thus gives judges ample discretion to allow leading direct examination questions as needed to elicit a witness's disclosure of self-impeaching information.

We turn now to specific impeachment techniques that are regulated by the evidence rules. We begin with general attacks on the witness's character for truthfulness, which are designed to suggest that a witness is not worthy of belief no matter what she says or on whose behalf she testifies. Next (in Section V) we discuss more particularized attacks on a witness's testimony tied to specific circumstances of the witness or case. Later (in Section VIII) we discuss special rules that govern the use—for impeachment as well as for other purposes—of character evidence in sexual assault and child molestation cases.

———

Problem V-24. Mike Mussel is charged with conspiracy to commit extortion. In sworn statements to the police (which are inadmissible hearsay if offered to prove the facts described in the statements), Asa Argent and Bobbie Bell each has described overlapping but only partial aspects of an extortion scheme they allegedly hatched with Mussel and started to carry out before being arrested. Together, the two statements give a full picture of the scheme. At trial, the prosecutor calls Argent as her first witness—with trepidation, having heard a rumor a week earlier that Argent was getting "cold feet." Sure enough, Argent takes the stand and denies knowing Mussel or anything about an extortion scheme. **In a jurisdiction where parties must vouch for their witnesses, may the prosecutor cross-examine Argent about his prior sworn**

---

[110] See, e.g., Chambers v. Mississippi, 410 U.S. 284 (1973) (discussed in Chapter Seven).

statement? How about in a jurisdiction that follows the Federal Rules? If the prosecutor is allowed to impeach Mussel in this manner, how should the jury be instructed? In either of the two jurisdictions, may the prosecutor present reputation evidence that Argent is a liar? Would the prosecutor want to do this? Assume the prosecutor is permitted (over objection) to impeach Argent with his sworn statement. Bell testifies next in accordance with her sworn statement, and the prosecution then rests. The jury convicts Mussel. **What is Mussel's strongest claim for reversing his conviction on appeal? Does your answer cause you to reconsider the propriety of allowing Argent to be cross-examined about his sworn statement? Why or why not?**

B. IMPEACHMENT BY EVIDENCE OF BAD CHARACTER

1. Impeachment by Reputation and Opinion Evidence

One way to suggest that a witness is lying is to show that he is generally disposed to lie. This might be done by showing that the witness has a reputation as a liar, that people who know him believe he cannot be trusted or that he has lied on particular occasions in the past. If you wonder about the admissibility of such evidence, your instincts are sound because these types of evidence all invite the jury to believe the witness is a liar and then to infer that when he testified he was acting in accordance with his untruthful character. As we have seen, FRE 404(a)(1) generally forbids that kind of inference. Recall, however, that subparagraph (3) of Rule 404(a) (quoted on p. 345) declares an exception for uses of character evidence permitted by Rules 607, 608 and 609. We already have discussed FRE 607, which lets parties impeach their own witnesses. Now we turn to FRE 608. It provides:

Rule 608. A Witness's Character for Truthfulness or Untruthfulness

> **(a) Reputation or Opinion Evidence.** A witness's credibility may be attacked or supported by testimony about the witness's reputation for having a character for truthfulness or untruthfulness, or by testimony in the form of an opinion about that character. But evidence of truthful character is admissible only after the witness's character for truthfulness has been attacked.

> **(b) Specific Instances of Conduct.** Except for a criminal conviction under Rule 609, extrinsic evidence is not admissible to prove specific instances of a witness's conduct in order to attack or support the witness's character for truthfulness. But the court may, on cross-examination, allow them to be inquired into if they are probative of the character for truthfulness of:

(1) the witness; or

(2) another witness whose character the witness being cross-examined has testified about.

By testifying on another matter, a witness does not waive any privilege against self-incrimination for testimony that relates to the witness's character for truthfulness.

FRE 608 allows a party to introduce evidence of a witness's propensity to lie (or, at times, to tell the truth) as the basis for an inference that a witness is behaving dishonestly (or honestly) on the witness stand. FRE 608 incorporates the same preference as FRE 405 for reputation and opinion testimony, as opposed to specific instances of conduct, when character evidence is offered to show a propensity.[111] That preference is tempered, however, by FRE 608(b)'s permission for limited cross-examination about specific instances of bad conduct and FRE 609's authorization to use a witness's prior convictions to impeach.

Unlike the exceptions to the propensity rule found in FRE 404(a)(2)(A) and (B), FRE 608 applies in all cases, civil as well as criminal, and may be invoked by all parties. This is not because there is good reason to believe that a propensity to lie or tell the truth is more predictive of conduct than other character traits. Indeed, to the extent that character traits best predict conduct in situations very like the ones in which the traits previously were revealed,[112] evidence of the witness's mendacity in family, community or business settings may not say much about her truthfulness in the courtroom. The oath, the stern eye of the black-robed judge, the flags, mahogany and other indicia of formality, the recording of what is said, and the threat of cross-examination and of prosecution for perjury may all inspire more than the usual degree of honesty. Or the stakes at a trial, the witness's interest in the outcome (if any) and the one-shot and highly scripted nature of courtroom testimony—which provides little basis for testing what is said there against what was said on other occasions—may permit more *dis*honesty than the witness would venture when talking to close associates. Either way, a witness's behavior outside the courtroom doesn't necessarily tell us much about how she will behave inside it. But in the 19th century, when the exception arose, people viewed character differently, and—particularly in small town settings—those who earned reputations for

---

[111] Common law jurisdictions would not allow the use of opinion testimony to show a witness's propensity to lie or tell the truth. They often accomplished the same thing, however, by allowing witnesses testifying about other witnesses' reputations to conclude by stating whether they would believe the testimony under oath of those witnesses. The step FRE 608(a) took in allowing opinion as well as reputation evidence was thus a small and sensible one. Courts continue to allow a witness who attacks another witness's character for truthfulness to testify hypothetically that she would not believe what the other witness says under oath, but do not permit her to say whether she believes the actual testimony the witness gave. See, e.g., United States v. Harris, 471 F.3d 507 (3d Cir. 2006).

[112] See supra, p. 352, note 12; supra, Section II.B.5, pp. 383–387.

mendacity may have been seen as unworthy of belief in any context. The interesting question is why when most other uses of character to show propensity were barred, character as evidence of credibility was welcomed.

One answer is that the danger of prejudice is lower when character evidence is used to attack or rehabilitate a witness than when it goes to the merits. Often, the character evidence does not pertain to a party whose fate is at issue. Moreover, character evidence on credibility only bears on the weight the jury should give to a witness's testimony; it does not speak directly to the merits of the claims. For this reason we regard it as *collateral*. But this does not entirely explain why FRE 608 and some parts of FRE 609 treat the parties' testimony the same as that of other witnesses. When a party's character for truthfulness is vilified after he testifies, there is a danger that the jury will generalize what it hears into an overall assessment of bad character.[113] Because parties may be close associates of the witnesses they call, attacks on a party's witnesses can reflect badly on that party as well. Character impeachment has still other costs, even when the witness is not a party or a party's friend. Honest witnesses may be reluctant to testify for fear of being made to look dishonest, and the jury may pay more attention to a witness's character in evaluating the accuracy of her testimony than to more important factors such as her opportunity to observe or any specific incentives she may have to be truthful or to lie.

Diminished prejudice is not, however, the only justification for the wider admissibility of character evidence on credibility than on the merits. Excluding character evidence creates incentives to search for better evidence. This search is more important, and likely to be more productive, when it is aimed at finding noncharacter evidence of what happened than when it seeks to uncover noncharacter evidence of credibility. Specific factors that relate directly to credibility, such as bias and the quality of an opportunity to observe, are usually obvious from the witness's story or from what the parties know about the witness. If, for example, a party has no reason to think a witness is biased against her, it is unlikely that interviewing 50 people who know the witness will uncover evidence of bias. By contrast, interviewing even a few additional people who know something about the matters at issue in the case is likely to tell a lawyer something. So incentives to search for noncharacter evidence (including those created by a ban on character evidence) have greater returns when they encourage exploration into the merits of cases rather than into collateral matters such as credibility. Where credibility is

---

[113] For these reasons, parties choosing to testify give up much of FRE 404(a)(1)'s protection. Some commentators have argued that this effect is justified by the need to counteract the strong incentives of parties (particularly criminal defendants) to commit perjury to further their causes. Because juries probably mistrust party testimony in proportion to how much rides on it, the need for additional, exceptional responses to self-interested testimony seems weak.

concerned, the preference for reputation and opinion evidence of a witness's character minimizes the cost of searching by letting a single character witness report or distill the views and information of others.

The preference for reputation and opinion testimony on direct examination reflects the same compromise we saw in our discussion of FRE 404(a)(2) and 405. Possibly unreliable character evidence is permitted, but it generally must take a form that jurors can see is potentially unreliable, that takes little time to introduce, and that is unlikely to arouse emotions. McCormick gives this version of the bloodless testimony that typically is given:

Q. Do you know the general reputation at the present time of William Witness in the community in which he lives, for truth and veracity? **A.** Yes.

Q. What is that reputation? **A.** It is bad.[114]

The same compromise has led nearly all courts to limit the "opinion" testimony allowed by FRE 608(a) to *lay* witnesses and to disallow expert testimony about a witness's disposition to lie or tell the truth.[115] Prior to the adoption of the Federal Rules of Evidence, some jurisdictions had assumed that general character is predictive of honesty and allowed reputation or opinion testimony about a witness's character as a whole. Adhering to the majority rule, FRE 608(a) includes a pertinence requirement, limiting testimony to "character for truthfulness or untruthfulness."[116] To testify to credibility, a character witness must know reasonably well the person whose credibility is at issue, or be acquainted with the person's current reputation for truthfulness or honesty in a residential, business or other community.

A witness who testifies to another witness's propensity to lie may be asked on cross-examination whether he "has heard" or "knows" about specific instances in which the original witness told the truth, preferably

---

[114] McCormick, § 43.

[115] The specific ground for exclusion is usually that expert opinion evidence on credibility is not *helpful* to the jury, as required by FRE 702, or sometimes that such testimony is unduly prejudicial under FRE 403. See infra, Chapter Nine. Occasionally, courts allow expert testimony about a witness's particular mental defect that undermines her perception, memory, narrative ability, or even her truthfulness. The explanation seems to be that the defect in credibility is sufficiently specific and predictable that, under the analysis in Section II. B.5., supra, pp. 383–387, it does not qualify as character evidence. Such testimony is not governed by FRE 608(a), which applies only to evidence of "*character* for truthfulness or untruthfulness," and instead is governed entirely by FRE 402, 403 and 702. See, e.g., United States v. Love, 329 F.3d 981 (8th Cir. 2003) (expert psychological testimony permitted on question of witness's memory loss); United States v. Gonzalez-Maldonado, 115 F.3d 9 (1st Cir. 1997) (expert testimony permitted on mental illness that rendered a witness "prone to exaggeration"). See also Section V.D, infra, pp. 459–465, discussing impeachment based on defects of perception, memory or narrative clarity.

[116] See, e.g., United States v. Meserve, 271 F.3d 314 (1st Cir. 2001) (trial court abused its discretion by permitting a witness to be impeached with testimony that he had a reputation in the community for violence and assaultive behavior).

in circumstances where telling the truth was embarrassing or costly to that witness. As with cross-examination of character witnesses under FRE 404(a)(2)(A) and (B), such questions are supposed to probe the standards the character witness is applying and test that witness's familiarity with the behavior of the witness being attacked. Questions about specific instances of truth telling rarely accomplish much, however. Several isolated acts of honesty are likely to have little impact on a jury's assessment of the credibility of a witness's testimony. Allowing such cross-examination, however, may serve to deter some unnecessary or inaccurate attacks on the character of generally honest witnesses.

Specific instance cross-examination does play an important role in one situation. Under FRE 608(a), a witness whose character for truthfulness has been attacked may be rehabilitated with reputation or opinion testimony from other witnesses who attest to the original witness's *good* character for truthfulness. But FRE 608(b)(2) then allows the opposing party to ask the rehabilitation witnesses about specific instances of *dishonest* behavior by the witness whose truthfulness they have affirmed. If bad acts are conceded, the jury may not only doubt the character witnesses' rehabilitation testimony, but may also treat the information as reason to doubt the original witness's veracity. This is a real deterrent to rehabilitation testimony because isolated acts of dishonesty are likely to have more impact on the jury than isolated acts of honesty.[117] We discuss this issue in Section VI, on rehabilitation.

Questions about specific instances take more time than reputation and opinion testimony and tend to be more dramatic. This threatens the compromise that admits character evidence in exceptional circumstances but only in a quick and weak form. FRE 608(b) (discussed in more detail in the next section) accordingly provides only that specific-instance questions "may" be permitted on cross-examination, implying broad judicial authority to exclude potentially prejudicial questions, including ones that the usual balancing test of FRE 403 might permit.

Problem V-25. In Proton Inc.'s action for breach of a contract by Electron, Ltd., Charmaine Proton testifies that she and Anita Electron shook hands on the deal in question at the Atomic Café on February 3. Electron testifies that no agreement was reached at the February 3rd meeting, or at any other time. In rebuttal, Proton calls Charles Neutron, until recently a business partner of Electron, to testify: (1) that in his opinion, based on close observation of Electron over many years, she is a "compulsive contract breacher"; (2) that during those same years, he repeatedly heard Electron lie to other employees and clients about her

---

[117] See supra, p. 396 for a general discussion of the greater probative value of specific acts as evidence of bad character than as evidence of good character.

weight, age, income and golf handicap; and (3) that Electron had a reputation around the office as a liar. **Is any of this testimony by Neutron admissible under FRE 608(a)? In response (assuming that some or all of this evidence is admitted), may Electron's attorney (relying on FRE 608 as a whole) ask Neutron if he is aware that Electron spends every weekend volunteering at a home for severely retarded children? May the attorney ask Neutron if he is aware that Electron recently found $1000 in a taxicab and turned it into the police? If Neutron's answer is "No, I don't know what Electron does in taxicabs," may Electron call the cab driver to describe the incident? May Electron call an employee to testify that, in her opinion, Electron is honest? That Neutron is a liar? Why or why not?**

2.   Impeachment by Bad Acts

Acts of lying or deceit may indicate a weak moral or psychological commitment to the truth, and suggest that the witness's testimony is untrustworthy. But jurors may easily overestimate the probative value of such conduct. The witness's prior actions may have been specific to a context very different from testifying in court, and even those who occasionally lie tell the truth most of the time. Moreover, the dramatic quality of bad-acts evidence makes it more likely than reputation or opinion testimony to waste time, distract the jury with collateral factual disputes, and risk other types of prejudice.

Because of the conflicting policy considerations that bear on bad-acts impeachment, evidence law has developed distinctions governing admissibility that are extraordinarily fine, even for an area that is full of subtle and complicated rules. If prior dishonest behavior has resulted in a felony conviction, evidence of that conviction is very likely admissible under FRE 609—if it is not too old. If the dishonest behavior has *not* resulted in a felony criminal conviction or is not a crime, FRE 608(b) gives the trial court discretion to allow the cross-examiner to inquire into the matter but does not allow "extrinsic" evidence that the bad act occurred. This means that a witness may be asked about her past dishonest acts, but if she denies them, even falsely, other evidence may not be introduced to prove that they occurred.[118] The cross-examiner, it is said, "must take

---

[118] Under the last sentence of FRE 608(b), taking the stand does not waive the witness's privilege against self-incrimination if the witness is asked about matters that relate only to character for truthfulness. This provision protects character witnesses generally, but especially criminal defendants, by letting them refuse to answer specific-act questions that might require them to admit crimes that have not resulted in convictions. Prosecutors or courts may avoid this limitation by granting the witness immunity from prosecution for the bad act or at least from the use of his testimony and evidence derived therefrom if he later is prosecuted for the crime about which he is asked. By filing a motion with the court before the witness is cross-examined, the party presenting the witness to another witness's character for truthfulness can secure a ruling forbidding the opposing party to ask about prior bad acts covered by the last sentence of FRE 608(b). This procedure avoids the prejudice that is likely if the witness is forced to invoke her Fifth Amendment privilege in front of the jury. Prior to 2003, FRE 608(b)'s last sentence

the witness's answer as given."[119] The rules are the same when witnesses are asked about the dishonest acts of other witnesses whose character for truthfulness they have affirmed.

By now, the logic (or pragmatic illogic) of this compromise should be apparent. Evidence of prior bad acts is allowed to impeach (or rehabilitate) a witness, but only in the relatively quick and weak form of cross-examination questions put to a witness who is testifying for another purpose. Wasted time, surprise, distraction by collateral issues and undue salience are avoided by forbidding what otherwise would seem to be the most reliable form of evidence, namely, independent testimony or documents describing the bad acts. FRE 608(b) further limits bad-acts evidence by requiring that the acts be probative of truthfulness or untruthfulness (a limitation that some common law jurisdictions did not apply), and by giving the trial court discretion over whether to permit bad-acts cross-examination. If a witness has been cross-examined about acts suggesting dishonesty, the court has discretion to let the opposing party on redirect examination ask questions about acts suggesting honesty.

The fact that FRE 608(b) bars extrinsic evidence to disprove a witness's denial of a prior act does not mean that a witness can lie with impunity about prior bad behavior. The opposing party can fall back on FRE 608(a) and present unfavorable reputation or opinion testimony about the witness's character for truthfulness based on general knowledge, or an opposing witness's personal knowledge, of the bad acts the witness has denied. A false denial also may lead to a perjury prosecution, and an ethical attorney will instruct her witnesses to correct any testimony she knows is false. In practice, lawyers often bring out a witness's impeachable bad acts on direct examination, to avoid ethical

---

extended this protection to any witness testifying about "matters that relate only to *credibility*." FRE 608 was amended that year to limit protection provided by the last sentence to witnesses whose "testimony . . . relates only to the witness's *character for truthfulness*." Because, as we will see below, attacks on another witness's character for truthfulness are only one (and a relatively rare) means of attacking another witness's credibility, the 2003 amendment greatly limited the scope of the protection afforded by FRE 608(b)'s last paragraph.

[119] Although the cross-examiner must take the answer she gets, she need not surrender without a fight. Most courts let her probe to be sure that the witness knows what prior incident is being asked about and that he firmly denies it. Judicial control is needed, however, to deter lawyers from unethically asking questions that have no purpose other than suggesting to the jury that the questioner knows certain facts to be true.

Notice that the limitation on extrinsic evidence of bad acts may adversely affect the party offering the witness whose honesty is being attacked as well as the party attacking the witness. When a witness admits a prior dishonest act, the jury is likely to focus on the witness's deceitfulness and not, for example, on the witness's possibly exculpatory mental state at the time the deceitful statement was made or the bad act occurred. (This is less of a problem when a prior conviction is used to impeach, because the issue will have been adjudicated and the mental elements of the crime will be known to the jury.) Although the courts generally allow the witness to give a brief explanation of the circumstances under which the deceitfulness occurred, FRE 608(b) forbids extrinsic evidence that might more successfully temper the effect of the witness's admission that she lied.

and legal problems, and preemptively to take the "sting" out of the expected cross-examination.

Perhaps the strongest argument in favor of bad-act evidence, even when limited by FRE 608(b)'s ban on extrinsic proof, is that it sometimes works effectively to expose dishonesty in the courtroom. Consider one classic instance:

> Henry E. Lazarus, a prominent merchant in [New York City] was indicted . . . by the Federal Grand Jury, charged with the offense of bribing a United States officer and violation of the Sabotage Act, but was honorably acquitted by a jury after a thirty minute deliberation. It was during the height of [World War I] and Mr. Lazarus was a very large manufacturer of rubber coats and had manufactured hundreds of thousands for the Government under contract. The government for its protection employed large numbers of inspectors, and in the heat and excitement of war times these inspectors occasionally tried to "make good." One of these efforts resulted in the indictment of Lazarus.

> The chief witness against Lazarus was Charles L. Fuller, Supervising Inspector attached to the Depot Quartermaster's Office in New York City. Fuller testified that Lazarus gave money to him to influence him in regard to his general duties as inspector, and to overlook the fact that Lazarus was manufacturing defective coats and thereby violating the Sabotage Act.

> Martin W. Littleton acted as chief counsel for the defense and was fully appreciative of Mr. Lazarus' high character and of his conscientious discharge of his duties in the manufacture of material for the Government. He was also well informed as to the general character and history of Fuller. After Fuller testified in chief, he was first questioned closely as to the time when he became an employee of the Government, counsel knowing that he was *required to make and sign and swear to an application as to his prior experience.*

> A messenger had been sent to the Government files to get the original of this application, signed by the witness, and came into court with the document in his hand just as counsel was putting the following question.

> **Q.** Did you sign such an application? **A.** I did, sir.

> **Q.** Did you swear to it? **A.** No, I did not swear to it.

> **Q.** I show you your name signed on the bottom of this blank, and ask you if you signed that? **A.** Yes, sir.

> **Q.** Do you see it is sworn to? **A.** I had forgotten it.

> **Q.** You see there is a seal on it? **A.** I had forgotten that also.

Q. This application appears to be subscribed on the 24th of May, 1918, by Charles Lawrence Fuller. **A.** It must be right if I have sworn to it on that date.

Q. Do you remember in May, 1918 that you signed and swore to this application? **A.** That is so, I must have sworn to it, sir.

Q. Do you remember it? **A.** Let me look at it and I can probably refresh my memory.

. . .

Q. Don't you remember you swore to it the date you signed it? **A. I** swore to it.

Q. Was your name Fuller? **A.** Yes, sir.

Q. Has your name always been Fuller? **A.** No, sir.

Q. What was your name?

The witness protested against any further inquiry along that line, but counsel was permitted to show that his name at one time was Finkler and that he changed his name, back and forth, from Finkler to Fuller.

Counsel then proceeded to bring the witness down to [the statements and oath he made] in his application [for a government job].

Q. You were asked when you sought this position, these questions: 'When employed, the years and the months,' and you wrote in, 'February, 1897 to August, 1917, number of years 20; Where employed—Brooklyn; Name of Employer—Vulcan Proofing Company; Amount of salary—$37.50 a week; also superintendent in the rubber and compound room.'

Q. You wrote that, didn't you? **A.** Yes, sir.

Q. And you swore to that, didn't you? **A.** Yes, sir.

Q. Now, were you employed from February, 1897, to August, 1917, twenty years, with the Vulcan Proofing Company? **A.** No, sir.

Q. And had you been assistant superintendent of the rubber and compound room? **A.** No, sir.

Q. That was false, wasn't it? **A.** Yes, sir.

Q. 'And through my experience as chief inspector of the rubber and slicker division,' that was false, wasn't it? **A.** Yes, sir.

Q. You knew it was false, didn't you? **A.** Yes, sir.

Q. And you knew you were swearing to a falsehood when you swore to it? **A.** Yes, sir.

Q. And you swore to it intentionally? **A.** Yes, sir.

Q. And you knew you were committing perjury by swearing and pretending you had been twenty years in this business? **A.** I did not look at it in that light.

Q. Didn't you know you were committing perjury by swearing and pretending you had been twenty years in this business? **A.** Yes, sir.

Q. And you are swearing now, aren't you? **A.** Yes, sir.

Q. In a matter in which a man's liberty is involved? **A.** Yes, sir.

Q. And you know that the jury is to be called upon to consider whether you are worthy of belief or not, don't you? **A.** Yes, sir.

Q. When you swore to this falsehood deliberately, and wrote it in your handwriting, and knew it was false, you swore to it intentionally, and you knew that you were committing perjury, didn't you? **A.** I didn't look at it in that light.

Q. Well, now, when you know you are possibly swearing away the liberty of a citizen of this community, do you look at in the same light? **A.** Yes, sir, I do.

Mr. Littleton then uncovered the fact that the witness, instead of having been twenty years superintendent of a rubber room with the Vulcan Proofing Company, as he had sworn in his own handwriting, was a stag entertainer in questionable houses, was a barker at a Coney Island show, was an advance agent of a cheap road show and had been published in the paper as having drawn checks that were worthless, the witness fully admitting all of the details of his twenty years of questionable transactions. The result was his utter collapse so far as his credibility was concerned, and the Government's case collapsed with him.

The . . . design of the cross-examiner was to get the witness at the outset of his cross-examination in a position from which he could not possibly extricate himself, by confronting him with this document, written in his own handwriting in which he would be obliged to admit that he had sworn falsely. The witness having been thoroughly subjugated by this process would then, as he actually did, confess to twenty years of gadding about in questionable employment, under different names, and thus completely destroy himself as a reliable witness in the eyes of the jury.[120]

Littleton's cross-examination of Fuller is a classic, not because it's a good example of the usual course of cross-examination on prior bad acts, but

---

[120] Francis L. Wellman, The Art of Cross-Examination 37–41 (4th ed. 1936). See also Johnson v. Brewer, 521 F.2d 556 (8th Cir. 1975).

because it worked so uncommonly well. Does the occasional utility of such cross-examinations justify the unfairness that is probably much more common when witnesses are cross-examined about isolated acts of unproven prior misconduct?

Problem V-26. Same facts as in Problem V-25, supra, pp. 418–419. **May Proton call Electron's neighbor, Pietro Prairie, to testify that three times in the last two years, Electron borrowed Prairie's lawn mower from his garage, then denied doing so? How else might Proton use the lawn mower incidents against Electron? May Proton's lawyer ask Electron on cross-examination if she lies about her golf handicap? If the golf handicap question is allowed and Electron denies lying about it, may Proton call Neutron to testify that she does? May Proton's lawyer ask Electron on cross-examination if she overstated her income on an application for a home mortgage five years ago? If the question is allowed and Electron denies doing so, may Proton introduce the mortgage application along with Electron's tax return for the same year, revealing her overstatement of income?**

3. Impeachment by Prior Convictions

Most common law jurisdictions allow a witness to be impeached with any conviction for a crime involving dishonesty or false statement. FRE 609 follows this practice, except that it places a presumptive ten-year limit on the age of convictions used to impeach. In regard to impeachment by convictions for crimes that do not involve dishonesty, the rules in different jurisdictions range from barring all such impeachment to allowing impeachment by all prior convictions no matter how minor the infraction or how old. Practice also varies in regard to balancing probative value against prejudice. Some jurisdictions require that such a balance be struck in all cases. Others admit convictions for impeachment purposes in all cases regardless of any such balance. Still others, including those following FRE 609, use a variety of practices, including (1) the automatic admissibility of recent convictions for crimes of dishonesty; (2) the admissibility of recent convictions for crimes not involving dishonesty subject to balancing rules that are more favorable to criminal defendants who testify than to other witnesses; and (3) the exclusion of all old convictions unless their probative value substantially outweighs their prejudicial potential. Within the broad outlines of a jurisdiction's applicable rules, appellate courts usually respect a trial judge's exercise of discretion.

We already have indicated why convictions for crimes of dishonesty may be used to impeach a witness's testimony. Such convictions have at least as much probative value as other forms of propensity evidence, and they may have less potential for unfair prejudice. Convictions are easy to prove, they rarely prompt time-consuming collateral disputes and they leave little room for doubt that the witness committed the dishonest act attributed to her. Although the possibility of prejudice remains high when it is the accused whose testimony is being impeached, that prejudice is moderated somewhat by the difference between the conviction the jury learns of and the crime with which the defendant is charged—unless the defendant is charged with a crime of deceit. Moreover, most crimes of deceit do not elicit as much fear or revulsion as serious crimes of violence provoke.

When, however, conviction of a crime that does *not* involve deceit is used to impeach, and particularly when it is used to impeach a criminal defendant, probative value declines substantially and the potential for unfair prejudice increases. If, for example, the state can impeach an alleged armed robber's testimony with a prior armed robbery conviction, he may be convicted because the jurors think he has a propensity to commit armed robbery and not because they think he has a propensity to lie. This use on the *merits* of evidence offered solely for its bearing on *credibility* constitutes unfair prejudice. On the one hand, the jury is likely to give a prior armed robbery conviction considerable probative weight (probably more than it deserves) on the question whether the defendant committed the charged armed robbery. On the other hand, the jurors are unlikely to see why a prior armed robbery conviction shows a predisposition to commit perjury in general. (Of course, they may well conclude that if he committed the prior robbery he's probably guilty of this one, and therefore is lying when he says he didn't commit it). Because the forbidden inference on the merits is intuitively much stronger than the permitted inference on credibility, a limiting instruction is unlikely to help. It's always hard to ask jurors to refrain from drawing inferences that they instinctively want to draw; it's harder still to try to tell them that they must do so in service of other inferences that they find inherently implausible.

Allowing a criminal defendant to be impeached with prior convictions—and especially with convictions that are similar to the crime charged—may keep the accused from testifying at all. Consider the unhappy dilemma facing the criminal defendant with a prior record. The privilege against self-incrimination gives him a right to remain silent. Exercise of that right usually is costly, however, because jurors expect innocent defendants to tell their stories, since they know that *they* would want to tell *their* stories if *they* were wrongly accused.[121] Although instructions to jurors not to draw adverse inferences from an accused's

---

[121] It does not follow, of course, that if the jurors were themselves defendants, they could testify and tell their stories. If they were wrongly accused of a crime, they would be forced to learn a great deal about the criminal justice system that otherwise most people happily ignore, and they might well be given—and follow—legal advice to stay off the witness stand.

silence are routinely given, they are just as routinely ignored.[122] On the other hand if the defendant decides to testify, he will be impeached with his prior record. In that event—and notwithstanding that he has a true exculpatory story to tell, and a constitutional right to tell it—his prior criminal record decreases the likelihood that he will be believed, not because the jurors will think the prior conviction relates directly to his credibility but rather because they will treat the conviction as further evidence that he committed the crime charged.

Professors Kalven and Zeisel gathered data measuring these disadvantages. They found that among criminal defendants who testified at trial, acquittal was about 40% less likely if the defendant was impeached with one or more prior convictions.[123] Interestingly, defendants who did not testify suffered about the same disadvantage as defendants who testified and were impeached by prior convictions. Because a defendant with a prior record evidently is as likely to be hurt by testifying as by keeping silent, he may well decide even if innocent to withhold testimony that the jury would benefit from hearing, and that a defendant has a constitutional right to give.[124]

---

[122] See Note, To Take the Stand or Not to Take the Stand, The Dilemma of the Defendant with a Criminal Record, 4 Colum. J.L. & Soc. Probs. 215, 221–22 (1968).

[123] Harry Kalven, Jr. & Hans Zeisel, The American Jury 160 (1966).

[124] For recent studies reaching equally disturbing conclusions, see John Blume, The Dilemma of the Criminal Defendant with a Prior Record—Lessons from the Wrongfully Convicted, 3 J. Empirical Stud. 477 (2008) (study revealing that subsequently exonerated, demonstrably innocent defendants, many of whom were arrested in part because of their criminal record, were no more likely to have testified at their original criminal trials than criminal defendants as a whole—most of whom are guilty—revealing the powerful effect the threat of impeachment by prior conviction has in keeping even innocent defendants from taking the stand and providing the trier of fact with important information); Theodore Eisenberg & Valerie P. Hans, Taking a Stand on Taking the Stand: The Effect of a Prior Criminal Record on the Decision to Testify and on Trial Outcomes, Cornell Law School Research Paper No. 07–012 (2007) (a study of 300 trials in four counties finding that, controlling for strength of evidence and other factors, (1) defendants with a prior criminal record are significantly more likely to forgo testifying than other defendants—sensibly, it seems, because, when they do forgo testifying, the probability that jurors will hear about their prior record is significantly lower; (2) in cases with weak evidence of guilt, the jury's knowledge of the defendant's record increased the probability of conviction, leading the authors to conclude that juries rely on criminal records to convict when the remaining evidence might not otherwise support conviction and that prior-convictions impeachment may lead to erroneous convictions).

The Supreme Court's decision in Luce v. United States, 469 U.S. 38 (1984), makes the defendant's decision whether to testify even more difficult. Prior to Luce, most federal courts allowed a defendant to file a motion in limine before testifying, asking the trial court to rule that particular prior convictions could not be used to impeach because the convictions were too prejudicial or too old. If the court ruled that the convictions could be used, the defendant could choose not to testify and, if convicted, could appeal the judge's decision on the motion in limine as an abuse of discretion or as procedurally flawed. Many state courts continue to follow this practice. Under Luce, however, federal criminal defendants may not appeal a ruling allowing the impeachment use of prior convictions unless they actually testify and are actually impeached with the prior convictions. As a result, many trial courts reserve rulings on motions to forbid impeachment by prior conviction until the defendant has begun testifying and the prosecutor seeks to impeach. Diminishing appellate protection even further, the Supreme Court more recently has ruled that objection to the convictions' use is waived if defense counsel brings them out on direct examination to "remove the sting." Ohler v. United States, 529 U.S. 753 (2000). Federal criminal defendants thus must decide whether to testify and whether to bring out the

What, then, accounts for a rule that "some suggest does not square with our supposed allegiance to the doctrine that all are innocent until proven guilty?"[125] It sometimes is said that English history provides the best explanation for permitting impeachment by any prior felony convictions. Historically, all felonies were capital offenses in England, so convicted felons were seldom around to testify. By the 16th century some felonies were not capital; by the 17th century the punishments for many felonies that still were capital were routinely commuted, and executions were often delayed. As felons became available to testify, the courts disqualified them from doing so, however, on the ground that conviction of an "infamous" crime rendered them untrustworthy as a class. This disability became untenable in the 19th century, as it became clearer that it often took the testimony of one thief to catch another. Felons accordingly were allowed to testify. They continued to be treated differently, however: The blanket rule of disqualification on the basis of a felony conviction was replaced with a blanket rule of impeachment based on their prior conviction of an infamous crime. Only later did the notion that a felony conviction reflects adversely on credibility take hold.

Because the rule's modern rationale appears to be so clearly contrived with respect to crimes that do not suggest dishonesty, it is fair to ask why the rule in its present form has persisted. One common answer is that the jury is "entitled" to know that a witness "with the appearance of an unblemished citizen" is actually an unworthy miscreant.[126] But *why* should jurors know this? Apparently so they won't make a propensity inference from the witness's supposedly good character to his likely honesty. There is no empirical proof, however, that jurors assume a person has good character when they hear no evidence of his bad character, or that they believe that people of generally good character tell the truth when (as is true of most criminal defendants) they have powerful motives to lie. Moreover, when the witness is the accused, the jury is sure to receive substantial evidence suggesting that his character is not good. And if a lawyer does try to suggest that a witness's character

---

prior convictions on direct examination, without knowing whether the trial court will allow the prosecutor to ask about the convictions on cross-examination. Because decisions to allow impeachment by prior convictions are discretionary and rarely are overturned on appeal, federal defendants generally must proceed on the assumption that the prior convictions (if less than ten years old) *will* be admitted to impeach. And the defendant must further assume that any decision to admit them will be affirmed on appeal if the defendant decides to test the ruling by testifying and then challenging the impeachment on appeal—and will not be appealable at all if defense counsel tries to reduce the prejudice by bringing out the prior conviction on direct examination. The effect of *Luce* and *Ohler*, therefore, is to increase the likelihood that defendants will decide *not* to testify for fear that impeachment by prior convictions will harm their chances more than testifying will help. An amendment to FRE 103 in 2000 states that the party on the losing end of a "definitive" pretrial evidentiary ruling need not revisit the issue at trial to preserve a claim for appeal. The Advisory Committee's Note on the amendment states, however, that it is not intended to undermine—or codify—the rule of *Luce*. See supra, Chapter Two, Section III. G.4., pp. 189–190.

[125] 3 Weinstein's Evidence ¶ 609[02].

[126] 120 Cong. Rec. 2376 (Feb. 6, 1974) (statement of Rep. Hogan in support of FRE 609).

is unblemished, the door could *then* be opened to evidence of prior convictions. All in all, routinely admitting prior convictions evidence is likely to cause more prejudice than it prevents, particularly when the witness is the defendant in a criminal case or a party to a civil case.

Other arguments in favor of impeachment by prior conviction focus on particular categories of cases or witnesses. It sometimes is said that such impeachment redresses an imbalance between prosecutor and accused.[127] Criminal defendants go free if the jury finds a reasonable doubt of their guilt. If they were freely able to testify falsely in order to establish doubt, more guilty defendants would go free. Using prior convictions to impeach reduces the likelihood of inaccurate acquittals based on perjury. Admittedly, it does so by implicitly inviting the jurors to rely on an impermissible propensity inference about the defendants' *conduct*, and by inappropriately reducing their anticipated regret at the prospect of convicting an innocent defendant. But this is a price worth paying to protect public safety—or so the argument goes.

Impeachment by prior conviction, however, is a clumsy way of evening the score between prosecutors and defendants. If it has the suggested effect, it penalizes prior offenders who tell the truth but has no impact on defendants with clean records who lie. Indeed, if jurors know of the impeachment rule, the absence of impeachment will perversely strengthen the previously unconvicted offender's credibility. Overall, this explanation simply makes a virtue of the principal vice of impeachment by prior convictions—that it undermines the requirement of proof beyond a reasonable doubt. It does emphasize that unjustified acquittals are a price of evidence rules that protect defendants from prejudicial information, but it ignores the other side of the equation. Allowing impeachment by prior felonies means that some innocent defendants will be convicted because of their criminal records.

---

[127] This argument proceeds on the assumption that criminal defendants and the witnesses who testify for them are disproportionately likely to have criminal records, so that impeachment by prior conviction disproportionately disadvantages criminal defendants. This assumption does not hold true for the many cases in which crimes are proved through the testimony of coparticipants and informants, including most drug trafficking, gambling and other "victimless" crimes. Here the *state's* witnesses are equally vulnerable to impeachment by prior felonies. In that situation, however, there is a nonpropensity reason to allow such impeachment. The past criminal involvements of such witnesses may make them vulnerable to pressure to cooperate with the state and to tell the prosecutor what they think she wants to hear. Evidence of prior conviction thus often raises an inference that the witness should be disbelieved because of a case-specific bias or motive to lie and thus is not forbidden by the propensity rule in the first place. See infra, Section V.A., pp. 440–446. An amendment to FRE 609(a) in 2006 confirmed this interpretation. By substituting the phrase "attacking a witness's *character for truthfulness*" for the phrase "attacking the *credibility* of a witness," the amendment made clear that Rule 609 regulates the use of prior convictions only as a basis for suggesting that a witness has testified falsely in accordance with bad character and not as a basis for other forms of impeachment, such as showing bias. The only exception is FRE 609(d)(3), which continues to refer to attacks on a witness's "credibility" and governs the use of juvenile adjudications for all types of impeachment. FRE 609(d) is discussed infra, p. 438 & note 136.

It also might be argued that prior crimes are more probative on the issue of the credibility of testifying criminal defendants than we have suggested. When a criminal defendant takes the stand, it almost always is to deny that she committed the charged crime. Proof that she committed crimes in the past tends to prove that she committed the charged crime and thus that she is lying when she says she did not. A similar argument can be extended to witnesses for the accused. Birds of a feather flock together. If the defendant's friendly witnesses are convicted felons, the defendant probably is one too, or she would not have associated with them. And if the defendant herself is a criminal, she probably committed the charged crime and her witnesses are probably lying to protect her. The problem with this theory is that it depends on the jurors' drawing precisely the propensity inference that they have been told *not* to draw—from the fact that the defendant committed prior crimes (or befriended known criminals) to the likelihood that the defendant committed the crime charged.

Or one might argue that courts have a special incentive to admit evidence of prior convictions because convictions are judgments by the judicial system itself. The thrust of the argument is that considerations of consistency and integrity—or, at least, of self-protection and self-promotion—prompt courts to pay special attention and give special prominence to their *own* character judgments. Historically, courts gave full force to those judgments by forbidding convicted felons to testify. When that practice gave way to the need for testimony by felons, courts instead allowed opposing parties to inform the trier of fact of the courts' prior negative judgment about the witness. Although this theory helps explain courts' affinity for impeachment by prior convictions, it does little to justify the practice.

There is another explanation for the felony impeachment rule that doesn't justify it but may say something about why we keep it. Although felony impeachment conflicts with other principles built into substantive law and evidence law, once history gave birth to it politics have sustained it. When a defendant has a felony record, and the jury knows it, the prosecution is more likely to get a conviction; defendants who know this are more likely to plead guilty. Prosecutors—classic repeat players in the judicial system, who often go on to serve as judges, legislators, attorneys general and governors—have enough political power to preserve that basic advantage no matter how many contradictions it poses for the system. At the same time the tension between the felony impeachment rule and the ideals of our legal system are sufficiently palpable to have generated a series of compromises that increasingly have complicated the old common law rule of blanket felony impeachment. Policy aside, it is those complications—to which we now turn—that mainly concern lawyers and judges applying modern felony impeachment rules.

As of the time Congress adopted the Federal Rules, most federal courts in the country had settled upon a compromise approach that was devised by the District of Columbia Circuit in its landmark decision in *Luck v. United States*.[128] The *Luck* approach was described as follows in a later decision:

> The rationale of our *Luck* opinion is important; it recognized that a showing of prior convictions can have genuine probative value on the issue of credibility, but that because of the potential for prejudice, the receiving of such convictions as impeachment was discretionary. The defendant who has a criminal record may ask the court to weigh the probative value of the convictions as to . . . credibility against the degree of prejudice which the revelation of his past crimes would cause; and he may ask the court to consider whether it is more important for the jury to hear his story than to know about prior convictions in relation to his credibility. We contemplated the possibility of allowing some convictions to be shown and some [to be] excluded; examples are to be found in those which are remote and those which have no direct bearing on veracity, and those which because of the peculiar circumstances at hand might better be excluded. The *Luck* opinion contemplated an on-the-record consideration by the trial judge whose action would be reviewable only for abuse of discretion, and that once the exercise of discretion appeared, the trial court's action be "accorded a respect appropriately reflective of the inescapable remoteness of appellate review." . . .
>
> *Luck* also contemplated that it was for the defendant to present to the trial court sufficient reasons for withholding past convictions from the jury. . . . The underlying assumption was that prior convictions would ordinarily be admissible unless this burden is met. [But] "[t]he trial court is not required to allow impeachment by prior conviction every time a defendant takes the stand in his own defense."
>
> The impact of criminal convictions will often be damaging to an accused and it is admittedly difficult to restrict its impact, by cautionary instructions, to the issue of credibility. The test of *Luck*, however, is that to bar them as impeachment the court must find that the prejudice "far outweigh[s]" the probative relevance to credibility, or that even if relevant the "cause of truth would be helped more by letting the jury hear the defendant's story than by the defendant's foregoing that opportunity because of the fear of prejudice founded upon a prior conviction."

---

[128] 348 F.2d 763 (D.C.Cir. 1965).

. . .

In considering how the District Court is to exercise the discretionary power we granted, we must look to the legitimate purpose of impeachment which is, of course, not to show that the accused who takes the stand is a "bad" person but rather to show background facts which bear directly on whether jurors ought to believe him rather than other and conflicting witnesses. In common human experience, acts of deceit, fraud, cheating, or stealing, for example, are universally regarded as conduct which reflects adversely on a man's honesty and integrity. Acts of violence on the other hand, which may result from a short temper, a combative nature, extreme provocation, or other causes, generally have little or no direct bearing on honesty and veracity. A "rule of thumb" thus should be that convictions which rest on dishonest conduct relate to credibility whereas those of violent or assaultive crimes generally do not; traffic violations, however serious, are in the same category. The nearness or remoteness of the prior conviction is also a factor of no small importance. Even one involving fraud or stealing, for example, if it occurred long before and has been followed by a legally blameless life, should generally be excluded on ground of remoteness.

A special and even more difficult problem arises when the prior conviction is for substantially the same conduct for which the accused is on trial. Where multiple convictions of various kinds can be shown, strong reasons arise for excluding those which are for the same crime because of the inevitable pressure on lay jurors to believe that "if he did it before he probably did so this time." As a general guide, those convictions which are for the same crime should be admitted sparingly; one solution might well be that discretion be exercised to limit the impeachment by way of a similar crime to a single conviction and then only when the circumstances indicate strong reasons for disclosure, and where the conviction directly relates to veracity.[129]

Although this passage describes the federal courts' practice prior to the adoption of the Federal Rules, it also serves as a useful guide to the rule Congress codified in FRE 609 in 1975, particularly as that rule was amended in 1990. As amended, FRE 609 provides:

Rule 609.   Impeachment by Evidence of a Criminal Conviction

---

[129] Gordon v. United States, 383 F.2d 936, 939 (D.C.Cir. 1967), cert. denied, 390 U.S. 1029 (1968).

(a) **In General.**   The following rules apply to attacking a witness's character for truthfulness by evidence of a criminal conviction:

(1) for a crime that, in the convicting jurisdiction, was punishable by death or by imprisonment for more than one year, the evidence:

(A) must be admitted, subject to Rule 403, in a civil case or in a criminal case in which the witness is not a defendant; and

(B) must be admitted in a criminal case in which the witness is a defendant, if the probative value of the evidence outweighs its prejudicial effect to that defendant; and

(2) for any crime regardless of the punishment, the evidence must be admitted if the court can readily determine that establishing the elements of the crime required proving—or the witness's admitting—a dishonest act or false statement.

(b) **Limit on Using the Evidence After 10 Years.**   This subdivision (b) applies if more than 10 years have passed since the witness's conviction or release from confinement for it, whichever is later. Evidence of the conviction is admissible only if:

(1) its probative value, supported by specific facts and circumstances, substantially outweighs its prejudicial effect; and

(2) the proponent gives an adverse party reasonable written notice of the intent to use it so that the party has a fair opportunity to contest its use.

(c) **Effect of a Pardon, Annulment, or Certificate of Rehabilitation.**   Evidence of a conviction is not admissible if

(1) the conviction has been the subject of a pardon, annulment, certificate of rehabilitation, or other equivalent procedure based on a finding that the person has been rehabilitated, and the person has not been convicted of a later crime punishable by death or by imprisonment for more than one year; or

(2) the conviction has been the subject of a pardon, annulment, or other equivalent procedure based on a finding of innocence.

(d) **Juvenile Adjudications.**   Evidence of a juvenile adjudication is admissible under this rule only if:

(1) it is offered in a criminal case;

(2) the adjudication was of a witness other than the defendant;

(3) an adult's conviction for that offense would be admissible to attack the adult's credibility; and

(4) admitting the evidence is necessary to fairly determine guilt or innocence.

(e) Pendency of Appeal. A conviction that satisfies this rule is admissible even if an appeal is pending. Evidence of the pendency of an appeal is also admissible.

The admissibility of prior convictions to impeach under FRE 609 largely depends on the considerations identified in *Luck:* whether the conviction is for a crime of dishonesty; whether the conviction is used to impeach a criminal defendant or some other witness; the similarity between the crime involved in the prior conviction and in the case at hand; and the age of the conviction. In place of *Luck*'s discretionary sliding scale, however, FRE 609 adopts a tiered set of admissibility rules. Under FRE 609(a)(2), convictions for all crimes involving a dishonest act or false statement—even a minor one—are automatically admissible to impeach if the convictions are not more than ten years old as defined in the rule. Under FRE 609(a)(1)(A), convictions for crimes punishable (even if not actually punished) by more than one year of imprisonment are admissible to impeach witnesses other than criminal defendants, if the convictions are not more than ten years old and if, under FRE 403, their probative value is not substantially outweighed by the danger of improper prejudice.[130] Under FRE 609(a)(1)(B), convictions for crimes punishable by more than one year are admissible to impeach criminal *defendants* if the convictions are not more than ten years old and if the court determines that their probative value outweighs any prejudice to the defendant. Finally, under FRE 609(b), a conviction that otherwise would be admissible is inadmissible if it is more than ten years old unless the court finds that the conviction's "probative value, supported by specific facts and circumstances, substantially outweighs its prejudicial

---

[130] Prior to the 1990 amendments, FRE 609(a) was poorly drafted, and seemed to make felony convictions automatically admissible to impeach all witnesses in civil cases, and to impeach prosecution witnesses in criminal cases, if the convictions were not more than ten years old. The Supreme Court reluctantly confirmed this interpretation in Green v. Bock Laundry Mach. Co., 490 U.S. 504 (1989). Before *Green*, practice varied, reflecting the anomalous nature of a rule that appeared to side-step not only the usual FRE 403 balance of probative value and prejudice but also the most basic rule of relevance. (In *Green*, for example, a civil plaintiff who had been injured by a washing machine was impeached with an arguably *irrelevant* marijuana conviction.) Many courts had applied FRE 403 to prior convictions used to impeach witnesses in civil cases, and a smaller number of courts had applied FRE 403 to prior convictions used to impeach prosecution witnesses. *Green* prompted the adoption of the 1990 amendment, which applied FRE 403's balancing test to all recent felony convictions for crimes not involving dishonesty and not used to impeach criminal defendants. The 1990 amendment thus brought the impeachment of defense witnesses other than the accused within the usual balancing rule, and replaced the more protective rule that FRE 609(a) had originally seemed to apply to *all* defense witnesses with a special balancing rule applicable only to the criminal defendant herself.

effect" (FRE 609(b)(1)), and unless the party seeking to use a conviction to impeach gives the opposing party advance notice (FRE 609(b)(2)). Although the ten-year rule in FRE 609(b) does not distinguish between crimes of dishonesty and other crimes, the requirement of substantially more probative value than prejudicial effect makes it unlikely that convictions for crimes other than ones of dishonesty will be admitted if they are more than ten years old.

The usual method of impeachment by prior conviction is to ask the witness whether she was convicted of crime A with elements B, C and D in a specified court on a specified date. Some courts allow questions about the sentence imposed; others do not.[131] Most courts forbid the impeaching examiner to ask questions about aggravating facts underlying the conviction unless the facts reveal dishonesty or false statement and thus are independently admissible, in the discretion of the court, under FRE 608(b). Typically, if the witness confirms the conviction, questioning ceases. If she denies the conviction, she may be confronted with a public record reflecting the judgment of conviction and sentence, and the record may be admitted into evidence. Most courts let the witness briefly explain the conviction or protest her innocence, although such explanations can be dangerous because they open the door to questions by the impeaching party about the facts underlying the conviction. Only the witness may provide an explanation. "Extrinsic" explanatory evidence is forbidden.

Prior to 1990, FRE 609(a) required that impeachment by prior conviction occur during cross-examination of the witness being impeached, and that it be limited to questions put to the witness and public records. By dispensing with the former requirement, the 1990 amendment confirmed the actual practice of nearly all courts which, despite the original rule's language, allowed the attorney presenting the witness to bring out her prior convictions on direct examination in order "to pull the sting." Although *any* "evidence" that the witness was convicted is admissible under the revised FRE 609(a), courts are impatient with "extrinsic" evidence of prior convictions other than judicial records. Once impeachment by prior convictions occurs, the party whose witness has been impeached has a right to an instruction limiting the jury's use of the prior conviction to evaluation of the witness's credibility and forbidding its use on substantive issues.

FRE 609(a)(2) makes recent prior convictions automatically admissible to impeach if the conviction is for a crime that has as an

---

[131] FRE 609(a) makes only the "conviction," not sentence, admissible. Opaque and inconsistent sentencing practices diminish the value of the information jurors can extract from the length of a sentence. Allowing evidence about the sentence also is inconsistent with the uniform interpretation of FRE 608(b) to limit questions about specific instances of dishonest behavior to the behavior itself and bar questions about consequences imposed for the behavior, such as being fired for lying on the job or paying a fine for filing a false tax return.

element some act of dishonesty or false statement.[132] Perjury, subornation of perjury, false report, false tax returns, fraud, knowingly passing a worthless check, forgery, embezzlement, counterfeiting and witness tampering are examples. Prior to 2006, the courts were divided on the admissibility under FRE 609(a)(2) of convictions for crimes that did not involve dishonesty as an essential element but were committed through dishonesty, such as rape committed by an assailant who gained entry by pretending to be a repairman. A desire to keep impeachment by prior conviction short and simple and to avoid thorny disputes about what actually happened led some courts to insist that the elements and not simply the facts of the crime involved deceit. On the other hand, the presumed high probative value of acts of dishonesty and false statement led other courts to allow impeachment whenever the crime actually involved dishonesty, whether revealed by the elements or the facts of the crime. A 2006 amendment to FRE 609(a)(2), as redrafted in the 2011 revision, adopted a middle position, allowing witnesses to be impeached with a conviction "if the court can *readily determine* that *establishing* the elements of the crime required proving—or the witness's admitting—a dishonest act or false statement" (emphasis added). The amended Rule 609(a)(2) permits the use of any conviction of a crime that either involves a dishonest act or false statement as an element, or as to which the charging documents, jury instructions, or plea colloquy or agreement formally required the prosecutor to prove (or in the event of a guilty plea, reveal that the defendant did or was required to admit) a dishonest act or false statement. Under the latter aspect of the amended rule, impeachment is automatically allowed using convictions for some crimes, such as obstruction of justice or bribery, that do not always involve deceit as an element, as long as dishonesty was formally charged or pleaded to in the run up to the conviction. This compromise makes good sense. It allows witnesses to be impeached with all crimes that have been formally adjudicated to include dishonesty or false statement, as long as that adjudication can be established quickly from the face of an easily accessible and formal statute, charging paper, jury instruction or guilty plea transcript. Little is lost in the compromise, moreover, because FRE 608(b) gives trial judges' discretion to permit cross-examination about specific deceitful acts, including those underlying convictions as to which there was no formal requirement of proof or any admission of an act of dishonesty, but deceit nonetheless was involved. If, for example, a witness had previously been convicted of a rape in which he in fact gained entry by false pretenses, although neither the criminal statute nor the indictment referred to false pretenses, the court might still exercise its

---

[132] As originally drafted, FRE 609(a)(2) referred to "dishonesty or false statement," which was redundant because "false statement" is a form of, not an alternative to, "dishonesty". The 2011 amendments removed the redundancy by referring to "a dishonest *act* or false statement" (emphasis added).

FRE 608(b) discretion to allow the opposing party to cross-examine the witness about the deceit, although not about the conviction that followed.

In the past, the federal courts also divided on the question whether crimes involving stealth or surreptitious behavior such as shoplifting or other forms of theft qualify as dishonesty crimes. The Advisory Committee Note to the 1990 amendment criticized as over broad a number of decisions characterizing all forms of larceny as "dishonesty" crimes falling within the rule, and the original legislative history indicates that dishonesty crimes were meant to encompass only crimes that involved lying, fraud and other forms of deceit. By now there is substantial agreement among federal courts that FRE 609(a)(2) does not apply to shoplifting, theft, burglary, robbery, smuggling, and drug dealing, despite the surreptitious behavior that typically accompanies them, but the courts remain divided on the crime of knowingly receiving stolen goods.

The *Luck* decision provides a helpful catalogue of the considerations that should govern the balance of probative value and prejudice when felony convictions are used to impeach under FRE 609(a)(1). Most courts treat the "seriousness" of the offense, as revealed by the *potential* sentence, as a proxy for probative weight. Courts also tie probative value to the likelihood that although the crime at issue is not a crime of dishonesty it nevertheless suggests that character trait. At one end of the spectrum are crimes that often rely upon concealment, such as theft and drug dealing. At the other end are crimes that are commonly committed without stealth, such as manslaughter and assault. By any standard, the recency and frequency of convictions contribute to probative weight, as does the importance of the particular witness's credibility under the circumstances of the case.

Prejudice is largely a function of how likely it is that the jury will use the prior convictions as substantive evidence of guilt and not just as evidence bearing on credibility. Such misuse is particularly likely when a criminal defendant is impeached with prior convictions for the same offense as is charged in the case. Prejudice is also a problem if the earlier crimes are especially heinous or numerous, for then the jury may want to lock the defendant up regardless of his guilt of the crime charged. Misuse is less likely, but may still be a cause for concern, when prior convictions are used to impeach criminal defense witnesses with a close enough connection to the defendant to create a "guilt by association" effect, or when the witness being impeached is a party to a civil case or someone closely connected to a party. Misuse is less likely still when the witness is testifying for the prosecution because the impact of the information is likely to be limited to its tendency to undercut the witness's credibility. In this last situation, moreover, credibility may be undermined not because of a propensity inference, but because a witness's prior troubles with the law may suggest that the prosecution has leverage over him. Nonetheless, the state may sometimes be prejudiced by the felony impeachment rule, as when jurors reject the state's case not because they disbelieve its witnesses, but because of their distaste for the people on whom it relies for evidence.[133]

Keep in mind that FRE 609 has three different balancing tests, which also imply different allocations of the burden of persuasion. When a recent felony conviction for a crime not involving dishonesty is offered as a basis for attacking the character for truthfulness of a witness other than a criminal defendant, the impeachment is presumptively permissible, and the court should allow it unless the party whose witness is being impeached can satisfy the usual FRE 403 balancing test by showing that prejudice substantially outweighs probative value (FRE 609(a)(1)(A)). If the witness being impeached with a recent felony conviction for a crime not involving dishonesty is the criminal defendant, the impeachment is presumptively impermissible and is forbidden unless the party offering the prior felony can demonstrate that probative value "outweighs its prejudicial effect to that defendant" (FRE 609(a)(1)(B)). Finally, if any crime more than ten years old as defined in the rule is offered as a basis for attacking any witness's character for truthfulness, it, too, is presumptively impermissible and will not be allowed unless the party offering the evidence shows that the conviction's "probative value, *supported by specific facts and circumstances*, substantially outweighs its prejudicial effect" (FRE 609(b)(1)).

The remaining provisions of FRE 609 are comparatively straightforward:

• FRE 609(b)'s presumptive bar to stale convictions is largely self-explanatory, but should be read with care. Notice that in many cases, the ten-year period runs from the date physical confinement under the conviction ends, not from the date on which the conviction occurred. For the purposes of this rule, at least, rehabilitation does not begin in prison.[134] There are conflicting views on the date backwards from which the expiration of the ten-year period is calculated. Some courts use the

---

[133] The trial judge role is difficult because the relevant considerations often are double-edged. For example, when a criminal defendant's testimony is particularly important to the jury understanding of what happened, prior convictions have considerable probative value (because of the importance of the defendant's credibility), but also can have considerable prejudicial effect (if the threat of prior-crimes impeachment is likely to cause the defendant to forgo testifying). Similarly, a lengthy history of serious crimes is both probative (under FRE 609's dubious assumption that a defendant disposition to tell the truth is inversely proportional to the seriousness of her prior record) and prejudicial (because it skews the regret matrix against the defendant). Only by carefully analyzing the particular circumstances of each case can a judge determine whether these double-edged considerations tip in favor of probative value or prejudice, or simply cancel each other out.

[134] Cf. United States v. Rogers, 542 F.3d 197 (7th Cir. 2008) (time spent outside physical custody on probation or parole does not delay commencement of the ten-year period unless that status is revoked and incarceration is (re)imposed).

date on which the trial where the testimony is offered began, others use the date on which the witness being impeached first testifies, and one court has used the date of the charged crime where the criminal defendant was the witness being impeached.[135] Because a conviction's freshness or staleness bears on the strength of the inference that the witness is disposed to lie under oath, the point at which the oath is given in the current case is the most sensible date from which to measure the ten years.

• Courts have also differed on whether pardons render convictions inadmissible. FRE 609(c) adopts a complicated compromise position that gives inflexible effect to considerations courts previously had used as a basis for discretion, such as the witness's criminal history since the pardon and the reason for the pardon (if it is known). Discretion remains, however, because pardons that do not justify the automatic exclusion of prior convictions under FRE 609(c) may affect the balance between probative value and prejudice that the court must strike under FRE 609(a)(1)(A) and (B) and 609(b).

• Prior to the adoption of the Federal Rules, the prevailing view had been that evidence of juvenile adjudications was not admissible for impeachment of any sort. FRE 609(d) makes such adjudications admissible in criminal cases if (1) the witness is not the defendant, (2) the adjudication is for a crime that could be used to impeach an adult following conviction, and (3) the evidence is necessary to a fair determination of guilt or innocence. Constitutional problems might arise if criminal defendants could not impeach prosecution witnesses in these circumstances.[136]

• Subdivision (e) of the rule tracks the common law in allowing impeachment on the basis of convictions under appeal and in providing that the pendency of the appeal may be disclosed to the jury.

———————

Problem V-27. Dan is charged with armed robbery of a hot dog vender on 116th Street and Amsterdam Avenue in New York. Dan wants to take the stand and testify that he was not the person wearing a ski mask who committed the offense and, indeed, that he was 1000 miles away that day,

———————

[135] See, e.g., United States v. Watler, 461 F.3d 1005 (8th Cir. 2006) (citing cases); United States v. Foley, 683 F.2d 273 (8th Cir. 1982).

[136] See Davis v. Alaska, 415 U.S. 308 (1974). FRE 609(d) is understood to codify the holding of *Davis*, that a criminal defendant may not be barred from using a pending juvenile adjudication to show that a prosecution witness was subject to pressure from the prosecutor and thus was likely to be biased in favor of the state. *Davis* may not require the same result if a juvenile adjudication is offered solely as proof of a witness's bad character for truthfulness. *Davis* itself notes that impeachment by showing bad character is a far weaker basis for attacking a witness's credibility than impeachment by showing bias. In addition, juvenile adjudications are weak indicators of ongoing bad character because they are not formal determinations of guilt and are associated with an expectation of rehabilitation.

in Kalamazoo, visiting his invalid aunt. Dan's aunt has since died, and Dan has no one besides himself to verify his whereabouts in Kalamazoo on the day in question. Dan was convicted of another armed robbery five years earlier. **As Dan's attorney, would you advise him to testify or not? Why?**

Problem V-28. Rocky Reid lost an arm when a three-wheeler he was driving turned over. Reid sues TWR, the vehicle's manufacturer, on a products liability theory, seeking $5,000,000 in damages. Reid, the only witness to the accident, testifies that the vehicle turned over when he was traveling 15 mph up a 30 degree incline—well within the range of safe operation of the vehicle. TWR claims Reid was traveling 35 mph down a 50 degree incline—contrary to a variety of warnings TWR gives owners and operators of the vehicle. Depositions reveal that each party will present apparently strong expert testimony supporting its version of the accident. In a bench conference after Reid's direct examination, his lawyer, citing FRE 402, 403 and 404, asks the judge to bar TWR's lawyer from asking Reid the following cross-examination questions: (1) "A year ago to this day, Officer Webb caught you with two ounces of marijuana at a picnic in Roosevelt Park, correct?" (2) "Four years ago to this day, you were convicted of misdemeanor possession of an ounce of marijuana and sentenced to half the maximum sentence, namely seven months in the county jail, correct?" (3) "Six years ago to this day, you were convicted of the felony of having sexual relations with a fourteen-year-old girl and given eighteen months, suspended, correct?" (4) "Thirteen years ago to this day, you were convicted of felonious possession of an ounce of marijuana and sentenced to a year and a day, suspended, correct?" TWR's lawyer responds that she believes Reid is lying, that his criminal record supports that belief, and that sustaining Reid's objections will cut the heart out of TWR's planned cross-examination. **How should the judge rule on Reid's objections to TWR's proposed questions? Assuming any of the questions is allowed and Reid answers "No," may TWR call Officer Webb to testify that the facts alleged in the question are true to his personal knowledge? What other evidence should the judge permit TWR to introduce in the event of a "no" answer? What logic supports the overall pattern of rulings FRE 609 requires in this case?**

"Will the witness please tell the court exactly
how long he's known the accused?"

V.   OTHER FORMS OF IMPEACHMENT

A. IMPEACHMENT FOR BIAS, INTEREST OR MOTIVE

So far we have discussed methods of attacking and defending the credibility of a witness by using evidence that bears on her character for truthfulness. More often than not, however, effective impeachment has little or nothing to do with general character traits, and instead focuses on issues that are of particular significance to the case at hand. One of the most important of these case-specific methods is impeachment for a bias, interest or motive that might color the witness's testimony.

Consider the Supreme Court case *United States v. Abel*.[137] Abel and two accomplices were indicted for bank robbery. The accomplices pled guilty, and Abel went to trial. At trial, one of the accomplices—Ehle— testified for the government and implicated Abel as one of the robbers. Abel then called one Mills, who knew both Abel and Ehle and spent time with both of them in prison. Mills testified that after the robbery Ehle told him in prison that he planned to implicate Abel falsely in the robbery

---

[137] 469 U.S. 45 (1984).

in order to get a lighter sentence.[138] The prosecutor was then permitted, over objection, to ask Mills on cross-examination whether Mills and Abel were members of a secret prison organization with a creed requiring members to lie for each other and to deny that the organization exists.[139] Mills denied knowing about such an organization. On rebuttal, the government recalled Ehle, who testified that he, Abel and Mills were indeed members of a secret prison organization whose members are required to deny its existence, and to "lie, cheat, steal [and] kill" to protect one another.[140]

After hearing all this testimony, a juror might conclude that Ehle is a liar by disposition, or that Mills is, and therefore that one or the other, or both, are untrustworthy on any issue. But that propensity argument is *not* the basis on which Abel tried to impeach Ehle, or on which the government tried to impeach Mills. Abel tried to show that Ehle lied because Ehle had a strong motive to incriminate Abel, regardless of the truth: to get a reduction in his own prison sentence. The prosecutor tried to show that Mills lied out of loyalty to his gang: to help a fellow gang member (Abel) and to thwart a traitor (Ehle). In each case, the argument is distinguished from propensity because it is specific to the context. A person may lie to get out of prison—or to keep a close associate from going to prison—and yet be honest in other situations.[141]

The motives that were raised in *Abel*, on both sides, are powerful bases for impeachment, if true. Most claims of bias, interest or motive (here, generically described as "bias") are less extreme. A witness may be biased because she has a stake in the outcome of the case, or is related to someone who does; because she is a friend of a party, or a former friend, or a neighbor, or an employer, or an employee, or a rival, or an enemy; because she was a party in a similar case, or might have been, or believes she might be in the future, or has a friend who was a party in such a case, or was a lawyer for a party; because she was involved in an accident or transaction similar to the one at issue, or expects to be, or has a friend or relative who has been in that situation; because she belongs to a group that has a strong position on an issue in dispute, or supports one of the parties, or opposes a party; and so on. Sometimes these potentially biasing events or associations suggest that the witness might lie—

---

[138] After you have studied the hearsay rule and its exceptions (Chapter Six), you might return to this case to see why Mills' report of Ehle's statement is not inadmissible hearsay. For the moment, take our word that it is admissible.

[139] The organization at issue was the "Aryan Brotherhood." The trial judge ruled, however, that the prosecutor could not use that name because it was unduly prejudicial. Id. at 48.

[140] Id.

[141] As we noted in discussing the distinction between propensity and nonpropensity inferences generally, the difference between impeachment by character and impeachment for bias is a matter of degree, not kind. The test for deciding whether a claim that a witness is disposed to shade the truth is an attack on her character ("she is a liar") or an accusation of bias ("she lies for her friends") is essentially the same as that described supra, Section II.B.5, pp. 383–386.

although not that she would necessarily do so. More often they suggest that she is likely to shade or unconsciously slant her testimony to help the side she favors. Evidence of basic compelling biases may not be excluded without error—a familial relationship between a witness and a party, for example, or a romantic relationship, or a direct interest in the verdict, or a bribe. When the apparent motive is weaker, judges have discretion to admit or exclude evidence of bias or to limit the exploration of bias to a few questions.

Bias is sometimes said to be a favored mode of impeachment. This can mean several things. In general, courts seem to believe that evidence of a specific reason why a witness should not be believed in a particular case is more probative than a global attack on the witness's character for truthfulness. At the same time, such evidence is frequently less embarrassing. It is less humiliating to be exposed as the wife of a police captain or as a former defendant in a similar lawsuit than as an ex-felon or a person with a bad reputation for truthfulness. Courts also seem to feel that evaluating the motives and biases of witnesses is a task that is particularly suitable for juries, but that general character evidence may more easily prejudice them. In short, the contrasting treatment of impeachment by character and impeachment for bias and the explanations for the difference parallel the distinction courts make between propensity and nonpropensity uses of character, more generally.

The favored status of impeachment for bias has three specific manifestations. First, such impeachment is constitutionally protected when a criminal defendant is doing the impeaching. In *Davis v. Alaska*[142] the Supreme Court wrote:

> One way of discrediting the witness is to introduce evidence of a prior criminal conviction of that witness. By doing so the cross-examiner intends to afford the jury a basis to infer that the witness' character is such that he would be less likely than the average trustworthy citizen to be truthful in his testimony. The introduction of evidence of a prior crime is thus a general attack on the credibility of the witness. A more particular attack on the witness' credibility is effected by means of cross-examination directed toward revealing possible biases, prejudices or ulterior motives of the witness as they may relate directly to issues or personalities in the case at hand. The partiality of a witness is subject to exploration at trial, and is "always relevant as discrediting the witness and affecting the weight of his testimony." We have recognized that the exposure of a witness' motivation in testifying is a proper and important function of the [criminal defendant's constitutional] right of cross-examination.

---

[142] 415 U.S. 308, 316 (1974).

Davis is one of several cases in which the Supreme Court has held that the cross-examination for bias is protected by a criminal defendant's Sixth Amendment right to confront adverse witnesses, even in the face of significant countervailing state interests.[143] In *Davis*, for example, the Court held that the constitutional right to impeach for bias overrode the state's interest in preserving the confidentiality of juvenile court records; and in *Olden v. Kentucky* [144] the Court gave precedence to this same right over the state's interest in avoiding potentially prejudicial testimony about the sexual activity of an alleged rape victim. There is no similar protection for cross-examination that is addressed to general attacks on the witness's character for truthfulness. As far as existing case law is concerned, states are at liberty to eliminate entirely cross-examination on character for truthfulness or impeachment by prior convictions, without offending the Sixth Amendment.

Second, courts often say that "bias is not collateral." "Collateral" is a term of art; to say that "bias is not collateral" means simply that bias may be proved with extrinsic evidence—i.e., with evidence (including documentary evidence) other than the testimony of the witness being impeached.[145] *United States v. Abel* is a good example. In *Abel*, the government could not get Mills to admit on cross-examination that he and Abel were members of the same prison gang who had pledged to commit perjury to defend each other. So the government presented extrinsic evidence on the point, namely, rebuttal testimony from Ehle. The Court upheld this procedure, noting that the absence of a specific federal rule of evidence on impeachment for bias does not mean that this type of evidence is inadmissible, even in an extrinsic form:

> Rule 402 provides that all relevant evidence is admissible, except as otherwise provided by the United States Constitution, by Act of Congress, or by applicable rule. A successful showing of bias on the part of a witness [is relevant because it] would have a tendency to make the facts to which he testified less probable in the eyes of the jury than it would be without such testimony.[146]

Applying the default principle of FRE 402—that relevant evidence is admissible unless explicitly forbidden by some other rule—and noting that FRE 608(b)'s ban on extrinsic evidence applies only to impeachment by character, the Court interpreted the Federal Rules to preserve the

---

[143] See also Alford v. United States, 282 U.S. 687 (1931); Smith v. Illinois, 390 U.S. 129 (1968); Giglio v. United States, 405 U.S. 150 (1972); Delaware v. Van Arsdall, 475 U.S. 673 (1986). See generally Chapter Seven.

[144] 488 U.S. 227 (1988).

[145] The term "extrinsic" is derived from the rules that govern impeachment by evidence that contradicts the witness's testimony. In that context, as we will see, infra, Section V.B, the rules of evidence permit the impeaching party to bring out *any* contradictory evidence on cross-examination, but the rules forbid the use of extrinsic evidence for this purpose if the contradiction concerns a merely "collateral" issue.

[146] 469 U.S. at 51.

common law approach to impeachment for bias. That approach permits "the showing of bias by extrinsic evidence, while requiring the cross-examiner to 'take the answer of the witness' with respect to less favored forms of impeachment"—such as character for truthfulness—subject, as always, to the discretion of the trial court to exclude evidence that is unduly prejudicial.[147]

Abel also illustrates a third way in which bias is a favored mode of impeachment. Abel argued on appeal that evidence of Mills' membership in the prison gang was admitted not to show bias but as past conduct that reflected badly on his truthfulness; that as such, it was governed by FRE 608(b); and that under FRE 608(b) it was error to admit the evidence of gang membership on two grounds: first because membership in an organization, by itself, is insufficiently probative of truthfulness; and second because, in any event, extrinsic evidence may not be used to show character for truthfulness under FRE 608(b).[148] The Court disagreed. Mills' membership in the organization showed a possible bias toward Abel; therefore, the evidence was admissible for that purpose, without regard to FRE 608(b), despite the fact that "because of the tenets of the organization described, it might also impeach his veracity directly [i.e., as character evidence]."[149] On its face, this holding is unremarkable. As the Court pointed out, even if this evidence did violate FRE 608(b) (an issue it did not decide), "there is no rule of evidence which provides that testimony admissible for one purpose and inadmissible for another purpose is thereby rendered inadmissible; quite the contrary is the case."[150] At another level, this apparently routine holding—especially coming from the Supreme Court—is telling. Mills' and Abel's

---

[147] Id. at 52. The *Abel* Court was somewhat chagrined by the Federal Rules' silence on impeachment for bias:

> Both parties correctly assume . . . that the question is governed by the Federal Rules of Evidence. But the Rules do not by their terms deal with impeachment for "bias," although they do expressly treat impeachment by character evidence and conduct, Rule 608, by evidence of conviction of a crime, Rule 609, and by showing religious beliefs or opinion, Rule 610. Neither party has suggested what significance we should attribute to this fact. Although we are nominally the promulgators of the Rules, and should in theory need only to consult our collective memories to analyze the situation properly, we are in truth merely a conduit when we deal with an undertaking as substantial as the preparation of the Federal Rules of Evidence.

Id. at 49. There is no reason for chagrin, however. Because impeachment for bias does not fall within the propensity or any other exclusionary rule, it is governed by the FRE's default principles, codified in FRE 402, that relevant evidence is (1) admissible (unless its prejudicial impact substantially outweighs its probative force); and (2) may take any form not otherwise forbidden, including specific instances of conduct developed either on cross-examination or through independent evidence. Because the Federal Rules' default principles basically mirror the common law approach to evidence of bias used to impeach, the drafters of the Federal Rules could (and evidently did) essentially codify the common law approach to this form of impeachment by saying nothing specific on the issue.

[148] Id. at 55.

[149] Id. at 56.

[150] Id. Of course, Abel's attorney could have (but didn't) asked for a limiting instruction. 469 U.S. at 48. See Chapter Two, Section III.F., pp. 184–186.

membership in a gang committed to lying and other bad behavior was almost certainly more powerful as evidence of Mills' bad character for truthfulness—*and*, by association, Abel's bad character for law-abiding behavior—than as evidence of Mills' bias; but at least as extrinsic evidence, and possibly on cross-examination, it was inadmissible for all of those propensity purposes. Nonetheless, the preferred status of bias as a means of impeachment helped the prosecution avoid the objection that the prejudicial potential of Ehle's rebuttal testimony—as proof of Mills' and Abel's bad character—substantially outweighed its probative force as evidence of Mills' bias. FRE 403 objections fail in many such cases because "bias" is such an open-ended concept, and because it is "favored" as a mode of impeachment. Still, we believe that the FRE 403 question in *Abel* deserved more attention than it got.

In most common law jurisdictions extrinsic evidence of bias could not be presented unless the witness was first questioned on that issue on cross-examination. If the witness admitted the facts suggesting a motivation to lie or shade the truth, the opposing party was precluded from introducing further evidence of those facts. If the witness denied or did not fully acknowledge the basis for impeachment, the examiner could present other evidence on the issue. Because the Federal Rules don't specifically mention impeachment for bias, they contain no such "foundation" requirement for extrinsic evidence. Some federal courts nevertheless require cross-examination on alleged bias as a foundation for impeachment by extrinsic evidence. This procedure saves time (because cross-examination is quicker), and avoids distracting the jury or unnecessarily compounding the embarrassment the process may cause witnesses.[151] In any event, the practicality of the common law rule leads most lawyers to follow it and cross-examine on facts suggesting bias. If the impeaching facts are admitted, or if their "sting" already has been pulled on direct examination, extrinsic evidence becomes cumulative and may be excluded for that reason under FRE 403.

Problem V-29. Barbara Chin was severely injured in a car accident at an intersection in Durham, North Carolina in July 2010. She sues General Motors, the manufacturer of the car she was driving, claiming

---

[151] The courts' authority to require such a foundation is probably best predicated on FRE 611(a), which gives the judge plenary control over "the mode and order of interrogating witnesses and presenting evidence." See Chapter Two, Section II.D., pp. 156–157. The closest analogous provision of the Federal Rules is FRE 613(b), governing impeachment with prior inconsistent statements, which states that extrinsic evidence may be introduced as long as the witness has "an opportunity to explain or deny" the statement at some point in the proceeding. Ordinarily, that opportunity comes on cross-examination; occasionally, the witness has to be recalled on rebuttal for that purpose. See infra, Subsection C., pp. 452–455. Even if it does not make sense to interpret the Federal Rules, as McCormick suggests, to impose the same foundational requirement for all impeachment for bias, FRE 611(a) gives judges ample authority to accomplish this in particular cases. See McCormick, § 39.

that because of a fault in the electronic ignition system the car suddenly lurched forward after she had come to a full stop at a red light, causing the collision. General Motors denies that there was a fault in the ignition system, and claims that Chin failed to come to a stop at the light. At trial, Chin calls Brooks Davis as a witness. Davis testifies that he saw the entire accident clearly from an overpass, and that the car Ms. Chin was driving (which he identifies) came to a full stop for at least ten seconds and then suddenly shot into the cross-traffic in the intersection. On cross-examination, the attorney for General Motors wants to ask Davis the following question: "Mr. Davis, isn't it true that in 2006 you were permanently laid off by the Ford Motor Company after working for Ford for twenty-two years"? **Is this line of examination permissible? Would it make a difference if Davis had been laid off by General Motors?**

Problem V-30. Cynthia Simon files suit against police officer Roy Cone claiming that he violently beat her during a drug raid in June 2013. She testifies to this effect, and calls a witness, Billy Rich, who testifies that he saw officer Cone drag the handcuffed Ms. Simon out of the house where the raid took place, that when he first saw her she was already bleeding from at least one head wound, and that he then saw Cone deliberately trip Simon as she stepped off the sidewalk and kick her in the side when she was on the ground. The defense wants to present evidence that Rich was arrested in 2009 for drunk driving (he eventually pled guilty to reckless driving); was arrested again in 2011 for public drunkenness and released without charges; was arrested in 2012 for outstanding traffic and parking fines (which he paid off); and was questioned in 2008 in connection with a robbery, but not arrested. The defense also wants to show that Rich's brother was arrested several times for misdemeanors and felonies and served two years in state prison for unarmed robbery. **May the defense explore these issues? If so, may it do so with extrinsic evidence or will it be limited to cross-examination?** The defense calls two police officers—John Flight and Rudy Gloves—who testify that they took part in the drug raid and that Officer Cone did not beat, assault or mistreat Simon. Simon wants to show that officers Flight and Gloves have been disciplined for the excessive use of physical force in connection with unrelated drug raids. The defense objects. **How should the court rule? If the court allows the impeachment, may Simon use departmental records showing that the officers had been suspended for unnecessary violence, or must Simon first question the officers about these suspensions?**

B. IMPEACHMENT BY CONTRADICTION; THE COLLATERAL MATTER RULE

Perhaps the most common way to discredit a witness and her testimony is by introducing contradictory evidence that is more convincing. The presentation of contradictory stories is, of course, the essence of trials, so this process often is not even seen as impeachment.

Suppose the plaintiff offers an eyewitness, Leslie Berg, who testifies about how an automobile accident occurred. The defendant offers a second eyewitness, Hannah Rose, who gives a different version of what happened that is more detailed, more internally consistent and delivered with more confidence. Hannah's testimony is, of course, relevant and admissible on the question of what happened. Her testimony, however, is also relevant and admissible on the question of Leslie's credibility. Assume, for example, that Leslie arrived at the scene slightly before Hannah and testifies about events that Hannah did not see. Hannah's convincing contradiction of Leslie's testimony where it overlaps with hers may lead the jury to be skeptical about *everything* Leslie reported, including facts Hannah knew nothing about.

When contradictory evidence is directly relevant to facts at issue, it presents no problem. Tricky issues occur only when the contradictory evidence that a party wishes to offer has no independent relevance in the case—i.e., when, but for its value for impeachment, there is no reason the jury should hear the evidence at all. Suppose, for example, that Leslie testified that she was stopped at a red light in her brand new baby blue Miata when the accident occurred. If the defendant happens to know that the witness's car is a ten-year-old pea green Corolla, may the defendant bring out that fact in order to cast doubt on Leslie's testimony as a whole? Under the usual common law rule of evidence, the theoretical answer is clear. The defendant may ask Leslie about the age, color and make of the car she was driving on cross-examination, and, if Leslie admits a misstatement, may use that admission as an argument that nothing she says can be believed. But, even if Leslie denies that her car is old, green and a Corolla, the defendant may not introduce a separate witness for the sole purpose of showing that Leslie misstated the age, color and make of her car. Under this so-called "collateral matter" rule, extrinsic evidence offered for the sole purpose of contradicting a prior witness is inadmissible if it is not relevant independently of the contradiction. This is because the evidence would tell the jury nothing if it did not differ from the adverse witness's testimony. (By contrast, evidence showing an adverse witness's biases, interests or motives, or his inability to observe and report coherently, is not considered "collateral." Although such evidence may have no relevance in the case except to impeach witness's testimony, it avoids the collateral matter rule because its relevance is independent of any tendency it might have to contradict what the witness said.)[152]

---

[152] In its original form, the collateral matter rule only allowed extrinsic evidence to impeach by contradiction if the impeaching party could have offered the evidence in her case-in-chief. See *Attorney-General v. Hitchcock*, 154 Eng. Rep. 38, 39 (1847). More recently, however, some common law courts have allowed evidence that, although independently relevant and admissible

The collateral matter rule applies to exclude testimony, however, only if the *sole* purpose of the later witness is to contradict some fact not independently relevant to which an earlier witness testified. If the defendant calls a witness to provide favorable testimony as to how an accident occurred, that witness may incidentally testify that the car stopped next to his was pea green, not baby blue, without violating the collateral matter rule.[153] The rule's goal is an eminently practical one—to keep each witness's testimony from becoming the occasion for another witness's time-consuming and distracting contradiction of the first witness on matters of no independent importance in the lawsuit.

There are, however, occasions on which collateral contradictions seem to have an important bearing on general credibility. If Leslie had said she was wearing a hat, and Hannah was confident Leslie was bareheaded, a jury that believed Hannah would nonetheless have little reason to question Leslie's credibility. Months or years after the event, Leslie may have forgotten a trivial, irrelevant detail of the kind people forget all the time, while remembering the essential facts of the accident. If, however, Leslie had said she was driving a new, blue Miata when she was actually in an old green Corolla, the kind of self-aggrandizement evident in her auto upgrade might lead the jury to question much of the relevant information she reported. The argument for admitting extrinsic evidence is stronger in the second context than in the first, especially if Leslie is a crucial witness.

Even at common law, judges often allowed extrinsic evidence to be used for collateral contradiction when it seemed to have substantial probative value. Such decisions were almost invulnerable to reversal because few appellate courts would order a new trial simply because the jury heard apparently valid impeaching evidence that did not relate to the merits. The emergence of an apparently strong collateral matter rule in certain appellate decisions, despite its discretionary abandonment by trial judges in many cases, may be an artifact of the type of cases most likely to be appealed: those in which the impeaching testimony was *excluded.* Even if an appellate court believed that excluded collateral testimony had some bearing on credibility, it had good reason not to reverse, given strong potential bases for the trial judge's decision to bar the impeachment. In our accident case, for example, had the contradictory testimony about the car's make and color instead been

as of the time the witness testifies, was not admissible in the impeaching party's case-in-chief because, for example, it had not yet become relevant. For instance, a plaintiff cannot present evidence in her case-in-chief showing that a particular person with no apparent relationship to the case is biased against her. If, however, that person testifies for the defendant, evidence of bias is independently relevant to the case, and, accordingly extrinsic evidence of bias may be offered to impeach the witness both by contradiction (if she denied on cross-examination the facts constituting bias) and by showing bias.

[153] Query: Can you think of any reason why an eyewitness to an accident would be allowed to testify about the color of the car stopped next to hers—a car which had no part in the crash—even if there were no issue of contradiction involved?

admitted, the jury might have had no basis for deciding between the opposing claims about Leslie's car; or the party that called Leslie might have been able to show that she owned both cars and had made a mistake that did not undermine the credibility of her description of the accident; or the jury might think that Leslie's self-aggrandizing misrepresentation was of little or no significance in evaluating the evidence as a whole. A trial judge is much better situated than an appellate court to evaluate such possibilities—and, because retrials are expensive, the trial judge's assessment of the value of collateral contradiction is almost always upheld on appeal. Appellate judges often explained this outcome, not by explicitly ceding the matter to the trial judge's discretion, but by citing the collateral matter rule. A better description of the common law rule might be that there was no *right* to impeach an opposing witness with extrinsic evidence of collateral contradictions; that to call contradictory testimony collateral was a valid objection which if true was likely to be sustained at trial without fear of reversal on appeal; that a trial judge's failure to sustain an objection of this sort was also almost never cause for reversal; and that there were situations in which trial judges could and did allow impeachment by extrinsic evidence on collateral matters.

The Federal Rules neither codify nor reject the collateral matter rule. True, FRE 608(b) provides that "extrinsic evidence is not admissible to prove specific instances of a witness's conduct in order to attack . . . the witness' character for truthfulness," but FRE 608, as it says, applies only to impeachment based on inferences from a witness's propensity to lie. Impeachment by contradiction relies on a different inference, more specific to the case at hand, i.e., that the witness's testimony deviates so substantially from accurate accounts of what happened that the witness must lack either the ability or the desire to tell the truth about the particular matter. Courts in Federal Rules jurisdictions do not, however, admit all extrinsic evidence offered to impeach by contradiction. Instead, they use the usual balance of probative weight against prejudice, distraction and waste of time to determine the admissibility of such evidence. This practice, like the discretion common law judges often exercised, makes good sense. If the plaintiff did not offer a witness to a particular fact during her case-in-chief because the fact, though relevant, was too minor to bother with, allowing her to present the fact through a rebuttal witness just to contradict a defense witness may unduly delay the proceedings or distract the jury's attention from the main issues. On the other hand, some contradicting facts that are *not* independently relevant may bear so strongly on a witness's credibility that the jury should be informed of the contradictory information, even through extrinsic evidence.

Problem V–31. Janetta Kerouac is charged with interstate transportation of a stolen vehicle. Merrilee Haggard testifies for the prosecution that she went to the Biograph Theater in Washington, D.C. on June 6, 2013 to see the movie *Paris, Texas*; that she parked her 1976 Ford F-10 pick-up truck directly in front of the doorway to the theater; that during the movie she came out to buy some Junior Mints, looked out the front door and saw Kerouac sitting in the front seat of Haggard's 1976 Ford pick-up truck, then bending under the dashboard, then driving off. During Kerouac's case, defense counsel calls Melanie Gibson, manager of the Biograph, to testify—contrary to Haggard's denials on cross-examination—(1) that the movie shown on June 6, 2013 was *China 9, Liberty 32*; (2) that Haggard purchased Milk Duds, not Junior Mints; and (3) that Gibson "never, but never" allows anyone to park in front of the doorway to the theater, which is a no parking zone. The prosecutor objects to all of Gibson's testimony. **What rulings?** Another prosecution witness, Wilhamina Nelson, testifies during the prosecution's case in chief that on the evening of June 6, 2013, she saw Kerouac shove a coat hanger between the frame and driver's side window of a 1976 Ford F-10 parked near the Biograph Theater. On cross-examination, Nelson denies knowing Kerouac except as the woman she saw breaking into the pick-up truck, and Nelson is not otherwise questioned. Defense counsel later offers the testimony of Patsy Fonda (4) that she and Nelson spent the evening of June 6, 2013 bowling together in Biloxi, Mississippi, and (5) that Nelson complained that "a gal named Jackie Kerouac had run off with her man, leaving her cryin' in the rain." Defense counsel also offers (6) the testimony of car mechanic Glenda Campbell who examined the allegedly stolen vehicle after it was recovered in Albuquerque and determined that the passenger side, not the driver's side, door lock had been tampered with. The prosecutor objects to Fonda's and Campbell's testimony. **What rulings?**

C. IMPEACHMENT BY PRIOR INCONSISTENT STATEMENTS

Another common method of impeaching a witness is by showing that her own prior statements on the subject contradict her testimony. As we have seen, effective cross-examination often depends on prior statements, which are used to fashion a series of leading questions that the witness must agree with, or be impeached by proof that she expressed agreement with the proposition at an earlier time.[154] As a result, a large portion of pretrial preparation consists of creating and collecting prior statements by witnesses. Testimony before grand juries, at preliminary hearings, suppression hearings and in pretrial depositions, and statements given to

---

[154] See Chapter Two, Section II.B., pp. 151–154.

the police and to investigators and insurance companies, all serve this purpose.[155]

Although impeachment by prior inconsistent statements is a form of impeachment by contradiction—the witness's prior statement contradicts her testimony—it does not, *in theory*, depend on the accuracy of the contradictory prior statement. When a person first says one thing and then another, the inconsistency casts doubt on *both* statements. Perhaps the witness has no recollection of the event and fabricates a story when asked about it. Or perhaps she says whatever people want to hear at the time, or lets other situation-specific motivations determine what she says. In either event, the inconsistency provides reason to believe that none of the witness's statements on the issue are fully credible. Often, of course, the jury will believe that the witness's prior statement is true and rely on it not only to impeach the witness's contradictory testimony but also as a basis for deciding what happened. Although this mixed use of the evidence may seem appropriate and unremarkable—it mirrors jurors' treatment of other contradicting evidence—it presents a serious problem. As we will see, the prior statement is very often hearsay and thus inadmissible for the truth of what it asserts if no exception to the hearsay rule applies.[156] If the prior statement *is* inadmissible hearsay, the possibility that the jury will consider the prior statement as evidence that what it says is true (despite being instructed not to do so) is a form of prejudice that weighs against admitting the statement for impeachment.

---

[155] The Supreme Court sometimes has allowed even illegally obtained statements and other illegally obtained evidence to be used to impeach, although the statements and other evidence are inadmissible on substantive issues. See, e.g., Kansas v. Ventris, 129 S.Ct. 1841 (2009) (allowing impeachment of a criminal defendant by prior statements to a police informant obtained in violation of the Sixth Amendment right to counsel); Harris v. New York, 401 U.S. 222 (1971) (allowing impeachment of a criminal defendant by prior statements to police obtained in violation of the *Miranda* rule). But see Mincey v. Arizona, 437 U.S. 385 (1978) (forbidding impeachment of a criminal defendant by prior statements obtained involuntarily). We leave these rulings and related issues to courses in criminal procedure. Compare Walder v. United States, 347 U.S. 62 (1954) (allowing the prosecutor to use illegally seized physical evidence to impeach a criminal defendant) with James v. Illinois, 493 U.S. 307 (1990) (forbidding the prosecutor to use illegally seized physical evidence to impeach a defense witnesses other than the defendant). Also compare, e.g., Fletcher v. Weir, 455 U.S. 603 (1982) (defendant's silence after arrest but before *Miranda* warnings may constitutionally be used to impeach his protests of innocence at trial) and Jenkins v. Anderson, 447 U.S. 231 (1980) (defendant's silence before arrest may be used to impeach) and United States v. Havens, 446 U.S. 620 (1980) (defendant may be asked about his possession of property and then, if he denies possessing it, may constitutionally be impeached by way of contradiction with proof that the government seized the property from him, even if the seizure was illegal and the property is inadmissible in the government's case-in-chief) with, e.g., Doyle v. Ohio, 426 U.S. 610 (1976) (under the Fifth Amendment Due Process Clause, defendant's silence *after* receiving *Miranda* warnings may not be used to impeach his testimony at trial).

[156] See Chapter Six, Section IV.D., pp. 757–770. A small minority of jurisdictions, egged on by many academic commentators, recognize a hearsay exception for *all* prior inconsistent statements by a testifying witness who can be examined about the prior statement. This rule avoids both the hearsay difficulty with prior statements used to impeach and the charade of telling jurors that they can rely upon the witness's prior statement to assess her credibility but not for the truth of the matter asserted; it also provides an incentive to place witnesses on the stand in order to elicit their out-of-court statements. See also infra, p. 454, note 159; infra, pp. 457–458.

At common law, extrinsic evidence of inconsistent statements could be used only if the proper foundation was laid in cross-examination. If the witness (1) was confronted with the prior statement, (2) had an opportunity to deny making it or to explain away the inconsistency, and (3) denied or did not forthrightly acknowledge the statement, then—and only then—might the impeaching party present extrinsic evidence of the inconsistent statement. The impeaching party usually could lay the foundation for extrinsic evidence simply by asking the witness whether or not she recalled making a specified statement at or about a certain time. By looking first to the witness's acknowledgment of the inconsistent statement, and by requiring a denial before resorting to extrinsic evidence, the common law emphasized the statement's nonhearsay use—to impugn the witness's credibility—and usually avoided time-consuming and distracting extrinsic evidence. A witness's qualified or tentative admission of a prior inconsistent statement did not, however, prevent extrinsic proof. The details of the previous statement were fair game for the examiner and had to be fully conceded before extrinsic proof was barred.

Also at common law, impeachment by prior inconsistent statements—like impeachment by contradiction—was subject to the collateral matter rule. To return to our automobile accident example, suppose that Leslie testified that she saw the accident on her way to pick up her children at church. If, on cross-examination, she denied telling a coworker that she saw the accident while on her way to place a bet with a bookie, the coworker's testimony would have been inadmissible. Although evidence contradicting this part of Leslie's testimony might have cast doubt on everything else she said, extrinsic evidence was inadmissible because her destination at the time of the accident was "collateral" to the issues in the case. After Leslie testified that she saw the accident on her way to church, the opposing party could not introduce a witness solely to *contradict* her by testifying that he saw her leave her car and walk into a gambling hall. Analogously, extrinsic evidence of Leslie's *prior statement* that she was going to the gambling hall was inadmissible because it merely established an inconsistency in her description of a collateral fact.

FRE 613, which governs the procedure for impeachment by prior inconsistent statement, changes common law practice somewhat. It provides:

Rule 613.   Witness's Prior Statement

   (a) Showing or Disclosing the Statement During Examination. When examining a witness about the witness's prior statement, a party need not show it or disclose its contents to the witness. But the party must, on request, show it or disclose its contents to an adverse party's attorney.

(b) Extrinsic Evidence of a Prior Inconsistent Statement. Extrinsic evidence of a witness's prior inconsistent statement is admissible only if the witness is given an opportunity to explain or deny the statement and an adverse party is given an opportunity to examine the witness about it, or if justice so requires. This subdivision (b) does not apply to an opposing party's statement under Rule 801(d)(2).[157]

FRE 613 modifies common law practice in two ways. First, FRE 613(b) substantially broadens the admissibility of extrinsic evidence of a witness's prior inconsistent statements. It does so by allowing the statements to be proven by extrinsic evidence even *before* the witness has a chance to explain or deny them, as long as *at some point* the witness gets to explain or deny and the opposing party gets to question the witness about the statements. Edward Cleary, Reporter of the Supreme Court's Advisory Committee on the Federal Rules and the principal drafter of the Rules, explained this modification as follows:

> The objectives of the [common law] procedure are: (1) to save time, since the witness may admit having made the statement and thus make the extrinsic proof unnecessary; (2) to avoid unfair surprise to the opposite party by affording him an opportunity to draw a denial or explanation from the witness; and (3) to give the witness himself, in fairness, a chance to deny or explain the apparent discrepancy. These are desirable objectives. The second and third can, however, be achieved by affording an opportunity to explain at any time during the trial, and no particular time sequence is required. Only the first of the objectives named above, saving time, points in the direction of the traditional foundation requirement on cross-examination, and even here countervailing factors are present: the time saved is not great; the laying of the foundation may inadvertently have been overlooked; the impeaching statement may not have been discovered until later; and premature disclosure may on occasion frustrate the effective impeachment of collusive witnesses. The argument may be made that the recalling of a witness for further cross-examination will afford an adequate solution for these difficulties and hence [that] the traditional procedure should be retained. The argument is not a sound one. In the first place, recall for cross-examination has traditionally been very much within the discretion of the judge and seems likely to continue so.

---

[157] The rule's last sentence withdraws the foundation requirement for prior statements made by a *party* and offered against the party. As Chapter Six, Section III.B., pp. 591–593, explains, such statements are always admissible for the truth of the matter asserted, so special rules aimed at limiting their use to impeachment are not necessary. Accordingly, when the prior statement was made by and offered against a party, no foundation of the sort covered by this rule is required, and the statement need not be shown to either the party witness or opposing counsel before it is used on cross-examination or offered through extrinsic evidence.

And secondly, the admissibility of prior inconsistent statements ought not to be enmeshed in the technicalities of cross-examination when all that is being sought is the presentation of an opportunity to deny or explain.

In view of these considerations, the Advisory Committee concluded that the objectives could better be achieved by allowing the opportunity to deny or explain to occur at any time during the trial, rather than limiting it to cross-examination.

Moreover, occasionally situations may arise where the interests of justice will warrant dispensing entirely with the opportunity to explain or deny. Thus if a witness becomes unavailable through absence or death, the judge ought to have discretion to allow the impeaching statement.

In my view, the existing practice would continue in general to be followed under the rule. It is convenient and effective to raise the matter on cross-examination, and doing so would avoid problems that might ultimately arise if witnesses become unavailable before the end of trial. The rule ought, however, to remain as drawn, leaving the practical approach to the good sense of the practitioner.[158]

Professor Cleary correctly predicted that lawyers and courts would generally continue to follow the common law practice of giving witnesses a chance to explain or deny before extrinsic evidence is offered. We wonder, however, about the wisdom of letting lawyers deviate from this practice. The Reporter acknowledges that allowing extrinsic evidence in cases in which the witness would have admitted the statement wastes time. More important, allowing extrinsic evidence of statements the witness would readily acknowledge may give the statements more impact than is warranted, because they will not be followed immediately by an explanation. Moreover, when a witness is confronted with a prior statement that contradicts her testimony, the statement's value for impeachment is obvious. When the witness being impeached is not on the stand, the main apparent value of the statement may be as evidence of its truth—for which it is usually impermissible hearsay.[159] Finally, the change inconveniences witnesses. Under FRE 613(b), the party calling a witness has a strong incentive to make the witnesses stay in court or

---

[158] Letter from Edward W. Cleary to Hon. William L. Hungate, May 8, 1973, in Supplement to Hearings Before the Subcomm. on Criminal Justice of the House Comm. on the Judiciary, 93rd Cong., 1st Sess. 74–75 (1973).

[159] The drafters proposed FRE 613 along with a provision establishing an exception to the hearsay rule for all prior inconsistent statements. (Strictly speaking, it would have been an *exclusion* from the hearsay rule. See Chapter Six, Section IV.D., pp. 757–770.) Although Congress retained FRE 613, it rejected the hearsay exception. FRE 613 made more sense in conjunction with the rejected hearsay exception because then no hearsay problem would arise, no matter when the prior statement was admitted. See supra, p. 451, note 156; infra, pp. 457–458.

remain available to return on short notice until the end of the opposing party's case. If a party does not take this precaution, the opposing party may introduce a prior statement that the witness will have no chance to explain or deny.[160] The reasons Professor Cleary gives for the modification—inadvertent failure to lay a foundation, late discovery of the inconsistent statement and premature disclosure to collusive witnesses— could be avoided by retaining FRE 613(b)'s "justice" exception to the foundation requirement. Even under FRE 613(b) as written, courts can and often do require cross-examination on prior inconsistent statements as a foundation for using extrinsic evidence, under FREs 611 and 403.[161]

FRE 613 contains no "collateral matter" rule barring extrinsic evidence of prior statements that are irrelevant apart from their use to impeach. Nonetheless, if the portion of the witness's testimony being impeached by a prior statement is "collateral," that provides an independent argument under FRE 403 for excluding extrinsic evidence of the prior inconsistent statement. The Federal Rules' treatment of extrinsic evidence of prior inconsistent statements for impeachment on collateral issues thus resembles their treatment of extrinsic evidence for impeachment by contradiction on collateral issues. In both cases, the issue is not mentioned by the rules, but common law practice continues under the general rules governing prejudice, probative value, waste of time and order of questioning.

The second way in which FRE 613 modifies the common law is by abandoning the rule in *Queen Caroline's Case*.[162] Under that rule, before a witness could be questioned about a prior written statement, the statement had to be shown to the witness. The rule was roundly criticized because letting the witness see her exact statement before being questioned about it made it easier for the witness to explain away

---

[160] If the party presenting a witness has notice that a prior inconsistent statement exists, the court may treat the party's failure or inability to recall the witness when extrinsic evidence of the statement is offered as waiving an objection to the evidence on the ground that the requirements of FRE 613(b) were not met. See, e.g., Rush v. Illinois Central R.R., 399 F.3d 705 (6th Cir. 2005). On the other hand, if a party is surprised by the prior statement, the court may either exclude the extrinsic evidence or grant a continuance to permit the party to recall the witness being impeached. See, e.g., Manley v. AmBase Corp., 337 F.3d 237 (2d Cir. 2003). Some courts, however, always give the party offering evidence of a prior inconsistent statement the duty to ensure that the witness is available to deny or explain it. A court that reads the rule this way may preclude impeachment by prior inconsistent statements after a witness has completed her testimony, unless the impeaching party has alerted the court to the need to have the witness remain accessible for re-examination. Once alerted, courts often order a witness to "step down" (instead of being "excused") and to remain available for recall to the stand. Of course, from the point of view of the witness, the inconvenience is the same whether she is tethered to the court at the request of the direct examiner, or of the cross-examiner.

[161] See United States v. Schnapp, 322 F.3d 564 (8th Cir. 2003) (upholding trial court discretion under FRE 611 to bar extrinsic evidence of a prior inconsistent statement that the witness wasn't asked about on cross-examination, even though there was no surprise and the witness could have been recalled).

[162] 2 Brod. & Bing. 284, 129 Eng. Rep. 976 (1820). The United States Supreme Court approved the rule in The Charles Morgan, 115 U.S. 69, 77–78 (1885).

inconsistencies between the earlier statement and the current testimony. Even before the adoption of the Federal Rules, most federal courts had abandoned the rule and required only that the examiner refer in general terms to a statement made at a particular time and place about a particular matter. Rule 613(a) adopts this practice, insisting only that the written prior statement or the substance of an oral statement be disclosed to opposing counsel when the witness is being examined about it.

A prior statement does not impeach a witness unless it actually contradicts her testimony. Sometimes, however, parties are tempted to offer as impeachment prior statements that differ from a witness's testimony without contradicting it, in the hope that the jury will, in violation of the hearsay rule, consider the statement as substantive evidence that the matter it describes is true. This practice forces courts to decide whether the prior statement is in fact "inconsistent" with the testimony. Courts sometimes say that the test is whether there is a "material" inconsistency between the two descriptions. This terminology is unfortunate. It does little to guide the judge's discretion, and it invites confusion between the requirement of "inconsistency" (whether the testimony and the statement differ in some significant respect), and the "collateral matter" problem (whether the issue on which the statement and the testimony differ is important to the lawsuit). A better approach is to ask whether the testimony and the statement—even if they are not logically incompatible—appear to be based on different beliefs about the truth. Thus, if a witness testified that she "saw George at 10 p.m. at the high school football game," she might be impeached with an earlier statement that she saw him at 9:50 on the same night at a bar two miles away. Although it is not impossible for both statements to be true, they appear to be based on different descriptions of the facts of that night. Likewise, details omitted from one statement but included in another can make the two statements inconsistent if the details are important enough that they "naturally would have been asserted" by someone who observed them.[163] An asserted lack of memory about an event and a description of the event can also be inconsistent if the asserted memory loss preceded the testimony giving the description, or if the asserted memory loss comes later, at trial, but the judge believes it is contrived.[164] In all of these cases, although the statements appear inconsistent, if they are not, the witness will have a chance to explain why.

Even if there is a significant inconsistency between the witness's testimony and her prior statement, the prior statement still may be excluded if its probative value is substantially outweighed by its likely

---

[163] Jenkins v. Anderson, 447 U.S. 231, 239 (1980).

[164] But cf. United States v. Hale, 422 U.S. 171 (1975) (silence at the time of arrest or during custodial interrogation is not inconsistent with exculpatory trial testimony about what happened, given the many reasons why even an innocent suspect might be scared or reluctant to talk to the police).

prejudice. Probative value depends on the extent of the inconsistency, the centrality of the issue on which the statements differ and the importance of the witness being impeached. Prejudice is largely a function of danger that the jury will rely on the prior statement for its truth, despite the hearsay rule. Waste of time and the danger of distracting disputes on subsidiary issues also may be weighed in the balance.

In discussing FRE 607, supra, p. 412 & note 108, we mentioned that it is improper to call a witness who is expected to give damaging testimony for the sole purpose of impeaching the witness with evidence that is inadmissible on substantive issues. This problem most frequently arises in criminal cases in which the government seeks to use a witness's prior statements implicating the defendant after the witness "turns coat" and refuses to repeat her statements in court. If the prior statements are inadmissible hearsay, and the government knows in advance that the witness will not provide favorable testimony, the government can benefit from calling the witness only if the jury ignores court's instructions and uses the impeaching prior statements for their truth. In this situation, most courts will not allow the prosecutor to impeach the witness with the prior inconsistent statements.[165] When the witness's failure to testify favorably to the government surprises the prosecutor, virtually all courts let the prosecutor impeach the witness with her prior statement, including courts that do not generally allow a party to impeach its own witness.[166] The proper outcome is less clear when the witness is expected to provide some testimony favorable to the government and some that is inconsistent with her prior statements. In this situation, some commentators have proposed a return to the practice prior to the adoption of FRE 607, which forbade impeachment by prior statement unless the particular testimony that is inconsistent with the statement surprised the party that called the witness. The courts are split, but some permit impeachment with all prior inconsistent statements if the government's "primary purpose" in calling the witness was not to impeach her. These courts seem to be saying that they won't tolerate the pretextual calling of witnesses to circumvent the hearsay rule, but if the witness was properly called, they will give the calling party considerable leeway to use inconsistent statements to impeach, because there is often good reason to believe that the inconsistent prior statement is more reliable than the in-court testimony.[167]

---

[165] But see United States v. DeLillo, 620 F.2d 939 (2d Cir. 1980) (permitting the government to call a witness for the sole purpose of impeaching him with prior inconsistent statements because the witness was crucial to government's case). We can see no justification for *DeLillo* under the Federal Rules. Some think those rules should include an exception to the hearsay rule for the prior inconsistent statements of crucial "turn coat" witnesses, but they do not.

[166] Criminal defendants, and both parties in civil cases, are also allowed to impeach their own witnesses by prior inconsistent statements when the witness's testimony comes as a surprise. See supra, Section IV.A, pp. 411–413.

[167] See, e.g., United States v. Burt, 495 F.3d 733 (7th Cir.), cert. denied, 552 U.S. 1063 (2007) (concerns about calling a witness as a subterfuge for impeaching him with otherwise

It is easy to understand why courts interpret FRE 607 so broadly, and to sympathize with their motives.   Nonetheless, many of these decisions are indefensible as a matter of evidence law. Nothing in FRE 607 trumps the usual balancing of probative value and prejudice.   The probative value of eliciting testimony on a particular point *not* with the goal of relying on it but solely to impeach the witness with her prior inconsistent statement, is nil.   The best that good faith impeachment can hope to accomplish is to neutralize the testimony completely, which— setting aside testimony that surprises the direct examiner—can more easily be achieved by not eliciting any testimony on that point in the first place.   At the very least, impeachment of one's own witness by prior inconsistent statements should be prohibited (absent surprise) if the probative value to the party of the witness's testimony as a whole, on all matters that are favorable to the government, is substantially outweighed by the likely prejudice from the jury's probable misuse of the prior inconsistent statements for the truth of the matter asserted.[168]

The reason many courts freely allow parties to impeach their own witnesses with prior inconsistent statements—even in apparent disregard for the balance of probative value and prejudice required by FRE 403—is no secret. Most commentators and many judges believe that prior inconsistent statements by witnesses who are available for cross-examination should be admissible for all purposes, as an exception to the hearsay rule. A few state jurisdictions follow this rule.[169] Freely admitting prior inconsistent statements to impeach one's own witnesses has nearly the same effect, as long as jurors disobey instructions to consider the statements for impeachment only. As we will see in Chapter Six, however, when Congress enacted the Federal Rules of Evidence it considered this exception to the hearsay rule and rejected it in all but a few circumstances.[170] Although the Federal Rules authorize courts in certain circumstances to declare *new* exceptions to the hearsay rule, that authority should not extend to this situation, where Congress specifically rejected an exception of the particular type.[171]   Moreover, even if the courts had the authority to create such an exception, there is no justification for doing so indirectly rather than directly.   If the purpose of the rule is to permit the jury to consider the prior statements for their truth, there is no reason to instruct them *not* to do so.   Yet, that is what happens in courts that admit such statements as "impeachment" under

---

inadmissible evidence do not arise if the presenting party derives significant favorable evidence from the witness).

[168] See, e.g., United States v. Buffalo, 358 F.3d 519 (8th Cir. 2004) (citing case law supporting the "primary purpose" approach and the competing FRE 403 approach and applying the latter).

[169] See, e.g., Calif. Evidence Code § 1235; supra, p. 451, note 156 and p. 454, note 159.

[170] See Chapter Six, Section IV.D., pp. 757–770.

[171] See Chapter Six, Section IV.B., pp. 746–755.

FRE 607 without acknowledging that they are creating a new hearsay exception.

————

Problem V-32.   Howard Hyde, a customer service representative for Challenge Airlines in San Diego, is charged with conspiracy to import heroin.   The prosecution presents evidence that Ivana Ifsher flew from Bangkok to San Diego on a Challenge flight, cleared customs, "discovered" she had left her cosmetics case on board the aircraft, and called the customer services office to ask if someone would retrieve the case and deliver it to her.   Before Hyde, who volunteered for the job, could reach the plane, a flight attendant discovered the case and its white powder contents (later identified as heroin), and gave it to customs officials.   At trial, Hyde testifies that he had nothing to do with Ifsher's scheme and had "never knowingly delivered drugs to anyone."   On cross-examination, the prosecutor asks, "In fact, you have delivered heroin in the past?," to which Hyde responds, "Never."   Over objection, the prosecution seeks to introduce five rebuttal witnesses: (1) Teresa Torres to testify that Hyde told her three years earlier that he had given heroin to a friend as a birthday present. (2) Chester Cartaret to testify that Hyde told him a year earlier, "I'd move cocaine in a New York minute, if the price was right." (3) Deborah Freeman to testify that Hyde told her two years earlier that he frequently went to a pharmacy and picked up morphine for his then-wife, for which she had a legal prescription. (4) Preston Pittman to testify that Hyde gave him a gram of heroin three years earlier as a birthday present. (5) Lucy Lassley to testify that she was on the same flight as Ifsher from Pakistan to San Diego a month before Ifsher's Bangkok trip; that she witnessed Ifsher make a call on her cell phone after clearing customs; and that twenty minutes later, she saw Hyde hand Ifsher a fanny pack and heard Hyde say, "Here you go. See you in a month."   **Is any of this evidence admissible?   Is any additional foundation needed to make it admissible? Review Problem V-24, supra, p. 413–414.**

D. IMPEACHMENT BY DEFECTS IN PERCEPTION, MEMORY AND DESCRIPTION

Our discussion of impeachment thus far has focused primarily on a single determinant of accurate testimony—the witness's sincerity, her desire to tell the truth.[172]   When a party attacks a witness's sincerity by claiming that the witness is generally disposed to lie, FRE 608 and 609

————

[172] The modes of impeachment we have considered so far are primarily, but not *exclusively*, relevant to arguments that turn on sincerity.   When a witness testifies that she saw the defendant at the mall, a prior statement by her—or evidence from other witnesses—that he was not at the mall at that time could suggest defects in the witness's perception or memory as well as intentional deception.   Likewise, a biased witness may *see* or *remember* things differently from an unbiased witness, even if she makes every effort to tell the truth.

apply. Under those rules, reputation and lay opinion evidence are the preferred forms of proof; expert opinion evidence is heavily disfavored; and specific instances of conduct may be a subject of cross-examination in the discretion of the court but may not be shown through extrinsic evidence except in the case of prior convictions. When a party attacks a witness's sincerity based on factors more specific to the case—such as the witness's bias against a party, her interest in the outcome, evidence convincingly contradicting her testimony or prior inconsistent statements—evidence of specific instances of behavior is generally preferred. Such evidence is almost always allowed on cross-examination, and is allowed as extrinsic evidence as well, unless the aspect of the witness's testimony being impeached is "collateral" or the evidence is unduly prejudicial.

In this section, we consider attacks on three other determinants of the accuracy of a witness's testimony: perception, memory and clarity of description. Did the witness have the ability to see or hear the event he is reporting? Does he remember what he perceived? And can he accurately describe what he remembers? Here, too, the inferences relied upon to impeach may be divided into two basic categories. A party might seek to impeach a witness based on a general disposition to misperceive, misremember or misdescribe things. Common expressions from everyday life suggest that we draw these kinds of dispositional inferences all the time: "I'm sure he didn't notice. He's a space cadet." "Of course she forgot. She's your typical absent-minded professor." "That's not what he meant. He's just gets tangled up in his words." Alternatively, a party might seek to impeach a witness based on more specific defects in perception, memory or description that were operating on the occasion in question. A witness might have been standing too far away to hear a whispered conversation on a noisy street; the event might have been so minor and so far in the past that accurate memory is unlikely; or the witness might be drunk on the stand and have trouble saying what he means and remembering what he heard. Evidence relevant to perception, memory and description can take the same forms as evidence that bears on sincerity. For example, a witness might be impeached on the basis of his *reputation* for being unobservant; or through a lay person's or an expert's *opinion* that his memory is defective; or through *examples* of specific things he has said that were intended to mean one thing but seemed to mean something else. In principle, all these bases for impeachment can be developed both on cross-examination and through extrinsic evidence.

Most courts and commentators assume that there is no Federal Rule governing impeachment by sensory or mental defects, and instead apply a set of common law principles.[173] Those principles, like most of the rules

---

[173] FRE 608 regulates impeachment aimed at testing "[a] witness's credibility" and (especially as amended in 2003) the witness's "character for truthfulness or untruthfulness."

governing impeachment for lack of sincerity, disfavor inferences based on general psychological traits. Courts do not like debates over the general quality of a witness's memory, the keenness of his hearing and so forth. Such evidence may sneak in on cross-examination, however, through questions that address the witness's limited education, poor command of English, history of misperception ("you don't hear so well these days, do you?") or poor memory. Such questions are sometimes allowed as "background" rather than impeachment per se, but—upon objection— most courts will stop a cross-examination that aims too directly and extensively to suggest misperception or faulty memory based upon nothing more than general psychological propensities. Extrinsic evidence of general psychological or perceptual traits, including expert testimony, is almost always forbidden.

Evidence that the witness lacked or lacks the *ability* to perceive, remember or describe the particular event in question, generally *is* admissible on cross-examination and may be presented through extrinsic evidence if the issue is important. Extrinsic evidence may be used, for example, to show that the witness was suffering from a temporary disability—for example, that a passing truck blocked her view of the accident she described, or that a concussion shortly after the event impaired her memory of it. Extrinsic evidence may also be used to show a specific ongoing condition—such as deafness, color blindness or long-term memory loss—that (unlike a general psychological or personality trait) invariably manifests itself in predictable ways. If a witness has a hearing loss, for example, it is predictable that particular stimuli (e.g., soft voices, low frequencies or conversations with substantial background noise) will lead to a particular outcome (inability to hear).[174]

The usual balance of probative value and prejudice determines the admissibility of evidence of particularized defects in perception or memory. Cross-examination on such matters (including simple courtroom experiments to gauge, for example, what a witness can see or hear from different distances) is rarely prohibited, and is ordinarily preferred to extrinsic evidence because it saves time. When a defect can be accurately described and understood by lay people—for example, if a witness has difficulty seeing without glasses—lay testimony is preferred to time-

---

Both of these phrases could refer to "accuracy" generally and not just to "sincerity." "Truthful" means "corresponding with reality" as well as "telling the truth, esp. habitually." Nonetheless, the general (if rarely defended) assumption has been that FRE 608 governs traits related to sincerity and not to perception, memory and clarity. Applying FRE 608 usually would lead to the same result as common law principles; occasionally, however, lay opinion testimony about another witness's general perceptive, mnemonic or narrative traits might be admissible under FRE 608(a) but not under common law rules.

[174] Notice the similarity between these admissible ongoing conditions affecting perception and memory, and the habits and routine practices discussed supra, Section II.B.4. Although all of these traits are used as a basis for inferring action in accordance with the trait, the trait is sufficiently definite, permanent and well understood that one can predict with great certainty how it will manifest itself under particular conditions.

consuming and potentially distracting expert testimony, if extrinsic evidence is allowed at all. In other cases, establishing the existence or explaining the effect of sensory or mental defects may require expert testimony. The probative value of such evidence depends on the importance of the testimony being impeached, the jury's ability to gauge the issue without expert assistance, the expert's opportunity to acquire information on the witness and the quality of scientific knowledge in the field. Medical and physiological testimony is more likely to be allowed than psychological testimony. Common topics (if the issue is disputed) include color blindness, near-sightedness, premature senile dementia and tone deafness. Prejudice consists primarily of wasted time, the possibility of a distracting battle of experts, the danger that jurors will give expert testimony more weight than it deserves and a reluctance to subject witnesses to the embarrassment of medical and psychological scrutiny in public. Overall, the treatment of situation-specific evidence of defects of perception, memory and description is similar to the treatment of situation-specific evidence of insincerity—except for a greater availability of relevant medical testimony (albeit *no* greater willingness to permit psychological testimony).

There is no "bright line" between evidence that indicates a general tendency to misperceive, misremember or misdescribe, and evidence that suggests an inability to do so on a particular occasion. The difference between these two forms of impeachment may be described using the same continuum from specificity to generality that we discuss above in connection with the propensity rule.[175] Plotting the locations of particular types of evidence on that continuum requires a comparison between the stimulus (e.g., red and green lights) and response (seen as the same) revealed by the evidence offered to impeach (the witness is color blind), and the stimulus and response that characterize the witness's testimony (witness said the light was red). The more similar, the better. The proper outcome in each case also will depend, as always, on case-specific considerations of probative value and prejudice.

Several issues recur in this area. Evidence of alcoholism or drug addiction is generally not permitted as a basis for inferring that the witness was "under the influence" at the time of a particular event and thus did not accurately perceive it or cannot accurately remember or describe it.[176] On the other hand, specific evidence of alcohol or drug use at the time of the event (which affects perception) or while testifying (which affects memory and clarity of description) generally is permitted through cross-examination and if necessary by extrinsic evidence.

---

[175] See supra, Section II.B.5, pp. 383–387.

[176] See, e.g., Kunz v. DeFelice, 538 F.3d 667 (7th Cir. 2008). A few courts allow cross-examination about drug use generally on the theory that it is surreptitious behavior and thus tends to show bad character for truthfulness, as is permitted in the court's discretion by FRE 608(b), but the trend is against permitting such cross-examination.

Although the principle is less well-established, expert evidence of brain damage or other physiological effects of chronic alcohol or drug abuse that permanently and predictably impair perception, memory or coherence should also be admissible, subject to FRE 403.

Evidence of general psychological tendencies arguably related to poor perception and memory is generally inadmissible, especially as extrinsic evidence.   On the other hand, evidence of an identifiable mental abnormality—such as brain damage or psychosis—may be admissible for impeachment if the condition manifests itself predictably in specific ways that obviously affect perception, memory or clarity; occasionally, expert witnesses are allowed to testify on this point.[177]   If there is reason to suspect abnormality, a court might order a civil party or a victim in a criminal case to undergo a psychiatric evaluation conducted by an expert for the opposing party, or the judge might authorize an expert to view the witness in court and testify about what is observed.   In fact, courts rarely take these steps.   For the most part, impeachment of this sort is conducted by cross-examination about the witness's psychological history and about documents revealing that history.

Another recurring issue is the admissibility of expert testimony on the unreliability of eyewitness identifications and (more recently) of confessions.[178] Legal history includes many examples of innocent people convicted on the basis of positive but false identifications and false confessions.   An impressive and consistent body of psychological research shows that certain conditions are particularly likely to result in

---

[177] See, e.g., United States v. Jimenez, 256 F.3d 330, 343 (5th Cir. 2001) (mental health records may be used to impeach if they reveal an " 'impairment of the witness ability to comprehend, know, and correctly relate the truth' "), and also see the cases on expert testimony cited supra, p. 417, note 115. Competence to testify should be distinguished from credibility. Under FREs 601–603 nearly all adults, even ones who are "insane," are competent to testify. Competence requires only that the witness actually have perceived the event at issue, have some ability to remember what he perceived, and have some capacity to communicate and understand the oath or affirmation that precedes testimony. Once these minimal requirements are satisfied, the issue becomes whether the probative value of what the witness has to say is substantially outweighed by the dangers of prejudice, confusion or waste of time. See Chapter Two, Section I.C., pp. 146–147.

[178] For discussions of the social scientific reasons for doubting eyewitness identifications and confessions under certain circumstances, and of the courts' traditional resistance but growing sympathy towards expert testimony informing jurors of those reasons, see Danielle E. Chojnacki, et al., An Empirical Basis for the Admission of Expert Testimony on False Confessions, 40 Ariz. St. L.J. 1 (2008); Richard A. Leo, False Confessions: Causes, Consequences, and Implications, J. Am. Acad. Psychiatry L. 332 (2009); Jacqueline McMurtrie, The Role of the Social Sciences in Preventing Wrongful Convictions, 42 Am. Crim. L. Rev. 1271 (2005); Jennifer L. Overbeck, Note, Beyond Admissibility: A Practical Look at the Use of Eyewitness Expert Testimony in Federal Courts, 80 N.Y.U. L. Rev. 1895 (2005); Edward Stein, The Admissibility of Expert Testimony about Cognitive Science Research on Eyewitness Identification, 2 Law, Probability & Risk 295 (2003); Gary L. Wells & Elizabeth F. Loftus, Eyewitness Memory for People and Events, in 11 Handbook of Psychology, Forensic Psychology 149 (Alan. M. Goldstein ed. 2002); Welsh White, False Confessions in Criminal Cases, 17 Crim. Just. 5 (Winter 2003); Richard Wise, et al., A Tripartite Solution to Eyewitness Error, 97 J. Crim. L. & Criminol. 807 (2007). See also John Schwartz,   Confessing   to   Crime,   but   Innocent,   N.Y.   Times,   Sept.   13,   2010, http://www.nytimes.com/2010/09/14/us/14confess.html?_r=1&ref=us.

inaccurate identifications, including stress caused by violent or threatening events, the lapse of even a comparatively short period of time between the event and the identification, reinforcement of the identification (as when a police officer tells a witness that she picked the "right guy" from a line-up), and racial and ethnic differences between the witness and the person she saw. A different set of circumstances has been found to predict false confession, especially a lengthy and aggressive interrogation, a young suspect, or a suspect who is mentally ill or impaired. One way to understand the traditional view barring expert testimony about the known foibles of identifiable categories of eyewitnesses and people who confess to crimes is that the testimony invites inferences that fall too far towards the propensity end of the spectrum, i.e., inferences from the frailty of human psychology in general rather than the uncertainty of a particular identification by a specific witness or a particular confession. Indeed, when expert testimony of this sort is offered and permitted, it is only as general scientific information that jurors might use to evaluate eyewitness identification testimony or confessions. The expert is not allowed to express an opinion about the accuracy of any particular identification or the truthfulness of any specific confession. Although this keeps the *expert* from saying that a particular person acted in accordance with the trait, it may invite the jury to draw that inference on its own—e.g., that a particular eyewitness falls into a category of people disposed to make inaccurate identifications and thus that she is more likely than otherwise to have done so on this occasion. Coupled with the (questionable) assumption that jurors know enough to evaluate eyewitness credibility and confessions on their own, this concern continues to lead many courts to exclude this type of expert testimony. The opposing view is that some particular types of errors of perception and memory in making identifications and confessions are so well understood by social scientists, yet so little understood by lay people, that expert evidence ought to be admitted to help jurors assess the evidence. The argument is that the inference the jury is invited to make—if the jurors conclude (unaided, in this respect, by the expert witness) that the particular witness or defendant falls into the relevant category—is sufficiently like an inference from a medical condition or habit to qualify as a nonpropensity judgment. The developing consensus among commentators, which is gradually gaining favor in the courts, at least with regard to eyewitness identification experts, is that such evidence should be admitted in cases in which an eyewitness identification or confession that is pivotal to the proof of the defendant's guilt was made under conditions known to be conducive to error.

———————

Problem V-33. Gene Bandy is charged with conspiring to distribute heroin. Two key government informers, Sydney Sharp and June Greedy, testify that they saw Bandy sitting in a car with several other defendants shortly before the other defendants delivered half a kilo of heroin to a warehouse where the police were waiting. Bandy wants to cross-examine Sharp and Greedy concerning their use of heroin. He wants to ask them: (1) whether they are or ever have been heroin addicts; (2) whether they had used heroin during the forty-eight hours prior to the time they allegedly saw him with the other defendants in the case; (3) whether they had used heroin at any time in the three days since the trial began; and (4) whether any drug agents have ever supplied them with heroin or the money to purchase it. **May Bandy ask these questions? If Sharp denies ever using heroin, may Bandy call one of Sharp's friends who will testify that Sharp is addicted to heroin; that Sharp took heroin (bought with money furnished by the police) on the morning that he claims to have seen Bandy in the car; and that Sharp injected heroin about twelve hours before he testified? If Greedy testifies that she was addicted to heroin but does not remember whether she had taken heroin about the time she saw Bandy in the car, may Bandy introduce one of Greedy's friends who will testify that Greedy had injected heroin on the morning of the day that she claims to have seen Bandy?**

Problem V-34. In the trial referred to in the preceding problem, Bandy's fiancée Jean Robinson is called by the defense to testify that she heard Bandy's codefendants talking about heroin, but that the topic never came up in front of Bandy, and Bandy himself never spoke of drugs. **May the codefendants impeach Robinson by showing that twelve years ago she was committed to a mental institution following her then-fiancé's death? May they show that one year ago she spent three weeks in a mental institution suffering from delusions, and that she has been under a psychiatrist's care ever since? What if, in the last-mentioned scenario, the alleged conspiracy was hatched fifteen months before trial?**

E. IMPEACHMENT BY RELIGIOUS BELIEFS

FRE 610 provides:

Evidence of a witness's religious beliefs or opinions is not admissible to attack or support the witness's credibility.

At ancient common law, only witnesses who were considered competent to take a Christian oath were permitted to testify. This religious qualification for testifying was never widely recognized in America, and would now be unconstitutional under the First and Fourteenth Amendments. A few states, however, have permitted impeachment by evidence that the witness does not believe in a God who punishes lying under oath, but most have long since abolished such impeachment, and FRE 610 expressly prohibits it.

McCormick explains the rejection of impeachment by religious beliefs on grounds of irrelevance: "[T]here is no basis for believing that the lack of faith in God's avenging wrath is today an indication of greater than average untruthfulness."[179]   As a factual proposition, McCormick's contention may be wrong. It may be that religious people are more truthful than average; and even a plausible argument that religion is associated with truthfulness is sufficient to meet the usual test for relevance. But notwithstanding that religious feelings are often powerful and may relate to truthfulness, there are several reasons why impeachment on this issue is properly forbidden. First, inferences based on propensities, including propensities grounded in religion, have limited probative value. Religion may seem to bear directly on the seriousness that people attach to oaths, but there are no systematic data to support this view; the religious hypocrite and the honest atheist are both familiar figures.   Second, allowing such impeachment offends the basic value, incorporated in Article VI of the Constitution [180] and reflected in the Establishment Clause of the First Amendment, that the government should not judge people by their religion. Third, evidence that a witness holds some particular religious beliefs, or is an adherent of some faiths, or lacks any religious faith at all, might prejudice the jury. Finally, many people consider matters of faith to be private, and the threat that they might have to discuss or defend their religious beliefs in court might deter them from coming forward to testify or embarrass or offend them if they do.

Like many of the rules we have discussed, FRE 610 does not make evidence—in this case, evidence of religious beliefs—inadmissible.   It merely forbids its use for a specific purpose—to attack or support a witness's general credibility. The same evidence might be admissible for a different purpose, subject to a balancing of probative weight against prejudicial impact. For example, the jury may be told that a witness is a member of the same sect as the accused, in order to suggest bias.

Problem V-35. Bill Miller is charged with murder in connection with the death of his former business partner. It is well known that there was considerable bitterness between the partners at the time their joint venture broke up, and the partner's death occurred soon enough after the termination of their association that Miller stood to collect a substantial sum from an insurance policy that each partner had taken out with the other as beneficiary. Miller wishes to introduce evidence that he is an active and devoted member of the Corinthians, a small, close-knit religious sect whose principal tenets include a commitment to

---

[179] McCormick § 46.

[180] "[B]ut no religious test shall ever be required as a Qualification to any office or public trust under the United States."

peacefulness and nonviolence. He also wishes to testify that except when he is ill he spends his Wednesday evenings from 6:00 p.m. until 9:00 p.m. at the Corinthian Church attending their Holy Wednesday religious services. Miller's partner was killed at 6:30 p.m. on a Wednesday. **Should this testimony by Miller be allowed?** Suppose that Miller does not testify and instead calls Saul Tarsus who testifies that he and Miller were fishing at a state park 100 miles from the murder scene when the murder occurred at 6:30 p.m. on a particular Wednesday. **May the prosecutor bring out on cross-examination, (1) that Tarsus is a member of Corinthians and that its teachings include the nonbinding effect of public oaths; (2) that Miller and Tarsus belong to the same Corinthians congregation; (3) that except when Tarsus is ill, he spends his Wednesday evenings from 6:00 p.m. until 9:00 p.m. attending services at the Corinthians Church?**

VI.   REHABILITATING IMPEACHED WITNESSES

Trials often turn on the relative credibility of opposing witnesses. To win this battle, trial lawyers work not only to undermine the credibility of the other side's witnesses but also to bolster the credibility of their own. Often they do this with evidence that is relevant for other purposes. Eliciting an expert witness's credentials is necessary to persuade the court that the witness should be permitted to offer an expert opinion, and is also a way of persuading the jury that the expert's testimony should be believed. Background information about lay witnesses may serve the same subsidiary function, as may evidence describing the vantage point from which a witness observed events or her peculiar reasons for remembering the matter well. Corroborating testimony from later witnesses simultaneously enhances the credibility of an earlier witness and provides additional evidence on the merits. More subtle cues such as dress, grooming, manner of speech and the use of honorific titles ("Dr.," "Sir," "Captain," etc.) may also affect a jury's judgment of a witness's credibility. Such aspects of testimony may seem inevitable and look unrehearsed, but experienced lawyers often work long hours with clients and witnesses to achieve an effective "natural" look.

For current purposes, these credibility-enhancing aspects of otherwise relevant evidence must be distinguished from evidence that has no function other than to shore up a witness's credibility. As with evidence offered to impeach credibility, evidence offered exclusively to support or (in the stock phrase) to "rehabilitate" credibility is subject to important limitations. The most basic restriction is that evidence that is admissible only to support a witness's credibility may not be offered until after her credibility has been attacked. FRE 608(a) makes this limitation explicit in the case of character evidence offered to support credibility: "evidence of truthful character is admissible only after the witness's character for truthfulness has been attacked." No similar provisions restrict other methods of supporting a witness's credibility, but the same limitation is understood to apply.[181] The logic of this rule is simple. If the testimony of one witness automatically became an occasion for another witness to testify to support the preceding witness's credibility, trials might never end. Moreover, if a witness's credibility is not attacked, evidence offered to support her credibility is likely to be a waste of time.

Matters are different once a witness's credibility has been impeached. Although impeachment enables the jury to learn important facts about the witness and her relation to the parties, it may be as one-sided as untested direct examination. The information used to discredit a witness may not be as well-established as the cross-examiner's confident questioning suggests. As a result, explanation and rebuttal may be necessary to place impeachment evidence in its proper context. The rules governing rehabilitation accordingly must be sufficiently flexible to achieve this goal while still avoiding needless waste of time. Usually, rehabilitation must respond directly to a form of impeachment that has already taken place. A witness who has been impeached with evidence of poor vision may be rehabilitated with evidence that her eyesight was corrected with contact lenses, but not with evidence that she has sharp hearing, or acute memory. This commonsense rule becomes slightly more complicated in two contexts: impeachment by character evidence and by prior statements.

A witness impeached by evidence of bad character—whether in the form of reputation or opinion, conviction of a crime or prior bad acts—may be rehabilitated by evidence of good character. This is true even when the witness has denied the prior bad acts on cross-examination, given the assumption that a witness's denial will not stop jurors from taking the accusation as true. FRE 608(a) limits evidence supporting a witness's character for truthfulness to testimony that the witness has a good reputation for honesty and to opinions that the witness is generally honest. Under FRE 608(b)(2), specific instances of honest behavior may be brought out only on cross-examination of a character witness who provides *unfavorable* reputation or opinion testimony about a prior

---

[181] Turncoat coconspirators and informants often testify for the government under agreements providing inducements (e.g., the prosecutor's promise to recommend leniency in pending criminal proceedings in return for the testimony). Such agreements typically admonish the witness to tell the truth and threaten to void the agreement and prosecute the witness in the event of perjury. Knowing the defense will use the agreement to claim that the witness has a strong self-interest in testifying favorably to the government, prosecutors try to "pull the sting" by revealing the agreement and emphasizing its "tell the truth" clauses on direct examination. Some federal circuit courts bar direct-examination references to those clauses, as bolstering in advance of an attack on credibility. Most courts allow the practice (subject to FRE 403 limits on the amount of emphasis given to the matter) on the grounds that "pulling the sting" doesn't constitute bolstering and that revealing the "tell the truth" clauses is necessary to provide a full picture. The risk in this situation is that the jury will understand the agreement to mean not only that the government is vouching for the witness's honesty (an especially strong form of bolstering) but also that the government has inside information about the truth and can be sure that what the witness says is true.

witness, or on redirect examination of a favorable character witness who has been impeached on cross-examination with specific instances of dishonesty on the part of the witness whose credibility is at issue.

If, instead, the witness was impeached by evidence suggesting bias, but not bad character, then, in general, only evidence rebutting the accusation of bias is admissible as rehabilitation. Sometimes, however, forms of impeachment that do not directly impugn the witness's character for honesty will have that effect indirectly. FRE 608(a) recognizes this possibility by allowing character rehabilitation when a witness's character for truthfulness "has been attacked," without limiting the triggering forms of attack to testimony about the witness's bad character for truthfulness. For example, evidence that the witness took a bribe is admissible to show bias, but also suggests that she is dishonest by disposition—as does evidence of inconsistent statements, or even sometimes a harsh and skeptical cross-examination or directly contradictory testimony by other witnesses. In such circumstances, the better (though not universal) rule is to treat these events as attacks on the witness's character and to permit rehabilitation through reputation or opinion testimony that the witness has a good character for truthfulness.[182]

Rehabilitation by prior consistent statements is governed by its own set of rules. Evidence sometimes suggests that a witness developed a motive to lie at some particular point in time prior to trial. For example, there may be evidence that on a particular date a witness was bribed to give favorable testimony; or that a once neutral witness developed a friendship with a party sometime after witnessing an accident. In common law jurisdictions, evidence that the witness made statements *consistent* with her testimony *before* her alleged motive to lie arose was admissible to show that she had told the same story that she testified to at trial before the alleged incentive to falsify came into existence. In most common law jurisdictions, prior consistent statements could be used only to rehabilitate a witness's credibility by rebutting express or implied charges of recent fabrication or of improper influence or motive, and then only if they predated the alleged incentive to deceive. FRE 801(d)(1)(B) makes prior consistent statements that rebut an express or implied charge of recent fabrication admissible *not only* to rehabilitate the witness's credibility *but also* as independent evidence of the matters asserted in the prior statements, and the rule says nothing about when the statements need to have been made.[183] In *United States v. Tome*,[184]

---

[182] See, e.g., United States v. Bonner, 302 F.3d 776 (7th Cir. 2002) (claim in defendant's opening statement that a witness was testifying for the government in hopes of securing VA benefits qualifies as an attack on character for truthfulness and permits the government to introduce evidence of the witness's good character).

[183] Apart from FRE 801(d)(1)(B), most prior consistent statements are inadmissible hearsay when offered for the truth of the matter asserted. See Chapter Six, Section IV.D., pp. 757–770. Unlike most rules admitting hearsay, this one hardly matters because if the prior statement is

the Tenth Circuit Court of Appeals read FRE 801(d)(1)(B) to permit the admission of consistent statements made after the motive to fabricate had arisen, as substantive evidence as well as rehabilitation, finding that despite their timing they had some tendency to rebut the alleged improper motive. The Supreme Court reversed,[185] concluding that the drafters of FRE 801(d)(1)(B) intended to maintain the prevailing common law practice limiting the admissibility of prior consistent statements to those made before a motive to fabricate arose.

A few jurisdictions admit a witness's prior consistent statements for rehabilitation in almost all situations in which prior inconsistent statements have been used for impeachment. The theory is that the existence of the prior consistent statements may counter the inference of untrustworthiness raised by prior inconsistent statements even if the consistent statements were made after the inconsistent statements and after a motivation to lie allegedly arose. Most courts reject this position on the ground that once it's established that a witness has given two inconsistent descriptions of an event, adding a third statement does little or nothing to help the jury evaluate his testimony.

The best reasoned approach is to permit a prior consistent statement whenever it tends to rebut a specific attack on the witness's credibility, subject to FRE 403. For example, if the opposing party claims that a witness's memory is faulty because the event in question occurred years before the trial, the court should admit evidence of consistent statements made near the time of that event, whether or not the witness ever developed a motive to lie. This evidence ought to be admissible, moreover, whether the challenge to the witness's memory is made by introducing a prior inconsistent statement, by skeptical questioning on cross-examination, by claims made in the opposing party's opening statement, or by other means.[186]

Problem V-36. Portia Poole, an avid Red Socks fan, sues Daphne Dayne, an avid Yankees fans, claiming that Dayne clobbered her with a beer bottle at the ball park during a dispute over an umpire's call. Poole's first witness is David Rhombus who describes the argument over the umpire's

---

consistent with the witness's in-court testimony, the latter may always be relied on as substantive evidence if the jury concludes on the basis of both statements that the witness is credible. The rule may make a difference when a statement that is admissible as a prior consistent statement says something more than the testimony it corroborates.

[184] 3 F.3d 342 (10th Cir. 1993).

[185] 513 U.S. 150 (1995).

[186] The Supreme Court's *Tome* decision does not address this issue; it merely holds that prior consistent statements that are offered for the truth of the matter asserted, under FRE 801(d)(1)(B), must rebut a charge of recent fabrication and must have been made before the motive to fabricate arose. *Tome* does not deal with prior consistent statements that are addressed to other issues and used to rehabilitate only.

call and testifies that the argument ended when Dayne hit Poole over the head with a beer bottle. Poole's second witness is Clemons Rocket, a business associate of Rhombus, who is prepared to testify that in his opinion Rhombus is "as honest as they come." **What ruling on Dayne's objection to Rocket's testimony? Would it make a difference if Dayne's lawyer had brought out on cross-examination of Rhombus that he is Poole's brother-in-law? That Poole paid him $2000 in "expenses" to travel the 40 miles to town to testify? That Rhombus told a business associate the day after the alleged incident that "I rushed my sister-in-law to the hospital yesterday after she got a gash in her head, but I didn't see how it happened"? What if Dayne's lawyer cross-examined Rhombus about understating his income on the previous year's tax returns, which Rhombus denied?** Instead, suppose that Dayne did not cross-examine Rhombus, that Poole rested her case after Rhombus testified and that Dayne's only witness is Divad Submohr. And suppose that Submohr testifies that she saw the argument over the disputed umpire's call, that Dayne never hit or tried to hit Poole with a beer bottle and that the argument ended when Poole, who had been drinking, swung at Dayne with her fist, only to slip and fall on the concrete bleachers and injure herself. **May Rocket now testify as described above?**

––––––––––

"Isn't it true that you did not love the victim, as you claim, but, in point of fact, feigned affection for the sole purpose of obtaining tuna fish?"

VII.   THE ETHICS OF IMPEACHMENT

Most witnesses testify honestly and accurately. Nonetheless, most important witnesses are cross-examined with visible displays of skepticism, or pointedly impeached, in an effort to persuade the jury to disbelieve them.   In other words, lawyers routinely try to discredit witnesses they believe—or ought to believe—are telling the truth. Sometimes a lawyer will attack a witness even though she *knows* the witness is telling the truth because her client has told her the same thing, in confidence. In either situation, impeachment raises significant ethical issues.

This problem can occur in any trial. Even when all information is shared by both sides, skillful attorneys can use undisputed evidence— prior felonies, inconsistent statements, a motive to lie—or simply careful, aggressive questioning—to discredit witnesses who are in fact telling the truth. The problem is aggravated, however, when the parties possess private information about the merits of the case.   In civil cases, this possibility is limited by each party's ability to compel the testimony of the other party and by discovery rules requiring each side to disclose facts that may permit the other side to corroborate or rehabilitate the testimony of its own witnesses. Even so, attorneys in civil cases often know things their opponents do not know, and sometimes can impeach truthful witnesses more successfully than would be possible if they shared their knowledge. This problem is more pronounced in criminal cases. There, the privilege against self-incrimination and the attorney-client privilege (which favor the defense), chronic imbalances in resources (which generally favor the government), and the limited nature of discovery [187] combine to create a context in which lawyers on both sides know things they know the other side will never learn. This enables them to impeach witnesses who might look far better if both sides put all their cards on the table.

These possibilities are troubling.   They suggest that truthful witnesses may be harassed or embarrassed. This is bad in itself, and it may deter them or others from testifying or from reporting serious

---

[187] Under the due process rule of Brady v. Maryland, 373 U.S. 83 (1963) and United States v. Bagley, 473 U.S. 667 (1985), prosecutors have a constitutional obligation to disclose exculpatory evidence to the defense—including evidence that could be used to impeach government witnesses—if there is a reasonable probability that disclosure would produce a different outcome. This standard gives prosecutors considerable leeway to withhold evidence that, while exculpatory, is not unambiguously supportive of a verdict in favor of the defendant, see, e.g., Strickler v. Greene, 527 U.S. 263 (1999), and, regrettably, prosecutors often call close questions in favor of nondisclosure, see, e.g., *id.*; Kyles v. Whitley, 514 U.S. 419 (1995). Defense lawyers have no similar disclosure obligation under the Constitution, although increasingly American jurisdictions provide for mutual discovery in criminal cases by statute or rule of court. Rule 3.8(d) of the Model Rules of Professional Conduct places prosecutors under a considerably stricter ethical obligation to "make timely disclosure to the defense of all evidence or information known to the prosecutor that *tends to negate* the guilt of the accused or mitigates the offense . . . ." (emphasis added).

misconduct in the future. Also, and more important in the context of the particular case, the jury may disbelieve truthful witnesses and reach the wrong verdict. But there are equally serious problems with rules that would prohibit lawyers from challenging witnesses whose testimony they believe or ought to believe. Rules that focus on what lawyers know or believe are bound to be difficult to apply and enforce. As a result, they will inevitably produce arbitrary and unfair consequences. Some lawyers will capitalize on their willingness to bend the rules; others might be investigated or punished for vigorously defending unpopular clients even though they played entirely by the book. Worse, such rules might discourage clients from revealing damaging information to their lawyers, for fear that if the lawyer knows too much she will be less effective in court. But a lawyer who is not fully informed will usually be a less effective advocate for the client at trial, and will always be less effective in other crucial contexts—in particular, in plea bargaining and settlement negotiations. Finally, lawyers who know they may face serious sanctions if they challenge the other side's witnesses too vigorously may grow timid in cross-examination, even when they *don't* believe an adverse witness. This would undermine the strong testing of evidence on which our adversarial system depends. These last two considerations led Professor Monroe Freedman to conclude in a famous article that "when a lawyer fails to cross-examine [a truthful witness] only because his client, placing confidence in the lawyer, has been candid with him, the basis for such confidence and candor collapses. Our legal system cannot tolerate such a result."[188]

Professor Cookie Ridolfi, a former criminal defense lawyer, reaches a similar conclusion. She focuses on rape cases in which consent is the defense and in which a vigorous, skeptical cross-examination of the victim is both particularly important to the defendant and particularly likely to humiliate the witness, and will perhaps deter others from reporting similar crimes:

> Some defense attorneys believe that effective cross-examination can be done in a way that does not demean the complainant. I disagree. No matter what tone of voice is used or how politely the questions are put, a good cross-examination must still ultimately demonstrate that the complaining witness is a liar.
>
> Moreover, if the defense attorney is respectful of the complainant's feelings, she lends credibility to the prosecution's case. The more successful the defense counsel is at cutting away at the complainant's credibility, the more effective the defense and, necessarily, the more damaged the complainant is. An attorney who is concerned about a complainant's feelings

---

[188] Monroe H. Freedman, Professional Responsibility of the Criminal Defense Lawyer: The Three Hardest Questions, 64 Mich. L. Rev. 1469, 1474–75 (1966).

necessarily compromises her client's right to an advocate with exclusive loyalty.[189]

Professor Ridolfi describes a case from her own practice. She represented a man charged with the assault and rape of a woman who was his dance partner at a club featuring provocative "live dancing." The victim alleged that the defendant broke into her home, dragged her to the basement and brutally beat and raped her. The defendant claimed the sex was consensual and that it was interrupted by the woman's husband, who beat her. The jury acquitted, apparently in part because some jurors felt that Ridolfi would not have fought so hard for her client unless he was innocent. Afterwards, the defendant was arrested and convicted in two later cases of rape and assault that resembled the alleged attack in Professor Ridolfi's trial.[190] Was it ethical for Ridolfi to sharply cross-examine the victim in the first case? Should the defense lawyer in the later cases have done so, despite her almost inevitable belief that the defendant was a violent rapist *and* a repeat offender?

The organized bar's strongest official statement on the subject is in a nonbinding set of standards for defense lawyers. It states:

(a) The interrogation of all witnesses should be conducted fairly, objectively, and with due regard for the dignity and legitimate privacy of the witness, and without seeking to intimidate or humiliate the witness unnecessarily. Proper cross-examination can be conducted without violating rules of decorum.

(b) Defense Counsel's belief or knowledge that the witness is telling the truth does not preclude cross-examination.

(c) Defense counsel should not ask a question which implies the existence of a factual predicate for which good faith is lacking.[191]

Former Federal District Judge Marvin Frankel proposed a different rule, which would require civil and criminal lawyers to:

> Question witnesses with a purpose and design to elicit the whole truth, including particularly supplementary and qualifying

---

[189] Cookie Ridolfi, Statement on Representing Rape Defendants, in Deborah L. Rhode, Professional Responsibility: Ethics by the Pervasive Method 206 (2d ed. 1998).

[190] Id.

[191] American Bar Association, Standards Relating to the Administration of Criminal Justice, The Defense Function, Standard 4–7.6 (3d ed. 1993). Language in the first edition of the Standards discouraging defense lawyers from using cross-examination "to discredit or undermine" truthful witnesses was weakened in the second edition and entirely discarded in the third edition. These same standards, however, forbid a prosecutor to use cross-examination to discredit a truthful witness. Id., The Prosecution Function, Standard 3–5.7(b).

matters that render evidence already given more accurate, intelligible, or fair than it otherwise would be.[192]

After much consideration, the American Bar Association came up with the following provision in its most recent set of ethical rules governing professional conduct:

> In representing a client, a lawyer shall not use means that have no substantial purpose other than to embarrass, delay, or burden a third person, or use methods of obtaining evidence that violate the legal rights of such a person.[193]

Notice that the American Bar Association rule makes no reference to Judge Frankel's concern for "the whole truth."

In our view, truth ought to be a matter of great concern at trial, always. But how that concern is manifested should depend on whether the case is civil or criminal and, if criminal, whether the cross-examiner is the defense attorney or the prosecutor. In criminal trials, a paramount objective is to minimize the one kind of deviation from "the whole truth" that we fear most—the conviction of innocent defendants. The most important rule aimed at that goal is the constitutional requirement that the government prove the defendant's guilt beyond a reasonable doubt. For that requirement to be meaningful, the state must face determined opposition. The policies underlying the Fifth Amendment privilege against self-incrimination and the Sixth Amendment right to confront adverse witnesses permit—indeed, require—criminal defense attorneys to put the state to its proof and to test that proof vigorously. Vigorous testing includes the tenacious (which is not to say abusive or disrespectful) cross-examination of prosecution witnesses. That sort of cross-examination would be less common if defense lawyers were required to censor their questions to keep them consistent with their information or their beliefs about the underlying events. By encouraging vigorous challenges to the state's case, the approach we propose protects individual liberty, discourages oppression, and encourages government investigators to search for evidence energetically but without conscripting the defendant and his lawyer in that process. This approach also may allow some guilty defendants to go free. But that is a cost we have to pay if we wish to keep innocent defendants from being convicted.

A different set of policies governs in civil cases. There, the privilege against self-incrimination is replaced by a mutual right to compel testimony from the other party and to discover whatever information the opponent has. There is no Sixth Amendment right to cross-examine adverse witnesses in civil cases; the likelihood of systematic oppression of

---

[192] Marvin Frankel, The Search for Truth: An Umpireal View, 123 U. Pa. L. Rev. 1031, 1058 (1975).

[193] American Bar Association, Model Rules of Professional Conduct MR 4.4(a) (2008).

individuals by large institutions is lower; and pro-plaintiff and pro-defendant errors are treated similarly, unlike wrongful convictions, which are far worse than wrongful acquittals. In the civil context, the ability to cross-examine a witness whom the examiner believes (or should believe) is telling the truth on the basis of information that is not known to the opposing side achieves an advantage that is not needed to protect individual liberty or to counter chronic imbalances of resources. In our view, a lawyer in a civil case should not cross-examine a witness when she believes, or reasonably should believe, that the witness is telling the truth, if the bases for that belief have not been disclosed to the other side and are not available for use in rehabilitating the witness. The case for such a restriction is even stronger for criminal prosecutors because errors that may be produced by prosecutorial overreaching are the kind we most want to avoid: erroneous criminal convictions.[194]

These views are controversial. They are likely to please no one, save perhaps a segment of the criminal defense bar. In thinking about how you would resolve this difficult problem—and, particularly, about the extent to which it ought to be treated as a problem for the profession to address rather than an issue for each individual lawyer—consider how Professor Ridolfi resolved it for herself, in rape cases:

> I remain firm in my belief that every person, no matter what the charge or circumstances of the case, deserves dedicated and competent counsel. I also know that some men are victims of a woman's false charges of rape and agree strongly that this defense [consent] must be pursued when a [rape] defendant makes this claim. I am not critical of any other woman who chooses to defend a man charged with rape. But for all of the reasons I have given, I would find it difficult to again be in the position where I would have to challenge a woman's claim of rape knowing that what she claims may be true.[195]

As Professor Ridolfi herself suggests, and as we discuss in the next section, rape cases may present a context in which special rules and practices should apply.

Problem V–37. Alma Goncalves is on trial for her life, charged with murdering Cal Cote, a restaurant owner, by shooting him in the chest with a .22 caliber pistol as he was entering the men's room of his restaurant just after closing time. Cote's wallet was never found.

----

[194] For this reason, among others, it is widely recognized that in criminal cases, the prosecution—unlike the defense—has an obligation not merely to represent its side but also to see that justice is done. See, e.g., ABA Standards, supra, note 191, The Prosecution Function, Standard 3–1.2(c): "The duty of the prosecutor is to seek justice, not merely to convict." See also supra, p. 472, note 187 and p. 474, note 191.

[195] Ridolfi, supra, note 189, at 222–23.

Eugenia Morales, a waitress at the restaurant, testifies that when she left the restaurant before the murder occurred, Cote was locking the front door for the night and that, at the time, only Cote, Goncalves and two truck drivers were in the restaurant. Two truck drivers testify that they left the restaurant five minutes after Morales did, when only Cote and a woman customer were present. An acquaintance of Goncalves testifies that he had recently seen her carrying a .22 caliber pistol. When Cote's body was discovered, the front door to the restaurant was locked but the back door was unlocked. Goncalves tells her lawyer in confidence that she shot Cote with a pistol she carries for self-protection when he sexually attacked her as she was about to go in the women's room. She then panicked and fled, grabbing Cote's wallet as an afterthought. Doubting that a jury would believe the extenuating parts of Goncalves's story, and knowing her testimony would be impeached by prior felony convictions, Goncalves and her lawyer decide she should not testify. Instead, the lawyer will rely on Raul Huerta, who attends church with Goncalves and was going into a convenience store next to the restaurant about five minutes after the truck drivers say they left. Huerta will testify that he saw Goncalves walk out of the restaurant, that the two chatted for several minutes before she walked to her car and drove away, and that she was calm and composed and wasn't carrying a wallet. The only other witness is Enid Otero, who testifies for the prosecution that Goncalves told her she killed Cote. **May defense counsel ethically impeach Otero with her record of felony convictions for sexually abusing her young son, operating a house of prostitution, perjury and cocaine dealing? Would it matter that Otero's convictions all are eight years old or older (though admissible under FRE 609), and all are unknown in the local community to which Otero recently moved to "start over?" Would it matter that the defense lawyer knows Otero is telling the truth because Goncalves confidentially admitted telling Otero about the killing? Would it matter if Goncalves instead confided in her lawyer that she planned the robbery and killed Cote to eliminate a witness? Should a defense lawyer in this situation discourage his client from telling him what really happened? Would it matter if the lawyer knows the prosecutor could effectively rehabilitate Otero but is too lazy and incompetent to do so? Is it ethical for defense counsel to present Huerta's testimony? Would it be ethical for the lawyer to cross-examine Otero about a damaging motive to lie based on information Goncalves's brother supplied that the lawyer suspects, but does not know, is false? If the ethical rules permit Otero to be impeached in these ways, would you do so? Would any of your answers change if Cote's surviving children instead were suing Goncalves for wrongful death?**

VIII.   CHARACTER AND CREDIBILITY IN SEXUAL ASSAULT AND CHILD MOLESTATION CASES

A. HISTORICAL INTRODUCTION

"Where rape is involved the rules of the game are simply different."[196]

The seriousness of the crime of rape cannot be overstated. Even compared to other violent crimes, rape is especially brutal, degrading and terrifying; the experience may haunt the victim for years. Many jurisdictions punish only deliberate homicide more severely. At the same time, rape is an unusual crime of violence in that it is defined in part by acts of sexual intercourse which, if both parties consent, are not criminal at all and are enjoyed by millions of people every day. Although the definition of rape is currently in a state of flux, it remains the case in many jurisdictions that the line that separates legal sex from sexual assault is free and intelligent consent.[197] In these jurisdictions, a defendant may only be convicted of rape if the jury finds both that the victim did not consent to sexual intercourse, and that the defendant intended to have sex with the victim without her consent. This allows an accused to counter a rape charge by showing that the woman[198] did consent, or by showing that he mistakenly thought she did and thus lacked the *mens rea* required for conviction. In most of these jurisdictions a defense of mistaken consent requires a mistake that was both honest and reasonable; in a few states, however, an honest mistake suffices to acquit, even if it was unreasonable. Unlike trials for other crimes, therefore, which usually focus on the defendant's conduct or on the defendant's state of mind, rape trials frequently turn on the *victim's* intentions—Did she consent or didn't she?—or on the defendant's interpretation of the victim's intentions, or on both.

Many people argue that the substantive law of sexual assault should be reformed to reduce or eliminate the focus on consent and on the victim's acts and mental state. Some jurisdictions have in fact changed their rape laws, and more may follow. In the meantime, trials must often be conducted under existing, consent- and victim-focused statutes. Considering the stakes, moreover, they need to be handled very carefully.

---

[196] Vivian Berger, Man's Trial, Woman's Tribulation: Rape Cases in the Courtroom, 77 Colum. L. Rev. 1, 10 (1977).

[197] In some circumstances consent or lack of consent is presumed. At common law, for example, a woman was usually presumed to consent to sex with her husband; as a matter of law, therefore, a man typically could not rape his wife. By now, marital exceptions to rape have largely been abandoned. In all jurisdictions, consent is immaterial in cases of sexual relations with children below a certain age—so-called statutory rape—because such children are presumed incapable of intelligent consent.

[198] Although men as well as women are raped, the great majority of rape trials involve charges that a man attacked a woman. In the discussion that follows, we focus on charges of heterosexual rape of women who are legally competent to consent to sexual intercourse. Most of the important evidentiary issues arise in such cases.

A mistaken rape conviction can ruin a man's life just as surely as being raped can ruin a woman's life (especially if the perpetrator goes free). As a result, the questions of consent and intent must be thoroughly explored in any case in which they are legitimately at issue, which creates difficult and unusual evidentiary problems. Historically, common law courts have dealt with these problems badly. The special rules we discuss in the two subsections that follow were intended to correct various aspects of this unhappy situation.

The special evidentiary rules in sexual assault cases are extremely important in their own right. They also raise, in a different context, the questions of character and credibility that the rest of this chapter addresses. Because the existing rules often resolve those questions differently from the evidence rules that apply in other cases, these special rules provide a useful opportunity to reconsider more generally the proper treatment of character and credibility in court.

The special rules that are the main subject of this section were developed recently to *protect* women who complain of rape. Before we get to those rules, it is important to recognize that rape trials have always been run under a different set of rules from those that have governed other criminal trials. Until the last thirty-five or forty years, however, most of those extraordinary rules reflected *mistrust* of women who complained of rape. For example, despite the rule in other criminal cases that "the testimony of a single witness [will] . . . legally suffice as evidence upon which the jury may found a verdict,"[199] some jurisdictions used to insist in rape cases that the testimony of the complaining witness be corroborated. Likewise, in many jurisdictions judges used to instruct jurors to be skeptical of rape charges. One common version of a cautionary instruction, based loosely on a passage from Sir Matthew Hale's eighteenth century *History of the Pleas of the Crown*, was used in California until 1975: "A charge [of rape] is one which is easily made and, once made, difficult to defend against, even if the person accused is innocent. Therefore the law requires that you examine the testimony of the female person named in the information with caution."[200] No similar instructions were ever used in trials of other felonies, and no reliable empirical support for the empirical claim in instructions such as these was ever developed.

What, then, led to this uncharacteristic skepticism about complaining witnesses when rape was the charge? Clearly gender bias was at work. The precise nature of that bias has been described in a number of ways, but one condition for its operation is clear: These rules

---

[199] 7 Wigmore § 2034, at 343.

[200] California Jury Instructions, Crim. No. 10.22 (3d ed. 1970), quoted in People v. Rincon-Pineda, 14 Cal.3d 864, 871, 123 Cal.Rptr. 119, 538 P.2d 247, 252 (1975) (rejecting use of this jury charge for future trials).

were written when judges, lawyers, commentators and jurors were all male, and in considering rape—unlike other charges—could only imagine themselves as defendants and not as victims. The upshot of the bias was a disposition to overprotect male defendants and to treat female victims as unreasonable and unstable, especially on matters of sex. In the 1930's, for example, Wigmore cited the claims of a prominent contemporary male psychiatrist that the "psychic complexes" of "errant young girls and women coming before the courts" led them frequently to "contriv[e] false charges of sexual offenses by men" as a result of women's "probably universal" "fantasies of being raped."[201]

Another hallmark of rape trials was the cross-examination of the complainant on her sexual history. The rules of evidence that now prohibit such questioning are the subject of the next subsection. As a prelude, however, it is useful to see the prior practice in context. First, although questioning about other sexual experiences was a particularly humiliating form of cross-examination of rape victims, it was probably never the most common. Much the same effect, or worse, was achieved simply by questioning the victim about the sexual encounter that was the basis for the prosecution—insinuating at each step of the way that the victim invited or willingly cooperated in the defendant's acts, and that the victim "enjoyed it."[202]

Second, this line of attack used to work with jurors, women as well as men.[203] Harry Kalven, Jr. and Hans Zeisel's classic study, *The American Jury*, which was published in 1966, includes forty-two "simple" rape trials—cases involving a single nonstranger assailant, with no proof of violence apart from the alleged rape.[204] The juries convicted the defendants of rape in only three of the cases; the trial judges would have done so in twenty-one of them. Kalven and Zeisel found that jurors were reluctant or unwilling to convict defendants of rape, even where there was strong evidence that the victim had not consented to sex, if they thought the victim was promiscuous or that she had "invited" the attack by flirtatious or seductive behavior. Given this extraordinarily low conviction rate, and considering how extremely unpleasant the process was for the victim, it is no surprise that most rapes were never reported to the police. (Notice, by the way, that the empirical evidence Kalven and Zeisel developed directly contradicts the assumptions by Hale and Wigmore that are discussed above.)

The historic mistreatment of the complaining witness, however, is not the only way that rape cases have differed from other criminal

---

[201] 3 A Wigmore § 924A, at 736, 744, quoting Letter by Dr. Karl Menninger dated Sept. 5, 1933.

[202] See, e.g., United States v. Thorne (D.D.C. 1969), quoted in Berger, supra note 196, at 13.

[203] See Barbara A. Babcock, et al., Sexual Discrimination and the Law 828 (1975).

[204] Kalven & Zeisel, supra, note 123, at 253.

prosecutions. The rules of evidence that apply to the *defendant's* sexual propensities have also been different. In some jurisdictions, courts or legislatures apply specific exemptions from the propensity rule in rape cases for evidence of the defendant's "lustful disposition." Until recently—and in most state jurisdictions even today—these explicit exceptions have been restricted to other incidents of sexual behavior by the criminal defendant with the victim in the case at bar, or to other instances of what courts considered aberrant or "unnatural" sexual behavior. In 1994, Congress adopted a similar but more expansive approach by enacting FREs 413–415, which make any evidence of prior similar offenses admissible against criminal and civil defendants for all purposes in cases involving charges of sexual assault and child molestation; these rules are discussed in Subsection C below. But even in jurisdictions that have never had "lustful disposition" or other explicit exceptions, courts in rape cases have frequently bent the propensity rule beyond recognition, usually by admitting evidence of prior sexual misconduct by the defendant to show "intent" or for some other supposed nonpropensity purpose. See infra, p. 503, note 248. The impulse may have been to give the prosecutor the means to attack the defendant in the same way the defense attorney was allowed to attack the victim. The upshot was that until the 1970's the propensity rule was often a dead letter in rape trials, for both sides.

Finally, there is the question of race. Racial issues pervade the American system of criminal justice, but few—perhaps none—are as incendiary and invidious as the racist stereotype of black males as sexual aggressors who prey on white women.[205] In fact, the great majority of rapes are intra-racial; most rape victims are attacked by men of their acquaintance and of their own race.[206] Nonetheless, preoccupation with inter-racial rape by black men produced extraordinary patterns of discrimination. Until 1977, for example, the death penalty was authorized for rape in a dozen states, all in the South;[207] in practice, however, it was reserved almost exclusively for black men who were convicted of raping white women.[208]

In general, American courts rarely discuss race explicitly as a factor in criminal behavior. Rape, as usual, has been the exception. Well into the middle of the twentieth century, reported opinions described race as evidence of rape. In some cases courts held that juries may rely on race as evidence of the defendant's intent to commit a sexual assault, or as

---

[205] See Jennifer Wriggins, Rape, Racism and the Law, 6 Harv. Women's L.J. 103 (1983).

[206] See id. at 114 & n.71.

[207] See Coker v. Georgia, 433 U.S. 584, 593 & n. 6 (1977).

[208] See Samuel R. Gross & Robert Mauro, Patterns of Death, 37 Stan. L. Rev. 27, 38 n.47 (1984); Marvin Wolfgang & Mark Riedel, Rape, Racial Discrimination and the Death Penalty, in Hugo A. Bedau & Chester M. Pierce, eds., Capital Punishment in the United States 99–121 (1976).

evidence that the alleged victim did not consent to sex with the defendant:

> [W]hite women in this part of the United States do not willingly submit to sexual intercourse with negroes, whatever may be their conduct in other parts, and when a negro expresses a desire for sexual intercourse with a white woman, it leads to the conclusion that he entertains a criminal intent, only awaiting an opportunity for the intended assault.[209]

In other cases, courts approved the use of evidence of prior inter-racial sexual attacks by creating a racially specific end run around the propensity rule:

> [T]he evidence of other acts was admitted not to indicate the defendant's bad character generally or disposition to commit crime, but to show his peculiar and unnatural lustful desire for white women as bearing on the intent with which he assaulted the white woman in that case and as tending to negative any other but the rape intent.[210]

The cases quoted above are old, and any judge who wrote today as these judges did then would certainly be reversed and perhaps be impeached. But old prejudices die hard and new ones are easily born. To judge by the uneven vigor with which crimes are prosecuted and sentences meted out, it is still the case in many areas of the country that crimes with white victims tend to be regarded as more serious than equally heinous crimes with black victims, and black on white crime is often disproportionately highlighted in discussions of the "crime problem."[211] Moreover, despite constitutional law barring the practice, examples continue to emerge of government attorneys prosecuting black defendants who use peremptory challenges to strike all blacks from juries for no discernible reason other than their race.[212] In particular, race continues to be a disturbing background factor in rape cases. For example, as late as 1989–2003, rapes of white victims by black offenders accounted for 5% to 6% of all rapes in the United States, but nearly half of all exonerations of innocent rape defendants who were convicted in error—a disproportion that is probably due largely to the high risk of error in eyewitness identifications across racial lines and may reflect

---

[209] White v. State, 137 Tex.Crim. 481, 131 S.W.2d 968, 970 (Tex.Ct.Crim.App. 1939). See Story v. State, 178 Ala. 98, 59 So. 480, 482 (Ala. 1912); Kelley v. State, 1 Ala.App. 133, 135, 56 So. 15, 16 (1910); Patrick v. State, 70 Ga.App. 530, 29 S.E.2d 103, 105 (Ga.Ct.App.1944); McCullough v. State, 11 Ga.App. 612, 76 S.E. 393 (1912).

[210] McKenzie v. State, 250 Ala. 178, 180, 33 So.2d 488, 491 (1947).

[211] See, e.g., David Cole, No Equal Justice: Race and Class in the American Criminal Justice System (1998); Marc Mauer, Race to Incarcerate (2006); Randall Kennedy, Race, Crime and the Law (1997).

[212] See Miller-El v. Dretke, 545 U.S. 231 (2005).

other biases as well.[213] In rape cases like *Olden v. Kentucky*, which you will encounter in Chapter 7, the importance of race to what happened is obvious and acknowledged.

Of course, stereotypes and prejudice affect others besides African-Americans, and the point is not to treat one form of bias as more serious than another. Rather it is to remind you that while recognizing that rape shield laws were enacted to protect women and the justice system from offensive stereotypes and degrading cross-examination, we must also recognize that rape defendants have legitimate interests that call for protection. In some circumstances prejudices and stereotypes besides those directed at women victims come into play and lead jurors to disbelieve honest stories of consent or of innocence and misidentification. As is so often the case, the search for justice is a search for balance.

B. RAPE SHIELD RULES[214]

As we have noted, until the 1970s, evidence of a rape victim's sexual history was often admissible for its supposed bearing on her consent and her credibility. For example, a 1970 California pattern jury instruction stated:

> Evidence was received for the purpose of showing that the female person named in the information was a woman of unchaste character.
>
> A woman of unchaste character can be the victim of a forcible rape, but it may be inferred that a woman who has previously consented to sexual intercourse would be more likely to consent again.
>
> Such evidence may be considered by you only for such bearing as it may have on the question of whether or not she gave her consent to the alleged sexual act and in judging her credibility.[215]

Under this instruction, evidence of prior consensual sex could be used to support two inferences. The first—that unchastity suggests consent—was widely accepted. As one court put it, "No impartial mind can resist the conclusion that a female who had been in the recent habit of illicit intercourse with others will not be so likely to resist as one who is

---

[213] Samuel Gross et al., Exonerations in the Unites States, 1989–2003, 95 J. Crim. L. & Criminology 523, 547–48 (2005).

[214] Some of the most troublesome issues encountered in applying rape shield rules implicate the Confrontation and Compulsory Process Clauses of the Sixth Amendment. These issues are discussed in Chapter Seven. The case of Olden v. Kentucky, 488 U.S. 227 (1988), discussed in Chapter Seven, Section II.E., pp. 866–869, is particularly relevant to this discussion. See also infra, text on pp. 486–496 accompanying notes 223, 227, 231, 234 and 238.

Although the statutes discussed here shield rape *victims*, not rape, we follow the legal convention and refer to "rape shield statutes."

[215] California Jury Instructions, Crim. No. 10.06 (3d ed. 1970).

spotless and pure."[216] A second use in a minority of jurisdictions was that past sexual behavior might be offered to suggest a general propensity to lie under oath. Our discussion focuses on the first inference, i.e., on the relationship between evidence of a victim's past sexual behavior and the likelihood that she consented to sex with the accused, or that he reasonably believed she did.

As usual, the admissibility of this category of evidence ought to turn on the balance between its probative value and the danger of prejudice. If that balance were struck sensibly, prior sexual history to show consent would be an unlikely exception to the general rule against propensity evidence; quite the opposite. You will recall that, in general, propensity evidence is excluded—in spite of its considerable probative value— because of the danger that jurors will overestimate its predictive force, and because it is likely to produce other types of prejudice.[217] Like other propensity evidence, a rape victim's sexual history tends to prejudice the jury—in this context, against the state rather than against the defendant. Indeed, as we discuss below, the aggregate prejudice from this type of propensity evidence is probably much greater than that from most other kinds of propensity evidence.[218]

Before we consider the problem of prejudice, however, there is a preliminary question presented by evidence of a rape complainant's sexual history that is not presented by other types of propensity evidence: Does this evidence have *any* significant probative value on the issue of consent? (Of course, under any view of its probative value, such evidence is only potentially relevant if consent—or mistaken belief about consent— is in fact at issue.) Many people find it intuitively plausible that a woman who has engaged in consensual sex in the past is more likely to have done so on the occasion in question than one who has not. This is a legitimate argument—at least in the sense that evidence is relevant if it advances the inquiry to any degree, however minuscule. But it is also a weak argument, because sexual behavior is notoriously dependent on context. Many people, women and men alike, are sexually active but only with a

---

[216] Lee v. State, 132 Tenn. 655, 179 S.W. 145 (1915). See State v. Wood, 59 Ariz. 48, 122 P.2d 416 (1942); People v. Collins, 25 Ill.2d 605, 186 N.E.2d 30 (1962).

[217] See supra, Section II.A., pp. 347–356.

[218] The fact that the prejudice is against the state changes the balance. As FREs 404(a)(2)(A) and 404(a)(2)(B) suggest, and consistent with constitutional protections accorded defendants, we are willing to disadvantage the state in ways that, at least in theory, we would not want to—or could not constitutionally—disadvantage the defendant. See Chapter Seven. There is, however, a further complication. Although it is the state that is officially prejudiced by evidence offered for its supposed bearing on a woman's propensity to consent to sex, it is the woman, the alleged and in most cases the actual victim of rape, who is degraded by the testimony, may suffer reputational and psychological harm and as a result may be disposed to forgo the law's protection and not report the rape rather than endure these disabilities. As we have noted, these harms to rape-victim witnesses are far more serious than similar harms inflicted on other victims who testify in criminal cases. Our official and noble aspiration to bend over backwards to prevent the conviction of the innocent clashes with the likewise important desire not to inflict additional harm on rape victims.

single partner or a small number of partners, and only under specific well-defined circumstances. Even so, if the question were "Did this woman have consensual sex with this man at a particular time?," evidence of her general sexual history might be probative, to some slight extent. But that simple question is rarely the issue in rape prosecutions.

Let's turn the tables for a moment. Consider a rape trial in which the prosecution seeks to introduce evidence that the *defendant* has engaged in consensual sex with several other women, to show that he raped the victim in the case at hand. You might well wonder why the prosecutor would want to do that,[219] given an obvious problem of probative value: How does *consensual sex* with woman A tend to show that the defendant *raped* woman B? It may suggest the opposite. The type of conduct at issue in the trial is fundamentally different from the past behavior. *But the same is true for evidence of other acts of consensual sex by the alleged rape victim.* When a rape defendant argues that the victim consented, the claim is not simply that she agreed to have sex with him, but that she did so *and then falsely accused him of rape.* The core of the argument is always that the victim has made a false accusation. The fact that the woman had consensual sex with other men whom she did *not* accuse of rape tends, if anything, to suggest that her accusation against the defendant is true. Even in so-called "date rape" cases where consent is not an obviously implausible defense, prior consensual sex by the complainant—in the absence of evidence of prior false accusations—is unpersuasive evidence that she consented to sex but later called it rape.[220]

On the other side of the balance, evidence of the victim's sexual past may be highly prejudicial. True, jurors probably misuse such evidence less than they did forty or fifty years ago, because pre-marital and extramarital sex, are now common and widely acknowledged. It seems less likely than in the past that most jurors will define a woman's character by her sex life or believe that if she has consented to have sex with some men, she will do so again with any man. But the transformation is far from complete. Double standards with regard to sexual activity by men and women outside of marriage remain, and some

---

[219] Even if the prosecutor wanted to offer the evidence, the propensity rule would bar it. But that does not keep us from wondering why the prosecutor cares.

[220] As a matter of logic, past consensual sexual conduct is just barely relevant. It rules out the possibility that under no circumstances would the complainant ever consent to sex, or do so outside a long-term relationship. But even on that theory its probative value is very low— probably no higher than that of evidence of the defendant's prior consensual sex offered to show he is a rapist. Exclusion of the evidence is easily justified—indeed, compelled—under FRE 403 by the strong potential for prejudice.

In some cases, there is evidence that the complainant had a motive to deny consenting to the sex in question (e.g., her jealous boyfriend found out about it) but had no similar motive to deny the prior sex. Even then, however, the probative weight of the *past sexual conduct* remains low. The real issue in such a case is the *motive to lie* about consent—which is plainly relevant and usually admissible without any need of rules inviting character attacks on alleged rape victims.

jurors may vastly overestimate the probative value of a rape victim's past sexual history, or be disposed to doubt truthful testimony because of it, or believe that forcible sex with an unmarried but sexually experienced woman is not a very serious offense.[221]

Prejudice to the jury's fact-finding is only one of the problems caused by admitting evidence of a woman's sexual history in rape trials. An even more important reason to exclude such evidence is its effect on the victim herself. Rape is inevitably traumatic for the victim, and a trial for rape may well cause additional trauma. At a minimum the woman will have to recount her experience and confront her alleged assailant. Exposure of the victim's sex life is *not* inevitable, however and neither is the attempt to portray her, by virtue of her past behavior, as someone who would consent to the degrading attack to which she was subjected. The victim who is forced to disclose her sexual history may not only suffer emotional pain, but may also find that her relationships with friends and family are disrupted. To avoid these consequences, some women may not report rapes or may withdraw complaints in order to avoid testifying, and those who follow through on prosecuting their assailants may suffer for doing so. The state, therefore, has a substantial interest in protecting the privacy of rape victims' sex lives for reasons that are unrelated to the quality of fact-finding at the particular trial in question.

During the past several decades all but one jurisdiction in the United States has enacted some sort of "rape shield" statute. These laws prevent defendants in rape cases from exploring various aspects of the sexual histories of their alleged victims and preclude the admission of specified types of sexual history evidence for specified purposes. They also commonly impose special procedures before evidence of sexual history can be introduced for any permitted purposes, often including a hearing at which the victim is represented. Such laws have been passed largely to protect the privacy interests of rape victims, but they have also been justified by their tendency to prevent the prejudice and estimation problems discussed above.

Despite their common purpose, rape shield statutes come in many forms, and some are far more protective of victims than others.[222] All of

---

[221] Generally speaking, of course, it takes only a few jurors with views of this sort to prevent a conviction. The fact that the jurors themselves may have engaged in sex outside of marriage does not necessarily mean that they will accept similar behavior in others. Sex is an aspect of social behavior that is notorious for hypocrisy. Jurors who practice pre-marital or extra-marital sex may never admit it in the jury room, and may preach a different morality for others.

[222] See J. Alexander Tanford & Anthony J. Bocchino, Rape Victim Shield Laws and the Sixth Amendment, 128 U. Pa. L. Rev. 544 (1980) (examining 46 of the earliest rape shield laws and finding "almost every conceivable use of sexual history evidence [was] . . . admissible under at least one rape victim shield law"). As of 2010, all but one state (Arizona) had a rape shield statute or rule, and case law in that state provided somewhat similar protection. The rape shield statutes in about three-quarters of the states roughly track FRE 412, either with or without that rule's constitutional catchall exception (see infra, pp. 495–496). Most of the remaining shield laws simply give judges discretion to admit or exclude evidence of the complainant's sexual

these statutes, however, are designed primarily to exclude evidence that otherwise might be offered by criminal *defendants*. By contrast, most of the other "relevance rules"—the categorical rules discussed in Chapter Four and this chapter that exclude relevant but potentially prejudicial evidence—either apply only to civil cases (subsequent remedial measures, offers of compromise, offers of medical or humanitarian assistance, liability insurance), or apply only to evidence offered by the prosecution in criminal cases (plea negotiations and withdrawn guilty pleas). Even the general propensity rule—which by its terms applies to both sides in all trials—is used in criminal cases primarily to limit the prosecution's evidence and is modified by two exceptions that benefit criminal defendants. Because the Bill of Rights includes several specific procedural guarantees to criminal defendants, the rape shield statutes' limitation of the evidence defendants can introduce raises constitutional questions that are not typically raised by the other rules considered in this chapter and in Chapter Four. A legislature cannot by fiat change the logical relevance of evidence in a case, nor can it by statute infringe on a defendant's constitutional rights to present relevant evidence. To the extent that rape shield laws preclude the introduction of evidence tending to exonerate the accused, they may interfere with his rights to compulsory process or to due process of law. To the extent that they bar inquiries into relevant facts on cross-examination, they may interfere with a defendant's rights under the Confrontation Clause of the Sixth Amendment.[223] Rape shield statutes must strike a difficult balance because the heinous nature of rape makes it particularly important not only that we protect victims and convict the guilty, but also that we protect defendants and acquit the innocent.

---

conduct based upon the usual considerations of probative weight and prejudice; the rest either bar evidence of past sexual conduct on the issue of consent but not on the issue of the complaining witness's credibility, or vice versa. For discussions and proposals, see, e.g., Michelle J. Anderson, From Chastity Requirement to Sexuality License: Sexual Consent and a New Rape Shield Law, 70 Geo. Wash. L. Rev. 51 (2002) (courts should more tightly restrict evidence of the complainant's prior sexual conduct, particularly prior encounters with the defendant and patterns of sexual behavior); Harriet R. Galvin, Shielding Rape Victims in the State and Federal Courts: A Proposal for the Second Decade, 70 Minn. L. Rev. 763 (1986) (rape shield laws should be replaced by an analog to FRE 404 treating the complainant's past sexual conduct as inadmissible to support an inference that a person who previously engaged in consensual sexual conduct is more likely for that reason to have consented to sexual conduct on another occasion, but permitting other uses of the evidence); Cristina Carmody Tilley, A Feminist Repudiation of the Rape Shield Laws, 51 Drake L. Rev. 45 (2003) (increases in the number of women jurors and other changes render rape shield laws obsolete and counterproductive); Frank Tuerkheimer, A Reassessment and Redefinition of Rape Shield Laws, 50 Ohio St. L.J. 1245 (1989) (existing rape shield laws should be replaced with a more broadly protective privilege of the complaining witness to bar evidence of her prior sexual conduct unless the defendant's constitutional rights require its admission). See also Stacy Futter & Walter R. Mebrane, Jr., The Effects of Rape Law Reform on Rape Case Processing, 16 Berkeley Women's L.J. 72 (2001) (statistical survey of the impact of different rape law reforms on case processing through 1992).

[223] See generally Chapter Seven, Section II.E., pp. 866–869, discussing Olden v. Kentucky, 488 U.S. 227 (1988).

FRE 412, the federal rape shield statute, was enacted in 1978 without any input from the Federal Rules Advisory Committee or from the Supreme Court.   It was the product of a coalition between congressional liberals, strongly influenced by the rise of feminism in the 1970's, and congressional conservatives with a law-and-order agenda.   It was, from the victim's standpoint, one of the country's most protective rape shield laws.   In 1994 Congress amended FRE 412 in the light of Advisory Committee recommendations, to broaden its coverage and to eliminate some potential constitutional problems in the original version. It remains a broadly protective statute and has been emulated by a significant number of state rape shield rules:

Rule 412.   Sex-Offense Cases: The Victim's Sexual Behavior or Predisposition

(a) Prohibited Uses. The following evidence is not admissible in a civil or criminal proceeding involving alleged sexual misconduct:

(1) evidence offered to prove that a victim engaged in other sexual behavior; or

(2) evidence offered to prove a victim's sexual predisposition.

(b) Exceptions.

(1) *Criminal Cases.*   The court may admit the following evident in a criminal case:

(A) evidence of specific instances of a victim's sexual behavior, if offered to prove that someone other than the defendant was the source of semen, injury, or other physical evidence;

(B) evidence of specific instances of a victim's sexual behavior with respect to the person accused of the sexual misconduct, if offered by the defendant to prove consent or if offered by the prosecutor; and

(C) evidence   whose   exclusion   would   violate   the defendant's constitutional rights.

(2) *Civil Cases.* In a civil case, the court may admit evidence offered to prove a victim's sexual behavior or sexual predisposition if its probative value substantially outweighs the danger of harm to any victim and of unfair prejudice to any party.   The court may admit evidence of a victim's reputation only if the victim has placed it in controversy.

(c) Procedure to Determine Admissibility.

(1) *Motion.* If a party intends to offer evidence under Rule 412(b), the party must:

(A) file a motion that specifically describes the evidence and states the purpose for which it is to be offered;

(B) do so at least 14 days before trial unless the court, for good cause, sets a different time;

(C) serve the motion on all parties; and

(D) notify the victim or, when appropriate, the victim's guardian or representative.

(2) *Hearing.* Before admitting evidence under this rule, the court must conduct an in camera hearing and give the victim and parties a right to attend and be heard. Unless the court orders otherwise, the motion, related materials, and the record of the hearing must be and remain sealed.

(d) Definition of "Victim." In this rule, "victim" includes an alleged victim.

As broadened in 1994, Part (a) of FRE 412 applies to any case involving "sexual misconduct," including criminal cases where crimes other than rape are charged, and civil actions where, for example, sexual harassment is alleged. It makes all evidence of the "sexual behavior" or "sexual predisposition" of any person who is an alleged victim of sexual misconduct presumptively inadmissible, whether or not that person's victimization is the basis for the case. The prohibited evidence of "sexual behavior" includes activities that only imply or are a consequence of sex, such as using contraceptives, contracting a sexually transmitted disease or having an illegitimate child;[224] the prohibited evidence of "sexual predisposition" includes such things as manner of speech, modes of dress and other matters reflecting "lifestyle". Ordinary witnesses are protected as well as parties and complaining witnesses. The only evidence of sexual behavior that subsection (a) does not presumptively bar is evidence of sexual activity that is part of the misconduct charged. FRE 412's exclusion is categorical. Unlike most of the other "relevance rules" we have considered—which prohibit the use of specified types of evidence for particular purposes only—FRE 412 excludes evidence of sexual conduct or sexual predisposition regardless of the purpose for which it is offered.[225] The main objective of the rule is to prohibit propensity inferences from evidence of sexual disposition or conduct, but it also prohibits any other use of such evidence that is not within one of the exceptions in subsection (b).

---

[224] See also United States v. Blue Bird, 372 F.3d 989 (8th Cir. 2004) (FRE 412(a)'s ban on evidence of "sexual behavior" bars the prosecution from introducing evidence of the victim's chastity or virginity prior to the incident in question).

[225] Only FRE 410, excluding evidence of plea negotiations or withdrawn guilty pleas, is similarly categorical. See supra, Chapter Four, Section I.A., p. 288, note 2.

The presumptive exclusion in FRE 412(a) is subject to the exceptions in FRE 412(b). FRE 412(b)(1), which applies to criminal cases, has two specific subsections, (A) and (B), and a catchall exception, subsection (C), for "evidence whose exclusion would violate the defendant's constitutional rights." Obviously, if the exclusion of evidence would violate the Constitution, that evidence must be admitted whether or not the rule says so. Subsection (C) does not change that requirement, nor does it answer the question whether there *is* any category of evidence that must constitutionally be admitted and is not already covered by subsections (A) and (B).

The first thing to notice about FRE 412(b)(1)(A) and (B) is that each allows only evidence of certain *specific instances* of an alleged victim's sexual behavior. Regardless of other circumstances, reputation and opinion evidence are not admissible under these exceptions.[226] As long as evidence of specific acts is admissible and is at least as probative as reputation or opinion evidence on the points for which it is offered, this ban should not pose constitutional problems. In some unusual situations, however, the admission of reputation or opinion evidence may be constitutionally required. One example is when the defendant's intent is in issue, and the alleged victim's reputation was not only known to the defendant but also may reasonably have affected his views about whether she consented to sex. In *Doe v. United States*,[227] for example, a soldier charged with rape was allowed to testify that several men had told him that the alleged victim was promiscuous, and that he had read a love letter she had written to another man. The Fourth Circuit held that Congress did not intend the original FRE 412 to exclude evidence of a victim's past sexual behavior when it was offered to show the defendant's state of mind. The Fourth Circuit's reading of congressional intent was problematic, to say the least; it contravened the apparently plain language of the prior rule, just as it would contravene the language of the current rule. The Fourth Circuit's opinion is easier to justify as an attempt to construe FRE 412 to avoid possible constitutional difficulties, or to apply its constitutional catchall exception. A reasonable but mistaken belief in consent is a defense to rape under federal law. Given that rule, if the other evidence in the case—apart from the complaining

---

[226] FRE 404(a)(2)(B), discussed supra, Section III.B, pp. 407–410, provides an exception to the propensity rule for reputation and opinion evidence about an alleged victim that is offered by a criminal defendant; one of the examples given in the Advisory Committee's original Note to the precursor to FRE 404(a)(2)(B) was the use of such evidence "in support of a claim . . . of consent in a case of rape." When FRE 412 was originally added to the Rules, it was universally understood to supersede the precursor to FRE 404(a)(2)(B) in sexual assault cases. A 2006 amendment codified that understanding by providing that the exception to the propensity rule for evidence of a victim's bad character in criminal cases was "subject to the limitations in Rule 412" (FRE 404(a)(2)(B)).

[227] Doe v. United States, 666 F.2d 43 (4th Cir. 1981). But see United States v. Saunders, 943 F.2d 388, 390 (4th Cir. 1991) ("The rule manifests the policy that it is unreasonable for a defendant to base his belief of consent on the victim's past sexual experiences with third parties. . . .").

witness's testimony—is consistent with the possibility of consensual intercourse, the defendant's Sixth Amendment right to compulsory process, and his Fifth Amendment right to due process, might be threatened if he were not allowed to show what *he* knew of the woman's reputation. If, however, the circumstances of the sexual assault clearly negate consent—as in cases involving a weapon, injurious violence or intentional deceit—or if the defendant's knowledge may be sufficiently proved without resort to reputation evidence, excluding evidence of reputation known to the defendant should pose no constitutional problem.

In cases like *Doe*, the goals of rape shield statutes seem to clash with the accused's right to present evidence that may negate an element of substantive rape law. Like FRE 412, most state rape shield laws do not make an explicit exception for evidence of the accused's prior knowledge of the complainant's sexual history to support a claim that he reasonably (if mistakenly) believed she consented to sex with him. And some commentators argue that it is per se unreasonable for a man to assume a woman has consented to sex based on what he knows or believes about her sexual experience.[228] (On the other hand, most rape shield statutes, like FRE 412(b)(1)(B), do permit evidence of the complainant's prior sexual conduct "with respect to the . . . accused," evidently based in part on the assumption—which also underlies the *Doe* analysis—that the defendant's knowledge about the complainant's prior sexual behavior with him may have reasonably affected his belief about consent.)[229] Certainly if the woman's refusal to consent to sex on the occasion in question is unambiguous, there should be no constitutional problem with excluding evidence of what the accused knew or believed at the time about the victim's prior sexual behavior. But in the face of ambiguity, people do honestly interpret other peoples' behavior in the light of facts they know or believe about them. If knowledge of a woman's past sexual experience is to be an impermissible basis for interpreting ambiguous behavior, it would be better to change the substantive law of sexual assault to make the defendant's belief immaterial (as a number of

---

[228] See, e.g., Sakthi Murphy, Rejecting Unreasonable Sexual Expectations: Limits on Using a Rape Victim's Sexual History to Show the Defendant's Mistaken Belief in Consent, 79 Cal. L. Rev. 541 (1991).

[229] This exception also reflects the belief that even though a woman's past consensual sexual behavior with others may say nothing about the likelihood she would have consented to sex with the defendant on the occasion charged as a crime, her past consensual sex with *him* does increase the likelihood that she consented to sex with him on the charged occasion. Even taking into account the fact that the woman complained of rape on this occasion and didn't before, there may be something to the intuition that past consensual sex with the defendant has more probative value on the issue of consent than past sexual conduct with others, because it tells us that the defendant is or once was the type of person with whom the complainant would consensually have sex. But given the fact that the woman *did* complain this time, the better justification will usually lie in what consensual sex between the complainant and the defendant says about the reasonableness of a defendant's belief in consent, rather than what it says about the woman's actual consent. See infra, p. 495, note 237.

reformers have proposed), rather than make that change indirectly through the rules of evidence.[230]

Notice that the reputation and opinion evidence that we have been discussing is relevant for a *nonpropensity* purpose—to show the defendant's intent. More generally, the constitutional analysis suggested by *Doe* may apply to *any* nonpropensity use that a criminal defendant proposes for any evidence of prior sexual behavior that bears on a closely contested issue in a rape case—including reputation, opinion or specific-instance evidence. Although FRE 412 appears on its face to have abandoned FRE 404's distinction between propensity and nonpropensity evidence when it comes to consent or belief in consent in rape cases, the Constitution may preserve a good bit of that distinction.[231]

A second thing to notice about the exceptions in FRE 412(b)(1)(A) and (B) is that they are both limited to evidence of sexual *behavior*. Sexual *predisposition* evidence remains absolutely precluded. The line between evidence of sexual behavior and evidence of sexual predisposition is sometimes hard to draw. The Advisory Committee Note, for example, says that an alleged victim's *statements* expressing an intent to have sexual intercourse with the accused, or voicing sexual fantasies involving the accused, may be considered sexual *behavior*. But for that Note, however, one might have thought that these examples were about as close

---

[230] We argue above that prior acts of consensual sex by the complaining witness that did not result in accusations of rape have little bearing on the likelihood that she has had consensual sex but falsely charged rape on the occasion in question, because the fact that she did charge rape on this occasion destroys its similarity to other consensual sexual encounters. That argument does not apply to the *defendant's* belief about consent at the time of the sexual encounter, when the woman had *not yet* accused him of rape—assuming she had not clearly indicated her unwillingness to have sex. Of course, one may deny that a woman should have the responsibility of unambiguously withholding consent; arguably, a disposition not to consent should be presumed and it should be the man's duty to establish consent before engaging in sex. See infra, p. 493, note 233. But as long as it *is* a defense that the accused mistakenly believed the woman consented, his knowledge of her prior sexual behavior may have significant probative weight on the issue of his belief—unless it is shown that she unambiguously did not consent.

[231] The courts' treatment of two recurring types of evidence of the alleged victim's prior behavior offered by criminal defendants in rape prosecutions—to suggest that the victim previously made false claims of rape in the wake of consensual sex and to show prostitution—reveals the relevance of the distinction between propensity and nonpropensity evidence in the interpretation of rape shield statutes and the constitutional exception. Compare, e.g., Boggs v. Collins, 226 F.3d 728, 739 (6th Cir. 2000), cert. denied 532 U.S. 913 (2001) (absent "an argument sounding in motive, bias or prejudice," the defendant's effort to cross-examine the alleged victim about prior false claims of nonconsent and rape amounted to an attack on the victim's "general credibility," and exclusion of such evidence did not violate the Constitution), with, e.g., Redmond v. Kingston, 240 F.3d 590 (7th Cir. 2001) (trial court's refusal to permit the defendant to show that the 15-year-old victim had previously used a false claim of nonconsent and rape to get her mother's attention violated the Constitution). And compare, e.g., Commonwealth v. Jones, 826 A.2d 900, 909 (Pa.Super. 2003) (alleged victim's convictions for prostitution were not admissible because they tended "solely to show she has a propensity to engage in sexual activity for hire") with Commonwealth v. Harris, 443 Mass. 714, 825 N.E.2d 58 (2005) (rape shield law gave the trial court discretion to admit evidence of the alleged victim's prostitution where the defendant presented a colorable defense that the alleged victim claimed rape because of a dispute with him over payment and the prosecutor argued that there was no evidence that the alleged victim was a prostitute).

to the literal meaning of "sexual predisposition" as one might get.[232] Excluded sexual predisposition evidence is apparently meant to be limited to lifestyle evidence—such as manner of speech or of dress—that some might think predict sexual proclivity. But even this exclusion could pose constitutional problems in some situations if it is applied to the complaining witness's conduct at or near the time of the alleged assault in the presence of the defendant; people sometimes communicate their intentions by means that the Advisory Committee seems to classify as predispositions. Provocative dress, conversation with the defendant that is laced with sexual innuendo, and the like might create a context in which a jury could find that the woman consented or at least that the defendant reasonably thought sexual advances would be welcome, and reasonably interpreted a woman's ambiguous behavior as consent. In that situation, assuming that consent is otherwise a plausible defense, an accused would have a constitutional argument that evidence of the complainant's dress and speech while she was with him, at or near the time of the events in question, cannot be barred.[233]

---

[232] We have no inside knowledge of the Advisory Committee's deliberations, but the language suggests that the Committee may have been divided on whether to exclude all sexual predisposition evidence. Those arguing that some such evidence should be admissible might have used expressed intentions to have intercourse with the accused, or sexual fantasies involving the accused, as compelling examples. The majority, rather than creating an exception to the ban that could have grown larger than intended, might have agreed to state explicitly in the "legislative history" that statements of these sorts qualify as sexual behavior under the rule rather than as predisposition. Creating a legislative history of this sort is a common form of compromise in the legislative process. In enacting its own version of the proposed amendments to FRE 412, Congress adopted the Advisory Committee Note. Courts, however, need not accept the Advisory Committee's characterization of stated intention to have sex with the accused or sexual fantasies involving the accused as "behavior," for they seem literally closer to prohibited "predispositions" regarding sex than the kinds of lifestyle examples the Advisory Committee gives. Moreover, the Advisory Committee was commenting on a draft rule rather than the rule Congress enacted. Nevertheless, we would not be surprised if courts endorsed the Advisory Committee's characterization, both because Congress revised the rule against the background of the Advisory Committee draft, and because excluding evidence of expressed sexual intentions and fantasies regarding the accused could raise constitutional problems. Indeed, another way to make sense of the Advisory Committee's peculiar take on the behavior/predisposition distinction is by interpreting it as a proxy for the distinction—which the Constitution may treat as important in this context—between nonpropensity and propensity uses of sexually-related evidence. Sexual statements to or about the defendant may *seem* more like predisposition than behavior, but they are sufficiently context-specific to count as nonpropensity rather than propensity evidence. See infra, p. 493, note 233.

[233] Whether stated verbally, or communicated less directly through manner of dress, the probative value of evidence of the complaining witness's apparent "intent" to have sex with the defendant depends on inferences that are specific to the time, place and people at issue in the case. As we have seen supra, Section II.B.5, pp. 383–387, such limited and specific inferences place the evidence at the nonpropensity end of the range. Again, although FRE 412(a) forbids both propensity and nonpropensity uses of prior sexual behavior, the fact that the evidence is offered for a nonpropensity purpose seems to count in favor of admissibility under the exceptions in FRE 412(b)(1).

All this may lead you to conclude that rape or other sexual crimes should be redefined so that a belief in consent to sex is no defense unless that consent was verbal and explicit. Then inferences from evidence suggesting sexual predisposition would be no defense, and the exclusion of such evidence would pose no constitutional issue. Courts, however, cannot assume that Congress intended to change the substantive law of rape and other sex crimes by changing a procedural rule.

In cases where consent is relevant and plausible, courts can avoid a constitutional problem by interpreting "sexual behavior," as opposed to "sexual predisposition," to include evidence that describes verbal or nonverbal statements or behaviors of the complainant that were particularly directed towards the defendant and immediately led up to or occurred during the alleged rape. The Advisory Committee's Note invites this interpretation when it states that the word "other" in FRE 412(a)(1) was "used to suggest some flexibility in admitting evidence 'intrinsic' to the alleged sexual misconduct." If "other" is given this reading, then either FRE 412(a)(1) or the exception in FRE 412(b)(1)(B), allowing evidence of specific instances of the alleged victim's sexual behavior "with respect to the person accused of the sexual misconduct," may allow evidence of how the alleged victim talked, dressed or otherwise behaved with the accused on the occasion in question.

In addition to the judicial desire to avoid constitutional problems, there is another reason to expect this broad interpretation. A striking distinction between the amended FRE 412 and the original federal rape shield rule is that the amended version bars evidence from the prosecutor on the same terms as evidence from the accused. Yet prosecutors often try to show that rape victims did not dress provocatively and did not do or say anything that could be interpreted as an invitation to sex. In addition to its probative value, such evidence has considerable narrative relevance, for it is an integral part of the sexual misconduct story that the prosecutor seeks to tell. Courts will almost certainly interpret FRE 412 to allow evidence of this sort to be introduced by prosecutors. If they do so, the symmetry of FRE 412 means that criminal defendants should be able to introduce similar evidence that points in the opposite direction.[234]

Subsections (A) and (B) of FRE 412(b)(1) permit evidence of an alleged victim's sexual behavior in two specific situations in which its probative value is likely to be high. FRE 412(b)(1)(A) is most important when a criminal defendant denies that he had sexual intercourse with the complainant, or when his claim of consent seems negated by injuries the woman has suffered. This exception lets the defense show that the alleged victim was sexually involved with others and to argue that this sexual involvement—and not his own alleged behavior—was the source of any semen, injury or other physical signs of sexual activity including pregnancy. The prior rule confined the exception to evidence offered to explain the presence of semen or injury. As a result, at least one court did not allow a rape defendant to introduce evidence of other sexual

---

[234] If a prosecutor has introduced what is arguably sexual propensity evidence in a particular case, banning defense evidence on such issues might contravene a criminal defendant's Sixth Amendment rights. See infra, p. 506 and note 255; Chapter Seven, Section II.E., pp. 866–869 (discussing Olden v. Kentucky, 488 U.S. 227 (1988)). Congress greatly increased the importance of this point when it adopted FRE 413–415, which greatly expand the occasions on which prosecutors may introduce sexual propensity evidence against criminal defendants. See infra, Subsection C, pp. 500–512.

activity by an alleged victim after the prosecutor elicited evidence that her hymen was ruptured. The court reasoned that a ruptured hymen was a normal incident of sexual intercourse and not an "injury."[235] FRE 412 now requires the opposite result.

FRE 412(b)(1)(B) allows a defendant accused of sexual misconduct to introduce evidence of other instances of sexual behavior between him and the alleged victim to show consent, and it allows prosecutors to introduce such evidence for any purpose otherwise permitted by the rules of evidence. Although some have argued that prior consensual sex between the alleged victim and the accused has little or no bearing on the likelihood that there was consent on a specific occasion,[236] the more prevalent view, as reflected by the many state rape shield statutes embodying a similar exception, is to the contrary. In addition to its possible probative value on the question of the complainant's actual consent, a past history of consensual sex between the accused and complainant may, as we note earlier, bear on whether the accused reasonably *thought* there was consent.[237] Moreover, such a history is likely to be integral to any story the defendant might offer to explain why the alleged victim would falsely accuse him of rape. Although neither of these last two uses is specifically permitted by FRE 412(b)(1)(B), which applies only to the use of the evidence "to prove consent," excluding such evidence where it forms part of a plausible "innocence story" is likely to be unconstitutional—or, put differently, the evidence is likely to be admissible under the constitutional catchall exception in FRE 412(b)(1)(C). Notice that FRE 412(b)(1)(B) applies to the alleged victim's prior sexual behavior not only *with* but also "*with respect to* the person accused of the sexual misconduct" (emphasis added). The Advisory Committee Note indicates that this language was meant to include an alleged victim's statements expressing an intention or desire to have sex with the defendant, even if it never occurred on that occasion. As with other issues under this rule, if the circumstances of the alleged sexual misconduct make the accused's claim of consent implausible—when, for example, other physical violence accompanied the sexual assault—courts are unlikely to recognize a right to offer evidence of a past sexual relationship between the accused and the alleged victim unless the prosecution opens the door by suggesting that the two had no prior sexual involvement.

As we note above, FRE 412(b)(1)(C), which provides that evidence about a victim's sexual activities is admissible whenever the Constitution

---

[235] United States v. Shaw, 824 F.2d 601 (8th Cir. 1987), cert. denied, 484 U.S. 1068 (1988). But see United States v. Begay, 937 F.2d 515 (10th Cir. 1991).

[236] See Anderson, supra note 222; David P. Bryden & Sonja Lengnick, Rape in the Criminal Justice System, 87 J. Crim. L. & Criminology 1194, 1369–73 (1997); Tuerkheimer, supra note 222.

[237] See generally supra, p. 491 and note 229. At a minimum, such evidence negates any implication that the alleged victim would never consent to sex with the accused.

requires its admission, states an inevitable legal fact. We have suggested that there are situations in which the Constitution might require the admission of evidence of sexual history, including evidence that is not covered by the specific exceptions in FRE 412(b)(1)(A) and (B). The Supreme Court reached the same conclusion in *Olden v. Kentucky*,[238] which held that under the Sixth Amendment Confrontation Clause sexual history evidence fairly suggesting that a key prosecution witness had a specific motive to lie could not be excluded by Kentucky's rape shield statute. More generally, the Constitution is likely to provide defendants with a right to introduce sexual history evidence—particularly for nonpropensity purposes—whenever it is crucial to a defense that is plausible given the circumstances of the case and the governing substantive law. On the other hand, where the defense theory is implausible, or the evidence appears to have only marginal value, or sexual history is peripheral to the case, the presumptive protections of FRE 412 should stand.

To summarize, one functional way to predict whether the Constitution requires admission of evidence of prior sexual conduct is to ask three questions: (1) Is the evidence relevant to an issue that is plausibly in dispute? (2) Is it offered for some purpose other than a propensity inference (as defined in Section II above)? (3) Does its probative value outweigh its prejudicial impact, including prejudice to the complainant? If the answer to any of the questions is "no," the Constitution is *not* offended if the evidence is excluded. But if the answer to all three questions is "yes," then the Constitution very likely does require admission of the evidence, even if a rape shield statute would otherwise bar it. This test is not spelled out in FRE 412, or stated explicitly in the case law, but it does seem to work. In practice it means that, subject to a somewhat more preclusive balance of probative weight and prejudice than usual, the Constitution tracks the substantive portions of FRE 404(b) when a rape defendant offers evidence of the complainant's sexual history.

May a court exclude defense evidence that is admissible under one of the exceptions in FRE 412(b)(1) because it has low probative value or is highly prejudicial? Under the prior rule, one court allowed the prosecution to attribute an injury to the charged rape of a ten-year-old, but precluded the defendant from showing that the alleged victim had intercourse with another man because the other man testified at an admissibility hearing that he never injured the victim while having sex with her, and that his acts of intercourse were not recent although the injuries seemed to be.[239] The Advisory Committee Note cites this case with apparent approval, pointing out that evidence admissible under FRE

---

[238] 488 U.S. 227 (1988) (discussed in Chapter Seven, Section II.E., pp. 866–869).

[239] United States v. Azure, 845 F.2d 1503 (8th Cir. 1988).

412(b)(1)(A) may still be excluded if it does not satisfy FREs 402 or 403. The Committee's imprimatur on the particular ruling in this case is unfortunate; even under the prior, more preclusive rule, the jurors probably should have been permitted to consider the evidence, given its appreciable probative value and the defendant's constitutional interest in having it admitted. There will, however, be times when evidence that qualifies under FRE 412(b)(1)(A) may properly be excluded under FRE 402 or 403. One is where evidence of sexual activity by an alleged victim is offered to show an alternative source of semen, and DNA or other serological evidence excludes the man or men named as possible alternative sources. The same result is arguably justified where DNA analysis indicates that the accused is a possible source of the semen, with a minuscule probability that someone else could be the source. In these situations, calling the jury's attention to an alleged victim's other sexual partners has little if any probative value and could bias or confuse the jury and defeat the privacy interests that FRE 412 is designed to protect.[240] Evidence that qualifies for the FRE 412(b)(1)(B) exception might also be excluded under FRE 403 if, for example, the defendant's prior sexual encounters with the complainant occurred long ago or under circumstances that were very different from those of the case at hand.

Subject to a defendant's constitutional rights, evidence covered by FRE 412(b)(1) is admissible only when it is not excluded by other rules of evidence. Thus, in the absence of an exception to the hearsay rule, hearsay evidence of a rape complainant's sexual history is unlikely to be admitted to show that history, regardless of how important it is to the accused's defense.

A recurring issue is whether in ruling on a FRE 403 objection to evidence admissible under one of the exceptions in FRE 412(b)(1), a court in a criminal case may consider harm to the victim as well as prejudice to the prosecution. Some courts took this approach even under the prior rule, finding implicit authority in the purpose for which the rule was passed and in the victim's right to participate in the FRE 412(c) hearing. Courts adopting this view may also take comfort in the Advisory Committee's Note to the revised rule, which states that the revision is proposed "to expand the protection afforded alleged victims of sexual misconduct," and that FRE 412 seeks to achieve its objective by barring

---

[240] When the alleged alternative semen donor is a close relative of the accused, even a test that strongly suggests that the accused is the source may not sufficiently reduce the probability that the relative left the semen to justify excluding evidence of the relative's sexual relations with the victim—assuming the relative has not been specifically excluded by a DNA test. Except in the case of identical twins, however, DNA technology has now advanced to the point that very often even close relatives may be eliminated as possible alternative donors. The strongest argument against permitting a DNA "identification" of the defendant to preclude evidence that others might be the source of semen is that in practice the strength of DNA evidence is limited by the chance of laboratory error, so that DNA evidence pointing to the defendant is not as powerful as prosecutors frequently argue. Even so, DNA matches are very strong evidence of an accused's involvement. See Chapter Nine, Section VI.E., pp. 1247–1260.

sexual behavior and predisposition evidence except in "designated circumstances in which the probative value of the evidence significantly outweighs possible harm to the victim." Finally, as we note above, prejudice to the complainant seems to play a role in the constitutional analysis that courts use under FRE 412(b)(1)(C).

On the other hand, the specific provision in FRE 412(b)(2) that in *civil* cases courts should weigh "the danger of harm *to any victim*" indicates that when Congress wanted harm to the victim to affect the decision on admitting sexual history evidence, it said so. Given the protections the Constitution extends to criminal defendants, a distinction between civil and criminal cases makes sense. Moreover, FRE 403 has always been understood to concern prejudice to the *parties*, and Congress should not lightly be assumed to have amended such a fundamental rule by implication. Despite these arguments, a number of courts do appear to consider harm to alleged victims in making FRE 403 rulings.

As we just noted, FRE 412(b)(2) applies in civil cases. It protects alleged victims from sexual behavior and sexual predisposition evidence, not by forbidding the use of this evidence on any issue, but by providing that to be allowed the evidence must (1) be admissible under the other applicable rules of evidence, including FRE 402 and 404 (thus barring all evidence offered to show propensity), and (2) have substantial probative value. The rule reverses the usual FRE 403 presumption. Evidence of sexual behavior or predisposition is admissible only if its probative value substantially outweighs both the danger of unfair prejudice to any party, and the danger of harm to the victim. Courts may well read the countervailing considerations as additive factors, so that if the evidence's probative value substantially outweighs the dangers of unfair prejudice and of harm to the victim, taken separately, but does not outweigh the two together, the evidence is inadmissible. Such fine analyses, however, are probably not necessary, for FRE 412(b)(2) gives discretion to the trial judge to do what she thinks best. The rule also precludes a civil litigant from introducing evidence of an alleged victim's reputation unless the alleged victim has placed her reputation at issue, which is most likely to happen when she seeks damages for reputational harm. Although civil litigants are entitled to due process of law, the Due Process Clause is unlikely to figure in the application of this rule. If a decision excluding evidence raises substantial due process issues, it is likely to be reversible as an abuse of discretion in balancing the probative value of the evidence against its tendency to prejudice a party and to harm the alleged victim. Notice, finally, that the civil-case exception in FRE 412(b)(2) is probably narrower than the catchall exception for criminal cases in FRE 412(b)(1)(C). The difference in the treatment of civil and criminal cases reflects the fact that a defendant's Sixth Amendment rights to present favorable evidence and to confront adverse witnesses apply only to criminal actions.

Subsection (2) of FRE 412(c) provides for an *in camera* hearing whenever a party seeks to present sexual history evidence under one of the exceptions in FRE 412(b). The alleged victim as well as the parties are entitled to be notified and to participate in the admissibility hearing. The court's task at the hearing is to decide whether a reasonable jury could possibly credit the sexual history evidence and, if so, whether the evidence is admissible under the rule.[241]

Problem V-38. Charles Dale is charged with the rape of Margaret Stover, a college senior. At trial, Stover testifies that Dale invited himself over to her dormitory room, brought a fifth of Scotch with him, got drunk, refused to leave, forced her onto her bed and raped her, then fled when an acquaintance of hers—Rick Jamison—heard her cries and rushed in. Jamison testifies that he was passing in the hall and heard Stover shout, "Don't! Stop!", that he rushed in and saw Dale and Stover on her bed unclothed from the waist down, that Dale then grabbed his pants and shoes from the floor, knocked Jamison over and ran out. Dale's attorney claimed in his opening statement that after sharing the Scotch, Dale and Stover had sex, but that it was consensual, and that what Stover shouted was, "Don't stop!" Dale wants to address the following issues on cross-examination of Stover, Jamison or both: (1) that Stover had consensual sex with three other men in her dorm room in the semester before this incident; (2) that Stover had consensual sex with Dale in her freshman year; (3) that Stover was involved in a longstanding sexual relationship with Jamison; and (4) that Dale knew of (1) and (3) before the alleged rape occurred. **Which of these issues, if any, may Dale explore, assuming that under the jurisdiction's rape statute, force, consent, and the defendant's reasonable belief that the complainant consented, are all material issues?**

Problem V-39. In February 2013, a mother discovered the bloodstained skirt and panties of her 9-year-old daughter hidden in the back of a closet. The girl was examined by a pediatrician who determined that she might have been the victim of vaginal penetration. Forensic tests on the panties were consistent with the presence of semen, but inconclusive on the genetic traits of the semen. The girl stated that Jones, who resided in the house with the girl's older sister, was responsible. Based on her description of the events, Jones was charged with digital penetration and with having or attempting to have sexual intercourse with the girl. In August 2013, six months after the alleged incident, the victim's sister discovered her alone in a room with a 17-year-old male, with her panties

---

[241] The previous version of FRE 412 gave the judge authority, notwithstanding FRE 104(b), to determine the existence of facts decisive of the relevance of evidence offered under the exceptions in FRE 412(b). That provision was deleted by the 1994 amendment because of the doubtful constitutionality of denying a jury trial on potentially critical factual questions.

pulled down. At trial Jones wants to cross-examine the victim about this latter incident. He argues that this line of questioning will reveal that he was not the source of the semen found on the victim's panties in February 2013, and is therefore permitted under FRE 412(b)(1)(A). **How should the judge rule?**

Problem V-40. Thomas Calhoun is the 40-year-old owner of a martial arts school. One of his female students, K.M., complains to the police that he had sex with her while they were attending a martial arts tournament when she was 15 years old. At trial, Calhoun attempts to call (1) several witnesses to testify that K.M. told them that she had sex with three other adult men, and (2) the three men to testify that they had never had sex with her. The prosecutor objects to all of this testimony. **How should the judge rule?**

C. PRIOR OFFENSES BY THE DEFENDANT

In 1994 Congress added three new rules to Article IV of the Federal Rules of Evidence, FREs 413–415. FRE 413 provides:

413. Similar Crimes in Sexual-Assault Cases

(a) Permitted Uses. In a criminal case in which the defendant is accused of an offense of sexual assault, the court may admit evidence that the defendant committed any other sexual assault. The evidence may be considered on any matter to which it is relevant.

(b) Disclosure to the Defendant. If the prosecutor intends to offer this evidence, the prosecutor must disclose it to the defendant, including witnesses' statements or a summary of the expected testimony. The prosecutor must do so at least 15 days before trial or at a later time that the court allows for good cause.

(c) Effect on Other Rules. This rule does not limit the admission or consideration of evidence under any other rule.

(d) Definition of "Sexual Assault." In this rule and Rule 415, "sexual assault" means a crime under federal law or state law (as "state" is defined in section 18 U.S.C. § 513) involving:

    (1) any conduct proscribed by 18 U.S.C. § 109A;

    (2) contact without consent, between any part of the defendant's body—or an object—and another person's genitals or anus;

    (3) contact, without consent, between the defendant's genitals or anus and any part of another person's body;

    (4) deriving sexual pleasure or gratification from inflicting death, bodily injury, or physical pain on another person; or

(5) an attempt or conspiracy to engage in conduct described in subparagraphs (1)-(4).

FRE 414 is the same as FRE 413, except that the words "child molestation" are substituted for the words "sexual assault," and the list of definitions in subsection (d) differs, although it follows the pattern of FRE 413(d).

FRE 415, which applies in civil cases, is as follows:

Rule 415. Similar Acts in Civil Cases Involving Sexual Assault or Child Molestation

(a) Permitted Uses. In a civil case involving a claim for relief based on a party's alleged sexual assault or child molestation, the court may admit evidence that the party committed any sexual assault or child molestation. The evidence may be considered as provided in Rules 413 and 414.

(b) Disclosure to the Opponent. If a party intends to offer this evidence, the party must disclose it to the party against whom it will be offered, including witnesses' statements or a summary of the expected testimony. The party must do so at least 15 days before trial or at a later time that the court allows for good cause.

(c) Effect on Other Rules. This rule does not limit the admission or consideration of evidence under any other rule.

FREs 413–415 were added at the last minute to the Violent Crime Control and Law Enforcement Act of 1994 in order to secure a favorable vote for the closely contested Act by a single member of the House of Representatives.[242] The rules are based on a 1989 proposal by the United States Department of Justice;[243] they were not drafted in the usual way by the Supreme Court's Advisory Committee on the Federal Rules of Evidence and endorsed by the Supreme Court itself; they were not considered in hearings in the Judiciary Committees of the two houses of Congress. Congress did delay the effective date of these rules to permit the Judicial Conference of the United States to submit a report to Congress recommending modifications of the Federal Rules of Evidence "as they affect the admission of evidence of a defendant's prior sexual assault or child molestation crimes in cases involving sexual assault or child molestation."[244] After soliciting public comments and receiving reports from two of its committees, the Judicial Conference opposed the adoption of FREs 413–415, concluding that "the concerns expressed by

---

[242] See James Joseph Duane, The New Federal Rules of Evidence on Prior Acts of Accused Sex Offenders: A Poorly Drafted Version of a Very Bad Idea, 157 FRD 95, 95–97 (1994).

[243] See Office of Legal Policy, Report of the Attorney General on the Admission of Criminal Histories at Trial, 22 U. Mich. J.L. Ref. 707 (1989). See also David J. Karp, Evidence of Propensity and Probability in Sex Offense Cases and Other Cases, 70 Chi.-Kent L. Rev. 15 (1994).

[244] Pub.L. No. 103–322, 108 Stat. 1796, 2137 (1994).

Congress and embodied in new Evidence Rules 413, 414, and 415 are already adequately addressed in the existing Federal Rules of Evidence," particularly FRE 404(b).[245] Alternatively, the Conference proposed that Congress "correct ambiguities and possible constitutional infirmities . . . in new Evidence Rules 413, 414, and 415, yet still effectuate Congressional intent" by recasting the three rules into a single exception to the propensity rule, to be codified along with the other exceptions in FRE 404(a). Under the terms of the 1994 Act, however, FREs 413–415 went into effect 150 days after Congress received the Judicial Conference's report because Congress failed to rescind or modify the new rules.[246]

Together, the three rules provide generically that "the court may admit evidence" of a criminal defendant's or a civil party's commission of another similar sexual assault or child molestation crime, and that "[t]he evidence may be considered on any matter to which it is relevant" in a criminal or civil case involving an allegation of sexual assault or child molestation. Of course, even before these new rules were enacted, evidence of prior sexual offenses could be used under FREs 404(a) and 404(b) for any purpose other than "proving action in accordance" with a character trait. The main effect of FREs 413–415, therefore, is to permit evidence of prior rapes and child molestations in support of a propensity inference. The statements of the member of Congress who secured the inclusion of these rules in the 1994 crime package suggest that this indeed was the rules' intended effect.[247]

As we have noted, a minority of American states have at one time or another had an exception to the propensity rule for evidence of "lewd and lascivious" character, or evidence of a propensity for unusual and abnormal sexual relations. Such exceptions, however, typically applied only to other sex crimes involving the same partner or victim as the crime charged, and were used primarily to prove adultery and fornication, crimes that have seldom been prosecuted in recent years and are no

---

[245] Report of the Judicial Conference of the United States on the Admission of Character Evidence in Certain Sexual Misconduct Cases, reprinted in 56 Crim. L. Rep. (BNA) No. 19, at 2140 (Feb. 15, 1995). "The overwhelming majority of judges, lawyers, law professors, and legal organizations who responded [to the Judicial Conference's request for comments] opposed new Evidence Rules 413, 414, and 415." Id. "It is important to note the highly unusual unanimity of the members of the Standing and Advisory Committees [of the Judicial Conference] composed of over 40 judges, practicing lawyers, and academicians, in taking the view that Rules 413–415 are undesirable. Indeed, the only supporters of the Rules were representatives of the Department of Justice." Id. See also James S. Liebman, Proposed Evidence Rules 413 to 415—Some Problems and Recommendations, 20 Dayton L. Rev. 753 (1995).

[246] Pub. Law No. 103–322, 108 Stat. 1796, 2137 (1994).

[247] "The past conduct of a person with a history of rape or child molestation provides evidence that he or she has the combination of aggressive and sexual impulses that motivates the commission of such crimes and lacks the inhibitions against acting on these impulses. A charge of rape or child molestation has greater plausibility against such a person." 140 Cong. Rec. 2433 (Apr. 19, 1994) (statement of Rep. Susan Molinari). See also id. at H8991 (Aug. 21, 1994) (statement of Rep. Susan Molinari in favor of admitting evidence of "the defendant's propensity to commit sexual assault or child molestation").

longer on the books in many states. The number of jurisdictions that recognized an exception for prior sexual misconduct dwindled during the latter half of the twentieth century.

Even in jurisdictions without special exceptions to the character rule for sexual assault or child molestation crimes, courts have been adept at admitting other evidence of prior sexual offenses. Consider, for example, the Iowa case of *State v. Schlak*.[248] There the defendant was accused of sexually molesting a fifteen year old girl, and the court upheld the admission of evidence of other attacks on different victims on the grounds that they showed a motive, namely, the defendant's "desire to gratify his lustful desire by grabbing or fondling young girls. . . . " Clearly this evidence is relevant only in that it suggests a propensity to assault young girls. Imagine the Iowa court's likely reaction to evidence of other thefts offered in a larceny trial to show the defendant's "desire to gratify his greedy nature by grabbing other people's belongings."

Why has the propensity rule been relaxed in sexual misconduct cases, either explicitly by rules such as FREs 413–415 or implicitly by cases such as *Schlak*? No doubt the main motive is the revulsion that rape and child molestation inspire. But there is a heavy cost to responding to this revulsion by attempting to secure convictions without regard to the value of the evidence or its potential for unfair prejudice. As the Judicial Conference wrote in its 1995 report criticizing FREs 413–415:

> [T]he new rules, which are not supported by empirical evidence, could diminish significantly the protections that have safeguarded persons accused in criminal cases and parties in civil cases against undue prejudice. These protections are a fundamental part of American jurisprudence and have evolved under long-standing rules and case law. A significant concern . . . was the danger of convicting a criminal defendant for past, as opposed to charged, behavior or for being a bad person.[249]

---

[248] 253 Iowa 113, 111 N.W.2d 289 (1961). More recent examples are Estelle v. McGuire, 502 U.S. 62 (1991) (discussed supra, p. 371 and note 44), Hart v. State, 57 P.3d 348 (Wyo. 2002) (admitting testimony about prior uncharged molestation occurring years before under different circumstances on theory that it demonstrated common plan, modus operandi and identity), and State v. Moore, 120 Idaho 743, 819 P.2d 1143 (Idaho 1991) (in case involving allegation that defendant sexually abused his six-year-old granddaughter, court approved admission of evidence that defendant had sexually abused his daughter and stepdaughter many years before because it showed a plan and motive "to exploit and sexually abuse an identifiable group of young female victims," namely, "young female children living within his household"). See Aviva Orenstein, Deviance, Due Process, and the False Promise of Federal Rule of Evidence 403, 90 Cornell L. Rev. 1487, 1497 n.31 (2005) (in addition to two states that still enforce "lustful disposition" exceptions, the author identifies twelve states with multiple recent decisions affirmatively giving trial courts wider latitude to admit prior bad acts evidence in sexual assault cases than the states' character rules would otherwise allow); People v. Donoho, 204 Ill.2d 159, 273 Ill.Dec. 116, 788 N.E.2d 707, 717–18 (2003) (citing cases).

[249] Report of the Judicial Conference of the United States, supra, note 245.

In other words, these rules increase the risk that innocent defendants will be convicted of rape and child molestation. This is not a farfetched possibility. Now that DNA identification is available, it is possible to go back and run tests to determine whether convicted defendants could have been the rapist in closed rape cases in which semen from the rapist was retrieved and has been preserved. From 1989 through the first two-thirds of 2010, about 240 men who had been convicted and imprisoned for rape in the United States were exonerated by DNA evidence, and the number continues to rise. The actual number of erroneous convictions is certainly higher—probably much higher—because in some cases DNA evidence was never available, in many others it was available but was not preserved, and in others it was never tested because the defendant had died by the time the technology became available, or had completed his sentence and was released, or simply never found out about this new scientific test or the evidence to which it could be applied.[250]

Advocates for the new rules make a different argument. They claim that rapists and child molesters are driven by perverted psychological compulsions, and that a history of such crimes is consequently a better predictor of future criminal behavior than a history of other crimes. The available empirical research does not support this argument. On the contrary, it shows that rapists and child molesters as a class do not have especially high rates of recidivism.[251] In any event, this argument

---

[250] According to the Innocence Project website, as of September 1, 2010, there were 258 DNA exonerations in the United States. http://www.innocenceproject.org/Content/351.php. Professor Brandon Garrett's study of the first 200 of those exonerations determined that 93 percent were for rape or rape-murder. Brandon Garrett, Judging Innocence, 108 Colum. L. Rev. 55, 74 (2008). Extrapolating the 93 percent from the first 200 exonerations to the remaining 58 suggests that about 240 of the known DNA exonerations as of 2010 were for rape or rape-murder. See also Edward Connors et al., Nat'l Inst. of Justice, Convicted by Juries, Exonerated by Science: Case Studies in the Use of DNA Evidence to Establish Innocence After Trial 20 (1996) (survey of 19 DNA laboratories in the United States, including the FBI's, showing that, in the nearly 22,000 rape cases in which pretrial tests were conducted between 1989 and June 1995, DNA excluded 23% of the suspects).

[251] One review of the literature by respected researchers suggests that sexual-offense and child-molestation recidivism (1) is generally lower than for other violent crimes; (2) may be higher for small categories of child molesters, especially over the long term; and thus (3) is more appropriately dealt with by targeted strategies, not blanket rules treating all alleged sexual and child-molester offenders, as a class, less favorably than all other alleged offenders. See George C. Woodworth & Joseph B. Kadane, Expert Testimony Supporting Post-Sentence Civil Incarceration of Violent Sexual Offenders, 3 Law, Probability & Risk 221, 223 (2004):

> An 11-state Bureau of Justice Statistics study (Beck & Shipley, 1989) indicated that rapists had a 51.5% three-year re-arrest rate for any charge and a 19.0% re-arrest rate for homicide, rape, or assault. The corresponding rates for prisoners convicted of [non-sexual] assault were 60.2% for any offence and 22.4% for homicide, rape, or assault. For prisoners convicted of any violent offence the corresponding re-arrest rates were 62.5%, and 21.8%.

See also Patrick A. Langan & David J. Levin, Bureau of Justice Statistics, U.S. Dep't of Justice, Recidivism of Prisoners Released in 1994, at 8–9 (2002) (in study of 272,111 prisoners during three years following their release from prison in 1994, same-offense recidivism rate (measured by rearrests) was 41.2% for drug offenders, 23.4% for burglars, 13.4% for robbers and 2.5% for rapists; only homicide offenders had a lower same-offense rearrest rate than rapists (1.2%)); id. at 8 (22.3% of released "other sexual" offenders, which includes child molesters, and 27.4% of

suggests at most that FRE 406 should be extended to admit evidence of demonstrably obsessive or compulsive misbehavior along with (and analogous to) evidence of habit and routine practice. It does not justify either FREs 413–415's wholesale admission of evidence of other sex crimes, or the ingenuity of many courts in finding ways to admit such evidence despite the propensity rule.

Other proponents of a relaxed propensity rule argue that evidence of prior crimes is necessary to convict guilty rapists because rape is unusually difficult to prove.[252] They point out that when the evidence shows incontrovertibly that the defendant shot the victim from behind and took her purse, we do know that a crime has been committed. We may have to resolve difficult questions about the mental state with which the defendant acted in order to determine the degree of offense, but the raw physical facts leave little doubt that the criminal threshold has been crossed. By contrast, when evidence shows that the defendant had sexual intercourse with a woman after the two of them spent the evening on a date, there are at least two competing descriptions: rape and consensual sex. Before the jury even considers the defendant's mental state, it must answer the thorny question: Did a crime occur? Sometimes all the jury has to go on is a swearing contest—He said vs. She said. Moreover, "blame the victim" defenses are unique to rape cases and, due to continuing gender bias, may carry weight with prosecutors making charging decisions and with jurors in their deliberations—unless the balance can be set right. Evidence that the alleged rape victim willingly engaged in sexual foreplay may suggest to some that later intercourse was consensual; it may also make prosecutors and jurors less sympathetic towards the victim and more willing to forego punishing even a guilty

---

released rapists were reconvicted within three years of *some* other crime (not necessarily the same one), compared to 46.5% of released robbers, 47% of released drug offenders, and 54.2% of released burglars; again, only former killers were less likely than former rapists and "other sexual" offenders to have been reconvicted of some crime (20.5%)); Franklin E. Zimring & Chrysanthi S. Leon, A Cite-Checker's Guide to Sexual Dangerousness, 3 Berkeley J. Crim. L. 65, 73 n.41 (2008) ("Sex offenders in general have low rates of recidivism."); Joseph A. Aluise, Note, Evidence of Prior Sexual Misconduct in Sexual Assault and Child Molestation Proceedings: Did Congress Err in Passing Federal Rules of Evidence 413, 414, and 415?, 14 J.L. & Pol. 153, 195 (1998) ("neither the available psychological data nor statistical comparisons demonstrate conclusively that sex offenders are any more likely to repeat their crimes than are other classes of criminals").

Recidivism studies provide only incomplete information on the relationship between prior offenses and subsequent behavior. They do not reveal repeated offenses that occurred before the offender's initial arrest, and their results may be skewed by the low rates at which sexual assault and child molestation crimes are reported. Nonetheless, the available evidence does not support the claim that the compulsion or disposition to commit sex crimes as a class is any stronger than that to commit other offenses. If the admission of evidence of prior crimes is justified on the theory that it focuses on the relatively small numbers of "career" offenders who commit most of the crimes and helps assure that they are convicted and subjected to lengthy incarceration, then the crimes of choice ought to be burglary and robbery, not rape and child molestation as a whole. See James Q. Wilson, Thinking About Crime 145–58 (rev. ed. 1983) (high proportions of burglaries and robberies are committed by career criminals).

[252] See Roger C. Park, The Crime Bill of 1994 and the Law of Character Evidence: Congress Was Right About Consent Defense Cases, 22 Fordham Urb. L.J. 271 (1995).

defendant. Other crimes evidence—which makes defendants seem less sympathetic—thus might correct an imbalance in sexual assault cases that does not occur in trials for homicide or purse snatching. More important, such evidence may resolve the unique ambiguity in rape cases over whether a crime in fact occurred. If the complainant says "rape" and the defendant says "consent," the victim's claim appears much more plausible when we find out that the defendant has raped in the past. Similar arguments may be made in the case of child molestation, in which even very violent acts can be hidden from view for long periods of time, and young witnesses are unable to come forward and provide convincing accounts of what happened.

There is more to this rationale than to the others, but it too is an unconvincing justification for FREs 413–415. First, those rules permit the use of evidence of prior crimes in *all* rape and child molestation trials, including those in which consent is not a defense and there is no question that a crime occurred. This argument, for examples, does not justify admitting evidence of prior rapes as proof that the defendant is the one who sexually assaulted a stranger on the street. In such cases, a crime clearly occurred, and the jury is unlikely to have too much sympathy for the defendant or too little for the victim.[253] Indeed, when consent is not an issue, the conjunction of FREs 404 and 413 can produce unsettling results. If a man is charged with raping and murdering a woman, evidence of an *uncharged prior rape* may be used to prove that he raped her, but evidence of a *prior murder conviction* may not be used to prove that he killed her. Second, in date rape cases and in child-molestation and other contexts where proof is difficult and bias is likely, *non*propensity uses of prior-crimes evidence are often available—to show a common scheme, for example, or to negate a defense of mistake or accident.[254] As we have noted, these uses tend to be significantly more probative and less prejudicial than propensity uses. Third, requiring courts to admit evidence of the defendant's prior sexual misconduct might increase their tendency to admit evidence of the *victim's* prior sexual conduct under one of the exceptions to the rape shield statute codified in FRE 412.[255] If FRE 413 turns out to have this effect, it might actually

---

[253] Professor Roger Park, an eloquent exponent of the need for special rules to cure imbalances of proof in rape cases, limits his approval of FRE 413 to cases in which consent is a defense. See id.

[254] For pre-FRE 413 decisions properly admitting evidence of prior similar acts to show that a rape defendant intentionally orchestrated the otherwise inexplicably recurring circumstances that he says prove consent, or to show that the defendant knew from experience that "no" means "no," see, e.g., United States v. Sneezer, 983 F.2d 920 (9th Cir. 1992); United States v. Link, 728 F.2d 1170 (8th Cir. 1984); Oliphant v. Koehler, 594 F.2d 547 (6th Cir.), cert. denied, 444 U.S. 877 (1979).

[255] See supra, p. 494 and note 234. In the background is the question whether FREs 413 and 414 have implications for the constitutionality of FRE 412, either generally or in specific cases. Suppose, for example, that a rape defendant is barred from showing a rape victim's promiscuous sexual history but the prosecutor in the same case is allowed to show that the defendant has twice before been arrested for rape. Does this make the application of FRE 412

aggravate proof and bias problems in acquaintance rape cases. Last, and most important, any attempt to counteract jurors' improper sympathies for defendants and against victims in sexual assault cases by admitting evidence designed to create equally improper sympathies running in the opposite direction is bound to fail; the tool is so imprecise that it will inevitably do more harm than good. When you shoot in the general direction from which shots have been fired, you're much more likely to hit innocent people on the other side of the street than to knock the bad guy's bullets out of the air.

In sum, we believe FREs 413–415 were produced by a combination of momentary political maneuvering and an understandable revulsion at rape and child molestation, rather than by thoughtful consideration of the need for the rules and of their consequences. Date rape, child molestation and crime in general were "hot button" issues in the late 1980s and early 1990s. No one wanted responsibility for releasing sex offenders and child molesters on "technicalities"—such as the propensity rule—and a majority in Congress in 1994 and 1995 could not resist voting to abolish such a "technicality." If there is a villain of the piece, it is the Justice Department in the administrations of the first President Bush and President Clinton. Rather than stand back from the fray and ask what is just, as prosecutors are supposed to do, Department lawyers in both administrations persistently lobbied for ill-considered rules whose prime virtue was that they might make it easier for some prosecutors to win cases, and, briefly, for some politicians to win elections.

We have taken a strong position on these controversial rules. You will, of course, form your own judgment, and it may be different from ours. Whatever it is, your judgment may be of more than academic interest in determining the reach of these rules. Federal prosecutions for sexual assault and child molestation are rare. In the fifteen years after they first went into effect, FREs 413–415 have been used in only a couple of dozen reported cases. If these rules have a significant impact on American law, it will be because states adopt similar provisions. Most Federal Rules of Evidence are widely copied by states.[256] FREs 413–415 are something of an exception; so far, fewer than ten states have imitated

---

constitutionally suspect? There are old Supreme Court cases under the Compulsory Process Clause of the Sixth Amendment which held state laws unconstitutional because they imposed evidentiary burdens on the defendant that did not apply to the state. See generally Chapter Seven. Would this line of authority undermine the constitutionality of FRE 412 or FRE 413? The answer is not clear because FREs 412 and 413 address different kinds of evidence (character of the victim and character of the defendant) rather than (as in the older precedents) the same or similar evidence offered by different parties, (e.g., an accomplice's testimony). Nevertheless, the unfairness in a particular case of rigorously eliminating a possible source of pro-defendant bias while overturning a longstanding principle that protected against pro-prosecution bias might induce a court to regard the situation as so lopsided that it violates due process. If so, the remedy is not likely to be any limitation on FRE 412; rather FRE 413, at least as applied in such contexts, would probably be found to be unconstitutional.

[256] See Chapter Two, Appendix 1.

them.[257] The Bar's views have a great deal of impact on debates of this sort in state legislatures. Moreover, as we discuss below, FREs 413–415 are so poorly drafted that Congress itself may eventually revisit the rules, and in so doing, may rethink their wisdom and breadth.

Part of this ameliorative process began with the 2011 recodification of the FRE as a whole. Although promoted by the Advisory Committee as an effort to improve the Rules' clarity and update their terminology without making substantive changes, the 2011 modifications to FREs 413–415 quietly removed language that had posed a difficult question of interpretation about the intended breadth of the three rules. In doing so, the revisers appear to have adopted the narrower—and clearly the more sensible—of the two previously available readings.

As originally written by Congress, all three rules had stated that "evidence of [a party's] commission of another offense or offenses of [sexual assault or child molestation] *is admissible,* and may be considered for its bearing on any matter to which it is relevant." This language could have been read to require courts to admit *any evidence* of prior sexual offenses, including, for example, statements made during settlement or plea negotiations, hearsay and highly prejudicial evidence that is only modestly probative, even though FREs 408 and 410, 802 and 403 would otherwise require exclusion. Even statements within the attorney-client privilege might conceivably have been deemed "admissible." This reading was plausible because when the Federal Rules make evidence admissible subject to exclusion by other provisions, they generally make that clear by stating that the evidence "is admissible *unless* any of the following provides otherwise" (FRE 402 (emphasis added), citing the Constitution, federal statute and other federal rules of evidence and procedure), or "is admissible if it is otherwise admissible under these Rules" (FRE 412(b)(2), prior to the 2011 recodification)[258] or "*may* be admissible" (e.g., FRE 404(b)(2) (emphasis added)).[259] On the other hand, the only rule

---

[257] See Alaska R. Evid. 404(b)(3); Ariz. R. Evid. 404(c); Cal. Evid. Code § 1108; Fla. Stat. ch. 90.404(2)(b) (child victims only); 725 Ill. Comp. Stat. 5/115–7.3; La. Code Evid. Ann. art. 412.2; Tex.Crim. Proc.Code Ann. § 38.37 (child victims only); West Vir. R. Evid. 413–415. Although Indiana and Missouri adopted similar legislation for child-molestation cases, Ind. Code Ann. § 35–37–4–15 (Burns 1994); Vernon's Ann. Mo. Stat. § 566.025 (1995), the courts in the former state have questioned the validity of its statute and have not thus far enforced it, see Mote v. State, 775 N.E.2d 687 (Ind. Ct. App.2002); Day v. State, 643 N.E.2d 1, 2–3 (Ind. Ct. App.1994), and the latter state's supreme court ruled its statute unconstitutional, see State v. Ellison, 239 S.W.3d 603 (Mo. 2007) (quoted supra note 17). See generally People v. Donoho, 204 Ill.2d 159, 273 Ill.Dec. 116, 788 N.E.2d 707, 717–18 (2003) (citing statutes); David P. Leonard, In Defense of Character Evidence Prohibition: Foundations of the Rule Against Trial by Character, 73 Ind. L.J. 1161, 1213 n.229 (1998); Orenstein, supra, note 248, at 1497 n.31.

[258] This language was adopted by Congress simultaneously with its adoption of FREs 413–415.

[259] It is possible that the awkward original phrasing of the three rules—"*is* admissible and *may* be considered for its bearing on any matter to which it is relevant"—was always intended to mean that prior crimes evidence is only *potentially* "admissible," i.e., that such evidence "*may* be" admitted, subject to other applicable exclusionary rules. As originally adopted, however, the rules did not say that, and the phrase stating that the evidence "may be considered for its

that is clearly intended to bypass other exclusionary rules is FRE 609(a)(1)(A), and the "*must* be admitted" language it uses to establish a rule of mandatory admissibility is more explicit than the "*is* admissible" language in FREs 413–415 as originally adopted. Moreover, the congressional proponents of FREs 413–415 consistently assumed that the other rules of evidence *would* apply, as did the Judicial Conference.[260] Of particular importance, of course, is FRE 403, which gives judges the discretion to exclude unduly prejudicial evidence for any reason, including the fact that it would be inadmissible under a more specific exclusionary rule. No matter how probative evidence of other sex crimes is thought to be as a general matter, there is no good reason to require its admission when its prejudicial effect substantially outweighs its probative value, or when the language and policies of one of the other exclusionary rules apply—except, of course, the propensity rule in FRE 404(a)(1), which FRE 413–415 are clearly intended to supersede.

Relying on these and other arguments, all federal circuit courts that considered the issue in the decade and a half between the new rules' adoption and the 2011 recodification had ruled that FRE 403 did govern the admissibility of evidence under FRE 413–415, and some had held that Rule 403's application was required to assure the new rules' constitutionality.[261] Additionally, the three rules themselves had always

---

bearing on any matter to which it is relevant" seemed not to govern the judge's actions prior to admitting the evidence and instead to refer to the jury's actions after the evidence was admitted. Complicating matters, FRE 413–415 are clearly intended to trump FRE 404 and permit propensity uses of prior sexual-assault and child-molestation crimes that would otherwise be barred by FRE 404, but the three rules provide no textual basis for identifying which of the Federal Rules of Evidence do (e.g., FRE 403, 802?) and do not (e.g., FRE 404, 405?) apply to evidence offered under the new rules. Although the 2011 recodification appears to have solved the former problem with regard to rules of evidence besides the propensity and allied rules, it remains silent as to which of the propensity and allied rules are trumped by FRE 413–415.

[260] See Duane, supra, note 242, at 102–03 & nn.49–51, 115 & n.102, 118–19 & n.118. The Judicial Conference thought that "serious constitutional questions would arise" if "Rules 413–415 free the prosecution from . . . the hearsay rule and Rule 403." See supra, p. 502, note 245. More broadly, it has been suggested that the new rules may violate the Equal Protection Clause because they treat criminal defendants differently based on the type of offense charged, and the Due Process Clause because they "offend some principles of justice so rooted in the traditions and conscience of our people as to be ranked fundamental." Patterson v. New York, 432 U.S. 197, 202 (1977). Cf. 1A Wigmore, § 58.2, at 1185 (the propensity rule is "firmly and universally established in [the] policy and tradition" of American law). For a suggestion in a child molestation case that the propensity rule is constitutionally protected, see Estelle v. McGuire, 502 U.S. at 76 (O'Connor, J., concurring in part and dissenting in part); supra, p. 356 and note 17. See generally Louis M. Natoli & R. Stephen Sigall, "Are You Going to Arraign his Whole Life?": How Sexual Propensity Evidence Violates the Due Process Clause, 28 Loy. U. Chi. L.J. 1 (1996).

[261] See, e.g., United States v. Hawpetoss, 478 F.3d 820 (7th Cir. 2007) (citing cases and factors to be considered in the balance); United States v. Charley, 189 F.3d 1251 (10th Cir. 1999) (FRE 403's applicability keeps FRE 413 from violating the defendant's constitutional rights); United States v. Larson, 112 F.3d 600 (2d Cir. 1997) (applying FRE 403 to exclude instances of molestation occurring 21–23 years earlier but to permit ones occurring 16–20 years earlier). See also Seeley v. Chase, 443 F.3d 1290, 1295 (10th Cir. 2006) (requiring trial court to make a "reasoned, recorded statement" of its FRE 403 analysis). Some commentators have suggested that Rules 413–415 imbue prior crimes evidence with presumptively more probative value than a court otherwise would find under FRE 403. This seems wrong. Although in sexual assault and

contained (and continue to contain) some modest limitations, including a presumptive 15-day pretrial notice requirement and a restriction of admissible evidence to proof that the defendant previously engaged in (even if he never was actually convicted for) conduct constituting a crime under the law governing the jurisdiction where the behavior occurred.[262] By replacing the "is admissible" language originally included in FRE 413–415 with the phrase "the court *may* admit," the 2011 recodification appears to have resolved this ambiguity in favor of requiring judges to apply the other rules of evidence (besides FRE 404(a)(1)) and, in so doing, to exercise their usual discretion under FRE 403 to exclude evidence that is substantially more prejudicial than probative.

Even after the 2011 recodification, however, FREs 413–415 continue to present difficult questions of interpretation, including:

(1) Do they afford the party against whom other-crimes evidence is admitted the right to rebut that evidence with evidence (including propensity evidence) of lawful behavior? The rules do not explicitly provide such an opportunity, but a concern for even-handedness would seem to require it.

(2) Do these rules only permit evidence of specific acts of sexual assault or child molestation, or are reputation and opinion testimony also admissible, as they are under the other exceptions to the propensity rule? FRE 405 suggests that reputation and opinion—the favored modes of proving character—should be admissible, but the unreliability of opinion evidence and the hearsay nature of reputation evidence present strong arguments for the opposite conclusion, especially when the evidence is used to establish the guilt of a criminal defendant. The federal courts have thus far limited the new rules to specific-instance evidence.

The Supreme Court has yet to address these questions or to confirm that the federal courts have the authority under FRE 403 to develop a common law of admissibility of evidence of prior sex and child-molestation crimes that strikes a balance between prejudice and probative value. In other contexts, the Court has been prone to interpret the Federal Rules of Evidence literally, even in the face of strong competing policy considerations and clear evidence of a contrary intent by the drafters and by Congress.[263] A blindly literalist reading of the rules could lead, for example, to the unfortunate conclusion that criminal defendants have no

---

child molestation cases, FRE 413–415 reject the policy bases for FRE 404's *categorical* judgment that prejudicial effect always substantially outweighs probative value, that judgment should not stop courts from conducting their own *case-specific* analyses of probative value and prejudice. See Orenstein, supra, note 248 (criticizing the "toothless and ineffectual" manner in which some courts have applied the FRE 403 balance in considering evidence offered under FRE 413–415 and proposing a stricter approach).

[262] See, e.g., United States v. Blue Bird, 372 F.3d 989 (8th Cir. 2004) (evidence of unwanted sexual advances that did not constitute a crime is not admissible under FRE 413).

[263] See, e.g., Green v. Bock Laundry Mach. Co., 490 U.S. 504 (1989); Huddleston v. United States, 485 U.S. 681 (1988); Bourjaily v. United States, 483 U.S. 171 (1987).

opportunity to rebut "other acts" evidence of sexual assault or child molestation with "other acts" evidence pointing in the opposite direction. On the other hand, the Court's tradition of interpreting statutes to avoid constitutional questions provides it with a basis for joining the lower federal courts in steering clear of unfortunate interpretations of FRE 413 and 414, by applying FRE 403 and other longstanding principles that assure the fairness of judicial proceedings, especially in criminal cases.[264]

* * *

When the Federal Rules of Evidence were enacted in 1975, the Advisory Committee's Note to FRE 404(a) included the comment that "an accused may introduce pertinent evidence of the character of the victim, as in support of a claim of . . . consent in a case of rape. . . . " In 1978, just three years later, Congress adopted FRE 412, the rape shield rule, which specifically prohibited the sort of character evidence described in that Note, reversing a longstanding policy of American courts. Sixteen years later, in 1994, Congress simultaneously revised and strengthened FRE 412, and passed FRE 413, under which admission of evidence of prior sex crimes by a rape defendant is not only permitted but arguably required. This rule also reverses a longstanding judgment by American courts on prejudice and probative value.[265] To like effect is FRE 414, which adopts the same approach to evidence of prior sexual-molestation crimes committed by defendants charged with that same offense.

The juxtaposition of FRE 412 and FREs 413 and 414 is most striking for what it tells us about changing political and social values. The adoption of FRE 412 reflected a desire to protect the victims of sexual assaults from a humiliating process and to prevent the state's case from being prejudiced by judgments about the victim's lack of "respectability." There is now wide agreement that these goals are important, and the rule has been amended in the light of experience to broaden its coverage and to reduce (if not eliminate) constitutional difficulties. FREs 413 and 414, on the other hand, suggest a lack of concern for the danger of prejudicing juries against sex-crime and child-molestation defendants with prior records, even though some are undoubtedly innocent. Any trend in this direction is troubling.

---

[264] On the relevant constitutional issues, see supra, text on pp. 503, 506 and 509 accompanying notes 249, 255 and 260. The constitutional considerations apply only to evidence admitted against criminal defendants and thus only to FRE 413 and 414, not FRE 415.

[265] These two policy changes—prohibiting character evidence on one side and welcoming it on the other—could both simultaneously make sense. It may be that a woman's sexual history and her manner of dress and speech have little or no value as evidence that she consented to sex on an occasion she claims was a rape. It could also be that evidence of prior sexual assaults by a rape defendant is so probative—regardless of the circumstances or issues in the case—that it should be admitted in evidence despite the strong policies that keep out analogous evidence in prosecutions for robbery, murder and kidnapping. We have expressed sympathy for the first claim and skepticism about the second. In both cases, however, the available empirical support is too thin to support confident factual judgments. Regrettably, when policy judgments become politically charged—as they certainly have on these issues—facts are rarely decisive.

Since the late 1960s, the American criminal justice system has become increasingly "tough" on criminal defendants. Most of the changes—longer prison sentences, reduction or elimination of parole, increased use of the death penalty—apply to people who have already been found guilty. FREs 413 and 414 were enacted as part of this general punitive trend, but also in response to the unjustifiable way that rape prosecutions in particular had long been conducted. Unlike other recent "anti-crime" measures, however, these rules do not increase the punishment for those who have been convicted, but reduce procedural protections for defendants at trial, when they are still supposedly presumed innocent. The long term impact of these rules is uncertain. If they remain limited to federal courts and a few states, they will become isolated and comparatively unimportant curiosities; if they eventually are widely copied by the states, they will set a national standard for sexual assault trials; and if they are applied to other crimes, they could help unravel the longstanding rule that the state may not rely on propensity evidence to prove guilt.

Problem V-41. In January 2012, a ten-year-old girl was abducted from her home. Her partially decomposed body was found in the woods nine weeks later, in March 2012; no useable DNA from the criminal could be recovered; the physical evidence of the events following the abduction was inconclusive. After an intensive and highly publicized 13-month investigation in which hundreds of suspects were questioned, Mordecai Asche was arrested and charged with burglary, kidnapping, rape and murder. Eventually, over a course of interrogation that lasted nearly 70 hours, Asche confessed to all charges. At trial, his attorney repudiates the confession and claims that it was involuntary and false. Asche does not testify. **Which of the following items, if any, may the prosecution use in evidence under the Federal Rules?**

1. Testimony by one Frank Patch (under a prosecutorial grant of immunity) that in 2012 he and Asche murdered an 18 year old woman and stole her money, together with corroborating evidence that the woman in question was in fact murdered. No one was ever tried for that crime.

2. A certified record of a 2003 conviction of Mordecai Asche for kidnapping, for which Asche served eight years in prison.

3. Testimony from a 37-year-old woman that in 2002 Asche, who was drunk, forced his way into her room in the hotel where they were both staying, pushed her down on the bed and tried to pull off her clothes; he left after she knocked him off the bed and kicked him several times.

4. Testimony from the landlady of the boarding house where Asche lived in 2003 and 2004, that in June 2013 her then 9-year-old daughter told her that "Mr. Asche did dirty things to her in the closet."

5. The same landlady's testimony that Asche had a reputation in the neighborhood as a "sex fiend."

ADDITIONAL PROBLEMS

1. Propensity and Nonpropensity Inferences

Problem V-42. Doe Latie is charged with murdering her husband. The prosecutor calls a neighbor of the Latie household, Wendall Noal, to testify that Doe has a reputation in the community as someone who hated her husband, beat him and wanted him out of her life. Defense counsel objects. **What ruling and why?** The prosecutor calls a different neighbor, Wilma Frank, to testify that she saw Doe beat her husband on two occasions and heard Doe say to her husband that "I wish you were dead." Defense counsel objects. **What ruling and why?**

Problem V-43. Bob Bullard, claiming to be a skilled and experienced bank guard, signs a contract to work for a period of four months as a guard at the Chapel Hill Last State Bank ("Last State"). The contract provides that he may be fired for dishonesty or incompetence. After two weeks Bullard is fired. He sues Last State for breach of contract. The bank offers a formal written evaluation of Bullard in which Steve Stricht, Bullard's supervisor at the bank where he worked before coming to Last State, states that, in Stricht's opinion, Bullard is entirely incompetent as a bank guard. Stricht wrote the evaluation two months before Bullard left to go work at Last State. Bullard objects, citing FRE 404(a). **How should the judge rule on the objection? What if Bullard saw the evaluation before signing his contract with Last State? What if he never saw the evaluation? What if the evaluation instead was prepared by Bullard's current supervisor at Last State but was never seen by Bullard? On which of these issues is it important that Bullard's character is "in issue"?**

Problem V-44. Martin Stubbs is charged with robbing the 20–20 Liquor Store in Saginaw, Michigan, at gun point, and taking $500 in cash and a fifth of Jim Beam bourbon. The prosecution offers the following evidence: (1) That Stubbs stole a 2011 Chevrolet in Lansing, Michigan, and drove it to Saginaw, presumably so he could commit the robbery. (2) That after the robbery, Stubbs drove the Buick back to Lansing, to his ex-wife's house. (3) That after arriving at his ex-wife's house, Stubbs finished what was left of the bourbon, banged on his ex-wife's door and yelled obscenities, kicked a hole in the door, threatened to kill everybody in the house, fired shots into the air, and had to be forcibly subdued by four police officers. **Are these items of evidence admissible? If so, for what purposes?**

Problem V–45. Sandy Sypher is charged with the armed robbery of a bank. She and her two accomplices allegedly escaped with about $25,000. The prosecutor wishes to place a government informer on the stand to testify that the day after the robbery Sypher gave him $1000 in new bills and told him to buy her "the best heroin money can buy." **Should this testimony be allowed? Should it be allowed if the informer had immediately turned the money over to the police, and if they discovered among the $1000 some of the "bait bills" taken in the bank robbery?**

Problem V–46. On July 17, 2012, Lyle Smith and Rudolph Shaeffer, two long-time prisoners in the Greenpine State Prison, are shot and killed as they crawl out of a tunnel that leads from a prison store room to a parking lot beyond the prison wall. In May 2013, Collin Trope is tried for attempted prison break for his alleged role in the failed escape. The evidence against Trope is circumstantial; the strongest items are that Trope's car was seen near the tunnel, and that a sweatshirt belonging to him was found in the tunnel. Trope denies that he had any role in the scheme. The prosecution offers the following evidence: (1) Prior to being released in March 2012, the defendant, Collin Trope, was imprisoned at Greenpine for seven years, on a rape charge, and worked as a trustee in the area that includes the store room where the tunnel opened into the prison. (2) Two picks, a shovel, a wheelbarrow and 50 yards of electrical extension cords that were found in the tunnel were all stolen from a nearby hardware store in May 2012 by two unidentified masked robbers. **Are these items admissible? If so, for what purposes?**

Problem V–47. Giuseppe Doaks is accused of burglary. Orestes Oro testifies that he surprised a burglar in his house, who escaped with some silver. A pawnshop owner testifies that she is "almost certain" Doaks is the man who pawned the silver that Oro testifies was taken from his house in the burglary. A handwriting expert testifies that the writing on the pawn ticket is "consistent with Doaks' writing, and there is about an 80 percent chance that Doaks is the person who filled it out." The prosecutor offers the testimony of Pilar Plata that Doaks is the intruder she surprised near her dining room credenza six days before, and a block and a half away from, the Oro burglary. Nothing was taken from Plata. As was true of the Oro burglary, Plata's back door had been jimmied in the early morning hours. **Should Plata be permitted to testify? Would it make a difference if Doaks previously was acquitted of the Plata burglary? If he previously was convicted of the earlier burglary? If he never was charged with that burglary?**

Problem V–48. In December 2012, thirty blank vehicle registration certificates were stolen from a state office building in Columbia, Missouri.

In February 2013, Defendant Hank Corcoran is arrested for selling a stolen automobile in Norman, Oklahoma, which had been registered in the name of Lloyd Ives on one of the purloined certificates. The state's evidence against Corcoran consists largely of the eyewitness testimony of the man who bought the stolen automobile. Corcoran defends on the ground that he was home with a cold the day the alleged sale took place. **Can the state introduce the testimony of another eyewitness who will identify Corcoran as the person from whom she bought a stolen car in Carson City, Nevada, which was also registered in the name of the Lloyd Ives on one of the stolen certificates? What would the state's theory be?**

Problem V-49. **On the same facts as the previous problem, will Corcoran be able to introduce an FBI agent who will testify that Corcoran was positively identified by two individuals in California as the person who sold them stolen cars that were registered on the stolen certificates under the name Lloyd Ives, but that charges were dropped when it turned out that the sale leading to the second identification had occurred at the very time the defendant was in court being arraigned on charges in connection with the first sale?**

Problem V-50. Farmer is charged with murdering Woody, his hired hand who disappeared in 1909. After Woody disappeared, Farmer took possession of Woody's horse and personal property. Ten years later, Woody's skeleton was found in Farmer's livery barn. During the trial, the prosecutor wants to introduce evidence that Farmer had two other hired hands who had disappeared, one in 1906 and one in 1913. In each case Farmer took possession of the workers' personal property after the disappearance. A search for their remains was made after Woody's skeleton turned up. One worker's skeleton was found in a cave on Farmer's property. The other worker's body was not found. **Should this evidence be admitted at Farmer's trial for Woody's death? Does it show anything besides Farmer's propensity to kill his help? Does it show that? Would the case for admission be stronger if the other two deaths involved not other farm hands but a neighboring farmer, whose skeleton was found, and an itinerant peddler, last seen on Farmer's property?**

Problem V-51. Quaalude is a Schedule II controlled substance. Its prescription by a physician is permitted if she believes it is for a legitimate medical purpose. Dr. April August, a physician, was charged with two counts of prescribing Quaalude to May March without a legitimate medical purpose. March, 45 years old, testified that she went to August, asked for Quaalude, and after a brief discussion with the doctor obtained a prescription for thirty pills. Dr. August charged March $75 for this visit and recommended that she take the prescription to

Glass Drugs if she had trouble filling it elsewhere. Dr. August said she prescribed the drug, a depressant, for March's insomnia. The jury acquitted Dr. August on this count. March testified that she scheduled a second appointment with Dr. August a month later, and upon arriving at the office was handed a second prescription, signed by Dr. August, for another thirty pills. The prescription was waiting at the receptionist's desk. March had no conversation with Dr. August. She again paid $75 for the visit. The jury convicted August on this count. In addition to March's testimony, the government introduced 478 prescriptions issued by Dr. August for Quaalude and other Schedule II drugs over a twenty-month period surrounding the events described above. All had been filed at Glass Drugs. Over one three-month period, Dr. August's prescriptions made up 47 percent of the Schedule II prescriptions filled by that pharmacy. Evidence showed that a number of the prescription holders had "track" marks on their arms and/or were under 21 years old. **Did the trial court commit reversible error in admitting the "other prescriptions" evidence?**

Problem V-52. Ralph Rakestraw was held up at gunpoint one night while returning home from work. He reported the crime to the police who showed him photographs from their "mug files." He identified a photograph of Dick Deadeye as a picture of the man who robbed him, and later picked Deadeye out of a lineup. At Deadeye's trial the prosecutor asked Rakestraw the following questions:

> **Q.** What happened next? **A.** The police showed me pictures from their files.

> **Q.** And did you recognize any of the pictures? **A.** Yes, I picked out one that belonged to the person I thought had robbed me.

> **Q.** [The prosecutor hands Rakestraw a card on which there are two pictures, one full face and one in profile, both of a man wearing a striped shirt with the number 057962 superimposed at shoulder level.] Do you recognize this picture? **A.** Yes, that's him. These are the pictures I picked out.

> **Q.** Will you show those pictures to the jury? **A.** (Rakestraw hands the pictures back to the prosecutor who hands them to the jury foreperson. They are passed from hand to hand.)

If you were Deadeye's attorney, would you have objected at any point in this questioning? On what theory? Do you think your objection would have been sustained? Why or why not?

Problem V-53. Pedro Gomez was an experienced pilot who worked for Alta Airlines, a seller of general aviation airplanes based in Denver, Colorado. Gomez was responsible for taking delivery of new airplanes manufactured by the Kadet Aeronautics Co. in Tacoma, Washington. When a new plane was ready for delivery, Gomez would travel to Tacoma, get in the plane along with one of Kadet's experienced test pilots, and fly to Denver. Gomez and a Kadet test pilot named Bill "Snoopy" Barron were killed when their plane crashed into a mountain in heavy cloud cover halfway between Tacoma and Denver. Gomez's widow sues Kadet, claiming Barron was operating the plane when it crashed and was negligent. Kadet agrees that pilot error caused the crash but contends Gomez was piloting the plane when the accident occurred. When the plane took off Gomez was in the left seat, Barron in the right. The plane had dual controls and could be flown from either seat. At trial, Gomez's widow offers the testimony of Ace Acrid that he and Barron kept private planes at an airstrip near Tacoma and frequently flew together in each other's and in other pilots' pleasure planes. Acrid will say that on these trips, Barron always insisted that the pilot with the most experience flying the type of plane in question operate the plane. Gomez's widow can show that Barron had more experience flying the type of airplane involved in the crash than Gomez. **Should Acrid's testimony be admitted?** At the same trial, Kadet wants to introduce evidence of an industry custom that the pilot in the left seat of a dual-control plane does the actual flying. Kadet also wants to introduce testimony that on each of the four previous occasions when Gomez picked up a Kadet plane for Alta he sat in the left seat and did the flying. **Is Kadet's evidence admissible? Does the answer to this question turn on the ruling on Acrid's testimony?**

Problem V-54. Mack Kennedy suffered unexpected complications in the course of an operation that left him paralyzed from the waist down. It is clear that the paralysis did not result from negligence but is a rare, unavoidable complication associated with the operation in question. Kennedy sues, alleging that the hospital breached a duty to him by not warning him that paralysis was a complication that might result from the operation. The hospital wants to introduce an internal practice manual that instructs its physicians to warn patients that the danger of paralysis is a possible complication of the operation in question. The physician, Sue Black, who described the operation to Kennedy, has since died. The hospital wants to introduce the testimony of the chief resident who will say that, although she was not present when the operation in question was described to Kennedy, she was present on at least fifty occasions when Dr. Black, an intern whose work she supervised, explained operations to patients. In each case she observed Dr. Black give whatever warnings were required by the hospital manual. **Should the hospital be allowed to introduce its manual or the testimony of its chief resident? Would it matter if none of the residents' observations of Dr. Black involved the operation that Kennedy had undergone or a danger of paralysis? Would it matter if the chief resident had only observed two situations in which Dr. Black was required to warn of an operation's complications and both times she did so?**

If the defendant hospital introduced the manual only, could Kennedy introduce one of the 150 or so patients whom Dr. Black had prepped for operations to say that he had to ask Dr. Black about side effects after she had risen to leave the room without mentioning them?

Problem V-55. Jeffrey Janowski is charged with a purse snatching in the Central Square subway station. The prosecution wants to call Officer Michael Mamlouk at trial to testify that Janowski confessed to grabbing the purse. Before trial, Janowski files a motion to suppress the alleged confession, claiming he was never given *Miranda* warnings, that he at first refused to talk to the police and asked for a lawyer and that he only confessed, falsely, after "the first officer told me to talk or he'd wring it out of me." At a pretrial hearing on the suppression motion, Mamlouk testifies that he came into the interrogation room in the middle of the questioning, when his partner, George Grillet, was asking Janowski questions about the purse snatching. After a minute, Janowski confessed. Grillet was killed later that night, before filing a report in Janowski's case. Mamlouk testifies that he had previously witnessed Grillet conduct twenty interrogations from beginning to end and that Grillet always started with *Miranda* warnings and always stopped asking questions if a suspect said he didn't want to talk or asked for a lawyer. The prosecutor also offers the police department interrogation manual, which requires all officers before interrogating suspects to read them their *Miranda* rights and stop asking questions when suspects either say they don't want to talk or ask for a lawyer. Defense counsel objects to Mamlouk's testimony about Grillet's interrogation practices, and to the police manual, and asks to strike both from the record. **What ruling? Should that ruling change if defense counsel offers an internal police department audit showing that, during the six months surrounding Janowski's interrogation, department officers conducting interrogations failed to give *Miranda* warnings, or continued questioning suspects who said they didn't want to talk, or ignored requests for counsel, twelve percent of the time? What if it was twenty-four percent of the time? Four percent of the time?** Janowski then takes the stand at the hearing and says that, "As is my habit, the moment Grillet started asking questions, I said, 'I'm not talking, and I want a lawyer.' " **What ruling on the prosecutor's motion to strike the part about his "habit"? May Janowski show that he has been arrested and interrogated on 15 prior occasions, and that each time he promptly refused to talk and asked for a lawyer?**

Problem V-56. The automobiles of Leslie Fosdick and Richard Tracy collide head-on at 60 mph, killing both. It is unclear who was responsible. Tracy's widow wants to bring a wrongful death action against Fosdick's estate, alleging that Fosdick's gross negligence was the cause of the collision, and that Fosdick was drunk at the time of the accident. An investigator working for Tracy's widow's attorney has discovered the following information: (1) Fosdick had a reputation in the town in which she lived as a drunkard and as a reckless driver. (2) Fosdick was ticketed ten times over the preceding two years for driving while under the influence of alcohol. Twice she was convicted of this offense and eight times she pleaded guilty to the lesser offense of reckless driving. (3) A local police officer is willing to testify that even when sober Fosdick was the worst driver he had ever seen. (4) A woman who owns a gas station next to a local bar could testify that on at least 15 occasions during the six months preceding the accident she saw Fosdick stagger to her car obviously drunk, get in and drive off. **If the case goes to trial, do you think Ms. Tracy will be able to get in any or all of the information that the investigator has found? The investigator reports that he has not yet been able to determine whether there were any eyewitnesses to the accident. Does it matter whether or not there were any?**

Problem V-57. Sam Smith is charged with having anal intercourse with a ten-year-old boy. He offers the testimony of a psychiatric social worker with a general practice who has counseled Smith in one-hour sessions each week for the last three years, of a psychologist and expert in sexual deviance who interviewed Smith once for five hours, giving him a battery of psychological tests, of Smith's personal physician (an internist) who has given Smith an annual physical examination in each of the preceding five years, and of a medical doctor specializing in sexual dysfunction who examined Smith once for three hours, performing a variety of physical tests. Each of these witnesses qualifies as an expert in his or her field and is prepared to say that Smith (1) is not a sexual deviate, and (2) could not have committed the alleged crime. **Is any of this testimony admissible? Should Smith's wife of thirty years be permitted to offer the same opinions?**

2. Substantive Exceptions to the Propensity Rule

Problem V-58. Robin Stryker is prosecuted for fraud in the sale of land. Wishing to introduce character testimony, she hires a private investigator to canvas the community and ascertain her reputation for honesty. The investigator interviews a substantial portion of the community, asking citizens if they know Stryker's reputation for honesty and also if they have an opinion as to her character for honesty. **Can the investigator testify as a character witness? If he can, what sort of cross-examination might be expected?**

Problem V-59. Sol Levine is an author who has had only limited success. He lives alone in a high-rise apartment on the income from a small inheritance that his grandparents left him. His one passion is bridge, which he plays three or four times a week at the Trump Bridge

Palace. **If he is accused of criminally assaulting his next-door neighbor, may he introduce testimony from others who play regularly at the Trump Bridge Palace that he has a good reputation for peacefulness and nonviolence? If he is accused of theft, may he introduce testimony from these individuals that he has a good reputation for honesty and truthfulness?**

Problem V-60. Assume in the preceding problem that the desired character evidence is admissible under the jurisdiction's established precedent. **Must the court hear from each of the fifteen Trump regulars whom Levine would like to have testify? Would the situation be any different if Levine had brought suit for libel and the defense called these witnesses to testify that, before the libel (which accused Levine of being dishonest and violent), Levine's reputation for peacefulness and honesty was terrible?**

Problem V-61. Donald Dauphin, the proprietor of a neighborhood grocery store, swore to a criminal complaint charging Meg Peters with shoplifting. A jury acquitted Peters of the charge, and Peters has sued Dauphin for malicious prosecution. As her first witness, Peters wishes to call a local banker to testify that her reputation for honesty is excellent in the community in which she lives and works. **Is this evidence admissible?**

Problem V-62. Demetrios Demos is charged with attempted murder after shooting Valentin Valov, paralyzing him from the waist down. Demos claims self-defense. The evidence shows that Demos got into a shoving match with several people at a raucous party next-door to his home after Demos complained about the noise. As Demos was flailing about, trying to keep his balance, he accidentally grabbed Ana Valov's hair. Seeing this, Valov (who is 6'3" and 250 lbs) said, "Nobody treats my sister Ana that way. Nobody!," and slugged Demos (who is 5'4" and 130 lbs) in the stomach. Demos cursed Valov and left. Valov followed Demos home and shouted for Demos to come outside, which Demos did, and shot Valov wounding him in the abdomen. In addition to testifying to the above facts, Demos offers the following evidence: (1) Demos's testimony that, after his encounter with Valov at the party, it was his opinion that Valov was an extremely violent person. (2) The testimony of William Watteaux that he met Valov at a party the week before and again at the party where the scuffle with Demos occurred and that: (a) Based on his observations on those occasions, it is his opinion that Valov is highly irritable and belligerent. (b) Valov pushed Hazel Han to the ground at the party the week before when Han made what Valov thought was a remark critical of Ana. And (c) Valov had a reputation for violence among the partygoers—who had partied together once weekly for the past month. (3) The testimony of Cecil Cedric, who works with Valov, that Valov has a reputation among his coworkers for starting fights. (4) The testimony of Demos's brother Nicholas that when he challenged Valov's right to enter Demos's property just before the shooting occurred, Valov punched Nicholas in the jaw. **(Does it matter whether defendant Demos saw this incident?)** (5) Demos's testimony that he saw Valov the day before—in the hallway outside the courtroom—and Valov said, "I'll get you for what you've done to me." **How should the judge rule on each item of evidence? May the prosecution respond to any of this evidence with evidence of Valov's reputation in the neighborhood where he lives for law-abiding behavior? With evidence of Demos's reputation for violence? How would your answers to any of these questions change if Valov instead was suing Demos for damages?**

Problem V-63. Ivan Skivar had just arrived in Dodge City after a twelve day trip by stagecoach from New York. He planned to stay for two days and see the sights (this was his first time in the West), before continuing on to San Francisco. However, his plans have been disrupted. He now finds himself in jail charged with murder. Skivar's story is that he had just arrived in town when Abdul Lamear stuck out a foot and tripped him. Lamear seemed to think that the sight of Skivar on the ground with his baggage scattered in all directions was very funny, for he laughed uproariously. Skivar responded with a few choice expletives (here deleted). At this point, Lamear pulled out his dagger and charged Skivar, stabbing him in the arm. Skivar tried to get away but Lamear placed a knife at his throat. Skivar, having been warned about the "Wild West," had a derringer up his sleeve. Fearing for his life, he shot Lamear. **May Skivar introduce witnesses who will testify that Lamear had a bad reputation for violence and hostility? May Skivar introduce witnesses who will testify about other occasions when Lamear played crude practical jokes on strangers? As to other occasions when Lamear flew into a murderous rage when cursed by another?** The stagecoach driver has told the prosecutor that on the trip from New York he witnessed several occasions when Skivar tried to pick fights and that he felt the other passengers were afraid of Skivar. **Is the prosecutor likely to get this evidence in? After Skivar testifies to the above story, may the prosecutor call Dodge City saloon owner Kitty Karson to say that Lamear always behaved calmly in her establishment even when others got in fights? What else might the prosecutor ask Karson to testify about?**

Problem V-64. R.J. Samuels, on trial for the murder of his ex-wife, claims in his opening statement that she was in fact killed by drug dealers with whom she was acquainted; he suggests that the killing may have been a punishment for her failure to pay for drugs the dealers delivered to her. In his defense, Samuels offers testimony from a local police detective that three men known to be cocaine dealers were seen in a parked car on the block where the murder occurred about 40 minutes before the victim is thought to have been killed. **(1) Is the evidence admissible? What objections may be made? (2) If this testimony is admitted, may the prosecutor on rebuttal call witnesses to testify that they knew the victim well, and that in their opinion she was not a drug user. (3) May Samuels present testimony from two witnesses who will say they knew the victim's reputation in her neighborhood and that she was reputed to be a heavy drug user? (4) If the evidence in (3) is admitted, may the prosecutor rebut with the testimony described in (2)? (5) If the evidence in (3) is admitted, may the prosecutor rebut with testimony that Samuels has a reputation in his neighborhood as a frequent cocaine user?**

3.   Impeachment Exceptions to the Propensity Rule

Problem V–65. Charles Fairfax is on trial for perjury. He takes the stand and denies the substance of the charges under oath. **Should the prosecution be allowed to introduce witnesses who will testify that Fairfax has a bad reputation for truth and veracity? Would your answer be the same if Fairfax were being tried for assault with a deadly weapon?**

Problem V–66. Fidel Ostrow is a prisoner in a federal penitentiary located at Lewisburg, Pa. He has sued two prison guards, claiming they assaulted him and thereby deprived him of his civil rights. During cross-examination of Ostrow, the guards' lawyer asks whether Ostrow had written a letter to another inmate telling him how to "set up" a suit against a guard. Ostrow admits only that he had written a letter telling another inmate how to file suit. The guards' attorney then offers into evidence a letter from Ostrow to another inmate which could be read as an explanation of how to "set up" a false brutality claim. Ostrow objects to the introduction of the letter. **Should it be excluded under Rule 608(b)?**

Problem V–67. Bernard Sugar, the district attorney for Lourdes Parish, is indicted for accepting bribes from local "numbers" operators in return for leaving them alone. At trial Sugar takes the stand and denies ever accepting money as payment for overlooking criminal activity. On cross-examination, the special prosecutor appointed to represent the state initiates the following exchange:

> **Q.** Did you ever mishandle a client's money while you were in the private practice of law? **A.** No, never.

> **Q.** Isn't it a fact that you commingled Sara Jane Dodley's trust funds with your own bank account just five years ago? **A.** That's a lie.

Q. Didn't Sara Jane Dodley file a complaint against you with the local bar association? **A.** I don't recall. She may have, but if she did she lied.

Q. Didn't the state bar association reprimand you for the way you handled the trust funds of Sara Jane Dodley? **A.** No, they never really reprimanded me.

Q. Let me show you this letter you received from the bar association to refresh your recollection. Now I repeat, were you reprimanded? **A.** No.

During the course of the colloquy, defense counsel persistently objects, but to no avail. **Would you have permitted this examination? Would you allow the prosecutor to introduce the letter that was handed to Sugar?**

Problem V-68. Maria Cox is charged with illegally importing marijuana and with possessing marijuana with the intent to distribute. Her version of the facts is that she went from Texas to Mexico to have her hair done and parked her car in a free customer lot, leaving the keys with an attendant. Unbeknownst to her, ten kilos of marijuana were in her car when she brought it back to the United States. During the cross-examination of Cox, the government offers two documents: First, a sworn statement made fourteen years earlier in which Cox states that she had used another name, had entered the United States with a false birth certificate and had worked as a prostitute in the United States and Mexico; second, an FBI rap sheet listing a 1999 violation of the immigration laws, a 2001 civil deportation proceeding, a 2001 fine for vagrancy, and the arrest for the marijuana offenses giving rise to the instant case. Cox objects to the use of the documents and to any questions concerning the matters they mention. **Should her objection be sustained in whole or in part?**

Problem V-69. Paul Parker sues his next door neighbor, Nix Nosey, for stealing a billfold from the glove compartment of Parker's car. Parker testifies that soon after he saw Nosey close the door of his car, he found his billfold missing. Nosey admits opening the car door, but says he did so only to turn off Parker's lights. He testifies he did not take any billfold or even open the glove compartment. Seven years earlier Nosey was convicted on three charges of receiving stolen goods. Parker offers these convictions for impeachment purposes. Nosey objects that their prejudicial effect outweighs any impeachment value. **How should the court rule?**

Problem V-70. Shirley Bassin is one of several defendants charged with conspiracy to violate the Food Stamp Act by pretending to have larger "families" than really existed. She testifies that the dependents she claimed actually were living with her and were dependent upon her. The prosecution wants to impeach her with a two-year-old conviction for petit larceny, a misdemeanor. The defendant objects. The following exchange takes place:

> **Prosecutor**: Your honor, we have a witness who will testify that the petit larceny involved the defendant's walking into a store to pick up a package that belonged to someone else who had already paid for it. This was a misrepresentation of identity and qualifies for admission under FRE 609(a)(2).

> **Defense Counsel**: Your honor, there is nothing on the face of the conviction to indicate that the defendant did anything but get involved in petty theft.

> **Court**: Well, I am inclined to permit the witness to inform the jury about the circumstances of the prior conviction and to allow the jury to consider the conviction in assessing the credibility of the defendant.

> **Defense Counsel**: Your honor, the rule does not permit any more than a mention of a conviction. Getting into a dispute about who did what and so on is going to be a waste of time and highly prejudicial. We think everything—all mention of the conviction and the details—should be excluded. But certainly if anything is to be allowed, it should only be the fact of the conviction. And we'll stipulate to that if you overrule our basic objection.

What should the judge do? Would it matter if the allegations about the misrepresentations Bassin allegedly used in the petit larceny were: (1) clear from the transcript of the trial for petit larceny; (2) alleged in the indictment for petit larceny; (3) described in Bassin's colloquy with the judge at the time she pled guilty to the petit larceny?

Problem V-71. Harold Levat is charged with the brutal attempted rape of Suzanne Shannon. He claims he is the victim of a mistaken identification and takes the stand to testify that at the time Ms. Shannon was raped, he was on a solitary backpacking trip in the Great Smokey Mountains. Ten years earlier, Levat was convicted of a felony, statutory rape, and the prosecutor plans to ask about that conviction on cross-examination. Levat objects under FRE 402, 403 and 404. **How should the judge rule on each objection?** Assume the conviction was for rape, not statutory rape. **Does this make Levat's objections stronger, weaker or do they remain the same?** Suppose the judge indicates that she will permit the prosecutor to ask Levat whether he has previously been convicted of a felony but will not allow the specific felony to be mentioned. **Does this affect the prejudice calculation? The probative value calculation? On balance, is this a better or worse procedure than those the parties propose?**

Problem V-72. Steven Stone and Prentice Pike were involved in a traffic accident in which Stone's truck demolished Pike's motorcycle. Pike sues Stone for damages. Stone claims Pike attempted to pass him on the right and that he did not see the motor bike. Pike claims Stone tried to run him off the road. Stone has a five-year-old conviction for child molesting; Pike has a five-year-old conviction for assaulting a police officer. **Both parties will testify. Each intends to impeach the other party with that party's conviction but asks the court to bar his own impeachment with his own conviction. How should the judge rule? Is there anything else the judge would want to know before ruling?**

Problem V-73. On Glen Gilcrist's way to The Walls Prison to visit an incarcerated friend, Gilcrist bought two ounce bags of marijuana. He put one bag in his boot, and smoked the other marijuana while driving to the prison. Guards discovered the marijuana in Gilcrist's boot before letting him into the visiting room. Gilcrist is charged with possession of marijuana with intent to distribute. He claims he had no intention of giving the marijuana to anyone else, and that he simply forgot that he had put it in his boot. Gilcrist wants to testify. In a pretrial motion, he asks the court to bar the prosecutor from cross-examining him about a twelve-year-old conviction for possession with intent to distribute cocaine for which he served 25 months in prison, and a nine-year-old conviction for possession of stolen goods for which he served 18 months. **How should the court rule? If the court denies the motion and Gilcrist consequently decides not to testify, is convicted, and later appeals his conviction based on the trial judge's ruling on his pretrial motion to bar cross-examination about his two prior convictions, what is the prosecutor's strongest response to the appeal? Would your answer to either question change if the two convictions were for assault with a deadly weapon and conspiracy to commit rape?** If the prior convictions were for assault and conspiracy to commit rape, suppose that after the judge overrules the pretrial motion to forbid the cross-examination questions, Gilcrist decides to testify anyway, and on questioning by his lawyer on direct examination, acknowledges the two convictions. Gilcrist is convicted. **May he appeal the judge's ruling on his pretrial motion? Why or why not?** Suppose that on cross-examination of Gilcrist, the prosecutor tries to bring out that the conspiracy to commit rape involved a scheme to lure a young woman to an empty warehouse on the pretext that there was a party there. **What ruling on Gilcrist's objection to this cross-examination?**

Problem V-74. Izzie Lawson is charged with hiring Tiger McGrath to assassinate his former business partner, Linda Day. According to the government's theory of the case, Lawson became upset with Day for switching partners and decided to seek revenge. Lawson denies hiring

McGrath and claims that someone, perhaps even Day, set him up. Lawson has previously been convicted of tax evasion. So has Day. The tax charges stem from a tax return the two filed on behalf of the partnership. Day testifies at trial that Lawson threatened her when she told him about her plan to switch business partners. Lawson wants to take the stand to deny the threat and to deny hiring McGrath, but he does not want his prior conviction used against him. He asks the judge to permit him to impeach Day, but to prevent the state from impeaching him, with the tax evasion conviction. **What should the judge do? Would your decision be the same if the convictions were for aggravated assault arising out of an incident when Lawson and Day jointly attacked a third party?**

Problem V-75. Sharon Dixon is charged with possession of marijuana with intent to distribute. She testifies that the suitcase with 20 pounds of marijuana that was found in her apartment was hidden there by a friend without her knowledge. The following cross-examination and colloquy ensues:

Q. Have you ever been convicted of a felony?

Defense counsel: Your honor, may we be heard outside the presence of the jury? [Continuing after the jury is excused:] Your honor, the only previous conviction suffered by the defendant is a prior conviction of possession of marijuana with intent to distribute. She was convicted ten years ago and was put on parole after serving two years. For eight years she has been clean. Her prior conviction should be excluded as more probative than prejudicial.

Prosecutor: Nonsense. The conviction is essential to show that this testimony about being an innocent victim is false.

Court: I believe that only if the jury knows about the prior conviction can it properly evaluate her defense. So I shall let it in.

Q. [after the jury returns]: Ms. Dixon, have you ever been convicted of a felony? **A.** Yes. Once

Q. When? **A.** Ten years ago.

Q. What was the charge? **A.** Possession of marijuana with intent to distribute.

Q. What sentence did you get?

Defense counsel: I object your honor. We don't care about the sentence. Just the crime.

Court: No, I will let her answer.

A. Five years.

Q. How much time did you serve?

Defense counsel: Again we object.

Court: Again you are overruled.

A. Two years. I was on parole for three.

Q. How much marijuana did you have when you were arrested before?

Defense counsel: That's irrelevant.

Court: No, I think it sheds light on the conviction. I'll allow it.

A. 80 pounds.

Q. Where did you keep it?

Defense counsel: That's irrelevant and even more prejudicial.

Court: That's enough from you, counsel. I have indicated that I am going to permit this line of questioning.

A. In a secret compartment in the attic of my house.

REDIRECT EXAMINATION

Q. Why did you get involved with marijuana ten years ago?

Prosecutor: That doesn't matter.

Court: Come here to sidebar and tell me what you are trying to prove.

Defense counsel: We are trying to show that when she committed the offense ten years ago her mother was dying of cancer and she needed money to pay medical bills.

Prosecutor: That's inflammatory and has nothing to do with the value of the evidence of the conviction offered for impeachment purposes.

Court: That is too prejudicial. You may ask her whether she had a need for money at the time and that's all.

Defense counsel: That's not good enough, your honor.

Court: That's all.

Which of the judge's rulings would you affirm? Which would you overturn? Under what theory was the prior conviction admitted? Under what theory was the attempted explanation of the conviction excluded?

4. Other Forms of Impeachment

Problem V-76. In 2013, Orville Wrong filed suit against the executor of the estate of defendant on a rejected creditor's claim, seeking an accounting and alleging that before defendant's death in 2011, he had wrongfully appropriated the design of a fuel-saving auto engine invented by Wrong. The executor's answer denied that Wrong had invented the engine and alleged as an affirmative defense that Wrong had sold any interest he had in the invention to defendant. A witness was called to testify on Wrong's behalf. The witness indicated that Wrong had engaged in a certain kind of research and had reached a certain stage of experimentation in 2010. On cross-examination, counsel asked: "Isn't it a fact that Wrong owes you a large sum of money and that he has been unable to pay?" Wrong objects to the question. **What ruling?** After that, counsel for defendant asks the witness: "Isn't it a fact that in 2010 you heard Wrong say to defendant, 'I'll sell you my interest in the engine for $500,000'?" Again Wrong objects. **What ruling?**

Problem V-77. Howard Constantine is charged with robbery, but claims he was elsewhere when it occurred. The prosecution calls Mario Mezzo to testify that Constantine admitted he was the robber when the two shared a jail cell after Constantine's arrest. **May defense counsel bring out on cross-examination of Mezzo that he was recently convicted of a serious felony and is awaiting sentence? What if the prosecutor, in objecting to this, assures the judge that there are no understandings between her office (which prosecuted Mezzo) and Mezzo that his testimony in Constantine's case will affect his own sentence? When cross-examining Mezzo, may defense counsel try to show that Mezzo has received favorable sentencing treatment in the past for testifying against cell mates? That Mezzo knows what it's like to serve time in jail because he has repeatedly done so on misdemeanor drug convictions? That the offense for which Mezzo is awaiting sentence is the sexual molestation of an eight-year-old girl? That it is part of the prison culture for inmates to commit acts of violence against other inmates convicted of sexually molesting children? If Mezzo denies any of these assertions, may defense counsel prove them through extrinsic evidence? May defense counsel make these points through extrinsic evidence if Mezzo was not asked about them on cross-examination? Suppose, instead, that the prosecution has entered into a written "cooperating witness" agreement with Mezzo in which the prosecutor promises to inform the sentencing judge in Mezzo's pending case of his cooperation in the Constantine prosecution, if Mezzo testifies truthfully, subject to penalty of perjury for lying, that Constantine planned and committed the alleged robbery. May the prosecutor ask Mezzo on direct-examination about the "cooperating witness" agreement? If she does ask about it, may she ask Mezzo about his promise in the agreement to testify truthfully and about a clause voiding the agreement and subjecting Mezzo to a possible perjury prosecution if he testifies**

falsely? May the prosecutor ask Mezzo to read the relevant "truth-telling" portions of the agreement? If the prosecutor does not ask Mezzo about the "cooperating witness" agreement on direct examination, may defense counsel do so on cross-examination? If Mezzo denies that any such agreement exists, may defense counsel introduce the written agreement? If Mezzo admits that such an agreement exists and accurately describes its terms, may defense counsel introduce the agreement itself? If the trial judge forbids the prosecutor to refer to the "truth-telling" portions of the agreement on direct examination, and if defense counsel asks about the agreement on cross-examination, may the prosecutor ask about the "truth-telling" portions of the agreement on redirect examination?

Problem V-78. Lester Higgins, a Los Angeles police officer, is sued by the widow of Gary Gardet for Gardet's wrongful death. Higgins claims he stopped Gardet for a traffic violation and on suspicion that Gardet committed a robbery moments before. When Higgins approached Gardet's car and asked him to get out, Gardet instead reached under the seat, then jerked back quickly, at which point Higgins shot him. Elliott Pearson, a 55-year-old carpenter is the chief witness for the plaintiff. Pearson testifies that he was stopped at a traffic light and saw Higgins pull over Gardet's car, approach the driver's side with gun drawn, then stumble and shoot Gardet through the open window. Higgins's attorney wants to impeach Pearson by showing (1) that in the preceding twelve years, Pearson has been arrested by L.A. Police Department officers for statutory rape, four traffic warrants, possession of narcotics, failing to appear on the traffic warrants and petty theft—although Pearson has never been convicted of a felony. (2) That Pearson told a coworker, Sally Garvanian, eight months before the Gardet incident that his family was being harassed by the police, that his son had been arrested in an auto theft ring and his wife had been arrested for drunk driving, and that "I'll get even with those goddam cops." (3) That a year before the Gardet incident, Pearson (along with 6,000 other citizens) signed a petition to the Mayor of Los Angeles to appoint an independent monitor to investigate police brutality by the LAPD. (4) That two years earlier, Higgins arrested Pearson's best friend, Charles Conklin, for drunken and disorderly conduct. **Are any of these bases for impeachment admissible? May Higgins's lawyer use police witnesses and records, and the testimony of Garvanian, to impeach Pearson, or is she limited to cross-examining Pearson? In considering item (4), does it matter that Conklin is unavailable and that Pearson testified in a pretrial deposition in the case that, although Conklin is his best friend and he knew Conklin had been arrested for disorderly conduct, this was the first he knew that Higgins was the arresting officer?**

Problem V-79. Toby Reich is charged with committing a robbery in Seattle on July 14, 2012. Barry Tender, a witness for the defense, testifies that Reich was a regular patron in his Portland, Maine, restaurant, and that he saw Reich in his restaurant at the time of the robbery in Seattle, Washington. On cross-examination, Tender states that he thinks Reich had been in the restaurant every day in June and July of 2012. To contradict this, the prosecutor offers the testimony of a police officer to the effect that he saw Reich in Seattle on July 10, 2012, and that Reich stated that he had been there for a couple of days. The police officer also states that Reich said that he had come from Portland, Maine. **Should this testimony be admitted? What if the officer testifies that he saw Reich in San Francisco on June 10, 2012? Assuming that it was error to admit this testimony, is it sufficiently harmful that an appellate court should reverse? What if it was Tender, not Reich, whom the police officer would testify to having seen in San Francisco on July 10, 2012?**

Problem V-80. Jack Man Wang is the proprietor of a martial arts school. Walter Skip Daley is a former student. In 2013, it was their custom to go out to dinner at a Chinese restaurant after martial arts classes, and at the end to pool any change from the dinner bill and use it to buy LOTTO lottery tickets in common. Defendant Daley would take the pooled money and buy the tickets using numbers they chose together. He would also usually buy additional LOTTO tickets for himself only. On June 15, 2013, Daley was in possession of a winning LOTTO ticket worth $58,000,000. Wang claims it was one of their joint tickets, and that he is entitled to $29,000,000. He testifies that the lottery numbers they chose jointly—3, 4 and 8—appeared only on the winning ticket. Daley claims the winning ticket was his only. He testifies that the numbers on the ticket came from his birthday (4/19/74) and his horse's birthday (3/28/06). **Which of the following items of Daley's testimony may be contradicted by extrinsic evidence, if any:**

  1. **He testified that he ordered steamed dumplings at dinner—but he didn't.**

  2. **His horse's birthday was really 4/28/06.**

  3. **He said they ate at China Gate, but in fact it was closed, and they had to walk four blocks to Asia Garden.**

Problem V-81. Richard Pisari is charged with robbing a postal installation with a knife, in 2012. Pisari testifies in his own behalf. He has no prior convictions. **As defense counsel, on what basis would you object to the following question on cross-examination:**

  "Mr. Pisari, a couple years ago, in 2010, you committed a robbery of a drug dealer with a knife, correct?"

Assume your client answers "No" before you get a chance to object. **How will that affect the ruling if you decide to object?** Assume that after your client answers "No," you decide not to object. On rebuttal, the prosecutor calls Detective Jones. On inquiry from the court, the prosecutor indicates that Jones will testify as follows:

Q. Detective Jones, do you know the defendant? **A.** Yes.

Q. How did you come to know the defendant? **A.** I met him while I was working in an undercover capacity in 2010.

Q. Now, Detective Jones, did there come a time in 2010 when you had a conversation with the defendant? **A.** Yes.

Q. Please relate to the jury the substance of that conversation? **A.** Basically, the defendant told me he robbed a drug dealer, name of Vincente, with a knife.

What objection would you make? How should the court rule?

Problem V-82. Green is charged with selling drugs. The prosecution's key witness is Porter, an addict who had told detectives months before Green's arrest that Green was his supplier. When Porter takes the stand, he cannot remember anything about the drug sales. **Should the prosecutor be permitted to introduce Porter's prior statements to impeach his testimony?** Assume that Porter remembers the events and shortly before the trial tells the prosecutor that it was Nolan, not Green, who sold the drugs. **May the prosecutor call Porter to testify that Nolan was his supplier, and then impeach Porter with his prior statements that it was Green? If Porter sticks with his statement that Green gave him the drugs but also testifies at trial that he received the drugs at Nolan's house, should the prosecutor be permitted to impeach him with pretrial statements that he had received the drugs at Green's house? Would you expect the defense to bring out the prior statements in any of these scenarios?**

Problem V-83. The defendant is arrested for selling narcotic drugs in Palo Alto, California. The sole witness against him is Smith, an undercover narcotics agent. At the trial Smith testifies to the circumstances of the sale. Cross-examination includes the following testimony:

Q. Were you a narcotics agent in Charlottesville, Virginia? **A.** Yes.

Q. You were the key witness there in several cases, weren't you?

A. Yes.

Q. Did you ever perjure yourself in a narcotics trial? **A.** No.

Q. Did you ever lie to the prosecutor about the circumstances of a so-called "buy?" **A.** No.

Q. Isn't it true that on October 14, 2009, after you testified in a case, the prosecutor made the following statement in a Charlottesville Court?

Your Honor, it is my duty to inform the court that this witness Smith lied when he said the defendant sold him the drugs. We have learned that Smith gave the money we supplied him with to a male friend to be transmitted to his girlfriend, and that the male friend supplied the drug. We move to dismiss the prosecution and guarantee we will never use this witness again.

A. No.

You are defense counsel. **Prepare an argument that might lead a judge who takes a strict view of the collateral issue rule to admit extrinsic evidence of this incident. How would you argue to a judge who views the rule less strictly?**

Problem V-84. Pedestrian is struck at an intersection by an automobile driven by Driver. In Pedestrian's suit for damages, he presents the testimony of a highway patrolman who states that he saw Driver's car shortly before the accident traveling at a speed in excess of the posted limit. **Can Driver ask the patrolman whether he gave Driver a ticket for speeding? Can Driver introduce the patrolman's accident report that does not mention Driver's speeding? How would he go about doing so?**

Problem V-85. Officer Stanke is standing on a street corner one evening when a man runs towards him yelling, "I've been robbed! There she goes!" Stanke sees a woman running around a corner in the direction the man points. Stanke gives chase and after losing sight of the woman for a few minutes comes upon Cathy Culler and her husband Winston Winower sitting on a stoop counting money. Stanke asks, "Where'd you get that?" Neither Culler nor Winower answers. Stanke thereupon arrests Culler and seizes $159 that Culler had in her hand. Culler is charged with robbery. At trial, the prosecutor calls the alleged robbery victim, who identifies Culler as the robber. The prosecutor also calls Stanke, who gives the above description of the incident, minus his question to Culler and Winower about where they got the money. Winower then testifies that the $159 was from a disability check he had cashed earlier that day and that he had counted it out and given it to Culler to purchase a money order. **In cross-examining Winower, may the prosecutor impeach him with his silence on the stoop when Stanke asked about the money? Could the prosecutor impeach Winower if his response to Stanke's question instead had been, "None of your business"? Or, "It's hers"? Or, "From some guy"? In each of these scenarios, may the prosecutor, instead of asking these questions when cross-examining Winower, call Stanke on rebuttal to describe what he said to Culler and Winower on the stoop, and what**

Winower did in response? May the prosecutor call Stanke to give that testimony if Winower says on cross-examination that he doesn't remember what he said to Stanke?

Problem V-86. Same facts as Problem V-85. Suppose Cathy Culler declines to testify at an initial trial at which the victim identifies her as the woman who stole $159 dollars from him. After the jury is unable to reach a verdict, Culler takes the stand at a second trial and testifies that her husband, Winston Winower, gave her the money. **May the prosecutor cross-examine Culler about her failure to give the same testimony at the first trial?**

Problem V-87. Same facts as Problem V-25, supra, pp. 418–419. **May Proton ask Electron on cross-examination: (1) Whether she likes a drink now and then? (2) Whether she is in the habit of drinking a bottle of gin a day? (3) Whether she was in that habit on February 3rd, the day of the crucial meeting in the case? (4) Whether she had three martinis for lunch before taking the stand to testify? (5) Whether she had three martinis for lunch on February 3rd, at the Atomic Cafe? May Proton instead call Neutron to testify that he saw Electron drink three martinis during lunch at the Atomic Cafe on February 3rd, or during lunch before Electron testified at trial? May Neutron give that testimony if, on cross-examination, Electron denies drinking any alcohol at either lunch? May Proton call a physician who has examined Electron to testify that Electron's heavy drinking has caused brain damage affecting her memory?**

5. Rehabilitation

Problem V-88. Varda Von Ronk is severely lacerated when she is thrown through the sunroof of her car in an accident. She sues the car maker, Traverse Motors, on products liability and negligence theories. Von Ronk's star witness is Wendell Wissel, who formerly was employed by Traverse as a design engineer. Wissel testifies that the car's sunroof was not made of shatter-proof glass, but could and should have been. On cross-examination, Wissel admits he recently was fired by Traverse. **May Von Ronk thereafter rehabilitate Wissel by presenting witnesses and documents establishing that he was fired for writing memos to the company criticizing it for failing to recall cars with nonshatter-proof sunroofs? For the same purpose, may Von Ronk introduce a letter Wissel wrote to Traverse a week after being fired, repeating his criticisms of the sunroof? How would your answers be affected by Traverse's demand to respond, if this evidence is admitted, by showing that Wissel was fired for incompetence, insubordination and chronic tardiness?**

Problem V-89. Arch Awry, famed beach volleyball player, sues Bronzetone Products for injuries allegedly suffered when Awry's leg became infected from using a Bronzetone sunblock while playing volleyball on the beaches of Baja California. Bronzetone calls Dr. Sabrina Sells, famed sports physician, who treated Awry's leg. She testifies that Awry told her he injured the leg when he dove on a piece of glass hidden in the sand while making a spectacular "save" that enabled his team to qualify for the All-World Beach Volleyball Tournament. **In rebuttal, may Awry call five friends, each of whom will testify about a separate occasion on which Awry told him or her that his leg became infected from Bronzetone's sunblock? What else might Awry try to show about these conversations to improve his chances of getting them admitted? If this rebuttal testimony is allowed, should it be limited to one witness? To less than all five?**

Problem V-90. The government's case against Sergio Stein, accused of masterminding drug trafficking in Cleveland, depends on the testimony of Reuben Lamb, a pusher who has turned state's evidence. Anticipating defense impeachment, the government brings out on direct examination of Lamb that he has been convicted of murder and extortion. After Lamb leaves the stand, the government calls three witnesses to testify that, despite Lamb's past violence, his reputation for truth and veracity is excellent. The defense objects. **How should the trial judge rule?**

Problem V-91. Elizabeth Souris is sued for damages arising from an automobile accident. She testifies in her own defense. The plaintiff, Peter Lapin, introduces two prior inconsistent statements allegedly made by Elizabeth to witnesses shortly after the accident. Thereafter, Elizabeth seeks to present two witnesses to testify to her good character for truth and veracity. Peter objects. **What ruling?** Assume that these witnesses are permitted to testify that Elizabeth has a good reputation for truth and veracity. **May Peter thereafter impeach the character witnesses for the defendant by showing that they have bad reputations for truth and veracity? May the character witnesses be asked on cross-examination if they have heard that Elizabeth was convicted of drunk driving, arrested for shoplifting, suspended from college (nine years earlier) for plagiarism, divorced on the grounds that she "cheated on her husband," and has claimed to be the head of a coven of witches?**

---

6. *Sexual Assault and Molestation Cases*

Problem V-92. On September 1, at 1:15 a.m. Ruth Romare phones the police to report a forcible rape. She says that she went out with Cal Carswell that evening and that, after walking her home, Carswell refused to leave, pushed his way into her living room and raped her. Romare says that Carswell left ten minutes earlier and that she called immediately after regaining her composure. Carswell admits having sex with Romare between midnight and 1:00 a.m. on September 1, but says Romare consented. **After Romare testifies, may the prosecutor play a tape of her phone call to the police to support her claim that she did not consent? May it do so after Carswell's lawyer brings out on cross-examination of Romare that she was convicted three years earlier of burglary? Of fraud? What if Carswell's lawyer instead suggests on cross-examination of Romare that she accused Carswell of raping her because she was afraid her steady boyfriend, Jonathan Tunstall, would hear that she had sex with Carswell on September 1? Would your answer to the last question change if Romare had waited twenty-four hours before calling the police?**

Problem V-93. A seventeen-year-old girl testifies that three youths pulled her 500 feet down an alley, forced her into a vacant building and raped her. The youths charged with this offense do not dispute much of what the girl says but claim that once inside the building she consented to sexual relations, or at least seemed to. They seek to present evidence that (1) six months before the alleged rape the girl had had sexual intercourse with her boyfriend, who now lives in another state; and (2) that a month before the alleged rape the girl moved into a motel with a forty-year-old man. **Is this evidence admissible? Would the ruling change if the evidence instead were that the youths *knew* of (1) and (2) when they had intercourse with the girl, and if they relied upon the Sixth Amendment? Would the ruling change if the evidence in regard to (2) were instead that the girl had told juvenile authorities that she was not living with a forty-year-old man in a motel when in fact she was? If the evidence in this last scenario is admissible, what form must it take?**

Problem V-94. Tracy Shire, aged 16, alleges that Frank Flaherty, aged 21, raped her, and she so testifies in court. **May Flaherty question Shire on cross-examination about the following alleged incidents?** (1) Shire falsely accused George Christianson of stealing a cell phone Shire's parents bought her that she promptly lost. (2) Shire falsely accused Celia Morrow of denting the fender of the BMW her parents gave Shire as a present for earning good grades in her junior year, though in fact it was Shire who ran into Morrow's car while it was parked at the mall. (3) Shire falsely accused Bruce Furman (aged 16) of getting her drunk at a party, taking her home and raping her, after her parents found out she spent the night with Furman, rather than at the home of the girlfriend who gave the party, as she had originally told her parents. (4) In fact, Shire has had intercourse with six young men, aged 16–19, over the last year (not including Flaherty), and has accused three of them of raping her—the same three her parents found out about. **Is any of this cross-examination permissible? Is any additional information needed to make it permissible? If the questions are**

permitted, and if Shire denies any of the allegations, may Flaherty call witnesses to verify them?

Problem V-95. Fred Howell is accused of raping Kay Cornish. Cornish reported the rape three days after it allegedly occurred and there was no physical evidence. Howell claims Cornish is a sex worker, that she willingly had sex with him for money on the night in question, and that she later became angry with him after he reneged on a promise to pay her $5000 to escort him around town over the next three days. **May Howell ask Cornish on cross-examination at trial whether she accepted $300 to have sex with him on the night in question? Whether she is a sex worker? Whether two other men paid her to have sex with them that same night? If any of these questions are allowed, and if Cornish denies the allegations, may Howell call those two men to testify? If they invoke their Fifth Amendment privilege against self-incrimination and decline to testify, may he call a police officer on the vice squad to express an opinion, based on substantial surveillance of Cornish, that she is a sex worker?**

Problem V-96. Charles Carson, a G.I. stationed at a Marine base in Lejune, North Carolina, is charged with raping Susan Sokol at her home on the night of July 7, 2013. Carson's defense is that Sokol consented to sexual relations or, at least, that he reasonably believed she did. Sokol testifies that she met Carson for the first time at a bar near the base on July 7, 2013, that he gave her a ride home, that she invited him in for a cup of coffee, and that when she asked him to leave he instead forced her into her bedroom, punched her several times in the chest and raped her, after which he fell asleep. When Carson left at 10:30 the next morning, Sokol went to the emergency room at a local hospital where a doctor examined her and called the police. The doctor testified that Sokol had two bruised ribs, although he could not say when the injuries occurred. Semen recovered during Sokol's examination matched Carson's DNA. At various points during the trial, Carson offers the following evidence:

> 1. The testimony of Lawrence Lawry, a social worker with Lejune Family Services Agency, that he has frequently provided counseling to Sokol, is familiar with her background and behavior, has visited her home on ten occasions to evaluate her and her children's living conditions, and that: (a) each of Sokol's three children has a different father, none of whom established a long-term relationship with Sokol; (b) on seven of the ten occasions he visited Sokol's home, he found her with a different man, and he never saw her with the same man on more than one occasion; (c) that the defendant, Charles Carson, was the last man he saw with Sokol at her home, when he visited between 8:30 and 9:30 a.m. on July 8, 2013, that Sokol said nothing to him about a rape or otherwise indicated that anything was amiss, and that her interaction with Carson "looked comfortable and

casual—about the same as her interaction with the other men I have seen her with on the previous six occasions"; and (d) that in his opinion, Sokol is sexually promiscuous.

2. Carson's own testimony, as follows: (a) On the evening of July 6, 2013, he and Fred Felter, a buddy from the base, saw Sokol at the bar in Tad's Tavern. The three struck up a conversation during which Sokol "flirted with both of us." The three had some beers at a table, where the flirting continued. After awhile, Felter made a sexual proposition to which Sokol responded, "I'd love to. Take me home." (b) The next morning, July 7, 2013, Felter saw Carson and told him that Sokol invited him into her home for a drink, asked him to stay the night and had consensual sexual relations with him. (c) That night, Carson went to Tad's alone and found Sokol at the bar. She remembered him from the night before, had some beers with him, asked him to drive her home, invited him in for coffee, asked him to stay the night and engaged in apparently consensual sexual relations with him. He never hit her or used any other force. (d) Felter has a reputation around the base as a brawler, though Carson has never seen him act violently.

3. The testimony of Nelson Newell that he met Sokol at Tad's Tavern on July 12, 2013, had some drinks with her, drove her home, and at her invitation joined her in her house for a cup of coffee, spent the night and had consensual sexual relations with her.

4. The testimony of Harley Hall and Jason James, each essentially as follows: Each witness met Sokol for the first time in a bar. The two chatted, flirted, had some drinks and drove to Sokol's home. Sokol invited the witness in, asked him to stay the night and had consensual sexual relations with him. He awoke the next morning to find "some social worker snooping around the place and appearing judgmental about Sokol and me." Sokol became upset, worrying that her children would be taken from her. Later in the day, each witness was approached by police officers investigating a complaint that he had raped Sokol. No charges were filed.

5. The testimony of Pamela Parnell that she met Carson two years earlier in a bar near the base; that he walked her home that evening, squeezed her hand at the door and left "like a perfect gentleman"; that she has been seeing Carson steadily since, and they plan to marry; that each time she has declined to be intimate with Carson he has respected her wishes; and that he has never made unwanted, violent or forcible sexual advances to her or to anyone else in her presence.

6. Cross-examination of Sokol about the events described in items 1(a), 1(c), 2(a), 2(b), 3 and 4 above.

How should the judge rule on the prosecution's objections to each aspect of this evidence?

Problem V–97. Same facts as Problem V–96. The prosecution offers the following evidence in its case in chief:

1. The testimony of Sergeant Manning Morrison, Carson's superior officer at the Lejune base, that: (a) Carson's military pay is being garnished to pay child support to three separate women; (b) Morrison has seen Carson on numerous occasions in the company of young women, but has never seen him twice with the same woman; (c) on four occasions, Morrison saw Carson approach women Carson apparently did not know, invite them to have a drink and then "put his hands all over them," causing one woman to throw her drink in his face and shout, "Until you get a personal invitation, keep your hands to yourself!"; (d) Morrison has heard Carson brag to other men on the base about his sexual conquests in the vein of "Well, gents, I got another notch in my belt last night"; (e) in Morrison's opinion, Carson is "lecherous and sexually out of control."

2. The testimony of Tad's Tavern owner Thaddeus Tudor, that (a) two years earlier he saw Carson shove a woman against the wall in the bar and forcibly grope her; (b) Tudor was told on the same occasion by another female customer (via inadmissible hearsay) that some weeks earlier Carson offered her a ride home, took her to his car in the alley behind Tad's and tried to rape her there, but she escaped and came back inside Tad's; (c) later that night, Tudor confronted Carson and told him to "stop forcing yourself on the ladies," to which Carson replied, "I've never pushed myself on any lady customers"; and (d) Carson has a reputation among Tudor's female customers as "a sexual bully who won't take 'no' for an answer."

3. The testimony of Rory Raley, that twenty-three years earlier when she and Carson were students at Franklin High School in Chester, Pennsylvania, he met her at a party, put some pills in her drink that made her dizzy, took her to a bedroom in the house where the party was taking place saying she should lie down, threw her on the bed, pinned her arms behind her back and unbuttoned her blouse—but then was interrupted by the owner of the house and sent home.

4. The testimony of Nancy Nedelsky that in August 2012, she met Carson at a bar; had some drinks with him and some friends of hers; accepted his offer to drive her home; invited him in for a nightcap; asked him to leave so she could go to bed; was forced by him into her bedroom and slugged in the stomach hard, then raped, after which Carson immediately drove away. Nedelsky did not call the police,

because she was embarrassed and angry at herself for letting Carson into her home.

How should the judge rule on Carson's objections to each aspect of this evidence? Would the prosecutor have a stronger case for admitting any of this evidence if she offered it on rebuttal after Carson testified that Sokol consented? Would any of it become admissible if used on cross-examination of Carson (assuming he testifies)? Would any of your answers change if the trial took place in a jurisdiction in which the Federal Rules *minus* FREs 413–415 were in effect?

Problem V-98. Reconsider Problem V-96 above, focusing particularly on the evidence offered by Carson that should be *excluded* under FRE 412. Also reconsider Problem V-97 above, focusing particularly on the evidence offered by the prosecution that should be *admitted* under FRE 413. **Would a judge's decision to admit any of the evidence the prosecution proffers in Problem V-97 change your mind about any of the evidence that you thought should be excluded in Problem V-96? Why or why not? Does FRE 404(a)(1) affect your answer in any way? In your judgment, would this case be more fairly tried in a jurisdiction that generally adheres to the FREs but: (1) omits FRE 412, while including FRE 413; (2) includes FRE 412, while omitting FRE 413; (3) omits both rules; (4) includes both rules?**

Problem V-99. The defendant is charged with sexually molesting his eleven-year-old stepdaughter Sandra. Sandra testified that on Sunday afternoon, December 12, 2012, the defendant took her to the basement of an unfinished home next to her own and tried to have sexual intercourse with her but failed. Sandra reported the incident to her aunt who reported it to the police. A medical examination showed evidence of sexual contact with Sandra but there was no clear evidence of when or with whom it occurred. The prosecutor offers the following evidence in his case in chief: (1) Sandra's testimony that during the previous year, at intervals of two to four weeks, the defendant had fondled her in the bathroom of their home and made her touch him. (2) Testimony by her sister Pamela, aged ten, and her brother Jason, aged 12, that the defendant had committed similar acts with them on several occasions during the preceding year or so. (3) Testimony by Sandra's aunt that the defendant was reputed among members of the extended family to be sexually perverted, especially when it came to young children. (4) A certified court record showing that the defendant was convicted of the rape of a twenty-one-year-old woman in 1997. **Is this evidence admissible under the common law approach to such evidence? Under the approach prescribed by FRE 404 prior to the adoption**

of FREs 413 and 414? Under FRE 413 and/or 414? Apart from particular rules, *should* it be admissible?

IX. BIBLIOGRAPHY

McCormick, Chs. 4, 5, 17.

Weinstein, Chs. 404–406, 412–415, 607–613.

Wigmore, §§ 52–144, 191–218, 244–383, 874–1046, 1100–1144.

Aiken, Jane Harris, Sexual Character Evidence in Civil Actions: Refining the Propensity Rule, 1997 Wis. L. Rev. 1221.

Anderson, Michelle J., From Chastity Requirement to Sexuality License: Sexual Consent and a New Rape Shield Law, 70 Geo. Wash. L. Rev. 51 (2002).

Baker, Katharine, Once a Rapist? Motivational Evidence and Relevancy in Rape Law, 110 Harv. L. Rev. 563 (1997).

Beale, Sara Sun, Prior Similar Acts in Prosecutions for Rape and Child Sex Abuse, 4 Crim. L.F. 307 (1993).

Bellin, Jeffrey, Circumventing Congress: How the Federal Courts Opened the Door to Impeaching Criminal Defendants with Prior Convictions, 42 U.C. Davis L. Rev. 289 (2008).

Berger, Vivian, Man's Trial, Woman's Tribulation: Rape Cases in the Courtroom, 77 Colum. L. Rev. 1 (1977).

Blume, John, The Dilemma of the Criminal Defendant with a Prior Record—Lessons from the Wrongfully Convicted, 3 J. Empirical Stud. 477 (2008).

Bobst, Christopher, Rape Shield Laws and Prior False Accusations of Rape: The Need for Meaningful Legislative Reform, 24 J. Legisl. 125 (1998).

Bryden, David P. & Sonja Lengnick, Rape in the Criminal Justice System, 87 J. Crim. L. & Criminology 1194 (1977).

Bryden, David P. & Roger C. Park, "Other Crimes" Evidence in Sex Offense Cases, 78 Minn. L. Rev. 529 (1994).

Chojnacki, Danielle E., et al., An Empirical Basis for the Admission of Expert Testimony on False Confessions, 40 Ariz. St. L.J. 1 (2008).

Colb, Sherry F., "Whodunit" Versus "What Was Done"; When to Admit Character Evidence in Criminal Cases, 79 N.C. L. Rev. 939 (2001).

Convis, Charles L., Testifying About Testimony: Psychological Evidence on Perceptual and Memory Factors Affecting the Credibility of Testimony, 21 Duq. L. Rev. 579 (1983).

Crump, David, How Should We Treat Character Evidence Offered to Prove Conduct?, 58 U. Colo. L. Rev. 279 (1987).

Davies, Susan M., Evidence of Character to Prove Conduct: A Reassessment of Relevancy, 27 Crim. L. Bull. 504 (1991).

Dodson, Robert D., What Went Wrong with Federal Rule of Evidence 609: A Look at How Jurors Really Misuse Prior Convictions Evidence, 48 Drake L. Rev. 1 (1999).

Duane, James Joseph, The New Federal Rules of Evidence on Prior Acts of Accused Sex Offenders: A Poorly Drafted Version of a Very Bad Idea, 157 FRD 95 (1994).

Eisenberg, Theodore & Valerie P. Hans, Taking a Stand on Taking the Stand: The Effect of a Prior Criminal Record on the Decision to Testify and on Trial Outcomes, 94 Cornell L. Rev. 1353 (2009).

Falkner, Judson F. & David T. Steffen, Evidence of Character: From the "Crucible of the Community" to the "Couch of the Psychiatrist," 102 U. Pa. L. Rev. 980 (1954).

Frankel, Marvin E., The Search for Truth: An Umpireal View, 123 U. Pa. L. Rev. 1031 (1975).

Freedman, Monroe H., Professional Responsibility of the Criminal Defense Lawyer: The Three Hardest Questions, 64 Mich. L. Rev. 1469 (1966).

Friedman, Richard D., Character Impeachment Evidence: The Asymmetrical Interaction Between Personality and Situation, 43 Duke L.J. 816 (1994).

Friedman, Richard D., Character Impeachment Evidence: Psycho-Bayesian[!?] Analysis and a Proposed Overhaul, 38 U.C.L.A. L. Rev. 637 (1991).

Galvin, Harriett R., Shielding Rape Victims in the State and Federal Courts: A Proposal for the Second Decade, 70 Minn. L. Rev. 763 (1986).

Green, Stuart P., Deceit and Classification of Crimes: Federal Rule of Evidence 609(a)(2) and the Origins of Crimen Falsi, 90 J. Crim. L. & Criminology 1087 (2000).

Graham, Michael H., Impeaching the Professional Expert Witness by a Showing of Financial Interest, 53 Ind. L.J. 35 (1977–78).

Hale, William G., Some Comments on Character Evidence and Related Topics, 72 So. Cal. L. Rev. 341 (1949).

Hale, William G., Specific Acts and Related Matters as Affecting Credibility, 1 Hastings L.J. 89 (1950).

Haxton, David, Comment, Rape Shield Statutes: Constitutional Despite Unconstitutional Exclusions of Evidence, 1985 Wis. L. Rev. 1219.

Hutton, Mary Christine, Commentary: Prior Bad Acts Evidence in Cases of Sexual Contacts with a Child, 34 S.D. L. Rev. 604 (1989).

Imwinkelried, Edward J., The Need to Amend Federal Rule of Evidence 404(b): The Threat to the Future of the Federal Rules of Evidence, 30 Vill. L. Rev. 1465 (1985).

Imwinkelried, Edward J., Reshaping the "Grotesque" Doctrine of Character Evidence: The Reform Implications of the Most Recent Psychological Research, 36 Southwestern U.L. Rev. 741 (2007).

James, Fleming, Jr. & John J. Dickenson, Accident Proneness and Accident Law, 63 Harv. L. Rev. 769 (1950).

Johnson, Denise R., Prior False Allegations of Rape: Falsus in Uno, Falsus in Omnibus, 7 Yale J. L. & Feminism 243 (1995).

Kaloyanides, David J., The Depraved Sexual Instinct Theory: An Example of the Propensity for Aberrant Application of Federal Rule of Evidence 404(b), 25 Loy. L.A. L. Rev. 1297 (1992).

Karp, David J., Evidence of Propensity and Probability in Sex Offense Cases and Other Cases, 70 Chi.-Kent L. Rev. 15 (1994).

Kuhns, Richard B., The Propensity to Misunderstand the Character of Specific Acts of Evidence, 66 Iowa L. Rev. 777 (1981).

Ladd, Mason, Credibility Tests—Current Trends, 89 U. Pa. L. Rev. 166 (1965).

Ladd, Mason, Some Observations on Credibility, Impeachment of Witnesses, 52 Cornell L. Q. 238 (1967).

Ladd, Mason, Techniques and Theory of Character Testimony, 24 Iowa L. Rev. 498 (1939).

Leonard, David P., In Defense of Character Evidence Prohibition: Foundations of the Rule Against Trial by Character, 73 Ind. L.J. 1161 (1998).

Leonard, David P., The Use of Character to Prove Conduct: Rationality and Catharsis in the Law of Evidence, 58 Colo. L. Rev. 1 (1987).

Leonard, David P., The Use of Uncharged Misconduct Evidence to Prove Knowledge, 81 Neb. L. Rev. 115 (2002).

Lewan, Kenneth M., Rationale of Habit Evidence, 16 Syracuse L. Rev. 39 (1964).

Liebman, James S., Proposed Evidence Rules 413 to 415—Some Problems and Recommendations, 20 Dayton L. Rev. 753 (1995).

Maguire, John M. & Charles W. Quick, Testimony: Memory and Memoranda, 3 How. L.J. 1 (1957).

McCormick, Charles T., The Scope and Art of Cross-examination, 47 Nw. U. L. Rev. 177 (1956).

McGowan, Carl, Impeachment of Criminal Defendants by Prior Conviction, 1970 Law & Soc. Ord. 1.

Mendez, Miguel A., California's New Law on Character Evidence: Evidence Code Section 352 and the Impact of Recent Psychological Studies, 31 UCLA L. Rev. 1003 (1984).

Mueller, Christopher B., Of Misshapen Stones and Compromises: *Michelson* and the Modern Law of Character Evidence, in Evidence Stories 75 (Richard Lempert ed. 2006).

Murphy, Sakthi, Rejecting Unreasonable Sexual Expectations: Limits on Using a Rape Victim's Sexual History to Show the Defendant's Mistaken Belief in Consent, 79 Cal. L. Rev. 541 (1991).

Myers, John E.B., Uncharged Misconduct Evidence in Child Abuse Litigation, 1988 Utah L. Rev. 479 (1988).

Natoli, Louis M. & R. Stephen Sigall, "Are You Going to Arraign his Whole Life?": How Sexual Propensity Evidence Violates the Due Process Clause, 28 Loy. U. Chi. L. J. 1 (1996).

Nichol, Gene R., Jr., Prior Crime Impeachment of Criminal Defendants: A Constitutional Analysis of Rule 609, 82 W. Va. L. Rev. 391 (1980).

Nicholas, Peter, They Say He's Gay The Admissibility of Evidence of Sexual Orientation, 37 Ga. L. Rev. 793 (2003).

Ordover, Abraham P., Balancing the Presumptions of Guilt and Innocence: Rules 404(b), 608(b) and 609(a), 38 Emory L.J. 135 (1989).

Orenstein, Aviva, Deviance, Due Process, and the False Promise of Federal Rule of Evidence 403, 90 Cornell L. Rev. 1487 (2005).

Overbeck, Jennifer L., Note, Beyond Admissibility: A Practical Look at the Use of Eyewitness Expert Testimony in Federal Courts, 80 N.Y.U. L. Rev. 1895 (2005).

Park, Roger C., The Crime Bill of 1994 and the Law of Character Evidence: Congress Was Right About Consent Defense Cases, 22 Fordham Urb. L.J. 271 (1995).

Park, Roger C., Eyewitness Identification: Expert Witnesses Are Not the Only Solution, 2 Law, Probability & Risk 305 (2003).

Polenberg, Richard, Law and Character: The Saintly Cardozo—Character and the Criminal Law, 71 U. Colo. L. Rev. 1311 (2000).

Reed, Thomas J., Reading Gaol Revisited: Admission of Uncharged Misconduct Evidence in Sex Offender Cases, 21 Am. J. Crim. L. 127 (1993).

Ridolfi, Cookie, Statement on Representing Rape Defendants, in Deborah L. Rhode, Professional Responsibility: Ethics by the Pervasive Method 206 (2d ed. 1998).

Sanchirico, Chris William, Character Evidence and the Object of Trial, 101 Colum. L. Rev. 1233 (2001).

Schrag, Joel & Suzanne Scotchmer, Crime and Prejudice: The Use of Character Evidence in Criminal Trials, 10 J.L. & Econ. Org. 319 (1994).

Seidelson, David E., Extrinsic Evidence on a Collateral Matter May Not Be Used to Impeach Credibility; What Constitutes "Collateral Matter"?, 9 Rev. Litig. 203 (1990).

Slough, M.C., Impeachment of Witness, Common Law Principles and Modern Trends, 34 Ind. L.J. 1 (1958).

Slough, M.C. & J. William Knightly, Other Views, Other Crimes, 41 Iowa L. Rev. 325 (1956).

Swancara, Frank, Impeachment of Non-Religious Witness, 13 Rocky Mt. L. Rev. 336 (1941).

Stein, Edward, The Admissibility of Expert Testimony about Cognitive Science Research on Eyewitness Identification, 2 Law, Probability & Risk 295 (2003).

Symposium: Perspectives on Proposed Federal Rules of Evidence 413–415, 22 Fordham Urb. L.J. 265 (1995).

Tanford, J. Alexander & Anthony J. Bocchino, Rape Victim Shield Laws and the Sixth Amendment, 128 U. Pa. L. Rev. 544 (1980).

Taslitz, Andrew E., Myself Alone: Individualizing Justice Through Psychological Character Evidence, 52 Md. L. Rev. 1 (1993).

Teitelbaum, Lee E., Gale Sutton-Barbere & Peder Johnson, Evaluating the Prejudicial Effect of Evidence: Can Judges Identify the Impact of Improper Evidence on Juries? 1983 Wis. L. Rev. 1147.

Thomas, Elwood L., Rehabilitating the Impeached Witness with Consistent Statements, 32 Mo. L. Rev. 472 (1968).

Tilley, Cristina Carmody, A Feminist Repudiation of the Rape Shield Laws, 51 Drake L. Rev. 45 (2003).

Tuerkheimer, Frank, A Reassessment and Redefinition of Rape Shield Laws, 50 Ohio St. L. J. 1245 (1989).

Uviller, H. Richard, The Advocate, the Truth and Judicial Hackles: A Reaction to Judge Frankel's Idea, 123 U. Pa. L. Rev. 1067 (1975).

Uviller, H. Richard, Credence, Character, and the Rules of Evidence: Seeing Through the Liar's Tale, 42 Duke L.J. 776 (1993).

Uviller, H. Richard, Evidence of Character to Prove Conduct: Illusion, Illogic, and Injustice in the Courtroom, 130 U. Pa. L. Rev. 845 (1982).

Uviller, H. Richard, Unconvinced, Unreconstructed, and Unrepentant: A Reply to Professor Friedman's Response, 43 Duke L.J. 834 (1994).

Weissenberger, Glen, Making Sense of Extrinsic Act Evidence: Federal Rule of Evidence 404(b), 70 Iowa L. Rev. 579 (1985).

Wells, Christina E. & Erin Elliott Motley, Reinforcing the Myth of the Crazed Rapist: A Feminist Critique of Recent Rape Legislation, 81 B.U. L. Rev. 127 (2001).

BIBLIOGRAPHY

CHAPTER 6

HEARSAY

■ ■ ■

I.   HEARSAY POLICY

A.   INTRODUCTION

Wigmore has called the hearsay rule "'that most characteristic rule of the Anglo-American law of evidence'—a rule which may be esteemed, next to jury trial, the greatest contribution of that eminently practical legal system to the world's methods of procedure."[1] While some scholars, judges, and practicing lawyers have argued that the hearsay rule, on balance, hinders rather than contributes to the practical resolution of legal disputes, virtually everyone would acknowledge the centrality of the hearsay rule to American evidence law.[2] In this chapter we discuss the nature and contours of the hearsay rule, the justifications supporting it, and the numerous situations in which courts admit hearsay evidence. Later in this chapter we will present several common definitions of hearsay and a detailed discussion of what hearsay actually is. But before doing this, there are points we wish to make that require us to have some idea of what we are talking about. So, for the moment, accept this overbroad version of the basic hearsay principle: *the trier of fact may be asked to believe only those statements made by witnesses testifying at the trial.* The fact-finder may not be presented with statements of non-witnesses and asked to believe they are true. Thus, testimony by one witness that another person said something may not be considered by the fact-finder as evidence that what that other person said is true.

The common law attitude toward hearsay developed as the jury was transformed from a group of neighbors chosen to resolve matters on the basis of what they knew or could learn to a group of uninformed citizens charged with deciding a case solely on the basis of information presented

---

[1]   WIGMORE § 1364, at 28.

[2]   The importance of the hearsay rule in England has substantially diminished with the demise of jury trials in most civil cases. In the United States, the hearsay rule is inapplicable or relaxed in the numerous cases litigated before federal and state administrative agencies. In theory, the rule applies in its full rigor to bench trials, but except when lower court decisions explicitly rely on inadmissible hearsay, appellate courts generally assume that the trial judge properly discounted inadmissible hearsay. Even when the trial judge excludes evidence on hearsay grounds, he has heard the hearsay before reaching a decision. In these circumstances, there is good reason to believe that if the hearsay is convincing, most judges cannot help but be influenced by it. If you know that an opponent's case would be substantially strengthened by convincing but inadmissible hearsay, you have reason to insist on a jury trial.

to them.　McCormick presents the following brief summary of these developments:[3]

> The development of the jury was, no doubt, an important factor [in the development of the hearsay rule].　It will be remembered that the jury in its earlier forms was in the nature of a committee or special commission of qualified persons in the neighborhood to report on facts or issues in dispute.　So far as necessary its members conducted its investigations informally among those who had special knowledge of the facts.　Attesting witnesses to writings were summoned with the jurors and apparently participated in their deliberations, but the practice of calling witnesses to appear in court and testify publicly about the facts to the jury is a late development in jury trial.　Though something like the jury existed at least as early as the 1100s, this practice of hearing witnesses in court does not become frequent until the later 1400s.　The changeover to the present conception that the normal source of proof is not the private knowledge or investigation of the jurors, but the testimony of witnesses in open court, is a matter of gradual evolution thereafter.　Finally, in the 1500s it has become, though not yet the exclusive source of proof, the normal and principal one.
>
> It is not until this period of the gradual emergence of the witness testifying publicly in court that the consciousness of need for exclusionary rules of evidence begins to appear.　It had indeed been required even of the early witnesses to writings that they could speak only of "what they saw and heard" and this requirement would naturally be applied to the new class of testifying witnesses.　But when the witness has heard at firsthand the statement of X out of court that he has seen and heard a blow with a sword, or witnessed a trespass on land, as evidence of the blow or the trespass, a new question is presented.　Certainly it would seem that the earlier requirement of knowledge must have predisposed the judges to skepticism about the value of hearsay.
>
> . . . And so through the reigns of the Tudors and the Stuarts there is a gradually increasing drumfire of criticism and objections by parties and counsel against evidence of oral hearsay declarations.　While the evidence was constantly admitted, the confidence in its reliability was increasingly undermined.　It was derided as a "tale of a tale" or "a story out of another man's mouth."　Parallel with this increasingly discredited use of casual oral hearsay was a similar development in respect to transcribed statements made under oath before a judge or judicial officer, not

---

[3]　MCCORMICK, EVIDENCE § 244 (footnotes omitted).

subject to cross-examination by the party against whom it is offered. In criminal cases in the 1500s and down to the middle 1600s the main reliance of the prosecution was the use of such "depositions" to make out its case. As oral hearsay was becoming discredited, uneasiness about the use of "depositions" began to take shape, first in the form of a limitation that they could only be used when the witness could not be produced at the trial. It will be noted that the want of oath and the unreliability of the report of the oral statement cannot be urged against such evidence but only the want of cross-examination and observation of demeanor.

It was in the first decade after the Restoration that the century or so of criticism of hearsay had its final effect in decisions rejecting its use, first as to oral hearsay and then as to depositions. Wigmore finds that the period between 1675 and 1690 is the time of crystallization of the rule against hearsay.[4]

> Whether the rule against hearsay was, with the rest of the English law of evidence, in fact "the child of the jury" or the product of the adversary system may be of no great contemporary significance. The important thing is that the rule against hearsay taking form at the end of the seventeenth century was neither a matter of "immemorial usage" nor an inheritance from Magna Charta but, in the long view of English legal history, was a late development of the common law.

The impetus for the final development and rather rigid interpretation of the hearsay rule came in part from a number of celebrated trials in which obvious injustice was wrought by a reliance on hearsay. One of the most famous was the trial of Sir Walter Raleigh. Raleigh was convicted of conspiracy to commit treason on the basis of the sworn, out-of-court statement of his alleged co-conspirator Lord Cobham.[5]

Raleigh protested:

> But it is strange to see how you press me still with my Lord Cobham, and yet will not produce him; it is not for gaining of time or prolonging my life that I urge this: he is in the house

---

[4] Professor Landsman dates the crystallization of the hearsay rule somewhat later. He finds that it was applied inconsistently through the beginning of the 18th century, but it was a firmly established rule of practice by the end of that century. Also, the principle deficiency attributed to hearsay changed over the course of the 18th century from the lack of an oath to the lack of cross-examination. Stephan Landsman, *The Rise of the Contentious Spirit: Adversary Procedure in Eighteenth Century England*, 75 Cornell L. Rev. 497, 565–72, 597–601 (1990). Landsman suggests that the hearsay rule was not only a product of the jury system, but also a product of the adversary system. As criminal defense counsel became a fixed part of the adjudicatory system, the rules of evidence they might evoke solidified. *Id.* at 543–44, 564–65. We have more faith in Landsman's historiography than in Wigmore's.

[5] PHILLIMORE, HISTORY AND PRINCIPLES OF THE LAW OF EVIDENCE 157 (1850).

hard by, and may soon be brought hither: let him be produced, and if he will yet accuse me or avow this confession of his, it shall convict me and ease you of further proof.[6]

Cobham was never produced.

The prosecution also introduced hearsay through the testimony of a live witness:

Attorney General.—"I shall now produce a witness viva voce:"

He then produced one *Dyer,* a pilot, who, being sworn, said, "Being at Lisbon, there came to me a Portuguese gentleman who asked me how the King of England did and whether he was crowned? I answered him, that I hoped our noble king was well, and crowned by this; but the time was not come when I came from the coast of Spain. 'Nay,' said he, 'your king shall never he crowned, for Don Cobham and Don Raleigh will cut his throat before he come to be crowned.' And this, in time, was found to be spoken in mid July."

Raleigh.—"This is the saying of some wild Jesuit or beggarly priest; but what proof is it against me?"

Attorney General.—"It must perforce arise out of some preceding intelligence, and shows that your treason had wings."

The attorney-general's response to Raleigh serves only to emphasize the weakness of Dyer's testimony.[7]

The injustices of Raleigh's case and other political trials had a substantial impact on the subsequent development of English criminal procedure: they justified a strict hearsay rule and influenced the framers of the United States Constitution to incorporate in the Sixth Amendment a right to confront adverse witnesses.[8]

---

[6] The accusation was later allegedly withdrawn, but the withdrawal was also allegedly recanted.

[7] PHILLIMORE, *supra* note 5.

[8] The "Confrontation Clause" and the most important cases interpreting it will be discussed in detail in Chapter Seven. For the present, note that this constitutional guarantee applies only in criminal cases, and that while it is designed to promote many of the same values as the hearsay rule, it does not necessarily follow the contours of this rule and its exceptions. *See, e.g.,* Crawford v. Washington, 541 U.S. 36 (2004).

FIGURE ONE
THE TESTIMONIAL TRIANGLE

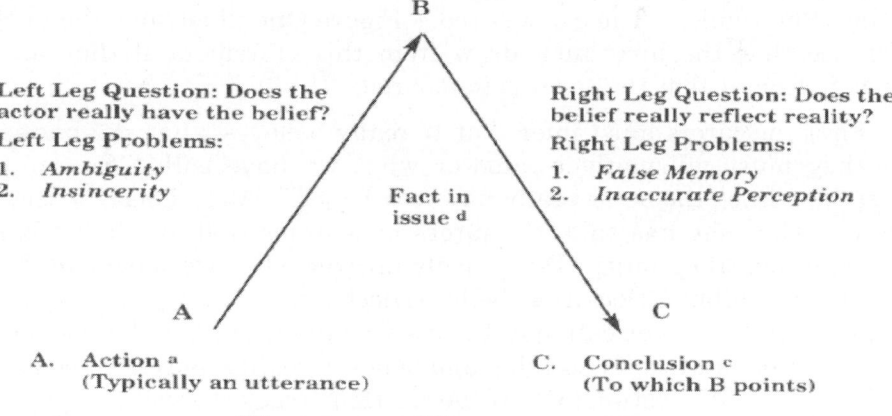

B.   Belief [b] (Of actor responsible for A)

B

Left Leg Question: Does the
actor really have the belief?

Left Leg Problems:
1. *Ambiguity*
2. *Insincerity*

Right Leg Question: Does the
belief really reflect reality?

Right Leg Problems:
1. *False Memory*
2. *Inaccurate Perception*

Fact in
issue [d]

A

C

A.   Action [a]
(Typically an utterance)

C.   Conclusion [c]
(To which B points)

[a] *W*'s statement "The car was red."
[b] *W*'s belief that the car was red.
[c] The fact that the car was red.
[d] The color of the car.

B.   INFERENCES FROM TESTIMONY

History provides one explanation for the hearsay rule. It explains how the rule and its exceptions arose out of earlier procedures or circumstances, and it depicts the ways in which past generations rationalized the rule. But history does not and should not bind us. To evaluate both the longstanding rationales that have been offered for the hearsay rule and the possible alternative justifications, one must understand what hearsay is and the dangers the rule is intended to avoid. This can best be done by first considering the ways in which jurors make inferences from testimony. In doing so we shall borrow Professor Laurence Tribe's testimonial triangle, which we will return to as our discussion of hearsay proceeds.[9]

---

[9]   Laurence H. Tribe, Triangulating Hearsay, 87 Harv. L. Rev. 957 (1974). Our version of the testimonial triangle is a modification of Tribe's presentation. One difference is that our triangles lack a base and thus are not actually triangles, although we shall refer to them as such. The base is removed because it suggests a link between the two base points that does not exist. A more informal display of this triangle might look as follows:

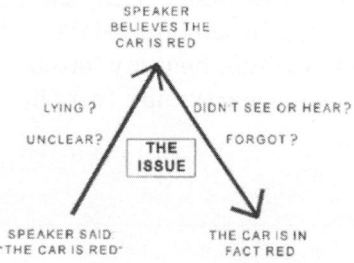

SPEAKER
BELIEVES THE
CAR IS RED

LYING?   DIDN'T SEE OR HEAR?

UNCLEAR?   THE ISSUE   FORGOT?

SPEAKER SAID
"THE CAR IS RED"

THE CAR IS IN
FACT RED

Consider a trial in which the owner of a red car is charged with leaving the scene of an accident. To establish that the defendant's car hit the victim, the prosecution calls an eyewitness, W, and after the usual preliminaries asks her if she noticed the color of the car that struck the victim. She replies, "The car was red." Figure One illustrates the double inference that the jury must draw from this statement if they are to conclude from it that the car was in fact red.

First the jurors must infer that W really believes what she has said: i.e., they must affirmatively answer what we have called the left leg question: "Does the actor really have the belief?" After inferring that W believes what she has said, the jurors must infer that W's belief is not mistaken; i.e., they must affirmatively answer what we have called the right leg question: "Does that belief reflect reality?" Only if the jurors are prepared to answer both questions affirmatively, and make the double inference from statement to belief and belief to reality, may they conclude on the basis of W's testimony that the car that struck the victim was red.

The triangle suggests that the jurors face two main problems in making each inference. To conclude that W really believed what she appeared to say, the jurors must first be sure that she and they interpret words in the same way. There should be no ambiguity in what was said. If the jurors discover that W only recently learned English and that she frequently confuses red with yellow, they will be wary of giving too much weight to her testimony. The jurors must also conclude that W was not trying to deceive them when she stated the car was red. If they learn that W hates the defendant, they are again likely to discredit her testimony.

In answering the right leg question, the jurors must decide whether a sincere belief is mistaken. Here, the major problems are mistakes of memory and of perception. The jurors, to continue with our example, are more likely to accept W's belief if her description is given one day, rather than one year, after the accident. If W were shown to be color blind, however sincere her belief, it would not count for much.

These problems of inference exist whenever jurors are asked to believe a witness's testimony. Obviously, we do not exclude ordinary testimony because there is a danger that the jurors may be deceived. While we are aware of this possibility, there are certain features of testimony given in the courtroom that are thought to minimize the danger: the testimony is given under *oath*, the jurors are able to observe the witness's *demeanor*, the testimony relays crucial information in the *context* of a larger story while hearsay often consists only of crucial statements, and the opposing party may test the witness's story by *cross-examination*.

Of these safeguards, the opportunity to cross-examine is the most important. Ideally, cross-examination may clear up ambiguity, expose insincerity, and reveal reasons to suspect a witness's memory or his ability to have observed clearly the events he describes. In practice, cross-examination rarely destroys a witness's testimony, but it often leads to the qualification of unqualified assertions, indicates motives to deceive, and suggests to jurors the kind of critical stance they should take toward a witness's testimony.

The oath is thought to have been effective in promoting honesty at a time when people were more religious and believed in an avenging God, more generally. Many think it now helps primarily insofar as it emphasizes the solemnity of the occasion and raises the threat of prosecution for perjury.

Appellate courts often rely on the trier's opportunity to view a witness's demeanor as justification for not reversing decisions below, but there is no good evidence that the opportunity to observe the demeanor of testifying witnesses aids in evaluating credibility, and there is some evidence to the contrary.[10] The shifty-eyed witness may be simply nervous or astigmatic, while the cool and collected one may be an experienced liar.

Most commentators on the hearsay rule do not mention a statement's context as an aid to evaluating courtroom testimony,[11] but hearing testimony in the context of a larger story aids in evaluating credibility. Even without cross-examination, jurors may spot inconsistencies between the various portions of a witness's testimony, and they may notice that not all pertinent facts were perceived or remembered—which could lead them to question the accuracy of those facts that were reported. Context, like cross-examination, aids jurors in evaluating all the testimonial dangers; oath and demeanor aid only in the evaluation of sincerity.

C. THE HEARSAY DANGERS

Consider our earlier example of the hit-and-run driver, but this time, assume that *W* arrived after the driver had fled but in time to hear an observer, *O*, state, "A red car hit the victim."

---

[10] Olin G. Wellborn, *Demeanor*, 76 Cornell L. Rev. 1075, 1078–91 (1991).

[11] This may be because a witness who is properly identified and shown to have firsthand knowledge will be allowed to testify to a single fact set in no context other than that which the adversary attempts to establish through cross-examination. But a witness usually will not be allowed to testify in court without taking an oath, without appearing in person before the factfinder, and without subjecting himself to cross-examination. In practice, however, important witnesses usually report facts in the context of larger stories, while reported hearsay more often consists of discrete factual statements.

FIGURE TWO

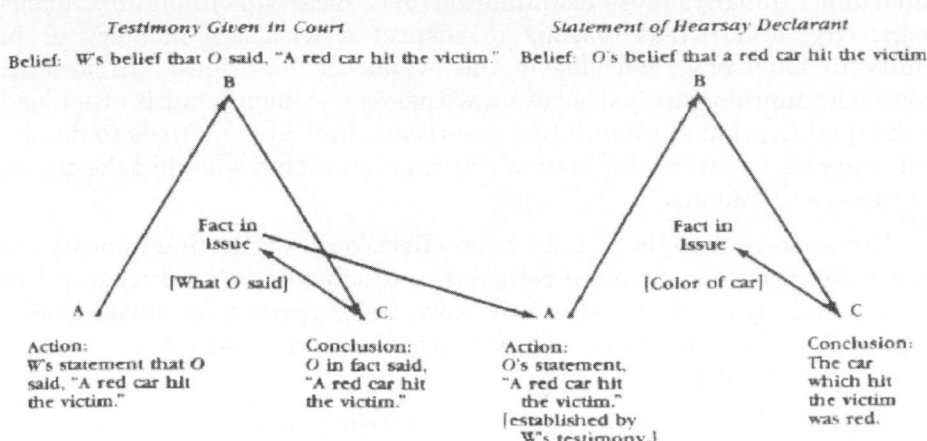

Figure Two depicts the series of inferences that the trier of fact will have to make to conclude from W's report of O's statement that a red car in fact hit the victim. The fact-finder will have to infer from W's testimony that W believes she heard O, the speaker, make the statement, "A red car hit the victim;" from W's belief, that O did make the statement; from O's making the statement, that O believed the car was red; and from O's belief, that the car was in fact red. These inferences respecting the meaning, veracity, and accuracy of O's statement have none of the safeguards that commonly exist when jurors are asked to evaluate courtroom testimony. Because O is an out-of-court speaker, the jurors cannot view his demeanor; they lack any assurance an oath brings, and they will not see him tested by cross-examination. These deficiencies constitute the most commonly mentioned hearsay dangers. To them we add the likelihood that the speaker's statement will be reported as a discrete item of information; hence it will not be subject to the consistency checks possible when a statement is part of a larger story.

To these dangers, which are all associated with the speaker's statement rather than the witness's testimony, some commentators have added the danger of mistaken transmittal. As the children's game of "telephone" illustrates, it is easy to misreport what another has said. Wigmore rejected this argument as a justification for the hearsay rule because testimony reporting an out-of-court statement is subject to the same safeguards that exist to maximize the reliability of all testimonial evidence. Wigmore's premise is correct, but he fails to appreciate important differences between ordinary testimony and reports of hearsay. First, honest mistakes about crucial matters may be more likely when statements are reported than when more complex events are described. The failure to hear the single word "not" can transform a statement from one of exculpation into an admission of guilt or liability. The failure to appreciate one detail of a complex scene is unlikely to be so crucial, particularly since other testimony may fill in details without forcing jurors to choose between inconsistent stories. If a mistake in reporting is an honest one, the witness will not be deterred by the oath, nor will the witness's demeanor suggest that he is lying.

Second, and more important, cross-examination is likely to be less effective in testing dishonest or mistaken reports of out-of-court statements than it is in testing most other erroneous testimonial claims. This seems particularly true of intentional deceit. A witness reporting hearsay seldom has to carefully fit a story into the context of facts too well established to deny. The witness need only testify to his good hearing and to what he heard. If asked how what he heard may be reconciled with other facts in the case, the witness may reply that he knows nothing beyond what some—perhaps unidentified—other has said. How, for example, does one deal on cross-examination with the victim's friend who claims to have heard, upon arriving at the scene of the accident, a stranger in the crowd say, "The red car was speeding"? If the friend testified that he saw the red car speeding, one could quiz him on his ability to judge speed, his vantage point, his failure to warn, and his failure to report the driver to the police. Inconsistency in answering such questions might convince the jury that the witness could not be trusted. Inconsistency is more difficult to show when only hearsay is reported.[12]

D. THE HEARSAY DILEMMA

We have now canvassed the reasons usually given for the exclusion of hearsay. We hope we have convinced you that, in many circumstances, hearsay evidence is less reliable than similar or identical testimony that is subjected to cross-examination before the trier of fact. It does not follow from this that hearsay evidence is valueless or that any and all hearsay should be excluded. While there may be a danger that jurors will be misled if hearsay evidence is admitted, jurors may be *more* likely to be misled if they never learn of the evidence. Consider the example we have used of the hit-and-run driver. Suppose some evidence connects the defendant, who drives a red car, to the scene of the crime: The day after the accident he took a freshly dented fender in for repair, and the accident occurred at 5:10 p.m. on a street the defendant travels while going to and from work. Are the jurors likely to reach a better decision if

---

[12] In addition to these arguments, the fact that hearsay involves inferences about the veracity and accuracy of two speakers may also complicate the jury's decision on the proper weight to be accorded a hearsay declaration. If a juror decides there is a 50 percent chance that a witness's statement is accurate, how much weight should that statement be given in the jury's deliberations? If the jury believes that a witness's report of an out-of-court declaration has a 50 percent chance of being accurate, and if accurate, the out-of-court statement has an 80 percent chance of being true, how much weight should be given to the out-of-court statement? Mathematically, the hearsay situation is as tractable as the other, but jurors, who will reach both conclusions on intuitive rather than mathematical bases, may be more likely to make mistakes in deciding the appropriate weight to be accorded hearsay statements than in evaluating the proper weight of disputable courtroom testimony.

they learn from *W*, a witness whose credibility is tested, that she heard *O*, an apparently disinterested observer, say that the car in the accident was red? Or, are they likely to reach a better result if this evidence is kept from them?

Perhaps hearsay should be routinely admitted. After all, even though people prefer to act on the basis of firsthand information, important decisions are often based entirely on secondhand and third hand reports. Can we not trust jurors to view hearsay with appropriate skepticism and accord it proper weight?[13] If we are not willing to go this far, should we perhaps trust judges to exclude the most dangerous hearsay and call the jury's attention to the limitations of what they admit? These are good questions that are often posed by critics of the hearsay rule. They raise somewhat different issues of whether hearsay should be grounds for excluding evidence and, if so, whether exclusion should be by rule or by discretion. As with many difficult questions, there are no clearly correct answers. We will discuss these issues in more detail in Section IV of this Chapter.

In the American legal system, hearsay is not routinely admitted, nor is the decision whether to admit hearsay left solely to judicial discretion. On the other hand, hearsay evidence is routinely offered and is often admitted. The common law has moderated the tension of a rule excluding potentially unreliable but perhaps helpful information by formulating a series of exceptions—really rules in themselves—that specify situations in which hearsay is admissible. The justifications for most hearsay exceptions reflect two criteria: necessity and reliability. When evidence of a particular type is not likely to be available unless hearsay statements are admitted, or when particular types of hearsay appear to carry special guarantees of reliability, exceptions to the hearsay rule are likely. We shall discuss these exceptions to the hearsay rule and the rationales commonly given for them in Section III of this Chapter.

For the present, it is sufficient to note that while scholars are agreed that the exclusion of all hearsay would be untenable, many see the proliferation of hearsay exceptions as part of the problem rather than as its solution. The Federal Rules list 28 specific exceptions and a general

---

[13] Social scientists and lawyers have recently begun to study hearsay experimentally. Generally speaking, studies find that hearsay evidence is discounted relative to eyewitness testimony. The studies done to date provide no good basis for policy recommendations because there are too few of them and there is a broad range of hearsay that remains unstudied. The stimulus materials are also simplified representations of trials presented to mock jurors who are sometimes just college students and do not deliberate. To point out these limitations on policy relevance is not to criticize the research. Some of these studies have been nicely designed and executed. It is just that we must know much more for responsible, empirically based, policy recommendations. *See, e.g.*, Margaret B. Kovera, Roger C. Park & Steven D. Penrod, *Jurors' Perceptions of Eyewitness and Hearsay Evidence*, 76 Minn. L. Rev. 703 (1992); Peter Miene, Roger C. Park & Eugene Borgida, *Juror Decision Making and the Evaluation of Hearsay Evidence*, 76 Minn. L. Rev. 683 (1992); Regina Schaller, *Expert Evidence and Hearsay*, 19 LAW & HUM. BEHAV. 345 (1995).

exception to the hearsay rule. Some commentators have spotted even more in the various states. One may wonder whether a rule that requires 29 exceptions should exist. Indeed, one may ask whether it makes sense to call something a rule when it has 29 codified exceptions. When you have mastered the exceptions, we will return to these questions. As you read about the hearsay rule and its exceptions, consider alternative ways in which our legal system might deal with hearsay, and ask yourself: How satisfactory are the compromises that the common law courts have evolved?

II.   DEFINING HEARSAY

A. GENERAL DEFINITIONS

In the preceding discussion of hearsay policy we did not attempt to precisely define hearsay because we needed to know only the general characteristics of hearsay evidence. A general appreciation of the concept of hearsay, however, is not enough when faced with close questions of admissibility at trial. Fine distinctions between different types of out-of-court statements and the uses to which they are put will frequently determine what evidence the jury will be allowed to hear. In this section we shall explain in detail what is and what is not hearsay, and alert you to some kinds of evidence whose hearsay status is not clear.

The definition which you will have to master is the definition set forth in FRE 801 which provides:

> **(a) Statement.** "Statement" means a person's oral assertion, written assertion, or nonverbal conduct, if the person intended it as an assertion.

> **(b) Declarant.**[14] "Declarant" means the person who made the statement.

> **(c) Hearsay.**[15] "Hearsay" means a statement that:

---

[14] The Federal Rules refer to the maker of hearsay statements as the *declarant*. Hearsay statements may be made by speaking, or by writing, or by pointing or communicating through any other type of action, so a declarant may do any of these things. In the text, we shall use the word *speaker* rather than *declarant* to refer to the maker of a hearsay statement because it is a less pretentious word and makes for simpler writing. Except when we refer to someone who is actually speaking, we use the word "speaker" in the same broad sense that the Federal Rules and most commentaries use the word "declarant."

[15] FRE 801 goes on in Section (d) to exclude certain types of statements from its hearsay definition. However the Federal Rules label the rules that govern these statements, they function as exceptions to what FRE 801(a), (b), and (c) would otherwise define as inadmissible hearsay. We will postpone our discussion of these exclusions from the hearsay definition until we reach the exceptions to the hearsay rule.

Rarely will anything turn on whether an out-of-court statement is excluded from the definition of hearsay under FRE 801(d) or is an exception to the hearsay rule under FRE's 803, 804, or 807. Occasionally a party will be entitled to a cautionary instruction with respect to statements admitted under a hearsay exception but will have no right to such an instruction for non-hearsay. FRE 807 allows the discretionary admission of hearsay only by reference to those

(1) the declarant does not make while testifying at the current trial or hearing; and

(2) a party offers in evidence to prove the truth of the matter asserted in the statement.

To introduce the topic, however, we shall organize our discussion around a definition that captures the essence of FRE 801(c) in shorter and simpler language:

Hearsay is an out-of-court "statement" offered for the truth of the matter asserted.

Three aspects of this definition require elucidation. First, what is meant by the word "*statement*"? (The quotation marks, which we shall now discard, no doubt alerted you to the fact that it means something more than "an oral or written declaration or remark.") Second, what does it mean for a statement to be "*offered for the truth of the matter asserted*"? And third, what does it mean for a statement to be "*out-of-court*"? These questions are best answered in reverse order.

B. "OUT-OF-COURT"

"Out-of-court" statements are any statements except those made by witnesses during the *current* trial while testifying before the trier of fact. Thus, assuming the other elements of the definition are met, any oral or written statement by someone other than the witness will be hearsay, as will all statements by the witness herself except testimony at the current trial. Hearsay thus includes earlier statements by witnesses under oath in depositions, statements made in earlier trials, and statements made during the current trial in the judge's chambers. This aspect of the hearsay rule is counter-intuitive and often confusing. If the witness herself made the out-of-court statement, why should we consider it hearsay when the jury can see her repeat it under oath and she can be cross-examined on it? There are, to be sure, differences between cross-examining a witness about what she said shortly after she said it and cross-examining the same witness about what she said some time ago. In the former situation, for example, the witness cannot credibly say, "I'm sure what I said was correct, but I don't remember exactly what it was." But many believe the differences are not substantial enough to justify a blanket rule of exclusion. This view is reflected in FRE 801(d)(1), which defines some prior statements of witnesses as non-hearsay. Some states go beyond the Federal Rules in this respect.

---

factors that justify hearsay exceptions, so in these small ways the distinction may have consequences. Usually, however, courts approach statements excluded from the hearsay definition under FRE 801(d) as if they were dealing with hearsay that qualifies for admission under an FRE 803 or an 804 exception. Moreover, the Supreme Court in its Confrontation Clause cases generally addresses the constitutional issues posed by statements covered by FRE 801(d) in the same way it addresses the constitutional issues posed by acknowledged hearsay exceptions.

C. "THE TRUTH OF THE MATTER ASSERTED"

A statement is "offered for the truth of the matter asserted" when its relevance to some fact in issue lies not in the fact that the statement was spoken or written, nor in some inference that can be drawn from the fact that the speaker believes it to be true, but rather in a conclusion that is justified only if the statement is true. In other words, a statement is not hearsay unless it is offered to establish the existence of a fact or facts therein asserted. To see why hearsay is defined in this way, consider the testimonial triangles I, II, and III in Figure Three.[16]

Triangle I portrays the situation where the relevant issue is whether a statement was spoken. Here, one can reason directly from the report of the statement to the fact in issue. Suppose, for example, the issue was whether Emma was conscious after she fell off a horse. That Emma said, while lying on the ground, "A snake spooked Beauty" is good evidence that Emma was conscious, and it is good evidence on that issue whether or not a snake in fact had spooked her horse. In deciding whether Emma's speech act was relevant, we have to ask neither the right nor the left leg question, so the four primary hearsay dangers do not exist.

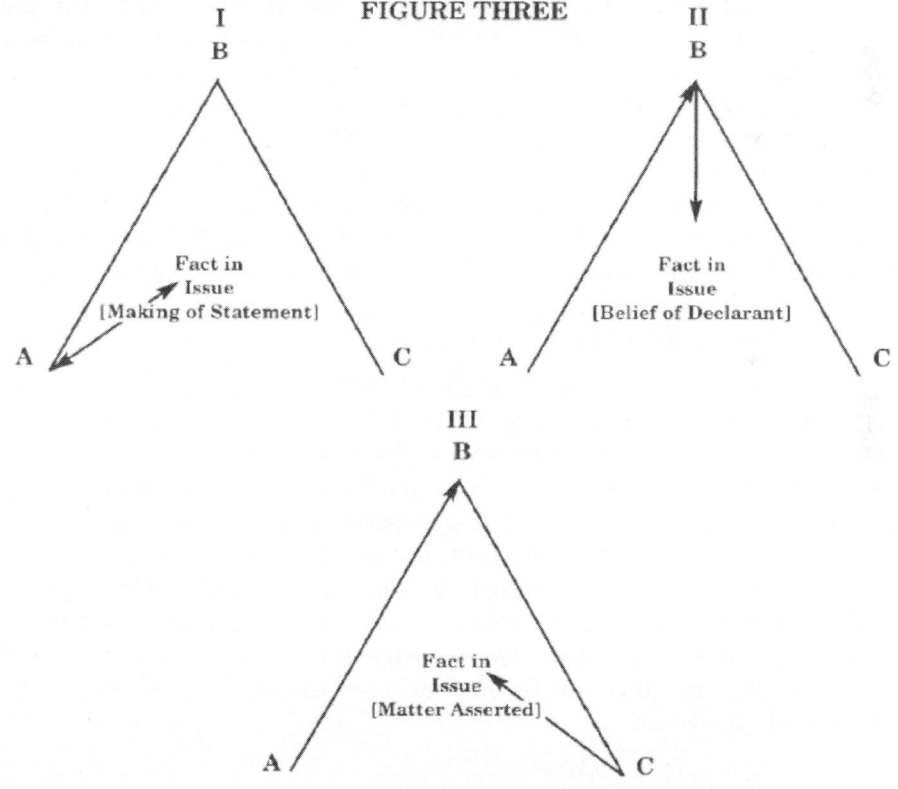

FIGURE THREE

---

[16] Note that we have dropped the triangular depiction of the witness's testimony; these triangles depict only the statement of the out-of-court speaker.

Triangle II portrays the situation which usually exists when a statement, regardless of its truth, supports some inference that bears on a fact in issue. Usually the inference is from the belief of the speaker to the fact. Suppose that after her fall from Beauty, Emma brings an action against the dude ranch where she was vacationing for giving her a skittish horse. To prove that the fall distressed her, she might introduce her statement that she said as she got up, "I'll never ride again." This statement suggests that Emma was distressed by the fall, even if a week later Emma was riding once more. Since the concern is whether a belief signifying distress existed and not whether the belief was true, we never have to ask the right leg question, "Does the belief reflect reality?" Thus the right leg's dangers of faulty memory and misperception do not exist. You might wonder whether the nonexistence of only two of the hearsay dangers justifies classifying a statement as not hearsay. Analytically, this follows from the definition of hearsay. Moreover, since the right leg problems are probably the most significant hearsay dangers, it makes sense to classify statements used so to eliminate right leg dangers as not hearsay. As we shall see, even lesser reasons to discount the right leg dangers can justify hearsay exceptions.

Triangle III depicts the situation where the relevance of a statement depends upon the truth of the conclusion the statement appears to reach. Here, all hearsay dangers are present, so a statement used this way is considered hearsay. If, for example, Emma had said, after refusing to remount her horse, "Beauty has been skittish since we started," what she said would be hearsay if offered to prove the horse had been skittish. On this point, a jury would be concerned that Emma both believed what she said and that her belief reflected reality. If Emma was paving the way for a lawsuit (from the time she fell), or if she thought normal, cautious walking was skittish behavior in a horse, a jury would be misled if it concluded from Emma's statement that the horse was skittish.

To define hearsay in terms of the triangle, *an out-of-court statement is hearsay if and only if the inference that the proponent seeks to establish depends upon an affirmative answer to both right and left leg questions.* This is true only of the last of our examples. In pictorial terms, a statement is not hearsay unless the proponent is asking the trier to travel up the left leg and down the right leg of the speaker's triangle as a prelude to applying the statement to a fact in issue. Such statements are excluded as hearsay because without the aid of the oath, demeanor, context, and—above all—the *opportunity* for cross-examination,[17] the trier of fact does not have sufficient basis for responding affirmatively to these crucial questions.

---

[17] Note that it is the opportunity for cross-examination that is crucial, not cross-examination itself. If the adversary chooses not to cross-examine, it is assumed that cross-examination would not have revealed substantial weaknesses in the offered assertions.

1. Verbal Acts

Concrete examples of out-of-court statements that are not hearsay show how these principles are applied. Perhaps the most important situation in which out-of-court statements are not hearsay is when an utterance has legal significance in itself. This is common; in many cases, whether or not certain words were spoken or written is the central issue in dispute. Consider an action disputing the formation of a verbal contract. The out-of-court statements allegedly constituting the contract are not hearsay because the issue is not whether the statements are in some sense *true*, but rather whether they were made. Legal rights and duties turn on whether words sufficient to constitute a contract were spoken.

Take another example: suppose Ken calls Bill "a liar" and Bill responds with an action for slander. Testimony by Bill that Ken called him "a liar" would not be reporting hearsay.[18] Bill is not repeating Ken's words to convince the jury that what Ken said is true. Quite the opposite; in most jurisdictions Bill would collect nothing if the jury was convinced of the truth of what Ken said. Bill reports Ken's accusation because a slander action requires proof that offensive words *were spoken*. The situation would be the same if Bill's action were for libel, and a newspaper column were introduced in which Ken said Bill was "a liar."

Finally, consider a suit in probate that turns on whether Bonnie is the surviving spouse of Clyde. Testimony that Bonnie and Clyde responded "I do" to the traditional questions of the marriage ceremony and that a minister then said, "I now pronounce you husband and wife" would not be objectionable hearsay because the quoted statements are part of the act of getting married. It doesn't matter whether the partners ever intended to love, honor, or cherish each other; having participated in the prescribed ceremony they are married just the same. Even if the ceremony had been so irregular as to establish no legal tie, testimony reporting the exchange of vows would not be hearsay. It would merely be some evidence that there was a legally sufficient ceremony; evidence in the hypothesized circumstances could be countered by other, stronger evidence.

Out-of-court statements that are not hearsay because the very fact that they were spoken or written carries legal consequences are generally called "*verbal acts*."[19] In terms of the testimonial triangle, verbal acts fit the situation depicted in Triangle I of Figure III. When statements are verbal acts, the speaking or writing of certain words relates directly to a

---

[18] Note that "hearsay" technically refers to the *out-of-court statements* that are reported in courtroom testimony. However, testimony reporting such statements is often objected to as "hearsay." In this Chapter, we use the term "hearsay" to refer both to out-of-court statements offered for the truth of what they assert, and to testimony reporting such statements.

[19] Some courts and commentators call such statements "operative facts" or "operative legal facts."

fact in issue and, indeed, often constitutes the very fact a party must prove to get legal relief. Verbal acts cannot be understood without a thorough understanding of relevant substantive law because it is substantive law that gives the speech constituting verbal acts legal significance.

2. Verbal Parts of Acts

In some situations conduct is ambiguous, but accompanying words clarify the conduct, indicating its proper legal significance. Such explanatory words are known as the "verbal part of the act" and are not considered hearsay. For example, one friend hands another $20 and says, "Sure, I can loan you twenty." Or a depositor hands a teller $10,000 with a note indicating that the money is to be placed in his child's trust account. Without the accompanying words, the legal status of the conduct would be unclear. With the words we know that the friend was not giving $20 away, and that the depositor was surrendering control over $10,000.

In many circumstances verbal parts of acts are relevant in the way Figure Three-I depicts, but in other situations they appear relevant in the sense depicted in Figure Three-II. A bank depositor may be bound by the objective indications he gave of creating a trust, regardless of what he may have believed he was doing. But in the case of the friendly loan, the statement appears relevant because it negates donative intent. This inference requires the jury to reason from the making of the statement to the donor's belief about the transaction. It is the donor's belief or intent that determines how the transaction should be characterized. Since reasoning from a statement to intent does not require a full trip around the triangle, explanatory statements that are relevant in this way are not hearsay. Most courts, however, do not engage in such fine analysis. They treat all clarifying statements as part of the acts they accompany and assume the jury can reason directly from them to facts in issue. Figure Three-I depicts the dominant analysis.

This assimilation of statement to act is reflected in declarations by some courts that such statements are not hearsay because they are part of the *res gestae*, that is part of the thing done. If this were the only way the phrase *res gestae* were used, it might be a convenient way to clarify why verbal parts of acts are not considered hearsay. But, as we shall see, this phrase has been used to encompass several different hearsay exceptions, all of which carry guarantees of reliability apart from their close relationship to a legally relevant act. The multiple meanings of the phrase *res gestae* invite confusion, so we shall try to avoid using this phrase in our discussion.

3. Statements Manifesting Awareness

Often a claim or defense rests to some extent upon the allegation that an individual was or should have been aware of a particular fact. When this is so, the fact that an individual made or heard a particular statement may be strong evidence that awareness existed. Consider a homicide case in which the defendant, Green, argues that he acted in self-defense when he shot Brown. In support of this defense, it would not be hearsay for Green to testify that he had overheard Brown say: "The next time I see Green, I am going to kill him." The statement gave Green reason to think Brown was out to kill him, and so makes a claim of self-defense more plausible than it would be if Green had no reason to believe that Brown was a threat to him. This is so regardless of whether the threat that led to Green's belief was one that Brown intended to carry out.

The use of statements to show awareness occurs also in negligence actions. Consider an auto accident traceable to a defect in the defendant, Spencer's, brakes. Since reasonable people seldom drive cars knowing their brakes are bad, information that Spencer knew (or should have known) he had bad brakes supports the plaintiff's charge of negligence. For this reason a mechanic's statement telling Spencer his brakes needed repair would not be hearsay if offered to show that Spencer was aware of his brake problems. Similarly, testimony reporting that Spencer had told a friend before the accident, "My brakes are bad," would not be hearsay on the issue of whether he knew that his brakes were bad. But each statement would be hearsay if offered to show that Spencer's brakes were, in fact, in need of repair.

When statements are offered to show *an effect on the listener*, the situation is that depicted by the triangle in Figure Three-I. Whether the out-of-court speaker believed what he said or whether what he said was in fact true is irrelevant for this purpose: the statement is offered only to show that the listener was or should have been alerted to certain facts. Thus, when a threat to kill is shown as part of a claim of self-defense, the issue the trier needs to resolve is whether the defendant was justified in taking the threat seriously, not whether the threat was made in earnest or in jest. When a mechanic advises a driver that his brakes need repair, the reasonable response is to have the repairs done or seek a second opinion, regardless of whether the mechanic was serious, intended a joke, or intentionally lied to increase his business.

But, one might object, if the mechanic was joking or lying, wouldn't this mean that Spencer's decision to ignore his warning was reasonable? The objection is sound only to the extent that Spencer had reason to suspect a joke or a lie. The reasonableness of discounting information or ignoring a warning will almost always affect only the weight of the evidence; it will not determine its admissibility.

It is easy to think that the resolution of an admissibility issue determines the outcome of the case. Occasionally this is true when essential evidence is excluded, but it is certainly not always true regardless of how crucial the issue on which the evidence bears. If Spencer could show, for example, that he knew the mechanic had not inspected his brakes, ignoring the warning would not suggest negligence. A judge is not inconsistent when she admits disputed evidence on a central aspect of a party's case and then directs a verdict for the opposing party because that aspect was not sufficiently proved. This might occur because the admissible evidence was insufficient to prove an essential point or was so refuted that a jury could not reasonably find in favor of the proponent on the crucial issue.

When a statement is offered to show the speaker's own knowledge or belief, the situation is usually that depicted in Figure Three-II. The speaker's belief, or point B on the triangle, is the fact in issue, so left leg problems will exist, but right leg ones will not. If a person believed his brakes needed repair—as evidenced by his statement to that effect—and he did nothing, he was acting unreasonably regardless of the actual condition of his brakes. Often when a speaker's belief is at issue, he will be available to testify to his beliefs at the time of the statement.[20]

Both the mechanic's warning and Spencer's own statement that his brakes are bad illustrate how statements that are not hearsay for certain purposes may be hearsay for others. Neither the warning nor Spencer's own statement is hearsay when offered to show that Spencer was or should have been *aware* of the defective condition of his brakes, but each would be hearsay if offered to show that the brakes were *in fact* defective.[21] For this latter purpose a full trip around the speaker's triangle would be necessary to reach the desired conclusion. The jurors would want to be sure that Spencer believed what he said, and that this belief reflected reality. When a statement supports both a permissible nonhearsay inference and a prohibited hearsay inference, the statement is (subject to FRE 403) admissible to prove the permissible inference. However, the opponent will be entitled to an instruction that the statement should not be considered for any hearsay purpose. Also, the statement's tendency to support the hearsay inference may not be considered on a motion for a directed verdict.

Occasionally, a statement is offered to show knowledge or awareness when awareness is not an issue in the case but is a fact tending to prove

---

[20] When a statement is offered to show the speaker's knowledge or belief, it will often be the statement of a party. If so, detailed analysis is not necessary, for we shall see that the statements of parties are routinely admitted under the admissions exception to the hearsay rule.

[21] As you will soon see, Spencer's own statement would be an "admission," which FRE 801(d) arbitrarily defines as "not hearsay." Admissions, however, are better conceived as exceptions to the hearsay rule—i.e., as hearsay, but admissible nonetheless—for they fit squarely within the FRE 801(c) definition. This is how we will treat admissions throughout this Chapter.

some other matter in dispute. In one well-known case, *Bridges v. State*,[22] a man was accused of sexually assaulting a seven year old girl. Both the victim's mother and several police officers were permitted to testify as to statements made by the victim describing the defendant's home and bedroom. The girl's out-of-court description of the exterior and interior of the defendant's home was held to have been properly admitted over a hearsay objection because it was offered not to show how the man's room *in fact* looked, but rather to show that the girl had *knowledge* of the room that could only have been acquired from seeing it. The girl's testimony tended to prove she had been in the defendant's room because there was other admissible evidence that showed the room did in fact match the girl's description. The obvious inference was that the girl could describe the room accurately because she had been there. Without non-hearsay evidence describing the room, the girl's recollection would have proved little. The probative value of her description turned on its accuracy, even though the description was not offered for its truth.

Problem VI-1. Morgan Banker sues the Tabloid Press for publishing in an editorial in one of its daily newspapers the following alleged libel: "Banker's nefarious career began when he embezzled $25,000 from the Macrosoft National Bank of which he was at the time cashier." **Can this statement be introduced by Banker over a hearsay objection?** Banker, alleging malice on the part of Tabloid in publishing the libel, seeks punitive damages. Tabloid's defense to the charge of malice is that at the time the statement was published, Tabloid reasonably believed it to be true. At trial, Banker produces a secretary who worked in Tabloid's editorial office at the time of the publication. She testifies, over Tabloid's objection, that the day before the editorial was published she overheard a conversation between the author of the editorial and Gates, the president of the bank in which Gates said: "I tell you, Banker did not steal the $25,000: it was loaned to him by the bank on my authority." **On what issues, if any, is the evidence hearsay? On what issues, if any, is it not?**

4. States of Mind

An individual's intent is relevant for so many purposes in so many different areas of the law that parties must often prove their own or another's mental outlook. When such proof is needed, we say that "state of mind" is a fact in issue.[23] State of mind may be proved

---

[22] 247 Wis. 350, 19 N.W.2d 529 (Wis. 1945).

[23] "Awareness," discussed above, is one kind of state of mind. We discuss awareness separately for three reasons: (1) this type of state of mind evidence is so common that it merits special attention; (2) statements that provide a listener with a reason to be aware of something will often be relevant as non-hearsay evidence without any need to determine the state of mind

circumstantially from statements made by the person whose mental outlook is in issue. These statements are not hearsay because the jurors are concerned with what the statements imply about a speaker's beliefs, but not with whether they reflect reality.[24]

This is most obvious when sanity is disputed. A lawyer would not want to introduce his client's statement "Little green Martians are following me" to prove that his client is being shadowed by extraterrestrial beings. The statement's relevance lies instead in the fact that its existence is a symptom of mental disorder. This does not mean it is dispositive on the issue of mental illness; maybe the client was joking, or possibly feigning mental illness because it was in her interest. However, making the statement is at least some evidence of mental illness, and, although the left leg dangers are real,[25] no right leg problems are posed.

A similar analysis applies to statements offered to prove other mental states, such as fear, intent to steal, alienated affections, and donative intent. For example, if Arthur sues Lancelot for alienating the affections of his wife, Guinevere, he would not introduce Guinevere's statement "Arthur, you're a bastard" to prove he was an illegitimate child or even to show that he treated his wife poorly, which is what the language implies. Rather he would introduce the statement as evidence that when Guinevere said it, she no longer loved him. Or consider a will contest triggered by ambiguous language that could be interpreted as giving all a testator's goods to either his son Paul or his daughter Susan. Susan would not introduce her father's statements "Paul hates me" and "Susan is my most devoted child" to prove her brother's hatred of her dad or her own devotion, but rather to show that if her father intended to give all his wealth to just one child, she was the one. It may be that the father was completely mistaken about his children's feelings toward him. The inference Susan wants the jury to draw from her father's statements—that he preferred her to Paul—is sustainable regardless of their truth.

Analytically, perhaps the most perplexing problem in identifying hearsay arises when statements assert exactly the state of mind that is in issue. Suppose in his suit for the alienation of affections, Arthur seeks to introduce Guinevere's statement "I don't love you anymore." The statement asserts one of the basic facts Arthur must prove, and the jury is asked to treat the assertion as true. At the same time, the very fact

---

in fact induced; and, (3) this kind of state-of-mind evidence seldom asserts the fact in issue and so does not pose the difficult analytic problems to be discussed below.

[24] By this point you should be able to apply the triangular analysis and figure out which of the Figure Three triangles apply. From now on, we will leave this to you as an exercise.

[25] If there are no self-interest motives for the statement, even the left leg dangers are small, for sane people don't ordinarily claim Martians are following them when they know this isn't so. Regardless of whether the client knows his claim is false, the utterance may indicate a mental disturbance.

that Guinevere said she didn't love Arthur is circumstantial evidence that she didn't, since people who love their spouses don't usually flatly deny it. One may reason from this statement to the fact that Guinevere's affection for Arthur was dead in exactly the same way one reasoned from the statement, "Arthur, you're a bastard."

There are at least two reasons why it makes sense to classify statements asserting the state of mind they are offered to prove as not hearsay. The first is that when a statement may be used for both a hearsay and a non-hearsay purpose, the statement will generally be admitted for the non-hearsay purpose regardless of the probability that the jurors, despite instructions, will treat the statement as support for the forbidden hearsay inference.[26] Second, it should be clear that the jurors are only being asked to conclude that the speaker has the belief reflected in the statement. There is no need for the jurors to decide whether the belief is well-founded, because there are no possible problems of perception or memory when a person describes her current feelings. If a woman believes that she hates her husband, then for the law's practical purposes she does, regardless of what several years of psychoanalysis might reveal. Thus we face the same Figure Three-II-type situation encountered with many other statements classified as not hearsay. On the other hand, such statements certainly sound like hearsay. The statement "I don't love you anymore" in our example is used to prove, albeit circumstantially, the truth of what it asserts. This suggests that the definitional problem will be less confusing if such statements are considered hearsay.

Fortunately, the question of how to classify such statements has little practical importance. As you will learn in the next section, there is a hearsay exception for statements describing a speaker's existing state of mind, so the kinds of statements we are talking about are admitted into evidence regardless of how they are classified. For the purpose of dealing with the problems in this book or examination questions, we suggest that you arbitrarily classify statements offered to prove precisely the state of mind asserted as hearsay. We do this both because it accords with the view of most commentators, and because most courts, if faced with a hearsay objection to such a statement, will more easily understand the argument that the statement comes within the state of mind *exception* than the more complicated argument that the statement is *not hearsay* in the first place.

---

[26] Under FRE 403, a court has discretion to exclude a statement if on balance the need for the statement in support of the non-hearsay inference is likely to be outweighed by the danger that the jurors will regard the statement as support for the hearsay inference. In practice, courts seldom exclude statements on these grounds.

5. Impeachment

Perhaps the most common non-hearsay use of out-of-court statements is impeachment. Prior inconsistent statements used to impeach the testimony of a witness are admitted not to prove the truth of what they assert, but rather to suggest that a witness's testimony should not be believed because he has said different things about the same event. From this perspective, it is the making of the inconsistent statement that is important and not whether it is true. A similar analysis applies to the use of prior consistent statements to disprove a charge of recent fabrication. Absent a hearsay exception, a party is entitled to have the jury instructed that it should not consider such statements as bearing on anything other than credibility.[27]

We have discussed impeachment by prior inconsistent statements in Chapter Five, and the matter will be touched on again in Section IV of this Chapter.

6. Opinion Surveys

Opinion surveys are another source of out-of-court statements admitted as non-hearsay. Statements generated by opinion surveys typically escape the hearsay objection because they are used to show a belief or state of mind and not the truth of the respondent's answers. For example, consider a trademark case in which respondents are shown the defendant's product and asked to name the manufacturer. The fact that some proportion of the respondents name the plaintiff corporation is not offered to show that the plaintiff manufactured defendant's product but rather to show that defendant's product looks so much like the plaintiff's trademarked design as to invite confusion. Or consider a survey offered in support of a change of venue motion. A report that 75% of those interviewed say the defendant is guilty is not offered by defense counsel to show that her client is guilty; rather it is offered to show that community opinion is such that the defendant cannot get a fair trial.

D. "STATEMENT"

Now we have only to define the word "statement," and our definition of hearsay will be complete. Consider the Federal Rule. FRE 801(a) tells us: "'Statement' means a person's oral assertion, written assertion, or nonverbal conduct, if the person intended it as an assertion." But what is an "assertion"? FRE 801(a) has simply replaced one definitional problem with another.

The best way to resolve this problem is to look at what most courts do in deciding whether an action or utterance amounts to an assertion.

---

[27] FRE 801(d)(1) creates hearsay exceptions for certain prior inconsistent and prior consistent statements, but it does so in the guise of defining such statements as not hearsay.

Typically, judges require the conjunction of two conditions. *First,* there must be, either implicitly or explicitly, a claim that some fact or circumstance exists. In other words, there must be an explicit or implicit *description* of some aspect of the world. *Second,* the speaker must intend to make such a claim. For example, suppose that after accidentally hitting his thumb with a hammer, Tim says, "My thumb hurts." If the issue is whether the blow hurt, we have here an assertion, and thus a statement for the purposes of the hearsay rule. Right after hitting his thumb, Tim is claiming and intends to claim that his thumb feels sore. Suppose, on the other hand, that Tim merely screams "ouch" after hitting his thumb. This is not an assertion. Although the word "ouch" is evidence of pain, it is an involuntary response to a blow and as such is uttered without any intent to claim that pain exists. Hence Tim has not made a "statement," and testimony that he said "ouch" when he hit his thumb would not be hearsay if offered to prove that the blow hurt.

Intentional claims need not take the form of declarative sentences. Had Tim looked up from hitting his thumb, seen an onlooker, and only then cried, "ouch," we might have a statement for purposes of the hearsay rule because in these circumstances it is plausible to suppose that Tim uttered "ouch" with the intent of telling the onlooker that his thumb hurt. Questions too may qualify as assertions, although it is easy to find examples of courts that have not realized this. For example, the question, "Sue, what did you do with the stolen money?" should be considered a "statement" if it is offered to prove that Sue once possessed stolen money. The question contains within it the claim that Sue had once possessed stolen money, and the speaker intended to tell Sue he believed this was so; indeed, his question to her is premised on it. Consequently, all the hearsay dangers are present.

Other claims that might appear implicit in declarations are not "statements" for hearsay purposes because intent is lacking. Suppose, for example, that while the police are at the site of a suspected bookie joint the phone rings, an officer picks it up, and a voice says, "This is Jonesy. I want to put ten dollars on Go Blue in the fifth at Jamaica." The second sentence, if offered to show that the establishment was a bookie joint, is not an FRE 801(a) "statement" and so is not hearsay. Arguably, no claim at all is being made; the most one can say is that implicit in the language is the caller's belief that he has reached a bookie. But even if one saw a claim here, it would not be intentional. The caller did not intend to tell the person answering the phone that he thought this was a bookie joint; he simply wanted to place a bet.[28]

---

[28] This analysis captures what courts most often do and provides a principle that seems to make sense of most cases and of the language of the Federal Rules in light of the Advisory Committee's notes. These notes first recognize the existence of non-assertive verbal conduct, and then go on to say: "When evidence of conduct is offered on the theory that it is not a statement and hence not hearsay, a preliminary determination will be required to determine whether an

FRE 801(a) also recognizes that speaking and writing are not the only ways to make intentional claims. Any action intended to claim that some fact or circumstance exists qualifies as an assertion, and hence as a statement for purposes of the hearsay rule. Such actions include pointing to a person in a lineup, nodding in response to a question, and the use of sign language. Equating actions and words in this way makes sense. Clearly the same hearsay dangers are present whether one points to an individual or says "the third from the left," whether one answers "yes" to a question or nods affirmatively, and whether one talks with one's voice or with one's hands.

1. Silence

It is difficult to determine whether some kinds of non-verbal conduct manifest the intention required for an assertion. Suppose, for example, that Tyrone accuses Mildred of stealing his wallet and Mildred says nothing. By not responding, does Mildred intend to agree with the charge? The following argument has been offered to support this view: If Mildred had not taken Tyrone's wallet, she would have risen in indignation and denied the charge; since Mildred said nothing, she must have intended to agree with Tyrone's claim (this step of the argument is somewhat strained). Therefore, by implication, silence asserts guilt. Thus silence becomes hearsay. It might appear more reasonable to classify silence in the face of an accusation as circumstantial evidence of guilt, but it should be recognized that, however one categorizes the evidence, the basic hearsay dangers are present. Silence is probative of guilt only if the implication of guilt reflects the accused's belief and only if the accused's belief reflects reality. The most severe hearsay danger is obviously the extreme ambiguity of the failure to respond to an accusation.

Most courts have treated silence in the face of an accusation as a "statement" and therefore hearsay.[29] However, classifying silence as hearsay rarely leads to exclusion since some exception to the hearsay rule, most often the admissions exception, is usually available.

---

assertion is intended. The rule is so worded as to place the burden upon the party claiming that the intention existed; ambiguous and doubtful cases will be resolved against him and in favor of admissibility." Many commentators, however, have questioned the Advisory Committee's note and the policies it seems to reflect; opinions differ about whether our betting example, even in a Federal Rules jurisdiction, should be considered hearsay.

[29] Often one sees trial judges determining whether an out-of-court statement is admissible by reference to whether it was made in the presence of the defendant or, in a civil case, a party. This rule of thumb is an analytically unsound reflection of the fact that some statements made in the presence of a party will, if not replied to, be admitted under the admissions exception to the hearsay rule (see infra, pp. 588–91), while many statements made in the presence of a party will be circumstantially relevant and not hearsay (e.g., a statement offered to show that the defendant was aware of something). Except in these instances, the fact that a statement was made in the presence of a party should not affect its admissibility. Thus a trial attorney must be prepared to point out why certain statements made in the presence of a party are hearsay assertions that fit into no available exception.

2.   Non-Assertive Conduct

Statements, we have seen, are hearsay only when their relevance depends upon the double inference from statement to belief, and from belief to reality. Scholars have for generations debated whether an act performed without any intent to claim that some fact is true (i.e., nonassertive conduct) should be treated as hearsay when its relevance depends upon the same double inference. Suppose, for example, that a well-known sea captain first inspects all parts of a vessel with great care and then embarks with his family on that same vessel. If the vessel sinks at sea, should the testimony of someone who viewed the captain's inspection be admitted to refute a claim of unseaworthiness, or is it objectionable as hearsay? If the captain upon leaving the vessel had said to the witness, "This ship is seaworthy," the witness's report of the statement would be hearsay. Should the result differ when the jurors are asked to infer from the captain's conduct that he would have declared the boat seaworthy had he only been asked? The relevance of both the direct assertion of seaworthiness and the assertion implied by the captain's conduct require a full trip around the testimonial triangle. First, the jurors must conclude that the captain held the belief asserted in his statement or allegedly implied by his conduct. Then they must conclude that his belief reflected reality. Why should the one situation be considered hearsay and not the other? In other words, why should the intention to make a claim be an element of the Federal Rules' hearsay definition?

The issue of how to treat nonassertive conduct received its earliest and most thorough discussion in the English case, *Wright v. Doe d. Sandford Tatham*.[30] The case involved a contest over a will by which a testator, John Marsden, bequeathed part of his estate to his steward, Wright. Admiral Tatham, Marsden's heir at law, attempted to void the will, claiming that Marsden was mentally incompetent when he wrote it. The case wound its way through eight years of litigation, including several trials and numerous appeals, before it was finally resolved by the House of Lords in 1838 in favor of Admiral Tatham. Virtually all the great English attorneys of the day were involved in the case, either as lawyers or as judges. The central evidentiary issue concerned the admissibility of letters written to Marsden by persons since deceased. There was nothing special about the letters, but their tone suggested that the writers believed they were corresponding with a person of ordinary understanding and intelligence. Wright sought to introduce the letters for their tendency to show that Marsden was mentally competent. The King's Bench and eventually the House of Lords decided that the hearsay rule prevented Wright from introducing the letters to prove Marsden's

---

[30]   7 Ad. & E. 313, 112 Eng. Rep. 488 (Ex.Ch. 1837), aff,'d 7 Eng. Rep. 559 (H.L. 1838). This case is reprinted in Section V of this Chapter.

sanity. In the words of Baron Parke: "[P]roof of a particular fact, which is not of itself a matter in issue, but which is relevant only as implying a statement or opinion of a third person on the matter in issue, is inadmissible in all cases where such a statement or opinion not on oath would be of itself inadmissible."[31]

At common law, most American courts dealt with the problem of whether to treat non-assertive conduct as hearsay by failing to recognize the hearsay problem.[32] The states that did recognize the problem generally sided with the English court and treated the conduct as hearsay. But most of the cases treating non-assertive conduct as hearsay are old,[33] and the trend, even before the Federal Rules, was probably in the opposite direction.[34] Where the case law is muddy, modern statutes are clear. The Uniform Rules, the New Jersey Evidence Code, the California Evidence Code, the Federal Rules of Evidence, and the states that have adopted evidence codes based on the Federal Rules, all exclude non-assertive conduct from their definitions of hearsay.[35]

There are arguments supporting both the older cases and the modern codes. In *Wright*, for example, the letters to Marsden posed each of the four basic hearsay dangers. The correspondents might not have been sincere. Even if they doubted Marsden's sanity, they might have written their letters as if Marsden were sane in order to spare his feelings. There is also considerable ambiguity regarding the import of the letters and whether, even if sincere, they reflect a belief in Marsden's sanity. For example, one letter suggests that Marsden have his lawyer meet with the attorney for the local parish to resolve a dispute. It is not a letter one

---

[31] *Id.* at 388–89, 112 Eng.Rep. at 516–17.

[32] In preparing the first edition of this book, the authors directed a research assistant to explore the case law in the states and determine which states treated non-assertive conduct as hearsay and which did not. The task of assigning positions to states proved impossible because only a few common-law states recognized the problem sufficiently well to state a position. Perhaps the issue would have disappeared entirely by now if the problem were not so intriguing to commentators and teachers of evidence.

[33] In 1992 the English high court reaffirmed *Wright,* perhaps because it was reluctant to overrule such a venerable decision. Regina v. Kearley, 2 All E.R. 345 (1992). However, changes in the English hearsay rule found in the Civil Evidence Act of 1995 and the 2003 Criminal Justice Act mean that today *Wright* is no longer good law in the land that gave it birth.

[34] The 1972 second edition of McCormick's hornbook stated that the trend "is in the opposite direction" [§ 250, at 598]; however, the cases cited indicate that the revisors did not fully understand the problem. For example, Belvidere Land Co. v. Owen Park Plaza, Inc., 362 Mich. 107, 106 N.W.2d 380 (Mich. 1960), is cited with the summary "evidence of receipt of telephone calls and visitors asking for Owen Park Plaza to show confusion with Owen Park Apartments." State v. Izzo, 94 Ariz. 226, 383 P.2d 116 (Ariz. 1963), is cited with the summary "evidence that wife did not return home night before her murder as proof of her fear of accused husband." Triangular analysis makes it clear that the classification of the evidence in these cases as not hearsay does not depend on its non-assertive character. The evidence is offered only to show belief and not to show the truth of what is believed, so in neither case does it pose right leg problems. If sophisticated evidence scholars such as the revisors of the McCormick hornbook could mis-analyze evidence questions in this way, it is no wonder that courts failed to appreciate the problem.

[35] Texas, however, treats non-assertive writings as hearsay.

would ordinarily write to someone of suspect mental capacity, but the writer may have expected the letter to be opened, read and answered not by Marsden but by his steward. Problems of perception and memory are also present. One letter, written by a cousin who some years earlier had emigrated to America, is fraught with such difficulties.

On balance, however, the decisions of recent codifiers to exclude nonassertive conduct from their definitions of hearsay are wise. As a practical matter, the difficulty of analyzing non-assertive conduct for its hearsay character is likely to lead to inconsistent decisions at the trial level and reversible error on appeal. More fundamentally, the hearsay dangers generally threaten the credibility of explicitly intended factual claims more than they threaten the credibility of implicit assertions (which we may think of as those assertions we would expect to hear if we asked the actor about the belief that motivated her action).[36] This is clearest with respect to the danger of insincerity, since the absence of assertive intent negates any motive to conceal true beliefs.[37]

Problems of memory and perception are also frequently attenuated when assertions are implied from action. Conduct often occurs soon after supporting facts are perceived. Moreover, the translation of a mistaken belief into action usually carries more adverse consequences than just the statement of a mistaken belief; hence, an individual who acts on a belief is more likely to have carefully checked her perception and memory than one who merely speaks her mind.

Ambiguity, unlike the other basic dangers, is more likely to exist when non-assertive conduct must be interpreted than when intended statements must be understood. Individuals who intend to make a point try to make themselves clear. Actions are much less likely to carry a clear message. The sea captain described at the beginning of this section might have been looking for a lost wallet. He is unlikely, however, to turn to an observer and proclaim that he is not conducting an inspection. But the likely ambiguity of non-assertive conduct does not necessarily mean that ambiguity is a greater threat with respect to assertions implied from nonassertive conduct than it is with respect to explicit assertions. The ambiguity of action is likely to be so evident that jurors will take this source of unreliability into account when asked to make inferences from conduct. Jurors are less apt to appreciate ambiguity when a hearsay statement appears clear on its face.

---

[36] These are often referred to in the literature as "implied assertions."

[37] Close questions may arise about whether an assertion is intended, e.g., if a person winces when a doctor touches a particular area, is the response involuntary or intended as an assertion of pain? If we know the person is seeing the doctor in connection with pending litigation, we may suspect an intent to assert.

3. Assertions Implied from Other Assertions[38]

The problem of assertions implied from non-assertive conduct has received considerable attention in the literature. Less attention has been paid to the problem of assertions implied from other assertions. Suppose, for example, that Able is found shot in the chest. When asked what happened, he says, "Adams killed me." If Able survives and Adams is tried for assault with a deadly weapon, would Able's statement be hearsay on the issue of whether it was Adams who shot him? According to our definition, Able's statement is not hearsay since it is not offered to prove that Adams *killed* Able, the matter asserted. But the statement is offered to show that a belief necessarily implied by it—namely the belief that Adams was the assailant—is true. In these circumstances anything that casts doubt on the sincerity, meaning, or reliability of the original statement is likely to cast similar doubt on that statement's implications. Thus, an out-of-court statement, offered not for its literal truth but for the truth of some proposition implicit in it, should be considered hearsay so long as the validity of the implicit proposition depends on the existence and accuracy of a belief that the speaker of the actual statement apparently *intended* to convey. Many courts, often without seeing any problem, have treated the implications of intended statements in this way. But other courts elevate form above substance, and if a statement does not fit the narrowest, most literal reading of the hearsay rule, they do not consider it hearsay. Thus, while all courts would treat a witness's testimony that Fred said to Susie, "I see you have the cash from the bank you robbed" as hearsay on the issue of whether Susie had loot from a bank robbery, one finds courts that would admit on this issue testimony that Fred asked Susie, "Is that the cash from the bank you robbed?" According to such courts, questions are not assertions and thus cannot be hearsay. These courts are wrong as a matter of both law and of English. A person who asks a question may in the process assert a fact, and the question may then be used as evidence of that assertion rather than as evidence of the speaker's doubt about some aspect of that fact. This is obvious from an equivalent form of the question, "That is the cash from the bank you robbed, is it not?"

We selected the bank robbery example because it is easy to see an intended assertion, even in the question form. Often, however, it is not so easy for a trial judge to decide whether a declaration should be read as intending to say more than what it literally asserts. If intent cannot be read into a declaration, a proposition implicit in it is not hearsay under the Federal Rules. Of course, as it becomes clearer that the speaker was

---

[38] For more detailed discussions of statements offered for assertions they imply rather than specifically assert and their status under the Federal Rules, see Roger C. Park, *"I Didn't Tell Them Anything About You": Implied Assertions as Hearsay Under the Federal Rules of Evidence,* 74 Minn. L. Rev. 783 (1990), and RONALD J. ALLEN & RICHARD B. KUHNS, AN ANALYTICAL APPROACH TO EVIDENCE 332–41 (1989).

not thinking about the proposition his statement is offered to prove, the statement becomes less probative of the proposition it allegedly implies. As with other non-assertive conduct, a diminution in sincerity problems may be accompanied by an increase in ambiguity.

E.   OTHER HEARSAY-RELATED PROBLEMS

1. Hearsay Distinguished from Lack of Personal Knowledge

Occasionally the hearsay rule is confused with the rule limiting testimony to matters a witness knows firsthand. If a witness who did not see an accident says, "Katsuko told me the accident was caused when the Porsche ran a red light," the witness is testifying from personal knowledge. She knows firsthand what Katsuko told her, and she is testifying to nothing more than Katsuko's statement. If the statement is offered to prove the Porsche ran a red light, the proper objection is hearsay. If the witness had instead said, "The accident happened because the Porsche ran a red light," the proper objection is lack of personal knowledge rather than hearsay. Here the witness is describing an event she did not see. When a witness testifies to matters she did not see, it is likely that she is merely reporting the statements of others without attribution. Thus, the personal knowledge objection is really an objection to anonymous hearsay.   But the personal knowledge objection also protects against statements based on dreams, crystal ball gazing, and deductions unsupported by what the witness knows.

The personal knowledge requirement applies even to hearsay speakers. If, for example, it is clear that a hearsay speaker did not speak from firsthand knowledge, evidence of what she said ordinarily is excluded even if a hearsay exception applies—except in the case of admissions. As we will see, admissions may be used in evidence even if the speaker had no personal knowledge of what she spoke.

––––––––––

Problem VI-2. One rainy day Eve slipped and fell on the floor of the Foxy-Loxy Supermarket, breaking a hip. Eve claims that the floor was dangerously slippery because of the rain and that the manager was negligent in not putting down some substance to soak up the water and improve the traction. The supermarket manager testifies that the floor always gets wet when it rains and that in twelve years at the same location no one has ever complained about the floor being slippery. **Should a hearsay objection to this testimony be sustained? What arguments, if any, could be made that the evidence is not hearsay? If the manager testifies that in the twelve years she has worked at the Foxy-Loxy neither she nor any of the employees of the store has ever slipped when the floor was wet, would this**

testimony be objectionable as hearsay? Would any other objection be available?

2. Multiple Hearsay

Occasionally one hearsay declaration will be embedded in another. This frequently happens when a party seeks to introduce a written report (the first level of hearsay) of another's out-of-court statement (the second level of hearsay). For example, an insurance company might want to introduce, on the issue of arson, a report in which a licensed investigator wrote, "I talked to the fire chief today and he said the fire resulted from arson." The report would be offered for the truth of what it asserts: that the fire chief made the reported statement. The fire chief's statement would also be offered for the truth of what it asserts—that the fire was due to arson. To be admissible both the chief's statement and the report's assertion that the chief made the statement must qualify under a hearsay exception, though they need not qualify under the same hearsay exception. When hearsay is two levels deep, it is called double hearsay; when it is more than two levels deep, it is called multiple hearsay. We leave it to you to conjure up an example of the latter. When you do, remember that the principle of admissibility is the same: a hearsay statement is admissible only if a) it meets some exception to the hearsay rule and b) only if each level of hearsay in which the statement is incorporated also qualifies under some exception to the hearsay rule. FRE 805 codifies this principle:

> Hearsay within hearsay is not excluded by the rule against hearsay if each part of the combined statements conforms with an exception to the rule.

3. Machine or Animal "Statements"

The hearsay rule reflects an assessment of both the frailties of reported perceptions and the degree to which these frailties can be better assessed if the perceiver testifies in person, before the trier of fact, subject to cross-examination. The rule does not apply to statements from nonhuman sources whose evidence is not given under oath and cannot be tested by cross-examination. Thus a speed-measuring device might flash numbers on a screen as cars speed by. The machine's reading is a kind of out-of-court "declaration," but a report of that reading is not hearsay. Although the admissibility of the reading depends on some evidence of the machine's accuracy and on evidence that it was used properly at the time in question, this kind of foundation testimony is not a response to the hearsay dangers. A similar analysis applies to the "statements" of animals, such as the "statement" an injured watchdog makes by growling at one of five men in a lineup. We think by now you can see why the hearsay objection would not apply to a report of a dog's out-of-court behavior. We leave to you the determination of the required foundation for receiving such evidence.

Occasionally a machine, usually a computer, will retrieve or compile statements people have made on a topic. In such cases there is a twofold problem. First, the proponent of the statements must show that the machine accurately compiles and reports the information it receives. Then, if the compilation or report is offered for the truth of what is therein asserted, the proponent must show that the statements reproduced in the report are either not hearsay or are admissible under a hearsay exception.

ADDITIONAL PROBLEMS

The problems that follow test your ability to identify hearsay. In trying to solve the problems, you may want to refer to the text. We encourage you to use triangular analysis because we think it helpful, but if you find some other approach works better for you, feel free to use it. See if you can spot examples of the kind of nonassertive conduct which was hearsay at common law but is not under the Federal Rules.

" . . . and do you smell that man anywhere in the courtroom?"

Problem VI-3. In the following vignettes **W** is always a witness testifying in court, **D** is a defendant in a civil or criminal action, **P** is the plaintiff in a civil action or the prosecutor in a criminal case, and **X** may or may not be a hearsay declarant. Read each problem and determine whether **W's** testimony is objectionable as hearsay.

1. On the issue of whether **D** struck **P**, **W's** testimony that she saw **D** strike **P**.

2. On the issue of whether **D** struck **P**, **W's** testimony that **X** told her that he saw **D** strike **P**.

3. On the issue of whether **D** struck **P**, **W** reads the entry that she made in her diary on the day of the alleged fight, "Today I saw **D** strike **P**."

4. On the issue of whether **D** struck **P** in self-defense, **W** testifies that she heard **X** say to **D** shortly before the fight, "You better watch out, **P** is out to get you."

5. The same testimony as in #4 on the issue of whether **P** was the first aggressor in his fight with **D**. **D** offers **W's** testimony.

6. On the issue of whether **X** was a citizen, **W's** testimony that she saw **X** swear allegiance to the United States as part of the citizenship ceremony.

7. On the issue of whether **Z** was **X's** sole devisee, **X's** will in which it is written, "**I** leave all my worldly possessions to **Z**, who is the most loving and honest of my seven children."

8. The same will as in #7 on the issue of whether **Z** was more honest than his six siblings.

9. The same will as in #7 on the issue of whether **X** loved **Z** more than he loved his other children.

10. On the issue of whether **X** had drunk a fifth of whiskey before leaving the Happy Hour Bar, **W's** testimony that just before he left she heard **X** say in a very slurred voice, "I got to go now—ha, ha, ha—did pretty good, killed me a fifth of Mountain Jack in—ha, ha—45 minutes—ha, ha, ha."

11. The same testimony as in #10 on the issue of whether **X** was drunk when he left the Happy Hour Bar.

12. On the same issue as in #10, **W's** testimony that she saw **X** enter a booth alone with a fifth of Mountain Jack Whiskey, and that when she next passed the booth about 40 minutes later she noticed that there was only about an ounce or two left in the bottle.

13. On the same issue as in #10, **W's** testimony that as **X** stood at the cash register she heard the cashier ask him, "Are you the one who downed that whole fifth of Mountain Jack?"

14. On the issue of whether **X**, a child, was saddened when the cat knocked over his goldfish bowl, **W's** testimony that **X** cried as he picked up the dead goldfish.

15. On the issue of whether **P** had suffered a disabling back injury in an auto accident, a movie taken by one of **D**'s investigators two months after the accident. The movie shows **P** shoveling snow and changing the tire on a car.

16. On the issue of whether a burglar had entered a house before daybreak, testimony by **W**, a farmer, that she heard the cock crow about 15 minutes after she had been awakened by the sounds of an intruder and that her cock always crows when the sun rises.

17. On the issue of whether **X** and **Y** had been involved in some sort of wager, **W**'s testimony that she saw **X** and **Y** shake hands and heard **X** say, "It's a bet."

18. On the issue of **D**'s loyalty to the United States, testimony that the FBI, after a security check, had cleared **D** for access to top secret information.

19. On the issue of whether **X**, who had moved to Hawaii some 12 months before, had the requisite domiciliary intent to qualify as a resident for voting purposes, **W**'s testimony that **X** had once said to her, "The tropical breezes, the sun, the sand, the perfume of plumerias, I know of no place that is nicer."

20. On the same issue as in #19, **W**'s testimony that **X** had told her, "Because I love Hawaii so much, I intend to live here forever."

Problem VI-4. Frank Farmer was driving his automobile south on First Street. Sue Smith was driving west on Second Avenue. Their vehicles collided in the intersection of First Street and Second Avenue. The intersection was not controlled by any traffic sign or signal, and is located in a jurisdiction in which a statute provides that upon simultaneous approach to an intersection in the absence of excessive speed, the vehicle on the right has the right of way. Smith brought an action against Farmer for personal injuries, alleging excessive speed and failure to maintain lookout or control. Farmer, in his answer to Smith's complaint, denied any negligence and alleged that Smith was contributorily negligent in failing to yield the right of way. Witnesses are available to testify as follows:

(a) A witness for Smith, who, like Farmer, was driving south, will testify that three miles north of the scene of the accident, Farmer passed her car at an estimated speed of 70 miles per hour, that Farmer's car rapidly disappeared, and that she saw it next a few minutes later badly damaged at the intersection of First Street and Second Avenue. **Is there any hearsay problem here?**

(b) A bystander will testify that after the accident she went to Smith's car. Smith was conscious and said, "I was already in the intersection when he came barging in." **Is this hearsay?**

(c) Suppose Smith dies and damages are sought for her pain and suffering during the brief period she remained alive after the accident. **Is there a nonhearsay purpose for which evidence of Smith's statement would be relevant?**

Problem VI-5. A widow sues a railroad to recover damages for the death of her husband, who was killed when armed robbers held up the railroad station where he worked. She claims the railroad should have been aware of the danger to her husband from robbers. To prove this, the widow offers to show that during the preceding four years there had been ten robberies or attempted robberies at railroad stations located between 4.7 and 29.8 miles from the deceased's station. She also wants to introduce witnesses to testify that there were conversations between the ticket agents' union and the railroad concerning the need for increased protection from armed robbers. However, none of these conversations specifically referred to the station of her husband. **Is any of the evidence hearsay? Would you admit it all?**

Problem VI-6. On February 3, Marsha Cook was attacked and severely beaten by some unknown assailant. She was in a coma for a week. When she came out of the coma, a nurse was sitting in the room reading a paper. The nurse, seeing Marsha open her eyes, went to her. Suddenly the color drained from Marsha's face, she pointed to the back of the newspaper, withdrew her hands, covered her eyes, and said, "He's the one." Harry Medford, the man whose picture was on the back of the page, was arrested and charged with assault. The prosecution, in its effort to prove that Medford was the assailant, puts the nurse on the stand to testify to Marsha's words and action. **If the defense objects that the nurse's testimony is hearsay, should an objection be sustained? Would you reach a different decision if the picture showed Medford being booked for armed robbery than you would if the picture showed Medford receiving the Jaycee's Young Man of the Year Award? Would your decision be any different if you knew that Marsha had later failed to pick Medford out of a lineup?**

Problem VI-7. Woods, Nichlaus's nephew and heir is contesting Nichlaus's will on the ground that Nichlaus was mentally incompetent to make a will. Garcia, who is fighting to support the will, wants to introduce a letter written by an old college friend of Nichlaus about the time the will was drafted. The letter begins, "It is some three years since we have last met, but you are still my wisest and most generous friend." The letter goes on to seek both a loan and advice about certain "delicate matters of business and family." Garcia also has a copy of Nichlaus's response denying the loan but giving four pages of detailed advice. **Are either or both of these letters admissible over a hearsay objection?**

Problem VI-8. Assume that during the early days of the television blacklist, producers would call a particular number, give a name, and then hear a voice state whether or not that individual was blacklisted as a communist or communist sympathizer. Warren Walters, a newspaper columnist, is being sued by Harry Harkness, an actor turned politician, for writing a column urging people not to vote for Harkness because "Harkness is either a communist or the next closest thing." Walters defends on the ground that (1) the accusation was true or (2) he (Walters) had good reason to believe the charge was true. He offers evidence that he received the number of "Blacklist Central" from a producer friend, that he called the number, and that when he spoke the name "Harry Harkness" into the phone a voice responded, "Harry Harkness doesn't check. You can't use him on any television show." **Is this evidence objectionable as hearsay when offered in support of either or both of Walters' defenses?** Suppose "the voice" is put on the stand to testify in support of the defense of truth. He says he can state unequivocally that Harkness is a communist because he remembers reading Harkness's name on a red colored paper headed "Known Communists." **Is this testimony objectionable? Why or why not?**

Problem VI-9. Vince Kearny is accused of arson. Near the burned house, rags were found, some of which were believed to have been soaked in oil and used to start the fire. The state called in "Old Boston," a bloodhound of distinguished pedigree. She sniffed the remaining rags and took off cross-country, eventually coming to Kearny's house. When Kearny's brother opened the door, she moved past him to Kearny and growled at him. **Is testimony by Old Boston's handler, reporting the dog's behavior admissible over the objection that it is hearsay? Prepare the questions you would ask before asking him to describe what Old Boston had done.**

Problem VI-10. Phil Morris sues Tobacco Company, alleging that their cigarettes caused the lung cancer from which his wife died. To prove that his wife was suffering from cancer, Morris offers x-rays showing cancerous lesions in his wife's lungs and a nurse's testimony that Ms. Morris's attending physician ordered chemotherapy, a common treatment for lung cancer. Defendant objects. **Are the x-rays hearsay? Is the nurse's testimony hearsay? Would the case for admitting the nurse's testimony about the chemotherapy change if Morris were seeking damages for his wife's pain and suffering as well as for her death?**

Problem VI-11. Plaintiff Fred Boyd was injured in an automobile accident. To demonstrate Boyd's disabilities, Boyd's attorney commissioned a 25-minute motion picture of Boyd performing various acts around the home and taking various medical tests. The acts were chosen to demonstrate particular aspects of Boyd's impairment. For example, one sequence shows Boyd attempting to touch his knees with his hands but being unable to do so. Another shows him grimacing with pain while reaching above his head to take a can of soup from a kitchen shelf. A third shows that he is unable to cut a steak without assistance. The defendant objects to the admission of the movie, claiming that it is hearsay. **Is the defendant's characterization of the film correct?**

Problem VI-12. David Cole is charged with possession of heroin. An informant named Mazor, after telling his contact in the Drug Enforcement Administration (DEA) that he would lead him to the source's home, went to Cole's house. Cole wasn't there, so he left. Later that day, the DEA agent secured a warrant to search Cole's home. A half ounce of heroin was found underneath the mattress of the bed in Cole's guest room. Cole claims that he regularly lets friends use his guest room and that a friend must have left the drug there. At trial, the DEA agent describes Mazor's behavior in explaining why he decided to search the house. Cole objects to the description as hearsay. **Is the objection well-founded? If Cole sued the DEA for a violation of his civil rights, alleging that their agent searched his home without probable cause, would the agent's description of Mazor's behavior be objectionable as hearsay?**

Problem VI-13. Harold Wolfman is on trial for selling crack cocaine. At his trial the state questions Phil Robinson, the arresting officer of the case, as follows:

Pros.: Now Officer Robinson, did you have the occasion to talk to Judy Rosen about with who supplied her with the crack cocaine you found on her?

Rob.: I did.

Pros.: Was she forthcoming with the information?

Rob.: Yes, she was.

Pros.: Now Officer Robinson, being careful not to tell the jury what Ms. Rosen told you, can you tell the jury what you did after you questioned Ms. Rosen?

Rob.: I went to Mr. Wolfman's house and arrested him.

Is any of Officer Robinson's testimony objectionable as hearsay?

Problem VI-14. Rita Rubini is on trial for bank robbery. Bank teller Fred Ninchi takes the stand to testify that Ms. Rubini pulled a gun on him and demanded cash. To support Mr. Ninchi's testimony, the prosecutor offers a "composite sketch" made by a police artist based on a conversation Mr. Ninchi had with her three days after the robbery. Defense counsel objects that the sketch is hearsay. **How should the court rule? How should it rule if Ninchi had died before the trial**

and the state offers the sketch which bears a striking resemblance to Rubini?

Problem VI-15. Roberta Martin and her daughter Anne are arrested for selling and conspiring to sell brownies laced with marijuana. At their trial, the government introduces the police officer who arrested them. She testifies that she went to the Martin's house, arrested Anne, and waited with Anne for Roberta to arrive home. As Roberta entered the door, Anne said to her, "Mom, I didn't tell them anything about you." Roberta appeals her conviction on both charges, arguing that the statement was hearsay. **Should the appellate court find for Roberta on this issue? If Anne appeals her convictions, would its ruling be any different?**

Problem VI-16. Carl Rhinehart is on trial for fraud in connection with a series of shady stock and real estate transactions. In each case the alleged swindler identified himself as Cale Hannibal of 675 Bathurst Avenue, North Arlington, New Jersey. Three of the victims of the fraudulent transactions have identified Rhinehart as the man who passed himself off as Cale Hannibal. Rhinehart claims that this is a case of mistaken identity. To establish that there is no Cale Hannibal of 675 Bathurst Avenue in North Arlington, New Jersey, the prosecution puts a police officer, Henry Johnson, on the stand. Johnson testifies that he visited North Arlington, a town of about 20,000 people located on one square mile of land in northern New Jersey, and that he looked in a city directory and a telephone directory and found no one listed with the last name of Hannibal. He also testifies that he went to a number of bars, two bowling alleys, both high schools, and a local football game and asked people if they had ever heard of Cale Hannibal. No one reported knowing or having heard of Hannibal. Finally he testifies that he cruised through the town for more than two hours going down every side street that he saw and he never found a street named "Bathurst Avenue." Rhinehart objected to each item of Johnson's testimony as hearsay and each objection was overruled. **Was the judge's decision to overrule these objections correct? How is this evidence relevant? What is the best argument that can be made that this evidence is hearsay? The best argument that it is not hearsay?**

Problem VI-17. Test your understanding of hearsay and review the chapter on relevance by considering the following transcript. **How would you rule on the points raised by counsel? What additional points would you make?**

THE DANGEROUS TOY CASE

For Christmas, a mother purchased a Matteline toy gun for her five-year-old child at Gambels Department Store. The gun is an advance on former cap guns, giving off smoke and a spark when fired. Plastic projectiles emerge from the gun. The fifth time the child fired the gun it exploded, shooting a plastic projectile into his right eye, causing permanent damage. The mother sued both Gambels and Matteline, the manufacturer. Her lawyer is not certain whether to urge negligence and breach of express warranties in addition to strict liability. **What impact, if any, will this choice have on the course of the trial?** The following is a transcript of testimony given at the trial.

THE MOTHER'S TESTIMONY DIRECT EXAMINATION

Q. State your name please. **A.** Mrs. Cecilia Jones.

Q. Your address? **A.** 104 Broad Street, Philadelphia, Pennsylvania.

Q. Mrs. Jones, are you married or single? **A.** Married.

Q. How many children do you have? **A.** Three.

Q. What does your husband do?

Defense Counsel: Objection, your Honor, why don't we get on with this case? All of this is immaterial and irrelevant. The jury ought to be able to hear the facts of the case and not the personal history of Mrs. Jones.

[How should the court rule? Why is this kind of testimony offered?]

Q. Mrs. Jones, would you please focus on the date of December 15, 1999? **A.** Okay.

Q. Have you some recollection of that date? **A.** Yes, a very clear recollection.

Q. Would you tell the jury and the court what, if anything, happened out of the ordinary that day? **[Why is this question phrased so awkwardly?]** **A.** Okay. Shortly after eating lunch on December 15, 1999, I decided to do some early Christmas shopping at the downtown Gambels store, in Center City, Philadelphia; I went down to the store and began looking for Christmas toys for my three children. One of the toys I saw was the gun made by Matteline, and it interested me.

Q. What, if anything, did you do after seeing the gun? **A.** I went over to one of the clerks in the store, and I said I would like to get some information about this gun.

Q. What, if anything, did he say?

[If the defense objects that this question will elicit hearsay what should the plaintiff's counsel argue? How should the court decide?]

A. He said, "Sure, ask anything you want." I said that I had been concerned about whether the gun was safe.

Q. Did he respond? **A.** Yes. He said, "Let me tell you the truth about these toys that we carry. Many of these guns are dangerous. The manufacturers are rushing to manufacture as many guns as possible before the Federal Trade Commission clamps down on manufacturers and requires them to make safe products. So for the most part these guns are not terribly safe, but the Matteline is the safest gun we have."

[Should Mrs. Jones be allowed to testify over objection to these statements of the employee?]

Q. What did you do after receiving this information? **A.** I was beginning to be satisfied that the Matteline gun was a good buy, but I really was interested in why the guns were dangerous. I asked the clerk just what it was about the Matteline gun that made it safe as compared with the other guns that he thought were so dangerous.

Q. What did he say? **A.** He said that the other guns would often splinter, crack, or break apart. Some, which utilized explosive smoke devices, would explode or burst apart, projecting particles at high speed that endangered children. He said the Matteline gun was well manufactured, well made, and was the kind of gun that would not break apart, that it could be battered about, dropped on the floor, kicked around, and fought over without much danger, if any, to children.

[Is this testimony objectionable as hearsay? On relevance grounds?]

Q. What, if anything, did you do then? **A.** I bought the gun in reliance on the statements made by the clerk.

Q. What did you do next with respect to the gun? **A.** Well, I took it home, wrapped it up, and put it with the Christmas gifts. It stayed with the presents till Christmas morning.

Q. What happened next? **A.** On Christmas morning, my children opened their presents and my youngest son took his gun and started playing with it. He fired a number of times, and then it exploded, shooting a projectile into his eye. I took him to the doctor and the doctor told me that there was permanent eye damage.

[Is there anything objectionable here?]

Q. Mrs. Jones, would you have bought the gun if it were not for the statements by the clerk? **A.** No.

Q. Mrs. Jones, did you rely on the statements by the clerk? **A.** Yes.

Q. Mrs. Jones, did you trust the clerk? **A.** Yes.

CROSS-EXAMINATION

Q. Mrs. Jones, do you remember that you are sworn to tell the truth? **A.** Yes.

Q. And you are doing so? **A.** Yes.

Q. Mrs. Jones, would you please tell the court precisely what it was that your older child said to the younger child when he unwrapped the gift?

Plaintiff's counsel: Objection. Such statement would be hearsay, and in any event it is immaterial.

[Following a conference with the attorneys, the court overrules the objection. **Is this ruling correct? Why? What went on during the bench conference?**]

A. My oldest son told my youngest son that it looked as though the gun was broken. There seemed to be a crack along the top of the gun, he said, and that maybe it ought to go back to the store.

Q. Did the youngest son take the gun to you and show it to you? **A.** Yes, he did, and I told him that that crack had been there when I bought the gun and that I did not think it was a crack; I thought it was just a part of the look of the gun.

[Should a hearsay objection to this answer be sustained?]

Q. Mrs. Jones, how many years have you shopped at Gambels? **A.** Oh, about fifteen years on and off.

Q. What do you know about the temporary clerks who work there prior to Christmas?

[Before the answer is rendered, counsel for the plaintiff objects and says, "Your Honor, I fail to see the relevance of this kind of question. Mrs. Jones is not an employee of Gambels, has no relationship with Gambels and cannot be expected to have knowledge concerning the employees of Gambels." The court overrules the objection. **Is the court's ruling correct? Why did defense counsel ask this question?**]

A. Well, I know that many of them are college students and many of them are young people.

Q. Did you know this prior to the time that you purchased the gun? **A.** Yes.

Q. Where did you get this knowledge? **A.** Well, I remember many friends of the family had children who had grown up and worked at Gambels, and I knew many of them and they told me that they had worked there only temporarily and that Gambels was very good about hiring people prior to Christmas. Many young people I know have talked to me about working at Gambels.

[Should this answer be stricken from the record if it is objected to as hearsay? Who would object to it?]

Q. Mrs. Jones, you receive the *Call-Bulletin*, don't you? **A.** Yes. We receive the newspaper every evening.

[Where did the lawyer get the information on which this question is based?]

Q. Do you regularly read it? **A.** Yes.

Q. Mrs. Jones, isn't it true that one week before you purchased the Matteline gun, the *Call-Bulletin* carried a story concerning an FTC investigation into all Matteline products, stating that the products were unsafe, they were likely to cause damage, and recommending that consumers be very wary of such products?

[Is counsel's reference to this story objectionable as hearsay? Is the decision to ask this question strategically wise?]

A. Well, I cannot say whether or not the newspaper carried such a story; all I know is I did not read it.

[Who has been cross-examining Mrs. Jones, counsel for Gambels or counsel for Matteline?]

REDIRECT EXAMINATION

Q. Mrs. Jones, have you ever heard or had occasion to hear any of your friends or neighbors or relatives talk about children's toy guns? **A.** No.

Q. Mrs. Jones, had you ever heard anything about the Matteline guns or other Matteline products prior to purchasing the toy for your child on December 15?

A. No.

Q. Mrs. Jones, between December 15 and Christmas 1999, had you occasion to hear or read or see anything that might have caused you to doubt the wisdom of your purchase? **A.** No.

[At this point defense counsel moves to strike the above testimony as hearsay. How should the court rule?]

Q. Mrs. Jones, what, if anything, did you do with respect to the Gambels store after your son's accident?

[Why did the lawyer wait until this point to ask this question? Should it be permitted over objection?]

A. Well, I phoned up the store after I got back from the doctor's office. I was furious. I don't know precisely who it was that I talked to, but I do know she was very apologetic, she said, "I'm sorry, Mrs. Jones, that you have had such difficulty, sometimes our people go overboard in trying to sell their products and we will certainly see that everything is taken care of."

Q. What did you take that to mean?

[Would you object to this inquiry? Is the prior answer hearsay?]

A. I thought that she meant she was sorry that the product was bad, that she knew I had relied on their advice, and that she would see that the doctor bills were paid. I thought she was very nice at the time.

Q. Were you surprised when the defendant resisted paying the bills?

[Should this question be allowed over objection?]

A. Yes, very surprised.

RE-CROSS-EXAMINATION

Q. Mrs. Jones, are you really trying to tell us that you called up Gambels and that Gambels admitted that it was wrong, although they had no idea who told you about the gun, they had no idea when you bought the gun, and they had no idea what gun it was? **A.** Yes, I am telling you just that.

Q. Mrs. Jones, are you telling us that you phoned up and have no idea whom you talked to, but an unnamed person guaranteed that everything would be taken care of? **A.** Well, that's the way I took it.

Q. That is all, Mrs. Jones.

[Why does the cross-examiner stop here? Is there any objection that might have been made to these questions?]

THE CHILD'S TESTIMONY

Q. State your name please. **A.** Michael Jones.

Q. Michael, where do you live? **A.** With my mother.

Q. How old are you? **A.** Five.

[Should such a young child be permitted to testify? How should the court proceed before reaching a decision?]

Q. Do you remember the accident to your eye? **A.** Yes, I remember.

Q. Would you please tell us the circumstances? **A.** Well, I opened my Christmas gift that my mom gave me. It was a gun. My brother, he said, "It looks like something is wrong with the gun." I asked my mom. My mom told me the man at the store said the gun was okay and I went and used it. Then it blew up and hit me in the face.

[Are there any hearsay problems here?]

Q. That's all. Thank you.

The defendants offered into evidence a written rule of Gambels Department Store that employees are not to give any written or oral warranties with respect to any products, nor are they to say that any product is especially good or especially bad. The plaintiff objects to the introduction of this into evidence.

[Is it hearsay? Is it relevant? How would you rule?]

Next the defendants seek to introduce a survey taken of all the persons who had worked in the toy department between September 1, 1999, and January 1, 2000. The survey shows that no person remembered Mrs. Jones or remembered ever giving any special advice regarding Matteline guns and that no person remembered telling any customer that these guns were safe or safer than any other guns sold in the toy department. The plaintiff objects.

[What is the likely basis for this objection to the introduction of this survey? How would you rule?]

The defendants rest.

Finally, on rebuttal, the plaintiff seeks to introduce evidence of the fact that when she sent the bill for the doctor's services to the defendant, the defendant did not respond for five months.

[How, if at all, is this evidence relevant?]

The trial ends. You are the judge. Would you change any of your rulings after the trial is over and you have an overview of the entire proceeding?

III. EXCEPTIONS TO THE HEARSAY RULE

A. INTRODUCTION

Judge Weinstein has written, "In the sea of admitted hearsay, the rule excluding hearsay is a small and lonely island."[39] In this section we shall discuss the principal exceptions to the hearsay rule—rivers of admissibility flowing together to create Weinstein's "sea of admitted hearsay." In the final section of this Chapter, we shall examine the ways in which judges and scholars have tried to modify or avoid the rigidities of the hearsay system.

The hearsay exceptions we shall examine in this section specify the situations in which hearsay statements are admissible for all relevant purposes. Morgan and Maguire have suggested that a picture of the

---

[39] Jack B. Weinstein, *Probative Force of Hearsay*, 46 IOWA L. REV. 331, 346 (1961). Judge Weinstein's observation is something of an exaggeration. Hearsay objections are frequently sustained at trial, and much evidence is never offered because it is hearsay.

hearsay rule and its exceptions "would resemble an old-fashioned crazy quilt made of patches cut from a group of paintings by cubists, futurists and surrealists."[40] This crazy quilt quality derives for the most part from the fact that no single rationale justifies the many hearsay exceptions. The admissions exception has been justified by the nature of the adversary system, the ability of a party to explain his own out-of-court statements, and the notion that a party can hardly claim that his own statements cannot be believed. Several exceptions, most notably the exceptions for prior testimony and past recollection recorded, are justified by the existence of some opportunity for cross-examination, either when the statements were made (but not in front of the current trier of fact) or in front of the current trier of fact (but at a time when the circumstances leading to the statement have been largely forgotten). The remaining exceptions, by far the largest group, are justified by the claim that some characteristic of the statement negates one or more hearsay dangers or because the hearsay evidence is believed to be more reliable than any other evidence that might be available.

The "quilt" is further complicated in two ways. First, some exceptions admit hearsay evidence only if the speaker is not available to testify at the trial, while other exceptions allow hearsay to be used regardless of the speaker's availability. Second, the Confrontation Clause of the Sixth Amendment guarantees that "in all criminal prosecutions, the accused shall enjoy the right to be confronted with the witnesses against him." This provision promotes some of the same values as the hearsay rule, but it can bar the admission of evidence that state or federal hearsay rules permit, and the hearsay rules commonly bar evidence that the Confrontation Clause does not forbid. Since the Confrontation Clause applies only in criminal cases and only to evidence offered by the prosecution, the scope of constitutionally permissible hearsay exceptions is, in some instances, different in criminal and civil cases.[41] We examine Confrontation Clause problems in detail in Chapter Seven.

Most courts and scholars believe that the probative value of hearsay evidence usually outweighs the danger that it will mislead the jury. This attitude leads to the liberal interpretation of hearsay exceptions, the creation of new exceptions, findings of harmless error when hearsay is mistakenly admitted, and the prevailing view that a fact finder may rely on otherwise inadmissible hearsay when it is received without objection.[42]

---

[40] Edmund M. Morgan & J.M. Maguire, *Looking Backward and Forward at Evidence*, 50 Harv. L. Rev. 909, 921 (1937).

[41] In some cases it might be so unreasonable or unfair for a civil jury to base a judgment on certain hearsay that the use of that evidence would violate the due process clause of the Fifth or Fourteenth Amendment. Thus, there might in rare instances be constitutional limitations on the admissibility of hearsay evidence even in civil cases. *Cf.* Willner v. Committee on Character & Fitness, 373 U.S. 96 (1963); Greene v. McElroy, 360 U.S. 474 (1959).

[42] This prevailing attitude is supported by the fact that the hearsay rule either does not apply or is greatly relaxed in many of the trial-type hearings conducted by arbitration panels, administrative agencies, and other quasi-judicial bodies. It has never been shown that fact-

As we look at the exceptions, you should ask yourself whether the dominant attitude is justified. Remember that if hearsay is admitted, the jurors are free to disregard or discount it. If hearsay evidence is excluded, not even the most cautious inferences from the evidence are possible.

B. ADMISSIONS

The statements of a party to the litigation, commonly referred to as the admissions exception, is a particularly important hearsay exception.[43] It is frequently invoked and often is the vehicle to admit hearsay that is crucial or even devastating. This is because *the admissions exception allows one party to introduce into evidence almost any nonprivileged statement made by an opposing party or by certain people with a special relation to the opposing party, such as a party's agents, employees, and co-conspirators.* The thrust of the admissions exception is simple: *if your opponent said it, you can use it.*

We have already suggested that the admissions exception is an anomaly among the hearsay exceptions. It is the only exception that admits statements that do not, at least in theory, carry some special guarantee of reliability or provide some extra test of the speaker's credibility. Some commentators have seen an extra guarantee of reliability in the fact that the opposing party may deny or explain his statement, but the admissions exception applies to statements made by a party's predecessors, associates, and agents, regardless of whether they are in court when their statements are offered.

Other commentators find a special guarantee of reliability in the fact that admissions are usually against the speaker's interest when made, but this is not required. A statement that was self-serving or neutral when made is as readily admitted as a statement that was against interest when made.[44]

---

finding before these bodies is inferior to the fact-finding that occurs in court, nor has it been shown that it is better.

[43] The language of the restyled rules no longer uses the terms "admission" or "admissions." The Advisory Committee notes state that referring to a statement as an admission could be confusing because some statements which were allowed under the exception were not admissions in the colloquial sense, i.e., they admitted nothing. Recently, some courts have abandoned the use of the term "admission," but this has neither changed the application of the rule nor overruled prior case law which referred to such statements as "admissions." See, e.g., United States v. Ndubuisi, 460 F. App'x 436, 439 (5th Cir. 2012). Meanwhile, other courts still routinely refer to statements as admissions. See, e.g., Hansen v. PT Bank Negara Indonesia (Persero), 706 F.3d 1244, 1249 (10th Cir. 2013); Trickey v. Kaman Indus. Technologies Corp., 705 F.3d 788, 805–06 (8th Cir. 2013); Wright v. Farouk Sys., Inc., 701 F.3d 907, 910 (11th Cir. 2012). Since the terms "admission" and "admissions" are deeply ingrained in the discussion of this exception to the rule against hearsay in practice and in the legal literature, we continue to refer to it, at least for now, as the admissions exception.

[44] There is a general hearsay exception for statements that, when made, are against the speaker's interests. Unlike the admissions exception, the exception for statements against interest limits the kinds of adversely affected interests that make a statement admissible. It usually requires that the speaker be unavailable, and it applies to statements that do not come from the opposing party or someone associated with him. Although the admissions and

Those who abandon the search for special indicia of reliability often assert that the admissions exception is justified by "the nature of the adversary system." Morgan, for example, writes: "The admissibility of an admission made by the party himself rests not upon any notion that the circumstances in which it was made furnish the trier means of evaluating it fairly, but upon the adversary theory of litigation. A party can hardly object that he had no opportunity to cross-examine himself or that he is unworthy of credence save when speaking under sanction of an oath."[45] Despite the frequency with which this statement is quoted or similar sentiments expressed, it is difficult to see why an admissions exception is inherent in the adversary theory of litigation. The adversary theory does not entail the admission against a party of anything he ever said; one might just as plausibly argue that the adversary system, resting as it does on a right to counsel, implies that a person should never be confronted with uncounseled out-of-court statements.[46] And however one views the adversary system and its implications, the adversary theory does not explain the admissibility of statements made by a party's agents, partners, co-conspirators, and predecessors in interest, all of which may be admissible as admissions.

If we discard Morgan's assertion about the adversary theory of litigation and focus instead on his second sentence—"A party can hardly object that he is unworthy of credence save when speaking under sanction of an oath"—we are closer to the probable rationale. This exception is best seen as rooted in ideas about the *responsibility* which individuals have for their actions. People are expected to tell the truth as a matter of course, not because the law requires veracity in everyday speech, but because accepted notions of morality require it.[47] The law recognizes in the hearsay rule the fact that people do not always speak the truth, but recognizing this does not mean that parties before the court will be assumed to have failed in their moral duty to tell the truth or be relieved of the responsibility for their actions if they have failed. Additionally, the frequency with which admissions are against a speaker's interest when

---

statement-against-interest exceptions are clearly distinguishable, many trial courts and some appellate courts confuse the two, referring to an exception for "admissions against interest," usually in situations in which the admissions exception is appropriate. To the purist, there is no "admissions against interest" exception, despite the fact that many lawyers and courts have used this phrase. We advise you to take the purist position. To do otherwise invites confusion between the rationales and the applicability of the two exceptions. Such confusion can lead to overlooking the availability of a valid hearsay exception or to citing the wrong exception and thus failing to preserve an important point for appeal.

[45] Edmund Morgan, Basic Problems of Evidence 266 (1963).

[46] Indeed, in criminal cases, certain statements by defendants that qualify as admissions will not be admissible unless before they were made there was a knowing and voluntary waiver of the right to counsel. *See, e.g.*, Miranda v. Arizona, 384 U.S. 436 (1966); Escobedo v. Illinois, 378 U.S. 478 (1964).

[47] "[A] man's acts, conducts, and declarations, wherever made . . . are admissible against him, as it is fair to presume they correspond with the truth; and it is his fault if they do not." Truby v. Seybert, 12 Pa. 101(1849).

made and the likelihood that the parties or their associates are available to explain statements offered as admissions provide a plausible basis for a hearsay exception. Include the special probative value which a party's own knowledge often gives his statements, and the case for the hearsay exception may be compelling.

The admissions exception is also peculiar in other respects. Other hearsay exceptions overcome only the objection that a statement is hearsay. If the speaker's statement is an otherwise inadmissible opinion[48] or is obviously not based on firsthand knowledge, the statement will be excluded on these grounds. A party, however, can always explain to the jury why his opinion was mistaken or his conclusions unreliable. Hence, in most jurisdictions, the opinion rule and firsthand knowledge objection are unavailable when hearsay is offered as an admission. The Advisory Committee's notes indicate that the Federal Rule is intended to follow general practice in this respect. In other words, if a statement was made by the opposing party, it not only is an "admission," it is, in effect, a ticket for *admission* in evidence that often is good against most objections, including hearsay.

The broad scope and special characteristics of the admissions exception are most easily justified when a party's own statements are offered by an opponent. But the justifications for admitting a party's statements begin to fade when the statements of a party's agents, employees, and co-conspirators are offered, for the party may have no special ability to explain or deny what these speakers said. The statements of agents and others are less likely to have been against interest when made, and the party is less responsible for their conduct than for his own. Yet exceptions for "vicarious" admissions are as firmly embedded in American evidence law as the exception for personal admissions. However, when a statement is by an agent or co-conspirator of a party, some courts re-impose on the speaker the personal knowledge requirement and are more reluctant to admit opinion. Other courts proceed as with personal admissions.

1.   Distinguished From Judicial Admissions

Hearsay admitted as admissions, like other hearsay evidence, may be disputed by the party who allegedly uttered it. In this respect, a hearsay or "evidential" admission differs from a "judicial admission;" that is, an admission made in the pleadings or in response to a request for admission under the rules of civil procedure. A judicial admission binds a party and may not be controverted except by amending or by withdrawing it, which

---

[48] Some courts apply the opinion rule less stringently when an opinion of marginal admissibility is embodied in hearsay. They relax the rule because the answer of an absent speaker cannot be reformulated in more concrete terms. Unless the court receives the opinion as embodied in the hearsay, it must do without the information that the speaker's opinion would have provided the fact-finder.

may require the approval of the court.[49] Because hearsay admissions may be disputed, some jurisdictions consider these statements as less binding than statements made by parties testifying in court. While the better rule allows a party to introduce evidence that contradicts his courtroom testimony, some states do not allow a person to dispute the factual assertions in his own testimony, and others forbid contradiction when a party testifies unequivocally to matters within his peculiar knowledge.[50]

2. The Federal Rule

The drafters of the Federal Rules, focusing on the admissions exception's unique rationale, chose to exclude statements that qualify as admissions from their definition of hearsay.[51] In practice, the drafters' decision should make no difference in the utilization of admissions, but it is confusing. For simplicity, we will speak of an admissions *exception* throughout this text, notwithstanding the Federal Rules' characterization of admissions and the many state courts that follow it.

Under both the Federal Rule and the common law, statements that qualify as admissions may be introduced to prove the truth of the matter

---

[49] *See, e.g.*, Fed.R.Civ.P. 36.

[50] In some jurisdictions, a party's version of important events, if adverse to his legal interest will be conclusive on the facts testified to even if other witnesses for the party testify to a different, more favorable version of the event. Thus, if the plaintiff testifies that he went through a stop sign, this testimony could justify a directed verdict against him even if other credible witnesses testify that the plaintiff did not go through the stop sign or that there was no stop sign at the intersection. Whether the testimony is conclusive would depend on whether the court finds that this is an event about which the party easily could be mistaken, a situation in which "no contradiction" jurisdictions make an exception and do not bind parties to their testimony. Other exceptions include situations in which a party's testimony appears to result from inadvertence or a mistake of language, is avowedly uncertain, or is merely negative in effect. A party is also free to contradict himself during the course of his own testimony; it is the unequivocal meaning of his own testimony taken as a whole that determines which facts have been so established by the party's own testimony that they may not be controverted. McCORMICK § 258 (4th ed. 1992).

[51] The Advisory Committee states in the notes accompanying FRE 801: "Admissions by a party-opponent are excluded from the category of hearsay on the theory that their admissibility in evidence is the result of the adversary system rather than satisfaction of the conditions of the hearsay rule."

This classification is a practical mistake regardless of the conceptual case that can be made for it. Lawyers still have to explain why out-of-court statements of parties are not hearsay. To state simply, "They are not defined as hearsay" explains nothing. Thus lawyers are left to argue that statements are admissions. Hence the exception lives on in the courtroom, even if eliminated in theory by the rules.

If the drafters of the Federal Rules of Evidence did make a mistake, they have considerable company among evidence scholars. For more than half a century, distinguished scholars have debated whether parties' statements are admissible under a hearsay exception or whether they are admissible as nonhearsay. Perhaps the most cogent argument that admissions are not hearsay is made by Professor Strahorn, who argues that they are relevant conduct of the speaker. John S. Strahorn Jr., *A Reconsideration of the Hearsay Rule and Admissions*, 85 U. PA. L. REV. 564 (1937). This argument reflects the position taken by Wigmore in the first edition of his treatise, in which he argues that admissions are admissible for their impeachment effect because they are inconsistent with the claims implicit or explicit in a party's case. 2 WIGMORE, EVIDENCE § 1048 (1st ed. 1904).

asserted. FRE 801(d)(2) specifies five kinds of statements that are admissible as admissions:

> **(d) Statements That Are Not Hearsay.** A statement that meets the following conditions is not hearsay:
>
> . . .
>
> > **(2) An Opposing Party's Statement.** The Statement is offered against an opposing party and:
> >
> > > **(A)** was made by the party in an individual or representative capacity;
> > >
> > > **(B)** is one the party manifested that it adopted or believed to be true;
> > >
> > > **(C)** was made by a person whom the party authorized to make a statement on the subject;
> > >
> > > **(D)** was made by the party's agent or employee on a matter within the scope of that relationship and while it existed; or
> > >
> > > **(E)** was made by the party's coconspirator during and in furtherance of the conspiracy.
> > >
> > > The statement must be considered but does not by itself establish the declarant's authority under (C); the existence or scope of the relationship under (D); or the existence of the conspiracy or participation in it under (E).

FRE 801(d)(2) follows the general contours of the common law admissions exception, but is slightly more liberal in certain respects and may be more limited in others.

3. Personal Statements

FRE 801(d)(2)(A) specifies the clearest kind of admission—a statement made by a party and offered against the party as an individual or in a representative capacity. The Federal Rule admits a party's statement against her in a representative capacity, even though the statement was not made in that capacity. For example, a trustee, while gossiping with a friend, may make statements pertaining to property in the trust she manages. If the trustee is sued as the trust's representative, what she said to her friend will be received as an admission. This makes sense, because as long as the trustee is sued in her representative capacity, she will usually be available to explain what she meant by the statement, regardless of the capacity it was made in, and disputes over the latter issue are avoided.

Since any statement by a party may be an admission, it is easy to deal with parties' statements so long as one is alert to the many different ways statements can be made and to the fact that a statement that constitutes an admission may be held inadmissible for reasons that have nothing to do with the hearsay rule. Statements made in the course of compromise negotiations are admissions, but they are excluded for the reasons specified in Chapter Four. Incriminating statements are a type of admission, but their admissibility depends on the circumstances in which they were received. Withdrawn guilty pleas are admissions, but other policies, like those expressed in FRE 410, may prevent the admission of withdrawn pleas of guilty or of statements made in connection with them. Guilty pleas not withdrawn are also admissions, as are civil pleadings later amended or a party's pleadings in one case when offered against the party in another.[52] However, when civil pleadings or guilty pleas to minor offenses are offered as admissions, they may have little probative value and so be objectionable under Rule 403. Thus, inconsistent or hypothetical pleadings allowed under rules of civil procedure are usually not admissible, and guilty pleas to traffic offenses are commonly excluded in related civil actions since the cost of contesting a traffic ticket is often greater than the fine.

Even where a jurisdiction's hearsay definition included conduct, a party's conduct could be admitted as an admission of any assertion implied. Thus, jurors may treat evidence of a defendant's flight after a crime or her attempt to bribe witnesses as an admission of guilt or consciousness of a weak case. A party's failure, in a civil case, to testify, or her failure to produce a witness close to her or some item of real evidence in her possession, and her refusal to submit to a requested physical exam will each justify the inference that had the party produced the evidence, it would have favored her opponent. The jury, however, is not compelled to draw inferences from such conduct. Except where the implications of conduct are almost indisputable, courts are generally unwilling to allow one party to prove an essential element of her case solely on the basis of inferences that may be drawn from the other party's conduct.

If a jurisdiction does not treat conduct as hearsay, evidence like the above poses no hearsay problem and should be admissible without special justification as long as it is relevant and does not contravene any other recognized policy. Nevertheless, courts in jurisdictions that do not recognize conduct as hearsay may still, in deciding to admit certain

---

[52] A party's pleadings in one case are admissions in that case, usually judicial admissions, meaning that except by amendment, which may require the permission of the court, a party cannot controvert facts pleaded. Where a party in arguing to the jury wants to use another's pleadings as a basis for some adverse inference not conceded on the face of the pleading, this may be done in most jurisdictions by simply quoting the pleading as part of the record. In some jurisdictions, the party must first introduce the relevant portion of the pleadings as part of her own evidence, giving the pleader an opportunity to explain why he has so pleaded. MCCORMICK § 257. On inconsistent pleadings in civil cases, *see* Sherman J. Clark, To Thine Own Self Be True: Enforcing Candor in Pleading Through the Party Admissions Doctrine, 49 Hastings L.J. 566, 585 (1998).

evidence, speak of "admissions by conduct." This characterization speaks to the way the evidence is relevant rather than to its hearsay status.

Statements made by defendants in criminal cases pose special values conflicts. Allowing the prosecution to admit incriminating statements made by the defendant puts substantial pressure on the accused to take the stand to explain away her statements. The pressure is particularly strong where a statement is fabricated, quoted out of context, or otherwise inaccurate, since in these circumstances the accused has something important to explain. Yet if the accused takes the stand to explain such a statement, even a fabricated one, she will be forced to forfeit some of the protection provided by the Fifth Amendment, and she will open herself up to cross-examination and impeachment. On the other hand, excluding an accused's statements may prevent the state from introducing important relevant evidence. Courts do not attempt to strike a balance. The admissions exception may be used against criminal defendants so long as the statements are, as a matter of constitutional law, otherwise admissible.

4.   Adoptive Statements

Subsection (B) of FRE 801(d)(2) refers to what the common law referred to as adoptive admissions. This exception recognizes that parties often agree with statements others make. More importantly, it holds parties responsible for statements they agree with or otherwise assent to in the same way that they are held responsible for their own assertions.

Where agreement is clear, the justification for admitting adoptive admissions is almost as strong as the justification for admitting a party's own assertions since explicit agreement is simply another way of making a statement. If Alice says, "X is true," and Bob, a party to the case, says, "Yes, that's right," it is difficult to see why Alice's statement should not be treated as if Bob had said it.

Problems arise, however, when it is not clear that a party's acquiescence in another's statement is a knowing and voluntary expression of agreement. Suppose, for example, that the beneficiary of a life insurance policy proves the insured's death by sending the insurance company the death certificate, as the insurance policy requires. If the death certificate attributes the insured's death to an excluded cause, like suicide, should the death certificate be admissible to prove the cause of death, or should the insurance company be required to place the maker of the certificate on the stand if it wishes to get his opinion into evidence? The company's claim that the beneficiary adopted the certificate maker's judgment is unrealistic. The beneficiary mailed the death certificate to prove that the insured died, not how he died. The beneficiary may not have chosen the doctor who filled out the death certificate; she almost certainly lacked the expertise to evaluate the doctor's judgment, and she is unlikely to have known that the certificate's attribution of cause would, if true, bar recovery under the policy. Yet most jurisdictions treat a cause-of-death statement in a death certificate as an adoptive admission unless the statement is disclaimed when the certificate is submitted. Exclusion is more likely—though by no means guaranteed—if the policy requires a specific mode of proving death or if an insurance agent helped the beneficiary provide the proof of death.

Even more difficult problems are presented when it is unclear whether a party has acquiesced in another's statement. The admission by silence—a classic example of the adoptive admission—poses this problem. If Sarah Black confronts Tom Green, saying, "You're the one who robbed me," does Green's silence indicate his acquiescence in the accusation? Green may not have heard what Black said; he may have thought Black was joking; or he may, by his silence, have intended to treat Black's false accusation with the disdain it deserved. Courts generally hold that unanswered statements are not admissible under an adoption rationale if the judge determines that the listener for some reason did not appreciate the accusation or if the statement was made in a context where an untrue accusation would probably not be denied. In other situations, courts feel that the probability a listener would contradict on untrue statement is sufficiently high that the jury should learn of the interchange and decide for itself whether the party's silence indicates acquiescence.

Perhaps the most disquieting feature of the admission by silence is that it allows a person who knows of the exception to generate favorable evidence. In the situation most prone to abuse, however—that of the arrestee—the right to silence and the requirement that an accused be warned of this right create a context where even innocent people may be unlikely to deny false accusations. Consequently, silence in the face of accusations by the police made while in their custody is not admissible to support an inference of guilt or to impeach a witness once *Miranda* warnings have been given.[53] Silence during the period after arrest but before *Miranda* warnings have been given is admissible for impeachment.[54] Pre-arrest silence in the face of a police accusation or breaking off voluntary cooperation without alluding to *Miranda* may also

---

[53] Doyle v. Ohio, 426 U.S. 610 (1976).

[54] Fletcher v. Weir, 455 U.S. 603 (1982) *per curiam*. The Supreme Court's rationale for the disparate treatment of silence depending on whether the *Miranda* warnings have been administered to the suspect is one of detrimental reliance. Because the police tell the suspect that she has the right to remain silent, it is unfair to then allow the prosecution to use post-*Miranda*-warning silence as evidence of guilt. On the other hand, an individual who has not been so warned does not have a similar reliance interest. You can, and should, question this reasoning given that many persons know they have the right to remain silent regardless of whether they are officially administered the *Miranda* warnings. The more likely answer for the disparate treatment is the Court's low commitment to the *Miranda* rule itself. The Court has not confronted the issue of whether such silence may be offered by the state in its case-in-chief as an adoptive admission. Since the accusation that defined the substance of the admission could, if a response were called for, be considered questioning in violation of *Miranda*, it is likely that the use of post-arrest but pre-warning silence will be confined to impeachment.

be used for impeachment if *Miranda* warnings have not been given, and if an innocent person would most likely have denied a direct or implicit accusation, the accused's silence may be used to support an inference of guilt as well.[55]

Problem VI-18.   Christina Santilukka and her child Dolly go to Dodi Hannah's beauty salon.   Hannah suggests that Dolly and Sara, the child of another woman having her hair done, play in the yard behind the salon.   A few minutes later the adults hear cries.   Hannah goes outside and brings in a crying Dolly.   According to Santilukka, Hannah said, "I'm so sorry, my dog has bitten your child."   According to Hannah the remark was, "I'm so sorry, Sara says my dog has bitten your child."   **For the purpose of determining admissibility, does it matter which version of Hannah's statement is correct?   Why or why not?**

Problem VI-19.   The testator, Harold Hawk, has just died and four beneficiaries are meeting with Erica Darling, executor for Hawk's estate. Darling opens Hawk's safe and pulls out seven bundles of money, saying there's $500.00 in each bundle.   At this point Susan Sparrow, one of the beneficiaries, says, "No, there's $5,000.00."   Darling doesn't respond to this statement but moves on to other matters.   Darling is later charged with the crime of not reporting as part of Hawk's estate the $32,500 in cash, taken from the safe.   **Can another beneficiary testify to the statements of Darling and Sparrow concerning the amount of money in the bundles, to show that the bundles contained $5,000.00 each?**

5.   Authorized Statements

Subsections C, D, and E of FRE 801(d)(2) refer to kinds of statements that the common law treated under the heading of *representative* or *vicarious* admissions.   Subsections C and D distinguish two kinds of vicarious admissions and, following the modern trend, liberalize the conditions of admissibility with respect to each.   Subsection E, dealing with the statements of co-conspirators, codifies the law with respect to a particularly important type of vicarious admission.

---

[55]   Jenkins v. Anderson, 447 U.S. 231 (1980); Silanas v. Texas, 133 S.Ct. 928 (2013). *Jenkins* dealt with the use of silence for impeachment, and *Salinas* with substantive inferences. In *Salinas*, Justices Scalia and Thomas indicated that they do not believe that silence constitutes testimony within the meaning of the Fifth Amendment, regardless.   Justices Alito, Roberts and Kennedy who signed the plurality opinion believe that it can amount to testimony when used to support an inference of guilt or a suggestion of how a question might have been answered.   They held, however, that so long as a person is talking voluntarily to the police and is free to leave the conversation, the Fifth Amendment will not preclude the state from using a person's refusal to answer a question and accompanying behavior (e.g. downcast eyes, signs of nervousness) to support an inference of guilt unless the person made it clear that breaking off the conversation was done with the intent of invoking the self-incrimination privilege.

Statements falling under Subsection C are called "authorized" statements. When a party has explicitly authorized another to speak for her with respect to some subject, the speaker's statements regarding that subject will be admitted as if they were the party's own statements. The case for admitting the speaker's statements is weaker than the case for admitting personal or adoptive admissions, since the authorizing party may lack personal knowledge of the facts the speaker admits and may have done nothing to manifest agreement with the speaker's statements. But the party presumably has chosen a trustworthy spokesperson, so it does not seem fundamentally unfair to allow the agent's statements into evidence. Furthermore, the speaker, unless dead or otherwise unavailable, is likely to be friendly to the party and willing to testify for her.

The exception for authorized admissions also means that corporate parties, which can speak only through designated individuals, regularly make statements that can be introduced as their admissions. Without the exception, incorporation would entail yet another special benefit, and people generally would be better off speaking through third parties than speaking for themselves. These are additional reasons to treat authorized statements as admissions.

The common law distinguished two kinds of authorized statements, those the speaker was authorized to make to third parties and those that were to be reported only to the authorizing party or others within a firm. Only statements of the first kind were admissible against the party. Thus, the common law admissions exception did not cover reports of internal reviews, inspections, and other investigations. Although the opposing party could call the investigator and, absent some privilege, ask him to tell the jury what he discovered, this procedure could prove perilous because the investigator was likely to be an unfriendly witness.

So long as one justifies the admissions exception solely on the basis of responsibility or other characteristics of the adversary system, a distinction based on who is authorized to receive a statement makes sense. When a party has taken precautions so that third parties will not learn what her agents have said, why should she be responsible for statements leaked out against her orders?

A much stronger case for admitting internal reports can be made if we discard the responsibility justification for admissions and look at the kinds of factors that justify most hearsay exceptions. Internal reports are likely to have such significant indicia of reliability that their admission makes sense for this reason alone. First, a person making an internal report seldom is motivated to falsely portray a situation as less favorable to those who sought the report than it in fact is.[56] Second, those who prepare internal reports usually have an insider's access to individuals and information, so their reports are likely to be based on the full and frank disclosure of their various informants. Finally, internal reports are usually prepared for business purposes and so may share the guarantees of reliability that inhere in routine business activity. Without specifying their reasons in detail, the drafters of the Federal Rules make it clear that Subsection C applies to all authorized statements regardless of what dissemination is authorized.

6. Vicarious Statements of Agents

FRE 801(d)(2)(D) treats the vicarious admissions of agents generally. It is usually used to admit the statements of business employees. The common law once admitted an agent's statement against a principal only if the principal had authorized the agent to speak about the matter. Thus, early common law cases usually excluded the post-accident statements of truck drivers offered against truck owners on the ground that the drivers had authority to drive for the owners but not to speak for them. FRE 801(d)(2)(D) avoids this result. Following what had become the dominant trend, it admits statements by agents as long as the statements relate to matters within the scope of the agency relationship. Specific authority to speak is not the test.

The theory of the admissions exception provides no good rationale for extending admissibility this far.[57] Nevertheless, the extension is wise. McCormick notes that there are reasons to believe that agents' statements made during and about their agency have some special likelihood of reliability: "Typically the agent is well informed about acts in the course of the business, the statements are offered against the employer's interest, and while the employment continues, the employee is not likely to make the statements unless they are true."[58]

In order to admit an agent's statement as an admission against the principal the judge must be persuaded as a preliminary question governed by FRE 104(a) that at the time the statement was made the speaker was the principal's agent and that her statement concerned a matter within the scope of her agency. Traditionally, in deciding whether an agency relationship existed, the judge could not consider the purported

---

[56] Since bearers of sad tidings sometimes suffer for their news, there might be an incentive to report a situation as being more favorable than it is, but a party confronted by a report she authorized can hardly complain that the facts reported may be distorted in her favor.

[57] McCormick writes, "[I]f admissions are viewed as arising from the adversary system, responsibility for statements of one's employee is consistent with that theory." McCORMICK § 259. Responsibility for the statements of agents may be consistent with vicarious liability, but we see no inevitable relationship between such responsibility and the adversary system; and, in any event, vicarious admissions are admissible for all purposes, not just to prove one type of liability.

[58] *Id.*

agent's own statements. This was considered improper "boot strapping." Thus, if Smith, upon crashing into the plaintiff said, "I ran a red light because I was rushing to make a delivery for White," his relationship to White could not be proved by that statement, unless it was admissible under some separate exception to the hearsay rule. To introduce a statement against White, Smith's statement that he ran a red light, the plaintiff must be able to show with admissible evidence that it was more likely than not that Smith was White's agent at the time of the accident.[59]

However, In 1987, the Supreme Court in *Bourjaily v. United States*,[60] reached the opposite conclusion in a case involving co-conspirator hearsay. The Court held that the last sentence of FRE 104(a)—which provides that in determining whether the conditions for admitting evidence are met, a court "is not bound by evidence rules, except those on privilege"—means that the judge in a FRE 104(a) hearing could consider a co-conspirator's hearsay statements in deciding whether the conspiracy that rendered one conspirator's statements admissible against others existed.

After *Bourjaily*, the federal courts were divided on whether the hearsay statements of agents might similarly be considered in deciding whether an agency relationship existed. In 1997, FRE 801(d)(2) was amended to codify this practice. The 1997 amendments also answered a question the Supreme Court had reserved in *Bourjaily*; namely, whether the conspiracy (or agency) relationship needed to trigger the exception could be established when *all* the evidence offered to establish the relationship was admissible only if the relationship existed. The amendment provides that it cannot.[61] Even in the FRE 104(a) hearing, some otherwise admissible evidence of the relationship must be presented.[62]

Many courts over the years have refused to treat statements by government agents in criminal cases as admissions admissible against the government. In the leading case, *United States v. Santos*,[63] the defendant, Santos, and two others were charged with and convicted of assaulting a federal officer with a deadly weapon. Santos appealed,

---

[59] There might, of course, be an exception to the hearsay rule other than the admissions exception that renders everything Smith said after the accident substantively admissible. Or, Smith's statement admitting agency might qualify as an excited utterance or under some other hearsay exception, in which case it would be admissible evidence of Smith's agency.

[60] 483 U.S. 171 (1987).

[61] FRE 801(d)(2) is reproduced supra, p. 595. The relevant portion reads:

The statement must be considered but does not by itself establish the declarant's authority under (C); the existence or scope of the relationship under (D); or the existence of the conspiracy or participation in it under (E).

[62] *Compare, e.g.*, Lopez v. State, 29 Ark.App. 145, 778 S.W.2d 641 (1989); Lloyd v. Delaware, 534 A.2d 1262 (Del.1987) (following Bourjaily) withRomani v. Florida, 542 So.2d 984 (Fla.1989); State v. Fink, 92 N.C.App. 523, 375 S.E.2d 303 (N.C.App. 1989) (rejecting *Bourjaily*).

[63] 372 F.2d 177 (2d Cir. 1967).

claiming that he should have been allowed to introduce as an admission a sworn affidavit by a narcotics agent identifying someone else as the third assailant. A panel of the Second Circuit recognized the apparent unfairness of allowing the government to introduce statements of a defendant's agents while not giving defendants reciprocal rights, but the judges nevertheless upheld the trial court's decision. They noted that the government's "many agents and actors are supposedly uninterested personally in the outcome of the trial and are historically unable to bind the sovereign."[64]

FRE 801(d)(2)(D) appears to reverse the *Santos* doctrine, for the rule does not distinguish criminal from civil cases or government employees from other agents.[65] Some courts have interpreted the rule this way,[66] but most courts still refuse to admit statements of government agents as admissions against the government.[67]

Problem VI-20. Belcher Power and Light Company owns a dam on the Huron River. On August 6, 2010, at about 3 A.M., following a heavy rainstorm, the dam gave way, sending water cascading through the town of Hutchins about 12 miles downstream. The residents of Hutchins sue Belcher for 50 million dollars in damages, alleging that it was negligent in building and maintaining the dam. **Can any of the following information be introduced against Belcher at trial?** (a) The statement of Rosita Sanchez, an engineer, who had been sent to repair a sluice gate, to an onlooker, who turned out to be the mayor of Hutchins, "This repair won't do much good if there's a heavy storm. The whole system is bad." (b) The same statement made by Sanchez to her husband when she went home that night. (c) The statement of the president of the company, upon being called by reporters at 3:20 A.M. and informed of the disaster, "Oh my God; the sluice system must have failed. We were negligent in maintaining it." (d) A report in the company files prepared by an outside consulting firm some twelve years earlier when the decision to build the dam was made, stating, "The soil at the suggested dam site is too porous. A series of heavy rain storms would create a danger of collapse." **Would your decision about the report be different if it**

---

[64] *Id.* at 180.

[65] Randolph N. Jonakait, *The Supreme Court, Plain Meaning, and the Changed Rules of Evidence*, 68 Tex. L. Rev. 745, 774–78 (1990).

[66] *See, e.g.*, United States v. Van Griffin, 874 F.2d 634 (9th Cir. 1989); United States v. Kattar, 840 F.2d 118 (1st Cir. 1988); and United States v. Morgan, 581 F.2d 933 (D.C.Cir. 1978) (dictum).

[67] *See, e.g.*, United States v. Kampiles, 609 F.2d 1233 (7th Cir. 1979); United States v. Durrani, 659 F.Supp. 1183 (D.Conn.), aff'd, 835 F.2d 410 (2d Cir. 1987). For a more in depth discussion of this issue, *see* Anne Poulin, Party Admissions in Criminal Cases: Should the Government Have to Eat Its Words, 87 Minn. L. Rev. 401 (2002).

were offered not to show negligent construction, but to justify punitive damages?

7. Partners and Co-conspirators

When business partners make statements relating to partnership activities, the statements of one partner are usually admissible against the partnership in suits arising out of partnership activity. Although a partnership, like any business, might authorize only certain of its members to speak for it, courts have generally assumed that partners who purport to speak for the partnership have the authority to do so.[68]

Subsection E of FRE 801(d)(2), treats statements made "by the party's coconspirator during and in furtherance of the conspiracy" as the party's admissions, and adopts a usually justified common law position that co-conspirators are "partners in crime" and that the statements of one co-conspirator, like the statements of any partner, should be admissible against the others. Despite the analogy between business partners and partners in crime, statements of co-conspirators are not treated like those of business partners. Even if one accepts the agency rationale for admitting statements of partners, one must conclude that the rationale breaks down when used to justify the admission of most statements by co-conspirators.

Statements of business partners are most often introduced when the partnership, as a firm, is involved in litigation, usually civil litigation arising out of some tort, contract, or property problem. A partner's statements are admitted *against the partnership*, a joint enterprise that has authorized its partners to speak for it, or is assumed to have done so. It is true that courts speak of the statements as being admitted against the fellow partners, but this reflects the substantive law of partnerships, which obligates partners personally when a partnership's assets do not cover judgments against it, and enables partners to share the proceeds when a partnership prevails as a plaintiff.[69] Except, insofar as a partner may be obligated by his relationship to the partnership, the out-of-court

---

[68] Questions sometimes arise about whether a partner is speaking for the partnership. A number of cases have held that the casual statements of partners, admitting liability in an accident, for example, do not bind the partnership.

[69] Consider the following example:

An ongoing partnership decides to make partner *A* its spokesperson with respect to litigation growing out of accidents. Partner *B* objects strenuously, saying that *A* will never speak for him, but *B* is outvoted and chooses not to leave the partnership. If there is an accident and *A* makes an improvident statement without which there would not be proof sufficient to find the firm liable, the statement will be introduced as an admission even if *B* is the only partner with assets sufficient to satisfy a judgment against the firm. *B* will have to pay the judgment not because he authorized *A*'s statement, but because he belongs to a firm that authorized that statement, and his relationship to that firm makes him ultimately responsible for the firm's debts.

statements of his partners are inadmissible against him.[70] This is best seen when one partner's statements implicate another partner in a crime. Unless the offense is one for which the firm might be held liable (e.g., a violation of some regulatory legislation), criminal activity is assumed to be beyond the scope of the partnership, and the statements of one partner are inadmissible against another because they do not relate to partnership business.

The situation of conspirators differs from that of business partners in that conspirators' liability does not derive from the unsatisfied obligations of an enterprise they joined for their common good. It derives instead from the fact that the activity of the enterprise they have joined is itself illegal. Statements of co-conspirators that are in furtherance of the conspiracy are verbal actions taken for illegal ends. As such, they need not be hearsay if offered against a conspirator on a conspiracy count, for they can be admitted not for their truth but simply to show what the conspirators did. Just as conspirators are each responsible for physical actions taken on behalf of the conspiracy, so are they responsible for verbal actions.[71] In other situations, however, the statements of conspirators pose the usual hearsay problems, and conspirator's statements may be offered for their truth rather than as verbal acts.

As an example consider the situation of Rogers and Brady, who are charged with conspiring to rob a bank. At trial, the government offers the testimony of a sporting goods salesperson that he sold two ski masks to Rogers, who said he was buying one for himself and the other for his friend Brady. The purchase of the masks might be offered as an overt act of the conspirators, and if so, evidence of the purchase, including the conversation, would be admissible if the conversation were deemed to be a verbal part of the purchase act. However, if the statement to the clerk is offered to prove that the second mask was for Brady, it is hearsay and poses the usual dangers of out-of-court statements offered for their truth.

FRE 801(d)(2)(E) provides an exception for statements of conspirators that are hearsay. It is, of course, unnecessary to rely on an exception when a statement is not offered for its truth, but some courts

---

[70] Of course, a partner's relationship to a firm may be such that a court would hold that she had in fact authorized another partner to speak for her. If, for example, one partner, as firm bookkeeper, noted that another earned $100,000, a court might admit this statement as an admission of the partner's earnings when the partner is prosecuted for reporting a gross income of $50,000. However, admissibility would turn not on the fact that the report on earnings was made by a partner, but rather that the partner, as a part owner of the firm, had authorized the bookkeeping partner to state her earnings for her. The situation would be the same if the bookkeeper were an employee and the partner a sole proprietor who had hired her.

[71] The theory of conspiratorial responsibility is that when individuals cooperate to achieve illegal ends, they should all be held liable for the illegality achieved since each in some way advanced or attempted to advance the illegal goals of the group. One may also be liable for the act of joining an illegal conspiracy. In this instance one is responsible only for one's own actions in joining. Statements that constitute joining an illegal conspiracy, as acts that are themselves illegal, are not hearsay if used to show membership.

confuse the hearsay and nonhearsay uses of conspirator's statements. You should not. If you are alert to the proper nonhearsay uses, you may avoid many of the problems that arise under this complicated hearsay exception.[72]

The Federal Rules follow the common law in providing that one conspirator's statements may be treated as the statements of another only if they were made in furtherance of their conspiracy and during its existence. Taking the "in furtherance" requirement seriously might lead a court to hold that the reference to Brady in our preceding example is inadmissible against him because it was not needed to induce the clerk to sell the masks and so did not further the ends of the conspiracy. However, courts routinely slight the "in furtherance" requirement. The co-conspirators' exception is often used to admit statements in which one conspirator points the finger at another or recounts in narrative fashion the past illegalities of the conspiracy, even though it is highly unlikely that the statements advanced the ends of the conspiracy.

The exception for co-conspirators' statements is not limited to cases in which conspiracy is charged. When a person is charged individually with a crime, the statements of fellow conspirators are admissible against him, provided the judge makes a preliminary finding that the speaker and the defendant were part of the same conspiracy and that the other conditions for co-conspirators' admissions are met.[73] Since conspiracy is not charged, the statements of fellow conspirators are immaterial if offered as acts of the conspiracy, but they may be quite incriminating if received for the truth of what they assert. To admit them for this purpose requires a hearsay exception.

The justification for an exception that admits the hearsay of one conspirator against a co-conspirator is unclear. Consider a situation in which there is evidence that Able, Baker, and Charley have conspired to kidnap Dugan, but Able alone is charged with kidnapping and attempting to murder Dugan. If Baker said to Charley after Dugan had been wounded trying to escape, "We should take away Able's gun; he shot Dugan last night and if his aim wasn't bad we'd all be up for murder," this statement would be admissible against Able as a vicarious admission that he shot Dugan.

Able need not have been present when Baker made the statement, and there need be no evidence that Able authorized Baker to make the statement on his behalf. The statement is irrelevant as an act of the

---

[72] For a more detailed discussion of the issues discussed above, see the first edition of Richard O. Lempert & Steven A. Saltzburg, A Modern Approach to Evidence (1977).

[73] In some jurisdictions the exception in these circumstances is referred to as an exception for "joint venturers," rather than "co-conspirators." To admit the statements of one against the other, the prosecution need only show by a preponderance of the evidence that a joint venture existed. A joint venture for criminal purposes is a conspiracy whether or not the crime of conspiracy has been charged or can be proved beyond a reasonable doubt.

conspiracy because the prosecution has chosen not to charge Able with conspiracy, and Baker may have had a strong motive to place the blame for the shooting on Able. Yet, the jury will hear Charley's testimony reporting Baker's statement. All the hearsay dangers are present in this situation.

An analogous example in the partnership context would be a situation in which Able, while on partnership business, is involved in an accident allegedly due to his drunk driving. Suppose that the victim of the accident chose to sue Able personally but not to sue the firm, and that the victim sought to introduce a statement that Able's partner Baker made to another partner Charley the day after the accident: "Charley, we shouldn't let Able drive on partnership business; he was drunk last night and is likely to be drunk again." Few courts would hold that the fact that Baker made the statement to further the partnership's business interests renders it admissible against Able, when Able is sued personally.

If the co-conspirators' exception cannot be justified on the traditional theory of authorized admissions and if it cannot be justified by analogy to the exception for statements of partners, how can this variant of the admissions exception be justified?

One might argue that reliability and necessity justify the exception. Active conspirators are likely to know who the members of the conspiracy are and what they have done. When speaking to advance the conspiracy, they are unlikely to describe nonmembers as conspirators; usually, they have no incentive to describe the actions of their fellow members inaccurately, and in fact, they often incriminate themselves.[74] Necessity exists because the members of a criminal conspiracy have a Fifth Amendment privilege to refuse to testify to anything pertaining to the conspiracy.[75] Thus, hearsay may be the only way to introduce the observations of one conspirator against another. Since much of the conspiratorial activity is likely to have been done secretly, the observations of the conspirators may be the only proof of certain crucial matters.

The problem with this analysis is that it takes us far from the common justifications for the admissions exception. The exception is traditionally justified in part because of the availability of the speaker to

---

[74] This analysis changes if a conspiracy has broken up in disagreement or through arrest; it is also inapplicable if a conspirator has a motive to misrepresent—for example, by claiming that a powerful figure is involved in the conspiracy in order to persuade others to join or cooperate.

[75] The prosecutor might circumvent the Fifth Amendment problems by granting use immunity. The value of such immunity to conspirators may be low, since conspirator A who has immunity for his statements may be convicted on the testimony of conspirator B who has immunity for his statements, and vice versa. This possibility may mean that conspirators will choose the penalties of contempt rather than testify under a grant of use immunity, in which case the necessity for a hearsay exception will still exist. An exception may also be necessary when conspirators are tried together, since neither defendant could be forced to take the stand at his own trial to testify against a codefendant under a grant of use immunity.

deny or explain the statements attributed to him. The argument from necessity turns on the likely unavailability of the speaker, and it cannot explain why the exception applies to statements heard or uttered by a conspirator who has turned state's evidence and is willing to testify. As for the reliability argument, the statements of conspirators advancing their conspiracy appear no more reliable than any other statements made by individuals in a position to know what they are talking about with no apparent motive to deceive. Yet in the general case this special reliability is not enough to overcome the hearsay objection.

Thus we must acknowledge the possibility that there is no good analytical justification for admitting the statements of co-conspirators in cases where conspiracy is not charged, or in cases in which, because the "in furtherance" requirement is not strictly construed, the statement is not a material act of the conspiracy. So, what is the explanation for widespread admission in such cases? Allowing the prosecution to use them makes it easier to secure criminal convictions. Prosecutors have pressed for interpretations of the rules of evidence that admit such statements, and when faced with criminal defendants presenting unsympathetic cases, courts have accepted the easy analogy to partnerships and have decided that co-conspirators' statements should be admitted without closely analyzing the situation. In reaching this position, courts have probably been misled by the fact that when conspiracy is charged and the conditions of the exception are taken seriously, co-conspirators statements are *acts* in furtherance of the conspiracy and so not excludable as hearsay in the first place. But even if courts have been misled in this way, usually no great injustice is done. When co-conspirator hearsay is offered, it is almost always intertwined with substantial non-hearsay evidence. So even apart from the hearsay there is likely to be considerable evidence pointing to the defendant's guilt.

There is, however, one development that should perhaps concern us. A number of recent cases involve conspirators' admissions that have been made to government agents or to conspirators who have already turned informant. These people are unlikely to be unbiased when recounting what they have been told. The conspirator's exception may allow the government to actively elicit or shape statements designed to incriminate individuals whom the government has targeted.

Our discussion of how the co-conspirators exception has been and should be analyzed is complicated because the issues it deals with are complicated. The *law* regarding conspirators' admissions is not so complicated. We will try to state it simply.

The first task faced by the proponent of a conspirator's hearsay is to show that the speaker and the defendant against whom the statement is offered were both members of an existing conspiracy. This issue, like the preliminary issues under FRE 801(d)(2)(C) and (d)(2)(D), is for the judge to decide under FRE 104(a) *by the preponderance of the evidence.* In deciding this issue, the court must, according to the last sentence of FRE 801(d)(2), consider the contents of the statements whose admissibility is at issue, but may not find that a conspiracy existed or that the speaker and the defendant were members of that conspiracy if those statements are the only evidence that supports those conclusions. This language, as we have already noted, clarifies and extends the Supreme Court's holding in *Bourjaily v. United States.*[76]

There is some question, however, about the amount of protection this extension of *Bourjaily* provides. The Advisory Committee's Note indicates that it did not mean to require that there always will be some evidence of a conspiracy (or agency) that is independent of the hearsay statement itself. Rather, it appears that evidence associated with the hearsay statement and admissible only in connection with it—such as evidence of the identity of the speaker or the context in which the statement was uttered—may be enough to allow a court to admit a coconspirator's or agent's hearsay despite the lack of other evidence of a conspiracy or an agency relationship beyond the hearsay whose admissibility is at issue. To the extent that courts interpret the last sentence of FRE 801(d)(2) this way, the additional protection that seems to be provided by the independent evidence requirement is likely to prove illusory.

A number of state courts, however, have rejected *Bourjaily* and have interpreted their versions of FRE 104(a) to preclude bootstrapping when the admissibility of a co-conspirator's hearsay is in issue. Some also require the conspiratorial relationship to be shown by more than a preponderance of the evidence. Unless the evidence codes in these states are amended, it will be more difficult to admit the hearsay of conspirators and of agents generally, in these states' courts than in the federal courts within these states.

The party that offers the hearsay of one conspirator as the statement of another must persuade the judge, by a preponderance of the evidence, that a conspiracy existed. Three methods of proving the conspiracy are common. First, the judge may conduct a "mini trial" out of the presence of the jury to determine whether it is more likely than not that the speaker and the defendant conspired together. Second, by the time the prosecutor wishes to offer the co-conspirator's statement, the government may have already introduced enough evidence to permit the judge to determine that a conspiracy probably existed. Finally, the co-conspirator's statement may be introduced subject to "connecting up," *i.e.,* to the later introduction of evidence sufficient to allow the judge to

---

[76]   483 U.S. 171 (1987).

determine that a conspiracy probably existed.[77] Should the government fail to offer evidence sufficient to support such a finding, the defendant may be entitled to a mistrial because a belated instruction to disregard a co-conspirator's incriminatory statements is unlikely to remove them from the jurors' minds. For this reason, the first two methods of establishing the preliminary fact of conspiracy are preferable to the third, but the third may be the only practical way to proceed in a case with many defendants and numerous statements.

Once two people are shown to have been participants in the same conspiracy, the statements of one are treated as admissions of the other if two conditions are met. The first condition is that the statements must have been made *in furtherance* of the conspiracy. However, as we noted earlier, courts often pay little attention to whether a conspirator's statement actually furthered the conspiracy. Statements that do no more than confess to illegal actions or inculpate fellow conspirators have often been introduced under this exception.

The second condition is one we have not yet discussed: A co-conspirator's statement is admissible only if it was made *during* the life of the conspiracy. Once a conspiracy has ended, statements by its former members are admissible only against themselves. In most jurisdictions this condition has been taken more seriously than the "in furtherance" requirement.

Conspiracies are considered over when the conspiracy has achieved its goal or when it has been broken up or conclusively disbanded. Thus, the arrest or indictment of the conspirators or a decision by the conspirators to disband, coupled with evidence that this has occurred, are typically treated as terminating the conspiracy.

There is some dispute over when a conspiracy has achieved its goal. Usually it is with the completion of the criminal act, but the exact point of completion may not be clear. Some courts have held that a conspiracy to rob a bank does not end with a successful getaway but only with the splitting up of the proceeds, whenever that occurs. If a criminal enterprise appears ongoing, the conspiracy will not be treated as over simply because an arrest intervenes before the next crime may be carried out. Some prosecutors have gone further and argued that any successful conspiracy gives rise to a second conspiracy: to conceal criminal involvement and escape punishment. If this argument were accepted, an arrest would not end a conspiracy for the purposes of the admissions exception because conspirators who plead not guilty often cooperate to

---

[77] Note that the defendant might be able to transform either the second or the third way of proceeding into a mini trial by requesting a FRE 104(c) hearing after the government has presented its case to the jury. If the defendant is not allowed to present evidence to the judge, the preponderance of the evidence standard is reduced to the requirement of a prima facie case, since there will be no evidence suggesting the *nonexistence* of a conspiracy except that which the defendant might adduce on cross-examination of the state's witnesses.

deny their involvement.   Most courts, however, do not perceive conspiracies in the "concealment phase."[78]

Individuals may also leave conspiracies before the conspiracy has ended. If a conspirator's involvement has clearly terminated, statements made by co-conspirators after the date of termination will not be admissible against him.   The opposite is not true, however.   When a conspirator enters an ongoing conspiracy, he is held to have adopted the earlier remarks of fellow conspirators. Their statements, made perhaps before the defendant even knew the conspiracy existed, may be introduced as the new co-conspirator's admissions. This view of adoption, like some other arguments used to justify the co-conspirators' exception, is pure fiction.

Problem VI-21. There is good evidence that Tinker, Evers, and Chance conspired to rob the Glendale Bank. Tinker, allegedly the brains behind the operation, recruited Evers, and Evers recruited Chance. Tinker and Chance have never met. Evers and Chance were arrested two weeks after the robbery when they tried to pass some marked bills.   Tinker was arrested a week later. Tinker was tried alone. He was charged with bank robbery, extortion by threat, and receipt of stolen property knowing it was stolen.   Chance has offered to turn state's evidence.   He is willing to testify to the following remarks that Evers made to him during the planning stage of the robbery. *"Tinker has this all set up. This is the map of the bank that he's drawn and here's a key to the alley door that he gave me. Tinker will be at the end of the alley with the getaway car."* Two days before the robbery it appeared that Evers was getting cold feet. He said to Chance, *"Maybe we shouldn't go through with this. Tinker is clever, but I'm not sure how well he will do his part. I don't think a VW has enough acceleration to be the getaway car, and with his noisy muffler and pink decals the cops can spot us a mile away.   Shall I tell Tinker it's off?"* Chance persuaded Evers to continue in the scheme. The night of the robbery, while getting soaked by the rain in a trench outside of town, Evers said, *"That bastard Tinker is responsible for our problems.   He never showed up in the car. We were lucky to escape on foot."* (It turned out that Tinker had been stopped a block from the bank about the time of the robbery and given a ticket for driving with a defective muffler.) After

---

[78] The Supreme Court specifically rejected the idea of an implied conspiracy to conceal for the purpose of determining the scope of the co-conspirator exception in Krulewitch v. United States, 336 U.S. 440 (1949). In a later case, however, the Court held that where this view does prevail, as in Georgia, admitting against the defendant statements made in the "concealment phase" does not necessarily violate the Confrontation Clause of the Sixth Amendment. Dutton v. Evans, 400 U.S. 74 (1970). Given recent developments in the Supreme Court's Confrontation Clause Jurisprudence discussed in Chapter Seven, there is reason to question whether the Court's holding in *Dutton* is still good law, but its results might still hold even if the analysis would be different.

Evers and Chance were arrested but before Tinker was arrested, Evers told Chance, *"I've gotten word to Tinker where we hid the money. He'll get us the best lawyer in the business."* In addition, during the robbery, Chance said to the bank president who was in his office when the break-in occurred, *"If you don't fill this sack with money, I will blow off your head."* This was contrary to Tinker's plans, since Tinker had planned the robbery for a time when no one was expected to be in the bank.

To which of Evers' statements will Chance be allowed to testify? Will he be allowed to repeat his own statement to the bank president? Does the admissibility of any of these statements depend on whether Tinker is charged with conspiracy to engage in the offenses charged?

8. Privity

The last major heading under which many courts admit statements as admissions is privity. If a person acquires an interest directly from another, statements made by the other person while possessing that interest may be introduced against the acquirer as admissions. But no such exception is found in the Federal Rules.

Some courts have justified the admission by privity of predecessor-in-interest statements with the argument that an individual adopts her predecessor's statements concerning an interest when she comes into possession of that interest. This justification is untenable as a description of what actually occurs when one person acquires another's interests, especially since courts will admit statements under the privity doctrine even though the successor in interest was unaware of her predecessor's comments. If a person "adopts" a predecessor's statements when succeeding to an interest, it is only because the law says that the statements will be adopted for purposes of the admissions exception, whatever the successor's intent.

There are two plausible justifications for admitting statements by predecessors in interest. The first is that if it were the predecessor rather than the successor who was litigating the matter, the predecessor's statements could be offered against him as personal admissions. If the statements had substantial probative value, the predecessor's chances of prevailing in the litigation would diminish accordingly. Why, courts have asked, should the transfer of a claim increase the probability that it will be effectively asserted?[79] The second reason is that admissions offered under the privity theory are often very likely to be reliable, since most

---

[79] In some circumstances, such as those covered by the holder-in-due-course doctrine, the legislature has decided that the transfer of a claim to another should have exactly this sort of effect by extinguishing a claim or a defense altogether. When this kind of decision has been made, admissions by privity are irrelevant and hence inadmissible.

will have been against the speaker's interest when made. If they are reliable, justice is served by making them available to the fact-finder.

The second reason is a powerful one, but it does not prove the need for an exception based on privity. Instead, it argues that there should be an exception for hearsay statements that are against interest when made. There is in fact such an exception. Reliance on this exception instead of the admissions exception has the virtue of excluding statements by predecessors that are of questionable reliability because they were not against interest when made. The drafters of the Federal Rules, following the decision of the drafters of the Model Code of Evidence and the Uniform Rules of Evidence, made no provision for admitting statements by predecessors in interest as admissions because they assumed that when such statements had particular probative value, they would be admissible under the declaration against interest exception. But one can imagine cases in which this would not happen.

Statements by individuals jointly sharing an identical interest have been treated in the same way as other statements of parties in privity. At common law statements of one came in as admissions of the other, but they are inadmissible as admissions under the Federal Rules. Despite the Federal Rules, in some joint interest situations it is impossible in any practical sense not to use the statements of one joint holder against another, since if either holder is liable, the relief ordered by the court will run against the jointly held property.

When an identity of interest is alleged to exist, either through a conjoint relationship or through succession, the technical analysis of what constitutes an identity of interest is important. For example, the statements of joint tenants or joint owners will be received against each other, but the statements of tenants in common or co-legatees will not be. The statements of an insured will be received against a beneficiary when the insured retained the power to change the designation of the beneficiary, but not otherwise. To deal with these evidence problems in practice, you must first master the substantive law that relates persons to property and other interests.

ADDITIONAL PROBLEMS

Problem VI-22. Hatfield and McCoy have long disputed the ownership of a pond that borders both of their farms. Hatfield claims the pond is his and has said so on many occasions. McCoy has done likewise. All this changed, however, the day that Sammy Smith dove into the pond, hit his head on a rock, and drowned. When the Smiths brought suit against Hatfield, his defense was that the pond belonged to McCoy, so he was not responsible for the injuries of those using it. Hatfield wishes to introduce the statements of McCoy as evidence that McCoy owns the pond. **May he do so?** The Smiths wish to introduce Hatfield's prior assertions of title to prove that he owns the land. **May they do so?** The Smiths would also like to introduce a witness who will testify that Hatfield's father, from whom Hatfield inherited the land, often claimed ownership of the pond. **May they do so?** Hatfield would like to introduce a witness who will testify that she heard Hatfield's grandfather, from whom his father inherited the land, say, "I sure wish I owned the pond that borders the McCoy's property. I tried to fool the kids once by telling them that their pappy had sold it to mine, but when I couldn't produce a deed they weren't buying." **May Hatfield introduce this witness?**

Problem VI-23. Lady Macbeth is charged with the murder of Duncan, King of Scotland. A physician is willing to testify that he saw her walk in her sleep one night, and that while she was still asleep she said, "Out, damned spot! Out, I say! . . . Yet who would have thought the old man to have had so much blood in him!" and "Here's the smell of the blood still. All the perfumes of Arabia will not sweeten this little hand." **Will the prosecutor be allowed to introduce the doctor's testimony over a hearsay objection?**

Problem VI-24. Carrie Bogart sues the driver of an automobile in which she was riding for damages arising out of an accident. Her husband, Peter, who was in the car but was not injured, sues for loss of consortium. The jurisdiction has a rule that guests like the Bogarts assume the risk that defects in the host's vehicle may lead to accidents, unless the host/driver knows or should know of the defective condition and fails to inform a guest of it. The defendant testifies that he thought that the tire that blew out and caused the accident was in good condition, that the tire was in fact in good condition, and that the blowout was caused by broken glass in the road. Peter testifies that he helped change the tire shortly before the accident and it appeared to be in good condition, but that when they took it to the garage to inflate it a man, whose tire gauge they had borrowed, said that the tire was in poor condition and that with the 38 pounds of air they had put in it, it might blow to pieces in a few miles. The defendant had replied that he would take a chance on the tire, and Peter, as he recounts it, said that he would do the same. **Are any of the statements at the garage admissible? Against which parties? On what issues?**

Problem VI-25. Doris Driver ran into and injured Walter Walker, a pedestrian. Petulia Passenger was with Driver in her car. Walker sues Driver, alleging that Driver was drunk and ran into Walker when Walker was in a marked crosswalk. Walker's counsel wants to have a police officer testify to a statement Passenger made privately to the officer: "We were returning from a party at which we had all been drinking." Driver objects.

What result? Would the result be any different if the statement had been made in Driver's presence? Suppose the officer had said to

Driver: "The accident was all your fault." When Driver failed to respond, the officer continued: "I'm putting you under arrest because you are drunk." Driver responded with an expletive. **Is any of this interchange admissible?**

Problem VI–26. Alfred Hitchcock claims to have bought a movie camera from the DeMille Camera Shop on June 12, 2009. The camera carries a guarantee from the manufacturer extending one year from the date of purchase. On May 15, 2010, the camera inexplicably stopped working, and Hitchcock sent it back to the manufacturer for repairs under the warranty. Two weeks later, Hitchcock received a note from the manufacturer stating that they will not repair the camera under the warranty without proof of purchase. Hitchcock, having lost his receipt, went back to DeMille and asked for a duplicate. The clerk made out a new receipt, which Hitchcock received and mailed to the manufacturer. Two weeks later he got another letter from the manufacturer stating that the camera would not be repaired for free because the warranty had expired before the camera had been sent in. Hitchcock sues the manufacturer for the cost of repairs. At the trial, the manufacturer wishes to introduce a copy of the receipt that Hitchcock had sent in. On the receipt, in the space marked "Date of Purchase," the clerk had written "5/12/09." **Is this receipt admissible? Would it be admissible if Hitchcock had not mailed the receipt himself but had instead requested the clerk to mail the receipt directly to the manufacturer?**

Problem VI–27. Fred Johnson sues Walt Wreckless after the cars they were driving collided. Johnson puts his passenger, Sam Schwartz, on the stand to testify to Wreckless's negligence. On cross-examination, Schwartz is asked if Johnson had been drinking before the accident. He responds, "Fred and I each had two beers before we set out in the car. Fred had been driving for about an hour when this other guy hit us." Johnson recovers $25,000 from Wreckless. A month later Ken Starr, the local prosecutor, brings charges against Johnson for "driving after drinking." **At the trial can the prosecutor introduce Schwartz's statement that Johnson had had two beers? Would the situation be any different if Schwartz's testimony had been in a deposition that Johnson introduced in the civil suit when Schwartz proved unavailable?**

Problem VI–28. Laura Morgan is charged with possessing phenmetrazine, a controlled substance, with intent to distribute. She was arrested in rather strange circumstances. The police had secured a warrant to search a single-family house after furnishing the judge with an affidavit from Detective Chang, which said that a reliable informant had told him that a man between 22 and 24 years of age known as Timmy had within the past 48 hours been selling drugs from inside the house.

When the police arrived to execute the warrant, Timmy was not there, but Morgan was present with a group of four others in the hallway. She was holding a snarling German shepherd on a leash. According to the police, they saw Morgan reach into a pocket just as they opened the door, throw twelve pink pills on the floor, and try to crush them with her feet. A search of the basement led to the seizure of 77 additional pink pills and $4,280 secreted in a hole in the ceiling. Chemical analysis revealed that the pink pills contained phenmetrazine.

At the trial, the government introduces the testimony of the owner of the house, who says that Morgan came to the house every day to feed and exercise her dogs, which were kept chained in the basement. The owner also testifies that no one has lived in the basement since she moved the dogs down there more than a year ago. On cross-examination, she admits that her son, Timmy, lives with her in the house. As part of her defense, Morgan would like to introduce the affidavit of Detective Chang, which was used to secure the search warrant. She would also like to ask a police officer whether Detective Chang said to him after Morgan's arrest, "I expect she just bought these. She's not the distributor." **Is evidence of Detective Chang's affidavit, or of the statement he made after Morgan's arrest, admissible against the government?**

Problem VI-29. Stanley Owner owned Greenacre, a 200-acre tract of land with a 23 room mansion located at one end. When Stanley died, he bequeathed a 50% interest in Greenacre to each of his two children, Fay and Ray. Mark Trueblood, Owner's trusted servant for 22 years, brings suit to void the bequest as it applies to Greenmansion and the surrounding five acres of land, alleging that some seven years earlier he had turned down an offer of more lucrative employment when Owner promised him that Greenmansion would be his if he stayed on for an additional five years. **In a suit against Fay and Ray, can Mark testify that Owner told him when he threatened to leave some seven years before, "I can't match the Vanderwink's salary offer, but if you stay with me another five years Greenmansion will be yours"? Can Mark testify that five years to the day after this conversation Owner had told him, "Well, it's five years since we made our deal, Mark; Greenmansion is yours. I'll continue to live in it, but we know that you've now earned the title. I'll be sure that legal title passes to you on my death"? Can Mark introduce against either Fay or Ray or both of them Ray's statement two days after Owner's death, "Well Mark, I understand that Greenmansion has been yours for two years now. I wish Dad had told me sooner. I'll really miss the place"?** (Disregard any Statute of Frauds or Dead Man's Statute problems in formulating your answers.)

Problem VI-30. Able sells land to Baker, who thinks that Able has good title to the land, free from all encumbrances. One day, when Baker is walking on the far corner of his land, he notices a man herding sheep. When Baker asks the man to leave his land, the man replies that he has an easement he purchased from Able that gives him the right to graze sheep on this portion of the land. Baker subsequently sues to eject the sheep from the land, but Able is no longer within the jurisdiction of the Court. The sheepherder wishes to introduce the testimony of Able's brother, who will testify that just before leaving the jurisdiction Able said, "I really put one over on old Baker. He won't discover the sheep and the easement until I'm long gone." **Is the statement admissible?** (Disregard any Statute of Frauds problems in formulating your answer.)

Problem VI-31. Ellen Masters, a police officer, shot and killed Fred Jacobs. Masters alleges that the killing occurred when Jacobs, despite being handcuffed, broke away and attempted to flee. She claims she fired one warning shot, and when Jacobs didn't stop she fired the shot that apparently killed him. Jacobs's family claims that he was intentionally shot through the back at close range. They bring a civil suit seeking damages for Masters' actions. In answering the third paragraph of plaintiff's complaint, which asserts that Masters fired a shot at close range killing plaintiff, Masters responds with an answer that "admits the third paragraph of plaintiff's complaint insofar as it claims that defendant fired a shot killing plaintiff, but neither affirms nor denies plaintiff's claim that the shot came from close range." The answer is filed by Masters' lawyer and is signed by her as attorney for the defendant, but it is not signed by Masters herself.

On the morning of the trial Master's attorney, who had breakfasted on martinis, says to her taxi driver on the way to the courthouse, "I think they're caving. I think they will settle for under $15,000. They'll be fools if they do. If they had decent experts, it would be clear to them that the shot was fired from less than four feet away." It turned out that Masters' attorney knew what she was talking about, for the case was settled for $10,000 during the recess following the selection of the jury. The Police Officers' Benevolent Association paid 95% of the settlement on Masters' behalf.

Later, following considerable political pressure, Masters is charged with murder based on the same incident. **At the trial may the prosecution introduce Masters' pleading in the civil case to show that Masters shot Jacobs? May the prosecution introduce the taxi driver's testimony as to what Masters' attorney said on the morning of trial to prove that the shot was fired from four feet or less? May evidence of the final settlement be introduced for any purpose?**

Problem VI-32. Charles Street, who works part time delivering groceries for the Foxy-Loxy Super Market, crashed into Marvin Gardens about five o'clock one evening. After the collision James Place, a passerby, came up to Street and asked what happened. Street replied, "I was speeding, trying to deliver my last bag of groceries for the F & L, when I missed the stop sign and collided with the car in the intersection." Later Street repeats the same story to the police officer sent to investigate the accident. **If Gardens sues Foxy-Loxy, can either of Street's statements come in on the issue of his negligence? Can either statement come in on the issue of whether Foxy-Loxy is liable for Street's negligence on the theory of respondeat superior? Is there any other information that you would wish to have before answering these questions? What might you do as Gardens' attorney if you thought the court would rule that these statements were inadmissible against the supermarket?**

Problem VI-33. On the same facts as the above, Street pleads guilty to tickets issued for speeding and for failing to stop at a stop sign. **Would Street's pleas be admitted against Foxy-Loxy? Against Street, if Gardens had sued him? Would the situation be any different if Gardens' heirs, suing Foxy-Loxy for wrongful death, wished to introduce the fact that Street had pleaded guilty to a charge of negligent homicide following the accident? If Street had pleaded innocent, could a jury verdict of "guilty" be introduced against either Street or Foxy-Loxy in a civil suit arising out of the same incident?**

Problem VI-34. Virgil Flame drives a truck for the Keepon Trucking Company, a sole proprietorship owned by Henry Keepon. One evening Virgil misjudges his distance while pulling into a rest area and scrapes a parked car. He offers Shayna Sonda, the irate owner, $350, saying, "Your damages can't be more than $150. If you don't call the cops, I'll give you $350." Sonda asks why and Virgil replies, "This rig's ten tons over the weight limit. I have Keepon's map to avoid the scales, but I never thought I might get caught up this way." **If Keepon is later charged with knowingly sending out trucks over the highway weight limit, may Sonda testify to any of the remarks that Virgil made to her?** Assume there is no other evidence that the map referred to exists or that Keepon knew the truck was over the weight limit, but it is admitted that Virgil was working for Keepon at the time he made these remarks.

Problem VI-35. Harry Tracy and Senator Coolidge are charged with offering and taking a bribe, respectively. At their joint trial, the prosecution seeks to introduce the testimony of an aide to the Senator who will testify that he overheard his boss saying on the telephone, "I just accepted some money from Tracy to vote for the farm bill." **Is this admissible or should it be excluded on the ground that it is hearsay? If it is admissible, should it come in against both parties? If not, what can counsel for the party entitled to**

protection do to ensure that the statement will not be used against her client?

Problem VI–36. Castor and Pollux are partners who operate the C-P Appliance Store in the Bronx. In early May of 2007, Castor, who has been thinking of moving to Florida, offers to sell his 50 percent share of the business to Ajax for "its market value of $150,000." Ajax declines, so Castor sticks with the business. Two months later the Discount Appliance Center opens an outlet across from C-P. C-P cannot meet the competition and in a month is driven out of business. Later it turns out that Discount had engaged in predatory pricing for the purpose of driving C-P out of business. Pollux brings a treble damage action against Discount in which he claims actual damages of $500,000, giving rise to treble damages of $1,500,000. **On the issue of the value of Pollux's interest in the partnership, can Discount introduce Ajax to testify that Castor offered him a 50% interest in the store for $150,000? If Castor had offered to sell Ajax the entire store for $300,000, would Ajax be allowed to testify to this?**

Problem VI–37. White and Black are the president and vice president of COLORS, a company they organized to "exploit the vast mineral wealth of the West." Green is called the company's "chief engineer." There are no other employees. COLORS holds the mineral rights to several thousand acres of land in Colorado and Wyoming, but the land has been thoroughly explored and, at current market prices, there are no minerals on the land worth extracting. Nevertheless, Green roams the country securing investors with promises of large returns from soon to be developed gold mining and oil shale operations. White and Black maintain a New York office. It is their task to maintain the semblance of an active energy exploration company and to entertain potential large investors whom Green lures to the city. One day when Green is in New York, he stops by the office while White and Black are together opening the mail. Black hands him a check from a letter he has just opened. It is made out to COLORS in the amount of $90,000. "Here's a nice return from your travels," says Black. "It's that sucker you met at the Kansas convention. What was he, a potato farmer?"

When the conspiracy is eventually broken up by the police, Black flees the jurisdiction, Green turns state's evidence, and White is tried alone for fraud. **At White's trial, may Green relate his conversation with Black to show that White was involved in a fraudulent activity? May it be introduced to show that White was involved in a conspiracy if White is charged with conspiracy to defraud?**

Problem VI–38. Moe and Joe are in a conspiracy to sell drugs. In an effort to expand operations, Joe seeks out new recruits from other gangs. As part of his strategy, he seeks to impress upon potential members Moe's reputation for toughness. He brags to one person, who turns out to be an undercover DEA agent, that "Moe is the biggest and meanest dealer around," and that he can "personally verify" that "Moe killed two dealers who tried to invade our gang's territory." Moe is a suspect in several murders of a rival gang's members. He is arrested. At trial, the prosecution seeks to introduce the DEA agent to testify to Joe's statements regarding Moe's involvement in murder. **May the agent testify to what Joe told him?**

Problem VI-39. Carol Pack, her husband, and her parents are charged with burning down a restaurant to collect insurance money and with conspiring with her parents and husband, Bruce, to do this. At trial, the state introduces a tape recording of the family discussing the restaurant fire, a recording made two days after the fire. On the tape Pack's father says, "Well Carol, having your restaurant burn was the best thing that has happened to us. You were killing yourself, and we couldn't have sold it for a third of the insurance money." And her mother added, laughing, "I'll bet the insurance company will be suspicious, but they will find there was no gasoline on the floor, just grease, and they'll never know you spilled it there or that Bruce was careless with his cigarettes." Pack's counsel objects that the recording is inadmissible hearsay, but the court overrules the objection.

At the close of the trial, defense counsel moves to dismiss all charges against the defendants for insufficient evidence. The court rules that there is indeed insufficient evidence of conspiracy, but that there is enough evidence that the defendants set the fire to take the case to the jury. Defense counsel then moves to have the tape recording excluded and a mistrial declared since the conspiracy charges were dismissed and the recording constitutes hearsay that was admitted only because it qualified under the conspirators' exception. The court denies the motion.

Carol and her husband are convicted and appeal, arguing that the tape recording should have been excluded. **How should the appellate court rule?**

Problem VI-40. *A, B, C, D,* and *E* are on trial for a conspiracy to defraud the United States Government and the Veterans' Administration by submitting false information to the VA with respect to certain requests for VA-guaranteed home mortgages. The first such request was on August 1, 2002, and the last on September 20, 2007. *A* was a VA loan reviewer from April 2000 until she resigned from the VA on September 30, 2007. *B, C, D,* and *E* were, respectively, officers for two banks, one insurance company, and a real estate agency. At the joint trial the prosecution seeks to introduce evidence of instances in which *B, C, D,* and *E* conspired with *X,* an official with the FHA, to submit fraudulent data to secure FHA-guaranteed mortgages. These instances occurred in October, November, and December of 2007. *A* seeks to have the jury instructed that this evidence has no bearing on her activity in the conspiracy and should not be considered by the jury on the issue of whether *A* is guilty of participating with *B, C, D,* and *E* in an illegal conspiracy to defraud the VA. The trial judge refuses to give the requested instruction. **Has the trial judge made a mistake?**

C. OTHER EXCEPTIONS

In theory the remaining exceptions to the hearsay rule may be justified on one of two grounds: Either the exception's conditions suggest the statements they admit are especially likely to be reliable, or the hearsay speaker has faced or may still face the test of cross-examination. Most hearsay exceptions are of the first type; they reflect psychological assumptions about circumstances that make for trustworthy assertions. Exceptions of the second type arise when cross-examination was possible immediately following the hearsay statement but not before the current trier of fact, or when the speaker may be cross-examined about a past statement before the current trier of fact. Exceptions of both types rest on circumstances that supposedly negate one or more of the hearsay dangers.

Most hearsay exceptions apply regardless of the speaker's availability at trial, but some exceptions exist only when the speaker isn't available. Exceptions do not require the speaker's unavailability when courts feel that the characteristics of the offered hearsay make it at least as trustworthy as similar testimony by the speaker from the witness stand, or when the difficulty of finding the speaker and bringing her to court is thought to outweigh the incremental benefits of having live testimony. Thus, judgments about requiring unavailability, like judgments about creating exceptions in the first place, are based on judicial intuitions about the situations in which out-of-court statements are likely to be trustworthy.

These intuitions and the exceptions they justify reflect the commonsense psychology popular at the time the exceptions were formed.[80] As psychology advances and we learn more about processes of narrative description, we are better able to appreciate the wisdom behind certain exceptions and the tenuous nature of others. The following extract from an article by Professor Daniel Stewart is an aid to critical evaluation of the hearsay exceptions. In the portion of the article reproduced here, Professor Stewart presents a psychological perspective on the processes of perception and description that helps explain the threats posed by those dangers we have thus far summarized with the

---

[80] Decisions to except statements from the hearsay rule have been very much a one-way ratchet. The creation of exceptions requires a plausible rationale, but once created, exceptions generally endure even if the justifications for their creations are discredited. This reflects widespread judicial and academic ambivalence over whether hearsay should be barred at all. For those who feel hearsay should not be barred, or that it should be barred only on FRE 403 grounds, a discredited exception yields better results than no exception at all.

words ambiguity, insincerity, false memory, and inaccurate perception. Although the article is old, the principles it reports are basic and consistent with more recent research.

Critiques like Professor Stewart's have led some scholars who do not want to abandon the hearsay rule entirely to reevaluate the relative merits of testimony with cross-examination and the situation-specific guarantees of most hearsay exceptions. They believe that the situation-specific guarantees generally deserve little weight and argue for a "best evidence" approach to the admission of hearsay. In situations where it is easy to bring speakers to court, these scholars would either bar their hearsay statements, requiring testimony instead, or they would allow the hearsay only if the speaker also testified or was available for testimony. Where a speaker is unavailable, or where the cost of securing a speaker's presence substantially exceed the likely benefits (as with many business records), they would allow the hearsay, subject to FRE 403, believing that if a hearsay statement's probative value is not substantially outweighed by unfair prejudice or other costs, a jury aware of the hearsay will reach a better informed decision than a jury that does not know of the out-of-court statements.[81]

PERCEPTION, MEMORY, AND HEARSAY: A CRITICISM OF PRESENT LAW AND THE PROPOSED FEDERAL RULES OF EVIDENCE

1970 Utah L. Rev. 1, 8–10, 14–23.[82]

Daniel Stewart, Jr.

. . .

The crucial questions in hearsay law concern the determinants of perception, memory, narration, and prevarication. Historically, exceptions to the law of hearsay have been founded upon assumptions of testimonial reliability based largely on the subjective and unsystematic study of human testimony, with more than a small touch of a highly rationalistic view of man. These assumptions have been carried forward in the . . . [Federal] Rules of Evidence.

. . .

Inconsistent perceptions and memories of the same events by different people arise out of complicated neurological, psychological, and physiological processes. Although functions of different

---

[81] *See, e.g.*, Dale Nance, *The Best Evidence Principle*, 73 Iowa L. Rev. 227 (1988); Michael L. Seigel, *Rationalizing Hearsay: A Proposal for A Best Evidence Hearsay Rule*, 72 Boston U. L. Rev. 893 (1992).

[82] The full article discusses the hearsay exceptions found in the Federal Rules of Evidence in the light of the observations reported in this excerpt. Although this article and the studies it cites are "ancient" as scholarly articles go, the research cited in portions we excerpt are still regarded as basic truths.

neurological processes, perception and memory are both interdependent aspects of cognition. Memory does not exist without perception, and there is no psychologically meaningful perception without memory.

. . .

In organizing raw sensory input, the central nervous system is not a passive or photographic recorder. Basic interpretative principles make an automobile headlight observed from an angle appear circular even though optically the image is elliptical, and the size of an object at a distance appears much the same size as when it is nearer, even though the size of the retinal image may change many times. Injury, pathology, drugs, youth, and senility can seriously impair the accuracy of these processes.

It is, however, the behavioral and motivational factors that are particularly powerful in producing distortion in testimony. The law has long been aware of the effect of bias on testimonial accuracy. But powerful intrapsychic processes also produce substantial distortion in testimony without influence from the type of bias generally recognized, and without any intent to falsify. Bartlett, in a landmark study of memory states:

The first notion to get rid of is that memory is primarily or literally reduplicative or reproductive. . . . In fact, if we consider evidence, rather than presupposition, remembering appears to be far more decisively an affair of construction rather than one of reproduction.

A number of studies illustrate the point and demonstrate the substantial degree of perceptual and memory error in recounting the types of events that frequently are the subject of litigation. . . .

C.S. Morgan concluded that a typical report of a casual, but somewhat out of the ordinary event would give a substantially accurate report of the event but would contain roughly 20% to 25% error. Morgan also found a significant incidence of reporting non-facts. For example, a question asking whether the 150 subjects had observed a nonexistent fact produced an affirmative response from 18%.

William Marston tested a group of 18 lawyers immediately after a staged event in which a boy entered a classroom, handed the instructor a large envelope, scraped his baseball glove with a knife while awaiting an answer, and then exited. Marston found that free recall reports rendered immediately after the event were 94.05% accurate, but mentioned only 23.2% of the details in the incident. Not one person, for example, mentioned the knife. In contrast, nonleading direct questions produced answers more complete but less accurate, *i.e.*, 31.2% complete and 83.2% accurate (with an individual high of 94.5% and individual low of 64.2%). Leading questions in the nature of cross-examination resulted in an average completeness of 28.5% of the details and an average accuracy of 75.5%.

Essentially, the same scene was portrayed a second time for another small group who had reason to expect a reenactment of the event. This group proved to be less accurate than the first. The reason may be found in the reduced incidence of caution (measured by "I don't know" answers) compared with the first group. Marston concluded that there may be an inverse correlation between the number of inaccuracies and the degree of caution exercised. Perhaps a valid explanation is that a person who is expected to provide an accurate description is more prone to guess.

Brown demonstrated the particular unreliability of eye witness identification of persons and also provided further evidence that people honestly testify to the occurrence of events they have not witnessed. A workingman appropriately dressed walked across a classroom passing in front of the instructor's desk to tinker with the radiator. He made some inquiry about the heat, retraced his steps, and left as unceremoniously as he had entered. The instructor treated the incident in a casual manner. Sixteen days later the workingman returned with five other men of similar appearance and dress, and the subjects were asked to identify the workingman from among those in the group. Thirty students who had had some experience with surprise tests were 76.6% accurate in their identification. Sixty-four students who had had no such prior experience were 65.5% accurate. Sixteen students who likewise had had no prior experience with surprise tests were presented with a lineup of workingmen which did not include the man who had entered the classroom. Ten, or 62.5%, identified the wrong man, and only four were correct in saying that he was not there. A group of seventeen students who also had had no prior experience with such tests and had actually not seen the event were treated by the experimenter as if they had. In effect they were asked to identify a man involved in an incident which they had never seen. Twelve or 70.5% said they didn't remember the incident, but five or 29.5% stated they recalled the incident and "identified" the man.

Perception of height, weight, age, and personal identification are especially vulnerable to inaccuracy. A drama of a startling and exciting nature was conducted before 150 sophomore college girls. Two high school boys chasing a third charged into a class that was in session. All three rushed about shouting and overturning furniture in full view of the girls. The duration of the incident was one minute and 30 seconds. The subjects rendered a free recall narration of their perceptions immediately after the event. One week later and seven weeks later (a much shorter period than it usually takes to get a trial) objective tests composed of true-false, completion, and multiple choice items were given. The range of judgments of height, weight, and age were after one week and seven weeks as follows:

HEIGHT

	First Week	Seventh Week
First Boy	4'8" to 7"	4' to 6'
Second Boy	4' to 6'4"	4'8" to 5'10"
Third Boy	4' to 5'10"	4'8" to 5'10"

WEIGHT

First Boy	90 lbs. to 170 lbs.	105 lbs. to 165 lbs.
Second Boy	100 lbs. To 160 lbs.	95lbs. To 150 lbs.
Third Boy	85 lbs. To 150 lbs.	80 lbs. To 145 lbs.

AGE

First Boy	11 years to 20 years	19 years to 19 years
Second Boy	12 years to 19 years	11 years to 19 years
Third Boy	10 years to 18 years	10 years to 19 years

As Bartlett stated, the reason memory is not primarily "reduplicative" and is more "an affair of construction rather than reconstruction" is because "every human cognitive reaction—perceiving, imagining, remembering, thinking, and reasoning—is "an effort after meaning." As the individual strives to organize and adjust to his environment, the meaning of his experiences is perceived and remembered in terms of cultural and emotional values, attitudes, habits, and anxieties. These factors act as powerful filters determining what and how an individual perceives and remembers.

At a basic level, the individual must be selective in both informational input from the environment and the retention of that input. Innumerable stimuli bombard each individual at any given moment. Purposeful behavior is possible only by selecting from among relevant stimuli and organizing them in a psychologically meaningful manner. Experimental studies demonstrate that individuals have limited spans of conscious apperception and cannot focus on more than a few stimuli at the same time. Memory also works on a principle of selectivity. Thus, what a person perceives and remembers "is apt to be a generalization. If this were not so, he might be hopelessly lost in detail."

Accordingly, a principle of economy influences people to perceive and remember by formulating a general overall impression, with only a few details standing out. The overall impression may produce an associated affective attitude. The impression and the affective attitude produced by it provide the framework for supplying details not observed or remembered, but which then appear in the guise of original perceptions. Memory of a poorly defined perceptual pattern is especially susceptible to substantial alteration by attitudes which shape the image of the event and conform it to preconceptions constructed from the associated affect. Such memories are very unfaithful to their originals. . . .

Stereotypes generally exert an important influence on cognitive functioning. A person may conform a percept to a stereotype because his mental set expects the usual or common event or because memory of the event is more easily retained if it fits a known pattern. Moreover, stereotypes are often the basis for supplying facts to fill in memory gaps and reconstruct details that were not perceived or are forgotten. Thus, a beard, for example, may appear on the face of a man who never wore one, or a gun in the hand of a person who never possessed one. A sour faced clergyman may become pleasant in his mien, and a woman the victim of aggression, not the aggressor.

The manner in which individuals encode visual and verbal perceptions in the brain also contributes to the plastic nature of memory and in particular to transference of details and fusion of memories. Perceived material may be stored by visual imagery or by verbal labels applied to the perceived object. Since visual imagery is the mode of dreaming, day-dreaming, and imagining as well as a mode of memory, confusion as to the source of images and the blending of different images is easily accomplished. Moreover, the more strongly one wishes that reality had been different, or the stronger the power of suggestion or of group pressure to conform, the easier it is for the daydream, suggestion, or imagined event to become "reality" in the mind of the witness. Verbalized memory may produce distortion in yet another way. Application of a verbal label to an ambiguous stimulus may result in modification of the perception to conform with the verbal label.

The difference between verbal and visual encoding may also have other significant legal consequences. Despite the great reliance placed on demeanor evidence by the courts, demeanor may in fact lead the trier of fact astray. Bartlett found that persons who remember by visual imagery are subjectively more confident that their reproductions are accurate than are verbalizers. Verbalizers, although generally no less accurate than visualizers, are more hesitant and uncertain in their reproductions and hence do not appear as confident.

Memory is also molded by the influence of rationalization which is sometimes an unconscious and sometimes a conscious process. Rationalization provides an explanation for an event so that the material can be satisfyingly dealt with. "The general function of rationalization is in all the instances the same. It is to render material acceptable, understandable, comfortable, straightforward; to rob it of all puzzling elements. As such it is a powerful factor in all perceptual and in all reproductive processes. The forms it takes are often directly social in significance." Over a period of time the mind easily traverses the course, "could it possibly have been X," to "it must have been X," to "it was X." In the initial stages, the process may be conscious; at a later stage the conclusion emerges as a remembered "fact."

Numerous other factors influence perception and memory. The mental "set" or expectation of an individual will tend to focus attention on particular objects to the exclusion of others. Favorable material is more readily remembered than unfavorable. Excitement, a factor evidence law relies upon as a warrant for trustworthiness, produces a significant degree of error, sometimes of the most bizarre type. . . .

Perception and memory are especially unreliable when, as is always the case when hearsay evidence is adduced, the initial stimulus is words. People generally retain verbal descriptions of events less accurately than they do visual perceptions. When a hearsay narrative of an event is rendered by one person to another, significant distortion is particularly likely, because the initial stimulus is filtered through two different cognitive processes. The point is illustrated by Allport and Postman in their classic study, *The Psychology of Rumor*:

[An] important source of invention and falsification comes about through verbal misunderstandings. When a person does not see the initial incident, and when he has no prior knowledge as to its nature, he becomes exclusively dependent upon his own auditory impressions for his understanding. The auditory apparatus is faulty in many people, but even those with normally acute hearing often mishear, or misinterpret, words for which they have no supporting mental context. Consider the following reproductions [which are related by one subject immediately to another]. . . .

Fourth Reproduction: Picture is of a subway or streetcar. There is a Negro in it and a laborer with a razor. They are going along a street. There are signs outside: *vote for somebody and for some camp.* On the right side there is a woman asleep, a man with a beard, and a priest.

Fifth Reproduction: Picture is of a streetcar or subway. There is—somebody or other—a Negro and a laborer with a razor. On the right side of the car there is a lady asleep, a man with a beard, *campaign* signs to vote for somebody, a priest.

Sixth Reproduction: Scene is a streetcar or subway. There is a Negro man and laborer with a razor in his hand. Sitting down are a lady sleeping, an old man with a beard, a priest. There are signs: A camp sign and a sign to vote for somebody.

Bartlett also studied the essential elements of hearsay. A short prose selection was presented to subjects who read the selection through twice. After an interval of 15 to 30 minutes, a subject reproduced the material to another (who had not read it) who in turn did the same. As the material passed through several phases of reproduction the distortions were increasingly magnified. It is infrequent that more than one step of hearsay is admissible in court, although not impossible, but Bartlett's findings also apply to one-step reproductions, although in a less extreme form. He found that proper names and titles are especially unstable; that there is a strong tendency to develop a concrete version of the account with the result that general opinions, reasoning, and arguments are transformed and omitted; that the language is transformed into more conventional and popular phrases; that in all cases there was much abbreviation; that rationalization resulted in changes in various types; and that the changes that are introduced may be radical.

At the same time, the subjects may be very well satisfied with their efforts, believing themselves to have passed on all important features with little or no change, and merely, perhaps, to have omitted unessential matters.

Allport and Postman built upon the earlier work of Bartlett. They found that the oral transmission of verbal material from one person to another is distorted by three basic processes. First, "leveling" eliminates details so that the account becomes shorter and easier to manage. Accounts having 20 or more details were reduced to five, with the process of elimination beginning with the first transmission. There is, however, a limit to leveling. Short concise statements are far less subject to distortion and are likely to be faithfully reproduced.

Second, "sharpening" produces selective perception, retention, and reporting of a limited number of details. This process relates to leveling in that focusing on selected stimuli results in the ignoring of other stimuli.[83] A special aspect of sharpening is "closure," or the tendency to make a report coherent and meaningful by supplying material even though the material was not perceived. Errors of this type usually occurred in the report of the first subject.

Finally, "assimilation" describes the process by which memory drops, transposes, imports, and falsifies details as a result of the "intellectual and emotional context existing in the listener's mind." Things are perceived and remembered as they usually are despite the nature of the stimulus. In one experiment, a Red Cross ambulance is recalled as carrying medical supplies rather than explosives. In another, a policeman is seen as arresting a Negro rather than protecting him. "In short, when an actual perceptual fact is in conflict with expectation, expectation may prove a stronger determinant of perception and memory than the situation itself."

In sum, cognitive processes of the human organism are not the equivalent of a photographic process which renders and preserves an essentially accurate counterpart of some event. Although the legal system uses the organism as a source of "facts," perception and memory operate in a way that enables a person to cope with his environment within the limitations that inhere in the neurological and psychological functioning of the organism. The degree of correspondence between the testimony of an event and the reality it purports to represent may, therefore, vary widely according to the effect of numerous factors. The imperatives of successful adaptation do not require that the individual's cognitive process operate in all instances to provide information having the degree of objective accuracy necessary for accurate, after-the-fact reconstruction which is attempted by judicial fact determination.

There is no reason to suppose that witnesses called to testify typically perceive and remember more accurately the type of events involved in the studies than the subjects in the experiments did. The studies discussed are based upon fact situations that in all instances provide a multitude of stimuli which transcend the normal span of apperception. Although not highly unusual, they were not routine occurrences of the kind that a person expects to happen periodically. Moreover, the studies did not involve the subjects personally as participants in the action, nor did the subject matter of the studies necessarily have a high degree of interest to the subjects because of related prior experiences. They did, however, evoke the attention of the subjects, they were not complicated, there was for the most part no distraction, and memory periods were short. In short, the studies were based on situations that are often similar to events which

---

[83] Names of places and persons are especially subject to being dropped.

become the subject matter of testimony admitted under various exceptions to the hearsay rule.

. . .

The right to cross-examine is of the greatest importance to the integrity of the fact-finding process and is the keystone of both the hearsay rule and the right of confrontation. Blunt though it may be for the discovery of subconscious distortion, cross-examination is the principal legal instrument for testing the accuracy of a witness's perception, memory, and communication. By means of cross-examination the witness may be required to explain ambiguous, unclear, or inconsistent testimony; personality traits that influence cognitive functioning may be disclosed; the effect of the witness's mental set at the time of perception, possible suggestive influences, and numerous other factors which affect a witness's mental processes may be investigated. Obviously, a witness who testifies to hearsay can usually provide the trier of fact with none of the same information.

A person who relates a hearsay is not obliged to enter into any particulars, to answer any questions, to solve any difficulties, to reconcile any contradictions, to explain any obscurities, to remove any ambiguities; he entrenches himself in the simple assertion that he was told so, and leaves the burden entirely on his dead or absent author.

. . .

Evidentiary reliability is also thought to be promoted by the oath and demeanor evidence. Despite skepticism regarding the value of the oath, some evidence exists that sworn testimony is more accurate than unsworn testimony. That result may follow, not from fear of divine sanction, but from the greater caution that witnesses probably exercise when under oath. Although highly regarded by the judges and attorneys, the value of demeanor evidence as a means of determining testimonial reliability has yet to be demonstrated factually. . . . Some evidence that demeanor may be deceptive is Bartlett's finding that a witness's feeling of certainty as to the accuracy of his testimony does not correlate with greater accuracy in fact.[84]

Of course, the appearance of a witness having firsthand knowledge is an essential condition of cross-examination, the oath, and demeanor evidence, but for pragmatic reasons the law has never excluded all hearsay. Since adjudication operates in a forced decision

---

[84] Since Stewart wrote, numerous studies of eyewitness testimony have revealed that there is no strong relationship between witness confidence and witness accuracy if there is any relationship at all, but jurors treat witness confidence as an important indicator of accuracy.

context and cannot indulge the luxury of the scientific world in putting off a decision to await better evidence (which rarely would be forthcoming anyway), doubt must be treated as a factor in decision making, not as a barrier to it. As Professor Kalven has observed, "[A] trial is an exercise in the management of doubt." Rules governing burden of proof are a chief means of determining the effect doubt is to have in adjudication, but the hearsay rule also bears on the issue. The more relevant the evidence excluded by the hearsay rule, the more likely it is that a factual dispute will be decided by a somewhat arbitrary rule governing the burden of proof rather than on the basis of some evidence.

. . .

An additional body of research, important to the evaluation of hearsay, was not published until some years after Stewart's article. This is the work on leading questions and eyewitness reports by Elizabeth Loftus and her associates.[85] In a series of experiments, Loftus found that the way questions are worded profoundly affects the answers received. In one experiment, Loftus found that subjects asked if they got headaches *frequently*, and if so how often, reported an average of 2.2 headaches per week. Subjects asked if they got headaches *occasionally*, and if so how often, reported an average of 0.7 headaches per week. In another study, 100 students viewed a short film showing a multiple car accident. Following the film, the students were queried about what they had seen. One group was asked "the" questions such as, "Did you see *the* broken headlight?" The other group was asked "a" questions such as, "Did you see *a* broken headlight?" The group asked the "the" questions was considerably more likely to report having seen the item inquired about regardless of whether it had actually appeared in the film. In a related experiment, subjects who viewed a series of accident films were asked to estimate how fast two cars were going when they *smashed* (collided, bumped, hit, or contacted) each other. Estimates of speed varied depending upon the word used. The range was from 40.8 m.p.h. for those hearing the word "smashed" to 31.8 m.p.h. for those hearing the word "contacted." Question effects were also found to persist over time. A week after viewing an accident film, without seeing it again, subjects who had been asked the "smashed" and "hit" forms of the question were asked a new series of questions about the accident. Subjects previously queried with "smashed" were more than twice as likely to report having seen

---

[85] *See e.g.*, Elizabeth F. Loftus, *Reconstructing Memory: The Incredible Eyewitness*, 8 Psychology Today, Dec. 1974, at 116, reprinted in 15 Jurimetrics J. 188 (1975); Elizabeth F. Loftus & John C. Palmer, *Reconstruction of Automobile Destruction: An Example of the Interaction Between Language and Memory*, 13 J. VERBAL LEARNING & VERBAL BEHAVIOR 585 (1974); Elizabeth F. Loftus & Guido Zanni, *Eyewitness Testimony: The Influence of the Wording of a Question*, 5 BULL. OF THE PSYCHONOMIC SOC'Y 86 (1975). In the text we discuss only the implications of this research for the hearsay rule, but it suggests also the wisdom of the rule forbidding leading questions on direct examination.

broken glass in the film as subjects queried with "hit." There was in fact no broken glass in the film. Those previously queried with "smashed" apparently remembered the accident as more severe and added details that accorded with a high-speed collision. This general finding is replicated in other research by Loftus. Thus, it appears that how people are questioned about an event, shortly after that event, can affect their descriptions of the event at later points in time.

For our purposes, the most important implication of this research is that out-of-court statements elicited by questions are prone to be distorted in ways suggested by the questioner. Yet unless the questions that elicited the statements are reported exactly as asked, there may be no way for the fact-finder or counsel to evaluate this possible source of distortion. Loftus suggests that the language of her questions implicitly conveyed information to her respondents that was incorporated into their memory images of the events they were asked to describe. She suggests that information conveyed about events by means other than questions may cause similar distortion.[86] Based on Loftus's research, it appears that we may add to the classic hearsay dangers the danger that perceptions reported in out-of-court statements may be distorted by the circumstances in which the statements were elicited. This danger is not completely cured by the substitution of a speaker's live testimony for her hearsay declaration, since the speaker's testimony may be affected by the circumstances in which the out-of-court statements were first elicited. However, when live testimony is presented, cross-examination is available to probe for distortion.

As you study the hearsay exceptions that follow, ask yourself how you would expect the evidence they admit to be distorted. Are any or all of the exceptions justified by the likelihood that if the conditions of the exception are met, distortions will either not occur or be revealed? Also consider the wisdom of admitting the hearsay of available speakers. Do the exceptions that allow this always, or even more often than not, leave the jury with a more accurate impression of what occurred than the impression they would receive from the speaker's testimony? Finally, consider the possibility of a middle ground between availability and unavailability. Are there situations in which it makes sense to admit the hearsay of available speakers, provided the proponent of the hearsay places the speaker on the stand for cross-examination?

---

[86] Recently there has been a trend toward more relaxed admission of hearsay of alleged victims of child abuse. Dana T. Blackmore, *The Tug of War Between the Confrontation Clause and Hearsay Exceptions in Child Abuse Cases: Implications of White v. Illinois*, 28 S.U.L. Rev. 93, 104–05 (2001). Often this hearsay has been elicited through questions directed at the child by a parent, psychological professional, or other person. Some jurisdictions have recognized the danger of distorting question effects, and encourage or require the recording of professional or police questioning of children if the hearsay is to be admitted in lieu of live testimony.

1. Availability Immaterial

a. *Present Sense Impressions*

We shall first examine those hearsay exceptions that apply without regard to a speaker's availability. FRE 803 lists 23 types of statements that "are not excluded by the hearsay rule, even though the declarant is available as a witness." It provides a convenient codification of these exceptions that we shall follow.

FRE 803(1) provides:

Present Sense Impression. A statement describing or explaining an event or condition, made while or immediately after the declarant perceived it.

At common law there was a general hearsay exception admitting spontaneous declarations.[87] However, most common law jurisdictions required some guarantee of spontaneity in addition to the coincidence of statement and event. Usually the guarantee was found in the fact that the event described so excited the speaker as to still his reflective capacity, thus reducing the likelihood of fabrication. For more than three quarters of a century commentators argued that requiring excitement as a guarantee against fabrication did more harm than good. Hutchins and Slesinger, reviewing the psychological literature in 1928, argued that excitement, even if it stilled reflection, so distorted perceptual processes that the conclusions of an excited onlooker were almost certain to be unreliable.[88] They went on to argue that it was the contemporaneous unexcited statement that should be admitted: "With emotion absent, speed present, and the person who heard the declaration on hand to be cross-examined, we appear to have an ideal exception to the hearsay rule."[89] The absence of emotion enhances the reliability of perception, speed avoids memory problems while limiting the time for reflection and falsification, and the presence of the person hearing the statement often means that an observer of the event described is present for cross-examination.

---

[87] There are still state common law jurisdictions, but most United States jurisdictions today have evidence codes modeled on the Federal Rules, and several have other modern systems of codification. Moreover, even in those jurisdictions that lack codes, a variety of evidentiary issues are regulated by statute or have been changed in the direction of the Federal Rules by court decision. It perhaps is premature to claim the death of the common law of evidence, especially since evidence codes are often interpreted in light of the common law. Nonetheless, for simplicity, we shall speak of the common law requirements surrounding the hearsay rule and its exceptions, and of the rules of common law jurisdictions, in the past tense.

[88] Robert M. Hutchins & Donald Slesinger, *Some Observations on the Law of Evidence*, 28 COLUM. L. REV. 432 (1928).

[89] Id. at 439.

Most states today have a present sense impression exception.[90] In other states, common law courts may admit contemporaneous but unexcited utterances under the rubric of *res gestae*, although the circumstances in which they do so are sometimes limited.

Professor Waltz identified 10 propositions that he termed the "undisputable" characteristics of the 803(1) exception.[91] They are: (1) the described event or condition need not have caused excitement; (2) the declaration need not directly relate to the principal litigated event; (3) the speaker need not have been a participant in the perceived event; (4) the speaker must have been a percipient witness; (5) the speaker need not be identified; (6) the speaker need not be shown to have been oath-worthy; (7) subject matter is restricted to a description of the observed event; (8) minimal time-lapse is permissible; (9) present sense impressions are not cumulative (i.e., a speaker's present sense impression is not inadmissible simply because the speaker is a witness who testifies to the described event from the stand); and (10) impressions in opinion form are admissible.

Tracing the history of the present sense impression and the cases and commentary that influenced the drafters of FRE 803(1), Professor Waltz argued that there should be a corroboration requirement, with sources of corroboration including not just the witnesses who heard the speaker's statement but also the circumstances surrounding the described event and witnesses who observed the event without hearing what the speaker said. The Federal Rules do not, however, require corroboration, and federal courts have generally not read such a requirement into the Rules. However, several states, including some with rules patterned on the Federal Rules, require present sense impressions to be corroborated by witnesses who also saw the event described.

b. *Excited Utterances*

FRE 803(2) codifies the common law rule on excited utterances:

---

[90] In Houston Oxygen Co. v. Davis, 139 Tex. 1, 161 S.W.2d 474 (Tex.Com.App. 1942), often cited as the leading case on this aspect of spontaneous exclamations, a passenger in one car was willing to testify that the driver had commented as another car sped by, "they must have been drunk, that we would find them somewhere on the road wrecked if they kept that rate of speed up." *Id.* at 476. The remark proved prescient; the car did crash four miles farther on. The occupants of the car sued the Houston Oxygen Company, which sought to introduce the statement in question. The court reviewed the arguments given on behalf of admitting unexcited spontaneous declarations, added to the above arguments the fact that a witness who heard a misstatement might have checked it at the time, and concluded, "[C]omments, strictly limited, to reports of *present* sense-impressions, have such exceptional reliability as to warrant their inclusion within the hearsay exception for Spontaneous Declarations." *Id.* at 477, citing MCCORMICK & RAY'S TEXAS LAW OF EVIDENCE, p. 548, § 430.

[91] Jon R. Waltz, *The Present Sense Impression Exception to the Rule Against Hearsay: Origins and Attributes*, 66 IOWA L. REV. 869 (1981).

Excited Utterance. A statement relating to a startling event or condition, made while the declarant was under the stress of excitement that it caused.

We have already mentioned the excited utterance in our discussion of present sense impressions. Even before most states adopted evidence codes modeled on the Federal Rules, they all had some variant of this exception. Some courts referred to it as the excited utterance exception, some as the spontaneous exclamation exception, and some did not distinguish excited statements from other statements that were admitted under the heading *res gestae*.

The primary justification for the excited utterance exception has been that excitement stills reflective capacity, so statements made by individuals feeling the stress of startling events are unlikely to be colored by motives to deceive. This may be true, but excitement also tends to distort perception and cloud memory. Excited utterances may, on balance, be less reliable than much hearsay we refuse to admit. Nevertheless, the excited utterance exception is not likely to be eliminated. The trend in evidence law is to expand the admissibility of hearsay, as commentators argue that we should trust juries to give hearsay evidence its proper weight. Perhaps allowing the presumed honesty of an out-of-court speaker to outweigh an added probability of misperception is not completely misguided. We may wish particularly to avoid jury verdicts tainted by a speaker's intentional deception, but mistakes due to errors of perception and memory may be accepted as an inevitable cost of the way we have chosen to resolve legal disputes.

The excited utterance exception requires both that the event giving rise to the statement be startling enough to still reflection and that the speaker be under the influence of the startling event when he makes his statement. Few questions are raised about the first issue. Accidents, injuries, assaults, and other extraordinary events are all thought to be sufficiently startling to still reflection. Courts differ when the only evidence that a startling event occurred is the statement of an obviously excited speaker. Most allow the speaker's excited statement to be used to establish the event;[92] some do not. Since this situation seldom exists except when the effect of the described event on the speaker is in issue, the better procedure is to admit the evidence. If the statement and surrounding circumstances provide sufficient evidence for a reasonable jury to conclude that the event in question has occurred, the matter should reach the jury; if not, a directed verdict is in order if proving the matter asserted is essential to a party's case. Thus, if a dying man claims that he stumbled down an open manhole and his heirs sue the city, the man's statement, coupled with the presence of an open manhole near

---

[92] Federal courts applying FRE 104(a) should consider the hearsay in deciding whether a startling event occurred.

where he was found, should be enough to get the case to the jury. If, however, no witnesses report seeing an open manhole, and the city's records reveal no activity that would require a manhole to be opened, the absence of any evidence of an open manhole other than the alleged victim's excited statement, should lead the judge to direct a verdict for the city, even after admitting the statement.

More difficulties have been caused by the requirement that the speaker be under the influence of the exciting event. Courts listen to testimony about the speaker's apparent state of excitement in determining admissibility, but they generally pay more attention to lapses of time. The shorter the lapse between the statement and the exciting event, the more likely it is that the statement will be admitted. Sometimes courts have found that lapses as short as 5 minutes provide enough time for excitement to end; sometimes lapses as long as half an hour are seen as too short to still excitement, and even longer lapses may be allowed when there is reason to believe that the stress of the exciting event has continued. When an exciting event creates a condition, such as the pain of an injury, that interferes with reflection and endures over time, courts are particularly receptive to claims that excitement has persisted. Recently the theory of enduring excitement has led some courts to admit as excited utterances statements of allegedly abused children made hours or even days after the alleged abuse, often in circumstances where the child has appeared calm in the interim. A theory of reawakened excitement has been invented to admit statements that appear reliable because of their content and spontaneity, rather than because of the stilling of reflection that excitement supposedly brings. In other cases time is, in effect, suspended. Courts have admitted statements made by people waking from comas, long after the event described, apparently on the theory that while the person was unconscious the excitement did not abate. At the other extreme, statements made shortly after a startling event have been excluded when it appears that the speaker had calmed down.

In determining whether an individual is speaking under the influence of an exciting event, courts look closely at the apparent spontaneity of the speech. Self-serving statements arouse judicial suspicion, and remarks made in response to questions are often excluded, although the response to a simple "What happened?" may be allowed. Courts are also reluctant to admit statements as excited utterances if the speaker's actions between the event and the statement suggest an ability to reflect on what happened. Thus a woman who coolly rescues her two children from a burning car may find that statements she makes after the rescue is complete do not qualify as excited utterances.

The excited utterance exception admits statements "*relating to* a startling event or condition." This means that statements admitted under 803(2) need not directly recount the event perceived so long as they relate to it in some way. For example, in one case a shopper in a supermarket slipped on some cottage cheese and fell. A bystander's remark, upon observing the fall, that about two hours earlier she had told the supermarket to clean its floor, was held to relate sufficiently to the exciting event to be admissible as an excited utterance.[93] Had the bystander remained calm after the fall, the remark could not have come in as a present sense impression, for FRE 803(1) is limited to statements "describing or explaining an event or condition." "Relating to" is not enough.

Some states do not follow the Federal Rule's "relating to" language. In these states, admissible excited utterances are only those that directly elucidate the exciting event. The battleground has been over the admission of excited utterances to prove agency. In jurisdictions following the federal approach, the excited post-accident statement of a truck driver that he worked for a particular company is admissible against that company to prove agency. Other states exclude such statements because they do not in some way explain the accident. When an agency relationship is asserted, the Federal Rule is preferable because agency usually reflects a continuing relationship likely to remain in a person's mind as long as he is working for a particular employer. When details of past activity are important, even details relating to agency, the Federal Rule raises the possibility of memory problems. These are unlikely to exist when the exception is limited to utterances describing or explaining the startling event.

———————

Problem VI-41. The argument for admitting unexcited statements describing present sense impressions has usually been based on a comparison between statements of this kind and excited utterances, which all would agree are admissible. The claim is that since excited utterances are admissible and since contemporaneous but unexcited utterances are likely to be more reliable than excited utterances, it follows *a fortiori* that there should be an exception for spontaneous but unexcited utterances. But this does not follow. One could just as easily conclude that neither excited utterances nor unexcited spontaneous statements should be admitted as exceptions to the hearsay rule. **Which do you think is the better position? Which of the hearsay dangers are substantially reduced when evidence is introduced under the exception for present sense impressions? Which of the dangers are substantially reduced when evidence is introduced under the exception for excited utterances? Should there be an exception for spontaneous unexcited utterances, or should we perhaps**

---

[93] David v. Pueblo Supermarket, Inc., 740 F.2d 230, 235 (3d Cir. 1984).

rethink our exception for excited utterances? Assuming we are to have a hearsay exception for unexcited utterances, should the exception apply regardless of the availability of the speaker? How does the extract from Stewart's article bear on this question? Would it make sense to require the proponent to show a speaker's unavailability before admitting such statements in the speaker's absence, but to allow the statements to be admitted if the proponent presents the speaker and puts him on the stand?

Problem VI-42. An anonymous caller phoned 911 to describe a burglary taking place at a restaurant he could see from his apartment. He described the burglars as a black man wearing tennis shoes and a Bulls T-shirt and a white guy with a crow bar. The police arrived within three minutes and arrested Ed Degnes, a black man who was hiding in an air conditioning duct on the roof wearing a Bulls T-shirt and tennis shoes. Then, as they left the roof, the 911 operator received another call from the same person saying, "They arrested the black guy, but the white guy's still on the roof." The police returned to the roof and arrested a white man, Salvadore De Silva as he was walking toward a ladder that led down from the roof on the side away from where the police car was parked. They later found a crow bar on the roof. **At the trial can tapes of either or both calls be introduced against Degnes or De Silva? Would it make any difference if the caller had identified himself but had died before the trial? Would it make a difference if the 911 tape recorder was not working, but the state placed the 911 operator on the stand to testify to what she had heard?**

c. Statements of Physical Condition

The admissibility of a speaker's statements concerning her own physical condition depends, in part, on the person to whom the statement is made. When the statement is made to a lay person, FRE 803(3) expresses the general rule:

> **Then–Existing Mental, Emotional, or Physical Condition.** A statement of the declarant's then-existing state of mind (such as motive, intent, or plan) or emotional, sensory, or physical condition (such as mental feeling, pain, or bodily health), but not including a statement of memory or belief to prove the fact remembered or believed unless it relates to the validity or terms of the declarant's will.

When the statement is made to a physician or other person in order to secure medical treatment, FRE 803(4) applies. Federal policy in this area is considerably more liberal than the old common law:

> **Statement Made for Medical Diagnosis or Treatment.** A statement that:

(A) is made for—and is reasonably pertinent to—medical diagnosis or treatment; and

(B) describes medical history; past or present symptoms or sensations; their inception; or their general cause.

Statements of physical condition made to lay persons are admissible under the general exception for spontaneous statements that reflect states of mind. Two basic requirements must be met before statements will be admitted under this exception. First, the statement must reflect a condition that exists when the statement is spoken. The statement, "I have a terrible headache" is admissible under this exception; the statement, "I had a terrible headache yesterday" is not. Second, the statement must be spontaneous. Under the Federal Rule, and in most courts, the mere concurrence of the statement and the condition described provides sufficient evidence of spontaneity unless the circumstances suggest that the speaker was trying to manufacture evidence in his favor.[94] Some courts, however, have held that certain kinds of statements are not spontaneous. Among the older cases, one finds judicial opinions that purport to exclude any self-serving statements, or, more commonly, self-serving statements made after the commencement of litigation. There are even opinions that hold involuntary expressions of physical condition such as grunts and groans admissible but exclude verbalizations such as "I hurt." Where courts have taken these views decisions are often inconsistent, and today, except possibly in the case of self-serving statements made pending litigation, both case law and evidence codes generally allow judges discretion to admit both self-serving statements and verbal descriptions of physical conditions.

Statements admitted under the exception for bodily condition are usually statements about pain or other bodily feelings. A statement to a lay person that one's kidney is infected or appendix inflamed would probably be excluded on personal knowledge or opinion rule grounds unless offered to show the speaker's pain. When statements recount a condition that the speaker can perceive and evaluate, such as the declaration, "I have red spots on my chest," the exception is likely to apply, although the case for it is somewhat weaker here than when the exception is used to admit statements of pain or discomfort, because the necessity element is not so great. Spots, unlike pain, are readily

---

[94] Under the Federal Rules, it is not clear that the judge has discretion to exclude statements describing existing bodily conditions even in these circumstances. It appears from the language of the rule that the evidence should come in for what it is worth. But if a judge did exclude it, it is unlikely that this would be held to be an abuse of discretion, since FRE 403 provides general authorization for balancing probative value against such dangers as unfair prejudice and misleading the jury. Even if it were so held, the error would almost certainly be found harmless, since statements made with the intent of manufacturing evidence have little probative value. Given FRE 803(3), the better procedure is for the federal judge to admit the statement. She can use her power to comment on the evidence to call the jury's attention to its deficiencies.

observable by third parties, and a possibility of misperception exists. When present pain is described, there are no memory problems, perception problems are unlikely, and there is, in theory, little chance of falsehood since the statement must be spontaneous. However, the difficulty of developing any judicial test for spontaneity other than the apparent coincidence of statement and feeling means that the spontaneity requirement offers little protection against a person who wishes to fabricate evidence of pain.

People seeing doctors usually know that the quality of their treatment depends in part on their candor in describing their physical condition. This added guarantee of reliability has led to a receptive judicial attitude toward statements made for treatment purposes to physicians. Any statement about physical condition that is admissible if made to a layperson is, of course, admissible if made to a treating physician. Even self-serving statements are not barred. The modern trend goes further, admitting descriptions of past symptoms made to secure treatment and statements about the causes of illness and injury, if the statement was made for diagnosis or treatment. Even states that exclude statements of past symptoms from the hearsay exception may allow a treating physician to recount such statements in telling the jury how she arrived at an opinion. Statements introduced only as the basis for an opinion are not considered hearsay.

Physicians employed both to testify and to treat are usually regarded as treating physicians, but most common law courts refused to apply the hearsay exception to statements made to physicians employed only to testify. The reason for the distinction between treating and testifying physicians is obvious. In talking to a physician hired only to testify, motives to falsify the extent of an ailment are not counterbalanced by the realization that treatment and health may depend upon the honesty of what is reported. Thus, even statements of then-existing physical conditions were usually barred in common law jurisdictions if they were made to physicians employed solely for their expert testimony, and a few states incorporated this restriction in their modern codes. But even where restrictions remain, non-treating physicians are usually allowed to recount statements of existing conditions and descriptions of past symptoms in explaining how they arrived at their conclusions.

FRE 803(4) takes a different view. In providing an exception for statements made for the purposes of medical diagnosis or treatment, it makes no distinction between the diagnoses of treating physicians and the diagnoses of doctors employed solely to testify. Admissible statements include statements describing past symptoms as well as statements about the cause or source of the ailment to the extent that these are pertinent to either diagnosis or treatment. Furthermore, because FRE 803(4) refers to statements made "for...medical diagnosis or treatment" it is not limited to statements made to a physician. Thus a statement made to a nurse, a medical student, an ambulance driver, someone masquerading as a physician, or a family member might qualify under this exception if the patient intended the statement to be for diagnosis or treatment. This makes sense, for it is the patient's belief in making the statement that provides a guarantee of truthfulness.

Problem VI-43. Do you think that the liberal view that FRE 803(4) takes toward the admission of statements made to physicians is wise? The drafters justify their decision to admit statements made to a physician solely for the purpose of securing his testimony in court on the ground that "[W]hile these statements were not admissible as substantive evidence, the expert was allowed to state the basis of his opinion including statements of this kind. The distinction thus called for was one most unlikely to be made by juries." Yet, not all jurisdictions allow physicians engaged only to testify to repeat those patient statements that figured in their diagnoses. **If the drafters were worried that jurors might not follow instructions to treat patients' statements solely as the basis of a diagnosis, would it have been wiser for them to preclude doctors from testifying to such statements regardless of purpose? Even if the drafters are correct about jury behavior, might not a party be better off if his opponent's statements to a physician are presented as the basis for an expert opinion rather than as substantive evidence of the cause of his condition? How?**

Problem VI-44. Kenneth Kasper is suffering from severe headaches and muscle spasms that lead him to consult a neurologist. He tells the neurologist the following story: "I work cleaning out old wells and mines and other places like that. Well, last Wednesday I was down in a well picking up debris when this guy who worked for the Ace Exterminating Company started to release this gas into the well. They were supposed to kill the rats and bugs that lived at the bottom. Well, they'd been told I would be by either that day or the next to clean out the debris, but they never even looked to see if I was there before they started pumping the gas. They should have seen my other ladder lying on the grass and my van that was parked outside. Well, I knew what was happening and I hightailed it up the ladder and chewed them out. I didn't feel so bad immediately, but by that night my hand was shaking and I began to get real severe headaches, so I went to see my doctor, but he couldn't see nothing. The headaches have continued; my head feels like it's splitting in two now, and occasionally my muscles will twitch so bad I can't hang on to anything. I had a two minute attack driving over here, and I had to stop the car. Can you help me?"

The neurologist was unable to help Kasper, so on the advice of a friend he went to see a physical therapist. The physical therapist, who was not an M.D., was also unable to help Kasper. On the advice of another friend he went to see a physician who had studied in China and was now a full-time acupuncture therapist. Kasper did not believe in acupuncture, but he thought the treatment could not hurt and he was desperate for help. Acupuncture did not help, but Kasper left convinced it was not the fraud that he thought it was. This experience led him to become interested in faith healing and non-Western medicine. Eventually he heard of a Dr. Quick, a man with no medical training, who healed by holding his hands above the affected parts and saying prayers in five languages to each of the four winds. Kasper was convinced Quick could help him. He went to Quick, was treated by him, and was cured. Before treating Kasper, the physical therapist, the acupuncture specialist, and the faith healer all asked him what had caused his problems. Kasper told each of them exactly what he had told the neurologist.

Assume that Kasper sues the Ace Exterminating Company. May Kasper call the neurologist, the physical therapist, the acupuncture specialist, or the faith healer to testify to any of the information Kasper gave them before they began their respective treatments?

d. Other Existing States of Mind

State of mind is often an issue in litigation. When this is so, statements that circumstantially suggest a speaker's state of mind are not hearsay.[95] However, if a statement asserts the very state of mind in question, most courts view the assertion as hearsay because the jury can take the statement at face value rather than try to reason circumstantially from it. Fortunately, the hearsay analysis seldom matters, because hearsay statements asserting relevant states of mind are admissible under FRE 803(3) and similar common law exceptions.[96] Thus, in a dispute over a will the testator's statement, "I want my son

---

[95] *See supra* pp. 563–65. Some courts, preferring a quick decision to close analysis, cite the "state of mind" exception as the reason to admit such statements and not the fact they are not hearsay. Usually nothing turns on this, but see the footnote that follows.

[96] The distinction between a statement that is not hearsay and a statement to the same effect admitted under a hearsay exception is not always meaningless. In some jurisdictions a party might be entitled to an instruction that hearsay evidence merits less weight than non-hearsay evidence. *See, e.g.,* Gu v. Gonzales, 454 F.3d 1014, 1021 (9th Cir. 2006), Glendale Unified Sch. Dist. v. Almsi, 122 F.Supp.2d 1093, 1101 (C.D. Cal. 2000), State v. Martinez, 290 Kan. 992, 236 P.3d 481, 490 (2010), State v. Veltre, 957 So.2d 47, 50 (Fla. App. 2007), Washington Post v. District of Columbia Dep-'t. of Employment Servs., 675 A.2d 37, 44 (D.C. 1996). There are also jurisdictions where substantive law occasionally requires corroboration of admissible hearsay but does not require corroboration of non-hearsay statements. *See, e.g.,* State v. Martinez, 290 Kan. 992, 236 P.3d 481, 490 (2010), Gehin v. Wisconsin Group Ins. Bd., 278 Wis.2d 111, 153–54, 692 N.W.2d 572 (2005), State v. Tucker, 317 Or. 188, 190, 855 P.2d 150 (1993), Augustine v. Berger, 88 Misc.2d 487, 388 N.Y.S.2d 537, 540 (1976).

Eldridge to have all my money," would be admitted under the state of mind exception on the issue of testamentary intent. An immigrant's statement, "I intend to stay here forever," offered to show domiciliary intent, or a husband's statement "I no longer love my wife" offered to prove absence of love in an alienation of affections lawsuit, is also admissible as a state of mind.

i.   To Show Feelings

FRE 803(3) admits statements describing a speaker's *then existing* state of mind. This means that assertions of states of mind qualify for the exception only if they purport to describe the speaker's feelings when she speaks. The statement, "I am happy now" qualifies, while, "I was happy yesterday" does not. Suppose a person's happiness on Tuesday is an issue in a case. The state of mind exception means that if the person said on Monday, "I am happy now," the hearsay rule will not keep it out. The court might exclude the statement if the judge feels there is little relationship between the person's feelings on Monday and her feelings on Tuesday—as for example, if tragedy struck shortly after the speaker spoke. Most often, however, the statement will be admitted on the theory that without an important intervening event, feelings often persist.

Whether a state of mind at one time tends to prove a state of mind at another time is a *relevance* and not a *hearsay* question. If a testator says on Monday, "I don't want Clarence to inherit a cent," and the following Tuesday goes to his safe deposit box, takes out his will leaving everything to Clarence, and rips the will up, it is his state of mind on Tuesday when he destroyed the will and not his state of mind on Monday that determines whether he destroyed the will with intent to revoke. Nevertheless, what the testator said on Monday is admissible to establish his feelings toward Clarence on Monday. The jury will be allowed to reason from his feelings that day to his probable state of mind a day later when he ripped up the will. If the destruction of the will followed the testator's statement by a year instead of a day, evidence of the statement might be excluded. However, this would not be because it is hearsay on the issue of what the testator intended when he tore up the will, but rather because the testator's state of mind on a Monday in one year seems not very probative of his state of mind a year later.

A similar analysis applies when the issue is the speaker's state of mind before he made the statement. Thus, if a testator rips his will up on Monday, and on Tuesday says, "I don't want Clarence to inherit a cent," the statement is admissible under the state of mind exception and would not be excluded as irrelevant because the testator's attitudes on Tuesday are likely to be much like they were the day before. If, however, the testator had said, "When I ripped up the will, I didn't want Clarence to inherit a cent," the statement would not qualify under the general state of mind principle because it does not refer to a *then existing* attitude.

However, the last clause of FRE 803(3), consistent with the practice in most states, creates a special exception for statements describing past states of mind or other past facts when those facts relate to the execution, revocation, identification, or terms of the speaker's will. In other circumstances, hearsay references to past states of mind are inadmissible.

The usual justification for the state of mind exception is that what we have called "right leg dangers" poses no threat. The *then existing* requirement eliminates memory problems, and the speaker is presumed to have no difficulty in perceiving his own feelings.[97] The exception does not require speaker unavailability, for if the speaker were to testify, "his own memory of his state of mind at a former time is no more likely to be clear and true than a bystander's recollection of what he then said."[98] Wigmore claims that the exception is also supported by a guarantee of sincerity, since statements describing then existing states of mind are often spontaneous.[99] However, the speaker's assertion is usually the only evidence that his declaration is coincident with an existing state of mind. Nothing prevents a designing speaker from asserting whatever feeling or other state of mind it is convenient to possess. Nevertheless, with the exception of statements relating physical conditions, courts seldom exclude statements relating states of mind because they were responses to questions or because of obvious motives to falsify. In this respect, the exception differs from other hearsay exceptions requiring spontaneity.

Suppose that the testator we have been discussing had said, "I don't want Clarence to inherit a cent because he is an alcoholic who spends all his money on whiskey." The testator's feeling that Clarence should not inherit a cent is an admissible state of mind, but neither the rationale for the state of mind exception nor the literal language of FRE 803(3) applies to the description of Clarence's drinking behavior. Yet courts generally admit statements that assert both a feeling and the circumstances giving rise to that feeling.

A primary justification for the admission of this type of statement is that descriptive statements that accompany assertions of feelings shed light on the strength of the asserted feelings. Consider, for example, a trial for extortion by threat in which the prosecution must prove that the victim was put in some fear. If a prosecution witness could testify only to the victim, Luke's statement, "I am afraid of Darth," Darth's counsel might soften the statement's impact by arguing that it was a single assertion based on mistake, that Luke's fear was unreasonable, or that Luke's other behavior suggested he didn't really fear Darth. If, however, the witness reported Luke's entire statement, "I'm afraid of Darth; he had

---

[97] Whatever the views of some schools of psychiatry, the law in this area does not entertain the question of whether the speaker really thought what he thought he thought.

[98] Mutual Life Ins. Co. v. Hillmon, 145 U.S. 285, 295 (1892).

[99] 6 WIGMORE § 1714 CHADBOURNE REV. 1976.

his henchmen torture me and now he threatens to kill me if I don't join the dark side," it would be difficult to convince a jury that Luke's fear was not real. The problem, of course, is that the reported statement would also lead the jury to believe that Darth's henchmen had tortured Luke and that Darth had threatened to kill Luke if he didn't change sides. On these issues, Luke's reported statements are inadmissible hearsay. The prejudicial impact of admitting the statements for the light they shed on Luke's state of mind is obvious. The law resolves this kind of conflict by vesting considerable discretion in the trial judge. She may sever the statements, admitting only those that directly assert feelings, or she may admit the entire declaration to show the strength with which the feeling in question was held. If the judge admits the entire statement, affirmance on appeal is likely provided the trial judge has instructed the jury that it may not use the statement to prove the truth of any assertions other than the claimed state of mind. Reversal becomes more likely when so much other evidence tends to prove the relevant state of mind that it appears that the purpose of introducing the declaration was to suggest the truth of the otherwise inadmissible hearsay it incorporates.

A statement that does not directly assert feelings may be offered as indirect evidence of a state of mind and not for the truth of what it asserts. For example, the testator's statement, "Clarence cannot be trusted with money because of his drinking problem," tends to show that the testator did not intend to leave his money to Clarence when he made his will. Statements used to imply a state of mind are not technically hearsay, and there is no way to eliminate the prejudicial aspects while still using them to establish the relevant mental condition. Where prejudice is extreme, exclusion under FRE 403 is possible, and where this relief is unavailable, counsel can perhaps avoid the evidence by offering to stipulate to the state of mind in issue.

———————

Problem VI-45. While showering after a squash game, Hank Sloan asked his friend Kyle Manbury how he was doing, "I feel great," said Kyle. "I've just beaten you 3 out of 4 times in squash. My divorce is final, Sue is out of my life at last; I just got a big raise so I can afford the alimony, and I'm dating the most marvelous woman. Also, I got a clean bill of health from my doctor last week, and I have a hunch those poems I sent to *The New Yorker* are going to be accepted. Spring is here, tra, la, la!" Two days later Kyle was found in his car in the garage, dead—a victim of carbon monoxide poisoning. His ex-wife, Sue, is the beneficiary under a $750,000 life insurance policy issued by the Honesty Insurance Company which Kyle had taken out three months before in connection with his alimony obligation. When Sue seeks to collect under the policy, Honesty rejects the claim, saying Kyle died of suicide, an excluded cause, during the first two years of the policy's existence. Sue sues. Honesty introduces e-mail messages which Kyle had written to friends during the preceding six months and up to two weeks before his death. The older messages complain about the likely cost of the divorce and how seriously he will be set back financially, and more recent messages express Kyle's fear that a mole is cancerous and that it has been ignored for too long. Sue seeks to put Hank on the stand to testify to everything Kyle told him after their squash game. **Can she do this? If so, for what purposes can the various statements Kyle made be introduced? Would your answer be the same if Honesty had not introduced the evidence it did? Does the fact that a letter from *The New Yorker* rejecting his poems was found open on Kyle's kitchen table affect the admissibility of Kyle's statement about the poems? Does the fact that the temperature went from 73° to 49° the day after the squash game (it being the Midwest in April) affect the admissibility of Kyle's expression of joy at the arrival of spring?**

ii.   To Show Behavior

Thus far we have been discussing situations in which a speaker's state of mind is at issue. More difficult problems arise when statements asserting or implying a state of mind are offered to establish *behavior* consistent with that state of mind. One can distinguish two situations in which state of mind evidence is offered to prove behavior. The first is to prove that the speaker has taken some action consistent with her state of mind, as when statements of intent are offered to show action in accord with intent, a matter discussed below. The second is when an existing state of mind is offered to show the behavior that caused it, as when the statement "I fear Darth because he threatened to kill me," is offered to show that Darth threatened to kill the speaker or that Darth did something to put the speaker in fear, or, to give a celebrated example, the statement, "Dr. Shepard has poisoned me," offered to show that the speaker believes Dr. Shepard poisoned her and, hence, that Dr. Shepard probably did poison her.

A speaker's belief that Dr. Shepard poisoned her is circumstantial evidence that Dr. Shepard did poison her, because people's beliefs about others' actions are often well founded. But if this were enough for a hearsay exception, the exception would swallow the hearsay rule since it involves the same reasoning process from statement to belief and from belief to reality as hearsay offered for its truth. The only difference is that we purport to be reasoning circumstantially from a belief rather than accepting the statement because we trust the speaker's accuracy. But the need for trust is the same because in both instances the conclusion that the speaker's statement is true depends on the accuracy of her perceptions and the quality of her memory.

Realizing that the hearsay rule would be undermined if statements were admissible to show beliefs when beliefs were relevant only as evidence of the facts that may have given rise to them, courts ordinarily do not admit out-of-court statements for this purpose. The case most often cited for this proposition is *Shepard v. United States*.[100] In that case, to show the defendant had poisoned his wife, the prosecution introduced as a dying declaration the wife's statement, "Dr. Shepard has poisoned me." On appeal the Supreme Court held that the statement did not meet the dying declaration hearsay exception. The prosecution also argued that the statement was admissible as evidence of the decedent's state of mind because it tended to negate the defendant's suggestion that his wife had committed suicide. The Court rejected this argument on two grounds. First, since the statement had been offered at trial for its truth, the state could not argue on appeal that it might have been admissible had the jury been instructed to use it in a narrower fashion. Second, even if the statement had been offered only to negate an implication of suicide, the jury would almost certainly have treated it as proof of what Dr. Shepard did.

Justice Cardozo put the matter as follows:

> It will not do to say that the jury might accept the declarations for any light that they cast upon the existence of a vital urge, and reject them to the extent that they charged the death to some one else. Discrimination so subtle is a feat beyond the compass of ordinary minds. The reverberating clang of those accusatory words would drown all weaker sounds. It is for ordinary minds, and not for psychoanalysts, that our rules of evidence are framed. . . . When the risk of confusion is so great as to upset the balance of advantage, the evidence goes out.[101]

Cardozo continued (and it is in this dictum that he makes the point for which the case is so often cited):

> There are times when a state of mind, if relevant, may be proved by contemporaneous declarations of feeling or intent. . . . So . . . declarations by an insured that he intends to go upon a journey with another, may be evidence of a state of mind lending probability to the conclusion that the purpose was fulfilled. *Mutual Life Ins. Co. v. Hillmon*. . . . The ruling in that case marks the high water line beyond which courts have been unwilling to go . . . Declarations of intention, casting light upon the future, have been sharply distinguished from declarations of memory, pointing backwards to the past.
>
> There would be an end, or nearly that, to the rule against hearsay if the distinction were ignored.[102]

---

[100] 290 U.S. 96 (1933). This case is reprinted in Section V of this Chapter.

[101] *Id.* at 104.

[102] *Id.* at 104–06.

Some courts, however, do not follow *Shepard* when a speaker's description of a defendant's activities is offered to show the speaker's fear. Rather they allow the inference from a speaker's fear of another person to the conclusion that that person did something to engender the fear. The California Supreme Court, in *People v. Merkouris,* [103] wrote in successive sentences:

> The declarations that defendant had threatened the victims were admissible, *not to prove the truth of that fact directly*, but to prove the victims' fear.

> Where, as here, the identification of defendant as the killer is in issue, the fact that the victims feared defendant is relevant because it is some evidence that they had reason to fear him, that is, that *there is a probability that the fear had been aroused by the victims' knowledge of the conduct of defendant indicating his intent to harm them rather than, e.g., that the victims' fear was paranoid.*[104]

In other words, the victims' statements about the defendant's threats were admitted not to show that threats were made but to show that the victims feared the defendant, which suggested that the defendant had indicated his intent to harm (i.e., threatened) them. If this rationale confuses you, don't worry; the fault is in the rationale and not you. This case is best understood as an example of the way in which appellate courts strain to approve evidentiary rulings below when they wish to affirm the results reached.

The rule of the *Merkouris* case was eliminated in California by the adoption of its current evidence code, but similar decisions emerge occasionally in other states when statements relate the cause of fear. In most instances, however, states follow federal practice and do not admit statements of memory or belief to prove the fact remembered or believed.[105] The one common exception, codified in FRE 803(3), is when

---

[103] 52 Cal.2d 672, 344 P.2d 1 (Cal. 1959), cert. denied, 361 U.S. 943 (1960).

[104] Id. at 6 (emphasis added).

[105] In United States v. Brown, 490 F.2d 758, 767 (D.C.Cir. 1973), as amended (1974), the court described three purposes for which statements admitting fear are commonly allowed in evidence. In each case the statements are, at least in theory, intended to describe a state of mind inconsistent with the activity that the defendant attributes to the speaker. They are not intended to be used as proof that the defendant's behavior was responsible for the speaker's state of mind: [T]he courts have developed three rather well-defined categories in which the need for such statements overcomes almost any possible prejudice. The most common of these involves defendant's claim of self-defense as justification for the killing. When such a defense is asserted, a defendant's assertion that the deceased first attacked him may be rebutted by the extrajudicial declarations of the victim that he feared the defendant, thus rendering it unlikely that the deceased was in fact the aggressor in the first instance. Second, where a defendant seeks to defend on the ground that the deceased committed suicide, the evidence that the victim had made statements inconsistent with a suicidal bent are highly relevant. A third situation involves a claim of accidental death, where, for example, the defendant's version of the facts is that the victim picked up the defendant's gun and was accidentally killed while toying with it. In such cases the deceased's statements of fear as to guns or of the defendant himself (showing

the memory or belief relates to the execution, revocation, identification, or terms of the speaker's will. This is because testators have peculiar knowledge about facts relating to their own wills, and since they are dead when their wills reach probate, their statements about their testamentary intent may be the most reliable available evidence. Yet, people lie about their wills to keep the peace in the family or to manipulate others, and a person reporting a testator's statement may have a substantial incentive to lie. This has led some jurisdictions to admit testators' will-related statements only when they are corroborated by other evidence.

The situation is different when one considers statements of intent introduced to show action in accord with intent. The leading case is *Mutual Life Insurance Co. v. Hillmon*,[106] an evidence law classic. The case arose out of a dispute between Sallie Hillmon and three companies that had insured the life of her husband, John Hillmon. Mrs. Hillmon claimed that a body found at Crooked Creek, Kansas, was her husband's. The insurance companies claimed that the body was that of a person named Walters, who had accompanied Hillmon to Crooked Creek. The evidence identifying the corpse was conflicting.[107] To support their theory that it was Walters' body that had been found at Crooked Creek, the insurance companies sought to introduce two letters that Walters had written his fiancée. In them he told her that he had met a John Hillmon and was going to accompany him on his trip to "parts unknown." The trial court excluded the letters, and the Supreme Court held that they should have been admitted under the state of mind hearsay exception. Mr. Justice Gray wrote:

> But whenever the intention is of itself a distinct and material fact in a chain of circumstances, it may be proved by contemporaneous oral or written declarations of the party.

> The existence of a particular intention in a certain person at a certain time being a material fact to be proved, evidence that he

---

he would never go near defendant under any circumstances) are relevant in that they tend to rebut this defense. Of course, even in these cases, where the evidence is of a highly prejudicial nature, it has been held that it must be excluded in spite of a significant degree of relevance.

[106] 145 U.S. 285 (1892). This case is reprinted in Section V of this Chapter.

[107] The litigation began in 1880 and continued until 1903. There were six trials in all. In the first two the jury hung 7–5 and 6–6. The Supreme Court's well-known decision was on review from a plaintiff's judgment rendered in the third trial. The remand resulted in two more trials to hung juries followed by a second verdict for plaintiff, which the Supreme Court also reversed. During the interim, however, most of the insurance company defendants settled, in part because in 1896 the State Insurance Commissioner of Kansas barred three companies from doing business in that state because of the public's disapproval of the companies' resistance to Mrs. Hillmon's claims. For a fascinating account of the facts of this case see Wigmore, Principles of Judicial Proof 856–96 (1913). For a classic analysis of the legal issues it raises *see* Maguire, *The Hillmon Case—Thirty-Three Years After*, 38 HARV. L. REV. 709 (1925). For a more recent and thorough treatment that suggests that quite a different story, see Marianne Wesson, *The Hillmon Case, The Supreme Court and the McGuffin*, pp. 277–306 in R. Lempert (ed.) EVIDENCE STORIES (2006).

expressed that intention at that time is as direct evidence of the fact as his own testimony that he then had that intention would be. After his death there can hardly be any other way of proving it, and while he is still alive, his own memory of his state of mind at a former time is no more likely to be clear and true than a bystander's recollection of what he then said, and is less trustworthy than letters written by him at the very time and under circumstances precluding a suspicion of misrepresentation.

The letters in question were competent not as narratives of facts communicated to the writer by others, nor as proof that he actually went away from Wichita, but as evidence that, shortly before the time when other evidence tended to show that he went away, he had the intention of going, and of going with Hillmon, which made it more probable both that he did go and that he went with Hillmon than if there had been no proof of such intention.[108]

The court's ruling makes sense. No right leg problems exist in reasoning from Walters' intentions to his actions because, when he was writing his fiancée, Walters would not have misperceived his own intentions or forgotten them. This does not, however, mean that the inference from intention to action is a strong one. Walters may have changed his mind after mailing his letter or intervening circumstances may have kept him from doing what he wanted. But these difficulties concern relevance rather than hearsay. Had Walters, for example, been cross-examined right after he wrote his letters, the examination could have revealed little about the probability that unanticipated future circumstances would lead Walters to change his mind or prevent him from carrying out his plan.[109] The situation was different in the *Shepard* case. While Mrs. Shepard could not have misperceived or forgotten her recollection, she might well have misperceived or forgotten the event she purported to recall. The likelihood of these dangers could have been assessed by cross-examination at the time Mrs. Shepard spoke.

In *Hillmon*, the Supreme Court said that Walters' statement of his intent to go to Colorado with Hillmon was admissible not only to show that he did go, but also to show that he went with Hillmon. Most courts follow the Supreme Court in this respect and allow a statement of an intention to do something with another to support not only the inference that the speaker did what he said he would do in the company of the other person, but also, since the two are not separable, to support the

---

[108] 145 U.S. at 295–96.

[109] Cross-examination would not have been entirely useless because it could have revealed something about the strength of Walters' intentions—a left leg issue. However, we have already seen that circumstances that eliminate the problems of either leg are enough to justify a hearsay exception, even though cross-examination might help assess problems associated with the other leg.

inference that the other person did what the speaker expected in the speaker's company. The House Committee in approving FRE 803(3) explicitly disavowed this aspect of *Hillmon*, but it is not clear what weight to accord this legislative history. Federal courts often ignore it or take a middle position. Thus, especially in criminal cases, some courts require corroboration before a hearsay statement of one person's intent to act jointly with another may be used to suggest the other's action. In these courts, Arnie's statement, "I am going to buy some cocaine from Jack," is, standing alone, inadmissible to show that Jack sold cocaine to Arnie. But it is admissible if other competent evidence corroborates it, such as evidence that shortly after Arnie spoke he and Jack were seen together.[110]

When statements of intent are used to show the actions of others in this way, they pose all the hearsay dangers. Arnie's statement, "I intend to do something with Jack," tends to prove that Arnie and Jack did something together only if the statement's implicit claim that "Jack intends to do the same thing with me" is correct. This depends on whether Arnie correctly perceived and remembered Jack's intentions. The right leg dangers are back. Therefore, the better policy is to exclude statements of intent like Arnie's to prove another's actions when the statements are the only evidence of the speaker's actions or when the speaker is likely to have acted as intended even if he was wrong about who else might be involved. For example, if Rick says, "I'm going to play poker with Sam, Deborah, Michael, Nick, Tom, Peter and Juliet," his statement should not be admitted to show that the others were gambling, even if we know Rick left to play poker, since his belief would have led him to leave to play poker even if he were wrong about who would be at the game. There is, however, good reason to allow a statement of intent to do something with another to show both the speaker's and the other's actions, if there is other evidence that the speaker did what she intended, and it is unlikely that she would have done so except in the company of the other person.

People v. Alcalde [111] provides an example. In *Alcalde* a woman told her roommate that she was going to have dinner with Frank. She left her house in the evening and the next morning was found murdered. Her statement sheds light on whom she was with the night before.

There is no dispute that the woman dressed for dinner and went out. It is unlikely, given her intentions, that while waiting for Frank to pick her up she would have left with someone else. Although she might have gone out on her own had Frank never come by, it seems at least as likely that she would have returned to her apartment had Frank not shown up. Thus, the fact that she went out and did not return to the apartment for

---

[110] *See, e.g.*, United States v. Cicale, 691 F.2d 95 (2d Cir. 1982), *cert. denied*, 460 U.S. 1082 (1983).

[111] 24 Cal.2d 177, 148 P.2d 627 (Cal. 1944).

dinner is probative of whether she went out with Frank.[112]   This probative value does not turn entirely on the accuracy with which she perceived Frank's intention when she stated she was going out with him. Even if the woman had mistaken Frank's intention, she might have called him to reconfirm the date or have gone to his apartment or bumped into him, with the same result. It is less likely that she would have sought the opportunity to go out with someone else.   Moreover, despite the theoretical existence of hearsay dangers, it is unlikely that Frank's intention was misperceived. People are usually careful about arranging dates.

The situation is similar in *Hillmon*. Given that Walters intended to leave Wichita with Hillmon and that he apparently disappeared from Wichita about the time he said he would leave,[113] it is likely that Hillmon left with him. Although Walters' implied recounting of Hillmon's intent has all the hearsay dangers, the fact that Walters apparently left Wichita makes it likely that none of these dangers were realized. This situation and that in *Alcalde* differ from the situation of Arnie and Jack in our earlier drug-dealing scenario. The fact that Arnie met with Jack provides no assurance that Arnie correctly perceived Jack's availability to deal, since whether Arnie was correct or not, he would have sought out Jack. However, in cases of this sort, the quality of the meeting is usually consistent with drug dealing (or with whatever behavior one person's intentions suggest the other would engage in). So with corroborating information on the character of the meeting, it may be wise to stretch *Hillmon* this far.

More troubling are cases like *United States v. Pheaster*.[114] In that case, a sixteen-year-old named Larry told several people he was going to meet "Angelo" in a parking lot and pick up some free marijuana. Ransom notes were later sent to Larry's parents, but the youth was never heard from again. An acquaintance named "Angelo" was tried for kidnapping, and Larry's statements were introduced to show that a meeting between the young man and Angelo did occur. The court cited *Hillmon* and *Alcalde* as precedent, but there are crucial differences. The likelihood of Larry's going to the parking lot was the same whether or not Angelo went, so we cannot find in Larry's behavior any extra reason to believe

---

[112] Recall the discussion of the likelihood ratio in Chapter Three. What is the likelihood the woman would have gone out had Frank not come by, given her intent? (Let us say 0.5.) What is the likelihood that she would have gone out with Frank had he come by? (Let us say almost 1.0.) Thus, if you accept our estimates, knowing that the woman intended to go out with Frank and in fact went out would almost double the prior estimate of the odds that she went out with Frank. The problem is that a jury that considered not just the woman's intent and action but also the implicit assertion that Frank intended to go out with her might increase its prior estimate that she went out with Frank by far more than the doubling we assume is reasonable. If this is likely, it provides justification for a corroboration requirement.

[113] Walters wrote to his family and fiancée regularly, but after his last letters from Wichita, he was not heard from again.

[114] 544 F.2d 353 (9th Cir. 1976).

that Angelo did what Larry expected.[115] All the hearsay dangers seem present, although one might argue that in acting on his intent Larry provided some assurance of his sincerity. However, since Larry might have acted the same way (i.e., left the group he was with) had he been lying about whom he was going to meet or where he was going, this is a thin reed on which to rest a hearsay exception. Requiring corroboration of the intended joint action in these circumstances is a policy that better respects the *Hillmon* precedent [116] and the hearsay rule.

ADDITIONAL PROBLEMS

Problem VI-46. Sammy Peoples and Alice Mooney, two nine-year old children, were trick-or-treating one Halloween night when they came to the house owned by "old Mr. Crabtree." Alice said to Sammy, "I'm afraid to get anything from him. I've heard he put a razor blade in Carol's apple last year." Sammy said he wasn't afraid and went to Crabtree's house. He came back shortly with a candy apple, looked it over closely, and said, "No razor blade in here." Then he took a bite and said, "This tastes strange, sweet but bitter." He took two more bites and threw the apple down. About two minutes later he complained to Alice, "My stomach hurts. I'd better go home." He came home and his mother asked him, "What is wrong?" He replied, "My stomach started hurting right after I ate old Crabtree's apple." Then he vomited. Ms. Peoples tried calling a doctor, and when she could not get one she took Sammy to the emergency room of the local hospital. She told the orderly who admitted them that "My son told me that his stomach began to hurt right after he ate an apple that Tyrone Crabtree had given him. He started throwing up and then went into convulsions, so I brought him here."

Assume that Crabtree is charged with poisoning Sammy Peoples and with attempted murder. **Will any of the following be admitted either to prove the facts asserted or for some other purpose: Sammy's testimony about what Alice said about her reasons for not going to Crabtree's house? Alice's testimony about what Sammy said about the taste of the apple and about his stomach's hurting? Ms. Peoples' testimony about what Sammy told her when she asked what was wrong? The orderly's testimony about what Ms. Peoples told him when Sammy was admitted to the hospital?**

---

[115] In contrast, the likelihood of Walters' leaving Wichita for country unknown to him and the likelihood of the victim in *Alcalde* getting dressed for dinner and going out was greater if their intended companions accompanied them.

[116] Since the circumstances of Walters' disappearance from Wichita lend some corroboration to his implicit assertion that Hillmon would be leaving with him, while Larry's action in leaving his friends does not corroborate his implicit claim that Angelo would be at the parking lot, it appears *Pheaster* surpasses the *Hillmon* "high water mark."

"We medical practitioners do our very best, Mr. Nyman. Nothing is more sacred to us than the doctor-plaintiff relationship."

Problem VI-47. The party was just getting under way when Fred was called to the telephone. Putting down the phone, Fred went quickly to get his coat. Sara, his date, looking rather annoyed, said, "Where are you going? The party's just begun." Fred took Sara into the hall with him and said in a low voice, "Don't tell anyone, but last week I was with Sam when he hooked a van full of cigarettes. He just called to say he's found a buyer. I'm going to meet him at the last truck stop on the Carolina Turnpike, and we're going to start for New York tonight. Do you remember Cary? He moved to New York a while back. We're going to deliver the cigarettes to him because he has some good connections up there. I'm sorry to spoil your fun, but I'll bring you back something really nice." With that Fred left.

Fred and Sam were arrested in a stolen truck three days later in North Carolina, just over the Virginia border. Fred's story is that the call he received at the party was from an "old flame" asking him to pick her up at a truck stop because her car had broken down. He says that when he got there he learned that a trucker had helped her fix the car, and she had gone off with him. The trucker who told him this was the partner of the trucker who had gone off with the girl, and he was furious because now he had no relief driver and was already behind schedule. This trucker offered Fred $1,000.00 if he would share the driving to New York and drive the empty van back. Fred said that he agreed to do this, but got out in New York before the cigarettes were delivered, meeting the trucker again at an agreed upon rendezvous point. Sam claims that he had hitchhiked to New York several days before to see a rock concert. He says he was sitting in a bar in New York when he was astonished to see his friend Fred enter the bar. Quickly, he arranged a ride back. Fred tells the same story of their meeting. When they were arrested, Fred had $600 in his wallet and a box containing a $950 cashmere woman's sweater from Saks Fifth Avenue. Sam had $300 in his wallet and the stub for a rock concert that had been held on Long Island some three days before Fred received the call at the party. About $20,000 was found stuffed into a hole in the driver's seat. Both Fred and Sam disclaim all knowledge of it. About a week after Fred and Sam were arrested, the police raided the drugstore in Manhattan that Cary manages. They found no sign of the cigarettes or of any other stolen goods. It is indisputable that the truck in which Sam and Fred were found had been hijacked with a load of cigarettes on board.

Fred, Sam, and Cary are charged with grand theft, the interstate transportation of a stolen vehicle, selling untaxed cigarettes, and conspiring to engage in these activities. **Is Sara's testimony reporting what Fred told her at the party admissible against Fred, Sam, or Cary on any of the following issues: (1) whether Fred, Sam, and Cary were members of the same conspiracy; (2) whether Fred had gone to the last truck stop on the Carolina Turnpike; (3) whether Fred had met Sam at this truck stop; (4) whether Sam and Fred drove to New York together; (5) whether the stolen van had been driven across state lines; (6) whether Sam had stolen the van; and (7) whether the cigarettes were delivered to Cary?**

Problem VI-48. Henry Lucas, a black man, is arrested for firing a gun at a car as it was driving down Sunset Street. In its case-in-chief, the prosecution presents witnesses who testify that Henry lives on Sunset Street near the place of the killing, that he owns a gun that could have fired the shots in question, and that Henry left a bar five blocks from the scene of the shooting with the gun in his pocket. In his defense Henry introduces two of his friends who testify that he did not have a gun with him, and that he left the bar only after hearing the shots. Henry then offers the tape of a 911 caller on a car phone who said, "I'm on Sunset Street and some white guy is firing at the car ahead of me." **Is this tape admissible? Would it make a difference if one could hear shots on**

the tape? Suppose the caller had said, "I was just on Sunset Street and some white guy was firing a gun at the cars driving by"?

Problem VI–49. James Glenn is charged with stabbing and killing Juanita Johnson. If allowed to testify over Glenn's hearsay objection, a police officer, Pearlman, will relate the following story:

> I was working at the counter when Ms. Johnson entered the station. As she approached, she appeared as though she might fall, but instead she lunged the several steps necessary to reach me. She leaned up against the counter and grasped my wrist, saying, "Please help me. Please help me. He did it." I responded, "Who is he and what did he do?" She replied, "James did it." I thought at first she said, "James Lynn," but I was certain only about the "James." I was unable to clearly make out the last name so I said, "Who?" She replied, "James Glenn." I then asked, "Where does he live?" and she replied, "3407 Sherman." Then I asked, "What did he do to you?" She replied, "I don't know because he got me in the back."

A deputy medical examiner for the government testified that there was such a large amount of whiskey in Ms. Johnson's blood that a normal person would have had to consume ten ounces of whiskey in one hour to reach that concentration. But there is also evidence that Ms. Johnson was a chronic alcoholic, with greater than average tolerance for alcohol. **Should Officer Pearlman's testimony be admitted?**

Problem VI–50. Harriet Jones was injured when the car she was driving collided with a truck. She was trapped in the car and in severe pain prior to her removal. Subsequently she brought an action for damages against the owner of the truck. At trial, a witness called by Jones testifies that he arrived at the scene minutes after the accident occurred. While comforting Ms. Jones, he heard her exclaim, "Why didn't he watch where he was going?" Defendant objects to the admission of this testimony. **What result?** Jones offers the witness's testimony that immediately after the accident the truck driver said, "It's all my fault. My employer, Daniel's Trucking, will pay." **Is this admissible?** Can it be used to show that the driver worked for Daniel's Trucking?

Problem VI–51. Eleanor Smith claims that she was raped by a police officer, named Tom Carl, who stopped her for running a red light. She says that after she was raped, she returned to her car and gave chase to Carl in his car, only giving up, to call in a complaint on her car phone, when she realized that she had no hope of catching him. She adds that Carl headed off at full speed with his headlights off, even though it was dark. Officer Carl, for his part, says that although he did stop Ms. Smith for running the light, neither a rape nor a subsequent chase took place.

At Carl's trial, the state puts on the stand a second police officer, Officer Small. Officer Small testifies that he was in the vicinity of the alleged rape and in fact heard Ms. Smith's complaint when it was broadcast over the police radio. He also testifies that shortly before Ms. Smith's complaint was broadcast, he picked up the following conversation on his CB radio:

> First person: Look at that police car! He's going at full speed, and he doesn't have his lights on.

> Second person: And look at that little car trying to catch up to him!

Defense counsel immediately objects to the testimony, charging that it is inadmissible hearsay. **How should the court rule?**

Problem VI-52. From behind a tree, Jack Medoff watched a bloody school-yard shooting in which 9 persons were killed and 29 wounded. No other observer had a good view, as those in the yard hit the ground, fainted, or fled. The wounded all have what are at best shaky memories about what occurred. Fifteen minutes after the shooting, in the midst of the carnage, Medoff told a police officer, Maria Fabrini, who had just arrived: "I saw what happened." He described the incident and the assailant, adding: "I'm pretty sure it was the Pogue's kid."

Medoff, it turns out, was a veteran observer of carnage. Fifty years ago, during World War II, Mr. Medoff had the unenviable job of "cleaning up" during and after battle. He would watch the bloodshed and, when it seemed safe, rush out to pick up the bodies of fallen comrades in arms. Needless to say, the work was grisly, but Medoff was good at the task, and was renowned for being able to do the job when all around were overcome by the sight of gore. He was also responsible for filling out reports of what had happened.

Three months after the school-yard shooting Medoff died at age 78. When John Pogue is put on trial for multiple murders, the state seeks to have officer Fabrini testify to what Medoff said, citing the excited utterance and present sense impression exceptions. Pogue's attorney objects, claiming that Medoff's background was such that watching the shooting would not have excited him and that his statement to Fabrini doesn't qualify as a present sense impression. **Setting aside any possible Confrontation Clause issues, how should the court rule?**

Problem VI-53. Officer Hassim is on routine patrol one morning when he sees a disheveled, seemingly hysterical woman running down the street. The woman seems afraid someone is following her, as she continually looks over her shoulder. Officer Hassim stops his car. Upon catching sight of the police car, the woman runs toward it and tries to open the door before the officer has a chance to unlock it.

Upon entering the car, the woman, Polly Draper, tells Officer Hassim that she has just been sexually assaulted at the house of a man she met earlier in the evening. Officer Hassim notices that the woman's hands shake and her voice trembles. He takes her immediately to the hospital, where the doctors confirm that the woman is suffering from a mild case of shock. After treatment the woman is released, whereupon she is taken to the police station to make a formal statement about the alleged assault.

The alleged assailant is apprehended. At trial several months later, the prosecutor puts Ms. Draper on the stand to testify to the assault, but once on the stand, the woman tells the prosecutor that she had not been sexually assaulted. Stunned, the prosecutor seeks to introduce Ms. Draper's statement to Hassim. **May he do so? Would your answer be different if there was evidence that before the trial Draper had been visited by friends of the defendant who had warned her to drop all charges or "face the consequences"?**

Problem VI-54. In early December, Phyllis Shingle was attacked and almost killed by a man who attempted to rob her. Fortunately her screams attracted a passerby, and the man fled. She was unable to identify her assailant from pictures in police files, and the man was never found. Six months later she opened her door to a pizza delivery man and let out a sudden scream. Her roommate came running. "That's the one who attacked me," she said, pointing to the door. But the delivery man had dropped the pizza and fled. **If the delivery man is tried for the robbery attempt, may Phyllis's roommate testify to Phyllis's statement of identification?**

Problem VI-55. Patrolwoman Stephanie Westerly arrived at the scene of an automobile accident between a Cadillac and a Volkswagen about five minutes after it had occurred. She is willing to testify that just after she extricated the plaintiff from the Volkswagen, a man who had just walked out of a drugstore saw the body and, becoming very agitated, said, "How horrible, I think I'm going to faint. I'm sure the Cadillac was going too fast." **May the plaintiff introduce Westerly's testimony at trial as evidence that the driver of the Cadillac was speeding?**

Problem VI-56. Cassidy claims that as she was being helped from her burning car after colliding with a red Ford, she heard a hysterical voice that she thinks was a man's but that she cannot further identify, say, "The red car went through the light. The driver must have been asleep." **Can Cassidy testify to hearing these statements as part of her effort to prove that the defendant drove his car through a red light because he was asleep?** After Cassidy was pulled out, the person aiding her asked what happened. Cassidy replied, "I'll tell you as soon as we get away from this car. If the gas tank ignites, it might explode." Once they were safely away Cassidy said, "That car went through a light and plowed into me." The helper asked, "Do you know why he missed the light?" Cassidy replied, "No", and the helper asked, "Are you sure? The police will want to know." Cassidy responded, "His head was slumped over. I think he was asleep." Assume Cassidy dies and her widower brings a wrongful death action. **Can he introduce the helper to testify to what Cassidy told him?**

Problem VI-57. Louie Fealafine sues Nora Johnson for personal injuries allegedly sustained in an automobile accident. It is undisputed that cars driven by Fealafine and Johnson collided at an intersection controlled by a traffic light. Each claims to have had the green light. Fealafine wishes to call to the stand Dr. Holmes, his personal physician. It was Dr. Holmes who treated Fealafine for injuries after the accident. Dr. Holmes would testify, "I examined Mr. Fealafine shortly after the accident. Louie Fealafine related to me the circumstances of the accident, including the fact that the other driver ran a red light and caused the accident. My examination revealed that pieces of windshield glass were lodged in plaintiff's forearm. I removed them, gave other treatment to plaintiff, and took down the history of the accident." Johnson objects to this testimony. **What result?**

Problem VI-58. Sheila Hauser is suing Dr. Lewis Coles, an anesthesiologist, for injuries suffered during the course of a routine appendectomy. Dr. Dorie Tallchief, an anesthesiologist, agrees to examine Hauser in order to give Hauser's attorney her opinion about whether there has been negligence, and to help him develop his theory of the case. She has stated, however, that she will under no circumstances testify in court in a malpractice action against another physician. Hauser tells Dr. Tallchief during the course of the examination that her left leg is entirely numb, that she never had any problems with the leg before the operation, and that she has had severe pains in her neck and head that have not left her since the operation. She also tells the doctor that when she awoke after the operation she heard Dr. Coles exclaim, "Thank goodness! I was afraid I hadn't given her enough oxygen!" After the examination, Dr. Tallchief writes a report for Hauser's attorney in which she notes what Hauser has told her and states that it is her opinion that the numbness Hauser reports is permanent and may eventually lead to the loss of the leg, that there is a 50% chance that the reported pains will disappear in time, and that she believes the disabilities were due to the fact that Dr. Coles negligently failed to administer a sufficient amount of oxygen during the operation. Lincoln Franks, Dr. Tallchief's nurse, was present during the entire examination and is willing to testify for Hauser. **Will a court allow him to testify to any of the statements that Hauser made to the doctor? May Hauser's attorney offer any or all of Dr. Tallchief's report into evidence? Would your answer to these questions be the same if Tallchief had agreed to testify for Hauser before conducting her examination? If Tallchief's report was helpful to Coles, could he secure its admission?**

Problem VI-59. When she decided to leave Hollywood, the sultry star Emily Garry surprised her fans by buying a bed and breakfast in a wooded area near Lake Superior in Michigan's Upper Peninsula. ("Because I like people, not publicity.") One April, after the winter skiing season and before she opened for the spring mushroom season, she was surprised when a man who had never stayed with her, named Harry Garbo, offered her three times her usual rate if she would give him a room for a week because, he said, "I want to be alone." "You'll hardly be alone," she warned him, "my six-year-old grand niece, Aimee Uffner, is visiting that week and bringing Baby, her new St. Bernard puppy."

Harry came anyway. He proved to be an agreeable guest, spending most of his days alone in a boat or in the woods and playing with Aimee and Baby in the evenings. One afternoon, Aimee came running into the house in tears, with Baby right behind her. "What happened?" asked Emily. "Mr. Garbo landed his boat," said Aimee, "and Baby ran up and jumped on him. He fell and a plastic package and white stuff, like sugar, fell out. Baby started eating it. When Mr. Garbo saw this he got up and kicked Baby and called him names and told me to take my dog away before he killed him. He won't really kill him, will he Nana?" "No dear," said Emily, "I'll talk to that man." But she never did. While they were talking, Harry had come in the back entrance, packed his things, placed the money he had promised to pay on the bed and left.

Shortly afterwards, Baby began moaning and behaving strangely. Emily took him to the vet and told the vet what Aimee had told her. The vet took blood tests because he couldn't find anything wrong. The test results, which came back long after Baby had recovered, showed that the dog had ingested cocaine. Harry Garbo was arrested and tried for cocaine possession. **At the trial may Emily testify to what Aimee told her? May the vet testify to what Emily told him?**

Problem VI-60. James Drifter has begun seeing a psychiatrist because "It's time I went to a shrink and straightened myself out." On his tenth visit to his psychiatrist, they are discussing one of Drifter's dreams when the psychiatrist says, "I think that you are trying to hide something that you are feeling very guilty about." Drifter replies, "I can't keep anything from you. I robbed the First National Bank two months ago so I would be able to afford these visits. Now I see that some innocent kid is going to take the rap." The next day Drifter takes his own life after first sending the doctor a note saying, "Tell the court what I've told you. The kid is innocent." **May the psychiatrist testify to what Drifter told him when "the kid" is tried for bank robbery? May Drifter's note to the psychiatrist be introduced?**

Problem VI-61. At the age of 16, Ross Cornwell was tragically injured on a railroad turntable, losing both his legs. This occurred on July 3, 2010. On July 31, his parents filed suit on his behalf against the railroad company.   On August 5, his older sister, who had just returned from Europe, saw him for the first time since the accident. She asked him how he was and he replied, "Terrible." He proceeded to list all the things he was never going to do again: play baseball, dance, ride, swim, etc. He then said that he also felt constant pain in his toes and in his calf, although he knew his legs had been amputated. Finally he confided in his sister, "I am going to kill myself." Ross did not kill himself, and at the trial six months later was getting around quite nicely on a pair of artificial legs. The Cornwells' lawyer seeks to have Ross's sister testify to what Ross told her on her first visit with him, claiming that it is relevant on the damage issue. **May the sister testify to everything Ross said, some of what he said, or none of what he said? Would the situation be any different if the visit had occurred on July 25 rather than August 5?**

Problem VI-62. Karen Ikeda, born and raised in the Midwest, chose to attend a state school in Florida. During her first year there she sent a series of glowing letters to her parents in which she described the school, the town it is located in, and above all the weather. Among other things, she wrote: "I am never so happy as when I feel the warm wind in my face; I intend never to face another Midwestern winter; I feel at home, and I don't believe I will ever leave Florida." Immediately upon graduating from college, Karen left Florida to do graduate work at the University of Michigan. The state of Florida, which had classified Karen as a resident at the end of her first year, sues to recover the difference between resident and non-resident tuition on the ground that Karen had falsely stated that she had intended to remain a Florida resident when in fact she was only there for the temporary purpose of attending college. Karen argues that at the time she applied for residency status she did intend to remain in Florida indefinitely. She seeks to introduce the letters she wrote to her parents during the first year. **Are any of the statements in these letters hearsay on the purpose for which they are offered? If they are hearsay, is there any exception available to justify their admission?**

Problem VI-63. Osa Johnson was walking through her living room one day when she happened to glance out the picture window and see her neighbor changing a tire on his car. "Well, I guess Smitty's back is better," she remarked to her husband, "He's changing the tire on their car." Martin Johnson merely grunted. He did not look up from the football game he was watching on television. Assume that two weeks after this, Henry (Smitty) Smith's case against the Flagship Trucking Company is brought to trial. Negligence is conceded and the only issue is damages. **In order to refute Henry's claim that he is unable to do even light physical work because of his back condition, may Flagship introduce Martin who will testify to his wife's**

statement? If Osa testifies to having seen Smitty change a tire, may she be asked by the defendant what she said at the time?

Problem VI-64. Abe Henderson, the surviving son of billionaire Paul Jetty's closest friend, is summoned to see the old man as he lies sick in the hospital. Jetty asks to see Abe alone. They are together for 20 minutes until the visit is broken up by a doctor. Leaving the room, Abe runs into Henrietta Jetty, Paul Jetty's only child and heir at law. "Your father's a remarkable man," Abe tells Henrietta. "Here he's pushing 90 and may be on his deathbed, but he's a complete gentleman and as alert as ever." Henrietta, without answering, brushes past Abe into her father's room. The next day Jetty dies. It turns out that three days before his death Jetty had made a will in which he left his entire fortune to Abe Henderson, the son of his old friend. In his will, Jetty states that he feels he provided sufficiently for his daughter while she was alive, that she was not grateful for what he had done, and that he was not going to provide for her upon his death. Henrietta sues to break the will, claiming that her father was not mentally competent to make a will at any time during the last three months of his life. **Can a doctor who overheard what Abe said to Henrietta upon leaving Jetty's room testify to Abe's statement? Would the case for admitting the statement be any different if Jetty had left all his money to the Cancer Society rather than to Abe Henderson? Can Abe testify to his own statement?**

e. Recorded Recollection

Sometimes a person sees or hears something, makes a written record of what he saw or heard, and then forgets what it was he recorded. This is a common experience for people such as inventory takers or accident investigators, who routinely record detailed information or numerous observations of a similar sort. It may also occur, given a long lapse of time, when events are unique and important. When a witness has forgotten relevant information that he put in writing, he may be allowed to read his recorded observations to the jury, and the jury may be allowed to treat this recorded recollection as if it were courtroom testimony. The exception invoked to admit the evidence was called at common law the exception for "past recollection recorded." FRE 803(5), the Federal Rule admitting recorded recollections, follows the general contours of the common law exception:

Recorded Recollection. A record that:

(A) is on a matter the witness once knew about but now cannot recall well enough to testify fully and accurately;

(B) was made or adopted by the witness when the matter was fresh in the witness's memory; and

(C) accurately reflects the witness's knowledge.

If admitted, the record may be read into evidence but may be received as an exhibit only if offered by an adverse party.

First, the record must relate to something the witness once knew firsthand. Second, the witness's memory of the event described must have faded to the point that he can no longer testify fully and accurately about the event in question. Third, the record must be shown to have been made or adopted by the witness when the matter was fresh in his memory. Finally, there is the requirement that the record accurately reflect the witness's knowledge at the time it was written. In practice, this means that the witness must testify either that she remembers making an accurate recording of the event in question although she no longer remembers the facts recorded, or, if the witness has entirely forgotten the situation in which the recording was made, that she is confident she would not have written or adopted some description of the facts unless that description truly described her observations at the time.[117]

Other records, such as Memoranda, may be introduced under this exception even when the witness did not make the record. It is sufficient that the witness adopted the record as a reflection of her knowledge. Thus, if a witness dictated an account of her observations to a third party and checked it for accuracy, or read and endorsed an account prepared by a third party that reported the same facts that the witness observed, the account will be admitted as the witness's recorded recollection as long as the other conditions for the exception are met. If the witness dictated an account while the matter was fresh in her mind but without checking the transcription for accuracy, courts generally admit the account if the witness testifies that her oral statements accurately reported what she observed and the transcriber testifies that the transcription accurately recounts what he heard the witness say. This is really a double hearsay problem. The witness's out-of-court statements are hearsay that, if the witness is believed, accurately portray what he observed. The transcription is hearsay that, if the transcriber is believed, accurately reports what he heard. The simultaneous transcription is crucial to this extension of the past recollection recorded exception, since an important justification for this exception is that there is little danger that the witness's words will be reported incorrectly. Most courts do not allow one witness to testify orally to a report of another, even if the other swears her report was accurate when made, and the testifying witness states that he has a clear memory of what the other said.

---

[117] The common law was somewhat more fastidious than the Federal Rule. Dominant views were that forgetting had to be more complete, that the writing had to be made soon after the event it described and that the maker had to "vouch for the accuracy" of the writing.

Several rules peculiar to writings apply when the exception for recorded recollection is invoked. The "original document" or "best evidence" rule[118] requires that the record introduced be the original memorandum unless the proponent can show that the original is unavailable through no fault of her own. In some jurisdictions, the memorandum is treated as an ordinary item of documentary evidence and may be taken to the jury room when deliberations begin. The drafters of the Federal Rule thought there was no reason to give recorded recollection potentially greater impact than ordinary testimony, so FRE 803(5) provides that the record may not be offered as an exhibit unless the adverse party requests it.

There is no single strong justification for the exception for recorded recollection, but the case for the exception is strong when one considers the variety of safeguards involved. The requirement of a recording ensures that the speaker's language will be accurately transmitted to the trier of fact. The requirement that the record be made when memory is fresh avoids problems of forgetting. The speaker's presence as a witness allows the attorneys to clear up ambiguities in the language of the hearsay statement and gives the fact-finder some sense of the speaker's integrity and an opportunity to evaluate her capacity to observe.

This exception is also unusual in that the speaker must be both present and, in a sense, unavailable at the same time. The speaker must be in court to testify to the circumstances that qualify the declaration for admissibility as recorded recollection. On the other hand, she must lack a clear memory of the event described, so, in effect, she is not available to be examined about it.

The hearsay exception for recorded recollection should not be confused with the use of recorded information to refresh recollection. A witness whose memory of an event is hazy may be given a copy of a statement, a picture, a map, a cartoon or some other item (even intangibles such as the smell of Madeleine's baking) to aid recall. If the witness's memory is jogged by the information, she is allowed to relate her refreshed recollection of the event. In theory there is no hearsay problem. Since the witness is testifying to a current, albeit revived, memory, she may be cross-examined on the story she has told. In practice, however, the witness's recollection is often remarkably similar to the information contained in the item used to refresh her memory, and it is apparent that the witness's memory is limited to what she has just read. This impression is enhanced in courts in which the witness is allowed to jog her memory throughout her testimony by consulting the memorandum used for refreshment.

---

[118] See our discussion of this rule, in Chapter Ten, pp. 1299–1309.

A few courts do not allow memory to be refreshed except from records that meet the test for recorded recollection. The prevailing practice, however, is to the contrary. Since witnesses with refreshed memory purport to be speaking from present recollection, the information used to revive their recollection never enters into evidence, is not seen by the jury, and is not hearsay. Thus, courts generally place few restrictions on the kinds of items that may be used to revive recollection. There need be no guarantee that the information is reliable; it need not have been prepared at or near the time of the events described; the witness is not required to have been involved in its preparation, and she is not required to have seen it before trial. Whatever is used to revive recollection must, however, be shown to opposing counsel and may be used by her as a basis for cross-examination. In the extreme case in which it appears that the item could not or has not refreshed recollection, the testimony of the witness may be barred by the court or, if already given, stricken from the record.

Counsel may also refresh a witness's recollection in private before she takes the stand. Here, FRE 612 and its state equivalents govern. Subject to certain limitations in criminal cases, FRE 612 gives opposing counsel a right to see any writings used before trial to refresh a witness's memory "if the court decides that justice requires the party to have those options."

Problem VI-65. Officer Joe Hetz answers a 911 call and finds Maria Santana lying on the floor stabbed in the back, apparently dying. While waiting for an ambulance to arrive Hetz asked Santana what happened. Santana, though obviously in pain and under the influence of alcohol nevertheless tells the following story: "I was drinking with three of my son's teenage friends when one of them, Carl Sampson, started to get nasty and talking filthy. I told him he had enough to drink and that he would have to go home. He used the 'F' word and hitched up his pants a bit so I could see a knife in his boot. I turned to call the police and then he stabbed me." Officer Hetz wrote this statement down as he rode in the ambulance with Ms. Santana to the hospital. Santana was immediately wheeled into the operating room. Three hours later, when the operation was over and Santana was emerging from the anesthetic, Hetz read Santana her statement, asked her if it was her own true recollection and after she nodded yes, had her sign each page of the statement. (Hospital records show that at the time of the signing, she had a blood alcohol level of .22, far in excess of the amount which makes one legally drunk.) However, she has since forgotten the details of the statement and remembers nothing of the stabbing itself. Her doctors think that the memory loss was a delayed response to the shock of the event and don't expect her ever to remember.

At Sampson's trial Ms. Santana is put on the stand. The prosecutor wants to admit Ms. Santana's statement as her past recollection recorded. **Setting aside any possible Confrontation Clause objection, may she? If so, what must she do to qualify the statement for admission?**

----

f. Business Records

i. The Shopbook Rule

Historically, business records, despite their hearsay nature, have been admissible under two distinct exceptions. The first, the "shopbook rule," is rooted in the early English custom that allowed a merchant doing business on account to enter his books into evidence to prove the defendant owed him money. This exception, as it developed in this country, was justified on the ground of necessity. In the eighteenth and early nineteenth centuries, the common law barred interested parties from testifying in their own behalf. Had there not been a hearsay exception for shopbooks, merchants might have had no way to establish legitimate debts.

To ensure reliability, different jurisdictions required one or more of the following guarantees: (1) a "supplemental oath" taken by the merchant as to the justness of his accounts, (2) inspection by the court to determine if the books were fairly kept in the regular course of business, (3) testimony that the merchant kept honest books, and (4) proof apart from the books that at least some portion of the goods charged to an account had been actually delivered.

ii. Regularly Kept Records

The second exception admits the regularly kept records of business establishments. Guarantees of reliability are found in three basic requirements: "(a) the entries must be original entries made in the routine of a business, (b) the entries must have been made upon the personal knowledge of the recorder or of someone reporting to him, [and] (c) the entries must have been made at or near the time of the transaction recorded."[119] One justification for the exception is that when an entry is made in the course of a business routine, the routine itself lends a guarantee of reliability since one is not likely to develop a routine of erroneous recording. Business records are also likely to be reliable because customers can be expected to complain about errors, and the firm can be expected to discipline those who make erroneous entries in disregard of the business routine. At common law this exception was also

----

[119] McCormick § 286.

rooted in necessity, for it could be invoked only after the recorder and any informants were shown to be unavailable.

iii. Statutory Reform

The common law exception for regularly kept records might have been gradually liberalized by the courts to meet the exigencies of modern business practice and to take account of various non-business situations in which routine records are likely to be as reliable as records kept in business. Some courts moved in this direction, but others did not. The aspects of the common law exception that caused the most difficulty were those that were particularly unsuited to large-scale businesses. Chief among these were the requirement that each entry be qualified in court by the person who made it and the related requirement that all employees transmitting information to the entrant be called as witnesses if the entrant did not have firsthand knowledge of the matter recorded. These requirements could be avoided only by evidence that the relevant persons were unavailable. The impracticability of these requirements is obvious. In a large business, there might be literally dozens of people responsible for making entries in a single account. Dozens of others might be involved in transmitting the information recorded in a single entry. Indeed, in a business in which numerous individuals report or record similar information, there might be no way to determine who among a group of employees was responsible for an entry.

Difficulties of this sort coupled with the restrictive interpretations some courts gave to the term "business" generated considerable pressure for reform. Interest in reform led to two model statutes, the Commonwealth Fund Act, first proposed in 1927, and the Uniform Business Records as Evidence Act, drafted in 1933. Most states adopted one or the other of these acts, although many states have now switched to language similar to that of FRE 803(6). While the two statutes differed somewhat in language, they were interpreted to mean about the same thing.

Both statutes eliminated the common law requirement that all individuals who prepared or furnished recorded information be in some way accounted for. Both acts eliminated the unavailability requirement, since neither act conditioned admissibility on the absence of witnesses who could testify to the events recorded. Also, both acts defined business very broadly to include all sorts of businesses, professions, occupations, and callings. Records were admissible under these acts if they had been made in the regular course of business following ordinary business procedures at about the time of the event or transaction recorded.

iv. Business Duty and Informants

Two cases interpreting the Commonwealth Fund Act set limits on the expansive language of that act. The first, *Johnson v. Lutz*,[120] involved an accident report prepared by a police officer based on the statements of those present at the scene of the accident. Despite language in the Act that the lack of personal knowledge by the entrant or maker should affect weight and not admissibility, the New York Court of Appeals held that the record was inadmissible when offered for the truth of the statements therein recorded. The Court interpreted the "lack of personal knowledge" language as applying only when those providing information incorporated in the record *had a business duty* to transmit information to the entrant or maker. Although some commentators criticized this decision as imposing limitations not found in the language of the Act, others, including the authors, believe the decision was both wise and in accord with the intended meaning of the Act. The language that *Johnson* is claimed by some to contravene was designed to eliminate the inconvenience of accounting for all employees who had played a part in transmitting the information recorded. This is justified because the same guarantees of reliability that apply to the person making the record apply to all employees in the chain of information. All are presumed to be acting in accord with some routine, and all are subject to the sanctions of superiors for mistakes in transmission. These safeguards do not apply to statements made by speakers in a non-business capacity. The statement of one who observed an accident would not be admissible if testified to by someone at the scene. There is no good reason that it should be more readily admitted if recorded in a police report. If the statement qualifies under some other exception to the hearsay rule, prevailing practice allows the report to be introduced to prove that the statement was made and allows the statement to be received under the applicable exception. For example, if the statements reported by the officer in *Johnson* had been made by the party against whom the report was offered, the report would have been admitted as a business record and the party's statements as recorded by the police officer would have been admitted as personal admissions.

v. Regular Course of Business

The second major case, *Palmer v. Hoffman*,[121] arose out of a grade-crossing accident in which the plaintiff was injured and his wife was killed. The defendant railroad sought to introduce statements made by the train's engineer (who had died before trial) to his superior in the presence of an official from the Massachusetts Public Utilities Commission. The question facing the Court was whether the engineer's

---

[120] 253 N.Y. 124, 170 N.E. 517 (N.Y. 1930).
[121] 318 U.S. 109 (1943).

statements were made "in the regular course" of business within the meaning of the federal statute (essentially the Commonwealth Fund Act). The railroad argued that it was part of their regular business to investigate accidents and to take the statements of employees involved, but the Supreme Court refused to admit the statements. "Their primary utility," wrote Justice Douglas, "is in litigating, not in railroading."[122]

From one perspective, the railroad's argument is clearly correct. A railroad could no more stay in business without investigating its accidents than it could without maintaining its locomotives. Nevertheless, there is considerable sense in the Court's position. Accident reports are not "typical of entries made systematically or as a matter of routine to record events or occurrences, to reflect transactions with others, or to provide internal controls."[123] Hence, they do not share the trustworthiness associated with established routine. In addition, it is not clear that inaccuracy in reporting accidents will be punished by the business, since whatever exonerates the employee tends to negate the company's liability as well.

The court of appeals had reached the same result as the Supreme Court, but the majority had justified exclusion largely on the basis of the self-serving nature of the engineer's statements.[124] This rationale has been criticized on the ground that many of the statements in a party's books are self-serving in character.[125] But the critics miss the point: debts recorded in a party's books serve that party's interests, but unless suit to collect that debt is contemplated, the party has no interest in overstating the amount owed. The situation is different when litigation appears likely. At this point the need to present one's case in the most favorable light is obvious, and even basically honest individuals may be tempted to distort evidence.[126] Moreover, in any large scale business, the benefits of misreporting accounts accrue to the company and not to the record keeper. However, when an employee fills out an accident report she has at least two reasons to attempt to exonerate herself. First, victims of the accident may choose to sue her personally. Absent some privilege, her report, if discovered, may be introduced against her as an admission. Second, an employee's job may be in jeopardy if the company attributes the accident to her carelessness.

---

[122] *Id.* at 114.

[123] *Id.* at 113.

[124] Hoffman v. Palmer, 129 F.2d 976 (2d Cir. 1942).

[125] Charles V. Laughlin, *Business Entries and the Like*, 46 IOWA L. REV. 276, 289 (1961). See also Judge Clark's dissent in *Hoffman, supra* note 124, 129 F.2d at 1002. ("I submit that there is hardly a grocer's account book which could not be excluded on that basis [a powerful motive to misrepresent].")

[126] As the extract from Stewart, reproduced supra in the text at note 82, indicates, a person may not even be aware of the way in which his interests have affected his memory and perceptions.

Most jurisdictions follow *Palmer v. Hoffman* when a business attempts to introduce accident reports or other self-serving records made at a time when litigation appeared likely. Courts differ, however, in the seriousness with which they take the Supreme Court's rationale. Absent some motive to misrepresent, records made for proper business purposes usually will not be excluded from evidence simply because the business rarely has the occasion to make such records. Most courts feel that an activity may be in the regular course of business without being so frequent as to be routine.

vi.   Opinions in Business Records

When an opinion is incorporated in a business record the court will examine the nature of the opinion to determine admissibility. The more speculative the opinion, the greater the probability of exclusion. Problems with opinions frequently arise when parties seek to introduce diagnoses contained in hospital records. As long as a diagnosis reflects a standard expert judgment based on a set of reasonably objective criteria, courts have little trouble in admitting it. A diagnosis of a fractured elbow or appendicitis would be admitted in most, if not all, jurisdictions. A court is less likely to admit a diagnosis when the diagnostic criteria are less certain, and it is unlikely to admit opinions that go beyond diagnosis into the cause or prognosis for a condition. Faced with an entry on a patient's chart that reads, "Diagnosis: substantial lung damage resulting from black lung disease due to working in a poorly ventilated coal mine," most courts would admit the entry to show lung damage, some would admit it to show black lung disease, but few, if any, would admit it to show that the disease was caused by poor working conditions.

Professor Laughlin suggests, "[I]f the person making the entry could have testified to his opinion, a record of that opinion should be admissible."[127] This suggestion makes considerable sense when lay opinions are recorded, since admissible lay opinion pertains to evaluations on which most people would not differ, or to events that cannot readily be described in more concrete terms. However, it is less satisfactory when expert opinion is involved, because the examination of experts is designed to do more than relate facts or illuminate hearsay dangers. Expert testimony should elucidate the bases of the expert's reasoning and indicate the way in which different facts affect the expert's ultimate conclusion. Cross-examination is a test of expertise and of the thoroughness and care with which the expert approached the problem before him. Without some understanding of how the expert reached his opinion, the jury is often unable to appreciate the full implications of the facts reported. It is also unable to evaluate the reasonableness of the expert's opinion vis-à-vis the opinions of experts giving conflicting

---

[127] Laughlin, *supra* note 125, at 304.

testimony. In these circumstances it seems that the prevailing view is a sensible one.

vii. Computer Records

Records stored on computers pose special problems. They require a more technical foundation than the typical business record and may necessitate providing the opposing counsel with programming information and/or the opportunity to run tests on the proponent's machine. In addition, there are technical objections that can be made to the introduction of computer printouts as business records. The printouts themselves are often prepared specifically for the litigation in question, and the information reported in the printouts may not have been entered into the computer at or near the time of the transactions to which the information pertains. These objections are generally dismissed by courts, and properly so. As long as the information on which a printout is based was entered before the prospect of litigation arose, the fact that the printout is prepared for use in court should not be disturbing. The printout simply reproduces stored information in a form that humans can appreciate. Ordinarily, there is little reason to be suspicious of the reproduction. The time at which information was entered on the computer is unimportant if the information accurately reproduces records made at or near the time of the transaction.

viii. Absence of an Entry

When, as a matter of business routine, an entry in a business record could be expected if an event occurred, most courts allow the absence of an entry to be shown as evidence of the event's non-occurrence. Thus, in a dispute over payment of debt, the fact that the creditor's books do not record a payment is usually admissible evidence that the debtor did not pay. When hospital records do not note that a patient's heart stopped, the lack of notation will be admitted as evidence that the patient's heart never stopped while she was hospitalized.

ix. Other Statutes—The Federal Rule

In addition to the basic business records exception, other statutes may affect the admissibility of business records in some jurisdictions. These statutes are particularly likely with respect to bank records, hospital records, and corporate records generally. Also, a few states retain versions of the shopbook exception. It is difficult to imagine a shopbook entry that would not be admissible under either the exception for business records or that for past recollection recorded, but where such statutes exist they may serve as alternative grounds of admissibility.

Until the Federal Rules of Evidence were enacted, the Federal Business Record Act was modeled on the Commonwealth Fund Act. FRE

803(6) replaces the rule modeled on this act. FRE 803(7) applies when the lack of an entry is offered to prove the nonoccurrence of some matter. The drafters saw fit to include the latter exception, although the lack of an entry seems not to fit in the Federal Rules' definition of hearsay because failing to make a business record almost never involves an assertive intent.

FRE 803(6):

Records of a Regularly Conducted Activity. A record of an act, event, condition, opinion, or diagnosis if:

(A) the record was made at or near the time by—or from information transmitted by—someone with knowledge;

(B) the record was kept in the course of a regularly conducted activity of a business, organization, occupation, or calling, whether or not for profit;

(C) making the record was a regular practice of that activity;

(D) all these conditions are shown by the testimony of the custodian or another qualified witness, or by a certification that complies with Rule 902(11) or (12) or with a statute permitting certification; and

(E) neither the source of information nor the method or circumstances of preparation indicate a lack of trustworthiness.

FRE 803(7):

Absence of a Record of a Regularly Conducted Activity. Evidence that a matter is not included in a record described in paragraph (6) if:

(A) the evidence is admitted to prove that the matter did not occur or exist;

(B) a record was regularly kept for a matter of that kind; and

(C) neither the possible source of the information nor other circumstances indicate a lack of trustworthiness.

The Federal Rules codified the most liberal preexisting practices with respect to business entries. Data compilations are specifically made admissible, leaving no question concerning the status of computer records. Business is defined to include institutions and associations as well as businesses, occupations, professions, and callings of every kind. In addition, opinions and diagnoses are specifically declared admissible. This last change has led the federal courts to adopt a more liberal attitude in admitting diagnoses and opinions than that which prevailed before their enactment. When, however, records are based on the statements of informants, the rule of *Johnson v. Lutz* applies and the record is admissible only if the statement was transmitted as part of a regular business activity.   The Supreme Court's argument in *Palmer v. Hoffman* is not, however, fully accepted.   Absence of routine renders records inadmissible under FRE 803(6) only when their non-routine nature indicates a lack of trustworthiness.   The existence of positive motives to misrepresent makes exclusion more likely.

Problem VI-66.   Michael Minton, a successful lawyer, died at the age of 63.   Minton had been interested in numismatics from the time he was a child and by his mid-30s he was known as much for the quality of his coin collection as for his legal skills.   Minton was continually buying, selling, and trading coins.   It is estimated that one-third of his $5,300,000 estate was represented by his coin collection or income he had earned from sales of his coins.   Shortly after Minton's death, the Midas Coin Company brought suit against the estate, alleging that Minton had neither paid for nor returned an 1803 silver dollar delivered on approval, along with an 1865 gold five-dollar piece and an 1861 silver three-cent piece.   The other two coins had been returned.   The estate defends on the ground that the silver dollar was never received.   In support of this defense the estate introduces Florence Minton, Michael's widow, who testifies to the regularity and care with which Michael kept track of his coins in a large leather-covered book that he called his "Coin Register."   She also testifies that whenever Michael received a coin on approval, he either wrote a check for the coin immediately or left the coin locked in a drawer for his chauffeur to pick up and return to the appropriate company.   The five-dollar gold piece and the silver three-cent piece were delivered the evening before Michael's death. Mrs. Minton also testifies that her husband dictated notes to her every night concerning his numismatic activities.   He had often expressed the hope of compiling them into a book that he had tentatively titled, *I Made a Mint on Coin Collecting: The Autobiography of a Numismatic Nut* [Minton's sense of humor left something to be desired.] Finally, Mrs. Minton testifies that she transcribed his words accurately and had never known Michael to lie. The estate, in order to prove that the silver dollar never was delivered, offers as a business record the final page of Minton's "Coin Register," which reads as follows:

Date	Coin		Cond.	Recd.	Ret'd	Bt.	Sd.	Am't.	Party
7/26	(1891cc)	$1 ag.	V.F.	X	X			($15.75)	Univ.
7/26	(1882)	Ind. 1¢	Unc.	X		X		($32.20)	Midas
7/30	(1796)	Ig. 1¢	V.F.				X	($400)	Reese
7/30	(1849)	$1 au.	Unc.			X		($300)	Reese
8/3	(1865)	$5 au.	Fine	X	X			($350)	Cn.X.
8/3	(1899)	$10 au.	V.F.	X		X		($140)	Cn.X.
8/3	(1917)	$20 au.	Unc.	X		X		($380)	Cn.X.
8/5	(1865)	$5 au.	V.F.	X	X			($550)	Midas
8/5	(1861)	3¢ ag.	Fine	X	X			($20.00)	Midas

The estate claims that the absence of any notation acknowledging receipt of the silver dollar should be admitted as evidence that the coin never arrived. **How should the court rule?**

The estate also wishes to introduce as a business record a portion of the material that Minton had dictated to his wife the night that he died. This extract reads: "I don't know why I do business with Midas. Their coins are seldom in the promised condition and the company is so unreliable. They were supposed to deliver the silver dollar with the coins that arrived today. If the dollar was truly uncirculated, it would be the prize of my collection. If they have sold it to another, I shall cease doing business with them." **Is this writing admissible?**

The estate also wishes to put Minton's chauffeur on the stand to testify that he went to the locked drawer where coins are left for him to return and he only found the five-dollar gold piece and the three-cent silver piece. **Should this testimony be allowed?**

g. Public Records and Reports

There was at common law an exception for official records and reports much like the exception for business records. The written report of a public official is admissible if the official had personal knowledge of the matter reported on as well as an official duty to report on it. Some common law courts used this exception to admit evaluative reports, that is, reports of factual conclusions reached following an investigation, but this was not the usual practice. However, various statutes make the results of specific evaluations admissible. At the federal level, for example, the findings of the Secretary of Agriculture are admissible as *prima facie* evidence of the true grade of grain, and bills of health that are prepared for ships embarking from foreign ports to the United States are, if properly executed by a consular official or other United States officer, admissible to show the sanitary history and condition of the vessel. As these examples indicate, statutes of this sort are usually narrowly focused.

FRE 803(8), the Federal Rule's hearsay exception for public records and reports, made two important changes to the prior law. First, evaluative reports are now generally admissible except when offered against the defendant in a criminal case. Those statutes that specifically authorize the admission of evaluative reports are no longer necessary except insofar as they allow evaluative reports to be used by the government in criminal cases.[128]   Second, the previous Federal Rule applied only to the reports of federal agencies. FRE 803(8) applies to the records of all public offices and agencies, state or federal, and has been interpreted by some courts to include the public records and reports of the agencies of foreign governments. The justifications for the rule—the assumptions that public records will be reliable because public officials perform their duties properly and that the records are often necessary because officials are unlikely to remember what they record—are presumed to apply abroad as well as at home.

These changes have made FRE 803(8) one of the most useful and widely used exceptions to the hearsay rule. The government is in the business of producing documents. Government agents investigate and report on a wide variety of incidents, many of which trigger litigation. When there is stock fraud, the SEC investigates. After an airplane crash, the FAA has someone on the scene immediately. Numerous agencies respond to complaints of job discrimination, and even an ordinary traffic accident inevitably generates at least one police report. In some instances, statutes that impose reporting requirements or authorize investigations provide that information collected or facts discovered are not admissible in evidence. Even when statutes do not prohibit disclosure, the results of governmental investigations were at one time often kept confidential by the investigating agencies. Today, however, many agencies have changed their policies, and the federal Freedom of Information Act and analogous state laws may give litigants access to material that agencies do not wish to reveal. Access to governmental reports is valuable to litigators because the government's investigative resources far outstrip those of most clients, and public investigations often begin long before lawyers are mobilized. In addition, the apparent neutrality of governmental investigators means that their factual findings are likely to carry great weight in litigation between private parties.

FRE 803(8) provides:

Public Records. A record or statement of a public office if:

(A) it sets out:

    (i) the office's activities;

    (ii) a matter observed while under a legal duty to report, but not including, in a criminal case, a matter observed by law-enforcement personnel; or

---

[128] As we shall see in Chapter Seven, the use of some evaluative reports against criminal defendants may create problems under the Confrontation Clause.

(iii) in a civil case or against the government in a criminal case, factual findings from a legally authorized investigation; and

(B) neither the source of information nor other circumstances indicate a lack of trustworthiness.

FRE 803(8)(A)(i) is orthodox and noncontroversial. An agency's report of its own activities may be used to show that the activities occurred. For example, the report of a building inspector that he inspected a house located at 901 Kaplan Boulevard may be introduced to show that the inspection occurred.

FRE 803(8)(A)(ii) captures the essence of the common law exception. The observations of public officials are admissible so long as they were made in the line of duty and there was a duty to report them. If the building inspector observed a crack in the foundation of the house at 901 Kaplan and reported this, the report would be admissible as proof of a structural defect. If, however, the inspector had observed a marijuana plant growing in the kitchen of the house, his report would not be admissible to show that marijuana was being grown because the inspector had no duty to report observations unrelated to the building's condition.

Suppose the building inspector had made his report orally to a supervisor and the supervisor had not written it down. Under the literal language of FRE 803(8), it might appear that the supervisor could testify to what the inspector told her because the exception extends to a "record or statement." However, the legislative history of the Federal Rule contains no suggestion that it does not require a writing, and one can argue that an official's statement is not the statement of an office or agency until it is written down and made part of the agency's record. Under this analysis, the supervisor could not testify to the inspector's oral statement, but if the supervisor had written down the inspector's statement as part of her official duties, the supervisor's report would be admissible. As with business records, the writing avoids both reporting errors and memory problems.[129]

Subsection (A)(ii) does not apply in criminal cases to matters observed by police officers and law enforcement personnel. This exception was added on the floor of the House of Representatives largely to ensure

---

[129] One district court, sitting without a jury, focused on the word "statement" to admit the *testimony* of a postal inspector who had conducted an investigation into an alleged lottery scheme. The exception was not needed to the extent that the investigator had personal knowledge of admissible evidence, but in this case several questions asked of the inspector called for hearsay answers. Since the specific questions are not reported, one cannot tell whether the exception was correctly applied, assuming that it applies to testimony in the first instance. The exception appears also to have been used to circumvent lay opinion problems (FRE 701), although the court does not recognize this. *See* United States Postal Ser. v. Thielbar, 5 Fed.R.Evid. Serv. (Callaghan) 1106 (N.D.Iowa 1980). A U.S. Tax Court case, on the other hand, said that oral testimony in court is not a "statement" under the rule. Little v. Commissioner of Internal Revenue, T.C. Memo. 1996–270, 71 T.C.M. (CCH) 3168.

that criminal defendants would not be tried on the basis of police reports. Given the Supreme Court's recent Confrontation Clause decisions, discussed in more detail in Chapter Seven, the exclusion seems prescient. Compare the language of 803(8)(A)(ii) with that of subsection (A)(iii), which protects criminal defendants by providing that factual findings resulting from investigations are admissible in criminal cases only "against the government." There is no obvious reason for the difference except that the language of subsection (iii) was drafted by the advisory committee subject to criticism and revision, while the language of subsection (ii) was first offered in a House debate. The House was concerned only with the use of reports against defendants. It could have achieved this goal with an exception that did not turn on whether the case was criminal. Some courts have refused to read the exclusion of FRE 803(8)(A)(ii) literally.[130] Relying on legislative history, they have interpreted subsection ii's exclusion of reported observations to conform with FRE 803(8)(A)(iii), and have allowed criminal defendants to introduce police reports.

The subsection (ii) exclusion requires courts to determine who are "law–enforcement personnel." A clear test has yet to emerge. In one case, building inspectors were held not to be law enforcement personnel, in part because the maximum penalty for violating the building code was a fine.[131] In another case, a Customs Service chemist who had identified a white powder as heroin was held to fall within the ban because Customs Service chemists "are, without question, important participants in the prosecutorial effort."[132] The same circuit that decided this case indicated that IRS agents who gather information routinely used in litigation are performing a law enforcement function,[133] but that employees of the medical examiner's office are not because, although they investigate unnatural deaths, they have no responsibility for enforcing laws.[134]

Subsection (iii) is the most controversial aspect of FRE 803(8) because it opens the door to so much evidence. In construing this section one must first determine what is meant by "factual findings." Had our building inspector filed a report saying, "Because of its cracked foundation, leaking roof, and rusting furnace, the house at 901 Kaplan is not fit for human habitation," would the assertion that the house is unfit for human habitation count as a factual finding or would it be better characterized as an "opinion?" "Opinion" is a word that because of its inclusion in FRE 803(6) is conspicuously absent in FRE 803(8). In Chapter Two we discussed the difficulty of separating fact from opinion.

---

[130] See, e.g., United States v. Smith, 521 F.2d 957 (D.C.Cir. 1975).

[131] United States v. Hansen, 583 F.2d 325, at 333 (7th Cir. 1978), cert.denied, 439 U.S. 912 (1978).

[132] United States v. Oates, 560 F.2d 45, 68 (2d Cir. 1977).

[133] United States v. Ruffin, 575 F.2d 346 (2d Cir. 1978).

[134] United States v. Rosa, 11 F.3d 315 (2d Cir. 1993).

Here it is impossible. A factual finding, unless it is a simple report of something observed, is an opinion as to what more basic facts imply: The building inspector is *of the opinion* that a house with a cracked foundation, leaking roof, and rusting furnace is not fit for human habitation; he has found *as a matter of fact* that the house at 901 Kaplan is not fit for human habitation.

Sometimes, when it is difficult to know the precise scope that should be accorded an evidence rule, legislative history provides a good guide to the spirit in which the rule should be interpreted. Here, however, the legislative history is confused. In the House of Representatives, the Committee on the Judiciary noted its intention that "the phrase 'factual findings' be strictly construed and that evaluations or opinions contained in public reports shall not be admissible under this Rule." The Senate Committee on the Judiciary, noting the House's comment, took "strong exception to this limited understanding of the application of the rule." The Conference did not address the matter. In an earlier edition, we suggested that the Senate had the better of this dispute. Not only is it impossible to separate factual findings from opinions, but, as the Senate points out, FRE 803(8)(B)[135] bars factual findings that appear untrustworthy. The Supreme Court confirmed our judgment in *Beech Aircraft Corp. v. Rainey*.[136] In *Rainey*, the Court held that a report containing an Air Force officer's admittedly speculative conclusions about the cause of a plane crash he had investigated had been properly admitted into evidence under FRE 803(8)(A)(iii).[137] The trial court's "obligation" to exclude reports that appeared untrustworthy was seen as an adequate guarantee of reliability.

Even before *Rainey,* most courts took a similarly broad view as to what 803(8) allowed. Thus, FRE 803(8)(A)(iii) has been used in a school desegregation suit to admit an HEW hearing examiner's finding that a particular school had been established and maintained as a black school for segregation purposes.[138] It has also been used in a civil rights action to admit a finding by a state human rights agency that the plaintiff's allegation of racially motivated job termination was not supported by the facts;[139] it has been used to admit a civic commission's report showing illegal practices of the New York City police;[140] and it has been used in a

---

[135] Despite the fact that the 2011 Advisory Committee notes stated that the changes to the rules were stylistic only, the new version of FRE 803(8) eliminated an ambiguity which existed in the prior version of the rule which did not demarcate the new section (b) as a separate subsection. The previous wording of the rule created an ambiguity as to whether the "lack of trustworthiness" language modified only what is now (a)(iii) relating to factual findings from a legally authorized investigation or the other public records exceptions as well. But, now FRE 808(8) is no longer ambiguous in that regard.

[136] 488 U.S. 153 (1988).

[137] FRE 803(8)(A)(iii) was formally known as 803(8)(C).

[138] United States v. School Dist. of Ferndale, Mich., 577 F.2d 1339 (6th Cir. 1978).

[139] Theobald v. Botein, Hays, Sklar & Herzberg, 493 F.Supp. 1 (S.D.N.Y.1979).

[140] White-Ruiz v. City of New York, 1996 WL 603983 (S.D.N.Y.).

wrongful death action to admit the conclusion of a shooting review board that the defendant officers had acted within departmental guidelines.[141] Lower courts, however, have been reluctant to characterize legal conclusions as "factual findings," so in admitting reports under FRE 803(8)(A)(iii), they often excise judgments of law. In *Rainey,* the Court left open the question of whether this was the proper line to draw.

Courts generally read the word "investigation" broadly. Administrative hearings resulting in factual findings are commonly treated as investigations under this rule.[142] Accident reports have also qualified.[143] Moreover, a duty to investigate is not needed for a report to be admissible. It is sufficient that the investigation be authorized by law; the decision to investigate may have been a matter of discretion.

FRE 803(8)(A)(iii) admits factual findings that are based, in part, on hearsay. There are two levels at which hearsay may occur. First, a government agent may report to some other agent who prepares an official report. The analogy to business records means that this should pose no problems, even if the final report quotes the first agent's statements. Second, the agency's conclusions may be based in whole or in part on the statements of those who had no duty to talk to government agents. Thus, the finding that a plane crash was due to pilot error may be based in part, as it was in *Rainey*, on the statements of people who saw the accident. The findings of a hearing examiner may be based entirely on testimony presented to him, testimony that would be hearsay if offered by transcript in a subsequent action. The fact that a report is based on the statements of those with no official duty to speak does not mean that the factual findings it contains will be inadmissible. But hearsay statements included in such reports are often excluded even though they are arguably relevant for the non-hearsay purpose of showing the basis for the agency's findings. Thus, a woman's statement that she saw a plane hit the ground at a 30° angle cannot be introduced to show the angle at which the plane hit the ground, and it is likely to be excised from the report given the jury no matter what its influence on the agent who investigated the crash. The hearing transcript that accompanies the findings of a hearing examiner will be similarly excluded.

Factual findings that rest in large part on hearsay are not necessarily inadmissible, but they are vulnerable to exclusion under the trustworthiness requirement imposed by section B of FRE 803(8). In deciding whether a hearsay source makes factual finding untrustworthy, courts usually look at all the information that supports the factual findings. If, for example, an airplane accident investigator concludes on the basis of the distribution of wreckage, communications with the control

---

[141] Perrin v. Anderson, 784 F.2d 1040 (10th Cir. 1986).

[142] Chandler v. Roudebush, 425 U.S. 840 (1976).

[143] Lubanski v. Coleco Indus., Inc., 929 F.2d 42 (1st Cir. 1991).

tower, and the observations of bystanders, that a crash was due to pilot error, the report would not be excluded because part of the evidence on which the investigator relied was hearsay. However, if the investigator's finding rested only on a bystander's statement, "The plane came in so low it was clear that the pilot had made a mistake," exclusion is likely because an official imprimatur does not increase the reliability of out-of-court statements. A similar decision might be reached where a factual finding is supported by non-hearsay as well as hearsay evidence, if the hearsay is important to the factual conclusion and comes from an untrustworthy source. When a factual finding is based on an evaluation of the conflicting out-of-court statements [144] of two parties and their witnesses, as often happens in administrative hearings, the examiner's ability to evaluate conflicting stories received in a court-like setting is typically thought to make the examiner's findings sufficiently trustworthy for admissibility under the rule.

Ordinarily the hearsay exceptions operate without reference to one another. If a statement is admissible under one exception, it is not excluded simply because it does not quite meet the conditions of another exception. It should be obvious that many of the records admissible under FRE 803(8) appear also to qualify under FRE 803(6). Some courts have held, however, that by enacting a separate exception for public records and reports, Congress meant to preclude recourse to the exception for business records when public records were offered. This is important in criminal cases. FRE 803(8)(A)(ii) bars the observations of law enforcement personnel in criminal cases and FRE 803(8)(A)(iii) protects criminal defendants from the introduction of factual findings resulting from investigations. FRE 803(6) contains no such limitations. The better procedure is to interpret the rules together, but not to read one as barring resort to the other. Thus, if a police report describes the suspicious behavior of a criminal defendant, a prosecutor should not be able to avoid Congress's specific judgment on the one occasion when it considered the admissibility of such evidence by offering the report as a business record. On the other hand, if the police record reports a routine matter that when recorded had no obvious relevance to any criminal action (e.g., a ledger containing the serial numbers of guns legally registered in a city), the record should be admitted to prove the truth of what it asserts. Since it is barred by the literal language of FRE 803(8)(A)(ii), a prosecutor should be able to resort to FRE 803(6) or, perhaps, FRE 807. Congress was not thinking of this kind of record when it enacted FRE 803(8), and the value judgments that are embodied in that rule are not undercut if such records

---

[144] Note that the statements are "out-of-court," and hence hearsay only in the context of the litigation in which the factual findings of the hearing examiner are offered. In the hearing before the examiner, the statements of the parties and their witnesses would have been given in court subject to cross-examination. It is in part because of the testimonial quality of the evidence presented in administrative hearings that courts have found the factual findings of hearing examiners admissible under FRE 803(8)(A)(iii).

are admitted. A number of courts have drawn such lines. Other courts have allowed reports that could not be admitted against criminal defendants under 803(8) to be admitted under 803(6) if the author of the report testifies.[145] They argue that the author's availability as a witness protects the defendant's confrontation rights, and so achieves what they see as the goal of the FRE 803(8)(A)(ii) and (8)(A)(iii) preclusions.

ADDITIONAL PROBLEMS

Problem VI-67. Early on the evening of September 19, 2012, a truck traveling west on U.S. Route 20 collided with a car traveling south on State Route 6, killing four of the five teenagers riding in the car. Route 20 is a four-lane divided highway, while Route 6 is a two-lane country road. The intersection is controlled by a light that is always red in the direction of Route 6 and green in the direction of Route 20, except when a car on Route 6 trips a sensor. When this occurs, if six seconds pass without any vehicle's tripping a sensor on Route 20, the light turns to amber on Route 20 for four seconds and then after one second of red on both roads it turns to green on Route 6 and red on Route 20.

At the time of the accident, Sergeant Bonny Hendricksmeyer, a 28-year veteran of the state highway patrol, was on duty at a local patrol office. She reached the scene of the accident about six minutes after the collision. She carefully examined the physical circumstances of the accident and noted the tire marks on the highway and the damage done to the vehicles. Several days later she interviewed the surviving passenger from the car and the truck driver. The passenger had no recollection of the event, and the truck driver said he could not say what color the light was because he had been blinded by the sun. He did say that he did not see any eastbound traffic on Route 20 stop or slow down and that he saw the car emerge from behind a house on Route 6. After finishing her investigation, Hendricksmeyer filled out an accident report. The report quoted what the truck driver had said verbatim. It also contained the observation that "apparently the car entered the intersection against a red light," and she had checked a box under the heading "contributing circumstances" which read "failure of vehicle #2 [the car] to yield the right of way." Nearby in the margin in her writing were the words, "teenage driver!"

At trial the defendant company, which is being sued on a *respondeat superior* theory, calls the truck driver, who repeats the observations he made to the officer and is vigorously cross-examined about them. The company also calls Hendricksmeyer and asks her to describe in detail the accident scene as it appeared to her and the investigation she conducted. However, the defense does not ask Hendricksmeyer whether she had

---

[145] United States v. Hayes, 861 F.2d 1225 (10th Cir. 1988); United States v. Sokolow, 81 F.3d 397 (3d Cir. 1996).

reached any judgments regarding the cause of the accident. Later in the trial, after Hendricksmeyer has been excused, the company offers her accident report. **Should it be admitted over the plaintiff's objection?**

Problem VI-68. Bob Sherill was arrested along with his girl friend, Phyllis Nowak for dealing in drugs and explosives. Nowak gave the police a detailed written statement describing Sherill's illegal activities as well as her own fear of him. A police stenographer took the statement down, and Nowak signed each page and initialed 11 changes in wording that she made when the statement was read back to her. Only Sherill was indicted. At trial Nowak admitted making the statement but said she didn't remember much about it or about what activities of Sherill's prompted it because she had been strung out on drugs at the time she made the statement and for some days before that. The state offers the statement as Nowak's past recollection recorded, and the judge allows it to be read to the jury, finding that Nowak's attempt to distance herself from the statement was "evasive" and "disingenuous," resulting from either her fear of Sherill or her newly professed desire to marry him. **Did the judge reach the right decision?**

Problem VI-69. At 11:30 P.M. on December 3, 2010, a car driven by Neil Nyland collided with one driven by Belinda Bryce, causing considerable damage to both vehicles and severely injuring Ms. Bryce. Rachel Duty, a passenger in Nyland's car, suffered minor injuries. The day after the accident Sam Kalven, an accident investigator for Nyland's insurance company, interviewed Nyland and Duty. Both told stories that tended to exonerate Nyland. Three days after the accident Kalven interviewed Bryce and took her statement. Bryce's story was somewhat mixed. She placed the responsibility for the accident on Nyland, but she stated that she had had several drinks shortly before the accident, that she had left a party early because she felt sleepy, and that she had left her eyeglasses at the party. Shortly after the interview, Bryce brought suit against Nyland alleging that his negligence was responsible for the accident. The case did not reach trial until two and a half years later. At the trial, Nyland's lawyer (DC) put both Duty and Kalven on the stand. The following material is extracted from their testimony:

TESTIMONY OF RACHEL DUTY

DC: [*after asking a series of preliminary questions*] Now Ms. Duty, can you tell the jury the way this intersection looked at the time of the accident?

Duty: Well, my memory is rather vague. I'm not sure I can describe it.

DC: Let me show you this picture, perhaps that will refresh your memory. [*He first hands a copy to plaintiff's counsel, who immediately rises to her feet.*]

PC: Your Honor, a picture can't be used to refresh memory. Besides, according to the date on the back, this picture was taken two weeks ago. It's now summer. The accident occurred two and a half years ago during the winter. This can't be used to refresh memory.

Court: It's only to refresh memory. I'll let that in.

[Is the court's ruling on this point correct?]

DC: Your Honor, I'd like to show this picture to the jury as well.

[How should the court respond to this request? How should it rule if plaintiff's counsel makes the request?]

. . .

DC: Thank you, Ms. Duty. That was a very complete description. Now I would like to call your attention to the accident itself. Can you tell the jury in your own words what happened as you approached the intersection?

Duty: I'm afraid I cannot. My mind is a complete blank. I only remember that I went into the dashboard, cutting my nose.

DC: Do you remember describing the accident to this man (pointing to Kalven) the day after it occurred?

Duty: Yes, I do.

DC: Will you read this please? [*He hands her two typed sheets of paper.*] Does that refresh your memory?

Duty: Well, it sounds familiar, but I can't say that I have a live memory of what it describes.

DC: Tell me, Ms. Duty, is that your signature at the bottom of this page? [*He hands her a handwritten page.*] Your Honor, the plaintiff has stipulated that the typed pages I previously handed Ms. Duty are a true copy of this original.

Duty: Yes, that's my signature.

DC: Did you sign this statement after it was taken down?

Duty: I must have, I haven't signed it since then.

DC: Your Honor, I would like to offer this paper in evidence either as a business record or as past recollection recorded.

PC: Your Honor, I would like to ask Ms. Duty just one question before you make your ruling.

Court: Proceed.

PC: Ms. Duty, did you read this paper before you signed it?

Duty: I don't remember.

PC: You couldn't swear that you read it, could you?

Duty: Why, no.

PC: In fact, you probably didn't read it, isn't that so?

Duty: I don't know. I guess there's a fifty-fifty chance I didn't read it.

PC: Ms. Duty, can you read the handwriting on this report for the jury right now?

Duty: [*hesitating and stumbling*] I . . . was a passenger . . . in the . . . cab, no car. . . .

PC: Thank you Ms. Duty, that will be all. Your Honor, this cannot be admissible as the witness's past recollection recorded, and it's not a business record. We object to its admission.

[How should the court rule? Why? Is there any way DC might have strengthened the case for admitting this as a business record? As past recollection recorded?]

Court: I'll admit that as recorded recollection.

DC: Thank you, Your Honor. May the clerk enter this in evidence as Defense Exhibit Three?

PC: Your Honor, she can read that to the jury, but the clerk can't enter it in evidence.

[How should the court rule?]

. . .

[*After some preliminary questions the following occurs:*]

DC: Now Mr. Kalven, will you tell the jury when you first saw the plaintiff Belinda Bryce?

Kal: I first saw her three days after the accident.

DC: How did you happen to see her?

Kal: I was sent to interview her.

DC: Were you sent on business?

Kal: Yes, I was.

DC: And did you interview her as part of your business responsibility?

Kal: Yes, I did.

DC: Now, do you often interview people in connection with your business?

Kal: Yes, I do.

DC: These interviews are routine for you?

Kal: Yes, they are.

DC: Did Ms. Bryce talk to you?

Kal: Yes, she did.

DC: Did you make a record of that interview?

Kal: Yes, I regularly make records when I interview people on business.

DC: Do you have the record with you?

Kal: Yes, I do. [*He produces five typed pages.*]

DC: Your Honor, we would like to introduce the second and third pages of this report, which has been marked Defense Exhibit Four, into evidence as a business record.

Court: Any objection counsel?

PC: Yes, let me state first that I don't think this report qualifies, but, if he wants to admit it, he should admit the whole report, not just selected pages.

DC: But only pages two and three are relevant to our case, Your Honor.

[How should a court respond to the claim that the whole report should be admitted if any of it is to be entered?]

Court: [*after ruling on the above claim*] Well, shall I admit the report now, counselor, or do you want to pursue your argument that none of the report should be admitted?

PC: I would like to ask Mr. Kalven a few questions, Your Honor. Mr. Kalven, this report was made three days after the accident, isn't that so?

Kal: Yes, it was.

PC: And it's possible that Ms. Bryce might have forgotten certain facts about the accident in the interim, is it not?

Kal: Yes, it is.

PC: Tell me, Mr. Kalven, is Ms. Bryce employed by the same company that employs you?

Kal: No, she is not.

PC: And just what company is it that employs you?

Kal: The Security Investigation Company.

PC: And that is a wholly owned subsidiary of what company?

DC: [*rising to his feet*] May we approach the bench, Your Honor? [*at the bench:*] Your Honor, that question was asked just to show that the Security Investigation Company works only for the Security Insurance Company. She asked that question just to alert the jury to the fact that the insurance company is the real defendant. There is no need for that question. It's already been established that the report was made in the regular course of Kalven's business as an investigator. It is irrelevant just whom the investigation was being conducted for.]

[How should the court rule on this argument?]

PC: Mr. Kalven, when Ms. Bryce made her statement to you she was under no business duty to tell you anything, was she?

Kal: That is correct.

PC: Your Honor, that report can't come in as a business record. The witness admitted that the report wasn't made at or even near the time of the accident, and the speaker Ms. Bryce was under no business duty to tell Mr. Kalven anything.

[How should the court rule on this question? Are PC's arguments good ones? Could PC have come up with any stronger arguments in support of her claim that the report is inadmissible as a business record? How should DC respond to the arguments PC has made?]

DC: [*After the court rules that the record does not qualify as a business record.*] Mr. Kalven, do you have a present memory of what Ms. Bryce told you when you interviewed her?

Kal: No, I do not.

DC: Now, when you record someone's statement, do you make an accurate record of what they have said?

Kal: Yes, I do.

DC: You transcribe what they say?

Kal: No, I do not.

DC: [*obviously surprised and disappointed*] You don't?

Kal: No.

DC: What do you do?

Kal: Well, I take down in my own words, summarizing as I go along, the gist of what was said.

DC: [*recovering*] Are these summaries accurate?

Kal: Yes, they are.

DC: You are positive that this summary, even though you don't remember it now, was, when you took it down, faithful to what Ms. Bryce had told you?

Kal: Yes, I am.

DC: Mr. Kalven, will you please read your notes to the jury as your past recollection recorded?

PC: Objection, Your Honor. This record wasn't made when the accident was fresh, and the witness has already said that it is not a transcription of what my client told him but rather a summary in his own words. This doesn't qualify for the exception.

[How should the court rule?]

Problem VI-70. Steve Kew was driving along Sloan Street when a little girl, Mary Ames, ran in front of him from between two parked cars. He tried to stop, but he could not stop before his car struck her. Seeing no one around, he picked her up, put her in his car, and sped to the emergency room of the local hospital. While at the hospital an attendant filled out an admission form. In the space labeled "cause of injury" the attendant wrote "Hit by car. Mr. Kew says that the patient jumped out from between two parked cars and that he couldn't stop because his brakes were bad." **If Mary's parents later sue Steve, may Steve introduce his copy of the form to show that Mary had suddenly jumped in front of his car? May the parents introduce the hospital's copy to show that Steve's brakes were bad?**

Problem VI-71. Following the accident described in the preceding problem, Mary Ames was given emergency treatment and admitted to the hospital. Mary's parents want to introduce the following extracts from her hospital chart under the business entry exception. **May they introduce any or all of this information to prove Mary's injuries?**

1. (By a doctor) X-rays reveal broken ribs and chipped collarbone. Patient complains of numbness in right leg. Nerve damage suspected.

2. (By a nurse) Patient in obvious pain. Administered sedative.

3. (By a doctor) Right foot still numb. Nerve damage caused when she was thrown on her back. Recommend physical therapy. Patient will never walk without a slight limp.

May the defendant Kew introduce the following extracts from the hospital records?

1. (By a nurse) Mary is remarkably cheerful. She brightens up life for everyone on the ward and is being showered with attention by

both patients and staff. Yesterday when she got the Teddy Bear, she said she didn't think she ever wanted to go home.

2.   (By a physical therapist) Numbness not serious. Only outpatient care is needed now. She will be walking normally within two years.

3.   (By a doctor) Patients and staff must not sympathize with Mary when she limps. I think she is exaggerating walking difficulties to get attention.

Problem VI-72. Rules of the Camden Chemical Company require all employees wishing to leave early to report to their supervisor, and require the supervisor to report the reasons the employee wishes to leave to the head supervisor, who has authority to grant permission. One day Shelley Fraser, the supervisor of the chemical lab, called Harry Armstrong, the head supervisor, to report that Alex Earnst had requested permission to leave early because he felt sick following an accident in the chemical lab that released a dense cloud of yellow gas. Permission was given. Two days later Earnst died. His widow sued for survivor's benefits under the state workers' compensation statute. There is some evidence that Earnst's death was caused by chemical burns to his lungs. **In order to prove that the cause of death was work-related, may Mrs. Earnst introduce Armstrong to report what Fraser said to him on the theory that this was a business record?**

Problem VI-73. Joan Sanders witnessed an auto accident and heroically helped two teenagers escape from a burning car. She was burned slightly in the effort and was in some pain when the police arrived 15 minutes later. She briefly told the police that she had seen a blue Lexus swerve across the center line into the car driven by the teenagers. She was then taken to the hospital for treatment. Five days later, at a friend's suggestion, she wrote down a more detailed description of what she had seen.

At the trial two years later, will the police report be admissible under the business records exception against the driver of the Lexus? Will the statement Sanders wrote five days after the accident be admissible as Sanders's past recollection recorded? What questions would you ask Sanders in an attempt to qualify this statement as past recollection recorded?

Problem VI-74. Salesperson A at the J.C. Nickels Department Store sold a television set to the defendant for $800 and wrote a receipt charging the T.V. to the defendant's account. The store's copy of the receipt went to floor manager B, who gave it to bookkeeper C, who copied it into a daybook. Daybook entries were given to bookkeeper D, who copied all information relating to sales on account into a ledger book. Ledger books were sent once a week to the chain's central data processing facility, where E coded the information and gave it to F, who punched it on machine-readable cards and then gave the cards to G, who entered them on the Nickels computer. The computer had been programmed by H, I, and J to send monthly bills to all those with open charge accounts and to print weekly lists of all accounts that were three months overdue. Names on this list and amounts owed were mailed to the credit managers of the stores where the transactions occurred and the credit managers wrote letters to the delinquent debtors. The weekly lists were then destroyed. Assume that the defendant's name has reached the credit manager in this way and the appropriate dunning letter has been written. Two days after the letter was mailed to the defendant, the central data processing facility was gutted by fire, destroying the ledger books stored there and the computer. **If Nickels sues the defendant for money due on the television, and the defendant states she never owed any money, may the letter from the credit manager be introduced as a business record to establish the existence and the amount of the debt? If you were the attorney for Nickels, what would you do to establish a foundation for admitting the letter as a business record? What is the minimum number of witnesses you would have to call?**

Problem VI-75. Paul Oakes is charged with possession of heroin. The government intends to call as its final witness Dr. Waterman, a chemist who analyzed the white powder taken from Oakes and identified it as heroin. Waterman is employed by the Customs Service. On the day of the trial Waterman is present, looking somewhat ill, but he is unable to testify because of unexpected delays in the presentation of the government's case. The next day Waterman is unable to testify because he is suffering from a high fever and severe bronchial infection. Rather than seek a continuance, the government calls Dr. Barrels, a chemist who works with Waterman in the Customs Service Laboratory. Dr. Barrels testifies to the routine procedures that are used in preparing worksheets and final reports. She identifies two government exhibits as a worksheet and a final report of a chemical analysis done by her colleague Waterman (whose handwriting she recognizes) in the Customs Service Laboratory. The documents describe the substance taken from an envelope marked "P. Oakes" as a white powder and identify it as heroin. The government seeks to introduce these documents as either business records or public records. **Setting aside any possible Confrontation Clause Objection, are they admissible under either or both theories?**

Problem VI-76. Hungate is charged with burglary. The strongest evidence against him is a fingerprint found on a sterling silver knife that was dropped by the burglar as he fled. The defense argues that the fingerprint was planted on the knife some two months after the robbery because Hungate testified against a police officer in a civil rights action charging police brutality. In its case in rebuttal, the government introduces a clerk who works in the FBI's fingerprint identification laboratory. She testifies that as soon as a print enters the office for analysis it is stamped with its date of receipt and a sequential identification number. The government then introduces the identification card that contains Hungate's print. It is dated eight days after the burglary. The government also introduces the ten identification cards that follow Hungate's card in numerical sequence. The first six have the same date as Hungate's card and the last four are dated nine days after the burglary. The government offers these cards to show the date on which the print was received as either a business record or a public record or report. **Should the cards be admitted?**

Assume that the fingerprint found on the knife did not belong to Hungate. He offers the FBI report containing the fingerprint found on the knife to prove the truth of what it asserts: namely, that "the instant print is not that of the suspect Hungate or of anyone living in the victim's house. It is consistent with the prints of Fred Smith, who according to our records has three convictions for petty larceny and an arrest for burglary, but there are too few points to make a definite match." In offering the evidence Hungate's attorney cites only FRE 803(8). The trial court refuses to admit the evidence under that exception and, following his conviction, Hungate appeals. **Did the trial judge commit reversible error?**

Problem VI-77. The police suspected that David Mendes was selling narcotics after an informant made a controlled buy of four rocks of crack cocaine and reported that drugs and guns were stored in his apartment. Officer Beatty sought a search warrant for the apartment at 12 Washington Place, noting the details of the controlled buy and indicating that the apartment was leased and lived in by one David Mendes. When the raid was conducted the police found not just Mendes in the apartment, but also a woman named Joyce Goslin. A search of the apartment turned up three guns, 36.12 grams of crack, some of which was in zip lock bags, men's and women's clothing, and letters addressed to both Goslin and Mendes. After the search, Beatty filled out arrest reports. In his report on Mendes he listed as the reason for arrest, "possession of crack cocaine for sale and unlicensed guns." On the form for Goslin he wrote, "suspicion, pending further investigation."

Later Goslin was also charged with possession of the crack cocaine and weapons. She argues that she had just come to the apartment to buy several rocks of crack and has no other connection to the guns or crack for sale. To support her case she wishes to introduce the sworn affidavit Officer Beatty submitted to get the search warrant and the arrest report on Mendes. **Are these admissible?**

Problem VI-78. In 1998 the Secretary of HEW, pursuant to authority granted him by law, ordered the Surgeon General to establish a task force to study problems associated with DES, a drug once used to prevent miscarriages and other purposes but now thought to cause cancer and chromosomal damage. The task force consisted of a group of doctors and other experts employed by various departments of the federal government. In addition a large group of consultants participated in the hearings of the task force and in the preparation of the final report. The consultants included both doctors and non-professionals, some of whom were active in organized efforts to expose the allegedly harmful effects of DES (e.g., the president of DES Action and the director of the Health Research Group, a Ralph Nader organization). No representative of the pharmaceutical industry was on the task force or among its consultants. The group did no original research, but reviewed the scientific literature relating to DES and met on eight occasions to talk about the health effects of DES. At these meetings a wide variety of persons, not otherwise associated with the project, presented their views and data to the task force. The final report of the task force finds that there are serious dangers associated with DES; it makes a number of "action recommendations" and discusses their scientific basis, and it recommends further research to fill in the gaps in what is known about DES.

Plaintiff brings an action against a manufacturer of DES. She alleges that she has certain deformities because her mother was given DES. She would like to introduce the report of the HEW task force to establish the dangers of DES and the fact that it can cause conditions such as hers. **Should the report be admitted?**

h.   Other Exceptions

We have now discussed the most important of the FRE 803 exceptions to the hearsay rule, but many other hearsay exceptions also do not require prior proof of the speaker's unavailability. The number and nature of these exceptions vary from state to state. We present the specific exceptions found in FRE 803 as examples of the kinds of additional exceptions that will be found in the various states. The Advisory Committee's notes (ACN) are included to give you some idea of the policies that lie behind these exceptions and of their relation to the common law.[146]

---

[146] The Advisory Committee prefaces its comments on the exceptions as follows: The exceptions are phrased in terms of non-application of the hearsay rule, rather than in positive terms of admissibility, in order to repel any implication that other possible grounds for exclusion are eliminated from consideration.

The present rule proceeds upon the theory that under appropriate circumstances a hearsay statement may possess circumstantial guarantees of trustworthiness sufficient to justify non-production of the speaker in person at the trial even though he may be available. The theory finds vast support in the many exceptions to the hearsay rule developed by the common law in which unavailability of the speaker is not a relevant factor. The present rule is a synthesis of them, with revision where modern developments and conditions are believed to make that course appropriate.

In a hearsay situation, the speaker is, of course, a witness, and neither this rule nor Rule 804 dispenses with the requirement of firsthand knowledge. It may appear from his statement or be inferable from circumstances. *See* Rule 602.

Most of these exceptions engender little controversy and more or less track the common law. However, a few are truly innovative. FRE 803(16) transforms a rule of authentication into a hearsay exception. At common law, an *ancient* document—defined as one that was at least 30 years old—was presumed genuine unless the circumstances in which it was found suggested otherwise. However, the statements it contained were not admissible for their truth unless they qualified under some hearsay exception. Now the appellation *ancient* attaches after 20 years, and the presumption of genuineness brings with it a hearsay exception.

FRE 803(18) broadens a rule of impeachment and transforms it into a hearsay exception. At common law, an expert witness could be impeached by statements in treatises or other scholarly literature inconsistent with her testimony, provided that (depending on the jurisdiction) she admitted that she had relied on that literature, or she acknowledged it to be authoritative, or the authoritativeness of the literature was otherwise established. A party could not, however, offer statements from scholarly works as substantive evidence to support its case. FRE 803(18) allows a party to read to the jury statements from any reliable authority on any science or art to prove what the statements assert. An expert must be on the stand when the work is offered and available to comment on what is read. The expert need not acknowledge the work as authoritative as long as the proponent can prove its authoritative nature by other means. The rule can be useful when a party has difficulty recruiting distinguished experts to testify on its behalf. In some localities this is reputed to be the case in tort actions for medical malpractice. Under the rule, a party may bolster an undistinguished expert's testimony by reading from treatises or other authoritative sources. Of course, a selective reading of what a source says, or a partisan expert's interpretation of it, may be confusing or misleading.[147]

FRE 803(22) creates a hearsay exception for felony judgments entered upon guilty pleas or guilty verdicts in criminal trials. Subject to certain limitations, such judgments are admissible to prove facts essential to the judgment. Guilty pleas are admissions when offered against the person making the plea, but the rule makes them more broadly admissible. Jury verdicts are hearsay when used to prove facts essential to the judgment because they are, in effect, the jurors' out-of-court assertions that particular facts have been found. The problem posed by this exception is how to determine what facts were essential to a judgment, for these are the only facts that one can be sure the jury found by proof beyond a reasonable doubt. Because FRE 803(22) is only a hearsay exception, a party can dispute the implications of a guilty plea or verdict that is offered against him. However, in some jurisdictions, rules

---

[147] See Chapter Nine, pp. 1142–1148.

of *res judicata* or collateral estoppel may make a guilty plea or verdict incontrovertible when offered in related litigation to prove certain facts.

With these comments by way of preamble, here are the remaining FRE 803 exceptions:

(9) Public Records of Vital Statistics. A record of a birth, death, or marriage, if reported to a public office in accordance with a legal duty.

[**ACN** Advisory Committee Note)], Records of vital statistics are commonly the subject of particular statutes making them admissible in evidence. The rule is in principle narrower than Uniform Rule 63(16) which includes reports required of persons performing functions authorized by statute, yet in practical effect the two are substantially the same. . . .

(10) Absence of a Public Record. Testimony—or a certification under Rule 902—that a diligent search failed to disclose a public record or statement if the testimony or certification is admitted to prove that:

(A) the record or statement does not exist; or

(B) a matter did not occur or exist, if a public office regularly kept a record or statement for a matter of that kind.

[**ACN**] The principle of proving nonoccurrence of an event by evidence of the absence of a record which would regularly be made of its occurrence, developed in Exception (7) with respect to regularly conducted [business] activities, is here extended to public records of the kind mentioned in Exceptions (8) and (9). Some harmless duplication no doubt exists with Exception (7). . . .

The rule includes situations in which absence of a record may itself be the ultimate focal point of inquiry, e.g. *People v. Love*, 310 Ill. 558, 142 N.E. 204 (1923), certificate of Secretary of State admitted to show failure to file documents required by Securities Law, as well as cases where the absence of a record is offered as proof of the nonoccurrence of an event ordinarily recorded.

The refusal of the common law to allow proof by certificate of the lack of a record or entry has no apparent justification. The rule takes the opposite position, as do Uniform Rule 63(17); California Evidence Code § 1284; . . . Congress has recognized certification as evidence of the lack of a record. 8 U.S.C. § 1360(d), certificate of Attorney General or other designated officer that no record of Immigration and Naturalization Service of specified nature or entry therein is found, admissible in alien cases.

(11) Records of Religious Organizations Concerning Personal or Family History. A statement of birth, legitimacy, ancestry, marriage, divorce, death, relationship by blood or marriage, or similar facts of personal or family history, contained in a regularly kept record of a religious organization.

[ACN] Records of activities of religious organizations are currently recognized as admissible at least to the extent of the business records exception to the hearsay rule, and Exception (6) would be applicable. However, both the business record doctrine and Exception (6) require that the person furnishing the information be one in the business or activity. The result is such decisions as *Dailey v. Grand Lodge*, 311 Ill. 184, 142 N.E. 478 (1924), holding a church record admissible to prove fact, date, and place of baptism, but not age of child except that he had at least been born at the time. In view of the unlikelihood that false information would be furnished on occasions of this kind, the rule contains no requirement that the informant be in the course of the activity.

(12) Certificates of Marriage, Baptism, and Similar Ceremonies. A statement of fact contained in a certificate:

(A) made by a person who is authorized by a religious organization or by law to perform the act certified;

(B) attesting that the person performed a marriage or similar ceremony or administered a sacrament; and

(C) purporting to have been issued at the time of the act or within a reasonable time after it.

[ACN] The principle of proof by certification is recognized as to public officials in Exceptions (8) and (10), and with respect to authentication in Rule 902. The present exception is a duplication to the extent that it deals with a certificate by a public official, as in the case of a judge who performs a marriage ceremony. The area covered by the rule is, however, substantially larger and extends the certification procedure to clergymen and the like who perform marriages and other ceremonies or administer sacraments. Thus certificates of such matters as baptism or confirmation, as well as marriage, are included. In principle they are as acceptable evidence as certificates of public officers. . . . When the person executing the certificate is not a public official, the self-authenticating character of documents purporting to emanate from public officials, see rule 902, is lacking and proof is required that the person was authorized and did make the certificate. The time element, however, may safely be taken as supplied by the certificate, once authority and authenticity are established, particularly in view of the presumption that a document was executed on the date it bears.

(13) Family Records. A statement of fact about personal or family history contained in a family record, such as a Bible, genealogy, chart, engraving on a ring, inscription on a portrait, or engraving on an urn or burial marker.

[ACN] Records of family history kept in family Bibles have by long tradition been received in evidence. . . . Opinions in the area also include inscriptions on tombstones, publicly displayed pedigrees, and engravings on rings.

(14) Records of Documents That Affect an Interest in Property. The record of a document that purports to establish or affect an interest in property if:

(A) the record is admitted to prove the content of the original recorded document, along with its signing and its delivery by each person who purports to have signed it;

(B) the record is kept in a public office; and

(C) a statute authorizes recording documents of that kind in that office.

[ACN] The recording of title documents is a purely statutory development. Under any theory of the admissibility of public records, the records would be receivable as evidence of the contents of the recorded document, else the recording process would be reduced to a nullity. When, however, the record is offered for the further purpose of proving execution and delivery, a problem of lack of firsthand knowledge by the recorder, not present as to contents, is presented. This problem is solved, seemingly in all jurisdictions, by qualifying for recording only those documents shown by a specified procedure, either acknowledgment or a form of probate, to have been executed and delivered. Thus what may appear in the rule, at first glance, as endowing the record with an effect independently of local law and inviting difficulties of an *Erie* nature . . . is not present, since the local law in fact governs under the example.

(15) Statements in Documents That Affect an Interest in Property. A statement contained in a document that purports to establish or affect an interest in property if the matter stated was relevant to the document's purpose—unless later dealings with the property are inconsistent with the truth of the statement or the purport of the document.

[ACN] Dispositive documents often contain recitals of fact. Thus a deed purporting to have been executed by an attorney in fact may recite the existence of the power of attorney, or a deed may recite that the grantors are all the heirs of the last record owner. Under the rule, these recitals are exempted from the hearsay rule. The circumstances under which dispositive documents are executed and the requirement that the recital be germane to the purpose of the document are believed to be adequate guarantees of trustworthiness, particularly in view of the non-applicability of the rule if dealings with the property have been inconsistent with the document. The age of the document is of no significance, though in practical application the document will most often be an ancient one.

(16) Statements in Ancient Documents. A statement in a document that is at least 20 years old and whose authenticity is established.

[ACN] Authenticating a document as ancient, essentially in the pattern of the common law, as provided in Rule 901(b)(8), leaves open as a separate question the admissibility of assertive statements contained therein as against a hearsay objection. Wigmore further states that the ancient document technique of authentication is universally conceded to apply to all sorts of documents, including letters, records, contracts, maps, and certificates, in addition to title documents, citing numerous decisions. Since most of these items are significant evidentially only insofar as they are assertive, their admission in evidence must be as a hearsay exception. The former position is believed to be the correct one in reason and authority. As pointed out in McCormick § 298, danger of mistake is minimized by authentication requirements, and age affords assurance that the writing antedates the present controversy.

(17) Market Reports and Similar Commercial Publications. Market quotations, lists, directories, or other compilations that are generally relied on by the public or by persons in particular occupations.

[ACN] Ample authority at common law supported the admission in evidence of items falling in this category. While Wigmore's text is narrowly oriented to lists, etc., prepared for the use of a trade or profession, authorities are cited which include other kinds of publications, for example, newspaper market reports, telephone directories, and city directories. The basis of trustworthiness is general reliance by the public or by a particular segment of it, and the motivation of the compiler to foster reliance by being accurate. . . .

    Uniform Commercial Code § 2–724 provides for admissibility in evidence of "reports in official publications or trade journals or in newspapers or periodicals of general circulation published as the reports of such [established commodity] market."

(18) Statements in Learned Treatises, Periodicals, or Pamphlets. A statement contained in a treatise, periodical, or pamphlet if:

(A) the statement is called to the attention of an expert witness on cross-examination or relied on by the expert on direct examination; and

(B) the publication is established as a reliable authority by the expert's admission or testimony, by another expert's testimony, or by judicial notice.

If admitted, the statement may be read into evidence but not received as an exhibit.

[ACN] The writers have generally favored the admissibility of learned treatises, with the support of occasional decisions and rules, but the great weight of authority has been that learned treatises are not admissible as substantive evidence though usable in the cross-examination of experts. The foundation of the minority view is that the hearsay objection must be regarded as unimpressive when directed against treatises since a high standard of accuracy is engendered by various factors: the treatise is written primarily and impartially for professionals, subject to scrutiny and exposure for inaccuracy, with the reputation of the writer at stake. Sound as this position may be with respect to trustworthiness, there is, nevertheless, an additional difficulty in the likelihood that the treatise will be misunderstood and misapplied without expert assistance and supervision. This difficulty is recognized in the cases demonstrating unwillingness to sustain findings relative to disability on the basis of judicially noticed medical texts. The rule avoids the danger of misunderstanding and misapplication by limiting the use of treatises as substantive evidence to situations in which an expert is on the stand and available to explain and assist in the application of the treatise if desired. The limitation upon receiving the publication itself physically in evidence, contained in the last sentence, is designed to further this policy.

The relevance of the use of treatises on cross-examination is evident. This use of treatises has been the subject of varied views. The most restrictive position is that the witness must have stated expressly on direct his reliance upon the treatise. A slightly more liberal approach still insists upon reliance but allows it to be developed on cross-examination. Further relaxation dispenses with reliance but requires recognition as an authority by the witness, developable on cross-examination. The greatest liberality is found in decisions allowing use of the treatise on cross-examination when its status as an authority is established by any means. The exception is hinged upon this last position, which is that of the Supreme Court, *Reilly v. Pinkus*, 338 U.S. 269 (1949), and of recent well considered state court decisions.

In *Reilly v. Pinkus*, supra, the Court pointed out that testing of professional knowledge was incomplete without exploration of the witness' knowledge of and attitude toward established treatises in the field. The process works equally well in reverse and furnishes the basis of the rule.

The rule does not require that the witness rely upon or recognize the treatise as authoritative, thus avoiding the possibility that the expert may at the outset block cross-examination by refusing to concede reliance or authoritativeness. Moreover, the rule avoids the unreality of admitting evidence for the purpose of impeachment only, with an instruction to the jury not to consider it otherwise. The parallel to the treatment of prior inconsistent statements will be apparent. See Rules 613(b) and 801(d)(1).

(19) Reputation Concerning Personal or Family History. A reputation among a person's family by blood, adoption, or marriage— or among a person's associates or in the community—concerning the person's birth, adoption, legitimacy, ancestry, marriage, divorce, death, relationship by blood, adoption, or marriage, or similar facts of personal or family history.

(20) Reputation Concerning Boundaries or General History. A reputation in a community—arising before the controversy— concerning boundaries of land in the community or customs that affect the land, or concerning general historical events important to that community, state, or nation.

(21) Reputation Concerning Character. A reputation among a person's associates or in the community concerning the person's character.

[ACN] Trustworthiness in reputation evidence is found "when the topic is such that the facts are likely to have been inquired about and that persons having personal knowledge have disclosed facts which have thus been discussed in the community; and thus the community's conclusion, if any has been formed, is likely to be a trustworthy one." On this common foundation, reputation as to land boundaries, customs, general history, character, and marriage have come to be regarded as admissible. The breadth of the underlying principle suggests the formulation of an equally broad exception, but tradition has in fact been much narrower and more particularized, and this is the pattern of these exceptions in the rule.

Exception (19) is concerned with matters of personal and family history. Marriage is universally conceded to be a proper subject of proof by evidence of reputation in the community. As to such items as legitimacy, relationship, adoption, birth, and death, the decisions are divided. All seem to be susceptible to being the subject of well-founded repute. The "world" in which the reputation may exist may be family, associates, or community. This world has proved capable of expanding with changing times from the single uncomplicated neighborhood, in which all activities take place, to the multiple and unrelated worlds of work, religious affiliation, and social activity, in each of which a reputation may be generated. The family has often served as the point of beginning for allowing community reputation. . . .

The first portion of Exception (20) is based upon the general admissibility of evidence of reputation as to land boundaries and land customs, expanded in this country to include private as well as public boundaries. The reputation is required to antedate the controversy, though not to be ancient. The second portion is likewise supported by authority, and is designed to facilitate proof of events when judicial notice is not available. The historical character of the subject matter dispenses with any need that the reputation antedate the controversy with respect to which it is offered. . . .

Exception (21) recognizes the traditional acceptance of reputation evidence as a means of proving human character. The exception deals only with the hearsay aspect of this kind of evidence. Limitations upon admissibility based on other grounds will be found in rules 404, relevancy of character evidence generally, and 608, character of witness. The exception is in effect a reiteration, in the context of hearsay, of Rule 405(a).

(22) Judgment of a Previous Conviction. Evidence of a final judgment of conviction if:

(A) the judgment was entered after a trial or guilty plea, but not a nolo contendere plea;

(B) the conviction was for a crime punishable by death or by imprisonment for more than a year;

(C) the evidence is admitted to prove any fact essential to the judgment; and

(D) when offered by the prosecutor in a criminal case for a purpose other than impeachment, the judgment was against the defendant.

The pendency of an appeal may be shown but does not affect admissibility.

[ACN] When the status of a former judgment is under consideration in subsequent litigation, three possibilities must be noted: (1) the former judgment is conclusive under the doctrine of res judicata, either as a bar or a collateral estoppel: or (2) it is admissible in evidence for what it is worth: or (3) it may be of no effect at all. The first situation does not involve any problem of evidence except in the way that principles of substantive law generally bear upon the relevancy and materiality of evidence. The rule does not deal with the substantive effect of the judgment as a bar or collateral estoppel. When, however, the doctrine of res judicata does not apply to make the judgment either a bar or a collateral estoppel, a choice is presented between the second and third alternatives. The rule adopts the second for judgments of criminal conviction of felony grade. This is the direction of the decisions, which manifest an increasing reluctance to reject in toto the validity of the law's fact-finding processes outside the confines of res judicata and collateral estoppel. While this may leave a jury with the evidence of conviction but without means to evaluate it, it seems safe to assume that the jury will give it substantial effect unless defendant offers a satisfactory explanation, a possibility not foreclosed by the provision. But see *North River Ins. Co. v. Militello*, 104 Colo. 28, 88 P.2d 567 (1939), in which the jury found for plaintiff on a fire policy despite the introduction of his conviction for arson. . . .

Practical considerations require exclusion of convictions of minor offenses, not because the administration of justice in its lower echelons must be inferior, but because motivation to defend at this level is so often minimal or nonexistent. Hence the rule includes only convictions of felony grade, measured by federal standards.

Judgments of conviction based upon pleas of nolo contendere are not included. This position is consistent with the treatment of nolo pleas in Rule 410. . . .

While these rules do not in general purport to resolve constitutional issues, they have in general been drafted with a view to avoiding collision with constitutional principles. Consequently the exception does not include evidence of the conviction of a third person, offered against the accused in a criminal prosecution to prove any fact essential to sustain the judgment of conviction. A contrary position would seem clearly to violate the right of confrontation. *Kirby v. United States*, 174 U.S. 47 (1899), error to convict of possessing stolen postage stamps with the only evidence of theft being the record of conviction of the thieves. The situation is to be distinguished from cases in which conviction of another person is an element of the crime, e.g. 15 U.S.C. § 902(d), interstate shipment of firearms to a known convicted felon, and, as specifically provided, from impeachment.

(23) Judgments Involving Personal, Family, or General History, or a Boundary. A judgment that is admitted to prove a matter of personal, family, or general history, or boundaries, if the matter:

(A) was essential to the judgment; and

(B) could be proved by evidence of reputation.

[ACN] A hearsay exception in this area was originally justified on the ground that verdicts were evidence of reputation. As trial by jury graduated from the category of neighborhood inquests, this theory lost its validity. It was never valid as to chancery decrees. Nevertheless the rule persisted, though the judges and writers shifted ground and began saying that the judgment or decree was as good evidence as reputation. The shift appears to be correct, since the process of inquiry, sifting, and scrutiny which is relied upon to render reputation reliable is present in perhaps greater measure in the process of litigation. While this might suggest a broader area of application, the affinity to reputation is strong, and paragraph (23) goes no further, not even including character.

The leading case in the United States, *Patterson v. Gaines*, 47 U.S. (6 How.) 550, 599 (1848), follows in the pattern of the English decisions, mentioning as illustrative matters thus provable: manorial rights, public rights of way, immemorial custom, disputed boundary, and pedigree.

———————

Problem VI-79. Anthony Gebippe died in August 2013 and left his entire estate to the Indiana University Foundation by a will dated six months before his death. It is alleged that part of the estate included a large house and land in Bedford, currently occupied by Harry Gebippe, Anthony's son.

Harry has challenged the will in probate court, alleging that on the date of death the property in Bedford belonged to him (Harry), not his father. He further challenged the will on the grounds that Anthony was not competent at the time he executed the will in question.

(1) Harry offers into evidence a certified copy of a deed, dated June 15, 2007, which appears to pass title to the Bedford property from Anthony to Harry. The certification indicates that the original is on file with the clerk of court. The lawyer for the Foundation objects on hearsay grounds. **Is the document admissible?**

(2) Harry offers into evidence a written court judgment finding Anthony to be dangerous because of mental disease and ordering him (Anthony) committed to the State Hospital. The judgment is dated the day after the will was signed. **Is it admissible over a hearsay objection?**

(3) To prove the value of several copyrights that are part of the estate, Harry offers a certified copy of Anthony's 2012 tax return obtained from the I.R.S. **Would this document be admissible over a hearsay objection?**

(4) Finally, Harry wishes to produce a certified copy of Anthony's death certificate on which the cause of death is listed as brain tumor, signed by Dr. Frank Stein of the State Hospital for the Insane. **Is it admissible over a hearsay objection?**

"I'm not going to make excuses. They were very tough today. They wanted this one more than we did, and they deserved to win."

2. Hearsay Exceptions Conditioned on Unavailability

a. *Requirement of Unavailability*

i. *The Meaning of "Unavailable"*

As a precondition to admitting certain kinds of hearsay evidence, the proponent must show that the speaker is not available to testify. One would suppose that hearsay that is admissible only if the speaker has been shown to be unavailable is less reliable than hearsay admitted without regard to availability. This is the prevailing view. In its commentary accompanying the federal hearsay rules the Advisory Committee writes:

> [Rule 803] is based upon the assumption that a hearsay statement falling within one of its exceptions possesses qualities which justify the conclusion that whether the declarant is available or unavailable is not a relevant factor in determining

admissibility. The instant rule [804] proceeds upon a different theory: hearsay which admittedly is not equal in quality to testimony of the declarant on the stand may nevertheless be admitted if the declarant is unavailable and if his statement meets a specified standard. The rule expresses preferences: testimony given on the stand in person is preferred over hearsay, and hearsay, if of the specified quality, is preferred over complete loss of the evidence of the declarant.

These comments make sense of the distinction between the FRE 803 and FRE 804 exceptions, but they are far from indisputable. After you have studied the exceptions discussed in this section, compare the exception for present sense impressions with the exception for former testimony, or the excited utterance exception with the exception for statements against interest. Many of the hearsay statements admitted by the FRE 804 exceptions have more indicia of reliability than some of the FRE 803 exceptions. But the drafters did not rethink the relative reliability of hearsay versus courtroom testimony; instead they relied on history and the common law to determine when unavailability would be required.

At common law, the requirement of unavailability was defined separately for each of the exceptions conditioned on it, but the Federal Rules take the sensible position that it is the fact of unavailability and not the reason for it that matters. FRE 804(a) specifies the circumstances in which a speaker is considered unavailable:

Criteria for Being Unavailable. A declarant is considered to be unavailable as a witness if the declarant

> **(1)** is exempted from testifying about the subject matter of the declarant's statement because the court rules that a privilege applies;
>
> **(2)** refuses to testify about the subject matter despite a court order to do so;
>
> **(3)** testifies to not remembering the subject matter;
>
> **(4)** cannot be present or testify at the trial or hearing because of death or a then-existing infirmity, physical illness, or mental illness; or
>
> **(5)** is absent from the trial or hearing and the statement's proponent has not been able, by process or other reasonable means, to procure:
>
> > **(A)** the declarant's attendance, in the case of a hearsay exception under Rule 804(b)(1) or (6); or
> >
> > **(B)** the declarant's attendance or testimony, in the case of a hearsay exception under Rule 804(b)(2), (3), or (4).

But this subdivision (a) does not apply if the statement's proponent procured or wrongfully caused the declarant's unavailability as a witness in order to prevent the declarant from attending or testifying.

The states generally follow the Federal Rule in accepting death, physical disability, mental illness, absence from the jurisdiction, and privilege as grounds for unavailability. The provision that unavailability is not established when the party offering the hearsay is responsible for the speaker's absence also codifies prior practice. A few states are unwilling to find unavailability when a speaker present at the trial refuses to testify. The fear is that the proponent of the hearsay has secured this refusal. More states balk when a witness claims lack of memory. The worry here is that forgetfulness is feigned to avoid cross-examination. The Federal Rule makes no mention of statutory incompetence as a ground of unavailability, an oversight in view of FRE 601.[148] In state courts, statutory incompetence is usually an accepted source of unavailability. The federal courts should reach the same result despite the codifiers' oversight.

State courts often find the unavailability requirement satisfied if a speaker can be shown to be absent from the jurisdiction and thus beyond the process of the state court. Under FRE 804(a)(5), showing a witness to be beyond the reach of process is not enough. One must be unable to secure the witness's attendance by means other than a subpoena and, except for the use of former testimony under FRE 804(b)(1), attempts to depose must have been unsuccessful before the witness's absence will be accepted as tantamount to unavailability.

ii. Constitutional Aspects

In civil cases the states may continue to accept absence from the jurisdiction as sufficient to establish unavailability. But in criminal cases, the right to confrontation guaranteed by the Sixth Amendment requires the state to do more than show mere absence as a precondition to invoking hearsay exceptions that require unavailability. How much more is required is not clear. Several decisions by the Supreme Court address this issue.

In 1968, in *Barber v. Page*,[149] the Court held that the speaker's absence from the jurisdiction did not by itself overcome Confrontation

---

[148] FRE 601, as transmitted to Congress, provided, "Every person is competent to be a witness except as otherwise provided in these rules." Had this been enacted, there would have been no reason to include incompetence as a ground for unavailability in Rule 804(a). However, Congress amended the rule in diversity actions, so now Dead Man's Statutes and other state rules of competence will render witnesses incompetent in federal court in some cases. The implications of this amendment for the unavailability requirement were no doubt overlooked when FRE 804(a) was approved.

[149] 390 U.S. 719.

Clause objections to the use of prior testimony. In *Barber,* the State of Oklahoma sought to introduce a transcript of testimony that one Woods had given at a preliminary hearing, against his codefendant Barber. At the trial, as a precondition to introducing the transcript, the prosecutor had shown that Woods was in a federal prison in Texas some 225 miles from the Oklahoma courthouse. Although there were serious questions about whether the conditions of the prior testimony exception had been met at the earlier hearing, the Court was willing to assume that there were no constitutional impediments to using Woods' testimony upon a sufficient showing of unavailability; but the Court held a sufficient showing had not been made. The Justices found that Oklahoma had made no effort to secure Woods' presence once it determined that he was located in another state. Yet the policy of the federal prisons to honor *subpoenas ad testificandum* virtually guaranteed that the state could have produced Woods' at trial had it tried.

Barber seemingly established a principle that was both simple and sensible: In a criminal case, a hearsay speaker outside the jurisdiction is unavailable for Confrontation Clause purposes only if the state makes a good faith effort to secure the speaker's attendance at trial, and fails. However, in *Mancusi v. Stubbs,*[150] decided four years after *Barber,* the Court indicated that it was not content with simplicity and sensibility.[151] *Mancusi* involved the validity of Stubbs's conviction for murder on retrial, after an earlier Tennessee conviction was overturned on constitutional grounds. In the interim, Holms, the key witness against Stubbs at the earlier trial, had moved to Sweden. Tennessee made no effort to contact Holms or to persuade him to appear at the retrial.[152] The Court held that even though Holms was a crucial witness, and even though no effort had been made to secure his attendance, admitting his prior testimony did not violate the Confrontation Clause. The Court justified its holding on two grounds. First, it found that had Holms been contacted and refused to attend the retrial he, unlike Woods, could not have been compelled to appear. So the state might not have been able to secure Holms' presence. Second, and more fundamentally, the Court found that Stubbs's earlier opportunity to examine Holms was substantially more conducive to a full and effective cross-examination than Barber's opportunity to examine Woods. Holms, who testified at a trial before a judge, was a crucial witness against Stubbs. Woods was Barber's codefendant, testifying at a

---

[150] 408 U.S. 204 (1972).

[151] From the tone of our comments you have no doubt gathered that we approve of *Barber*, and not of *Mancusi*. The opinions are both short; read them for yourself and decide if you agree with us. Justice Marshall, who wrote the opinion for eight members of the Court in *Barber*, dissented in *Mancusi*, but only Justice Douglas joined him. In the four years between *Barber* and *Mancusi*, Chief Justice Warren and Justices Black, Fortas, and Harlan left the Court and were replaced by Chief Justice Burger and Justices Blackmun, Powell, and Rehnquist.

[152] A subpoena had been mailed to Holms' last known United States address, in Texas. Tennessee called Holms' son to the stand to establish Holms' presence in Sweden, so it appears the state knew where Holms could be reached.

preliminary hearing before a magistrate. Stubbs had cross-examined Holms, since his defense depended largely on shaking Holms' testimony. Barber's attorney had not cross-examined Woods at the preliminary hearing, and it is not clear that he had reason to do so.

After *Mancusi* it appears that the Confrontation Clause allows a state to establish the unavailability required to introduce prior testimony either by failing in a good faith effort to secure the speaker's presence, or by showing that the speaker cannot be compelled to be present and that the speaker's prior testimony was thoroughly tested by cross-examination. Later cases, including, *Ohio v. Roberts* [153] and *Crawford v. Washington*,[154] which has replaced Roberts as the font of Confrontation Clause jurisprudence, cite both *Barber* and *Mancusi* with approval while affirming a good faith test more reminiscent of *Barber* than *Mancusi*. However, *Crawford*, also changes the reach of the Confrontation Clause so that the clause protects only statements that are *testimonial* in nature, a matter we explore in Chapter Seven. For the moment what you should know is that in criminal cases there will be instances where findings of unavailability that were once constrained by the Confrontation Clause are now only constrained by judicial interpretations of FRE 804(a), and other instances where a finding of FRE 804(a) unavailability that once was sufficient to admit hearsay meeting the conditions of one of the FRE 804 exceptions will now not overcome the Confrontation Clause bar.

One wonders why the Court came out as it did in *Mancusi*. The good faith standard of *Barber* is not too much to ask of prosecutors and is likely to generate less reversible error than the complicated balancing of the later case. *Mancusi* is particularly puzzling because it appears that the Court intentionally reached out to limit its holding in *Barber*. On the facts of *Mancusi*, the question the Court answered was of uncertain importance and perhaps moot.[155] In addition, the argument based on the quality of the earlier cross-examination is suspect since Stubbs's first conviction had been overturned because of inadequate assistance of counsel.[156] This case is best explained by the changing policy preferences

---

[153] 448 U.S. 56 (1980).

[154] 541 U.S. 36 (2004).

[155] The validity of Stubbs' second Tennessee conviction was not raised on an appeal from that conviction. It became an issue when Stubbs was convicted of a later offense in New York, because the Tennessee conviction, if valid, would have triggered a New York second-offender statute. However, Stubbs also had another earlier conviction on appeal. If that conviction had been sustained, it too would have triggered the second-offender statute, and there would have been no need to decide the validity of the Tennessee conviction.

[156] The basis for this decision was the fact that counsel had been appointed only four days before trial. Justice Rehnquist, who wrote the opinion in *Mancusi*, argued that Tennessee had apparently never really passed on the adequacy of Stubbs' counsel but had instead adopted a per se rule—not constitutionally required—that no one appointed four days in advance of a murder trial could give adequate representation. After getting this far in the evidence course, do you believe that cross-examination could adequately test a critical witness when the cross-examiner had at most three days to become acquainted with the client, learn about the case, investigate the facts, and prepare for a murder trial?

of Justices appointed to the Supreme Court. It is but one of a number of the Burger and Rehnquist Courts efforts to free state hearsay exceptions from Confrontation Clause constraints that the Warren Court decisions seemed to have imposed. These efforts, as well as the current counter-trend led by Justice Scalia and a possible retreat from his views, are discussed in more detail in Chapter Seven.

Barber, Mancusi, and *Roberts*, the three cases that most directly address the constitutional requisites for unavailability, all involve the prior testimony of speakers who were unavailable because they were absent from the jurisdiction. However, the Court's current cases make clear that Confrontation Clause problems are possible whatever the cause of a speaker's absence.

b. Former Testimony

FRE 804(b) lists several categories of evidence that "are not excluded by the rule against hearsay if the declarant is unavailable as a witness." The first is former testimony:

(1) Former testimony. Testimony that:

> **(A)** was given as a witness at a trial, hearing, or lawful deposition, whether given during the current proceeding or a different one; and

> **(B)** is now offered against a party who had—or, in a civil case, whose predecessor in interest had—an opportunity and similar motive to develop it by direct, cross-, or redirect examination.

The case for this exception is strong because the exception applies only to testimony, and it admits only statements made under oath in situations of some solemnity. These statements may often be proved by transcripts, which reduce the danger of misreporting, and they will frequently have been made much closer in time to the events described than would be possible with live testimony. This means that prior testimony may be more reliable than current testimony, both because the witness's memory may have been fresher,[157] and because there will have been less opportunity for anyone to try to influence the witness to change his story. Finally, the party against whom the statement is offered must have had an opportunity to test the speaker's credibility by direct or cross-examination and must have had a motive to do so similar to the motive at the current trial. The most apparent advantage of courtroom testimony over prior testimony lies in the jury's opportunity to view the witness's demeanor, but there is little reason to believe that demeanor helps in judging witness credibility.

---

[157] This last argument is not as powerful as it may appear. Studies indicate that most forgetting occurs within a few days after an event. Thus, the memory advantage of prior testimony will be most substantial when the earlier hearing occurred only a day or two after the event in question.

For these reasons commentators view the prior testimony exception favorably. Wigmore went so far as to argue that the earlier opportunity for cross-examination means prior testimony is not hearsay.[158] Others have wondered why prior testimony requires the speaker's unavailability when exceptions likely to admit less reliable hearsay require no such showing.[159] Most commentators support broadening the exception by expanding the category of individuals against whom prior testimony may be introduced.

The case for the exception is often less compelling in practice, however, than in theory. This is because courts typically ignore the realities of legal practice in interpreting two of the conditions that are designed to ensure the adequacy of the earlier cross-examination. The first is the requirement of an earlier opportunity for cross-examination, and the second is the need for similarity of issues.

i.   Opportunity for Cross-examination

Courts have interpreted the requirement of an earlier opportunity for cross-examination to mean only that. If there was an opportunity to cross-examine the speaker when he testified, the exception admits the earlier testimony regardless of whether the witness was actually cross-examined and regardless of the quality of whatever cross-examination occurred. Focusing on the opportunity for cross-examination rather than on its occurrence often makes sense, because waiving cross-examination is most likely when a lawyer believes that the witness is telling the truth or that further probing may hurt her case. But when an attorney's time or resources have not allowed her to adequately prepare a case, waiving cross-examination (or conducting a weak cross-examination) may only reflect the lawyer's inability to collect the information on which a successful cross-examination might have been based.

Attorneys do not always prepare well for trials. Nonetheless, except when an attorney's representation was professionally inadequate, it may not be unfair to hold a party responsible for his attorney's lapses.[160] The situation is different, however, if the earlier testimony was given in a nontrial setting such as a preliminary hearing. Here counsel might well

---

[158] 5 WIGMORE § 1370, at 55.

[159] One reason for this is that it would be possible to build an entire case out of prior testimony whenever an earlier trial was reversed or all important witnesses were deposed. It is very unlikely that one could similarly avoid all live testimony by means of other hearsay exceptions.

[160] As a practical matter, it may be very difficult to distinguish situations in which waiving cross-examination or a weak cross-examination, was attributable to an inability to adequately prepare, from situations in which a limited cross-examination, or none, reflected a belief that the witness was telling the truth or that cross-examination risked uncovering additional adverse information. Since the party is directly responsible for any failures of cross-examination at the trial in question, it does not seem unfair to extend this responsibility to a subsequent trial, as long as the stakes at the first trial were sufficiently high that the party could have been expected to make a serious effort to present a strong case.

have entered the case so recently that there was no time to prepare adequately for cross-examination. Indeed she may not have known who would testify for the prosecution or the theory of the prosecution's case until she heard the testimony at the exam. Yet most courts do not ask whether the opportunity to cross-examine witnesses in such settings is a realistic one. As long as the formal opportunity existed, the testimony at preliminary hearings of witnesses whose trial testimony cannot be secured is admitted as former testimony. Courts ordinarily ignore the fact that one basic safeguard supporting the former testimony exception is missing.

The opportunity for cross-examination is also likely to have been compromised when former testimony is offered against the party who presented the witness at the earlier hearing. Under the Federal Rule and in most states, the opportunity to develop testimony by direct and redirect examination is considered an adequate substitute for cross-examination; although in some jurisdictions, parties still face restrictions in attacking the credibility of their own witnesses, even if some portion of a witness's testimony has been damaging. Furthermore, if a witness's testimony is mostly favorable, the party presenting a witness may have no motive to attack her general credibility. Nevertheless, the majority's position here is probably a wise one. Even in restrictive jurisdictions, impeaching one's own witness is ordinarily allowed when her testimony has been surprising and harmful. If a party believes that favorable testimony from a witness is honest, her failure to clarify harmful matter by redirect examination carries the suggestion that she was not sure the matter would have been clarified in her favor.[161]

ii. Identity of Issues: Motive to Cross-Examine

The second requirement designed to ensure the adequacy of the earlier cross-examination was summarized at common law by the phrase "identity of issues." Although some courts applied this test literally to exclude earlier testimony when the later case involved different claims or defenses, courts today avoid such formalism. Judicial opinions refer to a "substantial" identity of issues. Substantial identity is usually found when "the issues in the first proceeding, and hence the purpose for which the testimony was offered, [were] such that, the present opponent . . . had an adequate motive for testing on cross-examination the credibility of the testimony."[162] However, courts also find the requirement met when the issues are formally similar but the motivations to cross-examine are

---

[161] In some jurisdictions, earlier testimony by a party's own witness will be admitted as an adoptive admission, thus avoiding the analytic difficulties of applying the former testimony exception to testimony offered against the party that called the witness at the prior hearing. Of course, the reliability of prior testimony does not depend on the theory used to justify its admissibility.

[162] 2 McCORMICK § 304, Professor McCormick's position that only the opponent's prior motive for examining the witness mattered was shared by the drafters of the Federal Rule.

markedly different. For example, since impeaching a prosecution witness at a preliminary hearing will seldom result in a case being dismissed, it is common practice to conduct a non-impeaching cross-examination—frequently using open ended questions—to discover the extent of the witness's knowledge and to commit the witness to a story that can be used in planning an impeaching cross-examination at trial. Yet courts usually find sufficient identity of issues in these circumstances to justify the admission of preliminary hearing testimony against a defendant, since the state's formal task is to show the defendant's likely responsibility for the crime, and the defendant can go free if he shows the state has no case. Courts also allow testimony recorded in discovery depositions to be introduced at trial if the speaker is unavailable. Here again a party may have had little reason to test the speaker's credibility when the evidence was taken, although she may have substantial reason to do so at trial.[163]

The focus of FRE 804(b)(1) on the similarity of motives for cross-examination—as opposed to the identity of issues—may lead the federal courts to pay closer attention to the party's actual motivation at the earlier trial. The Supreme Court emphasized the importance of this issue in *United States v. Salerno*.[164] In *Salerno*, the prosecutors had given immunity to two witnesses called before a grand jury investigating bid rigging in the cement trade in New York City. To the prosecutors' consternation, the witnesses gave testimony exculpating the targets of the investigation. During the trial, the defense called these men as witnesses. When the state refused to immunize their trial testimony, the witnesses refused to testify, citing their Fifth Amendment privilege against self incrimination, and the trial court refused to admit their prior grand jury testimony. The Second Circuit ruled that fairness required the admission of their grand jury testimony.[165] The Supreme Court reversed, holding that FRE 804(b)(1) allowed no such rule of thumb, but required a specific finding that the prosecutors' motives in examining the witnesses before the grand jury were similar to what they were at trial. On remand, a panel of the Second Circuit held that the identity of motive requirement had been met and indicated that in reaching this judgment perhaps the best clue was the quality of the examination that had in fact occurred.[166] The *en banc* court, however, disagreed, finding that similar motivation for examination at the grand jury hearing and at trial did not

---

[163] Generally speaking, testimony in depositions is treated as former testimony. Some jurisdictions have special rules relating to the taking of depositions and the situations in which evidence contained in depositions is admissible. For expert witnesses—especially in civil cases—parties often agree to use depositions at trial instead of live testimony. This practice is likely to become increasingly common with the advent of videotaped depositions, and there have been suggestions to amend the Federal Rules of Evidence or the Federal Rules of Civil Procedure to allow a party to introduce an expert's deposition in a civil case as a matter of right.

[164] 505 U.S. 317 (1992).

[165] United States v. Salerno, 937 F.2d 797 (2d Cir. 1991).

[166] United States v. Salerno, 974 F.2d 231 (2d Cir. 1992).

exist because: 1) the defendants had already been indicted, thus the government did not have a strong interest in proving the witnesses were lying; and, 2) the grand jurors had already indicated to the prosecutor that they did not believe the testimony exculpating the defendants.[167]

Despite *Salerno*, it is not clear that similar close scrutiny will extend to cases where prior testimony is offered *against* criminal defendants rather than on their behalf. In 1970, in *California v. Green*,[168] the Supreme Court held that the admission of preliminary hearing testimony at the defendant's trial did not violate the Confrontation Clause of the Sixth Amendment. *Green*—which pays little attention to the differences between motives for cross-examination at preliminary hearings and at trials—was cited with approval in the Advisory Committee Note for FRE 804(b)(1) as a case in which the same motive requirement was satisfied.

iii. *The Same Party Requirement*

Even before the Federal Rules, most courts had relaxed a third common law requirement—that there be an identity of parties—to avoid needless formalism. When mutuality was required, the offering party and the opponent both had to have been parties to the hearing in which the prior testimony was given. The requirement made little sense. It made the prior testimony, in principle, available to either party, but it is not mutual availability that justifies the exception. Rather it is justified by the testing of the speaker's story that occurred, or could have occurred, at the earlier hearing. Since the proponent of the former testimony would not be offering it if he were not satisfied with what was said, the opponent is the only person with reason to complain that the earlier testimony is unreliable. Thus, it is the opponent's opportunity and his incentive to test the witness at the earlier hearing that are crucial. The identity of the person first offering the evidence does not affect the rationale for the exception; only the identity of the person against whom the evidence is offered matters. Under FRE 804(b)(1) that person must be the person *against whom* the evidence was originally offered or, *in civil actions* and proceedings, a "predecessor in interest," which technically means someone in privity with that person.[169] In criminal cases, any relaxation of the same party requirement is seen as threatening the defendant's Confrontation Clause rights.

Consider the following example. Peter, a pest control specialist, sues Doreen for breach of contract, alleging that Doreen hired him to

---

[167] United States v. DiNapoli, 8 F.3d 909, 915 (2d Cir. 1993) (en banc).

[168] 399 U.S. 149.

[169] At one time, privity was accepted as a way of meeting the same party requirement for many of the same reasons that justified admissions by privity. Both reflected the tendency of the common law to merge the identity of parties with property when property interests acquired in certain ways were in dispute. The modern justification for holding that the participation by one in privity at the earlier hearing satisfies the same party requirement is the belief that the predecessor and successor in interest will have had the same motive to cross-examine.

exterminate termites and carpenter ants in buildings she owned and then never let him on the premises. Doreen claims she never hired Peter because she never had a termite or carpenter ant problem. During the trial, Peter calls an expert who testifies that he examined Doreen's building and found it severely infested with termites, but saw no signs of carpenter ants. Soon after this trial, Xavier, a cabinet maker, rents space in the building from Doreen, who covenants that the building is free from termites and carpenter ants. Later, Xavier sues Doreen, alleging that the building was infested by termites when he rented it. If the expert who testified for Peter in his suit against Doreen is unavailable, Xavier may introduce the expert's prior testimony since Doreen, the party against whom the testimony is offered, was a party to the earlier suit and in that trial had a motive to show the expert was wrong when he said there was a termite problem. The testimony also could have been introduced had the building been rented by Doreen's son who had inherited it from Doreen, since the son would be in privity with Doreen. If, on the other hand, Xavier had alleged that the building was infested by carpenter ants when he rented it, Doreen could not introduce the expert's testimony that there was no carpenter ant problem because Xavier was not a party to the case of Peter versus Doreen, nor was he in privity with a party.

Many commentators and several courts have supported the elimination of even this limited party identity requirement. If the party against whom the testimony was originally introduced was able to test the evidence at the earlier trial and had incentives similar to those of the party opposing the evidence at the subsequent hearing, the earlier testimony will have been sufficiently tested to justify its admission. The Federal Rule, as submitted to Congress, took this position, for it admitted former testimony whenever a person "with motive and interest similar" to the current opponent had participated in the earlier proceeding. The House Judiciary Committee changed the exception to its present form, believing that absent the privity implied by the phrase "predecessor in interest," it is unfair to make one party responsible for the way in which another handled a witness.

The question is a close one, but it seems to us that the congressional change reflects the better accommodation of the competing interests. Cross-examination is as much art as science. Different attorneys approach the examination of witnesses in different ways, and good attorneys assess the entire case in deciding whether to cross-examine. Fear of a devastating reply may lead some attorneys to waive cross-examination or to avoid a line of questioning despite a good chance that a witness's testimony will be qualified or shaken. Others may spare the impeachable witness to avoid arousing jury sympathy. Decisions to forego or limit cross-examination vary with the lawyer's skills and proclivities, her assessment of case strength, and the client's demands. Most members of the House Committee felt that it was unfair to hold a person who had played no role in determining the scope of the earlier examination—not even the vicarious role of client—to the tactics and skill that influenced whether and how cross-examination was conducted. The case for the House position is even stronger when the testimony in the earlier case was less critical than in the later action or when the stakes in the earlier case were insufficient to justify a searching cross-examination.[170]   In theory, when these circumstances apply, the opportunity or motives for cross-examination were not the same in the earlier trial, and the evidence should be excluded on these grounds. However, the tendency of courts to ignore reality when assessing opportunity and motive suggests that the "same opponent" requirement serves as a safeguard to prevent the admission of prior testimony that has not been adequately tested by cross-examination.

What makes the policy question difficult is that a powerful countervailing argument exists. Former testimony, even if elicited by an unrelated party, is often likely to be more complete and accurate than much of the testimony admitted under most other hearsay exceptions. If the choice is between accepting evidence that is imperfect, and forgoing the evidence entirely—as it always is when unavailability is shown—it is reasonable to conclude that acceptance is preferable. Some federal courts have done just that.[171]   They read the rule to mean that if a party to a prior suit was interested in achieving the same end as a party to a later suit, the prior party was a "predecessor in interest" of the second. For example, suppose that in one trial Able sought to show that Dale, whom he was suing for assault, started a fight, but Dale took the stand and said he wasn't present. If in later, unrelated litigation Edwards sued Baker for starting the same fight and Baker defended himself by blaming it on the now unavailable Dale, Edward could in these courts introduce the testimony Dale gave in the suit brought by Able.[172]   These courts reason that both Able and Baker were interested in showing that Dale was the aggressor, and that since Able's interest in making this showing *preceded* Baker's, Able was Baker's "predecessor in interest." The judicial logic is creative, but if this were how the phrase "predecessor in interest" were meant to be interpreted, Congress could have left the Advisory Committee's language unaltered and achieved the same result. Other

---

[170] This may be because funds were not available to conduct the kind of investigation needed for a successful cross-examination, or because there was insufficient money to pay counsel for more than a perfunctory effort. These conditions may, of course, also have existed at an earlier hearing involving the party against whom the evidence is later offered. At least in these circumstances the party can call the court's attention to the earlier deficiency. And perhaps it is not quite so unfair to make a party suffer the consequences of earlier poverty or an unwillingness to invest funds as it is to make one suffer the consequences of someone else's poverty or penuriousness.

[171] *See, generally,* Dennis J. Turner, *Federal Rules of Evidence 804: Will the Real Predecessor-in-Interest Please Stand Up,* 19 Akron L. Rev. 251 (1985).

[172] *See, e.g.,* Lloyd v. American Export Lines, Inc., 580 F.2d 1179 (3d Cir.), cert. denied, 439 U.S. 969 (1978).

courts have made a more particularized examination of whether it would be fair to hold one party to another's cross-examination of a witness, inviting the party in the later proceeding to point to additional questions she would have asked or lines of inquiry she would have pursued. This is a better solution, but it still appears that in substituting the phrase "predecessor in interest" for the Advisory Committee's "person with motive and similar interest," the House Judiciary Committee, which authored the amendment, wanted to invoke the strictures of the common law. Courts that loosen these strictures are ignoring likely congressional intent, even if one might argue that Congress's overriding concern was with fairness and that a broad reading of "predecessor in interest" is not unfair.[173]

iv. Proving Prior Testimony

Statements admitted as prior testimony have often been recorded in some way when made and can be played back or transcribed for presentation at the later hearing. When this is done, the danger that the earlier statements will be misreported is minimal. One might think that when recordings or transcripts are available, prior testimony must always be proved through them. There is, however, no such requirement in the Federal Rules, nor was there at common law. Certified transcripts admitted under the official records exception to the hearsay rule are just one way of proving prior testimony. Earlier testimony may also be proved by the testimony of an observer who purports to remember what was said in the earlier hearing, by the testimony of an observer with recollection refreshed from stenographer's notes or other memoranda, or by the notes of an observer, if the notes qualify as recorded recollection or a business record. In none of these situations is the witness required to report exactly what was said. As long as the witness claims to be reporting accurately the substance of what was said, the phrasing of the earlier testimony need not be reproduced.

v. Objections to Prior Testimony

McCormick summarizes the law on when objections to prior testimony may be made if they were not made at the earlier hearing: There are sweeping statements in some opinions that this may always be done, and in others that it is never allowable. The more widely approved view, however, is that objections which go merely to the form of the testimony—as on the ground of leading questions, unresponsiveness, or opinion—must be made at the original hearing, when errors can be corrected. On the other hand, objections that go to the relevancy or the competency of the evidence may be asserted for the first time when the former testimony is offered at trial.[174]

---

[173] *See,* MCCORMICK § 303.

[174] MCCORMICK § 306.

Problem VI-80. Jack Horner is a truck driver for the Royalle Pie Company. Returning from a delivery one evening, Horner's truck skidded on some ice and swerved into two men walking by the side of the road. Dave Fisher, one of the injured men, elected to sue Horner personally. At trial Fisher called Horner as a hostile witness. Under cross-examination, Horner admitted that he was returning from a delivery for the Royalle Pie Company and that he was probably driving five or ten miles over the speed limit when the truck went into the skid. Horner's lawyer, supplied by Royalle, failed to examine Horner further on this point. The trial resulted in a verdict for Fisher. Three months later, Ted Bunter, the other injured man, brings suit against Royalle on a respondeat superior theory. In the interim Horner has died. **May Bunter introduce Horner's testimony in the earlier trial to establish that Horner was acting in the course of his employment at the time of the accident? To show that he was driving in excess of the speed limit when the truck hit the ice? Does it matter whether Royalle is represented in the later action by the lawyer they had hired for Horner in the earlier action? Would your answers be different if Horner's lawyer had been retained privately by him rather than by the company?**

Problem VI-81. On the same facts as the preceding question, assume that Horner's lawyer had Horner testify on his own behalf. Horner testifies that the men he hit were both wearing dark clothes and facing away from traffic, that they were walking at the side of the road although there was a sidewalk by the road, and that his speed, though faster than the official limit, was about five miles an hour slower than the prevailing speed on the highway in question. **In the later action could Royalle introduce this testimony against Bunter? Could it be introduced against Fisher, if the earlier trial ended in a hung verdict and Fisher decided to sue Royalle after Horner had died?**

c. *Dying Declarations*

The dying declaration exception has been rationalized since its inception by the assumption that a person who knows death is imminent is unlikely to lie. At the time this exception was defined, this assumption may have been justified. Heaven and hell were real places to many people, bearing false witness was a serious sin, and if one died with a lie on one's lips there was no chance for repentance and absolution. In today's more secular society, the general validity of the assumption is doubtful, although there are people to whom it still applies.

i. Common Law Requirements

At common law, dying declarations were admitted only in homicide cases in which the speaker was the victim of the homicide charged.[175] The statements had to relate to the homicidal act or the circumstances surrounding it, and the proponent of the statement had to be able to show that the speaker was aware of his impending death. In addition to these requirements, the states were concerned that the deathbed statements be the witness's own good faith declarations. Some courts excluded dying declarations that appeared to tell only part of the speaker's story, or statements that implicated people against whom the speaker had special reasons for revenge. Although in most states dying declarations were sufficient to establish crucial facts in issue, in some states a party was entitled to an instruction that a dying declaration did not have the same value as sworn testimony. In others, however, it was appropriate to tell the jury that dying declarations "stand on the same plane of solemnity as statements made under oath." Some such differences still exist.

ii. The Federal Rule

FRE 804(b)(2), defines the scope of the federal hearsay exception for dying declarations:

> **Statement Under the Belief of Imminent Death.** In a prosecution for homicide or in a civil case, a statement that the declarant, while believing the declarant's death to be imminent, made about its cause or circumstances.

The most important change that this exception makes in the common law is that it allows the admission of dying declarations in civil cases as long as they concern the cause or circumstances of what the speaker believed was his impending death. An earlier draft would have admitted dying declarations in all cases to prove the circumstances of apparently impending death, but the House Committee on the Judiciary, doubting the reliability of deathbed statements, retained the restriction of dying declarations in criminal cases to homicide prosecutions, "where exceptional need for the evidence is present." Also, under the Federal Rule the speaker's statement may be offered even if he is not dead. Any of the causes of unavailability specified in FRE 804(a) will do.

Those who favor the admissibility of dying declarations in civil cases argue that if dying declarations are reliable enough to be admitted in homicide actions where a defendant's life may be at stake, it follows *a fortiori* that they should be admissible in civil actions, in which much less is at stake. This argument is vulnerable at two points. First, if we were writing on a blank slate, it is not clear that reliability alone would justify

---

[175] Some common law courts expanded the circumstances of admissibility to include criminal prosecutions for abortions that had resulted in a woman's death and, in a few states, some civil actions.

a dying declaration exception for homicide cases. Second, it may be that dying declarations are less reliable in civil cases than they are in homicide actions.

iii. A Justification for the Exception in Homicide Cases

The religious justification for the dying declaration exception may have largely disappeared in modern society, but it still appears that a person who believes she is about to die from a criminal assault has little interest in deceiving listeners about the cause of her impending death. Although in some situations a dying person might lie about what happened to implicate an enemy or protect a loved one, those who believe they are victims of homicide are likely to want their killers to be brought to justice. However, this likelihood alone is not a strong justification for the exception. It provides some guarantee of reliability, but countervailing factors suggest unreliability. Chief among these is the likelihood that the speaker will have been under great stress before, during and after the homicidal attack. Stress often interferes with accurate perception, and can lead to problems of memory or narration. Yet stress may not be the threat to perception in this area that it is in others. The most significant fact commonly proved by dying declarations—the identity of a previously known killer—seems unlikely to be either misperceived or forgotten. More troubling, is the possible absence of firsthand knowledge. We don't necessarily know what the victim saw. It may be that her accusation was a surmise based on her best guess about who was out to get her.[176]

If the case for the dying declaration in homicide cases were based entirely on the probable honesty of deathbed statements, discounted by the likelihood of misperception, it would be a weak one; perhaps defensible, perhaps not. But there are two other factors that have nothing to do with reliability: the special need we feel to bring murderers to justice, coupled with a desire not to let the victim's death improve the criminal's chances at trial.[177] Perhaps these factors properly sway the balance toward admissibility.

At best, however, this analysis is a rationale for the exception and not an explanation of why dying declarations are admitted today. The admissibility of dying declarations is rooted more in history than in reason. Courts have received dying declarations from the time that hearsay was first distinguished from courtroom testimony. They continue

---

[176] If other statements by the speaker indicate that she lacked firsthand knowledge of the identity of her assassin, the statement will be excluded. If no evidence suggests this, the statement will be admitted on the assumption that the speaker perceived what her statement indicates.

[177] The hearsay rule and the trial system give the criminal an interest in the victim's death. The dying declaration exception removes that interest only in limited circumstances, but these are probably the circumstances in which it would otherwise be most obvious that the criminal has gained by a deadly rather than a merely injurious assault.

to apply this exception—sometimes citing old rationales and only rarely wondering if they still apply—because most modern courts favor the wider use of hearsay, and, regardless of reliability, would view the exclusion of once acceptable hearsay as a step in the wrong direction.

iv. *Extension to Civil Cases*

The extension of the exception to civil cases is not legitimated by history. Although the argument that evidence reliable enough for homicide cases is reliable enough for civil actions is not unreasonable, it is, as we have seen, questionable whether the dying declaration exception in homicide cases can be justified on reliability grounds alone. Moreover, even if dying declarations carry special guarantees of reliability in homicide cases, similar reliability may not exist in civil actions. Dying declarations in civil cases usually relate not to an intentional assault on the speaker, but to an accident in which the speaker was involved. The accident victim may have incentives to misreport what happened that the assault victim lacks. The most obvious is the desire to protect her estate from liability, and to enhance the prospect that her heirs will have a cause of action. This can lead to conscious misrepresentation. Subconsciously, a dying accident victim may feel guilty about leaving her family or about the harm she may have done others. Denying or deflecting responsibility may help cope with guilt. Finally, explanations of the cause or circumstances of a speaker's impending death are more likely in homicide than in civil cases to involve straightforward accusations of responsibility or simple descriptions of attacks. In civil cases such explanations are more likely to recount the complicated details of accidents and their aftermath. Stress is likely to pose more of a threat to reliability the more complex the matters reported.

One might justify extending the dying declaration exception to civil cases with the argument that the rule excluding hearsay is fundamentally mistaken or that the need for hearsay when speakers are unavailable overrides any justification for excluding statements. A person might also argue that there is no clear evidence of gross injustice in jurisdictions that admit dying declarations in civil cases. But, if the concern is to limit new hearsay exceptions to situations of special reliability, a dying declaration exception in civil cases is a questionable candidate for innovation.[178]

---

[178] The dispute about whether dying declarations should be admitted in civil cases is not as important as it might seem since dying declarations are often admissible under other hearsay exceptions. Most commonly, they qualify as excited utterances since courts will often find that serious trauma, such as the trauma of thinking one is about to die, can extend an excited state caused by the trauma-inducing event.

Problem VI-82. Jim Short is found dying of stab wounds. A police officer accompanies him to the hospital in an ambulance. On the way the officer, who knows Short, says, "Jim, the driver tells me you lost too much blood.

He says he's never seen anyone in your condition survive. You know you don't have long to live, don't you?" Jim nods yes. The officer continues, "Now Jim, this is Sandy's doing isn't it?" Jim nods yes. "He pulled a knife on you, didn't he?" Jim nods yes. "He slashed you because he knew you were ready to testify against him on the drug case, isn't that the reason?" Jim nods yes. "He wanted to do more than scare you. He wanted to be sure you wouldn't live to tell your story. Isn't that what happened?" Jim nods yes and expires. **Setting aside any possible Confrontation Clause objections, if Sandy is charged with murdering Short, will the officer's questions and Jim's answers be admissible against Sandy at trial?** Suppose that the police officer, after establishing that Jim was aware of his impending death, had merely asked Jim what had happened and Jim had replied, "Sandy was out to get me because he knew I intended to spill on him," and then died before saying anything more. **If there was other evidence linking Sandy to the killing, would the statement be admissible to establish Sandy's motive? If there was no other evidence linking Sandy to the killing, would the statement be admissible to show that Sandy was the killer?**

d. *Statements Against Interest*

The Federal Rules, like the common law, contain an exception for statements against interest. The exception rests on the notion that unless there is some benefit to be gained, people seldom tell lies that make them appear worse off than they might otherwise seem. Thus if Susie, when asked whether she owns the house she lives in replies, "No, I rent it," she is likely to be telling the truth. While it's easy to see why a renter might falsely claim she owns the house—to secure a loan, to discourage others from seeking to buy or rent her place, or just generally to bask in the appearance of prosperity—it is hard to imagine why an owner would falsely claim to be a renter. Only if a specific reason for that deception could be shown—for example, that Susie was trying to hide assets from creditors—would one suspect a statement which makes the speaker appear worse off than she would otherwise seem to be. This is particularly so since the *making* of such statements may threaten a speaker's interests. Thus, if Susie, who claims fee simple ownership of her house, is sued by Jane, who also claims to own the property, Susie's statement that she rents the property can be used against her as an admission. For these reasons the fact that a statement is against interest when made provides considerable protection against the danger of prevarication. Although the exception provides less protection against the dangers of misperception and poor memory, there is some protection here as well since people are likely to double check those perceptions and memories that make them appear worse off than they otherwise might think they are.[179]

FRE 804(b)(3) is the federal exception for statements against interest:

Statement Against Interest. A statement that:

(A) a reasonable person in the declarant's position would have made only if the person believed it to be true because, when made, it was so contrary to the declarant's proprietary or pecuniary interest or had so great a tendency to invalidate the declarant's claim against someone else or to expose the declarant to civil or criminal liability; and

(B) is supported by corroborating circumstances that clearly indicate its trustworthiness, if it is offered in a criminal case as one that tends to expose the declarant to criminal liability.[180]

Except in so far as this rule admits statements against penal interest, a topic we shall discuss separately, the Federal Rule tracks the common law.

At common law, the basic requirements for the statement against interest exception were few: the speaker had to be unavailable,[181] the declaration when made had to have been against the speaker's pecuniary or proprietary interest, and the usual firsthand knowledge requirement applied. Some states added to these the further requirement that the speaker must have had no probable motive to falsify, a condition that could be subsumed under the requirement that a statement be against interest when made.

i.   The "Against Interest" Requirement

It is sometimes difficult to determine when a statement is sufficiently against interest to qualify under the exception. Statements often found to be against pecuniary or proprietary interest include: declarations acknowledging indebtedness, declarations acknowledging payment of a debt, declarations acknowledging contingent contractual liability, statements of agents acknowledging receipt of money on behalf of

---

[179] For example, the IRS reports that most arithmetic errors on tax returns favor the taxpayer. This doesn't require cheating by taxpayers; it merely means that normal humans are likely to check their addition when their tax bill is larger than expected, and to smile with relief when it is less than they thought they owed.

[180] The rule was amended in 2010 to require that both the government and the defendant show corroborating circumstances before a statement against interest is admitted. The prior version of the rule only required the defendant to demonstrate corroborating circumstances.

[181] Originally only death was an acceptable cause of unavailability, but other causes of unavailability became accepted over time.

principals, declarations admitting less than a fee simple interest in property, declarations by an heir acknowledging that property has been left by will to another, declarations by beneficiaries of insurance policies tending to defeat claims thereunder, and statements acknowledging tortious liability in specific amounts. Courts were divided on whether statements that tend to establish or extinguish tort liability qualify as statements against interest. The prevailing view, and that found in the federal rule, is that they do qualify.

Whether a statement was against interest will often depend on facts and circumstances that existed at the time the statement was made. Lisa's statement, "Last year George bought out my partnership interest in the Gambels Department Store," would be against interest if Gambels was flourishing, but not if it was in debt. Similarly, a statement by Alan that Betsy owns Blackacre can be considered a statement against interest only if Alan believes he has some colorable claim to Blackacre.[182] It is for the court, not the jury, to find the contextual facts that may condition the admissibility of statements offered as "against interest."

While the situation at the time of the trial cannot determine whether a statement was against interest when made, it may influence the decision on admissibility. First, it may be a clue to whether a statement was, in fact, against interest when made. For example, a statement acknowledging a life estate in land is generally assumed to be against interest because the law presumes that the possessor of land holds the fee. However, if the assignee of someone who once possessed property were sued for eviction by a plaintiff who alleges that she owns the land and that she rented it to the prior possessor whose leasehold interest has now expired, the prior possessor's statement to the assignee that he held a life estate would appear not to have been against interest when made. The subsequent suit makes it likely that when the possessor spoke, he knew that he had no colorable claim to the fee. It is not against interest to assert that one has a life estate when one either has a life estate or a leasehold interest.

Second, the situation at trial may be important because an earlier statement may be against interest only with respect to certain inferences. If the statement is offered to support those inferences it will be admitted; otherwise it will be excluded. Consider, for example, an income tax return that reports earnings of $100,000. The statement is admissible if offered to show that the taxpayer earned at least $100,000 since a

---

[182] Regardless of what Alan believes when he says Betsy owns Blackacre, should he later learn that he has a claim to the property, his statement would be admissible against him as a personal admission if he sues to acquire title. This has led some courts to admit such statements not just against those who spoke them, but also against third parties as declarations against interest. A better practice is not to admit such statements against third parties because the statements do not have the indicia of reliability that justify the exception. Thus Alan, not knowing he has some claim to Blackacre, might well be careless about the truth if he was arguing that his friend Betsy and not his enemy Carl was the rightful owner.

taxpayer has an incentive to minimize reported income. The same incentives mean that the tax return is inadmissible to show that the speaker earned no more than $100,000.

A declaration may have both self-serving and disserving aspects. When assertions are separable a court has three options: (1) to admit the entire declaration on the strength of the part which is disserving, (2) to admit the entire statement if the disserving part predominates and to exclude it entirely if the self-serving part predominates, or (3) to admit only those parts of the statement that are disserving. American courts usually choose either the second or third option, although the first option is reflected in some decisions. In the 1994 case of *Williamson v. United States*,[183] the Supreme Court endorsed the third option in interpreting the Federal Rules.[184] The Court first held that the word *statement*, as used in the rule, referred not to global disclosures by a person (as in, "she gave a statement"), but to each particular assertion a speaker made. A court's task, according to the Supreme Court, is to examine the assertions separately to determine whether each is so contrary to an interest specified in FRE 804(b)(3) that a reasonable person would not have made the statement unless she believed it was true. The fact that a statement that implicates another is closely associated with a self-implicating statement does not make it admissible, and a neutral statement also does not qualify under the exception. *Williamson* was a criminal case, so the Court spoke of "inculpatory" statements; but the same assertion-focused analysis should apply to statements against pecuniary, proprietary and other civil liability interests.

When a single assertion is both self-serving and disserving, the third option is not possible. Here courts commonly take the second approach. If the statement seems on balance self-serving, it will be excluded; if it is on balance disserving, it is admitted. This kind of balancing is commonly required when a creditor's statement acknowledges part payment of a debt. If when a creditor speaks the statute of limitations has run on the debt and part payment would revive it, the statement would be excluded in a later trial because the creditor's interest in reviving the legal obligation outweighs his interest in not acknowledging payments he has not received. If the statute has not run, an acknowledgment of part payment would be considered a statement against interest because it admits that a debt is not as large as it once was.

The inclusion of neutral observations will not result in the exclusion of those parts of a statement that are genuinely against interest. In the federal courts before *Williamson*, and still in many state courts, neutral

---

[183] 512 U.S. 594 (1994).

[184] The Court recognized that apparently neutral statements like "Sam and I went to Joe's house" might be against the declarant's interest if a reasonable person in the declarant's shoes would realize that being linked to Joe and Sam would implicate the declarant in Joe's and Sam's conspiracy. *Id.* at 603.

observations linked to statements against interest were more likely to be admitted than self-serving comments. In deciding whether to admit the neutral portions of a statement against interest, a court willing to do this will look at how closely related the neutral portion is to the disserving portion and at whether there are other indicia of reliability. If circumstances, including a close relationship to the disserving portion, suggest that the neutral portion is reliable, admission was once likely. Several states have refused to follow *Williamson*,[185] and, even in the federal courts, there has been some "slippage" from its seemingly clear mandate.[186]

Problem VI-83. Horton sues Prince to quiet title to a tract of land known as "Cold Bottom." Horton claims to own the land by virtue of 20 years of open and hostile adverse possession. It is admitted by all that Horton has lived openly on the Cold Bottom tract for 20 years. The issue is whether his possession was hostile throughout this period. Prince argues that up until two years before the date the suit was filed, Horton was paying her rent for use of the land. The rent was allegedly paid through a local real estate dealer who collected money from Horton, deducted a commission, and forwarded her own check for the remaining amount to Prince. The dealer is now deceased. To prove her claim, Prince seeks to present testimony by the dealer's husband that up until the time of his wife's death about two years ago, she would come home on the first day in every quarter complaining, "Well, I've gotten the money out of Horton again. I don't know why I put up with this. The commission isn't worth it. He's got to be the crookedest man I have met." The husband also remembers that his wife once told him, "When Horton gave me the rent today he said that he wouldn't be paying for long because he had a lawyer friend who told him how he could trump up a claim for adverse possession. I was going to tell him that he couldn't so long as he was paying me rent, but I figured that would make it harder than ever to collect." **May the husband testify to any of his wife's statements? May the defense introduce checks from the deceased real estate dealer on which she has written in the lower left-hand corner "Horton rent"? May the dealer's check stubs that say "Horton rent" on them be admitted on any theory?**

---

[185] *See, e.g.*, People v. Newton, 966 P.2d 563, 577 (Colo.1998) (rejecting *Williamson* in favor of prior state-law precedent), State v. Sonthikoummane, 145 N.H. 316, 769 A.2d 330, 334 (2000) (same), State v. Hills, 264 Kan. 437, 957 P.2d 496, 503 (1998) (same), Chandler v. Commonwealth, 249 Va. 270, 455 S.E.2d 219, 225 (1995) (same), People v. Beasley, 239 Mich.App. 548, 609 N.W.2d 581, 585 (2000) (same), State v. Julian, 129 Ohio App.3d 828, 719 N.E.2d 96, 100 (1998) (same).

[186] *See, e.g.*, United States v. Savoca, 335 F.Supp. 2d 385, 399, n5 (S.D.N.Y. 2004).

ii. Statements Against Penal Interests

The limitation of the common law exception for statements against interest to statements against pecuniary or proprietary interests was long criticized as too narrow. Many commentators argued that admissions of criminal responsibility or of disgraceful conditions or behavior carry guarantees of reliability much like those that exist for statements against fiscal interests. Before the Federal Rules opened the door to some statements against penal interests, Justice Holmes's brief but eloquent dissent in the case of *Donnelly v. United States* [187] persuaded some state courts to admit statements against penal interest.

Donnelly had been convicted and sentenced to die for a murder which he claimed one Joe Dick had committed. Some evidence suggested that Dick had committed the crime, and Dick had confessed to the crime before he died. But the trial court excluded Dick's confession because it did not qualify as a statement against interest. The majority in *Donnelly* held the exclusion proper because Dick's confession did not relate to a pecuniary or proprietary interest. Justice Holmes disagreed:

> The confession of Joe Dick, since deceased, that he committed the murder for which the plaintiff in error was tried, coupled with circumstances pointing to its truth, would have a strong tendency to make anyone outside of a court of justice believe that Donnelly did not commit the crime. I say this, of course, on the supposition that it should be proved that the confession really was made, and that there was no ground for connecting Donnelly with Dick. . . . [T]he exception to the hearsay rule in the case of declarations against interest is well known; no other statement is so much against interest as a confession of murder, it is far more calculated to convince than dying declarations, which would be let in to hang a man; and when we surround the accused with so many safeguards, some of which seem to me excessive, I think we ought to give him the benefit of a fact that, if proved, commonly would have such weight.

Yet, there are reasons to be wary of statements admitting criminal involvement. Publicized crimes can attract false confessions. If these confessions were admissible, the prosecutor might have to tell the jury in detail why each confessor could not have committed the crime charged. Also, a criminal on his deathbed or safely outside the jurisdiction might seek to protect his criminal cohorts by confessing to crimes they have committed.[188] Finally, the report of what an unavailable speaker said may itself be a lie. Although this is possible whenever a statement

---

[187] 228 U.S. 243, 277–78 (1913).

[188] Ironically, the police, to make their record look good, may also elicit confessions to crimes that the confessor did not commit. *See* JEROME H. SKOLNICK, JUSTICE WITHOUT TRIAL 164–81 (1966).

against interest is admitted, it may pose special dangers with statements in criminal cases because all the defendant needs to do is raise a reasonable doubt as to his guilt and a third party's confession might in itself be enough to raise such doubt. All three reasons become less persuasive when there is substantial independent evidence connecting the speaker to the crime. FRE 804(b)(3) relies on this in extending the exception to statements that implicate a speaker in crimes, for it requires the existence of corroborating circumstances that indicate trustworthiness when a statement against penal interest is offered either to exculpate an accused, or when the prosecution seeks to use one person's inculpatory statement against another person accused of a crime.

In jurisdictions that do not admit statements against penal interest, statements admitting crimes that are also torts may be admissible as statements against pecuniary interest. However, a number of courts that recognize the pecuniary implications of statements implicating their speakers in crimes admit such statements only in civil cases.[189]

Although the exception for statements against penal interest was passed with cases like *Donnelly* in mind, it is today far more commonly invoked by the prosecution than by the defense. Criminals often implicate others in the course of admitting their own criminal involvement. Before the Supreme Court's decision in *Williamson*, some federal courts rather freely admitted portions of a criminal's confession that implicated others, particularly if additional indicia of reliability were present. Today, federal courts more carefully parse confessions to see which portions that implicate others were truly against the confessor's interest when made, and if the statements are offered by the prosecution and were made to the police, a prosecutor, or at a hearing, the Confrontation Clause may bar the statement's use.

iii. Statements Against Social Interests

The Advisory Committee's draft of FRE 804(b)(3) admitted statements that tended to make the speaker "an object of hatred, ridicule or disgrace." The House Judiciary Committee deleted this language, but a number of states that modeled their evidence codes on the Federal Rules preferred the Advisory Committee's version, and a few common law decisions also extended the exception to comments against social interest. Where the extension is not authorized, courts sometimes find that statements against social interests have legal implications that make them admissible on traditional grounds. Thus, a court might admit a

---

[189] A criminal defense attorney in a jurisdiction that either does not admit or greatly restricts the admission of statements against penal interests may argue that the Compulsory Process Clause of the Sixth Amendment, as interpreted in Chambers v. Mississippi, 410 U.S. 284 (1973) and Holmes v. South Carolina, 547 U.S. 319 (2006), give the defendant a constitutional right to introduce third party admissions of criminal responsibility as long as other evidence connects the third party with the crime. These cases and their implications are fully discussed in Chapter Seven.

man's statement that he fathered a child out of wedlock, not because this is a disgraceful thing to do, but because in acknowledging fatherhood the speaker exposes himself to a suit for child support payments.

iv. Distinguished From "Admissions"

Often statements against interest are admissible under some other exception to the hearsay rule, usually one that has the advantage of not requiring unavailability. The most common alternative ground of admissibility is the exception for the statements of a party opponent, commonly referred to as the admissions exception, since parties are frequently alleged to have said things against their financial or penal interests, and all relevant statements by opposing parties qualify as admissions. Indeed, in offering the statements of opposing parties, lawyers often say they are presenting an "admission against interest." No such exception can be found in the Federal Rules or at common law, properly understood. The admissions exception, unlike the exception for statements against interest, does not require unavailability or firsthand knowledge, and admissions need not be against interest when made. In these ways it is broader than the statement against interest exception. It is narrower in that a statement is only admissible against the person who made it or against a person whose relation to the speaker makes her responsible for what the speaker has said.

———————

Problem VI-84. Sam Dovico and Ferdinand Gangi are jointly charged with selling narcotics. Dovico is tried and found guilty by a jury. Gangi pleads guilty. While in prison, Gangi tells another prisoner that he was solely responsible for the sale and that Dovico was innocent. On the strength of this disclosure, Dovico is granted a new trial. However, Gangi dies before the new trial can begin. **Should the prisoner who heard Gangi's confession be allowed to testify to it? Would the case for admission be stronger if Gangi had testified that he and his long time girlfriend and frequent visitor, Jane Gordon, were responsible for the sale, not he and Dovico? Would your answer to either of the above questions be different if you were in a progressive jurisdiction that had held that statements against social interest were sufficient to justify the statement against interest exception to the hearsay rule?**

e. Statements of Pedigree

One of the less frequently invoked federal hearsay exceptions is the exception for statements of pedigree or family history, FRE 804(b)(4):

(4) Statement of Personal or Family History. A statement about:

(A) the declarant's own birth, adoption, legitimacy, ancestry, marriage, divorce, relationship by blood, adoption, or marriage, or similar facts of personal or family history, even though the declarant had no way of acquiring personal knowledge about that fact; or

(B) another person concerning any of these facts, as well as death, if the declarant was related to the person by blood, adoption, or marriage or was so intimately associated with the person's family that the declarant's information is likely to be accurate.

The Federal Rule differs from the common law version in that the statement need not be *ante litem motam,* (made before the beginning of the controversy giving rise to the litigation) and the speaker need not be the person, or a relative of the person whose family status is at issue, but may be someone else—such as servant or close friend—who has been intimately associated with the person's family. The exception admits statements that are not based on firsthand knowledge, a necessity since knowledge of family history is typically based on secondhand information.

This exception was justified at common law on two grounds: the need for and likely accuracy of the special knowledge that relatives have of family history, and the protection against intentional deception inherent in the *ante litem motam* requirement.

The Federal Rule follows the lead of a number of states in dispensing with the requirement that the speaker be related to the subject of the statement. This change makes sense, for unrelated individuals intimately connected with a family often know as much about a family's history as family members. The elimination of the requirement insulating the statement from the instant controversy is more questionable. The failure of the proponent to produce family history statements made before a litigated controversy raises questions about the accuracy of statements made with knowledge of what was at stake, but the rule's drafters felt that juries could adequately take this cause for suspicion into account.

FRE 804(b)(4) overlaps FRE 803(19). When statements of family history are numerous enough to constitute a *reputation* for the matter in the family, among associates, or in the community, the unavailability of the speakers need not be shown and family history facts may be established by anyone familiar with that reputation. Not all states have an FRE 803(19) type exception, and some that do place restrictions on the reputation evidence that the Federal Rules do not impose.

Although FRE 804(b)(4) has not given rise to many reported cases, you should not ignore it. Whenever a family relationship is relevant in a case, this rule may provide a useful, efficient way of offering evidence.

Problem VI-85. When billionaire George Bigbucks died, Peter Mooch sought a share of the estate claiming he was Bigbucks's grandson, as his father was the product of a short-lived marriage that Bigbucks entered into when he was 19. To show this, Mooch wishes to introduce several witnesses who will testify that his deceased father often said he was Bigbucks's son and other witnesses who will testify that his deceased grandmother claimed she married Bigbucks when she was 17 because he had gotten her pregnant and divorced him 8 months later, 2 months after the baby, Mooch's father was born. He also wants to introduce a family tree he prepared as a class assignment in 4th grade in which Bigbucks is listed as his grandfather, but he wants to excise the teacher's comment, "You must not lie about your ancestors." **Is testimony as to what his father and grandmother had said about his father's relation to Bigbucks admissible? Is the family tree Mooch prepared admissible? If it is, should the teacher's comment be excised? Is this evidence sufficient to prove that Mooch is Bigbucks's grandson?**

f. Forfeiture by Wrongdoing

FRE 804(b)(6) provides an exception for:

Statement Offered Against a Party That Wrongfully Caused the Declarant's Unavailability. A statement offered against a party that wrongfully caused—or acquiesced in wrongfully causing—the declarant's unavailability as a witness, and did so intending that result.

The exception is arguably not necessary, for numerous courts have held that when it can be shown that a party has secured the absence of a potential witness through murder, intimidation, bribery, or otherwise, he has implicitly endorsed that person's likely testimony, thus qualifying it for admissibility as an adoptive admission.

There are several areas of concern. The first involves the determination of when a party is responsible for a potential witness's absence. This is for the judge to determine under FRE 104(a), and the burden of proof is almost certain to be by a preponderance of the evidence.[190] As with the preliminary proof of conspiracy needed to qualify a statement as a conspirator's admission,[191] allowing a judge to find by a preponderance of the evidence, without regard to the rules of evidence that a party has acted criminally has disquieting aspects, even if it also has practical virtues. But the rule poses additional problems. When a

---

[190] Some courts have required that a party's criminal responsibility for a potential witness's absence be proved by *clear and convincing evidence*, but several Supreme Court decisions suggest that all decisions made by judges under FRE 104(a) should be by a preponderance of the evidence.

[191] *See* Bourjaily v. United States, 483 U.S. 171 (1987), discussed *supra*, pp. 602, 609.

judge is asked to find as a preliminary matter that a conspiracy exists, it is usually in the context of a case in which much of the evidence, apart from the hearsay, bears on the question the judge must answer, and the judge may rest her determination to allow a conspirator's hearsay in large measure on what the other evidence in the case shows. FRE 804(b)(6) requires a judge to find, as a preliminary matter, that an entirely different crime—such as murder or witness intimidation—has occurred. Courts are understandably reluctant to devote much time to resolving preliminary questions of admissibility, yet a party may hotly contest the allegation that he is responsible for a witness's absence. There is substantial variability as to how much of a mini trial is permitted and what kind of evidence is sufficient to establish, by a preponderance of the evidence, a party's responsibility for a potential witness's absence.

Suppose, for example, three crucial witnesses against an accused mobster are found murdered, gangland style, shortly before the mobster's trial. In these circumstances it is hard to believe that the mobster was not responsible for their deaths. Yet with nothing else to connect the mobster to the deaths, is it reasonable for a court to hold that it is more likely than not that the mobster secured their deaths? Findings of legal responsibility, particularly findings of criminal responsibility, usually require more evidence than this. Even in civil cases, where the preponderance standard is regularly used, more than suspicions of this sort are usually required to support a verdict.

An ancillary issue is whether, when FRE 804(b)(6) hearsay is admitted, juries will be allowed to learn the reason for the speaker's absence. The prejudicial potential of such information is obvious. If a jury learns that someone who would have testified against the accused has been murdered, bribed, intimidated, or otherwise prevented or dissuaded from testifying, they are likely to attribute his absence to the party opposing the testimony. This counsels against telling the jury. Yet without knowing why they are getting hearsay rather than live testimony, the jury might discount the hearsay substantially, which is a good reason to inform the jury why the speaker is absent. That is a disquieting possibility, however, not just because of the prejudicial impact of the information, but also because the party will be labeled a criminal based on a finding by a judge, which reflects the preponderance of the evidence rather than by a jury finding of proof beyond a reasonable doubt. Moreover, much of the evidence that influences the judge may be inadmissible in court, and the party is likely to have only a limited opportunity to contest it. In a situation with no good solution, the best alternative may be to simply tell the jury that the witness could not get to the court and so her hearsay is offered instead, although this may leave the jury wondering why the hearsay of other unavailable witnesses has not been offered. The matter is sufficiently thorny that it is likely that the Supreme Court will eventually have to resolve it.[192]

Problem VI-86. Joey Grass is charged with involvement in a conspiracy to smuggle 50 tons of marijuana into the U.S. The only evidence that Grass is part of the conspiracy is that he purchased four trucks in which the marijuana was carried, and the government has a recording of him conversing with Salim Shah, the owner of the dealership that sold him the trucks, shortly before Shah was to testify before the grand jury. Grass had said to Shah, "Before that grand jury, Shah, you don't remember anything about me. You say nothing in reference to me because you're a smart guy and your memory ain't that good. Understand?" When Shah testified before the grand jury, he identified Grass as the person to whom he sold the trucks. Ten months later, on his way to the courthouse to testify against Grass, Shah was gunned down in a gangland style shooting. When word of Shah's death reached those in the courtroom, everyone who heard the news except for Grass seemed upset. Grass could barely keep from smiling. Nothing else ties Grass to Shah's death, though there is no one else who would obviously benefit from it. The government offers Shah's grand jury testimony under FRE 804(b)(6). **Does it qualify for admission under this exception?**

3. Impeaching a Hearsay Speaker

Hearsay speakers may be impeached with respect to their reported statements in much the same way as ordinary witnesses. Witnesses may testify to a hearsay speaker's biases, inability to observe, and bad reputation for truth and veracity. Difficulties potentially arise if the attempt is to impeach by inconsistent statements. You will recall that at common law this mode of impeachment requires a cross-examiner who wishes to introduce extrinsic evidence of an inconsistent statement to first direct the witness's attention to the alleged inconsistent statement, and that even under the Federal Rule the witness must be provided with some opportunity to explain or deny the allegedly inconsistent statement. These requirements cannot be met if the hearsay speaker is unavailable. Most states and the federal courts do not impose the traditional foundation requirements even if the hearsay speaker is available, or, as

---

[192] At first glance, the issue seems to resemble the use of other bad acts against a criminal defendant, under FRE 404(b), to prove motive, opportunity, knowledge, common scheme, etc. There, too, the jury learns about other misconduct by the defendant, and the standard for admissibility is even lower—merely evidence sufficient to support a finding that the defendant committed the acts. See Chapter Five, p. 376–377 (discussing Huddleston v. United States, 485 U.S. 681 (1988)). But since the defendant's commission of these prior acts admitted under FRE 404(b) bears on his guilt, he is allowed to present evidence and to argue to the jury that he did not in fact commit those acts. By contrast, parties are not generally allowed to dispute the foundational requirements for hearsay exceptions before the jury.

with former testimony, there once was an opportunity to lay a foundation for the impeachment, and it was not done. Also, when a witness is impeached by inconsistent statements, the statements will almost always have preceded the testimony, but a hearsay speaker may ordinarily be impeached by inconsistent statements made before or after the admitted hearsay.

The Federal Rules' receptive attitude toward hearsay is complemented by an equally receptive attitude toward evidence that tends to impeach the credibility of hearsay speakers. FRE 806 provides:

> When a hearsay statement—or a statement described in Rule 801(d)(2)(C), (D), or (E)—has been admitted in evidence, the declarant's credibility may be attacked, and then supported, by any evidence that would be admissible for those purposes if the declarant had testified as a witness. The court may admit evidence of the declarant's inconsistent statement or conduct, regardless of when it occurred or whether the declarant had an opportunity to explain or deny it. If the party against whom the statement was admitted calls the declarant as a witness, the party may examine the declarant on the statement as if on cross-examination.

As the range of admitted hearsay grows, this rule will likely continue to grow in importance. To judge by the case law, however, although parties often protest the admission of the hearsay of available declarants, they seldom call them to the stand for cross-examination, even when they have advance notice that hearsay will be offered. This is not surprising, for litigants will seldom have investigated hearsay speakers with the thoroughness that they might have investigated key witnesses, and not knowing what a person might say, it is dangerous to call him even for purposes of impeachment.

———————

Problem VI-87. Sarah Jay and Emma Swift are on trial with three others for conspiracy to distribute cocaine. Frank Hawk, an unidentified co-conspirator who has turned state's evidence, says that Swift told him that Jay had three kilos of cocaine stored in her house and that if he ran short of cocaine, she would give him some more. Jay testifies that she barely knows Swift, that she never stored cocaine or delivered it to anyone, and that she thinks Swift told Hawk she was in the conspiracy because her uncle was the chief of police and her involvement would have suggested that the conspiracy had police protection. In addition to her testimony, Jay seeks to impeach Swift by introducing evidence that Swift faces a murder charge when the current trial is over and has in the past been convicted once for attempting to smuggle cocaine into the country and another time of selling heroin. Swift, who has not testified and does not intend to, objects to the impeaching evidence. **How should the court rule?**

ADDITIONAL PROBLEMS

Problem VI-88. We have criticized the way in which the prior testimony exception is implemented on the ground that courts often do not look closely at whether the earlier situation provided a realistic occasion for effective cross-examination or at the quality of the incentives that existed for cross-examination. An argument can be made that the exception for prior testimony should apply regardless of the opportunity or motives that existed for earlier cross-examination. The earlier testimony will have been under oath, the situation will have been a solemn one, and the witness will have known how much was at stake for the parties. In addition, an exception for non-cross-examined prior testimony could require that the earlier testimony be proved by a trial transcript. **If you were a member of Congress, would you support a move to add such an exception to the hearsay rules? Why or why not?**

Problem VI-89. Peggy Jones sues Dr. Warren for malpractice, alleging that while he was treating her, he was suffering from chronic alcoholism and insane delusions. Ms. Jones has two affidavits available that were filed in the local probate court in an emergency commitment hearing. Each affidavit is by a local psychiatrist who knew Dr. Warren well, and each states that he is suffering from insane delusions brought on by chronic alcoholism and is likely to kill himself. They are dated January 15, 2010, the last day Dr. Warren treated Ms. Jones. The emergency commitment hearing was held *ex parte* and Dr. Warren was committed to a local mental hospital on the strength of the affidavits. Two days after the emergency commitment, the court, according to its usual practice, ordered a full hearing on whether Warren should remain committed. The psychiatrists who had signed the affidavits testified to the substance of their affidavits, and they were cross-examined by the counsel appointed by the court to represent Warren. Warren was not present, having refused to come to court. The court again ordered Warren committed, finding that he presented a danger to himself because of insane delusions stemming from chronic alcoholism. **At the trial for malpractice, may Ms. Jones introduce (1) the affidavits in which the psychiatrists reported their opinions; (2) the testimony of the psychiatrists given in the full hearing held by the probate court; and (3) the judgment by the court, after the full hearing, finding Warren a danger to himself, due to insane delusions stemming from chronic alcoholism, and ordering Warren committed?**

Problem VI-90. Nora Arnold has been indicted for perjury. She is charged with lying to a congressional committee when she told the committee that she had never been a member of the Communist Party.

May her statement "I was never a Communist," which she made at the hearing, be introduced against her at the perjury trial? On what theory? Rather than introducing a transcript of what was said, may the prosecutor place on the stand a staff assistant, who will testify that Nora "unequivocally denied having had anything to do with the communist party"?

Problem VI-91. Karen Peabody was an eyewitness to a robbery. She testified against the defendant at a preliminary hearing, identifying him as the man she had seen fleeing the Chicken Little convenience store with a drawn gun. She was questioned by the defense counsel at the preliminary hearing but did not change her story. When the case reached trial, Ms. Peabody was in the hospital with injuries suffered in an automobile accident. The doctor's estimate was that she would not be able to leave the hospital for two weeks. **In these circumstances may the prosecution introduce her testimony from the preliminary hearing? Would the situation be different if she was in intensive care following severe burns, and the doctor estimated that she would not be able to leave the hospital for six months?**

Problem VI-92. Esther Levy, a tourist in Hawaii, was injured on state property and sued the state under the Hawaii Tort Liability Act. At the first trial the state won a directed verdict, but the Hawaii Supreme Court reversed the trial court, entered judgment for Levy, and ordered a new trial on the issue of damages. Ms. Levy, who had returned to her home state of New York in the interim, never testified at the second trial. Instead a transcript of the testimony that she gave at the first trial was entered into evidence. At the second trial, damages in excess of 50 thousand dollars were awarded. The state appealed, claiming that the transcript of Levy's testimony in the earlier trial was improperly admitted. **How should the Court rule on appeal?**

Problem VI-93. Ralph Royster, who admits to being a member of the America First Movement, is charged, along with four other men, in the racially motivated assault on a young Cambodian immigrant, which occurred at about 11:00 p.m. on a Saturday evening. Tried in state court, he argues mistaken identity and presents his girlfriend, Judith Washington, as an alibi witness. She says that on the night of the assault they were at her house watching John Wayne films, a triple feature that they started watching at 6:30 p.m. and didn't finish until well after midnight. She presents video store receipts showing that she took out *The Searchers, Red River Valley*, and *The Kentuckian*, at 2:00 p.m. on the afternoon of the assault. The state cross-examines Washington vigorously, seeking to show that they began watching the films at about 3:00 p.m. and were finished by about 10:00 p.m., when Royster's buddies came by. Washington persists in her story and details a series of chores she had to do that afternoon. The jury acquits Royster, but convicts his four codefendants. Later the federal government tries Royster for violating the Cambodian immigrant's civil rights. When the case comes to trial, Washington is in the hospital, having just emerged from a coma following a serious automobile accident. She has no memory of what she and Royster did the night of the assault, and the doctors expect it will be four to six months before she might recover her memory, if she will at all. At his trial, Royster seeks to present a transcript of the testimony Washington gave in state court. **Should the judge admit the transcript over the U.S. Attorney's objection? Should the U.S. Attorney object?**

Problem VI-94. Harry Heston was tried for running an illegal numbers operation. At the trial, Heston's lieutenant, White, turned state's evidence and testified, "Heston raked in two hundred grand a year from the numbers operation." Despite White's testimony, Heston was acquitted. Shortly afterward, White was found shot once through the head. The police had a strong suspicion that Heston was responsible, but were never able to pin the crime on him. About a year later the IRS brought an action against Heston for taxes owed on $500,000 a year that the IRS claimed Heston had earned in his numbers racket but never reported. **May Heston, in an effort to minimize the claimed delinquency, introduce evidence that White, at the earlier trial, had stated that Heston only made $200,000 a year?**

Problem VI-95. Peter Prince sued Sharon Samuel in small-claims court, arguing that an electric heater that Sharon's Appliance Store had sold him was defective. He claimed that it did not regulate itself properly, sometimes failing to go on and sometimes failing to turn itself off when the desired temperature was reached. Sharon claimed that she had examined the heater once when Prince had returned it and had found nothing wrong. She argued that Prince either had not regulated it correctly or had abused it in some way after it had been examined in her store. Lawyers are not allowed to represent people in small claims court in the jurisdiction in question, but each party questioned the other vigorously, if not necessarily to great effect. Their testimony was given under oath. The judge ordered Sharon to pay Prince $10 to cover any problems with the heater that were the store's fault, and both went away feeling they had won. Three days later a fire broke out in Prince's room, killing him. Prince's estate brings suit against Sharon's Appliance Store and against the Kilowatt Company, which manufactured the heater, claiming it overheated and started the fire. Sharon is present at the trial. **Is the testimony that Prince gave in the small claims court admissible against either defendant? Is Sharon's testimony admissible against either defendant? Is Sharon's testimony admissible on behalf of either defendant? If Sharon were unavailable, would her former testimony be admissible for or against either defendant?**

Problem VI–96. Grant Will, an inventor, sues the Ford Motor Company for infringing on one of his patents in designing their anti-lock brake system. Ford defends by contesting the patentability of Will's invention, arguing that Will's ideas are an obvious extension of prior technology and do not constitute a substantial enough advance in the state of the art to have merited patent protection. Will's crucial witness is Dr. Thomas Panzer, Dean of the Engineering School at the National Institute of Technology and the world's leading expert on anti-lock braking systems. With great clarity, he explains to the jury the importance of Will's invention and why it was not, in his opinion, obvious from prior technology. Ford cross-examines Panzer for two days, but does not shake his testimony. Indeed, if anything, the cross-examination strengthens Will's case because it reveals why Ford's theories are mistaken. At least this appears to be what the jury concludes, for it awards Will $16 million. Will then sues General Motors for similar infringement, and G.M. interposes the same obviousness defense. In the time between the two trials, Dr. Panzer dies. Will seeks to introduce against G.M. a videotape of the testimony that Dr. Panzer gave in the Ford trial. G.M. objects, and the court sustains G.M.'s objections. **Is the court's ruling correct? Does it make sense?** Suppose in the Ford suit, Ford claimed that Will's invention was made possible by confidential data that he had secured by bribing an employee of Autolabs, a joint venture of the "Big Three" American auto companies designed to foster cutting edge automobile research. Will countered by calling Stanley Packard, the head of Autolabs, who testified that he had personally approved transferring the data, and that all he had asked was that Autolabs be cited in any publications that drew on the data. **If G.M. makes a similar claim when it is sued, and if Packard is unavailable, should Will be allowed to offer a videotape of Packard's testimony? Are the arguments for allowing the testimony stronger or weaker than they are for Panzer's testimony?**

Problem VI–97. Hancher is charged with assault with a deadly weapon. The charges stem from a bar fight in Iowa City in which Hancher pulled a knife on one Dick Druid. Hancher claims Druid was coming at him with a broken beer bottle and that he pulled the knife to scare Druid off. The crucial witness at the preliminary hearing was an eighteen-year-old girl named Sandy Struthers. She testifies that Druid didn't have a bottle in his hand and that Hancher first pulled his knife when Druid's back was turned. As Struthers finishes her testimony, Hancher leans over and whispers to his attorney, who had been appointed two days before the hearing, "Ask her whether she's Druid's girlfriend. I know her and she would say anything for him. Somebody told me she was in the bathroom when the fight started. She didn't see him break the bottle or me pull my knife." The attorney whispers back, "That's the kind of stuff we save for the trial. You're going to be bound over regardless."

A year later, and two weeks before trial, the prosecutor sends a subpoena to Sandy Struthers's house ordering her to show up at the trial. Struthers's parents call the prosecutor and tell him that their daughter left town six months before and they have no idea how to locate her. They say that they have heard from her only once, a month after she left, when she telephoned from Phoenix, and that they also had indirect contact some three months earlier when a social worker called from San Francisco to verify the fact that Sandy was no longer their dependent. The prosecutor tells them that if they should hear from their daughter during the next two weeks they should try to learn how she can be reached and they should be sure to call his office. At the trial, the prosecutor calls Struthers's parents to verify her unavailability and then offers a transcript of her testimony at the preliminary hearing. **Should the transcript be admitted? If it is admitted, can the defendant show that Struthers was Druid's girlfriend and that she was in the bathroom when the fight started? If this is allowed, how can he make this showing?**

Problem VI-98. Freddy Farmer farms land that borders on government property. One day Freddy is stopped for speeding. In his car the police spot a basket full of gold. Freddy claims to have found the gold on his property. The government claims the gold was illegally taken from government property and so should revert to the government. To support this claim, the government seeks to introduce a map, found in the basket that was drawn by Pauline Prospector shortly before her death five years earlier. The map purports to locate a cache of gold on government property near the border of Freddy's farm. **Is the map admissible to show the location of the gold?**

Problem VI-99. Sam Peck is charged with murder. He allegedly killed a bank guard in the course of an armed robbery. As he was leaving, he also shot a pedestrian, Carl Adams, on the sidewalk outside the bank. When the police arrived Adams was lying in a pool of blood. As they were placing him on a stretcher, Adams said to one of the officers, "That bastard who shot me was Sam Peck. We went to high school together, and he knew I recognized him. Well, I've had it and I'm going to heaven, but I hope he roasts in hell." In spite of what he said, Adams recovered. However, he died of a heart attack a year later while Peck was still at large. Eventually Peck was captured and brought to trial. **At the trial may the state offer Adams's statement to identify Peck as the bank robber? Had Adams died of the gunshot wound, could the state introduce his statement if Peck were tried for murdering him?**

Problem VI-100. A four-year-old child is found severely beaten. Lying in a hospital bed, the child asks the attending doctor to hold her hand. The doctor complies. The child asks the doctor how long the doctor will stay there. The doctor replies that he is willing to stay as long as she wants. The child responds, "I want you to hold my hand till I'm no longer here." The doctor asks the child what she means. The child responds, "I'm going away." The doctor replies, "Who did this to you, honey? Was it your mother?" The child nods her head, yes. The child dies 15 minutes later. At the mother's trial for beating the child to death, the prosecution seeks to have the doctor testify to the child's statements. **How should the court rule?**

Problem VI-101. Candy Young is found shot in the back. **Will her statement "Billy Olds shot me" be admitted if there is evidence that when she made this statement she knew she was about to die?** Assume that after stating that she expects to die, Candy made a more elaborate statement, "Billy Olds and I had a fight. I told him I never wanted to see him again. He slapped me. I kicked him. He pulled a gun and hit me on the shoulder with the butt. I gave him a karate chop to the stomach and he fell down. I turned and ran and then he shot me." **Is a court more or less likely to admit this statement than they are the simple statement "Billy Olds shot me,"? If Tom Novack is charged with Young's murder, will the statement be admissible on his behalf?**

Problem VI-102. Jennifer Weiss, Shirley Tomes, and some other graduate students were watching an episode of L.A. Law in which a dying declaration figured. Afterwards the following conversation ensued:

> Shirley: That seems like a reasonable exception to me. After all you wouldn't want to meet your maker with a lie on your lips.
>
> Jenny: I don't believe there is a 'maker.'
>
> Shirley: You don't? You know that's the kind of belief that leads people to Hell after they die.
>
> Jenny: And I suppose dying with a lie on your lips takes you to Hell, also?
>
> Shirley: Certainly.

Jennifer and Shirley were not exactly friends because their views on so many matters differed, and each had an abiding hatred of the other's spouse, for each had dated the other's spouse and suffered what she regarded as serious abuse at his hands. Jennifer and Shirley ran into each other at a park one day and were standing near a litter basket when a man with a trench coat that was pulled over his face came up and deposited a bag in the basket. A minute later it exploded, mortally wounding the two women. Before she died, Shirley told a doctor who had rushed to the scene, "I saw that man who did it. I know him well. It was Fred Weiss." Before she died, Jennifer told a doctor, "I saw the man who did it. I know him well. It was Al Tomes." Weiss and Tomes are tried separately for murder. **Assuming witnesses are available who will** testify in a 104(a) hearing to the conversation following L.A. Law, **can the state introduce Shirley's statements against Weiss and Jennifer's statements against Tomes? Can Weiss introduce Jennifer's statements? Can Tomes introduce Shirley's statements? If these statements are admitted, can any party introduce a witness to testify to the post-L.A. Law conversation?**

Problem VI-103. Pat Kelley was dying of cancer. She was in great agony and knew she had at most a week or two to live. One evening a nurse looked in and noticed that Pat was in a shallow sleep and looked particularly pale. He shook her awake and asked her if she had had her medicine for the evening. She replied that she did not remember having any of her hospital medicine but that her sister had given her two pills to swallow before she left. The nurse gave Pat her medicine and departed. That night Pat died. A routine autopsy showed that the cause of death was not cancer, but poison. Her sister is charged with manslaughter for this "mercy-killing." **May the state introduce Pat's statement that her sister gave her two pills to swallow as part of its effort to establish that the sister was responsible for the poison?**

Problem VI-104. Jill Hennesey, a notorious gambler, is being sued by the IRS for back taxes. The IRS claims that Hennesey failed to report as earnings $800,000 that she and a partner won in 2006 by gambling. To prove this, the IRS seeks to introduce entries on some papers seized from Hennesey that record winning bets totaling $800,000. Hennesey claims that at most she owes taxes on $300,000 in winnings because the partnership lost $500,000 wagering on the horses during 2006, and the tax law allows gambling losses to be subtracted from winnings. She seeks to introduce other entries on the papers seized by the IRS that note gambling losses totaling $500,000. The entries reporting losses are interspersed with those reporting winnings. **May the government introduce the entries reporting Hennesey's successful wagers? If the government is allowed to do this, may Hennesey introduce the entries that show her bad bets? If you were Hennesey's lawyer, what arguments would you make in support of your motion to admit the entries showing the losing bets?** Assume the entries were written by the partner, since deceased.

Problem VI-105. One day *A* tells her cousin, "I've just conveyed Whiteacre to *B* in exchange for Blackacre." Some years later, after both *A* and *B* have died, oil is discovered on Whiteacre, and a dispute arises between the heirs of *A* and those of *B* about who owns which property. **May B's heirs introduce A's cousin to testify to what A told him?**

Problem VI-106. Carol Pack, a 30-year-old woman, sues the estate of Butler Yates, claiming that she is the adopted daughter of Yates and entitled to a share in his estate. **May Pack introduce a witness who will testify that her natural father, now nowhere to be found,**

once said, "Well, I've done it. I've entered into a contract with Butler allowing him to adopt Carol. He's her father now. I no longer have the rights or the responsibility"? At the time of this statement Pack was five years old. **May the estate introduce copies of Yates's income tax returns for the years when Pack was 12, 13, and 14 years old to show that Carol's name is not listed among Yates's dependents?**

Problem VI-107. Harriet Duncan sues Randy Goshen, alleging that he is the father of her child. Randy claims he is not the father. Randy wishes to introduce a witness who will testify that she once heard Sam Davids state that he is the father of Harriet's child. **If Randy cannot find Davids to subpoena him, will the witness's testimony be admissible?**

Problem VI-108.   Tom Bergman arranged to buy Swampacre from George Fellini and to pay for it in a series of monthly cash installments beginning in June 2007. Bergman subsequently suffered a financial setback, which left him short of cash. He stopped making installment payments on Swampacre in August, and in October 2007 received a letter from Fellini which said, "Thank you for the $2,500 you have already paid me for the half-interest I sold you in Swampacre. I see, however, that you are no longer making payments. Do you have any idea when you are going to be able to resume the payments?" Beginning about the time the letter was written, Swampacre soared in value on rumors that a local developer had a permit to fill land and build apartments in the area. Within three weeks Swampacre was worth far more than what Bergman owed. In November 2007 Fellini died, and in January 2008 Bergman sent a check for all back payments and the current payment to Fellini's estate. The estate sought to avoid the transaction entirely and so returned the check. Bergman then sued to quiet title. At the trial, the estate claims, first, that Bergman forfeited his claims to the land by not paying the installments when they fell due, and, second, that Bergman, at most, has a claim to half the land. The estate holds a copy of a letter Fellini wrote to Bergman in October 2007. **Can Bergman introduce the letter to show his payment lapse did not forfeit his title? Can the estate introduce the letter to show that Bergman has at most only a half interest? If one party is allowed to use the letter to prove one of its points, can the other party use it to prove its own claims?**

Problem VI-109. Stephen Bird, noted bridge authority, wrote a column in which he accused Henry Hogg and his partner, Timothy Toucan, of cheating in major bridge tournaments over a 10-year period. Hogg sues Bird for libel. **At the trial, may Bird introduce evidence that Timothy Toucan, since deceased, had admitted before his death that he and Hogg had been cheating at bridge for many years?**

Would it matter whether the admission was made before or after Bird's column appeared?

Problem VI-110. Henderson, vice president and treasurer of the Mogg Corporation, is accused by a corporate auditor of embezzlement. Eventually she admits to having taken $540,000 over a three-year period. The company fires Henderson but does not press charges. Henderson leaves for a foreign country to be sure that the charges will not be brought despite the company's failure to press them. Later Mogg sues the company that had bonded Henderson for the $540,000. **In order to prove that this was the amount lost, may the company introduce Henderson's admission of this fact?**

Problem VI-111. Thompson, Ekols, and Meeks are charged with bank robbery. Ekols chose to plead guilty and turn state's evidence while Thompson and Meeks pled not guilty and were tried together. Ekols testified as follows:

> The day before the robbery Meeks approached me and asked me if I would like some easy money. I said "yes," and we went to his apartment and planned the robbery. It's only a small branch. We thought they wouldn't have much security. The next morning Meeks told me that he'd gotten Roland Thompson to drive for it. Later that day Meeks and I went to his apartment. Roland was there in the parking lot. He drove us downtown and circled the block the bank was on once or twice. Then he let us out. Meeks told him to meet us at the corner of First and Fifth, and he was there when we got out.

The cross-examination included the following:

Defense Counsel: You say you planned this robbery with Meeks. Was Thompson ever involved in the planning?

Ekols: No.

D.C.: Did you and Meeks ever discuss the robbery while you were in the car driving to the bank?

E: No.

D.C.: Did you ever hear Meeks mention the robbery in Thompson's presence?

E: No.

D.C.: After the robbery, what was Thompson's share of the proceeds?

E: He didn't get any of the money.

D.C.: Isn't it true that on the morning of the robbery Meeks said, "I've suckered Thompson into driving for it?"

E: No. He said, "I've gotten Thompson to drive for it." He meant Thompson agreed.

D.C.: Did Meeks use the word "agreed?"

E: No.

D.C.: Thank you. No more questions.

At the preliminary hearing in this case, right after pleading not guilty, Meeks had said within the hearing of the U.S. magistrate, the prosecuting and defense attorneys, a reporter, and Thompson, "They ought to let Thompson go. He didn't have anything to do with it." At the trial the government did not seek to introduce this statement against Meeks in its case-in-chief. It was also not used for impeachment since Meeks never took the stand. Thompson, however, wanted to introduce the statement. **Should he have been allowed to place any of the witnesses to the statement on the stand to testify to what Meeks had said?**

Problem VI-112. Phyllis Harris works as a bank teller at First National. One day a woman walks up to a window and passes through a note saying "I've got a gun. Put all your money in the bag." Phyllis puts $5,000 in the woman's bag and the woman flees. Later Phyllis is questioned by Special Agent Rebecca Kirshner of the FBI. Although Kirshner does not arrest Phyllis, she gives her *Miranda* warnings. She suspects Phyllis is involved in the robbery both because she delayed in pressing the switch that triggers the silent alarm and because she knows that Phyllis's brother Ed is a suspect in another bank robbery, at Bankers Trust. After several hours of questioning, Phyllis breaks down and confesses her complicity. She tells Kirshner:

"About five days ago Eddie called me. He said that he was one of those who robbed the Bankers Trust, but that his pictures weren't on the T.V. news because the surveillance cameras didn't catch him. I think he was proud of it. He asked me to meet him the next day, and I did. The next day he told me he wasn't really one of the robbers, but that he was outside the bank at the time, and he thought the police suspected him so he had better get out of town. He said he needed money and that his girlfriend, Karen, would stage a bank robbery if I would cooperate. I didn't want to do it, but he wore me down saying how it would kill mama if he got arrested. I stopped by Karen's yesterday morning to explain the layout of the bank, and you know the rest."

Eddie Harris was arrested four years later and tried for robbing Bankers Trust. The state's central witness is Simon Shuster, one of the robbers who was caught soon after the robbery and convicted. He identifies Eddie as a participant and says that because Eddie's location was near the bank's door, he was out of the field of the camera. The corroborating evidence is weak. One of Eddie's prints was found on the getaway car, and he was absent from work the day of the robbery. To further corroborate the accomplice's testimony, the state would like to introduce Phyllis's statement. Eddie's admission that he was one of the participants but that the camera didn't catch him is considered particularly important. Phyllis, who was indicted for the second robbery but never tried, is called as a witness. She says she no longer remembers the details of her conversation with agent Kirshner, and she specifically does not recall ever telling Kirshner that her brother said that he had helped rob the Bankers Trust but had not been photographed. She does say that she recalls answering all of Kirshner's questions truthfully. The state would like to call Agent Kirshner to testify to Phyllis' statement. **Setting aside any possible Confrontation Clause objection, is Kirshner's testimony admissible?**

Problem VI-113. On May 1, 2012, an abortion clinic in Laramie, Wyoming, was destroyed by a bomb. Hilda Coverly has been arrested as an accessory after the fact for sheltering Marcus Hayes, who is a suspect in the bombing. After receiving her *Miranda* warnings, Hilda told the following story to the officer interrogating her: "The day after the bombing, Marcus, who is a former boyfriend of mine, came to my house and said, 'You've got to help me; I'm wanted in connection with that Laramie bombing.' I said to him, 'Marcus, did you do it?' He said, 'No.' Then he said, 'I can't lie to you Hilda. Yes, I did it.' I thought for a bit, and then I thought he was honest with me, and we had parted friends, so I told him he could hide in my basement until the heat was off."

When Marcus is tried for the bombing, Hilda pleads the Fifth Amendment and refuses to testify. **Setting aside any possible Confrontation Clause objection, may the state introduce her statement to the officer who arrested her?**

Problem VI-114. Franz and Herman Lound attempted to rob a bank, but bungled it from the start. It ended in tragedy when the bank manager, despite being bound and gagged, was stabbed to death by one or both brothers after he kicked Franz. Helen Gomez, a teller who was tied up next to the manager was also stabbed several times, but survived. The brothers were soon arrested and face the death penalty. Herman refused to talk to the police, but Franz told them that he killed the manager with a knife after the manager kicked him. He added that Herman had nothing to do with the killing and, in fact, was not even in the back room at the time.

At trial, Herman testifies but Franz does not. Herman seeks to introduce Franz's statement taking full responsibility for the killing as a statement against interest. Corroborating the statement is a bruise on Franz's leg, Gomez's testimony that only one person stabbed her, her testimony that she saw the manager kick someone, and Herman's testimony that he was not in the room when the killing occurred. **Should** the judge admit Franz's statement? **Would it make a difference if Gomez also testified that she saw two men struggling with the manager, that she is sure it was Herman who stabbed her, and that she heard one person say to the other, "Just be sure he's dead"?**

Problem VI-115. Larry Grant sues Ted Hagler for alienating the affections of his wife, Carrie. Hagler replies that his wife never loved him, but had married him for his money. To prove this, Hagler offers a letter from Carrie's sister Sandra to their mother, in which Sandra writes, "Carrie is marrying Larry Grant only for his money. I think she will regret it." Grant objects to the letter as hearsay. Hagler responds that since the letter concerns a fact of family history, it is admissible under FRE 804(b)(4). **How should the court rule?**

Problem VI-116. Curly and Moe had just emerged from a restaurant when a black limousine drove by, spraying machine gun fire. Curly was killed instantly. Moe was still conscious when the police arrive. He asked them, "Is Curly dead?" "Yes," he was told. "Well," says Moe, "Curly always said we would die together. It was Stan Hardy who did this; he thought Curly was trying to move in on his territory, but why he went after me I don't know. I guess it's the company I keep."

Hardy was arrested and put on trial for Curly's murder. Moe survived but refused to testify; "I don't remember anything," he told the D.A., "And if I did, I don't think it would be very healthy for me." When asked about a recent $50,000 deposit in his bank account and how he could manage it when he had never earned more than $25,000 in a single year, Moe said, "All these years I have been saving money under my mattress. I thought it was time I should get some interest." **Can the state introduce the identification of Stan Hardy that Moe made after he was gunned down?**

Problem VI-117: Rory Epstein is charged with selling crack cocaine. Part of the state's evidence is that Rory's girlfriend, Amanda Stark, had told her girlfriend, Suellen Danning, that Rory took home as much as $3,000 a week from crack sales. **Can Suellen testify to what Amanda told her?** Suppose the state calls Amanda to the stand to ask her about Rory's crack dealings. Amanda has with her a certificate showing she married Rory two weeks before the trial and claims her privilege as a spouse not to testify against her husband. **Now can Suellen testify to what Amanda said? Would it make a difference if Suellen told the judge that she asked Amanda why Rory had after many years agreed to marry her and that Amanda had replied, "He wants to shut my mouth at trial"? Would it make a difference if Suellen told the judge that she asked Amanda why she had agreed to marry Rory after all the grief he had given her and Amanda had replied, "I was afraid of what he would do to me if I didn't"?**

IV. MODERN TRENDS

A. LOOKING BACKWARD AT PAST JUDGMENTS ON THE FUTURE OF HEARSAY

For many years, evidence scholars wrote about "the future of hearsay," and a glance at the future became the customary way of concluding the hearsay chapter in casebooks. For several generations, the consensus among scholars was that the future of the common law hearsay doctrine was bleak. The most common criticisms were that the exclusion of hearsay evidence too often hampered the search for truth, and that the proliferation of hearsay exceptions had created a system of unmanageable complexity. Suggested improvements ranged from abolishing the hearsay rule to the creation of new hearsay exceptions that would admit reliable evidence currently excluded.

Prior to the passage of the Federal Rules, the case most often cited as an example of what the future would and should bring was *Dallas County v. Commercial Union Assurance Co.*[193] This case grew out of an incident on July 7, 1957, when, "the clock tower of the Dallas County Courthouse at Selma, Alabama, commenced to lean, made loud cracking and popping noises, then fell, and telescoped into the courtroom."[194] Dallas County sued its insurance carrier alleging the collapse was caused by lightning. The carrier defended, claiming that the collapse stemmed from structural defects not covered by the policy. Perhaps the strongest evidence offered by the county was testimony that charred timbers had been found in the tower debris. To rebut the inference, supported by expert testimony, that the charred timbers were the result of lightning, the insurance company introduced a copy of the *Morning Times* of Selma for June 9, 1901, which carried an unsigned story reporting a fire in the courthouse, then under construction. The jury found for the defendant and the issue on appeal was whether this story had been properly admitted under the then governing rule, Fed. R.Civ.P. 43(a), which provided:

> All evidence shall be admitted which is admissible under the statutes of the United States, or under the rules of evidence heretofore applied in the courts of the United States on the hearing of suits in equity, or under the rules of evidence applied in the courts of general jurisdiction of the state in which the United States court is held. In any case, the statute or rule which favors the reception of the evidence governs. . . .

Rather than strain to fit the story under one of the existing hearsay exceptions, the appellate court looked at the two criteria that Wigmore thought sufficient for the creation of a hearsay exception—necessity and

---

[193] 286 F.2d 388 (5th Cir. 1961).

[194] *Id.* at 390.

circumstantial guarantees of trustworthiness. Admitting that witnesses to the fire still might be found, the court nevertheless saw the story as necessary to prove reliably the source of the charred timbers. The court assumed that it was unlikely that a witness could be found who clearly remembered events surrounding the courthouse's construction, and that no witness could give testimony as accurate and reliable as the contemporary news article. The court believed the story was trustworthy because the reporter had no motive to lie and would have been embarrassed to mistakenly report a matter so easily checked by readers. The court concluded:

> We do not characterize this newspaper as a "business record", nor as an "ancient document", nor as any other readily identifiable and happily tagged species of hearsay exception. It is admissible because it is necessary and trustworthy, relevant and material, and its admission is within the trial judge's exercise of discretion in holding the hearing within reasonable bounds.[195]

Despite the approval that greeted this opinion, it was not followed by any marked increase in the tendency of courts to ignore the parameters of the hearsay exceptions and look instead to the general character of the proffered hearsay. Predictions that the hearsay rule would be substantially relaxed continued to better indicate the hopes of the prognosticators than the behavior of courts.[196] Beginning in the mid-1960s, this changed when a number of states and the federal government decided to codify their rules of evidence. Suddenly, the numerous critics of the hearsay rule no longer had to convince courts how hearsay doctrine should develop. As reporters of, or advisers to, committees drafting evidence codes, the critics had the opportunity to write their preferences into law. Although some of the more extreme ideas for liberalizing the hearsay rule were never accepted or were eliminated in the enactment process, all the modern codes substantially liberalized traditional restrictions on hearsay evidence. With the enactment of the Federal Rules of Evidence and of the many state codes modeled on it, the "future of hearsay" is, upon us and here to stay.

There has been a significant expansion of the situations in which hearsay evidence is admissible. The increased admissibility of hearsay evidence has been accomplished in two ways: first, by the elimination of restrictive conditions that are part of the traditional exceptions; and, second, by the creation of new exceptions to the hearsay rule. In Section

---

[195] *Id.* at 397–98.

[196] Trial courts have always taken liberties with the hearsay doctrine, as they have with other rules of evidence. Their reasons range from a desire to get at the truth to mistakes about what the hearsay rule requires. Appellate courts affirming cases in which hearsay is not clearly admissible almost always justify free-wheeling trial court decisions by reference to a specific exception, or they treat error as harmless. Rarely do or did they take the approach seen in *Dallas County* and disclaim the need to look to particular exceptions.

III of this Chapter we noted the many ways in which the specific exceptions of the Federal Rules of Evidence differ from their common law counterparts. In almost all cases, deviation from tradition enhances the admissibility of hearsay evidence. Indeed, certain federal hearsay exceptions, such as the exception for statements in learned treatises, were unknown at common law.

B. RELIABILITY AS A PRIMARY JUSTIFICATION

Most of the hearsay exceptions that the Federal Rules of Evidence created or expanded are reactions to specific situations in which the drafters thought hearsay should be admitted. We have already discussed most of these new and changed rules. The exceptions that we discuss in this section are based on more general principles. Perhaps the most basic and potentially the most expansive principle is the one applied in the *Dallas County* case: *If an item of hearsay evidence has circumstantial guarantees of trustworthiness equivalent to the guarantees that justify the recognized exceptions, that evidence should be admitted whether or not it meets the requirements of an established hearsay exception.* This principle is most likely to be applied when it is difficult to develop nonhearsay evidence that bears on a fact in issue.

This principle was pressed to the fullest in the first published draft of the Federal Rules of Evidence. This draft contained only two exceptions to the hearsay rule. Proposed FRE 803(a) applied regardless of the speaker's availability:

> A statement is not excluded by the hearsay rule if its nature and the special circumstances under which it was made offer assurances of accuracy not likely to be enhanced by calling the speaker as a witness, even though he is available.

Proposed FRE 804(a) applied if the speaker was unavailable:

> A statement is not excluded by the hearsay rule if its nature and the special circumstances under which it was made offer strong assurances of accuracy and the speaker is unavailable as a witness.

The specific exceptions now found in these subsections were mentioned, but only as illustrations of situations in which hearsay should be admitted and not by way of limitation.

This dramatic subordination of specific hearsay exceptions to the principles of reliability and necessity was ultimately rejected as too drastic a change in established doctrine. The federal rules transmitted by the Supreme Court to Congress for codification contained specific hearsay exceptions. However, the principle that guided the original approach was embedded in two new rules, FRE 803(24) and FRE 804(b)(6), both of which provided exceptions for:

A statement not specifically covered by any of the foregoing exceptions but having comparable circumstantial guarantees of trustworthiness.

The Rules differed only in that "foregoing exceptions" were conditioned on unavailability in the case of FRE 804(b)(6). The House Judiciary Committee rejected these *catchall* exceptions, pointing to the uncertainty they injected into hearsay law and the fear that by diminishing the predictability of hearsay rulings they would impair the ability of litigants to prepare for trial.

The members of the Senate Judiciary Committee had a different fear. They were afraid that unless courts had discretion to admit reliable hearsay, the result in cases like *Dallas County* would be reversed. They proposed language giving courts discretion to admit apparently reliable hearsay when the need for it was great. With the addition in conference of a notice requirement, the Senate revision was enacted as FRE 803(24) and FRE 804(b)(5).[197] Later, the rules were consolidated and renumbered as FRE 807:

(a) In General. Under the following circumstances, a hearsay statement is not excluded by the rule against hearsay even if the statement is not specifically covered by a hearsay exception in Rule 803 or 804:

(1) the statement has equivalent circumstantial guarantees of trustworthiness;

(2) it is offered as evidence of a material fact;

(3) it is more probative on the point for which it is offered than any other evidence that the proponent can obtain through reasonable efforts; and

(4) admitting it will best serve the purposes of these rules and the interests of justice.

(b) Notice. The statement is admissible only if, before the trial or hearing, the proponent gives an adverse party reasonable notice of the intent to offer the statement and its particulars, including the declarant's name and address, so that the party has a fair opportunity to meet it.

The spirit of the rule that Congress enacted was quite different from the rules the drafters originally favored and from the catchall rules transmitted to Congress by the Court. Under the earlier versions, the decision to exclude hearsay was suspect; the goal was to avoid depriving the jury of evidence. Under the enacted version, hearsay evidence remains suspect; only in exceptional circumstances should a court admit hearsay that does not meet the conditions of a particular exception.

---

[197] The rule was enacted as FRE 804(b)(5) rather than (b)(6) because a draft FRE 804(b)(5) rule was eliminated in the enactment process.

However, there is considerable variation in the way in which the *catchall* or *residual* exception has been interpreted.[198] Some judges are faithful to congressional intent and use their discretion only in exceptional circumstances. Other judges, however, treat FRE 807 as a license to admit whatever hearsay they think essential to a just result. Consider, for example, the case of *United States v. Lyon*,[199] the trial of a man who allegedly built bombs in shoe boxes. A Mrs. Lorts, Lyon's landlady, told a police officer who had found a bomb in a shoe box that she had given a shoe box to Lyon. Shortly after this interview, Lyon jumped bail and remained free for 11 years. By the time of the trial, Mrs. Lorts had forgotten both the incident and her description of it. The trial judge admitted the police officer's transcription of his interview with Mrs. Lorts under the former catch-all exception, FRE 804(b)(5). The appellate court approved, noting that "[t]rustworthiness was guaranteed by Smith's detailed testimony about how he took Mrs. Lorts' statement and transcribed it."[200] But this justification relates not at all to the trustworthiness of Mrs. Lorts' statement. It means, at most, that whatever Mrs. Lorts said was accurately reported. This is an important consideration, but by this standard the recorded statements of any unavailable witnesses would be presumptively admissible. The court also noted that the shoe box, which was in evidence, bore the signatures of both Mrs. Lorts and the police officer and that it conformed to the description of the box that Mrs. Lorts had given the officer. Here the court was looking for circumstantial guarantees of trustworthiness,[201] but these guarantees are not akin to those that attach to other hearsay exceptions. Indeed, they are hardly guarantees at all. They just suggest that if we can believe the assertion that the state believes Mrs. Lorts made by signing the box, and believe that she described the box she gave Lyon accurately, the shoe box in court is the one Mrs. Lorts gave Lyon. But the point of the hearsay rule is that absent an exception, the jury should not be asked to believe a speaker's out-of-court assertions.

The Eighth Circuit in *Lyon* was arguably unfaithful to both the letter and the spirit of the residual exception. But a court may remain faithful to the letter of the rule and still use it in a way that Congress never intended. *Turbyfill v. International Harvester Co.*[202] is such a case. In *Turbyfill*, the plaintiff and two companions, while shopping on the

---

[198] Given the revisions to the Federal Rules of Evidence, we shall refer to a single catchall exception, FRE 807. We shall, however, freely cite case law interpreting FRE 803(24) and/or FRE 804(b)(5). This case law has the same precedential value with respect to FRE 807 as it had with the rules it originally interpreted.

[199] 567 F.2d 777 (8th Cir. 1977).

[200] *Id.* at 784.

[201] *Id.* If, as was probably the case, Mrs. Lorts signed the box to indicate that it was the box she gave Lyon, her signature was assertive conduct and is itself objectionable as hearsay. If she signed the box without intending to assert that it was the box she gave Lyon, it is hard to see how her signature is relevant.

[202] 486 F.Supp. 232 (E.D.Mich.1980).

defendant's used-car lot, were, with the aid of the defendant's mechanic, Anderson, trying to start a balky truck. While the plaintiff was pouring gasoline from a small can into the truck's carburetor, one of his companions attempted to start the engine. The engine backfired, the gas can caught fire, and the plaintiff was severely burned. Three hours later, Anderson's supervisor told him to go into a room and write down everything he knew about the accident. Anderson died before the suit that arose out of this event reached trial. The defendant offered his statement to show how the accident occurred, and the trial judge admitted it under the residual exception. The judge noted that the statement was offered to prove a material fact and that it was more probative on the points for which it was offered than any other evidence that the defendant could reasonably have obtained. Guarantees of trustworthiness were present because:

> He [Anderson] wrote the statement on the afternoon of the accident, while the circumstances were still fresh in his mind. Moreover, the fact that he made his written account while alone in a room indicates that the account accurately reflects his knowledge of the events transcribed.[203]

The judge in *Turbyfill* complied with the letter of the rule. After determining that the evidence is material and necessary, he found, as a matter of discretion, that the hearsay carried guarantees of trustworthiness equivalent to those that guarantee other hearsay exceptions.[204] The problem is with the exercise of discretion. If Anderson's hearsay is admissible, so is any other uncoerced statement written or uttered while an event is fresh in the speaker's mind and not amenable to duplication by other reasonably accessible evidence. Indeed, Anderson's statement is more suspect than most such statements, for Anderson was a potential defendant in Turbyfill's suit, and he might also have feared being fired by his employer if he admitted responsibility for the accident.[205] The judge's exercise of discretion in *Turbyfill* undercut a

---

[203] Id. at 235.

[204] The trial judge also cited FRE 803(5), the exception for past recollection recorded, as a justification for his decision. The judge pointed out that if Anderson had been present at the trial and had been unable to remember the circumstances of the accident, his written account would have been admissible. This is true, but this is because additional guarantees of trustworthiness are thought to attach to FRE 803(5) statements. First, Anderson would have had to swear to the accuracy of the statement when he made it. Second, he could have been cross-examined about his perceptual abilities and about his feelings at the time of the accident. He might have been asked, for example, whether his company disciplined employees who were responsible for accidents or whether it had ever occurred to him that he might be sued personally by Turbyfill. While he was being questioned the jury could have viewed Anderson's demeanor and judged whether he was the kind of person who might falsely describe an incident in order to protect himself. The availability of FRE 803(5) to admit hearsay similar to Anderson's actually emphasizes the degree to which Anderson's hearsay lacks the guarantees associated with other exceptions.

[205] In addition to Anderson's obvious motive to falsify there is the natural human instinct to deny one's responsibility for a tragic event. This may be the greater threat to accuracy.

considered congressional decision.[206] If *Turbyfill* were the standard for admissible hearsay, the hearsay rule would be all but destroyed. As long as hearsay was necessary, all but the most obviously contrived statements would be admitted.

Lyon and *Turbyfill* are extreme cases. *Lyon* itself would likely now come out differently due to changes in the Court's Confrontation Clause jurisprudence. They do not, however, stand alone. We could have drawn on many other cases for examples of courts disregarding such seemingly clear legislative history as the following:

> It is intended that the residual hearsay exceptions will be used very rarely, and only in exceptional circumstances. The committee does not intend to establish a broad license for trial judges to admit hearsay statements that do not fall within one of the other exceptions contained in rules 803 and 804(b).[207]

Other courts have taken Congress' intent seriously and cite the above language in construing the residual exception. Although the appellate courts have addressed issues on a case-by-case basis, no circuit has laid down a coherent framework to guide trial judges in their exercise of discretion, so the jurisprudence of the residual exception is, almost four decades after its enactment, still in flux.

In interpreting the residual exceptions, subsection (a)(2), that the statement be offered as evidence of a material fact and subsection (a)(4), that the purposes of the rules and the interests of justice be served, are not problematic. If a statement is not material, it is not admissible under any hearsay exception, and if the statement is material, trustworthy and necessary, the purposes of the rules and the interests of justice will almost certainly be served by its admission. It is also possible to read "material" not in a technical sense, but as signifying a congressional intent that the fact that the evidence is offered to prove be important to the outcome of the case. This reading does not limit the applicability of the exception when its availability matters. Subsection (a)(3), the requirement that the statement be "more probative on the point for which it is offered than any other evidence that the proponent can obtain through reasonable efforts" is substantively important. It suggests that

---

[206] One might argue that the guarantees in *Turbyfill* were no weaker than those that justify the admission of dying declarations or excited utterances. But, when those exceptions arose, their justifications appeared considerably stronger than they do now. Only twentieth century psychology makes us wonder whether the presumably enhanced sincerity these exceptions presume is more than offset by difficulties of perception. Congress was concerned with the trustworthiness of the hearsay that the residual exceptions might admit. Courts should not use exceptions attributable more to historical reasons and nineteenth century psychology than to current judgments of reliability as benchmarks for determining what circumstantial guarantees of trustworthiness are equivalent to the established exceptions.

[207] Notes of Committee on the Judiciary, S.Rep.No. 1277, 93d Cong., 2d Sess. 20 (1974). Because the House of Representatives would have eliminated the residual exceptions entirely, the quoted language from the Senate Committee's report indicates the most expansive reading that can be given to the residual exception consistent with its legislative history.

although unavailability is not a formal prerequisite to admissibility under FRE 807, it will often be required. Also, courts may require attempts to depose witnesses outside their jurisdiction before applying this exception. Probably the most common situation where FRE 807 has been used to admit the hearsay of available witnesses is when child abuse is alleged. Adults have been allowed under the rule to tell juries what available child abuse victims told them. Some states have enacted special exceptions to the hearsay rule for child abuse cases, so the Rule 807 exception is not needed to reach this result.

In applying the residual exception, courts have paid special attention to the requirement of circumstantial guarantees of trustworthiness equivalent to those that justify other hearsay exceptions. More hearsay has been refused for lack of trustworthiness than for any other reason, but, as in *Turbyfill*, the requirement is also, on occasion, empty. Courts searching for equivalent guarantees of trustworthiness have looked at what the statement says, the circumstances in which it was made, and the extent to which it is corroborated by other evidence. Given Congress's apparent intent to require indicia of trustworthiness like those of the other exceptions, the existence of corroborating evidence should play no part in applying FRE 807, since the trustworthiness of hearsay admitted under the specific exceptions is not guaranteed by its consistency with other evidence. Some federal courts, following the apparent congressional intent, refused to look to corroborating circumstances for guarantees of trustworthiness, but they were probably in the minority in 1990 when the Supreme Court decided *Idaho v. Wright*.[208]

In *Wright*, a trial court, applying Idaho's Rule 803(24), a rule identical to its then federal counterpart, admitted the hearsay of a two-and-a-half-year-old girl describing incidents of sexual abuse. The issue in *Wright* was not Idaho's interpretation of its hearsay exception, but the constitutionality of using this evidence against a criminal defendant. The Supreme Court, in deciding that the girl's statements had too few indicia of reliability to satisfy the Confrontation Clause, held that in searching for "particular guarantees of trustworthiness"[209] a court should look not at corroborating evidence, but at whether the circumstances surrounding the making of the statement made the speaker particularly worthy of belief. The Court quoted with approval the Ninth Circuit's conclusion in *Huff v. White Motor Corp.* that "[t]he circumstantial guarantees of trustworthiness on which the various specific exceptions to the hearsay rule are based are those that existed at the time the statement was made and do not include those that may be added by using hindsight."[210] Since

---

[208] 497 U.S. 805 (1990). The case is reprinted in part in Chapter Seven.

[209] This language was taken not from Rule 803(24) but from an earlier case, *Ohio v. Roberts*, 448 U.S. 56 (1980). *Roberts* is discussed in Chapter Seven.

[210] Huff v. White Motor Corp., 609 F.2d 286, 292 (7th Cir. 1979).

the *Huff* court was interpreting Rule 803(24), the citation suggests that the Supreme Court would interpret FRE 807 in the same way.

As a matter of federal statutory interpretation, the Ninth Circuit's views, as endorsed by the Supreme Court, are clearly correct, even though as a purely factual matter the best indicator of a hearsay statement's trustworthiness is likely to be its coincidence with the other evidence in the case. Coincidence with other evidence differs, however, from the circumstantial guarantees of trustworthiness that support the other exceptions, and is best seen as not a *circumstantial* guarantee at all.

Moreover, there are policy reasons not to use consistency as a guide to trustworthiness. This approach can easily blur the separate elements of a case. Assume, for example, that a state must prove elements A, B, and C to convict a criminal defendant. Elements A and B are proved by testimony while element C is proved only by hearsay. If hearsay tending to prove C is deemed trustworthy because it is consistent with the evidence supporting elements A and B, a court in admitting C is likely to be deciding *sub silentio* that if elements A and B exist, element C probably exists as well.[211] But if a state made C a separate element of a crime, its existence should be established separately from that of elements A and B.

Perhaps an even more serious flaw with the consistency test for trustworthiness is that it presumes that the evidence in a case points in one direction. Hearsay that is corroborated by one side's evidence is likely to conflict with evidence the other side presents. In deciding that corroboration makes hearsay trustworthy, the court is implicitly accepting as true the evidence one side presents. Indeed, if a court were convinced that one side's evidence was "a pack of lies," hearsay corroborating those lies would be less trustworthy on that account.

Finally, a court will often have to decide whether to admit hearsay under the residual exception when it has heard only a portion of the evidence that the plaintiff has to offer. Hearsay that appears to be consistent with other evidence at that point in the trial may appear inconsistent later on, even before the defense has presented its case.

In searching for "equivalent circumstantial guarantees of trustworthiness," courts must compare hearsay admissible only under the residual exception, if it is admissible at all, with hearsay admissible under the specific exceptions. Special problems arise if the hearsay in question is much like the hearsay that a specific exception admits. On the one hand, the hearsay in question is likely to share some of the indicia of trustworthiness that justify the specific exception. On the other hand, the hearsay may fail to qualify under the specific exception because

---

[211] Of course, it will often be the case that evidence that bears on the existence of A or B tends to prove C as well.

it is of a kind that Congress meant specifically to exclude. For example, dying declarations offered in armed robbery cases will have guarantees of trustworthiness similar to those of dying declarations offered in homicide cases. But using FRE 807 to admit a dying declaration in an armed robbery trial ignores Congress's intent that dying declarations be admissible only in homicide cases and civil actions.

What we believe courts should do is defer to legislative intent when it appears that Congress or the Advisory Committee had reasons for the lines they drew, and to use discretion when there is no evidence that a matter was considered. Not all courts do this. Particularly in dealing with the statements of alleged victims in sex abuse cases, courts tend to admit hearsay if the conditions of an established exception are almost met without regard to whether the exception's parameters were designed to exclude hearsay of the type offered. But Congress intended the residual exception to be rarely used; it did not think it was establishing a vehicle that would undermine the careful and sometimes hotly contested line drawing it engaged in when defining the specific exceptions.

If there is one portion of the residual exception that seems invulnerable to judicial discretion, it is the requirement that a statement "is admissible only if, before the trial or hearing, the proponent gives an adverse party reasonable notice of the intent to offer the statement and its particulars." Some courts read the requirement literally and say it is to be strictly construed. But other courts read it in light of its most obvious purpose, "so that the party has a fair opportunity to meet" the statement. One of the first cases construing the residual exception held that when the government had an unexpected need to present hearsay admissible only under the residual exception, a continuance was sufficient to meet the purposes of the notice requirement.[212] Other courts have implied that even a continuance is not necessary if the adverse party had reason to expect that information like that contained in the hearsay would be admitted.[213] In ruling this way, courts not only ignore what appears to be a clear congressional command, but also treat pretrial notice as if its sole function is to allow the adversary an opportunity to challenge the hearsay. Knowing before trial whether certain evidence is admissible may also affect a party's litigation strategy and proclivity to settle. In addition, if notice must be given before trial, hearsay cannot be resorted to when a party finds that other attempts to prove a point have not been convincing. It may even be that the requirement of pretrial notice was one means by which Congress meant to ensure that the residual exception would be used "very rarely, and only in exceptional circumstances."

---

[212] United States v. Iaconetti, 540 F.2d 574 (2d Cir. 1976), *cert. denied* 429 U.S. 1041 (1977).

[213] United States v. Lyon, 567 F.2d 777 (8th Cir. 1977), is one such case.

The future of hearsay is inextricably linked with the way in which courts interpret the residual exception. To date, interpretations have been mixed. On the one hand, judges want discretion to admit hearsay when they feel admitting it will enhance justice. On the other, there is the pull of the legislative history that, on any fair reading, means that the residual exception should be used sparingly and only in special circumstances. Indeed, Justice Stewart, in a dissent from a denial of certiorari, suggested that it is "open to serious doubt whether [former] Rule 804(b)(5) was intended to provide case-by-case hearsay exceptions, rather than only to permit expansion of the hearsay exceptions by categories."[214]

In this, we think Justice Stewart was mistaken. The rule's language and the legislative history described above make it clear that a court asked to apply FRE 807 should carefully consider the importance of the offered evidence and the justifications for admitting it. This kind of meticulous scrutiny does not lend itself to establishing new categories of exceptions. Evidence might be admitted in one case because of special circumstances that, if even slightly altered, would not justify admission in another case.

To secure or fight the admission of evidence under the residual exception, a lawyer must understand the policies underlying the hearsay rule and its exceptions. The proponent of hearsay should be ready with analogies to the policy justifications for other exceptions, and the opponent should be prepared to point out how hearsay dangers that other exceptions guard against are not removed in the particular case. Both sides should know the rule's legislative history, although it will usually be the opponent of the hearsay who draws the most comfort from it.

———————

Problem VI-118. In exchange for dropping a drug charge and lifting a detainer for a parole violation, Brown agreed to cooperate with agents from the Drug Enforcement Agency (DEA). He was particularly important in an investigation involving Charles East. On three occasions, Brown was strip searched to ascertain that he had no heroin in his possession, given money, and sent to meet East. Each time he returned from the meeting with heroin that he gave to the DEA agent in charge of the case. His phone calls to East to arrange his purchases were monitored, and on one occasion the DEA agents were able to photograph East and Brown together. After each purchase, the DEA agent prepared a statement summarizing what had occurred, and Brown read, corrected, and signed these statements. On March 16, 2012, Brown appeared before a grand jury and described his dealings with East and with others

---

[214] McKethan v. United States, 439 U.S. 936, 939 n. 3 (1978) (Stewart, J., dissenting), *denying cert. to* United States v. Garner, 574 F.2d 1141 (4th Cir. 1978).

involved in the heroin traffic. The statements signed by Brown were read to the grand jury and the government's attorney periodically asked him if they were correct. On March 19, Brown was found dead in his car with four bullets through the back of his head. A month later, a week before East's case was scheduled to come to trial, the government notified East that it intended to offer under FRE 807 a transcript of Brown's grand jury testimony, including the prepared statements that Brown had said were accurate. At the time this notice was given, the government stipulated that it had no evidence connecting East to Brown's death. **Setting aside any possible Confrontation Clause objection, should the judge admit the evidence?** Suppose that Brown had not died in the manner described, but had died of a heart attack on the third day of trial shortly before he was scheduled to be called as a witness. At that point the government stated its intention to offer the transcript of Brown's grand jury testimony under FRE 807. **Should the transcript be admitted?**

"Do you swear to tell the truth, the whole truth, and nothing but the truth, and not in some sneaky relativistic way?"

C. NECESSITY AS A PRIMARY JUSTIFICATION

The admission of the hearsay in *Dallas County* was justified primarily by its likely reliability. The necessity for the evidence, although a factor the court weighed, was of secondary importance. Although under FRE 807 the need for the hearsay rule is an important consideration, here too courts devote most of their attention to reliability issues. Some commentators would admit hearsay in almost all situations where a need for it exists. They argue that since the costs of excluding hearsay are clear, while the possibility that hearsay will mislead the jury is problematic, the statements of unavailable speakers should be admitted unless there are special reasons to suspect their reliability. But, as a factor to be weighed in creating hearsay exceptions, necessity cuts two ways. Hearsay is most necessary to a party when it is the only available evidence tending to prove an important aspect of her case. Yet, in these circumstances, the concern for reliability should be greatest, because the case's outcome may turn on whether the hearsay is admitted. What is necessary to the proponent of hearsay may be devastating for the opponent. When the need for hearsay carrying no special indicia of reliability is great, we cannot be certain whether justice is more likely to be advanced by the admission of the hearsay or by its exclusion.

Those who argue that necessity is a sufficient basis for a hearsay exception point to an exception available in civil actions in Massachusetts since 1898 and later copied in Rhode Island:

> No declaration of a deceased person shall be excluded as evidence on the ground of its being hearsay if it appears to the satisfaction of the judge to have been made in good faith before the beginning of the suit and upon the personal knowledge of the speaker.[215]

Despite a long and apparently favorable experience with this exception in two states, the proposal to admit necessary hearsay so long as it does not appear unreliable has not been well received. An exception embodying this principle is regarded as one of the features that doomed *The Model Rules of Evidence*, the first attempt to radically restructure the rules of evidence through codification. The principle is, however, accepted to a limited extent in certain states which, in abolishing their "Dead Man's Statutes," provided a hearsay exception for statements of decedents in actions involving their estates. The necessity principle was also embodied in the version of the Federal Rules transmitted by the Supreme Court to Congress. Proposed Rule 804(b)(2) of that version provided:

> *Statement of recent perception.* A statement, not in response to the instigation of a person engaged in investigating, litigating, or settling a claim, which narrates, describes, or explains an event

---

[215] Mass. Acts and Resolves 1898, ch. 535, p. 522.

or condition recently perceived by the speaker, made in good faith, not in contemplation of pending or anticipated litigation in which he was interested, and while his recollection was clear.

This proposed federal exception was both broader and more restrictive than the Massachusetts rule. It was broader in that it applied to criminal as well as civil actions, and whenever the speaker was unavailable, not only when the speaker was dead. It was more restrictive in that it was limited to statements of *recent* perception, and excluded statements that might be taken by insurance adjusters or other persons investigating claims. Despite the efforts of the drafters to include more indicia of reliability in the Federal Rule than are in the Massachusetts statute, Congress deleted the exception for fear that it would admit statements that did not bear "sufficient guarantees of trustworthiness to justify admissibility."[216] Statements that would have been admissible under this proposed exception are, however, not necessarily inadmissible under the Federal Rules. When the guarantees of reliability incorporated in the exception appear strong, courts may use FRE 807 to admit the hearsay this exception would have allowed. Also, several states have incorporated this exception in their evidence codes.

D. PRIOR STATEMENTS OF AVAILABLE WITNESSES: A PROBLEM IN POLICY ANALYSIS

The third basic principle that has transformed common law hearsay doctrine is the idea that the prior out-of-court statements of people available to testify should be admitted as substantive evidence. We shall discuss this principle in detail, particularly as it applies to prior inconsistent statements, because it provides an excellent example of the difficulties of policy analysis in the hearsay area. Our starting point is the observation that a rule permitting the substantive use of prior inconsistent statements is asymmetric in that its benefits accrue almost entirely to the party having the burden of proof, that is, the prosecution in criminal cases and the plaintiff in most aspects of civil actions. The defending party is likely to be content with the traditional rule, which allows prior inconsistent statements for impeachment only, since if the jury disbelieves crucial prosecutorial or plaintiff's witnesses, the defendant will prevail.

Proponents of a hearsay exception for prior statements by available speakers argue that the speaker's presence at trial provides an opportunity for cross-examination that protects against many of the same dangers the hearsay rule is designed to avoid. The jury can observe the speaker's demeanor and develop some notion of whether she is a person who usually tells the truth. Ambiguity in her earlier statement may be cleared up by the later cross-examination. Also, she will usually be able

---

[216] Report of Committee on the Judiciary, H.R. Rep. No. 650, 93d Cong., 1st Sess. 6 (1973).

to describe the context in which she spoke, so the jury may get some sense of her opportunity to observe and her motives to falsify. A hearsay exception for a witness's earlier statements is, however, rarely necessary when the witness adopts her earlier statement or repeats it from the stand, since the substance of the earlier statement is also proved by courtroom testimony. Yet, as we shall see, only when the witness adopts or reiterates the earlier statement is the opportunity for cross-examination likely to be fully effective as a means of testing the credibility of the earlier assertion.

An exception for a witness's out-of-court statements is most valuable when the substance of the earlier statements cannot be proved by the witness's testimony. If the witness has forgotten the incident described in the earlier statement, or if her testimony differs from her earlier statement, evidence of what she once said may be the only way to prove what she asserted. Yet in these circumstances, courtroom cross-examination is often of limited utility. The witness may forestall attempts to develop inconsistencies in or the implausibility of her earlier statements by saying, "I don't remember." She may deal similarly with efforts to have her admit that her vantage point was obscured or her judgment biased. Whether the witness's memory failure is feigned or honest, the jurors are likely to find they have only a bare accusation or simple description without any of the contextual information that might help them weigh the witness's out-of-court remarks. Although cross-examination still may help clarify ambiguous language and give the jurors an idea of the witness's general trustworthiness, the more significant hearsay dangers remain.

The opportunity for cross-examination appears more meaningful when the witness's story from the stand is inconsistent with what she said earlier than when she has forgotten the incident. Indeed, in the former situation, the witness has probably stated from the stand the version of the event the cross-examiner would have tried to elicit had she reiterated her earlier statement in court. Justice White, writing for the majority in a Confrontation Clause case called *California v. Green*, put the argument this way: "The most successful cross-examination at the time the prior statement was made could hardly hope to accomplish more than has already been accomplished by the fact that the witness is now telling a different, inconsistent story, and—in this case—one that is favorable to the defendant."[217]

This argument is, however, not as telling as it might appear, for it ignores those dramatic features that may determine the impact of the witness's recantation. Consider the following situations, in each of which the witness eventually withdraws a statement accusing Green of selling him marijuana. Situation B is most like that in *California v. Green*.

---

[217] 399 U.S. 149, 159 (1970).

Situation A:

The witness on direct examination accuses Green of selling marijuana and the cross-examiner gets the witness to repudiate the accusation.

Prosecutor [on direct examination]: And will you tell us who sold you the marijuana that was found in your possession?

W: It was Martin Green.

P: And how did this sale occur? Did he hand you the marijuana?

W: No, he pointed to some bushes near his parents' house and said I would find the baggies there. I did, I found twenty-nine.

P: Thank you. Your witness.

Defense Counsel [on cross-examination]: Is marijuana the only drug you have ever used?

W: No, it is not.

D: What other drugs have you used?

W: Well, I've dropped acid, that is, used LSD.

D: What are the effects of dropping acid?

W: Well, it makes you super high. It changes your sense of things, of time, of space. Your world is different, everything is alive.

D: In short, it distorts your perceptions considerably, isn't that right?

W: Yes.

D: You might be talking to someone and not remember who he is afterward?

W: Yes.

D: The features of the person you are talking to might be different; you might see a nose exaggerated or proportions changed?

W: Yes.

D: Now, when was the last time you had dropped acid before you arranged this marijuana purchase?

W: Well, actually I had taken some about twenty minutes before I got the call from Green telling me where to go to pick up the marijuana.

D: LSD distorts the perception of voices, does it not?

W: It may.

D: You really can't be certain it was Green's voice you heard on the phone, can you?

W: No.

D: It's quite possible that someone else had called you up, your best friend, for example; yet you might have thought it was Green who called you when the effects wore off?

W: Yes.

D: You then went to pick up the baggies. Did you not?

W: Yes, I guess so.

D: What do you mean, I guess so?

W: Well, I was still high, so fact and fantasy are really mixed up in my mind. If I hadn't had the baggies on me when the police came I wouldn't know what I had done.

D: You really aren't sure where you got the marijuana, are you?

W: No.

D: You wouldn't want to swear under oath that Green was your supplier, would you?

W: No.

D: In short, you have no idea where the marijuana came from, isn't that so?

W: Yes.

Situation B:

The witness acknowledges but repudiates and explains his earlier inconsistent statement.

Prosecutor [on direct examination]: Now can you tell us who sold you the marijuana?

W: No, I cannot.

P: Your honor, the witness's statement is inconsistent with his earlier statements on this subject. The prosecution is surprised by this testimony and would like to question him as if on cross-examination to clarify certain matters.

Judge: Go ahead.

P: Do you mean that you cannot swear that it was Green who gave you the marijuana?

W: No, I cannot.

P: Do you remember giving a statement to a police officer shortly after you were arrested with the marijuana?

W: Yes, I do.

P: And that was soon after you purchased the marijuana, at a time when your memory of the event was considerably fresher than it is now.

W: Yes.

P: Do you remember giving Officer Johnson, the officer who arrested you, the following statement, "I bought the dope off of Green. He had the baggies under a bush on his folks' property. I gave him the money and he told me where to look."

W: Yes, I said that.

P: Thank you.

Defense Counsel [on cross-examination]: You've just testified that you cannot be sure that Green sold you the marijuana, isn't that right?

W: Yes, it is.

D: In fact, you have no reason to believe it was Green who sold you the marijuana, do you?

W: No.

D: Could you explain why you're unsure about who sold you the marijuana?

W: Yes. You see, I had just dropped acid at the time I bought the marijuana. That's LSD. It distorts your perception. You can't be sure of anything. I had this call on the phone telling me about the dope. The voice might have sounded like Green's, but it could have been anybody's. Then I went out to pick the stuff up. But I was so high I couldn't tell fact from fantasy. When the police came I thought the police might go easy on me if I could name my supplier, so I just picked Green's name out because I knew him as an acquaintance. But he wasn't a friend.

D: Thank you.

P: **[on redirect examination]:** Just one more question. When you were arrested, you never told the officer that you had just been taking LSD did you?

W: No.

D: **[on re-cross-examination]:** Why didn't you tell the arresting officer you were high on LSD?

W: I was afraid I would get busted for that, too.

Situation C:

The witness denies making an earlier inconsistent statement.

Prosecutor [on direct examination]: Now, can you tell us who sold you the marijuana?

W: No, I cannot.

P: Your honor, the witness's statement is inconsistent with his earlier statements on this subject. The prosecution is surprised by this testimony and would like to question him as if on cross-examination to clarify certain matters.

Judge: Go ahead.

P: Do you mean you cannot swear that it was Green who sold you the marijuana?

W: No, I cannot.

P: Do you remember giving a statement to a police officer shortly after you were arrested with the marijuana?

W: No, I don't. I never gave a statement.

P: You are denying that you ever gave any statement to the arresting officer?

W: Yes, I never said anything.

P: That is all, thank you.

. . .

P: [Questioning Officer Johnson after he has described the circumstances of the arrest.]: What did you say next?

Johnson: I said that he was only a juvenile and if he would cooperate things might go easier for him.

P: What did he say?

J: He said, "I bought the dope off of Green. He had hidden the baggies under a bush on his folks' property. I gave him the money and he told me where to look."

P: You're sure he identified Green?

J: Yes, I'm certain.

P: Thank you, officer.

In each of these situations the witness has told two stories. One accuses the defendant of supplying him with marijuana; the other professes an inability to identify the supplier. Yet the situations differ substantially in their likely incriminatory effect. In situation **A**, the jury sees the prosecution's witness discredited on cross-examination. Here they are likely to discount the accusation entirely. In situation **B** there is no discrediting of the witness, just an explanation of why his earlier statement was inaccurate. If the jury accepts the explanation, it may discount the accusation; if it does not, the later courtroom repudiation is unlikely to help the defendant. In situation C there is no cross-examination because the witness has denied ever accusing Green, and he has said he cannot identify the person who gave him the marijuana.[218] The jury is faced with the simple question of whom to believe. If the witness is believed, the defendant was never identified as the supplier; if the police officer is believed, the identification stands with full force. These examples show that the repudiation of an earlier story on direct examination is not necessarily equivalent to the retraction of that story on cross-examination. For the advocate, the way in which a jury learns facts can be almost as important as the facts the jury learns.

But does this make the case against the exception? The right of cross-examination that is at the heart of the hearsay rule is not a right to discredit an opponent's testimony in the most dramatic way possible. Rather, it is a right to test an opponent's story so that the jury may better assess its validity. When a witness *remembers* making an earlier inconsistent statement, the cross-examiner's main disadvantage is that he cannot attack the witness's general credibility because he wants the jury to believe the witness's testimony. But the *substance* of the witness's inconsistent statement may be tested almost as thoroughly at the trial as it could have been at the time the statement was made. The California Law Revision Commission put the argument this way:

> The declarant is in court and may be examined and cross-examined in regard to his statements and their subject matter. . . . The trier of fact has the declarant before it and can observe his demeanor and the nature of his testimony as he denies or tries to explain away the inconsistency. Hence, it is in as good a position to determine the truth or falsity of the prior statement as it is to

---

[218] Although the defense would like the jury to believe that the witness has testified truthfully and never said anything to the police about Green, the likelihood that the jury would believe the police officer's story of what was said rather than the witness's denial might lead a sophisticated lawyer to conduct a different kind of cross-examination in which she would attempt to show, as in cross-examination A, that because the witness had taken LSD at the time of the incident, even if he mistakenly claims not to have identified Green, any identification that he made at the time would be almost worthless. A potential problem is that while the witness freely cooperates with the defense in cross-examination C, where his cooperation consists of denying that he made a statement, he might not cooperate by indicating he had taken LSD, if the cross-examiner tried to lead him in that direction after he denied saying anything. Also the defense, by questioning the credibility of a favorable witness, would risk losing the benefit of the denial.

determine the truth or falsity of the inconsistent testimony given in court.[219]

If testimonial repudiation of an earlier out-of-court statement is likely to be less convincing than the repudiation of direct testimony on cross-examination, it is because the jury may not believe that contemporaneous cross-examination would have shaken the earlier out-of-court statement. The crucial factor will be whether the witness can offer a satisfactory explanation for the discrepancy between her out-of-court statement and her courtroom testimony. Absent a convincing explanation, it is not irrational for the jury to believe that "the inconsistent statement is more likely to be true than the testimony of the witness at the trial because it was made nearer in time to the matter to which it relates and is less likely to be influenced by the controversy that gave rise to the litigation."[220] However, it does not necessarily follow that we want to allow convictions or judgments to rest largely on out-of-court statements that have been contradicted by sworn testimony. There is a troubling irony in resting a verdict on the judgment that someone who cannot be believed under oath was credible in an earlier unsworn statement. Also, the prior statement may have been elicited by leading questions that would have been barred on direct examination as unduly suggestive.

The case against a prior statement exception is considerably stronger when the witness denies making the inconsistent statement or says she does not remember making it. If the denial is coupled with a failure to remember the incident described in the earlier statement or with a claim to have never known anything about the incident, the opposing attorney is likely to have a good deal of difficulty testing the truth of the inconsistent statement on cross-examination,[221] since she cannot extract from a witness the details of an incident that she claims to have forgotten or to have never known about in the first place.[222] Virtually all the hearsay dangers are present, including the possibility that the person reporting the earlier statement is lying.

Prospects for a meaningful cross-examination are only slightly more favorable when the witness remembers the incident, but denies making the inconsistent statement. The witness has already told a story favorable to the cross-examining party, so that party has little incentive to question the witness's credibility or her opportunity to observe. It may

---

[219] California Law Revision Comm'n, Comment on Sec. 1235 of the California Evidence Code (1965).

[220] *Id.*

[221] It is questionable whether statements asserting lack of memory or noninvolvement in an event are inconsistent with earlier statements describing the event. Some courts have held that they are.

[222] Other modes of impeachment, like showing the witness has a bad reputation for truth and veracity, will still be available.

also be difficult for the cross-examiner to show that the earlier statement, if made, is not to be believed, since the witness has denied making the earlier statement. However cooperative the witness, it will be hard to draw from her an explanation for a discrepancy that is not acknowledged. The cross-examiner is at a similar disadvantage if the witness claims to have forgotten whether she ever told an inconsistent story.

When a witness denies making an inconsistent statement, the disputed issue is usually whether the statement was made. This issue is likely to be reduced to a swearing contest between the witness who claims she never made the alleged statement and some other witness who claims to have heard it. The report of a discrete statement is difficult to shake on cross-examination. Hearing a discrete statement is consistent with almost any context and with many different relationships between speaker and hearer. Only when the circumstances suggest difficulty in overhearing or bias on the part of the reporting witness is the opportunity for cross-examination likely to be meaningful. Rationally disproving a witness's claim that she said nothing is even more difficult absent a reliable recording of it or independent witnesses to the statement. Thus, in deciding whether an inconsistent statement was made, the jury will often have little to guide it apart from its evaluation of the general credibility of the witnesses who report and deny the statement.[223] When, as is often the case, the reporting witness is a police officer or the denying witness is someone who has been in trouble with the law, the jury is likely to believe that the earlier statement was made and to treat it as true. With the dispute focused on what, if anything, was said, the possibility that the statement was made but was inaccurate may be ignored.

Yet even when cross-examination cannot effectively test prior inconsistent statements, a strong case can be made for admitting inconsistent statements as substantive evidence. Recall situations **B** and **C**. Do they not suggest the possibility that the witness was in some way "reached" between the time he made the earlier statement and the trial? A witness may be threatened or bribed or the code that prohibits "squealing" may reassert itself once the pressure applied to elicit the earlier statement has disappeared. False testimony for any of these reasons not only leads to injustice but also threatens the integrity of the trial process and should be discouraged in every way possible.

Justice and the integrity of the trial may also be threatened when unacknowledged prior inconsistent statements are admitted as

---

[223] Some might argue that the jury's opportunity to observe the demeanor of the witnesses while they make their contradictory claims about whether anything was said is a good way to determine where the truth lies. Although a relationship between demeanor and credibility provides a convenient justification for a number of legal rules, existing evidence suggests that demeanor evidence is actually of little use in making credibility judgments. *See* Olin G. Wellborn, *Demeanor*, 76 CORNELL L. REV. 1075 (1991).

substantive evidence, for the allegedly inconsistent statements may have been misreported or fabricated to secure a criminal conviction or civil judgment. In some jurisdictions perjury has too often been a part of police work. A Chicago police officer put the matter this way:

> A vice officer spends quite a bit of time in court. You learn the judges, the things they look for. You become proficient in testifying. You change your testimony, you change the facts. You switch things around 'cause you're trying to get convictions. You figure he's only a criminal, so you lie about it. The judges are aware of it. The guy who works in plain clothes is usually ambitious and aggressive and will take the time to go to court.[224]

Lying under oath by individuals sworn to uphold the law offends the integrity of the criminal justice system as much as false recantations by bribed or threatened witnesses.

Given these competing factors, how should we resolve the difficult policy issue of whether to create a hearsay exception for prior inconsistent statements? At least two intermediate positions exist. The first—the position of the common law—is not intended as a compromise but, in effect, it is. At common law, prior inconsistent statements are admitted to impeach a witness but not to prove the substance of what she said. Although the jury may be instructed to consider these statements only on issues of credibility, few believe that the jurors entirely disregard the substantive implications of what they learn.[225] Thus, statements ostensibly admitted for impeachment purposes may advance a party's affirmative case. However, the formal limitation on admissibility provides the opposite party with two important safeguards. The first is that limitations on impeaching one's own witnesses mean that a witness may not be called just to present the jury with an inconsistent out-of-court statement.[226] This prevents a party from building a case largely on out-of-court statements, but it can also destroy a case in which a crucial

---

[224] Studs Terkel, Working 194 (1974). Police perjury is most frequent when police seek the admission of evidence, usually narcotics, gambling material or a weapon used in a violent crime. *See, e.g.*, Christopher Slobogin, Testilying: Police Perjury and What To Do About It, 67 U. Colo. L. Rev. 1037 (1996). It is not, however, confined to cases in which technical rules prevent the conviction of guilty defendants. There are documented instances in which police officers responded to charges that they used excessive force against an individual by filing and swearing to fabricated charges of resisting arrest, Paul Chevigny, Police Power (1969), as well as cases in which the police testified falsely to confessions or other inculpatory statements. *See, e.g.*, Veney v. United States, 344 F.2d 542 (D.C.Cir.), *cert. denied*, 382 U.S. 865 (1965).

[225] While some jurors may ignore limiting instructions, others take them seriously. If only one juror treats an instruction as strictly controlling, it may still have an impact on the deliberative process and the ultimate verdict.

[226] In practice, this limitation is often circumvented by courts that are uncritically receptive to claims of surprise. A party who knows an opponent's witness will tell a story more favorable to him than the witness's earlier story should try to have this made clear before the witness's testimony is presented to the jury, so that the opposing party may not claim surprise. However, a party is most likely to know this when he has played some part, proper or not, in securing the recantation of the witness's earlier story.

witness has changed an earlier honest account. Whether this limitation is wise is a difficult question. The second safeguard is that the distinction between substance and impeachment, however meaningless it may be to the jury, may be dispositive when a directed verdict is requested. If evidence of facts asserted only in statements admitted for impeachment is essential to a party's case, the other party will be entitled to a directed verdict. If the statement is admitted for substantive as well as impeachment purposes, the directed verdict will not issue.

This places a valuable limitation on the use of inconsistent statements. If a case is so weak that it cannot get to the jury unless a prior inconsistent statement is given substantive effect, the case probably should not get to the jury. The difficulties in cross-examining witnesses about earlier inconsistent statements coupled with the danger of mistake or fabrication are good reasons to ignore the substance of prior inconsistent statements in determining whether a party has presented sufficient evidence to reach the jury. We are approaching the situation in Sir Walter Raleigh's case when a conviction is allowed to turn on evidence of an out-of-court statement by a witness who denies making the statement, or who repudiates it under oath.[227]

FRE 801(d)(1) embodies a second intermediate position. It offers substantial protection against the danger that an out-of-court statement will be fabricated or misreported, and also provides whatever assurances are gained when statements are given under oath. Rather than create a new exception, FRE 801(d)(1) removes some prior inconsistent statements from the definition of hearsay. This reflects a debate among scholars about the essence of hearsay that we need not discuss. The same result could have been reached by the creation of a hearsay exception, and for ease of speech, we shall occasionally refer to the rule as an "exception."[228] FRE 801(d)(1) provides that a statement that meets the following conditions is not hearsay:

(1) A Declarant-Witness's Prior Statement. The declarant testifies and is subject to cross-examination about a prior statement, and the statement:

---

[227] One might object that if the jurors are persuaded that the witness's new story is attributable to a bribe or threat, they should be allowed to credit the earlier version. But, the jury can do this under the current system. If a party appears responsible for the bribe or threat, the statements that the party sought to change may be received against him as adoptive admissions, and bribes or threats may be used to show consciousness of guilt.

[228] The original draft of FRE 801(d)(1) made all prior inconsistent statements admissible. Congress added restrictions because it felt that prior inconsistent statements generally were subject to certain of the hearsay dangers. Congress did not, however, change the approach of the drafters and convert the rule into a hearsay exception. As with other instances in which Congress changed the draft rules, some states adopted the draft's position before Congress changed it or, if afterwards, notwithstanding Congress's different decision.

(A) is inconsistent with the declarant's testimony and was given under penalty of perjury at a trial, hearing, or other proceeding or in a deposition;

(B) is consistent with the declarant's testimony and is offered to rebut an express or implied charge that the declarant recently fabricated it or acted from a recent improper influence or motive in so testifying; or

(C) identifies a person as someone the declarant perceived earlier.

Subsection (1)(A) of the federal "exception" relates to inconsistent statements generally. When statements admitted under this provision were made in other trials, hearings, or depositions, there will often have been contemporary cross-examination; but neither actual cross-examination nor the opportunity for it are conditions of the exception. The Senate insisted that the rule admit inconsistent statements made under oath at "other proceedings" so that grand jury testimony would be admissible as substantive evidence when it contradicted a witness's testimony.[229] Because of its *ex parte* nature and the pressure prosecutors can put on witnesses, testimony before grand juries arguably should be regarded with *more* suspicion than other inconsistent statements, but this does not seem to happen in practice. This may cause some injustice, but it also makes the rule a bulwark against the so-called turncoat witness.

One problem courts face in interpreting this rule is deciding whether a witness's testimony at trial that she has forgotten an incident is inconsistent with an earlier statement describing it. When courts suspect that a witness's forgetfulness at trial is feigned, as it might be in response to a bribe or intimidation, they do not hesitate to find inconsistency.

Subsection (B) of FRE 801(d)(1) seems unnecessary. If a statement is consistent with trial testimony, the jury already has substantive evidence of the matter testified to. The earlier statement serves solely to enhance the credibility of the courtroom testimony. When used to enhance credibility, consistent statements are not hearsay under the traditional definition. However, some courts have used the rule to admit corroborating statements that add information to what the witness has testified to. Not all courts interpreting this subsection limited corroborating statements to those made before the alleged incentive for falsification arose, but the Supreme Court, in *Tome v. United States* [230] held that this was required: "The Rule," said the Court, "permits the introduction of a declarant's consistent out-of-court statements to rebut a charge of recent fabrication or improper influence or motive only when

---

[229] It should also apply to statements made to congressional committees and in other circumstances where testimony is under oath.

[230] 513 U.S. 150 (1995).

those statements were made before the charged recent fabrication or improper influence or motive."[231]

Before states began copying the Federal Rules, only a few admitted prior inconsistent statements for all substantive purposes,[232] but more than half had an exception akin to FRE 801(d)(1)(C). The justification for this exception is that out-of-court identifications are usually more reliable than the ritualistic courtroom identification of the person sitting next to defense counsel. If a lineup has been properly conducted and the defendant identified, the out-of-court identification should carry more weight with the jury than courtroom finger pointing. The exception also makes considerable sense when a witness has identified someone, either through photographs or in person, shortly after first perceiving him. Recollection can fade rapidly, so an identification made shortly after someone has been first perceived is more likely to be accurate than an identification made at some later time. The Federal Rule, however, is not limited to the situations in which the exception makes the most sense. Prior statements of identification are not barred by the language of this rule no matter how suggestive or casual the conditions under which they were made and no matter how great the length of time between the perception and an identification. In some circumstances, however, there may be constitutional problems that prevent the admission of out-of-court identifications, FRE 801(d)(1)(C) notwithstanding.[233]

Sections (A), (B), and (C) of FRE 801(d)(1) all require the speaker to testify subject to cross-examination at the trial or hearing at which the statement is offered. The cross-examination requirement is ordinarily satisfied by proffering the witness. In *United States v. Owens*,[234] the Supreme Court interpreted FRE 801(d)(1)(C) to allow the admission of a statement of prior identification by a prison guard who had been beaten with a metal pipe, despite the fact that at the time of the trial he could not remember anything that happened at the time he was struck, nor the circumstances surrounding his later hospital bed identification of the defendant as his assailant—except that he did identify him. The Court held that in limiting the statements admissible under FRE 801(d)(1) to those in which witnesses were "subject to cross-examination concerning the statement," Congress meant to demand no more than that the witness

---

[231] *Id.* at 167. *Tome* does not address a related issue: Whether and when prior consistent statements may be used to rehabilitate a witness on some basis other than rebutting a charge of recent fabrication or improper motive. If prior consistent statements are admitted for such a purpose, they will be inadmissible hearsay on substantive issues, and may be considered only in evaluating the witness's credibility.

[232] *See* Walter J. Blakey, *Substantive Use of Prior Inconsistent Statements Under the Federal Rules of Evidence*, 64 KY. L.J. 3 (1975–76), for a thoughtful analysis of the prior inconsistent statement problem.

[233] *See* Simmons v. United States, 390 U.S. 377 (1968); United States v. Wade, 388 U.S. 218 (1967); Gilbert v. California, 388 U.S. 263 (1967); Stovall v. Denno, 388 U.S. 293 (1967).

[234] 484 U.S. 554 (1988).

be placed on the stand, take an oath, and be willing to respond to the cross-examiner's questions to the extent he is able.

There are two final points we wish to make before concluding our discussion of admissible and inadmissible hearsay. First, in criminal cases the future of hearsay has to a significant event, especially in recent years, been constitutionalized. The Confrontation Clause of the Sixth Amendment may require the exclusion of certain kinds of hearsay evidence while the Compulsory Process Clause of the same Amendment may mandate the admission of certain hearsay. These matters are discussed in detail in Chapter Seven.

Second, other rules of evidence have implications for the treatment of hearsay. FRE 703, for example, can be read to relax the hearsay rule substantially in the case of experts. Since under FRE 703 the facts or data on which experts rely need not be admissible in evidence, experts can and often do rely on inadmissible hearsay in forming their opinions.[235] In a number of cases expert witnesses have been allowed to refer to hearsay not for the truth of the hearsay, but to give the jury the basis of their opinions. This can be carried to extremes. One state trial court, for example, allowed a psychiatrist to testify that he had consulted a more eminent psychiatrist about the defendant's sanity and that the more eminent psychiatrist agreed with his opinion. The state supreme court, refusing to read its rules on expert testimony as a conduit for otherwise inadmissible hearsay, reversed the trial court's decision.[236] In other state high courts, the decision might have been affirmed.[237]

ADDITIONAL PROBLEMS

Problem VI-119. A bartender received a counterfeit ten-dollar bill as payment for a drink. Realizing it was counterfeit, she told the manager to call the police. When the police arrived, she pointed to the man who gave her the bill, and he was arrested. At the defendant's trial a year later, the bartender says that she can no longer remember what the man who passed the ten-dollar bill looked like, but she does remember pointing out the culprit to the arresting officer. The arresting officer testifies that the defendant is the man whom the bartender pointed out. **Is the officer's testimony that the bartender pointed to the defendant admissible over defendant's hearsay objection? Would the situation be any different if the police officer testified to the earlier identification, but the bartender either denied making the identification or stated that she had forgotten the incident and**

---

[235] See Chapter Nine, pp. 1140–1141.

[236] State v. Towne, 142 Vt. 241, 453 A.2d 1133 (1982).

[237] See the cases collected in Peter J. Rescorl, Comment, *Fed. R. Evid. 703: A Back Door Entrance for Hearsay and Other Inadmissible Evidence: A Time for a Change?*, 63 TEMPLE L. REV. 543 (1990).

did not remember whether she had received a counterfeit bill or whether she had identified the person who passed it to her?

Problem VI-120. The defendant, in a jurisdiction that follows the Federal Rules of Evidence, introduces a witness who testifies that he was near Bill's Bar at the time it was robbed and that he never saw the defendant. On cross-examination the prosecutor calls the witness's attention to a statement the witness made under oath to a grand jury two months after the robbery. In this statement the witness said that he saw the defendant walk down a side street about 50 feet from the bar five minutes before the robbery. The witness remembers the statement but says that he now knows he was mistaken, and that it was someone else he saw. The defendant moves for a directed verdict, claiming that there is no credible evidence placing him near the scene of the crime. The prosecutor argues that under FRE 801(d)(1)(A) the inconsistent statement of the defendant's witness may be treated by the jury as substantive evidence that the defendant was near the scene of the crime. The defendant argues that FRE 801(d)(1)(A) does not apply and that because he had called the witness first he could only question the witness on redirect examination and not on cross-examination. He claims that FRE 801(d)(1) requires that a witness be subject to cross-examination concerning an earlier inconsistent statement before that statement may be used substantively. **Who should prevail?**

Problem VI-121. Professor Ellen Carter was a distinguished medical sociologist famous for her careful ethnographies of hospital life. In an article written shortly before her death and published in a major sociology journal, she described conditions at "Oceanview Hospital." She wrote that because of inadequate staffing at Oceanview it was customary for nurses and even orderlies to prescribe medicine for patients. According to Professor Carter, physicians usually initialed these prescriptions without seeing the patient and after the drug had been administered. The claim was supported by the detailed description of a case in which drugs were mistakenly prescribed by three different nurses before a doctor finally diagnosed the patient's disease correctly and prescribed the correct drug. The mistaken prescriptions resulted in serious injury to the patient. The article quotes the head of the hospital as saying, "Our nurses were responsible for those mistakes. We just don't have enough doctors to examine each patient every time we prescribe drugs."

Henry Moler sues Bayside General Hospital for injuries suffered following the administration of three different drugs, none of which was correctly prescribed. He claims that although prescriptions for the drugs were initialed by a staff doctor, they were in fact prescribed by nurses. He contends that the hospital was aware of this practice and so asks for punitive as well as actual damages. The details of Moler's case are precisely the details of the case described in Carter's article. The hospital administration reluctantly stipulates that "Oceanview Hospital" is the pseudonym that Professor Carter used for Bayside General Hospital in a series of articles based on her research at that institution. Moler offers Carter's article to prove that the drugs administered to him were prescribed by nurses and to show the kind of gross negligence on the part of the hospital that would justify punitive damages. The hospital objects to the introduction of this article on the ground that it is hearsay. **How should a court rule?**

Problem VI-122. Dorothy (Dotty) Smathers is seeking to collect on the insurance policy for her late husband, Alford. The insurance company is contesting the claim on the grounds that the policy was fraudulently procured. The company alleges that Ms. Smathers was having an affair at the time of her husband's death and took out the policy planning to murder him and then collect. The insurance company offers evidence that Alford died from eating poisoned mushrooms. Ms. Smathers was questioned about her husband's death after an autopsy revealed mushroom poisoning, but she was never charged with a crime. The prosecutor made a statement to the press shortly after the autopsy in which he said, "We're pretty sure we know who did it, but we lack the evidence we need to show guilt beyond a reasonable doubt so we must close this case without prosecuting."

In support of its case, the company would like to offer a newspaper story published in a national newspaper three months after the prosecutor's statement and two years before the current trial. The story, under the headline "Affair and Murder Shock Small Town," details the facts of Ms. Smathers' alleged affair and the subsequent death of her husband. It is based on interviews with towns folk and includes the prosecutor's statement as well as a statement by one man that, "Al told me his wife was cooking him wild mushrooms for dinner," and a statement by another, "Whenever I don't know if a woods mushroom is good, I always take it to Dotty. She knows about such things." The attorney for Ms. Smathers objects to the introduction of the article on the ground that it is hearsay. **How should the court rule? Would it matter if the paper were not a national newspaper, but the weekly newspaper of the town where the death occurred? Does it make a difference if the townspeople who spoke to the reporter are mentioned by name?**

Problem VI-123. L.B., a nine-year old girl, describes for the court three instances of sexual assault, involving the fondling of her genitals and digital penetration by a 17 year old neighbor boy. Her testimony is hesitant, embarrassed, and a bit vague when she is asked where the boy touched her. Only when asked leading questions ("Did he put his finger in your private parts") does she confirm the penetration, and this with a barely mumbled, "Ya." The state wishes to offer, under the residual exception, the testimony of Harrison Keller, a psychiatric social worker, whom L.B. was seeing for bed wetting problems. Keller will testify that at one session L.B. seemed very upset and that when he probed, but without using leading questions, since he had no idea what was the matter, she described an assault just two hours earlier.

Further questioning revealed that this was the third such incident. Keller will testify that L.B. was clear and forceful saying, "Johnny hurt me. He put his fingers in here" (pointing to her vagina). The medical evidence is consistent with L.B.'s claim of digital penetration, but it is not conclusive. Setting aside any possible Confrontation Clause objection, **should the court allow Harrison to testify?**

Problem VI-124. Stan Mead is indicted for bank robbery. During the trial the government sought to place William Carmel on the stand to testify as follows:

"I work at the bank that was robbed. About five minutes after the robbers fled, I was locking the entrance door when a customer knocked on the door. I recognized him as someone whom I had seen in the bank about once a month during the preceding five years, but I don't know his name and I haven't seen him since. Anyway, there was a kid of about 20 sitting in a car outside the door giving this customer the make and license plate number of the getaway car. I didn't hear what the kid said, but I saw the kid's lips move, and the customer relayed the information through the door. I didn't open the door because it's our policy to keep the building secure after a robbery. He told me the car was a "tan Dodge Valiant" with license plate number 700 QRS."

In addition to this testimony, the government has a witness who will testify that he worked for a while as a taxicab driver with Mead, and he used to see him driving an off-white Dodge with license plate number 700 QRS. This witness's testimony is, however, open to suspicion, for a car with plate number 700 QRS is registered to him. However, the witness claims that he once lost his wallet and when he regained it, it contained a registration certificate for a car with the plate number in question registered to his name by, he believes, Mead. The government investigation has verified that the registration was not in the witness's handwriting and that he does not drive a Dodge. The other evidence that significantly implicates Mead is the testimony of three eyewitnesses who viewed a photo spread. One of the eyewitnesses says that although Mead's face was masked, his eyes, mustache, ears, and part of his face were visible. This witness feels that he can identify Mead positively on that basis. A second eyewitness says that she saw Mead's face from the tip of his nose to his chin before it was masked and was able to see certain features through the mask because it did not distort them. A third witness says that Mead's picture closely resembles the appearance of the robber.

The trial judge elects to admit the evidence under FRE 807. He offers the defendant a five-day continuance to prepare for this evidence, but the defense counsel declines the offer saying that since the government claims it has searched thoroughly for the unknown speakers, she doesn't believe that a continuance would be of much help. The defendant appeals, arguing that the decision to admit Carmel's testimony was in error. On appeal, the state defends the decision under FRE 807 and claims the testimony was admissible under FRE 803(1) as well. **How should the appellate court rule?**

E. OVERALL EVALUATIONS: A CASE AGAINST LIBERALIZATION

As the lawyers, judges, legislators, and educators of tomorrow, the future of hearsay is in your hands. By now you should understand the current hearsay system and be aware of important considerations in evaluating proposals for change. In concluding this section, we present further arguments for and against change.

Among hearsay scholars, our position is a conservative one. We do not advocate radical changes in traditional hearsay doctrine. Those who oppose admitting more hearsay are often thought to distrust the jury system. But this is not where our conservatism is rooted. Rather, our position reflects beliefs about testimonial accounts of statements and about the system of justice in this country.

1.   The Danger of Hearsay

We believe that the chance that an out-of-court statement will be significantly distorted when recounted in court, though not great, is not negligible. Dangers include difficulties in perceiving speech, the natural tendency to translate what one hears into what one wants to hear, and perjury. We do not wish to overemphasize the danger of perjury, for it is probably the least common of the three. We suggest only that there are enough cases in which witnesses tell contradictory stories that the danger cannot be regarded as *de minimis*.[238]

Justifications like these for the hearsay rule are sometimes dismissed because these dangers exist whenever perceptions are reported and testimony reporting hearsay may, like other testimony, be tested through cross-examination. The argument is formally correct, but we feel that the dangers are greater with reports of statements than with reports of visual stimuli, and that the opponent's ability to correct for these dangers is

---

[238] When witnesses appear to contradict each other, the contradiction is often only a seeming one or due to honest mistakes in perception or to the unconscious reconstruction of events in ways that favor each witness's interests. It is, in part, because these possibilities exist whenever one testifies falsely under oath that prosecutions for perjury at trial are uncommon. However, a low rate of prosecution does not mean that perjury rarely happens.

lesser. First, small mistakes in overhearing statements may completely change their meaning. Consider, for example, the simple mistake of hearing "has" when the speaker said "hasn't." Since most witnessed events are more complex than statements, small mistakes in perceiving them are less likely to distort their meaning. Second, cross-examination is less likely to be effective in testing reports of statements than in testing reports of more complex events.[239] Third, legally significant statements are often directed at just one person, while legally significant events are more often observed by several people. Thus, the opportunity to question a misreported statement through the testimony of other witnesses will generally be less than the possibility of questioning an erroneous observation through the testimony of others. Furthermore, it is particularly hard to prove perjury when statements are attributed to an anonymous or unavailable speaker, so the temptation to lie may increase.

2. The Balance of Advantage

Our second reason for skepticism about proposals to liberalize the admission of hearsay is how liberalization might affect the balance of advantage in litigated cases. Despite the important rights enjoyed by accused criminals, we feel that the balance of advantage lies with the state in criminal cases [240] and with wealthy organizations in civil actions.[241] For organizations, litigation is often routine, so many have special agents, like detectives and insurance adjusters, who are assigned the job of collecting statements. They have a substantial capacity to generate evidence, and thus organized parties are likely to have available more hearsay evidence than the individuals they oppose. Moreover, there is reason to suspect the reliability of the statements organizations preserve, although this may not be evident on the face of those statements. An organization's agents may have elicited statements by asking leading questions or they may have recorded only what they

---

[239] We do not mean that the dramatic revelation of perjury is more likely when testimony reports events other than statements. Although this may be so, our concern is with cross-examination used more prosaically to demonstrate why a witness's account, whether honest or dishonest, may be doubted. This is largely due to the difficulties, which we mentioned in our discussion of prior inconsistent statements, of setting discrete statements in contexts that allow meaningful cross-examination. If a witness claims to have heard just statements, he may plausibly claim that that was all that was said or that the speaker then moved away or lowered his voice. An attorney who visits the scene is unlikely to find barriers to sound that would render claims to have heard a statement suspect, and if the witness cannot describe the scene of the statement very well, it does not suggest he wasn't listening closely. Investigations of visual observations are more likely to uncover sight barriers that make reports implausible, and if a witness on cross-examination has difficulty describing or misdescribes the scene of her observations, her report of what she saw becomes suspect.

[240] See, e.g., Abraham S. Goldstein, The State and The Accused: Balance of Advantage in Criminal Procedure, 69 Yale L.J. 1149 (1960). This thoughtful discussion is dated because of the many changes that have occurred in criminal procedure since it was written. However, we feel that Goldstein's conclusion, that the balance of advantage lies with the state, still holds today.

[241] See Marc Galanter, Why the "Haves" Come Out Ahead: Speculations on the Limits of Legal Change, 9 Law & Soc'y Rev. 95 (1974).

thought their superiors wanted to hear. In addition, an organization like a police department may have special claims on its hearsay informants that make their accounts suspect.[242]

Even if these problems did not exist, one might still have reservations about a change in evidence law that is likely to disproportionately advantage certain litigants. True, there is considerable disparity in the capacity of parties to uncover evidence and one would not, for example, want to bar eyewitness testimony simply because organized parties are more likely to find eyewitnesses than unorganized ones. But the fact that imbalance necessarily exists in our justice system does not justify its exacerbation.

Liberalizing the hearsay rule also changes the balance between those bearing the burden of proof, generally prosecutors and plaintiffs, and their opponents, generally defendants, since it makes it easier to introduce the evidence needed for a *prima facie* case. We do not see any need to make the prosecutor's task easier, and because of the dangers we perceive, we are reluctant to expand the situations in which hearsay enables a party to avoid a directed verdict.[243]

3.   Judicial Discretion

Most proposals for reforming the hearsay rule expand judicial discretion. This is obviously true of proposals to admit hearsay so long as some standard of reliability and necessity is met. It is also true of proposals to abolish the hearsay rule entirely, for much of what the hearsay rule excludes is arguably irrelevant or unduly prejudicial. This brings us to the third reason for our conservative stance toward hearsay

---

[242] Consider testimony by accused criminals who hope for easy treatment from a prosecutor's office, or testimony by insurance adjusters reporting statements they attribute to unavailable informants. People often have a few friends who can be pressed into stretching the truth, but they seldom have the range of influence that organizations may have. Organizations may even generate pressures for deceitful stories without overtly asking for them. A criminal may feel (correctly) that if he can offer the police or prosecution testimony of value to them, he will be treated better regardless of the veracity of his testimony. The police and prosecution may accept such reports as true without close investigation because they want to close cases and convict people they believe are guilty. Similarly, the insurance adjuster is likely to believe (again, perhaps correctly) that adjusters who report hearsay that favors the company are likely to do better with the company in the long run than adjusters who report hearsay that undermines the company's interests. True, the jury may discount such statements because they are recounted by interested witnesses, but even discounted hearsay leaves the opponent worse off than if the statement were excluded.

[243] A judge, ruling on a motion for a directed verdict, will view the evidence in the light least favorable to the movant. A judge may well find that a reasonable jury can credit hearsay that he himself does not believe. If that hearsay reports facts necessary for a *prima facie* case, a directed verdict will be avoided. The jury later may view the hearsay with the same skepticism as the judge but nonetheless find for its proponent. Sympathy may lead to a plaintiff's verdict when there is insufficient proof of negligence if hearsay is discredited. Knowing a defendant's criminal record or conclusions drawn from the defendant's failure to take the stand may lead to a conviction, even though at least some jurors do not believe hearsay that is essential for a *prima facie* case of criminal responsibility. There is even harm if the jury's verdict favors the hearsay's opponent, for a trial has been needlessly held.

reform. Put simply, we do not trust all trial judges. If we thought that the country's trial judges were almost always highly capable and completely impartial, we might support hearsay reform despite our reservations. The hearsay rule excludes considerable relevant evidence, a cost that must be acknowledged by its defenders. Unfortunately, the trial bench is not uniformly excellent. Although many trial judges in this country are capable and impartial, others are neither. In almost any large city and in many smaller ones, lawyers tell stories of judges noted for their incompetence or unfairness or both. Abraham Blumberg, a lawyer-sociologist, characterized one of nine judges of a criminal court he studied as an "Intellectual—Scholar." The other eight fell into the categories "Routineer-Hack," "Political Adventurer-Careerist," "Judicial Pensioner," "Hatchet Man," and "Tyrant-Showboat-Benevolent Despot."[244] The captions give you an idea of what Blumberg thought of their performance.

Furthermore, it appears that trial judges who are biased are more likely to favor the prosecution than the defense. There are a variety of institutional reasons for this, including the system of electing judges that prevails in most state court jurisdictions, the fact that many judges have had prosecutorial experience, and the need for cooperation between judges and prosecutors in the general administration of the criminal courts. These factors all suggest that increasing judicial discretion in the hearsay area will make it somewhat easier for prosecutors to secure convictions.

4. Systematic Effects

Finally, we believe the current system is working reasonably well, and we fear the long-run impact of substantially liberalizing the hearsay rule. In the literature criticizing the hearsay rule, examples are rarely given of cases in which the exclusion of hearsay has led to unjust results. Yet, this would surely be the strongest indictment that one could bring against the rule. One reason for the lack of outrageous cases is that the hearsay rule is already applied more liberally than it is written. Competent attorneys can usually find some way to introduce reliable hearsay essential to their case. When judicial creativity is added to the long list of exceptions, the hearsay rule becomes an even greater conceptual nightmare, but a nightmare that is probably more agonizing to those who contemplate it than to those who live with it. On aesthetic grounds alone, we can appreciate the desire of scholars to limit hearsay exclusions. But one should be wary of changing a messy system that apparently delivers justice, however elegant the suggested alternative seems to be.

---

[244] Abraham S. Blumberg, Criminal Justice 138 (1967).

Also, liberalizing the hearsay rule may affect attitudes in a harmful way. Today, hearsay is suspect, an attitude that is probably colored by the general rule excluding hearsay evidence. If the hearsay rule were formally or effectively abolished, attitudes toward hearsay might change. Judges who today strive to find some rationale for admitting reliable hearsay that does not clearly fit an established exception might, under a more liberalized system, admit "for what it's worth," hearsay they now exclude. This is the most common decision when evidence is of generally low probative value. However, hearsay evidence with low probative value differs from most other marginal evidence. The low probative value of hearsay usually stems from the fact that it is difficult to evaluate the trustworthiness of what is reported. Reported hearsay, *if believed*, may be quite probative of a fact in issue. The consequences of admitting suspect hearsay usually should be slight, for the jury is likely to dismiss such hearsay as incredible. In some cases, however, the consequences may be great, either because the hearsay enables a party to avoid a directed verdict or because the jury does not appreciate the weakness of the evidence. Furthermore, there is the danger that if judicial attitudes toward the hearsay rule change, the attitudes of lawyers will change as well. If hearsay evidence is easily accessible and readily admissible lawyers may devote less attention to finding nonhearsay evidence on the same point. This means that over time an increasing proportion of trial evidence will be hearsay rather than firsthand testimonial accounts.[245] Such a change, we believe, would not only decrease the appearance of fairness; it would also be likely to lead to substantial injustice as well. We are not saying that changes such as these necessarily would occur with hearsay reform. They are, however, possibilities that must be taken into account when evaluating the more radical proposals for admitting more hearsay.

Although we said that our position on hearsay reform is a conservative one, it should be obvious to you that its implications are in another sense "liberal." Most suggested hearsay reforms are likely to be of more benefit to prosecutors than defendants. A conservative view of reform is consistent with the civil libertarian position on the criminal process. Thus, it is not surprising that attitudes toward the criminal process are often related to attitudes toward the hearsay rule.

---

[245] Since courtroom testimony is usually more convincing than hearsay, regardless of the hearsay rule, attorneys have an incentive to find nonhearsay evidence to prove crucial elements of their cases. However, were the hearsay rule abolished, the incentive would be less than it is now. Currently, a failure to present nonhearsay evidence on a particular point may entitle an opponent to a directed verdict or mean that the jury learns nothing about a matter. Also, the bureaucratic pressures in the offices of prosecutors and public defenders may enhance the desirability of using hearsay in a system where hearsay is freely admitted, because hearsay evidence is easily routinized in advance of trial. Finally, there are witnesses whose presentation at trial is likely to be so shaky that the party calling them would prefer hearsay statements to testimony. The hearsay rule exists, in part, so that the weaknesses of such witnesses are exposed to the fact-finder.

When Congress enacted the Federal Rules of Evidence, the House's "liberal" Committee on the Judiciary consistently tried to restrict the scope of suggested hearsay exceptions, while the Senate's more "conservative" committee favored the expansive positions of the draft rules. Similarly, those who believe that many criminals escape conviction because of "technical" difficulties in proving guilt beyond a reasonable doubt are likely to favor hearsay reform. Those who believe that the danger of convicting innocent people is already significant, and who subscribe to the notion that it is better to acquit several people who are guilty than to convict one who is innocent, are more likely to oppose suggested reforms. To those who think that the integrity and competence of police, prosecutors, and judges is high and that witnesses almost always tell the truth, the hearsay rule may appear as an often archaic impediment to the search for truth. To those who think that the integrity or competence of police, prosecutors, and judges is at times suspect and that error, intentional or not, is common in testimony, the hearsay rule is more likely to appear as an imperfect but important guarantor of the integrity of the trial process.

F. OVERALL EVALUATIONS: THE CASE FOR REFORM

In this discussion of hearsay we have not hesitated to give you our own views on specific rules and proposals for change. We have at the same time tried to point out the ways in which our opinions differ from those of other writers, and we have tried to acknowledge the strength of the positions we ultimately reject. We regard many of the questions in this area as close ones. In trying to present our views in simplified fashion we may have overstated the conviction we feel. At the same time, we may have also failed to do justice to those who take a contrary position. The acknowledgment of an opposing view is not the same as the development of its argument. In closing this section, we shall let Judge Jack Weinstein, one of the most distinguished proponents of hearsay reform, speak for himself. After you have read his views on reform you will be in a better position to evaluate intelligently the conflicting arguments.

PROBATIVE FORCE OF HEARSAY
Jack B. Weinstein[246]

The present evidence rules fall short of providing a satisfactory solution to the hearsay problem. They exclude evidence that has a higher probative force than evidence they admit. They fail to provide adequate procedural devices to minimize the possibility of misjudging the probative force of hearsay admitted. . . .

---

[246] Jack B. Weinstein, *Probative Force of Hearsay*, 46 Iowa L. Rev. 331 (1961).

I.   NATURE OF HEARSAY PROBLEM

For the purpose of this discussion, the term hearsay is used broadly to encompass any action or declaration involving a hearsay danger. A hearsay danger exists when a trier of fact is asked to conclude that a proposition about a matter of fact is true because an extra-judicial speaker stated it was the case or did an act, verbal or otherwise, from which it can be inferred that he believed it to be true. To accomplish what is requested of him, the trier must rely upon one or more elements of the speaker's credibility—his ability and opportunity to observe, remember, or communicate accurately or his intention to state what he believes to be true. A person is an extra-judicial speaker unless, when he made the declaration or did the act, he was under oath, before the trier, and subject to cross-examination—in which case he is a witness. The probative force of a line of proof is its power to convince a dispassionate trier of fact that a material proposition, sometimes referred to as an "ultimate fact," is probably true or false. It may also be defined as the increment, resulting from admission of evidence, in the "degree of belief which it is *rational* to entertain" with respect to a proposition about a matter of fact. Convincing power or probative force of any statement is affected by the trier's assessment of the credibility of the speaker with respect to the specific statement. . . .

General credibility of a speaker depends upon his general attitude towards truth as well as his normal ability to observe, remember, and communicate his thoughts accurately. His specific credibility, while dependent upon general credibility, may vary depending upon the occasion he had to make the observation attributed to him, the circumstances surrounding his statement, and his relationship to the case—i.e., a generally honest man may yield to the temptation to exaggerate to help a dear friend or to hurt an enemy. Since specific credibility of the same witness or extra-judicial speaker may vary from one statement to another, it will also be determined by taking into account the statement's consistency with other information in the case, its internal consistency, and its conformity with the trier's preexisting general knowledge. This reasoning is reversible; where the trier finds that a particular declaration does not accord with his experience or other credible evidence, he finds the speaker's specific credibility low and may infer from this a low general credibility. The probative force of hearsay may, therefore, increase as it is fitted into a mosaic of other evidence. On the other hand, the increment of convincing power of hearsay may be reduced as the number of lines of proof tending to prove the same material proposition increases—i.e., as evidence becomes cumulative.

In sum, in order to determine how much weight should be given to any hearsay, a trier must be able to determine the credibility of the extra-judicial speaker when he made the statement attributed to him, and to do this the statement must be viewed as part of the other evidence in the case. It is obvious that the trier has exactly the same problem with respect to a witness. Hearsay is thus a special form of testimonial proof. The main justification for treating it differently from other testimonial proof must be that the trier can more readily come to a correct conclusion with respect to credibility if he observes the speaker making his statement, or doing the act, under the stress of a judicial hearing when he is under oath, being observed by an adverse party, and subject to almost immediate searching cross-examination to test the various elements of his credibility. This explains the theoretical justification—but not the practical absurdity in many instances—for treating the out-of-court statement of the witness himself as hearsay.

Since no one can read another man's mind or judge his capacities directly, evidence of specific credibility, including demeanor, is always circumstantial; and even the demeanor of an extra-judicial speaker may be described by the witness reporting his statement. Many kinds of evidence bearing upon credibility do not require the presence of the speaker. So, for example, reputation, inconsistent statements, prior bad acts, and motive to falsify are available in evaluating the veracity of the extra-judicial speaker. Even as to such discrediting evidence, however, there may be some advantage in introducing it when the speaker's reaction to it may be observed. This is one justification for the rule requiring a foundation by questioning the witness about certain kinds of evidence before using them in attacking him. . . . Does it follow, then, that all hearsay should be treated as testimonial proof and permitted to come in subject to proof and disproof of credibility?

II.   SOLUTIONS TO THE HEARSAY PROBLEM

A.   Admitting Hearsay Freely

There are three separable but related objections to free admission of hearsay. They do not, however, require the absolute exclusionary hearsay rule, for each of them may be considered by the court in determining when hearsay should be admitted and by the trier in deciding how much probative force to give hearsay once it is admitted.

First, lawyers assume that the ability of the trier to assess credibility is greater when he can observe demeanor and reaction to cross-examination. Even if this assumption is not subject to proof by acceptable psychological tests and theory, it is shared by jurors and it seems to accord with our common experience. In the trial of cases, if the trier feels more assurance that he can arrive at truth, and if the parties agree that this is the case, we are entitled to assume it to be true—in the absence of a demonstration to the contrary—in constructing procedural rules. Trials are designed to settle disputes in a way that gives the litigants and public a sense of fairness. Until, therefore, it is demonstrated that the reliability of a statement cannot be better assessed by observing the demeanor of the person while he is making it, we are justified in placing reliance on this first factor.

Assurance of the trier, however, dictates only a rule of preference, not of exclusion. Moreover, it suggests that the risks in using hearsay are exaggerated because the trier tends to recognize the difficulty in evaluating the probative force of hearsay and does not rely heavily upon it when he is aware that it is hearsay. Courts and many commentators, however, are probably correct in suggesting that juries are generally not as apt to be as critical of hearsay as trained judges. If this is true—and the danger is easily magnified—it can be met by permitting courts to comment on the weight to be given evidence. Lawyers can and do carry the main burden of showing the dangers by their arguments.

The second factor is one of trial convenience. Where credibility is assessed primarily on the basis of demeanor, an opposing attorney can see a witness for the first time and cross-examine solely on the basis of trial observation, hints from his client or expert, and what he believes about the witness's background and the facts of the case. It is better if he is prepared in advance, of course—and all the tactics books warn against the danger of unprepared cross-examinations. But the trial can go on without any extensive before-trial examination of the witness's background or preparation for proof and disproof of his credibility by other witnesses and documents. This permits cheaper preparation and a shorter trial, and by avoiding the need for continuances to permit investigation it makes the present form of dramatic jury trial more practicable.

A third factor is the possibility during the course of cross-examination of prevailing upon the honest witness to change his testimony or upon the craven one not to varnish the truth. While it is possible to cause the dishonest witness to contradict himself or change his demeanor, Professor Morgan has pointed out that "if a witness is willing to commit perjury and counsel is willing to cooperate, neither oath nor cross-examination will be of much avail to expose the wilful [sic] falsehood unless either witness or counsel is unusually stupid."

B.   Excluding Hearsay

What, then, of the other possible alternative—excluding hearsay? Obviously, this approach would deny to the trier much useful information which should be available if he is to have a substantial chance of coming to a correct conclusion on the facts. In view of the paucity of other information bearing on many issues of fact, much hearsay must be admitted. . . .

C.   Class Exceptions

Wigmore's rationale for the hearsay exceptions expresses a compromise position between allowing all hearsay or no hearsay. Where, he argues, there is great necessity for a class of hearsay and there are general circumstantial grounds for concluding that a class of hearsay is reliable, an exception for the class may be created. This analysis, made possible by treating admissions and former testimony as not requiring the test of cross-examination and by applying variable standards of need and credibility to different cases, has satisfied the conscience of the bar but not that of recent commentators. It should be emphasized that Wigmore's rationale— as well as that of most of the cases—makes admissible a class of hearsay rather than particular hearsay for which, in the circumstances of the case, there is need and assurance of reliability. Nevertheless, Wigmore's analysis might have supported an exception based upon the individual case rather than upon a class—although it would have compounded his difficulty in synthesizing the cases for his treatise.

The second factor underlying the hearsay rule referred to above—i.e., that of trial convenience—might be used to support a class theory of exceptions. Since the classes of hearsay are defined in advance, the argument would go, lawyers cannot claim surprise when they are used. This rationale is not persuasive because, in the individual litigation, a lawyer may be surprised by his opponent's reliance on particular hearsay even though it falls within a class recognized as an exception. He may not, in fact, have time to investigate and obtain data to attack the extra-judicial speaker's credibility. Having *a priori* classes does, however, cut down the amount of hearsay that may be offered and thus offers him some protection. It also permits the judge to rule mechanically on admissibility without having to think of the particular circumstances of the case—and, as with many of our procedural rules, a judge may, in refusing to think, find satisfaction in the knowledge that this self-denial is required of him.

D. Admission Based Upon Probative Force
With Procedural Safeguards

1. Greater Discretion in Judge

Apart from the greater burden on the judges, it would seem desirable to abandon the class exception system and substitute individual treatment if such a practice were to be combined with advance notice to the opponent when hearsay was to be introduced. Hearsay would then be admissible when it met the usual standard for admission of any line of proof—*i.e.*, a reasonable man might be appreciably more satisfied about the truth or falsity of a material proposition with the evidence than without it. To prevent burdening the trial with a great deal of evidence of small probative force, it would be well to permit the court a greater freedom to exclude than it normally exercises. Where its probative force was minimal because it was cumulative, other evidence would normally be preferred to hearsay.

The concept that admission should depend upon probative force weighed against the possibility of prejudice, unnecessary use of court time, and availability of more satisfactory evidence is an application of the well recognized principle embodied in Rule 45 of the Uniform Rules giving the court discretion to exclude admissible evidence. Where the extra-judicial speaker was available to the proponent but was not produced, the argument of spoliation could be permitted in evaluating probative force, but it would seem better to exclude the evidence or at least require that the extra-judicial speaker be made available for cross-examination, for the burden on the opponent to produce the witness for examination should be minimized. The right to treat such a witness as upon cross-examination with the right to attack credibility should, of course, be protected.

The circumstantial proof of credibility which gave rise to the class exception may continue to be utilized in the particular case in assessing probative force.   Nevertheless, a series of independent letters written by disinterested ministers who were eyewitnesses to an event and who are shown to have acute vision, sound memories, and clear powers of communication might well be given more weight than many dying declarations or implied admissions which may be made by a party having no knowledge of the event or may have been made many years before by a predecessor in interest who had every motive to lie. On the other hand, hearsay coming within one of the traditional exceptions may rightly be given greater weight by a trier than testimony on the witness stand. Some faith must be reposed in triers to assess the evidence as "responsible persons" engaged "in serious affairs."

2. Notice of Intention to Use Hearsay

Notice and a minimum standard of credibility as a basis for admission of hearsay is worth increased attention now in view of the widespread growth of discovery-disclosure procedures in civil cases and the availability of pretrial hearings in many jurisdictions. . .

It is not suggested that this warning procedure is wholly satisfactory. Often an attorney is surprised by testimony at the trial and wants to meet it with hearsay. Advance notice of such possible use is often not practical; where the case is tried with a jury an adjournment is often difficult. A notice requirement should not, of course, be strictly enforced for every mite of hearsay. Nevertheless, the law ought to have some regard for the pitiful plaint of one lawyer, when his opponent introduced damaging testimony regarding an alleged conversation with an agent: "We should have some opportunity to run it down."

3. Judge's Comment on Evidence

To minimize the possibility of overestimation of the probative force of hearsay under a rule of discretion, the trial court's power to comment freely on the weight of such evidence should be recognized. If the jurisdiction does not generally recognize this right in the judge, a specific rule to this effect should be embodied in any codification of the law of evidence.

4. Review by Appellate Court and Greater Trial Court Control over Jury

More explicit recognition of the power of appellate courts in evaluating hearsay should also be recognized if a new hearsay approach is adopted. Appellate courts have sought to insure reasoned consideration of hearsay by applying mechanical tests of probative force in reviewing verdicts and decisions as well as administrative orders. Reliance on such "rules of law" disguises the fact that courts are reviewing the reasonableness of findings of fact but, like other procedural subterfuges, often leads to indefensible results. There is no reason for appellate courts to be embarrassed about exercising a higher degree of control when a finding is based upon hearsay rather than upon testimony of a witness in court; since the credibility of the statement does not depend upon the trier's observation of the extra-judicial speaker's demeanor, but rather upon a calculated evaluation of the surrounding circumstances found in the record, the appellate court may well feel itself in as good a position as the trier to evaluate the probative force of a statement. If its force is slight or so questionable as to be entitled to little weight, the appellate court will feel strongly impelled to discount it.

This attitude of more stringent review is part of a general pattern in cases involving circumstantial proof. Appellate courts, while normally denying the exercise of any substantial degree of control, use mechanical tests such as the inference on an inference rule, and these tests are in truth applied selectively to insure what the court believes is a sound result. Care must therefore be taken in evaluating cases in which appellate courts have taken the position that hearsay has no probative force. The rule may have been applied selectively as a means of exercising control over a trial judge or jury which has made a finding of fact unacceptable to an appellate judge with limited powers to substitute his judgment for the trier's.

III. CURRENT TRENDS AND CRITICISMS OF HEARSAY RULE

The current tendency is clearly towards much freer admissibility of hearsay. But without frank recognition of the rapid change in our attitude towards the exclusionary rules, we abandon the possibility of providing reasonable procedural protections.

In addition to the tendency to ignore hearsay dangers by providing a narrow definition of hearsay and by expanding the exceptions [,] . . . . there is in the cases and in practice a tendency to admit hearsay where there can be no serious doubt of the credibility of the extra-judicial speaker—*i.e.*, where probative force is high. . . . So quickly has the exclusionary power of the hearsay rule waned that there are few cases today where the outcome of a well-tried case would have been different had it not been for the hearsay rule, where a good court was prevented from admitting persuasive hearsay. Not all lawyers and courts, of course, have fully exploited present tendencies.

Scholars have reached surprising agreement on the desirability of replacing our present hearsay rule with one based upon probative force in the particular case. In the last century Bentham in England and Appleton in this country recognized the ability of triers to assess the probative force of hearsay and proposed that the best-evidence concept be applied to hearsay. More recently Thayer declared that "the attempt to make the group [of classes], in the form in which they finally chanced to settle, fit into a scheme having any measure of theoretical consistency is an undertaking so Procrustean as to defy even the brilliant ingenuity of Professor Wigmore"; the class system he denominated as "crude and primitive." . . . McCormick has noted that "the values of hearsay declarations or writings, and the need for them, in particular situations cannot with any degree of realism be thus minutely ticketed in advance. . . . Too much worthless evidence will fit the categories, too much that is vitally needed will be left out." Morgan has repeatedly insisted that much of the hearsay excluded "raises the hearsay dangers to no greater extent than evidence now admitted under the hearsay exceptions." He has demonstrated by a series of devastating hypotheticals how much evidence of high probative force may be excluded and how much of low convincing power admitted under our present rules. The notes to the Model Code of Evidence state that in many exceptions "the necessity resolves itself into mere convenience and the substitute for cross-examination is imperceptible." . . .

IV. EVALUATION OF HEARSAY WHEN THE EXCLUSIONARY RULE IS NOT RECOGNIZED

In the sea of admitted hearsay, the rule excluding hearsay is a small and lonely island. No serious claim has been made that adjudications in which hearsay is received on a discretionary basis and given reasonable probative force fail to resolve satisfactorily issues of fact.

Continental systems manage well without our rules. The matter is left to the judge's *intime conviction*, his common sense. The lack of experience of lawyers from other countries with our exclusionary rules makes it impossible to use them before international tribunals.

In this country the hearsay rule is strictly applied in the order of one percent of the civil litigations commenced. Arbitrators are not bound by the rules and it is estimated that seventy percent or more of private civil litigation not involving accident cases are tried before arbitrators; lawyers appear in most of these cases and have shown no general dissatisfaction with the process. . . .

Workmen's accident cases, which clogged our courts earlier in this century, as well as the many other kinds of litigation handled by administrative agencies, have been resolved without utilizing mechanical rules excluding hearsay. . . . The probative force of hearsay should remain "constant at all levels of the adjudicatory process." It seems clear that the administrative process is having an ameliorative effect on court trials; the proper standards for decisions based upon hearsay in both is that of "convincing evidence."

Where our procedure is not adversary, as in grand jury proceedings and hearings on the issuance of search and arrest warrants, some of our courts have recognized convincing hearsay as a basis for action. When sentencing reports of probation officers or social workers' reports used in custody cases must be kept confidential, there is little doubt that the hearsay may be relied upon; the important problem is one of providing procedural devices which will permit the parties to meet the hearsay and so reduce its apparent force. . . .

When judges try cases which involve such small amounts that relaxation of the hearsay rule reduces the cost of trial to reasonable proportions, or so complex that admission of hearsay shortens the trial to acceptable lengths, the hearsay rule is ignored. Sitting without juries, judges have been told to err in favor of admission rather than exclusion of evidence. Experience with the ability of human beings to weigh hearsay should affect jury trials.

Even in the class of cases where courts might be inclined to enforce present rules of evidence strictly, the exclusionary hearsay rule has little direct impact. Only a small percent of commenced civil cases which are not terminated by defaults reach trial; most are settled and a few are disposed of by summary judgment or other motion. Hearsay may be elicited by deposition under the widely adopted Federal Rules [of Civil Procedure] and, for most cases, the sessions at which depositions are taken constitute the "trial," for the litigation is commonly terminated on the lawyer's evaluation of the depositions.

V.   EVALUATION OF HEARSAY WHEN NO OBJECTION IS MADE TO ITS ADMISSION

In all but a few jurisdictions, hearsay admitted without objection may be considered by the trier of facts and given whatever weight it is entitled to under the circumstances. One court has explained this sound approach by noting:

The hearsay rule is merely an exclusionary principle limiting admissibility and in no sense a canon of relevancy. It involves no assertion that hearsay statements are without probative force or that they furnish no logical basis for conclusions of fact. On the contrary, if relevancy were not assumed, no special rule of exclusion would be required. . . . [H]earsay testimony when admitted without objection is to be considered and given its logical probative effect. This position has also been supported on the theory that the hearsay rule is based on the right of the opposing party to cross-examine the speaker under oath and that this right is waived by the failure to object. . . .

VI.   CONCLUSION

There is no reason to believe that our judges are less able to assess the probative force of hearsay than are their civil counterparts or arbitrators or administrative hearing officers. There is little reason to believe that jurors—a much more highly educated and sophisticated group than their English seventeenth and eighteenth century predecessors—are not also capable of assessing hearsay's force without giving it undue weight. As Morgan has pointed out, the present hearsay rules rely upon "an entirely unrealistic assumption of naive credulity of jurors." The arguments of the opposing counsel in the case and caution of the judge—assuming the court is given necessary power to comment on the evidence—furnish sufficient guidance.

Much wider discretion should be vouchsafed the court to admit hearsay of high and assessable probative force. Exercise of discretion rather than mechanical rules requires more thought and consideration of such factors as surprise, possible prejudice through overestimation of force, and the availability of other evidence more easily assessed. Since it is desirable that the extra-judicial speaker be called to give evidence directly where important evidence is involved, rather forceful application of a best-evidence concept should be encouraged; it presents less dangers than does reliance on an argument of spoliation.

Discretion to admit hearsay should be exercised in advance of the trial wherever possible so that the opponent will have the opportunity to investigate and produce evidence in derogation of particular hearsay. The pre-trial hearing furnishes a useful opportunity for the court to exercise this discretion.

Since hearsay's probative force can be estimated on the record by the inferential methods used in estimating any circumstantial proof, appellate courts are in a position to exercise greater control over trial decisions based on hearsay. . . . [T]hey ought to assume the . . . power of reviewing the evidence—a review which, of course, ought to be exercised with restraint. . . .

ADDITIONAL PROBLEMS

Problem VI-125. You are on a legislative committee that is drafting a new code of evidence for your state. One member of the committee has proposed that the traditional hearsay rule be replaced with a rule that defines hearsay and then provides: The admissibility of hearsay evidence shall be within the discretion of the judge. In determining the admissibility of hearsay the judge shall consider the probable reliability of the hearsay declarations and the availability of the speaker for courtroom testimony. **Would you support such a hearsay rule? Why or why not? What is your ideal hearsay rule?**

Problem VI-126. Apparently in response to the O.J. Simpson murder trial, California has adopted a hearsay exception, contingent upon unavailability, for statements made in writing, electronically recorded, or communicated to law enforcement officials that narrate, describe, or explain the infliction or threat of physical injury, provided that the statements have been made at or near the time of the infliction or threat of physical injury, not more than five years before the filing of the instant action, and under circumstances that suggest the statement is trustworthy. **Assuming there is no Confrontation Clause problem, would you support the inclusion of an exception like this in the**

Federal Rules? Is such an exception necessary? What features render a statement like this trustworthy?

Problem VI-127. Professor Michael Seigel has proposed the following "Best Evidence" substitute for the current Hearsay Rule:[247]

> Hearsay is admissible if it is the best evidence available to the offering party from a particular declarant source, or if the best evidence has been or will be presented to the trier of fact.

The concept of *best evidence* is specified as follows:

> (1) Except as otherwise provided, the live testimony of an in court witness is the best evidence of the assertive content of such testimony.

> (2) Hearsay is the "best evidence" when the declarant is physically unavailable, as by reason of death, disability, assertion of privilege, or refusal to attend the proceeding from beyond the reach of process.

> (3) Hearsay is the best evidence when the identity of the declarant is unknown and cannot be discovered through diligent inquiry.

> (4) Hearsay is the best evidence when the court determines that the pertinent assertive materials will not be found in the memory of a reasonable number of declarants. If there is doubt on this issue, the court may require the hearsay proponent to present testimony from one or more knowledgeable declarants in addition to the hearsay. The court may also require such hearsay evidence to be introduced through an appropriate foundation witness.

> (5) Hearsay is the best evidence when it is an aggregate representation of the judgment of a large number of anonymous individuals. The court may require such hearsay to be introduced through an appropriate foundation witness.

> (6) Hearsay is the best evidence when the court cannot reasonably expect that the declarant will cooperate on the witness stand with the hearsay proponent because the declarant is an opposing party or is strongly identified with an opposing party.

What do you see as the strengths and weaknesses of Professor Seigel's proposal? Do you favor its adoption in lieu of the current system?

---

[247] Michael L. Seigel, *Rationalizing Hearsay: A Proposal for A Best Evidence Hearsay Rule*, 72 B.U.L.REV. 893, 893 (1992).

V. THREE CLASSIC CASES

In this book, we have deliberately eschewed using cases to teach settled principles of evidence law. Some cases, however, are so closely associated with certain evidentiary principles that they have become part of the culture of the legal profession. We mention these cases in the text, and sometimes we describe them in detail. We recognize, however, that some students may want to read classic cases themselves, and teachers may feel that the principles they embody will be better remembered if their seminal language is read along with our textual treatment. The three cases that follow would head almost everyone's list of hearsay classics. Their importance was obvious at the time they were handed down, and they continue to be associated with the principles they espouse.

Wright v. Doe d. Tatham grew out of a disputed bequest. John Marsden, a wealthy landowner, had left two manor houses, a rectory, and a large amount of land to his steward, Wright. Admiral Sanford Tatham, Marsden's heir at law, claimed that the bequest was a result of Wright's overreaching and that the will devising the properties was invalid because Marsden's mental state was, throughout his life, such that he was not competent to make a will. The case turned on the admissibility of three letters, all of which were of a kind that one might write to a person of ordinary intelligence. The judges who heard the case on a first appeal to King's Bench and a subsequent appeal to the Exchequer Chamber all thought that the letters could not be introduced to show that their authors had acted as if Marsden were competent. When used for this purpose the letters they held were hearsay, for their relevance depended on the truth of beliefs that the letters implied. Thus, *Wright* has come to stand for the proposition that what we call implied assertions or non-assertive conduct should be treated as hearsay. This proposition, as you know, has been abandoned in the Federal Rules and other modern evidence codes. As you read the case, consider whether it is wise to have abandoned the rule in *Wright* or whether that case should have come out differently. The judges in *Wright* were also unanimously of the view that if Marsden had acted in response to the letters, the letters could be introduced to help the jury evaluate the rationality of Marsden's response. The King's Bench judges did not believe that there was enough evidence that Marsden had reacted to the letters to render them admissible. The Exchequer Chamber judges split three-three on this issue, so a verdict for Tatham was affirmed by an equally divided court. The case generated numerous opinions, the most informative of which are those by Lord Denman speaking for King's Bench and by Baron Parke on review in Exchequer Chamber. We present the essential portions of each and follow them with the letters on which a fortune turned.

WRIGHT V. DOE D. SANDFORD TATHAM

7 Ad. & E. 313, 112 Eng. Rep. 488 (Ex. Ch. 1837).

LORD DENMAN C.J.

This case rests . . . on a single question—that of the admissibility of certain letters tendered on a trial [of] whether the testator was competent to make a will; which the plaintiff denied, alleging his entire natural incapacity.   Such an issue opens a wide door for the admission of evidence, as every transaction of the testator's life, every expression he ever used, and his manner of conducting himself in the most ordinary concerns, may have a bearing on the question.

The letters tendered, written . . . by respectable persons now deceased, who were acquainted with the testator, had been found in his house, with the seals broken, shortly after his death.   No other circumstance was proved relating to them: no act of the testator's was shown to have produced them, or to have followed upon them.

[I]t has been strongly contended before us, as it was at the trial, . . . that the contents of these letters ought to be laid before the jury, as showing in what manner the testator was treated by the writers; and such treatment, abstracted from all corresponding conduct on his part, was said to be evidence to disprove his alleged imbecility.

Without dispute, any . . . act done by the testator with reference to the letters would have made them evidence; for such act could not be properly explained without recourse to them: and, if received, no rule of law could have prevented their full effect from being produced on the minds of the jury. . . .

The manner in which a man is treated by persons ignorant of his intellectual character would be obviously of no value. But, even if well acquainted with him, their treatment does not prove their opinion. The respectful phrases may be ironical, or employed for the very purpose of circumventing the party addressed, on the presumption of his imbecility. . . .

The learned counsel will, however, remind us that they disclaim the letters as proofs of the opinion of the writers, or of any fact mentioned in them, and that their only object is to show the treatment which the testator received from other persons. But if it be admitted,—and we think it cannot be denied,—that the letters would prove absolutely nothing if they proceeded from persons unacquainted with the deceased, or if they were insincere and hypocritical, it inevitably follows that their relevancy to the question depends on their representing the real opinion of the writers. . . .

The hardship of excluding these letters was powerfully urged, since it was said that letters of a contrary tendency might undoubtedly have been given in evidence, and that the jury were in fact much influenced by the manner in which the testator was treated by children pursuing him in the street like one deprived of reason.[a] But the answer is, that. . . the insults offered to him as an idiot by boys, when he walked out, are not evidence as the acts of the boys: their treatment of him as such is nothing; but the manner in which he received that treatment falls within the scope of our rule, and may certainly furnish strong proofs in affirmance or refutation of the proposition under inquiry.

The argument for the defendant appears, indeed, to be founded on a fallacious use of the word treatment. The behavior of **A.** to **B.** may. . . be called treatment of him, though he be absent or asleep, and wholly unconscious of what is done. **A.** might thus evince his high or mean opinion of **B.**'s understanding and character; but such proof of his opinion is allowed to be no evidence in a Court of Justice. If such behavior were observed by **A.** towards **B.** in his presence, and while he was in a state of consciousness, his conduct in return, with reference to the forms of society and to the natural feelings of human nature in similar circumstances, may afford strong evidence of the state of his intellect. In this latter case, the treatment of **B.** by **A.** must be given in evidence, not as treatment, but because **B.'s** conduct thereupon cannot be understood without it. This bears an exact resemblance to letters sent and answered, or dealt with in any way: the former case is that of letters merely written and received, without proof that the party receiving them did anything in respect to them. . . .

This must be considered as the judgment of my brothers Littledale and Coleridge, and myself. Our two brothers, having been engaged in the cause while at the Bar, have taken no part in the deliberation. . . .

PARKE B. The question for us to decide is, whether all or any of the three rejected letters were admissible evidence . . . for the purpose of showing that Mr. Marsden was, from his majority in 1779 to and at the time of the making of the alleged will and codicil in 1822 and 1825, a person of sane mind and memory, and capable of making a will?

It is contended . . . that each of the three letters was evidence of an act done by the writers of them towards the testator, as being a competent person; and that such acts done were admissible evidence on this issue *proprio vigore*, without any act of recognition, or any act done thereupon by him.

. . .

First, then, were all or any of these letters admissible on the issue in the cause as acts done by the writers, assuming, for the sake of argument, that there was no proof of any act done by the testator upon or relating to

---

[a] The plaintiff, Tatham, had introduced at trial evidence that the boys of the town where Marsden lived would pursue him, calling out names such as "Silly Marsden" and "Crazy Jack."

these letters or any of them,—that is, would such letters or any of them be evidence of the testator's competence at the time of writing them, if sent to the testator's house and not opened or read by him?

Indeed this question is just the same as if the letters had been intercepted before their arrival at his house; for, in so far as the writing and sending the letters by their respective writers were acts done by them towards the testator, those acts would in the two supposed cases be actually complete. It is argued that the letters would be admissible because they are evidence of the treatment of the testator as a competent person by individuals acquainted with his habits and personal character . . . that they are more than mere statements to a third person indicating an opinion of his competence by those persons; they are acts done towards the testator by them, which would not have been done if he had been incompetent, and from which, therefore a legitimate inference may . . . be derived that he was so.

Each of the three letters . . . indicates that in the opinion of the writer the testator was a rational person. He is spoken of in respectful terms in all. Mr. Ellershaw describes him as possessing hospitality and benevolent politeness; and Mr. Marton addresses him as competent to do business to the limited extent to which his letter calls upon him to act, and there is no question but that, if any one of those writers had been living, his evidence, founded on personal observation, that the testator possessed the qualities which justified the opinion expressed or implied in his letters, would be admissible on this issue. But the point to be determined is, whether these letters are admissible as proof that he did possess these qualities?

I am of opinion that, according to the established principles of the law of evidence, the letters are all inadmissible for such a purpose. One great principle in this law is, that all facts which are relevant to the issue may be proved; another is, that all such facts as have not been admitted by the party against whom they are offered, or some one under whom he claims, ought to be proved under the sanction of an oath. . . .

That the three letters were each of them written by the persons whose names they bear, and sent, at some time before they were found, to the testator's house . . . are facts . . . proved on oath; and the letters are without doubt admissible on an issue in which the fact of sending such letters by those persons . . . is relevant to the matter in dispute; as, for instance, . . . on any issue in which it is the material question whether such letters or any of them had been sent. . . .

But the question is, whether the contents of these letters are evidence of the fact to be proved upon this issue,—that is, the actual existence of the qualities which the testator is, in those letters, by implication, stated to possess: and those letters may be considered in this respect to be on the same footing as if they had contained a direct and positive statement that he was competent. For this purpose they are mere hearsay evidence, statements of the writers, not on oath, of the truth of the matter in question, with this addition, that they have acted upon the statements on the faith of their being true, by their sending the letters to the testator. That the so acting cannot give a sufficient sanction for the truth of the statement is perfectly plain; for it is clear that, if the same statements had been made parol or in writing to a third person, that would have been insufficient; and this is conceded by the learned counsel for the plaintiff in error. Yet in both cases there has been an acting on the belief of the truth, by making the statement, or writing and sending a letter to a third person; and what difference can it possibly make that this is an acting of the same nature by writing and sending the letter to the testator? It is admitted, and most properly, that you have no right to use in evidence the fact of writing and sending a letter to a third person containing a statement of competence, on the ground that it affords an inference that such an act would not have been done unless the statement was true, or believed to be true, although such an inference no doubt would be raised in the conduct of the ordinary affairs of life, if the statement were made by a man of veracity. But it cannot be raised in a judicial inquiry; and, if such an argument were admissible, it would lead to the indiscriminate admission of hearsay evidence of all manner of facts.

Further, it is clear that an acting to a much greater extent and degree upon such statements to a third person would not make the statements admissible. For example, if a wager to a large amount had been made as to the matter in issue by two third persons, the payment of that wager, however large the sum, would not be admissible to prove the truth of the matter in issue. You would not have had any right to present it to the jury as raising an inference of the truth of the fact, on the ground that otherwise the bet would not have been paid. It is, after all, nothing but the mere statement of that fact, with strong evidence of the belief of it by the party making it. Could it make any difference that the wager was between the third person and one of the parties to the suit? Certainly not. . . .

Let us suppose the parties who wrote these letters to have stated the matter therein contained, that is, their knowledge of his personal qualities and capacity for business, on oath before a magistrate, or in some judicial proceeding to which the plaintiff and defendant were not parties. No one could contend that such statement would be admissible on this issue; and yet there would have been an act done on the faith of the statement being true, and a very solemn one, which would raise in the ordinary conduct of affairs a strong belief in the truth of the statement, if the writers were faith worthy. The acting in this case is of much less importance, and certainly is not equal to the sanction of an extra-judicial oath.

Many other instances of a similar nature . . . were supposed on the part of the plaintiff in error, which, at first sight, have the appearance of being mere facts, and therefore admissible, though on further consideration they are open to precisely the same objection. . . . To [this] class belong the supposed conduct of the family or relations of a testator, taking the same precautions in his absence as if he were a lunatic: his election, in his absence, to some high and responsible office; the conduct of a physician who permitted a will to be executed by a sick testator; the conduct of a deceased captain on a question of seaworthiness, who, after examining every part of the vessel, embarked in it with his family; all these, when deliberately considered, are, with reference to the matter in issue in each case, mere instances of hearsay evidence, mere statements, not on oath, but implied in or vouched by the actual conduct of persons by whose acts the litigant parties are not to be bound.

The conclusion at which I have arrived is, that proof of a particular fact, which is not of itself a matter in issue, but which is relevant only as implying a statement or opinion of a third person on the matter in issue, is inadmissible in all cases where such a statement or opinion not on oath would be of itself inadmissible; and, therefore, in this case the letters which are offered only to prove the competence of the testator, that is the truth of the implied statements therein contained, were properly rejected, as the mere statement or opinion of the writer would certainly have been inadmissible.

[Parke goes on to say that Marsden did not react to the letters in a way that would render them admissible for the light they shed on his reactions.]

The Letters

I.   From CHARLES TATHAM, Mr. Marsden's cousin, who, at
the time of writing, was in America.

"My Dear Cousin.—You should have been the first person in the world I would have wrote too had not. my time imployd been by affairs that called for my more imeadeate atention in the first place I am called upon by my Buseness it being the first consideration must by no means be neglected. As for my Brother his goodness is Such that I know he will Excuse me till I am more disengaged was I to write to him in my present Embarased situation I might perhaps only do justice to my own feelings & he might construe it deceit (so different an oppinion have I of him to Mankind in Genl. who above all things are fond of Flattery). I shall now proceed to give you a small Idea of what has passd. since my Departiure from Whitehaven as I supose Harry long ere now has told you the rest. We saild the 14th. July & had Good Weather the Chief of the Way but as you know nothing of Sea fareing matters it is not worth While to Dwell upon the Subject. We Reachd. the Cape of Verginia the 13th Septr. but did not get heare till the begining of the present Month so we were about twenty Days in coming 350 Miles. When I arivd. I was no little consirned to find the Town in a Most Shocking Condition the People Dieing from 5 to 10 per day & scarsely a Single House in Town cleare of Descease which proves to be the Putrid Fevour-I am going to Philadelphia in a few days if God Spares my Life and permits me my Health & their I intend to stay till Affairs here bare a more friendly Aspect & so the Next time you here from me will be I expect from that Place tho' Youl Please to direct to me heare as usual. God Bless You my Dear cousin and may You still be Blessd with health which is one of the greatest Blessings we require hear is the sinseare wish of Dr. cosn. Your Affect. Kinsman & verry Humble Servt.

"CHA. TATHAM.

"P.S. Pray give my kind Love to my Aunt My Brother & My Cousin Betty allso my Complements to all the rest of the Family and all others my former Aquintances, & c.

"Alexandria, 12th Octr. 1784."

Addressed "John Marsden Esquire Wennington Hall, Lancaster."

II. From the Rev. OLIVER MARTON, Vicar of Lancaster.

"Dear Sir.—I beg that you will Order your Attorney to Wait on Mr. Atkinson, or Mr. Watkinson, & propose some Terms of Agreement between You and the Parish or Township or disagreeable things must unavoidably happen. I recommend that a Case should be settled by Your and their Attorneys, and laid before Councill to whose Opinion both Sides should submit otherwise it will be attended with much Trouble and Expence to both Parties.—I am, Sr. with compliments to Mrs. Coockson, Your Humble Servant, & c.

"OLIVER MARTON.

"May ye 20th 1786.

"I beg the favour of an Answer to this.

"John Marsden, Esq. Wennington."

III. From the Rev. HENRY ELLERSHAW, on resigning the perpetual curacy of Hornby, to which Mr. Marsden had appointed him.

"Dear Sir.—I should ill discharge the obligation I feel myself under, if, in relinquishing Hornby, I did not offer you my most grateful acknowledgments for the abundant favours of your Hospitality and Beneficence. Gratitude is all that I am able to give you, and I am happily confident that it is all that you expect; I have only therefore to assure you, that no Circumstances in this World will ever obliterate from my Heart and Soul the remembrance of your benevolent Politeness. May the good Almighty long bless you with Health and Happiness, and when his Providence shall terminate your Xtian Warfare upon Earth, may the Angels of the Lord welcome you into Blessedness everlasting. It will afford me Pleasure to continue my Services during the Vacancy, if agreeable to you. With every sentiment of Respect and Affection to yourself and the worthy family at the Castle, I hope you will ever find me, Your grateful, faithful & obliged Servt.

"HENRY ELLERSHAW.

"Chapel le dale.

"3d Oct: 1799—Please to deliver the Inclosed to Mr. Wright."

Sallie Hillmon's efforts to recover on three insurance policies her husband had taken out became a cause célèbre in its time. The case was in litigation for more than two decades. It required six trials and two appeals to the Supreme Court. At trial, Mrs. Hillmon never lost, although on four occasions the jury was hung. In the Supreme Court, she never won. Popular sentiment, however, was in her favor—so much so that, for a short period, three insurance companies were barred from doing business in Kansas—and eventually she received most of what she sought. The *Hillmon Case*, by which we mean the opinion on the first appeal to the Supreme Court, stands for the proposition that statements of intent may be used for their tendency to show action in accord with intent. It also discusses the state of mind exception more generally and suggests that when one's intended actions are inextricably linked with the likely actions of another, statements of intent may be used to show that one acted with the other. These propositions, which have made the case a classic, were not essential to the Supreme Court's decision. The Court reversed the verdict at trial because in joining the three defendants the trial judge had improperly restricted them to the number of peremptory challenges that was available to a single party. The admissibility of Walters letters was discussed only because the issue was "so likely to arise upon another trial." We present only that portion of the opinion that bears on this issue.

MUTUAL LIFE INSURANCE CO. V. HILLMON
145 U.S. 285 (1892).

MR. JUSTICE GRAY, after holding for the Court that the judgment was reversed on other grounds, continued:

On July 13, 1880, Sallie E. Hillmon, a citizen of Kansas, brought an action against the Mutual Life Insurance Company, a corporation of New York, on a policy of insurance, dated December 10, 1878, on the life of her husband, John W. Hillmon, in the sum of $10,000, payable to her within sixty days after notice and proof of his death. On the same day the plaintiff brought two other actions, the one against the New York Life Insurance Company, a corporation of New York, on two similar policies of life insurance, dated respectively November 30, 1878, and December 10, 1878, for the sum of $5000 each; and the other against the Connecticut Mutual Life Insurance Company, a corporation of Connecticut, on a similar policy, dated March 4, 1879, for the sum of $5000.

In each case, the declaration alleged that Hillmon died on March 17, 1879, during the continuance of the policy, but that the defendant, though duly notified of the fact, had refused to pay the amount of the policy, or any part thereof; and the answer denied the death of Hillmon, and alleged that he, together with John H. Brown and divers other persons, on or before November 30, 1878, conspiring to defraud the defendant, procured the issue of all the policies, and afterwards, in March and April, 1879, falsely pretended and represented that Hillmon was dead, and that a dead body which they had procured was his, whereas in reality he was alive and in hiding. . . .

On February 29, 1888, after two trials at which the jury had disagreed, the three cases came on for trial, under the order of consolidation. . . .

At the trial the plaintiff introduced evidence tending to show that on or about March 5, 1879, Hillmon and Brown left Wichita in the State of Kansas, and travelled together through Southern Kansas in search of a site for a cattle ranch; that on the night of March 18, while they were in camp at a place called Crooked Creek, Hillmon was killed by the accidental discharge of a gun; that Brown at once notified persons living in the neighborhood; and that the body was thereupon taken to a neighboring town, where, after an inquest, it was buried. The defendants introduced evidence tending to show that the body found in the camp at Crooked Creek on the night of March 18 was not the body of Hillmon, but was the body of one Frederick Adolph Walters. Upon the question whose body this was, there was much conflicting evidence, including photographs and descriptions of the corpse, and of the marks and scars upon it, and testimony to its likeness to Hillmon and to Walters.

The defendants introduced testimony that Walters left his home at Fort Madison in the State of Iowa in March, 1878, and was afterwards in Kansas in 1878, and in January and February, 1879; that during that time his family frequently received letters from him, the last of which was written from Wichita; and that he had not been heard from since March, 1879. The defendants also offered the following evidence:

Elizabeth Rieffenach testified that she was a sister of Frederick Adolph Walters, and lived at Fort Madison; and thereupon, as shown by the bill of particulars, the following proceedings took place:

Witness further testified that she had received a letter written from Wichita, Kansas, about the 4th or 5th day of March, 1879, by her brother Frederick Adolph; that the letter was dated at Wichita, and was in the handwriting of her brother; that she had searched for the letter, but could not find the same, it being lost; that she remembered and could state the contents of the letter.

Thereupon the defendants' counsel asked the question: "State the contents of that letter." To which the plaintiff objected, on the ground that the same is incompetent, irrelevant, and hearsay. The objection was sustained, and the defendants duly excepted. The following is the letter as stated by witness:

Wichita, Kansas,

March 4th or 5th or 3d or 4th—I don't know—1879.

Dear sister and all: I now in my usual style drop you a few lines to let you know that I expect to leave Wichita on or about March the 5th, with a certain Mr. Hillmon, a sheeptrader, for Colorado or parts unknown to me. I expect to see the country now. News are of no interest to you, as you are not acquainted here. I will close with compliments to all inquiring friends. Love to all.

"I am truly your brother, FRED. ADOLPH WALTERS."

Alvina D. Kasten testified that she was twenty in Fort Madison; that she was engaged to be married to Frederick Adolph Walters; that she last saw him on March 24, 1878, at Fort Madison; that he left there at that time, and had not returned; that she corresponded regularly with him, and received a letter about every two weeks until March 3, 1879, which was the last time she received a letter from him; that this letter was dated at Wichita, March 1, 1879, and was addressed to her at Fort Madison, and the envelope was postmarked "Wichita, Kansas, March 2, 1879;" and that she had never heard from or seen him since that time.

The defendants put in evidence the envelope with the postmark and address; and thereupon offered to read the letter in evidence. The plaintiff objected to the reading of the letter, the court sustained the objection, and the defendants excepted.

This Letter was dated "Wichita, March 1, 1879," was signed by Walters, and began as follows:

"Dearest Alvina: Your kind and ever welcome letter was received yesterday afternoon about an hour before I left Emporia I will stay here until the fore part of next week, and then will leave here to see a part of the country that I never expected to see when I left home, as I am going with a man by the name of Hillmon, who intends to start a sheep ranch, and as he promised me more wages than I could make at anything else I concluded to take it, for a while at least, until I strike something better. There is so many folks in this country that have got the Leadville fever, and if I could not of got the situation that I have now I would have went there myself; but as it is at present I get to see the best portion of Kansas, Indian Territory, Colorado, and Mexico. The route that we intend to take would cost a man to travel from $150 to $200, but it will not cost me a cent; besides, I get good wages. I will drop you a letter occasionally until I get settled down; then I want you to answer it." . . .

The court, after recapitulating some of the testimony introduced, instructed the jury as follows: "You have perceived from the very beginning of the trial that the conclusion to be reached must practically turn upon one question of fact, and all the large volume of evidence, with its graphic and varied details, has no actual significance, save as the facts established thereby may throw light upon and aid you in answering the question, Whose body was it that on the evening of March 18, 1879, lay dead by the camp-fire on Crooked Creek? The decision of that question decides the verdict you should render."

The jury, being instructed by the court to return a separate verdict in each case, returned verdicts for the plaintiff against the three defendants respectively. . . .

MR. JUSTICE GRAY, after stating the case as above, delivered the opinion of the court. . . .

There is, however, one question of evidence so important, so fully argued at the bar, and so likely to arise upon another trial, that it is proper to express an opinion upon it.

This question is of the admissibility of the letters written by Walters on the first days of March, 1879, which were offered in evidence by the defendants, and excluded by the court. In order to determine the competency of these letters, it is important to consider the state of the case when they were offered to be read.

The matter chiefly contested at the trial was the death of John W. Hillmon, the insured; and that depended upon the question whether the body found at Crooked Creek on the night of March 18, 1879, was his body, or the body of one Walters.

Much conflicting evidence had been introduced as to the identity of the body. The plaintiff had also introduced evidence that Hillmon and one Brown left Wichita in Kansas on or about March 5, 1879, and traveled together through Southern Kansas in search of a site for a cattle ranch, and that on the night of March 18, while they were in camp at Crooked Creek, Hillmon was accidentally killed, and that his body was taken thence and buried. The defendants had introduced evidence, without objection, that Walters left his home and his betrothed in Iowa in March, 1878, and was afterwards in Kansas until March, 1879; that during that time he corresponded regularly with his family and his betrothed; that the last letters received from him were one received by his betrothed on March 3 and postmarked at Wichita March 2, and one received by his sister about March 4 or 5, and dated at Wichita a day or two before; and that he had not been heard from since.

The evidence that Walters was at Wichita on or before March 5, and had not been heard from since, together with the evidence to identify as his the body found at Crooked Creek on March 18, tended to show that he went from Wichita to Crooked Creek between those dates. Evidence that just before March 5 he had the intention of leaving Wichita with Hillmon would tend to corroborate the evidence already admitted, and to show that he went from Wichita to Crooked Creek with Hillmon. Letters from him to his family and his betrothed were the natural, if not the only attainable, evidence of his intention.

. . .

A man's state of mind or feeling can only be manifested to others by countenance, attitude or gesture, or by sounds or words, spoken or written. The nature of the fact to be proved is the same, and evidence of its proper tokens is equally competent to prove it, whether expressed by aspect or conduct, by voice or pen. When the intention to be proved is important only as qualifying an act, its connection with that act must be shown, in order to warrant the admission of declarations of the intention. But whenever the intention is of itself a distinct and material fact in a chain of circumstances, it may be proved by contemporaneous oral or written declarations of the party.

The existence of a particular intention in a certain person at a certain time being a material fact to be proved, evidence that he expressed that intention at that time is as direct evidence of the fact as his own testimony that he then had that intention would be. After his death there can hardly be any other way of proving it; and while he is still alive, his own memory of his state of mind at a former time is no more likely to be clear and true than a bystander's recollection of what he then said, and is less trustworthy than letters written by him at the very time and under circumstances precluding a suspicion of misrepresentation.

The letters in question were competent, not as narratives of facts communicated to the writer by others, nor yet as proof that he actually went away from Wichita, but as evidence that, shortly before the time when other evidence tended to show that he went away, he had the intention of going, and of going with Hillmon, which made it more probable both that he did go and that he went with Hillmon, than if there had been no proof of such intention. In view of the mass of conflicting testimony introduced upon the question whether it was the body of Walters that was found in Hillmon's camp, this evidence might properly influence the jury in determining that question.

The rule applicable to this case has been thus stated by this court: "Wherever the bodily or mental feelings of an individual are material to be proved, the usual expressions of such feelings are original and competent evidence. Those expressions are the natural reflexes of what it might be impossible to show by other testimony. . . . "

In accordance with this rule, a bankrupt's declarations, oral or by letter, at or before the time of leaving or staying away from home, as to his reason for going abroad, have always been held by the English courts to be competent, in an action by his assignees against a creditor, as evidence that his departure was with intent to defraud his creditors, and therefore an act of bankruptcy. . . .

So letters from a husband to a third person, showing his state of feeling, affection and sympathy for his wife, have been held by this court to be competent evidence, bearing on the validity of the marriage, when the legitimacy of their children is in issue.

. . .

Upon an indictment of one Hunter for the murder of one Armstrong at Camden, the Court of Errors and Appeals of New Jersey unanimously held that Armstrong's oral declarations to his son at Philadelphia, on the afternoon before the night of the murder, as well as a letter written by him at the same time and place to his wife, each stating that he was going with Hunter to Camden on business, were rightly admitted in evidence. Chief Justice Beasley said: "In the ordinary course of things, it was the usual information that a man about leaving home would communicate, for the convenience of his family, the information of his friends, or the regulation of his business. As the time it was given, such declarations could, in the nature of things, mean harm to no one; he who uttered them was bent on no expedition of mischief or wrong, and the attitude of affairs at the time entirely explodes the idea that such utterances were intended to serve any purpose but that for which they were obviously designed. If it be said that such notice of an intention of leaving home could have been given without introducing in it the name of Mr. Hunter, the obvious answer to the suggestion, I think, is that a reference to the companion who is to accompany the person leaving is as natural a part of the transaction as is any other incident or quality of it. If it is legitimate to show by a man's own declarations that he left his home to be gone a week, or for a certain destination, which seems incontestable, why may it not be proved in the same way that a designated person was to bear him company? At the time the words were uttered or written, they imported no wrongdoing to any one, and the reference to the companion who was to go with him was nothing more, as matters then stood, than an indication of an additional circumstance of his going. If it was in the ordinary train of events for this man to leave word or to state where he was going, it seems to me it was equally so for him to say with whom he was going." Hunter v. State, 11 Vroom (40 N.J. Law) 495, 534, 536, 538.

Upon principle and authority, therefore, we are of opinion that the two letters were competent evidence of the intention of Walters at the time of writing them, which was a material fact bearing upon the question in controversy; and that for the exclusion of these letters, as well as for the undue restriction of the defendants' challenges, the verdicts must be set aside, and a new trial had.

Shepard v. United States is important because it emphasizes the limits of *Hillmon*. Forward-looking statements of intent are admissible to show actions in accordance with intent. Backward-looking statements of memory or belief are not admissible to show actions consistent with a memory or belief. The case is also valuable for its discussion of the common law dying declaration exception, and it illustrates how a statement can be hearsay on one issue and not on another. In the latter instance, *Shepard* tells us that if a statement is erroneously admitted under an exception to the hearsay rule, reversal may not generally be avoided by showing on appeal a proper non-hearsay use of the statement. Finally, *Shepard* may be profitably read simply for the richness of Justice Cardozo's prose.

SHEPARD V. UNITED STATES
290 U.S. 96 (1933).

MR. JUSTICE CARDOZO delivered the opinion of the Court.

The petitioner, Charles A. Shepard, a major in the medical corps of the United States army, has been convicted of the murder of his wife, Zenana Shepard, at Fort Riley, Kansas, a United States military reservation. . . .

The crime is charged to have been committed by poisoning the victim with bichloride of mercury. The defendant was in love with another woman, and wished to make her his wife. There is circumstantial evidence to sustain a finding by the jury that to win himself his freedom he turned to poison and murder. Even so, guilt was contested and conflicting inferences are possible. The defendant asks us to hold that by the acceptance of incompetent evidence the scales were weighted to his prejudice and in the end to his undoing.

The evidence complained of was offered by the Government in rebuttal when the trial was nearly over. On May 22, 1929, there was a conversation in the absence of the defendant between Mrs. Shepard, then ill in bed, and Clara Brown, her nurse. The patient asked the nurse to go to the closet in the defendant's room and bring a bottle of whisky that would be found upon a shelf. When the bottle was produced, she said that this was the liquor she had taken just before collapsing. She asked whether enough was left to make a test for the presence of poison, insisting that the smell and taste were strange. And then she added the words "Dr. Shepard has poisoned me."

The conversation was proved twice. After the first proof of it, the Government asked to strike it out, being doubtful of its competence, and this request was granted. A little later, however, the offer was renewed, the nurse having then testified to statements by Mrs. Shepard as to the prospect of recovery. "She said she was not going to get well; she was going to die." With the aid of this new evidence, the conversation already summarized was proved a second time. There was a timely challenge of the ruling.

She said, "Dr. Shepard has poisoned me." The admission of this declaration, if erroneous, was more than unsubstantial error. As to that the parties are agreed. The voice of the dead wife was heard in accusation of her husband, and the accusation was accepted as evidence of guilt. If the evidence was incompetent, the verdict may not stand.

1.   Upon the hearing in this court the Government finds its main prop in the position that what was said by Mrs. Shepard was admissible as a dying declaration. This is manifestly the theory upon which it was offered and received. The prop, however, is a broken reed. To make out a dying declaration the speaker must have spoken without hope of recovery and in the shadow of impending death. The record furnishes no proof of that indispensable condition. . . . Fear or even belief that illness will end in death will not avail of itself to make a dying declaration. . . . The patient must have spoken with the consciousness of a swift and certain doom.

What was said by this patient was not spoken in that mood. There was no warning to her in the circumstances that her words would be repeated and accepted as those of a dying wife, charging murder to her husband, and charging it deliberately and solemnly as a fact within her knowledge. To the focus of that responsibility her mind was never brought. . . . She did not speak as one dying, announcing to the survivors a definitive conviction, a legacy of knowledge on which the world might act when she had gone. . . .

2.   We pass to the question whether the statements to the nurse, though incompetent as dying declarations, were admissible on other grounds.

The Circuit Court of Appeals determined that they were. Witnesses for the defendant had testified to declarations by Mrs. Shepard which suggested a mind bent upon suicide, or at any rate were thought by the defendant to carry that suggestion. More than once before her illness she had stated in the hearing of these witnesses that she had no wish to live, and had nothing to live for, and on one occasion she added that she expected some day to make an end to her life. This testimony opened the door, so it is argued, to declarations in rebuttal that she had been poisoned by her husband. They were admissible, in that view, not as evidence of the truth of what was said, but as betokening a state of mind inconsistent with the presence of suicidal intent.

(a) The testimony was neither offered nor received for the strained and narrow purpose now suggested as legitimate. It was offered and received as proof of a dying declaration. What was said by Mrs. Shepard lying ill upon her deathbed was to be weighed as if a like statement had been made upon the stand. There is no disguise of that purpose by counsel for the Government. They concede in all candor that Mrs. Shepard's accusation of her husband, when it was finally let in, was received upon the footing of a dying declaration, and not merely as indicative of the persistence of a will to live. Beyond question the jury considered it for the broader purpose, as the court intended that they should.

. . . A trial becomes unfair if testimony thus accepted may be used in an appellate court as though admitted for a different purpose, unavowed and unsuspected. . . .

(b) Aside, however, from this objection, the accusatory declaration must have been rejected as evidence of a state of mind, though the purpose thus to limit it had been brought to light upon the trial. The defendant had tried to show by Mrs. Shepard's declarations to her friends that she had exhibited a weariness of life and a readiness to end it, the testimony giving plausibility to the hypothesis of suicide. By the proof of these declarations evincing an unhappy state of mind the defendant opened the door to the offer by the Government of declarations evincing a different state of mind, declarations consistent with the persistence of a will to live. The defendant would have no grievance if the testimony in rebuttal had been narrowed to that point. What the Government put in evidence, however, was something very different. It did not use the declarations by Mrs. Shepard to prove her present thoughts and feelings, or even her thoughts and feelings in times past. It used the declarations as proof of an act committed by some one else, as evidence that she was dying of poison given by her husband. This fact, if fact it was, the Government was free to prove, but not by hearsay declarations. It will not do to say that the jury might accept the declarations for any light that they cast upon the existence of a vital urge, and reject them to the extent that they charged the death to some one else. Discrimination so subtle is a feat beyond the compass of ordinary minds. The reverberating clang of those accusatory words would drown all weaker sounds. It is for ordinary minds, and not for psychoanalysts, that our rules of evidence are framed.

They have their source very often in considerations of administrative convenience, of practical expediency, and not in rules of logic. When the risk of confusion is so great as to upset the balance of advantage, the evidence goes out.

These precepts of caution are a guide to judgment here. There are times when a state of mind, if relevant, may be proved by contemporaneous declarations of feeling or intent. Mutual Life Ins. Co. v. Hillmon, 145 U.S. 285, 295. Thus, in proceedings for the probate of a will, where the issue is undue influence, the declarations of a testator are competent to prove his feelings for his relatives, but are incompetent as evidence of his conduct or of theirs. . . . In damage suits for personal injuries, declarations by the patient to bystanders or physicians are evidence of sufferings or symptoms, but are not received to prove the acts, the external circumstances, through which the injuries came about. So also in suits upon insurance policies, declarations by an insured that he intends to go upon a journey with another, may be evidence of a state of mind lending probability to the conclusion that the purpose was fulfilled. Mutual Life Ins. Co. v. Hillmon, supra. The ruling in that case marks the high water line beyond which courts have been unwilling to go. . . . Declarations of intention, casting light upon the future, have been sharply distinguished from declarations of memory, pointing backwards to the past. There would be an end, or nearly that, to the rule against hearsay if the distinction were ignored.

The testimony now questioned faced backward and not forward. This at least it did in its most obvious implications. What is even more important, it spoke to a past act, and more than that, to an act by some one not the speaker. Other tendency, if it had any, was a filament too fine to be disentangled by a jury.

The judgment should be reversed and the cause remanded to the District Court for further proceedings in accordance with this opinion.

VI.   BIBLIOGRAPHY

McCormick, Charles T., Evidence Chs. 24–34.

Weinstein Chs. 801–807.

Wigmore Chs. 37; 45–61.

Wright, Charles A. and Kenneth W. Graham, Jr., Federal Practice and Procedure: Evidence §§ 6321–6354.

Bartels, Robert, The Hearsay Rule, the Confrontation Clause, and Reversible Error in Criminal Case 26 Ariz. State L.J. 967 (1994).

Bein, Freda F., Parties' Admissions Agents' Admissions: Hearsay Wolves in Sheep's Clothing, 12 Hofstra L.Rev. 393 (1984).

Bein, Freda F., Prior Inconsistent Statements: The Hearsay Rule, 801(d)(1)(A) and 803(24), 26 U.C.L.A.L.Rev. 967 (1979).

Bennett, Fred W., How To Administer the "Big Hurt" in a Criminal Case: The Life and Times of Federal Rule of Evidence 806, 44 Cath.Univ.L.Rev. 1135 (1995).

Callen, Craig, Hearsay and Informal Reasoning, 47 Vand.L.Rev. 43 (1994).

Chevigny, Paul, Police Power (1969).

Cordray, Margaret M., Evidence Rule 806 and the Problem of Impeaching the Nontestifying Declarant, 56 Ohio State L.J. 495 (1995).

Fenner, G. Michael, The Hearsay Rule (Carolina Academic Press 2009) (2nd Ed.).

Friedman, Richard, Route Analysis of Credibility and Hearsay, 96 Yale L.J. 667 (1987).

Gamble, Charles W., The Tacit Admission Rule: Unreliable and Unconstitutional—A Doctrine Ripe for Abandonment, 14 Ga.L.Rev. 27 (1979).

Hutchins, Robert M. and Donald Slesinger, Some Observations on the Law of Evidence: Spontaneous Exclamations—Memory, 41 Harv.L.Rev. 860 (1928).

Hutchins, Robert M. and Donald Slesinger, Some Observations on the Law of Evidence: Spontaneous Exclamations, 28 Colum.L.Rev. 432 (1946).

Imwinkelried, Edward J., Declarations Against Social Interest: The (Still) Embarrassingly Neglected Hearsay Exception, 69 So.Cal. L.Rev. 1427 (1996).

Imwinkelried, Edward J., Of Evidence and Equal Protection: The Unconstitutionality of Excluding Government Agents' Statements Offered as Vicarious Admissions Against the Prosecution, 71 Minn.L.Rev. 269 (1986).

Imwinkelried, Edward J., The Scope of the Residual Hearsay Exceptions in the Federal Rules of Evidence, 15 San Diego L.Rev. 239 (1978).

Jefferson, Bernard S., Declarations Against Interest: An Exception to the Hearsay Rule, 58 Harv.L.Rev. 1 (1944).

Jonakait, Randolph N., Text, Texts, or Ad Hoc Determinations: Interpretation of the Federal Rules of Evidence, 71 Indiana L.J. 551 (1996).

Jonakait, Randolph N., The Supreme Court, Plain Meaning, and the Changed Rules of Evidence, 68 Tex.L.Rev 745, 774–78 (1990).

Ladd, Mason, The Hearsay We Admit, 5 Okla.L.Rev. 271 (1952).

Charles V. Laughlin, Business Entries and the Like, 46 Iowa L. Rev. 276, 289 (1961).

Maguire, John M., The Hearsay System: Around and Through the Thicket, 14 Vand.L.Rev. 741 (1961).

Maguire, John M., The Hillmon Case—Thirty-three Years After, 38 Harv. L.Rev. 709 (1925).

Maguire, John M. and Robert C. Vincent, Admissions Implied from Spoliation or Related Conduct, 45 Yale L.J. 226 (1935).

McCormick, Charles T., The Borderland of Hearsay, 39 Yale L.J. 489 (1930).

Moorehead, James D., Compromising the Hearsay Rule: The Fallacy of Res Gestae Reliability, 29 Loyola L.A. L.Rev. 203 (1995).

Morgan, Edmund, Admissions, 12 Wash.L.Rev. 181 (1937).

Morgan, Edmund, Declarations Against Interest, 5 Vand.L.Rev. 451 (1952).

Morgan, Edmund, Hearsay Dangers and the Application of the Hearsay Concept, 62 Harv.L.Rev. 177 (1948).

Morgan, Edmund, The Rationale of Vicarious Admissions, 42 Harv.L.Rev. 461 (1929).

Mueller, Christopher B., Post-Modern Hearsay Reform: The Importance of Complexity, 76 Minn. L.Rev. 367 (1992).

Mueller, Christopher B., The Federal Coconspirator Exception: Action, Assertion, and Hearsay, 12 Hofstra L.Rev. 323 (1984).

Nance, Dale, The Wisdom of Dallas County (*Dallas County v. Commercial Unition Assurance Company*; FRE 807: Residual Exception), in Lempert, Richard, Evidence Stories (Foundation Press 2006).

Nesson, Charles, The Evidence or the Event? On Judicial Proof and the Acceptability of Verdicts, 98 Harv.L.Rev. 1357 (1985).

Park, Roger C., "I Didn't Tell Them Anything About You": Implied Assertions as Hearsay Under the Federal Rules of Evidence, 74 Minn.L.Rev. 783 (1990).

Park, Roger C., The Rationale of Personal Admissions, 21 Ind.L.Rev. 509 (1988).

Park, Roger C., A Subject Matter Approach to Hearsay Reform, 86 Mich.L.Rev. 51 (1987).

Quick, Charles W., Some Reflections on Dying Declarations, 6 How.L.J. 109 (1960).

Raeder, Myrna, The Effect of the Catchalls on Criminal Defendants: Little Red Riding Hood Meets the Hearsay Wolf and is Devoured, 25 Loy.L.A. L.Rev. (1992).

Rand, Joseph W., The Residual Exceptions to the Federal Hearsay Rule: The Futile and Misguided Attempt to Restrain Judicial Decision, 80 Georgetown L.J. 873 (1992).

Rice, Paul W., Should Unintended Implications of Speech be Considered Nonhearsay? The Assertive/Nonassertive Distinction Under Rule 801(a) of the Federal Rules of Evidence, 65 Temple L.Rev. 529 (1992).

Schum, David, Hearsay From a Layperson 14 Cardozo L.Rev. 1 (1992).

Slough, M.C., Spontaneous Statements and State of Mind, 46 Iowa L.Rev. 994 (1961).

Swift, Eleanor, The Story of *Mahlandt v. Wild Canid Survival & Research Center, Inc.*: Encounters of Three Different Kinds (FRE 801(d)(2)): Admissions, in Lempert, Richard, Evidence Stories (Foundation Press 2006).

Swift, Eleanor, The Hearsay Rule at Work: Has It Been Abolished De Facto by Judicial Decision?, 76 Minn.L.Rev. 473 (1992).

Swift, Eleanor, Abolishing the Hearsay Rule, 75 Calif. L.Rev. 495 (1987).

Swift, Eleanor, A Foundation Fact Approach to Hearsay, 75 Calif.L.Rev. 1339 (1987).

Tanford, J. Alexander, The Limits of a Scientific Jurisprudence: The Supreme Court and Psychology, 66 Ind.L.J. 137 (1990).

Travers, Arthur H. Jr., Prior Consistent Statements, 57 Neb.L.Rev. 974 (1978).

Tribe, Laurence, Triangulating Hearsay, 87 Harv.L.Rev. 957 (1975).

Waltz, Jon, The Present Sense Impression Exception to the Rule Against Hearsay: Origins and Attributes, 66 Iowa L.Rev. 869 (1981).

Weinstein, Jack, Probative Force of Hearsay, 46 Iowa L.Rev. 331 (1961).

Weissenberger, Glen, Hearsay Puzzles: An Essay on Federal Evidence Rule 803(3), 64 Temple L.Rev. 145 (1991).

Weissenberger, Glen, Reconstructing the Definition of Hearsay 57 Ohio State L.J. 1525 (1996).

CHAPTER 7

CONFRONTATION AND COMPULSORY PROCESS

■ ■ ■

I.   INTRODUCTION

Sometimes ordinary rules of evidence are supplemented or supplanted by constitutional doctrines. The most familiar of these arise out of the Fourth and Fifth Amendments and have to do with the admission of evidence acquired by police searches, the admission of confessions made to police officers and the privilege against self-incrimination. The admissibility of crucial evidence often turns on the interpretation of these doctrines.[1] Despite their importance, we do not treat them in this text. They are generally unrelated to the other evidence rules we discuss, and criminal procedure or constitutional law courses ordinarily cover them.

However, two clauses of the Sixth Amendment relate so closely to the rules of evidence and trial procedure that we cannot ignore them. The first, the Confrontation Clause, may mean that, in a criminal case, some hearsay evidence is not admissible against an accused even though it meets the conditions of a hearsay exception. The Confrontation Clause may also give defendants rights in joint trials when evidence is admissible only against one defendant and in some situations where the state seeks to alter the usual rules that govern the receipt of trial testimony. The second, the Compulsory Process Clause, may mean that evidence offered by the defendant in a criminal case must be received even though it is inadmissible under the jurisdiction's ordinary rules of evidence. The Compulsory Process Clause also has implications for criminal discovery and for the sanctions that may attach to rules requiring criminal defendants to notify the state of witnesses they intend to call or defenses they intend to present.

Cases that raise confrontation and compulsory process issues force courts to explore the relationship between rules of evidence and fairness

---

[1]   Generally speaking, it is in criminal cases that the admissibility of evidence will be controlled by these constitutional doctrines or by the Sixth Amendment protections discussed in this chapter, although they may also apply in cases that while nominally "civil," carry substantial adverse consequences for the subject of the action. Moreover some of these doctrines, the privilege against self-incrimination in particular, protect people in settings other than judicial trials, and the violation of constitutional restrictions on the gathering of evidence may give rise to civil actions.

at trial. As Supreme Court membership has changed and doctrines have evolved, so too have conceptions of what constitutes a fair trial, resulting in decisions inconsistent with or overruling prior case law.

II. THE CONFRONTATION CLAUSE

But it is strange to see how you press me still with my Lord Cobham, and yet will not produce him. . . . let him be produced, and if he will yet accuse me or avow this confession of his, it shall convict me and ease you of further proof.[2]

—Sir Walter Raleigh

[T]hese are accusations that I can't even answer. . . . You tell me I am from Al Qaida, but I am not an Al Qaida. I don't have any proof to give you except to ask you to catch Bin Laden and ask him if I am part of Al Qaida. . . . I don't have proof regarding this. What should be done is you should give me the evidence regarding these accusations because I am not able to give you any evidence. I can just tell you no, and that is it.[3]

—Mustafa Ait Idr, detainee at Guantanamo Bay Naval Base

A. HISTORICAL BACKGROUND

The Confrontation Clause provides that, in all criminal prosecutions, the accused shall enjoy the right "to be confronted with witnesses against him."[4] This language might only mean that an accused person has a right, when his case is tried, to be present and to hear the testimonial evidence the state offers; or, at the other extreme, it could be read to bar the introduction of all hearsay in criminal trials. The framers of the Bill of Rights never expressed clearly their intended construction of this clause, nor do any early Supreme Court cases interpret the provision.

Most scholars agree that the framers drafted the Confrontation Clause to curb abuses associated with such notorious English trials as that of Sir Walter Raleigh. We have already described this trial in our

---

[2]   Phillimore, History and Principles of the Law of Evidence (1850).

[3]   In re Guantanamo Detainee Cases, 355 F. Supp. 2d 443, 469 (D.D.C. 2005). The speaker and five other Algerians who had been living in Bosnia for 7 to 9 years had been cleared by Bosnian courts of terrorist involvement after evidence against them was proven false. But upon their release from jail they were placed in U.S. custody and taken to the United States' Guantanamo Bay Naval Base on Cuba and held there on the basis of secret evidence. Craig Whitlock, *At Guantanamo, Caught in a Legal Trap; 6 Algerians Languish Despite Foreign Rulings, Dropped Charges,* Washington Post, August 21, 2006, p. A1. Ultimately Mr. Idr and the other Algerian detainees were released and returned to Bosnia. William Glaberson, *U.S. Set to Release 3 Detainees from Base,* New York Times, December 16, 2008, p. A28.

[4]   The Supreme Court has held that the Due Process Clause requires that the values of confrontation and compulsory process also be preserved in certain proceedings that are not formally criminal. It appears that the scope of this due process right is narrower than the Sixth Amendment rights as applied in criminal cases. See, e.g., Greene v. McElroy, 360 U.S. 474 (1959); Morrissey v. Brewer, 408 U.S. 471 (1972); Wolff v. McDonnell, 418 U.S. 539 (1974).

discussion of hearsay in Chapter 6. By way of review, consider Professor Graham's description:

> On November 17, 1603, Sir Walter Raleigh . . . went on trial for high treason. His conviction for having conspired to deprive the King of his government, to alter religion and bring in "the Roman superstition," and to procure foreign enemies to invade the kingdom was eventually to cost Raleigh his head: but it gained him fame as the supposed cause of the Confrontation Clause of the Sixth Amendment.

> The principal, indeed the only, evidence to support Raleigh's conviction was the written confession of Lord Cobham, an alleged coconspirator. This document obtained by officers of the Crown in proceedings at which Raleigh was neither present nor represented by counsel, was used against Raleigh, though he was able to show that Cobham had later recanted. Raleigh, though not a lawyer and not permitted counsel, responded with an eloquent demand for confrontation:

>> "The proof of the Common Law is by witness and jury; let Cobham be here, let him speak it. Call my accuser before my face, and I have done."

> Raleigh's repeated demands for confrontation were answered by Justice Warburton in terms familiar to those who have heard the modern claims for law and order:

>> "I marvel, Sir Walter, that you being of such experience and wit should stand on this point; for so many horse-stealers may escape, if they may not be condemned without witnesses."

> The only witness produced to testify *viva voce* at Raleigh's trials was one Dyer, a pilot who had been in Portugal at the time the conspiracy was supposed to have been afoot. He testified:

>> "I came to a merchant's house in Lisbon to see a boy that I had there; there came a gentleman into the house, and inquiring what countryman I was, I said an Englishman. Whereupon he asked me if the King was crowned? And I answered, No, but that I hope that he would be so shortly. Nay, saith he, he shall never be crowned; for Don Raleigh and Don Cobham shall cut his throat ere that day come."

> Modern lawyers would recognize this as the rankest sort of hearsay; a concept that did not evolve until much later. Raleigh shrewdly responded in terms of weight rather than admissibility: "This is the saying of some wild Jesuit or beggarly priest; but what proof is it against me?" Although his contemporaries

tended to agree that none of the evidence proved Raleigh guilty, he was convicted.[5]

The United States Supreme Court had no occasion to interpret the Confrontation Clause until the case of *Mattox v. United States*[6] arose about a century after the clause's enactment. Clyde Mattox had been convicted of murder, but the conviction had been overturned by the Supreme Court. In the period between Mattox's original trial and retrial two crucial prosecution witnesses died. At the retrial the state introduced transcripts of the deceased witness's testimony at the earlier trial. Mattox claimed that this procedure violated his right to confrontation. The Court affirmed the conviction, making it clear that there were circumstances in which the Confrontation Clause did not prevent a prosecutor from introducing out-of-court statements. Speaking through Justice Brown, the Court wrote:

> The primary object of the constitutional provision in question was to prevent depositions or *ex parte* affidavits, such as were sometimes admitted in civil cases, [from] being used against the prisoner in lieu of a personal examination and cross-examination of the witnesses in which the accused has an opportunity, not only of testing the recollection and sifting the conscience of the witness, but of compelling him to stand face to face with the jury in order that they may look at him, and judge by his demeanor upon the stand and the manner in which he gives his testimony whether he is worthy of belief. There is doubtless reason for saying that the accused should never lose the benefit of any of these safeguards even by the death of the witness; and that, if notes of his testimony are permitted to be read, he is deprived of the advantage of that personal presence of the witness before the jury which the law designed for his protection. But general rules of law of this kind, however beneficent in their operation and valuable to the accused, must occasionally give way to considerations of public policy and the necessities of the case. To say that a criminal, after having once been convicted by the testimony of a certain witness, should go scot free simply because death has closed the mouth of that witness, would be carrying his constitutional protection to an unwarrantable extent. . . .

> Many of its provisions in the nature of the Bill of Rights are subject to exceptions, recognized long before the adoption of the Constitution, and not interfering at all with its spirit. Such exceptions were obviously intended [by the framers] to be respected. . . . For instance, there could be nothing more directly

---

5   Kenneth W.Graham, Jr., The Right of Confrontation and the Hearsay Rule: Sir Walter Raleigh Loses Another One, 8 Crim. L. Bull. 99 (1972), at 99–101.

6   156 U.S. 237 (1895).

contrary to the letter of the provision in question than the admission of dying declarations. They are rarely made in the presence of the accused; they are made without any opportunity for examination or cross-examinations; nor is the witness brought face to face with the jury; yet from time immemorial they have been treated as competent testimony. . . . They are admitted not in conformity with any general rule regarding the admission of testimony, but as an exception to such rules, simply from the necessities of the case, and to prevent a manifest failure of justice. . . . The sense of impending death is presumed to remove all temptation to falsehood, and to enforce as strict an adherence to the truth as would the obligation of an oath. If such declarations are admitted, because made by a person then dead, under circumstances which give his statements the same weight as if made under oath, there is equal if not greater reason for admitting testimony of his statements which were made under oath.[7]

Four years later, in the case of *Kirby v. United States*,[8] the Court made it clear that *Mattox* did not mean that the Confrontation Clause was to be narrowly interpreted. *Kirby* involved a statute making it a crime to receive stolen property with an intent to convert. The statute provided that judgments of conviction against the principal felons should be evidence that the property of the United States alleged to have been stolen was in fact stolen. In overturning this provision, the first Justice Harlan wrote:

The record showing the result of the trial of the principal felons was undoubtedly evidence, as against *them*, in respect of every fact essential to show *their* guilt. But a fact which can be primarily established only by witnesses cannot be proved against an accused—charged with a different offense for which he may be convicted without reference to the principal offender—except by witnesses who confront him at the trial, upon whom he can look while being tried, whom he is entitled to cross-examine, and whose testimony he may impeach in every mode authorized by the established rules governing the trial or conduct of criminal cases.[9]

In the six decades following *Kirby* the Supreme Court rarely considered the Confrontation Clause, and there is no significant Supreme Court interpretation of the clause[10] until 1965 when, in the case of

---

[7] Id. at 242–44.

[8] 174 U.S. 47 (1899).

[9] Id. at 55.

[10] Note, however, *Motes v. United States*, 178 U.S. 458 (1900), in which the Supreme Court refused, on Confrontation Clause grounds, to admit the preliminary hearing testimony of a government witness who at the hearing had been subject to cross-examination by at least some

Pointer v. State of Texas,[11] the Supreme Court for the first time applied the Confrontation Clause to the states.

Pointer arose out of a robbery in which Pointer and a co-defendant, Dillard, were arrested for allegedly robbing one Kenneth W. Phillips. At a preliminary hearing before a Texas judge, Phillips identified Pointer as the man who had robbed him. Pointer, who had no counsel, did not try to cross-examine Phillips, although Dillard did. By the time of the trial Phillips had moved to California. After showing that Phillips had moved from the jurisdiction, the state, over Pointer's objection, introduced a transcript of Phillips's preliminary hearing testimony into evidence. The Court held that this violated Pointer's right to confrontation. The case is most important for its holding that the Confrontation Clause applies to the states in the same way that it applies in federal proceedings. Justice Black, writing for the majority, noted that "a major reason underlying the constitutional confrontation rule is to give a defendant charged with a crime an opportunity to cross-examine the witnesses against him."[12] But Justice Black also speaks of "the right of confrontation and cross-examination,"[13] thus implying that the right of cross-examination does not necessarily exhaust the meaning of the Confrontation Clause.

B. THE FOUR FACES OF CONFRONTATION

The distinction that Justice Black articulated in *Pointer* was prescient. Cross-examination does not exhaust the right to confrontation. We can now identify in the case law four distinct ways in which the right to confrontation may be realized. First, *a defendant may be protected from the incriminatory effects of evidence that is not technically offered against him and that would be inadmissible hearsay if it were so offered.* Second, *a defendant may insist on the exclusion of certain hearsay offered against him.* Third, *the state cannot impose certain restrictions on the cross-examination or impeachment of prosecution witnesses.* Fourth, *witnesses against an accused may be compelled to testify in settings where they cannot easily avoid looking at the accused face to face.* Each of these protections has been advanced by some Supreme Court decisions and limited by others. Because this ebb and flow of Confrontation Clause protection will probably continue, you must keep up with current case law to be sure that what we write below is not superseded. We examine these uses of the Confrontation Clause in turn.

---

defendants. The witness had escaped, due to the negligence of the government, and it appeared that he might have left the jurisdiction by the time of the trial. See also *West v. State of Louisiana*, 194 U.S. 258 (1904).

[11] 380 U.S. 400 (1965).

[12] 380 U.S. at 406–07.

[13] Id. at 405.

1.   Evidence Not Against the Accused

Because juries cannot follow instructions perfectly, evidence may harm a defendant even though it is not technically offered against the accused. Two of the early decisions following *Pointer* protect defendants in these circumstances. The first case, *Douglas v. State of Alabama*,[14] decided the same day as *Pointer*, grew out of charges against two people, Lloyd and Douglas, for assault with intent to commit murder. At Douglas's trial, Lloyd, who had been tried separately and convicted, was called by the prosecution as a witness, but he refused to testify, invoking the Fifth Amendment despite the judge's ruling that the privilege's protection had ended with his conviction. The prosecutor, citing Lloyd's failure to cooperate, asked and received permission to examine Lloyd as a hostile witness. Under the guise of cross-examination to refresh memory, the prosecutor read a document that purported to be Lloyd's confession, pausing every few sentences to ask Lloyd, "Did you make that statement?" Lloyd continued in his refusal to answer, but the entire confession, including parts implicating Douglas, was read to the jury in this fashion. Later three law enforcement officers identified the prosecutor's document as a transcription of Lloyd's confession. The prosecutor never offered the document itself into evidence.

The Court, speaking through Justice Brennan, found that "[i]n the circumstances of this case, petitioner's inability to cross-examine Lloyd as to the alleged confession plainly denied him the right of cross-examination secured by the Confrontation Clause."[15] Yet the Confrontation Clause only gives a criminal defendant the right to be confronted with *witnesses against him*, and Lloyd's confession was never in evidence, so technically Lloyd was never a witness against Douglas, even as a hearsay declarant. The Court eschewed such formal analysis. It took the reasonable position that, although the confession was not technically testimony, the jurors might have regarded it as such, and that they might have read Lloyd's repeated invocation of the Fifth Amendment as an admission of the confession's accuracy.

The second case involving evidence technically not offered against the accused dealt with a situation common in joint trials: the use of a confession implicating two or more defendants but admissible against only one. This case, *Bruton v. United States*,[16] spawned numerous progeny that limited and qualified its protections.

Bruton grew out of a joint trial of Bruton and Evans for armed postal robbery. Evans had confessed to a postal inspector that he and Bruton committed the robbery in question. At the trial, evidence of Evans's oral confession was introduced against him as an admission, but the judge

---

[14]   380 U.S. 415 (1965).

[15]   Id. at 419.

[16]   391 U.S. 123 (1968).

instructed the jury not to treat the confession as evidence against Bruton since Evans had never taken the stand, and Bruton could not question him. This case resembles *Douglas* in that, technically, no evidence was introduced against the appellant, for the prosecutor offered Evans's confession as Evans's personal admission and not as evidence against Bruton. But, as in *Douglas,* the Court was unwilling to be bound by the formal posture of the case. Overruling an earlier decision, it held that despite the judge's limiting instruction the jury could not be expected to ignore Evans's confession when evaluating the evidence implicating Bruton. Because Bruton had not had an opportunity to examine Evans about statements the jury might rely on, the Court held that introducing Evans's confession in the joint trial violated Bruton's Confrontation Clause rights.[17]

In the ensuing years, the reach of *Bruton* has been limited, but the core right that *Bruton* announced stands. The jurisprudence following *Bruton* not only delineates the current status of a defendant's right when a co-defendant's confession is offered, but also offers an example of how the Court may shape a precedent so that it comes to stand for a far more specific and narrower set of propositions than those it originally seemed to embody.

The same year that *Bruton* was decided, the Court held that the decision should apply retroactively. This meant that those convicted at joint trials could have their cases reopened if *Bruton* violations had occurred.[18] However, the next year the Court limited the implications of this case as well as of *Bruton* itself when it held in *Harrington v. California*[19] that a *Bruton* violation could be harmless error. It is no coincidence that, in the time between these two cases, two liberal Justices in the *Bruton* majority resigned and were replaced by Justices identified more with the "law and order" side of the criminal procedure spectrum.

---

[17] The implications of *Bruton* are potentially great. In many areas judicial instructions are thought sufficient to cure trial errors or to ensure that evidence is used only for a permitted purpose. Where constitutional rights are not threatened by the impermissible use of evidence, the limiting instruction may be the best way to minimize improper impact while getting on with the practical business of finishing trials. The *Bruton* Court is probably correct in its conclusion that the jury cannot be expected to follow an instruction to completely disregard certain persuasive evidence, but this doesn't mean that limiting instructions are totally without effect. *Bruton*, read broadly, appears to stand for the proposition that where a natural but impermissible use of powerful prosecution evidence will violate a person's constitutional rights, the Court will not assume that an instruction limiting the evidence to permissible uses provides adequate protection for the person's constitutional rights. But in *Harris v. New York*, 401 U.S. 222 (1971), the Court held that statements taken from a defendant in violation of the *Miranda* rule could be used for impeachment, even though they are inadmissible as substantive evidence. It is at least as unlikely that a properly instructed jury would limit its use of a defendant's own inculpatory statements to impeachment purposes as it is that the *Bruton* jury would have considered Evans's confession only against him. However, except for the *Bruton* situation, the Court's rulings since *Harris* have tended to reflect faith in jury instructions, not *Bruton's* realism on the matter.

[18] *Roberts v. Russell*, 392 U.S. 293 (1968).

[19] 395 U.S. 250 (1969).

Indeed, the jurisprudence of the Confrontation Clause owes much to the fact that it was first applied to the states toward the end of the Warren Court era but was subsequently elaborated on by the increasingly conservative Burger and Rehnquist Courts. Nevertheless, not every post-*Bruton* decision has cut back on defendants' rights.

Two years after *Harrington*, in *Nelson v. O'Neil*,[20] the Court confronted a situation in which two men, O'Neil and Runnels, had been tried jointly for kidnapping, robbery and vehicle theft. Runnels's confession, which also implicated O'Neil, was introduced against Runnels, with an instruction not to consider it as evidence against O'Neil. O'Neil was thus in the same situation as Bruton except that Runnels, unlike Bruton's codefendant Evans, took the stand and denied having made the confession. The Supreme Court held that O'Neil's confrontation rights had not been violated, and it indicated that the result would have been the same had Runnels admitted making the confession. As the Court saw it, the fact that O'Neil could examine his codefendant on his confession, whereas Bruton had no such opportunity, was a crucial difference between the two cases.

In so deciding, the Court ignored factors affecting the adequacy of a cross-examination. O'Neil, for example, had no incentive to show that Runnels was mistaken, for Runnels had denied making the confession that implicated O'Neil. Yet if the jurors disbelieved Runnels's denial, as they apparently did, O'Neil's situation was much like Bruton's. He never had the opportunity to show that if the confession was made, it was untruthful insofar as it implicated him. Had Runnels admitted confessing, O'Neil might have faced a different bind. So long as codefendants are conducting a joint defense, as they might whether innocent or guilty, neither defendant has an incentive to destroy the credibility of the other on the witness stand because, in doing so, each defendant may undermine his own case as well. Also, cross-examining a codefendant on a confession may enhance the likelihood that a jury will ignore limiting instructions, since cross-examination makes no sense if the evidence doesn't implicate the cross-examining party in the first instance.

O'Neil means that the Court's assumption in *Bruton* that a limiting instruction cannot fully protect a defendant from the incriminatory aspects of a codefendant's confession is one that the defendant must evaluate as an all or nothing proposition. If the defendant believes the limiting instruction offers protection, he can refrain from cross-examining his codefendant and risk the possibility that the jury will use some portion of the confession against him. If, on the other hand, the defendant believes the jury will disregard the limiting instruction, he can cross-examine his codefendant at the risk of encouraging a jury not

---

[20]   402 U.S. 622 (1971).

swayed by the cross-examination to use the confession as evidence against him. What the defendant as a practical matter cannot insist on is the simultaneous realization of two rights: the right under the usual rules of evidence not to be implicated by evidence that has not been admitted against him and the Sixth Amendment right not to be incriminated by evidence he has been unable to confront through cross-examination. Instead of acknowledging the defendant's dilemma, the Court analyzes the *Bruton* problem as if codefendants' confessions were hearsay offered for substantive purposes. The Court's guiding principle is that if the admission of a codefendant's confession against a defendant would violate none of the defendant's Confrontation Clause rights, the Court will not find a Confrontation Clause violation when domestic law makes the evidence admissible only against the confessing codefendant.

The *Bruton* line culminates in four more recent cases.[21] The first of these, *Lee v. Illinois*,[22] grew out of a bench trial in which the judge admitted that he treated the confession of one non-testifying codefendant as substantive evidence of the other's guilt. The state argued that because the confessions overlapped substantially in the descriptions they provided, they corroborated each other to the point where each codefendant's confession was reliable enough for use against the other without violating the other's right of confrontation. The Supreme Court by a 5–4 majority held that in convicting the defendant Lee the trial judge had relied on constitutionally inadmissible evidence. For the majority, the fact that confessions interlocked did not necessarily indicate sufficient reliability to overcome Confrontation Clause barriers to admissibility.

A year later the case of *Cruz v. New York*[23] posed the same problem for the Court in the *Bruton* context. Cruz and his codefendant had both confessed. Their confessions shared many details: at their joint trial each confession was offered only against its maker, and the jury was instructed not to use the confession of one codefendant as evidence of the other's guilt. The Court held that, while an appellate court could consider evidence of the degree of interlock in determining whether a *Bruton* violation was harmless error, there was no *per se* exception to *Bruton* in cases where confessions interlocked. Rather, if a codefendant's confession

---

[21] In addition to the cases we discuss in the text, note also *Tennessee v. Street*, 471 U.S. 409 (1985), in which the defendant Street complained that his confession to a murder had been coerced and that he had been forced to provide a confession patterned on that of his alleged fellow conspirator, Peele. To rebut this claim, the trial judge allowed the sheriff to testify that Peele's confession had not been coerced and allowed the prosecutor to introduce Peele's confession so that the jurors could compare it to Street's and judge for themselves whether Street's confession might have been patterned on it. Peele did not testify at Street's trial and so could not be examined on the portions of his confession that implicated Street. A unanimous Court, including Justices Brennan and Marshall, who during their tenure invariably dissented from decisions limiting the scope of the Confrontation Clause, held that when a defendant raised an issue that made a codefendant's confession relevant for a legitimate non-hearsay purpose, a limiting instruction provided all the protection to which the defendant was entitled.

[22] 476 U.S. 530 (1986).

[23] 481 U.S. 186 (1987).

was not substantively admissible under *Lee*, it could not be admitted against its maker in a joint trial without violating a codefendant's rights under *Bruton*.

Cruz was something of a surprise. A number of circuit courts had carved out an "interlocking confessions" exception to *Bruton*, and even after *Lee* many Court watchers felt the Supreme Court would do the same, particularly since the conservative Justice Scalia had replaced a member of the *Lee* majority. However, Justice Scalia not only joined the Court's four most liberal Justices to form the *Cruz* majority, but he also authored the opinion in that case. The key to this puzzle, and the first indication of the nuanced perspective Scalia would bring to Confrontation Clause issues, lies in a second opinion authored by Scalia that appeared the same day as *Cruz* and immediately before *Cruz* in the *U.S. Reports*. In that case, *Richardson v. Marsh*,[24] the confession of Marsh's codefendant had been admitted against the codefendant in redacted form so that not only was all mention of Marsh's name eliminated from the confession, but there was no specific allusion to Marsh's existence. However, when Marsh testified, she mentioned a conversation in a car to which the codefendant had also alluded, thus indicating that she was the anonymous accomplice with whom her codefendant had conversed. Justice Scalia, with three members of the *Cruz* majority dissenting, held that the combination of the redacted confession and limiting instructions sufficiently protected Marsh's rights under the Confrontation Clause. Practicalities influenced Scalia, for he pointed out that one-third of all federal criminal trials had joint defendants, and that the efficiency and fairness advantages to joint trials were such that barring confessions in joint trials was too drastic a remedy.

Further elaboration came in *Gray v. Maryland*.[25] In *Gray*, two men, Anthony Bell and Kevin Gray, were tried jointly and convicted of involuntary manslaughter for their part in a gang of six people who had beaten to death a man named Stacey Williams. Bell had confessed to the police, implicating Gray and another. For example, at one point in his confession, when asked "Who was in the group that beat Stacey," Bell had replied, "Me, Kevin Gray, Tank Vanlandingham and a few other guys." At trial, Bell did not take the stand. His confession was introduced against him by a police officer who said the word "deleted" or "deletion" where the names of those Bell identified appeared.[26]

---

[24]   481 U.S. 200 (1987).

[25]   523 U.S. 185 (1998).

[26]   The officer was reading from a transcript in which there were blank spaces where the co-offenders had been identified. We have inserted the names of the two codefendants into the quote to reconstruct the original statement that the Court did not reproduce. We may have gotten the names reversed or used a nickname for Vanlandingham when Bell had used his given name.

So the portion of the confession we quoted would have been heard by the jury as, "Me, deleted, deleted and a few other guys." The *Gray* majority pointed out that in *Richardson* all reference to the codefendant, Marsh, had been omitted, and it was only Marsh's testimony that suggested she was the person with whom the confessing defendant had discussed a planned murder. They then held that redactions that simply replaced a co-offender's name with an obvious blank space or a word such as "deleted" so closely resembled the *Bruton* situation as to demand the same result. "To replace [the codefendant's name] with an obvious blank," the Court said, "will not likely fool anyone."[27] An acceptable redaction of Bell's response to the question of who was in the group is, for the Court, "Me and a few other guys." This is similar to the redacted remark in *Richardson*, for it does not suggest that Bell specifically identified anyone as a participant in the beating.

Putting *Cruz*, *Marsh* and *Gray* together, a message emerges that harks back to the "good faith" concerns of *Douglas* and *Bruton*. Prosecutors should not try to circumvent the hearsay rule when its mandate is required by the Confrontation Clause by admitting against defendant **A** (whom we shall call Alice) in a joint trial a confession that also implicates defendant **B** (whom we shall call Bob) when the confession is inadmissible against Bob. If a prosecutor offering Alice's confession is indifferent to or invites the possibility that Alice's confession will implicate Bob, the Confrontation Clause will protect Bob from this possibility by requiring the prosecutor either to sever Bob's case from Alice's or to forego using Alice's confession.[28] However, if the prosecutor does everything she reasonably can to ensure that Alice's confession will not be improperly used, which in practice means redacting Alice's confession to remove all mention of Bob as well as markers, like blank spaces or the word "deleted" that seem to refer to Bob, the Confrontation Clause will not demand more. Thus it appears that the law is that *confessions redacted in good faith may be freely used in joint trials even if they originally implicated the codefendant in the crime, but unredacted and incompletely redacted confessions may only be used if the confessing defendant testifies and is subject to cross-examination.*

As we shall see below, Confrontation Clause jurisprudence was fundamentally changed in 2004 in the case of *Crawford v. Washington*.[29] It did not appear from *Crawford* that the outcomes in the *Bruton* line of

---

[27] 523 U.S. at 193. In *Gray*, perhaps to ensure that no one was fooled, the prosecutor followed the reading of the confession with the repeated "deletions" by next asking the officer, "after he [Bell] gave you that information, you subsequently were able to arrest Mr. Kevin Gray; is that correct?" Id. The Court disapproved of this obvious charade but did not treat it as crucial to its holding.

[28] Another alternative used occasionally in recent years is to try codefendants' cases simultaneously to separate juries. When evidence admissible against only one codefendant is offered, the jury trying the other codefendant's case leaves the courtroom.

[29] 541 U.S. 36 (2004).

cases would be changed, for the key cases are cited favorably there. However recent cases, discussed below, cast doubt on *Bruton*'s vitality. Moreover, if a "confession" consisted of casual comments to a friend rather than statements to the police, the Confrontation Clause today would probably allow the introduction of the unredacted "confession" against the confessor even if it implicated a codefendant in a joint trial. Moreover, for reasons that will be clear when we discuss the *Crawford* case and its progeny, if otherwise applicable hearsay law permitted, the prosecutor would most likely be able to offer the confessor's statements to a friend *directly* against a codefendant whether or not the confessor takes the stand.

Returning to the *Bruton* line of cases, it follows almost *a fortiori*, and seems confirmed by *O'Neil* and *Cruz*, that if the Confrontation Clause would not prevent hearsay from being admitted against Bob, then Bob has no constitutional complaint when the evidence is admitted against Alice, and the judge, in accord with state hearsay law, tells the jury not to consider Alice's confession in judging Bob's guilt. Bob has no cause to complain, although only protected by a limiting instruction, because he is better off than if the state had pushed its hearsay exceptions to constitutional limits and made Alice's hearsay fully admissible against him. Thus, to understand the boundaries of *Bruton*, we must understand the limits the Confrontation Clause imposes on the admissibility of hearsay in general.

This brings us to the second purpose for which the Confrontation Clause has been invoked—as a limitation on a state's ability to admit hearsay evidence against criminal defendants. This is potentially a substantial limitation, for it might mean that the state in criminal cases is not free to create new hearsay exceptions or even that hearsay admissible under traditional exceptions is constitutionally suspect. We discuss this limitation on the use of hearsay in the next section.

Problem VII-1. The police arrived at State and Monroe to find Homer Hammer lying in a pool of blood. He had been shot by an armed guard in the Brinks truck he had tried to rob. "Bring a priest, quick," said Homer,

"I ain't long for this world."

"You're not going to confess to a priest until you confess to me," said the cop bending over Homer.

"OK," said Homer. "Me and Linda Sawyer dreamed up this scheme drinking coffee over there," he continued, pointing to a coffee house on Monroe. "We noticed that the Brinks guard made at least three trips into the bank with money and didn't lock the back door but just closed it. The idea was that Linda would go into the bank and faint right into the guard's arms to delay his return, and I would open the truck door, steal a money bag, run to Linda's car which is parked over there and make my escape. Linda even bought a gun and gave it to me in case there was trouble. But how was I to know that a second guard sat inside the truck with his gun drawn? Did Linda escape?"

"Not for long," said the cop.

Within an hour, the cop was knocking on Linda's door. Her eyes opened wide with fear when she saw him.

"Homer told us about your robbery scheme," said the cop.

"Homer did? That bastard!" responded Linda.

"Calm yourself," said the cop. He then proceeded to read her her *Miranda* rights, after which he said, "Now you might find it's easier on your conscience if you speak up." Linda responded with a confession that did not differ in any important details from what Homer had said.

Homer did not die, and a year later Homer and Linda were tried together for attempted armed robbery and a conspiracy to commit armed robbery. Neither took the stand to testify. You are the prosecutor. **At their joint trial will you be able to introduce Homer's confession against Homer? Against Linda? If you offered a redacted confession what would it say? Would you be able to introduce Linda's confession against her? Against Homer? If you offered a redacted confession what would it say? Would you be able to introduce against Linda the cop's first statement to her along with her reply "Homer did? That bastard!"? Would you be able to introduce this evidence against Homer? Could you introduce any version of this conversation against either defendant? What would the version you might be allowed to admit say?**

2. Hearsay Evidence

Two early cases, *Pointer v. Texas* [30] and *Barber v. Page* [31] involved efforts by states to introduce against criminal defendants the preliminary hearing testimony of declarants who at the time of trial were in other states. In each case the testimony was arguably admissible under an orthodox reading of the former testimony exception to the hearsay rule, but in each case the Supreme Court held that the use of the testimony violated the defendant's Confrontation Clause rights. In *Pointer*, the preliminary hearing testimony was that of a man named Phillips who accused Pointer of robbing him. The Court seemed particularly troubled by the fact that, because Pointer had no counsel at the preliminary hearing, Phillips's accusations had never been tested through cross-examination. In *Barber*, the Court felt that the state had not made a good faith effort to secure the hearsay declarant's presence and held that

---

[30]   380 U.S. 400 (1965).

[31]   390 U.S. 719 (1968).

the Confrontation Clause made such an effort a precondition to the invocation of the prior testimony exception in criminal cases.   The declarant in *Barber*, like the declarant in *Pointer*, had not been cross-examined at the preliminary hearing, but unlike the Court in *Pointer*, the *Barber* Court thought this detail hardly mattered. "Confrontation," wrote Justice Marshall, "is basically a trial right.   It includes both the opportunity to cross-examine and the occasion for the jury to weigh the demeanor of the witness.[32]"

A jurisprudence which built on *Barber* and took Marshall's dictum seriously could have substantially limited the ability of prosecutors to use a number of the traditional hearsay exceptions. How far the Court might have gone in this direction is impossible to say, for changes in Court personnel changed the direction of the Court's Confrontation Clause decisions. The about-face was signaled in 1970 in the case of *California v. Green*.[33] In *Green*, the Court both approved a then novel California rule of evidence that allowed a witness's prior inconsistent statements to be introduced as substantive evidence and held that there was no constitutional bar to the use of a witness's preliminary hearing testimony when the witness was produced in court. The Court noted by way of dictum that the preliminary hearing testimony would also have been admissible had the witness been unavailable, thereby disposing of *Barber's* dictum that confrontation is basically a trial right.[34]

During the decade following *Green* no case of enduring importance addressed the relationship of the Confrontation Clause to the hearsay rule. Then, in 1980, the Court decided *Ohio v. Roberts*,[35] which sought to establish general principles for interpreting the Confrontation Clause and became the touchstone of Confrontation Clause jurisprudence for the next 25 years.

Roberts grew out of a trial for credit card theft and check forgery in which the defendant argued that the victim's daughter had given him the check and credit cards while she was allowing him to stay in her parents' home. Unfortunately for the defendant, his counsel saw the daughter, Anita, in the courtroom hallway during the preliminary hearing and called her as the defense's only witness. But when Anita took the stand

---

[32]   390 U.S. 719, 725 (1968).

[33]   399 U.S. 149 (1970).

[34]   *Barber's* other strand, that a good-faith effort to procure the presence of a hearsay declarant was a precondition to the admission of former testimony, was undercut by the case of *Mancusi v. Stubbs*, 408 U.S. 204 (1972). In *Mancusi*, the defendant Stubbs's first trial had resulted in a guilty verdict, later reversed for ineffective assistance of counsel. When Stubbs was retried, the state made *no* effort to secure the presence of one of their crucial witnesses, but instead introduced a transcript of the witness's testimony at the first trial. The court held that, because the witness was in Sweden at the time of the second trial and could not have been compelled to appear in a Tennessee court, the state did not have to make any effort to secure his presence.

[35]   448 U.S. 56 (1980).

she denied rather than supported the defendant's claims. By the time the case went to trial, more than a year after the preliminary hearing, Anita could not be located, and pursuant to an Ohio statute the prosecutor offered a transcript of her preliminary hearing testimony to rebut the defendant's excuse.[36]

Although *California v. Green* might have been read to have allowed the admission of Anita's testimony for it seemed to have established the principle that the preliminary hearing testimony of an unavailable witness was admissible at a later trial, the Supreme Court of Ohio, chose to distinguish *Green*. Noting that normally there is little incentive to cross-examine a witness at a preliminary hearing, the appellate court ruled that since Anita had not been declared hostile at the preliminary hearing and cross-examined, the transcript of her testimony was inadmissible. The United States Supreme Court, in an opinion authored by Justice Blackmun, reversed. It held that the Confrontation Clause had been intended to exclude some but not all hearsay and endeavored to develop a set of principles that would tell trial judges where to draw the line. It held that:

> The Confrontation Clause operates in two separate ways to restrict the range of admissible hearsay. First, in conformance with the Framers' preference for face-to-face accusation, the Sixth Amendment establishes a rule of necessity. In the usual case (including cases where prior cross-examination has occurred), the prosecution must either produce, or demonstrate the unavailability of, the declarant whose statement it wishes to use against the defendant.

> The second aspect operates once a witness is shown to be unavailable. Reflecting its underlying purpose to augment accuracy in the fact finding process by ensuring the defendant an effective means to test adverse evidence, the Clause countenances only hearsay marked with such trustworthiness that "there is no material departure from the reason of the general rule."

The first principle that Justice Blackmun enunciated is procedural and appears almost absolute in its requirement that before the state can introduce hearsay the declarant has either to be produced or shown to be unavailable, though the Court dropped a footnote indicating that in exceptional circumstances where the defendant had no reasonable expectation of benefitting from confrontation the requirement might be relaxed. The second principle, that to be admissible hearsay has to have some "indicia of reliability," adds a substantive prong to the test. The required indicia, the Court held, could be inferred, *without more*, when

---

[36] A major issue dividing the majority and dissent in *Roberts* was whether the state's effort to find Anita and bring her to court was sufficient to satisfy the demands of the Clause. This aspect of the case did not set any important precedent.

the hearsay fell within a *firmly rooted* hearsay exception, but where hearsay did not fit a traditional exception it had to be excluded *absent a showing of particularized guarantees of trustworthiness*. The Court went on to hold that the hearsay in *Roberts* met these tests and reversed the judgment of the Ohio Supreme Court.

Roberts treated the Confrontation Clause as akin in its aims to the hearsay rule. It sought both to promote the appearance of fairness (hence available witnesses had to be produced) and to enhance truth-finding (hence hearsay was admissible only if it was likely to be reliable enough to enhance the search for truth.). These are important goals that may explain why a right to confrontation was incorporated into the Sixth Amendment. But it was immediately obvious that aspects of the decision were problematic.

The requirement that available witnesses be almost always produced would, if taken literally, have worked a dramatic change in the way criminal cases were tried. All hearsay exceptions offered against the accused in criminal cases would require unavailability. Excited utterances, present sense impressions, declarations evincing states of mind, statements in business records, and the rest of the 803 exceptions would be unavailable to prosecutors unless one of the conditions listed in FRE 804(a) was met. Given Confrontation Clause jurisprudence before *Roberts*, it was unlikely that the Court meant to go this far. In 1986, in *United States v. Inadi*,[37] a case involving a co-conspirator's admission, the Court made it clear that it had not. The Court's unwillingness to require unavailability where established hearsay exceptions did not was confirmed in *White v. Illinois*,[38] where the Court found no Confrontation Clause violation when the hearsay of an allegedly abused but not necessarily unavailable child was admitted under the spontaneous declaration and medical diagnosis exceptions.

Equally problematic is the proposition in *Roberts* that reliability can be inferred solely from the fact that a statement falls within a firmly rooted hearsay exception. Not only are some hearsay exceptions, like the admissions exception, not justified on reliability grounds, but hearsay can be of questionable reliability even if it fits the contours of a reliability-based exception. This possibility seems not to have troubled the courts, perhaps because this *Roberts* prong provided an easy means to apply a bright line rule that favored admissibility and aided the state. The Supreme Court confirmed its intention that this prong of *Roberts* be taken literally in *Bourjaily v. United States*[39] where, confronted with a co-conspirator's admission, it held that this "exception to the hearsay rule is

---

[37]   475 U.S. 387 (1986).

[38]   502 U.S. 346 (1992). *White* is arguably the only Supreme Court case decided in the wake of *Roberts* that might come out differently under a *Crawford* analysis, but this would not be because of its failure to meet a prong of the original *Robert's* test.

[39]   483 U.S. 171 (1987).

firmly enough rooted in our jurisprudence that, under this Court's holding in *Roberts*, a court need not inquire into the reliability of such statements."[40] If an offshoot of the admissions exception, not traditionally justified on reliability grounds, could nonetheless be assumed reliable without further inquiry, it followed that the same was true of exceptions that purported to carry indicia of reliability.

Roberts did have somewhat more bite when hearsay exceptions were novel, such as the catch-all exception and the exception for statements against penal interest. Thus in *Idaho v. Wright*,[41] by a 5 to 4 vote the Court refused to find guarantees of trustworthiness sufficient to justify the admission, under a catch-all exception, of a two-and-a-half year-old's statements to a pediatrician inquiring into possible abuse, and ruled that evidence corroborating the claims could not provide those guarantees. Nine years later in *Lilly v. Virginia*,[42] the Court unanimously rejected an attempt to introduce, under the new exception for statements against penal interest, a portion of a defendant's confession to the police that implicated an accomplice when the latter was being tried for murder. But even though the Supreme Court's holdings indicated that at least with respect to novel hearsay exceptions, *Roberts'* requirement of indicia of reliability had teeth, many lower court judges, particularly in state courts, were attempting to gum it to death. Indicia of reliability, it seemed, could be found in almost any surrounding circumstance if a judge so desired. Even *Lilly,* which seemed a firm precedent for the proposition that without confrontation statements during police interrogation by one accomplice could not be introduced against another, was often circumvented.

Roberts had always had its critics in the academy, and by the time of *Lilly* even its support on the Supreme Court was waning. Although the decision in *Lilly* was unanimous, only four Justices unequivocally endorsed the *Roberts* approach. Moreover, several scholars had by then offered general theories of the Confrontation Clause that resonated with themes that Justices Scalia and Thomas, in particular, had urged.[43] The time was clearly ripe for the Court to rethink its approach to the clause. It did so in *Crawford v. Washington,* which has replaced *Roberts* as the starting point for Confrontation Clause analysis.

---

[40] Id. at 183.

[41] 497 U.S. 805 (1990).

[42] 527 U.S. 116 (1999).

[43] The most important of these were A. Amar, The Constitution and Criminal Procedure, 125–131 (1997) and R. Friedman, Confrontation: The Search for Basic Principles, 86 Geo. L. J. 1011 (1998).

CRAWFORD V. WASHINGTON[44]
541 U.S. 36 (2004).

JUSTICE SCALIA delivered the opinion of the Court.

I

. . . On August 5, 1999, Kenneth Lee was stabbed at his apartment. Police arrested petitioner later that night. After giving petitioner and his wife Miranda warnings, detectives interrogated each of them twice. Petitioner eventually confessed that he and Sylvia had gone in search of Lee because he was upset over an earlier incident in which Lee had tried to rape her. The two had found Lee at his apartment, and a fight ensued in which Lee was stabbed in the torso and petitioner's hand was cut.

Petitioner gave the following account of the fight:

"Q. Okay. Did you ever see anything in [Lee's] hands?

"A. I think so, but I'm not positive.

"Q. Okay, when you think so, what do you mean by that?

"A. . . . I think, I think that he pulled somethin' out and I grabbed for it and that's how I got cut . . . but I'm not positive. I, I, my mind goes blank when things like this happen. I mean, I just, I remember things wrong, I remember things that just doesn't, don't make sense to me later."

Sylvia generally corroborated petitioner's story about the events leading up to the fight, but her account of the fight itself was arguably different—particularly with respect to whether Lee had drawn a weapon before petitioner assaulted him:

"Q. Did Kenny do anything to fight back from this assault?

"A. (pausing) I know he reached into his pocket . . . or somethin' . . . I don't know what.

"Q. After he was stabbed?

"A. He saw Michael coming up. He lifted his hand . . . his chest open, he might [have] went to go strike his hand out or something and then (inaudible).

"Q. Okay, you, you gotta speak up.

"A. Okay, he lifted his hand over his head maybe to strike Michael's hand down or something and then he put his hands in his . . . put his right hand in his right pocket . . . took a step back . . .

---

[44] Most internal citations and footnotes are omitted without notation. Omitted text is noted by ellipses. Retained Court footnotes are numbered with a lower case letter following. Ours are numbered only.

Michael proceeded to stab him . . . then his hands were like . . . how do you explain this . . . open arms . . . with his hands open and he fell down . . . and we ran (describing subject holding hands open, palms toward assailant) . . .

"Q. Did you see anything in his hands at that point?

"A. (pausing) um um (no)."

The State charged petitioner with assault and attempted murder. At trial, he claimed self-defense. Sylvia did not testify because of the state marital privilege, which generally bars a spouse from testifying without the other spouse's consent. In Washington, this privilege does not extend to a spouse's out-of-court statements admissible under a hearsay exception, so the State sought to introduce Sylvia's tape-recorded statements to the police as evidence that the stabbing was not in self-defense. . . .

Petitioner countered that . . . admitting the evidence would violate his federal constitutional right to be "confronted with the witnesses against him." According to our description of that right in *Ohio v. Roberts,* it does not bar admission of an unavailable witness's statement against a criminal defendant if the statement bears "adequate 'indicia of reliability.' ". . . .

The Washington Supreme Court reinstated the conviction, unanimously concluding that, although Sylvia's statement did not fall under a firmly rooted hearsay exception, it bore guarantees of trustworthiness: " '[W]hen a codefendant's confession is virtually identical [to, i.e.., interlocks with,] that of a defendant, it may be deemed reliable.'. . .

II

The Sixth Amendment's Confrontation Clause provides that, "[i]n all criminal prosecutions, the accused shall enjoy the right . . . to be confronted with the witnesses against him." We have held that this bedrock procedural guarantee applies to both federal and state prosecutions. As noted above, *Roberts* says that an unavailable witness's out-of-court statement may be admitted so long as it has adequate indicia of reliability—i.e., falls within a "firmly rooted hearsay exception" or bears "particularized guarantees of trustworthiness." Petitioner argues that this test strays from the original meaning of the Confrontation Clause and urges us to reconsider it.

A

The Constitution's text does not alone resolve this case. One could plausibly read "witnesses against" a defendant to mean those who actually testify at trial, those whose statements are offered at trial, or something in-between. We must therefore turn to the historical background of the Clause to understand its meaning. The right to confront one's accusers is a concept that dates back to Roman times. The founding generation's immediate source of the concept, however, was the common law. English common law has long differed from continental civil law in regard to the manner in which witnesses give testimony in criminal trials. The common-law tradition is one of live testimony in court subject to adversarial testing, while the civil law condones examination in private by judicial officers.

Nonetheless, England at times adopted elements of the civil-law practice. Justices of the peace or other officials examined suspects and witnesses before trial. These examinations were sometimes read in court in lieu of live testimony, a practice that "occasioned frequent demands by the prisoner to have his 'accusers,' i.e. the witnesses against him, brought before him face to face."

. . .

The most notorious instances of civil-law examination occurred in the great political trials of the 16th and 17th centuries. One such was the 1603 trial of Sir Walter Raleigh for treason. Lord Cobham, Raleigh's alleged accomplice, had implicated him in an examination before the Privy Council and in a letter. At Raleigh's trial, these were read to the jury. Raleigh argued that Cobham had lied to save himself: "Cobham is absolutely in the King's mercy; to excuse me cannot avail him; by accusing me he may hope for favour." Suspecting that Cobham would recant, Raleigh demanded that the judges call him to appear, arguing that "[t]he Proof of the Common Law is by witness and jury: let Cobham be here, let him speak it. Call my accuser before my face. . . ." The judges refused, and despite Raleigh's protestations that he was being tried "by the Spanish Inquisition," the jury convicted, and Raleigh was sentenced to death.

. . . Through a series of statutory and judicial reforms, English law developed a right of confrontation that limited these abuses. . . . Courts, meanwhile, developed relatively strict rules of unavailability, admitting examinations only if the witness was demonstrably unable to testify in person. Several authorities also stated that a suspect's confession could be admitted only against himself, and not against others he implicated.

One recurring question was whether the admissibility of an unavailable witness's pretrial examination depended on whether the defendant had had an opportunity to cross-examine him. In 1696, the Court of King's Bench answered this question in the affirmative, in the widely reported misdemeanor libel case of *King v. Paine*. The court ruled that, even though a witness was dead, his examination was not admissible where "the defendant not being present when [it was] taken before the mayor . . . had lost the benefit of a cross-examination." . . .

B

Many declarations of rights adopted around the time of the Revolution guaranteed a right of confrontation. The proposed Federal Constitution, however, did not. At the Massachusetts ratifying convention, Abraham Holmes objected to this omission precisely on the ground that it would lead to civil-law practices: "[W]e shall find Congress possessed of powers enabling them to institute judicatories little less inauspicious than a certain tribunal in Spain, . . . the *Inquisition*." . . . The First Congress responded by including the Confrontation Clause in the proposal that became the Sixth Amendment. . . .

III

This history supports two inferences about the meaning of the Sixth Amendment.

A

First, *the principal evil at which the Confrontation Clause was directed was the civil-law mode of criminal procedure, and particularly its use of ex parte examinations as evidence against the accused.* [Emphasis added.] It was these practices that the Crown deployed in notorious treason cases like Raleigh's; . . . that English law's assertion of a right to confrontation was meant to prohibit; and that the founding-era rhetoric decried. The Sixth Amendment must be interpreted with this focus in mind. Accordingly, *we once again reject the view that the Confrontation Clause applies of its own force only to in-court testimony, and that its application to out-of-court statements introduced at trial depends upon "the law of Evidence for the time being."* [Emphasis added] Leaving the regulation of out-of-court statements to the law of evidence would render the Confrontation Clause powerless to prevent even the most flagrant inquisitorial practices. Raleigh was, after all, perfectly free to confront those who read Cobham's confession in court.

This focus also suggests that *not all hearsay implicates the Sixth Amendment's core concerns. An off-hand, overheard remark might be unreliable evidence and thus a good candidate for exclusion under hearsay rules, but it bears little resemblance to the civil-law abuses the Confrontation Clause targeted.* [Emphasis added.] On the other hand, *ex parte* examinations might sometimes be admissible under modern hearsay rules, but the Framers certainly would not have condoned them.

The text of the Confrontation Clause reflects this focus. It applies to "witnesses" against the accused—in other words, those who "bear testimony." 1 N. Webster, An American Dictionary of the English Language (1828). "Testimony," in turn, is typically "[a] solemn declaration or affirmation made for the purpose of establishing or proving some fact." *An accuser who makes a formal statement to government officers bears testimony in a sense that a person who makes a casual remark to an acquaintance does not.* [Emphasis added] The constitutional text, like the history underlying the common-law right of confrontation, thus reflects an especially acute concern with a specific type of out-of-court statement.

Various formulations of this core class of "testimonial" statements exist: *"ex parte in-court testimony or its functional equivalent* [emphasis added]—that is, material such as affidavits, custodial examinations, prior testimony that the defendant was unable to cross-examine, or similar pretrial statements *that declarants would reasonably expect to be used prosecutorially,"* [emphasis added] Brief for Petitioner 23; *"extrajudicial statements . . . contained in formalized testimonial materials,* [emphasis added] such as affidavits, depositions, prior testimony, or confessions," White v. Illinois, 502 U. S. 346, 365 (1992) (THOMAS, J., joined by SCALIA, J.); *"statements that were made under circumstances which would lead an objective witness reasonably to believe that the statement would be available for use at a later trial,"* [emphasis added] Brief for National Association of Criminal Defense Lawyers et al. as *Amici Curiae.* These formulations all share a common nucleus and then define the Clause's coverage at various levels of abstraction around it. Regardless of the precise articulation, some statements qualify under any definition—for example, *ex parte* testimony at a preliminary hearing.

Statements taken by police officers in the course of interrogations are also testimonial under even a narrow standard. Police interrogations bear a striking resemblance to examinations by justices of the peace in England. The statements are not sworn testimony, but the absence of oath was not dispositive. Cobham's examination was unsworn, yet Raleigh's trial has long been thought a paradigmatic confrontation violation. . . .

In sum, even if the Sixth Amendment is not solely concerned with testimonial hearsay, that is its primary object, and interrogations by law enforcement officers fall squarely within that class.[1a]

[1a.] We use the term "interrogation" in its colloquial, rather than any technical legal, sense. . . .

B

The historical record also supports a second proposition: that *the Framers would not have allowed admission of testimonial statements of a witness who did not appear at trial unless he was unavailable to testify, and the defendant had had a prior opportunity for cross-examination.* [Emphasis added] The text of the Sixth Amendment does not suggest any open-ended exceptions from the confrontation requirement to be developed by the courts. Rather, the "right . . . to be confronted with the witnesses against him," is most naturally read as a reference to the right of confrontation at common law, admitting only those exceptions established at the time of the founding. As the English authorities above reveal, the common law in 1791 conditioned admissibility of an absent witness's examination on unavailability and a prior opportunity to cross-examine. The Sixth Amendment therefore incorporates those limitations. The numerous early state decisions applying the same test confirm that these principles were received as part of the common law in this country.

. . . This is not to deny . . . that "[t]here were always exceptions to the general rule of exclusion" of hearsay evidence. Several had become well established by 1791. But there is scant evidence that exceptions were invoked to admit *testimonial* statements against the accused in a *criminal* case.[2a] Most of the hearsay exceptions covered statements that by their nature were not testimonial—for example, business records or statements in furtherance of a conspiracy. We do not infer from these that the Framers thought exceptions would apply even to prior testimony.[3a]

IV

Our case law has been largely consistent with these two principles. Our leading early decision, for example, involved a deceased witness's prior trial testimony. *Mattox v. United States*, (1895). In allowing the statement to be admitted, we relied on the

---

[2a.] The one deviation we have found involves dying declarations. The existence of that exception as a general rule of criminal hearsay law cannot be disputed. Although many dying declarations may not be testimonial, there is authority for admitting even those that clearly are. We need not decide in this case whether the Sixth Amendment incorporates an exception for testimonial dying declarations. If this exception must be accepted on historical grounds, it is sui generis.

[3a.] We cannot agree with THE CHIEF JUSTICE that the fact "[t]hat a statement might be testimonial does nothing to undermine the wisdom of one of these [hearsay] exceptions." Involvement of government officers in the production of testimony with an eye toward trial presents unique potential for prosecutorial abuse—a fact borne out time and again throughout a history with which the Framers were keenly familiar. This consideration does not evaporate when testimony happens to fall within some broad, modern hearsay exception, even if that exception might be justifiable in other circumstances. [Chief Justice Rehnquist concurred in *Crawford in* an opinion joined by Justice O'Connor. Justice Scalia responds at several places in the text and in a number of footnotes to arguments the Chief Justice made. We have however excised references to the Rehnquist concurrence in the text, and most footnotes responding to aspects of the Chief Justice's opinion as well as the opinion itself have been eliminated.]

fact that the defendant had had, at the first trial, an adequate opportunity to confront the witness. . . .

Our later cases conform to *Mattox*'s holding that prior trial or preliminary hearing testimony is admissible only if the defendant had an adequate opportunity to cross-examine. See *Mancusi v. Stubbs* (1972); *California v. Green* (1970); *Pointer v. Texas* (1965). Even where the defendant had such an opportunity, we excluded the testimony where the government had not established unavailability of the witness. See *Barber v. Page* (1968). We similarly excluded accomplice confessions where the defendant had no opportunity to cross-examine. See *Roberts v. Russell* (1968); *Bruton v. United States* (1968); *Douglas v. Alabama* (1965). In contrast, we considered reliability factors beyond prior opportunity for cross-examination when the hearsay statement at issue was not testimonial. See *Dutton v. Evans* (1970—plurality opinion).

* * *

Our cases have thus remained faithful to the Framers' understanding: Testimonial statements of witnesses absent from trial have been admitted only where the declarant is unavailable, and only where the defendant has had a prior opportunity to cross-examine.[4a]

V

Although the results of our decisions have generally been faithful to the original meaning of the Confrontation Clause, the same cannot be said of our rationales. *Roberts* conditions the admissibility of all hearsay evidence on whether it falls under a "firmly rooted hearsay exception" or bears "particularized guarantees of trustworthiness." This test departs from the historical principles identified above in two respects. First, it is too broad: It applies the same mode of analysis whether or not the hearsay consists of *ex parte* testimony. This often results in close constitutional scrutiny in cases that are far removed from the core concerns of the Clause. At the same time, however, the test is too narrow: It admits statements that *do* consist of *ex parte* testimony upon a mere finding of reliability. This malleable standard often fails to protect against paradigmatic confrontation violations. . . .

[4a] . . . [W]e reiterate that, when the declarant appears for cross-examination at trial, the Confrontation Clause places no constraints at all on the use of his prior testimonial statements. It is therefore irrelevant that the reliability of some out-of-court statements " 'cannot be replicated, even if the declarant testifies to the same matters in court.' " The Clause does not bar admission of a statement so long as the declarant is present at trial to defend or explain it. (The Clause also does not bar the use of testimonial statements for purposes other than establishing the truth of the matter asserted. See *Tennessee v. Street*, 471 U.S. 409 (1985).)

A

Where testimonial statements are involved, we do not think the Framers meant to leave the Sixth Amendment's protection to the vagaries of the rules of evidence, much less to amorphous notions of "reliability." . . . *Admitting statements deemed reliable by a judge is fundamentally at odds with the right of confrontation. To be sure, the Clause's ultimate goal is to ensure reliability of evidence, but it is a procedural rather than a substantive guarantee. It commands, not that evidence be reliable, but that reliability be assessed in a particular manner: by testing in the crucible of cross-examination.* [Emphasis added] The Clause thus reflects a judgment, not only about the desirability of reliable evidence . . . , but about how reliability can best be determined.

The *Roberts* test allows a jury to hear evidence, untested by the adversary process, based on a mere judicial determination of reliability. It thus replaces the constitutionally prescribed method of assessing reliability with a wholly foreign one. In this respect, it is very different from exceptions to the Confrontation Clause that make no claim to be a surrogate means of assessing reliability. For example, *the rule of forfeiture by wrongdoing (which we accept) extinguishes confrontation claims on essentially equitable grounds; it does not purport to be an alternative means of determining reliability.* [Emphasis added] . . . Dispensing with confrontation because testimony is obviously reliable is akin to dispensing with jury trial because a defendant is obviously guilty. This is not what the Sixth Amendment prescribes.

B

The legacy of *Roberts* in other courts vindicates the Framers' wisdom in rejecting a general reliability exception. . . . Reliability is an amorphous, if not entirely subjective, concept. . . . For example . . . [t]he Virginia Court of Appeals found a statement more reliable because the witness was in custody and charged with a crime (thus making the statement more obviously against her penal interest), while the Wisconsin Court of Appeals found a statement more reliable because the witness was not in custody and not a suspect. The unpardonable vice of the *Roberts* test, however, is not its unpredictability, but its demonstrated capacity to admit core testimonial statements that the Confrontation Clause plainly meant to exclude. Despite the plurality's speculation in *Lilly* that it was "highly unlikely" that accomplice confessions implicating the accused could survive *Roberts*, courts continue routinely to admit them . . . [as well as] other sorts of plainly testimonial statements despite the absence of any opportunity to cross-examine. [Cites to cases involving plea allocutions, grand jury testimony and prior trial testimony.]

To add insult to injury, some of the courts that admit untested testimonial statements find reliability in the very factors that *make* the statements testimonial. . . . It is not enough to point out that most of the usual safeguards of the adversary process attend the statement, when the single safeguard missing is the one the Confrontation Clause demands.

C

Roberts' failings were on full display in the proceedings below. Sylvia Crawford made her statement while in police custody, herself a potential suspect in the case. Indeed, she had been told that whether she would be released "depend[ed] on how the investigation continues." In response to often leading questions from police detectives, she implicated her husband in Lee's stabbing and at least arguably undermined his self-defense claim. Despite all this, the trial court admitted her statement, listing several reasons why it was reliable. In its opinion reversing, the Court of Appeals listed several *other* reasons why the statement was *not* reliable. Finally, the State Supreme Court relied exclusively on the interlocking character of the statement and disregarded every other factor the lower courts had considered. The case is thus a self-contained demonstration of *Roberts'* unpredictable and inconsistent application.

Each of the courts also made assumptions that cross-examination might well have undermined. The trial court, for example, stated that Sylvia Crawford's statement was reliable because she was an eyewitness with direct knowledge of the events. But Sylvia at one point told the police that she had "shut [her] eyes and . . . didn't really watch" part of the fight, and that she was "in shock." The trial court also buttressed its reliability finding by claiming that Sylvia was "being questioned by law enforcement, and, thus, the [questioner] is . . . neutral to her and not someone who would be inclined to advance her interests and shade her version of the truth unfavorably toward the defendant." The Framers would be astounded to learn that *ex parte* testimony could be admitted against a criminal defendant because it was elicited by "neutral" government officers. But even if the court's assessment of the officer's motives was accurate, it says nothing about Sylvia's perception of her situation. Only cross-examination could reveal that.

* * *

We have no doubt that the courts below were acting in utmost good faith when they found reliability. The Framers, however, would not have been content to indulge this assumption. They knew that judges, like other government officers, could not always be trusted to safeguard the rights of the people. . . . They were loath to leave too much discretion in judicial hands. By replacing categorical constitutional guarantees with open-ended balancing tests, we do violence to their design. Vague standards are manipulable, and, while that might be a small concern in run-of-the-mill assault prosecutions like this one, the Framers had an eye toward politically charged cases like Raleigh's—great state trials where the impartiality of even those at the highest levels of the judiciary might not be so clear. It is difficult to imagine *Roberts* providing any meaningful protection in those circumstances.

* * *

Where nontestimonial hearsay is at issue, it is wholly consistent with the Framers' design to afford the States flexibility in their development of hearsay law—as does *Roberts*, and as would an approach that exempted such statements from Confrontation Clause scrutiny altogether. Where testimonial evidence is at issue, however, the Sixth Amendment demands what the common law required: unavailability and a prior opportunity for cross-examination. *We leave for another day any effort to spell out a comprehensive definition of "testimonial."* [Emphasis added] Whatever else the term covers, it applies at a minimum to prior testimony at a preliminary hearing, before a grand jury, or at a former trial; and to police interrogations. These are the modern practices with closest kinship to the abuses at which the Confrontation Clause was directed. . . .

The judgment of the Washington Supreme Court is reversed, and the case is remanded for further proceedings not inconsistent with this opinion.

———————

Crawford is a powerful statement of one view of the Confrontation Clause, and it has been generally well-received by the professorate, but Scalia's opinion is not without its weaknesses. Chief among these, though it may turn out to be of little consequence, is that its historical foundations appear shaky, at least if one can trust the devastating critique of Professor Davies.[45] Professor Davies musters evidence suggesting that Justice Scalia misinterpreted *King v. Paine,* the precedent on which he relies most heavily for his claim that common law courts would not receive uncross-examined deposition testimony and for the implication that when a deponent has been cross-examined his

---

[45] Thomas Y. Davies, What did the Framers Know and When Did They Know It? Fictional Originalism in Crawford v. Washington, 71 Brooklyn L. Rev. 105 (2005).

testimony is admissible if he is later unavailable to testify.[46] Davies argues that although the framers may well have erected the Confrontation Clause to bar certain statutory or continental procedures, this does not support the romantic notion, implicit in Scalia's argument, that the drafters treasured a return to classic common law procedures for their own sake. Professor Davies also makes a larger and a more important point. It is that the search for an originalist understanding of the Confrontation Clause is a futile quest. Unless one can channel the framers, something even Justice Scalia cannot do, there is no way of knowing precisely what the framers intended. Moreover, even knowing this would be of limited use because the criminal justice system in 1791 was very different from what it is now. For one thing police forces as we know them had yet to be invented. Thus the framers could not have intended to bar statements like those in *Crawford* simply because they were made during a police interrogation. The framers knew about official investigations but did not have the concept of police interrogation. Also, consider hearsay. Eighteenth Century juries heard considerable hearsay because testimony was not presented in a tightly controlled direct examination that facilitated objections to questions. Juries instead heard narratives in which witnesses told their stories of what had happened, and people narrating events often mix what they have heard with their first hand impressions. With a few rare exceptions, including, perhaps, some business records and dying declarations, juries were given a blanket instruction that any hearsay a witness might have recounted *was not evidence.* What does this imply for an originalist interpretation of the Confrontation Clause? Does it mean the clause was only intended to bar deposition hearsay because the framing generation did not consider other hearsay to be "evidence" and so had no cause to bar it? Or should we instead say the Clause bars most hearsay because the framers sought to preserve a common law aversion to almost all uncross-examined statements? *Roberts,* which looks to the purpose that even Scalia sees as underlying the Confrontation Clause—promoting the reliability of evidence—at least presents a coherent theory for dealing with issues and situations the framers would not have contemplated.

Despite the cogent critiques of Professor Davies and others, *Crawford* has its virtues, and the historical and jurisprudential failings of its originalist perspective are unlikely to undermine its core holding. The *Crawford* core, however, takes us only so far. It left many issues for

---

[46] Professor Davies disputes Justice Scalia's interpretation of the jurisprudence of the Marian Statutes in a portion of the *Crawford* decision that we have excluded from our text and points out that decisions in three of the cases that Justice Scalia relies on would not have reached U.S. shores in time to affect thinking about the need for or contours of The Confrontation Clause. Professor Jonakait in his own analysis of Scalia's historical arguments adds that it is dangerous to assume that the framers meant to enshrine English procedure at the time of ratification. He notes that certain portions of the Bill of Rights were designed specifically to reject the English way of doing things. Randolf N. Jonakait, The Too-Easy Historical Assumptions of Crawford v. Washington, 71 Brooklyn L. Rev 219 (2005).

another day.[47] Perhaps none is more fundamental than what statements qualify as testimonial, for *Crawford's* bar applies only to uncross-examined *testimonial* evidence offered in hearsay form. Rather than answer this question, Justice Scalia provided three suggested answers that we italicized in the text above. They range from a definition that only includes formalized testimonial material (for example, grand jury testimony, affidavits and recorded confessions) to any statement that a reasonable person might expect to be used to support an arrest or prosecution. Further specification, Scalia told us, would have to wait for another day.

That day has been arriving at the rate of a case or two each year, beginning on June 19, 2006 when the Court handed down a single opinion deciding two cases: *Davis v. Washington* and *Hammon v. Indiana*.[48] Both were domestic violence cases in which the victim, in one case a former girlfriend and in the other a spouse, refused to testify. In each the state had been allowed to admit statements the victim made in response to police questioning which identified the accused as the assailant and described his violent actions. In *Davis* the statements had been made in the course of a 911 call begun while the assailant was a present menace. In *Hammon* the statements were made to police officers called to the scene of ongoing domestic violence, apparently by someone other than the wife. By the time the police arrived or due to their arrival, the violence in *Hammon* had ceased, and the woman at first told the officers that nothing had happened. Not satisfied the police separated Ms. Hammon from her husband, and under questioning she described the assault that had occurred and signed a sworn affidavit containing the description.

The Court found the statements in *Davis* admissible but held that the Confrontation Clause barred the statements in *Hammon*. The salient difference for the Court was that in *Davis* even though the caller was responding to police (or, more precisely, a 911 operator's) questions, her purpose was not to describe what was going on or to implicate anyone in the assault but rather to get help when faced with immediate danger. Hence, although her statements were responses to official interrogation,

---

[47] There is already a large literature identifying and discussing issues that *Crawford* left open. One thoughtful treatment is, Robert Mosteller, *Crawford v. Washington*: Encouraging and Ensuring the Confrontation of Witnesses, 39 U. Rich. L. Rev. 511 (2004–2005). Also, for both general discussions and articles focusing on specific issues, see the Summer 2005 issue of Criminal Justice and the Fall 2005 issue of the Brooklyn Law Review. Articles discussing the implications of Michigan v. Bryant, 131S. Ct. 1143 (2011) the most recent case as we write, include Bellin, Jeffrey The Incredible Shrinking Confrontation Clause, 92 B.U.L. Rev. 1865 (2012) and Moreno, Joelle Anne, Finding Nino: Justice Scalia's Confrontation Clause Legacy From Its (Glorious) Beginning To (Bitter) End, 44 Akron L. Rev. 1211 (2011). See also a set of articles on Confrontation in the Fall 2012 (Vol. 45) issue of the Texas Tech Law Review with articles from a symposium on the Sixth Amendment.

[48] 547 U.S. 813 (2006). The next appearing case, *Whorton v. Bockting*, 549 U.S. 406 (2007), which we do not discuss, held that *Crawford* did not apply retroactively.

they were not, the Court concluded, testimonial in nature.[49] The woman in *Hammon*, on the other hand, was in no danger, and her statements to the officer that were memorialized in the affidavit were simply to tell the police what had happened in the same way she might later tell a court.[50] *Davis* no doubt means that statements in 911 calls and other cries for assistance will not be objectionable on Confrontation Clause grounds, at least while the assailant is present or the danger otherwise continues.[51] *Hammon* indicates that so long as police questioning is aimed at establishing the circumstances of a past crime, it doesn't have to be in a formal setting like the station house interrogation in *Crawford* for the protections of the Confrontation Clause to attach.

While not pretending to resolve all issues that can arise in deciding whether statements are testimonial, Scalia usefully summarized the principles that distinguished *Hammon* from *Davis*:

> Statements are nontestimonial when made in the course of police interrogation under circumstances objectively indicating that the primary purpose of the interrogation is to enable police assistance to meet an ongoing emergency. They are testimonial when the circumstances objectively indicate that there is no such ongoing emergency, and that the primary purpose of the interrogation is to establish or prove past events relevant to later criminal prosecution.[52]

Suppose, however, the police shout out to a man on the sidewalk "What's up" and the man replies, "Jones tried to break into my car." Will the police be barred by the Confrontation Clause from testifying to the man's statement? Does it make sense to consider the exchange an interrogation? And what is one to make of a situation in which the police

---

[49] The Court mentioned four features of the conversation in *Davis* that rendered the victim's statements non-testimonial: (1) the declarant was speaking about events "*as they were actually happening*, rather than 'describ[ing] past events.'" (2) the declarant's call was "plainly a call for help against a bona fide physical threat." (3) Viewed objectively, the questions and answers in *Davis* "were necessary to be able to *resolve* the present emergency, rather than to simply learn . . . what had happened in the past." (4) The declarant's statements were informal and made "in an environment that was not tranquil, or even (as far as any reasonable 911 operator could make out) safe." *Id.* at 827 (emphasis in original). Some courts following *Davis* required that all four factors be present before holding that statements are not testimonial for Confrontation Clause purposes, while other courts used a "totality of the circumstances" test. *Michigan v. Bryant*, 131S. Ct. 1143 (2011) discussed at note 58 *infra* suggests that even when the first two points and perhaps the third do not exist, there are circumstances where a court may find that a statement was not testimonial.

[50] The trial court had admitted the affidavit as Ms. Hammon's present sense impressions and her statements to the officer as excited utterances. These decisions are hard to reconcile with a fair reading of those hearsay exceptions, but they are the kinds of decisions that judges often make.

[51] The call in *Davis* continued after the alleged assailant departed, and the Court indicated that the Confrontation Clause protection might reassert itself after the danger had passed. The issue didn't arise in the case, however, because the later statements had not been admitted into evidence.

[52] 547 U.S. 813, 822.

seem to be neither concerned with dealing with an ongoing emergency nor seeking to prove past events relevant to a later criminal prosecution, but are making a general inquiry that might, as in the example, yield news of a crime? Davis does not resolve all issues and others sure to arise, even on the narrow question of what constitutes a police interrogation sufficient to make responses "testimonial."

Also open, despite Justice Scalia's use of the word *objectively*, is the relevance of the speaker's intent. If a person tells a friend that if anything happens to him he should "Tell the jury that Joe is responsible," is the statement nontestimonial because it was made to a friend or testimonial because the speaker intended his statement to be conveyed to the police and/or used in court should anything happen to him? Or suppose the speaker is a young child whom the police question in order to gather evidence to use in court, but the child is too young to know how her statements will be used. Is what she says admissible? Similarly unclear is how statements elicited by surrogates for the police will be treated. Pediatricians or child psychologists might seek to learn from a child patient or a parent who is responsible for an injury, knowing they are obligated by statute to inform the police if they learn of abuse, or an ER doctor may ask a rape victim if she knows her assailant. Will the admissibility of identifications in these circumstances turn on whether the declarant knew of the questioner's reporting obligation, and will it be affected by the treatment relevance of the questions posed or by whether the surrogate had a law enforcement intent in asking the question? If the police have already been involved will different lines be drawn?

Davis's importance extends beyond its specific holding, for it apparently resolves another question left open by *Crawford. Crawford* did not hold that the Confrontation Clause was never implicated when a witness's statements were not testimonial, nor did it explicitly overrule *Roberts.* So commentators had speculated that the *Roberts* test might be maintained to prevent the admission under novel exceptions of hearsay lacking indicia of reliability. In *Davis,* Scalia tells us that the Confrontation Clause applies only to testimonial hearsay, and later, in an almost offhand remark, he indicates that *Crawford* did overrule *Roberts.*[53] What in *Crawford* was a right that *focused* on testimonial evidence, in *Davis* becomes a right that offers no protection unless hearsay *is* testimonial. For Scalia and the Court, aided by an 1828 dictionary, the phrase "witnesses against" does not just encompass those who give testimony; *that is all it can mean,* albeit with "testimony" defined more

---

[53] This is made clear in *Bockting, supra* note 48, where Justice Alito writes for a unanimous Court: "the Confrontation Clause has no application to [nontestimonial hearsay statements] and therefore permits their admission even if they lack indicia of reliability." *Id.* at 420.

broadly than "statements in depositions or from the witness stand" and including at the least some statements made to the police.[54]

Davis was followed in the Supreme Court by *Giles v. California*,[55] another domestic violence case, but this one had ended in homicide when Dwayne Giles shot and killed his ex-girlfriend Brenda Avie. There was no dispute that Giles had shot and killed Avie. Even if Giles had not admitted the shooting, there were witnesses who had heard the shots and had seen Giles standing near the victim with his gun in his hand. Giles claimed he had shot Avie in self-defense. To refute this claim the prosecution sought to admit statements Avie had made three weeks before she was shot to a police officer responding to a domestic violence report. These statements described both threats Giles had made and violence he had done to her. To overcome Gile's Confrontation Clause claim the state accepted an invitation extended in *Crawford* and found that Giles had forfeited his Confrontation Clause rights because he had

---

[54] Scalia claimed that *Davis* forced the Court to decide whether the Confrontation Clause was limited to testimonial evidence because even though the statements at issue were not testimonial they were in response to a 911 operator's (hence police) interrogation. The argument is unconvincing. The Court could have reached the result it did without overturning *Roberts* since the Davis caller's statements easily qualify as excited utterances and so require no further guarantee of reliability. Scalia bases the Court's limitation of the Confrontation Clause's protection to testimonial evidence not just on the Clause's "witnesses against" language, but also on his analysis of precedent. He points out that in most if not all of the prior Supreme Court cases excluding evidence under the Confrontation Clause, the evidence was testimonial in nature, while in cases that allowed the admission of unconfronted hearsay, the statements were usually nontestimonial. But had the Court previously believed that only testimonial hearsay was protected by the Confrontation Clause, it would have disposed of the nontestimonial cases Scalia cites more simply and quite differently. Thus, while asserting continuity with precedent, the *Davis* opinion changes the prior Supreme Court understanding, which read the phrase "witnesses against" as potentially encompassing any hearsay declarant.

Justice Scalia's repeated references in *Crawford* to the influence of Sir Walter Raleigh's trial in establishing a right to confrontation also suggests that his was an outcome oriented historiography, for nowhere in *Crawford* does Scalia acknowledge that Raleigh protested against two kinds of hearsay evidence. One was the use of Cobham's letters and deposition that Scalia mentions, but the other was the ordinary non-testimonial hearsay of the Spanish merchant, as reported by Dyer the pilot, accusing Raleigh and Cobham of plotting to kill the king. Raleigh did not demand to confront the merchant, for unlike Cobham the merchant was not close at hand, but Raleigh was as dismissive of his reported testimony as he was of Cobham's accusation: "This is the saying of some wild Jesuit or beggarly priest; but what proof is it against me?" If the drafters of the Confrontation Clause had Raleigh's trial in mind, then shouldn't we assume that they intended to interpose the clause against both kinds of hearsay, testimonial and non-testimonial, that Raleigh so eloquently opposed? Justice Scalia is also selective in his reliance on the 1828 edition of Webster's Dictionary, for he mentions only the fifth of five meanings one finds in that edition. The first meaning is "Testimony; attestation of a fact or event," and the third is "A person who knows or sees anything; one personally present; as, he was witness; he was an eye-witness."

One can also ask whether what the drafters had specifically in mind, even if knowable, should matter. A different perspective on the Confrontation Clause is that it was designed to constitutionalize certain requisites of a fair trial. If so, *Roberts* may be closer to the mark than *Crawford* in holding that regardless of whether hearsay is testimonial, if the declarant is absent the Constitution demands at minimum reasons to believe the hearsay is reliable. It is possible that in some circumstances the Constitution will be read so as to demand this, but if the *Crawford* jurisprudence remains unaltered, the Due Process Clause will have to be the source of this right.

[55] 554 U.S. 353.

procured the declarant's absence through his own murderous wrongdoing. The majority in *Giles* told California it had misinterpreted the invitation.

The Court held that forfeiture was not an automatic consequence of a defendant's wrongful responsibility for a witness's absence. Rather it depended on the nature of that responsibility. If the defendant had acted with the *purpose* of preventing the witness from testifying then the right was forfeited. But if the defendant's action had another purpose, in *Giles* self-defense if one believes the defendant's story or a rage-driven desire to kill, if the state's version of what happened is accepted, the Confrontation Clause right is not forfeited even though the defendant might benefit from his crime by having closed the mouth of his victim. Justice Scalia, who wrote the majority opinion, was troubled by the fact that to decide otherwise would require the judge to determine that the accused was guilty of the charged crime as a prerequisite to admitting the testimony bearing on his guilt,[56] but this wasn't his primary motivation. Rather the decision was rooted in his understanding of how seventeenth and eighteenth century British courts interpreted the forfeiture doctrine and the way in which it had been applied in American courts since that time. In particular, Scalia pointed out, American courts had never routinely admitted the hearsay of murder victims on the theory that the alleged killer had forfeited a right to object. Justice Breyer, writing for himself and two other dissenters, took issue with Justice Scalia's analysis of the early case law. The academic nature of their dispute reminds one that these Justices are both former law professors, disposed sometimes to take interesting but speculative positions about what cases stand for and history teaches. It is also further testimony to the fact that when it comes to constitutional interpretation, history can seldom provide unequivocal answers.

Although Giles prevailed in the Supreme Court, the protection the case will ultimately provide him and other alleged killers of spouses or girlfriends is uncertain. In concluding his opinion, Scalia carves out a potential exception for domestic violence cases. He suggests that a purpose of domestic violence, discernible from a past history, may be to prevent, through intimidation, the report of further domestic violence. He writes, "Where such an abusive relationship culminates in murder, the evidence may support a finding that the crime expressed the intent to isolate the victim and to stop her from reporting abuse to the authorities or cooperating with a criminal prosecution—rendering her prior

---

[56] The differences between the judge's decision and the jury's are that the judge would have to make this determination by a preponderance of the evidence while a jury would have to find guilt beyond a reasonable doubt, and the judge may be able to hear evidence that would be kept from the jury. An analogous situation frequently arises in conspiracy trials when the judge must determine by a preponderance of the evidence whether there is enough evidence of conspiracy to admit the statement of one conspirator against another. The idea of trial by jury makes this situation an uneasy one, and the majority did not want to extend it beyond the one circumstance in which it is well rooted.

statements admissible under the forfeiture doctrine."[57] Perhaps in some cases the intent Justice Scalia hypothesizes will exist, but the motivations for domestic violence and murder are varied and the silencing of the victim would not seem to be among the most prominent. Nevertheless, it would not be surprising to see the jurisprudence of domestic homicide cases develop so that courts routinely, if fictively, hold that one of the killer's motivations was to prevent the reporting of violence to the police.

Giles dealt with a side issue in Confrontation Clause jurisprudence. Apart from seeming to resolve the question of when actions forfeit the right to confrontation, its primary significance seemed to be as a signal of the seriousness with which the Court's majority took the right to confrontation as enunciated in *Crawford*. *Hammon* and *Davis* were the more important cases, clarifying the difficult question of when statements were testimonial. Although these paired cases left open many questions regarding when statements to the police are testimonial, they seemed to establish a principle that would be easy to apply to common situations. If the primary purpose of a statement was to secure assistance in the face of an ongoing threat or to otherwise aid the police in their effort to eliminate such a threat, the statement was not testimonial. This was true even when what was said was not spontaneous but a response to police questions. If, however, a threat was no longer ongoing, statements describing what happened or who was involved were testimonial and would be barred by the Confrontation Clause unless the speaker was produced at the trial. Moreover, these cases confirmed that *Roberts* was a dead letter and reliability had nothing to do with Confrontation Clause analysis.

But certainty on these issues, or at least the certainty that Confrontation Clause protections are substantial when the police are questioning someone who is no longer threatened, was shattered by *Michigan v. Bryant*,[58] which, as we write, is the last of the line of cases seeking to flesh out what *Crawford* means by testimonial.[59] *Bryant* arose out of what appears to have been an aborted drug deal in which the victim Anthony Covington was fatally wounded by a shot fired through a closed door. After being shot he managed to drive to a gas station where he talked to the police who had been called to the scene. In the brief time between the arrival of the police and the EMTs he was questioned individually by five different officers. He told each of them that he had been shot by Rick Bryant, whom he recognized by his voice. The police went to Bryant's house, found a bullet hole in the back door and other evidence consistent with Covington's story and left after determining that

---

[57] *Id.* at 2693.

[58] 131 S. Ct. 1143 (2011).

[59] Justice Scalia, who wrote *Crawford*, vigorously dissented from the *Bryant* majority's view of when statements to the police are testimonial, which suggests that *Bryant* changes rather than merely fleshes out the *Crawford* conception.

Bryant was no longer there. It appears that no special effort was made to search for Bryant, and he was not arrested until a year later in California. The Michigan Supreme Court reversed Bryant's conviction at trial, likening Covington's statements to those given by the spouse in *Hammon* after the danger to her had passed. Two dissenters on that court saw the case as more like *Davis,* arguing that the primary purpose of the statements was to assist the police in addressing an ongoing emergency.

Justice Sonya Sotomayor, writing for herself and four other Justices,[60] sided with the Michigan dissenters. In doing so she struck so many different notes that it is difficult to identify a "test" emerging from *Bryant*. But the number of considerations mentioned and the way Sotomayor applied them make it easy to imagine that a court could find that except for station house interrogations most accusatory statements made to the police raise no Confrontation Clause problems. The Court first holds that an inquiry to determine whether a statement is primarily testimonial rather than an effort to deal with an ongoing emergency, requires an *objective* evaluation of "the circumstances in which the encounter occurs and the statements of the parties"[61] This means, "The relevant inquiry is not the subjective or actual purpose of the individuals involved in a particular encounter, but rather the purpose that reasonable participants would have had, as ascertained from the individuals' statements and actions and the circumstances in which the encounter occurred."[62] Thus the speaker's actual state of mind does not matter unless, perhaps, it is clear from what the speaker says.[63] Also the interrogator's purpose appears to figure into the Court's analysis for more than just the light it sheds on the speaker's intent.[64]

---

[60] The Justices who joined in the opinion, Roberts, Altio, Kennedy and Breyer have continually differed with Justice Scalia on the reaches of the Confrontation Clause. Justice Thomas also voted to overturn the decision below but he did so because he believed the statement was made in circumstances that lack the formality sufficient to trigger Confrontation Clause protections.

[61] *Bryant, supra* note 58 at 1156.

[62] *Id* at 1156.

[63] Presumably if the speaker said, "In case I can't make it to court I want the jury to know that Joe and Sally did it" that would be testimonial no matter what the other "objective" circumstances.

[64] Justice Sotomayor writes: "The existence of an ongoing emergency is relevant to determining the primary purpose of the interrogation because an emergency focuses the participants on something other than "prov[ing] past events potentially relevant to later criminal prosecution." *Bryant, supra* note 58 at 1157. The reason the police have for interrogating a person may, however, differ substantially from the reasons a person has for saying what he does. Indeed, the person questioned will often not be told and may not know the reason why police are asking questions, and when the police ask, "Who did it?" a person is likely to think that the purpose behind the question is to arrest the person and begin the legal process regardless of whether an emergency is ongoing. Still it would not be surprising if the police soon learn to begin questioning crime victims and other witnesses by telling them that they want to know who did it in order to stop the person from endangering others.

A judge's view about what objective circumstances indicate is a subjective judgment. Hence the *Bryant* analysis elevates the judge's subjectivity above that of the speaker's in determining the speaker's intent. To guide the judge's exercise of subjectivity the Court mentions a number of factors that it sees as potentially bearing on the issue of whether a statement was made with testimonial intent. Particularly important is the presence of an ongoing emergency. But whether an emergency is ongoing depends, the Court tells us, not just on whether the speaker is still threatened but also on whether the public is in danger. If a gun has been used and the gunman is on the loose, the Court's language invites trial judges to find that statements identifying an assailant are made primarily to assist the police in dealing with an emergency situation. This is particularly true if the speaker has been injured by an assailant. The reasonable victim in the majority's view is one who thinks as much about the public's welfare as her own or who is literally so traumatized that she cannot form an intention at all. Justice Sotomayor writes:

> During an ongoing emergency, a victim is most likely to want the threat to her and to other potential victims to end, but that does not necessarily mean that the victim wants or envisions prosecution of the assailant. . . . Alternatively, a severely injured victim may have no purpose at all in answering questions posed; the answers may be simply reflexive. The victim's injuries could be so debilitating as to prevent her from thinking sufficiently clearly to understand whether her statements are for the purpose of addressing an ongoing emergency or for the purpose of future prosecution.[65]

The existence of an ongoing emergency, the victim's condition and the apparent aim of the interrogation as evidenced by questions asked and answered are not the only factors that Justice Sotomayor thinks relevant to deciding whether the protections of the Confrontation Clause apply. Other factors are the location of the interrogation (near the crime scene or in the station house), the formality or informality of the statement taking and whether the speaker is likely to have had mixed motives. Perhaps most surprising is a statement that does not otherwise figure in the Court's analysis: "Implicit in *Davis* is the idea that because the prospect of fabrication in statements given for the primary purpose of resolving that emergency is presumably significantly diminished, the Confrontation Clause does not require such statements to be subject to the crucible of cross-examination."[66] *Davis* simply purported to follow *Crawford,* and the majority in both cases seemed to agree that the reliability concerns of *Roberts* had no role to play in Confrontation Clause analysis. Yet here we

---

[65] *Bryant supra* note 58 at 1161.

[66] *Id* at 1157

have reliability invoked as a justification. Perhaps as membership on the Court changes aspects of *Roberts* will enjoy a rebirth.

The Court's willingness to accept the state's claim that Covington's statements were not testimonial because they were made to deal with an ongoing emergency indicate how weak the *Bryant* standard can be. There was objectively no ongoing emergency. Covington had been shot not by a roving gunman but through a door, and there was no reason to believe that others would be targeted. The Court emphasized that when the police arrived on the scene they did not know whether the public was in any danger, but Covington whose intent is at issue certainly knew. Moreover, the police never acted as if there was an ongoing emergency. There is no mention of alerts being sent out for more officers or of the initiation of a search, and the police took their time before going to Bryant's home. Instead, five officers, at different times, asked what happened and who did it. Moreover, if the officers original lack of knowledge about the possibility of ongoing danger counts toward interpreting Covington's statements as nontestimonial, shouldn't their almost certain knowledge that what Covington said would, if he died, be admissible in court[67] count in favor of seeing his remarks as testimonial? It is true that Covington most likely had mixed motives when he spoke, for he repeatedly asked when medical help would arrive, but it is hard to see mixed motives when he identified Bryant as the shooter. Covington knew what he was doing, and he intended to tell officers of the law that Bryant had shot him.

Justice Scalia's strong dissent suggests that the meaning of "testimonial" in *Bryant* differs significantly from what it was thought to mean in *Crawford, Davis and Hammon*. In the latter two cases testimonial was not confined to statements that the speaker intended to be used in court but also had roots in the broader sense of testimony as a description of an event. If a statement was either made with the knowledge that it might be used in court or was offered to or elicited by law enforcement personnel primarily to inform them of some matter that might be at issue in a trial, the statement was testimonial for Confrontation Clause purposes. Although the *Bryant* opinion does not go so far as to remove all descriptive statements from the Clause's protection, it appears that when statements are made by crime victims in close proximity to the crime, the majority's vision of "testimonial" comes close to requiring an intent to make a statement that could substitute for court testimony.[68]

---

[67] The shooting in this case occurred before Crawford was decided, so it appears there would have been no problem in admitting Covington's statements as excited utterances under the then existing constitutional principles.

[68] Justice Alito, one of the *Bryant* majority said as much in *Giles v. California,* "The Confrontation Clause does not apply to out-of-court statements unless it can be said that they

No doubt this thread of Confrontation Clause jurisprudence will continue to develop, and it is impossible to say where it is headed. The swing voters on these issues may be heavily influenced by case facts. Conceivably in the next case the Court could retreat from *Bryant* and more broadly interpret Confrontation Clause rights. It is, however, interesting to note that although all the Justices seem to agree that the Confrontation Clause was created to prevent injustices like that which occurred in the trial of Sir Walter Raleigh, both of the out-of-court accusations introduced against Raleigh appear allowable under *Bryant*. The accusation relayed by Dyer, the pilot returned from Portugal, was gossip repeated without testimonial intent and could even be interpreted as an effort to warn of likely treachery. Lord Cobham's confession was probably written to avoid torture rather than to accuse Raleigh or it could be seen as a statement made to protect the king from the danger of releasing Raleigh. These were nontestimonial purposes even if the equivalent of testimony emerged.

A second line of cases beginning with *Melendez-Diaz v. Massachusetts*[69] raises the issue of what is testimonial and how much this should matter in a different context. In this case sworn laboratory certificates had been offered to prove that a substance the defendant possessed was cocaine. The certificates were entered into evidence without calling their maker under a Massachusetts evidence rule which provided that such certificates were "prima facie evidence of the composition, quality, and the net weight" of the analyzed substance. The defendant could have exercised his right under Massachusetts law or the Sixth Amendment's Compulsory Process Clause to call the scientist who prepared the report, but chose to rest instead on the claim that his Confrontation Clause rights had been violated. It is, on the one hand, hard to see the certificate's assertions as anything other than testimonial, and on the other hand it is difficult to imagine any hearsay evidence likely to be more reliable or less likely to be challenged effectively by cross examination.[70] Thus the case was a test of how seriously one should take the Court's assertion that reliability had no role to play in Confrontation Clause analysis.

A majority of the Court was willing to take it quite seriously. The Court held by a 5–4 vote that the prosecutor's introduction of the

---

are the equivalent of statements made at trial by "witnesses." *Giles supra* note 55 at 379. Justice Thomas appears to share this view.

[69] 557 U.S. 305 (2009).

[70] This is not to say that forensic evidence of this sort is necessarily reliable, but it is very hard to shake on cross-examination the testimony of an expert testifying to the result of an automated analytic process. Moreover, if the defendant had a specific reason to believe test results are unreliable, the Massachusetts procedure allowed the defendant to call the expert. Laboratory reports have, however, been used in some states to admit the results of forensic tests like ballistic examinations that involve more subjectivity and are more prone to error than the testing at issue on *Melendez-Diaz*.

certificates without calling their maker contravened the principles expressed in *Crawford*.[71]   The Court did not, however, place an affirmative duty on prosecutors to call forensic analysts when they sought to introduce their reports.   Rather it gave its imprimatur to rules requiring defendants to demand confrontation upon notice that a prosecutor intended to offer certificates or similar affidavits into evidence.

Although the new Confrontation Clause jurisprudence purports to ignore the reliability of out-of-court statements, neither the majority nor the dissent in *Menendez-Diaz* could resist a little skirmishing on this score.   The majority pointed to a National Academy of Science report[72] that documented frequent problems with the quality of forensic science evidence and occasional problems with the honesty of forensic scientists. The dissent dismissed the report's relevance, and without explicitly saying so seemed to proceed on the assumption that assertions in forensic drug reports are so reliable that confrontation serves little purpose. (The latter argument had under *Roberts*, with its focus on reliability, been used to justify certification statutes like the one Massachusetts enacted.) Both sides miss an important point.   The key virtue of requiring forensic scientists to personally present their reports lies not in the possibility that dishonesty will be revealed.   Not only are most forensic scientists honest, but cross-examination will only rarely trip up an experienced witness intent on deception.   The virtue lies instead in the fact that all tests, including tests for drugs, have an error rate, and the conditions of collection and storage may mean that a test is likely to be more or less reliable.   Moreover, the science behind an accepted test may be more equivocal than a report setting forth test results indicates, as when a legal drug has a test profile that resembles an illegal one.   If prosecutors must present forensic science reports through informed witnesses, these and other matters, including the integrity of the chain of custody, may be explored. The dissent also argued that given the way modern laboratories work, *Melendez-Diaz* will require crime scene specialists, lab technicians and others with a role in producing the final report to each appear in court.   There is logic to this claim, but the expense and disruption that this requirement would cause makes it unlikely that the Court will insist on such steps.

The majority and dissent further differed on the likely disruptive impact of the new requirement.   The majority thought the impact would be small and suggested that trial courts antagonized by the needless subpoenaing of forensic scientists would ensure this by punishing advocates with adverse rulings.   The dissent, pointing to the large

---

[71] Justice Thomas, who holds a narrower view of the Confrontation Clause than any other Justice in that he believes it protects only statements in affidavits offered in lieu of testimony, provided the crucial fifth vote.

[72] Strengthening Forensic Science in the United States A Path Forward, National Academies Press, Washington, D.C. (2009).

number of cases involving forensic evidence, felt the impact would likely be huge and saw the majority's punishment argument as a "stunning slur on the integrity of the Nation's courts."[73]

Even today it is not clear who is right about the case's impact. An amicus brief for the United States in *Briscoe v. Virginia* (discussed below) asserts that before the District of Columbia adopted a simple notice statute like the one approved in *Melendez-Diaz,* Drug Enforcement Agency analysts testified in District courts about seven to ten times a month. In the year after *Melendez-Diaz* and the District of Columbia's switch to the notice procedure the Court suggested, analysts were called on to testify about fifty times a month. A year later, however, the rate had fallen to twenty-four times a month, and it is too soon to tell where it will stabilize. An article in the *Boston University Law Review* describes other adaptations Massachusetts made after *Melendez-Diaz.* These included having a single analyst test substances from start to finish so that only one witness need be called, prioritizing drug cases so that laboratories losing analyst time to testimony prioritized the most important cases and taking waivers of *Melendez-Diaz* rights into account in offering plea or sentencing deals.[74] But the article goes on to note that some jurisdictions required forensic reports to be accompanied by analyst testimony before *Melendez-Diaz*, and it prefaces its review of state notice and demand statutes with Justice Scalia's judgment in that case: "The sky will not fall."

For the most part the argument over the impact of *Melendez-Diaz* has focused on the burdens forensic laboratories will face if their analysts must spend time testifying in court rather than doing forensic analysis. What is seldom noted is that this is in essence a dispute over money. If a laboratory will lose a year of analyst time to testimony[75] it can make up for this by hiring an additional analyst. Since the number of analysts in a crime lab is not fixed, much of the dispute over the burdens *Melendez-Diaz* places on forensic laboratories is a red herring. The real issue is how much we are willing to pay to maintain an effective criminal justice

---

[73] *Melendez-Diaz supra* note 69 at 2555. It is hard to see the majority's claim on this score as unrealistic. Trial courts, for example, have frequently punished defendants who insisted on their right to jury trial by imposing longer sentences than they did on those who pled guilty or chose bench trials. This was once regarded as a perversion of justice, but today it is so accepted that a "discount" for relinquishing trial rights is part of sentencing guidelines.

[74] Silberman, Valerie J., Testing The Testimonial Doctrine: The Impact Of Melendez-Diaz v. Massachusetts On State-Level Criminal Prosecutions And Procedure. 91 Boston U. L. Rev. 789 (2011).

[75] Silberman surveyed directors of three Massachusetts crime labs about how often their analysts were required to testify following *Melendez-Diaz*. One lab with 15 analysts estimated that testimony was required about 225 times over a six month period, which would be 450 times a year. Assuming that each occasion took an analyst away from the lab for a day and that before *Melendez-Diaz,* the lab's analysts never testified, then the laboratory would have to add one full time and one quarter time analyst to make up for the time lost. Another laboratory estimated that there were only 40 occasions on which one of its analysts appeared in court and although no number were given the burden on the third laboratory was apparently even smaller. *Id* at 815.

system while protecting a defendant's constitutional rights. In another respect, however, the impact issue is not a red herring. Under *Crawford* the Confrontation Clause applies regardless of the declarant's availability. It takes time, sometimes years, between the preparation of a forensic analysis and a defendant's trial. During that time an analyst may have moved or died or otherwise be unavailable. It remains to be seen how the Supreme Court will act when confronted with that situation. Moreover, memories fade and an analyst who does hundreds of tests each year is likely to have forgotten the results of any specific test and issues that arose during the test except to the extent that these matters are noted in her report. Thus we are likely to be treated to the spectacle of analysts who are required to testify but whose only testimony is a reiteration of their reports as past recollection recorded. When doctrines have as serious deficiencies as *Crawford* has when applied to some, *but not all*, laboratory reports, the law is vulnerable to change.

The first two cases following *Melendez-Diaz* suggested, however, that the *Melendez-Diaz* majority would hold firm to the principle the case espoused or even extend it. *Briscoe v. Virginia*[76] involved a Virginia procedure that as in *Melendez-Diaz* allowed the state to introduce a certified statement to prove forensic tests results. The statute differed from the Massachusetts law in that it gave the defendant the right to call the scientist who produced the report during the state's case-in-chief and to question the scientist as an adverse witness. The difference in the Massachusetts and Virginia statutes may appear small, but it is significant. Calling an experienced witness friendly to the prosecution after the prosecution has rested can play havoc with a defendant's effort to tell a coherent exonerative story and would give the state a second chance to advance its claim that the defendant possessed an illegal drug. This will not happen if the witness is called when the state is presenting its evidence. The Court decided *Briscoe per curium* with an order that the lower court reconsider its approval of the Virginia procedure in light of *Melendez-Diaz v. Massachusetts*, with the obvious implication that it did not survive.

Bullcoming v. New Mexico[77] involved a blood alcohol report generated by gas chromograph testing which was offered not as a bare report but through a witness familiar with laboratory procedures who could answer questions about how the report had been prepared, the reliability of the procedures used and what the numbers meant. The witness was not, however, the scientist who had prepared and certified the report, and he had not personally observed the test procedure. The Court by a 5-4 vote held that the availability of a scientist familiar with laboratory

---

[76] 130 S. Ct. 1316 (2010).

[77] 131 S. Ct. 2705 (2011).

procedures and able, assuming lab protocols had been followed,[78] to explain how the report was generated and what the report meant was not enough to satisfy the Confrontation Clause. Justice Sotomayor concurred to emphasize situations *Bullcoming* did not cover: tests done or offered for a dual purpose, testifying witnesses who had supervisory authority over the analyst conducting the test or other personal connection to the case, the raw data itself and cases where the analyst is not reporting the views of another but offering his own views of data not admitted into evidence.

Williams v. Illinois,[79] the next case in this line, and the most recent as we write, forced Justice Sotomayor to confront the last of the situations on her list. Forced to decide, she held that the Confrontation Clause applied to bar the evidence, but Sotomayor was in dissent. Unlike *Melendez-Diaz, Brisoce* and *Bullcoming,* the prosecution prevailed. *Williams* began when semen from a rape victim was sent by the police to Cellmark, a private forensic laboratory, for analysis. Cellmark extracted DNA from the semen, typed it, and returned the resulting DNA profile to the police, who entered it into a data base. Some months later Williams was arrested in an unrelated case. When his DNA was typed and run against the data base, it matched the DNA profile Cellmark had submitted. Williams was arrested. He opted for a bench trial and was convicted by the judge based largely on the testimony of a state laboratory analyst who had typed his DNA after he was arrested and then compared it to the DNA profiles in the data base. Finding that her profile matched the Cellmark profile, she testified that there was an infinitesimally small chance that anyone other than Williams was the source of the DNA taken from the victim. The Cellmark profile that the expert reviewed was, however, never entered into evidence. Its accuracy and the fact that was taken from the rape semen sample sent to Cellmark were crucial to the state's case, but Williams had no chance to question the Cellmark analyst who prepared it, and citing the Confrontation Clause he objected to the implicit introduction of its results via the state's expert.

Justice Alito wrote for himself and Justices Roberts, Bryer and Kennedy, all of whom had dissented throughout the *Melendez-Diaz* line of cases. He gave two reasons why the Cellmark report did not pose Confrontation Clause problems. First, it had not been introduced into evidence, and to the extent that it had been referred to at trial it was simply to acknowledge it as a basis for an expert opinion. It was never, according to Alito, offered for the truth of the matter asserted and thus,

---

[78] The analyst who generated the report was unable to testify because he was on unpaid leave. Both the majority and the dissent had their reasons for not wishing to make much of this, and their opinions give no hint as to why this was so. It is possible that the reason would have affected the analyst's credibility.

[79] 132 S. Ct. 2221 (2012).

he assumed, was not within the purview of the Confrontation Clause.[80] In this connection Justice Alito made much of the fact that Williams had been tried by a judge, arguing that although a jury might mistakenly treat evidence like the Cellmark report as an assertion of fact, a judge would recognize that the report was not offered for its truth and would only consider it as the basis for an expert opinion. Ultimately, however, Justice Alito thought this didn't matter. He argued that the report could have been introduced had it been offered because it was not testimonial. The report did not accuse anyone[81] and had been prepared not as testimony but to help identify the perpetrator.

Five members of the Court disagreed with both of Justice Alito's arguments and regarded the Cellmark report as testimonial regardless of whether it had been formally introduced into evidence. However, one of those holding this view, Justice Thomas, interprets the Confrontation Clause differently from most if not all of his colleagues. He believes that regardless of whether a statement is testimonial in nature, it is barred only if it takes a testimonial form, which requires indicia of formality. He distinguished the Cellmark report from the reports in the earlier forensic science cases in which he had concurred because the earlier cases involved statements that were notarized or certified by the analyst or the laboratory.

Hence five Justices in *Williams* reject the prevailing plurality's propositions that forensic laboratory reports relied on by experts are nontestimonial if they are not introduced into evidence or if they have been prepared both to identify an accused and to convict the accused once identified. But *Williams* is precedent for holding that if laboratory reports are not offered as evidence and neither presented as certificates nor sworn to be true, the Confrontation Clause will not prevent experts from assuming their accuracy and offering opinions based on this assumption, at least if trial is to a judge.

---

[80] Justice Alito was relying for his conclusion on *Tennessee v. Street, supra* note 21, which held that the Confrontation Clause did not bar the introduction of a non-testifying co-defendant's confession because the confession was not offered for its truth but rather to show that a codefendant's confession did not track the defendant's, thereby refuting the defendant's claim that he had been coerced into writing a confession based on what his codefendant had confessed to. The reliance on *Street* seems misguided. In *Street* not only did the value of the codefendant's confession not depend on its truth, but it was relevant, the Court pointed out, because of an issue the defendant had raised. In *Williams* if Cellmark had erred or its report had been altered after Williams had been identified as a suspect, an opinion based on it would be worthless. In formulating her opinion the testifying witness had to assume that the Cellmark profile reflected the results of a true and accurate analysis.

[81] Justice Alito's argument seems to mislead on this issue as well. The fact that the report makes no accusations is of little import. Although the cases the Court had heard all involved accusations, the Confrontation Clause applies to all evidence offered against an accused whether or not it is identification evidence or accuses him of a crime. Thus if the weather at the time of a crime is relevant, a defendant has a right to cross-examine a state's witness who describes the weather.

When we contrast *Bullcoming* with *Williams* we are thus left with a somewhat bizarre outcome. If a laboratory report has whatever extra guarantees of care and accuracy a formal certificate provides and is offered not by the person who prepared it but by a witness who knows the analyst and the laboratory's protocol, the Confrontation Clause precludes the report's admission unless, perhaps, the witness observed or supervised the person who did the analysis. Moreover, if the report is not admitted into evidence another expert cannot render an opinion which assumes the report's truth. If, however, a laboratory reports its findings in some less formal way, the Confrontation Clause does not bar an expert from offering opinions that assume the report's truth and does not require that the report be admitted at trial. The defendant may, consistent with FRE 703, question the testifying expert about the report on which she based her opinion, but the opinion will stand even if the expert knows little or nothing about the laboratory's analytic procedures, how the reporting analyst has fared on proficiency tests, whether the laboratory has had problems with sample mix-ups and the like. If the defendant wants to explore these issues, he will have to call the person who made the report, which is a burden that when reports are more formal *Melendez-Diaz, Briscoe* and *Bullcoming* puts on the prosecution. Moreover, if the plurality in *Williams* hews to its dissenting position in the earlier cases[82] and if the states relax whatever aspects of their forensic laboratory reports Justice Thomas sees as indicating formality, the Confrontation Clause may be again read so as to allow states to make forensic science reports presumptively admissible without accompanying witnesses.

Whatever the logical problems with the way *Williams* was resolved, almost certainly no injustice was done. The match in question was so unlikely that it is impossible to believe that the source of the Cellmark sample was anyone other than the defendant. About the only possible error would be a mix-up or mislabeling of crime scene samples resulting in the defendant's being linked to the wrong crime. But not all forensic evidence is as reliable or as probative as DNA evidence, and DNA evidence is more open to error when, unlike the situation in *Williams,* a defendant sample and a crime scene sample are analyzed by the same laboratory at the same time.

To judge from *Crawford* and its earliest progeny one might have thought that overruling *Roberts* in favor of a testimonial approach was a windfall for criminal defendants. Even before *Bryant* and *Williams* there was, however, reason to think this view was misleading—an artifact of the first cases to reach the Court. There is a vast range of hearsay that is clearly nontestimonial and hence admissible under *Crawford* that might

---

[82] Whether they would is open to question since *Williams* purports to endorse and distinguish *Melenedez-Diaz* and its progeny.

not have satisfied the *Roberts'* standard. Moreover, unless limited by the Due Process Clause, *Crawford* allows for substantial relaxation of the hearsay bar in criminal cases. In theory even base rumor could be admissible against defendants in criminal cases, since rumor is not testimonial in nature. This may be unlikely to happen, but some expansion of the range of admissible hearsay in criminal cases would surprise no one.

A driver of Confrontation Clause jurisprudence and practice, although judicial opinions and academic theorists seldom acknowledge it, is the aversion many prosecutors have for the right of confrontation. It is a non-reciprocal right that makes their task harder. Worse still, it can mean that a guilty person will go free. In *Hammon*, for example, it appears that Mr. Hammon did assault his wife, but if Amy Hammon will not or cannot testify, and if her statements to the officers are inadmissible, Mr. Hammon will not pay for his crime. This prosecutorial perspective is shared by many trial and appellate court judges in situations where they believe excluding evidence will thwart justice. No matter how seemingly adverse the precedent, prosecutors have frequently pushed against the Supreme Court's Confrontation Clause jurisprudence, often with considerable success. Often in state trials and appeals rules seem stretched to avoid excluding the state's evidence,[83] and in the Supreme Court, seemingly expansive protections have been reinterpreted and limited in later litigation. *Bryant* and *Williams* are recent examples.

Roberts often failed to guarantee defendants confrontation not because it was inconsistent with the goals of the Confrontation Clause nor because it established an unreasonable standard for Confrontation Clause jurisprudence, but because it could be so easily subverted. Either a trial judge could pigeonhole a statement into an exception it did not truly fit, thus automatically meeting the *Roberts* test,[84] or the court could find in almost any statement indicia of reliability that ostensibly met the *Roberts* requirement. *Crawford*, whatever its historical or other flaws as an opinion, seemed to have the virtue of clearly delineating kinds of hearsay—*ex parte* affidavits, grand jury testimony, accomplice confessions, certain statements to the police—that do not comport with Confrontation Clause requirements regardless. Constitutional conservatives approved of *Crawford* because these kinds of hearsay were clear targets of the Confrontation Clause's ban. Liberals liked *Crawford* because even if its reach was less than they thought it should be, it promised to be more effective than the easily subverted *Roberts* in protecting against the use of particularly egregious forms of unconfronted

---

[83] Appellate opinions present, however, a possibly skewed view since when defendants prevail at trial prosecutors cannot appeal those evidentiary rulings that may have unduly aided the defense.

[84] See text at notes 35–42, *supra*.

hearsay. As two commentators observed, the Confrontation Clause after *Crawford* had a "Smaller Mouth, Bigger Teeth."[85]

But as we have seen prosecutors have not ceased pushing against the Clause, and trial judges still want to resist the exclusion of what they see as probative evidence.[86] So *Crawford*'s bigger teeth are vulnerable to being worn down. In particular, the narrower the definition of "testimonial," the less *Crawford* will protect. Narrowing seems to be happening. After *Bryant* it would appear that few statements identifying an unapprehended gunmen will be considered testimonial if they are made in close temporal proximity to the shooting. Courts have been invited to assume that any reasonable person, even one who has been seriously injured, will want to help the police apprehend the shooter not with an eye to securing a criminal conviction but simply as a good citizen concerned for public safety. If five police officers ask the same question, and no one seems to feel it is urgent to find the shooter, it seems not to matter. But if statements that can help the police apprehend shooters are not testimonial why isn't the same true of robbers, burglars, muggers and others on the loose after committing crimes. All can be plausibly thought of as posing dangers to society which any good citizen would want to cooperate in forestalling. The teeth of the Confrontation Clause are further dulled, in the case of most hearsay almost down to the gums, if statements to authorities must be formal rather than conversational to qualify as testimonial. Justice Thomas seems to feel this way and Justice Alito may as well. Even Justice Sotomayor feels that formality is an important clue to whether the protections of the Confrontation Clause attach.

A serious problem with *Roberts* was its almost infinite malleability since judges as we have noted were adroit in fitting statements into established hearsay exceptions or finding "equivalent guarantees of reliability" when no traditional exception could be stretched. But not all judges played these games or played them in the same way. This made for considerable unpredictability. A major reason for *Crawford's* popularity among the legal professorate was that it promised greater predictability. But *Bryant*'s standards for determining when the primary purpose of a statement is testimonial appear so flexible that predictability is substantially diminished. *Williams*, for its part suggests that there is considerable scope for maneuvering out from under the strictures of the Clause.

The jurisprudence of *Crawford* is, however, still young and can go in many directions. The change of a seat or two on the Court could

---

[85] W. Jeremy Counsellor & Shannon Rickett, The Confrontation Clause after Crawford v. Washington: Smaller Mouth, Bigger Teeth, 57 Baylor L. Rev 1 (2005).

[86] *Lilly*, for example, contained language indicating that unconfronted accomplice confessions were almost always barred by the Sixth Amendment, yet a study by Kirst, cited in *Crawford*, indicates that even after *Lilly* more than a third of such confessions were admitted.

dramatically affect the standards for and the scope of the Clause's limitations on hearsay evidence. Recent cases and the views of recent Court appointees contain some tantalizing hints of directions that may be taken. Reliability, which Justice Scalia did his best to read out of Confrontation Clause jurisprudence, seems for some Justices to be a concern, and the unavailability of the declarant, or the cost of making declarants available, which Scalia also thought irrelevant, seem also to weigh heavily for some. Reliability and availability were the twin pillars of *Roberts*. Perhaps there will be a place for them in the post-*Crawford* Confrontation Clause jurisprudence after all.

*"As a matter of fact, I **have** read the Constitution, and, frankly, I don't get it."*

Problem VII-2. Henry Clark, desk clerk at the Sweetwater Motel, is found at 4:00 one morning sprawled dead behind his desk. He was shot in the course of an apparent robbery. The evidence shows that the death occurred between 2:45 and 3:15 a.m. David Dick, a former acting manager of the Sweetwater, is accused of the murder. At the trial the prosecutor wishes to introduce under FRE 803(6) an entry in the motel logbook that reads, "2:35 a.m., David, a former acting manager, has been here." As a foundation for this evidence, the prosecutor offers the testimony of the hotel manager, who states that desk clerks are instructed to note the presence of any suspicious individuals in the logbook and the time at which they are seen. The manager further states that, to his knowledge, Clark had been introduced to Dick on one occasion. The log entry is clearly in Clark's handwriting. Dick objects to the introduction of the log entry, stating that its use at trial would violate his right to confrontation under the Sixth Amendment. **How should the court rule?** Suppose below the logbook notation is the scrawled statement in the same handwriting, "Dick shot me." **Is this statement admissible?** Suppose it said. "If I don't survive, Dick shot me." **Would this change anything?**

Problem VII-3. Birch Harms and his companion, Rachel McMillan, are jointly tried for conspiring to blow up the Washington Monument. At their joint trial, recordings of statements that Birch made to an FBI undercover agent are introduced. The statements describe the scheme in detail as well as the leading roles that he and Rachel are to play in it. Birch's counsel cross-examines Agent Troutman, who was wired for sound. Troutman admits that he knows of no steps that were made to carry out the plot, but he responds "No" when he is asked, "Isn't it true that Birch's opening remark, which is drowned out by that truck noise in the background, was, 'Last week you asked me how I would call attention to the danger of nuclear war. I wouldn't do this, but let me tell you my wildest dream about how to get the nation's attention'?" Rachel's confession to the police is also introduced. The confession describes the plan in detail but doesn't mention Birch by name, referring instead to "my partner." Generally it is consistent with Birch's remarks, but it differs dramatically on some important details. Neither Birch nor Rachel testifies. Both are convicted. Rachel's conviction is reversed by the appellate court, citing *Bruton v. United States* and *Gray v. Maryland*. At her retrial Birch is called by the state. He points out that he faces additional charges growing out of his alleged plans to blow up the Washington Monument, and he refuses to testify, claiming his privilege against self-incrimination. The prosecution then offers that portion of the transcript of the earlier trial that includes the undercover agent's testimony and the tape of Birch's remarks as it was played for the jury. The prosecutor argues that the portion of the transcript offered is admissible under the state's former testimony exception, which is broader than the federal exception in that it admits former testimony "so long as the person against whom the testimony was first offered had an opportunity for cross-examination and the same motive to cross-examine as the person against whom the testimony is subsequently offered." The judge admits the transcript. **If Rachel argues that this violates her rights under the Confrontation Clause, will she win on appeal?** Suppose the prosecution had offered, as a statement against interest, only those portions of Birch's remarks that did not inculpate Rachel in order to establish that there was a scheme to blow up the landmark, and that Rachel protested and demanded that the state grant Birch use immunity rather than use his hearsay. Citing a statute that provides that a court cannot grant use immunity except upon the application of the Attorney General of the United States, the prosecutor told the judge that the Attorney General had considered the matter and decided that it was not in the national interest to grant use immunity to Birch. **With Birch thus unavailable to testify, should the Court admit his hearsay?**

Problem VII-4. Tiffany Johnson is sitting in a Starbucks sipping a vanilla latte when she receives a tweet from her friend Sy Gordon. Gordon's tweet reads, "*In U Street bank, 2 men robbing, 1 blond, 6 ft, nose scar, rose tattoo, don't see me under desk.*" Later Gibby Kluckhorn, who is about six feet tall, blond, and with a scar on his nose and a rose tattoo and his friend Tom Stewart are arrested for the robbery. Gordon is available to testify but rather than call him the state just offers his tweet. **Is it admissible? Would the situation be different if Gordon has left the state and his whereabouts are unknown? Would it be different if the tweet had ended, "Tell cops." If Johnson were a police officer who was in Starbucks on her break and one of 30 people who received Gordon's tweets would that affect the tweet's admissibility. Would you reach the same decision if Officer Johnson was the only person who received Gordon's tweets? Do your answers to any of the above questions change if rather than tweeting Johnson, Gordon had sent a text message saying he was hiding under a desk in a bank being robbed and it was only after Johnson had texted back, "Describe the robbers" that he gave his description of Kluckhorn?** Suppose that Kluckhorn was killed in a later robbery and only Stewart was being tried for the U Street robbery. The prosecution introduces other evidence that Stewart was drinking with Kluckhorn in a bar two blocks from the bank 15 minutes before the robbery and left the bar with him, that a witness saw him get into a car with Kluckhorn that went through a red light a block from the bank within 90 seconds of the time the robbers fled, and that he and Kluckhorn had each lost about $3000 on the horses the day after the robbery. **Would the tweet (or text message) describing Kluckhorn as the robber be admissible? Would anything be different if Gordon's tweet had said:** "*In U Street bank, robbers just fled, 1 blond, 6 ft, nose scar, rose tattoo, didn't see me under desk.*"**?**

Problem VII-5. On December 1, 2009 during a routine examination a pediatrician notices a black and blue mark on his three year old patient's thigh and redness in the area of her vagina. "Did someone hurt your leg?" he asks? "Yes," says Lily Harmon, the young patient. "Did he also touch you there?" asks the doctor pointing to her vagina. "Yes" is the reply. "Who touched you here?" asks the doctor? "Unca," replied Lily. The doctor notified the authorities and some weeks later a psychologist who was a specialist in child sexual abuse interviewed Lily. The interview was taped. A portion went like this: **Q:** "Did your daddy hurt your leg and touch your pee place?" **A:** "No." **Q:** "Did your brother Ned?" **A:** "No." **Q:** "Who touched you then?" **A:** [Silence] **Q:** "Was it your Uncle Joe?" **A:** [Silence] **Q:** "It was your Uncle Joe, wasn't it?" **A:** "Yes." Lily's Uncle Joe is arrested and charged with child sexual abuse. At the trial, the judge determines that Lily is too young to understand the nature of the oath and rules she cannot testify. **Can the state introduce either the pediatrician's testimony to what Lily told him or the videotape of the psychologist's questioning if Joe objects on Confrontation Clause grounds? Would your answer be different if by the time of the trial Lily were seven years old? Would you answer differently if Lily was seven years old at the time of the alleged abuse, but when Joe was tried two years later she said she didn't remember and didn't want to testify, and was excused from testifying after a psychologist who examined her said she had repressed the incident and could be psychologically damaged if forced to talk about it from the stand. Does it matter in any of these scenarios, whether Joe was the only uncle at Lily's house for Thanksgiving 2009 dinner, or whether six other uncles were present? If two of the uncles present were named "Joe"?**

Problem VII-6. In May of 2013 the following 911 call was received: **V(oice):** "Can you send someone quick, Larry's hitting me again."

O(perator): "Where are you?" **V:** "2617 Sheridan."

O: "A car is on the way. Is he hitting you now?" **V:** "No, I've locked myself in the bathroom. He's kicking at the door. . . . (screaming) I've called the cops you bastard."

O: "Who's Larry?" **V:** "My husband."

O: "Does he hit you often?" **V:** "Only when he's drunk."

O: "Is there any danger the door will break?" **V:** "No, he's stopped kicking. He's leaving in the car."

O: "How often has he attacked you?" **V:** "Four or five times."

O: "Are you going to need medical care?" **V:** "No, I'm fine."

O: "Has he ever hurt you?" **V:** "Three months ago he knocked out a tooth, and last year he threw a plate at me; I was black and blue where it hit."

O: "What happened this time?" **V:** "He started drinking in front of the tube, and when I said he could fetch his own beer because he had had enough already he came at me."

O: "Are you still upset, honey?" **V:** "Yeah, my nerves are frayed, but I'll calm down."

Larry was charged with felony assault, but his wife refused to testify against him. When pressed as to why she wouldn't testify she said, "I know what's best for me." **Can the prosecutor introduce a transcript of part or all of this 911 conversation if Larry objects to its admission on Confrontation Clause grounds? Assume the prosecutor decides to honor his wife's wishes and does not try Larry for spouse abuse. She does, however, charge Larry, who had been stopped by the police half an hour after his wife's call for driving erratically, with drunk driving. Because Larry's blood alcohol level when he was tested was in a marginal range, the prosecutor seeks to bolster the blood alcohol evidence with Larry's wife's testimony. However, his wife refuses to testify against Larry, citing the marital privilege. May part or all of the 911 tape be introduced against Larry? Would your answer be different if Larry's wife was willing to testify to his drinking that day, but Larry was able to and did invoke a marital privilege to keep her from testifying?**

Problem VII-7. (A) Lynwood Mayberry III is charged with the murder of Harry Ring, while robbing his jewelry store. Ring was taken to the hospital after the shooting and although his condition at first seemed to improve, he died after six days. At the trial the prosecutor seeks to introduce the following items: hospital records that say Ring was admitted for a gunshot wound, a list recording his vital signs every four hours from the time of Ring's admission to the time he died, and giving as a cause of death "shock attributable to gunshot wound"; an autopsy report that lists the cause of death as "damage to internal organs caused by .22 caliber bullet lodged in third rib"; a photograph showing a car with Mayberry's license going through a red light taken by an automated camera at an intersection three blocks from where the robbery occurred; time and date stamps indicate the photo was taken ten minutes after Ring had pressed a silent alarm; a report indicating that Mayberry's finger print "perfectly matches" a print taken from a glass case in Ring's store; a ballistics report indicating that bullets fired from a .22 caliber pistol in Mayberry's home "matches the bullet found lodged in Ring's rib"; and a photograph of rings, bracelets and necklaces found in a strong box in Mayberry's home with arrows pointing to twelve pieces and a note saying that Mrs. Ring identified the indicated pieces as "pieces Harry carried in his store." Mayberry, on the other hand, wishes to introduce a report from an expert he hired which says, "The bullet found in rib did minor damage to organs and could not have caused death. Death was caused by toxic shock following a hospital acquired bacterial infection. Earlier diagnosis and the administration of antibiotics would have prevented this death." Mayberry also seeks to introduce an estate appraisal dated some six years earlier which lists numerous pieces of jewelry that Mayberry inherited from his mother and describes in detail the most valuable pieces, four of these descriptions match pieces marked with arrow in the police photo. **Assuming there are no authentication problems, what may be admitted over Confrontation Clause objections? (B)** Suppose that instead of being shot Ring had died unexpectedly of apparently natural causes, but an autopsy report, done routinely in the case of unexplained deaths, revealed he had died from arsenic poisoning. **If Mrs. Ring was charged with murder, could she object on Confrontation Clause grounds to the introduction of the report without calling the medical examiner who did the autopsy? Could she object if the autopsy was not routine but was done at the instance of an insurance investigator who said he was suspicious because a million dollar policy on Ring's life, with Mrs. Mayberry as the beneficiary, had been taken out 9 months before his death? Would it make a difference if the investigator had asked the prosecutor or police to request the autopsy and they did? If the prosecutor or police requested the autopsy at their own initiative? Would your answer to any of the above questions change if the medical examiner who conducted the autopsy had retired and moved to Japan?**

3. Cross-examination and Impeachment

The cases we have discussed thus far involve efforts by defendants in criminal cases to prevent the admission of inculpatory evidence. We have seen that in some circumstances the Confrontation Clause bars the admission of out-of-court statements, but often it will not. The Confrontation Clause provides, however, not just a right to bar evidence. It also guarantees modes of trial procedure. Even those who, like the late Dean Wigmore, would give the clause no role in excluding hearsay believe it has important implications for trial procedure. The clause's procedural protections are of two types: a right to be present when evidence is offered against one and a right to cross-examine and impeach opposing witnesses.[87] These rights are reflected in the general rule, applicable in

---

[87] The defendant's rights with respect to evidence other than witness testimony are somewhat less clear. Presumably, documents can only be received subject to the defendant's right to examine them and challenge their authenticity. However, in *Snyder v. Commonwealth of Massachusetts*, 291 U.S. 97 (1934), the Supreme Court held, by a vote of 5 to 4, that a prisoner had no right under the Fourteenth Amendment to be present at a jury view of the scene of his alleged crime. *Crawford's* attempt to hew closely to the words "witnesses against" suggest that the current Court would not read the Confrontation Clause as providing any rights to examine physical evidence other than evidence offered for the witness statements it contains, but it seems likely that the Due Process Clause would give a defendant a right to examine physical evidence offered against him even if the Confrontation Clause did not. Cf. Gardner v. Florida, 430 U.S. 349 (1977) (finding a due process problem with a capital-sentencing judge's use against the defendant of documents and statements the defendant didn't have a chance to examine and refute). Moreover, a good defense counsel confronting the issue would do some historical research we have not done. If it could be shown that historically English and early American

both civil and criminal proceedings, that when an individual who has testified for one party refuses to answer questions on cross-examination, that individual's direct testimony shall, at the request of the other party, be stricken from the record.[88]

Confrontation Clause rights, as we have already noted, may be waived. At trial, cross-examination is often foregone, and the admission of the uncross-examined prior testimony of unavailable witnesses will not violate the Confrontation Clause so long as there was an opportunity for cross-examination at the hearing where the testimony was given. The right to be present at one's trial is, if anything, even more fundamental than the right to cross-examination, but it too may be forfeited even where it is not intentionally waived. In *Illinois v. Allen*,[89] the Supreme Court held that an obstreperous defendant could lose his right to be present at his own trial if, after being warned by the judge that he would be removed, he nonetheless persisted in disruptive behavior.[90]

The right to confront opposing witnesses does not mean that defendants in criminal cases have an unlimited or uncontrolled right to engage in cross-examination. Totally apart from statutory restrictions on cross-examination like rape shield laws, cross-examination must pertain to relevant matters, and ordinarily the scope of cross-examination is limited by rule to matters either covered in direct examination or relevant to credibility.[91] In addition, judges have discretion to control examinations that are unduly repetitive or argumentative or that involve the badgering or intimidation of witnesses. Nevertheless, a judge who takes a narrow view of proper cross-examination and seriously limits the

---

courts extended a right to examine nontestimonial physical evidence, this could motivate some Justices to see a right to examine such evidence implicit in the Confrontation Clause.

[88] Where a state's witness in a criminal case refuses to submit to cross-examination, the Confrontation Clause requires that his testimony be stricken from the record. In a civil case, the Due Process Clause of the Fourteenth Amendment may require a similar result. Problems arise where the refusal of the witness to submit to cross-examination is not willful, as where disability or death intervenes between direct and cross-examination, or where the refusal to submit to cross-examination is only partial, as where a witness submits to detailed cross-examination on the subject matter of his direct testimony, but pleads the Fifth Amendment when asked about matters that might impeach his credibility. *Giles* suggests that where no cross-examination is possible, the direct testimony would have to be stricken even if the impossibility of cross-examination is not the witness's or the prosecution's fault. Where there has been some cross-examination the situation is murkier. For a discussion of these issues see, McCormick § 19.

[89] 397 U.S. 337 (1970).

[90] Obstreperous behavior may also justify such measures as gagging or shackling a defendant. It has been suggested that the best way to deal with obstreperous defendants is to remove them to a room from where they can view the proceedings by closed-circuit television and communicate with their attorneys by telephone. This is now sometimes done.

[91] However, the defendant may have a right under the Compulsory Process Clause to call a prosecution witness as his own if he wishes to explore matters beyond the scope of the direct examination. And there may be the further right, an amalgam of confrontation and compulsory process rights, to question the witness as if on cross-examination, if the witness is "hostile". See *Chambers v. Mississippi, infra* § IV-B.

defendant's cross-examination risks reversal for violating the Confrontation Clause.[92]

The most interesting questions arise when the state, for policy reasons, forbids an admittedly relevant line of cross-examination. The Supreme Court, to date, has been reluctant to allow such limitations. In *Alford v. United States*,[93] a unanimous court held that it was error to bar the cross-examiner from asking a witness for the prosecution where he lived. The Court stated:

> It is the essence of a fair trial that reasonable latitude be given the cross-examiner, even though he is unable to state to the court what facts a reasonable cross-examination might develop. . . .

> The question "Where do you live?" was not only an appropriate preliminary to the cross-examination of the witness, but on its face, without any such declaration of purpose as was made by counsel here, was an essential step in identifying the witness with his environment, to which cross-examination may always be directed.[94]

The Court also pointed out that, on the facts of *Alford*, there was an additional reason why the question in dispute should have been allowed. The defense had reason to believe that the witness, although not convicted of a crime, was in the custody of federal authorities. The Court recognized that this fact might have suggested that the witness's testimony was "affected by fear or favor growing out of his detention,"[95] something the defense was "entitled to show by cross-examination."[96] The Court apparently decided *Alford* on the basis of its supervisory power over the lower federal courts. Nowhere does the Court's opinion mention the Confrontation Clause.

In *Smith v. Illinois*,[97] the Court overturned a conviction for the sale of narcotics because the trial judge had sustained objections to questions asking the state's principal witness for his true name and where he lived. The witness had admitted he was testifying under an alias. This reversal rested squarely on the Sixth and Fourteenth Amendments, and *Alford* is cited as setting the appropriate standard for the application of the Confrontation Clause. Justice White, in a concurring opinion joined by Justice Marshall, noted that the Court in *Alford* recognized that questions that tend merely to harass, annoy or humiliate a witness may

---

[92] This does not mean that undue restriction of cross-examination will always lead to the reversal of a conviction. In the light of other evidence and the cross-examination that did take place, the error may be judged harmless.

[93] 282 U.S. 687 (1931).

[94] Id. at 692–93.

[95] Id. at 693.

[96] Id.

[97] 390 U.S. 129 (1968).

go beyond the bounds of proper cross-examination. White suggested that inquiries tending to endanger the personal safety of the witness fall in the same category. Lower courts since *Smith* have sustained objections to questions seeking a witness's current address if providing the information might endanger the witness.[98]

Both *Alford* and *Smith* are cases in which a trial judge decided for case-specific policy reasons that a witness should not have to answer certain questions. *Davis v. Alaska* [99] and *Olden v. Kentucky* [100] are more interesting and difficult cases. In *Davis*, the policy decision was the state's, not a judge's. Furthermore, the Court did not challenge the state's assertion that when juveniles were witnesses it had good reasons for precluding certain lines of inquiry. In *Olden*, the judge was exercising discretion given to him by the state equivalent of FRE 403. Not only was the judge's exercise of discretion arguably reasonable, but his ruling closely accorded with legislative policy judgments embodied in the federal rape shield statute and the similar shield statutes of many states.

Davis involved a man tried for stealing a safe from a bar in Anchorage, Alaska. The safe had been discovered near the home of a youth named Richard Green, who said that some hours after the safe was stolen he had seen and spoken with two Negro men standing alongside a late-model metallic blue Chevrolet sedan near where the empty safe was later found. Green later identified Davis from a photo array as one of the men he had seen. At trial Green identified Davis as the man he saw with "something like a crowbar" in his hands standing next to a car parked where the safe was later found. Other evidence against Davis was that the trunk of a blue Chevrolet he had rented contained paint chips and particles identified as safe insulation, each of which could have come from the stolen safe.

At the time of the trial Green was on probation by order of the juvenile court because he had burglarized two cabins. The defense counsel wanted to probe these convictions to show Davis's testimony could have been biased since he himself was a likely suspect, and he might have feared that if he did not dispel suspicion his probation would be revoked. Before Green testified, however, the prosecutor invoked Alaska law to secure a protective order preventing mention of Green's delinquency status.[101] In a subsequent cross-examination by Davis, Green at first

---

[98] See, e.g., United States v. Battaglia, 432 F.2d 1115 (7th Cir. 1970), *cert. denied* 401 U.S. 924 (1971).

[99] 415 U.S. 308 (1974).

[100] 488 U.S. 227 (1988).

[101] Alaskan law then provided:

"No adjudication, order, or disposition of a juvenile case shall be admissible in a court not acting in the exercise of juvenile jurisdiction except for use in a presentencing procedure in a criminal case where the superior court, in its discretion, determines that such use is appropriate." [Alaska Rule of Children's Procedure 23]

denied ever feeling that he might be suspected of the crime but admitted it had crossed his mind that the police might have thought he had something to do with the crime. He also admitted the police had questioned him about the incident but denied he had ever been questioned in the same way before by law enforcement officers. At this point the prosecutor objected to the line of questioning, and the objection was sustained. The defense counsel was also precluded from introducing evidence about Green's juvenile convictions to suggest not just that Green was biased but also that his denial of having been similarly questioned before was most likely a lie.

The Supreme Court, speaking through Chief Justice Burger, reversed, citing the Confrontation Clause's guarantee of an accused's right to confront witnesses against him. After laying out the facts, the Court began by citing language in *Douglas v. Alabama* stating that "a primary interest secured by [the Confrontation Clause] is the right of cross-examination."[102] A trial judge could preclude repetitive and unduly harassing interrogation, but when a cross-examination suggested that a witness might be biased against an accused or have other specific motivations to lie, the exposure of such motivations was, in the Court's words, "a proper and important function of cross-examination."

It was thus not enough that the trial court had allowed Davis's attorney to ask Green whether he might be biased. Without being able to tell the jury why Green might be biased, Davis was, as the Court saw it, denied the right of effective cross-examination. Although the Justices acknowledged Alaska's interest in protecting the anonymity of juvenile offenders, they regarded that interest as outweighed by Davis's interest in showing that Green had a specific reason to testify falsely; namely, Green's record made him a likely suspect who might benefit if another person was convicted of the crime.

Olden v. Kentucky differs from *Davis*, and is arguably a stronger case for the prosecution because the trial court's concern in barring a line of cross-examination was not a state policy extraneous to the trial but a discretionary judgment, ordinarily entrusted to the trial judge, about when the probative value of evidence is outweighed by its prejudicial effect. The Court upheld the defendant's Confrontation Clause claim, however, perhaps in part because it disagreed with how the state court had struck the balance.

Olden arose when James Olden, a black man, was accused of forcibly raping Starla Matthews a young white woman. The alleged rape had

---

"The commitment and placement of a child and evidence given in the court are not admissible as evidence against the minor in a subsequent case or proceedings in any other court. . . . " [Alaska Stat. § 47.10.080(g) 1971.]

Such provisions were not unusual in state juvenile codes of the time.

102 380 U.S. 415, 418 (1965).

occurred when Olden and a friend offered to give Matthews a ride home from a "black bar" after the girl friend she had come with had left without her. One or more acts of sexual intercourse had occurred at several stops on the way home. This was admitted. The defense was consent.

Matthews was not the best witness a prosecutor could desire. She had been "somewhat intoxicated" when she accepted the ride; she had given inconsistent statements about what had occurred, at one time accusing Olden's friend as well as Olden of rape, and although she testified at trial that Olden had threatened her with a knife, she had never mentioned a knife to the police. There was also testimony that Matthews had not looked troubled when seen by others with Olden and his friend and that a policeman was present when she was seen in a store with them but she never approached the officer. Perhaps the strongest evidence supporting Matthews' allegation, was that when she had been dropped off near the home of her friend Bill Russell, she immediately and, so it seemed, spontaneously told Russell that she had just been raped. To counter the latter evidence, the defense wanted to show that although at the time of the rape both Russell and Matthews were married to others, they were most likely sexually involved, and by the time of the trial they had separated from their spouses and were living together. The defense theory was that Matthews concocted the story of the rape when Russell saw her disembark from the car because she feared that Russell would have suspected her of having had consensual sex with the men who drove her home. The defense may also have hoped to benefit from the Kentucky jury's reaction to the fact that Russell was black and Matthews was white.

At trial Olden had argued strenuously that in order to demonstrate Matthews' motive to lie, it was crucial, that he be allowed to introduce evidence of Matthews' and Russell's current cohabitation. Nevertheless, the trial judge granted the prosecutor's motion *in limine* to keep all evidence of Matthews' and Russell's cohabitation from the jury. In addition, when the defense attempted to cross-examine Matthews about her living arrangements, after she had claimed during direct examination that she was living with her mother, the trial court sustained the prosecutor's objection.

Olden was acquitted of the rape charge but convicted of forcible sodomy, and the Kentucky Court of Appeals upheld the conviction, holding that although evidence that Matthews and Russell were living together at the time of trial was not barred by the Kentucky's rape shield law "its probative value [was] outweighed by its possibility for prejudice." By way of explanation, the court stated: "[T]here were the undisputed facts of race; Matthews was white and Russell was black. For the trial court to have admitted into evidence testimony that Matthews and

Russell were living together at the time of the trial may have created extreme prejudice against Matthews."

The Supreme Court did not dispute the Kentucky court's view that prejudice was a possibility, but the Justices held that the state appeals court had nonetheless failed to accord proper weight to petitioner's Sixth Amendment right "to be confronted with the witnesses against him." *Davis*, and a case that followed it, *Delaware v. Van Arsdall* [103] were cited for the proposition that "a criminal defendant states a violation of the Confrontation Clause by showing that he was prohibited from engaging in otherwise appropriate cross-examination designed to show a prototypical form of bias on the part of the witness, and thereby 'to expose to the jury the facts from which jurors . . . could appropriately draw inferences relating to the reliability of the witness.' "[104] The Court thought it plain that a reasonable jury's judgment of Matthews' credibility would have been significantly different had the defense counsel been allowed to pursue the proposed line of cross-examination and so reversed the decision below. Speculation about the possibility the jury might be biased by the evidence could not, in the Court's view, justify excluding what it saw as strong impeaching evidence.

In *Delaware v. Van Arsdall*,[105] cited in *Olden*, the Court was unanimous (except for Justice Stevens, who did not address the issue) in finding a Confrontation Clause violation when, on Rule 403 grounds, the defendant in a murder trial was not allowed to ask a key prosecution witness whether he had had criminal charges for being drunk on the highway dismissed and was also barred from inquiring into the witness's connection with an unrelated murder.[106] *Davis*, *Olden* and *Van Arsdall* carry a similar message: *criminal defendants have a right to question prosecution witnesses about matters that fairly cast doubt on their credibility*. If policy reasons justify such preclusion, they will have to be stronger than the reasons given in the cases that have reached the Supreme Court to date.[107]

However, the protection of the Confrontation Clause seems to disappear if it is circumstances rather than the government (in the

---

[103] 475 U.S. 673 (1986).

[104] *Olden*, 488 U.S. at 231–32.

[105] 475 U.S. 673 (1986), cited in *Olden*, 488 U.S. at 231–32.

[106] *Van Arsdall* is independently important because it held that *Chapman v. California*, 386 U.S. 18 (1967) applies to cases in which cross-examination has been denied in violation of the Confrontation Clause. *Chapman* held that the erroneous denial of a constitutional right can be harmless error if the prosecution satisfies the court that the error was harmless beyond a reasonable doubt.

[107] The decided cases all involve questions aimed at revealing bias, which as we said in Chapter Five, pp. 440–445, is a "favored" mode of impeachment. The protection should be the same when questions are directed to opportunity to observe and similar matters that directly implicate the credibility of testimony. It may not extend to less direct and less powerful forms of impeachment such as the introduction of prior inconsistent statements that deal with collateral matters.

person of the judge) that preclude an effective cross-examination. This is the apparent message of *Delaware v. Fensterer*,[108] like *Olden*, a *per curiam* opinion rendered without the benefits of briefing on the merits or oral argument, hardly the most auspicious basis for what has become an important precedent. The defendant in *Fensterer* had been tried for murder, largely on the basis of circumstantial evidence. To support its theory that the victim had been strangled with a cat leash, the state introduced an expert who testified that two hairs on the leash were the victim's, and that one of them had been forcibly removed.[109] The expert further testified that there were three ways to identify forcibly removed hair, but that he had no notes about his method of identification and so could not recollect the basis for his conclusion. Thus the defendant was precluded from cross-examining the witness about how he had determined that the hair was forcibly removed and, in particular, from showing (if it were the case) that the witness's particular method was unreliable. Nevertheless, the Court held that the defendant's Confrontation Clause rights had not been violated. "Generally speaking," the Court said in language it has quoted several times since, *"the Confrontation Clause guarantees an opportunity for effective cross-examination, not cross-examination that is effective in whatever way, and to whatever extent, the defense might wish."* (emphasis ours)

Fensterer was the key precedent for the Court when it decided *United States v. Owens*.[110] *Owens* grew out of an attack on a prison guard, John Foster, who had been brutally beaten with a metal pipe. Among his injuries was a skull fracture that required nearly a month of hospitalization and left his memory seriously impaired. About three weeks after the attack, while Foster was still in the hospital, an investigating agent visited him. Foster described the attack to the agent, named Owens as the attacker and identified Owens from an array of photographs. At the trial Foster recounted his activities on the day of the attack up to the time he was struck and said he clearly remembered identifying Owens as the attacker during the hospital interview. On cross-examination he admitted that he could not remember seeing his assailant, that he could not remember any of his hospital visitors except the agent, and that he did not remember whether any person suggested

---

[108] 474 U.S. 15 (1985).

[109] Although the Justices may not have realized it, absent nuclear DNA, which can be extracted from a hair root, hair evidence cannot be used to make a unique identification. This is the conclusion reached in what is the most thorough scientific review of forensic science done to date. (Committee on Identifying the Needs of the Forensic Sciences Community, National Research Council, Strengthening Forensic Science in the United States: A Path Forward, The National Academies Press (2009).) Even at the time of *Fensterer*, the idea that a confident identification could be made from two hairs was preposterous. (Problems with the statistical basis of hair evidence had been highlighted in a 1989 National Research Council report: *Fienberg*, S.E., ed. (1989). The Evolving Role of Statistical Assessments as Evidence in the Courts. Springer-Verlag, New York.)

[110] 484 U.S. 554 (1988).

that Owens was the attacker. Despite an attempt to refresh Foster's memory with hospital records, including one indicating that Foster had attributed the assault to someone other than Owens, Foster's said his memory was not jogged. The Court, speaking through Justice Scalia, held that there was no Confrontation Clause violation, reiterating the statement from *Fensterer* italicized above.

The problem with Justice Scalia's analysis is that, unless Foster feigned his memory loss and Owens was convicted on perjured testimony, Owens did not have an opportunity for effective cross-examination. All he could hope to show was what the jury knew from the direct examination—that Foster had once identified Owens but could no longer remember the circumstances of the identification. While it is true, as the Court pointed out, that the memory loss might itself call Foster's testimony into question, cross-examination was not needed to show this. *Owens* differs from *Fensterer* in that in *Fensterer* the witness's failure to record his method of examining the hair itself called the expert's competence into question and may have led the jury to wonder whether the witness's perception that the hair had been forcibly removed was accurate in the first instance. Moreover, the expert in *Fensterer* could have been cross-examined about his familiarity with or the deficiencies in each of the three ways that he might have proceeded. In *Owens*, the circumstances surrounding Foster's initial perception of the assailant and his mental state during the later identification could not be explored, although these are the issues that bear most directly on the accuracy of identifications.

A jury might reasonably have concluded that if Foster's memory was gone at the trial, it might also have been poor at the time of the identification, but since Owens was convicted, we have to assume that this was not his jury's conclusion. Moreover, Owens could not have done anything by means of cross-examination to persuade the jury that Foster's memory failure at trial meant that he had little memory when he made the hospital bed identification.[111] The fact that a different jury might have doubted Foster's identification and acquitted does not mean that Owens had an opportunity for an effective cross-examination. Hence, it seems that, for some Justices, placing a witness on the stand for whatever confrontation is possible ordinarily, and perhaps always,

---

[111] The Court points out that other deficiencies in Foster's testimony, such as a pre-existing animus against Owens, might be shown if they existed, but it ignores the utility of cross-examination on the case facts in uncovering or demonstrating bias. Moreover, the same could be said of *Davis* or *Olden*. In these cases, the fact that some ways of testing the witness's credibility existed did not mean that the preclusion of other ways posed no Confrontation Clause problems.

Owens is also problematic because Foster's statement was admitted under FRE 801(d)(1)(c), which provides that statements of prior identification are admissible only when the declarant is subject to cross-examination concerning the statement. See Chapter Six, pp. 767–770. It appears from the Court's holding that cross-examination that satisfies the Confrontation Clause is sufficient to satisfy FRE 801(d)(1), even though Congress seems to have intended an opportunity for a more meaningful cross-examination.

satisfies the Confrontation Clause.[112] Justice Scalia seems consistently to take this position. Interestingly, as we shall see in the next section, this position is not necessarily pro-prosecution. It can have implications that favor defendants' interests. Perhaps if *Crawford* had been decided before *Owens*, the defendant's inability to probe the substance of what was clearly testimonial hearsay would have counted for more.

Problem VII-8. Harlan Chandler, a former hit man who has turned state's evidence as part of a plea bargain to avoid the death penalty, is testifying in the trial of Joey Gallo, the reputed head of the local Mafia. When asked, "Who ordered you to kill Solomon Schwartz," Chandler replies, "Joey Gallo." He makes the same reply when asked who ordered two other murders he admitted committing. His direct examination concludes at the end of the trial day, and cross-examination is scheduled for the next day. That night Chandler suffers a heart attack and dies. The next day Gallo moves for a mistrial or, in the alternative, that Chandler's testimony be stricken from the record. **Should either of Gallo's motions be granted? Would your answer be different if Chandler, along with the detective he was handcuffed to, was gunned down from a speeding car as he left the courthouse?** Suppose, under either of these scenarios, the defense argued only that Chandler's statements that Gallo ordered the killings should be stricken. The defense argues that the statements do not indicate that Gallo personally told Chandler to commit the murders, and so they may be based on hearsay or even made up. The prosecutor argues that the answer should stand because the defense made no hearsay or personal knowledge objections when the answers were given. Gallo's attorney says that he did not object because he thought he could more effectively refute all of Chandler's testimony if he showed, on cross-examination, as he was confident he could do, that on such a crucial issue Chandler presented rumors and suppositions as if they were his own firsthand knowledge. **How should a court rule?** Assume the court allows Chandler's testimony to stand. **May Gallo call the state's attorney to testify to the plea bargain that had been made with Chandler? May Gallo present witnesses who will testify that Chandler often pretended to have inside knowledge that he did not have? Would your**

---

[112] Even after *Fensterer* and *Owens*, the question remains whether the state could use against a criminal defendant the testimony of a witness who, after testifying on direct examination, refused to answer questions on cross-examination. The standard procedure, as noted earlier, is to strike a witness's direct testimony when he refuses to be cross-examined on it, but suppose a court refused to strike. If the government played no part in securing the witness's refusal, *Fensterer* would seem to say that allowing the testimony would not violate the Confrontation Clause. However, this has long been seen as a situation in which the Confrontation Clause would preclude use of the evidence, and *Crawford*'s emphasis on the need for cross-examination when evidence is testimonial seems to strengthen this traditional approach.

answers to any of these questions be different if, by the time the trial had adjourned for the day, Chandler had withstood an intensive cross-examination with his credibility unshaken, but the cross-examination had not been concluded and the statements saying Gallo had ordered the murders had not yet been touched on? Would it make a difference if Chandler's credibility had been substantially shaken by the cross-examination that had occurred?

4. "Look Me in the Eye" Protection

The fourth type of protection that the Confrontation Clause gives to criminal defendants is what might be called "look me in the eye" protection. As a general rule the Confrontation Clause requires the state's witnesses in criminal trials to testify in the defendant's presence, so that the defendant can scrutinize the witness, and the witness cannot, except with difficulty observable by the jury, avoid looking at the defendant. Justice Scalia regards this right as being at the very core of the Confrontation Clause, and except perhaps where the defendant forfeits this right by behavior so obstreperous that a trial cannot continue in his presence,[113] he seems to treat the protection accorded by this right as close to absolute. Scalia is right to regard the "look me in the eye" aspect of the Confrontation Clause as one its central protections. Not only does this protection come closest to the literal definition of "confrontation," but at a time when most of the protections of the Confrontation Clause were unknown in English criminal procedure, the requirement that witnesses against the defendant testify orally in the defendant's presence was a central aspect of the English common law, and, as we have seen, the one Sir Walter Raleigh invoked when he demanded that the court "[c]all my accuser before my face." Yet even this protection is not absolute.

The current bounds of "look me in the eye" protection are defined by two cases, both of which involved state rules designed to protect child abuse victims from having to look at and/or feel they are being seen by those they are testifying against. In the first of these, *Coy v. Iowa*,[114] the trial court placed a large fabric screen between the child victim and the defendant, with lighting making the screen transparent from where the defendant sat but opaque from the victim's perspective. Thus victim and defendant sat in the same room, and the defendant could see the victim while she testified. The victim, however, could not see the defendant. The seemingly opaque screen blocked her view. The Court reversed Coy's

---

[113] See *Illinois v. Allen*, 397 U.S. 337 (1970), where the Court held that a trial judge's decision to remove a defendant from the courtroom and have him watch the proceedings by closed-circuit television did not violate the Confrontation Clause when the removal was due to the defendant's disruptive behavior.

[114] 487 U.S. 1012 (1988).

conviction, holding that the state's effort to block the victim's view of the defendant violated the Confrontation Clause.

In so holding, Justice Scalia was eloquent. He wrote:

> The Sixth Amendment gives a criminal defendant the right "to be confronted with the witnesses against him." This language "comes to us on faded parchment, with a lineage that traces back to the beginnings of Western legal culture. There are indications that a right of confrontation existed under Roman law. The Roman Governor Festus, discussing the proper treatment of his prisoner, Paul, stated: "It is not the manner of the Romans to deliver any man up to die before the accused has met his accusers face to face, and has been given a chance to defend himself against the charges." Acts 25:16. . . .
>
> Most of this Court's encounters with the Confrontation Clause have involved either the admissibility of out-of-court statements, or restrictions on the scope of cross-examination. The reason for that is not, as the State suggests, that these elements are the essence of the Clause's protection—but rather, quite to the contrary, that there is at least some room for doubt (and hence litigation) as to the extent to which the Clause includes those elements, whereas, as Justice Harlan put it, "[s]imply as a matter of English" it confers at least "a right to meet face to face all those who appear and give evidence at trial." Simply as a matter of Latin as well, since the word "confront" ultimately derives from the prefix "con-" (from "contra" meaning "against" or "opposed") and the noun "frons" (forehead). . . .
>
> We have never doubted, therefore, that the Confrontation Clause guarantees the defendant a face-to-face meeting with witnesses appearing before the trier of fact. . . .
>
> President Eisenhower once described face-to-face confrontation as part of the code of his home town of Abilene, Kansas. In Abilene, he said, it was necessary to "[m]eet anyone face to face with whom you disagree. You could not sneak up on him from behind, or do any damage to him, without suffering the penalty of an outraged citizenry. . . . In this country, if someone dislikes you, or accuses you, he must come up in front. He cannot hide behind the shadow." The phrase still persists, "Look me in the eye and say that." Given these human feelings of what is necessary for fairness, the right of confrontation "contributes to the establishment of a system of criminal justice in which the perception as well as the reality of fairness prevails."
>
> . . . The Confrontation Clause does not, of course, compel the witness to fix his eyes upon the defendant; he may studiously

look elsewhere, but the trier of fact will draw its own conclusions. Thus the right to face-to-face confrontation serves much the same purpose as a less explicit component of the Confrontation Clause that we have had more frequent occasion to discuss—the right to cross-examine the accuser; both "ensur[e] the integrity of the fact-finding process."   The State can hardly gainsay the profound effect upon a witness of standing in the presence of the person the witness accuses, since that is the very phenomenon it relies upon to establish the potential "trauma" that allegedly justified the extraordinary procedure in the present case.   That face-to-face presence may, unfortunately, upset the truthful rape victim or abused child; but by the same token it may confound and undo the false accuser, or reveal the child coached by a malevolent adult.   It is a truism that constitutional protections have costs.[115]

Despite Justice Scalia's eloquence, it was clear when *Coy* was handed down that it would not be the last word on the right to physical confrontation.   Justices O'Connor and White, whose concurrences were necessary for the *Coy* majority, emphasized in a separate opinion written by Justice O'Connor, that even at its core the right to confrontation was not absolute.   O'Connor pointed out that Iowa's use of a screen to shield an abuse victim from the trauma of regarding an alleged assailant was idiosyncratic, and she strongly suggested that if instead the court had used closed-circuit television to achieve this goal, the Confrontation Clause would not stand in the way.   In *Maryland v. Craig* [116]   Justice O'Connor's view prevailed by a single vote.

MARYLAND V. CRAIG
497 U.S. 836 (1990).

JUSTICE O'CONNOR delivered the opinion of the Court.   This case requires us to decide whether the Confrontation Clause of the Sixth Amendment categorically prohibits a child witness in a child abuse case from testifying against a defendant at trial, outside the defendant's physical presence, by one-way closed-circuit television.

I

In October 1986, a Howard County grand jury charged respondent, Sandra Ann Craig, with child abuse, first and second degree sexual offenses, perverted sexual practice, assault, and battery.   The named victim in each count was Brooke Etze, a six-year-old child who, from August 1984 to June 1986, had attended a kindergarten and prekindergarten center owned and operated by Craig.

---

[115] Id. at 1015–1020.

[116] 497 U.S. 836 (1990).

In March 1987, before the case went to trial, the State sought to invoke a Maryland statutory procedure that permits a judge to receive, by one-way closed-circuit television, the testimony of a child witness who is alleged to be a victim of child abuse. To invoke the procedure, the trial judge must first "determin[e] that testimony by the child victim in the courtroom will result in the child suffering serious emotional distress such that the child cannot reasonably communicate." Once the procedure is invoked, the child witness, prosecutor, and defense counsel withdraw to a separate room; the judge, jury, and defendant remain in the courtroom. The child witness is then examined and cross-examined in the separate room, while a video monitor records and displays the witness' testimony to those in the courtroom. During this time the witness cannot see the defendant. The defendant remains in electronic communication with defense counsel, and objections may be made and ruled on as if the witness were testifying in the courtroom.

In support of its motion ... the State presented expert testimony that Brooke, as well as a number of other children who were alleged to have been sexually abused by Craig, would suffer "serious emotional distress such that [they could not] reasonably communicate," if required to testify in the courtroom.... Craig objected to the use of the procedure on Confrontation Clause grounds, but the trial court rejected that contention, concluding that although the statute "take[s] away the right of the defendant to be face to face with his or her accuser," the defendant retains the "essence of the right of confrontation," including the right to observe, cross-examine, and have the jury view the demeanor of the witness. The trial court further found that, "based upon the evidence presented ... the testimony of each of these children in a courtroom will result in each child suffering serious emotional distress ... such that each of these children cannot reasonably communicate." ...

The Court of Appeals of Maryland reversed and remanded for a new trial. The Court of Appeals rejected Craig's argument that the Confrontation Clause requires in all cases a face-to-face courtroom encounter between the accused and his accusers, but concluded: "[U]nder § 9-102(a)(1)(ii), ... [u]nless prevention of 'eyeball-to-eyeball' confrontation is necessary to obtain the trial testimony of the child, the defendant cannot be denied that right."

. . .

II

We observed in Coy v. Iowa that "the Confrontation Clause guarantees the defendant a face-to-face meeting with witnesses appearing before the trier of fact." ...

We have never held, however, that the Confrontation Clause guarantees criminal defendants the absolute right to a face-to-face meeting with witnesses against them at trial. Indeed, in Coy v. Iowa, we expressly "le[ft] for another day ... the question whether any exceptions exist" to the "irreducible literal meaning of the Clause: 'a right to meet face to face all those who appear and give evidence at trial.'"... We concluded that "[s]ince there ha[d] been no individualized findings that these particular witnesses needed special protection, the judgment [in *Coy*] could not be sustained by any conceivable exception." Because the trial court in this case made individualized findings that each of the child witnesses needed special protection, this case requires us to decide the question reserved in Coy.

. . .

[T]he right guaranteed by the Confrontation Clause includes not only a "personal examination," but also "(1) insures that the witness will give his statements under oath—thus impressing him with the seriousness of the matter and guarding against the lie by the possibility of a penalty for perjury; (2) forces the witness to submit to cross-examination, the 'greatest legal engine ever invented for the discovery of truth'; [and] (3) permits the jury that is to decide the defendant's fate to observe the demeanor of the witness in making his statement, thus aiding the jury in assessing his credibility."

The combined effect of these elements of confrontation—physical presence, oath, cross-examination, and observation of demeanor by the trier of fact serves the purposes of the Confrontation Clause by ensuring that evidence admitted against an accused is reliable and subject to the rigorous adversarial testing that is the norm of Anglo-American criminal proceedings.

. . .

In sum, our precedents establish that "the Confrontation Clause reflects a preference for face-to-face confrontation at trial," a preference that "must occasionally give way to considerations of public policy and the necessities of the case." ... Thus, though we reaffirm the importance of face-to-face confrontation with witnesses appearing at trial, we cannot say that such confrontation is an indispensable element of the Sixth Amendment's guarantee of the right to confront one's accusers.

. . .

That the face-to-face confrontation requirement is not absolute does not, of course, mean that it may easily be dispensed with. As we suggested in Coy, our precedents confirm that a defendant's right to confront accusatory witnesses may be satisfied absent a physical, face-to-face confrontation at trial only where denial of such confrontation is necessary to further an important public policy and only where the reliability of the testimony is otherwise assured.

III

Maryland's statutory procedure, when invoked, prevents a child witness from seeing the defendant as he or she testifies against the defendant at trial . . . [but] Maryland's procedure preserves all of the other elements of the confrontation right: the child witness must be competent to testify and must testify under oath; the defendant retains full opportunity for contemporaneous cross-examination; and the judge, jury, and defendant are able to view (albeit by video monitor) the demeanor (and body) of the witness as he or she testifies. . . . These safeguards of reliability and adversariness render the use of such a procedure a far cry from the undisputed prohibition of the Confrontation Clause: trial by ex parte affidavit or inquisition, . . .

[T]hese assurances of reliability and adversariness are far greater than those required for admission of hearsay testimony under the Confrontation Clause. We are therefore confident that use of the one-way closed-circuit television procedure, where necessary to further an important state interest, does not impinge upon the truth-seeking or symbolic purposes of the Confrontation Clause.

The critical inquiry in this case, therefore, is whether use of the procedure is necessary to further an important state interest. . . .

We have of course recognized that a State's interest in "the protection of minor victims of sex crimes from further trauma and embarrassment" is a "compelling" one. . . .

We likewise conclude today that a State's interest in the physical and psychological well-being of child abuse victims may be sufficiently important to outweigh, at least in some cases, a defendant's right to face his or her accusers in court. That a significant majority of States has enacted statutes to protect child witnesses from the trauma of giving testimony in child abuse cases attests to the widespread belief in the importance of such a public policy. . . . Thirty-seven States, for example, permit the use of videotaped testimony of sexually abused children; 24 States have authorized the use of one-way closed-circuit television testimony in child abuse cases; and 8 States authorize the use of a two-way system. . . .

Accordingly, we hold that, if the State makes an adequate showing of necessity, the state interest in protecting child witnesses from the trauma of testifying in a child abuse case is sufficiently important to justify the use of a special procedure that permits a child witness in such cases to testify at trial against a defendant in the absence of face-to-face confrontation with the defendant.

The requisite finding of necessity must of course be a case-specific one: the trial court must hear evidence and determine whether use of the one-way closed-circuit television procedure is necessary to protect the welfare of the particular child witness who seeks to testify. . . . The trial court must also find that the child witness would be traumatized, not by the courtroom generally, but by the presence of the defendant. . . . Finally, the trial court must find that the emotional distress suffered by the child witness in the presence of the defendant is . . . more than "mere nervousness or excitement or some reluctance to testify." [T]he Maryland statute, which requires a determination that the child witness will suffer "serious emotional distress such that the child cannot reasonably communicate," clearly suffices to meet constitutional standards.

. . .

In sum, we conclude that where necessary to protect a child witness from trauma that would be caused by testifying in the physical presence of the defendant, at least where such trauma would impair the child's ability to communicate, the Confrontation Clause does not prohibit use of a procedure that, despite the absence of face-to-face confrontation, ensures the reliability of the evidence by subjecting it to rigorous adversarial testing and thereby preserves the essence of effective confrontation. . . .

[In Part IV of the opinion, which is omitted, the Court held that the Confrontation Clause does not require the trial court to attempt to question a child witness in the defendant's presence before resorting to closed circuit television, nor does it require the trial court to find that the use of two-way closed-circuit television (both the witness and the defendant see the other on a TV) would cause the witness severe emotional distress as a precondition to using one-way closed-circuit television.]

JUSTICE SCALIA, with whom JUSTICE BRENNAN, JUSTICE MARSHALL, and JUSTICE STEVENS join, dissenting.

. . .

I

According to the Court, "we cannot say that [face-to-face] confrontation [with witnesses appearing at trial] is an indispensable element of the Sixth Amendment's guarantee of the right to confront one's accusers." . . . The Court makes the impossible plausible by recharacterizing the Confrontation Clause, so that confrontation (redesignated "face-to-face confrontation") becomes only one of many "elements of confrontation." The reasoning is as follows: The Confrontation Clause guarantees not only what it explicitly provides for—"face-to-face" confrontation—but also implied and collateral rights such as cross-examination, oath, and observation of demeanor (TRUE); the purpose of this entire cluster of rights is to ensure the reliability of evidence (TRUE); the Maryland procedure preserves the implied and collateral rights (TRUE), which adequately ensure the reliability of evidence (perhaps TRUE); therefore the Confrontation Clause is not violated by denying what it explicitly provides for— "face-to-face" confrontation (unquestionably FALSE). This reasoning abstracts from the right to its purposes, and then eliminates the right. It is wrong because the Confrontation Clause does not guarantee reliable evidence; it guarantees specific trial procedures that were thought to assure reliable evidence, undeniably among which was "face-to-face" confrontation. . . .

II

. . .

Unwillingness [to testify] cannot be a valid excuse under the Confrontation Clause, whose very object is to place the witness under the sometimes hostile glare of the defendant. "That face-to-face presence may, unfortunately, upset the truthful rape victim or abused child; but by the same token it may confound and undo the false accuser, or reveal the child coached by a malevolent adult."

. . .

III

. . .

The "special" reasons that exist for suspending one of the usual guarantees of reliability in the case of children's testimony are perhaps matched by "special" reasons for being particularly insistent upon it in the case of children's testimony. Some studies show that children are substantially more vulnerable to suggestion than adults, and often unable to separate recollected fantasy (or suggestion) from reality. The injustice their erroneous testimony can produce is evidenced by the tragic Scott County investigations of 1983–1984, which disrupted the lives of many (as far as we know) innocent people in the small town of Jordan, Minnesota. At one stage those investigations were pursuing allegations by at least eight children of multiple murders, but the prosecutions actually initiated charged only sexual abuse. Specifically, 24 adults were charged with molesting 37 children. In the course of the investigations, 25 children were placed in foster homes. Of the 24 indicted defendants, one pleaded guilty, two were acquitted at trial, and the charges against the remaining 21 were voluntarily dismissed. . . . A report by the Minnesota Attorney General's office . . . concluded that there was an "absence of credible testimony and [a] lack of significant corroboration" to support reinstitution of sex-abuse charges, and "no credible evidence of murders." . . . Children were interrogated repeatedly, in some cases as many as 50 times; answers were suggested by telling the children what other witnesses had said; and children (even some who did not at first complain of abuse) were separated from their parents for months.

. . .

The value of the confrontation right in guarding against a child's distorted or coerced recollections is dramatically evident with respect to one of the misguided investigative techniques the report cited: some children were told by their foster parents that reunion with their real parents would be hastened by "admission" of their parents' abuse. Is it difficult to imagine how unconvincing such a testimonial admission might be to a jury that witnessed the child's delight at seeing his parents in the courtroom? Or how devastating it might be if, pursuant to a psychiatric evaluation that "trauma would impair the child's ability to communicate" in front of his parents, the child were permitted to tell his story to the jury on closed-circuit television?

In the last analysis, however, this debate is not an appropriate one. I have no need to defend the value of confrontation, because the Court has no authority to question it. It is not within our charge to speculate that, "where face-to-face confrontation causes significant emotional distress in a child witness," confrontation might "in fact disserve the Confrontation Clause's truth-seeking goal." If so, that is a defect in the Constitution—which should be amended by the procedures provided for such an eventuality, but cannot be corrected by judicial pronouncement that it is archaic, contrary to "widespread belief" and thus null and void. For good or bad, the Sixth Amendment requires confrontation, and we are not at liberty to ignore it.

An interesting feature of the Court's opinion in *Craig* is how Justice O'Connor transforms the apparent concern of the Maryland legislature—that children would be so traumatized by the defendant's presence that they could not testify—to the concern that seems to have most troubled her—that children would suffer traumatically by being forced to confront the defendant. This transformation has important implications for the Court's holding. If the primary concern is that the defendant's presence will inhibit testimony, the best way to determine this is to see whether the child can testify in court, and only if she cannot to allow testimony over closed-circuit television. If, however, the concern is to spare the child the trauma of confronting an abuser, exposing the child to the defendant to see if she is traumatized could cause the very harm the procedures are designed to prevent.[117]

Craig is also interesting in that both the majority and dissenting opinions are based on unproven empirical suppositions. The majority believes that abused children will be traumatized not by the courtroom experience in general, but by the presence of the defendant in that setting and that psychologists can tell courts which children are likely to experience trauma. The dissent, on the other hand, thinks that face-to-face encounters between witnesses and defendants can help elicit truth. Neither of these propositions has been proven by empirical research or is self-evidentially correct.[118] Moreover, the majority's arguments implicitly assume that the defendant was an abuser, while the dissent's arguments assume that she was not. The presumption of innocence might suggest that the dissent is on firmer ground here, but, as in *O'Neil* and *Owens,* Confrontation Clause jurisprudence can leave innocent defendants with no effective weapons to prove their claims.

Even the *Craig* majority regards the Maryland procedures as hard to justify under the Confrontation Clause. Thus, there is a question about how far this precedent may be pushed. The majority seems motivated in part by its image of the psychological vulnerability of young children. It is not clear that *Craig* will support similar procedures designed to protect teen-age or adult sex crime victims from the trauma of in-court confrontations with their assailants. Yet older victims may suffer as much as younger ones by the proximity of their abusers, and since older victims may more reliably identify their assailants, accepting Justice Scalia's analysis suggests that less will be gained from confrontation in these cases.

---

[117] On remand the Maryland Court of Appeals persisted in its focus on what it saw as the fundamental question under Maryland law: whether the children would be able to testify. It again reversed, holding that before concluding that the children would be unable to testify because of trauma, the trial judge should have interviewed them. The prosecutor declined to retry Ms. Craig, citing parental desires to avoid subjecting their children to another trial, and counts involving 12 alleged incidents were dropped. Perhaps this was because while the case was on appeal, the hysteria that had swept the country about day care child abuse had subsided and elsewhere some cases had been dropped or convictions overturned. Ms. Craig claimed traumas of her own. She and her husband lost their house, felt forced to move out of state and exhausted their savings after having spent $200,000 on her initial defense. (An attorney who later entered the case said he did $350,000 worth of legal work for her *pro bono* because he believed her innocent.) At a news conference following the Maryland Court's reversal on remand, she described her experience this way: "It was sad. It was like living and walking through a nightmare and I was yelling for help and nobody heard." It is impossible for us to know whether Ms. Craig was guilty or not, but according to news reports a $1.2 billion civil case that 13 of the children in her care brought against her in 1987 was settled for $900 a child.

[118] On these issues see Ralph Underwager and Hollida Wakefield, Poor Psychology Produces Poor Law, 16 Law & Human Behavior 233 (1992); Gail Goodman, Murray Levine & Gary Melton, The Best Evidence Produces the Best Law, 16 Law & Human Behavior 244 (1992). The authors of these articles, several of whom helped write an amicus brief for the American Psychological Association supporting the Maryland procedure, differ on the accuracy and propriety of the American Psychological Association's amicus participation in *Craig.*

Whether *Crawford* and its progeny have implications for *Craig* is unclear. The thrust of Scalia's position in *Crawford* is consistent with the theme that underlies his dissent in *Craig*, that when the Confrontation Clause applies, it guarantees certain modes of procedure regardless of other concerns and values. No one disputes that the Confrontation Clause applies to the *Craig* situation, and today's Court might well have come out differently.

Problem VII–9. Candace Kline, a 31-year-old rape victim, tells the prosecutor that, as much as she would like to see the man who raped her brought to justice, she can't bear the idea of being in proximity to him, and will not testify if she has to be in the same room. The prosecutor asks the judge to allow Kline to testify from another room by two-way closed circuit television (meaning she could see the defendant and vice versa by looking at a monitor) or to place the defendant in the other room and let him watch Kline testify before the jury using a similar television arrangement. In either case, the defendant and his attorney would be able to converse privately by cell phone. The defendant argues that either procedure violates his rights under the Confrontation Clause. **How should the court rule? Does it matter if a psychiatrist testifies that Candace suffers post-traumatic stress disorder and could suffer serious, perhaps permanent, mental harm if forced to be in the same room as her alleged assailant? If the psychiatrist doesn't forecast serious harm, but opines that nerves will render Candace speechless or incoherent if the defendant is present? If the judge is willing to grant some relief, may the defense insist on determining who is in the courtroom with the jury and who is present via closed circuit? Do your answers to any of these questions change if Candace is 11 years old rather than 31? If the charge were not rape but spouse abuse and the defendant had allegedly battered Candace for three years? Would the defendant have cause to complain if rather than being placed in another room he was made to stand at the back of the courtroom behind the spectators while Candace testified? Suppose to give Candace a sense of security the judge had the defendant handcuffed and had a police officer sit next to him during Candace's testimony. Would this violate the defendant's Confrontation Clause or other rights?**

"What's so great about due process? Due process got me ten years."

C. CONCLUSION

We have seen in this section that the Confrontation Clause offers defendants four different kinds of protection. *First*, it can protect defendants from harmful inferences from evidence that is not technically offered against them and would be inadmissible hearsay if it were. The Court seems willing to extend this protection when, as in *Douglas*, a prosecutor seems to be offering evidence solely for its impermissible inferences. Moreover, in a joint trial, if the state wishes to offer the statements of a non-testifying codefendant against that codefendant, it must redact the offered statement so that it does not directly implicate another codefendant in the crime. If, however, a codefendant whose statement is offered testifies, the Court finds the demands of the Confrontation Clause satisfied by the formal opportunity that one defendant has to question the other. This ignores the reality of joint defenses and the futility of cross-examining if the making of a statement is denied, but a majority of the Court seems untroubled by these real world contingencies.[119]

Second, the Confrontation Clause prohibits the admission of some hearsay when then speaker cannot be cross-examined. The key is whether the hearsay is testimonial in nature, but what hearsay is testimonial has not yet been fully defined. At a minimum, however, testimonial hearsay seems to include grand jury testimony, *ex parte* affidavits including formal reports by forensic scientists and accomplice confessions in law enforcement contexts. Whether the Clause's protections extend to information the police solicit to aid in their investigations appears context dependent. Statements made shortly after a crime has been committed appear unlikely to be protected if a colorable claim can be made that the person on the loose poses a serious threat to public safety. Some statements made to people acting as surrogates for the police or with a responsibility to report to legal authority are likely to be treated as testimonial as perhaps will statements made to a person's friends and acquaintances for transmittal to the police. The Supreme Court has not, however, explored these boundaries. Even when hearsay is testimonial in nature, the right to confrontation may be forfeited. But so long as *Giles* is good law, simple responsibility for a witness's absence (as when it appears that the defendant has killed a declarant) will not by itself result in forfeiture. Some intent to preclude the declarant's testimony must have motivated the crime. Still to be decided are the standards by which forfeiture may be proved. Non-testimonial hearsay appears, after *Davis* to enjoy no Confrontation Clause protection, but it is possible that the Due Process Clause will be read to preclude the introduction of some unreliable hearsay. When a hearsay declarant is placed under oath, testifies in court and is offered to the other side for cross-examination, *Owens* indicates that Confrontation Clause requirements are, without more, satisfied.[120]

Third, the Confrontation Clause can be used to overturn restrictions on cross-examination even when the restrictions support legitimate state policies, at least in the context of impeachment for bias. We cannot, however, conclude that no state policies can justify restrictions on relevant exculpatory cross-examination. Rape shield statutes are an area where law and practice are to the contrary.

Where a defendant's ability to cross-examine effectively is hampered not by state action but by some condition of the witness, such as poor

---

[119] After *Williams* when a codefendant does not testify and his confession is admitted *only against him* one may ask whether redaction is still required, for the *Williams* plurality made much of the fact that the Cellmark Report had not been admitted into evidence, and in these circumstance the confession will not have been introduced against the accused codefendant. We find it doubtful that the rule will change in these circumstances, but the possibility is there.

[120] It is possible that the Court might view the situation differently if the declarant witness did not recall making the hearsay statement or if the witness could not understand the questions asked.

memory, offering either her trial testimony or otherwise admissible hearsay seems to pose no Confrontation Clause problems. Thus a prosecutor may offer a witness whose damaging testimony cannot be undercut by a defense cross-examination because she is unable to remember the context in which her observations were made. However, some exceptional circumstances, such as a witness's refusal to respond on cross-examination, may require the exclusion of testimony on Confrontation Clause grounds, even where the state has not interfered with the opportunity for cross-examination.

Finally, the Confrontation Clause ordinarily requires witnesses to testify in a setting in which a defendant and witness can regard each other face to face. In special circumstances, however, such as cases of alleged child sexual abuse, even this protection is not absolute.

It is difficult to predict how Confrontation Clause jurisprudence will develop from here, particularly since important cases have often been decided by bare majorities, and trends in interpretation have shifted with judicial appointments. A particularly interesting question is whether reliability will ever again be an important consideration in assessing the admissibility of hearsay evidence, either, under the Confrontation or the Due Process Clause. There are a signs that some Justices may not subscribe to the language in *Davis,* which indicates that neither *Roberts* nor any other test is available to contest the admission of nontestimonial hearsay, no matter how unreliable it may seem. At the moment formalism and what is arguably a discredited originalism prevail in interpretations of the Confrontation Clause. But the formalism and originalism are not excessively rigid, and it appears that certain kinds of hearsay which good faith applications of the *Roberts* test might not have excluded, in particular grand jury testimony and accomplice confessions to the police, are now without question inadmissible if offered against the accused in criminal cases.

ADDITIONAL PROBLEMS

Problem VII-10. Ok Lee, the wealthy owner of Lee's Auto Leasing, is charged in the state of Indiana with sideswiping a pedestrian and knowingly leaving the scene of an accident. She is also being sued by the alleged victim for substantial damages. The state's evidence includes an employee of Lee's who will testify that the day after the accident he removed a dent in the side of her car's right front fender and did some touch-up painting, and an expert who testifies that a fleck of red paint found on the victim's clothes is consistent with the paint on the red Buick convertible Lee drives. In addition, the victim testifies that the car that hit her was a large red convertible with its top down that could have been a Buick or an Oldsmobile, and she is sure Lee was the driver. As its final witness, the state wants to introduce a teenager, Kareem Johnston, who will testify that he was standing on a corner a block from the accident when someone, whom he later learned was named Ellen Dannin, came running up to the corner and yelled at a red convertible parked at a stoplight, "Lady, you just hit a woman, the least you can do is turn around and take her to the hospital." The woman in the car, whom Kareem feels he can identify as the defendant, turned around, looked at Dannin and, noticing the light had turned green, grinned and sped off.

When Lee objected to Johnston's evidence, the judge asked the prosecutor where Dannin was. The prosecutor said that he had contacted Dannin, who had moved to San Diego three weeks before the trial and asked her if she could come to Indiana for the trial. Dannin had said she couldn't afford the plane ticket and the salary she would lose by missing work. Therefore, the prosecutor said, she was offering the evidence only to show that Lee had reason to believe she had hit someone and not as evidence that she had actually hit the victim. The judge admitted the evidence for this purpose and instructed the jury that they were to consider Johnston's testimony only for its bearing on Lee's knowledge, and they should not treat it as evidence that Lee had in fact hit someone.

Lee, in her defense, testified that she was nowhere near the place of the accident on the day and time in question but was in a park walking her dog. Her witnesses include her housemaid, who testified that Lee drove off with her dog, a Saint Bernard, on the night in question and that anyone who saw Lee in the car would have been sure to have seen the dog, and the manager of her leasing company, who testified that he noticed a dent in the fender of Lee's car at least two days before the accident.

Lee was convicted. She appealed, claiming that the admission of Kareem's testimony violated her rights under the Confrontation Clause. **Should Lee prevail on appeal? Does anything turn on whether the trial was to a judge rather than to a jury?**

Problem VII-11. On August 7, 1982, Frank Head, the district attorney of Piedmont County, was killed when dynamite wired to the ignition system of his car exploded. A lengthy investigation culminated in the arrest of four people: Black, Shay, Pine and Stark. Shay and Black pled guilty to murder while Pine was convicted after trial. At Stark's trial, evidence was introduced that he, Pine and Black were involved in a conspiracy to distribute liquor illegally in Piedmont County, and that Head, at the time of his death, had been acting vigorously to break up the conspiracy. Head had seized large quantities of illegal alcohol, padlocked a building owned by Stark and filed criminal charges that resulted in fines of more than $100,000. There is also evidence that Stark is the leader of the conspiracy to distribute liquor and that Pine is his lieutenant and "enforcer." It appears that, on occasion, Stark was referred to by the conspirators as the "old man," and that he was known in some portions of the community by this sobriquet.

The only evidence that linked Stark to the conspiracy to murder Head, other than the evidence establishing motive, was the testimony of Shay. Shay said that he was approached by Pine and offered $5,000 if he would murder Head. He declined, saying he wanted at least $7,500. Pine responded saying he did not think "the old man" would pay more than $5,000 but that he would inquire. According to Shay, Pine returned an hour later, saying, "The old man won't go up anymore, but I'll add $500 to make it $5,500." Shay accepted the offer. Shay also testified that at one time he thought of pulling out, but Black told him that if he backed out, the "old man" would have "something done" to him and his family. Shay admitted on cross-examination that, other than what Pine told him, he knew nothing as to Stark's "having any connection" with the money given to him by Pine and that he had never had any contact with Stark regarding the killing. Shay's testimony reporting what Pine and Black had told him was admitted against Stark as a co-conspirator's admission. The state never called Pine or Black. Had Stark called them to offer testimony in his defense he would have forfeited his right under state law to make the last closing argument to the jury. Stark appealed his conviction for murder, claiming that his right to confrontation had been denied. **Should an appellate court reverse Stark's conviction?** Suppose the reported dialogue occurred not with Shay but with Smith, a police officer working undercover when approached by Pine. Assume that after hearing Pine's offer, Smith had asked to meet with the "old man" seeking to achieve a positive identification of Stark before arresting him but rather than arrange the meeting Pine had paid Shay to kill Head. **Would Smith be able to testify to what Pine had told him? Would your answer be different if Pine had approached Smith at the police station, revealed the plot, said he now regretted being the conduit of the money to Shay, and offered to "set up" Stark if his (Pine's) involvement in the plot were forgiven, but as they were talking the dynamite exploded?**

Problem VII-12. Harry Gebippe is charged with selling cocaine to an undercover police officer, Jane Kane, on the afternoon of September 2, 2013, while she was posing as a law student. Harry denies that the sale took place, and claims he was bird watching in Yellowwood State Forest at the time. The following facts are pertinent.

Adam Bentley and Cliff Davis were sitting in Nick's Coffee Shop on September 2 in the late afternoon when two cops came running up with guns drawn, pointed at the table next to them and yelled for everyone to freeze. One cop grabbed a guy sitting at the next table, threw him against the wall and took out a pair of handcuffs. Davis, while they attempted to cuff the guy, said, "My God, they've grabbed Gebippe. He's in my evidence class." Suddenly, the man being cuffed broke free, and escaped. Later Gebippe was arrested.

Kane, the undercover officer, died of a gunshot wound shortly before Gebippe's trial and soon after reporting a threat that if she didn't leave the jurisdiction, she would regret it. In a statement written on September 3, Kane described the September 2 cocaine purchase, saying that after securing the cocaine, she had pointed out the seller to the two cops who attempted the arrest and that the person whom the cops attempted to handcuff, whose name she did not know, was the person who sold her the cocaine. She described the seller as about 5 feet, 10 inches tall, about 170 pounds in weight, said he was a law student who had blond hair and blue eyes. The state offers this report under FRE 804(b)(5), and the judge, after finding it more likely than not that Gebippe was responsible for the officer's unavailability ("because no one else had a motive"), admits the report. **Have Gebippe's rights under the Confrontation Clause been violated? Does it matter that Gebippe is a blond, blue-eyed law student who is 5 feet 11 inches and weighs 180 pounds?** To nail down the identification, the prosecution, after admitting the officer's report, places Adam Bentley on the stand; he testifies to what Davis said. Gebippe objects on Confrontation Clause grounds. **Should Bentley's testimony be allowed? Would the situation be different if after the suspect had escaped one of the cops had asked Bentley and Davis if they knew who the escapee was and Davis had replied, "I think his name is Gebippe"? If Davis testifies that he remembers telling the officer that it was Gebippe who fled but the more he has thought about it the less certain he is, would his hearsay be admitted? If Davis's hearsay is admitted, could Gebippe be convicted if that and Kane's reports are the state's only evidence that Gebippe was the seller? Would your answer be different if the report had not described the seller beyond saying that he was a law student?**

Problem VII-13. Payne, who pled guilty to a conspiracy to pass counterfeit money, is called by the government as a witness in the trial of his brother for the same conspiracy. At the trial Payne claims to remember neither the event nor his guilty plea, and he states that he can neither confirm nor deny making a statement he allegedly gave to a federal agent several months before the trial. Payne explains his failure of memory by saying that he had a fall that caused memory problems, that he has recently been a patient at a state mental hospital, and that he is still on medication prescribed by psychiatrists at the hospital. The state then calls a federal agent who testifies that Payne admitted his involvement in the conspiracy in a statement given to the agent and that in that statement Payne also implicated his brother. The agent testifies further that at the time of the statement Payne seemed to be in good health and his memory seemed to be much better than it is at the trial.

The statement itself is in the agent's handwriting and unsigned. The agent explains that this is because the interview with Payne had to be terminated prematurely when Payne complained of dizzy spells and lapses of memory. The prosecutor then asks the agent to read the statement to the jury. At this point, the defendant, Payne's brother, objects, claiming that the statement is inadmissible hearsay under both the Federal Rules and the common law and that if the statement were admissible under some hearsay exception, its introduction would nonetheless violate the Confrontation Clause. **How should a court rule on the issues the defendant raises?**

Problem VII-14. Kienlen is charged with bank robbery. He presents an insanity defense. His chief witness is Dr. Gonzales, the psychiatrist who admitted him to State Mental Hospital three months before the robbery. Dr. Gonzales testifies that, in his opinion, Kienlen was suffering at the time of the robbery from a psychosis, which left him, at best, in tenuous contact with reality. The psychiatrist also testifies that, after reaching his conclusion, he examined the discharge records concerning Kienlen's various stays at State Hospital. On cross-examination the prosecutor reads to Dr. Gonzales from records, including discharge records, made during Kienlen's previous stays in the hospital. The general import of the records is that Kienlen was never diagnosed as psychotic while in the hospital, that his problem was poor social adjustment, and that he used hospitalization as a way to escape responsibility. After reading from each record, the prosecutor asks Dr. Gonzales whether the information in that record causes him to change his opinion, and the doctor responds in each instance that it does not. Counsel for the defendant objects to the reading of these letters on Confrontation Clause grounds. The trial judge overrules the objection, stating that he will instruct the jury to use the information only for impeachment purposes. Kienlen is convicted and appeals on Confrontation Clause grounds. **How should an appellate court rule? Are there procedures available that will permit adequate cross-examination of the witness?**

Problem VII-15. Wilma V., a four year old child, identifies the defendant, her Uncle Ray, when asked to "point to the person who touched you in a private place." When asked where Uncle Ray asked her to touch him, she murmurs "on his thing." Ray's attorney begins his cross-examination by saying to Wilma, "Now Wilma, I want you to look at your Uncle Ray, look him right in the eye." Wilma looks at her Uncle and begins crying. After that she won't say another word, and after ten minutes during which the judge, both attorneys and a psychologist who is present asked her to testify, she is taken from the stand in tears. Ray moves that Wilma's testimony be stricken. **How should the judge rule? Would it make a difference if Wilma's reticence had been triggered not by the cross-examination, but by the prosecutor's inquiry into yet more intimate details of what had occurred? If it**

were triggered by the prosecutor asking Wilma to look her uncle in the eye? If Wilma was 6 years old? 9 years old? 15 years old? Suppose before ever placing Wilma on the stand the prosecutor asks the court to allow Wilma to testify via closed-circuit television. He argues that it is common knowledge that a four-year old will be traumatized and most likely will be unable to testify coherently if forced to testify in the same room as the person who abused her and to look him in the eye. The prosecutor adds that he had arranged to have a child psychiatrist who had examined Wilma come to court to testify to these facts but the psychiatrist had had a family emergency that precluded his testifying. **If the judge grant's the prosecution's motion to have Wilma testify from another room via closed-circuit television have Ray's Confrontation Clause rights been violated? Would your answer be different if the judge had prefaced his decision by saying he knew the prosecution would not misreport what the psychiatrist had told him, and the defense counsel remained silent when the judge, following these remarks, asked her to speak up if she thought the prosecutor would lie?**

Problem VII-16. During the cross-examination of David Dan, who had allegedly been assaulted in a bar by Ted Anton, a former friend of his, the following occurred.

Defense Counsel: Mr. Dan, I noticed that not once in this cross-examination and at no time during the direct examination have you looked at Ten Anton, the defendant in this case. Can you tell the jury why this is?

Mr. Dan: The prosecutor told me that I didn't have to look at him if looking at him would make me nervous, and frankly it makes me very nervous.

Defense Counsel: Mr. Dan, I would like you to turn toward Mr. Anton now and look him right in the eye as you repeat your claims that he attacked you first and that you never pulled a knife.

Mr. Dan: [turning toward the judge] Your Honor, do I have to?

What should the judge say? Are any of Anton's constitutional rights violated if the judge answers "no" and Anton continues to look away?

Problem VII-17. Floyd Jones is on trial for a sexual assault on his young son, Colin, who was 3 1/2 years old at the time of the alleged assault. Colin's mother, Carol, testified at trial: "Floyd left Colin off rather early after a Saturday visit, and I still was playing bridge. I met Colin as he came in the door and brought him into the living room to say hello to the women I was playing with, and I remarked in jest as I did so, 'You're home early, did you and Daddy fight?' Colin answered, half crying,

'Mommy, Daddy licked my pee pee and asked me to lick his.' I said, 'Does Daddy do this all the time?' Colin answered, 'Yes.' "

Floyd Jones objected to this testimony on hearsay and Confrontation Clause grounds, but the judge let it in saying, "What a child says to a parent is not testimonial. Moreover, there are circumstantial guarantees of trustworthiness in that it was said spontaneously less than five minutes after his father dropped him off and in the presence of three other women, each of whom can verify what was said." After Carol was done testifying, Floyd's attorney said, "Your Honor, I request the state call Colin Jones and place him on the stand so that I may cross-examine him." The judge said, "The rule doesn't provide for that, he just has to be available. You'll have to call him as part of your own case, but if he proves hostile, I'll let you cross-examine him." Floyd again objected on Confrontation Clause grounds. Later, Floyd called Colin, who by the time of the trial was almost five years old, and the following dialogue ensued:

Atty: What happened when you saw your Dad that Saturday?

Colin: My Daddy tried to lick my pee pee?

Atty: How do you know?

Colin: My Mommy told me?

Atty: Has your Mommy told you this many times or just once?

Colin: Many times.

Atty: Colin do you remember what happened or just what your Mommy told you?

Colin: What Mommy told me.

At that point Floyd's attorney, citing the Confrontation Clause, moved to strike Colin's answer during the state's case-in-chief to the question "What happened?" and Carol Jones's report of what Colin had said to her. The Court denied the motion. Then the prosecutor asked Colin, "Now Colin, your Father took you to the bathroom and pulled down your pants and licked your pee pee; isn't that what happened?" Floyd's objection that the prosecutor shouldn't be allowed to use leading questions was overruled by the judge ("the boy ain't the state's witness") and Colin proceeded to answer, faintly, "Yes." The prosecutor continued, "Now Colin, close your eyes and imagine you are with your Father in the bathroom again. Can't you see what happened and not just what your Mommy told you?" Colin again answered, faintly, "Yes." **Floyd Jones was convicted and appealed, arguing that the admission of Colin's hearsay, the failure to strike Colin's testimony and allowing the prosecutor to use leading questions all violated his Confrontation Clause and Due Process rights. Should Floyd prevail?**

III. THE COMPULSORY PROCESS CLAUSE

A. APPLIED TO THE STATES

The Compulsory Process Clause of the Sixth Amendment provides that "[i]n all criminal prosecutions, the accused shall enjoy the right . . . to have compulsory process for obtaining witnesses in his favor." Together with the Confrontation Clause, which applies to witnesses against the accused, the Compulsory Process Clause gives criminal defendants the constitutional right to present available exculpatory evidence to the trier of fact. The clause is the culmination of centuries of development in English criminal procedure. Until the fifteenth century, jurors were chosen because of their familiarity with the event, and neither side could call witnesses. This was followed by a period extending until about 1600 when only the prosecution could call witnesses. During the seventeenth century the accused gained the right to call witnesses, but could neither compel their attendance nor have them testify under oath. Finally, by an act of Parliament in 1702, criminal defendants were given the right to have their witnesses sworn.[121] Although the Parliamentary act contains no mention of the subpoena power, it was interpreted to give a right of compulsory process as well.

The inability to call defense witnesses, like the inability to confront the prosecution's witnesses, resulted in clear injustice in a number of celebrated trials. William Penn, while in England, was one famous victim of tactics preventing the presentation of a full defense.[122] Trials like Penn's were well-known in the colonies and the procedures used were abhorred. Penn himself drafted provisions for the charters of the colonies of New Jersey and Pennsylvania designed to prevent tactics like those used against him in England.

Thus, by the time of the American Revolution, the right to subpoena defense witnesses was considered fundamental to the Anglo-American system of criminal justice. Nine of the newly independent colonies provided specifically in their constitutions or attached bills of rights for the defendant's right to produce witnesses in his favor. It is not surprising then that the Compulsory Process Clause, like the Confrontation Clause, was included in the Sixth Amendment without significant commentary or debate.

---

[121] The provision that witnesses could be sworn did not, however, apply to the accused, who was not allowed to testify under oath in his own favor until the nineteenth century.

[122] Penn was charged with delivering a sermon on London's streets to an unlawful assembly of Quakers. His effort to defend himself without counsel was interrupted by the court and he was forcibly removed to a walled-off corner of the courtroom while the trial proceeded in his absence. Penn was acquitted when the jury ignored the judge's instructions to convict. The jury was then ordered fined and imprisoned, giving rise to the celebrated *Bushell's Case*, in which the King's Bench determined that a jury could not be punished for reaching a verdict which the trial judge saw as unsupported by the evidence.

Unlike the Confrontation Clause, the Compulsory Process Clause was the focus of an early case that helps clarify the framers' intent. In 1807 Chief Justice Marshall had to interpret the clause while sitting as a circuit judge in the trial of Aaron Burr. The Chief Justice gave the clause a broad reading, consistent with the notion that the clause was intended to constitutionalize the accused's right to present the evidence needed for an effective defense.

Burr had attempted to subpoena a letter in the hands of President Jefferson. The government argued that this removed the case from the Sixth Amendment, which explicitly extends the right of process only to witnesses and not to their papers. Marshall rejected this "literal distinction" as "too much attenuated to be countenanced in the tribunals of a just and humane nation."[123] In addition, Marshall held that only a minimum showing of materiality was needed to justify production of the letter, since the accused could not be expected to know exactly what the letter contained or how trial testimony would make it relevant. Finally, Marshall held that Burr could subpoena the letter even though he had not yet been indicted because an indictment appeared imminent and an immediate trial could be reasonably anticipated. The Chief Justice felt that inherent in the Compulsory Process Clause was the right of process at an early enough stage so that the accused had an effective opportunity to prepare a defense.[124]

After this auspicious beginning, the jurisprudence of the Compulsory Process Clause lapsed into a 160-year decline. From 1807 until 1967, the Supreme Court addressed the clause only five times, twice in dictum and three times while declining to construe it.[125] Then in 1967 the Supreme Court decided *Washington v. Texas*.[126] *Washington* arose when a jealous youth, Jackie Washington, drove with a group of boys to the house of his former girlfriend. The group had invited Charles Fuller to join them because he possessed a shotgun. When they arrived at the house, where the girl, her mother and the girl's new boyfriend were having supper, the youths left the car and some of them threw bricks at the house. They then fled, leaving only Washington and Fuller. When the mother and the

---

[123] *United States v. Burr*, 25 Fed. Cas. 30, 35, No. 14,692D (C.C.D.Va. 1807).

[124] Marshall also held that the President could be the object of a *subpoena duces tecum*, and that even if the President had the right, by virtue of his office, to himself determine that certain portions of the subpoenaed material were too sensitive to be revealed (which Marshall found unnecessary to decide), where the government attorney made this decision on the President's behalf, a continuance would be ordered unless the entire letter was produced. These holdings do not tell us as much about the central meaning of the Compulsory Process Clause as the holdings mentioned in the text, but they emphasize the importance that Marshall attached to the clause and his broad reading of it.

[125] The brief history presented above is drawn from Westen, The Compulsory Process Clause, 73 Mich. L. Rev. 71 75B108 (1975) [hereinafter Compulsory Process I]. For a fuller history of the clause, refer to the cited portion of Westen's article and sources cited therein. See also Westen, Compulsory Process II, 74 Mich. L. Rev. 191 (1975).

[126] 388 U.S. 14 (1967).

boyfriend went to investigate, either Washington or Fuller fired the shotgun, fatally wounding the boyfriend.

At his trial, Washington testified that he had tried to persuade an intoxicated Fuller to leave before the shooting, and that when Fuller insisted on shooting someone, he, Washington, fled toward the car. Washington then called Fuller as his witness. Fuller would have testified that Washington pulled at him and tried to persuade him to leave, and that Washington began running before the shot was fired.However, Fuller was not allowed to testify because of a Texas evidentiary rule that persons charged or convicted as co-participants in the same crime could not testify for one another, even though either could testify for the state.

In reviewing the application of this rule, the Supreme Court, speaking through Chief Justice Warren, first held that the compulsory process guarantee of the Sixth Amendment applied to the states because it so essential to a fair trial that it was incorporated into the Due Process Clause of the Fourteenth Amendment. "Just as an accused has the right to confront the prosecution's witnesses for the purpose of challenging their testimony, he has the right to present his own witnesses to establish a defense. This right is a fundamental element of due process of law."

The Court then went on to hold that Washington's compulsory process rights had been violated. The Court had to overcome two hurdles in reaching this conclusion. The first was that when the Compulsory Process Clause was adopted the federal system did not allow defendants indicted together to testify and that, without addressing the compulsory process issue, the Supreme Court had upheld this rule in 1852.[127] The second was that the language of the Compulsory Process Clause only gives a defendant a right to "compulsory process for obtaining witnesses" and does not speak of a right to have witnesses testify. Washington had been able to subpoena Fuller and have him present in the courtroom at Washington's trial.

The Court never addressed the implications of the federal evidentiary rule for the understanding of the drafters of the Sixth Amendment. Instead, the Justices cited a later case overruling the ban on the testimony of co-indictees as a matter of federal evidence law [128] and held that its reasoning was required by the Sixth Amendment. They then cited this case for the proposition that "the Sixth Amendment was designed in part to make the testimony of a defendant's witnesses admissible on his behalf in court," claiming that "it could hardly be argued that a state would not violate the clause if it made all defense testimony inadmissible as a matter of procedural law."

In concluding, the Court held that Washington:

---

[127] United States v. Reid, 53 U.S. (12 How.) 361 (1852).

[128] Rosen v. United States, 245 U.S. 467 (1918).

was denied his right to have compulsory process for obtaining witnesses in his favor because the State arbitrarily denied him the right to put on the stand a witness who was physically and mentally capable of testifying to events that he had personally observed, and whose testimony would have been relevant and material to the defense. The Framers of the Constitution did not intend to commit the futile act of giving to a defendant the right to secure the attendance of witnesses whose testimony he had no right to use.[129]

B. PRE-EMPTING RULES OF EVIDENCE

It is clear from *Washington* that the reach of compulsory process is potentially broad. Some of this potential was realized in *Chambers v. Mississippi*. *Chambers* is now recognized, even by the Supreme Court, as a compulsory process case,[130] but it was written with an effort to avoid making constitutional law, and nowhere in it is the Compulsory Process Clause specifically mentioned.

CHAMBERS V. MISSISSIPPI
410 U.S. 284 (1973).

MR. JUSTICE POWELL delivered the opinion of the Court.

[*Chambers* arose when a police officer, Aaron Liberty, was shot in the back with four bullets from a .22 caliber revolver while trying to control an unruly Woodville, Mississippi crowd that was interfering with an attempted arrest. Before he died, Officer Liberty turned around and fired his shotgun down an alley, wounding Leon Chambers. One deputy sheriff testified at trial that he was standing several feet from Liberty when the shots were fired and he saw Chambers shoot him. Another deputy sheriff said that, although he could not see whether Chambers had a gun in his hand, he saw Chambers "break his arm down" shortly before the shots were fired.

Gable McDonald was one of three friends who helped take Chambers to the hospital after he was shot. Shortly after the killing, McDonald left his wife in Woodville and moved to Louisiana, taking a job in a sugar mill. He returned to Woodville some five months later when told by his wife that an acquaintance of his, Reverend Stokes, wanted to see him. After talking to Stokes, McDonald made a sworn statement in the office of Chambers' lawyers admitting that it was he and not Chambers who had killed Liberty. He said he did it with a nine-shot .22 caliber revolver he had discarded shortly after the shooting and admitted to having already told a friend of his, James

---

[129] Washington v. Texas, 388 U.S. 14, 23 (1967).

[130] See Rock v. Arkansas, 483 U.S. 44 (1987).

Williams, that he had killed Liberty. He was then turned over to the police and jailed.

A month later, at a preliminary hearing, McDonald recanted his testimony, saying Stokes had persuaded him to confess, promising him he would not go to jail and would share in the proceeds of a lawsuit that Chambers would bring against the town of Woodville. He said he had not been at the crime scene, but had been drinking beer down the street with a friend, Berkeley Turner, when the shots were fired. The local Justice of the Peace accepted McDonald's repudiation. After laying out these facts, Justice Powell's opinion continues:]

. . . At trial, [Chambers] endeavored to develop two grounds of defense. He first attempted to show that he did not shoot Liberty. . . .

Petitioner's second defense was the allegation that Gable McDonald had shot Officer Liberty. He was only partially successful, however, in his efforts to bring before the jury the testimony supporting this defense. Sam Hardin, a life-long friend of McDonald's, testified that he saw McDonald shoot Liberty. A second witness, one of Liberty's cousins, testified that he saw McDonald immediately after the shooting with a pistol in his hand. In addition to the testimony of these two witnesses. . . .Chambers attempted to prove that McDonald had admitted responsibility for the murder on four separate occasions, once when he gave the sworn statement to Chambers' counsel and three other times prior to that occasion in private conversations with friends.

In large measure, he was thwarted in his attempt to present this portion of his defense by the strict application of certain Mississippi rules of evidence. Chambers asserts in this Court . . . that the application of these evidentiary rules rendered his trial fundamentally unfair and deprived him of due process of law. . .

II

Chambers filed a pretrial motion requesting the court to order McDonald to appear. Chambers also sought a ruling at that time that, if the State itself chose not to call McDonald, he be allowed to call him as an adverse witness. . . . The trial court granted the motion requiring McDonald to appear but reserved ruling on the adverse-witness motion. At trial, after the State failed to put McDonald on the stand, Chambers called McDonald, laid a predicate for the introduction of his sworn out-of-court confession, had it admitted into evidence, and read it to the jury. The State, upon cross-examination, elicited from McDonald the fact that he had repudiated his prior confession. McDonald further testified, as he had at the preliminary hearing, that he did not shoot Liberty, and that he confessed to the crime only on the promise of Reverend Stokes that he would not go to jail and would share a sizeable tort recovery from the town. . . .

At the conclusion of the State's cross-examination, Chambers renewed his motion to examine McDonald as an adverse witness. The trial court denied the motion, stating: "He may be hostile, but he is not adverse in the sense of the word, so your request will be overruled." On appeal, the State Supreme Court upheld the trial court's ruling, finding that "McDonald's testimony was not adverse to appellant" because "[n]owhere did he point the finger at Chambers."

Defeated in his attempt to challenge directly McDonald's renunciation of his prior confession, Chambers sought to introduce the testimony of the three witnesses to whom McDonald had admitted that he shot the officer. The first of these, Sam Hardin, would have testified that on the night of the shooting he spent the late evening hours with McDonald at a friend's house after their return from the hospital and that, while driving McDonald home later that night, McDonald stated that he shot Liberty. The State objected to the admission of his testimony on the ground that it was hearsay. The trial court sustained the objection.

Berkley Turner, the friend with whom McDonald said he was drinking beer when the shooting occurred, was then called to testify. In the jury's presence, and without objection, he testified that he had not been in the café that Saturday and had not had any beers with McDonald. The jury was then excused. In the absence of the jury, Turner recounted his conversations with McDonald while they were riding with James Williams to take Chambers to the hospital. When asked whether McDonald said anything regarding the shooting of Liberty, Turner testified that McDonald told him that he "shot him." Turner further stated that one week later, when he met McDonald at a friend's house, McDonald reminded him of their prior conversation and urged Turner not to "mess him up." Petitioner argued to the court that, especially where there was other proof in the case that was corroborative of these out-of-court statements, Turner's testimony as to McDonald's self-incriminating remarks should have been admitted as an exception to the hearsay rule. Again, the trial court sustained the State's objection.

The third witness, Albert Carter, was McDonald's neighbor. They had been friends for about 25 years. Although Carter had not been in Woodville on the evening of the shooting, he stated that he learned about it the next morning from McDonald. That same day, he and McDonald walked out to a well near McDonald's house and there McDonald told him that he was the one who shot Officer Liberty. Carter testified that McDonald also told him that he had disposed of the .22 caliber revolver later that night. . . . The jury was not allowed to hear Carter's testimony. . . .

In sum, then, this was Chambers' predicament. As a consequence of the combination of Mississippi's "party witness" or "voucher" rule and its hearsay rule, he was unable either to cross-examine McDonald or to present witnesses in his own behalf who would have discredited McDonald's repudiation and demonstrated his complicity. . . .

III

The right of an accused in a criminal trial to due process is, in essence, the right to fair opportunity to defend against the State's accusations. The rights to confront and cross-examine witnesses and to call witnesses in one's own behalf have long been recognized as essential to due process. . . . Both of these elements of a fair trial are implicated in the present case.

A

Chambers was denied an opportunity to subject McDonald's damning repudiation and alibi to cross-examination. He was not allowed to test the witness' recollection, to probe into the details of his alibi, or to "sift" his conscience so that the jury might judge for itself whether McDonald's testimony was worthy of belief. . . . Of course, the right to confront and to cross-examine is not absolute and may, in appropriate cases, bow to accommodate other legitimate interests in the criminal trial process. But its denial or significant diminution calls into question that ultimate "integrity of the fact-finding process" and requires that the competing interest be closely examined.

In this case, petitioner's request to cross-examine McDonald was denied on the basis of a Mississippi common-law rule that a party may not impeach his own witness. The rule rests on the presumption—without regard to the circumstances of the particular case—that a party who calls a witness "vouches for his credibility."

. . .

Whatever validity the "voucher" rule may have once enjoyed, . . . it bears little present relationship to the realities of the criminal process. . . . [I]n modern criminal trials, defendants are rarely able to select their witnesses: they must take them where they find them. Moreover, as applied in this case, the "voucher" rule's impact was doubly harmful to Chambers' efforts to develop his defense. Not only was he precluded from cross-examining McDonald, but, as the State conceded at oral argument, he was also restricted in the scope of his direct examination by the rule's corollary requirement that the party calling the witness is bound by anything he might say. He was, therefore, effectively prevented from exploring the circumstances of McDonald's three prior oral confessions and from challenging the renunciation of the written confession.

In this Court, Mississippi argues that there is no incompatibility between the rule and Chambers' rights because no right of confrontation exists unless the testifying witness is "adverse" to the accused. The State's brief asserts that the "right to confrontation applies to witnesses '*against*' an accused." Relying on the trial court's determination that McDonald was not "adverse," and on the State Supreme Court's holding that McDonald did not "point the finger at Chambers," the State contends that Chambers' constitutional right was not involved.

The argument that McDonald's testimony was not "adverse" to, or "against," Chambers is not convincing. The State's proof at trial excluded the theory that more than one person participated in the shooting of Liberty. To the extent that McDonald's sworn confession tended to incriminate him, it tended also to exculpate Chambers. And . . . McDonald's retraction inculpated Chambers to the same extent that it exculpated McDonald. . . . The availability of the right to confront and cross-examine those who give damaging testimony against the accused has never been held to depend on whether the witness was initially put on the stand by the accused or by the State. We reject the notion that a right of such substance in the criminal process may be governed by that technicality or by any narrow and unrealistic definition of the word "against." The "voucher" rule, as applied in this case, plainly interfered with Chambers' right to defend against the State's charges.

B

We need not decide, however, whether this error alone would occasion reversal since Chambers' claimed denial of due process rests on the ultimate impact of that error when viewed in conjunction with the trial court's refusal to permit him to call other witnesses. The trial court refused to allow him to introduce the testimony of Hardin, Turner, and Carter. Each would have testified to the statements purportedly made by McDonald, on three separate occasions shortly after the crime, naming himself as the murderer. The State Supreme Court approved the exclusion of this evidence on the ground that it was hearsay.

The hearsay rule, which has long been recognized and respected by virtually every State, is based on experience. . . . Out-of-court statements are traditionally excluded because they lack the conventional indicia of reliability. . . . A number of exceptions have developed over the years to allow admission of hearsay statements made under circumstances that tend to assure reliability and thereby compensate for the absence of the oath and opportunity for cross-examination. Among the most prevalent of these exceptions is the one applicable to declarations against interest. . . . Mississippi recognizes this exception but applies it only to declarations against pecuniary interest. . . .

[Justice Powell then discusses the common law's limitation of this exception to declarations against pecuniary or proprietary interests and the then modern trend to admit declarations against penal interest as well. He also notes the reasons why in this case McDonald's confessions appear particularly reliable.]

Few rights are more fundamental than that of an accused to present witnesses in his own defense. E.g., *Webb v. Texas*, 409 U.S. 95 (1972); *Washington v. Texas*, 388 U.S. 14, 19 (1967); *In re Oliver*, 333 U.S. 257 (1948). In the exercise of this right, the accused, as is required of the State, must comply with established rules of procedure and evidence designed to assure both fairness and reliability in the ascertainment of guilt and innocence. Although perhaps no rule of evidence has been more respected or more frequently applied in jury trials than that applicable to the exclusion of hearsay, exceptions tailored to allow the introduction of evidence which in fact is likely to be trustworthy have long existed. The testimony rejected by the trial court here bore persuasive assurances of trustworthiness and thus was well within the basic rationale of the exception for declarations against interest. That testimony also was critical to Chambers' defense. In these circumstances, where constitutional rights directly affecting the ascertainment of guilt are implicated, the hearsay rule may not be applied mechanistically to defeat the ends of justice.

We conclude that the exclusion of this critical evidence, coupled with the State's refusal to permit Chambers to cross-examine McDonald, denied him a trial in accord with traditional and fundamental standards of due process. In reaching this judgment, we establish no new principles of constitutional law. Nor does our holding signal any diminution in the respect traditionally accorded to the States in the establishment and implementation of their own criminal trial rules and procedures. Rather, we hold quite simply that under the facts and circumstances of this case the rulings of the trial court deprived Chambers of a fair trial.

The judgment is reversed and the case is remanded to the Supreme Court of Mississippi for further proceedings not inconsistent with this opinion.

It is so ordered.

[The concurring opinion of JUSTICE WHITE, and the dissenting opinion of JUSTICE REHNQUIST are omitted.]

———————

The cases decided before *Chambers* in which the Court overturned criminal convictions on compulsory process grounds all involved evidentiary rules or judicial actions that were both somewhat aberrant and biased against the interest of defendants.[131] *Chambers* is significant because it found constitutional infirmities in trial court rulings that were consistent with well-established principles of evidence law. While one might argue that the voucher rule is a discredited anachronism,[132] there was nothing idiosyncratic about the trial court's refusal to declare McDonald a hostile witness. More important, the application of the Mississippi hearsay rule was entirely orthodox and on its face favored neither the defense nor the prosecution. The Court notes the modern trend expanding the declaration against interest exception to include statements against penal interest and suggests that such statements are particularly reliable if corroborated. But the Court fails to mention that even under a modern code, such as the Federal Rules of Evidence, McDonald's declarations would not have been admissible as statements against interest because the federal rule, like the rule in most states, requires the declarant's unavailability. When the declarant is available, evidence law prefers live testimony and thus excludes statements against interest. Apparently the Court is willing to find that a traditional application of a traditional hearsay exception violates a defendant's rights under the Due Process Clause. While the Court ultimately rests its determination that Chambers was denied a fair trial on the conjunction of two different rulings below, the opinion reads as if the hearsay ruling alone would justify reversal. It was the exclusion of the apparently reliable confessions that did the most to make the trial unfair.

Although the Court purports to reverse Chambers's conviction in the name of due process, the values protected by the Compulsory Process Clause are clearly implicated. Justice Powell cites the *Webb* and *Washington* cases as illustrating the proposition that "[f]ew rights are more fundamental than that of an accused to present witnesses in his

———————

[131] Cf. *Wardius v. Oregon*, 412 U.S. 470 (1973). This case overturned Oregon's "notice of alibi" statute. In *Wardius* the petitioner, who had not given the required notice of alibi, was prevented from putting an alibi witness on the stand and from giving alibi testimony himself. The petitioner cited the Compulsory Process Clause as grounds for reversal, but the Court chose not to explore that issue. Instead the conviction was reversed with a finding that the Oregon procedure violated due process because it forced the defendant to give notice of alibi witnesses without imposing any reciprocal discovery obligation on the state.

[132] If the second aspect of the voucher rule—that a party calling a witness is bound by what the witness says—means, as the Court seems to imply, that Chambers could not have disputed McDonald's testimony in his argument to the jury or through other witnesses, the Mississippi rule differed in this respect from prevailing evidence law.

own defense."[133] It is this element of due process that is violated by the Mississippi court's application of its hearsay rule.

Indeed, one may argue that the Court's rejection of the Mississippi voucher rule in Part II-A of this case, although couched in terms of the value of confrontation, is better analyzed in terms of compulsory process. The state did not call McDonald as a witness against Chambers. He was present because Chambers had subpoenaed him, exercising a right guaranteed under the Compulsory Process Clause. Once it became clear that McDonald would not testify voluntarily in Chambers' favor, Chambers could only extract favorable evidence from McDonald by examining him as a hostile witness and, if necessary, impeaching his testimony. So long as the techniques of confrontation are used by defendants attempting to gain favorable evidence from witnesses not offered by the prosecution, the Compulsory Process Clause, not the Confrontation Clause, seems the appropriate basis for any constitutional right to proceed as if on cross-examination.[134] Chief Justice Marshall made it clear in the trial of Aaron Burr that the Compulsory Process Clause was not intended to be a "dead letter," it was intended to guarantee to the accused an *effective* opportunity to present a defense. At times, the right to present testimony in one's favor may be ineffective without the opportunity to treat one's "own witnesses" as hostile. In these circumstances the Compulsory Process Clause may require that litigants have this opportunity.

One may ask why this case was decided on generalized due process grounds rather than on the more specific grounds of the Confrontation and/or Compulsory Process Clauses. Professor Westen suggests two reasons: First, Justice Powell, the author of the *Chambers* opinion, opposed incorporating the specifics of the Bill of Rights into the Due Process Clause of the Fourteenth Amendment. Second, the defendant had not mentioned the Compulsory Process Clause as the basis of his rights in the court below.[135] To these reasons we would add two others. The only Compulsory Process Clause precedent for holding invalid the Mississippi law was *Washington*, but that case struck down a restriction on witnesses without regard to the facts of the particular case. Certainly the Court would have had difficulty saying that the Mississippi rule regarding out-of-court statements was arbitrary in the way the Texas law was. Thus, the Court may not have believed the Compulsory Process Clause applied to Chambers' situation. Indeed, one can read *Chambers* not as an extension of *Washington*, but as a considered refusal to give

---

[133] 410 U.S. 284, 302.

[134] So long as the Court is willing to read the meaning of the phrase "witnesses against him" in the Confrontation Clause as broadly as it did in *Chambers*, the issue of whether a confrontation or compulsory process right is involved may have no practical importance. Close analysis will be similarly unimportant to the extent that the Court takes a generalized due process approach to questions of the kind posed in *Chambers*.

[135] Westen, Compulsory Process I, *supra* note 125, at 151, n. 384.

Washington a broad reading. Finally, the Court was aware that, in this case, it was invalidating the application of well-established rules of evidence. It felt the facts of *Chambers* made its decision appropriate,[136] but it did not want to suggest the creation of a rule that would generalize the results of this case. The due process approach allows the Court to tailor its decision to the facts presented.

The Court's concern with restricting the implications of *Chambers* is evident in the rather peculiar lines that close Justice Powell's opinion:

> In reaching this judgment we establish no new principles of constitutional law. Nor does our holding signal any diminution in the respect traditionally accorded to the States in the establishment and implementation of their own criminal trial rules and procedures. Rather, we hold quite simply that under the facts and circumstances of this case the rulings of the trial court deprived Chambers of a fair trial.[137]

But when the Court decides a case on constitutional grounds, it is difficult to avoid making constitutional law, however hard it tries. Although courts have usually declined the invitation to declare established exclusionary rules unconstitutional, either generally or in the context of a particular case, where the possibility of injustice is patent, courts have overturned traditional evidentiary limitations, although they are more likely to cite the Due Process Clause than the Compulsory Process Clause. In the years immediately following the decision, *Chambers* was cited in a case that said that Wisconsin could not, in a first-degree murder trial, preclude psychiatric testimony on the issue of intent;[138] in a case holding that a state cannot bar evidence that one of its undercover drug agents was involved in a "frame-up" in another state;[139] in a case suggesting that the statement against penal interest exception should be read broadly when the corroborated statements of an unavailable witness are offered to exonerate the accused;[140] in a state case holding that so long as a third party's confession bears "a semblance of reliability," a criminal defendant has a constitutional right to call that person as a witness and, if he denies responsibility for the crime of which the defendant is accused, to introduce that person's confession;[141] and in

---

[136] *Chambers* is rare among cases to reach the Supreme Court in that it appears likely that the defendant was innocent. Thus the majority may have been motivated in this case more by a desire to do substantive justice than by a notion of procedural justice. The case was posed, however, in procedural justice terms, and it had to be disposed of on procedural grounds. For a discussion of the facts underlying *Chambers* See Landsman, Chambers v. Mississippi: A New Justice Meets an Old Style Southern Verdict in Evidence Stories (R. Lempert ed.) Foundation Press (2006).

[137] 410 U.S. at 302–03.

[138] *Hughes v. Mathews*, 576 F.2d 1250 (7th Cir. 1978).

[139] *Johnson v. Brewer*, 521 F.2d 556 (8th Cir. 1975).

[140] *United States v. Benveniste*, 564 F.2d 335 (9th Cir. 1977).

[141] *Welcome v. Vincent*, 549 F.2d 853 (2d Cir. 1977).

a case holding that in certain circumstances where credibility is crucial a defendant has a due process right to introduce exonerative polygraph evidence.[142] Numerous other cases have cited and sometimes followed *Chambers* since then.[143]

The Supreme Court has also had occasion to follow *Chambers*. One case, *Holmes v. South Carolina*,[144] involving an alleged rapist, is strikingly similar. Holmes, the defendant in the case, claimed that another man, White, was the rapist. The state introduced considerable forensic evidence which suggested Holmes was guilty, but Holmes disputed the validity of the evidence, some of which he claimed had been planted. In his defense Holmes sought to introduce evidence that White had on several occasions admitted his involvement in the crime, that White could be placed in the vicinity of the crime, and that White had offered a false alibi. The trial judge refused to admit Holmes' evidence and the South Carolina Supreme Court affirmed, holding that the evidence inculpating Holmes was so strong that his exonerative evidence could not "raise a reasonable inference of . . . innocence."

A unanimous Court, speaking through Justice Alito, overturned Holmes' conviction, although it took pains to acknowledge the general validity of the exclusions for prejudice, confusion, waste of time and the like that FRE 403 and its state counterparts allow. The Court also cited with approval language from *Am. Jur.* 2d indicating that evidence that a third party committed a charged crime may be excluded where it does not sufficiently connect the other person to the crime, "as, for example, where the evidence is speculative or remote." The Court, however, regarded the evidence Holmes offered as far from speculative or remote, and regarded the South Carolina Court's focus on the strength of the state's case rather than the quality of Holmes' evidence as "arbitrary," unrelated to any legitimate state goals and aimed at resolving questions typically left for the jury.

Holmes is like *Chambers* not just on its facts but also because the Court refused to state a broad rule but instead issued a holding closely attuned to the circumstances of the case. *Holmes* differs from *Chambers*

---

[142] *State v. Dorsey*, 87 N.M. 323, 532 P.2d 912 (App.1975); cf. *McMorris v. Israel*, 643 F.2d 458 (7th Cir. 1981). For a case that invokes the Compulsory Process Clause rather than the Due Process Clause as the source of a right to submit to polygraph evidence see *State v. Sims*, 52 Ohio Misc. 31, 369 N.E.2d 24, 6 Ohio Op.3d 124 (Ohio Com.Pl. 1977). The court in *Sims* does not cite *Chambers*. But see *Commonwealth v. Tanso*, 411 Mass. 640, 583 N.E.2d 1247 (1992); *State v. Duntz*, 223 Conn. 207, 613 A.2d 224 (1992); *Dean v. Duckworth,* 748 F.2d 367 (7th Cir. 1984), *cert. denied* 469 U.S. 1214 (1985).

[143] Two Supreme Court cases later addressed issues similar to those addressed in two of the state cases cited above. In each of these cases, *United States v. Scheffer*, 523 U.S. 303 (1998) (polygraph evidence) and *Clark v. Arizona*, 548 U.S. 735 (2006) (psychiatric testimony going to *mens rea*) the Supreme Court approved the exclusion of evidence that state courts, relying on *Chambers* had ordered admitted. *Scheffer* is discussed at note 156 *infra* and we explain why we don't discuss *Clark* in note 161 *infra*.

[144] 547 U.S. 319 (2006).

in that it mentions the Compulsory Process Clause by name, but it also references due process and confrontation as bases for the right it is enforcing and so does not firmly assert a Compulsory Process Clause right.

Green v. Georgia,[145] an earlier post-*Chambers* decision similarly mentions only the Due Process Clause and avoids the creation of a general right. *Green* involved two men, Moore and Green, convicted in separate trials of rape and murder. At Moore's trial Thomas Pasby, one of the state's witnesses, testified that Moore had told him that he had killed the victim, shooting her twice after ordering Green to run an errand. At the death penalty phase of Green's trial, Pasby's testimony, which would have duplicated the testimony he had given for the state in Moore's trial, was ruled inadmissible hearsay. The unfairness was compounded when the prosecutor, while addressing the jury, had the temerity to argue:

> We couldn't possibly bring any evidence other than the circumstantial evidence . . . that we had pointing to who did it. . . . I don't know whether Carzell Moore fired the first shot and handed the gun to Roosevelt Green and he fired the second shot or whether it was vice versa or whether Roosevelt Green had a gun and fired the shot or Carzell Moore had the gun and fired the first shot or the second, but I think it can be reasonably stated that you Ladies and Gentlemen can believe that each one of them fired shots so that they would be as equally involved and one did not exceed the other's part in the commission of this crime.[146]

The Court, pointing out the disserving character of Moore's statement and the fact that the state had thought the statement sufficiently reliable to use in prosecuting Moore, held that Green's right to a fair trial on the issue of punishment had been denied and vacated his death sentence.

The Court would, no doubt, have reached the same result had the prosecutor not argued that there was no possible evidence on who killed the deceased, when in fact he had successfully objected to telling evidence on that precise point. However, the prosecutor's remarks highlight a feature that *Chambers* and many of its progeny share. When courts follow *Chambers* to reverse criminal convictions, it is often the case that a prosecutor's adversarial instincts have overcome her duty to promote justice. Prosecutors need not object to all evidence excludable under domestic rules of evidence. Indeed, they should not do so when evidence is sufficiently important and reliable that its consideration might be essential to a fair verdict. When the state relies on exclusionary rules to secure the conviction of a person whose guilt appears in the light of all

---

[145] 442 U.S. 95 (1979).

[146] *Id* at 442.

the evidence questionable at best, *Chambers* is a valuable precedent for securing justice on appeal.

It is possible to contemplate compulsory process challenges to almost any ruling excluding defense evidence, and some commentators have argued that most exclusionary rules should give way to a defendant's need to introduce evidence on her own behalf. But the history of the Compulsory Process Clause does not suggest that it was intended to supplant local evidence rules. The framers of the Sixth Amendment knew about rules of disqualification, rules of privilege and rules excluding hearsay. However broad the potential breadth of *Chambers* and *Washington*,[147] courts, given this history, have not used the Compulsory Process Clause to cut a wide swath through well-established evidentiary rules. Privileges, for example, often exclude reliable evidence, yet courts routinely rebuff compulsory process challenges to established privileges,[148] and they have almost unanimously held that, absent extraordinary circumstances, neither compulsory process nor due process requires the state to give immunity to witnesses who invokes their Fifth Amendment privilege against self-incrimination even if that is the only way the defendant might compel their testimony.[149]

Where evidence rules are invalidated on compulsory process related grounds, they are typically of specialized and limited applicability as in *Washington* or, as in *Chambers*, *Holmes* and *Green*, confined closely to the facts of cases in which unfairness or likely injustice is obvious. Another Supreme Court decision, *Rock v. Arkansas*,[150] has both these characteristics and nicely illustrates the point.

Rock grew out of a struggle between spouses, which ended in the husband's death from a bullet in the chest. Because the defendant had no memory of the details of the shooting, defense counsel sought the aid of a hypnotist. Under hypnosis, Rock remembered that during the struggle she had her thumb on the hammer of the gun but never pulled the trigger. Defense counsel then gave the gun to an expert who concluded that it was defective and could discharge without the trigger being pulled if it was hit or dropped.

---

[147] For one view of how drastic these changes may and should be, see the two articles by Westen *supra* note 125.

[148] See e.g., *United States v. Thornton*, 733 F.2d 121 (D.C.Cir. 1984); *United States v. Boyett*, 923 F.2d 378 (5th Cir. 1991). But see *United States v. Sanchez*, 988 F.2d 1384 (5th Cir. 1993) (the government informant's privilege must give way if it interferes with a criminal defendant's due process rights).

[149] See, e.g. *Stewart v. Amaral*, 626 F.Supp. 192 (D.Mass. 1985); *United States v. Drape*, 668 F.2d 22 (1st Cir. 1982); *United States v. Hooks*, 848 F.2d 785 (7th Cir. 1988); *United States v. Shirley*, 884 F.2d 1130 (9th Cir. 1989).

[150] 483 U.S. 44 (1987). See also infra, Chapter 11, pp. 1403–1409, excerpting *Rock* and discussing the Supreme Court's treatment in *Rock* of questions of "legislative fact" in deciding whether hypnotically enhanced memories can ever be reliable enough for admission in evidence.

At the trial, the expert was allowed to testify about the gun's condition, but Rock was not allowed to testify to her version of what happened. The trial judge ruled that a person who had been hypnotized could only recount her recollections before hypnosis.

On appeal, the Arkansas Supreme Court went further, ruling that testimony based on post-hypnotic memories was never permissible. Neither ruling was unreasonable. By the time of Rock's trial it was widely recognized that under hypnosis subjects often invent information to please the hypnotist or to fit their desired view of the world, and that they are later unable to distinguish their inventions from reality. A number of states had in various ways restricted the testimony of once-hypnotized witnesses, and at least one other state, California, refused to accept testimony from any once-hypnotized witness other than the accused.[151]

While the Arkansas courts' skeptical views of post-hypnotic testimony was reasonable, applying the view retrospectively to Rock was problematic. Since at the time she was hypnotized no state appellate court had ever ruled on the issue, Rock had no idea that her decision to undergo hypnosis would severely limit her right to testify.[152] Moreover, Rock's recollection under hypnosis was corroborated by the expert who examined the gun, indicating the accuracy of her hypnotically refreshed testimony.[153] Thus the Supreme Court concluded that, "a State's legitimate interest in barring unreliable evidence does not extend to *per se* exclusions that may be reliable in an individual case."[154] The Court, however, cannot mean this. If it did, the character, hearsay and almost all the other exclusionary rules of evidence, except rules of privilege, could not be applied *as rules* to bar evidence offered by criminal defendants. Rather, *Rock* should be seen as standing for the more limited proposition that when a state evidentiary rule bars apparently reliable and exonerative defense evidence that few if any other states would bar,

---

[151] *People v. Shirley*, 31 Cal.3d 18, 181 Cal.Rptr. 243, 723 P.2d 1354 (1982). One rationale for the California rule is that once-hypnotized witnesses may testify to information they recalled before the hypnosis with greater confidence than they would have had if they had never been hypnotized. Their demeanor could thus make their testimony more convincing than it would be if they had testified to the same information without having been hypnotized. Later California cases retreated somewhat from *Shirley*, allowing once-hypnotized witnesses to testify to events recalled and related prior to the hypnotic session, *People v. Hayes*, 49 Cal.3d 1260, 265 Cal.Rptr. 132, 783 P.2d 719 (1989), and holding that the improper admission of testimony to events recalled only after hypnosis can be harmless error. *People v. Alcala*, 4 Cal.4th 742, 15 Cal.Rptr.2d 432, 842 P.2d 1192 (1992).

[152] At the prosecutor's insistence, the trial judge limited Rock's testimony largely to a reiteration of her vaguely written pre-hypnosis description of what had occurred; she was precluded from elaborating on the recollections she had before she was hypnotized. The Court never had to decide whether this limitation violated the Compulsory Process Clause, but as the Court's majority describes the case, this limitation added to the unfairness of Rock's trial.

[153] Just as there was substantial evidence that information recalled under hypnosis could be distorted by suggestion or for other reasons, there was also evidence that accurate information inaccessible to conscious memory could be accessed through hypnosis.

[154] 483 U.S. at 61.

the rule as applied may violate an accused's rights under the Compulsory Process Clause.[155] The four justices who dissented in *Rock* would seemingly not grant even such limited protection. The fact that despite the strength of *Rock*'s case four justices dissented indicates the extent of the Court's reluctance to use the Compulsory Process Clause to rectify injustices that exclusionary rules of evidence sometimes engender.

When there has not been clear injustice, the Supreme Court is unlikely to treat the Compulsory Process Clause as a tool to remove what it sees as reasonable restrictions on a defendant's right to present evidence. If there were any doubts on this score, the Court removed them in the case of *United States v. Scheffer*.[156] The case arose when Scheffer, an airman who was working within the Air Force as an undercover drug informant, went AWOL and was later convicted of this offense along with drug use and other charges. Scheffer had sought to bolster his denial of drug use with lie detector evidence, but the Court upheld Military Rule of Evidence 707, which bans the introduction of polygraph evidence in court-martial proceedings.

Scheffer was a strong case for arguing that a *per se* ban on polygraph evidence was unconstitutional. The Armed Forces regularly use polygraphs for security and other administrative purposes, including criminal investigations. Their operators are well trained, and the triers of fact in courts martial are primarily officers who are likely to be relatively sophisticated consumers of this sort of evidence. Moreover, on the facts of the case, evidence of a polygraph test that "indicated no deception" when Scheffer denied using drugs since joining the Air Force was about the only evidence that Scheffer could provide to corroborate his testimony that he had not knowingly ingested the amphetamines that showed up in a urine sample he had given. The results of the urine test had not been reported at the time of the polygraph exam.

The eight-person majority in *Scheffer* was clearly influenced by the broader scientific controversy surrounding the utility and validity of polygraph evidence. But they agreed on several principles that they saw as governing compulsory process and related due process claims without regard to that controversy. "A defendant's interest in presenting [relevant] evidence," the Court wrote, "may ... bow to accommodate other legitimate interests in the criminal trial process."[157] Moreover, "state and federal rule makers have broad latitude under the Constitution to establish rules excluding evidence from criminal trials. Such rules do not abridge an accused's right to present a defense so long as they are not

---

[155] Another example is *Crane v. Kentucky*, 476 U.S. 683 (1986), in which the Court overturned a Kentucky rule that once a judge had determined that a confession passed the constitutional threshold for voluntariness, a defendant could not introduce evidence suggesting the confession was involuntary in order to try to persuade the jury that it was untrustworthy.

[156] 523 U.S. 303 (1998).

[157] Id. at 1264.

'arbitrary' or 'disproportionate to the purposes they are designed to serve.' "[158]   Finally, "the exclusion of evidence [is] unconstitutionally arbitrary or disproportionate only where it has infringed upon a weighty interest of the accused."[159]

Applying these tests, the Court found no support for Scheffer in *Washington v. Texas*, *Chambers* or *Rock*. In each of those cases, the Court said, the exclusion of critical evidence undermined the accused's defense. Scheffer's polygraph evidence, by contrast, was seen merely as an attempt to bolster his credibility, and its exclusion—in the Court's view—did not prevent Scheffer from telling the military jurors his full version of the events. Therefore, the Court did not believe that Scheffer's defense was "significantly impaired by the exclusion of polygraph evidence."[160] Justice Stevens, in dissent, shows the weakness of the majority's conclusion. Given Scheffer's strong interest in the outcome and the fact that he had gone AWOL several weeks after the urine test and polygraph exam, the polygraph results were probably his only hope of convincing the jury he was telling the truth when he denied having knowingly used drugs.[161]

C. ACQUIRING EVIDENCE AND SECURING TESTIMONY

Compulsory Process Clause rights are not confined to overruling limitations imposed by exclusionary rules of evidence. The clause's fundamental concern is with the ability of an accused to acquire evidence and put witnesses on the stand. A number of cases have addressed this aspect of compulsory process, with results as mixed as the results of Confrontation Clause jurisprudence.[162]

---

[158] Id.

[159] Id.

[160] Id. at 1269.

[161] The Court also denied a compulsory process claim in *Clark v. Arizona*, 548 U.S. 735 (2006). Justice Souter's opinion for the majority opinion is complex and confusing, seeming to turn more on a state's capacity to define the proof relevant to an insanity defense than it does on the compulsory process issue.

[162] In *United States v. Augenblick*, 393 U.S. 348 (1969), the Court held that the prosecution's failure at a court martial to produce lost Jencks Act material (the Jencks Act requires the state at trial to turn over to the accused prior statements made by its witnesses) was not a violation of constitutional dimensions, nor was the failure to call a witness who might have known where the material could be found but whose preliminary hearing testimony apparently suggested that he did not. In dictum, the Court acknowledged the possibility that, in some situations, the failure to produce a Jencks Act type statement might be a denial of compulsory process.

In *Webb v. Texas*, 409 U.S. 95 (1972), the Court found the Due Process Clause violated when a trial judge so harshly admonished a defense witness about the penalties for false testimony as to suggest a judicial expectation of perjury—which, in effect, drove the witness from the stand. *Webb* has since been followed in several circuit court cases in which prosecutorial or judicial behavior appears to have intimidated witnesses into refusing to testify for the defense. The case has not, however, availed defendants complaining that delays in sentencing convicted co-offenders discouraged these offenders from giving exculpatory testimony for fear that their own sentences would be enhanced. In *Cool v. United States*, 409 U.S. 100 (1972), a judicial instruction that the jury should disregard testimony by the defendant's alleged accomplice unless

The two most important post-*Chambers* compulsory process cases apart from *Scheffer* involved these aspects of compulsory process. In *Taylor v. Illinois* [163] the Court considered the constitutionality of a judge's ruling barring a witness's testimony as a sanction for a discovery violation. In *Pennsylvania v. Ritchie* [164] the Court addressed a defendant's claim that his compulsory process rights entitled him to access privileged information that might help him identify witnesses in his favor.

In *Taylor*, a defense witness was not allowed to testify that the target of an alleged attempted murder and his brother had been carrying guns and threatening the defendant, and that the witness had alerted the defendant to these facts. The trial judge barred the witness because defense counsel waited until the second day of trial, after the state's two principal witnesses had testified, to inform the prosecutor that the witness would testify, although the prosecutor had filed a pretrial discovery motion for a list of defense witnesses. The trial judge's decision was apparently a reaction not only to the late notice, but also to the defense counsel lying about when he was first aware of the witness's availability, and, allegedly, to the increasing use of late notice as a tactic by defense lawyers in his court.

In its decision, the Supreme Court first rejected the state's position, which, ignoring *Washington*, argued that the Compulsory Process Clause granted only a right of subpoena and had nothing to do with the introduction of evidence. The Court also recognized that a discovery sanction excluding the testimony of a material defense witness might contravene a defendant's compulsory process rights.

The Court, however, found no Compulsory Process Clause violation in *Taylor* because defense counsel had interviewed the witness during the week before trial, had not included the witness's name on an amended witness list he submitted the day the trial began, and had lied to the judge about when he first knew of the witness. The Court found that "the inference that [defense counsel] was deliberately seeking a tactical advantage is inescapable."[165] This and other language in the Court's

---

"convinced it is true beyond a reasonable doubt" was found to obstruct impermissibly the defendant's right, guaranteed in *Washington*, to present an accomplice's testimony. In *United States v. Valenzuela-Bernal*, 458 U.S. 858 (1982), the Court found no compulsory process violation when two illegal aliens, whom the defendant was charged with transporting into this country, were deported, making their testimony unavailable to him. The Court, however, suggests that the result might have been different had the defendant been able to make "some showing that the evidence lost would have been both material and favorable to the defense." Thus, *Valenzuela-Bernal* stands for the proposition that there is no compulsory process violation when the state has legitimate reasons for actions that render witnesses unavailable (here the interest in deporting aliens) and the defendant cannot show that testimony from those witnesses would have been important to his defense.

[163]   484 U.S. 400 (1988).

[164]   480 U.S. 39 (1987).

[165]   484 U.S. at 417.

opinion suggests that the Justices in the majority suspected that the late notice might have been designed to facilitate perjury. Because of the blatant nature of defense counsel's violation, the Court was not swayed by the possibility that other sanctions, like contempt charges, might deter late notices or by the possibility that alternative devices, like continuances, might alleviate any harm the prosecution suffered from being surprised. The majority was also unmoved by the argument that the defendant was apparently an innocent victim of his lawyer's tactics. Three dissenters would not have allowed the preclusion sanction unless the defendant could be shown to have been complicit in counsel's misbehavior.

On its face the majority's decision seems inconsistent with *Washington*. That case held that a state's fear of perjured testimony did not justify its rule excluding accomplice testimony in part because "the truth is more likely to be arrived at by hearing the testimony of all persons . . . who may seem to have knowledge of the facts involved in a case, leaving the credit and weight of such testimony to be determined by the jury." But in *Washington*, the Court was dealing with a *per se* rule that the Justices did not in fact believe was an effective tool against perjury. In *Taylor*, the majority thought that the late notice might well have been designed to hamper the state's efforts to discredit a lying witness. This attitude may account for the Court's quick dismissal of what was probably the defendant's strongest argument. Illinois' reciprocal discovery act provided the state with little information (name and address) that would help in discrediting an uncooperative defense witness. Voir dire of the witness before he testified and the possibility of a continuance to allow a police record check were likely to give the state as much or more ammunition to attack the witness's testimony as it would have had if the discovery rules had been complied with. The result in *Taylor* may not be troubling if one assumes the witness was bent on perjury, but if the witness was honest, the Court's decision denied Taylor evidence that might have exonerated him. The jury which we usually trust to distinguish between honest and dishonest witnesses was never given that opportunity.

Taylor built on *United States v. Nobles* [166] in which the Court held that the testimony of a defense investigator which would have impeached crucial prosecution witnesses was properly barred when the defense refused to provide the prosecution at trial with relevant portions of a report prepared by the investigator after interviewing the witnesses. *Taylor* in turn was precedent for *Michigan v. Lucas*.[167] *Lucas* held that compliance with a pretrial notice and hearing requirement was not

---

[166] 422 U.S. 225 (1975).

[167] 500 U.S. 145, 111 S.Ct. 1743 (1991).

necessarily an unconstitutional predicate to a defendant's ability to offer evidence of his prior sexual behavior with an alleged rape victim.

Taylor and *Nobles* indicate that the preclusion of defense evidence is a permissible sanction for discovery violations where it appears that the defense is resisting or avoiding discovery in order to hinder accurate fact-finding. *Lucas* suggests that a preclusion sanction may also be constitutional where discovery procedures are designed to foster important state policies that extend beyond the state's interest in promoting accurate fact-finding, like protecting the dignity of rape victims. However, in each case the Court also recognized that the total preclusion of a witness's testimony is a drastic step that strikes at the heart of the values the Compulsory Process Clause is designed to protect. Preclusion will probably not be allowed where non-compliance with discovery rules is inadvertent. Further, even when there is conscious non-compliance, it is not clear that preclusion will be allowed if a defendant's failure to reveal information in a timely fashion does not seem motivated by a desire to thwart the policies underlying the discovery rule.

Pennsylvania v. Ritchie[168] dealt not with the preclusion of defense evidence but with the defendant's ability to gather evidence in the first instance. *Ritchie* involved a defendant charged with sexual offenses against his minor daughter. The matter had been referred to Pennsylvania's Children and Youth Services (CYS), a state protective services agency charged with investigating offenses of this sort. During pretrial discovery, the defendant sought to subpoena the CYS's records, claiming the CYS file might contain the names of exculpatory witnesses as well as other unspecified exculpatory evidence. At trial the defendant was convicted largely on his daughter's testimony, leading him to claim on appeal that the unavailability of the CYS report violated his Sixth Amendment right to confrontation as well as his right to compulsory process, since the report might have contained information that would have made for a more effective cross-examination. The Pennsylvania Supreme Court agreed, and remanded the case with an order that the CYS file be revealed to Ritchie's attorney.

On review in the Supreme Court, Justice Powell, writing for a four judge plurality, dismissed the Confrontation Clause claim, stating that "[t]he ability to question adverse witnesses . . . does not include the power to require the pretrial disclosure of any and all information that might be useful in contradicting unfavorable testimony."[169] The Court

---

[168] 480 U.S. 39 (1987).

[169] Id. at 53. Three justices disagreed with this conclusion and two justices did not reach this issue because they believed the Pennsylvania Supreme Court decision did not constitute a final order in the case, meaning the matter was not ripe for review.

was, however, more hospitable to Ritchie's compulsory process claim. Speaking now for five justices, Justice Powell wrote:

> Our cases establish, at a minimum, that criminal defendants have the right to the government's assistance in compelling the attendance of favorable witnesses at trial and the right to put before a jury evidence that might influence the determination of guilt.

> . . .

> This Court has never squarely held that the Compulsory Process Clause guarantees the right to discover the identity of witnesses, or to require the government to produce exculpatory evidence. Instead, the Court traditionally has evaluated claims such as those raised by Ritchie under the broader protections of the Due Process Clause of the Fourteenth Amendment. Because the applicability of the Sixth Amendment to this type of case is unsettled, and because our Fourteenth Amendment precedents addressing the fundamental fairness of trials establish a clear framework for review, we adopt a due process analysis for purposes of this case. Although we conclude that compulsory process provides no greater protections in this area than those afforded by due process, we need not decide today whether and how the guarantees of the Compulsory Process Clause differ from those of the Fourteenth Amendment. It is enough to conclude that on these facts, Ritchie's claims more properly are considered by reference to due process.

> It is well settled that the government has the obligation to turn over evidence in its possession that is both favorable to the accused and material to guilt or punishment. Although courts have used different terminologies to define "materiality," a majority of this Court has agreed, "[evidence] is material only if there is a reasonable probability that, had the evidence been disclosed to the defense, the result of the proceeding would have been different. A 'reasonable probability' is a probability sufficient to undermine confidence in the outcome."

> . . .

> The Commonwealth . . . argues that no materiality inquiry is required, because a statute renders the contents of the file privileged. Requiring disclosure here, it is argued, would override the Commonwealth's compelling interest in confidentiality on the mere speculation that the file "might" have been useful to the defense.

> Although we recognize that the public interest in protecting this type of sensitive information is strong, we do not agree that

this interest necessarily prevents disclosure in all circumstances. This is not a case where a state statute grants CYS the absolute authority to shield its files from all eyes. Given that the Pennsylvania Legislature contemplated some use of CYS records in judicial proceedings, we cannot conclude that the statute prevents all disclosure in criminal prosecutions.[1a] . . . Ritchie is entitled to have the CYS file reviewed by the trial court to determine whether it contains information that probably would have changed the outcome of his trial. If it does, he must be given a new trial. If the records maintained by CYS contain no such information, or if the nondisclosure was harmless beyond a reasonable doubt, the lower court will be free to reinstate the prior conviction.

. . .

This ruling does not end our analysis, because the Pennsylvania Supreme Court did more than simply remand. It also held that defense counsel must be allowed to examine all the confidential information, both relevant and irrelevant, and present arguments in favor of disclosure. The court apparently concluded that whenever a defendant alleges that protected evidence might be material, the appropriate method of assessing this claim is to grant full access to the disputed information, regardless of the State's interest in confidentiality. We cannot agree.

A defendant's right to discover exculpatory evidence does not include the unsupervised authority to search through the Commonwealth's files. . . . We find that Ritchie's interest (as well as that of the Commonwealth) in ensuring a fair trial can be protected fully by requiring that the CYS files be submitted only to the trial court for in camera review. Although this rule denies Ritchie the benefits of an "advocate's eye," we note that the trial court's discretion is not unbounded. If a defendant is aware of specific information contained in the file (e.g., the medical report), he is free to request it directly from the court, and argue in favor of its materiality. Moreover, the duty to disclose is ongoing; information that may be deemed immaterial upon original examination may become important as the proceedings progress, and the court would be obligated to release information material to the fairness of the trial.

To allow full disclosure to defense counsel in this type of case would sacrifice unnecessarily the Commonwealth's compelling

---

[1a.] We express no opinion on whether the result in this case would have been different if the statute had protected the CYS files from disclosure to anyone, including law-enforcement and judicial personnel.

interest in protecting its child abuse information. . . . A child's feelings of vulnerability and guilt and his or her unwillingness to come forward are particularly acute when the abuser is a parent. It therefore is essential that the child have a state-designated person to whom he may turn, and to do so with assurance of confidentiality. Relatives and neighbors who suspect abuse also will be more willing to come forward if they know that their identities will be protected. Recognizing this, the Commonwealth—like all other States—has made a commendable effort to assure victims and witnesses that they may speak to the CYS counselors without fear of general disclosure. The Commonwealth's purpose would be frustrated if this confidential material had to be disclosed upon demand to a defendant charged with criminal child abuse, simply because a trial court may not recognize exculpatory evidence.

. . .

We agree that Ritchie is entitled to know whether the CYS file contains information that may have changed the outcome of his trial had it been disclosed. Thus we agree that a remand is necessary. We disagree with the decision of the Pennsylvania Supreme Court to the extent that it allows defense counsel access to the CYS file. An in camera review by the trial court will serve Ritchie's interest without destroying the Commonwealth's need to protect the confidentiality of those involved in child abuse investigations. The judgment of the Pennsylvania Supreme Court is affirmed in part and reversed in part, and the case is remanded for further proceedings not inconsistent with this opinion.[170]

In *Ritchie*, as in *Chambers*, Justice Powell transformed a claim that seems to fit naturally within the compass of the Compulsory Process Clause into a due process claim. Here, unlike *Chambers,* the transformation was clearly deliberate because the Compulsory Process Clause claim was not only argued by the parties in the Supreme Court, but also served as the basis of the decisions below. One reason for Powell's approach may be that the transformation fit *Ritchie* into a line of due process cases extending back to *Brady v. Maryland*,[171] which impose on prosecutors a duty to turn over exculpatory information to defendants. Cases following *Brady* have held that defendants have a right to exculpatory information in the hands of other state agencies as well, even when that agency has both a good reason and the legal authority to keep the information confidential. By relying on due process rather than compulsory process, however, *Ritchie* creates a precedent that will not

---

[170] Id. at 56–61.

[171] 373 U.S. 83 (1963).

necessarily extend to similar information in the possession of private agencies or individuals. It remains unclear whether courts will treat the private assertion of a state-created privilege as state action.

Due process also differs from compulsory process in that fairness rather than the ability to acquire exculpatory evidence is at its core. The Court may have had more difficulty justifying judicial screening of the CYS report had it given independent content to the Compulsory Process Clause. While a judge might be trusted to recognize evidence the withholding of which would be grossly unfair, only the defense counsel is likely to recognize the range of information that might aid the defense. This is particularly true when, unlike *Ritchie*, the judicial decision about what information to release is made not after the fact but at some stage in the pre-trial proceedings. It apparently never occurred to the Court that *Ritchie* decisions will ordinarily be made before trial, posing substantial problems for judges who must decide what information to order revealed while knowing little if anything about the parties' cases. The standard of materiality the Court articulates—"a reasonable probability that, had the evidence been disclosed to the defense, the result . . . would have been different"—is viable for after-the-fact judgments on appeal but is an unworkable *a priori* standard. A judge simply cannot know before trial what evidence has a reasonable probability of changing the result because she does not then know what evidence the parties will introduce. Although the decision also imposes on the judge a continuing obligation to make evidence available if trial proceedings make it material, this requirement is likely to be of little help. It assumes that the judge rather than a clerk perused the file in the first instance, that the judge remembers well what the file contains, and that the utility of the evidence to the defense does not depend on inquiries the evidence might trigger.

The *Ritchie* majority emphasizes the fact that CYS reports have no absolute privilege, and that courts might utilize them in some situations. Thus, the case does not stand for the proposition that absolute privileges must give way before a criminal defendant's compulsory process or due process claims. However, few privileges are absolute. There are invariably circumstances in which countervailing values abrogate privileges that otherwise would attach.

Fairness to possibly innocent criminal defendants is a value enshrined in Fifth and Fourteenth Amendment Due Process Clauses, as well as in the Sixth Amendment. A court could rely on *Ritchie* to abrogate most evidentiary privileges—at least to the point of allowing *in camera* review and the disclosure of clearly exculpatory evidence.[172]

---

[172] Two pre-*Ritchie* cases, themselves more than 150 years apart, make it clear that the Compulsory Process Clause might override certain claims of executive privilege. See *United States v. Burr*, 25 Fed.Cas. 30 (No.14,692D) (C.C.D. Va. 1807); *United States v. Nixon*, 418 U.S. 683 (1974).

However, just as the Court has been cautious about using compulsory process to mandate drastic inroads on longstanding exclusionary rules of evidence, so can we expect caution when the Court is asked to use due process or compulsory process to abrogate familiar privileges. A sign of that caution may be Justice Powell's decision to write *Ritchie* as a due process rather than as a compulsory process case.

Problem VII-18. The defendant is accused of robbing a supermarket. A witness who saw the getaway car testified that a small person or a child was in the car with the defendant when he drove away. The defendant claims he was hiking in the woods with his seven-year-old son at the time of the robbery. In support of this alibi, the defendant would like to put his son on the stand. The prosecution objects and the following dialogue ensues:

> **Judge:** Do you know what an oath is?
> **Child:** No.
> **Judge:** Do you know what a lie is?
> **Child:** Yes, it's not telling when you did something wrong.
> **Judge:** Do you know what God does to people who lie?
> **Child:** I don't know about God.
> **Judge:** Do you ever lie?
> **Child:** [squirms but says nothing.]
> **Judge:** Do you know what happens when you lie?
> **Child:** Sometimes you get spanked and sometimes no one knows.

At this point the judge rules that the child does not understand the nature of the oath and so will not be allowed to testify. The defendant claims this decision violates his rights under the Compulsory Process and Due Process Clauses. **How should the court rule?** Assume the prosecutor sought to introduce the child as a witness against the defendant in this case and the court ruled the child competent. **How should the court rule on the defendant's argument that putting this child on the stand violates his rights under the Confrontation Clause?**

ADDITIONAL PROBLEMS

The following problems suggest some situations in which you as an attorney may wish to advance compulsory process arguments. They also pose the question of where to set the limits of compulsory process. The problems refer specifically to the Compulsory Process Clause, but in answering them you should assume the defendant invokes the Due Process Clause as well.

Problem VII-19. Bowie and Keen are charged with bank robbery. A joint trial has been scheduled. Bowie asks that the court try her separately and after Keen. In support of her motion for a later separate trial she introduces an affidavit from Keen, which states: "If I am tried before Bowie and am either convicted or acquitted, I shall testify that I had never met Bowie until the time we were both arrested, and I shall offer further testimony in her favor. However, if we are tried jointly or if Bowie is tried first, I shall have to claim my Fifth Amendment right and refuse to testify." **Is the judge required by the Compulsory Process Clause to grant Bowie's motion?**

Problem VII-20. In the same circumstances as the preceding problem assume that the trial was severed, but that Keen's earlier trial had ended with the jury hung 8–4 for acquittal, and the prosecutor had tentatively decided not to seek a retrial. When Bowie called Keen, the prosecutor objected even to placing Keen on the stand because Keen had stated that, as long as she was subject to retrial, she would be forced to claim her right to remain silent. The judge determined that this was true and refused to place Keen on the stand. Bowie asked the judge to grant use immunity so that Keen could be forced to testify. After determining that the prosecutor had no desire to seek use immunity for Keen's testimony, the judge rejected Bowie's request, explaining (correctly) that use immunity was only authorized by statute at the behest of the Attorney General. Bowie argued that the judge's refusal to grant immunity and the prosecutor's refusal to request it violated her rights under the Compulsory Process Clause. **How should the court rule?** Bowie also argued that if the judge would not grant immunity, Keen should at least be placed on the stand so that the jury might see that she chose to claim her Fifth Amendment privilege. Bowie argued that since her case was built on the theory that she had been mistaken for someone else, her failure to put anyone on the stand who could apparently testify to this fact would result in an unjustified inference that no such person existed. Hence she argued, she had a right under the Compulsory Process Clause to put Keen on the witness stand, even if Keen intended to invoke her Fifth Amendment privilege. **How should the court rule on this argument?**

Problem VII-21. In the same circumstances as the preceding two problems, assume that Keen, instead of invoking the Fifth Amendment, stated that since she was not involved in the bank robbery, she had no idea whether or not Bowie was involved, having never met her until the time they were both arrested. Bowie requests permission to question Keen as a hostile witness. **Does either the Confrontation Clause or the Compulsory Process Clause require the court to grant this request?**

Problem VII-22. In the same circumstances as the preceding three problems, assume that Keen was put on the stand and refused to testify on Fifth Amendment grounds. Bowie then sought to introduce Keen's statement in the affidavit she had submitted to the trial court in Problem VII-19. The prosecutor objected that the statement was hearsay. **How should the court rule on Bowie's claim that she has a right under the Due Process Clause and under the Compulsory Process Clause to have this hearsay statement admitted on her behalf? Should the court's ruling be any different if Bowie had two witnesses who will testify that they saw Keen and an unidentified female partner (not Bowie) rob the bank? If she has two witnesses who will testify that while in jail Keen told them that the police had made a mistake when they arrested Bowie?**

Problem VII-23. Lee is accused of manslaughter and of leaving the scene of an accident in which two pedestrians were hit by a car. In the accident, one pedestrian was killed, and the other was knocked unconscious and was still in a coma at the time of Lee's trial. Lee moved for a continuance until such time as the victim in the coma recovered and could testify on his behalf. The judge, after hearing medical testimony that the victim in the coma might recover the next day, the next year, or not at all, refused to grant a continuance. **Did this decision violate Lee's rights under the Compulsory Process Clause? Would the situation be any different if the doctors had testified that within six months the victim would either be dead or fully recovered?** Assume that three months after Lee was tried and convicted the victim recovered. Lee seeks a new trial at which the victim's testimony could be taken. He claims to have this right under the Compulsory Process Clause. **How should a court rule? Should the court decide differently if Lee had obtained an affidavit from the victim stating that she was hit by a yellow car and Lee's car was blue?**

Problem VII-24. Consuela Gonzalez is accused of attempted extortion. The principal evidence against her is voiceprint evidence, a new scientific technique admissible in the jurisdiction in question but subject to challenge before the jury. Gonzalez seeks to subpoena a leading authority on voiceprints who has expressed considerable skepticism about their accuracy and has done studies that back up his claims. The expert ordinarily commands a fee of $10,000—ten times more than the fees demanded by less eminent, and presumably less persuasive, experts in this field. Gonzalez can afford to pay at most $200. Citing the Compulsory Process Clause, Gonzalez asks the trial court either to order the state to pay the expert's $10,000 fee or to order the expert, under threat of contempt, to testify as an ordinary witness with no special fee. There is a statute in the jurisdiction which provides that, "in the case of indigent defendants, the state will pay up to $500 in expert witness fees," and there is clear precedent that experts will not be required to testify to matters within their expertise unless they agree to do so. **How should the court rule on Gonzalez's request?** Assume the court denies her request and that Gonzalez then moves to order the state to pay a witness fee of $1000 since she is unable to identify any expert skeptical of voice prints who will testify for less than that amount. The prosecution in response to this motion admits that it knows of no voice print skeptic who charges less than $1,000 to testify but that the expenditure is unnecessary because its voice print witness is an expert who on cross-examination can explain and testify about the skeptics' claims. **How should the court rule?**

"RAPE SHIELD" PROBLEMS

We discussed the Federal Rape Shield Statute, FRE 412, in Chapter Five along with other types of character evidence. The application of the rule cannot, however, be fully understood without understanding what the Confrontation and Compulsory Process Clauses are likely to require. Now that you have read our discussion of the law in these areas we present several problems that probe the implications of these constitutional protections for the application of FRE 412.

Problem VII-25. Suppose that the state of Hutchins, "in order to protect the reputation of our beloved dead and to prevent the pain and suffering of their near kin," passes a statute that provides: "In a trial for homicide, reputation or opinion evidence of the past violent behavior of the deceased victim is not allowed. Evidence of past violent acts that the deceased perpetrated on persons other than the accused is inadmissible, but evidence of past violent acts by the deceased on the accused may be admitted on the issue of self-defense." **Is this statute unconstitutional on its face? Can you think of circumstances where it would be unconstitutional as applied? If the statute provided that evidence of violent acts by the deceased was inadmissible except where the evidence was constitutionally required to be admitted, would this be a wise legislative policy? What are the salient differences between this statute and the federal rape shield statute? What are the salient differences between rape victims and homicide victims?**

Problem VII-26. Josh Carvelle is accused of raping Sabrina Kowalski. He denies having had intercourse with Sabrina. To prove that Sabrina was raped, the state offers her testimony that she was raped, testimony of a rape crisis center counselor whom Sabrina called the morning after the alleged rape, and testimony of Sabrina's best woman friend, who saw Sabrina in tears the night of the alleged rape and asked what happened. The trial occurs seven months after the alleged rape, and when she takes the stand Sabrina, who is unmarried, is visibly pregnant. Josh, citing FRE 412(b)(1)(A), wants to offer evidence that she has been "living with" her boyfriend for the past year and that the two plan shortly to get married. The prosecutor argues that since the state has introduced no physical evidence that Sabrina was raped, evidence that Sabrina was living with her boyfriend is inadmissible. **How should a judge rule? Should the judge rule differently if Josh has admitted having intercourse with Sabrina on the night in question but claims consent? Should the judge rule differently if Josh wants to show not that Sabrina lived with a boyfriend, but that she was having sex with many different men about the time of the alleged rape?**

Problem VII-27. Bill and Monica, college students on spring break who just met on the beach that morning, were drinking their third or fourth Mai Tai and talking as the sun fell over the sea. "Did you hear the one about the chicken and the egg?" asked Monica. "No," said Bill. "Well," said Monica, "This chicken and egg were lying in bed. The chicken is smoking a cigarette and has a pleased look on its face. The egg, looking a bit disgruntled, says to no one in particular, 'Well, I guess we answered *that* question.' " They both broke up with laughter, and proceeded to share a number of other sexually themed jokes. Shortly afterward, Bill invited Monica to come to his room to watch a movie on television. At that point, their stories diverge except in one respect. They both agree they had sexual intercourse. Bill claims they started kissing, he helped Monica off with her clothes and with her consent they made love. Monica claims that Bill tried to kiss her, that she pushed him away saying she didn't feel good after all that alcohol, that Bill then stripped her clothes off and that, although she repeatedly said, "No," he raped her. Bill claims Monica said, "Oh," several times, but never "No." Bill says Monica never screamed for help and that she didn't try to hit or otherwise resist him physically. Monica says she didn't scream because she was afraid of what Bill might do, and that she did try to push him away but he was so heavy and she was feeling so poorly her efforts didn't have much force. Bill would like to introduce the chicken and egg and other jokes as some evidence that Monica had consented to the sex or that he reasonably thought she did. **Should the court admit evidence of the jokes Monica told on either of these issues?**

Problem VII-28. Three youths are accused of dragging a seventeen-year-old girl 500 feet down an alley, forcing her into a vacant house, and raping her. The youths argue that once in the building the girl consented to the sex act. They seek to present evidence that six months before the alleged rape the girl had had sexual intercourse with her boyfriend, who now lives in another state. They also wish to offer evidence that sometime after the alleged rape, the girl had moved into a motel with a forty-year-old man. When questioned about the last incident by the juvenile authorities, she had first denied having had sexual intercourse with the man, but later admitted it. **Is this evidence admissible in a jurisdiction without a rape shield law? Is it admissible in federal**

court? Does it matter that she never claimed that the forty-year-old man raped her?

Problem VII-29. Mack Lane is charged with raping a sixteen-year-old former friend, Jane Kenny. Jane testifies that she was walking home with him one evening when Mack lured her into a house where he and three friends had sexual intercourse with her. Jane claims that she struggled, but that she could do nothing as she was held down by the three youths during the acts. She says that when the last of the youths left the room where they had placed her, she telephoned her sister and asked her to come get her, but did not say that she had been raped. However, before her sister arrived a friend of hers opened the door, found her and escorted her outside. Jane immediately ran to a nearby police car screaming that she had been raped. The doctor who examined her found no signs of external bruises or injuries but he did find internal marks consistent with either normal or multiple intercourse. At the trial, Mack wants to introduce evidence that Jane had engaged in other acts of intercourse in the past and that she had a bad reputation for chastity. He claims that this is probative both of Jane's veracity and on the issue of her consent. Mack also wants to introduce evidence that on two other occasions Jane had run screaming to police cars claiming she had been raped by several men, and on each occasion she had later admitted that she had engaged in consensual intercourse with just one person. **Is any of the evidence that Mack wishes to offer admissible in a jurisdiction with no rape shield law? Is any of it admissible in federal court? Does it matter whether the witnesses to the other accusations are police officers or friends of Mack? Would you permit Mack to show that Jane's father has on a number of occasions beaten her because of his suspicion that she had been engaging in sexual activity?**

Problem VII-30. Fred is accused of raping Paula. There was no evidence of violence and Paula did not complain of the rape until two days after it allegedly occurred. Fred claims that Paula is a prostitute who filed the rape charge when it turned out that he had unknowingly paid her with a counterfeit $100 bill, and she thought this was intentional. Thus, Fred's defense is consent. **May Fred introduce the testimony of two men who will say that they had paid Paula to have sex with them? Does it matter how long before the rape complaint these acts occurred? If Fred's two witnesses plead the Fifth Amendment, would Fred be able to introduce the testimony of a vice squad officer to the effect that Paula has a reputation as a prostitute and that, in his opinion, Paula was a prostitute? Would your ruling on this question change if the officer testified in a preliminary hearing that in ten years in the business Paula had not once complained of rape? If Paula takes the stand to testify that Fred raped her and says that fear made her refrain from**

reporting the rape, may Fred ask her on cross-examination whether she has worked in the past as a prostitute? May Fred ask whether she didn't consent to sex with him on the condition that he pay $100.00? Assume that the judge refuses to admit any testimony regarding Paula's other sexual activities or alleged activities as a prostitute. **Have any of Fred's constitutional rights been violated? Would they be violated if, in trying to introduce the evidence, Fred had not complied with the applicable parts of FRE 412(c)? Do your answers to any of the above questions change if it was shown by the testimony of third parties that Paula had complained within hours of the alleged rape and that when Paula came to the police station she was badly bruised and cut in several places? If there were subsection (c) hearings on any of these issues, what would happen at such hearings?**

Problem VII-31. The EEOC Guidelines define sexual harassment as "[u]nwelcome sexual advances, requests for sexual favors, and other verbal or physical conduct of a sexual nature . . . " 29 C.F.R. § 1604.11(a) (1993). Harassment becomes cognizable under Title VII [of the Civil Rights Act of 1964] under the following conditions: when (1) submission to such conduct is made either explicitly or implicitly a term or condition of an individual's employment, (2) submission to or rejection of such conduct by an individual is used as the basis for employment decisions affecting such individual, or (3) such conduct has the purpose or effect of unreasonably interfering with an individual's work performance or creating an intimidating, hostile, or offensive working environment. Diane Dale sues the Zap Electric Company for sexual harassment. She claims (1) that the factory floor on which she works is a hostile work environment because many of her male coworkers have pictures of nudes taped to the walls in the areas where they work and that they tell sexually themed jokes in her presence; (2) that her foreman often refers to her not by her name but as "Babe" or "Sexy"; for example, he might say "Come here, Sexy" when he wants her attention; and (3) that the plant manager asked her on a date once and that when, after leaving the nightclub where they had been dancing, she declined an offer to go his house, he drove by it anyway, saying as he drove by, "I thought I would drive by so that you would know where to come if you ever want a promotion."

At the trial Zap wants to offer in its defense nude photos of Dale as: "Plaything of the Month" that appeared a year earlier in a nationally circulated "men's" magazine. The company also would also like to introduce a copy of the magazine, which features an interview with Dale. When asked what her favorite things were, she had answered, "ginger ice cream, a good joke and sex with handsome men." **Is the evidence Zap offers admissible? Would it be admissible on each of the counts of Dale's complaint if the counts were tried separately?** Suppose at the section 412(c) hearing on admissibility Dale testified that she posed for the magazine only because her mother was ill and she was desperate for money to care for her, and that a magazine staffer had changed her actual answer ("ginger ice cream, a good joke and detective novels") without telling her, explaining after the photo spread appeared that her answer had not been "sexy enough." **Would this affect the admissibility of the photo and interview evidence? Would any of your answers change if the pictures had appeared 5 years before?**

Problem VII-32. On the same facts as the preceding problem Dale wants to introduce a friend of hers, Esther Weiss, to testify that she has had the same experiences Dale reported. **Should Weiss's testimony be allowed?** Suppose Weiss had been the one who had posed for the pictures and given the interview. **Should the company be allowed to inquire into these matters on cross-examination? Would your answer to this question differ if, rather than report her own experiences, Weiss had testified that she had observed male workers insist that Dale listen to sexually themed jokes and had seen men pinch Dale or whistle at her as they walked by? If Weiss testified in either way could Zap ask her on cross-examination whether she and Dale were lesbians who at one time had been sexually involved with each other? Could Zap just ask her whether she and Dale were lesbians?**

IV. BIBLIOGRAPHY

Amar, Akhil, The Constitution and Criminal Procedure: First Principles, Yale University Press, New Haven (1997).

McCormick, § 252.

Weinstein § 802 App. 100.

Wigmore Ch.47.

Wright, Charles A. and Kenneth W. Graham, Jr., Federal Practice and Procedure: Evidence, vol. 30A, §§ 6355–6374 (2000).

Baker, Katharine K., Applying *Crawford's* Confrontation Rights in a Digital Age, 45 Tex. Tech L. Rev 33 (2012).

Baker, Katharine K., Once a Rapist? Motivational Evidence and Relevancy in Rape Law, 110 Harv. L. Rev. 563 (1997).

Bellin, Jeffrey, The Incredible Shrinking Confrontation Clause, 92 B. U. L. Rev. 1865 (2012).

Berger, Vivian, Man's Trial, Woman's Tribulation: Rape Cases in the Courtroom, 77 Colum. L. Rev. 1 (1977).

Counsellor, W. Jeremy & Shannon Rickett, The Confrontation Clause after *Crawford v. Washington*: Smaller Mouth, Bigger Teeth, 57 Baylor L. Rev 1 (2005).

Davies, Thomas Y., What did the Framers Know and When Did They Know It? Fictional Originalism in *Crawford v. Washington*, 71 Brooklyn L. Rev. 105 (2005).

Fisher, Jeffrey, Reclaiming Criminal Procedure, 38 Geo. L. J. Ann. Rev. Crim. Pro. 3 (2009).

Fisher, Jeffrey, What Happened—and What is Happening—to the Confrontation Clause, 15 J. Law & Policy 587 (2007).

Fishman, Clifford S., Consent, Credibility, and the Constitution: Evidence Relating to a Sex Offense Complainant's Past Sexual Behavior, 44 Cath. Univ. L. Rev. 709 (1995).

Flanagan, James F., Compelled Immunity for Defense Witnesses: Hidden Costs and Questions, 56 Notre Dame Lawyer 447 (1981).

Friedman, Richard D., Confrontation and Forensic Laboratory Reports, Round 4, 45 Tex. Tech L. Rev. 51 (2012).

Friedman, Richard D., Forfeiture of the Confrontation Right After Crawford and Davis, 19 Regent U. L. Rev. 487 (2006–2007).

Friedman, Richard D., Grappling with the Meaning of Testimonial, 71 Brooklyn L. Rev. 241 (2005).

Friedman, Richard D., The Story of *Crawford*, pp. 335–357 in Evidence Stories, R. Lempert (ed.) Foundation Press (2006).

Giannelli, Paul, Expert Testimony and the Confrontation Clause, 22 Capital Univ. L. Rev. 45 (1993).

Graham, Kenneth W., Jr., The Right of Confrontation and the Hearsay Rule: Sir Walter Raleigh Loses Another One, 8 Crim. L. Bull. 99 (1972).

Graham, Michael H., The Confrontation Clause, the Hearsay Rule, and the Forgetful Witness, 56 Tex. L. Rev. 151 (1978).

Jonakait, Randolph N., The Too-Easy Historical Assumptions of Crawford v. Washington, 71 Brooklyn L. Rev 219 (2005).

Landsman, Stephan, Chambers v. Mississippi: A New Justice Meets an Old Style Southern Verdict, pp. 359–383 in Evidence Stories, R. Lempert (ed) Foundation Press, (2006).

Lord, Daniel B., Determining Reliability Factors in Child Hearsay Statements: Wright and Its Progeny Confront the Psychological Research, 79 Iowa L. Rev. 1149 (1994).

Metzger, Pamela R., Confrontation Control, 45 Tex. Tech L. Rev. 83 (2012).

Monnin, Paul N., "Proving Welcomeness: The Admissibility of Evidence of Sexual History in Sexual Harassment Claims Under the 1994 Amendments to Federal Rule of Evidence 412," Special Project, Current Issues in Sexual Harassment Law, 48 Vand. L. Rev. 1155 (1995).

Moreno, Joelle Anne, Finding Nino: Justice Scalia's Confrontation Clause Legacy From Its (Glorious) Beginning To (Bitter) End, 44 Akron L. Rev. 1211 (2011).

Mosteller, Robert P., *Crawford v. Washington*: Encouraging and Ensuring the Confrontation of Witnesses, 39 U. Rich. L. Rev. 511 (2004–2005).

Mosteller, Robert P., Remaking Confrontation Clause and Hearsay Doctrine Under the Challenge of Child Sexual Abuse Prosecutions, 1993 Univ. Ill. L. Rev. 691 (1993).

Murthy, Sakthi, Comment: Rejecting Unreasonable Sexual Expectations: Limits on Using a Rape Victim's Sexual History to Show the Defendant's Mistaken Belief in Consent, 79 Cal. L. Rev. 541 (1991).

Silberman, Valerie J., Testing The Testimonial Doctrine: The Impact of Melendez-Diaz v. Massachusetts on State-Level Criminal Prosecutions And Procedure, 91 Boston U. L. Rev. 789 (2011).

Sklansky, David Alan, Confrontation and Fairness, 45 Tex. Tech. L. Rev. 103 (2012).

Sloan, Jacqueline H., Extending Rape Shield Protection to Sexual Harassment Actions: New Federal Rule of Evidence 412 Undermines Meritor Savings Bank v. Vinson, 25 S. W. U. L. Rev. 363 (1996).

Swift, Eleanor, Smoke and Mirrors: The Failure of the Supreme Court's Accuracy Rationale in White v. Illinois Requires a New Look at Confrontation, 22 Capital Univ. L. Rev. 145 (1993).

Tanford, J. Alexander and Anthony J. Bocchino, Rape Victim Shield Laws and the Sixth Amendment, 128 U. Pa. L. Rev. 544 (1980).

Taslitz, Andrew E., Patriarchal Stories I: Cultural Rape Narratives in the Courtroom, 5 S. Cal. Rev. L. and Woman's Studies 389 (1996).

Tuerkheimer, Frank, A Reassessment and Redefinition of Rape Shield Laws, 50 Ohio St. L. J. 1245 (1989).

Wallach, Shawn J., Protecting the Victim at the Expense of the Defendant's Constitutional Rights, 13 N. Y. L. Sch. J. Hum. Rts. 485 (1997).

Westen, Peter, Compulsory Process II, 74 Mich. L. Rev. 191 (1975).

Westen, Peter, Confrontation and Compulsory Process: A Unified Theory of Evidence for Criminal Cases, 91 Harv. L. Rev. 567 (1978).

Westen, Peter, The Compulsory Process Clause, 73 Mich. L. Rev. 71 (1974).

White, Welsh S., Accomplices' Confessions and the Confrontation Clause, 4 William and Mary Bill of Rights Journal 753 (1996).

CHAPTER 8

PRIVILEGES

∎ ∎ ∎

I.   INTRODUCTION

The evidence rules discussed in previous chapters are mostly designed to aid "the search for truth."[1] However evanescent truth may be, the law assumes that juries can find the truth if suitable rules govern the adversary process. The most basic rule is that relevant evidence is admissible, for it is felt that the more a jury learns about a situation, the better it will be able to reconstruct what occurred. Chief Justice Burger, speaking for a court that unanimously denied a claim of executive privilege in the case of *United States v. Nixon*, wrote:

> The need to develop all relevant facts in the adversary system is both fundamental and comprehensive. The ends of . . . justice would be defeated if judgments were to be founded on a partial or speculative presentation of the facts."[2]

Nevertheless, the jury is denied some evidence because it is feared that the jurors will be misled or biased by it. This may be done on an ad hoc basis by reference to FRE 403 or through exclusionary rules like the hearsay rule. The study of these exclusionary rules is at the core of evidence courses and encompasses most of what we have thus far discussed. No inconsistency is seen between these rules and the principle that Chief Justice Burger expressed. Like Burger's principle, these rules are believed to enhance the search for truth, for they exclude evidence that is thought likely to be prejudicial, unreliable or otherwise prone to interfere with the search for truth.

This chapter deals with another group of exclusionary rules—rules of privilege. The rationale for these rules differs from the rationale of most of the evidence rules we have encountered. The exclusionary rules of privilege mean that a person who has reliable, relevant information, may sometimes keep secret what she knows. No one pretends that this aids the search for truth. Privileges persist because some values are regarded as important enough to justify restrictions on how that search is conducted. These values are not peculiar to the United States. Many countries which regard most Anglo-American exclusionary rules of

---

[1]   See Chapter Two, pp. 157–161.

[2]   United States v. Nixon, 418 U.S. 683, 709 (1974).

evidence as quixotic if not perverse, nevertheless recognize a broad range of privileges, some of which are unknown in this country.[3]

Privileges are unusual in other ways as well. They are, for example, the only rules of evidence that bind judges when they are deciding preliminary questions of fact pursuant to FRE 104. Privileges, unlike the other exclusionary rules, are also presumptively applicable in a variety of non-judicial settings, such as grand jury proceedings and hearings before administrative agencies or legislative committees. In addition, objections under most other rules of evidence are made while the witness is testifying, and the jurors know of the objection and the fact that a party is trying to keep information from them. While this occasionally happens when only some of what a witness testifies to is privileged, often the issue is whether a witness can be made to testify at all or whether an allegedly privileged document should be admitted. In those situations courts often rule in advance so that the privilege claim need not be made in front of the jury. Even when only some of a witness's testimony is privileged, courts will often rule out certain lines of questioning on the basis of privilege before the witness takes the stand.[4] Finally, when a party does not present evidence in his control or a witness who might be expected to favor his story, it is generally permissible for opposing counsel to call attention to this omission and to suggest that the evidence was not presented or the witness not called because doing so would have harmed rather than advanced the party's case. This should not be done when the evidence or witness is protected by a privilege.[5]

A number of privileges involve a "professional" counselor and a "nonprofessional" seeking advice—most commonly the attorney-client privilege, the doctor-patient privilege, and the psychotherapist-patient privilege. These are thought to promote free communication on topics relevant to important professional services. Other privileges are designed to establish zones of private activity or private communication. Spouses may have a privilege so broad as to preclude any testimony from one spouse concerning the other. In addition, they often have one that protects their private communications. The Fifth Amendment gives criminal defendants the well-known privilege not to testify against

---

[3] The Taiwanese evidence code, for example, provides a privilege for testimony that may expose the witness, or a number of his relatives including aunts, uncles, in-laws and former in-laws, to humiliation. See James C. Liu, Morley Shih, Anthony M. Lo, Frank H. Lan, and Fullsoon Lin, Major Laws of the Republic of China on Taiwan, 811 (1991).

[4] Proposed Federal Rule of Evidence 513(b) would have required courts to keep juries from learning that a privilege had been claimed so far as practicable.

[5] Proposed Federal Rule of Evidence 513(a) would have precluded comments on the fact that privilege had been claimed, while subsection (c) of the same rule would have entitled a privilege claimant to a jury instruction that no adverse inference could be drawn from a claim of privilege. This rule implies that parties should be precluded from suggesting that juries draw adverse inferences from evidence that is not offered when the evidence has been withheld because of a privilege.

themselves.[6] The government has special privileges. It may in some circumstances conceal the identity of informants; it may refuse to reveal state secrets; and it may, to some extent, shield information used in governmental deliberations. News reporters in some states may claim a privilege to protect their sources similar to the government's privilege to protect informants, and businesses may claim a privilege to protect trade secrets similar to that which exists to protect official information. Most privileges are not constitutionally based. They exist in some places and not in others. They take different forms in different jurisdictions. Interest groups often seek privileges for information they believe should be held in confidence, and critics of the privilege system seek to limit or repeal existing privileges. In every state you will find some form of attorney-client privilege, priest-penitent (or clergy) privilege, spousal privilege, and governmental privileges. The privilege against self-incrimination also applies throughout the United States, because it is constitutionally required. The incidence of other privileges varies markedly.

SOME BASICS

A **privilege** is the right to prevent the disclosure in evidence of a confidential communication or other protected information.

A person who is entitled to assert a privilege is called a **holder** of the privilege. For example, for the attorney-client privilege the client is the only holder, but for the clergy-penitent privilege, in some states, both parties to a covered communication are holders.

Most privileges cover only communications, not the underlying events that are the subject of the communication. Thus, the attorney-client privilege covers confidential statements a client makes to her lawyer describing an automobile accident, but not other evidence about the accident—including (in a civil case) deposition or trial testimony from the client describing the accident. A communications privilege also does not generally cover events other than communications in the relationship that gave rise to the privilege. For example, the fact that a parishioner consulted with her priest is not a covered communication. But not every privilege is limited to communications. Some bar questions that seek certain information. The state secrets privilege and the informers privilege are examples. A few privileges, including the Fifth Amendment and one of the spousal privileges, preclude the calling of certain people as witnesses.

A communication is **confidential** if it was intended to be restricted to the parties to the privilege, and if reasonable steps were taken to keep it

---

[6] Because this privilege plays such an important role in the law of criminal procedure and is covered in criminal procedure courses, we discuss it only briefly in this chapter.

private. What a husband shouts to his wife in a train station does not qualify for a communications privilege.

Finally, privileges only protect against the disclosure of information as **evidence** in some legal proceeding such as a trial or grand jury hearing. Evidentiary privileges do not preclude all disclosure. Thus, the attorney-client privilege does not prohibit an attorney from disclosing her client's professional confidences to her drinking buddies in a bar or to the world on television, but a separate body of law—the rules of professional conduct—requires the lawyer to maintain the confidentiality of client information in all contexts. By contrast, while a husband (or an ex-husband) is entitled to prevent his wife (or ex-wife) from testifying to a confidential marital communication, neither the applicable evidentiary privilege nor any other law gives him the power to stop her from disclosing all in a kiss-and-tell biography.

Judges want the truth to emerge in their courts so that justice can be done. Claims of privilege can threaten this goal, for most privileges preclude testimony from people well situated to know the truth. Courts regularly see valuable evidence lost to claims of privilege. Thus, most judges are reluctant to create new privileges; they occasionally pierce new holes in old ones, and in deciding how far the protections of a privilege extend, they usually begin with the proposition "privileges should be strictly construed."

Many scholarly commentators have shared the view that privileges too frequently thwart justice. The utilitarian philosopher Jeremy Bentham would have abolished almost all privileges, including, especially, the one you shall enjoy as a lawyer. He wrote of the attorney-client privilege, which is widely regarded as one of the more defensible privileges:

> When, in consulting with a law adviser, attorney or advocate, a man has confessed his delinquency, or disclosed some fact which, if stated in court, might tend to operate in proof of it, such law adviser is not to be suffered to be examined as to any such point. The law adviser is neither to be compelled, nor so much as suffered, to betray the trust thus reposed in him. Not suffered? Why not? Oh, because to betray a trust is treachery; and an act of treachery is an immoral act.

> An immoral sort of act, is that sort of act, the tendency of which is, in some way or other, to lessen the quantity of happiness in society. In what way does the supposed cause in question tend to the production of any such effect? The conviction and punishment of the defendant, he being guilty, is by the supposition an act the tendency of which, upon the whole, is beneficial to society.... The good, then, that results from the conviction and punishment, in the case in question, is out of

dispute: where, then, is the additional evil of it when produced by the cause in question? Nowhere. The evil consists in the punishment: but the punishment a man undergoes is not greater when the evidence on which the conviction and punishment are grounded happens to come out of the mouth of a law adviser of his, than if it had happened to come out of his own mouth, or that of a third person.

But if such confidence, when reposed, is permitted to be violated, and if this be known, (which, if such be the law, it will be), the consequence will be, that no such confidence will be reposed. Not reposed?—Well: and if it be not, wherein will consist the mischief? The man by the supposition is guilty; if not, by the supposition there is nothing to betray: let the law adviser say everything he has heard, everything he can have heard from his client, the client cannot have anything to fear from it. That it will often happen that in the case supposed no such confidence will be reposed, is natural enough: the first thing the advocate or attorney will say to his client, will be,—Remember that, whatever you say to me, I shall be obliged to tell, if asked about it. What, then, will be the consequence? That a guilty person will not in general be able to derive quite so much assistance from his law adviser, in the way of concerting a false defense, as he may do at present.

Except the prevention of such pernicious confidence, of what other possible effect can the rule for the requisition of such evidence be productive? Either or none at all, or of the conviction of delinquents, in some instances in which, but for the lights thus obtained, they would not have been convicted. But in this effect, what imaginable circumstance is there that can render it in any degree pernicious and undesirable? None whatever. The conviction of delinquents is the very end of penal justice.[7]

Other scholars have been neither so passionate in their condemnation of privileges as Bentham nor so hostile, but they have nonetheless regarded privileges with considerable suspicion. More than half a century ago Professor Edmund Morgan wrote of the physician-patient privilege, "[T]he law reports and the experience of judges and lawyers furnish ample evidence that such a privilege operates to suppress the truth and to further injustice."[8] More recently, McCormick noted that the dominant attitude among bench, bar, and scholars is that "[T]he

---

[7] Jeremy Bentham, 5 Rationale of Judicial Evidence 302–04 (J.S. Mill ed., 1827).

[8] Some Observations Concerning a Model Code of Evidence, 89 U. Pa. L. Rev. 145, 151 (1940).

granting of a claim of privilege can serve only to shut out the light" as far as the party seeking to bring the matter into the lawsuit is concerned.[9]

Yet despite these views, privileges have endured for more than two centuries. If some privileges have been narrowed with the passage of time or even repealed, other privileges have been expanded and new privileges have been created. Why have privileges endured, and what justifies their creation and expansion? The dominant analysis, which courts still cite and commentators must either endorse or contend with, is Wigmore's. Focusing on privileges for confidential communications, he argues that before such privileges are granted, four requisites must be met:

(1) The communications must originate in a *confidence* that they will not be disclosed;

(2) This element of *confidentiality must be essential* to the full and satisfactory maintenance of the relation between the parties;

(3) The *relation* must be one that in the opinion of the community ought to be sedulously *fostered*; and

(4) The *injury* that would accrue to the relation by the disclosure of the communications must be *greater than the benefit* thereby gained for the correct disposal of litigation.[10]

Wigmore's position, like Bentham's, is utilitarian. The two differ in their approval of certain privileges only because they differ in their "armchair sociology." Wigmore thought that the conditions he set are met in the case of certain privileges, like the attorney-client privilege, while Bentham would have disagreed. Their putative disagreement highlights the indeterminate nature of Wigmore's fourth proposition.

Absent from Wigmore's analysis is any sense of values apart from the value of fostering socially desirable relationships. Wigmore does not recognize that for symbolic or other reasons we might want to define zones of interpersonal privacy that the law cannot touch, or that respect for human relationships might make us reluctant to compel people to betray the love or trust that special others have reposed in them. Many commentators have noted these deficiencies in Wigmore's analysis and sought to rest privileges on these less instrumental grounds.[11]

Privileges are also supported by two arguments that focus on the costs they impose. First, proponents point out, most privileges only

---

[9] McCormick (2nd ed.) § 77, at 156. The current edition of McCormick is far more nuanced. McCormick, (6th ed.) § 77.

[10] Wigmore § 2190, at 62.

[11] See David Louisell, Confidentiality, Conformity and Confusion: Privileges in Federal Court Today, 31 Tul. L. Rev. 101, 110–11, 113–14 (1956); Thomas Krattenmaker, Testimonial Privileges in Federal Courts: An Alternative to the Proposed Federal Rules of Evidence, 62 Geo. L.J. 61, 86–88 (1973); Charles Fried, The Lawyer as Friend: The Moral Foundations of the Lawyer-Client Relation, 85 Yale L.J. 1060 (1976).

protect communications; they do not protect the information those communications convey. Thus, Pamela Plaintiff may not be asked what she told her lawyer about an accident, but she may be asked in a deposition or at trial what she knows about the accident, and if her answers differ materially from what she told her attorney, the lawyer has an obligation to see that Pamela corrects her story. Moreover, as we shall see, almost all privileges offer only partial or qualified protection. These qualifications are such that many privileges do not apply or are deemed waived in situations where the information they protect are likely to have great probative value. For example, in many states with a physician-patient privilege, the privilege does not apply when a litigant places his health in issue, and to defend an action by asserting that it was done on advice of counsel is to waive the privilege for conversations pertaining to that advice.

Second, while the cost of a privilege invoked at trial appears clear, over the long run some privileges may cost the legal system little information, and they may even generate information that would otherwise be unavailable.[12] The news reporter's privilege is, for example, often justified on this ground. If a reporter has no privilege to protect a source's identity, valuable information may be provided in a particular trial. But sources may become more reluctant to talk confidentially to reporters, and so reporters in the future may publish stories that are less informationally rich. This may prevent future litigants from acquiring leads to admissible evidence they would otherwise find. If these suppositions are true, jurisdictions that allow reporters to keep sources confidential suffer no long-run informational cost, for the information courts cannot access would not have been available absent the privilege. Similar arguments are made with respect to other privileges, such as the attorney-client privilege and the psychotherapist-patient privilege.

No doubt, there is some truth to this argument, but it should not be oversold. One survey study, for example, reports that more than half of its 105 lay respondents said they would withhold information from their attorneys despite a lawyer's general assurance of confidentiality, if confidentiality could not be guaranteed, but nearly three-quarters of respondents were never told when they first talked to their attorneys that their conversations were privileged, and even those who would withhold information would still reveal much.[13] As for journalists, confidential sources are used in jurisdictions with and without a news reporter's privilege, and it has yet to be shown that the existence of a privilege makes a difference in their availability.

---

[12] See Stephen A. Saltzburg, Privileges and Professionals: Lawyers and Psychiatrists, 66 Va. L. Rev. 597 (1980).

[13] Fred C. Zacharias, Rethinking Confidentiality, 75 Iowa L. Rev. 601 (1990).

Privileges also sacrifice no information where witnesses would defy court orders to testify. This is a strong justification for the priest-penitent (or clergy) privilege, particularly as it applies to the sacrament of the confession, and this rationale, as well as fears of dishonest testimony, may have influenced those few jurisdictions that recognize a parent-child privilege. An additional reason to extend privileges to such relationships is because a court's efforts to coerce testimony from people like priests or parents may undermine the law's legitimacy for many people.

Finally, we should recognize that politics and ideology play a role in who gets privileges. There are few privileges as broadly protective and as firmly entrenched as the attorney-client privilege and the related work-product protection. Surely, this in some measure reflects the fact that almost all judges and many legislators—the creators and definers of privileges—are attorneys. Other groups must campaign for privileges, and they do. News reporters, accountants, medical doctors, social workers, and psychologists have all succeeded in claiming confidential communication privileges in some jurisdictions while being denied them in others. Usually when they succeed in arguing for a privilege, it is legislators rather than judges who have granted it. Courts, as we have noted, are reluctant to recognize new privileges, although it does happen.

The diversity of privileges across the various states reflects differences in substantive policy judgments. Because privileges give rights to specific classes of litigants rather than to all litigants offering or opposing the same type of evidence, many see them as aimed more at promoting substantive policies than at regulating trial procedures. When the proposed Federal Rules of Evidence were before Congress, not only was there considerable debate about the substantive policies embodied in the proposed privileges, but there was also a feeling that to impose federal privileges in diversity cases would violate the *Erie* Doctrine.[14] Ultimately Congress could neither accept the proposed federal privileges nor agree on amendments that would make them generally acceptable. Instead the Congress opted for FRE 501:

> The common law—as interpreted by United States courts in the light of reason and experience—governs a claim of privilege unless any of the following provides otherwise:
>
> - the United States Constitution;
> - a federal statute; or
> - rules prescribed by the Supreme Court.

---

[14] Erie R. Co. v. Tompkins, 304 U.S. 64 (1938).

But in a civil case, state law governs privilege regarding a claim or defense for which state law supplies the rule of decision. [15]

This rule allows courts to change the contours of privilege law in the context of specific case decisions. The Supreme Court and the federal courts of appeals have on occasion acted on this permission. The rule also recognizes the substantive nature of privilege law in providing that state privileges pertain where state law provides the rule of decision, but that the federal law of privileges applies in other cases brought in federal court.[16]

FRE 501 means that except when state and federal privileges are similar, Wigmore's requisites for extending privileges will not pertain since if either the state or the federal government can coerce testimony that the other would privilege, speakers cannot be confident that their communications will not be disclosed in some court. Other justifications for privileges are less threatened by FRE 501. The state and federal governments may, for example, differ in their willingness to coerce one party in a special relationship, like the marriage relationship, to participate in making a case against the other. FRE 501 respects this judgment in cases in which the jurisdiction's substantive law governs.

Although the privileges proposed for Article Five were never enacted into law, courts often cite them in resolving privilege issues. Much that is in the rules tracks the common law, and where they deviate, they usually reflect the dominant scholarly and judicial views about what the law should be. Judge Weinstein in his treatise, for example, proposes that

---

[15] Congress also added a new section to Title 28 of the United States Code: § 2076. Rules of evidence:

The Supreme Court of the United States shall have the power to prescribe amendments to the Federal Rules of Evidence. Such amendments shall not take effect until they have been reported to Congress by the Chief Justice at or after the beginning of a regular session of Congress but not later than the first day of May, and until the expiration of one hundred and eighty days after they have been so reported; but if either House of Congress within that time shall by resolution disapprove any amendment so reported it shall not take effect. The effective date of any amendment so reported may be deferred by either House of Congress to a later date or until approved by Act of Congress. Any rule whether proposed or in force may be amended by Act of Congress. Any provision of law in force at the expiration of such time and in conflict with any such amendment not disapproved shall be of no further force or effect after such amendment has taken effect. *Any such amendment creating, abolishing, or modifying a privilege shall have no force or effect unless it shall be approved by act of Congress. . . .* (emphasis added).

Note the special provision for privilege rules. Congress's action leaves the role of the courts slightly confused because the Rule permits the development of a law of privileges on a common law basis while the statute restricts the Court's power to change privileges. In *Trammel v. United States*, 445 U.S. 40 (1980), the Court concluded that the statute restricted only its formal rulemaking power and did not prevent it from redefining privileges in the context of specific cases. The Court has done this several times since *Trammel*.

[16] When federal courts are hearing state claims by virtue of pendent jurisdiction, most federal courts hold that the federal privilege law applies to all claims, although this appears to conflict with the literal language of FRE 501. The cases typically involve situations in which a state privileges information that federal law does not. It is commonly thought that once privileged information is revealed for its bearing on the federal claim, it is both pointless and impossible to keep a jury from considering the information when deciding the state claim.

federal courts should treat the rejected rules as standards to guide them, and some courts have used them in this way. Other courts have turned to state privilege law for guidance in determining how federal privileges apply. Judges who do this argue that when the scope of a federal privilege is unclear, comity counsels respect for a state's interests. Since a state's purposes in extending a privilege may be subverted if federal law is less protective,[17] the comity argument is a strong one. It is not, however, so strong as to lead the federal courts to recognize privileges new to federal law simply because states have them. In the cases where it has dealt with privileges, the Supreme Court has used the proposed federal privilege rules as one source of guidance, but in recent cases the proposed rules seem less important than widespread practice among the states and classic common law understandings.[18]

Notably, only one additional Federal Rule of Evidence governing privileges has been created. In 2008, Congress enacted Federal Rule of Evidence 502, Attorney-Client Privilege and Work Product; Limitations on Waiver, in order to regulate to some extent the significant problem of inadvertent waiver of privileged material during discovery, especially electronic discovery.

Problem VIII-1. New privileges are often proposed. **Would you favor any of the privileges described below? What factors would you want to weigh in deciding whether to create a new privilege? Is there any additional information that you would like to have? Is this information currently available? If a privilege is desirable, on what basis does one choose between an absolute privilege forbidding all testimony relating to privileged information regardless of the circumstances and a qualified privilege that might not apply to certain information or in all situations?**

A. News reporters claim that they must often give sources a promise of confidentiality in order to elicit important information. Indeed, even if explicit promises are not given, an unspoken understanding may be thought to exist. Reporters believe that if they are compelled to reveal the identity of individuals giving them information in confidence, their sources will dry up. **Should there be a privilege to protect the identity of sources promised confidentiality or the identity of sources generally?** Reporters also receive a good deal of information "off the record." This

---

[17] Where state and federal privileges differ, it is usually the federal privilege that is less protective. Where a federal privilege arguably protects more than state law, comity is no reason to follow the state interpretation, but a Wigmore-style utilitarian analysis will suggest that there is nothing to be gained from greater federal protection.

[18] See, e.g., Jaffee v. Redmond, 518 U.S. 1 (1996); Swidler & Berlin v. United States, 524 U.S. 399 (1998).

information often helps them to understand the background of a story or to develop leads to on-the-record sources. **Should reporters be privileged to refuse to reveal the contents of off-the-record information? Does it matter if the identity of the off-the-record informant is known?**

B.   In a number of cities throughout the United States, centers have been established to shelter drug addicts, runaways, pregnant teenagers, and other troubled individuals. Most such centers engage in informal counseling, and often intensive individual or group therapy sessions are available for the "guests." **Should information gained in informal counseling or in group therapy sessions be privileged? Should the identity of the guests at such establishments be privileged?**

C.   At times a party will seek to put the best friend of an opposing party on the stand. Honest testimony in these circumstances may strain even a close friendship. The best friend may be called upon to reveal information given in the strictest confidence. The temptation to commit perjury is obvious. **Should there be a privilege that enables an individual to keep his best friend from testifying against him? Should there be a privilege that enables an individual to prevent his best friend from testifying to anything the friend has learned from the individual in confidence engendered by the friendship?**

II. ATTORNEY-CLIENT PRIVILEGE

A. BASIC JUSTIFICATIONS

The attorney-client privilege, its roots extending to Roman law, is the oldest of the existing privileges for confidential communications. Until the end of the eighteenth century, the privilege was justified by its relationship to the honor of attorneys:

> After the retainer, they [attorneys] are considered as the same person with their clients and are trusted with their secrets, which without a breach of confidence cannot be revealed, and without such sort of confidence there could be no trust or dependence on any man. . . .[19]

In the early nineteenth century, a new justification emerged:

---

[19] Sir Geoffrey Gilbert, The Law of Evidence 138 (London ed., 1756), quoted in 8 Wigmore § 2290, at 543 n.3. See generally Max Radin, The Privilege of Confidential Communication Between Lawyer and Client, 16 Cal. L. Rev. 487 (1928); Geoffrey C. Hazard, An Historical Perspective on the Attorney-Client Privilege, 66 Cal. L. Rev. 1061 (1978), for a discussion of the development of the privilege to cover legal advice when litigation was not pending or necessarily contemplated.

This was the theory that claims and disputes which may lead to litigation can most justly and expeditiously be handled by practiced experts, namely lawyers, and that such experts can act effectively only if they are fully advised of the facts by the parties whom they represent. Such full disclosure will be promoted if the client knows that what he tells his lawyer cannot, over his objection, be extorted in court from the lawyer's lips.[20]

Both the emerging justification and the one it replaced were attacked, as we noted in the introduction, by the English lawyer-philosopher Jeremy Bentham. You will recall that his argument, reduced to its essence, was that the innocent would have nothing to fear from the abrogation of the privilege while no good came of the guilty getting more effective legal assistance. Many scholars have responded to Bentham's critique.[21] Both his premises are vulnerable.

First, Bentham is mistaken in his assumption that the innocent have nothing to fear from the revelation of their confidences. The honest disclosures of an innocent defendant, such as the admission by an accused embezzler that he was desperate for money, could form a central link in the state's case. Other disclosures, such as a man's confession that he was with his mistress at the time he allegedly robbed a bank, although exonerative, could severely disrupt a person's life, perhaps so much so that he would prefer risking a conviction to revealing the information. In civil cases, which Bentham does not consider, lawyers may acquire proprietary information, which, if publicly disclosed, could hurt their clients or help competitors—perhaps to a greater extent than the stakes of the litigation. In each of these situations, as in many others, the information conveyed in confidence may help a lawyer construct a sounder case, even if that information is itself never revealed.

Bentham is equally short-sighted when he suggests that no good may come from protecting the confidences of a guilty client. When lawyers know their clients have behaved illegally, they can encourage fair plea bargains and settlements, forestall perjury, and persuade their clients to cease ongoing illegal actions.[22] If the guilty do not confide in their attorneys because they know their attorneys may be forced to testify, lawyers are less able to achieve such outcomes.

---

[20] McCormick (2nd ed.) § 87, at 175. See also McCormick (6th ed.) § 87.

[21] See, e.g., James A. Gardner, A Re-Evaluation of the Attorney-Client Privilege (pt.1), 8 Vill. L. Rev. 279, 304–06 (1963); Radin, supra note 19; 8 Wigmore § 2291.

[22] More than three-quarters of 63 upstate New York attorneys polled by Professor Zacharias reported that at some point in their careers confidentiality helped them dissuade a client from wrongdoing. See Zacharias, supra note 13. On the other hand, more than one-third asserted attorney-client confidentiality in situations in which they personally believed that, as good citizens, they should have been required to make information public. See id.

In addition to these arguments, two considerations emphasized by Professor Saltzburg strengthen the case for an attorney-client privilege.[23] First, people who go to lawyers know that what they say may be legally consequential, and if there were no privilege lawyers would surely alert their clients to that fact. In this the attorney-client privilege differs, for example, from a reporter-source privilege, a psychotherapist-patient privilege or a husband-wife privilege. Few conversations in these settings pertain to contemplated litigation, and in these relations it is not part of one party's routine to alert the other to salient legal facts.

The informational consequences of abolishing the attorney-client privilege are suggested in a survey of 105 upstate New York residents.[24] Nearly 30% of those surveyed reported that they gave information to their attorneys that they "would not have given without a guarantee of confidentiality,"[25] and a majority of the respondents said that they would withhold information from an attorney who told them he could not guarantee confidentiality, even if the attorney promised that, except in unusual cases, he would keep the client's disclosures secret.[26] These results do not mean that people will not talk to their attorneys, for people often have little choice but to use lawyers, and where they do they must describe their cases to them. But they might nonetheless withhold or lie about crucial information, the kind of information that critics of the privilege point to when they suggest that if attorneys could be compelled to speak, the truth would surely be revealed. If this would occur, extending a privilege to attorney-client communications may not be that costly, for the most revealing information that attorneys now possess would often not be disclosed to them absent a privilege.

Professor Saltzburg's second point is that the attorney-client privilege protects the adversary system not just by fostering attorney-client communications but also by precluding one party from routinely calling her adversary's attorney as a witness. Obviously, if an attorney is forced to give testimony that damages her client, the trust necessary for a successful attorney-client relationship may be broken. Less obvious perhaps are other potential problems. If, for example, an attorney's credibility were severely challenged on cross-examination, she might not be able to function effectively as an advocate thereafter. Also since people cannot cross-examine themselves and may well miss what is objectionable about a question when focusing on how to answer it, effective advocacy would require a second attorney to protect a client's interests while the first was on the stand, thus increasing litigation costs. Finally, a testifying attorney has her own reputation as well as a client's interests to protect; the two may not be congruent.

---

[23] See Saltzburg, supra note 12, at 605–10.

[24] Zacharias, supra note 13.

[25] Id. at 381.

[26] See id. at 386.

For these and other reasons it has long been regarded as ethically problematic for a lawyer to testify in a case she is litigating. Although there may be some situations—particularly those involving discrete, uncontroversial facts such as the authentication of a document—in which a lawyer's testimony poses few ethical problems, the more central the lawyer's testimony, the greater those problems are likely to be. While the attorney-client privilege does not preclude calling an adversary's attorney, it does minimize the purposes for which this can occur, and by confining that testimony to nonprivileged information, it limits the likely importance of the lawyer's testimony to the opponent's case. In doing so, it prevents overzealous advocates from raising ethical conflicts in order to deprive opponents of the counsel they employ.

The attorney-client privilege applies not just at trials but also in administrative tribunals, before grand juries, and in other settings. This is important because in the early 1980s a new tactic emerged in federal grand jury investigations: summoning the attorney for the person targeted by the investigation.[27] This tactic poses some of the same problems for adversary system values as calling an opponent's attorney at trial. It imposes costs on attorneys and their clients that would not otherwise exist. It can create ethical conflicts that require attorneys to cease representing clients. And it may be even more potent in destroying attorney-client trust than calling an attorney at trial, because grand jury secrecy means that the client can never be certain what his attorney revealed.

Critics believe that the tactic of summoning attorneys before grand juries has sometimes been adopted not primarily because of the nonprivileged information attorneys might provide but to disrupt the legal representation of the target. Defenders of this tactic claimed that attorneys subpoenaed before grand juries were often knowing aids to ongoing crimes or frauds that the grand juries were investigating. This justification, however, could seldom be proven; if it could, the attorney would have been a defendant and not defense counsel. Many commentators were troubled by grand jury subpoenas and some courts limited the situations in which such subpoenas may be issued.[28] Also the ethics codes of some state bars were amended to treat subpoenaing defense counsel to testify before grand juries as an ethics violation unless done for a few, limited purposes. A Justice Department report of practices in the mid-1980s reveals that more than 400 grand jury subpoenas to attorneys were approved during twelve surveyed months after subpoena guidelines designed to restrict this procedure were in

---

[27] For a critical discussion of this tactic see Max. D. Stern and David A. Hoffman, Privileged Informers: The Attorney Subpoena Problem and a Proposal for Reform, 136 U. Pa. L. Rev. 1783 (1988).

[28] See, e.g., In re Grand Jury Proceedings (Schofield), 486 F.2d 85, 93 (3d Cir. 1973).

effect.[29] Today the attorney general must approve federal subpoenas to defense counsel, and their use has fallen off considerably. The example nevertheless illustrates how more than 150 years after Bentham, evaluations of the attorney-client privilege are still a matter of perspective.

B. THE PRIVILEGE IN DETAIL

It is difficult to evaluate arguments for and against the attorney-client privilege in the abstract, for the attorney-client privilege, like other privileges, is case specific. Some conversations between attorneys and clients are protected by the privilege, while others are not. Generally speaking, an instrumental view of the privilege has prevailed. The privilege ordinarily applies when it is thought to promote attorney-client communications about legal matters and not otherwise. Later, you will see that a similar orientation is evident in most other privileges.

If otherwise applicable, the attorney-client privilege in the United States applies whether an attorney is in private practice or is in-house counsel. This is not always the case elsewhere. On September 14, 2010, for example, the European Court of Justice held in *Akzo Nobel Chemicals Ltd. and Akcros Chemicals v. European Commission,* that under European Union law, the lawyer-client privilege does not extend to communications with corporate in-house counsel because in-house counsel are not "independent" lawyers.

PFRE 503, the attorney-client privilege that was proposed by the drafters of the Federal Rules of Evidence and approved by the Supreme Court but not enacted, tracks the common law in many respects, and varies from it in some others, making the proposed rule a helpful guide to understanding the scope of the privilege and certain issues that recur in applying it. Unless we indicate differently, you may assume that the law in most state and federal courts is consistent with the proposed federal rule's provisions.

Proposed Federal Rule of Evidence (PFRE) 503:

LAWYER-CLIENT PRIVILEGE

(a) *Definitions.* As used in this rule:

(1) A "client" is a person, public officer, or corporation, association, or other organization or entity, either public or private, who is rendered professional legal services by a lawyer, or who consults a lawyer with a view to obtaining professional legal services from him.

---

[29] See Stern & Hoffman, supra note 27 at 1788, n.191. Evidence gathered from attorneys often includes tax records and the like and tends to be used more in civil than in criminal cases.

(2) A "lawyer" is a person authorized, or reasonably believed by the client to be authorized, to practice law in any state or nation.

(3) A "representative of the lawyer" is one employed to assist the lawyer in the rendition of professional legal services.

(4) A communication is "confidential" if not intended to be disclosed to third persons other than those to whom disclosure is in furtherance of the rendition of professional legal services to the client or those reasonably necessary for the transmission of the communication.

(b) *General rule of privilege.* A client has a privilege to refuse to disclose and to prevent any other person from disclosing confidential communications made for the purpose of facilitating the rendition of professional legal services to the client, (1) between himself or his representative and his lawyer or his lawyer's representative, or (2) between his lawyer and the lawyer's representative, or (3) by him or his lawyer to a lawyer representing another in a matter of common interest, or (4) between representatives of the client or between the client and a representative of the client, or (5) between lawyers representing the client.

(c) *Who may claim the privilege.* The privilege may be claimed by the client, his guardian or conservator, the personal representative of a deceased client, or the successor, trustee, or similar representative of a corporation, association, or other organization, whether or not in existence. The person who was the lawyer at the time of the communication may claim the privilege but only on behalf of the client. His authority to do so is presumed in the absence of evidence to the contrary.

(d) *Exceptions.* There is no privilege under this rule:

(1) *Furtherance of crime or fraud.* If the services of the lawyer were sought or obtained to enable or aid anyone to commit or plan to commit what the client knew or reasonably should have known to be a crime or fraud; or

(2) *Claimants through same deceased client.* As to a communication relevant to an issue between parties who claim through the same deceased client, regardless of whether the claims are by testate or intestate succession or by *inter vivos* transaction; or

(3) *Breach of duty by lawyer or client.* As to a communication relevant to an issue of breach or duty by the lawyer to his client or by the client to his lawyer; or

(4) *Document attested by lawyer.* As to a communication relevant to an issue concerning an attested document to which the lawyer is an attesting witness; or

(5) *Joint clients.* As to a communication relevant to a matter of common interest between two or more clients if the communication was made by any of them to a lawyer retained or consulted in common, when offered in an action between any of the clients.

1. Being a Client

We see from the rule that the attorney-client privilege belongs to the client, who may be a natural person (like you, for example) or a corporation or other organized entity. What transforms a person or entity into a client is using or seeking to use a lawyer, or someone reasonably believed to be a lawyer, for professional legal services.

One need not actually hire an attorney to benefit from the attorney-client privilege. If Carrie Client approaches her friend Alice Attorney for legal advice, their conversation is privileged whether or not Alice charges for her services.[30] The situation would be similar if Alice were a lawyer who advertised free initial consultations, and if after the consultation Carrie decided that Alice was not for her or Alice decided that she did not want to take Carrie's case. Nor need Alice actually be a lawyer for the privilege to attach to Carrie's conversation with her. If Carrie looks up Alice's name in the yellow pages under "attorney" and describes her case, their conversation is privileged, even if Alice was disbarred after her phone number was listed or was never a member of the bar in the first instance. The key is the reasonableness of Carrie's belief that Alice was a lawyer. If, for example, Carrie knows that Alice is a recent law school graduate still awaiting her bar examination results, nothing that Carrie says to Alice will be privileged no matter what the quality of Alice's legal advice.

The proposed federal rule makes it clear that not everyone who consults a lawyer is a client for purposes of the privilege. To be a client, a person must be receiving or seeking "professional legal services." Moreover, under subsection (b) of PFRE 503 even when one is seeking professional legal services, communications not relating to such services are not privileged. If, for example, Carrie describes an injury in detail to Alice, a personal injury specialist, because she wants Alice to recommend a good doctor, nothing Carrie says would be privileged. What is more surprising, perhaps, is that Carrie would not enjoy a privilege for financial information she provided Alice if Alice were a tax attorney whom Carrie had hired to do her tax return. The courts say that filling out tax returns is an accountancy function, and those who hire attorneys

---

[30] There are, however, some scattered court decisions that have held that people seeking legal advice from close friends or relatives, who were attorneys, were consulting their friends or relatives as personal friends or relatives and not as attorneys so the privilege did not attach. One gets the impression in these cases that the courts involved were looking for excuses to pierce the privilege and that most such cases were incorrectly decided. Nevertheless, these cases suggest that special precautions should be taken to make the nature of the relationship clear when counseling a close friend or relative.

for this purpose are not seeking legal services. This view would, no doubt, surprise many people who hire tax attorneys for their knowledge of what the law requires, but courts argue that it would be anomalous to privilege communications to an attorney for a service when the same communications made to an accountant for the same services would not be privileged.[31] The same courts, however, will protect financial disclosures to attorneys involved in complicated tax planning without asking whether accountants engage in similar activities. What motivates courts seems to be more a conception of the kind of work that requires distinctively legal skills rather than a concern for whether some non-lawyers have and sell these skills, but the latter is not irrelevant. It influences courts in deciding whether an activity draws on skills that are distinctively legal. Thus, courts that deny the privilege to lawyers doing tax returns are influenced by the fact that people not qualified to practice law often do this work. We see a similar phenomenon in the patent law area, where the privilege is often denied communications involving purely technical disclosures even though the patent attorneys need this information to apply for patents.

The proposed federal rule allows public officers and government agencies to be clients for purposes of the privilege, and in other sections seems to protect their communications as it would those of any other client. In this, the rule is more protective than a somewhat confused common law or the rules in some states. Because public officials speak on behalf of all citizens, their ability to claim the attorney-client privilege has been disputed. Claims are commonly honored when those litigating against a state agency seek to learn what the most directly involved officials told the agency's attorneys regarding the litigation, and they may be honored where a party wants to learn about disclosures made and

---

[31] The argument can be reversed. In a few states accountants have secured a privilege for their clients' communications to them by arguing that they are performing the same services as attorneys who have a privilege. In jurisdictions with an accountant-client privilege, attorneys will enjoy a privilege for accountant-type work, but the protection they enjoy may not be as strong as that provided by the attorney-client privilege.

In the *IRS Restructuring and Reform Act of 1998* the argument that accountants should be treated like attorneys achieved partial success, as Congress included in the reform bill a privilege for clients of federally authorized tax practitioners, which in certain cases grants taxpayer clients of non-attorney practitioners the same privilege their communications would enjoy if their tax advisors were attorneys. But as the Senate Finance Committee's report makes clear, the old law precluding attorneys from claiming the privilege for ordinary tax accounting remains good law. Information disclosed to a tax practitioner to prepare a tax return is, for example, not made privileged by the new law because it is now not privileged when divulged to an attorney. The new privilege is also limited because it may not be claimed in criminal cases or before administrative bodies other than the IRS. This is a strange communications privilege because it protects confidential communications in one setting but not in other settings where it might be at least as valuable to the taxpayer. Thus it is difficult to see how it will promote communications that will not otherwise be made. Its motivations seem instead to achieve for CPAs, enrolled agents and others a kind of professional parity with attorneys in a setting where they often perform the same functions, or, more cynically but in keeping with much else in the bill, to make it more difficult for the IRS to prove taxpayers have unlawfully underpaid their taxes. For the text of this privilege see Problem 95 infra.

legal advice sought in connection with the matter giving rise to the litigation, as when a contract litigant seeks to learn what an official told the agency attorney who negotiated the contract. In other settings in which an individual might assert a privilege for communications seeking legal advice, such as before a legislative committee, the privilege is often not available to public officials or agencies. This makes sense, for one element of official performance, which voters and taxpayers should be entitled to assess, is the ability of their representative to handle legal matters and the quality of the legal advice they receive. The Uniform Rules of Evidence captures the ambivalence over whether a public official or agent should have recourse to the attorney-client privilege by making the privilege unavailable unless "the court determines that disclosure will seriously impair the ability of the public officer or agency to act upon the claim or conduct a pending investigation, litigation, or proceeding in the public interest."[32]

2.   Privileged Communications

Not every communication that a client makes to a lawyer is privileged. If a person asks a lawyer's advice in choosing a physician or on investing money, she does not, as we have seen, even become a client for purposes of the privilege. Under subsection (b) of PFRE 503, even if she is a client, communications about these and other matters that do not involve the provision of legal services are not privileged, even if they occur in the course of an ongoing lawyer-client relationship. In these respects, the proposed federal rule tracks the common law. Problems arise because a communication may have more than one purpose. A person who provides information to a lawyer regarding a complicated shopping center lease may want the lawyer's advice not just with respect to the legal import of the arrangement but also with respect to the financial soundness of the investment, and since one may depend on the other, the two kinds of advice often cannot be easily separated. In circumstances like these, if business advice appears to be the primary purpose of the communication, the privilege is unlikely to attach to any of the information conveyed. If the desire for legal advice clearly predominates, the court is likely to protect those aspects of the conversation related to the legal advice but not those relating only to business matters. If the same communications are relevant to both legal advice and business advice, close cases will be construed against the privilege claimant, although the protection of the privilege is likely to apply if the communicator's interest in the lawyer's business judgment appears largely incidental.

The law's treatment of dual purpose communications and its tendency to resolve close cases against privilege claimants pose ethical

---

[32]   Uniform Rule of Evidence 502(d)(7). Federal Rules of Evidence 2010–2011 West (2010).

and practical problems for lawyers who get themselves involved in business governance. Thus, if a lawyer is part owner of a business with particular responsibility for the corporation's legal work, communications to the lawyer—with the possible exception of communications relevant to litigation the lawyer is currently handling—are generally regarded as ineligible for the privilege. For similar reasons, the elevation of a lawyer from the position of counsel to a board of directors to membership on that board may risk the forfeiture of the privilege, even in cases in which the other directors want the lawyer-director's legal opinion.

3.   Identity as a Confidence

Questions of what constitutes protected communications recur in situations in which such details of the lawyer-client relationship as meeting dates, fee arrangements, or the client's name or address are sought. Ordinarily courts assume disclosures relating to such matters were not intended by the client to be confidential, or they deny that they relate to the provision of legal services. But occasionally courts protect such information. Consider, for example, cases involving a client's identity. Wright and Graham, in a useful analysis,[33] break them down into three types: *bagman, whistle blower,* and *sugar daddy.*

Baird v. Koerner,[34] the seminal case in this area, is also the prototypical *bagman* case. In *Baird,* a tax lawyer, Alva Baird, consulted with "certain accountants" about the tax liability of "certain undisclosed taxpayers," said to be "reputable and responsible businessmen," and about what steps might be taken should the IRS, which was not then pursuing these people, start a criminal investigation. Later, apparently following Baird's advice, the taxpayers' attorney gave Baird a cashier's check for $12,706.85, said to be the amount collectively owed plus interest. Baird mailed this to the IRS saying that it was to pay money owed by one or more taxpayers whose identity was unknown to him. The government sought to compel Baird to name those he did know, the accountants and the attorney, so that they, in turn, could be forced to reveal the taxpayers' names. Baird refused; he was held in contempt, and an appeal was brought. A three-judge panel of the 9th Circuit held that Baird could claim the privilege.

In re Kaplan is an example of a *whistle blower* case.[35] In *Kaplan,* an attorney representing a group of fruit buyers in a New York neighborhood was informed by one member of the association that although its members could not find parking in the neighborhood and could not arrange parking with the city, large trailer trucks parked illegally for long periods of time without any difficulty. The informing member, after

---

[33]   C.A. Wright & K.W. Graham, Jr., 24 Federal Practice and Procedure § 5484 (1986).

[34]   279 F.2d 623 (9th Cir. 1960).

[35]   8 N.Y.2d 214, 203 N.Y.S.2d 836, 168 N.E.2d 660 (1960).

investigating the matter, told the lawyer that the trucks had obtained their neighborhood parking privileges by paying off two powerful politicians. The lawyer then conveyed this information to the heads of certain city departments. Later he was jailed for contempt when he refused to reveal his client's name to the New York City Commissioner of Investigation. New York's highest court reversed the contempt citation.

In re Grand Jury Proceedings (Pavlick)[36] is a representative *sugar daddy* case. *Pavlick* grew out of an incident in which the U.S. Coast Guard boarded a vessel, found eighteen tons of marijuana, and arrested its three-man crew. Pavlick later represented them at the instance of a fourth man, who had approached Pavlick both to discuss his own situation and to arrange the representation. Pavlick's services apparently fulfilled a promise that had been made to at least one crew member that "he would be taken care of" if he were arrested. Pavlick invoked the attorney-client privilege in refusing to identify the crew members' benefactor. The trial judge denied the government's motion to compel disclosure, and a divided panel of the Fifth Circuit affirmed. The panel emphasized both that the benefactor had consulted Pavlick about his own legal situation and that there was no suggestion that the criminal enterprise in which the benefactor and the crew had been involved was ongoing.

The fact that clients' identities have been protected in these situations does not mean that claims of privilege always prevail. Courts are particularly reluctant to sustain claims of privilege in the sugar daddy situation if there is any suggestion that the third party payment was part of a criminal enterprise. Indeed, the Fifth Circuit, sitting *en banc*, later reversed *Pavlick* for this reason.[37]

When courts do sustain claims of privilege with respect to such matters as a client's identity or lawyer-client fee arrangements, they tend to rely on one or more of three overlapping rationales, all of which can be traced to *Baird*. The first and most popular is the "communication" rationale, which allows the privilege when disclosure would connect the client to an already disclosed but otherwise privileged communication. Thus, in *Baird* one knows the essence of what the unnamed taxpayers told their attorney, for in submitting the check Baird made it clear that his unknown clients had admitted a violation of the tax laws. Had these clients visited Baird themselves and described their situation without acting to correct it, Baird could not have been compelled to reveal their confidences.

The second, called the "legal advice" rationale, extends the privilege when the name of the client would show her guilt in the very matter for which the attorney was employed. Thus in *Baird*, to know the client's

---

[36] 663 F.2d 1057 (5th Cir. 1981) *rev'd en banc*, 680 F.2d 1026 (5th Cir. 1982).

[37] In re Grand Jury Proceedings (Pavlick), 680 F.2d 1026 (5th Cir. 1982) (en banc).

name would be to know who was guilty in the matter that led to Baird's employment.

The third rationale is the so-called "last link" rule. It holds that when the client's name or information about fee arrangements is the last link in a chain of incriminating evidence, the privilege attaches. Judge Gee, who dissented from the panel in *Pavlick* and wrote for the majority when the panel was reversed *en banc*, emphasized that even if the government knew who paid Pavlick, they would need more evidence to secure an indictment. But why it should matter whether a client's name is the last rather than a middle link in a chain of incriminating evidence is hard to fathom. Perhaps for this reason, the last link rule seems the least popular of the three rationales.

Professors Wright and Graham in their treatise criticize the application of the privilege in bagman and whistle blower cases not on the grounds that there is no confidential communication but rather because the communications are not for the purpose of securing legal services. Messengers deliver money and publicists convey information. They overstate the argument in cases like *Baird*, for Baird's actions followed his legal advice on the taxpayers' situations, but it is hard to refute their argument in a case like *Kaplan*. Yet McCormick, who wrote,

> One who reviews the cases in this area will be struck with the prevailing flavor of chicanery and sharp practice pervading most of the attempts to suppress the proof of professional employment, and the broader solution of a general rule of disclosure seems the one most consonant with the preservation of the high repute of the lawyer's calling,[38]

nevertheless cited *Kaplan* as a case where "protection of the client's identity is conceivably in the public interest." McCormick may be right, but it does not follow that the attorney-client privilege is being correctly applied when it is the vehicle used to protect that interest. If a state wants to create a whistle blower's privilege, it can always do so.

A similar analysis can be made of cases like *Baird* and *Pavlick*. It seems that under the guise of interpreting the attorney-client privilege, courts are creating a privilege akin in some cases to the informant's privilege that the government claims to protect its sources, and in other cases to the immunity prosecutors grant to circumvent the Fifth Amendment privilege against self-incrimination. By allowing lawyers to conceal their clients' identities, we allow individuals to reveal important or incriminating information without worrying that they will be adversely affected by disclosure. The issue is not so much whether this is desirable as it is whether this should be done by courts under the guise of

---

[38] McCormick (2nd ed.) § 90, at 187.

interpreting the attorney-client privilege rather than by legislatures deciding what privileges should exist.

Ultimately, we cannot state "the law" in this area. There are too many inconsistent decisions. What you should take away from this discussion is not the idea that there are situations in which you can assure a client that her identity will remain inviolate. Rather, you may not be able to promise confidentiality in certain situations in which your client wants to keep her identity confidential. But you will be able to tell her that there are issues and precedents that might make the matter worth litigating if someone seeks to require you to disclose her identity.

4.   The Privilege Holder

PFRE 503(b) follows the common law in giving the privilege to the client. In this, the attorney-client privilege differs from attorney work-product protection (discussed below) which, according to many courts, belongs to the lawyer. Because the privilege belongs to the client, she may claim the privilege or she may waive it. While the attorney may, and indeed is under an ethical obligation to, claim the privilege in a client's absence, a client may waive the privilege despite an attorney's strong objections. The same is true of a guardian, conservator or other person who has legal authority on behalf of a privilege holder or who succeeds to the legal authority of the person making the communication.

In some cases involving enterprises, authority to claim or waive the privilege is unclear, for the privilege belongs to the enterprise, and it is not obvious who has the legal authority of a client. In *Commodity Futures Trading Comm'n v. Weintraub*,[39] a case involving a bankrupt corporation, the Supreme Court held that the trustee in bankruptcy controlled a corporation's assertion of the attorney-client privilege. The privilege could not be claimed by the corporation's pre-bankruptcy managers who had made the confidential communications in question. Even before *Commodity Futures*, it had been long recognized that a corporation's management can waive the privilege for their predecessors' otherwise-protected disclosures to corporate counsel.

The question of who holds the privilege poses particularly difficult problems in shareholder derivative actions since there is often the suspicion that those actions are frivolous or are not actually in the interest of most of the shareholders on whose behalf suit is nominally brought. The leading case on this issue is *Garner v. Wolfinbarger*,[40] in which the Fifth Circuit qualified the protection management enjoys by allowing litigants to show good cause why management should not be allowed to invoke the privilege. Among the factors courts consider are the stakes of the shareholders actively participating in the litigation, the

---

[39]   471 U.S. 343 (1985).

[40]   430 F.2d 1093 (5th Cir. 1970), *cert. denied*, 401 U.S. 974 (1971).

nature of the claims they are making, and other evidence that management acted wrongly or not in the shareholders' interest. In most courts, the burden of showing that the privilege should not apply is on the shareholders, and, regardless of what they show, management can still claim a privilege for disclosures they make to counsel in their efforts to resist the shareholders' claims.

The *Garner* approach has been extended to other cases involving fiduciary relationships, such as those in which union members sue their officers, limited partners sue general partners, and beneficiaries of a trust sue the trustee. In the trustee cases, some courts have reversed *Garner*'s usual presumption and placed on the trustee the burden of showing that the privilege should apply. A few others hold that the mere existence of the fiduciary relationship justifies piercing the privilege.

Commodity Futures, *Garner*, and the general rule that a corporation's current management can waive the privilege for past management's disclosures mean that no corporate officer can ever be sure that privileged disclosures to corporate counsel will remain confidential. Thus a major rationale for the privilege—that the communication would not occur were there any danger of unwanted disclosure—is not fully applicable to disclosures made on behalf of corporations, trusts and other legal entities.

With certain exceptions, such as will contests, the privilege may be claimed under the proposed federal rule after the death of the client. The Supreme Court took this view in *Swidler & Berlin v. United States*.[41] In a few states the privilege's protection ends with the death of the client or when her estate has been wound up. But even where the privilege expires with the client, the lawyer ordinarily has an ethical obligation to keep a dead client's communications confidential unless ordered to disclose them by a court.

5. The Breadth of Protection

A communication, as indicated by PFRE 503(b), need not be between the client and lawyer to be privileged. In certain situations adequate representation requires that communications involve third parties. In these circumstances, whether the third party is seen as representing the lawyer or representing the client, conversations that pass through the intermediary do not lose the privilege on that account.

The simplest situation, and the one in which the intermediary rule is most easily justified, is when the lawyer and client speak different languages, and a translator is needed so that they can communicate. Communications to those who assist lawyers like secretaries and law clerks are also protected, whether they come directly from the client to

---

[41] 524 U.S. 399 (1998).

the assistant or are relayed to the assistant by the attorney. The privilege is also commonly extended to expert intermediaries needed to assess the legal implications of a client's disclosures. Thus, if an injured client describes her symptoms to a doctor who is to advise the lawyer on the client's prognosis, the description may be protected by the attorney-client privilege. A description of a business's marketing procedures given to an economist who is advising a lawyer on an antitrust claim may be similarly protected under the privilege, even though ordinarily there is no privilege for conversations with economists. Finally, when a client is cooperating in the joint prosecution or defense of a case, the privilege commonly protects a client's disclosures to someone else's lawyer or a lawyer's disclosure of a client's confidences to another's lawyer in the course of the cooperative action.

In the above respects PFRE 503(b) tracks the common law and the attorney-client privilege rules of most states. However, its protections are broader in other respects. First, it privileges what a client's lawyer or representative says to her. Surprisingly, the usual privilege is not so generous. It does not, for example, protect what lawyers tell clients about information from third parties, and in some formulations it does not protect anything the lawyer says to the client unless the lawyer's comments tend to reveal what the client told her. This makes sense in theory, if one believes the sole purpose of the privilege is to encourage clients to disclose information to attorneys that they would not disclose if confidentiality could not be guaranteed. It makes less sense if one takes seriously other justifications for the privilege, and in practice it is an unworkable formulation. So even in jurisdictions where the privilege in theory extends only to the client's confidences and the lawyer's remarks suggestive of client confidences, lawyers are seldom forced to reveal their side of confidential communications with clients; but they may be required to say whether they passed on specific information, such as a trial date, or to recount nonprivileged information, like accounts of witnesses, that they reported to their clients.

The proposed federal rule also provides unusually broad protection for conversations among representatives of clients. This could privilege an extraordinary amount of information, particularly in organizational contexts where many employees might be considered representatives of the client. What is unusual about the PFRE provision is that it does not require that discussions between the client's representatives be transmitted to a lawyer as long as they are made to facilitate the representation in some way. In the same vein is the wide privilege that PFRE 503 gives lawyers in talking to their representatives. The conversations need not be based on client confidences, nor need they be made for transmission to the client. These provisions do not, however, seem to have reshaped the privilege, even in federal courts. The classic common law understanding and the general practice in the states have more strongly influenced judicial interpretations. Thus, you should not assume that a privilege will attach to conversations between or among representatives of attorneys and representatives of clients simply because the conversations facilitate the representation. The only clearly privileged conversations in these circumstances are those necessary to transmit the client's confidences to the attorney.

6. The Intent of Confidentiality

Even if all other requisites for the attorney-client privilege are met, the privilege will not attach unless the client's communication to her attorney is intended to be confidential. Thus, if Carrie Client and Alice Attorney are out drinking with a group of friends and Carrie tells Alice, across the table, the details of an accident she was involved in, nothing Carrie says will be privileged even if Alice has already been retained to represent her in litigation growing out of the accident. If Carrie did not mind her friends knowing what she said, the court will not let her keep her remarks from the jury. The presence of bystanders negates the claim that confidentiality was intended.

The old common law was quite rigid about this. Even hidden eavesdroppers were allowed to testify. Courts said that if the attorney and client did not take steps to ensure no eavesdroppers were near, confidentiality must not have been important to them. This claim cannot be made today, when eavesdropping usually occurs through electronic surveillance. Thus, modern courts have consistently held that electronic surveillance does not defeat the privilege unless the speakers knew or should have known that they were being overheard.

Some courts have departed even further from the common law. The D.C. Circuit, for example, found that a corporate president intended confidentiality when he talked with the corporation's general counsel in normal tones in the first class compartment of a commercial airliner.[42] More typical, however, is an Eleventh Circuit decision that found no intention of confidentiality when a conversation took place in a courtroom corridor in tones loud enough for passersby to overhear.[43] One cannot help but note the class biases inherent in these inconsistent decisions.

The common law also denied the privilege for lack of confidentiality when unprivileged third parties, like close friends and relatives, were present when attorneys and clients conversed. Courts today, recognizing the need people have for psychological and other support, usually find that a close friend or relative is a person whose presence is needed for the client to communicate effectively or aids in the rendition of legal services. Nevertheless, when such people are present, one cannot be certain that a court will not see their presence as a reason to vitiate the privilege.

---

[42] In re Sealed Case, 737 F.2d 94 (D.C. Cir. 1984).

[43] United States v. Blasco, 702 F.2d 1315, *cert. denied*, 464 U.S. 914 (1983).

Another situation in which courts hold that confidentiality is not intended is when clients provide their lawyers with information they expect their lawyers to reveal. This is one reason why, when clients use lawyers as tax preparers, courts often hold that what they tell their lawyers is not confidential. It is intended to be revealed on the tax return. A similar analysis holds when business clients furnish lawyers with information to be given to the SEC in connection with stock offerings or other matters. The problem here should be obvious. A client may not know what has to be revealed and may intend to disclose as little as the law, according to her lawyer, permits. Moreover, the client may provide the lawyer with extensive background information, which does not have to be disclosed, so that the lawyer can better advise her on what must be revealed. Courts differ on how much protection they extend when clients make these claims.

Finally, even when a lawyer is consulted in confidence, courts may hold that aspects of the consultation or of a communication are not intended to be confidential and so must be revealed. We have already discussed at some length the presumption that clients do not intend their identities to be confidential and the situations in which this presumption can be defeated. Lawyers have also been required by some courts to testify to a client's physical appearance or mental state during a consultation or to turn over a letter from a client as a handwriting exemplar. The justification is that information about the appearance of oneself or one's handwriting is not communicated in confidence.

Before we turn to some special issues concerning the privilege, such as its application to corporations, exceptions to it, and ways it can be waived, we should reiterate a point made in our general introduction to the privilege. It protects only communications between the client and the attorney. It does not protect the facts communicated. Thus if Carrie Client tells Alice Attorney that she has money in a Swiss bank account, absent another privilege—like the Fifth Amendment privilege—Carrie may be required in a deposition, before a grand jury, or at trial to state whether or not she has money in a Swiss bank. She may claim the attorney-client privilege only if she is asked whether she told Alice she had money there. Moreover, should Carrie lie under oath in answering the question, the dominant view is that Alice has an ethical obligation to insist that Carrie correct her answer even though, but for Carrie's privileged communication, Alice would not know her client had lied.

————————

Problem VIII-2. Jones is charged with shooting her husband. She was arrested two days after she called the police to report she had come home and found her husband dead. At trial, the prosecution wishes to introduce evidence of the fact that Jones went to a noted criminal lawyer,

Joe Hetz, one hour after the coroner said her husband had been killed, and that prior to that visit Hetz had never represented Jones in any matter, nor had he ever been retained by Jones for any purpose. To prove these facts, the prosecution calls Hetz and asks: "Did the defendant come to your office at 1:30 p.m. on January 3, 2013 to seek legal counsel?" Jones objects to the question on the ground that her relationship with Hetz is privileged. The prosecution also asks: "Wasn't that the first time you ever met Jones?" The same objection is made. **How should the court rule?**

Problem VIII-3. In the above case, Wilson, an eyewitness, testifies that he saw Jones commit the murder. Hetz asks Wilson whether he talked to the prosecutor and Wilson answers, "Yes." The next questions are: "Is it not true that when you first approached the prosecutor you told him that you were not positive that you could make any identification of the perpetrator of the crime, even though you knew that the defendant had been charged with the offense and you knew her quite well? Isn't it also the case that the prosecutor advised you that someone murdered Mr. Jones, and that if it was not the defendant, then perhaps it was you, Mr. Wilson?" The prosecution objects to both questions on the ground that any advice given to the witness was given in confidence and is protected by the attorney-client privilege. **How should the court rule?**

Assume that there is a motion to suppress the murder weapon, a gun, taken from the defendant, because the search which led to the seizure violated the Fourth Amendment. A police officer testifies to the circumstances surrounding the arrest. Hetz asks, "Officer, prior to your testifying here today, did you seek legal advice from the prosecution as to the meaning of probable cause and the application of the legal definition to the facts of this case?"

Once again, an objection is made on the basis of the attorney-client privilege. **What is the proper ruling?**

7. Corporate Clients

When an individual consults an attorney, the identity of the client is clear. But the term "client" encompasses corporations and other organizations as well as natural persons. Only one federal court thought corporations did not enjoy the privilege, and it was soon reversed.[44] There has, however, been considerable dispute over when the privilege applies in the corporate setting and who can claim it. The privilege does not apply when an attorney is consulted for a reason other than securing legal advice, or if a communication to an attorney is treated by the corporation in a way that negates an intention of confidentiality. Nor does the privilege apply automatically whenever a corporation asks an

---

[44] Radiant Burners, Inc. v. American Gas Ass'n, 207 F. Supp. 771 (N.D. Ill. 1962), *rev'd*, 320 F.2d 314 (7th Cir. 1963), *cert. denied*, 375 U.S. 929 (1963).

employee to talk confidentially to a lawyer so that the corporation can secure legal advice. If, for example, an off-duty worker fortuitously witnesses an event affecting her employer's legal liabilities, the attorney-client privilege will not attach to what she tells the company's lawyer. Courts see no reason why the employment nexus should give the worker's statements greater protection than that accorded other witnesses.

When an employee's ability to give evidence is job-related, the question is whether the employee must have some particular status before her communications to the company's attorneys are privileged. The once dominant test limited the privilege to statements made by members of the corporate "control group," a group loosely defined as those individuals having authority to seek out and act on legal advice. This group includes at least the directors and executive officers of the corporation. A broader test applies the privilege to communications of lower-level corporate employees reporting information acquired and transmitted in the course of corporate duties. In federal courts during the 1960s the control group test was ascendant, but in 1970 the Seventh Circuit applied the broader test in *Harper & Row Publishers Inc. v. Decker*,[45] a decision affirmed by an equally divided Supreme Court. Because of uncertainty regarding of which test the Court would prefer, the drafters of the proposed federal rule did not specify a standard.

The Supreme Court indicated its preference in 1981 in the case of *Upjohn Co. v. United States.* The *Upjohn* opinion is valuable not only for its discussion of the attorney-client privilege but also for its analysis of the work-product doctrine. At the same time, there are problems with the Court's analysis, and many questions are left unanswered.

Upjohn Co. v. United States
449 U.S. 383 (1981).

Justice Rehnquist delivered the opinion of the Court.

We granted certiorari in this case to address important questions concerning the scope of the attorney-client privilege in the corporate context and the applicability of the work-product doctrine in proceedings to enforce tax summonses. With respect to the privilege question the parties and various *amici* have described our task as one of choosing between two "tests" which have gained adherents in the courts of appeals. We are acutely aware, however, that we sit to decide concrete cases and not abstract propositions of law. We decline to lay down a broad rule or series of rules to govern all conceivable future questions in this area, even were we able to do so. We can and do, however, conclude that the attorney-client privilege protects the communications involved in this

---

[45] 423 F.2d 487 (7th Cir. 1970) (per curiam), *aff'd per curiam by an equally divided Court,* 400 U.S. 348 (1971).

case from compelled disclosure and that the work-product doctrine does apply in tax summons enforcement proceedings.

I

Petitioner Upjohn manufactures and sells pharmaceuticals here and abroad. In January 1976 independent accountants conducting an audit of one of petitioner's foreign subsidiaries discovered that the subsidiary made payments to or for the benefit of foreign government officials in order to secure government business. The accountants, so informed Mr. Gerard Thomas, petitioner's Vice-President, Secretary, and General Counsel. Thomas is a member of the Michigan and New York bars, and has been petitioner's General Counsel for 20 years. He consulted with outside counsel and R. T. Parfet, Jr., petitioner's Chairman of the Board. It was decided that the company would conduct an internal investigation of what were termed "questionable payments." As part of this investigation the attorneys prepared a letter containing a questionnaire which was sent to "all foreign general and area managers" over the Chairman's signature. The letter began by noting recent disclosures that several American companies made "possibly illegal" payments to foreign government officials and emphasized that the management needed full information concerning any such payments made by Upjohn. The letter indicated that the Chairman had asked Thomas, identified as "the company's General Counsel," "to conduct an investigation for the purpose of determining the nature and magnitude of any payments made by the Upjohn Company or any of its subsidiaries to any employee or official of a foreign government." The questionnaire sought detailed information concerning such payments. Managers were instructed to treat the investigation as "highly confidential" and not to discuss it with anyone other than Upjohn employees who might be helpful in providing the requested information. Responses were to be sent directly to Thomas. Thomas and outside counsel also interviewed the recipients of the questionnaire and some 33 other Upjohn officers or employees as part of the investigation. On March 26, 1976, the company voluntarily submitted a preliminary report to the Securities and Exchange Commission on Form 8-K disclosing certain questionable payments. A copy of the report was simultaneously submitted to the Internal Revenue Service, which immediately began an investigation to determine the tax consequences of the payments. Special agents conducting the investigation were given lists by Upjohn of all those interviewed and all who had responded to the questionnaire. On November 23, 1976, the Service issued a summons pursuant to 26 U.S.C. § 7602 demanding production of:

> "All files relative to the investigation conducted under the supervision of Gerard Thomas to identify payments to employees of foreign governments and any political contributions made by the

Upjohn Company or any of its affiliates since January 1, 1971, and to determine whether any funds of the Upjohn Company had been improperly accounted for on the corporate books during the same period.

The records should include but not be limited to written questionnaires sent to managers of the Upjohn Company's foreign affiliates, and memorandums or notes of the interviews conducted in the United States and abroad with officers and employees of the Upjohn Company and its subsidiaries."

The company declined to produce the documents specified in the second paragraph on the grounds that they were protected from disclosure by the attorney-client privilege and constituted the work product of attorneys prepared in anticipation of litigation. On August 31, 1977, the United States filed a petition seeking enforcement of the summons under 26 U.S.C. §§ 7402(b) and 7604(a) in the United States District Court for the Western District of Michigan. That court adopted the recommendation of a magistrate who concluded that the summons should be enforced. Petitioner appealed to the Court of Appeals for the Sixth Circuit which rejected the magistrate's finding of a waiver of the attorney-client privilege, but agreed that the privilege did not apply "to the extent that the communications were made by officers and agents not responsible for directing Upjohn's actions in response to legal advice . . . for the simple reason that the communications were not the 'client's.'" The court reasoned that accepting petitioner's claim for a broader application of the privilege would encourage upper-echelon management to ignore unpleasant facts and create too broad a "zone of silence." Noting that Upjohn's counsel had interviewed officials such as the Chairman and President, the Court of Appeals remanded to the District Court so that a determination of who was within the "control group" could be made. In a concluding footnote the court stated that the work-product doctrine "is not applicable to administrative summonses issued under 26 U.S.C. § 7602."

II

Federal Rule of Evidence 501 provides that "the privilege of a witness . . . shall be governed by the principles of the common law as they may be interpreted by the courts of the United States in light of reason and experience." The attorney-client privilege is the oldest of the privileges for confidential communications known to the common law. Its purpose is to encourage full and frank communication between attorneys and their clients and thereby promote broader public interests in the observance of law and administration of justice. . . . Admittedly complications in the application of the privilege arise when the client is a corporation, which in theory is an artificial creature of the law, and not an individual; but this Court has assumed that the privilege applies when the client is a corporation. . . .

The Court of Appeals, however, considered the application of the privilege in the corporate context to present a "different problem," since the client was an inanimate entity and "only the senior management, guiding and integrating the several operations, . . . can be said to possess an identity analogous to the corporation as a whole." The first case to articulate the so-called "control group test" adopted by the court below, Philadelphia v. Westinghouse Electric Corp., 210 F. Supp. 483, 485 (E.D. Pa.), . . . reflected a similar conceptual approach:

> "Keeping in mind that the question is, Is it the corporation which is seeking the lawyer's advice when the asserted privileged communication is made?, the most satisfactory solution, I think, is that if the employee making the communication, of whatever rank he may be, is in a position to control or even to take a substantial part in a decision about any action which the corporation may take upon the advice of the attorney, . . . then, in effect, *he is (or personifies) the corporation* when he makes his disclosure to the lawyer and the privilege would apply." (Emphasis supplied.)

Such a view, we think, overlooks the fact that the privilege exists to protect not only the giving of professional advice to those who can act on it but also the giving of information to the lawyer to enable him to give sound and informed advice. . . .

In the case of the individual client, the provider of information and the person who acts on the lawyer's advice are one and the same. In the corporate context, however, it will frequently be employees beyond the control group as defined by the court below—"officers and agents . . . responsible for directing [the company's] actions in response to legal advice"—who will possess the information needed by the corporation's lawyers. Middle-level—and indeed lower-level—employees can, by actions within the scope of their employment, embroil the corporation in serious legal difficulties, and it is only natural that these employees would have the relevant information needed by corporate counsel if he is adequately to advise the client with respect to such actual or potential difficulties. This fact was noted in *Diversified Industries, Inc. v. Meredith*, 572 F.2d 596 (C.A.8 1977) (en banc):

> "In a corporation, it may be necessary to glean information relevant to a legal problem from middle management or non-management personnel as well as from top executives. The attorney dealing with a complex legal problem 'is thus faced with a "Hobson's choice." If he interviews employees not having "the very highest authority", their communications to him will not be privileged. If, on the other hand, he interviews *only* those

employees with the "very highest authority," he may find it extremely difficult, if not impossible, to determine what happened.' "

The control group test adopted by the court below thus frustrates the very purpose of the privilege by discouraging the communication of relevant information by employees of the client to attorneys seeking to render legal advice to the client corporation. The attorney's advice will also frequently be more significant to noncontrol group members than to those who officially sanction the advice, and the control group test makes it more difficult to convey full and frank legal advice to the employees who will put into effect the client corporation's policy.

The narrow scope given the attorney-client privilege by the court below not only makes it difficult for corporate attorneys to formulate sound advice when their client is faced with a specific legal problem but also threatens to limit the valuable efforts of corporate counsel to ensure their client's compliance with the law. In light of the vast and complicated array of regulatory legislation confronting the modern corporation, corporations, unlike most individuals, "constantly go to lawyers to find out how to obey the law," particularly since compliance with the law in this area is hardly an instinctive matter.[a] The test adopted by the court below is difficult to apply in practice, though no abstractly formulated and unvarying "test" will necessarily enable courts to decide questions such as this with mathematical precision. But if the purpose of the attorney-client privilege is to be served, the attorney and client must be able to predict with some degree of certainty whether particular discussions will be protected. An uncertain privilege, or one which purports to be certain but results in widely varying applications by the courts, is little better than no privilege at all. The very terms of the test adopted by the court below suggest the unpredictability of its application. The test restricts the availability of the privilege to those officers who play a "substantial role" in deciding and directing a corporation's legal response. Disparate decisions in cases applying this test illustrate its unpredictability. Compare, e.g., *Hogan v. Zletz*, 43 F.R.D. 308, 315–316 (N.D. Okl.1967), aff'd in part sub nom. *Natta v. Hogan*, 392 F.2d 686 (C.A.10 1968) (control group includes managers and assistant managers of patent division and research and development department), with *Congoleum Industries, Inc. v. GAF Corp.*, 49 F.R.D. 82, 83–85 (E.D. Pa. 1969), aff'd, 478 F.2d 1398 (C.A.3 1973) (control group includes only

---

[a.] The Government argues that the risk of civil or criminal liability suffices to ensure that corporations will seek legal advice in the absence of the protection of the privilege. This response ignores the fact that the depth and quality of any investigations to ensure compliance with the law would suffer, even were they undertaken. The response also proves too much, since it applies to all communications covered by the privilege: an individual trying to comply with the law or faced with a legal problem also has strong incentive to disclose information to his lawyer, yet the common law has recognized the value of the privilege in further facilitating communications.

division and corporate vice-presidents, and not two directors of research and vice-president for production and research).

The communications at issue were made by Upjohn employees[b] to counsel for Upjohn acting as such, at the direction of corporate superiors in order to secure legal advice from counsel. As the magistrate found, "Mr. Thomas consulted with the Chairman of the Board and outside counsel and thereafter conducted a factual investigation to determine the nature and extent of the questionable payments *and to be in a position to give legal advice to the company with respect to the payments.*"

Information, not available from upper-echelon management, was needed to supply a basis for legal advice concerning compliance with securities and tax laws, foreign laws, currency regulations, duties to shareholders, and potential litigation in each of these areas. The communications concerned matters within the scope of the employees' corporate duties, and the employees themselves were sufficiently aware that they were being questioned in order that the corporation could obtain legal advice. The questionnaire identified Thomas as "the company's General Counsel" and referred in its opening sentence to the possible illegality of payments such as the ones on which information was sought. A statement of policy accompanying the questionnaire clearly indicated the legal implications of the investigation. The policy statement was issued "in order that there be no uncertainty in the future as to the policy with respect to the practices which are the subject of this investigation." It began "Upjohn will comply with all laws and regulations," and stated that commissions or payments "will not be used as a subterfuge for bribes or illegal payments" and that all payments must be "proper and legal." Any future agreements with foreign distributors or agents were to be approved "by a company attorney" and any questions concerning the policy were to be referred "to the company's General Counsel." . . . Pursuant to explicit instructions from the Chairman of the Board, the communications were considered "highly confidential" when made, and have been kept confidential by the company. Consistent with the underlying purposes of the attorney-client privilege, these communications must be protected against compelled disclosure.

The Court of Appeals declined to extend the attorney-client privilege beyond the limits of the control group test for fear that doing so would entail severe burdens on discovery and create a broad "zone of silence" over corporate affairs. Application of the attorney-client privilege to communications such as those involved here, however, puts the adversary in no worse position than if the communications had never taken place.

[b.] Seven of the eighty-six employees interviewed by counsel had terminated their employment with Upjohn at the time of the interview. Petitioner argues that the privilege should nonetheless apply to communications by these former employees concerning activities during their period of employment. Neither the District Court nor the Court of Appeals had occasion to address this issue, and we decline to decide it without the benefit of treatment below.

The privilege only protects disclosure of communications; it does not protect disclosure of the underlying facts by those who communicated with the attorney. . . . Here the Government was free to question the employees who communicated with Thomas and outside counsel. Upjohn has provided the IRS with a list of such employees, and the IRS has already interviewed some 25 of them. While it would probably be more convenient for the Government to secure the results of petitioner's internal investigation by simply subpoenaing the questionnaires and notes taken by petitioner's attorneys, such considerations of convenience do not overcome the policies served by the attorney-client privilege. . . .

Needless to say, we decide only the case before us, and do not undertake to draft a set of rules which should govern challenges to investigatory subpoenas. Any such approach would violate the spirit of F.R.E. 501. . . . While such a "case-by-case" basis may to some slight extent undermine desirable certainty in the boundaries of the attorney-client privilege, it obeys the spirit of the Rules. At the same time we conclude that the narrow "control group test" sanctioned by the Court of Appeals, in this case cannot, consistent with "the principles of the common law as . . . interpreted . . . in the light of reason and experience," F.R.E. 501, govern the development of the law in this area.

III[46]

Our decision that the communications by Upjohn employees to counsel are covered by the attorney-client privilege disposes of the case so far as the responses to the questionnaires and any notes reflecting responses to interview questions are concerned. The summons reaches further, however, and Thomas has testified that his notes and memoranda of interviews go beyond recording responses to his questions. To the extent that the material subject to the summons is not protected by the attorney-client privilege as disclosing communications between an employee and counsel, we must reach the ruling by the Court of Appeals that the work-product doctrine does not apply to summonses issued under 26 U.S.C. § 7602.[c]

The Government concedes, wisely, that the Court of Appeals erred and that the work-product doctrine does apply to IRS summonses. This doctrine was announced by the Court over 30 years ago in *Hickman v. Taylor*, 329 U.S. 495, 67 S.Ct. 385, 91 L.Ed. 451 (1947). In that case the Court rejected "an attempt, without purported necessity or justification, to secure written statements, private memoranda and personal

---

[46] Full understanding of the situations in which attorneys can keep matters confidential requires an understanding of the work-product doctrine because when the attorney-client privilege is not available, the work-product doctrine still may be. **Upjohn is an important statement of the potential breadth of this protection.**

[c] The following discussion will also be relevant to counsel's notes and memoranda of interviews with the seven former employees should it be determined that the attorney-client privilege does not apply to them. See n. b, supra.

recollections prepared or formed by an adverse party's counsel in the course of his legal duties." The Court noted that "it is essential that a lawyer work with a certain degree of privacy" and reasoned that if discovery of the material sought were permitted:

> much of what is now put down in writing would remain unwritten. An attorney's thoughts, heretofore inviolate, would not be his own. Inefficiency, unfairness and sharp practices would inevitably develop in the giving of legal advice and in the preparation of cases for trial. The effect on the legal profession would be demoralizing. And the interests of the clients and the cause of justice would be poorly served.

The "strong public policy" underlying the work-product doctrine was reaffirmed recently in *United States v. Nobles*, 422 U.S. 225 (1975), and has been substantially incorporated in Federal Rule of Civil Procedure 26(b)(3).[d]

Nothing in the language of the IRS summons provisions or their legislative history suggests an intent on the part of Congress to preclude application of the work-product doctrine. Rule 26(b)(3) codifies the work-product doctrine, and the Federal Rules of Civil Procedure are made applicable to summons enforcement proceedings by Rule 81(a)(3). While conceding the applicability of the work-product doctrine, the Government asserts that it has made a sufficient showing of necessity to overcome its protections. The magistrate apparently so found. The Government relies on the following language in *Hickman*:

> We do not mean to say that all written materials obtained or prepared by an adversary's counsel with an eye toward litigation are necessarily free from discovery in all cases. Where relevant and nonprivileged facts remain hidden in an attorney's file and where production of those facts is essential to the preparation of one's case, discovery may properly be had. . . . And production might be justified where the witnesses are no longer available or can be reached only with difficulty.

The Government stresses that interviewees are scattered across the globe and that Upjohn has forbidden its employees to answer questions it considers irrelevant. The above-quoted language from *Hickman*,

---

[d] This provides, in pertinent part:

"A party may obtain discovery of documents and tangible things otherwise discoverable under subdivision (b)(1) of this rule and prepared in anticipation of litigation or for trial by or for another party or by or for that other party's representative (including his attorney, consultant, surety, indemnitor, insurer, or agent) only upon a showing that the party seeking discovery has substantial need of the materials in the preparation of his case and that he is unable without undue hardship to obtain the substantial equivalent of the materials by other means. In ordering discovery of such materials when the required showing has been made, the court shall protect against disclosure of the mental impressions, conclusions, opinions or legal theories of an attorney or other representative of a party concerning the litigation."

however, did not apply to "oral statements made by witnesses . . . whether presently in the form of [the attorney's] mental impressions or memoranda." As to such material the Court did "not believe that any showing of necessity can be made under the circumstances of this case so as to justify production. . . . If there should be a rare situation justifying production of these matters, petitioner's case is not of that type." Forcing an attorney to disclose notes and memoranda of witnesses' oral statements is particularly disfavored because it tends to reveal the attorney's mental processes.[e]

Rule 26 accords special protection to work product revealing the attorney's mental processes. The Rule permits disclosure of documents and tangible things constituting attorney work product upon a showing of substantial need and inability to obtain the equivalent without undue hardship. This was the standard applied by the magistrate. Rule 26 goes on, however, to state that "[i]n ordering discovery of such materials when the required showing has been made, the court shall protect against disclosure of the mental impressions, conclusions, opinions or legal theories of an attorney or other representative of a party concerning the litigation." Although this language does not specifically refer to memoranda based on oral statements of witnesses, the *Hickman* court stressed the danger that compelled disclosure of such memoranda would reveal the attorney's mental processes. It is clear that this is the sort of material the draftsmen of the Rule had in mind as deserving special protection. . . .

Based on the foregoing, some courts have concluded that *no* showing of necessity can overcome protection of work product that is based on oral statements from witnesses. Those courts declining to adopt an absolute rule have nonetheless recognized that such material is entitled to special protection.

We do not decide the issue at this time. It is clear that the magistrate applied the wrong standard when he concluded that the Government had made a sufficient showing of necessity to overcome the protections of the work-product doctrine. The magistrate applied the "substantial need" and "without undue hardship" standard articulated in the first part of Rule 26(b)(3). The notes and memoranda sought by the Government here, however, are work product based on oral statements. If they reveal communications, they are, in this case, protected by the attorney-client privilege. To the extent they do not reveal communications, they reveal the attorneys' mental processes in evaluating the communications. As Rule 26 and *Hickman* make clear,

---

[e.] Thomas described his notes of the interviews as containing "what I considered to be the important questions, the substance of the responses to them, my beliefs as to the importance of these, my beliefs as to how they related to the inquiry, my thoughts as to how they related to other questions. In some instances they might even suggest other questions that I would have to ask or things that I needed to find elsewhere."

such work product cannot be disclosed simply on a showing of substantial need and inability to obtain the equivalent without undue hardship.

While we are not prepared at this juncture to say that such material is always protected by the work-product rule, we think a far stronger showing of necessity and unavailability by other means than was made by the Government or applied by the Magistrate in this case would be necessary to compel disclosure. Since the Court of Appeals thought that the work-product protection was never applicable in an enforcement proceeding such as this, and since the Magistrate whose recommendations the District Court adopted applied too lenient a standard of protection, we think the best procedure with respect to this aspect of the case would be to reverse the judgment of the Court of Appeals for the Sixth Circuit and remand the case to it for such further proceedings in connection with the work-product claim as are consistent with this opinion.

Accordingly, the judgment of the Court of Appeals is reversed, and the case remanded for further proceedings.

CHIEF JUSTICE BURGER, concurring in part and concurring in the judgment.

I join in Parts I and III of the opinion of the Court and in the judgment. As to Part II, I agree fully with the Court's rejection of the so-called "control group" test, its reasons for doing so, and its ultimate holding that the communications at issue are privileged. As the Court states, however, "if the purpose of the attorney-client privilege is to be served, the attorney and client must be able to predict with some degree of certainty whether particular discussions will be protected." For this very reason, I believe that we should articulate a standard that will govern similar cases and afford guidance to corporations, counsel advising them, and federal courts.

[I]n my view the Court should make clear now that, as a general rule, a communication is privileged at least when, as here, an employee or former employee speaks at the direction of the management with an attorney regarding conduct or proposed conduct within the scope of employment. The attorney must be one authorized by the management to inquire into the subject and must be seeking information to assist counsel in performing any of the following functions: (a) evaluating whether the employee's conduct has bound or would bind the corporation; (b) assessing the legal consequences, if any, of that conduct; or (c) formulating appropriate legal responses to actions that have been or may be taken by others with regard to that conduct. Other communications between employees and corporate counsel may indeed be privileged—as the petitioners and several *amici* have suggested in their proposed formulations—but the need for certainty does not compel us now to prescribe all the details of the privilege in this case.

Upjohn rejects the control group test, but the majority takes pains to avoid specifying the test that replaces it. This is strange since the major flaw that the Court sees in the control group test is its unpredictability.[47] *Upjohn* is also less than satisfactory in its analysis of the reasons for extending the privilege to corporations. With individuals, the privilege is seen as necessary to motivate confidences because it is thought that people will not reveal embarrassing or incriminating information unless their lawyer can assure them that she cannot be compelled to reveal what they say. In corporations things do not work this way. Unless the lawyer, to whom a corporate employee talks , is representing the employee as well as the corporation, only the corporation holds the privilege. This means the corporation can waive the privilege, and it may be most likely to do so when it can avoid liability by scapegoating employees who have admitted careless or improper actions. Such scapegoating may be more likely the further removed employees are from the control group.

Moreover, not even those in control of the corporation can be sure their disclosures to attorneys will be kept confidential. As we have already noted, the Court held in the *Commodity Futures* case that a trustee in bankruptcy could waive the privilege for disclosures made by the corporation's former managers, and, more commonly, successor officers and directors can waive the privilege for the confidences of their predecessors. PFRE 503 was breaking new ground rather than restating existing law when it provided that the privilege could survive the dissolution of the corporation. Thus the extension of the attorney-client privilege to corporations cannot be justified with the claim that a guarantee of confidentiality is needed to induce corporate employees to speak. The corporate attorney-client privilege does not provide individual employees with that guarantee.[48] Nor is such a guarantee likely to be necessary. Corporations have many ways, including the threat of dismissal for noncooperation, of ensuring that employees talk. But such threats are rarely necessary. Since corporate rather than individual liability is usually at issue when corporate counsel seek information from employees, employees usually have little reason to care whether their disclosures are revealed in court.

---

[47] The Court's analysis is not persuasive on this point. Many corporate employees are clearly members of the control group, while other employees clearly are not. At the margin there may be difficult questions of interpretation, but this is often true of the law. Moreover, the apparently inconsistent decisions to which the Court refers may reflect the fact that people with similar titles may have different responsibilities in different corporations. Certainly, few courts were complaining about the difficulties of applying the control group test before *Upjohn*.

[48] On these issues see generally, Stephen A. Saltzburg, Corporate and Related Attorney-Client Privilege Claims: A Suggested Approach, 12 Hofstra. L. Rev. 279 (1984).

A better justification for extending the attorney-client privilege to corporations is that the guarantee of confidentiality helps induce corporations to conduct investigations that plumb the depths of employee knowledge. One might argue that a company like *Upjohn* would not launch the kind of investigation it did but for the attorney-client privilege. If so, the privilege does not cost the judicial system information because the information sought would not exist but for the privilege. This argument, however, fails in *Upjohn*, and it is likely to apply only rarely in other corporate contexts.

The argument fails in *Upjohn* because at the time *Upjohn* conducted its investigation, competent counsel would have told the company that there was a good chance that only communications from the Upjohn control group were privileged. Upjohn went ahead and conducted its investigation anyway.

The argument is weak generally because corporations are so enmeshed in the regulatory state that they often must investigate questionable conduct. Corporate officers would be risking civil, criminal, or shareholder liability if they did not learn whatever they could in a situation like *Upjohn's*. Moreover since sanctions ordinarily fall on the corporation rather than its officers, corporate officers, unlike individual clients, can seldom anticipate severely adverse personal consequences from the revelation of what investigators, like Upjohn's attorneys, uncover.

Moreover, applying the privilege to the communications of corporate employees can have considerable information costs. While the Court in *Upjohn* might have been influenced by the fact that Upjohn appeared to be a good corporate citizen trying to correct a past mistake and pay the IRS its due, Upjohn wanted to determine its tax debt itself. Its claim of privilege worked to thwart the IRS's effort to review Upjohn's determination that all but $700,000 of the $4,400,000 it had paid as bribes and kickbacks to employees of foreign governments had been paid by foreign subsidies, and so had no U.S. tax consequences. Indeed, Upjohn ordered its employees not to give the IRS any information about payments it claimed were not relevant to its U.S. tax liability. Moreover, while Upjohn provided the government with the names of those employees who had filled out questionnaires, it declined to make those employees located in foreign countries available for questioning.[49]

Even when a corporation's employee informants are amenable to process, litigants may find it too expensive to question them all, and if

---

[49] These details come from C.A. Wright and K.W. Graham, 24 Federal Practice and Procedure § 5483, which provides a fuller portrait of the case than does the Supreme Court's opinion.

they do question them all and receive the same answers[50] the corporation's lawyers received, expensive duplication of effort will have occurred. Loss of information and expense are exacerbated by the routines some corporations have of channeling considerable information to attorneys. Much of it is apparently unprivileged, for it will not have been produced primarily to secure legal advice. But when litigation arises, it can be difficult for a court to separate the chaff from the wheat, and contests over what is privileged add to litigation costs.

For these reasons and because work-product protection is ordinarily available to balance factors like the need for and the cost of acquiring information that the attorney-client privilege ignores, the Supreme Court may in some future case return to the control group test or something like it. *Upjohn* has, however, been on the books for a while, and although some states employ the control group or other tests—as of 2010, it appeared that approximately eight states still use the control group test— *Upjohn* guides federal courts. Since *Upjohn* does not lay down rules, courts apply it differently. Many have read it broadly, protecting not only disclosures by low-level corporate employees to corporate counsel but also disclosures by past employees, an extension of *Upjohn* that some find hard to justify. There seems, however, to be general agreement on certain core principles: (1) the communication should stem from a need to secure legal advice; (2) disclosure should reflect corporate policy or be at the instance of some high-level employee; (3) employees talking to a corporation's attorneys should know that confidentiality is intended; (4) the corporation should keep the disclosure confidential, which means not circulating it beyond those with a "need to know"; and (5) the communication should relate to a matter within the scope of the employee's business duties.

The proposed federal rule and most of the rules enacted by the states that have used it as a guideline assume that a client can be a government agency as well as a corporation. The Supreme Court has not yet decided whether the privilege should apply in the same way to all types of organizations. As we have noted, many jurisdictions substantially limit the availability of the privilege for information communicated to government employees. Thus, governmental agencies, and perhaps other organizational actors, may not enjoy the broad privilege extended to business corporations in *Upjohn*.

---

[50] Compare David M. Greenwald, Robert R. Stauffer, & Erin R. Schrantz, Testimonial Privileges § 1:33 (2010) with Edward J. Imwinkelried, The New Wigmore: A Treatise on Evidence—Testimonial Privileges 879, n. 299 (2010).

Problem VIII-4.

A. The Winkel Motor Company is thinking of marketing a new steering device but is concerned with potential liability should the device in any way contribute to accidents. To insulate the company as much as possible from successful lawsuits, the president of the company placed Winkel's General Counsel, Frank Edsel, in charge of the program to develop, evaluate, and market the device. The president orders that all employees submit to Edsel, in confidence, a memorandum prepared specially for the purpose of obtaining legal advice that describes all test data and other information about the steering device and that the employees destroy all other copies of the data and information they have described to counsel. She then instructs Edsel to give a legal opinion on the potential liability of the company should it market the device and to carefully scrutinize any advertising about the device to minimize claims based on advertising. Final authority to proceed with, abandon, or do anything else with the device rests at all times with the board of directors and company management. **Can Edsel ethically accept this assignment?**

B. Assume that Fielding, who purchased a car containing the steering device, is injured, and that the alleged cause of the injury is a defect in the device. **If Fielding sues the company, can he obtain copies of the test data and other reports the company produced regarding the device? If the reports have been shredded, may Fielding obtain a copy of the memorandum given to Edsel which summarizes the test data and other information? Would your answer be different in a state that used the control group test? Does it matter if Edsel, rather than being a company employee, is a partner in an outside firm?**

C. The company has employee-investigators who are assigned to investigate the Fielding accident. These investigators photograph both the car and the accident scene, and they interview the witnesses. They also prepare a report containing their conclusions regarding the accident. **Are the photographs, the witnesses' statements, or the report protected by the attorney-client privilege if they are transmitted directly to Edsel? If one of the witnesses was Doris Provine, a Winkel test driver on her way to work, who was ordered by her supervisor to talk to Edsel, would her statement enjoy greater protection than those of other witnesses? Would it make any difference if rather than being on her way to work, she was test driving the new Winkel SUV when she saw the accident? Would it make any difference if she was Winkel's president?**

8.   Physical Evidence

Physical evidence—such as guns, knives, counterfeit money, stolen property, tax returns, computer disks and photographs—poses special problems for attorneys and for the application of the attorney-client privilege. First, there is the question of when physical evidence can be considered a confidential communication made to secure legal advice. This depends on the nature of the evidence, how the attorney acquired it, and how the proponent intends to use the evidence at trial. If Carrie Client, on trial for killing Viola Victim, gave Alice Attorney a copy of a letter she had written to a friend in which she confessed her guilt, no privilege would attach to the information in the letter because Carrie had not intended to confine her confession to her attorney. Most courts treat photographs of generally accessible places, such as accident scenes, similarly. Since a photograph portrays what anyone could have seen, courts assume that a client who gives a picture of some public space to an attorney does not intend to keep the appearance of the scene confidential. If, however, Carrie gave Alice the knife she killed Viola with, her intent would almost certainly be that no one other than Alice and her assistants see it. But what exactly are the communicative elements of the act, and how do they pertain to the privilege? We shall return to this question shortly, when we consider the use the opponent wishes to make of the evidence.

Lawyers may acquire physical evidence in different ways. They may discover it independently of their client's disclosure. If they do, no privilege attaches. Thus if Alice, nosing around an alley behind Carrie's house, looks in a dumpster and finds the knife used to kill Viola, she can be compelled to describe at trial both the knife and how she happened to find it. If, however, Carrie tells Alice where the knife is and then Alice finds it, or if Carrie dumps the knife on Alice's desk, the state's ability to question Alice at trial is likely to be more circumscribed.

Also, there is the question of how the opponent—in our hypothetical, the prosecution—intends to use the evidence. If it seeks simply to present the knife as an item of physical evidence at trial, the attorney-client privilege will do Carrie little good, no matter how her attorney acquired the evidence. *As long as a party could have acquired and introduced evidence had the opponent's attorney not acquired it, the party may acquire and introduce evidence that the opponent gave to her attorney.* Thus if the state could, by subpoena, have required Carrie Client to turn over all the knives in her possession, it may require Alice Attorney, by subpoena, to turn over any knives that Carrie has given her. It makes no difference that Alice found the knife in a dumpster only because Carrie told her in confidence where it was. Had the knife remained in the dumpster, the state's investigators might possibly have found it, so the state will not be barred from introducing the knife simply because Carrie's attorney took possession before the state looked.

Physical evidence given by a client to an attorney in confidence in order to secure legal advice is, however, protected by the privilege if the evidence would have been privileged had it remained in the hands of the client. This principle is most often applied in cases involving "pre-existing documents." If a document was prepared before a legal controversy arose, it may ordinarily be subpoenaed from a party's attorney if it has been given to her, since the fact that it pre-existed the controversy usually means that it was not prepared to secure legal advice. However, if the party could have claimed a privilege to defeat the subpoena, such as a spousal privilege or the privilege against self-incrimination, the privilege will not be lost by turning the documents over to an attorney, in confidence, for the purpose of securing legal advice.[51]

An opponent may, however, not be content simply to introduce physical evidence acquired from the attorney. He may also seek to link the evidence to the client by showing that it was acquired from her attorney. Thus, the state may seek to have Alice testify that she acquired the knife that killed Viola from Carrie or by following Carrie's instructions. Here the protection of the privilege is usually available. Even if the object itself is not a communication, the act of providing the attorney with it includes communicative elements. At a minimum, the client is telling her attorney that she had the object in her possession, and most courts will protect that disclosure. In the criminal context, this protection is linked to the Fifth Amendment. While search warrants and other devices allow a state to secure incriminating evidence, a person cannot, unless granted legally sufficient immunity, be required to turn over self-incriminating evidence when to do so would be to admit the existence of the evidence, the fact that she possessed it or other incriminating information.[52] If there is a communication in turning over evidence in response to a subpoena, there is a similar communicative element when evidence is turned over to an attorney.

Some have seen a potential problem here, arguing that it allows people to enlist their attorneys as accomplices in breaking the chain that links incriminating evidence to them. As long as Carrie has the knife in her possession, the police may search her apartment and find it. But if the knife is in her attorney's office because Carrie gave it to her, and the police break in and find it, the privilege bars them from linking the knife to Carrie by showing Alice is her lawyer. The lawyer's role in breaking the chain of evidence may, however, not be as important as it might seem.

Even if the knife may not be linked to Carrie through Alice, Carrie is not home free. The police can get the knife, and it may be linked to her in

---

[51] See Fisher v. United States, 425 U.S. 391 (1976).

[52] Unites States v. Doe, 465 U.S. 605 (1984).

other ways. Perhaps there are fingerprints on the handle, or maybe it is the missing piece to a set in her home, or perhaps it is distinctive enough that someone recognizes it as hers. Moreover, a criminal seeking to destroy evidence has better ways of doing it than through her attorney—throwing a knife in a lake, for example. In fact, preventing physical evidence from being linked to a client through her attorney may, as we shall see, enhance rather than diminish the state's access to it.

Additional problems are posed when an attorney does not receive physical evidence from a client but instead finds it following a client's directions. If Alice, for example, removed the knife from a dumpster behind Carrie's house, the state can no longer find it in a location that would have linked it to Carrie. For this reason when evidence has been located through the confidence of a client and then removed by an attorney or her investigator, courts have conditioned the availability of the privilege on a disclosure, through stipulation or testimony, of the circumstances and condition in which the evidence was found.

The general rule that evidence given in confidence to an attorney may not thereby be linked to the client is not followed all the time or by all courts. Particularly in cases involving contraband (e.g., counterfeit money, illicit drugs, stolen goods and other objects that are unlawful to possess), courts often require attorneys to state how they acquired goods. It is not part of an attorney's business, courts say, to be a conduit for stolen property.

Instead of introducing the knife or asking Alice how she acquired it, the state might seek to put Alice on the stand to describe the knife on the theory that Carrie's act of giving it to her was not a communication. Ordinarily this will not work. As a general rule, a confidentiality privilege will not protect observations. However, if an object is intentionally shown or given to the attorney in confidence, there is little difference between this and confidentially describing the object, except that showing or giving is a more effective way of communicating how the object appears. Moreover, the attorney's testimony might link the object to the client, bringing the concerns discussed above into play. If, however, an object shown to an attorney later disappears, and it seems that the lawyer played a role in this, or that it was the client's plan to show the object to her attorney and then dispose of it, the attorney can be forced to testify. The theory is that showing or giving the object to the attorney was done as part of a plan to illegally dispose of it rather than for the protected purpose of securing legal advice.

Another special problem that physical evidence poses for attorneys is the problem of what to do with it. An attorney cannot ethically advise or participate in the destruction of evidence or maintain possession of material she knows is contraband. Once a lawyer has possession of an object that is evidence in a case, she should not return it to a client if she knows or has good reason to believe the client will dispose of it, and often she may have an obligation to turn the object over to an opponent or to the state. Thus, before a lawyer takes a tangible object from a client, she should be certain that her client knows what she might have to do with it. This information should not, however, be given in a way that encourages the client to dispose of evidence. These principles are easy to state, but you can imagine the difficulties that can arise in implementing them.

Almost all the cases that discuss what attorneys should do with physical evidence given to them by clients are criminal cases. They generally hold that a lawyer may keep an object that was used in a crime or is important evidence bearing on it, long enough to examine the object for whatever relevance it has to the defense. Then, so long as the object is not protected under the Fifth Amendment or some other privilege, she *must* turn it over to the state. With objects that are contraband, like drugs or stolen money, a case can be made that once the contraband is recognized as such, it should be turned over immediately since no one can legally possess it. Some courts, however, let even contraband be held briefly for examination, if the examination is needed to better advise the client.

When a lawyer turns over an object to the state, this should be done in such a way that the object is traceable to the attorney, so that a court, and not the attorney, may decide whether an object's link to a client is protected. If the lawyer were, for example, to return money taken in a bank robbery anonymously, she would be participating in a perhaps illegal effort to destroy her client's link to stolen goods.

Being gifted with objects used in crimes, or with the fruits of crimes, does not put a lawyer in a happy position. Not only may the lawyer be required to help the state gather its evidence, but the tug of war between loyalty to client and duty to state may place the lawyer in a situation in which her own professional status is in jeopardy. This is illustrated by the following case.

IN RE RYDER
381 F.2d 713 (4th Cir. 1967).

Before HOFFMAN, CHIEF JUDGE, and LEWIS and BUTZNER, JUDGES.

MEMORANDUM

PER CURIAM.

This proceeding was instituted to determine whether Richard R. Ryder should be removed from the roll of attorneys qualified to practice before this court. . . .

In proceedings of this kind the charges must be sustained by clear and convincing proof, the misconduct must be fraudulent, intentional, and the result of improper motives. . . . We conclude that these strict requirements have been satisfied. Ryder took possession of stolen money and a sawed-off shotgun, knowing that the money had been stolen and that the gun had been used in an armed robbery. He intended to retain this property pending his client's trial unless the government discovered it. He intended by his possession to destroy the chain of evidence that linked the contraband to his client and to prevent its use to establish his client's guilt.

On August 24, 1966 a man armed with a sawed-off shotgun robbed the Varina Branch of the Bank of Virginia of $7,583. Included in the currency taken were $10 bills known as 'bait money,' the serial numbers of which had been recorded.

On August 26, 1966 Charles Richard Cook rented safety deposit box 14 at a branch of the Richmond National Bank. Later in the day Cook was interviewed at his home by agents of the Federal Bureau of Investigation, who obtained $348 from him. Cook telephoned Ryder, who had represented him in civil litigation. Ryder came to the house and advised the agents that he represented Cook. He said that if Cook were not to be placed under arrest, he intended to take him to his office for an interview. The agents left. Cook insisted to Ryder that he had not robbed the bank. He told Ryder that he had won the money, which the agents had taken from him, in a crap game. At this time Ryder believed Cook.

Later that afternoon Ryder telephoned one of the agents and asked whether any of the bills obtained from Cook had been identified as a part of the money taken in the bank robbery. The agent told him that some bills had been identified. . . .

The next morning, Saturday, August 27, 1966, Ryder conferred with Cook again. He urged Cook to tell the truth, and Cook answered that a man, whose name he would not divulge, offered him $500 on the day of the robbery to put a package in a bank lockbox. Ryder did not believe this story. Ryder told Cook that if the government could trace the money in the box to him, it would be almost conclusive evidence of his guilt. He knew that Cook was under surveillance and he suspected that Cook might try to dispose of the money.

That afternoon Ryder telephoned a former officer of the Richmond Bar Association to discuss his course of action. He had known this attorney for many years and respected his judgment. The lawyer was at home and had no library available to him when Ryder telephoned. In their casual conversation Ryder told what he knew about the case, omitting names. He explained that he thought he would take the money from Cook's safety deposit box and place it in a box in his own name. This, he believed, would prevent Cook from attempting to dispose of the money. The lawyers thought that eventually F.B.I. agents would locate the money and that since it was in Ryder's possession, he could claim a privilege and thus effectively exclude it from evidence. This would prevent the government from linking Ryder's client with the bait money and would also destroy any presumption of guilt that might exist arising out of the client's exclusive possession of the evidence.

. . .

[Ryder had Cook sign a power of attorney giving him access to Cook's box and the power to dispose of the money. He did not, however, follow the advice of the attorney he consulted and tell Cook that when the case ended he would return the money to the bank.]

He testified about his omission:

". . . In the power of attorney, I did not specifically say that Mr. Cook authorized me to deliver that money to the appropriate authorities at any time because for a number of reasons. One, in representing a man under these circumstances, you've got to keep the man's confidence, but I also put in that power of attorney that Mr. Cook authorized me to dispose of that money as I saw fit, and the reason for that being that I was going to turn the money over to the proper authorities at whatever time I deemed that it wouldn't hurt Mr. Cook."

Ryder took the power of attorney which Cook had signed to the Richmond National Bank. He rented box 13 in his name with his office address, presented the power of attorney, entered Cook's box, took both boxes into a booth, where he found a bag of money and a sawed-off shotgun in Cook's box. He transferred the contents of Cook's box to his own and returned the boxes to the vault. He left the bank, and neither he nor Cook returned.

Ryder testified that he had some slight hesitation about the propriety of what he was doing. Within a half-hour after he left the bank, he talked to a retired judge and distinguished professor of law. He told this person that he wanted to discuss something in confidence. Ryder then stated that he represented a man suspected of bank robbery. The judge recalled the main part of the conversation:

". . . And that he had received from this client, under a power of attorney, a sum [of] money which he, Mr. Ryder, suspected was proceeds of the robbery, although he didn't know it, but he had a suspicion that it was; that he had placed this money in a safety deposit vault at a bank; that he had received it with the intention of returning it to the rightful owner after the case against his client had been finally disposed of one way or the other; that he considered that he had received it under the privilege of attorney and client and that he wanted responsible people in the community to know of that fact and that he was telling me in confidence of that as one of these people that he wanted to know of it."

. . .

The same day Ryder also talked with other prominent persons in Richmond—a judge of a court of record and an attorney for the Commonwealth. Again, he stated that what he intended to say was confidential. He related the circumstances and was advised that a lawyer could not receive the property and if he had received it he could not retain possession of it.

On September 7, 1966 Cook was indicted for robbing the Varina Branch of the Bank of Virginia. . . .

On September 12, 1966 F.B.I. agents procured search warrants for Cook's and Ryder's safety deposit boxes in the Richmond National Bank. They found Cook's box empty. In Ryder's box they discovered $5,920 of the $7,583 taken in the bank robbery and the sawed-off shotgun used in the robbery.

. . .

At the outset, we reject the suggestion that Ryder did not know the money which he transferred from Cook's box to his was stolen. We find that on August 29 when Ryder opened Cook's box and saw a bag of money and a sawed-off shotgun, he then knew Cook was involved in the bank robbery and that the money was stolen.

. . .

We also find that Ryder was not motivated solely by a certain expectation the government would discover the contents of his lockbox. He believed discovery was probable. In this event he intended to argue to the court that the contents of his box could not be revealed, and even if the contents were identified, his possession made the stolen money and the shotgun inadmissible against his client. He also recognized that discovery was not inevitable. His intention in this event, we find, was to assist Cook by keeping the stolen money and the shotgun concealed in his lockbox until after the trial. His conversations, and the secrecy he enjoined, immediately after he put the money and the gun in his box, show that he realized the government might not find the property.

We accept his statement that he intended eventually to return the money to its rightful owner, but we pause to say that no attorney should ever place himself in such a position. Matters involving the possible termination of an attorney-client relationship, or possible subsequent proceedings in the event of an acquittal, are too delicate to permit such a practice.

We reject the argument that Ryder's conduct was no more than the exercise of the attorney-client privilege. The fact that Cook had not been arrested or indicted at the time Ryder took possession of the gun and money is immaterial. Cook was Ryder's client and was entitled to the protection of the lawyer-client privilege. . . .

Regardless of Cook's status, however, Ryder's conduct was not encompassed by the attorney-client privilege. . . .

. . .

It was Ryder, not his client, who took the initiative in transferring the incriminating possession of the stolen money and the shotgun from Cook. Ryder's conduct went far beyond the receipt and retention of a confidential communication from his client. . . .

. . .

Not all papers in a lawyer's file are immune. The rule is summarized in McCormick, Evidence, § 93 at p. 188 (1954):

> "[I]f a document would be subject to an order for production if it were in the hands of a client, it would be equally subject if it is in the hands of an attorney."

Ryder, an experienced criminal attorney, recognized and acted upon the fact that the gun and money were subject to seizure while in the possession of Cook.

. . .

. . . In argument, it was generally conceded that Ryder could have been required to testify in the prosecution of Cook as to the transfer of the contents of the lockbox.

We conclude that Ryder violated Canons 15 and 32. His conduct is not sanctioned by Canons 5 or 37. . . .

> 5. *The Defense or Prosecution of Those Accused of Crime.* It is the right of the lawyer to undertake the defense of a person accused of crime, regardless of his personal opinion as to the guilt of the accused; otherwise innocent persons, victims only of suspicious circumstances, might be denied proper defense. Having undertaken such defense, the lawyer is bound by all fair and honorable means, to present every defense that the law of the land permits, to the end that no person may be deprived of life or liberty, but by due process of law.

> "15. *How Far a Lawyer May Go in Supporting a Client's Cause.*

> . . .

> "The lawyer owes 'entire devotion to the interest of the client, warm zeal in the maintenance and defense of his rights and the exertion of his utmost learning and ability,' to the end that nothing be taken or be withheld from him, save by the rules of law, legally

applied. . . . But it is steadfastly to be borne in mind that the great trust of the lawyer is to be performed within and not without the bounds of the law. The office of attorney does not permit, much less does it demand of him for any client, violation of law or any manner of fraud or chicane. He must obey his own conscience and not that of his client.

. . .

"32. *The Lawyer's Duty In Its Last Analysis.* No client, corporate or individual, however powerful, nor any cause, civil or political, however important, is entitled to receive, nor should any lawyer render any service or advice involving disloyalty to the law whose ministers we are, . . . When rendering any such improper service or advice, the lawyer invites and merits stern and just condemnation.

. . .

"37. *Confidence of a Client.* It is the duty of a lawyer to preserve his client's confidences. This duty outlasts the lawyer's employment, and extends as well to his employees; and neither of them should accept employment which involves or may involve the disclosure or use of these confidences, either for the private advantage of the lawyer or his employees or to the disadvantage to the client, without his knowledge and consent, and even though there are other available sources of such information. . . .

The money in Cook's box belonged to the Bank of Virginia. The law did not authorize Cook to conceal this money or withhold it from the bank. His larceny was a continuing offense. Cook had no title or property interest in the money that he lawfully could pass to Ryder. . . . No canon of ethics or law permitted Ryder to conceal from the Bank of Virginia its money to gain his client's acquittal.

Cook's possession of the sawed-off shotgun was illegal. Ryder could not lawfully receive the gun from Cook to assist Cook to avoid conviction of robbery. Cook had never mentioned the shotgun to Ryder. When Ryder discovered it in Cook's box, he took possession of it to hinder the government in the prosecution of its case, and he intended not to reveal it pending trial unless the government discovered it and a court compelled its production. No statute or canon of ethics authorized Ryder to take possession of the gun for this purpose.

. . .

In helping Cook to conceal the shotgun and stolen money, Ryder acted without the bounds of law. He allowed the office of attorney to be used in violation of law. The scheme which he devised was a deceptive, legalistic subterfuge—rightfully denounced by the canon as chicane.

Ryder also violated Canon 32. He rendered Cook a service involving deception and disloyalty to the law. He intended that his actions should remove from Cook exclusive possession of stolen money, and thus destroy an evidentiary presumption. His service in taking possession of the shotgun and money, with the intention of retaining them until after the trial, unless discovered by the government, merits the "stern and just condemnation" the canon prescribes.

Ryder's testimony that he intended to have the court rule on the admissibility of the evidence and the extent of the lawyer-client privilege does not afford justification for his action. He intended to do this only if the government discovered the shotgun and stolen money in his lockbox. If the government did not discover it, he had no intention of submitting any legal question about it to the court. If there were no discovery, he would continue to conceal the shotgun and money for Cook's benefit pending trial.

Ryder's action is not justified because he thought he was acting in the best interests of his client. To allow the individual lawyer's belief to determine the standards of professional conduct will in time reduce the ethics of the profession to the practices of the most unscrupulous. Moreover, Ryder knew that the law against concealing stolen property and the law forbidding receipt and possession of a sawed-off shotgun contain no exemptions for a lawyer who takes possession with the intent of protecting a criminal from the consequences of his crime.

. . .

We find it difficult to accept the argument that Ryder's action is excusable because if the government found Cook's box, Ryder's would easily be found, and if the government failed to find both Cook's and Ryder's boxes, no more harm would be done than if the agents failed to find only Cook's. Cook's concealment of the items in his box cannot be cited to excuse Ryder. Cook's conduct is not the measure of Ryder's ethics. The conduct of a lawyer should be above reproach. Concealment of the stolen money and the sawed-off shotgun to secure Cook's acquittal was wrong whether the property was in Cook's or Ryder's possession.

There is much to be said, however, for mitigation of the discipline to be imposed. Ryder intended to return the bank's money after his client was tried. He consulted reputable persons before and after he placed the property in his lockbox, although he did not precisely follow their advice. Were it not for these facts, we would deem proper his permanent exclusion from practice before this court. In view of the mitigating circumstances, he will be suspended from practice in this court for eighteen months.

There are relatively few cases involving attorneys whose clients have given them contraband or other incriminating physical evidence, so the case law leaves open important questions. For example, it seems clear that when attorneys take possession of physical evidence that is either contraband or the fruit or instrumentality of crimes, they must turn it over to the state or, in the case of stolen property, to its rightful owner. It is not clear, however, whether being handed an object by a client constitutes taking possession, or whether possession is transferred only when the client departs without asking for the object back. Similarly, it is clear that a lawyer must not advise or assist in the disposal of evidence or contraband, but it is unclear whether this obligation precludes an attorney from returning such objects to clients if they have been given with the understanding they would be wanted back. It is generally agreed that lawyers possessing objects they must turn over to the state may examine them before doing so, but it is not clear how long they may hold objects for examination.

Of course, not all evidentiary objects have figured in crimes. A letter to a friend that admits a murder may, for example, be highly probative, but it is not contraband. Under *Fisher v. United States*,[53] if a writing or physical object, such as a letter, could not be subpoenaed from a client because of the client's Fifth Amendment or other privilege, it cannot be subpoenaed from an attorney when it has been turned over to her in confidence to secure legal advice. If, however, the writing or object would not be protected in the hands of the client, it is not clear whether there are circumstances in which the lawyer, even without a subpoena, should turn the evidence over to the state, or whether the lawyer is obliged not to do this. Also, if a lawyer receives such evidence, it is not clear whether she must, after examining the item, return it to her client so that the lawyer plays no part in concealing the evidence.

The bottom line regarding physical evidence, the protection of the privilege, and an attorney's obligations is that the cases provide only partial guidance and are sometimes inconsistent. An attorney who receives physical evidence from a client can never be sure that she will not end up an unwilling contributor to her client's conviction. She may also, like Ryder, run risks of her own. Thus, a lawyer should be careful when dealing with physical evidence and be sure that when a client offers such evidence he knows exactly what the lawyer's obligations regarding it are.

Problem VIII-5. Assume that Anthony Harris is charged with willfully evading the payment of federal income taxes. **Does his lawyer have a duty to share information with the prosecutor under any of the**

---

[53]   425 U.S. 391 (1976).

following circumstances? Under which circumstances might the attorney be called to testify about the writing if it had been lost or destroyed?

A. Harris produces a bankbook showing a secret account that indicates he has received undeclared income. He gives it to his lawyer.

B. Harris tells his lawyer that, under a false name, he has money in a bank in a distant city and that he doubts the government knows this.

C. In response to his lawyer's request for a summary of his income, Harris prepares a detailed analysis of his receipts during the past several years.

D. In connection with the detailed report described in *C*, Harris delivers to the lawyer all the records he has kept in connection with his previous tax returns.

E. Harris drops the key to a safe deposit box on his attorney's desk. The attorney goes to the bank, opens the box, and finds $100,000 in large bills.

In the last situation should the attorney act differently if the client has consulted her as a suspect in a bank robbery in which $100,000 in large bills was taken rather than as someone suspected of concealing income?

C. COMMUNICATIONS THAT ARE NOT PRIVILEGED

Communications in certain settings or about certain matters are specifically exempted from the protection of the attorney-client privilege. The five exceptions found in PFRE 503(d) were intended to codify the common law.

When an attorney serves as an attesting witness, she is not acting as a lawyer and the client's obvious intent is to have her available to testify should the need arise.

When two persons are claiming through the same deceased client, as in a dispute over which of two wills is valid, the issue of who may properly claim the privilege as the deceased's successor is often tied up with the ultimate issue in the case. Some courts allow either side to claim the privilege. Better practice, codified in the proposed rule, is to hold the privilege inapplicable in such disputes. This exception is supported by the sensible fiction that the deceased client would have been willing to reveal confidential communications to ensure that her affairs were settled as she intended.

When two clients consult a lawyer jointly about a matter of common interest, there is no privilege if a dispute should arise between them since courts assume that the clients do not intend that their communications be kept secret from each other. The exception is most commonly invoked when insureds and their insurance companies fall out and sue each other. Since the exception applies only when the communication refers to a matter of common interest, not every statement that one party makes to a jointly retained attorney loses the privilege's protection if the parties later become antagonists in a legal dispute. For example, an insured may discuss with her attorney her responsibility for an accident and the tax consequences of any payment she might receive. In later litigation with the company, her statements about her responsibility for the accident would not be privileged, since she and the company were jointly concerned with defending her actions, but her discussion of her tax situation should retain its privileged status since what she was talking about was solely her concern. Some courts have not appreciated such distinctions.

Courts also get confused in "common case" situations, which arise when parties represented by separate counsel meet together to plan a common trial strategy. Many courts privilege what is said in such conferences, a decision that can be justified by the fact that the mutual disclosures are made to further the rendition of professional legal services to each lawyer's client. If this is so, each party should be able to claim the privilege for what she says or confidences her attorney reveals regardless of whether she later litigates against third parties or her erstwhile allies. Some courts, however, treat this situation like the jointly retained counsel situation and find an exception to the privilege when those who had been mounting a common claim or defense fall out and become legal antagonists. A justification for an exception is that the parties never intended their disclosures to each other to be confidential between them. Unlike the joint client situation, this rationale does not justify abrogating the privilege for disclosures relating to the common interest but made only to the party's own counsel.

There is also an exception for communications relevant to a breach of duty between lawyer and client. This is a polite way of saying that if a client forces a lawyer to sue for her fee, one price the client may pay is the revelation of relevant confidences. This principle also strips the privilege from relevant statements if a client sues her lawyer for malpractice. These situations are the ones that motivated the exception, but many courts extend the exception to other situations in which a client questions her lawyer's behavior. Thus the exception has been used to abrogate the privilege when a claim of ineffective assistance of counsel is made, though a waiver theory might better justify the result.

Probably the most difficult, and certainly the most frequently litigated, of the common law exceptions to the privilege arises when a lawyer's services are alleged to have been sought to aid in the commission of a crime or fraud. The language of the proposed federal rule suggests that what is crucial is the client's intent when the lawyer is employed. If the services are secured with the intent to commit what the client knows, or should know, is a crime or fraud, nothing the client says to her attorney is privileged.

Not all courts, however, read the privilege this way. Decisions both expand and contract the exception. On the one hand, some courts deny the privilege when the client consults a lawyer in good faith but the lawyer later suggests or carries out some illegal or fraudulent action on behalf of the client. On the other hand, regardless of why the lawyer was consulted, some courts abrogate the privilege only for statements relating to the criminal or fraudulent endeavor. In interpreting this exception, most courts give "crime or fraud" an expansive interpretation. It is, for example, commonly extended to communications relating to intentional torts, and "fraud" is often taken to mean lies or dishonesty of any sort.

For many years there was a debate over whether in determining the applicability of the crime or fraud exception a court could consider otherwise privileged statements. The issue arose because the determination of the exception's applicability is a preliminary question of fact for the judge to decide under FRE 104(a). FRE 104(a), as you recall, provides that in determining preliminary questions of fact, the judge is bounded by no rules of evidence except the rules of privilege. It might thus seem that the judge could consider the presumptively privileged material only if the crime or fraud exception applied, but this is precisely what the judge does not know.

In 1989 in the case of *United States v. Zolin*,[54] the Supreme Court confronted this dilemma. The Court held that FRE 104(a) did not preclude an *in camera* review of apparently privileged statements to determine whether the crime or fraud exception applied. However, to trigger an *in camera* review the proponent of the exception has to present enough unprivileged evidence to support a good faith belief by a reasonable person that the review might produce evidence supporting the exception's applicability, and even when such evidence is produced, *Zolin* gives the judge discretion to reach a decision without considering the allegedly privileged statements.

D. WAIVER

A client may always waive the protection of the attorney-client privilege. The lawyer, although presumed to have authority to waive the privilege on the client's behalf, may not do so over the client's objection. Nor may an attorney assert the privilege when the client agrees to waive it.

---

[54] 491 U.S. 554 (1989).

The simplest ways to waive the privilege are by expressly agreeing to do so, or by failing to assert the privilege when privileged information is requested. The privilege is also waived when a person voluntarily discloses, in a setting where a privilege does not apply, what she said to her attorney. Thus if Carrie Client, responding to a cross-examiner's charge of recent fabrication, says she told Alice Attorney during their first conversation that she had a green light, the opposing party will be able to examine Carrie in detail about exactly what she said about the light. By testifying to what she told Alice, Carrie will have waived the privilege. This waiver would apply not only in the current litigation but in any future lawsuit, grand jury investigation, or other proceeding, no matter who the opposing party. Moreover, Carrie might well find that she had waived the privilege with respect to everything she told Alice about the accident at their first meeting, and she would almost certainly find that she had waived the privilege with respect to everything she told Alice about the traffic light in any conversation.

The reason for this broad imputation of waiver is that the courts will not allow a selective waiver of the privilege to convey a misleading impression, as it would if Carrie, at a subsequent meeting with Alice, had admitted that she ran a red light, or as it might if Carrie, at her first meeting with Alice, had also said that she was speeding at the time of the accident.

Waiver may not be just unknowing, as in Carrie's case; it may be completely inadvertent. In one case, for example, a defendant was held to have waived the privilege with respect to drafts of letters to counsel that plaintiff's investigators found by searching a dumpster outside the defendant's office. The court reasoned that the defendant's failure to shred the drafts before depositing them in the trash indicated it had no desire to keep them confidential.[55] This is an extreme and probably bad decision. Far more common and less controversial are decisions holding that corporations have waived their attorney-client privileges for documents circulated beyond the range of persons who had a "need to know" in connection with the legal representation.

The principle that even an inadvertent disclosure of confidential information waives the privilege, together with the extension of waiver to all communications relating to the communication disclosed, poses considerable problems in the discovery process. When tens or hundreds of thousands or even millions of documents are to be given to an adversary, it is both costly and difficult to ensure that no privileged documents are turned over. The struggle of courts and parties with this issue has yielded a range of diverse decisions and solutions.[56] These

---

[55] Suburban Sew 'N Sweep, Inc. v. Swiss-Bernina, Inc., 91 F.R.D. 254 (N.D. Ill. 1981).

[56] See Richard L. Marcus, The Perils of Privilege: Waiver and the Litigator, 84 Mich. L. Rev. 1605 (1986).

include the traditional application of the doctrine, decisions that waive the privilege for the disclosed documents but not for related material, decisions that honor parties' agreements that inadvertent disclosure during discovery does not constitute waiver, and court-established discovery procedures that provide that inadvertent disclosure shall not constitute waiver.

Inadvertent waiver has become a substantial issue in the modern technological age. Faxes, emails, and texts are misaddressed and accidentally sent to people outside the privileged relationship. Far more likely, however, is the near certainty that privileged material will be accidentally disclosed in the transfers of vast numbers of documents that often take place in electronic discovery. No matter how careful counsel may be in privilege review of requested information, there is a strong likelihood that some, perhaps important, privileged information will be accidentally transferred to opposing counsel. The problem has become so significant that in 2008 Congress added a new privilege rule, FRE 502:

Rule 502. Attorney-Client Privilege and Work Product; Limitations on Waiver

The following provisions apply, in the circumstances set out, to disclosure of a communication or information covered by the attorney-client privilege or work-product protection.

(a) Disclosure Made in a Federal Proceeding or to a Federal Office or Agency; Scope of a Waiver. When the disclosure is made in a federal proceeding or to a federal office or agency and waives the attorney-client privilege or work-product protection, the waiver extends to an undisclosed communication or information in a federal or state proceeding only if:

(1) the waiver is intentional;

(2) the disclosed and undisclosed communications or information concern the same subject matter; and

(3) they ought in fairness to be considered together.

(b) Inadvertent Disclosure. When made in a federal proceeding or to a federal office or agency, the disclosure does not operate as a waiver in a federal or state proceeding if:

(1) the disclosure is inadvertent;

(2) the holder of the privilege or protection took reasonable steps to prevent disclosure; and

(3) the holder promptly took reasonable steps to rectify the error, including (if applicable) following Federal Rule of Civil Procedure 26(b)(5)(B).

(c) Disclosure Made in a State Proceeding. When the disclosure is made in a state proceeding and is not the subject of a state-court order concerning waiver, the disclosure does not operate as a waiver in a federal proceeding if the disclosure:

(1) would not be a waiver under this rule if it had been made in a federal proceeding; or

(2) is not a waiver under the law of the state where the disclosure occurred.

(d) Controlling Effect of a Court Order. A federal court may order that the privilege or protection is not waived by disclosure connected with the litigation pending before the court—in which event the disclosure is also not a waiver in any other federal or state proceeding.

(e) Controlling Effect of a Party Agreement. An agreement on the effect of disclosure in a federal proceeding is binding only on the parties to the agreement, unless it is incorporated into a court order.

(f) Controlling Effect of this Rule. Notwithstanding Rules 101 and 1101, this rule applies to state proceedings and to federal court-annexed and federal court-mandated arbitration proceedings, in the circumstances set out in the rule. And notwithstanding Rule 501, this rule applies even if state law provides the rule of decision.

(g) Definitions. In this rule:

(1) "attorney-client privilege" means the protection that applicable law provides for confidential attorney-client communications; and

(2) "work-product protection" means the protection that applicable law provides for tangible material (or its intangible equivalent) prepared in anticipation of litigation or for trial.

Although a full discussion of FRE 502 is beyond the scope of this text, a brief analysis is appropriate. FRE 502(a) deals with the scope of waiver. It declares that although disclosure of attorney-client or work product protected material may result in waiver as it affects the disclosed material, other, related, privileged material will not be at risk unless the other requirements of FRE 502(a) are met. This can substantially soften the impact of waiver. FRE 502(b) governs inadvertent waiver. If the privilege holder "took reasonable steps to prevent disclosure" and otherwise complied with the rule's requirements, FRE 502 may fully protect against inadvertent waiver. Notably, FRE 502 contains detailed provisions that govern both federal *and* state proceedings. In light of FRE 502 (e), we can expect lawyers who have adopted the increasingly frequent practice of joint party agreements to deal with accidental disclosure to ask the court to embody the agreement in a court order in order to ensure its effectiveness against other parties.

A party waives her privilege by revealing, in some non-privileged setting, a confidential communication to her attorney, but the privilege is not necessarily waived if the subject matter of the disclosure, rather than the communication, is discussed with friends or with others who cannot legally keep confidences. Thus, Carrie would waive her privilege if she told a friend that she told Alice, her attorney, that she was speeding. She would not necessarily waive it if she simply told the friend she was speeding. But, if a party talks too freely about a matter she discussed with her attorney, a court might take this to indicate that the client did not intend confidentiality when she talked to her attorney or, if she did initially, that she no longer seeks it.

People may also be held to have waived the privilege in situations in which they would very much like to retain it. Thus, if a person defends an action by claiming she was relying on advice of counsel, the privilege will be deemed waived for all conversations relating to that advice. Even when the advice claim is not explicit, the privilege may be found to have been waived, as in one case in which state officials asserted immunity as a defense and the court held that the defense put their good faith in issue and, in so doing, waived the privilege as to communications with counsel bearing on the issue.[57] Waiver can also be effected by preparing a prospective witness with the aid of privileged documents, since a lawyer doing so knows that if the witness testifies, the preparation materials may have to be provided the opposing party under FRE 612.

In short, it is easy to inadvertently waive the attorney-client privilege, and, even when a particular confidence is intentionally waived, the breadth of what has been waived may be wider than expected. Thus, attorneys, particularly those with organizational clients or in the discovery phase of litigation, must closely monitor how confidential information is maintained and used to avoid losing the protection of the privilege.

Problem VIII-6. Clara Davis, knowing she is under investigation for fraud, consults Sonja Kassebaum, an attorney, to secure legal advice. She tells Kassebaum of the scheme she has been using to sell small parcels of land at large profits. The scheme is ingenious but of questionable legality, and Kassebaum, citing her sense of ethics, refuses to take Davis as a client. Two weeks later at a cocktail party where people are talking about different get-rich-quick schemes, Kassebaum describes the scheme that Davis revealed to her. **Do Kassebaum's revelations in some way**

---

[57]   Mitzner v. Sobol, 136 F.R.D. 359 (S.D.N.Y. 1991).

violate the attorney-client privilege? Will they affect Davis's ability to claim the privilege with respect to Kassebaum's testimony if Kassebaum is subpoenaed after the case goes to trial? Would your answer to either of these questions be different if Kassebaum had agreed to take Davis on as a client? Suppose it was Davis rather than Kassebaum who had described the scheme at the party. Would Davis's revelations affect her right to claim the attorney-client privilege if asked before a grand jury to reveal what she told Kassebaum?

E. ATTORNEY WORK PRODUCT

The attorney-client privilege is one of two rules that help attorneys keep confidential information they acquire while serving clients. The other, as we are reminded in *Upjohn*, is work-product protection. Work-product protection has historically been regarded as something other than a privilege, perhaps because an early rationale for it was that in an adversary system, one party, absent special circumstances, should not be able to reap the fruits of an opponent's expenditures to secure and analyze information. However, work-product protection works much like a privilege and can be justified by the kinds of instrumental rationales that are used to justify most privileges. Courts recognize this, and today judges often speak of "the work-product privilege."

Because of its historical roots in a case probing the limits of discovery,[58] rules regarding work product have been codified in the Federal Rules of Civil Procedure (though work-product claims may be made in criminal cases as well), and the subject is typically explored in civil procedure courses. For this reason, our treatment of work-product will be brief despite the topic's importance, and it will focus on the differences between the attorney-client privilege and work-product protection.

Perhaps the most salient difference between work-product protection and the attorney-client privilege is that the attorney-client privilege protects only what attorneys learn in confidence from clients, while the work-product protection protects what attorneys learn, whether confidentially or not, from all sources. Thus, the work-product protection covers a far broader range of information. This does not, however, mean that work-product protection will suppress more information than the privilege.

First, one attorney can often duplicate another's efforts. Thus, if Carrie Client cannot learn on discovery what Oliver Opponent's counsel discovered in interviewing witnesses, she may at her own expense

---

[58]   Hickman v. Taylor, 329 U.S. 495 (1947).

interview the same witnesses Oliver did unless circumstances, such as the death of a witness, make this impossible.

Second, although the attorney-client privilege applies to all confidential communications made to secure legal advice, work-product protection applies only to information that attorneys collect in anticipation of litigation. Thus the routine work that attorneys do all the time for clients should not qualify for work-product protection. Some courts, however, pay little attention to the anticipation-of-litigation requirement, and in this respect work-product protection seems to be expanding.

Third, while the attorney-client privilege is generally absolute when it applies, work-product protection is supposedly conditional, depending on an opponent's need for evidence and the opponent's ability to acquire it. But this does not tell the full story. Work product that captures facts relevant to litigation, such as the story a witness tells or evidence about the damage a vehicle sustained in an accident, will usually be discoverable if the opponent can show the information is no longer available or can be had only at an exorbitant cost that is far higher than the first party had to bear. If, however, the work product captures the opinions or litigation strategy of an attorney such as an attorney's opinion of a witness's truthfulness, in federal practice the protection accorded work product is almost as absolute as that accorded a client's confidential communications. Knowing this leads some attorneys, almost always attorneys working for corporations and other large institutions, to interview witnesses and collect information themselves, and to do this in such a way that their opinions and judgments are intertwined with the facts they gather.

The work-product protection also differs from the attorney-client privilege in that the attorney is said to be the privilege holder when it comes to work-product while the client owns the attorney-client privilege. It is hard to see why this privilege should be the attorney's when she has been gathering information at the behest and expense of the client. Moreover, if a client does not want an attorney to reveal her work product, the attorney's professional obligations to her client, which include a general obligation of confidentiality with respect to what she learns during the course of the representation, should preclude the attorney from waiving work-product protection. Conversely, if it is in the client's interest to disclose work-product information, the attorney may have an ethical obligation to do so.

Over time the work-product and attorney-client protections seem to be becoming more alike. Work-product protection has come to apply in criminal as well as civil cases, courts are less careful than they once were in insisting on a litigation nexus, and the protection accorded opinion work-product is often almost absolute. Courts are also reading into the work-product doctrine some of the waiver rules and exceptions that condition the attorney-client privilege. Thus, most courts have read a "crime or fraud" exception into the work-product protection, often without regard to whether it is the attorney or client who has engaged in forbidden behavior. Other courts have found a waiver of work-product protection when an attorney's advice or conduct is in issue. From the other end, a few states and an occasional federal district court have held that the attorney-client privilege is not absolute but must give way when the need for disclosure is great enough. If these trends continue, perhaps one day we will have no attorney-client privilege or work-product protection, but will instead have a single defeasible privilege for information acquired by attorneys.

Problem VIII-7. The Winkel Motor Company has upcoming contract negotiations with the Motor Workers Union (MWU). Winkel's President, Bert Martin, calls General Counsel Herb Edsel into his office and says (1) "Herb, the union is killing us competitively. I want to use this round of negotiations to break them or put them in our pocket. I don't care how we do it; I just want to do it. Draw me up a plan." (2) Two weeks later Edsel submits a two-part plan to Martin. The first is "to hire replacement workers as soon as our P.R. people tell us the public will sympathize." The second is "to make unreasonable demands we know the union will reject. When it does, we declare the contract at an impasse, impose our terms and fire all workers who don't came back." (3) Martin sends back a memo; "I like it; proceed, you're in charge of everything."

Anticipating the possibility of vandalism or even violence against the strike breakers as the strike proceeds, Edsel asks Lisa Kahn, the most capable attorney in his office, to investigate various security agencies and prepare a report on them. (4) Kahn's report on a company called "First in Strike Trouble," says in part "FIST is the toughest agency out there. Replacement workers love them but that may be because they seem excessively prone to meet violence with violence." (5) Edsel interviews the head of FIST. He explains the strike may be a long one because the company wants to break the union. He talks about the need for FIST to protect workers and property, and says he wants FIST to be as tough as the law allows. He then explains the constraints the law imposes on Winkel and by extension, FIST. (6) Later Edsel decides to hire FIST. He sends FIST a letter saying the contract will follow and adding, "In addition to what the contract provides, Winkel will represent you and your employees in any tort or criminal action that grows out of your work for the company."

FIST is hired. The strike occurs and Winkel implements its plans. At one point FIST's guards charge into a group of picketers and beat them with truncheons, allegedly because they are preventing strike breakers from passing through their lines. Several union members are seriously injured. Edsel puts Kahn in charge of learning what happened. (7) She interviews the guard who did the most harm. He tells her, "I'm in this business because I like hurting people. Once I start hitting people, I just can't seem to stop." (8) She also interviews a guard who was merely a witness. She copies down in her own words what she thinks is important in what he says. Since what he said was not helpful to Winkel, she doesn't bother to write down his name. (9) She does the same thing in interviewing one of the injured picketers. (10) One of the paralegals who works under Kahn interviews another guard witness. The interview is tape recorded and transcribed, after which the tape is erased. Kahn reviews the transcript, annotating it with her views of its legal implications. (11) The same is true of a union witness interviewed by the paralegal. (12) Kahn and her paralegal each interview another dozen or so guards and other witnesses. All the witness interviews are tape recorded and transcribed, and the tapes are then erased. The witnesses' names and addresses are not always preserved. (13) Edsel asks for a report of what happened. Before they are called away for other urgent business, Kahn and her paralegal each summarize the gist of five or six of the interviews they conducted and forward them to Edsel along with the full transcripts. Edsel reads both, adds his comments to the summaries, files them and discards the transcripts.

Later MWU complains to the labor board that Winkel did not bargain in good faith, and the injured workers sue Winkel and FIST for their injuries. The FIST guards are not sued because they have low salaries and few assets. During the course of the unfair labor practice litigation, requests are made to discover evidence items (1) through (6) above. Winkel responds by asserting attorney-client privilege and work-product protection with regard to each. **Will Winkel prevail?**

During the discovery phase of the tort suit, the plaintiffs seek to discover items (4) through (13) above. Winkel and FIST resist, asserting the attorney-client privilege and work-product protection. All the guards interviewed also enter an appearance (by an attorney paid for by FIST) and claim the attorney-client privilege for whatever they told Kahn or her paralegal. **How should a court rule?**

"I never discuss my clients with their mothers."

F. ETHICAL ISSUES

Questions relating to the attorney-client privilege often merge with other questions about the duty that an attorney owes her client and the court. There are ways in which a client who has revealed information to an attorney may be disadvantaged even if the privilege is honored. One recurring issue is whether an attorney whose client has confessed to a crime may continue to defend the client as if no confession had been made. The American Bar Association at one time tried to prescribe in some detail how defense counsel should act.

ABA STANDARDS FOR CRIMINAL JUSTICE, THE PROSECUTION FUNCTION AND THE DEFENSE FUNCTION STANDARD 7.7 (APP. DRAFT [ENACTED RULE IN EFFECT FROM 1971 TO 1979])

Testimony by the defendant.

(a) If the defendant has admitted to his lawyer facts which establish guilt and the lawyer's independent investigation established that the admissions are true but the defendant insists on his right to trial, the lawyer must advise his client against taking the witness stand to testify falsely.

(b) If, before trial, the defendant insists that he will take the stand to testify falsely, the lawyer must withdraw from the case, if that is feasible, seeking leave of court if necessary.

(c) If withdrawal from the case is not feasible or is not permitted by the court, or if the situation arises during the trial and the defendant insists upon testifying falsely in his own behalf, the lawyer may not lend his aid to the perjury. Before the defendant takes the stand in these circumstances, the lawyer should make a record of the fact that the defendant is taking the stand against the advice of counsel in some appropriate manner without revealing the fact to the court. The lawyer must confine his examination to identifying the witness as the defendant and permitting him to make his statement to the trier or the triers of fact; the lawyer may not engage in direct examination of the defendant as a witness in the conventional manner and may not later argue the defendant's known false version of facts to the jury as worthy of belief and he may not recite or rely upon the false testimony in his closing statement.

Professor Monroe Freedman, a noted if controversial legal ethicist, took quite a different view:

THE ADVERSARY SYSTEM AND
THE NECESSITY FOR CONFIDENTIALITY

The adversary system has further ramifications in a criminal case. The defendant is presumed to be innocent. The burden is on the prosecution to prove beyond a reasonable doubt that the defendant is guilty. The plea of not guilty does not necessarily mean "not guilty in fact," for the defendant may mean "not legally guilty." Even the accused who knows that he committed the crime is entitled to put the government to its proof. Indeed, the accused who knows that he is guilty has an absolute constitutional right to remain silent. The moralist might quite reasonably understand this to mean that, under these circumstances, the defendant and his lawyer are privileged to "lie" to the court in pleading not guilty. In my judgment, the moralist is right. However, our adversary system and related notions of the proper administration of criminal justice sanction the lie.

Some derive solace from the sophistry of calling the lie a "legal fiction," but this is hardly an adequate answer to the moralist. Moreover, this answer has no particular appeal for the practicing attorney, who knows that the plea of not guilty commits him to the most effective advocacy of which he is capable. Criminal defense lawyers do not win their cases by arguing reasonable doubt. Effective trial advocacy requires that the attorney's every word, action, and attitude be consistent with the conclusion that his client is innocent. As every trial lawyer knows, the jury is certain that the defense attorney knows whether his client is guilty. The jury is therefore alert to, and will be enormously affected by, any indication by the attorney that he believes the defendant to be guilty. Thus, the plea of not guilty commits the advocate to a trial, including a closing argument, in which he must argue that "not guilty" means "not guilty in fact."

[The question is posed whether it is proper to put a witness on the stand when you know he will commit perjury.]

Perhaps the most common method for avoiding the ethical problem just posed is for the lawyer to withdraw from the case, at least if there is sufficient time before trial for the client to retain another attorney. The client will then go to the nearest law office, realizing that the obligation of confidentiality is not what it has been represented to be, and withhold incriminating information or the fact of his guilt from his new attorney. On ethical grounds, the practice of withdrawing from a case under such circumstances is indefensible, since the identical perjured testimony will ultimately be presented. More important, perhaps, is the practical consideration that the new attorney will be ignorant of the perjury and therefore will be in no position to attempt to discourage the client from presenting it. Only the original attorney, who knows the truth, has that opportunity, but he loses it in the very act of evading the ethical problem.

The problem is all the more difficult when the client is indigent. He cannot retain other counsel, and in many jurisdictions . . . it is impossible for appointed counsel to withdraw from a case except for extraordinary reasons. Thus, appointed counsel, unless he lies to the judge, can successfully withdraw only by revealing to the judge that the attorney has received knowledge of his client's guilt. Such a revelation in itself would seem to be a sufficiently serious violation of the obligation of confidentiality to merit severe condemnation. In fact, however, the situation is far worse, since it is entirely possible that the same judge who permits the attorney to withdraw will subsequently hear the case and sentence the defendant. When he does so, of course, he will have had personal knowledge of the defendant's guilt before the trial began. Moreover, this will be knowledge of which the newly appointed counsel for the defendant will probably be ignorant.

The difficulty is further aggravated when the client informs the lawyer for the first time during the trial that he intends to take the stand and commit perjury. The perjury in question may not necessarily be a protestation of innocence by a guilty man. Referring to the . . . hypothetical of the defendant wrongly accused of a robbery at 16th and P, the only perjury may be his denial of the truthful, but highly damaging, testimony of the corroborating witness who placed him one block away from the intersection five minutes prior to the crime. Of course, if he tells the truth and thus verifies the corroborating witness, the jury will be far more inclined to accept the inaccurate testimony of the principal witness, who specifically identified him as the criminal.

If a lawyer has discovered his client's intent to perjure himself, one possible solution to this problem is for the lawyer to approach the bench, explain his ethical difficulty to the judge, and ask to be relieved, thereby causing a mistrial. This request is certain to be denied, if only because it would empower the defendant to cause a series of mistrials in the same fashion. At this point, some feel that the lawyer has avoided the ethical problem and can put the defendant on the stand. However, one objection to this solution, apart from the violation of confidentiality, is that the lawyer's ethical problem has not been solved, but has only been transferred to the judge. Moreover, the client in such a case might well have grounds for appeal on the basis of deprivation of due process and denial of the right to counsel, since he will have been tried before, and sentenced by, a judge who has been informed of the client's guilt by his own attorney.

A solution even less satisfactory than informing the judge of the defendant's guilt would be to let the client take the stand without the attorney's participation and to omit reference to the client's testimony in closing argument. The latter solution, of course, would be as damaging as to fail entirely to argue the case to the jury, and failing to argue the case is "as improper as though the attorney had told the jury that his client had uttered a falsehood in making the statement."

Therefore, the obligation of confidentiality, in the context of our adversary system, apparently allows the attorney no alternative to putting a perjurious witness on the stand without explicit or implicit disclosure of the attorney's knowledge to either the judge or the jury. . . .

Of course, before the client testifies perjuriously, the lawyer has a duty to attempt to dissuade him on grounds of both law and morality. In addition, the client should be impressed with the fact that his untruthful alibi is tactically dangerous. There is always a strong possibility that the prosecutor will expose the perjury on cross-examination. However, for the reasons already given, the final decision must necessarily be the client's. The lawyer's best course thereafter would be to avoid any further professional relationship with a client whom he knew to have perjured himself.[59]

––––––––––––

The difficulty of getting agreement on the issues Freedman discusses is perhaps best indicated by the fact that the ABA standard you read was withdrawn when the *Standards* were revised in 1979, and for fourteen years the ABA's commentary on the defense function provided no guidance for the lawyer whose client seemed bent on perjury. The third edition of the *Standards*, published in 1993, seems to take a position. Standard 4–7.5 (a) provides: "Defense counsel should not knowingly offer false evidence, whether by documents, tangible evidence, or the testimony of witnesses, or fail to take reasonable remedial measures upon discovery of its falsity." The commentary adds:

> When evidence that a lawyer knows to be false is provided by a person who is not a client, the lawyer must refuse to offer it regardless of the client's wishes.

> When false evidence is offered by the client, however, a conflict may arise between the lawyer's duty to keep the client's revelations confidential and the duty of candor to the court. Upon ascertaining that material evidence is false, the lawyer should seek to persuade the client that the evidence should not be offered or, if it has been offered, that its false character should immediately be disclosed. If the persuasion is ineffective, the lawyer must take reasonable remedial measures.

> The advocate's proper course with respect to reasonable remedial measures, ordinarily, is to remonstrate with the client confidentially. If that fails, the advocate should seek to withdraw if that will remedy the situation. If withdrawal will not remedy the situation or is impossible, the advocate should make disclosure to the court. It is for the court then to determine what should be done—making a statement about the matter to the trier of fact, ordering a mistrial, or perhaps nothing.[a]

––––––––––––

[59] Monroe Freedman, Professional Responsibility of the Criminal Defense Lawyer: The Three Hardest Questions, 64 Mich. L. Rev. 1469, 1470–72, 1575–78 (1966).

[a] A separate standard relating to defense counsel's obligations when his or her client proposes to testify or testifies perjuriously was considered for inclusion in these Standards but was not adopted for lack of consensus as to the appropriate approach. Counsel should pay close attention to the ethics code rules adopted on this subject in his or her jurisdiction. [This footnote to the commentary suggests that the ABA means to take no position on a lawyer's obligation when a client lies or lets her lawyer know she intends to lie under oath, and renders the commentary ambiguous.]

Counsel's duty to rectify the presentation of false evidence continues only until the conclusion of the proceeding at which the evidence was offered.[60]

The Supreme Court addressed the client perjury issue in the 1986 case of *Nix v. Whiteside*,[61] and was unanimous in answering one important question. Neither a defendant's Sixth Amendment right to counsel nor his right to testify and present a defense is violated if counsel refuses to cooperate when she thinks her client will testify falsely. Under *Nix*, a defendant has no constitutional complaint if his lawyer threatens to reveal his perjury to the court, or to impeach his perjured testimony, even if this leads him to refuse to testify or to tell a less persuasive story than he otherwise might have told.

Although the *Nix* Court does not specifically address the issue, one can conclude from *Nix* that to the extent the attorney-client privilege in criminal cases is rooted in the Sixth Amendment's right to counsel, a defendant's constitutional interest in the confidentiality of her communications does not trump the lawyer's obligation to present truthful evidence. But the fact that a defendant has no constitutional claim if his counsel prevents him from committing perjury does not necessarily answer the lawyer's ethical question of how to act when it is only a client's confidences that allow her to conclude that her client proposes to lie, nor does it mean that she must prevent or reveal the lie. Five of the Justices who heard *Nix* clearly approved of the kinds of actions the defense attorney in that case took. Moreover, although it is not the Supreme Court's business to make ethical rules for the states, the same five Justices believed that a lawyer should not cooperate in the presentation of perjured evidence. Perhaps it is no coincidence that then Chief Justice Burger assigned the *Nix* opinion to himself. When Monroe Freedman's article suggesting that a lawyer might be obliged to present perjured testimony first appeared, Justice Burger, then a D.C. Circuit Court judge, reportedly wished to explore the possibility of disbarring Professor Freedman for publishing an article advocating unethical behavior.

The ethical dilemma we have discussed exists because the attorney-client privilege allows an attorney to elicit information from a client by assuring the client that he will not be hurt by what he says no matter how embarrassing or incriminating his disclosures. Yet the lawyer's obligation to the court may mean that the client's trust is betrayed, and that the client faces a worse outcome than he would have faced had he not trusted his lawyer and told her the truth.

Situations of potential perjury or the destruction of evidence are probably the most common situations in which lawyers must decide

---

[60] See ABA Model Rule of Professional Conduct 3.3(b).

[61] 475 U.S. 157 (1986).

whether the rules of professional conduct, or their own ethical standards, require them to reveal or threaten to reveal a client's confidences, but they do not pose the most difficult dilemmas of this sort that a lawyer can face. When perjury is the threat, an accepted solution exists, which often works—namely, to dissuade the client from the illegal course of action. This gives the client everything she is entitled to (i.e., an honest defense) and does not deceive the court.

In other situations the clash between professional duty and common morality is more fundamental. Suppose, for example, the confidential disclosures of a client whom the lawyer is defending on a murder charge indicate that he is a serial killer who is likely to kill again if he is acquitted. Should this information affect how the client is defended? Suppose an acquittal is secured; is that the end of the matter? If all the client revealed was a litany of his past murders, and he never indicated an intent to kill in the future, the attorney-client privilege should protect those confidences as long as the other requisites of the privilege are met. Ethical codes similarly obligate the attorney to maintain the client's confidences. But is silence a satisfactory solution? Attorneys are people as well as lawyers; surely a person who knows someone is a serial killer should turn him in. But what should the ethical person who is an attorney do?

If the dilemma posed above is not sharp enough, suppose the lawyer reads of a new killing and because of what she has learned in confidence recognizes that the crime bears her client's signature. What then should she do? Suppose the client is not a serial killer, but a serial rapist, or a serial "date rapist," or a professional burglar, or a drug wholesaler, or a con man who preys on the elderly, or an alcoholic who persists in driving drunk after her license has been revoked? Do the answers differ? Here we take refuge in being professors. We can pose the questions, but it is for you to answer them.

G. CLOSING REMARKS

In our discussion of the attorney-client privilege, we have not mentioned every situation in which the applicability of the privilege is problematic. There are a number of areas in which the principles that underlie the privilege do not provide clear guidance, and the courts are understandably split. For example, are discussions between an insured party and a lawyer working for an insurance company protected in a "direct action" state?[62] Do lawyers have peculiar duties to disclose information they learn in connection with mergers or the sale of stock?[63]

---

[62] See Gottlieb v. Bresler, 24 F.R.D. 371 (D.D.C. 1959) (rejecting the majority common law position and concluding that statement of insured to insurer is not privileged).

[63] See SEC v. National Student Mktg. Corp., 360 F. Supp. 284 (D.D.C. 1973) (raising the question of whether a lawyer has an obligation to disclose corporate violation of securities laws to the SEC).

When you are working in areas like these, where the implications of the general principles behind the privilege are unclear, you will want to learn how courts have dealt with similar situations. You will find that different courts reach different conclusions. You will also learn that when you face hard ethical decisions, you should not try to resolve them on your own, but should discuss them with ethical attorneys whom you trust and should strongly consider asking for assistance from the ethics experts of the bar of your jurisdiction. In some circumstances, these conversations will be privileged.

As we see it, four arguments strongly support the attorney-client privilege. Three of these, however, carry more force when clients are people than when they are businesses or other organized entities.

First, the attorney-client privilege may not suppress much information. The privilege does not prevent disclosure of what a person knows; it only protects actual communications with counsel. In most civil cases, discovery devices may be used to probe the knowledge of all witnesses, including the opposing party. It is true that in criminal cases the government may be barred from questioning the accused, but this is because of the privilege against self-incrimination, not the attorney-client privilege. If the Fifth Amendment results in inequities in the criminal process, this should be corrected at the constitutional level and not by interfering with the attorney-client relationship. Even in criminal cases, the privilege may not deny courts much evidence. If clients knew that whatever they told their attorneys might be revealed at trial, attorneys would not learn as much about their clients' activities as they do now. This is why the Sixth Amendment's "right to counsel" may mandate the privilege in criminal cases; without it, legal representation may be ineffective.

Second, the privilege is necessary for effective representation because it facilitates the kind of interview that ensures that nothing is overlooked. The effective interviewer endeavors to learn everything she thinks the client knows. The lawyer must insist that the client reveal incriminating or embarrassing information. People are understandably reluctant to reveal information that casts them in a bad light. The privilege helps the attorney convince the client to "come clean." Also clients might not speculate about facts of which they were unsure if their statements could be discovered by their opponents. Thus, the privilege can encourage clients to give their attorneys leads that might be crucial to a successful case, or, indeed, to the conclusion that there is no case worth litigating.

Third, without the privilege attorneys might routinely be called to testify at trials against the interests of their clients. Not only might this hamper the attorney's rapport with her client, but it could interfere with the attorney's ability to represent the client effectively before a jury. Even if an attorney's testimony revealed nothing that hurt her client's case, impeachment might have a devastating effect on the jury's view of an attorney's competence or character. Moreover, while a party's attorney was testifying, a second attorney would be needed to spot objectionable questions and to cross-examine and rehabilitate the attorney who testified. The attorney-client privilege protects against these possibilities.

Finally, there are less instrumental values. The lawyer-client relationship should be one of loyalty and can be one of intimate trust. One can argue that it is simply wrong to compel attorneys to reveal confidences that were gained only because of the rapport they were able to establish in the counseling relationship. Expecting attorneys to routinely reveal their clients' confidences is inconsistent with a system in which attorneys are defined as their client's zealous advocates. If there were no privilege, some attorneys, rather than risk a situation in which they might be forced to betray a confidence, would, no doubt, avoid certain information, even if this made them less able to negotiate fair settlements or pleas or to render the best possible assistance at trial. Some attorneys in whom clients reposed incriminating confidences might even choose to perjure themselves or go to jail for their silence.

Would we admire or condemn an attorney who preferred jail to revealing her client's confidences? If there are circumstances in which we would admire her, it suggests that the privilege is rooted in deeply held values. Furthermore, in a society in which government is too often intrusive and in which data on the web follows one throughout life, it is good to have zones of privacy—perhaps especially in the age of Facebook and other social networking sites. Should the relationship with an attorney be such a zone? Privacy values alone might not justify a privilege for this relationship. Indeed, personal privacy is probably threatened more by the compelled testimony of best friends than it is by that of lawyers. But, when privacy values are coupled with the other factors that support the privilege, they weigh heavily in the balance.

If the client is a corporate entity, the third point we make above appears to have the same force as it does with respect to natural persons. The identification of lawyer with client remains real, and the same potential for abuse would exist if communications to counsel were not privileged. It is not clear, however, that one should expect this potential to be realized. In the past, much of what was learned by counsel from low-level corporate employees enjoyed only work product protection. This protection seems to have been sufficient to prevent serious abuse.

The argument that the privilege encourages clients to be honest in communicating with counsel is weaker when corporations, particularly large ones, are clients.[64] Corporate employees, unlike individual parties,

---

[64] In an interview study done in Manhattan, Professor Vincent Alexander found that 62% of in-house counsel, 88.5% of outside counsel and 75% of the business executives interviewed felt that the privilege encouraged candor among those corporate representatives who knew about it.

are often not deeply involved in the matters they discuss with the corporation's attorneys and fear no personal harm however the corporation fares in the legal process. The situation is similar with respect to less instrumental values. The corporate setting typically depersonalizes the attorney-client relationship. Communications to counsel are often part of a job or, indeed, explicitly ordered. Furthermore, loyalty to business organizations is not regarded in the same way as loyalty to human beings. In closely held corporations, however, corporate-individual differences may disappear, and even when representing the largest corporations, corporate counsel can develop relationships of deep trust with the corporate representatives with whom they most frequently deal. These relationships, because of continued representation, may become more intimate or friendly than the relationships most attorneys have with "one shot" clients.

Finally, invocation of the privilege in the corporate setting has a greater potential for concealing information than does its invocation when individuals are clients. Determining who in a corporation has relevant information or deposing large numbers of individuals may be costly. The office of corporate counsel may be an efficient clearinghouse for corporate information. Moreover, employees performing routine functions may forget the details of events that they have described to the corporate attorney. Corporate counsel's records may be the only source of this information. Although opening up the attorney's files might deter the collection of some information, a business's needs for an attorney to have information is likely to outweigh the possible costs of potential disclosure, particularly since the work-product rule would still ensure a considerable degree of privacy. Moreover, organizations can structure their arrangements so that reports that do not have to go to counsel are sent there specifically to take advantage of the privilege. Even if this tactic does not work in court, it can impose substantial litigation costs on opponents who seek the information.

These figures are likely to be high estimates of the value of the attorney-client privilege in encouraging candor since the respondents, especially the lawyers, are likely to have wanted study results that would show the need for the privilege. While 89% of lawyers believed more than half of upper management knew of the privilege, only 46% believed more than half the middle managers did and less than 10% believed that more than half the employees below middle management did. The study contains several other findings that call into question *Upjohn's* extension of the privilege to the communications of those outside the control group, and particularly to employees below the level of middle management. Only one-third of the attorneys said that before *Upjohn* they had taken account of the control group test in their practice. While some lawyers said they had limited their communications to members of the control group before *Upjohn*, it is unclear how many of them needed to talk to lower ranking employees, and more lawyers had spoken before *Upjohn* to members not in the control group than had confined their communications to control group members. Indeed, fewer than 10% of the attorneys indicated that *Upjohn* had affected the frequency of their lower-level communications. See Vincent Alexander, The Corporate Attorney-Client Privilege: A Study of Participants, 63 St. John's L. Rev. 191 (1989).

We believe that, except in one circumstance, only a qualified privilege is desirable in the corporate setting.[65] The privilege should give way upon a substantial showing of need in much the same way as "work-product" protection. The full privilege should be reserved for situations in which the confidential communications are elicited under circumstances, including potential liability or severe personal embarrassment, similar to those facing natural persons. In these situations the privilege may be necessary to secure disclosures. The Supreme Court, as you have seen, was not attracted by the idea of a limited privilege in *Upjohn*. So do not mistake our policy preference for the law.

ADDITIONAL PROBLEMS

Problem VIII-8. The Grundy Commission, examining vice in New York City, notes that one lawyer, Maury Bricks, handles more than one-fourth of the cases in which streetwalkers are arrested for soliciting. They subpoena Bricks and ask him the following questions: "Have you been personally employed by each of the alleged prostitutes you have represented in New York City courts during the last year? Who pays your fees when you represent streetwalkers charged with soliciting? Are you paid a retainer by Nicole Lucier, known generally as "Madame Nicole"? During the past year how much money have you received from Madame Nicole?" Bricks (respectfully) declines to answer each of the above questions claiming that to do so would violate the attorney-client privilege. The Commission, according to the powers delegated to it, finds Bricks in contempt and orders him imprisoned until he responds to their questions or for sixty days, whichever comes first. Bricks appeals the order, again citing the attorney-client privilege. **How should the appellate court rule? Why?**

Assume that the appellate court rules against Bricks. Bricks answers the first question, but does not know whether he should respond to the other three. He is, in fact, paid a retainer by Lucier, and this retainer amounted to $180,000 during the previous year. However, he accepted the retainer only after he assured Lucier that he would keep both the fact and the amount of the retainer in the strictest confidence, and after he told her, in good faith, that if he were ever asked about his relationship with her, the attorney-client privilege would enable him to protect her identity. It is clear that Lucier would not have retained

---

[65] Almost 64% of the lawyers Professor Alexander interviewed said that a qualified corporate privilege that would give way when corporate attorney-client communications contained information that the opponent could not get with reasonable effort from non-privileged sources, would have no effect on the frequency with which corporate clients sought their legal advice. Nearly three-quarters said that a qualified privilege would not lead them to communicate less with lower-level employees. About 55% of the attorneys interviewed thought upper management would be less candid if the privilege were qualified, and 53% thought middle management would be; but only about 40% of management thought management would be less candid. Almost two-thirds of the attorneys felt that a qualified privilege would have no effect on the candor of employees below middle management. See id. 364–372.

Bricks but for these assurances. **How should Bricks respond to the questions pertaining to Madame Nicole? Should he choose jail?**

Problem VIII-9. Andy, Brian and Chris allege that they were unlawfully arrested, beaten, and denied adequate medical care by police officers in the city of Corrupt. Following the incident, the police charged all three with assault and resisting arrest. Andy and his father immediately consulted a local law firm with which Andy's father had business connections. The two spoke with Joe, a young associate at the firm, who accepted a $1,000 retainer from Andy's father and filed an appearance on his behalf in the criminal charges stemming from the incident. Several days later Joe informed Andy that he must withdraw from the case because his firm represents the city police department's insurer, a conflict of interest.

In a later civil rights suit brought by Brian and Chris against the Corrupt Police Department, the plaintiffs seek to have the city's law firm removed as counsel. Brian and Chris's lawyers argue that because they plan to call Andy as a witness and because the city's law firm previously represented Andy, Andy's attorney-client privilege rights mean that the firm has confidential information about Andy's version of the events that will make its representation of the police department either unfair to them if it is used in cross-examination or unfair to the department if the firm bends over backwards to avoid cross-examining on matters with respect to which it possesses confidential information. **How should the court rule on the motion to disqualify the city's law firm?**

Problem VIII-10. Jean Perry is a CPA and an attorney. She is hired by Hilda Grant, a wealthy jockey, to prepare her tax return so as to minimize her tax liability. **If the State Racing Commission should call Perry to testify to the sources of Grant's earnings, will Grant be able to claim a privilege to prevent Perry from testifying to what she had learned while preparing Grant's taxes? If Perry gave tax advice but Grant filed her own return, does this make any difference? Assume Perry was a CPA but not a lawyer; would Grant be able to prevent Perry's testimony if Perry had given the same advice that a competent tax lawyer would have given?**

Problem VIII-11. Assume that Grant had been in an auto accident shortly after seeing her attorney, Perry, about her taxes. **If the other party to the accident sues Grant on the theory that she was drunk at the time, could they call Perry to the stand and ask her whether she had smelled whiskey on her client's breath? Could they ask Perry whether Grant's discussion of her tax matters had revealed the kind of inattention and confusion which might be associated with intoxication? Could they ask Perry if she had served Grant any alcoholic beverages? Do your answers to any of**

the above questions depend on whether Perry is representing Grant in the tort action?

Problem VIII-12. Sam Tucker, a prominent attorney, will not take a case unless his potential clients' stories have been confirmed by a lie detector examination. Assume that in accordance with this policy Tucker sends Jimmy Jacobs, an accused forger, for a polygraph examination. **If the government seeks to question the polygraph examiner at trial, may Jacobs claim the attorney-client privilege to prevent the examiner from describing the examination? Could the privilege be claimed if the examiner was asked only two questions: "Did you administer a polygraph examination to Mr. Jacobs," and "Did you conclude Mr. Jacobs was lying"? Do your answers to these questions depend on whether Tucker had accepted Jacobs as a client? If Jacobs had not been indicted at the time of the examination but had approached Tucker fearing indictment, could he claim the attorney-client privilege to prevent the examiner from describing the examination to a grand jury? If Jacobs knew of Tucker's policy and sought out the examiner before consulting Tucker, would this make a difference?**

Problem VIII-13. Assume that in the previous question Tucker had told the examiner when he sent Jacobs for the examination, "I want you to be particularly careful with this examination. I am convinced Jacobs is telling the truth, and I intend to create a new law in this case by establishing a precedent that defendants have the right to introduce polygraph evidence which exonerates them." **Should this affect the court's ruling on whether the polygraph examiner may be called by the government and questioned about the test he administered to Jacobs?**

Problem VIII-14. Alan Kaufman, a professional basketball star, has hired Daniel Novack, an attorney, as his agent. Novack doesn't understand the tax implications of certain endorsement proposals so he refers Kaufman to a leading tax practitioner. Kaufman gives Novack a detailed account of his conversations with the tax specialist. After considering the tax consequences, the quality of the products Kaufman would be associated with, Kaufman's image, and the likelihood of future endorsement contracts, Novack advises Kaufman to sign with the Winkel Corporation. Later the IRS charges Kaufman with income tax evasion. They seek to put either the tax specialist or Novack on the stand in order to learn what Kaufman told the specialist about his tax situation. **May Kaufman claim the attorney-client privilege with respect to the testimony of either or both of them?**

Problem VIII-15. Lenny Loss and his secretary Sarah Gilson consulted a lawyer, Andrea Seligman, about their possible liability in a security fraud scheme involving the stock of Macrosoft Corporation. Lenny told Andrea that he would pay both his and Sarah's fees. At their first meeting on July 14, 2013, Lenny and Sarah described for Seligman behavior that might implicate each of them in the security fraud conspiracy. At their second meeting on July 26, 2013, Seligman told them she has considered their situation carefully and thinks their interests conceivably diverge, so she can only agree to continue to represent Lenny, her long-time client. Nevertheless the conversation continues about matters of mutual interest, though from time to time Seligman interrupts what one or the other says and cautions them that it relates to a matter on which their interests might diverge.

Later Seligman is called before a grand jury investigating securities fraud in high tech industries. She is asked the following questions:

1. Is Lenny Loss a client of yours?

2. Did Lenny Loss call you for an appointment the day the Macrosoft securities fraud investigation was reported to the press?

3. Did Lenny Loss ask you to represent someone other than himself?

4. Did Lenny agree to pay both his own fees and the other person's?

5. Who was the person whom Lenny brought with him?

Andrea refuses to answer each of these questions, citing the attorney-client privilege. The prosecutor asks the judge in charge of the grand jury to order Andrea to answer each of these questions and to hold her in contempt if she doesn't. **What should the judge do?**

Problem VIII-16. On the same facts as in the preceding question, Seligman is recalled before the grand jury three weeks later. She seeks to quash the subpoena arguing that she has no non-privileged information and that being continually summoned before the grand jury interferes with her relationship with her client. **How should the court rule?**

Assume the court orders Seligman to appear before the grand jury. She is then asked:

1. On July 14, 2013, did Lenny Loss and Sarah Gilson consult you jointly on a matter related to the Macrosoft stock fraud investigation?

2. What did they tell you about their possible involvement in that matter when they met with you that day?

3. Did you tell them at a meeting on July 26 that their interests might diverge and that you could not continue to represent both of them but would have to confine your representation to Lenny Loss?

4. Why did you think their interests might diverge?

5. Considering only what was said after you told them you could not represent them both, what did each tell you about their dealings in Macrosoft stock?

Seligman respectfully declines to answer these questions, citing the attorney-client privilege. **Which, if any, of these questions should the court compel her to answer?**

Problem VIII-17.

A.   Suppose that before Seligman's first grand jury appearance Gilson had been called before the grand jury and waived her attorney-client privilege with respect to all matters relating to her conversations with Seligman. **Would this affect your answers to the two preceding problems?**

B.   Suppose Gilson had brought a civil suit against Loss for involving her, without her realizing it, in fraudulent activity. In her suit, she called Seligman, and her attorney asked Seligman each of the questions the prosecutor had asked her before the grand jury. **Which, if any, can Seligman refuse to answer based on the attorney-client privilege? Could Loss be required to provide any information that his attorney could avoid providing?**

Problem VIII-18. In a securities fraud suit brought against the Metzger Insurance Company, its lenders and investors sought transcripts of interviews conducted by the company's law firm, Salvatore and Kelly, of two Metzger employees. During the interviews, conducted in connection with pending litigation, attorneys from Salvatore and Kelly assured the Metzger employees that their statements would remain confidential. As a result, the two employees revealed information helpful to the firm's case preparation, and then shortly after their interviews both employees resigned their positions. When the plaintiff sought to depose the same two employees, both refused to answer questions, invoking their fifth amendment privilege against self-incrimination. Claiming they could not get the information any other way, the plaintiff urged the court to overrule Metzger's claims of attorney-client privilege and work-product protection and order the defendant's lawyers to turn over to the plaintiff their copies of the Metzger employee interviews. **How should the court rule?**

Problem VIII-19. One day the president of the Allspice Music Company asks Ginger Posh, the general counsel, to come to her office. She outlines for Posh a major new sales campaign that the company is considering. The only difficulty with the campaign is that some of the material the company hopes to sell may infringe certain copyrights held by other companies and individuals. She describes the copyright situation in some detail and presents Posh with a memorandum of law prepared for the company by an outside copyright attorney, who has concluded that there is a substantial risk that some infringement suits against the company will be successful. She wants Posh's advice as to whether the profits from the campaign are likely to offset any costs associated with possible suits for copyright infringement and the bad publicity that may stem from being sued. **If Allspice is later sued for copyright infringement, will the president's statements to Posh concerning the copyright situation be protected by the attorney-client privilege? Will the memorandum prepared by the outside copyright attorney be protected?** Assume that Posh also is concerned about the company's potential liability for copyright infringement, but is uncertain about whether the conclusions of outside counsel are correct. Posh supplies company employees, who are veterans of the music business, with copies of both the songs the company plans to promote and previously copyrighted works that sound similar. She asks them for their opinions as to whether the company's music is essentially the same as or different from the copyrighted works. Each employee is told that his answers will be confidential and that the information is sought to enable the company to obtain legal advice. **If Allspice is sued for copyright infringement, will the employees' responses be privileged? Does it matter whether the company president knew of Posh's actions and approved them? Does it matter whether she ordered the employees to respond to Posh? If Posh provided similar material to independent music experts and asked them to provide their opinions about the similarity of Allspice's music and previously copyrighted material, would their responses be privileged?**

Problem VIII-20. The town of Cookville is being sued for injuries sustained by an elderly man who slipped on an icy city sidewalk and fell, breaking his hip. The plaintiff asks for actual and punitive damages. The mayor of Cookville tells the attorney who has been hired to defend the case that the town had not removed the snow from city sidewalks because a particularly hard winter had left it with no money in its snow removal account. The mayor admitted that $25,000 in a contingency fund, which might have paid for snow removal, had been spent instead on a trip to Florida for the mayor and council members so that they could attend a conference on the cash flow problems in small towns. **If the attorney is asked what reason, if any, the mayor gave for not covering snow removal expenses from the contingency fund, may she claim the attorney-client privilege on the town's behalf and refuse to answer? Does it matter if the attorney is hired not by the town but by the insurance company that writes the town's liability policy and has the contractual burden of defending any tort actions brought against the town? If she is sued personally for dereliction of duty, could the mayor claim the privilege for what she told the town's attorney?**

Problem VIII-21. During the 1960s, Smokes Corp. was under continuing public criticism by people claiming that its cigarettes caused lung cancer. To rebut these contentions, Smokes secretly commissioned a study by Chemicals Inc., a private research firm, to determine the carcinogenic effects of cigarette smoking. Smokes asked Chemicals Inc. to keep the results of the study confidential in case the results were not what the company hoped. If the results showed that smoking was not a health hazard, Smokes would, of course, have publicized the information and reassured smokers as to the safety of its product.

After the study was completed, Smokes convened a meeting of its top executives and two in-house lawyers to review the study's results. The study showed a strong correlation between smoking and lung cancer. In fact, it indicated that individuals increased their risk of contracting lung cancer by 35% if they smoked one pack a day over a three-year period.

Alarmed at these results, Smokes' executives agreed to bury the study's findings and to deny that such a study had ever been commissioned by the company, should the matter ever arise. They further decided that the company should maintain its official position that smoking has no significant health risks for otherwise healthy adults.

Maria Armijo and Danica Ray, Smokes' in-house attorneys, met privately after the meeting to discuss what had happened. "Don't you think the company is defrauding the public?" asked Danica. "Aren't they misleading it into believing that its cigarettes are not dangerous when, in fact, the study showed they are?" "Well, even if the company is misleading or lying to the public, we are in no position to reveal what we heard," replied Maria. "That meeting was confidential. The attorney-client privilege forbids us from speaking." "But if we don't say anything, people are gonna die," exclaimed Danica. "It's unethical for us not to violate the privilege—I mean peoples' lives are at stake!" **Who is right, Danica or Maria? Does the attorney-client privilege prevent Danica and Maria from speaking out? Does anything else prevent them? If Smokes is later sued, can the plaintiff call the two lawyers to prove that Smokes knew cigarette smoking was dangerous and concealed the information it had?**

Problem VIII-22. Henry Gray is suspected in the stabbing death of John Warren. His attorney, before Gray's indictment, learns of a knife that closely resembles the description of the switchblade knife that was used in the killing. **Does the attorney have an affirmative duty before trial to give the prosecutor the knife or tell the prosecutor how to find it in any of the following circumstances?**

    A.   Gray brings a knife to his attorney and asks him to hold the knife until after the trial.

    B.   The same as in *A*, except that after the attorney has examined the knife Gray asks for it back, and the attorney gives it to him. Later the police search Gray's house, but no knife turns up.

    C.   During an interview with his lawyer, Gray mentions that a knife is hidden in his neighbor's yard. The attorney goes to the yard, examines the knife, and leaves it there.

D.   The same as in C, but the attorney takes the knife back to his office.

E.   Gray, claiming to be innocent, gives his attorney permission to search his house.   Although Gray has said he does not own a switchblade knife, the attorney finds one.

F.   Gray tells his attorney that he has a switchblade knife that he has given to his best friend, Jeremiah Johnson.

Under which of these circumstances could the attorney be compelled to testify about the knife—e.g., its appearance or where it was when he saw it?

Problem VIII-23.   Charles Oakes approaches Joan Bennet, an attorney, for legal advice.   He tells Bennet that the police have been questioning him about a murder, and he wants Bennet to represent him.   Bennet agrees.   At first Oakes denies any involvement in the murder, but upon further questioning by Bennet, and with the assurance that the attorney-client privilege will protect the confidence of any communication, Oakes admits to the murder of a seventeen-year-old girl.   He tells Bennet that he hid the body in a cave near a lake in a state forest.   **Does Bennet have any responsibility to disclose this information to anyone? Would she be acting ethically if she did disclose this information?** The next weekend Bennet goes camping in the state forest with the goal of checking her client's story.   She finds the body in the place described. **Was Bennet acting wisely when she went in search of the body? Does Bennet's personal observation change her responsibilities regarding disclosure?   If the body had fallen from a ledge on which the client said he had placed it and now was visible from the entrance of the cave, would it be okay for Bennet to place the body back on the ledge?   Would she be acting properly if she left the body where it was but later told Oakes it had fallen?   What should Bennet say if she simply told Oakes she had visited the cave, and Oakes asked her if the body had fallen?**   Two months after agreeing to represent Oakes, Bennet receives a letter from the deceased's parents in which they describe their grief at not knowing whether their daughter is dead or alive and at the prospect that their daughter may be dead and unburied.   They ask Bennet if she can shed any light on these matters.   She responds that she knows nothing about these matters.   **Is Bennet's response proper?   If a grand jury calls Bennet to testify and asks if she knows where the body is, must Bennet answer?   Must Bennet refuse to answer?**

Problem VIII-24.   You are an attorney in a large city.   A man, whom you recognize as Clyde Bonnie, comes into your office and says that he expects to be picked up soon for armed robbery of a supermarket.   He wants you to defend him.   You tell him you will accept his case if he can pay your fee.   At that he lays down a shoe box in front of you and says that it contains a Colt revolver registered in his name which he doesn't want anyone to find. He then turns to leave, but you stop him because you still haven't discussed your fee. After he hears how much you expect to be paid, he asks you to "loan" him back his "box" because he has to "visit" another supermarket. You persuade him to leave the box in your custody, and he leaves, stating that he will raise the money somehow because he wants you as his "mouthpiece." Two days later, shortly after Bonnie has paid you your retainer, you read in the paper that the Foxy Loxy Supermarket has been robbed by a man armed with a knife. The general description of the robber resembles that of your client. The story also states that the same supermarket had been robbed a week before by a man armed with a Colt revolver. Two weeks pass and your client still has not been picked up for armed robbery.

Are you under any ethical duty to disclose all or part of the interchange that occurred between you and Bonnie on his first visit to your office? What should you do with the gun that is in the box? If your client is arrested and the prosecution calls you to the stand, is your client privileged to prevent you from revealing all or part of what he told you on his first visit to your office? Can you be forced, over your client's objection, to disclose that you have a Colt gun? To say that Bonnie gave it to you? To turn the gun over to the state?

Problem VIII-25. In a securities fraud suit, Burnham Corp. turns over to the Ruder law firm, as requested in discovery, all documents relating to the sale of one of Burnham's products to purchasers other than Ruder's client. Burnham's lawyers, however, have blacked out all references to their other purported clients and client representatives contained in the requested materials. Ruder objects to the omission of this information, but Burnham's firm claims the attorney-client privilege requires this. **How should the court rule?**

Problem VIII-26. Assume that in problem VIII-4 Doris Provine was sued along with the Winkel Corporation and that in the jurisdiction in question both Provine and the Winkel Corporation could claim the attorney-client privilege with respect to Provine's statements to the corporate attorney. **If Provine tells her husband what she told the corporate attorney, would this affect the availability of the privilege to her? The availability of the privilege to Winkel? If Provine tells her best friend what she told the corporate attorney, would this affect the availability of the privilege to her? The availability of the privilege to the corporation?**

Problem VIII-27. Dan Nostrum, newspaper columnist and author of the best selling book, *Washington's Seamy Side*, is sued for libel by Sam Senator, a powerful politician, whose private life was explored in some detail in Nostrum's book. At the behest of Joanne Betlem, his attorney,

Nostrum describes in detail how he researched the portion of the book pertaining to Senator. Although Nostrum is proud of his research methods, it is clear to Betlem that these methods were so slipshod that Nostrum might be fairly regarded as having acted in reckless disregard of the truth. Before Nostrum leaves, Betlem cautions Nostrum not to discuss their conversations with anyone. Nostrum replies, "But, I'm proud of my methods. Sam abused me in public. I have to defend my reputation by calling a press conference to defend myself." Betlem, after almost losing her client by bluntly describing the deficiencies in his research, convinces Nostrum not to hold the press conference and to keep the discussion between them confidential. **If Nostrum is later asked what he told Betlem about his research methods, may he refuse to respond on the basis of the attorney-client privilege? Do you think your answer would hold in practice as well as in theory? Why or why not? If Nostrum is asked in a deposition to describe his research methods, may he refuse to do so on the ground of attorney-client privilege? May Betlem refuse to respond if she is asked whether she advised Nostrum not to call a press conference? May Betlem refuse to respond if she is asked what she thought of Nostrum's research methods?**

Problem VIII-28. The FBI has a mail cover on Kent Kingston, a notorious gangster. The cover is authorized by a warrant. One item that is opened and copied is a letter by Kingston to his attorney, listing the income he has received from certain illegal ventures. Kingston wants to pay the taxes due but does not want the source of income to be revealed. He asks if this is legally possible and, if so, how this may be done. **May the letters be introduced by the prosecution if Kingston is tried for the illegal activities giving rise to this income? Would the situation be any different if the letters were to Kingston's accountant rather than to his attorney?**

Problem VIII-29. Carla Castenada, a Cuban who speaks no English, consults an attorney about a land dispute she is having with a neighbor. She brings along one Mary Sanchez, to act as a translator. During the conference with the attorney Carla discloses certain facts which under-cut her claim to title in the disputed land. Later, in one of those coincidences which happen in problems as well as real life, Mary marries Castenada's neighbor. The neighbor dies, of course, and Mary, the sole beneficiary of his will, brings suit against Castenada to quiet title in the disputed land. **May Mary testify at the trial concerning the conversation she translated between Castenada and her attorney?**

Problem VIII-30. Arnold and Baker are both concerned because their children have become devoted followers of the Reverend Luna's Galactic Church. They consult a lawyer together to learn about their legal options. Arnold describes an elaborate kidnapping and reprogramming plan to the attorney and asks if it would be legal. The attorney tells Arnold that it would not be and advises him not to implement it. They leave. Later Baker's son is accidentally killed during a kidnapping attempt that closely follows the plan Arnold described. **If Baker sues Arnold for the wrongful death of his son, will the attorney-client privilege prevent him from testifying to the plan Arnold disclosed in the lawyer's office? If the state prosecutes Arnold for kidnapping, will the attorney-client privilege prevent Baker from testifying as a witness for the state?**

Problem VIII-31. Thomas Dooley asked David Guard, an attorney, to represent him in a divorce action. During a series of interviews Dooley related to Guard the intimate details of his married life, including the fact that he had engaged in several adulterous affairs during the preceding five years. Dooley also acquainted Guard with the details of his financial condition, including the facts that: (a) he is the recipient of a trust fund paying $15,000 a year, (b) he owns a variety of stocks with a book value of $190,000 and a current market value of $310,000, (c) his earned income has increased during the preceding five years from $42,000 to $60,000 and he expects it to continue increasing at the rate of about $4,000 a year during the foreseeable future, and (d) he has earned an additional sum ranging from $10,000 to $25,000 during each of the preceding three years from the illegal sale of amphetamines. He is considering giving up this "business" because of the risk involved. After the divorce was completed, Dooley paid Guard $5000 for general services but refused to pay an extra $5000 which Guard claimed was due him for special tax advice. Dooley claimed that the tax advice he received from Guard was not worth more than $500. Guard sues for his fee. **If Guard takes the stand on his own behalf, may Dooley claim the attorney-client privilege to prevent Guard from testifying to the conversations relating to (a) his adulterous affairs, (b) his involvement in the illegal sale of amphetamines, and (c) the other details of his financial situation?**

When the divorce action mentioned above was tried, Dooley, after testifying on direct examination to his financial status, was asked by his wife's attorney, "Isn't it true that your trust paid $30,000 a year until the past month when, at your encouragement, the trustees shifted the corpus into more speculative stock?" **If Dooley answered, "No, why three months ago I told Mr. Guard the expected earnings were only $15,000 a year," would he be able to claim a privilege if his wife's attorney then asked him what else he told Mr. Guard about his finances?**

Problem VIII-32. Paul Peters sues the Foxy-Loxy Supermarket for injuries allegedly suffered when Peters passed through an electronically operated entrance door to the Foxy-Loxy. The complaint alleges that as Peters approached the entrance the door automatically opened, but that before Peters passed completely through the door closed suddenly and with great force, striking Peters in the face, breaking his eyeglasses, and causing blindness in his right eye. Foxy-Loxy calls Sarah Andrews, an attorney, who will testify that the day after the alleged accident, Peters consulted her and asked her to sue the defendant, but that she refused because Peters insisted on claiming that his right eye had been blinded by the accident, although he admitted that he had in fact lost the sight in that eye a year earlier in an industrial accident. Plaintiff objects to the testimony on the ground of privilege. **What is the proper ruling?**

Problem VIII-33. Reuben Mize was arrested for running an illegal gambling business, and a file cabinet of his records, including coded listings of his customer base and his runners' names, was taken from his office. Later the charges were dropped when the state could not decipher most of the records and could not prove that others were current, but the police refused to return the records to Reuben. Reuben went to José Gonzalez, an attorney, and asked José to help him get the records back. When José asked him why he wanted the records back so badly, Reuben replied, "That's my current customer base. They are how I make my living." José was able to secure the return of Reuben's records. Six months later, Reuben is again arrested. At trial the state seeks to ask José what Reuben told him when he hired him to secure his records. Reuben claims the attorney-client privilege to keep José from testifying. The state asks the judge to ascertain in chambers what Reuben had said and to decide whether Reuben's disclosures were protected by the privilege. **Does the judge need to do this to admit the evidence? Should the judge do this? Is what Reuben said protected by the privilege? Does it matter whether José knew that the business Reuben referred to was his gambling business rather than the dry cleaning business, which was the cover for his gambling operation?**

Problem VIII-34. Herb Edsel, General Counsel of the Winkel Corporation, writes a letter to outside environmental counsel, the firm of Wang and Lee, noting that the cost of equipment to eliminate all chromium from the company's waste water is some $9,000,000 dollars more than the cost of equipment that will eliminate 85% of the chromium from the company's waste water. He asks what Winkel's obligation is under the Clean Water Act and what the penalty is for the relatively small chromium discharges that will occur if Winkel uses the cheaper equipment. Judy Wang writes back that Winkel is required to remove all chromium to the extent feasible; that in her opinion, for a multi-billion dollar firm like Winkel, the need to spend an extra $9,000,000 to remove 100% of the chromium in its water does not make 100% removal infeasible, and that the fine for failing to remove all the chromium is up to $1000 a day if the failure is inadvertent and up to $50,000 a day if it is intentional.

Edsel writes back saying that the makers of the cheaper chromium recovery device claim it removes 100% of chromium from waste water, and it is only by experience that Winkel knows it does not. He asks Wang whether, if Winkel uses the cheaper machinery, its failure to eliminate all chromium is likely to be considered inadvertent. Wang responds that although it does not change Winkel's obligation to install the more expensive machinery, in all the cases she knows about where scrubber or recovery technology did not perform as well as advertised, failure to achieve advertised levels of pollution reduction were regarded as inadvertent, unless it was shown that the company knew that the technology it used did not perform as advertised and that better technology was available.

Edsel then writes back and asks how the EPA goes about showing actual knowledge. Wang replies that when knowledge has been shown, it has always been based on material in the company's own records.

Following this exchange of correspondence, Winkel installed the lower priced recovery equipment, and all information comparing the two types of equipment was purged from its files. About a year later, the EPA cited Winkel for willful discharge of chromium and sought a fine of $50,000 a day going back to the date when the zero discharge requirement was implemented, which was the day Winkel's recovery equipment became operational. Winkel argues that its fine should be no more than $1,000 a day because it had reason to believe that the equipment it installed would remove all chromium. The EPA seeks to acquire by subpoena "all correspondence between Winkel and outside counsel relating to Winkel's response to the new zero chromium discharge equipment." Winkel claims the correspondence is protected by the attorney-client privilege. **How should the court rule? Should the court examine the correspondence in chambers before making its ruling. If the EPA submits copies of the correspondence, which an anonymous, disillusioned lawyer at Wang and Lee had turned over to it, claiming the correspondence showed Winkel's fraudulent purposes, should the judge look at the correspondence before making his ruling? Is Judy Wang acting ethically if she asserts the claim of privilege for the corporation? If Edsel asserted the claim of privilege, would Wang be acting ethically if at her own initiative she wrote the trial judge saying that she did not believe the attorney-client privilege applied?**

Problem VIII-35. Netbest has brought an antitrust suit against the Macrosoft Corporation alleging that Macrosoft had integrated an Internet browser into its operating system with the express purpose of driving Netbest out of business. Netbest asks on discovery for copies of all Macrosoft documents that explain Macrosoft's decision to integrate an Internet browser in its operating system. In one of thirty-five file folders

Macrosoft turns over to Netbest, a letter marked on the front "Privileged attorney-client communication" is found stuck to the back of another document. The letter reads, in part, "Our aim is to develop an interface that is maximally incompatible with what Netbest offers. We hope that by doing this and by integrating our browser, we will drive Netbest out of business so that we can later raise our prices and make a killing. If we do succeed in driving Netbest out of business will we face antitrust problems?" Netbest would like to offer this letter at the trial. Macrosoft claims it is protected by the attorney-client privilege. **What result? Would it matter if Macrosoft's attorneys had had a team of lawyers and paralegals read through all the files for privileged materials before they were turned over to Netbest and had removed hundreds of documents? Would it matter if a routing slip attached to the letter showed that copies had been sent to the leaders of the engineering team that was developing the new operating system?**

Problem VIII-36. Kate Rist is charged with murdering a police officer. There were no eyewitnesses to the crime, but Rist's gun was found near the scene, and it can be proved that Rist harbored a grudge against the officer. During the first of several meetings with appointed counsel Rist admits the crime, but indicates that she wishes to put the prosecution to its proof. Independent investigation has turned up nothing for defense counsel. Shortly before trial, Rist tells counsel that she really did not kill the officer, but that she lent her gun to a recently deceased friend. Rist says that the friend was the killer and that she had been lying to protect her friend. The lawyer finds the story incredible and asks the court for leave to withdraw, which is refused. At the trial the lawyer puts Rist on the stand, and asks her only one question: "Please relate your story of the night in question." Rist is convicted, then she challenges her conviction on the ground that she was denied the effective assistance of counsel and that statements made in confidence to her attorney resulted in her being denied the right to testify like other witnesses. **Should she prevail?**

Problem VIII-37.

(a) You have been appointed as counsel to Abner Pogo who is charged with domestic terrorism. Among the evidence the state proposes to offer against him is a cache of arms and explosives found in a storage locker he had rented some years before in the town of Saline in southeast Michigan. When you interviewed him, Pogo steadfastly denied placing the arms in the locker. He claimed the locker was in his name only because he is treasurer of the Michigan People's Militia, and he told you that he is certain that the material must have been placed there by Alyssa Kendal, the head of the Militia, as she is the only one other than he who has a key. However, he is fiercely loyal to and in love with Kendal, and refuses to make her the scapegoat by naming her to the police. Upon further questioning he admits that records showing he purchased ten barrels of ammonium nitrate fertilizer, which can be used in making explosives, are accurate, but he says that these barrels were not the ones found in the storage locker. Rather, this fertilizer, cans of gasoline and a large cache of grenades and small arms that he has acquired are stored in a barn on a friend's property in Michigan's Upper Peninsula. His friend and at least six of the more militant members of the Michigan Militia know about these materials and could get access to them. You visit the U.P. and find that everything is in the barn as described. At this point you believe everything Pogo has told you, including his claim that he is innocent of the crime charged. You also know that if the material in the barn in the U.P. were discovered and linked to Pogo, he could be convicted of charges more serious than the ones he currently faces. **How do you advise your client?**

(b) At the trial arising out of the case described above, Pogo takes the stand and denies owning or ever having had possession of any of the material in the rented storage locker. On cross-examination, the following interchange occurs:

D.A.: You are aware that ten barrels of ammonium nitrate fertilizer were found in the locker, are you not?

Pogo: So I've been told; I've never seen the stuff.

D.A.: Mr. Pogo, here's a receipt you signed for ten barrels of ammonium nitrate fertilizer, dated March 13, 2013. This is a receipt for a purchase you made, isn't it?

Pogo: It's for nothing I bought; someone must have forged my signature.

D.A.: If you didn't place the guns and the explosives in the locker, do you know who did?

Pogo: No.

D.A.: Do you know of anyone who might possibly have done this?

Pogo: I have no idea.

D.A.: Who else has a key to the locker?

Pogo: I don't know.

D.A.: Do you have any caches of guns and explosives stored elsewhere than in Saline?

A.K.: Objection your Honor. That's irrelevant and inadmissible under Rule 404.

Pogo: (Before the judge can rule) No, I don't.

The court then takes a recess and you then have time to gather your thoughts. **What do you do?**

(c) Pogo is found guilty and sentenced to five years in prison. On his way out of the courtroom, he stops to shake hands with you and says, "Thanks for everything. I probably would have gotten ten years if not for you. I know I wasn't the easiest client, and I appreciate your loyalty. I suppose I won; after all, Uncle Pinko and the U.N. didn't Waco me. Goodbye, and don't tell anyone about that U.P. barn. I want that stuff to be there when I get out in five years, or to be available to my friends in the interim." **What should you do with your information about the weapons cache in the U.P. barn?**

III. PRIVILEGES FOR HEALTH CARE PROVIDERS

A. THE PHYSICIAN-PATIENT PRIVILEGE

1. Justifications

At common law a patient had no privilege to prevent his physician from testifying to information learned in confidence. In 1828, the New York legislature enacted the nation's first physician-patient privilege. Today some form of the privilege exists in almost all states. In the first half of the nineteenth century, when the attorney-client privilege was justified largely on the basis of professional honor, the case for a physician-patient privilege may have seemed strong: a patient's physical condition is a private matter that an honorable doctor should keep confidential. But as justifications for privileges became more instrumental, the case for the physician-patient privilege weakened. The argument was made that without the privilege people would be reluctant to seek treatment for loathsome or shameful diseases like leprosy and syphilis, but the difficulties with this argument are clear. Individuals are seldom thrust involuntarily into litigation requiring embarrassing disclosures about their medical histories. People seeing doctors, unlike those who see lawyers, do not usually fear that confidential disclosures might harm them in a lawsuit because they do not usually expect litigation. Above all, the desire for good health is a powerful incentive to seek treatment and to be honest with one's physician, whatever the potential for disclosure. There was, Wigmore pointed out, no evidence that jurisdictions without the physician-patient privilege have lower standards of medical care than those that have adopted it. Whether this is still true is unclear.

Dean Wigmore asserted that ninety-nine percent of the cases in which the privilege is claimed fall into one of three categories: actions on life insurance policies in which the deceased's health claims when he applied for the policy are challenged; tort actions for injuries, where the plaintiff's physical condition is at issue; and testamentary actions, where the testator's mental capacity is questioned. In these situations, a privilege is likely to prevent probative evidence that is not otherwise available from reaching the trier of fact. Further, in each of these situations the patient holding the privilege has knowingly become involved in a legal matter that makes his health a central issue. Wigmore comments:

> In all of these the medical testimony is absolutely needed for the purpose of learning the truth. In none of them is there any reason for the party to conceal the facts, except as a tactical maneuver in litigation.[66]

This argument, often reiterated by others, does not necessarily argue against a physician-patient privilege. It might, instead, make the case for exceptions to the privilege, and in many states exceptions that deal with Wigmore's concerns exist. Thus, a patient-litigant exception is common. Where this exception exists, the privilege will typically not protect information regarding any physical or emotional condition that the privilege holder makes relevant in litigation. If, for example, Mary brings suit for neck injuries she suffered in an auto accident, she could not, in most states, claim the privilege to protect medical records growing out of her post-accident diagnosis or treatment or to protect any medical records relating to her past neck problems. Even when a party's physical or mental condition is not the focus of the litigation, the patient-litigant exception ordinarily applies. Thus if Fred, who has been sued for assault and battery, claims that his arthritic hands would have prevented him from ever landing the blows described, most states will not allow him to use the privilege to withhold medical information relating to his hands.

Wigmore may have lost his battle against the physician-patient privilege, but he and those who took up his banner have, to a considerable extent, won the war, for their arguments against the privilege are reflected in many states in waiver rules or specific exceptions to the privilege. Moreover, in one jurisdiction their victory seems complete. Courts interpreting FRE 501 regularly hold that the physician-patient privilege is unavailable in federal criminal cases and federal question civil actions. Only when state law provides the rule of decision, as in diversity tort actions, are the benefits of the physician-patient privilege likely to apply in federal court. The drafters' choice not to include a physician-patient privilege is further testimony to the prevailing academic view of this privilege.

Although the physician-patient privilege probably owes its widespread adoption more to the lobbying power of state medical associations than to its legal defenders, some scholars have advanced strong privacy arguments for the privilege.[67] It may be a mistake to think that but for a powerful lobby those who oppose the privilege would

---

[66] Wigmore § 2380a, at 831.

[67] See Thomas G. Krattenmaker, Testimonial Privileges in Federal Courts: An Alternative to the Proposed Federal Rules of Evidence, 62 Geo. L.J. 61 (1973); Wright and Graham, Federal Practice and Procedure, Vol. 25 § 5522 (1989); Note, Developments in the Law—Privileged Communications, 98 Harv. L. Rev. 1450 (1985).

have carried the day. Revelations to physicians are often quite intimate and potentially embarrassing. Most people might well wish some protection for what their doctors learn in confidence.

Although almost every state has a physician-patient privilege, the contours of the privilege vary widely in terms of what is and is not protected. Since we cannot offer a proposed federal rule as a model, we offer instead California's version of the physician-patient privilege.

CALIFORNIA EVIDENCE CODE

ARTICLE 6. PHYSICIAN-PATIENT PRIVILEGE

§ *990.* *"Physician."* As used in this article, "physician" means a person authorized, or reasonably believed by the patient to be authorized, to practice medicine in any state or nation.

§ *991.* *"Patient."* As used in this article, "patient" means a person who consults a physician or submits to an examination by a physician for the purpose of securing a diagnosis or preventive, palliative, or curative treatment of his physical or mental or emotional condition.

§ *992.* *"Confidential communication between patient and physician."* As used in this article, "confidential communication between patient and physician" means information, including information obtained by an examination of the patient, transmitted between a patient and his physician in the course of that relationship and in confidence by a means which, so far as the patient is aware, discloses the information to no third persons other than those who are present to further the interest of the patient in the consultation or those to whom disclosure is reasonably necessary for the transmission of the information or the accomplishment of the purpose for which the physician is consulted, and includes a diagnosis made and the advice given by the physician in the course of that relationship.

§ *993.* *"Holder of the privilege."* As used in this article, "holder of the privilege" means:

(a) The patient when he has no guardian or conservator.

(b) A guardian or conservator of the patient when the patient has a guardian or conservator.

(c) The personal representative of the patient if the patient is dead.

§ *994.* *Physician-patient privilege.* Subject to Section 912 and except as otherwise provided in this article, the patient, whether or not a party, has a privilege to refuse to disclose, and to prevent another from disclosing, a confidential communication between patient and physician if the privilege is claimed by:

(a) The holder of the privilege.

(b) A person who is authorized to claim the privilege by the holder of the privilege; or

(c) The person who was the physician at the time of the confidential communication, but such person may not claim the privilege if there is no holder of the privilege in existence or if he or she is otherwise instructed by a person authorized to permit disclosure.

The relationship of a physician and patient shall exist between a medical or podiatry corporation as defined in the Medical Practice Act and the patient to whom it renders professional services, as well as between such patients and licensed physicians and surgeons employed by such corporation to render services to such patients. The word "persons" as used in this subdivision includes partnerships, corporations, limited liability companies, associations, and other groups and entities.

§ *995. When physician required to claim privilege.* The physician who received or made a communication subject to the privilege under this article shall claim the privilege whenever he is present when the communication is sought to be disclosed and is authorized to claim the privilege under subdivision (c) of Section 994.

§ *996. Exception: Patient-litigant exception.* There is no privilege under this article as to a communication relevant to an issue concerning the condition of the patient if such issue has been tendered by:

(a) The patient;

(b) Any party claiming through or under the patient;

(c) Any party claiming as a beneficiary of the patient through a contract to which the patient is or was a party; or

(d) The plaintiff in an action brought under Section 376 or 377 of the Code of Civil Procedure for damages for the injury or death of the patient.

§ *997. Exception: Crime or tort.* There is no privilege under this article if the services of the physician were sought or obtained to enable or aid anyone to commit or plan to commit a crime or a tort or to escape detection or apprehension after the commission of a crime or a tort.

§ *998. Exception: Criminal proceeding.* There is no privilege under this article in a criminal proceeding.

§ *999. Exception: Proceeding to recover damages on account of conduct of patient.* There is no privilege under this article as to a communication relevant to an issue concerning the condition of the patient in a proceeding to recover damages on account of the conduct of the patient if good cause for disclosure of the communication is shown.

§ *1000. Exception: Parties claiming through deceased patient.* There is no privilege under this article as to a communication relevant to an issue between parties all of whom claim through a deceased patient, regardless of whether the claims are by testate or intestate succession or by inter vivos transaction.

§ *1001. Exception: Breach of duty arising out of physician-patient relationship.* There is no privilege under this article as to a communication relevant to an issue of breach, by the physician or by the patient, of a duty arising out of the physician-patient relationship.

§ *1002. Exception: Intention of deceased patient concerning writing affecting property interest.* There is no privilege under this article as to a communication relevant to an issue concerning the intention of a patient, now deceased, with respect to a deed of conveyance, will, or other writing, executed by the patient, purporting to affect an interest in property.

§ *1003. Exception: Validity of writing affecting property interest.* There is no privilege under this article as to a communication relevant to an issue concerning the validity of a deed of conveyance, will, or other writing, executed by a patient, now deceased, purporting to affect an interest in property.

§ *1004. Exception: Commitment or similar proceeding.* There is no privilege under this article in a proceeding to commit the patient or otherwise place him or his property, or both, under the control of another because of his alleged mental or physical condition.

§ *1005. Exception: Proceeding to establish competence.* There is no privilege under this article in a proceeding brought by or on behalf of the patient to establish his competence.

§ *1006. Exception: Required report.* There is no privilege under this article as to information that the physician or the patient is required to report to a public employee, or as to information required to be recorded in a public office, if such report or record is open to public inspection.

§ *1007. Exception: Proceeding to terminate right, license or privilege.* There is no privilege under this article in a proceeding brought by a public entity to determine whether a right, authority, license, or privilege (including the right or privilege to be employed by the public entity or to hold a public office) should be revoked, suspended, terminated, limited, or conditioned.

2.   Exceptions and Waiver

In most jurisdictions, the physician-patient privilege is not as riddled with exceptions as it is in California, but every state privilege allows for at least some of the exceptions found in the California statute. Most, if not all, states abrogate the privilege when a patient has consulted a physician to facilitate the commission of a crime, in actions involving a breach of duty arising out of the physician-patient relationship, and when physicians are required to report diseases or conditions to public authorities for inclusion in public health databases A strong majority of states do not apply the privilege in criminal cases. At least fourteen states do so, however, and the treatise New Wigmore, reports that Louisiana and a few other states apply the privilege only in criminal cases. More than half the states do not allow it in disputes concerning workers' compensation.

California's exception for situations in which the patient has placed his condition in issue generally prevents plaintiffs from claiming the privilege in personal injury litigation. Some states follow California in this regard, while others hold that the plaintiff only waives the privilege by testifying about his physical condition. All hold it waived as to the plaintiff's testifying physicians, and doctors consulted jointly with testifying physicians, to the extent they are called to testify about the privileged matter. Some states maintain that calling one physician to testify waives the privilege with respect to all doctors consulted about the particular physical condition. Waiver may also be effected under state counterparts to Rule 35 of the Federal Rules of Civil Procedure. These rules provide that in certain cases one party may secure a doctor's examination of the other. If a party examined under the rule seeks a report of the opponent's examination or deposes the examining physician, she waives the privilege as to examinations conducted by her own physician.

3.   Other Features

The physician-patient privilege in California has other features generally characteristic of the privilege. The patient holds the privilege and may waive it. The privilege survives the death of the patient and may be asserted by heirs or representatives. The privilege extends to information that the physician learns from examining the patient even if the patient does nothing to actively communicate information to the doctor, apart from allowing the examination. The presence of third persons or the transmittal of information to others in order to facilitate treatment or diagnosis does not abrogate the privilege, but the presence of third persons not necessary to the consultation, or the patient's knowing transmittal of information to such persons, will vitiate the privilege. Finally, the privilege applies only to information that the physician receives for the purpose of diagnosis or treatment. Here the California statute, by using the disjunctive "or," creates a somewhat broader privilege than the one found in most jurisdictions. Usually, a diagnostic consultation is not privileged unless the patient seeks the diagnosis, at least in part, for the purpose of securing treatment. Thus, if a patient consults a physician only to secure an expert diagnosis at trial, confidential communications to that physician are not privileged. The theory is that the patient never intended to keep the results of the examination confidential. Of course, the abrogation of the privilege in these circumstances is meaningless unless the party, after receiving the diagnosis, chooses not to have the physician testify. Where this occurs, the party can sometimes claim that the physician was advising the lawyer, and the protection of the attorney-client privilege may apply as will the provisions of Fed. R. Civ. P. 26(b) and its state counterparts, which in large measure shield non-testifying experts from discovery.

4.   Contrasted With Attorney-Client Privilege

The contrast between the physician-patient and the attorney-client privileges reflects differences in those professional relationships. Although the attorney-client privilege is the more absolute, the physician-patient privilege applies in some circumstances where the attorney-client does not. The latter privilege, as we saw, applies only to communications that the client intended to be confidential, and so the court will seldom protect the attorney's observations of the client. The physician-patient privilege, by contrast, mostly protects observations. The patient need not have intended to communicate what the doctor saw. Indeed, some states have protected observations of or test results from unconscious patients. The attorney-client privilege, on the other hand, protects confidential communications. Although the physician-patient privilege is often similarly characterized, it is more accurately characterized as a privilege for revelations of a kind that both physician and patient would have expected to be held in confidence. Another difference is that the attorney-client privilege may be lost if third parties share with or observe communications. Medicine, however, often has a corporate quality. Various health care providers may be present at an examination or have access to a patient's medical records. As long as the patient could not easily exclude extraneous observers, like medical students accompanying doctors on rounds, courts typically allow the privilege despite their presence. Courts also often allow the privilege when the family or, in some circumstances, friends of the patient are present at an examination. The argument is that their presence provides supports to the patient and so facilitates the examination. During an examination of a child, the presence of parents is regarded as a matter of course.

Problem VIII-38. Ted Ohlin took his ten-year-old son to a pediatrician for a physical examination. Present at the examination were Ted and his child; the pediatrician; a young man in a white coat who was introduced to Ted after the examination as an anthropologist doing research on the medical profession; and a nurse. From time to time another nurse entered and left the examination room. The office was so small that whenever the nurse opened the door people in the waiting room could hear what the doctor said to Ted and his son. Thus, at least six people heard the doctor diagnose the son's illness as mumps and advise the youngster to stay out of school to avoid infecting others. Following an epidemic of mumps in the son's school, the parents of those children who caught the mumps sue Ted and his son for causing the epidemic by not heeding the doctor's advice to stay away from school. **May Ted or his son claim the physician-patient privilege to prevent the pediatrician from testifying to her diagnosis or advice? Will the claim of privilege prevent the anthropologist from testifying? The nurses? The people in the waiting room? Ted, if he is called as an adverse witness?**

B. PSYCHOTHERAPIST-PATIENT PRIVILEGE

The committee that drafted the federal rules did not include a physician-patient privilege, apparently persuaded by a long-standing, two-pronged academic attack against the privilege. First, the critics argued that a concern for health was sufficient to encourage people to confide in their physicians. Second, the critics claimed the privilege too often protected information central to litigation, or like the California privilege, its many exceptions negated its effect. The drafters did, however, feel that a convincing case could be made for a psychotherapist-patient privilege.

But when Congress failed to enact the Advisory Committee's recommendations, litigants in federal court were left without a psychotherapist-patient privilege. In the decades following the enactment of the Federal Rules, several federal circuits created a psychotherapist-patient privilege with the discretion they saw vested in them under FRE 501, but other circuits believed that if there was to be a psychotherapist-patient privilege, it should come through legislative action. The Supreme Court resolved this conflict in 1996 in the case of *Jaffe v. Redmond.*[68] *Jaffe* grew out of an incident in which a police officer, Mary Lu Redmond, shot and killed a young man as she attempted to quell a disturbance. The police officer claimed the victim was armed when she shot him and was about to stab a man he was chasing as they burst from a building, but other witnesses said the victim was unarmed when he emerged from the apartment building. Jaffe, the administrator of the

---

[68] 518 U.S. 1 (1996).

victim's estate, sued Redmond and others. During discovery Jaffe learned that Officer Redmond had had about fifty counseling sessions with Karen Beyer, a licensed social worker, following the incident, and he sought to get her notes to assist in cross-examining Redmond. When both the defendant and the social worker refused to turn over the notes, the judge instructed the jury that it could presume the notes contained information unfavorable to the defendant. The Seventh Circuit reversed a plaintiff's verdict, recognizing, under FRE 501, a psychotherapist-patient privilege that would protect the notes unless, "in the interests of justice, the evidentiary need for the disclosure of a patient's counseling sessions outweighs the patient's privacy interests." The Supreme Court, in affirming, strengthened the privilege's protection, as it held that the privilege applied with no need to strike a balance like that the Court of Appeals proposed.

The extracts from the majority opinion, per Justice Stevens and Justice Scalia's dissent that we present below, rehearse the arguments for and against the creation of a psychotherapist-patient privilege and of privileges in general. They are also the best example we have to date of how the Court interprets Congress's mandate in FRE 501 to extend privileges according to "The common law . . . *in the light of reason and experience*" (emphasis added).

JAFFEE, SPECIAL ADMINISTRATOR FOR ALLEN, DECEASED V. REDMOND ET AL.
518 U.S. 1 (1996).

JUSTICE STEVENS delivered the opinion of the Court.

II

Rule 501 of the Federal Rules of Evidence authorizes federal courts to define new privileges by interpreting "common law principles . . . in the light of reason and experience." . . . The Rule . . . did not freeze the law governing the privileges of witnesses in federal trials at a particular point in our history, but rather directed federal courts to "continue the evolutionary development of testimonial privileges."

. . . "For more than three centuries it has now been recognized as a fundamental maxim that the public . . . has a right to every man's evidence. When we come to examine the various claims of exemption, we start with the primary assumption that there is a general duty to give what testimony one is capable of giving, and that any exemptions which may exist are distinctly exceptional, being so many derogations from a positive general rule." Exceptions from the general rule disfavoring testimonial privileges may be justified, however, by a "'public good transcending the normally predominant principle of utilizing all rational means for ascertaining the truth.'"

Guided by these principles, the question we address today is whether a privilege protecting confidential communications between a psychotherapist and her patient "promotes sufficiently important interests to outweigh the need for probative evidence. . . . " Both "reason and experience" persuade us that it does.

III

Like the spousal and attorney-client privileges, the psychotherapist-patient privilege is "rooted in the imperative need for confidence and trust." Treatment by a physician for physical ailments can often proceed successfully on the basis of a physical examination, objective information supplied by the patient, and the results of diagnostic tests. Effective psychotherapy, by contrast, depends on an atmosphere of confidence and trust in which the patient is willing to make a frank and complete disclosure of facts, emotions, memories, and fears. Because of the sensitive nature of the problems for which individuals consult psychotherapists, disclosure of confidential communications made during counseling sessions may cause embarrassment or disgrace. For this reason, the mere possibility of disclosure may impede development of the confidential relationship necessary for successful treatment. . . .

By protecting confidential communications between a psychotherapist and her patient from involuntary disclosure, the proposed privilege thus serves important private interests.

Our cases make clear that an asserted privilege must also "serv[e] public ends." . . . The psychotherapist privilege serves the public interest by facilitating the provision of appropriate treatment for individuals suffering the effects of a mental or emotional problem. The mental health of our citizenry, no less than its physical health, is a public good of transcendent importance.

In contrast to the significant public and private interests supporting recognition of the privilege, the likely evidentiary benefit that would result from the denial of the privilege is modest. If the privilege were rejected, confidential conversations between psychotherapists and their patients would surely be chilled, particularly when it is obvious that the circumstances that give rise to the need for treatment will probably result in litigation. Without a privilege, much of the desirable evidence to which litigants such as petitioner seek access—for example, admissions against interest by a party—is unlikely to come into being. This unspoken "evidence" will therefore serve no greater truth-seeking function that if it had been spoken and privileged.

That it is appropriate for the federal courts to recognize a psychotherapist privilege under Rule 501 is confirmed by the fact that all 50 States and the District of Columbia have enacted into law some form of psychotherapist privilege. We have previously observed that the policy decisions of the States bear on the question whether federal courts should recognize a new privilege or amend the coverage of an existing one. Because state legislatures are fully aware of the need to protect the integrity of the factfinding functions of their courts, the existence of a consensus among the States indicates that "reason and experience" support recognition of the privilege. In addition, given the importance of the patient's understanding that her communications with her therapist will not be publicly disclosed, any State's promise of confidentiality would have little value if the patient were aware that the privilege would not be honored in a federal court. Denial of the federal privilege therefore would frustrate the purposes of the state legislation that was enacted to foster these confidential communications. . . .

The uniform judgment of the States is reinforced by the fact that a psychotherapist privilege was among the nine specific privileges recommended by the Advisory Committee in its proposed privilege rules. In *United States v. Gillock*, 445 U.S. [360 (1980)], at 367–368, our holding that Rule 501 did not include a state legislative privilege relied, in part, on the fact that no such privilege was included in the Advisory Committee's draft. The reasoning in *Gillock* thus supports the opposite conclusion in this case. . . . [W]e hold that confidential communications between a licensed psychotherapist and her patients in the course of diagnosis or treatment are protected from compelled disclosure under Rule 501 of the Federal Rules of Evidence.

IV

All agree that a psychotherapist privilege covers confidential communications made to licensed psychiatrists and psychologists. . . . Today, social workers provide a significant amount of mental health treatment. . . . We therefore agree with the Court of Appeals that "[d]rawing a distinction between the counseling provided by more readily accessible social workers serves no discernible public purpose."

We part company with the Court of Appeals on a separate point. We reject the balancing component of the privilege implemented by that court and a small number of States. Making the promise of confidentiality contingent upon a trial judge's later evaluation of the relative importance of the patient's interest in privacy and the evidentiary need for disclosure would eviscerate the effectiveness of the privilege. As we explained in *Upjohn*, if the purpose of the privilege is to be served, the participants in the confidential conversation "must be able to predict with some degree of certainty whether particular discussions will be protected. An uncertain privilege, or one which purports to be certain but results in widely varying applications by the courts, is little better than no privilege at all."

These considerations are all that are necessary for decision of this case. A rule that authorizes the recognition of new privileges on a case-by-case basis makes it appropriate to define the details of new privileges in a like manner. Because this is the first case in which we have recognized a psychotherapist privilege, it is neither necessary or feasible to delineate its full contours in a way that would "govern all conceivable future questions in this area."

V

. . .

JUSTICE SCALIA, with whom THE CHIEF JUSTICE joins as to Part III, dissenting.

The Court has discussed at some length the benefit that will be purchased by creation of the evidentiary privilege in this case: the encouragement of psychoanalytic counseling. It has not mentioned the purchase price: occasional injustice. That is the cost of every rule which excludes reliable and probative evidence—or at least every one categorical enough to achieve its announced policy objective. . . .

In the past, this Court has well understood that the particular value the courts are distinctively charged with preserving—justice—is severely harmed by contravention of "the fundamental principle that '"the public . . . has a right to every man's evidence.""' . . . Adherence to that principle has caused us, in the Rule 501 cases we have considered to date, to reject new privileges, see *University of Pennsylvania v. EEOC*, 493 U.S. 182 (1990) (privilege against disclosure of "legislative acts" by member of state legislature), and even to construe narrowly the scope of existing privileges, see e.g., *United States v. Zolin*, 491 U.S. 554, 568–570 (1989) (permitting *in camera* review of documents alleged to come within crime-fraud exception to attorney-client privilege); *Trammel, supra* (holding that voluntary testimony by spouse is not covered by husband-wife privilege). The Court today ignores this traditional judicial preference for the truth, and ends up creating a privilege that is new, vast and ill defined. . . .

I

. . .

II

. . . Effective psychotherapy undoubtedly is beneficial to individuals with mental problems, and surely serves some larger social interest in maintaining a mentally stable society. But merely mentioning these values does not answer the critical question: Are they of such importance, and is the contribution of psychotherapy to them so distinctive, and is the application of normal evidentiary rules so destructive to psychotherapy, as to justify making our federal courts occasional instruments of injustice? On that central question I find the Court's analysis insufficiently convincing to satisfy the high standard we have set for rules that "are in derogation of the search for truth."

When is it, one must wonder, that *the psychotherapist* came to play such an indispensable role in the maintenance of the citizenry's mental health? For most of history, men and women have worked out their difficulties by talking to, *inter alios*, parents, siblings, best friends, and bartenders—none of whom was awarded a privilege against testifying in court. Ask the average citizen: Would your mental health be more significantly impaired by preventing you from seeing a psychotherapist, or by preventing you from getting advice from your mom? I have little doubt what the answer would be. Yet there is no mother-child privilege.

How likely is it that a person will be deterred from seeking psychological counseling, from being completely truthful in the course of such counseling, because of fear of later disclosure in litigation? And even more pertinent to today's decision, to what extent will the evidentiary privilege reduce that deterrent? The Court does not try to answer the first of these questions; and it *cannot possibly have any notion* of what the answer is to the second, since that depends entirely upon the scope of the privilege, which the Court amazingly finds it "neither necessary nor feasible to delineate." . . .

Even where it is certain that absence of the psychotherapist privilege will inhibit disclosures of the information, it is not clear to me that that is an unacceptable state of affairs. Let us assume the very worst in the circumstances of the present case: that to be truthful about what was troubling her, the police officer who sought counseling would have to confess that she shot without reason, and wounded an innocent man. . . . [I see no] reason why she should be enabled to *deny* her guilt in the criminal trial—or in a civil trial for negligence—while yet obtaining the benefits of psychotherapy by confessing guilt to a social worker who cannot testify. It seems to me entirely fair to say that if she wishes the benefits of telling the truth she must also accept the adverse consequences. . . .

The Court confidently asserts that not much truth-finding capacity would be destroyed by the privilege anyway, since "[w]ithout a privilege, much of the desirable evidence to which litigants such as petitioner seek access . . . is unlikely to come into being." If that is so, how come psychotherapy got to be a thriving practice before the "psychotherapist privilege" was invented?

. . .

In its consideration of this case, the Court was the beneficiary of no fewer than 14 *amicus* briefs supporting respondents, most of which came from such organizations as the American Psychiatric Association, the American Psychoanalytic Association, the American Association of State Social Work Boards, the Employee Assistance Professionals Association, Inc., The American Counseling Association, and the National Association of Social Workers. Not a single *amicus* brief was filed in support of petitioner. That is no surprise. There is no self-interested organization out there devoted to pursuit of the truth in the federal courts. The expectation is, however, that *this Court* will have that interest prominently—indeed, primarily—in mind. Today we have failed that expectation, and that responsibility. It is no small matter to say that, in some cases, our federal courts will be the tools of injustice rather than unearth the truth where it is available to be found. The common law has identified a few instances where that is tolerable. Perhaps Congress may conclude that it is also tolerable for the purpose of encouraging psychotherapy by social workers. But that conclusion assuredly does not burst upon the mind with such clarity that a judgment in favor of suppressing the truth ought to be pronounced by this honorable Court. I respectfully dissent.

———————

We leave it to you to decide whether the majority or the dissent has the better of the argument, but one point Justice Scalia makes deserves attention. It is curious, though not unprecedented,[69] for the Court to use the need for certainty to justify a broad reading of a privilege and then leave so much undefined that it is impossible for those who benefit from the privilege to know precisely what disclosures will be protected.[70] But the situation is not quite so ill-defined as it may seem. As the contours of the privilege are further refined, the federal courts are likely to look at state practice and the proposed federal rule for guidance. Practices vary across states, but there are commonalities, and as about 40% of the states modeled their psychotherapist privilege on the proposed federal privilege, PFRE 504 is a good place to start:

PFRE 504: PSYCHOTHERAPIST-PATIENT PRIVILEGE

(a) *Definitions.*

(1) A "patient" is a person who consults or is examined or interviewed by a psychotherapist.

(2) A "psychotherapist" is (A) a person authorized to practice medicine in any state or nation, or reasonably believed by the patient so to be, while engaged in the diagnosis or treatment of a mental or emotional condition, including drug addiction, or (B) a person licensed or certified as a psychologist under the laws of any state or nation, while similarly engaged.

---

[69]   See Upjohn v. United States, supra in text following note 45.

[70]   This does not mean the majority is foolish, as Justice Scalia seems to charge. It has created a broad zone of protection such that most people have reason to be confident that disclosures to psychotherapists will be protected. Also, lawyers can predict and tell therapists who in turn can tell patients what kinds of disclosures are likely to be risky from the point of view of the privilege. Finally, courts are likely to make sounder judgments if they delineate the bounds of the privilege on a case-by-case basis rather than attempting to resolve in advance, and in the abstract, all issues that are likely to arise.

(3) A communication is "confidential" if not intended to be disclosed to third persons other than those present to further the interest of the patient in the consultation, examination, or interview, or persons reasonably necessary for the transmission of the communication, or persons who are participating in the diagnosis and treatment under the direction of the psychotherapist, including members of the patient's family.

(b) *General rule of privilege.* A patient has a privilege to refuse to disclose and to prevent any other person from disclosing confidential communications, made for the purposes of diagnosis or treatment of his mental or emotional condition, including drug addiction, among himself, his psychotherapist, or persons who are participating in the diagnosis or treatment under the direction of the psychotherapist, including members of the patient's family.

(c) *Who may claim the privilege.* The privilege may be claimed by the patient, by his guardian or conservator, or by the personal representative of a deceased patient. The person who was the psychotherapist may claim the privilege but only on behalf of his patient. His authority so to do is presumed in the absence of evidence to the contrary.

(d) *Exceptions*

(1) *Proceedings for hospitalization.* There is no privilege under this rule for communications relevant to an issue in proceedings to hospitalize the patient for mental illness, if the psychotherapist in the course of diagnosis or treatment has determined that the patient is in need of hospitalization.

(2) *Examination by order of judge.* If the judge orders an examination of the mental or emotional condition of the patient, communications made in the course thereof are not privileged under this rule with respect to the particular purpose for which the examination is ordered unless the judge orders otherwise.

(3) *Condition an element of claim or defense.* There is no privilege under this rule as to communications relevant to an issue of the mental or emotional condition of the patient in any proceeding in which he relies upon the condition as an element of his claim or defense, or, after the patient's death, in any proceeding in which any party relies upon the condition as an element of his claim or defense.

As written, PFRE 504 applies only to licensed physicians and psychologists, but we see in *Jaffe* that the federal common law privilege extends at least to licensed social workers doing therapeutic counseling. Whether it extends beyond social workers to lay counselors or to doctors treating physical conditions who are also concerned with their patients' emotional health remains to be seen.

The proposed federal rule and many state rules exclude from the privilege's protection communications relevant to hospitalization, communications in connection with judge-ordered mental examinations, and communications relating to mental conditions that a party is relying on as part of a claim or defense. These exceptions cover situations in which the potential court use of a psychotherapist's testimony is the most obvious. Yet patients are expected to talk to therapists anyway. The presence of these exceptions calls into question the instrumental case for the privilege.

In addition, the Court indicates in *Jaffe* that communications which psychotherapists have a duty to reveal—such as a serious intention to harm another—are not protected by the privilege. Also, in recent years many states have exempted statements acknowledging child abuse from their psychotherapist or other counseling privilege. It would be surprising if the federal courts did not follow prevailing practice in reading exceptions into the privilege *Jaffe* establishes.

The physician-patient and psychotherapist-patient privileges are in some measure a status symbol. From the outset, when the best argument for the physician-patient privilege seemed to be that lawyers had one, they have been the subject of concerted lobbying efforts by professional groups motivated, many think, at least as much by status concerns as by the necessity for a privilege. As Justice Scalia's dissent in *Jaffe* indicates, this lobbying extends even to the courts. At the same time, the professionals who claim these privileges often elicit, in an atmosphere of trust, intimate and potentially embarrassing information from those they serve. It is a mistake to think that lobbying alone is responsible for the spread of these privileges through the states or for the adoption of the psychotherapist-patient privilege by the Supreme Court. Without the widely shared sense that a physician or psychotherapist *should* keep client confidences, the lobbying efforts would probably have failed and the *amicus* briefs in *Jaffe* would have been ignored rather than relied on by the *Jaffe* majority.

Problem VIII-39. Sharon Riley visits a rape crisis center following a sexual assault. She spends an hour talking to Carissa Logan, a volunteer counselor in the Center with a bachelor's degree in psychology. Carissa recommends that Sharon see a psychotherapist, but Sharon cannot afford to do so, and Carissa sees her on twelve other occasions in the next three months, for periods ranging from twenty minutes to two hours. James Dickerson is charged with raping Sharon, and she testifies to this effect. She also testifies that although she kissed him, she did not consent to any further sexual activity and did nothing to lead him on. James testifies at the trial that Sharon had unbuttoned his pants as they kissed, taken off her blouse, and asked him to use a condom, but that as they both lay naked, Sharon said, "No." He claims that he respected this, stopped and didn't penetrate. He suggests that Sharon's strict upbringing made her feel guilty about what did happen and her role in it, and this led her to claim that he had coerced and raped her. James would like to call Carissa to the stand to recount what Sharon told her had happened, to discuss how Sharon's story had changed over time, and to talk about whether Sharon showed signs of extreme guilt at what had happened. Sharon claims the psychotherapist-patient privilege to keep Carissa from testifying. **How should the court rule? Would it make a difference if Carissa held a master's degree in social work and was a licensed therapist? Suppose she had an M.S.W., but no therapist's license?**

Suppose after each session with Sharon, Carissa had consulted with Phil Reed, a psychiatrist who served as a resource person for the Center's volunteer counselors. Sharon knew about these consultations. **Would this make a difference in the availability of the privilege to Sharon? Could Sharon claim the privilege to prevent Reed from revealing what Carissa told him? Would any of your answers be different if Sharon did not know about these consultations?**

Problem VIII-40. In an insurance fraud case a grand jury issued a subpoena for Karen Blue, a psychiatrist, ordering her to appear and to produce certain records including: patient files, progress notes, ledger cards, copies of insurance claim forms, and documentation supporting dates of service rendered and the identities of patients receiving said service for eighteen specific persons. Blue filed a motion to quash the subpoena, citing the psychotherapist-patient privilege, after which the district judge held that the records could be redacted of information other than the patients' names and the fact and length of treatment. **Was the district court judge correct in ordering Blue to reveal the identities of her patients as well as the length of their treatment?**

IV. MARITAL PRIVILEGES

A. TWO PRIVILEGES

At one time the common law forbade parties from giving testimony because of their interest in the case. The law regarded the interests of spouses as sufficiently close that neither spouse could testify when the other spouse was a party. As this bar disappeared from the common law, it was replaced, in part, by a privilege that protects one spouse against the harmful testimony of the other. We shall call this the *adverse testimony privilege.*[71]   In addition, courts and legislatures began in the middle of the nineteenth century to protect confidential communications between spouses.   We shall call this the *marital communications privilege.*

B. JUSTIFICATIONS

These privileges have each been justified on the instrumental ground that they promote marital well-being.   Many marriages, some argue, would be destroyed if one spouse's testimony harmed the other, particularly in a criminal case.   Hence there is need for an adverse testimony privilege.   Marriages also would be in trouble if spouses did not confide in each other.   Hence a marital communications privilege is needed so that spouses feel they can talk freely.   In addition, each privilege has noninstrumental justifications related to the privacy or sanctity of the marital relationship.

As with most instrumental arguments for privileges, those used to justify the marital privileges have never been put to an empirical test. Nonetheless, it is plausible to suppose that marital stress does increase if one spouse gives testimony that helps convict the other.   But the primary sources of marital stress in these circumstances probably are the trial and subsequent punishment.   It is seldom easy to be married to someone whose life is centered on a trial.   Maintaining a marriage over a lengthy incarceration can prove even more difficult.   But we surely are not going to exempt married folk from trials and punishment because we don't want to destroy marriages.

The instrumental case for the marital communications privilege is weaker still.   Few couples know of this marital privilege, and even if more did, it is unlikely that they would address each other differently because of the remote chance that a communication would later figure in a court case.   Indeed, in the situation in which the legal relevance of "pillow talk" is most obvious—when husband and wife jointly plan or carry out a crime—most jurisdictions with the marital communications privilege provide an exception.

Noninstrumental reasons for the two privileges are more substantial. Professor Gardner, speaking perhaps a bit extravagantly, described the basis for the marital privilege this way:

> This basis is the concept of human dignity in connection with an especially confidential relationship, one incidentally packed with "emotional dynamite" . . . In a personal and intimate sense the husband and wife relationship is the closest one known to man. Ideally, it involves a union of minds as well as bodies.   A spouse

---

[71]   This privilege has been referred to by many names, including spousal incapacity, spousal immunity, the privilege for anti-marital facts, and the spousal-witness privilege.

reveals himself to his marital partner in almost every way more thoroughly than to others—even when he does so unconsciously. This intimate relationship is of great worth in the promotion of the ultimate interests of society.

. . .

[S]omething in the spirit is shocked and hurt at the betrayal of former confidences, at the revelation of the secrets of the bedchamber, and perhaps at the vindictiveness of alienated ex-spouses. . . . [72]

McCormick, no fan of these privileges, reached the same conclusion as to their source but put a different spin on it. Writing about the privilege for marital communications, he noted:

It is a matter of emotion and sentiment. All of us have a feeling of indelicacy and want of decorum in prying into the secrets of husband and wife. . . . [T]his is the real source of the privilege.[73]

With the privilege (on his analysis) supported only by "emotion," "sentiment," and "a feeling of indelicacy," McCormick easily concluded:

When we [recognize the real source of the privilege], we realize at once this motive of delicacy, while worthy and desirable, will not stand in the balance with the need for disclosure in court of the facts upon which a man's life, liberty, or estate may depend.[74]

More than a century before, the utilitarian philosopher Jeremy Bentham had used harsher, more satirical language in reaching similar conclusions about the source and desirability of the adverse testimony privilege:

Hard—hardship—policy—peace   of   families—absolute necessity:—some such words as these are the vehicles by which the faint spark of reason that exhibits itself is conveyed.

. . .

Let us, therefore, grant to every man a license to commit all sorts of wickedness, in the presence and with the assistance of his wife: let us secure to every man in the bosom of his family, and in his own bosom, a safe accomplice: let us make every man's house his castle; and, as far as depends upon us, let us convert that castle into a den of thieves.[75]

---

[72] Gardner, supra note 21, Part II, at 489–90.

[73] McCormick (2nd ed.) § 86, at 173.

[74] Id. In the fifth edition of McCormick, the reviser is less critical and concludes that considerations like these argue for a qualified privilege. McCormick (5th ed.) § 86. In the later edition, the reviser is more critical. McCormick (6th ed.) § 86.

[75] Cited in David Louisell and Byron M. Crippin, Evidentiary Privileges, 40 Minn. L. Rev. 413, 417 (1956).

That these privileges have endured, however, testifies to the strength of McCormick's "motive of delicacy." Put another way, society does not want to place wives or husbands[76] either in a position where one will be an instrument of the other's undoing or where faith in marital confidences will be shattered by force of law. One important motivating force behind society's willingness to forgo evidence is a romantic view of the marital relationship that emphasizes the love, devotion, and closeness that the marriage ideal encompasses. As new, perhaps more realistic, views of marriage—and soaring divorce rates—highlight the fragility and temporary nature of marriage, McCormick, and Wigmore before him, seem to many more right than ever in regarding these privileges as "sentimental relics." Thus one encounters courts that have expansively interpreted the attorney-client privilege or the state secrets privilege, say of the marital privileges that they "are to be strictly construed." Many commentators applaud these results, although others say the very fragility of marriages today makes the marital privileges more important than ever. Our own view is that the key issue is neither nurturing marriages nor the reality of the romantic ideal, but rather respect for marriage as an institution. The question is to what extent does respect for marriage as an institution mean that it should be given unique privacy rights, and that the virtue of loyalty to a spouse should trump the needs that litigants or the state may have for information? We see privacy and the affection-born loyalty that spouses have for each other as at the very heart of the marital institution, and we respect that institution enough to believe that the noninstrumental case for the marital privilege justifies substantial protection.

Few courts, however, would write this way. In expanding on precedent or interpreting statutory privileges, judges typically follow a path we might call "as if" instrumentalism. This approach assumes that the marital privileges exist for the instrumental reasons of promoting marital confidences and marital stability. Further, this approach applies the privileges not only *as if* these were the only values to consider, but also *as if* the deciding court could envision how its decision would affect the viability of and flow of confidences in marriages of particular types. The Seventh Circuit took this perspective to an unjustifiable extreme in *Ryan v. Commissioner*,[77] which denied the adverse testimony privilege to a couple married forty years on the rationale that the marriage was so

---

[76] Until recently the marital privileges, especially the privilege for adverse testimony, have almost always been used to prevent wives from testifying against or revealing the confidences of their husbands. This, of course, reflects the greater involvement of men in serious criminality. As women have been "catching up" in this sphere in recent years, one finds more occasions in which a husband's testimony is precluded by claims of privilege.

[77] 568 F.2d 531 (7th Cir. 1977), *cert. denied*, 439 U.S. 820 (1978) ("The essential reason for the privilege against adverse spousal testimony is to foster family peace and harmony, for the benefit of husband, wife, children, and the public. . . . The Ryans, who were married for about 40 years, realistically do not contend that recognition of the marital privilege would have been necessary to protect their marriage").

strong that allowing one spouse to testify against the other would not destroy it. While few courts would follow this precedent, it illustrates nicely the different implications of the instrumental and noninstrumental cases for the privilege. From the latter perspective, a strong, loving marriage of forty years is the paradigmatic case for the application of the privilege and not a reason to abrogate it. *Ryan* also illustrates how lawyers need to know the policy behind evidence rules. In *Ryan*, a lawyer successfully turned a rule on its head by arguing policy rather than precedent. The fact that the court's decision contradicts long-standing precedent (and other cogent policy arguments) should not detract from our admiration of the lawyer's creative argument.

The instrumental perspective also profoundly influenced the drafters of the Federal Rules. The proposed rules on privileges contain a marital privilege, PFRE 505, for adverse testimony, but none for confidential communications. The Advisory Committee's note to PFRE 505 argues that the marital communications privilege, unlike the adverse testimony privilege, cannot be justified by the goals of preventing "marital dissension" or avoiding "the repugnancy of requiring a person to condemn or be condemned by his spouse;" nor, the drafters tell us, "can it be assumed that marital conduct will be affected by a privilege for confidential communications of whose existence the parties in all likelihood are unaware."

The Advisory Committee's decision surprised most observers. They would have predicted that if the drafters discarded one of the marital privileges, it would have been the one preventing adverse testimony. The case for the marital communications privilege seemed stronger, not only because more states had a privilege for confidential communications than had an adverse testimony privilege, but also because many view the adverse testimony privilege as a holdover from the common law's discredited bar on testimony by interested parties. The marital communications privilege, on the other hand, resembles a number of widely accepted confidential communications privileges. A countervailing consideration that possibly determined the fate of the two privileges is that less than two decades before the drafters began their work, the Supreme Court had specifically affirmed the adverse testimony privilege.[78] Thus the drafters may have wanted to abolish both privileges but felt constrained to allow the one that the Supreme Court had recognized.

C. THE ADVERSE TESTIMONY PRIVILEGE

The proposed federal privilege for adverse testimony, PFRE 505, was called in the suggested rules the "Husband-Wife Privilege." It reads as follows:

---

[78] Hawkins v. United States, 358 U.S. 74 (1958).

HUSBAND-WIFE PRIVILEGE

(a) *General rule of privilege.* An accused in a criminal proceeding has a privilege to prevent his spouse from testifying against him.

(b) *Who may claim the privilege.* The privilege may be claimed by the accused or by the spouse on his behalf. The authority of the spouse to do so is presumed in the absence of evidence to the contrary.

(c) *Exceptions.* There is no privilege under this rule (1) in proceedings in which one spouse is charged with a crime against the person or property of the other or of the child of either, or with a crime against the person or property of a third person committed in the course of committing a crime against the other, or (2) as to matters occurring prior to the marriage, or (3) in proceedings in which a spouse is charged with importing an alien for prostitution or other immoral purpose in violation of 8 U.S.C. § 1328, with transporting a female in interstate commerce for immoral purposes or other offense in violation of 18 U.S.C. §§ 2421–2424, or with violation of other similar statutes.

The proposed federal rule follows prevailing practice in some respects and is more restrictive in others. As in most states, it applies only to criminal cases, and the right to claim the privilege rests upon the existence of a valid marriage. The courts take a strict view of what constitutes a valid marriage for purposes of the privilege. Although the court will recognize common law marriages if valid under the relevant state's law, other marriages possibly valid under state law will in some courts not suffice. Thus if a foreigner has married a citizen solely to gain admission to this country, many courts would call the marriage a "sham" and no privilege would attach. More controversially, many courts withhold the privilege if the marriage seems to be "on the rocks." The instrumental rationale provides forceful justification: if a marriage is already on the rocks, there is nothing for the privilege to preserve. Moreover, noninstrumental reasons for the privilege lose their force as well. This makes sense as long as the marriage is truly in trouble, as when a legal separation exists. Some courts only abrogate the privilege in these circumstances. Other courts, however, will probe the marriage more closely, sometimes denying the privilege if the marriage appears in difficulty, even if the parties have not yet decided to separate. The federal courts have, on the whole, more aggressively probed the quality of marriages than have state courts.

Section (b) of the proposed federal rule—which makes the defendant spouse the holder of the privilege—now states the law in only a minority of jurisdictions. Most states and the federal courts now vest the privilege solely in the testifying spouse. The Supreme Court changed federal law in the case of *Trammel v. United States*.[79] *Trammel* overruled *Hawkins v. United States*,[80] which had reaffirmed the traditional rule that the privilege vests in the defendant spouse and so only he may waive the privilege. Instrumental thinking motivated the court's opinion in *Trammel*. Chief Justice Burger first noted the scope of the adverse testimony privilege:

> No other testimonial privilege sweeps so broadly. The privileges between priest and penitent, attorney and client, and physician and patient limit protection to private communications.
>
> . . .
>
> The *Hawkins* rule stands in marked contrast to these three privileges. Its protection is not limited to confidential communications; rather it permits an accused to exclude all adverse spousal testimony.

The Chief Justice then noted that the ancient foundations for the privilege, rooted in the presumed unity of husband and wife and the wife's implied subservience, had disappeared. He continued:

> The contemporary justification for affording an accused such a privilege is also unpersuasive. When one spouse is willing to testify against the other in a criminal proceeding—whatever the motivation—their relationship is almost certainly in disrepair; there is probably little in the way of marital harmony for the privilege to preserve. In these circumstances, a rule of evidence that permits an accused to prevent adverse spousal testimony seems far more likely to frustrate justice than to foster family peace.

The problem with the Chief Justice's analysis is that in *Trammel*, as in *Hawkins,* it is not clear that the wife's willingness to waive the privilege was voluntary. In *Trammel* the inducement to testify was an attractive plea bargain that Mrs. Trammel could avail herself of only if she agreed to testify against her husband. In *Hawkins* the wife had been held in jail as a material witness and told her release was contingent on her willingness to testify against her husband. Thus vesting the privilege in the witness-spouse gives the state an incentive to pressure spouses to testify, making the state a moving force in breaking up marriages.[81] Some courts, in an effort to remove this incentive, have considered the voluntariness of waivers.

One can argue that *Trammel* implies courts should no longer concern themselves with the viability of marriages when a party invokes the privilege. If the marriage is not viable, the witness-spouse should willingly waive the

---

[79] 445 U.S. 40 (1980).

[80] 358 U.S. 74 (1958).

[81] See generally Richard Lempert, *A Right to Every Woman's Evidence*, 66 Iowa L. Rev. 725, 734 (1981).

privilege.   *Trammel* also implicitly rejected the idea that the adverse testimony privilege should be denied spouses who have cooperated in a criminal enterprise. The lower court's decision had rested on this proposition, and the Supreme Court had been asked to affirm a "criminal partner" exception to this privilege.

The adverse testimony privilege endures only as long as the marriage endures, ending with annulment or divorce. Obviously it serves no purpose after death. The exception in the proposed federal rule for crimes committed by one spouse against the other or against the children of either is also standard. The extension to crimes committed jointly against a third party and the spouse codifies an accepted judicial gloss. Some states specifically deny the privilege when crimes against the marriage, such as bigamy or adultery, are charged. Had PFRE 505 been enacted, the federal courts would, no doubt, have treated such crimes as crimes against the spouse.[82] The drafters of the proposed rule cut back on the common law protection by not extending the privilege's protection to matters occurring before the marriage. This contradicts the rationale of the privilege, for the values it protects do not turn on whether the witness is asked to testify to events that occurred before or after her marriage. The change was motivated to prevent people from marrying to seal the lips of a witness. Although the PFRE does not follow the common law in this respect, some courts, particularly federal courts, will increasingly consider whether marriages were contracted to suppress testimony, and if so, deny the privilege, at least as to events occurring before the marriage. The last portion of PFRE 505, section (c)(3), reflects both Congress's decision to withdraw the privilege in any action involving the importation of aliens for immoral purposes and the Advisory Committee's extension of this policy to arguably analogous statutes. Federal courts follow the proposed rule in this regard.

D. THE PRIVILEGE FOR CONFIDENTIAL MARITAL COMMUNICATIONS

The marital communications privilege is mentioned with approval in *Trammel*, and is recognized under FRE 501 in all federal courts. Since no privilege was included in the Proposed Federal Rules, we turn to the California Evidence Code for an example:

CALIFORNIA EVIDENCE CODE

ARTICLE 5. PRIVILEGE FOR CONFIDENTIAL MARITAL COMMUNICATIONS

§ 980. Privilege for confidential martial communications

---

[82]   See, e.g., State v. Chrismore, 223 Iowa 957, 274 N.W. 3 (1937).

Subject to Section 912[83] and except as otherwise provided in this article, a spouse (or his guardian or conservator when he has a guardian or conservator), whether or not a party, has a privilege during the marital relationship and afterwards to refuse to disclose, and to prevent another from disclosing, a communication if he claims the privilege and the communication was made in confidence between him and the other spouse while they were husband and wife.

§ 981. Exception—Crime or fraud

There is no privilege under this article if the communication was made, in whole or in part, to enable or aid anyone to commit or plan to commit a crime or a fraud.

§ 982. Exception—Commitment or similar proceeding

There is no privilege under this article in a proceeding to commit either spouse or otherwise place him or his property, or both, under the control of another because of his alleged mental or physical condition.

§ 983. Exception—Proceeding to establish competence

There is no privilege under this article in a proceeding brought by or on behalf of either spouse to establish his competence.

§ 984. Exception—Proceeding between spouses

There is no privilege under this article in:

(a) A proceeding brought by or on behalf of one spouse against the other spouse.

(b) A proceeding between a surviving spouse and a person who claims through the deceased spouse, regardless of whether such claim is by testate or intestate succession or by inter vivos transaction.

§ 985. Exception—Certain criminal proceedings

There is no privilege under this article in a criminal proceeding in which one spouse is charged with:

(a) A crime committed at any time against the person or property of the other spouse or of a child of either.

(b) A crime committed at any time against the person or property of a third person committed in the course of committing a crime against the person or property of the other spouse.

(c) Bigamy.

---

[83] Section 912 relates to the waiver through disclosure of California's confidential communications privileges.

(d) A crime defined by Section 270 or 270a[84] of the Penal Code.

§ 986. Exception—Juvenile court proceedings

There is no privilege under this article in a proceeding under the Juvenile Court Law. . . .

§ 987. Exception—Communication offered by spouse who is criminal defendant

There is no privilege under this article in a criminal proceeding in which the communication is offered in evidence by a defendant who is one of the spouses between whom the communication was made.

As with the physician-patient privilege, California has created numerous exceptions to the privilege for confidential marital communications, not all of which exist in every jurisdiction. Because states differ in the contours of their privileges, in dealing with privilege issues you must refer to the law of the jurisdiction in which you practice. Indeed, even in federal practice you will find inconsistencies in privilege law between circuits, and within circuits; different district courts might reach different rulings on similar claims. Nevertheless, the same basic principles characterize the application of privileges in most courts. We shall highlight these in our discussion of the marital communications privilege, while pointing out the most important variations that exist. In doing so, we shall contrast the marital communications privilege with the adverse testimony privilege.

E. ADVERSE TESTIMONY AND MARITAL COMMUNICATIONS PRIVILEGES COMPARED

The adverse testimony and marital communications privileges differ in scope. In one important way the adverse testimony privilege is broader. It bars any testimony from one spouse that tends to harm the other. In most courts, it does not matter how or when the witness-spouse acquired her knowledge. Ordinarily the adverse testimony privilege means the prosecutor cannot place the witness-spouse on the stand. *The confidential communications privilege protects only communications by one spouse to another made in confidence during the marriage.* If a witness has other relevant information, the privilege poses no bar to her testimony.

In other respects the marital communications privilege is the broader of the two. The communicating spouse holds it, and, unlike the adverse testimony privilege, in most jurisdictions the witness-spouse may not waive it. It applies in all litigation settings, including cases in which the privilege holder is not a party. Most states, you will recall, confine the adverse testimony

---

[84] Sections 270 and 270a of the California Penal Code deal with child neglect and failure to support a spouse, respectively.

privilege to criminal cases, and a non-party spouse can seldom claim the privilege since he is unlikely to be hurt by his spouse's testimony against a third party. The adverse testimony privilege ends when the marriage ends, while the confidential communications privilege endures dissolution by divorce, and in some jurisdictions survives the death of the communicating spouse. This difference reflects the difference in the instrumental rationales for the two rules, though a noninstrumental argument can be made for it as well.[85] Finally the confidential communications privilege is more widespread. Virtually every American jurisdiction has one, but about a third of the states do not recognize the privilege for adverse testimony.

In some respects exceptions to the two privileges are similar, while in others they differ. The exception in Cal. Evid. Code § 985 for crimes against the spouse or children of either spouse applies to both privileges, although many jurisdictions, unlike California, do not extend this exception in the case of either privilege to crimes against a spouse's property. Also, a number of child abuse and related laws specifically abrogate both privileges. One must be careful not to miss such separate statutory exceptions, for the evidence codes do not contain them.

The exception in Cal. Evid. Code § 987 that allows a criminal defendant to defeat a spouse's claim of confidentiality and demand she testify needs no explicit counterpart in the adverse testimony privilege even when the witness-spouse is the privilege holder. If the defendant desires a spouse's testimony, it is presumably not adverse.

The exception for communications made to further a crime or fraud has been added to most modern codifications of the marital communications privilege. This reflects not just a judgment about what marital communication we seek to foster but also the influence of similar exceptions in the attorney-client, physician-patient, and other privileges for confidential communications. Some courts have pushed this exception beyond its arguably intended limits by charging spouses as accessories after the fact for keeping their partner's criminal involvement secret, although others have resisted this urge. When, however, one spouse actively aids the other to avoid justice—as when a wife, following her incarcerated husband's directions bribes a witness—the privilege will not protect communications relating to that misconduct.

There is no counterpart to this exception in the adverse testimony privilege, although a few courts have held that neither spouse can claim the privilege when they are partners in crime. These courts apparently feel a marriage of

---

[85] If a communication has been made in privacy because of the trust a marital relation engenders, it dishonors legitimate privacy expectations to reveal the communication simply because the trusting relationship that engendered the communication has now changed. There appears to be no comparable noninstrumental argument for maintaining the adverse testimony privilege after divorce. The fact that an ex-spouse is the instrument of her former partner's conviction undermines no obvious social values as long as her testimony does not reveal confidences entrusted to her during the marriage.

criminals is a criminal marriage, hence not worthy of preservation. The Supreme Court was invited to take this position in *Trammel*, but instead took the less drastic step of vesting the privilege in the witness-spouse.

The California exceptions for commitment, competence, and juvenile proceedings have no counterparts in the adverse testimony privilege, because the privilege seldom applies in these settings.

Some problems arise under the marital communications privilege that the adverse testimony privilege does not raise. For example, questions arise about what is confidential and what is a communication. Ordinarily the presence of a third party, even the couple's child, destroys the confidentiality that is a precondition for privileged marital communications. Courts commonly make exceptions, however, for children too young to understand what their parents are talking about and, presumably, the same rule would apply in the case of a senile parent.

At common law, eavesdroppers could testify to marital discussions they overheard unless they had been eavesdropping with the connivance of the spouse. With the plethora of sophisticated bugging devices available today, the rule regarding eavesdropping has changed for this as for other communications privileges, and eavesdroppers are generally forbidden from testifying if the communicants themselves could not testify. However, if a conversation between spouses is overheard by a person near them, courts often hold that the privilege never attached because the circumstances of the communication suggest that the spouses had no concern for confidentiality. Occasionally courts take this rationale to an unjustified extreme, as when one court allowed disclosure of a whispered conversation between spouses that a prison guard, who by prison rules had to be present, was able to hear.[86]

Communications include not only statements made by one spouse to the other, but also acts—such as pointing and nods of the head—that are intended to substitute for statements. Some argue they should also include acts done by one spouse in front of the other that would not be done but for the privacy of and trust engendered by the marital relationship. The classic example is when one spouse displays loot acquired in a crime to the other. Courts have gone both ways on whether this type of conduct is a protected communication. Some court decisions even apply the privilege when one spouse unexpectedly discovers information the other was trying to keep hidden. But the vast majority of courts would not find a communication in these circumstances.

Problem VIII-41. Peter Polk comes home one evening at 6 p.m. He empties a bag containing three rings, five watches and sixteen wallets

---

[86] See People v. Von Villas, 11 Cal. App. 4th 175, 15 Cal. Rptr. 2d 112 (1992).

onto the living room table. Sally Polk comes in, points to the pile and asks him where it came from. Peter responds, "These are the profits Wilkins and I made working the East end." **If Peter is tried for theft, may he or his wife claim a privilege to prevent his wife from testifying to what she saw or heard? If he is sued in tort for conversion by the owner of one of the watches, may he or his wife claim a privilege to prevent his wife from testifying to what she saw or heard? If Wilkins is tried alone for theft, may Peter or his wife claim a privilege to prevent his wife from testifying against Wilkins? If Peter refuses to claim a privilege, may Wilkins do so? Might he do so if Peter is in prison in a distant state?**

F. THE PARENT-CHILD PRIVILEGE

An argument sometimes made against the marital privileges is that no privilege protects the equally sacred relationship of parent-child. This is taken to suggest that privileges for intimate relationships are neither necessary nor desirable.[87] The argument, however, can be turned around. One might claim that the existence of the marital privileges argues for a parent-child privilege since it is hard to say which relationship is more precious or should be more sedulously fostered. Three states, Minnesota and Idaho by statute and New York by court decision, have allowed a parent-child privilege, although the codifiers in Minnesota and Idaho limit the privilege to communications from children to parents. Louisiana has a parent-child privilege of longer standing, rooted in its civil law tradition. At least two federal district courts have also allowed claims of parent-child privilege.[88] But it is misleading to emphasize the positive. Almost all states and virtually all federal courts, including all federal circuit courts of appeal that have considered the parent-child privilege, have declined to create this new protection. For this reason we shall say no more about this privilege but leave it to you to learn its dimensions if you practice in one of the few jurisdictions that recognize it. You should be able to see how arguments used to justify or criticize the marital privileges may be adapted to argue for or against a parent-child privilege, should an occasion for arguing the issue ever arise.

---

[87] The lack of a parent-child privilege may also reflect a historic reluctance by prosecutors to set parents against children, and vice versa, if the parent or child was unwilling to testify. Whatever the historical circumstances, recent years have seen increased efforts to coerce the testimony of parents against children and vice versa, a result perhaps of the same "war on crime" mentality that has led prosecutors to call attorneys before grand juries in order to acquire nonprivileged information about their clients. See the text supra, at note 27. Thus, the absence of a privilege preventing the acquisition of particular evidence may not mean there is no justification for the proposed privilege. Quite the contrary, the absence of a privilege may mean the noninstrumental case for the privilege is so strong that, until recently, widely shared norms of decency kept lawyers from seeking certain kinds of information from an opponent's close relatives unless they were willing to testify.

[88] In re Grand Jury Proceedings Witness (Agosto), 553 F. Supp. 1298 (D. Nev. 1983); In re Grand Jury Proceedings (Greenberg), 11 Fed. R. Evid. Serv. 579 (D. Conn. 1982).

Problem VIII-42. Joe and Alice Mineo are charged with the possession and sale of marijuana. They each face ten years in prison if convicted. The prosecutor wants to call their ten year old son, Fabian, to testify that they grew marijuana plants under lights in their basement; that people who were strangers to him came to buy marijuana seedlings from his parents; and that on weekends they regularly smoked marijuana with their friends. The defense counsel argues that the court should recognize a parent-child privilege and bar Fabian from testifying or, at least, tell him he does not have to testify if he doesn't want to. The prosecutor argues that there is no such privilege at common law and that Fabian's testimony is necessary for a conviction because someone apparently tipped off the Mineos about the police raid, and only dahlias were growing under the basement lights when they arrived. **Should the court recognize a parent-child privilege? If so, should the defendant or witness hold it? Would your answer be the same if Fabian were 16 years old? 30 years old? Would you apply a privilege if the Mineos had been charged with murder, and Fabian had allegedly seen them with the victim's ring, watch and wallet in their possession? If a privilege is created, should it apply in civil as well as criminal cases?**

"And, because a princess can't be forced to testify against her prince, they lived happily ever after."

V.   GOVERNMENT PRIVILEGES

Usually the government, in its role as prosecutor, is fighting the application or extension of privileges.   Courts, despite their formal independence from the executive, are a branch of government; so it is perhaps not surprising that they are often receptive to the state's arguments. If you peruse the case reporters, you will time and again find that "privileges are to be strictly construed," and you will encounter more than a few cases like *Trammel* that break from past law to create new ways around privileges, as well as cases that find exceptions on ad hoc bases that seem to turn privilege law on end.   The *Ryan* case, which refused to apply the adverse testimony privilege to a forty-year-old marriage because it was too strong to be destroyed by the wife's testimony, is a good example of judicial hostility to privilege claims.[89]

There are, however, some privileges only the government can claim. These include the state secrets privilege, official-information privilege, executive privilege, legislative privilege and the informer's identity privilege. Here, courts often seem not nearly so reluctant to honor claims of privilege or to broaden the protection they extend.   The following sections focus on the state secrets privilege, the official-information privilege, and the informer's identity privilege, but we begin with a brief introductory word about the others.

Executive privilege, which protects the deliberations and opinions of the President and his closest advisers, is almost exclusively asserted in contests between the President and Congress. The court cases it figures in may, however, be among the politically most important cases of a generation.[90]   President Bill Clinton tried to assert this privilege in a variety of contexts to prevent his advisors and protectors from being called before the grand jury investigating his relationship with Monica Lewinsky. What emerged from President Clinton's efforts to secure an expansive reading of executive privilege is what President Nixon discovered a generation before.   The courts are reluctant to allow a President to use claims of executive privilege to shield himself from an ongoing criminal investigation.   The case contexts in which claims of executive privilege are made are, however, so political that one can imagine that a future Supreme Court, more politically aligned with a politically strong President, might be more hospitable to claims of executive privilege than recent Courts have been. We may never know if this somewhat cynical view of politics and privilege is justified, for claims of executive privilege before grand juries or in court trials are rare. It is likely that few readers of this book will ever argue over this privilege in court, and for this reason we leave it to newspaper headlines.

---

[89]   Supra, note 77.

[90]   See United States v. Nixon, 418 U.S. 683 (1974).

The *legislative privilege* is rooted in the speech and debate clause of the Constitution. That clause gives legislators freedom to speak their minds on the floor of Congress without fear that they will have to answer in court for what they say. The clause can work as a true privilege—meaning that courts can rely on it to keep matters out of evidence—but more often it works as a substantive rule, protecting legislators from liability for official statements and actions without regard to the admissibility of evidence. This is another privilege that few readers of this book can expect to encounter.

A. STATE SECRETS PRIVILEGE

Proposed Federal Rule of Evidence 509 attempted to codify two of the three governmental privileges we shall discuss—the state secrets privilege and the privilege for official information. Perhaps no part of the federal evidence code was more controversial than this rule, and irreconcilable disputes over its bounds may have been the most important reason why Congress eventually decided to give up entirely on codifying privilege law. The controversy over PFRE 509 arose in part because the Justice Department successfully lobbied the drafters to broaden considerably the original draft privilege for state secrets and to add a privilege for official information that the drafters had originally not thought necessary.

At another time these changes might have coincided with a legislative interest in strengthening the state's position in litigation. But PFRE 509 was sent to a Congress that was just beginning to unravel the Watergate scandal and was acutely aware from the then recent Pentagon Papers case that an executive might claim the state secrets privilege to protect politically sensitive material that did not endanger national security.[91]

PFRE 509 reads as follows:

(a) *Definitions.*

(1) *Secret of state.* A "secret of state" is a governmental secret relating to the national defense or the international relations of the United States.

(2) *Official information.* "Official information" is information within the custody or control of a department or agency of the government the disclosure of which is shown to be contrary to the

---

[91] The Pentagon Papers contained a highly classified Pentagon study detailing the history of the United States' involvement in the Vietnam War. Daniel Ellsberg, who had access to the papers and later turned against the war, gave them to the *New York Times*, which published them despite efforts by the government to prevent publication. Early news stories about their release suggested that many state secrets had been compromised, but it later became clear that despite initial government claims, the Papers revealed almost nothing that affected national security, although there was much in them that raised questions about decisions made in the course of escalating the Vietnam War.

public interest and which consists of: (A) intragovernmental opinions or recommendations submitted for consideration in the performance of decisional or policymaking functions, or (B) subject to the provisions of 18 U.S.C. § 3500; [the Jencks Act] investigatory files compiled for law enforcement purposes and not otherwise available, or (C) information within the custody or control of a governmental department or agency whether initiated within the department or agency or acquired by it in its exercise of its official responsibilities and not otherwise available to the public pursuant to 5 U.S.C. § 522. [The Freedom of Information Act]

(b) *General rule of privilege.* The government has a privilege to refuse to give evidence and to prevent any person from giving evidence upon a showing of reasonable likelihood of danger that the evidence will disclose a secret of state or official information, as defined in this rule.

(c) *Procedures.* The privilege for secrets of state may be claimed only by the chief officer of the government agency or department administering the subject matter which the secret information sought concerns, but the privilege for official information may be asserted by an attorney representing the government. The required showing may be made in whole or in part in the form of a written statement. The judge may hear the matter in chambers, but all counsel are entitled to inspect the claim and showing and to be heard thereon, except that, in the case of secrets of state, the judge upon motion of the government, may permit the government to make the required showing in the above form *in camera.* If the judge sustains the privilege upon a showing *in camera*, the entire text of the government's statements shall be sealed and preserved in the court's records in the event of appeal. In the case of the privilege claimed for official information the court may require examination *in camera* of the information itself. The judge may take any protective measure which the interests of the government and the furtherance of justice may require.

(d) *Notice to government.* If the circumstances of the case indicate a substantial possibility that a claim of privilege would be appropriate but has not been made because of oversight or lack of knowledge, the judge shall give or cause notice to be given to the officer entitled to claim the privilege and shall stay further proceedings a reasonable time to afford opportunity to assert a claim of privilege.

(e) *Effect of sustaining claim.* If a claim of privilege is sustained in a proceeding to which the government is a party and it appears that another party is thereby deprived of material evidence, the judge shall make any further orders which the interests of justice require, including striking the testimony of a witness, declaring a mistrial, finding against the government upon an issue as to which the evidence is relevant, or dismissing the action.

PFRE 509 codifies two privileges: the privilege for state secrets, which is our current concern, and a privilege for official information, which we shall discuss shortly. Supporters of PFRE 509 argued that its state secrets privilege simply codified the law of the leading Supreme Court case defining the privilege, *United States v. Reynolds*.[92] Opponents of the proposed rule agreed it should do this, but they argued that it did more. With Congress's refusal to enact PFRE 509, *Reynolds* is still the place to begin a study of the privilege.

UNITED STATES V. REYNOLDS
345 U.S. 1 (1953).

MR. CHIEF JUSTICE VINSON delivered the opinion of the Court.

These suits under the Tort Claims Act arise from the death of three civilians in the crash of a B-29 aircraft at Waycross, Georgia, on October 6, 1948. Because an important question of the Government's privilege to resist discovery is involved, we granted certiorari.

The aircraft had taken flight for the purpose of testing secret electronic equipment, with four civilian observers aboard. While aloft, fire broke out in one of the bomber's engines. Six of the nine crew members and three of the four civilian observers were killed in the crash.

The widows of the three deceased civilian observers brought consolidated suits against the United States. In the pretrial stages the plaintiffs moved, under Rule 34 of the Federal Rules of Civil Procedure, for production of the Air Force's official accident investigation report and the statements of the three surviving crew members . . . [The government claimed privilege and the Secretary of the Air Force filed a formal claim that disclosure would not be in the public interest. The government did offer, however, to produce the survivors for plaintiffs' examination and said witnesses would be allowed to refresh their memories from any statement made by them to the Air Force, and authorized to testify as to all matters except those of a "classified nature."]

The District Court ordered the Government to produce the documents in order that the court might determine whether they contained privileged matter. The Government declined, so the court entered an order, under Rule 37(b)(2)(I), that the facts on the issue of negligence would be taken as established in plaintiffs' favor. After a hearing to determine damages, final judgment was entered for the plaintiffs. The Court of Appeals affirmed both as to the showing of good

---

[92] 345 U.S. 1 (1953).

cause for production of the documents and as to the ultimate disposition of the case as a consequence of the Government's refusal to produce the documents.

We have had broad propositions pressed upon us for decision. On behalf of the Government it has been urged that the executive department heads have power to withhold any documents in their custody from judicial view if they deem it to be in the public interest. Respondents have asserted that the executive's power to withhold documents was waived by the Tort Claims Act. Both positions have constitutional overtones which we find it unnecessary to pass upon, there being a narrower ground for decision.

The Tort Claims Act expressly makes the Federal Rules of Civil Procedure applicable to suits against the United States. The judgment in this case imposed liability upon the Government by operation of Rule 37, for refusal to produce documents under Rule 34. Since Rule 34 compels production only of matters "not privileged," the essential question is whether there was a valid claim of privilege under the Rule. We hold that there was, and that, therefore, the judgment below subjected the United States to liability on terms to which Congress did not consent by the Tort Claims Act.

We think it should be clear that the term "not privileged," as used in Rule 34, refers to "privileges" as that term is understood in the law of evidence. When the Secretary of the Air Force lodged his formal "Claim of Privilege," he attempted therein to invoke the privilege against revealing *military secrets*, a privilege which is well established in the law of evidence. . . .

Judicial experience with the privilege which protects military and state secrets has been limited in this country. . . . Nevertheless, the principles which control the application of the privilege emerge quite clearly from the available precedents. The privilege belongs to the Government and must be asserted by it; it can neither be claimed nor waived by a private party. It is not to be lightly invoked. There must be a formal claim of privilege, lodged by the head of the department which has control over the matter, after actual personal consideration by that officer. The court itself must determine whether the circumstances are appropriate for the claim of privilege, and yet do so without forcing a disclosure of the very thing the privilege is designed to protect. The latter requirement is the only one which presents real difficulty. As to it, we find it helpful to draw upon judicial experience in dealing with an analogous privilege, the privilege against self-incrimination.

The privilege against self-incrimination presented the courts with a similar sort of problem. Too much judicial inquiry into the claim of privilege would force disclosure of the thing the privilege was meant to protect, while a complete abandonment of judicial control would lead to intolerable abuses. Indeed, in the earlier stages of judicial experience with the problem, both extremes were advocated, some saying that the bare assertion by the witness must be taken as conclusive, and others saying that the witness should be required to reveal the matter behind his claim of privilege to the judge for verification. Neither extreme prevailed, and a sound formula of compromise was developed. . . . There are differences in phraseology, but in substance it is agreed that the court must be satisfied from all the evidence and circumstances, and "from the implications of the question, in the setting in which it is asked, that a responsive answer to the question or an explanation of why it cannot be answered might be dangerous because injurious disclosure could result." If the court is so satisfied, the claim of the privilege will be accepted without requiring further disclosure.

Regardless of how it is articulated, some like formula of compromise must be applied here. Judicial control over the evidence in a case cannot be abdicated to the caprice of executive officers. Yet we will not go so far as to say that the court may automatically require a complete disclosure to the judge before the claim of privilege will be accepted in any case. It may be possible to satisfy the court, from all the circumstances of the case, that there is a reasonable danger that compulsion of the evidence will expose military matters which, *in the interest of national security*, should not be divulged. When this is the case, the occasion for the privilege is appropriate, and the court should not jeopardize the security which the privilege is meant to protect by insisting upon an examination of the evidence, even by the judge alone, in chambers.

In the instant case we cannot escape judicial notice that this is a time of vigorous preparation for national defense. Experience in the past war has made it common knowledge that air power is one of the most potent weapons in our scheme of defense, and that newly developing electronic devices have greatly enhanced the effective use of air power. It is equally apparent that these electronic devices must be kept secret if their full military advantage is to be exploited in the national interests. On the record before the trial court it appeared that this accident occurred to a military plane which had gone aloft to test secret electronic equipment. Certainly there was a reasonable danger that the accident investigation report would contain references to the secret electronic equipment which was the primary concern of the mission.

Of course, even with this information before him, the trial judge was in no position to decide that the report was privileged until there had been a formal claim of privilege. Thus it was entirely proper to rule initially that petitioner had shown probable cause for discovery of the documents. Thereafter, when the formal claim of privilege was filed by the Secretary of the Air Force, under circumstance indicating a reasonable possibility that military secrets were involved, there was certainly a sufficient showing of privilege to cut off further demand for the documents on the showing of necessity for its compulsion that had then been made.

In each case, the showing of necessity which is made will determine how far the court should probe in satisfying itself that the occasion for invoking the privilege is appropriate. Where there is a strong showing of necessity, the claim of privilege should not be lightly accepted, but even the most compelling necessity cannot overcome the claim of privilege if the court is ultimately satisfied that military secrets are at stake. A *fortiori*, where necessity is dubious, a formal claim of privilege, made under the circumstances of this case, will have to prevail. Here, necessity was greatly minimized by an available alternative, which might have given respondents the evidence to make out their case without forcing a showdown on the claim of privilege. By their failure to pursue that alternative, respondents have posed the privilege question for decision with the formal claim of privilege set against a dubious showing of necessity.

There is nothing to suggest that the electronic equipment, in this case, had any causal connection with the accident. Therefore, it should be possible for respondents to adduce the essential facts as to causation without resort to material touching upon military secrets. Respondents were given a reasonable opportunity to do just that, when petitioner formally offered to make the surviving crew members available for examination. We think that offer should have been accepted.

Respondents have cited us to those cases in the criminal field, where it has been held that the Government can invoke its evidentiary privileges only at the price of letting the defendant go free. The rationale of the criminal cases is that, since the Government which prosecutes an accused also has the duty to see that justice is done, it is unconscionable to allow it to undertake prosecution and then invoke its governmental privileges to deprive the accused of anything that might be material to his defense. Such rationale has no application in a civil forum where the Government is not the moving party, but is a defendant only on terms to which it has consented.

The decision of the Court of Appeals is reversed and the case will be remanded to the District Court for further proceedings consistent with the views expressed in this opinion.

Reversed and remanded.

(Justices Black, Frankfurter and Jackson dissented.)

———————

Contrasting *Reynolds* with PFRE 509, we can see some of the differences that troubled members of Congress. *Reynolds* speaks only of military secrets while the proposed rule protects governmental secrets relating to the national defense or international relations. In this respect, *Reynolds* is narrower than the traditional privilege, and the proposed rule appears broader. The state secrets privilege traditionally applies to military or national defense secrets, such as the movement of troops or how to make an atom bomb, and to diplomatic secrets, such as the country's fallback position in delicate international negotiations. In speaking of secrets relating to international relations, the proposed rule uses language that may extend far beyond traditional notions of what must be kept secret for effective diplomacy, since the country's international relations may involve commercial trade, immigration, international environmental cooperation and the like. The volume of information that may "relate to" such issues is immense. Courts applying the state secrets privilege, however, ordinarily take a relatively strict view of what kinds of diplomatic secrets are protected.

Reynolds does not protect all military matters, but only those "which, in the interest of national security, should not be divulged." PFRE 509 is a poor guide to the state of the law because nothing about the definition of state secrets limits the rule's protection to information that, if released, would harm the United States. Read literally, for example, the rule might protect information about the number of potential job losses if an air base in a particular state shut down. This information clearly relates to the national defense, but its disclosure does not threaten national security. As such, it would not be protected under *Reynolds*, although it appears protected by the proposed rule.

Under both the proposed federal rule and *Reynolds*, the state secrets privilege is an absolute privilege. If it applies, no showing of need by the adversary will overcome it. In this respect, it is like the attorney-client and marital privileges. But in many ways it goes beyond other privileges we have encountered. The state secrets privilege is not riddled with exceptions. It protects not just communications but all information. The government can claim the privilege even when the information, in a sense, belongs to another. Thus, a scientist in litigation against either the government or a third party might be denied access to a report she herself has written if the report embodies state secrets. Indeed, one case privileged facts already widely known, sustaining the government's claim that an official affirmation of what everybody knew would harm the country's foreign relations.[93]

Because of the breadth of the state secrets privilege, special procedures must be followed to invoke it. First, under *Reynolds*, "[T]here must be a formal claim of privilege, lodged by the head of the department which has control over the matter, after actual personal consideration by

---

[93] Afshar v. Department of State, 702 F.2d 1125 (D.C. Cir. 1983).

that officer."[94] The requirement that the head of the relevant department (or agency) claim the privilege is preserved in PFRE 509, but *Reynolds*'s equally explicit language requiring personal consideration by the department head has been dropped. This appears to be a substantial change, for the personal consideration requirement is seen as a major guarantee that the state will not lightly or inappropriately invoke the privilege. In practice, however, "personal consideration" as required by *Reynolds* can mean almost anything, including rubber stamp approval of decisions made by others. The court will take the department head's word that the matter has been considered.

Reynolds recognizes that secrecy regarding some military matters may be so important that even the judge should not learn of them. The case also holds that in deciding how deeply to probe a privilege claim, a court should consider the opponent's need for the evidence. If this need is slight, as it arguably was in *Reynolds*, and if the appropriate official lodges what seems like a facially reasonable claim, no further judicial probing is required. PFRE 509 is less clear than *Reynolds* on the implications of litigant need and the appropriate extent of judicial probing. Federal courts today commonly hear state secrets privilege claims *in camera*, and sometimes *ex parte*, with only the government's attorney present. To sustain the privilege in an *in camera* or *ex parte* hearing, the government attorney need not necessarily reveal the secret information; she must only convince the judge that the information sought qualifies for the privilege. This is commonly done through an affidavit from the department head. Parties also occasionally use *ex parte* hearings to redact secret material from documents, so that the other party can acquire a portion of the information sought.

These procedures appear to give considerable discretion to the trial judges to probe claims of privilege and to reject those claims that do not seem adequately supported. However, for understandable reasons courts are reluctant to question the state secrets claims made by such agencies as the State Department, the Defense Department, and the CIA. If information is highly classified, and an executive department head asserts the need for continued secrecy, it is the rare judge who has the temerity to challenge the government's position. Thus, while most courts claim the authority to evaluate state secret claims, they rarely dispute the government's assertions. In some cases, courts have barred parties who knew military secrets from bringing claims because they accepted the government's argument that during the course of testifying a witness might inadvertently disclose confidential information.[95]

---

[94]   *Reynolds*, 345 U.S. at 12 (footnote omitted).

[95]   Farnsworth Cannon, Inc. v. Grimes, 635 F.2d 268 (4th Cir. 1980) (*en banc*); Fitzgerald v. Penthouse Int'l. Ltd., 691 F.2d 666 (4th Cir. 1982), *cert. denied*, 460 U.S. 1024 (1983).

The prospect of extreme judicial deference does not, however, make review of state secrets claims meaningless. The government may assert such claims less aggressively because they must justify them to a judge. Further, redaction of secret information is sometimes possible, making much of an otherwise secret document available to a party. Moreover, the need a party shows for the evidence not only affects the depth of the hearing, but it also relates to whether the state must pay a price if its privilege claim is sustained. This last possibility is unusual since valid privilege claims are supposed to be without cost, but the government is an unusual litigant. *Reynolds* recognizes the possible need for corrective steps to avoid unjust government victories and the possibility that such steps are constitutionally required in criminal cases in which the government claims a privilege to keep secret information that could materially help the defendant's case. *Reynolds* also suggests that corrective sanctions are ordinarily not needed when the government is a civil defendant. Nevertheless, courts occasionally make the government pay a price for a successful privilege claim, even as a civil defendant. They are more likely to make claiming the privilege costly when the state is a civil plaintiff, and they are most likely to do so when the state is prosecuting alleged criminals. Some possible costs of invoking the privilege are mentioned in PFRE 509(e). They range from striking a witness's testimony to dismissing the action. The latter is likely in a criminal case if the assertion of the privilege seriously undercuts a defendant's constitutional right to present a defense.

The costs that can be attached to valid claims of privilege are important not just to doing justice in particular cases, but also because they discourage the government from seeking to conceal privileged information when secrecy is not necessary. It counterbalances the judiciary's timidity in probing executive branch assertions that the state secrets privilege applies. The possibility that courts will sanction the government for valid privilege claims has, however, opened the door to the so-called "graymail" problem. Criminal defendants with access to state secrets seek to construct defenses that make secret information relevant. Their goal is to force the government to choose between prosecuting them and revealing secrets. In response to this problem, Congress in 1980, enacted the Classified Information Procedures Act (CIPA). On its face, CIPA says it does not alter the rules of evidence, but some of its procedures, such as a provision allowing the creation of document summaries as adequate substitutes for secret information, have implications for what may be offered at trial. Some courts have seen CIPA as providing a new privilege for classified information[96] or raising the threshold for relevance determinations.[97] CIPA, however, deals

---

[96] United States v. Yunis, 924 F.2d 1086 (D.C. Cir. 1991).

[97] United Stated v. Rewald, 889 F.2d 836 (9th Cir. 1989), *modified*, 902 F.2d 18 (9th Cir.) *cert. denied*, 498 U.S. 819 (1990).

primarily with pre-trial procedures; and for this reason we alert you to it but do not further discuss it.

Perhaps there is a lesson to be learned from the declassification in 2000 of documents relevant to the *Reynolds* crash. None proved to contain secret information, although they allegedly did substantiate Air Force negligence in not modifying the aircraft's engine to avoid the risk of fire.[98] The government clearly has a need to protect its true secrets, but the government privileges can also be used to shield embarrassing information the public has a right to know and a jury should be able to consider.

Problem VIII-43.

(A) Citizens Against Atomic Destruction (CAAD) sues the Consolidated Electric Company to prevent them from constructing a nuclear power generating station. They allege that the proposed station will be a nuisance because its emergency core cooling system is unsafe. They seek to discover the exact plans for the cooling system. The Atomic Energy Commission (AEC) presents the judge with a request signed by the chairperson of the Commission asking the court to deny discovery on the ground that the exact plans are a "national defense secret." **How should the court rule on this claim of privilege?**

(B) Assume that the government's claim of privilege is granted and the case goes to trial with discovery of the plans denied. At trial CAAD wishes to present the testimony of Leah Lempert, a nuclear engineer who had worked on the cooling system before leaving Consolidated Electric to campaign against the spread of unsafe nuclear power stations. The AEC through its chairperson claims a privilege on the ground of national defense to prevent Lempert from testifying to what she knows about the cooling system in the Consolidated Electric plant. **How should the court rule?** Assume that the judge believes the privilege must be granted because the court cannot in this area override the decision of the AEC concerning what is relevant to the national defense, but the judge also believes the privilege would not have been claimed if the core cooling system were unequivocally safe. **Is there any relief which the judge can grant CAAD consistent with PFRE 509?**

B. OFFICIAL INFORMATION PRIVILEGES

The United States has statutes specifically privileging certain kinds of official information, but it has never had a privilege for official

----

[98] Hampton Stevens, Supreme Court Filing Claims Air Force, Government Fraud in 1953 Case, Inside the Air Force, March 14, 2003, posted at http://www.fas.org/sgp/news/2003/03/iaf 031403.html (Visited August 9, 2010).

information broadly defined. PFRE 509 sought to create one by combining two established privileges with one new one. This effort, like the effort to broaden the state secrets privilege, met with substantial and ultimately fatal opposition from Congress.

The three privileges that make up the PFRE's official-information privilege are the *deliberative process* privilege, the *investigative files* privilege, and a new privilege for material exempt from Freedom of Information Act (FOIA)[99] disclosure. It is the *FOIA-exempt* privilege that expands PFRE 509's protection into a general privilege for official information. Although much official information is available under FOIA and therefore would not be protected by this privilege, nine broad categories of information enjoy FOIA exemptions, including a wide range of records and information compiled for law enforcement purposes, records relating to banking regulation, personnel and medical files in many instances, and records relating solely to the internal rules and practices of an agency.

If the drafters of the Federal Rules of Evidence have any reason to be embarrassed about their judgment in drafting rules of privilege, transforming the FOIA exemptions into an evidentiary privilege for official information is a leading cause. No Wigmore balancing test was applied here, nor are there any obvious non-instrumental reasons to want this privilege. FOIA permits *anybody* to obtain non-exempt information from the government. The FOIA exemptions do express congressional value judgments, but they express judgments about what the merely curious are entitled to learn from their government. Litigants are not merely curious; they need specific information to achieve justice. Congress could have made the FOIA exemptions into privileges had it wanted to; instead it expressed no judgment about litigants' rights to information. The Advisory Committee's invention of a FOIA-exempt privilege is a tribute more to political pressure from the Nixon administration's Justice Department than to reasoned evidentiary analysis.

One might argue, however, that the PFRE 509(a)(2) restriction on disclosing official information to information "the disclosure of which is shown to be contrary to the public interest" means that the FOIA exemptions would seldom have privileged official information that is not already privileged, since courts would have given paramount weight to a public interest in justice. We may never know because despite PFRE 509 the courts, by and large, have not looked to the FOIA exemptions as a source of new privileges.

This does not, however, mean that one can ignore FOIA when governmental privileges are at issue. First, if information is available

---

[99]   5 U.S.C. §§ 551 et seq. (1994).

under FOIA, it will not qualify for a governmental privilege. If everyone in the country can acquire certain governmental information, the courts will not, on official-information grounds, deny it to parties before them. Second, FOIA has exemptions that overlap the deliberative process and investigative files privileges. Since many more cases arise under FOIA than under these privileges, courts frequently look to FOIA precedent in interpreting these privileges—as they also do when other common issues arise, such as what it means for information to be within the custody or control of an agency of the government. Courts that look to FOIA in interpreting these overlapping privileges too often, in our view, blindly follow FOIA precedent, ignoring differences between the interests that FOIA balances and those in litigation.

The deliberative process privilege is usually justified by the need to promote candor and idea sharing among government officials engaged in decision making. As is true of other privileges, reliable empirical evidence has never supported this argument, and there are good reasons to think it unsound. First, the privilege is a qualified one—a litigant who shows sufficient need for the information is entitled to it. Second, a new administration can waive the privilege, perhaps scapegoating those in a prior administration who contributed to the decision. Thus a participant in government decision-making cannot rely on this privilege to ensure the confidentiality of her contribution. Better reasons for the privilege are that it prevents disruption that could be caused by interrupting government decision-making while it is in process, and it avoids the need to deal with the political fallout from discussions that lead to decisions not to act.

According to PFRE 509(a)(2)(A), the deliberative process privilege protects: "intragovernmental opinions or recommendations." Court decisions have added to these two terms words like "reasoning," "suggestions," and "advice." The privilege does not protect factual information the agency possesses, even if the information figures importantly in the decision-making process. Of course, disputes over what is fact and what is opinion are always possible.

The protected information must also be, according to the proposed rule, "submitted for consideration" in a decisional process. Court cases are more terse; they usually say the information must be "predecisional." The decision itself is not protected by the privilege, nor are opinions, recommendations or other information related to a decision but generated after it. Of course, an agency often can argue that opinions and recommendations regarding one decision also relate to the next.

The "investigative files" or "law enforcement" privilege is typically justified both by the need to facilitate the flow of information into governmental files and by the argument that secrecy facilitates ongoing investigations. Most of the case law interpreting the investigative files privilege is based on the overlapping FOIA protection, perhaps because once a criminal case reaches trial, statutory or due process rules often require the production of information in the government's files.[100] PFRE 509 places no time limit on the availability of the privileges. A completed investigation does not vitiate the privilege, although it may bear on the issue of whether the privilege should give way in the face of a litigant's interest. Some courts interpreting the FOIA exemption or the common law privilege have held that it applies to ongoing but not to completed investigations, while other courts take the view of the proposed rule. The requirement in the proposed rule that the report be compiled for "law enforcement purposes" can also be broadly or narrowly defined. But clearly the privilege is not limited to files generated in the course of criminal investigations. The rule will protect files generated by SEC investigations, IRS investigations, and the like, even when the agency aims only at civil sanctions.

The deliberative process privilege and the investigative files privilege have points in common. Both are qualified privileges, meaning that before allowing them a judge should weigh a litigant's need for the information against the interests that the privilege protects. If the former predominates, the privilege should be overridden. This possibility undercuts the most common instrumental arguments for both privileges because it means that those who participate in private deliberations, or provide law enforcement officials with information, can never be certain of the confidentiality of their statements.

PFRE 509(c) provides that the state's attorney can claim both privileges, but the courts have balked at this extension of existing law. Many still require the relevant agency head to claim the privilege, while others will allow a high ranking subordinate to claim the privilege. Personal consideration by the privilege claimant is also expected.

As PFRE 509(c) provides, both privileges, if sustained, can result in protective measures being taken against the government, if the government is a party. Often when a protective measure would be appropriate, the privilege's qualified nature means that it should give way. In a criminal case the government then has the option of revealing the information or dismissing charges, thus mooting all evidentiary issues.

Finally, unlike the state secrets privilege, the deliberative-process and the investigative-files privileges are not limited to the national government. State and local governments can claim the benefits of these privileges, even in federal court.

----

[100] See Wayne R. LaFave, Jerold H. Israel, Nancy J. King, and Orin S. Kerr, Criminal Procedure, 5th ed., § 20.3 (2009).

Problem VIII-44. Nancy Johnson, an attorney with the IRS, sues the agency because she feels she has been discriminated against and denied promotions because of her sex. She seeks copies of those evaluative memoranda which have been prepared regarding her work and the work of all attorneys who joined the IRS within the three years (before and after) surrounding the date she arrived. She also wants a copy of her personnel file and a copy of the files of all attorneys hired in the six year period. The government claims a privilege for official information. **How should the judge rule? If the judge favors the government on the privilege claim, should she give Johnson any relief in lieu of access to the information she seeks?**

C. INFORMER IDENTITY PRIVILEGE

1. Justifications

Informers seldom cut heroic figures. A few witness crimes fortuitously, but the vast majority witness crimes by design, and most are accomplices. Their tale-telling and betrayal may serve good ends, but this does not make their behavior admirable. Moreover, informers are often unsavory characters. They can be criminals who inform for cash, to avoid punishment or to be released early from incarceration. Ideally, the police could enforce the law without using informants other than fortuitous witnesses. But police agencies find informants essential to solving cases, particularly burglaries, and in combating drug offenses and other so-called victimless crimes. The informer identity privilege is designed to keep information from informers flowing. It is a qualified privilege. This means that although the government may prosecute some cases without revealing the identity or whereabouts of its informers, in other cases the government must choose between sacrificing a prosecution or "burning" an informer; that is, revealing the informer's identity.

The informer identity privilege has a two-fold rationale. The first is to protect informers from reprisals. Without protection, fear may deter potential informers from telling what they know. This is sometimes true, but attractive plea bargains or substantial financial rewards can often induce cooperation despite some danger, and in many cases informers' targets are in no position to take revenge on those who tattle. The second rationale for the privilege is to avoid "burning" informers. Some informers, particularly those who figure in cases involving drug trafficking and so-called victimless crimes,[101] are used again and again. If their identities had to be revealed so that defendants could call them to testify in court, word would quickly spread through local criminal communities, and their usefulness would end.

---

[101] E.g., prostitution and gambling.

In most jurisdictions, a state claiming the informer's privilege does not need to show that either privilege rationale applies. The state need only show that an informer gave information relating to some law violation with the expectation his identity would be held confidential. This already slight burden is further diminished in practice, for courts often presume informers intend confidentiality. The Supreme Court, for example, while rejecting a presumption that all informers value confidentiality, found it reasonable to suppose that paid FBI informants or witnesses to a gang-related murder expect their cooperation to be kept confidential.[102] More generally, the Court said that the type of crime and the informer's relation to it are factors a court should look to in deciding whether an informer probably gave information with the expectation that his identity would be protected. In particular, the Court suggested that informers whose relation to the crime might realistically lead them to fear reprisals could be presumed to have expected that their identities would be held confidential when they provided information on the crime. In an earlier case, the Court less plausibly suggested that whatever an informer's motivation, he would usually condition his cooperation on an assurance of anonymity.[103]

2.   Scope of the Privilege

Although some courts and commentators refer to the privilege we are discussing as the *informer identity privilege*, others speak of *the informer's privilege*. The former characterization is more accurate because the privilege belongs not to the informer but to the government to invoke as it sees fit. This undermines the first rationale for the privilege since an informer can never be sure that the government will not reveal his identity. Because the government holds the privilege, the informer cannot technically waive it, although he can destroy the privilege by revealing his identity and whereabouts. Both are important. When an informant, usually in the course of undercover activities, unavoidably or inadvertently reveals his identity, courts have applied the privilege to keep secret information about the informer's address. This can prevent a defendant from calling the informer as a witness.

Information supplied by an informer is not privileged except insofar as it would tend to identify the informer. To the extent it does not and is otherwise discoverable, a defendant can know what an informer told the police and, in appropriate circumstances, have the evidence admitted. Courts have also allowed the state to admit the statements of anonymous informers, if they are not hearsay or if an appropriate exception applies.

---

[102] U.S. Dept. of Justice v. Landano, 508 U.S. 165 (1993). In *Landano* the Court was interpreting FOIA exemption 7D, which provides that "information compiled for law enforcement purposes" is exempt from FOIA disclosure to the extent that it "could reasonably be expected to disclose" the identity of, or information provided by a "confidential source." At least with respect to the identity of informants, the FRE 501 standard should follow *Landano*.

[103] McCray v. Illinois, 386 U.S. 300 (1967).

The government most often invokes the informer identity privilege in criminal cases, but it applies in any circumstance in which someone gives information relevant to law enforcement. Thus people who inform on wages and hour violations, OSHA violations, and the like can also enjoy the protection of the privilege.

In the draft Federal Rules, PFRE 510 purported to codify the informer identity privilege:

IDENTITY OF INFORMER

(a) *Rule of privilege.* The government or a state or subdivision thereof has a privilege to refuse to disclose the identity of a person who has furnished information relating to or assisting in an investigation of a possible violation of law to a law enforcement officer or member of a legislative committee or its staff conducting an investigation.

(b) *Who may claim.* The privilege may be claimed by an appropriate representative of the government, regardless of whether the information was furnished to an officer of the government or of a state or subdivision thereof. The privilege may be claimed by an appropriate representative of a state or subdivision if the information was furnished to an officer thereof, except that in criminal cases the privilege shall not be allowed if the government objects.

(c) *Exceptions.*

(1) *Voluntary disclosure: informer a witness.* No privilege exists under this rule if the identity of the informer or his interest in the subject matter of his communication has been disclosed to those who would have cause to resent the communication by a holder of the privilege or by the informer's own action, or if the informer appears as a witness for the government.

(2) *Testimony on merits.* If it appears from the evidence in the case or from other showing by a party that an informer may be able to give testimony necessary to a fair determination of the issue of guilt or innocence in a criminal case or of a material issue on the merits in a civil case to which the government is a party, and the government invokes the privilege, the judge shall give the government an opportunity to show *in camera* facts relevant to determining whether the informer can, in fact, supply that testimony. The showing will ordinarily be in the form of affidavits, but the judge may direct that testimony be taken if he finds that the matter cannot be resolved satisfactorily upon affidavit. If the judge finds that there is a reasonable probability that the informer can give the testimony, and the government elects not to disclose his identity, the judge on motion of the defendant in a criminal case shall dismiss

the charges to which the testimony would relate, and the judge may do so on his own motion. In civil cases, he may make any order that justice requires. Evidence submitted to the judge shall be sealed and preserved to be made available to the appellate court in the event of an appeal, and the contents shall not otherwise be revealed without consent of the government. All counsel and parties shall be permitted to be present at every stage of proceedings under this subdivision except a showing *in camera*, at which no counsel or party shall be permitted to be present.

(3) *Legality of obtaining evidence.* If information from an informer is relied upon to establish the legality of the means by which evidence was obtained and the judge is not satisfied that the information was received from an informer reasonably believed to be reliable or credible, he may require the identity of the informer to be disclosed. The judge shall, on request of the government, direct that the disclosure be made *in camera*. All counsel and parties concerned with the issue of legality shall be permitted to be present at every stage of proceedings under this subdivision except a disclosure *in camera*, at which no counsel or party shall be permitted to be present. If disclosure of the identity of the informer is made *in camera*, the record thereof shall be sealed and preserved to be made available to the appellate court in the event of an appeal, and the contents shall not otherwise be revealed without consent of the government.

The first thing to note about the proposed federal rule is that subsection (a) does not require the informer to have given the information in confidence. This ignores language in the two leading federal cases, *Roviaro v. United States* [104] and *McCray v. Illinois*,[105] which assumes protected information is given in confidence, as well as an analogous exception to FOIA, which makes the need for confidentiality explicit. Some trial court decisions seem to follow the proposed rule and do not consider whether confidentiality was desired, but most courts would not protect the identity of an informer who did not seem concerned about concealing his identity.

Subsection (a) protects not only those who give law enforcers information but also those who assist police and law enforcement officials in other ways. Perhaps the most common form of assistance is introductions or vouching. An informer acquainted with a drug dealer may introduce an undercover officer to the dealer and vouch for the officer's reliability. After the officer has made a buy or an arrest, the informer typically disappears from the picture. The privilege may prevent the dealer from learning the informer's true name or address.

---

[104] 353 U.S. 53 (1957).

[105] 386 U.S. 300 (1967).

While common law courts often speak of the privilege as protecting only suppliers of information, most also protect informers who provide services like introductions and vouching.

Subsection (b) presents the orthodox view about who may claim the privilege, and subsection (c) lists situations in which the privilege does not apply. Subsection (c)(1) is a standard exception for situations where the defendant knows the informer's identity or when the informer will testify for the state. The privilege may persist although many people know the informer's identity, so long as those "who would have cause to resent the communication" do not know who the informer is. The quoted language is taken from the Supreme Court's decision in *Roviaro*.

Subsection (b) is also based on *Rovario*. In *Rovario* an informant secreted an FBI agent in the trunk of his car and then drove with Rovario to pick up a heroin stash. The Supreme Court held that because only the informer witnessed the entire transaction, the government's privilege had to give way before the defendant's need to examine the informer. *Rovario* established that the informer identity privilege is a qualified one. When a defendant's need for knowing an informer's identity outweighs the government's interest in keeping the informer's identity secret, the privilege must give. This will occur most often when the defendant wishes to call the informer as a witness.

Courts tend to follow *Rovario* when informers are the only non-police witnesses to an offense, or when they participated in the crime. In other instances, courts are likely to protect an informer's identity, as they weigh the government's (and the informer's) interest in secrecy against the defendant's need for the evidence. One distinction commonly encountered in the case law is the difference between a "mere tipster" and a participant in or witness to a crime. When informers have only targeted criminals for the police or introduced undercover agents to criminals and have then disappeared, courts call them "mere tipsters" and invariably protect their identities. Sometimes courts will label as mere tipsters and protect the identities of those who have witnessed more of the crime. As a general rule, the greater the informer's involvement in the crime and the fewer other people who have seen as much of the crime as the informer, the less likely courts are to protect the informer's identity.

Other factors weigh in the balance as well, particularly the likelihood that the informer will give exculpatory testimony, and the danger to the informer if his identity becomes known. Courts often explore the former issue *in camera*, as subsection (c)(2) of PFRE 510 provides. Often neither the defense attorney (as the proposed federal rule provided) nor the state's attorney attends the *in camera* hearing. Allowing the state's attorney to attend is probably more common than allowing both, even in federal courts. Defense counsel must submit questions in writing to the judge, because it is feared that the defense counsel might reveal the informer's identity to the defendant. When courts allow a defense counsel to participate in the *in camera* questioning of an informer, they commonly issue protective orders preventing counsel from disclosing the informer's identity to her client. This will hurt the defense when the client knows the informer and could supply useful leads for questioning him. If the court overrides the privilege, and the government refuses to comply, the state must drop the charges in criminal cases. The trial court's implicit finding that the informer's testimony is necessary for a fair defense gives these remedies roots in the Compulsory Process Clause of the Sixth Amendment and Due Process Clauses of the Fifth and Fourteenth Amendments. In civil cases where the government refuses to comply with a decision denying the informer's privilege, various corrective actions, including directed verdicts, may be ordered, depending on the informer's importance to the parties' cases.

Subsection (c)(3) of the proposed informer identity privilege provides special procedures when an informer's information bears only on the legality of a search. Here, the proposed rule requires that courts honor the privilege unless the judge doubts the informer's reliability or credibility. Even then the rule does not require the judge to order the informer's identity revealed. In *McCray*, the Supreme Court held that protecting an informer's identity does not violate the Sixth Amendment or the Due Process Clause when the judge, based on testimony in open court, trusts the reliability of an informer whose tip allegedly furnished probable cause for a search. The Court did not say that the judge could not or should not reveal the informer's identity in these circumstances, but simply that she need not. The drafters of the proposed rule transformed this "need not" grant of judicial discretion into a "should not," withdrawing discretion if the judge is satisfied from information the state provides in open court that the state's agents reasonably believed the informant was credible. In most courts this is not a hard burden to meet.

What is really at stake in subsection (c)(3) and in *McCray* is the extent to which courts will probe for police perjury in evaluating the reasonableness of searches that have turned up incriminating evidence. As Justice Douglas wrote for the four *McCray* dissenters, "There is no way to determine the reliability of Old Reliable, the informer, unless he is produced at the trial and cross-examined."[106] The constitutional concern is that there never was an informer, just an officer's lucky hunch or, worse yet, an illegal wiretap. Subsection (c)(3) of the proposed rule and the majority's opinion in *McCray*, are essentially "don't ask, don't tell" solutions.

---

[106] McCray v. Illinois, 386 U.S. 300 at 316 (1967).

Arguably, the informer identity privilege should apply differently today than it once did. In the past, if the defendant could not learn the informer's identity, he could not call him, and the government did not have to produce him because if the informer came to court his identity was likely to be revealed. But today, with remote testimony via videoconferencing and technology to scramble faces and disguise voices, the government has fewer legitimate reasons to resist producing informers for questioning. Courts need no longer require *ex parte, in camera* hearings on the likely value of an informer's testimony. Using the new technology, defense counsel can question informers without threatening the values the informer identity privilege is designed to protect. (Questions that might reveal the informer's identity could, of course, remain forbidden.) However, the anti-crime temper of the times is such that court decisions or statutes that expand criminal defendants rights to obtain potentially exculpatory evidence should not be expected any time soon.

D. CONCLUSION

Government privileges allow the state to try individuals or litigate against them in civil cases while withholding information these persons say they need for a fair case or defense. This is no more than what other privileges allow their holders to do, but the government has special obligations of fairness to its citizens—especially in criminal cases—that individual litigants lack, and the government has available special privileges that other litigants do not have. Moreover, the government litigates in its own courts before judges whom it pays and who hold office through its political processes. Perhaps this is why many of the same judges who cut into individual privacy or relationship interests by construing personal privileges strictly seem less strict when the government claims one of its unique privileges.

But if the government is often successful when it asserts its special privileges, it also must occasionally pay a price for its assertion of a privilege, a price that ordinary litigants asserting privileges do not pay. Sometimes the price is so high that the government cannot assert its privilege and simultaneously pursue the litigation. Moreover, the Supreme Court, on the few occasions it has visited government privileges, has written opinions sensitive to the power imbalance between individuals and government. In doing so, the Court has recognized, at least in principle, the importance of the individual interests involved.

Many of the problems posed by the exercise of government privileges are caused by excesses of the adversary system. On the one hand, if the exercise of government privileges comes at a price, individual litigants will try to make their need for privileged information appear great so as to exact that price whether or not the information is truly needed. Hence, the problem of "graymail" and the announced intention of many criminal defendants to call informers, even though their testimony—if they were called—would usually hurt the defense. On the other hand, some government attorneys invoke these privileges to secure litigation advantages, regardless of the information's importance to the opponents or the government's true interest in secrecy.

People implement evidence rules. Government privileges as abstract laws tend to strike a reasonable balance between individual and state interests. Many of the problems that arise stem not from how the privileges are defined but rather from the biases or zeal of those individuals who implement the privileges—prosecutors, defense attorneys and judges—and the incentives that stimulate zeal. These are, of course, difficulties with all evidence rules. But they may be at their worst when valid state and individual interests collide in a setting where both parties are passionate not about the validity of the opposing interests but about winning in court. Too often this is true of trials in which government privileges are claimed.

Problem VIII-45. With the help of a confidential informant, Kathy Barnes, a special agent in the Bureau of Narcotics and Dangerous Drugs, met Fred James, who took Barnes to Warren Bush on February 16, 2010. At that time Bush sold Barnes two ounces of cocaine. The sale took place in a house which James and Barnes entered, while the informer remained outside in an automobile. A week later Bush was arrested. At trial, Bush claimed entrapment, and demanded that the informer's identity be disclosed and that he be produced. He claimed that James had taken him aside before introducing Barnes and told him that if he could not supply his friend with cocaine, his "health would suffer." He said that while he possessed the cocaine, he was not a dealer but had had two ounces of cocaine left from cocaine he had purchased a week earlier from James for "recreational use." Bush contended that the informer might be able to support his defense. At no time prior to the trial did Bush seek to subpoena James, but James was a fugitive from justice during this period and no subpoena could have been served. The government claims a right to protect the informer's identity. **Should the government's claim be honored? How should the trial judge proceed to make a ruling?** Suppose the informer had entered the house with Barnes and James and been present at the sale. **How should the judge rule if the government said the informer was still working for them and claimed the informer's privilege? Would it matter if James was available and the government voluntarily produced him?**

VI.   OTHER PRIVILEGES

In the course of your practice you may encounter a number of privileges that we have not yet mentioned. State evidence codes or court decisions recognize some privileges; others stand alone or are incidental to other laws. For example, privileges are incorporated in laws requiring doctors to report certain illnesses, in tax laws and some administrative regulations. At least one privilege—that against self-incrimination—and arguably more—reporter's privilege, group membership privilege—have constitutional roots. In addition to these privileges, you might encounter privileges protecting trade secrets, communications to clergy, hospital and academic peer review material, communications to ombudspersons, the editorial discussions of news organizations, the location of police surveillance operations, self-critical reports, communications to accountants, judge-clerk communications, raw census data, and grand jury material. Many of these privileges, when they exist, are *qualified* privileges, meaning they give way if a party can demonstrate a need for information that outweighs the values the privilege promotes.

With the exception of the reporter's privilege, we shall not discuss any of these privileges in detail. This is not because these other privileges are unimportant or seldom applicable. Rather, except in the case of the Fifth Amendment, we feel that we have spoken at enough length about privileges to give you an idea of their common features and a sense of how to think and argue when privilege questions arise. If you encounter privileges we have not discussed, you should be able to apply what you have learned. Nevertheless, a few privileges merit an additional word before we leave them, if only to alert you to their likely importance.

A.   FIFTH AMENDMENT

The most important and frequently invoked privilege that we have not discussed is the Fifth Amendment's injunction that "[N]o person . . . shall be compelled in any criminal case to be a witness against himself," also known as the privilege against self-incrimination. This privilege allows a person in any setting to refuse to give testimony—indeed, to refuse to make any statement—that increases the individual's chances of criminal conviction. Ordinarily courts accept the individual's judgment of what statements will have this effect. When a Fifth Amendment claim is asserted, courts usually respect it without probing.

The privilege against self-incrimination does not, however, mean that the prosecution cannot use the threat of contempt to coerce a party into revealing incriminating information. If a court grants a person *testimonial* (also known as *use and fruits) immunity*—which means that the state will not use either her statements or any information derived from those statements in a criminal prosecution against her—the witness no longer has a right to remain silent. Some people, understandably, feel this is inadequate protection. They fear that any admissions of criminal involvement will spur the government to prosecute them, and they do not trust the government to ignore leads to other evidence that their testimony provides. These people desire, instead, *transactional immunity*—freedom from prosecution for any crimes associated with the transactions they admit. The Supreme Court has, however, long held that the Fifth Amendment requires only testimonial immunity.[107]

The Fifth Amendment also applies in special ways to different sorts of writings and tangible objects, and, in doing so, intersects with other privileges. For example, an attorney may have an obligation to turn over to the police the fruits or instruments of a crime. But a combination of the client's Fifth Amendment rights and the attorney-client privilege may prevent the state from linking these items to the client through the attorney.

The Fifth Amendment's protections are confined to testimonial communications, the contents of which would tend to incriminate the speaker. The Amendment does not preclude the state from compelling people to provide non-testimonial evidence that might be used against them. Thus, a woman can refuse to tell the police, a grand jury, or the courts whether she robbed a bank. She cannot, however, refuse to repeat the words the bank robber used ("Hand over all your money or I'll shoot"), even if her statement will facilitate a voice identification and be extremely helpful to the state's case against her. The reason is that the Fifth Amendment precludes only *testimonial compulsion*. The courts have held that in saying what the bank robber said, a suspected robber is not providing testimony. The situation is even clearer when a blood specimen rather than a voice specimen is sought. Similarly, suspects can be compelled to provide fingerprints, hair samples and handwriting exemplars, to appear and stand in lineups, to be photographed, and if arrested for a serious crime, or in some jurisdictions (until and unless the Supreme Court declares otherwise) for any crime, to provide a DNA sample.

The prosecution may also compel people to give the state certain records. Because corporations cannot claim the Fifth Amendment privilege, a corporate officer may be required to give the prosecutor a corporation's books that are in her custody, even though book entries show that she and not the corporation committed fraud.[108] Also, the privilege does not usually apply to records that the law requires a person to keep. However, when a person turns over records under compulsion, the state in a criminal case cannot, over the person's objection, use the fact that they obtained the records from the defendant to show the

---

[107] Kastigar v. United States, 406 U.S. 441 (1972).
[108] Braswell v. United States, 487 U.S. 99 (1988).

authenticity of the records or that the defendant possessed them. When the state uses a defendant's act this way, the act of production substitutes for testimony she might give—it is, in effect, a statement "These are the records you sought. I possess them."—and so the Fifth Amendment's protection attaches.

The preceding comments alert you to some key limitations of the Fifth Amendment privilege, but they barely tap the surface of Fifth Amendment jurisprudence and reveal few of its subtle intricacies.[109] We omit detailed discussion of the Fifth Amendment not because our discussion of other privileges alone equips you to deal with this one, but because the Fifth Amendment's constitutional basis makes it unlike the codified or common law rules of evidence this book focuses on and because there is simply too much to say. For both these reasons, courses on constitutional law and constitutional criminal procedure cover the Fifth Amendment. We leave more detailed discussion of this privilege to them.

B. OTHER PROPOSED FEDERAL PRIVILEGES

1. Required Reports

Several of the privileges we have not yet mentioned were the subject of proposed federal rules. PFRE 502 privileged reports required by law[110] if the law requiring them provided that they are privileged. Because this result would follow without PFRE 502 whenever a federal statute privileges a report it requires, the drafters must have intended the rule to extend similar protection in federal trials to reports privileged by state statutes. Since Congress did not enact PFRE 502, reports privileged by state law are ordinarily unprotected in federal question litigation. Occasionally, however, federal courts extend qualified privileges to reports privileged under state statutes. This occurs most often with respect to laws privileging state tax returns; here the federal courts seem influenced by an analogous privilege found in the federal tax code.

2. Communications to Clergy

PFRE 506 codifies the privilege for communications to the clergy, a widespread, long-standing evidentiary privilege, recognized in most if not all states and the federal courts. In its earliest version, this privilege, still often called the *priest-penitent privilege*, only protected communications in the nature of confessions that were made to clergy bound by church doctrine to preserve the secrecy of the confessional. Some state privilege laws still privilege little more than this. In most states, and under the proposed federal rule, a reluctance to distinguish

---

[109] For example, Miranda v. Arizona, 384 U.S. 436 (1966), and the countless cases applying and interpreting it, are all based on the privilege against self-incrimination.

[110] The privilege did not apply in court actions for failing to honestly comply with the law extending the privilege.

among religions, even by reference to their own doctrines, has led to a broader protection that clergy of all faiths and their communicants can enjoy. The privilege requires that the communication be confidentially made to a member of the clergy in the latter's religious capacity. Thus, the rule does not protect communications about business matters or personal grievances. Rather, it is intended to protect communicants seeking advice about religious matters or solace for the soul. As the role of the clergy has grown beyond the merely liturgical, the protections of the privilege have expanded as well. Thus, couples seeking marriage counseling from clergy can claim this privilege in some jurisdictions, although the jurisdiction might extend no privilege to communications to social workers or psychologically trained marriage counselors. During the Vietnam War, one court even went so far as to privilege conversations with draft counselors supervised by a clergyman.[111] This decision is hard to justify, except as a judicial protest against the war.

3. Voter's Privilege

PFRE 507 proposed a privilege giving individuals the right to refuse to disclose how they voted, unless they cast their vote illegally. This is a widespread privilege, which the federal courts are also likely to honor.

4. Trade Secrets

In civil litigation, the trade secrets privilege, codified in PFRE 508, can be quite important. This is a qualified privilege that protects business-relevant information of many sorts. Information pertaining to manufacturing processes, sales techniques, computer code, and customer preferences can all be trade secrets protected in litigation. The "qualified" nature of the privilege means that a court can deny it if the information it protects bears directly on the subject matter of the litigation, is needed for a fair resolution of the case, and cannot be acquired or replaced in any way. Judges have considerable discretion in determining if these conditions are met.

Businesses value their trade secrets highly, and, indeed, sometimes prefer trade secret protection to patent protection.[112] When trade secrets are financially important, one may expect fierce courtroom battles about the availability of the privilege. Although the privilege is qualified, courts knowing what is at stake for the secret's holder are often reluctant to find that the privilege should give. But, in some cases the interest of justice requires that this qualified privilege yield. For example, when the Coca-Cola Bottling Company introduced "'new Coke,'" some bottlers claimed that new Coke was really "'old Coke'" (now marketed as Coca-Cola

---

[111] In re Verplank, 329 F. Supp. 433 (C.D. Cal. 1971).

[112] Patent protection requires full disclosure of how an invention has been realized—perhaps facilitating inventions around the patent—and only protects the patent holder's exclusive rights to a process for a limited time.

Classic), renamed so the company could escape legal restrictions on the price it could charge for its syrup.[113] To litigate this claim, the bottlers had to know the formulas for new and old Coke.

"Interest of justice" claims are most powerful in cases such as tort claims, in which the party seeking disclosure has no interest in the secret independent of the litigation. Thus in one well-known case, a manufacturer had to disclose the "secret" ingredient in its soap powder when a waitress, using it to wash dishes, suffered severe chemical burns and sued the manufacturer of the powder.[114] Courts are more suspicious of requests for trade secrets in cases brought by competitors, who have reasons apart from the litigation to want to know the secret information.

When courts find that the need to prevent fraud or the interest of justice requires disclosure of a trade secret, PFRE 508 and general practice require the court to take steps to protect the privilege holder's interest in secrecy. When, as usually happens, the trade secret issue arises in discovery, the court may simply bar the adverse party from revealing the secret to anyone or, when a competitor requests the secret, the court may limit disclosure to the party's counsel and independent experts, who are enjoined not to pass the information on to their client. In some cases involving competitors, courts will take the more extreme measure of appointing a third party to receive and cull the secret information to determine its relevance or import. When a party must disclose a trade secret during a trial, however, steps like these are often not feasible. Still, judges may clear courtrooms of spectators, order those remaining, including jurors, not to reveal what they have learned, and seal that portion of the case record reporting trade secret evidence.

5. Other Proposed Rules

Before leaving the proposed federal rules on privilege we should note three other rules that were included in proposed Article V. One, PFRE 511,[115] establishes general principles of waiver that would have applied to all federal privileges. It provides that if the holder of confidential information (e.g., an informer's identity) or a confidential communications privilege *voluntarily* discloses any significant portion of the confidential matter or communication, except in another privileged relationship, he waives the privilege. Although Congress did not enact the proposed rule, cases across the range of confidential communication and information privileges hold that if the privilege holder freely discloses the matter or

---

[113] Coca-Cola Bottling Co. of Shreveport v. Coca-Cola Co., 107 F.R.D. 288 (D. Del. 1985).

[114] Putney v. Du Bois Co., 240 Mo. App. 1075, 226 S.W.2d 737 (1950).

[115] PFRE 511: Waiver of Privilege by Voluntary Disclosure [Not enacted].

A person upon whom these rules confer a privilege against disclosure of the confidential matter or communication waives the privilege if he or his predecessor while holder of the privilege voluntarily discloses or consents to disclosure of any significant part of the matter or communication. This rule does not apply if the disclosure is itself a privileged communication.

communication, he loses the privilege. Some cases apply a waiver theory as the proposed rule does, and others find the later disclosure to be convincing evidence that the privilege holder did not intend confidentiality. In the case of the secret information privileges, courts often find that the disclosure has destroyed the secrecy these privileges require. We discussed many of the issues this rule raises in connection with specific privileges.

Sometimes privileged information is disclosed because a person or organization is mistakenly told it has no privilege or because it is unable to claim the privilege, as when letters to an attorney are taken by the government in a search of the attorney's office. In a sense, allowing a claim of privilege in later litigation does no good, for the information the party wanted to keep confidential has been disclosed. One might ask why a court, which may have considerable need for the information, should not be able to use what might already be widely known information. One reason is that a party should not suffer because of an erroneous legal ruling by a magistrate or judge. A second is to remove incentives that parties would otherwise have to acquire privileged information illicitly. Responding to considerations like these, PFRE 512[116] allows a privilege holder to retain her privilege during litigation even though the privileged information has been disclosed—provided the disclosure was either erroneously compelled or made without the holder having an opportunity to claim the privilege. This rule is more protective than the common law, but similar rules apply in many jurisdictions today.

PFRE 513[117] provides that the fact-finder may draw no inference from a claim of privilege, that neither the judge nor counsel may comment on the invocation of a privilege, and that cases should be conducted so that as far as possible jurors do not know if parties or witnesses have claimed privileges. If the jury knows a privilege has been claimed, the party whom this information might hurt has a right to have the jury instructed not to draw any inferences from the privilege claim. Like FRE 512, the proposed rule protects more than the common law did, but it states principles that many jurisdictions apply today. PFRE 513's

---

[116] PFRE 512: Privileged Matter Disclosed Under Compulsion or Without Opportunity to Claim Privilege. A claim of privilege is not defeated by a disclosure that was (1) compelled erroneously or (2) made without opportunity to claim the privilege.

[117] PFRE 513: Comment Upon or Inference From Claim of Privilege Instruction [Not enacted].

(a) *Comment or inference not permitted.* The claim of a privilege, whether in the present proceeding or upon a prior occasion, is not a proper subject of comment by judge or counsel. No inference may be drawn therefrom.

(b) *Claiming privilege without knowledge of jury.* In jury cases, proceedings shall be conducted, to the extent practicable, so as to facilitate the making of claims of privilege without the knowledge of the jury.

(c) *Jury instruction.* Upon request, any party against whom the jury might draw an adverse inference from a claim of privilege is entitled to an instruction that no inference may be drawn therefrom.

protection makes privilege claims more valuable, because jurors who know a party has claimed a privilege may think (usually correctly) that the party has something to hide, and in some cases the context may give the jurors a good idea of what that something is. Nevertheless, and despite FRE 104(c), some federal courts have allowed prosecutors to call witnesses before the jury when they know the witnesses will assert their Fifth Amendment privilege and that the natural inference from their assertion will harm the defendant's case. Other federal courts do not allow this, and the Supreme Court has thus far declined to resolve the conflict among the circuits.[118]

ADDITIONAL PROBLEMS

Problem VIII-46. Shortly after being involved in an automobile accident, Smith goes to Drs. Jones, Schwartz, and Hood. Smith complains of pains in his lower back. Drs. Schwartz and Hood diagnose "whiplash" and, for a fat fee, agree to testify on Smith's behalf. Dr. Jones, after an exhaustive examination, finds absolutely nothing wrong with Smith and begins to suspect that perhaps Smith is faking his injuries. After further tests are conducted, Dr. Jones tells Smith:

> Smith, there is absolutely nothing wrong with you. I am convinced that you are feigning your injuries in order to bring a lawsuit. Therefore, I will refuse to treat you. In addition, I will volunteer my testimony at trial should you continue to complain about these imaginary injuries and to attribute them to the automobile accident in which you were involved.

Smith continues with his lawsuit, and Dr. Jones does just what she said; namely, she volunteers her services to the defense. When Dr. Jones seeks to testify, Smith objects. **What is the proper ruling? Does it depend on whether or not Smith has called Drs. Schwartz and Hood to testify?**

Problem VIII-47. The defendant is charged with first-degree murder. The trial judge believes the defendant is not competent to stand trial and orders a psychiatric examination to determine this. The defendant is found competent and the trial commences. The defense claims that the defendant is not guilty by reason of insanity and introduces psychiatric evidence to show the mental condition of the defendant. In response, the prosecution seeks to introduce testimony by the doctors who examined the defendant to determine his competency. The defendant objects, and urges that any statements or any information that he may have conveyed to the doctors during the competency examination is privileged. **How should the court rule?**

---

[118] See Lindsey v. United States, 484 U.S. 934 (1987) (denying cert. to No. 86–5339) (6th Cir. Apr. 17, 1987).

Problem VIII-48. Mr. and Mrs. Taylor are married on September 1, 2012. On March 2, 2013, Mrs. Taylor gives birth to a child. Shortly thereafter, Mr. Taylor files suit for divorce on the grounds that Mrs. Taylor was pregnant at the time of their marriage, that she did not disclose that fact to him, and that he is not the father of the child. To prove that the child was a full-term baby, Mr. Taylor calls the doctor who delivered the child. Mrs. Taylor's lawyer objects on behalf of the child, claiming that any information that the doctor may have obtained as a result of the delivery or post-natal care is privileged. **Should the objection be sustained? Would the decision be any different if the objection were entered on the mother's behalf?**

Problem VIII-49. While crossing the street, Susan Howe is hit by a car, breaking bones in both legs. From the hospital she contacts her lawyer, Ted White, who insists that Dr. Kildare, a famous orthopedic surgeon, attend her case. In the course of an initial diagnostic interview, Howe tells Dr. Kildare that she does not remember the details of the accident because she was drunk at the time, that she has always walked with a limp because one leg is shorter than the other, and that she hopes that the doctor will be able to correct that condition. After she is released from the hospital (without a limp), White sends her to Dr. Welby, another noted specialist. He asks Dr. Welby to evaluate her current condition with particular attention to the prognosis. He seeks Welby's opinion as an aid in estimating the value of the suit. White also intends to use Dr. Welby, as he has in the past, as a source of information on the technical medical details of the case. He has found that Welby's briefings aid him in presenting the plaintiff's case and in cross-examining the defendant's expert witnesses. Howe gave Welby the same information she gave Kildare. At trial, plaintiff Howe calls no expert medical witnesses, but the defendant seeks to call Kildare and Welby to testify to Howe's statements concerning her limp and her condition at the time of the accident and to her physical condition at the time each of the doctors examined her. **What testimony, if any, is likely to be admitted in a federal court? What testimony, if any, is likely to be admitted in a jurisdiction like California?**

Problem VIII-50. Jerry Crews was a voluntary patient in a psychiatric ward of a hospital where he saw the television movie "The Day After," depicting the nuclear annihilation of a Kansas town. After watching the movie as well as a panel discussion on the movie's implications, Crews became distraught and requested antidepressant medication. After taking the medicine, Crews told a psychiatric nurse on duty that if the President came to town he would shoot him. The nurse reported Crews's statement. Crews denied the statement, but admitted an extreme dislike of the President and said it would be in the best interest of the country if he were shot. During a trial in which Crews stood accused of threatening the life of the President, Crews argued against admission of his statement to the nurse, claiming it was protected by the psychotherapist-patient privilege. **How should the judge rule in this case?**

Problem VIII-51. In a wrongful death suit against the police department stemming from a violent confrontation between the police and one Don Dixon, who had been violently harassing his neighbors, Dixon's mother sought compensation for, among other claims, her son's emotional distress and suffering in the moments after the police shot him and before he died. The police department, asserting that in arguing emotional distress the plaintiff put her son's mental state in issue, then attempted to introduce into evidence records from Dixon's visit to a community mental health center one month before his death. At the center, Dixon admitted to using "street drugs," and said he had used "everything but heroin." Included in these records are statements by staff members of the center indicating Dixon's admitted propensity to engage in violent behavior to gain attention, including an incident in which he threatened to shoot his wife and himself. **Should the court allow this material in? Would it matter if Dixon's parents had testified that he was a happy, well-adjusted young man?**

Problem VIII-52. Joe Kanga brought a personal injury lawsuit pursuant to the Federal Tort Claims Act after he was injured in an accident involving his car and a United States postal vehicle. In his pretrial statements, Joe provided defense counsel with a complete copy of his hospital records from the Cleveland Clinic. He also provided the Postal Service with a witness list, which listed him as a witness but not Dr. MacDowell, his primary physician at the time of the accident. After receiving the list, the defense contacted Dr. MacDowell to interview him as a potential witness. MacDowell refused, saying an interview would violate Joe's physician-patient privilege. Dr. MacDowell said he would communicate with the defendant only if Joe waived the privilege by providing the defense with a complete set of his medical records. **Should a court order Dr. MacDowell to answer the deposition questions?**

Problem VIII-53. Following an automobile accident, Carl Kahn was brought unconscious to the emergency room of Lake City General Hospital. The admitting doctor, noticing that Kahn smelled of alcohol, thought he was drunk and ordered a blood test to be certain. The lab reported that Kahn had a blood alcohol level of .21, confirming the doctor's initial suspicions. On Kahn's patient chart, the doctor noted the blood alcohol level as well as the following diagnosis: inebriated, slight concussion, lacerations on the face and arms, broken wrist, shock. Treatment was ordered to deal with each of these conditions, and the chart was placed at the foot of Kahn's bed, where it was accessible to anyone who came by. **In a suit against Kahn by the other driver in the accident, will Kahn's claim of physician-patient privilege prevent the other driver from introducing Kahn's hospital record**

to show that Kahn was drunk? If the court rules that the record is protected by the privilege, may Kahn introduce the record to prove his injuries—in support of a counterclaim—without relinquishing the claim of privilege as to the diagnosis of inebriation?

Problem VIII-54. Karin Milgram goes to her doctor, Mai Liang, saying she is sure she has caught herpes from her boyfriend Randy Hayes. Now that they have broken up, she wants to know what steps she should take to keep from passing it on to her sex partners. Dr. Liang confirms the diagnosis, at which point Karin breaks out crying and says maybe she shouldn't date anymore and that she feels like killing herself. Karin and the doctor talk for half an hour about the guilt and depression she feels and about coping with the disease. She finally leaves with prescriptions for a new antiviral drug and an antidepressant. Later, a man sues Karin, claiming that she never alerted him to the fact that she had herpes when they had intercourse, and that he had gotten the disease from her. To prove that Karin had herpes before they began dating, the plaintiff wants either to question Dr. Liang about when she first diagnosed Karin's herpes, or to introduce Karin's medical records from that first visit. **Can Karin claim a privilege to prevent the doctor's testimony or the medical records from being received?** Suppose the woman who replaced Karin as Randy's girlfriend sues Randy for giving her herpes. To prove that he had herpes before they started dating, she wants to introduce Dr. Liang to testify to when she first diagnosed Karin with herpes and to what Karin said about how she contracted the disease during her visit. Karin is working with the Peace Corps in a remote village in Central Africa and is unreachable. Randy claims the doctor cannot testify because of Karin's privilege. **How should the court rule?**

Suppose the plaintiff has a telegram from Karin saying she is willing to waive the privilege, but Dr. Liang refuses to testify claiming the privilege on her own behalf. She says that had she been able to talk to Karin, Karin would not have waived the privilege because she would have realized that it was only destructive anger at her former boyfriend that led her to do so, and the doctor says she would have told Karin that if she testified about Karin's herpes, it could disrupt the close, trusting relationship they had built up when she was treating Karin. **How should the court respond to Dr. Liang's attempt to claim the privilege?**

Problem VIII-55. Hakeem Olanji, Chair of the English Department at Central State University, is charged with extortion. Abe Nunn, a member of the CSU English Department, claims that Hakeem said he would not promote him unless he donated $2,000 to the Chair's Discretionary Fund. Hakeem claims that although he was delighted (and astonished) when Abe made his donation, he had never requested the money or offered anything in exchange for it. He said the reason Abe had not been brought up for promotion sooner was because his record did not merit it, and that he started the promotion process for Abe shortly after receiving the donation because that is when Abe's book was accepted for publication. Hakeem claims that Abe has a history of delusionary thinking and that he has spent money for strange purposes in the past. To support his defense, Hakeem wishes to have turned over to him Abe's psychiatric records, including records of one hospitalization, and he wants to depose Abe's psychiatrist for discovery purposes. Abe claims the psychotherapist-patient privilege. **How should the court rule? Would the decision be different if Abe were suing Hakeem in civil court for extortion? Does it matter if Abe was asking damages for the shame and mental anguish he suffered from not being promoted at the normal time?**

Problem VIII-56. Sabrina Dunkett is charged with murdering her husband, George Clark, following a family squabble. Dunkett has retained F. Roy Bellow, a noted criminal lawyer, to defend her. Dunkett is wealthy, and money is of no concern in mounting a defense. Bellow calls Dr. Fredericka Phipps, the most respected psychiatrist in the city, and asks Phipps to examine Dunkett with an eye toward an insanity defense. Phipps is reluctant to get involved in a criminal case. But she agrees to participate when Bellow gives her a $15,000 retainer to "examine" Dunkett, to form an opinion of her mental condition on the night in question, and to gather information needed to advise on a course of psychiatric treatment for Dunkett if that proves proper. Phipps conducts the examination and submits a lengthy report to Bellow summarizing everything that Dunkett told her and noting her conclusion, which is "that your client was perfectly capable of understanding and controlling her actions when she shot her husband six times." The report also states that since the shooting Dunkett has developed some emotional disturbance, and asks whether she should prepare a report recommending treatment. Bellow says that advice is not needed. Knowing he cannot use Phipps as a witness, Bellow tries again. This time he retains Dr. Marvin Mageco, also a well-known psychiatrist. Mageco is retained for only $10,000 and does the examination. He concludes that Dunkett was suffering a dissociative reaction on the night of the shooting and was unable to control her behavior, because of the borderline paranoid schizophrenic condition from which she suffered. Happy to have this report, Bellow calls Mageco to testify as a witness. The government, which has learned that Dr. Phipps also examined the defendant, calls her as a witness. The prosecutor asks Dr. Phipps what Dunkett said about the night in question and whether she formed an opinion as to Dunkett's sanity. Dunkett objects and argues that anything said to Phipps was said to her as Bellow's agent and, as such, is protected by the attorney-client privilege. The government says that this privilege, like the doctor-patient privilege, should be disallowed since it relates to the results of a medical examination and the defendant has chosen to place her mental condition in issue. **How should a court rule?** Dunkett also claims that since she was told at the time of the examination that Dr. Phipps might be called upon to give advice concerning the treatment of any mental problem she might have, whatever she said to Phipps is protected by the psychotherapist-patient privilege. **How should a court rule?**

Problem VIII-57. Barry and Elissa Dunn were married for five years before they were divorced. During their marriage, they had three children. After their divorce, Elissa received custody of the children. She then married Stuart Chambers, who had two small children of his own. Furious over losing custody of his children, Barry investigates Stuart's background to see if he can learn anything that might discredit Stuart. Barry's detective work reveals that several years ago Stuart pleaded guilty to child molestation charges. Further, he learns that Stuart has a history of mental problems that have required several hospitalizations.

Armed with this new information, Barry seeks the counsel of an attorney to fight for custody of his children. Barry's attorney subpoenas Stuart's hospital records. The hospital complies with the request.

At the custody hearing, Stuart objects to the introduction of the hospital records claiming that they are confidential communications made by him to the hospital and hence the physician-patient privilege should attach. Further, he maintains that the hospital breached the physician-patient privilege since only he, as the patient, had the authority to waive the privilege and not the hospital.

Barry argues, however, that the hospital is merely the custodian of the records and that Stuart's communications were made confidentially to his physician and not to the hospital. **How should a California court rule?**

Problem VIII-58. Over the last six months Dr. Joanna Jenkins, a psychiatrist, has been seeing Earl Lancaster, a married man who is depressed because he has been diagnosed with AIDS. During one session, Earl admits to Dr. Jenkins that he has not told his wife, Rose, about his HIV-positive status. "It would just destroy her," he explains. "It would kill her to know that not only have I been cheating on her but that I have AIDS, too." Dr. Jenkins replies, "Well, if you're not going to tell her, at least make sure you're having protected sex so she doesn't get sick." "After twenty years of marriage, I can't start changing my ways now," says Earl. "She'd just get suspicious, she'd know something was wrong." "Are you having unprotected sex now?" asks Dr. Jenkins. "Of course," replies Earl. "I have no choice." **What should Dr. Jenkins do? If Earl is later prosecuted under a statute which makes it a crime to knowingly put another at risk of contracting AIDS without the**

other's knowledge, can the state call Dr. Jenkins to prove Earl had AIDS? Can they call him to prove that Earl violated the statute? Would it make any difference if Dr. Jenkins was a medical doctor treating Earl for his AIDS rather than a psychiatrist treating Earl's depression?

Problem VIII–59. Joy Smathers and her husband Gary were subpoenaed to testify before a United States grand jury investigating extortionate extensions of credit. Joy appeared, refused to testify and took the Fifth Amendment. She was not recalled. Gary also invoked the Fifth Amendment, but received full immunity, removing the self-incrimination danger. Gary then refused to answer certain questions asserting the adverse testimony privilege. **Should there be an adverse testimony privilege for testimony before a grand jury? Assuming arguendo that there should be, does the privilege disappear if the United States attorney in charge of the investigation states for the record the following:**

> On behalf of the United States government, I hereby represent and agree that no testimony of Gary Smathers before the Grand Jury, or its fruits, will be used in any way in any proceeding against his wife.

Problem VIII–60. A man tells his wife he has just robbed a grocery store. He doesn't see his ten-year-old son sitting in a chair. At the husband's trial the prosecution calls both the wife and child to testify to the man's statement. The husband seeks to exclude the testimony of both witnesses as privileged. Neither witness wants to testify. **Will the husband succeed in excluding the testimony of one or both of them? If so, on what ground? Would the situation be different if the man's wife had divorced him before the trial? If the wife had divorced him and the child were four years old? If the child were four months old?**

Problem VIII–61. Bill and Betty Smith, husband and wife, are on trial for smuggling cocaine in a jurisdiction that gives the adverse testimony privilege to the defendant spouse. They each want to testify on their own behalf and each intends to claim that the other was solely responsible for the crime. Each claims the adverse testimony privilege to keep the other off the stand. **Should the judge apply the privilege in this case? Are there ways of handling this case without abrogating the privilege?** Assume the Smiths are on trial in a jurisdiction that follows *Trammel* and each wants to testify as described above, but only in order to make out a defense. Neither wants to be a witness against the other. **Should the judge apply the privilege here? What would this entail?**

Problem VIII–62. Julie Adams is charged with armed robbery. She has fled, and the prosecutor thinks her husband knows her hiding place. She would like to force her husband to disclose it. The prosecutor subpoenas

Mr. Adams to appear before the grand jury. She asks Mr. Adams if he knows where his wife is hiding, and Mr. Adams replies that he believes he does. In response to the question of how he knows, Mr. Adams replies that his wife, fearing their phone was tapped, telephoned a friend and the friend passed the information to him. Claiming a marital privilege, Mr. Adams refuses to disclose the identity of the friend who relayed the message from his wife or the location of his wife. **In an action against Mr. Adams for contempt, should the claim of privilege be upheld? Could Mr. Adams have claimed the privilege at any earlier point? Could he have claimed any privilege if he had been divorced between the time he heard from the friend and the time he was subpoenaed before the grand jury? Would your answer to the previous question be different if it were Ms. Adams who had told Mr. Adams where she was?**

Problem VIII-63. A husband, sued for divorce in a fault jurisdiction, resists paying alimony, claiming his wife violated her marital vows. He testifies that his wife told him in secret that she had committed adultery with another man and was going to leave him. The wife objects to the introduction of this testimony on the ground that anything she may have told her husband in the confidence of the marriage was privileged. **Should the wife prevail? If she were prosecuted for adultery, could her husband be called to testify against her?**

Problem VIII-64. Van Duzek is charged with two counts of transporting aliens, knowing that the aliens were not legally present in the United States. The aliens allegedly transported include one who married Van Duzek one month after his indictment. She and two of her three children entered the United States at Brownsville, Texas, in October 2010, with a local border-crossing card. Van Duzek met her there, and they then traveled in his car to Laredo, Texas, and then to Chicago Heights, Illinois. One of the woman's children had preceded her there. She and her three children lived with Van Duzek's friends in Chicago Heights. They did not return to Mexico as planned because her fourth pregnancy made her ill. The prosecutor wants to call the wife as a witness against Van Duzek. She does not want to testify. **Does she have a right to refuse?**

Problem VIII-65. One morning Eileen Simpson awoke at 6 a.m. in order to get some milk for her baby. Entering the kitchen, she saw her husband sitting around the kitchen table with three other men. Her husband, Todd, is later charged with participating in a conspiracy with these other men. In order to prove Todd's association with the conspiracy, the prosecutor calls Ms. Simpson to testify to what she saw that morning. The Simpsons are divorced at the time of trial, but Todd still claims a marital privilege to prevent his wife from testifying to her observations. **How should a court rule? Should the court rule any differently if Todd**

had roused his wife, brought her downstairs and introduced her to the three men?

Problem VIII-66. Mrs. Conrad tells her husband that she wants him to be her agent in the sale of wheat from a farm she owns. Her husband sells the wheat, but before the delivery date has arrived the price of wheat rises $.40 a bushel. Mrs. Conrad then sells the same wheat to another buyer at a higher price. The original buyer sues Mrs. Conrad in contract for his lost profits. At the trial, he wishes to put Mr. Conrad on the stand and ask him whether Mrs. Conrad had told him that he was her agent for the sale of the wheat. Mrs. Conrad claims a marital privilege. **How should the court rule?**

Problem VIII-67. Sara Kemper operates a small jewelry store. One evening her husband comes home, tosses a diamond ring in her lap and says, "See what you can get for this; I won it in a crap game." It turns out the ring was stolen, and Sara is charged with the knowing sale of stolen property. She seeks to have her husband testify to what he told her, but the husband refuses, saying that whatever he told her was said in the confidence of the marriage relationship. **How should the judge rule on the husband's claim of privilege?**

Problem VIII-68. Argyle and Zanuk are both charged with bank robbery. According to the prosecution's theory of the case, they entered a bank wearing ski masks and robbed a teller at gunpoint. The prosecutor believes that Argyle's wife saw Argyle dispose of the ski masks and he wants to call the wife as a witness. Fearful of running into a spousal privilege, he calls Ms. Argyle to testify only against Zanuk. **Is this permissible? Does it matter whether Argyle and Zanuk are indicted together? Tried together? Whether Argyle has already been tried and convicted?**

Problem VIII-69. Bill and Jim are gay men who have been involved in a monogamous relationship for seven years. Five years ago they consecrated their relationship by getting married in a church with a minister. Bill and Jim reside in Michigan, a state that does not recognize gay marriages. Thus the couple is not eligible for state tax and health insurance benefits, which they would have access to if they had a traditional, heterosexual marriage. Ann Arbor, the city where they live, however, *does* recognize gay marriages in the form of registered domestic partnerships. Bill and Jim were among the first to register after the ordinance was passed. As Jim is a city employee, the couple was particularly pleased with the new law because it made Bill eligible to receive city health benefits as Jim's "domestic partner."

One day at work, Jim's supervisor, Buck, learns that Jim is gay and he immediately fires him. Outraged, Jim goes home to Bill and tells him what happened. They discuss the situation. Bill suggests that they seek the counsel of an attorney to sue the city for employment discrimination.

Jim disagrees saying, "Who does that Buck think he is? I'll get him, even if it means killing him!" Jim then grabs a gun and storms out of the house.

Jim hunts Buck down at work and shoots him. Jim is charged with first-degree murder. The prosecution alleges that the murder was premeditated. It wants to establish premeditation by discovering the contents of Jim's conversation with Bill immediately prior to his leaving the house with the gun in search of Buck. At trial, Jim invokes the adverse testimony privilege to prevent Bill from testifying against him. Jim argues that since their relationship is formally recognized by city ordinance as a domestic partnership, their communications should rightfully be protected under the spousal privilege. **How should the court rule?**

Problem VIII-70. Chuck Lawrence married Susanne Markus on September 5, 1992. The couple separated in 1994. In 1995, Chuck heard through the grapevine that Susanne had died in a car crash. Chuck believed what he heard, but Susanne had actually survived the crash. In 1996, Chuck married Katherine Taylor. They lived happily together thereafter under the false impression that they were legally married. Between 1996 and 2001, they had three children. Chuck and Katherine were zealous anti-abortion advocates. They had for years picketed and protested at the local Planned Parenthood office. In 2013, Planned Parenthood was finally able to secure a restraining order to keep Chuck and Katherine, as well as other abortion protesters, at least 50 feet from the clinic's entrance. This outraged Chuck.

"Why don't those courts understand?" exclaimed Chuck to his wife in the privacy of their home one evening. "They just don't get it. Those people are murderers. They've got to be stopped!"

Chuck then left their house with five gallons of kerosene and a box of matches. He went in turn to the local courthouse and to Planned Parenthood's headquarters, doused them each with kerosene, and set them ablaze. Shortly thereafter, Chuck was indicted on arson charges.

At trial, the state calls Katherine to the stand to learn what Chuck had told her before he left on his arson rampage. Katherine does not want to testify, and Chuck objects to Katherine's testifying, claiming that their communications were protected under both spousal privileges. The state proves that Susanne is still alive. **Given Chuck's good faith belief as to Susanne's death, can he successfully claim either spousal privilege?**

Problem VIII-71. In a plea agreement stemming from drug trafficking activities, Joe Coke agreed to cooperate with an ongoing drug investigation and also agreed to litigate the appropriateness of the forfeiture of a piece of land held in his wife's name. The government subsequently began civil forfeiture proceedings against the property, claiming Joe had held meetings in the home to organize his drug trafficking activities. Cindy Coke defended herself in the proceedings by claiming innocent ownership. During depositions, Cindy testified to conversations she had had with Joe prior to his arrest in an attempt to establish that she had not known of Joe's drug trafficking activities. When the government asked her about post-arrest conversations with Joe, Cindy's attorney advised her to assert the marital privilege. The district court denied Cindy's assertion of the privilege, and on appeal she argued that both the adverse testimony privilege and the confidential communications privilege should apply. **How should the court rule?**

Problem VIII-72. A fifteen-year-old boy, John Doe, was subpoenaed to testify in a grand jury proceeding inquiring into criminal acts alleged to have been committed by his mother and other family members. Doe refused to testify, claiming a parent-child privilege. As a result, the court ordered him held in contempt and confined him in a detention home for the eighteen-month term of the grand jury, or until he testifies as to what he saw, heard, and knows. In an appeal of his civil contempt order, Doe, a Mormon, claims that testifying against his family would violate his right to the free exercise of religion, in that his religious values place a premium on loyalty to one's family. Doe further says that testifying would violate his family's privacy and integrity anchored to the First Amendment, the common law and FRE 501. **How should the court rule?**

Problem VIII-73. Jane Myers, a freelance writer, and Dawn Patterson, an assistant city manager, are lesbians who have lived together for ten years. In June of 2008, they had a ceremony in their church in which they pledged themselves to each other as partners and were declared coupled. In September 2009, shortly after the city in which they lived passed an ordinance recognizing domestic partners, they registered as domestic partners, and since then Jane has been a beneficiary of Dawn's health insurance. In February 2010, Jane, who had been impregnated through artificial insemination, had a baby whom they have since been coparenting. Jane had endeavored to have Dawn listed as the baby's second mother on the birth certificate in the space provided for the father's name, but it was not allowed. Instead the father was listed as "unknown." In May 2011, Jane allegedly did some work ghostwriting a book for a university professor for $20,000. She did not report the earnings on her income tax. Later Jane is tried criminally for tax evasion. The government seeks to place Dawn on the stand to testify to what she saw of Jane's work and to what Jane told her about it. Jane claims the privilege for confidential marital communications to keep Dawn from revealing what she told her, and Dawn claims the adverse testimony privilege to keep from testifying altogether. **Should a court**

honor either claim? Would it matter if Jane wrote the book in January 2010? August 2009? May 2008?

Problem VIII-74. Jim Bonds is an electrical engineer. While working on military-related projects for various defense contractors, he possessed government security clearances. During a stint in Zurich, Switzerland, he shared an office with a Russian mathematician who asked him several times about United States military information. Bonds reported these incidents to the U.S. consulate, which resulted in several meetings between Bonds and consulate personnel. After returning to the United States, Bonds met with someone who identified himself as a CIA agent and who questioned Bonds about his contact with the Russian mathematician. Several months later, Bonds lost his security clearance and became the target of a campaign of harassment and psychological attacks. He was followed, unknown persons would enter and search his apartment, he received strange phone calls, and was on one occasion drugged with a substance that produced hallucinations. Bonds believed the U.S. government was using him for experimental research or as an informant of some kind. He filed suit against the United States, the CIA, the FBI, the Department of Defense, and the Department of State, alleging violation of his Fourth Amendment rights, assault and battery, and intentional infliction of emotional distress.

The government through the director of the CIA, claimed the state secrets privilege. The director asserted that to reveal anything about the alleged contacts between Bonds and government officers could pose a danger to the intelligence gathering capabilities of the U.S. After reviewing *in camera* a more particularized explanation of the government's assertion of privilege, the district court dismissed Bonds's complaint with prejudice. He appealed. **How should the appellate court rule?** Suppose Bonds's attorney suggests conducting the entire trial *in camera* so that all the privileged evidence can be heard. **Should the court implement this suggestion?**

Problem VIII-75. General Dynamics and Boeing sued the United States after the Department of the Navy terminated their contract to produce a stealth attack aircraft. In the suit, the plaintiffs sought access to certain classified material, called special access programs, controlled by the Air Force. The Acting Secretary of the Air Force claimed the state secrets privilege in regards to this material, providing a written statement that he had personally reviewed the material and found that its release would constitute a threat to national security. The Acting Secretary also provided the court, *in camera*, with a statement giving more particularized reasons for his claim of privilege.

The trial court, after examining the Secretary's statement and the nature of the material sought by the plaintiffs, denied the government's assertion of the privilege and ordered disclosure of the military secrets involved. The government appealed. **How should the appellate court rule?**

Problem VIII-76. Jim Turner filed a complaint with the Equal Employment Opportunity Commission (EEOC) after several incidents of what he felt was racial discrimination by his employer, the Kendall company. The EEOC investigated his claim, originally finding that Turner had cause to sue. After attempting conciliation between Turner and Kendall, the EEOC rescinded its original determination and found that Turner did not have reasonable cause to sue. Turner next filed suit directly against his employer, claiming he had been discriminatorily suspended and demoted because of his race and that Kendall displayed a pattern of practicing racial discrimination.

Kendall responded by subpoenaing the EEOC, requesting all files, records, papers, billings, personnel and/or employment records, and any other reports submitted by or related to Jim Turner. The EEOC provided Kendall with Turner's records from his first charge against the company, but denied access to all information connected with Turner's charges against other employers, agency memoranda containing staff evaluations and recommendations, and information related to the EEOC's conciliation efforts between Turner and Kendall. The district court ordered the EEOC to comply with the subpoena and the EEOC appealed. **Which of the official information privileges do you think the EEOC can best rely on in its appeal? How should the appellate court rule?**

Problem VIII-77. Benjamin Veola was arrested for drug trafficking after several undercover agents negotiated with him to buy $300,000 worth of cocaine. The agents had been introduced to Veola through a man known as "Vince," a drug dealer himself, who was paid $10,000 by the government for his services. Vince not only introduced the agents to Veola, but he was also present at their first two meetings. At trial, Veola's lawyer sought to elicit information about Vince, in order to show that both he and his police contacts were biased against Veola and had a special interest in making the charges against Veola stick. In addition to cross-examining the agents about their relationship with Vince, Veola moved to have the court order Vince to appear at trial. When the court refused to order Vince to appear after the government claimed the informer identity privilege, Veola asked for a "missing witness instruction" telling the jury that had Veola appeared his testimony would be adverse to the state's case. The court refused this request as well. **Were the trial judge's rulings correct?**

Problem VIII-78. Rachel Lindsey owns farmland that has been taken for a highway. She claims that the highest and best use of the land is for apartment dwellings, and that for this purpose the land is worth $6,000 per acre. The government has offered her $480 per acre, which it claims is the land's value as farmland. Rachel has heard that the government in choosing its highway routes attempts to evaluate the different potential uses of the land it would need to implement for different possible routes. She believes that government files contain the highway department's evaluation of likely uses for her land. She subpoenas all highway department documents relating to her land. **May the government resist the subpoena by claiming a privilege for official information? If it does, should the government be made to pay a "price" for withholding this information? If so, what should it be?** Assume Lindsey is attempting to enjoin the taking of the land entirely, claiming it is an abuse of discretion for the road to go through her land. She subpoenas all information in the highway department's files relating to possible routes that the highway might take. **May the government resist the subpoena by claiming a privilege for official information? If it does, should the government be made to pay a "price" for withholding this information? If so, what should it be?**

Problem VIII-79. The Army wishes to seize 20,000 acres of land owned by Hiram Brown. Brown resists the seizure on the ground that he has heard the land will be turned over to a private corporation and hence the seizure is not for a "public purpose." He demands to know the specific use to which the land will be put. The Army introduces a letter from the Secretary of Defense stating, "I must claim the privilege for state secrets and not specify the Army's intended use of this land since it relates closely to the national defense. It will be used for the benefit of the public." **What should the judge do? If this is the only evidence as to the Army's intended use, should the judge allow the condemnation?**

Problem VIII-80. Tom Tale testifies that he bought heroin from Stan Seller. On cross-examination Seller wishes to ask Tale whether he had informed on Seller twice in the past, whether he was a paid informant for the Bureau of Narcotics, and whether he was the anonymous informer who had turned in Frank Ravitz and Betty Bonds. Tale refuses to answer each of these questions, citing the informer's privilege. **Should the court order him to answer? What should the court do if Tale refuses to answer despite being ordered to do so?**

Problem VIII-81. Churder is charged with transporting stolen property knowing it was stolen. He defends on the ground that he took the property with the intent of turning it over to the police at his earliest convenience. He seeks the identity of the informant who told the police he was in possession of this property. **Should this request be granted?**

Problem VIII-82. Late one night the police burst into the Kitcheners' apartment without a warrant. They terrified the Kitcheners, turning the house upside down looking for narcotics, but they found nothing. The Kitcheners believe that Art Graham, with whom they had recently quarreled, falsely reported them out of spite. They sue the police, alleging reckless reliance on an unreliable informer. Interrogatories are issued to the chief of police. The first asks the chief to provide the name of the informer who told the police the Kitcheners were concealing narcotics. The second asks whether Art Graham was the informer. The chief refuses to answer either question, claiming the informer's privilege. **How should the court rule?**

Problem VIII-83. Jane Field is arrested for possession of narcotics, following a search of her apartment that reveals a package containing half a kilo of heroin. Field says the package had come in the mail that very morning. She says she opened it but had no idea of what it contained, since she had never seen heroin before. She also says she has no idea who sent it. She has a piece of brown wrapping paper with canceled stamps on it that could have fit the package. At trial she demands that the police reveal the name of the individual who informed on her. **When the police refuse, how should a court rule? Does it matter if the prosecution has three witnesses who will testify that they have bought heroin from Jane?**

Problem VIII-84. The state housing board brings an action to collect a civil fine of $2,000 from Ivan Tucker, a landlord. The claim is that for ten days during the month of February, Tucker failed to heat his apartments to the required minimum of sixty-two degrees. Tucker demands to know who complained about the lack of heat. **If the board can prove its charges without relying on the testimony of any tenant, must it nonetheless disclose the complainant's identity?**

Problem VIII-85. Stephen Silt is charged with selling narcotics. A government informant not only helped to arrange the alleged sales transaction, but also was present when it took place. Silt denies the sale, alleging that the two undercover officers who claim to have purchased the drugs have framed him. The government claims that Silt must show that the informant would support his version of the facts before the court orders disclosure. **Is this correct? If the government files an affidavit from the informant stating that the informant agrees with the government witnesses' version of the facts, is there any need to call the informant?**

Problem VIII-86. The 2012 election for Mayor of Cornwall, N.Y., was won by Sally Zoe, by one vote. After the election it turned out that seven recent residents, who lived in a part of a new subdivision that was in the township but not the town of Cornwall, had mistakenly but in good faith voted. Their subdivision, most of which was in the town, had overwhelmingly favored Zoe who was opposed to creating new subdivisions. Thomas Joy, the losing candidate, brings suit to have himself declared the winner, or if the court won't do that, to have a new election ordered. In addition to seeking the disallowances of two absentee ballots favoring Zoe, Joy wants the court to order each of the seven township residents to state how they voted. The voters claim a privilege not to disclose their ballots. **Should their privilege claim be sustained? Would you answer the same way if the voters had known or should have known that they were not eligible when they went to the polls?**

Problem VIII-87. Sam Hacket is part of a sect that believes God ordained polygamous marriages. He is prosecuted for bigamy after marrying Sandra Shell while still married to Belinda Strong. Belinda and Sandra not only knew about each other, but Belinda approved of Sam's second marriage and participated in the ceremony. **Can Reverend Clark, who counseled Sam and Sandra before their marriage and conducted the ceremony, be forced, over a claim of privilege, to say whether Sam admitted that he had an undissolved, valid marriage? Can he be asked if Belinda participated in the counseling sessions? If it can be shown that Belinda did participate in the counseling sessions, can Reverend Clark be forced to say whether Sam said he was married to Belinda? Can Reverend Clark be forced to say whether he married Sam and Sandra? Can he be forced to say whether Belinda participated in the ceremony and to describe her role in it? Can either of the women be forced to take the stand and testify against Sam? Can either woman be forced to disclose what was said in the counseling sessions?**

Problem VIII-88. One Saturday morning, a home in an all-white neighborhood that had just recently been purchased by a black family, the Cushmans, went up in flames. On the following Monday, the Cushmans' next-door neighbors, the Jones family, sought counseling with a priest. The Jones parents and their three adult children along with one of the children's fiancées, met with Lutheran pastor, Reverend Byron Williams, three times following the fire. Family members told Rev. Williams about their animosity towards blacks generally and their anger towards the particular black family that had just recently purchased the house next door to them. During one of the counseling sessions, several Jones family members admitted to having set fire to the Cushman home because the family was black and the family members did not want blacks living in the neighborhood. The state charged several members of the Jones family with arson. It subpoenaed Rev. Williams to testify before the grand jury about his family counseling sessions with the Jones family. Rev. Williams refused to testify claiming that the communications were protected by the clergy-communicant privilege. **Is Rev. Williams correct that the communications are privileged? Does the presence of many family members at the counseling sessions, each revealing his or her own personal feelings and prejudices, as well as the responsibility each had for the fire, negate the**

confidentiality necessary for the privilege to attach? Does it matter that one of the persons seeking counseling was a fiancée of a family member and was thus not related by blood to the Jones family? What if before the fire members of the Jones family had confessed during a family counseling session that they intended to burn down the black-owned home next door to them. Would their communications still be privileged? Would Rev. Williams have violated that privilege if he reported the potential arson to the police? Was he under any affirmative obligation to report the possible arson?

Problem VIII-89. The Wolverine Pen Company has a proprietary formula for an especially slippery ink that allows it to market the finest ballpoint pen on the market. It regularly buys its ink dyes in 1,000 pound lots from the Buckeye Ink Company, which manufactures ink dyes as well as a line of its own inks. In March 2010, Wolverine, after receiving complaints that its superfine pens were not writing darkly enough, found that two of the three lots of blue ink and one of the three lots of black ink it had purchased from Buckeye were defective because the colors were not adequately saturated. Wolverine sued Buckeye for the value of the three lots of ink and of an inventory of 100,000 pens already filled with ink from those batches that it had to destroy. In discovery, Buckeye sought disclosure of Wolverine's formula for the ink it uses in its superfine pen line. Wolverine sought to avoid giving Buckeye the formula, citing the trade secrets privilege. **What factors should the court weigh in deciding whether to allow the privilege? How should the court decide?**

VII. THE REPORTER'S PRIVILEGE

We conclude our discussion of privileges with material on the reporter's privilege.[119] Within the past two decades, a number of states (usually by statute but occasionally in a state's constitution or by court decision) and several federal courts have recognized this privilege. Where it exists, the reporter's privilege protects the identities of people who supply information to a reporter or the media on a confidential basis. Occasionally courts will extend the privilege to allow reporters to refuse to disclose confidential information as well. We shall provide you with enough material so that you can evaluate for yourself the wisdom of this privilege.

By now you should realize that there are often political aspects in the creation of new privileges and the redefinition of old ones. Legislatures

---

[119] You may find this privilege referred to by a number of names, including Newsman's Privilege, Journalist's Privilege, Media-Source Privilege, Journalist-Source Privilege, and so on. We choose "Reporter's Privilege" to emphasize that it applies to television and radio reporters as well as to journalists more narrowly defined.

are constantly wooed by professions that seek to have privileges attached to their business relationships. Usually the professions can honestly claim that their practitioners' professional relationships with others carry an expectation of confidentiality. However, many unprivileged relationships carry such an expectation. Privileges apply only to situations in which society feels the potential disclosure of confidential information would so threaten a valued relationship or so grossly invade personal privacy, that the harm outweighs the need for accurate information by litigants, judges, legislative committees, and grand juries. A privilege granted a profession represents, among other things, a legislative judgment affirming the social utility of that profession. Not surprisingly, an evidentiary privilege is something of a status symbol among professions. Pressure for new privileges may reflect professional pride as much as it reflects a need for the strong guarantees of privacy and confidentiality that privileges offer.

Perhaps the most interesting of the recently contested privileges is the reporter's privilege, found in some form in more than half the states. The privilege sought, and in some measure achieved, by news reporters is designed primarily to protect sources who provide reporters with confidential information. Usually this protection requires only that the identity of the source remain secret. The reporters print the information that these sources provide for all to see. Sometimes, however, a reporter must keep information confidential to protect the identity of a source, and on occasion a source will provide a reporter with information only on the understanding that she will not reveal it.

Professor Vince Blasi, who surveyed about one thousand reporters by mail in 1971, and conducted in-depth interviews with forty-seven others, reports the following findings:

> (1) [G]ood reporters use confidential source relationships mainly for the assessment and verification opportunities that such relationships afford rather than for the purpose of gaining access to highly sensitive information of a newsworthy character; (2) the adverse impact of the subpoena threat[120] has been primarily in "poisoning the atmosphere" so as to make insightful, interpretive reporting more difficult rather than in causing sources to "dry up" completely; (3) understandings of confidentiality in reporter-source relationships are frequently unstated and imprecise; (4) press subpoenas damage source relationships primarily by compromising the reporter's independent or compatriot status in the eyes of sources rather than by forcing the revelation of sensitive information; (5) only one

---

[120] Professor Blasi is referring here primarily to instances in which federal prosecutors in the late 1960s subpoenaed reporters who covered antiwar and other radical groups to testify before federal grand juries. Reporters have been similarly subpoenaed when their investigative reports document the extent of drug dealing in an area, reveal political corruption, expose consumer fraud, and in other similar circumstances.

segment of the journalism profession, characterized by certain reporting traits (emphasis on interpretation and verification) more than type of beat, has been adversely affected by the subpoena threat; (6) reporters feel very strongly that any resolution of their conflicting ethical obligations to sources and to society should be a matter of personal rather than judicial determination, and in consonance with this belief these reporters evince a high level of asserted willingness to testify voluntarily and also a very high level of asserted willingness to go to jail if necessary to honor what they perceive to be their obligation of confidentiality; (7) newsmen prefer a flexible ad hoc qualified privilege; (8) newsmen regard protection for the *identity* of anonymous sources as more important than protection for the *contents* of confidential information given by known sources; (9) newsmen object most of all to the frequency with which press subpoenas have been issued in what these reporters regard as unnecessary circumstances when they have no important information to contribute.[121]

The news reporter's privilege is unusual in two respects. First, because of the importance of the identity of the source, the right to assert the privilege must rest with the reporter rather than the source, although a source willing to reveal herself can waive it. Second, reporters have claimed that this privilege exists as a matter of constitutional law. They have argued that the First Amendment's guarantee of freedom of the press provides reporters with at least a qualified privilege to refuse to reveal the identity of their sources and other information gained under promises of confidentiality. In 1972, the Supreme Court, by a 5–4 vote, appeared to reject these claims. The Court's opinion, by providing a detailed description of circumstances in which reporters have felt that a privilege was necessary, is particularly helpful in understanding the values that clash in deciding whether to extend the privilege.

BRANZBURG V. HAYES
408 U.S. 665 (1972).

MR. JUSTICE WHITE delivered the opinion of the Court.

* * *

On November 15, 1969, the Courier-Journal carried a story under petitioner's by-line describing in detail his observations of two young residents of Jefferson County synthesizing hashish from marihuana, an activity which, they asserted, earned them about $5,000 in three weeks. The article included a photograph of a pair of hands working above a laboratory table on which was a substance identified by the caption as

---

[121] Vince Blasi, The Newsman's Privilege: An Empirical Study, 70 Mich. L. Rev. 229, 284 (1971).

hashish. The article stated that petitioner had promised not to reveal the identity of the two hashish makers. Petitioner was shortly subpoenaed by the Jefferson County grand jury; he appeared, but refused to identify the individuals he had seen possessing marihuana or the persons he had seen making hashish from marihuana. A state trial court judge ordered petitioner to answer these questions. . . .

. . .

In re Pappas originated when petitioner Pappas, a television newsman-photographer working out of the Providence, Rhode Island office of a New Bedford, Massachusetts television station was called to New Bedford on July 30, 1970, to report on civil disorders there that involved fires and other turmoil. He intended to cover a Black Panther news conference at that group's headquarters in a boarded-up store. Petitioner found the streets around the store barricaded, but he ultimately gained entrance to the area and recorded and photographed a prepared statement read by one of the Black Panther leaders at about 3 p.m. He then asked for and received permission to re-enter the area. Returning at about 9 o'clock, he was allowed to enter and remain inside Panther headquarters. As a condition of entry, Pappas agreed not to disclose anything he saw or heard inside the store except an anticipated police raid, which Pappas, "on his own," was free to photograph and report as he wished. Pappas stayed inside the headquarters for about three hours, but there was no police raid, and petitioner wrote no story and did not otherwise reveal what had occurred in the store while he was there. Two months later, petitioner was summoned before the Bristol County Grand Jury and appeared; answered questions as to his name, address, employment, and what he had seen and heard outside Panther headquarters; but refused to answer any questions about what had taken place inside headquarters while he was there, claiming that the First Amendment afforded him a privilege to protect confidential informants and their information. A second summons was then served upon him, again directing him to appear before the grand jury and "to give such evidence as he knows relating to any matters which may be inquired of on behalf of the Commonwealth before . . . the Grand Jury." His motion to quash on First Amendment and other grounds was denied by the trial judge who, noting the absence of a statutory newsman's privilege in Massachusetts, ruled that petitioner had no constitutional privilege to refuse to divulge to the grand jury what he had seen and heard, including the identity of persons he had observed. . . .

United States v. Caldwell arose from subpoenas issued by a federal grand jury in the Northern District of California to respondent Earl Caldwell, a reporter for the New York Times assigned to cover the Blank Panther Party and other black militant groups. A subpoena *duces tecum* was served on respondent on February 1, 1970, ordering him to appear before the grand jury to testify and to bring with him notes and tape recordings of interviews given him for publication by officers and spokesmen of the Blank Panther Party concerning the aims, purposes, and activities of that organization. Respondent objected to the scope of this subpoena, and an agreement between his counsel and the Government attorneys resulted in a continuance. A second subpoena, served on March 16, omitted the documentary requirement and simply ordered Caldwell "to appear . . . to testify before the Grand Jury." Respondent and his employer, the New York Times, moved to quash on the ground that the unlimited breadth of the subpoenas and the fact that Caldwell would have to appear in secret before the grand jury would destroy his working relationship with the Black Panther Party and "suppress vital First Amendment freedoms . . . by driving a wedge of distrust and silence between the news media and the militants." Respondent argued that "so drastic an incursion upon First Amendment freedoms" should not be permitted "in the absence of a compelling governmental interest—not shown here—in requiring Mr. Caldwell's appearance before the grand jury." . . . The Government filed three memoranda in opposition to the motion to quash, each supported by affidavits. These documents stated that the grand jury was investigating, among other things, possible violations of a number of criminal statutes, including 18 U.S.C. § 871 (threats against the President), 18 U.S.C. § 1751 (assassination, attempts to assassinate, conspiracy to assassinate the President), 18 U.S.C. § 21 (civil disorders), 18 U.S.C. § 2101 (interstate travel to incite a riot), and 18 U.S.C. § 1341 (mail frauds and swindles). . . . Also referred to were various writings by Caldwell about the Black Panther Party, including an article published in the New York Times on December 14, 1969, stating that "[i]n their role as the vanguard in a revolutionary struggle the Panthers have picked up guns," and quoting the Chief of Staff of the Party as declaring that: "We advocate the very direct overthrow of the Government by way of force and violence. . . . " On April 6, the District Court denied the motion to quash, . . . on the ground that "*every person* within the jurisdiction of the government" is bound to testify upon being properly summoned. Nevertheless, the court accepted respondent's First Amendment arguments to the extent of issuing a protective order providing that although respondent had to divulge whatever information had been given to him for publication, he "shall not be required to reveal confidential associations, sources or information received, developed or maintained by him as a professional journalist in the course of his efforts to gather news for dissemination to the public through the press or other news media." The court held that the First Amendment afforded respondent a privilege to refuse disclosure of such confidential information until there has been "a showing by the Government of a compelling and overriding national interest in requiring Mr. Caldwell's testimony which cannot be served by any alternative means."

Subsequently, the term of the grand jury expired, a new grand jury was convened, and a new subpoena *ad testificandum* was issued and served on May 22, 1970. . . . Upon his further refusal to go before the grand jury, respondent was ordered committed for contempt until such time as he complied with the court's order or until the expiration of the term of the grand jury.

Respondent Caldwell appealed the contempt order, and the Court of Appeals reversed. Caldwell v. United States, 434 F.2d 1081 (C.A.9 1970). Viewing the issue before it as whether Caldwell was required to appear before the grand jury at all, rather than the scope of permissible interrogation, the court first determined that the First Amendment provided a qualified testimonial privilege to newsmen; in its view, requiring a reporter like Caldwell to testify would deter his informants from communicating with him in the future and would cause him to censor his writings in an effort to avoid being subpoenaed. Absent compelling reasons for requiring his testimony, he was held privileged to withhold it. The court also held, for similar First Amendment reasons, that, absent some special showing of necessity by the Government, attendance by Caldwell at a secret meeting of the grand jury was something he was privileged to refuse because of the potential impact of such an appearance on the flow of news to the public. . . .

II

Petitioners Branzburg and Pappas and respondent Caldwell press First Amendment claims that may be simply put: that to gather news it is often necessary to agree either not to identify the source of information published or to publish only part of the facts revealed, or both; that if the reporter is nevertheless forced to reveal these confidences to a grand jury, the source so identified and other confidential sources of other reporters will be measurably deterred from furnishing publishable information, all to the detriment of the free flow of information protected by the First Amendment. Although the newsmen in these cases do not claim an absolute privilege against official interrogation in all circumstances, they assert that the reporter should not be forced either to appear or to testify before a grand jury or at trial until and unless sufficient grounds are shown for believing that the reporter possesses information relevant to a crime the grand jury is investigating, that the information the reporter has is unavailable from other sources, and that the need for the information is sufficiently compelling to override the claimed invasion of First Amendment interests occasioned by the disclosure. Principally relied upon are prior cases emphasizing the importance of the First Amendment guarantees to individual development and to our system of representative government, decisions requiring that official action with adverse impact on First Amendment rights be justified by a public interest that is "compelling" or "paramount," and those precedents establishing the principle that justifiable governmental goals may not be achieved by unduly broad means having an unnecessary impact on protected rights of speech, press, or association. The heart of the claim is that the burden on news gathering resulting from compelling reporters to disclose confidential information outweighs any public interest in obtaining the information.

. . .

Despite the fact that news gathering may be hampered, the press is regularly excluded from grand jury proceedings, our own conferences, the meetings of other official bodies gathered in executive session, and the meetings of private organizations. Newsmen have no constitutional right of access to the scenes of crime or disaster when the general public is excluded, and they may be prohibited from attending or publishing information about trials if such restrictions are necessary to assure a defendant a fair trial before an impartial tribunal. . . .

It is thus not surprising that the great weight of authority is that newsmen are not exempt from the normal duty of appearing before a grand jury and answering questions relevant to a criminal investigation. At common law, courts consistently refused to recognize the existence of any privilege authorizing a newsman to refuse to reveal confidential information to a grand jury. . . .

. . .

A number of States have provided newsmen a statutory privilege of varying breadth, but the majority have not done so, and none has been provided by federal statute. Until now the only testimonial privilege for unofficial witnesses that is rooted in the Federal Constitution is the Fifth Amendment privilege against compelled self-discrimination. We are asked to create another by interpreting the First Amendment to grant newsmen a testimonial privilege that other citizens do not enjoy. This we decline to do. Fair and effective law enforcement aimed at providing security for the person and property of the individual is a fundamental function of government, and the grand jury plays an important, constitutionally mandated role in this process. On the records now before us, we perceive no basis for holding that the public interest in law enforcement and in ensuring effective grand jury proceedings is insufficient to override the consequential, but uncertain, burden on news gathering that is said to result from insisting that reporters, like other citizens, respond to relevant questions put to them in the course of a valid grand jury investigation or criminal trial.

This conclusion itself involves no restraint on what newspapers may publish or on the type or quality of information reporters may seek to acquire, nor does it threaten the vast bulk of confidential relationships between reporters and their sources. Grand juries address themselves to the issues of whether crimes have been committed and who committed them. Only where news sources themselves are implicated in crime or possess information relevant to the grand jury's task need they or the reporter be concerned about grand jury subpoenas. Nothing before us indicates that a large number or percentage of *all* confidential news sources falls into either category and would in any way be deterred by our holding that the Constitution does not, as it never has, exempt the newsman from performing the citizen's normal duty of appearing and furnishing information relevant to the grand jury's task.

The preference for anonymity of those confidential informants involved in actual criminal conduct is presumably a product of their desire to escape criminal prosecution, and this preference, while understandable, is hardly deserving of constitutional protection. It would be frivolous to assert—and no one does in these cases—that the First Amendment, in the interest of securing news or otherwise, confers a license on either the reporter or his news sources to violate valid criminal laws. Although stealing documents or private wiretapping could provide newsworthy information, neither reporter nor source is immune from conviction for such conduct, whatever the impact on the flow of news. Neither is immune, on First Amendment grounds, from testifying against the other, before the grand jury or at a criminal trial. . . .

Thus, we cannot seriously entertain the notion that the First Amendment protects a newsman's agreement to conceal the criminal conduct of his source, or evidence thereof, on the theory that it is better to write about crime than to do something about it. . . . The crimes of news sources are no less reprehensible and threatening to the public interest when witnessed by a reporter than when they are not.

There remain those situations where a source is not engaged in criminal conduct but has information suggesting illegal conduct by others. Newsmen frequently receive information from such sources pursuant to a tacit or express agreement to withhold the source's name and suppress any information that the source wishes not published. Such informants presumably desire anonymity in order to avoid being entangled as a witness in a criminal trial or grand jury investigation. They may fear that disclosure will threaten their job security or personal safety or that it will simply result in dishonor or embarrassment.

The argument that the flow of news will be diminished by compelling reporters to aid the grand jury in a criminal investigation is not irrational, nor are the records before us silent on the matter. But we remain unclear how often and to what extent informers are actually deterred from furnishing information when newsmen are forced to testify before a grand jury. The available data indicate that some newsmen rely a great deal on confidential sources and that some informants are particularly sensitive to the threat of exposure and may be silenced if it is held by this Court that, ordinarily, newsmen must testify pursuant to subpoenas, but the evidence fails to demonstrate that there would be a significant constriction of the flow of news to the public if this Court reaffirms the prior common-law and constitutional rule regarding the testimonial obligations of newsmen. Estimates of the inhibiting effect of such subpoenas on the willingness of informants to make disclosures to newsmen are widely divergent and to a great extent speculative.[a] It would be difficult to canvass the views of the informants themselves; surveys of reporters on this topic are chiefly opinions of predicted informant behavior and must be viewed in the light of the professional self-interest of the interviewees.[b] Reliance by the press on confidential informants does not mean that all such sources will in fact dry up because of the later possible appearance of the newsman before a grand jury. The reporter may never be called and if he objects to testifying, the prosecution may not insist. Also, the relationship of many informants to the press is a symbiotic one which is unlikely to be greatly inhibited by the threat of subpoena: quite often, such informants are members of a minority political or cultural group that relies heavily on the media to propagate its views, publicize its aims, and magnify its exposure to the public.   Moreover, ... law enforcement officers are themselves experienced in dealing with informers, and have their own methods for protecting them without interference with the effective administration of justice. ... We doubt if the informer who prefers anonymity but is sincerely interested in furnishing evidence of crime will always or very often be deterred by the prospect of dealing with those public authorities characteristically charged with the duty to protect the public interest as well as his.

Accepting the fact, however, that an undetermined number of informants not themselves implicated in crime will nevertheless, for whatever reason, refuse to talk to newsmen if they fear identification by a reporter in an official investigation, we cannot accept the argument that

---

[a.] Cf., e.g., the results of a study conducted by James A. Guest and Alan L. Stanzler, which appears as an appendix to their article, The Constitutional Argument for Newsmen Concealing Their Sources, 64 Nw. U. L. Rev. 18, 57–61 (1969). A number of editors of daily newspapers of varying circulation were asked the question, "Excluding one-or two-sentence gossip items, on the average how many stories based on information received in confidence are published in your paper each year?   Very rough estimate."   Answers varied significantly, e.g., "Virtually innumerable," Tucson Daily Citizen (41,969 daily circ.), "Too many to remember," Los Angeles Herald-Examiner (718,221 daily circ.), "Occasionally," Denver Post (252,084 daily circ.), "Rarely," Cleveland Plain Dealer (370,499 daily circ.), "Very rare, some politics," Oregon Journal (146,403 daily circ.). This study did not purport to measure the extent of deterrence of informants caused by subpoenas to the press.

[b.] In his Press Subpoenas: An Empirical and Legal Analysis, Study Report of the Reporters' Committee on Freedom of the Press 6–12, Professor Vince Blasi discusses these methodological problems. Professor Blasi's survey found that slightly more than half of the 975 reporters questioned said that they relied on regular confidential sources for at least 10% of their stories. *Id.* at 21. Of this group of reporters, only 8% were able to say with some certainty that their professional functioning had been adversely affected by the threat of subpoena; another 11% were not certain whether or not they had been adversely affected. *Id.* at 53.

the public interest in possible future news about crime from undisclosed, unverified sources must take precedence over the public interest in pursuing and prosecuting those crimes reported to the press by informants and in thus deterring the commission of such crimes in the future.

We note first that the privilege claimed is that of the reporter, not the informant, and that if the authorities independently identify the informant, neither his own reluctance to testify nor the objection of the newsman would shield him from grand jury inquiry,. . . .

Of course, the press has the right to abide by its agreement not to publish all the information it has, but the right to withhold news is not equivalent to a First Amendment exemption from the ordinary duty of all other citizens to furnish relevant information to a grand jury performing an important public function. . . .

Neither are we now convinced that a virtually impenetrable constitutional shield, beyond legislative or judicial control, should be forged to protect a private system of informers operated by the press to report on criminal conduct, a system that would be unaccountable to the public, would pose a threat to the citizen's justifiable expectations of privacy, and would equally protect well-intentioned informants and those who for pay or otherwise betray their trust to their employer or associates. The public through its elected and appointed law enforcement officers regularly utilizes informers, and in proper circumstances may assert a privilege against disclosing the identity of these informers. But "[t]he purpose of the privilege is the furtherance and protection of the public interest in effective law enforcement. The privilege recognizes the obligation of citizens to communicate their knowledge of the commission of crimes to law-enforcement officials and, by preserving their anonymity, encourages them to perform that obligation." Roviaro v. United States, 353 U.S. 53, 59 (1957).

Such informers enjoy no constitutional protection. Their testimony is available to the public when desired by grand juries or at criminal trials; their identity cannot be concealed from the defendant when it is critical to his case. Clearly, this system is not impervious to control by the judiciary and the decision whether to unmask an informer or to continue to profit by his anonymity is in public, not private, hands. We think that it should remain there and that public authorities should retain the options of either insisting on the informer's testimony relevant to the prosecution of crime or of seeking the benefit of further information that his exposure might prevent.

We are admonished that refusal to provide a First Amendment reporter's privilege will undermine the freedom of the press to collect and disseminate news. But this is not the lesson history teaches us. As noted previously, the common law recognized no such privilege, and the constitutional argument was not even asserted until 1958. From the beginning of our country the press has operated without constitutional protection for press informants, and the press has flourished. The existing constitutional rules have not been a serious obstacle to either the development or retention of confidential news sources by the press.

It is said that currently press subpoenas have multiplied, that mutual distrust and tension between press and officialdom have increased, that reporting styles have changed, and that there is now more need for confidential sources, particularly where the press seeks news about minority cultural and political groups or dissident organizations suspicious of the law and public officials. These developments, even if true, are treacherous grounds for a far-reaching interpretation of the First Amendment fastening a nationwide rule on courts, grand juries, and prosecuting officials everywhere. The obligation to testify in response to grand jury subpoenas will not threaten those sources not involved with criminal conduct and without information relevant to grand jury investigations, and we cannot hold that the Constitution places the sources in these two categories either above the law or beyond its reach. . . .

The requirements of those cases, which hold that a State's interest must be "compelling" or "paramount" to justify even an indirect burden on First Amendment rights, are also met here. As we have indicated, the investigation of crime by the grand jury implements a fundamental governmental role of securing the safety of the person and property of the citizen, and it appears to us that calling reporters to give testimony in the manner and for the reasons that other citizens are called "bears a reasonable relationship to the achievement of the governmental purpose asserted as its justification." . . .

The privilege claimed here is conditional, not absolute; given the suggested preliminary showings and compelling need, the reporter would be required to testify. Presumably, such a rule would reduce the instances in which reporters could be required to appear, but predicting in advance when and in what circumstances they could be compelled to do so would be difficult. Such a rule would also have implications for the issuance of compulsory process to reporters at civil and criminal trials and at legislative hearings. If newsmen's confidential sources are as sensitive as they are claimed to be, the prospect of being unmasked whenever a judge determines the situation justifies it is hardly a satisfactory solution to the problem. For them, it would appear that only an absolute privilege would suffice.

We are unwilling to embark the judiciary on a long and difficult journey to such an uncertain destination. The administration of a constitutional newsman's privilege would present practical and conceptual difficulties of a high order. Sooner or later, it would be necessary to define those categories of newsmen who qualified for the privilege, a questionable procedure in light of the traditional doctrine that liberty of the press is the right of the lonely pamphleteer who uses carbon paper or a mimeograph just as much as of the large metropolitan publisher who utilizes the latest photocomposition methods. . . .

In each instance where a reporter is subpoenaed to testify, the courts would also be embroiled in preliminary factual and legal determinations with respect to whether the proper predicate had been laid for the reporter's appearance: Is there probable cause to believe a crime has been committed? Is it likely that the reporter has useful information gained in confidence? Could the grand jury obtain the information elsewhere? Is the official interest sufficient to outweigh the claimed privilege?

Thus, in the end, by considering whether enforcement of a particular law served a "compelling" governmental interest, the courts would be inextricably involved in distinguishing between the value of enforcing different criminal laws. By requiring testimony from a reporter in investigations involving some crimes but not in others, they would be making a value judgment that a legislature had declined to make, since in each case the criminal law involved would represent a considered legislative judgment, not constitutionally suspect, of what conduct is liable to criminal prosecution. The task of judges, like other officials outside the legislative branch, is not to make the law but to uphold it in accordance with their oaths.

At the federal level, Congress has freedom to determine whether a statutory newsman's privilege is necessary and desirable and to fashion standards and rules as narrow or broad as deemed necessary to deal with the evil discerned and, equally important, to refashion those rules as experience from time to time may dictate. . . .

In addition, there is much force in the pragmatic view that the press has at its disposal powerful mechanisms of communication and is far from helpless to protect itself from harassment or substantial harm. Furthermore, if what the newsmen urged in these cases is true—that law enforcement cannot hope to gain and may suffer from subpoenaing newsmen before grand juries—prosecutors will be loath to risk so much for so little. Thus, at the federal level the Attorney General has already fashioned a set of rules for federal officials in connection with subpoenaing members of the press to testify before grand juries or at criminal trials.[c] . . .

---

c. The Guidelines for Subpoenas to the News Media were first announced in a speech by the Attorney General on August 10, 1970, and then were expressed in Department of Justice Memo. No. 692 (Sept. 2, 1970), which was sent to all United States Attorneys by the Assistant Attorney General in charge of the Criminal Division. The Guidelines state that: "The Department of Justice recognizes that compulsory process in some circumstances may have a limiting effect on the exercise of First Amendment rights. In determining whether to request issuance of a

Finally, as we have earlier indicated, news gathering is not without its First Amendment protections, and grand jury investigations if instituted or conducted other than in good faith, would pose wholly different issues for resolution under the First Amendment. Official harassment of the press undertaken not for purposes of law enforcement but to disrupt a reporter's relationship with his news sources would have no justification. Grand juries are subject to judicial control and subpoenas to motions to quash. We do not expect courts will forget that grand juries must operate within the limits of the First Amendment as well as the Fifth.

. . .

[MR. JUSTICE POWELL, whose vote was crucial in *Branzburg*, expressed his understanding of the Court's opinion, in which he joined, in the following brief concurring opinion.]

I add this brief statement to emphasize what seems to me to be the limited nature of the Court's holding. The Court does not hold that newsmen, subpoenaed to testify before a grand jury, are without constitutional rights with respect to the gathering of news or in safeguarding their sources. . . .

As indicated in the concluding portion of the opinion, the Court states that no harassment of newsmen will be tolerated. If a newsman believes that the grand jury investigation is not being conducted in good faith he is not without remedy. Indeed, if the newsman is called upon to give information bearing only a remote and tenuous relationship to the subject of the investigation, or if he has some other reason to believe that his testimony implicates confidential source relationships without a legitimate need of law enforcement, he will have access to the court on a motion to quash and an appropriate protective order may be entered. The asserted claim to privilege should be judged on its facts by the striking of a proper balance between freedom of the press and the obligation of all citizens to give relevant testimony with respect to criminal conduct. The balance of these vital constitutional and societal interests on a case-by-case basis accords with the tried and traditional way of adjudicating such questions.

---

subpoena to the press, the approach in every case must be to weigh that limiting effect against the public interest to be served in the fair administration of justice" and that: "The Department of Justice does not consider the press 'an investigative arm of the government.' Therefore, all reasonable attempts should be made to obtain information from non-press sources before there is any consideration of subpoenaing the press." The Guidelines provide for negotiations with the press and require the express authorization of the Attorney General for such subpoenas. The principles to be applied in authorizing such subpoenas are stated to be whether there is "sufficient reason to believe that the information sought [from the journalist] is essential to a successful investigation," and whether the Government has unsuccessfully attempted to obtain the information from alternative non-press sources. . . .

In short, the courts will be available to newsmen under circumstances where legitimate First Amendment interests require protection.

MR. JUSTICE STEWART, with whom MR. JUSTICE BRENNAN and MR. JUSTICE MARSHALL join, dissenting.

. . .

[W]hen a reporter is asked to appear before a grand jury and reveal confidences, I would hold that the government must (1) show that there is probable cause to believe that the newsman has information that is clearly relevant to a specific probable violation of law; (2) demonstrate that the information sought cannot be obtained by alternative means less destructive of First Amendment rights; and (3) demonstrate a compelling and overriding interest in the information.

This is not to say that a grand jury could not issue a subpoena until such a showing were made, and it is not to say that a newsman would be in any way privileged to ignore any subpoena that was issued. Obviously, before the government's burden to make such a showing were triggered, the reporter would have to move to quash the subpoena, asserting the basis on which he considered the particular relationship a confidential one.

The crux of the Court's rejection of any newsman's privilege is its observation that only "where news sources themselves are implicated in crime or possess information *relevant* to the grand jury's task need they or the reporter be concerned about grand jury subpoenas." But this is a most misleading construct. For it is obviously not true that the only persons about whom reporters will be forced to testify will be those "confidential informants involved in actual criminal conduct" and those having "information suggesting illegal conduct by others." As noted above, given the grand jury's extraordinarily broad investigative powers and the weak standards of relevance and materiality that apply during such inquiries, reporters, if they have no testimonial privilege, will be called to give information about informants who have neither committed crimes nor have information about crime. It is to avoid deterrence of such sources and thus to prevent needless injury to First Amendment values that I think the government must be required to show probable cause that the newsman has information that is clearly relevant to a specific probable violation of criminal law.[d]

[d.] If this requirement is not met, then the government will basically be allowed to undertake a "fishing expedition" at the expense of the press. Such general, exploratory investigations will be most damaging to confidential news-gathering relationships, since they will create great uncertainty in both reporters and their sources. The Court sanctions such explorations, by refusing to apply a meaningful "probable cause" requirement. As the Court states, a grand jury investigation "may be triggered by tips, rumors, evidence proffered by the prosecutor, or the personal knowledge of the grand jurors." It thereby invites government to try to annex the press as an investigative arm, since any time government wants to probe the

Similarly, a reporter may have information from a confidential source that is "related" to the commission of crime, but the government may be able to obtain an indictment or otherwise achieve its purposes by subpoenaing persons other than the reporter. It is an obvious but important truism that when government aims have been fully served, there can be no legitimate reason to disrupt a confidential relationship between a reporter and his source. To do so would not aid the administration of justice and would only impair the flow of information to the public. Thus, it is to avoid deterrence of such sources that I think the government must show that there is no alternative means for the grand jury to obtain the information sought.

Both the "probable cause" and "alternative means" requirements would thus serve the vital function of mediating between the public interest in the administration of justice and the constitutional protection of the full flow of information. These requirements would avoid a direct conflict between these competing concerns, and they would generally provide adequate protection for newsmen. No doubt the courts would be required to make some delicate judgments in working out this accommodation. But that, after all, is the function of courts of law. Better such judgments, however difficult, than the simplistic and stultifying absolutism adopted by the Court in denying any force to the First Amendment in these cases.

The error in the Court's absolute rejection of First Amendment interests in these cases seems to me to be most profound. For in the name of advancing the administration of justice, the Court's decision, I think, will only impair the achievement of that goal. People entrusted with law enforcement responsibility, no less than private citizens, need general information relating to controversial social problems. Obviously, press reports have great value to government, even when the newsman cannot be compelled to testify before a grand jury. The sad paradox of the Court's position is that when a grand jury may exercise an unbridled subpoena power, and sources involved in sensitive matters become fearful of disclosing information, the newsman will not only cease to be a useful grand jury witness; he will cease to investigate and publish information about issues of public import. I cannot subscribe to such an anomalous result, for, in my view, the interests protected by the First Amendment are not antagonistic to the administration of justice. Rather, they can, in

---

relationships between the newsman and his source, it can, on virtually any pretext, convene a grand jury and compel the journalist to testify.

The Court fails to recognize that under the guise of "investigating crime" vindictive prosecutors can, using the broad powers of the grand jury which are, in effect, immune from judicial supervision, explore the newsman's sources at will, with no serious law enforcement purpose. The secrecy of grand jury proceedings affords little consolation to a news source; the prosecutor obviously will, in most cases, have knowledge of testimony given by grand jury witnesses.

the long run, only be complementary, and for that reason must be given great "breathing space."

[The separate dissenting opinion of MR. JUSTICE DOUGLAS is omitted.]

Society benefits when newspapers print stories like those written by Branzburg, Pappas, and Caldwell. Society also benefits when people are punished for the criminal behavior such stories disclose, or when courts avoid wrongful convictions because a reporter shows that the police have arrested the wrong person. But it is not clear that reporters need a privilege to gain the kind of access to information that Branzburg, Pappas, and Caldwell had.

For those who favor a reporter's privilege, distinguishing between the First Amendment rights of ordinary citizens and those of reporters can prove problematic. The First Amendment guarantees freedom of speech as well as freedom of the press. One can argue that forcing reporters to disclose sources invades the privacy of the reporter-source relationship and causes news to dry up, but one can also argue that forcing individuals to reveal others' confidences inhibits interpersonal communications and in this sense inhibits speech. Thus in arguing for the privilege, one must identify something about the role of the press in America that justifies a privilege for reporters and their sources when ordinary citizens and those who confide in them do not have one. This is particularly problematic in the age of the internet with its proliferation of blogs and privately managed sites devoted to breaking, or sometimes making up, news and with more mainstream publishers that extend to their on-line readers invitations to provide or comment on the news. In a real sense almost everyone today can become a news reporter. If we were today to establish a reporter's privilege how would we define its holders?

The Court's opinion in *Branzburg* suggests that the absence of a privilege "involves no restraint on what newspapers may publish or the type or quality of information reporters may seek to acquire." Surely this is disingenuous, at least if reporters are right in asserting that certain sources will refuse to talk without confidentiality. Indeed, ethical reporters might feel that if they are vulnerable to subpoena, they should not seek certain disclosures. But the Court is just as clearly correct when it asserts that sources and reporters often have a symbiotic relationship and the absence of a privilege should not cause most sources to dry up. But if some sources dry up, does it matter that most will not?

Despite the detail in the majority opinion, we cannot tell how strong the government's need for information was in *Branzburg* and its companion cases. An instrumental approach to the privilege would balance this consideration against the reporter's need for secrecy and society's likely benefit from extending a privilege. We do not know clearly whether the Court was unconcerned with this balance because it was not asking about the wisdom of a reporter's privilege but rather whether the First Amendment required it, or whether the Court assumed from its detailed recitation of the possible crimes that the reporters could help solve or forestall that the state greatly needed their testimony. Presumably the Court assumed the latter, for even on the question of whether the First Amendment implies a privilege, the government's need appears relevant. If the government interest is sufficiently weak, grand jury subpoenas might be seen as harassing. Even the majority suggests that under the First Amendment using subpoenas to harass the press is not permitted. Some have seen in this concession a basis for a more extensive privilege than the majority might contemplate.

It is not clear how much information the government would lose if reporters had an absolute privilege, at least so long as "reporter" could be confined to those who practice journalism as their main profession. In the short run, one can, as in *Branzburg*, point to information losses. In the long run, however, stories that might not be available absent a privilege may provide the government with more rather than fewer leads to crime. A qualified privilege would cost the government less short-run information but might have long-run costs. Arguably, however, these policy considerations have nothing to do with the merits of First Amendment claims.

The Court in *Branzburg* states that grand juries have a right to every citizen's evidence. This is a glib phrase but overly broad, as the Court itself concedes. Grand juries must bow to claims of the attorney-client, spousal, Fifth Amendment, and other recognized privileges. The fact that grand juries have a right, and indeed a need, to receive evidence does not determine whether the strength of other interests overrides that right and need. The Supreme Court did not decide that other interests did not override the grand jury's need for evidence. It simply decided that the First Amendment did not require a privilege that might frustrate grand jury investigations. Even if a reporter's privilege is desirable, the majority, perhaps wisely, did not want to create one as a matter of constitutional law.

One of the most interesting developments since *Branzburg* is the reading that lower courts have given it. Justice White may have thought he was putting an end to constitutionally based claims of a reporter's privilege, but many lower courts have seen in Justice Powell's separate opinion an invitation to protect the press on a case-by-case basis. Thus some federal cases refuse to extend the *Branzburg* holding to civil cases[122]; others uphold the privilege in a criminal context[123]; and some

---

[122] See, e.g., Riley v. City of Chester, 612 F.2d 708 (3d Cir. 1979).

cases require disclosures before grand juries only if the information sought bears a substantial relation to the grand jury investigation.[124] To defeat a reporter's privilege claim in federal court, a party seeking information from a reporter must, at a minimum, generally show that the information is important to the litigation and that it is not available from alternative sources. In diversity actions, more protective state privileges may apply.

The most surprising development of all is that some courts, applying FRE 501, have held that there is a common law reporter-source privilege. Although the Supreme Court did not address itself to common law claims, the history related by Justice White makes it doubtful that he would have found that reporters had or deserved a judicially created privilege. Since a common law privilege protects the flow of information, it resembles a constitutionally based privilege, especially if the privilege is conditional. Resting a conditional privilege on the First Amendment differs from finding one as a matter of federally recognized common law in that Congress can reject or change a common law privilege, but cannot limit or eliminate a constitutionally based one. The majority in *Branzburg* might have been motivated in part by the sense that the parameters of a reporter's privilege were better determined by a legislature than by a court.

A. A PROPOSED STATUTE

The following statute is the second tentative draft, dated June 1, 1975, of a Uniform Reporter's Privilege Act, considered but eventually rejected by the National Conference of Commissioners on Uniform State Laws. Now that you have read some of the policy and legal arguments concerning the privilege, ask yourself whether the proposed statute is too protective of the reporter's interests, or not protective enough. If this proposed statute were introduced in the legislature in your state, would you support it? What changes, if any, would you want to make? As you read this proposed statute ask yourself whether the distinctions made, between trials and other proceedings and between the disclosure of confidential sources and the disclosure of confidential information, are sensible.

---

[123] See, e.g., United States v. Cuthbertson, 630 F.2d 139 (3d Cir. 1980), *cert. denied*, 449 U.S. 1126 (1981).

[124] See, e.g., Lewis v. United States, 517 F.2d 236 (9th Cir. 1975).

Uniform Reporter's Privilege Act, Second Tentative Draft, June 1, 1975.

PREFATORY NOTE

. . .

Since 1969, the number of subpoenas issued to reporters has greatly increased. Several factors appear to have contributed to the rise. . . . Possibly the most important change is simply that the inhibitions (perhaps rooted in vague notions about the First Amendment) that used to deter litigants from subpoenaing reporters seem no longer to operate in the wake of a few well-publicized violations of the taboo and the Supreme Court's holding in Branzburg v. Hayes, 408 U.S. 665 (1972), that reporters do not have a general First Amendment privilege against compulsory process.

Whatever forces lie behind the increase in subpoenas, the phenomenon has created many instances of observed or articulated anxiety and noncooperation on the part of news sources, expressions of alarm from journalists and scholars, and a number of shield-law proposals in Congress and the state legislatures. In the last seven years alone, twelve different state legislatures have passed new shield laws and several other states have amended their preexisting laws.

. . .

The Uniform Reporter's Privilege Act is fashioned around two key distinctions. The first is the distinction between trials on the one hand, and investigative, accusatory, and preliminary proceedings on the other hand. Of the subpoenas that have been served on reporters in recent years, those that have been issued during the course of investigative, accusatory, and preliminary proceedings have tended to be the most numerous, most wide-ranging in scope, most dubious in motivation, most damaging to source relationships, and least justifiable in terms of evidentiary needs. From the reporter's point of view, these subpoenas comprise the crux of the problem. In providing for an absolute privilege against this type of subpoena, the Act grants reporters the essential protection they need in order to engage in the kind of in-depth investigative reporting that ultimately redounds to the benefit of law enforcement as well as most other societal interests.

The second important distinction comes into play with regard to trials. This is the distinction between evidence that discloses the identity of a confidential source and evidence that discloses only the content of confidential information that the reporter obtained from a source whose identity has already been published or remains undisclosed. In all proceedings except certain defamation and privacy actions, the Act grants reporters an absolute privilege to decline to give evidence that would disclose the identity of a confidential source; it is noteworthy that seventeen states already provide this much protection for the identity of a confidential source.   With regard to the content of confidential information, however, the Act provides that the privilege is superseded in a trial if the reporter's evidence is indispensable to the subpoenaing party's case.   In a libel case in which the plaintiff must prove that the defendant acted with negligence or reckless disregard for the truth, even the identity of a confidential source can be required to be disclosed if the source's identity is indispensable to the plaintiff's case and all other elements of the case have been established.

Although the basic privilege is limited to confidential sources and information, the Act also provides limited protection for non-confidential matter the disclosure of which would harm the future flow of information to the public to an extent unjustified by the likely evidentiary value of disclosure.

The Act defines "reporter" broadly to include authors of books, lecturers, pamphleteers, and other persons whose primary purpose in obtaining information is to contribute to public knowledge.

The most important procedural provisions are the requirement that every privilege claim be determined by a court of law and the requirement that a judge find reasonable grounds to believe that a reporter has relevant evidence before a subpoena can be issued to the reporter.

SECTION 1. [*Definitions.*]

As used in this Act:

(1) "Confidential information" means information which has been obtained by a reporter and withheld from publication pursuant to an express or implied understanding between the reporter and the source that the information would not be published.

This definition needs to be read in conjunction with Section 3, which provides that "confidential information" can under certain conditions be subpoenaed in a trial but cannot be subpoenaed in any other proceeding. . . .

(2) "Confidential source" means a source whose identity as a source of certain information has been withheld from publication pursuant to an express or implied understanding between the reporter and the source that his identity as the source of the information would not be published.

(3) "Give evidence" means to testify, produce tangible evidence, submit to a deposition, answer interrogatories, or otherwise make information available at any stage of a proceeding.

(4) "Information" means knowledge which is capable of being transmitted by oral, written, pictorial, electronic, demonstrative, or

other means. The term includes, but is not limited to, assertions and documentation of fact, expressions of opinion, fictional representations and portrayals, interpretations, predictions, eyewitness observations, and names of persons who might be able to furnish additional knowledge.

(5) "Proceeding" means any hearing or procedure in which or for which the power of compulsory process may be exercised.

(6) "Publish" means to disseminate by any means information in a form available to the public.

Comment

This definition includes the dissemination of highly specialized publications such as trade journals and foreign language, college, and underground newspapers which typically are read only in narrow circles but which are available to any member of the public who desires to have access to them. On the other hand, a restricted dissemination such as a private "house organ" newsletter, a commissioned survey, or a class limited to registered students is excluded. The definition includes a lecture open to the public, even if there is a charge for admission. However, information disseminated only in personal conversation is not regarded as "published." Information which has once been given in a public proceeding is "published," even if it was given under compulsion.

(7) "Reporter" means a person who had obtained, received, or processed the desired information primarily for the purpose of publishing it or using it to obtain, interpret, or prepare other information to be published.

(8) "Source" means an individual who communicates or transmits information to a reporter, or who expressly or impliedly authorizes a reporter to observe an activity or situation which the reporter would not otherwise be able to observe.

(9) "Trial" means the adversary proceeding in which a judicial or quasi-judicial body may make a final disposition of a claim of right for civil or administrative relief, or of a prosecution of a person who has been impeached, indicted, or otherwise formally bound over for final adjudication, for an offense punishable by fine, imprisonment, removal from office, revocation of license, or loss of other valuable privilege. The term includes a separate hearing at which the judicial or quasi-judicial body may make a final ruling on an issue in the proceeding.

Comment

This definition needs to be read in conjunction with paragraph 1(5), which defines "proceeding," and Section 3, which provides that confidential information can be subpoenaed under certain conditions in a trial. . . .

SECTION 2. [*Privilege Regarding Confidential Source.*]

In any proceeding, a reporter is privileged to decline to give evidence which would disclose or materially facilitate the discovery of the identity of a confidential source.

Comment

In making the privilege absolute with respect to the identity of a confidential source, the Act follows seventeen of the twenty-five states that have passed shield laws. (Two of these states have special qualifications limited to libel cases, which is the result provided by the Act if Section 5 is included.) In some instances criminal defendants would seem to be entitled under the Compulsory Process Clause of the Sixth Amendment to learn the identity of a confidential source. However, the Act does not incorporate any notion of what exceptions are required by the Sixth Amendment but rather leaves that question to case-by-case constitutional adjudication.

Evidence is considered to "disclose" the identity of a confidential source even if the subpoenaing party or the tribunal already has a good idea who the source is, for example, if the reporter is asked whether his source for a statement was a particular individual and a truthful answer would confirm the suspicion. Information is privileged under this section if its disclosure would not facilitate the discovery of a source's identity by the court or the subpoenaing party but would materially facilitate discovery by other persons who might retaliate against the source.

SECTION 3. [*Privilege Regarding Confidential Information.*]

(a) In any proceeding other than a trial, a reporter is privileged to decline to give evidence which would disclose confidential information.

(b) In a trial, a reporter is privileged to decline to give evidence which discloses confidential information unless the court determines that the evidence:

(1) will not disclose or materially facilitate the discovery of the identity of a confidential source, and

(2) is indispensable to the establishment of the offense charged, the claim pleaded, a defense raised, or the relief sought in the trial.

SECTION 4. [*Privilege Regarding Non-Confidential Matter.*]

In any proceeding, a reporter is privileged to decline to give evidence concerning non-confidential sources he has developed, non-confidential information he has obtained, opinions, or impressions he has formed, conduct in which he has engaged, or tangible material he has obtained or produced in the course of procuring and preparing information for publication, unless the court determines that the probable value of the reporter's evidence is sufficient to justify any detriment to the flow of information to the public that may ensue if the reporter is compelled to give the evidence.

Comment

This section protects a reporter from having to give evidence of a non-confidential nature when the flow of information to the public is likely to be harmed to an unjustifiable extent if the reporter is compelled to give the evidence. An example might be a dragnet subpoena to newspapers and television stations to acquire their films and photographs of a demonstration to identify persons who may have engaged in illegal conduct during the demonstration. In most instances even this kind of subpoena would be permissible, but if the Court determined that news coverage in the future would be harmed because of physical threats to photographers or retaliation by key sources against other journalists, the likely value of the documentary evidence could be found to be outweighed by the likely value of the future information that would be sacrificed if the evidence were to be compelled. This section gives a measure of protection to, among other things, the reporter's work product—tapes, notebooks, discarded drafts of stories, film "outtakes," lists of possible sources for stories, daily logs, and the like. One reason for providing a qualified privilege for these materials is to encourage reporters to preserve records that may have historical value.

In making the balancing determination required by this section, a court should take into account not only the importance of the evidence to the proceeding for which it is sought but also the importance of the proceeding itself.

SECTION 5. [*Exception to the Privilege in Defamation and Privacy Actions.*]

In a civil action for defamation or invasion of privacy in which the plaintiff must prove that the defendant had knowledge of the falsity of his statement or acted with reckless disregard or negligence concerning its truth or falsity, and in which the plaintiff may be hindered by a claim of privilege under this Act from proving the degree of fault required to establish liability, the plaintiff may have the issue of fault tried separately from and subsequent to the trial of all other issues in the case. After a finding for the plaintiff on all other elements of the [cause of action] [claim for relief] necessary to recovery, the issue of fault shall be tried and the privilege does not apply if the court determines that the reporter's evidence is indispensable to the establishment of the requisite fault.

SECTION 6. [*Procedures.*]

(1) A claim of privilege under this Act asserted in a judicial proceeding is determined by the judge hearing the case. A claim asserted in any other proceeding is determined by the [court of general jurisdiction].

(2) Compulsory process to give evidence shall issue against a reporter only upon an order by the judge who is conducting or ruling on preliminary motions for the proceeding for which the reporter's evidence is desired or, for a non-judicial proceeding, a judge of the [court of general jurisdiction]. The order shall be entered only upon a motion by the subpoenaing party supported by affidavit or sworn testimony and only upon a finding by the judge that there are reasonable grounds to believe that the reporter has evidence relevant to the proceeding.

(3) An order denying in whole or in part a claim of privilege under this Act is subject to an interlocutory appeal. If an appeal is taken, the order shall be stayed pending final disposition of the privilege claim. The appeal shall be given preference and heard at the earliest practicable date.

SECTION 7. [*Waiver.*]

A reporter waives the privilege with respect to particular items of evidence by voluntarily giving the evidence in any proceeding, but not by giving the evidence for the sole purpose of establishing his entitlement to the privilege. A source waives the privilege by submitting to the presiding officer of any proceeding a written notice of waiver specifying the particular items of evidence with respect to which the privilege is waived. If the reporter or the source waives the privilege with respect to particular items of evidence, the reporter may be examined regarding those items of evidence but not regarding other items of evidence for which the privilege has not been waived.

Comment

If either the reporter or the source waives the privilege in one proceeding with respect to particular items of evidence, the privilege is waived with regard to those items of evidence in all subsequent stages of that proceeding and in all subsequent proceedings. However, if a reporter is compelled to testify in one proceeding he is not considered to have waived the privilege for subsequent proceedings, although the evidence he gives under compulsion (but not that which he gives solely to establish his privilege claim) is considered "published" under Section 1(6) and hence no longer confidential so that only the limited protection provided by Section 4 would be available to the reporter. A reporter who is subpoenaed in one proceeding and does not contest the subpoena is considered to have given evidence "voluntarily."

If a reporter has more than one source for a particular item of evidence, one of the sources can waive the privilege without having to secure the consent of the other sources. However, a reporter cannot then be compelled to give particular items of evidence learned exclusively from a source who has not consented to the waiver.

If the privilege is waived with regard to a particular item of evidence, the judge should permit the reporter to be cross-examined only to the extent necessary for a fair assessment of the credibility and meaning of the particular item of evidence which the reporter has given.

An "item of evidence" is any unit of evidence which in the context of the proceeding had probative value standing alone.

In 2009, federal reporter shield laws were submitted in both the House (HR 985) and the Senate (S 448). The House bill passed unanimously on a voice vote. The Senate bill was reported out of the Judiciary committee in 2009 and had not been acted on at the time this new edition was prepared.

———————

Problem VIII-90. Sharon Michaels is an investigative author whose books address scandalous topics and expose frauds and corruption in the private and public sectors. Her upcoming book addresses one family's long and bitter feud over the control of Beauty Accessories, a large cosmetics corporation that grosses $1 billion in sales annually. The feud pits the company's founder and family patriarch, George Witherspoon, against his sons, Rick and Steve Witherspoon.

In the midst of this family dispute, Rick's wife, Lorraina, was found murdered in the family's log cabin in Durango, Colorado. While the police have not named any suspects yet, they are suspicious that a Witherspoon family member might be connected with the murder since Witherspoon family relations are so acrimonious and since family members are pointing to each other as the murderer.

Intrigued by the Witherspoon saga and the suspicious murder surrounding the dispute, Sharon Michaels decides to investigate the situation further and to make it the basis for a chapter in her upcoming book. She speaks with George Witherspoon and he agrees to an interview.

Rick and Steve subsequently learn that Sharon interviewed their father. They are suspicious of possible derogatory statements their father might have made to her about them regarding their role in Lorraina's murder. They want to learn exactly what he told her so that they can use this information in an ongoing defamation suit against him, which was based on George's telling reporters from the Associated Press and the *L.A. Times*, about six months before Sharon interviewed him, that he believed his sons to be mentally ill and probably responsible for Lorraina's murder.

The brothers served Sharon with a subpoena telling her to appear at a deposition to testify, and to produce any notes, documents, electronic recordings, or any other records in her possession that relate to Lorraina's death.

Sharon appeared at the deposition but refused to produce any documents or recordings or answer any questions concerning the substance of her interview with George. She claimed that the communications were protected under the "journalist-source" privilege, which she claims is a protection afforded by the First Amendment. **Is she right about the existence of this privilege? If this is a case of first impression and a state Supreme Court recognizes such a privilege under the state's constitutional guarantee of a free press, should it apply so that Sharon can resist all disclosure? If the state has adopted the draft Uniform Reporters Privilege Act, can Sharon be forced to comply with the subpoena?**

ADDITIONAL PROBLEMS

Problem VIII-91. If only a few reporters have the kind of source relationships that depend on the protection of a privilege, is a privilege for all reporters relying on confidential sources justified? Is there any way to extend the protection of a statute to only those reporters whose source relationships would "dry up" absent a statute? How should a privilege treat the many people who publish reports akin to news stories on the internet, either in personal blogs or in non-traditional and often politically slanted news sites like the Daily Kos.

Problem VIII-92. Many reporters regard the maintenance of promised confidentiality as a matter of personal and journalistic ethics. They feel so strongly that they will accept contempt citations and go to jail rather than breach the confidences of sources. **How should this fact be weighed in deciding whether to create a news reporter's privilege? Does it depend on the percentage of reporters who will eventually succumb to jailing or the threat of jailing and provide the information sought? Are there reasons to give this factor no weight, even if all reporters would serve out a sentence for contempt rather than breach a promised confidence?**

Problem VIII-93. Some reporters, particularly those dealing with alienated radical groups, believe that any obvious cooperation with authorities will lead their sources to distrust them. Assume that the following facts, which reflect the beliefs of these reporters, are true. Appearing before a grand jury, even if only to claim a privilege, will generate suspicion because sources will have no way of being sure about what in fact went on in the grand jury room. Participation in a "political trial" on behalf of the prosecution will cause source relationships to disappear and may destroy a reporter's ability to acquire any inside information on a particular radical movement. This is true even if the reporter gives testimony at trial only after threats of contempt, and even if she reveals no confidential information. **Do these facts justify the extension, to some or all reporters, of a privilege to refuse to testify to information not given in confidence and to refuse to submit documentary or photographic evidence not acquired without a promise that confidentiality would be maintained?**

Problem VIII-94. You have now seen a variety of privileges, some with constitutional roots and most arising out of a history of protecting certain relationships or certain kinds of information. We have focused our attention on how federal courts treat privileges, although we have noted the variety of approaches that exists throughout the United States. Often, requests are made of courts and legislatures to create new privileges. Analogies are drawn to existing privileges and claims of entitlement to equal treatment are not unusual. **How would you respond as a judge or as a legislator to proposals for the following privileges? Are your answers to Parts C and D the same as when you were asked to think about similar issues at the start of this Chapter?**

A. An Accountant-Client Privilege. Between one-third and two thirds of the states recognize this privilege. The argument can be made that information involving one's private records and financial dealings ought to be as protected in the same way as similar information transmitted to legal counsel. This is an especially strong argument when an accountant is giving complicated tax advice similar to that provided by lawyers. **Is there a valid distinction between the professions?**[125] **If there is an accountant-client privilege for tax matters, should it exclude the kind of information needed to fill out tax returns?**

B. Catholic Sisters and Irregularly Ordained Women-Penitent Privilege. As long as spiritual advisers provide religious counseling, they have a claim to protection under the communications-to-clergy privilege. This may be especially important when women are denied formal positions in the clergy but other women may seek them out for special counseling.[126] **Should such a privilege be extended?**

---

[125] Comment, Evidence: The Accountant-Client Privilege Under the New Federal Rules of Evidence—New Stature and New Problems, 28 Okla. L. Rev. 637 (1975).

[126] See Sister Simon Campbell, Catholic Sisters, Irregularly Ordained Women and the Clergy-Penitent Privilege, 9 U.C. Davis L. Rev. 523 (1976).

C. A Counselor-Counselee Privilege. A number of cities throughout the United States have centers to shelter drug addicts, runaways, pregnant teenagers, and other troubled individuals. Most such centers engage in informal counseling and often intensive individual or group therapy sessions for their "guests." **Should information gained in formal counseling or in therapy sessions be privileged? Should the identity of the "guests" at such establishments be privileged?**

D. Friend-Friend Privilege. At times a party will seek to put the best friend of an opposing party on the stand. Honest testimony in these circumstances may strain even a close relationship. The best friend may be called upon to reveal information given in the strictest confidence. The temptation to commit perjury is obvious. **Should there be a privilege that enables an individual to prevent his best friend from testifying to anything the friend has learned from the individual in confidence engendered by the friendship?**

E. Parent-Child Privilege. In a world in which families seem to have difficulty staying together, should a privilege protect the family relationship? If so, should it be a communications-type privilege, an incapacity-type privilege, or both? Is the parent-child or brother-sister relationship less worthy of a privilege than the husband-wife relationship?[127]

F. Peer Review or Business Judgment Privilege. If academics, doctors, other professionals, and business persons discuss their own work in confidence and review privately work done by their peers, the public, arguably, will benefit from the candid exchange of criticism. Such exchanges might be tempered or diminished if efforts at self-scrutiny must be shared with the public. **Should a privilege protect information exchanged in such peer review or confidential discussions? Should it protect the identities of those involved?**[128]

G. Social Science Research Privilege. Social scientists often promise their subjects or respondents that information communicated to them in the course of their research will be held confidential and published in a way that precludes the identification of individual responses. Researchers depend on voluntary participation. **Should they be able to offer the protection of a privilege? If there were such a privilege, how should courts define a social scientist? By an advanced degree? A teaching position? The nature of the research?**

---

[127] See Larry Michael Bauer, Recognition of a Parent-Child Testimonial Privilege, 23 St. Louis U. L.J. 676 (1979).

[128] See University of Pennsylvania v. Equal Employment Opportunity Commission, 493 U.S. 182 (1990).

Problem VIII-95. As part of the IRS Restructuring and Reform Bill, Congress enacted the following privilege for taxpayer clients of federally authorized tax practitioners:

"SEC. 7525. CONFIDENTIALITY PRIVILEGES RELATING TO TAXPAYER COMMUNICATIONS

"(a) UNIFORM APPLICATION TO TAXPAYER COMMUNICATIONS WITH FEDERALLY AUTHORIZED PRACTITIONERS.—

"(1) GENERAL RULE.—With respect to tax advice, the same common law protections of confidentiality which apply to a communication between a taxpayer and an attorney shall also apply to a communication between a taxpayer and any federally authorized tax practitioner to the extent the communication would be considered a privileged communication if it were between a taxpayer and an attorney.

"(2) LIMITATIONS.—Paragraph (1) may only be asserted in—

"(A) any noncriminal tax matter before the Internal Revenue Service; and

"(B) any noncriminal tax proceeding in Federal court brought by or against the United States.

"(3) DEFINITIONS.—For purposes of this subsection—

"(A) FEDERALLY AUTHORIZED TAX PRACTITIONER.— The term 'federally authorized tax practitioner' means any individual who is authorized under Federal law to practice before the Internal Revenue Service if such practice is subject to Federal regulation under section 330 of title 31, United States Code.

"(B) TAX ADVICE.—The term 'tax advice' means advice given by an individual with respect to a matter which is within the scope of the individual's authority to practice described in subparagraph (A).

"(b) SECTION NOT TO APPLY TO COMMUNICATIONS REGARDING CORPORATE TAX SHELTERS.—The privilege under subsection (a) shall not apply to any written communication between a federally authorized tax practitioner and a director, shareholder, officer, or employee, agent, or representative of a corporation in connection with the promotion of the direct or indirect participation of such corporation in any tax shelter (as defined in section 6662(d)(2)(C)(iii))."

How is this privilege like other privileges for confidential communications? How does it differ from them? Exactly what

will this privilege protect? Do you think Congress acted wisely in enacting this privilege? If you had been asked to draft a privilege for tax practitioners, would your draft have differed in any respect? How?

VIII.   BIBLIOGRAPHY

Greenwald, David M., Robert R. Stauffer, and Erin R. Schrantz, Testimonial Privileges (2010).

Imwinkelried, Edward J., The New Wigmore: A Treatise on Evidence— Testimonial Privileges (2010).

LaFave, Wayne R., Jerold H. Israel, Nancy J. King and Orin S. Kerr, Criminal Procedure, 5th ed. (2009).

McCormick, Chs. 8–13.

Wright, Charles A. and Kenneth W. Graham, Jr., Federal Practice and Procedure: Evidence, vols. 23-26A, §§ 5421–6000 (1980–1992) (with annual supplements).

Wigmore, Chs. 76, 79–83, 85–87.

Alexander, Vincent C., The Corporate Attorney-Client Privilege: A Study of the Participants, 63 St. John's L. Rev. (1989).

Allen, Ronald J., Mark F. Grady, Daniel D. Polsby, and Michael S. Yashko, A Positive Theory of the Attorney-Client Privilege and the Work Product Doctrine, 19 J. Legal Stud. 359 (1990).

Amar, Akhil Reed, Against Exclusion (Except to Protect Truth or Prevent Privacy Violations) 20 Harv. J.L. & Pub. Pol'y 457 (1997).

Barsdate, Lory A., Attorney-Client Privilege for the Government Entity, 97 Yale L.J. 1725 (1988).

Berger, Margaret A., The President, Congress and the Courts, 83 Yale L.J. 1111 (1974).

Berger, Margaret A., How the Privilege for Governmental Information Met Its Watergate, 25 Case W. Res. L. Rev. 747 (1975).

Blasi, Vince, The Newsman's Privilege, An Empirical Study, 70 Mich. L. Rev. 229 (1971).

Chafee, Zachariah, Privileged Communications: Is Justice Served or Obstructed by Closing the Doctor's Mouth on the Witness Stand?, 52 Yale L.J. 607 (1943).

Cohn, Sherman L., The Work-Product Doctrine: Protection not Privilege, 71 Geo. L.J. 917 (1983).

Fried, Charles, The Lawyer as Friend: The Moral Foundations of the Lawyer-Client Relation, 85 Yale L.J. 1060 (1976).

Gardner, James A., A Personal Privilege for Communications of Corporate Clients—Paradox or Public Policy, 40 U. Det. L.J. 299 (1963).

Gardner, James A., A Re-Evaluation of the Attorney-Client Privilege, 8 Vill. L. Rev. 279 (1963).

Goldstein, Abraham S. and Jay Katz, Psychiatrist-Patient Privilege: The GAP Proposal and the Connecticut Statute, 36 Conn. B.J. 175 (1965).

Hazard, Geoffrey C., Jr., Rectification of Client Fraud: Death and Revival of a Professional Norm, 33 Emory L.J. 271 (1984).

Hutchins, Robert M. and Donald Slesinger, Some Observations on the Law of Evidence: Family Relations, 13 Minn. L. Rev. 675 (1929).

Imwinkelreid, Edward J., An Hegelian Approach to Privileges Under Federal Rules of Evidence 501: The Restrictive Thesis, the Expansive Antithesis, and the Contextual Synthesis, 73 Neb. L. Rev. 511 (1994).

Imwinkelreid, Edward J. and James P. McCall, *Minnesota v. Philip Morris Inc.*: An Important Legal Ethics Message Which Neglects the Public Interest in Products Safety Research, 87 Ky. L.J. 1127 (1998–99).

Ladd, Mason, Privileges, Law and the Social Order 555–590 (1969).

Lefstein, Norman, Incriminating Physical Evidence and a Defense Attorney's Dilemma and a Need for Rules, 64 N.C. L. Rev. 897 (1986).

Lempert, Richard O., A Right to Every Woman's Evidence, 66 Iowa L. Rev. 725 (1981).

MacCarthy, Terence F. and Kathy Morris Mejia, Criminal Law: The Perjurious Client Question: Putting Criminal Defense Lawyers Between a Rock and a Hard Place, 75 J. Crim. L. 1197 (1984).

Marcus, Richard L., The Perils of Privilege: Waiver and the Litigator, 84 Mich. L. Rev. 1605 (1986).

Reese, Seward P., Confidential Communication to the Clergy, 24 Ohio St. L.J. 55 (1963).

Saltzburg, Stephen A., Corporate Attorney-Client Privilege in Shareholder Litigation and Similar Cases: *Garner* Revisited, 12 Hofstra L. Rev. 1817 (1984).

Saltzburg, Stephen A., Corporate and Related Attorney-Client Privilege Claims: A Suggested Approach, 12 Hofstra L. Rev. 279 (1984).

Saltzburg, Stephen A., Privileges and Professionals: Lawyers and Psychiatrists, 66 Va. L. Rev. 597 (1980).

Saltzburg, Stephen A., Communications Falling Within the Attorney-Client Privilege, 66 Iowa L. Rev. 811 (1981).

Sawyer, Craig T., The Physician-Patient Privilege: Some Reflections, 14 Drake L. Rev. 83 (1965).

Scheindlin, Shira A., Discovering the Discoverable: A Bird's Eye View of Discovery in a Complex Multi-District Class Action Litigation, 52 Brook. L. Rev. 397 (1986).

Sexton, John E., A Post Upjohn Consideration of the Attorney-Client Privilege, 57 N.Y.U. L. Rev. 443 (1982).

Shuman, Daniel W. and Myron S. Weiner, The Privilege Study: An Empirical Examination of the Psychotherapist-Patient Privilege, 60 N.C. L. Rev. 893 (1982).

Slovenko, Ralph, Psychiatry and a Second Look at the Medical Privilege, 6 Wayne L. Rev. 175 (1960).

Stedman, John C., Trade Secrets, 23 Ohio St. L.J. 4 (1965).

Stern, Max D. and David Hoffman, Privileged Informers: The Attorney Subpoena Problem and a Proposal for Reform, 136 U. Pa. L. Rev. 1783 (1988).

Stoyles, Robert L., The Dilemma of the Constitutionality of the Priest-Penitent Privilege—The Application of the Religious Clauses, 29 U. Pitt. L. Rev. 27 (1967).

Symposium on United States v. Nixon, 22 UCLA L. Rev. 1 (1974).

Waldman, Michael L., Beyond Upjohn: The Attorney-Client Privilege in a Corporate Context, 28 Wm. & Mary L. Rev. 473 (1987).

Waldron, Gerard J. and Jeff A. Israel, Developments Under the Freedom of Information Act-1988, 1989 Duke L.J. 686 (1989).

Zacharias, Fred C., Rethinking Confidentiality, 75 Iowa L. Rev. 601 (1990).

CHAPTER 9

EXPERT EVIDENCE

. . .

I.   INTRODUCTION

Juries and judges are supposed to apply their commonsense and common knowledge to the evidence in a trial; witnesses are supposed to provide the special knowledge which becomes that evidence. For an ordinary witness, special knowledge simply means personal knowledge of relevant facts—the sort of thing anybody could have picked up by listening and looking if she happened to have been present at the right place and time. An expert witness provides a different sort of special knowledge—"expertise" in some relevant area of human experience. An expert is a person who has learned, through training or experience, to evaluate phenomena that most other people do not understand and to notice things that untrained people are likely to miss.

Expert information is essential in most trials. A study of civil trials in California State Superior Courts in 1990–91, for example, found that one or more expert witnesses testified in 95% of the trials, and that, on average, four experts testified per case.[1]

Expert witnesses are important because science, technology, and other forms of specialized knowledge are pervasive in our culture, and they frequently deal with matters beyond the range of common understanding. Untutored commonsense may work as well as anything if the question is whether the driver or the pedestrian has given a more accurate description of the accident, but commonsense is close to useless when the issue is the meaning of the lines and shadows on an x-ray of a plaintiff's skull, or the temperature at which wheat dust in a silo might have exploded spontaneously, or the future medical expenses of a 24-year-old quadriplegic, or the friction coefficient of tires on wet asphalt. In this respect, litigation is similar to many other aspects of life. We all rely daily on the expertise of scientists, plumbers, doctors, translators,

---

[1]   Samuel R. Gross & Kent D. Syverud, Don't Try: Civil Jury Verdicts in a System Geared to Settlement, 44 UCLA L. Rev. 1, 31–32 (1996). Sixty percent of these witnesses were medical doctors or other medical witnesses. The rate at which experts testify may be increasing. An earlier survey of California civil jury trials (1985–86) found one or more expert witnesses in 86% of the cases, and an overall average of 3.3 experts per trial. The 1985–'86 survey included more detailed information on the specialties of the experts. As in the later survey, about 50% of the experts were medical doctors and an additional 9% were other medical witnesses—psychologists, physical therapists, nurses, dentists, etc. The two largest non-medical categories were engineers, scientists, and other similar specialists (20%); and business and financial experts (11%). Samuel R. Gross, Expert Evidence, 1991 Wis. L. Rev. 1113, 1119.

engineers, builders, computer programmers, and car mechanics—to name just a few. Perhaps in the distant past, in a technologically simpler culture, special expertise was less important. In our society it is a constant necessity.

Common law courts have long recognized the need for expert assistance and have granted expert witnesses special status. McCormick describes the basic common law requirements:

> A lay observer is qualified to testify because he has firsthand knowledge of the situation or transaction at issue. The expert has something different to contribute. This is the power—the knowledge or skill—to draw inferences from the facts which the jury could not draw at all or as reliably.

> . . . To warrant the use of expert testimony the proponent must establish at least two general elements. First, traditionally the subject of the inference must be so distinctively related to some science, profession, business or occupation as to be beyond the ken of laypersons. . . .

> . . . Second, on objection the witness's proponent must show that the witness has sufficient skill or knowledge related to the pertinent field or calling that his inference will probably aid the trier in his search for truth. The knowledge may derive from reading alone in some fields (education), from practice alone in some fields (experience), or as is more commonly the case, from both.[2]

FRE 702 restates this common-law rule, and adds that expert evidence must be based on adequate data and reliable methods:

> A witness who is qualified as an expert by knowledge, skill, experience, training, or education may testify in the form of an opinion or otherwise if:
>
> **(a)** the expert's scientific, technical, or other specialized knowledge will help the trier of fact to understand the evidence or to determine a fact in issue;
>
> **(b)** the testimony is based on sufficient facts or data;
>
> **(c)** the testimony is the product of reliable principles and methods; and
>
> **(d)** the expert has reliably applied the principles and methods to the facts of the case.

This sounds like a simple rule, but in practice it can be quite complicated. It is also an extremely important aspect of the law of evidence.

---

[2]   McCormick § 13 (footnotes omitted).

We will discuss the use of expert witnesses in five sections: *First*, the process of obtaining and preparing expert witnesses. *Second*, the rules of evidence that apply to expert testimony. *Third*, some special concerns that originally focused on scientific expertise but have now given rise to a general requirement that all expert evidence be "reliable." *Fourth*, the widespread dissatisfaction with our method of using experts, and the possibility of using court-appointed experts to improve that practice. *Fifth*, a few examples of expert evidence on particular issues.

II. OBTAINING AND PREPARING EXPERT WITNESSES

A. CHOOSING EXPERTS

In our adversarial system of litigation, the parties are responsible for the factual investigation of a case. This procedure has the advantage of assigning the responsibility for an investigation to those with the greatest incentive to conduct it thoroughly. Each side in a personal injury lawsuit, for example, will be anxious to locate any eyewitness who supports its theory of liability, and each side will want to know what witnesses are likely to be presented in opposition—in order to prepare to cross-examine them, and in order to predict the outcome at trial and evaluate the case for purposes of settlement. This arrangement gives an extraordinary amount of power to the attorneys who represent the parties. It is they who investigate the facts, and it is they who compel witnesses to appear at trials and depositions and to answer questions under oath, on pain of contempt of court. Cases do not exist on their own; attorneys create them.

For ordinary lay witnesses, however, the attorneys' power over the evidence is limited both by the facts of the case and by the structure of litigation. The only possible eyewitnesses to a car accident are those who happened to see the crash; both sides are forced to seek their evidence from this closed and usually well-known set of people. The power to compel testimony from this limited group is symmetrical: each side knows that the other can present any witnesses it chooses to ignore. And, although a party can use the court's subpoena power to compel an eyewitness to testify, it is unethical to offer the witness any fee or other inducement beyond the minimal witness fees and expenses provided by statute or rules of court,[3] and it is sometimes a crime as well.[4] In short, the paradigmatic eyewitness is a stranger to the dispute who happened to be present when an accident happened, whose testimony is equally

---

[3] See, e.g., Model Rules of Professional Conduct, Rule 3.4(b) and Comment (2010); American Bar Association, Standards Relating to the Administration of Criminal Justice, The Prosecution Function, Standard 3-3.2(a) (1993); American Bar Association, Standards Relating to the Administration of Criminal Justice, The Defense Function, Standard 4-4.3(b) (1993).

[4] See, e.g., 18 U.S.C. § 201(c)(2) (2010).

available to both sides, and who may be required testify as a civic duty for a nominal fee and no more.

Some lay witnesses do not fit this description. Some are parties to the litigation, or have other reasons to favor one side over the other. Also, in some cases a party may be able to choose from among many potential lay witnesses who could all testify to the same facts. If several dozen people witnessed a car crash and said that the defendant went through a red light, the plaintiff's attorney could decide which ones to use based on their likely demeanor and appeal. But this limited room for maneuvering is insignificant compared to the latitude the same lawyer has in her choice of medical experts to testify to the nature of the injuries her client suffered. For that task, the usual limitations on the power of a litigant to choose witnesses simply do not apply.

An expert need not have any previous contact with a case. In most cases, any minimally qualified practitioner of the expert discipline at issue is eligible to testify.[5] Typically, the expert's entire knowledge of the case is obtained after she has been enlisted as a witness. This is the single biggest difference between expert and lay testimony: *In many common contexts the parties and their lawyers have unparalleled power to select their expert witnesses from a large pool, and to do so on the basis of the likely content and the manner of their testimony.*

Moreover, the process by which experts are chosen is shielded from discovery. Under Federal Rule of Civil Procedure (FRCP) 26(a)(1)(A) a party must spontaneously disclose to its opponent the name, address and telephone number of "each individual likely to have discovered information relevant to disputed facts. . . . " This duty is backed up by FRCP 26(b)(1), which allows a party to request and obtain discovery from its opponent concerning "the identity and location of persons who know of any discoverable matter."

Expert witnesses, however, are handled separately. Under FRCP 26(a)(2)(A) and 26(b)(4)(A) both the duty of disclosure and the right to discovery are limited to experts the party "may use at trial to present [expert] evidence. . . . " Information from an expert who has been "retained or specially employed by another party in anticipation of litigation or to prepare for trial and who is not expected to be called as a witness at trial" need not be disclosed spontaneously, and may only be discovered "upon a showing of exceptional circumstances. . . . " FRCP 26(b)(4)(B). Experts who have been informally consulted but not retained are virtually undiscoverable secrets. A party who takes full advantage of these rules can "informally consult" with a dozen experts (a non-discoverable activity), retain the five experts who seem most promising (a generally non-discoverable activity), and, finally, at the last available

---

[5]   See infra, pp. 1134–1136.

date, designate the one of these five, whose opinion is most favorable, as an expert *witness*, whose information and opinions must be disclosed.[6]

Needless to say, this process has the power to degrade and distort evidence, as the Supreme Court noted as long ago as 1858:

> Experience has shown that opposite opinions of persons professing to be experts may be obtained to any amount; and it often occurs that not only many days, but even weeks, are consumed in cross-examinations, to test the skill or knowledge of such witnesses and the correctness of their opinions, wasting the time and wearying the patience of both court and jury, and perplexing, instead of elucidating, the questions involved in the issue.[7]

In addition to the power to select from a large pool, the process of obtaining expert witnesses has two other distinctive features.

First, expert opinion witnesses almost never testify under compulsion. The old English common law rule on this point was absolute; an expert, unlike an ordinary witness, was immune to compulsory process.[8] Most American jurisdictions have modified this rule, at least in theory, to allow parties to subpoena experts under some circumstances.[9] In practice, however, the formal rules on this issue make little difference; ordinary expert opinion testimony is hardly ever compelled. One reason that subpoenas are so rare is that the expert's cooperation in preparing and presenting testimony effectively cannot be compelled. While trial preparation is important for any witness, it is crucial for experts, to ensure that the jury understands the witness and to make the most of this opportunity to control the evidence. In addition, an unfriendly expert

---

[6] Discovery in criminal cases is much more limited than in civil cases, and extremely variable from one American jurisdiction to another. All jurisdictions require at least some discovery of expert evidence, but none as much as is provided by the Federal Rules of Civil Procedure. See, e.g., Paul C. Giannelli, Observations on Discovery of Scientific Evidence, 101 F.R.D. 622 (1983).

[7] Winans v. New York & Erie R.R., 62 U.S. (21 How.) 88, 101 (1858).

[8] The leading case on this issue is Webb v. Page, 1 Carr. & K. 23, 23–24 (1843), in which Mr. Justice Maule held that, "[t]here is a distinction between the case of a man who sees a fact and is called to prove it in court, and a man who is selected by a party to give his opinion on a matter on which he is peculiarly conversant from the nature of his employment in life. The former is bound, as a matter of public duty, to speak. . . . The latter is under no such obligation; there is no . . . necessity for his evidence, and the party who selects him must pay him."

[9] For example, Fed. R. Civ. Proc. 45, which governs subpoenas, provides in part:

To protect a person subject to or affected by a subpoena, the issuing court may, on motion, quash or modify the subpoena if it requires . . . disclosing an unretained expert's opinion or information that does not describe specific occurrences in dispute and results from the expert's study that was not requested by a party. . . .

Fed.R.Civ.Proc. 45(c)(3)(B)(ii). See Marjorie P. Lindblom, Note, Compelling Experts to Testify: A Proposal, 44 U. Chi. L. Rev. 851 (1977); Joe S. Cecil & Gerald T. Wetherington, Forward, Court-Ordered Disclosure of Academic Research: A Clash of Values of Science and Law, 59 Law & Contemp. Probs. No. 3, 1 (1996); Paul D. Carrington & Traci L. Jones, Reluctant Experts, 59 Law & Contemp. Probs. No. 3, 51 (1996).

can hurt a litigant (even without misrepresenting her views) and may well want to do so. Finally, and most important, there is rarely a need to run the risk of calling an unwilling expert: willing substitutes are almost always available.

By contrast, "occurrence experts"—those who happen to witness significant events in the course of their professional roles—do often testify in response to subpoenas. The typical witness in this category is an emergency room doctor who treated the plaintiff in a personal injury lawsuit, or who wrote the death certificate for the victim in a homicide prosecution. In Section VI we have reproduced the brief testimony of such a witness from The *Tellez* case, which was covered in Chapter One.

Second, expert witnesses are paid witnesses. An attorney may not pay ordinary witnesses anything beyond statutory witness fees and expenses and reasonable compensation for their time attending court,[10] but all common law jurisdictions have retained the old English rule that experts may contract for special fees both for their testimony and for time spent preparing to testify.

Because experts are paid to testify, and because they can be hired repeatedly to work on cases with similar or identical issues, they can become professional witnesses. Many do just that—they advertise their services (a practice that is unimaginable for lay witnesses), and earn substantial sums from this line of work. In years past, a typical issue of a law journal might have included pages of small and medium-sized ads with headings ranging from **BANKING EXPERT** ("Top Professional, 27 Years Experience . . . Excellent Communicator . . . GET THE BEST); to **BICYCLE EXPERT**; to **CARDIOVASCULAR THORACIC SURGERY** ("Skilled case review and testimony"); to **LEGAL MALPRACTICE EXPERTS** ("Excellent Reports, Articulate Witnesses").[11] Listings such as, "**A record \$2,250,000 security negligence settlement after testimony**. . . . "[12] were common. Now, of course, most of this traffic has migrated to the Internet, where a Google search quickly leads to entries such as "Since 1990, we have provided board-certified experts in over 10,000 malpractice and personal injury cases with a 92% win-rate compared to the industry average of 28%."[13] It's hard to imagine a similar practice for any other type of witness.

---

[10] E.g., it is a felony to offer or demand any consideration beyond statutory fees and expenses for lay testimony in federal court. 18 U.S.C. § 201(c)(2). See also Rule 5-310(B) of the Rules of Professional Conduct of the State Bar of California. See supra note 4.

[11] Nat'l. L.J., May 4, 1998, at B18-19. See also Expert Witnesses: Booming Business for Specialists, N.Y. Times, July 5, 1987, at 1. Increasingly, such advertisements are found on the internet.

[12] 21 Trial 103–07 (Dec. 1985).

[13] http://expertpages.com/details.php/2139_2201_239_121.htm (last visited July 2010).

B. EXPERT WITNESS PREPARATION

The usual process of witness preparation is vastly different for experts. The typical lay witness, of course, is prepared for testimony by the lawyer who intends to call her. In our car crash case, for example, the lawyer who intends to present an eyewitness will, if possible, meet with the witness, discuss the witness's testimony, explain the process of examination, go over lists of questions and answers, anticipate lines of likely cross-examination, identify or prepare any helpful exhibits, and (if the witness is willing) offer advice on the form, if not the content, of the testimony. But most lay witnesses who are not parties to a case have little incentive to prepare extensively for testimony. They will probably want to know in advance what will happen in court and to be prepared for the questions that will be asked, and they may be happy to assist the attorneys if it is not too much trouble. Most non-party witnesses, however, have little or no interest in the outcome of a case, and relatively little investment even in their own testimony; they believe what they say, of course, and they do not want to be contradicted or impugned, but it is not a central concern in their lives. As a result, the damage that these witnesses can suffer on cross-examination is, from their own point of view, limited. Occasionally a disinterested eyewitness will be impeached as a liar. This is unquestionably very unpleasant for the witness, whether or not she has lied, but even an attack of that type (and they are uncommon) focuses on testimony that is peripheral to the witness's own life. The common argument against an eyewitness is much less challenging—merely that she was mistaken. This may be irritating to the witness, it may make her angry, but it is hardly devastating. Finally, since lay witnesses are not paid, they may not be able to afford to spend a great deal of time preparing for court, and they certainly have no financial incentive to do so.

An expert witness is in an entirely different position. The most obvious difference is financial. Since the expert is paid she can afford to spend time preparing to testify, assuming that the party that hires her can foot the bill. Indeed, the time spent may be quite remunerative. If the expert values the role of witness, for financial reasons or otherwise, she will have an additional motive to spend time working with the attorney who calls her: Careful preparation and close collaboration are likely to increase the attorney's satisfaction, which may lead to more business from the same lawyer or his friends and acquaintances.[14] There is also a special need for careful preparation, since an expert—unlike a

---

[14] This is not an abstract consideration. Lawyers who are selecting experts are advised to remember that, "[b]esides being knowledgeable, the expert must be willing during the pendency of the case to spend the time necessary to review and analyze materials provided by counsel and to do so in a timely way. The expert should be accessible to counsel both by telephone and in person." Dennis R. Suplee & Margaret S. Woodruff, The Pretrial Use of Experts, 33 Prac. Law. 9, 13 (Sept. 1987).

lay witness—is called to testify about matters that are beyond the common knowledge of the judge or jury, and often beyond the ken of the lawyer who must examine the expert. It's one thing to get a clear story from a witness who saw two cars collide; it's quite another thing to get intelligible and persuasive testimony from a doctor who examined the spinal-cord injury of one of the drivers, and who has an opinion about the likely prognosis. It can be done, but it's not simple.[15]

Finally, the preparation of an expert witness differs from that of a lay witness because of the nature of the cross-examination and rebuttal that she faces. Experts are subject to much more wide-ranging cross-examination than ordinary witnesses.[16] Expert witnesses are also frequently contradicted by opposing experts,[17] who (unlike lay witnesses) will not be restricted to reporting their own observations and their opinions, but may also criticize the opinions of the experts on the other side. As result, an expert witness runs the risk of extraordinarily sharp attack. Many experts have written or testified about related matters previously. These materials may be used by the cross examiner in an attempt to challenge or contradict her present opinions. In some cases the opposing attorney may ridicule her entire discipline, or deny that any expert in that field can give useful evidence on the issue at hand. In all cases an expert witness risks being attacked as not merely wrong, but unqualified, ignorant, incompetent, biased, misleading or silly. Moreover, the attack is not directed to some passing observation but to her profession, her life's work.

To sum up: expert witnesses in well-financed cases are paid to spend time working to prepare their testimony with the attorneys who call them; there is a special need to prepare carefully, since their evidence is generally complex and technical; and they have a powerful motive to do so—the desire to construct defenses against opposing lawyers and opposing experts. The result is that the preparation of expert testimony often involves extensive detailed cooperative work by the expert and the attorneys who hired her, work that is done in anticipation of battle, under threat of attack. This type of preparation, perhaps even more than the processes of choice and payment, pushes the expert to identify with the lawyers on her side and to become a partisan member of the litigation team. The expert is not merely subject to the pull of the camaraderie that grows between co-workers on a difficult project, she is dependent on the lawyer for the preparation that will make her success possible, and for protection from the fearsome lawyer for the opposing side.

---

[15] Sometimes, of course, lawyers fail to take the time to carefully prepare the expert witnesses they call. This is a common complaint by expert witnesses, and a significant failure to conduct adequate pre-trial preparation.

[16] See infra pp. 1150–1155.

[17] See infra p. 1153.

The open-ended nature of the preparation of expert witnesses can affect the content of expert testimony in three ways. First, doing all this work takes time, time in which the biasing effects of partisan preparation can operate. Experienced lawyers are perfectly aware of how this process operates. They counsel beginners: "Do not press the expert to reach a conclusion, even orally, before he or she is thoroughly conversant with the case and an advocate of the client's cause."[18]

Second, the lawyer who retains an expert may be able to do more than choose his witness. Often, he can choose the issues on which the witness prepares and testifies as well. For example, a corporation facing charges of discrimination in both hiring and compensation might retain a statistician to rebut the hiring claim only—and give her data that is restricted to its hiring practices—because its lawyers fear that if that witness examined their payroll records, she would find evidence of wage discrimination. The corporation would then use a different witness (perhaps a less sophisticated expert) on the compensation issue.

Third, the information on which an expert bases her opinion is not entirely her own. Ordinarily, much of it will come from the attorney who hired her—hardly an unbiased source. As one experienced litigator put it:

Effective communication with experts has several objectives: to provide enough information so that the expert will be well-prepared, but to avoid providing materials that would open the door to otherwise unavailable lines of cross-examination; to give the expert leeway to develop ideas and conclusions with the requisite independence, but to provide sufficient guidance so that helpful opinions are reached; to make the expert a colleague while at the same time preserving objectivity.[19]

Problem IX-1. Juliet and Herbert Pren were badly injured in an automobile accident; both will be confined to wheelchairs for the rest of their lives. Juliet and Herbert sue for damages. One element of their damage claim relates to their inability to do housework after the accident. **May the Prens present an economist to testify to the value of various household services—e.g., cooking, cleaning, washing clothes, ser**

ving meals and caring for children? If yes, how would they go about obtaining such an expert?

---

[18] James E. Daniels, Managing Litigation Experts, A.B.A.J., Dec. 1984, 64, 66.

[19] Id. at 64–66. See also, e.g., Peter I. Ostroff, Experts: A Few Fundamentals, 8 Litig. 8, 9 (Winter 1982) ("Do not disclose facts or documents to the expert unless the opposition has already learned or seen them or you do not mind if the opposition does learn or see them.").

III.   THE RULES OF EVIDENCE FOR EXPERT WITNESSES

A. QUALIFICATIONS

A lay witness "may testify to a matter only if evidence is introduced sufficient to support a finding that the witness has personal knowledge of the matter." FRE 602. Expert witnesses are exempt from this rule, as the last sentence of FRE 602 spells out: "This rule does not apply to a witness's expert testimony under Rule 703." But expert witnesses must satisfy a different foundational requirement: They must be "qualified" as experts. Thus, FRE 702 says that if specialized knowledge will be helpful, "a witness who is *qualified as an expert* . . . may testify. . . ." about that special knowledge (emphasis added). Under the Federal Rules, the decision on an expert's qualifications is governed by FRE 104(a): "The court must decide any preliminary questions about whether a witness is qualified. . . ." In practice, courts are forgiving in applying this rule. Irving Younger, a trial court judge who became a prominent evidence teacher, once wrote that "It is almost impossible to fail to persuade the judge to let the expert give his opinion."[20] This is a bit of an exaggeration—there are reported cases of witnesses who were offered as experts but did not qualify—but not much. Although an expert's qualifications are an issue on which the judge must *make a finding*, the standard that many courts apply is closer to the requirements of FRE 104(b) (conditional relevance) or FRE 602 (personal knowledge)— demanding only evidence "*sufficient to support a finding*" of expertise. If it appears that the witness has at least the minimal qualifications for an expert in the field in which she is offered, she will usually be permitted to testify, especially if her credentials include an M.D. degree.[21]

If establishing a foundation were the sole purpose of evidence on qualifications, it would be a simple and quick matter. Indeed, in most cases the matter would be resolved by stipulation, since the proponent would be unlikely to call a witness who does not qualify with room to spare. But that is not the only purpose, and it is often an important and elaborate process.

---

[20] Irving Younger, Expert Witnesses, 48 Ins. Couns. J. 267, 274 (1981).

[21] See, e.g., Carroll v. Morgan, 17 F.3d 787, 790 (5th Cir. 1994) (cardiologist without training in pathology qualified to testify to cause of death, even in face of disagreement with three testifying pathologists); Wheeler v. John Deere Co., 935 F.2d 1090, 1100–1101 (10th Cir. 1991) (mechanical engineer permitted to testify as expert on consumer expectations despite lack of experience in consumer sampling); United States v. Viglia, 549 F.2d 335, 337 (5th Cir. 1977) (physician with no particular experience in area could testify on use of drug to treat obesity); Holmgren v. Massey-Ferguson Inc., 516 F.2d 856, 857 (8th Cir. 1975) (professor of mechanical engineering with little experience with corn pickers qualified as expert on corn picker design); Parker v. Gunther, 122 Vt. 68, 74, 164 A.2d 152, 156 (1960) (general practitioner could testify to brain damage). In the wake of Daubert v. Merrell Dow Pharmaceuticals, 509 U.S. 579 (1993), see infra pp. 1159–1163, some courts have become more demanding in their scrutiny of expert qualifications, but the basic pattern seems unchanged.

The proponent of an expert witness is entitled to produce evidence on the witness's qualifications to *bolster the weight* of the expert's testimony, as well as to establish its admissibility. Testimony on qualifications is offered to convince the jury that the witness should be believed not because *what she says* makes sense or sounds credible, but also—and sometimes primarily—because of *who she is*. This, of course, is *character evidence.*   In other contexts, character evidence may not be used to enhance a witness's credibility unless the opponent has first attacked her credibility; and even then the evidence is generally restricted to the witness's reputation for truthfulness and to other witnesses' opinions of her truthfulness. See FRE 608. Those general limitations do not apply to experts. So long as the evidence relates to the witness's expert qualifications, her credibility may be bolstered prior to any attack, and with a wide range of character evidence. The opportunity to present specific positive character evidence is a major asset for the proponent of the expert, who may present such evidence even if the opposition offers to stipulate that the witness is qualified. Indeed, experienced practitioners frequently warn the unwary novice to beware of an offer to stipulate to an expert's qualifications and thus obviate the need for testimony. After all, if the expert is good enough to use as a witness, the judge or jury should hear all the good things that can be said about her, in detail.

And evidence on qualifications can be quite detailed. An expert may be asked to describe where she went to school, from college on, what she studied, the degrees and any academic honors she received, the course of her entire professional career since she completed her schooling, all professional licenses she has earned, any publications she has authored or research she has conducted, any prizes she has been awarded, any other form of professional recognition she can claim, each professional association to which she belongs, any positions she has held in these associations, and any professional experiences that are particularly relevant to the case at hand—such as special training on the particular issues, similar tasks she has handled, and other cases in which she has testified as an expert. This recital can get boring, but that does not necessarily mean it is ineffective. The audience may not be interested, it may not appreciate all the details—it may not even hear them—but it cannot miss the message: We can sing this witness's praises for a long time.

The opposing attorney, of course, may cross-examine an expert witness about her qualifications. Because qualifications are a foundational requirement, he may do it under FRE 104 as a "voir dire" examination on that preliminary question before the witness is permitted to offer any substantive expert evidence—an option that is sometimes used to interrupt the direct examination and test the witness at an early stage. However, since the witness was chosen by the attorney who called her, the opposing attorney almost never has a realistic hope of convincing the judge that she is not qualified to testify. The standard is not high, and if it were a close call a different expert would have been hired in the first place.[22] As a result, the common functions of cross-examination on qualifications are more limited. The opposing attorney may try to embarrass the witness with negatives, such as, "You are not board certified in neurophysiology, are you Doctor?" Or a psychologist with a Ph.D. may be forced to admit that she is not a psychiatrist—i.e. not a "real" doctor with an M.D. And if possible, the cross-examiner may take this opportunity to run through a list of impressive sounding attributes of *his* expert witness which the opposing expert lacks.

This screening process—such as it is—turns almost entirely on credentials, which are a poor proxy for knowledge. The graduate student who knows more about the effects of a particular virus than anybody else in the world might not qualify as an expert witness on the topic—or if she did, she might appear less qualified than a run-of-the-mill Ph.D.—and so would probably never be called as a witness. The chairman of her department, on the other hand, will qualify easily no matter what he knows.[23]

Problem IX-2. Sue Stewart is resisting the state's effort to commit her to a mental hospital. She wishes to put Abigail Sanders on the stand to testify that although Sue is somewhat eccentric, she is perfectly capable of functioning in society without endangering herself or others, and that she is not suffering from any mental disease or defect. Sanders and Stewart have known each other as neighbors for more than fifteen years. Sanders holds a bachelor's degree in history, acquired some twenty years ago. For the past twelve years she has written a newspaper advice column which has been syndicated to over 300 newspapers. It is generally acknowledged that her column is one of the most sensible of its kind, that she "knows people" very well, and that she has an uncanny knack for understanding personal problems. **Should her testimony on Stewart's mental health be admitted? Is there any testimony she might give in addition to or instead of the testimony described?**

---

[22] The justification for allowing this examination on voir dire is that it goes to a preliminary question which the judge must decide before the witness is allowed to testify. Under FRE 104(c), this matter could be heard by the judge outside the presence of the jury. In practice, that rarely happens. Since the same questions could be asked before the jury on cross-examination, and since almost all experts do qualify and are cross-examined, it is more efficient to allow the jury to hear the initial cross on the issue of qualifications.

[23] There is a separate preliminary issue that, unlike the qualifications of the witness, sometimes is in serious dispute. When an expert witness is called to give "scientific" evidence, the court may conduct a hearing, outside the presence of the jury, on the validity of the underlying science. See infra, pp. 1157–1176.

B. EXPERT OPINION EVIDENCE

1. Expert Opinion Testimony, Generally

The subjects and the scope of lay testimony are infinitely variable. A witness may testify about an incident seen in passing, a series of related events, a sequence of business transactions over several years, or the signing of a single document. Some witnesses are called to describe their own actions; often a witness is asked to recall her reasons for doing some act or for neglecting to do it. But the general nature of lay evidence is always the same: A lay witness may testify about her own perceptions, and, if relevant, about her own state of mind at the time of the events at issue—and that is all. She may not openly guess or draw inferences about events that she did not perceive, or offer an explanation for events that she did perceive, or testify about the observations of others, or (with some exceptions) report the statements of others (or even her own past statements) describing past events, or comment on the testimony of another witness.

These restrictions reflect two fundamental concerns of common law fact-finding. The first is the division of functions. The trier of fact is supposed to have exclusive power to judge evidence; the role of the witness is to present evidence, not to evaluate it. The second concern is the reliability of evidence. The common law rules of evidence attempt to insure the reliability of the evidence presented at trials by a variety of exclusionary rules. The most important of these are the rule against hearsay and the requirement that a witness testify from personal knowledge. In this context, a particularly important manifestation of these two concerns is the common law's mistrust of lay opinion testimony. It is suspect on both grounds. Forming an opinion is seen as part of the process of evaluating evidence, which is the function of the judge or the jury and not that of the witness. In addition, a witness's opinions are, arguably, less reliable than her perceptions. As a result, traditional common law rules of evidence prohibited lay witnesses from testifying to "opinions" or "conclusions" and purported to limit them to "facts."

A rigorous rule against lay opinion evidence would be unenforceable. Many descriptions of observations have inferences and conclusions embedded in them. When a witness testifies that a person she saw across the room "was my friend Bob," that a conversations lasted "about five minutes," or that a car was parked "oh, maybe ten feet from the corner," she is expressing opinions. The witness, however, might be utterly unable to pare these statements down to the sensory data on which they are based—images, angles, the internal sense of the passage of time—and if she did manage, the resulting testimony would be awkward and uninformative. As a result, the common law rule was never literally enforced. Where it has been retained, it is compromised by exceptions,[24] and most American jurisdictions have repealed the traditional rule entirely.[25] FRE 701, for example, specifies that a non-expert witness may testify to those opinions that are (1) "rationally based on the witness's perception," and (2) "helpful" in resolving the case.[26] Both parts of this rule are important. If descriptions of concrete observations could provide information that the jury is able to evaluate as well as the witness, lay opinion testimony may be excluded even if it is based directly on the witness's perceptions.

With expert witnesses, none of the limiting rules we have mentioned applies in any meaningful sense: not the division of function between witness and jury, not the rule against hearsay, not restrictions on opinion testimony, not even the requirement of personal knowledge.

The core issue is the nature of expert opinion evidence. Expert evidence can only be used if it will "assist" the trier of fact to decide an issue that is beyond "common knowledge." Thus experts are almost never allowed to testify about the credibility of witnesses or the likelihood of a defendant's criminal or civil liability, since these are issues that we have specifically committed to the common sense of jurors. The boundaries of this restriction are sometimes contested. For example, most courts used to exclude expert evidence on the factors that affect the reliability of eyewitness identifications on the ground that this was a matter within the jury's common experience, and some courts still do so.[27] But for the usual expert issues this is not a problem; we know that we need expert assistance to understand most issues in medicine, engineering and science. Once that threshold is crossed an expert witness can offer opinions that are close to the core of the jury's task, and based on a wide range of first- and secondhand information.

Opinions are not the only type of testimony offered by expert witnesses, but they are the most common. Moreover, even when the testimony is couched in different terms, opinions are integral to all expert evidence. The Advisory Committee's comment on FRE 702 inadvertently illustrates this point. The Committee criticizes previous writers for assuming that "experts testify only in the form of opinions," when in fact an expert "may give a dissertation or exposition of scientific or other principles relevant to the case, leaving the trier of fact to apply them to the facts." The Committee is right that an expert witness may leave it to

---

[24]　See McCormick § 11; 7 Wigmore § 1917, p. 10.

[25]　See supra, Chapter Two, pp. 143–144.

[26]　FRE 701(c) includes a third qualification: that the opinion is "not based on scientific, technical or other specialized knowledge." The purpose of the amendment is to eliminate any overlap between expert opinion evidence (which is governed by FRE 702) and lay opinion evidence (which is governed by FRE 701), so as to prevent expert evidence sneaking in as lay opinion. See Chapter Two, pp. 143–144.

[27]　See Chapter Three, pp. 259–263.

the judge or jury to draw any ultimate factual conclusions from her testimony; most likely, the Committee hoped to encourage experts to testify in that form. It is also true that such testimony may not be called "opinion evidence." But a witness who gives the type of testimony the Committee describes must rely on her expert "opinion" (or, to use a word that is less loaded in this context, her expert *judgment*) to decide what the relevant scientific principles *are*, and she must make a host of lesser judgments to decide how to organize and present these principles. Even an expert who testifies only to a set of specialized observations—images produced by an MRI scan, for example—cannot avoid making an expert judgment that the technique she used was appropriate to the task at hand.

Many American courts once said that no witness—not even an expert—could give an opinion that encompassed an "ultimate issue" that was to be determined by the trier of fact. Under this rule an orthopedist might be prevented from testifying that an automobile accident "caused" the plaintiff's paralysis, since that opinion would "usurp the function" or "invade the province" of the jury. Instead, the witness would have to couch the opinion in artificially weak terms, and say that the accident "could have caused" the injury, that the "injury was consistent with" that cause, and so forth. This was not a useful limitation. Every expert opinion "usurps" the jury's function of evaluating evidence, to some extent. That is a primary purpose of expert evidence. The artificial line prohibiting opinions on a shifting collection of "ultimate issues" did not help either the witnesses or the jurors, and was increasingly abandoned in the second half of this century, even before American evidence law was largely codified.[28] FRE 704 explicitly renounces the ultimate issue rule, with one exception:

> **(a) In General—Not Automatically Objectionable.** An opinion is not objectionable just because it embraces an ultimate issue.

> **(b) Exception.** In a criminal case, an expert witness must not state an opinion about whether the defendant did or did not have a mental state or condition that constitutes an element of the crime charged or of a defense. Those matters are for the trier of fact alone.

FRE 704(b) reflects the continuing ambivalence of courts, legislatures, and the public toward the use of mental defenses in criminal cases. This particular manifestation was added to FRE 704 by Congress as part of the Insanity Defense Reform Act of 1984,[29] largely in response to the outcry that followed the acquittal by reason of insanity of John

---

[28] The shift seems to have begun in 1942, with Grismore v. Consolidated Products Co., 232 Iowa 328, 5 N.W.2d 646 (1942). See McCormick § 12.

[29] P.L. 98–473, Title II, ch. IV § 406.

Hinckley, who was tried in 1982 for the attempted assassination of President Ronald Reagan. Under 704(b) an expert witness may testify that a defendant was "psychotic" or "delusional" or "insane" at the time of a crime. But the expert may not testify that the defendant was "unable to distinguish right from wrong" or "unable to conform his actions to the requirements of law" if those latter mental states are elements of the jurisdiction's defense of "insanity" or "lack of criminal responsibility."

Even under FRE 704, opinion evidence will be excluded if the witness merely states how the jury should decide the case ("These injuries require a $5 million judgment"), or if the opinion is couched as a legal conclusion ("The defendant is clearly liable"). Such opinions are condemned either because they are not "helpful" to the trier of fact, or because they are not on an appropriate subject for expert testimony.

Problem IX-3. Stan Tucker is accused of murder. He admits killing the victim but pleads not guilty by reason of insanity. He introduces three psychiatrists who have examined him with the aid of numerous diagnostic tests and extensive interviews. They testify that he is a psychotic and that he has been suffering from psychotic episodes since his return from the war in Iraq three years before the killing. They testify that at the time of the killing he was deluded, that he did not have the mental capacity to know right from wrong, and that he could not have resisted the impulse to kill. **What objections, if any, could have been made to the testimony by these psychiatrists?** The prosecution counters the psychiatrists' testimony with the testimony of Tucker's former wife, who had been married to him for ten years and who had lived with him until a week before the killing. She testifies that Tucker's behavior did not change at all following his year of service in Iraq, that he always seemed normal to her, and that he was a very moral man with a firm sense of right and wrong. Indeed, she testifies that she finally decided to get a divorce because he thought it was immoral for her to drink, smoke, or play church Bingo. At the end of the spouse's rebuttal testimony the prosecutor rests her case and the defendant moves for a directed verdict, claiming that on the evidence the jury must acquit him by reason of insanity. **How should a court rule?**

---

2.   The Bases for Expert Opinion Evidence

In reaching an opinion, an expert, unlike a lay witness, is not restricted to relying on her own perceptions, or even on her own reasoning. Two types of second-hand information are allowed.[30] *First*, an expert may (indeed, *must*) rely on the general body of specialized knowledge that constitutes her field—published tables, reported experience, established principles, common lore. Typically, most of her expert knowledge is the residue of what she learned from others; sometimes she will have to go back and learn more to address the issues in a particular case. Expert witnesses have always been allowed to rely on the accumulated knowledge in their fields; it is essential to their function. As Wigmore put it, expert "generalizations which are the result of one man's personal observation exclusively are the least acceptable of all."[31]

Second, an expert witness may rely on other people's observations about the person or object or event at issue. This use of second-hand information has been controversial. Traditionally, common law rules of evidence required a witness to base her expert opinions solely upon her own observations, or on explicitly assumed facts drawn from evidence in the record. This practice was designed to keep the expert from basing her opinions on evidence about the case that had not been presented in court and tested before the jury. But despite its obvious logic, this restriction was criticized as unwarranted because in their day-to-day work, experts commonly form judgments based in part on numerous secondary factual sources, including reports and records, medical histories provided by patients and statements by other experts. As a result, the rule was increasingly compromised by exceptions.[32] Most modern codifications of the rules of evidence have abandoned this restriction entirely. The first part of FRE 703 provides:

> An expert may base an opinion on facts or data in the case that the expert has been made aware of or personally observed. If experts in the particular field would reasonably rely on those kinds of facts or data in forming an opinion on the subject, they need not be admissible for the opinion to be admitted. . . .

The argument for this rule, as illustrated in Advisory Committee Note to FRE 703, justifies this liberality as follows: "[A] physician in his own practice bases his diagnosis on information from numerous sources and of considerable variety. . . . The physician makes life-and-death decisions in reliance upon them. His validation . . . ought to suffice for judicial purpose." FRE 703 may be a good rule, but the Committee's argument is a non-sequitur. The issue is not whether the normally

---

[30] For a lucid description of the distinction between these two types of information, see Edward J. Imwinkelried, The "Bases" of Expert Testimony: The Syllogistic Structure of Scientific Testimony, 67 N.C. L. Rev. 1 (1988).

[31] 3 Wigmore § 687, p. 3. See also 2 Wigmore § 665(b), p. 919.

[32] See McCormick §§ 14–15; Paul D. Rheingold, The Basis of Medical Testimony, 15 Vand. L. Rev. 473 (1962); Marvin Katz, Comment, The Admissibility of Expert Medical Testimony Based in Part Upon Information Received from Third Persons, 35 S. Cal. L. Rev. 193 (1962).

restrictive rules of evidence should be loosened to let in evidence of a doctor's out-of-court medical *decisions* on medical diagnosis and treatment, even if they were based in part on inadmissible information. The question is whether the usual rules should be relaxed to let in opinion *testimony* based on otherwise inadmissible evidence—opinions that are generally offered by non-treating physicians who are often hired specifically to support or oppose the plaintiffs' claims for money.

C. HEARSAY IN EXPERT TESTIMONY

The Federal Rules of Evidence contain two specific exceptions to the hearsay rule that turn on the assumed reliability of information that is used by experts:

Statements Made for Purposes of Medical Diagnosis or Treatment. FRE 803(4) expands the traditional common law exception for statements "made for . . . medical diagnosis or treatment"[33] to include statements made to non-treating physicians who were consulted for the purposes of litigation only. The Advisory Committee noted that since "the [non-treating] expert was allowed to state the basis of his opinion, including statements of this kind" the common law rule required jurors to perform the unlikely mental gymnastics of considering diagnostically relevant hearsay statements in evaluating a non-treating medical expert's opinion, while erasing those statements from their minds when deciding what happened.[34]

"Learned Treatises." FRE 803(18)—a liberal version of the traditional "learned treatise" exception—encompasses all of the following:

A statement contained in a treatise, periodical, or pamphlet if:

> **(A)** the statement is called to the attention of an expert witness on cross-examination or relied on by the expert on direct examination; and
>
> **(B)** the publication is established as a reliable authority by the expert's admission or testimony, by another expert's testimony, or by judicial notice.

If admitted, the statement may be read into evidence but not received as an exhibit.

Under this rule, the expert may read or summarize passages or entire articles on direct examination, or the opposing attorney may do so on cross-examination.

---

[33] See Chapter Six, supra, pp. 638–641.

[34] This rationale made sense when FRE 803(4) was enacted in the original version of the Federal Rules, because FRE 703 permitted all experts to describe the bases for their opinions, including any inadmissible evidence if it was of "a type reasonably relied upon by experts in the particular field." As we will see, FRE 703 was amended in 2000 to limit this use of inadmissible evidence that is a basis for an expert opinion, but FRE 803(4) stands unchanged.

In addition to these specific exceptions, expert witnesses frequently operate under what amounts to a plenary exemption from the hearsay rule. As we have seen, under FRE 703, an expert witness is permitted to offer opinion evidence that is *based* on hearsay or other inadmissible evidence. Experts are also allowed to explain their opinions. FRE 705, which governs this process, permits an expert to "state an opinion—and give the reasons for it—without first testifying to the underlying facts or data," "[u]nless the court orders otherwise"—which suggests that the expert *may* testify to those underlying facts if she (and the lawyer who calls her) wishes to do so. The Advisory Committee Note to FRE 705 took that position: "The rule *allows* counsel to make disclosure of the underlying facts or data as a preliminary to giving an expert opinion, if he chooses. . . .   This is true whether the expert bases his opinion on data furnished him at secondhand [i.e., hearsay] or observed by him at firsthand." (Emphasis added.) FRE 705 also provides that "[T]he expert may be required to disclose those facts or data on cross-examination."

In 2000 FRE 703 was amended to add the provision that now appears in the last sentence of the current rule, italicized below:

> An expert may base an opinion on facts or data in the case that the expert has been made aware of or personally observed. If experts in the particular field would reasonably rely on those kinds of facts or data in forming an opinion on the subject, they need not be admissible for the opinion to be admitted. *But if the facts or data would otherwise be inadmissible, the proponent of the opinion may disclose them to the jury only if their probative value in helping the jury evaluate the opinion substantially outweighs their prejudicial effect.*

This amendment creates a presumption of exclusion for otherwise inadmissible evidence that forms basis for an expert opinion. It addresses the question as a balancing issue, like FRE 403, but sets the balance against admission. To be admitted, the probative value of the evidence must substantially outweigh its prejudicial impact, unlike FRE 403 which permits exclusion only if the prejudicial impact of evidence substantially outweighs its probative value. The 2000 amendment only limits the disclosure of inadmissible bases for expert opinions on direct examination, "by the proponent of the opinion or inference;" disclosure may still be required on cross-examination, as provided by FRE 705. See infra, p. 1144.

It is not clear how much the 2000 amendment to FRE 703 has changed practice in trial courts. Even before the amendment, federal courts sometimes excluded inadmissible evidence that was the basis for an expert opinion.[35] Some post-2000 cases suggest little or no change,[36]

---

[35] For example in Marsee v. United States Tobacco, 866 F.2d 319, 322–23 (10th Cir. 1989), a physician expert for the plaintiff was permitted to testify that in his opinion the plaintiff's oral

while in other cases evidence is excluded under the 2000 amendment, especially if it is evidence about the opinions of other, non-testifying experts.[37] Outside of federal courts, the last sentence of FRE 703 has not been widely adopted. Only 4 of the 43 jurisdictions that have codes of evidence patterned after the Federal Rules include that provision as worded in FRE 703, and at least 37 such jurisdictions have no similar provision at all.

In sum, in many (but not all) cases, statements of a patient describing her symptoms, or the results of tests conducted by laboratory technicians, or data gathered by a research assistant, may all be presented to the jury through the mouth of a testifying expert who relied on those items of information to reach an admissible expert opinion.

In theory, any otherwise inadmissible hearsay that an expert witness describes as a basis for her opinions may be considered only in evaluating the expert's opinion testimony, and not as substantive evidence of the underlying facts. In rare cases this limitation may be significant, usually when the party offering the evidence needs to rely on that information to defeat a motion for a directed verdict. In a jury case, the opposing party is entitled to a limiting instruction under FRE 105.[38] It is unrealistic, however, to expect this artificial distinction to have any impact on jurors: How can they accept an expert's opinion without concluding that the facts on which it is based are true?[39]

---

cancer was caused by his use of snuff (smokeless tobacco), and that this opinion was based in part on information about other snuff users who developed that disease; but the expert was not permitted to discuss the details of those other oral cancer cases, on the grounds that such information (from telephone conversations with other physicians) was "unnecessary and unreliable" for the purpose of understanding the testifying expert's opinion. For contrasting scholarly views on the issue, compare, e.g., Ronald L. Carlson, Policing the Bases of Modern Expert Testimony, 39 Vand. L. Rev. 577 (1986) (advocating limits on the jury's consideration of otherwise inadmissible evidence used as the basis for an expert opinion), and Paul A. Rice, Inadmissible Evidence as a Basis for Expert Testimony: A Response to Professor Carlson, 40 Vand. L. Rev. 583 (1987) (advocating unrestricted use of information reasonably relied upon by an expert).

[36] See, e.g., United States v. Floyd, 281 F.3d 1346, 1349 (11th Cir. 2002) ("[H]earsay testimony by experts is permitted if it is based upon the type of evidence reasonably relied upon by experts in the particular field.") (citing a pre-2000 11th Circuit case).

[37] See, e.g., Mike's Train House, Inc. v. Lionel, L.L.C., 472 F.3d 398, 409 (6th Cir. 2006).

[38] See, e.g., United States v. Madrid, 673 F.2d 1114, 1118, n. 4 (10th Cir. 1982) (instructing the jury that the testimony was being admitted to show the basis of the expert's opinion and not for the truth of the underlying source); American Universal Ins. Co. v. Falzone, 644 F.2d 65, 66, n. 1 (1st Cir. 1981) (instructing the jury that the expert's testimony about his colleague's investigation was being admitted only to show basis of opinion, not for the truth of the investigation); United States v. Sims, 514 F.2d 147, 149–50 (9th Cir. 1975) (recognizing the need for the court to instruct the jury that hearsay evidence is to be considered solely as a basis for the expert's opinion and not for its own truth).

[39] The Advisory Committee on the Federal Rules of Evidence addressed this exact issue with respect to statements made to non-treating physicians for purposes of diagnosis. In its Note to FRE 803(4) the Committee rejected the old rule that such statements were admissible as a basis for the expert's opinion but inadmissible as substantive evidence, because "The distinction thus called for was one most unlikely to be made by juries." See Rice, supra note 35.

Under the Federal Rules, the only limitation on an expert's right to rely on inadmissible evidence is the requirement that the expert's reliance on these "facts or data" be "reasonable" for an expert in her field. As we will see in Section IV, there is a recent trend to scrutinize the bases of some expert testimony more carefully. But this trend is largely limited to novel scientific evidence. For ordinary expert evidence, and especially for routine testimony by medical experts, the traditional requirement of evidence of "reasonable reliance" is usually satisfied by the expedience of asking the expert herself if her reliance was reasonable. The justification for this procedure is the belief that an expert is as competent to "judge the reliability of statements made to him by other investigators or technicians . . . " as "a judge and jury are to pass upon the credibility of an ordinary witness on the stand."[40] The logic of this argument is debatable, since expert witnesses (unlike judges and jurors) are permitted to make these judgments in proceedings in which their own credibility is at issue and for which they were hired by one side, perhaps because they believe and are willing to rely on crucial information supplied by their side that most experts would dismiss. The consequences of the rule, however, are clear. In many cases, expert witnesses are permitted both to draw inferences from evidence of which they have no personal knowledge and to determine the reliability of that evidence as a precondition to its use.

———————

Problem IX-4. Big Gill Springsten sues James Perkins claiming that he is entitled to a one-half partnership interest in Perkins' explosives business and for a percentage of past profits. Springsten calls a certified public accountant to testify. This accountant reviewed a financial report on the partnership prepared by another accounting firm at Springsten's request. The report has been marked as Exhibit One. The testimony is as follows:

Q. All right, sir. Let me show you what has been marked as Plaintiff's Exhibit Number One and ask you whether or not you recognize that instrument. **A.** I recognize it.

Q. All right, sir, and have you had occasion to familiarize yourself with that instrument? **A.** Yes, sir, I have and I have discussed certain matters in it with Mr. Steve Pena, who worked for Anderson & Co., an accounting firm hired to prepare the report.

Q. Can you tell me from this instrument what amounts of money that James Perkins took from the explosives business during the years covered by this accounting, which I believe is 1998 through April of 2006. **A.** Yes, sir.

———————

[40] McCormick § 15.

Q. What is that figure? **A.** The answer to your question involves two items, really. The total numbers, according to my computation, is $5,321,875.70.

Q. Now, that is your conclusion based upon your examination of this report marked as Plaintiff's Exhibit Number One, is that correct? **A.** Yes, sir. It is.

Q. And that is the moneys that that report shows actually came into James Perkins' possession from the James Perkins Explosives Company? **A.** Yes, sir.

Q. Are the figures in the report the type you usually rely on in making accounting judgments? **A.** Yes they are.

Perkins moves to have the testimony stricken on the ground that it is without a proper foundation because the witness did not himself examine Perkins' records. **Should he prevail? How might Springsten overcome the objection?**

"Is this really necessary, Your Honor? I'm an expert."

D. PRESENTING EXPERT TESTIMONY

Under traditional common law rules, a witness was not permitted to testify to an expert opinion without first specifying the information on which she relied. If some of that information was not personally known to her, the examining lawyer supplied it in the form of a hypothetical question, incorporating facts which had been or would be supported by admissible evidence.[41] This practice encouraged a conspicuous abuse: the examiner would ask the witness to "assume" the accuracy of the facts he was about to state, proceed to give a long, detailed and partisan summary of the evidence on the issue (both that which had been presented and that which was anticipated), and conclude by asking for the expert's opinion given that "assumption." This procedure enabled the lawyer to sum up the evidence in mid-trial, and to appear to receive an endorsement for his summation from the witness. It did little, however, to clarify the basis for the expert's opinion, both because the hypothetical questions used were often wonderfully complex, and because much of the hypothetical information in the question might have no bearing on the expert's conclusions. *Treadwell v. Nickel*, a 1924 case from California, is an amusing illustration of the bizarre extremes that are possible under this procedure: it describes an *eighty-three page* hypothetical question, followed by a *fourteen* page objection.[42]

The Federal Rules of Evidence, and other codifications of evidence law, have abandoned the hypothetical question as a requirement. As a corollary to allowing an expert to rely on inadmissible evidence in forming her opinions (FRE 703), FRE 705 provides:

> Unless the court orders otherwise, an expert may state an opinion—and give the reasons for it—without first testifying to the underlying facts or data. But the expert may be required to disclose those facts or data on cross-examination.

But while hypothetical questions are no longer required as a foundation for expert testimony, neither are they forbidden. They are now one of several methods of organizing expert testimony.

If the direct examiner does not use hypothetical questions, expert testimony under modern rules of evidence may follow a variety of formats. The witness may state a simple conclusion—"The plaintiff is permanently and totally disabled"—without any explanation; or she may go through the information she has acquired, item by item, explaining the significance of each piece, then give a lecture on general principles that apply to the issue, and conclude with her expert opinion; or she may start

---

[41]   See, e.g., Eisenmayer v. Leonardt, 148 Cal. 596, 84 P. 43 (1906).

[42]   194 Cal. 243, 228 P. 25 (Cal. 1924). See infra, pp. 1213–1214 for a modern example of a long hypothetical question to an expert psychiatrist, followed by an objection, in the capital case of People v. Orona, El Paso County District Court, Colorado (11/20/1990).

with her opinion and then justify it with whatever portion of the underlying facts and reasoning seems most useful. In theory, expert testimony is subject to those rules of evidence that dictate the form and manner of questioning of lay witnesses. In practice, these rules too are applied in diluted form. In particular, an expert witness may often be asked leading questions about disputed issues on direct examination—the traditional hypothetical question is a glaring example—and experts are usually given greater leeway than lay witnesses to testify in unbroken narratives.

E. RESPONDING TO EXPERT TESTIMONY

1. Cross-Examination

Cross-examination, as we have seen in Chapter Two, is a peculiar form of inquiry. Its goal is not to reveal information but to advance the cross-examiner's case. To score points through a hostile witness the cross-examiner must control the questioning tightly, which he can do by asking leading questions to which he already knows the answers. The archetypal cross-examination consists of nothing but leading questions that call for "yes" or "no" answers—a sequence of statements that the witness is required to admit or deny and nothing more. It is not really questioning at all, but an opportunity for the cross-examiner to present evidence in his own words.

This form of examination is possible only if the examiner knows in advance what the witness will say. With lay witnesses that is usually accomplished by taking a deposition or getting some other type of pretrial statement from the witness. If the witness is important, the cross-examiner may investigate the witness's background and perceptual capacities, explore the conditions of the witness's observations, and note how this witness's testimony compares to the likely testimony of other witnesses. For a lay witness, however, all of the information gathered in preparation for cross-examination—however extensive—will relate directly to the witness and the event: who she is, what she said, what she saw, what happened. This reflects the general limitations of cross-examination to "the subject matter of the direct examination and matters affecting the witness's credibility." FRE 611(b).

From the lawyer's point of view, the cross-examination of an expert differs from that of a lay witness in several respects that cut in different directions. On the one hand, the scope of permissible questioning is broader, which is an advantage to the examiner. On the other hand, because the expert has more status and authority than most lay witnesses, and because she will ordinarily know more about her subject than even the best prepared lawyer, it is more difficult for a lawyer to control the examination of a hostile expert, and control is essential for success on cross-examination. Moreover, many experts are experienced witnesses who have learned to parry predictable challenges to their credibility. From the point of view of the witness there are further differences. The subject of expert cross-examination is usually closer to the core of the witness's self-image and social identity, and the attack is often far more demeaning. Many experts experience cross-examination as a willful distortion of the scientific or other special knowledge on which their testimony is based, for the purpose of confusing the jury. The net result is that the cross-examination of experts is frequently more charged, messier, less predictable and less informative than the cross-examination of other non-party witnesses.

The cross-examination of an expert witness may include any move that can be used in cross-examining an ordinary witness. In particular, an expert witness may be impeached on all grounds that are available to impeach a non-expert witness—felony convictions, bias, inconsistent statements, errors of fact, etc. For experts, however, two of those grounds have a special bite.

First, since an expert witness is usually paid, she may be attacked as biased because of her fee, or because she has been hired repeatedly by the same party, or the same firm, or the same side.

Second, a lay witness is unlikely to have made any statements that might be inconsistent with her testimony except in the context of the case at hand and its surrounding events. An expert witness, however, may be vulnerable because of inconsistencies in statements on the same subject in testimony in unrelated cases, in speeches, in lectures, or in published books and articles.

In general, "Once an expert offers his opinion . . . he exposes himself to the kind of inquiry which ordinarily would have no place in the cross-examination of a factual witness. . . . [H]e may be 'subjected to the most rigid cross-examination' concerning his qualifications, and his opinion and its sources."[43] We have already considered one aspect of this extraordinary inquiry, the free use of any evidence concerning the witness's professional character in cross-examination on qualifications. In most cases, however, the major focus of this "most rigid cross-examination" is the expert opinion itself, and the latitude of the cross-examiner in attacking that opinion is as great as the expert's latitude in choosing information to form her opinion in the first place.

Under FRE 705, an expert witness may be cross-examined about the bases for her opinion whether or not she discussed them on direct. She can be asked to specify what she considered, and why, and to explain the significance of each item. She can also be required to answer questions

---

[43] Hope v. Arrowhead & Puritas Waters, Inc., 174 Cal.App.2d 222, 344 P.2d 428, 433 (Cal.Ct.App.1959) (quoting Forrest v. Fink, 71 Cal.App. 34, 234 P. 860, 863 (Cal.Ct.App.1925)); see also LeMere v. Goren, 233 Cal.App.2d 799, 43 Cal.Rptr. 898, 902 (Cal.Ct.App.1965); Ross v. Colorado National Bank of Denver, 170 Colo. 436, 446, 463 P.2d 882, 887 (1969).

about materials she did not consider—tests she did not conduct, data she did not review, etc.—and about the implications of these materials. She may be asked a series of hostile hypothetical questions, with items of information arranged (or rearranged) to suit the cross-examiner. She may be questioned about the reliability of her sources of information. She may be questioned about the opinions of other experts who have testified, or will testify, or even about those who have no expected role in the case. And last, but perhaps most important, under FRE 803(18) she may be cross-examined about the content of a published "treatise, periodical, or pamphlet" on the subject of her expert opinion.

This last form of cross-examination permits a lawyer to present his own expert evidence without calling a witness, including evidence on issues the expert on the witness stand never touched. If it is done at length the cross-examination can come to focus on the odd ritual of calling published material "to the attention" of the witness for the sole purpose of presenting it to the jury. The lawyer may also "call attention" to a series of unusual or exceptional cases that seem to contradict the expert's opinion, without letting the expert explain them. Sometimes, the cross-examiner can find an apparently relevant dispute in the expert's field and discuss it at length; more often the lawyer may try to seize upon the residual uncertainty that is inherent in most intelligent judgments, and magnify it. On some issues a lawyer can even trot out published statements by apparently well-credentialed authors who argue that no expert in the witness's field can offer evidence of value on the matter at issue[44]—an invitation to the jury to ignore all expert testimony that may become increasingly attractive as the evidence becomes increasingly confused.

This is one side of a coin: the special advantages the lawyer enjoys when cross-examining an expert. There is another side.

First, since the expert has great latitude to determine the content and the organization of her testimony, she can often structure it to thwart the cross-examiner. One common method is to present a small and elusive target: an expert who testifies to conclusions that are based solely on her "experience" and "expertise" is less vulnerable to attack than one who relies on explicit data or clearly specified lines of reasoning.[45]

Second, and more important, successful cross-examination depends on control, and expert witnesses are much harder to control than ordinary witnesses. In part this is due to the experience and preparation of the

---

[44] E.g., Jay Ziskin, Coping With Psychiatric and Psychological Testimony (5th ed. 1995) (psychiatric and psychological assessments are worthless); Michael McCloskey & Howard E. Egeth, Eyewitness Identification: What Can A Psychologist Tell A Jury?, 38 Am. Psychologist 550 (1983) (expert evidence on eyewitness identification is unreliable).

[45] See, e.g., Michael M. Nash, Parameters and Distinctiveness of Psychological Testimony, 5 Prof. Psychol. 239, 242 (1974) (recommending this method as a maneuver to avoid challenging cross-examination).

witnesses. Since experts are more likely than lay witnesses to have spent a great deal of time preparing for cross-examination, they have a better chance of anticipating and undermining the cross-examiner's intentions. In addition, many experts (but few lay witnesses) are repeat performers who have covered the exact same ground time and again, and have learned what questions to expect on cross-examination and how to take advantage of any openings.[46] Not surprisingly, novice attorneys are advised by their seniors to choose "an expert who has been cross-examined before [and] may sense any traps and be better able to avoid them . . . ."[47]

The main problem of control, however, concerns the content of expert testimony. Controlling any cross-examination can be difficult even with the best preparation. Any witness will sometimes be allowed to explain her answers on cross-examination, and most say some things that the cross-examiner does not foresee. An expert witness, however, has more power to frustrate the cross-examiner. Unlike a lay witness, she has greater authority in her own field than the attorney who confronts her or the judge who presides over her testimony. As a result, she will be given more leeway to explain herself or to refuse to answer a question in the terms in which it is asked. When a lawyer asks a radiologist a question about her specialty—"Isn't a CT scan the preferred method for diagnosing this condition?"—and the radiologist claims that the question cannot be answered without a good deal of background, or even that it misses the point entirely, how can he dispute her? The very fact that expert testimony is needed demonstrates that these are issues beyond the range of ordinary commonsense.

A similar difficulty is likely when an expert gives an unexpected answer. The attorney might not understand a detailed answer about the strengths and weaknesses of CT scans compared to MRI scans, ultrasounds and ordinary x-rays, and is even less likely to understand its implications. If the answer is incomprehensible—if the radiologist responds with three paragraphs of explanations and qualifications—the jury may blame the *lawyer* for confusing things by posing a stupid question to someone who knows more than he does. But that is not the worst risk. What if the radiologist surprises the cross-examiner by answering his question about CT scans with a simple "No"? Whatever they may think of expert witnesses, the jurors are not likely to assume that the lawyer is right and the doctor is wrong. To extricate himself the

---

[46] For example, in California civil jury trials in 1985–86, "For a particular [expert] appearance before a jury, the average number of times the same expert testified over a six-year period was 9.4, [not counting] testimony in criminal trials or in civil trials in courts other than California State Superior Courts, [or] the many cases in which the same experts were consulted, wrote reports, or even testified in depositions, but failed to testify in court because the cases were settled or dismissed before trial." Gross, supra note 1, at 1120.

[47] E. Eugene Miller & Charles M. Kolb, The Penologist as Expert Witness, 8 Litig. 30, 32 (Summer 1982).

lawyer must understand the answer; but how can he? In this context, the answer "No" could mean, among other things, that: (1) the terminology of the question was wrong, (2) there is a newer and better technique than the CT scan, (3) CT scans are not used for *initial* diagnosis, (4) CT scans are almost always used in *conjunction* with other diagnostic techniques, (5) opinions in the field differ, (6) the expert has a peculiar point of view, (7) the expert is ignorant, or (8) the expert is lying.

There is an obvious solution to this problem, the one that is used in ordinary consultations with experts: ask the expert to explain herself. But this may be a fatal trap. It destroys any vestiges of control the cross-examiner may hope to exercise, gives the witness an opportunity to bolster her opinions, and ratifies the authority of the witness. Worse, the answer may include some terribly damaging statement. Unfortunately for lawyers, it is often a hard trap to avoid. The impulse to ask for an explanation is difficult to resist, and the need for clarification may make the absence of a request conspicuous and damning. The safest way to avoid this danger is to drop the area of questioning entirely. Otherwise the cross-examiner risks repeated contradictions from the expert, and, ultimately, a lengthy explanation of the lawyer's own understandable ignorance of the expert's field. If the issue is important, this forces the lawyer to make a nasty choice: accept a cross-examination that has come to naught, or risk having it turned against him. As the laments of trial lawyers testify, both outcomes are common.[48]

The net effect of these cross currents is that the cross-examination of an expert witness is a high risk event for both sides. Either participant can get badly hurt—often in unforeseen ways—which may explain why lawyers and experts alike complain about the difficulty and the unpleasantness of the process. One experienced trial lawyer gives an inadvertently telling description of this conflict: "The expert will almost always know more about his field [the main issue of importance to the cross-examiner] than will trial counsel. Collateral or ad hominem attacks [the type most likely to wound the witness] may be the only available avenue of cross-examination."[49]

The best performers in this slippery arena are two somewhat unattractive characters. First, there is the *professional witness*. This is an expert who has become experienced enough in the role of witness to have perfected her performance. She knows how to use her position and authority to maximum effect; she is not upset by demeaning cross-examination (like the lawyers, she views testimony as a game) and,

---

[48] See, e.g., Francis L. Wellman, The Art of Cross Examination 74 (1904) ("Lengthy cross examination [of experts] . . . are usually disastrous and should rarely be attempted."); David B. Baum, Taking on the Opposing Expert, 20 Trial 74 (Apr. 1984) ("Many trial lawyers, in awe of opposing experts, conduct cross-examination by making the testimony far worse for their clients, . . .").

[49] Ostroff, supra note 19, at 8, 9.

therefore, she is hard to discredit. Second, there is the *lawyer-expert*. This is a lawyer who is highly knowledgeable in the field at issue; he may even be a qualified expert—a physician or an engineer. In his role as a lawyer, however, he uses his expertise not to instruct but to manipulate other experts and to undercut them.

2.   Rebuttal

Cross-examination is not the only way to discredit an expert witness: The opposing party may also call its own expert in rebuttal. In civil trials in California State Superior Courts in 1985–86, for example, two out of three expert witnesses faced opposing experts in their own fields, and 78% of medical experts faced opposing medical experts.[50] This is a predictable consequence of the power of the parties to choose their expert witnesses. Given the universe of possible choices, a lawyer can find some formally qualified witness to testify to any reasonable and many unreasonable expert propositions. When an opposing expert is called, the entire process is repeated in reverse: The direct and cross-examiner switch roles, and the new witness gives a contradictory opinion. In many cases the end result is that two qualified experts testify to diametrically opposing views, each is attacked by the other side, and a lay jury is told to sort out the truth on a question that is, by definition, beyond the reach of common knowledge.

3.   Criminal Cases: The Need for Opposition

On the other hand, in many criminal cases the main problem with expert evidence is the opposite: The only experts who are called testify by one side—the prosecution—and the defense makes no serious attempt to challenge their conclusions, or no attempt at all. The basic reason for this one-sided presentation is lack of resources. The great majority of criminal defendants are indigent; they are represented by public defenders or other court-appointed lawyers who have no funds to hire experts.[51] As a result, most expert evidence in criminal cases comes from state employees who are called by the prosecutors: police officers, medical examiners, technicians at state crime laboratories, psychiatrists at state hospitals, and so forth. Their findings are rarely subjected to review by defense experts. In many cases, the prosecution experts are hardly even

---

[50]   Gross, supra note 1, at 1120.

[51]   In Ake v. Oklahoma, 470 U.S. 68 (1985) the Supreme Court held that a defendant was constitutionally entitled to expert assistance to rebut psychiatric evidence offered by the state at the penalty phase of his capital trial. Some courts apply the constitutional principle in *Ake* broadly, and some jurisdictions provide expert assistance to indigent defendants by rule or statute. In other jurisdictions there are no such provisions, and the courts limit *Ake* to psychiatric expertise, to capital cases, or both. And some courts—when they do apply *Ake*— merely require that the defense have access to a report from an "independent court-appointed psychiatrist" whose evidence is available to both sides. Granviel v. Lynaugh, 881 F.2d 185 (5th Cir. 1989). See generally Paul C. Giannelli & Edward J. Imwinkelried, Scientific Evidence 109– 136 (2d ed. 1993).

cross-examined by the inexperienced, overworked and inadequately compensated court-appointed criminal defense lawyers. This might not be a problem if those experts could be counted on to do their jobs competently and fairly. Unfortunately, that is not always so. For example, Fred Zain worked as the West Virginia State Police serologist from 1979 till 1989, and from 1989 until 1993 he had a similar job in Texas. In 1992 a man convicted in part on Zain's evidence proved his innocence using a newly available DNA identification technique. The investigation that followed uncovered a massive pattern of fraud— perjury, fabricated reports of tests, altered laboratory records. In 1993 the West Virginia Supreme Court ordered a review of 134 convictions based in part on evidence supplied by Zain.[52] At least 9 defendants in West Virginia and 2 in Texas have been released after it was determined that they had been erroneously convicted on Zain's perjured evidence.

The Zain affair is not unique. There have been a disturbing number of similar scandals in the past two decades.[53] Even so, it's likely that comparatively few crime laboratory technicians deliberately falsify their evidence. Carelessness and ordinary incompetence, on the other hand, seem to be widespread. In the mid-1970s the Federal Law Enforcement Administration sent samples of known materials to police laboratories across the country for identification. The results were disheartening. Among other findings, the researchers reported that 75% of the laboratories provided "unacceptable" results (inaccurate or incomplete) on a blood test, 51% made errors matching paint samples, 36% erred in soil

---

[52] In the Matter of an Investigation of the West Virginia State Police Crime Laboratory, Serology Division, 190 W.Va. 321, 438 S.E.2d 501 (1993); "Court Invalidates a Decade of Blood Test Results in Criminal Cases," New York Times, Nov. 11, 1993 (p. A-20); Paul C. Giannelli, The Abuse of Scientific Evidence in Criminal Cases: The Need for Independent Crime Laboratories, 5 Virginia J. of Social Policy & the Law 439, 442–49 (1997).

[53] For example, Dr. Ralph Erdmann, a pathologist in Lubbock, Texas, supposedly performed some 450 autopsies a year for ten years in 40 counties—and testified to many of them. The authorities became suspicious when he filed an autopsy report that included the weight of the spleen of a man whose spleen had been surgically removed. Several of the corpses he claimed to have autopsied were exhumed, and found to have been untouched. A lawyer appointed to investigate concluded: "If the prosecution theory was that death was caused by a Martian death ray, then that was what Dr. Erdmann reported." Richard L. Fricker, Pathologist's Plea Adds to Turmoil, A.B.A.J., Mar. 1993, p. 24. Professor Giannelli's 1997 article, supra note 52, includes detailed descriptions of the Erdmann scandal, and of several additional cases of forensic science fraud. There have been a steady stream of them since. See, e.g., a 2010 editorial describing a report on misconduct at North Carolina's State Bureau of Investigation crime lab:

> Sickening. That's the word that comes to mind after the public release Wednesday of an audit of the State Bureau of Investigation's crime lab.

> Commissioned by Attorney General Roy Cooper, the audit found that the SBI had withheld or fudged blood evidence to help prosecutors in 190 cases over 16 years. The review found another 40 reports in which blood evidence was manipulated but no charges were filed.

> Among those convicted in the presence of tainted evidence include four people now on death row, five more who died in prison and three who were executed. . . .

Greensboro News & Record, Aug 20, 2010. See also Paul C. Giannelli, Wrongful Convictions and Forensic Science: The Need to Regulate Crime Labs, 86 N.C. L. Rev. 163 (2007).

examination, and 28% in firearms identification.[54] More recent attempts to gauge the overall accuracy of American crime laboratories suggest that they have improved.[55] Even so the error rates for some types of tests remain disturbingly high,[56] and reports of terrible mistakes continue to emerge.[57] This is extremely disturbing. Adversarial fact-finding may not be the best method of using expert knowledge, but it is the one we employ. As long as we rely on the adversarial process to guarantee the accuracy of expert evidence, we must actually have an adversarial process. When one side is missing, the result may be disastrous.[58]

Problem IX-5. Robin Marshall is charged with robbing a filling station with a .38 caliber revolver. The robber wore a mask, and (apparently accidentally) fired a bullet that lodged in the ceiling of the establishment. After his arrest, Marshall was identified as the robber by the attendant at the station and by a customer.

(1) Before trial, **Marshall's court-appointed defense attorney moves the court for funds** to employ a defense ballistics expert to counter the prosecution's anticipated expert evidence linking the slug recovered from the scene to a .38 caliber revolver found in Marshall's car when he was arrested.

(2) At trial, the prosecution presents a "forensic science officer"—Sgt. Gwen Schwartz of the state police—to testify that the slug fired by the robber is "a perfect match" to bullets that fired from Marshall's revolver.

---

[54] Joseph L. Peterson, et. al., Crime Laboratory Proficiency Testing Research Program 251 (1978).

[55] Joseph L. Peterson & Penelope N. Markham, Crime Laboratory Proficiency Testing Results, 1978–1991, I: Identification and Classification of Physical Evidence, 40 J. Forensic Sci. 994 (1995); Joseph L. Peterson & Penelope N. Markham, Crime Laboratory Proficiency Testing Results, 1978–1991, II: Resolving Questions of Common Origin, 40 J. Forensic Sci. 1009 (1995).

[56] For example, Peterson & Markham found that for several categories of testing— including identification of fibers, paints, body fluids, and hair—laboratory error rate was regularly over 10%. Id. at 1028. This may well be an underestimate of the true error rate, since only about 2/3 of United States crime laboratories participated in Peterson & Markham's voluntary proficiency testing program, and only about half of those provided data for their survey. More recent reports from specific labs suggest that the problem remains severe. See, e.g., The Associated Press, Detroit Crime Cases to Require Retesting, March 15, 2009 ("The authorities have identified 147 cases that will require the retesting of evidence handled by a police crime laboratory that is now closed because of test errors, and they say they expect to find more. The Wayne County prosecutor [said] that those cases had led to convictions and that the number represented the 'tip of the iceberg.'")

[57] See, e.g., George Castelle, Lab Fraud: Lessons Learned from the Fred Zain Affair, The Champion, May 1999, at p. 12 (DNA evidence misreported in sworn affidavit from nationally known laboratory).

[58] See generally Randolph N. Jonakait, Forensic Science: The Need for Regulation, 4 Harv. J. of L. & Tech. 109 (1991); Joseph L. Peterson & Penelope N. Markham, Crime Laboratory Proficiency Testing Results, 1978–1991, Paul C. Giannelli, "Junk Science": The Criminal Cases, 84 J. Crim. L. & Criminology 105 (1993). See generally National Research Council, Strengthening Forensic Science in the United States: A Way Forward, The National Academies Press (2009).

Marshall's defense attorney wishes to ask the following questions on cross-examination:

"You are not aware of any studies that measure the error rate for ballistics matching, are you?"

"You are an employee of the state police, right?"

"You always testify for the state, your employer, don't you?"

"In a murder case two years ago—*State v. Martin Johnson*—you testified, did you not, that the defendant's gun matched a bullet found at the scene?"

"But later it turned out you were wrong in the *Johnson* case, isn't that so?"

"Your highest degree in formal education is a B.A. in American Studies from North Central State College, right?"

"At North Central State, you flunked elementary physics in your sophomore year, and had to repeat the course, didn't you?"

"You went to North Central State because you were denied admission to the registered nursing program at Capitol State University, right?"

The prosecution objects to each of these questions.

(3) After the prosecution rests, the defense calls Dr. Betty Lofty, an experimental psychologist, to testify about the dangers of eyewitness misidentification—specifically: the difficulty of cross-racial identification (Marshall is black and the eyewitnesses are white); the effects of stress on accuracy; the damaging effects of suggestive pre-trial identification procedures; and the unreliability of eyewitness confidence as an indication of the accuracy of an identification. **The prosecutor objects to Dr. Lofty's testimony,** and announces that if she testifies he will call another experimental psychologist, Dr. Abe Ebberman, in rebuttal, to testify that:

(I) The studies on which Dr. Lofty based her opinions have serious methodological flaws.

(ii) Psychologists do not know enough to help jurors evaluate eyewitness identification evidence.

(iii) Dr. Lofty is known among her colleagues in psychology to be biased toward the defense in criminal cases, and to be "out to make a name for herself."

The defense objects to calling Dr. Ebberman, and to all these questions.

How should the court rule on all of these motions and objections?

Problem IX-6. As a judge, would you permit a plaintiff in a medical malpractice case to ask a defendant doctor for an opinion of the qualifications of the plaintiff's medical expert?

IV. SPECIAL ISSUES CONCERNING SCIENTIFIC EVIDENCE

A. *UNITED STATES V. FRYE*

In 1923 the United States Circuit Court of Appeals for the District of Columbia decided an appeal from the defendant's conviction in *United States v. Frye*.[59] The main issue was the trial court's ruling excluding expert evidence that the defendant had taken and passed a "systolic blood pressure deception test"—a primitive precursor of the modern polygraph or "lie detector." The Circuit Court's approach to this issue became the standard that governed the admissibility of evidence based on novel scientific techniques and theories in most American courts for the following 70 years:[60]

> Just when a scientific principle or discovery crosses the line between the experimental and demonstrable stages is difficult to define. Somewhere in this twilight zone the evidential force of the principle must be recognized, and while courts will go a long way in admitting expert testimony deduced from a well-recognized scientific principle or discovery, the thing from which the deduction is made must be sufficiently established to have gained general acceptance in the particular field in which it belongs.[61]

The problem identified in *Frye* is intrinsic to the use of scientific evidence. If courts are to admit expert scientific testimony, they must distinguish valid science from speculation and pseudo-scientific nonsense. Since judges and jurors are not scientists, they must make these distinctions by relying, in some manner, on the judgments of others who are. *Frye* described an apparently simple test for doing so: If the theory or technique has "gained general acceptance" in its own field, it can be used in evidence; if it is not "generally accepted," it must be excluded. The systolic blood pressure deception test flunked this test and its exclusion was affirmed.

---

[59] 293 F. 1013 (D.C.Cir. 1923).

[60] *Frye* did not immediately attract a wide following. It was not cited by a single court for a decade, and was only cited thirteen times in the first quarter century after it was issued. Eventually, however, it achieved prominence. See David Faigman, et al., Modern Scientific Evidence, Vol. 1 §§ 1.3–1.4, pp. 9–1 (2009).

[61] 293 F. at 1014.

By the mid-1970s, *Frye* was almost the only test that was used to screen the admissibility of novel scientific theories or techniques, in state and federal courts alike.[62] In practice, *Frye* was applied primarily in criminal cases, most often as a threshold test for evidence by the prosecution.[63] Over the years, this test was applied, among other issues, to the admissibility of polygraph "lie detector" evidence (almost universally excluded), blood type evidence (generally admitted), breath tests for intoxication (generally admitted), "voiceprint" identification (often admitted at first, later generally excluded), and DNA identification (almost universally admitted).

Despite this wide following, *Frye* had many critics. Some commentators thought it imposed an unnecessary condition on the admission of relevant evidence, and kept valuable information from juries. McCormick, for example, wrote: "General scientific acceptance is a proper condition for taking judicial notice of scientific facts, but it is not suitable as a determinant of the admissibility of scientific evidence."[64] Other critics pointed out that this apparently simple test conceals at least two factual decisions that judges are not well qualified to make: determining the *field* in which a scientific theory or technique belongs, and determining the collective *judgment* of the scientists who practice in that field.

After the Federal Rules of Evidence were enacted in 1975, some commentators and courts began to question the continued viability of the *Frye* test, at least in federal courts. Opponents argued that FRE 702 makes no mention of *Frye*'s "general acceptance" test, and, on its face, requires much less for the admissibility of any type of expert evidence, including scientific—merely that it "will assist the trier of fact."[65] *Frye*'s supporters responded that FRE 702 requires that the subject of the testimony under FRE 702 must be *scientific* (or other specialized) *knowledge*, and that the general acceptance requirement could be read into the definition of *scientific knowledge*. Increasingly, the courts were divided. Between 1975 and 1993, four federal circuits[66] and at least a dozen states [67] abandoned the *Frye* test.

---

[62] See Edward J. Imwinkelried, The Standard for Admitting Scientific Evidence: A Critique From the Perspective of Juror Psychology, 28 Vill. L. Rev. 554, 556–57 (1982–83): "*Frye* was not only the majority view among American courts; it was the almost universal view, with the overwhelming majority of federal and state courts following it. Indeed, at one point in the mid-1970s, *Frye* seemed to be the controlling test in at least forty-five states." See also Note, Betty K. Steingass, Changing the Standard for the Admissibility of Novel Scientific Evidence: State v. Williams, 40 Ohio St. L.J. 757, 769 (1979).

[63] See Paul C. Giannelli, "Junk Science": The Criminal Cases, 84 J. Crim. L. & Criminology 105, 111 (1993).

[64] McCormick § 203.

[65] See Paul Giannelli, The Admissibility of Novel Scientific Evidence: Frye v. United States A Half Century Later, 80 Colum. L. Rev. 1197 (1980).

[66] United States v. Baller, 519 F.2d 463, 465–466 (4th Cir. 1975), cert. denied, 423 U.S. 1019 (1975); United States v. Williams, 583 F.2d 1194 (2d Cir. 1978); United States v. Downing,

B. *DAUBERT V. MERRELL DOW PHARMACEUTICALS*

In 1993, the Supreme Court resolved the status of *Frye* in federal courts in *Daubert v. Merrell Dow Pharmaceuticals*.[68] Interpreting FRE 702, the Court held that "[n]othing in the text of this Rule establishes 'general acceptance' as an absolute prerequisite to admissibility. . . . That austere standard, absent from and incompatible with, the Federal Rules of Evidence, should not be applied in federal trials."[69] But the Court also held that the Federal Rules impose their own restrictions on the admissibility of scientific evidence:

> That the *Frye* test was displaced by the Rules of Evidence does not mean, however, that the Rules themselves place no limits on the admissibility of purportedly scientific evidence. Nor is the trial judge disabled from screening such evidence. To the contrary, under the Rules the trial judge must ensure that any and all scientific testimony or evidence admitted is not only relevant, but reliable.[70]

In other words, under FRE 702, the trial judge must decide two preliminary issues: "whether the expert is proposing to testify to (1) *scientific knowledge* that (2) will *assist the trier of fact* to understand or determine a fact in issue."[71] Or, to phrase it differently, the judge must decide "whether the reasoning or methodology underlying the testimony is scientifically *valid* and . . . whether that reasoning or methodology properly can be *applied* to the facts at issue."[72]

The Court recognized that this is a "flexible" inquiry, and that many factors will bear on it.[73] It then went on to list four: (1) Is the theory or technique testable, and has it been tested? If not, it probably does not qualify as science. (2) Has the theory or technique "been subjected to peer review and publication"? This is "a relevant, though not dispositive, consideration in assessing the scientific validity" of the evidence. (3) If the evidence concerns a particular scientific technique, what is its "known or potential rate of error"?   (4) Finally, "general" or "widespread" acceptance, while not a requirement, "can be an important factor in ruling particular evidence admissible. . . . " These are all preliminary factual issues that the judge must decide under FRE 104(a). Unlike the *Frye* test, the procedure described in *Daubert* applies to all scientific testimony

---

753 F.2d 1224, 1237–1240 (3d Cir. 1985); United States v. Piccinonna, 885 F.2d 1529, 1536–1537 (11th Cir. 1989).

  [67] See Samuel R. Gross, Substance and Form In Scientific Evidence: What Daubert Didn't Do, in Reforming the Civil Justice System, Larry Kramer ed., 234, 242 n.45 (1996).

  [68] 509 U.S. 579 (1993).

  [69] Id. at 588–589 (footnote omitted).

  [70] Id. at 589 (footnote omitted).

  [71] Id. at 592 (footnote omitted, emphasis added).

  [72] Id. at 592–593 (emphasis added).

  [73] Id. at 593–594.

whether novel or not. However, the Court noted that for "well established propositions" these requirements will be easy to satisfy, and may be subject to judicial notice.[74]

The context of *Daubert* is significant. *Daubert* was a product liability case, one of several hundred brought by plaintiffs who claimed that their birth defects were caused by the anti-nausea drug Bendectin which their mothers had taken while they were *in utero*. By the time *Daubert* was decided in federal district court, almost everybody—including most scientists and most judges—agreed that Bendectin *does not* cause birth defects, or at least that the overwhelming weight of credible scientific evidence was to the contrary.[75] Nonetheless, the plaintiffs in *Daubert* and other Bendectin cases were able to produce a few reputable doctors and scientists who would testify (contrary to prevailing scientific belief) that Bendectin could and did cause the birth defects suffered by those plaintiffs. The district court in *Daubert* excluded these expert opinions under *Frye,* and having done so granted the defendant pharmaceutical company's motion for summary judgment. The Ninth Circuit affirmed.

The actions of the lower federal courts in *Daubert* are probably best understood as a reflection of a growing concern by some corporate defendants, commentators and judges about the use of questionable scientific evidence in modern civil litigation in general, and in product liability suits in particular. Their argument runs as follows: Manufacturers mass-produce products that are distributed to tens of thousands, or hundreds of thousands, or millions of consumers. Inevitably, some of these consumers are injured or become sick and die. If all a consumer has to do in order to obtain compensation is find some foolish, shady, or idiosyncratic expert who will testify that the product *caused* the death or injury or sickness, then manufacturers will face catastrophic consequences. Under the prevailing legal doctrine of strict liability for injuries caused by an intended use of a product,[76] they would have to defend hundreds or thousands of expensive lawsuits, and risk dozens or hundreds of even more expensive verdicts from those rare juries that believe this evidence. The use of expert evidence in medical malpractice and other personal injury cases poses similar but less extreme risks. All these risks would, supposedly, be reduced by tightening the restrictions on scientific expert evidence—for example by applying *Frye* (or some similar test) with rigor. On the other side, the plaintiffs in *Daubert* and other cases argued that if qualified experts reach conflicting opinions on a scientific question, the jury should resolve

---

[74] Id. at 593, n.11.

[75] For an excellent description of the history of the Bendectin litigation and the scientific evidence that was used in it, see Joseph Sanders, Bendectin on Trial: A Study of Mass Tort Litigation (1998).

[76] See, e.g., W. Page Keeton, et al., Prosser & Keeton on the Law of Torts, §§ 97–100, pp. 690–707 (5th ed. 1984).

the debate as an issue of fact rather than the judge as a matter of law. Otherwise the right to trial by jury is eviscerated.[77]

The lower courts' attempt to use *Frye* as a basis for summary judgment in the *Daubert* case represented an unusual extension of that venerable precedent. The *Frye* test was designed as a screen for novel scientific *techniques* or *theories*, but there was nothing new or unusual about the techniques or theories of the plaintiff's witnesses in *Daubert*. The problem was simply that their *conclusions* appeared to be wrong. In general, American courts do little to screen the substance of expert opinion testimony, as long as the expert claims to follow traditional methods in arriving at those opinions. The Supreme Court could have reversed this extension of *Frye* while still affirming the use of the general acceptance test in its familiar sphere. Instead the Court constructed a new test, and at the same time cautioned the lower courts that in applying it they must focus "solely on principles and methodology, not on the conclusions they generate."[78]

The proponents of the *Frye* test saw it as an essential restriction on the use of unreliable expert evidence of dubious scientific value. If so, the rejection of *Frye*'s "austere standard" ought to have made the federal courts more willing to admit evidence based on novel scientific techniques and theories. In fact, *Daubert* had no such effect. For the most part, cases following *Daubert* seem to reach the same conclusions one would have expected under *Frye*. But it soon became clear that to the extent that they differ, *Daubert*—as it has been applied—is the more restrictive test.[79] The Supreme Court's opinion emphasizes the problematic nature of scientific evidence, and holds that trial judges must exercise a "gatekeeping role"[80] and exclude such evidence when they find it unreliable. This language has encouraged some judges to use their discretion to exclude scientific evidence they might otherwise have admitted.

Daubert has done little to change trial practice in most cases. The vast majority of expert witnesses, before and after *Daubert,* testify without objection. Nor was *Daubert* the first federal case to replace *Frye*'s "general acceptance" test with a list of factors. The Third Circuit had done so eight years earlier, in *United States v. Downing*,[81] a case cited

---

[77] There is little doubt that the worst abuses of scientific evidence occur in criminal cases, where—as we have discussed—there are repeated examples of inexcusable carelessness, incompetence, and outright fraud by prosecution experts. See supra, pp. 1150–1152, infra pp. 1167–1170. Some of these misuses have resulted in false convictions and long prison terms, or even death sentences. It is a telling comment on our legal system that proven erroneous criminal convictions, no matter how tragic, are a less influential impetus for reform than the risk of erroneous monetary judgments.

[78] 509 U.S. at 595.

[79] Gross, supra note 67, at 264–270.

[80] 509 U.S. at 597.

[81] 753 F.2d 1224 (3d Cir. 1985).

prominently in *Daubert*. Moreover, in operation, the tests in *Frye* and *Daubert* are more similar than they may at first seem. *Daubert* includes "general acceptance" as a factor to be considered, among others, in determining "reliability." *Frye* says that "general acceptance" is the only criterion for admission, but since there is rarely direct evidence on this point, judges must look for circumstantial indicia of "general acceptance"—including, conspicuously, "reliability." As the Sixth Circuit put it eighteen years before *Daubert*:

> [W]e deem, general acceptance as being nearly synonymous with reliability. If a scientific process is reliable, or sufficiently accurate, courts may also deem it "generally accepted."[82]

In other words, in practice, "general acceptance" is strong evidence of "reliability," and "reliability" is strong evidence of "general acceptance."

Frye was criticized because it required lay judges to make scientific judgments that are beyond their competence: How does a non-scientist determine the "general acceptance" of a scientific principle? And how does one choose the "field" within which a scientific technique is to be judged? The polygraph or "lie detector" is liable to fare much better by this test if "the field in which it belongs" is defined as "polygraphy" rather than "psychology" or "neurophysiology." *Daubert* is less specific than *Frye*, but it too requires such decisions—more of them. It has made the judge's task vaguer and more complex than it was under *Frye*. Many judges are uncomfortable passing on scientific questions, and most cases won't bear the weight of the type of inquiry that is necessary to do so competently. As a result, under *Daubert,* as under *Frye*, most decisions on the admission of scientific evidence are based on judicial precedent rather than science. Following a test-case hearing in a trial court, a federal court of appeals or state supreme court will determine that a type of scientific evidence—DNA identification evidence, for example—is admissible, and other courts in the jurisdiction will consider the issue settled as a matter of law.

Daubert does seem to have changed the uncommon test-case hearings in which the admissibility of scientific evidence is really determined—and those hearings, of course, are also uncommonly influential. Judging from reported cases, such hearings seem to have become less rare since *Daubert*, judges seem to be considering a wider range of evidence in making these decisions, and some judges also appear more willing to exclude the offered evidence. And those judges who do conduct elaborate *Daubert* hearings may have an easier time evaluating the scientific evidence at issue than they would have had twenty years ago. One consequence of the heightened attention to this area is a proliferation of articles and manuals that are designed to help lawyers and judges find

---

[82] United States v. Franks, 511 F.2d 25, 33, n. 12 (6th Cir. 1975).

their way through this thicket.[83]   Indeed, the single most important change in the use of scientific evidence over the past decade may be the great increase in the level of attention devoted to the subject.

Daubert has become the focus of debates over the admissibility of expert evidence, but ultimately it is more a symptom of increased attention to the issue rather than its cause.   Twenty-two briefs amicus curiae were filed in Supreme Court in *Daubert*, mostly by organizations of scientists and lawyers—an extraordinary number for a case that turned on the interpretation of a federal rule of evidence.   Clearly many people believed that change was in the wind, and that this case might determine the direction.   In fact, the Court's opinion in *Daubert* does little more than reaffirm the discretion of federal trial court judges to admit or exclude purportedly scientific evidence, and provide some guidance on how to make that decision.   Still, coming when it did, the break signaled by *Daubert,* whatever its formal content, accelerated a trend toward more careful scrutiny of expert evidence.   That *Daubert* is seen as a major decision reflects its timeliness more than its analytic significance.

Problem IX-7. Mary Nigel has sued the North American Insurance Cooperative (North American) for damages.   She claims that from June 2004, when she was hired by North American as an insurance adjuster, until November 2006, when she resigned, she was regularly sexually harassed by male supervisors who touched and fondled her buttocks and breasts and made frequent sexually suggestive remarks, and that complaints to higher-ups in the company led nowhere.

At trial, after the plaintiff testifies and describes the harassment she suffered, she calls Dr. Susan Tilden, a licensed clinical psychologist, who interviewed her repeatedly and gave her a variety of psychological tests. Dr. Tilden is prepared to testify to her expert opinion that: (1) As a result of her experiences at North American, Nigel has developed post-traumatic stress disorder (PTSD)—a recognized psychiatric syndrome—and low grade depression. (2) One of the tests she administered to Nigel—the Psychiatric Prognosis Protocol (PPP), which Dr. Tilden herself devised— indicates that Nigel is likely to suffer moderate to severe long-term psychiatric damage. **North American objects to Dr. Tilden's testimony on both points.**

In its defense, North American calls a psychiatrist, Dr. Lara Prichard, who conducted a court-ordered examination of Nigel. Dr. Prichard is prepared to testify to her expert opinion that: (3) Nigel has a hard time understanding social settings, and tends to confuse fantasy

---

[83] As far as judges are concerned, the most important publication for these purposes is probably the Federal Judicial Center's Reference Manual on Scientific Evidence (2nd ed. 2000).

with reality. (4) Nigel blames her difficulties at work at North American for problems that were caused by a variety of other conflicts. (5) Nigel is malingering and has "poor psychiatric credibility." **Nigel objects to all of this testimony by Dr. Prichard.**

How should the court rule on these objections? Is there additional information the court will need to make its rulings? Does it make a difference whether the court follows *Frye* or *Daubert?*

C. POST *DAUBERT* ISSUES

Daubert left several open questions, some of which have been answered by subsequent case law, and some of which have not.

1. *Kumho Tire Co., Ltd. v. Carmichael* (1): *Daubert* Governs Nonscientific Expert Testimony

FRE 702 applies to "technical, or other specialized knowledge" as well as to scientific expertise, but *Daubert* is more limited: "Our discussion is limited to the scientific context because that is the nature of the expertise offered here."[84] Initially, lower courts were divided on the implications of *Daubert* for nonscientific experts, but most agreed that they were obliged under FRE 702 to evaluate the reliability of all expert evidence, in some manner.[85] In 1999, the Supreme Court settled the issue in *Kumho Tire, Ltd. V. Carmichael*,[86] holding that:

> *Daubert*'s general holding—setting forth the trial judge's general "gatekeeping" obligation—applies not only to testimony based on "scientific" knowledge, but also to testimony based on "technical" and "other specialized" knowledge.[87]

The Court points out that FREs 702 and 703 grant exceptional testimonial latitude to all experts, not just to scientists, and that "there is no clear line that divides the one [category] from the others."[88] The

---

[84] 509 U.S. at 570. n.8.

[85] Compare, e.g., Berry v. City of Detroit, 25 F.3d 1342, 1350 (6th Cir. 1994) ("Although . . . *Daubert* dealt with scientific experts, its language relative to the 'gatekeeper' function of federal judges is applicable to all expert testimony offered under Rule 702"); with United States v. Starzecpyzel, 880 F.Supp. 1027, 1029, 1042 (S.D.N.Y.1995) ("the 'technical, or other specialized knowledge' branch of Rule 702 . . . is apparently not governed by *Daubert*," but, "the fact that *Daubert* does not apply to nonscientific expertise does not suggest that judges are without an obligation to evaluate proffered expert testimony for reliability"). See generally Edward J. Imwinkelried, The Next Step After Daubert: Developing A Similarly Epistemological Approach to Ensuring the Reliability of Nonscientific Expert Testimony, 15 Cardozo L. Rev. 2271 (1994).

[86] 526 U.S. 137 (1999).

[87] Id. at 141.

[88] Id. at 148. The Court adds: "Disciplines such as engineering rest upon scientific knowledge. Pure scientific theory itself may depend upon observation and properly engineered

general rule, therefore, is that regardless of the nature of the witness's discipline, "the trial judge must determine whether the [expert] testimony has 'a reliable basis in the knowledge and experience of [the relevant] discipline.' "[89]

2. *Kumho Tire, Ltd. v. Carmichael* (2): The Factors to Be Considered in Determining the Reliability of Expert Evidence

Daubert listed four of the "many factors" that bear on the "flexible inquiry" into the reliability of scientific evidence: testability, error rate, peer review and publication, and general acceptance. Although the Court was quite clear that it did not "presume to set out a definitive check list,"[90] before *Kumho Tires* some courts treated the *Daubert* factors as just that.[91] This is unfortunate, because the four *Daubert* factors are a peculiar and somewhat arbitrary collection. They are useful as a starting point in analyzing the value of scientific evidence, but they cannot be applied mechanistically to most types of scientific evidence; indeed, in many cases, one or more of them cannot be applied at all. If the question is the scientific validity of a hypothesis—"AIDS is caused by a virus," for example—"error rate" is not a meaningful test; the hypothesis is either correct or incorrect. On the other hand, if the issue is the value of a measurement technique—a breathalyzer test, for instance—the "error rate" is important, and can be determined, but "testability" has no meaning independent of error rate. Similarly, if the question is whether the expert correctly applied an established technique—gas chromatography—to a particular problem, "peer review and publication" are not meaningful criteria, since such questions almost never receive that sort of attention.

The Supreme Court's decision in *Kumho Tire* laid to rest any lingering belief that *Daubert*'s four factors were either exclusive or mandatory. Even if this four-factor inquiry could somehow be forced to fit all varieties of scientific evidence, it makes no sense as a universal test now that the process must be applied to all types of experts: What does "testability" mean for expert testimony on Chinese history? How do "peer review and publication" bear on an expert opinion on commercial mortgage financing? In any event, the Court's opinion in *Kumho Tire* makes the message explicit: "[W]e can neither rule out, nor rule in, for all cases and for all time the applicability of the factors mentioned in

---

machinery. And conceptual efforts to distinguish the two are unlikely to produce clear legal lines capable of application in particular cases." Id.

[89] Id. at 149, quoting *Daubert*, 509 U.S. at 592.

[90] 509 U.S. at 593.

[91] E.g., Stanczyk v. Black & Decker, Inc., 836 F.Supp. 565, 567 (N.D.Ill.1993) ("*Daubert* teaches that I must consider certain factors. . . . ")

Daubert. . . . "[92] "Rather, we conclude that the trial judge must have considerable leeway in deciding in a particular case how to go about determining whether expert testimony is reliable."[93]

Even before *Kumho Tire,* some courts had added to the list of *Daubert* factors. The most important additions concern the relationship between the expert witness's scientific work and her role in the litigation. Thus, in *Daubert* itself, on remand, the Ninth Circuit added the following consideration to those listed by the Supreme Court: whether experts are "proposing to testify about matters growing naturally and directly out of research they have conducted independent of the litigation, or whether they have developed their opinions expressly for purposes of testifying."[94] And the Seventh Circuit has listed a related consideration: whether the expert "is being as careful as he would be in his regular professional work outside his paid litigation consulting."[95] The implicit theme of these cases is familiar: Experts are apt to be less scrupulous and conscientious in testimony than in their ordinary work; as witnesses, they will say things in court that they would never say as scientists in their laboratories, clinics, or seminar rooms. The effect of such witness-oriented factors is to shift (and lower) the courts' aim from the quality of the science to the trustworthiness of the scientist, from the message to the messenger.

3. Applying *Daubert* to Nonscientific Expertise

Kumho Tire's extension of *Daubert*'s "reliability" requirement to nonscientific expertise created a new problem for courts in applying FRE 702. Over the past two hundred years, scientific disciplines have developed a widely accepted "scientific method" for evaluating theories and claims by observation, experimentation, dissemination of information, and replication. Over the long haul—and sometimes even in quite short order—this system has worked extremely well in sorting the valid from the invalid. But to what methods should courts look to evaluate the reliability of nonscientific expertise, on subjects that can range from civil engineering at one end of the spectrum to the professional ethics for bankruptcy lawyers at the other?

United States v. Starzecpyzel[96]—a pre-*Kumho Tire* case—is an interesting illustration of the relationship between these two issues: the status of an area of purported expertise as science or non-science, and the criteria by which it is evaluated to determine admissibility. In

---

[92]   *Kumho Tire,* supra note 86, 526 U.S. at 150.

[93]   Id. at 152.

[94]   Daubert v. Merrell Dow Pharmaceuticals, Inc., 43 F.3d 1311, 1317 (9th Cir. 1995).

[95]   Sheehan v. Daily Racing Form, Inc., 104 F.3d 940, 942 (7th Cir. 1997). See also *Kumho Tire,* 526 U.S. at 152 (trial court should assure itself that the expert witness "employs in the courtroom the same level of intellectual rigor that characterizes the practice of an expert in the relevant field").

[96]   880 F.Supp. 1027 (S.D.N.Y.1995).

Starzecpyzel—a criminal prosecution for theft, fraud, and related offenses—the prosecutor offered expert testimony by a forensic document examiner (FDE) that a signature in the name of the owner of the allegedly stolen items was not genuine. The trial-court judge conducted a hearing *in limine* to determine the scientific basis for the expert's testimony because "the Court originally considered *Daubert* to be controlling as to the admissibility of the forensic testimony at issue. . . . "[97] After hearing witnesses from both sides, the judge concluded that "the testimony at the *Daubert* hearing firmly established that forensic document examination, despite the existence of a certification program, professional journals and other trappings of science, cannot, after *Daubert*, be regarded as 'scientific . . . knowledge.' "[98] Nonetheless he decided to admit the evidence. First, he found that, despite its hollow scientific trappings, forensic document examination is not the sort of bad science that the Supreme Court was worried about in *Daubert*, but rather a "practical" expertise, "similar to that developed by a harbor pilot who has repeatedly navigated a particular waterway."[99] Therefore, the trial court held (pre-*Kumho Tire*) that *Daubert* "is largely irrelevant to the challenged testimony."[100] Second, the judge did recognize (also pre-*Kumho Tire*) that he had an obligation to "evaluate proffered [nonscientific] expert testimony for reliability,"[101] but the review he conducted was undemanding. The court found that professional FDE's develop a great deal of experience in determining the genuineness of signatures; that they seem to reach correct conclusions at least as often as lay people; that they have been used extensively by courts for decades; and that they are probably as reliable as some other types of admissible non-expert testimony, such as eyewitness identification.[102] Given that background, the court decided to admit the evidence by shifting the burden of persuasion to the defendants, the side challenging forensic document examination:

> Defendants presented no evidence, beyond the bald assertions of [their witnesses], that FDEs cannot reliably perform this task. Defendants have simply challenged the FDE community to prove that this task can be done reliably. Such a demonstration of proof, which may be appropriate for a scientific expert witness, has never been imposed on "skilled" experts.[103]

Starzecpyzel is obviously right when it holds that expert testimony on navigation routes by an experienced harbor pilot ought to be admissible

---

[97] Id. at 1028.

[98] Id. at 1038.

[99] Id. at 1029.

[100] Id. at 1028.

[101] Id. at 1042.

[102] Id. at 1043–47.

[103] Id. at 1046.

without any demonstration of its scientific basis. But forensic document examination is different. As Professor Michael Saks points out, "harbor pilots learn from the instant feedback they receive if they ground a ship or deliver it to the wrong wharf"—and those that continue in that line of work presumably learn well—but "neither handwriting examiners themselves, nor lay judges or jurors, can tell whether the identification is correct or not."[104] Moreover, Forensic Document Examiners (unlike harbor pilots) present themselves as scientists,[105] but they don't make the grade. As the court acknowledged, there is no scientific evidence that they possess any special skill in distinguishing genuine signatures from forgeries based on the style of writing.

The legal standard that the district court used in *Starzecpyzel* has been overruled by *Kumho Tire*. It is now clear that the proponent of expert evidence has the burden of establishing "reliability" under *Daubert* for any expert testimony, scientific or otherwise. Perhaps the District Court in *Starzecpyzel* would have excluded testimony from the forensic document examiner if it had applied the burden of persuasion that the Supreme Court prescribed in *Kumho Tire*. But probably not.

It is hard to believe that expert testimony on handwriting identification would have been admitted in federal courts under any evidentiary standard if it had been offered for the first time in the 1990s. But it wasn't; it is a venerable and widely-used type of expert evidence.[106] This is the key to the clearest lesson from *Starzecpyzel* and similar cases: *Expert evidence that has been admitted in the past is likely to be admitted in the future.* That conservative bias continues. In *Kumho Tire*, the Supreme Court recognized that trial courts have broad discretionary authority in considering challenges to expert evidence, including the authority "to avoid unnecessary 'reliability' proceedings in ordinary cases where the reliability of an expert's methods is properly taken for granted. . . . " 526. U.S. at 1176. Categories of expertise that have been routinely admitted for decades are often deemed appropriate for summary approval under this discretionary authority.

The unreliability of handwriting identification has received a good deal of attention since *Daubert*. In *United States v. Hines*,[107] a federal district court judge—while acknowledging her reluctance "to throw out decades of 'generally accepted' testimony"—ruled that an FBI Forensic Document Examiner could testify to specific similarities between known samples of the defendant's handwriting and the robbery note used in the crime at issue, but that the witness could not offer an expert opinion that

---

[104] Michael J. Saks, Merlin and Solomon: Lessons from the Law's Formative Encounters with Forensic Identification Science, 49 Hastings L.J. 1069, 1098 n.141 (1998).

[105] *Starzecpyzel*, 880 F.Supp. at 1044, n.18.

[106] See D. Michael Risinger et al., Exorcism of Ignorance as a Proxy for Rational Knowledge: The Lessons of Handwriting Identification "Expertise," 137 U. Pa. L. Rev. 731 (1989).

[107] 55 F.Supp.2d 62 (D.Mass. 1999).

the defendant was the author of that note. A few federal courts have followed suit and limited testimony from forensic document examiners,[108] and a couple have excluded handwriting identification testimony altogether,[109] but many more continue to admit such evidence,[110] most often no doubt without writing opinions or conducting preliminary hearings.

4. Forensic Science Evidence and the Difference Between the Impact of *Daubert* in Civil and in Criminal Cases

Handwriting identification is one of a set of "forensic sciences," areas of purported expertise in identifying samples, marks and traces to determine their composition or their origin. Other "forensic sciences" include fingerprint identification, ballistic and other "tool-mark" identification, hair and fiber identification, bite-mark identification, DNA identification, and "voiceprint" identification. Most forensic science evidence is used exclusively, or almost exclusively, in criminal trials; even handwriting expertise, which addresses issues of genuineness and authorship that are often in dispute in civil cases, seems to be offered primarily in criminal prosecutions.

As we mentioned,[111] the *Frye* test that preceded *Daubert* was mostly used in criminal cases. By the time *Daubert* was decided, challenges to expert evidence had become more common in civil litigation; after *Daubert* the balance shifted farther in that direction. A study of the first 18 months of federal cases after *Daubert* reported that while "[c]ases applying *Frye* were usually criminal. . . most of those applying *Daubert* are civil," and that "[a]mong reported decisions in federal criminal cases,

---

[108] Legacy Vision, LLC v. Yeamans, 2005 WL 6227149 (W.D. Okla. 2005); United States v. Van Wyk, 83 F. Supp. 2d 515 (D.N.J. 2000); United States v. Rutherford, 104 F. Supp. 2d 1190 (D. Neb. 2000); United States v. Santillan, 1999 WL 1201765 (N.D. Cal. 1999).

[109] United States v. Brewer, 2002 WL 596365 (N.D. Ill. 2002) (handwriting comparison testimony did not meet reliability standards of Fed. R. Evid. 702); United States v. Saelee, 162 F. Supp. 2d 1097, 1102–1103 (D. Alaska 2001) (expert testimony on handwriting comparison was not sufficiently reliable to be admissible under Fed. R. Evid. 702 and *Daubert*).

[110] See, e.g., United States v. Mooney, 315 F.3d 54, 61–63 (1st Cir. 2002) (handwriting expert's proffered testimony about similarities and differences between defendant's handwriting and that on incriminating letters, and ultimate opinion that defendant authored letters, was admissible as reliable and based on valid technical and specialized knowledge); United States v. Crisp, 324 F.3d 261, 270 (4th Cir. 2003) (admitting fingerprint and handwriting evidence as reliable based on "widespread and lasting acceptance in the expert community"); Deputy v. Lehman Bros., Inc., 345 F.3d 494, 508 (7th Cir. 2003) (district court committed reversible error by excluding expert's handwriting analysis testimony based on issues of credibility, and not on principles and methodology of handwriting analysis in general or witness's opinion in particular); United States v. Prime, 431 F.3d 1147, 1152–1154 (9th Cir. 2005), vacated on other grounds, 543 U.S. 1101, 125 S.Ct. 1005, 160 L.Ed.2d 1007 (2005) (testimony about handwriting analysis can be sufficiently reliable for admission under Fed. R. Evid. 702 and *Daubert;* thus, testimony of forensic document examiner, in wire fraud prosecution, that handwriting on counterfeit money orders and other documents was defendant's was admissible as reliable, based on high degree of accuracy shown in identification of writers, extensive peer review, and broad acceptance and use by law enforcement agencies).

[111] Supra note 63 and accompanying text.

Daubert has changed almost nothing."[112]   For the most part, that assessment is still accurate.

Most expert evidence in criminal cases is presented by the prosecution. Many criminal defense attorneys lack the resources, the skill, or the interest even to try to challenge the state's expert witnesses, let alone present their own. That was true under *Frye,* and has not changed since. A study published in 2005, twelve years after *Daubert,* found that "Despite the frequency of prosecution proffered scientific and expert testimony in criminal cases, *Daubert* is rarely invoked to challenge it."[113] Whatever effect *Daubert* has had on expert evidence in civil cases, in criminal practice it has had essentially none: it was a one-sided affair before *Daubert* and it remains a one-sided affair after.

This is unfortunate because the scientific basis for many "forensic sciences" is shaky, to say the least. DNA evidence is a conspicuous exception. Unlike other forensic sciences, DNA identification is based on scientific principles that were developed in biological laboratories for other scientific purposes, and employs technologies that are used by biological scientists daily. As a result, DNA tests (properly done) produce results that can be replicated by other scientists, and interpreted in accordance with general scientific principles, using data that are derived from systematic studies. Other forensic sciences, which were developed solely for use in court, don't come close—not even fingerprint identification, which was the pre-DNA gold standard for forensic evidence. There is no doubt that fingerprints often produce highly accurate evidence of identity. But fingerprint examiners have never done the studies that would lay a scientific foundation for their discipline, and many of them insist—despite famous errors—that their identifications are infallible.[114] Other forms of forensic trace identification—hair, fiber, ballistic and bite mark identification—are much less well grounded than fingerprint identification. Not surprisingly, false or misleading forensic evidence is common. Thus, for example, a study of 137 trials of criminal defendants who were falsely convicted and later exonerated by DNA evidence found that "in the bulk of these trials of innocent defendants— 82 cases or 60%—forensic analysts called by the prosecution provided invalid testimony at trial—that is, testimony with conclusions misstating empirical data or wholly unsupported by empirical data."[115]

---

[112] Samuel Gross, "Substance and Form in Scientific Evidence: What Daubert Didn't Do" in Reforming the Civil Justice System, Larry Kramer ed., 234 (1996).

[113] Peter J. Neufeld, The (Near) Irrelevance of *Daubert* to Criminal Justice and Some Suggestions for Reform, 95 Amer. J. of Public Health S107 (2005).

[114] Simon A. Cole, "More Than Zero: Accounting for Error in Latent Fingerprint Identification," 95 Journal of Criminal Law & Criminology 985 (2005).

[115] Brandon L. Garrett & Peter J. Neufeld, Invalid Forensic Testimony and Wrongful Convictions, 95 Virginia L. Rev.1, 2 (2009).

In 2009, after more than two years of work, a committee of the National Research Council of the National Academy of Sciences issued a major report on the state of forensic science in the United States.[116] The report is highly critical of the practice of forensic science, and suggests major reforms, but not in court procedure. On that score, the National Research Council's committee was gloomy:

> [T]he adversarial process relating to the admission and exclusion of scientific evidence is not suited to the task of finding "scientific truth." The judicial system is encumbered by, among other things, judges and lawyers who generally lack the scientific expertise necessary to comprehend and evaluate forensic evidence in an informed manner. . . . Judicial review, by itself, will not cure the infirmities of the forensic science community.[117]

The National Research Council's description of the judicial process speaks in terms that could apply equally to civil as well as criminal cases. But would the problem, let alone the solution, be the same in civil trials? Consider forensic odontology, or bite mark identification. The report has few kind words for this form of expertise: "Although the majority of forensic odontologists are satisfied that bite marks can [yield] positive identification, no scientific studies support this assessment. . . . In numerous instances, experts diverge widely in their evaluation of the same bite mark evidence."[118] Professor Michael Risinger has reviewed bite mark cases in detail, and his summary is even more depressing:

> Expert testimony identifying a person (usually a criminal defendant) as the source of bite marks . . . was noted [in] forty-seven criminal cases. . . . In only four or five of those cases is there any indication that the foundational reliability of such evidence was challenged [and] the challenges were generally brushed off by the courts. . . . [S]ome of the testimony involved in these cases went beyond mere identification to the timing of the bites, and even to the intent with which they were inflicted. In fact, only one opinion dealing with bite mark evidence even cited to *Daubert*. . . . [119]

But Risinger has a different view of the context than the National Academy committee:

> If, after *Daubert*, substantial liability of General Motors or Microsoft were dependent on the identification of bite marks . . . is it not clear that these issues would have been litigated

---

[116] National Research Council, Strengthening Forensic Science in the United States: A Way Forward, The National Academies Press (2009).

[117] Id. at 3–20.

[118] Id. at 5–37.

[119] Michael Risinger, Navigating Expert Reliability: Are Criminal Standards of Certainty Left on the Dock? 64 Albany L. Rev. 99, 135–36 (2000).

differently and more thoroughly than they have been, and that the results would have often been different?[120]

The courts, of course, cannot play the primary role in improving any scientific discipline, but they can do better than what we see here. At their best, courts can be intelligent consumers of scientific information, and they can create incentives for parties to improve the evidence that is presented. Would the National Academy have had more faith in the ability of courts to improve the quality of forensic science evidence if that type of expertise were used in the better financed, higher status and more competitive arena of civil litigation? Maybe. Would the courts actually do more in that context, as Professor Risinger believes? It seems likely. They could hardly do less.

5. The "Codification" of *Daubert* in the 2000 Amendment to FRE 702

In 2000 FRE 702 was amended to add what are now subsections (b) through (d), italicized below:

A witness who is qualified as an expert by knowledge, skill, experience, training, or education may testify in the form of an opinion or otherwise if:

     (a) the expert's scientific, technical, or other specialized knowledge will help the trier of fact to understand the evidence or to determine a fact in issue;

     (b) *the testimony is based on sufficient facts or data;*

     (c) *the testimony is the product of reliable principles and methods; and*

     (d) *the expert has reliably applied the principles and methods to the facts of the case.*

The Advisory Committee Note to this amendment states that it was enacted "in response to *Daubert* and the many cases applying *Daubert,* including *Kumho Tire.* . . . The amendment affirms the trial court's role as gatekeeper and provides some general standards the trial court must use. . . . Consistently with *Kumho,* the Rule as amended provides that [for] all types of expert testimony the trial court . . . [must decide] whether the evidence is reliable and helpful."

Daubert—applying and interpreting FRE 702 as it was written in 1993—rejected the *Frye* test and instead developed a more flexible system for implementing the judge's gatekeeping role for expert scientific evidence. *Kumho Tire* extended that role to nonscientific expertise. The 2000 amendment supersedes these cases. It was intended to reflect

---

[120] Id. at 143.

rather than change the law as developed by *Daubert, Kumho Tire,* and other cases following *Daubert*. All the same, the amended version of FRE 702 was promulgated by the Supreme Court and approved by Congress. Therefore the rule itself rather than *Daubert* and its case-law progeny is now the starting point for any discussion of the admissibility of expert evidence in federal courts.

The Advisory Committee Note to the 2000 amendment does a nice job of summarizing developments in the first seven years following *Daubert*: (i) The trial court's "gatekeeping function applies to all expert testimony, not just testimony based on science." (ii) "[T]he admissibility of all expert testimony is governed by the principles of Rule 104(a). Under that rule the proponent [of expert evidence] has the burden of establishing that the pertinent admissibility requirements are met by a preponderance of the evidence." (iii) "*Daubert* set forth a non-exclusive checklist for trial courts in assessing the reliability of scientific expert testimony." "Other factors may also be relevant." (Iv) "*Daubert* did not work a 'seachange over federal evidence law,' and 'the trial court's role as gatekeeper is not intended to serve as a replacement for the adversary system.' " [Citation omitted.] (v) Caselaw since *Daubert* "shows that the rejection of expert testimony is the exception rather than the rule." (vi) The 2000 "amendment is not intended to provide an excuse for an automatic challenge to the testimony of every expert." Rather, as the Court said in *Kumho Tire,* the trial court may "avoid unnecessary 'reliability' proceedings in ordinary cases where the reliability of an expert's methods is properly taken for granted. . . ."

6. The Standard for Appellate Review of Trial Court Decisions Admitting or Excluding Expert Testimony

As we discussed in Chapter Two, appellate review of evidentiary decisions is usually very forgiving.[121] This is particularly true where judges are required to weigh competing factors—for example, probative value and impermissible prejudice under FRE 403. In those situations, trial-court judges are said to have wide discretion to admit or exclude evidence, and will be reversed on appeal only for abuse of discretion—a high standard that is rarely met. *Daubert*, which requires judges to weigh multiple factors and emphasizes the "flexible" nature of their task, seems like a natural case for applying this abuse of discretion standard on review.

Despite this apparent fit, there are at least two substantial arguments for a more stringent form of review:

(1) In *In re Paoli R.R. Yard PCB Litigation (Paoli II),*[122] the Third Circuit reviewed a case in which the exclusion of scientific evidence

---

[121] Chapter Two, p. 164.

[122] 35 F.3d 717, 749–50 (3d Cir. 1994).

offered by civil plaintiffs led to a summary judgment for the defendants. Given this drastic consequence, the court held that such an exclusion should receive a "hard look" on appeal:

> [B]ecause the reliability standard of Rules 702 and 703 is somewhat amorphous, there is a significant risk that district judges will set the threshold too high and will in fact force plaintiffs to prove their case twice.[123]

(2) A more general argument can be made for a "hard look" on review of such issues, regardless of the direction of the decision—whether to exclude the scientific evidence, or to admit it.[124] The reliability of a scientific technique or the accuracy of a scientific theory—whether "voiceprints" may be used for identification,[125] for example, or whether Bendectin causes birth defects[126]—are issues that are likely to reappear, in case after case. Close appellate review of decisions on admissibility would help insure uniformity across a jurisdiction. Moreover, appellate courts are in a better position to judge the value of scientific evidence than of lay evidence, since questions of credibility and demeanor are far less important for scientific evidence, and published information on the state of scientific knowledge far more so.

Nonetheless, in 1997 in *General Electric v. Joiner*,[127] the Supreme Court held that abuse of discretion is the appropriate standard for appellate review of all decisions under *Daubert*, to admit or to exclude. The issue in *Joiner* was whether the plaintiff's exposure to a class of chemicals—"PCBs"—contributed to his lung cancer. The trial court found that the plaintiff's scientific evidence on this critical issue was inadmissible because "Joiner's experts had failed to show that there was a link between exposure to PCBs and small cell lung cancer."[128] The Eleventh Circuit reversed, and the Supreme Court, reversing the Court of Appeals, held that "it was within the District Court's discretion to conclude that the studies upon which the experts relied were not sufficient, whether individually or in combination, to support their conclusions. . . ."[129] Apparently, it would also have been within the trial court's discretion to decide that these studies *did* support the expert's conclusions, and other trial-court judges could also reach that conclusion. Under *Joiner*, appellate courts seem to have no authority to resolve such conflicts.

---

[123] Id. at 750 (citing *Daubert*).

[124] See David L. Faigman, Appellate Review of Scientific Evidence Under Daubert and Joiner, 48 Hastings L.J. 969 (1997).

[125] See Annotation, Admissibility and Weight of Voiceprint Evidence, 97 ALR.3d 294 (1980) and 1997 Supplement.

[126] See supra p. 1160.

[127] 522 U.S. 136 (1997).

[128] 522 U.S. at 140.

[129] 522 U.S. at 146–147.

The plaintiff in *Joiner* argued that his experts' *methodology*—reviewing published studies and applying them to the facts at hand—was unexceptional, and that the District Court was obviously really concerned about the experts' *conclusions*. If so, that would appear to violate *Daubert*, which says that in evaluating scientific evidence, the "focus, of course, must be solely on principles and methodology, not on the conclusions that they generate."[130] In *Joiner* the Court revises that statement:

> [C]onclusions and methodology are not entirely distinct from one another. Trained experts commonly extrapolate from existing data. But nothing in either *Daubert* or the Federal Rules of Evidence requires a district court to admit opinion evidence which is connected to existing data only by the *ipse dixit* of the expert. A court may conclude that there is simply too great an analytical gap between the data and the opinion proffered.[131]

The Court is certainly right that in evaluating scientific claims, methods and conclusions run together. Consider a professor of astronomy who is prepared to testify that using established scientific methods of observation and deduction, and extrapolating from published studies, he has concluded that the sun circles the earth. Given that conclusion, it's hard to believe that his methods were really scientifically acceptable. As the Advisory Committee Note to the 2000 amendment to FRE 702 says, "Under the Amendment, as under *Daubert*, when an expert purports to apply principles and methods in accordance with professional standards, and yet reaches a conclusion that other experts in the field would not reach, the trial court may fairly suspect that the principles and methods have not been faithfully applied."

Our conviction that an expert is wrong because others in the field disagree is a judgment about the *result*, not the process: He must have done it wrong, because the outcome is absurd. What this means, of course, is that in some cases trial judges applying FRE 702 are deciding the merits of the parties' scientific claims under the guise of determining admissibility. The trial court judge's conclusion in *Joiner* that "there is simply too great an analytical gap between the data and the opinion" is really a substantive judgment that the plaintiff's evidence was insufficient, masquerading as a procedural judgment that it was inadmissible. As a matter of policy it may make perfect sense to give trial courts that authority, and perhaps even to frame the issue as a question of "admissibility." But it is one thing to give trial-court judges the power to make such decisions, and quite another to do so and simultaneously all but eliminate oversight by appellate review.

---

[130] 509 U.S. at 595.

[131] 522 U.S. at 146.

In *Joiner* the issue at stake was a general one: the overall quality of the available scientific evidence on the relationship between exposure to PCBs and lung cancer. Two years later, in *Kumho Tire*, the Supreme Court extended that ruling to a more limited question: the value of the testimony of a particular expert on the cause of the failure of a particular tire. The Court noted specifically that all sides conceded that a qualified expert could draw that sort of conclusion from the type of examination the plaintiffs' expert relied on. "[T]he question before the trial court was specific, not general. The trial court had to decide whether this particular expert had sufficient specialized knowledge to assist the jurors. . . . "[132] After reviewing the record in detail, the Court concluded:

> In sum, Rule 702 grants the district judge the discretionary authority, reviewable for its abuse, to determine reliability in light of the particular facts and circumstances of the particular case. The District Court did not abuse its discretionary authority in this case.[133]

Kumho Tire's strong reaffirmation of the abuse of discretion standard of review indicates that the Supreme Court really did intend to cut to a bare minimum appellate authority over decisions to admit or exclude expert evidence.

———————

Problem IX-8. In September of 2005, Charlene Brack slipped on a film of mayonnaise that was negligently left on the floor of the Tiger Foods supermarket in Fort Worth, Texas. Immediately after the fall she complained of pain in her arm and lower back, headache and dizziness. When these symptoms persisted and common tests (MRI, EMG, diskogram) were uninformative, Ms. Brack was referred to Dr. James Reyes, who specializes in treating patients with persistent pain. Dr. Reyes diagnosed her condition as fibromyalgia, a syndrome that produces generalized pain, poor sleep, and an inability to concentrate. Brack sued Tiger Foods for personal injuries, and Tiger Foods removed the case to federal court on grounds of diversity.

At trial, Dr. Reyes testified to his diagnosis, and concluded that Brack's fibromyalgia was caused by hormonal changes, which in turn were caused by the trauma of her fall. He explained that he had eliminated other possible causes, and therefore, even though he didn't know the "real" cause, it had to be the fall at Tiger Foods.

The district court judge admitted Dr. Reyes' testimony over objection. **On appeal from a judgment for Brack, how should the circuit court rule on this issue?**

---

[132] 526 U.S. at 156.
[133] 526 U.S. at 158.

Problem IX-9. Fifteen former refinery workers have sued a variety of defendants—including the refinery at which they worked, two of its suppliers and several managers and owners individually—in federal court. They seek damages for injuries they claim to have suffered as a result of workplace exposure to the chemical benzene in concentrations up to 100 times the applicable OSHA (Occupational Safety and Health Administration) standard. Their symptoms included headaches, nausea, dizziness, diarrhea, and lack of energy.

At trial, they offer expert testimony from Dr. Stan Siegel, who has a Ph.D. in Environmental Science and extensive experience in toxicology and occupational hygiene and safety. Dr. Siegel testifies that although there is no direct evidence that benzene caused these symptoms, it is known to be a toxic substance; that there are several studies of benzene's toxic effects that are consistent with the symptoms reported by the plaintiffs; and that the facts that the workers first experienced these symptoms soon after their initial exposure to high levels of benzene, and that the symptoms subsided within two weeks after they left the refinery, strongly support his conclusion that exposure to benzene caused the plaintiffs' problems.

The district court judge excluded Dr. Siegel's testimony under *Daubert, Joiner* and *Kumho Tire,* and dismissed the plaintiffs' claims for lack of evidence that exposure to benzene caused their injuries. **How should the circuit court handle this issue on appeal?**

V.   DISSATISFACTION WITH EXPERT WITNESSES, AND THE USE OF COURT-APPOINTED EXPERTS

It seems that the use of expert witnesses in common law courts has always been troublesome. In his *Treatise on the Law of Evidence*, first published in 1848, Judge John Pitt Taylor describes several classes of witnesses whose testimony should be viewed with caution, including: enslaved people (which accounts for "the lamentable neglect of truth, which is evinced by most of the nations of India, by the subjects of the Czar, and by many of the peasantry in Ireland"); women (because they are more susceptible to "an innate vain love of the marvelous"); and "foreigners and of others . . . living out of the jurisdiction" (who have little fear of the consequences of perjury). But, "[p]erhaps the testimony which least deserves credit with a jury is that of *skilled witnesses.* . . . [I]t is often quite surprising to see with what facility, and to what extent, their views can be made to correspond with the wishes or the interests of the parties who call them."[134]   While others of Judge Taylor's insulting stereotypes have not stood the test of time, this last one has been remarkably durable. It was no novelty in 1848, and with a little effort one can find an abundance of similar comments from lawyers and judges in every decade since.[135] In fact, we have become thoroughly accustomed to this view of experts. And yet isn't it remarkable—isn't it, in fact, shocking—that casual observers and even interested partisans are treated by the legal profession with at least reasonable respect, but trained and experienced doctors, engineers and scientists are castigated?

Reading the comments of lawyers and judges, it is easy to get the impression that expert witnesses are intruders who disrupt the judicial search for truth. This is false, of course. As Karl Menninger, the eminent psychiatrist, pointed out, the expert "is not self invited to these parties. He is not a trespasser. He is called, then he is questioned, criticized, disputed, attacked, suspected, disregarded and ridiculed."[136] The expert witness that lawyers vilify is a creature of their own creation.

Needless to say, the contempt this process generates is not one-sided. Experts in other fields have equally strong feelings about the use to which their knowledge is put in court. In 1923 Wigmore wrote: "Professional men of honorable instincts and high scientific standards began to look upon the witness box as a 1178olgotha, and to disclaim all respect for the law's methods of investigation."[137] This was not a novel observation either; similar sentiments have been expressed regularly for over a century. To put it bluntly, in many professions service as an expert witness is not generally considered honest work. As one doctor explained over half a century ago: "Within the medical profession, where there is a reluctance to testify in court, there are sometimes heard derogatory remarks concerning those who testify frequently as expert witnesses. The attitude seems to be that such men must be hard pressed financially to be

---

[134] John Pitt Taylor, 2 Treatise on the Law of Evidence §§ 45–50, at 65–69 (3d ed. 1858) (emphasis in original).

[135] For example: "[I]t has often distressed and disturbed sensitive minds, when seeking to ascertain what the truth was, to be obliged to resort to the opinion of men who have seemed to regard their line of duty as lying in the direction of the success of the one who employed them. . . ." Emory Washburn, Testimony of Experts, 1 Am. L. Rev. 45, 48–49 (1866); "[I]f there was any kind of testimony not only of no value, but even worse than that, it was . . . that of medical experts." Rutherford v. Morris, 77 Ill. 397, 405 (1875); "[N]ow that they [expert witnesses] as a class have become retained agents of parties, (their utterances) have lost all judicial authority." Persons v. State, 90 Tenn. 291, 16 S.W. 726, 727 (Tenn. 1891) (excerpt from the trial court's charge to the jury, quoting Francis F. Wharton, 1 A Commentary on the Law of Evidence in Civil Issues § 454, at 425 (1888)); "Of all the cant that's canted in this canting world, expert medical cant is the most pernicious. . . . " Frank S. Rice, The Medical Expert as a Witness, 10 Green Bag 464 (1898); "The expert witness evil, which is a blight on judicial administration and a discredit to the medical profession, must sooner or later be faced." Lowder v. Standard Auto Parts Co., 136 Neb. 747, 287 N.W. 211, 215 (Neb. 1939) (opinion of Johnsen, J., concurring in part and dissenting in part).

[136] Karl Menninger, The Crime of Punishment 140 (1968).

[137] 2 Wigmore § 563, at 760.

coerced into this duty. . . . "[138] Probably the worst consequence of this view is that many of the best physicians, scientists and engineers refuse to participate in the process altogether.

These two points of view are complementary aspects of a common description of the use of expert evidence in American courts. Experts in other fields see lawyers as unprincipled manipulators of their disciplines, and lawyers and experts alike often see expert *witnesses*—those members of other learned professions who consort with lawyers—as whores.

Why does this system function so badly? The basic reason is that we have taken a form of investigation that was developed for lay witnesses, and applied it in a foreign context. Adversarial examination of sworn witnesses in the presence of the trier of fact may be an excellent tool in its usual sphere. But imagine how it would function under the following regime: the lawyers on each side of a dispute, acting in secret, choose people from an almost indefinitely large array and designate them as the witnesses; these witnesses are paid handsomely for their testimony; lawyers can preemptively hire witnesses in order to keep them from testifying when their honest testimony might help the other side; many witnesses make a business of testifying, and advertise their services; witnesses are allowed to testify to matters beyond their personal knowledge, and to evaluate as well as to present information; the existing rules of pre-trial discovery are curtailed so that the identity and the evidence of many potential witnesses can be concealed from the opposing party; the usual rules of evidence are largely inapplicable at trial; and, finally, the subject matter of the testimony by the witnesses is intrinsically confusing—if not incomprehensible—to judges and jurors. One would think the judicial system could not function in such circumstances. And yet, as we have seen, this is an accurate thumbnail sketch of how American courts use expert information.

We do not mean to say that expert evidence is always corrupt or confusing. There are many honest, helpful, informative expert witnesses, and there are many trials in which important medical, scientific or technical issues are resolved clearly and accurately, or are never in dispute. And trials are only the tip of the iceberg. Many more cases settle when experts honestly and accurately present the lawyers who hired them with unwelcome conclusions. The problem is that the system can go badly wrong, and often does. As Wigmore put it, "By any standard of efficiency, the orthodox method [of presenting expert evidence] registers itself as a failure, in cases where the slightest pressure is put upon it."[139]

---

[138] Samuel R. Gerber, Expert Medical Testimony and the Medical Expert, in Physician in the Courtroom 65, 72 (Oliver Schroeder, Jr. ed., 1957).

[139] 2 Wigmore § 563, p. 760.

Not surprisingly, there have been many calls for reform. The most frequently suggested reform by far is the use of neutral or court-appointed expert witnesses, either to the exclusion of other experts or, more commonly, in addition to experts presented by the parties. The attractiveness of this procedure is obvious. The most conspicuous dangers of adversarial expertise are (1) that partisan choice of witnesses will produce a biased selection of experts, and (2) that partisan compensation and preparation will further bias the evidence that these witnesses present. If the witnesses are chosen and compensated by the court, and responsible to it, these pitfalls are avoided. Calls for the use of neutral expert witnesses have been heard for well over a hundred years,[140] and have gained steadily in popularity since the early part of the twentieth century. In 1937 the National Conference of Commissioners on Uniform State Laws adopted a Model Expert Testimony Act that provided for court-appointed experts. In 1938, this Act was endorsed by the American Bar Association Committee on the Improvement of the Law of Evidence. In the following edition of his treatise, Wigmore was optimistic: "It would seem that the problem has now reached its final solution, assuming the Act is generally *adopted* and is *invoked* in practice when appropriate."[141] The first prerequisite for this final solution has been met. Explicit provisions for court-appointed experts have been adopted in the federal courts and in the great majority of states and territories.[142] Furthermore, many cases have held that judges have the inherent power to call expert witnesses, even without specific statutory authority.[143] On Wigmore's second condition, however, the matter has simply stalled. In most types of litigation, the authority to call court-appointed experts is hardly ever invoked.

FRE 706 is the model for most of the current provisions for the use of court-appointed experts. It includes five major elements:

(1) *Appointment.* An expert or experts may be appointed by the court on motion of a party or on its own motion, after notice. The court may ask the parties to submit nominations, and may encourage them to agree on the expert(s) to be appointed, but the actual selection is for the court.

---

[140] E.g., G. A. Endlich, Proposed Changes in the Law of Expert Testimony, 32 Am. L. Rev. 851, 854 (1898); Learned Hand, Historical and Practical Considerations Regarding Expert Testimony, 15 Harv. L. Rev. 40 (1901); Clemens Herschel, Services of Experts in the Conduct of Judicial Inquiries, 21 Am. L. Rev. 571 (1887); Emory Washburn, Testimony of Experts, 1 Am. L. Rev. 45, 61–62 (1866); 1 Wigmore § 563, at 966 (2d ed. 1923).

[141] 2 Wigmore § 563 (3d ed. 1940).

[142] See 6 Weinstein's Federal Evidence (2nd ed. 1997) T-136.

[143] E.g., Hall v. Baxter Healthcare, 947 F.Supp. 1387, 1393 n. 8 (D.Or.1996); Scott v. Spanjer Bros., 298 F.2d 928, 930–33 (2d Cir. 1962); Hart v. Community Sch. Bd. of Brooklyn, 383 F.Supp. 699 (E.D.N.Y. 1974), aff'd, 512 F.2d 37 (2d Cir. 1975). See John M. Sink, The Unused Power of a Federal Judge to Call His Own Expert Witness, 29 S. Cal. L. Rev. 195 (1956); R.E. Barber, Annotation, Trial Court's Appointment, in Civil Case, of Expert Witness, 95 A.L.R.2d 390 (1964).

(2) *Functions.* An appointed expert shall be informed of her duties either by a written court order or at a conference with the parties. The expert shall inform the parties of her findings, and may be called as a witness by the court or by any party. The expert shall also be available for deposition, and subject to cross-examination, by any party.

(3) *Compensation.* The court determines an appointed expert's compensation. In criminal cases, the expert will be paid from public funds; in civil cases, the court will order the parties to make payments as it sees fit, and the expert's fee will then be charged as a cost.

(4) *Disclosure.* The court has discretion to authorize disclosure to the jury of the fact of an expert's appointment.

(5) *Partisan Experts.* The court's power to appoint expert witnesses does not limit the parties' power to call their own.

The most conspicuous fact about FRE 706 is that it is rarely used. For example, in a 1986 survey of active federal district court judges, 80% said that they had never appointed an expert under Rule 706, and fewer than 10% said that they had done so more than once.[144] Similarly, a study of 529 Civil trials in California Superior Courts in 1985–86 found 1748 appearances by partisan experts, but not a single instance of testimony by a court-appointed expert,[145] despite the fact that the California Evidence Code (§§ 730–733) contains provisions for appointment similar to those in FRE 706.

Why is this power of appointment so neglected? One reason, no doubt, is that FRE 706 and similar provisions do nothing to help judges locate and select appropriate experts. If that is the problem, however, there is a solution: assemble panels of experts who are qualified and willing to accept court appointments. For medical testimony in personal injury cases, where the need is greatest, courts in some metropolitan jurisdictions have from time to time done just that, and even provided public funds to pay the appointed doctors. But these plans too, have had little effect. For example, a state-wide plan in New Jersey was used an average of six times a year from 1961 through 1975, and in Los Angeles in 1967 not a single expert had been appointed from the local panel in twenty-two months.[146]

Another possible explanation for the disuse of provisions for court-appointed experts is that the procedure is a bad idea, and judges know it. There are quite a few articulate proponents of this point of view, mainly

---

[144] Joe S. Cecil & Thomas E. Willging, Court-Appointed Experts: Defining a Role for Court-Appointed Experts Under Federal Rule of Evidence 706, Federal Judicial Center (1993).

[145] Gross, supra note 1, at 1191.

[146] Id. at 1192.

trial lawyers. Their main arguments fall into two categories. (1) Court-appointed experts have too much power. They are all but impossible to impeach or contradict, and, as a result, their testimony is dispositive of any issue they touch. Some couch this argument in strong rhetoric: The choice of an expert by the court compromises the impartiality of the judge (who associates her prestige with a particular witness) and destroys the parties' right to a jury decision (because the expert becomes the *de facto* fact-finder). (2) Court-appointed experts are misleading. They are not truly impartial—all experts have personal and professional biases—and they are as fallible as anyone else, yet they project a false aura of infallibility. This is particularly dangerous on issues where a discipline is divided into opposing camps; in that situation the choice of the appointed expert may amount to a judicial endorsement of one side of an unresolved dispute.

These arguments raise real concerns, but ultimately they are unpersuasive. Appointed experts may be more influential than adversarial experts, but that is as it should be. Other things being equal, the evidence of appointed experts *ought* to be given more weight for the very reason that they are not partisans of one side or the other. This does not mean that court-appointed experts have *undue* influence, and certainly not that judges or juries think they are infallible. In our everyday lives we all consult with nonpartisan accountants, doctors, builders, even lawyers; we rely on them, but we do not consider them infallible even when we have chosen them ourselves. There is no *a priori* reason to believe that this skepticism will somehow evaporate in court, and our limited experience with appointed experts suggests the opposite. For example, from June 1958 to September 1964, there were twenty-four jury verdicts in the United States District Court for the Eastern District of Pennsylvania in trials that included testimony by doctors from a panel of impartial experts. Fifteen of these verdicts were "consistent with the report of the neutral doctor"; nine were not.[147]

There are, of course, situations in which a field is divided into opposing camps. When that is true, any single expert may provide a misleading view of how experts think about the issues. But one should not exaggerate the problem. In many cases—probably most—the overwhelming majority of credible experts would reach the same conclusion, if they were not paid to support a particular position. *Daubert,* for example, was such a case.[148] Generally, appointed experts are not used in either situation. Moreover, an appointed expert might be particularly useful in a case where the field is split, if she is carefully chosen and her role is well-defined, since she need not be a partisan for one side or the other, and can explain the nature of the division to the

[147] Larry W. Myers, "The Battle of the Experts": A New Approach to an Old Problem in Medical Testimony, 44 Neb. L. Rev. 539, 573 (1965).

[148] Supra p. 1160.

jury. In the absence of such help the jurors are left to choose on their own between competing partisan experts who advocate incompatible positions. Is there any reason to suppose that they are likely to do as well in that situation as they would with the benefit of expert advice, albeit imperfect, from a non-partisan source?

Even to the extent that these arguments against appointed experts might be sound—or that judges believe them to be—they do not explain the pervasive failure to use court-appointed experts. The existing rules make it possible to avoid these issues entirely, at least in many cases. Under FRE 706, judges are encouraged to appoint experts whom the parties choose by mutual agreement; in jurisdictions with organized panels, the judge typically plays no part in the choice of the witness even in the absence of an agreement by the parties; if an issue divides a field into opposing camps, *two* experts can be appointed; and the jury need not be told of an appointed expert's status. Few judges even try to make use of these options. Besides, the main thrust of the arguments against appointed experts is that *juries* will be improperly deferential to them, but judges rarely appoint experts even in non-jury cases.

The true reasons for the failure to use court-appointed experts are probably social and structural, and the most obvious of these is the steadfast hostility of trial lawyers. Opposition by the organized trial bar is strong, and the public statements of prominent lawyers run to alarmism: the use of court-appointed experts "would fit well into . . . a non-adversary, almost communistic scheme," but we should "cling with liberty-loving, jealous loyalty to our system."[149] Such a system is "of its nature unjust, even totalitarian in its operation."[150] "[T]rial by jury . . . [would] become no more than an empty illusion, a shibboleth to which lip-service is paid while its destruction is endorsed."[151] Most lawyers, no doubt, are less heated about the topic, but no visible group of practitioners favors the practice, and (more important) very few trial attorneys ever ask judges to appoint experts.

At first this may seem surprising. After all, trials are zero-sum games: what hurts one side benefits the other. An appointed expert (if she has any effect) must ultimately help one party or the other. But to focus on the outcome ignores the nature of the attorney's work. A trial is a risky unpredictable event. The lawyer's main task is to attempt to control it, and the major method of achieving control is witness preparation. A good trial lawyer aims to know in advance all the answers his witnesses will give on direct and on cross-examination, and all the answers he will get on cross-examination of the opposing witnesses; to the

---

[149] Howard K. Berry, Impartial Medical Testimony, 32 F.R.D. 539, 545 (1962).

[150] M. N. Howard, P.C., The Neutral Expert: A Plausible Threat to Justice, 1991 Crim. L. Rev. 98, 101.

[151] Elwood S. Levy, Impartial Medical Testimony—Revisited, 34 Temp. L. Q. 416, 425 (1961).

extent possible, he also attempts to shape the testimony of the witnesses he calls. Partisan experts fit right into this scheme, but a court-appointed expert is different. She lacks the commitment to a party that would enable its attorney to shape and organize her testimony. Even if a lawyer knows in advance that a court-appointed expert's general position is likely to be favorable to his side, the appointed expert is dangerous since she is liable to give unanticipated answers to questions from either party. Trial lawyers cringe at risks like that. They would rather rely on adversarial experts, who may be less credible but will certainly be more tractable and predictable.

Judges of course, could appoint expert witnesses despite the opposition of trial attorneys. As we have seen, they seldom do. Some judges, no doubt, are persuaded by trial lawyers' criticisms of the practice, or continue to believe what they thought when they were trial lawyers themselves. However, a 1987 Harris Poll of 1000 judges found that 70% of state and 76% of federal judges favored the use of non-partisan experts in "cases involving technical or scientific issues."[152] Why then don't they do it?

Judges as well as lawyers want trials to be predictable and controlled. The judicial economy of adversarial jury trials requires careful advance preparation of the witnesses—to obtain evidence on all the issues that might come up in a single, one-shot proceeding, and to make the presentation of that evidence reasonably efficient. This is especially important for expert witnesses, whose testimony can be so wide-ranging and complex. The judge has no reason to worry about the preparation of a partisan expert; that is the responsibility of the attorney who calls the witness. To the extent that the judge views her role as overseeing the process of presenting evidence to the jury, partisan experts are the least of her problems, since they (unlike many lay witnesses) are likely to be experienced, well-prepared and well-spoken.

A court-appointed expert, however, is nobody's respon-sibility. Preparation by the parties' attorneys will not have the usual effect. The lawyers have no control over an appointed expert and are likely to be suspicious of the entire enterprise, if not overtly hostile, while the expert herself has no commitment to any one party and will probably be reluctant to compromise her neutrality by working too closely with either side. Worse, at least some authorities believe that *ex parte* communications between attorneys and court-appointed experts are improper.[153] This would mean that any pre-trial preparation by the

---

[152] Louis Harris and Associates, Judges' Opinions on Procedural Issues: A Survey of State and Federal Trial Judges Who Spent at Least Half Their Time on General Civil Cases, 69 B. U. L. Rev. 731, 741 (1989).

[153] See, e.g., Leesona Corp. v. Varta Batteries, Inc., 522 F.Supp. 1304, 1312 n. 18 (S.D.N.Y. 1981) ("The parties were not permitted to communicate directly with [the court-appointed expert]. All communication with the court expert was done through the Court, and copies of all

attorneys must take place (if at all) in the presence of the opposition—a procedure American lawyers will shun.

Nor can the judge fill the vacuum. Some judges clearly feel that witness selection and preparation are tasks they left behind when they were elevated to the bench. But even a judge who wants to undertake this responsibility is in a poor position to do it. The typical American judge has little or no advance information about the next case she will try, and little time to prepare for it. She could not possibly conduct the type of expert-witness preparation that an attorney for a party can afford. Moreover, out-of-court witness preparation by the judge is a concept foreign to American law; it runs counter to the prevailing norms of practice, and would probably be considered improper.[154] In other words, appointed experts are on their own, which makes judges reluctant to use them in all cases, and doubly reluctant to do so in jury trials, where the formalities, the ritual, and the need for preparation are all greatest.

In short, court-appointed experts are not used in American trials because they are beyond the control of lawyers. As a result, they are unpredictable, potentially under-prepared, and a threat to the power of trial attorneys. Appellate courts continue to refer to the use of court-appointed experts as one of the remedies that is available to alleviate the problems of expert evidence.[155] However, given the severe structural problems the procedure poses, it is unlikely to become common in American courts any time soon.[156]

---

materials sent by the Court [to the expert] were docketed by the clerk and placed in the court file."). See also Thomas E. Willging, Court Appointed Experts 8 (1986) ("ex parte communication between a party and the court's expert should . . . be prohibited.").

[154] Rule 706(b) provides that "[[t]he court must inform the expert of the expert's duties. The court may do so in writing and have a copy filed with the clerk or may do so orally at a conference in which the parties have an opportunity to participate." Otherwise, it makes no reference to discussion with the witness in preparation for her assigned tasks. The Canon 3(A)(4) of the Code of Judicial Conduct prohibits any ex parte communication by a judge "concerning a pending or impending proceeding," "except as authorized by law. . . . " This prohibition probably includes ex parte communications with a court-appointed expert. See United States v. Green, 544 F.2d 138, 146 n. 16 (3d Cir. 1976) ("the court should avoid ex parte communications with anyone associated with the trial, even its own appointed expert. . . . ").

[155] E.g., Daubert v. Merrell Dow Pharmaceuticals, 509 U.S. 579 (1993). In the wake of *Daubert* some judges have appointed experts, or expert panels, to assist them in making decisions on the admissibility of purportedly scientific evidence. E.g., Hall v. Baxter Healthcare, 947 F.Supp. 1387, 1393, n. 8 (D.Or.1996) (panel of experts appointed under the court's inherent power, to determine admissibility of scientific evidence of systemic injuries from silicone gel breast implants); see also id. at 1414–15 (referring to a FRE 706 panel appointed to study the same issue in a set of cases in Montgomery, Alabama). This sort of use of appointed experts— which does not require testimony before a jury—is easier to manage than presentation of evidence at trial. See Joe S. Cecil & Thomas E. Willging, Accepting Daubert's Invitation: Defining a Role for Court-Appointed Experts in Assessing Scientific Validity, 43 Emory L. J. 995 (1994). See infra note 156.

[156] Judges may be somewhat more willing to appoint experts to serve in roles that do not require them to testify. For example, a study of federal practice under Rule 706 found that for the most part, the few experts who were appointed were used for a variety of pre-trial and post-trial tasks, and not for "[w]hat one would expect to be the traditional function of court-appointed experts—the presentation of evidence at trial." Willging, supra note 153 at 3, n.11. In an

Problem IX-10. Gnatscope sues the Macrosoft Corporation for attempting to monopolize the browser market by designing its new desktop operating system to be incompatible with the Gnatscope browser, while at the same time incorporating Macrosoft's inferior Internet Executor browser as part of its desktop operating system's desktop. The parties disagree about almost everything, including: whether the browser market is confined to this country (where Macrosoft has been making great inroads) or includes other countries (where Gnatscope is by far the dominant player, and is the default browser on most competing operating systems); whether the code which renders Macrosoft's new desktop incompatible with Gnatscope is integral to important functional improvements in the operating system or whether the improvements have little value to consumers and were included just to create incompatibilities; whether Macrosoft has the market power to exclude Gnatscope when Gnatscope has established a "fix" which allows a compatible version of Gnatscope to be downloaded from the Internet provided the consumer is willing to forego what Gnatscope in its ad calls an "insignificant" feature of Macrosoft's operating system; whether the Internet Executor browser is inferior to Gnatscope; and whether polling data can be fairly interpreted as showing that when the functionality of the two browsers is described to them, consumers prefer Gnatscope to Internet Executor by a margin of 3 to 2. **Do you think the court should appoint an expert or experts in this case? If so, what should the expert(s) be asked to do? How should the expert(s) be compensated? What difficulties should the court foresee if it does appoint an expert (or experts)? If the court decides to appoint one or more experts, what orders, in relationship to this appointment, should the court enter?**

---

antitrust case, for example, a court-appointed expert might get the parties' experts to agree on a common database or on common terminology, or to focus on a particular set of questions. If the end result is not settlement, at least the evidence at trial is likely to be less confusing.

VI.   EXAMPLES OF EXPERT EVIDENCE

A. UNCONTESTED MEDICAL TESTIMONY IN A CRIMINAL TRIAL

It is important to remember that much expert testimony—like a great deal of evidence of every sort—is uncontroverted. A common example is medical testimony in a criminal case, to establish the fact that the victim of an alleged crime was injured or died, and the nature of the injury or the cause of death. The short excerpt that follows is from *People v. Tellez*, the aggravated assault and attempted escape trial that is presented in Chapter One, supra pp. 15–140.

. . .

SURANDER SINGHAL,

called as a witness on behalf of the People of the State of Illinois, having been first duly sworn, was examined and testified as follows:

DIRECT EXAMINATION

BY MR. REILLY:

Q.   Doctor, you have been sworn.

Would you please state your name and spell your first and last name for the benefit of our court reporter? **A.** My name is Surander, S-u-r-a-n-de-r, Singhal, S-i-n-g-h-a-l.

Q. Are you a licensed medical doctor here in the State of Illinois? **A.** Yes.

Q. When were you licensed, doctor? **A.** I was licensed in 1981.

Q. Where are you currently employed, doctor? **A.** Currently I am employed with the emergency medical services group called EMSCO.

Q. EMSCO? **A.** Right.

Q. Doctor, where did you attend college? **A.** I attended college in India.

Q. Did you obtain a degree at that college? **A.** That is right.

Q. Subsequent to coming, did you attend medical school in the country of India? **A.** That is right.

Q. Upon graduation from medical school, did you come to the United States? **A.** That's right.

Q. Did you serve a residency or internship program here in the United States? **A.** In the United States.

Q. Where was that residency served? **A.** St. Mary of Nazareth Hospital in Chicago.

Q. How long were you affiliated with St. Mary of Nazareth Hospital here in Chicago? **A.** From 1979 to 1982.

Q. Doctor, during the course of your time at St. Mary of Nazareth Hospital, did you do any teaching there? **A.** Yes.

Q. What type of teaching? **A.** I was teaching the family practice residents.

Q. Doctor, do you have any specialty at this time? **A.** Emergency medicine.

Q. Doctor, do you belong to any professional organizations? **A.** Yes. I do.

Q. What professional organization are you a member of? **A.** I belong to AMA, Chicago Medical Society, Illinois State Medical Society, American Academy of Family Physicians, and American College of Emergency Physicians.

Q. Are you board certified, doctor? **A.** I am board certified in family practice.

Q. Very briefly what does it mean to be board certified? **A.** It is an exam to qualify after you finish your residency.

Q. Doctor, in August of 1987, were you employed at St. Anthony's Hospital here in Chicago? **A.** That's right.

Q. In what area of the hospital were you employed? **A.** Emergency medicine.

Q. The five years prior to being at St. Anthony's, you were at St. Mary of Nazareth? **A.** That is correct.

Q. Again there you spent a great deal of your time in emergency medicine, is that right? **A.** Right.

MR. REILLY: Your Honor, at this time I would ask that the witness be qualified as an expert in the medical field and be allowed to render a medical opinion at this time.[157] I tender the doctor to the defense at this time.

MS. LYON: Your Honor, we are perfectly happy to stipulate to Dr. Singhal's qualifications.[158]

THE COURT: The witness is found to be qualified to testify as an expert as to medical matters. It is noted that he is board certified in family practice, that he is licensed to practice in the State of Illinois, that the proper foundation has been laid for him to testify as an expert in those areas.[159]

BY MR. REILLY:

Q. Doctor, I would like to direct your attention to a particular afternoon, Friday, August 28, 1987, shortly after 4:00 o'clock in the afternoon. Were you working in the emergency room at St. Anthony's Hospital?[160] **A.** If I can consult my records—

Q. Is your memory exhausted at this time as to the date? **A.** Well I have not gone through the records. If I could go through the records, I could look—

---

[157] As we will see, none of this witness's testimony is in dispute. Nonetheless, the proponent must go through the usual steps of qualifying the witness as an expert. The testimony that Mr. Reilly elicits on this issue is straightforward, a bit perfunctory, and more than sufficient; at this point, he is ready to ask the court to recognize Dr. Singhal as an expert.

[158] Ms. Lyon has no quarrel with the doctor's qualifications—or any other aspect of his presentation—but if she did, at this point she could ask to "voir dire" the witness on the subject of his qualifications.

[159] The judge makes it official. In the absence of an objection, Mr. Reilly could have gone ahead and asked Dr. Singhal to report his expert opinions and observations without a formal motion to qualify him as an expert. Which procedure is more useful to the side that calls the expert?

[160] Dr. Singhal is what is sometimes called an "occurrence expert:" a person with specialized knowledge or training who also has first-hand information about the case at hand, unlike the more common "opinion expert," who is called in after the fact to make observations, conduct tests, and offer opinions. Treating physicians, such as Dr. Singhal, are probably the most common type of "occurrence experts." Occurrence experts are an exception to the usual rule that expert witnesses can be chosen by the parties with few restrictions. When you need to know the opinion of the emergency room doctor, you're stuck with whoever was on duty when the victim was brought in.

MS. LYON: I have no objection if he needs to look at records to refresh his memory. That is fine. He can do it any time as far as I am concerned.

THE COURT: That is fine.[161]

BY MR. REILLY:

Q. Do you remember the date of August 28? **A.** Yes, sir.

Q. Did you have an opportunity while on duty there in the emergency room to examine a Mr. Nicholas Alfieri? **A.** Yes. I did.

Q. When you examined Mr. Nicholas Alfieri in the emergency room that afternoon, would you tell the ladies and gentlemen of the jury what you found when you examined Mr. Alfieri that afternoon? **A.** On Mr. Alfieri I noticed certain ecchymotic lesions involving the left inner thigh.

Q. Excuse me, doctor, if I could interrupt you for the benefit of the lay people. You observed certain ecchymotic lesions. Would you simplify that for us? **A.** It means contusions.

Q. Bruises or contusions? **A.** Yes.

Q. Where did you observe these bruises or contusions? **A.** They were noticed on the left inner thigh, right inner knee, left outer knee, and they were also noticed at the bottom of the scrotum.

Q. So the left inner thigh, the bottom of the scrotum and both knees, is that correct? **A.** That's right.

Q. Did these appear to be fresh to you at that time? **A.** Yes, sir.

Q. Doctor, after observing these injuries to Alfieri, you noted those injuries in your report, is that correct? **A.** That's right.

Q. Did you prescribe any treatment for Mr. Alfieri that afternoon? **A.** Yes. I did.

Q. What did you prescribe, doctor? **A.** We gave him a scrotum support to help him relieve his pain and to reduce swelling. He was asked to use ice packs for 48 hours. He was given pain medication, and he was advised to continue follow-up with his private physician.

Q. The scrotum support is something that he would wear? **A.** To relieve the pain and reduce the swelling.

Q. Doctor, based on your experience as a medical doctor, based on your training, based on your examination of Mr. Alfieri that afternoon at St. Anthony's Hospital, the injuries you noted, the injuries to the scrotum,

---

[161] Routine uncontested testimony from an occurrence expert may be comparatively unprepared. For one thing, unlike most experts, an occurrence expert whose connection with the case was incidental and fortuitous is not usually paid a professional fee for his services. Not surprisingly, Dr. Singhal—like the cop who's been brought in to testify to an arrest he made nine months earlier—needs to look at his records in order to answer questions.

to the inner thigh, and to both knees, are those injuries likely to have been caused by a kick?[162]

A.   That's right. That is possible.

Q.   By repeated and multiple kicks? **A.** That's right.

MR. REILLY: If I may have a moment, judge.

Nothing further from the doctor.

THE COURT: Cross.

CROSS-EXAMINATION

BY MS. LYON:

Q.   The pain medication you prescribed was Tylenol?[163] **A.** Tylenol. That's right.

Q.   You, of course, have no way of knowing why it was that he was kicked?

A.   No, ma'am.

Q.   You, of course, have no way of knowing who kicked him or the circumstances of it? **A.** No, ma'am.

Q.   Just that he had these injuries and you did this treatment? **A.** That's right.

MS. LYON: That is all. Thank you.

REDIRECT EXAMINATION

BY MR. REILLY:

Q.   Doctor, in treating Mr. Alfieri, you were aware that Mr. Alfieri stated that he was kicked by a prisoner. That is part of the medical history? **A.** That is a part of the medical history given to the nurses.

Q.   The statement was that he was kicked by a prisoner at approximately 12:05 p.m. that afternoon? **A.** That's right.[164]

MR. REILLY: Nothing further, judge.

THE COURT: Miss Lyon.

MS. LYON: I have no other questions.

---

[162] Note the use of leading questions on direct examination. This is common, despite the general prohibition against leading on direct. See FRE 611(c). An objection would be pointless. Even if it were sustained—and courts often permit leading on direct with experts—the direct examiner would rephrase the question and get the desired answer.

[163] Why does Ms. Lyon bring out that the drug prescribed was Tylenol?

[164] Would the fact that Mr. Alfieri said to "the nurses" that he was kicked by a prisoner be admissible as a statement for purposes of medical diagnosis or treatment, under FRE 803(4)?

THE COURT: Thank you very much, doctor. You are excused.

(Witness excused.)

NOTE

Did Dr. Singhal testify to anything that required expertise? If so, what?

B. EXPERT TESTIMONY ON CAUSATION IN A MEDICAL MALPRACTICE CASE

The following excerpt is a chapter from the book *Damages* by Barry Werth.[165] The book tells the story of *Sabia v. Norwalk Hospital,* a medical malpractice lawsuit that was filed in Bridgeport, Connecticut, in 1987, seeking damages for catastrophic brain damage suffered at birth by Anthony John Sabia. Anthony John Sabia (Little Tony) was one of twins born to Donna Sabia and Anthony Sabia, Jr. (Tony) on April 1, 1984. His brother, Michael, was still born; Little Tony was near death but survived, with permanent brain damage that stunted his growth and left him profoundly retarded and severely disabled—unable to walk, talk, dress, or feed himself. His parents, on his behalf, sued the Norwalk Hospital, where Donna Sabia received pre-natal care and delivered her children, and Dr. Maryellen Humes, the obstetrician who attended the delivery, alleging that these defendants were negligent both prior to and at the delivery, and that their negligence caused Little Tony's injuries.

In the process of pre-trial investigation and discovery, the plaintiffs in the *Sabia* case developed the following theory in support of their claims: Little Tony was injured following his brother's death in utero by a disastrous drop in blood pressure that was caused when he bled into his dead twin's body through blood vessels that connected them in the placenta they shared in their mother's womb. Given this scenario, the claim against Dr. Humes—who never saw Mrs. Sabia until mid-way through her labor—was that she should have recognized during labor that one twin was dead and delivered them immediately by a cesarean section, and that if she had Little Tony would have been born healthy. The Sabias settled their claim against Humes in February, 1992, for $1.35 million, well within the limits of her $2 million medical malpractice liability insurance policy. The claim against Norwalk Hospital went forward, with the plaintiffs (or rather, their lawyers) pressing the

---

[165] Simon & Schuster, New York: 1998, pp. 300–309. The footnotes are not part of the original text. Reprinted with the permission of Simon & Schuster, Inc., from Damages: One Family's Legal Struggles in the World of Medicine. Copyright ©1998 by Barry Werth.

potentially inconsistent theory that Michael Sabia's death was the end result of a process of deterioration that was underway for days before the delivery, that the danger to the twins should have been detected by hospital personnel in their pre-natal examination of Donna Sabia, and that if they had detected the problem both babies could have been delivered alive by cesarean section.

The expert whose testimony we see here is Dr. Kurt Benirschke, a world-famous authority on placental pathology. It was a major coup for the plaintiffs to enlist him on their side. His testimony for the plaintiffs focuses on the following points: that Michael Sabia's death caused Little Tony Sabia's injuries; Michael's death was the culmination of a slow process of diminished blood flow through his umbilical cord. The defense hopes to show that Michael's death was caused by a sudden and unforeseeable accident.

The testimony that's described here is in the form of a videotaped deposition. This is not a discovery deposition; that has already occurred. This is a testimonial deposition that is being conducted because Dr. Benirschke will not be available at trial (see Fed. R. Civ. Pro. 32(a)(3)).

Dramatis Personae:

Dr. Kurt Benirschke	A leading medical authority on placental pathology
Michael Koskoff	Lead attorney for plaintiffs Anthony John Sabia and his parents
Christopher Bernard	Second-chair plaintiffs' attorney
Bill Doyle	Lead attorney for defendant Norwalk Hospital
Beverly Hunt	Second-chair defense attorney
Michael Sabia (Twin B)	The still-born twin
Anthony John Sabia (Little Tony, Twin A)	The surviving, brain-damaged twin
Dr. Charles Lockwood	A medical expert for the defense

Glossary:

Velamentous cord insertion: A condition in which the umbilical cord is improperly attached to the placenta, without the usual coating of protective jelly, and vulnerable to accidents.

Anastomoses: Direct communication between the blood vessels of twins in the womb.

Monoamniotic twins: Twins who are carried in the womb in a single amniotic sac, by contrast to *diamniotic twins*, who are carried in two separate amniotic sacs.

Morbidity: Disease or injury.

Mortality: Death.

Monochorionic twinning: Gestation in which two twins share a single outer embryonic membrane.

. . .

SEPTEMBER 22, 1993

Kurt Benirschke glared at the video camera in front of him and fidgeted with his clip-on microphone wire. He wore a blue oxford shirt and no jacket, and his burgundy tie hung limply askew. He was sitting behind the desk in his windowless office across from the morgue at the UCSD Medical Center, waiting for Koskoff and Doyle to start questioning him about what had happened to the twins. Releasing the wire, he grabbed a pen, looked away, then leaned forward to scribble something. Next, he scooped up a pair of wirerim reading glasses and began twisting the stems in his large, liverspotted hands. When still nothing happened, he sank back in his chair, returned his gaze to the camera, steepled his index fingers, and assumed a look of murderous impatience, his dark eyes burning beneath the great cirrus of his brows. Finally, he reached for a coffee mug that said I LOVE YOU, GRANDPA and took a gulp.

Space was severely limited. Shoehorned in front of him, Koskoff and Bernard craned to stay out of the camera's view. Doyle and Hunt squeezed together off to the side. Beside them crouched a young court reporter and, just inside the closed door, a camera operator with a tripod. There was no way out for any of them without climbing over each other. Behind Benirschke's left shoulder, filling the only floor space left in the room, stood an easel supporting several schematics with overlays depicting the critical events that had led to Michael Sabia's death and Little Tony's brain damage.

The lawyers had flown to San Diego because Benirschke had said he was too busy to appear in court. Videotaping witnesses for trial was common, yet examining him here raised the stakes for both sides. Benirschke was the most important witness slated to testify. What he said regarding proximate cause—whether Norwalk Hospital's alleged negligence resulted directly in Little Tony's devastation—could well decide the trial's outcome. His storied independence, which Koskoff and Hunt had encountered at his first deposition, made him unpredictable. The lawyers had agreed to examine him prior to jury selection because afterward there would be no time. As a result, what the jurors saw of him, six weeks or so into the trial when both sides were laboring to establish their own themes while slashing away at the other's, would consist of a small-screen TV performance taped three thousand miles away and out of sequence.

The jury would see Benirschke, an austere-looking but surprisingly jolly German-accented doctor, but not the lawyers, who could be identified only by their disembodied voices, questions, and objections. These last a judge could rule on in the interim, which could lead to Benirschke's testimony being edited. The tape would be a static piece of crucial evidence in a dynamic proceeding, and how it played would depend in part on how well the lawyers could anticipate the courtroom events preceding its airing. For the lawyers, it was like shooting a movie climax on a soundstage before the cast and crew flew off on location. . . .

Koskoff still didn't know how much Benirschke would support him, but Benirschke was too central to the case not to testify and for Koskoff himself not to conduct his direct examination. What Koskoff knew was Doyle's defense strategy, as articulated by Lockwood, that what killed Michael Sabia was a sudden cord accident. Bernard had written him a long memo after returning from Lockwood's deposition five and a half weeks earlier. In it he'd urged Koskoff to find out whether Benirschke thought there was any "pathologic basis" for claiming that the cord compression that killed Michael Sabia occurred "over an extended period of time (at least several days; hopefully weeks)"—an opinion that would fortify their obstetrical experts' claim that his death had been preventable. Ever since, Koskoff had thought carefully about what—and, more decisively, what not—to ask Benirschke.[166]

Whatever apprehensions Koskoff harbored about his expert's opinions he now concealed behind a studied casualness. Benirschke was his witness, and he would let the jury know it by the obvious rapport between them. Unlike the procedure at depositions, experts at trial were questioned first by the lawyers who hired them, so Koskoff led off with a flattering walk-through of Benirschke's credentials. Benirschke answered dutifully at first, but soon seemed annoyed. Koskoff picked up the cue. After asking Benirschke whether he was listed in *Who's Who in Science and Engineering, Who's Who in the World, Who's Who in the East, Who's Who in the*

---

[166] Notice how the expert's role is defined in terms of the issues that have been framed in litigation, rather than by reference to the underlying events in the world. Dr. Benirschke does not support the plaintiffs' overall theory, but he is useful to them nonetheless because he also believes that the specific theory the defense has advanced is wrong.

West, Who's Who in America, and *Who's Who in Technology,* he apologized. "I'm sorry to embarrass you, doctor," he said with a laugh, "I have to do this." Benirschke tried to speed up the pace, interrupting Koskoff's listing of the chapters he'd contributed to textbooks with a bored, "and on and on and on." After twenty minutes the recitation ended with Benirschke chortling, then shaking his head in amazement at what lawyers will do to make a point.[167]

Formalities done, Koskoff moved on to the first major part of Benirschke's testimony—that Little Tony had been injured when his blood pressure dropped as he bled into his dead twin. In order to answer, Benirschke swiveled his chair to refer to the charts at his back, and pointed out the twins in utero, the sac, the placenta, the velamentous cord insertion. Using the overlays, he showed how the boys' circulatory systems communicated through the blood vessels in the placenta and speculated that they were connected artery to artery, the commonest form of anastomoses, he said. He also specified where the pathologist's report indicated there had been thrombi—blood clots. There were two—a small one in Michael's cord vessels indicating an earlier slowdown in his circulation, and a much larger one between the placenta and the uterine wall that had been caused by a partial separation called an abruption. This second clot, drawn by a medical illustrator Koskoff had hired to consult with Benirschke, was depicted as an angry red blot, much larger and more pronounced than the first.

Doyle objected to introducing the illustration as evidence.[168] He knew from the pathologist's report that there had been such a placental abruption, but no one had previously suggested that it was major, or that it had anything to do with the ultimate outcome. He suspected Koskoff of deliberately trying to make it seem more ominous than it was.

As Benirschke lectured, Koskoff questioned him gently. There had never been any doubt about how Little Tony was injured; Humes herself had seen it in the delivery room nine and a half years earlier, when Tony and Donna recall her saying that Little Tony was lifeless

---

[167] Dr. Benirschke, like many experts, thinks the process eliciting elaborate testimony on qualifications is ridiculous. That does not necessarily mean, however, that he thinks he is *not* an eminent physician and scientist, or that he does not expect people to pay close attention to his views and to yield to his authority. He might well expect that deference; but if so, in his own circle, where he is known, that attitude is quietly understood, not brashly advertised.

[168] The objection will be ruled on—if at all—by the trial-court judge before the deposition is used in evidence. The usual rule is that objections to the content of evidence need not be made at a deposition in order to preserve them for trial, but that objections to the form of a question are waived if not made when the question is asked, because doing so gives the examiner the opportunity to rephrase the question to avoid the problem. Fed. R. Civ. Pro. 32(d)(3). Can you tell the basis for this objection? Did it have to be made at the deposition?

and anemic because he "gave his blood" to his brother. The mystery—the center of the case—was what had killed Michael. That was the question upon which both sides' claims hinged, and to which Koskoff and Doyle most feared Benirschke's answer. Koskoff edged delicately toward it, then broached the point directly.

"Can you tell us, Doctor," he asked, "based on reasonable medical probability, whether Twin B died of a sudden cord accident?"[169]

Benirschke answered slowly, "No. It's a progressively . . . increasing . . . embarrassment, as it were, because of reduced flow through the circulation."

"How do you know it wasn't a sudden cord accident?"

Doyle interrupted. "I'm gonna object to that. He didn't say that."[170]

"Well, I'll withdraw. I thought he had said that."

Benirschke smiled ambiguously. Lawyerly gamesmanship both amused and dismayed him.

"Can you tell us," Koskoff began again, "based on reasonable probability, whether Baby B died of a sudden cord accident?"

"I see no evidence for that, so I don't think it's a sudden *cord* accident, a knot of the cord or something to that effect."

"Is there evidence that you see to the contrary?"

Benirschke paused. He'd been pinching a pencil and twirling it across his lips. Now he used it as an enumerator, tapping his unfurling fingers with each new point. "Well, in the first place," he said, "it's a common feature in the velamentous insertion of the umbilical cord to see that that baby is growth-retarded, and when one dies, it is that one rather than the other. Second, we find that there's a thrombus, which we see in other such babies is a common consequence of slowing of the circulation. To me, death is sudden anyway. I mean, you know, you're either living or you're dead. But it is a progressive injury that is exemplified by the thrombus. I don't conceive of this as a sudden twist in the umbilical cord"—he wrung his hands as if strangling a snake—"or knot"—he pantomimed tying a bow—"n the umbilical cord."

---

[169] "Reasonable medical probability" is a legal term of art. In most states, as a matter of substantive tort law, a medical malpractice plaintiff is required to present qualified expert evidence opinion "based on reasonable medical probability" that the plaintiff was injured by the defendant's negligence; in the absence of such evidence, the lawsuit will be dismissed. As a result, plaintiffs' lawyers (and sometimes defense lawyers) build the phrase into their questions like a catechism. What the term *means* is another matter entirely. Legal definitions are vague and uninformative, and physicians—the witnesses who have to answer these questions—don't use the expression in their own work at all.

[170] What's the objection here? Is it well taken? Is it worth making?

Here, it seemed, was the far edge of Benirschke's cooperation and of Koskoff's comfort level. There were other vital follow-up questions Koskoff could have asked: Could a velamentous cord insertion be detected by fetal monitoring? (The answer was no.) What about the reduced blood flow betrayed by the thrombus? (Possibly, but only if it occurred at the exact moment of the test.) But these would have muddied Koskoff's theory.[171] He chose not to ask them. Instead, apparently satisfied, he said he had nothing further and yielded his seat to Doyle, whose deliberateness as he approached the same uncertainties was palpable.

"Doctor," Doyle began funereally, "with respect to that retroplacental bleed"—the second, embellished blood clot that Doyle suspected Koskoff of throwing in as a ringer—"isn't it true that it's impossible for you to say that that was implicated in B's death?"

"Yes," Benirschke said.

"Okay. So when we're talking, in your opinion, about the *causes* of the death of Baby B, you're not saying that that was a cause?"

"That is correct."

Doyle spoke as if he was worrying every word. His voice was flat, less sonorous than Koskoff's, but deeper and slower. Each of his sentences seemed to have, like each of his cases, a simple theme, which Doyle reduced to a key word or words, then seemed to italicize.

"Now you also mentioned discordancy," he said slowing. "In that context, also, isn't it true that you're *not* saying that the growth retardation or the discordancy caused Baby B's death? Isn't that correct?"

"Correct, yes."

"In your opinion, based upon your training and experience, and your reading of the materials that was supplied to you, the cause of Baby B's death was the *pressure* on the blood vessels of the velamentous cord?"

"Correct."

"All right." He paused meaningfully. "And it's also true, isn't it Doctor, that you *cannot* say with reasonable medical probability how long that process of compression was present?"

Benirschke shook his head. "No, I cannot tell you exactly."

"And isn't it true that you cannot say with reasonable medical probability when that compression began?"

---

[171] These answers would have done more than "muddied" Mr. Koskoff's theory. They may have destroyed his clients' claim against the Norwalk Hospital.

"No, I do not know exactly, no."

"Let's talk a little bit about cord compression," Doyle said. "Even in cases of singletons, cord compression does happen."

Benirschke fiddled with his glasses, put them to his mouth. "Yes, *cord* compression occurs in prolapses of cords."[172]

"And in any pregnancy—I don't mean every pregnancy—but it's not unusual for there to be intermittent pressure on the cord. It comes and it goes."

"Ah, I don't think that's correct," Benirschke said. "I think that in labor perhaps it is, but not during the intrauterine state of affairs."

"Okay. Now in twin pregnancies, as opposed to singletons, is there an increased risk of cord pressure, from whatever source?"

"In monoamniotic twins there is, not in other twins." Little Tony and Michael, each held in their own sac, were diamniotic.[173]

"And, in cases where there's velamentous cord insertion, which is what we have here, isn't it true that the risk associated with that condition increases dramatically the mortality and morbidity rate?"

Benirschke's steepled forefingers played against his lips. "Yes," he said. "Twinning does. Monochorionic twinning does. And velamentous insertion does. All of them are incremental."

"All right," Doyle said. "And the reason there's more risk of undue pressure is that the cord of the twin is *not protected* with what's known, as you describe, as Wharton's jelly."

"No. The cord is. The blood vessels, from the point of insertion of the cord onto the membrane, are no longer protected."

"And that increases the risk of problems related to pressure on those vessels?"

"Yes."

Doyle sweated each new answer. He didn't know what Benirschke would say, only that he would "call it as he sees it." Like Koskoff, he wanted to take him as far as he could, then stop, but he was groping in the dark. He didn't know where the edge was. Measuring every word, he tiptoed on.

---

[172] Notice how Mr. Doyle has—up to this point—successfully conducted a careful, leading cross-examination of Dr. Benirschke. The witness has been restricted entirely to do short, predictable answers. For each of the preceding six questions, consider what the examiner would have to know to be confident that he would get the desired answer.

[173] Now the pattern has broken down. Dr. Benirschke has given two unexpected and unfavorable answers in a row. With the wisdom of hindsight, can you say how Mr. Doyle could have avoided these mishaps? And what sort of preparation (if any) would have prevented them in advance?

"Now, you've told us that it is your opinion, based on reasonable medical probability, that Baby B died on Saturday, March thirty-first. That's the day before delivery. Is that correct?"

"Yes."

"And isn't it true that, in your medical opinion, the sole cause of the injuries to Twin A—Tony—is related to the death of Twin B on Saturday, March thirty-first?"

"That's correct."

"Because of the process that you described to Mr. Koskoff."

"Yes," Benirschke said. He was suddenly grim.

"And isn't it true that prior to March thirty-first there is nothing in the medical records that you reviewed to indicate that there was a problem with this twin pregnancy?"

"I did not see any such evidence."

"Now something happened on Saturday that killed Baby B. Is that correct?"

Benirschke smiled at the obviousness of the question. "Sure."

"Because that's when he died. Right? Correct?"

"That's *apparently* when he died. Because two days before, somebody heard two heartbeats."

"You know from the records that the nurse-midwife heard two healthy heartbeats on March thirtieth."

"I know she heard two heartbeats," Benirschke said, quickly adding, "I don't know about the health."[174]

"And then something happened between that time and the time of Baby B's death on Saturday, March thirty-first."

"Yes."

Doyle so far had been "dancing on eggs," he says, but he now grew bolder. He still didn't know what Benirschke would say about the cause of Michael's death—the next obvious question—but he knew what he *had* said, at his deposition. Doyle seized on it. He handed Benirschke a copy of the transcript and asked him to follow along as he read aloud.

---

[174] Mr. Doyle tries to get Dr. Benirschke to agree that the heartbeats that were heard two days before the delivery were "healthy." This, of course, would lend support to his theory that the event that caused Twin B to die (and that, as a result, devastated the surviving twin) was sudden and undetectable. But Mr. Doyle has pushed too far; Dr. Benirschke won't agree, and emphasizes that Twin B might not have been healthy at that time. What should Mr. Doyle have done to prevent this?

"Mr. Koskoff asked you a question," Doyle said. He was pleased to discover that it was Koskoff, not Hunt, who'd asked it. " '*Can you tell me whether or not, aside from the thrombosis which ultimately killed Baby B, would it be likely that thrombi would develop in a velamentous cord insertion over a period of time?' Ms. Hunt: 'Object to the form. That wasn't his testimony. The Witness*'—this is you, Doctor—"

"I'm going to object to that question," Koskoff said.[175]

Doyle, ignoring him, kept on. "—'*Yeah, I don't think that the thrombosis killed the baby. I think it is the compression more likely of venous return that eventually led to so significant a hypoxia that the baby died, but the thrombus betrays the compression of the blood vessels.' Question: 'So that plays a part.' Answer: 'I believe the thrombosis signifies that there has been reduced blood flow through those blood vessels and that compression was the most likely cause and possibly . . . twisting . . . of . . . the . . . cord, but that this reduced venous return led to the death of that baby.'* Did I read that correctly?"

"Yes," Benirschke said.

Doyle lit up. "Isn't it true, Doctor, that you're not ruling out that what happened on Saturday, March thirty-first, was a cord accident, such as you described in your deposition, as a possible twisting of the cord? That could have happened, isn't that true?"

"It *could* have happened, but—"

"Right. And isn't it true that because you cannot tell us when the compression began that you can't rule that out?"

Koskoff interrupted: "I'll object to the point of that question. I don't think that—"

"I don't care what you think," Doyle snapped. "You can object to the form and it'll be ruled on at the time of trial."[176]

Benirschke clarified: "If a sudden twisting of the umbilical cord is what killed the baby, then there would have been no thrombi. The thrombi are clearly from some prior event."

"I understand that there were some thrombi," Doyle said, his voice ascending contemptuously. "But that thrombi didn't kill Baby B, did it?"

---

[175] Can you tell the basis for this objection? (As before, supra note 168, the judge will rule on it at trial—if there is a trial.)

[176] It's true, as Mr. Doyle seems to be saying, that other than objections to the form of the question, objections are not necessary at this point to preserve issues for decision by the trial judge. See supra, note 168. But both attorneys have been making objections that don't go to the form of questions. In this case, what (if anything) is the basis for the objection? And why, in your opinion, has Mr. Koskoff made it?

"It betrayed the slowing of the circulation."

"It betrayed that there was some pressure, earlier on; you can't exactly say when, but you described it as at a different time, two, three days. But we know this," Doyle asserted. "Whatever caused that thrombi two or three days before delivery did not kill Baby B?"

"The thrombi didn't."

"What killed Baby B was what happened on March thirty-first. Isn't that correct?"

"Sure. It died—"

"Right," Doyle snapped. "And something happened. And so, now, isn't it true that you can't sit here and tell us that based on reasonable medical certainty that there wasn't a sudden cord accident, a twisting of the cord, that led to Baby B's death? Isn't that correct?"

"I can only tell you what the medical probabilities are," Benirschke said, clearly frustrated. "Those probabilities are, because it happens in many other babies, that there is an *incremental* decrease in venous return because of compression of the velamentous vessels. That's all I can tell you. I was not there, I did not know the position of the baby; I have no evidence that there was a sudden twisting of the umbilical cord."

"And you don't have any evidence that there wasn't."

Benirschke shrugged and shook his head, his palms lifted. "I don't know," he said.

"You don't know," Doyle repeated.

"The obstetrician could tell you at the time of the delivery," Benirschke suggested.[177]

For fifteen seconds the camera's eye lingered on Benirschke as Doyle pondered his next move. The doctor nibbled on his half-folded plastic eyeglass temples, staring in anticipation. Then, when Doyle said nothing, Benirschke's expression changed. He didn't admire Doyle's gamesmanship, but he had to admit that it had worked. It was true, he didn't know what had killed the baby, and he couldn't exclude a sudden accident, though science and probability suggested a gradual demise. A faint smile flickered across his lips. Then, seeming to think better of it, he closed his mouth, shot a glance at the ceiling, and resumed his vigil.

---

[177] Mr. Doyle has gotten Dr. Benirschke to agree that he doesn't know for sure that Twin B didn't die from a sudden umbilical cord accident. But how impressed are you by this concession? How impressed do you think a jury would be?

"Doctor," Doyle began, slowly again, "in this case, the only evidence you found of cord compression prior to Saturday, March thirty-first, when Baby B died, was the thrombosis that you indicated was produced two or three days before birth. Is that correct?"

"Right." Benirschke looked glum. He picked up his mug and drained it.

"And there wasn't evidence, from what you saw, of thrombosis prior to that time?"

"No. There was none."

"Thank you," Doyle said. "I have nothing further."

Koskoff jumped in immediately. "Doctor," he said, "did you see if any *tests* were run by anyone in order to *detect* the presence of any such compression?"

"Objection," Doyle interrupted. "Beyond the scope of my cross-examination."[178]

Benirschke acknowledged that he hadn't.

Koskoff went on. "And you mentioned that the thrombus formed two to three days before delivery. Can you tell us whether or not the slowing of the circulation preceded that?"

"That's the commonest antecedent to thrombus formation."

"And you expressed the opinion to Mr. Doyle that that's what occurred in this case. Is that correct?"

"That's correct."

"And the cause of the slowing of the circulation was what?" Koskoff asked.

"My opinion is the compression of the branch vessels in the membrane."

"And the compression was caused by what?"

"By an expanding fetal mass," Benirschke said. "Commonly, it is the head, but it could be other portions of the body."

"The baby's getting bigger," Koskoff said.

"That's right."

"And is that a sudden process or an incremental process?"

"I'm going to object," Doyle said, "on the grounds that it's leading."

---

[178] *Is* the question beyond the scope of the cross-examination? Is that an objection to the form of the question?

"I'll withdraw the question. Earlier," Koskoff said to Benirschke, "you said that it was an incremental process. What does the word 'incremental' mean?"

"I stated earlier, as the baby grows, the pressure increases on those vessels."

"And you also mentioned that there was no evidence to support a sudden cord accident?"

"I'm gonna object," Doyle blurted, "on the grounds that the question is leading."[179]

"Is there any evidence of a sudden cord accident?"

Doyle repeated: "I object to the question on the grounds that the question is leading."

"I know of no such evidence." Benirschke generally regarded lawyers' objections as attempts to stanch the flow of truth. He suppressed a sneer.

"I have no further questions," Koskoff said.

"Nothing further," Doyle said.

Benirschke snickered, then plucked the microphone wire from his tie as if it were a leech. He was disgusted. All he'd wanted to do—all he ever wanted to do—was to say what, medically speaking, probably had occurred. But lawyers, he believed, "don't really want the truth, they just want to bend the truth to their party's interest." They were conspirators *against* the truth, he thought, asking narrow, partial, indirect questions from which they hoped certain assumptions would be inferred, then objected when the other side made the least effort to enquire further. "They never hear what you want to say," he says bitterly. "That's what hurts so much."[180]

Doyle left Benirschke's office worried that Koskoff had won. "Michael didn't get all he wanted," he would say, but he thought Koskoff had gotten most of it. Benirschke had clearly depicted a pregnancy gone sour, a progressively worsening situation in which Michael Sabia's death and Little Tony's injuries had been amply foreshadowed. With so much going wrong, how could a jury not conclude that the end was inevitable?

True, Doyle had kept Benirschke from ruling out a sudden cord accident, but the doctor had done so grudgingly, only conceding that in a case without a precise diagnosis anything was possible. His

---

[179] Is Mr. Doyle accomplishing anything by these objections to leading questions? Do they go to the form of the questions?

[180] If that is Dr. Benirschke's view, why has he agreed to be a witness in this case? And in particular—given that he believes that the tragedy the Sabias' have suffered was not preventable—why has he testified for the plaintiffs?

concession wasn't much to stand on, and Doyle feared Koskoff had more than made up for it with his drumbeat of dangerous anomalies—velamentous cord insertion, thrombi, unequal placentation, growth retardation, discordancy. He was miffed that Koskoff had even slipped in the placental abruption, which was a nonissue. "Michael's very clever," he says.

And yet both of them had stopped short of asking the real question—was Twin B's death preventable? Koskoff most likely avoided it because he knew what Benirschke's answer would be; Doyle, because he didn't.[181] Did the presence of the thrombi indicate an event that could have been diagnosed with fetal monitoring? And if so, could the outcome have been foreseen? These issues were the heart of the case.

Benirschke himself strongly believed that the answer to both questions was no, that what had happened, while gradual, was beyond anyone's ability to diagnose or arrest. He had no faith that the twins could have been saved. As competent perhaps as any expert in the world to say whether or not the hospital was at fault by not anticipating Michael Sabia's death, he was convinced that it wasn't. He says today that he regretted not being allowed to say so.

But the jury would never hear Benirschke's opinions. In a courtroom, unlike a morgue or a lab, truth emerges not from an accretion of carefully collected information but from a paradox: the only questions answered are those that are asked, yet the only ones asked are those to which the answers are already known, or at least suspected. Benirschke had hoped to tell the jurors what he thought about the issue of the hospital's blame. No one's views were more authoritative or crucial to their ability to reach a proper reckoning. But Doyle and Koskoff, joining preemptively to edit him, combined to bar him from addressing the subject.

On December 24, 1993, the Sabias settled their claim against Norwalk Hospital for $6.25 million, almost all of which was paid by the hospital's insurance carrier.[182] Dr. Benirschke, after hearing of the settlement, wrote in his file: "This is the second case of gross injustice in a twin case that I have seen."[183]

NOTES

(1) *Sabia v. Norwalk Hospital* was not a landmark case. It made no new rule of law, set no general precedent, and had no lasting impact on

---

[181] *Why* did Mr. Doyle not know the answer to this question? You should know that he was brought into the case at a late stage, after Dr. Benirschke's discovery deposition. Is that a sufficient explanation?

[182] Werth, supra note 165, at 365–370.

[183] Id. at 374.

anybody other than those immediately involved. Nonetheless, it was a big case, as medical malpractice lawsuits go. The total of the two settlements—$7.6 million—reflects the high cost of lifetime care for a nearly totally incapacitated newborn; for the defendants (the hospital and the obstetrician, and their insurance companies) the stakes were high, for the plaintiffs—a working-class family—they were huge. As a result, the expert testimony on which the case entirely depended was very carefully prepared. But it was never presented—since the case was settled—except for this deposition, which was recorded in advance, and which may have helped persuade the hospital to settle for a large amount rather than risk a trial.

(2) Dr. Bernirschke's testimony concerns a unique historical event: the circumstances of the tragic birth of Anthony John Sabia and his stillborn brother Michael Sabia, on April 1, 1984. It is impossible to *know*, after the fact, what killed Michael Sabia *in utero*, or exactly when he died, or whether the process could have been detected in time to save his brother. Dr. Benirschke had clear and persuasive opinions on both the cause of Michael's death and the possibility of saving Little Tony. Other doctors who were deposed had different views: **Why was Dr. Benirschke so important?** The plaintiffs' lawyer—Mr. Koskoff—took a great risk in using him as a witness. **Do you think Dr. Bernirschke was sufficiently persuasive on the issues on which he testified (cause of death) to be worth the danger and the fuss? What (if anything) made him so effective? Is that sort of presentation the best way to make use of medical knowledge to settle legal disputes?**

(3) On the second issue (the hospital's responsibility for Little Tony's injuries), Dr. Benirschke was equally clear: The hospital was not responsible. They couldn't have prevented this tragedy. Here too, other experts disagreed. But Dr. Benirschke had no doubt; he considered it a grave injustice that the hospital paid so much to settle the claim. **Why then did he agree to testify for the plaintiffs? And why did Mr. Koskoff use him? And, finally, how did Koskoff get away with it?**

C. PSYCHIATRIC TESTIMONY ON FUTURE DANGEROUSNESS AT THE PENALTY PHASE OF A CAPITAL MURDER TRIAL

The first excerpt in this section is from the opinions *Barefoot v. Estelle,* 463 U.S. 880 (1983), in which the Supreme Court addressed the admissibility of psychiatric testimony on the future dangerousness of a convicted capital murderer. Specifically, the issue was whether such testimony is unconstitutional because it is so unreliable that it is likely to produce "arbitrary" death sentences, which the Supreme Court has condemned.[184] One of the psychiatrists whose testimony was at issue in *Barefoot* was Dr. James Grigson. The second excerpt in this section is a transcript from *People v. Frank Orona,* a Colorado capital murder trial in which Dr. Grigson testified seven years after the *Barefoot* decision in the Supreme Court.

BAREFOOT V. ESTELLE
463 U.S. 880 (1983).

JUSTICE WHITE delivered the opinion of the Court.

On November 14, 1978, petitioner was convicted of the capital murder of a police officer in Bell County, Texas. A separate sentencing hearing before the same jury was then held to determine whether the death penalty should be imposed. Under Tex. Code Crim.Proc.Ann. § 37.071, two special questions were to be submitted to the jury: whether the conduct causing death was "committed deliberately and with reasonable expectation that the death of the deceased or another would result"; and whether "there is a probability that the defendant would commit criminal acts of violence that would constitute a continuing threat to society." The State introduced into evidence petitioner's prior convictions and his reputation for lawlessness. The State also called two psychiatrists, John Holbrook and James Grigson, who, in response to hypothetical questions, testified that petitioner would probably commit further acts of violence and represent a continuing threat to society. The jury answered both of the questions put to them in the affirmative, a result which required the imposition of the death penalty.

. . .

[Petitioner argues] that his death sentence must be set aside because the Constitution of the United States barred the testimony of the two psychiatrists who testified against him at the punishment hearing. There are several aspects to this claim. First, it is urged that psychiatrists, individually and as a group, are incompetent to predict with an acceptable degree of reliability that a particular criminal will commit other crimes in the future and so represent a danger to the community. Second, it is said that in any event, psychiatrists should not be permitted to testify about future dangerousness in response to hypothetical questions and without having examined the defendant personally. . . .

The suggestion that no psychiatrist's testimony may be presented with respect to a defendant's future dangerousness is somewhat like asking us to disinvent the wheel. In the first place, it is contrary to our cases. If the likelihood of a defendant committing further crimes is a constitutionally acceptable criterion for imposing the death penalty,

---

[184] See Furman v. Georgia, 408 U.S. 238 (1972). See generally Robert Weisberg, Deregulating Death, 1983 Supreme Court Review 305.

which it is, *Jurek v. Texas,* 428 U.S. 262, 96 S.Ct. 2950, 49 L.Ed.2d 929 (1976), and if it is not impossible for even a lay person sensibly to arrive at that conclusion, it makes little sense, if any, to submit that psychiatrists, out of the entire universe of persons who might have an opinion on the issue, would know so little about the subject that they should not be permitted to testify. . . .

[P]etitioner's view mirrors the position expressed in the amicus brief of the American Psychiatric Association (APA). . . . The amicus does not suggest that there are not other views held by members of the Association or of the profession generally. Indeed, as this case and others indicate, there are those doctors who are quite willing to testify at the sentencing hearing, who think, and will say, that they know what they are talking about, and who expressly disagree with the Association's point of view. Furthermore, their qualifications as experts are regularly accepted by the courts. If they are so obviously wrong and should be discredited, there should be no insuperable problem in doing so by calling members of the Association who are of that view and who confidently assert that opinion in their amicus brief. Neither petitioner nor the Association suggests that psychiatrists are always wrong with respect to future dangerousness, only most of the time. Yet the submission is that this category of testimony should be excised entirely from all trials. We are unconvinced, however, at least as of now, that the adversary process cannot be trusted to sort out the reliable from the unreliable evidence and opinion about future dangerousness, particularly when the convicted felon has the opportunity to present his own side of the case.

. . .

Whatever the decision may be about the use of psychiatric testimony, in general, on the issue of future dangerousness, petitioner urges that such testimony must be based on personal examination of the defendant and may not be given in response to hypothetical questions. We disagree. Expert testimony, whether in the form of an opinion based on hypothetical questions or otherwise, is commonly admitted as evidence where it might help the fact-finder do its assigned job. . . .

. . .

The judgment of the District Court is Affirmed.

. . .

JUSTICE BLACKMUN, with whom JUSTICE BRENNAN and JUSTICE MARSHALL join . . . , dissenting.

. . . The Court holds that psychiatric testimony about a defendant's future dangerousness is admissible, despite the fact that such testimony is wrong two times out of three. The Court reaches this result—even in a capital case—because, it is said, the testimony is subject to cross-examination and impeachment. In the present state of psychiatric knowledge, this is too much for me. One may accept this in a routine lawsuit for money damages, but when a person's life is at stake—no matter how heinous his offense—a requirement of greater reliability should prevail. In a capital case, the specious testimony of a psychiatrist, colored in the eyes of an impressionable jury by the inevitable untouchableness of a medical specialist's words, equates with death itself.

. . .

Doctor Grigson then testified that, on the basis of the hypothetical question, he could diagnose Barefoot "within reasonable psychiatric certainty" as an individual with "a fairly classical, typical, sociopathic personalty disorder." . . . He placed Barefoot in the "most severe category" of sociopaths (on a scale of one to ten, Barefoot was "above ten"), and stated that there was no known cure for the condition. . . . Finally, Doctor Grigson testified that whether Barefoot was in society at large or in a prison society there was a "one hundred percent and absolute" chance that Barefoot would commit future acts of criminal violence that could constitute a continuing threat to society. . . .

. . .

The American Psychiatric Association (APA), participating in this case as amicus curiae, informs us that "[t]he unreliability of psychiatric predictions of long-term future dangerousness is by now an established fact within the profession." . . . The APA's best estimate is that two out of three predictions of long-term future violence made by psychiatrists are wrong. . . . The Court does not dispute this proposition . . . and indeed it could not do so; the evidence is overwhelming. . . . John Monahan, recognized as "the leading thinker on this issue" even by the State's expert witness at Barefoot's federal habeas corpus hearing, . . . concludes that "the 'best' clinical research currently in existence indicates that psychiatrists and psychologists are accurate in no more than one out of three predictions of violent behavior," even among populations of individuals who are mentally ill and have committed violence in the past. J. Monahan, The Clinical Prediction of Violent Behavior 47–49 (1981) (emphasis deleted). . . .

The APA also concludes, see APA Brief 9–16, as do researchers that have studied the issue, that psychiatrists simply have no expertise in predicting long-term future dangerousness. A layman with access to relevant statistics can do at least as well and possibly better; psychiatric training is not relevant to the factors that validly can be employed to make such predictions, and psychiatrists consistently err on the side of overpredicting violence.

. . .

It is impossible to square admission of this purportedly scientific but actually baseless testimony with the Constitution's paramount concern for reliability in capital sentencing. Death is a permissible punishment in Texas only if the jury finds beyond a reasonable doubt that there is a probability the defendant will commit future acts of criminal violence. The admission of unreliable psychiatric predictions of future violence, offered with unabashed claims of "reasonable medical certainty" or "absolute" professional reliability, creates an intolerable danger that death sentences will be imposed erroneously.

. . .

Thus, the Court's remarkable observation that "[n]either petitioner nor the [APA] suggests that psychiatrists are *always* wrong with respect to future dangerousness, only most of the time," . . . (emphasis supplied), misses the point completely. . . .

DISTRICT COURT, COUNTY OF EL PASO, STATE OF COLORADO CASE NO. 89CR2945, DIVISION 2

THE PEOPLE OF THE STATE OF COLORADO, Plaintiff

v.

FRANK MICHAEL ORONA, Defendant

Reporter's Transcript of Proceedings on November 20, 1990, before the HONORABLE RICHARD V. HALL, Judge of the District Court [185]

Appearances:

For the Plaintiff:	Linda McMahan
For the Defendant:	Terri Brake

DIRECT EXAMINATION

BY MS. McMAHAN:

    Q. Good morning, Dr. Grigson. **A.** Good Morning.

---

[185] Because the proceedings that are included in this transcript were never the subject of an appeal, the transcript was never corrected by the court reporter and the parties. As a result, the available version contains a number of obvious errors. We have corrected some of these errors, in consultation with the attorney for the defendant in the case. Whenever the text has been modified, the printed version is placed in brackets. Omissions are indicated by ellipses.

Q. Would you please state your full name for the court reporter? **A.** James P. Grigson, G-r-i-g-s-o-n.

Q. And where are you employed, Dr. Grigson? **A.** Dallas, Texas.

Q. And what is your occupation? **A.** I am a medical doctor. I specialize in psychiatry, primarily forensic or legal psychiatry.

Q. Are you licensed to practice psychiatry in Texas? **A.** Yes, I am.

Q. And for how long have you been licensed? **A.** Since 1960, so a little over 30 years.

Q. Now please tell the jurors a little about your education and background? **A.** Yes, ma'am. I obtained my B.S. degree from Texas A & M University in Texas. I then attained my M.D. degree at Southwestern Medical School, a branch of the University of Texas located in Dallas. Then I spent one year in a rotating internship at the Baylor Medical Center. At the end of that time I decided to specialize in psychiatry, and I spent the next 18 months at Templeman Hospital in Dallas. I then completed the required three years of training, spending 18 months at Parkman Hospital in Dallas. I was chief of psychiatric residence at Parkman during my third year of residency training and I completed the three years. I then went into full-time teaching in the Department of Psychiatry at the Medical School in Dallas. I taught full-time for four and a half years. During that period, I was consultant to the state hospital system for two years. I was consultant to the Texas Women's University Health Center for two years. I was consultant to the Dallas County Health Department for three years. I have been out in private practice now for over 20 years. I have continued to teach throughout that period of time. However, it has been on a limited basis. I am certified by the American Board of Neurology and Psychiatry.

Q. Doctor, what do you do in private practice, what does your practice mainly consist of? **A.** It is almost entirely in the forensic or legal psychiatry.

Q. Would you explain to the jurors what forensic psychiatry means? **A.** Forensic psychiatry describes a branch of medicine primarily involving psychiatry and the law. The majority of the work that I do is at the request of various judicial district judges. I primarily [practice] in Dallas and in the State of Texas, to examine individuals to determine whether or not they are competent to stand trial. In other words, it does involve whether or not a person was sane or insane at the time of an alleged offense, whether the individual is, if given probation, in need of psychiatric treatment, whether or not the individual represents a continuing threat to society. That is most of the type of work that I do.

Q. Dr. Grigson, who usually calls upon you to give these kinds of expert opinions? **A.** It primarily comes from the various felony judges in the state.

Q. And are you often called upon by courts to also do psychiatric examination of people charged with serious criminal offenses? **A.** Yes, ma'am.

Q. Do you have any idea how many times you have done such evaluations and expert opinions in the criminal realm during the past 20 to 25 years? **A.** I have examined a little over 12,000 individuals that had criminal charges against them. Usually, it is about [510] psychiatric examinations a year.

Q. Now, concerning the criminal charged with murder, how often have you been called upon to render an expert opinion for that sort of crime? **A.** I have [examined] almost 1,300 individuals that were charged with offenses of murder.

Q. Concerning capital cases where the death penalty is being considered, how many times have you rendered an expert opinion in this area? **A.** I have examined over—well, to be exact, 396 individuals that were charged with the offense of capital murder.

Q. Now, do you only do this in the State of Texas? **A.** No, I have worked with attorneys in North Carolina, in the State of Louisiana, Arkansas, Oklahoma, New Mexico, Arizona, but most of it has been in the State of Texas.

Q. Doctor, do you normally testify for one side or for the other side, for the defense or the prosecution? **A.** I never do testify for anyone. Probably more frequently I'm called by the state, but I don't testify for the state or for the defense for those hearings.

Q. Would—could you explain that, please, to the jury? **A.** It means I look at an individual or examine an individual and take a look at the case and form an opinion based upon my experience, based upon the facts that are given to me and probably the majority—well, overwhelming majority of the time that opinion is probably beneficial to the state and the state will then call me to testify on behalf of the state. But I never testify for or against anyone.

Q. Dr. Grigson, have you ever rendered an opinion that was favorable for the defense and then called by the defense to testify, and I'm talking about capital murder cases? **A.** Well, the 396 individuals that I examined with capital murder charges, there were 176 that I said did not represent a continuing threat, that they were not dangerous, so that is about 40-something percent. Then in actual court cases, I have testified in four different occasions where it actually went for trial that the individual did not represent a continuing threat.

Q. Dr. Grigson, is it your experience sometimes that when you render an opinion that the person you have examined does not constitute a continuing threat to society it indicates those do not go to trial? **A.** Right. Only four out of [176] ever were tried as a capital murder case.

MS. McMAHAN: Your Honor, at this time I would offer Dr. Grigson as an expert in forensic psychiatry with the emphasis on death penalty cases.

. . .

THE COURT: The Court will allow the witness to testify [as an expert]. . . .

BY MS. McMAHAN:

Q. Dr. Grigson, did my office contact you and provide you information concerning this Defendant, Frank Orona? **A.** Yes, you did.

Q. Specifically, did you review the police reports concerning the homicide of John Cook? **A.** Yes, I did.

Q. Did you review police reports and arrest warrants that pertained to the crime committed against Sandy Harrell Bigelow in 1981? **A.** Yes, I did.

Q. Additionally, did you review the Colorado Department of Corrections records pertaining to this Defendant? **A.** Yes, I did.

Q. Did you review the reports of Dr. Alice Brill and Dennis Kleinsasser (sic) pertaining to this Defendant? **A.** Yes, I did.

Q. Doctor, are you familiar with the term "antisocial personality disorder"? **A.** Yes, I am.

Q. Are you familiar with the term "sociopath"? **A.** Yes.

Q. Could you tell us what the two terms means, and if it is one and the same? **A.** Antisocial personality disorder comes out of the [Diagnostic and Statistical Manual, Third] of the American Psychiatric Association. It is a—simply a term to describe individuals that have certain characteristics. It is the slang term for the prior term, which would be sociopath or psychopath, so all three of these terms are interchangeable. In trying to communicate to another person what you are talking about, what are the characteristics of a sociopath or antisocial personality disorder. The antisocial personality disorder is not an illness that is a disease. It is a defect, it is simply an individual that has certain characteristics, most notably is the fact that they do not have a conscience like the rest of us. At a fairly early age, most of us develop a conscience with feelings of guilt, shame, embarrassment, and we don't know why certain individuals do not develop consciences. They don't feel the guilt. They don't feel the shame. They don't feel the embarrassment that the rest of us feel. They are individuals who are only interested in their own self-pleasure, their own gratification. They continually manipulate. They continually break the rules. Some of them completely disregard, for instance, other people's property and on a small percentage of these people they have complete disregard for other human beings' lives, but there again, primarily interested in whatever they want, and no consideration or concern for what it might cost another person either in terms of their property of their lives.

Q. Dr. Grigson, are there varying degrees of sociopaths and, in other words, do people start out being antisocial or sociopathic or do they progress during their lives? **A.** No, there are different degrees. You have individuals that they will perhaps only break relatively minor rules, perhaps their entire life, but [they] don't escalate up in terms of violence. You have other individuals who would be considered your more serious sociopaths and that they have what is called an escalating scale of violence. They may start out breaking relatively minor rules, and then it becomes more and more major, more serious type of criminal offenses, and your most serious, of course, would be those individuals that end up killing people. That is really as severe as a sociopath can become.

Q. Can you treat someone who is a sociopath? **A.** Well, whenever you get them at a very early age, five, ten years of age, with the very best treatment plan and there is no medication that cures this or modifies this, but if you put them into a setting where there are very rigid rules and regulations are enforced and at an early age, one-third will show improvement, one-third will remain the same, one-third will actually get worse. After an individual has gotten to the point of adulthood, even that type of treatment setting is of no benefit, that they will conform for a given set of time and many doctors, psychiatrists and law enforcement agencies will think at that point that modification of their behavior has occurred, and as soon as the supervision is withdrawn, then they revert right back to the same type of behavior that they have been involved with previously.

. . .

Q. Doctor, you have testified before to your psychiatric opinion regarding someone's personality or makeup in a criminal case concerning maybe their past behavior or their future behavior? Is that a fairly common field of psychiatry? **A.** Well, particularly in my type of work, it is very common. Psychiatrists are making those types of predictions with regard to hospitalization, hospitals outside criminals area do a similar type of thing.

Q. Do you have any idea how many times you have done that in the past, predicted either past behavior or future behavior based on information you received? **A.** Well, probably in every one of these 12,000 cases I examined and certainly in the 1,400 courts that I have testified in, that came about, so almost in all of those that involved criminal charges.

Q. Doctor, so, is this your opinion that there is a way to predict future behavior of an individual by looking at past behavior of an individual? **A.** Oh, absolutely. You can't just take a person off the street and make some sort of prediction, but it is sort of like a horse race. If you look at the horse's background, you have a better indication of what he is likely to do in the future. The same is true with individuals, that their past history is of extreme importance.

Q. Are you called upon constantly, not just in sentencing-type hearings, to predict what someone might do in the future based on past behavior? **A.** Yes, I am.

Q. Can you give descriptions, examples of other types of commitment procedures or hearings where this information is called upon daily by psychiatrists? **A.** Right. Outside of the legal criminal field, psychiatrists often see a patient that comes in, and they are very depressed and they are thinking about giving up or they can't go on, you are going to consider the possibility of suicide, and whether the possibility of hospitalization is necessary or sometimes an antidepressant-type medication. That happens fairly frequently. An individual that is suffering from delusion or hallucinations, is hospitalization going to be required? Those are decisions that psychiatrists make pretty much every day. A lot of the types of decisions that I have to make is—about 40 percent [are questions of] incompetency, schizophrenics, and how dangerous are they to themselves and to others, do we really require commitment to the hospital.

Q. What kinds of information do you need, Dr. Grigson, before you can make those kinds of expert opinions? **A.** Well, preferably you know, I would like to be able to examine the individual. You get their childhood, early development, education history, marital, family, medical history and criminal areas. You—most important what type of criminal activity they have been involved in in the past and anytime psychiatric treatment or psychiatric hospitalization has occurred and then of paramount importance is the actual facts that are related to the particular charges that they are facing, what went on prior to the offense, during the offense, and then after the offense itself.

Q. Doctor, how about a hypothetical situation. Can you predict a hypothetical situation given to you if given enough—enough of what someone might do in the future? **A.** Sure, if you put enough information about them, then you can make a prediction based upon that information.

Q. At this time, doctor, I'm going to give you a hypothetical situation and with certain facts and I'm going to ask you to assume that the facts that I give you and the hypothetical are true and at the end of the hypothetical I'm going to ask your professional, expert opinion concerning whether or not the person in the hypothetical would be a continuing threat to society. Doctor, assume that a 29-year-old person murdered a 72-year-old gentleman for money, mainly to get his car out of the impound lot and to stay out of jail. Further assume that that person got the man, robbing him of cash, wallet and credit cards. Additionally, the person forced the man to write him two checks for cash as evidence by the elderly man's tremor, in the tremor in the writing, and the younger person's palm print on the back of the elderly man's check. Further assume that the younger man went to two banks, and wiped out the elderly man's bank account. Assume the elderly man had never ever overdrawn before on his account. Assume that the financial situation of this younger man, and I'm talking about two checking accounts were closed based upon overdrafts, that he was behind in his mortgage, utilities cut off, water cut off, no phone, a $6,000 debt to the court, and had not held a job for several years, so really had no source of income. Assume after stabbing the elderly man, 13 times, he dumped him in a deserted area of town without identification, and without his clothes, which he had burned after the murder. The younger man, over a span of a week, used the elderly gentleman's credit cards to purchase drinks, VCR, television, clothing, a black leather jacket, and to buy some new shoes. Further assume, Dr. Grigson, that at the time of this murder, this younger man was on probation for a Class Three felony of first degree burglary involving a deadly weapon. Also assume that in that case he took a woman, at gun point, drove her in her own car, forced her to open [Germer's] and took money out of the safe and eventually left her taped and gagged in her own car. Additionally assume that this same person has a pattern of drinking and driving and eluding police officers. Assume this same person has had a sawed-off shotgun found in his car. Additionally, this person has a history of early childhood theft, and this person has a history of manipulating others, lying to others, and making excuses for his behavior. Doctor, based upon this hypothetical and based upon information that you have been provided with in this particular case, do you have an expert opinion concerning the person in this hypothetical?

MS. BRAKE: Judge, I'm going to object to that hypothetical. It is the most crude set of facts that I have ever heard.

THE COURT: Would you like to add some items to the hypothetical?

MS. BRAKE: It is her question. I would be happy to cross, but she is the one who is obligated to give a correct statement of facts, and it is not.

THE COURT: The jury will evaluate the validity of the hypothetical for itself. And Defense counsel may pose a different hypothetical to the witness during cross-examination.

MS. McMAHAN: Thank you, Your Honor.

BY MS. McMAHAN:

Q. Dr. Grigson, based upon this hypothetical, and based on the information the People have provided to you concerning this case, do you have an expert opinion concerning whether or not the person in the hypothetical could be a continuing threat to society? **A.** Yes, I do.

Q. Now, I also want you—before I ask you what that opinion is, do you also have an expert opinion if that person was a member of the society of a prison population, I am also going to ask you whether he could be a continuing threat in that society, what is your expert opinion? **A.** It is my opinion, based on this information, that the person you described would represent a continuing threat, no matter what type of society they were in, a penal society, or out in the free world, that they would go—continue to commit future acts of violence.

Q. What is the basis of your opinion? Why do you say that, Dr. Grigson? **A.** Well, you have an individual that started at an early age with disregard to the rules in terms of stealing. Many kids do that. I mean, that is not uncommon, but then their behavior begins to conform, but you are describing an individual that goes from what I would consider small-type stealing, or petty theft-type up to kidnapping a woman, which is a very violent act, particularly whenever you are talking about with a weapon involved, you have got a robber-type of thing. That is a real major type of criminal type of offense, and then you have like the eluding of the police, you have got disregard for the law, disregard for authority figures. This is an extremely bad sign. Then, combined with the other acts of violence, then when you have like a 72-year-old man that only weighs 130 pounds that is stabbed 13 times, I mean, that is what you really call a senseless—totally, there is no reason—needless type of killing, and for the amount of dollars that are involved, I mean, that is not placing human life as very valuable, so that becomes extremely important in terms of what this individual would then do in the future, and it would be continuing acts such as that that you describe.

Q. Doctor, what if the person in the hypothetical has a long history of alcohol abuse. Would that change your opinion that that person could still be a continuing threat to society? **A.** No, absolutely not. You have many individuals that have addictions to alcohol or to drugs that do not go out and are involved in this type of goal-directed criminal behavior. Alcohol and drugs doesn't make you do this. This is a criminal-type mind that is at work.

Q. How about if you found out that person in the hypothetical lost his mother, his brother was killed around the same time frame, back in 1987, and his girlfriend and child deserted him in 1988. Would this change your opinion about whether or not this person would be a continuing threat to society? **A.** Absolutely not. In our society, that happens all too frequently, but it doesn't cause people to go out and become involved in this type of violent behavior. No, it would not change.

. . .

Q. Dr. Grigson, what if the person in the hypothetical had also taken steps at rehabilitation, had appeared interested in and self-motivated to change his drinking behavior in the past, would that change your opinion? **A.** No, that is quite typical, that type of behavior that you are describing and an individual will perhaps go to AA and do well for a period of time. They will get a job and pay taxes like the rest of us for a period of time. They will be seemingly responsible on the surface, and yet their mind continues to work in the criminal set, so they go right back to breaking the rules again.

Q. Thank you, doctor. I have nothing further, Your Honor.

. . .

CROSS-EXAMINATION

BY MS. BRAKE:

Q. Dr. Grigson, are you an ethical man? **A.** Absolutely.

Q. Have you ever been reprimanded by the American Psychiatric Association for giving testimony just like the testimony you are giving here today to this jury because it is unethical, is that true? **A.** No, that is not true. I have been censured on two occasions.

Q. Dr. Grigson, I'm sorry, just answer the questions. Thank you. Let me show you Defendant's Exhibit Nine, that is a letter of censure written to you by the American Psychiatric Association dated November the 1st, 1982? **A.** True.

Q. It is a letter stating you are reprimanded and this letter will serve as a reprimand. Let's talk about this. . . .

. . .

Q. You are known across the country as "Dr. Death," are you not? **A.** I have been referred to that.

Q. In fact, a lot of the publicity calls you Dr. Death? You are pretty notorious with that nickname, aren't you? **A.** It is somewhat.

Q. Are you aware of any publicity calling you Dr. Fair? **A.** Probably appropriate.

Q. Dr. Life? **A.** Dr. Life? Okay.

Q. Dr. Grigson, the letter of [reprimand], now this is something that was addressed to you, correct? **A.** Right, that is true.

. . .

Q. Now, this letter says that this complaint was filed against you for violation of ethics, correct? **A.** That is true.

Q. It alleges as a violation that you claimed 100 percent predicting dangerousness in the sentencing portion of a capital murder trial? **A.** That is what it says.

Q. I am right? Thank you, doctor. And further you testified at the trial without ever conducting an examination of the defendant, correct? **A.** That is true.

Q. And it says that you are found guilty of the ethical violation, correct? **A.** Correct.

Q. It also describes that you have—we will refer to this that I just read the principles of medical ethics, right? **A.** That is true.

Q. And it says that you have an appeal process, if you want to appeal that? **A.** That is not true.

Q. This is not the first time you have been censored, or reprimanded, cited for unethical conduct, is it? **A.** That was the second time that they were of the opinion that it was unethical.

Q. I take it your ethics are different from the American Psychiatric Association? **A.** I conform my behavior and the practice of medicine to the laws of the United States of America including the law that is handed down by the United States Supreme Court, which that does not conform to.

Q. Well, now, the opinion you are talking about, that is the *Barefoot* opinion, like I said we would get to [it] in a minute, what this really says, but—**A.** Yes, ma'am.

Q. But you were giving these types of opinions and this type of testimony in violation of the medical ethics long before the Supreme Court ever issued the *Barefoot* opinion, correct? Years before that? **A.** Yes, ma'am.

Q. Judges and the Supreme Court have? **A.** Yes, ma'am. I was.

Q. Now,—so, you said you were familiar with the principles of ethics? **A.** Yes, ma'am. I was.

Q. You said—it says that it is unethical for you to do this, correct, to give that kind of testimony? **A.** Well, the judges were saying it was correct. There was a conflict between the two.

Q. I'm asking about your sense of morality, Dr. Grigson, all right? Number one, do you agree with the principles of medical ethics? **A.** No, ma'am. I don't.

Q. So there—let's talk about where these come from. The principles of medical ethics have been in existence since 1957? **A.** Don't know, counsel.

Q. Probably even long before that there were principles involved? **A.** Sure.

Q. The American Medical Association and the American Psychiatric Association go through periodic revisions as to what is ethical and what is not ethical in the practice of medicine, right? **A.** That is true.

Q. And that is what they are all about, right? **A.** That is true.

Q. And so, when you decide how you are going to practice your practice of medicine, is it important for you or not to follow these principles? **A.** Only if they conform to the law that we are to abide by within the state, within the country. Now, if it conflicts with my religion, if it conflicts with the law of the state or the law in constitutionality of the United States, no, I would not abide by those rules.

Q. And it is your opinion that these principles of medical ethics back when you first started giving your testimony, just like the testimony in this case, it is your opinion this violates—that that violates the laws? **A.** That is what the U.S. Constitution states, yes, ma'am.

. . .

Q. Dr. John Monahan . . . you know him, don't you? **A.** No, I don't.

Q. Are you familiar with his studies? **A.** No, it doesn't ring a bell.

Q. You have never heard his studies. **A.** I didn't say that. I said it didn't ring a bell. I have read many studies over the past 25 years.

Q. Dr. John Monahan, upon whom one of the State's experts relied as "The leading thinker on this issue," now this is the Supreme Court, I think, concluded that the best clinical research currently in existence indicates that psychiatrists and psychologists are accurate in no more than one of three predictions of violent behavior over a several-year period. They said that in the opinion, did they not? **A.** That was based on a different type of study.

Q. Did they say that? **A.** If you read it, I will take your word that you are reading correctly.

Q. And you don't even remember Dr. Monahan's study? **A.** No, ma'am, I didn't.

Q. I'm sure you read this because you have had an interest in—**A.** Oh, years ago, sure.

Q. The Court also said ["]all of these professional doubts about the usefulness of psychiatric predictions can be called to the attention of the jury. Petitioners' entire argument is founded on the premise that a jury will not be able to separate the wheat from the chaff. We do [not] share in this low evaluation of the adversary process.["] **A.** Right, I will agree that certainly is true. The jury can separate the wheat from the chaff.

Q. So, the jury can listen to you, and the jury can listen to the authorities, and the jury can listen to other witnesses who the Supreme Court didn't hear their opinion and make an intelligent opinion about whether what you have to say holds any water? **A.** No question about it, they can.

Q. Now, the Supreme Court wasn't unanimous, were they? **A.** I don't recall what the split was, but it is rare that they are, so, I would assume it was not.

Q. So, there were three justices that said in their opinion what you had to say was totally unreliable and that this shouldn't be presented in any way, that a jury shouldn't even—**A.** They were the minority, that it true.

Q. And, in fact, those, three justices of the United States Supreme Court said in the opinion that anytime the Court, now they are talking about the majority of the United States Supreme Court, the ones that said, well, you come in but it is up to the jury to evaluate it, ["]the Court nor the State of Texas has cited a single reputable scientific source contradicting the unanimous conclusion of professions in the field that psychiatric predictions of long-term future violence are wrong more often than they are right.["] That is by—a statement that both the majority and minority agree to, correct? **A.** I think that is true.

. . .

Q. When—now, you have the right to appeal this reprimand that said you acted unethically? **A.** Yes, ma'am.

Q. Did you appeal? **A.** I did.

Q. When you appeal, it goes to the entire medical association, American Psychiatric Association, for a vote, correct? **A.** No, ma'am.

Q. When you—do you remember being in New Orleans, the general membership, where you stood up and you gave your position and said you were trying to explain to the general membership whether—why you said—**A.** But, you said the entire membership. That only goes to those who are present at the meeting.

Q. A meeting of the entire membership, if they wanted to come, correct? **A.** Right, the overwhelming majority are not there.

Q. And everyone who is there gets to vote? **A.** Right.

Q. On whether you are right or wrong, and they voted at that time the ethics committee was right, and you were wrong, didn't they? **A.**

When they sent it to the president of the American Psychiatric Association at that time,—

Q. The vote, Dr. Grigson, the majority vote was that you were unethical, these other colleagues? **A.** Right.

Q. And that is what they wrote in your letter at that time? **A.** Right, that is correct.

. . .

Q. When you come and testify in a capital murder case, you are not coming in at the request of the judge, are you? **A.** No, I am at the request of the defense or the state.

Q. And almost exclusively at the request of the government? **A.** Government overwhelming majority of the time, yes, ma'am.

Q. Now, on four cases that you have testified, capital murder trials that you have testified for defense lawyers in? **A.** Right.

Q. Did you actually testify that the person was not a threat of dangerousness in the future? **A.** Right, I did.

Q. And you gave all your credentials and told the jury your practice and all of that stuff that you have said in here? **A.** Right, I did.

Q. And the jury didn't believe you, did they? **A.** They found one of the guys guilty and that statute, sanity, was not even murder. It was way down below that.

Q. This wasn't capital murder, it wasn't a penalty phase? **A.** Yes, ma'am. That was the guilt or innocence, whether there were guilty of murder or not and they found him—

Q. If I could stop you for a minute? **A.** Okay.

Q. You understand that question, the penalty phase is where punishment is imposed? **A.** Yes, ma'am.

Q. And you don't get to that unless one is convicted of first degree murder? **A.** Yes, ma'am. You get to the penalty phase regardless. There is going to be a penalty phase even if they are convicted of criminal trespassing.[186]

Q. Okay. A penalty phase which deserves the death penalty couldn't occur unless first degree murder?[187] **A.** Right, that is—

Q. Okay. Now, in these three cases then, that you testified for the defense, that the person was not dangerous, in a life or death jury

---

[186] Texas, where Dr. Grigson primarily testifies, is one of just a few states in which juries sentence in non-capital criminal cases. Ms. Brake—who practices in Colorado—misses this point.

[187] And Ms. Brake recovers.

decision, they gave the death penalty in all three of those? **A.** Right, they did. That is true.

. . .

Q. Dr. Grigson, there is—do you follow all the publicity that surrounds your notoriety? **A.** It is impossible to follow [all of] it. Unfortunately, I have seen a lot of it.

Q. There is a stack of articles, some articles that talk about you and you have been in articles in Time magazine, again, lawyers' magazines and New York Times, and so on? Do you collect those? **A.** I have a few of them, yes, ma'am.

Q. You give lots of interviews to members of the press, don't you. **A.** Right, I do.

Q. And you talk a lot about what you do for a living. **A.** I do.

Q. In penalty cases? **A.** Right.

Q. Do you remember seeing an article by Richard Cohen called The Credentialing of America, December the 4th, 1988, marked as Defendant's Exhibit 110? **A.** Right, I have seen that article.

Q. You have seen that, haven't you? **A.** Yes.

. . .

Q. You are aware of lots of publicity and lots of opinions of professionals that say that your predictions of future dangerousness in the certainty that you purport to give to them is just unreliable? You are aware of those, right? **A.** I am.

Q. And this article in particular talks about that as do a whole lot of other articles and lots of professionals, correct? **A.** I don't specifically recall that article. I have read it, but, again, I don't recall which one it was.

Q. The criticism—one of the criticisms from your profession, Dr. Grigson, about you expressing an opinion on future dangerousness that you lend an aura of scientific or—you lend an aura of medicine to what is really just a lay judgment from—that the jury is to make, correct? **A.** No, ma'am. That is incorrect because I have a 25-year experience.

Q. Examining? **A.** Yes, ma'am.

Q. The criticism from your professionals, not your opinion, but your criticism from professionals in your field and these publications, The Credentialing of America, and a lot of others, the criticism, one of them is that you lend an aura of science and lend an aura of medicine to something that shouldn't have it. That is the criticism, isn't it? **A.** No, ma'am. That is incorrect because I have got more experience examining these individuals and—

Q. Would the Court instruct the question—the question is what the criticism, lawyer's opponents say about you? **A.** There is certainly many that say that, yes, ma'am.

Q. And Richard Cohen says that many psychiatrists are appalled by Dr. Death—

THE COURT: Excuse me. We don't wish the document in question to be read from. You may ask rhetorical questions of the witness, but you are not to read from that document unless Mr. Cohen comes and testifies, and then we have a different matter.

Q. Did you—well, you know that is what a lot of the criticism is, isn't it? **A.** I am sorry.

Q. You know that is in a lot of the publications, not just The Credentialing of America, but let me—may I ask him to look at it, Judge?

THE COURT: Yes.

Q. Would you read that part right there (indicating)? **A.** "Ability of Dr. Death to predict the future is beside the point. His real utility is lending his credentials to their hunch and ipso and sort of facto, turning it into a scientific finding."

Q. Thank you. One of the interviews that you gave not too long ago is with a Ron Rosenbaum? **A.** Yes.

Q. And that was in Vanity Fair magazine? **A.** That is true.

Q. Mr. Rosenbaum traveled around with you as you testified in three capital penalty cases in Texas in two days to make those predictions, is that right? **A.** No, it was over an eight-day period.

Q. Okay. Now, when—you talked to Mr. Rosenbaum, didn't you? **A.** Yes, ma'am. I did.

Q. And you told him a sort of a story about your practice and cases you have testified in? **A.** Right. That is true.

Q. And things that happened in court? **A.** Sure.

Q. And he watched you actually to testify, and he watched the defense attorney trying to cross-examine you, didn't he? **A.** Right, he did.

Q. Now, you talked to him—you like testifying in court, don't you? It is a challenge? **A.** It is.

Q. And one of the things you like about it is you like trying to get the best of defense lawyers on cross-examination? **A.** No, ma'am. That is not true. I think what I like the best is trying to get my point across to the jury in terms of why I feel the way I do.

Q. And you have read that article, haven't you? **A.** Yes, I have.

Q. And you said you have a favorite thing, which is to [save] something back for cross-examination to get the best of the defense lawyers, is that true? **A.** That does occur, yes, ma'am.

Q. And Mr. Rosenbaum says ["]the doctor told me of particular relish he has for doing damage to the defense—'I always hold something back for cross-examination.' He said once he was in Lubbock["]—that is your quote, isn't it? **A.** Right, that is true.

Q. And that is because you like it, it is kind of like a game trying to get the best of defense lawyers on cross-examination? **A.** In that what I'm trying to do is defend myself against opposing attorneys to convey my point to the jury in spite of what they are doing to me.

Q. Am I doing something to you? **A.** Oh, yes, ma'am.

Q. Good. You know Mr. Holter (sic), a defense lawyer, Floyd Holter? **A.** Yes, ma'am.

Q. He was one of the defense lawyers that was trying to cross-examine [you] in one of those cases? **A.** Right. That is true.

Q. And Mr. Rosenbaum watched that and wrote about it, didn't he? **A.** Yes, ma'am. He did.

Q. And he talked about Mr. Holter making a fatal mistake—

MS. McMAHAN: Judge, I'm going to object, if you are reading from the article, and strike that as hearsay. We don't have the right to cross-examine the author of this to find out what the full story may be as all we are being told in these reports are bits and pieces.

THE COURT: The witness was also there, and he can respond to your examination, if appropriate.

BY MS. BRAKE:

Q. And he wrote ["D]own Holter fell into a fatal mistake, he fell into a Dr. Death trap when there were two devastating counter punches. That is, after learning Dr. Death's reputation as a killing machine on cross-examination many lawyers told me the best thing to do is not cross-examine the doctor at all to minimize the damage that he can do." I guess I am not too smart—**A.** I think you are very brilliant.

Q. Well, thank you. When you set these traps on cross-examination, you are willing to deceive the jury, aren't you, to say things that aren't true just to get a set trap for defense lawyers and you—**A.** I've never tried to set a trap or anything, nor have I ever deceived juries. Usually, it is the person that is cross-examining me that is trying to deceive the jury, not me, because I'm under oath, and they are not.

Q. Well, let's—**A.** I don't lie.

Q. Let's talk about that. Mr. Holter was cross-examining you and asked the following question[: "I]n that case, the case of *Rodriguez v. Texas*, and did you say Mr. Rodriguez, no matter where he is, will kill again, that was always the question.["] Mr. Holter asked you, right? **A.** Right, that is true.

Q. And he asked you if you reached that question in many cases, didn't he? **A.** Right, that is true.

Q. Mr. Rosenbaum continues that ["T]his might have been a good question as it appeared that the doctor couldn't recall who the hell Rodriguez was[. But] the doctor, a poker player as well as a chess player, absolutely calculated that Holder didn't know the details, either, so he felt free to spring a trap of his own. The doctor remained as if searching his memory, and then suddenly upon a recollection 'Is Rodriguez the one that killed four women and raped 38?' Of course, he had no idea that Rodriguez had done, but what the jury heard was, killed four, raped 38. In the silence that followed, Holter had no idea whether Rodriguez allegedly had killed one or two hundred.["] That is a true account? **A.** Yes, ma'am. That is not a trap. Also, I did not mislead the jury.

Q. Is that simply freedom? Did you answer the question that way, right? **A.** Right.

Q. And you didn't know who Mr. Rodriguez was? **A.** No, I did not.

Q. What you were suggesting was not true, was it? **A.** No, ma'am. Rodriguez could have been the one that was filed in court and could rape 38 other women.

Q. You knew he didn't, didn't you? **A.** No, ma'am. I did not.

Q. You talked about making a prediction of future dangerousness. Now, you go into courts and you say you are 100 percent sure with your opinion of prediction, right? **A.** In terms of the giving an opinion, that is all I am doing, is giving an opinion, and if I felt like I am unable to do so, I would refuse, but if I give an opinion, certainly, I would certainly it or I am not going to share that.

Q. When you give an opinion, perhaps your judgment, you are 100 percent sure? **A.** Absolutely sure.

Q. No doubt at all? **A.** As far as the opinion goes, but it is only an opinion.

Q. But you believe it 100 percent? **A.** Absolutely. I believe my opinion that I give, sure.

Q. And that is one of the things for which you have been found to be unethical, predicting 100 percent certainty in the making it look like that is a medical opinion, correct? **A.** No, ma'am. That is my opinion alone.

Q. And you talk about it in terms of 100 percent accuracy and as a professional to 100 percent you are sure of your opinion? **A.** And the two are completely different.

Q. Well, that is because when you predict 100 percent accuracy, you are saying I'm 100 percent sure I am right. **A.** No, ma'am. I will say in terms of my opinion that I am giving as far as it is concerned I am 100 percent right or if I feel like I am 50, I would say that, or if I say, you know, I really can't give you an opinion, I don't know.

Q. And in that 100 percent figure, what about the 98, or if there's two percent remaining, and when that was, you would indicate? **A.** Right, that is true.

Q. So, you are certainly not telling this jury that you are 100 percent accurate in your predictions of future dangerousness, correct? **A.** I am telling the jury, I don't know of anyone who is 100 percent accurate about almost anything, so, that is true. I am not.

Q. And, in fact, you said that as we went over before all the literature and all the studies, people in your profession say that at best two out of three predictions of future dangerousness are wrong, correct? **A.** Well, that is—has nothing to do with the capital cases, but that is true that if you take all psychiatrists' general predictions, they don't have the experience to make those types of predictions.

. . .

Q. . . . And you talked, doctor, about people who may manipulate and con when you were describing your idea of a sociopath or an antisocial personality disorder, correct? **A.** Yes, ma'am.

Q. And a con man is a shortened term for a confidence man, correct? Is that con man, confidence man? **A.** I don't think of those two topics, I think of a con man as a manipulator, not a confidence man.

Q. Isn't it where it rises to a con? **A.** I don't really know.

Q. Okay. A con man is a person who will try to—well, say, finds a way to try to gain the confidence of the person that they are talking to. For instance, if I talk with you and I'm trying to con you, I'm going to say what I want to say to try to get you to agree with me, or to accept what I am saying, correct? **A.** Yes, ma'am. You have been doing so. You have been conning me, that is true.

Q. I would say you have been conning, too, doctor. There is an art of conning? **A.** Right.

Q. Okay. That is where you try—you watch someone and you want to convince them of something, and you change your behavior, or you change your words to try to get them on your side? **A.** Right.

Q. Is that what it is all about? **A.** Right.

Q. You can do that? **A.** Sure.

Q. When you testify that is what you do to the jury? **A.** I don't con the jury. I'm very honest with them.

Q. Very honest. You have never tried to con them? **A.** Not in terms of the negative sense, I have tried to convince them what I believe is true.

Q. And one of the things you have tried to do is, doctor, watch the jury and try to see who is on there that you think either believes what you are saying and do something directed at that particular juror, or to try to bring them over to your side, is that something that you do in terms of attempting to go up and down the row of jurors and getting their reactions, whether they are looking at you and trying to respond to your question, is that something you do when you testify? **A.** At times, you are right.

Q. And Mr. Rosenbaum, you told Mr. Rosenbaum, when he went around with you, a story about that, didn't you? A story about one time when you were testifying and you saw a juror and you classified that juror as a holdout juror, because you were watching a witness for the prosecution and that juror had her arms folded and had some body language that indicated that she wasn't buying the prosecution's case, right? **A.** That is true.

Q. Do you remember that? **A.** Absolutely, sure.

Q. And you watched that juror and then there was a recess in the courtroom? **A.** Right.

Q. And during the recess, you talked to the prosecutor and said—you said to the prosecutor that juror is not buying this, you are going to lose the case, she was going to hold out for a different opinion, so why don't we—let's talk about her and I want some personal information about her and we will see what we can do about it, and you and the prosecution then went and got the jury questionnaire, you knew what the jurors' responses were? **A.** Right. There was some discrepancies with what you said, but, we did.

Q. You got the jury questionnaires and read about that and you and the prosecution looked for something in that juror's questionnaire that you could use to try to win that juror over, is that—**A.** No, in terms of trying to make her aware of the type of person we were dealing with, I said she is the kind of person that we are dealing with.

Q. And you said that he was the kind of person that would rape a 14-year-old girl and she had a 14-year-old, he was just the kind who would rape? **A.** Sure.

Q. The reason that you went to the jury questionnaire was to get personal information about that juror? **A.** Right.

Q. Was to look for something that you could have the prosecution ask you in your testimony to try and unfold the juror's arms and have her listen? Right? **A.** No, to make her more aware of the type of person that we were dealing with. That was the purpose of it.

Q. So, you found in the questionnaire that she said she had a 14-year-old daughter and told the prosecutor, "Just ask me if he is the type of person that would go for a 14-year-old"? **A.** Right, he had before, right, he had.

Q. And this juror unfolded her arms and you won her over, didn't you? **A.** I didn't win her over, but she was aware of how dangerous he was, and she voted for the death penalty.

Q. You didn't think this was making—**A.** No, it was making her aware of the type of person. Before that point, she was not aware.

Q. Have you seen the questionnaires of these jurors to get information about them? **A.** No, ma'am. I haven't.

MS. BRAKE: I don't have anything further, Judge.

THE COURT: Ms. McMahan?

MS. McMAHAN: Thank you, Judge.

NOTES

(1) Dr. James Grigson used to be notorious. He was a poster child for irresponsible expert testimony.[188] As you see in the transcript, he was twice censured by the American Psychiatric Association, and was generally held in contempt by most of his colleagues. And yet, it was widely acknowledged that he was an uncommonly effective expert witness. **Can you explain why he was so impressive to juries? And can you explain why—considering how much ammunition was available—so few capital defense attorneys conducted the sort of devastating impeachment that you see here?**

(2) As we have mentioned,[189] the type of abuse of expert credentials that Dr. Grigson exemplifies seems to recur in criminal cases. For example, from 1976 until her death in 1987, Dr. Louise Robbins, an anthropologist from the University of North Carolina at Greensboro, testified as a prosecution witness in perhaps twenty cases in the United States and Canada. Her speciality was boot and shoeprint identification. "Give her a ski boot and a sneaker, for instance, and Robbins contended

---

[188] See, e.g., Ron Rosenbaum, Travels With Dr. Death 206–237 (1991); Paul C. Giannelli, "Junk Science": The Criminal Cases, 84 J. of Crim. L. & Criminology 105, 111, 113–117 (1993); George E. Dix, The Death Penalty, "Dangerousness," Psychiatric Testimony, and Professional Ethics, 5 Am. J. Crim. L. 151, 172 (1977); Charles P. Ewing, "Dr. Death" and The Case for an Ethical Ban on Psychiatric and Psychological Predictions of Dangerousness in Capital Sentencing Proceedings, 8 Am. J. L. & Med. 407 (1983).

[189] See supra, pp. 1150–1152.

that she could tell whether the two shoes had even been worn by the same person. Show her even a portion of a shoeprint on any surface, Robbins maintained, and she could identify the person who made it."[190] There was no scientific basis whatever for these claims. No other experts in any related field have ever said they could make such identifications. Nonetheless, Dr. Robbins apparently believed in her unique powers; she certainly was paid well to exercise them, and helped send at least a dozen defendants to prison, and at least one to death row. **In your opinion, why are these extreme cases of improper expert testimony more common in criminal prosecutions than in civil cases? And what can be done to prevent them?**

(3) **Does Dr. Grigson's testimony satisfy** *Daubert*'s **requirements for the admissibility of scientific expertise (or** *Kumho Tire*'s **requirements, if it is considered** *non-scientific* **expertise)? If it were admitted in a federal court, would that be error on appeal?** Of course, ordinary admissibility was not the issue in *Barefoot v. Estelle*. The question was whether it was constitutional error to admit such evidence at the sentencing phase of a capital case. Nonetheless, as Justice Blackmun pointed out in dissent, "reliability" is constitutionally required in capital sentencing hearings. The Court was probably influenced by the fact that psychiatrists (and psychologists and social workers) frequently make predictions about their patients' future behavior in other legal contexts: Civil commitment, child custody, adoption, etc. But perhaps the best explanation for the Court's unwillingness to exclude Grigson's testimony is contained in Justice White's appeal to the Court's own authority: Since the Court had already approved a capital sentencing statute that required lay jurors to make findings on future dangerousness, it could hardly prevent them from hearing testimony on the issue; and if juries must hear evidence on dangerousness, how could the Court exclude psychiatrists from the realm of witnesses who could provide that testimony? **Do you think that argument is persuasive? Could the court have excluded testimony such as Dr. Grigson's—on constitutional grounds—and still upheld the use of future dangerousness as a requirement for imposing the death penalty under the Texas capital sentencing statute?**

(4) **What motivated Dr. Grigson to testify as he did?** There's no easy way to tell, of course, but it's probably fair to assume that he felt he was telling the truth—that he honestly believed that the defendants against whom he testified *were* dangerous, or in any event, that they deserved to be sentenced to death. If so, he no doubt also felt that his appearances as a witness helped serve the cause of justice. But even so,

---

[190] Mark Hansen, Believe It or Not, 79 A.B.A.J. 64 (1993); see also Paul C. Giannelli, The Abuse of Scientific Evidence in Criminal Cases: The Need for Independent Crime Laboratories, 4 Va. J. Soc. Pol'y & L. 439, 457–462 (1997).

how would he justify the *manner* in which he went about presenting evidence? What were his goals, as a witness, and how did he go about achieving them? Consider Dr. Grigson's own description of his function: "Just take any man off the street, show him what the [defendant has] done, and most of them would say the same things I do. But I think the jurors feel a little better when a psychiatrist says it—somebody that's supposed to know more than they know."[191]

(5) Finally, it is important to distinguish the general issue—predictions of future violence—from the type of testimony that Dr. Grigson gave. As we mentioned, predictions of dangerousness are made in many legal contexts, from civil commitment to parole. Recent research suggests that psychiatrists and psychologists can do better at this task than they themselves believed in 1983, when *Barefoot* was decided.[192] Apparently, careful and well-informed professional predictions of future violence are somewhat better than lay predictions—which means that expert evidence from these professionals might improve lay judgments. Or it might not. Even the most optimistic researchers concede that psychiatric and psychological predictions of violence remain highly uncertain. Therefore, this evidence could be prejudicial, if juries rely excessively on unreliable expert opinions. In other words, this area of expertise presents an example of the common problem of balancing probative value against unfair prejudice—*if* the expert opinions are competent, responsible, and careful. The sort of testimony that Dr. Grigson offered, however, is another matter altogether. No respectable group of psychiatrists or psychologists has ever claimed to be able to predict with "100% certainty" that a person will commit future acts of violence, or to be able to make any useful predictions of future violence on the basis of hypothetical questions.

D. RAPE TRAUMA SYNDROME EVIDENCE IN A SEXUAL ASSAULT TRIAL

In the past few decades, American courts have been presented with expert evidence on several of psychological syndromes, including Post Traumatic Stress Disorder, Battered Women Syndrome, and Child Abuse Accommodation Syndrome. Rape Trauma Syndrome (RTS) was first described in the psychiatric literature in 1974,[193] and first presented in trial courts in the early 1980s. It is now generally categorized as a variant of Post Traumatic Stress Disorder (PTSD). Expert testimony

---

[191] John Bloom, Doctor for the Prosecution, American Lawyer, Nov. 1979, pp. 25–26.

[192] See John Monahan, Clinical and Actuarial Predictions of Violence, Scientific Status, in David L. Faigman, et al., Modern Scientific Evidence, vol. 2, §§ 10.9–10:21, pp. 129–154 (2009); John W. Parry, National Benchbook on Psychiatric and Psychological Testimony, 47–50, 222–225 (1998).

[193] A. Burgess & L. Holmstrom, Rape Trauma Syndrome, 131 Am.J. of Psychiatry 980 (1974).

describing RTS, or diagnosing a particular person as suffering from RTS, is commonly offered by the prosecution in sexual assault cases for one or both of two purposes: (1) To explain behavior by the alleged victim that may seem improbable for a person who has been recently raped. (2) To show that the alleged victim was in fact raped. Evidence of the *absence* of RTS is sometimes offered by the defense to show that the victim was not raped. American courts are divided on whether they will admit RTS evidence, and if so for what purpose. The case that follows illustrates both the type of testimony that may be admitted, and the divisions among judges over whether it should be admitted, and if so for what purpose.

UNITED STATES V. ALPHONSO O. HOUSER[194] UNITED STATES COURT OF MILITARY APPEALS
36 M.J. 392 (1993).

CRAWFORD, JUDGE:

The issue in this case is whether the military judge erred in overruling a defense objection to the testimony of a government expert on rape trauma, when the expert had not interviewed the victim.

> [Appellant was convicted of rape by general court-martial. He was sentenced to a dishonorable discharge, confinement for 30 years, and total forfeitures. The Court of Military Review affirmed.]

FACTS

The victim, 15-year-old W, knew appellant's spouse for 9–10 years and appellant for 5 to 6 years. She stayed with appellant and his family during the first few weeks of August 1988 to care for their children. She looked upon appellant and his spouse as her uncle and aunt.

On the evening of August 6, 1988, appellant's spouse went out for the evening. W testified that she fell asleep watching TV in the den; and that appellant woke her and asked her why she was asleep. Thereafter, she fell back asleep. She was awakened with appellant on top of her inserting his penis into her vagina. W testified that she told him to get off and tried to push him away, but he pushed harder and penetrated her. Appellant pulled his penis out of W's vagina only when he heard his spouse's car pull up outside the home. He immediately ran upstairs and got into the shower.

Mrs. Houser knocked on the door and W got up, unlocked the door, and unlatched the chain to let her in. Mrs. Houser testified that she thought it was unusual that the door was chained. W did not immediately tell Mrs. Houser that she had been raped by appellant.

---

[194] The published opinion in this case includes excerpts from the trial record, with omissions indicated by asterisks (* * *). In the edited version presented here, omissions from the published opinion are indicated by ellipsis (. . .), or by substituted text in brackets. The footnotes have all been added.

Rather, she waited until appellant and Mrs. Houser had gone to bed and then went to the bathroom to wash herself off. The next morning W told Mrs. Houser what had happened. When confronted, appellant denied raping W both to his spouse and the victim.

In his opening statement civilian defense counsel raised questions concerning the victim's failure to report and to resist the alleged rape. He further commented that she did not appear anxious. Additionally, he conducted a rigorous cross-examination of W, questioning her about inconsistent acts and statements.

Shortly after this cross-examination, the prosecution offered in rebuttal the testimony of an expert, Dr. Pamela P. Remer, a counseling psychologist and associate professor at the University of Kentucky, to explain rape trauma syndrome to the members. The defense objected to this testimony on the grounds that it "would be more prejudicial than probative." Defense counsel argued Dr. Remer "has not seen or diagnosed the alleged victim, cannot say that she particularly has any symptoms of rape trauma syndrome." Moreover, the defense asserted that Dr. Remer's testimony "can only serve to confuse and mislead the panel."[195]

. . . The judge overruled the defense objection and permitted Dr. Remer to testify. After the prosecution questioned Dr. Remer about her qualifications, the defense conceded that she was "an expert."

Dr. Remer testified as to six general stages of a rape trauma model. She labeled the first stage the "pre-rape stage" wherein: "Some of the common myths are things like that the victim is to blame, that rapes are committed by strangers." She continued:

> The major picture under the rape myth is of a stranger coming up to a woman in a dark alley who rapes her at gun point, and the typical rapist is not like that at all. The typical rape is more likely to be by an acquaintance, about 60% of rapes are done by an acquaintance, that is someone the victim knows. They are more likely to be done indoors than outdoors, and often in the victim's home, or in someone's home. And so we don't have—in lots of cases we don't have a stranger doing something awful and brutal to a woman with the use of a weapon. Most rapes are [by] someone the victim knows, the threat of force and in a protected place.
>
> . . .
>
> [If] it is more than a [sic] just a passing acquaintance, especially if she knows the rapist fairly well, there will usually be a good amount of trust in that relationship, and all of their interactions will be interpreted by the victim within that context of trust. . . . In

---

[195] In a military court martial, the "panel" or "court" is the functional equivalent of the jury in a civilian trial, and the "members" of the panel or court are service personnel who have a roles equivalent to that of jurors.

acquaintance rapes, when the victim and perpetrator [are] in a trusting relationship, the victim is much less likely to recognize she is in danger, because she will be viewing what happens from the aspect of having trust in this person. So that is one thing that—also if you are in an environment that you deem to be safe, your own home, a friend's home, . . . they are more likely not to recognize that it is a dangerous situation, because you have trust in the situation.

. . .

When the attack itself starts, she would then have a period of trying to make sense of what is going on, especially an acquaintance rape, where it is not expected at all, or it is against what she would normally expect from this person. So there would be now and actually throughout a period of—or a lot of confusion on the victim's part about what is happening to me; and of trying to make sense about that. This is happening at the same time that the victim is trying to figure out what do I do, how do I get myself out of this situation. There may be a period of struggling here for victims. There usually is a point at which the victim makes the decision, or realizes that she is not going to be able to stop the rape. . . .

Q. Might they experience some kind of paralysis or feeling of helplessness or—

A. About 45% of the victims in the recent survey that we did, said that they felt motionless; it is often described as a paralysis, [an] easy way to understand is being overwhelmed with fear and unable to move. And as I said, that coupled with the disassociation and the confusion makes it hard to respond.

Dr. Remer testified that the second stage "is the rape . . . itself" and that the third stage is the "crisis stage and it is the immediate period that follows the rape."

She explained that during the third stage the victim is faced with getting her safety and "how is she going to go about handling the aftermath of the rape." Because of what the victim has read or watched on television or in the movies about victims being "to blame," it is "difficult to tell anybody." She continued:

Victims of acquaintance rapes are much less likely to tell anyone, to tell anyone at all, much less to tell more than one person. And again I think it is because the acquaintance rape doesn't fit society's myth of what rape is; and because the victim expects to be blamed for it more, because it doesn't fit that definition. So delays are not uncommon; delays of days, weeks, months, even can occur before the victim—and that some studies, a victim 10 years, 15 years later, have never told.

. . .

Q. In the crisis stage . . . what are the victim's reactions, what does she want to do?

Q. [Sic] Well, she is still in shock, and somewhat still in disbelief about what has happened to her; and, [there is] very much a sorting out process about what just happened. She will be feeling overwhelming amount of fear still; afraid that the attacker might come back; afraid that she will be punished if she tells; afraid others will judge her; and, is just reliving often, over and over again in her own head the events of the attack that just took place; and, so that is the predominant reaction, is fear, and anxiety, and that leads to the victim not wanting to talk about what happened. There are two ends of a continuum, there is no one response to rape. I think one of the myths we have is, that rape victims would be crying hysterically, and that is not the case. There are a variety of responses to rape. On one end of the continuum, would be a super controlled state; that is the victim showing absolutely no emotion; and in fact, she would be characterized by the lack of any emotion on her, be that kind of a [taut], not letting anything out, to the other end of the continuum which can be somebody crying uncontrollably, unable to talk to anybody, that kind of thing.

Q. Within the third stage, would it be uncommon or common that the person would feel unclean after an attack?

A. Another major response, again, I fail to hear from any survivor, in other words, all survivors have said this, that following an attack they feel very unclean; that they have a sense of the rapist being on them and around them, and of wanting to get clean; it is part of needing to put the rape behind them and it is also a part of needing to reaffirm, hey I'm me again, and so it is very common for survivors to bathe, shower, wash clothes. If the attack for instance, occurred in their apartment or something, they would tidy the place up, often, unless they know—get some directions from somebody, the police or rape crisis center that says don't touch anything. The human response, I think, is to get clean, to do something.

. . .

Q. And in the second stage, would the victim's reactions to the rape be at all affected if the rape began while she was asleep?

A. Yes, and I'm going to hedge a little bit here, in terms of saying that it would depend on which stage of sleep the victim was awakened during [sic]. So there is some speculation here. But regardless of the stage of sleep, the victim would not have any forewarning of what was going to happen, if they were awakened while being raped. In other words, they wouldn't have any—see any behaviors of the other person that would give them warning about maybe I'm being in danger here; they wouldn't have any red flags to go for them. I think if a person is awakened out of sleep, again it doesn't matter what stage, they are going to be even more confused about what it is that is happening to me. And finally, if they are awakened in either REM sleep or in stage 4 of sleep, which is a deeper sleep, they are likely to be cognitively disoriented, have trouble processing their thoughts for a few moments, but it would add to the confusion that is normally a part of a rape, and if they are awakened in REM sleep they would even experience a temporary physical paralysis that all of us would experience if we are awakened while we are in REM sleep. That is, our body is unable—physically unable to respond for a few seconds.

Dr. Remer further explained that the third stage "lasts anywhere from a few minutes to up to a year, and it involves a bunch of crisis reactions by the victim in her immediate coping with rape." She also described the other stages. "The fourth stage is called a denial or a getting your life back together stage." The fifth stage is a "reliving stage." She testified that during this stage, there may be "flashbacks" to "the rape itself." She called the sixth stage "an integration or resolution stage, and at this point the victim has resolved most of the negative issues that come from the rape. . . . "

Dr. Remer then testified in response to hypotheticals as follows:

1.   A good caretaker would not want the children "to witness the attack."

2.   If there is "a trusting relationship," the victim would hesitate reporting the attack.

3.   If the victim woke up during an attack, she might fail to resist.

4.   The victim's first account may be distorted.

The concluding testimony was as follows:

Q. Doctor, if a person were experiencing the majority of the symptoms that you have talked about in your model, would they be suffering from a rape trauma syndrome?

A. Yes.   Most likely.   And it is the constellation of symptoms, . . .

. . .

Some of the typical symptoms in the crisis stage are: I talked about the fear; it is very usual for clients to be—for clients—for victims to be depressed and under depression; there are a whole bunch of symptoms, including: often there will be a change in their eating habits, either they eat a whole lot more or they are eating a lot less. Often there will be a change in their sleeping pattern; inability to sleep, nightmares especially, or they are sleeping all the time, and then it is an avoidance of being awake and thinking about the rape that is happening there. They feel sad, that is a part of depression; feel hopeless about the future, often, or feel helpless. They usually have some loss of interest in activities or a loss of energy from their normal way of being; they may be suicidal. The third major area of problems in the crisis stage and then on throughout is, some kind of sexual dysfunction. In one study, 60% of the rape survivors had some kind of sexual difficulty at the time the study took place, so it may be even higher than that actually, if you kept measuring over time. There is usually a disruption in interpersonal relationships, that has to do with the ability to trust others; and I've already talked about work disruption. Those are the major ones.

Q. And again, if the person is experiencing the majority of those types of symptoms, would they be suffering from a rape trauma—

A. What you do is look for a constellation of symptoms, and then assess that in terms of how has this person [sic] from when the trauma occurred, how has this person changed, which makes the symptoms and—since the symptoms come from research on thousands of victims, you can make a reasoned assessment, that this person has been raped.

On cross-examination, Dr. Remer admitted that her model was different from the original rape trauma syndrome model set up by Burgess and Holmstrom, that there are a number of models, and that these models do not contradict her model. Dr. Remer did not evaluate the victim and in fact never met the victim. Dr. Remer admitted that the rape trauma syndrome was not recognized in Diagnostic and Statistical Manual III. She also admitted that a number of the symptoms she had mentioned are caused by other disorders such as post-traumatic stress disorder and that many of these symptoms may also be the result of normal adolescent problems. She further testified that she did not know if the symptoms in her model were experienced by the victim and that she developed her model "to treat clients" so that she might "tailor" her counseling to better help what she termed "rape trauma survivors."

In its closing argument the prosecution said the following about Dr. Remer's testimony:

Dr. Remer, talking about Dr. Remer, you heard her, she was qualified as an expert in rape trauma, and she—and you heard her testimony concerning that there is acceptable reactions to rape, concerning whether you scream out; how much you resist; what sort of symptoms you are going to exhibit afterwards and every one of the symptoms that defense talks about, Dr. Remer said it was a possible reaction and acceptable reaction to being raped.

The judge instructed the court members on assessing the credibility of expert witnesses (there were two) as follows:

> While Dr. Remer was qualified as an expert in the treatment of rape victims, and rape trauma, and she has testified concerning her model and the stages that victims go through and the need to look and see if there is a constellation of symptoms and then try to determine what is the cause of these symptoms.
>
> Now, these witnesses are known as expert witnesses, because their knowledge, skill, training, or education may assist you in understanding the evidence, or in determining a fact in issue. Now, you are not required to accept the testimony of an expert witness, or give it more weight than the testimony of an ordinary witness; but you should consider the qualifications of the expert as an expert witness.
>
> Now, during the course of her testimony, Dr. Remer answered several questions in regards to a hypothetical question. Now, when an expert witness answers a hypothetical question, the expert assumes as true every asserted fact stated in that question. Therefore, unless you find that the evidence established the truth of the asserted facts in the hypothetical question, you cannot consider the answer of the expert witness to that hypothetical question.

DISCUSSION

A. [The court notes that: "Dr. Remer's qualifications are not at issue as defense counsel conceded that she was an expert."]

B. Subject Matter of Expert Testimony

Mil.R.Evid. 702 [like FRE 702] provides that the expert testimony is admissible when "scientific, technical, or other specialized knowledge will assist the trier of fact to understand the evidence or to determine a fact in issue." Mil.R.Evid. 702 is a very liberal standard. . . .

. . . In *United States v. Carter*, 26 M.J. 428 (1988), we held that "rape trauma syndrome evidence is probative . . . on the issue of consent by the victim. . . . " Id. at 429. In *Carter*, the Government qualified an expert on the treatment of rape victims to testify on "rape trauma syndrome," as a type of post-traumatic stress disorder (PTSD). The expert testified that she diagnosed the victim as having PTSD and the victim manifested rape trauma syndrome. See 22 M.J. 771, 772 (ACMR 1986). . . .

. . . In *United States v. Peel*, 29 M.J. 235, 241 (CMA 1989), cert. denied, 493 U.S. 1025, 110 S.Ct. 731, 107 L.Ed.2d 750 (1990), we held it was permissible for an expert to testify that the victim's failure immediately to report the crime "was not inconsistent behavior for a rape victim" and that a victim may act as if the rape never happened. . . .

. . . Thus rape-trauma-syndrome testimony by a properly qualified expert may be admissible to assist the trier of fact to understand the evidence. While in some cases it may be preferable that the prosecution wait until rebuttal, this Court has never limited rape-trauma-syndrome evidence to rebuttal because this would shift the focus to the question of appropriate rebuttal. [Footnote omitted.]

C.   Basis for Expert Testimony

Under Mil.R.Evid. 703, like Fed.R.Evid. 703, an expert's opinion may be based upon personal knowledge, assumed facts, documents supplied by other experts, or even listening to the testimony at trial. . . . Thus, there was no requirement for Dr. Remer to interview the victim before she could testify as to her six-stage model and the symptoms of typical rape survivors.

D.   Relevance

Section IV of the Military Rules of Evidence defines legal and logical relevancy.   Mil.R.Evid. 401 provides that the evidence is logically relevant if the evidence has "any tendency to make the existence of any fact that is of consequence to the determination of the action more probable or less probable than it would be without the evidence." Certain behavioral patterns such as failure to resist or delay in reporting a rape could be confusing to the fact-finders because these may be counter-intuitive. . . .   It is logically relevant for an expert to explain that certain behavior patterns occur in a certain percentage of rape cases or child abuse cases. Id. This is not to say that the offense occurred but, rather, that these events may happen to some victims. Without the testimony the members are left with their own intuition. For these reasons we conclude that Dr. Remer's testimony was relevant.

. . .

F.   Probative Value

Logically relevant and reliable expert testimony "may be excluded if its probative value is substantially outweighed by the danger of unfair prejudice, confusion of the issues, or misleading the members."   Mil. R.Evid. 403.

In determining whether the military judge abused his discretion in balancing probative value with the potential for unfair prejudice, we must examine Dr. Remer's testimony in the context of the entire case. The defense in its opening statement raised issues concerning a number of acts conceivably inconsistent for a victim of rape, e.g., the victim's failure to report, her failure to resist, and her apparent lack of anxiety. Additionally, trial defense counsel conducted a rigorous cross-examination of the victim during which he further questioned her behavioral conduct. Following this, trial counsel sought to introduce the expert testimony of Dr. Remer to put the behavioral evidence in perspective. Thus the Government argued that Dr. Remer's testimony was necessary to explain to the members the behavioral patterns of victims of rape.

Additionally, Dr. Remer's testimony was offered in rebuttal after the behavioral conduct of the victim was raised as an issue. The Government was careful to put her testimony into a proper framework for the members. The doctor was very careful not to confuse or mislead the court members. She did not testify that if certain behavioral conduct was present, a rape took place. She did, however, testify that in some rape cases the victim would fail to report the offense immediately, fail to resist and show no appearance of anxiety. Dr. Remer made it clear that her testimony was to give a framework within which to consider the arguments made by the defense in the context of what happens in some rape cases, but she would not usurp the role of the factfinder. Specifically, in order to avoid confusing the jury, she testified that she was seeking to aid the court members, but they had to determine whether an offense was committed. Furthermore, Dr. Remer did not violate our prohibition against expert witnesses' testifying about the credibility of the victim. . . .

. . . We conclude that the judge did not abuse his discretion in admitting Dr. Remer's testimony.

The decision of the United States Army Court of Military Review is affirmed.

JUDGE COX concurs.

SULLIVAN, CHIEF JUDGE (concurring):

I agree with the principal opinion in this case as well as the comment of Judge Wiss.

WISS, JUDGE (concurring):

I fully concur in the principal opinion and write only to comment on two aspects of it.

. . . [T]he principal opinion concludes that evidence of rape-trauma syndrome is not necessarily limited to rebuttal and may be introduced during the prosecution's case-in-chief. That is not an issue here, since Dr. Remer's testimony came in during the prosecution's case-in-chief but in obvious rebuttal to implications raised during the defense's earlier cross-examination of the prosecutrix. . . . However, I have no quarrel with that conclusion. . . .

I do caution, though, that relevance of testimony on rape-trauma syndrome seems to be limited to issues of whether there was consent and whether a rape did, in fact, occur. . . . Where one or the other or both are in dispute in the trial, it would seem unimportant when, during the trial, such expert testimony was offered. If, however, the trial revolves solely around the identity of the rapist, for example, the military judge should be especially cautious to ensure that the marginal probative value of rapetrauma-syndrome testimony under those circumstances is not "substantially outweighed by the danger of unfair prejudice, confusion of the issues, or misleading the members. . . . " . . .

GIERKE, JUDGE (concurring in the result):

I agree with the principal opinion that if placed in a proper, limited framework, expert testimony on the rape trauma syndrome is admissible to aid the factfinder in understanding the evidence and to rebut any misconceptions about a rape victim's behavior. . . . However, I take exception to the principal opinion's conclusion that Dr. Remer's expert testimony was placed into a proper framework by the Government. In my opinion, Dr. Remer was allowed to go too far in expressing her opinion that if certain behavioral conduct was present a rape took place. Considering the fact that this behavioral conduct matched that attributed to the victim, this conclusion was unfairly prejudicial, not very probative, and very misleading. Mil.R.Evid. 403. . . .

The record clearly indicates that trial counsel wanted more from Dr. Remer's testimony than simple use as rebuttal to explain the behavioral patterns of rape victims. The victim's mother and the victim testified on direct examination that, after the alleged rape, the victim cried a lot, had trouble sleeping, lost her appetite, and often had nightmares and flashbacks. Trial counsel also proffered testimony of the victim's high school counselor who was to discuss the "symptoms" the victim was exhibiting following the alleged rape and her impressions of how the victim was dealing with those symptoms. These "symptoms" included the victim's admission to her that she still had trouble concentrating and sleeping, bad dreams, flashbacks, and a loss of appetite. After a defense objection, trial counsel argued that the "impressions" of the counselor "are relevant in that they provide the basis for whether she . . . [the victim] was experiencing rape trauma syndrome or post-traumatic trauma syndrome. . . ." Noting that the counselor's testimony "would be cumulative with the prior testimony," the military judge disallowed her testimony.

Next, defense counsel objected to Dr. Remer's testimony, arguing, inter alia, that "Dr. Remer's testimony in this particular case would be more prejudicial than probative. . . . [It] will mislead the jury and invade the factfinding province of the jury." Without comment, the military judge overruled the objection and allowed Dr. Remer to testify as an expert on the rape trauma syndrome. Dr. Remer testified about general "symptomatic" behavioral traits of women who have been raped and answered "hypothetical" questions that identically matched the victim's testimony concerning her behavior immediately following the rape. Trial counsel concluded his questioning of Dr. Remer by asking her "if a person were experiencing the majority of these symptoms that you have talked about in your model, would they [sic] be suffering from a rape trauma syndrome?" Dr. Remer responded by saying, "Yes, most likely," and reminded trial counsel that she had not "finished telling" the members about the typical "constellation of symptoms." Not so coincidentally, she indicated that typical symptoms in the crisis stage of the rape trauma syndrome include "a change in . . . eating habits" (they eat more or eat less); "a change in . . . sleeping pattern" (they cannot sleep, have nightmares, or sleep all the time); depression (sadness, hopelessness); and "sexual dysfunction." Upon being asked again by trial counsel whether a person suffering from a majority of these "symptoms" would be suffering from rape trauma, Dr. Remer again suggested a "yes" answer and explained that upon examination of "a constellation of symptoms" and how a person has changed after a trauma, one "can make a reasoned assessment, that this person has been raped."

In my opinion, this is not limited, permissible testimony. It improperly allowed the members to infer that, if they believed that the victim exhibited certain behavioral conduct after an incident, then they could conclude she had been raped. The generalized behavior characteristics attributed to the victim and labeled as rape trauma "symptoms" could result from any number of stressful situations. . . . The rape trauma syndrome was developed from interviewing "thousands of victims" to help them better cope with the aftermath of their victimization. It presupposes the existence of a rape. It was not developed to determine whether a rape had, in fact, occurred. . . . Dr. Remer's conclusion that one can reasonably assess that a person has been raped based on "a constellation of symptoms" (a majority of which the victim possessed) "has meager scientific basis and minimum value but has substantial potential for misleading the factfinder." *United States v. Cameron*, 21 M.J. 59, 65 (CMA 1985). Cf. *State v. Taylor*, 663 S.W.2d 235 (fact that victim exhibited symptoms of rape trauma syndrome does not qualify expert to designate experience that gave rise to trauma). Moreover, contrary to the holding of the principal opinion, I do not believe that standard instructions of the type given in this case on the weight members may give to testimony of expert witnesses are adequate to protect against unfair prejudice to an accused. Such instructions place absolutely no parameters on how evidence of the rape trauma syndrome should be considered by the members.

Despite my belief that the military judge allowed the Government to improperly use expert testimony on the rape trauma syndrome, I would hold that his error was harmless under the unique circumstances of this case. . . . Trial counsel did not highlight Dr. Remer's improper conclusion in his closing argument. Appellant's defense was that he never had sexual intercourse with the victim and that she created the whole story. Yet, the victim's allegations were corroborated by medical evidence indicating that she suffered recent injuries caused by forceful penetration of her vagina. The victim, a 15-year-old girl, had no apparent motivation to make up her very plausible allegations. Therefore, I would hold that any error in allowing Dr. Remer's testimony in toto was harmless.

NOTES

(1) In *Houser v. Lowe*, 1996 WL 560232 (D. Kan. 1996) a federal district court dismissed a habeas corpus petition by Mr. Houser. In the process, the court reviewed the decision of the Court of Military Appeals in *United States v. Houser*, supra, under the standard announced in *Daubert v. Merrell Dow Pharmaceuticals*, supra pp. 1159–1163, and concluded that the Court of Military Appeals had properly found that the expert testimony on rape trauma syndrome was "relevant and reliable." Id. at *3.

(2) The use of Rape Trauma Syndrome evidence developed as part of a general reform in rape prosecutions that began in the 1970s. This issue is discussed in detail in Chapter Five in the context of the "rape shield" rules (e.g., FRE 412) and the special provisions of the Federal Rules of Evidence that permit the use of character evidence against defendants in sexual assault cases (FREs 413—415). For present purposes, it is sufficient to recall that until recently common law courts frequently treated complaining witnesses in rape cases with suspicion if not overt hostility. Their sexual behavior in other contexts was scrutinized; unless they could produce corroboration, their testimony—unlike that of other victims of violent crimes—was deemed legally insufficient to sustain a conviction; they were the subject of demeaning comments by judges and commentators; and jurors were given special instructions challenging their credibility. In that context, many advocates for rape victims welcomed Rape Trauma Syndrome evidence as a partial antidote. For example, Professor Toni Masaro wrote:

> A qualified expert who has examined the woman and detected signs of RTS can help to educate [the] fact finder in several ways. The expert can confirm the existence of trauma consistent with the woman's allegation of nonconsent. The expert can also, in explaining RTS, help the jurors to understand the psychological cost of rape—even when the victim is a nonvirgin or a prostitute, lacks physical injuries, met her assailant in a bar, or is married to him. Further, the expert can help to dispel the fact finder's confusion of seduction fantasies with the reality of rape. Hearing, perhaps for the first time, about the profound fear and long-term psychological trauma that rape can cause, the fact finder may overcome traditional disbelief of a complainant who was raped by

someone who was not a stranger wielding a weapon in a dark alley.[196]

(3) On the other hand, criticisms of RTS evidence have emerged from judges and scholars who are sympathetic to the general reform in rape prosecutions. Some critics complain that expert witnesses who testify about this syndrome often claim more than the underlying science will support. For example, Judge Gierke in his opinion concurring in the result in *Houser* points out that RTS was developed as a therapeutic concept for treating known rape victims rather than a forensic concept for determining whether a person was raped, and argues that evidence of RTS symptoms should not be permitted in support of an inference that a rape did occur. Professor Patricia Frazier points out that most RTS studies recruit their subjects through rape crisis centers, and therefore, "because many women [who have been raped] do not seek help at such centers, those that do may not be representative of most victims."[197] In an earlier piece with her colleague Eugene Borgida, Frazier discusses another common aspect of RTS evidence that was presented in *Houser*:

> Some expert testimony on RTS describes the "stages" of rape trauma. . . . Nonetheless, the notion that there are stages of rape trauma has not been well-documented in the research literature. The notion of stages originated with Burgess and Holmstrom, who described RTS as a two-phase reaction consisting of an acute and a reorganization phase. . . . [S]ubsequent longitudinal research has not conceptualized rape trauma in terms of an acute and a reorganization stage. Finally, the diagnostic criteria for PTSD [Post Traumatic Stress Disorder] make no mention of stages. In short, descriptions of the stages of RTS are not supported in the research literature and should be avoided in expert testimony.[198]

---

[196] Toni M. Masaro, Experts, Psychology, Credibility, and Rape: The Rape Trauma Syndrome Issue and Its Implications for Expert Psychological Testimony, 69 Minn. L. Rev. 395, 469–70 (1985). See also e.g., David McCord, The Admissibility of Expert Testimony Regarding Rape Trauma Syndrome in Rape Prosecutions, 26 B. C. L. Rev. 1143, 1187 (1985) (arguing that RTS should be admitted because: (1) it is reliable evidence tending to prove the element of lack of consent in rape cases; (2) may be helpful to a jury in overcoming certain prevalent misconceptions that can stand in the way of rational decision-making; and (3) is not violative of any rule of evidence); Morrison Torrey, When Will We Be Believed? Rape Myths and the Idea of a Fair Trial in Rape Prosecutions, 24 U.C. Davis L. Rev. 1013, 1067 (1991) (advocating expanded use of the concept of expert RTS testimony to permit introduction of expert testimony concerning the falsity of rape myths); Deborah A. Dwyer, Expert Testimony on Rape Trauma Syndrome: An Argument for Limited Admissibility, 63 Wash. L. Rev. 1063, 1064 (1988) (arguing that expert testimony on RTS is helpful and should be admissible because it is similar to other psychological testimony).

[197] Patricia A. Frazier, Rape Trauma Syndrome, Scientific Status, in David L. Faigman et al., supra note 192, vol. 2 § 15:14, p. 446.

[198] Patricia A. Frazier & Eugene Borgida, The Scientific Status of Research on Rape Trauma Syndrome, in David L. Faigman et al., Modern Scientific Evidence, vol. 1 p. 432 (1997) (footnotes omitted).

(4) Other critics take a different tack. Robert Lawrence sees RTS evidence as dangerous for rape victims:[199]

> If courts consistently permit the introduction of expert testimony on RTS, defendants will seek, under their sixth amendment rights, to introduce this evidence on their own behalf. The confrontation and compulsory process clauses of the sixth amendment are read together to guarantee the criminal defendant the right to present all probative evidence in his defense. If the RTS evidence is admitted to assist the state in making its case, the defendant must be allowed to introduce it to the extent that it may demonstrate innocence.
>
> In exercising this right, the defendant may seek to have a court-appointed psychiatrist examine the complainant. If the doctor concludes that the complainant does not suffer from RTS, the defendant may introduce testimony to that effect as evidence of consent. Although rape reform advocates have denounced compulsory psychiatric examinations of rape victims, the admissibility of expert testimony on RTS could reinstitute that practice. Rape trials once again would focus not on the defendant's conduct but on the psychological state of the victim.

Professor Susan Stefan elaborates on this line of criticism:[200]

> The presentation of rape trauma syndrome evidence does not solve the problem of women's lack of credibility; it concedes it. Women who accept and enact victimhood and have access to "objective" professionals who can vouch for their disturbance or disorder will be believed. Women who are not inclined to seek professional help or have no access to it because of economic or other pressures still have no credibility. The latter group could testify themselves that they were depressed, had headaches, and had difficulty sleeping since they had been raped—essentially the same testimony an expert would give. Without an expert, however, such women would still not have credibility on the question of whether they had been raped.[a] Thus, the old corroboration requirement, expelled from the letter of the law by feminists in the 1970s, still remains. . . .
>
> The problem with using rape trauma syndrome evidence is that it replaces one set of myths with another. The myth that a

---

[199] Robert Lawrence, Checking the Allure of Increased Conviction Rates: The Admissibility of Expert Testimony on Rape Trauma Syndrome in Criminal Proceedings, 70 Va. L. Rev. 1657, 1702–03 (1984) (footnotes omitted).

[200] Susan Stefan, The Protection Racket: Rape Trauma Syndrome, Psychiatric Labeling, and Law, 88 NW. U. L. Rev. 1271, 1333–39 (1994) (footnotes redesignated, and some omitted) Reprinted by special permission of Northwestern University School of Law, Law Review.

a. As Elizabeth Schneider put it, "Rape trauma syndrome . . . sets up the situation where a woman says, 'Believe me because an expert will show how badly I've been hurt.' "

woman who does not report being raped immediately has consented to sex has been replaced with the myth that delay in reporting is a "symptom" of a disorder. The myth that a woman or girl who continues to see or visit a man accused of raping her must have consented to sex has been replaced by the myth that such behavior is a product of a mental disorder. "Normal" women would still not react this way.

Expert testimony may be needed to explain a woman's failure to report rape, not as a symptom, but in terms of the likelihood of disbelief by police, retaliation by the rapist, hostility of family and support network, and the stress caused by the judicial proceedings and stigma of being a public rape "victim." Expert testimony can educate the jury that the very fact of the rape myth that rapists are strangers who leap out of bushes makes women reluctant to report rape by a previously trusted friend or (especially) an authority figure with power over her. Women may fear disbelief, or they themselves may be shocked or confused about what happened, especially if the attack does not fit into any known social category. The rape may be conceived as a major problem to be resolved in an ongoing relationship, rather than a crime. Meanwhile, the women act publicly as though nothing had happened. An expert can emphasize to the jury the courage and strength it takes to report being raped rather than the pathology that explains a delay in reporting. "Normal" women, defined as "typical" women, don't report being raped at all.

Professor Stefan suggests a remedy that is also illustrated in *Houser*:

The fact that courts have been willing to accept expert testimony for the purpose of correcting jurors' misconceptions points the way to alternatives to rape trauma syndrome evidence. "A growing number of courts have held that the use of expert testimony on social frameworks to correct jurors' beliefs that are erroneous does indeed 'assist the trier of fact.' "[b] This kind of testimony uses "general research results . . . to construct a frame of reference or background context for deciding factual issues crucial to the resolution of a specific case."

As part of "social frameworks" testimony, jurors might be told about rape myths, as suggested above; some experts are already beginning to incorporate information about rape myths into their testimony.[c] Much of this information would not be

---

b.   Laurens Walker & John Monahan, Social Frameworks: A New Use of Social Science in Law, 73 Va. L. Rev. 559, 580 (1987). Some have suggested that this information, rather than being presented by one side or the other, be included in the judge's charge to the jury. . . .

c.   See, e.g., United States v. Houser, 36 M.J. 392 (allowing expert testimony about rape myths, such as that the victim is to blame, that rapes are committed by strangers in dark alleys

controversial. For example, even government figures show that most women are raped by acquaintances, not strangers.

E. THE SCIENTIFIC BASIS FOR DNA IDENTIFICATION EVIDENCE

The following excerpt, an article by Professor William Thompson in the *Encyclopedia of Crime and Punishment*, describes the history and the major scientific and technical issues that are involved in forensic DNA identification testing.[201]

English geneticist Alec Jeffreys first described a method for "typing" human DNA in 1985. Since that time, DNA typing technology has advanced rapidly and the new DNA tests have been embraced eagerly by the criminal justice system. DNA tests are now routinely used to help identify the source of blood, semen and hair found at crime scenes and to establish family relationships in cases of disputed parentage. DNA tests have helped prosecutors obtain convictions in thousands of cases and have helped establish the innocence of thousands of individuals who might otherwise have become suspects.

How DNA Tests Work

The Nature of DNA

Deoxyribonucleic acid, or DNA, is a long, double-stranded molecule configured like a twisted ladder or "double helix." The genetic information of all organisms is encoded in the sequence of four organic compounds (bases) that make up the rungs of the DNA ladder. Most DNA is tightly packed into structures called chromosomes in the nuclei of cells. In humans there are 23 pairs of chromosomes; half of each pair is inherited from the individual's mother, half from the father. The total complement of DNA is called the genome.

---

at gunpoint, that most rapes are committed by acquaintances, indoors, and without weapons), cert. denied, 510 U.S. 864, 114 S.Ct. 182 (1993).

[201] Thompson, William C., DNA Testing, in David Levinson (Ed.) Encyclopedia of Crime and Punishment (Thousand Oaks, Calif.: Sage Publications, 2002), vol 2, pp. 537–44. Reprinted with permission. Copyright Sage Publications.

Figure 1: DNA from Blood

(From K. Inman & N. Rudin, An Introduction to Forensic DNA Analysis, CRC Press, 1997.)

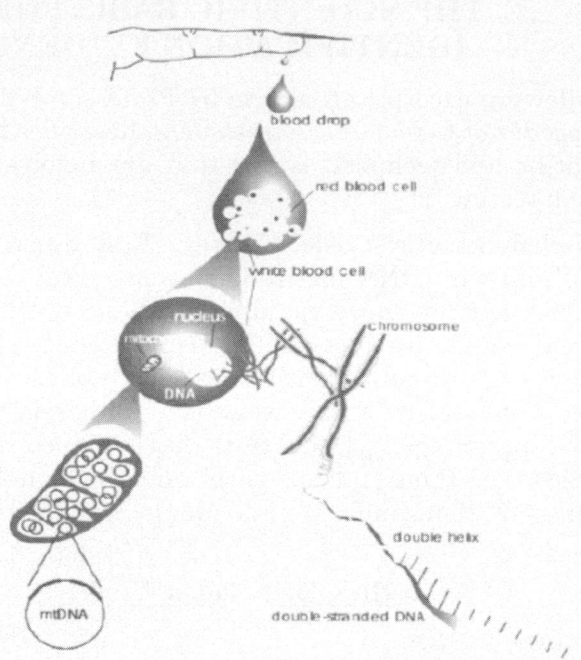

By some estimates, 99.9% of the genetic code is the same in all humans. To identify individuals, DNA tests focus on a few *loci* (plural of *locus*—a specific location on the human genome) where there is variation among individuals. These *loci* are called *polymorphisms* because the genetic code can take different forms in different individuals. Each possible form is called an *allele*.

Forensic DNA tests have examined two types of polymorphisms. *Sequence polymorphisms* vary only in the sequence of the genetic code. *Length polymorphisms* contain repeating sequences of genetic code; the number of repetitions may vary from person to person, making the section longer in some people and shorter in others.

Analysts begin the testing process by extracting DNA from cells and purifying it. They use test tubes, chemical reagents, and other standard procedures of laboratory chemistry.

In sexual assault cases, spermatozoa (containing male DNA) may be mixed with epithelial (skin) cells from the victim. Analyst generally try to separate the male and female components into separate *extracts* (samples) using a process called *differential lysis*, which employs weak detergents to liberate DNA from the epithelial cells followed by stronger detergents to liberate DNA from the tougher spermatozoa.

After the DNA is extracted, it can be "typed" using several different methods.

RFLP Analysis

When DNA tests were first introduced in the late 1980's, most laboratories employed a method called *RFLP analysis (restriction fragment length polymorphism analysis)*, which uses enzymes to break the long strands of DNA into shorter fragments (*restriction fragments*) and separates these by length (using a process called *electrophoresis*). A pattern of dark bands on an x-ray or photographic plate reveals the position (and hence the length) of target fragments that contain *length polymorphisms*.

Figure 2: RFLP Autorad in a Rape Case

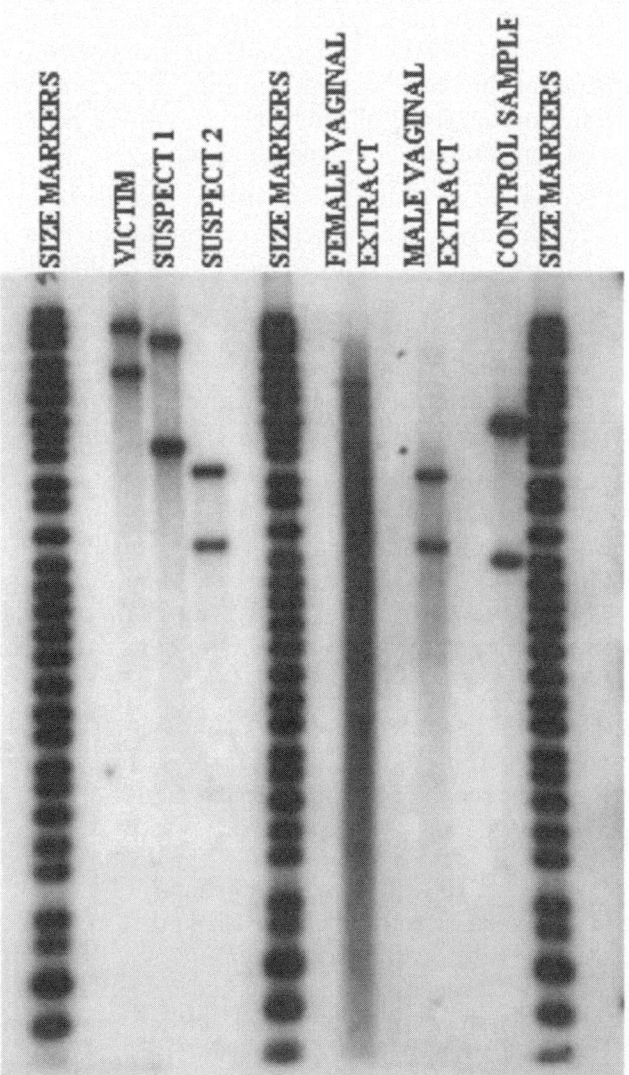

Figure 2 shows RFLP analysis of a single locus (containing a length polymorphism) in a case in which a woman was raped by two men. Each "lane" contains DNA from a different sample. The lanes labeled "size markers" contain DNA fragment of known size from bacteria and are used for calibration. Lanes on the left side show the band patterns produced by reference samples from the victim and two suspects. There are two bands in each lane because each individual has two copies of the relevant locus, one from the paternal half of the chromosome, the other from the maternal half.

Lanes on the right side of Figure 2 show the band patterns of evidence samples. The lane labeled "female vaginal extract" contains DNA from the female component (epithelial cells) of a vaginal sample taken from the victim. The DNA in this sample was too degraded to produce a distinct band pattern. The lane labeled "male vaginal extract" shows the band pattern of DNA from the male component (spermatozoa) of the same vaginal sample. This lane contains a band pattern similar to that of suspect 2, which indicates that the spermatozoa could have come from suspect 2.

In a typical case, four to six different loci (each containing a different length polymorphism) are examined in this manner. The full set of alleles identified in a sample is called its DNA profile. Because the probability of a "matching" pattern at any locus is on the order of one in hundreds to one in thousands, and the probabilities of a match at the various loci are assumed to be statistically independent, the probability of a match at four or more loci is generally put at one in many millions or even billions.

Although RFLP analysis is generally reliable, it sometimes entails subjective judgment. Whether the lane labeled "male vaginal extract" also contains bands corresponding to those of suspect 1 is a matter of judgment on which experts in this case disagreed. Dots to the left of the lane are felt-tip pen marks placed by a forensic analysis to indicate where he thought he saw bands matching those of suspect 1.

RFLP analysis requires samples that are relatively large (blood or semen stains about the size of a quarter) and well-preserved. It is also slow. A typical case takes four to six weeks.

DQ-Alpha and Polymarker Tests

In the early 1990s, newer methods of DNA testing were introduced that are faster (producing results in a day or two) and more sensitive (i.e., capable of typing smaller, more degraded samples). The new methods use a procedure called *polymerase chain reaction (PCR)*, which can produce billions of copies of target fragments of DNA from one or more loci. These "amplified" DNA fragments (called *amplicons*), can then be typed using several methods.

In 1991, Perkin-Elmer (PE), a biotechnology firm, developed a test kit for amplifying and typing a *sequence polymorphism* known as the DQ-alpha gene. Six distinct *alleles* (variants) of this gene can be identified by exposing the amplified DNA to paper test strips containing *allele-specific probes* (see Figure 3). The dots on the strip signal the presence of particular alleles. This test has the advantage of great sensitivity (DNA from just a few human cells is sufficient to produce a result) and allows more rapid analysis (1–2 days), but it is not as discriminating as RFLP analysis.

Figure 3: Test Strip Showing Polymarker (top) and DQ-Alpha (bottom) Test Results

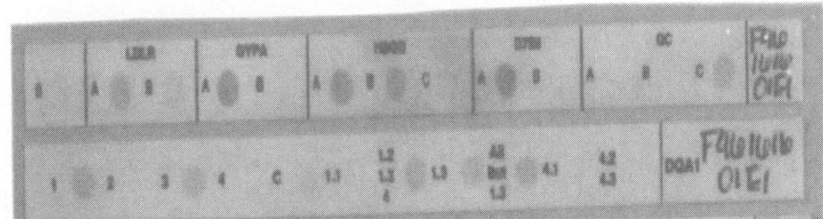

In 1993, PE introduced an improved kit that typed DQ-alpha and five additional genes simultaneously, thereby improving the specificity of this method (See Figure 3). With this new kit, known as the Polymarker/DQ-alpha test, individual profile frequencies are on the order of one in tens of thousands, however it still is not as discriminating as RFLP analysis. As with RFLP analysis, interpretation of the test strips may require subjective judgments. For example, experts disagreed on whether the dot labeled 1.3 in the lower strip shown in Figure 3 is dark enough to reliably indicate the presence of the allele designated 1.3.

STR Tests

The late 1990s saw the advent of *STR* (*short tandem repeat*) DNA testing. STR tests combine the sensitivity of a PCR-based test with great specificity (profile frequencies potentially as low as one in trillions) and therefore have quickly supplanted both RFLP analysis and the Polymarker/DQ-alpha test in forensic laboratories.

An *STR* is a DNA locus that contains a length polymorphism. At each STR locus, people have two alleles (one from each parent) that vary in length depending on the number of repetitions of a short core sequence of genetic code. A person with *genotype* 14, 15 at an *STR locus* has one allele with 14 repeating units, and another with 15 repeating units.

Figure 4: STR Test Results

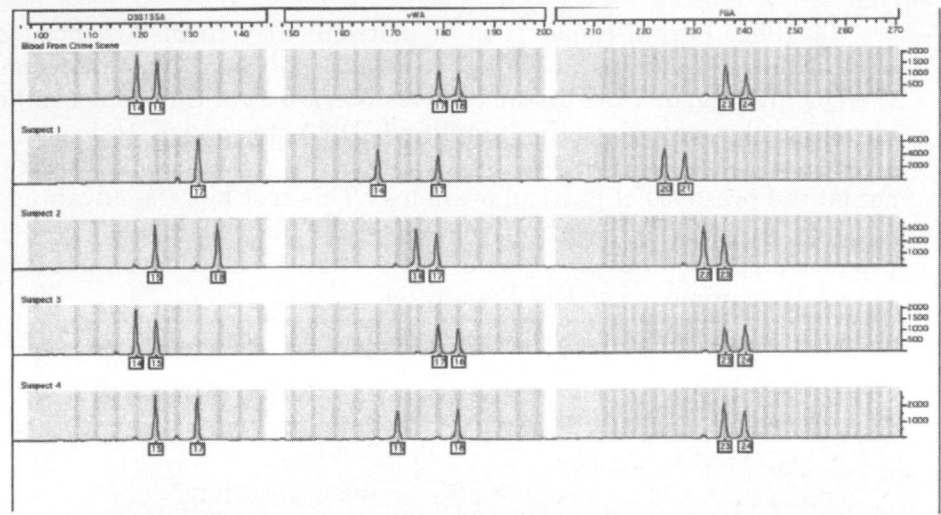

Figure 4 shows the results of STR analysis of five samples: blood from a crime scene and reference samples of four suspects. This analysis includes three loci, labeled "D3S1358," "vWA," and "FGA." Each person has two alleles (peaks) at each locus, one from the maternal portion and the other from the paternal portion of the chromosome. The position of the "peaks" on each graph (known as an electropherogram) indicates the length (and hence the number of core sequence repeats) of each STR. As can be seen, the profile of suspect 3 corresponds to that of the crime scene sample, indicating he is a possible source. Suspects 1, 2 and 4 are eliminated as possible sources.

In 1997, the FBI identified 13 STR loci that it deemed appropriate for forensic testing. Commercial firms quickly developed test kits and automated equipment for typing these STRs. The most popular test procedure, developed by Applied Biosciences International (ABI), a PE subsidiary, includes a PCR kit known as *ProfilerPlus* that simultaneously "amplifies" DNA from up to nine STR loci and labels the loci with colored dyes. An automated test instrument called the ABI 310 Genetic Analyzer then separates the resulting amplicons by length (using electrophoresis) and uses a laser to cause fluorescence of the dye-labeled fragments. A computer-controlled electronic camera detects the size and relative position of the fragments, identifies alleles, and displays the results as shown in Figure 4.

STR tests have greatly improved the capabilities of forensic laboratories, allowing highly specific DNA profiles to be derived from tiny quantities of cellular material. Test results generally allow a clear-cut determination of whether a particular individual could be the source of an evidentiary sample, although experts have differed over interpretation of results in some cases.

Mitochondrial DNA Tests

The tests described thus far examine DNA from cell nuclei (*nuclear DNA*). DNA is also found in *cell mitochondria*, which are *organelles* (structures) in which the process of cellular respiration occurs. Mitochondrial DNA (often designated *mtDNA)* contains *sequence polymorphisms*. In the late 1990s, forensic scientists began testing *mtDNA* by using a procedure known as *genetic sequencing* to produce a read-out of the genetic code from two polymorphic areas of the *mitochondrial genome*. Forensic scientists describe an mtDNA profile by stating how its sequence differs from that of a reference standard called the *Anderson sequence.*

Mitochondrial DNA tests are highly sensitive and can produce results on samples that are not suitable for other DNA tests, such as hair shafts, bone, and teeth. Because mtDNA is present in hundreds or thousands of copies per cell, it often survives much longer than nuclear DNA in old, degraded cellular samples. DNA tests on very old samples, such as the bones of Czar Nicholas II of Russia, have detected and typed mtDNA.

Mitochondrial DNA tests are far less discriminating than STR tests. The frequency of mtDNA profiles is generally put at one in hundreds. Additionally, because mtDNA is inherited maternally, mtDNA tests generally cannot distinguish between individuals in the same maternal line. Hence, sons of the same mother would be expected to have the same mtDNA profile, and this profile would also be found in daughters of the mother's sister and all of their children.

Minor variations are sometimes found in mtDNA profiles of different cells from the same person due to mutations. This phenomenon, known as *heteroplasmy*, complicates the process of determining whether two mtDNA profiles match. The appropriate standards for declaring an mtDNA match, and for estimating the rarity of matching profiles, are issues that have been debated in the courtroom.

Mitochondrial DNA tests are expensive and require special laboratory facilities and techniques. At this time only a few forensic laboratories perform these tests and they are used only where other types of DNA testing fail or cannot work. However, future technical improvements may lead to wider use of mtDNA tests.

Reliability and Quality Assurance

Although current DNA technology is capable of producing highly reliable results, questions are sometimes raised about the quality of laboratory work. Key issues include the potential for biased or mistaken interpretation of laboratory results and the possibility for error due to mishandling of samples. Acknowledging problems with the quality of early DNA testing procedures, a 1992 report of the National Research Council called for broader scrutiny of forensic DNA testing by a scientific body from outside the law enforcement community.

In response, the U.S. Federal Bureau of Investigation (FBI) created its own advisory body that was initially called the Technical Working Group for DNA Analysis Methods (TWGDAM) and more recently called the Scientific Working Group for DNA Analysis Methods (SWGDAM). The FBI director appoints its members. Although it has not satisfied all critics of forensic laboratory practices, this body has been credited with issuing guidelines that have improved the quality of forensic DNA work. For example, SWGDAM guidelines call for each analyst to take two proficiency tests each year.

Another quality assurance mechanism is laboratory accreditation. The American Society of Crime Laboratory Directors Laboratory Accreditation Board (ASCLAD-LAB) is a non-profit organization that reviews the protocols and procedures of forensic DNA laboratories and issues a certificate of accreditation to those meeting its standards. To help assure the competence of laboratory workers, a professional organization called the American Board of Criminology, has developed a certification programs for DNA analysts.

Despite these efforts, problems occasionally come to light. Errors have occurred in proficiency tests, although they are infrequent. Occasional errors arising from accidental switching and mislabeling of samples or misinterpretation of results have come to light in court cases. In one case, misinterpretation of a DNA test contributed to the wrongful rape conviction of a man who was later exonerated when more extensive DNA tests, by another laboratory, proved he could not have been the rapist.

A 1996 report of the National Research Council suggested that retesting of samples is the best way to address remaining concerns about the quality of laboratory work. The great sensitivity of PCR-based DNA tests makes it possible to split samples for duplicate analysis in most cases.

Databanks and Dragnets

The United Kingdom and all fifty American states now have government-operated *databanks* containing the DNA profiles of known offenders. Many crimes have been solved when a databank search revealed a match between the DNA profile of a blood or semen sample left by the perpetrator at a crime scene and the profile of a known individual in the databank. A databank match is called a *cold hit*.

The FBI maintains a national databank of DNA profiles known as *CODIS (Combined DNA Indexing System)*, which includes a Convicted Offender Index (containing profiles of offenders submitted by states) and a Forensic Index (containing DNA profiles of evidence related to unsolved crimes). CODIS allows government crime laboratories at a state and local level to conduct national searches which might reveal, for example, that semen deposited during an unsolved rape in Florida could have come from a known offender from Virginia.

Government databanks were initially limited to convicted violent or sex offenders. However, there has been serious discussion of expanding databanks to include arrestees[202], or even to make them universal (perhaps by sampling DNA from all citizens at birth), in the interest of better crime control.

Civil libertarians have expressed concern that government agencies could use the genetic information they collect in an intrusive or inappropriate manner. The information included in CODIS is limited to numerical data that designate RFLP and STR profiles. These profiles are useful for identifying individuals but are linked to no known medical or behavioral characteristics. However, most states have retained blood samples from those included in state databanks. State and federal statutes limit the disclosure of information contained in government databanks and generally specify that it be used solely for law enforcement purposes.

When police have the DNA profile of a perpetrator but cannot establish his or her identity, they sometimes conduct what has become known as a *DNA dragnet*, in which large numbers of individuals in the relevant community are asked to submit samples voluntarily for DNA testing. Police generally collect samples by

---

[202] Since Thompson wrote a number of states have begun this practice. In *Maryland v. King*, 569 U.S. ___ (2013) the Supreme Court by a 5-4 vote upheld a Maryland statute that allowed DNA to be taken via cheek swab from individuals arrested for serious crimes. The majority opinion appears to rest on the notion that DNA plays a role similar to fingerprints in ascertaining the true identification of suspects as part of the normal criminal booking process. Maryland, however, as the dissent makes clear, takes DNA samples from arrestees in order to query cold case data bases and link those they arrest to other unsolved crimes. This is what happened in the *King* case.

rubbing inside the individual's cheek with a cotton swab. Even if the guilty party does not submit a sample, the DNA dragnet may help police by narrowing the number of possible suspects. The first DNA dragnet, which was chronicled in Joseph Wambaugh's book "The Blooding," helped police solve two murders in Leicester England in 1987. The guilty man was identified when, in an effort to avoid suspicion, he asked a friend to submit a sample in his place. DNA dragnets have since been used repeatedly in Britain and are becoming more common in the U.S.

Prosecutors in some jurisdictions have developed a procedural innovation called a *DNA warrant* as a means of avoiding the statute of limitations in cases where they have DNA from the perpetrator but have not yet identified a suspect. Before the statute of limitations runs out, charges are formally filed in the case, but the "defendant" is identified by DNA profile rather than by name. The legality and constitutionality of this practice is still subject to debate.

DNA Evidence in the Courts

Judges in the United States have traditionally acted as "gatekeepers" for scientific evidence, excluding evidence that is deemed insufficiently reliable to be heard by a jury. Many state courts apply the *Frye* standard (first articulated in a 1923 appellate case called *Frye v. U.S.*), which requires that scientific testimony be based on a method or technique that is "generally accepted" by the "relevant scientific community." Since 1993, federal courts (and some state courts) have applied a standard articulated by the U.S. Supreme Court in a case called *Daubert v. Merrill Dow Pharmaceuticals*, which requires the judge to consider whether scientific testimony is "valid," based on such factors as whether the underlying method has been tested, is subject to error, has been published, has been performed in accordance with appropriate standards, and is generally accepted.

In the early 1990's, a number of state courts ruled DNA evidence inadmissible on grounds that the underlying methods were not yet "generally accepted." The key issue was the assumption of statistical independence of alleles that underlay the methods used for estimating the rarity of RFLP DNA profiles. A number of prominent scientists questioned whether sufficient research had been done to validate the independence assumption. Their major concern was that human populations might be *structured*, such that people of Italian ancestry, for example, would be unusually likely to have some profiles, while those of Norwegian ancestry would be likely to have other profiles, and so on. Forensic laboratories generally compute separate statistical estimates for major racial/ethnic groups (i.e., for those of Caucasian, Hispanic, African, and sometimes Asian ancestry), but they had insufficient data to generate reliable estimates for subgroups.

A 1992 report of the National Research Council gave credence to concerns about population structure and suggested that a conservative method called the *ceiling principle* be used for estimating the rarity of DNA profiles. A few appellate courts thereafter overturned convictions in cases in which the ceiling principle calculations had not been used. However, after further research found relatively little evidence of population structure for RFLP profiles, and a 1996 report of the National Research Council declared the ceiling principle no longer necessary, the admissibility of RFLP DNA tests was solidly established.

As each new generation of DNA technology reaches the courtroom, its reliability must be established under the *Frye* or *Daubert* standard. To make this determination, judges sometimes hold pretrial hearings in which the parties can present scientific testimony. Often there is scientific debate about the reliability of new procedures and the adequacy of the underlying validation, and hence there is a period of uncertainty over whether the "general acceptance" test will be met. The issue has been complicated by the tendency of some forensic laboratories to begin using new tests before the underlying validation research has been published and by the refusal of some commercial vendors to reveal complete scientific details of new methods on grounds that they are trade secrets.

Once the admissibility of a particular method is established by appellate ruling, courts in Frye jurisdictions generally admit the results of that method automatically. However, under the *Daubert* standard and in a few *Frye* states (California is a prominent example) judges may still rule DNA evidence inadmissible if they find that a laboratory failed to follow reliable scientific procedures in the case at hand.

DNA test results that are admitted into evidence can still be challenged in front of the jury. When lawyers attack DNA evidence, they generally try to show either that the results were misinterpreted, that the laboratory may have mixed up or cross-contaminated samples, or that an innocent transfer of DNA could have produced the incriminating results. In the OJ Simpson trial, for example, defense lawyers argued that the crime laboratory either inadvertently transferred Simpson's blood from a reference vial to samples collected at the crime scene, or, alternatively, that Simpson's blood may have been intentionally planted.

Post-Conviction DNA Testing

A number of convicted men in prison have sought to prove their innocence through DNA testing. As of early 2001, eighty-five men had been released from U.S. prisons after being exonerated by DNA tests. Several of these men had been facing execution. DNA exonerations prompted a number of states to pass laws requiring the government to afford convicted men access to biological evidence and to fund post-conviction DNA testing in cases where DNA testing was not done.

How were these innocent men convicted in the first place? Mistaken eyewitnesses were a key factor in the majority of these cases. Other factors that contributed to false convictions (in some but not all cases) include faulty forensic science (such as misleading conclusions from hair and fiber comparisons), fraudulent forensic science testimony (including the fabrication of serological test results in several cases), false confessions, lies told by so-called "snitches" (government informants), prosecutorial misconduct (such as failure to reveal exculpatory evidence) and incompetent defense lawyers.

The use of DNA testing to re-examine old cases was pioneered by the *Innocence Project*, a legal clinic at Benjamin Cardozo Law School in New York City. Lawyers Peter Neufeld and Barry Scheck, who codirect the Innocence Project, personally represented over forty of the exonerated men, and have played a key role in investigating the causes of these miscarriages of justice.

DNA Typing in the Future

Technical advances will continue to reduce the time and expense of DNA testing. Improvements in test kits should soon allow simultaneous PCR amplification of larger numbers of STRs, affording even greater speed and specificity to STR testing. Gene chip technology is already available that will allow typing of DNA within a few minutes on a custom-designed computer chip. In the near future this technology will make it feasible for police to perform STR typing of suspects and samples in the field using devices small enough to carry by hand.

The range of information that can be extracted from biological samples will also improve. New genetic probes that identify features on the Y-chromosome (which is possessed only by males) should help distinguish male from female DNA in sexual assault cases. Probes are also becoming available that can show what a DNA contributor looks like. The British Forensic Science Service has experimented with a probe that detects genes associated with red hair and a ruddy complexion.

Genetic tests capable of identifying behavioral propensities have been widely discussed due to their potentially profound ethical and social implications. However, because the association between genes and behavior is complex, the use of DNA tests to predict behavior is unlikely to be feasible in the near future.

Notes

(1) Having carefully read Dr. Thompson's excellent article, **do you have a clear general understanding of how DNA testing is performed? Could you focus in on the possible sources of error in such tests? Could you explain these issues to a jury?** Imagine that you are the defense attorney at a murder trial. The prosecution intends to introduce DNA evidence that purportedly shows that some of the blood on the deceased victim's shirt almost certainly came from your client. You believe there are serious concerns about the laboratory procedures used in the tests, and possibly about the impartiality of the prosecution's experts. **How would you go about preparing for the direct examination of your DNA expert? For the cross examination of the opposing expert?**

(2) DNA databases pose many ethical and policy questions, including: Whose DNA gets placed in a database? And under what conditions may investigators get access to it? For example, some people think that nobody should have his or her DNA in a databank unless that person "earned" that treatment by committing, and being convicted of, a serious crime. But if that policy is followed, how should investigators treat the fact that a near match with someone in the database may point a finger at a close relative of that person, whose DNA is not part of the registry? There are also issues posed about the statistical implications of a DNA match that is made by comparing a crime-scene sample to all the subjects in a large DNA database. Some statisticians worry that this procedure increases the risk of convictions of innocent defendants, but expert opinions differ as to whether and how the size of the database should be taken into account in evaluating the incriminatory implications of a match.

(3) DNA analysis is commonly a prosecutor's tool, or a tool of the mother (or welfare agency) in a paternity case. But not always. As Professor Thompson point out, many innocent people are excluded as suspects or fathers based on DNA analysis, and DNA analysis has been used during the past twenty years to prove that hundreds of people were convicted and imprisoned for felonies they did not commit. Defense counsel as well as prosecutors should regard DNA analysis as a useful tool.

(4) Despite its potential flaws, and the danger that it can be overvalued, DNA analysis is a powerful form of identification. It is, for

example, far more reliable than an eyewitness identification. Even so, DNA evidence will often only supplement eyewitness identifications, for prosecutors will want crime victims and bystanders to tell their stories, and to point their fingers at the defendant. In many cases in which it is used, DNA identification evidence is not essential to conviction. Rather, as with much forensic evidence, DNA identification is often introduced as much for its dramaturgical effect as for its evidentiary necessity. It helps erase residual doubts when other substantial evidence points to the defendant.

(5) One reason to believe that a DNA analysis has been correctly done, and that DNA match statistics may be relied on, is the consistency between DNA evidence and other evidence in the case. It is when DNA evidence stands alone or when it is contradicted by other evidence in a case—such as a credible alibi—that there is the greatest danger that a reported match results from inadvertent (or advertent) contamination, or unjustified subjective judgment, or laboratory error. So far, there are few cases where these dangers seem great, as other evidence usually points to a suspect. But DNA databases are expanding and dragnet DNA screening may spread as a police tactic. If so, more crimes will be solved, and there will be more cases in which DNA identification is the only evidence linking the defendant to the crime. DNA will become both more essential in identifying and convicting guilty defendants and a more likely source of occasional convictions of the innocent. It will also more frequently prevent trials of innocent suspects. On balance DNA identification to establish paternity and to make identifications is a great asset to the legal system. The trick is to use it correctly, and to make as few tragic errors as possible in the process.

ADDITIONAL PROBLEMS

Problem IX-11. Valentina Saltane, a graduate of the Grenada Medical College, was interning at the Bayside Hospital when Harold Haft, a 16-year-old boy, was brought into the emergency room following an auto accident. She stabilized the youth and prepared him for surgery, which the hospital's chief surgical resident conducted. Perhaps because of his pluckiness she developed a special interest in Haft. She accompanied him into surgery, watched the operation and made a special point of stopping in to see him during the two weeks he was in the hospital. Later Haft sued Ned Devine, the driver of the car he had been riding in at the time of the accident. The plaintiffs intended to call the chief surgical resident as an expert witness to testify to Haft's injuries and prognosis, but two days before his scheduled deposition, after submitting a report on Haft's condition, the resident died of a heart attack. So the plaintiffs called Dr. Saltane instead.

At the trial Dr. Saltane's deposition was offered, and hearsay objections to the use of a deposition were waived. At the deposition she had been asked to testify to what she knew about the case. She testified that Haft came to the hospital after having been thrown from a car driven by Devine, a friend of his who had been drinking and was speeding when he lost control of the vehicle. She then went on to say that he came to the hospital having lost two pints of blood, that he suffered a fractured knee cap and pelvis and a broken femur, that he was in considerable pain for two weeks after the accident which was not fully controlled by analgesics, and that his right leg was now an inch shorter than his left leg, that he would always suffer pain in his knee and that arthritis was a likely further complication probably entailing knee replacement surgery at some time in the future, and that he would always walk with a limp. Haft's attorney then asked her on what her testimony was based. Dr. Saltane replied: "I read the police report, I observed him when he entered the E.R., I talked to him then and later, while he was in the hospital, I went over his x-rays with the chief surgical resident, I observed the operation, I looked at his medical charts while he was in the hospital and I read a report the chief resident prepared on the case and the likely prognosis." Devine's attorney then objects to the entire deposition. **How should the court rule?** On cross-examination, Devine's attorney had asked Dr. Saltane "Now, these injuries would not have occurred had Mr. Haft been wearing his seat belt, isn't that right?" He wishes to read this question and Dr. Saltane's answer to the jury. Haft's attorney objects. **How should the court rule?**

Problem IX-12. Elizabeth Steinberg brought an action against a plastic surgeon for malpractice alleging that because the surgeon negligently failed to remove a plaster of paris splint when she complained of a burning sensation, her skin was severely damaged. She introduces as an expert a general practitioner who testifies that the plastic surgeon had enough evidence that the splint was doing damage that he should have been alerted to the need to remove it. The plastic surgeon objects to this testimony on the ground that plastic surgeons are not guilty of malpractice unless they fail to exercise the level skill expected by qualified plastic surgeons. He claims that the plaintiff's witness, as a general practitioner, is not competent to testify to the standard of care appropriate to plastic surgeons. **How should the court rule? Does it matter if the jurisdiction is one in which a prima facie case of medical malpractice may not be established without some expert testimony?** Assume that the plaintiff asked the doctor, "In your opinion, was there or was there not malpractice?" and that the doctor answered, "There was malpractice." **Should an objection to the question have been sustained? If an appellate court determines that the question was improper, should it reverse?**

Problem IX-13. Sylvia Swanson was injured when the door of a freight elevator in her employer's plant prematurely closed and struck her. She sued the manufacturer of the elevator claiming that the elevator's buttons were defectively designed because they could be activated inadvertently. She calls as her expert witness Maria MacDonald, a consulting engineer, who has a background not only in engineering, but in chemistry, machine guarding, toxicology and industrial hygiene and safety. On one occasion MacDonald designed machine guards for the buttons of a punch press. MacDonald never examined the elevator in question nor has she previously designed an elevator or any part thereof. As a consulting engineer her activities have principally related to fires, explosions, chemical poisoning, failures of materials, and failures of structural and hydraulic parts. The defendant objects that MacDonald is not an expert on elevators and should not be permitted to testify concerning alleged defects in the elevator's operating equipment. **Should MacDonald be permitted to testify as to the safety effects of leaving elevator buttons unguarded? Should she be permitted to give an opinion as to whether the absence of guards was a defect in the design?**

Problem IX-14. Paul Kettle is charged with robbing a grocery store. The theory of the prosecution's case is that Kettle is a narcotics addict who needed money to sustain his habit. To bolster the state's case, the prosecution seeks to introduce the testimony of a federal agent from the Bureau of Narcotics and Dangerous Drugs. The agent would testify that he has been working with the Bureau for 10 years, that he has investigated over 1,000 narcotics cases, that he has investigated and interviewed thousands of addicts, and that he considers himself to be an expert on narcotics addiction. In response to the question, "With respect to narcotics addicts, is there any generalization that you can make concerning their propensity to commit economic crimes," the witness would answer, "Yes, narcotics addicts have a difficult time holding jobs. Therefore, they have tremendous difficulty in securing sufficient funds to sustain their habit. This often results in their seeking money illegally. I personally have been involved in investigating hundreds of cases in which addicts have committed robberies, burglaries, and other crimes for the purpose of obtaining funds to purchase drugs." **Should this testimony be admitted?**

Problem IX-15. The State of Rhode Island condemns Bob Harris's land for a new elementary school. Harris and the state disagree on the value of the land and a condemnation suit is filed. To establish the value of the land Harris calls Sarah Burns, a local realtor who for twenty years has been selling property in the same area as the land in controversy. Before Burns testifies, the State questions her on voir dire concerning the basis of the testimony. She replies that she arrived at her opinion as to the value of Harris' property by relying on the prices at which land in the area similar to the land in question has sold recently, and on her knowledge of offers to buy or sell similar land. Since land is unique, no previous sale or offer is precisely analogous, so the realtor has reached a final opinion by estimating the value of particular features characterizing Harris' property and not the comparison properties, and vice versa. **Is the realtor a qualified expert? Should the court exclude the realtor's testimony but give evidence of the sale prices directly to the jury? What about evidence of the offers?**

Problem IX-16. Een sued Dulski for injuries resulting when Een's car collided with Dulski's truck. Dulski claimed that Een's car crossed the middle of the highway and caused the accident. To support this theory of causation, Dulski offered the testimony of a deputy sheriff and former city police officer with 17 years experience in investigating accidents. The officer arrived at the scene approximately 80 minutes after the accident occurred and before the damaged vehicles were moved. Dulski asked the officer for an opinion concerning the place of the impact. **Is this opinion admissible? What more would you want to know before you answer this question?** The Advisory Committee Note to FRE 703, states that "[t]he language would not warrant admitting in evidence the opinion of an 'accidentologist' as to the point of impact in an automobile collision based on statements of bystanders. . . . " **Why should such evidence be objectionable? Should the existence of eyewitness testimony support, impair, or have no effect on a claim that an accidentologist has useful information to convey to a jury?**

Problem IX-17. Sander Duchess is charged in Brooklyn, New York, with conspiracy to import and distribute cocaine in the period from 2008 through 2010. One of the witnesses against him is Ricky Charms, an FBI undercover agent who claims to have infiltrated Duchess's criminal organization. Charms testifies at length about the operation of Duchess's drug importation business. He authenticates and presents several audio tapes of surreptitiously recorded conversations in which Duchess apparently discusses plans to import and distribute cocaine. Much of what's said in these conversations, however, is obscure to say the least—such as Duchess's comment: "If they park the mattress one more time, whack'em!" The prosecutor offers Special Agent Charms as an expert in the underworld language used in the cocaine trade in New York in the first decade of the twenty-first century. **What foundation should the court require for such testimony? On what grounds might Duchess object to this expert testimony? Should it be admitted over objection?**

   Problem IX-18. A son is attempting to have his father committed to a mental institution. He presents witnesses who testify that his father has been acting "strangely"—he's been seen walking around his house naked, he seems impatient with his son, he constantly watches television, especially horror and detective and police shows, he has been buying a collection of "girlie" magazines, and he has an increasing tendency to go off by himself. The defendant father introduces the testimony of neighbors who have known him for years and who say that the old man's mind is quick, that he has always been pleasant, that his interest in television is shared by them, that he has always liked "girlie" magazines, and that his impatience with his son is understandable because the son is an irritating person. On rebuttal, the son introduces the testimony of two witnesses. The first, a salesman, testifies that the father commented while attempting to buy a handgun, "if Sergeant Friday were in this town, I might not need the gun." The second, a psychiatrist, is asked, "Based on everything that you have heard so far, and you have been here for all the testimony, have you an opinion as to whether the defendant is a danger to himself or to the community?" The defendant objects to the question. **Should the objection be sustained?**

VII.   BIBLIOGRAPHY

Cecil, Joe S. and Thomas E. Willging, Court-Appointed Experts: Defining a Role for Court-Appointed Experts Under Federal Rules of Evidence 706, Federal Judicial Center (1993).

Faigman, David, David H. Kaye, Michael J. Saks, and Joseph Sanders, Modern Scientific Evidence: The Law and Science of Expert Testimony (1997).

Faigman, David, Michael J. Saks, Joseph Sanders and Edward K. Cheng, Modern Scientific Evidence: The Law and Science of Expert Testimony, 2009–2010 ed. (2009).

Federal Judicial Center, Reference Manual on Scientific Evidence (2nd ed. 2000).

Giannelli, Paul C. and Edward J. Imwinkelried, Scientific Evidence (4th ed. 2007).

McCormick, Chs. 3, 20.

National Research Council, Strengthening Forensic Science in the United States: A Way Forward (2009).

Sanders, Joseph, Bendectin on Trial: A Study of Mass Tort Litigation (1998).

Taylor, John Pitt, Treatise on the Law of Evidence §§ 45–50, at 65–69 (3d ed. 1858).

Weinstein, Chs. 702–706.

Wigmore §§ 665(b), 672–688, 1917–1929, 2008–2015, 2023–2028, 2090.

Willging, Thomas E., Court Appointed Experts (1986).

Ziskin, Jay, Coping With Psychiatric and Psychological Testimony (5th ed. 1995).

Barber, R. E., Annotation, Trial Court's Appointment, in Civil Case, of Expert Witness, 95 A.L.R.2d 390 (1964).

Berry, Howard K., Impartial Medical Testimony, 32 F.R.D. 539, 545 (1962).

Burgess, A. and L. Holmstrom, Rape Trauma Syndrome, 131 Am. J. of Psychiatry 980 (1974).

Carlson, Ronald, Policing the Bases of Modern Expert Testimony, 39 Vand. L. Rev. 577 (1986).

Carrington, Paul D. and Traci L. Jones, Reluctant Experts, 59 Law and Contemp. Probs. No. 3, 51 (1996).

Castelle, George, Lab Fraud: Lessons Learned from the Fred Zain Affair, The Champion, May 1999.

Cecil, Joe S. and Gerald T. Wetherington, Forward, Court-Ordered Disclosure of Academic Research: A Clash of Values of Science and Law, 59 Law and Contemp. Probs. No. 3, 1 (1996).

Cecil, Joe S. and Thomas E. Willging, Accepting Daubert's Invitation: Defining a Role for Court-Appointed Experts in Assessing Scientific Validity, 43 Emory L. J. 995 (1994).

Cole, Simon A., "More Than Zero: Accounting for Error in Latent Fingerprint Identification," 95 Journal of Criminal Law & Criminology 985 (2005).

Dwyer, Deborah, Expert Testimony on Rape Trauma Syndrome: An Argument for Limited Admissibility, 63 Wash. L. Rev. 1063, 1064 (1998).

Faigman, David L., Appellate Review of Scientific Evidence Under Daubert and Joiner, 48 Hastings L. J. 969 (1997).

Frazier, Patricia A. and Eugene Borgida, The Scientific Status of Research on Rape Trauma Syndrome in David L. Faigman, et al., eds., Modern Scientific Evidence 414 (1997).

Garrett, Brandon L. & Peter J. Neufeld, Invalid Forensic Testimony and Wrongful Convictions, 95 Virginia L. Rev.1, 2 (2009).

Giannelli, Paul C., Wrongful Convictions and Forensic Science: The Need to Regulate. Crime Labs, 86 N.C. L. Rev. 163 (2007).

Giannelli, Paul C., "Junk Science": The Criminal Cases, 84 J. of Crim. L. and Criminology 105, 111 (1993).

Giannelli, Paul C., Observations on Discovery of Scientific Evidence, 101 F.R.D. 622 (1983).

Giannelli, Paul C., The Admissibility of Novel Scientific Evidence: Frye v. United States A Half Century Later, 80 Colum. L. Rev. 1197 (1980).

Gross, Samuel R., Expert Evidence, 1991 Wis. L. Rev. 1113.

Gross, Samuel R., Substance and Form In Scientific Evidence: What Daubert Didn't Do, in Reforming the Civil Justice System, L. Kramer ed., 234–279 (1996).

Gross, Samuel R. and Kent D. Syverud, Don't Try: Civil Jury Verdicts in a System Geared to Settlement, 44 UCLA L. Rev. 1, 31–32 (1996).

Herschel, Clemmens, Services of Experts in the Conduct of Judicial Inquiries, 21 Am. L. Rev. 571 (1886).

Howard, M. N., The Neutral Expert: A Plausible Threat to Justice, 1991 Crim. L. Rev. 98, 101.

Imwinkelried, Edward J., The "Bases" of Expert Testimony: The Syllogistic Structure of Scientific Testimony, 67 N.C. L. Rev. 1 (1988).

Imwinkelried, Edward J., The Next Step After Daubert: Developing A Similarly Epistemological Approach to Ensuring the Reliability of Nonscientific Expert Testimony, 15 Cardozo L. Rev. 2271 (1994).

Imwinkelried, Edward J., The Standard for Admitting Scientific Evidence: A Critique From the Perspective of Juror Psychology, 28 Vill. L. Rev. 554 (1982–83).

Katz, Marvin, Comment, The Admissibility of Expert Medical Testimony Based in Part upon Information Received from Third Persons, 35 S. Cal. L. Rev. (1962).

Koehler, J., Error and Exaggeration in the Presentation of DNA Evidence at Trial, 34 Jurimetics 21 (1993).

Lempert, Richard O., After the DNA Wars: Skirmishing with NRC II, 37 Jurimetrics J. 439 (1997).

Levy, Elwood S., Impartial Medical Testimony—Revised, 34 Temp. L. Q. 416 (1961).

Lindblom, Marjorie P., Note, Compelling Experts to Testify: A Proposal, 44 U. Chi. L. Rev. 851 (1977).

McCord, David, The Admissibility of Expert Testimony Regarding Rape Trauma Syndrome in Rape Prosecutions, 26 B. C. L. Rev. 1143 (1985).

Masaro, Toni, Expert, Psychology, Credibility, and Rape: The Rape Trauma Syndrome Issue and Its Implications for Expert Psychological Testimony, 69 Minn. L. Rev. 395 (1985).

Myers, Larry W., "The Battle of the Experts": A New Approach to an Old Problem in Medical Testimony, 44 Neb. L. Rev. 539 (1965).

Neufeld, Peter J., The (Near) Irrelevance of *Daubert* to Criminal Justice and Some Suggestions for Reform, 95 Amer. J. of Public Health S107 (2005).

Rheingold, Paul D., The Basis of Medical Testimony, 15 Vand. L. Rev. 473 (1962).

Rice, Frank S., The Medical Expert as a Witness, 10 Green Bag 464 (1898).

Risinger, D. Michael, et al., Exorcism of Ignorance as a Proxy for Rational Knowledge: The Lessons of Handwriting Identification "Expertise," 137 Univ. Pa. L. Rev. 731 (1989).

Risinger, Michael, Navigating Expert Reliability: Are Criminal Standards of Certainty Left on the Dock? 64 Albany L. Rev. 99, 135–36 (2000).

Saks, Michael J., Merlin and Solomon: Lessons from the Law's Formative Encounters with Forensic Identification Science, 49 Hastings L.J. 1069 (1998).

Sink, John M., The Unused Power of a Federal Judge to Call His Own Expert Witness, 29 S. Cal. L. Rev. 195 (1956).

Stefan, Susan, The Protection Racket: Rape Trauma Syndrome, Psychiatric Labeling, and Law, 88 N.W. L. Rev. 1271, 1333–39 (1994).

Thompson, William C., DNA Testing, in David Levinson (Ed.), Encyclopedia of Crime and Punishment, vol 2, pp. 537–44.

Torrey, Morrison, When Will We Be Believed? Rape Myths and the Idea of a Fair Trial in Rape Prosecutions, 24 U. C. Davis L. Rev. 1013 (1991).

Walker, Laurens and John Monahan, Social Frameworks: A New Use of Social Science in Law, 73 Va. L. Rev. 559 (1987).

Washburn, Emory, Testimony of Experts, 1 Am. L. Rev. 45, 48–49 (1866).

CHAPTER 10

EXHIBITS

■ ■ ■

I. INTRODUCTION

A. EXHIBITS VS. TESTIMONY

In America, unlike some other countries, testimony delivered orally in court is the iconic and most frequent form of trial evidence. The jurors hear the witness speak, under oath, typically in answer to questions, and they evaluate her statements. However, a great deal of evidence is presented in the form of *objects* that are marked as exhibits and received in evidence. The most common exhibits are documents—letters, contracts, payroll records, medical records, etc., or, increasingly, printouts or digital images of computer created "documents" and records. In many cases, documentary evidence overshadows testimony. But almost any object of reasonable size can become an exhibit in a trial—a gun, a bottle of pills, a railroad tie, fiber from a carpet, a map of a city, a plastic model of the human heart, a video recording of traffic at an intersection.

With testimony, the jury is ordinarily dependent on the witness to report accurately what she saw. Consider, for example, a homicide trial which turns on whether the defendant's use of a gun was a reasonable response to the deceased's movement for a knife. If an eyewitness testifies that the deceased "picked up a switch blade, about six inches long," the jury will have to decide whether the witness has accurately described the knife as well as the significance this fact may have for the case. However, if the knife is introduced as an exhibit the jurors can *see* and, if necessary, *feel* the knife for themselves. There is no issue of credibility with respect to the description of the knife. The only question is whether the exhibit is what the proponent claims it is—a knife the deceased picked up (and, if so, what significance that has for the case).

The proponent of any item of evidence must make a foundational showing that the offered evidence is what she claims it to be. In the case of testimony the witness must be shown to have been in a position to know what she is talking about, a fact that is usually established in the course of the witness's testimony. For an exhibit, the claim is that the object is in fact a gun found at the crime scene, a diagram of the building that burnt down, a contract signed by the defendant, or any other object that will (in itself or in conjunction with testimony) help the jury in its task. The process of establishing this claim is called authentication and will be discussed in Section II of this Chapter. For the moment we merely note that, in general, authentication requires some external evidence—usually, testimony from a witness—that a proffered exhibit is what it is said to be.

An exhibit may be objectionable on any ground that applies to testimony. If it's inflammatory or confusing, it may be unduly prejudicial; if it contains a description of an event and is offered to prove that the description is true, it is hearsay; if it records a confidential attorney-client communication, it is privileged; and so forth. But although the objections are the same, the procedure for making them is slightly different when the evidence is presented in a tangible form rather than in oral statements—as we will see in Section II.

B. REAL VS. DEMONSTRATIVE EXHIBITS—MAPS, DIAGRAMS, SCALE MODELS, ETC.

Exhibits can be of two basic types. Some are objects that played a role in the events giving rise to the litigation or that were formed or altered by those events or by such objects. These exhibits are often called *real evidence.* Common examples of real evidence include the weapon used in a homicide or an assault; a contract signed by the parties; blood or other tissue taken from a dead body or a living person; contraband that was seized by the police; surveillance photographs of a robbery; and the like. Other exhibits are prepared by a party in anticipation of trial for the purpose of explaining, demonstrating, or clarifying the testimony of a witness. These are called *demonstrative* or *illustrative* evidence. Common examples of demonstrative exhibits include a diagram of the floor plan of a building; a scale model of machinery; a plastic skeleton of the human body; a chart displaying the price of wheat over time; family income by race, or any other data; and so forth.[1]

Some courts do not distinguish between real and demonstrative evidence because the procedures governing the use of exhibits are similar in both cases. Regardless of the nature of the exhibit, the proponent must, as a foundational matter, present evidence that it is what she represents it to be. The difference between real and demonstrative or illustrative exhibits comes into play after that threshold is passed. If an

---

[1]   These categories, of course, do not exist in nature; they were created by courts. Professor Jennifer Mnookin argues persuasively that the terms "demonstrative evidence" and "illustrative evidence" were not generally used and had no fixed meanings in American law until the late 19th century when photographic evidence came into common use. Judges who had to decide how to treat photographs molded history to suit their purpose. They looked back at earlier cases in which maps, drawings, diagrams, and the like were presented in evidence, interpreted these uses as a general pattern permitting the use of "demonstrative" or "illustrative" evidence and held that photographs could be used on the same terms. The effect was not merely to create a new and apparently coherent category of evidence out of a disorganized pattern of prior practice but also to spur attorneys to make much greater use of all sorts of evidence that fit in this category—maps, diagrams and models as well as photographs. Jennifer L. Mnookin, The Image of Truth: Photographic Evidence and the Power of Analogy, 10 Yale J.L. & Human. 1 (1998).

exhibit is *real evidence* then, *once the jury decides what it is*, it has probative value in itself, independent of any witness. If an exhibit is merely *demonstrative* or *illustrative evidence*, its probative value (even after the jury decides what it is) depends entirely, or in part, on the credibility of one or more witnesses.

Thus, a plaster cast of a footprint is real evidence. Once the jury accepts the claim that it was created at the scene of a relevant event, the exhibit speaks for itself. A photograph of a footprint is also real evidence, for the same reason. But a hand-drawn picture is an illustrative exhibit because its value depends on the credibility of the artist—the jury must believe that she accurately perceived and accurately represented the matter in the picture. The mangled fender of a car after an accident is real evidence, even if expert testimony is necessary to identify it. A mangled fender created by a reconstruction of the accident is an illustrative exhibit—its probative value depends on the credibility of testimony that the reconstruction was similar enough to the actual accident for the fender to be useful in deciding the causes or consequences of that event. A film of a crash (if there happens to be one) is real evidence; a film of a reenactment, or a computer simulation, is merely demonstrative.

The fact that an exhibit is *real* evidence does not necessarily mean that it is especially compelling or unambiguous, or that it is more probative than a demonstrative exhibit. A plaster case of a footprint (real evidence) may be a crumbling mess, while a pencil drawing of the same print (demonstrative evidence) is highly revealing. A photograph of a building (real evidence) may be distorted (if, for example, it was taken through a lens with short focal length), while a scale diagram (demonstrative evidence) may be such a fair representation that all parties stipulate to its accuracy.

When a party creates an exhibit for illustrative or explanatory purposes, there is always some danger that the party will take unfair advantage. Courts are well aware of this. They require that the exhibit be relevant, just as any other evidence must be relevant. Moreover, the usual protections against unfair prejudice and confusion of the issues provided by FRE 403 are available to exclude exhibits that do more harm than good.

There is no requirement that evidence created for illustrative purposes be essential to the jury's understanding of testimony. If the exhibit evidence might be at all helpful in understanding testimony, it satisfies the basic test of relevance, and unless there is some countervailing consideration, the evidence will be admitted. One factor that will be considered is the time required to explain the exhibit. The objection that evidence is merely cumulative is often raised with exhibits prepared for illustrative purposes. These objections are not necessarily stronger or weaker than similar objections directed at testimony alone. A case-by-case approach to the evidence is required.

Objections that an exhibit distorts the facts, exaggerates an injury, or is misleading are more likely to succeed against demonstrative evidence than against real evidence because the former is subject to manipulation while the latter should be faithful to the condition in which it was found. You can see the difference if you compare a reenactment of an accident with a video recording of the accident itself that happens to be available. The reenactment may be created to emphasize what a party wants emphasized. The video recording, on the other hand, may suffer from problems of camera angle and the like, but except for editing out whole sections, there is nothing that a party can do to change it (absent major technical manipulation).

There are, however, situations in which courts prefer illustrative evidence to exhibits that were created by the actual events giving rise to the litigation. Consider a homicide or wrongful death case in which the cause of death is disputed. It might be possible to preserve and present the relevant portion of the corpse—a dismembered head, for example—as evidence of how the deceased died, but the emotional impact of doing so would be so disruptive that courts insist on models or diagrams. If the real thing is so dramatic or emotionally compelling that it will be excessively prejudicial or distracting, illustrative evidence may be required.

C. REAL VS. TESTIMONIAL EVIDENCE

Real evidence, then, is evidence that is available directly to the senses—that can be seen, heard, tasted, smelled, touched. Testimonial evidence, by contrast, is the report by another person—a witness—who has experienced such sensory impressions. The basic evidentiary requirement that all witnesses speak from personal knowledge recognizes that testimonial evidence begins as real evidence. What the witnesses see, feel, hear, or otherwise sense firsthand would be real evidence if the jurors were present at the event and able to share the witnesses' sense perceptions. It becomes testimonial because a need to assess credibility is interposed between the occurrence and the jury's assessment of its meaning.[2]

Testimonial evidence in its simplest form is a statement of a witness's observations—for example, a statement by W that the

---

[2] In one sense testimonial evidence remains real, since it must be perceived by a jury in some sensate manner, usually through the sense of hearing. But all evidence must be perceived through the senses, so there is no point in focusing on the way testimonial evidence is real if we are looking for a way to distinguish testimonial evidence from other forms of evidence. Analytically, however, one may argue that there is really only one form of evidence, although there may be different forms of proof. Jerome Michael and Mortimer Adler make this point in a perceptive and sophisticated article, Real Proof: I, 5 Vand. L. Rev. 344, 356 (1952).

defendant's car ran a red light. When a witness reports the statements of another (for example, *W*'s statement that *X* said that the defendant's car ran a red light) we have compound testimonial evidence—hearsay—if the other's statement is offered for its truth. In the latter case, the jury must assess the credibility of two individuals before reaching a conclusion about the fact in issue. FRE 806, which provides for the impeachment of hearsay declarants, implicitly recognizes the testimonial nature of reported hearsay. Statements offered for their truth are testimonial in nature even if reduced to writing and offered as exhibits.

When an out-of-court statement is offered to prove something other than the truth of what it asserts, the evidence can be either real or testimonial. For example, a police officer's oral or written report that the plaintiff spoke to him after an accident would be testimonial evidence that the witness was conscious at that time. But a note written by the plaintiff immediately after the accident would be real circumstantial evidence that the plaintiff was conscious when he wrote the note.

We have indicated a basic distinction between real and testimonial evidence, but there is no bright line to mark the boundary. Indeed, to the extent that demeanor is important in judging credibility, real and testimonial evidence merge, since demeanor evidence is real evidence: the jury perceives the witness's manner directly.[3] The two kinds of evidence also merge to the extent that the probative value of real evidence depends upon the foundation laid for the evidence by the testimony of a witness. A knife may be a very telling item of evidence *if* the jury believes the testimony that it was the weapon wielded by the deceased in a homicide case, but not otherwise.

D. SPECIAL RULES FOR EXHIBITS

The previous chapters have focused almost entirely on testimony. A number of the evidence rules you have learned, such as the relevance rules, apply to exhibits in much the same way as they apply to testimony. Others, such as the opinion and hearsay rules, do not apply to exhibits as such, although they may apply to statements contained in documentary exhibits. In this chapter we shall discuss special rules that apply only to real or demonstrative exhibits.

Because exhibits appeal directly to the jurors' senses and because such evidence may create impressions more vivid than any words, real

---

[3]   Demeanor evidence is an exception to the general rule that before something can become an item of evidence it must be offered by a litigant and admitted by a judge. Michael and Adler, supra note 2, argue that this is the only exception. 5 Vand. L. Rev. at 365–66 and n.65. Another possible exception is when a jury takes "judicial" notice of common experience, a phenomenon explored in several problems in Chapter Eleven, Section II.B, infra. Should a judge or a jury be permitted to consider the demeanor of a non-witness sitting in the courtroom? See e.g. Morrison v. People of State of California, 291 U.S. 82, 94 (1934); United States v. Schipani, 293 F. Supp. 156, 163 (E.D.N.Y. 1968), affirmed, 414 F.2d 1262, 1268 (2d Cir. 1969).

and demonstrative evidence have the potential to be particularly persuasive. However, real and demonstrative evidence may also be as weak or as questionable as the weakest testimonial evidence. It depends on how the evidence was developed and on what it purports to be.

In thinking about the persuasive power of evidence, whether testimonial or non-testimonial, it is important to keep two different aspects in mind: First, a jury must believe that certain evidence is credible before it will use the evidence to decide a case. Second, a jury must decide how to use what it finds credible.

Consider, for example, the prosecution of someone we shall call Howard Smith, for selling heroin. A witness testifies, "I called a telephone number listed as belonging to Howard Smith. The person who answered said he was Howard Smith. He said he had gotten hold of some heroin, so we arranged for a sale, and the heroin was delivered as arranged." When this evidence is offered against Smith, the jury must decide whether it believes that the witness is testifying truthfully. If it does not, the evidence will be dismissed as unhelpful (or perhaps even considered as evidence of innocence or prosecutorial bad faith). If it believes the witness, the jury's next step is to decide whether the defendant, Howard Smith, is the person who identified himself as the Howard Smith on the phone. The evidence may suggest that this is likely, but it could leave room for doubt, just as the credibility of the witness who testified about the conversation may be doubted. If the jury believes the witness and believes that the defendant is the Smith who agreed to sell the heroin, it will convict.

Now consider the situation where the witness has recorded the conversation with Smith. The jury must make the same two inferences. First, it must decide whether a conversation took place. The recording (real evidence) is likely to be particularly persuasive on this issue. Second, it must decide whether the defendant is the person who identified himself as Smith on the recording. Unless the recording is clear enough to allow an unequivocal identification of Smith's voice, there will be some degree of uncertainty on that issue. If the jury resolves the uncertainty by concluding that Smith is the voice on the recording, it will again convict. Otherwise, it will not.

In this example, real evidence is likely to lead the jurors to more readily accept certain facts as true—i.e., that the witness in fact conversed with someone who identified himself as Howard Smith. But it is also possible that testimonial evidence might be more persuasive evidence of certain facts. If the prosecution produced an apparently credible witness who had been with Howard Smith when he arranged the deal, that witness's testimony that the defendant was the person talking on the phone is likely to be more persuasive than a voice identification based on a tape that is hard to hear.

Why should special attention be given to exhibits if a jury is expected to use them the same way as testimony? There are several reasons.

First, neither lawyers nor judges can question exhibits. This makes the testimony of witnesses who set exhibits in context critically important. The Smith drug case is an illustration. The tape recording is only helpful if a jury can relate it to the charge made against Smith. In the usual case, a witness would testify to information such as how he placed the call and when the call was made, and he would then go on to say that the tape was an accurate recording of the ensuing conversation. If this witness is not believed, the tape is not likely to be useful. The foundation is vital. Neither real nor demonstrative exhibits are assumed to be helpful until a connection to the case is shown. Thus, many of the rules that relate to real and demonstrative evidence are concerned with the requisite foundation for admissibility. These rules are designed to ensure that such evidence meets minimal standards of reliability and that the jury can reasonably find that the evidence is what it purports to be.

Second, exhibits are sometimes dramatic. A jury might be heavily influenced (properly or improperly) by a blood soaked mattress or a video simulation of a plane crash as seen from the cockpit. The particularly vivid quality of some exhibits—together with the impossibility of cross-examining pictures or other objects, and the fact that intermediaries do not filter the information contained in real and demonstrative evidence—create a concern that such evidence will receive special, perhaps excessive, emphasis in the jury's deliberations. Special restrictions may be placed on real or demonstrative evidence when it is feared that such evidence might receive undue weight.

Third, many exhibits make their impact in an instant. Once the jury sees a photograph of a severed hand, there is not much anyone can do to minimize its impact. Therefore, a party must lay the foundation for an exhibit—and provide the opposing party with an opportunity to object and to present evidence on the foundational issue—*before* the exhibit may be shown to the jury.

II.   AUTHENTICATION

A.   THE GENERAL REQUIREMENT

FRE 901(a) provides that "[t]o satisfy the requirement of authenticating or identifying an item of evidence, the proponent must produce evidence sufficient to support a finding that the item is what the proponent claims it is." As the Advisory Committee Notes to FRE 901(a) point out, this requirement "falls in the category of relevancy dependent upon fulfillment of a condition of fact and is governed by the procedure set forth in Rule 104(b)." In other words, authentication under the federal rules is simply a special case of conditional relevance. The factual condition that must be fulfilled is the claim that the evidence "is what its proponent claims."

The requirement of authentication is most frequently applied to documents, and typically, what must be shown is the source or author of the document. We face the same issue constantly in everyday life, but our approach is different from that required by the rules of evidence. As McCormick notes:

> In the everyday affairs of business and social life, it is the custom to look merely at the writing itself for evidence as to its source. Thus, if the writing bears a signature purporting to be that of X, or recites that it was made by X, we assume, nothing to the contrary appearing, that it is exactly what it purports to be, the work of X. At this point, however, the law of evidence has long differed from the common sense assumption upon which each of us conducts her own affairs. Instead it adopts the position that the purported signature or recital of authorship on the face of a writing will *not* be accepted as sufficient preliminary proof of authenticity to secure the admission of the writing in evidence.[4]

What showing is required to authenticate an item of evidence? And who will determine its sufficiency, the judge or the jury? At common law, procedures varied. FRE 901(a) codifies the common law rule. As with any other issue of conditional relevance (see FRE 104(b)), the screening is by the judge, who simply decides if there is *sufficient* evidence to support a jury finding of authenticity. If the exhibit passes that test, the jury may consider it for whatever the jury believes it's worth. Recall, however, that under the procedures for FRE 104(b) (which govern decisions under FRE 901)[5] the required evidence, however slight, must be admissible (unlike determinations of admissibility that the judge makes under FRE 104(a), which are "not bound by evidence rules, except those on privilege").

Logically, FRE 901(a) is superfluous. It simply says that the "requirement of authenticating or identifying" imposes no demand beyond that already embodied in FRE 104(b). FRE 901(a) does not define "authenticating" or "identifying," or specify when they are required, it merely restates the general rule in FRE 104(b), and FRE 901(b) illustrates ways of establishing the necessary foundation when it is required. The specific illustrations that are given are drawn from contexts in which "authentication" or "identification" historically have been required; most deal with real evidence, but a couple deal with testimonial evidence concerning the identification of a voice or of a participant in a telephone conversation.

---

[4]   McCormick (6th ed.) § 221.

[5]   See Advisory Committee Note to FRE 901(a).

FRE 901. Authenticating or Identifying Evidence

(a) **In General.** To satisfy the requirement of authenticating or identifying an item of evidence, the proponent must produce evidence sufficient to support a finding that the item is what the proponent claims it is.

(b) **Examples.** The following are examples only—not a complete list—of evidence that satisfies the requirement:

(1) *Testimony of a Witness with Knowledge.* Testimony that an item is what it is claimed to be.

(2) *Nonexpert Opinion About Handwriting.* A nonexpert's opinion that handwriting is genuine, based on a familiarity with it that was not acquired for the current litigation.

(3) *Comparison by an Expert Witness or the Trier of Fact.* A comparison with an authenticated specimen by an expert witness or the trier of fact.

(4) *Distinctive Characteristics and the Like.* The appearance, contents, substance, internal patterns, or other distinctive characteristics of the item, taken together with all the circumstances.

(5) *Opinion About a Voice.* An opinion identifying a person's voice—whether heard firsthand or through mechanical or electronic transmission or recording—based on hearing the voice at any time under circumstances that connect it with the alleged speaker.

(6) *Evidence About a Telephone Conversation.* For a telephone conversation, evidence that a call was made to the number assigned at the time to:

> (A) a particular person, if circumstances, including self-identification, show that the person answering was the one called; or

> (B) a particular business, if the call was made to a business and the call related to business reasonably transacted over the telephone.

(7) *Evidence About Public Records.* Evidence that:

> (A) a document was recorded or filed in a public office as authorized by law; or

> (B) a purported public record or statement is from the office where items of this kind are kept.

(8) *Evidence About Ancient Documents or Data Compilations.* For a document or data compilation, evidence that it:

> (A) is in a condition that creates no suspicion about its authenticity;

> (B) was in a place where, if authentic, it would likely be; and

> (C) is at least 20 years old when offered.

(9) *Evidence About a Process or System.* Evidence describing a process or system and showing that it produces an accurate result.

(10) *Methods Provided by a Statute or Rule.* Any method of authentication or identification allowed by a federal statute or a rule prescribed by the Supreme Court.

Saltzburg, Martin and Capra's *Federal Rules of Evidence Manual* discusses the examples in subsection (b) of the rule:

> Subdivision (b) of Rule 901 contains ten illustrations of ways of authenticating evidence. It is plain that these are only illustrative; they are not limitations on the ways authentication can be accomplished. These examples are considered seriatim below.
>
> (1) Testimony of a witness who has personal knowledge as to a piece of evidence is a classic way of authenticating the evidence. Someone who is an eyewitness to the signing of a document may authenticate the document, for example.
>
> (2) A layperson can identify handwriting based upon familiarity with the handwriting, as long as the familiarity was not acquired solely for purposes of the litigation in which the testimony is offered.
>
> (3) Handwriting, fingerprints, blood, hair, clothing fibers, and numerous other things can be authenticated by comparison with specimens that have been authenticated. Sometimes the comparison can be done by the trier of fact; at other times an expert witness will be required, especially when scientific knowledge is needed to make a valid examination of the samples. Although the rule does not retain the common-law requirement that the exemplar's genuineness be established to the court's satisfaction, the trial judge still has discretion under Rule 403 to exclude specimens when questions as to their authenticity will be confusing and excessively time consuming.
>
> (4) Sometimes the characteristics of an item will themselves serve to authenticate the item. A letter may be authenticated, for example, by content and the circumstances indicating it was a reply to a duly authenticated letter.
>
> . . .
>
> (5) One who is familiar with the voice of another may authenticate a conversation or identify the speaker on a tape or other recording. However, if the tape or recording is offered for its truth, hearsay problems still will exist and must be solved following the satisfaction of the authentication requirement. Best evidence problems may likewise exist, and they too must be addressed. Authentication is thus just one hurdle among several to admissibility. Note that the person making the identification

may have become familiar with the voice for purposes of litigation, something not allowed in connection with handwriting.

(6) A speaker in a conversation may be identified other than by voice identification. For example, a telephone conversation might be authenticated in the case of a business by showing that a call was made to the number assigned to a business by the telephone company, that someone answered the phone purporting to represent the business, and that the conversation related to business reasonably transacted over the telephone. In the case of an individual, the fact that the number was assigned to the individual and that the person talking on the phone identified himself as being a certain person may be enough to authenticate the conversation, but ... most courts have required some circumstantial evidence in addition to self-identification.

(7) Public records are usually authenticated by proof of custody. This illustration extends the traditional thinking to cover data stored in computers.

(8) This is the traditional authentication by showing an ancient document. If evidence is presented that a document or data compilation (apparently including data stored in computers) is in such condition as to create no suspicion concerning its authenticity, is in a place where it would likely be if it were authentic, and has been in existence twenty years or more at the time it is offered, this is sufficient authentication. (Common law required 30 years.)

(9) Authentication may be accomplished by showing that a process or system produces an accurate result when it is employed. In order to introduce an X-ray, for instance, it may be necessary to demonstrate that the X-ray machine is accurate. Judicial notice may sometimes solve the problem here. Judges must be careful to differentiate, however, between authentication of a process generally and a showing that a particular machine works as intended.

(10) Any method of authentication or identification provided by an Act of Congress or by Rules prescribed by the Supreme Court shall be valid to authenticate. This is included to ensure that no one interprets the Rules of Evidence as superseding the established Civil and Criminal Rules of Procedure or Bankruptcy Rules.

. . .

Because subdivision (b) offers illustrations, it is arguable that some of the limitations—e.g., that the person identifying handwriting have been familiar with the writing prior to the litigation—are hortatory only and need not be honored. Whether they are binding or not, most Courts are following the limitations and seem to appreciate the guidance provided by the Rule.[6]

The fact that an exhibit (or voice, or telephone conversation) has been "authenticated" does not necessarily resolve the question of its identity. If the plaintiff testifies that Exhibit A is a contract that the defendant signed in his presence, that is sufficient authentication under FRE 901(b)(1) to admit the purported contract in evidence since the jury *could reasonably find* that the plaintiff is telling the truth. But the defendant may dispute its genuineness; she may testify and convince the jury that it's a forgery. If so, Exhibit A will remain in evidence, but the jury (we trust) will give it no weight and no legal effect.

Evidence of identity may be relevant or necessary for other evidentiary purposes in addition to fulfilling the foundational requirement of authentication. For example, a letter describing the hiring practices of Corporation X may be *relevant* in the trial of an employment discrimination complaint against Corporation X so long as it was written by a person with knowledge of these practices. If relevance were the only issue, the judge (under FREs 901 and 104(b)) would merely decide whether there is sufficient evidence from which the jury could reasonably conclude that the letter was written by some person—any person—who had such knowledge. Such authenticating evidence could consist of the appearance of the letter (e.g., the letter head), and its contents "taken in conjunction with circumstances" (e.g., whether the letter displays verifiable knowledge of other aspects of the company's operations) (FRE 901(b)(4)). But relevance alone will not make this letter admissible to prove how the company hired employees; for that purpose it is hearsay. To admit it the judge must find a hearsay exception. For example, if the letter is offered against the company, it would be admitted as an opposing party's statement (FRE 801(d)(2)) if it had been written by an authorized spokesperson for Corporation X, or by an "agent or employee on a matter within the scope of that relationship and while it existed." To decide whether the letter is admissible as an opposing party's statement, the judge (not the jury) must determine the identity and the status of the writer. Under *Bourjaily v. United States,*[7] the judge must make this decision (which may be based, at least in part, on otherwise inadmissible evidence) by a preponderance of the evidence.

Alternatively, consider a twenty-five year-old memorandum describing the hiring practices of Corporation X at the time it was written. Assuming these remote practices are relevant to show (for

---

[6] 3 Stephen A. Saltzburg, Michael M. Martin, & Daniel J. Capra, Federal Rules of Evidence Manual 1992–94 (7th ed. 1998). Reprinted from Federal Rules of Evidence Manual, 7th Edition with permission. Copyright 1998 Matthew Bender & Company, a part of LexisNexis. All rights reserved.

[7] 483 U.S. 171 (1987). See Chapter Six, p. 602, for a more extensive discussion of the implications of *Bourjaily.*

example) a history of intentional gender discrimination, the memorandum may be authenticated as an "ancient document" (FRE 901(b)(8)) simply by presenting evidence of its age, and showing that its condition raised no "suspicion" as to authenticity. Moreover, if authenticated, statements in the memorandum would be admissible under the "ancient documents" exception to the hearsay rule (FRE 803(16)) without regard to the identity of the author. Nonetheless, the identity of the author might bear on the *credibility* and the weight the jury gives those statements. Thus the plaintiffs may want to prove that it was written by the then chief executive officer of Corporation X, while the defendant corporation would prefer to show that it was written by a disgruntled employee with no knowledge of hiring practices.[8]

For demonstrative exhibits, the requirement of authentication is generally quite simple since the proponent's claim about the evidence is limited—merely that it is an accurate and helpful summary or illustration or diagram of relevant testimony by a witness. The possible foundational objections to the admission of a demonstrative exhibit are also limited: that it is *not* an accurate reflection of the testimony, or that it is misleading, confusing, or inflammatory. In this context, objections to authentication are swallowed up by general objections under FRE 403, since Rule 403 demands more. For example if a party attempts to introduce a scale model of a building, the judge should rule that it has been properly authenticated under FRE 901 if there is sufficient evidence from which the jury *could* conclude that it's an accurate model of the building in question. Nonetheless, if the quality of the model is doubtful, the judge might still exclude the exhibit under FRE 403 if she concludes that its probative value (as demonstrative evidence) is substantially outweighed by the dangers of confusing or misleading the jury, or wasting the jury's time.

Problem X-1. You are a plaintiff in a lawsuit against your law school. You wish to introduce in evidence the letter you received from the law school offering you admission as a law student to prove that you were admitted to the school. (For that purpose, the letter is not hearsay.)[9] **In how many different ways could you make a foundational presentation sufficient to authenticate the proffered exhibit?** Assume that your admission was conveyed to you by email. **In what ways could you make a sufficient foundational presentation in that context?**

---

[8] The plaintiffs would be allowed to put on evidence of the identity of the writer to show her personal knowledge, which is required despite the hearsay exception (see Advisory Committee Note to FRE 803); the defendant corporation could attempt to identify the author in order to impeach the hearsay declarant, under FRE 806.

[9] Why not?

Problem X-2. Federal narcotics agents suspected Gary Let of smuggling narcotics. The agents secured a warrant to wiretap the telephone in Let's home to "obtain evidence of the participation of Let and others unnamed in a conspiracy to smuggle heroin and other narcotic drugs into the United States in violation of federal law." In several of Let's conversations with unidentified persons they discussed "bringing in the stuff," but no mention of drugs was made. **Are the recorded conversations admissible at Let's trial for smuggling? What steps should the government attorney take in an attempt to lay a foundation?**

B. AUTHENTICATION PROCEDURE

Consider an item of testimonial evidence: for example, a statement by a witness that the defendant in a murder trial shouted at the deceased, "You're dead!" FRE 602 requires sufficient evidence "to support a finding that the witness has personal knowledge of the matter," but that evidence is not usually supplied in any special proceedings. Generally, evidence of personal knowledge is implicit in the context—as it would be, for instance, if a witness in a homicide trial had testified that she was in the same room as the defendant and the deceased. In unusual situations where personal knowledge appears to be lacking, opposing counsel may object.

For exhibits, there are three differences. *First*, the exhibit must be incorporated in the record as an object—unlike spoken testimony, which is simply recorded together with everything else that is said in court. *Second*, the foundational requirement (authentication) is considered more problematic. Therefore, the proponent is required to make a specific showing that the "item is what the proponent claims it is." FRE 901. *Third*, the proponent is generally required to move specially to admit the item in evidence, and the opposing party is routinely allowed to object in advance and to attempt to undercut the proponent's showing. The following example illustrates the process:

BROWN VS. WHITE

Transcript

By Plaintiff's Counsel (P.C.):

Q. Ms. Brown, after these negotiations, did you ever hear from Mr. White again?

A. Yes.

Commentary

There are seven stages to the process of admitting an exhibit in evidence, as illustrated by this transcript.

Transcript

Q.   How?

A.   I received a letter.

Commentary

P.C.: Mr. Clerk, please mark this document as Plaintiff's Exhibit No. 1, for identification. (Pause). Thank you.

1. *Marking.* This is the first step. The exhibit is now part of the record and available for review by the trial court or on appeal whether or not it is ultimately admitted in evidence. So far, the exhibit is not in evidence and may not be seen by the jury.

P.C.: May the record reflect that I am showing Plaintiff's Exhibit No. 1 to counsel for Mr. White. (Pause). Thank you.

2. *Showing.* Opposing counsel is entitled to see the exhibit in advance, in order to decide whether to object (and on what basis) before the jury sees the exhibit. In some courts, the judge will also want to see the exhibit at this point.

By P.C.: Q. Ms. Brown, I'm handing you a document marked Plaintiff's Exhibit 1, for identification. Do you recognize it?

3. *Authenticating.* The proponent of the exhibit must do two things at this point:

A.   Yes.

First, she must present evidence describing what the exhibit is, in general terms.

Q.   What is it?

A.   A letter from Mr. Ralph White to me, dated January 12, 2010.

In this case, it's a letter from the defendant to the plaintiff (or so the plaintiff claims). The text of the letter (which opposing counsel has now seen) presumably establishes its relevance. (Notice that the attorney is careful to refer to the document as "Plaintiff's Exhibit 1." That way the transcript is unambiguous.)

Q.   How do you know it's from Mr. White?

Second, she must present sufficient evidence to support a finding of "authenticity"— that the exhibit is what the proponent claims it to be. In this case the plaintiff appears to supply that evidence by testifying that she recognized Mr. Brown's signature and had seen it before this letter. See FRE 901(b)(2).

A.   It's on his stationery, and it's signed by him.

Transcript

Q. When you received this letter, were you already familiar with Ralph White's signature?

A. Yes. I'd had other letters from him.

P.C.: Your Honor, I move to admit Plaintiff's Exhibit No. 1 in evidence.

Defense Counsel (D.C.): I object, Your Honor. Insufficient authentication. May I voir dire the witness?

The Court: Proceed.

By D.C.: Q. You said that you had received "other letters" from Mr. White before this letter that you claim was from him. Actually, you only received one letter from Ralph White before January 12, 2010, isn't that correct, Ms. Brown?

A. I think you're right. I'm sorry.

Q. And that was over three years earlier, in the fall of 2006 right?

Commentary

4. *Motion.* Having laid the foundation (or attempted to do so), the proponent asks the judge to admit the exhibit in evidence.

5. *Opportunity to object and voir dire.* In this context, to "voir dire" the witness means to cross-examine the witness before cross is normally permitted in order to obtain information that can be used to clarify the admissibility of the evidence and, if appropriate, to object.

The opposing attorney objects on grounds of insufficient authentication, but he might also have objected at this point on other grounds, if appropriate: hearsay, undue prejudice, etc. The opponent is allowed to produce evidence on the objection. Here the objection is lack of authentication, and the standard the proponent must meet is merely "evidence sufficient to support a finding." Therefore, an opposing witness will be of no help; the opponent must try to show from the authenticating witness herself that she has insufficient knowledge. He is allowed to do that on "voir dire," a limited examination on a preliminary issue.

Defense counsel is trying to show the weakness of the authenticating testimony. He scores some points. They may not be enough to keep the document out—but even so, these concessions may help support a later argument to the jury that the letter is not genuine.

Transcript

A.   I believe that's correct.

DC: Your Honor, I renew my objection. She doesn't know enough to authenticate the exhibit.

The Court: That'll be for the jury to decide. I'll overrule the objection and admit Plaintiff's Exhibit No.1 in evidence.

By P.C.: Q. Ms. Brown, please read Exhibit 1 to the jury.

A.   It says: "Dear Janet, I thought over our discussion. . . . "

Commentary

6. *Ruling.* The court, evidently, concludes that despite the witness's limited knowledge, the minimal requirements of FRE 901 are met, presumably by non-expert opinion testimony identifying the defendant's signature. If that failed, the plaintiff might have tried to authenticate the letter by other means. Consider how she might have done so using the methods illustrated in 901(b)(1), (b)(3), and (b)(4).

7. *Publication.* Now, finally, the proponent can reveal the contents of the exhibit to the jury.

This step—which is called "publication"—can be accomplished in various ways. In this case, the witness reads the document. In addition, the attorney can read it, or it can be passed around the jury box, or a copy can be given to each juror, or the text can be shown on monitors or other displays. When a document is displayed electronically, counsel or a witness may electronically annotate the exhibit to clarify or to emphasize a point. Judges differ considerably in the level of control they exercise over the means of publishing exhibits to the jury. Some expect attorneys to ask for permission to publish an exhibit; some do not. Sometimes judges try to conserve time, especially with long documentary exhibits, by giving them to the jury during recesses or hearings from which the jury is excluded. Jurors may also be given books of exhibits to which they turn when instructed. This procedure is especially efficient if the admissibility of the exhibits has been determined in advance.

In theory, this is the procedure for admitting any exhibit. In practice, it will vary depending on the nature of the object. If the exhibit is a torn and blood-stained nightgown rather than a letter, the jury may become aware of its nature as soon as it is presented to the witness for authentication (if not when it is given to the court clerk for marking). If the opposing attorney has any objection based on the *appearance* of such an exhibit—for example that it is "inflammatory" (i.e., that its prejudicial impact substantially outweighs its probative value)—she must be given (or secure) an opportunity to view the exhibit and make the objection in advance, outside the presence of the jury.

Unlike testimony, exhibits can be directly available for the jury's consideration during deliberations. In some jurisdictions exhibits go to the jury room, unless for some reason the judge chooses to use a different procedure. In other jurisdictions the evidence actually involved in the case may go to the jury room but not the evidence prepared for explanatory or illustrative purposes. Some judges will not send exhibits to the jury room unless the parties agree. There are few hard and fast rules because there are conflicting policies. On the one hand, the jury might learn more from the evidence if it has it during deliberations. On the other hand, the jury does not have a transcript of the testimony, and may give the tangible exhibits disproportionate weight.[10]

Problem X-3. It is three years in the future. You represent Ms. Martha Sloan, a former classmate, who is suing your law school for educational malpractice. In the course of your client's direct examination, as evidence of such malpractice, you wish to present the syllabus (or course description) for the evidence course you are now taking to show that the law school, acting through its agent, your evidence professor, assigned *A Modern Approach to Evidence, Fifth Edition*, as the text for this course. **Plan and rehearse the examination through which you will introduce a copy of the syllabus or course description in evidence as an exhibit.**

---

[10] One reason why exhibits are sometimes sent to the jury room is that each juror does not always get sufficient time to examine an exhibit during the trial, whereas each juror ought to have an excellent opportunity to hear the complete testimony of the witnesses. When lawyers offer real or demonstrative evidence, they often want the jurors to use their own powers of observation to evaluate the evidence. This requires that jurors have an adequate opportunity to examine such evidence. The distinction in treatment may also be a vestige of history. Documents (e.g., contracts, wills, deeds) used to be at the core of most lawsuits and were given to the jury for examination. Transcripts are much more recent. For centuries they were not made at all; and even now, when most cases are recorded and many are transcribed, transcripts of the current case are not generally available at the time the deliberations begin, although real-time court reporters can produce such transcripts. Thus, we developed a tradition of sending exhibits but not transcripts to the jury room.

C. PROCEDURAL SHORTCUTS

The full-blown procedure for authenticating and admitting an exhibit into evidence is inefficient, to say the least. If it were followed, step-by-step, for each of the dozens (or hundreds) of exhibits that are used in many trials, it would take a vast amount of time and distract attention from the real issues in dispute. As a result, various procedural shortcuts have grown up around this practice. Perhaps the most important are procedures to resolve routine questions of authentication before trial. Thus, for example, Federal Rule of Civil Procedure 16(c)(2)(C) lists "obtaining admissions and stipulations about facts and documents to avoid unnecessary proof, and ruling in advance on the admissibility of evidence" among the agenda items for pretrial conferences; and Federal Rule of Civil Procedure 36, governing Requests for Admission, specifically lists among its purposes obtaining an admission of "the genuineness of any described documents." In civil cases, some judges routinely order a pre-trial exchange of all the exhibits that the parties plan to use in their cases-in-chief, and require them to make objections in advance outside the presence of the jury. When this is done, the exhibits can also be marked in advance (as well as shown to the opposition). Whatever steps are undertaken in advance—marking, showing, etc.—need not be repeated at trial. A stipulation or a ruling on *authenticity* resolves that issue but leaves open other possible objections. A stipulation or a ruling on *admissibility* ends the entire matter—although the proponent may have to present sufficient evidence of authenticity for the jury's consideration, and may want to present more if genuineness is actually disputed.

Some procedural steps can be completed in advance even without the assistance of the court or the opposing party. An attorney can almost always get the clerk (or the court reporter if it's her responsibility) to mark an exhibit, or several, ahead of time, generally at a recess. She may show it to the opposing attorney in advance, or alert the judge and solicit any objections. If the exhibit is a document, the lawyer may bring extra copies to give to the opposition and to the judge so the examination of the witness does not have to be interrupted while they examine the original.

D. SUBSTANTIVE SHORTCUTS: SELF-AUTHENTICATION

While the appearance and contents of a document are generally not sufficient to authenticate it, there are exceptions. Some documents may be authenticated without extrinsic evidence because under FRE 902 they are considered "self-authenticating." These include: foreign and domestic public documents, copies of public records, commercial paper and related documents, documents made self-authenticating by a federal statute, official publications, trade inscriptions and the like, and newspapers and periodicals.   In the case of foreign public documents, domestic public documents not under seal and copies of public records, there are special certification requirements before the documents will be treated as self-authenticating.

Specifically, FRE 902 provides:

The following items of evidence are self-authenticating; they require no extrinsic evidence of authenticity in order to be admitted:

(1) *Domestic Public Documents That Are Sealed and Signed.* A document that bears:

> (A) a seal purporting to be that of the United States; any state, district, commonwealth, territory, or insular possession of the United States;, the former Panama Canal Zone; the Trust Territory of the Pacific Islands; a political subdivision of any of these entities; or a department, agency, or officer of any entity named above; and

> (B) a signature purporting to be an execution or attestation.

(2) *Domestic Public Documents That Are Not Sealed but Are Signed and Certified.* A document that bears no seal if:

> (A) it bears the signature of an officer or employee of an entity named in Rule 902(1)(A); and

> (B) another public officer who has a seal and official duties within that same entity certifies under seal—or its equivalent—that the signer has the official capacity that the signature is genuine.

(3) *Foreign Public Documents.* A document that purports to be signed or attested by a person who is authorized by a foreign country's law to do so. The document must be accompanied by a final certification that certifies the genuineness of the signature and official position of the signer or attester—or of any foreign official whose certificate of genuineness relates to the signature or attestation or is in a chain of certificates of genuineness relating to the signature or attestation. The certification may be made by a secretary of a United States embassy or legation; by a consul general, vice consul, or consular agent of the United States; or by a diplomatic or consular official of the foreign country assigned or accredited to the United States. If all parties have been given a reasonable opportunity to investigate the document's authenticity and accuracy, the court may, for good cause, either:

> (A) order that it be treated as presumptively authentic without final certification; or

(B) allow it to be evidenced by an attested summary with or without final certification.

(4) *Certified Copies of Public Records.* A copy of an official record—or a copy of a document that was recorded or filed in a public office as authorized by law—if the copy is certified as correct by:

(A) the custodian or another person authorized to make the certification; or

(B) a certificate that complies with Rule 902(1), (2), or (3), a federal statute, or a rule prescribed by the Supreme Court.

(5) *Official Publications.* A book, pamphlet, or other publication purporting to be issued by a public authority.

(6) *Newspapers and Periodicals.* Printed material purporting to be a newspaper or periodical.

(7) *Trade Inscriptions and the Like.* An inscription, sign, tag, or label purporting to have been affixed in the course of business and indicating origin, ownership, or control.

(8) *Acknowledged Documents.* A document accompanied by a certificate of acknowledgment that is lawfully executed by a notary public or another officer who is authorized to take acknowledgments.

(9) *Commercial Paper and Related Documents.* Commercial paper, a signature on it, and related documents, to the extent allowed by general commercial law.

(10) *Presumptions Under a Federal Statute.* A signature, document, or anything else that a federal statute declares to be presumptively or prima facie genuine or authentic.

(11) **Certified Domestic Records of a Regularly Conducted Activity.** The original or a copy of a domestic record that meets the requirements of Rule 803(6)(A)-(C), as shown by a certification of the custodian or another qualified person that complies with a federal statute or a rule prescribed by the Supreme Court. Before the trial or hearing, the proponent must give an adverse party reasonable written notice of the intent to offer the record—and must make the record and certification available for inspection—so that the party has a fair opportunity to challenge them.

(12) **Certified Foreign Records of a Regularly Conducted Activity.** In a civil case, the original or a copy of a foreign record that meets the requirements of Rule 902(11), modified as follows: the certification, rather than complying with a federal statute or Supreme Court rule, must be signed in a manner that, if falsely made, would subject the maker to a criminal penalty in the country

where the certification is signed. The proponent must also meet the notice requirements of Rule 902(11).

Unlike the illustrations in FRE 901(b), the list of self-authenticating documents in FRE 902 is exclusive. In some states the class of self-authenticating documents is considerably more restricted.

The idea behind self-authentication is that the nature of these documents makes it sufficiently unlikely that they are not what they appear to be that a jury needs no additional basis for considering them as evidence. This is not an exception from the general requirement of authentication; it is a recognition that that requirement can sometimes be met by the appearance of a document together with past experience, which suggests that such documents usually are what they appear to be.

FRE 902 authentication does not mean that an exhibit is a domestic document under seal, or an official publication, or some other enumerated self-authenticating document. There is no way for a court to determine that issue without reference to other (extrinsic) evidence, which is what this rule is designed to avoid. Instead FRE 902 merely asks that the exhibit "purport" to be such a document—i.e., that it bear a seal that looks right, carry a printed masthead, etc. If the document meets this minimal requirement it is authenticated by its appearance. The opponent may argue to the jury that it is not genuine—perhaps even that it is a clear forgery—but the exhibit will remain in evidence. Of course the opponent may also object on other grounds—relevance, for example. In extreme cases the opponent may even exclude a self-authenticated exhibit on the ground that it is not genuine. Imagine, for instance, that a party to a lawsuit presents what appears to be the front page of a newspaper bearing the title "The New York Times." Under FRE 902(6), this exhibit is self-authenticating because it "purports" to be a newspaper and should be admitted without reference to any external information. This would be true even if it was obviously *not* a copy of The New York Times—if, for example, the name was printed in block letters rather than Gothic, and the usual statement in a box

"All the News

That's Fit to Print"

was missing. The opposing attorney could certainly convince the jury that this exhibit was not genuine. In addition, she might also object successfully under FRE 403 that the probative value of this exhibit (essentially, zero) is substantially outweighed by its tendency to confuse and mislead the jury or waste time.[11] More likely, the opposing attorney would let the exhibit go in and use it to embarrass her opponent.

---

[11] Remember that an objection under FRE 403 (unlike an objection to authenticity) is governed by FRE 104(a)—the court must determine whether the objection is valid and may consider inadmissible evidence in the process.

"Yes, I've seen it before. It's a double-dip, double-Dutch-chocolate ice-cream cone. I recognize the sprinkles."

Problem X-4.   Section (6) of FRE 902 makes newspapers self-authenticating.   Thus, in federal court in litigation arising out of an automobile accident there would be no need to authenticate an account of the accident in a local newspaper.   Yet the account would remain inadmissible as evidence of how the accident occurred. **Why?**

Problem X-5. What evidence would you present to authenticate each of the following exhibits?

A.   A video recording of Plaintiff changing a tire on his car, introduced by Defendant to show that Plaintiff had not been crippled in an automobile accident.

B.   An X-ray of Plaintiff's knee, introduced by him to show the damage done to his knee in an automobile accident.

C.   A can of peas, bearing the label Green Midget Company, introduced to show that the Defendant, Green Midget Company, was responsible for the presence in the can of a stone on which the Plaintiff broke a tooth.

D. Testimony that a voice on a recorded phone conversation demanded that the witness pay $100,000 to the Defendant or suffer the consequences, introduced to show that the Defendant is guilty of attempted extortion.

E. A bill, prepared by computer, introduced to show that the Defendant owed the Plaintiff oil company $900 for purchases charged to his credit card.

F. A copy of the Defendant's birth certificate, introduced to show that she is not a deportable alien.

G. A telegram reading, "Accept your offer of 8 a.m. this morning—stop—will buy 10,000 bushels at $10.69—stop—Grant Grain Company," introduced to show that the Grant Grain Company contracted to buy the Plaintiff's wheat.

H. Testimony that a voice on the other end of a phone call answered, "Police Headquarters," took the Defendant's oral account of an accident, and stated that there was no need for the Defendant to file a written report, introduced to show that the Defendant did not fail to report an accident.

E. ADDITIONAL REQUIREMENTS

1. Chain of Custody

Sometimes the minimal level of proof of authenticity demanded by FRE 901 is not the only requirement for admission of an exhibit in evidence. Perhaps the most common additional requirement is that for certain evidence the proponent must establish a "chain of custody." In the usual case, this requirement is applied to real evidence that is of significant importance to a criminal prosecution.

Suppose, for example, that a police officer arrests Jennie Jones and takes from her a substance that he thinks is cocaine. Later, a prosecution chemist analyzes the powder to determine its contents. In the criminal trial of *State v. Jones*, before the chemist is allowed to testify about the results of tests run on the substance, the state must show that the substance it has offered in evidence is not only that which was tested but also that which was seized from the defendant. In our example, the state would have to show that the powder that tested out as 90% pure cocaine is the same powder that was taken from Jennie Jones.

Suppose that the chemist testifies that the labels fell off several packets sent to him for analysis and that a powder he can identify as cocaine might have been seized from either Jones or Smith. Evidence about this substance would be excluded because it could not be shown to have come from Jennie Jones. This is so even though the chemist's testimony is logically relevant, for knowing that powder taken from either Jones or Smith was cocaine makes the conclusion that Jones possessed cocaine more likely than it would be if we knew nothing about the source of the powder, or if the substance taken from either Jones or Smith had turned out to be sugar.   Thus, the decision to exclude the chemist's testimony must be based on more than a concern for logical relevance.   In this case it reflects a judicial judgment that the jury could only guess whether the substance was taken from Jones, and that such guessing is impermissible when the narcotic quality of the substance is a matter that the prosecution must prove beyond a reasonable doubt.   Most courts would exclude the evidence in this situation even if the chemist testified that there was a 70% chance that the cocaine came from Jones—despite the fact that this testimony clearly would *support* a finding that the evidence is what the prosecution claims.

Now suppose the chemist identifies the substance offered in court as that which he tested but says that he does not know from whom the substance was taken.   If the arresting officer testifies that the substance is that which he took from Jones and that he kept careful control over it before giving it to the chemist for testing, the evidence will be admitted. What courts call a "chain of custody" has been established.   For a material like cocaine that has no distinctive markings, a chain of custody requires some system of identification and control.   It may be achieved, for example, by inserting the substance in a sealed envelope and having each person who handles the substance sign the envelope as evidence that he passed on what he took.

Obviously, a chain-of-custody requirement involves more than the usual showing of conditional relevance required by FRE 901.   It requires a high degree of care in the handling of evidence to avoid damage and tampering.   Tampering with evidence may not be a common problem, but the more sloppily evidence is handled, the greater the chances of tampering or of an unintentional mix-up, and the greater the likelihood that it will go undetected.   Fear of tampering has also led some courts to adopt rules requiring special care in the handling of audio recordings.[12]

---

[12]   See e.g., United States v. McMillan, 508 F.2d 101, 104 (8th Cir. 1974), where the court listed seven foundational requirements:

    (1) That the recording device was capable of taking the conversation now offered in evidence.

    (2) That the operator of the device was competent to operate the device.

    (3) That the recording is authentic and correct.

    (4) That changes, additions or deletions have not been made in the recording.

    (5) That the recording has been preserved in a manner that is shown to the court.

    (6) That the speakers are identified.

    (7) That the conversation elicited was made voluntarily and in good faith, without any kind of inducement.

(The last requirement on this list is not an evidentiary foundation but a reflection of constitutional rules that govern the admissibility of statements by defendants in criminal cases.) See also United States v. Oslund, 453 F.3d 1048, 1054 (8th Cir. 2006); United States v. Roach, 28 F.3d 729, 733 (8th Cir. 1994); United States v. Slade, 627 F.2d 293, 301 (D.C. Cir. 1980).

They think that the possibility of alteration is great enough, and alterations are difficult enough to detect that special rules are justified.

With respect to some types of physical evidence, tampering or alteration are not likely to be problems, so a chain of custody is less important and unlikely to be required. Consider, for example, a .45 caliber pistol seized from a suspect in a murder case. If the officer who seized it carves his initials into the base of the pistol, it is unlikely that he will have any trouble identifying the weapon in court, even if it has been in a place accessible to others between the time of seizure and the time of trial. The difference between the pistol and the cocaine is the difference between an object that is unique (or can be made so) and one that is not. For unique exhibits, a chain of custody is not generally required.

Prior to the enactment of the Federal Rules of Evidence, most jurisdictions required the judge to decide whether a sufficient chain of custody had been established for non-unique prosecution exhibits in criminal trials. The standard of proof that most courts required for this determination was a "reasonable probability" or "reasonable certainty" that evidence was unaltered—a standard that amounts in practice to much the same thing as proof by a preponderance of the evidence.[13] FRE 901 makes no reference to a chain-of-custody requirement in any type of case; chain of custody *is* mentioned in the Advisory Committee Notes, but merely as an *example* of authentication by a witness with knowledge under FRE 901(b)(1). Taken literally, FRE 901(a) can easily be read as doing away with any chain-of-custody requirement. Indeed, it is difficult to read the rule otherwise, although apparently neither the Advisory Committee nor Congress intended so sweeping a change. FRE 901 unambiguously provides that "[t]o satisfy the requirement of authenticating . . . the proponent must produce evidence *sufficient to support a finding* [of authenticity]." This rule cannot be read to impose a requirement, in any type of case, that the *judge* determine, to a *"reasonable probability"* or by any other standard, that physical evidence has not been altered. Nor is there any other provision of the Federal Rules of Evidence that speaks to this requirement, although some states have such rules.[14]

---

[13] See Paul C. Giannelli, Chain of Custody and the Handling of Real Evidence, 20 Am. Crim. L. Rev. 527, 553 (1983).

[14] E.g., Alaska Rule of Evidence 901(a)(1) provides that whenever the prosecution in a criminal case offers "real evidence which is of such a nature as not to be readily identifiable" or testimony describing such real evidence, it "must first demonstrate as a matter of reasonable certainty" that the evidence was not altered. The drafters believed that this rule is "similar to the chain-of-custody foundational requirement imposed by the common law." Id., commentary. Other states that have adopted the Federal Rules of Evidence have not modified Rule 901 in this manner.

Nonetheless, most Federal courts [15] (and most state courts in states that have adopted the Federal Rules) have continued to apply chain-of-custody requirements after the enactment of the Federal Rules.[16] Strictly speaking, their authority to do so must derive from FRE 403, which is the only provision of the Federal Rules that permits a court to exclude relevant evidence on a basis which is not explicitly spelled out elsewhere in the Rules. For the most part, however, the post-Federal Rule cases applying this requirement simply continue to follow the pre-Rules procedure, sometimes citing pre-Rules cases as authority.[17] A few cases do note the change enacted in FRE 901, but they too ultimately seem to apply something like the pre-Rules chain-of-custody requirement.[18]

Whatever the authority for requiring a chain of custody for nonunique physical evidence in criminal cases, there are excellent policy reasons for such a requirement. *First*, the defendant's interests in the outcome of a criminal case—liberty or even life—are considered greater than those for either side in civil cases, and the identification of physical evidence is often the critical part of the state's case against the defendant; in a drug case, for example, it is an essential element.[19] *Second*, as Professor Giannelli points out, in civil cases, litigants can effectively contest the genuineness of admitted exhibits because "depositions, interrogatories, requests for admissions, and pretrial conferences are available. In criminal cases, however, . . . the defendant . . . has no pretrial mechanisms for discovering what occurred during the period of custody [of the exhibit]."[20] Therefore, imposing a higher burden on the prosecution is appropriate. *Third*, careful handling requirements are most appropriate when litigation is clearly anticipated and when one side is in sole possession of important evidence. The requirement is also

---

[15] See, e.g., United States v. Combs, 369 F.3d 925, 938 (6th Cir. 2004) ("reasonable probability").

[16] See 5 Saltzburg et al., supra note 6, at 901–15.

[17] See, e.g. United States v. Williams, 809 F.2d 75, 89 (1st Cir. 1986) (trial court "must conclude that it was reasonably probable that the evidence had not been altered since the occurrence of the crime."); United States v. Howard-Arias, 679 F.2d 363, 366 (4th Cir. 1982) (prosecutor must "convince the court that it is improbable that the original item had been . . . tampered with."); United States v. Aviles, 623 F.2d 1192, 1198 (7th Cir. 1980), citing United States v. Bridges, 499 F.2d 179, 185 (7th Cir. 1974) (same).

[18] For example, in United States v. Mendel, 746 F.2d 155, 167 (2d Cir. 1984), the court says in one sentence that "the prosecution need only prove a *rational basis* from which to conclude that the exhibit did, in fact, belong to the appellants"; and in the next that "The ultimate question is whether the authentication testimony is sufficiently complete so as *to convince the court* of the improbability that the original item had been . . . tampered with." (Emphasis added.) Similarly, in United States v. Abreu, 952 F.2d 1458, 1467 (1st Cir. 1992) the court cites FRE 901 and then goes on to say that "the trial court 'must conclude that it was reasonably probable that the evidence had not been altered since the occurrence of the crime.'" (quoting United States v. Williams, 809 F.2d 75, 89 (1st Cir. 1986)). In United States v. Palella, 846 F.2d 977, 981 (5th Cir. 1988) the court says "we find sufficient evidence from which the jury could infer that the heroin samples were authentic." This sounds like a minimal FRE 901(a) showing, but in fact the evidence described laid out an adequate chain of custody.

[19] See Giannelli, supra note 13, at 556–57.

[20] Id. at 556 (footnote omitted).

manageable where an institution, such as a police department, can be expected to implement chain-of-custody rules as a matter of course. In many civil cases, it is unclear that an item will be used as evidence until it has been handled for a considerable period of time, and the people first possessing the evidence may know nothing about what the law requires. Viewed in this light, one of the major purposes of the chain-of-custody rule is to require police and prosecutors (as institutional investigators and litigators) to enforce careful procedures to guarantee the integrity of critical physical evidence over which they have exclusive control. Abandonment of the chain-of-custody requirement would remove an important incentive to be careful, and it might be taken as an invitation to tampering.

This focus on police procedure may explain why the chain-of-custody requirement is almost never applied to civil cases. It may also explain why courts frequently refuse to apply a chain-of-custody requirement, even in criminal cases, for those periods during which an exhibit was in hands other than those of the police. As one court said: "The chain-of-custody foundation is not required . . . for periods before the evidence comes into possession of law enforcement personnel."[21]

If there is a gap or a break in the handling of an object that cannot be accounted for, the question is whether the gap or break is serious enough to warrant exclusion. Courts typically require more than just a small break before excluding an exhibit. For example, no court would exclude evidence if an officer left it on a desk for a few moments while using the restroom. "Reasonable care" and a "reasonable showing" that there was no realistic opportunity for tampering are all a court is likely to require.

Some courts have become more lax, perhaps under the influence of the permissive language of FRE 901. In theory they continue to adhere to a chain-of-custody requirement, but in practice they hold that, absent positive evidence of tampering, even a substantial break in the chain goes to the weight of an exhibit rather than its admissibility.[22] This tendency is disturbing. The courts that admit these exhibits, and the juries that evaluate such evidence, may underestimate the damages involved by not noticing what we might call the "negative" aspects of relevance. If police typically follow a strict routine for preserving physical evidence, and if they know that courts prefer or require them to follow that routine, we ought to ask why the routine was not followed on a particular occasion. If no convincing explanation can be offered, the probability of tampering

---

[21] Williams v. State, 269 Ind. 265, 269–270, 379 N.E.2d 981, 984 (1978). See also, e.g., United States v. Smith, 893 F.2d 1573, 1579 (9th Cir. 1990); State v. Evans, 247 Mont. 218, 806 P.2d 512, 518 (Mont. 1991). Professor Giannelli takes the contrary position. He asserts that "This position misconceives the purpose of the chain-of-custody rule. The rule is not designed to hold the police 'accountable', but rather to ensure that evidence is relevant." Giannelli, supra note 14, at 539 (footnote omitted).

[22] E.g., United States v. Grant, 967 F.2d 81, 83 (2d Cir. 1992); United States v. Gelzer, 50 F.3d 1133, 1141 (2d Cir. 1995).

may be considerably greater than it would be if the routine had never been established in the first instance.[23]

Similar rules apply to the *condition* of an object. When that is important, it is not necessary to show that there is absolutely no possibility that its condition is unchanged. Except in the courtrooms of rather idiosyncratic judges, showing that there is no reasonable possibility that the object is changed is enough.

There are situations in which an object is offered in evidence even though its condition at the time of the trial is very different from its condition at the time of the relevant events. In some cases the changed condition is irrelevant and can be disregarded. For example, a gun may have been dropped and dented but the dent is clearly not relevant to the case. Even if the change is important, the evidence may be admitted. This is permissible as long as the decision-maker is able to understand, with the assistance of other evidence, how the exhibit has changed since the relevant event took place. For example, a machine that caused an injury may have been repaired before suit was filed. At the trial, the machine may be offered as evidence along with a description of how it appeared when the accident occurred. Such an exhibit, however, may be excluded under FRE 403 if the changes made in it are such that the jury is likely to be confused by seeing it or if the probative value of the evidence is likely to be substantially outweighed by unfair prejudice to the opposing party.

2. Attesting Witnesses

At common law, before any attested writing could be introduced the attesters had to be called or their absence explained.[24] According to Professor Morgan, "[t]his requirement which had its origin in the ancient Germanic transaction or business witness doctrine never had any basis in reason after the use of witnesses in open court became established in the common law. . . . "[25] At one time, whenever a writing was attested, the execution of that writing could only be proven through the attesters, unless they were shown to be unavailable. This rule was applied regardless of whether the writing was of a kind required by law to be attested.

---

[23] By moving away from rigid chain-of-custody requirements courts are also lowering the probative value of the fact that a chain-of-custody was broken. A good compromise between a rigid rule and a rule that relegates a break in the chain to weight only would be a rule that requires that either a chain-of-custody be shown or that a good reason for the break be given. For discussions of the probative value of what is not introduced into evidence see Richard O. Lempert, Modeling Relevance, 75 Mich. L. Rev. 1021, 1047–48 (1977) and Stephen A. Saltzburg, A Special Aspect of Relevance: Countering Negative Inferences Associated with the Absence of Evidence, 66 Calif. L. Rev. 1011 (1978).

[24] These requirements were waived if the opposing party admitted the genuineness of the writing. The general rule was that an admission of authenticity was valid only if found in the pleadings or in a stipulation. Wigmore, however, argued for authentication by extra-judicial admissions. 4 Wigmore § 1300, pp. 716–719. See also FRE 1007, discussed infra.

[25] Edmund Morgan, Basic Problems of Evidence 378 (1963).

Today, attesters do not have to be called unless the writing is one required by law to be attested. The modern view is embodied in FRE 903 which provides that "A subscribing witness's testimony is necessary to authenticate a writing only if required by the law of the jurisdiction that governs its validity." In many jurisdictions, existing attestation requirements are softened by various exceptions. One of the most common exceptions waives the requirement of authentication by attesting witnesses for writings that are only collaterally involved in the case being tried.[26] Rules softening this requirement do not signify a *lowering* of the basic relevance standard for evidence. Rather, they recognize that relevance can be demonstrated without calling these particular witnesses. When a jurisdiction adopts a rule requiring the testimony of a subscribing witness, it is signifying that it seeks a *stronger* guarantee of reliability as to certain documents than that which the normal rules of authentication ensure.

Problem X-6. The police arrest Sam Slade for possession of crack cocaine, and—in conjunction with the local prosecutor—secure Sam's cooperation as an undercover informant (i.e., "snitch") who will help them arrest crack dealers. On September 13, 2013 Sam is sent by the police into an apartment occupied by Miriam (Mimi) O'Neil, a suspected crack dealer, to buy crack cocaine. As he leaves Mimi's apartment ten minutes later Sam makes a prearranged signal, and Officers Gone and Wind rush in and arrest Mimi for selling crack. No crack is found in her apartment. At trial, Officer Wind produces a properly labeled evidence bag containing what has been determined to be a ten gram crystal ("rock") of crack cocaine. Officer Wind testifies that he saw Sam Slade give the "rock" to Officer Gone at Mimi's apartment about ten minutes after the bust; that Slade said to Gone "that's the rock she sold me"; that Gone put the crystal in his pocket; that an hour later—after they completed their fruitless search of the apartment—Officer Gone gave the "rock" to Wind; that he (Wind) bagged and labeled it on the spot; and that from then until trial, it has been in his locked evidence locker (for which there is only one key), or in his personal physical possession. Neither Officer Gone (who is on

---

[26] Along these lines, Weinstein and Berger say that "Only when the validity of the document is in issue need the state's law on execution be followed. . . . But if the will is to be admitted to prove a statement made in it as an admission, to show its contents for other purposes, or to show delivery, then the attesting witness is not required and authenticity can be demonstrated under Rules 901 and 902 rather than under the state statute." 5 Weinstein § 8.01. While this view is in accord with Wigmore's approach, 4 Wigmore § 1293, and has much to commend it as matter of policy, we find it difficult to interpret the words "unless required by the laws of the jurisdiction" in the manner suggested. The Advisory Committee's Note is not helpful. If a state were misguided enough to have a rule that "no will may be introduced into evidence for any purpose unless the attesting witnesses are first called to authenticate it," FRE 903 seems to require the federal courts to follow the state rule regardless of the purpose for which a will is offered, unless the final clause of the rule—"whose laws govern the validity of the writing"—is read as if it were qualified by the phrase "and only where the validity of the writing is material."

vacation)—nor Sam Slade (who skipped bail and can't be found) testifies. **Should the crack cocaine be admitted in evidence or excluded?**

III.   RESTRICTIONS ON SECONDARY EVIDENCE OF THE CONTENTS OF DOCUMENTS

A. THE ORIGINAL DOCUMENT OR "BEST EVIDENCE" RULE

There is no such thing as a "best evidence rule" in American evidence law. In the eighteenth and early nineteenth centuries, several English and American commentators argued that Anglo-American evidence law embodied a general "best evidence principle" to the effect that "the best evidence the nature of the case will admit shall always be required."[27] Several specific rules were offered as embodiments of this general principle, including the hearsay rule and the attested document rule.[28] By the late nineteenth century, however, this idea was rejected. As McCormick states: "While some modern opinions still refer to the 'best evidence' notion as if it were today a general governing legal principle . . . there is no such general rule."[29]

But while there is no general requirement that a party produce the best, or the best available evidence to prove a point, there is a common law rule of evidence that is generally *known as* the Best Evidence Rule. The name is a misnomer. In fact, the rule applies only to documents and is more accurately titled "The Original Document Rule." McCormick states the common law rule succinctly:

> [I]n proving the terms of a writing, recording or photograph, where the terms of the content are material to the case, the original document must be produced unless it is shown to be unavailable for some reason other than the serious fault of the proponent, or unless secondary evidence is otherwise permitted by rule or statute.[30]

In other words, if you want to prove what was said in a letter, you must, at common law, use the letter itself—rather than a copy of the letter, or notes taken from the letter, or a witness's recollection of the contents of the letter, or any other "secondary evidence" of the contents— unless there is an exception to the rule.

The Original Document Rule does not apply to objects other than documents. A witness can be called to testify about the appearance of a

---

[27] Blackstone, Commentaries 368, quoted in Thayer, Preliminary Treatise on Evidence at the Common Law 489 (1898).

[28] Simon Greenleaf, A Treatise on the Law of Evidence §§ 82–83 (1st ed. 1842).

[29] McCormick § 230 (6th ed. 2006). See generally Dale A. Nance, "The Best Evidence Principle" 73 Iowa L. Rev. 227 (1988).

[30] McCormick § 231 (6th ed. 2006) (footnotes omitted).

chair, radio, or dog without accounting for the original. When an inscription is attached to an object that is not considered a writing—a license plate on a car, or a name on a tombstone—the issue is closer. The consensus seems to be to follow Wigmore's suggestion that in such circumstances the judge has discretion to decide whether production of the object is required.[31]

Documents—especially legally operative instruments such as deeds, contracts and wills—are frequently critical in litigation. That was probably even more true two centuries ago when the Original Document Rule developed. At that time, however, accurate and reliable mechanical methods of copying—photographic, electronic, etc.—had not yet been developed. The primary purpose of the rule was to ensure that the exact contents of the writing were brought before the trier of fact—to prevent the distortions that may occur in copying (in those days, copying by hand) or in reporting only from memory, and to guard against fraud. A secondary purpose was to prevent a party from intentionally or unintentionally misleading the trier of fact by using selected portions of a larger set of writings.[32]

The Federal Rules of Evidence codify the Original Document Rule with two modifications that are appropriate to modern technology. *First*, the rule is applied to a wider range of items—"writings and recordings" of any sort, plus photographs, movies and videotapes. *Second*, copies made by reliably accurate processes receive special treatment as "duplicates."

FRE 1001 defines the types of exhibits that are subject to the rule:

In this article:

(a) A "writing" consists of letters, words, numbers, or their equivalent set down in any form.

(b) A "recording" consists of letters, words, numbers, or their equivalent recorded in any manner.

(c) A "photograph" means a photographic image or its equivalent stored in any form.

FRE 1002 presents the federal version of the original document rule which it calls, Requirement of the Original:

---

[31] 4 Wigmore, § 1182.

[32] McCormick § 231. Wigmore traces the evolution of the rule from "the primitive medieval conception [of] *a document* directly affecting rights of property or contract" where "[i]ts physical, material existence was what counted, and nothing else," to a more rational period when the rule began to have more of a procedural than substantive effect. 4 Wigmore § 1177, at 406. Also traced in Wigmore is the separation of the best evidence rule from the pleading rule of profert which "required that a certain *allegation be made in the written pleading,* namely, after the statement of title by document, the allegation that the document was hereby prolatum in curiam." Id. at 410. The rule of profert applied in civil cases only, to documents under seal and judicial records.

An original writing, recording, or photograph is required in order to prove its content unless these rules or a federal statute provides otherwise.

The term "original" is defined in FRE 1001d):

An "original" of a writing or recording means the writing or recording itself or any counterpart intended to have the same effect by the person who executed or issued it. For electronically stored information, "original" means any printout—or other output readable by sight—if it accurately reflects the information. An "original" of a photograph includes the negative or a print from it. [33]

FRE 1003 provides special treatment for "duplicates" of the original:

A duplicate is admissible to the same extent as the original unless a genuine question is raised about the original's authenticity or the circumstances make it unfair to admit the duplicate.

A "duplicate" is defined by FRE 1001(e):

A "duplicate" means a counterpart produced by a mechanical, photographic, chemical, electronic, or other equivalent process or technique that accurately reproduces the original. [34]

To illustrate the differences between an "original" writing and one that is not an "original," consider a photocopy. If parties to a contract embody their contract in a written instrument with four photocopies, they can make all four copies "originals" by executing the copies and treating them all as originals. What is crucial is the intent that each copy be an independent legally binding document rather than a copy of such a document. If, however, they only execute the typed copy, the four photocopies might be treated as secondary evidence—i.e., as something other than an "original."

When typewriters rather than computers and printers were how most legally relevant documents were produced, some common law courts admitted carbon copies as "duplicate originals" even if they were not

---

[33] FRE 1001(d) seems to eliminate any original document objection to a display of computer stored data "if it accurately reflects the information," whether viewed on a screen or a printout. Unfortunately, the rule's authors failed to consider the issue of "metadata"—sometimes defined as "data about data"—which includes information about a computer file which customarily is not displayed when the document is shown (or printed) in normal viewing mode. Metadata can include the date and time of creation of the file, the apparent author, notes and comments, even material that the author tried to delete. Accordingly, different versions of a computer file may yield identical hard copy printouts, but include quite different metadata that can be retrieved and viewed in the appropriate mode. Does that mean that the "normal" display of such a computer file does not "reflect the data accurately"? This question has not been authoritatively answered.

[34] There are not many cases in point, but it appears that a duplicate of a duplicate (e.g. a photocopy of a photocopy) is still a duplicate. Logically this ought to be so, as long as the entire process of creating the document that is used is sufficiently accurate and reliable. Indeed, some reproduction processes inevitably involve multiple duplication. For example, in offset printing the original is photographed to create a photographic plate, from which printed copies are made.

executed. In these courts, carbon copies were often treated more favorably than Xerox or other photocopies. The former were treated as originals, and the latter as secondary evidence. The distinction was based on the fact that a carbon is made with the same stroke of the key as the original, while a photocopy is made after the original. But a person bent on creating a false copy can do so with carbon paper almost as easily as with a Xerox machine. Nowadays, most jurisdictions have statutes modeled on the Uniform Photographic Copies of Business and Public Records as Evidence Act, that provide that regularly kept photographic copies of business and public records are admissible without accounting for the original. In this context, scanning is functionally a form of photocopying.

FRE 1003 eliminates the special treatment for carbon copies and makes all duplicates (as defined in FRE 1001(e)) presumptively admissible. Thus in federal court it is rarely necessary to decide whether a carbon or photocopy is an original. Handwritten copies do not benefit from the Rule 1003 presumption. The purpose of the federal rule is to eliminate best evidence objections to copies made in clearly reliable ways, except where the objecting party can offer a good reason to demand the production of the original.

Consider a claim based on a written contract. If counsel for the plaintiff asks her client, "What interest rate did the contract provide?" the question is objectionable under the Original Document Rule because it calls for secondary evidence—oral testimony—about the contents of a writing, the contract. In that situation, the objection should be sustained even in the absence of any real dispute or claim that the testimony will be inaccurate, since FRE 1002 says that the original is "required." Exclusion is equally clear if the attorney attempts to introduce a careful and apparently accurate handwritten copy of the contract. If, however, the attorney asks the witness to authenticate a *photocopy* of the contract, the opposition cannot exclude it so easily. If the photocopy has been executed, it constitutes an "original" and would meet the requirements of FRE 1002. If it has not been executed, it is a "duplicate." In that situation the opposition can still object under the Original Document Rule, but not simply by invoking it. Instead, the opposing attorney must present evidence of tampering, or other evidence that convinces the judge that there is "a genuine question" about the authenticity of the document from which the photocopy was made, or that other circumstances make use of a duplicate "unfair." See FRE 1003.

The Original Document Rule only applies when the evidence of a writing (or recording or photograph) is presented *to prove its contents*. It does not apply to evidence about the *existence* of writings, their location, their physical structure, etc. If, for example, the question arises whether a particular report was written and filed, a witness could testify that the report was made without accounting for the original. (Of course, if it were important to one party to show that the report existed, good trial tactics usually would motivate that party to produce the report or account for its absence.) Thus, the questions, "Did you receive a letter last week?", "When did you receive it?", "How many pages long was it?" and "Where is that letter now?" are all unobjectionable on this basis. But the questions "Who was the letter addressed to?", "What date appeared on the letter?" and "Who signed it?" are all objectionable, since they call for testimony about things written on the document in question. Similarly, "How many photographs did we show you?" is unobjectionable, but "Did the photographs show people?" and "Can you name those you recognized among the people pictured in those photographs?" are objectionable, although if the picture were produced and shown to the jury, the witness might then be allowed to identify those who were portrayed.

The advisory committee notes to the federal Original Document Rule (FRE 1002) make clear that it does not apply "to testimony that books or records have been examined and found not to contain any reference to a designated matter." Thus there is no objection under this rule to the following question (presumably, on cross-examination): "So, after examining the ledger carefully, you found not a single reference to my client, Mr. Brown, isn't that true?"

Some courts demand that an original document be produced, if possible, when there seems to be an important reason to require production, even though the contents of the document are not at issue. One such situation is a dispute over authenticity. Imagine a case in which a photocopy of a document is acknowledged by all parties to accurately reproduce its contents. The issue in dispute is whether the defendant is the author, and the plaintiff claims that the original was written on a particular type of bond paper that the defendant favored. In that situation, the judge might require that the original document be produced or accounted for before she allows a witness to testify that the document was in fact written on that type of paper, even though the only issue at stake is who wrote the document and not what it says. Situations like this rarely arise, however, because a sense of trial tactics generally leads counsel to produce or account for such documents.

Although a written record of an event is likely to be the most reliable evidence of what happened, the Original Document Rule does not require the production of such a record, if one exists, in preference to other evidence. For example, if a criminal defendant gives the police an oral confession which is recorded and transcribed, the prosecution is not required to produce either the recording or the transcript. Instead, the prosecutor, if she wishes, may prove the confession through the testimony of any witness who heard the defendant make it; what is at issue is what the defendant *said*, not what is contained in any written or electronic record of his statements. Needless to say, however, a transcript or a recording—while not required—will make for a stronger case. Similarly, when the content of past testimony is at issue, a litigant may prove what was said through the testimony of a witness who heard the original testimony, even if a transcript exists. Moreover, the Original Document Rule does not prevent the witness from summarizing what was said or giving the gist of it as she remembers it, even if the exact words are important, as in a perjury trial.

Consider a case in which there is a dispute about payment on a credit account. The debtor could introduce a receipt to prove payment. If so, the Original Document Rule would apply and an original receipt would be required, if it were available, because the debtor would be trying to prove that the receipt contained an acknowledgment of payment in order to prove that payment was made. Unless he could account for the unavailability of the original receipt, the debtor could not testify that *the receipt said,* "Paid in Full." However, the *fact of payment* is not *contained* in the writing, even if an acknowledgment of that fact is, and there is ordinarily no legal requirement that payment be proved by written acknowledgment. So the debtor might simply testify that payment was made and permit the trier of fact to rule on the credibility of his testimony.

However, in a case in which the applicable substantive legal rules make a writing indispensable—e.g., a case that turns on the terms of a written contract—the Original Document Rule may exclude the *only* available evidence on a critical issue. Some commentators have criticized the distinction between cases involving dispositive documents—deeds, judgments, or contracts—and cases where the fact that a writing has been made has no independent legal significance. Critics of the rule ask why a contract, which is nothing more than a written *expression of the agreement* of the parties, should be treated differently from a receipt, which is a written *record of a transaction* between the parties. McCormick suggests that the distinction should be abandoned in favor of a rule that permits the trial judge to exercise discretion in applying the Original Document Rule. The exercise of discretion would turn on such factors as the importance of the writing to the litigation and the reliability of the secondary evidence.[35]

Inability to produce an original or duplicate of a document does not ordinarily prevent proof of contents by other means. *The Original Document Rule is a rule of preference.* Original documents are preferred, but if there is a good reason why the original cannot be produced, secondary evidence, such as written copies or oral testimony, will be

---

[35] McCormick (6th ed.) § 234. But compare McCormick, supra, with McCormick (5th ed.) § 233 (suggesting that the authors of the more recent edition may be less committed to the suggestion than in the prior edition).

admitted. FRE 1004 lists the situations in which the production of the original is excused under the federal rules:

An original is not required and other evidence of the content of a writing, recording, or photograph is admissible if:

(a) all the originals are lost or destroyed, and not by the proponent acting in bad faith;[36]

(b) an original cannot be obtained by any available judicial process;[37]

(c) the party against whom the original would be offered had control of the original; was at that time put on notice, by pleadings or otherwise, that the original would be a subject of proof at the trial or hearing; and fails to produce it at the trial or hearing;[38] or

(d) the writing, recording, or photograph is not closely related to a controlling issue.[39]

These exceptions codify a basic truth about the modern version of the Original Document Rule: You should never have a significant item of evidence excluded on that basis. Why? Because if a document is important to your case, if it is not lost or destroyed, and if it is obtainable by judicial process and is not in the possession of your opponent, then *you should have it* in court. There is simply no excuse other than those listed that is compatible with good advocacy. Note also that the most important of these exceptions—FRE 1004(a)— has a good faith requirement. Thus, for example, in *Seiler v. Lucasfilm, Ltd.*[40] a copyright infringement

---

[36] What search should be required? Wigmore concludes that *"there is not and cannot be any universal or fixed rule to test the sufficiency of the search* for a document alleged to be lost." 4 Wigmore § 1194, at 440. The burden of proving the loss is on the proponent of the evidence, but the weight of the burden is unclear. More than a possibility of loss is required, but how much more depends on the jurisdiction.

[37] A deposition combined with a subpoena duces tecum may be used to obtain a writing from an absent non-party. It is unclear under the federal rule whether the prospect of great expense or difficulty in securing the original is enough to establish that the original is not obtainable.

[38] The Advisory Committee's Note states that:

The notice procedure here provided is not to be confused with orders to produce or other discovery procedures, as the purpose of the procedure under this rule is to afford the opposite party an opportunity to produce the original, not to compel him to do so.

[39] The prior wording of the Rule, echoing common usage, referred to "collateral matters," and judges may still use the expression. The word "collateral" is as difficult to interpret and as susceptible to misuse in this area as it is when used to limit the impeachment of witnesses, as discussed in Chapter Five. While the word may have "an exasperating indefiniteness about it" (Michael Martin, Basic Problems of Evidence § 14.08(a), at 451 (1988)), it softens the rule and "precludes hypertechnical insistence [upon it] . . . when production . . . would be impractical and [the writing's] contents are not closely related to any important issue in the case." Calif. Evid. Code § 1504, comment. Judges should examine the importance of the document to the issue in the case. Notice that this subsection is different from the first three. They require some attempt to get the original while this subsection requires nothing more than a finding that an issue is not controlling.

[40] 808 F.2d 1316 (9th Cir. 1986).

plaintiff was precluded from using reconstructions of drawings allegedly infringed upon by the movie "The Empire Strikes Back" because the judge found, under FRE 1004(a), that he had lost or destroyed the originals in bad faith. The text of Rule 1004 suggests that the opponent of the secondary evidence has the burden of showing that the original was lost as a result of bad faith.

In addition to these general exceptions FRE 1005 provides a specific exception for public documents. The contents of an official record, or of a document which may be recorded and filed and which is actually recorded and filed, may be proven by a copy. The justification, presumably, is that such copies are particularly reliable, and that it is important that the originals of such records not be removed from their usual places of safekeeping.

Under FRE 1007,[41] and in many jurisdictions that have not adopted the federal rules, the testimony, deposition or written admission of an opposing party may be offered to prove the contents of a writing without accounting for the nonproduction of the original. In some states ordinary oral admissions also may be used this way.

Finally, FRE 1006 codifies the common practice of using summaries in evidence when the original writings are voluminous. However, the originals or duplicates of the originals must be made available to the opposing party for examination or copying. The best practice is to provide an opportunity for inspection and examination of both the original and the summaries prior to trial. This saves time, prevents surprise and allows disputes about the evidence to be resolved before trial.

---

[41] FRE 1007 reads as follows:

The proponent may prove the content of a writing, recording, or photograph by the testimony, deposition, or written statement of the party against whom the evidence is offered. The proponent need not account for the original.

Saltzburg et al., supra note 6, at 1007–2, explain the rule as follows:

Although some cases have taken a different view, most American courts have held that if the secondary evidence offered consists of an admission of the contents by the opponent of the evidence, no showing is required of why the original is not produced. Prior to the enactment of the Federal Rules, it was not altogether clear whether all admissions would serve to prove the contents of an item otherwise covered by the Best Evidence Rule. Rule 1007 provides that the contents of writings and recordings may be proved only by admissions made in the course of giving testimony under oath or by written admissions. The policy underlying the Best Evidence Rule is to obtain an accurate version of the contents of writings and the other items covered by the Rule. If all oral admissions sufficed to prove the contents of writings, accuracy might be jeopardized. The Advisory Committee accepted the argument that the possibility of error was reduced if admissibility under this Rule was confined to written admissions or admissions under oath.

Admissions not covered by FRE 1007 might still be used under FRE 1004 to prove the contents of a writing. If A sues B for breach of contract, for example, and A satisfies Rule 1004 by showing that the original of the contract was destroyed and that there was no bad faith in A's doing so, then A can then offer as secondary evidence, admissions made by B concerning the contents of the contract. The difference between FRE 1004 and FRE 1007 is that the former requires an accounting for the original while the latter does not.

Since the purpose of the Original Document Rule is to get the best possible documentary evidence before the court, at one time most American jurisdictions required that the "next best" evidence be submitted when an original writing, recording or photograph was not available. Under this regime, there was a hierarchy of secondary evidence of the contents of writings. A certified or sworn copy was always preferred to other kinds of secondary evidence. A mechanical reproduction—typically a carbon copy—was usually considered the next best if a sworn copy could not be obtained. Other kinds of copies—such as a firsthand copy made while looking at the original—came next on the hierarchy and were preferred to oral testimony.

The Federal Rules follow the one-time minority position. They recognize no degrees of secondary evidence, and most jurisdictions that have codified their evidence rules have taken the same position. The Advisory Committee Note accompanying FRE 1004 states:

> While strict logic might call for extending the principle of preference beyond simply preferring the original, the formulation of a hierarchy of preferences and a procedure for making it effective is believed to involve unwarranted complexities. Most, if not all, that would be accomplished by an extended scheme of preferences will, in any event, be achieved through the normal motivation of a party to present the most convincing evidence possible and the arguments and procedures available to his opponent if he does not.

FRE 1008 specifies the roles of judges and jury when Original Document questions arise:

> Ordinarily, the court determines whether the proponent has fulfilled the factual conditions for admitting other evidence of the content of a writing, recording, or photograph under Rule 1004 or 1005. But in a jury trial, the jury determines—in accordance with Rule 104(b)—any issue about whether:
>
> (a) an asserted writing, recording, or photograph ever existed;
>
> (b) another one produced at the trial or hearing is the original; or
>
> (c) other evidence of content accurately reflects the content.

In other words, the judge (as usual) decides any factual questions that are essential to decide the technical application of this rule. See FRE 104(a). Saltzburg et al. list nine questions the judge may have to address before permitting a writing to go to the jury:

> (1) whether a given item of evidence is an "original";
>
> (2) whether a given item of evidence qualifies as a duplicate and is thus presumptively admissible;

(3) whether a genuine question is raised as to the authenticity of the original for purposes of Rule 1003;

(4) whether it would be unfair to admit a duplicate in lieu of an original as provided for in Rule 1003;

(5) whether an original is lost or destroyed, and whether a diligent search has been conducted for the original;

(6) whether the proponent lost or destroyed evidence in bad faith;

(7) whether an original can be obtained by any available judicial process;

(8) whether an adverse party has possession or control over the original and, if so, whether proper notice was given to that party;

(9) whether evidence goes to a collateral matter or to a controlling issue.[42]

In some cases, however, there is an actual controversy over a critical issue that goes beyond the technical rules of admissibility: (1) Did the asserted writing ever actually exist or is the exhibit a forgery? (2) Which of two or more exhibits is the true version of a document, recording, or photograph? (3) Does some other evidence—a copy perhaps, or oral testimony—accurately describe the real writing? In this situation, the judge must treat the factual question as one of conditional relevance under FRE 104(b), and admit the writing if there is sufficient evidence to support a jury finding in favor of the proponent. For example, consider a contract case in which the plaintiff claims that the original of its contract with the defendant was burned in a fire that destroyed the plaintiff's office. The defendant claims the contract never existed. In order to decide whether the original contract "was destroyed"—which would permit the plaintiff to put on secondary evidence of the contents of the contract (see FRE 1004(a))—the court must decide whether the contract in fact ever existed. If the judge did make that decision and found that the contract in fact never existed, the plaintiff would have no means to prove its contents and would lose by a directed verdict without reaching the jury. FRE 1008 prevents that outcome. Instead, the judge must merely decide whether the contract would have been destroyed on the assumption that it existed. If so, the court should admit secondary evidence of its terms, and let the jury decide (under FRE 1008) whether there ever really was a contract.[43]

Problem X-7. Sergeant Friday, a Los Angeles policeman, is placed in charge of an investigation into the identity of an armed robber terrorizing

---

[42] 5 Saltzburg et al., supra note 6, at 1008–2 to 1008–3.

[43] See Michael H. Graham, The Original Writing (Best Evidence) Rule, 26 Crim. L. Bul. 432, 448–50 (1990).

Hollywood families. He photocopies a composite description of the robber and distributes copies to all the officers under his command. Officer Monday possesses one of these copies when he encounters a suspect fitting the description. Aware that the description contains the notation that "suspect is believed to be armed and extremely dangerous," Monday panics when the suspect reaches into his pocket. He shoots the suspect, seriously wounding him. It turns out that the injured man is innocent of any wrongdoing, and was merely reaching for identification. The injured "suspect" sues for damages under state tort law and federal civil rights statutes. Monday defends on the ground that he reasonably believed that his life was in danger; he seeks to introduce the description given to him by Sergeant Friday. **As Officer Monday's lawyer, in a jurisdiction that interprets the Original Document Rule strictly, would you offer the original written description prepared by Friday, the photocopy sent to Monday, one of the other photocopies that were distributed to the officers in Friday's command, or a photocopy prepared from the original a week before the trial? Even in such a strict jurisdiction, do you think it would matter which document you offered?**

Problem X-8. Rudy Jacobs is charged with interstate transmission of child pornography. The chief witness at his trial is Agent Mark McEleroy of the FBI who testifies that: (1) He logged onto Rudy's world wide web homepage on the Internet, and saw "lewd and pornographic depictions of male and female children who appeared to be under 13 years of age." (2) Armed with a search warrant, he searched Rudy's home, and on his computer found a file containing 15 images of pornographic photographs of young children, which Agent McEleroy printed on Rudy's color laser printer. The prints are offered in evidence as Government Exhibits 1 through 15. **Rudy objects under the Original Document Rule both to the testimony describing his web site, and to the prints. What result?**

B. THE PAROL EVIDENCE RULE

Like the Original Document Rule, the Parol Evidence Rule has many facets, too many in fact. Thayer commented that "[f]ew things are darker than this, or fuller of subtle difficulties."[44] Wigmore agreed, complaining that "the so-called Parol Evidence rule is attended with a confusion and obscurity which make it the most discouraging subject in the whole field of evidence."[45]

---

[44] J. Thayer, A Preliminary Treatise on Evidence at the Common Law 390 (1898).

[45] 9 Wigmore § 2400, at 3.

What exactly is the rule?[46] One legal encyclopedia states it in the following manner.

> The well-established general rule is that where the parties to [an instrument] have deliberately put their engagement in writing in such terms as import a legal obligation without any uncertainty as to the object or extent of such engagement, it is conclusively presumed that the entire engagement of the parties, and the extent and manner of their undertaking, have been reduced to writing, and all parol evidence of prior or contemporaneous conversations or declarations tending to substitute a new and different contract for the one evidenced by the writing is incompetent. Stated otherwise the intention of the parties as evidenced by the legal import of the language of a valid written [instrument] cannot ordinarily be varied by parol proof of a different intention.[47]

Corbin's definition is similar:

> When two parties have made a contract and have expressed it in a writing to which they have both assented as the complete and accurate integration of that contract, evidence, whether parol or otherwise, of antecedent understandings and negotiations will not be admitted for the purpose of varying or contradicting the writing.[48]

As is Williston's:

> Briefly stated, this rule requires in the absence of fraud, duress, mutual mistake, or something of the kind, the exclusion of extrinsic evidence, oral or written, where the parties have reduced their agreement to an integrated writing.[49]

It is now generally understood that the Parol Evidence Rule is actually a rule of substantive contract law which provides that absent some exception the terms of a written contract constitute the entire agreement between the parties. If the Parol Evidence Rule is really a rule of contract law rather than an evidence rule, why is it mentioned here? Our answer is that despite its substantive nature, the policy of the rule is similar to the policies of true evidence rules previously examined. It is related, for example, to best evidence problems and hearsay concerns. But

---

[46] See generally Charles T. McCormick & Roy R. Ray, Texas Law of Evidence § 725, at 947–48 (1937):

The Parol Evidence Rule is the rule which, upon the establishment of the existence of a writing intended as a completed memorial of a legal transaction, denies efficacy to any prior or contemporary expressions of the parties relating to the same subject-matter as that to which the written memorial relates.

[47] 29A Am. Jur.2d Evidence § 1016, at 149–50.

[48] 3 Corbin, Contracts § 573, at 357 (1960).

[49] 4 Williston, Contracts § 631 at 948–49 (3d ed. 1957).

even more important for our purposes, and too often overlooked, is the relationship of the rule to the allocation of fact-finding functions to the jury.

> [The rule establishes a] reservation in the trial judge of a special and added authority over the question: Was this writing intended by the parties to displace this asserted oral term or agreement, if there was any such oral expression? Thayer was entirely aware that the parol evidence doctrine had been used by the judges to serve this purpose, but his main preoccupation was with the pioneer job of driving the parol evidence rule out of the "evidence" fold. Wigmore explicitly recognizes this special allocation of authority to the trial judge, but he cites no decisions to the point and apparently treats it as a minor and incidental feature of the subject. Williston, in his lucid and realistic treatment of the matter, follows, in the main, the lines laid down by Thayer and Wigmore. Like them, he touches but casually this question of "Who decides whether the document was intended to supersede that alleged oral agreement?"—a question which will be decisive of the result in most actual cases of competition between an alleged oral agreement and a written document. By couching his discussion of "collateral" oral agreements in terms of "admissibility," however, he reverts to the earlier "rule-of-evidence" phraseology.[50]

Elsewhere the same author joins another to develop the argument further:

> One of the chief motives in the development and preservation of the nexus of doctrines called the Parol Evidence Rule has been in the belief on the part of judges that the needs of the business world demand that contracts as written be guarded against claims of inconsistent oral agreements. But the extension of such protection has been none too easy in a legal system where disputed fact questions are usually left to the decision of untrained juries. In a contest involving choice between a writing and an alleged oral agreement the average juror's sympathy will ordinarily be with the one setting up the spoken against the written word. He will seldom take sufficient account of the high probability of error in the narrative of a witness (even disinterested, which is usually not the case) as to the purported substance of words, spoken months or even years before. The trial judge, on the other hand, is equipped by training and

---

[50] Charles T. McCormick, The Parol Evidence Rule As a Procedural Device for Control of the Jury, 41 Yale L.J. 365, 374–75 (1932) (footnotes omitted).

experience to take a long view and make proper allowance for such factors.[51]

Many cases still turn on the Parol Evidence Rule. Naturally most of them are state cases. If you examine the evidence headnotes in the published cases, you may be surprised at how often this rule is at issue.

Having discussed the rule briefly, we leave it. In the first edition of this book we treated the Parol Evidence Rule at great length because of the relationship it has to other rules of evidence and to issues involving the proper allocation of responsibility between judge and jury. Those who want to study the doctrine further should examine the sources cited in the first edition.

IV. PARTICULAR TYPES OF TANGIBLE EVIDENCE

A. VIEWS, DEMONSTRATIONS AND EXPERIMENTS

Sometimes the best way to present evidence to a court is to show the real thing. This happens whenever a "real evidence" exhibit is in itself an object of significance in the controversy—*the* contract, *the* bolt, *the* bottle of pills, etc. It can also happen when the thing the court sees (or hears or touches) cannot be marked and admitted into the record as an exhibit.

Views. Some objects—and all *places*—are simply too big to be admissible as exhibits. If important aspects of the object or place cannot be effectively captured through testimony or exhibits (photographs, drawings, scale models, maps, video recordings) the judge or jury may leave the courtroom to observe places or objects for themselves. We call such excursions "views." The decision to grant a view is within the discretion of the trial judge, who will consider the importance of the information to be gained and the extent to which such information can be

---

[51] McCormick & Ray, supra note 46, § 727, at 951. Writing alone, McCormick makes the same point in a slightly different way.

That the parol evidence rule chiefly stems from an anxiety to protect written bargains from rewriting by juries is confirmed by the comparative freedom which was allowed in chancery in respect to reformation, and in regard to oral variations asserted as a ground for denying specific performance. . . . It is true that other doors for jury intervention in support of oral variations have not been closed, as in the case of oral agreements that the writing shall not go into effect until the happening of a condition, and likewise oral agreements modifying the written terms after the execution of the document. Each of these escapes from the writing presents difficulties to the one who attempts it, and, in any event, the fact that protection in some situations has not been perfect, does not disprove the desire to furnish it generally.

It is not intended to suggest that these doctrinal devices were newly invented by the judges, consciously, to meet this need, in modern times. Thayer and Wigmore have traced too clearly the origin of the parol evidence formula against "varying the writing," to a primitive formalism which attached a mystical and ceremonial effectiveness to the carta and the seal. (5 Wigmore, Evidence § 2426). The writer merely ventures to submit that this formalism, abandoned elsewhere in so many areas of modern law, had here a special survival value—the escape from the jury—which led the judges to retain for writings the conception that they had a sort of magical effect of erasing all prior oral agreements.

McCormick, supra note 50, at 368, n.6 and 369, n.8 (footnotes omitted).

conveyed by other means. The fact that perfect information may not be available through secondary sources is not dispositive. The judge may also be influenced by the inconvenience of the excursion and by the extent to which the place or object to be viewed may have changed since the controversy arose.

In civil cases, the trial judge's presence at the view is usually not required, and it is not uncommon for the jury to be conducted to the scene by someone specially commissioned to show the jury the view.[52]   In criminal cases however, statutes usually require that the judge be present.   In addition, the constitutional right to confrontation may give the criminal defendant the right to be present at a view.[53]   There may also be a constitutional right to the judge's presence because the right to confront adverse evidence can only be secured if the accused is able to raise and preserve any objections—which will be difficult if not impossible in the judge's absence.[54]   Even if the trial judge's presence is not required, it is advisable. It helps ensure that no unauthorized comments are made to the jury during the view, that nothing improper is viewed, and that jurors are instructed not to talk about the case and do not do so.

Many jurisdictions hold that a view is not evidence; its purpose is to assist the trier of fact to understand and to evaluate other information which *is* in evidence.[55]   This rule reflects in part the difficulty of capturing a view for the record. If views are considered evidence, appellate courts may be unable to take them into account in reviewing the weight and sufficiency of the evidence, although with modern technology—including 360 degree images and immersive virtual reality—it might be possible to come close.   That problem, however, is not unique to views.   Absent a video record, which to date few courts use, a witness's demeanor is equally unavailable to a reviewing court, but jurors are regularly instructed that demeanor (if probative of truthfulness or untruthfulness) is evidence.   In both situations, appellate courts cannot know what the jurors perceived, and yet the jurors may have been influenced significantly by their perceptions.   In the case of a view, at least some of the experience can be captured by video recording.   In any event, it's one thing to *say* that a view is not evidence, and another to explain what this means, since the jury must be allowed to consider what they saw at least to the extent that it explains or clarifies other evidence.   Does anybody

---

[52]   See 4 Wigmore §§ 1162–1169. Certain statutes—e.g., in eminent domain cases—require a view upon request of a party. See McCormick (6th ed.) § 219.

[53]   But compare Snyder v. Commonwealth of Massachusetts, 291 U.S. 97 (1934) with State v. Garden, 267 Minn. 97, 125 N.W.2d 591 (1963), and People v. De Lucia, 20 N.Y.2d 275, 282 N.Y.S.2d 526, 229 N.E.2d 211 (1967).   See also Note, Confrontation, Cross-Examination, and the Right to Prepare a Defense, 56 Geo. L.J. 939, 959–60 (1968).   If the view is not evidence (a possibility discussed in the next paragraph of the text), do confrontation problems exist?

[54]   See 47 A.L.R.2d 1227 (1956) (necessity of judge's presence).

[55]   See generally, Note, Layne S. Keele, When Mohammed Goes to the Mountain: The Evidentiary Value of a View, 80 Ind. L. J. 1091, 1097 (2005).

really think that jurors who are instructed to consider a view as an aid in deciding a case, but not as evidence, treat the view differently than they treat other facts that are brought to their attention?[56]

Problem X–9. "Red" Zinger, a pedestrian, is hit by a car driven by Randy Gossip, at a main intersection in Middletown, and severely injured. Zinger sues Gossip to recover damages for negligence. Gossip contends that Zinger emerged from the sidewalk into the street from a position in which Zinger was invisible to Gossip, and that Zinger should have seen the moving automobile from the sidewalk. Zinger contends that Gossip should have seen him, and that he himself did not see Gossip's car. The case is tried to a judge, with no jury. **Is the judge allowed to visit the scene of the accident alone to inspect the features of this intersection? Does it matter if she knows the intersection well? Is she barred from going to the intersection unless counsel and the parties are also present? May the judge decide on her own motion that there should be a view? If a view is to be held, should the view take place before, during, or after the presentation of the parties' cases? If the case were tried to a jury and there had been no view, would it be proper for a juror who knows the intersection well to tell the other jurors during their deliberations what the intersection is like? How might such communications be prevented?**

Demonstrations and Experiments. Views are useful for locations and objects that cannot be brought into a courtroom. Some objects, however, can be brought to court even though they may not be made part of the record.[57] This applies to many perishable objects, to live animals, and, most important, to human bodies and to parts of bodies— injured limbs, scars, deformities, identifying marks, the appearance of a person's face, etc. In general, injuries and parts of the human anatomy may be displayed to the court. McCormick writes:

> The exhibition of the wound or physical injury, e.g., the injury sustained by a plaintiff in a personal injury action, will frequently be probative evidence of a material fact. Not surprisingly, therefore, exhibitions of physical injuries to the jury are commonly allowed.[58]

----

[56] See Helen D. Wendorf, Some Views on Jury Views, 15 Baylor L. Rev. 379 (1963).

[57] In most cases, photographs of the objects can be admitted in evidence, but they are often considerably less informative than the real thing. In some cases, a model and the like may be preserved as a physical addendum to the record, as real evidence is sometimes preserved in criminal cases.

[58] McCormick (6th ed.) § 217.

The trial judge has broad discretion to permit injuries to be displayed, even though the injuries may produce strong emotional reactions from the jury.

Sometimes what a litigant wants to show is not an object, but a process. In the case of an injury, that means demonstrating its consequences. Courts have been more reluctant to allow litigants to demonstrate the ways in which they are affected by their injuries than to permit the showing of the injuries themselves. They fear that the injury will be made to appear more debilitating than it in fact is: a limp will be exaggerated or tolerable pain made to appear excruciating. Nevertheless, the trial judge has discretion to allow such demonstrations where they promise to be more helpful than harmful.

"Oh-oh, we're in trouble!"

A litigant may wish to demonstrate an entirely different sort of process: how a locking mechanism on a cargo door works (or fails to work), that a certain type of fabric does not burn in an ordinary fire, that it is possible to open a particular type of container with no audible sound, etc. As with displays of injuries the judge has discretion to admit or exclude such demonstrations and experiments. Experiments conducted in the presence of the jury may be excluded if they involve considerable confusion and delay, but simple experiments by witnesses are usually permitted and more complicated experiments are sometimes allowed. Courtroom experiments may be strikingly effective, or conspicuously embarrassing. As a matter of adversarial tactics, they should not be attempted unless the results are sure to be favorable. Witnesses, usually experts, may also report the results of experiments conducted before trial, and may be allowed to present exhibits—charts, video recordings, digital images, samples—that depict or illustrate the processes or the results. This is the more common kind of experimental evidence. It allows for better testing of conflicting hypotheses in a more controlled fashion.

Regardless of whether an in-court or an out-of-court experiment is involved, the judge's decision on admissibility will turn on answers to questions like the following: How reliable is the experiment? How similar are the conditions under which the experiment was conducted to the conditions surrounding the event the experiment is designed to elucidate?[59] How helpful will the experimental evidence be to the jury? What is the likelihood that the jury will give the experimental evidence undue weight? For most experiments, expert testimony will be required either to establish as a foundational matter that the experiment is scientifically valid, or to explain the process and the results, or both.

Problem X-10. R.J. Samuels, a famous ex-basketball star, is on trial for murdering his wife. A bloody leather glove—allegedly belonging to R.J.— was found at the scene of the gruesome killing. At trial, one of R.J.'s defense lawyers—G. Rich Kelley—wants to have R.J. attempt to put on the glove in court, in the jury's presence, to show that it is too small and doesn't fit. **Should this be allowed?**

Problem X-11. In a personal injury action in which the plaintiff claims that he suffered severe injuries to his hands as a result of being burned, the plaintiff makes a motion in limine before trial for permission to have each juror touch his burned hands in order to feel their hardness. The defendant objects. **Should the motion be granted? If the judge is concerned with juror sensibilities, should he consider having only those jurors who *want* to touch the hands do so?**

---

[59] Depending on the issue, similarity may be more or less critical. For example, similarity is comparatively unimportant for a test to disprove an assertion that a given result is *impossible* under *any* set of circumstances.

B. PHOTOGRAPHS AND SOUND RECORDINGS

Photographs. Like maps and diagrams, photographs may be used as demonstrative evidence. They are admissible whenever a witness can testify from personal knowledge that they accurately portray relevant facts. Assume, for example, that a witness is present at the scene of a riot, and that while she is present photographs are taken. At a trial for crimes committed during the riot, relevant photographs of the riot will be admissible if the witness can state that they accurately represent what she saw at the scene. That is sufficient authentication under FRE 901(b)(1) ("Testimony of a witness with knowledge") or comparable provisions. The photographs need not have been taken by the witness who authenticates them, although they might have been. Black and white as well as color photographs and enlargements are normally admissible on the same foundation—i.e., the testimony of a witness that they accurately represent what she saw. Photographs that are unduly prejudicial may be excluded.[60]

On this theory, photographs, like other demonstrative exhibits, are "not in themselves evidence at all, but represent to the eye what the witness declares was the real appearance of the things at the times he saw it."[61] Or, as Wigmore put it a photograph "for evidential purposes [is] simply *nothing, except so far as it has a human being's credit to support it.*"[62]

This is not the only way to view photographs.[63] In a few early cases, judges extolled photography for its unparalleled power to produce exact images of reality. If that had become the general theory for admissibility, photographs would constitute independent evidence of unique significance. Unfortunately, by the late nineteenth century the dangers of photographic distortion and outright deception were already well known; it was impossible to argue that all photographs were per se accurate depictions of objects or events. Nonetheless, judges wanted to be able to admit photographs in evidence because, as Wigmore put it: "It would be folly to deny ourselves on the witness-stand those effective media of communication commonly employed at other times as a superior substitution for words."[64] The solution they devised was to make photographs readily admissible by reducing their status from independent evidence to mere illustrations of the oral testimony of witnesses. One effect of this shift was to greatly simplify the burden of authentication, and the judge's task of evaluating photographic evidence

---

[60] See Glenn W. Rosen, Admission into Evidence of Prejudicial Photographs, 31 J. Crim. L. & Criminology 604 (1941). Sometimes a color photograph may be more prejudicial than a black and white one, but no more probative.

[61] Baustian v. Young, 152 Mo. 317, 323, 53 S.W. 921, 922 (1899).

[62] 3 Wigmore § 790, at 218 (emphasis in original).

[63] The discussion in this paragraph is based on Mnookin, supra note 1, at 14–27, 43–45.

[64] 1 Wigmore § 790, at 219.

for admissibility. If any witness says she saw what the photograph shows, it's admitted. In fact, this procedure seems to have worked quite well, but the theory on which it's based does not do justice to the true nature of photographic evidence.

Suppose no pictures were taken during the riot, but the prosecution seeks to introduce posed pictures portraying what happened, according to the testimony of the prosecution's witness. Should those pictures be admitted? If all the photographs do is illustrate the witness's testimony— put her words into pictures—the process that produced them should be irrelevant. In theory, it wouldn't matter whether the pictures were taken at the actual riot in question, or staged, or taken at some other riot. In fact, of course, it does matter. Photographs frequently show quite a bit more than what any witness could see or remember, let alone describe. It's not just that they are more persuasive ("one picture is worth a thousand words"), but also that they can be more complete and detailed than any number of words. A photograph, we like to think, is not simply a pictorial *description* of reality, but a *copy* of reality—albeit an imperfect copy, and from a particular vantage point. Which is not to say that staged photographs will not be admitted. They might be,[65] but their value as evidence is more limited than photographs of the actual event.

The recognition that photographs have independent probative value led to the development of a second theory of admissibility, the "silent witness" theory, which gained wide acceptance in the mid-twentieth century.[66] Under this theory, a properly authenticated photograph is admissible "not merely as illustrated testimony of a human witness but as probative evidence in itself of what it shows,"[67] even if there is no human witness to contents of the photograph. Most surveillance photographs can only be admitted on this basis.[68] The "silent witness" theory of admissibility is now incorporated into the Federal Rules of Evidence in FRE 901(b)(9), which permits authentication of an exhibit by evidence that it has been produced by a "process or system and showing that it produces an accurate result." Under FRE 901(b)(9), all that is required is "evidence sufficient to support a finding" that the photographs

---

[65] Pictures of artificially reconstructed scenes are almost always admissible if the positions of the persons and objects reflect undisputed testimony. See McCormick (6th ed.) § 215. Thus, if there is no dispute that the defendants were at the scene at the spots indicated in the photograph, and that all the other people and things in the photograph are accurately represented, the photograph will be admitted. When facts are disputed, posed photographs may be admitted to illustrate one side of the case. See Dillard S. Gardner, The Camera Goes to Court, 24 N.C. L. Rev. 233, 245 (1946). The judge must balance their prejudicial effect against their probative value.

[66] See id. at 245.

[67] People v. Bowley, 59 Cal.2d 855, 861, 31 Cal. Rptr. 471, 382 P.2d 591, 595 (1963).

[68] See infra, pp. 1323–1324.

were produced by a process that created an accurate picture of a relevant scene.[69]

In many cases these two theories of admissibility merge. Suppose that the witness to the riot authenticates a photograph as an accurate depiction of what she saw, and the photograph is then used to corroborate her eyewitness testimony. Or consider a case in which a witness testifies that her deceased father was six feet, five inches tall and bearded, and a photograph of the dead man is used not only to *illustrate* her description, but also as independent evidence of his size and appearance. In these situations the photographs are presented not merely as illustrative evidence but as real evidence of relevant facts. For that second purpose, testimony that a photograph is an accurate picture of what the witness remembers (which could be true of a staged photograph or a hand-drawn sketch) should not suffice. The court should require evidence that authenticates it as a photograph taken at the time and place in question— testimony from the photographer (see FRE 901(b)(1)), distinctive characteristics of the photograph (see FRE 901(b)(4)), evidence of the process or system that produced the photograph (see FRE 901(b)(9)), or some other equivalent evidence. The additional burden, however, is slight—merely evidence from which a jury could reasonably conclude that the photograph does depict the event or person in question.

In most cases, courts do not pause to consider the range of purposes for which a photograph is used. If a picture of a crowd is admitted to "illustrate" the testimony of a witness who saw the scene, neither the judge nor the opposing attorney is likely to demand an additional foundation when a lawyer points out a significant detail (two policeman in the foreground) that the witness may have missed, or argues that the photo demonstrates the witness's accuracy. And why bother? In theory, of course, it could be a forgery; in practice, the upshot will simply be that the photographer will have to be called to testify to the uncontroversial fact that it really is a photograph of the scene in question. So far, the courts' liberality has worked satisfactorily because, with rare exceptions, photographs are what they seem to be—or close to it.

Some distortions have always been common in photographs. In pictures taken through lenses with focal lengths that are uncommonly long (telephoto) or short (wide angle), the relative sizes of objects may be misleading. The details of portraits or other pictures have long been "touched up" to improve their appearance. And, of course, the framing of an image can profoundly effect its interpretation, by including or excluding the context. It's one thing to see a picture of a house, shot from just beyond the corner of the front lawn, isolated against the sky; it's quite another to see it in a long view from down the street, as one of

---

[69] See United States v. Rembert, 863 F.2d 1023, 1026–28 (D.C. Cir. 1988) and cases cited therein.

fifteen identical tract homes. But these manipulations are well known, easily understood, and—for the most part—reasonably detectable, or at least predictable. (You may not be able to show that a publicity portrait was air brushed, but enough jurors will believe it was anyway.) They don't change the basic truth that most photographs do show what they appear to show, even if the images are sometimes deliberately arranged or gussied up.

Outright forgeries are a different matter. They have always been possible; there are famous examples going back to the early days of photography.[70] Until recently, however, high quality forgeries were quite a lot of trouble to produce. Computer technology has changed that entirely. In a 1998 Atlantic Monthly article, Kenneth Brower, describes the origin of a *Life* magazine cover from several decades ago:

> The image had begun in the mind of one of the magazine's editors. By a kind of redactional clairvoyance this editor, seated comfortably at his desk in Manhattan, had seen it all clearly: leopard and its kill in a thorn tree, branches framing a setting sun. The photographer set off in quest of this vision, traveling the East African savanna for weeks with a captive leopard, killing antelopes, draping the carcasses in the branches of various thorn trees, and cajoling the leopard to lie proudly on the "kill," a tableau that the photographer shot against a succession of setting suns. . . .
>
> . . . No photographer today would bother cruising the bush with trained leopards to fake a sunset shot. Anyone with Adobe Photoshop ($589 when I last checked; $599 with a scanner thrown in) could find a perfectly adequate leopard in the zoo, digitally edit out the bars of the cage, tree the cat with subtle movements of mouse, bloodlessly procure a dead antelope (if his computer held any in files), and then set the whole collage against a virtual setting sun.[71]

That was 1998. Thirteen years later Photoshop-like programs can be bought for less than $200, and a scanner is no longer necessary. Almost all photography is now digital, and digital images can be loaded directly onto a computer and manipulated, if necessary, pixel by pixel—and the alterations, done carefully, are all but absolutely undetectable.

Considering how easy it now is to alter photographs, should courts demand more than the minimal foundation that they have required in the past?[72] Some of the arguments that have led most American courts to

---

[70] Mnookin, supra note 1 at 26–41.

[71] Kenneth Brower, Photography in the Age of Falsification, Atlantic Monthly, May 1, 1998.

[72] See Benjamin v. Madison III, Seeing Can Be Deceiving: Photographic Evidence in a Visual Age—How Much Weight Does It Deserve? 25 Wm. & Mary L. Rev. 705 (1984); Christine Guilshan, A Picture Is Worth a Thousand Lies: Electronic Imaging and the Future of the

require a detailed foundation for the admission of sound recordings[73]—that alterations are easy to make and hard to catch—now apply with almost equal force to photographs. The same concerns could drive courts to require a comparable chain-of-custody-like foundation for the admissibility of photographs, at least in criminal cases, including evidence that describes the entire set of steps by which the picture that is presented in court was produced from the image that was initially formed in the camera. In most cases, this would mean that "the photographer himself [would] testif[y] that the photograph is what it appears to be and has not been manipulated."[74] So far, however, courts have continued to apply the same minimal standards for authentication of photographs that they used thirty years ago, and so far—although there have been some conspicuous disputes about the authenticity of particular photographs [75]—there is no evidence that the availability of digital-imaging technology has produced a rash of photographic forgeries. However, if forgeries are actually exposed in a few well-publicized cases, the rules on authentication of photographs could change rapidly.

We have focused on admissibility. Probative value is another matter. Almost all cameras these days are digital, and they are ubiquitous: embedded in cell phones, built into computer screens, sold separately as mini-webcams. Most stand-alone digital cameras are supplied with photo-correction software to fix "red eye," for example, or to crop the picture or change its contrast; most home computers can do the same to any image that is loaded into their hard drives. As a result, most people know that digital images are easily altered. In this context, the proponent of a digital image may have an easy time getting it admitted in evidence, but a hard time persuading skeptical fact finders to rely on it.

Sound Recordings. Recordings—while very important—are less commonly used in evidence than pictures. The main reason is probably that sounds are evanescent. If they are not recorded when they are made, they are not recordable. But pictures of relevant locales and objects may be made after the event at issue is over. Moreover, staged recordings are seldom useful for illustrative purposes because testimony about what a

---

Admissibility of Photographs into Evidence, 18 Rutgers Computer & Tech. L.J. 365 (1992); Dana Coleman, Photo Evidence: No Longer a Snap, New Jersey Lawyer, June 16, 1997.

[73] See supra, note 12, and infra pp. 1321–1323.

[74] Guilshan, supra note 72 at 379. Guilshan also argues that "stricter authentication could necessitate elimination of the silent witness theory of authentication altogether." Id. This latter argument seems to be based on the false assumption that under the "silent witness theory a photograph is 'taken at face value,' " id. Actually that mode of authentication requires evidence that a photograph is the product of a "process or system and showing that it produces an accurate result," FRE 901(b)(9)—which could be interpreted to require evidence that the photograph was not tampered with at any time up to its presentation in court. See infra pp. 1323–1324.

[75] See, e.g. B.J. Palermo, Appealing the O.J. Civil Case, The National Law Journal, February 10, 1997, p. A1 (defense in O.J. Simpson civil wrongful death suit claims photographs of defendant wearing shoes similar to those that left tracks at murder scene are fakes); Coleman supra note 72.

witness *heard* usually concerns a statement, a conversation, or some other form of speech by one or more people. In these circumstances, an accurate oral description of what was said can convey a much more complete impression of what the witness perceived than any oral testimony describing something the witness saw. We are often at a loss to describe a person, an event, or a place that we saw even if we remember it perfectly. A sketch, a drawing, or a photograph can *illustrate* what we cannot describe. But no witness should need a recording to *illustrate* the content of a speech or a conversation that she heard and remembers. In the case of visual perception, a photograph might be useful as an illustration, even if it were staged and the people in it actors. But it is hard to imagine how an audio recording (real or staged) would be useful to illustrate the testimony of a witness. If she remembers what was said, she can simply repeat it.[76]

Of course recordings are frequently used as *real* rather than illustrative evidence. They can corroborate the testimony of a witness about the occurrence or content of the speech, or (like photographs that are admitted under the "silent witness" theory) they can provide evidence about conversations or other auditory events for which no human witness is available. McCormick suggests that sound recordings ought to be treated the same way as visual exhibits, and should be admitted whenever a witness testifies that the recording is an accurate reproduction of the actual sounds she heard at the time and place in question.[77] By the same token, one could argue that audio recordings should be admitted whenever there is sufficient evidence of any sort to support a jury finding of authenticity, including, in particular, any of the methods suggested in FRE 901(b). However, as we pointed out earlier, some courts have been particularly strict in dealing with audio recordings, at least in criminal cases.[78] The major arguments for greater scrutiny in this situation are the same ones that support the "chain-of-custody" requirement for nonunique items of physical evidence offered by the prosecution in criminal cases: the dangers of error or tampering, the exclusive control of such evidence by the police, and the importance of avoiding wrongful convictions. These problems are becoming more acute for sound recordings, as digital electronic technology makes it increasingly difficult to detect editing and alteration. Most American courts have accepted these arguments. While the actual tests that are

---

[76] In theory, a recording could be useful to illustrate the *tone* and *manner* in which words were spoken—if the court is convinced that such an illustration has significant probative value, and is unlikely to be confused with an actual recording of the event in question. More likely the judge would simply allow the witness to illustrate the tone and manner herself. Illustrative recordings of sounds other than speech (an explosion, a crash, shots in quick succession, etc.) might also be useful and admissible to clarify what a witness means by vague terms such as "loud," "crashing," "one right after another," "rat-tat-tat!," and so forth—especially on cross-examination.

[77] McCormick (6th ed.) § 216.

[78] See discussion of United States v. McMillan, 508 F.2d 101 (8th Cir. 1974), supra note 12.

used vary from jurisdiction to jurisdiction, they require a stronger foundation for the admission of audio recordings than the minimal showing that is sufficient for authentication in general under FRE 901 and comparable rules.[79]   In some cases, the authenticity of audio recordings is the subject of elaborate testing and testimony by experts. For example, in *Gonzalez v. Trinity Marine Group, Inc.*,[80] the complaint was dismissed and other sanctions were imposed after the court determined, on the basis of expert testimony, that the plaintiff had altered an audiotape of conversations with officials of the defendant company.

Mechanical and Electronic Surveillance.   Surveillance—auditory or visual or both—is the common context in which photographs or recordings are admitted under the "silent" or "machine" witness theory of authentication. Audio recorders are frequently activated automatically in connection with wiretaps; video cameras record comings and goings in banks and liquor stores; surveillance cameras at automatic teller machines routinely photograph banking transactions that are otherwise conducted in private; and so forth. When no one can testify to the accuracy of what has been captured on film or recording media, courts insist on a foundation that shows how the machine was employed. See FRE 901(b)(9). This should include evidence that the recording was continuous and uninterrupted; or, if that is not the case, evidence of how the recording was turned on and off, and a description of any control devices that might have affected the sounds or images that the machine picked up. Those courts that apply a special standard of care for all audio recordings[81] will demand the same showing of freedom from editing or tampering for surveillance recordings that they require for other recordings. It may also be necessary to show that the machine was in good working order, although some courts will presume this if the recording or photographs appear to be adequate.   If admitted, a surveillance recording or picture may be the most powerful evidence of what happened on an occasion—indeed, it may be the only "witness" to critical events.

Many surveillance pictures and recordings are made under challenging conditions, and are difficult to understand and interpret. The critical part of a video recording taken by a hidden camera may be the

---

[79] See, e.g., United States v. McMillan, 508 F.2d 101 (8th Cir. 1974); United States v. McCowan, 706 F.2d 863 (8th Cir. 1983); (following *McMillan*); United States v. Starks, 515 F.2d 112, 121 (3d Cir. 1975) (following *McMillan*); United States v. Biggins, 551 F.2d 64, 66 (5th Cir. 1977) (rejecting *McMillan* and setting up parallel test); United States v. Rodriguez-Garcia, 983 F.2d 1563 (10th Cir. 1993) (rejecting *McMillan* but requiring chain of custody); United States v. Slade, 627 F.2d 293, 301 (D.C. Cir. 1980) (tapes must be found to be authentic, accurate, trustworthy, audible and comprehensible); United States v. Traficant, 558 F. Supp. 996 (N.D. Ohio, 1983) ("flexible" standard, accuracy is key); United States v. King, 587 F.2d 956, 961 (9th Cir. 1978) (*McMillan* factors useful but not dispositive).

[80] 1996 WL 495153 (E.D. La.).

[81] See supra note 79.

blurry image of a person in the background of a few frames; the critical conversation on a surreptitious recording may have taken place in a moving car, and may be virtually inaudible because of static and noise from the engine and from traffic. Courts usually allow the proponent of such evidence to present it with "enhancements" that are intended to make the relevant content more apparent—for example, enlargements or manipulations of color and contrast for pictures, or re-recordings made with electronic filters to screen out background noise on sound recordings.[82] Needless to say, an exhibit that depends on such a technique requires a foundational showing that it is in fact an accurately "enhanced" version of the original, which means that the proponent—if challenged—should be required to present expert testimony on that issue.

A court may also permit the proponent of a picture or a recording to provide aids to help the jury understand the original exhibit. These can range from earphones or magnifying glasses, to testimony by expert or lay witnesses that directs their attention to the important parts, to a transcript of a recording of a conversation that the jurors can read as they try to decipher the scratchy noisy tape itself. Some such aids may require their own evidentiary foundations—a sophisticated optical and electronic system for projecting enlarged images of microscopic particles, for example. And some aids to perception may be objectionable under FRE 403. For example, a transcript of a conversation may be extremely helpful to a juror who is struggling to follow a difficult audio recording—if it is accurate. But if it is inaccurate, it can be equally misleading. Ultimately, a transcript is a record of one listener's judgment on what was said, even if that listener is an expert with a great deal of experience analyzing surveillance tapes who has listened to the tape repeatedly using a variety of manipulations and techniques. If the contents of the conversation are in dispute, it may be unfairly prejudicial to the opposing party to present that interpretation in a format that makes it seem like an established fact—or worse, that deludes the jurors into thinking they heard it themselves.

Problem X-12. At R.J. Samuel's trial for murdering his wife, the prosecution presents evidence that bloody shoe prints found at the scene of the killing were made by an unusual style of expensive Primo Galleano loafers. The prosecution wants to introduce a black and white

---

[82] See, e.g., State v. Mora, 618 A.2d 1275 (R.I. 1993) (electronically enhanced audiotape of sexual assault admissible). Similarly the videotape of the beating of Rodney King by Los Angeles police officers on March 3, 1991, was presented unaltered at the state-court criminal trial of the officers who beat him, and they were acquitted. At a later federal trial of the same officers for violating King's civil rights, the prosecutors used an enhanced version of the videotape, and the improved visibility apparently contributed to the conviction of two of the defendants. See Henry Weinstein, Jury Relied Heavily on Tape of King Beating, L.A. Times, April 18, 1993, p. A1.

photograph of R.J. taken at an NBA awards ceremony two years before the murder. In the original print of the photograph—which was taken by a sports photographer but never published—R.J.'s shoes cannot be identified. However, an enlargement of the portion of the picture that shows R.J.'s feet, printed through a special filter on high-contrast photographic paper—appears to show that he was wearing similar-looking Primo Galleano loafers. **What foundation should be required in order to introduce the enlargement in evidence?**

Problem X-13. Gordon Stalker is charged with selling heroin to an undercover federal agent. Stalker presents a defense of entrapment, claiming that the idea for the sale originated not with him but with the government agent, that he (Stalker) was reluctant to become involved, that he only agreed to do it after tremendous pressure was put on him by the agent, and that he had no propensity to commit such a crime. In response the government introduces a digital audio recording made by the agent at the time of the sale. The recording contained the following conversation:

Agent: Where did you get the stuff?

Stalker: From a friend. What do you care?

Agent: I don't care. Just curious.

Stalker: All right. Where's the money?

Agent: Here it is.

Stalker: Thanks.

Agent: You're welcome, and thank you. I'll be in touch.

Stalker: Great.

Stalker objects to the recording on the grounds that it is likely to be misused by the jury because it only records the actual sale and not any previous meetings. He also argues that the recording could be misinterpreted by a jury as signifying more agreement and less pressure than in fact existed. **Should the court exclude the tape?**

C. COMPUTER-GENERATED EXHIBITS

The computer is a ubiquitous tool. Many trial-court exhibits are produced by computers, in one manner or another: charts, maps, diagrams, pictures, video displays, documents of every sort—contracts, letters, email, payroll records—and so on. For the most part, the foundational requirements for these various computer-generated exhibits are simply applications of the requirements for the admission of comparable exhibits prepared by other means.[83]

---

[83] See generally Fredric I. Lederer, The New Courtroom: The Intersection of Evidence and Technology: Some Thoughts On the Evidentiary Aspects of Technologically Produced or

If a computer is simply a tool that produces an exhibit, its use should be immaterial. We don't ordinarily care if a letter was typed or printed by a computer any more than we care whether it was written with a fountain pen or a ballpoint pen. A frequently cited 1984 opinion by a New York trial court expresses this position clearly:

> Whether a diagram is hand drawn or mechanically drawn by means of a computer is of no importance . . . A computer is not a gimmick and the court should not be shy about its use, when proper. Computers are simply mechanical tools—receiving information and acting on instruction at lightening speed. When the results are useful, they should be accepted, when confusing, they should be rejected. What is important is that the presentation be relevant . . . that it fairly and accurately reflect the oral testimony offered and that it be an aid to the jury's understanding of the issue.[84]

For many exhibits—especially illustrative exhibits—the fact that they were created by computer is indeed of no significance. A chart, diagram, or animated video that illustrates one party's theory of the direction from which shots were fired, can be produced either by hand or on a computer. The main difference is that the latter method is usually easier and cheaper—sometimes, by an enormous margin.

For other exhibits, however, the role of the computer is substantively important. This may be true for two different reasons. First, with real (as opposed to illustrative) exhibits there are sometimes disputes about genuineness: Is the computer-printed letter that is presented in court a genuine duplicate of a letter the plaintiff sent to the defendant, or was it altered? Is the computer-generated list of accounts receivable that was produced on discovery accurate, or was it doctored? To answer these questions, we need evidence about the process by which these exhibits were produced. That is also true if the disputed exhibit was produced by hand or on a typewriter. But when an exhibit is computer generated, evidence describing its origins will generally focus on computer technology.

Second, computers—unlike other tools—perform calculations and manipulate information, and these calculations and manipulations are often embedded in evidence. For example, an engineer who testifies about structural defects in the construction of a bridge, or an economist who testifies to the expected lifetime earnings of an adolescent plaintiff if he hadn't suffered a crippling injury, will inevitably rely on the results of computations performed by computers. In many cases these calculations

---

Presented Evidence, 28 Sw. U. L. Rev. 389 (1999); Stanley A. Kurzban, Authentication of Computer-Generated Evidence in the United States Federal Courts, 35 Idea: J. L. & Tech., 437 (1995). See also Lorraine v. Markel Am. Ins. Co., 241 F.R.D. 534 (D. Md. 2007).

[84] People v. McHugh, 124 Misc.2d 559, 476 N.Y.S.2d 721, 722–23 (Sup. Ct. Bronx Co. 1984).

are reflected in exhibits: a chart showing the future value of an investment, by year, at various interest rates; a graph of the average yearly temperature in a city over the course of the last decade; a map of projected population densities, by census tract, for a given state, twenty years in the future; and so forth. These results may depend not only on the underlying information but also on the mathematical formulae employed to calculate the numbers and the images that are displayed. A figure in an Excel spreadsheet, for example, may be generated by an algebraic formula embedded in the spreadsheet program. The process that produces the figure will be invisible to the naked eye unless intentionally revealed on direct or cross-examination. If such exhibits are admitted as substantive evidence, they must be authenticated—typically by showing, under FRE 901(b)(9), that they were created by "a process or system and showing that it produces an accurate result." If they are presented as a basis for an expert opinion (and are not otherwise admitted in evidence), they have to satisfy the requirement of FRE 703 that "experts in a particular field would reasonably rely on those kinds of facts or data in forming an opinion on the subject"—which requires evidence that the process that produced them is accurate and reliable. One way or the other, if the foundation for computer-generated exhibits that embody complex calculation is contested, the proponent will have to present expert testimony.[85]

With the possible exception of non-business emails, the most common computer-generated exhibits in American litigation are business records (including many business-generated emails). Virtually every adult member of this society is exposed to a constant stream of computer-generated information—bills, accounts, mailings, reports, etc. This is hardly surprising, since virtually all organizations in America maintain their records on computers and use computers to communicate and to create documents. Decades ago, computerized data was communicated primarily by producing paper printouts. These days our business and personal lives are increasingly dependent on electronic communication, including social media, and most computer data are never printed at all. Inevitably, computer-generated exhibits have become the dominant type of business records used in contemporary litigation. They can range from simple letters (for which the role of the computer is purely mechanical), to accounts (for which the computer must perform routine calculations), to complex analyses and summaries of vast computerized databases.

In most cases, computer-generated business records are used to prove that statements contained in them are true: that a customer does owe a specified sum for goods delivered, for example, or that the net worth of a company is what the company claims. For these purposes the exhibits

---

[85] The most elaborate example of this use of computer-generated evidence is computer-animated simulations, which we discuss in the next section.

must satisfy the requirements of the "business-records" exception to the hearsay rule: they must be shown to be based on information transmitted or recorded by people with knowledge of the events in question, at or near the time of those events, and kept as a regular practice by the business. See FRE 803(6).   In addition, in order to authenticate particular documents that are generated from these data, the proponent may have to present evidence on the reliability of the process by which they were produced. See FRE 901(b)(9).[86] There is no longer anything novel about this procedure. It simply requires step-by-step evidence on how the data are entered into the computer, how the computerized records are maintained, how information is retrieved from the database, what instructions are used to get the computer to perform particular computations, and—for each stage—how the accuracy and integrity of the process are assured.[87] For the most part, courts that have addressed the issue have held that computerized business records require no greater foundation than paper records, neither for authentication nor to satisfy the business-records exception to the hearsay rule.[88]

D. VIDEO RECORDINGS AND OTHER MOTION PICTURES

1.   The Range of Video Exhibits

Conceptually, video recordings are not different in kind from photographs and sound recordings. They typically include both audio and visual reproduction, and obviously show far more than any still photograph, but otherwise they are just an extension of the same processes. In the past two decades, however, video technology has become so inexpensive, convenient, powerful and flexible, that video recorded evidence has acquired a special place in American trial practice. Most likely, the importance of video evidence in litigation will continue to grow and the range of uses for such evidence will increase, especially given the video recording capabilities of modern digital cameras and cellphones. In 1988, Judge Eli Chernow of the Los Angeles County, California, Superior Court, gave a useful overview[89]:

---

[86] Under FRE 1000(d) such an exhibit will be considered an "original" of electronically stored information "if it accurately reflects the information." There may nonetheless be original document issues to address if the exhibit's "metadata" is at issue: information in the computer file that is generally not displayed in a printouts, including indications of authorship, dates of creation and modification, notes, deleted material, etc. See supra note 33.

[87] See, Note, Leah Vogt, Developments in the Law VI. Electronic Evidence and the Federal Rules, 38 Loy. L. Rev. 1745 (2005); Admissibility of Computerized Business Records, 15 Jurimetrics Journal 206, at 210–11, 224–46 (Spring 1975).

[88] See, e.g., United States v. Young Bros. Inc., 728 F.2d 682, 693 (5th Cir. 1984); United States v. Briscoe, 896 F.2d 1476 (7th Cir. 1990); Kurzban, supra note 83. Unfortunately, counsel often do not appear to understand how to apply the rules of evidence to electronic evidence. See Lorraine v. Markel Am. Ins. Co., 241 F.R.D. 534 (D. Md. 2007).

[89] Eli Chernow, Video in the Courtroom: More Than a Talking Head, 15 Litig. 3 (Fall 1988). Reprinted by permission of ABA Publishing.

You cannot appreciate the full impact of a courtroom video without seeing one. Nevertheless, it is important to suggest the variety and potential of such devices. Try to visualize the following videotapes:

Bus Accident: The plaintiff claims his arm was caught in a closing door as he left a bus. The defendant Transit Authority makes a videotape showing the inside and outside of the bus, the path described by plaintiff, the door, and the security devices designed to prevent this type of accident. The aims of the tape—which is offered in evidence—are clear: to show the plaintiff is shooting at the wrong target and that the defendant's bus had abundant safety features.

Motorcycle Accident: Here the defendant is charged with manufacturing a defective kickstand bolt, the failure of which caused a motorcycle to fall on the plaintiff. The motorcycle manufacturer introduces a videotape with an element of drama. A defense expert is shown next to a cycle with a standard bolt. He then removes the original bolt, and inserts a partially sawed-through bolt. The expert crouches in a vulnerable position beside the cycle. He twists and twists the bolt. It breaks—but the cycle barely moves.

Homicide Reconstruction: The defendant in a murder trial offers a video dramatization of his version of how the killing occurred. The tape, made with professional actors at the scene of the crime, illustrates an unintentional killing—manslaughter rather than murder.

Newspaper Plant Tour: A newspaper, defending a predatory pricing case, take the jury on a video tour of its publishing plant. The tape is narrated by the plant manager. It illustrates the operations involved in producing a newspaper, showing staffing patterns and the flow of work. The narrator describes the peak load demands on each department as deadlines approach. The video supports an important defense contention that the local paper at issue in the case was published at no added labor cost.

Truck Rollover: The key question in this case is whether the plaintiff, who was not wearing a seat belt, was injured because he came out of his seat, or because the roof of the truck collapsed on him. The defendant uses a silent animated video to show the cab of a small pickup truck in a rollover. A dummy is depicted behind the wheel. The dummy's head strikes the ceiling of the cab well before the cab supports begin to collapse.

Tire Rim Explosion: The plaintiff was injured when the truck tire he was filling with air exploded. In the video, a life-sized mannequin is crouched next to a truck. The tire and rim explode, hurling the mannequin 10 feet in a cloud of dust. There are two more showings of the explosion. The tape concludes with a close-up of the mannequin's face. See *Hale v. Firestone Tire & Rubber Co.*, 820 F.2d 928 (8th Cir. 1987).

To these efforts should be added the most familiar in-court video: the "day in the life" tape. It typically shows a quadriplegic plaintiff being cared for by his family and nurse. Usual scenes include the plaintiff being hoisted in and out of bed, being fed his meals, dealing in a limited way with his children, and attending, with difficulty, to his bathroom functions.

For most in-court videotapes, there is another important factor apart from their substance. They are not home movies. They are professionally packaged, crisply edited, and carefully presented. The narrator is often a professional with the kind of warm, expansive voice that could sell you the Brooklyn Bridge and would sound interesting reading the phone book. In current jargon, the production values are high.

Had I been the trial judge, I would not have allowed the audio portion of any of the tapes to be played to the jury, and I would not have admitted the bus or motorcycle tapes at all. I would have been especially dubious about the tire rim tape: The tire in the video was different from the tire in the accident, and the cameraman needed six takes to get the explosion offered at trial. But, except for the murder-manslaughter tape, each of these tapes and its audio track was admitted into evidence. Admission of the tire rim tape was affirmed by a federal appeals court.

All of this did not occur in the courtrooms of peculiar, avant-garde jurisdictions. These videos were received by state and federal judges described by both sides as conservative in such sober, solid places as Portland, Oregon, and Louisville, Kentucky.

. . .

How would the rules of evidence apply? Usually a videotape is offered as demonstrative evidence after an expert witness has testified. Once the expert has given his opinion and its basis, the tape is offered to illustrate the opinion. As a foundation for the tape's admissibility, the expert testifies that the video fairly and accurately illustrates the principles upon which he based his testimony, the application of those principles, and his conclusions. Of course, all this expert foundational testimony is subject to cross-examination.

. . .

Once the fighting over the tape's foundation is finished, the videotape's proponent will argue that it should be treated like a medical drawing or three-dimensional model of the human body. In other words, it should be received into evidence and shown to the jury.

Things are not always so simple, however. A trial lawyer facing his opponent's offer of a videotape will rarely agree with the evidentiary framework just outlined. He or she will likely argue that the tape constitutes hearsay, that it cannot be meaningfully cross-examined, that it lacks foundation, and that it is unduly prejudicial. Proponents counter that none of these objections has merit, and that treating a videotape differently from any other demonstrative or illustrative evidence is simply superstition, or fear of progress. All that is needed, the proponent will argue, is an adequate foundation provided by an expert witness who is available for cross-examination.

. . .

The fact is that the traditional rules of evidence cannot resolve all the controversy about videotapes. Even if the requirements of evidence law are satisfied a hundred times over, there remains this fact: A two-minute video, if well made, will make a greater impression on the minds and emotions of jurors than the world's best expert. Once jurors see the video, the images will be graven on their minds. In fact, opponents of videotapes argue that a jury will never be able to evaluate intellectual criticism of a video's validity, no matter how devastating the cross-examination of the sponsoring expert. The familiar power of television will shoulder everything else aside. The very value of using the videotape—its ability to impress and explain— is thus the source of the most persuasive arguments against its use.

Such concerns come down to one question: Is a video so fundamentally prejudicial that it should not be shown to the jury? Even though it satisfies the rules of evidence, is the videotape—like a picture of a plaintiff's wounds—*too* expressive and *too* persuasive?

. . . To appreciate how hard it can be to answer this question, consider the most dramatic video that I have seen—the Louisville hexane tape.

THE HEXANE TAPE

A series of early morning explosions destroyed miles of sewers and streets in Louisville, Kentucky. Plaintiffs contended that the explosions were caused by the release of the chemical hexane from a processing plant several miles away.

A videotape was prepared by the plaintiff Louisville Sanitation Districts shortly before trial and was then shown to the defendant during settlement discussions. In short order, there was a $20 million settlement.

Following this success, the hexane tape was sold by the Sanitation Districts to several private property owners. The trial in the suit they filed was mostly a battle over the admission of the tape. The judge and counsel viewed the tape several times during the course of plaintiff's expert testimony. There were certain deletions and a modification in the tape's narration. With these changes, the tape was ruled admissible. The trial promptly recessed for settlement talks. More settlements—this time estimated to range from $25 million to $50 million—followed.

What is the mysterious power of this video, you ask. And how can I get one of my very own?

The hexane video is a computer-generated animation narrated by an expert. It begins with a discussion of the dangerous properties of hexane. It shows the defendant's plant and its original containment system. The video then details the erosion of the safety protections over the years: a buildup of crust at the bottom of the containment vessel; the cracking of a pipe; the sealing of a previously open access port; and the effect of plant expansion.

What follows is a dramatic reconstruction of the accident. The narrator points out a clog causing hexane to build up in the containment vessel. The viewer then sees the failure of the designed safety features. In riveting animation, the vessel slowly fills and hexane spills inside the plant. An inspector is shown examining the sewers downstream from the plant. The narrator explains that the magnitude of the spill was not discovered during the inspection because of a blockage of the hexane outflow line, preventing hexane from immediately reaching the city sewers.

Ultimately, the viewer sees the blockage break, the hexane flow into the sewer lines, forming arteries of danger throughout Louisville. The narrator explains the hexane-to-air ratio necessary for an explosion. The scene then shifts to a map of Louisville showing major landmarks superimposed over the sewer lines. The animated explosive front of the hexane proceeds downstream from the plant and expands until it covers several miles of downtown Louisville. Finally, there is a series of simulated explosions between and around the landmarks of Louisville.

The hexane videotape has enormous impact. Contrast the traditional evidence needed to make the same points: the testimony of a chemical process engineer; diagrams of the plant; maps of the sewer system; eyewitness accounts; expert testimony on gas chemistry; and so on. It would be a mass of technical, overlapping, and interlocking material. The videotape ties it together unforgettably.

But is the hexane tape unduly prejudicial? Can any cross-examination of an expert impeach such powerful evidence? How can subliminal emotional land mines—perhaps the color of the animated gas flow or the depiction of landmarks—be detected? Can any amount of trial preparation and discovery ever provide an opponent enough of a preview to expose a charlatan video?

We can group the issues that videos present into three categories. (1) *Prejudice and probative value.* Under FRE 403 and analogous provisions the judge may have to decide whether the tape is inflammatory, whether it is misleading, whether it will confuse the jury or waste the court's time, and whether it has significant probative value on some material issue or issues. (2) *Other evidentiary objections.* In some cases other objections that are available for testimony may also be made against video presentations In particular, some videos, or portions thereof, are objectionable on the ground that they present hearsay or unqualified expert opinion evidence. (3) *Alternative methods of presenting evidence.* Often the court will have to decide whether a video is the best available method of presenting evidence on an issue, or at least whether it is no worse than some alternative method.

Problem X-14. Assume that all the information that is included in the Hexane tape is admissible in evidence through available expert and lay witnesses. **If you represented the Defendant Chemical Company, what arguments would you make to try to persuade the judge that the tape should be excluded? Which Federal Rules of Evidence would you rely on? If you represented the Plaintiffs, how would you respond to those arguments and try to persuade the judge to admit the tape?**

---

2.   Day-in-the-Life Videos

Any exhibition, demonstration or experiment can be video recorded, as an alternative to live presentation. Several of the videotapes Judge Chernow describes fall into this general category. A recorded event may be less dramatic than a live one, but it has great advantages. By prerecording the demonstration the attorney offering the evidence increases her control. She will *know* in advance how it will turn out—and so will her opponent, and so will the judge, who will be able to make a better informed decision on any objections that are raised. More important, many demonstrations are like views—they simply cannot be conducted in a courtroom. Video recording vastly expands the range of available evidence. The most common and important examples are Day-in-the-Life videos, which are frequently used as evidence of non-economic damages in personal injury cases. A documentary filmmaker who makes Day-in-the-Life videos describes their value:[90]

> I'm often asked by attorneys why they should hire a professional to produce a Day-in-the-Life video? Why spend money on a professional legal documentarian rather than on, for example, a camcorder that the attorney himself could use to do his own Day-in-the-Life? Why not buy or borrow a video camera, aim it at the client, and start filming? . . .

> Well, it isn't that simple. The technology that has made video equipment so much a part of our lives has also produced a very sophisticated audience. The judge and the defense attorney and the insurance claims adjusters . . . [are] savvy enough to know the difference between a professional production and an amateur one. And the professionally produced Day-in-the-Life signals to them all the seriousness of intent of the plaintiff's attorney.

> The well-crafted Day-in-the-Life film is cinema verite, and as such is unrehearsed. But the professional producer does a lot more than just point and shoot. *Unrehearsed* is not the same as *unplanned*. And the professionally shot Day-in-the-Life is carefully planned.

> . . .

> Let's start from the beginning and talk about equipment. The professional is not going to be using the same video camera you'd buy to make home videos. But not only will his cameras be of professional quality, so will his lighting and sound equipment. His plan for the day will include a substantial amount of setup time so that the video will be adequately lighted and so the sound will be clear. He'll know exactly how to light a bedroom or kitchen scene or how to handle white walls to keep the client from silhouetting. He'll know how to place the equipment to minimize interference in a classroom or therapy session. He'll also know how to adjust the mechanical requirements to suit the particular needs of the client; for example, I know that bright lights frequently make comatose patients sleepy, and so I adjust the lighting accordingly.

> Back at the studio, the professional will have editing equipment that will allow him to turn the four or so hours of Day-in-the-Life footage that he has shot into a clear, concise, cohesive production that will run approximately 20 minutes. . . .

---

[90] Bill Buckley, Day in the Life Videos, Why Hire a Professional? March, 1991, Nat'l Trial Lawyer. Reprinted by special permission of B & B Productions, Inc., 1991, Bill Buckley.

What the professional knows is that although editing technically takes place in the editing room, the process begins as the film is being shot. What this means is that throughout the filming he or she is thinking about shooting not only the action itself, but also the transitional shots that will provide a smooth flow. At the same time, the professional will be conceiving a story line that will give the finished product a clear beginning, middle and end.

. . .

The very number of Day-in-the-Life films that a professional has made will enhance his understanding of each type of case. . . . Not too long ago, I produced a Day-in-the-Life of a young man who had lost both legs below the knee in an automobile accident. I was well aware of the need to show his struggle to put on his prostheses. I knew how to shoot to demonstrate his difficulties in getting around. But I could also see that the young man did so well on his artificial legs that it was almost possible to overlook the tragedy of his disability. So I chatted with him and discovered that his exercise routine included swimming at the local YMCA. The scene of him diving into the water from his stumps became an emotional focal point of that Day-in-the-Life film.

Bear in mind, too, that the Day-in-the-Life producer does not have the luxury of rehearsing or reshooting scenes. When a client is severely injured, it is often all he can do to make an arduous effort once. The quadriplegic in physical therapy may be physically incapable of repeating a difficult action. So the producer most often has only one chance to get the shot and get it right. Even if rehearsals are not physically impossible, they are subject to being questioned by the defense. In a Day-in-the-Life film, nothing should be done "for the camera."

. . .

Finally, [a professional producer] will be helpful in the courtroom should it become necessary for him to testify in defense of the film's admissibility. For although Day-in-the-Life films are more common than they were 20 years ago, admissibility can still occasionally be a problem. The professional Day-in-the-Life producer will be capable of taking the stand to defend the manner in which the film was made. The defense attorney might ask if the producer wasn't intentionally trying to elicit sympathy by, for example, showing the client wince as he underwent physical therapy. The novice may deliberately zoom in for a close-up of that wince. The professional knows that objective distance is required—that, in any case, the wince will be visible in a medium shot and that the attorney can point it out if he feels it necessary.

The scene of the amputee diving into the pool that I spoke of earlier was admissible because it was not shot to overemphasize the client's disability. The drama came from the fact that such scenes are now an ordinary part of the client's life. The professional knows that and can speak to the point in the courtroom.

An experienced personal injury defense attorney presents another view[91]:

If there is one piece of damages evidence which does and rightly should cause the most apprehension for the defense, it is a well-done Day-in-the-Life (DIL) film. It will rivet the jury's attention like no other evidence and bring home to the most hardened heart the plight of a severely injured plaintiff.

. . .

In its purest form, a DIL video will begin as the injured party awakens, and continue until he or she has gone to sleep. In actuality, a DIL video presented in court consists of approximately fifteen to twenty minutes of edited tape which portrays limited segments of daily activities. As [a prominent plaintiffs' attorney] notes, "[u]sually the plaintiff will be required to do two days' activities in one, and perhaps repeat scenes due to equipment malfunction." . . .

Typical DIL videos consist of several segments:

> (1) waking—bathing, grooming, and dressing;
>
> (2) eating;
>
> (3) transportation—plaintiff getting around inside a house as well as outside, if he or she is able;
>
> (4) therapy—includes occupational as well as rehabilitative and recreational;
>
> (5) bowel/bladder care; and
>
> (6) going to bed—undressing, grooming, and positioning.

. . . Along with the above segments, the tape may show the plaintiff's difficulty in operating things we take for granted, such as a light switch or a telephone.

. . .

[P]laintiff's counsel use DIL videos to increase the size of the jury's verdict. Because of the power of these videos, however, defense counsel's worry is that they distort the value of a

---

[91] J. Ric Gass, Defending Against Day-in-the-Life Videos, 34 *For the Defense* (Defense Research Institute) 8–9, 15 (July, 1992). Reprinted by special permission of the Defense Research Institute.

plaintiff's case beyond its fair and reasonable value. Defense counsel's legitimate fear is that it is virtually impossible to show the jurors powerful, heart-wrenching, or gruesome videos, and then expect them to fairly determine liability, not to mention a fair and reasonable amount of damages.

While the first and foremost [defense] goal is to block completely the showing of the plaintiff's videotape presentation at trial, defense counsel cannot make this a knee-jerk reaction. For instance, there may occasionally be a tape that *ought* to be shown. It may be of such poor quality, be such a blatant exaggeration or play for sympathy, that defense counsel can turn it against the plaintiff and destroy his or her credibility.

The most obvious potential problem with Day-in-the-Life videos is that they might be inflammatory. In general, courts will admit even gruesome recordings that depict the plaintiff's physical condition accurately and without undue emphasis,[92] since testimony by the plaintiff and others is far less informative. Some videos, however, are excluded as unnecessarily disturbing. For example, in *Thomas v. C.G. Tate Construction*,[93] an otherwise acceptable film was excluded because of the manner in which it portrayed the plaintiff's painful physical therapy (a close-up shot showed his contorted face, while the soundtrack played his moans) and other graphic scenes, such as the removal of dead skin that was peeled back from the plaintiff's arm. Recordings may also be held inadmissible in whole or in part because they contain irrelevant and potentially prejudicial material.[94]

Defense attorneys frequently object to Day-in-the-Life videos on the ground that they are misleading because they were staged, or because they are an edited selection of the tape that was shot. These issues may occasionally result in exclusion, and can always be explored on cross-examination of the filmmaker. For this purpose, defense counsel will usually be entitled to obtain the "outtakes"—tape shot but not used—during pre-trial discovery. In addition, some courts allow defense attorneys, on request, to be present in the first instance, at the shooting of the tape.[95]

A common objection to Day-in-the-Life videos, and to other videotaped demonstrations, is that they are hearsay. The issue turns on

---

[92] Cf. Donathan v. Orthopaedic & Sports Med. Clinic., PLC, 2009 WL 3584263 (E.D. Tenn. 2009) (concluding that a day-in-the-life recording may be admissible but withholding final decision on a motion in limine pending witness testimony at trial).

[93] 465 F. Supp. 566 (D.S.C. 1979).

[94] E.g., Eckman v. Moore, 876 So.2d 975, 983 (Miss. 2004) (inclusion of decedent's stepson in video and still images was error).

[95] See Campbell v. Pitt County Memorial Hospital, Inc. 84 N.C. App. 314, 320, 352 S.E.2d 902, 906 (1987); Balian v. General Motors, 121 N.J. Super. 118, 296 A.2d 317 (1972). But see Cisarik v. Palos Community Hospital, 144 Ill.2d 339, 162 Ill. Dec. 59, 579 N.E.2d 873 (1991).

whether the tape contains verbal statements that are used to prove the truth of the matter stated, or assertive non-verbal conduct that is used to prove the matter asserted. See FRE 801. The extreme cases (as always) are clear. A candid shot of the plaintiff walking on crutches, or an unnarrated video of an assembly line, is not hearsay, since it contains no "statements." On the other hand, a tape of the plaintiff describing her physical problems, or a tape of a plant foreman describing the operation of a machine, does contain hearsay if it is offered to prove the truth of what the plaintiff or the foreman said. In between, there is an ambiguous gray area. If the plaintiff was aware of the filming, her non-verbal conduct might be interpreted as an assertion equivalent to the statement: "Look, this is how I get up, this is how I move, this is how I wash," and so forth. The more staged the conduct, the stronger the argument. A few courts have excluded Day-in-the-Life videos on this ground,[96] but most do not. Some courts have held that while hearsay, such videos are admissible under the residual exception to the hearsay rule (FRE 807) because they are more probative of the nature of the plaintiff's injuries than any other form of available evidence.[97]

3. Reconstructions, Reenactments and Simulations

Gregory Joseph has described the general nature of video reconstruction and reenactment[98]:

> Trial is an exercise in reconstructing facts. Ordinarily, this is done through the introduction of testimony and documents. It may be attempted to reconstruct pertinent events live before a jury. Video offers yet a third means of reconstruction, recreation or reenactment for the fact-finder. . . .

> Video affords the opportunity, at least conceptually, to visualize for the fact finder precisely how any incident in controversy occurred. Whether to admit or exclude reconstruction tapes is a matter committed to the discretion of the trial judge.

> . . .

> For example, in *Jenkins v. Snohomish County Public Utility District No. 1*, an action for injuries sustained by a boy who climbed into an electric utility substation, the defendant successfully offered a videotaped reenactment. The tape showed a boy of the minor plaintiff's age and size climbing into the substation over the fenced gate which the plaintiff had traversed and over a variety of other fences with and without barbed wire.

---

[96] E.g. Haley v. Byers Transp. Co., 414 S.W.2d 777 (Mo. 1967).

[97] See Grimes v. Emp'rs Mutual Liab. Ins. Co., 73 F.R.D. 607 (D. Alaska 1977).

[98] Gregory P. Joseph, Modern Visual Evidence §§ 4.05–4.05[2], pp. 4–49 (2008) (some citations omitted).

Conditions under which the tape was made were similar to those in issue, and the differences were explained to the jury. The trial judge instructed the jury to consider the tape only on the issue of the physical deterrent aspect of the fence with and without barbed wire, since that was the key issue raised by the plaintiffs. The Washington Supreme Court, while "sympathetic to the [plaintiffs'] concerns" about the impact of the tape on the jury, ruled that the trial judge had not abused his discretion in admitting the tape into evidence.[99]

Joseph notes, however, that:

> . . . [I]n contrast to the judicial reception accorded other forms of video-recorded evidence there has been considerable judicial reluctance to admit reconstruction videos offered for the purpose of demonstrating how an incident in issue occurred. . . . The courts are seriously concerned that reconstruction videos which are merely illustrative, may be so impressive to the jurors that they will disregard substantive evidence in reaching their verdicts.[100]

There is a danger that any video re-creation will be unconsciously viewed by the jury as an actual record of the event. In view of this danger, courts require a foundational showing that the conditions under which the videotape was made were substantially similar—or in some cases, *very* similar—to those involved in the event under litigation. Otherwise, as one court put it, "Whatever . . . counsel or experts said to the jury about differing circumstances, the drama of the filmed recreation could easily overcome the logic of the distinctions."[101] Courts tend to be more forgiving in applying this requirement if the tape is offered only as an "illustration" of a party's theory of how the accident might have occurred—usually to illustrate an expert witness's testimony—than if it is offered as a "reconstruction" to show how the accident *did* occur.[102] Some courts, however, recognize that even a videotape that is purportedly merely an "illustration" of a theory can *look* like a reconstruction, and require such tapes to meet the tougher foundational standards that apply to reconstructions.[103]

The most elaborate type of video reconstruction is computer animation, the technique used to create the Louisville sewer explosion video described by Judge Chernow.[104] In its simpler form, computer

---

[99] Id. pp. 4–51—4–52.

[100] Id., pp. 4–49—4–50.

[101] Fusco v. General Motors Corp., 11 F.3d 259, 264 (1st Cir. 1993).

[102] See Lopez v. Foremost Paving, Inc., 796 S.W.2d 473 (Tex. App. 1990); Green v. General Motors Corp., 104 Mich. App. 447, 304 N.W.2d 600, 601–602 (1981).

[103] See Randall v. Warnaco, Inc., 677 F.2d 1226 (8th Cir. 1982); Mechanick v. Conradi, 139 A.D.2d 857, 527 N.Y.S.2d 586, 588 (N.Y. App. Div. 1988).

[104] Supra pp. 1331–1333.

animation merely illustrates the testimony of a live witness, generally an expert. The animation can show things that are difficult to visualize and impossible to replicate. Consider this example[105]:

> Building owners and construction contractors throughout the country were bringing lawsuits against Dow Chemical Company. Masonry panels that adorned their buildings were cracking, and they argued that an additive supplied by Dow was the cause. Dow's claims manager . . . needed to find a way to demonstrate that Dow was not at fault. Drawing on his experience with forensic graphics . . . [he hired] a computer animation firm in Grand Rapids, Michigan, to help communicate his case.
>
> "We started with an actual video of the building . . . [t]hen we dissolved into an animation. We pulled a panel off the structure, rotated it onto its end, and showed the cracks in the panel which caused it to fall. Then we made the panel translucent, demonstrating the match between the cracks in the panel and the position of the support structures beneath it."
>
> Dow's attorneys argued that the support structures need to "breathe," to expand slightly when heated and contract slightly when cooled, to keep panels from cracking and falling out. The animation illustrated the argument.

The computational power of computers can also be used to generate and display new evidence. For example, in an airline crash case, known values of the airplanes' flight paths, velocities, headings, rates of climb or descent, turning radius, bank angles, etc., can be entered into a computer program. Based on these data, and applying accepted principles of optics and physics, the computer can calculate the trajectory of the planes in space and time. It can also generate an animated tape that provides views of the events leading up to the crash from the cockpit of each aircraft— showing what each pilot was able to see and for how long—and similar animated views from behind each aircraft, from the ground, and so forth.

One of the pioneering uses of computer-simulated animations was in the case of *In re Air Crash at Dallas/Fort Worth Airport on Aug. 2, 1985*,[106] which was tried in 1989:

> During the last few seconds of an otherwise routine descent into Dallas/Fort Worth airport one sultry August night in 1985, Delta Flight 191 flew suddenly into a killer thunderstorm. Wind-shear forces quickly dashed the craft to the ground, where it rolled violently across the airfield into some reservoir tanks, killing all

---

[105] Buck BloomBecker, "The Power of Animated Evidence," California Lawyer, May 1988, p. 47.

[106] 720 F. Supp. 1258 (N.D. Tex. 1989), aff'd, 919 F.2d 1079 (5th Cir. 1991).

137 people on board. Two years later, Delta sued both the Federal Aviation Administration and the National Weather Service for failing to warn the pilots that a storm of such severity had developed. Preparing to do battle with Delta's lawyers before a lone federal judge, Kathlynn Fadely, a young attorney with the U.S. Department of Justice, commissioned a series of computer-generated animations to simulate the Lockheed Tristar's performance and explain critical instrument readings in the last moments of flight. It soon became clear from the aircraft's maneuvers that the pilots knew at least as much about the weather as ground control did. "They were playing Russian roulette by flying into that storm," she says. "The judge said the animations were both helpful and powerful," Fadely recalls. By translating digital data from the aircraft's "black box" into striking images of the pilots, actions, and superimposing the cockpit soundtrack, she was able to weave a convincing narrative of pilot overconfidence and horrifying errors. She won the case, exonerating the federal government.[107]

The animated simulations in the Delta Flight 191 case were extraordinarily detailed and sophisticated. Four attorneys and six experts worked with the production company for nearly two years to create them, using forty different parameters to re-create the plane's flight—speed, acceleration, heading, pitch, roll, etc. The total cost was in the hundreds of thousands of dollars.[108] In the years since 1989, computer simulations have become much cheaper and much more widely available. The same procedure is now routinely used to re-create ordinary automobile accidents, although the input data are likely to be far less precise and detailed than those that are available for airplane crashes from inflight telemetry and voice recorders. A one-or two-minute animated simulation of a collision at an intersection, seen repeatedly from different angles, might now cost two thousand to five thousand dollars.

This type of computer-animated simulation may be extremely useful, if it is properly constructed. But that may be a very serious *if*, or rather a series of *if's*.

The underlying data may be full of errors or discrepancies, or it may, for one reason or another, be irrelevant or improper as evidence. The data may have been fed into the computer inaccurately. The computer may have been improperly programmed or not programmed to detect errors. The assumptions on which the

---

[107] Arielle Emmett, Simulations on Trial, 97 Tech. Rev. No. 4 (5/1/94).

[108] Paul Marcotte, Animated Evidence: Delta 191 Crash Re-Created through Computer Simulation at Trial, ABA J., Dec. 1989, pp. 52–54.

program was based may be wrong, illogical, or simply irrelevant to the issues sought to be proved.[109]

The scientific principles on which simulations are based are neither novel nor controversial. In general, they are straight-forward applications of Newtonian physics, and in most cases there is no dispute about the performance of the software packages that apply these principles. The usual problems concern the data. Data about an accident may have been reported in error (an eyewitness is wrong about speed or location), or recorded or entered in error, or based on an improper calculation (an expert incorrectly estimates speed from skid marks), or simply reflect an unsubstantiated theory or assumption. If so, the ultimate product may be deeply misleading.

Given the technical nature of these issues, the foundation that is required for computer animated simulations always includes expert testimony. Some witness, or witnesses, must be available to testify to the manner in which the data were collected, how they were entered, how the computer was programmed, what scientific assumptions were made, etc. Since these are matters beyond the ken of lay people, these witnesses will have to qualify as experts. In most cases, computer animated simulations are admitted (if at all) either as demonstrative exhibits that illustrate the expert testimony, or as a basis for expert conclusions, or both. In reported cases, computer-simulated videos are often admitted but are sometimes excluded, usually because the data on which they are based are not supported by evidence in the record.[110] The opposition, of course, is free to attack the data, the scientific and factual assumptions, or the computational process, on cross-examination or on rebuttal. In the absence of a competing video, however, the opposing party is likely to be at a severe disadvantage, with ambiguous and confusing testimony competing against vivid visual images.

Computer animation is rapidly becoming cheaper, more flexible, and more compelling. As this happens, legal disputes over computer-animated evidence will probably become more common. On the pro side, computer animation is *interesting*, it is (in itself) *succinct*, and it can *clarify* and *teach* things that would otherwise remain obscure. These are

---

[109] Martha M. Jenkins, Computer-Generated Evidence Specially Prepared for Use at Trial, 52 Chi.-Kent L. Rev. 600 (1976). See also John Selbak, Digital Litigation: The Prejudicial Effects of Computer-Generated Animation in the Courtroom, 9 High Tech. L. J. 337 (1994).

[110] Compare, e.g., Mintun v. State, 966 P.2d 954 (Wyo. 1998) (admission of computer animation of car crash upheld in criminal case), and Martin v. Kearfott Guidance and Navigation Corp., 1998 WL 1184107 (D.N.J. 1998) (computer-animated videos of helicopter accident admissible as illustrative evidence), with Sommervold v. Grevlos, 518 N.W.2d 733 (S.D. 1994) (computer animation of accident inadmissible because it misrepresented facts) and Exxon Corp. v. Halcon Shipping Co., Ltd., 1995 WL 20667 (D.N.J. 1995) (computer simulation stricken from record because images not in accord with evidence on possible collision between tugboat and fuel pipe).

considerable virtues. The arguments on the con side, however, are also strong:

1) Even now, computer-animated evidence can be *expensive*. Basic animations can be prepared on home computers, but high quality animations, especially those that depend on detailed data and complex scientific algorithms, may be very expensive. Their use confers an advantage on parties with greater wealth.

2) Computer-animated evidence is often *complex*. Although the final product may be short and interesting, the testimony that is necessary to lay the foundation may be long, confusing and boring. Indeed, for all practical purposes, the formulae that determine what a video simulation shows are indecipherable to a lay jury.

3) Computer-animated evidence is *seductive*. According to lawyers involved in the Delta Flight 191 case, for example, "the various animations created an eerie feeling of being there, of seeing and hearing what the crew experienced."[111] This uncanny realism reflects numerous editorial choices that are incorporated into the final product, perhaps deliberately in order to manipulate the audience. Even so, there is nothing wrong with the evidence *if* the re-creation is accurate. If not, a video animation may greatly exaggerate the persuasive force of a shaky argument. This problem is particularly worrisome since computer simulations are usually used in the course of expert opinion testimony—a notoriously malleable form of evidence in itself.

4) Finally, as we have already discussed, computer-animated evidence may be *inaccurate* and *misleading* in ways that are difficult to detect, and even more difficult to explain.

A study of the effects of video animations on mock jurors illustrates both the strengths and the dangers of this type of evidence—its ability to clarify, and its power to mislead.[112] Subjects were asked to judge a dispute over the cause of death of a man who fell from the roof of an eight-story building: Did he jump and commit suicide (in which case the defendant insurance company is not liable on his life insurance policy), or did he accidentally slip? The critical evidence is the distance at which his body landed from the edge of the building: if close (five to ten feet), that suggests that he slipped and fell; if far (twenty to twenty-five feet), that suggests that he ran and jumped. The researchers found that neutral videos illustrating the fall helped the subject-jurors—they were more likely to reach a decision that corresponded with the physical evidence on the position of the body. However, subjects who saw a video in which the

---

[111] Marcotte, supra note 108.

[112] Saul M. Kassin & Meghan A. Dunn, Computer-Animated Displays and the Jury: Facilitative and Prejudicial Effects, 21 L. & Human Beh. 269 (1997).

stick figure of the man visibly slips, waves his arms, loses his balance and falls, were more likely than those who saw no video to find that the fall was an accident—even when the body ended up twenty to twenty-five feet from the base of the building.[113]

How objections to computer animations are handled by judges depends on the nature and the use of the computer-animated evidence in each specific case. At one extreme, a computer-animated video might be used simply to *illustrate* an expert's opinion about the occurrence of a traffic accident. In that situation—where the animation includes no information that the expert could not provide orally without the aid of the computerized illustrations—the court must simply decide whether this demonstrative aid is helpful, and whether its potentially prejudicial impact substantially outweighs its probative value. This is a familiar discretionary ruling, governed by FRE 403, which gives the judge essentially unreviewable discretion to admit or exclude the tape. At the other end of the spectrum, a computer-animated simulation of a complex event—the collapse of a building in a storm, for example, or the diffusion of pollutants through soil—may constitute an essential basis for an expert opinion that is critical to a party's case. In such a case, the judge must first decide, under the applicable standard,[114] whether the expert's opinion is admissible as scientific expert evidence. If the judge decides to admit an expert opinion based in part on the information embodied in the simulation, she could still exclude the video itself under FRE 403 as unduly prejudicial, but at that point such a ruling is unlikely.

Video technology is a fast moving target. We routinely do things today that were uncommon or impossible 20 years ago: We place mini-cams in everything from pens to balloons to cash registers; we have video conversations with friends, colleagues and total strangers across the world; we make video recordings on cell phones and send them around the globe. Courts move more slowly, but eventually, as technology changes so will the visual evidence that is used in court.[115]

Problem X-15. Pamela Guest, a nine-year-old girl, fell head first off the balcony of the 43rd floor room of the Plaza Royale Hotel in New York City, where she was staying with her parents for Christmas, and was killed instantly on impact. One element of damages in the wrongful death lawsuit brought by her parents against the Plaza Royale Hotel is compensation for the emotional pain she suffered immediately before her death. As evidence on this issue, the plaintiffs' attorneys offer a computer

---

[113] See generally Neal Feigenson and Christina Spiesel, Law on Display (2009).

[114] See supra Chapter Nine, pp. 1157–1176, discussing FRE 702 and the *Frye* and *Daubert* cases.

[115] See infra, subsection F, p. 1351.

simulation that purports to show what a person would see falling head first from a 43rd story balcony to the pavement below, until the moment of impact, when the screen goes blank. **As an attorney for the plaintiffs, what points would you make in arguing that this tape should be admitted?   As an attorney for the defendant, what arguments would you make that it should be excluded?**

E. THE COURT RECORD; PREVIOUSLY RECORDED TESTIMONY

The traditional method of creating a record of a trial or a hearing is transcription by a certified court reporter who attends the hearing and takes notes of what is said on a stenographic machine. If a transcript is necessary the reporter uses those notes to dictate or type the transcript and certify it.   Most court reporters now use electronic stenographic machines on which they can produce transcripts as electronic files directly and efficiently, sometimes nearly simultaneously with the testimony. In some courts a "realtime" court reporter distributes a rough-draft of the transcript electronically, as it is produced, to the judge and to counsel on their computers; each recipient can make private annotations on his or her copy. "Voice writers" use voice recognition technology to produce similar transcripts. Using a flexible "mask" to ensure that his or her voice isn't audible to court participants, the reporter repeats what is said in the courtroom.   The computer, using software that has been "trained" to recognize the reporter's voice, produces text.

But court reporters (however they work) are expensive, and there is a limited supply of good ones.   Many courts now use electronic audio recordings instead, or audio and video recordings which are later transcribed if transcripts are required.   Electronic recording is comparatively inexpensive, especially audio recording, but it has disadvantages. If the recorder malfunctions or is accidentally turned off, there is no record whatever; and, if the recording includes no video, it is sometimes difficult to determine who is speaking.   On the other hand, electronic recording has a major advantage (in addition to its low cost) the attorneys and the judge can obtain copies of the recordings as they are produced.

Traditionally the court record is viewed as the means by which a party that chooses to appeal shows the appellate court what happened at trial. But, the lawyers and the judge often have a critical interest in having a court record available immediately, during the trial itself, in order to prepare for direct and cross-examination of later witnesses, decide what jury instructions to ask for or to give, discuss testimony in argument to the jury, or, in a bench trial, to help the judge determine her findings. Both electronic recording and realtime reporting make it easy to obtain records nearly simultaneously with the proceedings. (Interestingly, nearly all appellate courts require that electronically recorded proceedings to be transcribed for use on appeal. Kentucky is a notable exception; it permits counsel to rely on an electronic record directly.)

Video recording can also be used as the medium for the initial presentation of evidence to the trier of fact. This is done most often with video recorded depositions in cases in which the deposition is admissible within an exception to the hearsay rule (usually as an opposing party's statement under FRE 801(d)(2)(A) and Rule 32(a)(3) of the Federal Rules of Civil Procedure, or as prior testimony by an unavailable witness under FRE 804(b)(1) and Rule 32(a)(4) of the Federal Rules of Civil Procedure). Rule 30(b)(3) of the Federal Rules of Civil Procedure provides in part that a deposition "may be recorded by audio, audiovisual, or stenographic means," as specified by the party taking the deposition, and that any other party may designate another additional method. Needless to say, playing a video is a better method of presenting testimony than reading a transcript. It is likely to be more interesting, and it provides the jury with direct information on the witness's tone and demeanor. For example, in 2001, Bill Gates, the billionaire founder of Microsoft, attracted national attention for a "20–hour videotaped deposition in which he rocked back and forth in a chair as he claimed not to remember pertinent business deals and e-mails."[116]

A few courts have gone further, and experimented with using videotapes to present entire trials:

> On November 18, 1971 at approximately 4:30 pm, a jury in the Erie County, Ohio Court of Common Pleas returned a plaintiff's verdict for $9,600 in the case of *McCall vs. Clemons*, a routine personal injury case. There is nothing unusual about the date, the type of case, or the size of the verdict as it is recorded in the Office of the Erie County Clerk of Courts. What is unique in this case is that it was the first trial in Anglo-American jurisprudence in which all the testimony was pre-recorded on videotape, edited by the Judge, and then presented to the jury free of all objections and comments of counsel. This trial became known as a PRVTT (pre-recorded videotape trial).[117]

James L. McCrystal, the judge who presided over the *McCall* case, has written a "primer" on videotaped trials[118]:

> *What is a prerecorded videotaped trial?*

---

[116] Carolyn Said, The Microsoft Ruling; Score One for Bill Gates; Ruling Partially vindicates Mircosoft Chairman's take-no-prisoners strategy, S.F. Chronicle, June 29, 2001, at B1.

[117] James L. McCrystal, The Case for PRVTT's, 12 Trial 56 (July 1976).

[118] James L. McCrystal, Videotaped Trials: A Primer, 61 Judicature 250 (1978). Reprinted by special permission of Judicature, the Journal of the American Judicature Society.

A prerecorded videotaped trial (PRVTT) is a trial in which all of the testimony is prerecorded on videotape so that the judge can edit it before he shows it to a jury.   He deletes all the inadmissible questions, answers and comments from the videotape before the jury sees it.

How does a prerecorded trial differ from a conventional one?

The only difference is that all of the testimony is presented to the jury by videotape.   The impaneling of the jury, the voir dire, the closing arguments and the judge's instructions are conducted in a conventional way.

Where is the testimony recorded?

Anywhere that a videotape camera is available.   It is usually recorded in a studio, in a lawyer's or doctor's office, and sometimes at the scene of the incident which is the basis for the lawsuit.

Is the judge present when the testimony is recorded?

No. Usually only the witness and the two attorneys are present.   But many times counsel will want their clients present while the testimony is recorded.

How does prerecorded testimony differ from trial depositions?

It differs very little in format.   The principal difference is that prerecorded testimony is *trial* testimony and it will be shown to the jury.

When does the judge edit the testimony and where?

The judge may edit the testimony anywhere he wishes—in chambers, in his office, at home, or in any other convenient location.

How does he edit the testimony?

When the witnesses testify before cameras, a digital clock on the tape shows the hour, the minute and the second of their testimony.   As attorneys make objections or comments, a technician notes on a log sheet the exact times that attorneys spoke.   When the judge reviews the tape, he notes where these objections appear and he can advance the tape to the point of the objection.   In Ohio and Wisconsin, lawyers can object only after the witness has answered.   This policy eliminates many objections and it promotes orderly editing.   If the judge sustains an objection, he makes a notation so that the jury never sees or hears the question, the answer or the objection on the edited tape. If he overrules the objection, the jury will see the question and answer but not the objection itself.   But nothing is ever removed or erased from the original videotape. That tape remains intact until the case is ultimately concluded.

. . .

What are the advantages of a prerecorded trial over a live trial?

One advantage is that the trial can be conducted in one-half or one-third less time. Another advantage is that the jury never hears inadmissible comments, questions or answers. Prerecorded trials virtually eliminate the possibility of a mistrial. They enable a judge to make better use of his time, since he can take care of other business or preside at another trial while the jury watches the prerecorded trials. Trials don't have to be postponed or continued because parties or witnesses aren't available. Statistics show that prerecorded trials substantially reduce docket congestion.

How does a prerecorded trial save time?

It eliminates the objections of counsel, the side bar or bench conferences, the recesses in which lawyers and judge discuss the admissibility of certain testimony and the time spent waiting for witnesses to arrive.

What advantage does a prerecorded trial offer the litigant?

The main advantage is that his case can come to trial just as soon as the testimony has been recorded and edited. He doesn't have to wait his turn on the court calendar.

But how does a prerecorded trial help reduce docket backlog?

We know that 90 percent of all civil litigation is settled before trial.

But most disputes today are not settled until the judge assigns a trial date; the litigants wait to settle until very close to the day of the trial or they settle during the trial. When the judge orders a trial prerecorded, the day of recording becomes, in effect, the trial date, though it is not a date on the judge's calendar. Lawyers thus settle more quickly in those cases they would have settled eventually.

Despite these advantages—and despite generally favorable reactions on all sides in the few cases in which it has been used[119]—PRVTT has not caught on. Only a handful of jurisdictions permit the procedure described in the excerpts above, and many lawyers and judges are hostile to the idea of having an entire trial video recorded outside the jury's presence.[120] Some of the problems the opponents cite are technical:

> Several problems, however, probably make the judge's presence, during testimony-taking, in all but mildly contested cases, essential. First, in the absence of a judge, it is necessary to rely on the self-supervision and joint cooperation by counsel to maintain the decorum and dignity that attaches to testimony taken in courtroom

---

[119] Diane M. Hartmus, Videotrials, 23 Ohio N. U. L. Rev. 1 (1996).

[120] See Gregory P. Joseph, Modern Visual Evidence § 3.04, pp. 3–27—3–33 (1997).

surroundings. Second, a judge must be present to make immediate rulings on disputed points of relevance, prejudice, admissibility, competence and the like because subsequent examination of the witness could depend on the resolution of the dispute. For example, if question one of a long series of questions is ruled out, the tactics of the examiner in succeeding questions might be considerably different. It would seem that bench rulings are inextricable from the testimony-taking process itself, and that ex post [facto] rulings, contemplated by using videotape without the judge's presence, would be an unsatisfactory solution. At best such rulings could only delete material, and not reconstruct a line of questioning ultimately held improper as taped. Unfortunately, total retaping of the testimony might then become necessary, or, in the interest of avoiding duplication of efforts, a judge might be inclined to permit tainted material to remain.[121]

The main objection to PRVTT, however, is more basic. Opponents claim that too much is lost in the translation from live to recorded testimony. In theory, some of what's left out should not be missed. Under this system, jurors do not hear—and therefore cannot be influenced by—objections, excluded testimony, arguments on points of law, and the like. This restriction limits the tactical moves that attorneys can make, and might displease them even if it had no genuine drawbacks. On the other hand, there may be a real loss in comprehension, in judgment, in the sense of immediacy, when the jury only sees the witnesses on a video screen. And these effects may not be restricted to the evaluation of testimony.

The symbolism and ceremony of the trial process—the complex pattern of gestures comprising its ritualistic aspect—helps contribute to the sense of solemnity and dignity attached to the judicial process. This in turn contributes to the respect of the community toward that process and, ultimately, acceptance of its decisions. The courtroom, the judicial robe, the practice of standing upon the judge's entrance and exit, the oath taken by witnesses and, in general, the formalism attached to trial procedure are all part of the ceremony and drama—as Maitland said, the "picturesque garb"—of the process by which justice is rendered. These practices have symbolic value which transmutes their abstract nature into a more dramatic and easily understood form. Through the religious overtones in these symbols, the judicial process associates itself with the reverence ascribed to religion. In general, ritual and formality give the law authority, visibility and symbolic power. By severing testimony-taking from the court-room, and by fragmenting the unitary trial proceeding into a

---

[121] David M. Doret, Trial By Videotape—Can Justice Be Seen To Be Done? 47 Temp. L. Q. 228, 238 (1974).

series of mere "assembly line" inputs, videotape may undermine the trial's complex pattern of symbols and ceremonies and thus vitiate the support which the ritual power of the trial lends to acceptance of its decisions by the community.[122]

How much weight should we give these concerns? Most attorneys and judges would no doubt agree that the ceremonial functions of courtroom procedure matter more in criminal than in civil trials. In addition, constitutional considerations limit the manner in which testimony may be taken and presented in criminal cases. The confrontation clause of the Sixth Amendment requires that available prosecution witnesses testify in the defendant's presence (the constitutionality of live remote witnesses testifying via videoconferencing remains in dispute);[123] the jury trial clause could be interpreted to require that they testify in the presence of the jury; and the due process clause of the Fifth and Fourteenth Amendments could be read to require that they testify in the presence of a judge who is empowered to protect the defendant's rights. Not surprisingly, the only experiments in PRVTT of which we are aware are limited to civil cases.

The main advantage of PRVTT is that it saves time—or at least saves time for everybody except the lawyers. The largest component of this timesaving may be that this procedure encourages out-of-court settlements, which obviate the need for trials altogether. One major barrier to settlement is uncertainty about the testimony the witnesses will give in court: What exactly will they say, on cross as well as direct? And how will it look and sound? It is already common for settlements in civil cases to turn on the depositions of key witnesses.[124] As the use of videotape deposition testimony at trial becomes increasingly common, some judges—who are always eager for settlements to clear their dockets—might start using PRVTT as a way to reduce their civil trial load. In effect, the procedure amounts to the judge saying to the lawyers: "Look, you two, get the whole thing recorded, and *then* we'll see if we still need to bring in a jury to decide how to resolve it." So far, however, prerecorded trials remain rare.

---

[122] Id. at 256.

[123] Compare United States v. Yates, 438 F.3d 1307 (11th Cir. 2006) (en banc) (remote prosecution testimony in a federal case violated the Confrontation clause) with United States v. Abu Ali, 528 F.3d 210 (4th Cir. 2008) (live two-way video-conferenced deposition conducted from Saudi Arabia to Virginia in a terrorism case was constitutional).

[124] For example, in Chapter Nine, pp. 1192–1205, we reproduce the description of a deposition in a medical malpractice case that was influential in shaping the ultimate out-of-court settlement.

F. A FEW THOUGHTS ON TECHNOLOGY-AUGMENTED COURTROOMS

Increasingly, modern courtrooms are equipped with advanced electronic technology. A technology-augmented (or "high-tech") courtroom usually has equipment on which pictures and documentary evidence are displayed electronically to the fact-finder, and either an electronic system for recording the proceedings or a court reporter who uses technology to create the court record. It may also have the capacity to take testimony from witnesses in remote locations by videoconferencing (or "telepresence"), and technologies to assist those who have difficulty hearing, seeing, or moving.[125] Some courtrooms go even farther. The most advanced courtroom record system in the world may be that operated by the Center for Legal and Court Technology (CLCT) at William & Mary Law School. CLCT publishes to the web, in real time, a digital audio and video recording of the trial along with images of exhibits and a realtime transcript of the proceedings.[126]

When an attorney electronically displays an exhibit that is already is evidence, no evidentiary issues are posed. However, when an electronic image is displayed for the purposes of securing admission into evidence, it's important to remember that the image itself *is* the exhibit, and normal evidentiary requirements of authentication and the original document rule come into play.

Many if not most of the exhibits used in court today were created electronically, including e-mail, texts, spreadsheets, word processed documents, and digital photos. It makes little sense to print out those images for purposes of trial. Although technologically augmented trial practice often feels different from traditional practice, the change implicates few new evidentiary problems.[127]

---

[125] See generally Fredric Lederer, Wired, What We Have Learned About Courtroom Technology, ABA Criminal Justice (Winter, 2010); Fredric Lederer, The Potential Use of Courtroom Technology in Major Terrorism Cases, 12 Wm. & Mary Bill Rts. J. 887 (2004).

[126] In 2002, the William & Mary's Center for Legal and Court Technology (then the Courtroom 21 Project) tried an experimental Laboratory Trial that included the first known use in court of both holographic evidence and immersive virtual reality. For the latter procedure, witnesses who wore special glasses were, from their visual perspective, inserted into a computer recreation of an operating room suite. As they moved within the suite to demonstrate what would have been in their line of vision, the jury and other courtroom participants saw what the witnesses saw on a projection screen. As of 2013, the Center was awaiting delivery of its first 3D evidence technology.. See generally www.legaltechcenter.net.

[127] See Fredric Lederer, The New Courtroom: The Intersection of Evidence and Technology: Some Thoughts On the Evidentiary Aspects of Technologically Produced or Presented Evidence, 28 Sw. U. L. Rev. 389 (1999).

ADDITIONAL PROBLEMS

Problem X-16. Darcey Wayne is charged with using interstate wire communications to conduct a gambling enterprise. At trial, the Government presents evidence—including wiretap information and testimony from witnesses—that in the period from June 1 through October 15, 2012 (when Darcey was arrested) he would make phone calls to people who wished to place bets from the pay phone near the men's room at the Tip Top Lounge in Reno, Nevada. Apparently, potential bettors would call and leave their numbers on his pager, and he would return their calls from that pay telephone—as would several other bookies, according to the Government's evidence. The Government seeks to introduce as an exhibit a pad of paper found near the pay phone on October 12, 2012, with several names, dates, dollar amounts, and cryptic notations—such as "Dave G., MI/MS 10 $500." The Government claims that these notations are records of bets placed on that telephone line, although they cannot connect them to Darcey Wayne individually. Darcey objects. **What is the Government's best argument for admissibility? What foundational evidence would the Government have to present to get the pad admitted on that basis?**

Problem X-17. Someone enters the Big Seller department store and charges $1,000 to the account of John B. Jones, presenting Jones's credit card and signing Jones's name. When the bill is sent to Jones, he refuses to pay, stating in a letter that his credit card was apparently stolen and that he never bought the charged merchandise. Big Seller sues Jones, who demands and receives a jury trial. At the outset of its case, Big Seller opens by offering as evidence the $1,000 charge slip containing the signature "John B. Jones," together with the letter referred to above, as evidence that Jones himself made the $1,000 charge. Jones objects and argues that before either document is admitted, the judge must determine that Jones signed it. **Is Jones correct? What evidence might the department store use to authenticate these two documents?**

Problem X-18. Assume that Jones never wrote the letter referred to in the previous problem. Instead, Big Seller seeks to introduce as a handwriting exemplar a signature on another charge slip for which Jones had been billed. The charges on this bill had been paid by check after a bill was sent to Jones's house. **Could Jones successfully object to its introduction?**

Problem X-19. Sofa is accused of kidnapping the young daughter of a wealthy industrialist. Shortly after Sofa's arrest the police searched his car and found red threads, which looked like wool, in the trunk. The girl was wearing a red woolen sweater when she was kidnapped. When the prosecution offers the threads as evidence at Sofa's trial, defense counsel asks whether any tests were made comparing the girl's sweater and the threads. Receiving a negative answer, counsel moves to exclude the evidence. **Should the motion be granted? If the sweater was removed from the girl by the kidnapper and never found, could the threads be admitted? What foundation would you require?**

Problem X-20. Mayor Potter Plaindealer brings an action for libel against Joanne Mulvey and the Charlottesville Times. The complaint alleges that Mulvey was the author of a letter accusing the plaintiff of bribery and corruption in office; that Mulvey handed the letter to a reporter for the paper; and that it thereafter appeared in the paper. At trial, without any preliminary proof, the plaintiff offers in evidence a copy of the issue of the paper containing the allegedly libelous letter. Mulvey and the Times both object on the basis of the original document rule. They argue that the original letter to the paper should be produced. - **Would you sustain either objection?**

Problem X-21. Heavy brings an action against Stiles to set aside a mechanic's lien that Stiles has recorded for unpaid wages. Heavy claims that Stiles was paid in full for his services. As part of his case Heavy testifies that Stiles prepared time sheets for work performed and that he paid Stiles in accordance with the time sheets. Heavy produces and identifies the time sheets—which record payments received as well as hours worked—and offers them in evidence; they are admitted over Stiles' hearsay objection. **What hearsay exceptions are likely to cover these documents?** Stiles then testifies in defense that he actually spent more time working for Heavy than is shown on the sheets. Heavy objects, claiming that Stiles' testimony is inadmissible because the time sheets are the best evidence of the hours Stiles worked. **What is the proper ruling on the objection?**

Problem X-22. Stubbs is charged with auto theft. The prosecution seeks to introduce a witness, Cole, to testify that she saw Stubbs break into a white Chevrolet and drive away. During the course of Cole's testimony, the prosecution offers a photograph of a Chevrolet automobile and asks whether or not Cole can identify the picture. Cole replies that she can and says that it is a picture of the automobile she saw Stubbs take. The prosecution offers the photograph in evidence, and Stubbs objects on the ground that the photo is not the best evidence of the automobile. **Is there substance to the objection?**

Problem X-23. Greg Armand is arrested for the murder of Robert Peal. He is given appropriate *Miranda* warnings, signs a waiver of his rights, and—during five hours of audio-recorded questioning—admits to the killing and describes it in detail. A stenographer later types a transcript of the questioning, based on the audio recording. At trial, the prosecutor calls Sergeant Beattie, one of Armand's interrogators, to testify to Armand's confession. Armand objects that Beattie's testimony is not the best evidence of what he said: **Is the objection valid? If so, may the**

transcript be used or must the prosecution present the recording? What if the recording has been destroyed? What if both the recording and the transcript have been destroyed?

Problem X-24. During the first Iraqi war, Bleriot Leparre and Benny Morgan formed a corporation to produce parts used in army helicopters. After the war ended, the United States Senate created a special committee to investigate allegations of fraud, corruption, mismanagement, excessive profits, and inefficiency in the war effort. Morgan testified before that committee in executive session. The only people present were several Senators, their counsel Henry Adams, the clerk, a stenographic reporter, and Morgan. As a result of his testimony, Morgan was indicted for perjury. He requested a transcript of his testimony, but the court denied his request and sustained the government's claim of privilege to protect military secrets. At trial, the principal witness for the government is Henry Adams, who is prepared to testify to the substance of Morgan's testimony to the committee; the government then plans to offer other evidence to prove that what Morgan said in that testimony was false. Morgan objects under the original document rule and argues that the government is obliged to produce the transcript of his testimony as evidence, and that Adams should not be permitted to testify in lieu of the transcript. **Would you sustain his claim? Is there any other related claim that you would make if you were Morgan's attorney? If the government ultimately decides not to resist Morgan's claim, and provides the defense with a transcript of Morgan's testimony just before the defense began its case, would Morgan have any claim left to raise?** Assume that Adams had been out of the room during a portion of Morgan's testimony and had read the transcript of that portion. **Would Morgan's original document objection then be stronger? Would he have another objection?**

Problem X-25. Alex is charged with stealing a United States Treasury check from the mail. At trial the government seeks to introduce a photocopy of the check with the payee's name and address typed in because the copy machine failed to reproduce them. The prosecutor supports the offer with this statement: "We wish to offer this evidence to identify the stolen check and to illustrate what it looked like." The defense objects on original document grounds. **Should the objection be sustained?**

Problem X-26. Saltzer, an undercover agent for the United States Department of the Treasury, was wired for sound before a scheduled meeting with Darlene, a suspected counterfeiter. After Darlene made several incriminating statements and produced some counterfeit bills, Saltzer arrested her. At trial, the government offers as evidence a rerecorded tape of the meeting, and Darlene objects on the basis of original document rule. The government explains that the original recording is difficult to hear and somewhat garbled. By editing, some material has been deleted and some noise has been suppressed. **Should the rerecording be admitted? What if a portion of the conversation recorded on the original was so garbled as to be beyond comprehension? Should the re-recording still be admitted?** Suppose the original recording was perfectly clear, but instead of offering it, the government chose to have Saltzer testify to what was said. **Would there be any original document problem? What other protection might Darlene have against any unfairness that could be caused by this procedure? Would there be an original document problem if the government wanted to introduce a witness who had listened to the tape, to testify to what had been said?**

Problem X-27. In May 2013, a fire destroyed the home of Jerry and Camilla Prawn, which was insured by the Tri-State Insurance Company. Tri-State denied coverage, and the Prawns sued to collect damages under their policy. At trial, Tri-State presents circumstantial evidence linking the Prawns to the fire, in support of a defense that the Prawns set the fire themselves. In addition, Tri-State produces evidence of allegedly "material misrepresentations" by the Prawns in their insurance application, which, Tri-State claims, invalidate the insurance policy. Specifically, Tri-State produces evidence that Mr. Prawn earns his living from illegal gambling rather than as a real estate salesman, as he claimed in the application. To establish the significance of this misrepresentation, Tri-State calls John Strobe, one of its homeowners insurance underwriting managers, to testify that Tri-State would never have issued the insurance policy had it known the true source of Mr. Prawn's income. The Prawns object to Strobe's testimony and argue that Tri-State must produce the written insurance guidelines instead. **Is the objection well taken?**

Problem X-28. George Hockins is arrested in Mississippi for speeding, and two guns are found in his car. He is charged with illegal possession of firearms by an ex-felon. At trial, to prove his status as a convicted felon, the prosecution presents two exhibits. Exhibit 5 is a certified copy of a judgment of conviction for robbery on file in the Denver County, Colorado, Circuit Court, against a defendant named "Carl Smith." Exhibit 5a is an uncertified document that appears to be a "fingerprint card" from the Denver Police Department; it has a set of rolled fingerprints over the typed name "Carl Smith," lists the date, charge and court number of the robbery conviction described in Exhibit 5, and is signed "Carl Smith" at the bottom. A document examiner testifies that the defendant, George Hockins, wrote the signature "Carl Smith" on Exhibit 5a, and a fingerprint expert testifies that the fingerprints on that exhibit belong to Mr. Hockins. The defendant objects to both of these exhibits. **Are they**

admissible on the record described above? If not what additional evidence would do the trick?

Problem X–29. Pringle and Stangle share a two-bedroom apartment on the East Side of Manhattan in New York City. After an extensive investigation, the New York City police develop probable cause to believe that the two are selling heroin. The police obtain a warrant and search the apartment. In both bedrooms they find vials containing a white powdery substance that looks like heroin. To protect the evidence, the police place the vials in a pouch and label it. Unfortunately, all the vials are placed in the same pouch. When they learn of this, each defendant moves to suppress the use of the evidence against her. **Should the motions be granted? If not, what method of authentication would you suggest? Would there be any possibility of introducing this evidence if analysis revealed that some vials contained heroin and others did not?** Assume that instead of searching for and finding drugs, the police had suspected the two women of receiving stolen property, had searched both bedrooms, and had found jewelry, some of which was stolen, in each bedroom. **If the police had commingled all the jewelry, would the problem be the same? Would any jewelry be admissible at a joint trial? At separate trials? At a trial for conspiring to receive stolen property?**

Problem X–30. Smith is tried on an indictment charging him with bribery. The evidence for the state tends to show that Smith ran a gambling operation of the sort that is generally known as a "numbers racket," and that he paid protection money to 20 to 30 officers of the local police force. The state wants to call a former police officer who will testify that some person, whose name he does not remember, gave him a telephone number and told him it belonged to the defendant, Smith; that he is unable to remember that telephone number; that he called the number and asked to speak with Smith; that the person answering the call said he was Smith; that he (the officer) asked whether he was entitled to a pay-off; that the person on the phone said, "yes"; and that he then asked why he was entitled to the pay-off, and the other party said, "You are supposed to know why, and you will get $100 a month from the pay-off man at headquarters." The officer never met the defendant at any time either before or after the phone call. **Should the trial judge admit the officer's testimony?**

Problem X–31. Louie Lampa sues the defendant for injuries to his right sacral region and sacroiliac joint, his sciatic nerve, and his back. At trial, during the direct examination of a doctor who treated Mr. Lampa for his injuries, the following occurs:

Q. [By Mr. Green, plaintiff's attorney] Will you demonstrate this man up here before this jury, Doctor?

A. [By the Doctor] Demonstrate him?

MR. NORBLAD [defendant's attorney]: Just a minute; are you going to demonstrate that he couldn't bend over?

MR. GREEN: No, have the doctor explain what he did.

A. Is it all right?

COURT: Go ahead.

A. (To plaintiff) First thing stand with your heels in a military position, and you do as I do, stoop forward with your hands up, stoop over as far as you can.

MR. LAMPA: I can't stoop at all.

A. Try it.

MR. LAMPA: It hurts so bad I can't stoop.

A. Just try it.

MR. NORBLAD: I submit, Your Honor, that this is not proper; I can do the same thing; I submit it is improper.

COURT: No, objection overruled.

A. I am doing my best.

MR. NORBLAD: Please understand you are making no comments here: I am making my objection to the court, not you.

COURT: Both of you keep still.

A. Put your hands down and try stooping forward; I will measure how far you can stoop down.

MR. LAMPA: It hurts me right now like the dickens: it hurt me right now.

A. [Measuring] Thirty inches this time; the first time I examined him was within 17 inches; that was in February; on my second examination he acted about like he did now; he couldn't stoop forward very well.

Q. Go ahead and tell the result of your examination.

A. This is just one; try to stoop backwards like this.

MR. LAMPA: It is impossible.

MR. NORBLAD: This is certainly improper; there are comments being made by this man all the time; I would like to have the record show that the plaintiff is making statements here constantly that is [sic] absolutely improper.

COURT: Objection overruled.

A. Let us see what happens when you try to do this. (Bends backwards).

MR. LAMPA: I can't do it at all, Doctor; just like that, oh, oh, it hurts. Uh.

A. What side does that hurt?

MR. LAMPA: Right here; right here.

A. Try this motion (sideways bending). Now the other side as far as you can.

MR. LAMPA: It still hurts.

At the conclusion of the trial the defendant moves for a new trial because this demonstration was allowed. **Would you grant a new trial?**

Problem X-32. Claude Kagan is charged with murdering his wife. There were no witnesses to the shooting. The defendant told the police that he and his wife were alone in their house when he heard a shot from her bedroom. He ran into the room and found her bleeding on the bed with his .22 caliber pistol in her hand. She died from a wound to her chest. A chemist employed by the government examined the nightgown that the wife was wearing at the time of her death. He is prepared to testify that he found no gunpowder residue on the gown, although the material of the gown generally would retain residue if a shot were fired at it from between 18 and 24 inches away. The expert has also run certain tests. He fired the defendant's pistol at various distances into a test gown made of similar material, and with a weave pattern similar to that of the gown worn by the deceased wife. (Before doing this, he fired the gun into the wife's gown, which had been given to him by the police, to determine if the residue patterns on both materials were the same.) He will testify that these experiments support his conclusion that residue would be found if the gun were fired at the wife's gown at close range. He is prepared to present the wife's nightgown, and the test gowns, to illustrate and corroborate his testimony. The defendant objects to evidence of the experiment, claiming that the conditions of the experiment and the murder scene were not identical. He also objects to the presentation of the gowns on the grounds that they are unduly prejudicial and lack adequate foundation. **Should the expert be permitted to testify if no chain of custody is established for the wife's nightgown? Should he be permitted to testify about the experiment and present the gown to the jury, in any event?**

Problem X-33. Paul Fix, Judy Miller, and Frank Miller are accused of conspiring to help Martha Fix escape from a state penitentiary. The government's theory is that Paul Fix parked his car near the prison, leaving his keys under the seat, and then drove with the Millers to the airport where the three intended to rent a helicopter, fly it over the prison, and spray tear gas while Martha Fix escaped in the confusion. The plot was aborted when a police officer who had stopped Miller for speeding a quarter mile from the airport noted a tear gas canister partially hidden under the back seat. Even if the canisters had not been spotted, the stop would have effectively thwarted the plan for that day because there was only one fifteen minute period when the conspirators could count on Martha's being in the prison yard with the rope ladder she had made. The government wishes to introduce a map showing the airport where the helicopter the conspirators had arranged to rent was located, the place where Fix's car was found, and the spot where the three defendants were arrested. The defendants object that the map is not drawn to scale, does not include many of the existing streets and roadways, and shows the three particular locations with large red marks to unduly emphasize them. The government admits that its map is neither drawn to scale nor complete, but urges that it should be admitted as background evidence. **Who wins?**

Problem X-34. Sylvia Post was a student at the University of Stanton. One night, while studying at home, Sylvia was kidnapped by an underground revolutionary group. Later, Sylvia participated with members of the group in a bank robbery. Sylvia's parents and friends believed that she was coerced into participating, but one week after the bank robbery a recording was received by a Stanton radio station containing statements by Sylvia asserting that she voluntarily participated in the bank robbery and that she repudiated the capitalistic ideas and values of her parents and friends. Eventually, Sylvia is arrested and charged with bank robbery. Sylvia's defense is that she was coerced and "brainwashed" into participating in the bank robbery. To counter this defense and establish voluntary participation, the government wishes to introduce the recording received by the radio station. **Should the recording be admitted if its only authentication is evidence—which is not disputed—that the voice on it is Sylvia's? What might Sylvia demand by way of further authentication?**

Problem X-35. In December, 1999, How Sweet It Is, Inc., a confectionary manufacturer, shut down its marzipan plant in Orchard City, Wisconsin, as part of a general plan to restructure its Midwestern marzipan production operations. In the aftermath, some of the terminated employees in Orchard City were offered positions at How Sweet It Is's remaining Midwestern marzipan plant in Parchland, Illinois—but most were not. Margaret Jenkins, a forty-nine-year old confectioner with twenty years experience at the Orchard City plant, has sued How Sweet It Is, Inc., in federal court for age discrimination, claiming that regardless of experience and qualifications, the only Orchard City workers who were offered Parchland confectionary positions were under thirty-five years old. The following is a transcript of a portion of Ms. Jenkins's direct examination at trial. The exhibit that is mentioned in the transcript is reproduced on the page following this problem:

Q. (By Ms. Beasley, attorney for Plaintiff Margaret Jenkins) Ms. Jenkins, I'm showing you what has been marked as Plaintiff's Exhibit One for identification. Do you recognize it?

[How did the exhibit get marked? When might that have happened?]

A. (By Ms. Jenkins) Yes, I . . .

MR. SLACK (attorney for Defendant How Sweet It Is, Inc.): I object, Your Honor.

[Is there anything to object at this point? If so, what is the remedy?]

Q. [After the previous objection is handled] Do you recognize Plaintiff's Exhibit One?

A. Yes. That's the letter I got last December from Orville Hartchick, the CEO of How Sweet It Is, saying the plant would close and we'd all lose our jobs.

[What objection, if any, could be made to the last question, or to the answer?]

Q. Do you recognize the paper on which that letter is printed?

A. Yes. It's the company stationery from How Sweet It Is. I've seen it lots of times.

Q. And do you recognize the name of the person who signed it?

A. Yes. Orville Hartchick.

Q. How do you recognize Mr. Hartchick, his name?

A. He is the CEO of the company.

Q. Was he then, in December 1999, when you got the letter?

A. Oh yeah. And for the last fifteen years.

MS. BEASLEY: Your Honor, I move to admit Plaintiff's Exhibit 1 in evidence.

MR. SLACK: May I voir dire?

THE COURT: Please, proceed.

Q. (By Mr. Slack) Ms. Jenkins, this isn't the actual letter you got last December, is it?

A. I don't know what you mean.

Q. It's a photocopy, isn't it?

A. Oh, yeah. That's right.

Q. Is the original letter lost?

A.   No. I have it.

MR. SLACK: Your Honor, I object under the best evidence rule. They should have to produce the original letter.

MS. BEASLEY: Your Honor, I disagree.

THE COURT: Objection overruled.

[Is the Court's ruling correct?]

Q.   (By Mr. Slack) Ms. Jenkins, you had never seen Mr. Hartchick's signature before you got this letter, isn't that so?

A.   That's true.

Q.   And you haven't since.

A.   Right.

Q.   And the company stationery, you never used it yourself, like as a secretary, right?

A.   No. I didn't. That wasn't my job.

Q.   You just saw it once in awhile around the plant, didn't you?

A.   I guess so. And I got other letters from the company.

Q.   You mean you got other letters on that same stationery—but without Mr. Hartchick's name or his title, right?

MS. BEASLEY: I object, Your Honor, compound.

THE COURT: Ms. Jenkins do you understand the question?

MS. JENKINS: I think so, Your Honor.

THE COURT: Then overruled. You may answer.

A.   That's right. I never had another letter from Hartchick, the CEO, but I did get others on that sort of paper from the company.

MR. SLACK: Your Honor, I'm going to object to the admission of Exhibit One. Insufficient authentication.

MS. JENKINS: I think we've laid a sufficient foundation, Your Honor.

THE COURT: Exhibit One, for the Plaintiff, will be admitted as previously marked. Please mark that exhibit as admitted, Ms. Beasley.

[Is the Court's ruling, admitting the exhibit over objection, correct?]

MS. BEASLEY: Thank you, Your Honor.

Q.   (By Ms. Beasley) Ms. Jenkins, on what day did you receive this letter, Plaintiff's Exhibit One?

A. On December 18, 1999.

Q. What day of the week was that?

A. Saturday. A week before Christmas.

[What objection could Mr. Slack have made here? Should he have done so?]

Q. The next Monday, at work, did anything occur in connection with that letter?

A. Yes. For starts, at maybe 9:30 in the morning we got an announcement over the loudspeakers that at noon the manager would have a general meeting in the lunch room to talk about the letters that went out from headquarters saying the plant was gonna close.

Q. Ms. Jenkins, perhaps now you'd be kind enough to read Exhibit One to the jury.

MR. SLACK: Objection, Your Honor. The letter speaks for itself. There's no need to read it out loud. The jury can do that for themselves.

[How should the judge rule?]

How Sweet It Is, Inc.

Confectionary Sins
289 March Boulevard
Target City, Michigan 47392-1250

Orville J. Hartchick
President and Chief Executive Officer
Sweetsin@ail.com
www.sweetsin.com

1-734-989-4831, or
1-800-492 1831
Facsimile: 1-734-989-4892

```
┌─────────────────────────────────────────────┐
│   United States District Court                │
│   Middle District of Wisconsin                │
│                                               │
│   _Jenkins_ v. _How Sweet It Is, Inc._        │
│   No. Civ. _00-793- DC_                        │
│   Plaintiff's _X_  Defendant's _____         │
│   Exhibit Number __1__ For Idetification ____ │
│   In Evidence _____                         │
│   David Lynch, Clerk By: _BZB_ Deputy Date: 7/7/00 │
└─────────────────────────────────────────────┘
```

December 18, 1999

Ms. Margaret Jenkins
15392 Applesway
Ave.
Apt. 4K
Orchard City, WI

Dear Ms. Jenkins:

I'm afraid I'm obliged to confirm the rumors that have been flying around like boomerangs. It is true, as you may have heard, that in anticipation of a sizeable reduction in the demand for sweets in the aftermath of the third-millennial New Year, the Board of Directors of How Sweet It Is, Inc. has decided to consolidate our mid-western marzipan production in a single plant. In November of this year we undertook a careful study of the alternative courses of action open to us, and after long consideration have decided that it would be in the best interest of all concerned to close the Orchard City, Wisconsin and St. Paul, Minnesota marzipan lines, and retain only the plant in Parchland, Illinois. While this decision will no doubt cause some temporary dislocations, I am confident that if you were aware of all the factors we had to consider you would agree that it's a wise and compassionate plan.

Needless to say, we will do our utmost to provide alternative employment for those of you whose positions are discontinued and wish us to do so. Of course the positions we may be able to offer might require relocation within the mid-west territory, and quite possibly a change in compensation status. But it is too early to be concerned about that, especially since your plans in the year 2000 might lead your career in unforseen directions. For the moment, I only wanted to make you and all our loyal employees aware of these developments at the earliest possible moment.

With best wishes for the holiday season, I remain,

Very truly yours,

Orvill J. Hartchick

Orville J. Hartchick
President and CEO

OJC: mm
c:\files\dir.d\pers\gen\term.let

V.   BIBLIOGRAPHY

Feigenson, Neal, Christina Spiesel, Law on Display (2009).

Joseph, Gregory P., Modern Visual Evidence (2010).

McCormick, chs. 21–23, §§ 212–243.1 (6th ed. 2006).

Morgan, Edmund, Basic Problems of Evidence 378 (1963).

Saltzburg, Stephen A., Michael M. Martin, & Daniel J. Capra, Federal Rules of Evidence Manual chs. 901–1008 (9th ed. 2007).

Weinstein, chs. 901–1008.

Wigmore §§ 1150–1321, 2400–2478.

Buckley, Bill, "Day-in-the-Life" Videos, Why Hire a Professional? Nat'l Trial Lawyer (March, 1991).

Chernow, Eli, "Video in the Courtroom: More Than a Talking Head," 15 Litig. 3 (Fall, 1988).

Comment, A Reconsideration of the Admissibility of Computer-Generated Evidence, 126 U. Pa. L. Rev. 425 (1977).

Doret, David M., Trial By Videotape—Can Justice Be Seen To Be Done? 47 Temp. L. Q. 228, 238 (1974).

Gardner, Dillard S., The Camera Goes to Court, 24 N.C. L. Rev. 233, 245 (1946).

Gass, J. Ric, "Defending Against Day-in-the-Life Videos," 34 For the Defense 8–9, 15 (July, 1992).

Giannelli, Paul C., Chain of Custody and the Handling of Real Evidence, 20 Am. Crim. L. Rev. 527, 553 (1983).

Graham, Michael H., The Original Writing (Best Evidence) Rule, 26 Crim. L. Bul. 432, 448–50 (1990).

Jenkins, Martha M., Computer-Generated Evidence Specially Prepared for Use at Trial, 52 Chi.-Kent L. Rev. 600 (1976).

Klages, Karen, Court Reporters on the Way Out: Courts Experiment with Audio-Video Machines, 75 A.B.A. J. 28 (Feb. 1989).

Keele, Layne S., When Mohammed Goes to the Mountain: The Evidentiary Value of a View, 80 Ind. L. J. 1091, 1097 (2005).

Kurzban, Stanley A., Authentication of Computer-Generated Evidence in the United States Federal Courts, 35 Idea: J. L. & Tech. 437 (1995).

Lederer, Fredric I., The Potential Use of Courtroom Technology in Major Terrorism Cases, 12 Wm. & Mary Bill Rts. J. 887 (2004).

Lederer, Fredric I., The New Courtroom: The Intersection of Evidence and Technology: Some Thoughts on the Evidentiary Aspects of Technologically Produced or Presented Evidence, 28 Sw. U. L. Rev. 389 (1999).

McCormick, Charles T., The Parol Evidence Rule As a Procedural Device for Control of the Jury, 41 Yale L.J. 365, 374–75 (1932).

McCrystal, James L., Videotaped Trials: A Primer, 61 Judicature, the Journal of the American Judicature Society 250 (1978).

Michael, Jerome and Mortimer Adler, Real Proof: I, 5 Vand. L. Rev. 344, 356 (1952).

Mnookin, Jennifer L., The Image of Truth: Photographic Evidence and the Power of Analogy, 10 Yale J.L. & Human. 1 (1998).

Nance, Dale A., "The Best Evidence Principle" 73 Iowa L. Rev. 227 (1988).

Roberts, Jerome J., A Practitioner's Primer on Computer-Generated Evidence, 41 U. Chi. L. Rev. 254 (1974).

Rosen, Glenn W., Admission into Evidence of Prejudicial Photographs, 31 J. Crim. L. & Criminology 604 (1941).

Saltzburg, Stephen A., A Special Aspect of Relevance: Countering Negative Inferences Associated with the Absence of Evidence, 66 Calif. L. Rev. 1011 (1978).

Singer, Paula N., Proposed Changes to the Federal Rules of Evidence as Applied to Computer-Generated Evidence, 7 J. of Computers, Tech. & L. 157 (1979).

Wharton, Cory Dennis, Litigators Byte the Apple: Utilizing Computer-Generated Evidence at Trial, 41 Baylor L. Rev. 731 (1989).

CHAPTER 11

BURDENS OF PROOF: SHORTCUTS TO PROOF

■ ■ ■

Not all lawsuits involve disputed issues of fact. In some cases, mostly civil, the parties agree or the court rules that no material fact is in dispute. These cases depend entirely on how the court—guided by the parties' oral and written arguments—resolves legal questions. In most lawsuits, however, either the judge or the jury must decide whether certain facts existed, which often involves resolving evidentiary conflicts, and always requires that at least one party prove what happened to some requisite degree of certainty. That requirement is known as the *burden of proof*.

On closer analysis, the burden of proof can be broken down into three subsidiary burdens: (1) *pleading*—asserting the truth of legally significant facts; (2) *production*—presenting some evidence that tends to prove or disprove those facts; and (3) *persuasion*—convincing the fact-finder to some requisite degree of certainty that particular facts do or do not exist. In Section I, we discuss the rules that govern how these three burdens are allocated among the parties, and the scope of the burdens— how detailed, extensive and persuasive a party's factual allegations and evidence must be in order to succeed.

In some circumstances, judges may accept, or tell a jury to accept, a particular fact as true even though the parties have not offered any evidence of the fact, or have offered evidence that might logically be insufficient to prove it by the requisite burden of proof. These "shortcuts to proof" are designed for situations in which at least one of the following considerations apply: (1) Resources would otherwise be wasted proving facts that are hardly contestable. (2) A disputed issue so depends on matters of legal policy, or on factual patterns across many cases, that its resolution is as much a legal judgment as a factual one. (3) Important policy reasons favor a particular substantive outcome. We discuss these shortcuts in Section II.

I.   BURDENS OF PROOF

As noted, the law imposes three burdens that a party must satisfy to prove facts. The first is the burden of *pleading*; a party must identify those legally significant (material) facts it claims are true. The second is the burden of *production*; one party (identified by law) must present evidence that tends to prove or disprove a material fact, or else the opposing party will prevail on the issue. The third is the burden of *persuasion*; one party must persuade the trier that a material fact is probable enough to be taken as true, or the opposing party will prevail. This section discusses which party bears these burdens and explains the latter two.[1]

A. ALLOCATING THE BURDENS OF PLEADING, PRODUCTION AND PERSUASION

The law ordinarily places the burdens of pleading, production and persuasion on the party seeking to change the status quo. Usually that means that these burdens are borne by the plaintiff in a civil action, by the prosecution in a criminal case, and by the moving party in motions practice.[2] A burden may be allocated to a responding party in any of these settings, however, if that party—rather than just disputing the opponent's claims—advances affirmative claims of her own. Assigning burdens to the party seeking to mobilize the court to change the status quo is thought to deter groundless or wasteful litigation because it discourages lawsuits unless a moving party can muster substantial evidence in support of her claims. Placing the burden on the responding party might force her to disprove a general, uninformative claim (e.g., "the defendant owes me money") or suffer the consequences (e.g., a judgment for damages). Of course, in many cases the plaintiff could argue that the defendant knows full well the basis of his claim, and that it is the defendant who is trying to change the status quo and impose litigation costs, e.g., by refusing to pay a just debt. Still, someone has to start a case, keep it moving and bear the risk of losing if the trier is not sure what happened. Because filing suit, asserting a counterclaim or making a motion imposes costs that are justified only when they serve a valid purpose, the general rule allocates to the party taking those actions the burdens and risks associated with them. Accordingly, before the party opposing a lawsuit, counterclaim or motion is required to respond with evidence, the moving party typically must satisfy the pleading burden by identifying the material facts she claims are true, and satisfy the production burden by presenting evidence sufficient to make a "prima facie" showing that the facts alleged in the pleadings are true. And before a court will order a change in the status quo, the moving party usually must convince the trier of fact to some requisite level of certainty that the material facts are as she claims (thus satisfying the burden of persuasion).

---

[1] We do not explain the burden of pleading, which is governed by rules of civil and criminal procedure and is covered in courses on those subjects.

[2] See, e.g., Schaffer ex rel. Schaffer v. Weast, 546 U.S. 49, 56 (2005) ("the ordinary default rule [is] that plaintiffs bear the risk of failing to prove their claims").

Even under the general rule, however, the party initiating the suit is not required to satisfy all three burdens as to all disputed facts. Sometimes, the initiating party will know facts sufficient to establish the opposing party's liability as long as no other facts are true (the plaintiff may know, for example, that the defendant intentionally touched her without her consent) but may not know of other facts that negate liability (e.g., that the defendant is a plainclothes police officer who had probable cause, and was attempting, to arrest her). The substantive law of most jurisdictions deals with this problem by identifying: (1) facts that are necessary, even if not sufficient, to justify a particular outcome (e.g., in a negligence suit, a lack of due care, causation and damages); and (2) facts that may justify a different outcome even if the first set of facts is present (e.g., the plaintiff's assumption of the risk). Whether any given fact (e.g., a tort plaintiff's exercise of due care, or contributory negligence) is placed in the former category or the latter is a question of substantive law, which different jurisdictions answer differently. Once such distinctions are made, however, the party initiating the lawsuit is generally required to bear the burden of pleading, production and persuasion as to the former set of facts (often called *elements* of the cause of action or offense), and the opposing party, at least in civil cases, is generally required to bear those burdens as to the latter set of facts (generally called elements of an *affirmative defense*).

The allocation of burdens that we have described is common, but—in civil cases—it is not legally required. Legislatures and courts sometimes shift these burdens in order to rearrange the parties' rights and responsibilities because they believe the responding party has better access to relevant information than the moving party, or is less deserving of a favorable outcome under conditions of uncertainty.[3] For example, a state might require a tort defendant to allege and present "some evidence" of the plaintiff's negligence in order to raise a contributory negligence defense, but—once this is done—the plaintiff may bear the burden of showing that her injury was not attributable to her own carelessness. Allocating the burdens in this way means that a court will not waste time assessing contributory negligence unless the defendant provides some reason to believe it occurred, but that a defendant who satisfies that burden of production will avoid liability if contributory

---

[3] In Keyes v. School Dist. No. 1, 413 U.S. 189 (1973), for example, the Supreme Court relied on considerations of "access to information" and "unclean hands" to hold that proof by plaintiff schoolchildren (1) that the defendant school board had *intentionally* segregated schools in one part of the district, and (2) that schools in other parts of the district were *in fact* racially segregated, shifted to the defendant the burden of disproving the claim that the board intentionally segregated *all* the schools. (As you will see in Section II.C, pp. 1437–1477, below, *Keyes* in effect created a "rebuttable presumption" of intentional segregation of all schools following proof of intentional segregation of some schools.) See also Campbell v. United States, 365 U.S. 85, 96 (1961) (the "ordinary rule, based on considerations of fairness," is "not [to] place the burden upon a litiga[nt] of establishing facts peculiarly within the knowledge of his adversary").

negligence was as likely as not. The desirability of these outcomes is a legal policy judgment, and other ways of allocating the burdens may be equally defensible.

In criminal cases, the Due Process Clauses of the Fifth and Fourteenth Amendments require the prosecution to bear the burden of persuasion (and probably of pleading and production) as to every fact that the jurisdiction's substantive criminal law defines as an "element" of the offense. The Constitution does not, however, make the prosecution bear those burdens on matters that the governing law treats as "affirmative defenses" rather than as elements of the offense. For instance, if state law defines murder as "an intentional homicide committed by someone of sound mind," the Constitution requires the state to bear the burden of proving beyond a reasonable doubt not only that the defendant intentionally killed the victim but also that he was sane when he did so. But if state law defines murder as simply an "intentional homicide" and makes the absence of a sound mind an affirmative defense, the Constitution allows the burden of proving insanity to be placed on the defendant.[4] The Constitution thus gives the prosecution the same burden as the general rule described above but no greater burden.

---

[4] Compare Mullaney v. Wilbur, 421 U.S. 684 (1975) (because Maine defines murder as homicide committed with "deliberate and *unprovoked* cruelty," the absence of enough provocation to lower the offense to voluntary manslaughter is an element of the offense as to which the prosecution must bear the burden of proof), and In re Winship, 397 U.S. 358 (1970) (prosecution must the bear burden of proof of every element of the offense), with Martin v. Ohio, 480 U.S. 228 (1987) (because Ohio law treats self-defense as an affirmative defense to culpable homicide, rather than making the absence of self-defense an element of the offense, the Due Process Clause lets Ohio give the defendant the burden of proof on the issue), and Patterson v. New York, 432 U.S. 197 (1977) (because New York treats extreme emotional disturbance as a defense to intentional murder that reduces the punishment to that provided for voluntary manslaughter, rather than making the absence of emotional disturbance an element of murder, the Due Process Clause lets New York give the defendant the burden of proof on the issue), and Leland v. Oregon, 343 U.S. 790 (1952) (upholding state law giving the criminal defendant the burden of proving the affirmative defense of insanity beyond a reasonable doubt). There are strong arguments for making the government bear the burden of proving all facts decisive of the defendant's moral culpability, and for rejecting reliance on formalistic characterizations of issues affecting culpability as "elements" or "defenses." See, e.g., George Fletcher, Rethinking Criminal Law 524–35 (1978); Barbara Underwood, The Thumb on the Scales of Justice: Burdens of Persuasion in Criminal Cases, 86 Yale L.J. 1299 (1977). But cf. Francis Allen, The Restoration of *In re Winship*: A Comment on Burdens of Persuasion in Criminal Cases *After Patterson v. New York*, 76 Mich. L. Rev. 30 (1977). Although the Supreme Court has sometimes found these arguments persuasive as a matter of *federal* criminal law, and *Mullaney* suggested that the Court might also find them constitutionally persuasive and thus binding on the states, the Court's later constitutional cases have left to each state's substantive criminal law the decision whether to take the functional or formalistic approach.

As interpreted by the Court, the Constitution also lets states make criminal defendants prove facts dispositive of procedural rights, even rights protected by the Constitution, such as the due process right not to be tried while mentally incompetent. See, e.g., Medina v. California, 505 U.S. 437 (1992) (states may require criminal defendants to prove by a preponderance of the evidence that they are incompetent to stand trial). But cf. Cooper v. Oklahoma, 517 U.S. 348 (1996) (states may not require criminal defendants to prove incompetence to stand trial by clear and convincing evidence; discussed infra, Section B.2., pp. 1375–1376).

Mullaney, Patterson and *Martin* do however modestly constrain state law. If, for example, a state were to define first-degree murder as the deliberate and premeditated killing of another human being, and to define deliberation and premeditation as cool planning ahead of time, the

As a supervisory (i.e., nonconstitutional) matter in *federal* criminal cases, the Supreme Court has sometimes required the prosecution to bear the burden of persuasion not only as to elements of the offense but also— once a defendant has satisfied a burden of pleading and production—as to other matters that affect the defendant's liability, such as self defense. So in federal court, once a murder defendant pleads self-defense and supports his plea with credible evidence, the government must disprove that defense beyond a reasonable doubt. The same rule applies to certain other justifying or excusing conditions in federal courts (and, as a matter of substantive criminal law, in many states). But as we noted above, nothing in the Due Process Clauses keeps Congress from giving the defendant the burden of persuasion on affirmative defenses. Consider again the treatment of the burden of persuasion on the affirmative defense of insanity. Until 1984, the Supreme Court had given the *government* in federal criminal prosecutions the burden of persuading the trier of fact beyond a reasonable doubt that the defendant was sane at the time of the crime, as long as the defendant first pleaded that defense and produced some evidence to support it.[5] This was true, even where soundness of mind was not an element of the crime charged. In 1984, however, in the wake of a District of Columbia jury verdict of "not guilty by reason of insanity" for a defendant who wounded and attempted to kill President Ronald Reagan, Congress changed that rule and gave the

---

state could not, then, create an "affirmative defense" of, say, "impulsive murder" which would exonerate the defendant if he proved that he killed without cool reflection or preplanning. Where a fact (here, "impulsiveness") necessarily negates an element of an offense (here, the cool planning that premeditation and deliberation require), making the defendant bear the burden of proving that fact may lead the jury to think that the defendant bears the burden of disproving an element of the crime, in violation of the rule that the prosecution must prove all elements of a crime beyond a reasonable doubt. To perfect the suggested scheme, the state would have to redefine murder as merely intentional killing, then create a partial affirmative defense of "murder on impulse" which is available to a defendant who proves that his intent to kill was formed instantaneously and without reflection.

In Jones v. United States, 526 U.S. 227 (1999), the court first considered a related question: Must a factual finding that increases the maximum sentence that may be imposed on a defendant be made by the jury, on the basis of proof beyond a reasonable doubt, or may the issue be treated as a "mere sentencing factor" and given to the judge to resolve, say, by a preponderance of the evidence? The Court resolved the question as a matter of statutory construction, but in the process a majority of the Justices suggested (but did not adopt) the following legal standard: "[U]nder the Due Process Clause . . . and [the] jury trial guarantee[ ] of the Sixth Amendment, any fact (other than prior conviction) that increases the maximum [possible] penalty for a crime must be . . . submitted to a jury, and proven beyond a reasonable doubt." Id. at 243 n.6. In a number of subsequent cases, the Supreme Court adopted that general principle as a matter of federal constitutional law. See, e.g., Ring v. Arizona, 536 U.S. 584 (2002) (overturning a death sentence imposed under a state statute that made a finding of at least one statutorily specified aggravating circumstance a prerequisite for the death penalty but required the sentencing judge, not a jury, to determine whether at least one such factor was present beyond a reasonable doubt); Apprendi v. New Jersey, 530 U.S. 466, 490 (2000) (overturning a sentence imposed on a defendant under a state statute allowing the judge to increase the maximum possible penalty for the crime upon the judge's finding that the offense was motivated by racial animus, because, "[o]ther than the fact of a prior conviction, any fact that increases the penalty for a crime beyond the prescribed statutory maximum must be submitted to a jury and proved beyond a reasonable doubt"). Prior convictions are exempted from this rule because they are premised on facts previously found by a jury beyond a reasonable doubt.

  [5]   See Davis v. United States, 160 U.S. 469 (1895).

criminal defendant the burden of persuading the jury of his insanity, and defined the burden as proof by "clear and convincing evidence."[6] The federal courts have not found that this definition or allocation of the burden of persuasion violates due process. Indeed, as currently understood, nothing in the Due Process Clauses keeps Congress or a state legislature from defining "murder"—and the facts that a prosecutor must prove beyond a reasonable doubt—as "killing someone," leaving the absence of particular mental states (such as premeditation, intent or negligence) as affirmative defenses that the *defendant* must prove—even, perhaps, beyond a reasonable doubt.[7]

B. DEFINING THE BURDENS OF PRODUCTION AND PERSUASION

If the party with the burden of production as to a material fact presents *no* evidence tending to prove it, the opposing party has no duty to respond, and the trier of fact will not be asked to determine whether the asserted fact is true. Instead, the burden-bearing party's claim or defense will fail. The court will direct a verdict against the burden-bearing party or decline to present the unsupported claim or defense to the jury. But suppose the burden-bearing party offers *some* evidence of the material fact. How does the court decide whether that is enough evidence to require the opposing party to respond and the trier to resolve the issue? Or if enough evidence is produced to put the fact in issue, but the opposing party responds with contrary evidence, how does the court decide who prevails on the issue if, say, the opposing party's evidence is as strong as, or only modestly weaker than, the burden-bearing party's evidence? Knowing which party bears the burdens of production and persuasion does not tell us how much evidence it takes to satisfy those burdens. The answers to both questions—"Who bears the ultimate burden of persuasion?" and "What *is* that burden?"—come from the same source: the jurisdiction's substantive law.[8] Both answers depend on judgments about how to allocate between the parties the risk that the trier will reach an inaccurate decision.

---

[6] 18 U.S.C. § 17(a). See also United States v. Bailey, 444 U.S. 394 (1980) (holding that the criminal defendant bears the burden of production, and suggesting that he bears the burden of persuasion, on the affirmative defenses of necessity and duress in federal criminal prosecutions).

[7] Cf. Schad v. Arizona, 501 U.S. 624, 639 (1991) (plurality opinion) ("In the burden-shifting cases . . . , we have faced the difficulty of deciding, as an abstract matter, what elements an offense must comprise. Recognizing '[o]ur inability to lay down any "bright-line" test,' we have 'stressed that . . . the state legislature's definition of the elements of the offense is usually dispositive,' " but have also "recognized that . . . there are . . . constitutional limits beyond which the States may not go.").

[8] As we will see below, at least in criminal cases, the Due Process Clauses of the United States Constitution also sometimes dictate the answers to these questions.

1. The Relationship Between Burdens of Production and Persuasion

As we noted earlier, some burdens of production serve only to signal that an issue that is not usually contested, *is* contested in the case at hand. Having been alerted to the fact of a contest, the party that bears the burden of persuasion on the claim must produce evidence that responds to the issue her opponent's evidence has raised. Production burdens of this signaling sort generally are satisfied by the presentation of "any" evidence, or by evidence sufficient to show a genuine controversy. Consider a jurisdiction that gives tort plaintiffs the burden of proving the absence of contributory negligence. Because in many cases contributory negligence is not an issue, it would be wasteful to require plaintiffs to show their own due care in every case. The jurisdiction might accordingly require the defendant to produce "some evidence" of contributory negligence before requiring the plaintiff to show that she exercised due care.

In other situations, the party with the burden of production also bears the burden of persuasion. Here the production burden is usually more onerous—the burden-bearing party must present enough evidence to permit a rational trier to find that the requisite burden of persuasion is met. Although this burden of production is pegged to the burden of persuasion, the former is not as great as the latter. The persuasion burden requires evidence strong enough, when discounted by the opposing party's evidence, to *actually convince* the trier of fact to the requisite degree of certainty. The production burden requires only enough evidence to convince the judge, without considering any evidence the other side might or does present, that a reasonable trier of fact *could* find that the persuasion burden has been satisfied. In making this assessment, the trial judge should draw all reasonable inferences from the evidence in favor of the burden-bearing party and accord full credibility to that party's witnesses. In a theft case, for example, satisfying the prosecution's burden of production requires enough evidence to allow a rational juror to conclude beyond a reasonable doubt that the defendant took property belonging to another without the other's consent. If the judge concludes that a rational juror could find beyond a reasonable doubt that such a taking occurred, the production burden is met even though the judge believes that it would also be rational for a juror to harbor a reasonable doubt about the theft. Both assessments may be rational, not only because the same evidence can give rise to two opposing reasonable inferences, but also because the law assigns judgments of witness credibility almost exclusively to jurors, and the rationality of inferences depends heavily on what evidence is believed.

2. The Formal Definitions of the Burdens of Production and Persuasion

Generally speaking, in civil cases, the party bearing the burden of production satisfies it by producing enough evidence to *permit* a rational trier to find that the fact at issue is "more likely than not." The party bearing the burden of persuasion satisfies it by *actually persuading* the trier of fact that the evidence tending to show the fact is at least slightly stronger than the evidence suggesting the opposite.[9] The same often is true in criminal cases for those issues on which the *defendant* bears the burdens of production and proof.[10]

In theory, this "preponderance of the evidence" rule has two important consequences: It produces the verdict that is most likely to be factually correct;[11] and it allocates to each side an equal risk of an erroneous decision. This even-handed burden of persuasion is appropriate because we believe that in civil cases errors running against one class of parties are no more harmful than errors running against the opposing class. In practice, this symmetrical distribution of risks only occurs in cases where the rules of evidence and procedure are equally hospitable to the discovery, presentation and consideration of the evidence on both sides. In the rare case when the evidence supporting each side is equally probative, the burden-bearing party loses for the pragmatic reasons that (1) disposing of the litigation is more important than avoiding arbitrary tie-breaking rules, and (2) a default rule favoring maintenance of the status quo (thus modestly deterring litigation costs) is at least as sensible as any other arbitrary rule.

---

[9] The evidence presented by the burden-bearing party in a civil action may be so strong—despite the opposing party's attacks on it and contrary evidence—that a verdict will be directed in the first party's favor, and the issue will never go to the jury. This may occur, however, only if the judge, giving due deference to the jury's wide discretion in assessing probative force and credibility, and drawing all reasonable inferences in favor of the *non-moving* party, believes that any rational juror *must* find that the moving party's claims are more likely true than not. See Reeves v. Sanderson Plumbing Products, 530 U.S. 133 (2000). In criminal cases, however, directed verdicts in favor of the prosecution are not permitted. See infra, note 49.

[10] But see supra and infra, notes 4, 6 and 16, noting instances in which criminal defendants have been required to bear a stiffer burden of persuasion on affirmative defenses.

[11] Consider this conundrum, however. Suppose a tort plaintiff must prove by a preponderance of the evidence both that the defendant failed to exercise due care and that the defendant's lapse, rather than some other event, caused the plaintiff's injury. Suppose, as well, that the jury finds that there is a 60% probability both that the defendant failed to exercise due care, and a 60% probability that the defendant's lapse caused the plaintiff's injury. And suppose, finally (the most heroic assumption), that those two probabilities are entirely independent of each other, so that a change in one would have no effect on the other. In such a case, the plaintiff would win (having proved each material fact by more than a preponderance of the evidence) although the probability that *both* her factual claims are true (as must be the case for her to deserve to prevail) is only 36% (.60 x .60 = .36). Philosophers and legal scholars have puzzled over this problem for a long time. If you can solve it, you have a place waiting for you in their ranks (assuming you want it). See, e.g., L. J. Cohen, The Probable and The Provable (1977); Ronald J. Allen, A Reconceptualization of Civil Trials, 66 B.U. L. Rev. 401 (1986); David J. Kaye, The Paradox of the Gatecrasher and Other Stories, 1979 Ariz. St. L.J. 101; Richard O. Lempert, The New Evidence Scholarship: Analyzing the Process of Proof, 66 B.U. L. Rev. 439 (1986).

When, however, the *prosecution* in a criminal case bears the burden of proof, it generally cannot survive a motion to dismiss unless it produces enough evidence to permit a rational juror to accept its factual claims *beyond a reasonable doubt.* Then, to prevail and secure a guilty verdict at trial, the prosecution generally must convince the trier of fact that, even considering the defendant's evidence, these claims are *actually* true beyond a reasonable doubt. For the "elements" of a crime, proof beyond a reasonable doubt is not merely a convention but a requirement of the Due Process Clause of the Fifth and Fourteenth Amendments to the Federal Constitution. Juries, that is, are supposed to acquit some criminal defendants even though they believe those defendants are probably guilty.[12] This is the rule because the costs of a mistake running against the accused—the loss of an innocent person's liberty or life—are thought to be far worse than the cost of a mistake running against the State—the failure to punish a guilty person. Our legal creed and libertarian values demand that, before the sanction and stigma of a criminal conviction may be imposed, a person's guilt must be substantially certain. This heavy burden is also justified by the fact that the prosecution can usually command far greater resources than those available to the defendant. As summarized by the Supreme Court in *In re Winship*:[13]

> The beyond a reasonable doubt standard plays a vital role in the American scheme of criminal procedure. It is a prime instrument for reducing the risk of convictions resting on factual error. The standard provides concrete substance for the presumption of innocence—that bedrock "axiomatic and elementary" principle whose "enforcement lies at the foundation of the administration of our criminal law."
>
> . . .
>
> [U]se of the reasonable doubt standard [also] is indispensable to command the respect and confidence of the community in its applications of criminal law. It is critical that the moral force of the criminal law not be diluted by a standard that leaves people in doubt whether innocent men are being condemned.

The Court has even interpreted the Due Process Clause to impose on the government a heightened burden of persuasion—the intermediate, "clear and convincing evidence" burden—in certain *civil* actions in which the government seeks to deprive individuals of important liberties. As the Court explained in *Cooper v. Oklahoma*,[14] fleshing out *Winship*'s logic:

> The function of a standard of proof, as that concept is embodied in the Due Process Clause and in the realm of fact-finding, is "to

---

[12] How often do you think jurors *actually* acquit defendants they believe are probably guilty? See *infra*, Subsection 3, pp. 1377–1381.

[13] 397 U.S. 358, 363, 365 (1970) (citations omitted).

[14] 517 U.S. 348 (1996).

instruct the fact finder concerning the degree of confidence our society thinks he should have in the correctness of factual conclusions for a particular type of adjudication."

The "more stringent the burden of proof a party must bear, the more that party bears the risk of an erroneous decision." For that reason, we have held that due process places a heightened burden of proof on the State in civil proceedings in which the "individual interests at stake . . . are both 'particularly important' and 'more substantial than mere loss of money.' "[15]

In general, however, outside the criminal arena, the Constitution permits the use of the preponderance of the evidence test. In civil cases, most jurisdictions use that test for most purposes.

The Constitution also sometimes forbids imposing a heightened burden of proof on an individual from whom the government is trying to withdraw important liberties. In *Cooper*, for example, the Court forbade a state to require criminal defendants to prove by "clear and convincing evidence" that they were incompetent to stand trial. Imposing that burden, the Court concluded, created an excessively high risk of an erroneous competence determination, and of the "dire" consequence of the defendant proceeding to trial while unable to communicate effectively with counsel or to exercise other rights that are central to a fair trial.[16]

---

[15] Id. at 362–63 (citations omitted) (quoting Santosky v. Kramer, 455 U.S. 745, 756 (1982)) (termination of parental rights requires proof by "clear and convincing evidence"). See also Addington v. Texas, 441 U.S. 418 (1979) (involuntary civil commitment requires proof by "clear and convincing evidence"); Woodby v. INS, 385 U.S. 276, 285–86 (1966) (deportation requires proof by "clear and convincing evidence"); Chaunt v. United States, 364 U.S. 350, 353 (1960) (denaturalization requires proof by "clear and convincing evidence"); Schneiderman v. United States, 320 U.S. 118, 125 (1943) (same). The law of a minority of states also requires proof by "clear and convincing evidence" to prove civil claims, such as fraud, that are analogous to crimes and carry substantial moral opprobrium.

[16] 517 U.S. at 363–364. *Cooper* may be compared to cases in which the Court has permitted states to place heavy burdens of proof on citizens from whom the government is trying to take important liberties. For example, in Leland v. Oregon, 343 U.S. 790 (1952), the Court allowed a state to require criminal defendants to prove insanity beyond a reasonable doubt before excusing them from crimes for which they otherwise would be convicted. Although *Cooper* might seem to call *Leland* into question, the different outcomes of these two decisions may reflect significant differences between the risk that the defendant is incapable of defending himself *at all* against criminal charges, and the risk that he was insane at the time he committed an offense that the state has proved beyond a reasonable doubt. (In *Leland*, the insanity issue arose only after the state proved beyond a reasonable doubt that the defendant committed premeditated murder). In addition, the Court has recognized a constitutional right not to be tried while incompetent, Drope v. Missouri, 420 U.S. 162 (1975), but has not (as yet) recognized a right not to be convicted for a crime committed while insane. Cf. Atkins v. Virginia, 536 U.S. 304 (2002) (holding that states may not constitutionally *execute* mentally retarded offenders); Penry v. Lynaugh, 492 U.S. 302, 333 (1989) (suggesting in dicta that there is a right not to be *executed* for a crime committed while insane). See also supra, note 6 and accompanying text, discussing the federal statute governing the insanity defense in federal prosecutions, which gives criminal defendants the burden of proving insanity by "clear and convincing evidence."

Cooper, 517 U.S. at 363, distinguished two other prior decisions as follows:

In *Cruzan* [v. Director, Mo. Dept. of Health, 497 U.S. 261 (1990)], we held that the Due Process Clause does not prohibit Missouri from requiring a third party who seeks to

3.   The Meaning of Proof "Beyond a Reasonable Doubt"

It is clear that the burden of persuasion "beyond a reasonable doubt" is more onerous than proof by "clear and convincing" evidence, which in turn is more onerous than proof by a "preponderance of the evidence." But what content does each burden have beyond its relationship to the others? Only the preponderance burden, which requires a fact be more likely than not, has an obvious substantive meaning: The probability of the asserted fact must be greater than 50%. Given this, it is natural to ask whether the "clear and convincing evidence" translates into a probability greater than, say, 75%; and whether "beyond a reasonable doubt" requires a probability greater than 90%, 95%, or 99%. In fact, there are no settled definitions of these other burdens—not even verbal ones—as the courts' treatment of the meaning of "proof beyond a reasonable doubt" burden illustrates.

Although acknowledging that "the reasonable doubt standard is itself probabilistic,"[17] the courts have steadfastly declined to assign any particular probability to it. Indeed, because the "rule . . . often is[ ] rendered obscure by attempts at definition," the Supreme Court has suggested—and a number of federal circuit courts have approved—the practice of leaving the standard entirely undefined, at least unless the jury requests a definition and sometimes even if it does ask for guidance.[18]

---

terminate life-sustaining treatment to demonstrate by clear and convincing evidence that the incompetent person receiving such treatment would wish that step to be taken. 497 U.S., at 280. We reasoned that the heightened standard of proof was permissible because the decision maker was a surrogate for the incompetent individual, *id.* at 280–81, and because the consequences of an erroneous decision were irreversible, *id.*, at 283. In [Ohio v.] *Akron Center for Reproductive Health* [497 U.S. 502 (1990)], we upheld an Ohio statute that required an unmarried, unemancipated minor woman who sought to obtain an abortion without notifying a parent to prove by clear and convincing evidence that judicial bypass of the notification requirement was appropriate in her case. We approved the heightened standard of proof in that case largely because the proceeding at issue was *ex parte* [i.e., was held out of the presence of the parents, without any opposing evidence or argument being presented]. 497 U.S. at 515–16.

[17] Victor v. Nebraska, 511 U.S. 1, 14 (1994); see also In re Winship, 397 U.S. at 370 (Harlan, J., concurring) ("[I]n a judicial proceeding in which there is a dispute about the facts of some earlier event, . . . all the fact finder can acquire is a belief of what *probably* happened.").

[18] Hopt v. Utah, 120 U.S. 430, 440–41 (1887). See, e.g., Holland v. United States, 348 U.S. 121, 140 (1954) (" 'Attempts to explain the term "reasonable doubt" do not usually result in making it any clearer to the minds of the jury.' "); United States v. Wallace, 461 F.3d 15 (1st Cir. 2006) (trial judges in the First Circuit need not give instructions defining reasonable doubt); United States v. Walton, 207 F.3d 694 (4th Cir.), cert. denied, 531 U.S. 865 (2000) (trial judges in the Fourth Circuit may not define reasonable doubt unless the jury requests a definition, in which case the trial judge may, but is not required to, define the concept); United States v. Hanson, 994 F.2d 403, 408 (7th Cir. 1993) (trial courts in the Seventh Circuit need not define "beyond a reasonable doubt," because "an attempt to define [the phrase] presents a risk without any real benefit"). But cf. Note, Reasonable Doubt: To Define or Not to Define, 90 Colum. L. Rev. 1716, 1723 (1990) (studies suggest that the undefined words "reasonable doubt" confuse jurors). See generally Irwin A. Horowitz, Reasonable Doubt: Commonsense Justice and Standard of Proof, 3 Psychol. Pub. Pol'y & L. 285, 292–93 (1997) (studies suggest that, when "beyond a reasonable doubt" is defined, the relative leniency or strictness of the definition affects the likelihood that jurors will convict or acquit).

But how is the "reasonable doubt" standard applied? Consider a case in which the jury accurately concludes that there is an 80% chance that the defendant committed a brutal torture-murder. Although four out of every five people linked to a crime by such evidence would be guilty, an 80% probability is, in our view, insufficient to prove guilt beyond a reasonable doubt (or, put the other way around, a 20% probability of innocence is too high to justify a conviction).[19] The problem is that the unadorned phrase, "proof beyond a reasonable doubt," may not keep a jury from conviction, even so. Suppose that in the same case the jury believes that if the killer remains free, there is a 90% probability that he will kill again.[20] Do you think the undefined words "beyond a reasonable doubt" would keep the jury from convicting—i.e., from improperly deciding that a 20% doubt about guilt is too insignificant to warrant turning the defendant loose? (If you don't think the jury *should* turn the defendant loose, is your problem with our assumption that proof beyond a reasonable doubt requires a probability of guilt higher than 80%, or with the wisdom of the reasonable doubt standard itself?[21])

But even if the words "beyond a reasonable doubt" are unlikely to sufficiently constrain the jury's decision making, it is far from clear that adding more words will help. Consider whether any of the following definitions of reasonable doubt would effectively guide a jury:

Instruction 1: Reasonable doubt is such a doubt as would cause a reasonable and prudent person, in one of the graver and more important transactions of life, to pause and hesitate before taking the represented facts as true and relying and acting thereon. It is such a doubt as will not permit you, after full, fair, and impartial

---

[19] A few surveys have asked respondents in the general population to define "proof beyond a reasonable doubt" in numerical terms. They show that views differ greatly, but that there is a clustering around 85–90%. See Reid Hastie, Steven D. Penrod & Nancy Pennington, Inside the Jury (1983); Rita James Simon & Linda Mahan, Quantifying Burdens of Proof, 5 L. & Soc'y. Rev. 319 (1971). If, instead of being asked to attach a numerical probability of guilt to the words "beyond a reasonable doubt," mock jurors who have been instructed on that standard are asked to describe their relative tolerance for convicting the innocent and acquitting the guilty, their answers usually reveal a conviction standard of between a 51% and 65% probability of guilt. Some researchers believe that the latter, indirect measure of how jurors understand the words "beyond a reasonable doubt" is the best predictor of actual juror behavior, at least when the words are not further defined. See Reid Hastie, Algebraic Models of Juror Decision Processes, in Inside the Juror 81 (Reid Hastie ed., 1993). See also Chapter Three, Section II.B., pp. 249–255, where we discuss this issue in the context of the "regret matrix." In our view, "proof beyond a reasonable doubt" means at least a 90% probability of guilt, and even that standard may be low, depending on what proportion of those tried are in fact guilty and how persuasive evidence is when defendants are guilty compared to when they are innocent.

[20] Assuming the evidence supporting the two assessments was independent of each other, this would mean that there is a 72% chance—.80 x .90 = .72—that *this defendant* will kill again if left at large.

[21] Suppose the jury thought the murderer was *certain* to kill again if let loose, and that there was a 49% chance that this defendant was the murderer? Would you still expect the jury to acquit? Would it be unreasonable for the jurors to refuse to allow the defendant to return to their community? The point of this example is that proof "beyond a reasonable doubt" means something more than a state of evidence that might lead a reasonable, rational person to convict. It is a norm that is supposed to prohibit some judgments that might reasonably be made.

consideration of all the evidence, to have an abiding conviction, to a moral certainty, of the guilt of the accused. At the same time, absolute or mathematical certainty is not required. You may be convinced of a fact beyond a reasonable doubt and yet be fully aware that possibly you may be mistaken. You may find an accused guilty upon the strong probabilities of the case, provided such probabilities are strong enough to exclude any doubt of his guilt that is reasonable. A reasonable doubt is an actual and substantial doubt arising from the evidence . . . as distinguished from a doubt arising from mere possibility, from bare imagination, or from fanciful conjecture.

Instruction 2: If you entertain a reasonable doubt as to any fact or element necessary to constitute the defendant's guilt, it is your duty to give him the benefit of that doubt and return a verdict of not guilty. Even where the evidence demonstrates a probability of guilt, if it does not establish such guilt beyond a reasonable doubt, you must acquit the accused. This doubt, however, must be a reasonable one; that is, one that is founded upon a real tangible substantial basis and not upon mere caprice and conjecture. It must be such as would give rise to a grave uncertainty, raised in your mind by reasons of the unsatisfactory character of the evidence or lack thereof. A reasonable doubt is not a mere possible doubt. It is a doubt that a reasonable man can seriously entertain. What is required is not an absolute or mathematical certainty, but a moral certainty.

Instruction 3: Proof beyond a reasonable doubt is proof that leaves you firmly convinced of the defendant's guilt. There are very few things in this world that we know with absolute certainty, and in criminal cases the law does not require proof that overcomes every possible doubt. If, based on your consideration of the evidence, you are firmly convinced that the defendant is guilty of the crime charged, you must find him guilty. If on the other hand, you think there is a real possibility that he is not guilty, you must give him the benefit of the doubt and find him not guilty.

Each of the first two instructions was given to a jury that convicted a defendant of capital murder and sentenced him to die. The Supreme Court reviewed both instructions in the early 1990s to determine whether they permitted convictions on evidence less probative of guilt than due process requires. The Court unanimously rejected one of the instructions and overturned the resulting conviction, but it upheld the other instruction by a 7–2 vote over the dissenters' claim that there was no meaningful difference between the two instructions. The Court's different conclusions raise interesting questions. What are the differences between the two instructions? Is one preferable to the other? Would the instructions affect jurors differently in the case hypothesized above? Are the differences substantial enough to be of *constitutional* significance?

In *Victor v. Nebraska*,[22] the Supreme Court upheld a conviction imposed by a jury given the first instruction. In *Cage v. Louisiana*,[23] it overturned a conviction by a jury given the second instruction. These two decisions establish the following propositions: (1) Courts may use many formulations to instruct on the "beyond a reasonable doubt" standard, including reliance on those words alone; the Constitution neither requires any definition beyond those words nor prescribes a particular one. (2) The Due Process Clause requires proof "beyond a reasonable doubt" in order to assure a "very high level of probability" or "a subjective state of near certitude" of guilt before anyone is convicted of a crime, and it forbids "reasonable doubt" instructions that "undermine" that assurance.[24] (3) The terms "moral evidence" and "moral certainty" as used in the first two instructions tend to confuse jurors and convey a diluted sense of the requisite certainty, as does the second instruction's suggestion that a "reasonable doubt" must be a "substantial" or "grave" doubt. None of these phrases on its own is constitutionally fatal, although they may be impermissible in combinations—absent tempering by more acceptable language. (4) Defining a reasonable doubt as a doubt that would cause a reasonable person to hesitate to act in important affairs is acceptable to a majority, but not to all, of the justices. All of them, however, approve language requiring an "abiding conviction" of the defendant's guilt. Applying these propositions to the first two instructions reveals that both combine acceptable and unacceptable language, but that the mixture in the second instruction (from *Cage*) leans more heavily to the unacceptable side than that in the first instruction (from *Victor*).

Whether these finely nuanced differences would make much of a difference to lay jurors is highly questionable. So too is the capacity of either of the first instructions (including the one upheld in *Victor*) to constrain jurors faced with cases like the torture murder discussed above. Certainly, the third instruction, which the Federal Judicial Center developed for use in federal trials,[25] has the best chance of conveying an appropriate understanding of the standard.

In the end, it is hard to escape the conclusion that the courts have purposely left the meaning of "beyond a reasonable doubt" ambiguous. There are several reasons why courts might do so. Leaving the standard vague allows jurors to calibrate the meaning of "reasonable doubt" to the

---

[22] 511 U.S. 1 (1994).

[23] 498 U.S. 39 (1990) (per curiam).

[24] Victor v. Nebraska, 511 U.S. at 14, 15 (quoting Jackson v. Virginia, 443 U.S. 307, 315 (1979)).

[25] Federal Judicial Center, Pattern Criminal Jury Instructions, Instr. No. 21 (2008).

circumstances of the case, taking into account the seriousness of the offense, the danger the defendant poses to society and the severity of the punishment. Thus, for example, in *Adams v. Texas,*[26] the Supreme Court held that it is unconstitutional for a state to exclude jurors from service in capital cases simply because they would require a higher level of certainty in order to be convinced "beyond a reasonable doubt" in a case in which the defendant might be executed than they would require in a noncapital case.[27] A vague standard also allows jurors in practice to reduce the heavy burden that our system imposes on the state to secure convictions, while leaving the legal rule unchanged in theory. Finally, there is no escaping the fact that the term "reasonable doubt" is difficult to define. A vague definition, or none at all, may be better than a more specific one that doesn't capture the essence of the concept.

"You would rather let a guilty man go free than punish an innocent one? How do you figure that?"

----

[26] 448 U.S. 38 (1980).

[27] Id. at 50 ("Nor in our view would the Constitution permit the exclusion of jurors . . . who frankly concede that the prospects of the death penalty may affect what their honest judgment of the facts will be or what they may deem to be a reasonable doubt. Such assessments and judgments by jurors are inherent in the jury system. . . . ").

PROBLEMS

Problem XI-1. The General Assembly of the Land of Enchantment is revamping the Land's criminal laws. The Chair of the Assembly's Judiciary Committee has asked Oliver Louis Benjamin, Director of Legal Research for the Legislative Drafting Service, to draft proposed provisions (1) describing the crime of murder (which is to be defined, essentially, as the intentional killing of another human being) and the punishment for it; (2) providing for a lesser punishment if the killing (a) although intentional, was the product of provocation and passion, or (b) was not intentional, but was negligent, reckless or grossly reckless; and (3) providing for no punishment at all if the killing was intentional but (a) in self-defense, (b) the product of duress, (c) necessary in order to save two or more lives, (d) committed with the consent of the victim who was terminally ill, or (e) was the product of the perpetrator's severe mental disorder. **On which party should Benjamin propose placing the burden of persuasion as to the elements of murder; provocation and passion; negligence, recklessness and gross recklessness; self-defense; duress; necessity; mercy killing; and insanity? What should the burdens be—beyond a reasonable doubt; clear and convincing evidence; a preponderance of the evidence; something else? How should Benjamin go about answering these questions, and what factors are relevant? Is there any role for burdens of pleading and production, as opposed to burdens of persuasion? How should Benjamin propose that juries in the Land be instructed on the burdens of production and persuasion that he chooses?**

Problem XI-2. In the same situation as in the preceding problem, suppose that a different offense is under consideration: assault and battery (which is to be defined, essentially, as intentional touching without consent). And suppose that the bases for limiting or avoiding punishment are to be: a mental state less than intent; provocation and heat of passion; self-defense; duress; necessity; and insanity. **On which party should Benjamin propose putting the burden of persuasion as to the elements of assault and battery? As to the various bases for limiting or avoiding punishment? What should the burdens be? How should Benjamin go about answering these questions; what factors are relevant? How should Benjamin propose that juries in the Land be instructed on the burdens of production and persuasion that he chooses? Would your answers change if Benjamin instead were drafting a civil code and defining the intentional tort of assault and battery?** Suppose that Benjamin is drafting a code containing both the crime and the tort of assault and battery. **When, as in this scenario, the cause of action in a civil case parallels a criminal action recognized by the same jurisdiction, should the civil plaintiff have to prove wrongdoing**

beyond a reasonable doubt? Most American jurisdictions require only a preponderance of the evidence in a civil action in this situation. But a minority require a heavier burden, such as "clear and convincing evidence." **In this latter scenario, what are the strongest reasons for making the civil burden of persuasion a preponderance of the evidence? What are the strongest reasons for adopting a higher standard of proof in the civil action?**

Problem XI-3. Evan Elib (aka the "E-Bomber") is accused of sending viruses by e-mail in violation of the Virtual Viral Protection Act of 2013. The Act forbids "destroying or inhibiting the operation of another's computer by means of an electronic virus sent from a remote location with malice aforethought." In his opening argument, Elib's lawyer alleges that Elib was insane at the time the e-mail was sent, but the defense thereafter presents no evidence to support the allegation. **Should the jury be instructed on Elib's insanity defense? Should the defense go to the jury if Elib has testified that he sent the viruses at the command of an evil dog named Sam that inhabited his computer and periodically appeared on the screen, threatening to kill Elib, the President and the Secretary of Commerce if Elib did not send the virus? If the insanity defense does go to the jury, who should bear the burden of persuasion, and what should that burden be?**

Problem XI-4. Jeff Gordon rented a car from Lease-a-Heap on January 5. He undertook contractually to return the car five days later. On January 20, Lease-a-Heap wrote Gordon at the address on the rental agreement, demanding the return of the car. When there was no answer twenty days later, Lease-a-Heap sued Gordon for Conversion of a Rented Auto, and the local prosecutor charged Gordon with Grand Theft/Auto. At trial Gordon testifies that he drove the car to Lease-a-Heap's airport drop-off location on January 10 and, finding no attendant present, left the car with the keys in the glove compartment and ran to catch his airplane. On rebuttal, Hal Unser testifies that he saw Gordon driving a car matching the rental automobile on January 18. **Assume that Gordon is the defendant in a _civil_ action arising under each statute set out below. What instructions does each statute appear to require on (1) who bears the burden of persuasion with regard to the issue of intent to convert or steal the car, and (2) what that burden is? Would your answer change if Gordon is instead the defendant in a _criminal_ action arising under each statute?**

(1) Any person who rents an automobile from a commercial rental establishment and intentionally fails to return the automobile to the rental establishment on the date agreed upon is liable to the rental

establishment for the tort of Conversion of a Rented Automobile, and is also guilty of the criminal offense of Grand Theft of an Automobile.

(2) Any person who rents an automobile from a commercial rental establishment and fails to return the automobile to the rental establishment on the date agreed upon is liable to the rental establishment for the tort of Conversion of a Rented Automobile, and is also guilty of the criminal offense of Grand Theft of an Automobile. It is a defense to civil and criminal liability under this section that the failure to return the automobile was not intentional. **[Would it matter if this statute instead made the lack of intent an "affirmative defense"?]**

Problem XI-5. I. Nathan's automobile collides with Julissa's. Julissa files suit claiming Nathan was negligent. She alleges in her complaint that she is suffering from partial amnesia caused by the accident and is consequently unable to remember the details of the accident, or of any other events occurring during the past six years. **Given Julissa's allegation that she has amnesia caused by the accident, should the trial judge, in fairness, instruct the jury that Nathan has the burden of proving by a preponderance of the evidence that he is not liable for the accident or for any damages? Should the judge do so after satisfying himself that there is a substantial possibility that Julissa is suffering from amnesia as a result of the accident? Should the judge instead instruct the jury to find for Julissa if she (1) establishes by a preponderance of the evidence that she has amnesia caused by the accident, and (2) additionally establishes that there is a substantial possibility that Nathan negligently caused the accident—unless Nathan proves by a preponderance of the evidence that he did not negligently cause the accident or any damages? Or should some other allocation and definition of burdens be used, in fairness to Julissa?**

II.   Suppose, instead, that Nathan (twenty-five years old) is charged with molesting Julissa (five years old), who lives in the apartment next door to the one Nathan moved into six months ago. Julissa testifies that Nathan "touched her" but cannot coherently testify to much else. A medical doctor testifies that she has examined Julissa and found scarring that is consistent with—but not necessarily the product of—sexual molestation. The doctor testifies that in her expert opinion the scarring was caused by a wound suffered sometime during the previous three to six months. A psychiatric expert testifies that Julissa fits the profile of a child molestation victim—and that clinical trials have shown that this profile is accurate 78% of the time when it indicates that the child in question was a victim of molestation. **Should the judge lower the prosecution's burden of persuasion in any way to compensate for Julissa's young age, and the notorious difficulty of proving child molestation beyond a reasonable doubt?** Suppose the judge refuses to lower the burden of proof, Nathan is acquitted and several months later kills four-year-old Kirsty in the process of sexually molesting her. The state legislature thereafter adopts "Kirsty's Law" lowering the burden of persuasion in certain criminal child molestation cases to a requirement of proof that each element of the offense is "significantly more likely than not." **Is Kirsty's Law constitutional? Is it a good idea?**

Problem XI-6. Lee is charged with bank robbery and murder. Before the trial, Lee files a three-part motion to suppress evidence she expects the prosecutor to offer against her at trial. First, Lee moves to suppress money, ski masks and weapons seized in a search of her car conducted without a search warrant a half-hour after the robbery. She alleges that the police officer who conducted the search did so without probable cause, in violation of the Fourth Amendment. The Supreme Court has held that, although the Fourth Amendment protects the public against unreasonable searches and seizures, the exclusionary rule forbidding the introduction of illegally seized evidence at trial is *not* constitutionally mandated and instead is a judge-made "prophylactic" rule designed to create incentives for police officers to abide by the requirements of the Fourth Amendment. Second, Lee moves to suppress statements elicited from her by police officers at the station house shortly after her arrest, claiming that the statements were involuntary and thus violated her Fifth Amendment privilege against self-incrimination. The Supreme Court has held that the Fifth Amendment privilege against self-incrimination includes a constitutional privilege against the introduction at trial of statements involuntarily elicited from criminal defendants by police officers before trial. Third, Lee claims that these statements were made in violation of the *Miranda* rule, because no officer informed her during her custodial interrogation of her right to remain silent and to the assistance of a lawyer. The Supreme Court has held that the *Miranda* protections are constitutionally required "prophylactic" measures designed to help assure (among other things) that police officers respect suspects' Fifth Amendment privilege against self-incrimination. The Supreme Court has also held that the prosecutor has the burden of proving the *voluntariness* of a confession by a preponderance of the evidence when a defendant claims that it was extracted involuntarily in violation of the Fifth Amendment. **Do you think this allocation of the burden of persuasion is appropriate in the involuntary confession situation? Who should bear that burden—and what shall it be—when the basis for suppression is the Fourth Amendment exclusionary rule? When the basis for suppression is**

a violation of the *Miranda* rule? Would it matter if the *Miranda* rule were statutory or "supervisory," not constitutional? If a defense witness will testify that the bank teller who was killed in the robbery stated as he died, "Oscar Lukomnic killed me," should this evidence be admissible if there is only a reasonable possibility that the teller had the sense of imminent death required by the dying declaration exception to the hearsay rule? Or should the evidence be excluded unless Lee can demonstrate by a preponderance of the evidence that the requirements for a dying declaration are met? If the declaration instead identifies Lee, and is offered by the prosecutor, which standard of proof should the prosecutor have to satisfy before the hearsay statement is admitted as a dying declaration?

Problem XI-7. Examine the following two "pattern" jury instructions on burden of persuasion in a civil case. Is each satisfactory? Are they equally so? (Brackets indicate material a judge has discretion to use, or not to use, in a particular case.)

(1) I shall now explain to you the burden of proof which the law places on the parties to establish their respective claims. When I say that a party has the burden of proof, or, in this connection, use the expression "if you find" or "if you decide," I mean the evidence must satisfy you that the proposition on which that party has the burden of proof has been established by evidence that outweighs the evidence against it. You must consider all the evidence regardless of which party produced it.

(2) Whenever I say a claim must be proved, I mean that all of the evidence by whomever produced must lead you to believe it is more likely that the claim is true than not true. [If the evidence does not lead you to believe it is more likely that the claim is true than not true, then the claim has not been proved.] [Proof of a claim does not necessarily mean the greater number of witnesses or the greater volume of testimony. Any believable evidence may be a sufficient basis to prove a claim.]

Problem XI-8. In a negligence case involving a counterclaim by the defendant, is the following instruction satisfactory? What difference would it make if a written copy of the instruction is, or is not, provided to the jury during its deliberations? What changes would you make to improve the instruction? Start from scratch and prepare a better instruction:

In this action there is not only the claim of the plaintiff against the defendant, but also a claim by the defendant against the plaintiff. This is known as a counterclaim.

Because there is a counterclaim in this case, you may reach one of three results.

First, your verdict may be for the plaintiff on his claim and against the defendant on his counterclaim.

Second, your verdict may be for the defendant on his counterclaim and against the plaintiff on his claim.

Or, third, your verdict may be against both the plaintiff on his claim and the defendant on his counterclaim.

As to plaintiff's claim, he has the burden of proof on each of the following propositions:

(1) that the plaintiff was injured;

(2) that the defendant was negligent in one or more of the ways claimed by the plaintiff as stated to you in these instructions;

(3) that the negligence of the defendant was a proximate cause of the injuries to the plaintiff.

The defendant has the burden of proof on his defense that the plaintiff was negligent in one or more of the ways claimed by the defendant as stated to you in these instructions, and that such negligence was a proximate contributing cause of the injury to the plaintiff.

Your verdict will be for the plaintiff on his claim, if he was injured, and defendant was negligent, and such negligence was a proximate cause of his injuries—unless plaintiff himself was negligent and such negligence proximately contributed to his injuries.

Your verdict will be for the defendant on plaintiff's claim, if plaintiff was not injured, or if defendant was not negligent, or if negligent, such negligence was not a proximate cause of the injuries, or if the plaintiff himself was negligent and such negligence was a proximate contributing cause of his injuries.

As to the defendant's counterclaim, he has the burden of proof on each of the following propositions:

(1) that the defendant was injured;

(2) that the plaintiff was negligent in one or more of the ways claimed by the defendant as stated to you in these instructions;

(3) that the negligence of the plaintiff was a proximate cause of the injuries to the defendant.

The plaintiff has the burden of proof on his defense that the defendant was negligent in one or more of the ways claimed by the plaintiff as stated to you in these instructions, and that such negligence was a proximate contributing cause of the injuries to the defendant.

Your verdict will be for the defendant on his counterclaim if he was injured, and plaintiff was negligent, and such negligence was a proximate cause of his injuries—unless defendant himself was negligent and such negligence proximately contributed to his injuries.

Your verdict will be for the plaintiff on defendant's counterclaim if defendant was not injured, or if plaintiff was not negligent, or if negligent, such negligence was not a proximate cause of the injuries, or if the defendant himself was negligent and such negligence was a proximate contributing cause of his injuries.

If both plaintiff and defendant were negligent and the negligence of each was a proximate cause of the injuries received by the other, then your verdict will be no cause for action on both the plaintiff's claim and the defendant's counterclaim.

Problem XI-9. New York Supreme Court Judge Elena Sonia Ruth is presiding over an armed robbery case in which the identity of the defendant as the masked assailant is hotly contested. Believing that the outcome of the case may turn on the definition of "beyond a reasonable doubt," Judge Ruth has decided to scrap her usual jury instruction on that concept and devise a new one. She asks the prosecutor, defense counsel and her three law clerks to make proposals. The proposals for a definition of "a reasonable doubt" include: (1) "A doubt or uncertainty that might cause a reasonable person to refrain from acting on a matter of (great?) importance in her or his life." (2) "A real, not a speculative or imaginary, doubt." (3) "A probability, not a mere possibility." (4) "A 10% (5%?) (1%?) or greater chance that the defendant is innocent." Proposals are also made to define "beyond a reasonable doubt" as: (5) "To a moral certainty." (6) "The degree of certainty that a reasonable person requires before acting on a matter of (great?) importance in her or his life." (7) "More than a 90% (95%?) (99%?) certainty of guilt." (8) "Evidence so strongly suggestive that the defendant committed the robbery, that, if such evidence were encountered in the course of investigating 100 identical robberies, one would expect that the person implicated by the evidence was guilty of the crime committed in more than 90% (95%?) (99%?) of the cases." (9) "Evidence sufficient to convince you (or, to establish an abiding (strong?) conviction?) that the defendant committed the robbery." (10) "Evidence of guilt that is strong enough to justify putting the defendant in prison for life [the maximum sentence for the offense]." (11) "Evidence of guilt that is strong enough to justify putting the defendant in prison for at least fifteen years [the minimum sentence for the sentence, once parole possibilities are considered]." It also is proposed (12) that the phrase "beyond a reasonable doubt" be given no definition. **Which definition(s) should Judge Ruth use? Which would be constitutionally permissible? Which would be impermissible? Which favor the prosecution? Which favor the defense? In deciding whether any doubt of guilt that the evidence creates is less than a "reasonable" doubt, should the jury be affected by the punishment the defendant faces? Do you suppose that juries** *are* **(whether or not they** *should be***) affected by the possible or probable punishment? How much do jurors know, typically, about possible and probable punishments? How much do they think they know? How much should they be told about sentencing possibilities?**

Problem XI-10. Consider the following three jury instructions (taken from Louisiana, Nebraska and Nevada cases) defining the prosecutor's burden to prove a criminal defendant's guilt beyond a reasonable doubt. **Which instruction is most favorable to the defense? Are any of the instructions unconstitutional? As a prosecutor, how would you propose defining "beyond a reasonable doubt"? How would you do so as a defense lawyer?**

(1) A reasonable doubt is one that is founded upon a real and tangible substantial basis and not upon mere caprice and conjecture. It must be such doubt as would give rise to a grave uncertainty, raised in your mind by reasons of the unsatisfactory character of the evidence or lack thereof. A reasonable doubt is not a mere possible doubt. It is an actual and substantial doubt. What is required is not an absolute or mathematical certainty, but a moral certainty.

(2) Reasonable doubt is defined as follows: It is not a mere possible doubt, because everything relating to human affairs, and depending on moral evidence, is open to some possible or imaginary doubt. It is that state of the case which, after the entire comparison and consideration of all the evidence, leaves the minds of the jurors in that condition that they cannot say they feel an abiding conviction to a moral certainty, of the truth of the charge.

(3) A reasonable doubt is one based on reason. It is not mere possible doubt, but is such a doubt as would govern or control a person in the more weighty affairs of life. If the minds of jurors, after the entire comparison and consideration of all the evidence, are in such a condition that they can say they feel an abiding conviction of the truth of the charge, there is not reasonable doubt.

Problem XI-11. Daisy Dell is charged with stabbing to death her ex-boyfriend Rusty Rose. At trial, Lily Lake testifies that: "At 6:15 p.m., I was in Rusty's bedroom getting ready for a party; I couldn't hear much over the hair dryer. Around 6:30, I heard noises but thought it was something on one of those crazy DVD's Rusty listens to. But when I heard screams a couple of minutes later, I ran to the living room and saw

Rusty on the floor, all bloody. He was gasping for breath and screaming, 'It was Daisy! She has a key to the apartment. She saw the daisies I bought you and went crazy, yelling, "Daisies for Lily? What is this!!" and stabbed me.' That was the last thing he ever said to me." Later, Daisy testifies that she and Rusty had reconciled their differences two days before the stabbing, and that Rusty had told her he was going to break off his relationship with Lily. Daisy testifies that she did not stab Rusty and that, from 6:25 to 7:30 p.m. on the evening of the stabbing, she was walking her dog, Blue Bell, in the Municipal Botanical Gardens. Irwin Iris, who lives across the street from the Gardens, four blocks from Daisy's home, testifies that he saw Daisy walking her dog in the Gardens at 6:40 p.m. The Gardens are at least twenty minutes away from Rusty's house. The medical examiner estimates that the stabbing occurred between 6:15 p.m. and 6:30 p.m., but cannot be more specific. The trial judge instructs the jury: "You may find for the defendant based on her alibi only if you conclude that she has presented sufficient evidence to raise a reasonable possibility that she was elsewhere at the time of the homicide. If the defendant does present such evidence, you must find for her, unless the state proves beyond a reasonable doubt that the defendant was at the scene of the crime when the victim was killed." **Is this instruction appropriate? To which parties does the instruction assign the burdens of production and persuasion? Who *should* bear those burdens? Is the evidence sufficient to prove by a preponderance that Daisy was not at Rusty's house when the stabbing occurred? Is it sufficient to prove *beyond a reasonable doubt* that she was not there? Is it sufficient to prove beyond a reasonable doubt that Daisy *was* at Rusty's house when the stabbing occurred? Would it affect your views on who should bear these burdens of production and persuasion if case law in the relevant jurisdiction defines alibi as an "affirmative defense"?**

Problem XI-12. Dalton Dyer files a complaint alleging libel and slander against Morton MacDougall. The first count alleges that MacDougall said of Dyer at a directors' meeting of Awes, Inc., "You are stabbing me in the back." The second count alleges that MacDougall wrote a letter to Dorothy Gayle, Dyer's sister-in-law, stating, "Dyer has made false statements to my client in Wichita and presented bills for work not done." The third count alleges that MacDougall told Gayle that Dyer had sent out a "blackmailing letter." The fourth count alleges that MacDougall also told Allie Almirall, a lawyer, that Dyer had sent out a "blackmailing letter." At trial MacDougall denies uttering the libel and slanders attributed to him; Gayle denies receiving the letter that forms the basis for the second count; and Gayle and Almirall deny hearing the slander that MacDougall allegedly uttered to them. Dyer has no affirmative proof to support his complaint, not even his own testimony. He urges that a jury could find sufficient evidence to justify a verdict for him if it

disbelieves MacDougall, Gayle and Almirall. **Has Dyer produced
sufficient evidence to take any part of his case to a jury?**

Problem XI-13. Chamberlain was killed while working for a railroad.
His estate brought an action to recover damages for his death. The
federal district court held that the estate did not meet its burden of
producing sufficient evidence of negligence to warrant submitting the
case to the jury. The Court of Appeals reversed. The Supreme Court
agrees to review the case. **Should the Supreme Court find that the
burden of production was satisfied based on the following facts?**
(Chamberlain is referred to as "deceased"; the estate is referred to as "the
respondent".)

> That part of the yard in which the accident occurred contained a lead
> track and a large number of switching tracks branching from it. The
> lead track crossed a "hump," and the work of car distribution
> consisted of pushing a train of cars by means of a locomotive to the
> top of the "hump," and then allowing the cars, in separate strings, to
> descend by gravity, under the control of hand brakes, to their
> respective destinations in the various branch tracks. Deceased had
> charge of a string of two gondola cars, which he was piloting to
> branch track 14. Immediately ahead of him was a string of seven
> cars, and behind him a string of nine cars, both also destined for
> track 14. Soon after the cars ridden by deceased had passed to track
> 14, deceased's body was found on that track some distance beyond
> the switch. He evidently had fallen onto the track and been run over
> by a car or cars.

> The case for respondent rests wholly upon the claim that the fall of
> deceased was caused by a violent collision of the string of nine cars
> with the string ridden by deceased. Three employees, riding the
> nine-car string, testified positively that no such collision occurred.
> They were corroborated by every other employee in a position to see,
> all testifying that there was no contact between the nine-car string
> and that of the deceased. The testimony of these witnesses, if
> believed, established beyond doubt that there was no collision
> between these two strings of cars, and that the nine-car string
> contributed in no way to the accident. The only witness who testified
> for respondent was one Bainbridge; and it is upon his testimony
> alone that respondent's right to recover is sought to be upheld. This
> testimony is concisely stated, in its most favorable light for
> respondent, in the prevailing opinion of the court of appeals below by
> Judge Learned Hand, as follows:

> The plaintiff's only witness to the event, one Bainbridge, then
> employed by the railroad, stood close to the yardmaster's office, near
> the 'hump.' He professed to have paid little attention to what went
> on, but he did see the deceased riding at the rear of his cars, whose

speed when they passed him he took to be about eight or ten miles per hour. Shortly thereafter a second string passed which was shunted into another track and this was followed by the nine, which, according to the plaintiff's theory, collided with the deceased's. After the nine cars had passed at a somewhat greater speed than the deceased's, Bainbridge paid no more attention to either string for a while, but looked again when the deceased, who was still standing in his place, had passed the switch and onto the sorting track [no. 14] where he was bound. At that time his speed had been checked to about three miles, but the speed of the following nine cars had increased. They were just passing the switch, about four or five cars behind the deceased. Bainbridge looked away again and soon heard what he described as a 'loud crash,' not however an unusual event in a switching yard. Apparently this did not cause him at once to turn, but he did so shortly thereafter, and saw the two strings together, still moving, and the deceased no longer in sight. Later still his attention was attracted by shouts and he went to the spot and saw the deceased between the rails. Until he left to go to the accident, he had stood fifty feet to the north of the track where the accident happened, and about nine hundred feet from where the body was found.

. . . It is correctly pointed out . . . that Bainbridge was in no position to see whether the two strings of cars were actually together; that Bainbridge repeatedly said he was paying no particular attention; and that his position was . . . 900 feet from the place where the body was found and less than 50 feet from the side of the track in question.

Problem XI-14. Randy was convicted of first-degree murder for killing Frank during a robbery at the gas station where Frank worked. The jurisdiction does not have a felony murder rule, and Randy was convicted of premeditated and deliberate killing. At trial Bernice testified that she saw Randy running away from the gas station restroom just as she pulled into the station, that she looked for Frank to pay him for the gas she had pumped, and that she eventually found him lying on the floor of the restroom dead from three gunshot wounds. When Randy was arrested a day later, he had in his possession a credit card belonging to Frank. After his arrest Randy signed a statement—which was admitted at trial— saying that he saw Frank entering the gas station restroom with an oversized wallet in his back pocket; that he pulled a .22 caliber pistol from his coat pocket, followed Frank into the restroom and demanded Frank's wallet; that Frank grabbed the gun; that a struggle ensued; and that the gun fired three times—by accident—during the struggle. The state's theory is that Randy encountered Frank outside the restroom, "marched" Frank into the restroom, and shot him there "execution style." **How should an appellate court rule on Randy's claim that there was insufficient evidence to convict him beyond a reasonable doubt of**

first-degree (i.e., premeditated and deliberate) murder? Would it matter if only one shot had been fired? If there was no bullet damage on the floor but only on the wall opposite the entrance to the restroom? If the shooting occurred at the station's closing time, the station office was locked when the police arrived, and there was testimony that Frank's procedure for closing the station was to lock up the office, then clean up and lock the restroom, then shut down the pumps and get in his car and go home? What standard should the appellate court use in deciding whether there was sufficient proof to convict Randy beyond a reasonable doubt? How should it handle the possibility that the same evidence might support different inferences, some suggesting premeditation and deliberation, others suggesting accident? Given the level of control an appellate court is properly able to exercise over the sufficiency of the evidence in criminal cases, how important is it that the jury understand what "proof beyond a reasonable doubt" means?

II. SHORTCUTS TO PROOF

Usually parties satisfy their burdens of production and persuasion— or attempt to do so—by introducing testimony, documents or other evidence. But not always. Sometimes the law recognizes shortcuts that *permit* the trier to find a fact—or in some situations *require* the trier to find the fact—even though no evidence, or otherwise insufficient evidence, has been admitted. This section discusses three such shortcuts: stipulations and judicial admissions, judicial notice, and presumptions.

A. STIPULATIONS AND JUDICIAL ADMISSIONS

In almost every trial, there are some facts on which the parties agree. There may, for example, be no dispute that a particular document is the actual, original letter that one party sent to the other (thus establishing that the letter is "authentic" and the "best evidence," as required by FREs 901 and 1002); or that the defendant owns a 2013 green Subaru Outback station wagon; or that a witness is qualified to offer expert opinions; or that November 22, 1963 was a Friday. When such agreement exists, the parties can save time by "stipulating" to a particular fact in lieu of requiring the burden-bearing party to produce evidence to prove it. Going even further, a party can make a "judicial admission" that concedes an entire element of a cause of action or defense asserted by the opposition, removing the issue from controversy and requiring the trier of fact to assume that the element has been proven. In a contract action, for example, Defendant may judicially admit most of Plaintiff's claims—that Plaintiff and Agent entered into a contract that, by its terms, imposed obligations on Defendant; that Defendant did not fulfill these obligations; and that Plaintiff was damaged in the amount of $1,000,000—and dispute only Plaintiff's allegations that Agent had authority to bind Defendant, and that Plaintiff took appropriate steps to mitigate damages.

Sometimes parties stipulate to the testimony a witness would give if called and asked particular questions, or to the contents or characteristics of real evidence that might have been introduced.[28] For example, they might stipulate that "if Witness had been called to the stand, he would have testified that he saw the defendant eat a hamburger in the cafeteria of the James Madison High School in Queens County, New York City, at about 12:30 p.m. on Friday, November 13, 2012"; or that "if the jurors had viewed the defendant's car on February 21, 2010, they would have observed a red 2009 Ford Focus with Kansas license number BXT-972, and with a dented left front fender." These are stipulations to *evidence* rather than to *facts*. When such a stipulation is made, the parties retain the right to object to the stipulated evidence under applicable rules, to attack the evidence as insufficient or unbelievable and to introduce contrary evidence. A prosecutor who stipulates that a witness would testify that he saw the defendant on November 13 has not agreed that the Witness is telling the truth; a plaintiff who stipulates that defendant's car was dented on February 21, has not conceded that this fact is relevant or, if relevant, is sufficient to establish any fact of controversy. If stipulated evidence is admitted, the jury will be instructed to treat it as actual testimony or real evidence and to draw whatever inferences it deems appropriate. As with actual evidence, the jurors may choose to disregard the stipulated evidence entirely because they find it incredible, inconsistent with other evidence or otherwise unreliable.

On other occasions, the parties stipulate to the underlying fact itself: that "the defendant was present at James Madison High School, Queens County, New York City, on Friday, November 13, 2012, at about 12:30 p.m.," or that "on February 21, 2013, a red 2012 Ford Focus with Kansas license number BXT-972 was parked at 1312 Jackson Street in Wichita, between the hours of 8:30 and 11:30 a.m." This kind of stipulation serves as an "evidentiary admission" by both sides that the fact is true. Parties stipulating to a fact may not introduce evidence to contradict the fact or dispute its existence in argument to the jury, although they may argue about its implications—or even, about exactly what has been conceded. A stipulation to a fact is a sufficient basis for the trier of fact to find that the

---

[28] See, e.g., United States v. Mezzanatto, 513 U.S. 196, 203 (1995) (evidentiary stipulations in which parties "agree in writing to the admission of otherwise objectionable evidence, either in exchange for stipulations from opposing counsel or for other strategic purposes" are "a valuable and integral part of everyday trial practice" that are contemplated by the Federal Rules of Civil and of Criminal Procedure and "routinely honored by trial judges"); Diaz v. United States, 223 U.S. 442, 451 (1912) (a court may dispense with the right to confrontation and hearsay rule, "where, by the consent of the accused, the prosecution is permitted to read in evidence the testimony of an absent witness, given in some prior proceeding[,] or a statement of what such a witness would testify, if present, as embodied in an agreement made to avoid a continuance or to dispense with the presence of the witness[,] or the deposition of such a witness, taken within or without the jurisdiction" (citations omitted)).

fact has been proven by any burden of persuasion, but the trier is not required to do so. It may choose to ignore the stipulated fact if, for example, it is inconsistent with other evidence in the case.

Alternatively, a party against whom evidence otherwise would be presented may make a "judicial admission." For example, he may admit that he is a New York resident, or the owner of the car that struck the plaintiff, or that he failed to exercise due care at the time of an accident. Judicial admissions are more powerful than stipulations. Stipulations may concede only a *particular fact* from which a *fact of consequence* might be inferred (e.g., that the defendant owns a yellow shirt), while judicial admissions concedes the fact of consequence itself (e.g., that the defendant is the yellow-shirted man who killed the victim—thus admitting the "identity" and "act" elements of the crime and leaving open only the issues of mental state and self-defense). In addition, if a judicial admission is accepted, its effects are more far reaching. A stipulation may be contradicted by other evidence, or simply disbelieved by the trier of fact, but a judicial admission takes the issue away from the trier entirely, dispensing with the need for proof, and conclusively validating that portion of the claim for purposes of the lawsuit.

You might think that the party with the burden of proving a fact would always want the other party to stipulate to it—or better yet, to judicially admit it. Often, however, it is the party conceding the point that most wants the stipulation or judicial admission. For example, a murder defendant may offer to stipulate to the cause of the victim's death, or to judicially admit that an unnatural death occurred, in order to keep the jury from hearing a pathologist's graphic description of the violent cause of death, or viewing gruesome photographs of the body. The prosecutor, however, may resist the stipulation or admission and insist on presenting the evidence, hoping to achieve the very effect on the jury that the defendant wants to avoid.

You also might assume that if a stipulation or judicial admission is offered, the trial judge will routinely accept it in lieu of time-consuming evidence—even if the burden-bearing party objects. Our commitment to adversarial proceedings is so strong, however, that often the burden-bearing party, rather than the court, determines whether the stipulation or admission will be accepted. Of course, if *both* parties agree to the stipulation or admission, the court almost always goes along (although the judge isn't required to do so).[29] But if the burden-bearing party *refuses* to accept the proposed shortcut, the court will usually reject the proposal and allow the burden-bearing party to prove its case as it pleases, unless the party proposing the shortcut offers a very good reason

---

[29] See, e.g., United States v. James, 987 F.2d 648 (9th Cir. 1993) (rejecting an agreed to judicial admission removing an element of the crime from the case); Romero v. State, 493 S.W.2d 206 (Tex. Crim. App.1973) (refusing to accept the parties' stipulation to the admissibility of polygraph evidence).

to require its use. This is because a party seeking to introduce a particular item of evidence is presumptively entitled to every legitimate advantage that the evidence can provide, including in Wigmore's words, the "legitimate moral force of [the] evidence"—that is, the contribution the evidence makes to a complete and emotionally compelling narrative description of what actually happened.[30] In our homicide case, for example, the prosecution is entitled not only to show that a killing occurred and how it occurred (especially if the way it was committed suggests something about who may have committed it, and why), but also to convey a sense of why the event was important to the community—and why the community would want to convict and punish the perpetrator of any crime that occurred.[31] Accordingly, as Justice Souter explained in *Old Chief v. United States*,[32] a case we discuss in detail in Chapter Three,[33] much of the "gut" impact of evidence that a stipulation would neutralize counts as lost probative force, not as "unfair prejudice":

> [T]he accepted rule that the prosecution is entitled to prove its case free from any defendant's option to stipulate the evidence away rests on good sense. A syllogism is not a story, and a naked [stipulated] proposition in a courtroom may be no match for the robust evidence that would be used to prove it. People who hear a story interrupted by gaps of abstraction may be puzzled at the missing chapters, and jurors asked to rest a momentous decision on the story's truth can feel put upon at being asked to take responsibility knowing that more could be said than they have heard. A convincing tale can be told with economy, but when economy becomes a break in the natural sequence of narrative evidence, an assurance that the missing link is really there is never more than second best.[34]

---

[30] Wigmore § 2591, at 589.

[31] See, e.g., United States v. Sampol, 636 F.2d 621 (D.C.Cir. 1980) (in a prosecution for a political assassination, the trial court properly rejected the defendants' offer to stipulate that government witnesses would establish that the cause of the victim's death was wounds from an exploding bomb). In the "regret matrix" terms introduced in Chapter Three, Section II.B., pp. 249–255, the government is entitled to present evidence that will cause the jury to anticipate feeling a significant amount of regret if it erroneously acquits a guilty defendant (if not as *much* regret as if it erroneously convicts an innocent defendant).

[32] 519 U.S. 172 (1997).

[33] See Chapter Three, Section I.I., pp. 234–240, and Section IV, pp. 264–267.

[34] 519 U.S. at 189. The more of the burden-bearing party's case to which the other party offers to stipulate, the greater is the stipulation's adverse impact on the burden-bearing party's ability to tell a comprehensive and convincing story and, thus, the less likely a court is to force the stipulation. The rule against compelled stipulations is stronger in criminal than in civil cases. A civil defendant's answer can admit as little or as much of the plaintiff's complaint as the defendant chooses, but a criminal defendant can plead only "guilty" or "not guilty." The latter plea creates the expectation that the trial will cover all the elements. Moreover, the elements of criminal offenses typically parallel the elements of a story or narrative to a greater extent than the elements of many civil actions. See Nancy Pennington & Reid Hastie, Evidence Evaluation in Complex Decision Making, 51 J. Personality & Soc. Psychol. 243 (1986). Telling a convincing story about *any* of the elements of an offense will often require the prosecution to tell a story encompassing *all* of the elements.

Of course, if the burden-bearing party anticipates a ruling that the probative weight of the proffered evidence is substantially outweighed by its unfair prejudice, that party may feel compelled to accept the offered stipulation or admission to avoid ending up with *no* evidence—or insufficient evidence—on the point. Occasionally, moreover, the court may insist that the stipulation or admission be accepted because the shortcut would achieve most of the probative value of the evidence in question, including its valid narrative and emotive contributions, while avoiding most or all of its prejudicial effect. In other words, the court may conclude that the prejudicial impact that the shortcut avoids substantially outweighs the probative value that the shortcut sacrifices. Or, put still another way, in balancing probative value against prejudice, the trial judge should discount the former by the extent to which it can be obtained through a stipulation or other non-, or less, prejudicial device. As Justice Souter said in *Old Chief*, in concluding under the limited circumstances of the case that a prosecutor was obliged to accept a defendant's offer to stipulate:

> If an alternative [method of establishing a fact] were found to have substantially the same or greater probative value but a lower danger of unfair prejudice [than the evidence offered], sound judicial discretion would discount the value of the item . . . offered and exclude it if its discounted probative value were substantially outweighed by unfairly prejudicial risk.[35]

Sometimes, especially in civil cases, judicial admissions or stipulations emerge from the pleadings or from pretrial discovery. For example, a defendant's answer may admit to particular facts or elements of the cause of action, or a party to discovery may respond affirmatively to a request for an admission under Fed. R. Civ. P. 36, or the parties may distill a witness's deposition into an agreed stipulation to the testimony the witness would give if called. On other occasions—particularly in long trials or under pressure from the trial judge—the parties will meet just before trial or while the trial is in recess to work out the precise language of stipulations and admissions to be offered when the trial convenes or resumes. On still other occasions, the offer to stipulate or admit will be made in the midst of trial. This last procedure is likely to be more disruptive and less effective because it forces a halt to proceedings while the parties attempt to agree on language that precisely describes what is being stipulated to or admitted. Typically, unless the party offering the shortcut has been taken by surprise or is ill-prepared, a mid-trial offer to stipulate or admit is not intended to achieve an agreement but rather to bolster an objection to evidence on grounds of excessive prejudice, or to signal to the trier of fact that an issue is not contested

---

[35] 519 U.S. at 182–83.

PROBLEMS

Problem XI-15. Smith sues Jones for injuries suffered in a hit and run accident. Smith claims that Jones, driving a 1973 Ford Falcon, ran a red light, crashed into Smith's car, then abandoned the jalopy, hailed a taxi cab and fled. Jones denies he was the driver of the jalopy and claims that, in any event, it was Smith who ran the red light. Smith has subpoenaed Doe, who had told Smith's investigator that she saw a man with jet black hair leave the jalopy and hail a cab moments after the accident. (Jones has black hair.) Doe, however, was out of the country during the period set aside for depositions in the case, and more recently has told Smith's investigator (when he served the subpoena) that she is too busy to spend any time at the courthouse and will be extremely angry if forced to do so. Jones—who also interviewed Doe and found her to be a powerful witness against Jones—offers to stipulate that, "if called as a witness, Jane Doe would testify that she was at the intersection where the accident occurred at the time it occurred, and that she saw a black-haired man leave the Ford Falcon moments after the accident and flee the scene in a taxi." **As Smith's lawyer, would you advise Smith to accept the stipulation? What factors would influence your decision? Would you seek to rewrite the stipulation in any way? Would the stipulation bar Jones from calling Roe to testify that he was at the intersection when the accident occurred and that he saw a red-haired man leave the jalopy and hail a taxi? How can Smith permit Jones to keep Doe off the stand, and in the process, keep Roe off the stand as well? Under what circumstances would using such a device be in Smith's interest? Under what circumstances would using such a device be in Jones's interest? If Jones were to stipulate that a black-haired man was seen leaving the jalopy and hailing a cab, would that prevent him as a matter of law from presenting Roe's testimony?**

Problem XI-16. Thora Prometheus is on trial for intentionally setting fire to her ex-husband's Airstream mobile home. She claims she was elsewhere when the fire started, and her attorney believes she would make a convincing witness. The problem is that Prometheus has four prior convictions: one, ten years ago, for stealing cheap heirlooms from her invalid 87-year-old grandmother; two, seven years ago, for offering to share a cocaine cigarette with an elementary school student; and one, five years ago, for intentionally setting fire to the contents of a garbage can in the rectory of the historic-landmark church she had regularly attended since she was a child. The law of the jurisdiction permits prosecutors to inform the jury of the basic facts underlying prior convictions if the convictions are admissible for impeachment purposes. Defense counsel considers making the following stipulation: "The state and the defendant stipulate that the defendant, Thora Prometheus, was convicted ten years ago of petty larceny; seven years ago for possession of a small amount of cocaine and attempted contributing to the delinquency of a minor; and five years ago of fourth-degree arson." **As defense counsel, would you propose the stipulation? What factors would bear on your decision? What alternatives to this stipulation would you consider before proposing it? As prosecutor, would you accept the stipulation if defense counsel offered it? What factors would bear on your decision? Would it matter if you thought that declining the stipulation would probably cause Prometheus to refrain from testifying? How might you seek to amend the stipulation before accepting it? As trial judge, if defense counsel proposed the stipulation and the prosecutor refused to accept it, would you compel the prosecutor (on motion by defense counsel) to accept it? What factors are relevant to your decision? Would your answers to any of these questions change if the criminal record described above belonged not to Prometheus but to her star witness, Hera Hercules, who plans to testify that at the time the fire started, she and Prometheus were at Zeno Diner discussing politics over liver and onions?**

B. JUDICIAL NOTICE

1. Ordinary Judicial Notice of "Adjudicative" Facts

Suppose a party has the burden of proving a fact that is virtually beyond dispute—for example, that November 22, 1963 fell on a Friday. And suppose that the opposing party refuses to stipulate to the fact, perhaps in order to put the burden-bearing party to the trouble of proving it by locating a lay witness who remembers that November 22, 1963 was a Friday, or by presenting an historian or other expert witness, or producing documentary evidence that is not inadmissible hearsay. Should not the judge have an evidentiary tool that gives her the power to accept such a fact as true without evidence of any sort, even over objection?

There is such a tool. In lieu of requiring admissible evidence to prove an incontestable fact, the judge may "take judicial notice" of it. That means that the judge accepts the fact as true and requires (or, in criminal cases, *permits*) the jury to do the same. A judge may take judicial notice of a fact based on her own knowledge of its indisputable truth; for example, she might clearly remember that November 22, 1963 was a Friday and have confirmed her memory by looking at an old diary, or she may know that a crime committed at a certain location was within the jurisdiction of the court. Or she may do so based on a proffer of admissible evidence that could be produced to prove it (for example, the front page of a November 22, 1963 newspaper that identifies the day as

Friday[36]), or based on a reference tool that is itself inadmissible but accurately reflects what other admissible evidence would show (for example, a newspaper article from November 22, 2003, describing what happened on that date forty years earlier). Facts commonly noticed include days and dates verified by calendars, chemical or physical properties (e.g., that the formula for table salt is NaCl, or that diamond is the hardest known mineral), the natural light available at particular times (the time of sunrise, sunset, moonrise or moonset on particular days) and geographic locations (e.g., that Albuquerque, New Mexico, is in Bernalillo County, and Bernalillo, New Mexico, is in Sandoval County), but courts have also judicially noticed such facts as the comparative windiness of particular neighborhoods in San Francisco, the occasional dangerousness of mules, the ability of television sets to administer lethal voltages of electricity, the name of the office of the head of government of India, the association of colors with flavors of ice cream, and the traditional features of snow men.[37]

Under the Federal Rules of Evidence, judicial notice is governed by FRE 201, which states:

(a) Scope. This rule governs judicial notice of an adjudicative fact only, not a legislative fact.

(b) Kinds of Facts that May Be Judicially Noticed. The court may judicially notice a fact that is not subject to reasonable dispute because it:

(1) is generally known within the trial court's territorial jurisdiction; or

(2) can be accurately and readily determined from sources whose accuracy cannot reasonably be questioned.

(c) Taking Notice. The court:

(1) may take judicial notice on its own; or

(2) must take judicial notice if a party requests it and the court is supplied with the necessary information.

(d) Timing. The court may take judicial notice at any stage of the proceeding.

(e) Opportunity to Be Heard. On timely request, a party is entitled to be heard on the propriety of taking judicial notice and the nature of the fact to be noticed. If the court takes judicial notice

---

[36] Why is this document not inadmissible hearsay? See FRE 803(16); Chapter Six, Section III.C.1.h, pp. 692, 696. What would it take to authenticate the newspaper? See FRE 902(6); Chapter Ten, Section II., pp. 1275–1292. And why might a trial judge have a personal recollection that November 22, 1963 was a Friday?

[37] See, e.g., Dippin' Dots, Inc. v. Frosty Bites Distribution, LLC, 369 F.3d 1197 (11th Cir. 2004); Eden Toys, Inc. v. Marshall Field & Co., 675 F.2d 498 (2d Cir. 1982).

before notifying a party, the party, on request, is still entitled to be heard.

(f) Instructing the Jury.   In a civil case, the court must instruct the jury to accept the noticed fact as conclusive.   In a criminal case, the court must instruct the jury that it may or may not accept the noticed fact as conclusive.

FRE 201 is restricted by its own terms to judicial notice of "an adjudicative fact"—facts pertaining specifically to matters at issue in the litigation of the type we have been discussing thus far.   The other category of facts—"legislative facts"—is discussed in the next subsection.

FRE 201 strikes a balance between competing views about the desirability of judicial notice. Throughout the twentieth century and even before, judicial notice enthusiasts, led by Thayer, Wigmore and Kenneth Culp Davis, advocated wider reliance on this procedure—"an instrument of a usefulness hitherto unimagined by judges"[38]—to shorten and simplify trials, and to keep jurors from inadvertently reaching improbable conclusions or intentionally nullifying the law. These authors argued that judges should have discretion to judicially notice adjudicative facts that are merely *unlikely* to be challenged, as well as those that are entirely beyond dispute—or at least that judges should be able accept such facts as true unless the opposing party proves the contrary. On the other side, judicial-notice skeptics—led by Professors Morgan and Schwartz—argued that judicial notice threatens our adversarial commitment to resolving disputes based on evidence that is presented and tested in public and evaluated by jurors, rather than on information known privately to judges. They also have argued that judicial notice undermines the hearsay rule (the main reason why facts that are almost certainly true are sometimes difficult to prove), as well as the authentication and personal knowledge rules.   These authors argued that judicial notice should be limited to "indisputable" facts, or abandoned altogether.[39]

We are not entirely persuaded by the arguments on either side of this debate.   An inflexible commitment to adversarial testing and jury

---

[38]   Wigmore § 2583, at 585 (3d ed. 1940). See also James B. Thayer, A Preliminary Treatise on Evidence at the Common Law 309 (1898); Kenneth Culp Davis, Judicial Notice, 1969 L. & Soc. Order 513, 513–16 (advocating liberal use of judicial notice with a caveat that "convenience should always yield to the requirement of procedural fairness that parties should have [an] opportunity to meet in the appropriate fashion all facts that influence the disposition of the case").

[39]   See, e.g., Edmund M. Morgan, Judicial Notice, 57 Harv. L. Rev. 269 (1944); Warren F. Schwartz, A Suggestion for the Demise of Judicial Notice of "Judicial Facts", 45 Tex. L. Rev. 1212 (1967). Proponents of the Thayer-Wigmore-Davis approach to judicial notice qualified their broader view of what facts could be judicially noticed with a weaker view of the effect of judicial notice: the jury would be invited, but not required, to accept the judicially noticed fact as true, and the opposing party could present contrary evidence on the subject.   Proponents of the Morgan-Schwartz view advocated the opposite mixture of a narrow scope for judicial notice (only indisputable facts), but a more powerful effect (the jury would be required to accept the fact as true, and no contrary evidence could be offered).

consideration of all factual propositions in litigation would paralyze the judicial system. Many factual issues—even critical one—are resolved informally in motion practice. And even in formal proceedings, in ruling on objections, judges routinely exercise the authority granted by FRE 104(a) to make factual findings on the basis of inadmissible evidence or the judge's own knowledge.

More important, judges and jurors routinely make the most common factual judgments of all—so-called "evaluative inferences"—by informally "noticing" facts. Consider a case in which the central question is what caused an apartment building to burn down. Suppose the evidence in its entirety is that: (1) six months before the fire, the defendant purchased a fire insurance policy entitling him to recover $10 million if the building— which was worth $3 million—burned down accidentally; (2) an hour before the fire broke out in the building, the defendant was seen entering it with a five gallon container marked "gasoline" and a box of matches; and (3) the defendant swears he had nothing to do with the fire. This evidence is sufficient to support a jury decision—even by proof beyond a reasonable doubt—that the defendant set fire to the building. Yet, the jury could not possibly reach that decision without relying on numerous facts that were not formally proved by adversarially tested, admissible evidence: that containers marked with the word "gasoline" often contain that substance; that people rarely have reason to carry large quantities of gasoline into residential buildings; that when a match is struck and touched to gasoline, it usually starts a fire; that a $10 million "fire insurance policy on a house" entitles the insured individual to recover $10 million if the structure is accidentally destroyed by fire, no matter how recently the insured began paying premiums on the insurance policy; that insuring a building worth $3 million for $10 million dollars is unusual; that having $10 million provides access to advantages that most people want but cannot secure if they have substantially less money; that a witness with a substantial pecuniary or penal interest in the outcome of a lawsuit may lie; and so forth.[40] In other words, in order to understand and weigh the evidence, jurors necessarily take "jury notice" of an infinite variety of "evaluative facts" on which no evidence was—or realistically could be—introduced. This "use of non-evidence facts to appraise or assess the adjudicative facts of the case" is so basic and pervasive that FRE 201's drafters thought the matter inappropriate for formal regulation.[41]

In order to resolve lawsuits, therefore, courts routinely rely on facts that have not been proven with admissible evidence. They could not realistically do otherwise. But when courts do rely on unproven facts, it

---

[40] For a slightly different but consistent perspective on this issue, see our discussions of "conditional relevance," Chapter Two, Section III.E.3., pp. 179–181, and Chapter Three, Section I.E., pp. 223–228.

[41] See Advisory Committee Note to FRE 201.

is usually because the noticed facts are not controversial. Because even the most ardent supporters of judicial notice insist that this condition be met, the claim of opponents of judicial notice that it seriously threatens our adversarial system seems exaggerated.[42]

The skeptics' fear that judicial notice will be used to circumvent the hearsay rule is also overdrawn. Specific hearsay exceptions, such as those codified as FREs 803(6)-(23)[43] and the catchall exception codified in FRE 807, are likely to cover most matters susceptible to judicial notice. Indeed, these exceptions often have the same justification as judicial notice—that things almost "everybody knows" or that are almost certain to be true are reliable enough to be accepted at face value without following the usual rules. Moreover, judges can satisfy most of the fairness concerns about judicial notice by letting the opposing party be heard after being notified of the judge's intention to take judicial notice. This procedure reallocates the burden of production, but it makes good sense to place that burden on the party that seeks to challenge facts that very likely are true, in order to avoid formal proof in cases in which taking evidence is likely to be a waste of time and effort.

But it also is important not to oversell the virtues of judicial notice. On the one hand, if it is limited to genuinely incontrovertible facts, other procedures that are more compatible with adversarial fact-finding will usually be available. These include requests for admission, summary judgment, stipulations, judicial admissions—or spending a few moments hearing evidence, often admitted under the hearsay exceptions noted above. Indeed, parties often seek judicial notice to fill holes in their proof due to inadvertent failures to offer easily accessible evidence when they presented their case.[44] If, however, judicial notice is liberalized to cover facts that are more controversial and more difficult to prove, the dangers the skeptics point to become more worrisome. Moreover, when judicial notice is used for other-than-indisputable facts, there is a substantial risk of collateral litigation over the propriety of taking notice, which undercuts

---

[42] We are still concerned solely with judicial notice of "adjudicative facts." "Legislative facts" present a different set of considerations, which we discuss in the next subsection.

[43] The exceptions in FRE 803(6)-(23) cover such things as business records, government and market reports, vital statistics, marriage, baptismal and family records, reputation concerning personal and family history, documents affecting interests in property and boundaries, and various court records. FRE 807 covers other hearsay having "equivalent circumstantial guarantees of trustworthiness." See Chapter Six.

[44] Compare, e.g., McGinest v. GTE Service Corp., 360 F.3d 1103 (9th Cir. 2004) (appellate court may decline to take judicial notice of a fact a party easily could have established through evidence at trial), with, e.g., Capital Indemnity Corp. v. Russellville Steel Co., 367 F.3d 831 (8th Cir. 2004) (appellate court cures gap in trial record relating to diversity jurisdiction by taking judicial notice of how—and thus, by inference, where—insurance companies conduct their business), with, e.g., Central Green Co. v. United States, 531 U.S. 425, 434 (2001) ("The Government has asked us to take judicial notice of certain basic facts about the Friant Division of the Central Valley Project and about the waters flowing through that division and, more particularly, through the Madera Canal. Although petitioner will have an opportunity to challenge those details on remand, we accept them for purposes of this opinion.").

the advantages in time and trouble that justify using the shortcut in the first place.

Given these competing considerations, we conclude that a sensible set of common-law evidence rules would: (1) include a modest judicial notice mechanism for the occasional fact that, while formally in dispute, nonetheless is incontrovertible, or nearly so; (2) provide a reasonable opportunity for any party that opposes this procedure to show that judicial notice is inappropriate; and (3) make that opportunity available in most cases *before the fact*, while limiting costly *after-the-fact* procedures to unusual instances when fairness demands them. Such a mechanism would rarely remove from contention entire issues, or elements of causes of action or defenses. It would generally apply only to discrete facts that supply isolated building blocks for elements of claims, and it would be used especially sparingly over a defendant's objection in a criminal case, in consideration of the accused's constitutional right to trial by jury. The judicial notice rule we describe is, in essence, FRE 201. We believe it strikes the right balance.

FRE 201 is limited to judicial notice of adjudicative facts that are "not subject to reasonable dispute" because they either (1) are "generally known within the territorial jurisdiction of the trial court" (FRE 201(b)(1)) or (2) can be "accurately and readily determined from sources whose accuracy cannot reasonably be questioned" (FRE 201(b)(2)). The rule does not require that noticed facts be indisputable, but it does restrict the shortcut to two categories of noncontroversial facts that in all probability could be proved with admissible evidence. The first category encompasses facts that are so well-known in the community the court serves that proving them with evidence would waste time and contribute little or nothing to the acceptability of the verdict—facts that are "self-evident truths that no reasonable person could question."[45] It is not sufficient (nor is it necessary) that the judge herself have personal knowledge of the fact in question. Instead, the fact must be generally known to reasonably well-informed people in the community *and* must not be subject to reasonable dispute. FRE 201's drafters rejected a proposal to permit judicial notice of *all*, as opposed to *reasonably indisputable*, "propositions of generalized knowledge." Under FRE 201 as enacted, a court may not take judicial notice that most New Yorkers are rude, or that the University of Michigan has the best basketball team in the country—even if these propositions are universally accepted in a given jurisdiction—because they are nonetheless subject to reasonable dispute.

---

[45] Hardy v. Johns-Manville Sales Corp., 681 F.2d 334, 337 (5th Cir. 1982). Compare, e.g., United States v. Evans, 404 F.3d 227 (4th Cir. 2005) (taking judicial notice of fact that memories tend to fade over time) with United States v. Hoyts Cinemas Corp., 380 F.3d 558 (1st Cir. 2004) (in a suit for discrimination based on disability, the district court should not have taken judicial notice that movie patrons generally prefer to sit in the middle and back of the theater, not the front).

The second category includes facts that, although not generally known, are verifiable by consulting obviously reliable sources.[46] "Representative authoritative sources for verification include such reference materials as historical works, science and art books, language and medical journals and dictionaries, calendars, encyclopedias, commercial lists and directories, maps and charts, statutes and legislative reports."[47] Under this authority, a court may take judicial notice of: the fact that cocaine is derived from coca leaves; the chemical composition of clean air; the current membership of the United States Supreme Court; the use of radar to measure speed; the prime interest rate on June 17, 2013; the fact that January 20, 2013 was a Sunday; the county in which Albuquerque, New Mexico is located; the fact that Interstate Highways 25 and 40 intersect there; and so forth.

Under FRE 201(f), the effect of judicial notice differs in civil and criminal cases. In civil cases, judicial notice conclusively establishes the fact noticed, and the jury is instructed to accept that fact as true. In criminal cases (whether the fact noticed benefits the state or the defendant), the jury is instructed that it *may* accept a judicially noticed fact as conclusively proven, but that it need not do so. The limited effect of judicial notice in criminal cases reflects both the defendant's constitutional right to a jury trial—which includes the jury's power to acquit in the face of the evidence—and the defendant's constitutional right to confront the evidence offered against her, and to require the government to prove every element of the offense beyond a reasonable doubt. It also reflects our especially strong commitment to adversarial

---

[46] See, e.g., Daubert v. Merrell Dow Pharmaceuticals, Inc., 509 U.S. 579, 592 n.11 (1993) ("[T]heories that are so firmly established as to have attained the status of scientific law, such as the laws of thermodynamics, properly are subject to judicial notice under Federal Rule of Evidence 201.")

[47] Glen Weissenberger & James J. Duane, Federal Rules of Evidence: Rules, Legislative History, Commentary and Authority 69 (6th ed. 2009). Courts have struggled recently over whether sites on the World Wide Web where individuals or companies have posted information about themselves qualify as highly reliable sources. Compare O'Toole v. Northrop Grumman Corp., 499 F.3d 1218 (10th Cir. 2007) (citing cases) (the trial court abused its discretion in denying plaintiff's request for judicial notice of historical earnings by defendant company's retirement fund, as posted on the defendant's website) with Victaulic Co. v. Tieman, 499 F.3d 227, 236 (3d Cir. 2007) (in granting relief for plaintiffs, the district court abused its discretion in judicially noticing information on the defendant's website, including because websites are marketing tools that may be "full of puffery that no one should take a face value"). As these examples suggest, a case-by-case assessment of the likely (in)contestability of the information explains most decisions. Another recurring issue is a court's power to take judicial notice of actions of the same court in another case, or of a different court or public agency in another matter. The emerging rule is that courts may judicially notice that some official action by a court or agency *occurred* (e.g., that on a particular day a suit was filed, a trial commenced or a court resolved the dispute in favor of one party or the other), but, absent some other basis for judicial notice, the court may not notice, for their truth, the *facts the other court or agency found* as a basis for its action. See Kushner v. Beverly Enterprises, Inc., 317 F.3d 820 (8th Cir. 2003); Wyatt v. Terhune, 315 F.3d 1108 (9th Cir.), cert. denied 540 U.S. 810 (2003). Cf. United States v. Daychild, 357 F.3d 1082 (9th Cir. 2004) (based on the district court's familiarity with court records, it properly took judicial notice of the procedures used in the court to return and process indictments).

proceedings in criminal cases, and to the value of criminal-trial verdicts that reflect community beliefs.[48]

Under FRE 201(c), and (d), a judge *may* take judicial notice at any time, from the filing of the complaint to the conclusion of all appeals, even when not asked to do so. Under FRE 201(c)(1), a judge *must* take judicial notice after being asked to do so and being shown that the fact qualifies under FRE 201(a) and (b). In keeping with the goal of shortening proceedings, a party seeking judicial notice may do so orally and informally, during trial or on appeal (e.g., by showing the judge a book or calendar), as well as in a written motion or brief filed before, during or after trial, or on appeal. Allowing judicial notice of adjudicative facts on appeal in civil cases (e.g., in support of a claim that the evidence is sufficient to support the jury's verdict) promotes the goal of avoiding extended evidentiary proceedings—including futile remands for formal proof of essentially incontestable facts. This rational does not appear to hold for criminal cases, however, given FRE 201(g)'s recognition that even incontestable factual issues going to guilt or innocence may not be taken away from the jury.[49]

---

[48] The Advisory Committee Note to the original draft of what is now FRE 201(f) states that "there is to be no evidence before the jury in disproof [of judicially noticed facts] in civil cases," but that "[c]riminal cases are treated somewhat differently." This suggests that the rule does not bar the accused "from offering evidence rebutting the fact noticed." Christopher B. Mueller & Laird C. Kirkpatrick, Evidence § 2.11, at 92 & n.5 (3d ed. 2003) (citing United States v. Garland, 991 F.2d 328, 333 (6th Cir. 1993) (dicta))). See also Paul C. Giannelli, Understanding Evidence 679 & n.85 (2009) (Rule 201(g)'s (since recodified as Rule 201(f)'s) treatment of jury instructions in criminal cases "could be interpreted to recognize a right [on the part of the criminal defendant] to offer rebuttal evidence to the jury" (citing United States v. Horn, 185 F. Supp.2d 530 (D. Md. 2002))). Evidence offered by the accused has to be independently admissible, however, and evidence offered to rebut an "incontrovertible" fact often will be *in*admissible by virtue of FREs 402, 701, 702, and especially 403. As a result, the issue rarely arises. FRE 201(f) thus does little to protect the defendant's right to contest the noticed fact with evidence. It does, however, protect the jury's right to nullify the law and acquit even though the evidence against the defendant is incontestable. Although a number of states have judicial notice rules requiring criminal juries to accept judicially noticed facts as true, see Giannelli, supra, at 678 n.79 (citing state rules), the *Jones-Apprendi-Ring* line of Supreme Court cases cited supra, note 4, strengthens the argument that judges may not take even indisputable factual issues determinative of guilt or innocence from the jury without violating the Constitution. See Giannelli, supra, at 678–79 & nn.82, 83 (citing commentary on the question).

[49] In regard to civil cases, see the decisions cited supra, note 44. In regard to criminal cases, see Garner v. Louisiana, 368 U.S. 157, 173 (1961) (judicial notice may not be used as a vehicle for accomplishing "through argument to [an appellate court] what [the prosecution] is required by due process to do at the trial"). A restriction on appellate court judicial notice of facts determinative of guilt is supported by a long line of Supreme Court decisions forbidding trial courts to grant directed verdicts against criminal defendants, no matter how unreasonable it would be for the jury to acquit on the evidence of record. See, e.g., United States v. Martin Linen Supply Co., 430 U.S. 564, 572–73 (1977) ("[A] trial judge is prohibited from entering a judgment of conviction or directing the jury to come forward with such a verdict . . . regardless of how overwhelmingly the evidence may point in that direction."); United Brotherhood of Carpenters & Joiners of America v. United States, 330 U.S. 395 (1947). See also Crawford v. Washington, 541 U.S. 36, 62 (2004) (a state may not "dispens[e] with jury trial because a defendant is obviously guilty"). Judicial notice on appeal of facts threatens not only the constitutional right to a jury trial but also the rights to challenge incriminating evidence and to proof by the state beyond a reasonable doubt. If, notwithstanding these concerns, an appellate court is disposed to uphold a conviction based on judicially noticed facts that the jury didn't have

FRE 201(e) gives the party opposing judicial notice a reasonable opportunity to be heard on the appropriateness of taking notice, and on the precise contours of the fact to be noticed. This opportunity is least disruptive and most meaningful when that party has enough advance warning to allow her, before the fact, to muster any information that suggests that notice is inappropriate. If the opponent's case against judicial notice seems substantial, the better practice—especially during trial—is simply to require the fact to be proved in some other way. Because judicial notice is designed to save time, extensive hearings on the propriety of taking notice seldom make sense. However, when notice has been requested to fill a gap in the record after a case has closed, an extensive inquiry may be justified because this procedure may avoid even more extensive trial proceedings, and may determine which party prevails. In the absence of prior notification, the opportunity to be heard may be afforded after judicial notice has been taken. But this procedure can be awkward and ineffective—especially when it requires a "never mind" instruction to a jury that was previously told that it must or may treat a fact as conclusively proven. This procedure also can harm the party that sought judicial notice. If the judge reverses her decision allowing judicial notice, that party may find that an element of his case that could have been proven without resort to judicial notice is now unsupported by any evidence, entitling the other party to a directed verdict. None of these problems will occur for judicial notice of truly well-known and indisputable facts—that water at sea level boils at 100°C, for example, or that Cheyenne is the capital of Wyoming. But in less obvious cases, mistakes can occur—the judge may remember the wrong street name, or a map may include an error—and surprise requests for judicial notice should be disfavored.

PROBLEMS

Problem XI-17. A group of citizens brings an action challenging the most recent reapportionment of the state legislature. They claim that population disparities between districts are so great as to violate the principle of one-person, one-vote. **Can the district court hearing the challenge take judicial notice of the most recent U.S. Census**

---

a chance to reject, the court at the least should (1) give the defendant advance notice and an opportunity to respond, (2) satisfy itself that the requirements of FRE 201 are met, and (3) find that the government could have presented actually available and admissible evidence of the fact that would have compelled all rational jurors, even when presented with the defendant's contrary evidence, to find the fact beyond a reasonable doubt. Cf. United States v. Marks, 209 F.3d 577 (6th Cir. 2000) (the district court's failure to instruct the jury that it could reject the judicially noticed fact that Louisville, Kentucky lies within the jurisdiction of the United States District Court for the Western District of Kentucky was harmless error, because no rational juror could disagree with the fact).

figures reporting the populations of the various districts? Can it take judicial notice of the comparable figures from earlier U.S. Censuses? What is the actual effect of taking notice? What provisions should the court make for the party opposing judicial notice to present testimony by an expert demographer reporting rapid population shifts in the state between the last two Censuses? What should the effect of that testimony be?

Problem XI-18. Webb Peña brings an action in a Denver, Colorado court against Denver Rapid Transit (DRT) for injuries suffered when he was struck by a DRT bus. Peña was hit by a westbound bus while crossing the street after alighting from an eastbound bus. There is evidence that Peña was contributorily negligent in failing to notice the westbound bus, and that the driver of the westbound bus did everything possible to steer away from Peña. There is no evidence, however, that the driver of the westbound bus blew her horn. Peña's counsel requests that the jury be instructed that under the doctrine of "last clear chance," even if Peña had not exercised reasonable care in crossing the street, Peña is entitled to recover if the driver of the westbound bus realized or should have realized that the accident could have been avoided by blowing her horn. DRT objects to the instruction, correctly pointing out that Peña has introduced no evidence that the bus that hit him had a horn and that the horn, if blown, would have been loud enough to catch Peña's attention. Peña's counsel then asks the court to reopen the case and take judicial notice that all DRT buses are equipped with loud horns. **Should judicial notice be taken? If the motion to reopen is denied, may Peña's lawyer nonetheless invite the jurors to find the last clear chance doctrine satisfied based on their everyday experience that all *public* buses have loud horns? That all *DRT* buses have loud horns?**

Problem XI-19. Lucien is charged with grand larceny arising out of the theft of a 2011 Ford Taurus in March 2013. At the conclusion of the evidence, Lucien moves for a directed verdict because no evidence had been introduced to establish the value of the stolen car. The state's attorney could move to reopen the record, and with little difficulty could supply the missing evidence. She does not do so, however, but instead asks the court to take judicial notice of the value of the car. The court denies the defendant's motion, grants the prosecutor's motion and instructs the jury that, "Grand Larceny, so far as it might be material in this case, is committed when the property taken is of a value exceeding $500, and therefore the defendant, if he is guilty at all, is guilty of grand larceny." **Is it proper for the court to take judicial notice in this case? Is the court's instruction proper under FRE 201? Is judicial notice in these circumstances constitutional? Would you answer any of these questions differently if the car were a 1986 Ford Taurus?** Assume that there is evidence that the car was fourteen years old when stolen, and that it had been well cared for by its owner and was in perfect condition. Assume also that no evidence is offered at the trial on the value of the car, but that the court tells the jury that one element of the crime is that the property taken must have been worth more than $500. **If the jury convicts and the defendant appeals, may the appellate court take judicial notice of the "book value" of a "mint condition" Ford Taurus of that age? May it take judicial notice of the price range and going rate for well-preserved Ford Tauruses of that vintage as advertised on E-Bay and similar websites? If not, must the appellate court reverse the conviction?**

Problem XI-20. In this actual case (the names and facts of which have been altered to protect you from the fruits of too easy a Westlaw search), Albee Seltzer, a prison inmate serving a life sentence for a variety of crimes in Wisconsin, sues prison officials claiming they intentionally and maliciously implanted a device in his head to control his thoughts and actions. Seltzer files an affidavit stating that on July 27, last year, he woke up in his cell with bandages on each temple. The affidavit states that Seltzer has no knowledge how the bandages got there, and that he has no access to such bandages in his cell. The affidavit further states that when Seltzer removed the bandages a week later, there were matching scars on each side of his head, which are visible to this day. Shortly thereafter, the affidavit claims, Seltzer began to feel the effects of the mind control device, including a barrage of violent and confusing thoughts, and orders that he kick in the bars of his cell and of the cell next to his and kill his next-door neighbor. Seltzer asks for the appointment of counsel and of an expert medical doctor whom he claims, "on information and belief," would testify that such scars and bandages are indicative of brain surgery. He also asks for the resources necessary to conduct brain x-rays and scans to locate the device in his head. He requests a jury trial. The State of Wisconsin responds with an affidavit of the unit manager of the facility in which Seltzer is incarcerated stating that he received a similar administrative complaint from Seltzer a month before the court case was filed, that he checked the prison logs and determined that Seltzer had not visited the prison infirmary or any hospital—or, indeed, received medical services or medicine of any kind— in the last three years, and that bandages of the sort Seltzer described can only be applied in the infirmary or a hospital. **May the judge, without more, dismiss the complaint by taking judicial notice of the fact that intracranial thought control devices are beyond the reach of currently available medical technology? Should the judge do so?** Assume that a plaintiff in Seltzer's situation must show that he has a reasonable probability of succeeding on his claim or a related claim before a judge may appoint counsel and experts at state expense. **In order to find that the "nonfrivolous claim" requirement has been satisfied and, on that basis, to appoint**

counsel and medical and psychiatric experts to assist Selzter, may the judge take judicial notice of the fact that anyone making allegations of the sort Seltzer has made may well be in need of medical services of the sort the prison admittedly has denied Seltzer over the past three years? If either type of judicial notice is taken by the judge, and if the opposing party is permitted to and does appeal, what would be the strongest basis for overturning the trial judge's ruling? In resolving any of these questions, under what circumstances, if any, may the judge take judicial notice of the fact that: (1) in the last five years, Seltzer has filed fourteen prior suits alleging efforts to control his mind by various prison officials, employees of the State Department of Consumer Affairs, cell phone companies, the Russian Mafia and certain Teletubbies; (2) all fourteen suits were dismissed as frivolous; and (3) in dismissing the most recent suit, a judge found as fact, after an extensive hearing, that Seltzer is perfectly sane and files the suits for fun and to keep his mind active. (Would it matter if, instead, the finding was that Seltzer was schizophrenic and suffered from visual and auditory hallucinations?)

Problem XI-21. Daniel Pinchbeck is on trial for selling cocaine and for filing a false income tax return. The prosecutor wants to show that Pinchbeck has been seen in possession of large amounts of cash. Several of Pinchbeck's associates said so to an FBI agent before trial, but they are all unavailable to testify, having either recanted, fled the jurisdiction, asserted their privilege against self-incrimination or been found floating face down in the river. No written records are available, and Pinchbeck has declined to testify. At Pinchbeck's jury trial, the prosecutor asks the judge to take judicial notice of Pinchbeck's possession of large amounts of cash based on an article from a respected newspaper about the cocaine trade, which identifies Pinchbeck as a suspected major dealer and quotes an unidentified source stating, "Pinchbeck is usually loaded with cash. I seen him carrying around a trombone case filled to the brim with fifties and one hundred dollar bills." **In instructing the jury, should the judge take judicial notice of Pinchbeck's access to large amounts of cash? What more should the prosecutor be required to prove to justify the judge's taking judicial notice? What might the defense show to prevent the judge from granting the judicial-notice request? Would the prosecutor's case for judicial notice be strengthened by photographs posted on the Facebook pages of some of Pinchbeck's associates (also unavailable to testify) showing Pinchbeck flashing wads of cash? What if the prosecutor instead directs the court's attention to the website of a company that other evidence has shown is wholly owned by Pinchbeck, the company's Chief Executive Officer (CEO), which reports huge**

company profits and a large salary paid to its CEO during the last five years? Would it matter if the prosecutor instead offered four newspaper articles and one magazine article, all by different reporters and all quoting different named sources, stating that they had seen Pinchbeck with large amounts of cash? Would it matter if the prosecutor had introduced a receipt showing that Pinchbeck bought a yacht with cash six months before trial? Would it matter if the prosecutor also told the judge about the inadmissible hearsay statements that Pinchbeck's now unavailable associates had made to the FBI?

Problem XI-22. Suppose that the case in the previous problem is a civil suit, and that the issue is a claim that thirty-seven years ago, when Pinchbeck wrote his will, he had assets that are not accounted for in the will and are now hidden from the executor. And suppose that the "trombone case" newspaper article was written thirty-seven years ago. **May a trial judge judicially notice the newspaper article upon a showing that, despite diligent investigative efforts, it is the only available source of relevant information?**

Problem XI-23. African-American residents of Little Rock, Arkansas, bring a class action law suit in federal court to enjoin a recreational facility called the Lake Nixon Club from denying them admission because of their race. They allege a violation of Title II (the public accommodations title) of the Civil Rights Act of 1964. After a bench trial, the district court dismisses the complaint, finding that although plaintiffs were refused admission because of their race, the Lake Nixon Club is not a "public accommodation" as defined in the statute because it has not been shown to operate "in interstate commerce." Plaintiffs appeal. The Court of Appeals determines that there is no specific evidence that interstate travelers have been served at the Club, but there is evidence that the Club contains a snack bar serving 100,000 patrons each season and that the Club advertises its facilities in local hotels, motels and restaurants. **Based on these facts, may the Court of Appeals take judicial notice of the "fact" that the Club must serve food that has traveled in interstate commerce and must serve at least some interstate travelers? Should it do so?**

Problem XI-24. Mary Miley files suit against the Long Air airline company claiming that its rules regulating the permissible weight of "public contact" employees discriminate against women. After a bench trial, the judge finds for the defendant airline. Based on his personal experience of more than 100 flights on Long Air and more than 200 flights on twenty-four other airlines, the judge takes judicial notice of the fact that Long Air's employees have a reputation for both competence and "attractive looks," and that this reputation is "good for defendant's airline's business." **Is this a proper matter for judicial notice?**

Assume the restriction in question provides that no employee who regularly meets the public may exceed by 20% or more the appropriate weight with respect to their height and "build," as is given by the "Physician's Table of Appropriate Weights." The table lists appropriate weights for women which, depending on height and build, are between six and twenty-two pounds less than the weights for men in the same categories. **May the judge take judicial notice of the weights listed in the "Physician's Table," and of the fact that the proper weight specified for women is always less than the proper weight specified for men of the same height and "build?" May the judge take judicial notice of the fact (reported in the "Table") that a lower percentage of women than men in the population are within 20% of their specified weight?**

Problem XI-25. Bernhart Freis is charged with negligent homicide resulting from a car accident. At a jury trial, a highway patrol officer testifies that just before the accident he clocked Fries's car with a radar gun, and that it was traveling in excess of 90 miles per hour. Freis objects to the officer's testimony on the grounds that no evidence has been introduced that radar is an accurate method of measuring speed, or that the machine that clocked Freis was accurate. **May the state meet either ground for objection through judicial notice? If the judge takes judicial notice that radar is an accurate way to measure speed, may Freis introduce an expert to testify that radar is not an accurate way to measure speed: (1) in principle; (2) in practice, because of the sorry state of repair in which most radar machines are kept (a) by highway patrol departments across the United States, (b) by the highway patrol department of the state in question, or (c) by highway patrol officers in the relevant geographic division of the state highway patrol department; or (3) because of defects in the particular brand of radar gun the highway patrol officer was using? May Freis invite the jurors, based on logic and their own experiences, to conclude that radar often does not produce an accurate measurement of speed? Would your answers to any of these questions be different if this were a civil action?**

Problem XI-26. Benton Bainbridge sues Thurston Howell III for assault and battery, claiming that Howell was trying to drive him out of the Newport, Rhode Island neighborhood where they both summer. The first count of Bainbridge's complaint alleges that Howell hired Priscilla Stansbury and Eleanor Powell to beat up Bainbridge, breaking his arm and causing him $500,000 in damages. **If Howell defends against this count by claiming that he has never met or had any contact with Stansbury or Powell, could a state-court judge take judicial notice at a bench trial of the fact that Howell, Stansbury and Powell had pleaded guilty in federal court to a conspiracy to**

corner the trash hauling business in Providence through extortion? **Could the judge inform the jury of this fact in a jury trial? Could the judge, on request of Bainbridge's counsel, take judicial notice of the fact that six months earlier the lead story in the *Newport Plain Citizen*'s society page reported the marriage of Stansbury's daughter to Howell's son, and contained a picture of Stansbury and Howell together with the newlyweds?** The second count in Bainbridge's complaint alleges that Howell acquired a piece of Bainbridge's hair, took it to a practitioner of "voodoo" in Providence, and had the practitioner incorporate the hair into a doll image of Bainbridge. Howell then stuck silver spikes (otherwise used on the olives in Howell's trademark martinis) into the doll and broke the doll's leg, causing Bainbridge great pain, a broken leg, and damages of $500,000. Howell moves to strike count two of Bainbridge's complaint, asking the court to take judicial notice of the fact that one cannot cause physical injury by manipulating a doll image. **Should the court notice this fact? Is there any evidence that Bainbridge might present to the judge in support of an argument against judicial notice? Should the judge rule in the same way on Howell's motion if the voodoo doll allegations were offered in support of compensatory and punitive damages for the first count?**

Problem XI-27. When a trial judge is required to balance the probative weight of evidence against its prejudicial effect in order to determine whether or not to admit evidence, the judge must of necessity consider matters on which no proof has been offered. **Does such consideration amount to judicial notice? Should the judge inform the parties of any sources she has consulted in making her ruling? Of assumptions, experiences or general principles she has relied upon? Should she inform the parties of extra-record facts she intends to rely upon in reaching a decision on the merits of the case? Of the facts she relies upon in evaluating the credibility of witnesses in a bench trial? Why or why not?**

Problem XI-28. Gena Rowlan and Debbie Harris, both of Shreveport, Virginia, vacationed in Alaska, having driven there from Virginia in Rowlan's car. While in Anchorage, Rowlan struck a parked car, seriously injuring Harris. When the two return home, Harris sues Rowlan, claiming that Rowlan deliberately drove forty miles per hour inside the Anchorage city limits, despite knowing that the speed limit was thirty miles per hour. Rowlan admits driving forty miles per hour but denies the allegation that the speed limit was thirty miles per hour where the accident took place. The following colloquy occurs at trial [Hankins is Harris's lawyer; Randolph is Rowlan's lawyer]:

Judge: Now, Ms. Hankins, you ask me to take judicial notice that the relevant speed limit was thirty miles per hour. What authority do you have for that?

Hankins: Judge, it's the law of Alaska. There was no sign that anyone can remember clearly, but the law says that in unposted areas in cities in Alaska, the maximum speed limit is thirty miles per hour.

Randolph: I never heard of that law, Judge. I think she's wrong. And anyway, my client thinks the street they were on was a forty-miles-per-hour zone.

Judge: Well, I don't have anything in front of me that would enable me to decide the point. Perhaps I should just apply Virginia law, which makes twenty-five miles per hour the maximum in unposted areas of cities.

Randolph: Judge, that's ridiculous. What you should do is throw this case out.

What should the judge do? How might the parties convince the judge that the speed limit was less than, equal to, or more than thirty-five miles per hour at the relevant time and place? Would it matter if the accident took place in Guadalajara, Mexico, rather than Anchorage, Alaska (assuming miles per hour were properly translated into kilometers per hour)?

---

2. Legislative Fact-Finding

In *Hawkins v. United States*,[50] in 1958, the Supreme Court retained the common law privilege that prohibits one spouse from testifying against the other. It did so after concluding that "[a]dverse testimony given in criminal proceedings would, we think, be likely to destroy almost any marriage." This was a factual conclusion, but it was not based on evidence in the record; there was none on this point. Nor was it an appropriate subject for judicial notice as that procedure is commonly understood. The Court may have been right in its judgment, but the proposition is hardly indisputable. And yet no one seriously questions the appropriateness of this sort of fact-finding. On the contrary, a quick review of any set of appellate opinions that you have studied in any course will reveal that fact-finding like this occurs constantly, in almost every case in which a court makes new law, on issues that range from the deterrent effects of the exclusionary rule on police officers, to the impact

---

[50] 358 U.S. 74, 78 (1958).

of securities regulations on capital markets, to the effect of abortion and contraceptives laws on the sexual practices of teenagers.[51]

One of the fundamental principles of our system is that courts apply the law, and that in order to do so they must determine what the law is. In many cases the law is clearly set by precedent or statute or constitution, and the task is simple. But when the content of the law is up for grabs, a court must make a choice based at least in part on its judgment about the consequences of different formulations. That judgment will almost inevitably involve explicit or implicit factual findings—like the one from *Hawkins*—findings that in many cases are made without an evidentiary record. Because factual premises of this sort are used in the process of making law, they have become known as "legislative facts"; because judges usually determine these "legislative" facts without resort to adversarial fact-finding, the process of doing so is often described as a species of judicial notice. For example, as we have noted,[52] FRE 201 is explicitly limited to judicial notice of "adjudicative" facts, which—together with the Advisory Committee's Note on the rule, which we quote below—suggests that what courts do when they find legislative facts is to take a different (and uncodified) kind of judicial notice. We think this formulation is confusing, because in this context the essential attribute of judicial notice—actual, or at least near, indisputableness—is almost always missing. Calling this practice "judicial notice" suggests that what courts do about legislative facts is wrong, because it amounts to taking judicial notice when judicial notice is plainly inappropriate. We prefer a simple descriptive phrase: "legislative fact-finding." As you will see, we think legislative fact-finding is both inevitable and, if done well, appropriate. It is only rarely done well, however.

The 1987 Supreme Court case of *Rock v. Arkansas* [53] illustrates how very differently appellate courts treat questions of legislative fact and ordinary issues of adjudicative fact. In order to decide whether Arkansas could constitutionally exclude a criminal defendant's hypnotically refreshed testimony, the Court (as it saw the case) had to address two factual questions: (1) Are memories that are produced in hypnotic sessions ever reliable (and if so, under what conditions)? (2) Was the hypnosis of the defendant in this case, Vickie Rock, conducted under conditions that permit the recovery of reliable memories? The first is a question of legislative fact, the second of adjudicative fact. In reading the following excerpts from the majority and dissenting opinions in the case, consider how the Court approaches these two different issues.

---

[51] For an extensive survey of Supreme Court cases engaging in this sort of fact-finding in constitutional cases, see David L. Faigman, Constitutional Fictions: A Unified Theory of Constitutional Facts (2008).

[52] See supra, subsection 1, p. 1401.

[53] 483 U.S. 44 (1987).

ROCK V. ARKANSAS
483 U.S. 44 (1987).

JUSTICE BLACKMUN delivered the opinion of the Court.

The issue presented in this case is whether Arkansas' evidentiary rule prohibiting the admission of hypnotically refreshed testimony violated petitioner's constitutional right to testify on her own behalf in a criminal case.

I.

Petitioner Vickie Lorene Rock was charged with manslaughter in the death of her husband, Frank Rock, on July 2, 1983 . . . [A] fight [had] erupted when Frank refused to let petitioner eat some pizza and prevented her from leaving the apartment to get something else to eat. When police arrived on the scene they found Frank on the floor with a bullet wound in his chest. Petitioner urged the officers to help her husband, and cried to a sergeant who took her in charge, "please save him" and "don't let him die." . . . According to the testimony of one of the investigating officers, petitioner told him that "she stood up to leave the room and [Frank] grabbed her by the throat and choked her and threw her against the wall and . . . at that time she walked over and picked up the weapon and pointed it toward the floor and he hit her again and she shot him." [In another account, Vickie Rock had claimed that the gun went off accidentally when Frank hit her.]

Because petitioner could not remember the precise details of the shooting, her attorney suggested that she submit to hypnosis in order to refresh her memory. Petitioner was hypnotized twice by Doctor Betty Back, a licensed neuropsychologist with training in the field of hypnosis. Doctor Back interviewed petitioner for an hour prior to the first hypnosis session, taking notes on petitioner's general history and her recollections of the shooting. Both hypnosis sessions were recorded on tape. Petitioner did not relate any new information during either of the sessions, but, after the hypnosis, she was able to remember that at the time of the incident she had her thumb on the hammer of the gun, but had not held her finger on the trigger. She also recalled that the gun had discharged when her husband grabbed her arm during the scuffle. As a result of the details that petitioner was able to remember, Rock's attorney arranged for a gun expert to examine the handgun. . . . That inspection revealed that the gun was defective and prone to fire, when hit or dropped, without the trigger's being pulled. When the prosecutor learned of the hypnosis sessions, he filed a motion to exclude petitioner's testimony. The trial judge held a pretrial hearing on the motion and concluded that no hypnotically refreshed testimony would be admitted. The court issued an order limiting petitioner's testimony to "matters remembered and stated to the examiner prior to being placed under hypnosis." At trial, petitioner introduced testimony by the gun expert, but the court limited petitioner's own description of the events on the day of the shooting to a reiteration of the sketchy information in Doctor Back's notes. The jury convicted petitioner on the manslaughter charge and she was sentenced to 10 years' imprisonment and a $10,000 fine.

On appeal, the Supreme Court of Arkansas rejected petitioner's claim that the limitations on her testimony violated her right to present her defense. The court concluded that "the dangers of admitting this kind of testimony outweigh whatever probative value it may have," and decided to follow the approach of States that have held hypnotically refreshed testimony of witnesses inadmissible per se. Although the court acknowledged that "a defendant's right to testify is fundamental," it ruled that the exclusion of petitioner's testimony did not violate her constitutional rights. Any "prejudice or deprivation" she suffered "was minimal and resulted from her own actions and not by any erroneous ruling of the court." We granted certiorari, to consider the constitutionality of Arkansas' per se rule excluding a criminal defendant's hypnotically refreshed testimony.

II.

[In this section the Court examines the history, tradition and precedent regarding the accused's right to testify. The Court concludes that "[t]he right to testify on one's own behalf at a criminal trial has sources in several provisions of the Constitution."]

III.

. . .

Of course, the right to present relevant testimony is not without limitation. The right "may, in appropriate cases, bow to accommodate other legitimate interests in the criminal trial process." But restrictions of a defendant's right to testify may not be arbitrary or disproportionate to the purposes they are designed to serve. In applying its evidentiary rules a State must evaluate whether the interest served by a rule justify the limitation imposed on the defendant's constitutional right to testify.

IV.

The Arkansas rule enunciated by the state courts does not allow a trial court to consider whether posthypnosis testimony may be admissible in a particular case; it is a per se rule prohibiting the admission at trial of any defendant's hypnotically refreshed testimony on the ground that such testimony is always unreliable. Thus, in Arkansas, an accused's testimony is limited to matters that he or she can prove were remembered before hypnosis. This rule operates to the detriment of any defendant who undergoes hypnosis, without regard to the reasons for it, the circumstances under which it took place, or any independent verification of the information it produced.

In this case, the application of that rule had a significant adverse effect on petitioner's ability to testify. It virtually prevented her from describing any of the events that occurred on the day of the shooting, despite corroboration of many of those events by other witnesses. Even more importantly, under the court's rule petitioner was not permitted to describe the actual shooting except in the words contained in Doctor Back's notes. The expert's description of the gun's tendency to misfire would have taken on greater significance if the jury had heard petitioner testify that she did not have her finger on the trigger and that the gun went off when her husband hit her arm.

. . .

Although the Arkansas court concluded [as had the courts of a number of other States] that any testimony that cannot be proved to be the product of prehypnosis memory is unreliable, many [other] courts have eschewed a per se rule and permit the admission of hypnotically refreshed testimony. Hypnosis by trained physicians or psychologists has been recognized as a valid therapeutic technique since 1958, although there is no generally accepted theory to explain the phenomenon, or even a consensus on a single definition of hypnosis. See Council on Scientific Affairs, Scientific Status of Refreshing Recollection by the Use of Hypnosis, 253 J. Amer. Med. Ass'n 1918, 1918–19 (1985). The use of hypnosis in criminal investigations, however, is controversial, and the current medical and legal view of its appropriate role is unsettled.

Responses of individuals to hypnosis vary greatly. The popular belief that hypnosis guarantees the accuracy of recall is as yet without established foundation and, in fact, hypnosis often has no effect at all on memory. The most common response to hypnosis, however, appears to be an increase in both correct and incorrect recollections. Three general characteristics of hypnosis may lead to the introduction of inaccurate memories: the subject becomes "suggestible" and may try to please the hypnotist with answers the subject thinks will be met with approval; the subject is likely to "confabulate," that is, to fill in details from the imagination in order to make an answer more coherent and complete, and the subject experiences "memory hardening," which gives him great confidence in both the true and false memories, making effective cross-examination more difficult. See generally M. Orne et al., Hypnotically Induced Testimony, in Eyewitness Testimony: Psychological Perspectives 171 (G. Wells & E. Loftus, eds. (1984)); Diamond, Inherent Problems in the Use of Pretrial Hypnosis on a Prospective Witness, 68 Calif. L. Rev. 313, 333–42 (1980). Despite the unreliability that hypnosis concededly may introduce, however, the procedure has been credited as instrumental in obtaining investigative leads and identifications that were later confirmed by independent evidence. . . . See generally R. Udolf, Forensic Hypnosis 11–16 (1983).

The inaccuracies the process introduces can be reduced, although perhaps not eliminated, by the use of procedural safeguards. One set of suggested guidelines calls for hypnosis to be performed only by a psychologist or psychiatrist with special training in its use and who is independent of the investigation. See Orne, The Use and Misuse of Hypnosis in Court, 27 Int'l J. Clinical and Experimental Hypnosis 311, 335–36 (1979). These procedures reduce the possibility that biases will be communicated to the hyper suggestive subject by the hypnotist. Suggestion will be less likely also if the hypnosis is conducted in a neutral setting with no one present but the hypnotist and the subject. Tape or video recording of all interrogations, before, during, and after hypnosis, can help reveal if leading questions were asked. Id. at 336. Such guidelines do not guarantee the accuracy of the testimony, because they cannot control the subject's own motivation or any tendency to confabulate, but they do provide a means of controlling overt suggestions.

The more traditional means of assessing accuracy of testimony also remain applicable in the case of a previously hypnotized defendant. Certain information recalled as a result of hypnosis may be verified as highly accurate by corroborating evidence. Cross-examination, even in the face of a confident defendant, is an effective tool for revealing inconsistencies. Moreover, a jury can be educated to the risks of hypnosis through expert testimony and cautionary instructions. Indeed, it is probably to a defendant's advantage to establish carefully the extent of his memory prior to hypnosis, in order to minimize the decrease in credibility the procedure might introduce.

We are not now prepared to endorse without qualifications the use of hypnosis as an investigative tool; scientific understanding of the phenomenon and of the means to control the effects of hypnosis is still in its infancy. Arkansas, however, has not justified the exclusion of all of a defendant's testimony that the defendant is unable to prove to be the product of prehypnosis memory. The State's legitimate interest in barring unreliable evidence does not extend to per se exclusions [of evidence] that may be reliable in an individual case. Wholesale inadmissibility of a defendant's testimony is an arbitrary restriction on the right to testify in the absence of clear evidence by the State repudiating the validity of all posthypnosis recollections. The State would be well within its powers if it established guidelines to aid trial courts in the evaluation of posthypnosis testimony and it may be able to show that testimony in a particular case is so unreliable that exclusion is justified. But it has not shown that hypnotically enhanced testimony is always so untrustworthy and so immune to the traditional means of evaluating credibility that it should disable a defendant from presenting her version of the events for which she is on trial.

In this case, the defective condition of the gun corroborated the details petitioner remembered about the shooting. The tape recordings provided some means to evaluate the hypnosis and the trial judge concluded that Doctor Back did not suggest responses with leading questions. Those circumstances present an argument for admissibility of petitioner's testimony in this particular case, an argument that must be considered by the trial court. Arkansas' per se rule excluding all posthypnosis testimony infringes impermissibly on the right of a defendant to testify on his own behalf.

The judgment of the Supreme Court of Arkansas is vacated and the case is remanded to that court for further proceedings not inconsistent with this opinion.

CHIEF JUSTICE REHNQUIST, with whom JUSTICE WHITE, JUSTICE O'CONNOR, and JUSTICE SCALIA join, dissenting.

In deciding that petitioner Rock's testimony was properly limited at her trial, the Arkansas Supreme Court cited several factors that undermine the reliability of hypnotically induced testimony. Like the Court today, the Arkansas Supreme Court observed that a hypnotized individual becomes subject to suggestion, is likely to confabulate, and experiences artificially increased confidence in both true and false memories following hypnosis. No known set of procedures, both courts agree, can insure against the inherently unreliable nature of such testimony. . . .

. . .

This Court has traditionally accorded the States "respect . . . in the establishment of their own criminal trial rules and procedures." *Chambers v. Mississippi*, 410 U.S. 284, 302–03 (1973). . . .

The Supreme Court of Arkansas' decision was an entirely permissible response to a novel and difficult question. See National Institute of Justice, Issues and Practices, M. Orne et al., Hypnotically Refreshed Testimony: Enhanced Memory or Tampering with Evidence? 51 (1985). As an original proposition, the solution this Court imposes upon Arkansas may be equally sensible, though requiring the matter to be considered *res nova* by every single trial judge in every single case might seem to some to pose serious administrative difficulties. But until there is much more general consensus on the use of hypnosis than there is now, the Constitution does not warrant this Court's mandating its own view of how to deal with the issue.

———

Notice that the Supreme Court did not decide the case-specific questions of how Vickie Rock's recollections were hypnotically induced or whether her testimony based on those recollections was in fact admissible. Instead it remanded the case to the Arkansas courts to decide the issues. On remand, if a dispute arose over how Rock's memories were induced and whether testimony based on the memories qualified as reliable under the standards set forth in Justice Blackmun's opinion, the case would probably be sent back to the original trial court. Most likely, that court would hold an evidentiary hearing at which Dr. Back might be examined and cross-examined under oath about the hypnotic procedures she used, and her notes and tapes of the session might be admitted; independent evidence of the killing of Frank Rock that corroborated or contradicted Vickie Rock's "reclaimed" memories might be introduced through testimony of other sworn witnesses, and through exhibits; and expert witnesses might testify on whether this hypnotic session conformed to the standards set by the Supreme Court. In other words, because the resolution of these issues affects only a single case, it is treated as an ordinary question of "adjudicative" fact, and is resolved by the trial court using normal adversarial fact-finding procedures.

By contrast, consider how the *Rock* majority decided the more general and more important question raised by this case: whether posthypnotic testimony by a criminal defendant is so inherently unreliable that a state may constitutionally exclude all such evidence. In answering this question in the negative, the majority relied on facts that Justice Blackmun gleaned from five articles by four leading hypnosis researchers. Given that the dissenting Justices concluded that a contrary answer might reasonably be given to that "novel and difficult question"— citing a different report by Martin Orne, the researcher whom Justice Blackmun cited twice—it is clear that judicial notice would not have been appropriate under FRE 201 or any other standard typically used for judicial notice of *adjudicative* facts. Nor did the Court use any of the usual methods of adversarial factfinding—sworn testimony, direct and cross-examination in the presence of the fact-finder and so forth—that judicial notice replaces when the facts are "reasonably indisputable." Instead, the Court proceeded in an open-ended, haphazard and unconstrained manner that is typical of courts addressing questions of legislative fact. Indeed, Justice Blackmun's was slightly *more* careful than usual: he explicitly cited published data by scientific researchers, rather than simply relying on his own surmises or educated guesses.

Having in mind the Court's distinct treatment in *Rock* of these two kinds of factual questions, it is useful to reiterate the distinction between legislative and adjudicative facts. The Advisory Committee Note on FRE

201 provides an excellent formulation, derived from the pioneering work on this issue by Professor Kenneth Culp Davis:[54]

> Adjudicative facts are simply the facts of the particular case. Legislative facts, on the other hand, are facts which have relevance to legal reasoning and the lawmaking process. . . .

The many rules of evidence that are the subject of this book govern adjudicative fact-finding. But what rules govern legislative fact-finding? The clearest statement of the only procedural rule that applies in that setting is in *Chastleton Corp. v. Sinclair*,[55] a 1924 Supreme Court opinion by Justice Holmes: "The court may ascertain as it sees fit any fact that is merely a ground for laying down a rule of law." At first glance, this may seem odd. On the whole, legislative facts are *more* important than adjudicative facts, not less important. Why then are courts—which must follow elaborate rules of evidence and review in dealing with lesser facts— allowed to decide legislative facts in any manner they see fit? On reflection, the nature of the judicial process makes this liberality inevitable. Questions of legislative fact are usually resolved on appeal; frequently, they are addressed for the *first time* at that stage. Courts of appeal are awkward forums for the presentation of evidence, at best. Worse, a judge may not have occasion to frame a critical question of legislative fact until she is well into the writing of an opinion, at which point it is all but impossible to gather additional information from the parties. Nor is this a minor or occasional issue. The consideration of factual issues is an essential part of the process of legal reasoning by which judges decide open questions of law. Whether they rely on their own hunches, or articles they have read, or the parties' briefs, they will inevitably think not only about the meaning, but also about the real-world consequences, of the choices they must make. It would not work to place artificial limits on either aspect of this process. As Professor Davis put it:

> My opinion is that judge-made law would stop growing if judges, in thinking about questions of law and policy, were forbidden to take into account facts they believe, as distinguished from facts which are "clearly . . . within the domain of the indisputable."[56]

Because legislative fact-finding is used in the process of making law— as opposed to the process of deciding particular cases—findings of legislative fact have three important characteristics that set them apart from findings of adjudicative fact:

---

[54] See Kenneth C. Davis, An Approach to Problems of Evidence in the Administrative Process, 55 Harv. L. Rev. 364, 404–07 (1942); Kenneth C. Davis, Judicial Notice, 55 Colum. L. Rev. 945 (1955); Kenneth C. Davis, A System of Judicial Notice Based on Fairness and Convenience, Perspectives of Law 69 (1964).

[55] 264 U.S. 543, 548 (1924).

[56] Davis, A System of Judicial Notice Based on Fairness and Convenience, supra, note 54, at 82.

(1) *Legislative fact determinations are not subject to reconsideration by lower courts on the basis of new evidence.*

In *Brown v. Board of Education*,[57] the Supreme Court described the major issue before it as follows:

> Does segregation of children in public schools solely on the basis of race, even though the physical facilities and other 'tangible' factors may be equal, deprive the children of the minority group of equal educational opportunities?

Based on a variety of information, including social scientific studies, the Court answered this question affirmatively. In *Stell v. Savannah-Chatham County Board of Education*,[58] a district court judge handling a similar claim, held that the Supreme Court's holding in *Brown* embodied "a conclusion of fact rather than law." Based on that premise, the judge argued that the Court's judgment in *Brown* was not binding on a lower court if the record before that court was different—just as the conclusion of an appellate court that there was sufficient evidence to uphold a verdict of murder in one case would not bind a trial-court judge ruling on a motion to dismiss in a later murder case. Accordingly, the judge took evidence, concluded that the Supreme Court was wrong and that—as a factual matter—"education is best given in [racially] separate schools." Accordingly, he held that integration was not constitutionally required. The Fifth Circuit quickly reversed:

> The District Court was bound by the decision of the Supreme Court in *Brown*. We reiterate that no inferior federal court may refrain from acting as required by that decision even if such a court should conclude that the Supreme Court erred either as to its facts or as to the law.

> [W]e do not read the major premise of the decision of the Supreme Court in the first *Brown* case as being limited to the facts of the cases there presented. We read it as proscribing segregation in the public education process on the stated ground that separate but equal schools for the races were inherently unequal.[59]

(2) *Lower court findings on questions of legislative fact are not entitled to deference by higher courts.*

We saw an example of this second principle in *Rock v. Arkansas*: The Supreme Court remanded for findings on the *adjudicative* question of whether the particular post-hypnotic memories in that case were retrieved in a manner that was reliable; if there had already been a state-

---

[57]   347 U.S. 483, 493 (1954).

[58]   220 F.Supp. 667, 677 (S.D.Ga.1963).

[59]   333 F.2d 55, 61 (5th Cir. 1964).

court finding on that issue in the record, the Court would normally have deferred to it. But the Court considered the *legislative* fact issue—the reliability of post-hypnotic testimony in general—*de novo*, without deference to the Arkansas Supreme Court's contrary conclusion. This is common practice, if rarely discussed in opinions. In *Lockhart v. McCree*,[60] the Supreme Court dealt with this issue unusually explicitly, if in dicta. Normally, under Federal Rule of Civil Procedure 52(a), the factual findings of a district court that have been affirmed by a circuit court may be reversed by the Supreme Court only if they are "clearly erroneous"— which the Court has interpreted to be a very demanding standard of review. In the context of the issues in *Lockhart*, however, the Court said: "We are far from persuaded . . . that the 'clearly erroneous' standard of Rule 52(a) applies to the kind of 'legislative' facts at issue here."[61] The Court then proceeded to redetermine the issues, disregarding the lower courts' factual findings, and coming to the opposite conclusion on many questions.

(3) *A rule of law based on a determination of legislative fact may stand even if the court that originally decided the issue now believes its factual conclusion was wrong.*

In *Williams v. Florida*,[62] the Supreme Court upheld the constitutionality of six-person as opposed to twelve-person criminal juries, based in part on its conclusion "that there is no discernible difference between the results reached by the two different-sized juries." Three years later, in *Colgrove v. Battin*,[63] the Court upheld six-person federal civil juries, stating that "four recent studies have provided convincing empirical evidence of the correctness of the *Williams* conclusion. . . ." Most researchers who had studied this issue thought the Court was dead wrong, and the opinions in *Williams* and *Colgrove* stimulated a raft of new studies on jury size. Almost all of these studies compared six-and twelve-member juries, and almost all found that the verdicts of six- and twelve-person juries might diverge and that when they did the twelve-person jury verdict was likely to reflect better informed deliberations. Finally, in 1978, in *Ballew v. Georgia*,[64] the Supreme Court unanimously held that *five*-person criminal trial juries are unconstitutional. Justice Blackmun, writing for the majority, began his analysis by explaining that in 1970, when *Williams* was decided, "little empirical research had evaluated jury performance, [and] the Court found no evidence that the reliability of jury verdicts diminished with six-member panels."[65] He then

---

[60]   476 U.S. 162 (1986).

[61]   Id. at 170 n.3.

[62]   399 U.S. 78, 101–102 (1970).

[63]   413 U.S. 149, 160 (1973).

[64]   435 U.S. 223 (1978).

[65]   Id. at 230.

reviewed in detail the extensive body of post-*Williams* research showing that six-person juries are inferior. He concluded:

> While we adhere to, and reaffirm our holding in *Williams v. Florida*, these studies, most of which have been made since *Williams* was decided in 1970, lead us to conclude that the purpose and functioning of the jury in a criminal trial is seriously impaired, and to a constitutional degree, by a reduction in size to below six members.[66]

In other words, extensive and persuasive studies that six-person juries are not as good as twelve-person juries could not get the Court to reconsider the legal rule that six-person juries are permissible. But these same studies were influential on a related question that was being considered for the first time—the performance of five-person juries as compared to six-person juries—even though the studies did not directly address the issue at stake.

These three characteristics of legislative fact-finding reflect its function as an aspect of making law. They correspond to three structural attributes that legal rules (as opposed to factual findings) are supposed to have:

Hierarchy. The governing law is always the statement of the highest authority with the power to decide that has spoken on the issue: constitutional provisions trump statutes; statutes overrule rules of court; and so forth. Within the judicial system, higher courts make rules that bind lower courts. This allocation of power promotes uniformity (see below), and gives higher courts the final say on general legal questions that they are considered more competent to decide than are lower courts. Legislative facts are simply building blocks in the process of making these legal rules. We trust higher courts to handle them better than lower courts. And even if a lower court is correct in revising a factual premise of a higher court opinion, the legal consequences of that revision are uncertain. As a factual matter, the Supreme Court was wrong when it said in *Williams* that six-person juries perform as well as twelve-person juries; but the Court might have held that six-person juries are constitutional anyway, even if it had correctly found that they are not as effective as twelve-person panels. Because the court's factual and legal judgments are intertwined, a lower court cannot reject the former without (improperly) challenging the latter.

Uniformity. Legal rules are supposed to be the same across an entire jurisdiction; factual findings change from case to case. When two trial courts, or two intermediate courts of appeal, reach opposing conclusions on the same legal issue that is reason to appeal to a higher court to resolve the disagreement, and once resolved, further disagreement should

---

[66] Id. at 239.

cease. We do not want the constitutionality of six-person juries, or the availability of a marital privilege, to turn on the judge a litigant happens to get, or the district in which she happens to live. Consequently, such issues must be open to redetermination on appeal, and the judgment of the highest court must bind those below.[67]

Predictability. People arrange their affairs and privately settle disputes on the basis of a general assumption that yesterday's law will apply tomorrow. Sometimes, of course, old rules are overturned, but in general the assumption of legal stability is valid.[68] Because of the value of stability and predictability in the law, a legal rule—once announced—takes on a life of its own. Do not confuse a rationale that is given for choosing a legal rule with the rule itself. Even if the rationale is undermined, the rule may survive because there are other justifications for it—including sheer inertia.

The fact that courts, especially appellate courts, have the power to find legislative facts by any method they choose does not mean that all methods are equally good. Ideally, a court deciding an important question of legislative fact would have the best available information before it, but that ideal is rarely achieved. At one extreme, there are countless cases in which courts rely on hunches or "cracker-barrel folk wisdom."[69] For example, in *Jay Burns Baking Co. v. Bryan*,[70] the Supreme Court struck down a statute that required the weight of a loaf of bread to appear on the label because "it is contrary to common experience" that consumers might confuse a ten-ounce loaf with a pound loaf. (The dissent disagreed and cited facts to the contrary.) At the other end of the spectrum, there are occasional cases in which questions of legislative fact are the subject of elaborate trial-court hearings, at which extensive expert evidence is presented, followed by detailed analysis of the record on appeal.[71] In between, there are cases in which legislative fact-finding is based on published information extensively summarized in the parties' briefs, or submissions from amicus curia, or reports and articles the court itself discovers. Justice Blackmun, for example, is famously reported to have written *Roe v. Wade*,[72] the Supreme Court's landmark abortion decision, in the medical library of the Mayo Clinic, with many of the relevant sources at his fingertips. More recently, the Court based decisions barring the death penalty for juveniles and

---

[67] See Lockhart v. McCree, supra, note 60, 476 U.S. at 170 n.3 ("The difficulty with applying [the 'clearly erroneous' standard of review] to 'legislative' facts is evidenced here by the fact that at least one other Court of Appeals, reviewing the same social science studies as introduced by McCree, has reached a conclusion contrary to that of the [courts below].").

[68] Of course, appellate opinions that break new ground are over-represented in law school case books.

[69] McCormick § 334.

[70] 264 U.S. 504, 517 (1924).

[71] See, e.g., Lockhart v. McCree, supra; McCleskey v. Kemp, 481 U.S. 279 (1987).

[72] 410 U.S. 113 (1973).

mentally retarded individuals on detailed analyses of (and debates with the dissenting justices about) medical and psychological evidence of differences in the mental and moral functioning of youthful and mentally challenged individuals compared to adults of normal intelligence.[73] *Rock v. Arkansas*—another Blackmun opinion—falls into an intermediate category. The available information on post-hypnotic memory was not explored in detail, but the Court did rely on several articles reporting the results of scientific studies on the subject.

At first blush, it might seem that any use of systematic studies is superior to reliance on common knowledge and intuition. In fact, the Supreme Court's use of social scientific or medical data has sometimes made its legislative fact-findings more controversial, not less. If the Court does a poor job of using published studies, scholars in the relevant field may try to set the record straight, in print. Thus, when the Supreme Court in *Williams v. Florida* and *Colgrove v. Battin*[74] relied on social scientific studies to conclude that there are "no discernible differences" between six-and twelve-member juries, social scientists quickly pointed out that the research showed no such thing.[75] Such criticism can come from friends of a decision as well as from foes. For example, in 1955, Professor Edmond Cahn, an ardent supporter of school desegregation, disputed the view that the decision in *Brown v. Board of Education* depended on the Court's use of psychological and sociological evidence, "because I would not have the constitutional rights of Negroes—or of any other Americans—rest on any such flimsy foundation as some of the scientific demonstrations in these records."[76]

In a sense, the problem here is general to all decision making: the more explicit the justification, the easier it is to attack. In the legislative fact-finding context, however, that danger is worse, because the attack is likely to come from outside the legal profession, from people who understand the studies better than the judges who cited them. Folk wisdom may be a poor source of knowledge, but judges are about as good at using it as anybody. Safer yet, an opinion that appears to be based entirely on "legal" considerations ("We interpret 'due process of law' to mean. . . . ") is entirely immune to factual attack. It is hard to believe that judges make many such decisions without *thinking* about legislative facts—How will it work? Who will be affected? What really happens?—

---

[73] Roper v. Simmons, 543 U.S. 551 (2005); Atkins v. Virginia, 536 U.S. 304 (2002).

[74] See supra, pp. 1424–1425.

[75] See, e.g., Richard O. Lempert, Uncovering "Nondiscernible" Differences: Empirical Research and the Jury-Size Cases, 73 Mich. L. Rev. 643 (1975); Hans Zeisel & Shari S. Diamond, "Convincing Empirical Evidence" on the Six Member Jury, 41 U. Chi. L. Rev. 281 (1974).

[76] Edmond Cahn, Jurisprudence, 30 N.Y.U. L. Rev. 150, 157–58 (1955). Although *Brown's* use of social scientific evidence was severely criticized at the time and since, its conclusions have largely been validated by more recent research. See James S. Liebman, Desegregating Politics: "All-Out" School Desegregation Explained, 90 Colum. L. Rev. 1463, 1492–93, 1624–30 (1990).

but that thought process can be (and often is, even deliberately) hidden from view.

The difficulty and harmful effects of revising a finding of legislative fact on which a legal decision appears to rest adds to the problem: What should a court do when there is not enough information to answer an important legislative question adequately, but about which possibly, perhaps likely, we will someday know a good deal more? This is a plausible description of the situation that confronted the Supreme Court in *Williams v. Florida* in 1970. At that time, no one could say whether six-person criminal trial juries would perform less well than twelve-person juries, because few researchers had studied the issue. In science, there are two responses to this sort of uncertainty. First, a scientist could conclude that the available information suggests a tentative conclusion—perhaps that the two types of juries perform roughly the same—but keep open the possibility of revising that conclusion. As we have seen, courts don't usually do that. Legislative facts are used to make legal rules which—once made—should generally be stable, and should not lightly be unmade. Second, a scientist might say that the issue is open—that it is premature to decide how six-person juries compare to twelve-person juries, so the question must be deferred until more research has been completed. If a court did that, the immediate consequence would probably be that the legal status quo would be maintained—the party with the burden of proving facts sufficient to persuade the court to alter existing rules would have failed to carry its burden—but in the meantime the future of the rule in question would be in doubt. Courts almost never do that either, and for good reason.

Imagine what would have happened if the Supreme Court had said in 1970, "Six-person criminal juries *might* be unconstitutional, but we won't know until a good deal more research has been done." Over the next five, eight or ten years, there would have been a cloud of uncertainty over thousands of criminal judgments. This uncertainty could only be resolved by studies conducted by researchers over whom the courts have no control. Moreover, defining the legal issue as one that turns on empirical research would create a danger that studies would be generated for the purpose of securing one legal outcome or another. Could the Court accurately evaluate research conducted in this context? Finally, having said that *more* research is needed, the Court might have a hard time saying when there is *enough*. Will two more studies do? Are fifteen necessary? Does it matter how good they are? Can judges tell? Must this legal issue—once having been identified as controlled by empirical questions—*always* be open to revision as newer and better studies emerge? Given these worries, courts that want to postpone answering a question of legislative fact usually do so silently. They simply ignore the question until they believe they have enough information, and then they decide the issue, once and for all, on the first pass.[77]

The need to determine legislative facts when first presented suggests that courts should address these questions carefully and deliberately. At least four proposals made by scholars and judges suggest ways to do so. *First*, courts could identify in advance the disputable legislative fact questions that they consider important, and encourage the parties—and perhaps amicus curiae—to address them, and to present argument and information to the court.[78] Taking seriously the analogy to "legislative" activity, these proposals call for courts to behave more like legislative committees and administrative agencies—or perhaps like ideal versions of those bodies—which use legislative hearings and "notice and comment" procedures to enable interested parties and outside experts to identify important factual questions, supply data, back-up the parties' submissions with their own expert analyses and document their conclusions. *Second*, courts might employ experts and adopt evaluative standards that enhance their ability to identify and evaluate relevant

---

[77] There is one conspicuous exception to the usual pattern. In Witherspoon v. Illinois, 391 U.S. 510 (1968), a capital defendant argued that his conviction was unconstitutional because the state's practice of excluding opponents of the death penalty from capital trials—a procedure known as "death qualification"—created juries that were unduly prone to convict. The Court declined to rule on this issue because it found the available evidence to be "tentative and fragmentary," id at 517; but it explicitly anticipated that in some future case, with better information, a defendant might prevail on this claim. In Lockhart v. McCree, 476 U.S. 162 (1986), the issue was presented again, with a far more complete record—a dozen or more new studies, conducted after *Witherspoon*, that uniformly indicated that death-qualified juries are conviction prone. The Court did not bite. Overruling the district and circuit courts that handled the case, and contrary to the consensus of social scientists in the field, a five-Justice majority of the Court found that the evidence was still insufficient to prove the point. But that was not all the Court did in *Lockhart*. If it had stopped there, it might have faced a new challenge several years later, with even more new empirical studies. Instead, the Court slammed the empirical door shut, holding—contrary to *Witherspoon*—that the factual question did not matter: death qualification would not be unconstitutional even if it were shown that death-qualified juries are more likely to convict than ordinary juries. See Samuel R. Gross, Overruled: Jury Neutrality in Capital Cases, 21 Stanford Lawyer 11 (1986). Part of the explanation for this about-face is that by 1986 a majority on the Supreme Court had no interest in outlawing a major procedural aspect of capital punishment that an earlier Court, with a different composition and much greater qualms about the death penalty, considered suspect in 1968. In addition, however, it looks like the Court, having once tried to leave an issue of legislative fact open and invite further research and litigation to resolve it, was determined not to do so twice. For the view that the Court should conduct more experiments of the sort it tried in *Witherspoon* and recoiled from in *Lockhart,* see infra, notes 78–82 and accompanying text.

[78] See, e.g., Kenneth C. Davis, Judicial Notice, 1969 Law & Soc. Order 513, 527 (courts should inform the parties of plans to notice facts likely to be disputed, and permit the parties to apprise the court of available social science and other data); Peggy C. Davis, "There is a Book Out . . . ": An Analysis of Judicial Absorption of Legislative Facts, 100 Harv. L. Rev. 1539, 1603 (1987) (courts should "entertain or solicit special briefs, argument, affidavits or depositions of experts, or in the rare case, hearings, as to the propriety of taking judicial notice of a disputable fact"); Stephen A. Saltzburg, et al., Federal Rules of Evidence Manual 109 (6th ed. 1991) (court should give parties an opportunity to be heard on any "fact . . . likely to be critical to a decision on the law"); Robert E. Keeton, Legislative Facts and Similar Things: Deciding Disputed Premise Facts, 73 Minn. L. Rev. 1, 30–31 (1988) (courts should announce a tentative decision about "premise" facts, permit the parties to respond and invite factual submissions by interested individuals apart from the parties).

information.[79] *Third*, courts might carefully spell out the legislative facts on which they rely.[80] *Fourth*, appellate courts could undertake procedural as well as substantive review of legislative fact-finding by lower courts: Did the lower court give the parties notice? Did it consider evidence on both sides of the issue? And so forth.[81]

Innovations such as these would make the process of legislative factfinding more self-conscious and transparent, and more accurate. But they are not likely to happen. Legislative fact-finding is an adjunct of judicial lawmaking—sometimes called judicial *legislation*—which has a bad name. Although it is an absolutely necessary function, it sounds like an antidemocratic usurpation of power. In 1960, Beryl Levy wrote: "Appellate law making . . . is still typically covert and indirective, still half-apologetic and guilt-laden."[82] That is at least as true now as it was a half century ago. As a result, legislative fact-finding is treated like sex: judges do it regularly, but rarely talk about it in public. That may be just as well for sex, but not for a critical fact-finding function in which their conduct should be open, public and accountable.

---

[79] See, e.g., Kenneth Culp Davis, Judicial, Legislative, and Administrative Lawmaking: A Proposed Research Service for the Supreme Court, 71 Minn. L. Rev. 1, 15–16 (1986) (the Supreme Court should have access to a neutral research organization with scientific and social scientific experts, akin to the executive branch's General Accounting Office or the legislative branch's Congressional Research Service; the Court also should employ special court clerks with expertise in sciences or social sciences); John Monahan & Laurens Walker, Social Authority: Obtaining, Evaluating, and Establishing Social Science in Law, 134 U. Pa. L. Rev. 477, 499 (1986) (judges should only notice social science research that: "(1) has survived the critical review of the [relevant scientific] community; (2) has employed valid research methods; (3) is generalizable to the case at issue; and (4) is supported by a body of other research").

[80] See, e.g., Keeton, supra, note 78 (courts should carefully explain what legislative questions they considered, and how they resolved them).

[81] Compare Peggy C. Davis, supra, note 78 (advocating formal codification of "loose" controls on judicial notice of legislative facts that would require appellate courts to acknowledge their use of judicial notice of legislative facts and permit the parties to comment and supply relevant information) with Ann Woolhandler, Rethinking the Judicial Reception of Legislative Facts, 41 Vand. L. Rev. 111, 126 (1988) ("the current, haphazard method of receiving legislative facts, which creates its own incentives for counter-presentations over time, is preferable to a more rationalized approach to judicial reception that holds no promise of encouraging principled decisionmaking") with Michael C. Dorf, The Supreme Court 1997 Term, Foreword: The Limits of Socratic Deliberation, 112 Harv. L. Rev. 4, 11 (1998) (in order to avoid creating essentially permanent legal rules premised on findings of legislative fact that later prove to be dubious, the Court should "treat more of its precedents as provisional [i.e., as subject to more immediate and frequent revision] than is formally permitted under the doctrine of *stare decisis*?" (further elaborated, infra, notes 89–90 and accompanying text)).

[82] Beryl H. Levy, Realist Jurisprudence and Prospective Overruling, 109 U. Pa. L. Rev. 1, 2 (1960).

"Our best strategy may be to destigmatize embezzlement."

PROBLEMS

Problem XI-29. Penelope and Stan were married when a son Kristoff was born. Not long after the birth, Penelope left Stan for Gregory, CEO of Geneticus, a company that has pioneered a new genetic matching process, QNA, that is much cheaper and requires much less organic material than DNA testing. On Kristoff's second birthday, Gregory and his billions deserted Penelope. Gregory fled the country for an unknown destination, leaving behind only a lightly dandruff-flecked blue blazer and a bank account with enough money to set up someone for life. Penelope sues Gregory for child support, claiming that he, not Stan, is the biological father of Kristoff. Although there is not enough organic material tied to Gregory to permit DNA testing, his own invention, QNA, permits a single fleck of his dandruff to be tested, and that test shows that Gregory has biological traits that match those of Kristoff's father, and that fewer than 2% of men share those traits. (The test also rules out Stan as Kristoff's father.) Close to four-fifths of the twenty-six American jurisdictions that have considered the issue by the time of trial have accepted QNA testing as an alternative to DNA; the other jurisdictions have resisted. A leading journal, *Scientific Elite*, has just published an editorial emphasizing the need for caution and additional testing before accepting QNA analysis as a substitute for DNA testing. **May the trial court judicially notice the reliability of QNA tests under FRE 201? Or, should the trial judge use the standard provided by FRE 702? Does it make any difference? If the trial judge takes judicial notice of the reliability of QNA testing, may the appellate court reverse that judgment by taking judicial notice of three intervening scientific studies attacking the reliability of QNA testing?**

Problem XI-30. In *Furman v. Georgia*,[83] the Supreme Court reversed the death sentences that Georgia and Texas had imposed on two convicted rapists and one convicted murderer on the ground that these sentences constituted cruel and unusual punishment in violation of the Eighth Amendment. That judgment—which applied to several hundred other inmates as well, and which cleared death rows across America—was based on a conclusion that the sentencing procedures used in capital cases produced arbitrary, capricious or discriminatory results. Five concurring Justices joined a one-paragraph Per Curiam opinion stating the Court's judgment, and each also wrote a separate concurring opinion. The following excerpt from the concurring opinion of Justice Byron White illustrates a form of legislative fact-finding:

> I must arrive at judgment; and I can do no more than state a conclusion based on ten years of almost daily exposure to the facts and circumstances of hundreds and hundreds of federal and state criminal cases involving crimes for which death is the authorized penalty. That conclusion . . . is that the death penalty is exacted with great infrequency even for the most atrocious crimes and that there is no meaningful basis for distinguishing the few cases in which it is imposed from the many cases in which it is not.[84]

Is this a legitimate way to use facts on appeal? Can it be avoided? Should Georgia and Texas have been given the opportunity to demonstrate to White's satisfaction that there were grounds for distinguishing the few cases in which capital punishment was imposed from those in which it was not imposed? Should they have been given the opportunity to demonstrate that the sample of cases that White used to reach his conclusion was skewed, making it an invalid basis for the judgment he reached? How might such an opportunity have been provided?

---

[83]   408 U.S. 238 (1972).

[84]   Id. at 313. See also Baze v. Rees, 553 U.S. 35, 86 (2008) (Stevens, J., concurring in the judgment) ("[J]ust as Justice White ultimately based his conclusion in *Furman* on his extensive exposure to countless cases for which death is the authorized penalty, I have relied on my own experience in reaching the conclusion that the imposition of the death penalty represents 'the pointless and needless extinction of life with only marginal contributions to any discernible social or public purposes. A penalty with such negligible returns to the State [is] patently excessive and cruel and unusual punishment violative of the Eighth Amendment.' ").

Problem XI-31. About sixteen months after President Bill Clinton was elected President in 1992, Paula Jones filed a complaint against him in the United States District Court for the Eastern District of Arkansas. Her complaint described:

> events said to have occurred on the afternoon of May 8, 1991, during an official conference held at the Excelsior Hotel in Little Rock, Arkansas. The [then] Governor [of Arkansas, Bill Clinton] delivered a speech at the conference; respondent [Jones]— working as a state employee—staffed the registration desk. She alleges that [an Arkansas State Police Officer] persuaded her to leave her desk and to visit the Governor in a business suite at the hotel, where he made "abhorrent" sexual advances that she vehemently rejected. She further claims that her superiors at work subsequently dealt with her in a hostile and rude manner, and changed her duties to punish her for rejecting those advances. Finally, she alleges that after petitioner was elected President ... various persons authorized to speak for the President publicly branded her a liar by denying that the incident had occurred.[85]

President Clinton moved to dismiss or postpone the lawsuit while he was in office, alleging that permitting the suit to go forward would violate the constitutional separation of powers principle by inviting judicial interference with his duties as Chief Executive. The federal district court postponed the suit insofar as it affected the President, but the Eighth Circuit Court of Appeals reversed, holding that the President was little different from any other citizen for purposes of defending a civil lawsuit. A dissenting court of appeals judge contended that the suit should be stayed, predicting that otherwise the President's discharge of his constitutional duties would likely be impaired by this and other private suits. In response, a concurring judge opposed delay, predicting that it would create a significant risk of irreparable harm to litigants suing the President. The Supreme Court agreed to hear the case. Justice Stevens's opinion for the eight-person majority described—and rejected—the President's principal contention, as follows:

> As a factual matter, [the President] contends that this particular case—as well as the potential additional litigation that an affirmance of the Court of Appeals judgment might spawn—may impose an unacceptable burden on the President's time and energy, and thereby impair the effective performance of his office.
>
> [The President's] predictive judgment finds little support in either history or the relatively narrow compass of the issues raised in this particular case. . . . [I]n the more than 200-year

---

[85] Clinton v. Jones, 520 U.S. 681, 685–86 (1997).

history of the Republic, only three sitting Presidents have been subjected to suits for their private actions. If the past is any indicator, it seems unlikely that a deluge of such litigation will ever engulf the Presidency. As for the case at hand, if properly managed by the District Court, it appears to us highly unlikely to occupy any substantial amount of [the President's] time.[86]

In a separate opinion, Justice Breyer wrote:

The majority points to the fact that private plaintiffs have brought civil damage lawsuits against a sitting President only three times in our Nation's history; and it relies upon the threat of sanctions to discourage, and "the [trial] court's discretion" to manage, such actions so that "interference with the President's duties would not occur." I am less sanguine. Since 1960, when the last such suit was filed, the number of civil lawsuits filed annually in Federal District Courts has increased from under 60,000 to about 240,000 . . . ; the time and expense associated with both discovery and trial have increased . . . ; an increasingly complex economy has led to increasingly complex sets of statutes, rules and regulations, that often create potential liability, with or without fault. And this Court has now made clear that such lawsuits may proceed against a sitting President. The consequence . . . , given "the visibility of his office," [is that the President] could well become "an easily identifiable target for suits for civil damages[.]" . . . [S]ome lawsuits (including highly intricate and complicated ones) could resist ready evaluation and disposition; and individual district court procedural rulings could pose a significant threat to the President's official functions.

I concede the possibility that district courts, supervised by the Courts of Appeals and perhaps this Court, might prove able to manage private civil damage actions against sitting Presidents without significantly interfering with the discharge of Presidential duties—at least if they manage those actions with the constitutional problem in mind. Nonetheless, predicting the future is difficult, and I am skeptical.[87]

List all of the factual predictions on which the Court of Appeals judges and Supreme Court Justices based their conclusions in the *Clinton v. Jones* case. Given what you remember or have otherwise learned about the events that followed the Supreme Court's decision in the case, how successfully would you say that the court majorities (and the disagreeing judges) predicted the future with regard to President Clinton himself and with regard

---

[86] Id. at 701–02.

[87] Id. at 722–23.

to subsequent presidents?[88] What, if anything, could the courts have done to improve their predictive powers? What evidence could they have developed, and how could they have developed it? Does the frailty of such predictions, and the difficulty of designing information-gathering techniques to improve them, suggest that the Supreme Court should "treat more of its precedents as provisional [i.e., as subject to more immediate and frequent revision] than is formally permitted under the doctrine of *stare decisis*?"[89] In other words, would it help to treat each of the Court's legislative-fact conclusions as merely an experimental resolution of the problem—with the results of the experiment providing a basis for the Court to revise the relevant constitutional standard or rule when the issue next arises, and so on *ad infinitum*?[90] How much would such an approach modify

---

[88] The Jones lawsuit was pending for five of the eight years of President Clinton's term of office. Although originally brought by lawyers without apparent political affiliations, it subsequently was taken over by two law firms with strong ties to causes and groups opposed to President Clinton and his Administration's policies. A financier with similar ties donated over $1,000,000 to support investigations of Clinton's sex life before and while he was President. During a deposition in the *Jones* case, Clinton denied having "sexual relations" with a young White House intern named Monica Lewinsky. (The district judge later ruled that the Lewinsky matter was immaterial to the Jones suit; still later, but while the President remained in office, the judge ruled that Clinton had knowingly lied about Lewinsky in the deposition and accordingly found him in contempt and fined him.) Special prosecutor Kenneth Starr, who three years earlier had been appointed to investigate certain financial dealings of the President and his wife while he was Governor of Arkansas, concluded that the President may have perjured himself in answering questions about Lewinsky in the deposition in the separate *Jones* matter, and was given permission to expand his investigation to consider that possibility. Starr subsequently concluded that the President had indeed committed perjury in denying sexual relations with Lewinsky. He supported his conclusions in a report describing in graphic detail more than a dozen sexual encounters that allegedly occurred between the President and Lewinsky in the White House. The report concluded that the President's deposition testimony and related events, including subsequent grand jury testimony, established eleven potential grounds for impeaching Clinton. The Republican majority in the House of Representatives promptly voted to disseminate Starr's sexually explicit report to the public, and then impeached the Democratic President. Following a trial in the Senate, the President was acquitted. Meanwhile, the district court granted summary judgment in favor of the President in the *Jones* suit, ruling that there was no evidence that Jones's alleged encounter with Clinton had any adverse job-related effects on her. While that decision was on appeal, Jones and the President settled the case for $750,000. At least a year of the Clinton Presidency was consumed with the Jones and Lewinsky matters. Among the fall-out were allegations that the President very nearly involved the nation in a war with Iraq in order to distract the public from the Jones and Lewinsky matters and, conversely, that he dangerously temporized in response to Iraqi provocations out of fear that the public would perceive a stronger response as a ploy to distract its attention from those matters.

[89] Dorf, supra, note 81, at 11.

[90] Cf. id. at 75–76:

Consider an example. [I]n Morrison v. Olson, [487 U.S. 654 (1988),] the Court upheld severe restrictions on the President's power to remove an independent counsel because it found that the restrictions were not "of such a nature that they impede the President's ability to perform his constitutional duty. . . . " [Id. at 691.] This conclusion appeared to be little more than a guess, given the lack of experience under the statute at the time.

Suppose that the Court were now to regard *Morrison* as merely provisional. What lesson should be gleaned from the ferocity of Independent Counsel Kenneth Starr's investigation of President Clinton's efforts to conceal his sexual encounters with a former White House intern? See supra, note 88. Is Starr's zeal attributable to his own peculiar (perhaps politically partisan)

the usual common law method of constitutional and other adjudication? How well would the approach serve the parties to the initial, "experimental" decision? What else might the courts do when faced with legislative-fact judgments of the sort presented by the *Clinton v. Jones* case?

Problem XI-32. In 1980, in *Trammel v. United States*,[91] the Supreme Court held that the federal "spousal testimony" privilege—which prevents one spouse from testifying against the other in a criminal trial—could only be claimed by the witness-spouse, and not by the defendant-spouse. This holding was a change in the federal common law of evidence, contrary to the trend in most American states, and inconsistent with the version of the privilege in Proposed FRE 505, which the Court approved but Congress failed to adopt. The Court held that the purpose of the spousal testimony privilege is the preservation of marital harmony. Given that purpose, it decided that there is no reason to continue to give a criminal defendant the power to prevent his or her spouse from testifying against the defendant because, in the Court's view, "When one spouse is willing to testify against the other in a criminal proceeding—whatever the motivation—their relationship is almost certainly in disrepair; there is probably little in the way of marital harmony for the privilege to preserve."[92] Of course, another court could have viewed the world differently. It might have said: "When one spouse actually *does* testify against the other in a criminal case—regardless of the witness-spouse's motivations or expectations—the damage to the relationship is bound to be devastating, and will probably be irreparable." Based on that description, such a court might have held that giving the defendant-spouse the power to prevent such testimony helps preserve marital harmony by insuring that this fateful step is not taken except when both spouses agree to it at the outset.

Suppose that by 1985 it had become apparent from a couple of systematic studies and several highly-publicized trials that the Supreme Court had been wrong, as a factual matter, in *Trammel*. Assume that by then it was pretty clear that permitting spousal testimony in criminal cases over the defendants' objections *did* wreck a fair number of otherwise sustainable marriages, either because the witness-spouse did not anticipate the consequences, or because that option creates an

---

desire to drive President Clinton from office? Alternatively, is the Starr investigation a reflection of the incentives that any independent counsel faces? According to this latter view, the independent counsel is a Frankenstein's monster because he acts without the constraint of scarce resources that confronts ordinary prosecutors. If the Court were to draw this broader inference, it would be appropriate to overrule *Morrison*.

Instead of, or perhaps in addition to, revisiting *Morrison*, might the Court appropriately reconsider its . . . decision in *Clinton v. Jones*. . . . It was, after all, discovery conducted in *Jones* that led to the widening of Starr's investigative authority to include the President's extramarital sex life.

   [91]   445 U.S. 40 (1980). See Chapter Eight, Section IV.C., pp. 1038–1041.

   [92]   Trammel v. United States, 445 U.S. at 52.

incentive for law enforcement personnel to try to drive a wedge between spouses. **Should the Court at that point have reconsidered and reversed *Trammel*? What difference, if any, would it make if it was not until the year 2015 that the Court's error in *Trammel* became apparent? Is the question of reconsideration in light of new evidence the same here as in the context of the issues in *Clinton v. Jones*, which we discuss in the previous problem?**

C. PRESUMPTIONS

The law sometimes permits or even requires the fact-finder to "presume" that a consequential fact exists if some other fact has been proven. In a contract case, for example, if a consumer signed a contract, it sometimes is presumed that she read and understood it. In a torts case, if Alan was driving Betty's car, Alan is presumed to have had Betty's permission to do so. In an action to settle an estate, if the person who owns the estate has been missing without "tidings" for seven years, she not only is presumed to be dead, but she also is presumed to have died at the last moment of the seventh year. And in a variety of actions, if some result is a natural and probable consequence of something a person did, that person may be presumed to have intended the result.

As these examples indicate, presumptions generally take the form: *If the existence of fact X has been proven, fact Y may [or sometimes should, or always should] be considered proven.* Whether proving fact **X** means that fact **Y** *may, sometimes should be,* or *always should be* considered proven depends on the nature of the presumption and the evidence the party opposing the presumption offers. Because proof of fact **X** is the basis on which the fact-finder presumes the existence of fact **Y**, fact **X** is generally called the *basic* fact, and fact **Y** is called the *presumed* fact.[93]

The existence of a basic fact is usually reason to believe a presumed fact is true. Nevertheless, the two facts may not be so closely connected that, without a presumption, the basic fact alone would justify finding that the presumed fact exists. The more tenuous the inferential connection between the basic fact and the presumed fact, the more work the presumption does. For example, the presumption that a prisoner possessed contraband if he was present in a cell where it was discovered does more work when applied to a holding pen, which scores of prisoners pass through each day, than when applied to a cell the prisoner alone occupies. In the latter instance, one might infer possession without the aid of the presumption, but in the case of the holding pen, without a

---

[93] As we discuss below, the modern practice is to reserve the term "presumption" for devices that at least sometimes *require* jurors to find **fact Y** based on **fact X**, and to use the term "inference" or "permissive inference" to refer to devices that *invite* or *allow*, but don't *require*, the jury to make that finding. For the moment, however, we will use the word "presumption" to refer to both types of devices.

presumption it would appear more likely than not that the contraband did not belong to any particular prisoner.

Presumptions differ in the degree to which they bind the fact-finder to find the presumed fact regardless of the other evidence in the case. Consider the following six descriptions of how presumptions may work. They describe progressively stronger (in the sense of "more binding") presumptions. As one goes down the list, once the basic fact **(fact X)** is proved, the fact-finder's ability to find anything other than the presumed fact **(fact Y)** diminishes. We speak of juries in these examples, but the fact-finder could as well be the judge.

1.   If the jury finds that fact **X** exists, it may, but is not required to, find that when **X** is considered along with all the other evidence tending to prove fact **Y**, **Y** also is true.

2.   If the jury finds that fact **X** exists, it may, but is not required to, find that fact **Y** is true, even if **X** is the only evidence that suggests **Y** exists.

3.   If the jury finds that fact **X** exists, it must also find that fact **Y** is true unless the opposing party *claims* that **Y** is not true—in which case, no presumption arises, and the implications of **X** for **Y**'s existence depend on the degree to which **X** tends to prove **Y**. In other words, if the opposing party disclaims fact **Y**, fact **X** is treated the same as any other evidence of **Y**.

4.   If the jury finds that fact **X** exists, it must also find that fact **Y** is true unless the opposing party introduces sufficient evidence that **Y** is not true. If the opposing party does this, no presumption arises, and the implications of **X** for **Y**'s existence depend on the degree to which **X** tends to prove **Y**. How much evidence is required in order to prove **Y** untrue depends on the presumption. It may be *some* evidence of **Y**'s untruth, *substantial* evidence of **Y**'s untruth, or evidence that would *permit a rational fact-finder* to conclude that **Y** is untrue.

5.   If the jury finds that fact **X** exists, it must find that fact **Y** is true unless the opposing party *proves* that **Y** is not true. The burden that the opposing party faces in proving **Y** untrue varies with the presumption. It may be (a) by a *preponderance* of the evidence, (b) by *clear and convincing* evidence, or (c) *beyond a reasonable doubt*, or it may be (d) that the opposing party need only prove that **Y** is *as likely to be true* as **X**.

6.   If the jury finds that fact **X** exists, it must find that fact **Y** is true, no matter what.[94]

---

[94] Names that have sometimes (but not always) been attached to these six ways of connecting proof of fact **X** to proof of fact **Y** are: (1) "Permissive inference"; (2) "Permissive presumption"; **X** is treated as legally "sufficient" evidence of **Y**; (3) "Mandatory burden-of-

All but the first two presumptions on this list modify the burdens of pleading, production or persuasion that would otherwise apply. For this reason, modern legal usage typically refers to the first two as "permissive inferences," not presumptions. Presumptions that modify the burdens of production or persuasion (the latter four types listed above) are rules of substantive law as much as they are rules of evidence. Below, we discuss the difference between these six types of evidentiary devices, the policies they serve and the constitutional problems they may create.

In fact, only types (3)–(5) are true *presumptions* because only they give the basic fact an influence beyond its normal probative value without having conclusive effect. Type (1) and (2) presumptions ("permissive inferences" in modern parlance) alert the jury to the potential strength of the association between two facts but leave it to the jury to determine if that association exists.[95] Type (6) presumptions, called *conclusive presumptions*, seem to require a party to prove fact **Y**, but actually only require her to prove another fact, **X**. Conclusive presumptions mean that although proof of **Y** appears to be indispensable to making out a party's case, proof of **X** can substitute for proof of **Y**, and the burden-bearing party can choose which to prove.

The many situations in which courts have spoken of presumptions, and the murkiness of their definitions, explain Professor Morgan's observation more than seventy years ago that "[e]very writer" who has tried to make sense of presumptions "has approached the topic . . . with a sense of hopelessness and has left it with a feeling of despair."[96] The term *presumption* is unruly because it can be applied whenever one fact is used as a bridge to finding another, legally relevant fact. But this is true of many facts proven in litigation because legally dispositive facts (e.g., that the defendant was speeding) often can only be proved by establishing *other* facts (e.g., the length of skid marks). Morgan sought to domesticate the term by insisting that the link a *presumption* forges between a basic and a presumed fact be *artificial*, in the sense that the presumption requires or "permit[s] the trier of fact to give to the evidence [establishing

---

pleading-shifting presumption"; (4) "Mandatory burden-of-*production*-shifting presumption"; (5) "Mandatory burden-of-*proof*-shifting presumption"; (6) "Conclusive presumption." Types (3) and (4) are sometimes called "bubble-bursting" presumptions. Sufficient proof of **X** creates the possibility that the trier will be required to presume **Y** based on **X**. But that possibility is removed—the bubble bursts—if the other party either pleads that **Y** is not true (type (3)), or produces the specified amount of evidence that **Y** is not true (type (4)). See Sandstrom v. Montana, 442 U.S. 510, 516 & n.5 (1979).

[95] Presumptions of this sort are similar to judicial comments on the weight of the evidence. Federal judges and judges in some states are authorized not only to summarize the evidence in a case for their juries, but also—as long as they maintain their judicial neutrality—to comment on the weight of the evidence. Most American judges do not comment on the weight of the evidence, even when they have the power to do so.

[96] Edmund M. Morgan, Presumptions, 12 Wash. L. Rev. 255 (1937). See, e.g., Edmund M. Morgan, Further Observations on Presumptions, 16 S. Cal. L. Rev. 245, 247–49 (1943) (cataloguing six types of presumptions); Charles V. Laughlin, In Support of the Thayer Theory of Presumptions, 52 Mich. L. Rev. 195, 196–209 (1953) (eight types).

the basic fact] more than its inherently logical value [as proof of the presumed fact]."[97] We build on Morgan's insight by classifying the six types of "presumptions" we have identified by the likelihood that the link each instructs the jury to draw between basic fact **X** and presumed fact **Y** will be artificial in the sense that it will be stronger than the link a jury would draw if it were not told of the presumption.

At one extreme are the two types of so-called "permissive inferences," which permit but do not require a jury to find a presumed fact, **Y**, upon proof of the basic fact, **X**, alone. For example, jurors may be instructed that, if they find that Anne properly addressed and posted a letter to Bruce, they may, but need not, conclude that Bruce received the letter. As the modern preference for the term "permissive inference" suggests, the word "presumption" is arguably inappropriate here, because the so-called presumption simply permits the trier to "infer," but never requires it to find, **Y** based on **X**. Yet even permissive inferences may encourage stronger links between **X** and **Y** than logic or experience would suggest.[98] This is because a jury instructed on the evidentiary device may be influenced in its fact-finding by knowing that the law and the judge place their official imprimatur on the link between **X** and **Y**. Also, a permissive presumption (type 2) allows the party that must prove **Y** to avoid a directed verdict at the close of its case-in-chief as long as it has introduced evidence sufficient to prove **X**.[99] If the jury, or the judge on a motion for a

---

[97] Edmund M. Morgan, Further Observations, supra, note 96, at 246; see also Tot v. United States, 319 U.S. 463, 468 (1943) (presumptions raise constitutional questions when used against the accused in criminal cases insofar as they encourage jurors to take "a view of the relation between [**X** and **Y**] broader than that" they would take absent the instruction). To show that courts tolerate devices of this sort, Morgan cited decisions enforcing statutorily created presumptions that proof of **X** suffices to establish **Y**, though the same courts had concluded before the statute establishing the presumption was adopted that **X** was *not* sufficient to prove **Y**.

[98] This example illustrates the second of our six types of "presumptions." The conceptual distinction we introduce between what we call type 1 and type 2 devices tends to go unrecognized by courts, and both may be referred to as "permissive presumptions" or "permissive inferences." Almost never do true permissive inferences, our type 1 presumption, "artificially" bridge the gap between **X** and **Y**. An instruction that the jury may find that **X**, along with other evidence, establishes **Y** gives artificial weight to **X** only if **X** provides no logical evidence of **Y**, i.e., only if **X** is irrelevant. The idea that **X** may be sufficient, but only along with the other evidence in a case, to justify finding **Y** is, in federal courts, more likely to be communicated to juries through judicial comments on the weight of the evidence than by formal instruction on a "presumption." Professor Allen usefully discusses the relationship that exists among various devices for encouraging juries to think in certain ways about the evidence they have heard, including presumptions and judicial comment.   Ronald Allen, Structuring Jury Decisionmaking in Criminal Cases: A Unified Constitutional Approach to Evidentiary Devices, 94 Harv. L. Rev. 321 (1980).

[99] What we call a type 1 presumption, (i.e., a permissive inference that justifies finding **Y** only in conjunction with other evidence of **Y**) should not forestall a directed verdict if **X** is the only evidence of **Y**, as long as it is not reasonable in the context of the case to find **Y** from proof of **X** alone. But when a so-called "presumption" has been established, even if it is one that only exists to emphasize a permitted inference, courts typically leave it to juries to determine if the inference is justified. In criminal cases, however, on some facts it might be unconstitutional to allow a jury to find the presumed fact against the accused from evidence of just the basic fact. For example, if contraband is found in a cell, the law may provide that a prisoner who has been in that cell is "presumed" to have possessed that contraband. Although it might be acceptable to allow a case charging a prisoner with possessing contraband like drugs to go to the jury without

directed verdict, would not have considered **X** sufficient to prove **Y** without the permissive presumption, the party's case has been strengthened. Most troubling, jurors hearing words such as "the law presumes **Y** from **X**," which frequently are used when instructing even on *permissive* devices, may believe that they *must* find **Y** if they find **X**, even though other parts of the instruction explicitly tell them that they "*may* but need not find **Y** based on **X**."

At the other extreme are *conclusive* (or *irrebuttable*) *presumptions*— rules requiring a trier who finds the basic fact, **X**, to also find the presumed fact, **Y**. Conclusive presumptions may be attacked by disproving **X**, but if **X** exists, **Y** is presumed to exist as well, no matter how weak the actual link between **X** and **Y**. Thus, even though **Y** is supposedly the crucial issue in the case, evidence offered to disprove **Y** is not even admissible once **X** has been shown. Most authorities now recognize that so-called conclusive presumptions are not evidentiary presumptions at all, but rather substantive laws making **X**, irrespective of **Y**, decisive of the parties' rights and duties through the *irrebuttable* fiction that **X**'s existence always establishes **Y**. For example, if a law that says title passes only when the owner of property consensually transfers it to another person also provides that an owner is conclusively presumed to have consensually transferred property to anyone who has "openly and notoriously" possessed it, without consent, for seven years, the law actually is that title passes *either* upon consensual transfer *or* upon adverse possession for more than seven years. Conclusive presumptions often exist only temporarily before the law gives up the fiction that only **Y**, and not **X**, is decisive.[100]

---

other evidence that the prisoner possessed the drugs if the prisoner had been the only person occupying the cell, it almost certainly would be unconstitutional to allow a jury to convict the prisoner without other evidence of possession if the cell the prisoner occupied was a holding pen at a courthouse through which twenty prisoners had passed in the course of a day. However, one seldom encounters convictions based on evidence and permissive devices as weak as this, perhaps because such cases are not brought or, if they are brought, don't result in conviction. Neither type of permissive presumption forbids (though they often will deter) the judge from granting a directed verdict against the moving party after *all* the evidence is in. A directed verdict is required at that point if the opposing party's evidence that **Y** does not exist is so strong that, despite the legally recognized inference of **Y** from **X** and other evidence that may support the inference, no rational juror could find **Y**. A directed verdict against the moving party will also be in order if proof of fact **X** is a necessary predicate to finding fact **Y** and, after considering all the evidence, no rational juror could find **X**. If either of these situations arises in a criminal case, moreover, reversal of the conviction on appeal would be required under the rule of Jackson v. Virginia, 443 U.S. 307 (1979) (a conviction violates the Due Process Clause if a rational jury could not find one or more of the elements of the crime present beyond a reasonable doubt based on the evidence of record after drawing all reasonable inferences in favor of guilt).

[100] For a time, the Supreme Court perceived a constitutional problem with so-called conclusive presumptions even in civil cases. See, e.g., Vlandis v. Kline, 412 U.S. 441 (1973) (invalidating conclusive presumption of nonresidence for purposes of in-state college tuition if a student had a legal residence outside the state at any time during the year preceding admission); Stanley v. Illinois, 405 U.S. 645 (1972) (invalidating a statutory irrebuttable presumption that unmarried fathers are unqualified to raise children); see also Cleveland Bd. of Educ. v. LaFleur, 414 U.S. 632 (1974) (voiding a school board requirement of mandatory maternity leave commencing five months before the expected birth, which the Court treated as an irrebuttable

Mandatory but *rebuttable* presumptions also *require* the trier to find **Y** upon proof of **X**, but only on some, not all, occasions. These presumptions operate to place on the party opposing the presumption a burden of pleading or, more commonly, either a production burden or the burden of persuasion. When only the burden of *pleading* is affected, the party benefited by the presumption is entitled to have the presumed fact (**Y**) taken as proved unless the opposing party contends that it is not true. Such presumptions typically are used when **Y**, although technically an element of a cause of action or of an offense a party must prove, is generally not contested. The presumption of the defendant's sanity in a criminal case is an example. By "presuming" that the defendant is sane unless he pleads insanity, the law saves the state the trouble of proving sanity in the many cases in which it is not contested, trial time is shortened, money is saved, and the possibility of confusing the jury is avoided.

Mandatory presumptions that impose a burden of *production* on the opposing party require the jury, upon proof of fact **X**, to find fact **Y**, unless the opposing party *introduces evidence* tending to disprove **Y**. FRE 301

---

presumption of incapacity upon reaching the fifth month of pregnancy). The Court soon realized, however, that almost any law may be characterized as a conclusive presumption. For example, a law against driving more than 65 mph on the freeway may be characterized as a conclusive presumption of recklessness from high speed; a law against reckless driving may be characterized as a conclusive presumption of harm from recklessness, etc. See Note, Irrebuttable Presumptions: An Illusory Analysis, 27 Stan. L. Rev. 449 (1975). Lest the conclusive or irrebuttable presumption doctrine become an "engine of destruction for countless legislative judgments which have heretofore been thought [constitutional]," Weinberger v. Salfi, 422 U.S. 749, 772 (1975), the Court scrapped the doctrine and reinterpreted its prior cases as traditional applications of equal protection and due process law. (In retrospect the conclusive presumption cases were seen as banning discrimination against recent residents (*Vlandis*) and men (*Stanley*), and as forbidding undue burdens on the right to procreate (*LaFleur*)). This process began in *Salfi*, supra, which upheld a statute that both established a policy denying social security survivor benefits to any widow or widower of a marriage contracted so that the survivor could collect these benefits and created a conclusive presumption that any marriage contracted within nine months of a beneficiary's death was contracted so that the survivor could collect benefits. Under the conclusive presumption doctrine, the law was suspect because many—probably most—marriages that end within nine months because of a spouse's death are not contracted to create a social security entitlement in the survivor. As a matter of due process or equal protection, however, the law is less suspect, because it is reasonable to deny benefits to widows and widowers who have not been married long enough to have become completely dependent financially on their spouse, regardless of the motivation for the marriage. And while nine months may be an arbitrary line for assessing financial dependency, it is not an unreasonable one, and bright lines often are needed in the law. Because Congress could have passed a less-than-nine-month cut-off rule without establishing a presumption—and might well have done so had the Court overturned the statute in *Salfi*—the Court thought it made sense to uphold the presumption rather than force Congress to reenact the same rule with different words.

The conclusive presumption doctrine did not effectively distinguish permissible from impermissible legislation, but it did have one important virtue: it prevented one kind of legislative obfuscation. In the *Salfi* situation, for example, most people would probably agree that a person should not collect social security survivor benefits when a marriage was contracted with a person who did not have long to live just so the new spouse could collect benefits. But more might disagree with a policy denying survivor's benefits to those who had married for love but whose marriages had not lasted long. By establishing a conclusive presumption, a legislature can enact a statute which reads as if it is instituting the former rule when it is actually instituting the latter, with the effect of deflecting opposition that otherwise might have kept the proposal from being enacted.

treats all presumptions in civil cases in this manner, unless the presumption is explicitly given some other effect by the federal statute or rule creating it (or, under FRE 302, by state law in diversity cases).[101] FRE 301 provides:

> In a civil case, unless a federal statute or these rules provide otherwise, the party against whom a presumption is directed has the burden of producing evidence to rebut the presumption. But this rule does not shift the burden of persuasion, which remains on the party who had it originally.

FRE 301 might be read to say that *any* "evidence" that **Y** is untrue will rebut the presumption. Or it might be treated as silent on the question of the amount of required rebuttal evidence. Taking the latter approach, most federal courts have interpreted FRE 301's silence as signaling that the common law remains in force on the issue, and that the production-burden-shifting presumption should govern the outcome unless the opposing party presents "sufficient" (or, sometimes, "satisfactory" or "substantial") evidence to the contrary. "Sufficient evidence" is usually taken to mean evidence that, if believed, would permit a rational finder of fact to conclude that the presumed fact is not present.[102]

A mandatory burden-of-production-shifting presumption has different effects depending on whether a case is criminal or civil. FRE 301, which defines most federal presumptions as burden-of-production-shifting devices and governs their operation, applies only to civil cases; the drafters of the Rules initially proposed a different rule for criminal cases—Proposed Rule 303, quoted infra, note 115. Congress rejected Proposed Rule 303, however, leaving the treatment of presumptions in criminal cases to federal common law where the presumed fact (**Y**) is not an element of a crime, and to regulation by federal common and constitutional law where **Y** *is* an element of a crime. For the most part,

---

[101] Although Rule 301 says it governs the effect of all federal law presumptions in civil cases unless they are given a different effect by a statute or rule that formally codifies the presumption, some federal courts have also given a different effect to presumptions that are not formally codified but are endorsed by longstanding federal common law. See, e.g., Hood v. Knappton Corp., 986 F.2d 329 (9th Cir. 1993) and James v. River Parishes Co., 686 F.2d 1129 (5th Cir. 1982) (both following longstanding federal admiralty law in giving stronger effect than Rule 301 would do to a presumption that a vessel found adrift was negligently operated or secured). This approach seems reasonable as long as it is confined to contexts (such as admiralty law) where federal law comprehensively governs and where Congress has not occupied the field and instead has largely left federal common law to control.

[102] See, e.g., St. Mary's Honor Center v. Hicks, 509 U.S. 502, 507 (1993) (to rebut a burden-of-production-shifting presumption, the opposing party must offer " 'admissible evidence' . . . which *if believed by the trier of fact*, would support a finding that" the presumed fact is not true (emphasis in original)); ITC Ltd. v. Punchgini, Inc., 482 F.3d 135, 149 (2d Cir.), cert. denied, 552 U.S. 827 (2007) ("such contrary evidence as, when viewed in the light most favorable to [the rebutting party], would permit a reasonable jury to infer" that the presumed fact is not true; "sufficient evidence to permit a reasonable jury to conclude" that the presumed fact is not true); In re G-I Holdings, Inc., 385 F.3d 313, 318 (3d Cir. 2004) ("sufficient evidence"); A.C. Aukerman Co. v. R.L. Chaides Construction Co., 960 F.2d 1020, 1037 (Fed. Cir. 1992) ("sufficient to support a finding of the nonexistence of the presumed fact").

burden-of-production-shifting presumptions in criminal cases that run against the prosecution, and those that run against the criminal defendant on matters as to which it is appropriate to give the accused the ultimate burden of persuasion (see supra, Section I)—receive the same treatment as civil burden-of-production-shifting presumptions. The treatment of presumptions that run against the accused on matters as to which the Constitution gives the ultimate burden of persuasion to the prosecution are discussed below.

A mandatory burden-of-production-shifting presumption also has different effects depending on the other evidence introduced. To illustrate how different outcomes are contingent on the evidence introduced, assume that the presumption that a properly addressed and posted letter is received shifts the production burden. The basic fact, or fact **X**, in this presumption is that a correctly addressed letter with the right amount of postage was mailed. The presumed fact, or fact **Y**, is that the letter was received by the addressee.[103] If Anne introduces persuasive evidence that she stamped and mailed a letter to Bruce, and if Bruce neither contests her evidence of mailing or the implication that the letter was received, the judge will direct the jury to find that Bruce received the letter. If, instead, Bruce offers evidence tending to show that Anne did not mail the letter but introduces no evidence on whether he received it, the judge will tell the jurors that they should determine whether Anne mailed the letter to Bruce, and that if they find she did, they must conclude that Bruce received the letter. If the jury finds that Anne did not mail the letter but there is other evidence that Bruce received it (e.g., Anne testifies that she either mailed the letter or had it delivered by messenger but can't remember which), the jury must determine on the basis of all the evidence whether Bruce received the letter. The usual preponderance of the evidence standard will apply. If, finally, Bruce doesn't dispute Anne's testimony that she mailed the letter but says he looked for a letter from Anne and it never arrived, the outcome depends on the kind of presumption from which Anne benefits. If under the jurisdiction's rule, *any* "evidence" suffices to neutralize the presumption, then Bruce's testimony that the letter never arrived negates the presumption, and the jury should not be told of the presumption. The jury should simply decide whether the evidence that Bruce received Anne's letter (Anne's testimony of mailing it, and any other evidence of Bruce's receipt) preponderates over the evidence that Bruce did not receive the letter (Bruce's denial and any other evidence suggesting nonreceipt).[104] If instead "sufficient

---

[103] See Rosenthal v. Walker, 111 U.S. 185 (1884).

[104] Occasionally, judges in this situation will instruct the jury that it may, but is not required, to "infer" fact **Y** from fact **X** (here, receipt from mailing). Cf. Retail Services, Inc. v. Freebies Publishing, Inc., 364 F.3d 535 (4th Cir. 2004) (even after a presumption evaporates, a permissive inference remains); Nunley v. City of Los Angeles, 52 F.3d 792, 796 (9th Cir. 1995) ("Even after the 'bubble' of presumption has 'burst,' the factual question of receipt . . . may be decided in favor of receipt by a fact finder who may choose to draw inferences of receipt from the evidence of mailing, in spite of contrary evidence.").

evidence" is required to neutralize the presumption, most federal courts will still treat the presumption as negated, because a reasonable jury could find, based on Bruce's testimony (assuming the jury chooses to credit it), that the letter never arrived. In this instance, again, the jury should simply decide whether Anne's evidence on the point preponderates.[105] In any of these scenarios, Anne avoids a directed verdict at the end of her case-in-chief as long as she has produced enough evidence to allow a reasonable jury to find that she mailed to Bruce a correctly addressed and properly stamped letter.

As originally proposed by the drafters of the Federal Rules (but rejected by Congress), FRE 301 would not only have shifted the burden of production but also would have shifted the burden of persuasion in civil cases:

> In all civil actions and proceedings not otherwise provided for by statute or by these rules, a presumption imposes on the party against whom it is directed the burden of proving that the nonexistence of the presumed fact is more probable than its existence.[106]

---

[105] In some jurisdictions that require "sufficient" or "substantial" evidence to rebut the presumption, the judge will actually inform the jury of the presumption. In other words, if Bruce has not disputed Anne's evidence of mailing, the judge may instruct the jurors that receipt is "presumed" upon mailing, and that they must find that Bruce received the letter unless they regard Bruce's denial as "sufficient" or "substantial evidence" of nonreceipt. If the jurors regard the denial as sufficient or substantial, they should disregard the presumption and decide whether it was more likely than not that Bruce received the letter based on all the evidence in the case. Other courts, however, leave the issue whether the responding evidence is strong enough to neutralize the presumption to the *judge alone*, and never mention the word "presumption" to the jury. If the judge is satisfied that enough rebutting evidence has been offered, she instructs the jury to resolve the underlying question—whether the letter was received—under the usual preponderance of the evidence test. If no, or what the judge believes is insufficient or insubstantial, rebutting evidence is offered, the judge instructs the jury that it must find that the presumed fact is true. The virtue of this latter practice is that it keeps the beneficiary of the presumption from gaining from having invoked a presumption that has been rebutted and (by law) should have no effect. When, instead, the jury is instructed on the "presumption" and how it works, the judge inevitably calls attention to the link between **X** and **Y** and indicates that it is strong enough that, absent evidence disputing **Y**'s existence, fact **X** is a sufficient basis for concluding that fact **Y** also exists. Although the presumption is supposed to disappear once it is rebutted, the jury may overweight the tendency of fact **X** to prove fact **Y** because the judge has used the strong word "presumption" to emphasize the link that might exist between them. In these latter jurisdictions, rather than thinking of rebutted presumptions as bubbles that have burst or bats that have flitted away in the night (metaphors that courts and commentators have used to describe them), it would be more appropriate to think of them as Cheshire cats. Although the cat has gone, its grin remains.

[106] The enacted and superseded versions of FRE 301 represent different resolutions of a disagreement between James Bradley Thayer (writing at the end of the 19th century) and Edmund M. Morgan (writing during the 1930s). In Thayer's view, a presumption should always have a "bubble-bursting" or burden-of-production-shifting effect: If the trier of fact finds that **X** is true, then it also must find that **Y** is true unless the opposing party presents evidence sufficient to convince a rational individual that **Y** is not true, in which case the presumption does not arise. In Morgan's view, the effect Thayer accorded presumptions was too "slight and evanescent," Edmund M. Morgan & John M. Maguire, Looking Backward and Forward at Evidence, 50 Harv. L. Rev. 909, 913 (1937), and, indeed, "little short of ridiculous," Edmund M. Morgan, Instructing the Jury Upon Presumptions and Burden of Proof, 47 Harv. L. Rev. 59, 82–83 (1933). "If a policy is strong enough to call a presumption into existence," Morgan argued, "it is hard to imagine it so weak as to be satisfied by the bare recital of words on the witness stand

Burden-of-*persuasion*-shifting presumptions of this sort work the same way as burden-of-*production*-shifting presumptions except in one important situation—when the opposing party introduces evidence contesting **Y**, the presumed fact.   When this happens, the jury is instructed to find **Y** unless the *opposing* party's evidence convinces it that **Y** is not true by the appropriate standard of proof (usually a preponderance of the evidence, but sometimes higher).   In the dispute between Anne and Bruce, if the "mailing presumption" shifted the burden of persuasion, Anne's persuasive testimony that she properly addressed and posted the letter to Bruce would require Bruce not only to introduce evidence that he did not receive the letter but also to persuade the jury of this fact by a preponderance of the evidence—or by clear and convincing evidence, or any other standard the law required the party fighting the inference to meet.

Finally, we come to conclusive presumptions.   As we have already seen these are really rules of law that equate proof of the basic fact with proof of the presumed fact.   There is no way they can be rebutted; hence, they are sometimes called *irrebuttable presumptions*.

Chart 11–1 summarizes much of what we have discussed thus far.   It combines what we have called type 1 and 2 presumptions as *permissive inferences*, and it ignores type 3 presumptions, which are contested not with evidence but through pleading.

CHART 11–1

Types of Presumptions

The beneficiary of the presumption (*B*) introduces evidence of the basic fact. The presumption:	The party opposing the presumption (*O*) introduces:	The consequences of the presumption are that the jurors will be instructed that:
I. Is conclusive.	No evidence bearing on the presumption.	If they find the basic fact, they must find the presumed fact. A directed verdict may be in order.
	Evidence tending to contradict the basic fact.[a] Evidence tending to contradict the presumed fact (probably inadmissible).	If they find the basic fact, they must find the presumed fact. If they find the basic fact, they must find the presumed fact. A directed verdict may be in order.

or the reception in evidence of a writing [contending to the contrary]." Id. Morgan thought presumptions should have a burden-of-proof-shifting effect: if the trier of fact finds that **X** is true, then it also must find that **Y** is true, unless the opposing party proves by a preponderance of the evidence that **Y** is not true. The Supreme Court sided with Morgan when it sent the Proposed Federal Rules to the Congress, but Congress chose Thayer's position as the default rule. State codes based on the Federal Rules are split on this issue. Because FRE 301 is a default rule that operates only when the law creating a presumption does not specify its effect, one must always research the law creating a presumption to determine its effects.

The beneficiary of the presumption (*B*) introduces evidence of the basic fact. The presumption:	The party opposing the presumption (*O*) introduces:	The consequences of the presumption are that the jurors will be instructed that:
II. Shifts the risk of nonpersuasion (the burden of persuasion).	No evidence bearing on the presumption.	If they find the basic fact, they must find the presumed fact. A directed verdict may be in order.
	Evidence tending to contradict the basic fact.	If they find the basic fact, they must find the presumed fact.
	Evidence tending to contradict the presumed fact.	If they find the basic fact, they must find the presumed fact unless *O* convinces them by a preponderance of the evidence (or, in certain cases, by some higher standard) that the presumed fact does not exist.[b]
III. Shifts the production burden.	No evidence bearing on the presumption.	If they find the basic fact, they must find the presumed fact. A directed verdict may be in order.
	Evidence tending to contradict the basic fact.	If they find the basic fact, they must find the presumed fact.
	Evidence tending to contradict the presumed fact.	*Majority rule*: If the judge finds the evidence is "sufficient," there is no jury instruction relating the basic fact to the presumed fact.[b] The jurors decide the case based on the preponderance of the evidence. *Alternative rule #1*: Same outcome if *any* evidence is presented. *Alternative rule #2*: The jury is instructed to determine whether the evidence is "sufficient" or "substantial"; if so, the presumption dissolves and the jury decides the case based on the preponderance of the evidence; if not, the jury must find the presumed fact.
IV. Is a permissive inference.	No evidence bearing on the presumption.	If they find the basic fact, they must decide whether it, together with any other evidence presented in the case, justifies finding the presumed fact.[b] If *B* has the burden of proving the presumed fact and offers no evidence tending to prove the presumed fact except that which tends to prove the basic fact, *B* will probably be able to avoid a directed verdict.
	Evidence tending to contradict the basic fact.	The same as if *O* introduces no evidence bearing on the presumption.[b]
	Evidence tending to contradict the presumed fact.	The same as if *O* introduces no evidence bearing on the presumption, except that if *O*'s evidence contradicting the presumed fact is beyond dispute, a verdict will be directed against *B*.[b]

a.   Whenever evidence contradicting the basic fact is beyond dispute, the court will give a peremptory instruction, and the presumption will not help *B*. This is true throughout the chart.
b.   In some jurisdictions the jurors may be told that the law permits, but does not require, an inference from the basic to the presumed facts.

The many varieties of what we call "presumptions" reflect the many reasons why a legislature or court might want to treat proof of one fact as if it were in some measure, if not entirely, proof of another. As Professor James concludes, "the bases upon which courts or legislatures will create presumptions"

> may be summed up as reasons of convenience, fairness, and policy. What is *likely* is often presumed. Most [people] are sane, as the law reckons sanity, and most properly sent letters reach their destination. In the absence of any evidence pointing to an opposite conclusion in the case at hand, it is both convenient and fair to assume that *this* testator, or *this* man accused of crime, was sane when he made the will or did the act charged as criminal; or that *this* properly mailed letter reached the addressee. If nothing else, these assumptions will save a lot of time and trouble in making ponderous proof in every case of matters which will be controverted in only a small minority of cases.
>
> Access to evidence is often the basis for creating a presumption. When goods are damaged in a bailee's possession, for instance, the bailee can more easily find out what happened to them than the bailor, so it is fair to presume the bailee's negligence as an initial matter and put [the bailee] to the production of exculpatory evidence if he has any. . . . [107]

Professor Morgan adds:

> In some cases a presumption may be necessary to avoid a procedural impasse. Where a court has a fund to be distributed, and the determination of the rights of conflicting claimants depends upon the date of the death of X, it may be established that X disappeared more than seven years before the action was brought; this raises a presumption of his death, but by the orthodox view raises no presumption as to the date of death. If he died soon after the disappearance, A will take. If he died between four and six years after his disappearance, B will take; if later, C will take. In the absence of evidence and of any presumption as to date of death, the court simply cannot decide the case. This has led some courts to raise a presumption of death on the last instant of the seventh year. . . . [Other] presumptions express the result that the courts creating them deem socially desirable . . . in the absence of any showing to the contrary. The stock illustration . . . [is] that a right enjoyed by usage for a long period is presumed to have had a legal origin. . . . Finally, many, if not most, of the generally recognized presumptions are

---

[107] Fleming James, Civil Procedure § 7.9 (1965).

supported by two or more of the foregoing. The presumption that a child born in wedlock is the legitimate child of the husband, for instance, is supported by a heavy preponderance of probability, by the consideration of difficulty in producing legally competent evidence of paternity of a child born to a married woman, and by considerations of policy predicated upon a society in which the marriage and a birth during its existence create an institution by which the devolution of property is determined, and as to the intimate aspects of which accepted notions of decency and propriety demand a discreet secrecy.[108]

In criminal cases, an additional justification traditionally given for establishing presumptions running against the accused is that they rectify an imbalance created by the government's high burden of proof and its inability to force defendants to testify. Presumptions lighten the prosecution's burden of proof by removing some issues (e.g., sanity) from the case unless they are contested, by allowing evidence of an easy to prove fact to substitute for evidence of a more difficult to prove fact, and by calling the jury's attention to the likelihood that a difficult to prove fact is true if an easier to prove fact exists. Over the last fifty years and more, however, the Supreme Court has increasingly questioned the appropriateness of these effects based on the view that the Constitution forbids efforts to diminish the prosecution's demanding burden of persuasion in criminal cases. Depending upon how much of an evidentiary shortcut is taken, that is, these devices may undermine the government's burden under the Due Process Clause to prove, and the criminal defendant's Sixth Amendment right to have a jury actually find, the existence of all the elements that define a crime beyond a reasonable doubt.[109] In the following case, the Supreme Court grapples with these constitutional issues.

ULSTER COUNTY COURT V. ALLEN
442 U.S. 140 (1979).

JUSTICE STEVENS delivered the opinion of the Court.

A New York statute provides that, with certain exceptions, the presence of a firearm in an automobile is presumptive evidence of its illegal possession by all persons then occupying the vehicle. The United States Court of Appeals for the Second Circuit held that respondents may challenge the constitutionality of this [state] statute in a federal habeas corpus proceeding and that the statute is "unconstitutional on its face."

---

[108] Morgan, Presumptions, supra, note 96, 12 Wash. L. Rev. at 257–59. To illustrate the social contingency of the justifications for presumptions, consider whether any of the reasons Morgan gives for the paternity presumption remain valid today, when DNA evidence can usually resolve paternity questions.

[109] See Supreme Court decisions cited supra, note 4.

. . .

Four persons, three adult males (respondents) and a 16-year-old girl (Jane Doe, who is not a respondent here), were jointly tried on charges that they possessed two loaded handguns, a loaded machine gun, and over a pound of heroin found in a Chevrolet in which they were riding when it was stopped for speeding on the New York Thruway shortly after noon on March 28, 1973. The two large-caliber handguns, which together with their ammunition weighed approximately six pounds, were seen through the window of the car by the investigating police officer. They were positioned crosswise in an open handbag on either the front floor or the front seat of the car on the passenger side where Jane Doe was sitting. Jane Doe admitted that the handbag was hers. The machine gun and the heroin were discovered in the trunk after the police pried it open. The car had been borrowed from the driver's brother earlier that day; the key to the trunk could not be found in the car or on the person of any of its occupants, although there was testimony that [the owner of the car only recently had cleaned out the trunk and that] two of the occupants had placed something in the trunk before embarking in the borrowed car. The jury convicted all four of possession of the handguns and acquitted them of possession of the contents of the trunk.

Counsel for all four defendants objected to the introduction into evidence of the two handguns, the machine gun, and the drugs, arguing that the State had not adequately demonstrated a connection between their clients and the contraband. The trial court overruled the objection, relying on the presumption of possession created by the New York statute. Because that presumption does not apply if a weapon is found "upon the person" of one of the occupants of the car, the three male defendants also moved to dismiss the charges relating to the handguns on the ground that the guns were found on the person of Jane Doe. Respondents made this motion both at the close of the prosecution's case and at the close of all evidence. The trial judge twice denied it, concluding that the applicability of the "upon the person" exception was a question of fact for the jury.

. . .

Inferences and presumptions are a staple of our adversary system of fact-finding. It is often necessary for the trier of fact to determine the existence of an element of the crime—that is, an "ultimate" or "elemental" fact—from the existence of one or more "evidentiary" or "basic" facts. The value of these evidentiary devices, and their validity under the Due Process Clause, vary from case to case, however, depending on the strength of the connection between the particular basic and elemental facts involved and on the degree to which the device curtails the fact finder's freedom to assess the evidence independently. Nonetheless, in criminal cases, the ultimate test of any device's constitutional validity in a given case remains constant: the device must not undermine the fact finder's responsibility at trial, based on evidence adduced by the State, to find the ultimate facts beyond a reasonable doubt.

The most common evidentiary device is the entirely permissive inference or presumption, which allows—but does not require—the trier of fact to infer the elemental fact from proof by the prosecutor of the basic one and which places no burden of any kind on the defendant. In that situation the basic fact may constitute prima facie evidence of the elemental fact. When reviewing this type of device, the Court has required the party challenging it to demonstrate its invalidity as applied to him. Because this permissive presumption leaves the trier of fact free to credit or reject the inference and does not shift the burden of proof, it affects the application of the "beyond a reasonable doubt" standard only if, under the facts of the case, there is no rational way the trier could make the connection permitted by the inference. For only in that situation is there any risk that an explanation of the permissible inference to a jury, or its use by a jury, has caused the presumptively rational fact-finder to make an erroneous factual determination.

A mandatory presumption is a far more troublesome evidentiary device. For it may affect not only the strength of the "no reasonable doubt" burden but also the placement of that burden; it tells the trier that he or they must find the elemental fact upon proof of the basic fact, at least unless the defendant has come forward with some evidence to rebut the presumed connection between the two facts.[a] In this situation, the

---

a. This class of more or less mandatory presumptions can be subdivided into two parts: presumptions that merely shift the burden of production to the defendant, following the satisfaction of which the ultimate burden of persuasion returns to the prosecution; and presumptions that entirely shift the burden of proof to the defendant. The mandatory presumptions examined by our cases have almost uniformly fit into the former subclass, in that they never totally removed the ultimate burden of proof beyond a reasonable doubt from the prosecution.

To the extent that a presumption imposes an extremely low burden of production—e.g., being satisfied by "any" evidence—it may well be that its impact is no greater than that of a permissive inference, and it may be proper to analyze it as such.

In deciding what type of inference or presumption is involved in a case, the jury instructions will generally be controlling, although their interpretation may require recourse to the statute involved and the cases decided under it. . . .

The importance of focusing attention on the precise presentation of the presumption to the jury and the scope of that presumption is illustrated by a comparison of United States v. Gainey with United States v. Romano. Both cases involved statutory presumptions based on proof that the defendant was present at the site of an illegal still. In Gainey the Court sustained a conviction "for carrying on" the business of the distillery in violation of 26 U.S.C. § 5601(a)(4), whereas in Romano, the Court set aside a conviction for being in "possession, or custody, or . . . control" of such a distillery in violation of § 5601(a)(1). The difference in outcome was attributable to two important differences between the cases. Because the statute involved in Gainey was a sweeping prohibition of almost any activity associated with the still, whereas the Romano statute involved only one narrow aspect of the total undertaking, there was a much higher probability that mere presence could support an inference of guilt in the former case than in the latter.

Of perhaps greater importance, however, was the difference between the trial judge's instructions to the jury in the two cases. In Gainey, the judge had explained that the

Court has generally examined the presumption on its face to determine the extent to which the basic and elemental facts coincide. To the extent that the trier of fact is forced to abide by the presumption, and may not reject it based on an independent evaluation of the particular facts presented by the State, the analysis of the presumption's constitutional validity is logically divorced from those facts and based on the presumption's accuracy in the run of cases.[b] It is for this reason that the Court has held it irrelevant in analyzing a mandatory presumption, but not in analyzing a purely permissive one, that there is ample evidence in the record other than the presumption to support a conviction.

Without determining whether the presumption in this case was mandatory, the [United States] Court of Appeals analyzed it on its face as if it were. In fact, it was not, as the New York Court of Appeals had earlier pointed out.

The trial judge's instructions make it clear that the presumption was merely a part of the prosecution's case, that it gave rise to a permissive inference available only in certain circumstances, rather than a

---

presumption was permissive; it did not require the jury to convict the defendant even if it was convinced that he was present at the site. On the contrary, the instructions made it clear that presence was only " 'a circumstance to be considered along with all the other circumstances in the case.' " As we emphasized, the "jury was thus specifically told that the statutory inference was not conclusive." In Romano, the trial judge told the jury that the defendant's presence at the still " 'shall be deemed sufficient evidence to authorize conviction.' " Although there was other evidence of guilt, that instruction authorized conviction even if the jury disbelieved all of the testimony except the proof of presence at the site. This Court's holding that the statutory presumption could not support the Romano conviction was thus dependent, in part, on the specific instructions given by the trial judge. Under those instructions it was necessary to decide whether, regardless of the specific circumstances of the particular case, the statutory presumption adequately supported the guilty verdict.

b. In addition to the discussion of Romano in [note a,] supra, this point is illustrated by Leary v. United States. In that case, Dr. Timothy Leary, a professor at Harvard University, was stopped by customs inspectors in Laredo, Tex., as he was returning from the Mexican side of the international border. Marihuana seeds and a silver snuffbox filled with semirefined marihuana and three partially smoked marihuana cigarettes were discovered in his car. He was convicted of having knowingly transported marihuana which he knew had been illegally imported into this country in violation of 21 U.S.C. § 176a (1964 ed.). That statute included a mandatory presumption: "possession shall be deemed sufficient evidence to authorize conviction [for importation] unless the defendant explains his possession to the satisfaction of the jury." Leary admitted possession of the marihuana and claimed that he had carried it from New York to Mexico and then back.

Mr. Justice Harlan for the Court noted that under one theory of the case, the jury could have found direct proof of all of the necessary elements of the offense without recourse to the presumption. But he deemed that insufficient reason to affirm the conviction because under another theory the jury might have found knowledge of importation on the basis of either direct evidence or the presumption, and there was accordingly no certainty that the jury had not relied on the presumption. The Court therefore found it necessary to test the presumption against the Due Process Clause. Its analysis was facial. Despite the fact that the defendant was well educated and had recently traveled to a country that is a major exporter of marihuana to this country, the Court found the presumption of knowledge of importation from possession irrational. It did so, not because Dr. Leary was unlikely to know the source of the marihuana, but instead because "a majority of possessors" were unlikely to have such knowledge. Because the jury had been instructed to rely on the presumption even if it did not believe the Government's direct evidence of knowledge of importation (unless, of course, the defendant met his burden of "satisfying" the jury to the contrary), the Court reversed the conviction.

mandatory conclusion of possession, and that it could be ignored by the jury even if there was no affirmative proof offered by defendants in rebuttal.[c] The judge explained that possession could be actual or constructive, but that constructive possession could not exist without the intent and ability to exercise control or dominion over the weapons. He also carefully instructed the jury that there is a mandatory presumption of innocence in favor of the defendants that controls unless it, as the exclusive trier of fact, is satisfied beyond a reasonable doubt that the defendants possessed the handguns in the manner described by the judge. In short, the instructions plainly directed the jury to consider all the circumstances tending to support or contradict the inference that all four occupants of the car had possession of the two loaded handguns and to decide the matter for itself without regard to how much evidence the defendants introduced.

Our cases considering the validity of permissive statutory presumptions such as the one involved here have rested on an evaluation of the presumption as applied to the record before the Court. None suggests that a court should pass on the constitutionality of this kind of statute "on its face." It was error for the Court of Appeals to make such a determination in this case.

As applied to the facts of this case, the presumption of possession is entirely rational. Notwithstanding the Court of Appeals' analysis, respondents were not "hitchhikers or other casual passengers," and the guns were neither "a few inches in length" nor "out of [respondents'] sight." The argument against possession by any of the respondents was predicated solely on the fact that the guns were in Jane Doe's pocketbook. But several circumstances—which, not surprisingly, her counsel repeatedly emphasized in his questions and his argument—made it highly improbable that she was the sole custodian of those weapons.

Even if it was reasonable to conclude that she had placed the guns in her purse before the car was stopped by police, the facts strongly suggest that Jane Doe was not the only person able to exercise dominion over them. The two guns were too large to be concealed in her handbag. The bag was consequently open, and part of one of the guns was in plain view,

---

c. "Our Penal Law also provides that the presence in an automobile of any machine gun or of any handgun or firearm which is loaded is presumptive evidence of their unlawful possession.

"In other words, these presumptions or this latter presumption upon proof of the presence of the machine gun and the hand weapons, you may **[Note how much weight the Court places on the nondirective nature of this single word, "may."]** infer and draw a conclusion that such prohibited weapon was possessed by each of the defendants who occupied the automobile at the time when such instruments were found. The presumption or presumptions is effective only so long as there is no substantial evidence contradicting the conclusion flowing from the presumption, and the presumption is said to disappear when such contradictory evidence is adduced.

"The presumption or presumptions which I discussed with the jury relative to the drugs or weapons in this case need not be rebutted by affirmative proof or affirmative evidence but may be rebutted by any evidence or lack of evidence in the case."

within easy access of the driver of the car and even, perhaps, of the other two respondents who were riding in the rear seat.

. . . Under these circumstances, it was not unreasonable for her counsel to argue and for the jury to infer that when the car was halted for speeding, the other passengers in the car anticipated the risk of a search and attempted to conceal their weapons in a pocketbook in the front seat. The inference is surely more likely than the notion that these weapons were the sole property of the 16-year-old girl.

Under these circumstances, the jury would have been entirely reasonable in rejecting the suggestion—which, incidentally, defense counsel did not even advance in their closing arguments to the jury—that the handguns were in the sole possession of Jane Doe. Assuming that the jury did reject it, the case is tantamount to one in which the guns were lying on the floor or the seat of the car in the plain view of the three other occupants of the automobile. In such a case, it is surely rational to infer that each of the respondents was fully aware of the presence of the guns and had both the ability and the intent to exercise dominion and control over the weapons. . . . The application of the statutory presumption in this case therefore comports with the standard laid down in [the Court's prior cases]. For there is a "rational connection" between the basic facts that the prosecution proved and the ultimate fact presumed, and the latter is "more likely than not to flow from" the former.

Respondents argue, however, that the validity of the New York presumption must be judged by a "reasonable doubt" test rather than the "more likely than not" standard. . . . Under the more stringent test, it is argued that a statutory presumption must be rejected unless the evidence necessary to invoke the inference is sufficient for a rational jury to find the inferred fact beyond a reasonable doubt. Respondents' argument again overlooks the distinction between a permissive presumption on which the prosecution is entitled to rely as one not necessarily sufficient part of its proof and a mandatory presumption which the jury must accept even if it is the sole evidence of an element of the offense.[d]

In the latter situation, since the prosecution bears the burden of establishing guilt, it may not rest its case entirely on a presumption unless the fact proved is sufficient to support the inference of guilt beyond a reasonable doubt. But in the former situation, the prosecution may rely on all of the evidence in the record to meet the reasonable-doubt

---

d. The dissenting argument rests on the assumption that "the jury [may have] rejected all of the prosecution's evidence concerning the location and origin of the guns." Even if that assumption were plausible, the jury was plainly told that it was free to disregard the presumption. But the dissent's assumption is not plausible; for if the jury rejected the testimony describing where the guns were found, it would necessarily also have rejected the only evidence in the record proving that the guns were found in the car. The conclusion that the jury attached significance to the particular location of the handguns follows inexorably from the acquittal on the charge of possession of the machine gun and heroin in the trunk [notwithstanding that the jury was told that the same presumption applied to those items].

standard. There is no more reason to require a permissive statutory presumption to meet a reasonable-doubt standard before it may be permitted to play any part in a trial than there is to require that degree of probative force for other relevant evidence before it may be admitted. . . .

. . .

JUSTICE POWELL, with whom JUSTICE BRENNAN, JUSTICE STEWART and JUSTICE MARSHAL join, dissenting.

. . .

In the criminal law, presumptions are used to encourage the jury to find facts, with respect to which no direct evidence is presented, solely because other facts have been proved. The purpose of such presumptions is plain: . . . Through the use of presumptions, certain inferences are commended to the attention of jurors by legislatures or courts.

Legitimate guidance of a jury's deliberations is an indispensable part of our criminal justice system. Nonetheless, the use of presumptions in criminal cases poses at least two distinct perils for defendants' constitutional rights. The Court accurately identifies the first of these as being the danger of interference with "the factfinder's responsibility at trial, based on evidence adduced by the State, to find the ultimate facts beyond a reasonable doubt." If the jury is instructed that it must infer some ultimate fact (that is, some element of the offense) from proof of other facts unless the defendant disproves the ultimate fact by a preponderance of the evidence, then the presumption shifts the burden of proof to the defendant concerning the element thus inferred.[e]

But I do not agree with the Court's conclusion that the only constitutional difficulty with presumptions lies in the danger of lessening the burden of proof the prosecution must bear. As the Court notes, the presumptions thus far reviewed by the Court have not shifted the burden of persuasion; instead, they either have required only that the defendant produce some evidence to rebut the inference suggested by the prosecution's evidence, or merely have been suggestions to the jury that it would be sensible to draw certain conclusions on the basis of the evidence presented. Evolving from our decisions, therefore, is a second standard for judging the constitutionality of criminal presumptions which is based—not on the constitutional requirement that the State be put to its proof—but rather on the due process rule that when the jury is encouraged to make factual inferences, those inferences must reflect some

---

e. The Court suggests that presumptions that shift the burden of persuasion to the defendant in this way can be upheld provided that "the fact proved is sufficient to support the inference of guilt beyond a reasonable doubt." As the present case involves no shifting of the burden of persuasion, the constitutional restrictions on such presumptions are not before us, and I express no views on them. It may well be that even those presumptions that do not shift the burden of persuasion cannot be used to prove an element of the offense, if the facts proved would not permit a reasonable mind to find the presumed fact beyond a reasonable doubt. My conclusion . . . infra, makes it unnecessary for me to address this concern here.

valid general observation about the natural connection between events as they occur in our society.

. . .

In sum, our decisions uniformly have recognized that due process requires more than merely that the prosecution be put to its proof. In addition, the Constitution restricts the court in its charge to the jury by requiring that, when particular factual inferences are recommended to the jury, those factual inferences be accurate reflections of what history, common sense, and experience tell us about the relations between events in our society. Generally, this due process rule has been articulated as requiring that the truth of the inferred fact be more likely than not whenever the premise for the inference is true. Thus, to be constitutional a presumption must be at least more likely than not true.

. . .

Undeniably, the presumption charged in this case [in the instruction quoted in footnote c of the majority opinion] encouraged the jury to draw a particular factual inference regardless of any other evidence presented: to infer that respondents possessed the weapons found in the automobile "upon proof of the presence of the machine gun and the hand weapon" and proof that respondents "occupied the automobile at the time such instruments were found." I believe that the presumption thus charged was unconstitutional because it did not fairly reflect what common sense and experience tell us about passengers in automobiles and the possession of handguns. People present in automobiles where there are weapons simply are not "more likely than not" the possessors of those weapons.

. . .

As I understand it, the Court today does not contend that in general those who are present in automobiles are more likely than not to possess any gun contained within their vehicles. It argues, however, that the ["permissive"] nature of the presumption here involved requires that we look, not only to the immediate facts upon which the jury was encouraged to base its inference, but to the other facts "proved" by the prosecution as well. . . .

It seems to me that the Court mischaracterizes the function of the presumption charged in this case. As it acknowledges was the case in Romano, supra, the "instruction authorized conviction even if the jury disbelieved all of the testimony except the proof of presence" in the automobile. The Court nevertheless relies on all of the evidence introduced by the prosecution and argues that the "permissive" presumption could not have prejudiced defendants. The possibility that the jury disbelieved all of this evidence, and relied on the presumption, is simply ignored.

. . .

The Court's novel approach in this case appears to contradict prior decisions of this Court reviewing such presumptions. Under the Court's analysis, whenever it is determined that an inference is "permissive," the only question is whether, in light of all of the evidence adduced at trial, the inference recommended to the jury is a reasonable one. The Court has never suggested that the inquiry into the rational basis of a permissible inference may be circumvented in this manner. Quite the contrary, the Court has required that the "evidence necessary to invoke the inference [be] sufficient for a rational juror to find the inferred fact. . . . " Under the presumption charged in this case, the only evidence necessary to invoke the inference [of possession] was the presence of the weapons in the automobile with respondents—an inference that is plainly irrational.

Some points in *Allen* are clear. First, presumptions can take many forms depending not simply on their statutory or common law formulation but also, and more importantly, on the instructions through which they are conveyed to the jury. Thus, one must pay careful attention to the precise words used to describe a "presumption" to the jury.[110] As we note above, the commendable practice has arisen among lawyers and judges since *Allen* was decided of reserving the word "presumption" for mandatory devices (types 3–6 in our list of six devices above at pp. 1438–1439), and using the less directive word "inference" to refer to permissive devices (types 1 and 2).[111] The result of this practice is that jurors almost never hear the word "presumption," either in civil cases (for reasons noted above) or in criminal cases (for reasons discussed

---

[110] Consider whether the Court itself paid close enough attention to the instructions in *Allen*. Those instructions, quoted in footnote c, include a statement that "[t]he presumption . . . is effective only so long as there is no substantial evidence contradicting the conclusion flowing from the presumption, and the presumption is said to disappear when such contradictory evidence is adduced." Given this statement, it is not as "clear" to us as it was to the majority "that the presumption . . . gave rise to a *permissive* inference available only in certain circumstances, rather than a mandatory conclusion of possession, and that it could be ignored by the jury even if there was no affirmative proof offered by defendants in rebuttal." What matters, of course, is how the jury was likely to have understood the instructions in the context of the trial. See infra, note 113. Although not sufficient in itself, the modern practice of avoiding the word "presumption" in instructions like these, and using only the word "inference," helps to avoid the risk that jurors will believe their freedom to find the facts as they see them has been curtailed.

[111] The Federal Judicial Center's Pattern Jury Instructions and at least one federal circuit court have gone further and recommended that trial judges refrain from instructing criminal juries on "inferences" (especially if they run against the accused) and "leav[e] inferences to arguments of counsel." United Sates v. Hill, 252 F.3d 919, 923 (7th Cir. 2001); Federal Judicial Center, Pattern Criminal Jury Instructions, Commentary to Instr. 34, 39, 43–45 (2008). See also State v. Belcher, 385 S.C. 597, 685 S.E.2d 802 (2009) (citing cases) (a number of states now bar instructions in criminal cases that tell jurors they are permitted, even when the instructions do not tell jurors they are required, to infer the element of malice from the use of a deadly weapon, reasoning that such instructions impermissibly invade the province of the jury).

below). Second, as we suggested earlier, two factors are important in evaluating and classifying inferences and presumptions: (a) the quality of the logical connection between the basic fact **X** and the presumed fact **Y**; and (b) the leeway the device gives a trier who believes that **X** is true to find, nonetheless, that **Y** is *not* true. Third, in a criminal case in which the presumed fact is an element of the offense, a shortcut device of this sort is unconstitutional if it creates too high a risk that a guilty verdict will be premised on more of a tie between the basic and presumed facts than experience and logic together allow. This may happen if: (a) the device encourages the jury to believe that fact **Y** has been proven beyond a reasonable doubt because of the message that fact **X** provides strong evidence of **Y**, and not because of the jury's *own* assessment of the strength of the link between **X** and **Y**; or (b) the device leads the jury to believe that it is legally required to find the defendant guilty, although the government did *not* convince it beyond a reasonable doubt that **Y** was present. The first of these deficiencies undermines the defendant's right to a jury as opposed to a legislative or judicial determination of his guilt. The second undermines the defendant's right to an acquittal unless the prosecution proves his guilt beyond a reasonable doubt. Fourth, whenever the devices run against a criminal defendant in regard to an element of a crime, "mandatory" presumptions raise substantially more serious constitutional problems than "permissive" inferences because of their effect on the burden of proof.

The Court emphasized the fourth point in *Sandstrom v. Montana*, announced a few weeks after *Allen*. *Sandstrom* held that a *mandatory conclusive presumption* requiring the jury to find element **Y** upon proof of fact **X** is unconstitutional because it substitutes a requirement that the state prove fact **X** beyond a reasonable doubt for the constitutional duty to prove every statutory element of the offense, including **Y**, beyond a reasonable doubt.[112]

---

[112] 442 U.S. 510, 517 (1979) (instruction that "the law presumes that a person intends the ordinary consequences of his voluntary acts" violates the Due Process Clause because a reasonable juror could interpret the instruction as "an irrebuttable direction by the court to find intent once convinced of the facts triggering the presumption"). Earlier, we pointed out that conclusive presumptions actually are substantive rules of law in evidentiary disguise. For example, a rule that the jury must find intentional killing before convicting of murder, but also must presume that the defendant intended the natural consequences of his act, is really a rule that engaging in acts that lead as a natural consequence to death constitutes murder irrespective of an intent to kill. In *Sandstrom*, the presumption was judge-made, not statutory. The outcome might have been different if the legislature rather than the trial court had imposed the "conclusive" presumption, for then one could argue that the legislature had substituted "voluntary actions with death as a natural consequence" for "intent" as the mental element of murder, and that proof beyond a reasonable doubt of the former fact satisfied the state's constitutional burden of proof.

The Court's mechanical reliance on the formal statutory elements of offenses in cases such as *Patterson* and *Mullaney*, discussed supra, Section I, note 4, suggests that the legislature could not avoid *Sandstrom* as long as it formally listed "intent" as the mental element of murder (even while treating "actions with death as a natural consequence" as conclusive proof of intent). The constitutional "legality" requirement, that crimes be transparently defined by statute, points in the same direction. In Carella v. California, 491 U.S. 263 (1989) (per curiam), a unanimous Supreme Court seemed to reach this conclusion. *Carella* overturned a grand theft conviction

Later in *Francis v. Franklin* the Court ruled that a *mandatory-burden-of-proof-shifting presumption* requiring the jury to find element **Y** upon proof of

---

based on Carella's failure to return a rental car on time. The jury that convicted the defendant received instructions reciting verbatim two presumptions that the California legislature had adopted for use when theft was alleged as a result of a patron's failure to return a rented vehicle within the time period specified in the rental agreement:

1. Intent to commit theft by fraud is presumed if one who has leased or rented the personal property of another pursuant to a written contract fails to return the personal property to its owner within 20 days after the owner has made written demand by certified or registered mail following the expiration of the lease or rental agreement for return of the property so leased or rented.

2. Whenever any person who has leased or rented a vehicle wilfully and intentionally fails to return the vehicle to its owner within five days after the lease or rental agreement has expired, that person shall be presumed to have embezzled the vehicle.

Id. at 264. In *Carella*, the Court did not pause to consider the possibility that, by adopting this "mandatory conclusive presumption" of intent to steal (presumed fact **Y**) from a failure to return the car within twenty days (basic fact **X**), the legislature implicitly changed the substantive law of theft by allowing either "voluntary failure to return the vehicle within twenty days" or "intent to steal" to suffice as the mental element of the crime. Instead, the Court unanimously concluded that "[t]hese mandatory directions directly foreclosed independent jury consideration of whether the facts proved established certain elements [i.e., the *explicit* "intent to steal" elements] of the offenses with which Carella was charged. The instructions also relieved the State of its burden of proof articulated in [*In re*] *Winship,* namely, proving by evidence every essential element of Carella's crime beyond a reasonable doubt. The two instructions violated the Fourteenth Amendment." Id. at 266.

Carella would seem to be have disposed of the matter but for the Court's subsequent decision in Montana v. Egelhoff, 518 U.S. 37 (1996). There, the Court upheld a Montana statute defining murder as knowing or purposeful killing but forbidding evidence of voluntary intoxication to be "taken into consideration in determining the existence of a mental state which is an element of [a criminal] offense." Four members of the Court voted to affirm the severely intoxicated defendant's murder conviction on the ground that a sufficient number of states followed Montana's rule to avoid any due process problem. And four members of the Court (in three opinions) concluded that Montana's rule deprived the defendant of his constitutional right to adduce relevant exculpatory evidence admissible under generally established evidence rules. This left Justice Ginsburg's opinion concurring in the result to control the outcome. Justice Ginsburg first concluded (expressing a view apparently accepted by all members of the Court) that there is no constitutional rule forbidding a State to define the mental element of murder as *either* knowledge and purpose *or* the commission of acts that, absent voluntary intoxication, would establish intent beyond a reasonable doubt. Id. at 57–58 (Ginsburg, J., concurring in the judgment). She then concluded (expressing a view disputed by the dissenters and not addressed by the plurality) that the Montana Legislature had done just that by *indirection*—through a rule excluding consideration of evidence of intoxication on mental-element questions. Compare id. at 58–59, with id. at 80 (Breyer, J., dissenting) ("If the legislature wanted to equate voluntary intoxication, knowledge, and purpose, why would it not write a statute that plainly says so, instead of doing so in a roundabout manner. . . . "). If, as Justice Ginsburg suggests, the legislature may constitutionally change its substantive definition of the mental element of a crime from **Y** to **X** by indirection, through a statutory provision purporting to exclude evidence refuting **Y** (which, in *Egelhoff*, was intent) but not evidence refuting **X** (a mental state short of **Y**—in *Egelhoff*, intoxication), there is no reason to think that it could not do the same through a statutory provision identifying element **Y** as necessary for conviction but making **X** conclusive of it. Neither Justice Ginsburg nor any other member of the *Egelhoff* Court mentioned *Carella*, and as of this writing (late 2013) the discrepancy in the analysis in the two cases remains unacknowledged and unresolved. For the reasons discussed in the last paragraph of note 100, supra, *Carella* appears to us to have the better of the argument. Given the weight the Due Process Clause and Sixth Amendment place on a state's statutory definition of the elements of a crime, state legislatures ought to be required to define determinative facts as elements in a straightforward, transparent manner as a prerequisite to according constitutional significance to those facts. Defining a crime's elements by "indirection" cannot satisfy this "clear statement" requirement.

fact **X** unless the defendant proved the contrary violated the same constitutional principle.[113] *Francis* also confirmed a related proposition suggested by *Allen*. Permissive presumptions *never* raise constitutional questions based on a shifting of the burden of proof because they do not shift that burden (although they may raise constitutional questions if they encourage jurors to see more of a link between the basic and presumed facts, **X** and **Y**, than the jurors otherwise would). The *Supreme Court has not resolved the constitutional status of mandatory presumptions that are not conclusive and do not shift the burden of persuasion, but do shift the burden of* production.[114]

There is a good argument that a presumption that shifts a burden of production to the defendant *is* unconstitutional. Such a presumption requires the jury to find element **Y** if it concludes (1) that fact **X** is true, and (2) that the defendant has not produced the requisite amount of evidence (e.g., "sufficient evidence") that **Y** is not true. By providing that

---

[113] 471 U.S. 307, 315–20 (1985) (invalidating instructions that " '[t]he acts of a person of sound mind and discretion are presumed to be the product of the person's will, but the presumption may be rebutted,' " and that " '[a] person of sound mind and discretion is presumed to intend the natural and probable consequences of his acts but the presumption may be rebutted' "; these presumptions violate the Due Process Clause because they "could reasonably be read as telling the jury that it was required to infer intent to kill as the natural and probable consequence of firing the gun unless the defendant persuaded the jury that such an inference was unwarranted" and, thus, as "creat[ing] a[ ] . . . burden shifting presumption with respect to the element of intent"); see Sandstrom, 442 U.S. at 517 (dicta) (an instruction violates the Due Process Clause if a reasonable juror could interpret it "as a direction to find intent upon proof of the defendant's voluntary actions . . . unless the defendant proved to the contrary by some quantum of proof . . . —thus effectively shifting the burden of persuasion on the element of intent"). Dissenting Justices in both *Sandstrom* and *Francis* argued that, considered together with other instructions, the challenged instructions could have been interpreted as merely *permissive* inferences, i.e., as permitting but not requiring the jury to find intent, and as requiring the state to prove intent beyond a reasonable doubt under all circumstances. Instructions very often are susceptible to multiple interpretations, requiring a reviewing court to decide whether the risk that the jurors gave the instructions the forbidden interpretation was unconstitutionally high. In *Sandstrom* and *Francis*, the Court invalidated the instructions although it found only that a rational juror "*could*" have given them the forbidden interpretation. In subsequent cases, however, the Court increased the level of risk needed to establish a constitutional violation by requiring proof of a "reasonable likelihood" that a rational juror *would* have given the instruction the forbidden interpretation. Boyde v. California, 494 U.S. 370, 380 (1990). Note, though, that a "reasonable likelihood" is present if the forbidden interpretation was more than "a mere possibility"; the standard does not require that the forbidden interpretation be "more likely than not." Johnson v. Texas, 509 U.S. 350, 367–68 (1993).

[114]

A permissive [presumption] does not relieve the State of its burden of persuasion because it still requires the State to convince the jury that the suggested conclusion should be inferred based on the predicate facts proved. . . . A permissive [presumption] violates the Due Process Clause only if the suggested conclusion is not one that reason and common sense justify in light of the proven facts before the jury.

* * *

We are not required to decide in this case whether a mandatory presumption that shifts only a burden of production to the defendant is consistent with the Due Process Clause, and we express no opinion on that question.

Francis, 471 U.S. at 314–15 & n.3. Before *Sandstrom*, the Court approved or applied burden-of-production-shifting presumptions, but it has not done so since, and it has never considered whether such devices unconstitutionally relieve the state of the burden of persuasion. Cf. Turner v. United States, 396 U.S. 398 (1970); Roviaro v. United States, 353 U.S. 53, 63 (1957).

the jury *must* find element **Y** present, whether or not the government has proved **Y** beyond a reasonable doubt, burden-of-production shifting presumptions appear to violate the requirement that the government prove every element of a crime beyond a reasonable doubt.[115] They also violate the reasonable doubt requirement if fact **X** can trigger the presumption even when it has not been proved "beyond a reasonable doubt." Following this logic, most commentators have concluded that *Sandstrom* and *Francis* invalidate burden-of-production shifting presumptions. The fact that the issue almost never comes up in court suggests that legislatures and trial judges have reached the same conclusion and removed such devices from federal and state criminal law and jury instructions.

Other implications of *Allen* are not so clear. Consider the issue that divided the Court, namely, the constitutional status of a presumption in a criminal case that invites, but does not require, a jury to infer fact **Y**, an element of the crime, from fact **X**. The majority appears to have concluded that a permissive inference like this violates the Constitution "only if, *under the facts of the case*, there is no rational way the trier could make the connection permitted by the inference." The majority felt that only this modest safeguard was necessary, because the jury was told that it could reject any link between **X** and **Y**, either in the abstract or given all the evidence. Thus, the instruction on the permissive inference did little more than tell the jury that the **X-Y** connection might deserve *some* credence under the circumstances, leaving it to the jury to decide how much credence, if any, was due.[116] By contrast, Justice Powell, writing

---

[115] *Sandstrom* and later cases make clear that juries in criminal cases should not be instructed on mandatory presumptions from basic fact **X** to presumed fact **Y**, where **Y** is an element of an offense. Even where the link between basic fact **X** and element of the crime **Y** is merely a permissive inference, we think that trial judges should generally refrain from instructing juries on the inferential link, leaving the strength of the **X-Y** connection to the argument of counsel and the deliberations of jurors. See supra, note 111 for developing federal practice in this regard. Of note, Proposed FRE 303(c), which Congress deleted from the Federal Rules of Evidence, would have treated all presumptions running against the accused in criminal cases as merely "permissive presumptions," i.e., as a type-2 device in our list of six devices at p. 1438 above. This is true even if presumed fact **Y** is not an element of the crime or is an element of an affirmative defense. Additionally, Proposed Rule 303 would have required the prosecution to prove the basic facts **X** beyond a reasonable doubt before most presumptions running against the accused would have been given any effect. Proposed Rule 303(c) provides:

> Whenever the existence of a presumed fact against the accused is submitted to the jury, the judge shall give an instruction that the law declares that the jury may regard the basic facts as sufficient evidence of the presumed fact but does not require it to do so. In addition, if the presumed fact establishes guilt or is an element of the offense or negatives a defense, the judge shall instruct the jury that [the presumption's] existence must, on all the evidence, be proved beyond a reasonable doubt.

By banning burden-of-production-shifting presumptions running against the accused in *all* situations, not just when **Y** is an element of the crime, and by suggesting that the prosecution should bear a burden of proof beyond a reasonable doubt as to facts necessary to negative affirmative defenses, Proposed Rule 303(c) goes beyond the Court's current holdings under the Due Process Clause. Compare supra, Section I.A., pp. 1368–1372; supra, pp. 1457–1458.

[116] Although the Court did not say so in *Allen*, its willingness to let trial judges recommend that jurors infer **Y** from **X** may depend in part on whether the presumption in question is (as in *Allen* itself) statutory. If so, the legislative judgment that **X** tends to prove **Y** may deserve special deference. Somewhat analogously, the Court also has suggested that the common law's

for the dissent, feared that the jury would see the instruction as an invitation to find **Y** based on **X** alone, and so might find a stronger connection between fact **X** and element **Y** than it would have done if left to its own devices.

To avoid having the judge's mention of a presumption artificially bridge the **X-Y** gap, Justice Powell would have required that, without regard to the other evidence in the case, "the truth of the inferred fact be more likely than not whenever the premise for the inference is true." On Justice Stevens's case-specific, rationality analysis, the Constitution was satisfied because, as between the 16-year-old girl and the men, it was rational to think that they and not she had stuffed the large guns into her open pocketbook and had control over them. On Justice Powell's more-likely-than-not analysis, with its focus on the **X-Y** relationship abstracted from all other evidence, the Constitution was violated because regardless of who controlled the guns in *Allen*, guns in cars are usually exclusively controlled by a particular passenger—thus making a presumption that *everyone* in a car possesses *all* the guns found in it inaccurate as a general matter, and likely to mislead.

The presumption stood in *Allen*, under Justice Stevens's case-specific approach, because the gender and ages of the car's occupants and their proximity to the guns made it more likely than not that the men possessed the guns. Had this not been the case—had the guns, for example, been in a briefcase chained to the wrist of one of the men—it is possible that the presumption that all the occupants possessed the weapons would not have been saved even by showing, for example, that each of the men had later told the police that all the guns were his; for Justice Stevens emphasizes that facts *specific to the situation giving rise to the presumption* allowed the jury to conclude beyond a reasonable doubt that the men possessed the guns. The Court has not confronted a case in which the facts specific to the incident did not by themselves justify finding the presumed fact beyond a reasonable doubt but did justify such a finding when coupled with other evidence in the case (e.g., in *Allen*, testimony that the men had been seen a week earlier pooling their money to purchase guns that looked exactly like those found in the car). We cannot say whether the *Court* would broaden the *Allen* rule in these circumstances to allow a court to consider the probative implications of evidence unrelated to the situation giving rise to the presumption in determining the presumption's constitutionality.

We believe that allowing only situational facts to bear on the constitutionality of a permissive inference is sensible. Otherwise the jury might reject the evidence of the additional facts (e.g., not credit the witness who says he saw the men purchase the guns) and convict solely

---

long use of a presumption deserves deference in assessing the rationality of the **X-Y** link. See Wright v. West, 505 U.S. 277 (1992); Barnes v. United States, 412 U.S. 837 (1973).

on the basis of a presumption which, unlike the presumption in *Allen*, arises from a factual situation found by the jury that does not justify finding that the presumed fact exists beyond a reasonable doubt. Happily, these open questions are becoming less important as a result of the developing practice in criminal cases of using the less directive words "permissive inference" in lieu of "presumption," and beyond that of discouraging trial judges from instructing on inferences at all when the device runs against the accused. See supra pp. 1457–1458 & notes 93, 111.

As we note above, the Court has reserved judgment on whether *mandatory* burden-of-*production*-shifting devices unconstitutionally lower the government's burden of proof. If, contrary to our view, such devices are not per se unconstitutional on burden of proof grounds, they may still exert an unconstitutionally excessive influence on the jury's assessment of the strength of the **X-Y** connection. Both opinions in *Allen* suggest that, when dealing with mandatory burden-of-production-shifting presumptions (as opposed to the permissive device the Court actually analyzed there), a court should look beyond the facts of the instant case and ask whether *"in the run of cases"* fact **X** is sufficient by itself to permit a rational juror to find element **Y** *beyond a reasonable doubt*. If fact **X** and element **Y** are not invariably that strongly connected (as often will be the case), the presumption is unconstitutional.

Taken together, the Supreme Court's decisions from *Allen* through *Francis* suggest that, in criminal cases, the overriding constitutional question is whether a presumption creates too high a risk that a jury's guilty verdict will be based on an "artificial" link between fact **X** and element **Y**, i.e., a link rational jurors would not have made but for the presumption. Presumptions may do this in one of two ways. They may compel the jury to assume that element **Y** is present if fact **X** is present, when absent the presumption, even knowing of fact **X**'s existence, the jury would not otherwise have found **Y** established beyond a reasonable doubt. This unconstitutionally relieves the government of its burden of proving element **Y** to a jury beyond a reasonable doubt. Or, they may cause the jury to think that **Y** is present beyond a reasonable doubt only because the jurors weigh not only their own views of the strength of the **X-Y** connection, but also the legislature's or court's perception. This unconstitutionally substitutes a legislative or judicial judgment for a jury verdict. Presumptions that do no more than specify a permissive inference avoid the first defect entirely and, under the majority rule in *Allen*, avoid the second defect as long as the existence of fact **X** is sufficient, under the circumstances of the case, to permit a jury rationally to infer element **Y**. At the other extreme, where a presumed fact is one that the State must prove beyond a reasonable doubt, conclusive and mandatory burden-of-proof-shifting presumptions are always invalid as a result of the first defect and, accordingly, need not be evaluated for the second. In between are mandatory burden-of-production-shifting presumptions, which appear to invalid for the first reason though the Court has not yet addressed the issue, and are invalid for the second reason unless fact **X** *always* is sufficient, whatever the other case facts, to permit a rational juror to find element **Y** beyond a reasonable doubt. The chart below, which reports some important features of the Court's criminal presumption cases, should help you to understand and evaluate the constitutional rules the Court applies. The first seven cases (through *Allen*) focus on the possibility that devices will excessively influence juries in assessing the strength of the link between facts **X** and **Y**; the last three cases focus on the possibility that presumptions will diminish the government's burden of proof.

The complex constitutional rules that we have abstracted to make our chart do not apply in most civil cases,[117] nor in criminal cases to presumptions that favor the accused or that favor the government on issues on which the accused bears the burden of proof. Because the Constitution seldom controls which party should bear the burden of proof in a civil case, legislatures and courts have considerably more freedom to use presumptions to determine the burdens that civil parties bear. The "hallmark of civil presumptions" is that "they shift to the party against whom they operate the burden of production and sometimes even the burden of persuasion."[118] In a criminal case, shifting such burdens from the state to the accused renders them, at a minimum, constitutionally suspect where the fact at issue is an element of the crime.

Unlike rules governing what *counts* as evidence (e.g., the rules governing stipulations, judicial admissions and judicial notice), rules telling the trier of fact what to *do* with the admitted evidence (i.e., burdens of pleading, production and persuasion, and the combinations of those burdens called "presumptions") are not evidentiary rules at all but rules of substantive law, subject to constitutional constraints on the same basis as other substantive legal rules. Because the substantive policies affecting the appropriate allocation, definition and intermixture of burdens of pleading, production and persuasion are as varied as the substantive legal disciplines to which they apply, the two most useful lessons one can learn from studying them are the following: First, *refrain from overarching assumptions about how burdens and presumptions ought to work. Instead, analyze carefully the statute, judicial decisions and jury instructions that specify how they work in the case at hand.* Second, *consider whether the actual or projected allocations and definitions of the burdens of production and persuasion conflict with the*

---

[117] As is discussed supra, Section I.B.2., pp. 1375–1376, there are a small set of civil cases in which the Due Process Clause requires the government to bear the burden of proof by clear and convincing evidence. Presumptions that undermine that burden of proof assumedly would encounter the same constitutional problems as ones that undermine the government's beyond-a-reasonable-doubt burden in criminal cases.

[118] Mueller & Kirkpatrick, supra, note 48, at 141.

constitutional allocation and definition of the burden of proof in the important but relatively small segment of cases in which the Constitution applies (i.e., mainly, in regard to proof of elements of criminal offenses). Where this second constraint does not exist, policy makers—courts and legislatures and parties arguing before them—should structure statutes, decisions, instructions and arguments so as to further the governing or relevant substantive policies.

CHART 11–2

Case	Basic fact (X)	Presumed fact (Y)	Constraint on the jury	Ruling
Tot v. U.S (1943)	Prior conviction of violent crime and current possession of firearm	Defendant received firearm in interstate commerce	X proves Y unless D comes forward with contrary evidence	Invalid
U.S. v. Gainey (1965)	Unexplained presence at illegal still	Carrying on unbonded business of distiller	X may but need not suffice to prove Y	Valid
U.S. v. Romano (1965)	Unexplained presence at illegal still	Possession, custody, control of still	X "shall be deemed sufficient evidence" of Y unless D produces "satisfactory" explanation of X	Invalid
Leary v. U.S. (1969)	Possession of marijuana	Knowing importation from abroad	X "shall be deemed sufficient evidence" of Y unless D produces "satisfactory" explanation of X	Invalid
Turner v. U.S. (1970)	Possession of heroin	Knowing importation from abroad	X "shall be deemed sufficient evidence" of Y unless D produces "satisfactory" explanation of X	Valid: nearly all heroin in U.S. is imported
	Possession of cocaine	Knowing importation from abroad	X "shall be deemed sufficient evidence" of Y unless D produces "satisfactory" explanation of X	Invalid: much cocaine in U.S. is made there
	Heroin not in stamped package when found in D's possession	D handled drug knowing it was not originally in stamped package	X may but need not suffice to prove Y	Valid: heroin has no legal uses
	Cocaine not in stamped package in D's possession	D handled drug knowing it was not originally in stamped package	X may but need not suffice to prove Y	Invalid: at the time, cocaine had many legal uses
Barnes v. U.S. (1973)	Possession of recently stolen property	Knowing possession of stolen property	X may but need not suffice to prove Y	Valid
Ulster County Ct. v. Allen (1979)	Presence in car with guns or drugs	Possession of guns or drugs	X may but need not suffice to prove Y	Valid

Case	Basic fact (X)	Presumed fact (Y)	Constraint on the jury	Ruling
Sandstrom v. Montana, (1979)	V's death was the natural and probable consequence of D's voluntary act	D intended to kill V	Jury must presume Y based on X	Invalid
Francis v. Franklin, (1985)	Same as *Sandstrom*	D intended to kill V	Jury must presume Y based on X unless D disproves Y	Invalid
Carella v. California (1989)	Failure to return a rental car within 20 days of contractual return date	D intended to steal the car	Jury must presume Y based on X	Invalid

PROBLEMS

Problem XI-33. During its consideration of the original Federal Rules of Evidence, the House Subcommittee on Criminal Justice proposed the following version of FRE 301:

> In all civil actions and proceedings not otherwise provided for by Act of Congress or by these rules, a presumption imposes on the party against whom it is directed the burden of going forward with the evidence, and, even though met with contradicting evidence, a presumption is sufficient proof of the fact presumed to be considered by the trier of the facts.

In its report on the Rules, the Subcommittee explained:

> With respect to the weight to be given a presumption in a civil case, the Subcommittee agreed with the conclusion reflected in the Court's version [i.e., the version the Supreme Court had sent to Congress based on proposals made by the Federal Rules Advisory Committee] that the so-called "bursting bubble" theory of presumptions, whereby a presumption vanishes upon the appearance of any contradicting evidence by the other party, gives to presumptions too slight an effect. On the other hand, the Subcommittee believed that the rule proposed by the Court, whereby a presumption permanently alters the burden of persuasion [shifting it to the opposing party], no matter how much contradicting evidence is introduced—a view adopted by only a few courts—lent too great a force to presumptions. The Subcommittee accordingly adopted an intermediate position under which a presumption does not vanish upon the introduction of contradicting evidence, and does not change the burden of persuasion; instead it is merely deemed sufficient evidence of the fact presumed to be considered by the jury or other finder of fact.

What exactly would the effect of this proposal have been? How does it differ from FRE 301 as enacted and as currently applied by a majority of federal courts? As between FRE 301 as enacted, the Subcommittee's proposal, and a rule that shifts the risk of nonpersuasion to the opposing party, which is preferable? In thinking about these questions, consider the presumption in negligence cases that a car owned by the defendant but driven by someone else was being operated at the time of an accident with the defendant's consent. Assume that a tort plaintiff proves that a car that ran her over was owned by the defendant, but the defendant testifies that the car had previously been stolen. **Is the fact that the defendant owned the car sufficient under FRE 301 as adopted and interpreted by most federal courts to take the plaintiff's case to the jury? Under the Subcommittee's proposal?**

Problem XI-34. Anders Arthurson & Partners contracts with Shady Enterprises to handle all of Shady's accounting business for a flat fee of $10,000 per week. The written retainer agreement provides that the agreement shall remain in effect until either party terminates it by giving written notice thirty days prior to the effective date of the termination. In January 2013, Arthurson demands payment of $200,000 plus interest for work done from August through December, 2012. Shady refuses to pay, claiming that it terminated the contract as of August 1, 2012, by letter to Arthurson mailed on June 25, 2012. Arthurson denies receiving any such letter, and sues. The jurisdiction in question adheres to a presumption that a letter that is properly addressed and posted is received, and uses the burden-of-persuasion-shifting definition of a presumption. Arthurson points out that, as plaintiff, it already bears the burden of proving that it received no notice of any termination of the agreement, and proposes that the trial court instruct the jury on that burden but not on the presumption of receipt of a mailed letter. Shady responds by asking the court, based on the presumption's mandatory "step-up" effect, to increase the usual, preponderance of the evidence burden of proof to a requirement that Arthurson prove by "clear and convincing evidence" that it received the letter. **How should the trial court rule on Arthurson's and Shady's proposals regarding the presumption of receipt of a mailed letter? How, if at all, should the trial judge instruct the jury on the presumption?**

Problem XI-35. Julian Atencio sues Marissa Romana, the owner of a toy store in Baltimore, for damages occurring when Atencio slipped and fell outside the store. Atencio, who has brought the action in Maryland state court, seeks $95,000 in damages. Liability turns in part on whether Romana knew before the accident that a particular portion of the sidewalk outside her store became slippery in light rain. Atencio testifies that he walks past the store every day on his way from the bus stop to work, and that after twice slipping on the sidewalk in the drizzle, and before slipping and injuring himself, he dashed off an angry letter describing the unsafe condition of the sidewalk and mailed it to Romana's store. Having so testified, Atencio is the beneficiary under state law of a presumption that a properly addressed letter that is placed in a mailbox arrives at its intended destination.   Romana has available three witnesses whose testimony might help her on the issue. One is Atencio's ex-wife who, following a bitter divorce, has only slight credibility. She would testify that she heard Atencio say after the accident, "If only I had sent that letter to the toy store, this never would have happened." The second witness is Romana's sister-in-law, Emilia, who for years (until moving to the West Coast on the eve of trial) had managed Romana's store. Emilia has only moderate credibility, given her relationship to Romana. Emilia will testify that, during the relevant period, she opened all of Romana's mail but never opened a letter from Atencio. The third witness, the country's leading expert on operations of the U.S. Postal Service, has no prior involvement with the parties. She will testify that during the relevant period postal operations in and around Baltimore had deteriorated to the point where it was common for mail never to arrive at its destination, particularly mail sent from one location to another within the city. All three witnesses live in Seattle, Washington. Romana can afford to pay for only one witness to fly to Baltimore for the trial. **Which witness should Romana choose if the presumption is (1) a permissive inference; (2) one that shifts the production burden; (3) one that shifts the risk of nonpersuasion; (4) conclusive?**

Problem XI-36.   Rhoda Riley brings an action in state court against Southeastern State Law School to have her transcript corrected to reflect an A in Evidence, not the C that the record now contains. Riley claims that Hannah Wallis, her professor, actually awarded her the higher grade, and that the record is erroneous. Wallis is now deceased. The state courts have long recognized a common law presumption that records of public agencies, including schools such as Southeastern, are recorded and maintained in a regular, accurate form. Southeastern relies upon this presumption when it calls its records custodian to testify that C is the grade that was recorded in the ordinary course of Southeastern's record-keeping. **Which of the following pieces of evidence would be sufficient to rebut the presumption under a rule similar to FRE 301:   a properly authenticated letter from Wallis to Riley congratulating her on having received the highest grade in the class; a witness who heard Wallis tell another professor that Riley had surprised her on the exam; a witness who heard Wallis tell another professor that Riley had done surprisingly well on the exam; proof that Wallis wrote Riley a letter of recommendation for federal court clerkships after filing Riley's Evidence grade; testimony that the records custodian had been involved in frequent arguments with Riley concerning the way the school's**

records were kept and that the custodian had been heard to say that she did not think well of Riley; testimony by another employee of the records office that in the school term in question an unusual number of errors on transcripts had been detected and corrected?

Problem XI-37. Phillip South was married for twenty-one years before his wife, Mary North, told him she would file for divorce. Phillip was shocked, but did not contest the divorce because Mary agreed to take all the steps necessary, and pay, for the divorce, agreed not to demand any of Phillip's millions, and agreed to let him have custody of their two children, Amy (16) and Daniel (17). Mary left the house and, at some point in 2008, informed Phillip that their divorce had become final. Phillip married Sheri West in 2010, the same year in which they had their first child, Nancy. During a vacation trip to Costa Rica, Phillip and Sheri were killed in an automobile crash. The children were at home with relatives at the time. Neither parent had left a will. Thus, under state law, each legitimate child would take equally from Phillip. Amy and Daniel claim, however, that the second marriage was invalid and that Nancy is not Phillip's legitimate child. In the probate proceeding, Nancy's guardian offers a marriage certificate containing the names of Phillip South and Sheri West. The guardian also claims the benefit of a presumption that a marriage duly performed is valid. In response, Amy and Daniel offer into evidence the certificate solemnizing the earlier marriage of Phillip South and Mary North and rely on the presumption that a marriage once in effect continues in effect. **If both sides rest at this point, without producing any other evidence, who should prevail?** Assume that Nancy's guardian calls Sheri's best friend, Ruth Padoo, to testify that Sheri told her just before her wedding to Phillip that he had received a divorce decree that very day. **Now who wins?** Assume instead that in response to the marriage certificate offered by Nancy's guardian, Phillip's best friend, Howard Rafkin, is called to testify that he saw a certificate granting a divorce to Phillip South and Mary North. **Now does Nancy prevail? Do any of your answers depend on whether the Federal Rules or the burden-of-persuasion-shifting view of presumptions prevails in the jurisdiction in question?**

Problem XI-38. FRE 302 provides:

> In a civil case, state law governs the effect of a presumption regarding a claim or defense for which state law supplies the rule of decision.

Assume that under the doctrine of pendent jurisdiction, common law fraud claims are joined with federal securities claims in a federal court action for damages arising out of a corporation's sale of shares of its stock. Plaintiff claims that the directors of the corporation failed to disclose important information about the company's financial condition. But Plaintiff can prove the financial condition of the company only during a six-month period ending three months before the actual sale. **If under both state and federal law there is a presumption that a state of affairs shown to be continuous over a period of time continues beyond that period, and if the state law adopts the burden-of-persuasion-shifting view of presumptions, what should a federal judge say to the jury with respect to how this presumption bears on Plaintiff's state and federal causes of action? How should the judge instruct the jury if federal law does not recognize the presumption, but state law recognizes it and follows the burden-of-persuasion-shifting view of presumptions?**

Problem XI-39. In *Western & Atlantic R.R. v. Henderson*,[119] the Supreme Court held the following Georgia statute unconstitutional:

> A railroad company shall be liable for any damages done to persons, stock, or other property by the running of the locomotives, or cars, or other machinery of such company, or for damages done by any person in the employment or service of such company, unless the company shall make it appear that their agents have exercised all ordinary and reasonable care and diligence, the presumption in all cases being against the company.

The case arose when a woman sued for damages resulting from the death of her husband in a collision at a railroad crossing between her husband's truck and defendant's train. After she proved that her husband's death resulted from the operation of railroad equipment, the trial judge instructed the jury that in order to win the case, the railroad had to overcome a presumption of negligence by "showing" that its employees exercised ordinary care and diligence. The Supreme Court said:

> Legislation declaring that proof of one fact or group of facts shall constitute prima facie evidence of an ultimate fact in issue is valid if there is a rational connection between what is proved and what is to be inferred. A prima facie presumption casts upon the person against whom it is applied the duty of going forward with his evidence on a particular point to which the presumption relates. A statute creating a presumption that is arbitrary or that operates to deny a fair opportunity to repel it violates the due process clause of the Fourteenth Amendment. Legislative fiat may not take the place of fact in the judicial determination of issues involving life, liberty or property.

> The mere fact of a collision between a railway train and a vehicle at a highway grade crossing furnishes no basis for any inference

---

[119] 279 U.S. 639 (1929).

as to whether the accident was caused by negligence of the railway company or of the traveler on the highway or of both or without fault of anyone. And the presumption [in this case] was used to [resolve] conflicting allegations of negligence. Plaintiff claimed that the engineer failed to keep a lookout ahead, that he did not stop the train after he saw the truck on the crossing, and that his eyesight was so bad that he could not see the truck in time to stop the train.

Appellee relies principally upon *Mobile, J. & K.C.R.R. v. Turnipseed*, 219 U.S. 35. That was an action in a court of Mississippi to recover damages for the death of a section foreman accidentally killed in that State. While engaged about his work he stood by the track to let a train pass; a derailment occurred and a car fell upon him. A statute of the State provided: ". . . Proof of injury inflicted by the running of the locomotives or cars of such [railroad] company shall be prima facie evidence of the want of reasonable skill and care on the part of the servants of the company in reference to such injury." That provision was assailed as arbitrary and in violation of the due process clause of the Fourteenth Amendment. This court held it valid and said "The only legal effect of this inference is to cast upon the railroad company the duty of producing some evidence to the contrary. When that is done, the inference is at end, and the question of negligence is one for the jury upon all of the evidence. . . . The statute does not . . . fail in due process of law, because it creates a presumption of liability, since its operation is only to supply an inference of liability in the absence of other evidence contradicting such inference." That case is essentially different from this one. Each of the state enactments raises a presumption from the fact of injury caused by the running of the locomotives or cars. The Mississippi statute created merely a temporary inference of fact that vanished upon the introduction of opposing evidence. That of Georgia as construed in this case creates an inference that is given [the] effect of evidence to be weighed against opposing testimony and is to prevail unless such testimony is found by the jury to preponderate.

Did the Court accurately describe the character or effect of the Georgia statute? How would you describe the statute's character or effect? Did the Court accurately describe the character or effect of the Georgia provision "as construed in this case" by way of the trial court's instruction? How would it affect the proper description of the "presumption" if the Georgia trial judge had used the word "presents evidence," instead of "showing"? What if, instead, the trial judge had read the statute to the jury, then said, "So if you find by a preponderance of the evidence that the

running of the defendant's locomotive or cars caused injury to the plaintiff or damage to his truck, then the law of this state treats that as sufficient proof of defendant's negligence; and you may find for the plaintiff if you conclude that defendant or any of its employees was negligent." What accounts for the different treatment the Supreme Court gave to the Georgia presumption in this case and the Mississippi presumption in *Turnipseed*? How important in this regard are (1) the statutory formulations of the two presumptions; (2) the instructions given to the juries in the two cases (What do you imagine the instructions were in the *Turnipseed* case?); and (3) the facts of the two cases? This case arose during a period in which the Court was more likely than today to find that state regulatory statutes violated due process by "arbitrarily" interfering with owners' use of their property. Would the Georgia statute itself, or the jury instruction based on it, be upheld today? Suppose the case instead involved a charge of criminal negligence, and the word "guilty" were substituted for the word "liable" in the Georgia statute and the trial court's instructions to the jury. Would that statute or that jury instruction be upheld today?

Problem XI-40. Geoff Gordon rented a car from Lease-a-Heap on January 5. In the rental agreement Gordon signed, he undertook contractually to return the car five days later. On January 20, Lease-a-Heap wrote Gordon at the address on the rental agreement, demanding the return of the car. When there was no answer twenty days later, Lease-a-Heap sued Gordon for Conversion of a Rented Automobile, and the local prosecutor charged Gordon with Grand Theft of an Automobile. Gordon testifies that he drove the car to Lease-a-Heap's airport drop-off location on January 10 and, finding no attendant present, left the car with its keys in the glove compartment and ran to catch his airplane. On rebuttal, Kiley Bush testifies that she saw Gordon driving a car matching the rental automobile on January 18. **Assuming that Gordon is the defendant in a *civil* action arising under each of the four statutes set out below, what instructions does each statute appear to require on (1) who bears the burden of persuasion with regard to the issue of intent to convert or steal the car, and (2) what that burden is? Does your answer change if Gordon is instead the defendant in a *criminal* action arising under each statute? In either the civil or the criminal action, are there any constitutional objections to the instructions on the burden of persuasion that each statute appears to require?**

(1) Any person who rents an automobile from a commercial rental establishment and intentionally fails to return the automobile to the rental establishment on the date agreed upon is liable to the rental establishment for the tort of Conversion of a Rented Automobile, and is also guilty of the criminal offense of Grand Theft of an Automobile.

It is a defense to civil and criminal liability under this section that the failure to return the automobile was not intentional. **[Would it matter if this statute instead made the lack of intent an "affirmative defense"?]**

(2) Any person who rents an automobile from a commercial rental establishment and intentionally fails to return the automobile to the rental establishment on the date agreed upon is liable to the rental establishment for the tort of Conversion of a Rented Automobile, and is also guilty of the criminal offense of Grand Theft of an Automobile. Intentional failure to return is presumed if the person renting the automobile fails to return it within ten days of the agreed upon return date, and within five days of receiving a subsequent written demand for the automobile from the commercial rental establishment. The presumption shall be conclusive unless the person alleged to have converted or stolen the automobile establishes by a preponderance of the evidence that he or she did not intend convert or steal it.

(3) Any person who rents an automobile from a commercial rental establishment and intentionally fails to return the automobile to the rental establishment on the date agreed upon is liable to the rental establishment for the tort of Conversion of a Rented Automobile, and is also guilty of the criminal offense of Grand Theft of an Automobile. Intentional failure to return is conclusively presumed if the person renting the automobile fails to return it within ten days of the agreed upon return date, and within five days of receiving a subsequent written demand for the automobile from the commercial rental establishment.

(4) Any person who rents an automobile from a commercial rental establishment and fails to return the automobile to the establishment within ten days of the agreed upon return date, and within five days of receiving a subsequent written demand from the commercial rental establishment to return the automobile, is liable to the rental establishment for the tort of Conversion of a Rented Auto, and is also guilty of the criminal offense of Grand Theft of an Automobile.

Problem XI-41. Evelyn East is charged with the theft of three Depression-era green glass vases from a summer home owned by Carol Cloisonne. Cloisonne discovered that the vases were missing when she arrived at her summer home for the season in early June and noticed that a window had been pried open. No fingerprints or other evidence was found at the scene. Three weeks later, Cloisonne saw her vases in a booth rented by East at a local flea market. Cloisonne informed the sheriff, who immediately arrested East. At her jury trial, East testifies that Potter Porcelain sold her the green glass vases the day before she was arrested.

According to East, Porcelain said he had purchased the vases at a garage sale the previous weekend. Porcelain testifies in rebuttal that, although he knows East and frequently sells her "junk," he did not sell her the green vases, which he saw for the first time in court. **Which of the seven instructions set out below may the trial judge constitutionally give to the jury? What defects are there in the other instructions? In answering these questions, consider whether it would matter if, in addition to the evidence described above, there was testimony that the green glass vases were seen in East's car in April of the same year as the other events?**

(1) If you find from the evidence beyond a reasonable doubt that property of a value of $100 or more was stolen from Carol Cloisonne, and that it was recently thereafter found in the exclusive and personal possession of the defendant, Evelyn East, and that such possession has been unexplained or falsely denied by the defendant, then such possession is sufficient to raise an inference that the defendant was the thief; and if such inference, taking into consideration the whole evidence, leads you to believe beyond a reasonable doubt that the defendant committed the theft, then you shall find the defendant guilty.

(2) If you find from the evidence beyond a reasonable doubt that property of a value of $100 or more was stolen from Carol Cloisonne, and that it was recently thereafter found in the exclusive and personal possession of the defendant, Evelyn East, and that such possession has been unexplained or falsely denied by the defendant, then those determinations are sufficient as a matter of law to establish beyond a reasonable doubt that the defendant was the thief; and if you make those determinations, and if those determinations lead you to believe beyond a reasonable doubt that the defendant committed the theft, then you shall find the defendant guilty.

(3) If you find from the evidence beyond a reasonable doubt that property of a value of $100 or more was stolen from Carol Cloisonne, and that it was recently thereafter found in the exclusive and personal possession of the defendant, Evelyn East, and that such possession has been unexplained or falsely denied by the defendant, then a presumption arises that the defendant was the thief; and if such presumption, taking into consideration the whole evidence, leads you to believe beyond a reasonable doubt that the defendant committed the theft, then you shall find the defendant guilty.

(4) In order to find the defendant, Evelyn East, guilty, you must find beyond a reasonable doubt that she committed the theft. If you find from the evidence beyond a reasonable doubt that property of a value of $100 or more was stolen from Carol Cloisonne, and that it was recently thereafter found in the exclusive and personal possession of

the defendant, and that such possession has been unexplained or falsely denied by the defendant, then the law presumes that the defendant was the thief.

(5) In order to find the defendant, Evelyn East, guilty, you must find beyond a reasonable doubt that she committed the theft. If you find from the evidence beyond a reasonable doubt that property of a value of $100 or more was stolen from Carol Cloisonne, and that it was recently thereafter found in the exclusive and personal possession of the defendant, and that such possession has been unexplained or falsely denied by the defendant, then the law presumes that the defendant was the thief, unless it appears from the rest of the evidence that the defendant did not commit the theft.

(6) In order to find the defendant, Evelyn East, guilty, you must find beyond a reasonable doubt that she committed the theft. If you find from the evidence beyond a reasonable doubt that property of a value of $100 or more was stolen from Carol Cloisonne, and that it was recently thereafter found in the exclusive and personal possession of the defendant, and that such possession has been unexplained or falsely denied by the defendant, then the law presumes that the defendant was the thief, unless there is other credible evidence that the defendant did not commit the theft.

(7) In order to find the defendant, Evelyn East, guilty, you must find beyond a reasonable doubt that she committed the theft. If you find from the evidence beyond a reasonable doubt that property of a value of $100 or more was stolen from Carol Cloisonne, and that it was recently thereafter found in the exclusive and personal possession of the defendant, and that such possession has been unexplained or falsely denied by the defendant, then the law presumes that the defendant was the thief, unless the defendant rebuts that presumption by establishing by a preponderance of the evidence that she did not commit the theft.

Problem XI-42. Elaria Blago, a Massachusetts state patrol officer on duty at the Callahan Tunnel, heard one of the automatic toll collection machines signal that a vehicle had passed through without a deposit of $5.00 or an equivalent token. She noted the license plate number of the car, and that the male driver of the car had shoulder length hair and wore glasses. She did not attempt to stop the car. From the license plate number it was learned that the car was registered to the defendant Joseph C. Pauley. Blago accordingly swore out a complaint in the East Boston District Court charging that Pauley had deposited a copper slug in the toll collection machine at the end of the Callahan Tunnel intending to evade payment of the toll. At the trial in the Municipal Court, Blago was the only witness. She testified to the incident at the tunnel as recounted above. Pauley, who was present in court, had short hair and was not wearing glasses. Blago said she could not positively identify Pauley as the person who had deposited the slug. Pauley stipulated that he was the registered owner of the car and that whoever was driving the car at the time and place testified to had attempted to evade payment of the toll in violation of the tunnel regulation. The Commonwealth offered the tunnel rules and regulations in evidence, directing the court's attention to a section providing that

> [i]f a vehicle is operated within tunnel property in violation of any provision of these rules and regulations and the identity of the operator of such vehicle cannot be determined, the person in whose name such vehicle is registered shall be deemed prima facie responsible for such violation.

The regulation was received over Pauley's objection. The defendant offered no evidence. The judge found him guilty and fined him $500. No findings were made. Pauley appealed. Massachusetts case law provides that: "The trier of fact may convict in a criminal case if a 'prima facie' case is made out. No other evidence is necessary." **Should an appellate court overturn the conviction and declare the "prima facie" device unconstitutional? Would your answer change if the words "deemed prima facie" were removed from the quoted regulation? What if the word "may" in the passage quoted from Massachusetts case law were instead "shall"?**

Problem XI-43. Quentin Soffit, a carpenter and building contractor, is charged with criminal fraud. Margot Thums hired Soffit to renovate her home, giving him $35,000 to cover the cost of securing architectural plans and engaging subcontractors to perform plumbing, electrical and plaster work. When no work took place over the succeeding five months, and Thums was unable to reach Soffit, she contacted the police who discovered Soffit on an extended ski vacation and arrested him. Evidence shows that Soffit's only bank account had a balance of less than $300 for the five months prior to, and throughout, the period when he was on his ski vacation; that he cashed Thums' $35,000 check at a bank in the town where he was vacationing; and that he used cash to purchase goods and services in the amount of $31,789 during his vacation. Following his arrest and release on bail, Soffit telephoned Thums and informed her that he had engaged an architect, plumber, electrician, and plasterer, and asked when they could begin work on her home. Thums responded, "Don't waste my time!" and hung up. At trial, Soffit testifies he had always planned to perform the work for Thums and at no time intended to defraud her. In the instructions to the jury, the trial judge describes the elements of fraud and the prosecution's burden of proof beyond a reasonable doubt. Over Soffit's objection, the judge then instructs the jury as follows:

> Proof that the defendant failed to pay for such labor, services or materials for any specific improvement from the proceeds of any

payment made to him for such specific improvements shall constitute prima facie evidence of intent to defraud. Prima facie evidence means evidence of such a nature as is sufficient to establish a fact which, if unrebutted, remains sufficient for that purpose.

The jury convicts. **How should an appellate court rule on Soffit's claim on appeal that this instruction unconstitutionally required the jury to find intent to defraud unless Soffit produced evidence to rebut the finding? What difference would it make if Thums had brought the case against Soffit as a civil action for fraud?**

III.   BIBLIOGRAPHY

McCormick, § 254 (stipulations and judicial admissions), ch. 35 (judicial notice), ch. 36 (burdens of proof and presumptions).

9 Wigmore §§ 2483–2550 (presumptions); §§ 2565–2583 (judicial notice), 2588 (stipulations).

Allen, Ronald J., Presumptions in Civil Actions Reconsidered, 66 Iowa L. Rev. 843 (1981).

Allen, Ronald J., Presumptions, Inferences and Burden of Proof in Federal Civil Actions—An Anatomy of Unnecessary Ambiguity and a Proposal for Reform, 75 Nw. U.L. Rev. 892 (1983).

Allen, Ronald J., Structuring Jury Decisionmaking in Criminal Cases: a Unified Approach to Evidentiary Devices, 94 Harv. L. Rev. 321 (1980).

Barger, Coleen M., On the Internet, Nobody Knows You're a Judge: Appellate Courts' Use of Internet Materials, 4 J. App. Prac. & Process 417 (2002).

Cappalli, Richard B., Bringing Internet Information to Court: Of "Legislative Facts," 75 Temp. L. Rev. 99 (2002).

Cheng, Edward K., Independent Judicial Research in the Daubert Age, 56 Duke L.J. 1263 (2007).

Cleary, Edward W., Foreword to Symposium on Proposed Rules of Evidence, 1969 Law and Soc. Order 509.

Cleary, Edward W., Presuming and Pleading: An Essay on Juristic Immaturity, 12 Stan. L. Rev. 5 (1959).

Comment, The Presently Expanding Concept of Judicial Notice, 13 Vill. L. Rev. 528 (1969).

Davis, Kenneth Culp, An Approach to Problems of Evidence in the Administrative Process, 55 Harv. L. Rev. 364 (1942).

Davis, Kenneth Culp, Facts in Lawmaking, 80 Colum. L. Rev. 931 (1980).

Davis, Kenneth Culp, Judicial Notice, 55 Colum. L. Rev. 945 (1955).

Davis, Peggy C., "There is a Book Out . . . ": An Analysis of Judicial Absorption of Legislative Facts, 100 Harv. L. Rev. 1539 (1987).

Faigman, David L., Constitutional Fictions: A Unified Theory of Constitutional Facts (2008).

Falkner, Judson F., Notes on Presumptions, 15 Wash. L. Rev. 71 (1940).

Gross, Samuel R., Substance and Form in Scientific Evidence: What *Daubert* Didn't Do, in Reforming the Civil Justice System 234–279 (Larry Kramer ed. 1996).

James, Fleming, Burdens of Proof, 47 Va. L. Rev. 51 (1961).

Jeffries, John and Paul Stephan, Defenses, Presumptions and Burdens of Proof in the Criminal Law, 88 Yale L.J. 1325 (1979).

Karst, Kenneth, Legislative Facts in Constitutional Litigation, 1960 Sup. Ct. L. Rev. 75.

Keeffe, Arthur John, William B. Landis, Jr., and Robert B. Shaad, Sense and Nonsense About Judicial Notice, 2 Stan. L. Rev. 664 (1944).

Keeton, Robert E., Legislative Facts and Similar Things: Deciding Disputed Premise Facts, 73 Minn. L. Rev. 1 (1988).

Laughlin, Charles V., In Support of the Thayer Theory of Presumptions, 52 Mich. L. Rev. 195 (1953).

Lempert, Richard O., The New Evidence Scholarship: Analyzing the Process of Proof, 66 B.U. L. Rev. 439 (1986).

Levin, Leo and Robert J. Levy, Persuading the Jury with Facts Not in Evidence: The Fiction-Science Spectrum, 105 U. Pa. L. Rev. 139 (1956).

Louisell, David W., Construing Rule 301: Instructing the Jury on Presumptions in Civil Actions and Proceedings, 63 Va. L. Rev. 281 (1977).

Mansfield, John H., Jury Notice, 74 Geo. L.J. 395 (1985).

McBaine, James P., Burden of Proof: Degrees of Belief, 32 Cal. L. Rev. 242 (1944).

McBaine, James P., Burden of Proof: Presumptions, 2 U.C.L.A. L. Rev. 13 (1954).

McNaughton, John T., Burden of Production of Evidence: a Function of a Burden of Persuasion, 68 Harv. L. Rev. 1382 (1955).

McNaughton, John T., Judicial Notice—Excerpts Relating to the Morgan-Wigmore Controversy, 14 Vand. L. Rev. 779 (1961).

Michael, Jerome and Mortimer J. Adler, The Trial of an Issue of Fact, 34 Colum. L. Rev. 1224 (1934).

Miller, Arthur Selwyn and Jerome A. Barron, The Supreme Court, the Adversary System, and the Flow of Information to the Justices, 61 Va. L. Rev. 1187 (1975).

Monahan, John and Laurens Walker, Social Authority: Obtaining, Evaluating, and Establishing Social Science in Law, 134 U. Penn. L. Rev. 477 (1986).

Morgan, Edmund M., Judicial Notice, 57 Harv. L. Rev. 269 (1944).

Morgan, Edmund M., Presumptions, 12 Wash. L. Rev. 255 (1937).

Nesson, Charles, Rationality, Presumptions and Judicial Comment: a Response to Professor Allen, 94 Harv. L. Rev. 1574 (1991).

Newman, Jon O., Beyond "Reasonable Doubt," 68 N.Y.U. L. Rev. 979 (1993).

Note, Judicial Admissions, 64 Colum. L. Rev. 1121 (1964).

Note, Reasonable Doubt: To Define or Not to Define, 90 Colum. L. Rev. 1716 (1990).

Onstott, Christopher, Judicial Notice and the Law's "Scientific" Search for Truth, 40 Akron L. Rev. 465 (2007).

Roberts, E. F., Preliminary Notes Toward a Study of Judicial Notice, 52 Cornell L.Q. 210 (1967).

Saltzburg, Stephen A., Standards of Proof and Preliminary Questions of Fact, 27 Stan. L. Rev. 271 (1975).

Schwartz, Warren F., A Suggestion for the Demise of Judicial Notice of "Judicial Facts," 45 Tex. L. Rev. 1212 (1967).

Shapiro, Barbara J., "Beyond a Reasonable Doubt" and "Probable Cause": Historical Perspectives on the Anglo-American Law of Evidence (1991).

Shapiro, Barbara J., "To a Moral Certainty": Theories of Knowledge and Anglo-American Juries 1600–1850, 38 Hastings L.J. 153 (1986).

Solomon, Gus J., Techniques for Shortening Trials, 65 F.R.D. 485 (1975).

Sundby, Scott E., The Reasonable Doubt Rule and the Meaning of Innocence, 40 Hastings L.J. 457 (1989).

Thayer, James B., A Preliminary Treatise on Evidence at Common Law, Ch. 8 (1898) (presumptions).

Turner, Dennis J., Judicial Notice and Federal Rule of Evidence 201—A Rule Ready for Change, 45 U. Pitt. L. Rev. 181 (1983).

Underwood, Barbara, The Thumb on the Scales of Justice: Burdens of Persuasion in Criminal Cases, 86 Yale L.J. 1299 (1977).

Woolhandler, Ann, Rethinking the Judicial Reception of Legislative Facts, 41
Vand. L. Rev. 111 (1988).

INDEX

References are to Pages